SEX DISCRIMINATION AND THE LAW
Causes and Remedies

SEX DISCRIMINATION AND THE LAW
Causes and Remedies

BARBARA ALLEN BABCOCK
Stanford Law School
Stanford, California

ANN E. FREEDMAN
Attorney
Philadelphia, Pennsylvania

ELEANOR HOLMES NORTON
Chairperson, Commission on Human Rights
New York City

SUSAN C. ROSS
Attorney
New York City

Little, Brown and Company
Boston   1975   Toronto

KF
4758
.A7
S4

68891

INTRODUCTION

This is not a usual law school text. It did not, for instance, grow out of the scholarly or other interests of law professors, but rather had its genesis in student-generated courses in Women and the Law. The first such course was taught in the fall of 1969 at New York University Law School, and Susan Ross was one of the initiators. Women students at Yale, including Ann Freedman, learned about the N.Y.U. course, taught it themselves in the spring of 1970 and, for the spring of 1971, prevailed upon the faculty to hire Barbara Babcock, who had been teaching the course at Georgetown University. She and Ann Freedman then taught the course together at Georgetown in the fall of 1971. Meanwhile, Susan Ross had started teaching a course at George Washington. From the experience of teaching with an array of mimeographed materials, and from the increasing requests for copies of the syllabus and advice on materials, the need for a text became apparent. Ann Freedman and Barbara Babcock asked Susan Ross and Eleanor Norton, who was then teaching the course at New York University Law School, to join in the enterprise of book writing.

A grant was secured from the Carnegie Corporation of New York to help in the preparation of this book, and to hold a conference on teaching Women and the Law. The conference at New Haven in the fall of 1971 gathered most of the students, professors, and attorneys who were interested in teaching or had taught the fledgling course, and provided an ideal method of exchanging information and ideas about the contents of the proposed book. People in the feminist movement within and outside of the legal profession continued to be a source of inspiration and strength throughout the writing of the book. Also during the book's preparation, the developing materials were used in many courses, particularly by Ann Freedman at Georgetown in the spring and fall of 1973 and at Villanova in the spring of 1974, and by many other teachers and students who offered valuable criticism and suggestions.

In addition to its unusual inception, the book differs from most other law texts in that, on the whole, it was not written by full-time law professors. During most of the three years this book has been in production, two of the authors were engaged in work to eliminate sex discrimination — Eleanor Norton as Chairperson of the Human Rights Commission in New York City; Susan Ross as a lawyer in the General Counsel's Office of the Equal Employment Opportunity Commission, and later as a partner in a feminist law firm. In the first year of our work, Barbara Babcock was the Director of the Public Defender Service in the District of Columbia; later she became an associate professor at Stanford Law School, where she introduced the first Women and the Law course and a clinical program in the subject. In the last year, Ann Freedman has helped found a feminist law firm in Philadelphia, the Women's Law Project. Although our full-time professional responsibilities made the task of writing the book more difficult, we hope that our experiences with the practical application of feminist law are reflected in and contribute to this book.

A third way in which the text differs from traditional casebooks is in content. Although it contains many cases and statutory materials, there are also popular magazine articles, historical, economic, and sociological materials, practice manuals, and notes designed to provoke discussion or to answer rather than raise questions. But equal in importance to innovations in content is the explicit bias inherent in our approach. We believe that women suffer inequality, reinforced and at times created by laws, and that law can also be used to remedy many of these inequities. We also believe that American life would be immensely improved were women to enjoy a social, economic, and legal status truly equal to men's. These convictions have necessarily influenced our reading and explication of cases and our selection of materials. We have presented a feminist view of most of the issues raised in the chapters which follow. Although this is contrary to the purportedly objective presentation which many casebooks adopt, our experience in teaching from this perspective has been that it is a stimulating pedagogical method. Confronted by openly partisan materials, the law-trained student, especially, often resists, and in so doing learns valuable critical thinking and advocacy skills.

Finally, as to content, there is clearly more here than could be covered in one course. The constitutional law chapter alone could supply material for an entire semester, as could the chapter on employment law. Teachers of survey courses may want to cover selected portions from each chapter, however, in order to show the interrelation of sex discrimination problems in every area of the law. Some may want to expand Women and the Law courses to a full year in order to give in-depth treatment to all areas. Others may prefer to cover only two areas during one semester in order to study the practice implications of the materials. Whatever the choice, we think there are sufficient materials here to allow for a variety of approaches.

For all the differences we perceive between our effort and law texts generally, we do share the desire of most authors to convey our warmest gratitude to the many people who contributed to this work, without fixing upon them any responsibility for errors or misinterpretations which may have occurred.

First, of course, we thank the Carnegie Corporation, without which we would not have had the resources to initiate this project at all, and particularly Eli N. Evans, Executive Associate, who guided us through the granting process. Deep expressions of gratitude go also to our associates and students who have been critics and inspiration, largely without financial compensation: J. Starr Babcock, Edith Barnett, Francine Blau, Barbara A. Brown, Heidi Cochran, Carin Clauss, Prudence Clendenning, Nancy L. Davis, Mary C. Dunlap, Catherine East, Thomas I. Emerson, Gail Falk, Ann Corinne Hill, Harriet Katz, Douglas McGlashan, Maud Pervere, Rand Rosenblatt, Edward Sparer, and Susan Watkins. These expressions of gratitude are separate from and in addition to the implicit recognition involved in the reprinting of published and unpublished materials by our friends and colleagues, which appear throughout the book with what we trust is appropriate attribution.

We wish to thank the administration and staff of the Stanford Law School for the extraordinary support services rendered in the final production of the book, involving costly communication between co-authors who were by this time in Philadelphia, New York, and San Francisco. In particular, Patricia Nichter deserves great credit for the precision with which she dealt with these disparate materials. We also wish to thank Georgetown University Law Center for its early and continuous support of the course and the materials. Our special thanks go finally to our most patient publishers, who saw us through the inevitable missed deadlines without ever taking their eyes from the goal of quality.

We are also grateful to one another for the benefits of shared thinking and labor. Our method was for each author to be responsible primarily for certain chapters or sections, but in the final analysis, this division of labor was not completely maintained. Chapter One (constitutional law) was mainly the work of Ann Freedman and Barbara Babcock, with valuable editorial aid from Susan Ross; the first draft of the Equal Rights Amendment section was written by Eleanor Norton. Chapter Two (employment law) was Susan Ross's responsibility, with Ann Freedman working with her on Part I, the economic introduction, and Part IV, the executive order section. Ann Freedman had primary responsibility for Chapter Three (family law), with substantial editorial assistance from Barbara Babcock and some assistance from Susan Ross. Ms. Babcock wrote

Chapter Four (criminal law). Chapter Five's public accommodation section was Eleanor Norton's. Ms. Freedman, Babcock and Norton wrote the abortion section, and Ms. Freedman, Ross and Norton wrote the education section. Throughout, Ann Freedman and Barbara Babcock have borne primary administrative and editorial responsibility for producing the book.

August 1974

ACKNOWLEDGMENTS

The authors gratefully acknowledge permission to reprint the selections indicated below.

Chapter One

Anne Koedt, Ellen Levine & Anita Rapine, eds. — for The Trial of Susan B. Anthony, Radical Feminism, New York Times Books (Quadrangle), 1973. Reprinted by permission of the editors.

The Harvard Law Review — for the selections from Frankfurter, "Hours of Labor and Realism in Constitutional Law." Copyright © 1916 by The Harvard Law Review Association; and for selections from "Developments in the Law — Equal Protection." Copyright 1969 by The Harvard Law Review Association.

Quadrangle/The New York Times Book Company — for the selections from Up From the Pedestal, edited by Aileen S. Kraditor. Copyright © 1968 by Aileen S. Kraditor; for the selections from O'Neill, Everyone Was Brave, also excerpted in Chapter II. Copyright © 1969, 1971 by William O'Neill; and for the selections from Winick & Kinsie, The Lively Commerce, excerpted in Chapter IV. Copyright © 1971 by Charles Winick. Reprinted by permission of Quadrangle/The New York Times Book Company.

Barbara Brown, Thomas Emerson, Gail Falk & Ann Freedman, and The Yale Law Journal — for the selections from "The Equal Rights Amendment: A Constitutional Basis for Equal Rights for Women," also excerpted in Chapters II, III and IV. Reprinted with the permission of the authors, Yale Law Journal Company, and Fred B. Rothman & Company.

The California Law Review and Fred B. Rothman & Company — for selections from Tussman & tenBroek, The Equal Protection of the Laws. Copyright © 1949, California Law Review, Inc.; and for selections from Rosenheim, "Vagrancy Concepts in Welfare Law."

Harper & Row, Publishers, Inc. — for the excerpts abridged from pp. 1073–1078 in An American Dilemma, Twentieth Anniversary Edition, by Gunnar Myrdal. Copyright © 1944, 1962 by Harper & Row. By permission of the publisher.

The Harvard Civil Rights–Civil Liberties Law Review — for the selections from Freund, "The Equal Rights Amendment is Not the Way." Copyright © Harvard Civil Rights–Civil Liberties Law Review, 1971.

The Yale Law Journal and Fred B. Rothman & Company — for selections from "The Equal Rights Amendment and the Military."

Mariclaire Hale, Leo Kanowitz and the Hastings Law Journal — for selections from "Women and the Draft: A Response to Critics of the Equal Rights Amendment."

John Johnston & Charles Knapp — for the selections in this chapter and Chapters II and III from "Sex Discrimination By Law: A Study in Judicial Perspective." Reprinted by permission of the authors and the New York University Law Review.

Oxford University Press — for selections from The American Woman: Her Changing Social, Economic and Political Role, 1920–1970, by William H. Chafe, also excerpted in Chapter II. Copyright © 1972 by Oxford University Press, Inc.

Chapter Two

Lexington Books — for the selections from "Exploitation From Nine to Five," Report of the Twentieth Century Fund Task Force on Working Women, background paper by Adele Simmons, Ann Freedman, Margaret Dunkle & Francine Blau, Lexington, Mass. Copyright © 1974, Lexington Books, D.C. Heath & Company.

Norma Briggs — for the selection from Guess Who Has the Most Complex Job?

Francine D. Blau — for the selection from "Women's Place" in the Labor Market.

Myra Strober — for the selection from Lower Pay For Women: A Case of Economic Discrimination?; and for the selection from Some Thoughts on the Economics of Child Care, excerpted in Chapter III.

Carolyn Shaw Bell — for the selection from Age, Sex, Marriage and Jobs; and for the selection from Women and Social Security: Contributions and Benefits, from Chapter III.

The Johns Hopkins University Press — for the selections from A Sociologist's Skepticism by Oppenheimer in *Corporate Lib*, edited by Eli Ginzberg and Alice M. Yohalem. Copyright © by the Johns Hopkins University Press.

Monthly Labor Review — for the selection from Women Workers and Manpower Demands in the 1970's, by Janice Neipert Hedges.

Avon Books — for selections from The Rights of Women, by Susan C. Ross, also excerpted in Chapter V.

John Kenneth Galbraith and New York Times Magazine — for the selection from The Galbraith Plan to Promote the Minorities, by Galbraith, Kuh and Thurow.

George Cooper & Harriet Rabb — for the selections from Equal Employment Law and Litigation, Materials for a Clinical Law Project, produced under a grant from the Equal Employment Opportunity Commission.

The New York Times — for the selection from Voluntary Overtime Puts Snag in Auto Negotiations, by William K. Stevens; and for the article in Chapter III, "The Poor and the Work Ethic." Copyright © 1973 by the New York Times Company.

New York Law Forum — for the selections from Childbirth and Child Rearing Leave: Job Related Benefits, by Elizabeth Duncan Koontz.

American Civil Liberties Union — for the selections from Punishing Pregnancy: Discrimination in Education, Employment and Credit by Trudy Hayden.

Gail Falk and the Women's Rights Law Reporter — for the selection from Women and Unions: A Historical View.

New York Law Journal — for a selection from the issue of January 31, 1974.

Ms. Magazine — for the selection from Liberating Ma Bell, by Lisa Cronin Wohl; and for the selections from Confessions of a House-Husband, by Joel Roach and from Up From Under, by Susan Edmiston, excerpted in Chapter III; for the selection from Giving Women a Sporting Chance, by Brenda Feigan Fasteau, excerpted in Chapter V; and for the selection from How the Economy Hangs on her Apron Strings by John Kenneth Galbraith, excerpted in Chapter III. Reprinted with permission from Ms. Magazine.

Women's Rights Law Reporter — for the selection from The A T & T Settlement, by Diane Crothers.

University of Cincinnati Law Review — for the selections from Female Wage Discrimination: A Study of the Equal Pay Act 1963–1967, by Murphy.

Valparaiso University Law Review — for the selection from Equal Pay, Equal Employment Opportunity and Equal Enforcement of the Law for Women, by Caruthers Gholson Berger.

Business Week — for the selection from Equal Pay for Women Hits Retailers. Reprinted from the January 29, 1972 issue of Business Week by Special Permission. © 1972 by McGraw-Hill, Inc.

J. Stanley Pottinger and Change Magazine — for the selection from The Drive Toward Equality.

Carnegie Commission on Higher Education — for selections from Opportunities for Women in Higher Education: Their Current Participation, Prospects for the Future, and Recommendations for Action, A Report and Recommendations by The Carnegie Commission on Higher Education, also excerpted in Chapter V. Reprinted with permission. Copyright © 1973 by The Carnegie Foundation for the Advancement of Teaching. All rights reserved.

Bernice Sandler — for the selections from Help From Our Government: WEAL and Contract Compliance, from Letters from Readers: The Pottinger Papers, and from the speech A Feminist Approach to the Women's Colleges.

Commentary — for the selection from HEW and the Universities by Paul Seabury. Reprinted from Commentary by permission. Copyright © 1972 by the American Jewish Committee. Reprinted with the permission of the author.

Basic Books — for the selection from Help From Our Government: WEAL and Contract Compliance by Bernice Sandler in *Academic Women on the Move,* edited by Alice S. Rossi and Ann Calderwood. Copyright © 1973 by the Russell Sage Foundation.

Chapter Three

Thomas Y. Crowell Company, Inc., publisher — for selections from The Future of Marriage. Copyright © 1972 by Jesse Bernard, with permission of the publisher.

The New York University Law Review & Professor John D. Johnston — for the selection from Johnston, "Sex and Property: The Common Law Tradition, the Law School Curriculum, and Developments Toward Equality."

Richard Rapaport — for the selections from Relationship of the Women's Movement to the Passage of the Married Women's Property Acts in the Mid-Nineteenth Century, unpublished paper, Stanford Law School, 1971.

Little, Brown & Company — for selections from Foote, Levy & Sanders, Cases and Materials on Family Law. Copyright © 1966 by the authors. Also for the excerpts from Wigmore, Evidence (3d ed., 1940) appearing in Chapter IV.

The New York University Law Review & Judith Younger — for the selections from Younger, Community Property, Women and the Law School Curriculum.

Grace Blumberg & Carlyn McCaffrey — for the selections from Tax Law Materials, prepared for the AALS Symposium on the Legal Rights of Women, Oct. 20-21, 1972.

Suellen Plover — for the selections from her paper on Trusts and the Mistrusted Widow, prepared at George Washington University Law School, 1971.

The Saturday Review and Marya Mannes — for selections from Mannes & Sheresky, A Radical Guide to Wedlock. Copyright © 1972 by The Saturday Review.

Professor Lenore Weitzman — for selections from A Proposal for Legal Partnerships, in the form used, an unpublished paper prepared at Yale Law School, 1969, later published as Legal Regulation of the Marriage Contract: Tradition and Change; A Proposal for Individual Contracts and Contracts-In-Lieu of Marriage, 62 Calif. L. Rev. (June, 1974).

The publishers of Res Ipsa Loquitur, a publication of Georgetown University Law Center — for the selections from Knisely, The Marriage Contract: A Blueprint (1971).

Kathryn A. Walker — for the selections from Walker & Gauger, The Dollar Value of Household Work, New York State College of Human Ecology, Cornell University, June 1973.

Speiser, Recovery for Wrongful Death, Economic Handbook (1970) — reproduced with the permission of the copyright owner, The Lawyer's Cooperative Publishing Company, Rochester, N.Y.

Johns Hopkins University Press — for selections from Kreps, Sex in the Market Place. Reprinted from American Women at Work (1971).

The Buffalo Law Review — for selections from Blumberg, Sexism in the Code: A Comparative Study of Income Taxation of Working Wives and Mothers (1971).

The University of Pennsylvania Law Review & Fred B. Rothman & Company —

for selections from The Failure of the Work Incentive (WIN) Program; and for the excerpts from Comment: The Purposes of the Corroboration Requirement, appearing in Chapter IV.

The Hastings Law Journal — for selections from Walker, Sex Discrimination in Government Benefit Programs.

The Center for the Study of Public Policy, Cambridge, Massachusetts — for selections from Toward New Arrangements for Child Rearing, Impact Study of Day Care (1971).

The New Republic — for selections from Bourne, What Day Care Ought To Be. Reprinted by permission of the New Republic. Copyright © 1972, Harrison-Blaine of New Jersey, Inc.

Macmillan Publishing Company, Inc. — for the selections from Goode, Women in Divorce. Copyright © 1956 by William J. Goode; and for the excerpt from Goldstein & Katz, The Family and the Law (Tompkins, Report of the Subcommittee on the Family Law Process — Marriage Insurance). Copyright © 1965 by The Free Press, a Division of Macmillan Publishing Company, Inc.

The Wall Street Journal — for selections from Klein, Breaking Up. Excerpted with permission. Copyright © 1970, Dow Jones & Company, Inc. All rights reserved.

The University of Mexico Press — for selections from Kanowitz, Women and the Law. Copyright © 1969, Leo Kanowitz, by permission.

The Northwestern University Law Review (published from 1906 to 1952 as the Illinois Law Review) — for selections from Bradway, Why Pay Alimony.

Edward V. Sparer — for the use of his materials on Income Maintenance.

The Center for Social Welfare Policy and Law, New York — for the selections from Cases and Materials on Welfare Law (1972).

The Vanderbilt Law Review & Margaret J. Gates — for selections from Credit and Discrimination Against Women: Causes and Solutions.

Pantheon Books — for selections from Dorson, ed., The Rights of Americans, What They Are, What They Should Be, New York © 1970.

Chapter Four

Yale Law Journal Company — for selections from "Forcible and Statutory Rape: An Explanation of the Operation and Objectives of the Consent Standard." Reprinted by permission of the Yale Law Journal Company and Fred B. Rothman & Company; and for the selections from "The Rape Corroboration Requirement: Repeal Not Reform" and from "The Sexual Segregation of American Prisons."

American Law Institute — for the selections from The Model Penal Code. Reprinted with permission. Copyright © 1955.

Susan Griffin — for the selection from "The Politics of Rape." Copyright © 1972 by the author.

Criminal Law Review — for selections from Williams, Consent and Public Policy. Copyright © 1962.

The Michigan Law Review & Professor B.J. George, Jr. — for selections from "Legal, Medical and Psychiatric Considerations in the Control of Prostitution."

American Bar Foundation — for the selections from McIntyre, ed., Law Enforcement in the Metropolis. Copyright © American Bar Foundation, 1967.

The University of Chicago Press — for the selections from Levi, An Introduction to Legal Reasoning. Copyright © 1944 by the author and the University of Chicago Press.

Basic Books, Inc. — for the selection from Millet, Prostitution: A Quartet for Female Voices, in Women in Sexist Society (Garrick & Moran, eds., 1971).

Gail Sheehy — for the selections from "Cleaning Up Hell's Bedroom," New York Magazine. Copyright © 1972, Gail Sheehy.

The Editors of the American Criminal Law Review and the American Bar Association — for the selections from Kadish, The Crisis of Overcriminalization; Singer, Women and the Correctional Process; and Rosenbleet & Parriente, Prostitution of the Criminal Law. All copyrighted © by the American Criminal Law Review.

The National Council on Crime and Delinquency — for the selections from Lindsay, Delinquency's Time Bomb (1970).

The Law & Society Review and Kristine Olson Rogers — for selections from "For Her Own Protection. . . .": Conditions of Incarceration for Female Offenders in the State of Connecticut.

Chapter Five

The University of Buffalo Law Review — for selections from O'Neil, Private Universities and Public Law (1968).

Science Magazine, a publication of the American Association for the Advancement of Science, and P.A. Graham — for selections from Women in Academe (1970).

Doubleday & Company, Inc. — for selections from "Feminism, Masculinism and Coeducation," from The Academic Revolution by Christopher Jencks & David Reisman. Copyright © 1968 by Christopher Jencks and David Reisman. Reprinted by permission of Doubleday & Company, Inc.

The University of Minnesota Law Review — for selections from Note, Sex Discrimination in High School Athletics.

New York Magazine — for selections from Harkins, Sex and the City Council. Copyright © 1970 NYM Corp. Reprinted with Permission of New York Magazine.

SUMMARY OF CONTENTS

TABLE OF CONTENTS

Chapter Two. Employment Discrimination

Chapter Three. Sex Role Discrimination in the Law of the Family

Chapter Four. Women and the Criminal Law

Chapter Five. Women's Rights to Control Their Reproductive Capacities, Obtain Equal Education, and Gain Equal Access to Places of Public Accommodation

TABLE OF CASES

Italics indicate principal cases.

SEX DISCRIMINATION AND THE LAW
Causes and Remedies

CHAPTER ONE

Constitutional Law and Feminist History

I. THE PRIVILEGES AND IMMUNITIES OF CITIZENS OF THE UNITED STATES, 1848-1890

AMENDMENT XIV
[Proposed by Congress on June 16, 1866; ratified July 21, 1868]

Section 1. All persons born or naturalized in the United States, and subject to the jurisdiction thereof, are citizens of the United States and of the State wherein they reside. No State shall make or enforce any law which shall abridge the privileges or immunities of citizens of the United States; nor shall any State deprive any person of life, liberty, or property, without due process of law; nor deny to any person within its jurisdiction the equal protection of the laws.

Section 2. Representatives shall be apportioned among the several States according to their respective numbers, counting the whole number of persons in each State, excluding Indians not taxed. But when the right to vote at any election for the choice of electors for President and Vice President of the United States, Representatives in Congress, the Executive and Judicial officers of a State, or the members of the Legislature thereof, is denied to any of the male inhabitants of such State, being twenty-one years of age, and citizens of the United States, or in any way abridged, except for participation in rebellion, or other crime, the basis of representation therein shall be reduced in the proportion which the number of such male citizens shall bear to the whole number of male citizens twenty-one years of age in such State.

DECLARATION OF SENTIMENTS — ADOPTED BY THE
FIRST WOMEN'S RIGHTS CONVENTION
SENECA FALLS, N.Y., JULY 19, 1848
Stanton, Anthony, and Gage, History of Woman Suffrage 70-71 (1881)[1]

The history of mankind is a history of repeated injuries and usurpations on the part of man toward woman, having in direct object the establishment of an absolute tyranny over her. To prove this, let facts be submitted to a candid world.

He has never permitted her to exercise her inalienable right to the elective franchise.

1. Reprinted in Kraditor (ed.), Up From the Pedestal 184-186 (Quadrangle Books 1970).

He has compelled her to submit to laws, in the formation of which she had no voice.

He has withheld from her rights which are given to the most ignorant and degraded men — both natives and foreigners.

Having deprived her of this first right of a citizen, the elective franchise, thereby leaving her without representation in the halls of legislation, he has oppressed her on all sides.

He has made her, if married, in the eye of the law, civilly dead.

He has taken from her all right in property, even to the wages she earns.

He has made her, morally, an irresponsible being, as she can commit many crimes with impunity, provided they be done in the presence of her husband. In the covenant of marriage, she is compelled to promise obedience to her husband, he becoming, to all intents and purposes, her master — the law giving him power to deprive her of her liberty, and to administer chastisement.

He has so framed the laws of divorce, as to what shall be the proper causes, and in case of separation, to whom the guardianship of the children shall be given, as to be wholly regardless of the happiness of women — the law, in all cases, going upon a false supposition of the supremacy of man, and giving all power into his hands.

After depriving her of all rights as a married woman, if single, and the owner of property, he has taxed her to support a government which recognizes her only when her property can be made profitable to it.

He has monopolized nearly all the profitable employments, and from those she is permitted to follow, she receives but a scanty remuneration. He closes against her all the avenues to wealth and distinction which he considers most honorable to himself. As a teacher of theology, medicine, or law, she is not known.

He has denied her the facilities for obtaining a thorough education, all colleges being closed against her.

He allows her in Church, as well as State, but a subordinate position, claiming Apostolic authority for her exclusion from the ministry, and, with some exceptions, from any public participation in the affairs of the Church.

He has created a false public sentiment by giving to the world a different code of morals for men and women, by which moral delinquencies which exclude women from society, are not only tolerated, but deemed of little account in man.

He has usurped the prerogative of Jehovah himself, claiming it as his right to assign for her a sphere of action, when that belongs to her conscience and to her God.

He has endeavored, in every way that he could, to destroy her confidence in her own powers, to lessen her self-respect, and to make her willing to lead a dependent and abject life.

Now, in view of this entire disfranchisement of one-half the people of this country, their social and religious degradation — in view of the unjust laws above mentioned, and because women do feel themselves aggrieved, oppressed, and fraudulently deprived of their most sacred rights, we insist that they have immediate admission to all the rights and privileges which belong to them as citizens of the United States.

In entering upon the great work before us, we anticipate no small amount of misconception, misrepresentation, and ridicule; but we shall use every instrumentality within our power to effect our object. We shall employ agents, circulate tracts, petition the State and National legislatures, and endeavor to enlist the pulpit and the press in our behalf. We hope this Convention will be followed by a series of Conventions embracing every part of the country.

A. A Brief History of the Early Feminist Movement[2]

The remarkable document reprinted in part above was approved at a meeting attended by about three hundred people, called by Elizabeth Cady Stanton and Lucretia Mott. These two also drafted the declaration, basing it on the Declaration of Independence. As was the case with virtually all of the founders of the women's rights movement, these two women were first abolitionists. In fact, the idea for a women's rights convention was born when the two met each other in 1840 at the World Anti-Slavery convention in London, where women who had been fighting beside men for the same cause were excluded from participation. The Motts had come to the abolitionist movement from their ardent Quaker faith; Lucretia Mott, who had been ordained a minister at the age of twenty-eight by her Quaker meeting and was a founder of the first Female Anti-Slavery Society, was already a public figure when she went to the 1840 convention. Elizabeth Cady had married Henry B. Stanton, an abolitionist leader, earlier that year. Through him she became friends with other abolitionists, including the Grimké sisters from South Carolina. The sisters had already caused controversy by speaking publicly against slavery to audiences composed of both men and women.

It is an interesting historical note that Elizabeth Stanton's inclusion of the ballot in the list of proposed reforms attached to the Declaration of Sentiments was "so advanced that Mrs. Mott feared its inclusion would hurt the infant movement."[3] But Frederick Douglass supported Stanton, and the demand for woman suffrage was not deleted.

Following Seneca Falls, other women joined the young feminist movement and helped with the arduous work of winning political support for their cause through speaking tours, the gathering of thousands of signatures on petitions to the state legislatures, and the calling of women's rights conventions across the country. Two of the most important leaders who emerged from this work were Susan B. Anthony and Lucy Stone.

Susan B. Anthony came from an abolitionist and temperance background and joined the movement in 1851 after she met Elizabeth Cady Stanton. A superb organizer, Anthony's talents complemented Stanton's as thinker, writer, and speaker in a working partnership that was to last for half a century. Lucy Stone, who became famous for her courage and oratorical ability, was in 1847 one of the first women to graduate from the "regular" as opposed to the "literary" course at Oberlin. She became a paid lecturer for the Anti-Slavery Society, with whom she had a compromise arrangement allowing her to lecture on women's rights if she spoke about abolition on Saturdays and Sundays. In 1855 she married Henry Blackwell, but kept her own name. Rather then ending her career as a feminist, her marriage "made two advocates for women's rights where there had been one."[4]

Many of the women who joined the movement in this period worked for women's rights as well as for those of black men, and urged the logical nexus between the two. But not all abolitionists believed in joining the two issues, and there was substantial opposition to allowing women to speak on women's rights from abolitionist platforms. In fact, the argument that the abolitionist cause would be hurt by linking its credibility with the impractical and unpopular notion of women's rights repeatedly split the abolitionist movement in many states.[5]

---

2. This account is largely based on Flexner, Century of Struggle 45-50, 68-77, 84-90, 142-153 (Atheneum ed. 1970).

3. Kraditor, Ideas of the Woman Suffrage Movement 1890–1920, 1 (Anchor Books ed. 1971).

4. Flexner, supra, at 70.

5. Kraditor, Means and Ends in American Abolitionism, Introduction and ch. 3 (1965).

B. The Civil War Amendments

When the Civil War started, most women temporarily abandoned convention-going and other efforts to achieve their own rights and were concerned only with helping the war effort and ending slavery. As Kraditor records, "After the war's end they resumed their demands for equal rights and the vote, expecting the Republican Party, out of gratitude for the women's war activities, to respond more favorably than before. To their dismay and disillusionment, the party leaders informed them that 'this is the Negro's hour,' and that the women must wait for their rights."[6]

So grave was their disappointment at the attitude of the men in power that some feminist leaders, including Stanton and Anthony, opposed passage of the Fourteenth Amendment, which in Section 2 wrote the word "male" into the Constitution for the first time.

However, in the view of Eleanor Flexner, a leading historian of the early women's movement in America, the rights of women and the rights of blacks were politically quite different kinds of issues, although, as Stanton and Anthony argued, they were logically and morally very similar.[7]

> Slavery and the condition of the Negro had been a boiling national issue for thirty-five years; a war had been fought over it. No such intensity of feeling existed yet regarding the status of women, even among the women themselves, excepting in a still relatively small group. Opinion in Congress and throughout the North was concerned with assuring the vote for the Negro; it was relatively uninterested in how such a controversial measure would affect women.

Of course, as Flexner also points out, the Republican party expected to reap two million votes from the newly enfranchised blacks; joining black suffrage with the unpopular issue of woman suffrage would only jeopardize this windfall. Politically, the issue of women's rights was simply unappealing, and there was no reason to expect political leaders to put the justice of the women's cause above practical considerations.

Two years after the Fourteenth Amendment was introduced in Congress, the Fifteenth Amendment was proposed as a further protection of Negro suffrage. Feminists argued that the word "sex" should be added after "on account of race, color, or previous condition of servitude." But, again, the attempt to draw the attention of the national legislature to the parallel between the status of blacks and of women was fruitless.[8]

1. Occupational Choice

Having failed in political efforts to be included expressly in the Fourteenth and Fifteenth Amendments, feminists next turned to seeking the benefit of the privileges and immunities clause by arguing that it must include, for *all* citizens, a broad spectrum of civil rights, including the right to choose one's occupation and the right to vote. One of the first women to bring a case making such arguments was Myra Colby Bradwell.[9] Bradwell studied law under her husband's tutelage from the time of their marriage in

6. Kraditor, Ideas of the Woman Suffrage Movement 1890–1920, 2 (1971).

7. Flexner, supra, at 145.

8. The decision of Stanton and Anthony to lobby against the passage of the Fourteenth Amendment, though unsuccessful in preventing the insertion of the word "male" into the Constitution or obtaining woman suffrage at the same time as black suffrage, had important consequences for the women's movement. Their disagreement with other suffrage leaders over this and other issues led in 1869 to the formation of two separate organizations: the National Woman Suffrage Association, led by Stanton and Anthony, and the somewhat more conservative American Woman Suffrage Association, led by Lucy Stone and Henry Ward Beecher. The split lasted until 1890, when respectability triumphed over radicalism, and the two merged into the National American Woman Suffrage Association. For a discussion of the split and its consequences, see Flexner, supra, chs. X and XVI; O'Neill, Everyone Was Brave 14-30 (1969).

9. 1 James, James, and Boyer (eds.), Notable American Women 1607–1950, 223-225 (1971), is the source for all the biographical material on Myra Bradwell, who lived from 1831 to 1894.

1852. In 1868, after bearing four children, running a private school in Tennessee with her husband, and doing civic work during and after the Civil War, she started a weekly legal newspaper. Called the Chicago Legal News, it quickly became the most important legal publication in the West and Midwest. Bradwell was an avowed feminist, active in suffrage organizations and instrumental in obtaining the passage in Illinois of legislation removing women's legal disabilities.

In 1869, Myra Bradwell applied for admission to the Illinois bar. She passed the examination but was denied admission by the state supreme court because she was a woman, despite the precedent of Arabella Mansfield of Iowa, who earlier that year had become the first woman regularly admitted to practice law in the United States. Bradwell then took her case to the Supreme Court of the United States under the Fourteenth Amendment, arguing through her counsel, Senator Matthew H. Carpenter (R. Wis.), that:[10]

> . . . the profession of the law . . . is an avocation open to every citizen of the United States. And while the Legislature may prescribe qualifications for entering upon this pursuit, they cannot, under the guise of fixing qualifications, exclude a class of citizens from admission to the bar. . . . [A] qualification, to which a whole class of citizens never can attain, is not a regulation of admission to the bar, but is, as to such citizens, a prohibition.
>
> If this provision [the Privileges and Immunities Clause of the Fourteenth Amendment] does not open all the professions, all the avocations, all the methods by which a man may pursue happiness, to the colored as well as the white man, then the Legislatures of the States may exclude colored men from all the honorable pursuits of life, and compel them to support their existence in a condition of servitude. And if this provision does protect the colored citizen, then it protects every citizen, black or white, male or female.

BRADWELL v. ILLINOIS
83 U.S. (16 Wall.) 130, 21 L. Ed. 442 (1873)

Mr. Justice MILLER.

We agree . . . that there are privileges and immunities belonging to citizens of the United States, in that relation and character, and that it is these and these alone which a State is forbidden to abridge. But the right to admission to practice in the courts of a State is not one of them. This right in no sense depends on citizenship of the United States.

The opinion just delivered in the Slaughter-House Cases renders elaborate argument in the present case unnecessary; for, unless we are wholly and radically mistaken in the principles on which those cases are decided, the right to control and regulate the granting of license to practice law in the courts of a State is one of those powers which are not transferred for its protection to the Federal government, and its exercise is in no manner governed or controlled by citizenship of the United States in the party seeking such license.

Concurring Opinion of Mr. Justice BRADLEY Joined by Justices FIELD and SWAYNE.

I concur in the judgment of the court in this case . . . but not for the reasons specified in the opinion just read.

The claim that, under the Fourteenth Amendment of the Constitution, which declares that no State shall make or enforce any law which shall abridge the privileges and immunities of citizens of the United States, the statute law of Illinois, or the common law prevailing in that State, can no longer be set up as a barrier against the right of females to pursue any lawful employment for a livelihood (the practice of law included),

---

10. 2 Stanton, Anthony, and Gage, History of Woman Suffrage 620 (1887).

assumes that it is one of the privileges and immunities of women as citizens to engage in any and every profession, occupation, or employment in civil life.

It certainly cannot be affirmed, as an historical fact, that this has ever been established as one of the fundamental privileges and immunities of the sex. On the contrary, the civil law, as well as nature herself, has always recognized a wide difference in the respective spheres and destinies of man and woman. Man is, or should be, woman's protector and defender. The natural and proper timidity and delicacy which belongs to the female sex evidently unfits it for many of the occupations of civil life. The constitution of the family organization, which is founded in the divine ordinance, as well as in the nature of things, indicates the domestic sphere as that which properly belongs to the domain and functions of womanhood. The harmony, not to say identity, of interests and views which belong, or should belong, to the family institution is repugnant to the idea of a woman adopting a distinct and independent career from that of her husband. So firmly fixed was this sentiment in the founders of the common law that it became a maxim of that system of jurisprudence that a woman had no legal existence separate from her husband, who was regarded as her head and representative in the social state; and, notwithstanding some recent modifications of this civil status, many of the special rules of law flowing from and dependent upon this cardinal principle still exist in full force in most States. One of these is, that a married woman is incapable, without her husband's consent, of making contracts which shall be binding on her or him. This very incapacity was one circumstance which the Supreme Court of Illinois deemed important in rendering a married woman incompetent fully to perform the duties and trusts that belong to the office of an attorney and counselor.[11]

It is true that many women are unmarried and not affected by any of the duties, complications, and incapacities arising out of the married state, but these are exceptions to the general rule. The paramount destiny and mission of woman are to fulfil the noble and benign offices of wife and mother. This is the law of the Creator. And the rules of civil society must be adapted to the general constitution of things, and cannot be based upon exceptional cases.

The humane movements of modern society, which have for their object the multiplication of avenues for woman's advancement, and of occupations adapted to her condition and sex, have my heartiest concurrence. But I am not prepared to say that it is one of her fundamental rights and privileges to be admitted into every office and position, including those which require highly special qualifications and demanding special responsibilities.[12]

---

11. This argument about married women's common law disabilities was totally inapplicable to Myra Bradwell, who had been given a special charter which enabled her to become president of both the Chicago Legal News and a printing, binding, and publishing company, and, of course, to do the necessary contracting and other business transactions for both. 1 James, James, and Boyer, supra, at 224. — Eds.

12. In 1872, between Myra Bradwell's appeal to the Supreme Court of the United States and the unfavorable decision, the Illinois legislature had passed an act giving all persons, regardless of sex, freedom in selecting an occupation. Although Myra Bradwell did not again apply for admission to the bar, in 1890, when she was fifty-nine, the Illinois Supreme Court, acting on her original motion of 1869, admitted her to the practice of law in that state; two years later she was admitted to practice before the Supreme Court of the United States. 1 James, James, and Boyer, supra, at 225.

When she died in 1894, the American Law Review, 28:278-283, wrote in memoriam:

"A gentle and noiseless woman, her tenderness and refinement making her character all the more effective, Mrs. Bradwell was one of those who lived their creed instead of preaching it. She did not spend her days proclaiming on the rostrum the rights of woman but quietly, none the less effectively, set to work to clear away the barriers."

Two of her children, a son and a daughter, were lawyers. — Eds.

NOTES: FREEDOM OF OCCUPATIONAL CHOICE
AS A PRIVILEGE AND IMMUNITY OF CITIZENSHIP

1. The extremely conservative view in *Bradwell* of the meaning inherent in the words "privileges . . . of citizens" was presaged only the day before by the Slaughter-House Cases, 83 U.S. (16 Wall.) 36, 21 L. Ed. 394 (1873), in which butchers sought federal court protection from Louisiana legislation creating a monopoly of the slaughterhouse trade. The statute required all butchers in an extensive district to use a particular slaughterhouse and pay a toll for the use. The plaintiff butchers argued that this requirement meant they could not work at all, and that it was a privilege of all citizens to pursue their professions, immune from unreasonable government regulation. The majority of the Court ruled that the privileges and immunities of United States citizens, protected by the Fourteenth Amendment, were only those rights which owed their existence to the existence of the federal government, its national character, its Constitution, or its laws. These rights included free access to seaports; the right to come to the seat of government to assert any claim one may have against it, to seek its protection, to share in its offices, and to engage in administering its functions; and the right to use the navigable waters of the United States — but not freedom of enterprise and occupational choice, a right which predated the federal Constitution and was therefore within the constitutional and legislative power of the states, and beyond that of the federal government. The Fourteenth Amendment, according to the Court, could not conceivably have been intended by Congress to transfer the protection of basic civil rights from the states to the federal government. In passing, the Court stated its belief about the coverage of the Equal Protection Clause of the Fourteenth Amendment: "We doubt very much whether any action of a State not directed by way of discrimination against the negroes as a class, or on account of their race, will ever be held to come within the purview of this provision."[13] Justice Field, who joined Justice Bradley's comments about the privileges of women citizens in *Bradwell*, dissented in the Slaughter-House Cases, stating:[14]

> The first clause of the Fourteenth Amendment changes this whole subject [the issue of who is a citizen of the United States]. . . . A citizen of a State is now only a citizen of the United States residing in that State. The fundamental rights, privileges, and immunities which belong to him as a free man and a free citizen, now belong to him as a citizen of the United States, and are not dependent upon his citizenship of any State.

Even more vigorously, Justice Bradley wrote in dissent:[15]

> In this free country, the people of which inherited certain traditionary rights and privileges from their ancestors, citizenship means something. It has certain privileges and immunities attached to it which the government, whether restricted by express or implied limitations, cannot take away or impair. . . . In my view, a law which prohibits a large class of citizens from adopting a lawful employment, or from following a lawful employment previously adopted, does deprive them of liberty as well as property, without due process of law. Their right of choice is a portion of their liberty; their occupation is their property. Such a law also deprives those citizens of the equal protection of the laws, contrary to the last clause of the section.

Can Bradley's argument in the Slaughter-House Cases be reconciled with his position in *Bradwell*? Compare the argument made by the plaintiff in Minor v. Happersett, infra, subsection 2-b.

13. 21 L. Ed. at 410.
14. 21 L. Ed. at 414.
15. 21 L. Ed. at 423.

2. The Slaughter-House Cases were argued on January 11, 1872, and *Bradwell* on January 18, 1872. The opinion in *Bradwell* was scheduled to be handed down at the same time as *Slaughter-House,* but was actually announced the next day. Because the cases were *sub judice* during the fourteen-month period of decision, it is not farfetched to speculate that the restriction of the Privileges and Immunities Clause in *Slaughter-House* was influenced by the Court's realization that a broad interpretation would necessarily change the status of women.

Another interrelationship between *Slaughter-House* and *Bradwell* is that Matthew Carpenter, one of the great advocates of the day, was involved in both, although on opposite sides of the issue. He argued against the butchers that the Privileges and Immunities Clause did not protect that common calling, and for Myra Bradwell that the Constitution must include the right of a citizen to practice law. The fact that he was arguing these inconsistent positions, practically at once, may partially account for the narrowness of the approach he took in *Bradwell.* See footnote 29 infra.

Carpenter's ability to argue these two cases so close together without the Court's, or any historian's, remarking the inconsistency, may well be a reflection of the lightness with which Myra Bradwell's case was regarded. Fairman points out:[16]

> While Chicago lawyers could not fail to respect "our Myra's" remarkable attainments, their profession was inclined, the Illinois court had remarked, "if not to stand immovable upon the ancient ways, at least to make no hot haste in measures of reform. . . ." Her serious effort to win recognition as a lawyer was commonly treated as somewhat whimsical.

3. A number of commentators have suggested that, as Justice Field contended, decisions such as *Bradwell* and the Slaughter-House Cases frustrated the intent of Congress to change drastically the balance of power between the federal and state governments by transferring the protection of basic civil rights from the states to the federal government. For example, Carr states:[17]

> The meaning and purpose of these Civil War Amendments has been the subject of much controversy. But one can build a strong case contending that their congressional framers meant them to serve as a basis for a positive, comprehensive federal program — a program defining fundamental civil rights protected by federal machinery against both state and private encroachment. Perhaps the best evidence supporting this contention is that during and just after the period when the Amendments were framed, Congress passed seven statutes establishing just such a federal program.

Many of these statutes were invalidated by the Supreme Court. For further historical and legal materials on the Civil War Amendments and their interpretation by the Supreme Court during the Reconstruction era, see 2 Emerson, Haber, and Dorsen, Political and Civil Rights in the United States 1004-1034 (student ed. 1967).

2. Woman Suffrage

At about the same time as Myra Bradwell was bringing suit to gain her right to practice law, other feminists were trying a more direct tactic to use the new constitutional provisions: going to the polls on election day and attempting to cast their ballots.

History of Woman Suffrage records the efforts of women to vote in 1871 and 1872 in Missouri, New Hampshire, Connecticut, New York, Ohio, Illinois, Pennsylvania, California, and Michigan.[18] The most notorious case that resulted was that of Susan B. Anthony. She and thirteen other women voted on November 5, 1872, in Rochester, New

16. Fairman, History of the Supreme Court of the United States, Vol. VI, Reconstruction and Reunion, 1864–88 (The Oliver Wendell Holmes Devise), p. 1365 (part one, 1971).
17. Carr, Federal Protection of Civil Rights 36 (1947).
18. 1 Stanton, Anthony, and Gage, History of Woman Suffrage 586-756 (1882).

York. Within two weeks, they were arrested on the federal criminal charge of "having voted without the lawful right to vote," which carried a possible three-year jail term.[19]

a. The Trial of Susan B. Anthony

The trial of the United States of America v. Susan B. Anthony, 24 F. Cas. 829 (No. 14459) (N.D.N.Y. 1873), opened on June 17, 1873. Anthony's defense was that the Fourteenth Amendment's Privileges and Immunities Clause gave all citizens, including women, the right to vote regardless of state law. The judge would not allow Anthony to testify on her own behalf. After five hours of argument by her attorney and the district attorney, the judge — without leaving the bench — drew a previously prepared written opinion from his pocket and read it. He ruled that the Fourteenth Amendment was inapplicable and directed the all-male jury to bring in a guilty verdict. When Anthony's counsel, protesting this clearly unconstitutional procedure, requested that the jury be polled, the judge instead summarily discharged the jurors.

The next day the following interchange occurred in court:[20]

> *Judge Hunt:* (Ordering the defendant to stand up), Has the prisoner anything to say why sentence shall not be pronounced?
>
> *Miss Anthony:* Yes, your honor, I have many things to say; for in your ordered verdict of guilty, you have trampled under foot every vital principle of our government. My natural rights, my civil rights, my political rights, my judicial rights, are all alike ignored. Robbed of the fundamental privilege of citizenship, I am degraded from the status of a citizen to that of a subject; and not only myself individually, but all of my sex, are, by your honor's verdict, doomed to political subjection under this, so-called, form of government.
>
> *Judge Hunt:* The Court cannot listen to a rehearsal of arguments the prisoner's counsel has already consumed three hours in presenting.
>
> *Miss Anthony:* May it please your honor, I am not arguing the question, but simply stating the reasons why sentence cannot, in justice, be pronounced against me. Your denial of my citizen's right to vote, is the denial of my right of consent as one of the governed, the denial of my right of representation as one of the taxed, the denial of my right to a trial by a jury of my peers as an offender against law, therefore, the denial of my sacred rights to life, liberty, property and —
>
> *Judge Hunt:* The Court cannot allow the prisoner to go on.
>
> *Miss Anthony:* But your honor will not deny me this one and only poor privilege of protest against this high-handed outrage upon my citizen's rights. May it please the Court to remember that since the day of my arrest last November, this is the first time that either myself or any person of my disfr. ~chised class has been allowed a word of defense before judge or jury —
>
> *Judge Hunt:* The prisoner must sit down — the Court cannot allow it.
>
> *Miss Anthony:* All of my prosecutors, from the 8th ward corner grocery politician, who entered the complaint, to the United States Marshal, Commissioner, District Attorney, District Judge, your honor on the bench, not one is my peer, but each and all are my political sovereigns; and had your honor submitted my case to the jury, as was clearly your duty, even then I should have had just cause of protest, for not one

19. Section 19 of the Civil Rights Act of 1870, 16 Stat. 144. The purpose of this law was to make it a federal offense for white voters to cancel out black votes by voting more than once. The use against Anthony of a statute for a never-intended purpose is typical of political trials. Another indication of the political nature of the Anthony case was the watchful presence, throughout the prosecution, of Roscoe Conkling, the senator from New York and close political aide to President Grant. Burnham and Knight, The United States v. Susan B. Anthony, Ms. Magazine, Nov. 1972, pp. 99, 100.

20. Koedt, Levine, and Firestone (eds.), Radical Feminism 17-19 (Quadrangle/New York Times Book Co. 1973).

Versions of the trial of Susan B. Anthony also appear in the following works: 2 Stanton, Anthony, and Gage, History of Woman Suffrage 648-691 (1882); 1 Harper, The Life and Work of Susan B. Anthony 431-441 (1898); Catt and Shuler, Woman Suffrage and Politics 99-106 (American Library Paperback ed. 1970); Schneir (ed.), Feminism: The Essential Historical Writings 133-136 (1972). See also Susan B. Anthony's Constitutional Argument in Kraditor (ed.), Up From the Pedestal 243 (Quadrangle ed. 1970).

of those men was my peer; but, native or foreign born, white or black, rich or poor, educated or ignorant, awake or asleep, sober or drunk, each and every man of them was my political superior; hence, in no sense, my peer. Even, under such circumstances, a commoner of England, tried before a jury of Lords, would have far less cause to complain than should I, a woman, tried before a jury of men. Even my counsel, the Hon. Henry R. Selden, who has argued my cause so ably, so earnestly, so unanswerably before your honor, is my political sovereign. Precisely as no disfranchised person is entitled to sit upon a jury, and no woman is entitled to the franchise, so, none but a regularly admitted lawyer is allowed to practice in the courts, and no woman can gain admission to the bar — hence, jury, judge, counsel, must all be of the superior class.

Judge Hunt: The Court must insist — the prisoner has been tried according to the established forms of law.

Miss Anthony: Yes, your honor, but by forms of law all made by men, interpreted by men, administered by men, in favor of men, and against women; and hence, your honor's ordered verdict of guilty, against a United States citizen for the exercise of *"that citizen's right to vote,"* simply because that citizen was a woman and not a man. But, yesterday, the same man made forms of law, declared it a crime punishable with $1,000 fine and six months' imprisonment, for you, or me, or any of us, to give a cup of cold water, a crust of bread, or a night's shelter to a panting fugitive as he was tracking his way to Canada. And every man or woman in whose veins coursed a drop of human sympathy violated that wicked law, reckless of consequences, and was justified in so doing. As then, the slaves who got their freedom must take it over, or under, or through the unjust forms of law, precisely so, now, must women, to get their right to a voice in this government, take it; and I have taken mine, and mean to take it at every possible opportunity.

Judge Hunt: The Court orders the prisoner to sit down. It will not allow another word.

Miss Anthony: When I was brought before your honor for trial, I hoped for a broad and liberal interpretation of the Constitution and its recent amendments, that should declare all United States citizens under its protecting aegis — that should declare equality of rights the national guarantee to all persons born or naturalized in the United States. But failing to get this justice — failing, even, to get a trial by a jury *not* of my peers — I ask not leniency at your hands — but rather the full rigors of the law.

Judge Hunt: The Court must insist — (Here the prisoner sat down.)

Judge Hunt: The prisoner will stand up. (Here Miss Anthony arose again.)

The sentence of the Court is that you pay a fine of one hundred dollars and the costs of the prosecution.

Miss Anthony: May it please your honor, I shall never pay a dollar of your unjust penalty. All the stock in trade I possess is a $10,000 debt, incurred by publishing my paper — The Revolution — four years ago, the sole object of which was to educate all women to do precisely as I have done, rebel against your man-made, unjust, unconstitutional forms of law, that tax, fine, imprison and hang women, while they deny them the right of representation in the government; and I shall work on with might and main to pay every dollar of that honest debt, but not a penny shall go to this unjust claim. And I shall earnestly and persistently continue to urge all women to the practical recognition of the old revolutionary maxim, that "Resistance to tyranny is obedience to God."

Judge Hunt: Madam, the Court will not order you committed until the fine is paid.

Before trial, Anthony had been briefly imprisoned, and would have been able to take her case directly to the United States Supreme Court by writ of habeas corpus if her counsel had not, without her knowledge and against her wishes, paid her bail of $1,000. Likewise, Judge Hunt's refusal to enforce his judgment against her prevented her from going to prison a second time and seeking direct Supreme Court review of the case. The fine was never paid.

b. A Woman's Suffrage Case in the Supreme Court

The only case arising from the attempts of women to vote under the authority of the Fourteenth Amendment that reached the Supreme Court was brought by Virginia Minor.[21] Minor had actively supported the Union in the Civil War, working in a women's auxiliary of the Western Sanitary Commission, and helping destitute freedmen and white refugees who swarmed to St. Louis. When the auxiliary disbanded in 1865, Minor and several other women turned to their own rights. She was the first woman in Missouri to take a public stand for suffrage; after an unsuccessful petition to the state legislature to include women in a proposed constitutional amendment extending suffrage to black men, she served as the first president of the Woman Suffrage Association.

In 1872, Virginia Minor with her husband, Francis, filed suit against a St. Louis registrar who, acting under a clause of the state constitution that specifically barred women from voting, refused to register her. The Missouri Supreme Court ruled that the states had had the power to deny women the vote before the Fourteenth Amendment, and that the amendment's passage had not changed that power.

In the brief for their appeal to the Supreme Court, the Minors made both practical and legal arguments.[22] They began with the practical:[23]

> We think the chief difficulty in this case is one of fact rather than of law. The practice is against the plaintiff. The States, with one exception, which we shall notice hereafter more in detail, have uniformly claimed and exercised the right to act, as to the matter of suffrage, just as they pleased — to limit or extend it, as they saw proper. And this is the popular idea on the subject. Men accept it as a matter of fact, and take for granted it must be right. So in the days of African slavery, thousands believed it to be right — even a Divine institution. But this belief has passed away; and, in like manner, this doctrine of the right of the States to exercise unlimited and absolute control over the elective franchise of citizens of the United States, must and will give way to a truer and better understanding of the subject. The plaintiff's case is simply one of the means by which this end will ultimately be reached.

In the remainder of their brief, the Minors invoked a broad range of constitutional provisions, including the First Amendment (with the intriguing argument that voting is a form of free expression) and the Thirteenth Amendment (arguing that to be deprived of the franchise is to be placed in a condition of involuntary servitude). However, their main contention was that voting was one of the privileges and immunities of United States citizenship, both under the original Constitution and under the newly adopted Fourteenth Amendment. To support this interpretation of the Constitution, they used several arguments. One concentrated on the fundamental nature, in a democratic system, of the right to vote. A second was that voting for national officers was a right which depended for its existence on the existence of the federal government itself, and therefore must be a privilege of national rather than state citizenship. (Although they did not make an explicit reference, presumably this argument was based on the definition of privileges and immunities set forth in the Slaughter-House Cases; see Notes: Freedom of Occupational Choice as a Privilege and Immunity of Citizenship, supra.) A third strand of argument contended that the Fourteenth Amendment was the sole piece of affirmative legislation that could possibly be interpreted as conferring suffrage on black people, and that if it conferred suffrage on blacks, it must, by the same token, have conferred suffrage on women. The selections which follow illustrate the interplay of these arguments:[24]

21. 2 James, James, and Boyer (eds.), Notable American Women 1607–1950, 550-551 (1971), is the source of all the biographical material on Virginia Minor.

22. Excerpts from this brief are included in Kraditor, Up From the Pedestal, supra, at 230-243. Quotations from the brief will be cited to both the official version and the Kraditor anthology.

23. Brief for Plaintiff in Error at 11, Minor v. Happersett, 88 U.S. (21 Wall.) 162, 22 L. Ed. 627 (1875); Kraditor, id. at 233.

24. Brief for Plaintiff in Error at 26 et seq.; Kraditor, id. at 238-241.

. . . In voting for Federal officers he [the citizen] exercises the freeman's right to take part in the government of his own creation, and he does this . . . in his . . . capacity of [sic] a citizen of the United States. . . . Clearly, then, the right of a citizen of the United States to vote for Federal officers can only be exercised under the authority or sovereignty of the United States . . . and consequently the citizen of the United States could not justly have been deprived of such right by the State, even before the adoption of the XIV Amdnement.

But whatever doubt there may have been as to this, we hold that the adoption of the XIV Amendment put an end to it and placed the matter beyond controversy. The history of that Amendment shows that it was designed as a limitation on the powers of the States, in many important particulars, and its language is clear and unmistakable. "No State shall make or enforce any law which shall abridge the privileges and immunities of citizens of the United States." Of course all the citizens of the United States are by this protected in the enjoyment of their privileges and immunities. Among the privileges, that of voting is the highest and greatest. To an American citizen there can be none greater or more highly to be prized; and the preservation of this privilege to the citizens of the United States respectively is, by this Amendment, placed under the immediate supervision and care of the Government of the United States, who are thus charged with its fulfillment and guaranty. . . .

Whence, then, does [the Negro] derive [the ballot]? There is but one reply. The XIV Amendment conferred upon the negro race in this country citizenship of the United States, and the ballot followed as an incident to that condition. Or, to use the more forcible language of this Court, in the Slaughter-house cases (16 Wall., 71), "the negro having, by the XIV Amendment, been declared a citizen of the United States, is thus made a voter in every State of the Union." If this be true of the negro citizen of the United States, it is equally true of the woman citizen. . . .

. . . if the Fourteenth Amendment does not secure the ballot to woman, neither does it to the negro; for it does not in terms confer the ballot upon any one. As we have already shown, it is the altered condition of citizenship that secures to the negro this right; but this plaintiff might well reply, I was born to that condition and yet am denied its privileges. . . .

They also emphasized the relationship of this basic right to other rights and duties of citizenship that women admittedly shared:[25]

. . . There can be no division of citizenship, either of its rights or its duties. There can be no half-way citizenship. Woman, as a citizen of the United States, is entitled to all the benefits of that position, and liable to all its obligations, or to none. Only citizens are permitted to pre-empt land, obtain passports, etc., all of which woman can do; and, on the other hand, she is taxed (without her "consent") in further recognition of her citizenship; and yet, as to this chief privilege of all, she is forbidden to exercise it.

Besides the problem recognized by the Minors at the outset — that the practice of almost all states had long been against them — they had to deal with two other difficulties in order to establish their interpretation of the Privileges and Immunities Clause. First, passage of the Fifteenth Amendment undercut their theory that it was the Fourteenth Amendment that conferred suffrage on Negroes. Second, the power to fix qualifications for federal electors remitted to the states by Article I, §2, of the Constitution was apparently unlimited (except for the limitations imposed by the Fifteenth Amendment). The Minors' argument with regard to the Fifteenth Amendment was short: they remarked in passing that it had no direct bearing on their case,[26]

25. Brief for Plaintiff in Error, id. at 13; Kraditor, id. at 235.
26. Brief for Plaintiff in Error, id. at 31; Kraditor, id. at 239.

... inasmuch as this Amendment (the Fifteenth) is merely prohibitory — not conferring any right, but treating the ballot in the hands of the negro as an existing fact, and forbidding his deprivation thereof.

Later they observed:[27]

... as we desire to meet every possible objection, we think this a proper place to notice an argument sometimes put forward, based upon the XV Amendment. ... As this Amendment says, that the right of citizens of the United States to vote shall not be denied or abridged by the United States, or by any State, on account of race, color, or previous condition of servitude, it is claimed by some that it may be abridged on other grounds. But ... the IX Amendment to the Constitution effectually puts an end to the application of this principle by declaring that the enumeration in the Constitution of certain rights shall not be construed to deny or disparage others retained by the people. ...

As to Article I, §2, they argued that there was an important distinction between the power to set qualifications for voting, which the states admittedly possessed, and the power to restrict or limit suffrage, which they argued was beyond state authority. They explained the distinction as follows:[28]

It is to this Constitution ... we must look for the limitations, if any, that may be placed upon the political rights of the people or citizens of the United States. A limitation not found there, or authorized by that instrument, cannot be legally exercised by any lesser or inferior jurisdiction.

But the subject of suffrage (or the qualifications of electors, as the Constitution terms it) is simply remitted to the States by the Constitution, to be regulated by them; not to limit or restrict the right of suffrage, but to carry the same fully into effect. It is impossible to believe that anything more than this was intended. In the first place, it would be inconsistent and at variance with the idea of the supremacy of the Federal government; and, next, if the absolute, ultimate, and unconditional control of the matter had been intended to be given to the States, it would have been so expressed. It would not have been left to doubt or implication. In so important a matter as suffrage, the chief of all political rights or privileges, by which, indeed, life, liberty, and all others are guarded and maintained ... we repeat, it is impossible to conceive that this was intended to be left wholly and entirely at the discretion of the States. ...

We say, then, that the States may regulate, but they have no right to prohibit the franchise to citizens of the United States. They may prescribe the qualifications of the electors. They may require that they shall be of a certain age, be of sane mind, be free from crime, etc., because these are conditions for the good of the whole, and to which all citizens, sooner or later, may attain. But to single out a class of citizens and say to them, "Notwithstanding you possess all these qualifications, you shall never vote, or take part in your government," what is it but a bill of attainder? ...

A proper construction of Art. 1, Sec. 2 of the Constitution of the United States will further demonstrate the proposition we are endeavoring to uphold. That section is as follows:

"Article 1, Section 2. The House of Representatives shall be composed of members chosen every second year by the people of the several States; and the electors in each State shall have the qualifications for electors of the most numerous branch of the State Legislature."

This section consists of two clauses, but in neither is there a word as to the sex of the elector. He, or she, must be one of the people, or "citizens," as they are designated in the Constitution, that is all. ...

The right to vote is very different from the qualification necessary in a voter. A person may have the right to vote, and yet not possess the necessary qualifications

27. Brief for Plaintiff in Error, id at 31 et seq.; Kraditor, id. at 241.
28. Brief for Plaintiff in Error, id at 21 et seq.; Kraditor, id. at 234-237.

for exercising it. In this case, the right to vote is derived from the Federal Constitution, which designates the class of persons who may exercise it, and provides that the Federal elector shall conform to the regulations of the State, so far as time, place, and manner of exercising it are concerned. But it is clear that under this authority the State has no right to lay down an arbitrary and impossible rule.[29]

MINOR v. HAPPERSETT
88 U.S. (21 Wall.) 162, 22 L. Ed. 627 (1875)

Mr. Chief Justice WAITE delivered the opinion of the Court:

This was an action brought in the Circuit Court of St. Louis County, Missouri, by the plaintiffs in error, against the defendant, a registering officer, for refusing to register Virginia L. Minor as a lawful voter. . . .

It is admitted by the pleadings that the defendant refused to register the plaintiff, solely for the reason that she is a female; and that she possesses the qualifications of an elector in all respects, except as to the matter of sex as before stated. . . .[30]

. . .The direct question is, therefore, presented whether all citizens are necessarily voters.

The Constitution does not define the privileges and immunities of citizens. For that definition we must look elsewhere. In this case we need not determine what they are, but only whether suffrage is necessarily one of them. . . .

The amendment did not add to the privileges and immunities of a citizen. It simply furnished an additional guaranty for the protection of such as he already had. No new voters were necessarily made by it.

[There follows an outline of the various voting requirements in the states at the time of the adoption of the Constitution, showing that many classes of people, e.g., nonproperty owners, were excluded from suffrage.]

In this condition of the law in respect to suffrage in the several States it cannot for a moment be doubted that if it had been intended to make all citizens of the United States voters, the framers of the Constitution would not have left it to implication. So important a change in the condition of citizenship as it actually existed, if intended, would have been expressly declared. . . .

And still again, after the adoption of the fourteenth amendment, it was deemed necessary to adopt a fifteenth, as follows: "The right of citizens of the United States to vote shall not be denied or abridged by the United States, or by any State, on account of race, color, or previous condition of servitude." The fourteenth amendment had

---

29. Senator Mathew Carpenter, in arguing Myra Bradwell's case before the Supreme Court, chose to sacrifice the argument that suffrage is a privilege and immunity of citizenship for the sake of winning Bradwell the right to practice law. He assured the Court that "female suffrage, which, it is assumed, would overthrow Christianity, defeat the ends of modern civilization, and upturn the world" (Brief for Plaintiff in Error at 2, Bradwell v. Illinois, 83 U.S. (16 Wall.) 130), would *not* necessarily follow from the interpretation of the Fourteenth Amendment he was advancing:

". . . not because I feared that this court would deny one, even if the other would follow, but to quiet the fears of the timid and conservative." 2 Stanton, Anthony, and Gage, History of Woman Suffrage 618 (1882).

Carpenter argued that voting was a political right rather than a privilege and immunity of citizenship. To support his position, he pointed out that the Fourteenth and Fifteenth Amendments each explicitly recognize that the right to vote can be infringed, in one case providing a sanction for its infringement (an absolute ban on abridgment would be self-executing) and in the other prohibiting abridgment on the grounds of race, color, and previous condition of servitude (by implication suggesting that other grounds for abridgment are not prohibited). He also pointed out that if the Fourteenth Amendment had the claimed effect of granting suffrage to all citizens, the Fifteenth Amendment would not have been necessary, and further, that the basis of political representation in §2 of the Fourteenth Amendment — male citizens twenty-one years of age — assumed that females are not part of the voting population of the state. History of Woman Suffrage reports his argument without any comment on the senator's willingness to trade the right to follow an occupation for the right to vote. — Eds.

30. These two paragraphs are from the Lawyers' Edition version of the case. — Eds.

already provided that no State should make or enforce any law which should abridge the privileges or immunities of citizens of the United States. If suffrage was one of these privileges or immunities, why amend the Constitution to prevent its being denied on account of race, etc.? . . .

If suffrage was intended to be included within [the obligations of the amendment which declares that no person shall be deprived of life, liberty, or property without due process of law], language better adapted to express that intent would most certainly have been employed. The right of suffrage, when granted, will be protected. He who has it can only be deprived of it by due process of law, but in order to claim protection he must first show that he has the right.

But we have already sufficiently considered the proof found upon the inside of the Constitution. That upon the outside is equally effective.

The Constitution was submitted to the States for adoption in 1787, and was ratified by nine States in 1788, and finally by the thirteen original States in 1790. Vermont was the first new State admitted to the Union, and it came in under a constitution which conferred the right of suffrage only upon men of the full age of twenty-one years, having resided in the State for the space of one whole year next before the election, and who were of quiet and peaceable behavior. This was in 1791. The next year, 1792, Kentucky followed with a constitution confining the right of suffrage to free male citizens of the age of twenty-one years who had resided in the State two years or in the county in which they offered to vote one year next before the election. Then followed Tennessee, in 1796, with voters of freemen of the age of twenty-one years and upwards, possessing a freehold in the county wherein they may vote, and being inhabitants of the State or freemen being inhabitants of any one county in the State six months immediately preceding the day of election. But we need not particularize further. No new State has ever been admitted to the Union which has conferred the right of suffrage upon women, and this has never been considered a valid objection to her admission. On the contrary, as is claimed in the argument, the right of suffrage was withdrawn from women as early as 1807 in the State of New Jersey, without any attempt to obtain the interference of the United States to prevent it. Since then the governments of the insurgent States have been reorganized under a requirement that before their representatives could be admitted to seats in Congress they must have adopted new consitutions, republican in form. In no one of these constitutions was suffrage conferred upon women, and yet the States have all been restored to their original position as States in the Union. . . .

Certainly, if the courts can consider any question settled, this is one. For nearly ninety years the people have acted upon the idea that the Constitution, when it conferred citizenship, did not necessarily confer the right of suffrage. If uniform practice long continued can settle the construction of so important an instrument as the Constitution of the United States confessedly is, most certainly it has been done here. Our province is to decide what the law is, not to declare what it should be.

We have given this case the careful consideration its importance demands. If the law is wrong, it ought to be changed; but the power for that is not with us. The arguments addressed to us bearing upon such a view of the subject may perhaps be sufficient to induce those having the power, to make the alteration, but they ought not to be permitted to influence our judgment in determining the present rights of the parties now litigating before us. No argument as to woman's need of suffrage can be considered. We can only act upon her rights as they exist.

NOTES:

DOCTRINAL DIFFICULTIES POSED BY MINOR AND ANTHONY

In interpreting the Privileges and Immunities Clause of the Fourteenth Amendment in *Minor* and *Anthony,* the courts faced a dilemma. On the one hand, there was no doubt that Congress had not intended to enfranchise women by the passage of the Fourteenth Amendment. On the other hand, it turned out to be fairly difficult to interpret the broad language of the amendment so that it extended to only one of two similarly situated groups — blacks and women — and still produce a plausible and internally consistent theory of the amendment's meaning. The courts chose to abide by the intent of Congress rather than the logic of the language Congress used to express its intent, and a good deal of doctrinal confusion resulted.[31] Some of the theoretical inconsistencies between *Minor* and *Anthony* and Supreme Court decisions on other topics are discussed below.

(1) *Minor and the Slaughter-House Cases.* Corwin once described the Privileges and Immunities Clause of the Fourteenth Amendment as being "unique among consitutional provisions" in "having been rendered a 'practical nullity' by a single decision of the Supreme Court rendered within five years after its ratification" — the decision in the Slaughter-House Cases.[32] However, even the narrow definition of privileges and immunities set forth in that historic opinion was seemingly broad enough to support Virginia Minor's claim. The *Slaughter-House* definition, which still stands today, was that privileges and immunities of national citizenship are only those rights that owe their existence to the Constitution or the laws of the federal government. Two years after *Slaughter-House,* the Supreme Court failed to address the Minors' argument that voting for a national officer, as a right which obviously owed its existence to the existence of the federal government, was necessarily a privilege and immunity of national citizenship. The conflict between the two cases would have been difficult to resolve if the Court had chosen to address it, so it is not surprising that Chief Justice Waite relied solely on historical evidence to establish that voting was never intended to be a privilege and immunity of national citizenship.

(2) *The Minor Case and Congressional Power To Supervise the Voting Process.* Another problem that the courts were unable to solve was finding a constitutional doctrine that allowed them both to exclude voting from the list of privileges and immunities of national citizenship and yet also to assert broad federal power to supervise the voting process. Ironically, the *Anthony* case itself was an attempt by the federal government to use the Fourteenth Amendment to do both things simultaneously. (It was never challenged on the inconsistency because Anthony was prevented from taking her case to the Supreme Court by the failure of the lower court to enforce its judgment.) The federal statute under which Anthony was prosecuted prohibited "any person" from knowingly voting "without having a lawful right to vote" in any election for representative or delegate in the Congress of the United States. If, as the *Minor* Court asserted, the federal constitutional aspects of voting were confined to the rights set forth in the Fifteenth Amendment, then where did Congress get constitutional authority to punish Anthony for a violation of a *state* constitutional provision? Certainly, there had been no state infringement of the right to vote, either on the grounds of race, color, or previous condition of servitude, or on any other grounds.

The same problem arose a decade later in Ex parte Yarbrough, 110 U.S. 651, 4 S. Ct. 152, 28 L. Ed. 274 (1884). The defendants were charged with intimidating a "citizen of African descent" in order to prevent him from voting for a member of Congress. Counsel for the defendants cited *Minor* and argued that since the right to vote depended on state law, Congress lacked constitutional power to pass laws protecting citizens in their exercise of that right. The Court described this argument as "a proposition so startling as

31. If one accepts the theory, discussed supra in Notes: Freedom of Occupational Choice as a Privilege and Immunity of Citizenship, that Congress had intended the Privileges and Immunities Clause to transfer the protection of basic civil rights from the states to the federal government, it becomes even more paradoxical that Congress did not mean thereby to enfranchise women.

32. Library of Congress, The Constitution of the United States of America, Analysis and Interpretation 965 (Corwin ed. 1952).

to arrest attention and demand the gravest consideration,"[33]and went on at length to discuss the constitutional foundation and practical necessity for congressional power in this regard. The effort to distinguish *Minor* is, however, unconvincing; excerpts from the opinion follow:[34]

> If this government is anything more than a mere aggregation of delegated agents of other States and governments . . . it must have the power to protect the elections on which its existence depends from violence and corruption. . . .
> . . . The power [to protect the parties in exercising the right to vote] . . . arises out of the circumstance that the function in which the party is engaged or the right which he is about to exercise is dependent on the laws of the Unites States. . . .
> The proposition answers also another objection to the constitutionality of the laws under consideration, namely that the right to vote for a member of Congress is not dependent upon the Consitution or laws of the United States, but is governed by the law of each State respectively. . . .
> . . .[I]t is not correct to say that the right to vote for a member of Congress does not depend on the Constitution of the United States.
> The office, if it be properly called an office, is created by that Constitution and by that alone. . . .
> The States in prescribing the qualifications of voters for the most numerous branch of their own legislature, do not do this with reference to the election for members of Congress. Nor can they prescribe the qualification for voters for those eo nomine. They define who are to vote for the popular branch of their own legislature, and the Constitution of the United States says the same persons shall vote for members of Congress in that State. It adopts the qualification . . . of its own electors for members of Congress.
> It is not true, therefore, that electors for members of Congress owe their right to vote to the State law in any sense which makes the exercise of the right to depend exclusively on the law of the State.
> Counsel for petitioners, seizing upon the expression found in the opinion of the court in the case of Minor v. Happersett, 21 Wall. 162, that "the Constitution of the United States does not confer the right of suffrage upon any one," without reference to the connection in which it is used, insists that the voters in this case do not owe their right to vote in any sense to that instrument.
> But the court was combating the argument that this right was conferred on all citizens, and therefore upon women as well as men.
> In opposition to that idea, it was said the Constitution adopts as the qualification for voters of members of Congress that which prevails in the State where the voting is to be done; therefore, said the opinion, the right is not definitely conferred on any person or class of persons by the Constitution alone, because you have to look to the law of the State for the description of the class. But the court did not intend to say that when the class or the person is thus ascertained, his right to vote for a member of Congress was not fundamentally based upon the Constitution, which created the office of member of Congress, and declared it should be elective, and pointed to the means of ascertaining who should be electors.

Although the Court did not cite the constitutional provision on which the right to vote for a member of Congress is "fundamentally based," later decisions rely on *Yarbrough* for the proposition that voting for a federal official is a privilege and immunity of national citizenship.[35]

If the gloss put on *Yarbrough* by later cases is accepted, the question arises whether

33. 110 U.S. at 657.
34. Id. at 657-658, 662-664.
35. See Twining v. New Jersey, 211 U.S. 78, 29 S. Ct. 14, 53 L. Ed. 97 (1908), citing also Wiley v. Sinkler, 179 U.S. 58, 21 S. Ct. 17, 45 L. Ed. 84 (1900). See also Ex parte Siebold, 100 U.S. 371, 25 L. Ed. 717 (1880), United States v. Classic, 313 U.S. 299, 61 S. Ct. 1031, 85 L. Ed. 1368 (1941), and Harper v. Virginia Board of Elections, 383 U.S. 663, 86 S. Ct. 1079, 16 L. Ed. 2d 169 (1966).

Minor was overruled sub silentio, or whether it can be reconciled with *Yarbrough.* If, according to *Yarbrough,* voting is a privilege or immunity of federal citizenship that cannot be abridged by the states, and yet states have the power to set qualifications for exercise of the franchise, it is necessary to distinguish state abridgment of a citizen's right to vote from the establishment of qualifications. According to this interpretation, the paragraph from *Yarbrough* which attempts to distinguish *Minor* implies that the requirement that electors be male is a qualification for voting rather than an abridgment of women's right to vote.

The Minors had anticipated such an argument and set about to differentiate qualifications from abridgments. They argued that a qualification must be at least theoretically capable of achievement by all citizens. For example, individuals may acquire property and education, and the passage of time will enable them to meet age and residency requirements, so these are properly described as qualifications. In contrast, individuals have no power to change their sex, nor will the passage of time enable them to meet the requirement of being male. This "arbitrary and impossible" requirement was, properly speaking, not a qualification but an abridgment, and thus a violation of the Privileges and Immunities Clause.

The Supreme Court did not discuss this argument in the *Minor* opinion, and was not forced to confront it directly in *Yarbrough* because of the facts of the case, which involved private abridgment of voting rights and the question of federal power to prohibit such private actions, not state abridgment or regulation of voting rights. If the Court had recognized that the logic of its opinion required it to overrule *Minor,* women might not have had to get a special constitutional amendment to protect their right to vote against abridgment by the states. However, this was neither the first nor the last time that the Court merely distinguished one of its earlier decisions (albeit unconvincingly) rather than overruling it. Furthermore, it would be expecting too much to ask the Court to enfranchise women by judicial fiat — and in a case which did not raise the issue directly, at that.

Another alternative is that, later Supreme Court interpretations to the contrary, *Yarbrough* itself was consistent with *Minor.* This position derives from the contention that the Privileges and Immunities Clause, which applies in terms only to state action, could not serve as the basis for federal intervention to protect voters against private violence and intimidation. This argument requires finding other constitutional authority for the statute which was upheld in *Yarbrough,* and discounting much of the *Yarbrough* opinion, especially the approach the Court took in distinguishing the Minor case.

The question whether or not voting is a privilege and immunity of national citizenship, and the distinction between abridgment and the setting of qualifications, are of primarily academic concern today. The enfranchisement of women by the Nineteenth Amendment and the expansion of equal protection theory to shield civil rights, especially through strict scrutiny of laws abridging fundamental rights — one of which is suffrage — have taken the urgency out of any scheme to persuade the Court to resurrect the Privileges and Immunities Clause.

(3) *Minor and Dred Scott v. Sandford.* Dred Scott v. Sandford, 60 U.S. (19 How.) 393, 15 L. Ed. 691 (1857), is the famous case in which Chief Justice Taney ruled that persons of African descent, whether free or slave, were not and could not be made citizens of the United States, either by action of any state or by the federal government. Taney argued that the framers could not possibly have intended blacks to be included in the term "citizens" because citizenship would entitle them to such broad privileges, and supported his argument by pointing out that blacks were everywhere denied important civil and political rights. Dred Scott's counsel had argued, however, that one need not have first-class citizenship to be a citizen, pointing out that white women were denied the vote and were still considered to be citizens. Taney conceded that[36]

---

36. 15 L. Ed. at 707.

> Undoubtedly, a person may be a citizen, that is, a member of the community who form the sovereignty, although he exercises no share of the political power, and is incapacitated from holding particular offices. Women and minors, who form a part of the political family, cannot vote. . . .

Thus, Taney simultaneously asserted that citizenship necessarily entailed broad privileges, and admitted that women could be denied the most fundamental rights without any infringement of their rights as citizens. He refused to concede the similarities between the legal position of blacks and of women, and excluded blacks even from second-class citizenship.

Because of the *Dred Scott* decision, the passage of a constitutional amendment conferring citizenship on former slaves was an immediate priority after the Civil War. However, even the Fourteenth Amendment did not totally invalidate Taney's interpretation of the Constitution. Despite the fact that blacks and women were both now accorded citizenship, they were not yet equal before the law. The special category of "women as citizens," which Taney had recognized before the Civil War, and which was reaffirmed by the Supreme Court in *Bradwell* and *Minor,* insured the continuation for over a century of the artificial distinction between the legal status of women and the legal status of blacks.

II. THE FEMINIST MOVEMENT, "PROTECTIVE" LABOR LAWS, AND THE DUE PROCESS CLAUSE, 1900–1940

A. The Beginning of Substantive Due Process

This section deals with legislation especially designed to protect women workers:[1] the politics and philosophy that produced it, the constitutional doctrines that upheld it, and the societal attitudes toward women revealed in its passage and judicial sanction. At first protective legislation was sought for all workers because, even before the Civil War, industrialization and urbanization had brought such wretched working conditions that unions and social reformers urged legislation regulating conditions of work, hours, and wages. By the turn of the century, several such protective laws had been passed, and as the movement grew for state regulation of the conditions of employment, employers became increasingly concerned and turned to the courts for protection of their property rights.

As discussed in the previous section, the Supreme Court, in gutting the Privileges and Immunities Clause of the Fourteenth Amendment in the Slaughter-House Cases, implied the broadest kind of power in the states to enact laws protecting the health, welfare, safety, and morals of the public. According to Dowling and Gunther, in the three decades following the Civil War, the Court continued giving the states free rein:[2]

> . . . [D]ue process remained simply an assurance of fair procedures. . . . [T]he Contract Clause continued to be the major barrier to state economic legislation. Toward the close of the century, however, there were increasing pressures — off the Court as well as on it — to broaden the meaning of due process and equal protection. In Santa Clara County v. Southern Pac. R.R., 118 U.S. 394 (1886), the Court held, without discussion, that corporations were "persons" within the meaning of the Fourteenth Amendment. And in Mugler v. Kansas, 123 U.S. 623 (1887), the Court,

---

1. "Protective" legislation means laws regulating the terms and conditions of labor for women workers — such as laws limiting the weights they can lift or the hours they can work, laws establishing a minimum wage, laws excluding them from certain occupations, and other laws ostensibly enacted to protect the health and safety of workers or a particular class of workers. The recent history, present legal status, and contemporary impact of "protective" laws for women workers are discussed in Chapter Two, II-B. The term "protective" is placed in quotation marks whenever it refers to laws for women only to emphasize that such laws are often not in fact protective but discriminatory.

2. Dowling and Gunther, Cases and Materials on Constitutional Law 862-863 (7th ed. 1965).

though sustaining a law prohibiting intoxicating beverages, announced that it was prepared to examine the substantive reasonableness of state legislation. Justice Harlan stated that not "every statute enacted ostensibly for the promotion" of "the public morals, the public health, or the public safety" would be accepted "as a legitimate exertion of the police powers of the State." The courts would not be "misled by mere pretenses": they were obligated, he insisted, "to look at the substance of things." Accordingly, if a purported exercise of the police powers "has no real or substantial relation to those objects, or is a palpable invasion of rights secured by the fundamental law, it is the duty of the courts to so adjudge." And facts "within the knowledge of all" would be relied on in making that determination. Ten years later, in [Allgeyer v. Louisiana, 165 U.S. 578, 17 S. Ct. 427, 41 L. Ed. 832 (1897)] the Court for the first time invalidated a state statute on substantive due process grounds. . . .

In *Allgeyer,* the Court invalidated a Louisiana state law prohibiting marine insurance companies not licensed by the state from insuring Louisiana property. The first case in which the Supreme Court used substantive due process to invalidate state protective labor legislation was Lochner v. New York, reprinted below.

Before *Allgeyer* and *Lochner,* the Court had always, at least in theory, protected the people against legislation that was arbitrary in effect, even though passed in a procedurally correct manner. But in practice there had been a strong presumption of the validity of state laws, and the burden of proof of arbitrariness was on the challenger of the law. In these two cases, the Court shifted the analysis from whether the law was duly enacted or arbitrary in effect to whether it was a proper, reasonable law. One technique the Court used in importing substance into due process was "judicial notice." The Court would hold the law invalid unless it was reasonable according to "common understanding" or "common knowledge," i.e., was supported by facts so well known that they could be judicially noticed. Initially at least, "common knowledge" was virtually indistinguishable from the personal world view of the justices.

As you read *Lochner,* note the use of "judicial notice," particularly on p. 21.

LOCHNER *v.* NEW YORK
198 U.S. 45, 25 S. Ct. 539, 49 L. Ed. 937 (1905)

Mr. Justice PECKHAM delivered the opinion of the Court.

[The New York labor law prohibited employment in bakeries for more than sixty hours a week or more than ten hours a day. Lochner was fined $50 for requiring an employee to work more than sixty hours in one week.]

[The labor law of the State of New York] is not an act merely fixing the number of hours which shall constitute a legal day's work, but an absolute prohibition upon the employer permitting, under any circumstances, more than ten hours work to be done in his establishment. The employe may desire to earn the extra money, which would arise from his working more than the prescribed time, but this statute forbids the employer from permitting the employe to earn it.

The statute necessarily interferes with the right of contract between the employer and employes, concerning the number of hours in which the latter may labor in the bakery of the employer. The general right to make a contract in relation to his business is part of the liberty of the individual protected by the Fourteenth Amendment of the Federal Constitution. Allgeyer v. Louisiana, 165 U.S. 578. Under that provision no State can deprive any person of life, liberty or property without due process of law. . . . There are, however, certain powers, existing in the sovereignty of each State in the Union, somewhat vaguely termed police powers [which] relate to the safety, health, morals and general welfare of the public. . . .

It must of course be conceded that there is a limit to the valid exercise of the police power by the State. . . . In every case that comes before this court . . . where legislation of this character is concerned . . . the question necessarily arises: Is this a fair, reasonable and appropriate exercise of the police power of the State, or is it an unreasonable, unnecessary and arbitrary interference with the right of the individual to his personal liberty or to enter into those contracts in relation to labor which may seem to him appropriate or necessary for the support of himself and his family? . . .

The question whether this act is valid as a labor law . . . may be dismissed in a few words. There is no reasonable ground for interfering with the liberty of person or the right of free contract, by determining the hours of labor, in the occupation of a baker. There is no contention that bakers as a class are not equal in intelligence and capacity to men in other trades or manual occupations, or that they are not able to assert their rights and care for themselves without the protecting arm of the State. . . . They are in no sense wards of the State. . . . [W]e think that a law like the one before us involves neither the safety, the morals nor the welfare of the public. . . . The law must be upheld, if at all, as a law pertaining to the health of the individual engaged in the occupation of a baker. It does not affect any other portion of the public. . . . Clean and wholesome bread does not depend upon whether the baker works but ten hours per day or only sixty hours a week. . . .[3]

. . . The mere assertion that the subject relates though but in a remote degree to the public health does not necessarily render the enactment valid. The act must have a more direct relation, as a means to an end, and the end itself must be appropriate and legitimate. . . .

. . . This case has caused much diversity of opinion in the state courts. . . . [T]he Court of Appeals has upheld the act as . . . a health law. One of the judges of the Court of Appeals, in upholding the law, stated that . . . the regulation in question could not be sustained unless they were able to say, from common knowledge, that working in a bakery and candy factory was an unhealthy employment. The judge held that, while the evidence was not uniform, it still led him to the conclusion that the occupation of a baker or confectioner was unhealthy and tended to result in diseases of the respiratory organs. Three of the judges dissented from that view, and they thought the occupation of a baker was not to such an extent unhealthy as to warrant the interference of the legislature with the liberty of the individual.

We think the limit of the police power has been reached and passed in this case. . . .

. . . To the common understanding the trade of a baker has never been regarded as an unhealthy one. Very likely physicians would not recommend the exercise of that or of any other trade as a remedy for ill health. . . . There must be more than the mere fact of the possible existence of some small amount of unhealthiness to warrant legislative interference with liberty. It is unfortunately true that labor, even in any department, may possibly carry with it the seeds of unhealthiness. But are we all, on that account, at the mercy of legislative majorities? . . . No trade, no occupation, no mode of earning one's living, could escape this all-pervading power, and the acts of the legislature in limiting the hours of labor in all employments would be valid, although such limitation might seriously cripple the ability of the laborer to support himself and his family. . . .

It is also urged, pursuing the same line of argument, that it is to the interest of the State that its population should be strong and robust, and therefore any legislation which may be said to tend to make people healthy must be valid as health laws, enacted under the police power. If this be a valid argument and a justification for this kind of legislation, it follows that the protection of the Federal Constitution from undue interference with liberty of person and freedom of contract is visionary. . . . Scarcely any law but might find shelter under such assumptions. . . . Not only the hours of employes, but the hours

---

3. Later in the opinion, the Court rejected, without giving any reason, a specific argument that an overworked baker would not be "cleanly" in his habits. — Eds.

of employers, could be regulated, and doctors, lawyers, scientists, all professional men, as well as athletes and artisans, could be forbidden to fatigue their brains and bodies by prolonged hours of exercise, lest the fighting strength of the State be impaired. We mention these extreme cases because the contention is extreme. . . . [W]e think that such a law as this, although passed in the assumed exercise of the police power, and as relating to the public health, or the health of the employes named, is not within that power, and is invalid. . . . Statutes of the nature of that under review, limiting the hours in which grown and intelligent men may labor to earn their living, are mere meddlesome interferences with the rights of the individual. . . . All that it could properly do has been done . . . with regard to the conduct of bakeries, as provided for in the other sections of the act. . . . These several sections provide for the inspection of the premises where the bakery is carried on, with regard to furnishing proper washrooms and water-closets, apart from the bake-room, also with regard to providing proper drainage, plumbing and painting. . . .

Mr. Justice HARLAN, with whom Mr. Justice WHITE and Mr. Justice DAY concurred, dissenting.

Granting . . . that there is a liberty of contract which cannot be violated . . . but . . . assum[ing] that such liberty of contract is subject to such regulations as the State may reasonably prescribe for the common good and the well-being of society, what are the conditions under which the judiciary may declare such regulations to be in excess of legislative authority and void? . . . [T]he rule is universal that a legislative enactment, Federal or state, is never to be disregarded or held invalid unless it be, beyond question, plainly and palpably in excess of legislative power. . . . If there be doubt as to the validity of the statute, that doubt must therefore be resolved in favor of its validity. . . . If the end which the legislature seeks to accomplish be one to which its power extends, and if the means employed to that end, although not the wisest or best, are yet not plainly and palpably unauthorized by law, then the court cannot interfere. In other words, when the validity of a statute is questioned, the burden of proof, so to speak, is upon those who assert it to be unconstitutional. McCulloch v. Maryland, 4 Wheat. 316, 421.

Let these principles be applied to the present case. . . .

It is plain that this statute was enacted in order to protect the physical well-being of those who work in bakery and confectionery establishments. It may be that the statute had its origin, in part, in the belief that employers and employes in such establishments were not upon an equal footing, and that the necessities of the latter often compelled them to submit to such exactions as unduly taxed their strength.

Be this as it may, the statute must be taken as expressing the belief of the people of New York that, as a general rule, and in the case of the average man, labor in excess of sixty hours during a week in such establishments may endanger the health of those who thus labor. . . . I submit that this court will transcend its functions if it assumes to annul the statute of New York. It must be remembered that this statute does not apply to all kinds of business. It applies only to work in bakery and confectionery establishments, in which, as all know, the air constantly breathed by workmen is not as pure and healthful as that to be found in some other establishments or out of doors.

Professor Hirt in his treatise on the "Diseases of the Workers" has said: "The labor of the bakers is among the hardest and most laborious imaginable, because it has to be performed under conditions injurious to the health of those engaged in it. It is hard, very hard work, not only because it requires a great deal of physical exertion in an overheated workshop and during unreasonably long hours, but more so because of the erratic demands of the public, compelling the baker to perform the greater part of his work at night, thus depriving him of an opportunity to enjoy the necessary rest and sleep, a fact which is highly injurious to his health." Another writer says: "The constant inhaling of flour dust causes inflammation of the lungs and of the bronchial tubes. The eyes also suffer through this dust, which is responsible for the many cases of running eyes among the bakers. The long hours of toil to which all bakers are subjected produce rheumatism, cramps, and swollen legs. The intense heat in the workshops induces the workers to resort to cooling drinks, which together with their habit of exposing the greater part of their bodies to the change in the atmosphere, is another source of a number of diseases of various organs. Nearly all bakers are pale-faced and of more delicate health than the workers of other crafts, which is chiefly due to their hard work and their irregular and unnatural mode of living, whereby the power of resistance against disease is greatly diminished. The average age of a baker is below that of other workmen; they seldom live over their fiftieth year, most of them dying between the ages of forty and fifty. During periods of epidemic diseases the bakers are generally the first to succumb to the disease. . . ."

A decision that the New York statute is void under the Fourteenth Amendment will, in my opinion, involve consequences of a far-reaching and mischievous character; for such a decision would seriously cripple the inherent power of the States to care for the lives, health and well-being of their citizens. Those are matters which can be best controlled by the States. . . .

The judgement in my opinion should be affirmed.

Mr. Justice HOLMES dissenting.

. . . This case is decided upon an economic theory which a large part of the country does not entertain. If it were a question whether I agreed with that theory, I should desire to study it further and long before making up my mind. But I do not conceive that to be my duty, because I strongly believe that my agreement or disagreement has nothing to do with the right of a majority to embody their opinions in law. It is settled by various decisions of this court that state constitutions and state laws may regulate life in many ways which we as legislators might think as injudicious or if you like as tyrannical as this, and which equally with this interfere with the liberty to contract. Sunday laws and usury laws are ancient examples. A more modern one is the prohibition of lotteries. The liberty of the citizen to do as he likes so long as he does not interfere with the liberty of others to do the same, which has been a shibboleth for some well-known writers, is interfered with by school laws, by the Post Office, by every state or municipal institution which takes his money for purposes thought desirable, whether he likes it or not. The Fourteenth Amendment does not enact Mr. Herbert Spencer's Social Statics. The other day we sustained the Massachusetts vaccination law. Jacobson v. Massachusetts, 197 U.S. 11. United States and state statutes and decisions cutting down the liberty to contract by way of combination are familiar to this court. Northern Securities Co. v. United States, 193 U.S. 197. Two years ago we upheld the prohibition of sales of stock on margins or for future delivery in the constitution of California. Otis v. Parker, 187 U.S. 606. The decision sustaining an eight hour law for miners is still recent. Holden v. Hardy, 169 U.S. 366. Some of these laws embody convictions or prejudices which judges are likely to share. Some may not. But a constitution is not intended to embody a particular economic theory, whether of paternalism and the organic relation of the citizen to the State or of laissez faire. It is made for people of fundamentally differing views, and the accident of our finding certain opinions natural and familiar or novel and even shocking ought not to conclude our judgment upon the question whether statutes embodying them conflict with the Constitution of the United States. . . .

B. Work Conditions, Sex Segregation, and "Protective" Legislation

1. Discrimination by Employers

The next case dealing with remedial social legislation to reach the Supreme Court, Muller v. Oregon, 208 U.S. 412, 28 S. Ct. 324, 52 L. Ed. 551 (1908), involved a state labor law for women only. To understand how special laws for women came to be passed, the reader needs some understanding of the conditions of labor in the late nineteenth and early twentieth centuries, and some knowledge about organizations that were attempting to change these conditions.[4] Most striking is the fact that the labor market was as sex-segregated then as it is today; that is, two-thirds of all women workers would have had to change jobs in order to produce a sex-neutral distribution of workers among occupations.[5]

> "Men's industries" and "men's work" in general were classified as those requiring greater physical strength and higher skills, such as mining, processing of metals and manufacturing of machinery. "Women's work" in industry closely paralleled the type of work [women] had been required to do prior to the industrial revolution, such as weaving, sewing, laundering and canning. Generally, the skill level of women's work was considered low and their occupations considered less dangerous to the health than certain men's jobs.[6]

From the time of their entrance into the nonagricultural labor force in large numbers in the 1880s, women were paid lower wages than men. At the turn of the century, they comprised only 20 percent of the nonagricultural labor force, and were confined almost entirely to a few low-paid occupations, which they shared with equally destitute children. Working women were predominantly single and young — the average period spent by women in industry was from age fifteen to age twenty-five — and married women who worked were generally forced into it by circumstances such as the death, disability, or desertion of their husbands.[7]

By working, a woman "risked all sorts of suspicions as to her womanliness and moral character, and was subject to accusations that she was undermining basic social institutions and ideals,"[8] even if she worked to support herself and her family, as the vast majority of women did. Women were simply not "supposed" to work; it was a society that prescribed different spheres for men and women, and saw the increasing numbers of women workers as a cause for civic concern and moral outrage. Women workers did not need equal pay, or equal access to jobs; they needed to return to the home and the protection of a breadwinning husband, father, or son.

Because of their marginal status in the work force, women were a reserve force of cheap labor, available to replace more expensive males when mechanization made jobs simpler, or to break nascent unions. These uses of women meant that they were often a threat to the pay levels and jobs of male workers, which was another motive behind the chivalrous suggestion that women stay home. The fundamental sex segregation of the labor market was not, however, affected by the occasional use of women to replace men, mainly because in the majority of industries there were too few women to replace men in any substantial numbers. In any case, the general belief that women were inferior workers meant that women workers were used only when men were unavailable.

2. Discrimination by Unions

Unionization was the obvious answer to the problems of unhealthy working conditions, long hours, and starvation wages for workers of both sexes; unionization

4. This discussion of the position of women in the labor market is based generally on the following works: Flexner, Century of Struggle, chs. 9, 14, and 18 (Atheneum ed. 1970); Eisenstein, Bread and Roses: Working Women's Consciousness Develops, 1905-1920, 10 The Human Factor, Journal of the Graduate Sociology Student Union of Columbia University No. 1, 33 (1970); Hill, Protective Labor Legislation for Women: Its Origin and Effect (unpublished paper, Yale Law School 1970).

5. Edward Gross, Plus Ca Change . . . ? The Sexual Structure of Occupations Over Time, Social Problems 198, 202 (Fall 1968).

6. Hill, supra, at 8-9.

7. Eisenstein, supra, at 37.

8. Ibid.

would also help end the possibility of destructive competition between male and female workers. Unfortunately, the unions often discriminated against women as much as did employers.[9] Some union constitutions simply excluded women from membership. Others limited women to the positions of apprentices or helpers. Still others set quotas on women's union membership. When women tried to form independent locals to counter the sex discrimination of existing locals, the American Federation of Labor refused to charter them, nor would it take action against discriminating locals, despite a rhetorical commitment to the unionization of women workers. A few unions organized women into separate, and usually unequal, locals. Although such separate organizations enabled women to develop their own leadership and programs, when negotiations with employers by men's and women's unions occurred the women's union was the certain loser. Inexplicit exclusionary tactics were also common: high dues could be and were exclusionary in a period when women's wages averaged about half of men's.[10] Many unions that had lower dues for women also paid them lower strike, sickness, and death benefits. Unions often negotiated contracts for women to be paid lower wages than men, and for women to be excluded altogether from "men's" jobs. Some unions went so far as to lobby for and win passage of laws excluding women from certain trades. Even the most liberal unions, including several in which women members predominated, failed to hire women organizers in any significant numbers or to give women more than token representation in the leadership.

Several factors explain the attitudes and practices of unions, including" the disinclination of the majority of [the] unions [affiliated with the American Federation of Labor] to spend money organizing low-paid unskilled trades far removed from their own immediate interests."[11] Perhaps more important, the ideology that prevented employers from integrating their work forces had a powerful influence on unions as well. One labor historian has described the attitudes of unions as "a tacit understanding in the great brotherhood of man, that woman's place was in the home."[12] An American Federation of Labor pamphlet spelled out this view in greater detail: "Just in proportion as the woman is transferred from the home to the workshop is her refinement and elevating influence in the domestic circle destroyed, and hence the social environment, and therefore the character of the child, the family, and ultimately that of the whole industrial community is thereby lowered."[13]

Despite discrimination by male trade unions, and the inexperience, lack of funds, and double burdens of job and housework carried by most women workers, women did make sporadic attempts to form unions, generally parallel to, but independent of, male workers' unionization efforts. The earliest strikes by women were called in the 1820s in the New England textile mills. These and other strikes were almost uniformly unsuccessful. Yet through the 1870s women continued to attempt to unionize and strike, which is "evidence not so much of optimism as of the desperation of their plight. "[14] Although women succeeded in setting up unions for varying lengths of time during the 1890s and early 1900s in "meat packing, glove making, retail, domestic and janitor work, textiles, men's and women's garments, knit goods, shirtwaists, millinery and men's hats, cleaning

9. The discussion of union treatment of working women is based on Falk, Women and Unions: A Historical View, Women's Rights L. Rep., Spring 1973, p. 54. See also Chafe, The American Woman, ch. 3 (1972).

10. Falk, id. at 16.

11. Flexner, supra, at 201.

12. Wolfson, Trade Union Activities of Women, 143 Annals of the American Academy of Political and Social Science 123 (May 1929).

13. George Guston, quoted in 3 Foner, History of the Labor Movement in the United States 224 (1947).

14. Flexner, supra, at 137.

and dyeing, paper boxes, twine, rubber, boots and shoes, laundries, cigar and cigarette making, tobacco, printing, teaching, and many other fields,"[15] an estimate (made in 1924) counted fewer than 77,000 women trade union members as late as 1910, "a mere 1.5 percent of all women wage earners at that time, and only 5.2 percent of the women in manufacturing establishments. . . ."[16]

C. The Role of Women's Reform Groups in Seeking "Protective" Laws

Paralleling the efforts of working women themselves to improve their circumstances was the interest of the suffrage movement. In the 1890s, suffrage conventions began to adopt yearly resolutions expressing "[t]he doctrines that equal work should be rewarded with equal pay, that working women could protect their special interests only with the ballot, that women's lack of the vote had weakened their bargaining power, and that women's disenfranchisement had dragged down men's wages and weakened men's unions. . . ."[17] In the first decade of the twentieth century, the rhetorical linkage of suffrage with the interests of working men and women was augmented by the formation of organizations of wealthy women and working women who proposed to fight together for labor reform (and who also became involved in suffragist work, which had previously been largely a middle-class activity). One of the best known of these groups was the National Women's Trade Union League, formed in 1903 to assist working women in organizing unions. The NWTUL never considered the possibility of setting up unions of its own where organized labor was unwilling to cooperate. Instead, the league concentrated on organizing women workers for existing unions and assisting unions that had a large number of women members. In its early years, the league was led by women of independent means, who had the money, time, energy, and concern to devote themselves to the exhausting task of organizing community support for strikes of women workers all over the country. These women had sufficient social standing and influence so that the AFL leadership could not comfortably ignore the NWTUL. "On the other hand, the League's feminism and its middle- and upper-class membership enabled the AFL to keep it at arm's length," [18] giving it only minimal financial aid and being unresponsive to its demands to organize women more intensively and to force restricted affiliates to open up their membership to women.[19]

There is no way to know what would have happened if the NWTUL had from the outset challenged AFL hegemony, and used its ability to rouse public support to get independent women's unions organized. However, it is unlikely that a group of wealthy women, already operating outside the boundaries of their traditional spheres — both as women and as members of their social class — would have been able to poach successfully in the preserve of the male craft unions that dominated the labor movement, even if the idea had occurred to them.

In any case, the league rendered some valuable services to working women. "There was hardly a strike of women workers from 1905 on, in which the Women's Trade Union League was not to be found taking an active part in organizing the strikers, or picketing,

15. Id. at 200.

16. Id. at 246. According to Chafe, by the late 1920s the labor movement had reached 1 in 9 male workers, but only 1 in 34 female workers. Chafe, supra, at 68.

17. Kraditor, Ideas of the Women Suffrage Movement, 1890-1920, 120 (Anchor ed. 1971).

18. O'Neill, Everyone Was Brave 101 (1969).

19. The design of the NWTUL by its founders had included a plan for its ultimate control by working women. According to O'Neill, in 1921, when this came about, the organization fast lost its influence, because the male leaders of the AFL did not respect women of their own class as they had the original upper-class leaders, nor did the NWTUL represent enough organized working women to give it much clout of its own. O'Neill, id. at 116-117.

raising bail or strike funds, mobilizing public opinion or running relief kitchens and welfare committees."[20]

The league was also interested early in the "protective" labor laws, and at its 1909 convention "produced a legislative code (to guide local leagues in their work for the eight-hour day, a minimum wage in the 'sweated' trades, and the elimination of night work), as well as a handbook on conditions in the trades represented in the League's membership."[21]

The General Federation of Women's Clubs also participated in the "protective" law effort, especially after the election of Sarah Platt Decker as president in 1904. O'Neill reports:[22]

> . . . She reorganized the federation's committee structure and among many good appointments made Rheta Childe Dorr, a progressive journalist, chairman of the Committee on the Industrial Conditions of Women and Children. Mrs. Dorr, in turn, recruited an outstanding body of women, including Mary McDowell, the great settlement headworker from Chicago.
>
> The committee's methods showed what clubwomen could do when properly led. It decided to promote a federal report on the condition of working women and children which social workers and reformers had been urging on Congress for years without success. The committee began by securing the approval of President Roosevelt. Then it started pressuring Congress directly. The women wanted an appropriation of $1 million. Speaker Joe Cannon was determined not to give them a cent. In the end they got $350,000 for the project. . . .

Eleanor Flexner describes the final report:[23]

> The investigation and preparation of the nineteen-volume report took four years, from 1908 through 1911, and covered the condition of child as well as women wage earners. The report ranged over a wide area, covering not only conditions in a variety of industries employing women, but the history of women in trade unions, family budgets, the mortality of children in relation to the employment of mothers, and related topics. The report, a landmark when it was issued, is still required material for the student today.

A third group, the one that played the major role in the movement among middle and upper class reformers, was the National Consumers' League. Originally organized to improve the working conditions of women through consumer pressure on the employers, the first consumers' league "grew out of a mass meeting organized in New York City in 1890 by retail shop girls to publicize their low pay, long hours, and deplorable working conditions."[24] During the 1890s, the league worked out the idea of[25]

> . . . contacting individual store owners whose labor practices were sub-standard, promoting a White List of employers whose policies were more enlightened in the hopes that buyers would patronize them exclusively, and publicizing the abuses created by "the rage of the purchasing public for cheap goods." . . . By 1899, other leagues had been established in large cities, and the National Consumers' League was organized to coordinate their efforts. Florence Kelley, formerly Chief Factory Inspector of Illinois, became its general secretary. . . . In a few years there were ninety local leagues, twenty state leagues, thirty-five auxiliary leagues, and numerous college branches.

20. Flexner, supra at 245.
21. Flexner, supra at 246.
22. O'Neill, supra at 150-151.
23. Flexner, supra at 213.
24. O'Neill, supra at 95.
25. Id. at 96-97.

Some of the conditions that the league protested were indeed horrendous: "Wages of $2.00 a week for women not living at home; hours from 7:45 A.M. till midnight, with only a few minutes off for lunch; a six-day work week, with sometimes stocktaking on Sundays at no additional pay; no seats behind the sales counters; no lockers; no vacations; and no place to eat lunch except in the toilets and stockrooms."[26] In the face of such exploitation, "moral public suasion" was not enough; the league increasingly turned its attention to lobbying for "protective" legislation, in cooperation with like-minded groups. By 1908, nineteen laws setting maximum hours for women or prohibiting night work had been passed. Although all the social reform groups were active in this effort, the NCL was the leader.

Muller v. Oregon was the first of many decisions over two decades upholding "protective" laws for women only, for which the NCL as amicus curiae, or co-counsel with state attorneys general, could justifiably claim virtually the entire responsibility. Decided by the Supreme Court in 1908, *Muller* arose after a number of state courts had dealt with the validity of "protective" laws for women only. In 1895, in Ritchie v. People, 155 Ill. 98, 40 N.E. 454, an Illinois court had ruled that an eight-hour law for women was unconstitutional, first because it was "a purely arbitrary restriction upon the fundamental rights of the citizen to control his or her own time and faculties," and second because it treated equals unequally — i.e., it covered women in some occupations and not in others. This reasoning was followed in a 1907 New York decision, People v. Williams, 189 N.Y. 131, 81 N.E. 778, in which the court stated:[27]

> . . . an adult woman is not to be regarded as a ward of the state, or in any other light than the man is regarded, when the question relates to the business, pursuit or calling. She is entitled to enjoy unmolested her liberty of person and her freedom to work for whom she pleases, where she pleases, and as long as she pleases, within the general limitations operative on all persons alike. . . . She is not to be made the special object of the paternal power of the state. Under our laws men and women now stand alike in their constitutional rights, and there is no warrant for making any discrimination between them with respect to the liberty of person or of contract.

On the other hand, an 1876 Massachusetts decision, Commonwealth v. Hamilton Mfg. Co., 120 Mass. 383, upheld a ten-hour law for women and children, without reference to the fact that the limitation applied to adult women but not to adult men, on the unlikely ground that it was not a limitation on a woman's right to labor as many hours per day or per week as she wished, but only prohibited her employment continuously by the same employer more than a certain number of hours per day or per week. An 1895 Massachusetts decision reaffirmed this position; it was followed in 1902 with favorable court decisions on similar maximum hours laws for women in Pennsylvania, Nebraska, and Washington State.[28] By the time *Muller* was argued, the proponents of state "protective" legislation for women had a clear picture of what they faced. "A victory in *Muller* could be sought in two ways: first, by displacing the 'common understanding' in *Lochner* about the lack of health dangers in bakeries and other non-hazardous occupations with scientific evidence that all industrial jobs, when performed more than ten hours a day, were dangerous to a worker's health";[29] and, second, by making a case

26. Flexner, supra; at 208, n. 12

27. 189 N.Y. at 135-136, 81 N.E. at 780. See also Burcher v. People, 41 Colo. 495, 93 P. 14 (1907).

28. Opinion of the Justices, 163 Mass. 589 (1895); Commonwealth v. Beatty, 15 Pa. Super. 5 (1902); Wenham v. State, 65 Neb. 394, 91 N.W. 421 (1902); State v. Buchanan, 29 Wash. 602, 70 P. 52 (1902).

29. Hill, Protective Labor Legislation for Women: Its Origin and Effect 39 (unpublished paper, Yale Law School 1970). The usefulness of scientific evidence in convincing the Court of the need for state "protective" labor legislation may have been suggested to Brandeis by Holmes's discussion in the *Lochner* dissent about the hazards of the baking occupation. Judge Venn, dissenting from the New York Court of Appeals decision in *Lochner*, had also cited medical treatises. Interestingly, the lawyers for *Lochner* responded to this by themselves citing medical treatises to the effect that baking was not a particularly hazardous occupation, and that whatever hazards there might have been in the past were unrelated to long hours and had been eliminated by the New

that there was something about this law that justified an exception to the *Lochner* doctrine of liberty of contract. The latter tack was based on the fact that the Court had distinguished cases prior to *Lochner,* such as Holden v. Hardy,[30] which had upheld an hours limitation law for miners, by categorizing them as measures for exceptional or unusual situations, easily distinguishable from the "ordinary trades and occupations of the people." [31] Since the Oregon statute applied only to women, one obvious way to do this was to argue "for women's need for 'special' protection, based on something special or different about [them]."[32]

The NCL chose to combine these approaches. Louis D. Brandeis filed a 113-page brief on its behalf that was a compilation of evidence about (1) physical differences between men and women, (2) changed industrial conditions due to the introduction of machinery, (3) the "bad effects" of long hours on women workers' health and morals, on job safety, and on the health and welfare of future generations, (4) the conditions in laundries (Muller had been convicted of requiring a female employee to work more than ten hours a day in his laundry), (5) the reasonableness of the limit chosen (ten hours), and (6) the need for uniform restriction (i.e., without provisions for exceptions such as overtime at premium rates of pay). The evidence, much of it from European sources, was assembled by Josephine and Pauline Goldmark, Florence Kelley, and other volunteers. It included data applicable to all workers as well as allegations about the impact of overwork on women in particular, especially on their "female functions" and childbearing capacity; it ranged from quasi-scientific studies on infant mortality among the children of women workers, and the comparative mortality of men and women in particular industries, to undocumented assertions by doctors, state and foreign officials, working women, and others about the nature and functions of women, and the disastrous impact of overwork on their health and the health of their children.

For example, this statement, made by Jules Simon in the French Senate in 1891, was included under the heading "The State's Need of Protecting Women": "[W]hen we ask . . . for a lessening of the daily toil of women, it is not only of the women that we think; it is not principally of the women, it is of the whole human race. It is of the father, it is of the child, it is of society, which we wish to re-establish on its foundation, from which we believe it has perhaps swerved a little."[33]

Under the heading "Specific Evil Effects on Childbirth and Female Functions," the remarks of a British surgeon from the 1873 Report of the British Chief Inspector of Factories and Workshops, on the effect of women's work on infant mortality, were reprinted:[34]

> Shorten their hours of labor, for I believe that scores of infants are annually lost under the present system. As things now stand, a mother leaves her infant (say of two months old) at 6 A.M., often asleep in bed, at 8 she nurses it, then until 12:30 the child is bottle fed, or stuffed with indigestible food. On her return at noon, overheated and exhausted, her milk is unfit for the child's nourishment, and this state of things is again repeated until 6 P.M.; the consequence is, that the child suffers from spasmodic diarrhea, often complicated with convulsions and ending in death.

Under the same heading, an 1875 report from the Massachusetts Bureau of Labor Statistics was quoted:[35]

York sanitary regulations mentioned in the Supreme Court's majority opinion. The attorneys for the State of New York did not introduce contrary evidence on this point in their brief to the Supreme Court.

30. 169 U.S. 366, 18 S. Ct. 383, 42 L. Ed. 780 (1898).
31. Lochner v. New York, 198 U.S. at 63.
32. Hill, supra; at 38-39.
33. Brief Amicus Curiae for the National Consumers' League at 48, Muller v. Oregon, 208 U.S. 412.
34. Id. at 38.
35. Ibid.

It seems to be the back that gives out. Girls cannot work more than eight hours, and keep it up; they know it, and they rarely will, — and even this seems to "pull them down," so that it is extremely rare that a girl continues more than a few years at this business.

Mr. B._____, a foreman of a large printing establishment, says: "Girls must sit at the 'case'. I never knew but one woman, and she a strong, vigorous Irishwoman, of unusual height, who could stand at the case like a man. Female compositors, as a rule, are sickly, suffering much from backache, headache, weak limbs and general 'female weakness.' "

An excerpt from an 1871 report from the same Massachusetts bureau is presented under the heading "The Effect of Women's Overwork on Future Generations":[36]

14. *Progressive physical deterioration produced by family labor in factories.* It is well known that like begets like, and if the parents are feeble in constitution, the children must also inevitably be feeble. Hence, among that class of people, you find many puny, sickly, partly developed children, every generation growing more and more so.

15. *Connection between continuous factory labor and premature old age.* It is a fact, patent to every one, that premature old age is fully developed, in consequence of long hours of labor and close confinement. Very few live to be old that work in a factory.

Few of the numerous items presented were scientific in a modern sense, and most were far less authoritative than the medical treatises of which the dissenting judges and justices had taken notice in *Lochner.* However, the quantity of evidence amassed and the number and variety of "experts" and laymen whose views were quoted made a strong impression on the Court. By its cumulative nature and broad scope, the evidence demonstrated that the bad effects of long hours on women workers and on their children were "facts of common knowledge." The excerpts from the Supreme Court opinion that follow show how effective this first "Brandeis brief" was.

MULLER v. OREGON
208 U.S. 412, 28 S. Ct. 324, 52 L. Ed. 551 (1908)

Mr. Justice BREWER delivered the opinion of the court.

On February 19, 1903, the legislature of the State of Oregon passed an act (Session Laws, 1903, p. 148), the first section of which is in these words:

"Sec. 1. That no female (shall) be employed in any mechanical establishment, or factory, or laundry in this State more than ten hours during any one day."

Section 3 made a violation of the provisions of the prior sections a misdemeanor, subject to a fine of not less than $10 nor more than $25. On September 18, 1905, an information was filed in the Circuit Court of the State for the county of Multnomah, charging that the defendant ". . . require[d] a female, to wit, one Mrs. E. Gotcher, to work more than ten hours. . . ."

A trial resulted in a verdict against the defendant, who was sentenced to pay a fine of $10. The Supreme Court of the State affirmed the conviction, State v. Muller, 43 Oregon 252, whereupon the case was brought here on writ of error.

The single question is the constitutionality of the statute under which the defendant was convicted so far as it affects the work of a female in a laundry. That it does not conflict with any provisions of the state constitution is settled by the decision of the Supreme Court of the State. The contentions of the defendant, now plaintiff in error, are thus stated in his brief:

"(1) Because the statute attempts to prevent persons, sui juris, from making their own contracts, and thus violates the provisions of the Fourteenth Amendment.

36. Id. at 51.

"(2) Because the statute does not apply equally to all persons similarly situated, and is class legislation.

"(3) The statute is not a valid exercise of the police power."

It is the law of Oregon that women, whether married or single, have equal contractual and personal rights with men. . . .

It thus appears that, putting to one side the elective franchise, in the matter of personal and contractual rights they stand on the same plane as the other sex. Their rights in these respects can no more be infringed than the equal rights of their brothers. We held in Lochner v. New York, 198 U.S. 45, that a law providing that no laborer shall be required or permitted to work in a bakery more than sixty hours in a week or ten hours in a day was not as to men a legitimate exercise of the police power of the State, but an unreasonable, unnecessary and arbitrary interference with the right and liberty of the individual to contract in relation to his labor, and as such was in conflict with, and void under, the Federal Constitution. That decision is invoked by plaintiff in error as decisive of the question before us. But this assumes that the difference between the sexes does not justify a different rule respecting a restriction of the hours of labor.

In patent cases counsel are apt to open the argument with a discussion of the state of the art. It may not be amiss, in the present case, before examining the constitutional question, to notice the course of legislation as well as expressions of opinion from other than judicial sources. In the brief filed by Mr. Louis D. Brandeis, for the defendant in error, is a very copious collection of all these matters, an epitome of which is found in the margin.[1]

The legislation and opinions referred to in the margin may not be, technically speaking, authorities, and in them is little or no discussion of the constitutional question presented to us for determination, yet they are significant of a widespread belief that woman's physical structure, and the functions she performs in consequence thereof, justify special legislation restricting or qualifying the conditions under which she should be permitted to toil. Constitutional questions, it is true, are not settled by even a consensus of present public opinion, for it is the peculiar value of a written constitution that it places in unchanging form limitations upon legislative action, and thus gives a permanence and stability to popular government which otherwise would be lacking. At the same time, when a question of fact is debated and debatable, and the extent to which

---

1. The following legislation of the states imposes restriction in some form or another upon the hours of labor that may be required of women: Massachusetts: 1874, Rev. Laws 1902, chap. 106, §24; Rhode Island: 1885, Acts and Resolves 1902, chap. 994, p. 73; Louisiana: 1886, Rev. Laws 1904, vol. 1, §4, p. 989; Connecticut: 1887, Gen. Stat. Revision 1902, §4691; Maine: 1887, Rev. Stat. 1903, chap. 40, §48; New Hampshire: 1887, Laws 1907, chap. 94, p. 95; Maryland: 1888, Pub. Gen. Laws 1903, art. 100, §1; Virginia: 1890, Code 1904, title 51A, chap. 178A, §3657b; Pennsylvania: 1897, Laws 1905, No. 226, p. 352; New York: 1899, Laws 1907, chap. 507, §77, subdiv. 3, p. 1078; Nebraska: 1899, Comp. Stat. 1905, §7955, p. 1986; Washington: Stat. 1901, chap. 68, §1, p. 118; Colorado: Acts 1903, chap. 138, §3, p. 310; New Jersey: 1892, Gen. Stat. 1895, p. 2350, §§66, 67; Oklahoma: 1890, Rev. Stat. 1903, chap. 25, art. 58, §729; North Dakota: 1877, Rev. Code 1905, §9440; South Dakota: 1877, Rev. Code (Penal Code, §764), p. 1185; Wisconsin: 1867, Code 1898, §1728; South Carolina: Acts 1907, No. 233.

In foreign legislation Mr. Brandeis calls attention to these statutes: Great Britain, 1844: Law 1901, 1 Edw. VII, chap. 22. France, 1848: Act Nov. 2, 1892, and March 30, 1900. Switzerland, Canton of Glarus, 1848: Federal Law 1877, art. 2, §1. Austria, 1855; Acts 1897, art. 96a, §§1-3. Holland, 1889; art. 5, §1. Italy, June 19, 1902, art. 7. Germany, Laws 1891.

Then follow extracts from over ninety reports of committees, bureaus of statistics, commissioners of hygiene, inspectors of factories, both in this country and in Europe, to the effect that long hours of labor are dangerous for women, primarily because of their special physical organization. The matter is discussed in these reports in different aspects, but all agree as to the danger. It would, of course, take too much space to give these reports in detail. Following them are extracts from similar reports discussing the general benefits of short hours from an economic aspect of the question. In many of these reports individual instances are given tending to support the general conclusion. Perhaps the general scope and character of all these reports may be summed up in what an inspector for Hanover says: "The reasons for the reduction of the working day to ten hours — (a) the physical organization of women, (b) her maternal functions, (c) the rearing and education of the children, (d) the maintenance of the home — are all so important and so far-reaching that the need for such reduction need hardly be discussed."

a special constitutional limitation goes is affected by the truth in respect to that fact, a widespread and long continued belief concerning it is worthy of consideration. We take judicial cognizance of all matters of general knowledge. . . .

That woman's physical structure and the performance of maternal functions place her at a disadvantage in the struggle for subsistence is obvious. This is especially true when the burdens of motherhood are upon her. Even when they are not, by abundant testimony of the medical fraternity continuance for a long time on her feet at work, repeating this from day to day, tends to injurious effects upon the body, and as healthy mothers are essential to vigorous offspring, the physical well-being of woman becomes an object of public interest and care in order to preserve the strength and vigor of the race.

Still again, history discloses the fact that woman has always been dependent upon man. He established his control at the outset by superior physical strength, and this control in various forms, with diminishing intensity, has continued to the present. As minors, though not to the same extent, she has been looked upon in the courts as needing especial care that her rights may be preserved. Education was long denied her, and while now the doors of the school room are opened and her opportunities for acquiring knowledge are great, yet even with that and the consequent increase of capacity for business affairs it is still true that in the struggle for subsistence she is not an equal competitor with her brother. Though limitations upon personal and contractual rights may be removed by legislation, there is that in her disposition and habits of life which will operate against a full assertion of those rights. She will still be where some legislation to protect her seems necessary to secure a real equality of right. Doubtless there are individual exceptions, and there are many respects in which she has an advantage over him; but looking at it from the viewpoint of the effort to maintain an independent position in life, she is not upon an equality. Differentiated by these matters from the other sex, she is properly placed in a class by herself, and legislation designed for her protection may be sustained, even when like legislation is not necessary for men and could not be sustained. It is impossible to close one's eyes to the fact that she still looks to her brother and depends upon him. Even though all restrictions on political, personal and contractual rights were taken away, and she stood, so far as statutes are concerned, upon an absolutely equal plane with him, it would still be true that she is so constituted that she will rest upon and look to him for protection; that her physical structure and a proper discharge of her maternal functions — having in view not merely her own health, but the well-being of the race — justify legislation to protect her from the greed as well as the passion of man. The limitations which this statute places upon her contractual powers, upon her right to agree with her employer as to the time she shall labor, are not imposed solely for her benefit, but also largely for the benefit of all. Many words cannot make this plainer. The two sexes differ in structure of body, in the functions to be performed by each, in the amount of physical strength, in the capacity for long-continued labor particularly when done standing, the influence of vigorous health upon the future well-being of the race, the self-reliance which enables one to assert full rights, and in the capacity to maintain the struggle for subsistence. This difference justifies a difference in legislation and upholds that which is designed to compensate for some of the burdens which rest upon her.

We have not referred in this discussion to the denial of the elective franchise in the State of Oregon, for while it may disclose a lack of political equality in all things with her brother, that is not of itself decisive. The reason runs deeper, and rests in the inherent difference between the two sexes, and in the different functions in life which they perform.

For these reasons, and without questioning in any respect the decision in Lochner v. New York, we are of the opinion that it cannot be adjudged that the act in question is in conflict with the Federal Constitution, so far as it respects the work of a female in a laundry, and the judgment of the Supreme Court of Oregon is affirmed.

Note: The Impact of the Muller Decision

The immediate impact of the *Muller* decision on lower courts is well illustrated by a comparison between People v. Williams, 189 N.Y. 131, 81 N.E. 778, a 1907 New York decision, discussed supra, in which a state law prohibiting night work for women was held invalid, and People v. Charles Schweinler Press, 214 N.Y. 395, 108 N.E. 639 (1915) a later New York decision upholding a state law prohibiting night work for adult women. The court in *Schweinler* commented as follows on its decision in *Williams:*[37]

> While theoretically, we may have been able to take judicial notice of some of the facts and some of the legislation now called to our attention as sustaining the belief and opinion that night work for women in factories is widely and substantially injurious to the health of women, actually very few of these facts were called to our attention, and the argument to uphold the law on that ground was brief and inconsequential.

Blanche Crozier, writing in 1934, said the *Muller* decision "ended the controversy, so far as courts are concerned."[38] Not only ten-hour laws for women in laundries, but eight-hour laws,[39] laws governing numerous other occupations,[40] laws prohibiting night work,[41] and laws involving innovations in the methodology of enforcement, such as the posting of a schedule of hours of women's employment and punishing deviations therefrom,[42] were all upheld on the authority of *Muller*. Other states besides New York, which had previously taken an antiprotective stand, reversed themselves,[43] and some states began to extend the doctrine of sex differences to uphold minimum-wage laws for women, or for women and minors.[44]

The National Consumers' League continued to play a leading role in these cases, and O'Neill reports that[45]

> . . . logistical support for court tests became its special province. In 1908–1909, with a grant from the Russell Sage Foundation, it supplemented its foreign data with American evidence. When the Illinois maximum-hour law was tested, the NCL was ready with a six-hundred-page brief. In April 1910 Brandeis won the case, enabling Mrs. Kelley to tell her followers that this one event alone justified the league's existence. The NCL next took up minimum-wage laws, sponsoring bills to that effect in a number of states in 1911. When Brandeis was elevated to the Supreme Court, Felix Frankfurter replaced him as the league's chief counsel. The minimum-wage campaign was less successful than the maximum-hour effort. . . . Nonetheless, the legal research, lobbying, and propagandizing the league did on behalf of both principles paid off handsomely in the end. The NCL sustained this work, in addition to its many other functions, on a budget that never exceeded $10,000 before World War I,

---

37. 214 N.Y. at 411.

38. Comment, 13 Boston U. L. Rev. 276, 278 (1933).

39. Ten-hour law: Withey v. Bloem, 163 Mich. 419, 128 N.W. 913 (1910); eight-hour laws: Miller v. Wilson, 236 U.S. 373, 35 S. Ct. 342, 59 L. Ed. 628 (1915) and Bosley v. McLaughlin, 236 U.S. 385, 35 S. Ct. 345, 59 L. Ed. 633 (1915), both dealing with the California law; State v. Somerville, 67 Wash. 638, 122 P. 324 (1912).

40. E.g., pharmacist, Bosley v. McLaughlin, 236 U.S. 385, 35 S. Ct. 345, 59 L. Ed. 633 (1915).

41. Radice v. New York, 264 U.S. 292, 44 S. Ct. 325, 68 L. Ed. 691 (1924); People v. Charles Schweinler Press, 214 N.Y. 345, 108 N.E. 639 (1915).

42. Riley v. Massachusetts, 232 U.S. 671, 34 S. Ct. 469, 58 L. Ed. 788 (1914).

43. E.g., Ritchie v. Wayman, 244 Ill. 509, 91 N.E. 695 (1910). *Accord:* People v. Bowes Allegretti Co., 244 Ill. 557, 91 N.E. 701 (1910).

44. Stettler v. O'Hara, 69 Ore. 519, 139 P. 743 (1914), *aff'd without opinion,* by an evenly divided court, *sub nom.* Simpson v. O'Hara, 243 U.S. 629, 37 S. Ct. 475, 61 L. Ed. 937 (1917); State v. Crowe, 130 Ark. 272, 197 S.W. 4 (1917); Williams v. Evans, 139 Minn. 32, 165 N.W. 495 (1917); Holcombe v. Creamer, 231 Mass. 99, 120 N.E. 354 (1918) (in terms not mandatory). See also Hawley v. Walker, 232 U.S. 718, 34 S. Ct. 479, 58 L. Ed. 813 (1914) (affirming Ohio decision on the basis of *Muller).*

45. O'Neill, supra; at 152-153.

and with a membership of perhaps two thousand people. Dollar for dollar and woman for woman, it was the best buy in the history of social feminism.

The impact of *Muller* was not limited to state "protective" laws that applied to women workers only. Despite the *Lochner* decision, which was ostensibly still good law, between 1908 and 1917 at least three state courts upheld laws regulating the hours of labor of all workers regardless of sex,[46] while courts in three other states followed *Lochner* in invalidating such laws.[47]

One of these cases, Bunting v. Oregon, 243 U.S. 426, 37 S. Ct. 435, 61 L. Ed. 830 (1917), came before the Supreme Court in 1916. It dealt with an Oregon law forbidding employment of any person for more than ten hours per day in manufacturing establishments but providing that up to three hours overtime per day could be worked if paid for at the rate of time and one-half the regular wage. An official of a flour mill was prosecuted for employing a man for thirteen hours without paying the prescribed overtime rate. In an amicus brief for the NCL, Louis Brandeis and Josephine Goldmark used the same techniques pioneered in *Muller* and presented hundreds of pages of scientific studies and reports from European countries and various states to demonstrate that (1) men's health and family life were destroyed by long hours, especially in the hazardous conditions of modern industry; (2) long hours had a bad effect on safety and morals; (3) shorter hours had a good effect on morals (i.e., less drinking of alcohol), on the general welfare, and on citizenship (voting, Americanization of the foreign-born, and capacity for military duty); (4) a uniform requirement of shorter hours was the only protection against these hazards; and (5) a reduction in hours was economically beneficial —it increased output, improved efficiency and management, lowered the cost of production, and increased regularity of employment. The studies cited were considerably more scientific than those used in *Muller,* and included many statistical tables, graphs, and sophisticated analyses of the hazards of long hours and the benefits of shorter hours. Some of the headings under "The Nature and Effects of Fatigue," for example, were "The Chemical Nature of Fatigue," "The Toxin of Fatigue," and "The Physiological Function of Rest." Under "Superior Output in Shorter Hours" they included data on eight separate occupational categories, such as "Metal Trades: Iron and Steel, Tin Plate" and "Glass and Optical Instruments."[48] The brief in *Bunting* was two volumes totaling 1020 pages, including a thirty-five-page appendix of sources. *Bunting* was thus certainly litigated as a major case.

The opinion did not cite *Lochner,* and discussed principally the argument that the statute was unconstitutional because it really regulated wages rather than hours. Counsel had argued that, whichever it regulated, the statute was justified. While the Court passed over this contention, it upheld the law, stating:[49]

> There is a certain verbal plausibility in the contention that it [the statute] was intended to permit thirteen hours' work if there be fifteen and one-half hours' pay, but the plausibility disappears upon reflection. The provision for overtime is permissive, in the same sense that any penalty may be said to be permissive. Its purpose is to deter by its burden and its adequacy for this was a matter of legislative judgment under the

46. State v. Lumber Co., 102 Miss. 802, 59 So. 923 (1912), and State v. Bunting, 71 Ore. 259, 139 P. 731 (1914), each sustaining a ten-hour law for workers in manufacturing; People v. Klinck Packing Co., 214 N.Y. 121, 108 N.E. 278 (1915), sustaining a law requiring one day of rest in seven for all workers.

47. State v. Miksicek, 225 Mo. 561, 125 S.W. 507 (1910), invalidating a six-day act; State v. Barba, 132 La. 768, 61 So. 784 (1913), invalidating an eight-hour law for stationary firemen; Commonwealth v. Boston and Main R.R., 222 Mass. 206, 110 N.E. 264 (1915), invalidating a law limiting certain railroad workers to nine hours' work in ten hours' time.

48. Brief of the State of Oregon, Defendant in Error, Bunting v. Oregon, 243 U.S. 426, 37 S. Ct. 435, 61 L. Ed. 830 (1917). Between the preparation of the evidentiary portions of the brief and its submission, Brandeis was appointed to the Supreme Court. Felix Frankfurter carried the case to the highest court.

49. 243 U.S. at 436-437.

particular circumstances. It may not achieve its end, but its insufficiency cannot change its character from penalty to permission.

The Court briefly speculated on possible explanations of the legislative choices embodied in the statute, but concluded that it "need not cast about for reasons for the legislative judgment. We are not required to be sure of the precise reasons for its exercise or be convinced of the wisdom of its exercise. . . . It is enough for our decision if the legislation under review was passed in the exercise of an admitted power of government. . . ."[50]

The Court also dismissed the contention that the law was not a health measure, stating that the record contained no facts to support that contention, and briefly reviewed the judgment of the legislature and the state supreme court on that point, as well as statistics on average hours of work in other countries. Chief Justice White and Justices Van Devanter and McReynolds dissented without opinion, making it a 5 to 3 decision, since Mr. Justice Brandeis took no part in the consideration of the case.

NOTE: THE POSITION OF LABOR UNIONS
ON PROTECTIVE LAWS FOR MEN AND WOMEN

Unfortunately, *Bunting* had little or no practical impact, probably because the labor unions had lost interest in protective laws for men as a tool for improving working conditions. In 1914, the AFL reversed its previous position and adopted a resolution that specifically opposed maximum-hours legislation for men. The favorable decision in *Bunting* did not influence this position or stimulate a movement to pass protective laws for men in states other than Oregon.[51]

Why did union leaders and workers accept "protective" laws for women only, when they had originally sought protection for all workers? Ann Hill researched this question and found that the roles of unions changed according to the situations of their membership.[52] As Florence Kelley, the head of the National Consumers' League and a major advocate of protective legislation for men and women, explained:[53]

---

50. Id. at 437.

51. According to historian Elizabeth Brandeis, who studied labor legislation in this period,

"This reversal of position by the A. F. of L., combined with the general reaction against labor legislation, effectually put an end to the movement for general enforceable hour legislation for men and even reduced the amount of legislation sought for special groups. . . . A few more laws were passed for men in especially unhealthful occupations. . . . But up to 1933 Alaska was the only part of the United States to adopt a more general statute. . . . [She went on to explain that the eight-hour law passed in Alaska was so extreme that it was invalidated by the Alaska Supreme Court and never reached the United States Supreme Court.]

"Judging by the paucity of any kind of hour legislation for men enacted between 1918 and 1932, there was little desire to use the power of the state to reduce the length of the working day for adult men. . . . There is no ground for thinking that it was the courts which were retarding this kind of legislation. Rather it appears that no group was interested in conducting the campaigns necessary to secure it. . . . The chief force behind the movement for such laws was always organized labor. . . . From 1918 to 1932 organized labor apparently felt it had secured virtually all the legislative protection as to hours that it wanted. For the rest it preferred to gain the shorter work day by direct trade union action." Brandeis, Hour Laws for Men, in 3 History of Labor in the United States, 1896-1932, 540, 557-558 (Commons ed. 1935).

Brandeis also discussed the charge that the decision not to seek protective legislation was a selfish one on the part of the well-organized craft unions who did not themselves need the protection and refused to work to get it on behalf of other workers. She concluded that "the labor leaders were probably sincere, and in a measure correct, in their belief that the protection apparently secured for unorganized workers through hour laws might prove somewhat illusory." Id. at 559. Although Brandeis reviewed protective legislation for women favorably in another section of the book, she did not explain why the conclusions of male union leaders relative to the effectiveness of hours laws for men did not apply equally to hours laws for women.

Another explanation for the AFL's failure to seek further protective legislation lies in Samuel Gompers' general theory that government aid would weaken the trade union movement.

52. This discussion is based primarily on Hill, Protective Labor Legislation for Women: Its Origin and Effect 34-35 (unpublished paper, Yale Law School 1970).

53. Kelley, Some Ethical Gains through Legislation 133 (1905), as quoted in Hill, id. at 34.

In many cases, men who saw their own occupations threatened by unwelcome competitors, demanded restrictions upon the hours of work of those competitors for the purpose of rendering women less desirable as employees. In other cases, men who wished reduced hours of work for themselves, which the courts denied them, obtained the desired statutory reduction by the indirect method of restrictions upon the hours of labor of the women and children whose work interlocked with their own.

For this latter reason, the first Massachusetts ten-hour law, which covered only women and children in the textile industry, was equally beneficial to the men in the same industry, who were responsible for much of the agitation in its favor. Other union leaders pointed out that a reduction in working hours in one industry helped to fortify the demands of unions elsewhere for shorter working hours, whether the reduction was gained through legislation or through economic pressure. Often protective legislation and the use of economic force by the workers were interdependent; the textile industry is again a good example: "Each time the workers had fought for and won a reduction in hours (through legislation) the textile manufacturers had threatened a comparable reduction in wages. In 1912, when the 54-hour work week took effect, they carried out their threat, and 20,000 textile workers went on strike."[54]

As time passed, however, "protective" laws for women only were used increasingly by unions as tools to keep women out of "men's" jobs. For example:[55]

At the close of World War I, women street car conductors were displaced by returning soldiers with the aid of "protective" legislation that restricted their hours to make employment infeasible. . . . Women workers were dumped from jobs as messengers with the telegraph service and as elevator operators by restrictive hours and laws passed in 1918 and 1919, respectively. . . . Women in the printing trade lost their employment when the 1913 maximum hours law prescribing a 54 hour week and forbidding night work for women was interpreted to cover newspaper offices. The women in this trade, who had been extremely well paid in comparison to their sisters elsewhere, spent the next eight years lobbying for exemption from this law, which was finally granted in 1921.

After 1914, the American Federation of Labor turned almost entirely away from legislative action, in favor of the use of economic force as a means of obtaining shorter hours for men. In 1913, Samuel Gompers, the head of the AFL, took the position that protective laws for women only were "fetters from which they would have to free themselves in addition to the problems that now confront them" and that "[t]he industrial problems of women . . . are inextricably associated with those of men."[56] Unfortunately, this change in official position did not mean the end of special laws for women only. First, because the AFL was not pushing extension of hours laws to men, laws which covered only women remained on the books and continued to be used to reinforce sex segregation of the labor force. Second, the AFL failed to follow through on Gompers' rhetorical commitment to the organization of women into trade unions, and in fact "exhibited an unnecessarily hostile approach toward the unionization of women."[57] This hostility was manifested in the exclusion of women from male unions, coupled with the refusal to charter separate unions for women, the lobbying of AFL member unions to get "protective" legislation for women for the explicit purpose of keeping them out of "men's" jobs, the sanctioning of unequal pay for men and women, and the establishment

54. Hill, id. at 25.
55. Id. at 34-35, citing Baker, Protective Labor Legislation 227, 258, 265; 138-139, 233, 332; 242-244, 362-366; Beyer, History of Labor Legislation for Women in Three States 2 (1932); Winslow, The Effects of Labor Legislation on the Employment Opportunities of Women 247-267 (1928).
56. Gompers, Woman's Work, Rights and Progress, in American Federationist 624 (1913). See also Mandell, Samuel Gompers 179-180 (1963).
57. Chafe, The American Woman 88 (1972).

of separate seniority lists for men and women, which were used to keep women from competing on an equal basis with men for jobs.[58]

NOTE: THE LITIGATIVE STRATEGY
OF THE NATIONAL CONSUMERS' LEAGUE

The marshaling of scientific or quasi-scientific facts, which were outside the legislative history and the lower court record, in order to document a legal argument, was an important innovation in constitutional litigation. In *Muller,* the rationale for presenting such evidence was that it was "common knowledge" that the Court could judicially notice. But this characterization of facts licensed the Court to also set forth its own "common knowledge" about the nature of women, with disastrous results. The *Muller* opinion has been "one of . . . [the] most frequently cited authorities for the general proposition that sex is a valid basis for legislative classification"[59] and operates even today as a "roadblock to the full equality of women."[60] By its sweeping language about male supremacy and its invocation of the allegedly numerous and fundamental differences between the sexes, the decision crystalized the prejudices of the age and thus achieved a far greater impact on constitutional history than its holding warranted.

But it is only hindsight that enables us to question the result of the Brandeis-Goldmark strategy in *Muller.* At the time the case was brought, it appeared that the use of evidence about the impact of long hours on women workers was a means to force the Court to face the realities of the workplace for all laborers. In a 1916 Harvard Law Review article,[61] Frankfurter described what he saw as the progress from empty theorizing about liberty of contract to "realism in constitutional law," which all started with *Muller:*[62]

> Prior to 1908 the decisions [of various courts in cases dealing with social legislation] disclose certain marked common characteristics:
> (1) Despite disavowal that the policy of legislation is not the courts' concern, there is an unmistakable dread of the class of regulation under discussion. Intense feeling against the policy of the legislation must inevitably have influenced the result in the decisions. . . .
> (2) Legislation is sustained as part of the prevailing philosophy of individualism, as an exceptional protection to certain individuals as such, and not as a recognition of a general social interest. Thus legislation is supported either because women and children are wards of the state, are not sui juris, or to relieve certain needy individuals in the community from coercion. The underlying assumption was, of course, that industry presented only contract relations between individuals. That industry is part of society, the relation of business to the community, was naturally enough lost sight of in the days of pioneer development and free land.
> (3) The courts here deal with statutes seeking to affect in a very concrete fashion the sternest actualities of modern life: the conduct of industry and the labor of human

---

58. The unions sometimes defended their poor performance on the grounds that women could not be organized. This claim is questionable. By 1915, at least 80 percent of all workers in manufacturing, trade, and transportation — both male and female — were still unorganized. Frankfurter and Goldmark, The Case for the Shorter Work Day, The Brief for the U.S. Supreme Court in Bunting v. Oregon, October Term 1915, reprinted by the National Consumers' League (1916), as cited in Hill, supra, at 21. Yet the argument identifying economic force with male workers and legislative reform with women and children dates back at least to the 1870s, when it was certainly too early to make a definite statement that women could not be organized to seek labor reform through union activity. Hill, id. See supra Section B-2, and infra Chapter Two, II-D, for discussion of union practices toward women workers. See also Chafe, The American Woman, ch. 3. especially pp. 77-79, 83-88 (1972), for a critical discussion of AFL policies between 1910 and 1950.

59. Johnston and Knapp, Sex Discrimination By Law: A Study in Judicial Perspective, 46 N.Y.U.L. Rev. 675, 699 (1971).

60. Murray, The Rights of Women, in Dorsen (ed.), The Rights of Americans 521, 525 (1971).

61. Frankfurter, Hours of Labor and Realism in Constitutional Law, 29 Harv. L. Rev. 353 (1916).

62. Id. at 362-367, 369-370.

beings therein engaged. Yet the cases are decided, in the main, on abstract issues, on tenacious theories of economic and political philosophy. There is a lack of scientific method either in sustaining or attacking legislation. . . .

The courts decided these issues on a priori theories, on abstract assumptions, because scientific data were not available or at least had not been made available for the use of courts. But all this time scientific data had been accumulating. Organized observation, investigation, and experimentation produced facts, and science could at last speak with rational if tentative authority. There was a growing body of the world's experience and the validated opinions of those competent to have opinions. Instead of depending on a priori controversies raging around jejune catchwords like "individualism" and "collectivism," it became increasingly demonstrable what the effect of modern industry on human beings was and what the reasonable likelihood to society of the effect of fixing certain minimum standards of life.

The *Muller* case, in 1908, was the first case presented to our courts on the basis of authoritative data. For the first time the arguments and briefs breathed the air of reality. . . .

[T]here can be no denial that the technique of the brief in the *Muller* case has established itself through a series of decisions within the last few years, which have caused not only change in decisions, but the much more vital change of method of approach to constitutional questions. . . .

. . . [R]ecent cases, dealing with regulation of the hours of labor . . . illustrate two dominant tendencies in current constitutional decisions:

(1) Courts, with increasing measure, deal with legislation affecting industry in the light of a realistic study of the industrial conditions affected.

(2) The emphasis is shifted to community interests, the affirmative enhancement of the human values of the whole community—not merely society conceived of as individuals dealing at arm's length with one another, in which legislation may only seek to protect individuals under disabilities, or prevent individual aggression in the interest of a countervailing individual freedom.

As a result we find that recent decisions have modified the basis on which legislation limiting the hours of labor is supported. As science has demonstrated that there is no sharp difference in kind as to the effect of labor on men and women, courts recently have followed the guidance of science and refused to be controlled by outworn ignorance. . . .

. . . [O]nce we cease to look upon the regulation of women in industry as exceptional, as the law's graciousness to a disabled class, and shift the emphasis from the fact that they are *women* to the fact that it is *industry* and the relation of industry to the community which is regulated, the whole problem is seen from a totally different aspect.

(a) It is now clearly enough recognized that each case presents a distinct issue; that each case must be determined by the facts relevant to it; that we are dealing, in truth, not with a question of law, but the application of an undisputed formula to a constantly changing and growing variety of economic and social facts. Each case, therefore, calls for a new and distinct consideration, not only of the general facts of industry but the specific facts in regard to the employment in question and the specific exigencies which called for the specific statute.

(b) The groundwork of the *Lochner* case has by this time been cut from under. The majority opinion was based upon "a common understanding" as to the effect of work in bakeshops upon the public and upon those engaged in it. "Common understanding" has ceased to be the reliance in matters calling for essentially scientific determination.

Later events proved Frankfurter's optimism premature. True, maximum-hours laws for men and women were upheld, but such laws ceased to be the issue, at least for male workers, by 1920 at the latest. The unwillingness of the Court to extend its line of "progressive" decisions to encompass minimum-wage laws was a decisive setback for the National Consumers' League and other advocates of "protective" labor legislation; almost no further progress was made until the second half of the 1930s.

It is highly unlikely that any strategy other than the one chosen would have been more successful, given the conservative character of the Court, and certainly Brandeis, Goldmark, Frankfurter, and the NCL had a lot of new legal precedents to their credit by 1920. On the other hand, they were apparently blind to the reactionary implications of the *Muller* decision. Frankfurter emphasizes the *Muller* Court's acceptance of the factual authorities cited in the Brandeis-Goldmark brief, but fails to remark the grounds on which the Court itself places so much rhetorical emphasis: the common understanding of mankind about "woman." Elsewhere, he indicates that he sees the importance of persuading the courts to switch from concentrating on sex differences to concentrating on the problem of regulating industry in its relation to society. The article as a whole, however, creates the impression that the problem of differential treatment of the sexes would easily be erased by later, more progressive decisions, and ignores the possibility that its impact as an obstacle to the equality of the sexes might well be as great as its implications for the methodology of approaching constitutional questions.[63] And later, during the debate between the social reformers and the National Woman's Party over the Equal Rights Amendment, Frankfurter made it clear that if it came to a choice between equality and "protection", he would favor the continuation of special "protection" for women.[64]

NOTE: ATTITUDES OF SUFFRAGISTS AND WOMEN REFORMERS TOWARD SPECIAL "PROTECTIVE" LAWS FOR WOMEN

That Brandeis, Frankfurter, and other legal scholars hailed the *Muller* decision with no notice of its antifeminist implications is less surprising than that women as farsighted as Florence Kelley and Jane Addams, who were active in the labor reform movements but also worked for suffrage,[65] accepted "protection" for women only, and later fought against the Equal Rights Amendment to the Constitution primarily because it would invalidate their hard-won gains.[66] To understand the position of social reformers who supported suffrage and suffragist leaders, some information about changes in the ideology of the suffrage movement may be helpful.

The early suffrage movement relied on an argument based on "justice"; women spoke of natural right and God-given liberty, and contended that all human beings, regardless of sex, have a right to self-government, and that men and women were created equal, and should have equal rights under law.[67] With the start of the twentieth century, however, there was a "change from justice to expediency as the chief argument of the suffragists,"[68] although the change was gradual: some versions of the expediency argument had been used as early as 1848.[69] The argument of expediency was that women, especially middle-class white women, would use the ballot to improve society. Some

---

63. In this, Frankfurter was not alone; even today most constitutional law texts do not mention the implication of the *Muller* case for women's rights.

64. In 1923, Frankfurter wrote that "Only those who are ignorant of the law . . . or indifferent to the exacting aspects of women's life can have the naïveté, or the recklessness, to sum up women's whole position in a meaningless and mischievous phrase about 'equal rights'." Chafe, supra at 124. Frankfurter also wrote the opinion in Goesaert v. Cleary, 335 U.S. 464, 69 S. Ct. 198, 93 L. Ed. 163 (1948), upholding against a Fourteenth Amendment challenge a law excluding women from the occupation of bartending unless they were the wives or daughters of male owners of licensed liquor establishments. See infra, Part V of this chapter.

65. For an account of the activities of Kelley and Addams in the suffrage movement, see Kraditor (ed.), Up From the Pedestal 273 ff; O'Neill, Everyone was Brave 134; Flexner, Century of Struggle, 262-263, 219.

66. A full description of the split in the women's movement over the issue of "protective" laws and the effect of the Equal Rights Amendment is given in Chapter Two, II-B.

67. Kraditor, Ideas of the Woman Suffrage Movement 1890–1920, ch. 3 (Anchor ed. 1970); Kraditor (ed.), Up From the Pedestal 220-252.

68. Kraditor, Ideas, supra, at 43. Chafe, supra, at 1-47, describes this change and titles it "A Narrowing of Vision."

69. O'Neill, supra, at 49-50.

suffragists argued that votes for women would advance such diverse causes as temperance, peace, the abolition of prizefighting, and the defeat of machine government, as well as all other political corruption, and bring about solutions to the problems of adulterated food, urban overcrowding, air pollution, juvenile crime, prostitution, unhealthful factory conditions, and long hours and low wages for workers, especially women and children.[70] Racist and nativist arguments were also frequently invoked, calling for the enfranchisement of white women to counterbalance the votes of "illiterate and uneducated" foreign immigrants in the North and black men in the South.

Adoption by suffragists of the arguments of social reform came in the context of major political changes during the decade of the 1890s. One was the growing political importance of the Progressive Movement, which meant that different men were in or near power. The success of the suffrage movement thus depended on the support of a new group of men, who were oriented to social reform. Expediency arguments were much more likely to convince reform-minded men to give political support to the suffrage movement than the appeal to their notions of justice and democratic fair play. While such men were not otherwise committed to women's equality, they would support it once they saw that it would help them achieve their other goals.

Second and perhaps more important, there was a sharp upswing in the activism and social consciousness of middle- and upper-class women, who in large numbers joined organizations like the Women's Christian Temperance Union and the General Federation of Women's Clubs. If suffrage was to become a reality, the support of these social reform organizations was essential because their membership far exceeded that of strictly feminist groups such as the National American Woman Suffrage Association and the Woman's Party, especially in the early 1900s.[71] Suffrage leaders thus used arguments of expediency to convert female social reformers to the suffrage cause.

Female social reformers such as the leaders of the NWTUL, the NCL, and the GFWC have sometimes been viewed as an important part of the women's movement (e.g., O'Neill calls them social feminists), and indeed, in many ways they were. They typified what a large number of women were doing in the public sphere at that time, and toward the end, they became a force in the achievement of suffrage. Fundamentally, however, they were not feminists; their first and primary concern had never been an effort to change women's position in society vis à vis men, and they had joined the suffrage movement not because of the essential justice of granting women the vote, but because they believed that the women's vote would help them enact the social reforms which were their essential concern. In pursuing this latter desire, they helped change the basic strategy of the women's movement.

The change from justice to expediency had more profound implications than the suffragists realized. The argument that women should have the vote because of the good they could do implied that women were fundamentally different from men — otherwise, why would they vote differently?[72] The argument made by social reformers that women

---

70. Kraditor (ed.), Up From the Pedestal, supra, at 253-287.

71. O'Neill, supra, at 77.

72. Alice Duer Miller wryly commented on the suffragists' position, caught between the conflicting arguments of their opponents, in Our Own Twelve Anti-suffragist Reasons, from her book Are Women People? A Book of Rhymes for Suffrage Times (1915):

"1. Because no woman will leave her domestic duties to vote.

"2. Because no woman who may vote will attend to her domestic duties.

"3. Because it will make dissension between husband and wife.

"4. Because every woman will vote as her husband tells her to.

"5. Because bad women will corrupt politics.

"6. Because bad politics will corrupt women.

"7. Because women have no power of organization.

"8. Because women will form a solid party and outvote men.

"9. Because men and women are so different that they must stick to different duties.

workers were different and needed "special protection" was thus perfectly consistent with the suffragist view of women in the last decades before the vote was won. Furthermore, as we have seen, women's position in the labor force *was* different from men's position.

It soon became clear, moreover, that the opposition of employers, and hence legislators and the courts, coupled with the lack of enthusiasm of male labor unions, made the passage of protective legislation for all workers highly unlikely. Laws that at least "protected" women and children were seen as the proverbial half loaf rather than as a compromise potentially harmful to working women's equality.

In addition to the ideological compatability of the suffrage and "protective" labor law movements, the limited class composition of both played a significant role in their mutual allegiance. Most working women did not have the time to work in suffrage organizations, did not see the relevance to themselves, and were repelled by the movement's class prejudice. Had more of them been involved either in suffrage organizations or in labor reform groups, the fact that working women did not all have the same needs might have been brought to public attention more clearly.

On the other hand, even if the discriminatory effects of some "protective" laws had been more widely understood, the social reformers would have had to accept the idea that equal competition between women and men was a desirable and practical goal (which it might not in fact have been at that point in history), and then to persuade the rest of society to adopt the view of women that this entailed, an unlikely scenario at best.

D. Minimum Wages For Women

After *Muller,* the National Consumers' League and other reform groups turned to "a nationwide crusade to place a floor under women's wages as well as a ceiling over their hours."[73] In 1912 Massachusetts enacted the first minimum-wage law, and by 1920 fourteen more states had followed suit. The issue of minimum wages reached the Supreme Court with Adkins v. Children's Hospital, 261 U.S. 525, 43 S. Ct. 394, 67 L. Ed. 785 (1923), in which the NCL again used the famous Brandeis-Goldmark approach. There were two statistical briefs in that case and its companion, Adkins v. Lyons, one prepared by Frankfurter and Josephine Goldmark, and the other by Frankfurter with Mary Dewson, the secretary of the National Consumers' League. Each ran to more than 1000 pages, and was filled with tables and charts demonstrating the impact of poverty and malnutrition on the health of workers, on their productivity, and on their children, as well as numerous calculations of the "living wage," and evidence as to the numbers of women workers receiving far less income than necessary for subsistence. Reports of state officials and commissions were also quoted, and arguments very much like those made in *Muller* about the relationship of women's health to the future of the race were presented. To the statements about the relationship of a "living wage" for women to the health of future generations, the brief for Children's Hospital replied:[74]

> . . . [I]t does not follow from this, that those who have more than a living income can be compelled by law to hand over a part of that income directly to those who have less. This Government does not operate in that way. . . . If they are in need of charity,

---

"10. Because men and women are so much alike that men, with one vote each, can represent their own views and ours too.
"11. Because women cannot use force.
"12. Because the militants did use force."
Against this kind of reasoning neither arguments of expediency nor arguments of justice were of much avail.
73. Chafe, The American Woman 80 (1972).
74. Brief for the Appellee at 42-43, Adkins v. Children's Hospital, 261 U.S. 525 (1923).

the state, of course, has the power to help them and levy taxes upon all equally for this purpose, or individuals more fortunately situated may voluntarily, out of their abundance, give to them. But it is voluntary; it can not be made a criminal offense not to make the contribution.

ADKINS v. CHILDREN'S HOSPITAL
OF THE DISTRICT OF COLUMBIA
261 U.S. 525, 43 S. Ct. 394, 67 L. Ed. 785 (1923)

Mr. Justice SUTHERLAND delivered the opinion of the Court.

The question presented for determination by these appeals is the constitutionality of the Act of September 19, 1918, providing for the fixing of minimum wages for women and children in the District of Columbia, 40 Stat. 960, c.174 (Comp. St. Ann. Supp. 1919 §§3421 1/2a - 3421w).

The act provides for a board of three members to be constituted, as far as practicable, so as to be equally representative of employers, employees and the public. . . .

The act . . . provides (section 10) that if the board, after investigation, is of opinion that any substantial number of women workers in any occupation are receiving wages inadequate to supply them with the necessary cost of living, maintain them in health and protect their morals, a conference may be called to consider and inquire into and report on the subject investigated. . . .

The conference is required to make and transmit to the board a report. . . .

The board is authorized (section 12) to consider and review these recommendations and . . . to make such order as to it may appear necessary to carry into effect the recommendations, and to require all employers in the occupation affected to comply therewith. It is made unlawful for any such employer to . . . employ any woman worker at lower wages than are thereby permitted. . . .

Any violation of the act (section 18) by an employer or his agent or by corporate agents is declared to be a misdemeanor, punishable by fine and imprisonment. . . .

The appellee in the first case is a corporation maintaining a hospital for children in the District. It employs a large number of women in various capacities, with whom it had agreed upon rates of wages and compensation satisfactory to such employees, but which in some instances were less than the minimum wage fixed by an order of the board made in pursuance of the act. The women with whom appellee had so contracted were all of full age and under no legal disability. . . .

In the second case the appellee, a woman 21 years of age, was employed by the Congress Hall Hotel Company as an elevator operator, at a salary of $35 per month and two meals a day. She alleges that the work was light and healthful, the hours short, with surroundings clean and moral, and that she was anxious to continue it for the compensation she was receiving, and that she did not earn more. Her services were satisfactory to the Hotel Company, and it would have been glad to retain her, but was obliged to dispense with her services by reason of the order of the board and on account of the penalties prescribed by the act. The wages received by this appellee were the best she was able to obtain for any work she was capable of performing, and the enforcement of the order, she alleges, deprived her of such employment and wages. She further averred that she could not secure any other position at which she could make a living, with as good physical and moral surroundings, and earn as good wages, and that she was desirous of continuing and would continue the employment, but for the order of the board. An injunction was prayed as in the other case. . . .

The statute now under consideration is attacked upon the ground that it authorizes an unconstitutional interference with the freedom of contract included within the guaranties of the due process clause of the Fifth Amendment. That the right to contract about one's affairs is a part of the liberty of the individual protected by this clause is settled by the decisions of this court and is no longer open to question. . . . Within this liberty are contracts of employment of labor. In making such contracts, generally speaking, the parties have an equal right to obtain from each other the best terms they can as the result of private bargaining. . . .

There is, of course, no such thing as absolute freedom of contract. It is subject to a great variety of restraints. But freedom of contract is, nevertheless, the general rule and restraint the exception, and the exercise of legislative authority to abridge it can be justified only by the existence of exceptional circumstances. Whether these circumstances exist in the present case constitutes the question to be answered. It will be helpful to this end to review some of the decisions where the interference has been upheld. . . .

Statutes fixing hours of labor. . . . In some instances the statute limited the hours of labor for men in certain occupations, and in others it was confined in its application to women. No statute has thus far been brought to the attention of this court which by its terms applied to all occupations. In Holden v. Hardy, 169 U.S. 366, the court considered an act of the Utah Legislature, restricting the hours of labor in mines and smelters. This statute was sustained as a legitimate exercise of the police power, on the ground that the Legislature had determined that these particular employments, when too long pursued, were injurious to the health of the employees, and that, as there were reasonable grounds for supporting this determination on the part of the Legislature, its decision in that respect was beyond the reviewing power of the federal courts.

That this constituted the basis of the decision is emphasized by the subsequent decision in Lochner v. New York, 198 U.S. 45, 25 S. Ct. 539, 49 L. Ed. 937, 3 Ann. Cas. 1133, reviewing a state statute which restricted the employment of all persons in bakeries to 10 hours in any one day. The court referred to Holden v. Hardy, supra, and, declar[ed] it to be inapplicable. . . .

In Bunting v. Oregon, 243 U.S. 426, . . . since the state Legislature and state Supreme Court had found such a law necessary for the preservation of the health of employees in these industries [mills, factories, and manufacturing establishments], this court . . . accept[ed] their judgment, in the absence of facts to support the contrary conclusion. . . .

In addition to the cases cited above, there are decisions of this court dealing with laws especially relating to hours of labor for women. Muller v. Oregon, 208 U.S. 412; Riley v. Massachusetts, 232 U.S. 671; Miller v. Wilson, 236 U.S. 373; Bosley v. McLaughlin, 236 U.S. 385.

In the *Muller* Case the validity of an Oregon statute, forbidding the employment of any female in certain industries more than 10 hours during any one day, was upheld. The decision proceeded upon the theory that the difference between the sexes may justify a different rule respecting hours of labor in the case of women than in the case of men. It is pointed out that these consist in differences of physical structure, especially in respect of the maternal functions, and also in the fact that historically woman has always been dependent upon man, who has established his control by superior physical strength. The Cases of *Riley, Miller,* and *Bosley* follow in this respect the *Muller* Case. But the ancient inequality of the sexes, otherwise than physical, as suggested in the *Muller* Case [208 U.S.] (p. 421), has continued "with diminishing intensity." In view of the great — not to say revolutionary — changes which have taken place since that utterance, in the contractual, political, and civil status of women, culminating in the Nineteenth Amendment, it is not unreasonable to say that these differences have now come almost, if not quite, to the vanishing point. In this aspect of the matter, while the physical differences must be recognized in appropriate cases, and legislation fixing hours or conditions of work may properly take them into account, we cannot accept the doctrine that women of mature age, sui juris, require or may be subjected to restrictions upon their liberty of contract which could not lawfully be imposed in the case of men under similar circumstances. To do so would be to ignore all the implications to be drawn from the present-day trend of legislation as well as that of common thought and usage, by which woman is accorded emancipation from the old doctrine that she must be given special protection or be subjected to special restraint in her contractual and civil relationships. In passing, it may be noted that the instant statute applies in the case of a woman employer contracting with a woman employee as it does when the former is a man.

The essential characteristics of the statute now under consideration, which differentiated it from the laws fixing hours of labor, will be made to appear as we proceed. It is sufficient now to point out that the latter . . . deal with incidents of the employment having no necessary effect upon the heart of the contract; that is, the amount of wages to be paid and received. A law forbidding work to continue beyond a given number of hours leaves the parties free to contract about wages and thereby equalize whatever additional burdens may be imposed upon the employer as a result of the restrictions as to hours, by an adjustment in respect of the amount of wages. Enough has been said to show that the authority to fix hours of labor cannot be exercised except in respect of those occupations where work of long continued duration is detrimental to health. This court has been careful in every case where the question has been raised, to place its decision upon this limited authority of the Legislature to regulate hours of labor and to disclaim any purpose to uphold the legislation as fixing wages, thus recognizing an essential difference between the two. It seems plain that these decisions afford no real support for any form of law establishing minimum wages.

If now, in the light furnished by the foregoing exceptions to the general rule forbidding legislative interference with freedom of contract, we examine and analyze the statute in question, we shall see that it differs from them in every material respect. It is not a law dealing with any business charged with a public interest or with public work, or to meet and tide over a temporary emergency. It has to do with the character, methods or periods of wage payments. It does not prescribe hours of labor or conditions under which labor is to be done. It is not for the protection of persons under legal disability or for the prevention of fraud. It is simply and exclusively a price-fixing law, confined to adult women (for we are not now considering the provisions relating to minors), who are legally as capable of contracting for themselves as men. It forbids two parties having lawful capacity — under penalties as to the employer — to freely contract with one another in respect of the price for which one shall render service to the other in a purely private employment where both are willing, perhaps anxious, to agree, even though the consequence may be to oblige one to surrender a desirable engagement and the other to dispense with the services of a desirable employee. The price fixed by the board need have no relation to the capacity or earning power of the employee, the number of hours which may happen to constitute the day's work, the character of the place where the work is to be done, or the circumstances or surroundings of the employment, and, while it has no other basis to support its validity than the assumed necessities of the employee, it takes no account of any independent resources she may have. It is based wholly on the opinions of the members of the board and their advisors — perhaps an average of their opinions, if they do not precisely agree — as to what will be necessary to provide a living for a woman, keep her in health and preserve her morals. It applies to any and every occupation in the District, without regard to its nature or the character of the work.

The standard furnished by the statute for the guidance of the board is so vague as to be impossible of practical application with any reasonable degree of accuracy. What is sufficient to supply the necessary cost of living for a woman worker and maintain her in good health and protect her morals is obviously not a precise or unvarying sum — not even approximately so. The amount will depend upon a variety of circumstances: The individual temperament, habits of thrift, care, ability to buy necessaries intelligently, and whether the woman lives alone or with her family. To those who practice economy, a given sum will afford comfort, while to those of contrary habit the same sum will be wholly inadequate. The co-operative economics of the family group are not taken into account, though they constitute an important consideration in estimating the cost of living, for it is obvious that the individual expense will be less in the case of a member of a family than in the case of one living alone. The relation between earnings and morals is not capable of standardization. It cannot be shown that well-paid women safeguard their morals more carefully than those who are poorly paid. Morality rests upon other considerations than wages, and there is, certainly, no such prevalent connection between the two as to justify a broad attempt to adjust the latter with reference to the former. As a means of safeguarding morals the attempted classification, in our opinion, is without reasonable basis. No distinction can be made between women who work for others and those who do not; nor is there ground for distinction between women and men, for, certainly, if women require a minimum wage to preserve their morals men require it to preserve their honesty. For these reasons, and others which might be stated, the inquiry in respect of the necessary cost of living and of the income necessary to preserve health and morals presents an individual and not a composite question, and must be answered for each individual considered by herself and not by a general formula prescribed by a statutory bureau. . . .

The law takes account of the necessities of only one party to the contract. It ignores the necessities of the employer by compelling him to pay not less than a certain sum, not only whether the employee is capable of earning it, but irrespective of the ability of his business to sustain the burden, generously leaving him, of course, the privilege of abandoning his business as an alternative for going on at a loss. Within the limits of the minimum sum, he is precluded, under penalty of fine and imprisonment, from adjusting compensation to the differing merits of his employees. It compels him to pay at least the sum fixed in any event, because the employee needs it, but requires no service of equivalent value from the employee. . . . The law is not confined to the great and powerful employers but embraces those whose bargaining power may be as weak as that of the employee. It takes no account of periods of stress and business depression, of crippling losses, which may leave the employer himself without adequate means of livelihood. To the extent that the sum fixed exceeds the fair value of the services rendered, it amounts to a compulsory exaction from the employer for the support of a partially indigent person, for whose condition there rests upon him no peculiar responsibility, and therefore, in effect, arbitrarily shifts to his shoulders a burden which, if it belongs to anybody, belongs to society as a whole.

The feature of this statute, which perhaps more than any other, puts upon it the stamp of invalidity, is that it exacts from the employer an arbitrary payment for a purpose and upon a basis having no causal connection with his business, or the contract or the work the employee engages to do. The declared basis, as already pointed out, is not the value of the service rendered, but the extraneous circumstance that the employee needs to get a prescribed sum of money to insure her subsistence, health, and morals. The ethical right of every worker, man or woman, to a living wage may be conceded. One of the declared and important purposes of trade organizations is to secure it. And with that principle and with every legitimate effort to realize it in fact, no one can quarrel; but the fallacy of the proposed method of attaining it is that it assumes that every employer is bound at all events to furnish it. The moral requirement implicit in every contract of employment, viz. that the amount to be paid and the service to be rendered shall bear to each other some relation of just equivalence, is completely ignored. . . .

It is said that great benefits have resulted from the operation of such statutes, not alone in the District of Columbia but in the several states, where they have been in force. A mass of reports, opinions of special observers and students of the subject, and the like, has been brought before us in support of this statement, all of which we have found interesting, but only mildly persuasive. That the earnings of women are now greater than they were formerly, and that conditions affecting women have become better in other respects, may be conceded; but convincing indications of the logical relation of these desirable changes to the law in question are significantly lacking. They may be, and quite probably are, due to other causes. We cannot close our eyes to the notorious fact that earnings everywhere in all occupations have greatly increased — not alone in states where the minimum wage law obtains but in the country generally — quite as much or more among men as among women, and in occupations outside the reach of the law as in those governed by it. No real test of the economic value of the law can be had during periods of maximum employment, when general causes keep wages up to or above the minimum; that will come in periods of depression and struggle for employment, when the efficient will be employed at the minimum rate, while the less capable may not be employed at all. . . .

It follows, from what has been said, that the act in question passes the limit prescribed by the Constitution, and accordingly the decrees of the court below are [a]ffirmed.

Mr. Justice Brandeis took no part in the consideration or decision of these cases.

Mr. Chief Justice Taft, dissenting.

Legislatures in limiting freedom of contract between employee and employer by a minimum wage proceed on the assumption that employees, in the class receiving least pay, are not upon a full level of equality of choice with their employer and in their necessitous circumstances are prone to accept pretty much anything that is offered. They are peculiarly subject to the overreaching of the harsh and greedy employer. The evils of the sweating system and of the long hours and low wages which are characteristic of it are well known. Now, I agree that it is a disputable question in the field of political economy how far a statutory requirement of maximum hours or minimum wages may be a useful remedy for these evils, and whether it may not make the case of the oppressed employee worse than it was before. But it is not the function of this court to hold congressional acts invalid simply because they are passed to carry out economic views which the court believes to be unwise or unsound. . . .

The right of the Legislature under the Fifth and Fourteenth Amendments to limit the hours of employment on the score of the health of the employee, it seems to me, has been firmly established. . . . [T]he line ha[s] been pricked out so that it has become a well formulated rule. In Holden v. Hardy . . . it was applied to miners and rested on the unfavorable environment of employment in mining and smelting. In Lochner v. New York . . . it was held that restricting those employed in bakeries to 10 hours a day was an arbitrary and invalid interference with the liberty of contract secured by the Fourteenth Amendment. Then followed a number of cases . . . beginning with Muller v. Oregon . . . sustaining the validity of a limit on maximum hours of labor for women to which I shall hereafter allude, and following these cases came Bunting v. Oregon. . . . In that case, this court sustained a law limiting the hours of labor of any person, whether man or woman, working in any mill, factory, or manufacturing establishment to 10 hours a day with a proviso as to further hours to which I shall hereafter advert. The law covered the whole field of industrial employment and certainly covered the case of persons employed in bakeries. Yet the opinion in the *Bunting* Case does not mention the *Lochner* Case. No one can suggest any constitutional distinction between employment in a bakery and one in any other kind of a manufacturing establishment which should make a limit of hours in the one invalid, and the same limit in the other permissible. It is impossible for me to reconcile the *Bunting* Case and the *Lochner* Case, and I have always supposed that the *Lochner* Case was thus overruled sub silentio. Yet the opinion of the court herein in support of its conclusion quotes from the opinion in the *Lochner* Case as one which has been sometimes distinguished but never overruled. . . .

However, the opinion herein does not overrule the *Bunting* Case in express terms, and therefore I assume that the conclusion in this case rests on the distinction between a minimum of wages and a maximum of hours in the limiting of liberty to contract. I regret to be at variance with the court as to the substance of this distinction. In absolute freedom of contract the one term is as important as the other, for both enter equally into the consideration given and received, a restriction as to one is not any greater in essence than the other, and is of the same kind. One is the multiplier and the other the multiplicand.

If it be said that long hours of labor have a more direct effect upon the health of the employee than the low wage, there is very respectable authority from close observers, disclosed in the record and in the literature on the subject quoted at length in the briefs that they are equally harmful in this regard. Congress took this view and we cannot say it was not warranted in so doing. . . .

. . . I respectfully submit that Muller v. Oregon . . . controls this case. . . .

I am not sure from a reading of the opinion whether the court thinks the authority of Muller v. Oregon is shaken by the adoption of the Nineteenth Amendment. The Nineteenth Amendment did not change the physical strength or limitations of women upon which the decision in Muller v. Oregon rests. The amendment did give women political power and makes more certain that legislative provisions for their protection will be in accord with their interests as they see them. But I do not think we are warranted in varying constitutional construction based on physical differences between men and women, because of the amendment. . . .

I am authorized to say that Mr. Justice SANFORD concurs in this opinion.

Mr. Justice HOLMES, dissenting.

The question in this case is the broad one. Whether Congress can establish minimum rates of wages for women in the District of Columbia, with due provision for special circumstances, or whether we must say that Congress had no power to meddle with the matter at all. To me, notwithstanding the deference due to the prevailing judgment of the Court, the power of Congress seems absolutely free from doubt. . . .

The earlier decisions upon the same words [the Due Process Clause of the Fifth Amendment] in the Fourteenth Amendment began within our memory and went no farther than an unpretentious assertion of the liberty to follow the ordinary callings. Later that innocuous generality was expanded into the dogma, Liberty of Contract. Contract is not specially mentioned in the text that we have to construe. It is merely an example of doing what you want to do, embodied in the word liberty. But pretty much all law consists in forbidding men to do some things that they want to do, and contract is no more exempt from law than other acts. Without enumerating all the restrictive laws that have been upheld I will mention a few that seem to me to have interfered with liberty of contract quite as seriously and directly as the one before us. Usury laws prohibit contracts by which a man receives more than so much interest for the money he lends. Statutes of frauds restrict many contracts to certain forms. Some Sunday laws prohibit practically all contracts during one-seventh of our whole life. Insurance rates may be regulated. . . .

I confess that I do not understand the principle on which the power to fix a minimum for the wages of women can be denied by those who admit the power to fix a maximum for their hours of work. I fully assent to the proposition that here as elsewhere the distinctions of the law are distinctions of degree, but I perceive no difference in the kind or degree of interference with liberty, the only matter with which we have any concern, between the one case and the other. The bargain is equally affected whichever half you regulate. Muller v. Oregon, I take it is as good law today as it was in 1908. It will need more than the Nineteenth Amendment to convince me that there are no differences between men and women, or that legislation cannot take those differences into account. I should not hesitate to take them into account if I thought it necessary to sustain this Act. Quong Wing v. Kirkendall, 223 U.S. 59, 63, 32 S.Ct. 192, 56 L. Ed. 350. But after Bunting v. Oregon, . . . I had supposed that it was not necessary, and that Lochner v. New York . . . would be allowed a deserved repose. . . .

I am of the opinion that the statute is valid and that the decree should be reversed.

NOTE: MINIMUM WAGES, MAXIMUM HOURS, AND HEALTH

The ground on which the *Adkins* Court invalidated the District of Columbia minimum-wage law for women without overruling Muller v. Oregon was that of the "obvious" relationship between hours of work and health and the lack of relationship between minimum wages and health. The dissenters contended that as far as liberty of contract was concerned, the distinction had no merit; as Justice Holmes said, "The bargain is equally affected whichever half you regulate."

Holmes's argument, although accurate, is not wholly responsive to several concerns expressed in the majority opinion. First, the majority argued that the biological justifications advanced in *Muller* for infringing women's liberty of contract did not apply equally to a minimum-wage law. The sharp distinction they insisted on drawing between the direct relationship between the physical frailty of women and the physical strain of long hours under poor working conditions and the indirect relationship between women's health and low wages is an indication of their continued preference for the "common understanding" approach that they had used in both *Lochner* and *Muller,* but departed from in *Bunting.* Although the end result of long hours and low wages on the health of workers might be the same, the majority seem to have focused on the "common sense" idea that the concrete intervention of sending women home early was quite different from a law requiring employers to give women enough money so that they would not starve. A similar "common sense" perception, which reinforced the distinction the Court drew between maximum-hours laws and minimum-wage laws, was that if wages were too low, men would starve as quickly as women.

NOTE: THE ECONOMIC BURDEN OF PROTECTION

The second concern expressed by the majority is more troubling. According to Justice Sutherland, the effect of a maximum-hours law on a contract is not necessarily the same as the effect of a minimum-wage law, because "a law forbidding work to continue beyond a given number of hours leaves the parties free to contract about wages and thereby equalize whatever additional burdens may be imposed upon the employer as a result of the restrictions as to hours, by an adjustment in respect of the amount of wages."[75] If a woman worker's wages are decreased to compensate for the decrease in the number of hours she is able to work by law, she bears the economic burden of the decision of the legislature that the mothers of the race must be protected from overwork. If the employer is required to give a set rate per hour or per day, and is prohibited from increasing her hours to make up the increased cost, the employer bears the economic burden of protection. The implication of the Court's position, then, is that it is constitutional to force women to pay the economic price of protecting the state's interest in healthy children, but that placing the same burden on the employer is unconstitutional.

Finally, the slippery slope from minimum-wage legislation to income redistribution concerned the Court — not only employers, but the wealthy as a class, might be forced to contribute to the support of indigent workers. An argument then in vogue was that employers who paid less than subsistence wages were actually parasitic, forcing society to make up the deficit and forcing fair employers out of business. But this analysis apparently did not move the Court.

NOTE: THE "FEMINISM" OF THE ADKINS COURT

The Court in *Adkins* was clearly influenced by the passage of the Nineteenth Amendment in reaching its conclusion that, as to minimum-wage legislation, women and men had equal rights to full freedom of contract. And at this historical point, there were many former suffragists who were arguing against the unequal effects and implications of "protective" laws for women only.[76]

75. 261 U.S. at 569.
76. The account of the split in the women's movement over "protective" laws after suffrage was won

In evaluating the feminism of the Court, however, it is important to note that the *Adkins* case was decided at a time when the Supreme Court was invalidating on substantive due process grounds an unusually high percentage of state statutes regulating economic and social relations. One commentator, writing in 1927, found that, in cases decided under the Due Process Clause involving such state statutes, "from 1868 to 1912 the Court held against the legislation in a little more than 6 percent of the cases; [while between 1920 and 1927] . . . the Court . . . held against the legislature in 28 percent of the cases."[77] This trend continued through the middle of the next decade, with increasing percentages of Supreme Court invalidations of social and economic legislation.[78]

Even given this trend, the new policy of equal treatment of men and women workers with regard to liberty of contract was accepted by a bare majority of the Court (unlike the *Muller* decision, which was unanimous). Furthermore, although the *Adkins* case was followed by lower courts and the U.S. Supreme Court for almost fifteen years before being overruled, its application was strictly limited to laws fixing minimum wages.[79] By 1936, in the last case in which the Supreme Court followed the *Adkins* holding, Morehead v. New York ex rel. Tipaldo, 298 U.S. 587, 56 S. Ct. 918, 80 L. Ed. 1347, the majority ruled only on the argument presented in the petition for certiorari: that the statute in question was distinguishable from that considered in *Adkins.* Chief Justice Hughes dissented on the ground that the two statutes were in fact dissimilar;[80] Justice Stone, in an opinion joined by Brandeis and Cardozo, rejected the ruling of the majority that the question of the continuing constitutional validity of *Adkins* was not before the Court, and argued strongly for reversal of the lower court decision on the grounds of deference to legislative judgment as to the wisdom of the New York law. The view of these three dissenters was shortly to prevail, as part of the massive reconsideration and reversal of many substantive due process decisions under the increasing pressure of the Depression, unfavorable popular opinion, and President Roosevelt's threatened plan to expand the Court and pack it with more liberal justices. The first major case to indicate the Court's change in attitude toward state economic and social regulation was Nebbia v. New York, 291 U.S. 502, 54 S. Ct. 505, 78 L. Ed. 940 (1934), upholding a state law creating a board with power to fix milk prices. West Coast Hotel Co. v. Parrish was next.

---

is given in Chapter Two, II-B. In *Adkins,* counsel for Children's Hospital referred to the position of the National Woman's Party as follows:

"The National Woman's Party stands for equality between men and women in all laws. This includes laws affecting the position of women in industry, as well as other laws. The Woman's Party does not take any position with regard to the merits of the minimum wage legislation but demands that such legislation, if passed, shall be for both sexes. It is opposed to all legislation having a sex basis and applying to one sex alone."

He also quotes Carrie Chapman Catt, president of NAWSA, saying: "It is more important than any other consideration at this time, that every human being who is obliged to earn his or her living have absolute freedom to find any employment which seems suitable and profitable, without discrimination or restrictions of any kind." Oral Argument at 6, Adkins v. Children's Hospital, 261 U.S. 525 (1923).

77. Brown, Due Process of Law, Police Power, and the Supreme Court, 40 Harv. L. Rev. 943, 944-945 (1927).

78. See Wright, The Growth of American Constitutional Law 154 (1942). A summary of the laws invalidated in this period appears in Corwin, The Constitution of the United States 1431-1485 (1964 ed.); for a survey of laws sustained, see id. at 973-985, 1093-1146, 1284-1300.

79. Murphy v. Sardell, 269 U.S. 530, 46 S. Ct. 22, 70 L. Ed. 396 (1925); Donham v. West-Nelson Mfg. Co., 273 U.S. 657, 47 S. Ct. 343, 71 L. Ed. 825 (1926); Topeka Laundry Co. v. Court of Industrial Relations, 119 Kan. 12, 237 P. 1041 (1925); Stevenson v. St. Clair, 161 Minn. 444, 201 N.W. 629 (1925).

80. However, although the majority limited its holding to this question, the opinion reaffirmed the *Adkins* position in forceful dicta that were later quoted by the dissenters in West Coast Hotel v. Parrish, 300 U.S. 379, 57 S. Ct. 578, 81 L. Ed. 703 (1937), infra. The National Woman's Party filed a brief in this case urging the correctness of *Adkins;* they were joined by the National Association of Women Lawyers, the Bookbinders Union, the Brooklyn-Manhattan Transit Women's League, the Business Women's Legislative Council of California, and the Women's Equal Opportunity League of New York.

WEST COAST HOTEL CO. v. PARRISH
300 U.S. 379, 57 S. Ct. 578, 81 L. Ed. 703 (1937)

Mr. Chief Justice Hughes delivered the opinion of the Court.

This case presents the question of the constitutional validity of the minimum wage law of the state of Washington. . . .

"Sec. 3. There is hereby created a commission to be known as the 'Industrial Welfare Commission' for the State of Washington, to establish such standards of wages and conditions of labor for women and minors employed within the State of Washington, as shall be held hereunder to be reasonable and not detrimental to health and morals, and which shall be sufficient for the decent maintenance of women."

Further provisions required the commission to ascertain the wages and conditions of labor of women and minors within the state. Public hearings were to be held. If after investigation the commission found that in any occupation, trade, or industry the wages paid to women were "inadequate to supply them necessary cost of living and to maintain the workers in health," the commission was empowered to call a conference of representatives of employers and employees together with disinterested persons representing the public. The conference was to recommend to the commission, on its request, an estimate of a minimum wage adequate for the purpose above stated, and on the approval of such a recommendation it became the duty of the commission to issue an obligatory order fixing minimum wages. Any such order might be reopened and the question reconsidered with the aid of the former conference or a new one. . . .

The appellant conducts a hotel. The appellee Elsie Parrish was employed as a chambermaid and (with her husband) brought suit to recover the difference between the wages paid her and the minimum wage fixed pursuant to the state law. The minimum wage was $14.50 per week of 48 hours. The appellant challenged the act as repugnant to the due process clause of the Fourteenth Amendment of the Constitution of the United States. . . .

The appellant relies upon the decision of this Court in *Adkins* v. Children's Hospital, 261 U.S. 525. . . .

The Supreme Court of Washington has . . . refused to regard the decision in the *Adkins* Case as determinative and has pointed to our decisions both before and since that case as justifying its position. We are of the opinion that this ruling of the state court demands on our part a re-examination of the *Adkins* Case. . . .

. . . [R]egulation which is reasonable in relation to its subject and is adopted in the interests of the community is due process.

This essential limitation of liberty in general governs freedom of contract in particular. . . .

The point that has been strongly stressed that adult employees should be deemed competent to make their own contracts was decisively met nearly forty years ago in Holden v. Hardy,[169 U.S. 366] . . . where we pointed out the inequality in the footing of the parties. We said (id., 397):

> The legislature has also recognized the fact, which the experience of legislators in many states has corroborated, that the proprietors of these establishments and their operatives do not stand upon an equality, and that their interests are, to a certain extent, conflicting. The former naturally desire to obtain as much labor as possible from their employes, while the latter are often induced by the fear of discharge to conform to regulation which their judgment, fairly exercised, would pronounce to be detrimental to their health or strength. In other words, the proprietors lay down the rules, and the laborers are practically constrained to obey them. In such cases self-interest is often an unsafe guide; and the legislature may properly interpose its authority.

And we added the fact "that both parties are of full age, and competent to contract, does not necessarily deprive the state of the power to interfere, where the parties do not stand upon an equality, or where the public health demands that one party to the contract shall be protected against himself." "The state still retains an interest in his welfare, however reckless he may be. The whole is no greater than the sum of all the parts, and when the individual health, safety, and welfare are sacrificed or neglected, the state must suffer."

It is manifest that this established principle is peculiarly applicable in relation to the employment of women in whose protection the state has a special interest. That phase of the subject received elaborate consideration in Muller v. Oregon (1908) 208 U.S. 412, 28 S. Ct. 324, 326, 52 L. Ed. 551, 13 Ann. Cas. 957, where the constitutional authority of the state to limit the working hours of women was sustained. . . . Again in Quong Wing v. Kirkendall, 223 U.S. 59, 63, in referring to a differentiation with respect to the employment of women, we said that the Fourteenth Amendment did not interfere with state power by creating a "fictitious equality." We referred to recognized classifications on the basis of sex with regard to hours of work and in other matters, and we observed that the particular points at which that difference shall be enforced by legislation were largely in the power of the state. In later rulings this Court sustained the regulation of hours of work of women employees in Riley v. Massachusetts, 232 U.S. 671 (factories), Miller v. Wilson, 236 U.S. 373 (hotels), and Bosley v. McLaughlin, 236 U.S. 385 (hospitals).

This array of precedents and the principles they applied were thought by the dissenting Justices in the Adkins Case to demand that the minimum wage statute be sustained. The validity of the distinction made by the Court between a minimum wage and a maximum of hours in limiting liberty of contract was especially challenged. 261 U.S., p. 564. That challenge persists and is without any satisfactory answer. . . .

We think that the . . . *Adkins* Case was a departure from the true application of the principles governing the regulation by the state of the relation of employer and employed. Those principles have been reenforced by our subsequent decisions. Thus in Radice v. New York, 264 U.S. 292, we sustained the New York statute which restricted the employment of women in restaurants at night. . . .

. . . What can be closer to the public interest than the health of women and their protection from unscrupulous and overreaching employers? And if the protection of women is a legitimate end of the exercise of state power, how can it be said that the requirement of the payment of a minimum wage fairly fixed in order to meet the very necessities of existence is not an admissible means to that end? The Legislature of the state was clearly entitled to consider the situation of women in employment, the fact that they are in the class receiving the least pay, that their bargaining power is relatively weak, and that they are the ready victims of those who would take advantage of their necessitous circumstances. The Legislature was entitled to adopt measures to reduce the evils of the "sweating system," the exploiting of workers at wages so low as to be insufficient to meet the bare cost of living, thus making their very helplessness the occasion of a most injurious competition. The Legislature had the right to consider that its minimum wage requirements would be an important aid in carrying out its policy of protection. The adoption of similar requirements by many states evidences a deepseated conviction both as to the presence of the evil and as to the means adapted to check it. Legislative response to that conviction cannot be regarded as arbitrary or capricious and that is all we have to decide. Even if the wisdom of the policy be regarded as debatable and its effects uncertain, still the Legislature is entitled to its judgment.

There is an additional and compelling consideration which recent economic experience has brought into a strong light. The exploitation of a class of workers who are in an unequal position with respect to bargaining power and are thus relatively defenseless against the denial of a living wage is not only detrimental to their health and well being, but casts a direct burden for their support upon the community. What these workers lose in wages the taxpayers are called upon to pay. The bare cost of living must be met. We may take judicial notice of the unparalleled demands for relief which arose during the recent period of depression and still continue to an alarming extent despite the degree of economic recovery which has been achieved. It is unnecessary to cite official statistics to establish what is of common knowledge through the length and breadth of the land. While in the instant case no factual brief has been presented, there is no reason to doubt that the state of Washington has encountered the same social problem that is present elsewhere. The community is not bound to provide what is in effect a subsidy for unconscionable employers. The community may direct its lawmaking power to correct the abuse which springs from their selfish disregard of the public interest. The argument that the legislation in question constitutes an arbitrary discrimination, because it does not extend to men, is unavailing. This Court has frequently held that the legislative authority, acting within its proper field, is not bound to extend its regulation to all cases which it might possibly reach. The Legislature "is free to recognize degrees of harm and it may confine its restrictions to those classes of cases where the need is deemed to be clearest." If "the law presumably hits the evil where it is most felt, it is not to be overthrown because there are other instances to which it might have been applied." . . . This familiar principle has repeatedly been applied to legislation which singles out women, and particular classes of women, in the exercise of the state's protective power. . . . Their relative need in the presence of the evil, no less than the existence of the evil itself, is a matter for the legislative judgment.

Our conclusion is that the case of Adkins v. Children's Hospital, supra, should be, and it is, overruled. The judgment of the Supreme Court of the state of Washington is affirmed.

Affirmed.

Mr. Justice SUTHERLAND, dissenting.

Mr. Justice VAN DEVANTER, Mr. Justice McREYNOLDS, Mr. Justice BUTLER, and I think the judgment of the court below should be reversed. . . .

The Washington statute, like the one for the District of Columbia, fixes minimum wages for adult women. Adult men and their employers are left free to bargain as they please; and it is a significant and an important fact that all state statutes to which our attention has been called are of like character. The common-law rules restricting the power of women to make contracts have, under our system, long since practically disappeared. Women today stand upon a legal and political equality with men. There is no longer any reason why they should be put in different classes in respect of their legal right to make contracts; nor should they be denied, in effect, the right to compete with men for work paying lower wages which men may be willing to accept. And it is an arbitrary exercise of the legislative power to do so. In the *Tipaldo* case [Morehead v. New York ex rel. Tipaldo], 298 U.S. 587, 615, it appeared that the New York Legislature had passed two minimum-wage measures — one dealing with women alone, the other with both men and women. The act which included men was vetoed by the Governor. The other, applying to women alone, was approved. The "factual background" in respect of both measures was substantially the same. In pointing out the arbitrary discrimination which resulted, pp. 615-617, we said:

> These legislative declarations, in form of findings or recitals of fact, serve well to illustrate why any measure that deprives employers and adult women of freedom to agree upon wages, leaving employers and men employees free to do so, is necessarily arbitrary. Much, if not all that in them is said in justification of the regulations that the act imposes in respect of women's wages apply with equal force in support of the same regulation of men's wages. While men are left free to fix their wages by agreement with employers, it would be fanciful to suppose that the regulation of women's wages would be useful to prevent or lessen the evils listed in the first section of the act. Men in need of work are as likely as women to accept the low wages offered by

unscrupulous employers. Men in greater number than women support themselves and dependents and because of need will work for whatever wages they can get and that without regard to the value of the service and even though the pay is less than minima prescribed in accordance with this act. It is plain that, under circumstances such as those portrayed in the "factual background," prescribing of minimum wages for women alone would unreasonably restrain them in competition with men and tend arbitrarily to deprive them of employment and a fair chance to find work.

. . . Since the contractual rights of men and women are the same, does the legislation here invoked, by restricting only the rights of women to make contracts as to wages, create an arbitrary discrimination? We think it does. Difference of sex affords no reasonable ground for making a restriction applicable to the wage contracts of all working women from which like contracts of all working men are left free. Certainly a suggestion that the bargaining ability of the average women is not equal to that of the average man would lack substance. The ability to make a fair bargain, as every one knows, does not depend upon sex.

If, in the light of the facts, the state legislation, without reason or for reasons of mere expediency, excluded men from the provisions of the legislation, the power was exercised arbitrarily. . . .

Finally, it may be said that a statute absolutely fixing wages in the various industries at definite sums and forbidding employers and employees from contracting for any other than those designated would probably not be thought to be constitutional. It is hard to see why the power to fix minimum wages does not connote a like power in respect of maximum wages. . . .

NOTE

Although West Coast Hotel was limited in its holding to minimum-wage legislation affecting women and minors only, it was later to encompass minimum-wage legislation in general. In United States v. Darby, 312 U.S. 100, 61 S. Ct. 451, 85 L. Ed. 609 (1941), the Court upheld the validity of the Fair Labor Standards Act, which prescribed minimum wages and maximum hours for all workers employed in the production of goods for interstate commerce. In striking the fatal blow to substantive due process, the Court escaped at last from the constitutional need to establish a difference between men and women:[81]

> . . . Since our decision in West Coast Hotel Co. v. Parrish, 300 U.S. 379, it is no longer open to question that the fixing of a minimum wage is within the legislative power and that the bare fact of its exercise is not a denial of due process under the Fifth more than under the Fourteenth Amendment. Nor is it any longer open to question that it is within the legislative power to fix maximum hours. Holden v. Hardy, 169 U.S. 366; Muller v. Oregon, 208 U.S. 412; Bunting v. Oregon, 243 U.S. 426; Baltimore & Ohio R. Co. v. Interstate Commerce Comm'n [221 U.S. 612]. Similarly, the statute is not objectionable because applied to both men and women. Cf. Bunting v. Oregon, 243 U.S. 426.

81. 312 U.S. at 125.

III. THE NINETEENTH AMENDMENT

A. THE STRUGGLE FOR PASSAGE AND THE EFFECT OF THE AMENDMENT ON AMERICAN SOCIETY

AMENDMENT XIX
[Proposed by Congress on June 5, 1919; ratified August 26, 1920]

The right of citizens of the United States to vote shall not be denied or abridged by the United States or by any State on account of sex. Congress shall have the power to enforce this article by appropriate legislation.

Fantastic human effort finally gained passage of the Nineteenth Amendment:[1]

> To get the word male in effect out of the Constitution cost the women of the country fifty-two years of pauseless campaign. . . . During that time they were forced to conduct 56 campaigns of referenda to male voters; 480 campaigns to urge Legislatures to submit suffrage amendments to voters; 47 campaigns to induce State constitutional conventions to write woman suffrage into State constitutions; 277 campaigns to persuade State party conventions to include woman suffrage planks; 30 campaigns to urge presidential party conventions to adopt woman suffrage planks in party platforms, and 19 campaigns with 19 successive Congresses. Millions of dollars were raised, mainly in small sums, and expended with economic care. Hundreds of women gave the accumulated possibilities of an entire lifetime; thousands gave constant interest and such aid as they could. It was a continuous, seemingly endless, chain of activity.

A number of excellent works, some recent and some by the suffragist leaders themselves, record the full history of the final decades of the fight for the vote.[2] Here, because it sheds light on later efforts to change women's legal status, follows a brief discussion, based primarily on William Chafe's excellent history, The American Woman, Her Changing Social, Economic and Political Roles, 1920–1970 (1972), of explanations for the duration and difficulty of the suffrage campaign and for the rapid decline in feminist activity after the vote was won.

Historians of the suffrage movement often focus on the tactical and strategic decisions of suffrage leaders and organization — whether to take militant action, whether to suspend suffrage agitation during World War I, whether state referenda or a federal constitutional amendment was a better route to victory, whether to follow the British lead and hold the party in power responsible for the failure to grant suffrage. For the present-day reader the accounts of inspiring conventions, grueling campaigns, and leadership and factional disputes have a tendency to blur together. In reading them, one can lose sight of the most striking feature of the fight — that it took so long to win.

Numerous explanations have been offered for the high cost in time and effort of the suffrage struggle. Some historians hold that organizational flaws were responsible, such as the early focus on state rather than national campaigns, the small number of full-time workers, and the inadequate financing characteristic of most state suffrage campaigns. A second explanation is the active, though often undercover, opposition by liquor and business interests who believed that women would vote for sweeping re-

---

1. Catt and Shuler, Woman Suffrage and Politics 107-108 (Americana Library ed. 1970).
2. In addition to the works by Chafe, Flexner, Kraditor, and O'Neill cited in Parts I and II of this chapter, see Grimes, The Puritan Ethic and Woman Suffrage (1967); Catt and Shuler, supra; Stanton, Anthony, Gage, and Harper, History of Woman Suffrage (6 vols. 1881–1922); Schneir (ed.), Feminism: The Essential Historical Writings (1972); and Scott, The Southern Lady (1972).

forms, a belief reinforced by suffrage propaganda aimed at winning the support of reform-minded people. A third factor related to this is the corruptibility of politicians and of ignorant immigrant voters, which enabled the liquor and business interests to buy votes both in the legislature and at the polls. Often cited also is the opposition of white southerners, because of both their long-standing support of states' rights and their unwillingness to enfranchise black women. In fact, nine of the ten states which rejected the Nineteenth Amendment were below the Mason-Dixon line; among southern states, only Texas, Tennessee, Kentucky, and Arkansas voted to accept it.[3]

However, the most important single cause of the duration of the suffrage struggle was probably feminism's radical challenge to the status quo. At the time of the Seneca Falls Convention in 1848, women had very few legal and political rights, and the young movement advocated sweeping reforms. As long as there was a great gap between feminist demands and the reality of women's situations, the feminist platform appeared threatening to the whole social order. But through the efforts of women[4] and through other economic and historical forces, the legal position of women changed greatly in the years from 1848 to 1920. "Common law restrictions had largely been removed. Educational opportunity was available at a variety of private colleges and public universities."[5] There had been a large increase in the number of women working outside the home: "during World War I, thousands of women had moved into jobs formerly held by men, causing many observers to assert that a revolution in the economic role of women had occurred."[6]

At the same time, suffrage leaders further narrowed the gap between women's demands and reality by a "strategy of compromise."[7] Part II of this chapter described the process of "tempering those ideas most likely to offend public sensibilities and playing up the social utility of the ballot,"[8] which enabled leaders like Carrie Chapman Catt to build a national consensus for suffrage. By the close of World War I, the feminism of the early leaders had been sufficiently transformed by the drive to win suffrage that votes for women were less likely to be associated in the public consciousness with more threatening ideas like free love and the concomitant destruction of the home. And millions of women had rallied to the suffrage banner; the National American Women's Suffrage Association (NAWSA) alone boasted two million members by the time suffrage was won.[9]

Thus, because of the radicalism of 1848, the suffrage battle was long and arduous. Yet as women became necessarily more conservative and their societal position improved for various reasons, the vote seemed by 1920 the last step toward formal legal equality with men. But the process of mutual compromise was costly for the feminist movement because in some sense the vote was won while the platform for its exercise was lost. As Chafe explained:[10]

> . . . if women were to fulfill the expectations of female leaders, they had to vote together, organize on the basis of sex and demonstrate a collective allegiance to common ideals and programs. The validity of suffragist claims thus turned ultimately on the question of whether women would create a separate "bloc" in the electorate, committed to a distinctive set of interests and values.

3. Catt and Shuler, supra, at 462; Scott, supra, at 184.
4. The activities of the women's movement in bringing about legal reforms in the nineteenth century are detailed in Chapter Three, III-B.
5. Chafe, supra, at 22.
6. Ibid.
7. Id. at 20.
8. Ibid.
9. Id. at 37.
10. Id. at 26.

Immediately after woman suffrage was won, this seemed to be what was happening. In several state and local campaigns, women were able to mobilize female votes to defeat candidates and measures they opposed, and to win victories for their side.[11] Both state and federal legislators feared the opposition of the newly enfranchised women, and enacted a number of reform statutes which suffrage leaders supported, both in the women's rights area (e.g., jury service statutes) and in other areas (e.g., the Sheppard-Towner maternal and child health bill).[12] But by 1925 it became clear that women were not performing at the polls as suffragists had predicted. Women voters accounted for less than 40 percent of the total in most of the elections in the 1920s for which tabulations were available, and studies showed that there was little or no distinction between the political behavior of men and women.[13] Nor did organized women's groups fare any better. The League of Women Voters, for instance, which was organized to carry on where the National American Woman Suffrage Association left off, claimed to represent all the former members of NAWSA, but in fact it kept only a fraction. "Cleveland contributed 80,000 women to the suffrage fight, only 8,000 to the League."[14] "By mid-decade . . . the woman's movement had regressed to its earlier status as a small cadre of activists."[15]

The explanations that most suffrage historians have offered for the abrupt decline in women's movement activity after victory, and for the failure of women to use the vote to carry on the struggle, focus on various features of the suffrage movement itself:

— its mistaken faith that the franchise represented real political power;
— its tendency to exaggerate the good that women would do with the vote and the resulting disappointment when the heralded reforms did not occur;
— its middle-of-the-road, middle-class character and politics;
— the compromise it made from its original radical feminist position to its final narrow focus on the vote;
— its failure to develop a broad theoretical analysis of the weaknesses of American society and the position of women within it;
— dissension between radical feminists and social feminist reformers within the women's movement about the goals of the postsuffrage struggle, exacerbated by the postwar reaction against social change, attacks on the patriotism of reformers, including feminists, and red-baiting by right-wing groups.

However, the suffragists' limitations in foresight, political strategy, and ideology can not wholly account for the failure to use the vote effectively. They probably would not have been able to change the course of history even if they had been more farsighted or militant, and they might not have changed it as much as they did, had they been discouraged by knowing in advance that woman suffrage was ". . . a reform, not a revolution."[16] Furthermore, it is just as likely that the failure of the large majority of women to become politically active accounted for many of the problems within feminist organizations, as that the problems of feminist organizations account for lack of political activism among women — or that the same factors which explain one also explain the other.

The most persuasive explanation for the political inactivity of women in the postsuffrage era is that their social and legal position was still not strong enough for effective action. It is true that World War I was a watershed in women's history, increasing beyond any previous level their participation in the labor force, their emanci-

11. Ibid.
12. Id. at 27-29.
13. Id. at 30-32.
14. Id. at 37.
15. Ibid.
16. Id. at 47.

pation from traditional roles, and their role in public life. But although they were working in increasing numbers, women were confined to the lowest-paid, lowest-status jobs. Furthermore,[17]

> Only 5 percent of the women workers joined the labor force for the first time in the war years. The rest had transferred from lower paying jobs and were expected to return to them when the emergency passed. . . .
> More important, whatever positive impact the war did have was short lived. . . .
> . . . [Even] the federal government itself continued to discriminate against female employees. . . . Neither the labor movement nor the government was ready to accept a permanent shift in women's economic role.

Some observers point to the facts that the women working in the 20s were older, on the average, than women workers in earlier periods and that more of them were married, and interpret these changes as a sign of greater emancipation of women within marriage. According to Chafe, however, the changes in the age and marital status of women workers[18]

> . . . had little if anything to do with female freedom to pursue a life outside the home on a basis of equality with men. The greatest jump in employment among wives after 1910 occurred during the Depression. . . . Married women worked, not because they sought liberation from the burdens of domesticity or enjoyed a new equality with men in the job market but so that their families could survive economically. Moreover, the jobs they filled were of the most menial sort. Thirty-six percent of married women were employed in domestic and personal service, and another 20 percent worked in apparel and canning factories. . . . The poorest states . . . had the highest proportion of married women working.

The Depression also brought widespread demands that men be given preference for jobs over married women, whether or not the women's families needed the money or the women were better qualified for the jobs. The willingness of many employers to fire women employees in favor of men, and the public support for such policies, indicate how tenuous the position of women in the labor market was.

Thus, in the 1920s and 1930s, although women were more emancipated from traditional roles than they had been in the nineteenth century, they were not yet sufficiently economically independent to be able to organize politically. Moreover, the social position of women was such that there was no consensus upon which the use of the vote could be based. As noted before, in the course of the long struggle for the vote, the suffragists themselves had lost much of the sense of the justice of the women's cause as the rationale for their efforts, and were therefore in no position to unify women around a radical feminist banner. And the expediency argument of the social feminist justification for the suffrage movement — that women should seek the vote in order to use it altruistically to bring social change — could not galvanize the mass of women voters. It is one thing to organize in one's own self-interest, with the additional motive of reforming the world; it is another to defy cultural norms to vote for social changes which are only distantly related to personal concerns. Although the vote had been hailed by feminists as the key to the solution of many of the problems of women workers, it, like most legal reforms, was merely a tool for social change, depending for its efficacy on the degree of popular support.

Chafe analyzes the postsuffrage situation as follows:[19]

17. Id. at 52-54.
18. Id. at 56-57.
19. Id. at 46.

... the suffragists had correctly assumed that all females shared a common experience based on their sex. But they failed to realize that, unlike some other minority groups, women were distributed throughout the social structure and had little opportunity to develop a positive sense of collective self-consciousness. More important, they underestimated the barriers obstructing the creation of such consciousness. One of the central experiences which women shared was their relationship with men, yet nothing did more to discourage the growth of an independent female constituency. . . . Occasionally an issue like the suffrage focused overriding attention on the identity of women as women and generated a heightened sense of sex solidarity. But such issues emerged only rarely, and in the normal course of events women responded to political questions in the manner dictated by the men in their lives. Females did behave alike, but the sameness of their actions represented conformity to the role of helpmate rather than an assertion of their independence as a sex.

The final analysis, then, must acknowledge the ironic aspects of the suffragist victory and its aftermath. The mass of women were too little liberated in 1920 to use the vote to free their sisters and themselves; and the suffragists were too little feminist at the end of the 72-year struggle to lead a new campaign against sexism. That would have to wait until 40 years had passed, and economic and political forces independent of organized feminist agitation had changed women's situation.

B. The Effect of the Amendment on the Laws

The Nineteenth Amendment failed to revolutionize American society through the cleansing and reforming agency of women's votes. However, its impact on the law was substantial. In addition to changing the constitutional provisions and voting laws of all states that did not already grant full suffrage to women, the amendment caused alterations in laws about jury duty and office holding, and influenced judicial opinions and legislative actions in other areas.

1. Voting and Qualifications for Voting

State courts were unanimous in holding that the Nineteenth Amendment automatically extended the franchise to women. Almost immediately after its passage, however, the courts divided on the impact of the amendment on voter qualification statutes, especially qualifications related to marital status and the family.

a. Age and Literacy Qualifications

The two cases considered in this section, one of which arose in Ohio in 1920, and the other in Kentucky in 1932, both held that the qualifications for voting must be the same for both sexes. In the first case, a woman who had filed an affidavit stating that she was qualified to vote and that she was over the age of twenty-one sued for a writ of mandamus to compel the election officials to register her without requiring her to state her exact age, as required by Ohio voting law. The court had no problem in ruling that "the Nineteenth Amendment . . . conferred upon women no greater or different right with respect to the exercise of the elective franchise than had theretofore been possessed and enjoyed by men under the constitutions and laws of the states."[20] Thus, the case was "to be considered without regard to the sex of the relator," and the woman was required to state her age.

The second case was a suit brought by an unsuccessful school board candidate to contest the election results on the ground, inter alia, that several of the women who had

20. State ex rel. Klein v. Hillenbrand, 101 Ohio 370, 372, 130 N.E. 29 (1920).

cast their votes for his opponent were illiterate. Prior to the passage of the Nineteenth Amendment, Kentucky had passed a statute permitting women to vote in school elections, provided they could read and write and possessed the legal qualifications of male voters. In rejecting this challenge the court stated:[21]

> The validity of the Nineteenth Amendment was sustained in Leser v. Garnett, 258 U.S. 130, 42 S. Ct. 217, 66 L. Ed. 505. It is in the exact language of the Fifteenth Amendment, with the substitution of the word "sex" for the words "race, color, or previous condition of servitude," which, during its testing time, was consistently and uniformly held not to confer the right to vote upon the negro, but having the effect ex proprio vigore of striking from the laws of all states the word "white." Neal v. Delaware, 103 U.S. 370, 26 L. Ed. 567. Upon the same reasoning and following [the authorities interpreting the Fifteenth Amendment], the courts before whom the Nineteenth Amendment has come for interpretation have given it the same construction, and held that it is self-executing and became automatically operative by its inherent force. Under it women are politically emancipated and are not and may not be disqualified from voting on account of being women. [Citations omitted.] Therefore all of the laws of this commonwealth which denied or abridged the right of suffrage to women have yielded to the superior mandate, and it must be held that they have constructively, though very effectually, been repealed or rendered nugatory.
>
> But it is said by the appellant that the terms of this statute granting a limited right of suffrage to women in school elections is not discriminatory because of sex, but merely sets up a test of literacy. The argument is a specious one, for male voters are not required to meet the same test. Its limitation only applies to women, and it is therefore discriminatory against them. Illiterate women, no less than illiterate men, may exercise the right of suffrage in Kentucky, and such votes cast for the appellee were properly counted.

b. Poll Taxes

Courts were divided as to whether the Nineteenth Amendment required that women pay poll taxes where they had not previously been required to do so. The reasoning of the courts which required payment was that the Nineteenth Amendment "protects the men and women alike, and a burden cannot be placed upon one sex that is not put upon the other, nor can a privilege, benefit, or exemption be given one to the exclusion of the other. . . ."[22] The United States Supreme Court, however, held that women were not required to pay the tax.

BREEDLOVE v. SUTTLES
302 U.S. 277, 58 S. Ct. 205, 82 L. Ed. 252 (1937)

Butler, J., delivered the opinion of the Court.

A Georgia statute provides that there shall be levied and collected each year from every inhabitant of the State between the ages of 21 and 60 a poll tax of one dollar, but that the tax shall not be demanded from the blind or from females who do not register for voting. . . .

[Appellant] asserts that the law offends the rule of equality only to persons between the ages of 21 and 60 and to women only if they register for voting and in that it makes payment a prerequisite to registration. He does not suggest that exemption of the blind is unreasonable. . . .

[The Court first found that the age exemption did not offend equal protection. As

21. Prewitt v. Wilson, 242 Ky. 231, 234-235, 46 S.W.2d 90, 92 (1932). See also In re Graves, 325 Mo. 888, 30 S.W.2d 149 (1930), striking down a law that required separate ballots for women.
22. Graves v. Eubank, 205 Ala. 174, 87 So. 587 (1921).

to women, they] may be exempted on the basis of special considerations to which they are naturally entitled. In view of burdens necessarily borne by them for the preservation of the race, the State reasonably may exempt them from poll taxes. Cf. Muller v. Oregon, 208 U.S. 412, 421, et seq. Quong v. Kirkendall, 223 U.S. 59, 63. Riley v. Massachusetts, 232 U.S. 671. Miller v. Wilson, 236 U.S. 373. Bosley v. McLaughlin, 236 U.S. 385. The laws of Georgia declare the husband to be the head of the family and the wife to be subject to him. §53-501. To subject her to the levy would be to add to his burden. Moreover, Georgia poll taxes are laid to raise money for educational purposes, and it is the father's duty to provide for education of the children. §74-105. Discrimination in favor of all women being permissible, appellant may not complain because the tax is laid only upon some or object to registration of women without payment of taxes for previous years. . . .

To make payment of poll taxes a prerequisite of voting is not to deny any privilege or immunity protected by the Fourteenth Amendment. Privilege of voting is not derived from the United States, but is conferred by the State and, save as restrained by the Fifteenth and Nineteenth Amendments and other provisions of the Federal Constitution, the State may condition suffrage as it deems appropriate. Minor v. Happersett, 21 Wall. 162, 170 et seq. Ex parte Yarbrough, 110 U.S. 651, 664-665. McPherson v. Blacker, 146 U.S. 1, 37-38. Guinn v. United States, 238 U.S. 347, 362. The privileges and immunities protected are only those that arise from the Constitution and laws of the United States and not those that spring from other sources. Hamilton v. Regents, 293 U.S. 245, 261.

The Nineteenth Amendment . . . applies to men and women alike and by its own force supersedes inconsistent measures, whether federal or state. Leser v. Garnett, 258 U.S. 130, 135. Its purpose is not to regulate the levy or collection of taxes. The construction for which appellant contends would make the amendment a limitation upon the power to tax. Cf. Minor v. Happersett, supra, 173. . . . It is fanciful to suggest the Georgia law is a mere disguise under which to deny or abridge the right of men to vote on account of their sex. The challenged enactment is not repugnant to the Nineteenth Amendment.

Affirmed.[23]

c. Domicile

In 1938, the Supreme Court of Alabama stated its opinion in dicta on the question of whether the Nineteenth Amendment abrogated state rules which treat married women differently than married men in regard to domicile for voting purposes. The case, Wilkerson v. Lee, concerned two candidates for town council who contested election returns; one of the candidates protested the failure of voting officials to count the votes of two women who had recently married and left town. The court stated the rules governing a married woman's domicile for voting purposes and their relationship to the Nineteenth Amendment as follows:[24]

> Miss Dorothy Lee was a native of Columbia, Houston county; registered and paid her poll tax there for the year of this election. In the summer before the election she married Robert Stevens in St. Clair county . . . and thereafter lived with her husband in St. Clair county.
>
> When a woman marries and enters in the family relation at the domicile of the husband, this domicile becomes the domicile of the wife. We do not think the Nineteenth Amendment disturbs this normal incident of family life.

23. Poll taxes are now unconstitutional, both by judicial decision, Harper v. Virginia State Board of Elections, 383 U.S. 663, 86 S. Ct. 1079, 16 L. Ed. 2d 169 (1966); United States v. Texas, 252 F. Supp. 234 (W.D. Tex. 1966), *aff'd mem.*, 384 U.S. 155, 86 S. Ct. 1383, 16 L. Ed. 2d 434 (1966); United States v. Alabama, 252 F. Supp. 95 (M.D. Ala. 1966); and by the Twenty-fourth Amendment, which was ratified February 4, 1964. — Eds.

24. Wilkerson v. Lee, 236 Ala. 104, 107, 181 So. 296, 298 (1938).

But, if the husband, at the time of marriage, has merely a temporary abode in the county where they live, being a resident and qualified voter of another county, and husband and wife establish no family residence facto et animo prior to the date of the election, the wife would still be a legal voter in her home town. The evidence supported a finding to this effect by the trial court.

As of 1974, only 4 states allowed married women to have separate domiciles from their husbands for all purposes; another 15 allowed women to have separate domiciles for purposes of voting, 6 for election to public office, 5 for jury service, 7 for taxation, and 5 for probate. Other domicile rules are discussed in Chapter Three, III-A. When *Wilkerson* was decided, the concept of "divisible" domicile had not yet been developed. Thus, a holding allowing separate domicile would have implied the right to live apart from the husband without cause or consent, an idea which still is not widely accepted. In any case, the only right being asserted for the two women in the case was the maintenance of their previous domiciles until such time as their husbands established permanent domiciles. If the domicile rules were challenged today under the Nineteenth Amendment by a married woman who had lost her right to vote in a situation in which a married man would not have similarly forfeited his right to vote, what would the result be?

Some states have laws requiring women who marry to reregister for voting because, as a matter of law, their surnames change. If a woman who wishes to retain her premarriage surname sues the registrar of voters under the Nineteenth Amendment to compel him to maintain her prior registration, on the grounds that a man's registration is not affected by marriage, would she be successful?

2. The Fifteenth Amendment as a Model

The Nineteenth Amendment was intended to serve the same functions for women as its counterpart had for blacks. The texts of the two amendments track each other exactly, providing:

> *Section 1.* The right of citizens of the United States to vote shall not be denied or abridged by the United States or by any state on account of [race, color or previous condition of servitude] [sex].
> *Section 2.* The Congress shall have power to enforce this article by appropriate legislation.

In an early test of the Nineteenth Amendment, Justice Brandeis directly stated: "This Amendment is in character and phraseology precisely similar to the Fifteenth. For each the same method of adoption was pursued. One cannot be valid and the other invalid."[25] Yet in many state cases, the Nineteenth Amendment was not given the full implementation accorded the Fifteenth. Compare the next two cases, as an example.

NEAL v. DELAWARE
103 U.S. 370, 26 L. Ed. 567 (1881)

Mr. Justice HARLAN delivered the opinion of the court.

The plaintiff in error, a citizen of the African race, was, on the 11th May, 1880, indicted in the court of General Sessions of the Peace and Jail delivery of New Castle County in the State of Delaware for the crime of rape, an offense punishable, under the laws of that State, with death. . . .

A trial was had before a jury composed wholly of white persons, and a verdict of guilty having been returned, it was on the 27th May, 1880, adjudged that the accused

25. Leser v. Garnett, 258 U.S. 130, 136, 42 S. Ct. 217, 66 L. Ed. 505, 511 (1922).

suffer death by hanging. From that judgment this writ of error has been prosecuted. . . .

The essential question . . . is, whether . . . citizens of the African race, otherwise
qualified, were, by reason of the Constitution and laws of Delaware, excluded from
service on juries because of their color. . . .

The Constitution of Delaware, adopted in 1831 . . . , restricts the right of suffrage
at general elections to free *white* male citizens, of the age of 22 years and upwards [and
who possessed various other qualifications]. . . .

The Statutes of Delaware, adopted in 1848, and in force at the trial of this case,
provided for an annual selection, by the levy court of the county, of persons to serve
as grand and petit jurors, and from those so selected the prothonotary and clerk of the
peace were required to draw the names of such as should serve for that year, if summoned. They further provided that all qualified to vote at the general election, being
sober and judicious persons, shall be liable to serve as jurors, except public officers of
the State or of the United States, counselors and attorneys at law, ordained ministers of
the gospel, officers of colleges, teachers of public schools, practicing physicians and
surgeons regularly licensed, cashiers of incorporated banks, and all persons over 70 years
of age.

It is thus seen that the statute, by its reference to the constitutional qualifications
of voters, apparently restricts the selection of jurors to *white* male citizens, being voters,
and sober and judicious persons. And although it only declares that such citizens shall
be *liable* to serve as jurors, the settled construction of the State Court, prior to the
adoption of the Fifteenth Amendment, was that no citizen of the African race was
competent, under the law, to serve on a jury.

Now, the argument on behalf of the accused is, that since the statute adopted the
standard of voters as the standard for jurors, and since Delaware has never, by any
separate or official action of its own, changed the language of its Constitution in reference to the class who may exercise the elective franchise, the *State* is to be regarded, in
the sense of the Amendment and of the laws enacted for its enforcement, as denying
to the colored race within its limits, to this day, the right, upon equal terms with the
white race, to participate as jurors in the administration of justice; and this, notwithstanding the adoption of the Fifteenth Amendment and its admitted legal effect upon
the Constitutions and laws of all the States of the Union.

But to this argument, when urged in the court below, the State Court replied, as
does the Attorney-General of the State here, that although the State had never, by a
convention, or popular vote, formally abrogated the provision in its State Constitution
restricting suffrage to white citizens, that result had necessarily followed, as matter of
law, from the incorporation of the Fourteenth and Fifteenth Amendments into the
fundamental law of the Nation; that since the adoption of the latter Amendment neither
the legislative, executive nor judicial authorities of the State had, in any mode, recognized, as an existing part of its Constitution, that provision which, in words discriminates against citizens of the African race in the matter of suffrage; and, consequently,
that the statute prescribing the qualification of jurors by reference to the qualifications
for voters should be construed as referring to the State Constitution, as modified or
affected by the Fifteenth Amendment.

The question thus presented is of the highest moment to that race, the security of
whose rights of life, liberty and property, and to the equal protection of the laws, was
the primary object of the recent Amendments to the National Constitution. Its solution
is confessedly attended by many difficulties of a serious nature, which might have been
avoided by more explicit language in the statutes passed for the enforcement of the
Amendments. Much has been left by the legislative department to mere judicial construction. But upon the fullest consideration we have been able to give the subject, our
conclusion is that the alleged discrimination in the State of Delaware, against citizens
of the African race, in the matter of service on juries, does not result from its Constitution and laws.

Beyond question the adoption of the Fifteenth Amendment had the effect, in law, to remove from the State Constitution, or render inoperative, that provision which restricts the right of suffrage to the white race. Thenceforward, the statute which prescribed the qualification of jurors was itself enlarged in its operation, so as to embrace all who by the State Constitution, as modified by the supreme law of the land, were qualified to vote at a general election. The presumption should be indulged, in the first instance, that the State recognizes, as is its plain duty, an Amendment of the Federal Constitution, from the time of its adoption, as binding on all of its citizens and every department of its government, and to be enforced, within its limits, without reference to any inconsistent provisions in its own constitution or statutes. In this case that presumption is strengthened, and, indeed, becomes conclusive, not only by the direct adjudication of the State Court as to what is the fundamental law of Delaware, but by the entire absence of any statutory enactments or any adjudication, since the adoption of the Fifteenth Amendment, indicating that the State, by its constituted authorities, does not recognize, in the fullest legal sense, the binding force of that Amendment and its effect in modifying the State Constitution upon the subject of suffrage.

This abundantly appears from the separate opinions, in this case, of the Judges composing the court of Oyer and Terminer. Comegys, C.J., alluding to the Fifteenth Amendment, and the Act of March 1, 1875, 18 Stat. at L., 335, said:

> . . . There is . . . an excision or erasure of the word "white" in the qualification of voters in this State; and the Constitution is now to be construed as if such word had never been there. We have, then, no law of this State forbidding the levy court to select negroes as jurors, because they are negroes, if in their judgment they are otherwise qualified.

Wales, J., said:

> We know, from actual and personal knowledge of the history of the times, that since the adoption of the Fifteenth Amendment to the Federal Constitution, the provision in the Constitution of Delaware limiting the right to vote to free white male citizens, has been virtually and practically repealed and annulled, and that persons of color, otherwise qualified, have exercised and continue to exercise the elective franchise in all parts of this State with the same freedom as the whites. . . . But there is really no difficulty in reaching the conclusion that under the law regulating the selection of jurors the colored citizen is not excluded. That law was intended by its authors to be prospective in its operation and effect and to include all who would become voters after its passage, as well as the class of persons who were then entitled to vote. It was not a temporary statute, intended only to provide for the then existing state of things, but to reach forward and make one unvarying standard for the qualification of a juror, to wit: that he should be qualified to vote at the general election. . . . Whoever, thereafter, might become qualified voters in the State, whether by virtue of amendment to its Constitution or by virtue of "the supreme law of the land," that overrides and supplants state constitutions and state laws, eo instanti became qualified for selection and service as jurors. . . .

The remaining question relates to the denial of the motions to quash the indictment and the panels of jurors . . . [on the ground that] colored persons have always been excluded from juries in the courts of Delaware [which] was conceded in argument, and was likewise conceded in the court below. The Chief Justice, however, accompanied that concession with the remark in reference to this case, "That none but white men were selected is in nowise remarkable in view of the fact — too notorious to ignored — that the great body of black men residing in this State are utterly unqualified by want of intelligence, experience or moral integrity, to sit on juries." The exceptions, he said, were rare.

. . . [W]e are of opinion that the motions to quash . . . should have been sustained. . . . The showing thus made, including, as it did, the fact (so generally known that the court felt obliged to take judicial notice of it) that no colored citizen had ever been summoned as a juror in the courts of the State — although its colored population exceeded twenty thousand in 1870, and in 1880 exceeded twenty-six thousand, in a total population of less than one hundred and fifty thousand — presented a prima facie case of denial, by the officers charged with the selection of grand and petit jurors, of that equality of protection which has been secured by the Constitution and laws of the United States. It was, we think, under all the circumstances, a violent presumption which the State Court indulged, that such uniform exclusion of that race from juries, during a period of many years, was solely because, in the judgment of those officers, fairly exercised, the black race in Delaware were utterly disqualified, by want of intelligence, experience or moral integrity, to sit on juries. The action of those officers in the premises is to be deemed the act of the State; and the refusal of the State Court to redress the wrong by them committed, was a denial of a right secured to the prisoner by the Constitution and laws of the United States. . . .

The judgment of the Court of Oyer and and Terminer is reversed, with directions to set aside the judgment and verdict. . . .

[Dissenting opinions of Chief Justice WAITE and Justice FIELD omitted.]

COMMONWEALTH v. WELOSKY
276 Mass. 398, 177 N.E. 656 (1931)

RUGG, C.J.

As the jurors were about to be impaneled for the trial of this complaint, the defendant filed a challenge to the array. . . . The ground on which that challenge rests is that there were no women on the lists from which the jurors were drawn. . . .

. . . By its own self-executing force [the Nineteenth Amendment] struck from the Constitution of this commonwealth the word "male" wherever it occurred as a limitation upon the right to vote. . . .

. . . The statute here under examination [dealing with jury service] is a re-enactment of a long line of statutes of the commonwealth running back to a time shortly after the adoption of the Constitution as well as through all intermediate revisions dealing with qualifications for jury service. Laws of the colony and of the province are in effect the same. In the earlier and later statutes, the same essential and almost the identical words have been employed. The word "person" occurs in them all. The selection of jurors has constantly been required to be from those qualified to vote; . . . the right to vote was confined to male inhabitants, male persons, and finally to male citizens. . . . Manifestly, therefore, the intent of the Legislature must have been, in using the word "person" in statutes concerning jurors and jury lists, to confine its meaning to men. That was the only intent constitutionally permissible. . . .

Possession of property of specified value and payment of taxes as qualifications for voters were required in earlier days and from time to time, but these were gradually eliminated by Amendments to the Constitution until the last of such limitations disappeared with the approval of Amendment 32 in 1891. When the suffrage has been thus widened among male citizens, there has followed, without further legislation and without change in the phrase of the statute, a like extention of citizens liable to service as jurors. These concurring enlargements of those liable to jury service were simply an extension to larger numbers of the same classification of persons. Since the word "person" in the statutes respecting jurors meant men, when there was an extension of the right to vote to other men previously disqualified, the jury statutes by specific definition included them. No amendment to the statute can be conceived which could have made that meaning more clear. This is the force and effect of Neal v. Delaware, 103 U.S. 370, at page 389, 26 L. Ed. 567.

Changes in suffrage and in liability for jury service in the past differ in kind from the change here urged.

The Nineteenth Amendment to the federal Constitution conferred the suffrage upon an entirely new class of human beings. It did not extend the right to vote to members of an existing classification theretofore disqualified, but created a new class. It added to qualified voters those who did not fall within the meaning of the word "person" in the jury statutes. No member of the class thus added to the body of voters had ever theretofore in this commonwealth had the right to vote for candidates for offices created by the Constitution. The change in the legal status of women wrought by the Nineteenth Amendment was radical, drastic and unprecedented. While it is to be given full effect in its field, it is not to be extended by implication. It is unthinkable that those who first framed and selected the words for the statute now embodied in G.L. c. 234, §1, had any design that it should ever include women within its scope. . . . The words of Chief Justice Gray in Robinson's case . . . are equally pertinent to the case at bar: . . . "the whole course of legislation precludes the inference that any change in the legal rights or capacities of women is to be implied, which has not been clearly expressed." . . .

. . . The second argument of the defendant on this branch of the case is that, since the General Laws are enacted on December 22, 1920 (about four months subsequent to the ratification of the Nineteenth Amendment) the Legislature, although using the same essential words theretofore used to describe those liable to service as jurors, namely, "person qualified to vote for representatives to the general court," must have intended to include women. . . . [The court notes that the only change in the actual wording of the general laws was in regard to suffrage.]

. . . [A] subcommittee [to study law revision] to which was assigned the legislation of 1920 recommended that the laws relating to intoxicating liquors and woman's suffrage, affected by the Eighteenth and Nineteenth Amendments to the Federal Constitution, be redrawn to conform to these amendments. . . .

The draft of the General Laws reported by the joint special committee shows that they conformed to this paragraph of their report and made changes touching the right of women to vote. . . . They made no changes respecting women in any other particular. No change was made touching jury lists. . . . It is most unlikely that the Legislature should, for the first time, require women to serve as jurors without making provision respecting the exemption of the considerable numbers of women who ought not to be required to serve as jurors and without directing that changes for the convenience of women be made in courthouses, some of which are notoriously overcrowded and unfit for their accommodation as jurors.

. . . The question of the effect of granting the suffrage to women on statutes providing for the selection of jurors from the members of the electorate has arisen in several states. The conclusion here reached is supported in principle by a respectable body of authority. [Citations omitted.] There are decisions to the contrary. [Citations omitted.]

The contention of the defendant is that, by reason of the exclusion of women from the jury list, she has been denied the equal protection of the laws contrary to the guaranty contained in the Fourteenth Amendment to the federal Constitution. It hardly needs to be repeated that no provision of a state Constitution or statute in conflict with the paramount Constitution of the United States as interpreted by the Supreme Court of the United States has any validity. . . . This contention of the defendant in the main rests upon four decisions of the United States Supreme Court concerning the meaning and effect of the Thirteenth, Fourteenth and Fifteenth Amendments, adopted shortly after the close of the war between the states for the preservation of the Union, with respect to the rights of the colored race. The scope of those decisions can best be determined by certain quotations from them. . . .

[Discussion of Strauder v. West Virginia, 100 U.S. 303, Virginia v. Rives, 100 U.S. 313, and other cases is omitted.]

The intent and design of those amendments as thus authoritatively declared, were utterly different from the reasons leading to the adoption of the Nineteenth Amendment. Giving to those four decisions the widest scope, they all rest expressly upon the purpose and effect of the Thirteenth, Fourteenth and Fifteenth Amendments with respect to a race, up to that time enslaved in several of the states but thereby created citizens, made freemen and clothed with full civil and political rights. They were transformed from slaves to citizens of a free nation. The situation under those amendments then confronting the persons theretofore held as slaves was utterly different from that arising under the Nineteenth Amendment. Women had not been enslaved. They had been recognized as citizens and clothed with large property and civil rights. Woman has long been generally recognized in this country as the equal of man intellectually, morally, socially. Opportunities in business and for college and university training had been freely open to her. Education of the youth of the land had been largely intrusted to her. In many respects laws especially protective to women on account of their sex had been enacted. Most of those formerly imposing limitations, even upon married women with respect to property and business, had disappeared. Those were not changed by the Nineteenth Amendment. Current discussion touching the adoption of the Nineteenth Amendment related exclusively to the franchise. . . . The statement in Strauder v. West Virginia, 100 U.S. 303, at page 310, 25 L. Ed. 664, seems to us still vital and apposite to the present case: "We do not say that within the limits from which it is not excluded by the amendment a State may not prescribe the qualifications of its jurors, and in so doing make discriminations. It may confine the selection to males, to freeholders, to citizens, to persons within certain ages, or to persons having educational qualifications." This conclusion is fortified by decisions of the Supreme Court of the United States holding that the denial to woman by state statutes or laws of the right to practice law, Bradwell v. State of Illinois, 16 Wall. 130, 21 L. Ed. 442; In re Lockwood, 154 U.S. 116, 14 S. Ct. 1082, 38 L. Ed. 929, to vote (before the adoption of the Nineteenth Amendment); Minor v. Happersett, 21 Wall. 162, 22 L. Ed. 627, and to make contracts to perform labor by themselves more than specified numbers of hours within designated periods; Muller v. Oregon, 208 U.S. 412, 28 S. Ct. 324, 52 L. Ed. 551, 13 Ann. Cas. 957; Riley v. Massachusetts, 232 U.S. 671, 34 S. Ct. 469, 58 L. Ed. 788; Miller v. Wilson, 236 U.S. 373, 35 S. Ct. 342, 59 L. Ed. 628, L. R. A. 1915F, 829, violates no rights or privileges secured to women by the Fourteenth Amendment. Those rights appear to us quite as essential to the privileges and immunities of citizens and equal protection of the laws as the duty to serve as jurors. . . .

Exceptions overruled.

NOTE: PRINCIPLES OF CONSTRUCTION FOR THE FIFTEENTH AND NINETEENTH AMENDMENTS

In cases concerning the impact of the Fifteenth Amendment on discriminatory laws relating to voting, the initial question was whether the court would strike down the statute as invalid or extend it to cover the excluded group. The analytical tool for "extension" is usually a look at the legislative intent behind the statute:[26]

> Whether the statute falls completely or is modified in some way depends upon the court's assessment of what the legislature itself would have done had it known that all or part of its original enactment would be invalid. Of course, such legislative intent is often not easily ascertained. Where legislative history is scant, or lacking altogether, there is little for courts to rely on except their own judgment about what the legislature must have intended. Then, too, the further question arises as to which legislature's intent is relevant — the one which passed the bill originally, or an amending legislature, if any, or the one currently in session.

26. Brown et al., The Equal Rights Amendment: A Constitutional Basis for Equal Rights for Women, 80 Yale L.J. 871, 913-914 (1971).

The difficulty that some courts have felt in "extending" statutes in conformity with legislative intent is that "rewriting" is involved — and the work of drafting legislation is not for the courts. Thus, some courts have claimed that they cannot harmonize statutes with the Constitution by, in effect, reading words of qualification into them, although they *can* excise words or interpret them freely. When excision is performed, the courts sometimes describe the saving construction as having taken place without judicial intervention. By their account, the amendment, being self-executing, by "operation of law," magically erased the offending words from the previously unconstitutional legislation. In Fifteenth Amendment cases, saving nonconforming statutes by construction usually involved the excision of the offending adjective "white" modifying some race-neutral word like "person" or "citizen."

The "magic erasure" technique was also used on statutes which based liability for some other right or duty, such as jury service, on the status of being an elector. In such a case, the court would hold first that the constitutional amendment had erased the offending word from the law prescribing qualifications for electors. It would then go on to hold that since the word of limitation in the primary statute was gone, the term "elector," "person qualified to vote," or "voter" in the secondary statute was thereby automatically broadened to include the previously excluded cases. Neal v. Delaware is a good example of the technique. The Court there did not explicitly consider the legislative intent of the Delaware legislature. It is certainly possible that had the legislature known, when it was considering the statute on jury service, that the franchise would eventually be extended to blacks, it would have decided to base jury service on being a white male elector. Thus, in *Neal,* if the Court had followed the traditional method of surveying legislative intent in deciding the effect of the Fifteenth Amendment on the jury statute, the statute might well have been struck down. But this result was avoided through the concept of "magic erasure."[27]

The same technique of construction was freely used for the Nineteenth Amendment in interpreting suffrage statutes. See the wording of Prewitt v. Wilson, subsection 1-a. But in situations where a statute made some duty or right contingent on the status of being an elector, the magic erasure methodology that had been used in Fifteenth Amendment cases posed real problems for courts that did not want to extend the contingent right or duty (e.g., jury duty) to women electors. Returning to "legislative intent" as the analytical tool, some judges found themselves writing elaborate opinions to justify their conclusions that the enacting legislature, had it known that women would become electors, would not have wanted the contingent right or duty extended to women. Their task was often made more difficult because, in order to reach the chosen result, they had to read words of limitation or qualification into a statute that was neutral on its face.

The important point here, however, is not that opinions like *Welosky* were silly, but that in interpreting the Nineteenth Amendment, some courts simply refused to follow Neal v. Delaware, which should logically have created a strong basis for expansion of the duties and responsibilities of women's citizenship. This, of course, was not true of all courts; in many jurisdictions the Nineteenth Amendment was given a broad meaning.[28]

---

27. A statute denying jury service to blacks would also necessarily be struck down under Fourteenth Amendment analysis, Strauder v. West Virginia, 100 U.S. 303, 25 L. Ed. 664 (1880), for which the court would, of course, be responsible. Note that in *Neal* the Supreme Court found a prima facie violation of the Equal Protection Clause in Delaware's long exclusion of blacks from juries, even though the Court accepted the state court's conclusions that Delaware's law accorded with the Fifteenth Amendment.

28. In the following states, which based jury duty on elector status, the courts declined to extend liability to women after the passage of the Nineteenth Amendment:

Idaho: State v. Kelley, 39 Idaho 668, 229 P. 659 (1924).

Illinois: People ex rel. Fyfe v. Barnett, 319 Ill. 403, 150 N.E. 290 (1926).

Massachusetts: Commonwealth v. Welosky, 276 Mass. 398, 177 N.E. 656 (1931), *cert. denied,* 284 U.S. 684 (1932). Cf. In re Opinion of the Justices, 237 Mass. 591, 130 N.E. 685 (1921) (advisory opinion on proposed bill to extend liability for jury service to women).

3. Jury Duty in States in Which Liability Was Not Based on Enfranchisement

In six states that did not base jury duty on elector status, cases raising Nineteenth Amendment claims were brought. Four of these cases were appeals by male defendants who protested the exclusion of women from their juries; one was an appeal by a female defendant on the same basis;two were civil suits by women seeking to get their names placed on the jury list, and one case was an appeal by a man protesting the inclusion of women on the jury that had convicted him.[29] The main questions presented in these cases were (1) whether or not jury service was a right rather than a duty and therefore whether or not women denied a place on jury lists had standing to sue; (2) whether or not a man, who was not a member of the excluded class, could be heard to complain about the exclusion of women from his jury; (3) whether or not liability for jury service was implied in, or necessarily or historically related to, the right to vote; (4) whether or not the term "men" in jury statutes was generic and therefore included women as well; and (5) whether or not the Nineteenth Amendment had any bearing on these questions. The courts uniformly answered these questions in the negative. A typical ruling on the Nineteenth Amendment issue follows:[30]

> With us . . . liability to jury duty is not an incident to the right of suffrage, as in some of the States. . . . It is a far cry from elector to juror. The qualifications of the one are quite different from those of the other. . . .

South Carolina: State v. Mittle, 120 S.C. 526, 113 S.E. 335 (1922).

A similar result was reached in Washington Territory after the passage of a territorial law granting woman suffrage, which was invalidated in the same opinion. Harland v. Territory, 3 Wash. T. 131, 13 P. 453 (1887), overruling Rosencrantz v. Territory, 2 Wash. T. 267, 5 P. 305 (1884).

In the following states, which also based jury duty on elector status, the courts extended liability to women after the passage of the Nineteenth Amendment. (Both the earliest state case and the decision by the highest state court are cited, if different.)

Indiana: Palmer v. State, 197 Ind. 625, 150 N.E. 917 (1926).

Iowa: State v. Walker, 192 Ia. 823, 185 N.W. 619 (1921).

Michigan: People v. Barltz, 212 Mich. 580, 180 N.W. 423 (1920).

Nevada: Parus v. District Court, 42 Nev. 229, 174 P. 706 (1918) (under state constitutional amendment granting suffrage to women).

Ohio: Thatcher v. Pennsylvania, O & D R.R. Co., 33 Ohio App. 242, 168 N.E. 859 (1928); Browning v. State, 120 Ohio 62, 165 N.E. 566 (1929).

Pennsylvania: Commonwealth v. Maxwell, 271 Pa. 378, 114 A. 825 (1921).

All of the above cases, except the ones from Massachusetts and Illinois, were appeals by male defendants who had been either indicted by a grand jury or convicted by a petit jury which included women. Commonwealth v. Welosky involved a woman defendant protesting the exclusion of women from her jury; People ex rel. Fyfe v. Barnett was a suit by a woman seeking to compel the state jury commissioners to place her name on the jury lists.

29. The following reported cases deal with the Nineteenth Amendment and jury service statutes not based on elector status:

Arizona: McDaniels v. State, 62 Ariz. 339, 158 P.2d 151 (1945).

Georgia: Powers v. State, 172 Ga. 1, 157 S.E. 195 (1931).

North Carolina: State v. Emery, 224 N.C. 581, 31 S.E. 2d 858 (1944).

New Jersey: State v. James, 96 N.J.L. 132, 114 A. 553 (1921).

New York: In re Grilli, 110 Misc. 45, 179 N.Y.S. 795 (1920).

Texas: Glover v. Cobb, 123 S.W.2d 794 (Tex 1938); Harper v. State, 90 Tex. Crim. 252, 234 S.W. 909 (1921).

Suits by women and the earliest reported case in each state are both cited, if different. For further discussion of the issue of women's right and obligation to serve on juries see Part V.

30. State v. Emery, 224 N.C. 581, 583, 31 S.E.2d 858, 861 (1944).

4. *The Right of Women To Hold Elected or Appointed Office*

In Opinion of the Justices, 119 Me. 603, 113 A. 614 (1921), six of the eight justices of the Supreme Judicial Court answered in the affirmative an inquiry about the constitutionality of a Maine statute, based on the Nineteenth Amendment, enabling women to hold office. The particular office in question was that of justice of the peace:[31]

> The privileges conferred upon women by the Nineteenth Amendment are precisely the same as those conferred upon the colored race by the Fifteenth. Hence it follows that under the Constitution of Maine to-day, as amended and modified by the Nineteenth Amendment, male and female citizens of the United States have equal political rights so far as voting is concerned, and while it might still be said, as in the majority opinion in 1874, that there was nothing in the original Constitution indicating any transfer of political power to those who had never possessed it, that power at the present time has been transferred and shared by express and imperative command....
>
> It is true that the case of Neal v. Delaware, supra, involved the status of a juror, and not of a justice of the peace. But there can be no vital distinction. The broad principles of constitutional law laid down by the Supreme Court of the United States apply equally well to the problems before us.
>
> While a juror might not be regarded in the strictest technical sense as a public officer, yet that official is recognized by our Constitution and fills a most important part in the administration of justice. He is sworn to the faithful discharge of his duty, has within his keeping to a great extent the liberty and property of our citizens, and during his term of service is a component part of the judicial system of our state....
>
> At common law it was the general rule that a woman could not hold office and take part in the administration of government. But the common law can be changed at the will of the Legislature in the absence of constitutional inhibition, and it has been changed by our Legislature by the passage of the act of August 31, 1920, which provides that:
>
> "No citizen of the United States having a right to vote in this state shall be denied the right to hold civil office under this state or any subdivision thereof on account of sex."
>
> This act but carries out the legal effect of the Nineteenth federal Amendment. True, that amendment grants in terms only the right of suffrage to women, and not the right to hold office, and the one may not always be equivalent to the other. But so far as we have been able to ascertain, while the courts have frequently held constitutional a woman's right to hold certain offices for which she had no power to vote, we have discovered no case in which her right to hold office was denied where she possessed the right to vote therefor.
>
> When the ballot was conferred upon the colored race by the adoption of the Fifteenth Amendment, it is common knowledge that it was followed by the election of persons of that race to office in various sections throughout the Southern States, and we are unable to find that their right to hold office was ever questioned....
>
> [Two justices, while contending that the right to hold elected or appointed office is not a corollary of the franchise, based their agreement with the majority result on a statute passed by the Maine State Legislature removing women's disability with respect to office holding.]

The Supreme Court of North Carolina reached the same result as the Supreme Judicial Court of Maine in Preston v. Roberts, about a year later.[32] In an advisory opinion, the Massachusetts Supreme Court also decided that, although "the right to hold office is not necessarily coextensive with the right to vote,"[33] the Nineteenth Amendment indirectly had the effect of making women eligible to hold office.

31. 119 Me. at 605, 113 A. at 616-617 (1921).
32. 183 N.C. 62, 110 S.E. 586 (1922).
33. In re Opinion of the Justices, 240 Mass. 601, 606, 135 N.E. 173, 174 (1922).

The finding of the Massachusetts court (which paralleled that of the Maine court in most respects) appears inconsistent with Commonwealth v. Welosky, supra, in which the same court ruled in 1931 that, although jury duty was based on elector status, the legislature could never have meant that if women should become electors, they should also serve on juries — in effect reading words of sex qualifications into an apparently sex-neutral statute. Is there any logical distinction between the two issues aside from the lapse of time between one case and the other? One possible explanation might have been that the courts were focusing on the common law rights of defendants with regard to jury composition (i.e., trial by a jury of twelve *men*), a factor not present in the office-holding cases. However, the *Welosky* case involved a female defendant, who could hardly have reason to complain if her jury had included women. A second reason why the court treated the two issues differently might be found in the fact that holding or seeking office is optional, while jury service is not (at least in the absence of sex-based statutory exemptions for women).

The most curious decision on this subject is the advisory opinion of the Supreme Court of New Hampshire in 1927.[34] The court ruled that the intent of the legislature in limiting eligibility for elective office to voters was to make enfranchisement rather than sex the determining factor. Thus, the Nineteenth Amendment had the effect of making women eligible for elective office. However, eligibility for appointive office was not limited to voters. The court stated, therefore:[35]

> The matter is left as it was at common law. . . . [W]hile women are now eligible to all elective offices as to all other offices the common law rule excludes women. . . . This common law rule may be abrogated by the Legislature. . . . No such action has been taken as to the office of justice of the peace. It follows that women are now excluded from that office by virtue of the common law rule.

5. Other Consequences

UNITED STATES v. HINSON
3 F.2d 200 (S.D. Fla. 1925)

CALL, District Judge.

At common law it is probable that the plea of coverture would state a cause of abatement, on account of the unity of husband and wife; the husband being the responsible party for joint crimes committed by husband and wife. And this rule would prevail in states adopting the common law and having made no change by statute. As I understand it, there is no common law prevailing in the United States, and since the adoption of the Nineteenth Amendment to the Constitution, it seems to me that the rule of common law has no application to crimes committed against the United States.

The demurrer to the said plea will therefore be sustained.

————————

See also Adkins v. Children's Hospital of the District of Columbia, 261 U.S. 525, 43 S. Ct. 394, 67 L. Ed. 785 (1923), supra Part II, in which the majority cited the Nineteenth Amendment as one of the factors that had reduced the differences between the sexes (which had been relied upon in Muller v. Oregon to justify state protective labor legislation for women only).

34. In re Opinion of the Justices, 83 N.H. 589, 139 A. 180 (1927).
35. 83 N.H. at 593-594. See also In re Cavellier, 159 Misc. 212, 287 N.Y.S. 739 (1936), and Boineau v. Thornton, 235 F. Supp. 175 (D.S.C.), aff'd, 379 U.S. 15, *rehearing denied*, 379 U.S. 917 (1964), cases which deal with provisions about the sex of candiates and the Nineteenth Amendment.

IV. THE DEVELOPMENT OF MODERN EQUAL PROTECTION THEORY, 1945-1973

Many people believe that sex discrimination can be successfully challenged through litigation under the Fourteenth Amendment guarantee that no state shall "deny to any person within its jurisdiction the equal protection of the laws." In order to develop effective strategies under this clause, one must understand current equal protection theory, which is outlined briefly herein with illustrative materials and cases. Actual language from a number of the famous cases is included so that the reader may get the flavor of decisions upholding or striking down legislation. Section V will deal with the application of the theory to sex discrimination problems.

A. Outline of Equal Protection Theory

Central to an understanding of equal protection cases are two concepts: classification and legislative purpose. The following excerpt from a classic article, worth reading in its entirety, explains these concepts.

TUSSMAN AND TENBROEK, THE EQUAL PROTECTION OF THE LAWS
37 Calif. L. Rev. 341 (1949)

[The authors begin by describing the central paradox of the Equal Protection Clause.]
. . . The equal protection of the laws is a "pledge of the protection of equal laws." But laws may classify [because] . . . [t]he legislature, if it is to act at all, must impose special burdens upon or grant special benefits to special groups or classes of individuals. . . . And "the very idea of classification is that of inequality." In tackling this paradox the Court has neither abandoned the demand for equality nor denied the legislative right to classify. It has taken a middle course. It has resolved the contradictory demands of legislative specialization and constitutional generality by a doctrine of reasonable classification.
    The essence of that doctrine can be stated with deceptive simplicity. The Constitution does not require that things different in fact be treated in law as though they were the same. But it does require in its concern for equality, that those who are similarly situated be similarly treated. The measure of the reasonableness of a classification is the degree of its success in treating similarly those similarly situated. . . .
    We begin with an elementary proposition: To define a class is simply to designate a quality or characteristic or trait or religion, or any combination of these, the possession of which, by an individual, determines his membership in or inclusion within the class. A legislature defines a class, or "classifies," when it enacts a law applying to "all aliens ineligible for citizenship," or "all persons convicted of three felonies," or "all citizens between the ages of 19 and 25" or "foreign corporations doing business within the state." . . .
    It is also elementary that membership in a class is determined by the possession of the traits which define that class. Individual X is a member of class A if, and only if, X possesses the traits which define class A. Whatever the defining characteristics of a class may be, every member of that class will possess those characteristics.
    Turning now to the reasonableness of legislative classifications, the cue is to be taken from our earlier reference to the requirement that those similarly situated be similarly treated. A reasonable classification is one which includes all who are similarly situated and none who are not. The question is, however, what does that ambiguous and crucial phrase "similarly situated" mean? . . .

. . . The inescapable answer is that we must look beyond the classification to the purpose of the law. A reasonable classification is one which includes all persons who are similarly situated with respect to the purpose of the law.

The purpose of a law may be either the elimination of a public "mischief" or the achievement of some positive public good. To simplify the discussion we shall refer to the purpose of a law in terms of the elimination of mischief, since the same argument holds in either case. We shall speak of the defining character or characteristics of the legislative classification as the trait. We can thus speak of the relation of the classification to the purpose of the law as the relation of the Trait to the Mischief.

A problem arises at all because the classification in a law usually does not have as its defining Trait the possession of or involvement with the Mischief at which the law aims. For example, let us suppose that a legislature proposes to combat hereditary criminality — an admitted mischief — and that the sterilization of transmitters of hereditary criminality is a permissible means to that end. Now if the legislature were to pass a law declaring that for the purpose of eliminating hereditary criminality, all individuals who are tainted with inheritable criminal tendencies are to be sterilized, and if it provided for proper administrative identification of transmitters of hereditary criminality, our problem would largely disappear. The class, being defined directly in terms of the Mischief, automatically includes all who are similarly situated with respect to the purpose of the law.

This procedure requires, however, delegation of considerable discretion to administrators to determine which individuals to sterilize. Legislators, reluctant to confer such discretion, tend to classify by Traits which limit the range of administrative freedom. Suppose then, that they pass a law providing for the sterilization of all persons convicted of three felonies. The "reasonableness" of this classification depends upon the relation between the class of three-time felons and the class of hereditary criminals.

In other words, we are really dealing with the relation of two classes to each other. The first class consists of all individuals possessing the defining Trait; the second class consists of all individuals possessing, or rather, tainted by, the Mischief at which the law aims. The former is the legislative classification; the latter is the class of those similarly situated with respect to the purpose of the law. We shall refer to these two classes as T and M respectively.

Now, since the reasonableness of any class T depends entirely upon its relation to a class M, it is obvious that it is impossible to pass judgment on the reasonableness of a classification without taking into consideration, or identifying, the purpose of the law. . . .

There are five possible relationships between the class defined by the trait and the class defined by the Mischief. These relationships can be indicated by the following diagrams.

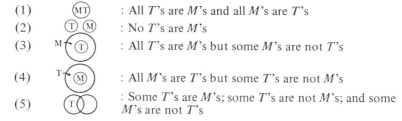

(1)   (MT)   : All *T*'s are *M*'s and all *M*'s are *T*'s

(2)   (T) (M)   : No *T*'s are *M*'s

(3)   M (T)   : All *T*'s are *M*'s but some *M*'s are not *T*'s

(4)   T (M)   : All *M*'s are *T*'s but some *T*'s are not *M*'s

(5)   (T)   : Some *T*'s are *M*'s; some *T*'s are not *M*'s; and some *M*'s are not *T*'s

One of these five relationships holds in fact in any case of legislative classification, and we will consider each from the point of view of its "reasonableness."

The first two situations represent respectively the ideal limits of reasonableness and unreasonableness. In the first case, the classification in the law coincides completely with the class of those similarly situated with respect to the purpose of the law. It is perfectly reasonable. In the second case, no member of the class defined in the law is tainted with the mischief at which the law aims. The classification is, therefore, perfectly unreasonable. . . .

Classification of the third type may be called "under-inclusive." All who are included in the class are tainted with the mischief, but there are others also tainted whom the classification does not include. Since the classification does not include all who are similarly situated with respect to the purpose of the law, there is a prima facie violation of the equal protection requirement of reasonable classification.

But the Court has recognized the very real difficulties under which legislatures operate — difficulties arising out of both the nature of the legislative process and of the society which legislation attempts perennially to reshape — and it has refused to strike down indiscriminately all legislation embodying the classificatory inequality here under consideration. . . .

The fourth type of classification imposes a burden upon a wider range of individuals than are included in the class of those tainted with the mischief at which the law aims. It can thus be called "over-inclusive." Herod, ordering the death of all male children born on a particular day because one of them would some day bring about his downfall, employed such a classification. It is exemplified by the quarantine and the dragnet. The wartime treatment of American citizens of Japanese ancestry is a striking recent instance of the imposition of burdens upon a large class of individuals because some of them were believed to be disloyal. . . .

But in spite of the flagrant injustice of over-inclusive classifications, there are circumstances in which legislation of this character has been, and perhaps must be, sustained. The circumstances are those of emergency, which must be grave and imminent if the impositions are harsh and onerous — as in the case of the wartime evacuations of Japanese-Americans — or less grave but still "emergency" if the impositions are relatively mild — as in the case of a police road block. . . .

The final situation to be considered is one in which the previously discussed factors of under-inclusiveness and over-inclusiveness are both present. . . .

For example, . . . the classification of "American citizens of Japanese ancestry" for the purpose of meeting the dangers of sabotage can be challenged both on the grounds that it is under-inclusive, since others — American citizens of German or Italian ancestry — are equally under the strain of divided loyalties, and that it is over-inclusive, since it is not supposed that all American citizens of Japanese ancestry are disloyal. The sustaining of this classification, therefore, requires both the finding of sufficient emergency to justify the imposition of a burden upon a larger class than is believed tainted with the Mischief and the establishment of "fair reasons" for failure to extend the operation of the law to a wider class of potential saboteurs. . . .

The bearing of the equal protection clause on the problem of classification is not exhausted by the reasonable classification requirement. The assertion of human equality is closely associated with the denial that differences in color or creed, birth or status, are significant or relevant to the way in which men should be treated. . . .

. . . We now suggest the possibility that there are some traits which can never be made the basis of a constitutional classification. . . .

Two possible forms of this doctrine must be distinguished. The first is the assertion that there are some traits which never in fact bear a reasonable relation to any legitimate public purpose and are consequently always "irrelevant" in this sense. Such an a priori assertion of universal irrelevance would be difficult to defend. Moreover, if there are such traits, their use in classifications would never pass the reasonable relation test. This form of the doctrine is both indefensible and gratuitous.

The significant formulation, suggested by the Rutledge dissent in the *Kotch* case [see infra Section B — Ed.], is that even if the classification is reasonably related to a legitimate public purpose, the employment of a forbidden trait invalidates it.

If the forbidden classification doctrine seems too extreme to give promise of further judicial development, there is a milder form of that doctrine which is in effect. It is the doctrine which establishes a presumption of unconstitutionality against a law employing certain classifying traits.

Speaking for the Court in the *Korematsu* case, Mr. Justice Black said, "It should be noted, to begin with, that all legal restrictions which curtail the civil rights of a single racial group are immediately suspect. That is not to say that all such restrictions are unconstitutional. It is to say that the courts must subject them to the most rigid scrutiny." [323 U.S. at 216.]

Presumably, this "rigid scrutiny" is also called for by classifications other than those which curtail the civil rights of any single racial group. But an attempt at an exhaustive listing of suspect classifications would be pointless. It suffices to say that this is of necessity a rather loose category. Its content, at any particular time, will depend upon the area in which the principle of equality is struggling against the recurring forms of claims to special and unequal status — whether along racial, religious, economic, or even political, lines.

But if there are "suspect" classifications requiring "rigid scrutiny," of what are they suspect and for what are they rigidly scrutinized? The answer leads in two directions. On the one hand, the reasonable relation test must be strictly applied. On the other hand, the Court must satisfy itself on the question of the discriminatory character of the regulation. . . .

Tussman and tenBroek's article was prescient in predicting developments of the next twenty years. With time, it became clear that the Supreme Court would use two tests to determine whether or not a law violated the Equal Protection Clause. In general, it applied the reasonableness test. This consisted of asking (1) did the legislature have a constitutionally permissible purpose in view in passing the law in question, and (2) is the classification used reasonably related to accomplishing that purpose? In dealing with legislative distinctions based on race or ethnic origin, the Court began taking a closer look, generally referred to as "strict scrutiny" of the contested law. Strict scrutiny has also been applied to restrictions on certain rights designated "fundamental," such as voting. Scrutinizing strictly, the Court asks (1) did the legislature have a purpose of overriding public importance for passing this law, and (2) were the means chosen by the legislature (the use of a suspect classification or of a classification affecting a fundamental interest) *necessary* to accomplish that purpose?

Thus, both halves of the test are strengthened when the Court looks at a law with strict scrutiny. The legislative purpose must be of overwhelming public importance, not merely constitutionally permissible. And the use of the classification, as well as the burden imposed on the members of the class, must be necessary to achieve that purpose, not merely rationally related. In other words, this means that there must be no less drastic alternative available to accomplish the legislative purpose[1] and, in the terms used by Tussman and tenBroek, that the class employed must come close to being neither under- nor overinclusive.[2]

The difference in outcome, depending on which test is used, is increased by two other factors. These are the requirements under the reasonableness test that "if any state of facts reasonably can be conceived that would sustain [the law], the existence of that state of facts at the time the law was enacted must be assumed" and that the person who assails the statutory classification "must carry the burden of showing that it does not rest upon any reasonable basis, but is essentially arbi-

---

1. I.e., a statutory design that would be less onerous to the people restricted, would affect fewer people or areas, or would not use a "suspect" basis for classification at all.

2. However, there is some evidence that if the state interest involved in the legislation is sufficiently compelling (e.g., national defense), and especially if there is an emergency situation, the Court will allow the use of an under- or overinclusive classification. See, e.g., Korematsu v. United States, 323 U.S. 214, 65 S. Ct. 193, 89 L. Ed. 194 (1944).

trary."[3] When the Court uses strict scrutiny, facts necessary to sustain the law will not be assumed, but must be demonstrated to the Court. Furthermore, the state bears the burden of proof on all issues: whether the legislative purpose is of overwhelming public importance, whether the chosen classification is necessary to accomplish that purpose, and whether less drastic alternatives for accomplishing that purpose are unavailable. Needless to say, the party with the burden of proof is more apt to lose, especially if a factual showing must be made; so the test of reasonableness favors the state, and the strict scrutiny test favors the party challenging the state law.

The cases that follow illustrate the application of the "reasonableness" test and the development of strict scrutiny in the Supreme Court in suspect classification and fundamental interest cases.

B. The Reasonableness Test

RAILWAY EXPRESS AGENCY v. NEW YORK
336 U.S. 106, 69 S. Ct. 463, 93 L. Ed. 533 (1949)

[New York City traffic regulations prohibited motor carriers from selling advertising space on trucks, but allowed companies to advertise for themselves on their own delivery trucks. The state courts upheld the ordinance as a valid safety regulation on the grounds that advertising on vehicles could distract drivers and pedestrians. To the Supreme Court, the Railway Express Agency argued that the regulation violated the Equal Protection Clause because it differentiated between advertisements not on the basis of what they said or how distracting they were, but on the irrelevant and therefore impermissible basis of whose trucks carried them. Justice DOUGLAS, for the majority, characterized this as superficial analysis:]

The local authorities may well have concluded that those who advertise their own wares on their trucks do not present the same traffic problem in view of the nature or extent of the advertising which they use. It would take a degree of omniscience which we lack to say that such is not the case. If that judgment is correct, the advertising displays that are exempt have less incidence on traffic than those of appellants. We cannot say that that judgment is not an allowable one. Yet if it is, the classification has relation to the purpose for which it is made and does not contain the kind of discrimination against which the Equal Protection Clause affords protection. It is by such practical considerations based on experience rather than by theoretical inconsistencies that the question of equal protection is to be answered. . . . And the fact that New York City sees fit to eliminate from traffic this kind of distraction but does not touch what may be even greater ones in a different category, such as the vivid displays on Times Square, is immaterial. It is no requirement of equal protection that all evils of the same genus be eradicated or none at all. . . .

Affirmed.

[Justice JACKSON, concurring, rejected the rationale advanced by the majority, stating, "There is not even a pretense here that the traffic hazard created by the advertising which is forbidden is in any manner or degree more hazardous than that which is permitted." Instead, he focused on the differing interests of those who advertised their own products and those who held advertising space out for hire.] . . . [T]he hireling may be put in a class by himself and may be dealt with differently than those who act on their own. But this is not merely because such a discrimination will enable the lawmaker to diminish the evil. That might be done by many classifications, which I should think

3. Lindsley v. Natural Carbonic Gas Company, 220 U.S. 61, 78-79, 31 S. Ct. 337, 340, 55 L. Ed. 369, 377 (1911).

wholly unsustainable. It is rather because there is a real difference between doing in self-interest and doing for hire, so that it is one thing to tolerate action from those who act on their own and it is another thing to permit the same action to be promoted for a price. . . .

NOTE: THE REASONABLENESS TEST IN PRACTICE

Notice that the Court applies the "reasonableness" test only cursorily. Justice Douglas first defines the legislative purpose as the prevention of traffic problems, presumably a constitutionally permissible purpose. He then states, in effect, that the classification is related to accomplishing this purpose, because those who advertise products on their own trucks may use a different "nature or extent of . . . advertising" than those who buy space for advertising on the trucks of others. If the first group advertises in a less distracting fashion than the second, it would be reasonable to allow the first to advertise but not the second. This is a clear example of the Court's "assuming the existence of a state of facts" in order to support a classification. In actuality, it seems highly unlikely that those who advertise products on their own trucks use less distracting advertising methods than those who buy space on other people's trucks. As the example shows, an assumption of facts can be used to uphold almost any law.

Note also that the classification used by New York City was both under- and overinclusive in relation to the purpose of the regulation. Many who advertise wares on their own trucks will do so in distracting ways, and the classification is thus underinclusive. Many who rent space will advertise in nondistracting ways, and the classification is thus overinclusive.

Readers should analyze the opinions which follow to see how thoroughly the Court applies either of the two equal protection tests. They should also check for over- and underinclusiveness and consider what degree of either should lead a court to find that a classification is not reasonably related to achieving the purpose of the law. Is it ever just for the courts to allow an over- or underinclusive classification?

KOTCH v. BOARD OF RIVER PORT PILOT COMMISSIONERS, 330 U.S. 552, 67 S. Ct. 910, 91 L. Ed. 1093 (1947). Louisiana's pilotage laws required that state pilots guide all ships going through the Mississippi River approaches to New Orleans. New pilots were appointed by the governor upon certification of names by a board composed of pilots. Only those with six months' apprenticeship under an incumbent pilot were eligible for certification. Administration of the system was attacked on the ground that the board certified only relatives and friends of the incumbents.

Justice BLACK, writing for the majority in a 5 to 4 decision, rejected the equal protection challenge, relying on the "entirely unique" nature of pilotage "in the light of its history in Louisiana." The object of the system "is to secure . . . the safest and most efficiently operated pilotage system practicable. We cannot say that the method adopted . . . is unrelated to this objective." He mentioned "the benefits to morale and esprit de corps which family and neighborly tradition might contribute" as one of the useful functions that "a closely knit pilotage system may serve." Four justices dissented, arguing that even if family ties made the system more efficient, a standard of "race or consanguinity" was impermissible.

MOREY v. DOUD
354 U.S. 457, 77 S. Ct. 1344, 1 L. Ed. 2d 1485 (1957)

Mr. Justice BURTON delivered the opinion of the Court.

This case concerns the validity of a provision in the Illinois Community Currency

Exchanges Act, as amended, excepting money orders of the American Express Company from the requirement that any firm selling or issuing money orders in the State must secure a license and submit to state regulation. . . . [W]e hold that the Act is invalid as applied [to appellees, a partnership for selling money orders in drug and grocery stores] because of this discriminatory exception. . . .

During the early 1930s, the closing of many banks in the Chicago area led to the development of simple banking facilities called currency exchanges. The principal activities of these exchanges were the cashing of checks for a fee and the selling of money orders. The fact that many of these exchanges went into business without adequate capital and without sufficient safeguards to protect the public resulted in the enactment of the Illinois Currency Exchanges Act in 1943. . . .

The American Express Company . . . is relieved of these licensing and regulatory requirements, and appears to be exempt from any regulation in Illinois. . . .

In determining the constitutionality of the Act's application to appellees in the light of its exception of American Express money orders, we start with the established proposition that the "prohibition of the Equal Protection Clause goes no further than the invidious discrimination." Williamson v. Lee Optical of Oklahoma, 348 U.S. 483, 489. The rules for testing a discrimination have been summarized as follows:

> 1. The equal protection clause of the Fourteenth Amendment does not take from the State the power to classify in the adoption of police laws, but admits of the exercise of a wide scope of discretion in that regard, and avoids what is done only when it is without any reasonable basis and therefore is purely arbitrary. 2.A classification having some reasonable basis does not offend against that clause merely because it is not made with mathematical nicety or because in practice it results in some inequality. 3.When the classification in such a law is called in question, if any state of facts reasonably can be conceived that would sustain it, the existence of that state of facts at the time the law was enacted must be assumed. 4.One who assails the classification in such a law must carry the burden of showing that it does not rest upon any reasonable basis, but is essentially arbitrary. Lindsley v. Natural Carbonic Gas Co., 220 U.S. 61, 78-79.

To these rules we add the caution that "Discriminations of an unusual character especially suggest careful consideration to determine whether they are obnoxious to the constitutional provision." . . .

The purpose of the Act's licensing and regulatory provisions clearly is to protect the public when dealing with currency exchanges. Because the American Express Company is a world-wide enterprise of unquestioned solvency and high financial standing, the State argues that the legislation classification is reasonable. It contends that the special characteristics of the American Express Company justify excepting its money orders from the requirements of an Act aimed at local companies doing local business, and that appellees are in no position to complain about competitive disadvantages since the "Fourteenth Amendment does not protect a business against the hazards of competition." . . .

The provisions in the Illinois Act, such as those requiring an annual inspection of licensed community currency exchanges by the State Auditor, make it clear that the statute was intended to afford the public continuing protection. The discrimination in favor of the American Express Company does not conform to this purpose. The exception of its money orders apparently rests on the legislative hypothesis that the characteristics of the American Express Company make it unnecessary to regulate their sales. Yet these sales, by virtue of the exception, will continue to be unregulated whether or not the American Express Company retains its present characteristics. On the other hand, sellers of competing money orders are subject to the Act even though their characteristics are, or become, substantially identical with those the American Express Company now has. Moreover, the Act's blanket exception takes no account of the characteristics of the local outlets that sell American Express money orders, and the distinct possibility that they in themselves may afford less protection to the public than do the retail establishments that sell competing money orders. That the American Express Company is a responsible institution operating on a world-wide basis does not minimize the fact that when the public buys American Express money orders in local drug and grocery stores it relies in part on the reliability of the selling agents.

The effect of the discrimination is to create a closed class by singling out American Express money orders. . . . Although statutory discriminations creating a closed class have been upheld, a statute which established a closed class was held to violate the Equal Protection Clause where, on its face, it was "an attempt to give an economic advantage to those engaged in a given business at an arbitrary date as against all those who enter the industry after that date." . . .

. . . The fact that the activities of the American Express Company are far-flung does not minimize the impact on local affairs and on competitors of its sale of money orders in Illinois. This is not the case in which the Fourteenth Amendment is being invoked to protect a business from the general hazards of competition. The hazards here have their roots in the statutory discrimination.

Taking all of these factors in conjunction — the remote relationship of the statutory classification to the Act's purpose or to business characteristics, and the creation of a closed class by the singling out of the money orders of a named company, with accompanying economic advantages — we hold that the application of the Act to appellees deprives them of equal protection of the laws. . . .

The judgment of the District Court is affirmed.

Mr. Justice BLACK, dissenting.

The Illinois statute involved here provides a state-wide regulatory plan to protect the public from irresponsible and insolvent sellers of money orders. . . . [W]hatever one may think of the merits of this legislation, its exemption of a company of known solvency from a solvency test applied to others of unknown financial responsibility can hardly be called "invidious." . . . I feel it necessary to express once again my objection to the use of general provisions of the Constitution to restrict narrowly state power over state domestic economic affairs.

I think state regulation should be viewed quite differently where it touches or involves freedom of speech, press, religion, petition, assembly, or other specific safeguards of the Bill of Rights. It is the duty of this Court to be alert to see that these constitutionally preferred rights are not abridged. But the Illinois statute here does not involve any of these basic liberties. . . .

Mr. Justice FRANKFURTER, whom Mr. Justice HARLAN joins, dissenting.

The more complicated society becomes, the greater the diversity of its problems and the more does legislation direct itself to the diversities. Statutes, that is, are directed to less than universal situations. Law reflects distinctions that exist in fact or at least appear to exist in the judgment of legislators — those who have the responsibility for making law fit fact. . . . To recognize marked differences that exist in fact is living law; to disregard practical differences and concentrate on some abstract identities is lifeless logic. . . .

. . . [I]t is suggested that the American Express Co. may not continue to retain "its present characteristics," while sellers of competing money orders may continue to be subject to the Act, even though their characteristics become "substantially identical with those the American Express Co. now has." What is this but to deny a State the right to legislate on the basis of circumstances that exist because a State may not in speculatively different circumstances that may never come to pass have such right? Surely there is time enough to strike down legislation when its constitutional justification is gone. Invalidating legislation is serious business and it ought not to be indulged in because in a situation not now before the Court, nor even remotely probable, a valid statute may lose its foundation. . . .

DANDRIDGE v. WILLIAMS
397 U.S. 471, 90 S. Ct. 1153, 25 L. Ed. 2d 491 (1970)

Mr. Justice STEWART delivered the opinion of the Court.

This case involved the validity of a method used by Maryland, in the administration of an aspect of its public welfare program, to reconcile the demands of its needy citizens with the finite resources available to meet those demands. Like every other State in the Union, Maryland participates in the Federal Aid to Families With Dependent Children . . . which originated with the Social Security Act of 1935. Under this jointly financed program, a State computes the so-called "standard of need" of each eligible family unit within its borders. . . .

The operation of the Maryland welfare system is not complex. By statute the State participates in the AFDC program. It computes the standard of need for each eligible family based on the number of children in the family and the circumstances under which the family lives. In general, the standard of need increases with each additional person in the household, but the increments become proportionately smaller. The regulation here in issue imposes upon the grant that any single family may receive an upper limit of $250 per month. . . . The appellees all have large families, so that their standards of need as computed by the State substantially exceed the maximum grants that they actually receive under the regulation. . . .

. . . Maryland says that its maximum grant regulation is wholly free of any invidiously discriminatory purpose or effect, and that the regulation is rationally supportable on at least four entirely valid grounds. The regulation can be clearly justified, Maryland argues, in terms of legitimate state interests in encouraging gainful employment, in maintaining an equitable balance in economic status as between welfare families and those supported by a wage earner, in providing incentives for family planning, and in allocating available public funds in such a way as fully to meet the needs of the largest possible number of families. The District Court, while apparently recognizing the validity of at least some of these state concerns, nonetheless held that the regulation . . . violates the Equal Protection Clause "because it cuts too broad a swath on an indiscriminate basis as applied to the entire group of AFDC eligibles to which it purports to apply. . . ." "A statutory discrimination will not be set aside if any state of facts reasonably may be conceived to justify it." . . .

To be sure, the cases . . . enunciating this fundamental standard under the Equal Protection Clause, have in the main involved state regulation of business or industry. The administration of public welfare assistance, by contrast, involves the most basic economic needs of impoverished human beings. We recognize the dramatically real factual difference between the cited cases and this one, but we can find no basis for applying a different constitutional standard. . . . It is a standard that has consistently been applied to state legislation restricting the availability of employment opportunities. Goesaert v. Cleary, 335 U.S. 464; Kotch v. Board of River Port Pilot Comm'rs, 330 U.S. 552. . . . And it is a standard that is true to the principle that the Fourteenth Amendment gives the federal courts no power to impose upon the States their views of what constitutes wise economic or social policy.

Under this long-established meaning of the Equal Protection Clause, it is clear that the Maryland maximum grant regulation is constitutionally valid. We need not explore all the reasons that the State advances in justification of the regulation. It is enough that a solid foundation for the regulation can be found in the State's legitimate interest in encouraging employment and in avoiding discrimination between welfare families and the families of the working poor.

It is true that in some AFDC families there may be no person who is employable. It is also true that with respect to AFDC families whose determined standard of need is below the regulatory maximum, and who therefore receive grants equal to the determined standard, the employment incentive is absent. But the Equal Protection Clause does not require that a State must choose between attacking every aspect of a problem or not attacking the problem at all. . . .

We do not decide today that the Maryland regulation is wise, that it best fulfills the relevant social and economic objectives that Maryland might ideally espouse, or that a more just and humane system could not be devised. Conflicting claims of morality and intelligence are raised by opponents and proponents of almost every measure, certainly including the one before us. But the intractable economic, social, and even philosophical problems presented by public welfare assistance programs are not the business of this Court. . . .

The judgment is reversed. . . .

[The concurring opinions of Mr. Justice BLACK and Mr. Justice HARLAN are omitted. The dissenting opinion of Mr. Justice DOUGLAS is omitted.]

Mr. Justice MARSHALL, whom Mr. Justice BRENNAN joins, dissenting.

The classification process effected by . . . Maryland's maximum grant regulation produces a basic denial of equal treatment. Persons who are concededly similarly situated (dependent children and their families), are not afforded equal, or even approximately equal, treatment under the maximum grant regulation. Subsistence benefits are paid with respect to some needy dependent children; nothing is paid with respect to others. . . .

In the instant case, the only distinction between those children with respect to whom assistance is granted and those children who are denied such assistance is the size of the family into which the child permits himself to be born. The class of individuals with respect to whom payments are actually made (the first four or five eligible dependent children in a family), is grossly underinclusive in terms of the class that the AFDC program was designed to assist, namely, all needy dependent children. Such underinclusiveness manifests "a prima facie violation of the equal protection requirement of reasonable classification," compelling the State to come forward with a persuasive justification for the classification.

The Court never undertakes to inquire for such a justification; rather it avoids the task by focusing upon the abstract dichotomy between two different approaches to equal protection problems that have been utilized by this Court.

Under the so-called "traditional test," a classification is said to be permissible under the Equal Protection Clause unless it is "without any reasonable basis." . . . On the other hand, if the classification affects a "fundamental right," then the state interest in perpetuating the classification must be "compelling" in order to be sustained. . . .

This case simply defies easy characterization in terms of one or the other of these "tests." The cases relied on by the Court, in which a "mere rationality" test was actually used, . . . are most accurately described as involving the application of equal protection reasoning to the regulation of business interests. The extremes to which the Court has gone in dreaming up rational bases for state regulation in that area may in many instances be ascribed to a healthy revulsion from the Court's earlier excesses in using the Constitution to protect interests that have more than enough power to protect themselves in the legislative halls. This case, involving the literally vital interests of a powerless minority — poor families without breadwinners — is far removed from the area of business regulation, as the Court concedes. Why then is the standard used in those cases imposed here? We are told no more than that this case falls in "the area of economics and social welfare," with the implication that from there the answer is obvious.

In my view, equal protection analysis of this case is not appreciably advanced by the a priori definition of a "right," fundamental or otherwise. Rather, concentration must be placed upon the character of the classification in question, the relative importance to individuals in the class discriminated against of the governmental benefits that they do not receive, and the asserted state interests in support of the classification. . . .

C. STRICT SCRUTINY

The cases that follow are examples of the application of strict scrutiny by the Supreme Court to state action. While reading them, remember that the existence of two standards of review is the result of a theory developed by legal scholars and advocates to explain a series of decisions of the Court, not a description of its own logic accepted by all the members of the Court. The most controversial question is what factors account for findings that particular classifications are "suspect" or particular rights are "fundamental."

Suspect classifications and fundamental rights are recently developed concepts in legal theory and judicial practice, although "[t]he concept of a suspect classification possesses historical roots which date back into the nineteenth century."[4] Justice Black's famous statement in the *Korematsu* case about "suspect" classifications and "rigid scrutiny," quoted by Tussman and tbe Broek above, was made in 1944. Likewise, "Skinner v. Oklahoma, decided in 1942, appears to be the first case to introduce the notion [of fundamental interests] in an equal protection decision."[5] As late as 1949, Tussman and tenBroek could say:[6]

> The equal protection clause of the Fourteenth Amendment appears thus to be *entering* the most fruitful and significant period of its career. Virtually strangled in infancy by post-civil-war judicial reactionism, long frustrated by judicial neglect, the theory of equal protection may yet take its rightful place in the unfinished constitutional struggle for democracy.

The next twenty years saw a tremendous expansion of the use of strict review under the Fourteenth Amendment. For general historical background on the Equal Protection Clause, and cases decided under it, see 2 Emerson, Haber, and Dorsen, Political and Civil Rights in the United States (student ed. 1967).

After reading this section, you may want to refer to Developments in the Law — Equal Protection, 82 Harv. L. Rev. 1065 (1969) for a more detailed view of equal protection theory.

HERNANDEZ v. TEXAS
347 U.S. 475, 74 S. Ct. 667, 98 L. Ed. 866 (1954)

Mr. Chief Justice WARREN delivered the opinion of the Court.

The petitioner, Pete Hernandez, was indicted for the murder of one Joe Espinosa by a grand jury in Jackson County, Texas. He was convicted and sentenced to life imprisonment. The Texas Court of Criminal Appeals affirmed the judgment of the trial court. 251 S.W.2d 531. Prior to the trial, the petitioner, by his counsel, offered timely motions to quash the indictment and the jury panel. He alleged that persons of Mexican descent were systematically excluded from service as jury commissioners, grand jurors and petit jurors, although there were such persons fully qualified to serve residing in Jackson County. . . .

In numerous decisions, this Court has held it is a denial of the equal protection of the laws to try a defendant of a particular race or color under an indictment issued by a grand jury, or before a petit jury, from which all persons of his race or color have, solely because of that race or color, been excluded by the State, whether acting through its legislature, its courts, or its executive or administrative officers. Although the Court has

---

4. Developments in the Law — Equal Protection, 82 Harv. L. Rev. 1065, 1131 (1969).
5. Ibid.
6. Tussman and tenBroek, The Equal Protection of the Laws, 37 Calif. L. Rev. 341, 381 (1949) (emphasis added).

had little occasion to rule on the question directly, it has been recognized since Strauder v. State of West Virginia, 100 U.S. 303, that the exclusion of a class of persons from jury service on grounds other than race or color may also deprive a defendant who is a member of that class of the constitutional guarantee of equal protection of the laws. The State of Texas would have us hold that there are only two classes — white and Negro — within the contemplation of the Fourteenth Amendment. . . .

Throughout our history differences in race and color have defined easily identifiable groups which have at times required the aid of the courts in securing equal treatment under the laws. But community prejudices are not static, and from time to time other differences from the community norm may define other groups which need the same protection. Whether such a group exists within a community is a question of fact. . . .

As the petitioner acknowledges, the Texas system of selecting grand and petit jurors by the use of jury commissions is fair on its face and capable of being utilized without discrimination. . . . [B]ut the petitioner alleges that those administering the law [discriminate].

The petitioner's initial burden in substantiating his charge of group discrimination was to prove that persons of Mexican descent constitute a separate class in Jackson County, distinct from "whites." One method by which this may be demonstrated is by showing the attitude of the community. Here the testimony of responsible officials and citizens contained the admission that residents of the community distinguished between "white" and "Mexican." The participation of persons of Mexican descent in business and community groups was shown to be slight. Until very recent times, children of Mexican descent were required to attend a segregated school for the first four grades. At least one restaurant in town prominently displayed a sign announcing "No Mexicans Served." On the courthouse grounds at the time of the hearing, there were two men's toilets, one unmarked, and the other marked "Colored Men" and "Hombres Aqui" (Men Here). No substantial evidence was offered to rebut the logical inference to be drawn from these facts, and it must be concluded that petitioner succeeded in his proof. . . .

The petitioner [next] established that 14 percent of the population of Jackson County were persons with Mexican or Latin American surnames, and that 11 percent of the males over 21 bore such names. The County Tax Assessor testified that 6 or 7 percent of the freeholders on the tax rolls of the County were persons of Mexican descent. The State of Texas stipulated that "for the last twenty-five years there is no record of any person with a Mexican or Latin American name having served on a jury commission, grand jury or petit jury in Jackson County." The parties also stipulated that "there are some male persons of Mexican or Latin American descent in Jackson County who . . . are eligible to serve as members of a jury commission, grand jury and/or petit jury."

. . . To rebut the strong prima facie case . . . thus established, the State offered the testimony of five jury commissioners that they had not discriminated against persons of Mexican or Latin American descent in selecting jurors. They stated that their only objective had been to select those whom they thought were best qualified. . . . [I]t taxes our credulity to say that mere chance resulted in there being no members of this class among the over six thousand jurors in the past twenty-five years. The result bespeaks discrimination, whether or not it was a conscious decision on the part of any individual jury commissioner. The judgment of conviction must be reversed.

MCLAUGHLIN v. FLORIDA
379 U.S. 184, 85 S. Ct. 283, 13 L. Ed. 2d 222 (1964)

Mr. Justice WHITE delivered the opinion of the Court.

At issue in this case is the validity of a conviction under §798.05 of the Florida statutes, F.S.A., providing that: "Any negro man and white woman, or any white man and negro woman, who are not married to each other, who shall habitually live in and occupy in the nighttime the same room shall each be punished by imprisonment not exceeding twelve months, or by fine not exceeding five hundred dollars."

Because the section applies only to a white person and a Negro who commit the specified acts and because no couple other than one made up of a white and a Negro is subject to conviction upon proof of the elements comprising the offense it proscribes, we hold §798.05 invalid as a denial of the equal protection of the laws guaranteed by the Fourteenth Amendment. . . .

Normally, the widest discretion is allowed the legislative judgment in determining whether to attack some, rather than all, of the manifestations of the evil aimed at; and normally that judgment is given the benefit of every conceivable circumstance which might suffice to characterize the classification as reasonable rather than arbitrary and invidious. . . . But we deal here with a classification based upon the race of the participants, which must be viewed in light of the historical fact that the central purpose of the Fourteenth Amendment was to eliminate racial discrimination emanating from official sources in the States. This strong policy renders racial classifications "constitutionally suspect," Bolling v. Sharpe, 347 U.S. 497, 499; and subject to the "most rigid scrutiny," Korematsu v. United States, 323 U.S. 214, 216; and "in most circumstances irrelevant" to any constitutionally acceptable legislative purpose, Hirabayashi v. United States, 320 U.S. 81, 100.

We deal here with a racial classification embodied in a criminal statute. In this context, where the power of the State weighs most heavily upon the individual or the group, we must be especially sensitive to the policies of the Equal Protection Clause. . . .

Our inquiry, therefore, is whether there clearly appears in the relevant materials some overriding statutory purpose requiring the proscription of the specified conduct when engaged in by a white person and a Negro, but not otherwise. . . . The State in its brief in this Court . . . says that the legislative purpose . . . was to prevent breaches of the basic concepts of sexual decency. . . .

We find nothing in this suggested legislative purpose, however, which makes it essential to punish promiscuity of one racial group and not that of another. There is no suggestion that a white person and a Negro are any more likely habitually to occupy the same room together than the white or the Negro couple or to engage in illicit intercourse if they do. Sections 798.01-798.05 indicate no legislative conviction that promiscuity by the interracial couple presents any particular problems requiring separate or different treatment if the suggested over-all policy of the chapter is to be adequately served. . . . That a general evil will be partially corrected may at times, and without more, serve to justify the limited application of a criminal law; but legislative discretion to employ the piecemeal approach stops short of permitting a State to narrow statutory coverage to focus on a racial group. . . .

Reversed.

[The concurring opinion of Mr. Justice HARLAN is omitted.]

Mr. Justice STEWART, with whom Mr. Justice DOUGLAS joins, concurring.

. . . [T]he Court implies that a criminal law of the kind here involved might be constitutionally valid if a State could show "some overriding statutory purpose." This is an implication in which I cannot join, because I cannot conceive of a valid legislative purpose under our Constitution for a state law which makes the color of a person's skin the test of whether his conduct is a criminal offense. . . . There might be limited room under the Equal Protection Clause for a civil law requiring the keeping of racially segregated public records for statistical or other valid public purposes. . . . But we deal here with a criminal law which imposes criminal punishment. And I think it is simply not possible for a state law to be valid under our Constitution which makes the criminality of an act depend upon the race of the actor. Discrimination of that kind is invidious per se.

DUNN v. BLUMSTEIN
405 U.S. 330, 92 S. Ct. 995, 31 L. Ed. 2d 274 (1972)

Mr. Justice MARSHALL delivered the opinion of the Court.

Various Tennessee public officials (hereinafter Tennessee) appeal from a decision by a three-judge federal court holding that Tennessee's durational residence requirements for voting violate the Equal Protection Clause of the United States Constitution. The issue arises in a class action for declaratory and injunctive relief brought by appellee James Blumstein. Blumstein moved to Tennessee on June 12, 1970, to begin employment as an assistant professor of law at Vanderbilt University in Nashville. With an eye towards voting in the upcoming August and November elections, he attempted to register to vote on July 1, 1970. The county registrar refused to register him, on the ground that Tennessee law authorizes the registration of only those persons who, at the time of the next election, will have been residents of the State for a year and residents of the county for three months. . . .

Durational residence laws penalize those persons who have traveled from one place to another to establish a new residence during the qualifying period. Such laws divide residents into two classes, old residents and new residents, and discriminate against the latter to the extent of totally denying them the opportunity to vote. . . .

To decide whether a law violates the Equal Protection Clause, we look, in essence, to three things: the character of the classification in question; the individual interests affected by the classification; and the governmental interests asserted in support of the classification. Cf. Williams v. Rhodes, 393 U.S. 23, 30 (1968). In considering laws challenged under the Equal Protection Clause, this Court has evolved more than one test, depending upon the interest affected or the classification involved. First, then, we must determine what standard of review is appropriate. In the present case, whether we look to the benefit withheld by the classification (the opportunity to vote) or the basis for the classification (recent interstate travel), we conclude that the State must show a substantial and compelling reason for imposing durational residence requirements.

Durational residence requirements completely bar from voting all residents not meeting the fixed durational standards. By denying some citizens the right to vote, such laws deprive them of " 'a fundamental political right, . . . preservative of all rights.' " Reynolds v. Sims, 377 U.S. 533, 562 (1964). . . .

Tennessee urges that this case is controlled by Drueding v. Devlin, 380 U.S. 125 (1965). *Drueding* was a decision upholding Maryland's durational residence requirements. The District Court tested those requirements by the equal protection standard applied to ordinary state regulations: whether the exclusions are reasonably related to a permissible state interest. 234 F. Supp. 721, 724-725 (Md. 1964). We summarily affirmed per curiam without the benefit of argument. But if it was not clear then, it is certainly clear now that a more exacting test is required for any statute that "place[s] a condition on the exercise of the right to vote." [Citing Bullock v. Carter, 405 U.S. 134 (1972); Kramer v. Union Free School District, 395 U.S. 621 (1969).]

This exacting test is appropriate for another reason, never considered in *Drueding:* Tennessee's durational residence laws classify bona fide residents on the basis of recent travel, penalizing those persons, and only those persons, who have gone from one jurisdiction to another during the qualifying period. Thus, the durational residence requirement directly impinges on the exercise of a second fundamental personal right, the right to travel.

. . . We considered such a durational residence requirement in Shapiro v. Thompson [394 U.S. 618 (1969)], where the pertinent statutes imposed a one-year waiting period for interstate migrants as a condition to receiving welfare benefits. Although in *Shapiro* we specifically did not decide whether durational residence requirements could be used to determine voting eligibility, id. at 638 n.21, we concluded that since the right to travel was a constitutionally protected right, "any classification which serves to penalize the exercise of that right, unless shown to be necessary to promote a *compelling* governmental interest, is unconstitutional." Id. at 634. . . .

In sum, durational residence laws must be measured by a strict equal protection test: they are unconstitutional unless the State can demonstrate that such laws are *"necessary* to promote a *compelling* governmental interest." Shapiro v. Thompson, supra, at 634 (first emphasis added); Kramer v. Union Free School District, 395 U.S. at 627. Thus phrased, the constitutional question may sound like a mathematical formula. But legal "tests" do not have the precision of mathematical formulas. The key words emphasize a matter of degree: that a heavy burden of justification is on the State, and that the statute will be closely scrutinized in light of its asserted purposes.

It is not sufficient for the State to show that durational residence requirements further a very substantial state interest. In pursuing that important interest, the State cannot choose means which unnecessarily burden or restrict constitutionally protected activity. Statutes affecting constitutional rights must be drawn with "precision." . . .

Tennessee tenders "two basic purposes" served by its durational residence requirements:

"(1) *Insure purity of ballot box* — Protection against fraud through colonization and inability to identify persons offering to vote, and

"(2) *Knowledgeable voter* — Afford some surety that the voter has, in fact, become a member of the community and that as such, he has a common interest in all matters pertaining to its government and is, therefore, more likely to exercise his right more intelligently." . . .

We consider each in turn. [As to purity of ballot box, the] main concern is that nonresidents will temporarily invade the State or county, falsely swear that they are residents to become eligible to vote, and, by voting, allow a candidate to win by fraud. . . .

Durational residence laws may once have been necessary to prevent a fraudulent evasion of state voter standards, but today in Tennessee, as in most other States, this purpose is served by a system of voter registration. . . . Given this system, the record is totally devoid of any evidence that durational residence requirements are in fact necessary to identify bona fide residents. The qualifications of the would-be voter in Tennessee are determined when he registers to vote, which he may do until 30 days before the election. . . . His qualifications — including bona fide residence — are established then by oath. . . . As long as the State relies on the oath-swearing system to establish qualifications, a durational residence requirement adds nothing to a simple residence requirement in the effort to stop fraud. The nonresident intent on committing election fraud will as quickly and effectively swear that he has been a resident for the requisite period of time as he would swear that he was simply a resident. . . .

It has been argued that . . . durational residence requirements are justified because they create an administratively useful conclusive presumption that recent arrivals are not residents and are therefore properly barred from the franchise. . . .

. . . The State's legitimate purpose is to determine whether certain persons in the community are bona fide residents. A durational residence requirement creates a classification which may, in a crude way, exclude nonresidents from that group. But it also excludes many residents. Given the State's legitimate purpose and the individual interests that are affected, the classification is all too imprecise. . . . In general, it is not very difficult for Tennessee to determine on an individualized basis whether one recently arrived in the community is in fact a resident, although of course there will always be difficult cases. . . .

Our conclusion that the waiting period is not the least restrictive means necessary for preventing fraud is bolstered by the recognition that Tennessee has at its disposal a variety of criminal laws which are more than adequate to detect and deter whatever fraud may be feared. At least six separate sections of the Tennessee Code define offenses to deal with voter fraud. . . .

In Kramer v. Union Free School District, supra, we held that the Equal Protection

Clause prohibited New York State from limiting the vote in school-district elections to parents of school children and to property owners. The State claimed that since nonparents would be "less informed" about school affairs than parents, id. at 631, the State could properly exclude the class of nonparents in order to limit the franchise to the more "interested" group of residents. We rejected that position, concluding that a "close scrutiny of [the classification] demonstrates that [it does] not accomplish this purpose with sufficient precision. . . ." Id. at 632. That scrutiny revealed that the classification excluding nonparents from the franchise kept many persons from voting who were as substantially interested as those allowed to vote; given this, the classification was insufficiently "tailored" to achieve the articulated state goal. Ibid. See also Cipriano v. City of Houma, [395 U.S. 701] at 706.

Similarly, the durational residence requirements in this case founder because of their crudeness as a device for achieving the articulated goal of assuring the knowledgeable exercise of the franchise. The classifications created by durational residence requirements obviously permit any long-time resident to vote regardless of his knowledge of the issues — and obviously many long-time residents do not have any. On the other hand, the classifications bar from the franchise many other, admittedly new, residents who have become at least minimally, and often fully, informed about the issues. Indeed, recent migrants who take the time to register and vote shortly after moving are likely to be those citizens, such as appellee, who make it a point to be informed and knowledgeable about the issues. Given modern communications, and given the clear indication that campaign spending and voter education occur largely during the month before an election, the State cannot seriously maintain that it is "necessary" to reside for a year in the State and three months in the county in order to be knowledgeable about congressional, state, or even purely local elections. . . .

It is pertinent to note that Tennessee has never made an attempt to further its alleged interest in an informed electorate in a universally applicable way. Knowledge or competence has never been a criterion for participation in Tennessee's electoral process for long-time residents. Indeed, the State specifically provides for voting by various types of absentee persons. These provisions permit many long-time residents who leave the county or State to participate in a constituency in which they have only the slightest political interest, and from whose political debates they are likely to be cut off. That the State specifically permits such voting is not consistent with its claimed compelling interest in intelligent, informed use of the ballot. If the State seeks to assure intelligent use of the ballot, it may not try to serve this interest only with respect to new arrivals. Cf. Shapiro v. Thompson, supra at 637-638. . . .

Mr. Chief Justice BURGER, dissenting.

. . . It is no more a denial of equal protection for a State to require newcomers to be exposed to state and local problems for a reasonable period such as one year before voting, than it is to require children to wait eighteen years before voting. Cf. Oregon v. Mitchell, 400 U.S. 112 (1970). In both cases some informed and responsible persons are denied the vote, while others less informed and less responsible are permitted to vote. Some lines must be drawn. To challenge such lines by the "compelling state interest" standard is to condemn them all. So far as I am aware, no state law has ever satisfied this seemingly insurmountable standard, and I doubt one ever will, for it demands nothing less than perfection.

The existence of a constitutional "right to travel" does not persuade me to the contrary. If the imposition of a durational residency requirement for voting abridges the right to travel, surely the imposition of an age qualification penalizes the young for being young, a status I assume the Constitution also protects.

NOTE: FUNDAMENTAL INTERESTS

Interests that have been identified as fundamental and therefore deserving of special treatment under the Equal Protection Clause include voting,[7] procreation,[8] and travel.[9] Other interests,[10] such as freedom of religion and freedom of speech, would likely call forth this same strict scrutiny in the equal protection context, but courts commonly use other provisions of the Bill of Rights to safeguard them. Why are these "personal" interests deemed fundamental by courts, and why are they treated differently from those involved in cases of economic regulation? The Harvard Law Review "Developments in the Law" article on equal protection lists, as one possible justification, the close relationship between economic regulation and conditions "about which a local legislative or administrative body would be better informed than a court," but concludes that "the different treatment of personal interests seems to rest upon the belief that they are simply more important than others."[11] Nevertheless it is certainly difficult to state a formulation that distinguishes fundamental personal interests from others.[12] In light of Goesaert v. Cleary, 335 U.S. 464, 69 S. Ct. 198, 93 L. Ed. 163 (1948), infra, Part V-B, and Dandridge v. Williams, 397 U.S. 471, 90 S. Ct. 1153, 25 L. Ed. 2d 491 (1970), supra Section B, can you accept the contention that economic and personal rights can readily or validly be distinguished? Is the balancing test set forth in Marshall's dissent in the Dandridge case a viable alternative?

NOTE: SUSPECT CLASSIFICATIONS

"Several types of classification have triggered active review by the courts. Classifications based on race have received the strictest treatment, but national ancestry (lineage) and alienage have been given close attention as well."[13] Recent cases have divided on the treatment of classifications based on wealth[14] and the marital status of one's parents.[15] It is possible that, because the Court is divided, other explanations must be sought to reconcile the contradictory decisions, such as whether or not fundamental interests are involved in each case. The Harvard Law Review article listed four possible

7. E.g., Harper v. Virginia Bd. of Elections, 383 U.S. 663, 86 S. Ct. 1079, 16 L. Ed. 2d 169 (1966); Reynolds v. Sims, 377 U.S. 533, 84 S. Ct. 1362, 12 L. Ed. 2d 506 (1964); Williams v. Rhodes, 393 U.S. 23, 89 S. Ct. 5, 21 L. Ed. 2d 24 (1968).

8. Skinner v. Oklahoma ex rel. Williamson, 316 U.S. 535, 62 S. Ct. 1110, 86 L. Ed. 1655 (1942).

9. Shapiro v. Thompson, 394 U.S. 618, 89 S. Ct. 1322, 22 L. Ed. 2d 600 (1969).

10. The question of whether education was also a fundamental right, raised by cases such as Brown v. Board of Education, 347 U.S. 483, 74 S. Ct. 686, 98 L. Ed. 873 (1954), was answered in the negative by the Supreme Court in Rodriguez v. San Antonio Independent School District, 411 U.S. 483, 94 S. Ct. 1278, 36 L. Ed. 2d 16 (1973), a case upholding the financing of schools by local property taxation. The right to pursue a particular occupation has ambiguous status under the Fourteenth Amendment. Compare Truax v. Raich, 239 U.S. 33, 36 S. Ct. 7, 60 L. Ed. 131 (1915), with Goesaert v. Cleary, 335 U.S. 464, 69 S. Ct. 198, 93 L. Ed. 163 (1948), infra, Part V-B. Access to criminal procedures, when available to the rich and denied to the poor, has apparently been considered fundamental in some cases; see, e.g., Griffin v. Illinois, 351 U.S. 12, 76 S. Ct. 585, 100 L. Ed. 891 (1956) (state must provide indigent a transcript for appeal).

11. Developments in the Law — Equal Protection, 82 Harv. L. Rev. 1065, 1128 (1969).

12. Id. at 1130.

13. Id. at 1124.

14. Compare Harper v. Virginia Bd. of Elections, 383 U.S. 663, 86 S. Ct. 1079, 16 L. Ed. 2d 169 (1966); Griffin v. Illinois, 351 U.S. 12, 76 S. Ct. 585, 100 L. Ed. 891 (1956); and Boddie v. Connecticut, 401 U.S. 371, 91 S. Ct. 780, 28 L. Ed. 2d 113 (1971), with Dandridge v. Williams, 397 U.S. 471, 90 S. Ct. 1153, 25 L. Ed. 2d 491 (1970), supra Section B.

15. Compare Levy v. Louisiana, 391 U.S. 68, 88 S. Ct. 1509, 20 L. Ed. 2d 436 (1968); Glona v. American Guar. & Liab. Ins. Co., 391 U.S. 73, 88 S. Ct. 1515, 20 L. Ed. 2d 441 (1968); and Weber v. Aetna Casualty & Surety Co., 406 U.S. 164, 92 S. Ct. 1400, 31 L. Ed. 2d 768 (1972), with Labine v. Vincent, 401 U.S. 532, 91 S. Ct. 1017, 28 L. Ed. 2d 288 (1971); cf. Kotch v. Board of River Pilot Comm'rs, 330 U.S. 552, 67 S. Ct. 910, 91 L. Ed. 1093 (1947), supra Section B.

explanations for the treatment of some classifications as suspect: (1) the historical basis of the Fourteenth Amendment; (2) the need for judicial protection of politically disadvantaged minority groups; (3) the undesirability of making congenital and unalterable traits the basis for legal classifications; and (4) the opprobrium that attaches to the fact of classification in a particular case. The article discounts the historical explanation, on the grounds that "this formulation does not explain why other traits have been accorded treatment similar to that given race or even why some racial classifications may be permissible while others are 'invidious' and therefore invalid."[16] The authors comment in a footnote that "the fact that lineage and, to a lesser extent, alienage are popularly thought of as closely akin to race has likely contributed to this development [cases finding classification according to these traits suspect]. Indeed, the language of the cases reveals that courts themselves readily make this association."[17] The review also discounts the explanation of political disadvantage, since that argument applies with equal force to minority economic interests, and the explanation of congenital and unalterable traits, since many classifications may validly be based on such congenital and unalterable traits as height, vision, or hearing. A fifth possibility, which the Harvard article does not discuss, is that suspect classification status depends on the presence of a combination of the four factors. The application of strict scrutiny to sex classifications is discussed in Part V, infra.

NOTE: STATE ACTION

Since the Civil Rights Cases, 109 U.S. 3, 3 S. Ct. 18, 27 L. Ed. 835 (1883), the Supreme Court has held that the Fourteenth Amendment applies only to "state action," because of the phrasing of the Equal Protection Clause ("No *state* shall . . . deny . . . the equal protection *of the laws*"). Thus private entities are not subject to equal protection standards, and the line between state and private action becomes very significant. A law review article briefly summarized the tests which the Court has used to determine whether or not there is state action as follows:[18]

> Constitutional doctrines pertaining to state action have developed mainly in the area of race discrimination. They are intricate and confusing, but in essence they embody two concepts. One is that the existence of state action depends upon the nature and degree of state involvement. This may range all the way from a direct criminal prohibition of certain conduct to the maintenance of conditions in the society that permit private activity to exist; from direct action to apparent inaction; from de jure to de facto responsibility. The second is that state action depends upon the function being performed. The activity out of which the claim for equal protection arises may range from a clearly governmental operation, such as the election of public officials, to purely personal relationships, such as a private social gathering.

Since 1944, there has been a vast expansion of activities in which the courts have found state action; "seldom in recent years has a decision found none."[19] Charles Black has called the current doctrine of state action "a conceptual disaster area," and other commentators have been equally critical;[20] nevertheless, this doctrine can be an important limitation on judicial intervention based on the Fourteenth Amendment. Chapter Five will return to the question of when "private" action is really private for Fourteenth

16. Developments in the Law — Equal Protection, supra, at 1125.
17. Id. at 1124 n.266. Cf. the comparisons between discrimination on the basis of race and on the basis of ethnic origin in Strauder v. West Virginia, 100 U.S. 303, 308, 25 L. Ed. 664, 666 (1879), and Korematsu v. United States, 323 U.S. 214, 65 S. Ct. 193, 89 L. Ed. 194 (1944).
18. Brown, Emerson, Falk, and Freedman, The Equal Rights Amendment: A Constitutional Basis for Equal Rights for Women, 80 Yale L.J. 871, 905 (1971).
19. Developments in the Law — Equal Protection, supra, at 1072.
20. Ibid.

Amendment purposes. For a brief summary with references to the major articles on the subject, see Developments in the Law — Equal Protection, 82 Harv. L. Rev. 1065, 1069-1072 (1969). Major cases in the area include Burton v. Wilmington Parking Auth., 365 U.S. 715, 81 S. Ct. 856, 6 L. Ed. 2d 45 (1961) (private premises in a state building); Evans v. Newton, 382 U.S. 296, 86 S. Ct. 486, 15 L. Ed. 2d 373 (1966) (a state-run privately donated park); Marsh v. Alabama, 326 U.S. 501, 66 S. Ct. 276, 90 L. Ed. 265 (1946) (a company town); Terry v. Adams, 345 U.S. 461, 73 S. Ct. 809, 97 L. Ed. 1152 (1953) (a privately run political primary); Shelley v. Kraemer, 334 U.S. 1, 68 S. Ct. 836, 92 L. Ed. 1161 (1948) (judicial enforcement of a discriminatory contract); and Moose Lodge No. 107 v. Irvis, 407 U.S. 163, 92 S. Ct. 1965, 32 L. Ed. 2d 627 (1972) (a private club with a state liquor license).

V. THE EQUAL PROTECTION CLAUSE AS A TOOL FOR WINNING EQUAL RIGHTS FOR WOMEN

This section presents the arguments and evidence supporting the proposition that sex should be declared a suspect classification. This is followed by an examination of the way the Supreme Court has traditionally handled equal protection challenges to sex-discriminatory laws, and a discussion of developments since 1966 in the Supreme Court and lower federal and state courts.

A. THE RACE–SEX PARALLEL

As the cases in the previous section illustrated, race is the paradigmatic suspect classification. Thus, to the extent that sex can be analogized to race, the chances are increased that it will be definitively declared a suspect classification. The classic statement of the parallels between the two was made by the great Swedish sociologist Gunnar Myrdal in An American Dilemma, originally published in 1944.

MYRDAL, AN AMERICAN DILEMMA
1073-1078 (Twentieth Anniversary ed. 1962)

In every society there are at least two groups of people, besides the Negroes, who are characterized by high social visibility expressed in physical appearance, dress, and patterns of behavior, and who have been "suppressed." We refer to women and children. Their present status, as well as their history and their problems in society, reveal striking similarities to those of the Negroes. . . .

. . . The ideological and economic forces behind the two movements — the emancipation of women and children and the emancipation of Negroes — have much in common and are closely interrelated. Paternalism was a pre-industrial scheme of life, and was gradually becoming broken in the nineteenth century. Negroes and women, both of whom had been under the yoke of the paternalistic system, were both strongly and fatefully influenced by the Industrial Revolution. For neither group is the readjustment process yet consummated. Both are still problem groups. The women's problem is the center of the whole complex of problems of how to reorganize the institution of the family to fit the new economic and ideological basis, a problem which is not solved in any part of the Western world unless it be in the Soviet Union or Palestine. The family problem in the Negro group, as we find when analyzing the Negro family, has its special complications, centering in the tension and conflict between the external patriarchal system in which the Negro was confined as a slave and his own family structure.

As in the Negro problem, most men have accepted as self-evident, until recently, the doctrine that women had inferior endowments in most of those respects which carry prestige, power, and advantages in society, but that they were, at the same time, superior in some other respects. The arguments, when arguments were used, have been about the same: smaller brains, scarcity of geniuses and so on. The study of women's intelligence and personality has had broadly the same history as the one we record for Negroes. As in the case of the Negro, women themselves have often been brought to believe in their inferiority of endowment. As the Negro was awarded his "place" in society, so there was a "woman's place." In both cases the rationalization was strongly believed that men, in confining them to this place, did not act against the true interest of the subordinate groups. The myth of the "contented women," who did not want to have suffrage or other civil rights and equal opportunities, had the same social function as the myth of the "contented Negro." In both cases there was probably — in a static sense — often some truth behind the myth.

As to the character of the deprivations, upheld by law or by social conventions and the pressure of public opinion, no elaboration will here be made. As important and illustrative in the comparison, we shall, however, stress the conventions governing woman's education. There was a time when the most common idea was that she was better off with little education. Later the doctrine developed that she should not be denied education, but that her education should be of a special type, fitting her for her "place" in society and usually directed more on training her hands than her brains.

Political franchise was not granted to women until recently. Even now there are, in all countries, great difficulties for a woman to attain public office. The most important disabilities still affecting her status are those barring her attempt to earn a living and to attain promotion in her work. As in the Negro's case, there are certain "women's jobs," traditionally monopolized by women. They are regularly in the low salary bracket and do not offer much of a career. All over the world men have used the trade unions to keep women out of competition. Woman's competition has, like the Negro's, been particularly obnoxious and dreaded by men because of the low wages women, with their few earning outlets, are prepared to work for. Men often dislike the very idea of having women on an equal plane as co-workers and competitors, and usually they find it even more "unnatural" to work under women. White people generally hold similar attitudes toward Negroes. On the other hand, it is said about women that they prefer men as bosses and do not want to work under another woman. Negroes often feel the same way about working under other Negroes.

In personal relations with both women and Negroes, white men generally prefer a less professional and more human relation, actually a more paternalistic and protective position — somewhat in the nature of patron to client in Roman times, and like the corresponding strongly paternalistic relation of later feudalism. As in Germany it is said that every gentile has his pet Jew, so it is said in the South that every white has his "pet nigger," or — in the upper strata — several of them. We sometimes marry the pet woman, carrying out the paternalistic scheme. But even if we do not, we tend to deal kindly with her as a client and a ward, not as a competitor and an equal.

In drawing a parallel between the position of, and feeling toward, women and Negroes we are uncovering a fundamental basis of our culture. Although it is changing, atavistic elements sometimes unexpectedly break through even in the most emancipated individuals. The similarities in the women's and the Negroes' problems are not accidental. They were, as we have pointed out, originally determined in a paternalistic order of society. The problems remain, even though paternalism is gradually declining as an ideal and is losing its economic basis. In the final analysis, women are still hindered in their competition by the function of procreation; Negroes are laboring under the yoke of the doctrine of unassimilability which has remained although slavery is abolished. The second barrier is actually much stronger than the first in America today. But the first is more eternally inexorable.

An article on the parallels between race and sex makes the point graphically.

HACKER, WOMEN AS A MINORITY GROUP
30 Social Forces 60 (1951)

CASTELIKE STATUS OF WOMEN AND NEGROES

Negroes	*Women*

1. High Social Visibility

Negroes	Women
a. Skin color, other "racial" characteristics.	a. Secondary sex characteristics.
b. (Sometimes) distinctive dress — bandana, flashy clothes.	b. Distinctive dress, skirts, etc.

2. Ascribed Attributes

Negroes	Women
a. Inferior intelligence, smaller brain, less convoluted, scarcity of geniuses.	a. Ditto.
b. More free in instinctual gratifications. More emotional, "primitive" and childlike. Imagined sexual prowess envied.	b. Irresponsible, inconsistent, emotionally unstable. Lack strong super-ego. Women as "temptresses."
c. Common stereotype "inferior."	c. "Weaker."

3. Rationalizations of Status

Negroes	Women
a. Thought all right in his place.	a. Woman's place is in the home.
b. Myth of contented Negro.	b. Myth of contented woman — "feminine" woman is happy in subordinate role.

4. Accommodation Attitudes

Negroes	Women
a. Supplicatory whining intonation of voice.	a. Rising inflection, smiles, laughs, downward glances.
b. Deferential manner.	b. Flattering manner.
c. Concealment of real feelings.	c. "Feminine wiles."
d. Outwit "white folks."	d. Outwit "menfolk."
e. Careful study of points at which dominant group is susceptible to influence.	e. Ditto.
f. Fake appeals for directives; show of ignorance.	f. Appearance of helplessness.

5. Discriminations

Negroes	Women
a. Limitations on education — should fit "place" in society.	a. Ditto.
b. Confined to traditional jobs — barred from supervisory positions. Their competition feared. No family precedents for new aspirations.	b. Ditto.
c. Deprived of political importance.	c. Ditto.
d. Social and professional segregation.	d. Ditto.
e. More vulnerable to criticism.	e. E.g., conduct in bars.

6. Similar Problems

Roles not clearly defined, but in flux as result of social change. Conflict between achieved status and ascribed status.

A law review notewriter made a case that race and sex are coming to be considered parallels for legal purposes because this attitude promotes wiser social policies.[1]

> . . . Through a process of social evolution, racial distinctions have become unacceptable. The old social consensus that race was a clear indication of inferiority has yielded to the notion that race is unrelated to ability or performance. Even allegedly rational attempts at racial classification are now generally rejected outright. The burden of showing that these attempts are based on something other than prejudice is enormous.
>
> There are indications that sex classifications may be undergoing a similar metamorphosis in the public mind. Once thought normal, proper, and ordained in the "very nature of things," sex discrimination may soon be seen as a sham, not unlike that perpetrated in the name of racial superiority. Whatever differences may exist between the sexes, legislative judgments have frequently been based on inaccurate stereotypes of the capacities and sensibilities of women. In view of the damage that has been inflicted on individuals in the name of these "differences," any continuing distinctions should, like race, bear a heavy burden of proof. One function of the fourteenth amendment ought to be to put such broad-ranging concerns into the fundamental law of the land.

B. The Reasonableness Test Applied to Sex Classifications, 1910-1970

QUONG WING v. KIRKENDALL
223 U.S. 59, 32 S. Ct. 192, 56 L. Ed. 350 (1912)

Mr. Justice Holmes delivered the opinion of the court.

This is an action to recover ten dollars paid under duress and protest for a license to do hand laundry work. . . . The law under which the fee was exacted imposed the payment upon all persons engaged in laundry business other than the steam laundry business, with a proviso that it should not apply to women so engaged where not more than two women were employed. The only question is whether this is an unconstitutional discrimination depriving the plaintiff of the equal protection of the laws.

The case was argued upon the discrimination between the instrumentalities employed in the same business and that between men and women. . . . It is to be observed that in 1900 the census showed more women than men engaged in hand laundry work in that State. Nevertheless we agree with the Supreme Court of the State so far as these grounds are concerned. A State does not deny the equal protection of the laws merely by adjusting its revenue laws and taxing system in such a way as to favor certain industries or forms of industry. . . . It may make discriminations, if founded on distinctions that we cannot pronounce unreasonable and purely arbitrary. . . . If the State sees fit to encourage steam laundries and discourage hand laundries that is its own affair. And if again it finds a ground of distinction in sex, that is not without precedent. It is recognized with regard to hours of work. Muller v. Oregon, 208 U.S. 412. It is recognized in the respective rights of husband and wife in land during life, in the inheritance after the death of the spouse. Often it is expressed in the time fixed for coming of age. If

---

1. Sex Discrimination and Equal Protection: Do We Need a Constitutional Amendment? 84 Harv. L. Rev. 1499, 1507-1508 (1971). See also the discussions of the similarities between sex and race discrimination in Johnston and Knapp, Sex Discrimination By Law: A Study in Judicial Perspective, 46 N.Y.U.L. Rev. 675, 738-741 (1971); and Murray, The Negro Woman's Stake in the Equal Rights Amendment, 6 Harv. Civ. Rights–Civ. Lib. L. Rev. 253, 257 (1971).

Montana deems it advisable to put a lighter burden upon women than upon men with regard to an employment that our people commonly regard as more appropriate for the former, the Fourteenth Amendment does not interfere by creating a fictitious equality where there is a real difference. The particular points at which that difference shall be emphasized by legislation are largely in the power of the State.

Another difficulty suggested by the statute is that it is impossible not to ask whether it is not aimed at the Chinese, which would be a discrimination that the Constitution does not allow. Yick Wo v. Hopkins, 118 U.S. 356. It is a matter of common observation that hand laundry work is a widespread occupation of Chinamen in this country while on the other hand it is so rare to see men of our race engaged in it that many of us would be unable to say that they ever had observed a case. But this ground of objection was not urged and rather was disclaimed when it was mentioned from the Bench at the argument. . . . It rests with counsel to take the proper steps, and if they deliberately omit them, we do not feel called upon to institute inquiries on our own account. Laws frequently are enforced which the court recognizes as possibly or probably invalid if attacked by a different interest or in a different way. Therefore without prejudice to the question that we have suggested, when it shall be raised, we must conclude that so far as the present case is concerned the judgment must be affirmed.

Judgment affirmed.

Mr. Justice HUGHES concurs in the result.

Mr. Justice LAMAR dissenting.

I dissent from the conclusions reached in the first branch of the opinion, because, in my judgment, the statute which is not a police but a revenue measure makes an arbitrary discrimination. It taxes some and exempts others engaged in identically the same business. It does not graduate the license so that those doing a large volume of business pay more than those doing less. On the contrary, it exempts the large business and taxes the small. It exempts the business that is so large as to require the use of steam, and taxes that which is so small that it can be run by hand. Among these small operators there is a further discrimination, based on sex. It would be just as competent to tax the property of men and exempt that of women. The individual characteristics of the owner do not furnish a basis on which to make a classification for purposes of taxation. It is the property or the business which is to be taxed, regardless of the qualities of the owner. A discrimination founded on the personal attributes of those engaged in the same occupation and not on the value or the amount of the business is arbitrary. "A classification must always rest upon some difference which bears a reasonable and just relation to the act in respect to which the classification is proposed." Connolly v. Union Sewer Pipe Co., 184 U.S. 560.

NOTE: INTRODUCTION TO GOESAERT V. CLEARY

In 1945, Michigan passed a statute providing in essence that women could not pour or dispense drinks from behind a bar unless they were the wives or daughters of male bar owners. Statutes such as Michigan's were passed at about the same time in other states, and seem to have sprung from a common motivation and lobbying effort by bartenders' unions, which excluded women.[2]

For several years, the Michigan statute was not enforced, but the Liquor Control

2. This explanation for the passage of the statute was given by plaintiffs' counsel at the hearing on the motion for a preliminary injunction and was never denied on the record. 29 Transcripts of Records, Goesaert v. Cleary, 335 U.S. 464, 69 S. Ct. 198, 93 L. Ed. 163 (1948). See also the dissent in the Supreme Court opinion itself, infra, which hints that there must have been an economic motivation by somebody for the passage of such statutes. In addition, see The Union Role: Good Faith Protection of Women or Self-Interested Protection of Men?, Chapter Two, II-B-3-b, which quotes material from a convention and the official journal of the Hotel and Restaurant Employees and Bartenders International Union, detailing the union's work on passage of anti-barmaid legislation.

Commission announced that as of May 1, 1947, they would move to effect its purposes. Immediately, four women, represented by a woman lawyer, filed class action suits on behalf of themselves and other women similarly situated, seeking to have the law declared unconstitutional as a taking of property without due process and as a denial of equal protection of the laws. The Goesaerts were a mother and daughter, the mother a bar owner and the daughter her main employee. The co-plaintiffs were Gertrude Nadroski and Caroline McMahon, a bar owner and her employee. With the complaint were filed twenty-four affidavits from women who either owned bars or were employed as barmaids, who would no longer be able to run their businesses economically or pursue their occupations unless the statute was struck down.

The affidavits describe such situations as that of a woman bar owner who lived with her invalid husband in a room adjoining the bar and could not make enough money to care for him unless she ran the bar herself. A number of bar owners swore that their life savings were invested in the bars, and that they had always operated them themselves, and did not want to and could not economically hire male bartenders. One affidavit stated: "Deponent further says that she has tried to employ male bartenders, but has found it very unsatisfactory because the male bartenders she has had would drink upon the premises, and she has not had any of this difficulty with a barmaid." Other women, who worked in bars, alleged that they had trained as bartenders, progressing from the lower-paid jobs of waitresses, and that they had no other training or way of making an adequate living.[3]

The plaintiffs' papers in the case are exceedingly well drafted. The federal district court granted a temporary restraining order on the basis of the original papers, but ultimately a three-judge court denied interlocutory relief, with one judge dissenting. Goesaert v. Cleary, 74 F. Supp 735 (E.D. Mich. 1947). The suit was litigated in a careful, lawyerly way on behalf of clients who were severely hurt. The complaint and subsequent briefs clearly reveal that this was in no sense a symbolic or educative suit, but was brought by plaintiffs desperately and immediately concerned about the impact of the statute on their ability to make a living. In light of this background, consider the Supreme Court's treatment of the plaintiffs' contentions.

GOESAERT v. CLEARY
335 U.S. 464, 69 S. Ct. 198, 93 L. Ed. 163 (1948)

Mr. Justice FRANKFURTER delivered the opinion of the Court.

As part of the Michigan system for controlling the sale of liquor, bartenders are required to be licensed in all cities having a population of 50,000, or more, but no female may be so licensed unless she be "the wife or daughter of the male owner" of a licensed liquor establishment. Section 19a of Act 133 of the Public Acts of Michigan 1945, Mich. Stat. Ann. §18.990(1), Cum. Supp.1947. The case is here on direct appeal from an order of the District Court of three judges, . . . denying an injunction to restrain the enforcement of the Michigan law. . . . To ask whether or not the Equal Protection of the Laws Clause of the Fourteenth Amendment barred Michigan from making the classification the State has made between wives and daughters of owners of liquor places and wives and daughters of non-owners, is one of those rare instances where to state the question is in effect to answer it.

We are, to be sure, dealing with a historic calling. We meet the alewife, sprightly and ribald, in Shakespeare, but centuries before him she played a role in the social life of England. See, e.g., Jusserand, English Wayfaring Life, 133, 134, 136-37 (1889). The Fourteenth Amendment did not tear history up by the roots, and the regulation of the liquor traffic is one of the oldest and most untrammeled of legislative powers. Michigan could, beyond question, forbid all women from working behind a bar. This is so despite

3. Goesaert Transcripts, supra, at 19-42.

the vast changes in the social and legal position of women. The fact that women may now have achieved the virtues that men have long claimed as their prerogatives and now indulge in vices that men have long practiced, does not preclude the States from drawing a sharp line between the sexes, certainly, in such matters as the regulation of the liquor traffic. See the Twenty-First Amendment and Carter v. Virginia, 321 U.S. 131. The Constitution does not require legislatures to reflect sociological insight, or shifting social standards, any more than it requires them to keep abreast of the latest scientific standards.

While Michigan may deny to all women opportunities for bartending, Michigan cannot play favorites among women without rhyme or reason. The Constitution in enjoining the equal protection of the laws upon States precludes irrational discrimination as between persons or groups of persons in the incidence of a law. But the Constitution does not require situations "which are different in fact or opinion to be treated in law as though they were the same." Tigner v. State of Texas, 310 U.S. 141, 147. Since bartending by women may, in the allowable legislative judgment, give rise to moral and social problems against which it may devise preventive measures, the legislature need not go to the full length of prohibition if it believes that as to a defined group of females other factors are operating which either eliminate or reduce the moral and social problems otherwise calling for prohibition. Michigan evidently believes that the oversight assured through ownership of a bar by a barmaid's husband or father minimizes hazards that may confront a barmaid without such protecting oversight. This Court is certainly not in a position to gainsay such belief by the Michigan legislature. If it is entertainable, as we think it is, Michigan has not violated its duty to afford equal protection of its laws. We cannot cross-examine either actually or argumentatively the mind of Michigan legislatures nor question their motives. Since the line they have drawn is not without a basis in reason, we cannot give ear to the suggestion that the real impulse behind this legislation was an unchivalrous desire of male bartenders to try to monopolize the calling. . . .

Nor is it unconstitutional for Michigan to withdraw from women the occupation of bartending because it allows women to serve as waitresses where liquor is dispensed. The District Court has sufficiently indicated the reasons that may have influenced the legislature in allowing women to be waitresses in a liquor establishment over which a man's ownership provides control. . . .

Mr. Justice RUTLEDGE, with whom Mr. Justice DOUGLAS and Mr. Justice MURPHY join, dissenting.

While the equal protection clause does not require a legislature to achieve "abstract symmetry" or to classify with "mathematical nicety," that clause does require lawmakers to refrain from invidious distinctions of the sort drawn by the statute challenged in this case.

The statute arbitrarily discriminates between male and female owners of liquor establishments. A male owner, although he himself is always absent from his bar, may employ his wife and daughter as barmaids. A female owner may neither work as a barmaid herself nor employ her daughter in that position, even if a man is always present in the establishment to keep order. This inevitable result of the classification belies the assumption that the statute was motivated by a legislative solicitude for the moral and physical well-being of women who, but for the law, would be employed as barmaids. Since there could be no other conceivable justification for such discrimination against women owners of liquor establishments, the statute should be held invalid as a denial of equal protection.

NOTE: OCCUPATIONAL EXCLUSION

The majority opinion in the Supreme Court and the two opinions filed by the three-judge district court were concerned only with discrimination among different classes of women. Goesaert v. Cleary, 74 F. Supp. 735, 738 (E.D. Mich. 1947). The dissenters in the Supreme Court focused on the discrimination against female bar owners, whom they apparently felt could provide moral protection for their daughters and could hire males to provide physical protection as good as that provided by a husband or father. However, they too failed to discuss the issue of discrimination between women and men desiring employment as bartenders, although this issue was clearly raised in the case by the barmaid plaintiffs who were nonowners.

Evidently if the prohibition on women being employed as bartenders applied only to women who neither owned a bar nor were related to the bar owner (regardless of the bar owner's sex), it would have been constitutional even in the eyes of the dissenters. Given the extreme consequences such a law would have for women who had previously been earning a living as bartenders, the various courts might have been a little more specific about the "moral and social problems" which arise when women tend bar. The record is devoid of any proof or specific allegations concerning the actuality of such problems. On the contrary, the affidavits of barmaids allege that they have tended bar for periods of four to seventeen years without incident. Justice Frankfurter notes that "the District Court has sufficiently indicated the reasons that may have influenced the legislature [in passing the statute]," but, as the dissenting judge on the three-judge court pointed out, the "reasons" given by the lower court were entirely speculative and not based on any facts in the record.

Another feature of the law which should be questioned and which none of the courts mentioned is the method chosen by the legislature to protect the barmaids (whom the court had defined as the victims of antisocial behavior) — depriving them of jobs, rather than penalizing customers who behaved antisocially. In any case, it seems unlikely that protection of barmaids was the purpose of the law in the first place.

State cases both before and after *Goesaert,* with few exceptions, sustained statutes prohibiting or regulating sale of liquor by women, "brushing aside constitutional challenges with expressions of deference to legislative judgment in matters of 'public morality.' "[4] Nine states and an unknown number of municipalities still have laws prohibiting women from being bartenders, and there are also a wide variety of sex-based laws regulating other aspects of the behavior of men and women in places of public accommodation where liquor is served.[5]

Note: Goesaert and United States v. Dege

Justice Frankfurter's allusion to the "sprightly and ribald" alewife of Shakespeare hardly supports the decision that the legislative power to regulate liquor traffic includes the power to exclude women from their "historic calling" of tending bar. But it was apparently an irresistible line at this point.

Compare the opinion in *Goesaert* with Frankfurter's opinion in United States v. Dege, 364 U.S. 51, 80 S. Ct. 1589, 4 L. Ed. 2d 1563 (1960), in which he held, to the disadvantage of the husband and wife in question, that the common law rule that a husband and wife could not be guilty of conspiring with each other did not bar their prosecution under the federal anticonspiracy statute. He explained his holding as follows:[6]

> The question raised by these conflicting views is clearcut and uncomplicated. . . . The claim that husband and wife are outside the scope of this . . . enactment of Congress

4. Johnston and Knapp, Sex Discrimination By Law: A Study in Judicial Perspective, 46 N.Y.U.L. Rev. 675, 685 (1971)
5. See Chapter Five, III, for a discussion of sex discrimination with and without the sanction of law in places of public accommodation, and Chapter Two, II-B-3-b, for a discussion of state laws excluding women from particular occupations and the impact of Title VII of the Civil Rights Act of 1964.
6. 364 U.S. at 52–54.

. . . must be given short shrift once . . . "we free our minds from the notion that criminal statutes must be construed by some artificial and conventional rule" . . . and therefore do not allow ourselves to be obfuscated by medieval views regarding the legal status of woman and the common law's reflection of them. . . . Such an immunity to husband and wife as a pair of conspirators would have to attribute to Congress one of two assumptions: either that responsibility of husband and wife for joint participation in a criminal enterprise would make for marital disharmony, or that a wife must be presumed to act under the coercive influence of her husband and, therefore, cannot be a willing participant. The former assumption is unnourished by sense; the latter implies a view of American womanhood offensive to the ethos of our society. . . .

For this Court now to act on . . . the medieval view that a husband and wife "are esteemed but as one Person in Law" . . . would require us to disregard the vast changes in the status of woman — the extension of her rights and correlative duties — whereby a wife's legal submission to her husband has been wholly wiped out, not only in the English-speaking world generally but emphatically so in this country.

The two cases can be harmonized if both are viewed as examples of judicial deference to other branches of government; the difference in their approaches to sex differentiation in the law was, according to this view, primarily a result of the different attitudes of the legislative and executive bodies involved, not a change of attitude on Frankfurter's part.

HOYT v. FLORIDA
368 U.S. 57, 82 S. Ct. 159, 7 L. Ed. 2d 118 (1961)

Mr. Justice Harlan delivered the opinion of the Court.

Appellant, a woman, has been convicted in Hillsborough County, Florida, of second degree murder of her husband. On this appeal . . . we consider appellant's claim that her trial before an all-male jury violated rights assured by the Fourteenth Amendment. The claim is that such jury was the product of a state jury statute which works an unconstitutional exclusion of women from jury service.

The jury law primarily in question is Fla. Stat., 1959, §40.01 (1), F.S.A. This Act, which requires that grand and petit jurors be taken from "male and female" citizens of the State possessed of certain qualifications, contains the following proviso: "provided, however, that the name of no female person shall be taken for jury service unless said person has registered with the clerk of the circuit court her desire to be placed on the jury list."

Showing that since the enactment of the statute only a minimal number of women have so registered, appellant challenges the constitutionality of the statute both on its face and as applied in this case. For reasons now to follow we decide that both contentions must be rejected.

At the core of appellant's argument is the claim that the nature of the crime of which she was convicted peculiarly demanded the inclusion of persons of her own sex on the jury. She was charged with killing her husband by assaulting him with a baseball bat. . . . As described by the Florida Supreme Court, the affair occurred in the context of a marital upheaval involving, among other things, the suspected infidelity of appellant's husband, and culminating in the husband's final rejection of his wife's efforts at reconciliation. It is claimed, in substance, that women jurors would have been more understanding or compassionate than men in assessing the quality of appellant's act and her defense of "temporary insanity." . . .

Of course, these premises misconceive the scope of the right to an impartially selected jury assured by the Fourteenth Amendment. That right does not entitle one accused of crime to a jury tailored to the circumstances of the particular case, whether relating to the sex or other condition of the defendant, or to the nature of the charges to be tried. It requires only that the jury be indiscriminately drawn from among those eligible in the community for jury service, untrammelled by any arbitrary and systematic exclusions. See Fay v. New York, 332 U.S. 261, 284-285, and the cases cited therein. The result of this appeal must therefore depend on whether such an exclusion of women from jury service has been shown. . . .

In the selection of jurors Florida has differentiated between men and women in two respects. It has given women an absolute exemption from jury duty based solely on their sex, no similar exemption obtaining as to men. And it has provided for its effectuation in a manner less onerous than that governing exemptions exercisable by men: women are not to be put on the jury list unless they have voluntarily registered for such service; men, on the other hand, even if entitled to an exemption, are to be included on the list unless they have filed a written claim of exemption as provided by law. Fla. Stat., 1959, §40.10, F.S.A.

In neither respect can we conclude that Florida's statute is not "based on some reasonable classification," and that it is thus infected with unconstitutionality. Despite the enlightened emancipation of women from the restrictions and protections of bygone years, and their entry into many parts of community life formerly considered to be reserved to men, woman is still regarded as the center of home and family life. We cannot say that it is constitutionally impermissible for a State, acting in pursuit of the general welfare, to conclude that a woman should be relieved from the civic duty of jury service unless she herself determines that such service is consistent with her own special responsibilities.

Florida is not alone in so concluding. [Other States have similar laws.] It is true, of course, that Florida could have limited the exemption, as some other States have done, only to women who have family responsibilities. But we cannot regard it as irrational for a state legislature to consider preferable a broad exemption, whether born of the State's historic public policy or of a determination that it would not be administratively feasible to decide in each individual instance whether the family responsibilities of a prospective female juror were serious enough to warrant an exemption.

Likewise we cannot say that Florida could not reasonably conclude that full effectuation of this exemption made it desirable to relieve women of the necessity of affirmatively claiming it, while at the same time requiring of men an assertion of the exemptions available to them. Moreover, from the standpoint of its own administrative concerns the State might well consider that it was "impractical to compel large numbers of women, who have an absolute exemption, to come to the clerk's office for examination since they so generally assert their exemption." Fay v. New York, supra, at 277. . . .

Appellant argues that whatever may have been the design of this Florida enactment, the statute in practical operation results in an exclusion of women from jury service, because women, like men, can be expected to be available for jury service only under compulsion. In this connection she points out that by 1957, when this trial took place, only some 220 women out of approximately 46,000 registered female voters in Hillsborough County — constituting about 40 per cent of the total voting population of that county[10] — had volunteered for jury duty since the limitation of jury service to males, see Hall v. Florida, 136 Fla. 644, 662-665, 187 So. 392, 400-401, was removed by §40.01 (1) in 1949. Fla. Laws 1949, c. 25,126.

This argument, however, is surely beside the point. Given the reasonableness of the classification involved in §40.01(1), the relative paucity of women jurors does not carry the constitutional consequence appellant would have it bear. "Circumstance or chance may well dictate that no persons in a certain class will serve on a particular jury or during some particular period." Hernandez v. Texas, [347 U.S. 475] at 482.

We cannot hold this statute as written offensive to the Fourteenth Amendment. . . .

Appellant's attack on the statute as applied in this case fares no better.

10. 114,247, of which some 68,000 were men.

In the year here relevant, 1955, Fla. Stat. §40.10 in conjunction with §40.02 required the jury commissioners, with the aid of the local circuit court judges and clerk, to compile annually a jury list of 10,000 inhabitants qualified to be jurors. In 1957 the existing Hillsborough County list had become exhausted to the extent of some 3,000 jurors. The new list was constructed by taking over from the old list the remaining some 7,000 jurors, including 10 women, and adding some 3,000 new male jurors to build up the list to the requisite 10,000. At the time some 220 women had registered for jury duty in this county, including those taken over from the earlier list.

The representative of the circuit court clerk's office, a woman, who actually made up the list testified as follows as to her reason for not adding others of the 220 "registered" women to the 1957 list: "Well, the reason I placed ten is I went back two or three, four years, and noticed how many women they had put on before and I put on approximately the same number." She further testified: "Mr. Lockhart [one of the jury commissioners] told me at one time to go back approximately two or three years to get the names because they were recent women that had signed up, because in this book [the female juror register], there are no dates at the beginning of it, so we can't — I don't know exactly how far back they do go and so I just went back two or three years to get my names." When read in light of Mr. Lockhart's testimony, . . . it is apparent that the idea was to avoid listing women who though registered might be disqualified because of advanced age or for other reasons.

Appellant's showing falls far short of giving this procedure a sinister complexion. It is true of course that the proportion of women on the jury list (10) to the total of those registered for such duty (some 220) was less than 5%, and not 27% as the trial court mistakenly said and the state appellate court may have thought. But when those listed are compared with the 30 or 35 women who had registered since 1952 . . . the proportion rises to around 33%, hardly suggestive of an arbitrary, systematic exclusionary purpose. Equally unimpressive is appellant's suggested "male" proportion which we are asked to contrast with the female percentage. The male proportion is derived by comparing the number of males contained on the jury list with the total number of male electors in the county. But surely the resulting proportion is meaningless when the record does not even reveal how many of such electors were qualified for jury service, how many had been granted exemptions . . . and how many on the list had been excused when first called.

This case in no way resembles those involving race or color in which the circumstances shown were found by this Court to compel a conclusion of purposeful discriminatory exclusions from jury service. E.g., Hernandez v. Texas, [347 U.S. 475]; Norris v. Alabama, 294 U.S. 587; Smith v. Texas, 311 U.S. 128; Hill v. Texas, 316 U.S. 400; Eubanks v. Louisiana, 356 U.S. 584. There is present here neither the unfortunate atmosphere of ethnic or racial prejudices which underlay the situations depicted in those cases, nor the long course of discriminatory administrative practice which the statistical showing in each of them evinced. . . .

The CHIEF JUSTICE, Mr. Justice BLACK and Mr. Justice DOUGLAS, concurring.

We cannot say from this record that Florida is not making a good faith effort to have women perform jury duty without discrimination based on sex. Hence we concur in the result, for the reasons set forth in [the second part] of the Court's opinion.

ALEXANDER v. LOUISIANA
405 U.S. 625, 92 S. Ct. 1221, 31 L. Ed. 2d 536 (1972)

Mr. Justice WHITE delivered the opinion of the Court.

After a jury trial in the District Court for the Fifteenth Judicial District of Lafayette Parish, Louisiana, petitioner, a Negro, was convicted of rape and sentenced to life imprisonment. His conviction was affirmed on appeal by the Louisiana Supreme Court, and this Court granted certiorari. Prior to trial, petitioner had moved to quash the indictment because (1) Negro citizens were included on the grand jury list and venire in only token numbers, and (2) female citizens were systematically excluded from the grand jury list, venire, and empaneled grand jury. Petitioner therefore argued that the indictment against him was invalid because it was returned by a grand jury empaneled from a venire made up contrary to the requirements of the Equal Protection Clause and the Due Process Clause of the Fourteenth Amendment. Petitioner's motions were denied. [The Court then set aside the conviction on the ground of invidious racial discrimination.]

Petitioner also challenges the Louisiana statutory exemption of women who do not volunteer for grand jury service. Article 402, La. Code of Crim. Proc. This claim is novel in this Court and, when urged by a male, finds no support in our past cases. The strong constitutional and statutory policy against racial discrimination has permitted Negro defendants in criminal cases to challenge the systematic exclusion of Negroes from the grand juries that indicted them. Also, those groups arbitrarily excluded from grand or petit jury service are themselves afforded an appropriate remedy. Cf. Carter v. Jury Commission of Greene County, 396 U.S. 320 (1970). But there is nothing in past adjudications suggesting that petitioner himself has been denied equal protection by the alleged exclusion of women from grand jury service. Although the Due Process Clause guarantees petitioner a fair trial, it does not require the States to observe the Fifth Amendment's provision for presentment or indictment by a grand jury. . . .

Against this background and because petitioner's conviction has been set aside on other grounds, we follow our usual custom of avoiding decision of constitutional issues unnecessary to the decision of the case before us. Burton v. United States, 196 U.S. 283, 295 (1905). See Ashwander v. Tennessee Valley Authority, 297 U.S. 288, 346-348 (1936) (Brandeis, J., concurring). The State may or may not recharge petitioner, a properly constituted grand jury may or may not return another indictment, and petitioner may or may not be convicted again. See Ballard v. United States, 329 U.S. 187, 196 (1946).

Reversed.

Mr. Justice POWELL and Mr. Justice REHNQUIST took no part in the consideration or decision of this case.

Mr. Justice DOUGLAS, concurring.

While I join [the first part] of the Court's opinion, I am convinced we should also reach the constitutionality of Louisiana's exclusion of women from jury service. The issue is squarely presented, it has been thoroughly briefed and argued, and it is of recurring importance. The Court purports to follow "our usual custom" of avoiding unnecessary constitutional issues. But that cannot be the sole rationale, for both questions are of constitutional dimension. We could just as well say that deciding the constitutionality of excluding women from juries renders it unnecessary to reach the question of racial exclusion.

It can be argued that the racial exclusion admits of the "easier" analysis. But this Court does not sit only to decide "easy" questions. And even when faced with "hard" constitutional questions, we have often decided cases on alternate grounds where a decision on only one would have been dispositive. See, e.g., Dunn v. Blumstein, 405 U.S. 330.

Petitioner complains of the exclusion of blacks and women from the grand jury which indicted him. Conceivably, he could have also complained of the exclusion of several other minority groups. Would he then be relegated to suffer repetitive reindictment and reconviction while this court considered the exclusion of each group in a separate lawsuit?

I believe the time has come to reject the dictum in Strauder v. West Virginia, 100 U.S. 303, 310, that a State "may confine" jury service "to males." I would here reach the question we reserved in Hoyt v. Florida, 368 U.S. 57, 60, and hold that Art. 402, La. Code Crim. Proc., as applied to exclude women as a class from Lafayette Parish jury rolls, violated petitioner Alexander's constitutional right to an impartial jury drawn from a group representative of a cross-section of the community. [The remainder of Justice Douglas's lengthy opinion is omitted.]

NOTES: DISCRIMINATION IN THE JURY SELECTION PROCESS

1. The Court's statement in *Hoyt* that "at the core of appellant's argument is the claim that the nature of the crime of which she was convicted peculiarly demanded the inclusion of persons of her own sex on the jury" does not accurately reflect the tack taken by the appellants. The major argument in the Supreme Court was that the systematic exclusion of women from the jury rolls denied the defendant an opportunity for a fair and impartial jury. The argument was made on a straight analogy to cases concerning racial exclusion, which create, in effect, a presumption of partiality from the mere absence of a substantial number of minorities on the lists. But, as a secondary argument, Hoyt attempted to show that in the circumstances of her case there was a demonstrable need for a jury which included women.[7]

The case was one in which Florida's second-degree murder statute required a finding of a depraved mind, and the defense was absence of this mental state and temporary insanity. In light of this factual situation, Hoyt argued that it was unfair for an "all-male jury [to be] involved in the determination of a woman's state of mind."[8] Given the facts in *Hoyt,* do you think women would be more sympathetic than men in evaluating the state of mind of the defendant? The imponderables of jury selection may make it impossible to state with certitude that any woman would be better than any man juror in a particular situation. Yet if such a statement could ever have validity, it would be in the *Hoyt* case.

To support her argument that women would have had a better insight into the facts of this case, Hoyt also cited sociological material demonstrating that women on juries have more "social and emotional specialization" than men, and that "sex-type differentiation in the interaction between men and women in jury deliberations can be reliably demonstrated," quoting from Strodtbeck and Mann, Sex Role Differentiation in Jury Deliberations, 19 Sociometry 3 (March 1956).[9]

2. *Hoyt* was litigated as a women's rights case in many respects. Two women representing the American Civil Liberties Union filed an amicus brief directed to the changing role of women in society and the importance of their assumption of all the privileges and duties of citizenship. And certainly the State of Florida was very much concerned with the status of women in its argument for preserving the system. The following passage from its brief is typical:[10]

> Appellee notes that nowhere within the confines of appellant's brief is any statistic cited which would, even in the slightest, tend to do away with the very practical and material reasons for the differences in responsibilities assigned to men and women in our society.
> Ever since the dawn of time conception has been the same. Though many eons may have passed, the gestation period in the human female has likewise remained unchanged. Save and except for a number of beneficial precautions presently available, parturition is as it well may have been in the Garden of Eden. The rearing of children, even if it be conceded that the socio-psychologists have made inroads

7. Brief for Appellant at 19-20, Hoyt v. Florida, 368 U.S. 57 (1961).
8. Id. at 5.
9. Id. at 19-20. For a more recent sociological study purporting to show that women on juries are more sympathetic toward women litigants, and men jurors more sympathetic to men, see Nagel and Weitzman, Women as Litigants, 23 Hast. L.J. 171, 192-197 (1971).
10. Brief for Appellee at 11, Hoyt v. Florida, 368 U.S. 57 (1961).

thereon, nevertheless remains a prime responsibility of the matriarch. The home, though it no longer be the log cabin in the wilderness, must nevertheless be maintained. The advent of "T.V." dinners does not remove the burden of providing palatable food for the members of the family, the husband is still, in the main, the breadwinner, child's hurts are almost without exception, bound and treated by the mother.

　　3. Although the Court in *Hoyt* fails to find systematic exclusion of women from juries, and the concurring justices state that there does not appear to be evidence of bad faith on Florida's part, the statistics presented at the evidentiary hearing and in the briefs are quite startling. At the time Gwendolyn Hoyt was tried, there were 10 women and 9990 men in the jury list of 10,000 from which the venire would be drawn. Over a ten-year period, about 220 to 275 women had filled in forms actually volunteering for jury service. One judge, dissenting from the opinion of the Florida Supreme Court denying a rehearing in the case below, observed from many years on the trial bench that, even among men, those most qualified to serve on juries were usually the ones who most actively sought to be excused, and that no system involving anything as onerous as jury duty could possibly run on volunteers.[11]

　　Traditionally, the Court has found discrimination in the jury selection process against blacks by comparing the number of blacks on jury lists to the number of eligible blacks, and has rejected the selection process if the resulting percentage seemed unreasonably low.[12] The Court repeated this process in *Hoyt,* when it pointed out that of the 220 registered women electors (the eligible female population for the jury list), 10 —or approximately 5 percent — were on the jury list. Similarly, by selecting from the eligible population only those women who had registered in the five years preceding the trial (30 to 35 women), it came up with a percentage of 33. The dishonesty of this approach as applied to sex discrimination is that the discrimination in *Hoyt* occurred at the point of *defining eligibility* for the jury list (when women had to affirmatively register in order to be eligible), rather than at the point of picking from among the eligible to place them on the jury list (as has been true for blacks).

　　The Court dismissed statistics which would have revealed discrimination at the point of defining eligibility, saying[13]

> Equally unimpressive is appellant's suggested "male" proportion which we are asked to contrast with the female percentage. The male proportion is derived by comparing the number of males contained on the jury list with the total number of male electors in the county. But surely the resulting proportion is meaningless when the record does not even reveal how many of such electors were qualified for jury service, how many had been granted exemptions . . . and how many on the list had been excused when first called.

While such statistics would have been imperfect, they would certainly have been more meaningful in revealing discrimination at the point of defining eligibility than the ones used by the Court. For example, the male proportion was 9,990 men on the jury list to 68,000 male electors, or roughly 15 percent, compared to the female proportion of 10 women on the jury list to 46,000 female electors, or roughly 0.02 percent. Differently stated, although women constituted 40 percent of the registered voters (roughly equivalent to the eligible population but for the discriminatory registration system), they constituted only 0.1 percent of the jury list. Compare this to Whitus v. Georgia, 385 U.S. 545, 87 S. Ct. 643, 17 L. Ed. 2d 599 (1967), in which the Court invalidated a jury selection process where blacks were 42 percent of the eligible population because blacks constituted only 9 percent of the jury list.

　　11. Dissent filed in petition for rehearing, 119 So. 2d 691, 702 (Fla. 1960).
　　12. See Kuhn, Jury Discrimination: The Next Phase, 41 S. Cal. L. Rev. 235, 250-257 (1968).
　　13. 368 U.S. at 68.

The Court dismissed the importance of the disproportion of women to men on the jury list as carrying "no constitutional significance" because "proportional class representation is not a constitutionally required factor." Yet, as Hernandez v. Texas, 374 U.S. 475, 74 S. Ct. 667, 98 L. Ed. 866 (1954), Part IV-C supra, demonstrates, proportional class representation is viewed as an important index of the overall fairness of the jury selection process — at least in non-sex discrimination cases. Surely a system which invariably produces a jury list composed of 0.1 percent women and 99.9 percent men has *some* constitutional significance.

4. Because the facts of *Alexander* involved a brutal rape of a young girl by two strangers, it was difficult to argue that there could be some actual prejudice from the absence of women on either the grand or petit jury. But in the general argument that a grand jury which had no women could not meet Fourteenth Amendment standards, a straight feminist line was taken. The Supreme Court brief, handled by the NAACP Legal Defense Fund, argued against the stereotypic view of women which assumes that they are all "so enmeshed in domestic duties" that they cannot serve on juries.[14] It further pointed out that the Supreme Court itself rejected this view of women in Phillips v. Martin Marietta Co, 400 U.S. 542, 91 S. Ct. 446, 27 L. Ed. 2d 613 (1971), Chapter Two, II-B-2, when it held that a woman who was automatically refused a factory job on the ground that she had preschool-age children had suffered illegal sex discrimination.

5. The treatment accorded by the Supreme Court to cases involving the exclusion of women from juries differs sharply from the Court's treatment of jury exclusion on other bases. As early as 1879, the Court decided, in Strauder v. West Virginia, 100 U.S. 303, 25 L. Ed. 664, that a state statute excluding blacks from jury duty violated the Equal Protection Clause of the Fourteenth Amendment. The Court asked,[15]

> . . . how can it be maintained that compelling a colored man to submit to a trial for his life by a jury drawn from a panel from which the State has expressly excluded every man of his race, because of color alone, however well qualified in other respects, is not a denial to him of equal legal protection?

and analogized the legislation to a hypothetical statute excluding "all naturalized Celtic Irishmen," which would also undoubtedly be inconsistent with "the spirit of the amendment."[16] Then the Court limited its holding as follows:[17]

> We do not say that within the limits from which it is not excluded by the amendment a State may not prescribe qualifications of its jurors, and in so doing make discriminations. *It may confine the selection to males,* to freeholders, to citizens, to persons within certain ages, or to persons having educational qualifications. We do not believe the Fourteenth Amendment was ever intended to prohibit this. . . . Its aim was against discrimination because of race or color.

The *Hernandez* case, supra, dealt with the exclusion of Mexican-Americans from jury duty, and speaks in the same broad terms as *Strauder*.

In an opinion earlier than *Hoyt* and quite different in tone, the Supreme Court held that the deliberate exclusion of women from federal juries violated the federal jury statute, stating:[18]

---

14. Brief for Appellant at 18, Alexander v. Louisiana, 405 U.S. 625 (1972).
15. 100 U.S. at 309.
16. Id. at 308.
17. Id. at 310. Emphasis added.
18. Ballard v. United States, 329 U.S. 187, 193-194, 67 S. Ct. 261, 264, 91 L. Ed. 181, 186 (1946).

The truth is that the two sexes are not fungible; a community made up exclusively of one is different from a community composed of both; the subtle interplay of influence one on the other is among the imponderables. To insulate the courtroom from either may not in a given case make an iota of difference. Yet a flavor, a distinct quality is lost if either sex is excluded.

The Court relied on this language in *Ballard* in Peters v. Kiff, 407 U.S. 493, 92 S. Ct. 2163, 33 L. Ed. 2d 83 (1972), its most far-reaching jury exclusion opinion to date. In reversing the conviction of a white man who claimed that blacks were excluded from his grand and petit juries, the Court held:[19]

> When any large and identifiable segment of the community is excluded from jury service, the effect is to remove from the jury room qualities of human nature and varieties of human experience, the range of which is unknown and perhaps unknowable. It is not necessary to assume that the excluded group will consistently vote as a class in order to conclude as we do that their exclusion deprives the jury of a perspective on human events that may have unsuspected importance in any case that may be presented.

It is a short step from the language and holding of Peters v. Kiff to a holding, reversing *Hoyt,* that laws which operate substantially to exclude women from juries violate the Fourteenth Amendment. (The Florida legislature itself reversed *Hoyt* by passing a statute which makes men and women equally liable to be called for service. See Fla. Stat. Ann. §40.01, as amended, Laws 1967, ch. 67-154, §1.) And in fact the rationales of *Hoyt* and *Peters* cannot coexist. *Peters* finds that a representative cross section is lacking when any identifiable group with different life experiences is excluded, and *Hoyt* finds that women are such a group (centers of homes, with special interests in childrearing and other unique attributes), yet allows their exclusion.

Less than a year after *Alexander,* a Louisiana federal court recognized that statutes like the one upheld in *Hoyt* and *Alexander* could no longer stand.[20] The court dealt with a petit jury (not, as in *Alexander,* a grand jury) selection statute exactly like the one in *Hoyt.* The opinion dealt with *Hoyt* by saying: "When today's vibrant principle is obviously in conflict with yesterday's sterile precedent, trial courts need not follow the outgrown dogma. Hence we consider that *Hoyt* is no longer binding."[21] The court went on to find that requiring women to file a written declaration of desire to serve has "resulted in jury panels that . . . have never included more than 5 percent females, and frequently less." The holding is that equal protection is denied female litigants in civil actions in the Louisiana courts, and that due process is denied all litigants.

6. The current state of the law on jury service may be briefly summarized as follows. The Federal Jury Selection Act specifically forbids discrimination against women in jury selection. 28 U.S.C. §1862. A three-judge court held Alabama's total exclusion of women inconsonant with the Equal Protection Clause of the Fourteenth Amendment. White v. Crook, 251 F. Supp. 401 (M.D. Ala. 1966). In the same year, however, a state court found Mississippi's total exclusion of women from juries constitutional. State v. Hall, 187 So. 2d 861 (Miss.), *appeal dismissed,* 385 U.S. 98 (1966).

By 1970, no state had a law which totally excluded women from jury service, but about half of the states retained statutory patterns which distinguished between men and women in regard to jury service;[22] few had reached such sex-neutral language as

19. 407 U.S. at 503-504. Note that this case directly decides the issue deemed novel by Justice Stewart in *Alexander,* where a man challenged the exclusion of women from the jury.

20. Healy v. Edwards, 363 F. Supp. 1110 (E.D. La. 1973), *prob. juris. noted,* — U.S. — , 94 S. Ct. 1405 (1974).

21. Id. at 1117.

22. Report of the Legislative Reference Service, American Law Division, Hearings on S.J. Res. 61 Before the Subcomm. on Constitutional Amendments of the Senate Comm. on the Judiciary, 91st Cong., 2d Sess.

New Jersey's law, which exempts any "person" who has the actual physical care of a minor child. N.J. Stat. Ann. §2A: 69-2g. Of course, in any particular case claiming the exclusion of women from juries, a lawyer must look not only at the statute but at the practice under it, for the experience of minorities demonstrates that discrimination in jury selection often occurs in practice even though the statute itself is adequate. It is clear that the Equal Rights Amendment would require both redrafting of statutes on jury selection to make them sex-neutral, and a close look at actual practices within the states, followed by reform where necessary.

NOTE:
FUNDAMENTAL INTERESTS IN SEX DISCRIMINATION CASES

Quong Wing, Goesaert, and *Hoyt* share a failure to recognize a possible fundamental interest claim; Frankfurter goes so far as to state that Michigan could "beyond question" forbid all women from working behind a bar. In this respect, however, the *Hoyt* opinion is probably most surprising since serving on a jury has long been seen as an important duty of citizenship, while the right to pursue one's calling has only intermittently been treated as a right of constitutional stature.

NOTES:
THE JUDICIAL RATIONALIZATION OF SEX DISCRIMINATION

Quong Wing, Goesaert, and *Hoyt* illustrate a number of forms of rationalization that are commonly used by courts at all levels to uphold sex-discriminatory state legislation. These include:[23]

> (1) express reliance on a mythology of male supremacy, which confines women to a subordinate social role and then patronizingly "protects" them against even their own attempts to change that role; (2) total deference to the legislature, despite serious assertions that its discriminatory enactments violate specific constitutional guarantees; and (3) cursory dismissal of these serious constitutional issues, on the basis of inadequately supported conclusions that rational connections do exist between sex discrimination and the promotion of some vaguely articulated state interest.

In addition, the courts have continued to base decisions on the average characteristics of both sexes. This results in gross injustice to the many individuals who do not conform to the "average."

The following are a few selections further illustrating the use of these forms of rationalization; quotations from lower court cases upholding sex-discriminatory legislation have been used to indicate that such attitudes have continuing effect.

(1) The Mythology of Male Supremacy and Female Inferiority

STATE v. HALL, 187 So. 2d 861 (Miss. 1966), *appeal dismissed,* 385 U.S. 98 (1966). In upholding a statute (later repealed) excluding women from jury service, against a

---

725-727 (1970). As of 1973, challenges to various types of exemptions for women had not been particularly successful. DeKosenko v. Brandt, 63 Misc. 2d 895, 313 N.Y.S.2d 827 (Sup. Ct. 1970) (upholding automatic exemptions for women jurors); Archer v. Mayes, 213 Va. 633, 194 S.E.2d 707 (1973) (upholding jury exemption for women but not men, with responsibilities for the care of children or dependent adults, in the face of a Fourteenth Amendment and state equal rights amendment challenge). *Accord:* Marshall v. Holmes, 42 L.W. 2206 (N.D. Fla. 9/28/73) (Fourteenth Amendment challenge only). See also Ammer v. Cataldo, Civ. No. 72-806-G (D. Mass. April 17, 1972) (order denying injunction against automatic state exemption for mothers of children under sixteen).

23. Johnston and Knapp, Sex Discrimination By Law: A Study in Judicial Perspective, 46 N.Y.U.L. Rev. 675, 697 (1971). See also Eastwood, The Double Standard of Justice: Women's Rights Under the Constitution, 5 Valparaiso L. Rev. 281, 285 (1971).

Fourteenth Amendment challenge by a woman who had been indicted for murder by an all-male grand jury, the Supreme Court of Mississippi thus stated the sole justification for the statute: "The legislature has the right to exclude women so they may continue their service as mothers, wives, and homemakers, and also to protect them (in some areas, they are still upon a pedestal) from the filth, obscenity, and noxious atmosphere that so often pervades a courtroom during a jury trial."[24]

LEIGHTON v. GOODMAN, 311 F. Supp. 1181 (S.D.N.Y. 1970). Finding a man's constitutional challenge to the automatic exemption from jury duty granted all women in New York to be "patently insufficient as a matter of law," the court stated this justification for the exemption:[25]

> Granted that some women pursue business careers, the great majority constitute the heart of the home, where they are busily engaged in the 24-hour task of producing and rearing children, providing a home for the entire family, and performing the daily household work, all of which demands their full energies. Although some women now question this arrangement, the state legislature has permitted the exemption in order not to risk disruption of the basic family unit. Its action was far from arbitrary.

UNITED STATES v. ST. CLAIR, 291 F. Supp. 122 (S.D.N.Y. 1968). The court held that it was not unconstitutional to draft men and not women. Congress exempted women from involuntary military service "presumably because they are 'still regarded as the center of home and family life.' Hoyt v. Florida"; Congress thus "followed the teachings of history that if a nation is to survive, men must provide the first line of defense while women keep the home fires burning."[26]

HOLLANDER v. CONN. INTERSCHOLASTIC ATHLETIC CONFERENCE, INC., No. 12497 (Super. Ct. Conn., New Haven County, Mar. 29, 1971). The court held it was not unconstitutional to exclude girls from a high school's only cross-country running team, stating that:[27]

> The present generation of our younger male population has not become so decadent that boys will experience a thrill in defeating girls in running contests, whether the girls be members of their own team or of an adversary team. It could well be that many boys would feel compelled to forego entering track events if they were required to compete with girls on their own teams or on adversary teams. The mere fact that cross-country running and indoor track do not involve bodily contact, a point stressed by the plaintiffs, is not the answer. In the world of sports, there is ever present as a challenge, the psychology to win. With boys vying with girls in cross-country running and indoor track, the challenge to win, and the glory of achievement, at least for many boys, would lose incentive and become nullified. Athletic competition builds character in our boys. We do not need that kind of character in our girls, the women of tomorrow, by the conduit of putting them in athletic competition with the opposite sex. That girls in the public school system may have their own teams, consisting of their own sex, in proper sphere of sport such as track, swimming, tennis — to name but a few — is not questioned if facilities and equipments are available and a sufficient number of girls manifest an interest. But this is a far call from the issues in the case at bar.

24. 107 So. 2d at 863.
25. 311 F. Supp. at 1183.
26. 291 F. Supp. at 124-125.
27. Mem. Op. at 8-9.

(2) Excessive Deference to the Legislature

JACOBSON v. LENHART, 30 Ill. 2d 225, 195 N.E.2d 638 (1964). In upholding a sex-based statutory distinction in the age of majority (males twenty-one, females eighteen) which in the instant case worked to the disadvantage of a female tort complainant, the Supreme Court of Illinois found that "legislative and judicial recognition that females mature physically, emotionally and mentally before male persons" is a reasonable basis for legislative classification. In reaching this conclusion, it considered the fact that the laws had stood unchallenged for almost 100 years; "the common acceptance by legislatures, judiciaries and public alike" that there are many areas in which females become competent to be freed from legal disabilities before males; and the principle that, although the statutes were passed a long time ago and times have changed, "the question whether the two sexes now develop to maturity and the age of discretion on a par with one another, should and must be committed to the wisdom and judgment of the legislature rather than to our courts."[28]

STATE v. HUNTER, 208 Ore. 282, 300 P. 2d 455 (1956). The Supreme Court of Oregon thus stated the rational basis for a statute which totally excluded females from participating in wrestling exhibitions:[29]

> We believe that we are justified in taking judicial notice of the fact that the membership of the legislative assembly which enacted this statute was predominately masculine. The fact is important in determining what the legislature might have had in mind with respect to this particular statute, in addition to its concern for the public weal. It seems to us that its purpose, although somewhat selfish in nature, stands out in the statute like a sore thumb. Obviously it intended that there should be at least one island on the sea of life reserved for man that would be impregnable to the assault of woman. It had watched her emerge from long tresses and demure ways to bobbed hair and almost complete sophistication; from a creature needing and depending upon the protection and chivalry of man to one asserting complete independence. She had already invaded practically every activity formerly considered suitable and appropriate for men only. In the field of sports she had taken up, among other games, baseball, basketball, golf, bowling, hockey, long distance swimming, and racing, in all of which she had become more or less proficient, and in some had excelled. In the business and industrial fields as an employee or as an executive, in the professions, in politics, as well as in almost every line of human endeavor, she had matched her wits and prowess with those of mere man, and, we are frank to concede, in many instances had outdone him. In these circumstances, is it any wonder that the legislative assembly took advantage of the police power of the state in its decision to halt this ever-increasing feminine encroachment upon what for ages had been considered strictly as manly arts and privilges? Was the Act an unjust and unconstitutional discrimination against woman? Have her civil or political rights been unconstitutionally denied her? Under the circumstances, we think not.

(3) Sex-Based Averaging

WARK v. STATE, 266 A.2d 62 (Me.), *cert. denied,* 400 U.S. 952 (1970). In upholding a statute which authorized imprisonment "for any term of years" as punishment for a male prisoner who had escaped from the State Prison, although a female escapee was punishable only by additional imprisonment of not more than eleven months, the Supreme Court of Maine found that the "varying behavioral patterns of the two sexes" justified the statutory distinction:[30]

28. 195 N.E.2d at 640.
29. 208 Ore. at 287-288, 300 P.2d at 457-458.
30. 266 A.2d at 65.

The Legislature could on the basis of long experience conclude that women, even those sentenced to the State Prison for serious offenses, tend for the most part to be more amenable to discipline and custodial regulation than their male counterparts and can therefore be effectively confined in an institution which lacks the high walls, armed guards and security precautions of a prison. By the same token the Legislature could reasonably conclude that the greater physical strength, aggressiveness and disposition toward violent action so frequently displayed by a male prisoner bent on escape from a maximum security institution presents a far greater risk of harm to prison guards and personnel and to the public than is the case when escape is undertaken by a woman confined in an institution designed primarily for reform and rehabilitation. Viewing statutory provisions for punishment as in part a deterrent to criminal conduct, the Legislature could logically and reasonably conclude that a more severe penalty should be imposed upon a male prisoner escaping from the State Prison than upon a woman confined at the "Reformatory" while serving a State Prison sentence who escapes from that institution.

Johnston and Knapp comment as follows on this decision:[31]

One indication of the tenacity of sex sterotyping is the fact that an opinion like that in *Wark* will so often seem sensible on first reading — at least to a male reader. After all, men are bigger and stronger on the average than women; if we were prison guards, we would probably be more afraid of an escaping male prisoner than a female. Isn't the court's reasoning therefore correct?

They go on to answer their own questions:[32]

The trouble with the court's approach is that, in its preoccupation with group characteristics, it ignores the fact that the law punishes *individuals.* . . .

　　[The statute] distinguishes between defendants not on the basis of their *individual* characteristics, but solely on the basis of the extent to which two groups differ in *average* size and strength — differences which may not at all apply to particular individuals within either group.[33]

---

　　31. Johnston and Knapp, Sex Discrimination By Law: A Study in Judicial Perspective, 46 N.Y.U.L. Rev. at 730 (1971).

　　32. Id. at 730, 731 (emphasis in the original). The authors also argue that even if all males were more dangerous than females, they could not appropriately be punished for this difference, since no male chose his sex, a point which supports the proposition that sex should be declared a suspect classification, discussed supra.

　　33. The following are some additional cases upholding sex classifications against constitutional challenges; the error in reasoning involved is listed where appropriate.

　　Maternity regulations: Schattman v. Texas Employment Commission, 459 F.2d 32 (5th Cir. 1972), *cert. denied,* 409 U.S. 1107, *rehearing denied,* 410 U.S. 959 (1973) (mandatory leave of two months before delivery does not deny equal protection); Gutierrez v. Laird, 346 F. Supp. 289 (D.D.C. 1972); Struck v. Secretary of Defense, 460 F.2d 1372 (9th Cir. 1971), *vacated and remanded,* 409 U.S. 1071 (1972) (upholding requirement that pregnant officers be discharged from the military; remand in *Struck* was for consideration of "the issue of mootness" in light of "the position presently asserted by the government," after Air Force had granted a waiver of discharge to the plaintiff); Miller v. Industrial Commission, 173 Colo. 476, 480 P.2d 565 (1971) (full employment compensation may be denied a woman willing and able to work solely because of her pregnancy; excessive deference to the legislature).

　　Government benefits: Gruenwald v. Gardner, 390 F.2d 591 (2d Cir. 1968), *cert. denied,* 393 U.S. 982 (1968) (method of computing Social Security payments preferential to women upheld; sex-based averaging of earning capacity of men and women); Duley v. Caterpillar Tractor Co., 44 Ill. 2d 15, 253 N.E.2d 373 (1969) (workmen's compensation benefits tied to husband's dependency on wife but not to wife's dependency on husband upheld).

　　Selective service: United States v. Dorris, 319 F. Supp. 1306 (W.D. Pa. 1970); United States v. Clinton, 310 F. Supp. 333 (E.D. La. 1970); Suskin v. Nixon, 304 F. Supp. 618 (N.D. Ill. 1969); United States v. Cook, 311 F. Supp. 618 (W.D. Pa. 1968) (all holding that males are not denied equal protection of the laws by the exclusion of females from the draft).

　　Criminal sanctions: Lamb v. State, 475 P.2d 829 (Okla. Crim. App. Ct. 1970) (upholding Oklahoma's sex-age differential for juvenile offender treatment, which was later invalidated in Lamb v. Brown, 456 F.2d 18 (10th Cir. 1972); excessive deference to the legislature, sex-based averaging); State v. Bearcub, 1 Ore. App.

C. Sex Discrimination Cases in the 1970s

REED v. REED
404 U.S. 71, 92 S. Ct. 251, 30 L. Ed. 2d 225 (1971)

Mr. Chief Justice BURGER delivered the opinion of the Court.

Richard Lynn Reed, a minor, died intestate in Ada County, Idaho, on March 29, 1967. His adoptive parents, who had separated sometime prior to his death, are the parties to this appeal. Approximately seven months after Richard's death, his mother, appellant Sally Reed, filed a petition in the Probate Court of Ada County, seeking appointment as administratrix of her son's estate. Prior to the date set for a hearing on the mother's petition, appellee Cecil Reed, the father of the decedent, filed a competing petition seeking to have himself appointed administrator of the son's estate. The probate court held a joint hearing on the two petitions and thereafter ordered that letters of administration be issued to appellee Cecil Reed upon his taking the oath and filing the bond required by law. The court treated §§15-312 and 15-314 of the Idaho Code as the controlling statutes and read those sections as compelling a preference for Cecil Reed because he was a male.

Section 15-312 designates the persons who are entitled to administer the estate of one who dies intestate. In making these designations, that section lists 11 classes of persons who are so entitled and provides in substance, that the order in which those classes are listed in the section shall be determinative of the relative rights of competing applicants for letters of administration. One of the 11 classes so enumerated is "[t]he father or mother" of the person dying intestate. Under this section, then, appellant and appellee, being members of the same entitlement class, would seem to have been equally entitled to administer their son's estate. Section 15-314 provides, however, that "[o]f several persons claiming and equally entitled [under §15-312] to administer, males must be preferred to females, and relatives of the whole to those of the half blood." In issuing its order, the probate court implicitly recognized the equality of entitlement of the two applicants under §15-312 and noted that neither of the applicants was under any legal disability; the court ruled, however, that appellee, being a male, was to be preferred to the female appellant "by reason of Section 15-314 of the Idaho Code." In stating this conclusion, the probate judge gave no indication that he had attempted to determine the relative capabilities of the competing applicants to perform the functions incident to the administration of an estate. It seems clear the probate judge considered himself bound by statute to give preference to the male candidate over the female, each being otherwise "equally entitled."

579, 465 P.2d 252 (1970), reprinted infra, Chapter Three, V-C (upholding criminal statute prohibiting an adult male from habitually accepting lodging with female welfare recipient; excessive deference to the legislature).

Recovery for loss of consortium: Miskunas v. Union Carbide Corp., 399 F.2d 847 (7th Cir. 1968), *cert. denied,* 393 U.S. 1066 (1969); Krohn v. Richardson-Merrell, Inc., 219 Tenn. 37, 406 S.W.2d 166 (1966), *cert. denied,* 386 U.S. 970 (1966) (upholding rules permitting husband but not wife to recover). See Chapter Three, III-C-2-d.

Employment: Calzadilla v. Dooley, 29 A.D.2d 152, 286 N.Y.S.2d 510 (4th Dept. 1968) (ban against female wrestling not unconstitutional); Vintage Society Wholesalers Corp. v. State Liquor Authority, 63 Misc. 2d 287, 311 N.Y.S.2d 735 (Sup. Ct. 1970) (requiring fingerprinting of male but not female employees of wholesale liquor dealers not unconstitutional; sex-based averaging); Wells v. Civil Service Commission, 423 Pa. 602, 225 A.2d 554, *cert. denied,* 386 U.S. 1035 (1967) (oral examination may be required of female applicants for police promotions, although not required of male applicants). All of the above probably violate Title VII of the Civil Rights Act of 1964. See Chapter Two, II.

Jury service: See cases cited in Notes: Discrimination in the Jury Selection Process, supra.

Domestic relations: Clarke v. Redeker, 259 F. Supp. 117 (S.D. Iowa 1966) (law basing wife's domicile on husband's, and not vice versa, upheld).

Education: Bucha v. Illinois High School Ass'n, 351 F. Supp. 69 (N.D. Ill. 1972) (upholding sex segregation in high school athletics), reprinted in Chapter Five, II-A-3. — Eds.

Sally Reed appealed from the probate court order, and her appeal was treated by the District Court of the Fourth Judicial District of Idaho as a constitutional attack on §15-314. In dealing with the attack, that court held that the challenged section violated the Equal Protection Clause of the Fourteenth Amendment and was, therefore, void; the matter was ordered "returned to the Probate Court for its determination of which of the two parties" was better qualified to administer the estate.

This order was never carried out, however, for Cecil Reed took a further appeal to the Idaho Supreme Court, which reversed the District Court and reinstated the original order naming the father administrator of the estate. . . . The Idaho Supreme Court then proceeded to examine, and reject, Sally Reed's contention that §15-314 violates the Equal Protection Clause by giving a mandatory preference to males over females, without regard to their individual qualifications as potential estate administrators. 93 Idaho 511, 465 P.2d 635. . . . [W]e have concluded that the arbitrary preference established in favor of males by §15-314 of the Idaho Code cannot stand in the face of the Fourteenth Amendment's command that no State deny the equal protection of the laws to any person within its jurisdiction.

Idaho does not, of course, deny letters of administration to women altogether. Indeed, under §15-312, a woman whose spouse dies intestate has a preference over a son, father, brother, or any other male relative of the decedent. Moreover, we can judicially notice that in this country, presumably due to the greater longevity of women, a large proportion of estates, both intestate and under wills of decedents, are administered by surviving widows.

Section 15-314 is restricted in its operation to those situations where competing applications for letters of administration have been filed by both male and female members of the same entitlement class established by §15-312. In such situations, §15-314 provides that different treatment be accorded to the applicants on the basis of their sex; it thus establishes a classification subject to scrutiny under the Equal Protection Clause.

In applying that clause, this Court has consistently recognized that the Fourteenth Amendment does not deny to States the power to treat different classes of persons in different ways. Barbier v. Connolly, 113 U.S. 27 (1885); Lindsley v. Natural Carbonic Gas Co., 220 U.S. 61 (1911); Railway Express Agency, Inc. v. New York, 336 U.S. 106 (1949); McDonald v. Board of Election Commissioners, 394 U.S. 802 (1968). The Equal Protection Clause of that Amendment does, however, deny to States the power to legislate that different treatment be accorded to persons placed by a statute into different classes on the basis of criteria wholly unrelated to the objective of that statute. A classification "must be reasonable, not arbitrary, and must rest upon some ground of difference having a fair and substantial relation to the object of the legislation, so that all persons similarly circumstanced shall be treated alike." Royster Guano Co. v. Virginia, 253 U.S. 412, 415 (1920). The question presented by this case, then, is whether a difference in the sex of competing applicants for letters of administration bears a rational relationship to a state objective that is sought to be advanced by the operation of §§15-312 and 15-314.

In upholding the latter section, the Idaho Supreme Court concluded that its objective was to eliminate one area of controversy when two or more persons, equally entitled under §15-312, seek letters of administration and thereby present the probate court "with the issue of which one should be named." The court also concluded that where such persons are not of the same sex, the elimination of females from consideration "is neither an illogical nor arbitrary method devised by the legislature to resolve an issue that would otherwise require a hearing as to the relative merits . . . of the two or more petitioning relatives. . . ." 93 Idaho at 514, 465 P.2d at 638.

Clearly the objective of reducing the workload on probate courts by eliminating one class of contests is not without some legitimacy. The crucial question, however, is whether §15-314 advances that objective in a manner consistent with the command of the Equal Protection Clause. We hold that it does not. To give a mandatory preference to members of either sex over members of the other, merely to accomplish the elimination of hearings on the merits, is to make the very kind of arbitrary legislative choice forbidden by the Equal Protection Clause of the Fourteenth Amendment; and whatever may be said as to the positive values of avoiding intrafamily controversy, the choice in this context may not lawfully be mandated solely on the basis of sex. . . .

The judgment of the Idaho Supreme Court is reversed and the case remanded for further proceedings not inconsistent with this opinion.

Reversed and remanded.

FRONTIERO v. RICHARDSON
411 U.S. 677, 93 S. Ct. 1764, 36 L. Ed. 2d 583 (1973)

Mr. Justice BRENNAN announced the judgment of the Court and an opinion in which Mr. Justice DOUGLAS, Mr. Justice WHITE, and Mr. Justice MARSHALL join.

The question before us concerns the right of a female member of the uniformed services to claim her spouse as a "dependent" for the purposes of obtaining increased quarters allowances and medical and dental benefits under 37 U.S.C. §§401, 403, and 10 U.S.C. §§1072, 1076, on an equal footing with male members. Under these statutes, a serviceman may claim his wife as a "dependent" without regard to whether she is in fact dependent upon him for any part of her support. 37 U.S.C. §401(1); 10 U.S.C. §1072(A). A servicewoman, on the other hand, may not claim her husband as a "dependent" under these programs unless he is in fact dependent upon her for over one-half of his support. 37 U.S.C. §401; 10 U.S.C. §1072 (2) (C). Thus, the question for decision is whether this difference in treatment constitutes an unconstitutional discrimination against servicewomen in violation of the Due Process Clause of the Fifth Amendment. A three-judge District Court for the Middle District of Alabama, one judge dissenting, rejected this contention and sustained the constitutionality of the provisions of the statutes making this distinction. 341 F. Supp. 201 (1972). We noted probable jurisdiction. 409 U.S. 840 (1972). We reverse.

I

In an effort to attract career personnel through re-enlistment, Congress established, in 37 U.S.C. §401 et seq., and 10 U.S.C. §1071 et seq., a scheme for the provision of fringe benefits to members of the uniformed services on a competitive basis with business and industry. Thus, under 37 U.S.C. §403, a member of the uniformed services with dependents is entitled to an increased "basic allowance for quarters" and, under 10 U.S.C. §1076, a member's dependents are provided comprehensive medical and dental care.

Appellant Sharron Frontiero, a lieutenant in the United States Air Force, sought increased quarters allowances, and housing and medical benefits for her husband, appellant Joseph Frontiero, on the ground that he was her "dependent." Although such benefits would automatically have been granted with respect to the wife of a male member of the uniformed services, appellant's application was denied because she failed to demonstrate that her husband was dependent on her for more than one-half of his support.[4] Appellants then commenced this suit, contending that, by making this distinction, the statutes unreasonably discriminate on the basis of sex in violation of the Due Process Clause of the Fifth Amendment.[5] In essence, appellants asserted that the dis-

4. Appellant Joseph Frontiero is a full-time student at Huntingdon College in Montgomery, Alabama. According to the agreed stipulation of facts, his living expenses, including his share of the household expenses, total approximately $354 per month. Since he receives $205 per month in veterans' benefits, it is clear that he is not dependent upon appellant Sharron Frontiero for more than one-half of his support.

5. "[W]hile the Fifth Amendment contains no equal protection clause, it does forbid discrimination that is 'so unjustifiable as to be violative of due process.'" Schneider v. Rusk, 377 U.S. 163, 168 (1964); see Shapiro v. Thompson, 394 U.S. 618, 641-642 (1969); Bolling v. Sharpe, 347 U.S. 497 (1954).

criminatory impact of the statutes is two-fold: first, as a procedural matter, a female member is required to demonstrate her spouse's dependency, while no such burden is imposed upon male members; and second, as a substantive matter, a male member who does not provide more than one-half of his wife's support receives benefits, while a similarly situated female member is denied such benefits. Appellants therefore sought a permanent injunction against the continued enforcement of these statutes and an order directing the appellees to provide Lieutenant Frontiero with the same housing and medical benefits that a similarly situated male member would receive.

Although the legislative history of these statutes sheds virtually no light on the purposes underlying the differential treatment accorded male and female members, a majority of the three-judge District Court surmised that Congress might reasonably have concluded that, since the husband in our society is generally the "breadwinner" in the family — and the wife typically the "dependent" partner — "it would be more economical to require married female members claiming husbands to prove actual dependency than to extend the presumption of dependency to such members." 341 F. Supp., at 207. Indeed, given the fact that approximately 99% of all members of the uniformed services are male, the District Court speculated that such differential treatment might conceivably lead to a "considerable saving of administrative expense and manpower." Ibid.

II

At the outset, appellants contend that classifications based upon sex, like classifications based upon race, alienage, and national origin, are inherently suspect and must therefore be subjected to close judicial scrutiny. We agree and, indeed, find at least implicit support for such an approach in our unanimous decision only last Term in Reed v. Reed, 404 U.S. 71 (1971).

In *Reed,* the Court considered the constitutionality of an Idaho statute providing that, when two individuals are otherwise equally entitled to appointment as administrator of an estate, the male applicant must be preferred to the female. . . .

[Discussion of appellee's argument and the Idaho Supreme Court decision in Reed v. Reed is omitted.]

. . . the Court held the statutory preference for male applicants unconstitutional. In reaching this result, the Court implicitly rejected appellee's apparently rational explanation of the statutory scheme, and concluded that, by ignoring the individual qualifications of particular applicants, the challenged statute provided "dissimilar treatment for men and women who are . . . similarly situated." Reed v. Reed, supra, at 77. The Court therefore held that, even though the State's interest in achieving administrative efficiency "is not without some legitimacy," "[t]o give a mandatory preference to members of either sex over members of the other, merely to accomplish the elimination of hearings on the merits, is to make the very kind of arbitrary legislative choice forbidden by the [Constitution]. . . ." Id., at 76. This departure from "traditional" rational basis analysis with respect to sex-based classifications is clearly justified.

There can be no doubt that our Nation has had a long and unfortunate history of sex discrimination.[13] Traditionally, such discrimination was rationalized by an attitude of "romantic paternalism" which, in practical effect, put women not on a pedestal, but in a cage. Indeed, this paternalistic attitude became so firmly rooted in our national consciousness that, exactly 100 years ago, a distinguished member of this Court was able to proclaim:

> Man is, or should be, woman's protector and defender. The natural and proper timidity and delicacy which belongs to the female sex evidently unfits it for many of the

---

13. Indeed, the position of women in this country at its inception is reflected in the view expressed by Thomas Jefferson that women should be neither seen nor heard in society's decisionmaking councils. See M. Gruberg, Women in American Politics 4 (1968). See also A. de Tocqueville, Democracy in America, pt. 2 (Reeves tr. 1840), in World's Classic Series 400 (Galaxy ed. 1947).

occupations of civil life. The constitution of the family organization, which is founded in the divine ordinance, as well as in the nature of things, indicates the domestic sphere as that which properly belongs to the domain and functions of womanhood. The harmony, not to say identity, of interests and views which belong, or should belong, to the family institution is repugnant to the ideas of a woman adopting a distinct and independent career from that of her husband. . . .

. . . The paramount destiny and mission of woman are to fulfil the noble and benign offices of wife and mother. This is the law of the Creator. Bradwell v. Illinois, 83 U.S. [16 Wall.] 130, 141 (1873) (Bradley, J., concurring).

As a result of notions such as these, our statute books gradually became laden with gross, stereotypical distinctions between the sexes and, indeed, throughout much of the 19th century the position of women in our society was, in many respects, comparable to that of blacks under the pre–Civil War slave codes. Neither slaves nor women could hold office, serve on juries, or bring suit in their own names, and married women traditionally were denied the legal capacity to hold or convey property or to serve as legal guardians of their own children. See generally, L. Kanowitz, Women and the Law: The Unfinished Revolution 5-6 (1969); G. Myrdal, An American Dilemna 1073 (2d ed. 1962). And although blacks were guaranteed the right to vote in 1870, women were denied even that right — which is itself "preservative of other basic civil and political rights" —until adoption of the Nineteenth Amendment half a century later.

It is true, of course, that the position of women in America has improved markedly in recent decades.[15] Nevertheless, it can hardly be doubted that, in part because of the high visibility of the sex characteristic,[16] women still face pervasive, although at times more subtle, discrimination in our educational institutions, on the job market and, perhaps most conspicuously, in the political arena.[17] See generally, K. Amundsen, The Silenced Majority: Women and American Democracy (1971); The President's Task Force on Women's Rights and Responsibilities, A Matter of Simple Justice (1970).

Moreover, since sex, like race and national origin, is an immutable characteristic determined solely by the accident of birth, the imposition of special disabilities upon the members of a particular sex because of their sex would seem to violate "the basic concept of our system that legal burdens should bear some relationship to individual responsibility. . . ." Weber v. Aetna Casualty & Surety Co., 406 U.S. 164, 175 (1972). And what differentiates sex from such nonsuspect statutes as intelligence or physical disability, and aligns it with the recognized suspect criteria, is that the sex characteristic frequently bears no relation to ability to perform or contribute to society.[18] As a result, statutory distinctions between the sexes often have the effect of individiously relegating the entire class of females to inferior legal status without regard to the actual capabilities of its individual members.

We might also note that, over the past decade, Congress has itself manifested an increasing sensitivity to sex-based classifications. In Tit. VII of the Civil Rights Act of 1964, for example, Congress expressly declared that no employer, labor union, or other organization subject to the provisions of the Act shall discriminate against any individual

15. See generally, The President's Task Force on Women's Rights and Responsibilities, A Matter of Simple Justice (1970); L. Kanowitz, Women and the Law: The Unfinished Revolution (1969); A. Montague, Man's Most Dangerous Myth (4th ed. 1964); The President's Commission on the Status of Women, American Women (1963).

16. See, e.g., Note, Sex Discrimination and Equal Protection: Do We Need a Constitutional Amendment?, 84 Harv. L. Rev. 1499, 1507 (1971).

17. It is true, of course, that when viewed in the abstract, women do not contstitute a small and powerless minority. Nevertheless, in part because of past discrimination, women are vastly underrepresented in this Nation's decisionmaking councils. There has never been a female President, nor a female member of this Court. Not a single women presently sits in the United States Senate, and only 14 women hold seats in the House of Representatives. And, as appellants point out, this underrepresentation is present throughout all levels of our State and Federal Government. See Joint Reply Brief of Appellants and American Civil Liberties Union (Amicus Curiae) 9.

18. See, e.g., Developments in the Law — Equal Protection, 82 Harv. L. Rev. 1065, 1173-1174 (1969).

on the basis of "race, color, religion, *sex,* or national origin."[19] Similarly, the Equal Pay Act of 1963 provides that no employer covered by the Act "shall discriminate . . . between employees on the basis of *sex.* "[20] And §1 of the Equal Rights Amendment, passed by Congress on March 22, 1972, and submitted to the legislatures of the States for ratification, declares that "[e]quality of rights under the law shall not be denied or abridged by the United States or by any State on account of sex."[21] Thus, Congress has itself concluded that classifications based upon sex are inherently invidious, and this conclusion of a coequal branch of Government is not without significance to the question presently under consideration. Cf. Oregon v. Mitchell, 400 U.S. 112, 240, 248-249 (1970); Katzenbach v. Morgan, 384 U.S. 641, 648-649 (1966).

With these considerations in mind, we can only conclude that classifications based upon sex, like classifications based upon race, alienage, or national origin, are inherently suspect, and must therefore be subjected to strict judicial scrutiny. Applying the analysis mandated by that stricter standard of review, it is clear that the statutory scheme now before us is constitutionally invalid.

III

The sole basis of the classification established in the challenged statutes is the sex of the individuals involved. Thus, under 37 U.S.C. §§401, 403, and 10 U.S.C. §§2072, 2076, a female member of the uniformed services seeking to obtain housing and medical benefits for her spouse must prove his dependency in fact, whereas no such burden is imposed upon male members. In addition, the statutes operate so as to deny benefits to a female member, such as appellant Sharron Frontiero, who provides less than one-half of her spouse's support, while at the same time granting such benefits to a male member who likewise provides less than one-half of his spouse's support. Thus, to this extent at least, it may fairly be said that these statutes command "dissimilar treatment for men and women who are . . . similarly situated." Reed v. Reed, supra, at 77.

Moreover, the Government concedes that the differential treatment accorded men and women under these statutes serves no purpose other than mere "administrative convenience." In essence, the Government maintains that, as an empirical matter, wives in our society frequently are dependent upon their husbands, while husbands rarely are dependent upon their wives. Thus, the Government argues that Congress might reasonably have concluded that it would be both cheaper and easier simply conclusively to presume that wives of male members are financially dependent upon their husbands, while burdening female members with the task of establishing dependency in fact.[22]

The Government offers no concrete evidence, however, tending to support its view that such differential treatment in fact saves the Government any money. In order to satisfy the demands of strict judicial scrutiny, the Government must demonstrate, for example, that it is actually cheaper to grant increased benefits with respect to *all* male

19. 42 U.S.C. §§2000e-2(a), (b), (c). (Emphasis added.) See generally, Sape & Hart, Title VII Reconsidered: The Equal Employment Opportunity Act of 1972, 40 Geo. Wash. L. Rev. 824 (1972); Developments in the Law — Employment Discrimination and Title VII of the Civil Rights Act of 1964, 84 Harv. L. Rev. 1109 (1971).

20. 29 U.S.C. §206 (d). (Emphasis added.) See generally, Murphy, Female Wage Discrimination: A Study of the Equal Pay Act 1963–1970, 39 U. Cin. L. Rev. 615 (1970).

21. H.J. Res. No. 208; 92d Cong., 2d Sess. (1972). In conformity with these principles, Congress in recent years has amended various statutory schemes similar to those presently under consideration so as to eliminate the differential treatment of men and women. See 5 U.S.C. §2108, as amended, 85 Stat. 644; 5 U.S.C. §7132, as amended, 85 Stat. 644; 5 U.S.C. §8341, as amended, 84 Stat. 1961; 38 U.S.C. §102 (b), as amended, 86 Stat. 1074.

22. It should be noted that these statutes are not in any sense designed to rectify the effects of past discrimination against women. See Gruenwald v. Gardner, 390 F.2d 591 (CA2 1968), *cert. denied,* 393 U.S. 982 (1968); cf. Jones v. Alfred H. Mayer Co., 392 U.S. 409 (1968); South Carolina v. Katzenbach, 383 U.S. 301 (1966). On the contrary, these statutes seize upon a group — women — who have historically suffered discrimination in employment, and rely on the effects of this past discrimination as a justification for heaping on additional economic disadvantages. Cf. United States v. Gaston County, 395 U.S. 285, 296-297 (1969).

members, than it is to determine which male members are in fact entitled to such benefits and to grant increased benefits only to those members whose wives actually meet the dependency requirement. Here, however, there is substantial evidence that, if put to the test, many of the wives of male members would fail to qualify for benefits.[23] And in light of the fact that the dependency determination with respect to the husbands of female members is presently made solely on the basis of affidavits, rather than through the more costly hearing process, the Government's explanation of the statutory scheme is, to say the least, questionable.

In any case, our prior decisions make clear that, although efficacious administration of governmental programs is not without some importance, "the Constitution recognizes higher values than speed and efficiency." Stanley v. Illinois, 405 U.S. 645, 656 (1972). And when we enter the realm of "strict judicial scrutiny," there can be no doubt that "administrative convenience" is not a shibboleth, the mere recitation of which dictates constitutionality. See Shapiro v. Thompson, 394 U.S. 618 (1969); Carrington v. Rash, 380 U.S. 89 (1965). On the contrary, any statutory scheme which draws a sharp line between the sexes, *solely* for the purpose of achieving administrative convenience, necessarily commands "dissimilar treatment for men and women who are . . . similarly situated," and therefore involves the "very kind of arbitrary legislative choice forbidden by the [Constitution]. . . ." Reed v. Reed, supra, at 77, 76. We therefore conclude that, by according differential treatment to male and female members of the uniformed services for the sole purpose of achieving administrative convenience, the challenged statutes violate ι Due Process Clause of the Fifth Amendment insofar as they require a female member to prove the dependency of her husband.[25]

Reversed.

Mr. Justice STEWART concurs in the judgment, agreeing that the statutes before us work an invidious discrimination in violation of the Constitution. Reed v. Reed, 404 U.S. 71.

Mr. Justice REHNQUIST dissents for the reasons stated by Judge Rives in his opinion for the District Court, Frontiero v. Laird, 341 F. Supp. 201 (1972).

Mr. Justice POWELL with whom The CHIEF JUSTICE and Mr. Justice BLACKMUN join, concurring in the judgment.

I agree that the challenged statutes constitute an unconstitutional discrimination against service women in violation of the Due Process Clause of the Fifth Amendment, but I cannot join the opinion of Mr. Justice Brennan, which would hold that all classifications based upon sex, "like classifications based upon race, alienage, and national origin," are "inherently suspect and must therefore be subjected to close judicial scrutiny." Supra, at 5. It is unnecessary for the Court in this case to characterize sex as a suspect classification, with all of the far-reaching implications of such a holding. Reed v. Reed,

23. In 1971, 43% of all women over the age of 16 were in the labor force, and 18% of all women worked full-time 12 months per year. See U.S. Women's Bureau, Dept. of Labor, Highlights of Women's Employment & Education 1 (W. B. Pub. No. 71-191, March 1972). Moreover, 41.5% of all married women are employed. See U.S. Bureau of Labor Statistics, Dept. of Labor, Work Experience of the Population in 1971 4 (Summary Special Labor Force Report, August 1972). It is also noteworthy that, while the median income of a male member of the armed forces is approximately $3,686, see The Report of the President's Commission on an All Volunteer Armed Force 51, 181 (1970), the median income for all women over the age of 14, including those who are not employed, is approximately $2,237. See U.S. Dept. of Commerce, Bureau of the Census, Statistical Abstract of the United States Table No. 535 (1972). Applying the statutory definition of "dependency" to these statistics, it appears that, in the "median" family, the wife of a male member must have personal expenses of approximately $4,474, or about 75% of the total family income, in order to qualify as a "dependent."

25. As noted earlier, the basic purpose of these statutes was to provide fringe benefits to members of the uniformed services in order to establish a compensation pattern which would attract career personnel through re-enlistment. . . . Our conclusion in no wise invalidates the statutory schemes except insofar as they require a female member to prove the dependency of her spouse. See Weber v. Aetna Casualty & Surety Co., 406 U.S. 164 (1972); Levy v. Louisiana, 391 U.S. 68 (1968); Moritz v. Commissioner of Internal Revenue, — F.2d — (CA10 1972). See also 1 U.S.C. §1.

404 U.S. 71 (1971), which abundantly supports our decision today, did not add sex to the narrowly limited group of classifications which are inherently suspect. In my view, we can and should decide this case on the authority of Reed and reserve for the future any expansion of its rationale.

There is another, and I find compelling, reason for deferring a general categorizing of sex classifications as invoking the strictest test of judicial scrutiny. The Equal Rights Amendment, which if adopted will resolve the substance of this precise question, has been approved by the Congress and submitted for ratification by the States. If this Amendment is duly adopted, it will represent the will of the people accomplished in the manner prescribed by the Constitution. By acting prematurely and unnecessarily, as I view it, the Court has assumed a decisional responsibility at the very time when state legislatures, functioning within the traditional democratic process, are debating the proposed Amendment. It seems to me that this reaching out to pre-empt by judicial action a major political decision which is currently in process of resolution does not reflect appropriate respect for duly prescribed legislative processes.

There are times when this Court, under our system, cannot avoid a constitutional decision on issues which normally should be resolved by the elected representatives of the people. But democratic institutions are weakened, and confidence in the restraint of the Court is impaired, when we appear unnecessarily to decide sensitive issues of broad social and political importance at the very time they are under consideration within the prescribed constitutional processes.

KAHN v. SHEVIN
42 U.S.L.W. 4591 (U.S. April 24, 1974)

Mr. Justice DOUGLAS delivered the opinion of the Court.

Since at least 1885, Florida has provided for some form of property tax exemption for widows. The current law granting all widows an annual $500 exemption, Fla. Stat. §196.191(7), has been essentially unchanged since 1941. Appellant Kahn is a widower who lives in Florida and applied for the exemption to the Dade County Tax Assessor's Office. It was denied because the statute offers no analogous benefit for widowers. Kahn then sought a declaratory judgment in the Circuit Court for Dade County, Florida, and that court held the statute violative of the Equal Protection Clause of the Fourteenth Amendment because the classification "widow" was based upon gender. The Florida Supreme Court reversed, finding the classification valid because it has a "fair and substantial relation to the object of the legislation,"[3] that object being the reduction of "the disparity between the economic capabilities of a man and a woman." . . . We affirm.

There can be no dispute that the financial difficulties confronting the lone woman in Florida or in any other State exceed those facing the man. Whether from overt discrimination or from the socialization process of a male dominated culture, the job market is inhospitable to the woman seeking any but the lowest paid jobs.[4] There are of course efforts underway to remedy this situation. On the federal level Title VII of the Civil Rights Act of 1964 prohibits covered employers and labor unions from discrimination on the basis of sex, 42 U.S.C. §§2000e-2 (a), (b), (c), as does the Equal Pay Act of 1963, 29 U.S.C. §206(d). But firmly entrenched practices are resistant to such pressures, and indeed, data compiled by the Woman's Bureau of the United States Department of Labor shows that in 1972 woman working full time had a median income which was only 57.9% of the male median — a figure actually six points lower than had been

---

3. Quoting Reed v. Reed, 404 U.S. 71, 76.

4. In 1970 while 40% of males in the work force earned over $10,000, and 70% over $7,000, 45% of women working full time earned less than $5,000, and 73.9% earned less than $7,000. U.S. Department of Commerce, Bureau of the Census: Current Population Reports, P-60, No. 80.

achieved in 1955.[5] Other data points in the same direction.[6] The disparity is likely to be exacerbated for the widow. While the widower can usually continue in the occupation which preceded his spouse's death in many cases the widow will find herself suddenly forced into a job market with which she is unfamiliar, and in which, because of her former economic dependency, she will have fewer skills to offer.[7]

There can be no doubt therefore that Florida's differing treatment of widows and widowers "rest[s] upon some ground of difference having a fair and substantial relation to the object of the legislation." Reed v. Reed, 404 U.S. 71, 76, quoting Royster Guano Co. v. Virginia, 253 U.S. 412, 415.

This is not a case like Frontiero v. Richardson, 411 U.S. 677, where the Government denied its female employees both substantative and procedural benefits granted males *"solely* for administrative convenience." Id., at 690 (emphasis in original).[8] We deal here with a state tax law reasonably designed to further the state policy of cushioning the financial impact of spousal loss upon the sex for whom that loss imposes a disproportionately heavy burden. We have long held that "[w]here taxation is concerned and no specific federal right, apart from equal protection, is imperiled, the States have large leeway in making classifications and drawing lines which in their judgment produce reasonable systems of taxation." Lehnhausen v. Lake Shore Auto Parts Co., 410 U.S. 356,

5. The Women's Bureau provides the following data:

| Year | Median earnings | | Women's median earnings as percent of men's |
	Women	Men	
1972	$5,903	$10,202	57.9
1971	5,593	9,399	59.5
1970	5,323	8,966	59.4
1969	4,977	8,227	60.5
1968	4,457	7,664	58.2
1967	4,150	7,182	57.8
1966	3,973	6,848	58.0
1965	3,823	6,375	60.0
1964	3,690	6,195	59.6
1963	3,561	5,978	59.6
1962	3,446	5,794	59.5
1961	3,351	5,644	59.4
1960	3,293	5,417	60.8
1959	3,193	5,209	61.3
1958	3,102	4,927	63.0
1957	3,008	4,713	63.8
1956	2,827	4,466	63.3
1955	2,719	4,252	63.9

Note. — Data for 1962-72 are not strictly comparable with those for prior years, which are for wage and salary income only and do not include earnings of self-employed persons.

Source: Table prepared by Women's Bureau, Employment Standards Administration, U.S. Department of Labor, from data published by Bureau of the Census, U.S. Department of Commerce.

6. For example, in 1972 the median income of women with four years of college was $8,736 — exactly $100 more than the median income of men who had never even completed one year of high school. Of those employed as managers or administrators, the women's median income was only 53.2% of the men's, and in the professional and technical occupations the figure was 67.5%. Thus the disparity extends even to women occupying jobs usually thought of as well paid. Tables prepared by the Women's Bureau, Employment Standards Administration, U.S. Department of Labor.

7. It is still the case that in the majority of families where both spouses are present, the woman is not employed. A. Ferris, Indicators of Trends in the Status of American Women 95 (1971).

8. And in *Frontiero* the plurality opinion also noted that the statutes there were "not in any sense designed to rectify the effects of past discrimination against women. On the contrary, these statutes seize upon a group — women — who have historically suffered discrimination in employment, and rely upon the effects of this past discrimination as a justification for heaping on additional economic disadvantages." Frontiero v. Richardson, 411 U.S. 677, 689 n.22 (citations omitted).

359. A state tax law is not arbitrary although it "discriminate[s] in favor of a certain class . . . if the discrimination is founded upon a reasonable distinction, or difference in state policy," not in conflict with the Federal Constitution. Allied Stores v. Bowers, 358 U.S. 522, 528. This principle has weathered nearly a century of Supreme Court adjudication,[9] and it applies here as well. The statute before us is well within those limits.[10]

Affirmed.

Mr. Justice BRENNAN, with whom Mr. Justice MARSHALL joins, dissenting.

The Court rejects widower Kahn's claim of denial of equal protection on the ground that the limitation in §196.191(7), which provides an annual $500 property tax exemption to widows, is a legislative classification that bears a fair and substantial relation to "the state policy of cushioning the financial impact of spousal loss upon the sex for whom that loss imposes a disproportionately heavy burden." Ante, p. 4. In my view, however, a legislative classification that distinguishes potential beneficiaries solely by reference to their gender-based status as widows or widowers, like classifications based upon race, alienage, and national origin, must be subjected to close judicial scrutiny, because it focuses upon generally immutable characteristics over which individuals have little or no control, and also because gender-based classifications too often have been inexcusably utilized to stereotype and stigmatize politically powerless segments of society. See Frontiero v. Richardson, 411 U.S. 677 (1973). The Court is not therefore free to sustain the statute on the ground that it rationally promotes legitimate governmental interests; rather, such suspect classifications can be sustained only when the State bears the burden of demonstrating that the challenged legislation serves overriding or compelling interests that cannot be achieved either by a more carefully tailored legislative classification or by the use of feasible less drastic means. While, in my view, the statute serves a compelling governmental interest by "cushioning the financial impact of spousal loss upon the sex for whom that loss imposes a disproportionately heavy burden," I think that the statute is invalid because the State's interest can be served equally well by a more narrowly drafted statute.

Gender-based classifications cannot be sustained merely because they promote legitimate governmental interests, such as efficacious administration of government. Frontiero v. Richardson, supra; Reed v. Reed, 404 U.S. 71 (1971). For "when we enter the realm of 'strict judicial scrutiny,' there can be no doubt that 'administrative convenience' is not a shibboleth, the mere recitation of which dictates constitutionality. See Shapiro v. Thompson, 394 U.S. 618 (1969); Carrington v. Rash, 380 U.S. 89 (1965). On

9. See Bell's Gap R. Co. v. Pennsylvania, 134 U.S. 232, 237; Madden v. Kentucky, 309 U.S. 83, 87-88; Lawrence v. State Tax Comm'n, 286 U.S. 276; Royster Guano v. Virginia, 253 U.S. 412.

10. The dissents argue that the Florida Legislature could have drafted the statute differently, so that its purpose would have been accomplished more precisely. But the issue of course is not whether the statute could have been drafted more wisely, but whether the lines chosen by the Florida Legislature are within constitutional limitations. The dissent would use the Equal Protection Clause as a vehicle for reinstating notions of substantive due process that have been repudiated. "We have returned to the original constitutional proposition that courts do not substitute their social and economic beliefs for the judgment of legislative bodies, who are elected to pass laws." Ferguson v. Skrupa, 372 U.S. 726, 730.

Gender has never been rejected as an impermissible classification in all instances. Congress has not so far drafted women into the Armed Services, 50 App. U.S.C. §454. The famous Brandeis Brief in Muller v. Oregon, 208 U.S. 412, on which the court specifically relied, id., at 419-420, emphasized that the special physical organization of women has a bearing on the "conditions under which she should be permitted to toil." Id., at 420. These instances are pertinent to the problem in the tax field which is presented by the present case. Mr. Chief Justice Hughes in speaking for the Court said:

"The states, in the exercise of their taxing power, as with respect to the exertion of other powers, are subject to the requirements of the due process and equal protection clauses of the Fourteenth Amendment, but that Amendment imposes no iron rule of equality, prohibiting the flexibility and variety that are appropriate to schemes of taxation. . . . In levying such taxes, the State is not required to resort to close distinctions or to maintain a precise, scientific uniformity with reference to composition, use or value. To hold otherwise would be to subject the essential taxing power of the State to an intolerable supervision, hostile to the basic principles of our Government and wholly beyond the protection which the general clause of the Fourteenth Amendment was intended to secure." Ohio Oil Co. v. Conway, 281 U.S. 146, 159.

the contrary, any statutory scheme which draws a sharp line between the sexes, *solely* for the purpose of achieving administrative convenience, necessarily commands 'dissimilar treatment for men and women who are . . . similarly situated,' and therefore involves the 'very kind of arbitrary legislative choice forbidden by the [Constitution]. . . .' Reed v. Reed, 404 U.S., at 77, 76." Frontiero v. Richardson, supra, 411 U.S., at 690. But Florida's justification of §196.191(7) is not that it serves administrative convenience or helps to preserve the public fisc. Rather, the asserted justification is that §196.191(7) is an affirmative step toward alleviating the effects of past economic discrimination against women.

I agree that, in providing special benefits for a needy segment of society long the victim of purposeful discrimination and neglect, the statute serves the compelling state interest of achieving equality for such groups.[5] No one familiar with this country's history of pervasive sex discrimination against women[6] can doubt the need for remedial measures to correct the resulting economic imbalances. Indeed, the extent of the economic disparity between men and women is dramatized by the data cited by the Court, ante, pp. 2-4. By providing a property tax exemption for widows, §196.191(7) assists in reducing that economic disparity for a class of women particularly disadvantaged by the legacy of economic discrimination.[7] In that circumstance, the purpose and effect of the suspect classification is ameliorative; the statute neither stigmatizes nor denigrates widowers not also benefited by the legislation. Moreover, inclusion of needy widowers within the class of beneficiaries would not further the State's overriding interest in remedying the economic effects of past sex discrimination for needy victims of that discrimination. While doubtless some widowers are in financial need, no one suggests that such need results from sex discrimination as in the case of widows.

The statute nevertheless fails to satisfy the requirements of equal protection, since the State has not borne its burden of proving that its compelling interest could not be achieved by a more precisely tailored statute or by use of feasible less drastic means. Section 196.191(7) is plainly overinclusive, for the $500 property tax exemption may be obtained by a financially independent heiress as well as by an unemployed widow with dependent children. The State has offered nothing to explain why inclusion of widows of substantial economic means was necessary to advance the State's interest in ameliorating the effects of past economic discrimination against women.

Moreover, alternative means of classification, narrowing the class of widow beneficiaries, appear readily available. The exemption is granted only to widows who complete and file with the tax assessor a form application establishing their status as widows. By merely redrafting that form to exclude widows who earn annual incomes, or possess assets, in excess of specified amounts, the State could readily narrow the class of beneficiaries to those widows for whom the effects of past economic discrimination against women have been a practical reality.

Mr. Justice WHITE, dissenting.

The Florida tax exemption at issue here is available to all widows but not to

5. Significantly, the Florida statute does not compel the beneficiaries to accept the State's aid. The taxpayer must file for the tax exemption. This case, therefore, does not require resolution of the more difficult questions raised by remedial legislation which makes special treatment mandatory. See Note, Developments in the Law — Equal Protection, 82 Harv. L. Rev. 1065, 1113-1117 (1969).

6. See Frontiero v. Richardson, 411 U.S. 677 (1973); Sail'er Inn, Inc. v. Kirby, 5 Cal. 3d 1, 485 P.2d 529 (1971). See generally The President's Task Force on Women's Rights and Responsibilities, A Matter of Simple Justice (1970); L. Kanowitz, Women and the Law: The Unfinished Revolution (1969).

7. As noted by the Court, *ante,* pp. 2-4:

"[D]ata compiled by the Woman's Bureau of the United States Department of Labor shows that in 1972 a woman working full time had a median income which was only 57.9% of the male median — a figure actually six points lower than had been achieved in 1955. . . . The disparity is likely to be exacerbated for the widow. While the widower can usually continue in the occupation which preceded his spouse's death in many cases the widow will find herself suddenly forced into a job market with which she is unfamiliar, and in which, because of her former economic dependency, she will have fewer skills to offer." (Footnotes omitted).

widowers. The presumption is that all widows are financially more needy and less trained or less ready for the job market than men. It may be that most widows have been occupied as housewife, mother and homemaker and are not immediately prepared for employment. But there are many rich widows who need no largess from the State; many others are highly trained and have held lucrative positions long before the death of their husbands. At the same time, there are many widowers who are needy and who are in more desperate financial straits and have less access to the job market than many widows. Yet none of them qualifies for the exemption.

I find the discrimination invidious and violative of the Equal Protection Clause. There is merit in giving poor widows a tax break, but gender-based classifications are suspect and require more justification than the State has offered.

I perceive no purpose served by the exemption other than to alleviate current economic necessity, but the State extends the exemption to widows who do not need the help and denies it to widowers who do. It may be administratively inconvenient to make individual determinations of entitlement and to extend the exemption to needy men as well as needy women, but administrative efficiency is not an adequate justification for discriminations based purely on sex. Frontiero v. Richardson, 411 U.S. 677 (1973); Reed v. Reed, 404 U.S. 71 (1971).

It may be suggested that the State is entitled to prefer widows over widowers because their assumed need is rooted in past and present economic discrimination against women. But this is not a credible explanation of Florida's tax exemption; for if the State's purpose was to compensate for past discrimination against females, surely it would not have limited the exemption to women who are widows. Moreover, even if past discrimination is considered to be the criterion for current tax exemption, the State nevertheless ignores all those widowers who have felt the effects of economic discrimination, whether as a member of a racial group or as one of the many who cannot escape the cycle of poverty. It seems to me that the State in this case is merely conferring an economic benefit in the form of a tax exemption and has not adequately explained why women should be treated differently than men.

I dissent.

Note: The Evolution of New Constitutional Standards for Reviewing Discriminatory Classifications

Between 1961, when *Hoyt* was decided, and 1973, there were a series of cases in the lower courts which challenged the idea that sex classifications were always reasonable, and helped change the legal climate enough to make the *Frontiero* decision possible. The first step was taken in a case which involved both race- and sex-based discrimination. In White v. Crook, 251 F. Supp. 401 (M.D. Ala. 1966), plaintiffs challenged jury selection procedures in Lowndes County, Alabama, on the grounds that blacks and women were excluded from jury service, the former by the practices of the jury commissioners and the latter by an Alabama statute. Having found for plaintiffs on the racial discrimination issue, the court prospectively invalidated the statutory exclusion of women. Then in 1968 and 1969, there were a series of cases finding a denial of equal protection in the unequal treatment of female prisoners, including, in four of the cases, longer periods of incarceration.[34] Personal liberty has long been a fundamental concern of the constitutional law and the courts, and it is not surprising that sex-discriminatory laws in this area were among the first to receive more careful judicial review.

---

34. Commonwealth v. Daniels, 430 Pa. 642, 234 A.2d 400 (1968); United States ex rel. Robinson v. York, 281 F. Supp. 8 (D. Conn. 1968); United States ex rel. Sumrell v. York, 288 F. Supp. 955 (D. Conn. 1968); Liberti v. York, 28 Conn. Supp. 9, 246 A.2d 106 (1968); Commonwealth v. Stauffer, 214 Pa. Super. 113, 251 A.2d 718 (1969).

In the course of deciding these cases, however, the courts began to examine more closely the states' justifications for differential treatment. For example, in invalidating longer sentences for women than for men for certain crimes, the Supreme Court of Pennsylvania found a denial of equal protection even though "a classification by sex alone would not, per se, offend the Equal Protection Clause."[35] Although the court believed, for example, that "there are undoubtedly significant biological, natural and practical differences between men and women which would justify under certain circumstances the establishment of different employment qualification standards,"[36] it nonetheless failed to discern "any reasonable and justifiable difference [of] deterrents between men and women which would justify a man being *eligible* for a shorter maximum prison sentence than a woman for the commission of the same crime especially if there is no material difference in their records and the relevant circumstances."[37] Thus, the court found that the law in question was "devoid of reasonable grounds of difference and is arbitrary, discriminatory and invalid under the Fourteenth Amendment of the Constitution of the United States."[38]

In the next few years, this approach was used in cases that involved rights less fundamental than jury duty and freedom from incarceration. In Mollere v. Southeastern Louisiana College, 304 F. Supp. 826 (E.D. La. 1969), a three-judge court ruled that single women under twenty-one could not be required to live in dormitories when the state college said its own finances demanded the arrangement, because no similar requirement was imposed on men. In Estate of Legatos, 1 Cal. App. 3d 657, 81 Cal. Rptr. 910 (1969), a California court invalidated a sex-discriminatory inheritance law.

The new approach of carefully reviewing the facts advanced to support sex-discriminatory classifications was skillfully used in Seidenberg v. McSorley's Old Ale House, 317 F. Supp. 593 (S.D.N.Y. 1970), and Kirstein v. Rector and Visitors of the University of Virginia, 309 F. Supp. 184 (E.D. Va. 1970). In *Seidenberg,* the court, in sharp contrast to the *Goesaert* case, refused to assume the existence of "moral and social" problems in order to justify the exclusion of women from a bar. "Outdated images of bars as dens of coarseness and iniquity and of women as peculiarly delicate and impressionable creatures in need of protection from the rough and tumble of unwashed humanity will no longer justify separatism."[39] Similarly, the court in *Kirstein* recognized that the educational opportunities at the all-male University of Virginia at Charlottesville were in fact superior to any offered women elsewhere. On this ground it invalidated the sex segregation at Charlottesville, even though it would not declare all single-sex state schools unconstitutional.

Beginning in 1971, an increasing number of courts invalidated sex-discriminatory state laws.[40] The Supreme Court of California was the first to cast its decision in terms

35. Commonwealth v. Daniel, 430 Pa. 642, 649, 243 A.2d 400, 403 (1968).

36. Ibid.

37. 430 Pa. at 650, 243 A.2d at 404 (emphasis in the original).

38. Ibid.

39. 317 F. Supp. at 606.

40. The following are further examples of cases striking down sex classifications on constitutional grounds before the *Frontiero* decision:

Criminal sanctions: Lamb v. Brown, 456 F.2d 18 (10th Cir. 1972) (Oklahoma's sex-based differential age requirement (boys — sixteen, girls — eighteen) to receive benefits of juvenile court proceedings); A. v. City of New York, 31 N.Y.2d 83, 335 N.Y.S.2d 33 (1972) (New York's sex-age differential (boys — sixteen, girls — eighteen) for "supervision" of juveniles for behavior that would not be criminal for an adult).

Maternity regulations: LaFleur v. Cleveland Board of Education, 465 F.2d 1184 (6th Cir. 1972), *aff'd,* 414 U.S. 632, 94 S. Ct. 791, — L. Ed. 2d — (1974);Bravo v. Board of Education, 345 F. Supp. 155 (N.D. Ill. 1972); Williams v. San Francisco School Dist., 340 F. Supp. 438 (N.D. Cal. 1972); Heath v. Westerville Board of Education, 345 F. Supp. 501 (S.D. Ohio 1972); Pocklington v. Duval County School Board, 345 F. Supp. 163 (M.D. Fla. 1972); Robinson v. Rand, 340 F. Supp. 37 (D. Colo. 1972); Jinks v. Mays, 332 F. Supp. 254 (N.D. Ga. 1971).

Education: Crews v. Cloncs, 432 F.2d 1259 (7th Cir. 1970) (hair length regulation for male but not female high school students); Brenden v. Independent School Dist., 342 F. Supp. 1224 (D. Minn. 1972), Chapter Five,

of a clear holding that sex was a suspect classification. The case was Sail'er Inn, Inc. v. Kirby, 5 Cal. 3d 1, 485 P.2d 529 (1971), a Fourteenth Amendment challenge to the state's law excluding women from the occupation of bartending. In a lengthy and well-written opinion, the court invalidated the laws on the grounds of the California Constitution, Title VII of the Civil Rights Act of 1964, and the Equal Protection Clause of the Fourteenth Amendment.

There are parallels between the evolution of the Supreme Court's positions on racial discrimination in education and this series of sex discrimination cases in the lower courts. In both instances, the courts gradually became convinced of the injustice of a whole class of legislation by a process of close examination of the facts in individual cases. In cases which came before the Supreme Court between 1890 and 1954 dealing with racial discrimination in state-supported education, there was a gradual progression from an almost irrebuttable presumption that racial segregation was not discriminatory to the opposite presumption. In 1896, in Plessy v. Ferguson, 163 U.S. 537, 16 S. Ct. 1138, 41 L. Ed. 256, the Court upheld a Louisiana state law providing for separate facilities on railroad trains for black and white passengers, on the condition that the separate facilties were "equal." The doctrine of "separate but equal" was applied in education cases only a few years later,[41] not to be officially repudiated until Brown v. Board of Education, 347 U.S. 483, 74 S. Ct. 686, 98 L. Ed. 873 (1954).

Between *Plessy* and its progeny in the field of education and Brown v. Board, there were three highly significant Supreme Court cases: Missouri ex rel. Gaines v. Canada, 305 U.S. 337, 59 S. Ct. 232, 83 L. Ed. 208 (1938), in which the Court held invalid a plan whereby whites attended a state law school and blacks had their tuition paid at an out-of-state law school; Sweatt v. Painter, 339 U.S. 629, 70 S. Ct. 848, 94 L. Ed. 1114 (1950), in which the Court struck down arrangements for the segregation of the races by the creation of a separate law school for blacks only; and McLaurin v. Oklahoma State Board of Regents, 339 U.S. 637, 70 S. Ct. 139, 94 L. Ed. 1149 (1950), which struck down a plan for the separation of the races in the use of the facilities of a single law school. The Court was still using the "separate but equal" formula, but instead of assuming the existence of facts demonstrating the equality of the segregated facilities, the justices took a closer look at the actual facts of the case. Of course, in practice, separate was by no means equal, and the Court held that Texas and Oklahoma must integrate state-supported legal education to satisfy the constitutional command that the state not deny the equal protection of the laws.[42]

A similar progression from minimal review to strict reasonableness and, for some justices, to strict scrutiny is evidenced in the Supreme Court opinions in *Hoyt, Reed,* and *Frontiero,* and the dissenting opinions in *Kahn.*[43] The majority opinion in *Kahn,* however, illustrates that looking at the facts has not (so far) been enough to bring the majority

---

II-A-3, infra, and Reed v. Nebraska School Activities Ass'n, 341 F. Supp. 258 (D. Neb. 1972) (both admitting individual girls to previously all-male varsity interscholastic athletic teams where there was no all-female interscholastic team); Shull v. Columbus Municipal School Dist., 338 F. Supp. 1376 (N.D. Miss 1972) (unwed mothers may not be barred from high school); Bray v. Lee, 337 F. Supp. 934 (D. Mass. 1972) (higher admission standard for women at Boston Latin public high school).

State "protective" law: Mengelkoch v. Industrial Welfare Comm'n, 442 F.2d 1119 (9th Cir. 1971) (reversing and remanding district court's denial of motion for three-judge court; maximum hours law applicable to women only presents substantial federal question).

For recent cases upholding sex classifications against Fourteenth Amendment challenges, see footnote 33 supra.

41. Cumming v. Board of Education, 175 U.S. 528, 20 S. Ct. 197, 44 L. Ed. 262 (1899); Berea College v. Kentucky, 211 U.S. 45, 29 S. Ct. 33, 53 L. Ed. 81 (1908); Gong Lum v. Rice, 275 U.S. 78, 48 S. Ct. 91, 72 L. Ed. 172 (1927).

42. This doctrinal evolution is discussed in detail in Emerson, Haber, and Dorsen, Political and Civil Rights in the United States 1230-1252 (student ed. 1967).

43. The evolution of judicial and administrative interpretations of the BFOQ (bona fide occupational qualification) standard under Title VII of the Civil Rights Act of 1964, which prohibits sex discrimination in employment, is another example of the influence of fact patterns on legal doctrines. See Chapter Two, II-B, infra.

of the Justices to see the fundamental injustice of all sex-based averaging. It may be that, as with race, only a separate constitutional amendment will be an adequate basis for eradicating sex discrimination from the law.

NOTE: A CRITIQUE OF KAHN V. SHEVIN

In Kahn v. Shevin, the Supreme Court considered explicitly and at some length an equal protection challenge to a sex-based legislative classification, and for the first time in a major opinion since Hoyt v. Florida thirteen years before, upheld the statute's validity. Despite the similarity of outcomes, the Court had not quite come full circle. The numerous lawsuits challenging sex discrimination which had been brought during the intervening years, and the women's movement to which they were often related, succeeded to some extent in raising judicial consciousness about sex discrimination, or at least injecting a new vocabulary into judicial opinions. Thus Justice Douglas's opinion for the Court in *Kahn* tied employment discrimination against women to "overt discrimination or . . . the socialization process of a male dominated culture"[44] — concepts totally unrecognized in the *Hoyt* opinion in 1961. At the same time — indeed, virtually in the same breath — Justice Douglas maintained a continuity of judicial paternalism by invoking Muller v. Oregon's justification of broad sex classifications in employment on the basis of women's "special physical organization."[45]

There is no doubt that the special tax exemption granted to all women under the Florida law challenged in *Kahn* is a benefit to all of them. This distinguishes the case from *Hoyt, Goesaert,* and *Muller,* in which the supposed sex-based benefits were at best debatable and at worst illusory. There is also little doubt in *Kahn* (as in *Hoyt*) that the sex-based average on which the legislation relies is substantially accurate. Widows on the average are less likely than widowers on the average to be or to have been employed, or, if employed or employable, are likely to earn less money. The relative accuracy and beneficence of Florida's sex classification raised a seldom confronted set of problems in equal protection jurisprudence. The Court's failure to consider them explicitly and adequately underscores the limitations of equal protection doctrine in remedying sex discrimination.

The Court might have been expected to approach the Florida statute with the concepts articulated in *Frontiero,* which was decided the previous term. In *Frontiero,* Justice Brennan, speaking for a plurality of four justices (Douglas, White, and Marshall joined in his opinion), accepted the principle that classifications based on sex, like those based on race, alienage, and national origin, are suspect classifications which must be subjected to close judicial scrutiny. The Court thus appeared to be moving in a fashion similar to the racial segregation cases discussed above, toward a categorical or per se judgment that sex classifications were discriminatory and hence could be justified, if at all, only by a showing of compelling state interest.

The *Kahn* opinion sharply halted this trend. The immediate seeds of *Kahn* lay in *Frontiero* itself, and in its much cited predecessor, *Reed,* supra. Despite Justice Brennan's acceptance of sex as a suspect classification and his eloquent renunciation of paternalistic discrimination, his analysis of the statute at issue relied almost exclusively on concepts of reasonableness and arbitrariness which figured so prominently in *Reed.* Indeed, when it came to explaining why Congress's denial of dependents' benefits to women in the armed forces violated the Equal Protection Clause, Brennan quoted the opaque language of *Reed* that sex classifications made solely for administrative convenience constitute "the very kind of arbitrary legislative choice forbidden by the [Constitution]."[46]

The question of what standard to apply to sex classifications was again raised in

44. 42 U.S.L.W. at 4592.
45. Id. at 4593 n.10.
46. 404 U.S. at 76.

Kahn, and the plurality represented by Brennan's opinion in *Frontiero* collapsed. Justice Douglas, writing for a majority of six, had difficulty perceiving that a special tax exemption for women constituted "discrimination" at all. He suggested that tax classifications are in a sense inherently arbitrary and therefore exempt from the finer standards of the Equal Protection Clause. Arbitrariness, in a constitutional sense, does not occur if the discrimination is "founded upon a reasonable distinction . . . not in conflict with the Federal Constitution."[47] Thus Douglas seemed to abandon his earlier agreement with the suspect classification position, and hold that sex classifications were not in conflict with the Constitution as long as they were rationally related to a permissible state policy. Not surprisingly, he was joined by the four justices who had concurred in the *Frontiero* judgment on the basis of the *Reed* strict reasonableness approach (Stewart, Burger, Blackmun, and Powell), and by Rehnquist as well. Hopefully, in subsequent cases, it will be possible to distinguish away the majority opinion as a decision more about state power to tax than about sex classifications.

Although the rationality of the legislative classification upheld by Douglas in *Kahn* is certainly questionable, the quality of the majority's inquiry is not markedly lower than many of the Court's previous decisions applying the test of rational relationship to non-sex-based classifications. In contrast, Justice Brennan's analysis, purporting to apply strict scrutiny, uses a weaker version of this test than has been customary in race cases. The weakness lies in Brennan's conception of what would constitute a compelling justification for a sex classification.

Brennan, like Douglas, was impressed by the general disparity between women's and men's wages, and argued that the state could provide special benefits for a "segment of society long the victim of purposeful discrimination and neglect," namely, widows in financial need.[48] But, as Justice White pointed out in his separate dissent, was this presumption of discrimination and concomitant need sufficiently accurate to justify a broad sex classification?

It is important that courts and legislatures be free to compensate the victims of discrimination for their losses. However, the paradox of remedies for sex and race discrimination is that often they must take sex and race into account. In individual cases, the need to remedy the discrimination is sufficiently acute, and the factual evidence of who suffered how much loss as a result of discrimination sufficiently strong, that remedial sex and race classification is appropriate. See, for example, the decisions designing new seniority systems to remedy the effects of past sex or race discrimination, discussed in Chapter Two, II-G, infra. In contrast, Brennan's hypothetical law involves sex averaging on such a grand scale that it undermines the concept of individual treatment without regard to sex. In effect, it substitutes discrimination against men for discrimination against women rather than substituting individual treatment for overbroad sex classification.

Such overclassification by sex is unjust. It is also a dangerous precedent. It creates the possibility that the rationale of remedying past discrimination will replace the rationale of "protecting" women as constitutional justification for statutory sex classifications which, in the guise of benefiting women, actually discriminate against them.

Another point is that it is unlikely that women can obtain benefits in one area of the law or the society without paying a high legal or social price elsewhere. It is quite common to hear discrimination against women justified on the grounds of the special benefits women get: until women are subject to the draft and give up sex-based alimony, why should they get equal rights in employment or politics? If the price of having men open doors for women, or of a tax exemption limited to widows and not to widowers, is continued inequality throughout the law and the society, it is too high.

Furthermore, as some commentators have suggested, partial equality—equality in

47. 42 U.S.L.W. at 4593.
48. Id. at 4594.

some areas of the law and not in others — may be an illusory gain. For example, Brown, Emerson, Falk, and Freedman comment as follows in arguing for the adoption of the Equal Rights Amendment:[49]

> To the extent that any exception [to the absolute principle of equality] is made,
> . . . women as a group are thrust into subordinate status and women as individuals
> are denied the basic right to be considered in terms of their own capacities and
> experience. And . . . the interrelated character of a system of legal equality for the sexes
> makes a rule of universal application imperative. No one exception, resulting in
> unequal treatment for women, can be confined in its impact to one area alone. Equal
> rights for women . . . is a unity.

NOTE: OTHER SUPREME COURT DECISIONS

In addition to *Alexander, Reed, Frontiero,* and *Kahn,* the Supreme Court has decided four other Fourteenth Amendment sex discrimination cases since 1970. Two upheld sex-discriminatory state laws through affirmance of three-judge district court decisions. Two invalidated such laws, one reversing a state supreme court decision and one simultaneously reversing the Fourth Circuit and affirming the Sixth Circuit. The first decision was Williams v. McNair, 401 U.S. 951, 91 S. Ct. 976, 28 L. Ed. 2d 235 (1971), *aff'g mem.* 316 F. Supp. 134 (D.S.C. 1970), infra Chapter Five, II. In this case, the Supreme Court found no denial of equal protection of the laws in the maintenance by South Carolina of a state college for women only. South Carolina maintained a large number of coeducational colleges and universities, of which two, the Citadel for men and Winthrop College for women, were sex-segregated. The lower court applied the rational relationship test and held that it was reasonable for the state to maintain Winthrop because (1) there is a respectable body of educators who favor single-sex institutions; (2) other state-supported schools were available to plaintiffs; and (3) there is no "special feature connected with Winthrop"[50] that would make it more advantageous educationally than any number of other state schools.

After *Reed* and *Alexander* were decided, the next sex discrimination case was Stanley v. Illinois, 405 U.S. 645, 92 S. Ct. 1208, 31 L. Ed. 2d 551 (1972). *Stanley* concerned the Illinois practice of denying unwed fathers custody of their children without a hearing on their fitness as parents. Such hearings were granted to married parents and unwed mothers. The Supreme Court ruled that, under the Due Process Clause,[51]

> all Illinois parents are constitutionally entitled to a hearing on their fitness before their
> children are removed from their custody. It follows that denying such a hearing to
> Stanley and those like him while granting it to other Illinois parents is inescapably
> contrary to the Equal Protection Clause.

The next case, which preceded *Frontiero,* was Forbush v. Wallace, 401 U.S. 970, 92 S. Ct. 1197, 31 L. Ed. 2d 246 (1972), *aff'g mem.* 341 F. Supp. 217 (M.D. Ala. 1971). *Forbush* was an equal protection challenge to an Alabama regulation which required that each married female applicant use her husband's surname in seeking and obtaining a driver's license. According to the three-judge court, Alabama took the position that as a matter of law a woman had to adopt her husband's surname upon marriage, unless she obtained a court order changing her surname.

The lower court held that the law was reasonable in that it was based on "a

49. The Equal Rights Amendment: A Constitutional Basis for Equal Rights For Women, 80 Yale L. J. 871, 892 (1971).
50. 316 F. Supp. at 138.
51. 405 U.S. at 658.

tradition extending back into the heritage of most western civilizations";[52] it was common to all fifty states, and uniformity among the several states in this area was important; and it avoided administrative inconvenience and the cost of a change in policy for the state. The court concluded that, in light of the simple, inexpensive means by which a married woman could change her name through the courts, "plaintiffs' injury, if any, through the operation of this law is de minimis."[53]

The fourth decision, which was handed down between *Frontiero* and *Kahn*, was Cleveland Board of Education v. LaFleur, 414 U.S. 632, 94 S. Ct. 791, — L. Ed. 2d — (1974). The Court held unconstitutional the rules of two school districts, one in Cleveland, Ohio, and one in Chesterfield County, Virginia, requiring pregnant teachers to take unpaid maternity leave commencing five and four months respectively before the expected childbirth. The rules were invalid because they were an unjustifiable burden on the exercise of "freedom of personal choice in matters of marriage and family life,"[54] protected by the Due Process Clause of the Fourteenth Amendment.

The asserted justifications for these policies were that "firm cut off dates are necessary to maintain continuity of classroom instruction"[55] because of the time needed to find a qualified substitute, and that "at least some teachers become physically incapable of performing certain of their duties during the latter part of pregnancy."[56] The Court ruled that the arbitrary cutoff dates were not rationally related to the valid state interest of preserving continuity of instruction. As to the state interest in insuring that a physically capable instructor is with the students at all times, the Court ruled:[57]

> While it might be easier for the school boards to conclusively presume that all pregnant women are unfit to teach past the fourth or fifth month or even the first month, of pregnancy, administrative convenience alone is insufficient to make valid what otherwise is a violation of due process of law. The Fourteenth Amendment requires the school boards to employ alternative administrative means, which do not so broadly infringe upon basic constitutional liberty, in support of their legitimate goals.

Both school districts also restricted a teacher's eligibility to return to work after giving birth, for which they offered the same justifications as for the firm cutoff dates in the second trimester of pregnancy. Both schools required a physician's certificate of physical fitness or a medical examination prior to the teacher's return. The Cleveland district also prohibited the teacher from returning to work until the next regular semester after her child became three months old. Chesterfield County guaranteed the teacher's re-employment no later than the beginning of the next school year following a determination of eligibility; in addition to the physician's certificate, the district also required assurances from the teacher that care of the child would not unduly interfere with her job duties. The Court upheld all of the above restrictions with the exception of the Cleveland rule relating to the age of the child.[58]

It is difficult to see what, if anything, distinguishes the three cases upholding sex classifications from the four invalidating them. One theory is that the Court is less likely

52. 341 F. Supp. at 222.
53. Ibid.
54. 414 U.S. at 639.
55. Id. at 640.
56. Id. at 641.
57. Id. at 647.
58. In a footnote, the Court commented with regard to the assurances required in Chesterfield County: "While such a requirement has within it the potential for abuse, there is no evidence on this record that the assurances required here are anything more than those routinely sought by employers from prospective employees — that the worker is willing to devote full attention to job duties. Nor is there any evidence in this record that the school authorities do not routinely accept the woman's assurances of her ability to return." 414 U.S. at 650.

to find a denial of equal protection of the laws based on sex when the party seeking that result is a man rather than a woman; the *Stanley* decision, arguably an exception, is more properly viewed as a due process, rather than an equal protection, decision. A second theory, that three-judge court actions, currently disfavored in the Supreme Court,[59] are more likely to receive summary treatment, is rendered questionable by the *Frontiero* decision.

One obvious explanation for the results in *LaFleur* and *Stanley* is the Court's increasing concern with the right to personal privacy in decisions relating to childbearing and childrearing. See also Roe v. Wade, 410 U.S. 113, 93 S. Ct. 756, 35 L. Ed. 2d 147 (1973), and Doe v. Bolton, 410 U.S. 179, 93 S. Ct. 739, 35 L. Ed. 2d 201 (1973), infra Chapter Five, I, and cases cited therein.

A further possibility is that differences in the way these five cases were litigated account for the different results. Both *Reed* and *Frontiero* were litigated as women's rights cases of paramount importance. For example, in *Reed,* excellent amici briefs were filed by the National Organization of Women's Legal Defense Fund jointly with the American Veterans Committee, Inc., by the American Civil Liberties Union, by the National Federation of Business and Professional Women's Clubs, and by the City of New York. Using a broad range of arguments, the amici sought a definitive statement from the Court on the status of women in twentieth-century America. The City of New York noted, for instance, that the absence of leadership by the Court in striking down statutes embodying sex discrimination made it difficult for New York to enforce effectively its own antidiscrimination policies.

While the effect of the briefs was not that evident in the *Reed* decision, apart from the favorable result, in *Frontiero* Justice Brennan relied heavily on the brief amicus curiae of the American Civil Liberties Union in his discussion of "our Nation['s] . . . long and unfortunate history of sex discrimination"[60] and in explaining his conclusion that sex is a suspect classification which merits strict scrutiny under the Equal Protection Clause.

Forbush, Stanley, and *Williams,* in contrast, were not pursued as effectively, and in none of the three were national feminist or civil rights organizations involved. There were other problems as well. In oral argument, counsel for Peter Stanley took the position that the central issue was not the statutory discrimination between unwed fathers and unwed mothers, but that between suitable and unsuitable unwed fathers.[61] Likewise, the facts in the *Forbush* case were not developed at the trial court level in the form most favorable to the plaintiff. For example, the record was allowed to stand with the patent misrepresentation that the laws of all fifty states require married women to use their husband's surnames.[62] In addition, no adequate record was ever developed on the actual availability and cost of the name change procedure when the person seeking the change was a married woman wishing to regain her premarriage name. In the Supreme Court, appellants were thus reduced to noting that the name change procedure was discretionary and would not be "without cost"[63] — hardly a persuasive statement. Similarly, the plaintiffs did not make an adequate record on the actual administrative cost of allowing married women to use their premarriage names on driver's licenses and other records.

Such criticisms should not, however, obscure the fact that the Supreme Court has been plodding rather than rushing down the road to eradicating sex discrimination. As *Kahn* illustrates, even with careful litigation and briefing by experts in the field, the Supreme Court does not always rule in favor of sex equality. In any event, it should not come as a surprise that there are defeats as well as victories among the Court's decisions

59. See, e.g., Younger v. Harris, 401 U.S. 37, 91 S. Ct. 746, 27 L. Ed. 2d 669 (1970).
60. 411 U.S. at 684.
61. Tr. of Oral Argument, Stanley v. Illinois, 405 U.S. 645 (1972).
62. See Chapter Three, III-A-2, for a discussion of the law relating to married women's surnames.
63. Brief for Appellee, n.1, Forbush v. Wallace, 401 U.S. 970 (1972).

in this field, nor is it surprising that a fairly large number of cases must be brought to the Court's attention before it completely repudiates the centuries-old tradition of sexism.

Note: The New "Strict Reasonableness"

Gunther has suggested that the Burger Court, while declining to expand the use of strict scrutiny, is beginning to put "bite" in the old "traditionally toothless minimal scrutiny standard" in other areas, as well as in sex discrimination cases.[64] Thus, the state must show a stronger state interest than previously to justify a challenged law. The Supreme Court decision in *Stanley* is a good example of this. One argument made by Illinois in that case was that since most illegitimate fathers are unfit and disinterested, exclusion of all of them from parenthood, unless they take the affirmative action of formally adopting their children, is administratively the most feasible course. Rejecting this argument summarily, the Court finds that "the Constitution recognizes higher values than speed and efficiency" and decries "procedure by presumption." *Stanley* should be compared in this respect to Hoyt v. Florida, in which the state argued that since most women will be tied up with domestic duties, they should all be exempted from jury service unless they take the affirmative action of volunteering. To that argument the Court responded that "from the standpoint of its own administrative concerns the State might well consider that it was 'impractical to compel large numbers of women, who have an absolute exemption to come to the clerk's office for examination.'"[65] Reed v. Reed is another good example of a case where the Court found expressly that the legislative purpose of the classification — i.e., the administrative convenience of avoiding a hearing on the merits of an appointment — although a legitimate state interest, was not sufficient to justify the sex discrimination of the Idaho statute.

With the *Frontiero* decision, the Court appeared to be moving beyond a general "strict reasonableness" standard toward expanding the use of strict scrutiny, contrary to Gunther's prediction. However, the *Kahn* case demonstrates that the view that sex is a suspect classification is still unquestionably a minority one. It thus behooves attorneys litigating sex cases to continue to develop factual records that clearly show the imprecision of the classification used, the weaknesses in the state interests asserted to justify discrimination, and hence the irrationality of the statute.

Note: Application of Due Process Analysis to Sex Discrimination Cases

Although in the *Stanley* and *LaFleur* cases the sex-discriminatory laws were invalidated, the use of due process rather than sex discrimination reasoning poses serious problems. The *LaFleur* case provides an excellent example. In using a due process approach, the Court was treating pregnancy as a unique problem, rather than comparing the school districts' rules relating to pregnancy-based disabilities to their rules relating to other temporary disabilities, as an equal protection approach would mandate. Because the case was decided only on the due process issue, the school boards can still discriminate against women by requiring them to show their capacity to continue work or to return to work while not requiring employees with other potentially disabling physical conditions to make the same showing.

A second problem with the Due Process Clause is that it implies a balancing test,

64. Gunther, Forward: In Search of Evolving Doctrine on a Changing Court: A Model for a Newer Equal Protection in the Supreme Court, 1971 Term, 86 Harv. L. Rev. 1, 18-19 (1972).
65. 368 U.S. at 64.

whereas an equal protection approach based on sex as a suspect classification would have triggered strict scrutiny. Thus, discrimination may be upheld more readily under the former than under the latter. A third is that considering the issue on either a due process or an equal protection–fundamental rights basis rather than on an equal protection–sex discrimination basis tends to obscure the question of the justice or injustice of the pervasive sex discrimination in our legal system and public institutions.

VI. THE EQUAL RIGHTS AMENDMENT

PROPOSED AMENDMENT XXVII
[Proposed by Congress on March 22, 1972]

Section 1. Equality of rights under the law shall not be denied or abridged by the United States or by any State on account of sex.

Section 2. The Congress shall have the power to enforce, by appropriate legislation, the provisions of this article.

Section 3. This amendment shall take effect two years after the date of ratification.

A. THE HISTORY OF THE EQUAL RIGHTS AMENDMENT, 1923–1973

After 1923, when the original version[1] was offered to the House Judiciary Committee, the Equal Rights Amendment was introduced in Congress every year. However, except in the years 1946, 1950, and 1953, little attention was paid to the proposal until the 1970s. Beginning in 1970, heightened effort brought about passage by the Senate on March 22, 1972, ending a half-century campaign for congressional enactment of a constitutional guarantee of equal rights for men and women.

In the 1920s and 1930s, the Equal Rights Amendment was urged as a corollary to the Nineteenth Amendment.[2] The National Woman's Party struggled for enactment of the resolution, arguing that the vote did not suffice to make American women full citizens. The party contended that full citizenship would not be accomplished until the inequalities in many other provisions of the law, such as those treating jury service, property rights, and marriage and divorce, were eradicated. The Woman's Party pointed out that none of the terrible evils predicted by antisuffragists had materialized with the passage of the voting amendment, and they argued that the ERA would have a similarly benign effect.

But there was profound disagreement among politically active women about the need for, and the probable consequences of, the Equal Rights Amendment. According to Chafe:[3]

> No issue divided women's organizations more than the Equal Rights Amendment to the Constitution. Endorsed by one wing of the suffrage movement and opposed by the other, it immediately became a focal point of controversy. Mary Anderson of the Women's Bureau denounced it as "vicious," "doctrinaire," and "a kind of hysterical feminism with a slogan for a program." Other suffragists viewed it as a direct threat to all the special legislation passed to protect women. . . .

1. The language of the original amendment, changed in 1943, was: "Men and women shall have equal rights throughout the United States and every place subject to its jurisdiction." This language was purportedly revised to avoid the possibility that it might be interpreted to require uniformity in laws among the states.

2. 80 Cong. Rec. E9287-9288 (daily ed. June 8, 1936) 74th Cong., 2d Sess. (Mr. Ludlow).

3. Chafe, The American Woman 112-113 (1972).

In some ways, the conflict represented an extension of the split between the Woman's Party and NAWSA [The National American Women's Suffrage Association] during the suffrage campaign. The Woman's Party (formerly the Congressional Union) adopted radical tactics, chaining themselves to fences, picketing the White House, and engaging in hunger strikes in prison. NAWSA, on the other hand, sought to cooperate with the government and to work from within to achieve its goals.

The Woman's Party was made up primarily of "hard core feminists," in O'Neill's terms,[4] while NAWSA and its successor, the League of Women Voters, were dominated by "social feminist" reformers and pragmatic organizers like Carrie Chapman Catt. The positions taken and strategies employed by these groups in their factional disputes about the Equal Rights Amendment reflected those differences of personal and organizational makeup:[5]

By [the mid-1920s], the two opposing camps were engaged in a bitter war. One side fought for the exclusive goal of female equality; the other side for social reform. One side believed that suffrage was only the first step in the campaign for freedom; the other that the Nineteenth Amendment had substantially finished the task of making women equal to men. Protective legislation became the crux of the differences between the two groups, but the issue was as much a symbol as a cause of the antagonism. . . .

One side was committed to the philosophy that women were exactly the same as men in all their principal attributes, the other to the position that females were a weaker sex whose rights would be destroyed unless safeguarded by special legislation. The division of opinion could hardly have been greater.

Both Chafe and O'Neill provide detailed accounts of the bitter disputes between the Woman's Party and the remainder of the women's movement during the 1920s and 1930s, accounts which illustrate not only the philosophical differences described above, but the extremes to which personal and political antagonisms drove both factions. The controversy operated to divert congressional attention from the amendment itself to the ideological divisions among women. It is thus hardly surprising that the amendment did not pass before the 1970s and that no clear theory of its meaning emerged until five years before passage.

In the early 1940s, the Senate Committee on the Judiciary began to report the amendment for favorable action on the floor.[6] America's experience in World War II provided strong evidence in the case for the amendment. That war had taken women out of the home in far greater numbers than ever before, and women had shown that they could perform successfully many jobs formerly considered appropriate only for men. There was a sense that by their service to the country women had proved themselves deserving of equal pay for equal work and other legal rights.

The amendment was debated and defeated on three occasions between 1946 and 1953.[7] Each time it was considered, similar issues were raised, with the opponents by far the more coherent in their position. They claimed that the standards to be used in adjusting the differences in legal treatment between the sexes, such as different ages of majority, were not indicated, that rights should be treated differently from duties and

4. O'Neill, Everyone Was Brave: The Rise and Fall of Feminism in America 5 (1969).

5. Chafe, supra, at 119, 129.

6. The material on legislative history from 1940 to 1956 relies heavily on an unpublished manuscript prepared by Barbara A. Brown as background research for Brown, Emerson, Falk, and Freedman, The Equal Rights Amendment: A Constitutional Basis for Equal Rights for Women, 80 Yale L.J. 871 (1971).

7. *1946:* 92 Cong. Rec. 9223-9229, 9293-9297, 9303-9335, 9397-9405, Vote: 38/35 (Sen.), 79th Cong., 2d Sess.; *1950:* 96 Cong. Rec. 738-744, 758-762, 809-813, 826, 828-834, 861-873, Votes: 51/31 (Sen.; Hayden Amend.); 18/65 (Sen; Kefauver Amend.); 63/19 (Sen.; ERA, as amended), 81st Cong., 2d Sess. *1953:* 99 Cong. Rec. 1386, 4313, 8884-8885, 8951-8974, 9118, Votes: 58/25 (Sen.; Hayden Amend.); 73/11 (Sen.; ERA, as amended), 83d Cong., 1st Sess.

yet were not distinguished in the amendment, and that protective legislation and support and divorce laws, which were properly biased in favor of women, were endangered by the amendment. Generally, they opposed the use of a constitutional amendment to effect change: "Using the constitution for a broom with which to sweep away indiscriminately the good with the bad is neither sound law nor sane behavior."[8]

The sponsors never set forth a comprehensive theory of the amendment. Instead they replied to the questions of their colleagues with piecemeal or intuitive responses which were sometimes mutually inconsistent. In many instances, the proponents had not really accepted the practical implications of the theoretical positions they took, and were therefore unable to dispose finally of issues. Because there was no unitary theory of the amendment, proponents were constantly entangled in arguments about their inconsistencies on minor points, while the attention of the Senate was drawn away from the major areas of concern.

For example, the proponents in 1946 argued that certain rights ought to be guaranteed by the federal government in order to give them dignity and permanence. This was certainly one good reason for an amendment, but no one seemed able to explain why federal and state statutory reform could not accomplish the same end. Similarly, although the proponents supported total equality in principle, they nevertheless sought to create exceptions. Yet when political and intuitive judgments were set aside, there were no legal distinctions between the exceptions that the amendment's sponsors approved and those they would not permit. It was therefore literally impossible to predict the effects that the amendment would be likely to have on existing laws. For example, Senator Pepper, a proponent of the ERA, suggested that if the courts found it to be a reasonable classification, women could be excused from combat duty, even though some women were stronger than some men. On the other hand, he asserted that under the ERA men would not be able to have exclusive control of community property, although they, on the average, had more business experience than women.[9]

In 1950, the Senate considered two important additions to the amendment. Senator Hayden proposed the following sentence: "The provisions of this article shall not be construed to impair any rights, benefits or exemptions conferred by law upon persons of the female sex." Senator Kefauver moved that the amendment be in the form of a bill, with a policy section stating "that it is the declared policy of the United States that in law and its administration, no distinctions on the basis of sex shall be made except such as are reasonably justified by differences in physical structure or maternal function." The bill provided for a commission on the status of women, which would report to the President. He would then convey its recommendations to the Congress for consideration. The commission itself would have no power to implement change. The states were expected to follow the lead of the federal government in revising their laws after review by a commission. According to Kefauver, distinctions, to be justified under his standard, would have to be based on real differences between the sexes, not custom or prejudice. However, he declared his belief that protective laws and other special state laws for women, which his bill would leave standing, were reasonably related to such real differences between the sexes.

The Kefauver amendment was rejected, and the ERA with the Hayden rider was passed by the Senate both in 1950 and in 1953; the House ignored the proposal entirely in both years.

Between 1953 and the amendment's next serious consideration in 1970, the women's movement, which had subsided after passage of the Nineteenth Amendment, again became a serious force in American politics. Simone de Beauvoir had published The Second Sex in 1949; it first appeared in the United States in 1953. Ten years later, Betty Friedan's book, The Feminine Mystique, appeared. President Kennedy appointed

8. H.R. Rep. No. 907, House Comm. on the Judiciary, Minority Views, p. 4, 79th Cong., 1st Sess. (1945).
9. 92 Cong. Rec. 9310 (1946).

the first Commission on the Status of Women in 1961, and in 1966 the National Organization for Women (NOW) was founded. But the time for the Equal Rights Amendment had not yet come. Due to the great expansion of judicial concern with civil rights under the Warren Court, most people believed that equality for women would finally be achieved through a new, broader interpretation of the Fourteenth Amendment.

By 1970, this development no longer seemed imminent, and the drive for passage of the Equal Rights Amendment was revived. In March, the Citizen's Advisory Council on the Status of Women issued a cogent memorandum on the ERA prepared by Mary Eastwood, which moved toward a coherent theory of the Equal Rights Amendment.[10] When Senate hearings were held in 1970, the Harvard Civil Rights-Civil Liberties Law Review prevailed upon Norman Dorsen, Thomas I. Emerson, Paul A. Freund, and Philip B. Kurland, four of the law professors who testified (on both sides of the issue), to expand their testimony for publication in a symposium on the ERA, to which Dr. Pauli Murray, Susan C. Ross, and Barbara Kirk Cavanaugh also contributed.[11] In addition, Barbara A. Brown, Professor Emerson, Gail Falk, and Ann E. Freedman collaborated on the previously mentioned article in the Yale Law Journal, which offered a definitive explanation of the impact of the amendment in the four areas of the law which had been the most controversial.[12]

Probably the key to the final passage of the Equal Rights Amendment was the organizations which supported it, many of which had been opposed for many years. The proponents in the 1970s ranged from the American Home Economics Association, the General Federation of Women's Clubs, and the Ladies Auxiliary of Veterans of Foreign Wars, to the International Brotherhood of Teamsters, the Women's Bureau of the U.S. Department of Labor, and the United Automobile Workers; and from the National Federation of Republican Women and President Nixon's Task Force on Women's Rights and Responsibilities, to the Women's Christian Temperance Union. Even the League of Women Voters, which had long been a leader of the opposition, adopted a resolution permitting state chapters to evolve their own positions on the amendment.

Many of the women's groups which supported the amendment, such as the National Organization of Women and the National Federation of Business and Professional Women's Clubs, organized massive letter-writing campaigns and lobbying efforts to make their views known to Congress, and to win national support for the measure. With the aid of this political pressure, the main congressional sponsors, Representative Martha Griffiths, Senator Birch Bayh, and Senator Marlow Cook, were finally able to persuade Congress to pass the amendment.

The hearings, debates, and scholarly articles which filled two years before the final Senate vote did not, however, persuade a number of influential individuals and groups. Senator Sam Ervin was the most active opponent in the Senate. The AFL-CIO and the

10. Citizen's Advisory Council on the Status of Women, The Proposed Equal Rights Amendment to the United States Constitution (1970).

11. Equal Rights for Women: A Symposium on the Proposed Constitutional Amendment, 6 Harv. Civ. Rights–Civ. Lib. L. Rev. 215-288 (1971).

12. Brown, Emerson, Falk, and Freedman, The Equal Rights Amendment: A Constitutional Basis for Equal Rights for Women, 80 Yale L.J. 871 (1971). See also Note, Sex Discrimination and Equal Protection: Do We Need a Constitutional Amendment? 84 Harv. L. Rev. 1491 (1971), for a pointed examination of three alternative ways to eliminate sex-discriminatory laws, one of which is the Equal Rights Amendment. Eastwood, The Double Standard of Justice: Women's Rights Under the Constitution, 5 Valparaiso U.L. Rev. 281 (1971), is an interesting anlysis proposing a "five-point guide" to applying the amendment to major areas of the law.

Gilbertson, Women and the Equal Protection Clause, 20 Clev.-Mar. L. Rev. 351 (1971), criticizes the Equal Protection Clause without particularly advocating the amendment. But Rawalt, Equal Justice for Women — Update the Constitution, 17 N.Y.L. Forum 528 (1971), makes out her case for the amendment by analyzing the Supreme Court's treatment of sex inequality via the Fourteenth Amendment. Note, The "Equal Rights" Amendment: Positive Panacea or Negative Nostrum?, 59 Ky. L.J. 953 (1971), argues that adoption of the amendment is undesirable. But see Bayh, The Need for the Equal Rights Amendment, 48 Notre Dame Law. 80 (1972); Lexcen, The Equal Rights Amendment, 31 Fed. B.J. 247 (1972); Martin, The Equal Rights Amendment: An Overview, 17 St. Louis U.L.J. 1 (1972).

International Ladies Garment Workers Union remained staunch in opposition, and Myra Wolfgang spoke strongly against the amendment for the Hotel and Restaurant Employees and Bartenders International Union.[13] Some law professors argued that chaos would result if the amendment were passed, because of both uncertainty as to its meaning and the great wave of litigation it would produce; they argued for the alternative solutions of litigation under the Fourteenth Amendment and the passage of new federal and state legislation to solve the problems of sex discrimination in each area one by one. As the amendment proceeded to the states for ratification, the opposition was led by different groups in different states; labor unions, fundamentalist church groups, and the John Birch Society were active in many areas, in struggles reminiscent of the freewheeling campaigns against the Nineteenth Amendment described by Carrie Chapman Catt in Woman Suffrage and Politics. Nevertheless, in state after state, the amendment's supporters have been able to obtain legislative ratification. As this book goes to press, the amendment has been ratified by 33 of the necessary 38 states, and it appears that after fifty years of debate, the Equal Rights Amendment's time has finally come.[14]

B. THE DEBATE THAT PRECEDED PASSAGE OF THE AMENDMENT

1. The Case for a New Amendment

BROWN, EMERSON, FALK, AND FREEDMAN
THE EQUAL RIGHTS AMENDMENT:
A CONSTITUTIONAL BASIS
FOR EQUAL RIGHTS FOR WOMEN
80 Yale L.J. 871, 875-885 (1971)

There are three methods of making changes within the legal system to assure equal rights for women. One is by extending to sex discrimination the doctrines of strict judicial review under the Equal Protection Clause of the Fourteenth Amendment. A second is by piecemeal revision of existing federal and state laws. The third is by a new constitutional amendment. These alternatives are not, of course, mutually exclusive. The basic question is what method, or combination of methods, will be most effective in eradicating sex discrimination from the law.

A. Extension of the Equal Protection Clause

In the past years many proponents of equal rights for women believed that the goal could be achieved through judicial interpretation of the Equal Protection Clause, as applied to both state and federal governments. Thus the President's Commission on the Status of Women argued in 1963 that "the principle of equality [could] become firmly

---

13. Wolfgang argued for the need to preserve protective labor legislation, despite the increasing trend under Title VII of the Civil Rights Act of 1964 for such legislation to be invalidated or extended to men. 118 Cong. Rec. S4416, S4426 (daily ed. Mar. 21, 1972). Her arguments, and the general issue of state protective labor legislation for women only, are discussed in Chapter Two, II-B. The AFL-CIO reversed itself and came out in favor of the amendment at its annual convention in October 1973.

14. For a fragmentary history of the fight for the amendment, see Martin, Equal Rights Amendment: Legislative Background, 11 J. Family Law 363 (1971).

The legislative history of the amendment from 1923 to 1971 is cited in Brown, Emerson, Falk, and Freedman, The Equal Rights Amendment: A Constitutional Basis for Equal Rights for Women, 80 Yale L.J. 871, 981-985 (1971). The following debates and reports developed after the Yale article was written: H.R. Rep. No. 92-259, House Judiciary Comm., 92d Cong., 1st Sess. (1971); Senate Rep. No. 92-689, Senate Comm. on the Judiciary, 92d Cong., 2d Sess. (1972).

The final vote in the House was 354 to 23, 117 Cong. Rec. H9392 (daily ed. Oct. 12, 1971). The final three days of debate in the Senate are recorded at 118 Cong. Rec. S4247-4272 (daily ed. Mar. 20, 1972); S4372-4430 (daily ed. Mar. 21, 1972), S4531-4613 (daily ed. Mar. 22, 1972). The final Senate vote was 84 to 8, the opponents including Senators Bennett, Buckley, Cotton, Ervin, Fannin, Goldwater, Hansen, and Stennis.

established in constitutional doctrine" through use of the Fourteenth and Fifth Amendments, and concluded that "a constitutional amendment need not now be sought." At the present time that viewpoint has been abandoned by active supporters of women's rights. This shift in position is fully justified. An examination of the decisions of the Supreme Court demonstrates that there is no present likelihood that the Court will apply the Equal Protection Clause in a manner that will effectively guarantee equality of rights for women. More important, equal protection doctrines, even in their most progressive form, are ultimately inadequate for that task.

The Supreme Court's approach to women's rights has been characterized, since the 1870s, by two prominent features: a vague but strong substantive belief in women's "separate place," and an extraordinary methodological casualness in reviewing state legislation based on such stereotypical views of women.. . .

On this state of affairs one cannot say that the possibility of achieving substantial equality of rights for women under the Fourteenth and Fifth Amendments is permanently foreclosed. But the present trend of judicial decisions, backed by a century of consistent dismissal of women's claims for equal rights, indicates that any present hope for large-scale change can hardly be deemed realistic.

B. Piecemeal Revision of Existing Laws

Over the years, some proponents of women's rights have thought sex discrimination could be ended most effectively if legislatures prepared women and men gradually for equality by a series of step-by-step reforms. There is no constitutional obstruction to the elimination of discrimination in our legal system by the piecemeal revision or repeal of existing federal and state laws. However such suggestions unrealistically assume a delicacy and precision in the legislative process which has no relationship to actual legislative capability. More importantly, the process is unlikely to be completed within the lifetime of any woman now alive. Such a method requires multiple actions by fifty state legislatures and the federal congress, by the courts and executive agencies in each one of these jurisdictions, and by similar government authorities in numerous political subdivisions as well. This government machinery would have to be mobilized to repeal or modify the statutes and practices in scores of different areas where unequal treatment now prevails. To be comprehensive such efforts would require a tremendously expensive, sophisticated, and sustained political organization, both nationally and within every state and locality. Campaigns to change the laws one by one could drag on for many years, and perhaps in some areas never be finished.

Even if it were possible to mobilize the nation's political machinery, legislative change alone would fail to provide an adequate foundation for the attainment of full legal equality for women. Any plan for eliminating sex discrimination must take into account the large role which generalized belief in the inferiority of women plays in the present scheme of subordination. As noted above, there is need for a single coherent theory of women's equality before the law, and for a consistent nationwide application of this theory. This is scarcely possible through legislative change alone, for the creation of basic policy would be divided among multiple federal, state, and local agencies.[31] Moreover, so long as they believe the laws against discrimination are subject to derogation at the option of the current legislature, many individuals and institutions will not undertake wholeheartedly the far-reaching changes which genuine sex equality requires. An unambiguous mandate with the prospect of permanence is needed to assure prompt compliance.

In essence, piecemeal legislative reform is what has been going on for the past century. Considered realistically, this approach, at least by itself, simply lacks the

---

31. For a discussion of the limits of congressional power to prohibit sex discrimination in areas traditionally reserved to the states, such as inheritance, domestic relations, and criminal law, see Note, 84 Harv. L. Rev. 1499, 1516-1518 (1971).

breadth, coherence, and economy of political effort necessary for fundamental change in the legal position of women.

C. The Case for a Constitutional Amendment

If expansion of the Equal Protection Clause and piecemeal legislation will not result in effective action, there remains the third alternative: a new constitutional amendment. Passage of a new amendment is a serious and difficult step, but we believe that it is a sensible, necessary means of achieving equal rights for women. A major reform in our legal and constitutional structure is appropriately accomplished by a formal alteration of the fundamental document. Claims of similar magnitude, such as the right to be free from discrimination on account of race, color, national origin, and religion, rest on a constitutional basis. The amending process is designed to elicit national ratification for changes in basic governing values, and those who feel that the Supreme Court has gone too far in recent years in effectuating constitutional change through interpretation should especially welcome the amending process.

Many of the reasons why piecemeal legislation is inadquate are also positive advantages in proceeding by amendment. The major political action — passage and ratification of the Amendment — can be accomplished by a single strong nationwide campaign of limited duration. Once passed, the Amendment will provide an immeditate mandate, a nationally uniform theory of sex equality, and the prospect of permanence to buttress individual and political efforts to end discrimination. The political and psychological impact of adopting a constitutional amendment will be of vital importance in actually realizing the goal of equality. Discriminatory laws, doctrines, attitudes and practices are set deep in our legal system. They are not easily dislodged. The expression of a national commitment by formal adoption of a constitutional amendment will give strength and purpose to efforts to bring about a far-reaching change which, for some, may prove painful.

There are likewise strong reasons for developing a consistent theory and program for women's equality under the aegis of an independent Equal Rights Amendment, rather than by judicial extension of the Equal Protection Clause. An amendment that deals with all sex discrimination, and only sex discrimination, corresponds roughly to the boundaries of a distinct and interrelated set of legal relationships. As already noted, woman's status before the law in one area, such as employment, relates both practically and theoretically to her status in other areas, such as education or responsibility for family support. Coming to grips with the dynamics of discrimination against women requires that we recognize the indications of, the excuses for, and the problems presented by women's inferior status. An understanding of these dynamics in any one field informs and enlightens understanding of sex bias elsewhere in the law. This is because, in the past, the legal and social systems have been permeated with a sometimes inchoate, but nevertheless pervasive, theory of women's inferiority.

Moreover, the achievement of equality under the law for women presents its own special problems. These problems differ in many ways from those involved in eliminating discrimination in other spheres where equal protection theory has been applied. They are closest to those which are raised in the area of race discrimination. Yet even here there are significant differences. Women are not residentially segregated from men. The socioeconomic connections which link different aspects of sexism are not necessarily the same as those that link the many facets of racism. Women are a majority, not a minority; thus, changes in the status of women may affect most of the population, rather than a small part. Furthermore, without a constitutional mandate, women's status will never be accorded the special concern which race now receives because of the history of the Fourteenth Amendment. For these reasons it is important to have a constitutional amendment directed to this specific area of equality, out of which a special body of new law can be created.

The adoption of a constitutional amendment will also have effects that go far beyond the legal system. The demand for equality of rights before the law is only a part of a broader claim by women for the elimination of rigid sex role determinism. And this in turn is part of a more general movement for the recognition of individual potential, the development of new sets of relationships between individuals and groups, and the establishment of institutions which will promote the values and respect the sensibilities of all persons. Adoption of an Equal Rights Amendment would be a sign that the nation is prepared to accept and support new creative forces that are stirring in our society.

2. The Views of the Amendment's Chief Opponent in the Senate

Senator Ervin of North Carolina led the fight in the Senate against the Equal Rights Amendment. The following excerpt from his statement at the hearings is significant because of the combination of legal and analytical arguments with religious and emotional views. Thus, his statements span the spectrum of the opposition to the amendment.

STATEMENT OF SENATOR SAM ERVIN
Hearings on S.J. Res. 61 and S.J. Res. 231 Before the Senate Comm.
on the Judiciary, 91st Cong., 2d Sess. at 2-4, 6-8 (1970)

. . . I am convinced that most of the unfair discriminations against them arise out of the different treatment given men and women in the employment sphere. . . .

Let me point out that Congress has done much in recent years to abolish discriminations of this character insofar as they can be abolished at the Federal level. . . .

Moreover, State legislatures have adopted many enlightened statutes in recent years prohibiting discrimination against women in employment.

If women are not enjoying the full benefit of this Federal and State legislation and these Executive orders of the Federal Government, it is due to a defect in enforcement rather than a want of fair laws and regulations. . . .

[The senator then argues that the Equal Protection Clause of the Fourteenth Amendment could and should be used to abolish sex discrimination. But he notes that this alternative may not be viable, and argues that while there should be a constitutional amendment, it should not be as far-reaching as advocates of the Equal Rights Amendment proposed.]

While I believe that any unfair discriminations which the law makes against women should be abolished by law, I have the abiding conviction that the law should make such distinctions between the sexes as are reasonably necessary for the protection of women and the existence and development of the race.

When He created them, God made physiological and functional differences between men and women. These differences confer upon men a greater capacity to perform arduous and hazardous physical tasks. Some wise people even profess the belief that there may be psychological differences between men and women. To justify their belief, they assert that women possess an intuitive power to distinguish between wisdom and folly, good and evil. . . .

The physiological and functional differences between men and women empower men to beget and women to bear children, who enter life in a state of utter helplessness and ignorance, and who must receive nurture, care, and training at the hands of adults throughout their early years if they and the race are to survive, and if they are to grow mentally and spiritually. From time whereof the memory of mankind runneth not to the contrary, custom and law have imposed upon men the primary responsibility for providing a habitation and a livelihood for their wives and children to enable their wives to make the habitations homes, and to furnish nurture, care, and training to their children during their early years.

In this respect, custom and law reflect the wisdom embodied in the ancient Yiddish proverb that God could not be everywhere, so he made mothers.

The physiological and functional differences between men and women constitute earth's important reality. Without them human life could not exist.

For this reason, any country which ignores these differences when it fashions its institutions and makes its law is woefully lacking in rationality.

Our country has not thus far committed this grievous error. As a consequence, it has established by law the institutions of marriage, the home, and the family, and has adopted some laws making rational distinctions between the respective rights and responsibilities of men and women to make these institutions contribute to the existence and advancement of the race. . . .

Congress and the legislatures of the various States have enacted certain laws based upon the conviction that the physiological and functional differences between men and women make it advisable to exempt or exclude women from certain arduous and hazardous activities in order to protect their health and safety.

Among Federal laws of this nature are the Selective Service Act, which confines compulsory military service to men; the acts of Congress governing the voluntary enlistments in the Armed Forces of the Nation which restrict the right to enlist for combat service to men; and the acts establishing and governing the various service academies which provide for the admission and training of men only.

Among the State laws of this kind are laws which limit hours during which women can work, and bar them from engaging in occupations particularly arduous and hazardous such as mining. . . .

The common law and statutory law of the various States recognize the reality that many women are homemakers and mothers, and by reason of the duties imposed upon them in these capacities, are largely precluded from pursuing gainful occupations or making any provision for their financial security during their declining years. To enable women to do these things and thereby make the existence and development of the race possible, these State laws impose upon husbands the primary responsibility to provide homes and livelihoods for their wives and children, and make them criminally responsible to society and civilly responsible to their wives if they fail to perform this primary responsibility. Moreover, these State laws secure to wives dower and other rights in the property left by their husbands in the event their husbands predecease them in order that they may have some means of support in their declining years. . . .

There are laws in many States which undertake to better the economic position of women. I shall cite only one class of them; namely, the laws which secure to women minimum wages in many employments in many States which have no minimum wage laws for men, and no other laws relating to the earnings of women. . . .

In addition, there are Federal and State laws and regulations which are designed to protect the privacy of males and females. Among these laws are laws requiring separate restrooms for men and women in public buildings, laws requiring separate restrooms for boys and girls in public schools, and laws requiring the segregation of male and female prisoners in jails and penal institutions.

Moreover, there are some State laws which provide that specific institutions of learning shall be operated for men and other institutions of learning shall be operated for women.

If the House-passed equal rights amendment should be interpreted by the Supreme Court to forbid legal distinctions between men and women, it would annul all existing laws of this nature, and rob Congress and the States of the constitutional power to enact any similar laws at any time in the future. . . .

For these reasons, I have drafted a substitute Federal equal rights amendment which will accomplish the undoubted purpose of the advocates of the House-passed equal rights amendment:

"Equality of rights under the law shall not be denied or abridged by the United States or by any State on account of sex."

The second sentence states that — "This article shall not impair, however, the validity of any law of the United States or any State which exempts women from compulsory military service or which is reasonably designed to promote the health, safety, privacy, education, or economic welfare of women, or to enable them to perform their duties as homemakers or mothers."

Candor compels me to confess that I cannot comprehend how any rational being in America can find any objection to this provision. . . .

I respectfully submit that the Senate of the United States ought to act with great deliberation in writing a proposed constitutional amendment for submission to the States. When an amendment is added to the Constitution it has an infinite capacity to bless America if it be wise, and an infinite capacity to curse America if it be unwise. . . .

NOTE

Under Senator Ervin's substitute amendment, quoted above, which provides that laws remain unimpaired that enable women "to perform their duties as homemakers or mothers," would a law excluding women from jury service be unconstitutional? Would a law that prohibited participation of women in dangerous sports survive the amendment?

3. Legislation as an Alternative to the Amendment

a. An Opponent's Preference for Legislation

The idea of approaching sex discrimination through various pieces of legislation —in conjunction with the Fourteenth Amendment — was the alternative most often put forth by those who opposed the Equal Rights Amendment. The best-known and most scholarly analysis preferring legislative to constitutional change was offered by the amendment's long-time opponent Paul A. Freund, during Senate hearings. The material reprinted here is taken from Freund's expansion of his testimony for a symposium on the Equal Rights Amendment.

FREUND
THE EQUAL RIGHTS AMENDMENT IS NOT THE WAY
6 Harv. Civ. Rights–Civ. Lib. L. Rev. 234-242 (1971)

The issue has always been over choice of means, not over ends. The objective is to nullify those vestigial laws that work an injustice to women, that are exploitative or impose oppressive discriminations on account of sex. Although such laws have been progressively superseded or held to be violative of equal protection,[2] some of these laws still disfigure our legal codes. Beyond this, the Women's Rights Movement seeks to achieve equal opportunity and equal treatment for women in business, professional, domestic, and political relationships, but unless equality is denied by a public agency

---

2. E.g., United States ex rel. Robinson v. York, 281 F. Supp. 8 (D. Conn. 1968); Commonwealth v. Daniel, 430 Pa. 642, 243 A.2d 400 (1968). Both cases invalidated statutes providing for more severe penalties for women than for men convicted of certain offenses.

or because of a law the Equal Rights Amendment by its terms has no application. If we want to see more women in law firms, in the medical profession, in the Cabinet —and I, for one, do — we must turn elsewhere than to the proposed amendment. The point is not the smug argument that we must change hearts and minds and attitudes (though that too is involved) rather than look to law; the point is that within the realm of law we have to compare the effects and effectiveness of a constitutional amendment on the one hand and the mandate of congressional legislation and judicial decisions on the other.

The proposed amendment attempts to impose a single standard of sameness on the position of the sexes in all the multifarious roles regulated by law — marital support, parental obligations, social security, industrial employment, activities in public schools, and military service — to mention the most prominent. . . . The alternative legal course is to achieve changes in the relative position of women through paramount federal standards or to overcome invidious classifications on the ground that they are presently unconstitutional. The choice resembles that in medicine between a single broad-spectrum drug with uncertain and unwanted side-effects and a selection of specific pills for specific ills.

In comparing the problem of choice twenty-five years ago and today, I concluded that so far from the case for amendment being strengthened, the choice of the alternative course was even more strongly indicated. The reason is that during the intervening years both the scope of congressional power and the promise of judicial redress have been made clearer, while the dangers implicit in the amendment remain as before. Congressional power under the commerce clause, as the civil-rights legislation shows, is adequate to deal with discrimination (whether private or governmental) based on sex, as on race. . . .

The paucity of contemporary Supreme Court decisions can be ascribed partly to the failure of women's groups to mount a series of selected test cases challenging forms of discrimination, and in part to the fact that some discriminatory laws have been held invalid by lower courts, without further appeal.[8] One Supreme Court decision, however, is a target of indignation by proponents of the amendment: Hoyt v. Florida.[9] The Court held by a divided vote that a state law might relieve women of jury duty unless they signified their willingness to serve, while requiring men to present specific reasons for excusal. Experience had shown that a much higher percentage of women than of men had in fact secured excusal on an individual basis, because of household duties, and the law was tailored to reflect this experience in a differentiated procedure based on a differentiated presumption of fact. As the Justices were divided, so, it seems to me, can reasonable persons of good will disagree among themselves on the decision. But to regard the decision as an invidious discrimination or a degrading affront to women that calls for redress by a constitutional amendment is surely far-fetched and obsessively sensitive. The classification more nearly resembled a factual generalization based on age or height than on race or color.

. . . The energies that have been spent for forty years in a effort to secure the submission of the amendment by Congress to the states would have to be followed, even if ultimately successful, by efforts to revise the laws in a satisfactory way. It is hard to believe that this preliminary struggle to obtain the support of two-thirds of Congress and three-fourths of the states is other than a diversion of energy from the essential task of revising the laws themselves. . . .

Still, it may be suggested, the amendment would serve importantly as a symbol

8. See note 2 supra. See also Kirstein v. Rector and Visitors of the Univ. of Va., 309 F. Supp. 184 (E.D. Va. 1970) (requiring admission of women to all-male campus of the University of Virginia, where facilities open to women were not equal); White v. Crook, 251 F. Supp. 401 (M.D. Ala. 1966) (holding invalid the exclusion of women from jury service).

9. 368 U.S. 57 (1961).

— a symbol that the nation has made a commitment to justice for women under law. One gets the impression that much of the drive for the amendment owes its force to this psychological wellspring. The value of a symbol, however, lies precisely in the fact that it is not to be taken literally, that it is not meant to be analysed closely for its exact implications. A concurrent resolution of Congress, expressing the general sentiment of that body, would be an appropriate vehicle for promulgating a symbol. When, however, we are presented with a proposed amendment to our fundamental law, binding on federal and state governments, on judges, legislatures, and executives, we are entitled to inquire more circumspectly into the operational meaning and effects of the symbol. Lawyers, in particular, have an obligation to ask these questions and to weigh the answers that are given. For if the amendment is not only a needless misdirection of effort in the quest for justice, but one which would produce anomalies, confusion, and injustices, no symbolic value could justify its adoption. We turn, then, to these issues of meaning and effect. . . .

A doctrinaire equality . . . is apparently the theme of the amendment. And so women must be admitted to West Point on a parity with men; women must be conscripted for military service equally with men (though classification on an individual basis for assignment to duties would be valid, it is asserted);[12] girls must be eligible for the same athletic teams as boys in the public schools and state universities; Boston Boys' Latin School and Girls' Latin School must merge (not simply be brought into parity); and life insurance commissioners may not continue to approve lower life insurance premiums for women (based on greater life expectancy)[13] — all by command of the Federal Constitution. . . .

Special scrutiny should be given to the field of domestic relations, with its complex relationships of marital duties and parental responsibilities. Every state makes a husband liable for the support of his wife, without regard to the ability of the wife to support herself. The obligation of the wife to support her husband is obviously not identical to this; if it were, each would be duty bound to support the other. Instead, the wife's duty varies from state to state. In some jurisdictions there is no obligation on the wife, even if the husband is unable to support himself. In others, the wife does have a duty of support in such a case.

In 1968 a recommendation on the subject was made by a Task Force on Family Law and Policy of the Citizen's Advisory Council on the Status of Women, a group that supports the amendment. The recommendation was a progressive and equitable one: "A wife should be responsible for the support of her husband if he is unable to support himself and she is able to furnish such support."[14] So far, so good. But what would be the effect on the rule fixing the husband's duty? Some members of the Task Force, but only some, took a position of reciprocity consistent with the principle of the amendment: "Some of the task force members believed that a husband should only be liable for the support of a wife who is unable to support herself due to physical handicap, acute stage of family responsibility or unemployability on other grounds."[15] This solution, dictated by the Equal Rights Amendment, would be contrary to the law of every state. Moreover, the support owed solely to "a wife who is unable to support herself" might be further eroded by the establishment of child-care centers. Where such centers are created, presumably a wife with small children would no longer be "unable" to support herself through employment, and so under the constitutional rule of reciprocity would lose the right of support from her husband. Thus child-care centers could by a reflexive effect

12. Citizens' Advisory Council on the Status of Women, A Memorandum on the Proposed Equal Rights Amendment to the Constitution, 116 Cong. Rec. E2588, E2590, E2591 (daily ed. Mar. 26, 1970).

13. Cf. Gruenwald v. Gardner, 390 F.2d 591 (2d Cir.), *cert. denied,* 393 U.S. 982 (1968) (higher Social Security retirement benefits for women sustained). Presumably the amendment would require a different result.

14. Citizens' Advisory Council on the Status of Women, Report of the Task Force on Family Law and Policy 9 (1968).

15. Ibid.

on the mother's ability to work outside the home, constitute a threat rather than an opportunity. Of course the spouses would be free to enter into an agreement regarding support, but the law is necessarily concerned with rules and presumptions in the absence of agreement. . . .

It is sometimes said that a rigid requirement of equality is no less proper for the sexes than for the races, and no less workable. But the moral dimensions of the concept of equality are clearly not the same in the two cases. To hold separate Olympic competitions for whites and blacks would be deeply repugnant to our sensibilities. Do we — should we — feel the same repugnance, that same sense of degradation, at the separate competitions for men and women? A school system offering a triple option based on race — all-white, all-black, and mixed schools — would elevate freedom of choice over equal protection in an impermissible way. Are we prepared to pass that judgment as readily on a school system that offers a choice of boys', girls', and coeducational schools? . . . One of the prime targets of the equal-rights movement has been the color-segregated public rest room. Whether segregation by sex would meet the same condemnation is at least a fair question to test the legal assimilation of racism and "sexism."

The answer proffered is that a counter-principle, a constitutional right of privacy, would be invoked at this point.[16] But this is only to restate the problem, which is whether there are not considerations other than identical treatment that ought to be taken into account in the various contexts of relations between the sexes. If privacy is one such consideration, though unexpressed in the amendment, when will it prevail and when will it not? Is privacy in fact the only unexpressed countervailing interest? Freedom of association is a constitutional right enjoying recognition even longer and firmer than privacy. It has been invoked without avail, as has the interest in privacy, to blunt the force of equal protection in the field of racial separation. Is it to have greater recognition (as in the area of public education) where relations between the sexes are concerned? Moreover, interests more social, less individual, than privacy or association are actually involved. If a public school conducts separate physical education classes for boys and girls, or a prison maintains separate cells for men and women, would the validity of the separation depend on a claim of privacy? If the pupils or prisoners waived any interest in privacy and wished to amalgamate the classes or the cells, would the school or the prison be required to conform? Or could the law respect a wider community sentiment that separateness was fitter and not invidious?

Constitutional amendments, like other laws, cannot always anticipate all the questions that may arise under them. Remote and esoteric problems may have to be faced in due course. But when basic, commonplace, recurring questions are raised and left unanswered by text or legislative history, one can only infer a want of candor or of comprehension.

I would not wish to leave the subject on a purely negative note. My concern, as I have said, is with the method proposed, which is too simplistic for the living issues at stake. It remains, then, to suggest alternative approaches. A great deal can be done through the regular legislative process in Congress. Concrete guidelines are set forth in an April 1970 Report of the President's Task Force on Women's Rights and Responsibilities. After recommending support of the proposed amendment, the Report urges that

— Title VII of the Civil Rights Act of 1964 be amended to empower the EEOC to enforce the law, and to extend coverage to state and local governments and to teachers;

— Titles IV and IX of the Civil Rights Act be amended to authorize the Attorney General to assist in cases involving discrimination against girls and women in access to public education, and to require the Office of Education to make a survey on that subject;

— Title II of the Civil Rights Act be amended to prohibit discrimination because of sex in public accommodations;

16. Emerson, In Support of the Equal Rights Amendment, 6 Harv Civ. Rights–Civ. Lib. L. Rev. 225, 231 (1971).

— the jurisdiction of the Civil Rights Commission be extended to include denial of civil rights because of sex;

— the Fair Labor Standards Act be amended to extend coverage of its equal pay provisions to executive, administrative, and professional employees;

— liberalized provisions be made for child-care facilities.[17]

It is an extensive, important, and thoughtful set of proposals. If a two-thirds majority can be found for the abstraction of the Equal Rights Amendment, it would be puzzling to know why a simple majority could not even more readily be found to approve this concrete program.

In addition, Congress would give a vigorous and valuable lead by enacting model laws for the District of Columbia in the fields of labor legislation and domestic relations.

Moreover, a few significant decisions of the Supreme Court in well-chosen cases under the fourteenth amendment would have a highly salutary effect. And decisions under Title VII of the Civil Rights Act will clarify the role of state laws regulating employment in light of the statutory concept of bona fide occupational qualifications.[18]

Finally, Congress can exercise its enforcement power under the fourteenth amendment to identify and displace state laws that in its judgment work an unreasonable discrimination based on sex.

NOTES

(1) Does Freund Support the Eradication of Sex-Discriminatory Laws and Practices? Freund introduces his argument with the idea that "[t]he issue has always been over choice of means, not over ends." In fact, although he alleges that he is in agreement with ERA proponents on ends, a careful reading of his examples and rhetoric reveals that often he is not. Sex integration of public high schools is an example. Most proponents of ERA favor the total sex integration of public schools; Freund holds it up as a clearly undesirable consequence, and implies that proponents must be unaware of the likely impact of the amendment in this and other areas — otherwise they would agree with him and oppose the ERA. It is typical of debates on the amendment that there is alleged but unreal agreement on goals between opponents and proponents.

(2) Ignoring Alternate Solutions. Notice how Freund first narrows the options and then attacks the amendment on the basis of his own narrow interpretation. Thus, his argument on support hinges on acceptance of a recommendation made by some of the members of the Citizen's Advisory Council on the Status of Women that husbands and wives should each be responsible for the support of the other only if that person is unable to support himself/herself. Stating that the ERA would dictate the result proposed by the council members, he attacks their suggestion. Of course there are other possibilities for conforming support laws to the ERA; see Chapter Three, VII. Freund presents no explanation of why the judiciary would be expected to reach the result he hypothesizes. And legislatures are free to select among many alternatives — the only requirement is that the solution be sex-neutral.

b. Conflicting Views Within One Bar Association

Scholarly and professional differences on the appropriateness of the Equal Rights Amendment are sharply illustrated by conflicting reports issued by three subject matter

17. President's Task Force on Women's Rights and Responsibilities, A Matter of Simple Justice iv-v (1970).

18. See Phillips v. Martin Marietta Corp., 39 U.S.L.W. 4160, 4160-61 (U.S. Jan. 25, 1971) (Marshall, J., concurring).

committees of the Association of the Bar of the City of New York. Two of the association's committees, the Committee on Civil Rights and the Special Committee on Sex and Law, issued a joint report strongly preferring the Equal Rights Amendment — in contrast to and in part stimulated by the earlier report of the Committee on Federal Legislation recommending a legislative approach to curing sex discrimination.

Significantly, the association originally referred the Equal Rights Amendment to its Committee on Federal Legislation instead of its Committee on Civil Rights. In its report, the Federal Legislation Committee succinctly stated its reasons for preferring the statutory approach.[15]

> The problems to which the proposed amendments direct themselves are substantially better dealt with by a broad statutory declaration of principle, coupled with specific, carefully drafted legislation directed at specific types of discrimination, and developed by judicial decision. Constitutional amendments afford an unsatisfactory remedy; at the same time, the alteration of the Constitution for this purpose threatens the integrity of the Fourteenth Amendment in other areas.
>
> Considering the nature of the existing discriminations and the judicial treatment being accorded to them, we have concluded that:
>
> Those discriminations which would be clearly invalidated by both of the proposed amendments could be stricken under the equal protection clause of the Fourteenth Amendment without the need for further constitutional amendment, particularly if the development of the law in this area were encouraged by a statute embodying a Congressional declaration of principle.
>
> Congress has already taken some action with respect to discrimination in employment and recent decisions show that such legislation has been having a beneficial effect. . . .

But the association's Civil Rights Committee finally did study the amendment, after a new study was initiated by the Special Committee on Sex and Law, formed under pressure from lawyers and law students within the association. Within the context of a more general pro-amendment analysis, these two committees responded to the views of the Federal Legislation Committee that a statutory approach was to be preferred:[16]

> Section 5 of the Fourteenth Amendment, which empowers Congress to enforce the provisions of that Amendment "by appropriate legislation" would probably be the basis for federal legislation in the equal rights area, although civil rights enactments have also been based on the Commerce Clause.
>
> It has been suggested that an Act of Congress pursuant to Section 5 would be preferable to the Equal Rights Amendment, because it would be more "specific" and therefore lead to less litigation. That such a statute might be more specific and therefore limited to particular areas (for example, employment), hardly recommends it as a vehicle for eliminating sex role determinism which pervades all areas.
>
> Moreover, a federal statute would lead to more litigation than the Amendment, not less. First, it is indisputable that challenges to its constitutionality could be made. Second, passage of a statute would lead to the customary search for exceptions to the rule, which the breadth of a constitutional amendment avoids.
>
> The Section 5 approach is less suitable than the Amendment for the further reason that sex-based laws involve many areas of traditional state concern, such as property and divorce laws. A state-based concurrence to the commitment to equal rights is therefore of particular importance to insure implementation.
>
> Doubt as to the feasibility of the statutory route has also arisen because the Supreme Court has recently held in Oregon v. Mitchell [400 U.S. 112 (1971)] that

15. Committee on Federal Legislation, Amending The Constitution To Prohibit State Discrimination Based on Sex, 26 Record of the Association of the Bar of the City of New York 77, 77–78 (1971).

16. Committee on Civil Rights and Special Committee on Sex and Law, The Equal Rights Amendment, 27 id. 172, 174–175 (1972).

Congress had no power under Section 5 of the 14th Amendment to pass legislation lowering the voting age in state elections to 18, since the legislation was not aimed at eliminating racial discrimination. This decision suggests that Section 5 may not authorize legislation in areas traditionally reserved to the states in their regulation of conduct, unless specifically directed to the elimination of racial discrimination.

C. THE EFFECT OF THE AMENDMENT

The heart of the debate concerning the Equal Rights Amendment has always been whether it would lead to a truly desirable equality or to irrational results, even causing hardships to women. The argument over results necessarily looks to the courts as arbiters of the amendment's meaning. Indeed, one of the arguments against the amendment was that litigating its meaning would unjustifiably burden the federal courts. Furthermore, according to the opponents of the ERA, uncertainty as to its meaning would produce absurd and inconsistent judicial decisions. But legislatures may well choose to conform statutory law to the amendment's command without judicial intervention. The remaining discriminatory statutes will inevitably be challenged, but the process need not be chaotic or uncertain. Fortunately, in the last few years, legislators, feminists, and legal scholars have developed theories of the amendment's meaning to guide judicial construction, making interpretation more certain and reducing the burden on courts and legislatures alike. What follows is an interpretation of the amendment that is likely to be influential because it presents a cohesive theory of the amendment's meaning which figured prominently in the congressional debates.

1. A Broad Theory of the Meaning of the Amendment

BROWN, EMERSON, FALK, AND FREEDMAN
THE EQUAL RIGHTS AMENDMENT:
A CONSTITUTIONAL BASIS
FOR EQUAL RIGHTS FOR WOMEN
80 Yale L.J. 871, 888-920 (1971)

III. THE CONSTITUTIONAL FRAMEWORK

The Equal Rights Amendment embodies fundamental principles which are derived from the purposes the Amendment is designed to achieve, the operational conditions necessary to attain those objectives, and the existing context of constitutional doctrine. It is not possible here to do more than examine these principles in a general and preliminary way. They can be fully developed only by the usual process of constitutional adjudication.[41]

A. The Basic Principle

The basic principle of the Equal Rights Amendment is that sex is not a permissible factor in determining the legal rights of women, or of men. This means that the treatment of any person by the law may not be based upon the circumstance that such person is of one sex or the other. The law does, of course, impose different benefits or different burdens upon different members of the society. That differentiation in treatment may

41. Discussions of the legal foundations of equal rights for women which we have found particularly helpful, and upon which we have attempted to build in this article, include Murray & Eastwood, Jane Crow and the Law: Sex Discrimination and Title VII, 34 Geo. Wash. L. Rev. 232 (1965); Citizens' Advisory Council on the Status of Women, The Proposed Equal Rights Amendment to the United States Constitution (1970); and the testimony of several witnesses in Hearings on S.J. Res. 61 and S.J. Res. 231 Before the Senate Comm. on the Judiciary, 91st Cong., 2d Sess. (1970).

rest upon particular characteristics or traits of the persons affected, such as strength, intelligence, and the like. But under the Equal Rights Amendment the existence of such a characteristic or trait to a greater degree in one sex does not justify classification by sex rather than by the particular characteristic or trait. Likewise the law may make different rules for some people than for others on the basis of the activity they are engaged in or the function they perform. But the fact that in our present society members of one sex are more likely to be found in a particular activity or to perform a particular function does not allow the law to fix legal rights by virtue of membership in that sex. In short, sex is a prohibited classification.

This principle is already widely accepted with respect to many activities. To take an example, virtually everybody would consider it unjust and irrational to provide by law that a person could not be admitted to the practice of law because of his or her sex. The reason is that admission to the bar ought to depend upon legal training, competence in the law, moral character, and similar factors. Some women meet these qualifications and some do not; some men meet these qualifications and some do not. But the issue should be decided on an individual, not a group, basis. And in such a decision, the fact of being male or female is irrelevant. This remains true whether or not there are more men than women who qualify. It likewise would remain true even if there were no women who presently were qualified because women potentially qualify and might do so under different conditions of education or upbringing. The law owes an obligation to treat females as persons, not statistical abstractions.

What is true of admission to the bar is true of all forms of legal rights. If we examine the various areas of the law one by one most of us will reach the same conclusion in each case. Sex is an inadmissible category by which to determine the right to a minimum wage, the custody of children, the obligation to refrain from taking the life of another, and so on. The law should be based on the right to a living wage for each person, the welfare of the particular child, the protection of citizens from murder, and not on a vast overclassification by sex.

This basic principle of the Equal Rights Amendment derives from two fundamental judgments inherent in the decision to eliminate discrimination against women from our legal system. First, the Amendment embodies the moral judgment that women as a group may no longer be relegated to an inferior position in our society. They are entitled to an equal status with men. This moral decision implies a further practical judgment — that such an equal status can be achieved only by merging the rights of men and women into a "single system of equality." By this we mean that the decision to eliminate women's historically inferior social position requires the prohibition of sex classification in the law. We reject an alternative conception of "equality" — that women's separate place should be "upgraded" in social status and material rewards. As already noted, such a dual system, in which women would have a different but "equal" status, has proven to be illusory. There is no reason to suppose that the present inferior status of women would materially change through adoption of a constitutional amendment which attempted to maintain a dual system of sex-based rights and responsibilities.

Second, the basic principle of the Equal Rights Amendment flows from the set of moral and practical judgments that have been made with respect to the fundamental rights of the individual in our society. Classification by sex, apart from the single situation where a physical characteristic unique to one sex is involved (as will be discussed in the next subsection), is always an overclassification. A permissible legislative goal is always related to characteristics or functions which are or can be common to both sexes. But in a classification by sex all women or all men are included or excluded regardless of the extent to which some members of each sex possess the relevant characteristics or perform the relevant function. Such a result is in direct conflict with the basic concern of our society with the individual, and with the rights of each individual to develop his or her own potentiality. It negates all our values of individual self-fulfillment.

To achieve the values of group equality and individual self-fulfillment, the principle of the Amendment must be applied comprehensively and without exceptions. Arguments that administrative efficiency or other countervailing interests justify limiting the Amendment contradict its basic premises.

First, the decision to protect the value of individual self-fulfillment embraces the judgment that efficiency in government operations is not a sufficient reason to ignore individual differences. In other words, the government cannot rely upon the administrative technique of grouping or averaging where the classification is by sex. There are some situations where it is permissible for the law to operate on the basis of groups or averages. For example, individuals can be classified by age — under 21 or over 65 —even though there are individual differences as to maturity or senility.[42] In such cases individual rights are sacrificed to administrative efficiency. But the Equal Rights Amendment makes the constitutional judgment that this is not acceptable where the factor of sex is concerned. Here, whatever the price in efficiency, the classification must be made on some other basis.[43]

Examples of this judgment appear frequently in our law today. Thus the assertion that some women leave jobs to marry or to move with their husbands does not constitute ground for discrimination on account of sex in government employment under Executive Order 11478, or in private employment under Title VII of the Civil Rights Act of 1964.[44] A balance of values has been struck. The decision has been made not to penalize all women because of a behavior pattern characteristic of some women. And any greater efficiency in a classification based on sex, rather than on an individual basis, has been excluded as a justifying factor. The Equal Rights Amendment makes the same judgment, but on a broader scale and in constitutional terms.[45]

Second, the Equal Rights Amendment embodies the moral and practical judgment that the prohibition against the use of sex as a basis for differential treatment applies to all areas of legal rights. To the extent that any exception is made, the values sought by the Amendment are undercut; women as a group are thrust into a subordinate status and women as individuals are denied the basic right to be considered in terms of their own capacities and experience. And, as noted above, the interrelated character of a system of legal equality for the sexes makes a rule of universal application imperative. No one exception, resulting in unequal treatment for women, can be confined in its impact to one area alone. Equal rights for women, as for races, is a unity.

A third, equally decisive consideration leads to the same conclusion. There is no objective basis available to courts or legislatures upon which differential treatment of men and women could be evaluated. As already pointed out, such judgments can be made only in terms of a dual system of rights, the rights of women being grounded in one set of values and the rights of men in another. Not only is such a system inevitably repressive of one group, but it affords no standard of comparison between groups. For example, in Hoyt v. Florida[46] the Supreme Court accepted a value system for women which viewed them as "the center of home and family life," and undertook to be "fair" to women by excusing them from jury service, a "benefit" not given to men. Upon what basis can it be said, however, that this outcome puts men and women upon a level of

42. But see Note, Too Old To Work: The Constitutionality of Mandatory Retirement Plans, 44 S. Cal. L. Rev. 150 (1970).

43. It seems highly probable that, as to most characteristics which the law takes into account, the differences within each sex are greater than the differences in average between the sexes. The justification for the Equal Rights Amendment, however, stands without regard to this factual assumption.

44. Executive Order 11478, 3 C.F.R. 133 (1969 Comp.), 42 U.S.C. §2000e (Supp. V, 1969); Title VII of the Civil Rights Act of 1964, 42 U.S.C. §§2000e to 2000e-15 (1964).

45. For discussion of the problem as it arises in the determination of insurance rates based on statistical differences between men and women, see Developments in the Law — Employment Discrimination and Title VII of the Civil Rights Act of 1964, 84 Harv. L. Rev. 1109, 1172-76 (1971) [hereinafter cited as Developments — Title VII].

46. 368 U.S. 57 (1961). . . .

"equality"? Nor did the Court, in making that decision, attempt to weigh the countless other legal differentiations between the sexes in order to strike an overall balance of "equality."

Fourth, the judgment as to whether differential treatment is justified or not would rest in the hands of the very legislatures and courts which maintain the existing system of discrimination. The process by which they make that judgment involves the same discretionary weighing of preferences as has resulted in the present inequality. This is true whether the standard of judging is "reasonable classification," "suspect classification," or "fundamental interest." There is no reason to believe that such a decision-making apparatus will end up in a substantially different position from what we have now. Only an unequivocal ban against taking sex into account supplies a rule adequate to achieve the objectives of the Amendment.

From this analysis it follows that the constitutional mandate must be absolute. The issue under the Equal Rights Amendment cannot be different but equal, reasonable or unreasonable classification, suspect classification, fundamental interest, or the demands of administrative expediency. Equality of rights means that sex is not a factor. This at least is the premise of the Equal Rights Amendment. And this premise should be clearly expressed as the intention of Congress in submitting the Amendment to the states for ratification.

It is argued that this position is naive, impractical, and leads to absurd results. Various examples of supposedly outlandish consequences are given. Most of these examples, such as those relating to public toilet facilities, are dramatic but are diversions from the major issues. On the central problems — property rights, marriage and divorce, the right to engage in an occupation, freedom from discrimination in employment and education — the burden of persuasion is on those who would impose different treatment on the basis of sex. Before a judgment on the feasibility of the Equal Rights Amendment can be made, however, it is necessary to pursue the legal analysis somewhat further.

B. Laws Dealing with Physical Characteristics Unique to One Sex

The fundamental legal principle underlying the Equal Rights Amendment, then, is that the law must deal with particular attributes of individuals, not with a classification based on the broad and impermissible attribute of sex. This principle, however, does not preclude legislation (or other official action) which regulates, takes into account, or otherwise deals with a physical characteristic unique to one sex. In this situation it might be said that, in a certain sense, the individual obtains a benefit or is subject to a restriction because he or she belongs to one or the other sex. Thus a law relating to wet nurses would cover only women, and a law regulating the donation of sperm would restrict only men. Legislation of this kind does not, however, deny equal rights to the other sex. So long as the law deals only with a characteristic found in all (or some) women but *no* men, or in all (or some) men but *no* women, it does not ignore individual characteristics found in both sexes in favor of an average based on one sex. Hence such legislation does not, without more, violate the basic principle of the Equal Rights Amendment.

This subsidiary principle is limited to *physical* characteristics and does not extend to psychological, social or other characteristics of the sexes. The reason is that, so far as appears, it is only physical characteristics which can be said with any assurance to be unique to one sex. So-called "secondary" biological characteristics and cultural characteristics are found to some degree in both sexes. Thus active or passive attitudes, or interests in literature or athletics, like degrees of physical strength or weakness, appear in members of each sex. Differences in treatment attributable to such shared traits must be based upon their existence in the individual, not upon a classification by sex.

Instances of laws directly concerned with physical differences found only in one sex are relatively rare. Yet they include many of the examples cited by opponents of the Equal Rights Amendment as demonstrating its nonviability. Thus not only would laws concerning wet nurses and sperm donors be permissible, but so would laws establishing medical leave for childbearing (though leave for child*rearing* would have to apply to both sexes). Laws punishing forcible rape, which relate to a unique physical characteristic of men and women, would remain in effect. So would legislation relating to determination of fatherhood.

Application of this subsidiary principle raises questions which should be carefully scrutinized by the courts. For one thing, while differentiation on the basis of a unique physical characteristic does not impair the right of a man or a woman to be judged as an individual, it does introduce elements of a dual system of rights. That result is inevitable. Where there is no common factor shared by both sexes, equality of treatment must necessarily rest upon considerations not strictly comparable as between the sexes. This area of duality is very limited and would not seriously undermine the much more extensive areas where the unitary system prevails. But the courts should be aware of the danger.

The danger is increased by the possibility of evasion in the application of the subsidiary principle. Unless that principle is strictly limited to situations where the regulation is closely, directly and narrowly confined to the unique physical characteristic, it could be used to justify laws that in overall effect seriously discriminate against one sex. A court faced with deciding whether a law relating to a unique physical characteristic was a subterfuge would look to a series of standards of relevance and necessity. These standards are the ones courts now consider when they are reviewing, under the doctrine of strict scrutiny, laws which may conflict with fundamental constitutional rights. It is possible to identify at least six factors that a court would weigh in determining whether the necessary close, direct, and narrow relationship existed between the unique physical characteristic and the provision in question.

These factors can be explained most easily in terms of a hypothetical case: a government regulation to reduce absenteeism at policy-making levels by barring women from certain jobs. Such a regulation might be defended by the government as being based on a unique physical characteristic of women, namely, the potential for becoming pregnant, and the consequent need for leaves of absence for childbearing.[47] In considering whether to sustain this rule, a court would weigh the following factors on the basis of factual evidence presented by the party attempting to justify the regulation:

First, the proportion of women who actually have the characteristic in question. In this case, the issue would be the number of women eligible for the jobs who were actually capable of becoming pregnant.

Second, the relationship between the characteristic and the problem. In this example, the court would inquire about the proportion of women who were likely actually to become pregnant and also choose to bear the child; the length of time most women would require for childbearing; and the extent to which a leave of this duration would actually interfere with an important governmental function.

Third, the proportion of the problem attributable to the unique physical characteristic of women. Here the court would consider the fact that only a small proportion of the total problem of long-term absenteeism and job transfer was caused by pregnancy; it would inquire into the proportion which was attributable to other factors, such as military duty, political disagreements, childrearing, job mobility, and disability due to illness or accidents, all of which cause absenteeism among workers of both sexes.

Fourth, the proportion of the problem eliminated by the solution. Here it would seem clear that the solution of not hiring women would eliminate absenteeism caused by pregnancy, but as indicated in the third factor, this would only be a small proportion of the overall problem of absenteeism.

Fifth, the availability of less drastic alternatives. "Less drastic" in this sense may

---

47. The possibility that a woman who became a mother might leave the workforce altogether for child-*rearing* is not based on a unique physical characteristic of women, and therefore would not even be considered in relation to the unique physical characteristics tests.

mean first, less onerous to the person being restricted; second, more limited in the number of persons or opportunities affected; or third, not based on sex at all, or "sex neutral." To determine whether less drastic alternatives were available to deal with the problem, the court would inquire into the feasibility of individualized procedures for screening out those who were likely to be absent, and the possibility of alternative devices such as job pairing and substitution.[48]

Sixth, the importance of the problem ostensibly being solved, as compared with the costs of the least drastic solution. Here the question would be the seriousness of the harm and dislocation that would actually result if an employee in one of the covered positions were absent for the length of time necessary for childbearing. The problem as thus measured would be balanced against the costs of the solution, in this case the continuation of sexual stereotyping and overbroad discrimination that would be caused by excluding all women from the jobs covered by the regulation.

How the courts would balance each of these factors is difficult to predict in advance of actual adjudication, although in the example given it is obvious that the combined weight of the overbroad classification by sex and the marginal relationship of the unique physical characteristic of pregnancy to the problem of absenteeism would require invalidation of the regulation. In any case, all of these considerations are of the kind that courts constantly deal with in similar cases where reliance upon a legitimate factor is used to achieve illegitimate ends. And however the borderline cases are resolved, the margin of error is not likely to be so large as to jeopardize the basic principle.

C. Classifications Based on Attributes Which May Be Found in Either Sex

Classifications are a necessary part of lawmaking and the Equal Rights Amendment does not, of course, require an end to all classifications based on recognition of the differences among people. The Amendment forbids the use of sex as a basis for legal differentiation, but it permits the legislature to continue to classify on the basis of real differences in the life situations and characteristics of individuals. It is important to keep in mind the nature and uses of these legitimate classifications as well as to note the possibility of their being employed to evade or nullify the prohibition against sex classification.

As pointed out above, classifications based upon sex necessarily include members of one sex who should not be covered, or exclude members of the other sex who should be covered, by a given law. Unfortunately, legislatures have traditionally used sex classifications as shorthand for other classifications which, although they are more precise, are also somewhat more difficult to administer. Because sex classifications were acceptable, they were often employed merely because members of one sex actually or apparently predominated in the smaller group to whom the law was really directed, whether or not a narrower more equitable classification was practicable. This common practice reinforced the pre-existing majority of one sex in the regulated or protected activity; for example, if only women can get extensive leaves for childrearing, it becomes economically impossible for men to stay home to care for children while thier wives work. Hence sex classifications begin to seem both natural and essential to sound legislation in many areas of public concern.

Elimination of sex classifications by the Equal Rights Amendment, however, does not prohibit the legislature from achieving legitimate purposes by other methods of

---

48. One commentator has suggested that at least in the First Amendment area, the doctrine of "less drastic means" has little viability beyond traditional legal assumptions about the impact of vague criminal statutes. See Note, Less Drastic Means and the First Amendment, 78 Yale, L.J. 464, 472-74 (1969). On the other hand, the U.S. Court of Appeals for the District of Columbia Circuit has used the concept of less drastic means in reviewing the problems of confinement in mental institutions; see Covington v. Harris, 419 F.2d 617 (D.C. Cir. 1969), and Lake v. Cameron, 364 F.2d 657 (D.C. Cir. 1966). See also the development of judicial concepts of "job validation" of tests under Title VII in Griggs v. Duke Power Co., 401 U.S. 424 (1971), and cases discussed in Developments — Title VII, supra note 45, at 1120-1140.

classification. In 1965, Pauli Murray and Mary Eastwood proposed the substitution of realistic "functional" classifications for sex classification. They argued that:

"If laws classifying persons by sex were prohibited by the Constitution, and if it were made clear that laws recognizing functions, *if performed,* are not based on sex per se, much of the confusion as to the legal status of women would be eliminated."[49]

This analysis need not be limited to literal "functions." It also applies to classifications based on prior education and training, experience, skills, or other measurable traits and abilities. The term "functional classifications" can thus be used to refer to all non-sex-based classifications.

A legislature taking this approach would make laws which reflected and related to the changing reality of individual lives and potentials, regardless of sex, instead of legislating women into conformity with each other, and pretending that all men are different from all women in terms of a given legislative purpose. For example, a legislature could use a non-sex-based classification to provide job retraining to the class of individuals who had been absent from the labor force for a specified number of years, for whatever reason. The functional basis would allow both men and women in that situation to get necessary encouragement to re-enter the labor force, unlike a blanket sex preference which would unfairly select out for special treatment individuals of one sex to the exclusion of the other. Likewise, a rule allowing workers to take sick leave when any member of their household was sick would be an appropriate functional classification. Unlike a rule allowing such leave only to mothers, which denies parents the opportunity to choose which of them will stay home, the functional rule is neutral, allowing workers to choose whether they wish to follow traditional sex-roles or share childrearing and other familial responsibilities. A system of functional classification may thus be utilized in ways which achieve important social objectives without discriminating against individuals on account of their sex.

On the other hand such classifications, though formulated without explicit sex reference, may in practice fall more heavily on one sex than the other. This opens the possibility that non-sex-based classifications can be used to circumvent the Equal Rights Amendment. The fact that women's life situations, on the average, are different from those of men, partly or largely because of past discrimination, makes such an outcome more than a remote possibility. For example, today most women have little choice about whether or not to give up full-time jobs outside the home in order to care for any children they bear, at least while the children are young. This lack of choice is one important reason why women predominate among the housekeepers and childrearers of our society. Consequently, to use a modified form of our previous example, a law might prohibit adults with primary responsibility for child care from working in managerial jobs, on the grounds that the function of caring for children was inconsistent with substantial occupational responsibility. Such a law or government regulation would constitute a serious evasion of the Equal Rights Amendment. Its practical effect would be to exclude the majority of women and very few men in certain age groups from a whole range of relatively well-paid jobs which most people consider desirable.

The problem of formally neutral laws which may have a discriminatory impact arises under any law which attempts to eradicate discrimination based upon a single prohibited factor in a context where many other factors may legitimately be taken into account. The same issues have consistently appeared in the enforcement of laws prohibiting discrimination because of race, religion, national origin, and labor organizing activity. The courts have responded by looking beyond the adoption of the "neutral" classification into the realities of purpose, practical operation, and effect. Where the classification is seen to be a subterfuge, or to nullify the objectives of the anti-discrimination law, the courts have not hesitated to strike it down. As one court has stated: "A

49. Murray & Eastwood, [Jane Crow and the Law] at 241.

procedure may appear on its face to be fair and neutral, but if in its application a discriminatory result ensues, the procedure may be constitutionally impermissible."[50]

And recently the Supreme Court, in holding a North Carolina literacy test invalid under the Voting Rights Act of 1965, said: "From this record we cannot escape the sad truth that throughout the years Gaston County systematically deprived its black citizens of the educational opportunities it granted to its white citizens. 'Impartial' administration of the literacy test today would serve only to perpetuate these inequities in a different form."[51]

In applying these principles to the Equal Rights Amendment the courts would follow standards similar to those set forth in the preceding section with respect to laws which propose to base differentiation upon a unique physical characteristic of one sex. Of those standards, only one would be different for functional classifications. Since a functional classification is necessarily limited to those individuals who actually perform a given task or share a given characteristic, the first question — the proportion of women who actually have the characteristic in question — would not be asked by the reviewing court. However, unlike unique physical characteristic classifications, in which by definition some or all of one sex and none of the other are included, the extent of the disproportion between the numbers of women and the numbers of men included in a functional class may vary. A given functional classification may include 100,000 women and 10 men, or a disproportion of 10,000 to 1, while another may affect 45,000 women and 40,000 men, or a disproportion of 9 to 8. The first classification would obviously be a more likely vehicle for perpetuating sex inequality than the second, and the presence of this factor would thus go far to weight the balance against the law.

Protection against indirect, covert or unconscious sex discrimination is essential to supplement the absolute ban on explicit sex classification of the Equal Rights Amendment. Past discrimination in education, training, economic status and other areas has created differences which could readily be seized upon to perpetuate discrimination under the guise of functional classifications. The courts will have to maintain a strict scrutiny of such classifications if the guarantees of the Amendment are to be effectively secured.

D. The Privacy Qualification

The Equal Rights Amendment must take its place in the total framework of the Constitution and fit into the remainder of the constitutional structure. Of particular importance for our purposes is the relation of the new amendment to the constitutional right of privacy.

In Griswold v. Connecticut[52] the Supreme Court recognized an independent constitutional right of privacy, derived from a combination of various more specific rights embodied in the First, Third, Fourth, Fifth and Ninth Amendments. This constitutional right of privacy operates to protect the individual against intrusion by the government upon certain areas of thought or conduct, in the same way that the First Amendment prohibits official action that abridges freedom of expression. Thus in the *Griswold* case the right was held to invalidate a Connecticut statute which prohibited the use of

---

50. Penn v. Stumpf, 308 F. Supp. 1238, 1244 (N.D. Cal. 1970).

51. Gaston County v. United States, 395 U.S. 285, 296-97 (1969). Other cases invalidating ostensibly neutral classifications which operated to discriminate against the right of blacks to vote include Lane v. Wilson, 307 U.S. 268 (1939); Gomillion v. Lightfoot, 364 U.S. 339 (1960). Pupil assignment laws, under which assignment of students to schools is ostensibly based upon non-racial factors, have not been allowed to operate so as to maintain segregation of races in the school system. See Green v. County School Board, 391 U.S. 430 (1968); United States v. Jefferson County Board of Education, 372 F.2d 836 (5th Cir. 1966), *cert. denied,* 389 U.S. 840 (1967). For rejection of an ostensibly neutral classification which abridged freedom of religion, see Sherbert v. Verner, 374 U.S. 398 (1963). On "neutral" classifications which operate to discriminate against blacks in employment, see Griggs v. Duke Power Co., 401 U.S. 424 (1971). Generally on the problem see Ely, Legislative and Administrative Motivation in Constitutional Law, 79 Yale L.J. 1205 (1970).

52. 381 U.S. 479 (1965).

contraceptives even by married couples and thereby infringed upon intimate relationships in marriage and the home. The position of the right of privacy in the overall constitutional scheme was not explicitly developed by the Court. Presumably the point at which the right of privacy cuts off state regulation will be determined by a test which balances the two interests at stake. Or it may be that the right of privacy, where found to be applicable, will be held to afford an absolute protection against government intrusion. In either event laws or other official action implementing the Equal Rights Amendment would have to be applied in a manner that was consistent with individual privacy under the consitutional guarantee.[53]

The exact scope of the right of privacy was likewise not spelled out by the Court in the *Griswold* case. Yet it is clear that one important part of the right of privacy is to be free from official coercion in sexual relations. This would have a bearing upon the operation of some aspects of the Equal Rights Amendment. Thus, under current mores, disrobing in front of the other sex is usually associated with sexual relationships. Hence the right of privacy would justify police practices by which a search involving the removal of clothing could be performed only by a police officer of the same sex as the person searched.[54] Similarly the right of privacy would permit the separation of the sexes in public rest rooms, segregation by sex in sleeping quarters of prisons or similar public institutions, and appropriate segregation of living conditions in the armed forces.

In such situations, the facilities provided for the sexes would have to be equal in quality, convenience and other respects. Likewise an employer could not refuse to hire women because he did not want to build or remodel rest rooms for them. Failure to provide separate facilities for one sex would not be permissible when the presence of such facilities is related to the exercise of some other right, such as the right to be free of discrimination in employment. Moreover, the separation of facilities for reasons of privacy would not mean that individuals or groups would be foreclosed from making flexible and various arrangements for the common use of facilities such as bathrooms. In the same way, hospitals could allow patients to choose a ward with individuals of the same sex or of both sexes. Such noncoerced decisions, springing from individual values and preferences in areas of private conduct, would not be affected by the Amendment.

It is impossible to spell out in advance the precise boundaries that the courts will eventually fix in accommodating the Equal Rights Amendment and the right of privacy. In general it can be said, however, that the privacy concept is applicable primarily in situations which involve disrobing, sleeping, or performing personal bodily functions in the presence of the other sex. The great concern over these matters expressed by opponents of the Equal Rights Amendment seems not only to have been magnified beyond all proportion but to have failed to take into account the impact of the young, but fully recognized, constitutional right of privacy.

It should be added that the scope of the right of privacy in this area of equal rights is dependent upon the current mores of the community. Existing attitudes toward relations between the sexes could change over time — are indeed now changing —and in that event the impact of the right of privacy would change too. . . .

F. State Action

The Equal Rights Amendment as proposed provides that equality under the law shall not be denied or abridged "by the United States or by any State." Like the Fourteenth and Fifteenth Amendments, therefore, the legal effect of the Amendment is confined to "state action." How does this much-debated and increasingly complex concept apply in the context of women's rights?

53. The balancing test for the right of privacy is used by Mr. Justice Goldberg in his concurring opinion, Griswold v. Connecticut, 381 U.S. 479, 486 (1965). For discussion of the full protection or absolute approach see T. Emerson, The System of Freedom of Expression, 544-550 (1970).

54. The constitutional right of privacy in the search situation was recognized in York v. Story, 324 F.2d 450 (9th Cir. 1963), *cert. denied,* 376 U.S. 939 (1964).

Constitutional doctrines pertaining to state action have developed mainly in the area of race discrimination. They are intricate and confusing, but in essence they embody two concepts. One is that the existence of state action depends upon the nature and degree of state involvement. This may range all the way from a direct criminal prohibition of certain conduct to the maintenance of conditions in the society that permit private activity to exist; from direct action to apparent inaction; from de jure to de facto responsibility. The second is that state action depends upon the function being performed. The activity out of which the claim for equal protection arises may range from a clearly governmental operation, such as the election of public officials, to purely personal relationships, such as a private social gathering. Both the "state involvement" and the "public function" concepts lead in the same direction and ultimately to the same conclusion: "state action" takes place in the public sector of society and not in the private sector.[60]

The Supreme Court has not decided whether the "state action" required is the same for all kinds of constitutional rights involved, or even whether it is the same for all kinds of claims made under the Equal Protection Clause. In other words it is not clear whether the same showing of "state action" is necessary to assert a right under the Equal Protection Clause as under due process or freedom of speech guarantees; or whether "state action" is identical in cases alleging discrimination on account of race as discrimination on account of religion, wealth, nationality or politics. In general it may be assumed, however, that while the basic principles for determining state action remain the same, the relevant factors may apply differently in different situations.

So far as the Equal Rights Amendment is concerned the problem would be to determine what should be held part of the public sector, in which different treatment on account of sex is forbidden, and what is part of the private sector, in which different treatment is allowed. In some areas the factors relevant to that determination would tend toward a broad application of state action. Thus in the areas of voting (already covered by the Nineteenth Amendment), employment (including the right of representation by the collective bargaining agent), and education, the public character of the function would lead to the requirement that the state assume extensive responsibility. There are other areas where the private sector would extend more broadly and the scope of "state action" would be correspondingly diminished. Such would be the case as to social, recreational and fraternal associations; facilities such as hotels, restaurants and theaters; and the right to dispose of property by will. Here the public effects of sex differentiation are less significant and a wider realm of individual choice is acceptable.

The application of the state action concept under the Equal Rights Amendment has been most widely discussed in connection with the area of education. There is no doubt that the Equal Rights Amendment would eliminate differentiation on account of sex in the public schools and public university systems. The decision of the Supreme Court in Williams v. McNair, noted previously,[61] could not stand. The question has been raised, however, as to how the Amendment would affect private schools and universities. The courts have so far consistently ruled that even the large private universities are not within the sphere of state action.[62] The decision of the Supreme Court in Walz v. Tax Commission of the City of New York,[63] upholding tax exemption for religious institutions, indicates that state-conferred tax exemptions alone would not bring private schools and universities into the state action realm. Thus it appears that, in the absence of special factors, under present court decisions on state action private educational

---

60. Cf. Black, Foreword: "State Action," Equal Protection, and California's Proposition 14, 81 Harv. L. Rev. 69 (1967).

61. Williams v. McNair, 401 U.S. 951 (1971). . . .

62. *See* Guillory v. Administrators of Tulane University, 203 F. Supp. 855 (E.D. La.), *vacated,* 207 F. Supp. 554, *aff'd,* 306 F.2d 489 (5th Cir. 1962); Greene v. Howard University, 271 F. Supp. 609 (D.D.C. 1967), *remanded,* 412 F.2d 1129 (D.C. Cir. 1969); Grossner v. Trustees of Columbia University, 287 F. Supp. 535 (S.D.N.Y. 1968); Powe v. Miles, 294 F. Supp. 1269 (W.D.N.Y.), modified, 407 F.2d 73 (2d Cir. 1968).

63. 397 U.S. 664 (1970).

institutions would remain within the private sector, not subject to the constitutional requirements of the Equal Rights Amendment.[64]

The current state of the law on state action in the field of education, however, will be subject to further development as the goals of the Equal Rights Amendment are pressed upon the courts. It would seem clear that the basic principles of state action would, as a general proposition, require that the state eliminate male domination from the educational system. What this would demand in specific instances cannot be spelled out in detail at this point. To the degree that large private institutions, functioning in a quasi-public capacity, provide a significant share of the education which counts most heavily toward achievement in our society, they will be required to operate without discrimination against women. The public sector in education would never be construed to embrace all private schools or colleges. Nevertheless, under present conditions, the Equal Rights Amendment will operate to expand the area in which different treatment of the sexes is impermissible in the area of education.

In general, it may be said that the concept of state action would be rigorously applied up to the point necessary to achieve the objectives sought by the Equal Rights Amendment. In the long run, as discrimination against women disappeared, however, it would be desirable for the public sector, in which state action prevailed, to diminish, and the private sector, in which individual preferences were recognized, to expand.

G. Others Matters of Interpretation and Wording

Several other questions of interpretation, as to which no serious problems arise, remain to be noted. One is the meaning of the word "rights" as used in the Amendment. The proponents have always made it clear that the exercise of rights entails the performance of duties and that the term "rights" includes all forms of privileges, immunities, benefits and responsibilities of citizens. By 1971, even the Amendment's opponents grant this, abandoning Senator Hayden's distinctions.

Consensus has also been reached on the meaning of the enforcement clause of the Amendment. In 1943, the Senate Judiciary Committee used the language of the Eighteenth Amendment, that "Congress and the several States shall have power, within their respective jurisdictions, to enforce this article by appropriate legislation."[65] The committee intended that this provision be construed as limiting Congressional authority in implementing the Amendment to that already provided by some existing federal constitutional power. Such is not, however, the intention of the present proponents. And the ambiguity has been clarified in the resolution introduced in this session by Representative Griffiths.[66] The enforcement provision is now similar to that in the Thirteenth, Fourteenth, and Fifteenth Amendments, and reads: "The Congress shall have the power to enforce, by appropriate legislation, the provisions of this article."[67] The states, not operating under a system of delegated powers, need no further grant of authority to implement the provisions of the Amendment.

There remains the question whether the present wording of the substantive provisions of the Amendment, which has been stable since 1943, can be clarified or improved. There is no persuasive reason to make any change. In the first place, the present language states the central idea succinctly. Its wording is similar to other consitutional amendments establishing and protecting fundamental rights, notably the Fourteenth, Fifteenth, and Nineteenth. Like them, the Equal Rights Amendment states a general principle

---

64. Of course, significant government aid, financial or otherwise, would involve state action. See, e.g., Simkins v. Moses H. Cone Memorial Hospital, 323 F.2d 959 (4th Cir. 1963), *cert. denied,* 376 U.S. 938 (1964). See also Green v. Kennedy, 309 F. Supp. 1127 (D.D.C. 1970).

65. S. Rep. No. 267, 78th Cong., 1st Sess. at 1 (1943).

66. H.R.J. Res. 208, 92d Cong., 1st Sess. (1971). Many resolutions embodying the Equal Rights Amendment have been introduced in the House of Representatives in the 92d Congress. They vary in their provisions on ratification, effective date, and enforcement. However, the version proposed by Representative Griffiths is the one which has received the endorsement of most of the proponents of the Amendment.

67. H.R.J. Res. 208, 92d Cong., 1st Sess. §2 (1971).

rather than spelling out the concept of equal rights in detail. This permits development of more specific doctrines through constitutional litigation and adaption of the basic mandate to unforeseen situations and new conditions, a process which has proved generally successful throughout our history.

Second, a search for more appropriate wording in the constitutions of other countries has not yielded positive results. Provisions granting equal rights for women do occasionally exist. Thus, Article 3, Section 2 of the Constitution of the German Federal Republic provides: "Men and women are equal before the law." This formulation, however, does not seem preferable to the Equal Rights Amendment.

Finally, use of this wording does not bind proponents to older, unacceptable theories sometimes advanced in previous debates. On the contrary, the responsibility rests upon the present Congress to attach to the Amendment the meaning it now intends.

H. Summary

We believe that the Equal Rights Amendment, broadly construed in the manner set forth above, furnishes a viable structure for achieving equality of rights for women. The basic proposition — that differences in treatment under the law shall not be based on the quality of being male or female, but upon the characteristics and abilities of the individual person that are relevant to the differentiation — is founded in the fundamental values of our society. Most of the objections which have been addressed to the absolute form of the Amendment are answered by the fact that the Amendment is inapplicable to laws dealing with unique physical characteristics of one sex or by application of the constitutional right of privacy. Such other objections as have been advanced simply run counter to the major premises upon which the concept of equal rights for women stands. Furthermore, they must fall before the intransigent fact that no system of equal rights for women can be effective which attempts to litigate in each case the judgment whether the differentiation is "reasonable" or "justified" or "compelled." As a matter of consitutional mechanics, therefore, the law must start from the proposition that all differentiation is prohibited.

IV. PROBLEMS OF TRANSITION. . . .

B. The General Rules for Judicial Application of the Equal Rights Amendment

To the extent that Congress and the state legislatures have expressly indicated the impact the Equal Rights Amendment is meant to have on existing law, that legislative history will govern later judicial interpretation. However, in many instances there may be no clear legislative mandate available, and the courts will have to determine the impact of the Amendment in light of its general legislative history and settled principles of constitutional adjudication. The doctrines developed by the courts for this task have given them broad authority to make sensible and practical adjustments in conforming current laws to the requirements of the constitutional mandate. Thus, the courts have the power to construe legislation to avoid unconstitutionality or even to avoid constitutional doubts; they may hold certain sections or applications of a law to be separable from others in order to save parts of the law; they may extend the scope of a statute to reach those wrongfully excluded; or they may invalidate the law in toto. The considerations governing the use of these various methods of construction have not always been made explicit in judicial opinions. Nevertheless patterns emerge from an examination of the cases, and it is possible to predict with considerable accuracy what the courts will do in most situations.[72]

72. For more detailed discussion of problems of statutory construction when constitutional questions are involved, see J. Sutherland, Statutory Construction (3d ed. F. Horack ed. 1943) [hereinafter cited as Sutherland]; Sedler, Standing to Assert Constitutional Jus Tertii in the Supreme Court, 71 Yale L.J. 599 (1962); Stern, Separability and Separability Clauses in the Supreme Court, 51 Harv. L. Rev. 76 (1937) [hereinafter cited as Stern]; Note, Supreme Court Interpretation of Statutes to Avoid Constitutional Decisions, 53 Colum. L. Rev. 633 (1953); Note, The Effect of an Unconstitutional Exception Clause on the Remainder of a Statute, 55 Harv. L. Rev. 1030 (1942).

In cases challenging statutes under the Equal Rights Amendment the courts will be faced with essentially two alternatives: either to invalidate the statute or to equalize its application to the two sexes. If the latter alternative is selected, there may sometimes be a question as to the proper basis for equalization. However, the more difficult problems posed in the application of other constitutional doctrines, such as vagueness or chilling effect, are unlikely to arise here.[73]

In determining the impact of a constitutional provision upon a non-conforming statute, courts look primarily to the legislative intent behind the statute in question. Whether the statute falls completely or is modified in some way depends upon the court's assessment of what the legislature itself would have done had it known that all or part of its original enactment would be invalid. Of course, such legislative intent is often not easily ascertained. Where legislative history is scant, or lacking altogether, there is little for courts to rely on except their own judgment about what the legislature must have intended. Then, too, the further question arises as to which legislature's intent is relevant — the one which passed the bill originally, an amending legislature, if any, or the one currently in session.[74]

In these circumstances, critics have charged that legislative intent and the policy judgment of the reviewing court are nearly indistinguishable. However that may be, the courts have tended to structure their judgment in terms of certain standard factors which are thought to provide at least rough guides to probable legislative intent and, equally important, to rational results in adjusting statutes to constitutional requirements. Since several of these factors are often present in one case, it is useful to describe the factors briefly and then, by way of illustrating their operation, analyze selected cases.

The first of these interpretive factors is a practical consideration of the *importance* of the legislation and the *feasibility* of retaining it in the altered form required by the constitutional mandate. If the challenged statute deals with a subject of major significance, the court will attempt to find a saving construction, even if that requires a strained interpretation of the statutory language on its face. On the other hand, if the saving construction produces a result which is not workable as a practical matter, or requires drastic changes in other areas to be viable, the court will be inclined to strike down the statute. For example, a court would be most unwilling to invalidate a revenue law or a voting qualifications statute, because taxes and voting are crucial to the political system. However, it might refuse to extend a law prohibiting night work for women to cover men, because such extension of coverage would not be feasible without fundamental changes in industrial organization, and because the subject matter is one that could readily await legislative action.[75]

Second, the courts are influenced by the *proportional difference* between what the original enactment was designed to cover relative to how much it can or must constitutionally include. This factor may be reflected either in terms of the number of persons who would be added or excluded relative to the original number, changes in geographical area covered, the number of original provisions which remain, or other indices of the percentage of the statute added or subtracted. Thus if the class added by construction is small in comparison with the classes already included, the court will generally assume

73. For reasons why vagueness and chilling effect problems are unlikely to arise, see notes 78 & 85 infra.

74. For the maxim that, assuming any legal effect can be given to the remaining provisions of the statute, legislative intent is determinative, see Dorchy v. Kansas, 264 U.S. 286, 289-90 (1924). See also Note, supra note 72, 53 Colum. L. Rev. at 642. For the proposition that the amending legislature's intent may be relevant, see Note, supra note 72, 55 Harv. L. Rev. at 1033.

75. See Note, supra note 72, 55 Harv. L. Rev. at 1032 n.20, 1033 nn.21 & 22, citing cases concerning tax statutes from which exceptions were removed, e.g., State ex rel. Bolens v. Frear, 148 Wis. 456, 134 N.W. 673 (1912), *appeal dismissed,* 231 U.S. 616 (1914); State ex rel. v. Baker, 55 Ohio St. 1, 44 N.E. 516 (1896), demonstrating the importance of when the legislature will be able to meet and enact a new statute; State ex rel. Wilmot v. Buckley, 60 Ohio St. 273, 54 N.E. 272 (1899); Anderson v. Wood, 152 S.W. 2d 1085 (Tex. 1941), indicating the significance of an existing law of similar substance. McLaughlin v. Florida, 379 U.S. 184, 195-96 (1965), also deals with this latter issue.

that the legislature would prefer the statute to stand despite a minor change and will probably extend the law to conform with the new constitutional mandate. If the proportion is reversed, the court might, by invalidating the law, refer the matter back to the legislature for decision.[76]

A third factor which strongly influences the courts is whether the statute in question is *civil* or *criminal*. Courts have long observed a maxim that penal laws are to be strictly construed. To avoid judicial creation of new crimes beyond those established by the legislature, courts will refuse to extend a criminal law to cover groups of people implicitly or explicitly excluded on the face of the law. In other words, the courts will not presume that the legislature, faced with the problem of unconstitutionally under-inclusive penalties, would have chosen to extend them to a new group.[77] As one court put it, in the process of invalidating an entire penal statute:

"By striking out the exemption as unconstitutional, it leaves subject to criminal prosecution those the Legislature expressly intended should be exempt.

"As to them it would be making that a crime which was never intended should be. The exemption renders it impossible to enforce the legislative will."[78]

The three factors discussed so far are the principal ones which guide the courts in determining legislative intent when the legislative history of the statute or the constitutional provision itself does not explicitly resolve the issue. There are two additional considerations which may influence judicial resolution of a constitutional challenge, but they operate with less force and clarity.

The first is related to the criminal–civil distinction. If a saving construction has the effect of extending a *burden* to a previously excepted class, the courts are somewhat less likely to adopt it than if the new construction extends a *benefit* previously denied those excepted. Thus a statute prohibiting women from being bartenders would be stricken down rather than extended to men; but a law giving only mothers of illegitimate children a right to custody would be extended to fathers.[79] There are two kinds of ambiguities, however, in the benefit-burden analysis, both of which may make it difficult for courts to appraise the benefits and burdens involved. First, a law may have a variable impact within the covered classification. Thus, a law providing a lower age of termination of parental support and control for women than men, or a law setting maximum hours for female workers, provides benefits to some of the class covered by the law (those who

76. See Note supra note 72, 55 Harv. L. Rev. at 1030 n.3, citing 22 Calif. L. Rev. 228 (1934), and 1030 n.6, 1031 n.7 and cases cited therein. State statutes which exclude noncitizens from benefits are usually interpreted to extend benefits to them, while statutes which impose burdens on them are almost invariably struck down, to avoid unconstitutionality under the Privileges and Immunities Clause of Article IV §2. The fact that the number of non-citizens burdened by a statute or excluded from a benefit-conferring act is usually small in proportion to the number of citizens may account for these results, although this is not stated explicitly in the cases. See Note, supra note 72, 55 Harv. L. Rev. at 1034 n.40, 1035 nn.41-44; Quong Ham Wah Co. v. Industrial Accident Commission, 184 Cal. 26, 192 Pac. 1021 (1920), appeal dismissed 225 U.S. 445 (1921) (workman's compensation benefit privilege extended to nonresidents).

77. See for discussion and authorities, 3 Sutherland, Ch. 56, esp. §§5604-5606, at 44-67; 2 Sutherland §2418, at 196-97; cf. Stern, supra note 72, at 88 nn.56-58, 89 nn.59-61; Note, supra note 72, 55 Harv. L. Rev. 1030, 1031, n.11; Yu Cong Eng v. Trinidad, 271 U.S. 500, 515-23 (1926) (citing cases). *Contra*, McCreary v. State, 72 Ala. 480 (1883); cf. Skinner v. Oklahoma ex rel. Williamson, 316 U.S. 535, 543 (1942) (dictum). . . .

78. State v. Gantz, 124 La. 535, 543, 50 So. 524, 526 (1909). Judicial revision of criminal statutes often raises a problem in addition to the one discussed. If a court, to avoid unconstutitional overbreadth, must read specific words of exception into a statute, the statute may be unconstitutionally vague as well. As the Supreme Court stated in Smith v. Cahoon, 284 U.S. 553, 564 (1931):

"Either the statute imposed upon the appellant obligations to which the State had no constitutional authority to subject him, or it failed to define such obligations as the State had the right to impose with the fair degree of certainty which is required of criminal statutes."

This problem is acute where the saving construction of the court, in "discovering" an implicit exception, raises the possibility that there may be other exceptions of a similar nature as yet hidden. Since the Equal Rights Amendment deals with the inclusion or exclusion of either of two well-defined groups, this problem is unlikely to arise.

79. See Note, supra note 72, 55 Harv. L. Rev. at 1031-32, 1034-35, and cases cited at 1035 nn.42-44.

want to be free of parental supervision and those who do not want to be forced to work long hours) and burdens to others (those who want to be supported through college by their parents and those who want to earn high overtime wages). Second, a law which provides a benefit to one class may entail a cost to another class. Thus, a law providing overtime pay for female employees may be intended to benefit them but also burdens the employer. Where the burden falls on the general public, as in the case of a benefit supported by tax funds, the court may be inclined to ignore the burden or cost aspect of the equation and extend the benefit to improperly excluded classes. But where the burden is borne by private individuals or groups the court may react differently.[80] For these reasons the benefit-burden dichotomy will often require further analysis.

The final consideration, which is probably the most frequently mentioned by judges, is actually the least important. In a series of cases dating back at least to United States v. Reese[81] in 1875, courts have claimed that they lack the power to add words to statutes, although they possess the power to excise words or to interpret them freely. Several commentators have rightly been critical of this semantic distinction on the ground that the answer to the question of what the legislature would have wanted to happen is not contingent on whether the result requires the addition or removal of words.[82] An examination of the cases in which courts have refused to reach a given result for methodological reasons suggests that alternative bases exist for most of these decisions, including hostility on the part of the court to the substantive policy embodied in the challenged statute.[83] In other words, semantic considerations appear to play more of a role in the courts' description of what they are doing than in the actual results. This factor can therefore be largely ignored as a basis of decision, although it may tip the scales one way or another in an unusually close case.[84]

The factors outlined above do not exhaust all the possibilities. But they do suggest the principal guidelines for judicial determination of "legislative intent." Since these factors sometimes militate against each other in particular cases, judicial interpretation of the Equal Rights Amendment can only be predicted if the relative weights accorded each are taken into account. The way in which these considerations operate in the actual process of judicial decision can best be seen from a brief examination of cases in areas most comparable to the Equal Rights Amendment.[85]

In several cases arising under the Fifteenth Amendment, state voting statutes which discriminated on their face against blacks were automatically extended to cover

---

80. See, e.g., Burrow v. Kapfhammer, 284 Ky. 753, 145 S.W.2d 1067 (1940), noted at 54 Harv. L. Rev. 1078 (1941). But cf. Butte Miners' Union No. 1 v. Anaconda Copper Mining Co., 112 Mont. 418, 118 P.2d 148 (1941), noted at 55 Harv. L. Rev. 1052 (1942).

81. 92 U.S. 214 (1875).

82. See, e.g., Stern, supra note 72, at 94-97.

83. See the discussion in id., at 102. Cases reflecting hostility on the part of the Court to the substantive policy involved in the statute include Carter v. Carter Coal Co., 298 U.S. 238 (1936) and United States v. Reese, 92 U.S. 214 (1875), discussed in Stern, supra note 72, at 99. An example of a different "alternative basis" is Illinois Cent. R.R. v. McKendree, 203 U.S. 514 (1906), where the Court cast is decision in methodological terms perhaps to avoid reaching another constitutional issue on which it was divided. See Stern, supra note 72, at 102 n. 116.

84. One indication of the accuracy of this analysis is the frequency with which the same courts follow the rule against addition of words on some occasions and violate it on others, avoiding open conflict with the *Reese* line of cases by neglecting to discuss the methodology implicit in their result. See, e.g., Holy Trinity Church v. United States, 143 U.S. 457 (1892), and Stern, supra note 72, at 80-82, 96.

85. In this survey we do not discuss statutes challenged on First Amendment grounds. Where statutory language has been found to be overinclusive on First Amendment grounds, a court will ordinarily refuse to limit the enactment to its constitutional applications in order to preserve the statute. The explanation is that a limiting construction will not eliminate the vice of the statute, which is that the over-broad language on its face will chill the exercise of protected First Amendment freedoms. Analogous Equal Rights Amendment cases are unlikely to arise, for it is the direct rather than the chilling effect of statutes which will be called into question. Similarly, we will not discuss challenges on grounds of vagueness, since the extension required in Equal Rights cases is likely to involve well-defined groups.

blacks as well as whites.[86] In those cases, the number added by the court was small in proportion to the number of people already included; in addition voting statutes are of prime importance to the operation of government and the inclusion of the new group did not raise administrative problems. Under the Nineteenth Amendment, prohibiting denial of the right to vote on account of sex, the same result was reached even though a large number of new voters (potentially over 50 per cent) was added to the rolls.[87] In these cases the subject matter — voting — was clearly the dominant factor. Courts are unwilling to invalidate such laws, thereby leaving the state without a statute on voting qualifications and procedures. Even when the number added by the change is large in comparison to the number covered by the original enactment, the importance of the law requires extension rather than invalidation.

The equal protection decisions probably provide the closest analogies to the cases likely to arise under the Equal Rights Amendment. Dealing with discrimination against specified classes of individuals, they have usually resulted in the extension of benefits to the previously excluded group. For example, in Sweatt v. Painter[88] and McLaurin v. Oklahoma State Regents[89] the right of access and treatment substantially identical to that accorded white students in state institutions of higher education was extended to black students. Such extension of benefits has not been limited to cases involving racial discrimination. In Levy v. Louisiana[90] the right to recover wrongful death benefits was extended to illegitimate children, and in Shapiro v. Thompson[91] the right to receive welfare benefits was extended to cover residents who had recently moved from another state. Extension in these cases was consistent with the general principles of construction discussed above: the statutes were civil, their subject matter was important, and the number of people added to the coverage of the law was small in comparison to the number already included. But even when the number of people affected is large, a statute involving an important civil benefit or duty is often extended. In White v. Crook,[92] the Alabama statute excluding women from jury duty was held to violate the Fourteenth Amendment; it was not struck down, but instead the right and duty of serving was extended to women.

On the other hand, when the discrimination is part of a criminal law, the coverage of the law is rarely if ever extended.[93] Thus, a criminal law providing special penalties for interracial cohabitation was struck down rather than extended to all cohabitation in McLaughlin v. Florida.[94] And the courts have invalidated state laws providing greater criminal penalties for women than for men, rather than extending the increased penalties to men.[95] Since persons prosecuted under a law are unlikely to urge that the law be extended to cover those discriminatorily excluded, and since individuals not prosecuted cannot urge this result, it might seem that the alternative of extension is not even before the court. However, in Skinner v. Oklahoma, a law which arbitrarily selected one class of habitual offenders for sterilization was remanded to the Oklahoma Supreme Court because, as Justice Douglas said,

"It is by no means clear whether, if an excision were made, this particular constitu-

---

86. Neal v. Delaware, 103 U.S. 370 (1880); Ex parte Yarborough, 110 U.S. 651 (1884); Guinn v. United States, 238 U.S. 347 (1915); Myers v. Anderson, 238 U.S. 368 (1915).

87. See. Leser v. Garnett, 258 U.S. 130, 136 (1922); Breedlove v. Suttles, 302 U.S. 277, 283 (1937); Graves v. Eubank, 205 Ala. 174, 87 So. 587 (1921); Foster v. Mayor & Council of College Park, 155 Geo. 174, 117 S.E. 84 (1923); Matter of Cavellier, 159 Misc. 212, 215, 287 N.Y.S. 739, 742 (1936).

88. 339 U.S. 629 (1950).

89. 339 U.S. 637 (1950).

90. 391 U.S. 68 (1968).

91. 394 U.S. 618 (1969).

92. 251 F. Supp. 401 (M.D. Ala. 1966).

93. See authorities cited in note 77 supra.

94. 379 U.S. 184 (1964).

95. U.S. ex rel. Robinson v. York, 281 F. Supp. 8 (D. Conn. 1968); Commonwealth v. Daniel, 430 Pa. 642, 243 A.2d 400 (1968).

tional difficulty might be solved by extending on the one hand or contracting on the other . . . the class of criminals who might be sterilized."[96]

Apparently, the Oklahoma Supreme Court did not feel it could take upon itself the decision to extend the penalty to a class of offenders not included by the legislature, and therefore invalidated the law by failing to take action on remand.

Taken as a whole, the principles used by the courts have operated to produce results that are probably what the legislature would have done had it known of the new constitutional mandate. While no one can say that the outcome of every issue will be the same in every state, it can be said with some assurance that the courts have the powers, doctrines and experience to handle Equal Rights Amendment cases without wholesale invalidation of viable laws or other absurd results. The main problem which we have discovered is the necessity for state legislatures to direct particular attention to their criminal laws, as the courts are least likely to correct defects in this area.

NOTE: PROBLEMS WITH THE PRIVACY DOCTRINE

Brown, Emerson, Falk, and Freedman argue that[17]

> . . . [T]he right of privacy would permit the separation of the sexes in public rest rooms, segregation by sex in sleeping quarters of prisons or similar public insitutions, and appropriate segregation of living conditions in the armed forces.

They arrive at this definition by focusing on privacy as it relates to sexuality under current mores. Disrobing, sleeping, and performing personal bodily functions in front of persons of the opposite sex are all currently defined as having sexual connotations and the authors thus limit the privacy doctrine to situations involving one of the three.

However, there is a basic problem with this process. The doctrine might encourage the development of exceptions to the ERA beyond those contemplated by the authors — such as a requirement that only male policemen guard males, a prohibition against male nurses caring for female patients, or an exclusion of women from private men's clubs. According to the Yale Law Journal analysis, these results would not be permitted, yet some courts might be persuaded to permit them under the "current sexual mores" test. Cf. the questions about the relationship of the right to privacy to the Equal Rights Amendment raised by Freund, supra Section B-3-a.

Discuss the political and tactical implications of the "current sexual mores" approach, and consider whether or not there is any other way to solve the "bathroom problem."

2. Application of the Theory: Maternity Leave

Throughout this book, the possible and predicted effects of the amendment are treated in the context of specific areas such as criminal law, family law, and employment discrimination law.[18] However, in order to illustrate the operation of a theory of inter-

---

96. Skinner v. Oklahoma ex rel. Williamson, 316 U.S. 535, 543 (1942) (citations omitted).

17. Supra, at 901.

18. The following is a partial list of laws which discriminate on the basis of sex and would therefore be affected by the ERA, taken from the 1970 Memorandum on the ERA by the Citizen's Advisory Council on the Status of Women.

"1. State laws placing special restrictions on women with respect to hours of work and weightlifting on the job;

"2. State laws prohibiting women from working in certain occupations;

"3. Laws or practices operating to exclude women from State colleges and universities (including higher standards required for women applicants to institutions of higher learning and in the administration of scholarship programs);

pretation at this point, the Yale article's exposition on the topic of mandatory maternity leave is presented here.

BROWN, EMERSON, FALK, AND FREEDMAN
THE EQUAL RIGHTS AMENDMENT:
A CONSTITUTIONAL BASIS
FOR EQUAL RIGHTS FOR WOMEN
80 Yale L.J. 929-932 (1971)

Compulsory Maternity Leave Regulations. Laws which require employers to impose leave on pregnant employees for a specified period before and after childbirth, without providing job security or retention of accrued benefits, such as seniority credits, are similarly exclusionary. Seven jurisdictions have enacted such restrictions into law; the stage of pregnancy at which mandatory leave is imposed varies between three weeks to four months before expected delivery.[112] None of these laws provides for any compensation by either state or employer, or job security, during the compulsory leave period, except that of Puerto Rico, which requires the employer to pay one-half salary during leave for temporary disabilities, including eight weeks compulsory leave for pregnancy, and provides job security during the required absence.[113] In addition to state laws, many state agencies have more restrictive regulations for their own employees; school board regulations are particularly significant, since a large number of women workers teach school.

"4. Discrimination in employment by State and local governments;
"5. Dual pay schedules for men and women public school teachers;
"6. State laws providing for alimony to be awarded, under certain circumstances, to ex-wives but not to ex-husbands;
"7. State laws placing special restrictions on the legal capacity of married women or on their right to establish a legal domicile;
"8. State laws that require married women but not married men to go through a formal procedure and obtain court approval before they may engage in an independent business.
"9. Social Security and other social benefits legislation which give greater benefits to one sex than to the other;
"10. Discriminatory preferences, based on sex, in child custody cases;
"11. State laws providing that the *father* is the natural guardian of the minor children.
"12. Different ages for males and females in (a) child labor laws, (b) age for marriage, (c) cutoff of the right to parental support, and (d) juvenile court jurisdiction;
"13. Exclusion of women from the requirements of the Military Selective Service Act of 1967;
"14. Special sex-based exemptions for women in selection of State juries;
"15. Heavier criminal penalties for female offenders than for male offenders committing the same crime."
For other discussions of impact in specific areas see Eastwood, The Double Standard of Justice: Women's Rights Under the Constitution, 5 Valparaiso U.L. Rev. 281, 301-317 (1971); Brown, Emerson, Falk, and Freedman, supra, at 920-967.
112. See 1969 Handbook 276-77. The jurisdictions are Connecticut, Massachusetts, Missouri, New York, Vermont, Washington, and Puerto Rico. The statutory prohibition on employment lasts until three to six weeks after childbirth. Id. The standard in the state of Washington is established by minimum wage orders, some of which provide that special permission may be granted for continued employment upon employer's request and with a doctor's certificate. In addition, the Oregon Mercantile and Sanitation and Physical Welfare Orders recommend that an employer should not employ a female at any work during the six weeks preceding and the four weeks following the birth of her child, unless recommended by a licensed medical authority. Id.
113. In addition, thirty-seven states and the District of Columbia disqualify women from collecting unemployment insurance during a specified period before and/or after childbirth, whether or not pregnancy is the reason for their unemployment. 1969 Handbook 52-54. Cf. Report of the Task Force on Social Insurance and Taxes, supra note 2, at 25-30, 44-46. On the other hand, Rhode Island's general temporary disability program provides cash benefits for unemployment due to maternity leave for a fourteen-week period around childbirth, and New Jersey's program provides cash payments for disabilities existing during the four weeks before and the four weeks following childbirth. However, New York and California, the only other states with state temporary disability programs, do not include disabilities based on pregnancy except in special circumstances. Id. at 44-46.

These regulations commonly require leaves to commence much earlier in pregnancy than the state laws discussed above.[114]

Under the Equal Rights Amendment, it will probably be argued in defense of these laws and state regulations that they deal with unique physical characteristics of women. It is true that the state may regulate conditions of employment for women in a physical condition unique to their sex, but the kind of regulation imposed would be subject to careful judicial review, utilizing the kinds of standards set forth previously in Part III. Two recent federal court decisions provide a preview of the kind of close scrutiny which the Equal Rights Amendment will require. One struck down a compulsory maternity leave regulation under Title VII; the other reached the same result under the Equal Protection Clause of the Fourteenth Amendment. Both courts recognized that compulsory maternity leave provisions are not genuinely protective either of women's health or of their employment rights.[116]

In Schattman v. Texas Employment Commission,[117] a woman challenged the imposition of compulsory leave in her seventh month of pregnancy. Following the *Weeks* doctrine that Title VII prohibits sex-based employment practices unless the employer can demonstrate a strong factual basis for the policy in terms of safety and efficiency, the court found no such evidence supporting compulsory maternity leave from the plaintiff's desk job.

This decision parallels an application of the Equal Rights Amendment's tests for regulations purporting to deal with unique physical characteristics. The maternity leave regulation in the *Schattman* case would satisfy only the most elementary of the unique physical characteristics tests: that the sex-based classification (i.e. pregnant women) be based in fact on a physical characteristic unique to one sex. The regulation would fall, however, if the state could not show the existence of a "problem" of legitimate legislative concern (such as the danger of job-related injuries to pregnant women) and a sufficiently close relationship between the problem and the physical characteristic in question. The state made neither showing in the *Schattman* case; if it *had* demonstrated a job-related problem which was tied to the condition of being seven months pregnant, the court might then have considered whether the regulation imposed was the least drastic solution to the problem demonstrated, and have balanced the importance of the problem against the costs of the least drastic solution.[119]

114. See, for statistics on women's employment as teachers, 1969 Handbook 90. A survey conducted by the National Education Association showed that in 1965-1966, a large number of school systems required maternity leave to begin between the fourth and sixth month of pregnancy, and extend until three or more months after childbirth. Research Div'n, National Education Assoc., Leaves of Absence for Classroom Teachers 1965-66 20-26 (1967). See also speech by Jacqueline G. Gutwillig, Chairman, Citizens' Advisory Council on the Status of Women, to Conference of Interstate Association of Commissions on Status of Women, St. Louis, Mo., June 19, 1971.

116. The legislative purpose of compulsory maternity leave legislation is not entirely clear; the central obscurity is the failure to specify what and who is being "protected," and why the legislature thinks the protection is necessary. Assuming that the primary purpose of such laws is to protect women's health, they can only be rationalized if one accepts as true the proposition that pregnant women, in contradistinction to all other workers, are unable or unwilling to seek or to heed medical advice about the safety and desirability of their continued performance of their jobs in light of the temporary change in their physical condition. Alternative explanations are available, however, and we are not in a position to say which of the possibilities is the actual legislative justification. One can suppose, for example, that the legislature was trying to design genuinely protective legislation and failed to think through fully the operative effect of lengthy compulsory leave without job security either in terms of women's rights as workers or in terms of the relationship between physical health and income and employment rights. Another possibility is that the legislators were willing to sacrifice women's roles as workers, which they considered relatively unimportant, to the supposed demands of pregnancy and motherhood, without much investigation either of medical evidence or alternative legislation with less impact on women's rights as independent adults. Or perhaps male legislators were acting on the basis of Victorian beliefs about the impropriety of women who are "in the family way" appearing in public at all. Since denying pregnant women the right to work when they are medically able and willing to work means that they cannot support themselves, this type of legislation, whatever its ostensible purpose, embodies an unrealistic assumption that all pregnant women have men to support them during their forced confinement.

117. 3 FEP Cases 311 (W.D. Tex. Mar. 4, 1971), 3 FEP Cases 468 (W.D. Tex. April 16, 1971).

119. The definition of the "problem," whether by explicit legislative history or by judicial interpreta-

A similar state regulation was struck down in Cohen v. Chesterfield County School Board,[120] in which a female teacher challenged a school board regulation imposing maternity leave at least four months prior to the expected birth of her child. The district court reviewed the supposed medical and administrative reasons for the school board's policy, and found them to have no empirical basis or persuasive force. The argument that mandatory leave was justified by frequent "incapacitation" at that stage of pregnancy was found to be medically incorrect; the idea that pregnant teachers had to be protected from such physical hazards of employment as "pushing with resulting injury to the fetus" was found to be entirely speculative, as was the allegation of increased inefficiency on the job, such as inability to perform duties during the fire drills.[121] The court concluded that "[b]asically, the four month requirement . . . was arbitrarily selected," and that "since no two pregnancies are alike, decisions of when a pregnant teacher should disconinue working are matters best left up to the woman and her doctor."[122] More broadly, the court held that "pregnancy, though unique to women, is like other medical conditions, and the failure to treat it as such amounts to discrimination which is without rational basis, and therefore is violative of the Equal Protection Clause of the Fourteenth Amendment."[123]

This decision, if cast in terms of the Equal Rights Amendment standards, would be similar to the *Schattman* decision discussed above: the state was unable to make an elementary showing of a job-related problem linked to the physical characteristic at issue. In addition, the court made two other findings that parallel the application of Equal Rights Amendment standards. First, the court held that in its relation to employment, pregnancy was only a small part of the larger problem of temporary disabilities which could not constitutionally be dealt with separately. Second, the imposition of compulsory leave was found to be impermissible where a rule letting a woman and her doctor decide when optional leave should commence would meet any medical need for leave and would be less onerous to pregnant women. In other words, the regulation discriminatorily selected out a small sex-linked part of a larger problem, and imposed a more drastic solution than was necessary. A court operating under the Equal Rights Amendment might also find that a sex-neutral rule, allowing any temporarily disabled worker and his or her doctor to determine the duration and timing of leave, would also be an available less drastic alternative.[19]

3. The Effect of the Amendment on the Military

The Equal Rights Amendment's clear requirement that women be fully integrated into the nation's military forces was at the core of the opposition in Congress, where there was particular concern about women in combat. Senator Ervin even offered an

---

tion, is central to setting the standards by which the legislation is to be judged. The more narrowly defined the problem is, the easier it is for the party defending the legislation to prove that the measures the law imposes solve a significant proportion of the problem. On the other hand, a narrow definition might cast doubt on the legislation under other tests, such as the importance of the problem to be solved or the adequacy of measures to select those contributing to the problem from the larger group with the unique physical characteristic. Although the focus of judicial scrutiny would thus shift from one factor to another depending on the definition of the "problem," the burden of proof on those defending the law would remain nearly the same.

120. 39 U.S.L.W. 2686 (E.D. Va. May 17, 1971). Contra, La Fleur v. Cleveland Board of Education, 39 U.S.L.W. 2686 (N.D. Ohio May 12, 1971).

121. 39 U.S.L.W. at 2686.

122. Id.

123. Id. at 2687 (citations omitted).

19. After the Yale article was written, the decisions in *Schattman, Cohen* and *LaFleur* were all reversed by the circuit courts of appeal. The Supreme Court then denied certiorari in *Schattman,* reversed *Cohen,* and affirmed *LaFleur.* Schattman v. Texas Employment Comm'n, 459 F.2d 32 (5th Cir. 1972), *cert. denied,* 209 U.S. 1107, *rehearing denied,* 410 U. S. 959 (1973); Cohen v. Chesterfield County School Board, 474 F. 2d 395 (4th Cir. 1973), Chapter Two, II-B, infra, *rev'd sub nom.* LaFleur v. Cleveland Board of Education, — U.S. —, 94 S. Ct. 791, — L.Ed. 2d — (1974); LaFleur v. Cleveland Board of Education, 465 F.2d 1184 (6th Cir. 1972), *aff'd,* — U.S. —, 94 S. Ct. 791, — L. Ed. 2d — (1974). — Eds.

amendment to the amendment providing: "This article shall not impair, however, the validity of any laws of the United States or any state which exempts women from compulsory military service."[20]

With the end of the compulsory draft in 1973, the emphasis of the debates in the states over the amendment has shifted somewhat from the congressional concentration on women forced into the military. However, many of the arguments about the difficulties of integrating women in the armed forces are still being raised, and often there is an assumption that the draft may be renewed in the near future.

LETTER FROM THE DEFENSE DEPARTMENT
TO SENATOR BAYH
Dated Feb. 24, 1972, 118 Cong. Rec. S4402 (daily ed. Mar. 21, 1972)

We, like the Department of Justice, believe it important that full consideration be given to the complications and litigation that might result should the amendment be adopted.

Depending on how the amendment was interpreted, the Department of Defense feels that two basic types of problems might arise — (1) those related to a requirement for assigning women to all types of duty, including combat duty, and (2) those related to whether or not separate facilities would be allowable and/or feasible to protect the privacy of both men and women.

At the request of the House Subcommittee Chairman, Mr. Rehnquist sent a letter dated May 7, 1971 to the Subcommittee detailing the effect of the enactment of the Equal Rights Amendment on several areas of law including the military draft. With respect to the draft, the letter stated:

> The question here is whether Congress would be required either to draft both men and women or to draft no one. A closely related question is whether Congress must permit to volunteer on an equal basis for all sorts of military service, including combat duty. We believe that the likely result of passage of the equal rights amendment is to require both of those results. As has been pointed out by many of the amendment's supporters, that would not require or permit women any more than men to undertake duties for which they are physically unqualified under some generally applied standard.
>
> To what extent such integration of the services would extend to living conditions and training and working units is uncertain. Proponents have indicated that some segregation would be permissible.

Further, there is the possibility that assigning men and women together in the field in direct combat roles might adversely affect the efficiency and discipline of our forces.

On the other hand, if women were not assigned to duty in the field, overseas, or on board ships, but were entering the armed forces in large numbers, this might result in a disproportionate number of men serving more time in the field and on board ship because of a reduced number of positions available for their reassignment.

If this amendment allowed no discrimination on the basis of sex even for the sake of privacy, we believe that the resulting sharing of facilities and living quarters would be contrary to prevailing American standards.

Even if segregation of living quarters and facilities were allowed under the amendment, during combat duty in the field there are often, in effect, no facilities at all, and privacy for both sexes might be impossible to provide or enforce. . . .

20. See 118 Cong. Rec. S4395, S4408 (daily ed. Mar. 21, 1972).

STATEMENT OF SENATOR BAYH
SUPPORTING MILITARY SERVICE FOR WOMEN
118 Cong. Rec. S4389 (daily ed. Mar. 21, 1972)

. . . [I]t is entirely possible that Congress would establish an exemption in which any parent could be exempted from the draft. Ridiculous, you say? Well, throughout most of the 1950s and 1960s . . . [a]ny father was exempted. So that exemption could exist under the equal rights amendment. Any parent, mother or father, could claim that exemption and not be subjected to the draft.

Congress could also provide that the parent who has the primary duty of rearing the children or caring for the home would be exempt. In the judgment of the Senator from Indiana, this would be perfectly constitutional under the equal rights amendment. . . .

Congress could take a further look and provide that no more than one parent in any family would be subject to conscription.

Then, let us move past the exemptions. Let us look at those who are not able to claim an exemption and those who are subject to the draft. What size burden are we really talking about? Does every 17-, 18-, or 19-, or 22-year-old woman feel that she is going to be drafted?

Let us look at the facts as they are today as far as men are concerned. Let us take the 1971 draft call, the most recent draft call. There were, in 1971, 1.9 million men in this country eligible for the draft; 50.5 percent, over half of those, were rejected for induction for one reason or another; 24.9 percent were rejected at induction.

So when we get right down to it, less than 25 percent of the men of this country were ever subjected to the draft in the first place. That number was between 400,000 and 500,000. Of this almost 500,000-man pool of men subjected to the draft after the various rejections, only 98,000 were ever called, and only 94,000 of those were ever inducted.

In other words, 5 percent of the eligible males in the country were inducted into the Army last year. Less than 15 percent — and I wish the Senator from Mississippi were here to verify this, because we are concerned about combat — out of that pool of 5 percent out of almost 2 million men were assigned to combat branches. That means that less than 1 percent of the eligible males in the whole country that were ever assigned to a combat unit.

It might be fair to say that is about the same risk women would be subjected to, except it would be fairer to assume that the sex-neutral standards that would be established by the Armed Forces on the basis of physical competence would exclude an even greater percentage of women because of the ordinary physical standards required, such as pushups, chins, running, and other physical and combat characteristics that are necessary for any member of the armed services.

Now, of this less than 1 percent — and if you look at all of the physical rejections that could occur, you would get down to significantly less than 1 percent of all the women in the pool who would be drafted in the first place — would they be assigned to combat duty?

Admittedly, there is no way we can guarantee they would not be, but in the judgment of the Senator from Indiana, they would be assigned to duty as their commanders thought they were qualified to serve. Just as 85 percent of those who are now in the armed services and who are men and not assigned to combat duties, so the commander would not need to send a woman into the front trenches if he felt that it would not be in the best interests of the combat unit to make such an assignment.

I want to suggest that I hope the time will not come when we have women drafted and sent into combat. I hope the time will not come when they are drafted, very frankly. But I suggest that right now we have a significant number of women in all of our military services who are serving with distinction, and many of them are serving in combat zones.

At the end of his statement, Senator Bayh quoted a letter from Colonel Stella Levy of the Israeli armed forces, which said that women in that country did not actually engage in combat, nor did they receive the same combat training as men. The senator implied that the same conditions could prevail in American armed forces were the amendment to pass. This position illustrates the tendency of advocates of the amendment, of whom Bayh was one of the most ardent, to "waffle" on the issue of equal military service for women. Apparently they were themselves uncomfortable with the idea of women in combat, or at least saw this as the most politically sensitive question of ERA interpretation. It is interesting to note that in the three congressional debates on the amendment between 1946 and 1953, immediately after World War II, the prospect of equal military service for women appeared much less unsettling to Congress. This was probably due to a combination of factors, particularly the performance of women in new roles in World War II, to the point where plans had been made for the conscription of women if the war continued, as well as the widespread belief that the next war would involve nuclear rather than conventional warfare.

Would the "sex-neutral" draft exemption for parents with primary responsibility for child care be constitutional according to the Yale theory of the ERA, if it exempted more women than men (as Bayh suggests it would)?

HALE AND KANOWITZ
WOMEN AND THE DRAFT: A RESPONSE
TO CRITICS OF THE EQUAL RIGHTS AMENDMENT
23 Hast. L. Rev. 199, 201-204 (1971)

. . . [To] evaluate the military implications of the Equal Rights Amendment, it is necessary to consider whether women could serve effectively as fighting members of the military. If they are qualified then it can be demonstrated that there is no legal or social reason for excluding them from equally sharing the benefits and the burdens of military service.

WOMEN AS COMBATANTS

The arguments that women are incapable of serving in the military have centered around two main themes — first, that women are physically incapable of serving in the military and, second, that they have historically demonstrated their unsuitability as soldiers. Both of these arguments are specious at best.

Physical Ability

Dr. Margaret Mead has an interesting view which raises some novel questions as to why women have not traditionally been warriors.

> Recent work on aggression in the animal world emphasized the amount of ritual combat between males of the same species, in which competitive and rivalrous behavior was kept within biologically structured bounds. The females of the same species, when they fight, fight in defense of their young and fight to the death.
>
> The controls which operate on male aggression seem to be lacking in females. Among human beings where cultural controls replace biological controls, the ability to use violence in a disciplined way seems to be dependent upon early experiences and learning how to subject aggressive physical behavior to rules of fair play and appropriateness.
>
> The historical and comparative material at least suggests that it may be highly

undesirable to permit women, trained to inhibit aggressive behavior, to take part in offensive warfare. Defensive warfare, on the other hand does not have the same disadvantages, as it invokes, the biological basis of defense of the nest and the young.[9]

Is the implication, then, that women might be altogether too deadly when turned loose in aggressive warfare? One can hardly believe that much of the warfare presently being waged is guided by principles of appropriateness and fair play even though it is waged exclusively by men. Perhaps fighting to the death in defense of one's young and otherwise inhibiting aggression is not such a bad idea. Ritual combat is wasteful and extremely dangerous in a world with nuclear weapons.

An alternative explanation for the limited role women play in warfare is put forward by anthropologist Lionel Tiger who thinks the reasons are primarily physiological, aggressive behavior depending upon testosterone stimulation.

> In experiments on primates, when both males and females are given extra testosterone, they show much more aggressive, hyper-male activity. Humans have similar reactions under artificial manipulation of hormone levels. Among boys and girls before puberty, boys show more testosterone than girls. But at adolescence the changes are startling: Testosterone in boys increases at least tenfold, and possibly as much as 30 times. On the other hand, girls' testosterone levels only double, from a lower base to begin with. These levels remain stable throughout the life cycle.[10]

. . . Rather than lacking an ability to control their aggressive instincts within the bounds of fair play, women are, Lionel Tiger suggests, simply not as chemically aggressive as are men. But, even if this is true, is it significant? We must question whether, with warfare so technical and destructive potential so great, there is a proven value in having military personnel who are as much as sixty times as aggressive as others. We must also consider whether natural and instinctive behavior is controlling when military personnel undergo extensive physical and psychological conditioning.

Physiologically, women have certainly been greatly handicapped as fighters by the demands of motherhood. Now, however, for the first time in history, women can effectively control their fertility. With the advent of sophisticated birth control techniques, the threat of pregnancy is no longer an obstacle to the effectiveness of a military woman.

Perhaps the most important factor facilitating the effective use of women in the armed forces is the technological revolution in warfare that has taken place over the last generation. The changes include the use of bombs, missiles and high-powered guns which minimize the strength required and maximize the precision and technological ability needed. Such changes make women more fit to wage war than ever before. . . . The extent of the technological revolution in warfare is illustrated by the fact that only 14 percent of the United States armed forces personnel now actually serve in combat units.[12] An examination of the present armed forces job categories reveals that

9. Mead, A National Service System as a Solution to a Variety of National Problems, in The Draft 99,107 (S. Tax ed. 1967).

10. Tiger, Male Dominance? Yes, Alas. A Sexist Plot? No, N.Y. Times, Oct. 25, 1970 (Magazine) at 124.

12.

Occupation Group	Percent Distribution 1967
Ground combat	14.1
Electronics	14.7
Other Technical	7.7
Administrative and Clerical	18.4
Mechanics and Repairmen	26.1
Craftsmen	6.8
Services	12.0

Bureau of the Census, U.S. Dep't of Commerce, Statistical Abstract of the United States 260 (1970) [hereinafter cited as Statistical Abstract].

at least half of the jobs being done in the military could be handled by women of no more than average endurance, strength, and abilities.[13] Moreover, women in particularly fit condition could qualify for any combat position.

Admittedly, present physical standards might have to be modified, but that should be encouraged in any event. Since so few military personnel are assigned to combat units, it is evident that many current physical standards are unrealistic. Frequently, they work to the disadvantage of the physically perfect, the unsophisticated, the poor, and the honest. At present, a high proportion of physical deferments go to young men in the highest educational brackets.[14] While this might suggest that education is a process dangerous to one's health, it is more likely that many physical deferments of an exotic nature go to those who have the ability to research the physical standards and the money to pay for high-class medical testimony. If a system were worked out whereby physical standards were relaxed and draftees were assigned according to their physical limitations, the justice of the requirements would be greater. Ninety-pound women could serve efficiently as supply clerks, as could ninety-pound men, and under the equal rights principle both would be equally draftable. . . .

————————

The attempts by proponents and opponents of the amendment to come to grips with its effect on the military illustrates particularly well the social attitudes and values inherent in the debate, as well as the impact the elimination of sex discrimination in one major institution can have on women's status in others. A 1973 law review article surveyed in detail the practices and regulations which would have to be changed if women were fully integrated into the armed forces. As you read the following excerpts from the article, consider whether the changes the Equal Rights Amendment would bring in the military are really so different from those that would be required under Title VII of the Civil Rights Act of 1964 to integrate other predominantly male occupations.

NOTE
THE EQUAL RIGHTS AMENDMENT AND THE MILITARY
82 Yale L.J. 1533, 1539-1554 (1973)

A. Getting In

1. Enlistment

In all the services women are subject to more exacting enlistment criteria relating to minimum age and parental consent requirements.[41] They must also have higher scores on mental aptitude tests and more educational credentials than their male counterparts.[42] Although women in the Army are barred from strenuous training and from

————————

13. See id.

14. " 'There are definite data to indicate higher disqualification rates for medical reasons among [college graduates] . . . which seemingly may be attributed to these candidates being more 'sophisticated' about . . . medically disqualifying defects.' " Newsweek, Aug. 3, 1970, at 42 (quoting an official report).

41. 10 U.S.C. §505 (1970) sets out the qualifications for original enlistment in the Army, Navy, Air Force, Marine Corps, and Coast Guard. Men applying must be not less than 17 years of age, whereas women must be not less than 18. Written parental consent is necessary to enlist a male under the age of 18 or a female under the age of 21. These distinctions are defended as a means of "protecting" young women from "making rash and immature" decisions and of providing the services "with a screening device by requiring wise and objective judgment of the interested parent or guardian." . . . [Hearings Before the Special Subcommittee on the Utilization of Manpower in the Military of the House Committee on Armed Services, 92d Cong., 1st & 2nd Sess. 12498 (1972)] (testimony of General Bailey) [hereinafter cited as Utilization Hearings].

A bill to make the minimum age of enlistment in the armed forces the same for both males and females was introduced in Congress on October 4, 1971, H.R. 11064, 92d Cong., 1st Sess. (1971), and received great attention from the branches of the service. See, e.g., Utilization Hearings, at 12500 (testimony of Captain Quigley). However, it died in the Armed Services Committee of the House and would have to be reintroduced.

42. To enlist in the Army men need only to meet the educational requirements of the specific option for which they are enlisting, not all of which require completion of high school. Women, however, must

various occupational specialities which require "heavy" labor, they must meet a minimum physical standard stated in more stringent terms than that imposed on males.[45] Finally, men who have dependent children may enlist under the normal Army procedures, but women must first obtain a waiver.[46]

Most of these enlistment differentials are justified on a theory of supply and demand: Since more women, but fewer men, apply than are desired by the services, the standards for women are set at higher levels.[47] This reasoning, based as it is upon judgments concerning the usefulness of an entire sex rather than of the individuals that comprise it, would be unacceptable under the ERA. Instead, minimum standards with regard to age, education, and mental and physical ability would have to be identical for men and women. Both sexes would have to be subjected to the same tests, except to the extent that certain medical criteria would be permitted to deal with the unique physical characteristics of each sex.

The courts might decide, as they have in employment discrimination cases under Title VII of the Civil Rights Act,[49] to supplement this rule of identical treatment with safeguards against more subtle forms of discrimination. Thus intelligence tests would have to be carefully scrutinized to insure that they are actually testing general intelligence—or skills specifically needed by the military—rather than a familiarity with male-oriented items in our present culture.[50] High physical standards or skill requirements which eliminated a large proportion of women might also be challenged as unnecessarily restrictive at a time when eighty-five percent of military jobs are noncombatant.[51] With regard to such a challenge, the services and ultimately the courts would

---

possess either a high school diploma or certification of passage of the equivalency exam. In addition, women are given a different battery of mental aptitude tests, and it is argued that since the scores are not comparable, the minimum qualifying scores are not required to be equal. Williams, Army Fact Sheet, Army Enlistment Standards for Men and Women, Aug. 7, 1972, on file with the Yale Law Journal. An attorney in the office of the General Counsel of the Secretary of Defense stated:

"All of the services have indicated to me that in general the minimum standards on test results and educational level required in order for a person to enlist or be an officer are generally higher for women than for men."

Speech by Carole L. Frings, DACOWITS Fall Meeting, Colorado Springs, Colorado, Nov. 12-16, 1972, at 11. See also . . . [Central All-Volunteer Force Task Force, Utilization of Military Women vi (1972)] at 14 [hereinafter cited as Task Force Report].

45. The consistency with which minimum physical standards are applied—with respect to both men and women—may be open to doubt. But the regulations are stated in undeniably different terms. For example, potential women Army enlistees must be able to perform with maximum effort for "indefinite" periods, to take "long" marches, and to withstand long periods of standing. Men are only ineligible if they have defects which would prevent "moderate" marching, and their ability to perform with maximum effort need only be for "long" rather than "indefinite" periods. The psychiatric standards for women are also more stringent. See Appexdix VIII, Physical Profile Functional Capacity Guide, C22, AR 40-501, June 19, 1968 (in document dated Aug. 7, 1972), on file with the Yale Law Journal. In the Marine Corps the physical profile for entry of women is also higher than that required for men. The Navy and Air Force have the same physical profile requirements for females as for males. Task Force Report, supra [note 42] at 16.

46. Task Force Report, supra [note 42] at 17. This differential also exists in the Marine Corps. Id. Until recently, both services also required a waiver for all married women, id., but the Army cancelled this restriction, effective April 20, 1973. N.Y. Times, March 27, 1973, at 26, col. 3.

47. Speech by Frings, supra note 42, at 11.

49. 42 U.S.C. §2000e (1970).

50. See Brown, Emerson, Falk & Freedman, [The Equal Rights Amendment: A Constitutional Basis for Equal Rights for Women, 80 Yale L.J. 871 (1971)], at 971. For example, the Armed Forces Qualifying Test is presently being revised because it was found to be male oriented. Interview with Col. Bette Morden, Special Assistant to the Director of the WAC, Washington, D.C., Dec. 6, 1972. (Col. Morden retired on Dec. 31, 1972.) By stressing areas, such as mechanics, which are unfamiliar to many women, the test eliminates qualified women. On the other hand, a test specifically designed to examine an applicant's skill in a particular field would be legitimate under the ERA, if narrowly drawn to fit the needs of the services.

Courts have already struck down allegedly "race-neutral" tests and educational requirements which were found to be discriminatory in effect. See Griggs v. Duke Power Co., 401 U.S. 424 (1971); Hicks v. Crown Zellerbach Corp., 319 F. Supp. 314 (E.D. La. 1970); Broussard v. Schlumberger Well Services, 315 F. Supp. 506 (S.D. Tex. 1970). See also Quarles v. Phillip Morris, Inc., 279 F. Supp. 505 (E.D. Va. 1968) Hholding unlawful a seniority system neutral on its face which perpetuated the effect of an employer's past discriminatory acts).

51. 118 Cong. Rec. S4390 (daily ed. March 21, 1972).

have to determine whether the legitimate needs of the military justified the maintenance of standards that barred virtually all women from the substantial educational and vocational opportunities in the armed forces.[52]

2. *Officer Procurement*

With undisguised bluntness the military services discriminate against women in the procurement of officers. Female applicants to the Army Officer Candidate School (OCS) are required to have completed two years of college, whereas male applicants need only have a secondary school education.[53] Direct appointments to a number of positions in the Navy and Marines are statutorily restricted to males.[54] Custom and regulation prohibit women from being considered for admission to the three major military academies,[55] even though they are not barred by statute.[56] Finally, the military's ROTC program was until recently completely closed to women,[57] and even now is available only on a limited, experimental basis.[58] . . .

B. *Fitting In*

1. *Structure of the Services*

The Army is organized into a number of functional units, such as the Infantry, the Medical Corps, and the Corps of Engineers, all of which are open to men. Women, on the other hand, are restricted to a single unit, the WACs, although they may be temporarily detailed to other units.[63] The other services do not have separate women's corps per se, but they still handle women separately for a number of administrative purposes.[64] For example, in the Marines, if there are an appreciable number of women at one base, a separate women's company will be created within a battalion.[65]

52. Cf. Griggs v. Duke Power Co., 401 U.S. 424 (1971) (Court sustained black employees' contention that an employer's requirement of a high-school education or passing of a standardized general intelligence test as a job condition violated Title VII, because neither of these requirements was related to the jobs in question); 2 CCH Employ. Prac. Guide §6286 (1971) (employer who applied a minimum-height rule to job applicants of both sexes found to have violated Title VII of the Civil Rights Act, since evidence revealed that the height requirement would be satisfied by the average male but by only twenty percent of the females and that such a requirement was not justified as a business necessity).

53. House, Fact Sheet, Procurement of WAC Officers Compared with Procurement of Male Officers, on file with the Yale Law Journal. In addition, females must have a G.T. (mental) score of 115 as compared with a G.T. score of 110 for males.

54. 10 U.S.C. §§5575, 5576, 5577, 5587 (1970). These restricted career areas in the Navy are the Supply Staff Corps, the Chaplain Staff Corps, the Civil Engineer Staff Corps, and officers designated for engineering, aeronautical engineering, and special duty. Women in the Navy and Marines also may not be limited duty officers. 10 U.S.C. §5589 (1970).

Women similarly are barred from the aviation cadet program, into which civilians and enlisted members of the Navy and Air Force can be commissioned. See 10 U.S.C. §§6911, 6913, 8257 (1970). The Navy has recently selected eight women for its aviation cadet program as "a test program established as a part of the Navy goal of equal rights and opportunities for women." N.Y. Times, Jan. 11, 1973, at 77, col. 1.

55. Interview with Col. Morden, supra note 50. Several Senators have nominated women for admission to the academies, see, e.g., 118 Cong. Rec. S4860 (daily ed. March 28, 1972), but none has been accepted.

56. See 10 U.S.C. §§4346, 9346, 69581 (1970).

57. This restriction was by custom rather than by statute. 10 U.S.C. §§2102-11 (1970) refers only to the admission of "persons" into ROTC.

58. A WAC ROTC program was initiated in September 1972 at ten colleges to test the effectiveness of ROTC as a procurement source for women officers. In conjunction with this program, twenty ROTC scholarships were to be made available to female students. Utilization Hearings, supra [note 41], at 12449 (testimony of Gen. Bailey); House, Fact Sheet, supra note 53. The Air Force ROTC program for women began in 1969 and is now open to women at 156 of the 170 colleges with Air Force units. See The Lady is an Air Force General, Airman Magazine, Sept., 1971, at 45. There are presently 17 women enrolled in Navy ROTC at four colleges. See Speech by Frings, supra note 42, at 15; N.Y. Times, Dec. 4, 1972, at 1, col. 3.

63. 10 U.S.C. §3071 (1970).

64. Speech by Frings, supra note 42, at 21. See also Task Force Report . . . at B-26.

65. Interview with Colonel Sustad, former Director of Women Marines, Washington, D.C., Dec. 5, 1972 (Col. Sustad retired on Jan. 30, 1973).

Under the ERA the WACs and all other remnants of separate women's corps would have to be eliminated.[66] Although the Supreme Court has never found sexually "separate but equal" facilities to violate the Fourteenth Amendment, such facilities would be impermissible under the ERA. The proponents of the Amendment have pointed out that the separate treatment of two groups, one of which has previously been treated as inferior by the law, can never in fact be equal.[67] Moreover, separation by sex is indisputably classification by sex — and that is forbidden by the ERA.[68]

Congress evidently did not intend, however, that sexual integration encompass integrated living facilities. The legislative history shows that the constitutional right to privacy was thought to permit the military to maintain separate living quarters for men and women, so that they would not be forced to undress or perform personal functions in the presence of the opposite sex.[69] This argument is dependent on two unsettled legal conclusions: that the right to privacy protects individuals from the embarrassment that would result from forced cohabitation and that the right so interpreted extends to military personnel. Neither conclusion, however, is unreasonable. First, the Ninth Circuit has held that the Fourth Amendment privacy right encompasses "[t]he desire to shield one's figured [sic] from view of strangers, and particularly strangers of the opposite sex. . . . "[71] Second, while the military may legitimately deprive its personnel of much

66. When questioned by the House Appropriations Committee, the Judge Advocate General of the Army commented on the effect that the ERA would have on the structure of the WACs:

"The primary function of maintaining a separate Women's Army Corps will probably be eliminated. Whether those distinctions based on sex that would remain permissible under the amendment will be continued through a separate label for female members is primarily a question of policy. However, the impact of the equal rights amendment, in my opinion, will so limit the permissible distinctions that it would be inaccurate to designate female members as belonging to a separate corps, as that term is used to designate separate branches within the Army."

Reprinted in Speech by Frings, supra note 42, at 21-22.

67. See Brown, Emerson, Falk & Freedman, supra note 50, at 902-03; Emerson, In Support of the Equal Rights Amendment, [6 Harv. Civ. Rights-Civ. Lib. L. Rev. 225 (1971)] at 231.

Congresswoman Martha Griffiths recognized the inadequacy of a dual system:

"I am not for 'separate but equal' because there is no such thing. The 'separate but equal' schools that we were sending blacks to were not equal. The 'separate but equal' schools that you are sending women to are not equal."

[Hearings on H.J. Res. 208 Before Subcomm. 4 of the House Committee on the Judiciary, 92d Cong., 1st Sess. 75-76 (1971) (remarks of Senator Ervin)] at 47. Dr. Bernice Sandler observed that sex-segregated colleges, particularly when operated by the same governing body, are reminiscent of race-segregated facilities. Id. at 272.

The case law under the Fourteenth Amendment has been mixed. Compare Kirstein v. Rector & Visitors, 309 F. Supp. 184 (E.D. Va. 1970) and Bray v. Lee, 337 F. Supp. 934 (D. Mass. 1972) with Williams v. McNair, 316 F. Supp. 134 (D.S.C. 1970).

68. "The law may operate by grouping individuals in terms of existing characteristics or functions, but not through a vast overclassification by sex." H.R. Rep. No. 92-359, [92d Cong., 1st Sess.] at 6 (Separate Views). . . .

69. See 117 Cong. Rec. H 9368 (daily ed. Oct. 12, 1971) (remarks of Congressman Ryan):

"An argument which has been made against the original language of the equal rights amendment is that it would violate common sense and public standards by prohibiting the separation of sexes in the sleeping quarters of such public institutions as coeducational colleges, prisons, and military barracks. . . . The constitutionally guaranteed right to privacy affords grounds for reasonable separation of the sexes in these instances." . . .

71. Ford v. Story, 324 F.2d 450, 455 (9th Cir. 1963) (police officer held to have violated the Fourth Amendment right of a woman who had come to the police station to report an assault. Over her objection, the officer had taken photographs of her in the nude and circulated them among the police personnel at the station. The court stated that "[w]e cannot conceive of a more basic subject of privacy than the naked body," the shielding of which is "impelled by elementary self-respect and personal dignity." Id. at 455). Although the right to privacy is arguably broad enough to encompass all such serious intrusions upon basic human dignity, see Bloustein, Privacy as an Aspect of Human Dignity: An Answer to Dean Prosser, 39 N.Y.U. L. Rev. 962 (1964), the courts have been well advised to proceed cautiously, with an eye to the established doctrines surrounding the express constitutional provisions from which the privacy right was derived. See Ely, The Wages of Crying Wolf: A Comment on Roe v. Wade, 82 Yale L.J. 921 (1973). In this regard, it should be noted that the right to segregated sleeping quarters propounded by Congress is the closest corollary in the military context to the privacy of home and sexual relations already protected by Supreme Court decisions. . . . Stanley v. Georgia, 394 U.S. 557 (1969).

of the privacy guaranteed to civilians, such deprivations must always be justified by compelling interests of discipline or morale.[72] Since living quarters are now segregated throughout the military, it is unlikely that the services would assert, or the courts declare, that the protection of sexual privacy through such an arrangement contravenes the doctrine of military necessity. Thus the courts would be justified in validating Congress' conclusion that the right to privacy, when balanced against the ERA, would permit the limited separation of the sexes for sleeping and toilet purposes.[73] The precise degree to which entire housing facilities could be kept separate is not clear,[74] but Professor Emerson has suggested that courts and administrators may look to the current mores of the community regarding relations between the sexes in determining the scope of the privacy exception.[75]

2. Basic Training

All enlisted recruits receive some form of basic training before being trained in their occupational specialties. In each of the services such training for males stresses discipline and physical development, while that of women is focused on administrative subjects.[76] A similar disparity characterizes officer basic training.[77] Moreover, training units are sexually segregated,[78] frequently at different bases.

These differences undoubtedly reflect the disparate utilization of men and women

72. A finding that the right to privacy bars forced cohabitation in military housing would not require the services to provide individual bedrooms and showers for every soldier. For one thing, there is no reason to believe that forcing men and women to disrobe in the presence of the *same* sex violates the "elementary self-respect and personal dignity" shielded by the right to privacy. . . . Moreover, it could probably be shown that the provision of individual living quarters, at least in basic training and combat situations, would seriously jeopardize the preparation and utilization of an effective fighting force, in violation of the doctrine of military necessity. . . .

73. Since privacy is an individual right, the possibility of waiver raises special problems. Presumably, if a group of service personnel waived thier right to be housed separately, the Equal Rights Amendment would require that they be assigned quarters on the basis of sex-neutral criteria, which might result in voluntary coeducational sleeping facilities. While the content of the privacy right may be determined by reference to societal mores, such mores in the *absence* of the privacy right are not of constitutional dimension and cannot be used to defeat the Amendment's ban on sex classifications. . . . However, it is possible that individual rights which require detailed government regulation—such as the rights to privacy and the equal protection of the laws in the military, public school, or prison context—cannot be waived.

74. In planning housing facilities the military could follow the model of universities which have established coeducational dormitories, while maintaining the right to privacy by designating separate floors or separate parts of the same building for each of the sexes. See Hearings, supra [note 67] at 274 (testimony of Dr. Sandler).

75. Brown, Emerson, Falk & Freedman, supra note 50, at 902. This conclusion is not unreasonable in light of the fact that social traditions and mores have been used to determine the very existence of the right to privacy. See Roe v. Wade, 93 S. Ct. 705, 735 (1973) (Stewart, J., concurring); Griswold v. Connecticut, 381 U.S. 479, 493 (1965) (Goldberg, J., concurring).

76. In the Army women are trained in professional development (benefits of military service, community services, leadership, personnel policies, etc.) but are not trained to be "traditional" military professionals. Watson, Fact Sheet, [Expansion of the Women's Army Corps, on file with the Yale Law Journal]. Although physically qualified, see note 45 supra, they do not take long marches or utilize their hand-to-hand combat potential. The closest that WACs come to combat training is two days of field training that "has the air of a well-disciplined group of girl scouts on a camp-out." Phillips, On Location with the WACs, Ms., Nov., 1972, at 62. In the Navy shipboard organization and rugged physical training are excluded from the female program. Interview with Captain Quigley, Assistant Chief of Naval Personnel for Women, Washington, D.C., Dec. 5, 1972. Instruction for women in the Marines includes subjects such as the application of make up, how to avoid trouble, and how to wear a uniform. Interview with Colonel Sustad, supra note 65. Air Force training follows a similar pattern. Interview with General Holm, supra note 62.

77. Interviews with Colonel Sustad, supra note 65, and Captain Quigley, supra note 76.

78. See, e.g., Interview with Colonel Sustad, supra note 65; Priem, Fact Sheet, Expansion of the Women's Army Corps, on file with the Yale Law Journal. Continental Army Command (CONARC) is currently studying a proposal to shorten the WAC Officer Basic Course from eighteen to nine weeks, after which the WAC officer would attend the basic officer course of one of the male branches. Priem, Fact Sheet, supra. The Air Force officer program already permits some mingling of the sexes during periods not set aside for physical training. Interview with General Holm, supra note 62.

in the military. After ratification of the ERA the services would still be permitted to adapt basic training to probable later assignments if they so desired, but placement in a particular training program could not be based on an overbroad sex classification. . . .

. . . A few differences in the physical training of all women might be justified by the unique physical characteristics of the sexes, but such differences would have to correlate closely with the characteristics in question and could not be based on the generalization that women are weaker than men.[81] . . .

3. Occupational Specialties

The military occupational classification (MOS) system is designed to identify, classify, and relate skills and personality characteristics to military job requirements.[86] In the Army women are specifically excluded from those MOS associated with combat, close combat support, hazardous duty, and strenuous physical activity, as well as those that would require their assignment to an isolated area.[87] As of July 1972, medical and dental specialties and administrative personnel accounted for the occupational specialties of 94.6 percent of the enlisted women in that service.[88] Similarly, women are excluded from more than half of the army officer MOS.[89]

Although the "Navy's intrinsic mission [is] as a seagoing operating force,"[90] women cannot be assigned to duty on naval vessels other than hospital ships and transports.[91] Furthermore, sea duty or even "eligibility for command at sea" is often an important

81. Brown, Emerson, Falk & Freedman, supra . . . at 893-94.

86. For example, factors that are to be considered in the training classification of an individual in a particular MOS in the Army are: (1) needs of the Army, (2) existing grade and MOS imbalances (both local and Army-wide), (3) budgetary or travel restrictions, (4) medical condition and physical limitations, (5) enlisted commitments, (6) training and experience (both civilian and military), (7) education, (8) test scores, (9) preference of individual, (10) avocation and hobbies, and (11) normal pattern of career progression. GAO, Improper Use of Military Personnel (1971), reprinted in Utilization Hearings, supra [note 41] at 12410.

87. Morden, Fact Sheet, WAC Utilization, Aug. 15, 1972, on file with the Yale Law Journal. Out of a total of 482 enlisted MOS, 434 are available to women. Id. Until August 1972, only 140 MOS had been open to women. The integration of women into these areas has been slow. Interview with Col. Morden, supra note 50. The only positions which are closed to men are WAC Commander, WAC recruiter, and certain jobs in the medical field involving the care and treatment of female patients. Utilization Hearings, supra [note 41], at 12443 (testimony of General Bailey).

88. Task Force Report, supra . . . at 26. Prior to July 17, 1972, women generally enlisted in the Administrative, Supply and Medical Fields. Women can now enlist for the following additional career fields: air defense missiles, wire maintenance, precision devices, textile and leather repair, automotive maintenance, motor transport operator, printing, law enforcement, and radio code. Since July 17, approximately twenty-five women have enlisted in these new career fields. The Army anticipates that with more publicity many more women will enlist in these areas that had been exclusively male career fields. Elder, Fact Sheet, Career Field Enlistments, Aug. 7, 1972, on file with the Yale Law Journal.

89. The total number of officer MOS in the Army is 365. Of the 188 from which women are excluded, eighty-one are medical officer MOS, thirty-five are male command MOS, forty-nine involve railroad, marine, or aviation operations, and twenty-three others involve strenuous physical labor or assignment to a combat or hazardous duty area. Morden, Fact Sheet, supra note 87. As a result, 46 percent of the women now serving as army officers are in the field of administration and personnel, while another 14.3 percent are in positions commanding other women. One of the MOS from which women are excluded is Post Commander. Women command organized WAC units consisting of approximately 100 women. Groups of less than fifty women at a station are called WAC contingents and are administered and commanded by men. Morden, Fact Sheet, supra note 87. Some classifications are particularly obtuse: women may be military police officers, but not correctional officers. Numerical List of Occupational Specialties, Section III, C31, AR 611-101, June 13, 1972, on file with the Yale Law Journal.

90. Utilization Hearings, supra [note 41] , at 12455.

91. 10 U.S.C. §6015 (1970). Women have served aboard Navy ships only with medical staffs on hospital vessels and transports belonging to the Military Sealift Command. Washington Post, Feb. 15, 1972, at A3, col. 5. Admiral Zumwalt's Z-gram 116, CNO msg 071115Z Aug. 72, noted that a limited number of officer and enlisted women were being assigned to the regular ship's company of the U.S.S. Sanctuary, a recommissioned hospital ship, as a pilot program. Although Z-gram 116 also authorized "limited" entry of enlisted women into all ratings, the statutory prohibition against assigning women to combat ships still exists, so that actual assignment policies are unclear.

qualification in the selection for officer shore assignments.[92] Finally, the "restricted line," a broad officer classification encompassing the more technical occupational specialties, is statutorily closed to women.[93] As a result of these restrictions, Navy women are concentrated in personnel jobs.[94]

Enlisted women Marines may serve on an interchangeable basis with men in about two-thirds of the enlisted Marine MOS.[95] Women Marine officers are also restricted to two-thirds of the available MOS fields.[96] Moreover, a regulation specifically states that women officers may succeed to command only over those activities which have the administration of women Marines as their primary function.[97]

By contrast, only five officer career fields in the Air Force are closed to women, and these are all associated with aircraft which might be engaged in combat missions.[98] However, half of the male officers are concentrated in the pilot and navigator categories,[99] which are two of those closed to women as a matter of Air Force policy.[100] The number of specialty fields open to enlisted women has recently been expanded, but few women have yet been assigned to these new fields.[101]

The primary reasons for the exclusion of women from various occupational fields, whether by law or regulation, are physiological and cultural. Some jobs are considered to be beyond the physical capabilities of women.[102] Others, most notably combat and sea duty,[103] are simply thought to be male activities.[104] Since women have proven their

92. NR-0836 (1948) states that "the officer detailed as Commandant of a naval district shall be an officer of the line in the Navy eligible for command at sea." Thus, women officers, whose career patterns should qualify them for just such leadership assignments, are arbitrarily excluded. Denby, Command Opportunity and Flag Grade for Women Officers, June 19, 1972, at 23-24 (unpublished thesis at U.S. Naval War College).
93. See note 54 supra. Theoretically, women in the "unrestricted line," encompassing most other officer assignments, can be designated for temporary duty in a restricted line community not involved in sea duty.
94. Coye [The Restricted Unrestricted Line Officer: The Status of the Navy's Woman Line Officer, Naval War College Rev. (March 1972), reprinted in Utilization Hearings, supra note 41], at 12484, citing Bureau of Naval Personnel Computer Printout, April 29, 1971. Commander Denby concluded after studying the opportunities for female officers that there was "irrefutable evidence that women officers have stagnated in a relatively limited number of career paths primarily in administrative areas." Denby, supra note 92, at 61. See also Coye, [id.] at 12476.
95. Utilization Hearings, supra [note 41], at 12462 (testimony of Colonel Sustad). Thirteen of the thirty-six enlisted MOS are completely closed to women. Limited duty and combat ship assignments are also closed to women Marines. See notes 54 & 91 supra.
96. Utilization Hearings, supra [note 41], at 12461 (testimony of Colonel Sustad). The twenty-three MOS available to female officers are not the same as the twenty-three considered suitable for enlisted women. For example, enlisted female personnel may be trained in logistics, but officers may not; officers may be in the Supply Services, but enlisted women may not.
97. Interview with Colonel Sustad, supra note 65.
98. 10 U.S.C. §8549 (1970) prohibits the Air Force from assigning women to duty in aircraft engaged in combat missions.
99. Interview with General Holm, supra note 62.
100. Id. Thus, as in the Navy, women "airmen" are excluded from one of the primary missions of the branch of the service of which they are considered full members.
101. Although, as of June, 1971, 98 percent of enlisted career fields were technically open to women. Task Force Report supra [note 42] at 25, as of July of the following year three-quarters of enlisted women were still administrative specialists and clerks. Id. at 26.
102. The Air Force excludes women from such jobs as telephone lineman for this reason. Utilization Hearings, supra [note 41] , at 12451 (testimony of General Holm).
103. When asked about the justification for restricting women from seagoing positions, Captain Quigley replied: "I would say first of all that you have to look at the sociological picture, and I do not think that this country, societally speaking, is ready for women sailing submarines under the sea and commanding aircraft carriers across the waters." Id. at 12495. See also id. at 12469 (testimony of General Bailey).
104. These justifications parallel those that have long been asserted in defense of occupational exclusion in other areas of employment. Under the Fourteenth Amendment and Title VII of the 1964 Civil Rights Act, the courts have outlawed exclusionary employment practices based on such sexual stereotypes. See, e.g., Phillips v. Martin Marietta Corp., 400 U.S. 542 (1971); Bowe v. Colgate-Palmolive Co., 416 F.2d 711 (7th Cir. 1969); Weeks v. Southern Bell Tel. & Tel. Co., 408 F.2d 228 (5th Cir. 1969); Ridinger v. General Motors Corp., 325 F. Supp. 1089 (S.D. Ohio 1971); Cheatwood v. South Central Bell Tel. & Tel. Co., 303 F. Supp. 754 (M.D. Ala. 1969); Rosenfeld v. Southern Pacific Co., 293 F. Supp. 1219 (D.C. Cal. 1968); Sail'er Inn v. Kirby, 5 Cal.

usefulness as administrators and personnel officers, the services may also feel that they are needed to provide a skilled continuity base.[105] Finally, women may be excluded from some training programs because, in the places where that skill is needed, a woman cannot be sent for other reasons.[106] Most revealing is the attitude that women would serve in a much larger number of service positions (as they did during World War II) if there were a national emergency.[107]

Under the Amendment all occupational specialties would have to be open equally to men and women. . . .

III. MOVING UP

Although many statutory limitations on the promotion of women to high ranking positions have been repealed,[115] the proportion of such positions actually filled by women is far smaller than the proportion of women in the military as a whole.[116] This discrepancy may be explained, at least in part, by continuing discrimination against women in promotion law and policy.[117]

Although enlisted women compete with enlisted men for Army promotion, separate promotion eligibility lists are maintained for WAC officers.[118] Navy and Marine

---

3d 1, 485 P.2d 529, 95 Cal. Rptr. 329 (1971). See generally Note, Developments in the Law—Employment Discrimination and Title VII of the Civil Rights Act of 1964, 84 Harv. L. Rev. 1109 (1971).

Title VII provides that it shall be an "unlawful employment practice" for an employer engaged in an industry affecting interstate commerce, who has twenty-five or more employees, to "discriminate against any individual with respect to his compensation, terms, conditions, or privileges of employment, because of such individual's race, color, religion, sex, or national origin. . . ." 42 U.S.C. §2000e-2(a)(1) (1970). Although the statute's basic proscription against sex descrimination is absolute on its face, one significant qualification is included. The provisions do not apply "in those certain instances where religion, sex, or national origin is a bona fide occupational qualification reasonably necessary to the normal operation of that particular business enterprise. . . ." 42 U.S.C. §2000e-2(e) (1970). This "bfoq" test is similar to the Equal Rights Amendment's "unique physical characteristics" exception. See Brown, Emerson, Falk & Freedman, supra [note 94] , at 926.

105. Coye, supra [note 94] at 12480.

106. Utilization Hearings, supra [note 41] , at 12486 (testimony of General Bailey). These reasons include: (1) In an "emergency" it might be necessary to send the person filling a particular job slot to a combat area, and (2) housing or grade restrictions might preclude transfer of a woman to an area that requires a particular MOS.

107. Utilization Hearings, supra [note 41] , at 12445, 12467, 12486 (testimony of General Bailey); id. at 12502 (testimony of General Holm).

115. Until 1967, WAC promotion to the grades of captain, major, and lieutenant colonel could be made only to fill vacancies in those grades, whereas male officers could be considered without regard to vacancies. 10 U.S.C. §§3299(f), (g) (1964), *as amended,* 10 U.S.C. §3299 (1970). Also repealed at that time was Act of Sept. 2, 1958, Pub. L. 85-861, §1(80)(E), 72 Stat. 1479, which prohibited WAC reserve officers from being promoted above the grade of lieutenant colonel, and 10 U.S.C. §3215 (1964), *as amended,* 10 U.S.C. §3215(a) (1970), which placed a two percent limit on the percentage which the prescribed authorized strength in female warrant officers bore to the total authorized strength of the Army in warrant officers. 10 U.S.C. §5462 (1970) still gives the Secretary of the Navy power to prescribe the number of women officers who may hold appointments in each grade above lieutenant junior grade in the Navy and above first lieutenant in the Marines.

116. See Utilization Hearings, supra [note 41] at 12440 (testimony of Congressman Pike):

"There are roughly a million people in the Army of which [sic] only 13,000 are women, about one woman for every 80 men. There is one woman brigadier general for 255 Army brigadier generals, one woman colonel for 500 Army colonels, one woman lieutenant colonel for every 190 Army lieutenant colonels, one woman major for every 120 Army majors, one woman captain for every 140 Army captains. Down in the realm of lieutenant, the women approach, but do not reach their proportionate share. The Army treats its women better than the Navy and the Air Force in terms of rank. There are still no female Major Generals."

See Special Subcomm. on the Utilization of Manpower in the Military of the House Comm. on Armed Services, 92d. Cong., 2d Sess., Report H.A.S.C. No. 92-58, at 14660 (1972).

117. Only the Air Force has no separate promotion lists or quotas for men and women, yet even in that service there is a comparatively low number of female officers. Air Force General Holm stated that the large ratio in the lower grades was "due in large part to the expansion of the force in recent years," and that because of past promotion restriction there are few women coming up through the system who have the time in service and the grade necessary for promotion. *Utilization Hearings,* supra [note 41] at 12488-89; Telephone Interview with General Holm, Director Secretary of the Air Force Personnel Council, April 16, 1973. See Utilization Hearings . . . at 12488 for a breakdown by sex of each rank in the Air Force.

118. Fact Sheet, WAC Promotion Policies, on file with the Yale Law Journal; 10 U.S.C. §§3283, 3296,

enlisted women compete for promotion with their male counterparts in their skill specialty.[119] Females may not, however, be considered for selection as limited duty officers,[120] an officer designation to which enlisted men who have served for a number of years in a specific technical field may be promoted. Navy and Marine women officers are considered for promotion through the rank of captain by separate selection boards.[121] Although the selection boards for male officers continue to supervise promotion to the highest ranks, women may only be appointed above the grade of captain (to flag rank) by order of the Secretary of the relevant service, and then only when there is a position of sufficient importance and responsibility to warrant such a designation and it is determined that the person best qualified to fill that position is a woman. Moreover, any woman officer so appointed reverts to her permanent grade when she is detached from the flag position,[122] although men retain their rank.

Since separate but equal treatment would be forbidden by the Amendment unless required by privacy considerations or military necessity, all vestiges of separate promotion systems would have to be eliminated, even if the military could demonstrate that the requirements for advancement were equal for each sex.[124] . . .

HALE AND KANOWITZ
WOMEN AND THE DRAFT: A RESPONSE
TO CRITICS OF THE EQUAL RIGHTS AMENDMENT
23 Hast. L. Rev. 199, 207-210 (1971)

BENEFITS OF MILITARY SERVICE

Since women are qualified to serve, there is no reason to deny them the many benefits available in the military. During the past decades, the military has been an avenue to acceptance and social betterment in this country. Minorities such as the American Indian, Americans of Japanese ancestry, Mexican Americans, and black Americans have served competently and even heroically. In fact the experience of black men in the American military service may provide an interesting parallel for the experi-

---

3311 (1970). The Director of the WACs is not automatically appointed a lieutenant or major general upon selection, as are the chiefs of the various male corps, and she alone is statutorily said to serve "normally for not more than four years." Compare 10 U.S.C. §3071 (1970) with 10 U.S.C. §3036 (1970).

    119. When Captain Quigley noted this fact at the Utilization Hearings, Representative Pike replied that nevertheless:

    "If you are an enlisted man in the Navy you are six times as likely to be an E-6 as an E-1 [the lowest rank]. If you are an enlisted woman, you are more than twice as likely to be an E-1 as an E-6. There are almost as many commanders in the Navy as there are ensigns, unless you're a woman, in which case there are three ensigns for every commander."

    Utilization Hearings, supra [note 41] at 12440.

    120. 10 U.S.C. §5589 (1970).

    121. 10 U.S.C. §5764 (1970), *as amended by* Pub. L. No. 90-130 §§1(19)(J.), (K), 81 Stat. 378 (1967). The appointment and promotion of women officers are governed by laws separate from those dealing with male officers. See, e.g., 10 U.S.C. §§5703, 5704, 5760, 5767(c), 5771 (1970). A statute which specified the number of years a male officer in the Navy or Marines had to serve in one grade before he could be considered for promotion to the next higher grade was suspended by Exec. Order No. 11,437, 3 C.F.R. 142 (1968 Comp.), but a similar section pertaining to women officers has not been suspended. See 10 U.S.C. §5752 (1970). Another statute provides for the temporary promotion of officers in time of war or national emergency. Male officers in the Navy in the grade of ensign *or above* and in the Marines in the grade of second lieutenant *or above* may be so promoted. Only female ensigns and second lieutenants may be promoted in this manner. 10 U.S.C. §§5787, 5787(b) (1970).

    122. 10 U.S.C. §5767 (1970), *as amended by* Pub. L. No. 90-130, §1(19)(N), 81 Stat. 379. This applies to women in the grade of rear admiral in the Navy and major general or brigadier general in the Marine Corps.

    124. Cf. Loving v. Virginia, 388 U.S. 1 (1967) (Virginia's antimiscegenation law prohibiting interracial marriages held to violate the Fourteenth Amendment's Equal Protection Clause despite the fact that it affected the races equally).

ence of women in the service. The United States military began to use black men as combat soldiers during the American Revolution.[21] In the First World War, large numbers of blacks served but they were relegated primarily to positions such as cooks, valets, and trench diggers[22] — jobs behind the lines not unlike those now assigned to women. During the Korean War, the supposed inability of blacks to serve as effective combat soldiers was dramatically disproved after the armed forces were desegregated by law.[23] The reappraisal of the fighting ability of this group has been so drastic that it is now a matter of concern that blacks constitute such a high proportion of the combat troops in Vietnam.[24]

With this reappraisal, minority group persons have gained access to many benefits of military service. They have received at least temporary recognition as equals by their fellow soldiers and have sometimes found less prejudice and greater economic opportunity in the armed forces than in civilian society. Military service has extended economic independence to many such Americans. While the compensation is hardly high, it includes "three squares," a place to live, and medical care, and for some Americans that is more than they ever were assured outside the military. At the same time, it affords many individuals their first opportunity for extensive travel and contact with the outside world. . . .

Military services also offer numerous educational benefits and even the most unqualified are given a chance to better themselves through the military. Marguerite Rawalt, former Chairman of the Task Force on Family Law and Policy of the Citizens Advisory Council on Status of Women, notes that:

> Military service benefits, especially for the young with limited education or training, accompany the responsibility. Since October 1966, some 246,000 young men who did not meet the normal mental or physical requirements, have been given opportunities for training and correcting physical problems, while such opportunities are not open to their sisters.[25]

Many young men who were unable to finish high school in civilian life are given the aid necessary to receive their diploma while in the military. Each of the services is also authorized to grant 5,500 ROTC scholarships to young men in colleges and universities.[26] These scholarships provide tuition, instructional fees, and an allowance for books. For the veteran, the G.I. Bill provides an educational assistance allowance which covers many expenses.[27] If he has a wife and dependents, the sum of the stipend is increased to absorb some of the financial burden.[28] Some individuals are allowed to continue their college or professional training while serving in the military and often the cost is financed by the government. Without these programs many young men might never be able to continue their educations.

Additionally, job training and experience is extended to many through the military services. Over half of the veterans questioned in one survey indicated that their military

21. The American Negro Reference Book 613 (J. Davis ed. 1966).

22. Of the 200,000 black soldiers who were overseas in World War I, 150,000 were assigned to labor and stevedore batallions. Id. at 616.

23. Exec. Order No. 9981, 3 C.F.R. 722 (1948).

24. 113 Cong. Rec. 10000 (1967) (remarks of Congressman Hawkins). See also Report of the National Advisory Commission on Selective Service, [In Pursuit of Equity: Who Serves When Not All Serve? (Feb. 1967)] at 9-10.

25. Hearings [on S.J. Res. 61 and S.J. Res. 231 Before the Senate Comm. on the Judiciary, 91st Cong., 2d Sess.], at 426.

26. Blue Ribbon Defense Panel, Report to the President and the Secretary of Defense on the Department of Defense at 142 (1970).

27. "The Administrator shall pay to each eligible veteran . . . an educational assistance allowance to meet, in part, the expenses of his subsistence, tuition, fees, supplies, books, equipment, and other educational costs." 38 U.S.C. §1681(a) (Supp. V, 1970).

28. Id. §1682(a)(1).

experience had resulted in a better job title or increased pay.[29] Norman Dorsen, a professor of constitutional law at New York University Law School, states that:

> Women are denied the opportunity to obtain the job training and experience available to servicemen from the working class and minority group backgrounds. It is well known that the armed forces serve as a "college" for many of the nations poor; I fail to see why women should be deprived of this opportunity.[30]

Another significant benefit of military service is the training in self-defense. Offering women the same minimum physical training as is offered to every male draftee would have enormous psychological effects. . . .

Frequently, the armed forces are also prescribed as the cure for aimless young men guilty of anti-social behavior. The prescription is sanctioned to the extent that it is not uncommon for a judge to give a young man the choice between enlisting or being sentenced for some minor offense.[33] Such an alternative is rarely, if indeed, ever, offered to young women in similar circumstances. . . .

Another benefit considered by the authors from inclusion of women as equals in the military is that millions of young women who are currently drawn into early marriage by economic inferiority and by an absence of alternative roles would gain financial and educational independence by military service. Hale and Kanowitz also postulate that military-sponsored training for formerly "male" jobs, if widely available to both sexes by virtue of the draft, could erode the barrier of differential skills-training that now stands between many women and equal employment opportunity.

NOTE: JUDICIAL DEFERENCE TO THE MILITARY

Assuming that the amendment is ratified, political and legal showdowns on the military status of women seem inevitable. Opponents of women in the military at all, and particularly in combat, would find solid comfort in sex discrimination cases under the Equal Protection Clause showing the Supreme Court reluctant to interfere in the affairs of the military.[21] Moreover, the Court defers to the military even in the area of racial discrimination. The most famous case is Korematsu v. United States, 323 U.S. 214, 65 S. Ct. 193, 89 L. Ed. 194 (1944). There the Court found that concentration camps for Americans of Japanese ancestry withstood equal protection strict scrutiny because of the government's compelling interest in national security. Given the Court's willingness to accept the idea that enough Americans of Japanese ancestry were potential traitors to justify incarcerating virtually all Japanese-Americans, it is unfortunately not difficult to imagine a Court willing to presume that enough women are incapable of using guns, or that enough women combat soldiers at the front would become pregnant, or that enough women would choose not to

---

29. Weinstein, Occupational Crossover and Universal Military Training, in The Draft 23, 30 (S. Tax ed. 1967).

30. Hearings, supra [note 25], at 325 (statement of Prof. Norman Dorsen).

33. This is largely an unspoken practice that is somewhat difficult to document. But see Army Reg. 601-270, para. 3-9c(1) (Mar. 18, 1969): "Men who have criminal charges filed and pending against them alleging a violation of a State, Federal, or territorial statute, and who as an alternative to trial for such violation are granted a conditional release from the charge by a court on the condition that they will apply for induction into the Armed Forces, are unacceptable. Waivers will not be granted in these instances." However, when a draftee refuses induction it is no defense that prosecuting authorities had dismissed criminal charges against him in order to permit his induction. Sumrall v. United States, 397 F.2d 924, 926-27 (5th Cir.), *cert. denied,* 393 U.S. 991 (1968).

21. See United States v. St. Clair, 291 F. Supp. 122 (S.D.N.Y. 1968) and the cases cited supra, Part V, n.33.

serve in the field rather than face the embarrassment of lack of privacy, and therefore to rule that national security requires the exclusion of all women from certain areas of military service.[22]

4. The Equal Rights Amendment and Discrimination Against Homosexuals

The question of the legality of state action which discriminates against homosexuals is in considerable flux.[23] Two constitutional theories for challenging such discrimination have been widely advanced. The first is that discrimination against homosexuals is sex discrimination: but for sex, a female could marry a female, or a male could marry a male; and but for the gender of her sexual partner, a divorced mother who is a lesbian could marry and regain custody of her children. A second argument is that the constitutional right to privacy prohibits state intervention in the private sexual behavior of consenting adults. In opposition to these contentions, it has been argued that discrimination on the basis of sexual preference is different from discrimination on the basis of gender. As long as all homosexuals are treated alike, regardless of whether they are male or female, the argument goes, there is no sex discrimination. A corollary of this argument is that the state may distinguish between heterosexual and homosexual relationships because only heterosexual relationships present the possibility of procreation.

There are a number of obvious problems with the latter argument. Regulation of marriage based on an asserted state interest in procreation is surely overbroad, since many heterosexual couples who are allowed to marry choose not to procreate, or are not

22. For other cases in which the doctrine of military necessity has been considered in light of the constitutional requirements of the First Amendment and due process, see Dash v. Commanding General, 307 F. Supp. 849 (D.S.C. 1969); United States v. Howe, 17 U.S.C.M.A. 165, 37 C.M.R. 429 (1967); United States v. Tempia, 16 U.S.C.M.A. 629, 37 C.M.R. 249 (1967). It is said in these cases that the rights admittedly involved must be balanced against the peculiar needs of the military because the doctrine of military necessity is also of constitutional dimension, deriving from the authorization to raise and maintain armed forces. U.S. Const., art. I, §8, clauses 12, 13, 14, 18.

23. Decisions relevant to the rights of homosexuals include:

Immigration and naturalization — Matter of Schmidt, 56 Misc. 2d 456, 289 N.Y.S.2d 89 (Sup. Ct. 1968); In re Labady, 326 F. Supp. 924 (S.D.N.Y. 1971); Kovacs v. United States, 476 F.2d 843 (2d Cir. 1973); Bouteiller v. Immigration and Naturalization Service, 387 U.S. 118, 87 S. Ct. 1563, 18 L. Ed. 2d 661 (1967).

Employment — Morton v. Macy, 417 F.2d 1161 (D.C. Cir. 1969); Scott v. Macy (II), 402 F.2d 644 (D.C. Cir. 1968); Gayer v. Laird, 332 F. Supp. 169 (D.D.C. 1971); Dew v. Halaby, 317 F.2d 582 (D.C.Cir. 1963); Adams v. Laird, 420 F.2d 230 (D.C. Cir. 1969); Richardson v. Hampton, 345 F. Supp. 600 (D.D.C. 1972); Wentworth v. Schlesinger, 42 U.S.L.W. 2271 (D.C. Cir. Nov. 15, 1973); Brass v. Hoberman, 295 F. Supp. 358 (S.D.N.Y. 1968); Society for Individual Rights v. Hampton, — F. Supp. — (N.D. Cal. 1973); Morrison v. State Board of Education, 1 Cal. 3rd 214, 461 P.2d 375, 82 Cal. Rptr. 175 (1969); McConnell v. Anderson, 451 F.2d 193 (D. Minn. 1971); Acanfora v. Montgomery City Board of Education, 42 U.S.L.W. 2439 (4th Cir. Feb. 7, 1974); In re Kimball, 33 N.Y. 2d 586, 301 N.E.2d 436 (1973).

Gay Bars (see generally 27 A.L.R. 3d 1254) — One Eleven Wine & Liquor v. Division of Alcoholic Beverage Control, 50 N.J. 329, 235 A.2d 12 (1967); Stoumen v. Reilly, 37 Cal. 2d 713, 234 P.2d 969 (1951); Vallerga v. Department of Alcoholic Beverage Control, 53 Cal. 2d 313, 347 P.2d 909, 1 Cal. Rptr. 494 (1959); Morell v. Department of Alcoholic Beverage Control, 204 Cal. App. 2d 504, 22 Cal. Rptr. 405 (1962); Kerma Restaurant Corp. v. State Liquor Authority, 21 N.Y.2d 111, 233 N.E.2d 833 (1967); Becker v. State Liquor Authority, 21 N.Y.2d 289, 234 N.E.2d 443 (1967).

Child custody — Nadler v. Superior Court, 255 Cal. App. 2d 523, 63 Cal. Rptr. 352 (1967); Bennett v. Clemens, 230 Ga. 317, 196 S.E.2d 842 (1973); Spence v. Durham, 283 N.C. 671, 198 S.E.2d 537 (1973); A. v. A., 514 P.2d 358 (Ore. 1973).

Marriage — Baker v. Nelson, 291 Minn. 310, 191 N.W.2d 185 (1971); Jones v. Hallahan, 42 U.S.L.W. 2270 (Ky. Ct. App. Nov. 9, 1973); Anonymous v. Anonymous, 67 Misc. 2d 1014, 325 N.Y.S.2d 499 (1971) (sex change); Corbett v. Corbett, 2 All E.R. 33 (1970) (sex change).

Organizations — Owles v. Lorenzo, 31 N.Y.2d 965, 293 N.E.2d 255 (1973); In re Thom, 33 N.Y.2d 609, 301 N.E.2d 548 (1973); Gay Students Organization of University of New Hampshire v. Bonner, 42 U.S.L.W. 2411 (D.N.H. Jan. 16, 1974).

This list of cases was prepared by Barbara Levy, P.O. Box 332, Grand Central Station, New York, N.Y. 10016.

in fact capable of procreation. Further, many types of state regulation which discriminate against homosexuals are far removed from any relationship to procreation: for example, discrimination in government employment against homosexuals seems to be more related to opinions about the morality of such conduct, and the susceptibility of homosexuals to blackmail because of the presumed disgrace of such tendencies, than to any state interest in childbearing. A second problem with the argument is that the net effect of the Supreme Court rulings in the abortion and contraception cases is that the only state interest in procreation which is compelling is its interest in the protection of fetuses who have survived into the third trimester of pregnancy.[24]

The effect that the Equal Rights Amendment will have on discrimination against homosexuals is not yet clear. The legislative history suggests that it was not the intent of Congress to prohibit such discrimination.[25] On the other hand, it is hard to justify a distinction between discrimination on the basis of the sex of one's sexual partners and other sex-based discrimination.[26]

In addition to the constitutional questions, state action penalizing homosexuality raises many social policy issues. Some lesbian feminists have argued persuasively that discrimination against lesbians is one way to keep individual women tied to individual men, and hence tied into a sexist and oppressive social and economic system. Male homosexuals have argued that the discriminatory treatment accorded them is fundamentally related to the misogyny of the society, and the fear "normal" men have of the "feminine" side of themselves. It has also been argued that all individuals are fundamentally bisexual, and that only in a society in which individuals were free to select sexual partners regardless of gender would it be possible to eliminate rigid sex-role polarities and move toward androgyny.[27]

These arguments highlight the connection between discrimination based on sexual preference and other forms of sex discrimination. Aside from such direct ideological connections these two overlapping kinds of discrimination both represent the tendency of society to be intolerant of human diversity, and to force individuals to conform to the moral norms of the majority, whether or not the public interest is in fact involved. The failure to challenge such invasions of individual liberties reinforces the notion that the law can be freely used as a tool of repression against all "deviations," and has disturbing implications for the civil liberties of all citizens.

D. The Campaigns for Ratification

The debates over ratification have varied greatly from state to state, with local issues and personalities largely creating the differences. There have, however, been three major consistent themes: the effect on state protective laws (particularly in states which have well-developed labor legislation), the effect on marriage and divorce laws, and the effect on the image of American womanhood. An illustrative account follows of the form the debates took over these issues.

24. See Roe v. Wade, 410 U.S. 113, 93 S. Ct. 756, 35 L. Ed. 2d 147 (1973) and Doe v. Bolton, 410 U.S. 179, 93 S. Ct. 739, 35 L. Ed. 2d 201 (1971) (state regulation of abortion); and Griswold v. Connecticut, 381 U.S. 479, 85 S. Ct. 1678, 14 L. Ed. 2d 510 (1965), and Eisenstadt v. Baird, 405 U.S. 438, 92 S. Ct. 1029, 31 L. Ed. 2d 349 (1972) (state regulation of contraception); and infra Chapter Five, Part A.

25. See the discussion of this issue by Senator Birch Bayh, the chief sponsor of the ERA in the Senate at 118 Cong. Rec. §4389 (daily ed. March 21, 1972), and the opinion expressed by Professor Thomas Emerson as reported in Note, The Legality of Homosexual Marriage, 82 Yale L.J. 573, 584 n.50 (1973).

26. For an argument that the ERA should be interpreted to prohibit a state ban on homosexual marriage, see Note, The Legality of Homosexual Marriage, supra.

27. Works discussing some of these issues include Martin and Lyon, Lesbian/Woman (1972); Rainone, Shelley, and Hart, Lesbians Are Sisters, in Tanner (ed.), Voices from Women's Liberation 349 (1970); Shelley, Notes of a Radical Lesbian, in Morgan (ed.), Sisterhood is Powerful 306 (1970).

LINKER AND MILLER, THE EQUAL RIGHTS AMENDMENT:
AN ANALYSIS OF THE CAMPAIGNS FOR RATIFICATION
IN CALIFORNIA AND UTAH
(Student paper, Stanford Law School, May 1973)[28]

PROTECTIVE LABOR LAWS

This issue was most intensely debated in California, perhaps because that state has the most comprehensive protective laws in the United States. Organized labor was at the heart of the opposition. The AFL-CIO newsletter urged its members to write their congressmen to defeat the ERA; women labor leaders testified in opposition before both the Assembly and the Senate committees. The Amalgamated Clothing Workers of America (AFL-CIO), the Hotel and Restaurant Employees and Bartenders International (AFL-CIO), and the Union Women's Alliance to Gain Equality (WAGE), an organization of working women from different unions and occupations, organized for the purpose of enhancing women's rights, all sent *women* representatives to speak against the amendment. Those groups recognized that women are discriminated against in employment, yet they feared the ERA would nullify the existing laws providing minimal protection for women. The opposition pointed out that some 2.5 million women and minors are now covered by the protective orders of the State Labor Code and the fourteen wage orders issued by the Industrial Welfare Commission. These state protective laws serve as additional safeguards to minimum federal standards. For example, under California protective wage laws, no woman, whether employed in inter or intra-state commerce, can receive less than $1.65 per hour. Without these protective laws, women engaged in interstate commerce would be subject to the federal level of $1.60, suffering a loss of 5 ¢ per hour, while women who were not engaged in interstate commerce and, therefore, not subject to federal regulations, would lose all minimum protections. Labor opposition also pointed to the possible plight of farm workers if state protective laws were nullified. Women farm workers are subject to the $1.65 state protections while federal minimums for those engaged in interstate commerce under the 1966 amendments to the Fair Labor Standards Act brought the minimum farm worker wage to only $1.30 per hour. Thus, even for those women lucky enough to be engaged in interstate commerce, nullification of state protective laws would mean a loss of 35¢ per hour.[1]

Other protections that the state laws provide are: time-and-a-half overtime pay after eight hours of work per day, as opposed to a federal law of after forty hours per week, and rest periods every four hours, as opposed to no federal provision for rest periods. The protective orders for women also include some fifty "health, welfare, and safety" measures covering lighting, ventilation, seats on the job, elevator services, toilets, and other measures related to job safety.

Unions were particularly concerned about the passage of ERA in view of the erosion of protective laws through enforcement of Title VII.[29] [Far from accepting the argument that this meant the laws were doomed anyway, ERA opponents argued that the only way to save the protective measures was through defeat of the amendment.]

In supporting protective laws, labor representatives . . . relied heavily on the view of woman as homemaker [with a] dual role in society as worker and primary homemaker. A good example of this underlying traditional view is seen in Ruth Miller's testimony:

---

28. This paper, prepared for the course in Women and the Law, closely covers the campaigns in California and Utah, but also contains much information about the debates in other states. The excerpts herein have been edited and reorganized, with the permission of Helene Linker and Margaret Miller.

1. Testimony by Ruth Miller, National Representative of Amalgamated Clothing Workers of America; AFL-CIO, before House Committee on the Judiciary on HJ Res. 208.

29. For a more in-depth analysis of the state labor law controversy, see Chapter Two, Part II-b-3, "State Labor Laws and the BFOQ." In particular, Note: Analysis of Restrictive State Laws, explores the California maximum-hour laws at length and reveals that generally they do not improve federal overtime pay coverage and in fact often reduce federal overtime pay for women workers. — Eds.

... A woman who works eight hours at the job is away from home from nine to ten hours each day. In most cases, she carries the responsibility for home, husband, children. She is the one who does the marketing, food preparation, cleaning, laundry. Extension of the work-day for her simply means endless hours of labor.[2]

The proponents of the ERA which were most active in responding to the arguments on protective laws were the local chapter of the National Organization of Women, Common Cause, the American Civil Liberties Union, Women's Equity Action League, and the United Auto Workers (the one union that felt the ERA would benefit women). On the issue of the benefits of protective laws, the proponents felt the situation was not as clear-cut as the unions would make it seem. They agreed that some of the protective laws were actually beneficial. Among these were the laws requiring a minimum wage, rest periods, and ventilation. [The basic position of the proponents was that these laws could be extended to men, either by the courts or by the legislature, and that certainly the amendment would not operate automatically to strike them down.] But, [the proponents argued, many other] "protections" [were actually] restrictions upon women, and urged that laws like those against night work in certain jobs actually tended to keep women out of desirable occupations, and should be struck down.

When legal arguments did not [give pause to] the strong labor opposition, the N.O.W., the A.C.L.U., W.E.A.L., National Women's Business and Professional Association, Common Cause, and the U.A.W. issued a joint statement denouncing labor's real motives for opposition to the ERA.

... The objection of labor camouflages the real opposition to ERA. That is, that women should be placed on an equal footing with men in competing for well-paid jobs and overtime.[3]

It should be noted that after passage of the ERA, the California legislature enacted a bill to extend all existing protective legislation to men.[4] Responding to the pressures of business interests which objected to the financial burden of extending wage and rest hours, Governor Reagan vetoed the measure.

ERA'S EFFECT ON FAMILY LAWS

To date, Utah is the state in which there has been the greatest focus on the effect of the ERA on the family. Leading the opposition was a group calling themselves Humanitarians Opposed to the Degradation of our Girls (HOTDOGS), apparently sponsored and financed by the John Birch Society.[5]

[T]he HOTDOGS' vehement opposition to the ERA was primarily inspired by the belief that the amendment would compel a radical change in the conventional structure of American family life and by the concomitant belief that women are not currently discriminated against by the laws of the country. While supporters of the amendment see American society and its laws as restricting women from enjoying a full life as citizens, the HOTDOGS believed the ERA would force most women to give up their preferred way of life.

The HOTDOGS insisted that the ERA would "inhibit childbearing and would cause youngsters to be put in 'day-care centers.'"[6] They believed that the amendment

2. Testimony by Ruth Miller, supra.
3. Joint statement released for Assembly floor debate, April, 1972.
4. AB 478.
5. During the HOTDOG campaign many of the Amendment's proponents felt the HOTDOGS represented the John Birch Society, but could not document their beliefs. However, the April, 1973 issue of *American Opinion*, the Birch Society's monthly magazine, identifies the leaders of the HOTDOGS as Society's members and credits the Birch Society with the efforts of a California organization, Happiness of Womanhood, as well. All legislators interviewed who voted against the Amendment in Utah also indicated their belief that all, or some of the HOTDOGS were Birchers.
6. Reba Lazenby in *The Utah Independent*, January 4, 1973, p. 10.

would compel mothers to seek employment to support themselves and their families: "ERA will wipe out a woman's freedom of choice to take a paying job or to be a fulltime wife and mother supported by her husband."[7] ERA would accomplish this by requiring alterations in family support laws that not only "make every wife in the U.S. legally responsible to provide 50 percent of the financial support of her family," but which also "abolish a woman's right to child support and alimony."[8] The opponents feared that under ERA women would not only lose their babies to day-care centers while mothers take jobs to support their families, but also, they would lose some of their children to their husbands in divorce cases as well. They objected to the fact that the amendment would remove the presumption from some state laws that the children of divorced parents should remain with their mothers unless overwhelming evidence of neglect, mistreatment, or bad character exists.

The proponents of the Amendment argued that ". . . the ERA will only require that men be eligible for alimony under the same conditions as women (as they are now in more than one third of the states), that the welfare of the child be the criterion in awarding custody in contested cases (as it is now in many states) and, that mothers be responsible for child support within their means."[9] Under the amendment, the courts would allocate family finances and determine child custody on a case by case basis according to fairness and the best interests of the children. The proponents additionally pointed out that studies by a committee of the American Bar Association show women's legal rights to support are presently more limited than the opponents indicate and the enforcement of these rights are currently very inadequate: ". . . in practically all cases the wife's ability to support herself is a factor in determining the amount of alimony; . . . alimony is granted in only a very small percentage of cases; . . . fathers, by and large, are contributing *less than half the support of their children* in divided families; . . . alimony and child support awards are very difficult to collect."[10] Opponents believed, however, that "under present American laws, the man is *always* required to support his wife and each child he caused to be brought into the world." "Why," they asked, "should women abandon these good laws — by trading them for something so nebulous and uncertain as the 'discretion of the Courts'?"[11]

THE IMAGE OF WOMEN

[A "scare" tactic which has been used by the opponents in many states is the association of] the amendment with the women's liberation movement, [which allegedly] represents a total assault on . . . the family as the basic unit of society. Phyllis Schlafly, . . . [a] former speech writer for Senator Barry Goldwater, now spearheads much of the national opposition to the ERA. Schlafly claims in her literature that:

> Women's libbers are trying to make wives and mothers unhappy with their career, make them feel that they are "second-class citizens" and "abject slaves." Women's libbers are promoting free sex instead of the "slavery of marriage." They are promoting Federal "day-care centers" for babies instead of homes. They are promoting abortions instead of families.
>
> Women's libbers do not speak for the majority of American women . . . we do not want to trade our birthright of the special privileges of American women — for the mess of pottage called the Equal Rights Amendment.
>
> If the women's libbers want to reject marriage and motherhood, it's a free country and that is their choice. But let's not permit these women's libbers to get away with pretending to speak for the rest of us. Let's not permit this tiny minority to

7. The Utah Independent, January 25, 1973, p. 10.
8. Id.
9. Statements in a pamphlet on the ERA put out by Common Cause, Washington, D.C. and used by the proponents in California.
10. Id.
11. The Phyllis Schlafly Report, Vol. 5, No. 7, February, 1972, p. 2.

degrade the role that most women prefer. Let's not let these women's libbers deprive wives and mothers of the rights we now have.[12]

Schlafly believes that women's liberationists reveal the true goals of the ERA when their speakers cite Russia as an example of a country where women have equal rights.

> Equal rights in the Soviet Union means that the Russian Woman is *obliged* to put her baby in a state-operated nursery or kindergarten so she can join the labor force. Under Soviet law, a woman (as well as a man) can be jailed for refusing to engage in "socially useful labor". . . .[13]

While Schlafly's literature merely makes innuendos about the communist nature of the consequences of the ERA, other groups have claimed forthrightly that the Amendment represents a communist plot. In Utah, for example, the characteristic political stance of the John Birch Society made the HOTDOGS naturally predisposed to oppose the ERA. The Society's view of American politics is wholly conspiratorial; the group was founded in 1959 solely to combat the "communist conspiracy" which they viewed as an internal threat. Birchers have attacked every change in the status quo in the sixties from the civil rights movement to flouridation as a communist plot. The ERA represents just one of the many recent changes in society that the communists have proposed in order to engineer American society a little closer to a total communist state. While their public literature astutely soft-peddled this belief in the communist origins of the amendment (outrageous charges of communist connections and plots have lost sympathizers before), when questioned in private, the chairman of the HOTDOGS confirmed her belief in the communist origins of the amendment. She complained that American women are being "pushed to follow the same pattern as Russia and China," and she suggested that the state governors' committees on the status of women which supported the ERA in many other states besides Utah have been established by communists to work for the passage of this amendment at the taxpayers' expense.[14]

E. STATE IMPLEMENTATION OF STATE AND FEDERAL EQUAL RIGHTS AMENDMENTS

By the fall of 1973, eleven states had passed state equal rights amendments, ten of which used language which was amenable to strict interpretation.[30] Two more states had begun the process of constitutional amendment.[31] At least eleven states had begun the work of reform of sex-discriminatory laws through the legislative process,[32] and lower court cases interpreting state amendments had been reported in at least four

12. Id., p. 4.

13. Id., p. 3.

14. January 19, 1973 interview with Reba Lazenby, president of the HOTDOGS.

30. Equal rights provisions which use language similar to the proposed federal Equal Rights Amendment or to the Fourteenth Amendment's Equal Protection Clause are Alaska Const., art. I, §3; Colorado Const., art. II, §29 (Laws 1972, p. 647); Hawaii Const., art. I, §4; Illinois Const., art. I, §§2 and 18; Maryland Declaration of Rights, art. 46 (Laws 1972, ch. 366); Montana Const. art. II, §4 (1973); Pennsylvania Const., art. I, §27 (1971); Texas Const., art. I, §3a (1972); and Washington Const., art. XXXI, §1 (1972). Virginia's new constitution provides that "the right to be free from any governmental discrimination upon the basis of religious conviction, race, color, sex, or national origin shall not be abridged, except that the mere separation of the sexes shall not be considered discrimination." Virginia Const. art. I, §11.

31. Wisconsin's amendment passed the legislature in 1972, the first step in a three-step process. Connecticut's citizens will vote on a constitutional amendment in 1974. Of these fourteen states, Illinois and Virginia had not ratified the federal Equal Rights Amendment by the time this book went to press.

32. All the states with state equal rights amendments except Pennsylvania, plus Wisconsin, Georgia, and Arizona. Arizona had not yet ratified the federal Equal Rights Amendment by the time this book went to press.

states.[33] Those undertaking the task of analyzing state laws and drafting new legislation included commissions on the status of women, the legislative reference service or legislative council, committees of the state bar association, women legislators, and special committees appointed by the governor or the legislative council.

One interesting development in a number of states has been the extension, or proposed extension, of forcible and statutory rape laws to cover heterosexual assaults regardless of the sex of the assailant and the victim.[34] While the legislative history of the federal Equal Rights Amendment suggests that forcible rape laws which applied only to male attackers and female victims would be upheld under the new amendment because such laws relate to unique physical characteristics of men and women, it will not be necessary for this question to be resolved in the courts if the present trend continues.[35]

The equalization of marriage ages has caused controversy. In Wisconsin, the legislative council was sufficiently concerned about the possibility that their age equalization proposal would be controversial that they introduced it separately from their omnibus equal rights bill.[36] Both the omnibus bill and the separate legislation are still under consideration as of this writing. Ages were not equalized in either Arizona or Maryland, although in Maryland an age equalization bill had been introduced; nor was action taken in Illinois or Texas.[37] The ages for marriage were already the same in Washington and were equalized by the legislature in New Mexico as part of the ERA reforms.[38] Equalizations bills generally made, or would have made, it possible for men to marry at younger ages than before.

Another difficult problem for state legislatures under the ERA may be deciding how to handle sex segregation in state prisons and other state residential facilities, such as mental hospitals.[39] Wisconsin's legislative council explicitly excluded this problem from their deliberations, while the proposed Maryland reforms apparently would have integrated at least some of the state's prisons.[40] Washington passed a statute providing that no member of one sex under arrest should be confined in the same cell of a city jail with any member of the other sex, to replace a law which had protected women from

33. See the discussion infra this section.

34. Ch. 241, §3-4, N.M. Laws 1973, amending N.M. Stat. Ann §§40A-9-2 and 40A-9-3 (1953); ch. 154, §§122, 123, Wash. Laws 1973, amending Wash. Rev. Code §§9.79.010 and 9.79.020 (1961). In Maryland and Wisconsin, similar laws were introduced but not passed. S.B. 383 (Md. 1973), which would have amended Md. Ann. Code art. 27, §12 (1957); and S.B. 386 (Md. 1973), which would have amended Md. Ann. Code art. 27, §461 (assault with intent to have carnal knowledge of a female under fourteen years of age and forcible rape); 1973 Assembly Bill 23, §§173-176 (Wis.), which would amend Wis. Stat. Ann. §§944.01, 944.02, 944.10, and 944.11(1). No action has been taken in Arizona, Illinois, or Texas. The new laws still distinguish between heterosexual and homosexual assaults, however. A law which covers male and female perpetrators and victims and both forcible sexual intercourse and forcible sodomy has been proposed for the District of Columbia. See Report to the D.C. City Council of the Public Safety Committee Task Force on Rape, Recommendations 24 and 25, pp. 10, 47-48 (July 9, 1973).

35. See, e.g., S. Comm. on the Judiciary, Equal Rights for Men and Women, S. Rep. No. 92-689, 92d Cong., 2d Sess. 16 (1972). A more detailed explanation is given in Brown, Emerson, Falk, and Freedman, The Equal Rights Amendment: A Constitutional Basis for Equal Rights for Women, 80 Yale L.J. 871, 955-961 (1971).

36. 1973 Assembly Bill 21 (Wis. 1973), to amend Wis. Stat. Ann. §245.02 (Supp. 1973).

37. S.B. 303 (Md. 1973), which would have amended Md. Ann. Code, art. 62, §§9a and 9b (1957 and Supp. 1971). Both Texas and Illinois have unequal marriage ages with and without parental consent. Tex. Family Code §§1.51, 1.52 (Pamphlet 1972); Ill. Rev. Stat. ch. 89, §3 (1969).

38. Wash. Rev. Code §26.04.010 (Supp. 1972); ch 51, §1, N. M. Laws 1973, amending N.M. Stat. Ann. §57-1-5 (1953).

39. Sex integration of state college dormitories and other voluntary state facilities will not pose similar problems for two reasons: first, individual choice can easily be substituted for institutional decision; and second, the constitutional right to privacy allows sex segregation of facilities such as bathrooms and bedrooms where disrobing, sleeping, and personal bodily functions are customarily performed. See S. Comm. on the Judiciary, Equal Rights for Men and Women, S. Rep. No. 92-689, 92d Cong., 2d Sess. 17 (1972), and Brown, Emerson, Falk, and Freedman, supra, at 900-902.

40. Wisconsin Legislative Council, Report to the 1973 Legislature on Equal Rights 6-7 (February 1973).

confinement in the same cell with men; Washington did not, however, confront the larger problem of sex-segregated state institutions for prisoners.[41] The equal rights bill proposed in Texas dealt with whether the obligation of male prisoners to do manual labor "upon the public roads, bridges or other public works of the county" should be extended to female prisoners, who had previously been exempted from manual labor outside the workhouse. The bill would extend the requirement to women, but introduce a new protection for both men and women by providing that any prisoner who has insufficient strength to do manual work shall not be required to do so.[42]

New Mexico, Washington, and Arizona all enacted statutes extending to women the obligation to support their spouses and minor children, and extending the criminal penalties for nonsupport and desertion to women.[43] In Wisconsin, extension of the husband's duty to support the wife was proposed in the omnibus bill, while in Texas, the limitation on the husband's right to receive support (that he be unable to support himself) will be extended to both spouses if the equal rights bill passes.[44] In Maryland, various bills extending support obligations to women and making them criminally liable for desertion and nonsupport were introduced and defeated. A prominent group of feminist lawyers took the position that mechanical extension of all such laws was not the wisest way to produce sex neutrality. For example, they argued that criminal penalties for desertion and the obligation of men to support their spouses in state insane asylums should be eliminated rather than extended, and that the uncodified as well as the statutory law should be carefully studied before reforms were proposed. They were successful in having a committee appointed by the governor to study the matter and report back to the legislature.[45] In 1973, Hawaii eliminated the requirement that unemployment compensation claimants who had left work because of homemaking obligations supply more evidence of availability for work than other claimants.[46] The legislature also deleted the pregnancy disqualification from the unemployment compensation statute,[47] eliminated special requirements relating to maternity leave for public employees,[48] and amended the exclusion of pregnancy from temporary disability insurance.[49]

Routine changes in state law have also been proposed or enacted in all of the

41. Ch. 154, §53, Wash. Laws 1973, amending Wash. Rev. Code §35.66.050 (1965).

42. S.B. 784, §11, 63rd Leg., reg. sess. (1973), which would have amended Tex. Code of Crim. Proc. Ann. art. 43.10 (1966).

43. Ch. 172, Ariz. Laws 1973, §§46-50, 110, amending Ariz. Rev. Stat. Ann. §§13-801, 13-802, 13-803, 13-804, 13-821.A.1(m), and 46-295 (1956); and ch. 139, Ariz. Laws 1973, §§1, 2, amending or repealing inter alia Ariz.Rev. Stat. Ann. §§25-315, 25-318, 25-319, 25-321, 25-321, 25-333, 25-341, 25-342, and 25-351 (1956). Cf. Taylor and Herzog, Impact Study of the Equal Rights Amendment, Preliminary Report of 1973 Equal Rights Legislation 2 (Sept. 25, 1973), The preliminary report can be obtained by writing to the authors at 1433 East Broadway, Tucson, Ariz. 85719. Chs. 42, 103, 241, 319, and 376, N.M. Laws 1973, amending N.M. Stat. Ann. §§13-1-27.1, 22-4, 22-7, and 40A-6-2 (1953). Ch. 154, Wash. Laws 1973, §§34-36, 112-113, amending Wash. Rev. Code. §§26.20.030, 26.20.050, 26.20.080, 74.20.220, and 74.20.230 (Supp. 1972, 1961). Cf. ch. 157, Wash. Laws 1973, an act relating to divorce and extending alimony on a sex-neutral basis. All three states also extended alimony rights without regard to sex.

44. 1973 Assembly Bill 23, §§51, 57, to amend subsections of Wis. Stat. Ann. §52 (Supp. 1973). Alimony rights are already equal in Wisconsin, but see Wis. Stat. Ann. §247-265 (1957). S.B. No. 784, §§2-4, 63rd Leg., reg. sess. (Tex. 1973), which would have amended Tex. Family Code §§3.59, 4.02 (Pamphlet 1972) and Tex. Pen. Code Ann. art. 602, 602-A, and 603-605 (Supp. 1972, 1952). The Texas reforms would not include alimony.

45. Telephone conversation on Oct. 9, 1973, with Ellen Luff, a Maryland attorney who is a member of the Women's Law Center, P.O. Box 1934, Baltimore, Maryland, 21203. The bills in question include S.B. 293, 343, 344, 348, and 353, first introduced by Senator Steers, Jan. 15, 1973.

46. Act 53, [1973] Sess. Laws Hawaii, *amending* Hawaii Rev. Stat. §383-29 (1968) (codified at Hawaii Rev. Stat. §383-29 (Supp. 1973)).

47. Act 75, [1973] Sess. Laws Hawaii, *amending* Hawaii Rev. Stat. §383-30 (1968) (codified at Hawaii Rev. Stat. §383-30 (Supp. 1973)).

48. Act 60, [1973] Sess. Laws Hawaii, repealing Hawaii Rev. Stat. §76-34 (1968).

49. Act 61, §3 [1973] Sess. Laws Hawaii, amending Hawaii Rev. Stat. §392-21 (Supp. 1969) (codified at Hawaii Rev. Stat. §392-21 (Supp. 1973)).

states mentioned, such as laws making the married women's property acts sex-neutral; extending pension and other survivor's benefits to spouses of female office holders, government employees, and veterans; extending prostitution laws to cover male prostitutes; eliminating sex discrimination in domicile laws, parental rights, homestead exemptions, and head of household provisions; and eliminating unnecessary sex-specific language.[50] Several states have also been prompted by the equal rights movement to extend antidiscrimination laws to prohibit denial of rights based on sex.[51] However, in several instances, the state legislatures have as yet failed to act to end serious sex-based inequities or have enacted sex-discriminatory statues as part of their law reform efforts. For example, in Illinois and Maryland, proposed laws relating to discrimination in the granting of credit were not drafted sex-neutrally; in Maryland, the bill passed.[52] However, the effect of the Maryland statute was ambiguous; one section protected the contract rights and power of single and married women, but did not mention men, while the others prohibited discrimination in retail installment sales or retail credit accounts on the basis of sex or marital status.[53] Likewise, although Arizona, California, and Texas have amended their laws to eliminate sex discrimination in provisions relating to the management and control of community property during marriage,[54] in 1973 the New Mexico legislators stubbornly refused to take similar action. Instead, they sought to retain a statutory presumption that the husband was the sole manager of the community property unless there was an agreement to the contrary or unless the wife had filed a written statement with the county clerk stating that she has assumed her rights to manage such property. The stated purpose of this presumption was "to provide temporary procedures by which the four hundred year tradition of husband management can be maintained in those families where the desires of the wife are not made known. . . ."[55] After a difficult floor fight, the statute was amended so that this presumption was limited to "commercial community personal property, personal property which is part of a community business enterprise or community personal property used in a business, the proceeds of which support the family in whole or in part."[56] Apparently these provisions refer to personal property used in family businesses. The rest of the new community property law is sex-neutral, requiring the spouses to consult on the management of jointly owned and community real property (joint management), allowing either to manage community personal property other than that used in family business (joint and several management), and allowing each to manage

50. See, e.g., ch. 154, Wash. Laws 1973.

51. See, e.g., ch. 557, Md. Laws 1973, amending Md. Ann. Code, art. 49B, §23 (a) (1972 Replacement Volume), to add sex and marital status to the prohibited bases of discrimination in home financing.

52. H.B. 1356, 78th Gen. Assembly, State of Illinois, 1973 and 1974, passed by the House and sent to the Senate, to amend Ill. Rev. Stat., ch. 121 1/2 (1969). Although this bill would prohibit discrimination on the basis of sex or marital status in the awarding of credit, this bill includes sex-specific language such as the following provision: "Sec. 4. When requested to do so by an applying married woman, the credit card issuer shall consider such married woman's financial status alone in making a determination of whether to allow her credit as an individual." Ch. 131, Md. Laws 1973, amending Md. Ann. Code, art. 45, §5 (1971 Replacement Volume), art. 83, §153C(b) (1969 Replacement Volume), and adding a new section, art. 83, §128(e).

53. The latter is art. 45, §5; the former are art. 83, §§128 (e) and art. 153C(b), id.

54. Ch. 172, Ariz. Laws 1973, §§61-64, amending Ariz. Rev. Stat. Ann. §§25-211, 25-213(C), 25-214, 25-215, and 25-216(B) (1956); cf. Taylor and Herzog, supra; ch. 987, Cal. Stats. 1973, amending, inter alia, Cal. Civ. Code §§5102, 5105, 5123, 5125, 5127 (West 1970) and repealing, inter alia, Cal. Civ. Code §5124 (West 1970); Tex. Family Code §5.22 (Pamphlet 1972). The Arizona statute now provides that the spouses have joint and several management of their community property except that both must join in actions respecting real estate or contracts of guaranty, indemnity, or suretyship. The California law now provides, inter alia, that the wife has the same powers over the community personal property as the husband had under prior law. The Texas law provides for sole management, control, and disposition by each spouse of the community property that he or she would have owned if single.

55. Senate Floor Substitute for Senate Judiciary Committee Substitute for Senate Bill 8, State of New Mexico, 31st leg., 1st sess. 1973, §2.

56. Ch. 320, §9, N.M. Laws 1973, creating a new section, N.M. Stat. Ann. 57-4A-7-1.

alone his or her separately owned real and personal property (separate management).[57]

The early judicial decisions interpreting state equal rights amendments are of varying quality. In Virginia, the state supreme court has ruled, in upholding a jury exemption for women but not men with responsibilities for the care of children or dependent adults, that the state equal rights amendment[58]

> . . . is no broader than the equal protection clause of the Fourteenth Amendment to the Constitution of the United States. Where a statute is based on a reasonable classification that bears a rational relationship to the objective of the State, as here, there is no impermissible discrimination under the Constitution of Virginia.

Of course, Virginia's ERA, which contains a provision authorizing sex separation, is the weakest in wording of the state equal rights amendments. The Colorado courts have affirmed the conviction of a man for statutory rape.[59] The Texas appellate courts have decided to continue to recognize a cause of action for breach of promise to marry because "it is just as reasonable to say [the state] removed discrimination by recognizing the right of both men and women to bring such suits"[60] and have similarly upheld a cause of action for criminal conversation.[61]

In Pennsylvania, the supreme court has decided one case under the Commonwealth Equal Rights Amendment, extending the common law duty of child support, which had previously fallen primarily on the father, to both parents, according to their ability.[62] As of June 1, 1974, the court had under consideration nine cases raising a variety of issues, including whether the right to sue for negligent invasion of consortium should be extended to wives as well as husbands, whether the right to alimony pendente lite and counsel fees should be extended to husbands, whether the exemption of married women from civil arrest under a tax statute should be eliminated, and whether the use of indeterminate minimum sentences for women, and determinate minimums for men, violates the state Equal Rights Amendment.[63] A number of other cases have been decided by lower courts, under various theories, many of them mutually inconsistent.[64] On the other hand, the Attorney General of Pennsylvania has issued two opinions construing the state ERA in accordance with the legislative history of the federal ERA.[65] The decisions by the Supreme Court will

---

57. Ch. 320, N.M. Laws 1973, enacting N.M. Stat. Ann. 57-4A-lff. For an explanation of the forms of management chosen, written by one of the bill's drafters, see Bingaman, The Effects of an Equal Rights Amendment on the New Mexico System of Community Property: Problems of Characterization, Management and Control, 3 N.M.L. Rev. 11, 36-55, (1973), and the discussion of community property, infra, Chapter Three, III-B.

58. Archer v. Mayes, 213 Va. 633, — , 194 S.E.2d 707, 711 (1973).

59. People v. Green, 514 P.2d 769 (Colo. 1973).

60. Scanlon v. Crim, 500 S.W.2d 554, 556 (Tex. Civ. App. 1973.)

61. Felsenthal v. McMillan, 493 S.W.2d 729 (Tex. Sup. 1973).

62. Conway v. Dana, No. 63 March Term 1973, Mar. 26, 1974.

63. Hopkins v. Blanco, No. 7 January Term 1974, *appeal allowed* Aug. 14, 1973; Wiegand v. Wiegand, No. 64 March Term 1974, *appeal allowed* Dec. 13, 1973; Henderson v. Henderson, No. 467 January Term 1973, *appeal allowed* July 3, 1973; Commonwealth of Pennsylvania v. Staub, No. 505 January Term 1973, *appeal allowed* July 30, 1973; Commonwealth v. Newsome, No. 182 January Term 1973, *appeal allowed* Dec. 12, 1972; Commonwealth of Pennsylvania v. Butler, No. 410 January Term 1971, *appeal filed* June 16, 1971; Commonwealth of Pennsylvania v. Piper, No. 27 January Term 1973, *appeal allowed* June 8, 1972; Commonwealth of Pennsylvania v. Hampton, No. 79 January Term 1973, *appeal allowed* Sept. 6, 1972; City of Philadelphia v. Percival et al., No. 464 January Term 1974, *appeal allowed* May 3, 1974.

64. Murphy v. Murphy, 95 Montg. County L.R. 61, *aff'd per curiam,* 224 Pa. Super. 460, 303 A.2d 838 (1973); Commonwealth ex rel Lukens v. Lukens, 224 Pa. Super. 227, 303 A.2d 522 (1973); Rogan v. Rogan, Luzerne C.P. Court, No. 1934 October Term 1972; Kehl v. Kehl, 120 P.L.J. 296 (Allegheny County 1972); Corso v. Corso, 120 P.L.J. 183 (Allegheny County 1972); Green v. Freiheit, October Term 1972, No. 1015, D.R. 260259, reported in the Legal Intelligencer, July 3, 1973; Digorolamo v. Apanavage, 293 A.2d 96 (Pa. Super. 1973).

65. 1973 Opinions of the Attorney General No. 41 (ruling that a state law barring females from being

thus be of considerable importance in charting the future course of ERA interpretation in Pennsylvania.

Many of these early efforts to conform state laws to equal rights provisions are encouraging. Nonetheless, both the technical and factual problems which have arisen in the legislative drafting, and the inconsistencies among early judicial decisions should encourage feminists, especially those in the legal field, to remain active in law reform and litigation after ratification of state and federal equal rights amendments has been obtained. Careful analysis of the legal problems and factual situation by those committed to progressive legislation *and* equal rights is the best way to maximize the positive effects of the recasting of laws which is now in progress across the nation.

---

boxers or wrestlers was repealed by the commonwealth ERA) and No. 62 (ruling that under the commonwealth ERA, the common law, and the motor vehicle code, a married woman can use her birth-given name after marriage and can continue or change her operator's license or vehicle registration to her birth-given name).

CHAPTER TWO

Employment Discrimination

I. INTRODUCTION: ECONOMIC AND SOCIOLOGICAL MATERIALS

This chapter presents information a lawyer needs for litigating employment sex discrimination cases. Judicial opinions, excerpts from statutes and regulations, case studies, and commentary alert the reader to substantive and procedural issues. Yet, in employment law particularly, legal materials alone cannot fully equip a lawyer. The litigator must understand the economic position of women workers, the causes of that position, and the changes needed. The effectiveness of employment litigation as a tool for improving the position of women workers depends entirely on the relationship of legal change to social and economic change.

The material which follows identifies the root causes of women's inferior position in the labor market as sex segregation, undervaluation of women's work, and the structure of supply and demand for women workers. Given this information, the lawyer should be better able to evaluate alternative remedies for discrimination against women workers. The introductory materials also highlight the relationship of sex discrimination in employment to other social problems such as poverty, the health of the economy, and the position of women in the family.

The facts about women workers are often dramatically different from the stereotypes, and can be used to challenge the thinking of employers, unions, lawyers, and judges about women workers, both informally and in sex discrimination litigation. The economic and sociological materials are divided into four parts. The first describes the position of women workers: the sociological characteristics of working women; their distribution across occupations and industries; their low pay and status as compared to that of men; their concentration in part-time jobs, jobs which do not require overtime, and jobs with a high risk of unemployment; and the causes of their inferior position. It is necessary to understand the present situation in order to measure progress and evaluate proposals for change. The second and third parts focus on the stereotypes about women workers that support sex discrimination, and the relationship of sex discrimination in employment to women's position in the family. The fourth presents predictions and proposals for the future.

In reading the following materials, and the rest of Chapter Two, students should think about how women workers themselves can use the law to challenge discrimination against them, and how the law can facilitate the organization of working women which is critical to the goal of ending sex discrimination in employment.

A. The Inferior Status and Pay of Women Workers

The article which follows is an overview of the position of women in the labor force. It presents demographic information about women who work for pay and describes the industrial and occupational distribution of women, income differences between men and women, evidence that men and women are paid unequally for equal work, the undervaluation of jobs in which women predominate, and the invalidity of some common excuses for sex discrimination.

SIMMONS, FREEDMAN, DUNKLE, AND BLAU
EXPLOITATION FROM 9 TO 5
Background Paper for the Twentieth Century Fund Task Force
on Women and Employment, ch. 1 (1974)

Women have always been indispensable to the American economy. During the colonial period, women produced many of the essentials for daily living. They spun and wove, and made clothing, soap, shoes, and candles. In addition, they cared for their households and families.[1] Spurred by the Puritan ethic, which condemned idleness as a sin, and the continual labor shortages of this early period, women also pursued a wide range of market activities. They were tavern keepers and store proprietors, traders and speculators, printers and publishers, as well as domestic servants and seamstresses.[2]

The involvement of women in industry in this country is as old as the industrial system itself. During the birth of the manufacturing industry in the textile mills of New England in the late eighteenth and early nineteenth centuries, women comprised the overwhelming majority of industrial workers. [3] But from the beginning, women factory workers held jobs that were quickly identified as "women's jobs." The results of this long tradition of sex-segregation in the labor market are apparent today.

This chapter reviews the current status of women in the labor market, describes the distribution of women among different industries and occupations, and shows how this distribution limits women's access to prestigious and highly paid jobs. It examines the income differences between men and women, and explores some of the popular myths that perpetuate discrimination against workingwomen. Finally, the future prospects for women in the labor market are investigated.

A PROFILE OF WORKINGWOMEN

During the past fifty years, an increasing number of women have entered the labor market. In 1920, 22.7 percent of the female population was employed; by 1970, this figure had risen to 42.8 percent. . . . Between 1940 and 1945, over 5.5 million women entered the labor force in order to meet the defense needs of the country. While considerable ground was lost immediately after the war, the number of workingwomen over the past thirty years more than doubled. In this period, the number of women in the total civilian labor force rose from 25 to nearly 40 percent; by 1970, nearly 50 percent of all women between the ages of sixteen and sixty-four were either working or seeking work.

As impressive as this increase has been, the change in the composition of this group has been even more significant. In 1940, the typical female worker was young and single; most older women were married and worked only in their own homes. Within the next ten years, this pattern began to change as older married women entered or reentered the

1. Eleanor Flexner, Century of Struggle: The Women's Rights Movement in the United States (New York: Atheneum, 1968), p. 9.
2. Edith Abbott, Women in Industry (New York: D. Appleton and Co., 1910), p. 11.
3. Ibid., Chapters IV and V.

labor force in increasing numbers. This trend continued and, by 1960, the contours of the "age profile" of the female labor force had undergone a major shift (see [Chart 2-1]). The percentage of women in the forty-five to fifty-four year-old age bracket who were in the labor force rose dramatically. During the last ten years, women have continued to enter the labor force in increasing numbers with the most rapid increases in participation occurring among women in the twenty to thirty-four year-old group, many of whom are mothers of preschool children.

These postwar changes have brought the profile of the female labor force more in agreement with the profile of the total female population. That is, women who engage

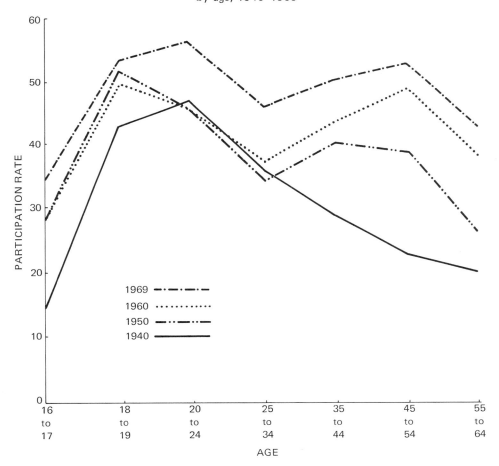

[Chart 2-1]
LABOR FORCE PARTICIPATION RATES OF WOMEN,
by age, 1940-1969

Source: Manpower Report of the President, 1972, p. 254 and 1969 Handbook on Women Workers, p. 18

in the work market have been drawing closer to the total female population in terms of their racial composition, age, educational attainment, marital and family status, and other characteristics.[4] Thus, it is rapidly becoming more difficult to consider working-women as in some sense an unrepresentative or atypical group. In 1969, the median age of workingwomen was thirty-nine, only slightly below the median age of forty-two for the entire female population. Similarly, 55 percent of the workingwomen had children under seventeen as compared to 57 percent of all women.

For obvious economic reasons, single, widowed, divorced, and separated women are more likely to work than married women. However, because married women are by far the largest group in the adult female population, the postwar increases in their labor market activity have meant that the majority of workingwomen are now married. Married women living with their husbands comprised 36.4 percent of the female labor force in 1940 and 59 percent in 1970.[5]

One major factor in determining whether or not a married woman participates in the labor force is the presence of children. In March 1971, 29.6 percent of wives with preschool children were in the labor force as compared to 49.4 percent with children between the ages of six and seventeen years.[6] Since married women between the ages of twenty-five and thirty-four are the most likely to have young children, their labor force participation rate is still relatively low. However, it is rising rapidly. The absence of these mothers from the labor force may stem not only from the conviction that a small child needs its mother at all times, but from difficulties in obtaining and paying for adequate alternative child care in addition to the fact that part-time work is hard to find. According to a recent study, mothers of small children are more likely to work if a relative is available to look after their children.[7]

Education is another major factor in determining if a married woman will seek employment. The more education a woman has, the more likely she is to work. In March 1969, 33 percent of all women with less than four years of high school, 43 percent of wives who had graduated from high school, and 51 percent of wives with four or more years of college were in the labor force.[8] Among both male and female workers educational attainment generally affects employment opportunities and pay scales.

The better a woman's educational credentials, the greater her chances of finding a desirable job that pays enough to help her provide for the maintenance of essential goods and services to ease the "double burden" of home and work. The correlation between educational attainment and employment also may reflect a process of self-selection; those women who earn diplomas may be more strongly motivated, ambitious, and career-oriented than those who do not. Although the educated woman also meets with discrimination that keeps her from better-paid, more prestigious jobs, her opportunities are still greater than those of a less educated woman, and to the extent that she has prepared herself through her education for a particular career, she is willing to try to pursue it.

Financial need, as measured by a husband's income, may also affect a wife's decision to enter the labor force. Married women most frequently give economic reasons for their decisions to seek work.[9] Whether or not husband and wife perceive the hus-

4. Janet Neipert Hedges, "Women Workers and Manpower Demands in the 1970's," Monthly Labor Review, June 1970, p. 21.

5. U.S. Department of Labor, Manpower Administration, Manpower Report of the President, April 1971 (Washington, D.C.: U.S. Government Printing Office), p. 234.

6. Department of Labor, Manpower Administration, Manpower Report of the President, March 1972 (Washington, D.C.: U.S. Government Printing Office), p. 195.

7. Elizabeth Waldman, "Marital and Family Characteristics of the U.S. Labor Force," Monthly Labor Review, May 1970, p. 25.

8. Ibid.

9. "Why Women Start and Stop Working: A Study in Mobility," Monthly Labor Review, Sept. 1965, pp. 1077-1082, cited in Vera C. Parella, "Women and the Labor Force," Special Labor Force Report No. 93, February 1968, p. 4.

band's income as adequate depends, among other things, on the size of the family, the standard of living to which they aspire, and their stage in the life cycle. Thus, the same level of income may meet the needs of one family but not another. Moreover, the response of a married woman to insufficient family income may depend on the kind of employment opportunities available and whether her earnings will cover the cost of services such as child care.

Proportionately, more black women than white participate in the labor force; in recent years, the differential has been declining. In 1948, 31 percent of all white women and 46 percent of all nonwhite women sixteen years of age and over were working. By 1971, 43 percent of white women and 49 percent of nonwhite women were working.[10]

There are several reasons for these differences. A higher proportion of black women are widowed, divorced, or separated from their husbands. These women rely heavily on their own earnings to support themselves and their families. Furthermore, the lower average earnings of black men increase the importance of a wife's contribution to family income.

But these factors do not explain all of the differences in labor force participation between black and white women. Even when marital status, age, children's ages, and husbands' incomes are held constant, black women are still more likely to work outside the home than white women. In March 1969, among families in which the husband's income was $10,000 or more, half of the black wives, but only one-third of the white wives, were in the labor force. Forty-four percent of black wives with preschool children were in the labor force in March 1969, as compared to 28 percent of white wives.[11]

The labor force participation rates of women, particularly of married women and teenagers, are very sensitive to the general level of economic activity. The impact of economic conditions on female labor force participation can take either of two forms. In times of economic downturn, if the male family head becomes unemployed, the wife or other members of the household may enter the labor force. These "additional workers" often leave the labor force once the major breadwinner is reemployed on a regular basis. At the same time, if a workingwoman loses her job and finds it impossible to locate a new one after prolonged search, she may become a "discouraged worker" and leave the labor force. Women, especially wives and teenagers, who are not yet working but have been planning to look for jobs, may wait until economic conditions improve.

Studies show that the second group of discouraged workers predominates so that the female labor force either declines or grows more slowly during periods of high unemployment.[12] Unemployment statistics then tend to underestimate the extent of female unemployment, particularly during periods of low economic activity.

Thus the gap between women's and men's unemployment rates tends to decline during recessions as women leave the labor force and to widen when the economy is buoyant as women are drawn into the labor force by increased employment opportunities. However, regardless of the stage in the business cycle, the incidence of unemployment among women is considerably higher than among men. For example, in April 1972, the unemployment rates were 5.7 percent for white women and 9.6 percent for nonwhite women; these figures may be compared with 7.4 percent for white men and 8.4 percent for nonwhite men.[13]

INDUSTRIAL AND OCCUPATIONAL DISTRIBUTION OF WOMEN

Once a women decides to work, she will find only a limited number of jobs available. Despite the rapid growth of the female labor force in recent years, women are

10. Manpower Report of the President, 1972, p. 162.
11. Waldman, "Marital and Family Characteristics," p. 12.
12. Gertrude Bancroft McNally, "Patterns of Female Labor Force Activity," Industrial Relations, May 1968, p. 209.
13. Manpower Report of the President, March 1973 (Washington, D.C.: U.S. Government Printing Office).

still primarily concentrated in certain industries and occupations. In 1968, more than 73 percent of all workingwomen were employed in the service sector, broadly defined to include wholesale and retail trade, finance, insurance, real estate, and public administration, as well as professional, personal, entertainment, business, and repair services.[14] An additional 20 percent worked in the manufacturing sector including public utilities. This distribution of women among industries is essentially the same as it was in 1940, when 71 percent of all workingwomen were employed in the service sector and 25 percent in manufacturing.[15]

Within the service sector, women tend to be concentrated in specific industries that have traditionally employed them. For example, in 1968, women made up 45 percent of the employees in retail trade, but only 22 percent in the wholesale trade; more than 81 percent of the workers in hospitals; and 59 percent of the employees in elementary and secondary schools, but only 41 percent in colleges and universities.[16]

In manufacturing also, certain industries are "women's industries." In 1968, when women comprised 28 percent of all manufacturing workers, they were 45 percent of the work force in textile mill products, 80 percent in apparel and related products, 40 percent in electrical equipment and supplies, 56 percent in leather, and 43 percent in tobacco industries, but less than 10 percent in the petroleum refining, primary metal, and lumber industries.[17]

The industrial distribution of women workers shows that some industries rely more heavily on women workers and employ them more readily than others. But the representation of women in an industry gives an incomplete picture of the opportunities open to them. Within a given industry women may fill a broad or narrow range of jobs and have full or limited opportunities for career advancement. In fact, throughout the United States virtually every industry, occupation, and firm in which women are represented at all, regardless of the specific ratio of male to female workers, employs disproportionately many women at the bottom and disproportionately few at the top.

An industry in the service sector may have a high proportion of women in its work force simply because it employs large numbers of clerical workers, not because it provides opportunities for women in professional, technical, and managerial positions. Similarly, manufacturing firms may welcome women into their operative and clerical categories, but exclude them from their skilled craft and supervisory jobs. Thus the occupational distribution of women workers reflects the differences in employment opportunities between male and female workers more accurately than does the industrial distribution (see Table [2-1]).

The distribution of female and male workers by major occupation reveals striking differences between the two groups. In 1971, over 60 percent of female white-collar workers (more than one-third of all employed women) worked in clerical jobs. Yet almost 70 percent of male white-collar workers (28 percent of the male work force) were in either the professional and technical or the managerial category.

Men also have the highest status, highest paying blue-collar jobs. Only 8 percent of women blue-collar workers were craftsmen or foremen in 1971. Yet over 43 percent of the men in this group were categorized as craftsmen and foremen. Data collected by the Equal Employment Opportunity Commission indicates that even in industries where women represent a large proportion of operatives, they may be excluded from craft jobs. For example, in the printing and publishing industry in Cleveland, over 60 percent of

14. This definition is similar to that used by Victor Fuchs in The Service Economy (New York: National Bureau of Economic Research, 1968).

15. U.S. Department of Labor, Women's Bureau, 1969 Handbook on Women Workers, Bulletin 294 (Washington, D.C.: U.S. Government Printing Office, 1969), p. 110 and U.S. Department of Labor, Women's Bureau, Background Facts on Women Workers in the United States, 1970, p. 14.

16. U.S. Department of Labor, Women's Bureau, 1969 Handbook on Women Workers, (Washington, D.C.: U.S. Government Printing Office), p. 116.

17. Ibid., p. 114.

TABLE [2-1]. OCCUPATIONAL DISTRIBUTION OF THE LABOR FORCE
by sex and race

		Percent Distribution			
				Females	
	Males		Total		Nonwhite
Major occupation group	1971		1971		1968
Total employed[a]	100.0		100.0		100.0
White collar workers	40.9		60.6		31.2
Professional & Technical		13.7		14.5	10.2
Managers, Officials & Proprietors		14.6		5.0	1.5
Clerical workers		6.7		33.9	17.4
Sales workers		5.9		7.2	2.1
Blue collar workers	45.9		15.4		18.2
Craftsmen & Foremen		19.9		1.3	0.8
Operatives		18.3		13.3	16.9
Non-farm laborers		7.7		0.8	0.5
Service workers	8.2		22.2		48.6
Private household workers		0.1		4.9	24.4
Other service workers		8.1		17.4	24.2
Farmworkers	5.1		1.7		2.1
Farmers and Farm Managers		3.2		0.3	0.2
Farm laborers and Foremen		1.9		1.4	1.9

a. Figures may not add to totals because of rounding.

Source: Cols. 1 and 2—U.S. Department of Labor, Manpower Administration, Manpower Report of the President, March 1972, p. 172; col. 3—U.S. Department of Labor, Women's Bureau, 1969 Handbook on Women Workers, p. 106.

the operatives, but only one percent of the craftsmen, were women. Similarly, in the electronics industry of that city, 57 percent of the operatives, but just 3 percent of the craftsmen, were women.[18]

The employment distribution of nonwhite women is particularly skewed toward the lower rungs of the occupational ladder. Almost half (49 percent) of nonwhite workingwomen worked in service jobs in 1968, compared to 22 percent of all women workers. One quarter of all nonwhite women were in the lowest paying occupation of private household worker; they comprised 64 percent of all women in this occupation. Less than a third (31 percent) of nonwhite women held white-collar jobs.

In analyzing the distribution of female employment by detailed occupations, two aspects of the employment problems of women are further highlighted. First, women are heavily concentrated in an extremely small number of occupations. One indication of the limited job opportunities open to women is that half of all workingwomen were employed in just twenty-one of the 250 occupations listed by the Bureau of the Census in 1969. Male workers were more widely distributed throughout the occupational structure, with half in sixty-five occupations. One-quarter of all employed women worked in only five jobs: secretary-stenographer, household worker, bookkeeper, elementary school teacher, and waitress.[19]

Second, most women work in predominantly female jobs. Women's share of total employment increased from 18 percent in 1900 to 33 percent in 1960, but the proportion of women in predominantly female occupations, occupations in which 70 percent or more of the workers were women, declined only slightly from 55 percent to 52 percent.

18. Computed from Equal Employment Opportunity Commission, Report No. 1: Job Patterns for Minorities and Women in Private Industry, 1966, and Manpower Report of the President, 1972, p. 172.
19. Hedges, "Women Workers," p. 19.

It is doubtful that such a small change can be interpreted as reflecting a trend toward reduced segregation.[20]

Another way of approaching the issue of the concentration of women in sex-segregated occupational categories is to construct an "index of segregation" based on the percentage of women in the labor force who would have to change jobs in order for the occupation distribution of women workers to match that of men. This "index of segregation" has remained virtually the same since 1900; it was 66.9 in 1900 and 68.4 in 1960. Thus, at any given time in this century, about two-thirds of all workingwomen would have had to change jobs in order to achieve the same occupational distribution as men. It is interesting to note that the figure for racial segregation in 1960 was 46.8, less than three-fourths of the figure for sex-segregation, showing that sex-segregation has been unaffected by the vast social and economic changes of the present century.[21]

These figures suggest that the growing number of workingwomen have entered the labor force not through an across-the-board expansion of employment opportunities but rather through an expansion of traditionally female white-collar and service jobs, through the emergence of entirely new occupations that were originally defined as female, and occasionally through a shift in the sex composition of some occupations from male to female.

Geography has been another important factor in determining the sex composition of occupations. For example, in the Midwest, cornhuskers are traditionally women, while trimmers are almost always men. In the Far West, cornhuskers are men and trimmers are women.[22] In addition to this complete reversal of sex labels, the concentration of women in a category may also vary geographically. For example, in 1960, 64 percent of spinners in textile mills were female in the Northeast as compared with 83 percent in the South.[23]

Furthermore, since women are not evenly distributed among industries, an occupation which is predominantly female in one industry may be predominantly male in another. Census categories that report averages and tabulations across all industry groups often underestimate the extent of sex segregation because they are not sensitive to this wide variation among industries. For example, in 1960 the census reported that 44 percent of all assemblers were women. This included assemblers in electrical machinery equipment and supplies, of whom 67 percent were women, as well as assemblers in motor vehicles and motor vehicle equipment, of whom only 16 percent were women.

Additional examples of regional and industrial differences may be drawn from data collected by the Equal Employment Opportunity Commission. For example, the occupation of salesworker in manufacturing exhibited a great deal of variation. In the textile industry in 1966, women composed 31 percent of sales personnel in Cleveland, but less than 1 percent in Chicago. Moreover, the mere representation of women in an industry is frequently not a very good predictor of their access to higher level jobs. For example, in the Chicago apparel industry 68 percent of all workers and 30 percent of the sales workers were women, while in Atlanta, where over 80 percent of apparel workers were women, they held only 9 percent of sales positions.[24] It is doubtful that such large differences can be explained in terms of differences in industry composition or in the availability of qualified women among the cities.

Within the same industry, the sex-typing of a job often varies from one business

20. Valerie Kincade Oppenheimer, "The Sex-Labeling of Jobs," Industrial Relations, May 1968, p. 220.

21. Edward Gross, "Plus Ca Change . . . ? The Sexual Structure of Occupations Over Time," Social Problems, Fall 1968, p. 202.

22. National Manpower Council, Woman Power, p. 91, cited in Valerie Kincade Oppenheimer, The Female Labor Force in the United States (Berkeley: University of California Press, Institute of Industrial Studies, 1970), p. 66.

23. Oppenheimer, "The Sex-Labeling of Jobs," p. 222.

24. Computed from Equal Employment Opportunity Commission, Report No. 1: Job Patterns for Minorities and Women in Private Industry, 1969, p. 164.

establishment to another. One department store may hire only men as elevator operators while another may hire only women; many restaurants employ either waiters or wait-resses, but not both. A recent study of employment patterns of workers in office and factory jobs shows that men and women in nine of the eleven job categories studied worked for companies that hired only one sex in that occupation.[25]

The U.S. census figures on the occupational distribution of women and men may so greatly underestimate sex-segregation that reversals in sex-typing of jobs — from one region, industry, or firm to another — cancel each other out on a nationwide basis.

The variations discussed also reveal the extremely arbitrary way in which occupations are sex-typed. Efforts to justify the exclusion of one sex from a job on the basis of differences in training or ability will have to be reconciled with the evidence that in different locales, industries, or companies, a man's job may be a woman's job.

INCOME DIFFERENCES BETWEEN MEN AND WOMEN

The pay differentials between men and women parallel the occupational differ-ences. Statistics for full-time, year-round employees show that, in 1971, the median annual income was $9,399 for men and $5,593 for women. Thus, women earned only 59.5 percent of the male median.[26] In 1968, the median income of white men was $8,014; of nonwhite men, $5,603 (69.9 percent of the white male median income); of white women, $4,700 (58.6 percent); and of nonwhite women, $3,677 (45.9 percent).[27]

Furthermore, the gap between women's and men's incomes increased between 1956 and 1969 and has narrowed only slightly since that time. In 1970, 12 percent of all year-round, full-time working women earned less than $3,000, while only 7 percent of the women, as compared to 40 percent of the men, earned $10,000 or more.[29]

Earning differentials by sex persist even when we control for major occupation group. In 1971, the ratio of the median earnings of full-time, year-round men workers to that of full-time year-round women workers was 66.4 percent for professional and technical workers; 53.0 percent for managers, officials, and proprietors; 62.4 percent for clerical workers; 42.2 percent for sales workers; 56.4 percent for craftsmen and foremen; 60.5 percent for operatives; and 58.5 percent for service workers.[30] These pay differences are in large part due to sex-segregation in employment, which means that even within broad occupational groups, men and women tend to be concentrated in different detailed occupational categories or to work in different industries.[31]

The data on earnings of female and male workers suggest that the "separate but equal" doctrine has consequences for the sexes in employment not unlike those for the races in education. The artificial division of occupations into "men's" and "women's" jobs results in substantially higher earnings for men than for women. This is because the demand for women workers tends to be restricted to a small number of occupational categories that are segregated by sex. At the same time, the supply of women available for work is highly responsive to small changes in the wage rate as well as to employment opportunities in general. Moreover, employers can often attract more women into poorly paid jobs simply by increasing the flexibility of work schedules. Thus, in most predomi-nantly female jobs there exists a reserve pool of qualified women outside the labor market who would be willing to enter it if the price or job were right. The abundance of supply relative to demand, or what has been termed the "over-crowding" of female

25. U. S. Department of Labor, Bureau of Labor Statistics, Wages and Related Benefits, Part II, p. 79.
26. Economic Report of the President, January 1973, p. 103.
27. U.S. Department of Commerce, Bureau of the Census, Current Population Survey, Series P-60, No. 66 and No. 80.
29. U.S. Department of Labor, Women's Bureau, Fact Sheet on the Earnings Gap.
30. Economic Report of the President, January 1973, p. 104.
31. In addition, full-time hours for women tend to be less than those of men on the average. For the effect of adjustment for this factor on the earnings differential see Economic Report of the President, January 1973, Table 28, p. 104.

occupations results in a lower determination of earnings for women's jobs.[32] This is not to say that men and women never receive different pay for the same work within an establishment. However, since men and women seldom work together in the same occupational classification, such instances of "unequal pay for equal work" account for a relatively small proportion of the aggregate earnings difference. Moreover, the limited job opportunities open to women give them little defense against such wage discrimination short of litigation. The problem is further complicated by the use of nominal differences in job titles to disguise existing inequalities.

One of the most popular explanations for the difference between men's and women's incomes is that women are merely secondary earners or, as one economist put it, "assistant breadwinners." This reason for paying women less is not valid, even if one is able to ignore the principle of equal pay for equal work. Of the women in the labor force in March 1971, 23 percent were single, 19 percent were widowed, divorced, or separated from their husbands, and 23 percent had husbands whose incomes were below $7,000.[33] Thus, a substantial proportion of the female labor force has little or no alternative means of support for themselves or their dependents. The economic plight of families headed by a female is particularly serious. In 1971, 6 million American families, about 11.5 percent of all the families in the population, were headed by women. More than a third of these families, including over half of the families headed by nonwhite women, lived in poverty. Only seven percent of the families headed by men had incomes below the low income level.[34]

The financial contribution of the "assistant breadwinner," the working wife of a working husband, can frequently mean the difference between poverty and a decent standard of living for her family. In 1966, 11 percent of white families in which only the husband worked lived in poverty, but only 3 percent of the white families in which both spouses worked were below the poverty line. Among nonwhite families in which only the husband was in paid employment, 34 percent lived in poverty. In nonwhite families in which both spouses worked, 19 percent were below the poverty line.[35] That a fifth of the nonwhite families lived in poverty even with both spouses working is a testimony to the severity of the combined effects of racial and sexual segregation in employment. . . .

Another frequently heard explanation of the difference between women's and men's incomes is that men are better trained. However, a recent study of the starting salaries of 1970 college graduates indicates that employers of professional and managerial workers intended to pay women less than men, even when these workers had the same college major. Employers planned to pay women 90 percent of a man's salary in accounting, 92 percent in liberal arts fields, 95 percent in chemistry, and 97 percent in economics, engineering, and mathematics.[37] Because these plans preceded any actual hiring, this pay differential could in no way reflect differences in job performance.

Among professional and technical workers, women's median earnings are 66 percent of that of men's. The heavy concentration of women in the traditional women's jobs of teacher, nurse, librarian, and social worker undoubtedly contributes to this differential. Occupations in which women predominate are often dismissed as unskilled or unimportant, even for men. Although it is extremely difficult to compare skill levels across occupations, educational attainment provides a crude index. A recent study compared the levels of educational attainment and earnings of men and women workers within a number of predominantly female jobs categories in which the educational attainment of both men and women was higher than the median for the total male

32. Barbara Bergmann, "The Effect of White Incomes on Discrimination in Employment," Journal of Political Economy, March–April 1971.

33. U.S. Department of Labor, Women's Bureau, Why Women Work, July 1972, p. 1.

34. Economic Report of the President, January 1973, p. 108.

35. Handbook on Women Workers, p. 130.

37. Frank S. Endicott, "Trends in Employment of College and University Graduates in Business and Industry," Northwestern University, 1970.

experienced civilian labor force (11.1 years). According to the study, the median income of the male workers was slightly above the median for the male labor force in six of the eleven cases; it was less in five cases; and in none was it commensurate with their educational attainment. However, in no case did the median earnings of female workers approach either those of the total male experienced civilian work force or those of their own male counterparts in the same occupation. To put it another way, men were somewhat underpaid and women were grossly underpaid, relative to their educational attainment, in these predominantly female occupations.[38]

A growing body of research into the question of male-female pay differences supports the view that discrimination accounts for a significant share of the differential. After controlling for education, experience, and other factors that might tend to cause productivity differences between men and women, the proportion of the differential attributable to discrimination has been estimated at between 29 and 43 percent.[39]

ABSENTEEISM AND TURNOVER

Somewhat different issues are raised when we consider the argument that lower salaries for female employees are justified on the grounds that women workers are a "poor investment," less likely than men to stay on the job. This view is also used as a rationale for the failure to hire or promote women in certain occupations. Before considering the empirical evidence on this question, one point deserves special emphasis. Even if it were true that women are *on the average* more likely to quit their jobs than men, this does not justify treating *individual* women as if they all conform to the average. In the absence of discrimination against women as a group, each female applicant would be entitled to consideration on the basis of her own job history or work aspirations.

But is this view correct? Certainly there is some evidence that would tend to support it. According to the Bureau of Labor Statistics, in 1968 the average voluntary turnover rate for male factory workers was 2.2 per hundred compared to 2.6 for female factory workers.[40] Further, in 1966, men averaged 5.2 years of continuous employment at one job and women averaged only 2.8 years. In comparable age groups, though, the job stability of single women was as great as that of all men; the job stability of married men was greater and that of married women was less. Single women aged 45 and over averaged more time in one job (15.5 years) than all men in this age group (13.1 years). The youngest workers of both sexes had the shortest job tenure, and young married women had the shortest of all. However, the job stability of married women increased with age.

Age is an important factor in labor turnover. Younger workers of both sexes change jobs more often than older workers. They can engage in occupational experimentation because generally they have fewer financial responsibilities than older workers, and, having little seniority to lose, they risk less by changing jobs. In addition, their turnover rate imposes little burden on an employer because on the average they have not received as much training as older workers.

Conversely, the longer a worker stays in a job, the more likely he is to continue. Length of service increases a worker's stake in a job in the form of nontransferable fringe benefits and seniority rights. Jobs that require substantial on-the-job training have a lower turnover rate, in part because the job skills acquired may not be transferable. Good prospects for promotion and high salary levels also diminish the worker's incentive to change jobs.

A U.S. Civil Service Commission study of the voluntary turnover rates of full-time

38. Oppenheimer, The Female Labor Force in the United States, pp. 100-101.
39. See Isabell Sawhill, "The Economics of Discrimination Against Women: Some New Findings," Journal of Human Resources, Summer 1973, for a review of this research.
40. U.S. Department of Labor, Bureau of Labor Statistics, Facts on Absenteeism and Labor Turnover Among Women Workers, August 1969, p. 2.

employees in the federal government found that, overall, women had a higher turnover rate than men.[41]The study also showed that many more women than men were in the low-grade jobs that have always had the highest total turnover rates. These data indicate that the overall turnover rates of female and male workers are misleading. Such things as age, grade level, type of job, and length of service are much more predictive of job success and retention than the single factor of sex. For example, women over thirty years of age had substantially lower turnover rates and were better employment risks than men between the ages of nineteen and twenty-four. The authors of the study conclude that:

> Much better predictions about the probability of loss can be made when age, grade level, etc., are taken into consideration than simply to assume that (1) probability of loss is the same for all women, and (2) probability of loss will be much greater for a woman than it would be for a man.[42]

The same variables also affect the rate of absences due to illness. A 1967 Public Health Service study indicates that the average work time lost by men and women seventeen years and over due to illness or injury was 5.6 days for women and 5.3 days for men. Men were more likely to be absent because of chronic conditions, while women were more plagued by acute illnesses that kept them away from work for shorter periods of time. Another survey of a large federal agency found that women employees with children had more absences than women without children, but single women took fewer sick days than single men. The survey also found that employees in high level jobs had fewer absences, *regardless of sex,* than those at lower levels.

The American public's opinion of workingwomen evolved when the typical woman worker was young, single, and apt to leave the work force permanently upon marriage. Today, the typical woman worker is forty years old, married, and a mother. Women with children under six are the least represented but fastest growing group in the labor force. As young workingwomen become pregnant, the lack of guaranteed maternity leave forces many of them out of their jobs. If they take new jobs after their children are born, they still lose their seniority rights. Because child-care facilities are both scarce and unreliable, mothers of young children often find themselves forced to drift in and out of jobs, continually losing seniority and the right to fringe benefits. In spite of these difficulties, the growing numbers of these women in the labor force suggest that their motivation is strong enough to override these obstacles.

In short, employer practices that restrict women to low-paying, dead-end jobs and deny them access to training encourage their turnover and absenteeism rates. The sex-segregated nature of the labor force lessens the chance for improved opportunities, for in general women presently compete with other women for jobs in the few occupations that our society defines as female jobs. The belief that women workers are a poor investment may indeed be a self-fulfilling prophecy.

———————

The following article presents further evidence that "women's" jobs are under-valued as compared to "men's" jobs.

———————

41. U.S. Civil Service Commission, President's Commission on the Status of Women, Report of the Committee on Federal Employment, Appendix F, October 1963.
42. Ibid., p. 24.

BRIGGS, GUESS WHO HAS THE MOST COMPLEX JOB?
Unpublished manuscript (1971)[1]

PREJUDICE: "being down on something you are not up on."

As a recent neophyte in the field of training women for jobs in the skilled trades, I was introduced, with due ceremony, to the Dictionary of Occupational Titles. This two volume product of the U.S. Department of Labor — sometimes alluded to as the Bureaucratic Bible — defines some 23,000 different occupations in over 230 different industries and becomes the basis on which a whole range of public and private agencies evaluate prerequisites, career-ladder criteria and salaries for the world of work. Early in my work as Wisconsin State Coordinator for Women in Apprenticeship, I was astonished that so many so-called "women's occupations" had the lowest possible ratings in this book.

This Federal Government best seller is used religiously not only by the Federal-State Employment Service, but by 65 other governmental agencies, as well as by private employment offices, military services and organizations, professional societies, industrial organizations, schools and libraries at home and abroad. . . .

. . .[T]he D. O. T. . . . is used in interviewing and referral, counseling, in occupational research and filing systems, in establishing job classification and training programs. . . .

A complexity-skill rating in the D.O.T. indirectly affects wages in that it (1) helps place a particular job in the classified hierarchy in relation to other jobs, (2) gives some indication of the amount of formal education necessary as a prerequisite for doing the job, and, (3) indicates the extent of on-the-job training necessary for successful performance.

Take a look, for a moment, at how the classification system works: the updated 1965 third edition uses a six-digit code to classify the 36,000 job titles by occupation and the skill and complexity level demanded by the job. The last three digits of the code [consult the tabulation] rate each job for complexity in relation to data, people, and things. The scale used assigns zero to the most complicated functioning and eight to indicate that there is no significant functioning demanded by the job in this area. An 878 rating for a particular job indicates that it involves no significant function with data (8), "serving" in relation to people (7), and no significant function with things (8). "Serving" is defined as "Attending to the needs or requests of people or animals or expressed or implicit wishes of people. Immediate response involved." The implication is that a job so defined can be performed successfully by anyone with minimal prerequisites, almost no training, and that it involves little responsibility.

[EXPLANATION OF JOB COMPLEXITY CODE USED IN THE
DICTIONARY OF OCCUPATIONAL TITLES]

Data	*People*	*Things*
0 - Synthesizing	0 - Mentoring	0 - Setting up
1 - Coordinating	1 - Negotiating	1 - Precision working
2 - Analyzing	2 - Instructing	2 - Operating/controlling
3 - Compiling	3 - Supervising	3 - Driving/operating
4 - Computing	4 - Diverting	4 - Manipulating
5 - Copying	5 - Persuading	5 - Tending
6 - Comparing	6 - Speaking/Signalling	6 - Feeding/offbearing
7 - _____	7 - Serving	7 - Handling
8 - No significant function	8 - No significant function	8 - No significant function

1. Available from the author, Division of Apprenticeship and Training, 310 Price Place, Madison, Wis. 53701. Published in different form in Forum, No. 2, pp. 15–17 (Wisconsin Psychiatric Institute 1971).

A casual perusal of the D.O.T. reveals that there is a cluster of traditionally women's jobs that are grossly underrated in complexity — partly, no doubt, because in the past women's "unpaid" work was taken for granted, looked simple, and was not thought to need any particular formal education or training. Partly this low rating comes because of an earlier cultural assumption that there was little skill involved in raising children, who, it seems, could be regarded as passive packages, to be "served" (digit 7, under people), at least until they were of school age, where they might be "instructed" (digit 2) by their teachers. And partly, I fear, the interpersonal skills which our society ascribes to women as their forte are less valued than the object manipulation of the more prestigious male domain.

Here are some revealing and felicitous juxtapositions as they are rated in the D.O.T.:

foster mother, 878
"Rears children in own home as members of family.

child care attendant, 878
". . . House parent, special school counselor, cares for group of children housed in . . . government institution."

home health aide, 878
Cares for elderly, convalescent or handicapped persons.

nursemaid, 878

nursery school teacher, 878*
"Organizes and leads activities of pre-kindergarten children, maintains discipline . . ."

nurse, mid-wife, 378

homemaker, (cross-reference maid-general) 878

kindergartner, 878
Entertains children in nursery.

nurse, practical, 878
(cares for patients and children in private homes, hospitals)

nurse, general duty, 378
(". . . Rotates among various clinical services of institution such as obstetrics, surgery, orthopedics, outpatient and admitting, pediatrics, psychology and tuberculosis. May assist with operations and deliveries.)

rest room attendant, 878
"Serves patrons of lavatories in store . . ."

parking lot attendant, 878
". . . parks automobiles for customers in parking lot . . ."

public bath maid, 878
. . . not quite as skilled as . . . *pet shop attendant, 877.*

delivery boy (newspaper carrier) 868
or closer in complexity and skill level to a *mud-mixer-helper, 887*

marine mammal handler, 328
"Signals or cues trained marine mammals . . ."

hotel clerk, 368

barber, 371

strip-tease artist, 878
(entertains audience by . . .)

offal man, poultry, 887
(shovels ice into chicken offal container)

cosmetology, 271
cosmetologist apprentice, 271
"provides beauty services for customers"

---

*In Wisconsin, a "3 year license will be granted (a nursery school teacher) upon evidence of completion of a 4-year course in a school accredited for providing a professional major in the teaching of nursery school children."

nurse, private duty, 378
(contracts independently to give nursing care . . . administers medications (and) independent emergency measures to counteract adverse developments . . .)

undertaker, 168
(arranges and directs funeral services . . .)

A parent or parent substitute, even a Nursery School teacher (878) does not rate with the dog trainer (228) — job analysts having presumably observed that children are rarely or never spoken to (6), persuaded (5), diverted (4), supervised (3), instructed (2), negotiated with (1) or mentored (0). Neither does a parent or nursery school teacher have need of data (8 being no significant function). Any foreman — of toy assembly or a rug cleaning crew, for instance, rates a 1 on data, because he coordinates. Crews of children (being "packages" rather than people) don't need their activities to be coordinated, it seems, even in groups of 18+.

As for the category of "things" — parents, parent substitutes and homemakers in fact juggle a combination of jobs along with the human interaction — namely:

Cooking	short order cook	38 *1*
Sewing	sewing machine operator	78 *2*
	seamstress	88 *4*
Laundry	laundry operator	88 *4*
Ironing	mangler	88 *5*
Cleaning	cleaner, furniture	88 *7*
Driving	chauffeur	88 *3*

along with tending or operating a number of machines (mixers, heaters, furnaces, polishers, ovens, etc.).

NOTE: OTHER SOURCES

For a detailed history of women's participation in the labor force, particularly of the effects of World Wars I and II and the depression on women workers, see Chafe, The American Woman, Her Changing Social, Economic and Political Roles, 1920–1970 (1972). The 1969 Handbook on Women Workers, put out by the Women's Bureau of the Department of Labor, is an excellent source of statistical information, including numerous charts and tables. The Women's Bureau also publishes short fact sheets which give more recent data on particular topics and which can be obtained by writing to the Women's Bureau, U.S. Department of Labor, 14th & Constitution Ave. N.W., Washington, D.C. 20210. The Monthly Labor Review, also published by the Department of Labor, is another good source of current data and analytic material on the status of women workers. Juanita Kreps' book, Sex in the Marketplace: American Women at Work (1971) also contains some useful discussions of sex discrimination in employment.

It is quite clear from the preceding material that women workers as a group occupy an inferior position in the labor force. What are the causes of this situation? Blau suggests that occupational segregation is one cause. She explains:[2]

---

2. Blau (under Weisskoff), "Women's Place" in the Labor Market, 62 Am. Econ. Rev. 161, 165–166 (1972).
    Footnotes which were omitted in the version published in the American Economic Review have been reinserted with the permission of the author.

The concentration of women in predominantly female jobs and the likelihood that even within relatively integrated occupations women and men tend to work in different industries or establishments results in a virtual "dual labor market" for female and male labor. The dual labor market analysis enables us to explain the pay differentials between female and male workers in terms of supply and demand analysis. Demand is greatly restricted by the sex-typing of jobs. At the same time, the supply of women available for work is highly responsive to changes in the wage rate and employment opportunities in general.[15] The abundance of supply relative to demand, or what has been termed the "overcrowding" of female occupations, would tend to result in a lower determination of earnings for "women's jobs."[16] Thus, we may replace the familiar statement that women earn less because they are in low paying occupations with the statement that they earn less because they are in *women's jobs.*

Similarly, the common complaint that women are restricted to low status occupations could also be restated in terms of the concentration of the female labor force in *women's jobs.* As long as the labor market is divided on the basis of sex, it is likely that the tasks allocated to women will be ranked as less prestigious or important, reflecting women's lower social status in the society at large. . . .

I would conclude that the elimination of occupational segregation by sex is essential to the attainment of economic equality for women.

In addition to causing undervaluation, there is another quite simple way that sex segregation contributes to the lower pay and lower status of women workers. As discussed earlier, women are "sex segregated" out of jobs which require more skill and into jobs which require less. Therefore they are paid less on the average than male workers.

Another result of sex segregation is the channeling of women into part-time or part-year jobs, jobs that do not require overtime, and jobs with a high risk of unemployment. In 1965, 66 percent of all men in the labor force worked full-time, full-year, while only 39 percent of all women workers did so. About 29.5 percent of women workers worked full-time less than a full year and 31.3 percent worked part-time for all or part of the year.[3] By 1968, the figures had changed only slightly: 41.4 percent of women workers worked full-time, full-year, while 29 percent worked full-time less than a full year and 29.7 worked at part-time jobs for all or part of the year.[4] The unemployment rates of women, which are higher than those for men, were discussed above. Statistics showing that women work proportionally less overtime than men, particularly less overtime at premium pay, are discussed below in Part II-B-3-b, Note: Analysis of Maximum Hours Laws as the Primary Example of Protective Legislation.

Those figures are important for three reasons. First, they cause the attachment of many women to the labor force to be discounted. For example, labor force participation rates are often determined by the percentage of women who work full-time, full-year. Since women are disproportionately represented among part-time and part-year workers, reliance on statistics about full-time, full-year workers exaggerates the role of men as breadwinners and workers and downplays the extent to which women work outside the home. As Waldman explained,[5]

15. It also seems likely that an individual employer can attract more women, frequently from outside of the labor force, by such nonpecuniary measures as more flexible work schedules.

16. See Bergmann [The Effect on White Incomes of Discrimination in Employment, J. Polit. Econ. (March-April 1971), and Occupational Segregation, Wages and Profits When Employers Discriminate by Race or Sex (unpublished paper, Jan. 1971)] for a rigorous development of the overcrowding thesis. The argument presented here is very general but could be extended to take into account differences in quality both within and between the female and male work force. Some of the quality differences between the two groups could be considered as deriving from the dual labor market itself.

3. Ginzberg, Paycheck and Apron — Revolution in Womanpower, 7 Ind. Rel. 193, 194 (1968), as cited in Goldberg, The Economic Exploitation of Women, in Gordon (ed.), Problems in Political Economy: An Urban Perspective 113, 114 (1971).

4. Waldman, Changes in the Labor Force Activity of Women, Monthly Labor Rev., June 1970, at p. 14. See also the discussion in Goldberg, supra at 114-116.

5. Waldman, supra.

Data on work experience over a calendar year provide one of the best measures of the strength of women's attachment to the labor force, because a larger number of them work at some time during a year than in any 1 month of the year. The 12-month record accounts for *all* women who were in the labor force at any time during the year by how many weeks they worked or looked for work and many other characteristics. For example, out of the 72 million women in the civilian population 16 years old and over in March, 1969, 30 million, or 42 percent, were in the labor force in March, but 37 million (52 percent) had worked at one time or another in 1968.

Likewise, Bell reports:[6]

Along with the notion of women as a "reserve army" of manpower goes the conviction that most women look for part-time jobs, which are somehow peripheral both to the economy and to the family. This idea provides a rationale for the conviction that the economic role of working women differs significantly from that of men. But . . . the facts contradict the myth. While more women than men work only part of the year or less than 40 hours a week, only one out of five does so by choice. Of the 33 million women in the labor force, only six million are on a *voluntary* part-time basis, and the proportion seeking full-time work has not varied much over the past 15 years. *Involuntary* part-time work, including short workweeks, layoffs for a day or two, and the like, greatly exceeds 20 per cent; like recent rates for unemployment, these figures run considerably higher among women workers than men.

A second reason these figures are important is that part-time and part-year workers generally receive status and pay lower than a pro rata share of a full-time, full-year worker's pay, fringe benefits, and opportunities for promotion.[7] Since the majority of part-time and part-year workers are women, unfair treatment of such workers is sex-discriminatory.

Third, to the extent that women hold part-time jobs, do not work overtime, or are unemployed out of necessity rather than choice, these statistics are another indication of women's inferior position in the labor market. According to Bell's statistics, reported above, the percentage of women working part-time involuntarily is quite high. Ginzberg's analysis further supports the idea that the large proportion of women working part-time or part-year is a result of discrimination against them. He discusses the statistics as follows:[8]

. . . Of the 17.6 million women who [worked less than full-time throughout the year in 1965] just over half (52 percent) indicated that they were out of the labor force for part of the year in order to take care of their homes. The second largest group, about 22 percent, were going to school. The remaining 26 percent were about evenly divided between those who could not find jobs and those who were kept from working because of illness, disability, or other reasons.[6]

It would be easy to conclude that a weakness in the demand for labor is a factor of relatively minor importance in explaining why women work part rather than full time. But before making this deduction, we must note that for 2.2 million women, unemployment was identified as the key variable and that another 900,000 women wanted to work, but could not find jobs. Some part of the 2.5 million who worked less than full time because of disability or other reasons might have worked full time had the demand for labor been stronger. The proof of the sensitive relations between the strength of demand for labor and the full time employment of women is found in the following four-year trend. From 1962 through 1965 the total number of women who worked increased by 2.4 million. The corresponding increase in those working full time, full year was 1.5 million. The proportion of women who worked full time

6. C.S. Bell, Age, Sex, Marriage and Jobs, The Public Interest, Winter 1973, at 79.
7. See Simmons et al., Background Paper for Exploitation From 9 to 5, ch. 3 (1974).
8. Ginzberg, supra footnote 3, at 194.
6. [Work Experience of the Population in 1965, Monthly Labor Rev., Dec. 1966] 1373.

increased from 36.8 percent to 38.8 percent, which suggests that many women will respond to the opportunity to shift from part- to full-time employment.[7]

As figures noted above attest, the trend toward an increase in the percentage of women working full-time, full-year which he reported has continued.[9]

One more factor which causes low wages for women was mentioned above: unequal pay for equal work. The pervasiveness of this kind of discrimination is documented in Part III, The Equal Pay Act, infra, this chapter.

B. The Sex Stereotypes That Make Sex Discrimination Acceptable[10]

Despite the federal laws prohibiting sex discrimination in employment, many forms of discrimination against women workers are still socially acceptable. For example, the widespread belief that women should get equal pay for equal work co-exists with the idea that women work for different reasons than men (i.e., for luxuries or out of boredom, rather than to earn a living) and therefore do not "need" or deserve equal treatment. Stereotypes like this must be challenged, both on the ground that women (and men) should be judged as individuals rather than on the basis of averages and stereotypes, and on the ground that the stereotypes are inaccurate. Identifying specific prejudices is useful, because it is only when they have been reduced to concrete terms that they can be challenged on factual grounds. This section therefore outlines some of the more common stereotypes about working women that are used to justify discrimination against them.

One common stereotype is that a woman's primary commitment is to her family and not to her job. Valerie Oppenheimer listed a number of factors which help account for the sex segregation of the labor market. Several are related to the belief that women workers are unreliable because of their family commitments: (1) that women's work life will be characterized by interruptions rather than career continuity; (2) that women will lack the geographical mobility necessary for many jobs; (3) that women will have lower career aspirations than men and therefore be less productive; and (4) that for the three reasons just listed, women will not be good candidates for on the job training.[11] On the basis of the assumption that women will or should place home and family first, employers also conclude that women will have high rates of turnover and absenteeism, and that they work best at jobs which draw upon the same skills as homemaking and family.

7. Ibid., p. 1370.

9. 1969 statistics on reasons why women not in the labor force did not have jobs lend further support to Ginzberg's analysis. According to the Bureau of Labor Statistics, "Of the 40.9 million women who were not in the labor force in 1969, 32.5 million were not working because of home responsibilities, 3.5 million because of school attendance, and 2.3 million because of ill health. Women and girls accounted for about half of all persons out of the labor force because of school attendance or ill health.

"While reasons for nonparticipation in the labor force in 1969 varied for women of different ages, home responsibilities were cited by the great majority of women 20 years of age and over. . . . More than two-thirds of all girls 16 to 19 years and about one-sixth of women in their early twenties were not working because they were in school. Ill health was the reason for nonparticipation of 8 percent of women 60 years of age and over but was not a significant factor among younger women.

"About 3.2 million, or 8 percent of all women who were not working or looking for work in 1969, reported that they wanted jobs. Of these, 39 percent were not looking for work because of home responsibilities, including women who reported inability to arrange child care. Seventeen percent were students and 12 percent did not seek work because they thought they would not be able to get jobs." U.S. Dep't of Labor, Women's Bureau, Background Facts on Women Workers in the United States 1 (1970). See also id. at 6, Table 2.

10. In preparing the discussion at the beginning of this section, the authors have relied heavily on Simmons et al., Background Paper for Exploitation From 9 to 5, ch. 3 (1974).

11. Oppenheimer, The Female Labor Force in the United States: Demographic and Economic Factors Governing Its Growth and Changing Composition 109-114, 104-105 (1970).

Because of these beliefs, women are considered to be generally less qualified workers and are excluded from jobs which require on the job training, career continuity, geographical mobility, strong motivation, or skills outside the traditional female realm. Thus top-level jobs are viewed as male jobs and jobs at all levels come to be sex-segregated.

Another assumption that causes sex segregation in the labor market is that women are suited by temperament and skill for certain jobs and not for others. As Oppenheimer explains:[12]

> [The sex-linked traits in question] may not even be proven traits of one sex or the other — it is sufficient that employers believe that they are, or believe that one sex has an advantage over the other in some important respect. . . . Women are supposed by many employers to have greater manual dexterity than men. This may or may not be true, but that is not particularly important. What is important is the extent to which employers believe it, and let this belief guide their hiring policies.

It is ironic that dexterous female hands are required for the manufacture of transistor radios but not for surgery. Similarly, women are told that they should not apply for some jobs because the jobs require working at night, yet female telephone operators and nurses routinely work at night. The inconsistencies are apparent, but the same excuses persist. Caroline Bird wryly observed that employers justified the sex typing of jobs "in the tone of voice a teller of fairy tales uses to warn his audience that what he says is not to be taken literally."[13] It is not surprising, therefore, that following a 1962 order requiring federal appointing officers to give reasons for requesting an employee of a particular sex, the number of requests for applicants of a specific sex dropped to one percent of their former volume.[14]

Georgina Smith, in Help Wanted — Female,[15] studied changes in the supply and demand of women workers in a large New Jersey county between 1953 and 1961. One of her goals was to identify reasons that specific jobs shifted from men's jobs to women's jobs in this period. The explanations given by employers were surprisingly uniform. A spokesman for a large manufacturing firm said:[16]

> [M]ost technological changes were of a type that would tend to increase the percent of women. For example, we have broken down the alignment of components and simplified [the] job and, *as the jobs called for less skill, they became women's work.*

Another manufacturer explained:[17]

> In assembly, we have one job . . . which was formerly performed by men. We decided that the job was simple enough so that there was no point in continuing to recruit men for it. So we made it a woman's job. We couldn't redesign it; it was already too simple.

A third employer stated:[18]

> We feel that jobs requiring manual dexterity call for women. Also this work is particularly tedious and painstaking — definitely a woman's job.

---

12. Id. at 103.
13. Bird, Born Female 69 (1969).
14. Ibid.
15. Smith, Help Wanted — Female: A Study of Demand and Supply in a Local Job Market for Women (1964).
16. Id. at 11 (emphasis supplied).
17. Id at 24.
18. Ibid.

Similarly, Oppenheimer noted:[19]

> Jobs entailing much physical strength tend to be automatically labeled male. Noland and Bakke found, for example, in their study of hiring practices in New Haven and Charlotte, that about 90 percent of employers preferred men for common laboring jobs — those in which physical strength is more likely to be needed — and about 75 percent required men; women were preferred only for cleaning jobs.[17]

She also pointed out that[20]

> [S]heer feminine (and masculine too, I presume) appeal is considered an important factor at times. For example, in a 1960 National Office Management Association study, about 28 percent of the 2,000 companies surveyed indicated that sex appeal is a qualification on some office jobs and that it is given serious consideration in the employment of receptionists, switchboard operators, secretaries, and stenographers.[21]

Two additional social beliefs about women and work were identified by Theodore Caplow in his examination of the relationship between cultural attitudes and the inferior position of women in the labor force. According to Caplow,[21]

> Women are barred from four out of every five occupational functions, not because of incapacity or technical unsuitability, but because the attitudes which govern interpersonal relationships in our culture sanction only a few working relationships between men and women, and prohibit all the others on grounds that have nothing to do with technology.

Caplow believes that, except in family or sexual relationships, social values dictate that men should not be subordinate to women, and that "intimate groups, except those based on family or sexual ties, should be composed of either sex but not both."[22] These deeply embedded perceptions explain the tenacity with which some companies have insisted on keeping certain jobs sex-segregated, and the emotion that is often aroused when the question of a female supervising male workers is discussed. The desire to prevent women from moving to positions of responsibility where they would be supervising men becomes in some cases a justification for defining whatever work a woman does as low-level work. If the same work were done by a man, instead, it might qualify him for a promotion.

The discouraging thing about these stereotypes is that they color people's perceptions of reality and skew their thinking. When one female employee conforms to the stereotype, an employer is likely to generalize his experience and conclude that all women will exhibit behavior like hers. Paradoxically, however, the deviation of individual women employees from the stereotypes does not undercut the mythology. For example, Smith reported that even when individual women held "men's" jobs and did them well, they were often not fully accepted by their employers and co-workers. In fact, the successes of these women were sometimes held against them. More than half of the firms Smith surveyed answered that women currently held jobs that the employer would

19. Oppenheimer, The Sex-Labeling of Jobs, 7 Ind. Rel. 226-227 (May 1968).
17. Noland and Bakke [Workers Wanted: A Study of Employers' Hiring Policies, Preferences and Practices in New Haven and Charlotte (New York: Harper, 1949)] pp. 184-185. In a study of job opportunities for women as technicians, the Women's Bureau found that in the electronics field, for example, "firms producing large electronic units often require their technicians to lift and move heavy equipment; they may, therefore, refuse to hire a woman for such work if they think it is beyond her strength." Careers for Women as Technicians, Women's Bureau Bulletin 282 (Washington, D.C.: 1962), p. 3.
20. Oppenheimer, supra footnote 19, at 227.
21. Ginder, [Factors of Sex in Office Employment, 36 Office Executive (Feb. 1961)] p. 11.
21. Caplow, The Sociology of Work 237 (1954) — Eds.
22. Id. at 238.

prefer to fill with men.[23] This opposition to a woman in a high-paying "male" position was evident for both blue- and white-collar jobs. One employer said, of a relatively highly paid blue-collar woman who had been employed by his company since World War II:[24]

> "The men want us to get rid of her. They want her out because she's too good; she's a pace-setter. I would say that the day she quits, all the men are going to go out and get cockeyed drunk."

Popular beliefs that women workers have higher rates of turnover and absenteeism are another example of the persistence of sex stereotypes in the face of alternative explanations of reality. They also illustrate the self-reinforcing nature of sex stereotypes. Consider the following.

STROBER, LOWER PAY FOR WOMEN: A CASE OF ECONOMIC DISCRIMINATION?
11 Ind. Rel., 279-280 (May 1972)

. . . [S]eparation rates for men and women of similar age and skill employed on similar jobs are about the same. This is the conclusion which emerges from several studies cited by the Woman's Bureau pamphlet, Facts About Women's Absenteeism and Labor Turnover.[4] For example, "A private study[5] conducted among 65 large chemical and pharmaceutical laboratories revealed only moderate differences in the labor turnover of men and women chemists when they were grouped by type of degree required for the grade of work performed. A majority of the surveyed laboratories reported that in comparisons made on this basis, women's turnover rates were 'about the same as men's.' No more than 10 percent of the laboratories reported them much higher."[6]

In a study of 1,298 female and 1,329 male lawyers, James White found virtually no difference in the percentages (30 percent for men, 29 percent for women) remaining at their first job three years after graduation from law school.[7] This study also points out the tremendous amount of turnover, for both sexes, in the first few years of employment.

Even in studies unadjusted for age and occupation, separation rates are similar for men and women. In 1968, a BLS study for manufacturing production workers showed a 2.6 percent quit rate for women, a 2.2 percent rate for men.[8] A recent survey by the Merchants and Manufacturers Association[9] of 664,321 employees in a wide variety of manufacturing and nonmanufacturing industries in California revealed that women were responsible for 34.4 percent of all quits and discharges. Since women represent 36.68 percent of California's labor force, the report concludes, "It appears as if sex has little bearing upon the area occupational turnover."[10]

Absenteeism rates for men and women also appear to be similar. According to a

23. Smith, supra footnote 15, at 25.
24. Id. at 26.
4. U.S. Department of Labor, Wage and Labor Standards Administration, Women's Bureau, Facts About Women's Absenteeism and Labor Turnover (Washington, D.C.: 1969).
5. John B. Parrish, "Employment of Women Chemists in Industrial Laboratories," Science, April 30, 1965.
6. Facts About Women's Absenteeism . . . , p. 5.
7. James J. White, "Women in the Law," Michigan Law Review, LXV (April, 1967). At the end of seven years, 14.5 per cent of men and 11.1 per cent of women were still at their first job. However, a significantly larger percentage of women than men left their *second* job in four of the eight classes studied.
8. Facts About Women's Absenteeism . . . , p. 2.
9. Merchants and Manufacturers Association, Labor Turnover Handbook (Los Angeles: 1970).
10. Ibid., p. 32.

Public Health Service study, work time lost because of illness or injury was 5.6 days for women and 5.3 days for men during 1967.[11] A U.S. Civil Service Commission study of sick leave records in 1961 showed that among persons earning $9,000–$10,000 a year, 6.9 sick leave days were used by women, 6.3 by men.[12]

I do not mean to imply that the question of differential turnover rates or absentee rates is closed. . . . I cite the above studies, however, because I believe [the] turnover hypothesis needs to be tested with the turnover data available. And at the present reading, employers are, in fact, discriminatory if they exclude women from certain occupations or hire them at lower rates of pay because they think women will leave the job sooner than men.

BLAU (UNDER WEISSKOFF)
"WOMEN'S PLACE" IN THE LABOR MARKET
62 Am. Econ. Rev. 161, 164 (May 1972)[25]

THE LABOR COST ARGUMENT

The widely held belief among employers that women have higher average rates of absenteeism and voluntary labor turnover than male workers might also tend to produce occupational segregation by sex. These differences in average labor costs would imply different pay rates for the same job. Insofar as it is frequently not optimal for legal, administrative, and industrial relations reasons to have different pay scales for the same occupation, this consideration might lead to occupational segregation within the establishment.[11] This factor would also tend to make employers unwilling to invest in firm specific training for women for fear of losing their investment. Indeed, it does appear that many predominantly female jobs are those in which general and transferable skills rather than firm specific training are required.

One point should be emphasized at the outset. Even if employer views regarding the average probability of loss of employing women were correct, their actions would still constitute a form of discrimination.[12] Discrimination is the process of forming stereotyped views that all members of a particular group are assumed to possess the characteristics of the group. Thus, the case of an individual female applicant is not considered on the basis of her particular job history or aspirations. Such treatment of women may reduce the cost of screening applicants, but it cannot be considered equitable.

But is the employer view correct? First, employer views formed at a time when most women workers were young and single and apt to leave the labor force permanently upon marriage have not responded to the changing composition of the female labor force. . . . The increase in the average age of women workers has had the effect of increasing the job stability of the female work force. Moreover, the rise in the labor force participation rates of young married women in the childbearing ages suggests that new work patterns are in the process of being forged.

Second, women are frequently denied the incentives given to male workers to

---

11. U.S. Department of Health, Education, and Welfare, Public Health Service, Vital and Health Statistics Current Estimates from the Health Interview Survey, United States, 1967, PHS Publication No. 1000, Series 10, No. 52, Tables 8 and 16, May 1969.

12. U.S. Civil Service Commission, unpublished data, cited in Facts About Women's Absenteeism . . . , p. 6. If salary level is not standardized, however, women do tend to use more sick leave. Women with children also tend to have more absences than women without children.

25. Footnotes which were omitted in the version published in the American Economic Review have been reinserted with the permission of the author.

11. I am referring here to pay differentials that are not based on length of service or merit ratings.

12. Piore has labeled this "statistical discrimination." Piore, The Dual Labor Market: Theory and Implications, in D. M. Gordon, ed., Problems in Political Economy: An Urban Perspective 90, 91 (1971).

remain on the job. Substantial investment in firm specific training, good prospects for promotion, and high pay levels decrease the probability of loss of an employee, regardless of sex. Employer practices that restrict women to low paying, dead-end jobs and deny them access to training serve to raise their turnover and absenteeism rates. Thus, a vicious circle may exist whereby employer views are constantly reaffirmed without giving women an opportunity to respond to a different structure of incentives.[13]

C. The Functions and Consequences of Sex Discrimination in Employment

Another way to analyze discrimination against women workers is to consider its function in the society, i.e., its relationship to other social structures. In choosing strategies to challenge sex discrimination on the job, it is useful to know what other social institutions it supports.

One function that sex discrimination serves is reinforcing the traditional sexual division of labor between husbands and wives. In the stereotypical family, the man is supposed to support his wife and children, and the woman is supposed to stay home and keep house. One way in which sex discrimination encourages families to conform to this pattern is by limiting women's work opportunities outside the home. When their outside opportunities are less attractive, women are more likely to stay home. Conversely, when more or better paying jobs open up, women are drawn out of the home into the labor force. Blau described as follows how sex segregation has limited the number of women who enter the labor force:[26]

> Occupational segregation by sex has important implications for other aspects of women's economic status. I would like to discuss . . . the relationship between occupational segregation and female labor force participation. . . .
>
> Occupational segregation may be the limiting factor on the growth of the female labor force. A study by Valerie Kincade Oppenheimer [The Female Labor Force in the United States: Demographic and Economic Factors Governing its Growth and Changing Composition (1970)] cited the increase in the *sex-specific demand* for women workers as the crucial factor in explaining the growth of the female labor force and its changing composition between 1940 and 1960. Oppenheimer points out that the expansion in the demand for women workers greatly exceeded the potential supply of the young, single women who were the backbone of the female labor force in the pre-1940 period. Under the pressure of an insufficiency in their preferred source of supply, employers were forced to abandon their prejudices against employing older, married women. Thus, Oppenheimer sees the great influx of these women into the labor force primarily as a *response* to increased job opportunities.
>
> Further research may show that a similar process was in operation in the years since 1960. In order to meet their needs for female labor, some employers may have found it necessary to discard their reservations about hiring mothers of young children, thus making possible the rapid increase in the labor force participation of women in this group that has occurred in recent years.
>
> This analysis which focuses primarily on *demand* factors in explaining changes in female labor force participation at least raises the possibility that had employment

13. Despite these factors, the differences in absenteeism and voluntary labor turnover between female and male workers are not as great as frequently imagined, see U.S. Dept of Labor, Women's Bureau, Facts About Women's Absenteeism and Labor Turnover, August 1969.

26. Blau (under Weisskoff), "Women's Place" in the Labor Market, supra, at 164-165. The theory that women enter the labor market in response to increases in demand for their services (and, presumably, concomitant increases in the prices employers are willing to pay for those services) is also supported by Smith's study, Help Wanted — Female, supra. See also Kreps, Sex in the Marketplace: American Women at Work, ch. 2 (1971), and Oppenheimer, Demographic Influence on Female Employment and the Status of Women, 78 Am. J. Soc. 946 (1973).

opportunities not been restricted to predominantly female jobs, even larger numbers of women might have entered the labor force. The extreme responsiveness of women to the demands exerted by the emergency conditions of World War II and the evidence that the female labor force tends to grow more quickly during the upswing in the business cycle and contract or grow more slowly during recessions would also support this view.[14]

In other words, if women were able to get better wages, and better jobs, more of them would probably enter the labor force. Since they cannot, they choose not to work, or to limit themselves to part-time or less demanding work. As a result, more women are available to care for children (especially very young children) and do housework. If, instead, women had the same choices men do, perhaps fewer of them would be willing to stay home with the children.

Similarly, sex discrimination gives men first priority on the jobs that are available. This is functional in a society in which men are supposed to do the breadwinning. Sex segregation as a means to this end has the advantage of protecting men from competition from women, while enabling employers to draw women into the labor force when they are needed. Women workers become a cushion for the economy, joining the labor force when extra workers are needed because of economic expansion or war mobilization, and returning home when employment is cut back at the end of a war or in a recession.

Sex discrimination also helps to distribute income among workers according to their sex. This makes it more feasible for male workers to support a wife and children in conformity with the traditional ideal.

One ground for challenging discrimination against women workers is that it is unjust; a person's life options should not be determined by the immutable trait of sex. A more effective challenge can be made, however, if it can be shown that sex discrimination is not only unjust but a cause of other serious social problems. In fact, there is considerable evidence that sex discrimination is a major cause of poverty. The "ideal" family structure posited above, with its rigidly divided sex roles and high male income, is not the reality for many families. Even with sex discrimination artificially increasing their wages, many men cannot earn enough to support a wife who stays home to care for their children, and many families have only one parent living at home. Sex discrimination penalizes these families, as well as single, divorced, separated, and widowed women without dependents, by depressing the earning power of the female wage earner.

The following selection from an article by Carolyn Shaw Bell presents further data on the economic roles of women workers. It is followed by an excerpt from a Woman's Bureau fact sheet, which suggests a strong link between sex discrimination and poverty. If these analyses are correct, and if economic planners wish to eradicate poverty, they must begin to consider the impact of their policies on women workers, and design government programs so as to decrease sex discrimination.

BELL, AGE, SEX, MARRIAGE AND JOBS
The Public Interest 76-84 (Winter 1973)

Over the past three years, while the unemployment rate has soared from 3.5 to 6 percent and stubbornly refuses to decline significantly, the role of women in the

14. I am referring to studies of the cyclical behavior of the labor force which generally indicate that the labor force participation rate, particularly of married women, is very elastic with respect to employment opportunities. Studies of female labor force participation using cross section data also point to the importance of such indicators of demand as the female wage rate and the level of unemployment. See McNally [Patterns of Female Labor Force Activity, 7 Ind. Rel. 204-218 (May 1968)] for a summary of this extensive literature. Of particular interest is the employment of the "feminist index" by Bowen and Finegan as an explanatory variable. [Bowen and Finegan, The Economics of Labor Force Participation (1969).]

economy has received special attention. The spectacular rise in the number of women who have joined the labor force has been singled out as an important structural change in the supply of labor — a change which explains, or helps to explain away, the existence of large numbers of people without jobs. . . .

. . . [T]he argument about the significance of women's unemployment which follows from the notion that the economic role of working women differs essentially from that of men contains a basic fallacy. This is exemplified in the point of view of former Secretary of the Treasury Connally. Testifying before the Joint Economic Committee in February, he pointed out that a 6 percent unemployment rate is not as critical today as in earlier decades, because many of the jobless then were homeowners, while today most of the people without jobs are women. This particular juxtaposition of homeowners versus women defies economic analysis. . . .

WOMEN'S EARNINGS AND FAMILY INCOME

The . . . oversight consists of ignoring the impact of women's earnings on family income. . . .[T]here have been more or less subtle attempts to minimize the sums involved or their critical importance to particular families. In his Life article, after his one-sentence dismissal of female unemployment, Mr. Connally turned to what he clearly believes to be the dominant contributor to economic welfare, asking: "Meanwhile, what's happening to the working man and his family?" The implication is clear: The working *man* has a family to support; his employment does not stem from attempts to be liberated or other suspect lures. Nor is this kind of interpretation confined to members of the Administration; the equation of "married men" with "breadwinners" is almost as widespread among economists as the equation of "woman" with "housewife," "wife and mother," or (whether or not she fulfills this potential) "prospective wife and mother." This persistence of the simplistic notion that women's earnings are merely supplementary does great harm not only to attempts at understanding the present unemployment situation, but also to the design of economic policy in many spheres.

It is true that married men account for 47 percent of the total labor force; they number 39 million. But aside from the 18 million married women in the labor force, there are another 13 million women who maintain households of their own, and who lack husbands to provide any income. In these cases, the woman is head of the household. In March 1972 such families included 10 million children under 18, and reported a median income of $4,456, compared to a median income of $11,810 for families with two parents as well as children. In the face of such data, it is difficult to countenance the repeated assertions that married men constitute some sort of "primary economic group," at least as far as human welfare is concerned.

As for the financial responsibilities of married men, in 1970 over half of those in the labor force had wives who contributed earnings from employment. Married working women provide over 25 percent of the total income in this country, but to most of their families, of course, they bring much more. For example, in 1970 over five million wives earned between $3,000 and $5,000; more than half of them were married to men whose own employment brought in less than $8,000. One out of four working wives provides over 40 percent of her family's total income; two and one-half million husband-wife families rely on the woman's earnings for over half the total income. Given these figures, what sense does it make to refer to married men as the "breadwinners"?

Moreover, aggregate figures necessarily blur details which can be crucial to individual families. A wife's earnings, even though they amount to less than half the total family income, can forestall debt and bankruptcy in the case of emergency. Depending on the size and composition of her family and on the other income available, a wife's wages can lift a family out of poverty. Since 1959 the number of poor families headed by a man has decreased by over half, while the number of poor families dependent on a woman has increased. The reason becomes clear from a simple comparison, over this time period, of families at various levels of income. In each of the census years 1950,

1960, and 1970, about 12 percent of the families in the lowest fifth of the income distribution consisted of married couples with a wife earning some income. But among families higher up on the economic scale, this percentage changed drastically over these 20 years. Among those in the *top* three fifths of the income distribution, the number of families with working wives grew by over 75 percent. Women who work have moved their families out of the "middle income" classes; in the top 5 percent of the income distribution, women earners now contribute to 40 percent of the households as compared to about 15 percent 20 years ago. . . .

. . . [T]he economic pressures on women who have families to support have been intensified by the many months of high unemployment coupled with rising prices. In April 1972, White House spokesmen for the first time abandoned their emphasis on unemployment figures for married men, and began commenting on the rate for all household heads, whether men or women. This figure, while higher than the former one, still understates the hardship for the women involved. For men, wives represent an income-producing resource to the family whether or not they are currently in the labor force: They may have property income, they may be potential earners if conditions change, they may be able to add unpaid labor to a family business or make a given income stretch farther by using more of their unpaid labor at home. But for women who are heads of households, no such additional income-producing resource exists because, by definition, there is no man in the household — not even a disabled husband who could at least babysit while the wife earned income outside the home.

It should also be realized that job opportunities for women are concentrated in lower-paying occupations; a full-time, year-round female worker earns 58 percent of what a full-time, year-round male worker does. Add to this the difficulties (both in time and money) of maintaining a household for single women with families, and the possibilities of their actually taking advantage of a job opportunity become even more circumscribed. Low-income people probably become skilled at "marginal analysis" fairly quickly, so that the difference between working and becoming eligible for welfare by not working often leads women with families to support to the second choice. Even for those who have been employed, any period of unemployment may settle the question in favor of going on welfare. Yet unemployment rates for women who are household heads, while available in a Bureau of Labor Statistics reference publication, have never been widely publicized. From 1969 to 1971, this figure rose from 2.8 to over 6 percent; in August of last year it was 5.9 compared to a 2.6 percent figure for adult men who are household heads and whose families may in fact be partially or largely supported by their wives. . . .

UNITED STATES DEPARTMENT OF LABOR,
WOMEN'S BUREAU, FACT SHEET ON
THE AMERICAN FAMILY IN POVERTY
1-2 (1971)[27]

FAMILIES IN POVERTY

About 5.2 million families, or 10 percent of the 51.9 million families in the United States, were living in poverty in 1970. (This was 264,000 more than in 1969 but 3.1 million less than in 1959, the first year for which poverty data are available.) Of the 2.3 million families living on farms, 436,000 or 19 percent were living in poverty.

Poor families included 3.7 million white, 1.4 million Negro, and 68,000 of other

27. The poverty level is based on the Social Security Administration's poverty thresholds, adjusted annually in accordance with the Department of Labor's Consumer Price Index. Currently classified as poor are those nonfarm households where total money income is less than $1,954 for an unrelated individual; $2,525 for a couple; and $3,968 for a family of four.

minority races.[2] The percentages of all families of each racial group who were poor were 8 percent, 29 percent, and 14 percent, respectively.

The sex of the family head is an increasingly important factor in the poverty status of families. The number of families headed by a woman who were living in poverty in 1970 was 1.9 million, the same as in 1959, whereas the 3.3 million poor families headed by a man in 1970 represented about half the 1959 figure. Although families headed by a woman constituted only 11 percent of all families in 1970, they accounted for 37 percent of all poor families. The proportion of all poor Negro families that were headed by a woman was even greater — 57 percent.

About 1 out of every 3 families headed by a woman lived in poverty in 1970 as compared with 1 out of 14 families headed by a man. The poverty rate was highest among Negro families headed by a woman — 54 percent, more than double the 25 percent for white families headed by a woman. The proportions for Negro and white families headed by a man were 18 and 6 percent, respectively.

The employment of women family heads takes many such families out of poverty. Among white families headed by a woman in 1969 (latest data available), 15 percent were poor where she was in the labor force; 37 percent where she was not. The comparable proportions for Negro families headed by a woman were 38 and 69 percent, respectively.

The depth of poverty suffered by poor families can be measured by the difference between the actual income and the poverty threshold for a family of similar composition. The median income deficits in 1970 for poor families headed by a man were $955 for white and $1,109 for Negro. The comparable amounts for families headed by a woman were $1,219 and $1,492, respectively. The difference in the median deficits between white and Negro poor families is accounted for in part by the smaller average size of the white families.

For further information on the economic position of female-headed as versus two-parent families, see The Economic Impact of Divorce on the Individual, Chapter Three, V-D.

D. The Future: Predictions and Proposals

The following materials illuminate the prospects for change from two perspectives: one predicting the future from currently observable trends, and the other concerning the design of mechanisms for promoting change.

Economic and social factors influence the amount of impact which legal changes have on women's position in the labor market. For example, if a particular industry is declining, sex integration may be both harder to obtain and less significant than the sex integration of an expanding industry. Similarly, the likelihood of eliminating sex discrimination may be greatly increased if certain social and economic policies are followed. For example, a full employment economy may make sex integration much easier to achieve. Or perhaps providing quality day care is a necessary prerequisite to ending sex discrimination in the labor market. In some cases, the connection between other economic and social changes and the legal action contemplated may be even more direct. If women do not have the training necessary for certain "men's" jobs, merely eliminating barriers at the hiring gate will not be enough. A coordinated strategy to eliminate overt sex discrimination and to make job training available might be the most effective. In some cases, coordinating economic and social changes with legal strategy may involve political alliances with other groups in the society to influence public policy. At other

2. Data for minority races other than Negro are included under "all races" when not reported separately.

times, coordinated litigation campaigns in several areas of sex discrimination may be necessary. At the least it can be important to choose litigation targets with economic and social consequences in mind. In any event, lawyers and legal workers need to be aware of economic and social trends to maximize the impact of legal change.

1. Social and Economic Trends and the Future for Women Workers: Some Predictions

OPPENHEIMER, A SOCIOLOGIST'S SKEPTICISM
in Ginzberg and Yohalem (eds.), Corporate Lib 30, 32-38 (1973)

I would like to explain why I think these pressures to admit women into men's occupations will continue. . . .

[M]y perspective is that of a sociologist-demographer involved in the analysis of female labor force participation. It seems to me that a greater familiarity with the changes that have occurred in female labor force participation will help us understand why pressures for the expansion of job opportunities for women are not likely to be a passing fad. Let me begin by reviewing some of the overall trends.

The extent of women's contribution to the national economy has changed considerably over the past ten years. The change has been particularly great since 1940 which marked the beginning of an accelerated growth in women's labor force participation. So great has this growth been that by 1970, 50 percent of American women aged 18 to 64 were in the labor force compared with 30 percent in 1940 and 20 percent in 1900.

Even more impressive is the changing relationship between female labor force participation and the family life cycle. In fact, this latter change overshadows the increase in the work rates for women as a whole. In 1900, if the average woman worked at all during her lifetime — and not a great many did — it was before marriage and children. A very small proportion were working later on in life. By 1940, the rates showed some changes in the *degree* of labor force participation, but the *pattern* by age was very similar to that of 1900. At both dates the peak work rates were among women in their early twenties and labor force participation declined sharply thereafter, never to rise again.

Starting sometime in the 1940s, however, there began to be a growing break with this traditional pattern of female labor force participation. The first great departure was the entrance or return of women past the age of 35 into the labor force — women whose children, by and large, had reached school age. Census data show a sharp increase between 1940 and 1950 in the work rates of women in the 35 to 64 age group. Furthermore, this pattern has persisted to this day — so much so that in 1970 between 49 and 54 percent of women between 35 and 59 years of age were in the labor force!

A second trend, starting in the 1950s but picking up considerable steam since 1960, has been the increased labor force participation of younger married women, including women with pre-school children. The 1940 work rates for married women between 20 and 34 years of age indicate that at that time work was a rather rare occurrence. The peak rate was for 20- to 24-year-old women, yet only 26 percent of them were in the labor force. However, by 1970, the Census reports work rates that ranged from a low of 38 percent for women aged 25 to 29 to a high of 47 percent for women aged 20 to 24. There were striking increases in the work rate of wives with preschool children, as well as of childless wives and those with older children.

As a consequence, in 1970, just under one third of mothers with preschoolers were working and 49 percent of mothers of school age children were in the labor force. In sum, work is becoming an increasingly important part of women's entire lives, not just during the period before they marry and start raising children. In other words, the presence of children, whatever their age, is becoming less and less of a deterrent to female labor force participation.

Now, there is very little reason to believe that these increases in female labor force participation are occurring because American women suddenly became uppity and decided they wanted to have that grand thing, a career with a capital C. On the contrary, studies in the mid-1960s of the potentially most career-minded group — college students — indicate that very few girls planned to have careers. Moreover, the kinds of jobs most working women hold certainly do not fall into the career category. Rather, to date, women's increased labor force participation seems to be largely a product of two main factors — a considerable postwar growth in the demand for female workers, that is, increasing job opportunities for women, coupled with women's desire to raise their families' standard of living. An indication of the latter is the continuing influence of the size of a husband's income upon his wife's decision to work and the increasing labor force participation of mothers whose husbands' incomes cannot keep up with that most devastating of combinations — rising aspirations coupled with rising inflation.

As a consequence of these trends many American families are becoming increasingly dependent on the incomes of two earners rather than on the earnings of the husband alone. To the extent that this situation becomes even more common, it cannot help but have an effect on women's job aspirations. For if women at all stages of the family life cycle are working in ever greater numbers, it is inevitable that many are going to stop viewing work as a brief interlude in a long life devoted to their families. Instead, they will start to look upon work as a possible lifetime activity, interrupted at times, perhaps, but nevertheless one of their major adult roles.

Thus, it is unlikely that women will continue to be satisfied with the kinds of jobs that used to be good enough for an interim period. As long as work was of secondary importance, women's work goals remained limited and the characteristics of women's jobs that make them most unattractive to men — poor pay and poor advancement opportunities — did not cause a great deal of dissatisfaction. However, as work becomes more important to women, and to their families as well, the more irritating will become the poor pay and the lack of opportunities so typical of female jobs.

Dissatisfaction with women's traditional occupations is likely to grow among all women workers but will be particularly acute among women who do not have the financial benefits derived from having a husband within the home, namely, the divorced and separated, whose economic welfare often depends entirely or very extensively on their own earning capacities. For many of these women a broken marriage coupled with their own low earning potential consigns them to a lifetime of economic marginality, not to mention the adverse effect of lowered incomes on the education of their children.

The situation is further aggravated by rising divorce rates and by the fact that a divorced woman's chances of remarriage are considerably less than those of a divorced man. As a consequence, the number of divorced and separated women rose 30 percent between 1960 and 1970, from 3.9 to 5 million, while the number of divorced men who did not remarry rose only 23 percent.

There are two other trends that will intensify the pressures for women to break away from traditional female jobs. These are the rising educational attainment of American women and the decline from the very high fertility of the postwar baby boom period. Both of these trends can be expected to have a multiplicity of effects on female labor force participation and on the increasing pressure for an expansion in job opportunities for women.

While there is considerable debate as to just how much our fertility is declining, there is little doubt that — for the present, at least — birth rates are considerably below those of the 1950s and early 1960s. With regard to educational attainment, there has been a substantial increase in the proportion of women completing high school and the proportions entering and finishing college. As a result, the percent of very poorly educated women has declined sharply. Now what are some of the implications of these trends?

One important effect of a lowered birth rate is that it is likely to increase the number of women who want to work. This is because children still remain an important deterrent to female labor force participation in spite of the fact that they don't deter quite as much as they used to. Lowered fertility will, therefore, probably increase the number of women competing for the traditionally female jobs. This competition is likely to be considerably aggravated by the rising educational level of women and other consequences of the fertility decline.

As far as education is concerned, the increased proportion of women with a college degree will mean a rising demand for high level jobs. College women — quite understandably — have not been very interested in clerical work, much less in the poorly paid blue-collar female occupations. Their main job opportunities have been in the female professions, primarily teaching. Thus in 1970, 80 percent of women with four or more years of college were in the professions. However, with declining fertility, the school age population will not be expanding so opportunities for female employment in elementary and secondary education will not be on the rise. Furthermore, the decline of the female college, or at least its lack of expansion, means that a traditional source of jobs for women with graduate degrees may also be drying up.

Thus, at a time when the number of highly educated women is on the rise, the traditional source of jobs for such women is not expanding and may even be contracting. While some of these women may marry prosperous husbands and not need or care to work, many are going to want to work and I doubt whether they will be satisfied with the lower level professional and clerical jobs that may be open to them. These women are well-educated and verbal and often quite knowledgeable about how things get done in this world. Personally I do not think they will quietly fade out of the job market when things get rough. In my opinion, they are going to make a fuss — in fact they have already started to do just that.

Another factor that is likely to aggravate the job situation for women is that an increase in female educational attainment does not mean only an increase in the proportion of well-educated women but also means a decline in the poorly educated and a rise in the moderately educated. As a consequence, an increasing proportion of women workers from a broad socioeconomic spectrum are squeezing into the clerical job market. Although the proportion of all employed women who were clerical workers rose considerably in the 1960-70 period (from 25 to 35 percent), the rise was particularly marked for wives of blue-collar workers. For example, the proportion of wives of craftsmen and foremen employed in clerical occupations rose from 31 to 35 percent; for operatives' wives the rise was from 24 to 29 percent; and even for laborers' wives there was an increase from 14 percent in 1960 to 21 percent in 1970. In spite of the rapid postwar expansion in job opportunities in clerical work, it is hard to see how such occupations can continue to provide most of the job opportunities for the increasing number of female high school graduates being produced by our society. If office automation should cut into the demand for clerical workers in the 1970s and 80s, the job situation for women will be even more difficult.

To sum up, my point is that a rapid postwar increase in job opportunities for women in the traditional female occupations has served to partially transform the economic role of women in the family. To the extent that this transformation is taking place, and to the extent that work is becoming an important role for mature women, women's job aspirations are bound to rise. The rising aspirations will be intensified by women's rising educational attainment. Yet at the same time that aspirations are on the rise, it is unlikely that the traditional female occupations can continue to provide the jobs necessary to maintain women's changing economic role. Moreover, in the case of the higher level female occupations, most notably teaching, the job opportunities are actually likely to shrink rather than expand in the foreseeable future at least. As a consequence, there will be increasing pressure on the part of women to break away from traditional female jobs into male jobs at all levels. But the pressure to enter male occupations is likely to be the greatest, I suspect, with respect to men's occupations at the highest levels because the traditional female job market for college women is exceedingly unlikely to expand nearly as much as is the population of college educated women who would like to work.

————————

Oppenheimer points out that teaching, the profession which has traditionally absorbed the largest proportion of educated women, is no longer an expanding occupation. Other commentators have highlighted the problem of declining demand for workers in "women's" occupations. For example, Hedges reports that[28]

> The manpower projections of the Bureau of Labor Statistics for the years from 1968 to 1980 indicate that the number of persons seeking to enter elementary and secondary school teaching during the period could be nearly three-fourths above the projected requirements, based on past patterns of entry.[3]

Examining manpower demands in professional nursing, social work, library work, home economics, nutrition, dietetics, and medical laboratory work, she concludes:[29]

> [These] are the largest of the "women's professions." Together they accounted for almost two-thirds of all professional women in 1969. A number of smaller professions predominantly filled by women are expected to grow rapidly from 1968 to 1980. But the "women's professions" together do not offer sufficient opportunities for the number of college educated women who are expected to seek employment in the 1970's.

Hedges points out that there are large demands for more workers in a number of rapidly growing professions from which women have previously been virtually excluded, such as medicine, dentistry, and engineering, and in skilled trades, such as appliance and business machine service work, and automotive repair work. Hedges states the implications of the data she has reported as follows:[30]

> Prospects are that the employment of women will accommodate to manpower needs in the 1970's better than in the past. First, what has been called the "framework" for improved use of women's abilities is in place.[15] Equality for women in employment, training, advancement, and pay are legally required by the Civil Rights Act of 1964 and the Equal Pay Act of 1963.
>
> Second, the need for highly skilled workers in the professions and trades, together with the growing acceptance of full occupational equality for women, is encouraging employers to recruit from as broad a base as possible. Reports from more than 100 business and industrial firms surveyed in late 1969, for example, indicated that they planned to hire one-fifth more women college graduates from the class of 1970 than from the previous class. Two-fifths or more of the firms indicated that more women would be hired in engineering, data processing, or accounting positions if qualified women could be found.[16] In addition, women graduates recently have been

28. Hedges, Women Workers and Manpower Demands in the 1970's, Monthly Labor Rev. at 22 (June 1970).

3. These projections are based on the continuation of recent trends in birth rates, college graduates, and re-entrants, and pupil-teacher ratios. They are an estimate of "effective demand," that is, the number of teachers required to fill and keep filled the number of teaching jobs needed for moderate advances in education. A larger number of teachers would be required to meet educational goals such as providing high quality education to all children, compensatory education for disadvantaged children, or specialized education for additional handicapped children.

29. Hedges, supra footnote 28, at 24.

30. Id. at 28-29.

15. Helen B. Schleman, "Women Might Have Helped: Some Problems Ahead," Vital Speeches of the Day, August 15, 1969, pp. 663-668.

16. Frank S. Endicott, Trends in Employment of College and University Graduates in Business and Industry (Evanston, Ill., Northwestern University, 1970), p. 7.

reported to be getting entry-level executive jobs that were closed to their predecessors.[17]

Third, the indications that women will strive to make the necessary occupational adjustments may be even more significant than public laws and employer attitudes. Women's attachment to the labor force seems strong as the 1970's open. The lengthening worklife of women; the increasing percent of women working full time, and year round; rising labor force participation rates for mothers of young children even in the face of inadequate child-care facilities; and the significant contribution working women are making to family income — all described elsewhere in this issue — testify to the strength of that attachment. Work is becoming an ongoing way of life for a growing proportion of women in the United States.

And finally, the increasing capacity of women to adjust to changing manpower needs, as well as their determination, is evidenced by the growing proportion of advanced degrees earned by women since 1960 and the growing number of women enrolled in continuing education.

For women, the initial result of continued concentration in the period ahead would be increasing competition in the "women's occupations" (particularly, perhaps, between young women and older women seeking to reenter employment) and rising unemployment. Depressed wage rates in occupations overcrowded by women and a decline in women's labor force participation rates might follow.

For the Nation, the results could include a lower standard of living and continued shortages in a number of occupations in which men predominate, with attendant pressures on costs and prices.

The diversity in women's employment that is necessary to achieve a balance between the supply and demand for labor in the years ahead will not be accomplished without improvements in the counseling and in the occupational preparation of women. Individual aptitudes and interests (not outmoded attitudes), together with changing manpower needs, must be the guiding factors in occupational choice. Furthermore, at every level of education and training, and in every educational and occupational curriculum, women applicants should be admitted without regard to sex. In addition, it is important that women fully use existing opportunities.

In sum, the occupational dispersion of women, long desirable on the score of improving skill levels and earnings, has become urgent in view of the manpower outlook for individual occupations in the 1970's. The strong attachment of women to the labor force and the pressures for a new source of manpower in certain professional occupations and skilled trades augur well. But a satisfactory outcome depends on improved counseling and occupational preparation of women, and on the will of women themselves.

For a more sophisticated analysis of various economic and social factors which could influence women's work opportunities, see Gold, Alternative National Goals and Women's Employment, 179 Science 656 (1973). Gold suggests that if economic growth does not continue at a relatively high rate, if women's labor force participation rates rise more quickly than predicted, and if productivity increases, reducing demand for personnel in many fields, several negative consequences might follow. For example, there is danger that public policies seeking to discourage women from working would again be adopted, that women would bear the brunt of higher unemployment rates, or that work hours and incomes would be reduced for both men and women workers.

All three predictions make it clear that equitable treatment for women depends on labor market trends, awareness among women of manpower demands, and efforts by women to challenge sex discriminatory policies on the part of employers and the government. If the discounting of the contribution of women workers to family incomes and national productivity and sex-based counseling and educational tracking are allowed to continue, the goal of equality for women workers will certainly suffer.

17. "For Women, A Difficult Climb to the Top," Business Week, August 2, 1969, pp. 42-44.

2. Mechanisms for Promoting Change

a. Decreasing Women's Responsibility for Housekeeping and Child Care

Earlier, the stereotype that women workers are unreliable because they place family commitments ahead of employment responsibilities was mentioned as a cause of sex discrimination. It has also been pointed out that such beliefs can become self-reinforcing. However, although it is clear that the stereotype is not valid for all women, and that employers' actions contribute to its validity for some women, it is, like most stereotypes, not totally without foundation in reality. Many women do carry heavy burdens of housework and child care on top of their outside jobs. Of course, this fact does not justify allowing employers to limit women's job opportunities. Each individual woman must be free to allocate her time between home and work. Nonetheless, because of family commitments women on the average may be less likely than men to accept certain work responsibilities. Those who favor sex equality on the job must therefore consider ways in which women's family roles can be changed.

A number of possibilities for change have been suggested. For example, Margaret Benston discusses industrialization or communalization of housework (with a long quotation from Lenin) in the Political Economy of Women's Liberation,[31] as does John Kenneth Galbraith.[32] Ideas range from relatively popular suggestions, like increasing the quality and quantity of day care centers, to communal living on a grand scale. Other alternatives include wages for housewives, which might draw men into the occupation, and greater sharing of both household and occupational roles between men and women. These ideas are discussed in detail in Chapter Three, IV-B and C, infra.

b. The Establishment of Self-Reinforcing Cycles of Change

Since workers *are* segregated by sex in this country, women must shift their focus from equal pay, as it is now defined, and concentrate on the integration of jobs and on increasing the wage level of the "female" jobs.

Integrating jobs will open up more interesting work to women, who will then command the higher pay that goes with such work. Real integration will also help change the wage structure because as men enter traditionally female jobs the pay level of these jobs should rise. The classic example is the rise in pay and status of secondary school teachers and social workers as men entered these fields.

It is not enough, however, to hope for a better wage structure as a side-effect of integration. The wage structure itself must also be attacked in order to help, right now, the women who have already been shunted into the low pay of "women's work." Traditionally female jobs do not pay less because the work is inherently worth less; they pay less because women do this work. It is the wage structure itself that is discriminatory, and women must seek court decisions that will end wage segregation by forcing employers to raise the pay scale for traditionally female jobs. Of course, this will also have the effect of attracting more men to these jobs, thus promoting integration of jobs. The cycle goes full circle.[33]

[The claim that occupational segregation is an obstacle to the attainment of economic equality for women] is hardly surprising in that there is no reason to assume that the doctrine of "separate but equal" should be any more valid for women than

31. Monthly Review, Sept. 1969, at 13.
32. Edmiston, While We're At It, What About Maid's Lib? New York Magazine, June 28, 1971, at 38, reprinted in Chapter Three, IV-A, infra.
33. Ross, The Rights of Women 36-37 (1973).

[Chart 2-2]
WOMEN AS A PERCENT OF TOTAL EMPLOYMENT
IN MAJOR OCCUPATION GROUPS,
1969 and projected 1980

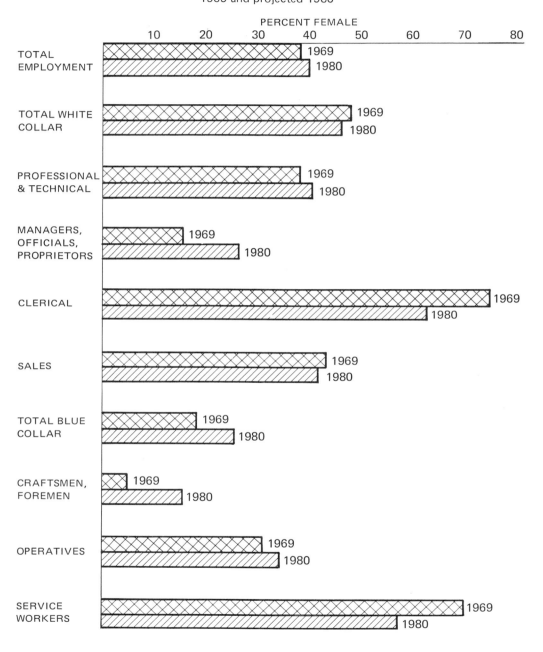

it is for other groups. Yet, defining the problem in these terms is extremely useful in that it points to policies that would affect the whole female work force and not just those at the upper levels. It means, for example, that we must have more women salesworkers in wholesale trade, more electricians and chefs as well as more female doctors, lawyers, and economists. It also means that more men must move into predominantly female jobs.

Since women presently comprise nearly two-fifths of the civilian labor force and are so heavily concentrated in predominantly female jobs, the attainment of integration is a task of enormous proportions. However, if the preceding dual labor market analysis is correct, a substantial movement of women into the male sector should have the effect of raising incomes of women in predominantly female occupations as well. This should also ease the task of attracting men into presently female pursuits. Thus, the payoff to sizable movements *toward* increased integration could be quite high.[34]

The size of the effort needed to substantially change the occupational distribution of women workers should not be underestimated. Not only are women heavily concentrated in a small number of occupations, they comprise nearly two-fifths of the labor force. Nonetheless, the projections shown in [Chart 2-2] indicate that a great deal can be accomplished by concentrating on the *new* jobs that will open up in the next ten years due to the growth and replacement needs of the economy. For the purposes of this example, we have allocated 40 percent of the new jobs in each occupational category to women and 60 percent to men. The particular ratio employed is, of course, purely illustrative, but the results can give us some indication of what the impact on the occupational distribution of women workers would be if new jobs were distributed differently from the way they have been in the past.

It appears as though fairly large changes would be forthcoming. The proportion of managers, officials and proprietors who are women would increase from 16 percent to 26 percent as would the proportion of craftsmen and foremen from 3 percent to 16 percent. Similarly, women would decline from 74 percent to 61 percent of all clerical employees and from 66 percent to 56 percent of service workers.[35]

c. A Frontal Attack on Sex Segregation in the Upper Echelons of Management

GALBRAITH, KUH, AND THUROW
THE GALBRAITH PLAN TO PROMOTE THE MINORITIES
New York Times Magazine, Aug. 22, 1971, pp. 9, 35-38, 40

In the last ten years, concern for equality in employment has been all but exclusively confined to what may be called entry-level jobs — jobs, good or bad, that a man or woman gets coming off the street or upon leaving school, as an alternative to unemployment. That blacks, Puerto Ricans, Mexican Americans and (where they are not disbarred for clear physical reasons) women should be equally prepared for such jobs and have an equal chance to obtain them is now widely agreed in principle and extensively affirmed by law. Much remains to be done about equality in hiring as the current statistics on black and female unemployment graphically affirm. But it is far from being the worst area of discrimination. The worst discrimination is not in the jobs at which the many enter but in the better jobs beyond. In the better salary brackets of the business corporation, women, blacks, Spanish-speaking citizens and American Indians have only token representation. For all practical purposes, jobs here are monopolized by white males. The figures are uncompromising. In 1969, white males accounted for only 52 per

34. Blau, "Women's Place" in the Labor Market, 62 Am. Econ. Rev. 161, 166 (May 1972).
35. Simmons, Freedman, Dunkle, and Blau, Background Paper for Exploitation From 9 to 5, Report of the Twentieth Century Fund Task Force on Working Women, ch. 1 (1974).

cent of all wage and salary earners in private and public employment. They had 96 per cent of the jobs paying more than $15,000 a year. Women comprise about 30 per cent of the full-time labor force; only two per cent of the women so employed had incomes over $15,000.

The occupational classifications show an equally striking discrimination. Of the male labor force in 1969, eight per cent had jobs as salaried managers and officials. Only two per cent of the female labor force had jobs that were so classified. Of the male managers and officials, thirty per cent — not far short of a third — earned more than $15,000. Of the women managers and officials, only four per cent — one in twenty-five — earned that much.

But even these figures give an unduly favorable picture of private industry. The various levels of government, though no model of equality, give women and minorities a much better break than private corporations. In the public sector in 1969, white males had "only" 89 per cent of the good jobs, i.e., those paying more than $15,000. Women had six per cent and non-white males had five per cent. In the private economy, by contrast, white males had 98 per cent of the good jobs. Non-white males and women divided the remaining two per cent. (In the Federal government last November, blacks, Spanish, Indians and Oriental Americans held 53.4 per cent of the jobs in the G.S. 1, or lowest white collar category, and 2 per cent of those in the G.S. 18, or highest classification.) . . .

We propose that the Congress now enact legislation declaring it to be national policy that employment of women, blacks, American Indians and Spanish-speaking minorities be in accord, throughout the various salary brackets in industry and government, with the numbers in the working force. To enforce this we propose that there be created a competently staffed body, fully representative of the minority groups to be assisted, called the Minorities Advancement Commission.

The law would empower the Commission to require any firm that has employed 5,000 people during the previous five years to submit a plan for bringing the distribution of women, blacks, and Spanish-speaking workers in its salary hierarchy into conformity with the representation of these groups in the working force of the community or communities in which it operates. The time allowed for full compliance would be ten years. Firms with fewer employees and, in consequence, somewhat less flexibility in promotion and employment, would be given more time — we suggest an extra year for each thousand fewer employees so that a firm with four thousand workers would have eleven years; one with three thousand, twelve years; one with two thousand, thirteen years. Firms with fewer than two thousand employees would be exempt from the application of the law. A similar requirement, as presently noted, would be made binding by law on the Federal government.

State and local governments would be invited similarly to bind themselves by law and be encouraged to this end by educational assistance to be mentioned presently. Educational institutions in the above employment categories — in practice, the very large ones — would be subject to similar inducement. In the case of private corporations, we would suggest exempting a maximum of three top positions from the operations of this legislation on the theory that, in the very senior positions, selection of talent should be subject to a minimum of constraint.

In the case of corporations, legislation would apply from just under the top positions down to a salary level set at 160 per cent of the national average earnings of fully employed male workers. (In 1969, this was $10,000 so $15,000 would now be the lower limit.) This part of the corporate hierarchy would be divided into five layers, or quintiles, each with one-fifth of the total salary payments. Compliance would be achieved when the appropriate share of salary in each quintile is paid to female, black or Spanish-speaking executives or other salaried workers.

Geographically, women are distributed fairly evenly over the population and also over the working population. For compliance here, we suggest using the expected proportion of women in the full-time labor force. This is now approximately thirty per cent. In the last ten years this proportion has risen by four percentage points so, assuming a similar increase in the next ten years, this requirement would be satisfied by paying 34 per cent of the salary income in each quintile to women.

Blacks and Spanish-speaking minorities are not uniformly distributed throughout the country. Here we propose that executive and other salary payments conform to the proportion of the minority group members in the working force (those employed and seeking employment) in the principal areas of operation of the firm in question. These figures, based on the Standard Metropolitan Statistical Areas as defined by the U.S. Bureau of the Census, would be supplied by the Commission.

We are sensitive to a reaction that this proposal will already have elicited from many executives including some who are not hostile to the objective. Surely, it will be said, this puts an impossible straitjacket upon the hiring of executives, specialists and other salaried personnel. Not merit but sex, color and ethnic origins would become the overriding considerations. Accordingly, we come now to the elements of flexibility in [Minority Advancement Plan] which, we believe, meet any such legitimate objection.

The firm, it has already been noted, is given ten years to comply, with added time for smaller (although by no means small) concerns. But we further propose that each firm be allowed to file with the Commission its preferred track for meeting this objective ten years (or more) hence. Subject to a minimum level of progress — after two years, not less than five per cent of the eventual goal in each of the quintiles — the corporation would be permitted to follow any route to ultimate compliance that it deemed desirable. The early years could thus be devoted to recruiting, training and promoting the women and minority group members whose advancement, at the end of the period, would put the firm in full compliance.

Having filed its track, the firm would be subject to penalties for failing to meet its requirements — the fine should be something more than the difference between what it is actually paying to women and minority group members and what is required under its plan. However, we would favor a hearing procedure that would allow a corporation, after notice and for good reason, to petition for an alteration in its track, providing always that it reached its required goal in the specified time and did not fall below its minimum annual rate of improvement. American Indians, in many respects the most disadvantaged of minorities, are too few in most areas to be dealt with as a special category. We suggest, as a partial solution, that salary paid to American Indians might count double for compliance in any of the three categories — women, blacks, or Spanish-speaking — that we do recognize. Black or Spanish-speaking women could count for compliance as women or as members of the relevant minority, whichever category the firm prefers. Overcompliance in a higher quintile would always be a credit for the same amount (measured by salary) of undercompliance in the next lower quintile. For smaller employers (those with fewer than 5,000 employees) the number of salary categories, i.e., the quintiles, might well be reduced. Without damaging the ultimate outcome, we believe that these provisions eliminate any legitimate complaint based on the rigidity of the procedures here employed. What remains is the need for aggressive planning and effort to develop executive and other talent among women and the minorities. But that, precisely, is our purpose.

MAP would be binding on all departments and agencies of the Federal Government, subject to special regulations for women in the Armed Forces and a declaration of intent as to minority representation instead of compelled procedures in the case of the judiciary. As with corporations, each department or agency, in conjunction with the Civil Service Commission, would file a track designed to bring it into compliance in the 10-year period.

A word need now be said about the development of the requisite talent. More may be available than is commonly imagined. As long as it is assumed that the better jobs belong to white males, the search for talent is extensively confined to white males. But certainly there will be need for an increase in executive and specialized training to fill the demand for women, blacks and Spanish-speaking personnel that MAP would create. To this we would expect business, engineering and law schools to respond. But we also propose a system of grants by the Federal Government to states for the support of such training by public and private institutions, and for the special recruitment and preparation that the black and Spanish-speaking students would require. We see these grants as the device for overcoming Constitutional difficulties in compelling compliance by state governments and educational institutions. Such aid would be contingent on legislation by the state governments applying MAP to their own employment policies and to the localities with employment large enough to bring them within the range of MAP. States forgoing such assistance and the resulting training would be subjecting corporations and other employers within their boundaries to a possible shortage of executive and specialized personnel, and prejudicing their own development. Acceptance of MAP by state and local governments and the filing of a track could also be a condition for the receipt of other Federal aid. . . .

It will be asked why we confine MAP to firms (and governmental units) employing more than 2,000 people. That is because larger firms and institutions have more flexibility in their employment policies than smaller firms, and have more highly organized procedures for executive development. Also, in these firms, owners and members of owning families have given way to professional executives. And we are exceedingly conscious of the political resistance we would encounter with a measure that would seem to interfere with the prerogatives of the small-business man. As proposed here, MAP would apply to somewhat fewer than 2,000 corporations, but those 2,000 account for roughly half of all production of goods and services in the private sector of the economy.

It will be suggested that 10 years for the big firms is too long. If equality is right, why not now? We think it important to differentiate between solid progress and appealing rhetoric. Ten years to equality is far better than never, which is the present prospect. . . .

It will be asked why MAP is confined to the higher income jobs. Why not make it applicable to the shop floor? The answer is that no reform can accomplish everything. Existing government legislation and union rules are all but exclusively focused on the production worker and we seek to avoid conflict with these regulations, including any tangle with the unions. It is also important that our present willingness to act at the bottom be matched by a similar willingness to act at the top. As things now stand, a white construction worker can be kept out of a job by regulations that require the contractor to employ blacks. He must wonder, if he stops to think about it, why the white executive has no similar worry. Also, if women and members of the minority groups are properly represented at the top, it would seem reasonably certain that they will suffer less discrimination at the bottom. . . .

NOTES

(1) Is it possible to achieve real change without strict quotas like those proposed in the Galbraith plan? It may be that the self-reinforcing cycle of change envisioned by Ross will never begin without such drastic action.

(2) One criticism of the Galbraith plan is that it departs from the principle of individual treatment. Since women are denied equality by being judged on the basis of group averages instead of individual characteristics, individual determinations of employability are important to ending sex discrimination, it is argued. Galbraith and his co-authors comment on this argument as follows:[36]

36. Galbraith et al, supra, at 40.

There is, we suggest, no clear evidence that women, blacks or Spanish-speaking people are intellectually inferior to white males. There will have to be accelerated development of executive and specialist talent in these groups. But that is an important purpose of MAP and it is for this that time is provided.

Is this a convincing argument? One problem with some affirmative action programs for minority groups in education has been that in many cases the support necessary to bring talented minority students who have been denied educational opportunity up to the educational level of students admitted by conventional standards has been lacking. The costs in frustration and anxiety for the minority students in such a situation can be severe. The importance of coordinating legal reforms with other economic and social changes must not be underestimated.

II. TITLE VII OF THE CIVIL RIGHTS ACT OF 1964

A. INTRODUCTION

Title VII of the 1964 Civil Rights Act is the most comprehensive and important of all federal and state laws prohibiting employment discrimination. It will thus be the main focus of this chapter. Cooper and Rabb describe its main features.

*COOPER AND RABB, EQUAL EMPLOYMENT LAW
AND LITIGATION
33-36 (1972)*

Title VII of the Civil Rights Act of 1964, 42 U.S.C. Sec. 2000e et seq., was enacted by Congress as a comprehensive prohibition on private acts of employment discrimination. As amended by the Equal Employment Opportunity Act of 1972, Title VII also now covers virtually all state and local government employees and previously-exempt employees of educational institutions. The law authorizes the Equal Employment Opportunity Commission (EEOC) to process, investigate and conciliate employment discrimination complaints and, if necessary, to bring suits against respondents in federal court. Between 1972 and 1974, the Attorney General also has authority to bring "pattern and practice" employment suits concurrently with EEOC. After 1974, EEOC assumes exclusive government authority for enforcement of the law. Title VII also creates a cause of action enforceable in federal court by aggrieved persons or classes of persons. The law provides for injunctive and affirmative relief as well as back pay, and the granting of attorneys' fees to a prevailing party.

Title VII forbids discrimination by an employer of fifteen or more persons engaged in an industry affecting commerce, including employment agencies and labor unions. The most notable employers exempt from coverage are the federal government and private clubs.

Although federal employees are not brought within the jurisdiction of the EEOC, Sec. 717(d) of the new Title VII obliges the federal government to undertake an affirmative program of equal employment opportunity for all employees and applicants. Under this section the Civil Service Commission is given authority to investigate complaints of discrimination in hiring and to execute appropriate remedies. An individual employee or applicant who is dissatisfied with the government's disposition of his complaint has the same right as an employee in the private sector to bring a court action.

For those persons substantively covered by Title VII, the dictates are broad in that Title VII forbids all discriminatory employment practices based upon race, color, religion, sex or national origin. There are, however, exceptions. The law permits classification or employment referral on the basis of religion, sex or national origin (but not race) in certain very narrow instances where religion, sex or national origin are bona fide occupational qualifications. Section 703(h) of Title VII states that it is not an unlawful employment practice for an employer to act upon the results of "any professionally developed ability test" provided that such test is not designed or used to discriminate, nor is it an unlawful employment practice for an employer to apply different conditions of employment or rates of pay pursuant to a bona fide seniority or merit system. The significance of these provisions in Sec. 703(h) is, however, very limited if not nonexistent after [the] court decision in Griggs v. Duke Power Co. [401 U.S. 424, 91 S. Ct. 849, 28 L. Ed. 2d 158 (1971)]. . . . Finally, Sec. 703(j) states that preferential treatment shall not be required merely because of the existence of a statistical imbalance within a group of employees. Despite these exceptions, the substantive coverage of Title VII is still quite broad.

In addition to the substantive limitations on Title VII, there are several very crucial procedural requirements which must be complied with as prerequisites to the filing of a complaint in federal court. Generally, these procedural prerequisites require the filing of a discrimination charge first with a state fair employment practices agency and then with the EEOC. Coupled with these prerequisites are rather strict time limitations.

B. Facial Discrimination and the BFOQ Defense

Discrimination in violation of Title VII occurs not only through distinctions based on sex, race, etc., but through application of apparently neutral policies, which have a disparate effect on a particular group. Minority workers have now moved beyond the stage of attacking policies which are discriminatory on their face (e.g., blacks in one cafeteria, whites in another) to raising the disparate impact argument, or challenging apparently evenhanded policies as giving present-day effect to past discrimination, without business necessity, e.g., Griggs v. Duke Power Co., 401 U.S. 424, 91 S. Ct. 849, 28 L. Ed. 2d 158 (1971). Women workers, on the other hand, still face open job segregation and other overt discriminatory practices, because employers and unions have not yet generally accepted the fact that sex discrimination is illegal. But as the obvious barriers fall, women will also begin to challenge apparently neutral policies with discriminatory effect. This section of Part II will explore facial sex discrimination and the Bona Fide Occupational Qualification (BFOQ), the chief substantive defense to such a charge. Section C will explore facially neutral policies with a discriminatory impact on women workers and "business necessity," the chief substantive defense to this charge.

1. Standards for Measuring the BFOQ

The principal antidiscrimination provisions of Title VII are found in Section 703, 42 U.S.C. §2000e-2 (1972). Section 703(a) forbids employers:

> . . . (1) to fail or refuse to hire or to discharge any individual, or otherwise to discriminate against any individual with respect to his compensation, terms, conditions, or privileges of employment, because of such individual's race, color, religion, sex, or national origin; or
> (2) to limit, segregate, or classify his employees or applicants for employment in any way which would deprive or tend to deprive any individual of employment opportunities or otherwise adversely affect his status as an employee, because of such individual's race, color, religion, sex, or national origin.

Section 703(e) provides an exception — for sex, religion, and national origin discrimination (but not race or color) — to the above prohibition. It allows

. . . an employer to hire and employ employees . . . on the basis of his [sic] religion, sex, or national origin in those certain instances where religion, sex, or national origin is a bona fide occupational qualification reasonably necessary to the normal operation of that particular business or enterprise. . . .

This exception is generally referred to as the BFOQ exception. In most sex discrimination cases to date, employers have raised the BFOQ as their chief defense. Thus, to understand how much freedom to discriminate employers will have, students must study the various standards which the courts have used to construe Section 703(e). The cases which follow illustrate three different standards.

CHEATWOOD v. SOUTH CENTRAL BELL TELEPHONE & TELEGRAPH COMPANY
303 F. Supp. 754 (M.D. Ala. 1969)

ORDER AND JUDGMENT

In this action Mrs. Claudine B. Cheatwood charges her employer, South Central Bell Telephone & Telegraph Company, with discrimination on the basis of sex in filling a vacancy for the job classification of commercial representative in Montgomery, Alabama, in violation of Title VII of the Civil Rights Act of 1964, 42 U.S.C. §2000e et seq.

It is admitted that the plaintiff and two other female employees submitted timely bids for the vacancy, that Employer declined to consider the bids of the female employees without considering their individual qualifications, and that the job was awarded to the only male applicant. . . .

Employer has, in effect, admitted a prima facie violation of §703(a) of the Civil Rights Act of 1964, 42 U.S.C. §2000e-2(a) which provides in pertinent part:

Employer Practices
    (a) It shall be an unlawful employment practice for an employer — (1) to fail or refuse to hire or to discharge any individual, or otherwise to discriminate against any individual with respect to his compensation, terms, conditions, or privileges of employment, because of such individual's . . . sex . . . ; or
    (2) to limit, segregate, or classify his employees in any way which would deprive or tend to deprive any individual of employment opportunities or otherwise adversely affect his status as an employee, because of such individual's . . . sex. . . .

Employer has consistently contended, however, that the position of commercial representative fits within the exception to the general prohibition of discrimination against women set forth in §703(e)(1), 42 U.S.C. §2000e-2(e)(1) which provides in pertinent part:

    (e) Notwithstanding any other provision of this subchapter, (1) it shall not be an unlawful employment practice for an employer to hire and employ employees, . . . on the basis of his . . . sex, . . . in those certain instances where . . . sex, . . . is a *bona fide occupational qualification* reasonably necessary to the normal operation of that particular business or enterprise. . . . (Emphasis added.)

In a recent case quite similar to the one sub judice, the Court of Appeals for the Fifth Circuit made clear that the burden of proof is on the employer to demonstrate that a given position fits within the bona fide occupational qualification exception. Weeks v. Southern Bell Telephone & Telegraph Co., 408 F.2d 228 (5th Cir. 1969). The court in *Weeks* went on to explain the extent of the showing required to satisfy that burden:

In order to rely on the bona fide occupational qualification exception, an employer has the burden of proving that he had reasonable cause to believe, that is, a factual basis for believing, that all or substantially all women would be unable to perform safely and efficiently the duties of the job involved.

The only issues in this case, then, are determining the duties of a commercial representative and determining whether or not all or substantially all women would be unable to perform those duties safely and efficiently.

The official job description in effect at the time this dispute arose provides:

COMMERCIAL REPRESENTATIVE — (9/49) Handles commercial matters primarily outside the Company's office, such as visits to customers' premises in connection with criticisms, facilities, securing signed applications where required, credit information, deposits, advance payments, coin telephone inspections, and visits in connection with live and final account treatment work. May also be assigned to work inside the office pertaining to service and collections.

The testimony at trial produced more specific descriptions of these duties and revealed certain additional duties that go with the job in Montgomery, Alabama:

1. Rural canvassing for new customers and mileage checks for billing purposes.

2. Relief of the coin telephone collector on an average of about two days per week.

3. Destroying certain of employer's records on a monthly and annual basis.

4. Handling current records of billing stubs and handling supply requisitions in the office.

5. Performing the biennial furniture inventory.

Defendant contends that several features of these duties make them inappropriate for performance by women. With respect to the rural canvassing, it suggests the possibilities that tires will need to be changed[1] and that restroom facilities are occasionally inaccessible. These contentions can be regarded as little more than makeweights. There is no proof that all or nearly all women would be unable to cope with these difficulties. They do, of course, render the position somewhat unromantic. But as was said in *Weeks,* Title VII "vests individual women with the power to decide whether or not to take on unromantic tasks."

Employer also contends that the duties of commercial representative would subject a female employee to harassment and danger. This is based partly on problems arising from the collection of over due bills and partly on the fact that when acting as a substitute coin collector, the employee must make collections in bars, poolrooms, and other such locations. Again, however, there is nothing in the record to indicate that these features of the position are functionally related to sex. They mean nothing more than that some women, and some men, might not wish to perform such tasks. Here, however, the record is clear that one obtains this position by bidding for it and that if one is dissatisfied it is possible to request a transfer or a return to the former position.

Employer has consistently placed principal reliance on the fact that certain aspects of the job as performed in Montgomery require lifting of weights. Although other aspects of the job require occasional lifting, the alleged strenuousness of the position relates primarily to the work involved in relieving the coin collector. The evidence reflects that other commercial representatives in Montgomery have spent an average of two days per week on this relief work. In a normal day of this work a commercial representative would collect approximately 45 coin boxes from pay stations on his route. As they are collected, these coin boxes are placed in a small metal case which is compact and relatively easy to handle. Each case will hold up to nine coin boxes. A case weighs approximately 6 pounds empty, and the estimates of its weight when full varied from

---

1. A former commercial representative testified that he had to change tires on the job 11 times in 13 years.

45 to 80 pounds. An actual random sample indicated that the average on a particular day in Montgomery was 60 ¾ pounds. Occasionally, a case will weigh over 90 pounds. In a given day, from five to nine cases must be handled, and each case must be lifted and/or carried full in, out or around the collection truck four times a day.

In an effort to generate the desired inferences from these facts, the parties engaged in a battle of experts. Defendant produced Dr. Wood Herren, a doctor who, subsequent to the complained-of events, was appointed defendant's medical director.[2] Dr. Herren is an internal medicine specialist which, according to his testimony, is a modern-day general practitioner. He did not purport to be an expert on either industrial medicine or the care and treatment of women, and his observations were based largely on his experience in 16 years of private practice. Plaintiff produced Dr. Nace R. Cohen, an obstetrician and gynecologist for more than 20 years.

These medical experts agreed, and, through their testimony, enlightened this Court to the effect that there were certain genetic and musculo-skeletal differences between the sexes: Males tend to have a heavier muscular and ligamentous structure; males tend to have a higher aerobic metabolism rate; females tend to have greater lordosis, or curvature of the spine; females only are susceptible to osteoporosis, a softening of the bones from hormonal changes associated with menopause; and females only are subject to pregnancy.

The doctors did not agree, however, on all the effects of these differences. Both doctors agreed that the differences in muscular and ligamentous structure and in aerobic metabolism meant that men can perform greater amounts of work than women, i.e., men can lift more, more often, for longer periods of time than women. Dr. Herren testified that the lordosis makes the low back of the female more prone to stress and strain from lifting; Dr. Cohen testified that he knew of no such tendency and suggested that the greater curvature makes it easier for women to bend forward and pick up objects.[3] Dr. Herren seemed to feel that osteoporosis would be quite significant in preventing women from safely performing this job; Dr. Cohen, with considerable experience on this particular subject, testified that only about 5 percent of the female population has a significant degree of osteoporosis prior to age 65. The doctors agreed that in most cases osteoporosis can be modified or avoided altogether with hormonal treatment. The doctors also agreed that little lifting should be done during pregnancy. Finally, Dr. Cohen testified that in his opinion between 25 and 50 percent of the female population could perform the coin collector relief work; Dr. Herren, while not asked by Employer whether all or substantially all women could perform the job, admitted on cross examination that some women, depending upon the individual, could perform the lifting without hazards.

A thorough consideration of the evidence makes clear that it is "rational," rather than merely capricious, for the employer to discriminate against women as a class in filling this position, i.e., on the average, men can perform these tasks somewhat more efficiently and perhaps somewhat more safely than women. Employer relies upon a statement in Bowe v. Colgate-Palmolive Co., 272 F. Supp. 332, 365 (S.D. Ind. 1967), for the proposition that such a showing is sufficient to rely upon the bona fide occupational qualification exception: "Generally recognized physical capabilities and physical limitations of the sexes may be made the basis for occupational qualifications in generic terms." As indicated above, however, Employer faces a more substantial burden. The language quoted from *Bowe* was specifically rejected in *Weeks* for the Fifth Circuit and the [Equal Employment Opportunity] Commission is urging on appeal that it be rejected by the Seventh Circuit — in both instances for the very good reason that if it were

2. It was thus not upon his advice that the male sex was made an occupational qualification for the position of commercial representative.

· 3. Here, and in other instances where the testimony of the doctors conflict, this court finds that the experience of Dr. Cohen is more specifically related to the problem at hand, that his testimony tends to be more detailed and relevant, and that his conclusions are more persuasive.

followed the bona fide occupational exception would swallow the rule against discrimination.[1]

Weeks requires Employer to show that all or substantially all women would be unable to perform safely and efficiently the duties of the position involved. While it may be that, in terms of lifting weights, the duties of this position begin to approach the outer limits of what women should undertake, this Court firmly concludes that Employer has not satisfied its burden of proof. Dr. Cohen's testimony that 25 to 50 percent of the female sex could perform the job, while not standing alone, is accepted by this Court and fully rebuts Employer's contention. Nor is the fact that pregnant women should not perform the job of crucial importance. Employer can have a rule against pregnant women being considered for this position,[2] but Title VII surely means that all women cannot be excluded from consideration because some of them may become pregnant.

It is not inappropriate to observe in conclusion that it appears to this Court that it will not impose a hardship on this Employer to determine on an individual basis whether a person is qualified for the position of commercial representative. On the other hand, it is manifest that the use of this class distinction deprives some women of what they regard as a lucrative and otherwise desirable position.

Accordingly, this Court now specifically finds and concludes that the male sex is not a bona fide occupational qualification for the position of commercial representative in Montgomery, Alabama.

The *Cheatwood* test was first set forth in Weeks v. Southern Bell Telephone & Telegraph Co., 408 F.2d 228 (5th Cir. 1969). Another district court attempted to apply the *Weeks* BFOQ standard in the following case.

DIAZ v. PAN AMERICAN WORLD AIRWAYS, INC.
311 F. Supp. 559 (S.D. Fla. 1970)

[Celio Diaz wanted to become an airline flight attendant and challenged Pan Am's limitation of the job to women. The court described the airline's reasons:]

Reviewing its own experience with the thousands of male and female cabin attendants it had hired over the preceding years, Pan Am determined in 1959 that the overall level of service provided by the females it had hired was superior to that provided by the males it had hired. While the males were found capable of satisfactorily performing what Pan Am (like other airlines) describes as the "mechanical" functions of the flight attendant's job, such as the stowage of coats and the preparation and service of meals and beverages, the male stewards were found, as a group, not to be the equal of the females in the "non-mechanical" functions which had now become more important — providing reassurance to anxious passengers, giving courteous personalized service, and in general, making flights as pleasurable as possible within the limitations imposed by aircraft operations. . . .

[Pan Am backed up its case with an expert witness:]

Pan Am sought, through a psychiatrist, Dr. Eric Berne, author of the "Structure and Dynamics of Organizations and Groups", to explain in psychological terms why, as the other evidence indicated, most airline passengers of both sexes prefer to be served by female stewardesses. There was no challenge to Dr. Berne's qualifications as an expert, and the Court found a considerable part of his testimony persuasive. Dr. Berne explained that the cabin of a modern airliner is, for passengers, a special and unique psychological

---

1. The district court *Bowe* decision was reversed on appeal, Bowe v. Colgate Palmolive Co., 416 F.2d 711 (7th Cir. 1969). — Eds.

2. Later legal developments cast doubt on this statement. See Section B-4-b, infra, Pregnancy-Related Discrimination.

environment ("sealed enclave"), characterized by the confinement of a number of people together in an enclosed and limited space, by their being subjected to the unusual physical experience of being levitated off the ground and transported through the atmosphere at high speed, by their being substantially out of touch with their accustomed world, and by their own inability to control events. That environment, said Dr. Berne, creates three typical passenger emotional states with which the air carrier must deal; first and most important, a sense of apprehension; second, a sense of boredom; and third, a feeling of excitement. Dr. Berne expressed the opinion that female stewardesses, because of the nature of their psychological relationship as females to persons of both sexes, would be better able to deal with each of these psychological states. He specially emphasized, however, that the relief of passenger anxiety, due to apprehended but non-imminent dangers, represents the most important psychological factor to be dealt with by airlines, and that females are themselves psychologically better suited for that role than males because passengers of both sexes would, in this context, respond better to the presence of females than males. He explained that many male passengers would subconsciously resent a male flight attendant perceived as more masculine than they, but respond negatively to a male flight attendant perceived as less masculine, where as male passengers would generally feel themselves more masculine and thus more at ease in the presence of a young female attendant. He further explained that female passengers might consider personal overtures by male attendants as intrusive and inappropriate, while at the same time welcoming the attentions and conversation of another woman. He concluded that there are sound psychological reasons for the general preference of airline passengers for female flight attendants.

     . . . On the basis of Dr. Berne's testimony and common sense, and on the basis of testimony by industry witnesses who described the problems of passenger apprehension, experienced over many decades, this Court finds that an airplane cabin does indeed represent a unique environment in which an air carrier is required to take account of special psychological needs of its passengers. On the record, therefore, the Court must find not only that under the conditions of modern air travel most Pan Am passengers do in fact prefer female stewardesses to male stewards, but also that there are basic psychological reasons which explain that preference. . . .

     [A psychologist also offered testimony:]

     Pan Am offered evidence as to the personal qualifications conducive to the optimum performance of the flight attendant's function, as Pan Am currently defines it, and as to the difficulties of determining whether individual applicants have those qualities. This included testimony by its own management and by officials of Eastern and United Air Lines. It also included testimony by Dr. Raymond A. Katzell, an industrial psychologist, Chairman of the Department of Psychology of New York University, past President of the Division of Industrial Psychology of the American Psychological Association, co-author of Testing and Fair Employment (N.Y.U. Press 1968), and a frequent consultant to government agencies and industrial institutions in his specialty. Dr. Katzell defined that specialty as the analysis of the factors which affect the work motivation and performance level of employees, and the pursuit of methods of fixing employment qualifications which will increase the probability that the employee selected for hire will perform "at a high level", and reduce the probability "of failure or poor performance." Noting that the flight attendant's work involves not only a "mechanical" aspect but an "intangible" aspect concerned with those "interpersonal activities" which are designed to contribute to passenger comfort and a physical and psychological sense of well-being, and noting that the work was performed without supervision, Dr. Katzell stated that a high level of job performance requires not only mechanical competence but also sincere interest and motivation in providing for the comfort and ease of others in the working environment of that position. Dr. Katzell concluded that the aggregate of separate personal characteristics which would produce such interest and motivation constitute what we commonly describe as "femininity"; that while some men possess one or more of these qualities (e.g., benevolence, genuine interest in the comfort of others, lack of perceived aggressiveness) to a greater degree than some women, or even than most women, "it would be quite infrequent to find a man possessing each of these traits to at least as high a degree as the average woman"; that while it may in theory be possible to determine which individual male applicants for employment are among the few who possess the aggregate of those traits to a satisfactory level, it is not possible to make such individual determinations in any reliable way in the actual pre-employment situation with the psychological or personality testing methods now available; that the best available initial test for determining whether a particular applicant for employment is likely to have the personality characteristics conducive to high-level performance of the flight attendant's job as currently defined is consequently the applicant's biological sex; that to eliminate the female sex qualification would simply eliminate the best available tool for screening out applicants likely to be unsatisfactory and thus reduce the average level of performance. . . .

[The court concluded:]

On the basis of this and other evidence, the Court finds that at the time of the plaintiff's application for employment and at the time of trial, there were few men who possessed the aggregate of personality characteristics which Pan Am was entitled to seek in its flight attendants; that it was not practically possible to identify in the hiring process those few men who did; that given the present requirements of the job, the admission of men to the hiring process, in the present state of the art of employment selection, would have increased the number of unsatisfactory employees hired, and reduced the average level of performance of Pan Am's flight attendants; and that the requirement that one be of the female sex was reasonably designed to improve the average performance of Pan Am's complement of flight attendants and was accordingly a bona fide occupational qualification reasonably necessary to the normal operation of Pan Am's business.

The Fifth Circuit responded to this application of the *Weeks* BFOQ standard with a new test.

DIAZ v. PAN AMERICAN WORLD AIRWAYS, INC.
442 F.2d 385 (5th Cir. 1971), cert. denied, 404 U.S. 950 (1971)

We note, at the outset, that there is little legislative history to guide our interpretation. The amendment adding the word "sex" to "race, color, religion and national origin" was adopted one day before House passage of the Civil Rights Act. It was added on the floor and engendered little relevant debate. In attempting to read Congress' intent in these circumstances, however, it is reasonable to assume, from a reading of the statute itself, that one of Congress' main goals was to provide equal access to the job market for both men and women. Indeed, as this court in Weeks v. Southern Bell Telephone and Telegraph Co., 5 Cir., 408 F.2d 228 at 235 clearly stated, the purpose of the Act was to provide a foundation in the law for the principle of nondiscrimination. Construing the statute as embodying such a principle is based on the assumption that Congress sought a formula that would not only achieve the optimum use of our labor resources but, and more importantly, would enable individuals to develop as individuals.

Attainment of this goal, however, is, as stated above, limited by the bona fide occupational qualification exception in section 703 (e). In construing this provision, we feel, as did the court in *Weeks,* supra, that it would be totally anomalous to do so in a manner that would, in effect, permit the exception to swallow the rule. Thus, we adopt the EEOC guidelines which state that "the Commission believes that the bona fide occupational qualification as to sex should be interpreted narrowly." 29 CFR 1604.1(a)

Indeed, close scrutiny of the language of this exception compels this result. As one commentator has noted:

> The sentence contains several restrictive adjectives and phrases: it applies only *"in those certain instances"* where there are *"bona fide"* qualifications *"reasonably necessary"* to the operation of that *"particular"* enterprise. The care with which Congress has chosen the words to emphasize the function and to limit the scope of the exception indicates that it had no intention of opening the kind of enormous gap in the law which would exist if [for example] an employer could legitimately discriminate against a group solely because his employees, customers, or clients discriminated against that group. Absent much more explicit language, such a broad exception should not be assumed for it would largely emasculate the act. (emphasis added) 65 Mich. L. Rev. (1966).

Thus, it is with this orientation that we now examine the trial court's decision. Its conclusion was based upon (1) its view of Pan Am's history of the use of flight attendants; (2) passenger preference; (3) basic psychological reasons for the preference; and (4) the actualities of the hiring process.

Having reviewed the evidence submitted by Pan American regarding its own experience with both female and male cabin attendants it had hired over the years, the trial court found that Pan Am's current hiring policy was the result of a pragmatic process, "representing a judgment made upon adequate evidence acquired through Pan Am's considerable experience, and designed to yield under Pan Am's current operating conditions better *average* performance for its passengers than would a policy of mixed male and female hiring." (emphasis added) The performance of female attendants was *better* in the sense that they were *superior* in such non-mechanical aspects of the job as "providing reassurance to anxious passengers, giving courteous personalized service and, in general, making flights as pleasurable as possible within the limitations imposed by aircraft operations."

The trial court also found that Pan Am's passengers overwhelmingly preferred to be served by female stewardesses. Moreover, on the basis of the expert testimony of a psychiatrist, the court found that an airplane cabin represents a unique environment in which an air carrier is required to take account of the special psychological needs of its passengers. These psychological needs are better attended to by females. This is not to say that there are no males who would not have the necessary qualities to perform these non-mechanical functions, but the trial court found that the actualities of the hiring process would make it more difficult to find these few males. Indeed, "the admission of men to the hiring process, in the present state of the art of employment selection, would have increased the number of unsatisfactory employees hired, and reduced the average levels of performance of Pan Am's complement of flight attendants. . . ." In what appears to be a summation of the difficulties which the trial court found would follow from admitting males to this job the court said "that to eliminate the female sex qualification would simply eliminate the *best* available tool for screening out applicants *likely* to be unsatisfactory and thus reduce the *average* level of performance." (emphasis added)

Because of the narrow reading we give to section 703(e), we do not feel that these findings justify the discrimination practiced by Pan Am.

We begin with the proposition that the use of the word "necessary" in section 703(e) requires that we apply a business *necessity* test, not a business *convenience* test. That is to say, discrimination based on sex is valid only when the *essence* of the business operation would be undermined by not hiring members of one sex exclusively.

The primary function of an airline is to transport passengers safely from one point to another. While a pleasant environment, enhanced by the obvious cosmetic effect that female stewardesses provide as well as, according to the finding of the trial court, their apparent ability to perform the non-mechanical functions of the job in a more effective manner than most men, may all be important, they are tangential to the essence of the business involved. No one has suggested that having male stewards will so seriously affect the operation of an airline as to jeopardize or even minimize its ability to provide safe transportation from one place to another. Indeed the record discloses that many airlines including Pan Am have utilized both men and women flight cabin attendants in the past and Pan Am, even at the time of this suit, has 283 male stewards employed on some of its foreign flights.

We do not mean to imply, of course, that Pan Am cannot take into consideration the ability of *individuals* to perform the non-mechanical functions of the job. What we hold is that because the non-mechanical aspects of the job of flight cabin attendant are not "reasonably necessary to the normal operation" of Pan Am's business, Pan Am cannot exclude *all* males simply because *most* males may not perform adequately.

Appellees argue, however, that in so doing they have complied with the rule in *Weeks.* In that case, the court stated:

> We conclude that the principle of nondiscrimination requires that we hold that in order to rely on the bona fide occupational qualification exception an employer has the burden of proving that he had reasonable cause to believe, that is, a factual basis for believing, that all or substantially all women would be unable to perform safely and efficiently the duties of the job involved. Id. 408 F.2d at 235

We do not agree that in this case "all or substantially all men" have been shown to be inadequate and, in any event, in *Weeks,* the job that most women supposedly could not do was necessary to the normal operation of the business. Indeed, the inability of switchman to perform his or her job could cause the telephone system to break down. This is of an entirely different magnitude than a male steward who is perhaps not as soothing on a flight as a female stewardess.

Appellees also argue, and the trial court found, that because of the actualities of the hiring process, "the *best* available initial test for determining whether a particular applicant for employment is likely to have the personality characteristics conducive to high-level performance of the flight attendant's job as currently defined is consequently the applicant's biological sex." Indeed, the trial court found that it was simply not practicable to find the few males that would perform properly.

We do not feel that this alone justifies discriminating against all males. Since, as stated above, the basis of exclusion is the ability to perform non-mechanical functions which we find to be tangential to what is "reasonably *necessary*" for the business involved, the exclusion of *all* males because this is the *best* way to select the kind of personnel Pan Am desires simply cannot be justified. Before sex discrimination can be practiced, it must not only be shown that it is impracticable to find the men that possess the abilities that most women possess, but that the abilities are *necessary* to the business, not merely tangential.

Similarly, we do not feel that the fact that Pan Am's passengers prefer female stewardesses should alter our judgment. On this subject, EEOC guidelines state that a BFOQ ought not be based on "the refusal to hire an individual because of the preferences of co-workers, the employer, clients or customers. . . ." 29 CFR §1604.1(iii).

As the Supreme Court stated in Griggs v. Duke Power Co., 400 U.S. 424, 91 S. Ct. 849, 28 L. Ed. 2d 158 (1971), "the administration interpretation of the Act by the enforcing agency is entitled to great deference. . . ." While we recognize that the public's expectation of finding one sex in a particular role may cause some initial difficulty, it would be totally anomalous if we were to allow the preferences and prejudices of the customers to determine whether the sex discrimination was valid. Indeed, it was, to a large extent, these very prejudices the Act was meant to overcome. Thus, we feel that customer preference may be taken into account only when it is based on the company's inability to perform the primary function or service it offers.

Of course, Pan Am argues that the customers' preferences are not based on "stereotyped thinking," but the ability of women stewardesses to better provide the non-mechanical aspects of the job. Again, as stated above, since these aspects are tangential to the business, the fact that customers prefer them cannot justify sex discrimination.

The judgment is reversed and the case is remanded for proceedings not inconsistent with this opinion.

_____

The Ninth Circuit is even more stringent than the Fifth Circuit.

ROSENFELD v. SOUTHERN PACIFIC COMPANY
444 F.2d 1219 (9th Cir. 1971)

HAMLEY, Circuit Judge:

Leah Rosenfeld brought this action against Southern Pacific Company pursuant to section 706(f) of Title VII of the Civil Rights Act of 1964 (Act), 42 U.S.C. §2000e-5(f). Plaintiff, an employee of the company, alleged that in filling the position of agent-telegrapher at Thermal, California, in March, 1966, Southern Pacific discriminated against her solely because of her sex, by assigning the position to a junior male employee. . . .

On the merits, Southern Pacific argues that it is the company's policy to exclude women, generically, from certain positions. The company restricts these job opportunities to men for two basic reasons: (1) the arduous nature of the work-related activity renders women physically unsuited for the jobs; (2) appointing a woman to the position would result in a violation of California labor laws and regulations which limit hours of work for women and restrict the weight they are permitted to lift. Positions such as that of agent-telegrapher at Thermal fall within the ambit of this policy. The company concludes that effectuation of this policy is not proscribed by Title VII of the Civil Rights Act due to the exception created by the Act for those situations where sex is a "bona fide occupational qualification."

While the agent-telegrapher position at Thermal is no longer in existence, the work requirements which that position entailed are illustrative of the kind of positions which are denied to female employees under the company's labor policy described above. During the harvesting season, the position may require work in excess of ten hours a day and eighty hours a week.[6] The position requires the heavy physical effort involved in climbing over and around boxcars to adjust their vents, collapse their bunkers and close and seal their doors. In addition, the employee must lift various objects weighing more than twenty-five pounds and, in some instances, more than fifty pounds.

The critical question presented by this argument is whether, consistent with Title VII of the Civil Rights Act of 1964, the company may apply such a labor policy. The pertinent provision of Title VII is section 703(a) of the Act. . . .

Southern Pacific's employment policy under which, for example, it has denied Mrs. Rosenfeld an employment assignment on the ground that women, considered generically, are not physically or biologically suited for such work, results in distinguishing employees, thus discriminating against some because of sex, within the meaning of subsection (1) of this provision. It also constitutes a limitation upon, segregation of, or classification of the company's employees in a way which would deprive or tend to deprive an individual of employment opportunities because of such individual's sex, within the meaning of subsection (2) of the quoted section.

There is therefore no doubt that the type of discrimination against women broadly prohibited by Title VII occurs under Southern Pacific's personnel policy. However, appellants contend that section 703(e) of the Act, 42 U.S.C. §2000e-2(e), provides specific authority for Southern Pacific's described employment policy. . . .

_____

6. It was, indeed, this opportunity to earn overtime pay that made this position attractive to plaintiff.

We deal first with Southern Pacific's argument that the strenuous physical demands of the position, both as to the hours of work and the physical activity required, render sex "a bona fide occupational qualification [hereinafter BFOQ] reasonably necessary to the normal operation of that particular business or enterprise. . . ." The company contends that under the formulation put forward by the Fifth Circuit in *Weeks v. Southern Bell Tel. & Tel. Co.*, 408 F.2d 228 (5th Cir. 1969), if Southern Pacific could prove it "had reasonable cause to believe, that is, a factual basis for believing, that all or substantially all women would be unable to perform safely and effectively the duties of the job involved," Id. at 235, it could properly rely on the BFOQ exception as a legal basis for excluding women generically from position such as that of agent-telegrapher at Thermal. Southern Pacific contends that it should not have been denied the opportunity to present such proof by the mechanism of summary judgment.

The *Weeks* case involved, among other issues, a challenge to a company-imposed weight-lifting restriction for female employees. The case had gone to trial below. The Fifth Circuit thus decided only that the company had not met the burden of proof for establishing a BFOQ below. There was no need for it to consider the basic issue of whether employment restrictions based upon characterizations of a sex group's physical capabilities are, by their nature, capable of fitting within the BFOQ category. Since this case reaches us after summary judgment, we must decide this question.

The crucial language of section 703(e), 42 U.S.C. §2000e-2(e) . . . provides an exception to Title VII's prohibition of discrimination when "sex . . . is a bona fide occupational qualification." The Equal Employment Opportunity Commission (Commission) has interpreted the particular exception to some extent in its published Guidelines. In pertinent part, the Guidelines provide that:

> (a) The Commission believes that the bona fide occupational qualification exception as to sex should be interpreted narrowly. . . .
> (1) The Commission will find that the following situations do not warrant the application of the bona fide occupational qualification exception: . . .
> (ii) The refusal to hire an individual based on stereotyped characterizations of the sexes. Such stereotypes include, for example, that men are less capable of assembling intricate equipment; that women are less capable of aggressive salesmanship. The principle of non-discrimination requires that individuals be considered on the basis of individual capacities and not on the basis of any characteristics generally attributed to the group. . . .
> (2) Where it is necessary for the purpose of authenticity or genuineness, the Commission will consider sex to be a bona fide occupational qualification, e.g., an actor or actress. 29 C.F.R. §1604.1.

In the case before us, there is no contention that the sexual characteristics of the employee are crucial to the successful performance of the job, as they would be for the position of a wet-nurse, nor is there a need for authenticity or genuineness, as in the case of an actor or actress. 29 C.F.R. §1604.1(a)(2). Rather, on the basis of a general assumption regarding the physical capabilities of female employees, the company attempts to raise a commonly accepted characterization of women as the "weaker sex" to the level of a BFOQ. The personnel policy of Southern Pacific here in question is based on "characteristics generally attributed to the group" of exactly the same type that the Commission has announced should not be the basis of an employment decision. 29 C.F.R. §1604.1(a)(1)(ii). Based on the legislative intent and on the Commission's interpretation, sexual characteristics, rather than characteristics that might, to one degree or another, correlate with a particular sex, must be the basis for the application of the BFOQ exception. See *Developments in the Law — Title VII*, 84 Harv. L. Rev. 1109, 1178-1179 (1971). Southern Pacific has not, and could not allege such a basis here, and section 703(e) thus could not exempt its policy from the impact of Title VII. There was no error in the granting of summary judgment on this issue.

The premise of Title VII, the wisdom of which is not in question here, is that women are now to be on equal footing with men. Weeks v. Southern Bell Tel. & Tel. Co., 408 F.2d 228, 236 (5th Cir. 1969). The footing is not equal if a male employee may be appointed to a particular position on a showing that he is physically qualified, but a female employee is denied an opportunity to demonstrate personal physical qualification. Equality of footing is established only if employees otherwise entitled to the position, whether male or female, are excluded only upon a showing of individual incapacity. See Bowe v. Colgate-Palmolive Co., 416 F.2d 711, 718 (7th Cir. 1969). This alone accords with the Congressional purpose to eliminate subjective assumptions and traditional stereotyped conceptions regarding the physical ability of women to do particular work. See Weeks v. Southern Bell Tel. & Tel. Co., 408 F.2d 228, 235-236 (5th Cir. 1969); Bowe v. Colgate-Palmolive Co., 416 F.2d 711, 717 (7th Cir. 1969). See also, Shultz v. First Victoria Nat'l Bank, 420 F.2d 648, 656 (5th Cir. 1969), (interpreting the Equal Pay Act of 1963, 29 U.S.C. §206(d)(1)). . . .

We have considered the meaning which appellants would ascribe to BFOQ, as provided for in the Act. We conclude, however, that the Commission is correct in determining that BFOQ establishes a narrow exception inapplicable where, as here, employment opportunities are denied on the basis of characterizations of the physical capabilities and endurance of women, even when those characteristics are recognized in state legislation.

Under the principles set forth above, we conclude that Southern Pacific's employment policy is not excusable under the BFOQ concept . . .

NOTES

(1) Rights of the Individual. Technically, the *Weeks* standard allows employers to discriminate against qualified women workers if the employer can prove that most women workers would not be qualified. Should the principle of nondiscrimination be interpreted to allow this result?

(2) Practical Consequences of Different Standards. As a practical matter, it seems unlikely that many employers will be able to meet the *Weeks* burden of proof. Does this negate the value of the stricter *Rosenfeld* standard? In answering this question, students should consider the trial strategy, time, and expense necessary under each of the tests.

Many courts — and apparently practitioners as well — have not been aware of the different BFOQ standards, and have cited *Weeks* as *the* BFOQ test. Since women can use the strict *Rosenfeld* and EEOC standard to defeat most BFOQ claims as a matter of law on a motion for summary judgment, and thus avoid costly discovery procedures and trials, practitioners should obviously press for adoption of this standard in other circuits. See also Bowe v. Colgate Palmolive Co., 416 F.2d 711 (7th Cir. 1969); Sprogis v. United Air Lines, Inc., 444 F.2d 1194 (7th Cir. 1971), *cert. denied sub nom.* United Air Lines, Inc. v. Sprogis, 404 U.S. 991 (1971).

(3) Sex Segregation of Jobs. Notice that all three cases dealt with openly sex-segregated job categories. This has been true of almost all decisions construing the BFOQ exception to date, and evidences the prime role that sex segregation has played in limiting women's employment opportunities.

(4) Are There Any Valid BFOQ's? Is the *Rosenfeld* standard too loose, too strict, or just right? One might argue that there should be no jobs for which sex is a BFOQ. After all, companies do not in fact employ wet nurses or sperm donors. Moreover, Shakespeare provides historical precedent for the use of boys to portray women, and it seems that, if individual men or women can convincingly portray people of the opposite sex in acting

or modeling, they should be allowed to compete for such jobs; insisting on same-sex portrayal merely perpetuates narrow sex role stereotypes and exaggerates the differences between the sexes.

On the other hand, some might contend that other considerations, such as maintenance of cultural norms or privacy, require BFOQ's not justifiable under the *Rosenfeld* standard. Why can't an employer employ only short-haired men even though he hires long-haired women employees, or insist that men wear pants although he allows women to wear dresses? Should not male and female restrooms be staffed exclusively by same-sex attendants? How about fitters of clothing in men's and women's store clothing departments? Or nurses and orderlies providing intimate care in hospitals and nursing homes? Yet even in such areas, the perpetuation of sex role stereotypes can be a countervailing argument, and it must be remembered that the definition of privacy can change. For instance, in some countries (e.g., France) integrated bathrooms are common, and in the United States the same woman patient who objects to being washed by a male orderly accepts a gynecological examination by a male doctor.

If one rejects the cultural norm or privacy arguments, the *Rosenfeld* standard takes care of other conceivable BFOQ's: escorts provided by a dating service, topless waitresses in a nightclub, prostitutes in those places where selling sex is legalized. Here sexual characteristics of one sex or the other are indeed crucial to job performance. Yet if public accommodation laws prohibiting sex discrimination are passed and enforced, even in this area employers might be forced to hire both men and women in order to cater to customers of both sexes.

For court decisions on these borderline areas, see Joseph v. House, 353 F. Supp. 367 (E.D. Va. 1973), *aff'd sub nom.* Joseph v. Blair, 6 FEP Cases 257 (4th Cir. 1973), in which the court awarded a preliminary injunction against enforcement of a local ordinance forbidding massage parlors to employ persons of one sex to give massages to the opposite sex, after finding that the plaintiffs were likely to succeed on their Title VII claim; and City of Philadelphia v. Pennsylvania Human Relations Commission, 5 FEP Cases 649 (Pa. Commonwealth Ct. 1973), in which the court required certification of same-sex BFOQ's for city youth center supervisor jobs, purportedly under the *Rosenfeld* standard. In the latter case, the court found:[3]

> There is no question that a woman is equally qualified (or disqualified) to conduct a search for contraband as well as is a man. However, the vital factor that the Commission here disregards is "who are the people being searched?" If sex is not "relevant" in the supervision of children who range in age from seven to sixteen in various stages of undress, where can it be?
>
> To subject a girl in this age group to a thorough search of her body by a male supervisor could cause not only a temporary traumatic condition, but also permanent irreparable harm to her psyche. It is no different where females supervise male juveniles. To have a woman supervisor observe daily showers of the boys at a time in life when sex is a mysterious and often troubling force is to risk a permanent emotional impairment under the guise of equality.
>
> The children at the Youth Study Center have a history of troubled and varied backgrounds. Emotional and social problems are the rule and not the exception. It is the role of the Supervisor to gain the confidence and the respect of the children in order to aid them in regaining a proper perspective of the trying problems of growing up in a dangerous, hostile, competitive world. The Commission cannot expect the City to produce cold, empirical facts to show that girls and boys at this age relate better to supervisors of the same sex. It is common sense that a young girl with a sexual or emotional problem will usually approach someone of her own sex, possibly her mother, seeking comfort and answers. For girls in the Youth Center, their Supervisors are their only advisors. A like situation prevails for the boys. To expect a female or a male supervisor to gain the confidence of troubled youths of the opposite sex in

3. 5 FEP Cases at 652-653.

order to be able to alleviate emotional and sexual problems is to expect the impossible.

This is clearly a situation in which the sexual characteristics of the employee are crucial to the successful performance of the job. The Commission has failed to delineate the difference between discrimination based on sex, and the situation where sex and certain inherent biological traits are essential to the performance of a task.

For law review commentary, see Note, Developments In The Law — Employment Discrimination and Title VII of The Civil Rights Act of 1964, 84 Harv. L. Rev. 1109, 1176-1186 (1971).

(5) The Scope of the BFOQ. It is important to contrast the language of §703(a) with that of §703(e). Section 703(a) covers discrimination in regard to failure to hire; discharge; compensation and terms, conditions, or privileges of employment; and any limitation, segregation, or classification of employees affecting their employment opportunities or status. However, the §703(e) definition of a bona fide occupational qualification is limited to hiring and employing on the basis of sex. Similarly, the definition of illegal employment agency discrimination in §703(b) is broader than the §703(e) BFOQ definition for employment agencies, and likewise for the labor union prohibitions of §703(c). Obviously, this difference should be pressed in any case where an employer asserts a "BFOQ" defense for a policy *not* relating to hiring and employing. For instance, employers presumably could not justify sex discrimination in pension plans or health insurance (see Part B-4-b, Pregnancy-Related Discrimination, *infra*) under the BFOQ, since this discrimination relates to the compensation, terms, conditions, or privileges of employment.

2. The Short-Lived "Sex-Plus" Exception — and Its Implications for the BFOQ

The Martin Marietta Corporation refused to hire women with pre–school-age children, although it would hire fathers of pre–school-age children. In an early Title VII case, Ida Phillips challenged this policy. The company, however, chose *not* to raise the BFOQ defense, and instead contended that its policy was not discriminatory within the meaning of §703(a) of the act.

This accident of litigation strategy led to a strained decision by the Fifth Circuit, and Ida Phillips's case quickly became a cause célèbre. The court accepted the company's argument, holding that Ida Phillips was discriminated against because of *sex plus* another factor: having pre–school-age children. This, the court said, was not discrimination based on sex, and therefore was not prohibited by the act. Phillips v. Martin Marietta Corp., 411 F.2d 1 (5th Cir. 1969).

Chief Judge Brown's dissent to the denial of a rehearing best expresses the problems with this reasoning.

PHILLIPS v. MARTIN MARIETTA CORPORATION
416 F.2d 1257 (5th Cir. 1969)

[Brown, C.J., dissenting:]
The full Court should look at the issue here posed. And now in the light of the standard erected — sex if coupled with another factor is acceptable — it is imperative that the full Court look at it.

II

Equally important, the full Court should look to correct what, in my view, is a palpably wrong standard.

The case is simple. A woman with pre-school children may not be employed, a man with pre-school children may.[5] The distinguishing factor seems to be motherhood versus fatherhood. The question then arises: Is this sex-related? To the simple query the answer is just as simple: Nobody — and this includes Judges, Solomonic or life tenured —has yet seen a male mother. A mother, to oversimplify the simplest biology, must then be a woman.

It is the fact of the person being a mother — i.e., a woman — not the age of the children, which denies employment opportunity to a woman which is open to a man.

How the Court strayed from that simple proposition is not easy to define. Not a little of the reason appears to be a feeling that the Court in interpreting §703(a)(1), 42 U.S.C.A. §2000e-2(a)(1), prohibiting sex discrimination, is bound to accept the contention of one of the parties, rather than pick and choose, drawing a middle line, or for that matter reaching independently an interpretation sponsored by no one. Thus, after noting that in the Trial Court and here the Employer did not "choose to rely on the 'bona fide occupational qualification' section of the Act, but, instead, defended on the premise that their established standard of not hiring women with pre-school age children is not per se discrimination on the basis of 'sex' " (Phillips v. Martin Marietta Corp., 5 Cir., 1969, 411 F.2d 1, 2-3), the Court virtually acknowledges the patent discrimination based on biology. The Court states: "Where an employer, as here, differentiates between men with pre-school age children, on the one hand, and women with pre-school age children, on the other, there is arguably an apparent discrimination founded upon sex. It is possible that the Congressional scheme for the handling of a situation of this kind was to give the employer an opportunity to justify this seeming difference in treatment under the 'bona fide employment disqualification' provision of the statute." 411 F.2d at 4.

But in what immediately followed the Court then does a remarkable thing. Referring to EEOC (appearing only as amicus), it states: "The Commission, however, in its appearance before us has rejected this possible reading of the statute. It has left us, if the prohibition is to be given any effect at all in this instance, only with the alternative of a Congressional intent to exclude absolutely any consideration of the differences between the normal relationships of working fathers and working mothers to their pre-school age children [under the BFOQ provision], and to require that an employer treat the two exactly alike in the administration of its general hiring policies. If this is the only permissible view of Congressional intention available to us, [as distinct from concluding that the seeming discrimination here involved was not founded upon "sex" as Congress intended that term to be understood], we have no hesitation in choosing the latter." 411 F.2d at 4.

It is this self-imposed interpretive straightjacket which, I believe, leads the Court to the extremes of "either/or" outright per se violation with no defense or virtual complete immunity from the Act's prohibitions. This it does through its test of "sex plus": "[1] A per se violation of the Act can only be discrimination based solely on one of the categories i.e., in the case of sex; women vis-a-vis men. [2] When *another* criterion of employment *is added* to one of the classifications listed in the Act, there is no longer apparent discrimination based solely on race, color, religion, sex, or national origin." 411 F.2d at 3-4 (Emphasis supplied).

Reducing it to this record the Court characterizes the admitted discrimination in this way. "The discrimination was based on a *two-pronged* qualification, i.e., a woman with pre-school age children. Ida Phillips was not refused employment because she was a woman nor because she had pre-school age children. It is the *coalescence* of these *two elements* that denied her the position she desired. In view of the above, we are convinced that the judgment of the District Court was proper, and we therefore affirm." 411 F.2d at 4 (Emphasis supplied).

---

5. The man would qualify even though as widower or divorcé he had sole custody of and responsibility for pre-school children.

If "sex plus" stands, the Act is dead. This follows from the Court's repeated declaration that the employer is not forbidden to discriminate as to non-statutory factors. Free to add non-sex factors, the rankest sort of discrimination against women can be worked by employers. This could include, for example, all sorts of physical characteristics, such as minimum weight (175 lbs.), minimum shoulder width, minimum biceps measurement, minimum lifting capacity (100 lbs.), and the like. Others could include minimum educational requirements (minimum high school, junior college), intelligence tests, aptitude tests, etc. And it bears repeating that on the Court's reading, one of these would constitute a complete defense to a charge of §703(a)(1) violation *without* putting on the employer the burden of proving "business justification" under §703(e). . . .

In addition to the intrinsic unsoundness of the "sex plus" standard, the legislative history refutes the idea that Congress for even a moment meant to allow "nonbusiness justified" discrimination against women on the ground that they were mothers or mothers of pre-school children. On the contrary, mothers, working mothers, and working mothers of pre-school children were the specific objectives of governmental solicitude.

In the first place, working mothers constitute a large class posing much discussed problems of economics and sociology. And with this large class and the known practice of using baby-sitters or child care centers, neither an employer nor a reviewing Court can — absent proof of "business justification" . . . — assume that a mother of pre-school children will, from parental obligations, be an unreliable, unfit employee.

In this and the related legislation on equality of *compensation* for women one of the reasons repeatedly stressed for legislation forbidding sex discrimination was the large proportion of married women and mothers in the working force whose earnings are essential to the economic needs of their families.

Congress could hardly have been so incongruous as to legislate sex equality in employment by a statutory structure enabling the employer to deny employment to those who need the work most through the simple expedient of adding to sex a non-statutory factor.

A mother is still a woman. And if she is denied work outright because she is a mother, it is because she is a woman. Congress said that could no longer be done.

PHILLIPS v. MARTIN MARIETTA CORPORATION
400 U.S. 542, 91 S. Ct. 496, 27 L. Ed. 2d 613 (1971)

PER CURIAM. . . .

Section 703(a) of the Civil Rights Act of 1964 requires that persons of like qualifications be given employment opportunities irrespective of their sex. The Court of Appeals therefore erred in reading this section as permitting one hiring policy for women and another for men — each having pre–school-age children. The existence of such conflicting family obligations, if demonstrably more relevant to job performance for a woman than for a man, could arguably be a basis for distinction under §703(e) of the Act. But that is a matter of evidence tending to show that the condition in question "is a bona fide occupational qualification reasonably necessary to the normal operation of that particular business or enterprise." The record before us, however, is not adequate for resolution of these important issues. See Kennedy v. Silas Mason Co., 334 U.S. 249, 256-257 (1948). Summary judgment was therefore improper and we remand for fuller development of the record and for further consideration.

Vacated and remanded.

[Concurring opinion of Mr. Justice MARSHALL omitted.]

NOTES

(1) It is difficult to imagine what evidence would show that conflicting family obligations are more relevant to a woman's job performance than a man's. Perhaps the Court meant such evidence as the average absentee rate of mothers as compared to that of fathers. Even in dictum, this is a disturbing suggestion since it reveals a Court prepared to penalize an individual woman worker whose job performance is excellent because of the average job performance of members of her class — some of whom perform well and some of whom do not. Read Justice Marshall's concurring opinion for a more enlightened view of the issue and compare his view with that of the Ninth Circuit in *Rosenfeld.*

(2) The invalidation of the sex-plus standard was fortunate, for other companies had already tried to justify discrimination against similar subclasses of women. The airline industry, in particular, often fired women flight cabin attendants who married or were older than thirty-two, although no men employees were under restrictions. See Cooper v. Delta Airlines, Inc., 274 F. Supp. 781 (E.D. La. 1967) (upholding a no-marriage rule before the *Phillips* decision); Lansdale v. United Air Lines, Inc., 437 F.2d 454 (5th Cir. 1971) (invalidating a no-marriage rule after the *Phillips* decision); Sprogis v. United Air Lines, Inc., 444 F.2d 1194 (7th Cir. 1971), *cert. denied sub nom.* United Air Lines, Inc. v. Sprogis, 404 U.S. 991 (1971) (invalidating a no-marriage rule); Gerstle v. Continental Airlines, Inc., 5 FEP Cases 976 (D. Colo. 1973) (finding no Title VII violation even assuming the no-marriage rule was invalid, on holding that two individual plaintiffs voluntarily resigned); Jurinko v. Wiegand Co., 331 F. Supp. 1184 (W.D. Pa. 1971) (finding illegal sex discrimination based on no-marriage rule), *aff'd on other grounds,* 5 FEP Cases 925 (3rd Cir. 1973). See also EEOC Case No. 7038, 2 FEP Cases 165 (1969) (invalidating no-marriage and under-thirty-two rules); EEOC Decision No. 71-1413, 3 FEP Cases 547 (1971) (invalidating a no-marriage and no-children rule); Laffey v. Northwest Airlines, Inc., 6 FEP cases 902, 911-912 (D.D.C. Nov. 12, 1973) (discussing no-marriage and under-thirty-two rules which had previously been removed by the employer).

3. State Labor Laws and the BFOQ

After passage of Title VII in 1964, the discriminatory effect of state labor laws regulating women's employment became a major issue. A chronological history of the development of these laws, and of the controversy over them, which begins in detail where the material presented in Part II of Chapter One concludes, is presented here for several reasons.

First, the controversy over these laws is not new but has continued for over half a century. It has always been based in large part on conflicting ideologies about sex roles and the family. It is important to understand these because they remain at the heart of the present conflicts over ratification of the Equal Rights Amendment and the effect of Title VII on the state laws. Thus, the study of the half-century battle over "protective" state labor laws aids evaluation of today's arguments. The view of the opposing forces at work on this one issue and of the results they obtained also offers fascinating insights into the interdependence of social ideology, law reform, and economics.

a. A History of the Controversy over "Protective" State Labor Laws[4]

(1) 1900-1940

As described in Chapter One, Parts I and II, the women's movement started with broad questions of women's role in society. By the early 1900s, however, it had become concentrated on obtaining the vote. Accompanying this change was a shift in focus from the justice of granting women the vote to the usefulness of women's vote to social reform. Chafe explains that, by the turn of the century,[5]

> Instead of emphasizing the inalienable rights of females as individuals, the feminists tended to emphasize the utility of the ballot as an agent for reforming society. And rather than base their appeal on the similarity of men and women as human beings, they underlined the immutable differences which distinguished the sexes and gave to each a unique role to play in politics.

As the following account shows, this change was crucial to the battles about the desirability of state "protective" laws for women only which broke out after the vote was won among women who had been active in the suffrage movement. The social reform women did not consider their goals in the framework of the need radically to challenge the sexism of the society, and thus ran head on into the opposition of the feminist side of the women's movement — and never really understood the reasons for that opposition. Their failure of understanding was to last into the 1970s.

The state labor law movement had begun in the mid-nineteenth century with agitation by reformers and workers for shorter work days. Although the movement originally concentrated on bargaining power to achieve this end, after the Civil War it turned increasingly to state maximum hours laws to set limits on workers' hours. As was detailed in Chapter One, the effort to achieve such legislation was led by social reform groups composed largely of women, such as the National Consumers League (NCL) and the General Federation of Women's Clubs (GFWC).

By the time of the decision in Muller v. Oregon, 208 U.S. 412, 28 S. Ct. 324, 52 L. Ed. 551 (1908), supra Chapter One, Part II, the social reform effort had already paid off. Nineteen states had passed laws setting maximum hours for women workers or prohibiting night work. The *Muller* decision gave added impetus to the campaign; by 1917, nineteen more states had passed hours laws covering women workers, and old laws were strengthened. And in that same year, the Supreme Court approved maximum hours laws for both men and women in Bunting v. Oregon, 243 U.S. 426, 37 S. Ct. 435, 61 L. Ed. 830 (1917). But the maximum hours movement had basically come to a halt — probably in part because the AFL, led by Samuel Gompers, reversed its earlier support of the laws in 1914.

The reform forces, led by the National Consumers League, were by then concentrating on minimum wage laws for women; fifteen states passed these laws from 1912 to 1923. In 1919, the NCL adopted an ambitious ten-year program for work and welfare reform.[6] However, the social reform forces were at that point just entering a period of decline. World War I hurt them, as the nation's attention turned to the war effort and as they lost many of their most prominent leaders to government posts.[7] In fact, much

---

4. The chronology that follows is based on three works: Chafe, The American Woman, Her Changing Social, Economic and Political Roles, 1920-1970 (1972); W. O'Neill, Everyone Was Brave (1969); and Ann Corinne Hill, Protective Labor Legislation For Women: Its Origin and Effect (unpublished paper, Yale Law School 1970).

5. Chafe, supra footnote 4, at 12.

6. O'Neill, supra footnote 4, at 233.

7. Id. at 219-221.

of their legislative battle during the war was simply " 'to hold the ground that was already gained.' "[8]

The reformers were soon weakened by other events — caused in part, strangely enough, by ratification of the Nineteenth Amendment in 1920, which gave women the vote. Initially, the minimum wage movement and other social reform causes were helped by suffrage, because "politicans moved quickly to win the support of the new voters."[9] Included in the social reform bills passed in a number of states to win the women's votes were night work laws and wage and hour legislation. The Congress was similarly responsive. However,[10]

> Beginning in mid-decade . . . women's standing in the eyes of politicans dropped precipitously. . . . Congressmen seemed as intent on rebuffing the requests of female reformers in the second half of the decade as they had been in granting them during the first half.
>
> The abrupt reversal of fortune bewildered and demoralized women leaders. Just a few years before, their reform coalition had wielded considerable influence over Congress and state politicans. Now they were an embattled minority fighting a rear-guard action against the destruction of programs already established. To some extent, the decline could be attributed to a conservative shift in national affairs [including the Supreme Court decisions] ruling against a federal child-labor law and minimum-wage legislation for women [the latter in Adkins v. Children's Hospital, 261 U.S. 525, 43 S. Ct. 394, 67 L. Ed. 785 (1923)].

Another cause of the reformers' decline was the increasingly strong evidence that there was no pro-reform "women's vote," as the suffragists and social reformers had claimed.[11] In addition, a new force had entered the scene. With suffrage achieved, the feminist wing of the women's movement turned its attention to other legal reforms. In 1921, a new National Woman's Party (NWP) was formed, and in 1923 the party introduced the Equal Rights Amendment, hoping to achieve legal equality all at once and to give the women's movement a new focus. As part of its stress on equality, the party opposed laws that "protected" one sex only, and advocated laws applying to both sexes. The NWP was responding in part to the complaints of women workers, many of whom lost jobs because of "protective" laws, especially in the aftermath of World War I when men wanted to get rid of the women war workers who had made small inroads into formerly all-male jobs. The issue arose at the 1919 convention of the National Women's Trade Union League (NWTUL):[12]

> Miss Fincher, a fraternal delegate from Typographical Union No. 2 in Philadelphia . . . had lost her job when New York banned night work for women or, as she told the delegates "this Women's Trade Union League became active in amending the laws of New York and confined my working hours between six in the morning and six in the evening and legislated me out of a position, while you gave the twenty-four hours to the men working in the industrial field."[5] Miss Finch [sic] was admonished and stripped of her credentials. . . .

Hill describes such events in more detail.[13]

> The struggle to pass protective labor legislation for women blossomed into a controversy within the women's movement over the efficacy of such laws after World

8. Id. at 218.
9. Chafe, supra footnote 4, at 27.
10. Id. at 29.
11. Id. at 29, 33, 37, 45-47.
12. O'Neill, supra footnote 4, at 241-242.
5. Proceedings of the 1919 Convention, Papers of the NWTUL, p. 226. See also Henriette R. Walter, "Women as Workers and Citizens," Survey, June 21, 1919, pp. 465-466.
13. Hill, supra footnote 4, at 43-44.

War I. The first women to oppose protective labor legislation were workers in male-dominated trades — printing, polishing and grinding, coremaking, streetcar conducting — who had lost their jobs because of so-called "protective" laws. . . . Numerically, the number of women affected in all the trades, where such restrictive regulations were enforced, was not large, but they were a determined group.[2] The women driven out of the printing trade fought for 8 years to secure an exemption for them from the maximum hours law for women in factories that had included them. Women who were replaced by men after World War I as streetcar conductors and elevator operators, with the help of a maximum hours law, and women forced out of the metal trades by "protective" regulations gained support for their cause from the National Woman's Party, which advocated the substitution of "person" for "woman" in all protective labor measures.[1] Two other women's organizations, the Women's League for Equal Opportunity, started in 1915 by women in the printing trade, and the Equal Rights Association, formed in 1917 (also by a printer), agitated for equal treatment of men and women workers.[2]

Like the NCL, the National Woman's Party took the battle to the court, and filed a brief in the *Adkins* case opposing minimum wage laws for women only.[14] The decision partly reflected the feminist arguments for legal equality, and thus the NWP won its first court battle with the NCL. Faced with the opposition of the Supreme Court, the mood of the country, and the feminist desire for legal equality, the movement for further minimum wage laws was temporarily halted.

The feminist–social reformer battle had just begun, and it would continue in much the same terms for the next half-century. On the surface, this may seem surprising, because only a few years previously the two sides had been united in their campaign for women's suffrage. Given their opposing views on women's nature and role in society, however, the controversy was entirely natural. The "narrowing of vision"[15] of the suffrage movement had served to obscure the opposing aims of the two wings, but with suffrage out of the way they came to light once more. The ERA controversy, and the litigation battle over equality under the Due Process Clause, were merely the focal point for these divergent views.

Thus, only one year after *Adkins* and after the National Woman's Party had introduced the ERA, the social reformers had lined up in opposition to legal equality for men and women. O'Neill reports:[16]

> By 1924 the Women's Joint Congressional Committee and every important social feminist organization had attacked the equal-rights amendment as a threat to protective legislation for working women. The Woman's party's response was evasive. When Florence Kelley asked Alice Paul if she was opposed in principle to protective

2. Winslow, Mary Nelson. The Effects of Labor Legislation on the Employment Opportunities of Women (a report sponsored by the Women's Bureau of the U.S. Department of Labor, printed by the U.S. Government Printing Office, 1928), p. xvii.

1. Baker, [Protective Labor Legislation] pp. 193-194 [(1925)]. Two present day writers have also advocated the change from "woman" to "person" in existing protective labor legislation. See Murray and Eastwood, "Jane Crow and the Law: Sex Discrimination and Title VII" 34 G.W.L. Rev. 232 (1965).

2. The motto of the Women's League for Equal Opportunity was: "Give a Woman a Man's Chance — Industrially." (Baker, [supra,] p. 190.) This group and the Equal Rights Association unequivocally opposed all protective labor legislation that applied only to women. This position placed them against all the women's organizations that belonged to the Women's Joint Legislative Conference (a coalition of about 30 groups, formed by the W.T.U.L. to lobby for protective laws for women). They found themselves on the same side with Associated Industries, the strong pressure group for manufacturers and employers. Industrial Commissioner Shientag described their efforts as "playing into the hands of an element and group in this state which has always stood against progress, which has always stood against every bit of legislation for the protection of working women and children and for the advancement of the cause of humanity." (Baker, [supra,] pp. 190, 193-94).

14. Chafe, supra footnote 4, at 127.

15. Id. at 3.

16. O'Neill, supra footnote 4, at 278-279.

legislation, Miss Paul refused to answer, saying only that her board was evenly divided on the question. Some WP leaders were more direct. Gail Laughlin, first president of the National Federation of Business and Professional Women's Clubs and an officer of the WP, opposed all legislation based on sex. "The so-called eight-hour laws for women, glibly called 'protective,' mean the shutting of the door of opportunity to women. If we are to have legislation concerning hours of labor — and I believe we should have that legislation — it should be based along lines of industry, not along lines of sex." The argument that protective legislation was desirable when equally applied to men and women was made so often by the militants that their sincerity on the point seems hardly open to question. Equal Rights, their well-edited journal, insisted that sweeping protective laws dated from the period when women as a group were inferior to male workers, but as this was no longer the case such laws had ceased to protect and now limited the opportunities of many women employees.

"We agree fully that the mother and unborn child demand special consideration. But so does the soldier and the man maimed in industry. Industrial conditions that are suitable for a stalwart, young, unmarried woman are certainly not equally suitable to the pregnant woman or the mother of young children. Yet 'welfare' laws apply to all women alike. Such blanket legislation is as absurd as fixing industrial conditions for men on a basis of their all being wounded soldiers would be."

In another editorial Equal Rights pointed out there would be no reason to fear the effect of an equal-rights amendment on mothers' pensions if fathers were included in the system of family allowances, as was done in France, Belgium, Germany, and other countries. The party resented being called anti-labor. Alice Paul had once helped organize a milliners' union; Josephine Casey, chairman of its Industrial Council, was a wage-earner and a former organizer of the ILGWU; and the party took the same position on protective legislation for working women that Samuel Gompers did for working men.

Moreover, other liberals supported the ERA:[17]

Judge Ben Lindsey, whose enthusiasm for social welfare was never in question, supported the equal-rights amendment, believing that "what is known as special legislation for women is in fact not for women at all, but for children." The Minnesota Farmer-Labor party endorsed the amendment at its convention in March 1924 thanks to the efforts of Myrtle Cain, a Farmer-Labor member of the state legislature as well as past president of the Minnesota WTUL. Among the La Follette candidates for Congress in 1924 were a number of social feminists pledged to support the equal-rights amendment.

The social reformers responded to the NWP position by name-calling. Mary Anderson, the head of the Women's Bureau, called it " 'a kind of hysterical feminism with a slogan for a program' ";[18] Florence Kelley, with the evidence against her, claimed that the feminists were backed by " 'powerfully organized exploiting employers of women and children' ";[19] and Raymond Robins claimed that they had " 'been used to a finish by the intelligent members of the Property Minded interests of the country and have been secretly financed by the Plunderbund.' "[20] Neither side understood the one way out of the feud — to combine the ERA campaign with an extensive and united effort to

17. Id. at 280-281.
18. Id. at 281.
19. This comment is quoted by O'Neill at p. 285. O'Neill points out that although many employers naturally sympathized with the NWP's position on the laws, the NWP was very careful to avoid any identification with such employers. (Id. at 286.) The principal source of financial support for the NWP was a wealthy widow, Mrs. Oliver Hazard Belmont (id. at 274-275), who had earlier been the leading NWTUL fund raiser in support of the women garment workers' great 1909 strike; as such, she was part of the group called "uptown scum" by the employers' association (id. at 153-154) and could hardly be described as an ally of exploitative employers. Given Ms. Belmont's prominent role in both the NWTUL and the NWP, it is difficult to believe that Florence Kelley did not deliberately try to smear the feminists rather than deal with the issues they raised.
20. Id. at 286.

extend all state laws to cover men workers. One can only speculate why. The most likely explanation is that unions would not support maximum hours limits for men. One piece of evidence supporting this theory is that the unions were later able to get minimum wage laws for men, so it seems logical that had they wanted maximum hours laws they could have gotten them. The reformers presumably thought that they had to go along with the unions on this, while the feminists might have thought that sex-neutral protection would be more easily achieved once the ERA had been ratified. And the feminists certainly thought that the most important thing was to get the ERA passed, and only later to turn to other efforts.

In any event, the disagreement continued to grow. In 1926, controversy erupted over a meeting on the needs of women workers scheduled by the pro-reformers Women's Bureau (headed by Mary Anderson, from the NWTUL). The bureau ignored the ERA and labor laws for women in its agenda; the NWP objected vociferously and publicly; and an investigation of the labor laws was scheduled. Since the bureau was biased from the start, the report when it finally was issued unsurprisingly supported single-sex laws.[21] Hill discusses the report, and its disregard of the relationship between the laws and sex segregation.

HILL, PROTECTIVE LABOR LEGISLATION FOR WOMEN: ITS ORIGIN AND EFFECT
44-48, 53 (Unpublished paper, Yale Law School 1970)

In the introduction to its report, the Women's Bureau disclaimed any conflicting interest that would impair their ability to be objective in studying protective labor legislation. However, the Chairman of the study, Mary van Kleeck had published a study in 1906 of the unenforceability of early protective labor legislation in New York, that spurred the state labor department and legislature to consider more effective legislation. Van Kleeck had worked with the College Settlement Association, the Women's Trade Union League, and the Consumers' League, all ardent advocates of protective labor legislation for women.

The report focused on five industries in depth — hosiery, clothing, paper boxes, women's shoes and electrical products — all of which employed both men and women. Women were generally in the majority in the first three industries and represented 40-55% of the workers in the shoe industry, and 20-35% of the employees of the electrical products companies.

The main interest of the study was "the possible curtailment of opportunities for women through the substitution of men, due to the labor laws applying to women only."[1]

The question sounds reasonable, but the Women's Bureau provides the answer at the outset when it concludes that women have practically no employment opportunities anywhere in industry.[2] They work in women's industries at low-skill, low-pay jobs, that offer no training and no advancement. Four of the industries selected for the study typify

21. Id. at 285 n.3.
1. [U.S. Dep't of Labor, Women's Bureau, The] Effects of Labor Legislation [on the Employment Opportunities of Women], p. xvii [(1928)]. One major premise of the report is that protective labor laws for women have "accomplished their ends," i.e. they have helped establish "constantly better conditions of employment for women." As the report notes, "no one claims that legislation is at the root of the inequalities that exist in the present-day attitude toward the two sexes." But the aim of the study is to find out "whether special legislation for women, by crystallizing certain attitudes, may be one of the forces that are keeping alive outdated and outworn theories and precedents and thus needlessly restricting women's opportunities" and placing them "at a disadvantage in competing with men" for a job. Id., pp. 2-3.
2. Id., pp. 89-96. The report concluded that, in comparison with the opportunities made available to men in the five industries under investigation, "women's opportunity is very slight and is dependent not on the limitations, legal or otherwise, that surround women's work, but on the individual attitude of the employer and what he thinks is the attitude of their fellow workers." Id., p. 91.

women's work. In the fifth, electrical products, women were employed at three specific jobs: "light assembling, packing, and some riveting" while men operated the machines.[3] Though the sex-segregated nature of the work force in the industries under investigation was rather blatant, the Women's Bureau report never explicitly acknowledges that its existence makes a study of women being replaced by men futile, if not absurd. It is safe to assume that before protective labor legislation for women was passed, women in the five industries did not have the higher paying positions. Protective labor laws did not tend to propel women up the job ladder, but rather to make their life more bearable at the jobs they held.[1]

Protective labor laws certainly did not enhance women's jobs in a way that would interest men. They were still mainly unskilled, low-paying, monotonous jobs. In short, protective labor laws did not turn at non-competitive situation between men and women into a competitive one.

In contrast, in those men's industries where women began to get a foothold and to gain enough skills to begin competing with male co-workers — such as printing and coremaking — the effect of protective labor legislation for women only was to turn a newly competitive situation back into one free of competition from women. Elizabeth Baker draws a similar conclusion in her study of protective labor legislation for women in New York: "in occupations or industries where men greatly predominate, protective laws for women are likely to prohibit rather than protect their employment, or in other words, to relieve men of the competition of women."[2]

The Women's Bureau Report stresses that the number of women injured by such restrictive legislation was small; on the other hand, they comprised a large percentage of the skilled women workers in industry in the early 20th century. To deny them the opportunity to practice their skills was to halt "the economic standard bearers in the progress of women," Baker contends. All women workers suffered when the most skilled in their ranks were driven out of printing, coremaking, transportation, and polishing and grinding, and forced to seek unskilled, low-paying work in women's industries, thus further glutting the labor market in those industries and further depressing women's wages overall.[1] . . . Clearly, a sudden elimination of all protective labor legislation for women that restricts their employment and extension of those measures that benefit women to men as well will not abolish the sex-segregated job market overnight. But at least such action would remove the first barrier to women's advancement; in addition, a heavy blow would be struck to the monstrous myths about woman's nature and functions that protective laws have helped to perpetuate.[21a]

---

3. Id., p. 88.

1. It is almost as if women were being forced to trade off opportunities for advancement or for work in "men's industries" for meager protections in their own unskilled, low-paying positions. The struggle for seats with backs can be seen as a mere diversion from the core problems of prejudice against women in industry, below-living wages and refusal to include women in training programs that would increase their skills and their job opportunities.

2. Baker, [supra,] p. 426.

1. Baker, [supra,] p. 433.

Baker describes the vicious cycle created by those discriminatory laws as follows: "the result [of such laws] automatically throws them back into occupations most of which are already overcrowded by women and in which women, chiefly because of their numbers, are underpaid. The economically necessary result of this increased pressure for employment is depression of the bargaining power which is already weak, rendering women less able to keep themselves in the struggle for decent working conditions and a living wage. In turn, it is this very lack of power among working women that forms one of the principal bases of special laws for their protection. Thus, there is formed a vicious circle from which women are not permitted to escape."

21a. Note that the enforcement mechanisms of these laws may accentuate their negative impact on women workers. While there is no conclusive evidence available, it appears that the state agencies charged with enforcement of the laws were understaffed and underbudgeted. This probably meant that the laws were not strictly or widely enforced. In such a situation, both employers (and unions) who wanted to use the laws to justify maintaining sex segregation and employers who wanted to force women to lift heavy weights, work overtime, or accept substandard pay would be free to do what they wanted.—Eds.

Despite the favorable Women's Bureau Report, progress toward new minimum wage laws had been effectively halted by the 1923 *Adkins* decision:[22]

> The *Adkins* decision thoroughly demoralized reform groups because it removed the principal grounds on which they had sought legislative help. In the wake of the judicial action, minimum-wage statutes were struck down in Arizona, Arkansas, Kansas, and Wisconsin, while in other states similar laws fell into disuse due to fear of legal challenge by employers.

On the other hand, the ERA also did not make any real progress in the next decade, despite the nearly $800,000 the Woman's Party spent on it.[23] By the 1930s, the Depression and the New Deal had their impact on both issues, according to O'Neill:[24]

> At home, unemployment occasioned such widespread misery as to make pleas on behalf of women's special difficulties seem irrelevant, while the New Deal infused the flagging social welfare movement with new vigor. Militants [O'Neill's term for feminists] experienced one shock after another. President Roosevelt personally appealed to the governors of thirteen states to sponsor minimum wage laws for women and children. The codes of the National Recovery Administration permitted employers to maintain wage differentials for men and women doing the same work. That Mr. Roosevelt also appointed the first woman cabinet member, the first woman director of the Mint, the first woman minister (to Denmark), and gave more scope to feminine talents than any previous President did not console the WP. After the Hundred Days Doris Stevens told her followers, "All about us we see attempts being made, buttressed by governmental authority, to throw women back into that morass of unlovely dependence from which they were just beginning to emerge."[5] But her call to battle went unheard.

The Women's Bureau, too, lobbied for the laws,[25] under the jurisdiction of Frances Perkins, FDR's woman Secretary of Labor and formerly one of the NCL activists working with Florence Kelley.[26] In response, fourteen new minimum wage laws were passed in the 1930s. Chafe reports on this development:[27]

> For a brief period, the Supreme Court continued to block the implementation of such laws. Within one eighteen-month span in 1935-36, it struck down the NRA, a federal law regulating the pay of miners, and New York's statute setting a minimum wage for women. The Court abruptly reversed itself, however, when public outrage and the decisive re-election of President Roosevelt indicated that popular opinion was running in a different direction. A few weeks after the Chief Executive announced his plan to enlarge the Supreme Court, the judges overruled their own decision in the *Adkins* case and upheld a minimum-wage law which duplicated in almost every respect the New York measure they had invalidated nine months earlier. The Court followed its action in the West Coast Hotel v. Parrish case with a series of positive rulings on other New Deal measures. . . .

Since the National Woman's Party had filed a brief opposing single-sex laws in the 1936 New York minimum wage case, Morehead v. New York ex rel. Tipaldo, 298 U.S.

---

22. Chafe, supra footnote 4, at 80.
23. Most of this money probably came from Mrs. Oliver Hazard Perry Belmont, see footnote 19 supra.
24. O'Neill, supra footnote 4, at 293.
5. "Tribute to Alva Belmont," Equal Rights, July 15, 1933, p. 189. Miss Stevens was especially irritated by the President's economy bill which stipulated that when both husband and wife were employed by the government, one should be discharged, because that one invariably turned out to be the wife.
25. Koontz, The Women's Bureau Looks to the Future, 93 Monthly Labor Rev. 3, 6-7 (June 1970).
26. O'Neill, supra footnote 4, at 97.
27. Chafe, supra footnote 4, at 81-82.

587, 56 S. Ct. 918, 80 L. Ed. 1347 (1936), which had immediately preceded *West Coast Hotel*, the latter decision could be viewed as a defeat in the battle for legal equality. Other events of the 1930s were also ominous for the cause of women's equality with men:[28]

> The Depression especially sharpened public disapproval of work by married women. Employed wives were "thieving parasites of the business world," a Kansas woman wrote to President Roosevelt. A Chicago-based organization urged that married women workers be forced back to the home because "they are holding jobs that rightfully belong to the God-intended providers of the household," and the executive council of the AF of L resolved that "married women whose husbands have permanent positions . . . should be discriminated against in the hiring of employees." Almost all Americans agreed. When the pollster George Gallup asked in 1936 whether wives should work if their husbands were employed also, a resounding 82 per cent of the respondents said no. Gallup reported that he had "discovered an issue on which voters are about as solidly united as on any subject imaginable — including sin and hay fever."
>
> Consistent with such opinion, employers increasingly denied married women the right to work. A National Education Association study in 1930-31 showed that, of 1500 school systems surveyed, 77 per cent refused to hire wives and 63 per cent dismissed women teachers if they subsequently married. A San Francisco wife was told when applying for a teaching job that she would have to get a divorce first. From 1932 to 1937, federal legislation prohibited more than one member of the same family from working in the civil service. Designed to combat nepotism, the law in fact discriminated almost exclusively against women. In nearly every state, bills were introduced to restrict the employment of married women, and at times whole cities embarked on crusades to fire working wives. The Federation of Labor in Cedar Rapids, Iowa, called on every merchant to dismiss any married woman whose husband could support her, and the City Council of Akron, Ohio, resolved that the school board, the Goodyear Tire Company, and all local department stores should deny employment to wives.

And O'Neill reports that the 1930s witnessed the effective demise of the Woman's Party and of "feminism as a distinctive force in the national life."[29]

Even so, there were some positive events to report. In 1938, Congress passed the Fair Labor Standards Act, 29 U.S.C. §§201 et seq., providing a minimum wage and overtime pay for workers of both sexes, and the Supreme Court found the law constitutional in 1941.[30] Thus, the constitutional rationale for single-sex laws, founded on the long-outmoded *Lochner* and *Muller* decisions, had completely disappeared. And although the Woman's Party was no longer as powerful, it was still persuasive enough to keep the ERA before the Congress.[31]

> As the amendment fight wore on, the feminists slowly gained ground despite their lesser numbers. A League of Women Voters official noted in 1937 that the Women's Party made such a fuss on Capitol Hill that some congressmen were willing to send the amendment to the floor just to secure peace and quiet. A House Sub-Committee endorsed the amendment in 1936, the Senate Judiciary Committee reported it to the floor two years later, and the Republican party officially supported it in 1940.

Of course the social reformers, with their traditional view of women's role in society, remained bitterly opposed to the ERA because of its supposed effect on the labor laws they had worked so hard to achieve. Chafe explores at length the then 20-year conflict between the two forces on this issue.

28. Id. at 108.
29. O'Neill, supra footnote 4, at 294-295.
30. United States v. Darby, 312 U.S. 100, 61 S. Ct. 451, 85 L. Ed. 609 (1941) (see Chapter One, supra).
31. Chafe, supra footnote 4, at 130-131.

CHAFE, THE AMERICAN WOMAN:
HER CHANGING SOCIAL, ECONOMIC,
AND POLITICAL ROLES, 1920-1970
124-128 (1972)

. . . At the root of the conflict was the issue of whether protective legislation helped or hindered the quest for equality. From the feminists' point of view, laws which singled out women for special treatment represented a conspiracy to deny them their economic rights. "Whatever the effects on women of sex legislation aimed to protect them," Alma Lutz declared, "it has been a real protection to men by slowing down the competition of women for their jobs." As early as 1836, the New England Association of Farmers, Mechanics and Other Workingmen had advocated special labor legislation for women in order to control the size of the work force, and in 1923 the AF of L offered a similar rationale for its renewed interest in protective statutes. If women were prohibited from lifting certain weights or from working long hours, male workers could feel safe in their jobs. The feminists were convinced that, under the guise of concern for women's health and safety, unions actually sought special wage and hour legislation for females as a way of preventing women from taking work away from men. The only purpose of protective legislation in the age of the new woman, Maud Younger wrote, was "to lower women's economic status, keep them in the ranks with little chance for advancement . . . and perpetuate the psychology that they are cheap labor and inferior to other adult workers."

To support their contention that special labor laws discriminated against women, the feminists marshalled an impressive array of evidence. In New York City over 700 women employees of the Brooklyn Rapid Transit System lost their jobs when a statute prohibiting split shifts for women prevented them from working the morning and evening rush hours. Waitresses, clerks in drug stores, women printers, and reporters all suffered when New York declared that women could not work after 10 p.m. One study concluded that, if it were not for protective legislation, 2 to 5 per cent more women would be gainfully employed, many of them in jobs which represented "frontiers" in women's work. The case of Mollie Maloney, a bookbinder who earned $46.50 working the night shift in 1919, illustrated the feminists' argument. After passage of New York's night work statute, she was forced to move from her former job to the less remunerative day shift. When another law limiting women's hours of overtime prevented her from filling rush orders, she lost her job entirely. From Maloney's point of view, protective legislation was manifestly unfair. "We working women can protect ourselves if we have equality of opportunity under the law," she declared.

The feminists singled out minimum-wage laws for special condemnation. Establishing a set rate for women's services, they argued, placed an unfair value on women's work and invited men to undercut them by accepting lower pay. In Ohio, women's employment declined by over 14 per cent after a minimum-wage law was passed. At Harvard University, twenty scrubwomen were fired when the state ordered their pay to be increased by two cents an hour. And in California, the director of finance reported in 1932 that thousands of women were out of work because men were willing to accept less pay than the legal base set for women. "In not a single state having minimum wage legislation . . . do women receive a living wage," the feminist Jane Norman Smith declared. "On the other hand, whenever this legislation has been enforced . . . women have lost their jobs and been replaced by men."

Ultimately the feminists objected to special labor legislation because it symbolized the evil of a social system which set women apart as a separate class and assigned them a place less equal than that of men. The phrase "protective legislation" carried the distinct connotation that women lacked the ability to care for themselves and were second-class citizens. "Under the common law, women were 'protected' from themselves in being placed under the guardianship of father and husband," a New York equal rights pamphlet declared, "[but] modern women do not wish 'protection' as inferior beings." Special labor laws, the feminists argued, categorized the whole sex as weak and dependent — the equivalent of classifying all men as disabled because a few were wounded veterans. Only when females ceased to be grouped with children as helpless creatures could they enjoy the full status of mature persons that was their birthright.

Within such a context, the real purpose of the Equal Rights Amendment was to obliterate sex as a functional classification within the law. The feminists argued that women could not achieve real freedom until they were treated as individuals, not members of a sexual group. "It is time sex be forgotten and men and women become co-workers in all that concerns the destiny of the human race," Mary Woolley of Mount Holyoke wrote. Not every member of the Women's Party agreed with Alice Paul that equality meant absolute identity with men, but most joined in the conviction that women should be accorded the same legal status as men. "We are not asking for any special rights," Anita Pollitzer told a Senate hearing. "We are not asking for anything but the same opportunity [as men] to be human beings in this land of ours."

As they had on other issues, the reformers rejected both the specific claims and underlying premise of the feminists' argument. Legislation regulating women's hours, wages, and working conditions, they contended, had ameliorated the horrors of sweatshop labor and given workers protection against unprincipled employers. Far from undermining female equality, such laws were responsible for "bringing the women's standard up a little toward the standards of men." Passage of the Equal Rights Amendment might correct a few instances of discrimination, but it would also wipe out years of progress and restore the intolerable factory conditions of the late nineteenth century. For the sake of giving an individual woman the right to drive a taxi in Ohio, the feminists were willing to junk the rights of almost all female industrial workers to decent working conditions. The historian Mary Beard summed up many of the reformers' arguments when she declared that supporters of the Equal Rights Amendment "ran the risk of positively strengthening anachronistic competitive industrial processes; of supporting . . . ruthless laissez-faire; [and] of forsaking humanism in the quest for feminism." In service to an abstract theory, the well-being of millions would be endangered.

Indeed, the reformers believed that the entire feminist drive was motivated by the desire of a few business and professional women to advance their own interests at the expense of the rest of the sex. In a brilliant article analyzing the class bias of feminism, Mary Van Kleeck pointed out that the Women's Party and its allies were concerned primarily with liberating the individual woman. The feminists placed special emphasis on personal freedom and accomplishment — values which appealed to career women who aspired to success in positions which were competitive with men. The nature of industrial labor, on the other hand, barred individualistic competition. The factory was a collective institution, and the women working in it cared more about economic security than personal liberty. The two classes thus had distinctly opposite economic interests, but the feminists refused to acknowledge the difference and instead attempted to impose their own point of view on all women. The result, Van Kleeck declared, was that in the name of freedom a small number of career women were undercutting the only protection which female factory workers had.

Subsequent events seemed to confirm the accuracy of Van Kleeck's analysis. The Women's Party filed a legal brief in the 1923 *Adkins* case urging the Supreme Court to invalidate Washington, D.C.,'s minimum-wage law for women. Thirteen years later, it repeated its performance in the celebrated New York State minimum-wage case. In both instances, the Court appeared to endorse the feminists' contention that placing a floor beneath the wages of women amounted to a denial of their freedom of contract. To the feminists, such decisions represented a bold advance toward equal rights, but to social reformers the opposite was true. Mary Anderson asserted that the Court's ruling in the New York case had about as much to do with freedom for women as the right-wing Liberty League had to do with liberty. The feminist position on equality, the *Nation* commented, "is as always logically sound and theoretically progressive. Humanly, however, it is impractical and reactionary."

Chafe here seems to side with the analysis of Mary Van Kleeck and the reformers. However, his explication ignores the fact that the plaintiff in one of the two *Adkins* cases (decided in one opinion) was a woman elevator operator who alleged she would lose her job if she gained the "protection" of a minimum wage; this confirmed the feminists' argument that legislation for one sex (women) often resulted only in a loss of jobs for that sex.[32] But this result was not necessary since the Supreme Court had already approved maximum hours legislation protecting both sexes, Bunting v. Oregon, 243 U.S. 426, 37 S. Ct. 435, 61 L. Ed. 830 (1917) — and under such laws it would, of course, be impossible for men to underbid women. Thus, it is difficult to understand why the social reformers fought so bitterly to preserve single-sex legislation from 1917 on. After all, they could have achieved their own aims without promoting the discrimination the feminists complained of by working for protection for all workers, rather than putting their energies into the fight against the Equal Rights Amendment. The union stand is easier to comprehend, since the single-sex laws did help protect male jobs against female encroachment. Perhaps the reformers' unwillingness to face the discriminatory impact of these laws simply reflected the human tendency to stick with a position once a lot of energy has been placed in it. From 1908 to 1917 (the years of the *Muller* and *Bunting* decisions) it is true that single-sex legislation seemed the only way around a conservative court.

Another hypothesis is that the reformers knew unions would join employers in opposition to legislation covering both sexes, and were unwilling to fight the unions in the open for the sake of those working women who were undeniably hurt by single-sex laws. Moreover, they had never analyzed the problem of sex segregation in the labor market and were unwilling or unable to see its connection with the state laws.

Chafe also ignores at this point a very fundamental misstatement of the reformers, which they carried through into the 1960s and 1970s — namely, that the feminists were primarily interested in business and professional women. True, many people in the Woman's Party were career women, but so were many of the reformers, and the discrimination which the feminists cited, as reported by Chafe himself, was directed against subway employees, waitresses, drugstore clerks, printers, reporters, bookbinders, scrubwomen, and chambermaids, hardly elite career jobs.

However, Chafe clearly understood the ultimate cause of the controversy:[33]

> Whatever the merits of the specific arguments, however, the conflict ultimately centered on the reformers' assumption that women *did* differ fundamentally from men and *should* be treated as a separate class. Summarizing the reform point of view, the Consumers League declared that, while women had the same rights as men, they were "not identical in economic or social function or in physical capacity" and hence could not be dealt with in the same way. . . .
>
> For the most part, reformers accepted such a definition of women's identity as a necessary prerequisite for achieving social-welfare legislation. Rose Schneiderman of the Women's Trade Union League observed that most women could not do the same work as men and needed safeguards to protect their health. In particular, Schneiderman rejected the idea that women should be employed as absolute equals with men. Those who "want to work at the same hours of the day or night and receive the same pay," she declared, "might be putting their own brothers or sweethearts, or husbands out of a job." Full-time work, by implication, remained the exclusive prerogative of men. The Court's interpretation in the *Muller* case coincided with the

32. It may be, of course, that the particular plaintiff in *Adkins* was recruited for the litigation and paid for her role in it by the employer. Otherwise, how could an unemployed elevator operator meet the expenses of a case which was finally concluded in the Supreme Court? But this possibility does not undercut the argument that protective laws often hurt rather than helped women, as the feminists' statistics on loss of jobs demonstrated.

33. Chafe, supra footnote 4, at 128-129.

reformers' own conviction that the two sexes had separate roles to play in life. "Nature made men and women different," Felix Frankfurter asserted; "the law must accommodate itself to the immutable differences of Nature."

Consistent with Frankfurter's reasoning, the reformers placed special emphasis on woman's role within the family in their campaign against the Equal Rights Amendment. "No law . . . can change physical structures that make women the child-bearers of mankind," a group of reformers asserted. Nature had decreed that women should devote their lives to caring for children. A man could not nurse a baby, Al Smith observed. Consequently, the two sexes could not be treated identically. The clear inference of the reformers' argument was that any effort to obliterate sexual differences in the law was a direct assault on God's creation. "To deny that women require care and protection," one writer charged, "is equal to a denial of their physical mission of motherhood."

The reformers and feminists thus held diametrically opposite conceptions of female equality. The Women's Party and its allies were convinced that protective legislation discriminated against females and that women could not be free until they achieved absolute identity with men in all areas of public policy regulated by the law. The reformers, in turn, believed that differences of physical and psychological make-up prevented women from ever competing on a basis of total equality with men and that special labor laws were required if females were to be protected against exploitation and given just treatment in their economic activities.

In the end, the reformers' belief in women's special nature seemed to take them beyond the point of reason. Rather than seeing how their protective legislation argument had lost its force with explicit Supreme Court approval of worker protection for both sexes in the 1941 *Darby* decision, they continued to oppose the ERA. In fact, "They formed a 'Committee of Five Hundred Against the Equal Rights Amendment' and attempted to counter the Women's Party's initiative by proposing an omnibus 'Women's Charter' which would establish the principle of equality while recognizing the differences between men and women."[34]

(2) 1940-1950

With the advent of World War II, the labor law–ERA controversy ceased —at least temporarily — and women workers poured into the nation's work force, particularly into many formerly all-male jobs.[35] The government encouraged this development, Chafe reports.[36]

> The War Manpower Commission itself attempted to facilitate the process by issuing guidelines designed to end sex discrimination. Employers were told to hire and train women "on a basis of equality with men," to "remove all barriers to the employment of women in any occupation for which they are or can be fitted," and to use "every method available" to ensure women's complete acceptance. The Office of War Information conducted a vigorous public relations campaign in support of the WMC's policies, and urged both employers and women to answer the call to national service. Although the government's pronouncements about non-discrimination were not always followed in practice, the war and the effort to legitimize women's work did succeed in changing the average citizen's attitude toward female employment. At the height of the Depression, over 80 per cent of the American people strongly opposed work by married women. By 1942, in contrast, 60 per cent believed that wives should be employed in war industries (only 13 per cent were opposed), and 71 per cent asserted that there was a need for more married women to take jobs.
>
> As a result of the manpower shortage and the aggressive campaign to recruit

34. Id. at 131.
35. Id. at 140-143.
36. Id. at 147-148.

female workers, women's economic status changed significantly for the first time in thirty years. During the war, the proportion of women who were employed jumped from slightly over 25 per cent to 36 per cent — a rise greater than that of the preceding four decades. By V-E Day, the female labor force had increased by 6.5 million, or 57 per cent. For the first time, more wives were employed than single women, more women over thirty-five than under thirty-five. Manufacturing took the largest number of new workers — 2.5 million — but an additional 2 million entered the clerical field, and the only areas of female employment to suffer a relative decline were those of domestic servant and professional. At the close of hostilities, nearly 20 million women were in the labor force — 35 per cent of all workers in contrast to 25 per cent in 1940.

Chafe concluded, however, that[37]

> Despite some important advances, therefore, many women workers continued to suffer from wage discrimination. In 1945 as in 1940, females who were employed in manufacturing earned only 65 per cent of what men received. The NWLB made a brave start toward redressing some of the inequalities which women experienced, but subsequent decisions weakened the impact of the Board's action. In addition, the government's anti-inflationary policies discouraged aggressive implementation of the equal-pay doctrine. Significantly, the NWLB refused to consider the most important source of discrimination against women — the differential in wage rates paid to females doing women's work. Impressive gains had been made in some war industries, especially those with strong unions, but, as long as female employment was judged by a different standard than men's, inequality was inevitable. A wage geared to the job rather than the sex of the worker offered the best solution, but at the end of the war such a goal remained almost as far away as it had been at the beginning.

After the war was over, however, women were once again expected to return to the home.[38]

> Under the Selective Service Act, veterans took priority over wartime workers in the competition for their old jobs. As war plants reconverted to peacetime production, women who were last hired were also first fired.

And while many of the new women workers remained in the labor market, many had to leave the more desirable "male jobs" they had entered and return to the less lucrative "female jobs." For example,[39]

> Women fell from 25 per cent of all auto workers in 1944 to 7.5 per cent in April 1946. The last figure was only one point higher than the percentage employed in October 1939. Overall, females comprised 60 per cent of all workers released from employment in the early months after the war and were laid off at a rate of 75 per cent higher than men. With the manpower crisis over, some employers revised their age requirements, throwing women over forty-five out of work, and large companies like Detroit Edison, Thompson Aircraft, and IBM reimposed earlier restrictions on the hiring of wives.
> An appreciable number of women retained positions in the labor force, however, confounding the expectations of those who believed that female employment would decline precipitously with the end of the fighting. The Bureau of Labor Statistics had predicted that 6 million people would lose their jobs in the year after the war, a substantial proportion of them women. In fact, only a small percentage of that number remained permanently out of work. A great many women left their former jobs, creating the impression of widespread unemployment, but a majority rejoined the

37. Id. at 158.
38. Id. at 179.
39. Id. at 180, 181.

labor force at a later date. . . . Thus while women lost some of their better-paid war positions, they did not disappear from the labor market as some had anticipated.

"Protective" laws once again played a role in forcing women out of desirable "men's jobs." The Labor Department promoted an 18-point program for "transition to a peacetime economy," designed to increase jobs and expand the economy, that included two points concerning women workers:[40]

> Revocation of all permits for the work of women beyond eight hours and for the work of women on the graveyard shifts.
>   Retiring women who are merely pin-money workers and come into the labor market only because of the war need in order to make opportunity for girls who must work regularly.

Contemporary cases still mention such practices. A New York State night work law which had been ignored during the war was suddenly reimposed on women inspectors at Corning Glass Works, forcing them out of the more lucrative night-shift work they had undertaken. See Hodgson v. Corning Glass Works, 474 F.2d 226 (2d Cir. 1973), infra Part III. And the Hotel and Restaurant Employees and Bartenders International Union was typical, if more open, in its campaign to pass antibarmaid laws in order to force women out of bartenders jobs gained during the wartime shortage of male bartenders (see Note: The Union Role — Good Faith Protection of Women or Self-Interested Protection of Men? infra Section B-3-b). This campaign was given added impetus by the Supreme Court's 1948 approval of these laws in the Goesaert v. Cleary decision; Frankfurter, one-time counsel for the NCL, authored the cavalier decision that refused even to take notice of the law's obviously discriminatory intent, thus continuing the social reform attitude towards sex discrimination.

Meanwhile, feminists continued to press for the ERA, and the social reformers remained adamantly opposed:[41]

> For a brief period during and after the war, the outlook appeared promising. Congressmen talked of approving the amendment as a vote of thanks to women for their "magnificent wartime performance"; both parties endorsed the measure; and luminaries such as Homer Cummings, Henry Wallace, and Harry Truman added their voices in support. The amendment involved a fundamental division of opinion over the meaning of equality, however, and provoked as much opposition as praise. Prominent women like Eleanor Roosevelt and Mary Anderson insisted that protective legislation was more valuable than the establishment of an abstract principle of legal rights, and in the end their viewpoint prevailed despite the increased backing won by the feminists. The Senate first considered the amendment in August 1946 and by a margin of 38 to 35 denied it the two-thirds approval needed for adoption. (The New York Times praised the vote, saying "motherhood cannot be amended.") Four years later, the measure passed by a sweeping majority of 63 to 11, but this time it contained a rider introduced by Senator Carl Hayden of Arizona specifying that no protective legislation was to be affected. The Hayden rider in effect voided the operative intent of the feminist bill and rendered it meaningless. "My amendment is a revolving door," Hayden boasted. "We come in one side and go out the other." One Washington reporter observed that Hayden "could put a rider on the Ten Commandments and nullify them completely." Although the Equal Rights Amendment was passed by the Senate one more time in 1953, with the Hayden rider, the Senate's action effectively buried hopes for its adoption until the late 1960's.

---

40. Rawalt, The Equal Rights Amendment and the Draft, National Business Women (November 1972), citing the New York Times, June 2, 1944, p. 10.
    41. Chafe, supra footnote 4, at 187-188.

(3) 1950-1971

During the 1950s states started enacting minimum wage laws that covered men workers, or amended existing laws to extend them to men.[42] No parallel development occurred for maximum hours laws, however. It was clear that the unions and social reformers were still not interested in limiting men's overtime work (and premium pay). From 1955 to 1968, 11 new minimum wage laws were passed — all protecting both men and women workers, and 13 existing laws were amended to cover men. By 1968, out of the 41 state minimum wage laws, 31 protected both men and women, 7 protected women only, and 3 protected women only but were inoperative. In contrast, maximum hours law coverage had not changed significantly since 1920; of the 42 laws, 39 covered women only. The social reformers had worked for other laws, too, so by the 1960s there was a plethora of special labor laws, most of it applicable to women only. These laws could be broken into two categories: those that restricted women's job opportunities and those that provided valid benefits which some men workers also wanted.[43] In general, as with the maximum hour and minimum wage laws, by the late 1960s the restrictive laws were still limited to women and the benefit laws had become widely available to men workers.[44] For example, 26 states prohibited women from working in mining, bartending, or other occupations; 11 states set weight limits on the amount women workers could lift; 19 states prohibited or regulated women working at night; and 7 states prohibited work before or after childbirth. None of these restrictions applied to men workers. In contrast, 14 out of 18 state laws providing for overtime pay applied to both men and women workers, as did the nationwide federal law; and 28 out of 42 laws providing for a day of rest did so.[45]

Meanwhile, other forces were at work affecting the labor market and society. Although the 1950s were a time of strong antifeminist propaganda, more and more women entered the labor market, and by 1968 the female percentage of the labor market — 37 — had surpassed the previous peak of 36 percent achieved at the end of World War II.[46] The 1960s also saw the revitalization of feminism as a force, and one of the major demands was job equality. Feminists played a key role in amending Title VII to cover sex discrimination; and in fact, the National Woman's Party, still led by the indomitable Alice Paul, lobbied strongly in Congress for this result.[47] So, with the passage of Title

42. The amendment process started in some states from 1941 to 1954, but the major activity was from 1954 on. U.S. Dept. of Labor, Women's Bureau, 1969 Handbook on Women Workers 263. Both the unions and the Women's Bureau appear to have played roles in these developments. Koontz, The Women's Bureau Looks to the Future, 93 Monthly Labor Rev. 3;7 (June 1970).

43. The distinction between restrictions and benefits is somewhat artificial, since a condition imposed by law can often be seen as either. Indeed, this was the source of the union and reformers' quarrel with the feminists — e.g., the former saw mandatory maximum hours for women as a benefit; the latter saw it as a serious detriment. However, the distinction will be used here for two reasons. First, the Equal Employment Opportunity Commission (EEOC) used it in its guidelines. Second, it does reflect accurately the division between laws which women workers have sought to abolish under Title VII (see Note: Impact of *Rosenfeld* and of the EEOC Regulations, infra) and those which they have not challenged or which men workers have sought to extend to themselves. Thus, workers in sex discrimination lawsuits have viewed one set of laws as restrictive, the other set as beneficial.

44. See the chart listing these laws in S. Ross, Sex Discrimination and "Protective" Labor Legislation, printed in Hearings on Section 805 of H.R. 16098 before the Special Subcomm. on Education of the House Comm. on Education and Labor, 91st Cong., 2d Sess., pt. 1, at 592, 595-96 (1970), and in Hearings on H.J. Res. 35,208, and Related Bills and H.R. 916 and Related Bills Before Subcomm. No. 4 of the House Comm. on the Judiciary, 92d Cong., 1st Sess., Serial No. 2, at 178 (1971). (Hereinafter cited to latter hearings.) The chart is based on data from U.S. Dept. of Labor, Women's Bureau, 1969 Handbook on Women Workers at 261-279, which lists laws in force as of January 1, 1969, for the 50 states, the District of Columbia, and Puerto Rico.

45. However, meal periods (22 laws for women; 3 for men and women), rest periods (13 for women; none for men), and seats (46 for women; 1 for men and women) were still provided predominantly for the female sex.

46. U.S. Dept. of Labor, Women's Bureau, 1969 Handbook on Women Workers 9.

47. See, generally, C. Berger, Equal Pay, Employment Opportunity and Equal Enforcement of the Law

VII and renewed efforts to pass and ratify the ERA in the late 1960s,[48] the discriminatory effect of the "protective" laws once again became a major issue. Once again social reformers and some labor unions lined up to preserve the laws, while feminists and other unions sought a declaration that Title VII invalidated some laws and extended others to men.

The argument soon focused on the EEOC guidelines dealing with the meaning of the statutory allowance of discrimination when based on a "bona fide occupational qualification." Each side urged the EEOC to adopt its viewpoint in the guidelines. Less than a month after the effective date of Title VII (July 2, 1965), several reform, church-women's, labor, and professional organizations[49] wrote the chairman of the EEOC urging that differential legislation applying to women workers be preserved under Title VII because "it has greatly improved their economic position, has provided essential protection from exploitation, and promoted their health, safety and well-being. There are still many differences between men and women which amply justify existing differential legislation."[50]

The EEOC responded to the diverse pressures by taking an ambiguous stand:[51]

> The development of the final [EEOC] position can be traced in the regulations the EEOC has issued under 29 C.F.R. Section 1604.1. The first was issued on December 2, 1965, and was based on the assumption that Congress had not intended to override state laws. In effect, the regulation allowed restrictive state laws to be used as a BFOQ defense, provided that the employer acted in good faith and that the state law effectively protected women rather than discriminated against them. This last proviso begged the question, of course, since the EEOC did not explain what was protection and what discrimination. The "benefit" type laws (minimum wage, overtime pay, rest periods, or physical facilities) could not be used as a BFOQ however, and in fact, in its case law, the EEOC requires not only that women be hired under these laws but that the benefit be extended to men.
>
> Less than a year later, on August 19, 1966, the EEOC announced in a press release, incorporated in all pertinent Commission decisions, that where there was a square conflict between Title VII and the state laws, it would refrain from making a decision, since EEOC interpretations could not insulate employers against state liability for violation of state statutes and since the EEOC could not institute suits to challenge the state law. It would, however, advise complainants of their right to bring suit, reserving the right to appear as amicus curiae because it thought litigation was necessary to resolve the conflict. It was apparent that the EEOC was beginning to be troubled by the state laws, for it dealt at length with the hours laws and a case then before the Commission which challenged the California version. A more realistic appraisal of state laws is now evident, when the Commission states:
> ". . . the facts indicate that the female charging parties are being denied promotional opportunities to earn premium pay for overtime. . . . There is no suggestion in the facts before us that the health or welfare of the charging parties would be adversely affected by permitting them to work in excess of 48 hours a week. . . .

for Women, 5 Valparaiso U.L. Rev. 326, 332-337 (1971). Some anti–civil rights Congressmen also supported the inclusion of sex discrimination in Title VII in the hopes of weakening the overall support for the proposed bill; this motive is generally played up in commentary, while the genuine feminist support is ignored.

48. See Chapter One, Part VI supra.

49. The groups: Young Women's Christian Association; American Association of University Women; National Consumers League; American Nurses Association; National Council of Catholic Women; United Church Women; National Federation of Settlements and Neighborhoods Centers; Americans for Democratic Action; American Civil Liberties Union; National Council of Jewish Women; National Council of Negro Women; Women's Division, The Methodist Church, Department of Christian Social Relations; International Union of Electrical Radio and Machine Workers; Amalgamated Meat Cutters and Butcher Workmen of North America.

50. Letter from Olga Margolin, Washington Representative, National Council of Jewish Women, to Franklin D. Roosevelt, Jr., Chairman, EEOC (July 30, 1965).

51. Ross, Sex Discrimination and "Protective" Labor Legislation, supra footnote 44, at 180-181.

"Over 40 states have laws or regulations which, like California's, limit the maximum daily or weekly hours which women employees may work. . . . The Commission believes that in fact these laws in many situations have an adverse effect on employment opportunities for women."

When pressure continued to mount, the commission scheduled public hearings on the issue for May 2 and 3, 1967. The list of organizations that testified on each side seemed to indicate that opinion was starting to swing against the state laws. Most groups emphasized their discriminatory effect, especially that of maximum hours, weight limit, and job prohibition laws, and urged the commission to rule that they were superseded by Title VII. Some groups added a more sophisticated analysis pointing out that, in addition, the commission could require employers to provide men workers with benefits under the other state laws. The groups testifying on the discriminatory effects of restrictive laws included unions (the United Auto Workers, the Columbia Typographical Union Local 101, AFL-CIO, and the International Chemical Workers); feminists (the National Organization for Women, sociologist Cynthia Epstein, Congresswoman Martha Griffiths, and the National Woman's Party); professional organizations (the National Association of Women Lawyers, the Soroptomist Federation, and the National Federation of Business and Professional Women's Clubs, Inc.); employer associations (the Metropolitan Washington Board of Trade and the Illinois State Chamber of Commerce); and one of the state commissions on the status of women (the Delaware Governor's Commission). A smaller number of groups testified in favor of the state labor laws and urged the commission to retain its current guidelines. They included two of the old reform groups (the National Consumers League and the National Federation of Settlements and Neighborhood Centers), a union (the International Union of Electrical Workers), and the National Council of Negro Women.[52] After the hearings were over, two other labor organizations (the AFL-CIO and the International Ladies' Garment Workers) and Congressman Celler submitted pro–state labor law testimony. Groups which took a neutral stand at the hearings included another union (the United Packinghouse Workers) and three state agencies (the Wisconsin Industrial Commission, the Michigan Department of Labor, and the Missouri Commission on Human Rights).

The testimony revealed the same deep split between the two sides that had prevailed in the 1920s and 1930s. Each saw women's nature and their role in society differently; each emphasized different effects of the state labor laws.

STATEMENT OF THE INTERNATIONAL UNION, UAW
Public hearing of the Equal Employment Opportunity Commission
(Washington, D.C., May 2 and 3, 1967), pp. 2, 4-5, 9-10

The contracts we negotiate with employers provide for equal pay, equal job opportunity, equal seniority, training, etc., but I couldn't begin to estimate the number of grievances we have taken all the way to arbitration in an effort to enforce a contract only to be stymied by one or another of the so-called state "protective" laws.

Because employers have used these laws to circumvent our collective bargaining contracts and to discriminate against the women who are members of our union, the UAW has taken the position that so-called "protective" state laws — that is, those based on stereotypes as to sex rather than true biological factors — are undesirable relics of the past.

---

52. The council was also authorized to testify on behalf of the Amalgamated Meat Cutters, the American Nurses Association, Church Women United, the National Council of Catholic Women, the National Council of Jewish Women, the National Committee on Household Employment, the Amalgamated Clothing Workers, the National Association of Social Workers, the Women's Division of the Methodist Church, and the Young Women's Christian Association.

At the end of World War II and the Korean conflict we first encountered the management practice of invoking state laws in order to bypass women's job rights. During war periods, management had been more than happy to employ females in practically any capacity and to ignore these state laws. They were honored only in the breach. Yet, when men were again available, the employers resorted to the technique of combining two jobs into one so that it was beyond the state maximum weight law, or scheduling hours of work beyond the statutory limit for women in order to avoid hiring women employees. Delegates to our biennial convention in 1946 spoke out against these practices. . . .

Now what has happened since Title VII became law? More and more employers have been able to discriminate against women because of anachronistic, so-called "protective" state laws regulating the employment of women. Because of state laws and regulations limiting the weights a woman may lift, or the hours a woman may work, employers have been able to deprive women of jobs, promotions and overtime. Provisions in UAW collective bargaining contracts prohibiting discrimination and regulating seniority are avoided and evaded through employer reliance on these outmoded laws.

It has been our experience that women work because they need the money —to make a living or to supplement a too meager family income. They are entitled to the same breaks in employment as men — a chance — (1) to share equally in overtime; (2) to bid on the basis of seniority for any job they can perform and (3) to the same promotion opportunities as men.

It is axiomatic that *some* women can lift more than *some* men. So it is that *some* women can work longer hours than *some* men. In Japan, the pearl divers who dive six hours a day to depths of 40 feet or more in icy waters are almost all women because, in that culture, women are thought to be stronger than men. A nostalgic view of women may seem romantic but when that societal view, enforced by law, operates to the economic detriment of women, it is nothing more than a state operated system of discrimination.

Any law regulating weight lifting or hours of employment should affect *all* workers equally instead of being based on an arbitrary, stereotyped and prejudicial view as to the sexes. We urge that the Congress meant to supersede such state laws and we urge the Commission to adopt that view forthrightly and forcefully and to support it in appropriate court tests. . . .

We are unhappy with the EEOC's performance in this area of the law. Its lack of courage here has brought long neglected laws and regulations out of the woodwork. This Commission's interpretation of "bona fide occupational qualifications" in Section 703(e) of Title VII is too broad. The states are even worse. They pass new civil rights legislation dealing with sex and add caveats that employers may, nevertheless, discriminate if they use the cover of a discriminatory state law. It is a vicious cycle. . . .

It is a plain fact of life that the discrimination against women in the employment market is class discrimination almost as gross and as evil as race discrimination. It cannot be rectified through a faint-hearted approach. We urge the Commission to take a more positive approach to the problems presented by state "protective" legislation and to cause Title VII to have real meaning for the women of America.

We strongly recommend that the Commission:

1. Reconsider its interpretation of Congressional intent with respect to state "protective" laws to make it clear that state laws that provide an umbrella for the protection of employers who discriminate are superseded.

2. Revise its guidelines and its definition of "bona fide occupational qualification" to prohibit reliance on state "protective" laws as a means of denying employment opportunities to women.

3. Rule on the merits of cases presenting conflicts between Title VII and state "protective" legislation, particularly where the legislation contains no exceptions. . . .

7. Make clear that the only protective legislation compatible with Title VII is that

based on real biological factors, such as that dealing with maternity leaves, separate rest rooms, pregnancy, and the like.

The AFL-CIO saw the issue differently:[53]

> Historically the state labor legislation initially enacted for the benefit of women has served not only as direct protection for women, but also as a means of abating abuses for men, increasing the acceptability of legislative standards for all workers and aiding union progress in bettering the conditions of work in the face of unfair competition on the part of non-union employers seeking to maintain their position by underpaying and overworking their workers.
>
> We have a major concern that benefits available to women under state labor laws be retained and that they be extended to men to the maximum extent possible.
>
> EEOC has followed this principle of retaining and extending benefits in rulings involving several types of legislative or other benefits heretofore applying only to women, for example, minimum wages and overtime pay. It has also ruled that rest periods provided for women must similarly be provided for men.
>
> EEOC has faced a more difficult problem in types of women's legislation that protect by *prohibiting* work under certain circumstances, such as limits on weights to be lifted and absolute maximums on hours worked per day or per week. The women's hours law in California (8 hours per day and 48 hours per week) was the immediate cause of the Commission's present "hands off" policy with respect to direct conflict between "employment opportunity" (for overtime pay or promotion) and state hours law limits.
>
> Where an existing law serves a valid protective purpose but is in a form not readily appropriate for direct extension to men, our position is that such a law, benefiting significant portions of the female work force, should not be invalidated because of adverse effects on particular individuals or groups bringing charges of denial of "equal employment opportunity."

The AFL-CIO thus conceded that maximum hours and weight limit laws could not be extended to men; presumably, laws prohibiting women from doing work like bartending were also in this category, but the AFL-CIO apparently saw no reason to mention these laws. Without any further discussion of why or how laws prohibiting women from holding jobs requiring lifting weights as light as 15 pounds or from being bartenders served a "valid protective purpose" which benefited "significant portions of the female work force," it turned to more extended discussions of maximum hours laws. Its first argument was that the invalidation of maximum hours laws "would deprive many women of much needed protection in the lowest paid and least organized segments of the work force."[54] That is, since many low-paid women workers are not protected by union contracts (which often provide for lucrative overtime pay rates), the state hours laws at least keep their hours down. The testimony did not mention that the laws also keep women's salaries down — because the "protected" women are barred from collecting straight-time pay for longer hours, the premium pay which is often received for overtime hours (under union contracts, state overtime pay laws, and the Federal Fair Labor Standards Act), and the higher pay of jobs requiring overtime hours. (For further analysis of this argument, see Note: Analysis of the Maximum Hours Laws as the Primary Example of Protective Legislation, infra.)

However, recognizing that some believe FLSA overtime is sufficient protection against long hours, the AFL-CIO testimony shifted to explaining why it is not. First "[c]overage of the Fair Labor Standards Act is not universal."[55] Many women are

---

53. Statement of Andrew J. Biemiller, Director, Dep't of Legislation, AFL-CIO, Before the Equal Employment Opportunity Commission on Guidelines on Discrimination Because of Sex (June 2, 1967) p. 2.
54. Id. at 3.
55. Id. at 4.

excluded from its coverage.[56] Second, "[t]he FLSA penalty overtime requirement of time and one-half for hours worked after 40 a week does not serve as a strong protection against long work days and long work weeks."[57] Because of the cost of fringe benefits, employers now find that time and one half only costs them 20 percent more than a straight-time hour, not 50 percent more. This is cheap enough to justify working trained employees longer hours rather than hiring new workers.

Then comes the crux of the argument:[58]

> We have no evidence that women *generally* prefer extended opportunity for overtime work to a clear hours limitation, even though obviously there are a number who do. In particular, most working women with family responsibilities, whether unmarried or with husbands who help with the household work, still face a "double work" schedule — additional hours of work and responsibility in the home after the day's job is done. Except for the privileged few, this remains a current reality in American life.

Thus, although men workers are theoretically harmed by long hours (and must indeed take on more than their fair share since women are barred from doing so — thereby placing, incidentally, additional pressure on women to take on more than their fair share of household work), the maximum hours laws must be preserved so that women can fulfill their household duties!

The National Consumers League — the champion of hours laws since the early 1900s — conveyed a similar viewpoint: "While men may also require protection from overtime hours, as a group their need is less than that of women, who usually spend more time on family and home responsibilities."[59] The feminist National Organization of Women, on the other hand, thought that Title VII could be interpreted to require benefits such as minimum wage, meal periods, and seats for men. But[60]

> . . . NOW strongly opposes . . . 3 types of state laws . . . which conflict with the guarantee against sex discrimination under the Federal law, namely: laws imposing arbitrary hours restrictions, laws restricting night work and weight lifting limits, imposed only upon women workers. Such laws prevent women from being hired, promoted, transferred, and recalled to work after lay-off. In addition to excluding them from jobs, such laws on hours deprive them of earning overtime pay.

NOW focused not on women's household work, but on their role as sole or co-supporters of families. Discussing the case of Mengelkoch v. North American Aviation Co., 284 F. Supp. 950 (C.D. Cal. 1968), *appeal dismissed,* 393 U.S. 83 (1968), NOW concluded:[61]

> . . . Mrs. M and other women in suit and not, work as assembly line workers for North American and because overtime is required, they cannot be employed in better paying jobs for which they have the skills, such jobs as operating functional test equipment, final assembly work, or work as supervisor on the Assembly line. Secondly, they are denied opportunity to earn time and a half for overtime; they would like to earn extra pay to feed, clothe, and send their children to school.

56. Many men are also excluded, of course, though once again the AFL-CIO seemed to believe this unimportant.

57. AFL-CIO Statement, supra footnote 53, at 4.

58. Id. at 6.

59. Statement of Katherine P. Elickson, Committee on Labor Standards of the National Consumers League on State Labor Standards Legislation, Before the Equal Employment Opportunity Commission (May 2, 1967) p. 5.

60. Statement by Marguerite Rawalt, Legal Counsel, National Organization for Women, to Equal Employment Opportunity Commission at Public Hearings (May 2, 1967) p. 1.

61. Id. at 2.

The commission did not take immediate action once the hearings were over, but[62]

. . . on February 24, 1968 . . . rescinded the 1966 policy and reaffirmed the original 1965 guideline — that is, that the EEOC would decide whether state legislation was superseded by Title VII in cases where the effect of state law is discriminatory rather than protective. Again, "discriminatory" and "protective" were not defined, although the Commission did announce that it would consult with state authorities about the purpose and effect of the laws.

The practical effect of the announced approach was that the commission began finding "reasonable cause" in cases where women workers charged loss of employment opportunities due to the state laws. And in September 1968, the General Counsel's Office submitted a brief amicus curiae in the district court *Rosenfeld* case, arguing that California's weight and hour law was superseded by Title VII. In November 1968 the district court issued a decision upholding this position, Rosenfeld v. Southern Pacific Co., 293 F. Supp. 1219 (C.D. Cal. 1968). Armed with the first court decision on point, the EEOC finally took a momentous stand — one that would ultimately lead to the resolution of the 50-year-old reformer–feminist controversy but in favor of the feminists this time.[63]

. . . [O]n August 19, 1969, the EEOC confronted the issue head on, and issued a complete new regulation, revoking 29 U.S.C. Section 1604.1(a)(3), (b), and (c), and substituting a new subsection (b). All mention of the "benefit" type law was omitted, and it was made clear that no *prohibitory law* could now be used as a BFOQ. The new regulation reads as follows:

"(b)(1) Many states have enacted laws or promulgated administrative regulations with respect to the employment of females. Among these laws are *those which limit the employment of females,* e.g., the employment of females in certain occupations, in jobs requiring the lifting or carrying of weights exceeding certain prescribed limits, during certain hours of the night, or for more than a specified number of hours per day or per week.

"(2) The Commission believes that *such state laws and regulations, although originally promulgated for the purpose of protecting females, have ceased to be relevant to our technology or to the expanding role of the female worker in our economy.* The Commission has found that *such laws and regulations do not take into account the capacities, preferences, and abilities of individual females and tend to discriminate rather than protect.* Accordingly, the Commission has concluded that such laws and regulations conflict with Title VII of the Civil Rights Act of 1964 and will not be considered a defense to an otherwise established unlawful employment practice or as a basis for the application of the bona fide occupational qualification exception." [Emphasis added.]

(4) Summary

A few years later, both the federal courts and state law forces had accepted this view (see Note, Impact of *Rosenfeld* and of the EEOC Regulations, infra). So for all practical purposes, the era of "protective" legislation for women only has come to an end, although as materials in the previous chapter demonstrated, remnants of the controversy continue in the struggle for state ratification of the Equal Rights Amendment. Hopefully, this new view of Title VII's effect on state laws will force the social reformers to direct their energies toward truly protective legislation — to protect all workers of both sexes who labor under unhealthy conditions or for longer hours than they wish to work — rather than continuing their anachronistic anti-ERA stance.[64]

Although the controversy has finally been resolved, it is important to understand

---

62. Ross, Sex Discrimination and "Protective" Labor Legislation, supra footnote 44, at 181.

63. Id. at 181.

64. In fact, in October 1973, the AFL-CIO ended its historic anti-ERA stand by passing a resolution in favor of its passage at its annual national convention.

the reasons for its intensity and duration because the history has implications for the present. The feminists were committed first and foremost to a society formed on sexually egalitarian lines; for them, discrimination caused by single-sex labor laws was another proof of how far from equality women workers were, and the ERA was a significant step on the road toward that equality. The social reformers were committed to improving the present society, not to changing one of its fundamental divisions; for them, single-sex laws helped ease the lot of the poor women worker by helping her get home to her children, so she could be a better mother. They did not realize that this narrow view of the woman worker's problems reinforced women's lowly position in the labor market because a society rigidly divided along sex lines demanded the same hierarchy in the labor market as in the home. In all the years of the struggle to get and keep single-sex labor laws, the reformers never confronted the essential nature of sex discrimination in the labor market — sex segregation and the undervaluation of the so-called "women's jobs." Thus the reformers actually helped preserve the status quo for the woman worker — low-paid, menial jobs with no chance for advancement out of the female labor ghetto.

The contemporary lesson of the whole controversy, then, is the importance of evaluating the social ideologies that lie behind demands for legal reform, because the law in turn will affect economic and societal conditions. And this lesson has relevance to the continuing struggle for ratification of the ERA, whose opponents still — amazingly — raise the "protective" law bugaboo. The Title VII issue, however, has already been resolved, as the following materials show.

b. The Invalidation of Restrictive State Laws

Labor unions, feminists, and social reformers were not the only forces making a major issue of the effect of Title VII on the state labor laws. Verifying the feminist position, women workers — principally blue-collar workers — launched an attack on the laws because employers were using them to exclude women from better-paying jobs. The law on the issue soon became clear-cut.

ROSENFELD v. SOUTHERN PACIFIC COMPANY
444 F.2d 1219 (9th Cir. 1971)

[The Rosenfeld case raised the issue of laws restricting women's work hours and the weights they could lift. After disposing of the company's contention that the job Leah Rosenfeld wanted was too arduous for women (see that portion of *Rosenfeld* reproduced in Section B-1 supra), the court turned to the issue of the state laws.]

But the company points out that, apart from its intrinsic merit, its policy is compelled by California labor laws. One of the reasons Mrs. Rosenfeld was refused assignment to the Thermal position, and would presumably be refused assignment to like positions, is that she could not perform the tasks of such a position without placing the company in violation of California laws. Not only would the repeated lifting of weights in excess of twenty-five pounds violate the state's Industrial Welfare Order No. 9-63, but for her to lift more than fifty pounds as required by the job would violate section 1251 of the California Labor Code. Likewise, the peak-season days of over ten hours would violate section 1350 of the California Labor Code.[65]

It would appear that these state law limitations upon female labor run contrary to the general objectives of Title VII of the Civil Rights Act of 1964, as reviewed above, and are therefore, by virtue of the Supremacy Clause, supplanted by Title VII. However,

65. The court had noted earlier that "[d]uring the harvesting season, the season may require work in excess of ten hours a day and eighty hours a week," and that it was "this opportunity to earn overtime pay that made this position attractive to plaintiff. — Eds.

appellants again rely on section 703(e) and argue that since positions such as the Thermal agent-telegrapher required weight-lifting and maximum hours in excess of those permitted under the California statutes, being a man was indeed a bona fide occupational qualification. This argument assumes that Congress, having established by Title VII the policy that individuals must be judged as individuals, and not on the basis of characteristics generally attributed to racial, religious, or sex groups, was willing for this policy to be thwarted by state legislation to the contrary.

We find no basis in the statute or its legislative history for such an assumption. Section 1104 of the Act, 42 U.S.C. §2000h-4, provides that nothing contained in the Act should be construed as indicating an intent to occupy the field in which the Act operates, to the exclusion of State laws or the same subject matter, nor be construed as invalidating any provision of state law ". . . unless such provision is inconsistent with any of the purposes of this Act, or any provision thereof." This section was added to the Act to save state laws aimed at preventing or punishing discrimination, and as the quoted words indicate, not to save inconsistent state laws. (H.R. Rep. No. 914, 88th Cong., 1st Sess. [1963], additional views of Hon. George Meader).

Still more to the point is section 708 of the Act, 42 U.S.C. §2000e-7, which provides that nothing in Title VII shall be deemed to exempt or relieve any person from any liability, duty, penalty, or punishment provided by any present or future state law ". . . other than any such law which purports to require or permit the doing of any act which would be an unlawful employment practice under this title." This section was designed to preserve the effectiveness of state antidiscrimination laws (110 Cong. Rec. 7243, 12721 [1964], comments of Senators Case and Humphrey).

The Commission, created by the provisions of Title VII of the Act, through its published Guidelines and Policy Statements has, albeit after considerable hesitation, taken the position that state "protective" legislation, of the type in issue here, conflicts with the policy of non-discrimination manifested by Title VII of the Act. On August 19, 1969, the Commission revoked a portion of its Guidelines on Discrimination because of Sex, formerly appearing as 29 C.F.R. §1604.1(a)(3), (b) and (c), and inserted a new subsection (b), quoted in the margin. It is implicit in this Commission pronouncement that state labor laws inconsistent with the general objectives of the Act must be disregarded. The Supreme Court has recently observed that the administrative interpretation of the Act by the enforcing agency "is entitled to great deference." Griggs v. Duke Power Co., 401 U.S. 424, 91 S. Ct. 849, 28 L. Ed. 2d 158 (1971). . . .

We have considered the meaning which appellants would ascribe to BFOQ, as provided for in the Act. We conclude, however, that the Commission is correct in determining that BFOQ establishes a narrow exception inapplicable where, as here, employment opportunities are denied on the basis of characterizations of the physical capabilities and endurance of women, even when those characteristics are recognized in state legislation.

Under the principles set forth above, we conclude that Southern Pacific's employment policy is not excusable under the BFOQ concept or the state statutes.

NOTE: IMPACT OF ROSENFELD AND OF THE EEOC REGULATIONS

To date, the largest single source of Title VII sex discrimination litigation has been the controversy over maximum hours, weight limits, and job prohibition laws. Like the EEOC, the federal courts were initially hesitant to face the issue:[66]

In Coon v. Tingle, 277 F. Supp. 304 (N.D. Ga. 1967), the court dismissed the constitutional challenge to the Georgia law — which prohibits women from working in retail

66. Ross, supra footnote 44, at 182.

liquor stores — on procedural grounds, but implied in dictum that it would abstain on this issue in any case. In Mengelkoch v. Industrial Welfare Commission, 284 F. Supp. 950, 956 (C.D. Cal. 1968), *appeal dismissed,* 393 U.S. 83, the court actually adopted the abstention approach. The women plaintiffs were seeking an injunction against the enforcement of California's maximum hours law, but the court wanted to avoid unnecessary friction in the federal system. And in Ward v. Luttrell, 202 F. Supp. 165 (E.D. La. 1968), 14 women engineers, framemen, and telephone operators sought an injunction against the enforcement of the Louisiana maximum hours laws. The three-judge district court dismissed the constitutional equal protection and due process claims on the ground that they were unsubstantial, but remanded the case to a one-judge court for a hearing on the supremacy issue under Title VII.

However, the District Court Rosenfeld decision in December 1968 marked a turning point, and by mid-1973, the decision of the highest courts to rule on each case had found state hours, weight, and job prohibition laws invalid under Title VII. The citations are given here to show the variety of laws attacked, the kinds of work involved and the roles of the employers and labor unions that were sometimes caught in the middle. Most of the cases were class actions.

Manning v. General Motors Corp., 3 FEP cases 968 (N.D. Ohio 1971) (job prohibition, weight and hour laws; GM employees seeking jobs reserved for men), *appeal on this issue withdrawn, and aff'd on other grounds,* 466 F.2d 812 (6th Cir. 1972), *cert. denied,* 410 U.S. 946 (1973);

Ridinger v. General Motors Corp., 325 F. Supp. 1089 (S.D. Ohio 1971) (job prohibition, weight and hour laws; GM employees at the Frigidaire and Inland Manufacturing Divisions seeking overtime work and better-paying jobs), *appeal on this issue withdrawn and remanded on other grounds,* 474 F.2d 949 (6th Cir. 1972);

Rinehart v. Westinghouse Electric Corp., 3 FEP Cases 851 (N.D. Ohio 1971) (job prohibition and weight laws; Westinghouse employees laid off in favor of junior males, seeking bumping privileges, recalls, and access to jobs reserved for men);

Kober v. Westinghouse Electric Corp., 325 F. Supp. 467 (W.D. Pa. 1971) (hours law; machine operator applying for computer console operator job);

Garneau v. Raytheon Co., 323 F. Supp. 391 (D. Mass. 1971) (hours law; Class 10 precision inspectors seeking advancement to Class 6 and overtime work);

Le Blanc v. Southern Bell Tel. & Tel. Co., 333 F. Supp. 602 (E.D. La. 1971) (hours law; assignment clerk and outside plant clerk seeking promotions to test deskman position), *not appealed on this issue, and aff'd on other grounds,* 460 F.2d 1228 (5th Cir. 1972), *cert. denied,* 409 U.S. 990, (1972);

General Electric Co. v. Young, 3 FEP Cases 561 (W.D. Ky. 1971) (hours law; GE, and intervening plaintiffs, the International Union of Electrical Workers and Reynolds Metal Company, seeking right to assign overtime work and jobs requiring overtime work to women employees);

Vogel v. Trans World Airlines, 346 F. Supp. 805 (W.D. Mo. 1971) (hours law; mechanic seeking overtime work);

McCrimmon v. Daley, 2 FEP Cases 971 (N.D. Ill. 1970) (job prohibition law; barmaids seeking employment and protesting arrests for employment as barmaids in violation of ordinance and bar owners and operators arrested for employing barmaids or seeking to employ women), *on remand from* 418 F.2d 366 (7th Cir. 1969);

Local 246, Utility Workers Union v. Southern Cal. Edison Co., 320 F. Supp. 1242 (C.D. Cal. 1970) (weight and hours laws; clerk typist seeking promotion to junior clerk position);

Caterpillar Tractor Co. v. Grabiec, 317 F. Supp. 1304 (S.D. Ill. 1970) (hours law; Caterpillar Tractor and Illinois Bell seeking right to assign women to overtime work paid at premium rates and to promote and assign women to jobs requiring overtime work, as a result of complaints from female employees that they were denied same);

Richards v. Griffith Rubber Mills, 300 F. Supp. 338 (D. Ore. 1969) (weight law; stock cutter seeking promotion to press operator position);

Sail'er Inn, Inc. v. Kirby, 485 P.2d 529, 95 Cal. Rptr. 329 (1971) (job prohibition law; bar owner employing women bartenders in violation of state law seeking to prevent revocation of liquor license for said offense);

Krause v. Sacramento Inn, 479 F.2d 988 (9th Cir. 1973) (job prohibition law; woman seeking job as bartender);

Schaeffer v. San Diego Yellow Cabs, Inc. (not officially reported) (S.D. Cal. 1970 or 1971) (hours law; taxicab driver seeking to work a nine-hour day), *appeal withdrawn on this issue and reversed in part on other grounds*, 462 F.2d 1002 (9th Cir. 1972);

Jones Metal Products Co. v. Walker, 29 Ohio St. 2d 173, 281 N.E.2d 1 (1972) (hours, weight and job prohibition laws; employers seeking invalidation of laws in order to avoid Title VII lawsuits by their employees or fines and imprisonment by state authorities enforcing state laws);

Evans v. Sheraton Park Hotel, 5 FEP Cases 393 (D.D.C. 1972) (hours law; banquet waitress seeking more lucrative work assignments).

Thus, less than a decade after passage of Title VII, federal courts had invalidated the hours laws of nine jurisdictions, as well as the weight laws of three jurisdictions, and two job prohibition laws. The issue seemed so well settled that the validity of these laws was no longer raised on appeal in many cases.[67]

The laws — particularly the hours laws — were also attacked in other ways. A Labor Department report[68] indicates that by 1973, 14 states had repealed their hours laws,[69] the attorneys general of 21 jurisdictions had ruled that the laws did not apply to employers covered by Title VII,[70] 3 states had amended the laws to provide for voluntary overtime for women,[71] and 3 states had exempted employees from maximum hour coverage if they were protected by FLSA premium pay.[72] This left only one state maximum hours law — Nevada's — without major exclusions or changes in status since 1964.

And the EEOC completed its invalidation of restrictive laws by adding laws prohibiting employment before and after childbirth to this category in its March 1972 amendments to the sex discrimination guidelines. They now provide:[73]

(1) Many States have enacted laws or promulgated administrative regulations with respect to the employment of females. Among these laws are those which prohibit or limit the employment of females, e.g., the employment of females in certain occupations, in jobs requiring the lifting or carrying of weights exceeding certain prescribed limits, during certain hours of the night, for more than a specified number of hours per day or per week, *and for certain periods of time before and after childbirth.* The Commission has found that such laws and regulations do not take into account

---

67. *Manning,* supra; *Ridinger,* supra; *Le Blanc,* supra; *Schaeffer,* supra.

68. Women's Bureau, U.S. Dept. of Labor, Status of State Hours Laws For Women Since Passage of Title VII of the Civil Rights Act of 1964 (July 1, 1972), updated for the authors on August 30, 1973 by Ruth Shinn, Division of Legislation and Standards, Women's Bureau.

69. Arizona (1970), Colorado (1971), Delaware (1965), Maryland (1972), Missouri (1972), Montana (1971), Nebraska (1969), New Jersey (1971), North Carolina (1973), New York (1970), Oregon (1971), South Carolina (1972), South Dakota (1973), and Vermont (1970).

70. Arkansas (1973) (by Department of Labor), California (1971), Connecticut (1972), District of Columbia (1970), Illinois (1970), Kansas (1969) (by Commissioner of Labor), Kentucky (1972), Maine (1973), Massachusetts (1970, 1971), Michigan (1969), Minnesota (1972) (by Department of Labor), Mississippi (1969), Missouri (1971), New Hampshire (1971) (by Commissioner of Labor), North Dakota (1969), Oklahoma (1969), Pennsylvania (1969), Rhode Island (1970), South Dakota (1969), Washington (1970, 1971), and Wisconsin (1970).

71. New Mexico (1969), Texas (1971), and Utah (1973).

72. North Carolina (1967), Tennessee (1969), and Virginia (1966).

73. 29 C.F.R. §1604.2 (b)(1) (1972) (emphasis added).

the capacities, preferences, and abilities of individual females and, therefore, discriminate on the basis of sex. The Commission has concluded that such laws and regulations conflict with and are superseded by Title VII of the Civil Rights Act of 1964.

NOTE: ANALYSIS OF THE MAXIMUM HOURS LAWS AS THE PRIMARY EXAMPLE OF "PROTECTIVE" LEGISLATION

Each kind of restrictive law operated differently and posed different problems. But, though proponents and opponents often spoke generally of "protective" laws, in fact conflict frequently centered on maximum hours laws alone. One reason for the conflict was the tacit agreement that, since employers must be able to schedule overtime work, maximum hour limits could not be extended to men, unlike other protective laws. Therefore, the choice was posed as one between maximum hours laws for women only or no protection against overtime for any workers. Second, proponents of the laws made shorter hours for women a prime concern because of what they believed to be women's unique need for time to meet their family responsibilities. Opponents, on the other hand, concentrated on the discrimination suffered by women who needed the extra money for themselves and their families. They argued that if premium overtime pay adequately protected men from overwork, it should be sufficient for women, and that many women did not need the extra time at home because they could make alternative arrangements for getting household work done or had no children.

With this background, the operation of maximum hours laws and their relationship to the Fair Labor Standards Act and other overtime pay provisions can be examined. Maximum hours laws do not provide for overtime pay; they simply place a flat limit on the number of hours an employer may work an employee. In contrast, the Fair Labor Standards Act (FLSA) places no flat limit, but provides that any hours worked after 40 per week shall be paid at the premium rate of one and one half times the normal wage. State overtime pay laws (sometimes combined with the maximum hour laws) and many union contracts make the same provision, although the hours limits or premium rates may vary. Premium pay was, of course, intended to compensate for long hours, but reformers originally hoped that it would also deter employers from requiring overtime work. The theory was that employers would prefer new employees at the straight-time rate for extra work, and this would lessen overtime while spreading employment opportunity. However, the deterrent lost some of its effect as fringe benefits became a higher percentage of employment costs, because the overtime pay did not include these costs, while the base salary for new employees did. Also, overtime work requirements were often seasonal, and employers found it easier to pay trained workers overtime than to find and train new part-time workers. In addition, many employees came to desire premium pay as a fast way to increase their incomes; unions which supported maximum hours laws for women only did not publicly acknowledge this factor.

Thirty-nine out of the 42 maximum hours jurisdictions covered women alone (see footnote 44, supra). In stark contrast, premium pay was generally available to men: the FLSA covered both men and women nationwide; 14 out of the 18 state overtime pay laws covered both men and women; and since men were (and are) more heavily unionized than women, union contracts providing premium pay covered more men than women. When the maximum hours provisions are added to the overtime pay provisions, of course, the net effect is to prohibit women from earning overtime pay. A second major effect, as the case annotations show, was that an employer could bar women from any job or promotion which he defined as requiring overtime work. This could also affect women's seniority rights and thus layoffs and recalls; for example, if a job required overtime, the employer could forbid a woman to bump back into that position during layoffs, thereby forcing her layoff over that of a junior male employee. A third major effect was to force many women into moonlighting on a second job for longer hours in order to earn the amount of money they could have received in shorter hours with premium pay;[74] for the laws in specific terms generally applied to *employers,* not to women workers. Finally, even where overtime pay was not available because of state or federal law exemptions or nonunion coverage, women working under maximum hour provisions were barred from earning extra money at straight-time rates.

Of course, these effects were not uniform. The states varied wildly in the number of hours considered necessary for a woman worker's protection, and thus a woman in one state might have some access to FLSA overtime pay where her sister working the same number of hours in another state would not.[75]

Moreover, the laws often had numerous exemptions, especially for agricultural and domestic workers. Since these same workers were excluded from FLSA coverage and were generally not unionized, it seems that the lowest-paid workers of both sexes were denied both shorter hours and premium pay for long hours — an interesting commentary on the thoroughness of the reform efforts.

A California legislative background study of California's labor laws shows in detail how the system can work. First it indicated the different kinds of maximum-hour coverage:[76]

> There are two different categories of maximum hours law in California, creating 3 categories of coverage:
> (1) Those exempt from any hours limitation under either law:
>
>> (a) government employees
>> (b) agricultural employees
>> (c) household domestics
>> (d) executive, professional, and administrative employees.
>
> (2) Those covered by the "10 and 58 law," i.e., Sec. 1350.5 provides that some women workers may work up to 10 hours per day and 58 hours per week, if they are paid 1½ times their regular rate of pay for time worked over 8 hours per day and 40 hours per week. These women workers are defined as those covered by the federal Fair Labor Standards Act except those exempted from Sec. 7 [the overtime pay section]

---

74. Ellen Lewis from Illinois wrote the Civil Service Commission in 1967 complaining that:

"However, the laws should go one step further. It could help us even more, if it could abolish the 48-hour per week work law. This is quite a handicap for us now, preventing us from working much overtime that seniority and job classification makes available to women.

"In order for a woman to make enough bring home pay to support herself and her children, she finds it necessary to take a second job rather than take advantage of extra pay hours on her regular job, (the second job being just straight time pay). This second job will take more hours away from her family than overtime on her normal job, thus denying her children the supervision of their mother that is necessary to keep them off the streets and out of trouble.

"In the past 2 months where I am employed, I have been eligible for 3 double time work days. Because I am a woman, the law says "No, only 48 hours!" — so the work went to a man who was next in seniority. It made no difference that I'm raising 4 children alone.

"The cost of living does not stop for women who support themselves and/or their children after 48 hours. The price of housing is not based on 48 hours a week or whether it is a woman or a man buying or renting. The cost of operating an automobile is no less for a woman than a man. There is no differential made in the expenditures we encounter in the normal daily life — just because we are women. Why then should we be denied the means of making the wages necessary to maintain the standards for ourselves and our children in daily life that are available to men — just because we are women?

"A friend of mine was denied a position she was well qualified to fill for the reason that the job would require more than 48 hours a week. This was a good position in an office in the data processing field, but since she could only work 48 hours a week, she was forced to take a lesser paying job and then take a second job at straight time. Now she is working 70 hours a week — just to make the same salary that could have been hers for 50-55 hours a week — just because she is a woman!"

75. See the chart listing the hour limits for each state in U.S. Dep't of Labor, Women's Bureau, 1969 Handbook on Women Workers 271. State limits varied from 8 hours per day and 40 hours per week (2 states) to 10 per day and 60 per week (4 states). Common limits were "8 + 48" (16 states) and "9 + 54" (5 states).

76. Staff Report for California Legislature Assembly Commission on Labor Relations, California's Protective Laws for Women 18-19 (2d printing November 18, 1969).

of the act by either Sec. 7 or Sec. 13 of the act and those in the clothing industry —
manufacture, drycleaning, laundering or repair. In addition, employees of airlines and
railroads, while not subject to the federal act, may work the 10 and 58 also. Although
the definition is quite complicated and technical, most women covered by either hours
limitation are covered by this one, including most women working in manufacturing,
the larger retail establishments, and much of the service industry.

(3) Those covered by the "8 and 48 law," i.e., Sec. 1350 provides that any woman
worker not exempt and not subject to the "10 and 58 law" may not work over 8 hours
per day and 48 hours per week. There is no overtime pay provision, of course, because
there is no overtime permitted. This law covers hotel, motel, and restaurant employees, the clothing industry, the motion picture theater industry, the smaller retail
establishments, some of the canning industry and a few others.*

The study then explored the number of women workers in each category:[77]

Who is covered by the maximum hours limitation? Certain women workers are
not covered at all by the State's hour limitation laws:

Government employees	559,300
Agricultural workers	106,900
Household Domestics	142,300
Executive, Professional	
and Administrative†	160,926
	969,426

These 969,426 women workers who are exempt from any hours limitation under
California law, comprise 36.2% of the total female work force.

The other 63.8%, then, 1,712,674 working women, are covered by an hours
limitation. California has two different hours limitations. . . .

The Wage and Hour and Public Contracts Division of the U.S. Department of
Labor, the agency which enforces the Fair Labor Standards Act, estimates that roughly
60% of total national work force is subject to the overtime provisions of the act. Using
this estimate for convenience,[78] 1,027,604 working women in California are covered
by the "10 and 58 law" — 60% of all women covered by either law, 38.3% of the total
female work force in California.

The other hours limitation law in California prohibits any woman subject to it
from working more than 8 hours per day and 48 hours per week. Again, based on the
same estimate used above, 685,070 women are subject to this provision — 40% of all
women covered by either law and 25.5% of the total female work force.

Finally, the study explored FLSA coverage to determine the areas of overlap. The
FLSA excludes some employees under its definition section, and also exempts numerous
employees from its overtime pay requirement. As a result, most public employees, all
domestic workers, all agricultural employees and all executive, administrative, and
professional employees (among other categories) are excluded from FLSA overtime pay
coverage. Some others excluded are hotel, motel and restaurant employees, the motion
picture theater industry, small retail establishments (with an annual gross volume of

* It is the difference in coverage between these three categories which has raised a legal problem. The
judge in the *Mengelkoch* Case suggested that there is no reasonable basis for the differences, that is, no basis
related to health, safety or welfare.

77. California's Protective Laws for Women, supra footnote 76, at 33-35.

† The figure for executive, professional and administrative female employees is 6% of the total work
force. It is an arbitrary guess. The Labor Code definition is a woman " . . . engaged in work which is
predominantly intellectual, managerial, or creative; which requires exercise of discretion and independent
judgment; and for which remuneration is not less than . . . $400 per month" or "licensed or certified by the
State of California and is engaged in the practice of one of the following recognized professions: law, medicine,
dentistry, architecture, engineering or accounting." (Sec. 1352.1)

78. This is used because the "10 and 58" law coincides roughly with FLSA coverage. — Eds.

sales less than $250,000), firms which retail prepared food, and seasonal employees. This gives roughly the following result for each California category:

1. The category of women workers who were not covered by either of the California maximum hours laws were also almost entirely exempted from FLSA overtime pay coverage; that is, California allows over one third of its female labor force to work long hours, but does not require premium pay for these long hours.

2. Women workers covered by the "10 and 58" law — again, over one third of the California female labor force — were mostly workers already covered by FLSA overtime pay. These women, however, were barred from FLSA overtime pay above 58 hours per week, unlike their male peers. (It was this law that Leah Rosenfeld attacked, since she wanted the overtime work during the harvesting season which sometimes ran over 10 hours a day and 80 hours a week; see *Rosenfeld,* supra p. 239, court's footnote 6.) Overtime is measured after 8 hours per day or 40 hours per week, however — which is a slight advantage over the FLSA standard, which uses only 40 hours per week.[75]

3. Women workers covered by the "8 and 48" law were not covered by FLSA overtime pay provisions (with the exception of employees in the clothing industry). Thus, about one quarter of California's female labor force was prohibited from working long hours, but neither did they earn any FLSA or state overtime pay, even above 40 hours a week, although they might earn premium rates under union contracts or from employers who routinely provide it. (Mary Lou Schaeffer attacked this law in her effort to work the 9-hour days allowed male taxicab drivers. Schaeffer v. San Diego Yellow Cabs, Inc., 462 F.2d 1002 (9th Cir. 1972).)

Thus, the California laws were never used to extend overtime pay coverage to women workers exempted from FLSA overtime pay coverage. Instead, the state laws left many FLSA-exempt women in the same position (category one), decreased the amount of overtime pay FLSA-covered women could earn (category two), and flatly limited the number of hours the other FLSA-exempt women could work without granting overtime pay for hours above 40 (category three). The California pattern thus contradicts the pro-maximum hours legislation claim that these laws are needed precisely because they help women unprotected by the FLSA or union contracts. In fact, California law provides no "protection" in either sense of the word (a limit on hours or premium pay) for agricultural and domestic workers (category one) and fails to provide premium pay for the 8 hours of overtime work allowed employees in small businesses (category three). Although undoubtedly appreciated by some women, California's maximum hours laws do not stand careful analysis of claims about why they are needed. Similar points could doubtless be made upon close examination of the operation of maximum hours laws in other states. Thus, the supporters of these laws can be criticized for overstating their benefits, sacrificing the interests of the women workers who are discriminated against, overlooking men workers who do not want overtime labor, taking a short-range and stereotypical view of sex roles within the family, and fighting fundamental legal changes such as the Equal Rights Amendment rather than working for voluntary overtime for all workers.

On the other hand, it is important to recognize that the invalidation of maximum hours laws hurts women who do not want to work overtime, and will continue to do so until there is some form of voluntary overtime. In the fall of 1973, the successful UAW bargaining for voluntary overtime showed that this can be accomplished, thus aiding both the men and women who want to avoid overtime.

Meanwhile, nationwide statistics seem to support the proposition that maximum hours have, in fact, limited women's overtime work, and given men a greater share of it. Department of Labor surveys for several years have shown greater percentages of men workers than women on overtime. In May 1964, 32.5 percent of the male labor force

79. Of course, it is only an advantage if the employer schedules overtime on a daily basis, rather than saving it up for the sixth day of the week.

worked over 40 hours a week, while only 14.4 percent of the female labor force did. The comparable figures for May 1965 were 34.9 percent and 15.2 percent; for May 1967, 33.2 percent and 12.6 percent; for May 1969, 32 percent and 12 percent; and for May 1970, 29.4 percent and 10.5 percent.[80] Thus, over the last few years, the percentage of overtime workers for both sexes has declined.

However, for the women who do work overtime, one would at least expect that they would earn premium pay in the same proportion as men. This is not true: a smaller percentage of women overtime workers received premium pay than did men overtime workers. This is probably a reflection of the fact that more men are covered by union collective bargaining agreements than are women,[81] and that proportionately more men workers are covered by the FLSA.[82] And as we have seen in the case of California, the state laws do not operate to increase premium pay coverage for women. Thus, in May 1964, 33.2 percent of the men overtime workers received premium pay, but only 21.2 percent of the women overtime workers did; in May 1965 the comparable figures were 37.4 percent and 25.7 percent; in May 1967, 40.2 percent and 30 percent; in May 1969, 44.2 percent and 38.5 percent, and in May 1970, 42.5 percent and 34.7 percent.[83] It would appear then, that while state maximum hours laws exempt some women workers or allow them to work more than 40 hours a week, they do not bring these women up to the premium pay standards which men overtime workers get through union, FLSA, or state law coverage. It is interesting to speculate to what extent these differences in the opportunity to work overtime and to receive premium pay account for the growing disparity in the income of year-round, full-time men and women workers. See Part I-A, supra.[84]

The statistics also indicate other social patterns. The percentage of married men with wives present working overtime has always been higher than that of any other marital group,[85] thus supporting the thesis that one-sex maximum hour laws may be a force in preventing fathers from engaging in home and child care. This effect appears to be strongest for men in the age bracket of twenty-five–fifty-four, when many couples are raising children.[86] This possible effect of the laws on traditional family sex roles is seldom discussed, but ought to be examined more closely. Another item to explore is the toll of race discrimination. Both minority men and women are less likely to work overtime than white men, and minority women who work overtime are less likely to earn premium pay than are white men (although a *greater* percentage of minority men earn premium pay than do white men).[87]

The foregoing analysis can be applied to the other kinds of restrictive "protective"

80. 1964 — Wetzel, Long Hours and Premium Pay, Monthly Labor Rev., Sept. 1965, p. 3; 1965 — Wetzel, Overtime Hours and Premium Pay, May, 1965, Monthly Labor Rev., Sept. 1966, p. 976, Table 2; 1967 — Fenlon, Overtime Hours and Premium Pay, May, 1967, Monthly Labor Rev., Oct. 1969, p. 45, Table 5; 1969 and 1970 — Fenlon, Recent Trends in Overtime Hours and Premium Pay, Monthly Labor Rev., Aug. 1971, p. 34, Table 5.

81. About one fourth of all men workers belong to a union, while only one seventh of all women workers do. U.S. Dept. of Labor, Women's Bureau, 1969 Handbook on Women Workers 82.

82. In 1968, of the 11.8 million workers excluded from the coverage of the FLSA, 5.4 million were women. In other words, while women were only 37 percent of the labor force, they were 46 percent of those not covered by the FLSA. U.S. Dept. of Labor, Women's Bureau, Women in Poverty: Jobs and the Need for Jobs 5 (April 1968).

83. 1964 — Wetzel, Long Hours, supra, at 3; 1965 — Wetzel, Overtime Hours, supra, at 976, Table 2; 1967, 1969, 1970 — Fenlon, Recent Trends, supra, at 34, Table 5.

84. See also Ginzberg, Paycheck and Apron — Revolution in Womanpower, 7 Ind.Rel. 193, 196 (1968), suggesting that women's lower earnings are in part explained by the fact that "they are less likely than men to work overtime."

85. In May 1970, 32 percent of males with wives present worked overtime, while only 9.7 percent of females with husbands present did so. In contrast, among single persons only 17.4 percent of the men worked overtime and 9.4 percent of the women. For all other marital categories (e.g. married, spouse absent), 30 percent of the men worked overtime and 14.6 percent of the women. Fenlon, Recent Trends, supra, at 34, Table 5.

86. Ibid. In May 1970, 32.8 percent of these men worked overtime versus 14 percent of the men aged 20-24, and 25.3 percent of the men aged 55 and over.

87. Ibid.

laws as well. But one salient deficiency runs through all the laws — from weight limits to prohibitions on bartending, night work, and work prior to childbirth. As one of the authors of this book noted in 1969:[88]

> The reality is that such laws simply do not accomplish their aim — *real protection.* Real protection would not bar a 5 foot 10 inch woman who weighs 180 pounds from lifting 15 pounds (which will enable her to earn $1,000 more per year) nor could it force a 5 foot 4 inch man who weighs 130 pounds and has a hernia to lift 100 pounds on a regular basis. Real protection would not bar from overtime and premium pay hours a single girl who is trying to save money for college or a widow who is the sole support of two teenage sons; nor would it limit a family which prefers an arrangement whereby the father cares for his children and does not work overtime while his wife works at night, for instance, as a nurse.
>
> The point is that sex as a criterion cannot predict with sufficient accuracy who needs what protection. If injury due to lifting weights is a problem the answer is to find out what every *individual* can safely lift with modern techniques and then forbid employers to fire individuals who refuse to lift weights above that limit. If some men and some women don't want to work overtime, laws should be passed forbidding employers to fire those who refuse overtime, but those men and women who *do* want overtime pay should not be penalized because of the desires of those who do not want it. . . .
>
> In conclusion, analysis of state laws applying to women only does not support the idea that they protect women in any important way. In fact, these laws do not protect women in the one area clearly applicable to women only — maternity benefits and job security; they are ineffective in dealing with the exploitation of women through lower pay than men; they are used to discriminate against women in job, promotion, and higher-pay opportunities; and in those few areas where they might be said to have real value, they exploit men by subjecting them to bad working conditions. Even more important, the existence of these laws reflects a basic perception that all women and men are inherently different in the amount and kind of work they can do. This difference is in turn used to justify "protective" treatment — but, as should be clear from the statistics, the crucial fact in the job market today is the exploitation of women, not their protection. As long as women argue for separate protective legislation, they reinforce the idea of a crucial difference and help to insure that the exploitation based on this idea will continue. Women simply are not a monolithic class with identical physical strengths, intellectual capacities, or job motivations, any more than men are.

NOTE: THE UNION ROLE — GOOD FAITH PROTECTION OF WOMEN OR SELF-INTERESTED PROTECTION OF MEN?

Many people have questioned the union motivation in pushing for "protective" labor laws for women — both in the initial drive for the laws, and in the controversy over passage and ratification of the Equal Rights Amendment and over the Title VII BFOQ guidelines.[89] The questionable politics of the union role in the controversy over

---

88. Ross, Sex Discrimination and "Protective" Labor Legislation, supra footnote 44, at 179-180.

89. See generally Discrimination by Unions, Chapter One, I, supra. A student who conducted interviews with representatives of several major companies (such as Aluminum Company of America, General Electric, and U.S. Rubber) in 1966 and 1967 found that many of them believed the real motive behind "protective" laws was the "protection and advancement of the male's status at work. . . ." Cromer, Sex Discrimination in Private Employment: The Conflict Between the Civil Rights Act of 1964 and State Labor Laws for Women, 37-38 (unpublished M.B.A. study project, Wharton School, 1967). Even the pro–labor law Women's Bureau was forced to concede in a 1928 report that male unions sometimes sought "protective" laws to protect their own jobs:

"During the course of this study instances have been found where the desire for self-protection led craft unions to attempt by restrictive legislation to keep women from working at the trade. The instances in which "protective" state labor laws in the first half of this century has already been discussed. In the 1960s and 1970s, strong reasons existed for continuing to suspect union motivations. In this period, even more than in earlier years, unions had the resources to mount a major campaign to pass laws providing for voluntary overtime for all workers and extending benefits like a rest period and seats to men workers. This would have eliminated the discrimination of which women workers complained, while preserving better labor standards. Instead, however, the pro–labor law unions put their major energies into fighting passage and ratification of the Equal Rights Amendment, and into preserving restrictive laws under Title VII. Nor did the unions help men file lawsuits under Title VII to press for the extension of maximum hours laws to men — although men workers had readily sued for other benefits available to women, such as paid rest periods (Burns v. Rohr Corp., 4 FEP Cases 939 (S.D. Cal. 1972)); a minimum wage (Bastardo v. Warren, 20 Wage & Hour Cas. 381, 4 EPD ¶7635 (W.D. Wis. 1971)); early retirement options (Rosen v. Public Service Electric & Gas Co., 2 FEP Cases 1090 (D.N.J. 1970), *on remand from* 409 F.2d 775 (3rd Cir. 1969), Bartmess v. Drewrys U.S.A., Inc., 444 F.2d 1186 (7th Cir.), *cert. denied*, 404 U.S. 939 (1971)); parental leave (Danielson v. Board of Higher Education, 4 FEP Cases 885 (S.D.N.Y. 1972)); and "female" jobs (Diaz v. Pan American World Airways, Inc., 442 F.2d 385 (5th Cir. 1971), *cert. denied*, 404 U.S. 950 (1971) (airline steward), supra). Union members, it would appear, still thought maximum hours laws suitable for women only. And many of the major unions leading the pro–labor law fight had strange histories if they were really so pro-women. For example, the Hotel and Restaurant Employees and Bartenders' International Union figured prominently in the anti-ERA movement and testified passionately on the virtue of state labor laws for women, particularly maximum hours laws. In Senate committee hearings on the ERA, the union's vice president testified as follows.

Statement of Myra Wolfgang
Hearings on S.J. Res. 61 and S.J. Res. 231
before the Senate Comm. on the Judiciary, 91st Cong., 2d Sess. (1970)
as reprinted in 118 Cong. Rec. S4416, S4417, S4419
(daily ed. March 21, 1972)

. . . I had seen the equal rights amendment run through the House of Representatives like a herd of stampeding cattle on a discharge petition maneuver. Never have so few business and professional women been so effective and done so much harm. The hysteria created by bra-burning and other freak antics is not a justification for the action taken by the House of Representatives, not is the fear of political reprisal. Let me assure you the threat is not born of reality.

There are various kinds of protection for women workers provided by State laws and regulations. . . . It would be desirable for some of these to be extended to men, but the practical fact is that an equal rights amendment is likely to destroy the laws altogether rather than bring about coverage for both sexes. Those State laws that are

---

this motive determined legislation are three: The New York law of 1899, secured by the metal polishers, prohibiting women from operating or using machines for buffing and polishing; and the laws of Massachusetts and New York, of 1912 and 1913, respectively, regulating the work of women in core rooms. In the second and third of these the molders did not secure the exclusion of women from the core rooms, but the regulations passed in lieu of exclusion were designed, at least in New York, to have that effect. . . ."
U.S. Dep't of Labor, Women's Bureau, History of Labor Legislation for Women in Three States and Chronological Development of Labor Legislation in the United States, Bull. No. 66, p. 2 (1928). According to the 1969 Handbook on Women Workers, at 277-278, Massachusetts and New York explicitly prohibited women from working on cores or in connection with coremaking as of January 1, 1969, although the metal polishers' prohibition had apparently disappeared.

outmoded or discriminatory, should be repealed or amended and should be handled on a case-by-case basis.

I am appalled by leaders of social institutions working hand in glove with industry leaders who wish to repeal the above-mentioned laws. . . .

The chief conflict between those who support the equal rights amendment and those of us who oppose it is not whether women should be discriminated against, but what constitutes a discrimination. We, who want equal opportunities, equal pay for equal work and equal status for women, know that frequently we obtain real equality through a difference in treatment rather than identity in treatment. . . .

For an example, the passage of an hours limitation law for women provided them with a shield against obligatory overtime to permit them to carry on their life at home as wives and mothers. While all overtime should be optional for both men and women, it is absolutely mandatory that overtime for women be regulated because of her double role in our society.

At the time that State protective legislation was initiated, there were relatively few women in the labor force, yet society recognized the need to protect women workers. At present, there are more than 30 million women in the labor force. Almost 60 percent of them are married and living with their husbands. Working mothers constitute 38 percent of all working women. Obviously, the majority of women workers have domestic responsibilities, and a very substantial number of them, almost 11 million, have children under the age of 18 years. Even with the 40-hour workweek, such women — between their paid employment and their many hours of cooking, cleaning, shopping, child care and other household duties — work arduously long hours. While "the double income economy" has forced millions of women [out of the] home and into the labor force, millions more to be the sole or major breadwinners for their families, it has not released them from home and family responsibilities.

To deprive women of protective legislation, for as long as 1 second, frustrates their basic constitutional right to safety and the pursuit of happiness and denies to them the fundamental reason for their participation in a government of law.

You must understand that the overwhelming portion of women who work, need to work. They need their job and the income it produces. Where women are unorganized, and that means 85 percent or more of them, they depend solely upon their employer's understanding of their home responsibilities. In most cases, he is a man more concerned with meeting production standards than he is for his female workers' children's safety and well-being. The records are replete with his answer posted on the bulletin board: "Beginning Monday, the new schedule will be 6 A.M. to 4 P.M., Monday through Saturday" — maybe even Sunday. . . .

. . . The "take it or leave it" attitude of most employers on this matter is notorious. . . . This is especially true during periods of recession and a shrinking labor market. With unemployment on the increase, labor standards are under attack. The person who glibly states that no one has to work overtime, if they don't want to, does not understand that when there are not enough jobs to go around, people fight to keep those that are available. Thousands of women, because of economic necessity will submit to excessive hours without a law to protect them in order to keep or hold a job. Thousands will work excessive hours, particularly when they see their employers calling for the nullification of protective legislation by urging passage of the equal rights amendment. They accede to this excessive overtime or quit the job. . . .

. . . Those who have testified before the subcommittee . . . and said that if the equal rights amendment were passed, women's protective laws would "automatically be extended to men," please take note. The attorney general of Michigan . . . didn't extend the 54-hour maximum law to men. . . . He invalidated it for women as attorney generals in other States are doing. Try running a household and raising three children working under that condition, gentlemen. It may be fine for lady lawyers and it may be fine for me, I haven't got the responsibilities, but it isn't fine for the woman who is working in a laundry, in a hotel, in a restaurant, in a convalescent home, and on the assembly lines. . . .

The impact on the number of hours a woman can be worked, resulting from the attorney general's order, would be catastrophic were it not for our being in a period of business recession, but with or without a recession, the impact of the passage of the equal rights amendment will reach into endless areas of working conditions.

Wolfgang was speaking for a union with an unusual history of sex discrimination; the Bartenders had struggled long and hard to secure explicit laws preventing women from working at all as bartenders. A 1946 issue of the union's official journal, Catering Industry Employee, explored the subject in an article titled "Bartending Must Revert to Bartenders, Says the G.E.B." (April 12, 1946, pp. 4–5). The article set forth a new postwar policy of the Bartenders' General Executive Board, to revert to the prewar policy of excluding women from bartender jobs and from the union. Until 1942, the union had, from its beginning more than fifty years prior, "persistently held and proclaimed that the bartenders' work was a cloister for the male gender." This policy was abandoned in 1942, because the wartime manpower shortage required that male bartenders transfer to work needed in the war effort, thus forcing bars to hire women in order to stay in business. The union accepted women members in order to maintain control of working standards. However, with the war's conclusion, the union wanted to revert to the prewar policy. At the February 1946 meeting of the General Executive Board in Los Angeles, the board adopted a resolution proposed by International Vice-President Miller, of Kansas City. In essence, the resolution proposed that since the war emergency was over, the occupation of bartending must revert to the exclusion of women. The article concluded by pointing out that the "progressive" states of California, Ohio, and Pennsylvania had already passed anti-barmaid legislation and exhorting all members to work toward the restoration of the union's "traditional principle" that "bartending is a man's job!"

By 1949, the union policy had met great success, it was reported at the Bartenders' 32nd Convention:[90]

> There is another arena in which the politics of Prohibition affords us a means of sharpening labor's political weapons. I refer to our anti-Prohibition work in the state legislatures.
> A good illustration of this phase of our political work versus the Drys is to be found in the many efforts being made under sponsorship of our locals and state councils to gain adoption by the states of anti-barmaid laws. These we conceive as direct support to our anti-Dry position because they eliminate one of the sources of Dry propaganda activity. You will recall receiving from the International Union in December a survey in which it was revealed that 17 states have some form of law banning employment of women behind the bar, and how at the same moment the United States Supreme Court declared that such laws are quite constitutional and are not discriminatory within the meaning of the 14th Amendment. Thereupon in Arizona, New Mexico, Washington, Montana, Colorado, Missouri, Ohio, New York and perhaps other states, our people went to work to mobilize support for similar measures. In hearings before legislative committees, in the marshalling of support for these measures back home, in the buttonholing of representatives and senators, we gained invaluable experience in the techniques of political operating required to gain adoption of other laws demanded by labor as well — housing bills, health and education measures, civil rights and minimum wage and hour laws and the rest.

---

90. From report of Fred Sweet, Director, Anti-Prohibition Dept., Proceedings of the Thirty-Second General Convention of Hotel and Restaurant Employees and Bartenders International Union 54 (April 25-29, 1949).

By 1972, the union had apparently ceased pressing this particular campaign,[91] but not its practice of sex discrimination. See Evans v. Sheraton Park Hotel, 5 FEP Cases 393 (D.D.C. 1972), infra Section D-2 (holding both the Bartenders International and two sex-segregated locals jointly liable under Title VII for favoring waiters over waitresses in lucrative assignments and in maintenance of sex-segregated locals; the hotel tried to justify the sex discrimination under the local maximum hours law — the very kind of law defended so strongly by Myra Wolfgang, the Bartenders' chief spokesperson in Congress).

The Amalgamated Clothing Workers union was another defender of state "protective" legislation — and another defendant in an employment sex discrimination case. See Hodgson v. Sagner, Inc., 326 F. Supp. 371 (D.Md. 1971), infra Part III-E (holding the international and the local jointly liable with the company for illegal payment of Equal Pay back wages due its women members to its men members). The International Ladies' Garment Workers Union (ILGWU), with an 80 percent female membership, wrote to the EEOC to preserve state labor laws — on a letterhead showing 22 men and one woman on its board of directors. A commentator on union sexism notes:[92]

> Perhaps all that needs to be said about the ILGWU is that a house history of the union written in the 1940's when the union was three-fourths women is titled Tailor's Progress: The Story of a Famous Union and the Men Who Made It. The book is just what the title suggests. Page after page of biography of men leaders of the ILGWU with not more than five or six women mentioned by name.

When these concrete examples are added to the union movement's general lack of concern for women workers,[93] one is forced to conclude that while some of the union support for restrictive labor laws stemmed from a good-faith belief that women need to get home to their babies, a good part of that support was based on plain, old-fashioned sex discrimination.

In this light, it was especially interesting to note that the UAW, which had testified against state labor laws, launched a major drive in 1973 to obtain voluntary overtime for all its workers. On the other hand, the AFL-CIO, an ardent supporter of the state labor laws,[94] made no major effort on this issue. The following news stories describe the concerns of each side in the dispute over voluntary overtime, and indicate that while unions cannot win it automatically, nevertheless success is possible.

> After six weeks of talks and 14 days before a possible strike deadline, negotiations over a new contract between the United Automobile Workers and the Chrysler Corporation appeared today to have hit their first major snag — voluntary overtime.
>
> Union leaders, who have been sporting lapel buttons that read "Overtime: Ask Me, Don't Tell Me," insisted yesterday that they would sign no contract that did not free auto workers from compulsory overtime provisions. The provisions have bound many workers to their jobs seven days a week, nine or more hours a day.
>
> Today, bargainers for Chrysler said that the company was prepared to endure a strike if the union did not come up with a more acceptable form of voluntary overtime than it has so far.

91. When Wolfgang was questioned about her union's role in promoting anti-barmaid legislation, in the Hearings on S.J. Res. 61 and S.J. Res. 231, supra, she commented only that in 1952 the union president had directed all bartenders' unions to admit women to membership. Id. at 68-69. This section of Wolfgang's testimony was not reprinted in the Congressional Record.

92. Falk, Women and Unions: A Historial View, 1 Women's Rights L. Rep. 54, 58 (Spring 1973), infra Section D-1.

93. See Falk, ibid., and Chapter One, II, discussing, for example, the unions' general failure to organize women workers.

94. In October 1973 the AFL-CIO at long last reconsidered the state labor law issue, and decided to support the ERA.

Each side, in a separate news conference, said that it was sure neither party wanted a strike when the current three-year contract expires at midnight Sept. 14. Each side said that enough time remained to reach an accord. But each side also said that it saw no accommodation on voluntary overtime in the offing.

William M. O'Brien, a Chrysler vice president who has been a party to the talks, told newsmen, "I think there's going to be a strike" over voluntary overtime unless U.A.W. proposals on the issue contain two safeguards.

One safeguard, Mr. O'Brien said, would be aimed at preventing workers from using voluntary overtime as a means of banding together, staying out of work and, in effect, pulling a wildcat strike under cover of the union contact. The second safeguard would assure that production would not be interrupted because of legitimately exercised refusals to work overtime.

So far, Mr. O'Brien said, the union proposals had not fulfilled these requirements to Chrysler's satisfaction. . . .

The emergence of voluntary overtime as a major sticking point ran true to the early form of the auto talks, in which noneconomic issues were widely viewed as being paramount to economic ones.[95]

It was one of the shortest labor disputes in United Auto Workers history. While UAW members were officially on strike pending the expected ratification of their new contract, the union resolved its differences with Chrysler Corp. last week a scant 60 hours after the walkout began. The new three-year pact will probably set the pattern for settlements with Ford and General Motors; . . . . UAW president Leonard Woodcock hailed the settlement as "precedent-setting," and a GM executive said that Chrysler "gave them the store." But as fat as the contract was, a close look showed that Chrysler got as well as it gave. For example, the union compromised on its demand for voluntary overtime — which no one expected it would fully get. Under the agreement, workers cannot be forced to work more than nine hours a day or on Sundays; they are also entitled to have every third Saturday off, but they must give advance notice if they want to take the day and must not be absent from work without an excuse during the preceding five days. In addition, voluntary overtime will be suspended during new-model start-up periods and for plants on Chrysler's "critical list" of factories — for example, a plant that is the only source of an important component. Not only was the union victory a qualified one but, as a practical matter, overtime may not be a major consideration next year if car production and sales drop as predicted.[96]

c. The Extension of Beneficial State Laws To Cover Men

Women workers have not attacked every kind of state labor law. Some laws provide for a minimum wage, overtime pay, a day of rest, lunch and rest periods, or seats for women workers. As to these provisions, the EEOC hesitated even longer than over the restrictive laws in ruling on the effect of Title VII. In March 1972 it finally issued regulations declaring that such laws were not invalidated, but that employers would have to provide men with such benefits in order not to violate Title VII.[97] The advantage

---

95. Sevens, Voluntary Overtime Puts Snag in Auto Negotiations, New York Times, Sept. 3, 1973, p. 27.

96. Labor: Quick Decision, Newsweek, Oct. 1, 1973, pp. 84-85.

97. 29 C.F.R. §§1604.2(b) (3), (4), and (5) (1972). The regulations provide:

"(3) A number of States require that minimum wage and premium pay for overtime be provided for female employees. An employer will be deemed to have engaged in an unlawful employment practice if:

"(i) It refuses to hire or otherwise adversely affects the employment opportunities of female applicants or employees in order to avoid the payment of minimum wages or overtime pay required by State law; or

"(ii) It does not provide the same benefits for male employees.

of this interpretation from a constitutional law viewpoint was that it preserved the validity of state laws, while on a practical level it upheld improved labor standards. Notice that such an approach would have been impractical for restrictive laws, for it would have required employers to eliminate weightlifting, overtime, and night work — and jobs like bartender would have ceased to exist.[98]

The EEOC stand influenced the courts, as the following case demonstrates.[99]

HAYS v. POTLATCH FORESTS, INC.
465 F.2d 1081 (8th Cir. 1972)

HEANEY, Circuit Judge.

We are asked on this appeal to determine the validity of an Arkansas statute which requires the appellant, Potlatch Forests, Inc., to pay its female employees time and a half for all hours worked in excess of eight hours per day.

Potlatch is an Arkansas employer of both male and female employees, who are admittedly covered by both Title VII of the Civil Rights Act of 1964, 42 U.S.C. §2000e et seq. and by the Equal Pay Act, 29 U.S.C. §206(d). Potlatch brought this suit to have the Arkansas statute declared invalid and to have its enforcement enjoined because of the effect of the Civil Rights Act of 1964. The District Court dismissed Potlatch's complaint. Potlatch Forests, Inc. v. Hays, 318 F. Supp. 1368 (E.D. Ark. 1970).

We agree with the District Court that Congress expressly disclaimed any general preemptive intent in enacting Title VII, and that the Arkansas statute can be held invalid only if it is in conflict with the Civil Rights Act. See, 42 U.S.C. §§2000e-7 and 2000h-4.

Insofar as the Arkansas statute results in discrimination against men, we also agree with the trial court that conflict with Title VII can be avoided by requiring Potlatch to pay its male employees the same premium overtime rate which it is compelled to pay its female employees. As the trial court pointed out:

"(4) As to other kinds of sex-oriented State employment laws, such as those requiring special rest and meal periods or physical facilities for women, provision of these benefits to one sex only will be a violation of title VII. An employer will be deemed to have engaged in an unlawful employment practice if:

"(i) It refuses to hire or otherwise adversely affects the employment opportunities of female applicants or employees in order to avoid the provision of such benefits; or

"(ii) It does not provide the same benefits for male employees. If the employer can prove that business necessity precludes providing these benefits to both men and women, then the State law is in conflict with and superseded by title VII as to this employer. In this situation, the employer shall not provide such benefits to members of either sex.

"(5) Some States require that separate restrooms be provided for employees of each sex. An employer will be deemed to have engaged in an unlawful employment practice if it refuses to hire or otherwise adversely affects the employment opportunities of applicants or employees in order to avoid the provision of such restrooms for persons of that sex."

Note that an employer may have a business necessity defense for failure to provide meal or rest periods or physical facilities for all workers. 29 C.F.R. §1604.2(b) (4) (ii). The commission had in mind a situation where an employer could not comply with the State law without a very serious disruption to some industrial process, such as a continuous-line assembly operation. The commission did not consider that mere cost or inconvenience in complying would create a business necessity defense.

98. Technically, the doctrine the commission used requires it to consider what the state legislature would have intended to do had it known that a law it passed would be unconstitutional as written. Clearly it would be unreasonable for the commission to conclude that a state legislature would have eliminated bartending or all overtime work to avoid the constitutional problem. For a more thorough discussion of this doctrine, see Brown et al., The Equal Rights Amendment: A Constitutional Basis For Equal Rights For Women, 80 Yale L.J. 871, 912-920 (1971).

99. Once again, attorneys from the EEOC's General Counsel's office appeared in a trial court to argue the case for extension, without benefit of formal guidelines; and once again, the EEOC gathered courage from a court declaration of extension to issue guidelines incorporating that position.

Discrimination with respect to pay between two classes of employees can be eliminated in either one of two ways. One class can be paid more or the other class can be paid less. . . .

As far as Act 191 of 1915 [Ark. Stat. Ann. §81-601] is concerned, an employer can comply with it and with the Civil Rights Act by paying daily overtime to both men and women. . . . The Arkansas statute does not say that women must be paid more than men; it simply says that they must be paid daily overtime without making a similar requirement as to men.

While Title VII of the Civil Rights Act was not passed to raise wages generally, it certainly does not 'impede' or 'frustrate' the purpose of the Act to require an Arkansas employer to eliminate discrimination by paying its male employees more than it would pay them ordinarily in order to equalize their pay with that of women. Potlatch Forests, Inc. v. Hays, 318 F. Supp. at 1375.

In the present case, Potlatch insists that it has been paying its male employees, as well as its female employees, the same premium overtime rate. Furthermore, Potlatch has conceded that the anti-sex discrimination provisions of Title VII will compel it to continue doing so if we uphold, as we do, the validity of the Arkansas statute.

There is ample support for the position that any discrimination against men resulting from the Arkansas statute is to be cured by extending the benefits of that statute to male employees rather than holding it invalid. As the District Court pointed out, this position is in accord with the express policies of the Equal Pay Act, 29 U.S.C. §206(d)(1).[4] See, Shultz v. American Can Company–Dixie Products, 424 F.2d 356, 359 (8th Cir. 1970); Murphy v. Miller Brewing Company, 307 F. Supp. 829, 836-837 (E.D. Wis. 1969); 29 C.F.R. §§800.60 and 800.61 (1972); L. Kanowitz, Woman and the Law, 121, 147 (1969); 7 A.L.R. Fed. 707, 713, 751-753 (1971). While the Equal Pay Act is not as far reaching as Title VII, it is of considerable help in interpreting the latter act. See, Ammons v. Zia Company, 448 F.2d 117 (10th Cir. 1971); Hodgson v. Brookhaven General Hospital, 436 F.2d 719 (5th Cir. 1970); Shultz v. Wheaton Glass Company, 421 F.2d 259, 266 (3rd Cir. 1970); Kanowitz, supra at 133; 7 A.L.R. Fed. 707, 713 (1971).

Before the trial court, the Equal Employment Opportunity Commission (E.E.O.C.), appearing as amicus curiae, also took the position that the benefits of the Arkansas statute should be extended to male employees. Subsequently, the E.E.O.C. has formalized its position in its current regulations. The administrative interpretation of the Act by the E.E.O.C. is entitled to great deference. Griggs v. Duke Power Co., 401 U.S. 424, 433-434, 91 S. Ct. 849, 28 L. Ed. 2d 158 (1971); Rosenfeld v. Southern Pacific Company, 444 F.2d 1219, 1227 (9th Cir. 1971). In addition, the position of the E.E.O.C. finds support in recent scholarship. Kanowitz, supra at 120-124, 189; Developments in the Law, Employment Discrimination and Title VII of the Civil Rights Act of 1964, 84 Harv. L. Rev. 1109, 1188-1190 (1971).

In arguing that the Arkansas statute must be declared invalid, Potlatch relies on the decisions of several federal courts which have invalidated state protective statutes, regulating the number of hours women could work or the number of pounds they could lift, or prohibiting their employment in specified occupations. The invalidated statutes differ from the Arkansas statute because their effect is to prohibit the employment of all members of one sex, in certain occupations. Potlatch Forests, Inc. v. Hays, supra, 318

---

4. 29 U.S.C. §206 reads in part: "(d)(1) No employer having employees subject to any provisions of this section shall discriminate, with any establishment in which such employees are employed, between employees on the basis of sex by paying wages to employees in such establishment at a rate less than the rate at which he pays wages to employees of the opposite sex in such establishment for equal work on jobs the performance of which requires equal skill, effort, and responsibility, and which are performed under similar working conditions, except where such payment is made pursuant to (i) a seniority system; (ii) a merit system; (iii) a system which measures earnings by quantity or quality of production; or (iv) a differential based on any other factor other than sex: *Provided, That an employer who is paying a wage rate differential in violation of this subsection shall not, in order to comply with the provisions of this subsection, reduce the wage rate of any employee.*" (Emphasis added)

F. Supp. at 1373, 1375. It would place an unreasonable burden upon employers to require them to extend the "benefits" of such protective laws to both sexes. Cf., Local 189, United Papermak. & Paperwork., A.F.L.-C.I.O., CLC v. United States, 416 F.2d 980, 989 (5th Cir. 1969). See, Developments in the law, *supra* at 1186-1195; Brown, et al., The Equal Rights Amendment: A Constitutional Basis for Equal Rights for Women, 80 Yale L.J. 872, 934-936 (1971).

In this case, no such unreasonable burdens are imposed by extending the benefits of the Arkansas statute to male employees.

> The financial burden thus placed upon Potlatch may seem onerous, but federal labor legislation enacted over the last thirty odd years has placed many onerous burdens on employers. It is open to Arkansas employers generally to seek repeal of Act 191 of 1915. It is open to Potlatch as an individual employer to rearrange its working schedules so that nobody works more than eight hours a day until all employees have worked their first forty hours in a workweek. Potlatch Forests, Inc. v. Hays, *supra*, 318 F. Supp. at 1375.

Affirmed.

NOTE: OTHER CASES

To date, no other federal appellate court has ruled on this issue. Several district court opinions have been handed down, but they are conflicting and in general badly reasoned. Three cases were decided prior to issuance of the 1972 EEOC guidelines on extending certain state laws to men.[100] In Ridinger v. General Motors Corp., 325 F. Supp. 1089 (S.D. Ohio 1971), *rev'd and remanded on other grounds*, 474 F.2d 949 (6th Cir. 1972), women plaintiffs had attacked Ohio's weight, hours, and occupation laws; General Motors' defense added the issue of the validity of the state laws requiring seats, lunch periods, and a separate lunchroom for women. The court held that the latter laws were valid, partly because no one had attacked their validity (GM sought a declaratory judgment that they were valid) and partly because there was "no showing that these statutes compel a classification of employees on the basis of sex which deprives females of employment opportunities because of their sex."[101] This position accords partially with the current EEOC guidelines, but not completely since the decision did not explicitly require that GM provide men with seats and lunch periods.

In another lawsuit against the same defendants and involving the same laws, another federal court struck down all of Ohio's protective laws, without considering the differences between the weight and hours laws on one hand and the seat and lunch period laws on the other. Manning v. General Motors Corp., 3 FEP Cases 968 (N.D. Ohio 1971), *aff'd on other grounds sub nom.* Manning v. Automobile Workers, Local 913, 466 F.2d 812 (6th Cir.), *cert. denied*, 410 U.S. 946 (1973). The conflict in the district courts was not resolved on appeal, because the issue was mooted by the Ohio Supreme Court ruling declaring all the Ohio laws invalid, again without much thought about the differences between the two kinds of laws. Jones Metal Products Co. v. Walker, 29 Ohio St. 2d 173, 281 N.E.2d 1 (1972).

In the period after issuance of the EEOC guidelines, two California courts have squarely rejected extending benefits to men. Burns v. Rohr Corp., 346 F. Supp. 994 (S.D. Cal. 1972) (formal ten-minute rest periods); Homemakers, Inc. v. Division of Industrial

---

100. See also Bastardo v. Warren, 20 WH Cases 381, 4 EPD ¶7635 (W.D. Wis. 1971) (denying defendant's motion to dismiss and plaintiff's request under the Fourteenth Amendment for a permanent injunction requiring the state to provide the protection of Wisconsin's minimum wage law to men), and 332 F. Supp. 501 (W.D. Wis. 1971).

101. 325 F. Supp. at 1098.

Welfare, 356 F. Supp. 1111 (N.D. Cal. 1972) (overtime pay). *Homemakers* specifically refused to apply the EEOC guidelines — a very unusual event, given the Supreme Court's command that the guidelines are entitled to great deference, Griggs v. Duke Power Co., 401 U.S. 424, 433-434, 91 S. Ct. 849, 28 L. Ed. 2d 158, (1971). In both cases, the courts seemed most uneasy about exercising "legislative authority," although there is ample support for the doctrine that state statutes should be construed to preserve their constitutionality where possible. See Brown, Emerson, Falk, and Freedman, The Equal Rights Amendment: A Constitutional Basis for Equal Rights for Women 80 Yale L.J. 871, 912-920 (1971), supra Chapter One. Technically, where benefit laws are challenged, courts do not have to resort to this doctrine. They need only declare, as the court did in Hays v. Potlatch Forests, that there is no conflict between state and federal law, since the employer can comply with both laws by providing overtime pay, a seat, etc., to both men and women. However, if the principles of statutory construction which apply when a state statute conflicts with a federal statute or constitutional provision are used, the same result would be reached. The main question would be what result would the state legislature have chosen had it considered the conflict between the sex-based law it passed and Title VII. As to benefit laws, it seems likely that the legislature would have chosen to give benefits to both sexes rather than denying them to both. As to restrictive laws, however, it would be unreasonable to require employers to comply with both laws (framing the issue as in *Potlatch Forests*) or to extend the restrictive laws to men (framing the issue in terms of statutory construction doctrine), since this would force employers not to hire men bartenders or to eliminate overtime work. Since the legislature is presumed to wish to avoid absurd or unreasonable results, the barmaid and overtime laws are invalidated.

The *Burns* Court was also uncertain about "the characterization of the rest-break period regulation as beneficial."[102] It pointed out that

> . . . since the net effect of the regulation is to reduce the number of work hours for women by one hundred minutes per forty-hour week it would appear that it could equally well be characterized as restrictive.

On this issue, the court was correct; the benefits-restriction analysis is not an adequate theoretical justification for invalidating some laws and preserving others. However, the criterion of the feasibility of retaining the statute in altered form — as the state legislature would have analyzed the situation — is adequate, coupled with the other standards summarized by Brown et al. in the article on the ERA, 80 Yale L.J. 871 (1971). Unfortunately, the courts have not adopted that framework for resolution of the issue.

Steelworkers, Local 1104 v. U.S. Steel Corp., 4 FEP Cases 1103 (N.D. Ohio 1972), *aff'd*, 479 F.2d 1255 (6th Cir. 1973), another case from the Northern District of Ohio, involved the application of Ohio's lunch break law to defeat women workers' claims for back pay under Title VII. The state law required that women receive an uninterrupted thirty-minute lunch break. Although in fact most men workers had an uninterrupted thirty-minute lunch break, some of them were occasionally called away from their lunches to work, after which they were allowed to return and finish their lunches. The company paid all the women for seven and one half hours a day while paying all the men for eight hours a day, because the men's break could be interrupted, regardless of whether or not individual men actually had uninterrupted thirty-minute lunch breaks. A few months after the EEOC ruled that Title VII preempted the state law in question, the state official responsible for enforcing the lunch break law announced that employers would no longer be prosecuted for violations thereof, and the company announced that "female employees will be provided the same hours of work and pay as is provided similarly placed and qualified male employees."[103] In denying the women workers' claim

102. 346 F. Supp. at 997.
103. 4 FEP Cases at 1111.

for back pay during the period that the state law was enforced, the court upheld the company's defense of good faith reliance on state law. The Sixth Circuit Court of Appeals affirmed in a brief opinion on the grounds that the district court had not abused its discretion.

The reasoning of the court throughout the decision is extremely weak. First, the court did not fully consider the possibility that the company could have extended the benefit of uninterrupted lunch periods to men workers. Under the EEOC guidelines, state laws providing benefits are invalid only if business necessity precludes their extension. In *Steelworkers,* the court did not require U.S. Steel to prove that there was a business necessity for men to be on call during lunch. From the facts in the opinion, it appears that the few occasions on which men's lunch breaks were interrupted could have been handled by a split shift for lunch, so that at least some workers in each job would be on call at all times. Second, the court discounted the fact that all men were paid during their lunch hour every day, whether or not they were interrupted. The court's position was that an interruptible lunch period is materially different from one that cannot be interrupted, whether or not interruptions actually occur, but there was no evidence on this point, and it appeared that the lunch breaks of many male workers were seldom if ever interrupted. The court also contended that the company could not "equitably" guarantee uninterrupted lunch breaks to some men while denying such privileges to others, or grant thirty-minute lunch periods to some and twenty-minute lunch periods to others. It would seem that the extra pay provided those who had interruptible lunch breaks (if it was not possible to solve the problem with split shifts) would be sufficient compensation for the different treatment. The opinion also does not explain why female and male workers who in fact take the same lunch breaks can be treated differently, but male workers must all be treated the same.

The company's defense of good faith reliance on state law is also untenable. The company could certainly have paid women for their lunch breaks without risking prosecution under state law, which required only that lunch breaks be granted, not that they be breaks without pay. While the company could argue that paying women for uninterrupted lunch breaks would have opened it to charges of Title VII violation, since men's lunch breaks were interruptible, a court faced with a Title VII suit would presumably have looked past the official policy to the fact that the vast majority of the men were not interrupted most of the time. If the court found any liability under Title VII on that set of facts, it would certainly have been less (because of the small number of workers involved) than the back pay liability which should rightly have been imposed on the company as the result of its denial of pay for lunch breaks to women workers.

All of the above problems with the *Steelworkers* opinion suggest that these issues may not have been properly litigated by plaintiffs. The case also illustrates another important fact about state protective legislation: even benefit laws are as often used to discriminate against women workers as to benefit them. In fact, the union contract for the men on this issue was much better than the state law "protecting" women. In light of the pattern of facts in this and other "benefit" cases, how important is the issue of extension versus invalidation of state protective law under Title VII? One reason it is significant is that it provides a model for how courts can handle conflicts between state laws and the Equal Rights Amendment, and in some of those areas, the availability of the remedy of extension is important. A second possible reason is that extension benefits workers who are not protected by union contracts. Since extension eliminates the problem of sex discrimination — regardless of whether the "benefit" under the challenged law has in fact previously inured to the benefit of women workers or to the benefit of men workers — lawyers should continue to seek this remedy. However, the cases will have to be litigated more carefully if the issue is to be pursued, or the result will be more bad law.

4. Specific Policies

a. AT&T: A Study in Sex Segregation

Section B-1, Standards for Measuring the BFOQ, has already pointed out that most BFOQ cases deal with openly sex-segregated job categories. The cases to date, however, have not used the term "sex segregation" when discussing the problem of the exclusion of women from one job, nor have they explored to what extent segregation is carried out throughout entire companies. The following materials represent the first case in which the sex segregation of an entire company was thoroughly explored.

In the fall of 1970, the Equal Employment Opportunity Commission started proceedings before the Federal Communications Commission against the American Telephone and Telegraph Company, which had just petitioned the FCC for an increase in long-distance telephone rates. The EEOC opposed the rate increase because of AT&T's "pervasive, system-wide, and blatantly unlawful discrimination in employment against women, blacks, Spanish-surnamed Americans, and other minorities."[104] Given this discrimination, the EEOC contended that granting a rate increase would violate numerous federal laws and the United States Constitution.

In response, the FCC scheduled a separate hearing on AT&T's employment practices. The EEOC established a special task force which began a year-long process of compiling statistics on AT&T employment patterns and analyzing company documents and policies. The following excerpt is taken from the EEOC Prehearing Analysis and Summary of Evidence, an EEOC summary of what it considered the salient features of AT&T discrimination. Only Chapter 2, detailing the statistics of segregation, is given here; the entire report is well worth reading for its across-the-board analysis of a major company's employment policies.[105]

EEOC PREHEARING ANALYSIS AND SUMMARY OF EVIDENCE,
A UNIQUE COMPETENCE, A STUDY OF EQUAL
EMPLOYMENT OPPORTUNITY IN THE BELL SYSTEM
In the Matter of Petitions filed by the Equal Employment Opportunity
Commission Before the Federal Communications Commission
Docket No. 19143, 32-64 (1972)

INTRODUCTION

Not only is the Bell System the nation's largest private employer, it is far and away the largest employer of women. Females, moreover, are employed in the Bell System at a much greater rate than in industry in general. It has become a cliche that the telephone company is "a good place" for a young girl to get a job.

In this chapter we will see the total sex segregation of the telephone company jobs and the resulting lower pay, poor working conditions, and fewer opportunities afforded to females. . . .

In 1968, when AT&T Vice President Walter Straley spoke of the Bell System's "unique competence to play a leading role in the improvement of employment opportunity," he referred, myopically, only to "disadvantaged minorities." If such a unique competence did in fact exist, it ought to apply with even greater force to women. But in 1971 it must be said that the System has failed to meet the challenge; the Bell companies must be characterized as uniquely *in*competent. Although women continue

104. Petition for Intervention at 1, EEOC v. American Telephone & Telegraph Co., Docket No. 19143 (Federal Communications Commission Dec. 10, 1970).
105. It is reprinted in the Congressional Record for Feb. 17, 1972 at pages E1243-E1272.

to be employed in very large numbers, they are confined to the most stifling and repetitive jobs. Their compensation is so meager as to make them doubt their own self worth. Their prospects for promotion are in the distant future, if at all. It is little wonder, therefore, that many women flee from telephone jobs almost as quickly as they are attracted to them.

EMMA NUTT TO THE PRESENT — NOT A VERY LONG WAY

The infant Bell companies, like most of their contemporaries in the 19th century, employed only males. Male Operators, however, were considered to be "noisy, boisterous and often rude to subscribers." As a bold experiment, the Telephone Dispatch Company (the predecessor of New England Tel.) employed Emma Nutt as the first female Operator in September, 1878.

The experiment proved to be quite a "success." Women very quickly took over the Operator's job and began to expand their areas of interest into what were then considered strictly male jobs. Female secretaries were employed "because girls would work for a third of the going $30-a-week salary for a male secretary." Ms. Nutt, having pioneered in the Operator's job, set the pace for telephone women by advancing to Chief Operator, the first supervisory job for women, in 1883, and retiring after 33 years of service.

The number of female employees grew with the rapid expansion of the telephone industry in the 20th century. They were limited, however, to a narrow spectrum of positions in the male dominated world of work. The jobs available to women remained those which were opened experimentally over 90 years ago. Operator and clerical jobs, together with their immediate supervisors, came to be reserved exclusively for females. Whole sections of the Bell System became the women's domain, "where men are managers, customers or husbands." By 1971 more than 400,000 women worked in the Bell System, thus constituting more than half of all operating company employees.

THE SEGREGATION OF JOBS

By way of introduction to sex segregation in the Bell System, it is instructive to examine the myriad of official company documents which deal with employment and employees. A total sex segregation of jobs is reflected in virtually all such Bell System documents. Through pictures of males or females, pronoun reference or through straight-forward identification, all jobs are strictly classified as either male or female. This sex denotation of jobs is carried consistently throughout company personnel manuals, collective bargaining agreements, job descriptions, company publications, general company advertisements, requisitions for employees, forms relating to employment, memoranda and letters, speeches, bill inserts, turn-over studies, testing studies, orientation materials, interviewer's aids, training manuals, community wage studies, award programs, annual reports, and even reports on affirmative action efforts to improve employment of minorities.

These documents unequivocally identify the following jobs as female: Operator, Plant and Accounting Department clerical jobs, Service Representative, inside sales jobs in the Commercial and Marketing Departments, and first level management jobs in the Traffic and Commercial Departments. Craft jobs, outside sales jobs, and middle and upper level management jobs are always identified as male jobs.[106]

---

106. Chapter 1 of the EEOC report described "The Bell System, its major departments, major jobs, and their functions, wage rates, and characteristics." A Unique Competence at 1. Readers interested in these details should consult the Congressional Record reprint. The major features are summarized at the end of Chapter 1 as follows:

" — The Bell System is the largest private employer in the world with over half its work force located in 30 major SMSA's [Standard Metropolitan Statistical Area].

" — Bell employees are divided into five major departments, the largest of which are Plant and Traffic. More than two-thirds of all Bell employees are in these two departments.

" — There are four major types of non-management jobs in the Bell System: (1) craft workers in the Plant

Public image. The rigid differentiation between the sexes in employment at Bell has become a trade mark of the System. The Operator's job in particular has come to be recognized by almost everyone as especially suited to women. The telephone company has been described in the press as "the great historical bastion of feminine employment" and the Operator's job as "a female stronghold" of long standing. A newspaper article in February, 1971, reported that, "The idea that Telephone Operators are — must be — women is firmly planted into the public mind." Similarly, the public conceives of all craft workers and all managers as being male. The public's close identification of females with Operators and males with craft workers and management is no accident. It is the direct result of a calculated System-wide sex segregation.

Only when one sex is totally unavailable for work has Bell resorted to "opposite sex" employment. During World War II women replaced men on most inside craft jobs, particularly Frameman. During strikes and service emergencies men have staffed the Operator's switchboards. These instances were certainly the exceptions, however, and as soon as the crisis had passed, the "normal" sex again took over the job.

A UNIFORM PICTURE

Perhaps the most striking feature of the Bell System's sex segregation is its absolute uniformity. All the operating companies are apparently subject to an immutable law of sex segregation in almost all jobs. The same jobs are allocated to the same sex in every company with the same result — women are consistently locked into the lowest paying jobs with practically no prospect for upward mobility, regardless of their skill or ambition. Every city, irrespective of its size or geographical location, reflects the same segregation. Minor variations only serve to highlight the pervasive pattern throughout the Bell System.

This consistency is most apparent in the degree to which the major jobs are sex segregated in the operating companies. For the purposes of this report, any major job (a job employing 20 or more persons) that is 90% one sex or the other will be considered to be sexually identifiable and segregated. In the 30 SMSA's, 92.4% of all employees in major job classifications are in sex-segregated jobs. (See Table [2-2].) There are no cities which may be categorized as "good" on this index. In New York City, the city with the least segregation, 86.0% of all employees are in classifications in which one sex is 90% predominant. An even more distressing statistic is the fact that in the 30 SMSA's, 54% of all employees in major job classifications are in *100%* sex-segregated jobs. In seven of the 30 SMSA's *all* of the 25 largest jobs are readily identifiable as belonging to one sex or the other. At least 21 of the 25 largest jobs are segregated in every one of the SMSA's.

Departmental segregation. Because virtually all jobs are sex segregated, whole departments may be designated as male or female in all the companies. Almost half of all females employed in the 30 SMSA's are in the Traffic Department while less than two

---

Department; (2) clerical workers in the Plant and Accounting Departments; (3) Operators in the Traffic Department; and (4) Service Representatives in the Commercial Department.

" — Operator is the lowest-paying major job in the Bell System, closely followed by the clerical positions. Service Representatives are moderately well paid, but the highest-paying non-management jobs are craft jobs in the Plant Department. In fact, craft wages exceed the pay of many first level management jobs.

" — The Operator's job is the least desirable major job in the System, largely because of the extremely undesirable working conditions. Consequently, turnover rates among Operators are quite high.

" — Virtually all of the 200,000 persons hired each year possess little or no skills and are completely trained within the System. The high turnover significantly magnifies recruiting and training costs.

" — Nearly one-fourth of all Bell employees are classified as management. A very large share of these are in the Plant Department.

" — Management personnel for third level and above in all departments are drawn primarily from craft employees or from college graduates hired into the IMDP [Initial Management Development Program] program. Other college graduates are hired into first level management jobs." Id. at 28-30. — Eds.

TABLE [2-2]. SEX SEGREGATION OF JOBS WITH 20 OR MORE EMPLOYEES,
by SMSA, December 31, 1970

Standard Metropolitan Statistical Area	Percent of All Employees in 100% Sex Segregated Jobs	Percent of All Employees in 90% Sex Segregated Jobs
Atlanta	79.8	92.7
Baltimore	61.9	96.3
Birmingham	91.7	92.7
Chicago	36.9	90.0
Cleveland	57.3	95.9
Dallas	81.0	99.2
Denver	58.6	94.4
Detroit	75.1	97.7
El Paso	96.0	100.0
Greensboro	97.7	97.7
Houston	83.1	97.9
Indianapolis	79.4	95.3
Jacksonville	83.6	96.3
Kansas City	87.1	99.3
Los Angeles	27.3	94.7
Memphis	82.2	93.9
Miami	72.0	92.2
Mobile	100.0	100.0
New Orleans	95.2	96.6
New York	38.6	86.7
Newark	74.6	88.7
Norfolk	91.4	100.0
Philadelphia	84.2	95.0
Phoenix	73.9	95.3
Richmond	50.5	91.8
St. Louis	77.1	95.3
San Antonio	96.3	100.0
San Diego	54.1	96.0
San Francisco	27.9	92.5
Washington	58.4	92.9
Total (30 SMSA's)	53.9	92.4

Source: EEOC C-661–EEOC C-690.

percent of all males are assigned to that Department. The Traffic Department has been appropriately described by Bell officials as a "nunnery."[107] In contrast, three-fourths of all males are employed in the Plant Department, but only one-eighth of all females. . . . Graphic and statistical presentations of the sex composition of all departments for each of the 30 SMSA's have been prepared.

Those data very clearly show the sex-segregated nature of all major departments in every location.

The concentration of females in Traffic and males in Plant has two immediate implications. First, because the wages in the Plant Department are much higher than in the Traffic Department, males make more money. Second, the opportunities for promotion within non-management, into management and within management are infinitely better in Plant and, therefore, for males. Later sections will quantify both the wage and promotional disadvantage suffered by women in the Bell System. First, however, a

107. 97.3 percent of Traffic Department employees are female. A Unique Competence, supra, Chart 4. — Eds.

detailed examination will be made of the specific jobs which are sex segregated. [See Table 2-3.]

TABLE [2-3]. SUMMARY OF FEMALE PARTICIPATION IN THE BELL SYSTEM, December 31, 1970

	Total Employment		Female Employment		Percent Female	
Officials and Managers	88,301		36,295		41.1	
Professionals	58,756		12,051		20.5	
Technicians	4,791		3,052		63.7	
Sales Workers	12,113		3,168		26.2	
Mgmt.		5,814		661		11.4
Non-mgmt.		6,299		2,507		39.8
Office and Clerical	359,119		348,071		96.9	
Secretaries (Mgmt.)		4,929		4,919		99.8
Clerical and Stenog.		141,394		131,677		93.1
Telephone Operators		165,372		165,148		99.9
Supvs./Serv. Assts.		13,440		13,437		100.0
Service Repres.		33,093		32,740		98.9
Other Bus. Off. Empls.		891		150		16.8
Craft Workers	192,328		2,120		1.1	
Operatives	7,437		119		1.6	
Service Workers	9,605		4,648		48.4	
Total	732,450		409,524		55.9	

Source: EEOC W-659

THE MAJOR FEMALE NON-MANAGEMENT JOBS

Nationwide, eight out of ten female employees are in three major groups of jobs: Operator (40% of all female employees), Service Representative (8% of all female employees), and clerical and stenographic (32% of all female employees). For almost a century the Bell companies have considered these jobs to be reserved for females.

Operator. At the end of 1970, the operating companies employed over 165,000 Operators, but only 224 (0.1%) were male. Were it not for the token effort of Pacific Tel. there would be almost none. Twelve companies have no male Operators.

Service Representative. Bell's recruitment literature says of the Service Representative, "She is the telephone Company." This is a particularly apt description since 99% of all Service Representatives are females. Five companies have *no* male Service Representatives. In only two companies and four of the surveyed SMSA's does the percentage of male Service Representatives exceed one percent. . . .

Clerical. The third major "female" job group is clerical. In the operating companies 93% of these low-paying jobs are held by women. Although 7% of these jobs are held by men, it should not be assumed that these are the same clerical jobs held by females. Consistent with the over all pattern, most companies reserve a certain few clerical jobs — Utility Clerk, Construction Clerk, etc. — for males. These classifications are usually paid more than "female" clerical jobs. In every SMSA almost all clerical jobs continue to be identifiable as "women's" jobs.

Inside sales. A fourth "female" job group, somewhat smaller than the three discussed above, illustrates the Bell System's segregation of even functionally-related jobs. As observed in Chapter 1, there are two basic categories of sales jobs — inside sales which handles smaller equipment and advertising orders and outside sales which contracts for major customer purchases. Despite the functional relationship between the jobs, they continue to be distinguishable by the sex of the incumbents. Of 1369 inside sales workers in the 30 SMSA's, 95.2% are females; of 4000 outside sales workers, only 8.1% are females. . . . In 1971 Southwestern Bell continues to designate its inside sales workers "Telephone Saleswomen."

In short, in 1971 almost every major low-paying job in the Bell System is a "female" job. The introductory description of low-paying jobs (Operator, clerical jobs in Plant and Accounting, Service Representative and inside sales jobs) is also a perfect description of jobs which are almost totally female. The fact that exactly the same jobs are female in city after city and company after company is obviously the result of System policy. The fact that these jobs are also the lowest paying jobs everywhere in the System is also no accident. The contrary situation exists, of course, with respect to the jobs which the Bell System has allocated to males. These jobs are discussed below.

THE MAJOR MALE NON-MANAGEMENT JOBS

One-fourth of the operating company employees are in telephone craft positions. Except for the upper level management jobs, these classifications are the most desirable in the System. Not only is the pay a great deal higher and the opportunity for promotion much greater, the job itself is much more challenging and satisfying than the Operator and clerical jobs.

These more attractive craft jobs have never been open to females on the same basis as males. Prior to the effective date of Title VII of the Civil Rights Act of 1964, there were virtually no females in any of the telephone crafts. In 1966 *only three companies* (New England Tel., Ohio Bell and Michigan Bell) employed *any* females in craft jobs.

The passage of Title VII has not, however, been a significant spur to the utilization of females in the telephone crafts. In 1971, although all the companies had at least one female craft worker, in only five companies did the proportion of female craft workers exceed 1%.

Two observations make this gross underutilization particularly distressing. First, it should be recalled that since the Bell System trains for every job, the absence of female craft workers cannot possibly be explained by the lack of "qualified applicants."

Second, each Bell company employed females in craft jobs at a rate far below that of other companies in its area. . . . In 1971, only Michigan Bell managed to employ female craft workers at a rate greater than area employers. In most of the operating companies, females are employed in the crafts at a rate only 10-15% of the area all-industries rate.

Of 190,000 telephone craft workers in the operating companies at the end of 1970, 99% were male. The "outside" crafts (Lineman, Installer-Repairman, PBX Installer-Repairman and Cable Splicer) were virtually 100% male. In the 30 surveyed SMSA's there were only nine females in outside crafts (three Repairmen, one Installer-Repairman, one Transmission Man, one Installer, two Station Installers and one Cable Splicer). . . .

The Bell System's employment of women in the "inside" crafts (Frameman, Switchman and Test Deskman) is hardly better; all are substantially sex segregated.

Michigan Frameworkers. The Frameman classification is a particularly interesting case study of the Bell System's penchant for classifying *every* job by sex. Prior to 1965 only one company, Michigan Bell, employed women in Framework. At Michigan Bell this classification, titled Switchroom Helper, was *totally* female and had been so for at least 20 years. The job was treated in every respect as a "female" *clerical*-type job. The "female" (clerical) test battery was administered to applicants; applicants were required to be between 5'3" and 5'10" tall; the rate of pay was within the clerical range rather than the craft range; promotional opportunities were into lateral clerical jobs rather than to higher-rated crafts or management. The Switchroom Helper's job, though craft in function and identical to the all-male Frameman's job in other companies, was typed in every way as a female classification by Michigan Bell.

After 1965, some companies (though by no means all) realized that females could no longer be excluded from the Frameman's job. . . . Southern Bell and South Central Bell, to a limited extent, began what amounts to a conversion of a "male" job into a "female" job. By the end of 1970, over 60% of the Framemen in Atlanta, Birmingham and Greensboro/Winston-Salem were "Framedames." The evidence also tends to show that the rate of pay for Framework relative to other crafts also began to reflect its "female" designation in these companies.

In January, 1970, Illinois Bell gave serious consideration to "an all female Frame force similar to Michigan Bell." They concluded, however, that their "hiring problems [among males] were not so critical that they should break toward an all female Frame force." Illinois Bell observed, nevertheless, that, "The Michigan people do still believe this is the way to go."

Most other companies, despite the examples in Michigan Bell and Southern Bell, continued to defend the male craft fortress. At the end of 1970, there were no female Framemen in six SMSA's, and less than 5% of all Framemen were female in eight other SMSA's. Despite the fact that Framemen in some cities were all female, only 12% of all Framemen in the 30 SMSA's were female.

The other major inside craft jobs continue to be exclusively male with little indication of any female participation to date. The Switchman classification was only 0.6% female at the end of 1970. Eleven of the 30 SMSA's had no female Switchmen. Females were similarly excluded from the Test Deskman's position, comprising only 1.7% of all employees in that position. In New York, for instance, of 1600 Deskmen, none were female.

In summary, on December 31, 1970, virtually all craft jobs in the Bell System were held by males. Outside craft positions were exclusively male. Females had entered only one inside craft job, Frameman, and that only very selectively. As noted before, males held 92% of the outside sales jobs.

Thus, the description of the sex composition of major Bell System non-management jobs comes full circle. All low-paying, high-turnover, dead-end jobs are female. High-paying, desirable jobs with substantial chances for promotion to middle and upper management are male. It is no surprise, therefore, to find very few females in management jobs above the first level. The following section describes this exclusion from management.

FEMALES AND MALES IN MANAGEMENT

The exclusion of females from Plant craft positions and their concentration in the Traffic Operator's job has serious implications for their respective opportunities for promotion into management. . . . [T]he chance for promotion into management within the Plant Department is twice as great as the chance for promotion to management in the Traffic Department. In the operating companies a woman's chances of reaching management are approximately one in eight while a man's chances are one in three. . . . The chances for a male to reach management are thus consistently two or three times the chances for a female.

Even these statistics, however, exaggerate a female's potential for achieving positions of responsibility and commensurate compensation. Of all male managers in the 30 SMSA's, 45% are in management level two or above; a meager 6.3% of all female managers have progressed above the initial plateau of management. . . . Even fewer females make it to the highest levels. Of 2650 employees above third level management in the 30 SMSA's, only 31 (1.2%) were female.

Most staggering are the departmental management figures. . . . [M]ost middle and upper level Bell System managers in all departments are either promoted up from craft jobs in the Plant Department or hired directly into management through the IMDP [Initial Management Development Program]. Chart 7 [not reproduced here] records the effect of this Bell System policy on the chances of women being promoted to middle management. It is almost inconceivable that in the 30 SMSA's, 99.6% of all non-management employees in Traffic are females, 92.4% of all first level managers in Traffic are female, but only 25.3% of all managers in levels two through five are female. Equally staggering disparities exist in the Commercial and Accounting Departments. It is now clear that in Traffic, Commercial, and Accounting, "men are managers, customers, or husbands." Females fill virtually all low-level jobs but are shut out of management jobs above the first level. For women, the Bell System's fabled "up from the ranks" promotion policy is the height of hypocrisy.

Even the law has not been a significant stimulus to promotion of women within management levels at the Bell System. After examining the distribution of women in management levels for the period between 1966 and 1969, AT&T's task force on women concluded in August, 1970, that,

> Movement during this four year period has been quite slow; for all practical purposes, the only change has been a slight increase in second level jobs held by women.

Staff roles. Moreover, within management levels, females find themselves confined to staff positions and not in the mainstream of management. For instance, 9.1% of all females in management (as defined by the operating companies) are classified as Secretaries, a position that would not be considered management in almost any other context.

Those females in more traditional management jobs are still confined to advisory, support positions. Of the 31 females above District level in the surveyed cities, only three are located in the operating departments. The others fill legal, medical or other specialized support roles. This same finding was emphasized in the report of the AT&T task force on women.

> Only a few of the District and above women managers are *functioning* in line management jobs. The job titles of the vast majority of these managers, regardless of department, indicate either a specialist assignment or a staff role. The few women that do progress in management, do not move into the general management mainstream.

The Bell System's failure to promote females must be classed as one of the most monumental inequities in private industry. Even so, AT&T Chairman of the Board, H. I. Romnes, on December 11, 1970, labeling as "outrageous" the EEOC's charges of "pervasive, system-wide" discrimination against women, stated that the Bell System "recruits, hires, assigns and promotes without discrimination." Romnes reported that females make up 33.5% of the System's managers and professionals. The hollowness of these statements is self-evident.

FEMALE AND MALE WAGES

Although by 1971 all the operating companies had ceased to officially label wage schedules as male or female, the total segregation of jobs had the same inevitable effect. This is not a case of unequal pay for equal work. Females are paid less because they are excluded from all jobs classified at a higher wage.

In the 30 SMSA's, 80% of all female employees are in classifications whose maximum basic annual wage is less than $7000; only 4% of all males are in such classifications. . . . At the more lucrative end of the scale the differences are equally disparate. While 34% of all males are in classifications with a maximum annual salary of at least $13,000, only 3% of all females are so situated.[108] The chance that a female will earn over $13,000 per year is less than one-tenth that of her male counterpart.

---

108. The percentages based on total number of employees are similar: 96.1 percent of all employees earning less than $7000 a year are women; and 89.5 percent of all employees earning more than $13,000 a year are men. A Unique Competence, supra, Chart 8. — Eds.

Furthermore, males begin at higher wages than females and continue to maintain a greater wage throughout their tenure in the Bell System. The average maximum wage for males in entry level jobs in the 30 SMSA's was $8,613; the average maximum wage for beginning females was $6,114 or only 71% of the male wage. A female in first level management averages $11,194. Should she compare herself to a male in first level management, she would discover that her wage is only 79% of his. When measured in terms of total "occupational position," females' wages were only 75% of the average wage for all employees and only 60% of the average wage of male employees. . . .

By any standard, the exclusion of females from craft jobs and middle and upper management positions is tragic. The psychological toll is incalculable. The toll in turn-over is fantastic. The loss in wages is astronomical. The conclusion is inescapable that, in terms of providing equality of opportunity for females, the Bell System has been uniquely *in*competent.

NOTE: AT&T'S BFOQ CLAIMS

Chapter 3 of the Prehearing Analysis and Summary of Evidence explores the various BFOQ claims made by different operating companies (these are the companies that actually supply telephone services; AT&T owns or has the majority stock in all of them, and thus controls all of them). This overview of an entire system of companies, all controlled by one nationwide corporation, provides a fascinating insight into BFOQ claims, because while the companies offered different and conflicting BFOQ rationales, the invariable result of each claim was maintenance of the sex segregation of jobs. The conflicting claims showed up particularly in the BFOQ claims based on state labor laws, because different laws governed different companies. Eight companies could not use the state laws to exclude women from craft jobs because either there was no applicable law or the law specifically excluded telephone company operations. However, these companies excluded women just as completely from craft jobs as did the twelve companies that were able to rely upon the state laws. The EEOC sums up the reactions of the companies which used the state laws:[109]

> *Challenging state laws.* There were four major reactions to the apparent conflict between state and federal law. First, Mountain Bell and Illinois Bell made a frontal [and successful] attack on the state law's validity, but only after they had been found in violation of either state or federal civil rights laws. In December, 1966, Mountain Bell challenged the Arizona protective law as "archaic" and in conflict with state and federal anti-discrimination laws. In June, 1968, the offending Arizona statute was revised to eliminate the conflict with Title VII. Similar laws existed in Utah, Montana, New Mexico and Texas, but the Company made no effort to have them removed by the courts. . . .
>
> *Exemptions from state law.* A second alternative was pursued by Bell of Pa., which sought exemptions from the state law for the classifications of Facilities Assigner and Frameman. The exemption was granted by the Pennsylvania Bureau of Labor Standards in March, 1968, for *all jobs* in Philadelphia and not just those for which exemption was sought. Unaccountably, the Company continued to rely on the state law. Even though they had a legal exemption, they continued to exclude women from other inside and outside crafts until January, 1970. Similar exemptions were allowed in other states, but they were not applied for by the Bell companies. . . .
>
> *Restriction of overtime.* A third major policy toward state protective laws was adopted by Southwestern Bell, Pacific Tel. (Frameman only), Ohio Bell (Frameman only) and Wisconsin Tel. These companies allowed women into certain craft positions but restricted their overtime. Wisconsin Tel. presents a particularly compelling example. After initially excluding women from all craft jobs on the basis of the state law,

109. Id. at 86-87, 89-90, 91-93.

the Company revised its position in 1968 to "allow" women into these jobs but to restrict the overtime they could work. The effect of this change in policy has been negligible. On December 31, 1970, Wisconsin Tel. employed 2864 craft workers, of whom 99.4% were male. . . .

The following companies spurned all of the above alternatives and excluded women from most traditionally male classifications based on state protective legislation: C&P (D.C.), Michigan Bell, New England Tel., Pacific Northwest Bell, and South Central Bell.

A summary of the various companies' policies concerning exclusion of females from craft jobs based on state protective laws is obviously difficult since so many inconsistent claims were being made within the System. Two conclusions can be reached with some confidence, however. First, if the operating companies had truly desired to place females in craft jobs, they could have. The companies could have attacked the state law; they could have sought exemptions from the laws; or they could have placed women in the jobs but restricted their overtime. All of these alternatives are viable as indicated by the fact that some companies claimed to use them. It appears reasonable to conclude that the failure of most companies to pursue these alternatives vigorously can be attributed to their continued desire to sex segregate craft jobs.

This observation is reinforced by the second conclusion which can be confidently made. The fact that some companies attacked state laws, obtained exemptions, or "allowed" females into craft jobs but restricted their overtime made virtually no difference in actual practices. All companies continued to exclude females from craft positions.

The second major source of BFOQ claims was stereotyped characterizations of the sexes (specifically prohibited by the EEOC guidelines, see 29 C.F.R. §1604.2(a)(1)(ii)). Cheatwood v. Southern Bell Telephone & Telegraph Co., 303 F. Supp. 754 (M.D. Ala. 1969), supra Section B-1 of this part, supplies examples of typical assertions. The EEOC study investigates the claims used to exclude women from jobs and adds examples of, and also explores the rationale for, excluding men from "female" jobs, such as the operator's position. The reasons offer an insight into the psychology of the males running AT&T:[110]

> . . . AT&T corporate headquarters circulated a position paper in January, 1966. The paper, entitled "Application of Title VII of Civil Rights Act to Traffic Operating Jobs in the Telephone Industry," awkwardly attempted to rationalize the exclusion of males. Three basic rationales were proposed. First, the paper argued that men were by nature unsuited to the Operator's job. The initial telephone company experience with rambunctious males was cited and the specter of deteriorating service was raised. "The present high level of service," AT&T contended, "is largely due to the employment of women as telephone operators."
>
> Second, the close nature of the work necessitated a segregated work force.
>
> "Many times operators' knees, elbows, hands and arms brush their neighbors' bodies. To have men and women (even those with the best intentions and good will) working side by side under these conditions would created an intolerable situation."
>
> The possibility of segregating men and women at the switchboards was rejected as "possibly a violation of Title VII"!
>
> Third, the Operators' chairs, switchboards, lounge and rest room facilities were designed for women, and the expense of accommodating males would be "too much for any management to consider or the public to pay for."

110. Id. at 74-75.

NOTE:
RECRUITMENT, HIRING, AND PROMOTION — THE SPECIFIC
POLICIES THAT PRODUCED AT&T's SEX SEGREGATION

Chapter 4 of the EEOC Prehearing Analysis and Summary of Evidence analyzes the specific discriminatory policies used by AT&T. The results are summarized here to illustrate the kind of analysis that must be undertaken in all employment discrimination cases — for the policies producing segregation constitute part of the plaintiff's case just as the segregation itself does. This analysis is also important because the plaintiff will need to know how the segregation is produced in order to know what remedies are needed to achieve integration. The Chapter 4 results are also given to indicate further examples of facially discriminatory policies that companies will try to justify under the BFOQ standard.

(1) Recruitment Policies. The Bell system used two principal facially discriminatory recruiting methods. The first was the use of high school recruiting materials that identified all jobs by sex; since high school recruiting is one of the three major Bell recruitment methods, this had obvious impact. The EEOC described some of these materials:[111]

> . . . In April 1969, they launched a nationwide campaign, including full color ads in women's magazines, to recruit Service Representatives. In a letter to all General Commercial Managers in the operating companies, AT&T Assistant Vice President Lee Tait described the program as follows:
> "It provides an excellent vehicle for selling the Service Representative job to young women in today's tight labor market. . . . Many think that the only job opportunities for women in the telephone company are clerical or switchboard operators." . . . Pamphlets describing Operator, Service Representative and clerical positions openly follow the dictum of a C&P (Va.) personnel manual that recruitment literature should be "fresh, feminine and applicant-centered." Two major brochures ("The Modern Telephone Operator" and "But She Doesn't Look Like a Telephone Company"), prepared by AT&T and used by every operating company, are illustrative. Both picture only females as Operators and Service Representatives and both use only the feminine gender to describe these employees. "Male" brochures used in 1971 ask, "Do you have jobs for young men?" and answer resoundingly, "Yes. . . ." Of the hundreds of brochures used in the 30 surveyed SMSA's only one or two picture females or males in "opposite sex" jobs. Films, talks, and slides used in high school recruitment parrot the same sexist theme.

A second related recruitment policy was the use of single-sex help-wanted advertisements in newspapers. The EEOC had Dr. Sandra Bem and Dr. Daryl Bem, two Stanford University professors, do a study on this practice:[112]

> The subject sample consisted of high school seniors, most of whom planned to seek a job upon graduation. They were given a booklet of actual and simulated recruiting advertisements and were asked to indicate their interest in applying for the jobs of Operator, Service Representative, Lineworker and Frameworker in the Bell System.
>   The results, presented in Chart [2-3], show the dramatic change for both males and females when the traditional sex designations [in the language of the ads] are eliminated or reversed. Though almost no females expressed an interest in Frame or Line work while these jobs carried the male stigma, one-fourth of the women would apply for this work when recruited through neutral advertisements. One-half of the surveyed women would seek these traditionally male jobs if the sex designation of

111. Id. at 109-110.
112. Id. at 110-112.

Chart [2-3]
POTENTIAL APPLICANTS FOR SEX-TYPED, NEUTRAL
AND SEX-REVERSED ADVERTISEMENTS

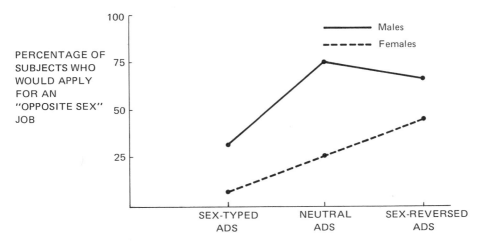

Note: Both curves show statistically significant effects at .01 level by X^2 test;
male decline is NOT significant.

the advertisements were reversed. A similarly dramatic pattern occured for males by simply eliminating the feminine connotations of the Operator and Service Representative advertisements.

(2) Hiring Policies. The EEOC report summarizes the entire hiring process:[113]

The applicant, either by telephone or in person, is first interviewed in a "gross pre-screen." This brief interview is intended to discourage those persons whose work requirements (salary, location, type of work) are inconsistent with the company's available jobs. No applicant who wishes to proceed, however, is rejected at this stage. The applicant is then given one or more of several batteries of tests based on the interviewer's evaluation of her or his interests and experience. If the test is completed successfully, a detailed application is filled out and an intensive interview is conducted. If the applicant's abilities and interests (as determined by the tests and the interview) "match" the company's job opening and the applicant passes security, reference and physical checks, a job is offered. Each of these stages may be defined in terms of gender and each contributes to the funneling of females and males into different jobs.

Discrimination first occurs in the employment offices, which were still generally sex-segregated because each department had its own hiring office and the departments in turn were segregated. By 1971, some companies had switched to centralized hiring offices, but all other steps remained as separate as in the segregated hiring offices. In both, segregated interviewers were used — women interviewing women applicants for the "women's" jobs, and men interviewing men. Women and men applicants each got a separate test — there was a "female test battery" and a "male test battery." And finally, different employment criteria were used:[114]

113. Id. at 119-121.
114. Id. at 122-123.

Females are asked about their child care arrangements (even though Bell's own studies indicate that turnover for females with children is not substantially different from those without children), their plans for marriage, their families' attitude toward their work, their husbands' permanency, and whether they are pregnant. Females may also be the subject of a "home visit" to acquaint the parents or family with the requirements of the job and determine the applicant's employability.

Males, on the other hand, are required to meet an entirely different set of standards. They must have a valid driver's license and a good driving record, must have the physical ability and willingness to do craft work, and must pass a security clearance, none of which are required of females. Further, while female college graduates are recruited and employed in non-management positions, there has been, at least through 1970, a "well-known" Bell System policy of not hiring male college graduates into non-management jobs.

A particularly incisive example of dual hiring criteria is found in the high school reference check forms used by New England Tel. in 1971. The form for females (headed "Miss") asks for grades in English, math, bookkeeping, typing, stenography, business machines and art. The comparable form for males (headed "Mr.") asks for the applicant's grades in English, algebra, plane geometry, solid geometry, trigonometry, physics, mechanical drawing, shop courses and languages.

(3) Promotion Policies. The principal kind of facially discriminatory promotion policy was segregated lines of progression, described by EEOC as follows:[115]

> The second major barrier to female promotion is the segregation of lines of progression. The operating companies uniformly contend that there are no fixed promotion ladders in the sense that one job is an absolute prerequisite for another. The companies' practice of training for all jobs following a promotion makes it unnecessary to have had work experience in a specific area prior to assignment to the job. Company job descriptions, personnel manuals and recruitment brochures do, however, describe lines of progression in non-management jobs. These are *inevitably* sex-segregated. . . . Although promotions often occur between departments, only in abnormal cases do promotions occur between "male" and "female" jobs.
>
> A particularly apt example of promotion channels based on sex occurs at Michigan Bell. As indicated in Chapter 2, the Switchroom Helper's job (Frameman in other companies) is an all-female craft job in Michigan. . . . [T]he normal promotion for Frameman or Switchroom Helper would be to Installer-Repairman, Lineman or Switchman. In Michigan Bell, however, the normal progression for female Switchroom Helpers is gerrymandered to require promotion to Installation Order Clerk, a clerical job with a top rate of slightly less than Switchroom Helper. One's career is virtually predestined by the line of progression into which she or he is hired.

Promotion standards also prohibited women's entrance into craft jobs; thus, the Bell companies require employees who wish to transfer into craft jobs to have successfully completed the craft ("male") test battery, but of course, the Bell System does not give women the craft test battery. Finally, an additional though more subtle factor influencing women to stay out of the craft jobs was the total absence of role models. The EEOC describes this problem:[116]

> Women (and men) are often quite reluctant to be the first pioneer in a new field. A Pacific Tel. Frameman said, "I knew there were several Framewomen so the idea of being the only girl didn't concern me." That concern, unfortunately, is quite real in most of the operating companies.
>
> It is not at all surprising that few women have been willing to take on the entire male hierarchy of the Bell System. Most women who have advanced to "male" jobs have done so only after a lengthy struggle. Lorena Weeks, just such a woman, encoun-

115. Id. at 130-131.
116. Id. at 143-144.

tered all the might of Southern Bell when she bid on a Switchman's vacancy in March, 1966. It was to be five years before she would be awarded the job. Her story epitomizes women's collective struggle for promotion.

"In March, 1966, a job was put up for bid for Switchman in the Louisville and Wadley exchanges. Since a Switchman's work is inside and involved equipment, some of which I had become familiar with as a telephone operator, I decided to bid on the job. . . . My bid for the Switchman's job in Wadley was returned. The only reason the Company gave for not letting me have the job was that I am a woman. The job went to the only other bidder, a man with less seniority then me."

Ms. Weeks then took her case to court and finally, in November, 1970, Southern Bell was ordered to place her on the job of Switchman.

"Every day I thought the Company would tell me to report for work in Wadley. Time drug on all through Christmas and the Holidays. Each day I hoped to be placed on my new job. Nothing happened — finally my attorney was able to get another hearing before Judge Bell in March, 1971. I told him how pressed we were for funds to keep our now three children in college. . . . He told me that before I left his chambers that day that he would issue an order and put me on the job the next day. He did and I went to work on March 3, 1971. . . .

"I am enjoying my work and am happier than I have ever been since working with the Telephone Company. During the time I was waiting for a final decision I was criticized by both males and females. They seemed to think I was trying to take something from 'the breadwinner' while I was only trying to prove that all men aren't breadwinners and that a loaf of bread costs a woman as much as it does a man."

It is little wonder that many women are discouraged from seeking "male" jobs by such examples. . . .

(4) Wage Policies. When a man receives a promotion, his new salary is based on length of service with the company, while a woman in the same position receives a new salary based on amount of money earned. The EEOC report gives an example:[117]

An example from the Pacific Tel. collective bargaining agreement in effect on January 1, 1971, is illustrative of the wage treatment procedures in all the companies following promotion. . . . A male with 72 months service as a Frameman who is promoted to Station Installer will receive an increase from $152.50 per week to $156.50 per week. Should a female Operator with identical service be promoted to the same job and perform the same duties, her new wage will be only $124.00. Her wage, relative to the male Framemen with whom she was hired, has increased only slightly.

This same disparity continues through a hypothetical promotion to PBX Installer after 18 months.[118] In this example, it will take the female four and one-half years to achieve parity with her male counterpart, and during that time she will have lost $6500 when compared to a male in the same classification and with the same company seniority.

This issue was treated in a 1967 arbitration award involving Southwestern Bell. The subject was broached following an Arbitrator's order to place a female clerk in a Plant craft job with appropriate back pay. The union subsequently grieved when the female was paid at a rate of only $95.50 per week rather than the $136.00 per week paid to her male predecessor. The Arbitrator held as follows:

"The Company, in calculating the back pay for Bernita Brock, has not complied with the existing award in this case. It should accept the award as determining that women in the situation of [clerks promoted to craft jobs] are qualified for the positions the Arbitrators awarded them. Miss Brock's wage rate should be calculated on that basis."

(5) Policies Affecting Management Jobs. So far, this discussion has concentrated on employment policies affecting nonmanagement jobs. As might be expected, the EEOC

117. Id. at 145-147.
118. The male would then earn $183 per week; the female, $142. Id. at Chart B — Eds.

found similar policies for management jobs that explained women's exclusion from the high-paying jobs above level two. Lines of progression into and through management continue to be sex-segregated, with the result that women managers are confined to the Traffic, Accounting, and Commercial Departments. Moreover, until the 1960s, the Bell System maintained a Management Assessment Program that was limited to consideration of men. This program formally assessed male employees for promotions to a wide spectrum of management jobs; women within AT&T were considered only informally, and then only for promotion within their own area.

Segregation also characterized the Bell policies for outside hiring of management personnel, most of whom are college graduates. The EEOC report describes the special programs for recruiting management that AT&T developed:[119]

The most ambitious program is the Initial Management Development Program (IMDP). This program was developed in the early 1960's after AT&T realized that,
"Most college recruits were not put on assignments which challenged themor which allowed the companies to evaluate their potential. The expectations and goals of new college hires declined during their early years with the Company. This was especially true of those on restricted jobs and unsatisfying training programs."
The IMDP was designed, therefore, to provide immediate supervisory experience to the outstanding college graduate. He (never she) was hired with the understanding that continued employment after the first year was conditioned on his performance. If, after one year, he did not evidence the potential to progress to District level (third level) within five years, his employment would be terminated.
This high risk/high gain program was, as one would expect, limited to men. . . .
Although Bell would not consider women for its most ambitious management program, they were willing, according to Assistant Vice President Mercer, to consider them for lesser programs.
". . . [C]ollege women should continue to be employed in training programs with less occupational objectives, where the training program is shorter and where the requirement for career coverage is not so acute."
Thus, parallel "women's IMDP" programs were established, and women were actively recruited. . . .
The lesser program may have pacified the conscience of Bell managers, but it was no favor to college women. They were treated as second class employees, paid less and challenged less, solely because of their sex.

Finally, promotion from the first level of management to higher levels is almost impossible for women; while a first-level male manager has a chance of "about one in four or five" to reach district level, the odds for the woman in the same position are "less than one in 300." This results from several factors:[120]

The two "essential opportunity factors" which are denied to women are (1) special schools or training programs and (2) rotational assignments. According to [a] 1970 study, "most management jobs filled by women are viewed as terminal hire or staff assignments."
Men readily transfer between management jobs in the several operating departments, gaining experience which will be valuable in higher assignments. Women are confined to single departments, often in a staff role.

In addition, lack of female role models for higher-level management jobs plays its part, as does the pervasive belief in female role stereotypes held by Bell male managers. (Samples from Table 6 of the study: "Women are not as competent as men." "Men and women should not work together too closely.")

119. Id. at 160-161, 162-163, 164.
120. Id. at 167-168.

This completes the discussion of Bell policies that openly discriminate against women employees. However, other policies that are apparently neutral and apply to both male and female employees have effectively discriminated against women employees; these policies are listed in Section C-4-b of this part, infra.

NOTE: UNDERVALUATION OF "WOMEN'S" WORK

As discussed above, the EEOC report documents the fact that women earn far less in the Bell system than do men. Chart [2-4] illustrates this further by showing the

Chart [2-4]
NATIONWIDE WAGE DISTRIBUTION FOR
PLANT AND TRAFFIC DEPARTMENTS

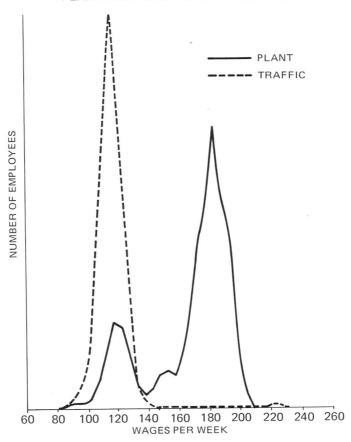

comparative wage distribution for the traffic department (predominantly female) and the plant department (predominantly male); thus, most women earn in the range of $80 to $140 a week, while most men earn in the range of $160 to $210 a week. Table 2-4 indicates the maximum annual salary range for each job; clearly the male jobs all pay a great deal more than the female jobs. In examining Table 2-4 it should be remembered that craft and outside sales jobs (Commercial and Communications Representatives) are virtually all male, while operator, clerical, service representative and inside sales jobs are

TABLE 2-4. SUMMARY OF MAJOR JOBS AND DEPARTMENTS

Department	Job Classification	Estimated Number of Persons in 30 SMSA's	Maximum Salary Range ($000)
Plant		153,000	
	Craft Workers	93,000	
	Inside Crafts	38,000	
	Switchman (Central Office Repairman)		9.0–10.0
	Test Boardman (Toll Test Deskman)		9.0–10.0
	Entry Level: Frameman		7.5– 8.5
	Outside Crafts	55,000	
	Cable Splicer		9.0–10.0
	PBX Installer-Repairman		9.0–10.0
	Entry Level: Cable		
	Splicer's Helper		7.5– 8.5
	Installer-Repairman		8.5– 9.5
	Lineman		8.5– 9.5
	Clerical Workers		6.0
	Service Workers		5.5
Traffic		105,000	
	Operator		5.0– 6.0
	Clerical Workers		6.0
Commercial		35,000	
	Service Representative		6.0– 7.0
	Commercial Representative		8.5– 9.5
Marketing		20,000	
	Communications Representative and Consultant		10.0–14.0
	Inside Sales		6.0
Accounting	—	27,000	—

virtually all female. The only low-paying job which is not all female is Service Worker (48 percent of these jobs are held by women, and 37 percent by blacks).

One major factor in the wage disparity, of course, is women's exclusion from the higher-paying male jobs. This factor is dramatically documented:[121]

> Because women in the 30 SMSA's are not distributed equitably through the whole range of available jobs, they lose $422 million every year.[122]. . . Nationwide in the Bell System women lose $950 million annually.
>
> Dr. Ronald Oaxaca, an economist at the University of Western Ontario, has calculated that, if differences in the personal characteristics (i.e., age, education, etc.) of females and males are taken into consideration, "the effects of discrimination account for roughly 55% of the observed male-female wage differential in the telephone industry." Thus, Bell's incumbent female employees, given their age, education and experience, are paid an aggregate of $500 million per year less than males with comparable personal characteristics.

However, approaching wage disparity as a problem caused solely by exclusion from "male" jobs ignores a second major factor causing the wage disparity: undervaluation of the women's jobs. The evidence of the frameworker job strongly suggests that Bell does not set the salary scale of jobs by their inherent value, but rather by the sex of the person doing the job. Thus, Michigan Bell, the one company that employed

121. Id. at 174-176.
122. As of December 31, 1970, the expected annual female wages in the 30 SMSAs, based on an equitable distribution of women through all jobs, were $1,859,337,719. However, actual female wages were $1,436,818,405. This left a male surplus of $422,519,314. Id. at Chart 16. — Eds.

women in the frameworker job, classified the job as clerical and paid it at the clerical rate rather than the craft rate (see Table 2-4), while all the other companies classified and paid it at the craft rates because they maintained it as an all-male job. Given the fact that it will take years to integrate fully all jobs within the Bell system, it is very important to increase the valuation of the female jobs. Otherwise, the women who of necessity will remain in those jobs for many years while waiting an opportunity to transfer into the formerly all-male (and sought-after) jobs will be condemned to the same low wages for years. The same is true of those women who will not seek transfer because they have been conditioned to believe that craft jobs are unfeminine. Raising the wage level of the female jobs is also important because it should make those jobs more attractive to men and thus speed up the process of integration; as men flow into female jobs, male jobs should become more accessible to women.

The EEOC Task Force ignored undervaluation completely. While this is understandable, in that the issue has not yet been litigated anywhere, it is particularly unfortunate because this kind of discrimination will be very difficult to prove, and the Michigan Bell handling of the frameworker job, measured against the uniform policy of other companies with the same job, offered unusual evidence that the companies are rating jobs by sex, not by skill. Moreover, the Task Force had access to such an enormous amount of AT&T documents that they found other kinds of evidence that lawyers in smaller cases might not. For example, in discussing the reasons Pacific Tel. hesitated to hire men as operators, the report notes that Pacific Tel. executives objected on the grounds that "if males were in Operators' jobs there might be some pressure to equalize the Operator's pay with Plant craft pay since men would then be serving in both positions."[123]

For further discussion of possible legal standards and evidence for proving discriminatory undervaluation of women's jobs, see Note: Equal Pay for Different Jobs if the Woman's Job Requires Equal Skill, Effort and Responsibility, *infra* Part III-B-2-b.

NOTE: THE EFFECT OF AT&T EMPLOYMENT POLICIES ON MINORITY WOMEN AND MEN

The EEOC report documents the discrimination suffered by blacks and Spanish-surnamed Americans in the AT&T system. The summary concluded:[124]

— Black employment in the Bell System increased steadily from the virtual exclusion of the 1930's and 1940's to an all-time high at the end of the 1960's. Yet, even at that time, most Bell companies had still not reached the average level of black employment for all major companies in their respective operating areas.
— Most of the increase in black employment from the 1940's to the end of the 1960's came in a low-paying, dead-end, and otherwise highly undesirable job, that of Operator. Very few blacks obtained jobs as craft workers.
— Even this increase has not been uniform throughout the System; the Southern companies — Southern Bell, South Central Bell, Southwestern Bell, and C&P (Va.) — continued their exclusionist policies up to the mid-1960's and consequently lagged far behind the rest of the System.
— Even the companies with the best and most sustained efforts of black employment (New York Tel., Ohio Bell, Bell of Pa., Michigan Bell, Illinois Bell, and Pacific Tel.) did not, after decades of hiring blacks, have a significant number of black workers in management. . . .
— The requirement of a high school diploma has a disparate impact upon blacks, artificially reducing the proportion of qualified applicants who are black. . . .
— The test batteries, both "male" and "female," reject a greatly disproportionate number of blacks, and changing the content of the test batteries has not signifi-

---

123. Id. at 73.
124. Id. at 209-210, 269-270, 286-287.

cantly changed the rate at which blacks are disqualified.

    — There is no reason to believe the Bell System test batteries reliably predict job performance, and their continued use is indefensible.

    — The urgent need to fill and re-fill the Operator vacancies has compelled the System virtually to abandon its test requirements in order to get enough blacks to fill the job at wages which are unattractive to whites. . . .

    — Spanish-surnamed Americans are employed by Bell at a rate significantly lower than their proportion in the population or their proportion in the work force of area employers.

    — The Spanish-surnamed Americans who have found employment at Bell are in the lowest paying classifications and are virtually excluded from management.

    — Bell's current employment pattern with regard to Spanish-surnamed Americans is analogous to the position of blacks in the Southern companies during the 1960's.

    — Bell's recruitment and hiring policies [such as the high school diploma and testing requirements] which restrict black employment have an even greater impact on Spanish-surnamed Americans. Irrelevant language and height requirements further impede Spanish-surnamed employment.

The black employment patterns are particularly interesting to study because they demonstrate the effect of superimposing racism on a basic sexist structure. In the 1930s blacks were excluded from all but service (janitors, porters) and laborer jobs, so that a mere 0.7 percent of telecommunications workers were black in 1930. Beginning in the 1940s, Bell companies began hiring black women as operators, with the result that black employment in the system grew to 1.3 percent by 1950, and 2.5 percent by 1960. In the 1960s there was a dramatic jump in black employment, up to 9.8 percent by 1970; but much of this jump remained attributable to Bell's willingness to hire black women as operators. Since the operator job was among the lowest paying in the system, this was the "logical" job for which to hire blacks; and since the Bell system was already committed to maintaining the operator job as a female job, only black women, not black men, were hired in that position.

The initial policy of hiring fewer black men than women also explained the exclusion of blacks from management in the 1960s. Since management jobs are male jobs in the Bell system, it was entirely predictable that an influx of black women into the system would not lead to a later black penetration of management. Thus, by 1971, in the 30 SMSA's blacks held only 3.4 percent of all management jobs, although they held 15.3 percent of all jobs; Anglos held 95.5 percent of all management jobs, but 81.3 percent of all jobs. Above the first-level low-paying management jobs, the figures became even more skewed: at level-two management, blacks held 0.8 percent of the jobs, and Anglos 98.7 percent.[125]

The EEOC report examines only one aspect of disparate treatment accorded combined sex-ethnic groups — that is, that the Bell System hired fewer black men than black women. However, in EEOC Exhibit 1: Charts and Tables,[126] several tables indicate that, once within the system, black women receive less favorable treatment than all other groups, including black men.

One example comes from Section H of EEOC Exhibit 1,[127] which gives a sex-ethnic breakdown for the 25 job titles with the greatest number of employees in the 30 SMSA's.

    125. These figures are presented in In the Matter of Petitions Filed by the Equal Employment Opportunity Commission Before the Federal Communications Commission, Docket No. 19143, EEOC Exhibit 1: Charts and Tables 423 (Table entitled 30 SMSA Totals — Race or National Origin as Percent of Job Group). The table does not give a sex breakdown of the management jobs held by blacks, but the rigid sex segregation throughout the company suggests that most black managers are male. The text infra, discussing operator and installer-repairman breakdowns, supports this hypothesis.

    126. This document, cited fully supra, is a 515-page compendium of various charts and tables showing statistical evidence of discrimination for each of the 30 SMSA's studied.

    127. EEOC Exhibit 1: Charts and Tables, supra, Section H, pp. 361-391, Twenty-Five Jobs With Greatest Numbers of Employees.

The information is too lengthy to reproduce in its entirety here, but some indication of the overall impact can be gained by looking at two major jobs in three major SMSA's. (See Table 2-5.) The jobs are operator, the largest "female" job, paying $5000 to $6000 per year, and installer-repairman, one of the largest "male" or outside craft jobs, paying $9000 to $10,000 per year. The cities — Birmingham, Chicago, and New York — are selected for geographic diversity.

TABLE 2-5

	Number of Employees		
	Operator	Installer-Repairman	
Birmingham, Ala.			
(South Central Bell Tel.)			
Black Men	0	12	
SSA Men[a]	0	0	
Anglo Men	0	178	
Black Women	334	0	
SSA Women	1	0	
Anglo Women	494	0	
Chicago, Ill.			
(Illinois Bell Tel.)			
Black Men	1	217	
SSA Men	0	24	
Anglo Men	0	1009	
Black Women	1675	0	
SSA Women	64	0	
Anglo Women	4160	1	
New York, N.Y.			
(New York Tel.)			
Black Men	0	504	413
SSA Men	0	193	169
Anglo Men	0	5166	3145
Black Women	8718	0	1
SSA Women	487	1	0
Anglo Women	6631	0	1

[a]Spanish-surnamed American.

Source: Data from EEOC Exhibit 1: Charts and Tables, supra, Section H, Twenty-Five Jobs with Greatest Numbers of Employees at 364,365 and 381. It reflects employment as of Dec. 31, 1970. Information on Indians and Orientals is omitted because the numbers are so small.

Thus, minority women hold approximately 50 percent of the operator jobs in these three cities (11,279 minority and 11,285 Anglo women), while minority men hold only 26 percent of the installer-repairmen jobs (1531 minority and 4332 Anglo men). However, minority *and* Anglo women hold none of the higher-paying craft jobs, thus insuring that their salaries will be much lower than either minority or Anglo men. And in fact, nationwide wage figures confirm the fact that sex segregation combined with race discrimination keeps minority women in the worst position of all groups. In the 30 SMSA's, the average wages for all Bell workers broken down by sex-ethnic groups were[128]

Anglo men	$11,940
SSA men	9,140
Black men	8,788
Anglo women	7,228
SSA women	6,471
Black women	6,342

128. Id. at 440, Table entitled Average Wages.

It appears, then, that in the Bell system those who suffer from both sexism and racism take the worst consequences, measured by wages, and that sexism alone takes a somewhat more severe toll in wages than racism alone.

It is unfortunate that the EEOC report did not further explore the combined effects of racism and sexism on different sex-ethnic groups, because such data is needed to develop adequate remedies. One would like to know, for example, the sex-ethnic breakdown for all craft jobs and all levels of management. The figures for the operator and installer-repairman jobs certainly suggest that different hiring and transfer goals will have to be set for each sex-ethnic subgroup.

b. Pregnancy-Related Discrimination

In the early 1970s, women workers began challenging on a major scale employment policies relating to pregnancy. Teachers in particular brought many cases, because school boards across the country retained old-fashioned policies forcing pregnant teachers to quit work.

COHEN v. CHESTERFIELD COUNTY SCHOOL BOARD
474 F.2d 395 (4th Cir. 1973)

HAYNSWORTH, Chief Judge:
In this action brought under 42 U.S.C. §1983, the plaintiff challenges the maternity leave regulation of the Chesterfield County School Board on the ground that it deprives her of her rights to due process and to equal protection of the laws guaranteed under the Fourteenth Amendment to the Constitution.[1] The challenged rule requires, with limited flexibility, that teachers who become pregnant must go on maternity leave at the end of the fifth month of pregnancy.[2] This appeal is taken from the District Court's decision that the maternity leave rule deprived Mrs. Cohen of equal protection: "Because pregnancy, though unique to women, is like other medical conditions, the failure to treat it as such amounts to discrimination which is without rational basis, and there-

1. Mrs. Cohen's complaint sought relief also under the Equal Employment Opportunity Act, Title VII of the Civil Rights Act of 1964, 42 U.S.C. §2000e-2(a). . . . At the time of the proceedings below, however, state agencies and educational institutions were specifically exempted from the Act. 42 U.S.C. §2000e(b); 42 U.S.C. §2000e-1. Subsequent to oral argument, these exemptions were repealed by the Equal Employment Opportunity Act of 1972, P.L. 92-261, signed by the President March 24, 1972 and effective immediately. Rules and practices of the defendant in effect when the defendant was exempt from the Equal Employment Opp. Act cannot be the basis for a violation of that Act. This opinion accordingly is limited to consideration of the rights and liabilities of the parties under the Equal Protection Clause of the Fourteenth Amendment.

2. The maternity leave provisions of the Chesterfield County School Board provides:

"a. Notice in writing must be given to the School Board at least six (6) months prior to the date of expected birth.

"b. Termination of employment of an expectant mother shall become effective at least four (4) months prior to the expected birth of the child. Termination of employment may be extended if the superintendent receives written recommendations from the expectant mother's physician and her principal, and if the superintendent feels that an extension will be in the best interest of the pupils and school involved.

"c. Maternity Leave

"1. Maternity leave must be requested in writing at the time of termination of employment.

"2. Maternity leave will be granted only to those persons who have a record of satisfactory performance.

"3. An individual will be declared eligible for re-employment when she submits written notice from her physician that she is physically fit for full-time employment, and when she can give full assurance that care of the child will cause minimal interference with job responsibilities.

"4. Re-employment will be guaranteed no later than the first day of the school year following the date that the individual was declared eligible for re-employment.

"5. All personnel benefits accrued, including seniority, will be retained during maternity leave unless the person concerned shall have accepted other employment.

"6. The school system will have discharged its responsibility under this policy after offering re-employment for the first vacancy that occurs after the individual has been declared eligible for re-employment."

fore is violative of the equal protection clause of the Fourteenth Amendment." Cohen v. Chesterfield County School Board, E.D. Va., 326 F. Supp. 1159, 1161.

When Mrs. Cohen became pregnant she was a social studies teacher at Midlothian High School in Chesterfield County. Her contract with the School Board required her to comply with all state and local school laws and regulations. In compliance with the Board's maternity provisions, Mrs. Cohen notified the Board on November 2, 1970 that she was pregnant and that her estimated date of delivery was April 28, 1971. With the written opinion of her obstetrician that she could work as long as she chose, she requested an extension until April 1, 1971 of the date she would stop teaching. The School Board denied this request, granting her leave effective December 18, 1970. In a subsequent personal appearance before the Board, Mrs. Cohen made an alternate request of an extension until January 21, 1971 — the end of the semester. This request, supported by a recommendation of her principal, was also denied. The District Court found that the basis of the denials of the requested extensions was that "the School Board had a replacement available, and felt it proper to abide by its regulation."

The plaintiff . . . stands squarely on a broader constitutional claim which would entirely exclude school officials from participation in the decision on the date of the maternity leave. That is for her, alone, to determine, she says, else she is subject to impermissible discrimination based upon sex.

We conclude, first, that the regulation is not an invidious discrimination based upon sex. It does not apply to women in an area in which they may compete with men. Secondly, school officials have a duty to provide, as best they can, for continuity in the instruction of children and, to that end, they have a legitimate interest in determining reasonable dates for the commencement of maternity leaves and a right to fix them.

We do not accept Mrs. Cohen's premise that the regulation's provision which denies her, with the advice of her doctor, the right to decide when her maternity leave will begin is an invidious classification based upon sex which may be justified only by some compelling state interest. Such invidious discriminations are found in situations in which the sexes are in actual or potential competition. A statutory preference for men over women in the appointment of administrators was recently stricken by the Supreme Court as quite unjustified by considerations of administrative convenience.[3]

Only women become pregnant; only women become mothers. But Mrs. Cohen's leap from those physical facts to the conclusion that any regulation of pregnancy and maternity is an invidious classification by sex is merely simplistic. The fact that only women experience pregnancy and motherhood removes all possibility of competition between the sexes in this area. No man-made law or regulation excludes males from those experiences, and no such laws or regulations can relieve females from all of the burdens which naturally accompany the joys and blessings of motherhood. Pregnancy and motherhood do have a great impact on the lives of women, and, if that impact be reasonably noticed by a governmental regulation, it is not to be condemned as an invidious classification.

We are not accustomed to thinking, as sex classifications, of statutes making it a crime for a man forcefully to ravish a woman, or, without force, carnally to know a female child under a certain age. Military regulations requiring all personnel to be clean shaven may be suspect on other grounds, but not because they have no application to females. Prohibition or licensing of prostitution is a patent regulation of sexual activity, the burden of which falls primarily on females, but it has not been thought an invidious sex classification. What of regulations requiring adult women sunning themselves on a public beach to keep their breasts covered? Is that an invidious discrimination based upon sex, a denial of equal protection because the flat and hairy chest of a male lawfully may be exposed?

The situation confronting us is not unlike that which occasioned the memorable

3. Reed v. Reed, 404 U.S. 71, 92 S. Ct. 251, 30 L. Ed. 2d 225.

lament of Anatole France, "the law, in its majestic equality, forbids the rich as well as the poor to sleep under bridges, to beg in the streets, and to steal bread."[4] Concern that the weight of the law falls more heavily upon the poor has been with us for years. Undoubtedly, some laws are directed to offenses which are unlikely to be committed by the wealthy, but there are also crimes which no poor person could commit. If the rich are unlikely to find spaces beneath bridges havens of rest, poor people are unlikely to find an opportunity to embezzle the funds of a national bank or to perpetrate a stock fraud. There are some laws which are not likely to be violated by the rich; there are others which are not likely to be violated by the poor. France stated his lament as he looked at some of such laws from the perspective of the poor, but the law may hold all of us accountable for antisocial conduct despite the differences in the temptations which confront us.

How can the state deal with pregnancy and maternity in terms of equality with paternity? It cannot, of course. The disabilities and preoccupations of maternity are visited but slightly upon the father. However sympathetic he may be, it is she who must shoulder the principal problems of pregnancy, the labors of childbirth and the care and feeding of the child in the early months of its life.

Pregnancy and maternity are sui generis, and a governmental employer's notice of them is not an invidious classification by sex.

Still, the regulation must serve some reasonable objective. We think it does.

Here we may take note of the fact that Mrs. Cohen attempts to confine her attack to the rules under which the time of commencement of maternity leave is determined. There she likens pregnancy to illness and other physical disability, contending that failure to treat pregnancy as other disabilities is an unwarranted discrimination.[7]

We think our view should encompass the whole regulation.

There are obvious difficulties in the way of drawing a perfect analogy, as Mrs. Cohen would, between the several conditions contemplated by the maternity leave regulations and physical disabilities.

In the first place, the maternity leave policy of this school system covers an indefinite period of time, after delivery, when the young mother may wish to breast feed her baby or otherwise devote herself primarily to its care. A few weeks after a normal delivery, a healthy young mother is suffering no physical disability. If she chooses to remain on maternity leave for some months thereafter, she does so because of a temporary preference for child-care over a return to teaching and not because of anything remotely resembling illness or physical incapacity.

Even pregnancy is not like illnesses and other disabilities. In this age of wide use of effective contraceptives, pregnancy is usually voluntary. No one wishes to come down with mononucleosis or to break a leg, but a majority of young women do wish to become pregnant, though they seek to select the time for doing so. Female school teachers, like other young women, plan to become pregnant.[8]

Unlike most illnesses and other disabilities, too, pregnancy permits one to foresee its culmination in a period of confinement and to prepare for it. The employer of the pregnant woman need not wait until the clock has struck to search for a replacement. Unexpected illnesses and disabilities may compel resort to a pool of substitute teachers available for short periods of employment, but pregnancy assures an opportunity to secure a more permanent replacement. As planning precedes most pregnancies, planning for the arrangements they necessitate may go hand in hand with them.

That circumstance supplies the justification for the rule that puts the starting of

---

4. A. France, The Red Lily (1894).

7. Her reasoning would seem to invalidate the provision for extended post-delivery leave during which the teacher-mother has a continuing guarantee of reemployment.

8. Of course, all pregnancies among teachers, as with other women, are not voluntary. See Love's Labor Lost: New Conceptions of Maternity Leave, 7 Harv. Civ. Rights–Civ. Liberties L. Rev. 260, 283-84, 288.

maternity leave, after the fifth month of pregnancy, within the control of school officials rather than in that of each pregnant teacher.[9]

Eighty per cent of the teachers employed in this school system are women. The system is large enough that the Board knows that a certain number of its teachers will become pregnant each year.[10] It knows that many of them will be unable to perform teaching duties over a period of several or many months, while some will be unwilling to do so for several months after the baby's delivery. The pregnant teacher's absence is not only predictable; it is of much longer duration than absences caused by such relatively transitory things as respiratory infections and digestive upsets.

Extended absences of teachers can occasion highly objectionable discontinuity in the education of children. When an extended absence is foreseen, the interest of the children is served by the employment of a regular replacement rather than dependence upon a succession of substitutes. That interest is furthered by the rule which starts the maternity leave at the end of the fifth month of pregnancy with the provision that the superintendent may postpone the time upon the teacher's request and with the approval of her doctor and her principal. Placing ultimate control in school officials rather than in each individual teacher, affords an opportunity for useful planning and specific commitments to replacement teachers, who, otherwise, might not be available.

Mrs. Cohen, in her contract, agreed to abide by the regulations.[12] Her effort to avoid them insofar as she dislikes them in their application to her should not prevail, for the regulations are not without reason. Their purpose may reasonably be regarded as contributing to the better education of the pupils by enabling school officials to arrange a larger degree of continuity in their instruction.[14]

Reversed.

Winter, Circuit Judge (dissenting):

Because I disagree with the conclusion of the majority and because the majority's decision, if it prevails, may well be relied on to invalidate an aspect of the implementation of the Equal Employment Opportunity Act, Title VII of the Civil Rights Act of 1964, 42 U.S.C.A. §2000e-2(a),[1] I respectfully dissent.

The majority concludes that the regulation does not discriminate against women as such; it only discriminates between pregnant teachers and other teachers. "It [the regulation] does not apply to women in an area in which they compete with men." As

9. Since we conclude that continuity in instruction reasonably supports the rule we need not consider other personalized reasons advanced in support of the regulation.

10. In addition to Mrs. Cohen, two others began maternity leave in December, 1970.

12. Concurring in Healy v. James, 408 U.S. 169, 202, 92 S. Ct. 2338, 2356, 33 L. Ed. 2d 266, Mr. Justice Rehnquist wrote:

"Cases such as United Public Workers v. Mitchell, 330 U.S. 75, 67 S. Ct. 556, 91 L. Ed. 754 (1947), and Pickering v. Board of Education etc., 391 U.S. 563, 88 S. Ct. 1731, 20 L. Ed. 2d 811 (1968), make it equally clear that the government in its capacity as employer also differs constitutionally from the government in its capacity as the sovereign executing criminal laws."

14. The point is being widely litigated with diverse results. See, e.g., Schattman v. Texas Employment Commission, 5 Cir., 459 F.2d 32; LaFleur v. Cleveland Bd. of Educ., N.D. Ohio, 326 F. Supp. 1208; Doe v. Osteopathic Hospital of Wichita, D. Kansas, 333 F. Supp. 1357; Robinson v. Rand, D. Colo., 340 F. Supp. 37; Williams v. School District, N.D. Calif., 340 F. Supp. 438; Monell v. Dept of Social Services, S.D.N.Y.; Danielson v. Bd. of Educ. of the City Univ. of N.Y., S.D.N.Y.; Bravo v. Bd. of Educ., N.D. Ill., 345 F. Supp. 155; Cerra v. East Stroudsburg Area School District, 3 Pa. Cmwlth. 665, 285 A.2d 206.

1. . . . On April 5, 1972, the Equal Employment Opportunity Commission adopted guidelines (a) declaring that exclusion of employees "from employment . . . because of pregnancy is in prima facie violation of Title VII" (29 C.F.R. §1604.10(a), and (b) requiring employers to treat disabilities caused by pregnancy and childbirth like other temporary disabilities (29 C.F.R. §1604.10(b)).

Although rules and practices of the defendant in effect when the defendant was exempt from the Act cannot be the basis for a violation of that Act, even though, as the amicus correctly points out, they are entitled to "great deference" in interpreting the Act, Griggs v. Duke Power Co., 401 U.S. 424, 434, 91 S. Ct. 849, 28 L. Ed. 2d 158 (1971), the majority's holding is to the effect that constitutionally discrimination between pregnant women and other women and men, on account of pregnancy, is permissible. It would seem to follow that a contrary regulation would be in excess of the statutory grant of authority.

to the pregnant school teacher, so the argument runs, the discrimination is permissible because of the need to provide continuity of education in the classroom.[2] Stated otherwise, a uniform date for the beginning of maternity leave is necessary to avoid disruption in the classroom by a sudden and unpredictable need to replace a teacher who delivers prematurely or who suffers a complication of pregnancy necessitating her absence from the classroom.

While superficially appealing, I am not persuaded by this argument and I think it a disingenuous one to be advanced on this record. The record is clear that there is not a high incidence of risk of premature delivery or complications of pregnancy in the beginning of the third trimester of pregnancy — the date that the regulation establishes as the beginning of maternity leave. And on the facts of this case, one can reasonably infer that continuity of the educational process would have been better preserved had Mrs. Cohen been permitted to complete the semester rather than to subject her students to a new teacher at an illogical and avoidable breaking point in the curriculum.

But there is a more fundamental defect in the majority's opinion. That the regulation is a discrimination based on sex, I think is self-evident. The inescapable truth is as Chief Judge Brown of the Fifth Circuit has stated . . . in Phillips v. Martin-Marietta Corporation, 416 F.2d 1257, 1259 (5 Cir. 1969) . . .:

> The distinguishing factor seems to be motherhood versus fatherhood. The question then arises: Is this sex-related? To the simple query the answer is just as simple: Nobody — and this includes Judges, Solomonic or life tenured — has yet seen a male mother. A mother, to oversimplify the simplest biology, must then be a woman.

Chief Judge Brown's analysis was echoed by Judge Wisdom, also in dissent in Schattman v. Texas Employment Commission, 459 F.2d 32, 42 (5 Cir. 1972), a case asserting the validity of a Texas regulation requiring a pregnant state employee to begin maternity leave not later than two months before her predicted delivery date: "Female employees are the only employees . . . who become pregnant; it follows that they are provisionally dismissed from work on account of their sex. . . ."

I need not concern myself with the applicable test to discriminate validly on the basis of sex. . . — because under either [test], I think the regulation denies equal protection. The record is literally devoid of any reason, medical or administrative, why a pregnant teacher must accept an enforced leave by the end of the fifth month of pregnancy if she and her doctor conclude that she can perform her duties beyond that date. Of course her employer is entitled to reasonable notice of when the teacher and her doctor conclude her leave should begin, so as to enable the employer to provide an adequate substitute, but it would seem that in most instances notice of not more than thirty days would be ample for that purpose. If I put aside instances where a teacher, male or female, suffers a sudden illness or the need for emergency surgery, and where presumably the teacher has little or no notice of impending prolonged absence, I cannot find in the record, nor can I imagine, any justification for requiring greater certainty as to the effective leave date of a pregnant teacher than of any other teacher, male or female, who may be absent for a prolonged period as a result of elective surgical procedure.

---

2. The record belies the benevolent purpose of the school officials ascribed to them by the majority: The principal of Mrs. Cohen's school had previously requested that she be permitted to teach until the end of the first semester, January 21, 1971. From the standpoint of minimizing disruption of the education process of her students, this would seem to have been a sensible request. However, blind adherence to the regulation, or the board's convenience in providing a replacement, or possibly the replacement's convenience in beginning work, was permitted to prevail. The board itself never articulated the reason for rejecting the recommendation of one who could be expected to have more intimate and accurate knowledge of the needs of the pupils affected than it.

To give an example of my last statement, prostatitis is peculiarly a male disease and in this sense sex related. A prostatectomy which may be required as a result of prostatitis or other chronic disease of the prostate, is rarely performed as an emergency surgical procedure. Rather, within a reasonable time range, the date for a prostatectomy is scheduled for a date suiting the availability of the hospital and the convenience of the surgeon and the patient. Under general sick leave regulations, a male teacher planning to undergo a prostatectomy is not required to give advance notice of the contemplated operation or to begin sick leave at any specific date, even at a semester break if one should intervene, prior to the operation, or to seek permission to continue work until the operation. Lest it be thought that an elective prostatectomy among male teachers is a rare event, I stress that the general sick leave requirements contain no requirement of notice, a mandatory beginning of sick leave or continuation of employment after notice until surgery for *any* elective surgery for *any* teacher, male or female. Yet it cannot be said that the disruptive effect on the students or the burden on the school administration is any less in the case of any elective surgery than the disruption and burden occasioned by a pregnant teacher's absenting herself to deliver. Indeed, it would be greater since the pregnant teacher would have been required to give notice of her impending confinement and thus school officials would have had ample time in which to find a replacement. To me, the discrimination is obvious.

I agree with the Sixth Circuit's decision in LaFleur v. Cleveland Board of Education, 465 F.2d 1184 (1972) holding invalid, as a denial of equal protection of the laws, a maternity leave regulation which, like that in the case at bar, required a teacher to begin maternity leave not later than five months before the expected date of normal birth of her child, but which, incidentally, required only two weeks notice of the fact of pregnancy and prohibited the teacher's return to her duties earlier than three months after the child's birth. Both the enforced leave before and after birth were held impermissible, because there was lacking, as here, medical evidence or any other valid reason to support the extended period of mandatory leave. While the court recognized that continuity of classroom instruction and relief of burdensome administrative problems would both be served if the regulation were upheld, it concluded that these problems were no more acute with respect to pregnant teachers than other teachers, male or female, who suffered other actual disabilities; and moreover, that administrative convenience could not be permitted to override "the determinative issues of competence and care" (Stanley v. Illinois, 405 U.S. 645, 657, 92 S. Ct. 1208, 1215, 31 L. Ed. 2d 551 (1972)). Rejected also was the argument that the teacher was bound by her employment contract which required adherence to the regulation because "constitutional protection does extend to the public servant whose exclusion . . . is patently arbitrary or discriminatory." Wieman v. Updegraff, 344 U.S. 183, 192, 73 S. Ct. 215, 219, 97 L. Ed. 216 (1952).

Additional support for my views is found in Robinson v. Rand, 340 F. Supp. 37 (D. Colo. 1972); Doe v. Osteopathic Hospital of Wichita, 333 F. Supp. 1357 (D. Kan. 1971); Williams v. School District (N.D. Cal. 1972); Monell v. Dept. of Social Services (S.D.N.Y. 1972); Bravo v. Board of Education, 345 F. Supp. 155 (N.D. Ill. 1972); Heath v. Westerville Board of Education, 345 F. Supp. 501 (S.D. Ohio 1972). There is a contrary dictum in the split decision in Schattman v. Texas Employment Commission, supra, indicating that a maternity leave regulation requiring leave to begin not later than two months before the expected delivery date would be valid; but, without expressing any view on the correctness of the dictum, I agree with the Sixth Circuit in *LaFleur* that *Schattman* is distinguishable from the instant case on its facts.

Craven and Butzner, JJ., authorize me to say that they join in this opinion.

NOTE: THE SUBSEQUENT HISTORY OF COHEN

Cohen and *La Fleur,* the Sixth Circuit case mentioned in the excerpt from Judge Winter's opinion, were decided together by the Supreme Court, 414 U.S. 632, 94 S. Ct. 791, — L. Ed. 2d — (1974), reversing the circuit court in *Cohen* and affirming *LaFleur.* Although both cases had been decided below on interpretations of equal protection, the Supreme Court relied on the possible chilling effect of such regulations on the procreative right, and on the Due Process Clause. The implications of the decision for constitutional doctrine are discussed in Chapter One, Section V supra. As for employment law, the opinion throws little light on how pregnancy is to be regarded. The only issue certainly decided was that "sweeping mandatory regulations". . ."cannot pass muster under the Due Process Clause of the Fourteenth Amendment, because they employ irrebutable presumptions that unduly penalize a female teacher for deciding to bear a child."[129] In a footnote, the Court stated that on this record it had no occasion to decide whether more reasonable regulations would be justifiable and specifically disclaimed any intent "to say that the only means for providing appropriate protection for the rights of pregnant teachers is an individualized determination in each case and every circumstance." Finally, in the same note, the Court intimates that it might view as reasonable a requirement that employment be terminated "at some firm date during the last few weeks of pregnancy."[130]

NOTE: PREGNANCY DURING EMPLOYMENT —
A THEORETICAL CONFLICT

The opinions of Judges Haynsworth and Winters nicely demonstrate the conflict over how to view pregnancy in the context of employment discrimination law, a subject which the Supreme Court's opinion in *Cohen* did not illuminate. One view concentrates on the uniqueness of pregnancy as a medical condition; the other on its similarities to other medical conditions. Jacqueline Gutwillig, the Chairperson of the Citizens' Advisory Council on the Status of Women, has forcefully explained why the second view is preferable.[131]

> We also found in our review of background materials that absence due to childbirth is sometimes treated as a temporary disability and sometimes as a special condition warranting special arrangements.
> The Council concluded that childbirth and complications of pregnancy are temporary disabilities *for employment purposes* because they have all the significant characteristics of temporary disabilities–(1) loss of income due to temporary inability to perform normal job duties, and (2) medical expenses. Additionally, childbirth has two other characteristics which are associated with only the more severe temporary disabilities — hospitalization and possible death.
> The theory that pregnancy is a "normal physiological condition" [unlike other temporary disabilities] has been advanced as a reason for treating pregnancy as a *special* condition warranting *special* arrangements. I don't know what "normal physiological condition" means; the more one analyzes the words, the more confusing they become, but I'm sure of one thing — medical care, hospitalization, and death are not normally associated with this phrase. I also know as a fact that the *result* of applying this concept has generally been to deny women benefits to which they are justly entitled. [Emphasis added.]

129. 414 U.S. at 648.
130. Id. at 647 n.13.
131. Quoted in Koontz, Childbirth and Child Rearing Leave: Job-Related Benefits, 17 N.Y.L. Forum 480, 496 n.88 (1971).

Cohen's denial of work to a woman willing and able to continue her job clearly demonstrates the truth of this last statement. In this respect, it is interesting to note an obvious comparison with the "protective" state labor laws. The view that women workers were special and had different needs than men workers led to passage of single-sex laws and to discrimination against women under these laws. Likewise, the view that pregnancy is special and unique generally leads to discrimination against pregnant women workers — and, like the state laws, this discrimination is often couched in the language of protection. For example, one lower court justified mandatory unpaid maternity leave of at least eight months on the grounds that pregnant teachers must be protected against the possibility of assault and injury; the court never dealt with the economic injury of the eight-month salary loss it was imposing on women workers. La Fleur v. Cleveland Board of Education, 326 F. Supp. 1208 (N.D. Ohio, 1972), *rev'd,* 465 F.2d 1184 (6th Cir. 1972), *aff'd,* 414 U.S. 632, 94 S. Ct. 791, — L. Ed. 2d — (1974). It is important that feminists understand the historical parallel and consequences of special treatment — because some feminists have supported special programs of aid to pregnant workers without realizing that their theory supporting such aid could just as easily support discrimination against pregnant workers. For example, laws requiring that employers pay pregnant women a maternity allowance while on leave from work could foster discrimination. If the law did not provide that other employees receive monetary allowances while on sick leave, employers would have a financial incentive not to hire women workers. Or if other employees did receive sick leave, the "special" maternity allowance might be less than the sick pay allowance or be restricted in other "special" ways. Another deficiency of the "pregnancy is unique" approach is that it ignores the needs of all workers; if workers need sick pay, all workers should get it, including men and both pregnant and nonpregnant women. Finally, this approach encourages the notion that women workers really *are* different, and thus reinforces the traditional sex role ideology that keeps women workers tied to their low-paying, low-status jobs. Since the importance of the experience of pregnancy is central to the sex role mystique, attacks on the "pregnancy is unique" approach are central to eradicating sex discrimination; because of the close analysis of the facts about pregnant women workers such actions contain, they help erase the core ideology that leads to all discrimination against women.

The importance of a factual approach is highlighted by the errors of fact in Judge Haynsworth's opinion. He states that however sympathetic the father may be, it is the mother "who must shoulder the . . . care and feeding of the child in the early months of its life"; and later, that many pregnant teachers "will be unable to perform teaching duties over a period of several or many months." The first statement is obviously false, and the second one is also. See generally Note: Expert Testimony in Pregnancy Cases, *infra.* These blatant errors are compounded by less obvious ones, as, for instance, the implication that all illnesses and disabilities except pregnancy are nonvoluntary. Clearly, Haynsworth's preconceptions have precluded him from exploring the subject in any depth, since elective plastic surgery, lung cancer caused by smoking, and injury caused by a failed suicide attempt could all be considered voluntary and are all conditions normally covered in various disability and sick leave plans.

Note: The EEOC Guidelines on Pregnancy.

In 1972, the EEOC issued pregnancy guidelines that specifically rejected the "pregnancy is unique" approach. In 29 C.F.R. §1604.10, the guidelines provide:

>   (a) A written or unwritten employment policy or practice which excludes from employment applicants or employees because of pregnancy is in prima facie violation of Title VII.
>   (b) Disabilities caused or contributed to by pregnancy, miscarriage, abortion,

childbirth, and recovery therefrom are, for all job-related purposes, temporary disabilities and should be treated as such under any health or temporary disability insurance or sick leave plan available in connection with employment. Written and unwritten employment policies and practices involving matters such as the commencement and duration of leave, the availability of extensions, the accrual of seniority and other benefits and privileges, reinstatement and payment under any health or temporary disability insurance or sick leave plan, formal or informal, shall be applied to disability due to pregnancy or childbirth on the same terms and conditions as they are applied to other temporary disabilities.

(c) Where the termination of an employee who is temporarily disabled is caused by an employment policy under which insufficient or no leave is available, such a termination violates the Act if it has a disparate impact on employees of one sex and is not justified by business necessity.

They also invalidate state laws prohibiting the employment of women for certain periods of time before and after childbirth. 29 C.F.R. §1604.2(b)(1). And §1604.9(d) prohibits an employer from providing benefits to the wives of male employees if he does not provide them to female employees.

Section 1604.10 of the guidelines was based on recommendations of the Citizens Advisory Council on the Status of Women. The council studied the effect of pregnancy on work opportunities and concluded that the term "maternity leave" was inadequate and misleading. Elizabeth Duncan Koontz, former director of the Women's Bureau, explains why.[132]

Discussions of maternity leave in the United States have been characterized by semantic confusion, much emotion, and few facts. Maternity leave is sometimes used to refer to leave for a period encompassing all of pregnancy and six months to a year following childbirth. To some the term means a period of four months or so prior to childbirth and six months to a year following childbirth. Others use the phrase to include only the period during which a woman is actually disabled by childbirth for paid employment outside the home — a very short period for most women.[2] To some it means a period during which the employee is paid; others are referring to leave without pay.[3] Most persons concerned with women's rights include in their concept of maternity leave some right to reemployment without loss of seniority.

The confusion arose, no doubt, because in earlier years many women were required by employers to stop work as soon as they knew they were pregnant and were not permitted to return for a year or two following childbirth, if they were permitted to return at all. Thus, liberalization of limits on the pregnant woman's right to work has varied according to the views of legislators and private employers.

The Citizens' Advisory Council on the Status of Women[6] studied this subject and concluded that for job-related purposes, maternity leave should be defined as that period (or periods) of time a woman is unable to perform her job because of childbirth or complications of pregnancy.[7] The Council concluded that it is irrational to require pregnant women to take leaves of absence while they are still able to work. Such policies are left over from the days, extending into this century, when pregnant women were forced to remain at home — when pregnancy was viewed as "obscene".

132. Id. at 480.

2. This is a standard often applied in state legislation providing for maternity coverage under temporary disability programs. See . . . U.S. Dep't of Labor, Growth of Labor in the United States 294 (1967); U.S. Dep't of Labor, 1969 Handbook on Women Workers 276-77. A number of states prohibit employment of women in one or more occupations for several weeks preceding and following childbirth. Id. at 276.

3. See generally Citizens' Advisory Council on the Status of Women, Report of the Task Force on Labor Standards 32 (1968).

6. The Council was established on Nov. 1, 1963, by Exec. Order No. 11,126, 3 C.F.R. 971 (1964), by President John F. Kennedy on the advice of the President's Commission on the Status of Women, and is composed of twenty private citizens who are appointed by the President for indeterminate terms. U.S. Dep't of Labor, 1969 Handbook on Women Workers, supra note 2, at 294.

7. Citizens' Advisory Council on the Status of Women, Women in 1970, at 4 (1971).

This feeling is still widespread, frequently disguised as concern for the protection of women's interests. Perhaps it would help to alleviate the semantic confusion if a new term were adopted to refer to leave for childbirth and complications of pregnancy — a term such as *childbirth leave.*

The subject of *child rearing* is a separate topic, requiring separate consideration and treatment. Only women can bear children, but both men and women are capable of rearing children. The conceptual framework of childbearing and child rearing fits both present and future reality better than a conceptual framework that assumes that childbearing and child rearing are both solely the responsibility of women. The young women feminists insist, quite logically, that assumption by men of a full share in the rearing of children would contribute to the welfare of the whole family.

Notice that the EEOC Guidelines treat the subject of pregnancy and childbirth only, not that of childrearing. And note further that the guidelines do not state that pregnancy *per se* disables women from working, but that for the period of time a woman is actually disabled from working, she is entitled to receive the same benefits as any other worker — male or female — who is actually disabled from working. The distinction is important because many employers think the cost of providing fringe benefits to disabled pregnant workers will be enormous, but their fears are based on the assumption that pregnant women are disabled from working for most of the pregnancy. Modern medical practice defines the disabled period as about three to six weeks for the average normal pregnancy, though of course problem pregnancies may disable any individual woman for longer periods of time.

The validity of the EEOC guidelines was not at issue in the *Cohen* and *La Fleur* cases, because they were instituted before Title VII was amended to cover schoolteachers. The Supreme Court did take note of the guidelines, however, stating that they were a development which would "lessen" the "practical impact of our decision in the present cases."[133] Unfortunately, a later Supreme Court pregnancy decision, Geduldig v. Aiello (discussed in the next note), appears to adopt the "pregnancy is unique" approach and may thus threaten the guidelines by rejecting their underlying theory. However, the issue is far from settled, since *Geduldig* was not decided under strict Title VII standards but rather under the Fourteenth Amendment.

NOTE: OTHER PREGNANCY DISCRIMINATION ISSUES

Most pregnancy litigation to date has centered on the issue of forced, unpaid leave for fixed periods of the pregnancy. The National Education Association has been particularly active in pursuing such cases, because many school boards have forced pregnant teachers off the job. Most of these cases are cited in Judge Winter's dissenting opinion in *Cohen*. See also Green v. Waterford Board of Education, 473 F.2d 629 (2d Cir. 1973) (the most clearly reasoned of the pregnancy decisions to date), and Buckley v. Coyle Public School System, 476 F.2d 92 (10th Cir. 1973).

Women have also begun litigating other issues, especially with the encouragement of the new EEOC guidelines. One important issue is the denial of health insurance or sick leave benefits to pregnant women. There are many variations on this general scheme. Companies may provide medical insurance benefits, for example, but limit them to a flat maximum for pregnancy, although no limits are set on recovery for treatment for any other medical condition.[134] Or the company may provide temporary disability

133. 414 U.S. at 639 n. 8.
134. For other common discriminatory features of medical insurance policies, see Hayden, Punishing Pregnancy: Discrimination in Education, Employment, and Credit, Women's Rights Project, American Civil Liberties Union (October 1973) at 52-53. This report is an excellent compilation and discussion of discriminatory policies related to pregnancy, and is available from the ACLU, 22 East 40th St., New York, N.Y. 10016.

benefits[135] to workers disabled by pregnancy, but limit their recovery to a smaller period of time than for any other disability. In Gilbert v. General Electric Co., 7 FEP Cases 796 (E.D. Va. 1974), denial of sickness and accident benefits to women disabled by pregnancy was held to be a violation of Title VII. A similar issue is being pursued in Grogg v. General Motors Corp., 73 Civ. 63 (S.D.N.Y.) (limitation of sickness and accident benefits to a maximum period of 6 weeks for disabilities caused by pregnancy and childbirth, but to 52 weeks for all other disabilities).

Another pregnancy discrimination issue concerns state unemployment insurance programs[136] and state temporary disability insurance programs. The former commonly provide that a pregnant woman may not recover unemployment insurance payments even though she is available for and able to work (the standard for other workers); in other words, the state laws assume that pregnant women are automatically unable to work for the entire period of pregnancy.[137] The latter programs also frequently regulate or limit coverage for pregnancy-related disabilities differently than for other disabilities.[138] An important Supreme Court decision upholding such a limitation is Geduldig v. Aiello, 42 U.S.L.W. 4905 (June 17, 1974). The Court upheld a California temporary disability insurance program which denied benefits for pregnancy-related disabilities, on the grounds that the exclusion was not sex discriminatory. The case was decided under the Fourteenth Amendment, since a state insurance program cannot be reached under Title VII (which only covers employers, unions, and employment agencies). The thrust of the opinion was deference to state economic regulation. Thus, the Court commented that "[p]articularly with respect to social welfare programs, so long as the line drawn by the State is rationally supportable, the courts will not interpose their judgment as to the appropriate stopping point."[139] The reasoning the Court used to reach the conclusion that excluding pregnancy was an "appropriate stopping point" rather than an invidious discrimination based on sex was (1) that the inclusion of temporary disabilities related to pregnancy would greatly increase the costs of the program, (2) that "there is no risk from which men are protected and women are not" and vice versa[140] and (3) that "[n]ormal pregnancy is an objectively identifiable physical condition with unique characteristics."[141] Therefore, "[a]bsent a showing that distinctions involving pregnancy are mere pretexts designed to effect an invidious discrimination against the members of one sex or the other, lawmakers are constitutionally free to include or exclude pregnancy from the coverage of legislation such as this on any reasonable basis, just as with respect to any other physical condition."[142]

Justice Brennan, joined in dissent by Justices Douglas and Marshall, saw the exclusion of pregnancy differently. He observed:[143]

> Despite the [California] Act's broad goals and scope of coverage, compensation is denied for disabilities suffered in connection with a "normal" pregnancy — disabilities suffered only by women. . . . Disabilities caused by pregnancy, however, like other physically disabling conditions covered by the Act, require medical care, often include

135. These are payments which compensate workers for loss of income due to inability to work because they are physically disabled. Another commonly used and similar concept is paid sick leave.
136. Unemployment insurance compensates people who are available for work but who cannot find a job, and have previously worked for a specified period in insured employment.
137. For a discussion of the case law on these programs, see Auchincloss, Unemployment Benefits, 1 Women's Rights L. Rep. 38 (Spring 1973).
138. For a full discussion of both unemployment and temporary disability insurance programs, see Citizens' Advisory Council on the Status of Women, Report of the Task Force on Social Insurance and Taxes (1968) (available from the Superintendent of Documents, U.S. Government Printing Office, Washington, D.C. 20402).
139. 42 U.S.L.W. at 4908.
140. Ibid.
141. Id. at n.20.
142. Ibid.
143. Id. at 4909-4910.

hospitalization, anesthesia and surgical procedures, and may involve genuine risk to life. Moreover, the economic effects caused by pregnancy related disabilities are functionally indistinguishable from the effects caused by any other disability: wages are lost due to a physical inability to work, and medical expenses are incurred for the delivery of the child and for post-partum care. In my view, by singling out for less favorable treatment a gender-linked disability peculiar to women, the State has created a double standard for disability compensation: a limitation is imposed upon the disabilities for which women workers may recover, while men receive full compensation for all disabilities suffered, including those that effect only or primarily their sex, such as prostatectomies, circumcision, hemophilia and gout. In effect, one set of rules is applied to females and another to males. Such dissimilar treatment of men and women, on the basis of physical characteristics inextricably linked to one sex, inevitably constitutes sex discrimination.

The reasoning in the Supreme Court decision, like that in Kahn v. Shevin, 42 U.S.L.W. 4591 (April 24, 1974), supra Chapter One, Part V, harks back to the old pattern of judicial deference to legislative classifications based on sex. Hopefully, the Court's failure to comprehend the similarities for almost all legislative purposes of temporary disabilities caused by pregnancy and other temporary disabilities will be limited in its impact by the fact that many challenges to such discrimination will be litigated under Title VII, and in the future, under the Equal Rights Amendment. In the interim, anyone interested in this area of the law or in the Supreme Court's attitudes toward sex discrimination should read the Supreme Court decision in its entirety.

Another recent pregnancy discrimination issue is the denial of child*rearing* leaves of absence to men. And although the EEOC guidelines do not explicitly cover childrearing leaves of absence, they do provide that an employer may not "discriminate between men and women with regard to fringe benefits"; fringe benefits are in turn defined broadly, and specifically include "leave." 29 C.F.R. §§1604.9(a) and (b). A case in point litigated under the Fourteenth Amendment is Danielson v. Board of Higher Education, 4 FEP Cases 885 (S.D.N.Y. 1972).

The combined effect of all the pregnancy programs discussed above was concisely summarized in a recent ACLU report:[144]

> The problem of unemployment compensation neatly illustrates the bind in which so many pregnant working women find themselves. First a woman whose income from employment is vital to her own survival or that of her family is laid off for several months on an involuntary maternity leave. But if she looks for another job, she runs full tilt into the wall of prejudice which decrees that pregnant women are unemployable. Then, if she turns as a last resort to unemployment benefits [to which she may have been contributing during her years as a wage-earner], she is sent away because pregnancy is deemed to render her "unavailable" for employment.

The same bind continues in other forms even if she is allowed to keep her job, and is not forced out on an unnecessary leave of absence. For she will still be unable to work for a certain period of time, and may find herself unable to collect temporary disability or full medical insurance payment (to which she has also been contributing during her years as a wage earner). Thus, just when her expenses increase due to loss of salary, high medical bills, and the costs of clothing and feeding a new child, all the fringe benefit programs that are supposed to decrease these problems for other workers are declared unavailable to her.

---

144. Hayden, Punishing Pregnancy, supra footnote 134, at 43-44.

NOTE:
THE BFOQ DEFENSE IN PREGNANCY DISCRIMINATION CASES

Until 1972, most pregnancy discrimination cases were litigated under the Equal Protection Clause because of the role of teachers in pursuing this issue. With the extension of Title VII to cover teachers in 1972, plus the issuance of specific EEOC pregnancy discrimination guidelines in the same year, attention is now turning to the Title VII standard, rather than the equal protection standard. Since the two are different, it is important to focus specifically on possible Title VII employer defenses to pregnancy discrimination issues.

Within this context, one must first note that discrimination directed toward pregnant women is facial discrimination. It necessarily applies to women only, and treats them differently than men, because only women become pregnant. Section C, infra, discusses facially neutral employment policies that, however, have a discriminatory impact on a protected class of workers; the defense to such a policy is called business necessity, and it is a looser standard than the BFOQ defense for facially discriminatory policies. Thus, it is of some importance to understand that discrimination directed against pregnant women is facial discrimination, and not a neutral policy producing a discriminatory effect.

This brings the discussion to the specifics of a BFOQ defense. Under a strict reading of Section 703(e) of Title VII, an employer can use the BFOQ defense only to justify discrimination in hiring and employment. Thus, an employer could only justify a refusal to hire or to employ a pregnant woman under the BFOQ; he could not justify something like a denial of sickness *benefits* to pregnant women because such benefits are either compensation or a privilege, term, or condition of employment. And even a refusal to hire pregnant women as a class would be difficult to establish under the strict *Rosenfeld* BFOQ standard.[145]

The EEOC had adopted the strict reading of the BFOQ as applying only to "hiring and employing" discrimination charges, for its guidelines specifically disallow a cost defense to a charge of sex discrimination in the furnishing of fringe benefits.[146] Of course, it is possible that the courts will not accept this narrow reading of the BFOQ. It is already clear that employers intend to fight the EEOC guidelines all the way, and their main BFOQ argument will be the increased cost of providing benefits for all temporary disabilities, including those caused by pregnancy. This argument may appeal to some courts and in fact was given considerable credence by the Supreme Court in Geduldig v. Aiello, 42 U.S.L.W. 4905 (June 17, 1974), discussed in the previous note. The three-judge district court in *Aiello* evidenced a greater understanding of the problems with the cost defense than did the Supreme Court, as the following selection indicates.

Aiello v. Hansen
359 F. Supp. 792, 797-800 (N.D. Cal. 1973), rev'd sub nom.
Geduldig v. Aiello, 42 U.S.L.W. 3362 (Dec. 17, 1973)

The question whether the exclusion of pregnancy-related disabilities from the program is arbitrary or rational depends upon whether pregnancy and pregnancy-related illness

145. There might be defenses other than the BFOQ to a refusal to hire charge. The employer could refuse to hire any individual pregnant woman who was actually unable to perform the job in question because of her physical condition, just as he could refuse to hire a man with a broken leg or a bad heart who could not do a particular job. However, to establish that the employer was not discriminating under §703(a), he would have to prove that he screened for and refused to hire men with such medical conditions. A mere *claim* that he did so would not suffice.

146. "It shall not be a defense under Title VII to a charge of sex discrimination in benefits that the cost of such benefits is greater with respect to one sex than the other." 29 C.F.R. §1609(e).

substantially differ from the included disabilities in some manner relevant to the purposes of the disability insurance program.

The search for the purposes that actuated the legislature is a difficult one. The only purpose expressly stated for the enactment of the disability insurance program is "to compensate in part for the wage loss sustained by individuals unemployed because of sickness or injury and to reduce to a minimum the suffering caused by unemployment resulting therefrom." Calif. Unemp. Ins. Code §2601. Clearly the exclusion of pregnancy-related disabilities does not promote this purpose; the economic hardship pregnant women suffer when they cannot work is identical to the hardship of other disabled workers. Thus, the court must look to those unexpressed purposes that, according to the defendant, are promoted by excluding pregnancy-related disabilities from the program.

The principal argument the defendant has made in this court is substantially the same argument accepted in Clark v. California Employment Stabilization Comm'n, 166 Cal. App. 2d 326, 331–332, 332 P.2d 716 (1958)—that the exclusion of pregnancy-related disabilities is necessary to protect the solvency of the disability insurance program. As discussed, the program is financed entirely from employee contributions. To pay benefits for pregnancy-related disabilities, defendant argues, would be so costly that this mode of financing the program would be impracticable.

Clearly it is a legitimate interest for a state to attempt to preserve the fiscal integrity of its programs. Shapiro v. Thompson, 394 U.S. 618, 633, 89 S. Ct. 1322, 22 L. Ed. 2d 600 (1969). More particularly, a state may properly seek to make a program self-sustaining and paid for by those who use it rather than by tax revenues drawn from the public at large. United States v. Kras, 409 U.S. 434, 93 S. Ct. 631, 34 L. Ed. 2d 626 (1973); James v. Strange, 407 U.S. 128, 141, 92 S. Ct. 2027, 32 L. Ed. 2d 600 (1972). "But a State may not accomplish such a purpose by invidious distinctions between classes of its citizens." Shapiro v. Thompson, supra at 633 of 394 U.S., at 1330 of 89 S. Ct.; see James v. Strange, supra at 141-142 of 407 U.S., 92 S. Ct. 2027; Rinaldi v. Yeager, 384 U.S. 305, 309–310, 86 S. Ct. 1497, 16 L. Ed. 2d 577 (1966). Thus, the fact that excluding pregnancy-related disabilities saves costs is only a first step; the state also must show that the exclusion of pregnancy-related disabilities rests upon some ground of difference having a fair and substantial relation to the object of the legislation.

Defendant argues that pregnancy-related disabilities are unique in that coverage of these disabilities is so extraordinarily expensive that it would be impossible to maintain a program supported by employee contributions if these disabilities are included. Unfortunately, it is impossible to determine if the cost of including these disabilities is substantially greater than the cost of including other disabilities, because, according to defendant, no statistics are available indicating the cost to the program of paying benefits on account of various disabilities presently covered. Even using defendant's estimate of the cost of expanding the program to include pregnancy-related disabilities, however, it is clear that including these disabilities would not destroy the program. The increased costs could be accommodated quite easily by making reasonable changes in the contribution rate, the maximum benefits allowable, and the other variables affecting the solvency of the program. For example, the entire cost increase estimated by defendant could be met by requiring workers to contribute an additional amount of approximately .364 percent of their salary and increasing the maximum annual contribution to about $119.

Moreover, regardless of the effect the inclusion of pregnancy-related disabilities would have, these disabilities cannot be excluded merely because the cost of including the entire group might be prohibitive. While some women suffering pregnancy-related disabilities will have large claims, not all pregnant women will. As the court noted in Heath v. Westerville Bd. of Educ., 345 F. Supp. 501, 505 (S.D. Ohio 1972), in its discussion of an analogous problem:

> Pregnancies, like law suits, are sui generis. While there are certain general similarities between each pregnancy, no two are entirely identical. While it may be quite true that

some women are incapacitated by pregnancy and would be well advised to adopt regimens less strenuous than those borne by school teachers, to say that this is true of all women is to define that half of our population in stereotypical terms and to deal with them artificially. Sexual stereotypes are no less invidious than racial or religious ones. Any rule by an employer that seeks to deal with all pregnant employees in an identical fashion is dehumanizing to the individual women involved and is by its very nature arbitrary and discriminatory. [Citations and footnote omitted.]

Similarly, by excluding all pregnancy-related disabilities on the grounds that these claims will be large, the state denies pregnant women benefits on the basis of generalities and stereotypes contrary to the requirements of the equal protection clause.

Like the forced maternity leave in *Heath,* the denial of benefits for pregnancy-related disabilities seems to have its roots in the belief that all pregnant women are incapable of work for long periods of time, and therefore, they will submit large disability claims. The truth of this belief is certainly suspect. As the *Heath* court pointed out, the treatment of pregnancy in other cultures shows that much of our society's views concerning the debilitating effects of pregnancy are more a response to cultural sex-role conditioning than a response to medical fact and necessity. 345 F. Supp. at 505 n. 1. Indeed, a realistic look at what women actually do even in our society belies the belief that they cannot generally work throughout pregnancy. See Struck v. Secretary of Defense, 460 F.2d 1377, 1379 (9th Cir. 1972) (Duniway, J., dissenting), vacated and remanded to consider mootness, 409 U.S. 1071, 93 S. Ct. 676, 34 L. Ed. 2d 660 (1972). Nevertheless, the belief that pregnant women are disabled for substantial periods results in their being denied the opportunity to work, unemployment compensation benefits designed to aid those able to work, and — because of the belief that they will submit large claims — disability insurance benefits. See generally Walker, Sex Discrimination in Government Benefits Programs, 23 Hastings L.J. 277, 282–284, 285 (1971). Thus, the apparently solicitous attitude that pregnant women are in a "delicate condition" has the effect that they often cannot earn an income or obtain the usual social welfare benefits for the unemployed. The only way to assure that this irrational result is not simply the product of mistaken stereotypical beliefs is to require, as the equal protection clause does, that each pregnant woman be considered individually. Cf. Sail'er Inn, Inc. v. Kirby, 5 Cal. 3d 1, 19-20, 95 Cal. Rptr. 329, 485 P.2d 529 (1971).

Therefore, if the state wishes to prevent or limit large claims, it must do so directly by excluding or limiting all claims in excess of certain amounts, not by excluding a disability that, in the opinion of the legislature, is likely to result in large claims. Then, to the same extent a heart attack victim or one suffering from sickle cell anemia is limited in the benefits he can receive, a woman disabled by pregnancy who makes a large claim will be limited.[5] Pregnant women with smaller claims, however, would then be able to collect disability insurance benefits rather than be denied any relief on account of a stereotypical belief about women.[6]

The court, therefore, concludes that pregnancy-related disabilities cannot constitutionally be excluded solely because of the cost of adding these benefits. Defendant has failed to point to any rational ground of difference that would lead the court to conclude that it is not merely saving expense by arbitrarily denying benefits to a class of citizens. Thus, this case is like the hypothetical situation once suggested by the Supreme Court

5. In such a nondiscriminatory system, if the contribution rate generated too much or too little income, increases or decreases in benefits would be spread across the entire work force. In the past, when excess income was generated the legislature increased the benefits to all workers except pregnant women.

6. Although plaintiffs have argued that §2626 is the result of stereotypical beliefs, others have suggested that pregnancy-related disabilities were excluded because women are a politically weak group, and reducing budgets by denying social welfare benefits to groups of women is, therefore, politically expedient. Walker, supra at 285. Precluding discrimination based upon political expediency is, of course, one of the traditional functions of the equal protection clause. See Railroad Express Agency, Inc. v. New York, 336 U.S. 106, 112-113, 60 S. Ct. 463, 93 L. Ed. 533 (1949) (Jackson, J., concurring).

of a state reducing expenditures for education by barring indigent children from the schools. See Shapiro v. Thompson, supra at 633 of 394 U.S., 89 S. Ct. 1322. Accordingly, the saving of cost cannot justify the classification.

The most important aspect of this discussion for Title VII purposes is clarification of the point that the employer should not be able to save costs by forcing a protected class of workers to take fewer benefits than other classes. This point would probably be obvious in the context of racial discrimination (e.g., an employer could not provide health insurance that provided monetary benefits for the treatment of all illnesses but sickle-cell anemia), but the mysticism with which pregnancy is traditionally viewed somehow obscures the sexually discriminatory aspect of such policies when applied to pregnancy. People accept sex divisions as more natural and right than other class distinctions. A recent study of the costs of the Boston Federal Reserve Bank's sick pay program found, for example, that it would cost less to provide sick pay for all employees under thirty-five, including pregnant women, than it would for all employees over thirty-five;[147] yet somehow it does not occur to anyone to save money in such programs by excluding all people over thirty-five from receiving sick pay. In other words, people generally accept the idea that insurance programs should operate by spreading the costs of all physical contingencies for financial loss except for losses caused by pregnancy.

Another point is that the additional costs for including pregnancy-caused disabilities in health and temporary disability insurance plans may not be that high in any case. An ACLU report cites the following data, first for temporary disability insurance, and then for medical insurance coverage.[148]

> In Wisconsin, where in 1971, 46.46 percent of 45,000 employees of the state government were women, it was calculated that out of each $100 that the state incurred in employee costs, 7¢ would be for temporary disability premiums attributable to pregnancy. True, this 7¢ represented a 30 percent increase over income continuation premiums excluding pregnancy (22¢) but only .07 percent of each $100 in employee costs. Thus, when private employers cried that to follow suit would raise their costs by 30 percent, what they actually meant is that their premiums would rise by thirty percent, still a negligible fraction of their real employee costs.[13] . . .
>
> The Citizens' Advisory Council on the Status of Women, a body of private citizens whose members are appointed by the President, estimates that the cost to

147. Greenwald, Maternity Leave Policy, New England Econ. Rev. 13, 18 (Jan./Feb. 1973). The author did a case study of the Federal Reserve Bank of Boston; the figures cited are a projection based on the bank's actual employment statistics, the nature and cost of its sick leave plan, and two different assumptions about how long a leave a pregnant worker would take. Assumption A was one month of leave prior to birth and six weeks after; Assumption B was for all accumulated sick leave (giving average leave of fourteen to sixteen weeks). Both assumptions are somewhat higher than the three to six weeks doctors believe are medically necessary; thus, projections based on these assumptions overstate the costs. But even under the more expensive Assumption B, the projected costs for those under thirty-five remained lower than for those over thirty-five. The figures for 1971 were:

men under 35	$0.09/hour
women under 35	.13/hour
men over 35	.17/hour
women over 35	.19/hour

The figures for 1972 were:

men under 35	$0.08/hour
women under 35	.12/hour
men over 35	.20/hour
women over 35	.17/hour

Id. at 18.
148. Hayden, Punishing Pregnancy, supra footnote 134, at 49, 50, 53-54, 62.
13. Fact sheet from Wisconsin Commission on the Status of Women.

employers of including claims arising from pregnancy under existing temporary disability insurance would be a 10 percent increase in premiums for a six-week benefit. Consider this figure against the fact that the total cost of *all* health, disability, life, and accident insurance premiums is 5.5 percent of the total wage and salary cost in private industry. The Council stresses that the cost of covering pregnancy-related disability can be held down only if there are no artificial pressures or requirements forcing women to stay off the job longer than necessary.[15] . . .

What would it cost to provide maternity payments [in medical insurance]? The Citizens' Advisory Council on the Status of Women sought the answer from the insurance industry itself, and came up with a representative estimate for a work group of whom 31-40 percent are women. These estimates showed that a good hospital, surgical, and major medical package for such a group (*before* discounting for larger employers, who pay less, and without regional and industrial adjustments) would cost $42 per month in premiums for each family without pregnancy benefits, a little less than $1 more per employee to include pregnancy benefits for female employees, and another $4 more per employee to include pregnancy benefits for the wives of male employees.[17]

Thus, if litigators do not succeed in obtaining a narrow reading of the BFOQ, under which the costs of benefits would not be a defense to a charge of sex discrimination, an alternative approach would be to explore the real costs of increased benefits. In doing so, litigators would have to examine the insurance company assumptions underlying cost estimates; one suspects that costs are often calculated on the basis of long leave times, rather than the much shorter period of actual physical disability allowed by the EEOC guidelines.

NOTE: EXPERT TESTIMONY IN PREGNANCY CASES

Because pregnancy is an emotionally charged event in our society, often thought of in semimystical terms, it becomes especially important in pregnancy discrimination litigation to help judges view the issue in terms of facts. The use of expert medical testimony has been useful in achieving this result. Excerpts from the following brief demonstrate the use of this tactic. The brief was filed in the United States Supreme Court by the International Union of Electrical Radio and Machine Workers (IUE) — as amicus curiae in the *La Fleur* and *Cohen* cases. In its Motion . . . For Leave To File Brief As Amicus Curiae, the IUE explained its interest as follows:[149]

1. The applicant is an international labor organization which has as members, and represents, more than 100,000 women employed in the electrical equipment manufacturing industry.
2. During the past two years the IUE has been engaged in negotiations with approximately 400 employers in an effort to obtain collective bargaining provisions which would assure each female employee the right to continue to work at her usual job during pregnancy for as long as she is able to perform her job without injury to herself or her future offspring and the right to be accorded the same terms and conditions of employment as any other disabled employee during any period she is unable to work because of childbirth or other pregnancy-related disability.
3. The IUE is a party plaintiff in the following two cases pending in the federal

15. "Job-Related Maternity Benefits," Remarks by Jacqueline G. Gutwillig, Chairman of Citizens' Advisory Council on the Status of Women, before the Kentucky Hospital Personnel Association, Louisville, Kentucky, April 16–18, 1973.
17. "Information from Insurance Industry Relating to Coverage of Childbirth in Health Insurance and Temporary Disability Insurance," Citizens' Advisory Council on the Status of Women, CACSW Item 20-N, July 2, 1971.
149. Brief of the IUE as Amicus Curiae, pp. 2-3, 4, 5, LaFleur v. Cleveland Board of Education, 414 U.S. 632, 94 S. Ct. 791, — L. Ed. 2d — (1974).

district courts presenting issues which may be materially affected by the decision in this case: Grogg v. General Motors Corp., U.S.D.C. S.D.N.Y. 73 Civ. 63 . . . , [and] Gilbert v. General Electric Co., 5 FEP Cases 989 (U.S.D.C. E.D. Va. 1973). . . .

    4. In addition to the above described cases, the IUE, its affiliated local or a member, with the assistance of the IUE, has filed, and there are presently pending, . . . charges of discrimination because of sex with the Equal Employment Opportunity Commission or a state fair employment practice agency which raise one or more related issues respecting unpaid leave for periods of absence from work because of childbirth or other pregnancy-related disability. . . .

    The IUE believes that the following questions of fact and law have not been, and there is reason to believe they will not be , adequately presented in the briefs of the parties.

    1. Whether there is any medical basis for a rule which requires a female employee because she has reached a specified month of pregnancy and without regard to her actual physical condition, to cease work at any time before the onset of labor. . . .

Much of the IUE brief was in fact devoted to a discussion of medical evidence in other pregnancy discrimination cases that clearly indicated that there is no medical basis for requiring all pregnant women to cease work at a specified month of pregnancy. In an Appendix, the IUE reprinted the testimony and cross-examination of several doctors in pregnancy discrimination cases. The following excerpt was taken from the proceedings in the AT&T case, supra.

Brief of the IUE as Amicus Curiae
Appendix A at 1a-10a, LaFleur v. Cleveland Board of Education,
414 U.S. 632, 94 S. Ct. 791, — L. Ed. 2d — (1974)

TESTIMONY OF ANDRE E. HELLEGERS . . .

My name is Andre E. Hellegers. I am presently Professor of Obstetrics-Gynecology, Professor of Physiology-Biophysics as well as the Director of Population Research at Georgetown University. In addition I am currently president of the Perinatal Research Society. A listing of my further qualifications can be found in the complete curriculum vitae attached hereto.

    There are to my knowledge no physiological data which warrant a rule that women in pregnancies should cease working. It should be recognized that if a woman were to develop diabetes, hypertension, or certain other conditions in pregnancy, then it would be possible that a stoppage of work would become necessary, but this in no way differentiates pregnancy from nonpregnancy, since this statement would be equally true for nonpregnant women, or indeed for men. No medical evidence can be adduced for the need to cease working in pregnancy. Indeed this may be deleterious in some circumstances in which:

    1. Loss of income would occur, which might decrease the quality of the diet consumed in pregnancy.

    2. A woman has several children, in which case her house work is likely to put more strain on her than a regular job in the labor force.

    3. The psychological stress of doing nothing could be worse than that of being gainfully employed.

    The Georgetown Obstetrical Service's advice regarding the desirability of working in pregnancy is individualized for every patient as it would be for nonpregnant patients, male or female, who ask whether they are capable of doing a particular job.

    It is of some significance that women doctors and nurses, who are working on the obstetrical and other services at the hospital often continue working right up to the day of delivery. This of course would not be so if the medical profession thought that working in pregnancy was contraindicated.

Finally, in the only large-scale analysis of work in pregnancy, involving close to four million women, women without incomes had a poorer outcome of pregnancy than women with incomes. The positive correlation between higher social classes and incomes with better pregnancy outcome, and lower social classes and income with worse pregnancy outcome is of course well known.

Knowingly, and in the absence of disease, to remove the opportunity for the income-producing activity from women is therefore to expose women and their unborn children to unnecessary reproductive stresses, unless financial compensation is given. . . .

Cross-Examination By Mr. Levy [the lawyer for AT&T]:

Q. At pages one and two of your testimony, you mention diabetes, hypertension or certain other conditions in pregnancy as making it possible that a work stoppage would become necessary.

Wouldn't such conditions as diabetes and hypertension make it probable if not mandatory to stop work?

A. It would depend on how you would define the diabetes and the hypertension.

There are a lot of non-pregnant men and women with diabetes and hypertension working. That in itself is not a contra-indication to work. If it were, I think a lot of executives would be out of jobs.

Presiding Examiner: How about lawyers.

The Witness: Yes, and doctors.

By Mr. Levy:

Q. Can you identify for us the certain other conditions to which you refer in that sentence?

A. Congenital heart disease, heart failure, cancer, any kind of thing that would make anybody stop working. Let me put it that way.

Presiding Examiner: Are those types that would be aggravated by a pregnancy?

The Witness: No, not necessarily. I am sorry, I did not have in mind a particular aggravation by pregnancy. I had in mind there are obviously pregnant women who should not work as obviously there are men who should not work.

By Mr. Levy:

Q. Dr. Hellegers, at page two, you seem to state categorically that there is no medical evidence for the need to cease working in pregnancy on the one hand and yet, you make reference to the Georgetown Obstetrical Services policy of being individualized for every patient. Are these two statements not inconsistent?

A. No, I don't think so. Perhaps I can explain it a little lower down, even.

One has to individualize in every man and in every woman who comes to consult you, whether they should or should not work. What I am trying to say here is there is nothing inherent in the pregnant state that prevents some from working and the individualization simply means I would say to someone with a massive brain tumor who cannot see straight they might be better off not driving a car.

That is what I meant by individualization.

Q. What are the bases on which the Georgetown Obstetrical Services make an individualized determination whether a patient is capable of doing a job?

A. I would say if a patient has hypertension which is out of control, if a person has diabetes which is out of control, and requires [admission] to a hospital and administration of insulin, then obviously, you would admit her to a hospital. You would do the same thing for a man.

Q. Does pregnancy commonly put stress on such organs as the kidney and the liver?

A. No, it doesn't; I think it is more by virtue of weight and not by virtue of pregnancy. It is akin to an obesity situation.

Q. Couldn't continuation at a job involve exposure to toxic substances which would produce no harm to a normal non-pregnant woman prove to be harmful to a pregnant woman?

A. It is an interesting question. My answer to that would be factually yes, providing that the exposure be in the first 12 weeks of pregnancy which is namely when the organs are being formed.

The difficulty with obstetrical practice is that we have yet to see patients after the time for the damage of irradiation in chemicals has gone by. It is an embryological problem that arises in the first 12 weeks.

Q. I was asking that question as to harm to the pregnant woman herself rather than the fetus she was carrying.

A. I don't think that pregnancy increases the harm which a noxious agent can do to a woman. Let me put it that way.

Q. But you would say that continuation of jobs involving potential exposure to various kinds of radiation or toxic matters or ultra-sound could be potentially harmful to the fetus? . . .

Q. Can't factors associated with normal pregnancy such as increased fluid retention, nausea, swollen ankles, bladder pressure, generally lessen agility because of this 25-pound weight?

Can't some or all of these result in serious diminution in the speed and efficiency required for the performance of certain jobs?

A. Let me put it this way: The water retention in pregnancy is amniotic fluid is 1000 CCs which would be two pounds of water sitting there and then by and large something like five pounds of water which is excess retained in pregnancy and excreted afterwards, so we are talking about something like seven pounds of water which is a heck of a sight less than is carried by most obese men.

I cannot ascribe it to pregnancy but I can ascribe seven pounds of water retained in pregnancy. I cannot ascribe any differences than from men who have had nephritis, to beer drinkers, whatever else retains water, or even salt eaters.

If someone has a particular predilection for salt, they are going to stash away a few pounds of water.

Q. What about some of the other factors that I mentioned? Is morning sickness or nausea fairly common or at least not uncommon in the first trimester of pregnancy?

A. That is correct, yes.

Q. Could that result in diminution of the efficiency required for the satisfactory performance of certain jobs?

A. Yes, I would think it would be in the same ball park as men with ulcers, burping, nausea. Understand me, I am in favor of good health. My testimony was not directed to whether there aren't changes in a woman's body in pregnancy. Obviously there are. My testimony was directed to the question of work.

Q. I am just trying to explore certain parameters of your views.

What about bladder pressure? Is it not uncommon for the developing fetus to impose greater pressure on the bladder than in the normal non-pregnant state?

A. Yes, it does but women, by and large, void less than men. If voiding in frequency and quantity of urine becomes an issue, then people would say men are in more trouble than women because they void more. That is in terms of CCs of urine produced per day is more than women. I cannot ascribe that to a disease.

Q. If there were a job that required continued attendance at a station for let us say hour-long intervals and a normally pregnant woman could not sustain the bladder pressure for that long. This could interfere, could it not, with the efficiency of that operation?

A. Yes, if you have to go to the john, you have to go to the john, man, woman, pregnant woman or anyone else. I must agree.

Q. Again, Doctor, are swelling of the ankles fairly common in pregnancy?

A. Yes, it is.

Q. Can that not possibly have an effect on the satisfactory performance of certain jobs which would call for speed of movement, locomotion?

A. It is impossible to answer that.

Q. You are using void in a different sense.

A. Yes. It is a kind of theoretical statement which asks are our ankles which are four inches in circumference any better than ankles which are six inches in circumference. It is an impossible question for me to answer. I don't know if any job specification goes to the circumference of ankles except in the chorus line.

Q. At page 2 of your testimony, Doctor, you suggest that it is of some significance that women doctors and nurses at the hospital often continue right up to the day of delivery.

Are not the job requirements and potential hazardous exposures quite different from those of telephone workers than doctors and nurses?

A. That is not within my competence to answer. That would mean I know the full telephone business which I do not.

I am saying there is nothing inherently in the pregnant state that eliminates work as a factor and it is best shown that those who most deal with pregnancy, namely obstetricians, nurses, pediatric interns, continue right up to delivery time.

By Mrs. Baker [a lawyer for the Federal Communications Commission]:

Q. You mentioned in your responses earlier that during the first trimester the danger seemed the greatest. Was that to the child or to both the mother and the child?

A. To the child.

Q. I think we are talking perhaps about three different areas of possible danger and harm. One would be to the baby, one would be to the mother and the third one might be others resulting from the mother's condition.

For instance, a woman who may be operating and might faint, might cause some harm to her fellow workmen. The question is: Would this harm be any greater than if a man fainted on a job?

Is there something particular about pregnancy which means when something happens to the woman it is any worse than if it happens to a non-pregnant human being?

A. Let me answer two ways: For the pregnant woman to faint and fall is to herself apart from the fetus no more dangerous than it is for a man to fall.

Q. To those around her?

A. My sort of crazy mind would say would you rather have a 100 pound woman fall on top of you or a 250 pound man?

More to the point would be your third category which is the fetal category and from the falling point of view, if fainting or falling in the first trimester could make you miscarry or something like that, you know we wouldn't have the abortion legislation fights that we have now today because every woman would drop down and abort it.

Unfortunately, or fortunately, one cannot expel a fetus by falling or all legal abortionists would be out of business.

Q. Do you find that all women lose tremendous amounts of dexterity, stamina, during pregnancy, or is this subject to individual variation?

A. It is individual. It depends on the weight gained and it depends on the starting weight.

Let me try to explain this. If a woman is pregnant and weighs 150 pounds to start with, the 20-pound weight gain on her represents obviously much less of a problem than if the 20-pound weight were to start in a girl who weighed 80 pounds.

It is a fraction of weight carried so one can already begin to individualize on that one in very much the same way as sudden weight gain among men.

A 100 pound man who turns obese is affected more than the man who is obese to start with.

Q. Are all pregnant women subject to a tremendous amount of edema?

A. No, it is usually that category of women who have what is called toxemia.

Q. Is exercise contraindicated in edema?

A. No.

Q. Can a pregnant woman lift, let us say, 20 pounds when pregnant if she is capable of doing so?

Will it harm her or her child if she is lifting 20 pounds four times a day and she keeps lifting 20 pounds four times a day, should she be able to do this through her pregnancy? . . .

A. I am bothered by the generality of the question. Lifting 20 pounds of weight is different for the 80-pound woman from the 160-pound woman.

Now let me answer it is contraindicated to lift children anyone can go into any American home where there is a first child and the second child and you see pregnant women lifting children.

Or, you can go to the supermarket and find pregnant women holding onto two pounds. There are pregnant nurses who lift their patients. They are some savvy, of course, about lifting.

Q. Can pregnant women overreach with their arms? Is there anything about pregnancy that would indicate that a woman should not reach right through pregnancy?

A. There is nothing in the pregnancy that tells she could not reach but I remind you again she does carry the weight in front of her and that is an obvious fact.

Nothing can happen to her. She can't have the baby or go into labor.

Q. And that would depend on the women's own feeling to do it every day? Provided they can get up to the desk or whatever, if they are physically capable because of the weight in front of them —

A. There is nothing short in the pregnancy other than the physical mass that contraindicated bending, lifting, and so on.

Q. Just because a woman is nine months pregnant, there is tremendous variation on how much incapacitated, if any, they are?

A. So many women have babies of which we say, gosh, I hardly knew she was pregnant. She does not show, is the common expression. Others show very clearly.

Q. Would the same thing go for bending or spending a number of hours sitting?

A. Sure. Pregnant women do hardly anything but that when they are home, bend, lift — that is the common state of a pregnant woman.

In the brief itself, the IUE summarized the testimony of the doctors. One excerpt, discussing necessary leave time for pregnancy and childbirth, follows.[150]

> Dr. Keetels in his testimony stated that the practice of allowing pregnant women to continue to work till term represents a change in accepted medical views which has occurred within the last four or five years but that the majority of the medical profession today is engaged in regularly advising normal patients that they may continue on their usual jobs until the onset of labor, with more and more doctors shifting continually to this practice. . . . Dr. Donovan . . . and Dr. Wilbanks . . . expressed their agreement with Dr. Keetels that the majority of doctors had now

150. Brief of the IUE as Amicus Curiae, supra footnote 149, at 29, 30, 33.

accepted the view that pregnant women could properly be advised to work until the onset of labor and that the medical profession was engaged in shifting to this view.

Women employed outside the home throughout pregnancy had no greater evidence of complications than those who stayed home. . . . Indeed none of the doctors knew of any instance where working had a detrimental effect on either mother or offspring. . . . All four doctors pointed out that the hospitals were full of female doctors, interns and nurses who worked until they went to the delivery room, in many instances during the shift on which they were working. . . .

These doctors also agreed that it was today accepted medical practice to advise patients to continue throughout pregnancy their usual horseback riding, tennis, swimming, bowling and other sports activities. . . . Dr. Wilbanks mentioned an instance when a pregnant patient's golfing was improved by her pregnancy. . . .

With respect to period of disability following childbirth, all the doctors were agreed on a minimum of 7 to 10 days, an average of two to three weeks, and a maximum of six weeks. . . .

c. Other Facially Discriminatory Policies

To date, most Title VII sex discrimination litigation has centered around openly discriminatory policies because employers and unions were so slow to recognize that sex discrimination really is illegal and had to be discontinued. The following list indicates the wide variety of policies which women have successfully challenged. While most of these cases do not deal with the root causes of women's low economic position, they are important because they have firmly established the fact that employers can no longer afford to treat sex discrimination issues lightly.

(1) *Different pension benefits and retirement ages based on sex.* Rosen v. Public Service Electric & Gas Co., 477 F.2d 90 (3d Cir. 1973) (pension benefits); Rosen v. Public Service Electric & Gas Co., 2 FEP Cases 1090 (D.N.J. 1970), *on remand from* 409 F.2d 775 (3d Cir. 1969) (pension benefits and retirement age); and Bartmess v. Drewrys U.S.A., Inc., 444 F.2d 1186 (7th Cir.), *cert. denied,* 404 U.S. 939 (1971) (retirement age). See also the EEOC Guidelines, 29 C.F.R. §1604.9.

(2) *Sex-segregated help-wanted advertising columns.* Pittsburgh Press Co. v. The Pittsburgh Comm'n on Human Relations, 413 U.S. 376, 93 S. Ct. 2553, 36 L. Ed. 2d 175 (1973) (holding that local agency order under city FEP law, prohibiting newspapers from using sex-segregated help-wanted advertising columns, does not violate the First Amendment). But cf. Brush v. San Francisco Newspaper Printing Co., 469 F.2d 89 (9th Cir. 1972), *cert. denied,* 410 U.S. 943 (1973), and Greenfield v. Field Enterprises, Inc., 4 FEP Cases 548 (N.D. Ill. 1972) (both holding that newspapers are not employment agencies within the meaning of Title VII, and therefore cannot be prohibited under Title VII from providing sex-segregated columns); *contra,* Morrow v. Mississippi Publishers Corp., 5 FEP Cases 287 (S.D. Miss. 1972) (holding somewhat ambiguously that a newspaper which *develops* sex-segregated columns may be an employment agency subject to Title VII proscriptions). The local agency ruling in the first case was based on language in a Pittsburgh law prohibiting action by "any person, whether or not an . . . employment agency" who *aids* another in an unlawful employment practice; Title VII has no such provision. The way around the narrow Title VII construction is to sue the class of defendant employers and employment agencies that advertise in these columns, under Fed. R. Civ. P. 23, which provides that "members of a class may sue or *be sued* as representative parties." [Emphasis added.] In a successful suit, the judge could order the class not to use the columns, thereby forcing the newspapers to stop providing sex-segregated columns for want of advertisers. The device is worth trying, given the lack of success in suing newspapers directly as employment agencies, especially since the law is clear that the practice of advertising in these columns is illegal.See Hailes v. United Airlines, 464 F.2d 1006 (5th Cir. 1972) (finding violation by individual airline for such advertising), and the EEOC guidelines, 29 C.F.R. §1604.5.

(3) Seniority systems based on sex. Bowe v. Colgate-Palmolive Co., 416 F.2d 711 (7th Cir. 1969); Laffey v. Northwest Airlines, Inc., 6 FEP Cases 902 (D.D.C. 1973); 29 C.F.R. §1604.3.

(4) Policies requiring women employees only to remain single. Sprogis v. United Airlines, Inc., 444 F.2d 1194 (7th Cir.), *cert. denied sub nom.* United Airlines, Inc., v. Sprogis, 404 U.S. 991 (1971); Lansdale v. United Airlines, Inc., 437 F.2d 454 (5th Cir. 1971).

(5) Giving priority to unemployed male parents for entry into job training program. Thorn v. Richardson, 4 FEP Cases 299 (D. Wash. 1971).

(6) Refusal to assign male nurses to female patients. Sibley Memorial Hospital v. Wilson, 6 FEP Cases 1029 (D.C. Cir. 1973).

(7) Short hair rules for men but not for women. The case law is unsettled on whether this policy violates Title VII. See Willingham v. Macon Tel. Publishing Co., 5 FEP Cases 1329 (5th Cir. 1973) (holding the policy to be sex discrimination, but remanding for determination of whether it is justifiable under the BFOQ); *contra,* Dodge v. Giant Food, Inc., 6 FEP Cases 1066 (D.C. Cir. 1973) (holding the policy does not constitute sex discrimination).

(8) Wage differences based on sex. Laffey v. Northwest Airlines, Inc., 6 FEP Cases 902 (D.D.C. 1973).

(9) Different work conditions based on sex. Laffey v. Northwest Airlines, Inc., 6 FEP Cases 902 (D.D.C. 1973) (holding that Northwest's policies of requiring stewardesses, but not male pursers, to wear contact lenses rather than eyeglasses, to share hotel rooms on layover, to have weight prescriptions and be monitored for weight maintenance, and to use only certain kinds of luggage, violated Title VII; other invalid policies included imposing a shorter height restriction on the women than on the men, giving only men a cleaning allowance, and imposing a "chain of command" on planes under which all male cabin attendants were superior to all female cabin attendants, regardless of classification or length of service).

C. Neutral Policies with a Discriminatory Impact and the Business Necessity Defense

1. The Legal Standard

There has been one major difference between the litigation of sex discrimination issues and of race and ethnic discrimination issues under Title VII. Most sex cases have concerned openly discriminatory policies, while most race and ethnic cases have concerned apparently neutral policies that, on closer examination, have a discriminatory impact. This may reflect the differing national consenses when Title VII was passed on the importance of prohibiting race and sex discrimination. The sex discrimination prohibition was initially seen as a joke, and most employers made little effort to eradicate openly sexist policies. The same employers took seriously the prohibition on racial discrimination. This did not mean that racial discrimination ceased — only that it took on a more subtle form, while the obvious forms, segregated cafeterias, for instance, were discontinued fairly rapidly. Moreover, the employers who were sued for overt discrimination had no obvious statutory defense such as the BFOQ to such policies (the BFOQ being limited to religion, sex, and national origin discrimination), and thus no ready reason to engage in prolonged litigation in order to continue these policies. Consequently, race discrimination litigators began attacking the more subtle forms of discrimination. Griggs v. Duke Power Company is the leading case on the "neutral rule" doctrine that evolved in these cases.

GRIGGS v. DUKE POWER COMPANY
401 U.S. 424, 91 S. Ct. 849, 28 L. Ed. 2d 158 (1971)

Mr. Chief Justice Burger delivered the opinion of the Court.

We granted the writ in this case to resolve the question whether an employer is prohibited by the Civil Rights Act of 1964, Title VII, from requiring a high school education or passing of a standardized general intelligence test as a condition of employment in or transfer to jobs when (a) neither standard is shown to be significantly related to successful job performance, (b) both requirements operate to disqualify Negroes at a substantially higher rate than white applicants, and (c) the jobs in question formerly had been filled only by white employees as part of a long-standing practice of giving preference to whites.

Congress provided, in Title VII of the Civil Rights Act of 1964, for class actions for enforcement of provisions of the Act and this proceeding was brought by a group of incumbent Negro employees against Duke Power Company. All the petitioners are employed at the Company's Dan River Steam Station, a power generating facility located at Draper, North Carolina. At the time this action was instituted, the Company had 95 employees at the Dan River Station, 14 of whom were Negroes; 13 of these are petitioners here.

The District Court found that prior to July 2, 1965, the effective date of the Civil Rights Act of 1964, the Company openly discriminated on the basis of race in the hiring and assigning of employees at its Dan River plant. The plant was organized into five operating departments: (1) Labor, (2) Coal Handling, (3) Operations, (4) Maintenance, and (5) Laboratory and Test. Negroes were employed only in the Labor Department where the highest paying jobs paid less than the lowest paying jobs in the other four "operating" departments in which only whites were employed. Promotions were normally made within each department on the basis of job seniority. Transferees into a department usually began in the lowest position.

In 1955 the Company instituted a policy of requiring a high school education for initial assignment to any department except Labor, and for transfer from the Coal Handling to any "inside" department (Operations, Maintenance, or Laboratory). When the Company abandoned its policy of restricting Negroes to the Labor Department in 1965, completion of high school also was made a prerequisite to transfer from Labor to any other department. From the time the high school requirement was instituted to the time of trial, however, white employees hired before the time of the high school education requirement continued to perform satisfactorily and achieve promotions in the "operating" departments. Findings on this score are not challenged.

The Company added a further requirement for new employees on July 2, 1965, the date on which Title VII became effective. To qualify for placement in any but the Labor Department it became necessary to register satisfactory scores on two professionally prepared aptitude tests, as well as to have a high school education. Completion of high school alone continued to render employees eligible for transfer to the four desirable departments from which Negroes had been excluded if the incumbent had been employed prior to the time of the new requirement. In September 1965 the Company began to permit incumbent employees who lacked a high school education to qualify for transfer from Labor or Coal Handling to an "inside" job by passing two tests — the Wonderlic Personnel Test, which purports to measure general intelligence, and the Bennett Mechanical Aptitude Test. Neither was directed or intended to measure the ability to learn to perform a particular job or category of jobs. The requisite scores used for both initial hiring and transfer approximated the national median for high school graduates.[3]

---

3. The test standards are thus more stringent than the high school requirement, since they would screen out approximately half of all high school graduates.

The District Court had found that while the Company previously followed a policy of overt racial discrimination in a period prior to the Act, such conduct had ceased. The District Court also concluded that Title VII was intended to be prospective only and, consequently, the impact of prior inequities was beyond the reach of corrective action authorized by the Act.

The Court of Appeals was confronted with a question of first impression, as are we, concerning the meaning of Title VII. After careful analysis a majority of that court concluded that a subjective test of the employer's intent should govern, particularly in a close case, and that in this case there was no showing of a discriminatory purpose in the adoption of the diploma and test requirements. On this basis, the Court of Appeals concluded there was no violation of the Act.

The Court of Appeals reversed the District Court in part, rejecting the holding that residual discrimination arising from prior employment practices was insulated from remedial action.[4] The Court of Appeals noted, however, that the District Court was correct in its conclusion that there was no finding of a racial purpose of invidious intent in the adoption of the high school diploma requirement or general intelligence test and that these standards had been applied fairly to whites and Negroes alike. It held that, in the absence of a discriminatory purpose, use of such requirements was permitted by the Act. In so doing, the Court of Appeals rejected the claim that because these two requirements operated to render ineligible a markedly disproportionate number of Negroes, they were unlawful under Title VII unless shown to be job-related. We granted the writ on these claims. 399 U.S. 926.

The objective of Congress in the enactment of Title VII is plain from the language of the statute. It was to achieve equality of employment opportunities and remove barriers that have operated in the past to favor an identifiable group of white employees over other employees. Under the Act, practices, procedures, or tests neutral on their face, and even neutral in terms of intent, cannot be maintained if they operate to "freeze" the status quo of prior discriminatory employment practices.

The Court of Appeals' opinion, and the partial dissent, agreed that, on the record in the present case, "whites fare far better on the Company's alternative requirements" than Negroes.[6] This consequence would appear to be directly traceable to race. Basic intelligence must have the means of articulation to manifest itself fairly in a testing process. Because they are Negroes, petitioners have long received inferior education in segregated schools and this Court expressly recognized these differences in Gaston County v. United States, 395 U.S. 285 (1969). There, because of the inferior education received by Negroes in North Carolina, this Court barred the institution of a literacy test for voter registration on the ground that the test would abridge the right to vote indirectly on account of race. Congress did not intend by Title VII, however, to guarantee a job to every person regardless of qualifications. In short, the Act does not command that any person be hired simply because he was formerly the subject of discrimination,

4. The Court of Appeals ruled that Negroes employed in the Labor Department at a time when there was no high school or test requirement for entrance into the higher paying departments could not now be made subject to those requirements, since whites hired contemporaneously into those departments were never subject to them. The Court of Appeals also required that the seniority rights of those Negroes be measured on a plantwide, rather than a departmental, basis. However, the Court of Appeals denied relief to the Negro employees without a high school education or its equivalent who were hired into the Labor Department after institution of the educational requirement.

6. In North Carolina, 1960 census statistics show that, while 34% of white males had completed high school, only 12% of Negro males had done so. U. S. Bureau of the Census, U. S. Census of Population: 1960, Vol. 1, Part 35, Table 47.

Similarly, with respect to standardized tests, the EEOC in one case found that use of a battery of tests, including the Wonderlic and Bennett tests used by the Company in the instant case, resulted in 58% of whites passing the tests, as compared with only 6% of the blacks. Decision of EEOC, CCH Empl. Prac. Guide. ¶17,304.53 (Dec. 2, 1966). See also Decision of EEOC 70-552, 2 FEP Cases 539. CCH Empl. Prac. Guide, ¶6139 (Feb. 19, 1970).

or because he is a member of a minority group. Discriminatory preference for any group, minority or majority, is precisely and only what Congress has proscribed. What is required by Congress is the removal of artificial, arbitrary, and unnecessary barriers to employment when the barriers operate invidiously to discriminate on the basis of racial or other impermissible classification.

Congress has now provided that tests or criteria for employment or promotion may not provide equality of opportunity only in the sense of the fabled offer of milk to the stork and the fox. On the contrary, Congress has now required that the posture and condition of the job seeker be taken into account. It has — to resort again to the fable — provided that the vessel in which the milk is proffered be one all seekers can use. The Act proscribes not only overt discrimination but also practices that are fair in form, but discriminatory in operation. The touchstone is business necessity. If an employment practice which operates to exclude Negroes cannot be shown to be related to job performance, the practice is prohibited.

On the record before us, neither the high school completion requirement nor the general intelligence test is shown to bear a demonstrable relationship to successful performance of the jobs for which it was used. Both were adopted, as the Court of Appeals noted, without meaningful study of their relationship to job-performance ability. Rather, a vice president of the Company testified, the requirements were instituted on the Company's judgment that they generally would improve the overall quality of the work force.

The evidence, however, shows that employees who have not completed high school or taken the tests have continued to perform satisfactorily and make progress in departments for which the high school and test criteria are now used.[7] The promotion record of present employees who would not be able to meet the new criteria thus suggests the possibility that the requirements may not be needed even for the limited purpose of preserving the avowed policy of advancement within the Company. In the context of this case, it is unnecessary to reach the question whether testing requirements that take into account capability for the next succeeding position or related future promotion might be utilized upon a showing that such long range requirements fulfill a genuine business need. In the present case the Company has made no such showing.

The Court of Appeals held that the Company had adopted the diploma and test requirements without any "intention to discriminate against Negro employees." We do not suggest that either the District Court or the Court of Appeals erred in examining the employer's intent; but good intent or absence of discriminatory intent does not redeem employment procedures or testing mechanisms that operate as "built-in headwinds" for minority groups and are unrelated to measuring job capability.

The Company's lack of discriminatory intent is suggested by special efforts to help the undereducated employees through Company financing of two-thirds the cost of tuition for high school training. But Congress directed the thrust of the Act to the *consequences* of employment practices, not simply the motivation. More than that, Congress has placed on the employer the burden of showing that any given requirement must have a manifest relationship to the employment in question.

The facts of this case demonstrate the inadequacy of broad and general testing devices as well as the infirmity of using diplomas or degrees as fixed measures of capability. History is filled with examples of men and women who rendered highly effective performance without the conventional badges of accomplishment in terms of certificates, diplomas, or degrees. Diplomas and tests are useful servants, but Congress had mandated the common-sense proposition that they are not to become masters of reality.

7. For example, between July 2, 1965, and November 14, 1966, the percentage of white employees who were promoted but who were not high school graduates was nearly identical to the percentage of nongraduates in the entire white work force.

The Company contends that its general intelligence tests are specifically permitted by §703(h) of the Act. That section authorizes the use of "any professionally developed ability test" that is not "designed, intended, *or used* to discriminate because of race. . . ." (Emphasis added.)

The Equal Employment Opportunity Commission, having enforcement responsibility, has issued guidelines interpreting §703(h) to permit only the use of job-related tests.[9] The administrative interpretation of the Act by the enforcing agency is entitled to great deference. See, e. g., United States v. City of Chicago, — U.S. — (No. 386, O.T. 1970); Udall v. Tallman, 380 U.S. 1 (1965); Power Reactor Co. v. Electricians, 367 U.S. 396 (1961). Since the Act and its legislative history support the Commission's construction, this affords good reason to treat the Guidelines as expressing the will of Congress. . . .

Nothing in the Act precludes the use of testing or measuring procedures; obviously they are useful. What Congress has forbidden is giving these devices and mechanisms controlling force unless they are demonstrably a reasonable measure of job performance. Congress has not commanded that the less qualified be preferred over the better qualified simply because of minority origins. Far from disparaging job qualifications as such, Congress has made such qualifications the controlling factor, so that race, religion, nationality, and sex become irrelevant. What Congress has commanded is that any tests used must measure the person for the job and not the person in the abstract.

The judgment of the Court of Appeals is, as to that portion of the judgment appealed from, reversed.

Note: Testing

The Court prohibited the high school completion requirement and general intelligence test because there was no evidence that either bore "a demonstrable relationship to successful performance of the jobs for which it was used." The EEOC guidelines explore in great detail the kind of data needed to show such a relationship. The process is generally referred to as validating a test or employee selection procedure, and is based on standards developed by the American Psychological Association. For further information, see the EEOC guidelines, 29 C.F.R. Part 1607. George Cooper and Harriet Rabb explore the subject in depth in Equal Employment Law and Litigation 91-154 (Employment Rights Project, Columbia Law School 1972). See also Cooper and Sobol, Seniority and Testing under Fair Employment Laws: A General Approach to Objective Conditions of Hiring and Promotion, 82 Harv. L. Rev. 1598 (1969).

Note: Analysis of the Duke Power Company Policies

Note that the *Griggs* case initially involved both facially discriminatory and facially neutral employment policies. The court of appeals ruled that blacks hired at the same time as whites could not be subjected to hiring standards which were never imposed on

9. EEOC Guidelines on Employment Testing Procedures, issued August 24, 1966, provide: "The Commission accordingly interprets 'professionally developed ability test' to mean a test which fairly measures the knowledge or skills required by the particular job or class of jobs which the applicant seeks, or which fairly affords the employer a chance to measure the applicant's ability to perform a particular job or class of jobs. The fact that a test was prepared by an individual or organization claiming expertise in test preparation does not, without more, justify its use within the meaning of Title II."

The EEOC position has been elaborated in the new Guidelines on Employee Selection Procedures, 35 Fed. Reg. 12333 (August 1, 1970). These Guidelines demand that employers using tests, have available "data demonstrating that the test is predictive of or significantly correlated with important elements of work behavior comprising or relevant to the job or jobs for which Guidelines are being evaluated." Id., at §1607.4(c).

whites, see *Griggs,* n.4, supra. This was a facially discriminatory policy with no possible defense, since there is no race BFOQ. The decision on this issue was not appealed. See Griggs v. Duke Power Company, 420 F.2d 1225 (4th Cir. 1970).

To prove a case under the neutral rule doctrine, litigators must first show that the policy disparately affects a protected class. This is usually done by statistics, see The Use of Statistics, Section F, infra. Civil rights cases in other areas provided a precedent for statistical proof:[151]

> In the area of discrimination "statistics often tell much, and courts listen." State of Alabama v. U.S., 304 F.2d 583, 586 (5th Cir., 1962), *affirmed per curiam,* 371 U.S. 37 (1962).
> The use of statistical proofs of discrimination has been widespread in jury,[18] school[19] and voting cases.[20] These cases have relied primarily on the so-called "rule of exclusion" which originated in Morris v. Alabama, 294 U.S. 587, 55 S. Ct. 579 (1935). Under this rule, the plaintiff is required to show a disparity between the percentage which his class represents in the relevant population sample and the percentage which his class represents on the jury, in a given school, or in the electorate.

Once the plaintiff has shown that the neutral policy disproportionately rejects or affects members of the protected class, the burden of proof shifts to the employer to try to justify this effect as a "business necessity." Robinson v. Lorillard sets forth the standard for business necessity.

ROBINSON v. LORILLARD CORPORATION
444 F.2d 791 (4th Cir. 1971)

Sobeloff, Senior Circuit Judge: — This is a class action arising under Title VII of the Civil Rights Act of 1964, 42 U.S.C. §§2000e, et seq. Plaintiffs are representative members of the class comprised of those Negro employees hired prior to May 31, 1962, into the blending, cutting, service, and shipping and receiving departments of the Lorillard Corporation plant in Greensboro, North Carolina. . . . At issue is the validity, as applied to the above class, of the departmental seniority system provided by the collective bargaining agreement for the plant.

From 1956, when Lorillard's Greensboro plant began operation, until May 31, 1962, Lorillard practiced overt racial discrimination in hiring. Five departments were all-white; Negroes were hired only into blending, cutting, service, and shipping and receiving — the four departments containing the lowest paying, least desirable jobs in the plant. The first collective bargaining agreement, negotiated in 1957, adopted a departmental and job seniority system which determined all important employment rights on the basis of length of service within a department and within a job classification in the department. Transfers between departments were explicitly prohibited.[1]

This departmental seniority system remained in effect unaltered until 1962 when

---

151. Pre-Hearing Memorandum of the Equal Employment Opportunity Commission On the Law of Discrimination, at 17, In the Matter of Petitions filed by the Equal Employment Opportunity Commission Before the Federal Communications Commission, Docket No. 19143 (April 15, 1971).

18. See, e.g., Turner v. Fouche, 396 U.S. 346, 90 S. Ct. 532 (1970); Muniz v. Beto, 434 F.2d 697 (5th Cir. 1970).

19. See, e.g., U.S. v. Hinds County School Board, 417 F.2d 852 (5th Cir., 1969), *cert. denied,* — U.S. —, 90 S. Ct. 612 (1970).

20. See, e.g., State of Alabama v. U.S., supra.

1. The original collective bargaining agreement also provided for certain jobs to be held only by the members of one sex or the other. These restrictions were subsequently dropped and are not at issue here.

it was amended to allow interdepartmental transfers to employees willing to forfeit accumulated seniority and begin as new employees in the department to which they were transferring. The 1962 agreement also abolished job seniority, providing instead for job openings to be filled by the most senior interested employee within the department, regardless of what specific jobs he had previously held.

In 1965, the provisions governing transfer between departments were further modified to allow a transferring employee, laid off because of low seniority in his new department, to return to his old department and maintain his original departmental seniority there. Otherwise, the 1962 transfer restrictions were retained — allowing transfer only when openings were available and only to the lowest paying, entry level jobs. The new collective bargaining agreement negotiated in 1968 made no further changes in the seniority and transfer provisions.

The District Court found the departmental seniority system in violation of the law because it poses a continuing discriminatory barrier to those Negroes who began work at the plant subject to Lorrillard's discriminatory hiring policy prior to May 31, 1962. Therefore, the Court ordered (1) modification of the transfer restrictions to permit employees to transfer to a different department to fill vacancies which may occur and, after a residency period of thirty days in the new department, to exercise their full employment seniority for all purposes, (2) adoption of "red circling" to allow a transfer-ring employee to continue his old wage rate in effect until rising in his new department to a position paying an equal or greater wage rate, and (3) payment of back pay to members of the affected class. . . .

The defendants appeal the finding of discrimination and the award of damages. . . . We affirm the judgment of the District Court with regard to those issues raised by the defendants. . . .

I. THE EXISTENCE OF UNLAWFUL RACIAL DISCRIMINATION

The Civil Rights Act of 1964 does not prohibit or provide a remedy for acts of discrimination which occurred prior to July 2, 1965. Thus, Lorrillard's present hiring policies are not at issue here because there is no evidence of record to establish the existence of a discriminatory hiring policy any later than the spring of 1962. However, "[w]hile it is true that the Act was intended to have prospective application only, relief may be granted to remedy present and continuing effects of past discrimination." Griggs v. Duke Power Co., 420 F.2d 1225, 1230, 2 FEP Cases 310 (4th Cir. 1970).[2] The seminal opinion on this subject is Quarles v. Philip Morris, Inc., 279 F. Supp. 505, 1 FEP Cases 260, 67 LRRM 2098 (E.D. Va. 1968). In that case Judge Butzner of our court, sitting as a district judge by designation, considered carefully the arguments to the contrary and concluded:

> The plain language of the act condemns as an unfair practice all racial discrimina-
> tion affecting employment without excluding present discrimination that originated
> in seniority systems devised before the effective date of the act. . . .
>   . . . The history leads the court to conclude that Congress did not intend to
> require "reverse discrimination"; that is, the act does not require that Negroes be

---

2. The Griggs case was partially reversed by the Supreme Court. Griggs v. Duke Power Co., —U.S. — , 3 FEP Cases 175, 39 LW 4317 (1971). However, the portion of the Fourth Circuit's opinion quoted in the text was not at issue on appeal. See also Parham v. Southwestern Bell Telephone Co., 433 F.2d 421, 427, 2 FEP Cases 1017 (8th Cir. 1970); Jones v. Lee Way Motor Freight, Inc., 431 F.2d 245, 248-49, 2 FEP Cases 895 (10th Cir. 1970), *cert. denied,* 3 FEP Cases 193, 39 LW 3388 (1971); United States v. Dillon Supply Co., 429 F.2d 800, 803-04, 2 FEP Cases 875 (4th Cir. 1970); United States v. IBEW, Local 38, 428 F.2d 144, 149-51, 2 FEP Cases 716 (6th Cir.), *cert. denied,* 400 U.S. 943, 2 FEP Cases 1121 (1970); Local 189, United Papermakers and Paperworkers v. United States, 416 F.2d 980, 991-94, 1 FEP Cases 875, 71 LRRM 3070 (5th Cir. 1969), *cert. denied,* 397 U.S. 919, 2 FEP Cases 426 (1970); United States v. Sheet Metal Workers Int'l Assoc., Local 36, 416 F.2d 123, 131-32, 2 FEP Cases 127 (8th Cir. 1969); Local 53, International Association of Heat and Frost Insulators and Asbestos Workers v. Vogler, 407 F.2d 1047, 1054-55, 1 FEP Cases 577, 70 LRRM 2257 (5th Cir. 1969).

preferred over white employees who possess employment seniority. It is also apparent that Congress did not intend to freeze an entire generation of Negro employees into discriminatory patterns that existed before the act.

279 F. Supp. at 515-16, 1 FEP Cases 268-269, 67 LRRM 2106-2107.

The record amply supports the findings of the District Court that Lorillard's departmental seniority system has a continuing discriminatory impact on the class represented by the plaintiffs. First, because the "white" departments are the better paying ones, the whites hired into those departments under the discriminatory hiring policy are presently receiving higher rates of pay than Negroes hired at the same time into the other four departments. Furthermore, if all barriers to transfer were removed, under a departmental seniority system the plaintiffs will always suffer a real economic handicap in the better paying departments. As transferees they are treated as new hires for departmental seniority purposes, while white coworkers hired at the same time have departmental seniority coextensive with their total employment seniority.

Nor have all barriers to transfer been removed. Since transferees are treated as new hires in the departments to which they are transferring, they start in entry level jobs at entry level pay rates. Thus, while a new department may offer a better long-range future, the immediate effect of transferring is acceptance of a substantial reduction in rate of pay, possibly for an extended period.

The defendants raise several arguments to counter the reasoning of *Quarles* and the numerous cases that have followed *Quarles.* Chief among them is the assertion that Lorillard's departmental seniority system is dictated by business necessity and intended to serve a legitimate business purpose. The terms "business necessity" and "business purpose" — used interchangeably in the briefs — do not represent identical concepts; nor are they equally relevant in assessing the validity of an employment practice. The distinction between them is best explained and understood by examining, first, the Title VII intent requirement, and second, the range of practices prohibited as unlawfully discriminatory under Title VII.

A. Intent

Employment discrimination suits initiated by private individuals are governed by §706 which provides in §706(g) for equitable relief if the court finds that a defendant "has intentionally engaged in or is intentionally engaging in" an unlawful employment practice. Although defendants in Title VII case have sought to establish that this portion of the statute requires that plaintiffs prove the existence of a discriminatory intent, the correct interpretation is that which Judge Wisdom gives in Local 189, United Papermakers and Paperworkers v. United States, 416 F.2d at 996:

[T]he statute, read literally, requires only that the defendant meant to do what he did, that is, his employment practice was not accidental. The relevant legislative history . . . bears out the language of the statute on that point.

The Supreme Court has conclusively adopted this interpretation in Griggs v. Duke Power Co., — U.S. — , 39 LW 4317 (1971). . . . Thus the presence in a respondent's mind of a "business purpose" rather than a discriminatory motive for maintaining a challenged employment practice is not alone determinative of the validity of the practice.

This is not to say that actual intent or motive is irrelevant to determining whether rights assured by Title VII have been infringed. In some instances the reasons for taking particular action may determine whether the action is unlawfully discriminatory. However, if a respondent's actions are otherwise determined to constitute an unlawful employment practice, the existence of a business purpose for continuing the practice will not negate its illegality. . . .

B. Unlawful Employment Practices

It is in determining whether a practice is unlawfully discriminatory that the business necessity test does come into play. The courts have recognized that respondents are sometimes justified in continuing an employment practice regardless of its differential racial impact. The classic example of an acceptable practice is an employer's policy, in filling secretarial positions, of hiring only applicants who can type even though, especially in a limited geographical area, it may be much more difficult for Negroes than for whites to obtain the necessary training and experience.

The business necessity test has evolved as the appropriate reagent for detecting which employment practices are acceptable and which are invalid because based on factors that are the functional equivalent of race. For example, Local 189, United Papermakers & Paperworkers v. United States, supra, was concerned with the validity of a seniority system which, as in our case, was itself neutral but perpetuated the effects of previous racial discrimination in hiring. The Fifth Circuit formulated this expression of the governing test:

> The controlling [sic] difference between the hypothetical typing requirement and the nepotism rule rejected in *Vogler* is *business necessity*. When an employer or union has discriminated in the past and when its present policies renew or exaggerate discriminatory effects, those policies must yield, unless there is an overriding legitimate, non-racial business purpose.

416 F.2d at 989 (Emphasis in original). The Tenth Circuit has framed the test a little differently in Jones v. Lee Way Motor Freight, 431 F.2d 245, 2 FEP Cases 895 (1970), which also involved a neutral transfer policy which perpetuated the effects of prior racial hiring practices: "When a policy is demonstrated to have discriminatory effects, it can be justified only by a showing that it is necessary to the safe and efficient operation of the business." 431 F.2d at 249.

Griggs v. Duke Power Co., supra, presented a slightly more complicated factual situation. . . . [Discussion of decision omitted.]

Collectively these cases conclusively establish that the applicable test is not merely whether there exists a business purpose for adhering to a challenged practice. The test is whether there exists an overriding legitimate business purpose such that the practice is necessary to the safe and efficient operation of the business. Thus, the business purpose must be sufficiently compelling to override any racial impact;[5] the challenged practice must effectively carry out the business purpose it is alleged to serve;[6] and there must be available no acceptable alternative policies or practices which would better accomplish the business purpose advanced, or accomplish it equally well with a lesser differential racial impact.[7]

---

5. The desire of a union to insure family security by restricting new membership to the sons and close relatives of present members may constitute a legitimate "business purpose." But it cannot override the racial impact where present union membership is all-white. See Local 53, International Association of Heat & Frost Insulators and Asbestos Workers v. Vogler, 407 F.2d 1074, 1 FEP Cases 577, 70 LRRM 2257 (5th Cir. 1969).

6. In the *Griggs* case the Supreme Court held that "Congress has placed on the employer the burden of showing that any given requirement must have a manifest relationship to the employment in question." 39 LW at 4319. The Court concluded that Duke Power failed to carry that burden in arguing that its educational standards were necessary to upgrade the quality of the work force:

"On the record before us, neither the high school completion requirement nor the general intelligence test is shown to bear a demonstrable relationship to successful performance of the jobs for which it is used." 39 LW at 4319.

7. It should go without saying that a practice is hardly "necessary" if an alternative practice better effectuates the intended purpose or is equally effective but less discriminatory. Thus, with regard to testing, the Equal Employment Opportunity Commission guidelines stipulate that "where technically feasible, a test should be validated for each minority group with which it is used; that is, any differential rejection rates that may exist, based on a test, must be relevant to performance on the jobs in question." 29 C.F.R. §1607.4(a).

Lorillard advances three "cogent business interests" for maintaining its department seniority system. The first is captioned "Industry Practice and Previous Experience." The substance of this point is that the Greensboro plant was the successor to an earlier Jersey City plant, and the practices at the old site were simply transplanted into the new operation. Lorillard further asserts that its seniority system is similar to those in other collective bargaining agreements in the tobacco industry. These submissions might have some force were it necessary to establish a bad motive or discriminatory intent as one element in a Title VII suit. But neither maintenance of the status quo nor conformance to precedent is a legitimate business purpose that will vindicate an otherwise unlawful practice.

Lorillard's second argument is that the seniority system was only adopted under union pressure, and that, "A company would probably never establish a seniority system of its own accord. . . ." At first blush this appears to be a rather forceful statement that the seniority system serves no business purpose. But Lorillard's apparent point is that it was forced either to accept the system or endure a strike.

Avoidance of union pressure also fails to constitute a legitimate business purpose which can override the adverse racial impact of an otherwise unlawful employment practice. The rights assured by Title VII are not rights which can be bargained away — either by a union, by an employer, or by both acting in concert. Title VII requires that both union and employer represent and protect the best interests of minority employees. Despite the fact that a strike over a contract provision may impose economic costs,[8] if a disciplinary contract provision is acceded to the bargainee as well as the bargainor will be held liable.

Lorillard's third argument, entitled "Efficiency, Economy and Morale," comes closest to stating a legitimate business purpose. The most forceful point under this heading is the assertion that employees will perform a job more efficiently if they have prior experience at other jobs within the same department. However, this "efficiency" business purpose fails to withstand scrutiny for a number of reasons. First, the record is barren of any real evidence that the jobs in the formerly all-white departments are so complex and inter-related that progression through a series of jobs is necessary to efficient performance of the more difficult tasks.

Second, there is direct evidence to the contrary in the fact that the seniority system ordered into effect by the District Court had been originally proposed *by Lorillard* in the course of negotiating the 1968 collective bargaining agreement. The District Court added only the red-circling requirement to remove the wage rate barrier to transfers. Third, Lorillard's efficiency argument is clearly inconsistent with its earlier argument that the seniority system would never have been adopted if the union had not forced it upon the company. Fourth, the order of the District Court specifically provides for a preliminary trial period on the job. If the transferee is unable to perform satisfactorily, the transfer does not become final and the employee returns to his old job.

Finally, it is difficult to imagine how even the necessity for job progression could constitute the business necessity which would justify a departmental seniority system that perpetuated the effects of prior discriminatory practices. For, after all, seniority is necessarily an inefficient means of assuring sufficient prior job experience. It may take only six months to learn a job well and become qualified for advancement. Yet the vagaries of chance may present an opportunity for advancement in only six weeks or not for six years. When some employees have been discriminatorily denied entry to the

---

8. While considerations of economy and efficiency will often be relevant to determining the existence of business necessity, dollar cost alone is not determinative. For example, although there undoubtedly are significant costs involved in validating tests, *Griggs* requires that employment tests be abandoned if not specifically validated as job-related. Analogous is Diaz v. Pan American World Airways, — F.2d — , 3 FEP Cases 337, 469 (5th Cir. 1971), where the court explicitly held that mere customer preference would not justify continuation of a discriminatory hiring policy, even in the context of a sex discrimination case which, unlike race cases, is subject to a "bona fide occupational qualification" exception. Slip opinion at 9.

department, an alternative promotion system could advance the employee who has been discriminated against if he has the greatest employment seniority and has served a necessary minimum time in his present job or has satisfactorily established his capacity to handle the job. Such an alternative plan would accomplish the business purpose "equally well with a lesser differential racial impact."[9]

We recognize Lorillard's point that changing the seniority system may frustrate the expectations of employees who have established departmental seniority but not employment seniority in the preferable departments. However, Title VII guarantees that all employees are entitled to the *same* expectations regardless of "race, color, religion, sex, or national origin." Where some employees now have lower expectations than their coworkers because of the influence of one of these forbidden factors, they are entitled to have their expectations raised even if the expectations of others must be lowered in order to achieve the statutorily mandated equality of opportunity.

We also recognize that some additional administrative costs may be imposed by the order of the District Court. But we have already noted that avoidance of the expense of changing employment practices is not a business purpose that will validate the racially differential effects of an otherwise unlawful employment practice. See note 8, supra.[152]

NOTE: DEPARTMENTAL AND PLANT SENIORITY

To understand the discrimination stemming from departmental seniority systems, it is necessary to know how employment rights are related to seniority. Seniority is the length of time a worker has been with a particular company. If it is measured by the date of hire into the company, it is referred to as employment or plant seniority. If it is measured by the date of assignment to a department within the company, it is referred to as departmental seniority. If it is measured by the date of assignment to a particular job, it is referred to as job seniority.

Employment benefits, such as pay, right to transfer to a higher-paying department, opportunity for promotion, preferential day shifts, avoidance of layoff when plant production requires fewer workers, or choice of vacation time, are often tied to seniority.

As the *Robinson* opinion pointed out, departmental seniority locks blacks (or women) into poorly-paid departments because it gives them incentives to stay in those departments rather than transfer to a department with better long-range possibilities. The incentive mentioned was avoiding the sacrifice in pay entailed in becoming an entry-level employee in the new department. Layoff furnishes another concrete example. Ordinarily, the worker with the longest seniority — whether under a plant or department seniority system — is the last worker laid off when there is a work shortage. Thus, if a woman or minority worker operating under a departmental seniority system has acquired a lot of seniority in one department, she or he is relatively protected against layoff. By transferring to another, better department, however, she or he will have no departmental seniority and thus may be laid off first if a work shortage develops. Few workers will want to risk this, and thus they are locked into the low-paying department. The essential injustice of this scheme can be seen by comparing the plant seniority of various workers. If a woman or black with twenty years plant seniority transfers into a high-paying Anglo male department, she or he will be laid off prior to the Anglo male with five years of plant seniority and five years of department seniority (i.e., the Anglo male who was initially hired into that department). Thus, even though she or he has been working with the company for fifteen years more than the Anglo male, the Anglo male

---

9. Text at note 7, supra.

152. Other decisions on the neutral rule doctrine are cited in the court's footnote 2, supra; see also United States v. Bethlehem Steel Corporation, 466 F.2d 652 (2d Cir. 1971), and Head v. Timken Roller Bearing Co., 6 FEP Cases 813 (6th Cir. 1973). — Eds.

will retain his job when the woman or black does not. Note that this injustice is only illegal under Title VII if the two departments were once sex or race segregated. If they were integrated, departmental seniority does not have an adverse impact on either women or blacks, for it would be likely that Anglo males would be injured by the system as often as women or blacks, and women or blacks would be just as likely as Anglo males to benefit from the system.

One concluding remark about departmental seniority is that it can have some advantages. As the *Quarles* court noted,[153]

> Operation of the company's business on departmental lines with restrictive departmental transfers serves many legitimate management functions. It promotes efficiency, encourages junior employees to remain with the company because of the prospects of advancement, and limits the amount of retraining that would be necessary without departmental organization.

Employment or plant seniority can also be discriminatory, but it is more difficult to attack since the victims of the discrimination are not always readily identifiable. An EEOC Handbook explains:[154]

> Providing a remedy for discrimination where the employer has utilized plant-wide seniority is extremely difficult and there are as yet no cases directly bearing on the point. The closest analogy would be those situations which arise in the building trades. In these cases . . . the collective bargaining agreement will establish preference referral categories based, inter alia, on length of service in the trade. For example, in order to get into the most preferred referral category an individual may be required to have had five years of prior experience under the collective bargaining agreement. Where protected classes have been denied prior opportunities for employment, no or few members of the class can meet the five year experience requirement. The Courts have uniformly ordered qualified blacks or Spanish-Surnamed Americans (there are no cases as yet dealing with sex discrimination in the building trades) to be placed in the most preferred referral category. The effect of this remedy is to give the previously excluded employee a five year seniority credit which makes him competitive with the employees who had previously benefited from the discrimination.
> We noted, however, that in the construction trades, unlike industrial plants, seniority was simply meeting minimum time requirement, whereas in the industrial situation seniority involves a strict ranking of employees depending upon length of service in the seniority unit. Thus, in an industrial plant where there had been past exclusion, the white anglo male workers would all have different seniority dates and would all have different relative rights based on seniority. How then do we provide a remedy where there is past exclusion and plant-wide seniority?
> For example, suppose the employer has a plant seniority system and practiced exclusion on sex until July 2, 1965. During a period of business expansion the employer hired a number of female employees. In a period of business contraction the employer begins to lay off based on plant seniority. Inevitably the female employees are hit the hardest, since none of them have a seniority date earlier than July 2, 1965, whereas the bulk of the male work force may have an earlier date.
> What relief then can we give the charging party who was laid off under a plant seniority system where the hiring practice has been to exclude female employees prior to July 2, 1965? To this time, no Court has dealt specifically with this question except by the analogy which we pointed out in the building trades. It appears to us that the analogy applies also to the industrial scene with appropriate modifications with respect to industrial seniority systems. In other words, it appears to us that a proper remedy would be to give a seniority credit.
> How is such a credit computed? Assuming, in the absence of a contrary proof

153. Quarles v. Philip Morris, Inc., 279 F. Supp. 505 (E.D. Va. 1968).
154. Equal Employment Opportunity Commission, Theory of Relief, A Handbook for Compliance Personnel of the Equal Employment Opportunity Commission 5-7 (November 1971).

that there have been in the community at all times qualified female workers, the appropriate answer would be that a seniority credit could be based on the average seniority of male incumbents. Since, if the employer had not discriminated on the basis of race or sex, the class of female employees would tend to have the same distribution of seniority as the class of male employees. The only way to generate such equality in the face of a practice of exclusion is to vest the class of female employees with average seniority.

In any given case, this might serve as a windfall to any specific employee. For example, if the employee were 22 years old and was given a 10-year seniority credit, it would mean that she would have had to have been eligible for work at age 12. This, of course, is absurd. However, in formulating class relief we are not so much concerned with the specific rights of any individual, but with creating equality for the class. Accordingly, unless the situation is like the example we gave, all of the employees should receive the same credit. Specific circumstances which would diminish any individual's rights have to be established by the employer. Where evidence compels that an adjustment be made then such adjustment should be based on giving a credit which would not exceed the individual's entry into the labor market. But seniority may be computed from the date of first employment in any job.

2. The Development of the Doctrine

a. Discriminatory Impact

One important distinction between *Robinson* and *Griggs* is the cause of the neutral rule's discriminatory impact. In *Robinson,* the company itself had discriminated in the past by segregating departments, and it was only because of the prior company discrimination that the departmental seniority system operated to discriminate against blacks. In *Griggs,* however, although the company itself had indeed discriminated in the past, the current discrimination against blacks arose from societal, not company, discrimination: fewer blacks than whites had completed high school and passed the standardized tests necessary for work in the better-paying departments.

In the development of Title VII law, the *Robinson* situation was the first to arise and was the source of the "neutral rule" doctrine. As the *Robinson* court indicates, Quarles v. Philip Morris, Inc., 279 F. Supp. 505 (E.D. Va. 1968), was the first to deal with a company's argument that[155]

> . . . the present departmental seniority system is not unlawful because it limits on a nondiscriminatory basis the transfer privileges of individual Negroes assigned to the [lower-paying] department years ago pursuant to a policy of segregation which has long since been abolished. . . . [T]he present consequences of past discrimination are outside the coverage of the act.

In rejecting this argument, the court pointed out that[156]

> Present discrimination may be found in contractual provisions that appear fair upon their face, but which operate unfairly because of the historical discrimination that undergirds them.

In Local 189, United Papermakers & Paperworkers v. United States, 416 F.2d 980 (1969), *cert. denied sub nom.* Papermakers and Paperworkers, Local 189 v. United States, 397 U.S. 919 (1970), another important opinion, the Fifth Circuit expanded on this concept, using prior civil rights case law in other areas to buttress the point that "facially neutral but needlessly restrictive tests may not be imposed where they perpetuate the effects of

155. 279 F. Supp. at 515.
156. Id. at 518.

previous racial discrimination."[157] *Griggs* then expanded the application of the "neutral rule" doctrine from systems that perpetuated the effects of past company discrimination to systems that had a discriminatory impact because of general societal conditions. Further expansion of the doctrine takes it beyond a disparate impact produced by general conditions to any disparate impact. For example, a minimum height requirement might be invalidated under the doctrine because it falls more heavily on women and members of certain ethnic groups.

b. Business Necessity

The development of the business necessity aspect of the "neutral rule" doctrine began with the *Local 189* decision, supra. The term business necessity came from a pre–Title VII case, Whitfield v. United Steelworkers, Local 2708, 263 F.2d 546 (5th Cir. 1958), in which the court had upheld a seniority system against a claim of race discrimination, partly on the ground that the "system was conceived out of business necessity, not out of racial discrimination."[158] In *Local 189,* the Fifth Circuit invalidated a seniority system under Title VII; in doing so, it distinguished its prior *Whitfield* decision on the basis of the supposed business necessity of the *Whitfield* system. The difference between the two decisions is more probably explained by the different judicial climates in 1958 (pre–Title VII) and 1969 (post–Title VII), but the "business necessity" distinction survived and became an important part of Title VII law, as *Griggs* and *Robinson* demonstrate.

3. Other Neutral Rule Decisions

There are many policies besides testing requirements and seniority systems that have been invalidated under the neutral-rule doctrine. Cooper and Rabb cite many cases.

COOPER AND RABB
EQUAL EMPLOYMENT LAW AND LITIGATION
6, 9-12 (1972)

The first practice challenged was nepotism and related rules giving preference to the family or friends of incumbent workers. These nepotic practices are not necessarily motivated by discriminatory intent, since it is a common human desire to protect one's family and friends regardless of one's prejudices. However, in offices or plants which have a predominantly white work force, the effect of a nepotic preference was to preserve the whiteness of the employee work force. This effect was ruled unlawful in Local 53, Asbestos Workers v. Vogler, 407 F.2d 1047 (5th Cir. 1969), United States v. Local 86, Ironworkers, 315 F. Supp. 1202 (W.D. Wash. 1970), *aff'd,* 443 F.2d 544 (9th Cir. 1971) and Lea v. Cone Mills Corp., 301 F. Supp. 97 (M.D.N.C. 1969), *rev'd on other grounds,* 438 F.2d 86 (4th Cir. 1971). These recent Federal court decisions were anticipated many years ago by the New York courts in State Commission for Human Rights v. Farrell, 43 Misc. 2d 958, 965-66, 252 N.Y.S.2d 649, 657 (Sup. Ct. 1964), a decision which ruled that nepotic practices in a construction trade local violated the New York Human Rights Law.

The next context in which discriminatory practices were challenged was that of seniority systems. . . .

Related to these seniority decisions are cases involving union referral systems. Many unions, particularly in the construction trades, operate hiring halls or other systems whereby skilled persons are routed to jobs. These referral systems typically gave preference to persons who had previously worked under the union's jurisdiction, which

157. 416 F.2d at 991.
158. 263 F.2d at 550.

operated to perpetuate the traditional exclusion of blacks and ethnic minorities from construction trade work. The courts, in several cases, refused to accept this result and barred further use of such preferences. United States v. Sheet Metal Workers Local 36, 416 F.2d 123 (8th Cir. 1969); United States v. Local 86, Ironworkers, 315 F. Supp. 1202 (W.D. Wash. 1970), *aff'd,* 443 F.2d 544 (9th Cir. 1971).

One common aspect of all these cases, whether involving nepotism, seniority or union referral, is that the discriminatory effect stemmed from the union's or the employer's past discrimination. A somewhat different issue was presented in cases challenging employer use of standardized aptitude tests. These tests have a discriminatory effect because educationally deprived groups (including blacks and ethnic minorities) are at a disadvantage in taking them. However, this disadvantage is not the result of the employer's past discrimination but rather general societal practices. Nonetheless, the courts have made it clear that the discriminatory effects of tests make them vulnerable under Title VII. Griggs v. Duke Power Co., 401 U.S. 424 (1971); Hicks v. Crown Zellerbach Corp., 319 F. Supp. 314 (E.D. La. 1970), *order entered* 321 F. Supp. 1241 (E.D. La. 1971); Chance v. Board of Examiners, 458 F.2d 1167 (2d Cir. 1972). On the same theory, other courts have barred employers from imposing minimum educational requirements (Griggs v. Duke Power Co., supra) and refusing to hire persons with arrest records (Gregory v. Litton Systems, Inc., 316 F. Supp. 401 (C.D. Cal. 1970)). In non–Title VII cases, courts have barred employers from refusing to hire women with illegitimate children (Cirino v. Walsh, 66 Misc. 2d 250, 321 N.Y.S.2d 493 (Sup. Ct. 1971)) and from imposing minimum height and weight requirements which operate adversely on women and Spanish surnamed groups (New York State Division of Human Rights v. New York-Pennsylvania Baseball League, 36 App. Div. 2d 364 (1971), *aff'd,* 29 N.Y.2d 921 (1972)).

The most recent development in this pattern of expanding coverage is that courts have begun to make it clear that subjective practices as well as objective requirements are covered by the strictures of Title VII. Thus, in Rowe v. General Motors Corp., 457 F.2d 348 (5th Cir. 1972), the court ruled that a system of allowing foremen virtually unfettered discretion in selecting employees for promotion was unlawful insofar as it imposed no check against the possibility of biased judgments by foremen. See Brown v. Gaston County Dying Mach. Co., 457 F.2d 1377 (4th Cir. 1972).

The EEOC describes other policies:[159]

> A closely related and equally unlawful employment practice is a "neutral" rule which prohibits transfers between different departments at a plant where the departments were formerly sex — or race — segregated. While the no-transfer rule applies to Anglo males as well as females and minorities, it is unlawful if it locks incumbent employees into formerly segregated departments. The Tenth Circuit recently banned the no-transfer rule as commonly used throughout the trucking industry to prevent city drivers to transfer to long-distance driver jobs:
> "To summarize, we hold that the no-transfer policy, as applied to plaintiffs, is an unlawful employment practice within the meaning of §2000e-2(a) because it perpetuates past discrimination, by preventing them from having jobs which were formerly denied to them because of their race, and because it does not satisfy the business necessity test." Jones v. Lee Way Motor Freight, 431 F.2d 245, 250 (10th Cir., 1970), *cert. denied,* — U.S. —, 3 EPD ¶8139, 3 FEP Cases 193 (1971).
> . . . [T]he courts have held recruitment practices directed largely towards attracting white males unlawful because they produce few, if any, women, blacks, or Spanish-surnamed American applicants.[28]

---

159. Pre-Hearing Memorandum of the Equal Employment Opportunity Commission on the Law of Employment Discrimination at 12, 23-25, In the Matter of Petitions Filed by the Equal Employment Opportunity Commission Before the Federal Communications Commission, Docket No. 19143 (April 15, 1971).
28. See, e.g., Parham v. Southwestern Bell Telephone Co., [433 F.2d 421 (8th Cir. 1970)]; Clark v.

A common recruitment device, for example, is to rely heavily on referrals from current employees to produce a flow of job applicants. Where, however, the employer already has a predominantly white male work force, such a system will produce few, if any, female, black, or Spanish-surnamed American applicants since referrals from employees tend to reflect the ethnic and sexual composition of the work force. The recruiting-through-employees system, in such a case, although a "neutral" practice, has a disparate impact on women and minorities and is not compelled by business necessity. It is therefore unlawful. . . . For similar reasons, the courts have held that word of mouth recruitment systems[30] and a policy of giving hiring preference to friends and relatives of employees[31] were unlawful employment practices.[32]

Other standard recruiting practices, such as visits to schools and advertising campaigns, are also unlawful if they do not reach all groups protected by Title VII. The Alabama State Personnel Board, for example, was found to discriminate by administering state employment examinations only at predominantly white schools and by failing to send its information mailings to newspapers or radio stations with predominantly black audiences. United States v. Frazier, — F. Supp. — , 63 LC ¶9502, 2 FEP Cases 847 (M.D. Ala., 1970).

4. Neutral Policies That Discriminate Against Women

a. A Minimum Weight Requirement

MEADOWS v. FORD MOTOR COMPANY
5 FEP Cases 665 (W.D. Ky. 1973)

ALLEN, District Judge: — Plaintiff, Dolores Marie Meadows, suing on behalf of herself and other women similarly situated, the scope of whose class has previously been fixed by this Court, has filed a renewed motion for summary judgment on liability. . . .

It appears from the evidence that 54 women have applied for employment on the production line of the Kentucky Truck Plant since plaintiff filed her application on October 10, 1969. None of these applicants have been employed, and it is admitted by defendant Ford that it has hired 935 production workers between October, 1969 and October, 1971. It is admitted also by Ford that it maintains an employment policy which requires a minimum weight of 150 pounds. An exhibit attached by plaintiff to her memorandum establishes that 80 per cent of all females from 18 to 24 years of age in the population of the United States cannot meet the 150 pound requirement, while 70 percent of the men in this age bracket do meet that requirement.

It is further established by the deposition of Dr. Charles E. Allen, Ford's physician, that Ford has made exceptions to its minimum 150 pound requirement for men who weighed between 135 and 150 pounds but has made no exceptions for women. It is also established from Dr. Allen's deposition that neither the company nor he has made any studies or tests to determine the strength of people weighing over 150 pounds as contrasted with those who weigh 150 pounds. Dr. Allen admits that at no time, although

American Marine Corp., [304 F. Supp. 603 (E.D. La. 1969)]; Lea v. Cone Mills Corp., 301 F. Supp. 97 (M.D.N.C., 1969).

30. Clark v. American Marine Corp., supra, 304 F. Supp. at 606.

31. Lea v. Cone Mills Corp., supra, 301 F. Supp. at 102.

32. Even if an employer employs a substantial number of females, blacks, and Spanish-surnamed Americans, employee referral systems and other like recruitment practices are still unlawful if the women, black, and Spanish-surnamed American employees are concentrated in certain particular jobs. Parham v. Southwestern Bell Telephone Co., supra, 433 F.2d at 427, n.5. Male employees, for example, are likely to refer their male friends and relatives for the "male" jobs and their female friends and relatives only for the "female" jobs.

he is the person who is designated by the Company to make physical examinations of all persons seeking employment on Ford's production line, has he been asked to perform a physical examination on a woman seeking such a job.

In the case of Rosenfeld v. Southern Pacific Company, 444 F.2d 1219, 3 FEP Cases 604 (9th Cir. 1971), summary judgment was rendered by the district court for the plaintiff woman employee bringing suit under Title 7, the Civil Rights Act of 1964. The specific position involved was that of an agent-telegrapher and the work requirements which that position entailed could have involved as much as 10 hours a day and 80 hours a week. The position required the heavy physical effort involved in climbing over and around box cars to adjust their vents, collapse their bunkers, and close and seal their doors. In addition, the employees were required to lift various objects weighing more than 25 pounds and in some instances more than 50 pounds.

The Railroad argues that it was their policy to exclude women generically from such positions for two basic reasons, one of which was the arduous nature of the work related activity which rendered women physically unsuited for the jobs, and the other reason is not applicable here. The court, in upholding the summary judgment in the district court, stated, in part, on page 1225, 3 FEP Cases at 608:

> The premise of Title VII, the wisdom of which is not in question here, is that women are now to be on equal footing with men. Weeks v. Southern Bell Tel. & Tel. Co., 408 F.2d 228, 236, 1 FEP Cases 656, 70 LRRM 2843 (5th Cir. 1969). The footing is not equal if a male employee may be appointed to a particular position on a showing that he is physically qualified, but a female employee is denied an opportunity to demonstrate personal physical qualification. Equality of footing is established only if employees otherwise entitled to the position, whether male or female, are excluded only upon a showing of individual incapacity. See Bowe v. Colgate-Palmolive Co., 416 F.2d 711, 718, 2 FEP Cases 121 (7th Cir. 1969). This alone accords with the Congressional purpose to eliminate subjective assumptions and traditional stereotyped conceptions regarding the physical ability of women to do particular work.

In Parham v. Southwestern Bell Telephone Company, 433 F.2d 421, 2 FEP Cases 1017 (8th Cir. 1070), at page 426, the court pointed out that "[i]n cases concerning racial discrimination, 'statistics often tell much and Courts listen'." The court held that where the statistics revealed an extraordinarily small number of black employees, except for the most part as menial laborers, there was a violation as a matter of law of Title 7, the Civil Rights Act of 1964.

In Bowe v. Colgate-Palmolive Company, 416 F.2d 711, 2 FEP Cases 121, the Seventh Circuit struck down a job restriction imposed by appellee which confined women to jobs not requiring the lifting of more than 35 pounds. The Appellate Court held that the trial court should have entered an injunction prohibiting the company from continuing the weight requirement limitation confined to women only. The court did allow the Colgate-Palmolive Company to retain a 35 pound weight lifting limitation as a general guide-line for all its employees, male and female, however, it required Colgate-Palmolive to notify all of its workers that such of them who desire to do so would be afforded a reasonable opportunity to demonstrate his or her ability to perform more strenuous jobs on a regular basis. In discussing the trial court's error in not granting a preliminary injunction, the court stated that had the trial court correctly perceived the meaning of BFOQ, it would have issued an injunction.

In the light of these decisions, it now becomes apparent to this Court that the 150 pound minimum weight requirement as it is administered by Ford, although neutral on its face, is highly discriminatory in practice and violative of the Civil Rights Act, Title 42 U.S.C §2005(e). The plaintiff is entitled to an injunction prohibiting Ford from continuing its 150 pound minimum weight requirement policy, especially as it is now administered.

NOTE: THE DIFFERENCE BETWEEN THE BUSINESS NECESSITY AND THE BFOQ DEFENSES

Note that Ford practiced two forms of discrimination: one facially discriminatory policy of making hiring exceptions for men, but not for women weighing between 135 and 150 pounds; and one neutral policy requiring that workers weigh 150 pounds. The court did not treat the two issues separately, however, and a subsequent decision in the same case indicates that the court was somewhat confused about the relationship between the "BFOQ" and "business necessity" defenses. In awarding final judgment to plaintiff, the court stated:[160]

> The establishment of policies or practices by an employer that are neutral on their face, but discriminatory in their effect, and that have no valid relationship to the accomplishment of the particular job, have been thoroughly condemned by the Supreme Court in Griggs v. Duke Power Company, 401 U.S. 424, 3 FEP Cases 175 (1971) and by the Seventh Circuit in Bowe v. Colgate-Palmolive Company, 416 F.2d 711, 2 FEP Cases 121, 223 (1969). The 150 pound restriction, as applied by the defendant, does not have a valid relationship to the ability of a person weighing less than 150 pounds to perform the task required of him and, therefore, does not constitute a bona fide occupational qualification, and, hence, defendant may not vindicate its policy by relying on that defense. See Bowe v. Colgate-Palmolive Company, supra.

In fact, the court misstated the holding of the *Bowe* decision, which invalidated a facially discriminatory policy, not a facially neutral policy. It is important not to confuse the two kinds of discrimination and their respective defenses, since the business necessity defense conceivably allows the employer more latitude to discriminate than does the BFOQ defense. Compare, for example, the standard for the BFOQ defense under Rosenfeld v. Southern Pacific Co., 444 F.2d 1219 (9th Cir. 1971) supra, with that for the business necessity defense under Robinson v. Lorillard, 444 F.2d 791 (4th Cir. 1971), supra. Employers' attempts to raise a cost defense to pregnancy-related discrimination provide a further illustration. Since cost is probably not a BFOQ defense, but might be a business necessity defense,[161] it will be an important element of pregnancy discrimination litigation to limit employers to the BFOQ defense. See Note: The BFOQ Defense in Pregnancy Discrimination Cases, supra, explaining why cost is not a BFOQ defense and discussing employers' attempts to justify the exclusion of pregnancy-related disabilities from health and temporary disability insurance plans because of the costs of including these disabilities.

An EEOC lawyer has explained at length some differences between business necessity and the BFOQ defenses:[162]

> The BFOQ is a statutory defense, written explicitly into Section 703(e) of the Act. It provides that when an employer has an *explicit* policy of hiring or employing employees on the basis of sex, national origin or religion (e.g., a refusal to hire women as airplane pilots or a refusal to hire a Mexican-American as a cook in a Chinese restaurant), he may justify that policy if he can show that being male (or Chinese) is in fact, in the words of the statute, "reasonably necessary to the normal operation of that particular business or enterprise."
>
> Under the express wording of the statute, the BFOQ is a defense to discrimination on the basis of religion, sex or national origin, never to discrimination on the basis of race. Thus, in enacting Section 703(e), Congress made a judgment that overt dis-

160. Meadows v. Ford Motor Co., 6 FEP Cases 797, 802 (W.D. Ky. 1973).
161. The distinction may be more theoretical than real; see *Robinson,* supra, specifically disallowing a business necessity cost defense.
162. Nancy Stanley, Memorandum to Beatrice Rosenberg, Chief, Appellate Division, Business Necessity and BFOQ Defense, Equal Employment Opportunity Commission, Feb. 13, 1973. (Emphases in the original.)

crimination against blacks is *never* permissible. An employer cannot, for example, refuse to hire blacks as door-to-door insurance salesmen in a white suburban neighborhood on the grounds that being white is a BFOQ for the job. . . .

Business necessity, on the other hand, is a judicial doctrine, articulated by the Supreme Court in Griggs v. Duke Power Co., 401 U.S. 424 (1971) as a defense in *neutral rule* situations when unintended[163] discrimination takes place. For example, an employer may have a recruitment system which, though fair on its face, relies heavily on referrals from white male employees and therefore operates to produce only other white males as applicants for available jobs. The system is *neutral,* but it has a disparate effect on women and blacks. In such a situation an employer can defend his neutral policy by arguing that "business necessity" compels it.

Unlike the BFOQ, business necessity is a defense to race discrimination, as well as to discrimination on the basis of religion, sex and national origin. . . .

A good discussion of both the BFOQ and business necessity defenses and of the confusion between them can be found in Oldham, "Questions of Exclusion and Exception Under Title VII — 'Sex-Plus' and the BFOQ," 23 Hastings Law Journal 55, 71-91 — see especially footnote 84, p. 72.

b. Other Policies

There are a growing number of neutral-rule sex discrimination cases, although they still constitute a distinct minority of all sex cases. The neutral-rule doctrine will become increasingly important in Title VII sex cases as employers realize that overtly discriminatory policies are illegal and thus turn to more subtle forms of discrimination. See, e.g., Danner v. Phillips Petroleum Co., 447 F.2d 159 (5th Cir. 1971) (reprinted in Note: A Refusal to Grant Class-Wide Relief, Section F-4 infra; holding that the policy of granting seniority and bumping rights only to holders of unionized jobs discriminated against women in violation of Title VII); Leisner v. New York Telephone Co., 5 FEP Cases 732 (S.D.N.Y. 1973) (discussed in the Note following Liberating Ma Bell, Section G-1-c infra; holding the women plaintiffs were entitled to a preliminary injunction under Title VII against defendant's use of such nonvalidated criteria for management jobs as prior supervisory experience, including military experience, and technical degrees); Feinerman v. Jones, 5 FEP Cases 901 (M.D. Pa. 1973) (upholding under the Fourteenth Amendment the state veteran's preference statute for awarding civil service jobs, in a poorly reasoned decision); Rose v. Bridgeport Brass Co., 6 FEP Cases 837 (7th Cir. 1973) (holding it was error to grant summary judgment to employer under Title VII where the job reclassification systems disproportionately eliminated women from the press operator position); Andrews v. Drew Municipal School District, 6 FEP Cases 872 (N.D. Miss. 1973) (holding that policy of barring from employment teachers who had illegitimate children violated Fourteenth Amendment); Smith v. City of East Cleveland, 6 FEP Cases 493 (N.D. Ohio 1973) (holding that minimum height and weight requirements for police officer position violated Fourteenth Amendment).

Another source of information on neutral policies that discriminate against women workers is the EEOC Prehearing Analysis and Summary of Evidence in the AT&T case. See AT&T: A Study in Sex Segregation, Section B-4-a supra. This document reveals that AT&T companies use almost as many neutral policies that discriminate against women as the overt policies discussed supra. For example, they use word-of-mouth recruitment policies, refuse to hire persons with illegitimate children, set minimum height requirements, use departmental seniority systems, give preference to new hires over transfers in promoting, and require prior craft experience for promotion to certain craft jobs.

---

163. The neutral rule doctrine is not of course limited to unintentional discrimination. A facially neutral policy which was adopted because the employer knew it would exclude disproportionate numbers of blacks, women, or other minorities is also prohibited. — Eds.

D. UNION LIABILITY

1. The History of Sex Discrimination by Unions

The following article will give the reader some idea of the dimensions and background of union sexism in the United States. In reading it, note the specific practices discussed to get ideas about the kinds of changes in unions women workers and feminist lawyers should seek today.

FALK, WOMEN AND UNIONS: A HISTORICAL VIEW
Women's Rights L. Rep. 54-65 (Spring 1973)

A. THE EARLIEST TRADE UNIONS

To have an understanding of the present-day sexism of labor unions, it is necessary to go back to the anti-woman origins of the earliest trade unions.[1] The earliest trade unions in America derived from working men's social clubs, which were thought of as a refuge from the worries of home and family. The trade unions that developed out of these clubs used men's jargon, and the meeting place was most often a thoroughly male location — the neighborhood saloon.[2]

The first American trade unions were established in the 1820's among the printers, cordwainers and carpenters, occupations in which there were no women. At this same time about 66,000 women were employed in the New England cotton mills.[3] The fact that these women had serious grievances and an ability to organize themselves was demonstrated as early as 1828 when the cotton mill workers of Dover, New Hampshire, marched out of work to protest a reduction of wages. They paraded, carried signs, held protest meetings, and eventually won their strike. The growth of labor activity among women during the next three decades was parallel to but independent of the growth of men's trade unions. Walkouts of women workers followed the Dover strike in mill towns all over the East Coast — in Lowell, Pittsburgh, Manchester, Taunton and Chicopee.[4] For the most part the men's unions took no interest in working women, though a few segregated "sister" unions were formed. In Philadelphia, a union of female cigarmakers was formed in 1835, separate from the Journeymen Cigarmakers.[5] The Daughters of St. Crispin, an organization of female shoe workers, was formed in 1869 after male shoe and bootmakers had organized the Knights of St. Crispin.[6] The Female Labor Reform Association founded in Lowell spread to other mill towns, but died out in a few years. Separate women's unions were formed among the collar workers, tailoresses, seamstresses, umbrella sewers, capmakers, textile workers, printers, launderesses and furnishers.[7]

None of the unions of women was able to sustain itself very long. Working women then, as now, frequently carried a double burden — responsibility for a home and family as well as for a job. Women lacked money for organizations, for dues, strike funds, and the expense of spreading the word to other women since they were generally paid only a fraction of what men were paid for the same work, and they were employed almost entirely in unskilled jobs.[8] Women had been traditionally isolated from one another in

---

1. Beatrice and Sidney Webb, Industrial Democracy 495, go back even farther, to the 14th Century guilds which excluded women.
2. T. Wolfson, The Woman Worker and the Trade Unions 56 (1926).
3. Id. at 58.
4. Flexner, Century of Struggle 55 (1959); Foner, History of the Labor Movement, vol. I at 108 (1947).
5. Foner, supra note 4, at 111.
6. Wolfson, supra note 2, at 60.
7. Foner, supra note 4, at 383.
8. Flexner, supra note 4, at 57-60.

the home; they were inexperienced in organizations and were unused to thinking of themselves as workers.[9] Moreover, far more than men, women workers who attempted to organize were met with strong disapproval. For instance, in 1831 when New York tailoresses were trying to organize, the *Boston Transcript* denounced their efforts as, "clamorous and unfeminine declarations of personal rights which it is obvious a wise Providence never destined her to exercise."[10] Thus a vicious circle was set up which continues today: men exclude women workers from full participation in their unions. Women, lacking bargaining power, were forced to work at lower wages under inferior working conditions. Employers could use women workers to undercut the wages and organizational efforts of men.

B. 1865 TO 1885

Very slowly a few enlightened men trade unionists began to see that women were in the work force to stay and that the interests of men workers lay in joining with their women co-workers, rather than excluding them.

At its first convention in 1866, the National Labor Union, a short-lived federation of national unions, had solicited the "hearty co-operation of women" but had not offered to organize them.[11] In 1867 the Cigarmakers admitted women to their union.[12] The National Typographical Union had passed a resolution in 1854 condemning the employment of women compositors. Women continued to be employed in the trade, however, and in 1869 Women's Typographical Union No. 1 was granted a charter by the international union. Three years later, at the 1870 convention, the typographers concluded that dual unionism led to two wage levels — one for men and a lower one for women — and decided not to charter any more women-only locals.[13] Up to 1880 the printers and cigarmakers were the only two of more than thirty national unions to admit women.[14]

Even more so than today, women workers in the nineteenth century were confined to unskilled and semi-skilled jobs. Thus it is not surprising that the first wide-scale organizing of women was done through the Knights of Labor, a national organization dedicated to the organizations of all workers, unskilled as well as skilled, which grew quickly in the 1880's. The history of the early years of the Knights indicates the chauvinism inherent even in an organization philosophically committed to the interests of all workers. In 1879, a resolution admitting women to membership and permitting them to form assemblies on the same basis as men was defeated[15] even though the preamble to the Constitution adopted in 1878 listed as one of the Order's principal objectives, "to secure for both sexes equal pay for equal work."[16] Not until 1882 did the convention vote to permit the initiation of women.[17]

The Knights organized men and women in the same assemblies and also chartered separate women's assemblies. Flexner claims that most efforts of the Order to organize women workers were sparked by a small group of women within the organization.[18] In

9. S. C. Hewitt, an organizer of the Fall River Mechanics Association, was far ahead of his time in 1844 in believing that women should be members of every labor movement. He discovered that he had to mention women explicitly in his writing and speaking because when he put out a call for "workingmen" women did not understand themselves to be included. Foner, supra note 4, at 204.

10. Quoted in Dickason, *Women in Labor Unions,* 251 Annals of the American Academy of Political and Social Science 70 (May 1947).

11. Wolfson, supra note 2, at 59.

12. Foner, supra note 4, at 383.

13. Id. at 384.

14. Id. at 388. This was at a time when the female workforce numbered 2,647,000 and was 15.2 per cent of the total labor force. Flexner, supra note 4, at 193.

15. Wolfson, supra note 2, at 61.

16. Quoted in Foner, supra note 4, vol. II at 61.

17. Id. Even then, the very name of the organization must have discouraged some women.

18. Flexner, supra note 4, at 195.

any case, by 1886, at the height of the Knights of Labor's membership, 121 women's assemblies existed and the Order had about 50,000 women members who formed eight to nine per cent of its total membership.[19] Women formed between 15 and 17 per cent of the total work force at this time.[20] However, in the peak year, 1886, only 16 of the 660 delegates, or between two and three per cent, to the annual convention were women.

The Knights were more strongly committed to organizing women than any other labor organization and their swift decline in the late 1880's put a serious damper on labor organizing among women.

c. 1885 to 1930[21]

The American Federation of Labor (AFL) began to grow in the late 1880's just as the Knights of Labor were declining. Perhaps because of competition with the Knights of Labor, the Federation showed a certain interest in women in its early years. In 1891 the AFL endorsed Women's suffrage.[22] In the late 1880's and early 1890's the AFL chartered some all-women Federal Labor Unions, some of which formed effective nuclei for organizing women workers by craft. A few special women organizers were appointed, and in 1892 Mary Kenney, a Chicago bindery worker, was appointed the AFL's first female general organizer. However, despite Gomper's recommendation, her post was discontinued by the Executive Council after five months, not because she had done a bad job, as her efforts were deemed "worthy of commendation," but because the Executive Council declared the Federation was "not in a condition financially to keep a woman organizer in the field,[23] Nor was the recommendation that the women organizer be seated on the Executive Council accepted.[24]

As the threat of competition from the Knights of Labor died out, the pattern of the AFL's position toward women solidified into occasional convention resolutions and statements by President Samuel Gompers giving lip service to the AFL's concern for women workers. Existing side by side with this rhetoric was a failure to impose any sanctions on the anti-women member unions, failure to adopt affirmative programs for organizing women, and a continuing policy of neglecting the interests of unskilled and semi-skilled workers, which had the effect of leaving out most women workers. The policy of outright exclusion of women, practiced by many AFL member unions, was the most overtly discriminatory practice against women. Although the practice gradually died out by the mid-twentieth century, it died hard and generally for economic reasons rather than because the unions recognized morally or philosophically that women should have equal rights.

The history Wolfson tells of the end of the sex ban in the Barber's Union is illuminating. In the early 1920's the International Journeymen Barber's Union was one of the unions that did not admit women. Up until that time there had been few women barbers, but when bobbed hair came into style in the 1920's, beauty parlors boomed and the number of women hairdressers grew. In 1922 several hundred women barbers in Seattle applied to the Seattle local of the Barber's Union and were refused admission. They applied to the AFL for an independent charter, but after it had been initially granted, a separate charter was denied them because of the vehement protests of the Barber's International. By 1924, however, the Barbers were losing control of shops because of the growing number of women barbers, and the subject of admitting women came up at the 1924 convention. Wolfson quotes the objections of one delegate:

19. Foner, supra note 4, vol. II at 61.
20. Flexner, supra note 4, at 193.
21. I have emphasized this period because of the comparative richness of source material and because of my belief that patterns developed in this period are particularly significant in shaping the present situation.
22. Foner, supra note 4, vol. II at 190.
23. Id. at 194.
24. Henry, Women and the Labor Movement at 54 (1923).

Do female barbers as a whole compare favourably as workmen with male barbers?

Do you think their sense of honour from a pecuniary standpoint would be as strong as a man's in protesting against a cut in wages or the lengthening of working hours?

Do you think the presence of, say, three or four ladies in a shop of ten or twelve chairs would be conducive to good discipline?

In view of the fact of her physical makeup, is it *not a fact that if she were comely to look upon, and possessed extreme charm, would it not have* a tendency to create discord among the men, who, up to the time of her admittance to membership, *were real working brothers?*

Is it not a fact that the real reason for employing women in barber shops is the questionable worth or drawing power as a physical attraction, and not on account of their workmanship?

Allowing for her attractiveness, and also for her workmanship, would she be as capable at forty-five or fifty years of age, with her drawing power limited, and her attractiveness practically gone, as a man at the same age?

In view of the fact that we will probably pass on a pension fund or provide in some way for our older members, when they are no longer able to stand at the chair, at this coming convention, does the female barber figure as an asset or a liability?

Finally, brothers, will it pay to have built up an organisation to where it is today, running smoothly, gaining slowly but surely, and admit an unknown quality, who from the first of it will be nothing but a *blithering liability?*[25]

In the delegate's speech, Wolfson says, are "to be found every objection employed by trade unionists to the admission of women workers: inferiority of workmanship, inability to organise, Lorelei propensities of women workers and the danger of intrusion by 'blithering liabilities'."[26]

Nevertheless, chauvinist myths gave way to economic reality. Another delegate argued: "Now, listen, brothers — give us a chance. It isn't a moral question. It is merely a question of business control. It is an economic question, a question of putting yourself in a position to control the labour power in your organisation, to control the business in your community, and bring it into your own shop."[27] The Barbers ended up voting to admit women.

Rules excluding women from membership fell slowly, and then only union by union. In 1924 seven AFL internationals still officially opposed admission of women members: the Teamsters, United Mine Workers, Brotherhood of Blacksmiths and Drop Forgers, Elastic Goring Weavers' Association, United Brotherhood of Carpenters and Joiners and the Pattern Makers' League and International Moulders Union.[28] Women were working in virtually all of the industries covered by these unions.

The list does not include unions with quotas and partial exclusions such as the Journeymen Tailors which constitutionally prohibited women from becoming custom tailors, limiting them to the position of helpers or apprentices. The pervasive use of the masculine gender in the naming and functioning of unions must have had at least a subliminally discouraging effect on women workers.

Even more explicit, the International Moulder's Union constitution said, "Any member, honorary or active, who devotes his time in whole or in part to the instruction of female help in the foundry, or in any branch of the trade shall be expelled from the union."[29] Sarah Simpson wrote in protest to Gompers, "It is an evil combination. Lack of skill keeps many of us from entering the unions of skilled craftsmen, and rigid apprenticeship regulations prevents (sic) us from becoming apprentices to the trade and

25. Proceedings of Journeymen Barbers' International Union Convention, 1924, quoted in Wolfson, *supra* note 2, at 77-78.

26. Wolfson, *supra* note 2, at 78-79.

27. Proceedings of Journeymen Barbers' International Convention, 1924, *supra* note 26, at 79.

28. Wolfson, *supra* note 2, at 75.

29. Henry, *supra* note 24, at 100.

thereby rising to the rank of skilled workers."[30] Even when union policy was nonexclusionary on its face women were widely excluded by local union policies and what Wolfson calls "a tacit understanding in the great brotherhood of man, that woman's place was in the home."[31]

High dues could be and were exclusionary in a period when women's wages averaged about half of men's. This is illustrated by correspondence between a group of women shoe makers in Pontiac, Illinois, and Frank Morrison, AFL national secretary-treasurer. The women explained that they wanted to join the Boot and Shoe Worker's Union but that the dues were too high, and they requested the AFL to pressure the Boot and Shoe Workers to lower their dues. The AFL did not do so. The women then organized their own local and asked the AFL to charter them as a mixed local. But the Boot and Shoe Workers vigorously protested, and the AFL refused to charter the group.[32]

Foner quotes the following two letters from the archives of the AFL. The first was written to Gompers in 1904 by the president of the largely female Shirt, Waist, and Laundry Worker's Union:

> A major handicap to our already exceedingly difficult task of organizing our craft throughout the country arises from the fact that in many localities the Central Labor bodies dominated by unions composed almost exclusively of men refuse to recognize our locals and the women delegates duly elected by them. We feel that no results can be accomplished unless this is satisfactorily adjusted, as the female members of our craft are naturally timid about joining the labor movement, and with the evidence now apparent that the unions of men in the Central Bodies are hostile to them and unwilling to support them, they are even more timid. This condition does not have a tendency to increase their desire to become active in the labor movement. On the contrary, it is causing many of our members to think of leaving organized labor. Hence our appeal to you that you take this up at your earliest convenience.[33]

The second was written by the President of District 5, United Mine Workers, also in 1904:

> Several groups of the working women of the Pittsburgh area requested me to give them information on how they could get organized. I contacted the various unions of the trades involved after which the women themselves approached them. I have learned that these women were told that there was no room for them in the unions they approached. Most of the women are so discouraged that they are ready to abandon the plan to organize and I wonder if there is not some way that they could be attached to the American Federation of Labor directly.[34]

Foner says the archives of the AFL contain many similar complaints with requests to the Federation to impose some control sanctions on the discriminating locals. In spite of its announced anti-discrimination policy the AFL consistently refused to take action against what O'Neill calls the "baronial chiefs"[35] on the grounds that the member internationals were autonomous. The subject came to a head in 1921, when the Women's Trade Union League, a group founded in 1903 to promote the organizing of women workers into trade unions, made a strenuous effort to persuade the AFL Executive Council that they should at least grant separate charters to women in industries where the affiliated internationals refused membership to women. The W.T.U.L. representa-

---

30. Quoted in Foner, supra note 4, vol. III at 227.
31. Wolfson, Trade Union Activities of Women, 143 Annals of the American Academy of Political and Social Science 123 (May 1929).
32. Foner, supra note 4, vol. III at 221-2.
33. Walter Charriere to Gompers, quoted in Foner, supra note 4, vol. III at 225-6.
34. P. Dolan to Gompers, quoted in Foner, supra note 4, vol. III at 226.
35. O'Neill, Everyone Was Brave 218 (1969).

tives pointed out that the AFL had occasionally waived its policy of exclusive jurisdiction in this way for Negro workers. The Council refused and responded with a variety of insults instead. Vice President James Duncan said he opposed all-women locals because women were not permanent workers; locals, he said, should be integrated and officered by men who were committed to their trade. Treasurer Daniel Tobin announced that he would fight to the end to keep out women coal-team drivers, who were dirty, unkempt and shoeless.[36]

A few unions, notably the International Brotherhood of Bookbinders, had a policy of organizing women in separate locals. In many ways this was a positive policy. It permitted women to develop their own leadership and develop programs to serve their own interests. In the case of the Bookbinders, Wolfson reports it was part of an affirmative policy of organizing women,[37] and such a policy was certainly preferable to the refusal of many unions to recognize women who had already gotten themselves together. But predictably, separate had a tendency to mean unequal. Foner reports complaints about the system of segregated locals in a single workplace with a joint committee to conduct negotiations with employers. Women complained that they got the short end of the deal because "the men think that the girls should not get as good work as the men and should not make half as much money as a man."[38]

Exclusionary policies were only the most clear-cut of the anti-women policies. Once women were committed to trade unions, they were generally treated as unwanted poor relations. In the 1920's a number of international unions required lower dues and lower initiation fees from women,[39] a recognition of the fact that unions negotiated lower wages for women. However, there was a catch to this beyond the fact that the practice indicated acceptance of the discriminatory status quo: strike benefits, sickness benefits and other incidentals were often tied to the amount of dues paid. The Bakery Workers carried the policy to its logical extreme. They organized women in female auxiliaries, exempted the women from assessments and also exempted them from benefits.[40] Some unions specifically excluded women who lost time because of pregnancy or menopause from sick benefits. No mention was made, says Wolfson, of the type of illness men must suffer in order to get sick benefits.[41]

In terms of benefits won through strikes and negotiations the women usually lost, sometimes resoundingly. In 1918 a three-day strike of streetcar workers was settled by an agreement between the Cleveland Railway Company and the Street Railwaymen that no more women would be employed.[42] The dues difference noted above was a tacit admission that the wage differential continued with a union on the scene. In the 1920's, wages for women averaged a little more than half the wages for men. In April, 1926, the average weekly pay for men was $32.75 and for women $18.60.[43] The income gap between male and female workers grew between 1923 and 1929.[44]

Away from the negotiating table unions were sometimes women's worst enemies. Elizabeth Faulkner Baker reports that the Wisconsin Federation of Labor resolved in 1918 to press for legislation to keep women out of the polishing and buffing trades.[45] The Building Trades Material Council of Chicago asked the state factory in-

---

36. Id. at 247.

37. Wolfson, The Woman Worker, supra note 2, at 123.

38. Mary Meenin to Chris Evans, June 20, 1892, AFL Correspondence, quoted in Foner, supra note 4, vol. II at 190.

39. Wolfson, The Woman Worker, supra note 2, at 80-1. Wolfson lists 12 international unions with such a policy.

40. Id. at 83.

41. Id. at 89.

42. Baker, Protective Labor Legislation 445.

43. Wolfson, The Woman Worker, supra note 2, at 44.

44. O'Neill, supra note 35, at 247. The differential for skilled and semi-skilled workers grew from 22.8 cents an hour in 1923 to 26.9 cents in 1929. For unskilled workers the difference jumped from 6.3 cents to 10.2 cents.

45. Baker, supra note 42, at 446.

spector to bar women from their trades on the ground that the work was unhealthy.[46] Many unions were active in the fight for protective legislation in the early 20th century and considered this a pro-woman position to take. But Baker claims that Gompers opposed the establishment of hours laws for men[47] and then as now it was an open question whether the support of protective legislation for women only was evidence of a pro-woman policy.

Little has been written about access to leadership positions for women in this period, but what there is suggested that women were generally kept out of the leadership. In 1923 Alice Henry was able to list on one and a half pages of a small paged book the women who were or had been national officers of international unions.[48] In 1918 women delegates to the AFL convention proposed an amendment to the Federation constitution which would have reserved two seats on the Executive Council for women. The proposal was not passed. As of 1926 the AFL had never had a woman on its Executive Council.[49]

Of much greater contemporary concern was the disproportionately small number of women organizers. The fact that women, rather than men, organizers were crucial if large numbers of women were to be unionized does not seem to have been seriously disputed. A male organizer explained that he was handicapped in reaching women workers after working hours.

> If a girl is living at home it is not quite so awkward, but if she is in lodgings, I can't possibly ask to see her in her own room. If I talk to her at all, it will be out in the street, which is not pleasant, especially if it is snowing or freezing or blowing a gale. It is not under these conditions that a girl is likely to see the use of an organization or be attracted by its happier or more social side.[50]

Note, incidentally, this organizer's use of the term "girl". The term is commonly used in union literature up to the present day even though male workers are not referred to as "boys". At best, calling women workers "girls" communicates the stereotype that women only work until they get married; at worst it indicates the labor movement's lack of respect for the dignity and maturity of women who work.

By 1924 only eight national unions employed women organizers.[51] Even unions like the International Ladies Garment Workers Union, Amalgamated Clothing Workers, and Cap Makers, which put a certain amount of emphasis on female leadership and had a heavily female jurisdiction, hired only one woman organizer for every three men organizers in the 1920's.[52] The AFL was essentially without a female general organizer until the time of World War I.[53]

The Women's Trade Union League was established in 1903 as an alternative means of organizing women. It saw its role as organizing women into existing unions, primarily those of the AFL. Considering the W.T.U.L.'s longstanding loyalty to the AFL, it received precious little support or response from the Federation's leadership. The AFL didn't give the League any votes at conventions or any money to speak of.[54] In 1912 the W.T.U.L. voted to lend support to the I.W.W.-led Lawrence strike, which included many women

46. Foner, supra note 4, vol. III at 224.

47. Baker, supra note 42, at 444.

48. Henry, supra note 24, at 97-98.

49. Wolfson, The Woman Worker, supra note 2, at 67-68.

50. Joan J. May to Gompers, Dec. 22, 1892, AFL Correspondence, quoted in Foner, supra note 4, vol. II at 193.

51. Wolfson, The Woman Worker, supra note 2, at 104.

52. Id. at 140.

53. Foner, supra note 4, vol. III at 232. Henry says that between 1908 and 1923, 38 women worked as organizers for the AFL, but evidently most of these were special organizers, many of them working for only a few weeks or months. Women and the Labor Movement supra note 24, at 95.

54. O'Neill, supra note 35, at 99, 101.

workers. The AFL, which was doing its best to sabotage the strike, ordered the W.T.U.L. to pull out, and the W.T.U.L. knuckled under, even after United Textile Workers (AFL) leader John Golden explained that the reason the U.T.W. could not help rank and file textile workers was that most of them were women and children who did not earn enough to be charged full dues and it did not pay the U.T.W. to organize them.[55]

In 1918 the AFL hired eight or nine women organizers for a campaign to organize women; the campaign ended before achieving much success. In 1926 the Federation sponsored a drive to recruit women workers in Newark, which Folson describes as "so puny and half-hearted in its efforts that practically nothing was accomplished,"[56] Up through the 1920's these two campaigns comprised the AFL's affirmative organizing campaign for women.[57]

The issue of hiring women organizers was intimately tied to the general union attitude toward women. Organizers applied what they called "common sense" techniques to the organizing of women, but the basis for this "common sense" lay in their experience organizing skilled male workers. Their conclusion that women were unorganizable was thus based on the fact that women did not respond to techniques that had been successfully used to organize skilled men workers.[58]

This conclusion masked a structure of antiwomen myths and prejudices sprinkled with occasional social realities that shaped trade union attitudes toward women. Officially the AFL justified its position by claiming that women were only temporary workers who worked for "pin money" and left the work force as soon as they got married, thus the organizing had to be done all over again, wasting both money and energy.[59] This belief in the way things were was undoubtedly colored by the labor leaders' views of the way things should be. Samuel Gompers, who was more pro-women than many, was asked in 1905 whether he thought that a married woman should contribute to the support of her family by working. Gompers answered,

> No! . . . In our time, and at least in our country, generally speaking, there is no necessity for the wife contributing to the support of the family by working . . . the wife as a wage-earner is a disadvantage economically considered, and socially is unnecessary.[60]

Feminine frailty was occasionally resorted to as a justification for not including women in unions on an equal basis with men. Take, for instance, this collection of comments to Theresa Wolfson explaining why women couldn't be organizers:

> "The woman organiser can't stand the strain of living away from home and being constantly on the go. It's a man's job," stated one official. "Organising is selling unionism. It means being on the road like a travelling salesman, and women just can't stand it," offered another official. "College women take the job too seriously. They work at organising with too much intensity and at the end of a couple of years they are all knocked out, nervous, sensitive, unable to stand the rebukes of officials of the union, or even of the employers they have to deal with."[61]

But they were damned if they did and damned if they didn't. Employers had long used attacks on union women's femininity as a way of attacking organization among working women, but some union men used the same level of sexist attack. In a letter to Agnes Nestor, who was at the time secretary-treasurer of the International Glove

55. Id. at 160.
56. Wolfson, Trade Union Activities of Women, supra note 31, at 124.
57. Id. at 125.
58. Wolfson, The Woman Worker, supra note 2, at 128.
59. Foner, supra note 4, vol. III at 223.
60. Id. at 224.
61. Wolfson, The Woman Worker, supra note 2, at 142.

Workers' Union, an AFL leader asked, "Do they (unions) not tend to unsex them (female members) and make them masculine?"[62]

Very likely the most accurate of the myths was the frequent observation that women workers couldn't be active union members because they had, in effect, two jobs, a job at work and a job at home. But if this burden was the main thing standing between women and active union membership, and if the unions were interested in having woman members, they showed a singular lack of concern for demands such as daycare that might have eased that burden and even less concern for encouraging their male members to share the home burdens.

The result of all these sexist policies was that women were broadly discouraged from joining unions. In 1929, Wolfson estimated that one in nine wage earners was organized, but only one in 34 women workers was a union member.[63] If anything this was an overestimate.[64] In 1933 Elizabeth Christman estimated that about twice as many working women were members of the Young Women's Christian Association (YWCA) as were members of the AFL.[65] There were certainly other reasons besides the unions' anti-woman practices why the number of women organized into labor unions was small at this time. Large numbers of women worked in occupations traditionally thought of as hard to organize, such as housekeeping, clerical and agricultural. Women were mostly unskilled and semi-skilled workers, and the labor movement generally neglected these classes of workers, regardless of sex. Further, women often failed to think of themselves as permanent workers, considered working a cause for shame and feared that identifying with a union was, or would be considered, unfeminine. Nevertheless, the unions' anti-women attitudes had the effect of a self-fulfilling prophecy. Unions did not on the whole want women, and women did not join in large numbers. So the myth that women cannot be organized became perpetuated through its own momentum.

The union that has consistently had the largest proportion of women members in the 20th century is the International Ladies' Garment Workers Union (ILGWU). At the turn of the century the needle trades were one of the largest employers of women, and the origins of the ILGWU go back to 1900. . . . [M]ore than 95% of the ILGWU's leaders are men.[66] Nor was the situation much better on a local level; Wolfson says that in 1926 only three of the ILGWU's local unions even had women secretaries.[67] An ILGWU pamphlet from the late 1940's[68] was perhaps not so far off base when it listed women as one of the "minority groups" whose interest the ILGWU defended. Judged by the standards of a minority group, women have done pretty well in the ILGWU. The union made efforts to hire women organizers and develop methods of organizing appropriate to women workers. One of the most important women's strikes of the twentieth century was the Uprising of the Twenty Thousand of 1909, a mass walkout by women needle trades workers in New York started by the women workers in spite of advice to the contrary from their male leaders. In the 1920's the ILGWU was torn by political factionalism according to Wolfson and women were the bastions of the left wing, which gave them opportunities for leadership.[69]

D. 1930-1950

In 1930 women comprised 7.7 per cent of all American trade union members. By 1944 the figure had jumped to 21.8 percent.[70] The 1944 figure is somewhat inflated

---

62. Foner, supra note 4, vol. III at 224.

63. Wolfson, Trade Union Activities of Women, supra note 31, at 120. She estimates that 8,500,000 women were gainfully employed in 1927 and that 260,095 of these women were union members.

64. Dickason estimates 10,697,000 women in the labor force and 260,000 women trade union members in 1930. This comes to about one woman in 40. (See Appendix A for figures covering the years 1910–1946.)

65. Quoted in Hutchins, Women Who Work 260.

66. Stolberg, Tailor's Progress 218 (1944).

67. Wolfson, The Woman Worker, supra note 2, at 179.

68. The Story of ILGWU, 1947 (rev. ed. 1951).

69. Wolfson, Trade Union Activities of Women, supra note 31, at 125.

70. Dickason, Women in Labor Unions, supra note 10, at 71.

because of the war but trade union membership of women did not fall back in later years to its pre-war level. Several factors account for the increased proportion of women joining unions in this period.

Dickason, writing in 1949, suggested some reasons for the increase.[71]

1. Emphasis in the 1930's on organizing workers on an industrial basis rather than by craft. This resulted in more emphasis on organizing unskilled, semi-skilled and white collar workers, the categories into which most women workers fell. This was undoubtedly a significant shift.

2. The large influx of women into the work force because of World War II, and particularly into the largely unionized manufacturing trades. The proportion of women workers jumped from one in four workers in 1940 to one in three in 1945.[72] While the proportion of women fell off in the post-war period, the war experience opened up many unions to women for the first time and increased the responsiveness of unions to women.

3. Federal legislation, which began to recognize and protect the rights of union members. The National Labor Relations Act passed in the 1930's recognized and in effect gave national approval to the rights of workers to organize. This may have helped to make union membership seem more respectable and thus more acceptable for women to join trade unions.

4. The end of most unions' constitutional exclusion of women. In 1942 the United Mine Workers removed its ban against women; in 1944 the Boilermakers did the same. These two were the last internationals to have sex bans.[73] In 1946 Summers found only eight unions which constitutionally barred women: Air Line Dispatchers Association (AFL), International Union of Operating Engineers (AFL), Brotherhood of Railroad Trainmen (Independent), Railroad Yardmasters of America (Independent), Railway Mail Association (AFL), Switchmakers Union of North America (AFL) and American Ware Weavers Protective Association (AFL). However, there were still a good many unions which lacked constitutional bans against women, but excluded them in fact.[74] In 1943 the American Civil Liberties Union counted 25 national unions which excluded women.[75]

Unions represented their female members better during the war years than in earlier decades. The subject of equal pay for equal work received considerable attention, and women's position in this regard seems to have improved. A Women's Bureau survey of 80 union contracts in a large midwestern war industry area revealed that half the contracts had clauses establishing equal pay for equal work.[76] The AFL and the Congress of Industrial Organizations (CIO) endorsed equal pay for equal work legislation which had been passed in seven states by 1949.[77]

The United Auto Workers (UAW), which was 28 per cent women by 1945, brought a case against General Motors before the War Labor Board that established the principle that wage rates for women should be at a rate equal to the rate for men. Other unions pressed other women's issues before the War Labor Board. The National Federation of Telephone Workers got a ruling that anti-woman discrimination based on marital status was illegal.[78]

Much less was done, according to Dickason, to diminish sex segregation of jobs.[79] The Women's Bureau study cited above found that 20 per cent of the union contracts studied had separate seniority lists for men and women.

The war stimulated some greater sensitivity to the problems and interests of

71. Id.
72. Dickason, supra note 10, at 71.
73. Summers, Admission Policies of Labor Unions, Quarterly Journal of Economics 66, 74 (Nov. 1946).
74. Id. Table 1 at 92-105.
75. A.C.L.U., Democracy in Trade Unions, at 16 referred to in Summers, supra note 73, at 78, n.3.
76. Dickason, supra note 10, at 73.
77. Id.
78. Id.
79. Id.

women within unions. The UAW's Women's Bureau dates from World War II. In 1944 the UAW held a national conference of its women members. Some unions got maternity leave clauses written into contracts. The Amalgamated Clothing Workers included maternity benefits in its insurance plan and worked for decent daycare. Women continued to be underrepresented in administrative and leadership positions in unions. In 1947 Dickason was able to count only 20 women officers of state labor organizations and 20 directors of education and research — which was the traditional woman's job.[80]

. . . The [legal] struggle over sex discrimination within trade unions continues. However many of the important political questions that must be answered about the roles of women in the work force and particularly within the union movement are still factual questions. For example, is it the pressures of a double job (homemaker and employee) or union discrimination that keeps women from positions of leadership within unions? Answers to this type of question are needed before broader considerations such as whether women should go it alone in their struggle as workers seeking to form independent women's unions or separate bargaining units within a larger sexually integrated union can be considered.

2. Sex-Segregated Locals under Title VII

EVANS v. SHERATON PARK HOTEL
5 FEP Cases 393 (D.D.C. 1972)

GESELL, District Judge: — This is a civil action alleging sex discrimination in violation of Title VII of the 1964 Civil Rights Act, 42 U.S.C. 2000e et seq. After extensive pretrial proceedings . . . the complaint was tried to the Court without a jury. Plaintiff is a regular banquet waitress employed at the Sheraton Park Hotel and a member of [the Hotel and Restaurant Employees and Bartenders International Union]. Her grievances were presented to the Hotel, to the unions and finally to the Equal Employment Opportunity Commission (EEOC). Suit was authorized by the EEOC on May 14, 1971, after its efforts to conciliate failed and the complaint was eventually filed in June, 1971, within the statutory time period. Plaintiff seeks damages against both the unions and the Hotel for the period beginning October, 1968, to the present . . .

The International Union at all times here relevant maintained two locals in the District of Columbia; an all-male Local 781 and an all-female Local 507. These locals supplied banquet waiters and waitresses to a number of establishments in the city, including approximately 20-25 employed at the Hotel. There have been about twice as many regular banquet waiters as waitresses working at the Hotel. Each local was represented at the Hotel separately by a different shop delegate who dealt with and presented grievances in the first instance to the banquet captain, who represented the Hotel.

Plaintiff claims that because locals segregated by sex were maintained and recognized it was possible for the Hotel to favor regular banquet waiters over regular banquet waitresses, and that in fact the banquet captain, himself a member of Local 781, discriminated by making more favorable assignments to the waiters. To understand this contention, it is necessary to explain the prevailing system governing compensation and assignments at the Hotel.

Waiters and waitresses were all paid the same hourly rates for participation in varying types of duties, but these rates varied depending on the nature of the work. . . . A significant and substantial portion of total compensation came from dividing an obligatory 16 percent gratuity among the waiters and waitresses participating in a particular function. The most lucrative work involved serving bar and food receptions because

80. Id.

the number of waiters and waitresses required for these functions was relatively small, while the bill and the resulting gratuity received were relatively high.

The records of the Hotel reveal that as a group waiters worked more hours than waitresses, received a larger total hourly compensation as a result and also received larger gratuities. Plaintiff asserts that this difference, which has been consistent over recent years, reflects decisions by the banquet captain to assign waiters rather than waitresses to lucrative receptions, as well as other discrimination against waitresses. She testified that waitresses were often given more menial assignments to types of work that were either less remunerative or carried no remuneration at all, and that waitresses were often passed over when well-paid work was available. The compensation differential between waiters and waitresses and testimony from other banquet waitresses supports the position taken by plaintiff to a considerable degree. . . .

. . . Proof submitted by the Hotel in explanation of compensation differentials reflected by its records indicates that the eight-hour law governing female employment in the District of Columbia, the acquiescence of the Hotel in certain stated customer preferences for waiters over waitresses, the unwillingness of some waitresses, notably plaintiff, to accept less attractive assignments or to work on their days off and a general willingness of the men to work longer hours and not ask for special considerations were all factors bearing on the situation.

The Court has resolved the controversy in favor of the plaintiff whose testimony, particularly as to receptions, is well supported by other credible witnesses. While the various factors mentioned by the Hotel may well have had some influence on the level of banquet waitresses' compensation, certainly discrimination based on eight-hour laws or customer preference cannot be offered in justification. . . . The Court is satisfied, . . . that from plaintiff's employment in October, 1968, at least through August, 1969, and probably longer, preference was given to banquet waiters for reception assignments, that women were not allowed to reserve receptions with the same regularity as men, and that this was a substantial factor in creating the compensation differential disclosed by the records. . . .

The discrimination in reception assignments is a classic example of the abuse inherent in maintaining and recognizing separate female and male locals for co-workers performing the same duties. It is inevitable in such a situation that not only will controversy and suspicion arise between males and females, but that the more dominant group, in this case the males, will gain privileges of various kinds. The failure of Local 507 to support plaintiff's justifiable official complaints concerning uneven and unfair assignments demonstrates the inability of a Janus-headed union to safeguard sex equality.

Such segregation is not and cannot be a bona fide occupational qualification. Maintenance of the two sex-segregated locals, which has now been eliminated by a post complaint merger, constituted a per se violation of the Civil Rights Act, 42 U.S.C. 2000e-2(c). See United States v. International Longshoremen's Association, 460 F.2d 497, 4 FEP Cases 719 (4th Cir.), *cert. denied,* 5 FEP Cases 149, 41 LW 3269 (U.S. Nov. 13, 1972). Moreover, under the practices present in this case, no bona fide occupational qualification having been shown by the defendants, 42 U.S.C. 2000e-2(a) and (c) have been violated. Both the International, the locals and the Hotel must be held jointly and severally liable for the consequences. . . .

In addition to her claim of damages for this discrimination, plaintiff claims damages for harassment, again invoking the Act, 42 U.S.C. 2000e-3(a). This harassment allegedly took two forms. In late 1970, plaintiff claims that the banquet captain complained and threatened to beat her up because she had gone to the EEOC. While the banquet captain insists that no such threat was made, the Court finds the testimony of the plaintiff far more credible. In addition, the proof showed that after plaintiff filed the EEOC complaint, a member of the management of the Hotel circulated a petition among the banquet waitresses to have plaintiff removed as shop delegate. The inference is inescapable that this apparently unfair labor practice resulted from the EEOC complaint. In light of all the circumstances and proof, an award of additional damages for harassment in the amount of $500 will be made. This is to be paid by the Hotel. There is no showing that the Union in any way was responsible in this phase of the case. The banquet captain was not a Union representative but functioned in a supervisory management capacity for the Hotel. . . .

NOTE: THE APPLICABILITY OF TITLE VII
SEX DISCRIMINATION CONCEPTS TO UNION PRACTICES

The provisions of Title VII prohibiting sex discrimination by employers and by labor organizations are somewhat different. The act provides as to employers that[164]

> It shall be an unlawful employment practice for an employer —
> (1) to fail or refuse to hire or to discharge any individual, or otherwise discriminate against any individual with respect to his compensation, terms, conditions, or privileges of employment, because of such individual's race, color, religion, sex or national origin; or
> (2) to limit, segregate or classify his employees or applicants for employment in any way which would deprive or tend to deprive any individual of employment opportunities or otherwise adversely affect his status as an employee because of such individual's race, color, religion, sex, or national origin.

As to labor organizations, the act states that[165]

> It shall be unlawful employment practice for a labor organization —
> (1) to exclude or to expel from its membership, or otherwise to discriminate against, any individual because of his race, color, religion, sex, or national origin; or
> (2) to limit, segregate, or classify its membership, or applicants for membership or to classify or fail or refuse to refer for employment any individual, in any way which would deprive or tend to deprive any individual of employment opportunities, or would limit such employment opportunities or otherwise adversely affect his status as an employee or as an applicant for employment, because of such individual's race, color, religion, sex, or national origin; or
> (3) to cause or attempt to cause an employer to discriminate against an individual in violation of this section.

Section 703(d), concerning discrimination in connection with apprenticeship and training programs, and §703(e), setting forth the BFOQ exception, govern both employers and labor organizations. Section 703(d) imposes identical obligations on each. Section 703(e) provides in part that:

> (1) It shall not be an unlawful employment practice for an employer to hire and employ employees . . . [or] for a labor organization to classify its membership or to classify or refer for employment any individual . . . on the basis of his religion, sex, or national origin in those certain instances where religion, sex, or national origin is a bona fide occupational qualification reasonably necessary to the normal operation of that particular business or enterprise. . . .

Although the provisions are worded somewhat differently, the language with regard to both labor organizations and employers is sufficiently broad to reach all forms of sex discrimination (except for the negligible discrimination allowed under the BFOQ provision). Therefore, while cases involving unions may sometimes concern practices

164. Section 703 (a) of Title VII, 42 U.S.C. §2000e-2(a).
165. Section 703(c) of Title VII, 42 U.S.C. §20003-2(c).

which probably would not be raised in suits against employers — such as discrimination in access to union membership — the legal concepts explained in Sections B and C supra, can be used to reach union as well as employer discrimination.

Note that Falk's suggestion in the historical article reprinted above, that women workers might form independent women's unions or separate bargaining units within sexually integrated unions, would violate Title VII. Given the history of sex discrimination by male-dominated unions, is this a problem for women workers?

NOTE: OTHER CASES

Thus far, there has been very little litigation against unions on the grounds of sex discrimination. Interestingly enough, there have also been relatively few complaints to the EEOC about unions as compared to employers. For example, in fiscal 1972, the EEOC received a total of 419 complaints against union practices and 335 joint complaints against unions, employers, or employment agencies, as compared with 9056 complaints against employers.[166]

The tactical question of whether or not women workers should sue unions which discriminate is discussed below in Part III-E. Those considering such litigation may want to familiarize themselves with the race discrimination cases which have been brought against unions under Title VII. See, e.g., United States v. Sheetmetal Workers, Local 36, 416 F.2d 123 (8th Cir. 1969); United States v. IBEW, Local 38, 428 F.2d 1144 (7th Cir.), cert. denied, 400 U.S. 943 (1970); Dobbins v. Local 212, IBEW, 292 F. Supp. 413 (S.D. Ohio 1968); and Asbestos Workers, Local 53 v. Vogler, 407 F.2d 1047 (5th Cir. 1969).

The *Asbestos Workers* case raises an interesting question about judicial sensitivity to sex discrimination issues. The second footnote of the court's opinion states:

> 2. It is the policy of the defendant Local 53 to restrict its membership to the sons or close relatives of other members. Local 53 does not admit new men as mechanics, regardless of their qualifications. In the past four years the defendant has accepted 72 first-year improvers as members. Sixty-nine of these are sons or stepsons of members: each of the other three is a nephew who was raised by a member as a son. Only such sons are even considered for membership. Finding of Fact No. 4(f).

3. Other Remedies for Sex Discrimination by Unions: The National Labor Relations Act

SIMMONS, FREEDMAN, DUNKLE, AND BLAU
EXPLOITATION FROM 9 TO 5;
Background Paper for the Twentieth Century Fund
Task Force on Women and Employment, ch. 4 (1974)

NATIONAL LABOR RELATIONS ACT AND THE RAILWAY LABOR ACT

The National Labor Relations Act (NLRA) and its major amendments, the Labor Management Relations Act of 1947 (Taft-Hartley Act) and the Labor Management Reporting and Disclosure Act of 1959 (Landrum-Griffin Act), define the structure and nature of federal regulation of labor relations. The Railway Labor Act supplements the NLRA by regulating labor-management relations in the railroad and airline industries. Federal Labor law has preempted regulation of labor relations in all the areas it touches, so that state labor regulation has relatively little vitality now.

---

166. Equal Employment Opportunity Commission, Sixth Annual Report (1972).

Major responsibility for administering the NLRA lies with the National Labor Relations Board (NLRB). The Board's many responsibilities include determining bargaining units, holding elections, and adjudicating disputes. Policing labor union discrimination against individual workers or classes of workers takes up only a small part of the Board's total attention, and for the most part is not even an explicit part of the authority delegated to the Board by Congress. However, as the governmental agency most responsible for shaping the development of labor union practices, as well as the agency with the largest staff and resources for regulating labor unions, the NLRB is in a special position to regulate sex discrimination by labor unions if it so chooses.

Coverage

The NLRA does not cover all workers, and most of the job categories it excludes are areas with a high percentage of women workers. Workers in agricultural labor and domestic service are explicitly excepted from the NLRA's definition of employee.[79] [In 1968,] two percent of all women workers [did] farm work; only 7.2 percent of all women workers [were] paid private household workers (domestic service). However, 97.6 percent of all paid private household workers [were] women.[80] Also excluded from the NLRA's definition of employers are the federal government, state and municipal governments, and nonprofit hospitals. The exclusion of governmental bodies is particularly significant since government is the fastest growing area of employment for women.[81] In 1968 there were 5.3 million women on government payrolls and women were 43.5 percent of all government workers.[82] In addition to the huge number of clerical and receptionist jobs filled by women in government, this figure includes school teachers (elementary school teaching is the fourth highest occupational category for women) and state, local, and federal hospital workers.

Taken together with the exclusion of nonprofit hospital workers, the exclusion of state, federal, and municipal hospital workers means that most workers are excluded from the NLRA, since there are relatively few private proprietary hospitals. This too is a very significant exception since 81.3 percent of all hospital workers, more than 1.3 million workers, were women in 1968.[83]

Altogether, the few categories of workers that are excluded from the NLRA and the Railway Labor Act manage to exclude more than one-fourth of all women workers. The NLRA and the Railway Labor Act provide important protections for workers in their attempts to organize, so these exceptions are discriminatory in and of themselves.

Administrative and Judicial Interpretation of
the NLRA's Duty of Fair Representation

Under the NLRA and the RLA there are extensive legal attempts to clarify the duty of unions to represent their members. A union that has been certified as the recognized agent of a bargaining unit has the power to represent and define the terms and conditions of employment of all employees in the unit, whether or not they are members of the union. All employees are bound by the collective agreement which the union negotiates, and they may not contract independently for other terms with the employer. From this power that is granted to unions under the NLRA and the Railway Labor Act, courts have derived a duty of unions to represent all employees fairly.

The duty of fair representation, not explicitly required by statute, was first enunciated by the Supreme Court in a case under the Railway Labor Act, Steele v. Louisville & N.R. Co.[84] Steele, a black man, was a locomotive fireman; he sued for an injunction

79. 49 Stat. 449 Sec. 101(2)(3) (1935).
80. [U.S. Dept of Labor,] Women's Bureau, [1969 Handbook of Women Workers 92, Table 40].
81. Handbook, [supra, at] 113.
82. Id. at 113.
83. Id. at 116.
84. 323 U.S. 198 (1944).

and damages against the all-white Brotherhood of Locomotive Firemen and Enginemen, which was trying to replace black firemen with white, and thus force the blacks out of jobs. The Supreme Court held that federal courts had jurisdiction to entertain such a suit and explained in the majority opinion of Chief Justice Stone that:

> So long as a labor union assumes to act as the statutory representative of a craft, it cannot rightly refuse to perform the duty which is inseparable from the power of representation conferred upon it, to represent the entire membership of the craft . . . (The statute requires the union) to represent non-union or minority members of the craft without hostile discrimination, fairly, impartially, and in good faith.

In the *Miranda Fuel Co.*[85] case in 1962, the NLRB carried the logic of *Steele* farther and found that violation of the duty of fair representation was an unfair labor practice. Since *Miranda,* the NLRB has found that unfair representation violates the NLRA in a number of cases.[86]

No particular limits have been set to what activities the duty of fair representation covers. *Steele* required fair representation in negotiation of the collective agreement. Conley v. Gibson[87] extended the duty to fair administration of the contract, which includes fair processing of grievances arising under the collective agreement. In Local Union No. 12, United Rubber, Cork, Linoleum and Plastic Workers of America,[88] the Fifth Circuit held that the union was required to process grievances even if they were not specifically subjects of the collective agreement; in the *Rubberworkers* case the court ordered the union to process grievances concerning segregated restrooms, showers, dining rooms, and a white-only golf course.

The extent to which the duty of fair representation obligates a union to refuse a discriminatory contract and strike is still uncertain. At least in cases of racial discrimination, the NLRB would probably go as far as to hold that a union may not accept a contract which conditions its benefits on discriminatory classifications.[89] Breach of the duty of fair representation has been found and prohibited in nonracial cases where the discrimination has been hostile or arbitrary — for instance, in cases of unfair allocation of seniority where two companies merge.

One might think that union discrimination against women would be considered "hostile" or "arbitrary" and therefore a violation of the duty of fair representation. However, the duty of fair representation has not yet been applied in any case to protect women, and in at least one state case[90] a [state] court has found that discrimination against women came within the "wide range of reasonableness" which the Supreme Court said it would allow to unions in deciding the best way to represent their members.[91]

. . . Moreover, while no federal court has ever said that sex discrimination *does not* violate the duty of fair representation, no federal court has ever said that discrimination against women *does* violate the duty either.

There is no particular reason to think that sex discrimination should not be a violation of the duty of fair representation.[92] . . . [In fact], in deciding the proper limits

---

85. 140 NLRB 181 (1962).

86. See, e.g., Independent Metal Workers Union, Local No. 1 (Hughes Tool Co.) 147 NLRB 1573 (1964) theory approved in Local Union No. 12, United Rubber Cork, etc. Workers, 150 NLRB 312; *enforcement granted*, 368 F.2d. 12 (5th Cir. 1966); *cert. denied*, 380 U.S. 837 (1967).

87. 355 U.S. 41 (1957).

88. Rubber Workers, supra n.70.

89. See, e.g., Local 1367, International Longshoremen's Assoc., 148 NLRB 44 (1967): "[C]ollective bargaining agreements which discriminate invidiously are not lawful under the Act . . . and both unions and employers are enjoined by the Act from entering into them."

90. Cortez v. Ford Motor Co., 349 Mich. 108, 84 N.W. 523 (Sup. Ct. Mich. 1957). See also Hartley v. Br. of Ry. and Steamship Clerks, 283 Mich. 201, 277 N.W. 885 (1938).

91. Ford Motor Co. v. Huffman, 345 U.S. 330 (1953).

92. A. Cox, "The Duty of Fair Representation," 2 Vill. L. Rev. 151, 160-61 (1957). . . .

of a bargaining unit, the NLRB has refused in a few cases to approve bargaining units established along sex lines. The Board refused a request for bargaining units made up of all women on the first and second shifts in *Cuneo Eastern Press, Inc.*[93] and said that bargaining units split on the basis of sex alone were inappropriate unless significant differences in skills were shown between the men and the women.[94]

The crucial question is not so much whether sex discrimination violates the duty of fair representation, but how blatant the discrimination must be and how far the NLRB and the courts will be willing to go in enforcing remedies against sex discrimination. The answer to this will lie in the development of the case law and in the generally inscrutable politics of the NLRB and labor relations law.

NOTE: THE NLRA AND TITLE VII

The Supreme Court has ruled that an aggrieved individual may pursue parallel remedies both in court under Title VII and through union grievance and arbitration procedures. *Alexander v. Gardner-Denver Co.*, — U.S. — , 94 S. Ct. 1011, 39 L. Ed. 2d 147 (1974). Plaintiffs may also join a claim of a union breach of the duty of fair representation to a Title VII claim in a federal lawsuit. There are some theoretical advantages to doing this:[167]

> Suits based upon the duty of fair representation may be brought in either federal or state courts.[108] Because there is no statute of limitations specifically applicable to such suits, the governing limitation period would be that provided by an appropriate state statute of limitations. Such a suit has the advantages of not involving the time consuming resort to the E.E.O.C., and avoiding the short limitation periods of Title VII, but, as compared with an action under that Act, it must be recognized that attorneys' fees and all other expenses of preparation of a suit based on the duty of fair representation will be the responsibility of the plaintiffs, as in civil litigation generally.
> The relief generally available in such a suit is limited by the fact that the suit must be brought against a union for action taken in its capacity as a bargaining representative, with remedies limited to those appropriate for redressing harm done by the union or for preventing recurrence of such breaches in the future.[110]

However, such suits are generally not thought to be very effective; sex discrimination has not yet been construed to be a violation of the duty of fair representation, and Title VII does cover sex discrimination in union practices. There seems little reason to add such a claim to a Title VII suit.

Another labor law remedy is resort to the NLRB for an unfair labor practice hearing on a claim of sex discrimination. Since Title VII is broad enough to cover any discriminatory practice that might be reached under the NLRA, there is usually no reason to proceed under the NLRA as well. The main reason for using the NLRA is to get the NLRB to decertify or refuse to certify a discriminating union as the bargaining representative of a particular group of workers. Simmons, et al point out that[168]

93. 106 NLRB 343 (1953).

94. See also Underwriters Salvage Co. of New York, 99 NLRB 337 (1952); Tom Thumb Stores, 123 NLRB 99 (1959); U.S. Baking Co, 165 NLRB 931 (1961).

167. Peck, Remedies for Racial Discrimination in Employment: A Comparative Evaluation of Forums, 46 Wash. L. Rev. 455, 480-481 (1971).

108. See, e.g., Humphrey v. Moore, 375 U.S. 335 (1964).

110. For discouraging reports on the effectiveness of suits based upon the duty of fair representation, see Herring, The "Fair Representation" Doctrine: An Effective Weapon Against Union Racial Discrimination? 24 Md. L. Rev. 113 (1964); Sovern, Racial Discrimination and the National Labor Relations Act: The Brave New World of Miranda, N.Y.U. Sixteenth Annual Conference on Labor 3-6 (1963).

168. Simmons, Freedman, Dunkle, and Blau, Exploitation from 9 to 5, supra, ch. 4, TAN 96.

For a weak union this is a serious sanction because an employer has no duty to bargain with a union that is not certified, nor are competitor unions prohibited from trying to take over under the usual "contract bar" rule.

However, as Cooper and Rabb point out,[169]

> [The NLRB] offers the advantage of government enforcement manpower and a unique remedy of decertification. But the jurisdiction of the Board is limited in fair employment cases and such cases run the risk of being given second priority to labor disputes more traditionally within the Board's competence. The individual complainant has relatively little control over the handling of his case.

In conclusion, it must be mentioned that as women workers begin to organize, they will increasingly turn to the NLRB — but for help in organizing, rather than in remedying sex discrimination per se. It is here that the NLRB's responsibilities in determining bargaining units, holding elections, and adjudicating disputes will become important to women workers.

NOTE: THE UNION AS AN ALLY

If unions are sympathetic to the needs of women workers, there are many actions they can take. In addition to bringing actions under Title VII and the Equal Pay Act on behalf of their members, they can press for contract clauses that prohibit discrimination on the basis of sex and that provide remedies for aggrieved individuals. Union contracts can also be used to achieve genuine protection for workers of both sexes, ranging from voluntary overtime provisions and sex-neutral weight-lifting limits to temporary disability protection and health plans which cover medical costs and disabilities arising from pregnancy on an equal basis with other medical costs and disabilities. Unions can work for benefits of special interest to women workers, such as child care. It will also be important for unions to employ women as organizers, to take affirmative action to get women into leadership positions, and to organize industries and occupations where women workers are concentrated. Finally, unions should support legislation to promote the cause of equality for women, such as the Equal Rights Amendment (endorsed by the AFL-CIO National Convention in 1973 after decades of opposition).

Of course, most unions are still a long way from such concerted action on behalf of women workers. And it should not be forgotten that even unions which are trying to help women members can have conflicts of interest in representing other women members. See Air Line Stewards and Stewardesses Ass'n, Local 550 v. American Airlines, Inc., 42 U.S.L.W. 2371 (7th Cir. Dec. 12, 1973) (holding that union controlled by currently employed stewardesses was an inadequate representative of formerly employed stewardesses in a class action challenging the airline policy of discharging pregnant stewardesses).

Much of the material that follows in Sections E through G is excerpted from Cooper and Rabb, Equal Employment Law and Litigation, Materials for A Clinical Law Course (Employment Rights Project, Columbia Law School, 1972). This book, produced under a grant from the Equal Employment Opportunity Commission, is designed as a casebook for a clinical law course and emphasizes litigation problems. It is an excellent source of information and is available, at no charge, from the Equal Employment Opportunity Commission, Office of State and Community Affairs, 1800 G Street, N.W., Washington, D.C. 20506. An updated version will be available from the EEOC in late 1974,

169. Cooper and Rabb, Equal Employment Law and Litigation, supra, at 58-59.

along with a companion Cooper and Rabb volume, Litigation Manual (also available free of charge). The manual includes sample Title VII litigation documents, e.g., complaints, interrogatories, class action motions and memos, Rule 37 motions and memos, and should be an invaluable aid for practitioners. Cooper and Rabb will also publish a casebook in 1975 on the law of equal employment opportunity, Litigating Fair Employment Cases: Documents and Materials for Student and Practitioner (West Publishing Co.).

E. Title VII Procedure and Administrative Process

1. The Statutory Requirements

Workers who seek to take advantage of Title VII must comply with several procedural requirements set forth in the act. Employers often defend against Title VII actions on the basis of a failure to comply with these requirements. Thus, lawyers should know what the procedures are in order to advise clients who have not yet been to the EEOC how to proceed with their cases. And if clients come to a lawyer after they have filed with the EEOC, the lawyer will also have to check for compliance with all the statutory requirements in order to suggest remedial action if it is necessary.

As a backdrop for understanding these procedural requirements, the next excerpt, from a legal handbook for laypersons, describes the outlines of the administrative process.

ROSS, THE RIGHTS OF WOMEN
64-68 (1973)

How does a woman enforce her rights under Title VII?
The initial steps are easy. You visit an EEOC office and fill out a simple form, called a "charge" form because you are "charging" the company with discrimination. The main question on the charge form is to "explain what unfair thing was done to you" and "how were other persons treated differently." The EEOC will then investigate your charge. If it believes you, the commission will try to get the company to stop discriminating; and if that doesn't succeed, you have the right to go to court to enforce your rights.

What process does the EEOC go through to enforce your rights?
If you live in a state or city that has passed a law against sex discrimination in employment . . . , usually called a fair-employment practice law (FEP law), the commission's first step will be to send a copy of your charge to the state or city agency. This is called deferring your charge to the other agency. It is done because Title VII requires that any person filing a charge with the commission must first file the charge with such a state agency; to insure that this is done, the commission files your charge for you. After this, the commission usually must wait sixty days before it has any power to act on your charge. Then it sends a notice of your charge to the person you charged with discrimination and starts its investigation. Someone will either be sent to the place where you work to look at company records and talk to people, or a list of questions will be sent to the company to fill out. After the investigation, the EEOC may either try to settle the case at once — by getting the company to agree to take steps to end the discrimination and reimburse you for any losses — or it may wait until a later stage. If no satisfactory settlement is reached, the EEOC writes a final decision on whether "reasonable cause exists to believe there is discrimination." Where the commission finds "reasonable cause," EEOC personnel make a final effort to settle the case, technically referred to as

conciliation efforts. If conciliation fails, either because you cannot accept what the company offers or because the company will not offer anything, the commission will give you a "notice of right to sue," and you may then take the company to court. You may also sue even if the commission finds "no cause," although it will be more difficult to find a lawyer in this instance. Other possibilities — both currently somewhat remote — are that the EEOC will itself bring a lawsuit on your behalf or that the Justice Department will in certain even more remote instances.

How long will this procedure take?

Unfortunately, the EEOC has a very large backlog of cases, and it will probably take two to three years for EEOC personnel to take all these steps.

Is there any way to shorten the process?

Yes. You have an automatic right to bring your lawsuit one hundred eighty days after EEOC acquires the power to act on your charge (i.e., one hundred eighty days from the time you go to the EEOC in a state without an FEP law and one hundred eighty days after the deferral period is over in a state with an FEP law). If you want faster action than the EEOC can give you, and you can find a lawyer to take your case, request the EEOC letter giving you the right to sue (the "notice of right to sue"). Don't ask for this notice until you have a lawyer, though, because she or he must start the lawsuit within ninety days of your receipt of the notice and will need time to prepare the case.

Are there any timing problems to watch out for?

Definitely, and they are extremely important. You can even lose your lawsuit if you don't comply with certain time requirements under Title VII, even though you were really discriminated against.

The first timing problem involves the date you file your charge with the commission. Title VII says you must do so within one hundred eighty days of the date you were discriminated against in a state with no FEP law, and within three hundred days in a state with an FEP law. Even if you think you have missed the time deadlines, you may still be able to comply with this requirement. Several courts have said that if the discrimination is of a continuing nature, such as a policy the company has never countermanded, then a charge is always filed within the time limits because the discrimination is still going on. You should, therefore, always write on the charge form that the discrimination is continuing, instead of limiting your charge to a particular date. When you think about it, almost every form of discrimination can be viewed in this manner. Thus, if the company refuses to promote you on August 11, 1972, because you are a woman, you can visualize the situation in two ways. You can either say you were personally discriminated against on August 11, 1972, or you can say that the company has a continuing policy of refusing to promote women into certain jobs, which you became aware of on August 11! The second way is always better, not only because it avoids this timing problem but also because it makes the point that other women besides yourself are affected by the policy.

Another reason to file your charge as soon as possible is to increase the amount of money you can win in a lawsuit. Under Title VII, you can win back wages, that is, the amount of money you would have earned if you had not been discriminated against. But you can collect back wages only for a period of time dating from two years prior to filing the charge up to the end of your lawsuit. The later you file your charge, the later the date from which the judge will compute the back pay due you. For instance, if you file on January 1, 1972, and ultimately win your lawsuit, you will collect back wages from January 1, 1970, up to the date you win the lawsuit, and the company will be ordered to increase your future wages to what you should be earning. If you wait to file until September 1, 1972, the back wages will be computed from September 1, 1970, and you will lose eight months of back wages that you are really entitled to.

The second timing problem posed by Title VII involves going to court. You have only ninety days after the day you receive your EEOC "notice of right to sue" to file the court complaint that starts the lawsuit. Never ask for the notice until you have a lawyer and make sure that your lawyer understands that the complaint must be filed within that time period, or you will lose your case. (If by some chance this happens to you, your lawyer has been extremely negligent, and you should go to another lawyer to sue the first one for malpractice.)

––––––––––––––––

The following excerpt describes Title VII's procedural requirements with a discussion of legal strategies for dealing with the requirements.

COOPER AND RABB
EQUAL EMPLOYMENT LAW AND LITIGATION
50-51, 60-74 (1972)

STATE ANTI-DISCRIMINATION AGENCIES

Almost every state in the union except those in the Deep South have employment anti-discrimination laws. . . .

The procedures governing the agencies vary from one to another. Title VII provides however that "[i]f any requirement for the commencement of such State or local proceeding is imposed by a State or local authority other than a requirement of the filing of a written and signed statement of the facts upon which the proceeding is based, the proceeding shall be deemed to have been commenced for the purposes of the subsection at the time such statement is sent by registered mail to the appropriate State or local authority." The only major decision of the United States Supreme Court regarding Title VII's procedural requirements, and specifically deferral of jurisdiction initially to State or local agencies, is Love v. Pullman, 404 U.S. 522 (1972). That decision suggests that complainants will not be held to a rigorous and inflexible standard in complying with deferral and State jurisdiction requisites prior to pursuance of their remedies at EEOC or in federal court. . . .

INSTITUTING A TITLE VII PROCEEDING
AGAINST A PRIVATE EMPLOYER

Time Requirements

When an unlawful employment practice occurs in a State which does not have its own anti-discrimination law, the aggrieved person must file a complaint [or charge][170] with the Equal Employment Opportunity Commission within 180 days of the discriminatory act.[1]

When an unlawful employment practice occurs in a State which has its own anti-discrimination law and enforcement agency, persons wishing to invoke their Title VII rights must first file their [charge] with the State agency.[2]

The statutes of limitations for filing claims with State agencies vary roughly from 90 days to one year. The liberal one year statutes are limited however by the Title VII requirement that when a charge has been first filed at a State human rights agency, the charge must further be filed with the EEOC no more than 300 days after the occurrence

––––––––––––––––

170. The EEOC calls its form a *charge* form, and this term is substituted in the text for complaint, to avoid confusion of the form used by the administrative agency with the judicial complaint used in federal court. — Eds.

1. 42 U.S.C. 2000e-5(e).

2. 42 U.S.C. 2000e-5(c). It should be noted that only state agencies having enforcement powers come under this provision.

of the discriminatory act or within 30 days after receipt of notice that the State agency has terminated its proceeding, whichever first occurs.[3]

Once a charge has been filed with a State agency, the State has exclusive jurisdiction over the matter for 60 days.[4] At the end of 60 days, EEOC may assume concurrent jurisdiction.

In order to insure that all necessary procedural steps are taken, the best practice is to simultaneously file State and federal charges. The charge filed with EEOC should be accompanied by a covering letter noting the simultaneous filing and requesting that 60 days from receipt of the charge the EEOC automatically assume jurisdiction.

Note that it is not strictly necessary that EEOC take jurisdiction 60 days after a [charge] has been filed with the State. As a matter of practice, however, nothing is lost by perfecting EEOC's jurisdiction at that time, and a possible oversight which would defeat EEOC jurisdiction at a later stage is avoided.

In the event that a violation is continuing, the discriminatory "act" does not occur on a given date from which the statutory period for filing begins to run. When this is the situation, a charge may initially be filed any time during the violation. Once the [charge] is filed, though, [all other] time limitations do apply. . . . Cox v. United States Gypsum Co., 409 F.2d 289 (7th Cir. 1969); Tippet v. Liggett and Meyers Tobacco Co., 316 F. Supp. 292 (M.D.N.C. 1970).

If a complainant wishes to proceed to federal court rather than await EEOC's efforts to investigate and conciliate, he or she must obtain an authorizing letter from the EEOC, commonly known as a "right to sue" letter. This may be obtained, as a matter of right, at any time after the EEOC has had jurisdiction over the charge for 180 days.[5] The right to sue letter may be demanded and issued even if neither the State agency nor the EEOC has taken any action on the charge.[6] The letter may be issued when the EEOC has found no reasonable cause to believe that the charge is true as well as when reasonable cause has been found.[7] The letter may issue and the court action commence despite EEOC's failure to attempt conciliation among the parties[8] and/or the charging party's refusal to submit to an attempted conciliation.[9] The only exception to the charging party's right to request this right to sue letter arises when the EEOC has actually taken the step of filing a civil action in a federal district court. In such a situation the charging party may privately intervene in the EEOC action, but may not seek to file a separate action as his own.[10]

In determining when and whether to demand the right to sue letter, primarily two factors weigh in the balance. One: Only in rare instances will EEOC be able, given its present work load, to complete action on a matter within something just over 180 days. If there is reason to proceed without delay, the case should be taken to court promptly without waiting for the EEOC to fully process the [charge]. Two: Many charges lodged at EEOC raise factual questions which require extensive investigation. If private parties finance the necessary data collection, the process may be very costly. Leaving the pre-trial discovery to EEOC saves money, at the expense of time and control over the discovery process. The decision to take the case to court at a given time will usually turn on a balancing of these time and money factors.

Having received a permission to sue letter, the charging party has only 90 days in

3. 42 U.S.C. 2000e-5(e).

4. 42 U.S.C. 2000e-5(c).

5. 42 U.S.C. 2000e-5(f)(1).

6. Carr v. Conoco Plastics, Inc., 423 F.2d 57 (5th Cir.), *cert. denied,* 400 U.S. 951 (1970).

7. Flowers v. Laborers International Union, Local 6, 431 F.2d 205 (7th Cir. 1970); Fekete v. United States Steel Corp., 424 F.2d 331 (3rd Cir. 1970); Beverly v. Lone Star Lead Construction Corp., 437 F.2d 1136 (5th Cir. 1971).

8. Rosen v. Public Service Electric & Gas Co., 409 F.2d 775 (3rd Cir. 1969); Choate v. Caterpillar Tractor Co., 402 F.2d 357 (7th Cir. 1968); Watson v. Limbach,___F. Supp.___ (S.D. Ohio 1971), 4 EPD Par. 7648.

9. Cox v. United States Gypsum Co., 409 F.2d 289 (7th Cir. 1969).

10. 42 U.S.C. 2000e-5(b)(1).

which to commence litigation in a federal district court.[11] If the action is not filed in federal court within the 90 day period, the Title VII cause of action may be dismissed.[12] Therefore, prudent counsel will never request a right to sue letter unless he or she is fully prepared to promptly commence action in federal district court. In order to allow charging parties to seek and secure counsel who will be able to move rapidly to prepare court papers, EEOC is normally willing to notify charging parties when the agency has concluded its determinations and will wait to send the letter until the party has retained counsel.

Contents of the Administrative Complaint

Both State and EEOC [charge] forms are simple questionnaires which require that the charging party "Explain what unfair thing was done to you." A simple statement such as "I believe I was fired because I am a Negro" is adequate to support a claim of racial discrimination.

It is advisable for a lawyer preparing a [charge] to plead in somewhat broader terms. If a charging party believes herself to have been discharged due to sex discrimination, she should charge the respondent with sex discrimination in recruiting, hiring and terms and conditions of employment, noting that her own grievances resulted from that pattern and practice. The charging party should complain on behalf of herself and all similarly situated past, present and future employees. No evidence need be submitted and no other pleadings need be made to support the allegation. Of course if the charging party has information which buttresses the claim, that information should be relayed to the agency and/or EEOC.

Charging parties should think big not only in the terms of their complaints but also in naming respondents. For example, where a complainant charges that he was excluded from an apprenticeship program established between a union and an employers' collective, he should name as respondents not only the local union whose officers personally rejected his application, but the international of the union, the prospective employer (if known), the employer's association, a contractor and the contractors' association, if they are all responsible for the apprenticeship program.

It is not uncommon for a complainant to be reluctant to sue his union as well as his employer or to have filed charges in which all of the possibly responsible respondents were not named. If the charge has not been filed when the attorney is first consulted, it should be checked to guarantee that all possible respondents are named. If the attorney is brought into a case after the initial charge is filed and if the charge is deficient due to failure to name all respondents, the deficiency is rarely fatal, although it may cause some time delay. Presuming a continuing violation, the charging party may at any time file a [charge] against the previously neglected respondents. This supplemental [charge] can contain precisely the same allegations as the earlier [charge] and will doubtless be consolidated with the earlier [charge] for investigation and action by the agency.

Again presuming a continuing violation, even if the initial [charge] has progressed to the stage of active litigation in federal district court, it is not too late to add respondents. Counsel simply files a charge on behalf of the charging party (plaintiff) at the State agency and/or EEOC and at the end of the requisite period moves to amend the complaint in district court to include the now-named defendants.

If the violation is not continuing, needless to say, a charge against an omitted respondent can always be made if the omission is discovered within the 180 day or 300 day EEOC rule or within the applicable State limitation if it is less than 300 days. In instances where the Title VII time limitations have been exceeded, the complainant in a race case can rely upon a claim under 42 U.S.C. Sec. 1981 to give jurisdiction over the omitted respondent.

---

11. 42 U.S.C. 2000e-5(f)(1).
12. Sanders v. Dobbs Houses, Inc., 431 F.2d 1097 (5th Cir. 1970), *cert. denied*, 401 U.S. 948 (1971).

ADDING A CLAIM UNDER 42 U.S.C. SEC. 1981

Racial employment discrimination actions against private employers are quite commonly bottomed on at least two causes of action: Title VII and 42 U.S.C. Sec. 1981. In a case where 42 U.S.C. Sec. 1981 has been pleaded as a basis for the action, the Title VII administrative procedures are not applicable. The Third[13] and Fifth[14] Circuits have held that the Sec. 1981 cause of action is not subject to the time limitations of a Title VII cause of action and permit the filing of Sec. 1981 claims without any showing of a reason for bypassing Title VII. The Seventh Circuit, while not disagreeing with the principle that Title VII time periods are inapplicable to Sec. 1981 claims, has held that charging parties must plead a reasonable excuse for bypassing Title VII and its administrative prerequisites before they will be permitted to proceed solely under 42 U.S.C. Sec. 1981.[15] This requirement will hopefully be satisfied by a showing that ignorance or oversight led to the omission of the missing respondent and that it is too late to correct the defect.

Section 1981 may broaden the scope of an employment discrimination action in another important respect. There are limits on the extent to which Title VII can be used to challenge the present effects of a discriminatory act which occurred prior to July, 1965, the effective date of Title VII. The 1866 effective date of 42 U.S.C. Sec. 1981 may avoid this problem. The statute of limitations which is most likely applicable to Sec. 1981 actions is drawn from the law of the State in which the federal action is brought. The State law consulted is that most analogous to Title VII.[16]

The comparison between Title VII and Section 1981 is not complete without pointing out certain respects in which Section 1981 is less broad. Most important, Section 1981 is basically a provision directed only against racial discrimination, not the broader range of classes protected by Title VII. For example, two recent decisions[17] have held that the provisions of Sec. 1981 may not be invoked as a basis for court action in sex discrimination cases. Also worth considering on a more mundane level is that Section 1981 contains no specific authorization of counsel fees comparable to that in Title VII.

RELYING UPON OTHER REMEDIAL ALTERNATIVES

If a complainant wishes to pursue not only multiple causes of action in a federal suit but also multiple or alternative remedies outside of litigation, he is probably free to do so. The courts have been fairly liberal in not forcing any particular choice of remedies. Thus, it has been specifically held that Title VII complainants may pursue remedies before the N.L.R.B.[18] or under the Railway Labor Act[19] without waiving any rights under Title VII. As for private contractual grievance procedures, such as those provided under a union collective bargaining agreement, it has been held that a Title VII complainant need not exhaust private grievance procedures.[20] . . . [W]here he has pursued those procedures to an unsuccessful conclusion, his rights to shift to Title VII [were] in serious doubt.[21] [However, in 1974 the Supreme Court ruled that resort to

---

13. Hackett v. McGuire Bros. Inc., 445 F.2d 442 (1971).

14. Sanders v. Dobbs Houses, Inc., 431 F.2d 1097 (5th Cir. 1970), *cert. denied,* 401 U.S. 948 (1971), and Boudreaux v. Baton Rouge Contracting Co., 437 F.2d 1011 (5th Cir. 1971).

15. Waters v. Wisconsin Steel Works, 427 F.2d 476 (7th Cir. 1970), *cert. denied sub nom.* United Order of American Bricklayers and Stone Masons, Local 21 v. Waters, 400 U.S. 911 (1970).

16. The issue of which statute of limitations is applicable to Sec. 1981 employment discrimination cases was raised in King v. Georgia Power Co., 3 EPD Par. 8318 (N.D. Ga. 1971) now on appeal to the Fifth Circuit, Case No. 71-3229.

17. Fitzgerald v. United Methodist Community Center, 335 F. Supp. 965 (D. Neb. 1972), 4 EPD Par. 7659; Williams v. San Francisco Unified School District et al., 340 F. Supp. 435 (N.D. Calif. 1972), 4 EPD Par. 7771.

18. Taylor v. Armco Steel Corp., 429 F.2d 498 (5th Cir. 1970).

19. Norman v. Missouri Pacific R. R., 414 F.2d 73 (8th Cir. 1969).

20. Bowe v. Colgate-Palmolive Co., 416 F.2d 711 (7th Cir. 1969).

21. Compare Culpepper v. Reynolds Metals, Inc., 421 F.2d 888 (5th Cir. 1970); Malone v. North American Rockwell Corporation, 457 F.2d 779 (9th Cir. 1972) [with] Dewey v. Reynolds Metals Co., 429 F.2d 324 (6th Cir. 1970), *aff'd by an equally divided court,* 402 U.S. 689 (1971).

union grievance arbitration does not bar a subsequent Title VII action. Alexander v. Gardner-Denver Company, — U.S. —, 94 S. Ct. 1011, 39 L. Ed. 2d 147, 42 U.S.L.W. 4212 (1974).]

INSTITUTING AN ACTION AGAINST A PUBLIC EMPLOYER

At the State Level

The recent amendments to Title VII have extended its reach to include state and local governments, departments, agencies, and political subdivisions. (An exemption for elected officials and their assistants is intended to be construed narrowly and does not affect the broad scope of the new law.) In 1972, only those governmental departments and agencies which employ 25 or more people in each of 20 or more calendar weeks may be subject to suit under Title VII; thereafter, public employers with 15 or more employees will be covered by this section.

The procedure for instituting a charge against a public employer is the same as that described . . . supra, regarding private employers, with the important exception that the Attorney General takes over for the EEOC at the court level. Thus, if the EEOC investigation of a public employer reveals discriminatory practices which are not conciliated, the case is referred to the Attorney General, who may bring a civil suit against respondent in the appropriate federal district court. If the EEOC determines that there is no basis for the aggrieved person's charge or if the Attorney General has not effectively conciliated or prosecuted the action, the complainant may institute a private suit against respondent on his own initiative. It is the statutory obligation of the Attorney General rather than the EEOC to notify a complainant at the expiration of the 180 day period, and the complainant has only 90 days after receipt of this notice to commence proceedings in federal court.

At the Federal Level

Federal employers (and those employers of the District of Columbia who are bound by the requirements of the federal competitive service) are not covered by the standard Title VII provisions, but are instead subject to the procedures outlined in Sec. 717, relating to non-discrimination in federal employment. A federal employee or applicant complaining of discrimination must file charges with the department or agency whose discriminatory practices he is contesting. He may appeal an unfavorable administrative decision to the Civil Service Commission which has the ultimate responsibility for enforcing equal employment in federal departments and agencies. If a complainant is dissatisfied with the final disposition of the complaint or with administrative inaction, he may file a civil action within 30 days of receipt of notice of final action, or after 180 days from the initial filing of the complaint with the department or agency. In such civil action, the head of the department or agency whose employment practices are disputed is named as the defendant, and the procedural requirements are the same as for suits against private employers.

In addition to these new Title VII remedies which may be pursued against public employers, the preexisting causes of action under the Constitution (Fifth and Fourteenth Amendments) of course remain available. These constitutional causes may be pursued separately and directly in court or may be joined with a Title VII cause. See 42 U.S.C. Sec. 1983.

NOTES

1. Employers' attempts to raise the procedural requirements of Title VII as jurisdictional bars to suit have been largely unsuccessful. Thus, in responding to countless motions to dismiss based on a plaintiff's failure to comply with one of these requirements, the courts have basically replied that plaintiffs must be given a chance to develop their case on the merits. See generally Hebert and Reischel, Title VII and the Multiple Approaches to Eliminating Employment Discrimination, 46 N.Y.U.L. Rev. 449, 461-483 (1971), for a discussion of the different defenses raised and the leading cases. In fact, the courts have established only two jurisdictional requirements to a Title VII suit: (1) that plaintiff file a timely charge with EEOC; and (2) that plaintiff institute timely suit after receiving a notice of right to sue. McDonnell Douglas Corp. v. Green, 411 U.S. 792, 93 S. Ct. 1817, 36 L. Ed. 2d 668 (1973).

2. As Cooper and Rabb note, 42 U.S.C. §1981 has some important advantages over Title VII, but is generally not available to contest sex discrimination. For a scholarly discussion of how §1981 could be interpreted to reach sex discrimination, see Stanley, Sex Discrimination and Section 1981, 1 Women's Rights L. Rep. 2 (Spring 1973). Ms. Stanley contends that §1981 implements the Thirteenth Amendment, that the Thirteenth Amendment applies to sex discrimination, and that therefore §1981 applies to sex discrimination. Her thesis that the Thirteenth Amendment, abolishing slavery, applies to sex discrimination as well finds some support in the recent Supreme Court decision, Frontiero v. Richardson, 411 U.S. 677, 93 S. Ct. 1764, 36 L. Ed. 2d 583 (1973), in which the Court noted that[171]

> [T]hroughout much of the 19th century the position of women in our society was, in many respects, comparable to that of blacks under the pre–Civil War slave codes. Neither slaves nor women could hold office, serve on juries, or bring suit in their own names, and married women traditionally were denied the legal capacity to hold or convey property or to serve as legal guardians of their own children.... And although blacks were guaranteed the right to vote in 1870, women were denied even that right — which is of itself "preservative of other basic civil and political rights" — until adoption of the Nineteenth Amendment half a century later.

2. A Case Study: Women Law Students Versus Wall Street Law Firms

The following materials demonstrate the typical procedural development of a Title VII suit. They include the initial charge filed with a local fair employment practice commission (the New York City Commission on Human Rights), the commission's probable cause decision, the court complaint, and court decisions on defendant's motion to dismiss, and plaintiff's motion for determination of a class action. The EEOC charge is not included, since it is virtually identical to the city commission charge (although the forms differ somewhat).

171. 411 U.S. at 685.

COOPER AND RABB
EQUAL EMPLOYMENT LAW AND LITIGATION
266-283 (1972)

[THE AGENCY CHARGE]

CITY OF NEW YORK
_____

Commission on Human
Rights on the
Complaint of

                         Complaint No. _____

     MARGARET
       Complainant

    against

       Respondent
_____

I, ... Margaret . . . .
residing at . . 420 West 119th Street, New York, N.Y. . . . . .
charge . . . . ‾‾‾‾‾‾ . . . .
whose address is . . . Park Avenue, New York, N.Y. . . . .
with an unlawful discriminatory practice relating to
. . . . employment . . . .
at . . . . . Columbia Law School . . . .
on or about . . . Fall, 1970 and continuing . . . .
by . . . . . a representative of said firm . . . .
because of my RACE ( ), COLOR ( ), CREED ( ),
                NATIONAL ORIGIN ( ), AGE ( ),
                PHYSICAL HANDICAP ( ), SEX (X).

The particulars are:

1. I am a second year law student at Columbia Law School. During the Fall of 1970, respondent conducted interviews of law students for the purpose of hiring law associates for summer positions to commence the following June. I was qualified for such a position with the firm. (See resume attached hereto.)

2. Although the respondent interviewed and/or gave job offers to men with equal or lesser qualifications than mine, the firm failed and refused to offer to hire me.

3. I believe that the respondent has discriminated against me on the basis of my sex. The following facts are submitted in support of my allegation:

4. Respondent _____, is a law partnership of approximately 45 partners and 36 associates. The firm engages in a general practice with a special emphasis on corporate law. Upon information and belief, _____ presently employs 1 female attorney. She is an associate assigned to work in Trusts and Estates, an area of law traditionally designated as women lawyers' work. None of respondent's partners are female.

5. On November 17, 1970, I had an interview at Columbia University Law School with Mr. L_____ of _____. During said interview the following transpired:

A) During the initial part of the interview I asked Mr. L__ some general questions about the firm, and he asked me a few questions about my resume. Then he said, "Do you have any questions you'd like to ask me?" Before I had a chance to answer he said, "I bet you want to know how many girls we have?" I said, "I would be interested, although that's not my only concern."

B) He said the firm had one woman, in his department, Trusts and Estates. She had been with them for four years.

He said, "I don't know exactly why, but for some reason women are really good at Trusts and Estates; they really love the detail work and they're very competent at it." He said, "Most men don't like this kind of work, though I am an exception."

Then I asked, "Don't you think there is a lot of specificity and detail in other types of legal work?" He said, "No, in Trusts and Estates it is different" and then he gave me a short description of what Trusts and Estates work entailed.

C) At this point I said, "Your firm does a lot of litigation work, doesn't it? I thought that discovery matters were highly detailed." He said that that was true but in litigation you are not dealing with detail all the time. "There are bigger issues involved whereas in Trusts and Estates there is detail all the time." He also said, "I don't know about you, but most women really like this detail."

D) Toward the end of the interview he said, "If a woman came to us and wanted to work in Trusts and Estates and we had an opening in this area, we would encourage her to go into Trusts and Estates." The implication of the statement was that (i) the firm would not encourage a man to go into the field of Trusts and Estates whereas they would a woman, and (ii) a woman would not be hired unless the firm had an opening in Trusts and Estates. I was not offered a position with the firm.

6. I charge that the respondent has discriminated against me because I am a woman in violation of the Administrative Code of the City of New York, and that as a result of respondent's unlawful discriminatory practices, I have suffered or may suffer loss of earnings, humiliation, outrage and mental anguish for which I claim compensatory damages and/or any such other legal or equitable relief as is necessary and appropriate.

I have not commenced any action, civil, criminal or administrative based upon the above allegation.

. . . .
. . . .
. . . . Margaret . . . .
(Signature of Complainant)

CITY OF NEW YORK
                                        SS.:
COUNTY OF NEW YORK

. . . . Margaret . . . ., being duly sworn, deposes
and says: that . . . . is the Complainant herein;
that . . . . she . . . . has read the foregoing complaint and
knows the contents thereof; that the same is true of
. . . . her . . . . own knowledge, except as to the matters
therein stated on information and belief and that as
to these matters . . . . she . . . . believes the same to be true.

Subscribed and sworn to before me
this ____ day of _____.

                          Margaret _____
                          (Signature of Complainant)

[THE AGENCY DECISION]

COMMISSION ON HUMAN RIGHTS OF
THE CITY OF NEW YORK ON

The Complaint of

MARGARET
           Complainant

against   Complaint No. 5207-JS

           Respondent

DATE OF ALLEGED VIOLATION: November 1970 and
                              continuing

DATE OF FILING: May 27, 1971

DATE OF SERVICE OF CHARGE: August 13, 1971

Probable Cause Decision

Summary of Charge

On May 27, 1971, a complaint was filed against the above-named law firm by Ms. Margaret _____, then a second year law student at Columbia University, alleging that said respondent had discriminated against her in violation of the Administrative Code of the City of New York, Section B1-7.0, by denying her summer employment because of her sex. Complainant alleges that respondent's campus interviewers for summer employment express a discriminatory preference for men except for positions in Trusts & Estates.

Summary of Investigation

(1) Respondent is a law firm in general practice, largely for corporate clients in diverse fields. Extensive work is done in the fields of securities, anti-trust, taxation and trusts and estates. Considerable work is also done in labor law, libel, commercial arbitrations, and real estate transactions. As of November 1971, the firm consisted of 86 attorneys, 43 partners and 43 associates. During the summer respondent also employs first and second year law students as summer associates or interns.

(2) Respondent sent a representative to Columbia Law School on November 17, 1970 for the purpose of recruiting prospective summer associates. Complainant registered for an interview and was interviewed by respondent's recruiter, Mr. Jack L_____. Complainant was not invited for an in-house interview or hired for summer employment although three male applicants from Columbia were offered in-house interviews and were subsequently hired. An examination of complainant's resume shows her qualifications to be equal to and no less than the three successful male applicants. Moreover, Mr. L_____ admitted to a Commission representative, during a meeting held on March 30, 1972, that complainant was the second best applicant he interviewed at Columbia for 1971 summer employment.

(3) Respondent denies any discrimination against complainant because of her sex. Mr. L_____ denies the substance of remarks attributed to him by charging party in her complaint.

(4) Respondent's pattern of employment of partners and permanent associates over a ten year period was examined in great detail. Of the 86 permanent attorneys presently employed by respondent only one is a female. She works in the Trusts and Estates Department. Since 1961 only 2 females have been employed on a permanent basis; their periods of employment never overlapped so that at no time in the past ten years has respondent employed more than one female attorney.

(5) Respondent denies that Trusts and Estates is a department to which women

are traditionally assigned and also denied that female associates are encouraged to enter Trusts and Estates.

(6) The pattern of promotion and advancement was examined. Of the 43 partners, none are female. Neither of the two female attorneys employed by respondent since 1961 achieved partnership status. The present female attorney graduated in 1963 and was hired in 1965. All four male attorneys graduating in 1963 are now partners. Three of the 36 attorneys graduating in later years are partners. All but four attorneys graduating before the one female attorney are partners and three of these four male associates were hired from two to five years after the female associate.

(7) Respondent's pattern of hiring was examined. As to permanent employment, respondent hired 129 persons from 1961-71. Only one of these new attorneys was female, representing .8% of all new hires.

(8) As to summer associates, respondent employed 83 persons in this capacity from 1961-71. Two of these (2.4%) have been female. Of the 83, 26 eventually were employed by respondent on a permanent basis, representing 22% of the 129 permanent employees hired between 1961-1971. All 26 summer attorneys subsequently hired as permanent staff were males.

(9) In the last ten years, females represented approximately 5% of the applicant flow for summer and permanent employment (306 of 6297). Respondent offered employment to only 3 of these women, representing 2% of all offers made. Females interviewed attended essentially the same law schools as the male applicants attended. The percentage of applicants with honors was the same for both males and females (35%). In 1961, women were 3% of the applicants, 50% of whom had honors; in 1962, 7% of the applicants, 36% with honors and in 1967, 7% of the applicants, 55% having honors. No women were offered jobs during these years. Finally, 2.4% of all the male applicants were offered employment whereas 1% of all the female applicants were offered employment.

(10) Respondent's recruitment patterns were reviewed. Approximately 95% of the applicants are male and 5% female. This ratio has not changed significantly in the last ten years. Female enrollment in law schools has increased in recent years.

(11) Male applicants are encouraged to continue seeking employment at respondent firm even though no jobs are available, females are not. A review of respondent's files revealed that some male and female applicants were sent different letters of rejection. Males and females were told that respondent was not in a position to make an offer. The letters to male applicants contained an invitation to come in for an interview anyway. The letters to females contained no such reference.

(12) Respondent was barred from recruitment on the University of _____ campus for the academic year 1970-71 as a result of statements allegedly made by its representative on that campus indicating a discriminatory hiring policy toward women. Respondent chose not to grieve the issue and to refute the charges. Instead, respondent voluntarily discontinued recruitment at the University of _____. Respondent's expulsion is known to women law students in New York City.

(13) Respondent pays the initiation fees of several partners for membership in the Sky Club. The Sky Club excludes women from membership.

Finding:

(1) Complainant was not invited for an in-house interview and was not hired although she was considered by respondent's interviewer to be the second most qualified applicant interviewed at Columbia. Three male applicants from Columbia, at least two of whom must have been less qualified than the complainant, were offered in-house interviews and were hired. Even though one of the eight 1971 summer employees was female, only two of the eighty-three summer employees since 1961 were female. In light of these facts, there is probable cause to believe that respondent rejected the complainant because of her sex.

(2) Analysis of employment statistics, job resumes and respondent's patterns and practices, indicates a virtual exclusion of female attorneys. This exclusion is attributed to the following factors:

(a) Almost without exception, respondent has rejected women applicants for permanent and summer employment although women with qualifications equal to and better than the male applicants have applied.

(b) Since 31% of summer employees are subsequently hired as permanent associates (representing 22% of all permanent hires), and almost all women are rejected for such employment, respondent denies women equal access to permanent employment.

(c) Respondent, since 1965, has restricted its female representation to one division, Trusts and Estates, an area of law for which women have been traditionally viewed as well-suited.

(d) Respondent has failed to advance women to partnerships although men with equal or inferior tenure and experience to the women have been so promoted.

(e) Respondent's interviews are conducted in such a manner as to express a preference for men and to discourage women from pursuing employment with respondent firm.

(f) Respondent's correspondence with applicants to whom no job offer is tendered encourages men to continue seeking employment and contains no such encouragement for the women.

(g) The absence of an increase in the percentage of female applicants while female enrollment in law schools is increasing may be attributed in part to respondent's reputation, as a result of an uncontested exclusion from interviewing at the University of _____ because of alleged discriminatory practices toward women, which deter women from applying for employment at respondent firm.

(h) Respondent pays the initiation fees of several partners for membership in a club that excludes women.

The Commission finds that probable cause exists to believe that respondent discriminated against the complainant because of her sex, and that respondent engages in patterns and practices of recruitment, selection, hiring, assignment and promotion of women attorneys which discriminates against them because of their sex, in violation of the Administrative Code of the City of New York, Section B1-7.0.

Preston David
Executive Director

4/27/72

[THE FEDERAL COURT COMPLAINT]

UNITED STATES DISTRICT COURT
SOUTHERN DISTRICT OF NEW YORK

MARGARET _____, individually
and on behalf of all other
persons similarly situated,

      Plaintiff

against

      Defendant

Complaint____
Class Action

I. Nature of Claim

1. This is a proceeding for declaratory and injunctive relief and damages to redress the deprivation of rights secured to the plaintiff by Title VII of the Civil Rights Act of 1964 (42 U.S.C. Sec. 2000e et seq.). Plaintiff seeks a declaratory judgment and injunction to restrain defendants from maintaining practices, policies, customs and usages which discriminate against plaintiff and members of her class because of their sex with respect to hiring and conditions of employment.

II. Jurisdiction

2. The jurisdiction of this Court is invoked pursuant to 28 U.S.C. Secs. 1331 and 1343(4) and 28 U.S.C. Secs. 2201 and 2202. Jurisdiction to grant injunctive and declaratory equitable relief as well as damages is invoked pursuant to 42 U.S.C. Sec. 20003-5(f) and (g). The amount in controversy exceeds $10,000.

III. Class Action Allegations

3. Plaintiff brings this action pursuant to Rule 23(a) and (b)(2) of the FRCP on her own behalf and on behalf of all other persons similarly situated. The members of this class, which has at least five hundred members, are too numerous to be joined in one action. The class is composed of all women qualified for legal positions at _____ who have been or would be denied employment because of their sex.

4. Defendant _____ (hereinafter sometimes "the firm") acquires its lawyers by hiring summer associates, permanent associates and partners. The firm follows a practice of interviewing law students on selected law school campuses during each Fall for positions as summer associates. In due course, plaintiff Margaret _____, a woman, applied for a position as a summer associate and was interviewed by the firm's representative in November, 1970. Upon information and belief, plaintiff _____ was qualified for a position as a summer associate at _____ during the summer of 1971. Plaintiff _____ was considered, by the firm's interviewer, to be the second most qualified applicant interviewed by him at Columbia. Despite that rating three male Columbia students, none of whom have higher grades than plaintiff and some of whom had lower grades, were hired by the firm for the Summer. Upon this information plaintiff _____ alleges that she was denied an "in-house" interview and summer employment because of her sex. For these reasons, the claims of plaintiff _____ are typical of the claims of the other members of the class whose interests she can fairly and adequately represent.

5. The question of law common to the above-described class is whether the interviewing, hiring, placement and promotion practices of the defendant deprive the members of the class of the civil rights secured to them by 42 U.S.C. Secs. 2000e et seq. by denying them positions, placements, promotions and other conditions of employment granted to similarly qualified males seeking legal positions at the firm.

The defendant has acted, or refused to act, on grounds generally applicable to the class, thereby making appropriate injunctive relief with respect to the class as a whole.

IV. Plaintiff

6. Plaintiff Margaret _____ is a graduate of the Columbia Law School class of 1972. In the Fall semester of 1970, her second year in law school, plaintiff was interviewed for a position at _____. Her grade average was Very Good/Good, which is the equivalent of a high "B" in standard grading computation. She had been awarded the Charles Bathgate Bech prize for the best examination in Property during her first year in law school. She was also honored by an appointment as a research assistant to a professor at Columbia Law School in the Summer of 1970 and again the following Fall.

V. Defendant

7. Defendant _____ is a law partnership of 43 partners and 43 associates. The firm engages in a general practice with a special emphasis on corporate law. The firm does extensive work in the fields of securities, anti-trust, taxation and trusts and estates. Defendant also has a substantial practice in labor law, libel, commercial arbitrations and real estate transactions. During the Summer defendant employs about eight students as summer associates. _____ is an employer within the meaning of Title VII of the Civil Rights Act of 1964.

VI. Statement of Claim

8. Defendant firm has a history of failing and refusing to hire women. The defendant firm has eighty-six permanent attorneys, forty-three partners and forty-

three associates. Of the eighty-six attorneys one is a woman and she is an associate. Between 1961 and 1971, only two females have been employed on a permanent basis. Their periods of employment never overlapped so that at no time in the past ten years has _____ employed more than one full-time female attorney. The single current woman associate is assigned to work in Trusts and Estates, a traditionally female job.

9. None of the partners in defendant firm is a woman. The firm has had no woman partner between 1961 and 1971. Neither of the female associates employed by defendant during this ten year period was offered a partnership, although all males in the firm who graduated from law school in the same year as the one current female associate became partners before June, 1971. Three of the firm's male attorneys who are now partners, graduated from law school after the female associate did. Thirteen male attorneys hired after the female associate have achieved partnership status.

10. A substantial number of permanent associates are hired from the firm's pool of summer associates. In addition to its permanent legal staff, the defendant employed 83 summer associates from 1961-1971. Two of these were women. Of the 83, 26 were subsequently hired as permanent associates. All 26 were male; neither of the two women summer associates was hired as a permanent associate.

11. Female applicants for employment are discouraged by the firm from seeking other than trusts and estates work. During plaintiff's interview, she was encouraged to consider working for the firm only if she would accept an assignment to trusts and estates work. Statements made by the interviewer as well as recruitment material prepared by the firm describe general opportunities within the firm as reserved to male lawyers.

12. A substantial number of male applicants who are not offered positions with the firm receive letters encouraging them to continue seeking employment at the firm at a later date. These male applicants are offered an invitation to come for an in-house interview. No women applicants have received such a letter. Females not offered employment are simply rejected.

13. Defendant _____ sponsors and maintains facilities, functions and benefits of employment from which the firm's summer and permanent female associates are excluded. These include but are not limited to all-male office functions and use of the partnership assets to maintain memberships for ten partners in a club which does not admit women.

14. The facts alleged in paragraphs 8-13 establish that _____ engages in a pattern and practice of sex discrimination by defendant law firm that constitutes a violation of 42 U.S.C. Sec. 2000e-2(a) and the interdictions of that statute against hiring, discriminating with respect to compensation, terms, conditions, or privileges, and against limiting, segregating, or classifying employees on the basis of their sex by consistently and continuously:

(a) failing and refusing to hire qualified women for legal positions while hiring similarly qualified men;

(b) offering substantially less opportunity to female associates than to male associates for promotion, advancement and the concomitantly higher salaries which accompany such status;

(c) utilizing recruitment procedures, interviewing techniques and differential rejection letters which actively discourage women applicants;

(d) considering women for employment primarily or exclusively in an area designated as suitable for women attorneys;

(e) maintaining conditions of employment which limit the extension of certain privileges and benefits exclusively to the firm's male attorneys.

VII. Procedural Requirements

15. Plaintiff filed a timely complaint at the New York City Commission on Human Rights and at the Equal Employment Opportunity Commission. Plaintiff _____ received a permission to sue letter from the EEOC on June 26, 1972.

VIII. Relief

WHEREFORE plaintiff respectfully requests that this Court:
A. Rule that the matter is properly maintained as a class action.

B. Enter a judgment declaring that the acts and practices of defendant law firm are in violation of the laws of the United States.

C. Issue a permanent injunction.

(i) Ordering defendant to refrain from using selection criteria for hiring, promoting and assigning legal employees that have a differential impact on women and which are not validated, and specifically to use only job related criteria which do not require women to possess other or higher qualifications than any male employed by the defendant at the time the order is issued;

(ii) Requiring defendant to use "Male/Female" or "he/she" where appropriate in all of their hiring materials and advertisements;

(iii) Requiring defendant to request referrals for vacant positions from groups specializing in the placement of women attorneys, specifically the Women's Bar Association and New Women Lawyers, and stating to all referral sources that the firm is interested in employing women attorneys;

(iv) Ordering the firm to select its female interviewees on the same basis as it selects male interviewees;

(v) Ordering the firm to conduct its interviews with men and with women in substantially the same manner, specifically refraining from informing women applicants that women are placed in certain departments or otherwise treated differently from male attorneys;

(vi) Ordering defendant to hire a woman for one out of every two positions each year as a summer associate and one out of every three positions each year as a permanent associate until such time as between 10% and 20% of the firm's associates and partners are women;

(vii) Requiring defendant firm to establish immediately reasonable goals and timetables for promotion of female associates to partnership status;

(viii) Ordering defendant to make all terms and conditions of employment equally available to women employed by the firm and their families as to men employed by the firm and their families;

(ix) Ordering defendant firm to pay plaintiff _____ the salary she would have earned during the Summer of 1971, plus interest, minus her actual earnings during that period.

D. Retain jurisdiction over this action and order _____ to report periodically to the appropriate authority on the firm's progress in compliance with the terms of the Court's order.

E. Grant plaintiff and the class she represents such other and further relief as may be necessary and proper.

F. Award plaintiff the costs of this action together with attorney's fees as provided in 42 U.S.C. Sec. 2000e-5(k).

Respectfully submitted,

Carol Bellamy
36 West 44th Street
New York, N.Y.

Harriet Rabb
435 West 116th Street
New York, N.Y. 10027
(212) 280-4291

KOHN v. ROYALL, KOEGEL & WELLS
59 F.R.D. 515 (S.D.N.Y. 1973)

Lasker, District Judge: During her second year in law school, plaintiff, Margaret Kohn, applied to Royall, Koegel & Wells, a large New York law firm, for a summer job. The latter interviewed her at the law school on November 17, 1970, but did not invite her to the firm for further interviews and did not extend her an offer of employment. On May 27, 1971, Kohn filed a complaint with the New York City Commission on Human Rights alleging that the firm's failure to hire her resulted from sex discrimination. On November 19, 1971, she filed a complaint with the Federal Equal Employment Opportunities Commission ("EEOC" or "Commission"). Kohn finally brought suit in this court on June 26, 1972.

The firm has moved to dismiss or, in the alternative, for summary judgment dismissing the complaint on the ground that this court lacks jurisdiction because Kohn's complaint with the EEOC was not timely. Kohn moves for a class action determination.

I. MOTION TO DISMISS

Section 706(d) of Title VII of the 1964 Civil Rights Act, 78 Stat. 259, *as amended*, 42 U.S.C. §2000e-5(e), required, as a jurisdictional prerequisite to federal suits alleging job discrimination, the filing of a complaint with the EEOC within a specified period of time. Since New York City has a commission which handles charges of discriminatory employment practices, the statutory time limit which is applicable to this case[1] is 210 days from the act complained of.[2] Since Kohn filed her EEOC complaint on November 19, 1971, it would normally be timely only if the act complained of occurred no earlier than April of that year.

Kohn argues that her EEOC complaint was timely for the following reasons: 1) The occurrence which is the basis of her complaint happened in April, 1971, or later; and 2) her complaint alleges a continuing violation.

The first ground is clearly without merit. During her interview by the firm on November 17, 1970, Kohn was informed that, if the firm was interested in her application, it would notify her by letter within the following week. (Affidavit of John B. Loughran.) Furthermore Robert A. Lingren, a member of the firm, has submitted an affidavit documenting the practice commonly followed by large New York firms of conducting interviews and extending offers for the following summer by the 15th of December. (Affidavit in support of motion to dismiss.) It is extremely likely that, as would most well informed law students, Kohn concluded from the firm's failure to contact her by the end of the year that they did not intend to extend her an offer. At any rate, her common sense must have intimated that fact to her well before the following April. Accordingly, unless the basis of Kohn's complaint is a continuing violation, rather than an isolated act, it must be dismissed as untimely filed.

We agree with defendant that, ordinarily, refusal to hire is not a continuing violation. Molybdenum Corp. v. EEOC, 457 F.2d 935, 4 FEP Cases 522 (10th Cir. 1972). However, where, as here, the complaining party alleges that the refusal of employment results from an ongoing pattern and practice of discrimination and seeks to represent the entire class of persons allegedly discriminated against, his or her individual grievance provides merely the springboard from which to investigate the employer's alleged continuing violation with respect to the class as a whole. The refusal to hire, which is isolated as to the individual, forms one item in an ongoing series of violations with respect to the class, the many elements of which are linked by their common source — employer discrimination. Defining continuing violation in this fashion does not thwart the purpose of the 210 day statute of limitations that the EEOC should have an opportunity to investigate and seek voluntary compliance and "should only be required to investigate fresh discriminatory acts." Hecht v. Cooperative for American Relief Everywhere, Inc., 351 F. Supp. 305, 310, 5 FEP Cases 352, 356 (S.D.N.Y. 1972). The discriminatory pattern of which plaintiff complains is by definition "fresh," since it is alleged to be continuing to this very day. This result is not a perversion of the class action device permitting an individual to revive a time barred claim by asserting the grievances of others.[3] Rather, it is a way of defining the jurisdiction-conferring con-

1. In 1972, section 706(d) was amended to extend the time for filing with the EEOC. 42 U.S.C.A. §2000e-5(e) (Supp. 1973). The parties do not claim that the new provision applies.

2. Section 706(d) required filing an EEOC charge within 210 days of the act complained of or 30 days of receipt of notice that the local agency had terminated its proceedings, whichever was earlier. Since the local agency proceedings continued well beyond the 210 days period the former time limit applies.

3. Although the statute of limitations is not a defense against a claim of continuing violation, the concept of laches is available to protect defendants from prejudicial delay. The firm, however, cannot claim

cept of continuing violation[4] so as to carry out the underlying purposes of the Act.

Title VII contemplates the elimination of the major social ill of job discrimination through suits by individuals acting as private "attorneys general".[5] Jenkins v. United Gas Corp., 400 F.2d 28, 31-32, 1 FEP Cases 364, 69 LRRM 2152 (5th Cir. 1968); cf. Newman v. Piggie Park Enterprises, Inc., 390 U.S. 400, 401-2 (1968). This method of enforcement makes an individual grievance the spearhead of an attack of larger proportions, since the individual claimant takes on the mantle of the state in seeking to rectify wrongs against himself and others.[6] Accordingly, an individual's claim, when it results from a pervasive discriminatory attitude, cannot be considered in isolation. As was held in Watson v. Limbach Co., 333 F. Supp. 754, 3 FEP Cases 1176 (S.D. Ohio 1971), a case which is exactly on point, the statute requires "at least an opportunity for plaintiff to prove that the alleged discrimination is of a continuous and ongoing variety." Id. at 766-67. See also Jamison v. Olga Coal Co., 335 F. Supp. 454, 458-59, 4 FEP Cases 532 (S.D. W.Va. 1971);[7] Culpepper v. Reynolds Metal Co., 296 F. Supp. 1232, 1235-36, 1 FEP Cases 590, 70 LRRM 2360 (N.D. Ga. 1968), *rev'd on other grounds,* 421 F.2d 888, 2 FEP Cases 377, 506 (5th Cir. 1970).[8]

We recognize that the notion of continuing violation contains some danger of abuse. To prevent its being used to inflate the importance of frivolous or unrepresentative claims, an individual plaintiff who alleges a continuing violation against a class of persons should be required to have a clearly demonstrable stake in the class position, whether or not the case is brought as a class action.[9] Kohn has met this requirement.

---

to have been prejudiced since they were given notice of the claim against them by the filing of a timely complaint before the New York City Commission on Human Rights on May 27, 1971.

4. Undeniably, existence of a continuing violation tolls the statute of limitations, satisfying the jurisdictional prerequisite of timely filing of EEOC charges. See, e.g., Bartmess v. Drewrys U.S.A., Inc., 444 F.2d 1186, 1188, 3 FEP Cases 795 (7th Cir.), *cert denied,* 404 U.S. 939, 3 FEP Cases 1218 (1971); Cox v. United States Gypsum Co., 409 F.2d 289, 1 FEP Cases 714, 70 LRRM 3278 (7th Cir. 1969); Watson v. Limbach Co., 333 F. Supp. 754, 765, 3 FEP Cases 1176 (S.D. Ohio 1971); Sciaraffa v. Oxford Paper Co., 310 F. Supp. 891, 896, 2 FEP Cases 398 (D. Maine 1970); Moreman v. Georgia Power Co., 310 F. Supp. 327, 1 FEP Cases 702, 70 LRRM 3112 (N.D. Ga. 1969); Hutchings v. United States Industries Inc., 309 F. Supp. 691, 2 FEP Cases 599 (E.D. Texas 1969), *rev'd on other grounds,* 428 F.2d 303, 2 FEP Cases 725 (5th Cir. 1970); Culpepper v. Reynolds Metal Co., 296 F. Supp. 1232, 1236, 1 FEP Cases 590, 70 LRRM 2360 (N.D. Ga. 1968), *rev'd on other grounds,* 421 F.2d 888, 2 FEP Cases 377, 506 (5th Cir. 1970): King v. Georgia Power Co., 295 F. Supp. 943, 946, 1 FEP Cases 357, 69 LRRM 2094 (N.D. Ga. 1968).

5. As a result, dismissal of Title VII suits for procedural irregularities is not favored since the statutory scheme contemplates achievement of its goals through the largely informal efforts of laymen. See Voutsis v. Union Carbide Corp., 452 F.2d 889, 4 FEP Cases 74 (2d Cir. 1971).

6. As was stated in Hutchings v. United States Industries, Inc. 428 F.2d 303, 311, 2 FEP Cases 725 (5th Cir. 1970), "once the judicial machinery has been set in train, the proceeding takes on a public character in which remedies are devised to vindicate the policies of the Act, not merely to afford private relief to the employee."

7. In Jamison, the court said:

"In asserting that the discriminatory conduct complained of occurred prior to the effective date of the Act and more than 90 days before plaintiff filed his charge with the EEOC, defendants completely ignore the fact that plaintiff Jamison's charge before the EEOC involved two separate areas of discrimination, one general and one specific. While it is true that the specific charge of discrimination with respect to the promotion of Jamison to the position of motorman apparently relates to conduct on the part of the defendants prior to the effective date of the Civil Rights Act of 1964, and to an incident occurring more than 90 days before the filing of the charge with the EEOC, nevertheless, the general charge of a denial of promotions to Negroes to better jobs and the failure on the part of the defendant unions to seek redress of such discrimination is not confined to the same time period as was the specific charge. Indeed, the complaint in this action and the charge before the EEOC both allege a pattern of conduct apparently continuing to the time of filing the charge with the EEOC and beyond, which would obviously meet the requirement that the discrimination complained of must occur subsequent to the effective date of the Civil Rights Act of 1964 and that the complaint must be filed with the EEOC within 90 days of the alleged unlawful practice." 335 F. Supp. at 458, 4 FEP Cases at 534.

8. If plaintiff fails to demonstrate the violation's continuous nature, the motion to dismiss can obviously be renewed. Watson v. Limbach Co., 333 F. Supp. 754, 766, 3 FEP Cases 1176 (S.D. Ohio 1971); King v. Georgia Power Co., 295 F. Supp. 943, 946, 1 FEP Cases 357, 69 LRRM 2094 (N.D. Ga. 1968).

9. Of course, this requirement is met if the plaintiff satisfies the prerequisites of Rule 23, especially Rule 23(a)(3) and (4). Cf. Calhoun v. Riverside Research Institute, 4 EPD ¶7825 (S.D.N.Y. 1972); Hyatt v. United

Accordingly, defendant's motion to dismiss or for summary judgment dismissing the complaint is denied.

II. MOTION FOR A CLASS ACTION DETERMINATION

Kohn seeks a determination that the suit may proceed as a class action on behalf of "all women qualified for legal positions at Royall, Koegel and Wells who have been or would be denied employment because of their sex." (Complaint, III, 3.) Since the requirements of Rule 23(a) and (b)(2) (Fed. R. Civ. P.) are satisfied, the motion is granted.

A. *Numerosity (Rule 23(a)(1))*

Kohn claims that the putative class contains approximately 500 women who are recent graduates of or are currently enrolled in the nation's leading law schools or are members of the bar admitted to practice in the New York area.

The firm maintains that this definition is too broad and that, properly defined, the class is not too numerous to permit joinder. In support of this proposition, it advances several arguments.

First, the firm contends that since it extends offers to only 2.6% of all applicants, if the entire proposed class actually applied, only 13 of its members could complain of failure to receive an offer. A corollary to this argument is that only rejected women applicants who can be shown to have been superior to the males hired in their place are proper members of the class.

The argument misses the point. The intended effect of Title VII is to give each applicant an equal *opportunity* to be hired. To the extent that an employer discriminates on the basis of a forbidden classification, he reduces the probability that any single member of that class will find employment with him. Discrimination makes competition for the limited number of positions more difficult for the entire class by use of a tougher standard as to all of its members. As a result, all applicants handicapped by the double standard have less opportunity for employment than persons not discriminated against. Accordingly, all are harmed, although not all could have been employed.

Second, the firm contends that the class cannot include women who will seek employment with it in the future. The case relied on, Gerstle v. Continental Airlines, Inc., 50 F.R.D. 213, 2 FEP Cases 830 (D. Colo. 1970), is inapposite. There, the employer eliminated the discriminatory rule before commencement of the suit, and so no case or controversy could exist as to present and future employees. Id. at 217. Here, on the contrary, the discriminatory practice is alleged to be continuing, and the class properly includes future as well as past applicants who will be affected by it. Rios v. Enterprise Association Steamfitters, Local 638, 3 FEP Cases 897, 3 EPD ¶8312 (S.D.N.Y. 1971); Black v. Central Motor Lines, Inc., 1 FEP Cases 586, 70 LRRM 2325, 1 EPD ¶9956 (W.D.N.C. 1968).[10]

Aircraft Corp., Sikorsky Aircraft Division, 50 F.R.D. 242, 2 FEP Cases 722 (D. Conn. 1970). As discussed infra, Kohn's claim meets these demands.

10. The firm contends that the class definition is excessively broad in another respect, since Kohn cannot represent those presently employed by the firm, as she is not a member of that class. Since the firm employs only two female attorneys, the effect of this argument on numerosity is too inconsequential to warrant further discussion. However, the firm also informally requests us to strike those portions of the complaint which concern the firm's internal employment policies (Defendant's Memorandum of Law opposing class action determination at 33) for the reason that "neither plaintiff nor the class she seeks to represent are employees of defendant, and therefore are not, and could not be, affected by these alleged policies." (Id. at 32.) The suggestion is without merit, since the terms and conditions of employment concern applicants for employment as well as employees. An employer, especially one as well known in its field as is defendant here, develops a reputation as to its attitudes respecting the employment of women professionals which is an important factor in a potential female applicant's decision whether or not to apply to it for employment. Discriminating against women in internal employment policies limits a woman applicant's employment opportunities by reducing the number of positions in which she would reasonably be interested. Further, by non-advancement an employer artificially limits the number of women it employs. As a result, an applicant has standing to complain of internal employment practices.

Accordingly, although Kohn's figure of 500, representing the labor pool from which the firm must draw its female employees, may be overbroad in that not all persons in the pool are necessarily interested in employment with the firm, it is reasonable to conclude that the number of persons who are interested is sufficiently large to justify class treatment. In 1970 alone (the year that Kohn applied for a position), the firm received 78 applications from women. (Affidavit of Robert Lindgren opposing motion for a class action determination, par. 20.) Since the firm is receiving an increasing number of applications from women (id. at par. 22), it is clear that the number of women applicants eligible for membership in the class exceeds that which would permit joinder of all members. Korn v. Franchard Corp., 456 F.2d 1206, 1209 (2d Cir. 1972) (district court ordered to allow class action for a class of seventy).

B. Common Question of Law or Fact (Rule 23(a)(2))

The firm contends that there are no questions of law or fact common to the class or, alternatively, that Kohn's claims are not typical of the claims of the class, because "[s]ince the process of selection is and must be to a great extent selective, the number of variables involved is infinite and the questions of fact involved are entirely unique in each case." (Defendant's Memorandum of Law opposing class action motion at 14.)

There is no doubt that hiring a professional requires weighing many subjective factors contributing to the applicant's qualifications *as a whole,* above and beyond the more objective academic qualifications. We cannot agree, however, that this fact immunizes discriminatory practices in professional fields from attack on a class basis. See Hecht v. Cooperative for American Relief Everywhere, Inc., 351 F. Supp. 305, 5 FEP Cases 352 (S.D.N.Y. 1972), which involved female employees at the executive level. The common question in both professional and nonprofessional employment situations is not whether one individual is better qualified than another, but whether that individual is considered less qualified, not because of his or her own worth, but because of discrimination forbidden by Title VII. Hecht, supra, at 312. Put another way, although a law firm is undoubtedly free to make complex, subjective judgments as to how impressive an applicant is, it is not free to inject into the selection process the a priori assumption that, as a whole, women are less acceptable professionally than men.

C. Representative Parties' Claims Typical of the Claims of the Class (Rule 23(a)(3))

Kohn, whose academic qualifications are not disputed, claims that she was denied employment because of her sex. Therefore, her claim is exactly typical of the claims of the class.

D. Fair and Adequate Protection of the Class' Interests (Rule 23(a)(4))

Kohn is represented by counsel experienced in this area of the law and can be expected diligently to represent the interests of the class.

E. Generally Applicable Grounds for Injunctive or Declaratory Relief (Rule 23(b)(2))

As discussed above, the essential allegation, here, is that the firm discriminates against all women applicants in its hiring procedure. If this allegation can be sustained — a matter on which we express no view — the class would be entitled to injunctive and declaratory relief to remedy past and prevent future discrimination. Accordingly, the requirements of Rule 23 are satisfied.

The firm also suggests that the fact that no one has come forward to join Kohn's suit indicates that no class of interested persons exist. We disagree. It is understandable and, in fact, predictable that fear of being labelled a troublemaker would deter most potential class members from sticking their necks out unnecessarily.

F. General Considerations

Finally, the firm contends that, even if the elements of a class action are present, it would be inequitable to allow the suit to proceed in class form because Kohn's claims are devoid of merit.

As noted by defendant itself, the requirement that a plaintiff seeking a class action determination demonstrate likelihood of success on the merits has not been uniformly accepted. Sunrise Toyota, Ltd. v. Toyota Motor Co., Ltd., 55 F.R.D. 519, 534 (S.D.N.Y. 1972). Such a showing should not be necessary in Title VII suits, or should be required only to the extent of screening out cases which are clearly frivolous, because "class actions are favorably viewed by the courts as a means of seeking redress for civil rights violations — the class action is the method which Congress has established for the vindication of the public interest through private actions."[11] Gerstle v. Continental Airlines, Inc., 50 F.R.D. 213, 216, 2 FEP Cases 830, 832 (D. Colo. 1970) (footnote omitted). As the Court of Appeals for the Seventh Circuit said in Bowe v. Colgate-Palmolive Co., 416 F.2d 711, 719, 2 FEP Cases 121, 126 (7th Cir. 1969): "A suit for violation of Title VII is necessarily a class action as the evil sought to be ended is discrimination on the basis of a class characteristic, i.e., race, sex, religion or national origin." See also Jenkins v. United Gas Corp., 400 F.2d 28, 33, 1 FEP Cases 364, 69 LRRM 2152 (5th Cir. 1968); Oatis v. Crown Zellerbach Corp., 398 F.2d 496, 499, 1 FEP Cases 328, 68 LRRM 2782 (5th Cir. 1968). The firm does not cite any case which imposed a prerequisite demonstration of probable success on a civil rights suit[12] in which a class determination was sought, and we decline to do so here.

At any rate, it is not clear that Kohn's claim is so insubstantial that it would not pass a reasonable threshold test. While we do not believe such a test is applicable, we have considered the question, because defendant has raised the subject. Having studied with care the statistics and arguments submitted by the parties, we note that the approaches of both raise interesting and often difficult questions. However, if a threshold showing were necessary, as defendant contends, we find that it has been made. It goes without saying that our holding indicates no view as to the merits of the case.

Furthermore, it is unlikely that a class action determination will prejudice or injure the defendant. If it should prevail against the class action, the broad vindication of its policies would surely discourage subsequent suits for discrimination, although it would not make them res judicata. On the other hand, if it lost against Kohn alone, we are certain it would abide by the spirit of the individual ruling, even though it would not be subject to sanction with regard to anyone other than Kohn.

Defendant's motion to dismiss is denied. Plaintiff's motion for a class action determination is granted.

It is so ordered.

Lasker, District Judge: — By memorandum filed March 7, 1973, 5 FEP Cases 725,

---

11. The many securities cases cited by the firm must be distinguished from other class actions, because of the heightened possibility of prejudice that exists in such cases. As the court said in Dolgow v. Anderson, 43 F.R.D. 472, 501 (E.D.N.Y. 1968): "So much of the stock market depends upon faith and reputation that the Court should be reluctant to lend its weight to any unnecessary publicity in connection with a pending lawsuit." On the other hand, we do not think that the harm which the firm stands to suffer, here, from such adverse publicity as may accompany this motion is greater than that which is incidental to the ordinary class action determination.

12. None of the civil rights cases cited by the firm are apposite. In Chance v. Board of Examiners, 330 F. Supp. 203, 3 FEP Cases 672 (S.D.N.Y. 1971), *aff'd,* 458 F.2d 1167, 4 FEP Cases 596 (2d Cir. 1972), consideration of the class action motion was, indeed, deferred until after the decision on preliminary injunctive relief, but merely to allow defendants, on consent of all parties, more time to answer the motion. 330 F. Supp. at 206, n.8, 3 FEP Cases at 674, N.2. Calhoun v. Riverside Research Institute, 4 FEP Cases 1006, 4 EPD ¶7825 (S.D.N.Y. 1972), denied a class action determination for failure to fulfill the requirements of Rule 23, which we have already found to have been met here. Black v. Central Motor Lines, Inc., 1 FEP Cases 586, 70 LRRM 2325, 1 EPD ¶9956 (W.D.N.C. 1968) made the class action order conditional on plaintiff's demonstrating that discrimination had occurred after the effective date of Title VII as a basis for the application of the statute.

we denied Royall, Koegel & Wells' motion to dismiss and granted Kohn's motion for a class action determination. The firm now presents a motion which it designates as a motion for reargument. It also moves for certification pursuant to 28 U.S.C. §1292(b) to permit an immediate appeal of the denial of its motion to dismiss.

The first motion presented is rejected as a motion to reargue. General Rule 9(m) of the rules of this court permit motions to reargue only where it is claimed that the court overlooked matters in issue or controlling decisions. No such claim is made here. The application put before us is rather that the court "reconsider the following two points:

"1. Whether the claim of the plaintiff is typical of the claims of the persons who comprise the class the plaintiff seeks to represent; and

"2. Whether the plaintiff has standing to complain of internal employment practices when she was never employed by defendant and does not seek such employment."

Ordinarily, especially where, as here, the motion was not timely made, we would deny it without further action. We believe, however, that the first point which we are asked to reconsider indicates a clear misunderstanding of the import of our earlier decision and the material in this memorandum is intended to clarify that ruling.

In our earlier decision, we did not hold, as claimed by the firm, that the class action determination brought Kohn's otherwise time-banned claim within the statute of limitations, but, rather, we found that Kohn's claim was itself timely, because it alleged a continuing violation. As we stated therein, an allegation of a continuing violation would have conferred jurisdiction on the EEOC, even if Kohn had not sought to represent other aggrieved persons.

The firm is, of course, correct that Kohn must have standing herself in order to bring a representative suit. Our earlier decision, by which we abide, found that she did and that, as a result (since her claims were typical in other respects), Kohn could represent the class.

We turn to defendant's second ground for its motion, namely, that Kohn does not have standing to complain of the firm's internal employment practices, because 1) she was never employed by it and 2) she does not now seek employment with it. The first point, that only an employee has standing to challenge internal employment practices, is not without its conceptual difficulties and has never been passed on in this Circuit.[1] The problem, however, has been considered by the Court of Appeals for the Fifth Circuit in Carr v. Conoco Plastics, Inc., 423 F.2d 57, 2 FEP Cases 388, 836 (5th Cir.), *cert. denied,* 400 U.S. 951, 2 FEP Cases 1120 (1970), which found that a class of applicants for employment had standing to challenge a prospective employer's allegedly discriminatory internal employment practices. The court said:

> The plaintiffs here seek equal opportunity for employment, and charge defendants with discriminating against them on account of race. There can be no serious question but that plaintiffs have the right to bring the action for themselves and others similarly situated. Envisioning an equal opportunity for employment plaintiffs have the correlated right to enjoy nondiscriminatory practices within the plant.
>
> It is foolhardy to say that once plaintiffs have removed racial discriminatory practices at the door, they are required to start anew in order to remove those that exist on the inside. Such a practice would result in a multiplicity of suits and a waste of time and money for all interested parties. Id. at 65.

---

1. The cases from other circuits relied on by the firm (Huff v. N.D. Cass Co., 468 F.2d 172, 4 FEP Cases 741 (5th Cir. 1972); Heard v. Mueller Co., 464 F.2d 190, 4 FEP Cases 1119 (6th Cir. 1972); and White v. Gates Rubber Co., 4 FEP Cases 293, 4 E.P.D. ¶7711 (D. Colo. 1971)) do not support its contention that only an employee has standing to challenge internal employment practices. They involve discharged employees who were not eligible for or were not seeking reinstatement and, therefore, were not potential employees of the defendant. Kohn, like the plaintiffs in Carr v. Conoco Plastics, Inc., 423 F.2d 37, 2 FEP Cases 388, 836 (5th Cir.), *cert. denied,* 400 U.S. 951, 2 FEP Cases 1120 (1970), asserts that, as an applicant for employment, she has standing to challenge internal employment practices.

We agree with the reasoning of the Fifth Circuit and adopt its approach.

As to the firm's contention that Kohn does not have standing to bring such a challenge because she no longer seeks employment with the firm, there is nothing properly in the record which supports this finding[2] and accordingly must be denied.

The firm wishes to take an immediate appeal from our order denying its motion to dismiss. Certification of the question based on that order[3] would be proper only if it "involves a controlling question of law as to which there is substantial ground for difference of opinion and . . . an immediate appeal from the order may materially advance the ultimate termination of the litigation" (28 U.S.C. §1292(b)).

Assuming arguendo, that denial of the motion to dismiss involves a "question of law as to which there is substantial ground for difference of opinion" and that "an immediate appeal . . . may materially advance the ultimate termination of the litigation", the motion must nonetheless be denied, because the question involved is clearly not "controlling", as that term has been interpreted.

The decisions in this Circuit leave no doubt that the phrase "controlling question of law" is not equivalent merely to a question of law which is determinative of the case at hand. To the contrary, such a question is deemed controlling only if it may contribute to the determination, at an early stage, of a wide spectrum of cases. In Brown v. Bullock, 294 F.2d 415, 417 (2d Cir. 1961), for example, Judge Friendly, writing for the Court en banc stated that a §1292(b) appeal was appropriate, not only because of the possibility of avoiding a lengthy trial, but because of its "precedential value for a large number of other suits." See also Atlantic City Elec. Co. v. General Elec. Co., 337 F.2d 844 (2d Cir. 1964); Sperry Rand Corp. v. Bell Telephone Laboratories, Inc., 272 F.2d 29 (2d Cir. 1959); Gottesman v. General Motors Corp., 268 F.2d 194 (2d Cir. 1959); Ratner v. Chemical Bank New York Trust Co., 309 F. Supp. 983 (S.D.N.Y. 1970); Leighton v. New York, S. & W. R.R. Co., 306 F. Supp. 513 (S.D.N.Y. 1969). Although the question presented here is intellectually intriguing and its determination favorably to the firm would save it considerable trouble and expense, we are bound to abide by the established policy of the Circuit against piecemeal appeals (Union Can Co. v. Isbrandtsen, 416 F.2d 96 (2d Cir. 1969); Petition of World Tradeways Shipping, Ltd., 373 F.2d 860 (2d Cir. 1967)).

Accordingly, defendant's motions for reargument of the class action motion and to amend the court's order to permit §1292(b) certification are denied.

It is so ordered.

---

2. This ground for reargument is based on a statement contained in the affidavit of Norman Ostrow in support of the motion to amend the order, par. 7, which says:

"During the proceedings which occurred prior to the filing of the complaint herein, I was informed by Ms. Kohn's attorney that Ms. Kohn did not seek employment by Royall, Koegel & Wells and would not accept such employment if it were offered."

This statement has no relevance to the motion to amend and is obviously addressed to the motion to reargue. General Rule 9(m) of the rules of this court provides that in support of a motion to reargue, which the motion before us purports to be, "[n]o affidavits shall be filed by any party unless directed by the Court." To allow the rule to be circumvented in this fashion would destroy its effectiveness whenever a motion to reargue is coupled with another motion. Therefore, we decline to consider this statement as properly part of the record before us. Furthermore, unless Kohn's attorney was authorized by her to make such statement on her behalf, it would not constitute an admission on her part.

3. Defendant wishes to certify the following question to the Court of Appeals:

"Whether the allegation by Ms. Kohn that the refusal of defendant to offer her employment resulted from an ongoing pattern and practice of discrimination and the designation by Ms. Kohn of her action as a class action are sufficient standing alone, to bar dismissal of the complaint for lack of subject matter jurisdiction since Ms. Kohn failed to file a complaint with the Equal Employment Opportunity Commission within the statutory period." Memorandum in Support of defendant's motion to amend at 2.

Even if the firm's motion to amend the order were not denied on the grounds discussed in the opinion, we would decline to certify this question since it does not accurately state the holding of our earlier opinion. As discussed above, that decision held that Kohn filed her complaint with the EEOC within the statutory period since running of the statute of limitations was tolled.

NOTE: HISTORY AND LESSONS OF THE CASE

This case originated in the school year of 1969–1970, when women law students at Columbia and New York University became angry at the discriminatory attitude they encountered in job interviews with several law firms. At the beginning of the next school year, they decided to do something about the problem, and women students were asked to write down any discriminatory incidents or attitudes they encountered during their fall job interviews. In the spring of 1971, charges were filed against the law firms with the New York City Commission on Human Rights; one of these charges is reproduced above. The charges were accompanied by a covering memorandum,[172]

> prepared as general background for the filing of specific [charges] against several law firms. The only information as to particular firms [was] in the [charges] themselves and supporting affidavits and much of this [was] allegation rather than evidence.

The covering memorandum consisted of a factual but general description of law firm practices that the women contended were discriminatory, along with statistics and other information designed to refute some of the stereotyped views held by male law firms. The memo summarized the net effect of these practices and the practices themselves as follows:[173]

> Women who work for many years in a firm, who are bound in by restrictions on the areas of law in which they may work, who do not see clients, who cannot handle cases that may involve travel, who make less money than their male colleagues and for whom partnership is not a likelihood, may be forced, in frustration, or anger or simple boredom, to abandon their coveted positions in law firms. Their doing so, however, reinforces the myth that women are "emotional," "unreliable" or truly uninterested in a large corporate practice. The result will be greater difficulty encountered by young women applying for positions in the firms which will recall that they "had women associates in the past but they didn't work out."
>
> The self-fulfilling prophecy just described will doubtless survive until women are given equal opportunity for employment and full status in law firms. In brief, the elements of discrimination which presently are obstacles to the attainment of that status are:
>
> 1. (A) Firms interview only the women with the highest academic qualifications while interviewing men with less spectacular grades or law review status; *or* (B) Firms may interview only women whose academic qualifications do not measure up to the firm's standards — refusing to interview the best ranked women in the class in order to assert that the firm has indeed considered some women applicants and found them unacceptable;
>
> 2. Women are not seriously interviewed but rather are quizzed on their plans for motherhood, and any assertions of intention to continue working even with small children are met with skepticism and disbelief;
>
> 3. While men are interviewed generally for a place in the firm, women are interviewed only for women's jobs if and when they are available;
>
> 4. Women may not be interviewed at all because firms erroneously believe that female attorneys are likely to stay only a short time and then change jobs for frivolous reasons or because they follow their husbands whose work requires moving to other cities;
>
> 5. Women, not allowed to attain partnership status, do not command salaries equivalent to their male colleagues who do become partners;
>
> 6. Women are assigned when hired, without the option to transfer, to traditionally women's areas of law which usually include much research and writing and little client contact;

172. Cooper and Rabb, supra, at 242.
173. Id. at 261-263.

7. Women lawyers are infrequently allowed to meet and deal directly with clients;

8. Women are excluded from firm lunches or dinners or business meetings which are very often held in clubs which exclude women or relegate to a limited area parties of diners which include women;

9. Women are generally not allowed to travel in conjunction with their work or are not assigned to matters which may involve travel; and

10. Women rarely are accorded partnership status in their firms.

Generally, charging parties do not file such memos with their charges, and the practice is not required by statute or regulation. Its use in this instance demonstrates how flexible and innovative approaches can achieve results before an administrative agency. The memo undoubtedly contributed to the in-depth agency investigation that followed filing of the charges, for it described the kinds of practices the investigation should look for and supplied answers to some of the stereotyped attitudes that law firms might advance in support of their practices. In fact, the investigation was one of unusual scope for either a local agency or the EEOC itself.

The EEOC never investigated the case, even though the women students had filed similar charges with the federal agency in the fall of 1971. By the time the EEOC was ready to start its investigation, the city commission was well into its own investigation. The women's attorney therefore suggested to EEOC personnel that they contact the city commission and defer action until the city had issued findings, in order to avoid duplication of effort. By the summer of 1972, the city commission issued very strong findings — reproduced above — against one of the law firms, Royall, Koegel and Wells. However,[174]

> . . . even the Commission's strong findings did not produce settlement and — rather than await Commission enforcement proceedings — the parties decided to avail themselves of their Title VII rights in Federal court.

The papers reprinted above should be examined carefully, for they illustrate several typical features of a Title VII proceeding. First, compare the original charge with the court complaint. Notice how the parties used the evidence which the city commission uncovered in its investigation in writing their complaint, and also how the scope of the charge has been expanded. Ms. Kohn originally charged sex discrimination as to the refusal to hire her for a summer position. In the complaint, she expands from one person being affected to a class of women victims, from one incident to a policy, and from hiring discrimination to other forms of discrimination affecting women employees as well as applicants. Employers have attempted to limit court complaints to the scope of the original charge, but the courts have allowed expansion into any discrimination which is like or related to the original charge, or which the EEOC might reasonably uncover in its investigation. See Sanchez v. Standard Brands, Inc., 431 F.2d 455 (5th Cir. 1970). This makes sense because charging parties will ordinarily have little access to the facts showing more pervasive patterns of discrimination than they have personally encountered, while the EEOC can easily uncover such evidence. Moreover, it would be a waste of legal and court resources and money to force parties to bring a new suit every time a new party suspected discrimination, rather than resolve all issues of discrimination practiced by a company in one lawsuit.

Despite this principle of law, charging parties would be better protected by pleading broad violations of Title VII in their charges. This avoids the invitation to the employer to raise the expansion point in a motion to dismiss. For example, compare the language of the charge reprinted above with the language advised by Cooper and Rabb, supra, Section E-1, under the heading Contents of the Administrative Complaint.

174. Id. at 242-243.

Another interesting feature about the law firm case is the charging parties' preference for the local agency proceeding rather than that of the EEOC. Since local agencies are often biased toward respondents, many parties will prefer to wait for EEOC action, even though it often takes much longer to act than the local agency.

Another point to note about the case study above is the law firm tactics in the court litigation. Employers typically commence by raising innumerable procedural defenses in a motion to dismiss. Motions to permit reargument and opposition to declaration of a class action, as in the *Kohn* case, further protract litigation, of course, and then an employer can always try an appeal of the procedural points if it loses the initial motion. Some Title VII cases go up and down from trial to appellate court so many times that the litigation continues for years. After losing on appeal of a procedural point, for example, the actual trial must still be held, and a favorable result can be appealed again. After a remand from this appeal, the question of relief will still have to be litigated, offering the chance for yet another appeal. Of course, some cases proceed to one favorable decision and the employer is then willing to settle, but since settlements are generally not reported it is difficult to know how many cases end this way. Hopefully, as the legal issues become more and more defined, employers will become more willing to settle, since protracted litigation and appeals are very expensive and will only add to the final bill for remedying the employment discrimination.

However, the *Kohn* case is proceeding along the former lines, for after losing on the procedural issues in district court, the law firm filed an appeal to the Second Circuit, reraising all the issues it had litigated in district court, even though the district court had denied certification for an interlocutory appeal. As this book goes to press, argument on the appeal has been postponed pending the outcome of settlement discussions.

Meanwhile, the New York City Commission has been continuing the investigation as to the other law firms. By early 1974, it produced more strong findings:[175]

> The city Commission on Human Rights has found probable cause that two law firms — Sullivan & Cromwell and Aranow, Brodsky, Bohlinger, Benetar & Einhorn — discriminate against women.
>
> The findings came as the result of complaints filed in 1971 by law school students against ten firms. The cases of seven others still are pending before the Commission. . . .
>
> A spokesman for Sullivan & Cromwell said the firm "vigorously denied" that it had discriminated against women, would consider the Commission's findings and then decide on "appropriate action."
>
> A spokesman for Aranow, Brodsky also denied the charges and said his firm "probably would ask for a conference."
>
> Under Commission procedures, the firms can ask for conciliation conferences to adjust the matter. The firms have until Feb. 7 to request conferences. If they do not, a public hearing is held before the commission, which then makes findings. Either side then can appeal the findings in State Supreme Court.
>
> The complaints were filed by two women who were then seniors at the New York University School of Law. They are Edith Barnett, now believed to be an attorney with the U.S. Department of Labor in Washington, D.C., and Diane Blank, now a partner in the all-female law firm of Bellamy, Blank, Goodman, Kelly, Ross & Stanley. They were represented by the Columbia University Law School's Employment Rights Project.
>
> The finding against Aranow, Brodsky on Monday concerned its alleged refusal to interview women. The firm has hired only one woman as an attorney between 1961 and 1971, according to the Commission, and has no female partners.
>
> "The record indicates," the Commission stated, "that individuals are selected or rejected for interviews for a wide variety of reasons. The fact that no women were

175. *Probable Cause Seen in Complaint by Women Against 2 Law Firms*, New York L.J. 1, 5 (Jan. 31, 1974).

initially considered as interviewees strongly suggests that the basis for exclusion in this case was sex.

"The records furnished by respondent, rather than refuting this inference of discrimination, substantiate complainant's individual allegations."

The Commission said the record in the allegation against Sullivan & Cromwell "indicated a virtual exclusion of females from the positions of partner and permanent associate. . . . The record further contains sufficient evidence to indicate that these statistics are the result of discriminatory practices in the selection, promotion and conditions of employment of women associates."

The Commission stated that the firm had never had a female partner, utilized social clubs that excluded women from membership thereby depriving them of equal conditions of employment and that prior to 1971, it had never assigned a woman to its tax or litigation divisions.

"The record indicates," the Commission said, "that the absence of full-time female associates may be attributed to the virtual exclusion of females as summer associates."

Of 113 summer associates at Sullivan & Cromwell from 1963 to 1972, according to the Commission, only 4.5 per cent were women and there were none during six of the summers. During the same period, twenty-one summer associates were offered permanent employment, of whom only one was a woman.

As of November, 1970, according to the Commission, the law firm had only two females among more than 100 associates.

F. Proving Discrimination

1. Evidence

a. An Approach to Investigating the Case

COOPER AND RABB
EQUAL EMPLOYMENT LAW AND LITIGATION
80-81 (1972)

The initial step in investigating a charge of discrimination against an employer is to isolate any identifiable practices having a discriminatory impact. This is true whether an individual claim is being investigated or a broader pattern and practice inquiry is being made. If specific practices can be singled out as the primary media of discrimination, it will be much easier to prove unlawful discrimination, and it will be easier to fashion an effective remedy. Thus the investigation of a complaint should not probe merely the facts of the complainant's case, but rather the overall practices and policies of the employer. The complainant's case is merely one part of the picture and it cannot be realistically evaluated out of context.

The best approach for an investigation (or use of discovery procedures if the matter is in litigation) is to seek to:

(1) identify each and every step in the employers' hiring and promotional process;

(2) catalogue all criteria used at each stage, both objective (e.g., "must have high school diploma") and subjective (e.g., "selections are made on the basis of judgments by our personnel interviewers");

(3) determine the impact of each criterion on protected minority groups [or women] as compared to its effect on others.

This information can be used in several ways. On the simplest level, it will permit an evaluation of the credentials of the persons hired or promoted to determine whether any exceptions are being made to the purported standards. If so, of course, the reasons for these exceptions should be determined and scrutinized for discriminatory impact. The exceptions are, in effect, another criterion in the employment pattern to be evaluated in the same manner as any other criterion.

Beyond identifying exceptions, full information on employment practices will identify those practices which are having a discriminatory impact on minorities [or women]. These are the practices which, pursuant to the *Griggs* principle, the employer must show to be properly justified by business necessity.

NOTE

The discussion above concerns a neutral policy with a disparate impact, but it is equally valid for overtly discriminatory practices. See, for example, in AT&T: A Study in Sex Segregation, supra, the discussion of facially discriminatory policies for several steps in AT&T's recruitment, hiring, and promotion processes. The investigator should also explore a company's structure, including, for example, its various departments and their hierarchical relationship to each other, in order to understand fully the various steps of the employment process.

b. The Use of Statistics

Statistics play a crucial role in employment discrimination cases. The first step in proving that a supposedly neutral employment policy violates Title VII is always to show its discriminatory impact on a protected class. This is a point litigators should especially note, for some have assumed that certain kinds of neutral employment policies, such as educational testing requirements, are automatically discriminatory. This is simply not so. Disparate impact must always be proved — and statistics furnish this proof. The following excerpts explore the use of statistics, both when the litigators know what specific policy produces a disparate impact and when they only know that something in the overall employment process adversely affects a protected class. Most of the cases discussed concern race discrimination but they apply equally to sex discrimination.

(1) To Show the Discriminatory Impact of Specific Policies

COOPER AND RABB
EQUAL EMPLOYMENT LAW AND LITIGATION
81-89 (1972)

... [S]tatistical data that one or more protected groups fare relatively poorly under the selection practice . . . may frequently be derived from the employer's own experience. . . . Thus in Hicks v. Crown Zellerbach Corp., 319 F. Supp. 314 (E.D. La. 1970), *order entered*, 321 F. Supp. 1241 (E.D. La. 1971), a study was made of average scores and pass-fail rates for whites and blacks who took the tests at Crown's facilities. This study showed whites passing the tests at approximately four times the rate of blacks and thereby clearly established the adverse racial effect of the tests. See also Arrington v. Mass. Bay Transp. Co., 306 F. Supp. 1355 (D. Mass. 1969), where 80% of the white applicants scored in the top two-thirds while only 25% of the blacks did so, and Carter v. Gallagher, 3 EPD Par. 8205 (D. Minn. 1971), where the district court found minority groups did less well on the basis of statistics indicating that 27% of minority group members passed compared with an overall pass rate varying between 40% and 60%.

There has been no need to seriously question that blacks have performed less well than whites in most job testing cases to date. But the disparity may not always be so apparent and courts may face difficult questions as to what degree of disparity in scores is necessary to establish a prima facie case of discrimination. While this issue has not yet been resolved with precision, it is clear that a much smaller discrepancy than that in the above cases will be sufficient. In Chance v. Board of Examiners, 330 F. Supp. 203 (S.D.N.Y. 1971), *aff'd,* 458 F.2d 1167 (2d Cir. 1972), test use was stayed after a court-ordered study of comparative minority and non-minority performance on the tests indicated in the aggregate that 31.4% of minority candidates and 44.3% of non-minority candidates achieved passing scores. This is not only the smallest discrepancy that has been found sufficient for a prima facie case, but also the smallest discrepancy in any of the cases litigated to date. It should be noted, however, that the court's finding of discriminatory impact in *Chance* was based on another factor along with the raw disparity in pass rates. The court concluded that the disparities revealed by the statistics constituted an underestimate of the discriminatory impact of the examination system because the promotional process involved a series of steps, each subject to an examination. This resulted in a cumulative multiplier effect which compounded the rate at which minority candidates were effectively screened out of positions at the top of the promotional ladder. Thus it is not certain whether the figures in *Chance* represent a sufficient discrepancy without the added factor of this multiplier effect. Also, the smaller the sample analyzed, the less significant is a discrepancy of a given percentage. The statistics should be drawn from a large enough sample and should show sufficient disparity that the differences cannot be explained by chance. Nevertheless, no court has yet found plaintiff's evidence insufficient on this ground, and in Carter v. Gallager, supra, the court accepted as relevant statistics summarizing the performance of twenty-two minority group applicants for the positions of fireman in Minneapolis when over 2,400 persons had taken the test in recent years.

In many situations, unfortunately, it will not be possible to rely on data directly derived from an employer's plant. There may have been too few applications of the standard on which to base a statistical study. Another reason for not relying on data directly obtained from the employer is that such data may be distorted because the employer's policies may cause an unusual group of whites or blacks to apply at his plant. For example, discrimination against blacks for managerial jobs may lead to a superior group of black applicants for clerical positions, and the "cultural bias" of the test may be masked by the superior abilities of this particular group of black applicants. Similarly, if the fact becomes widely known that an employer imposes a high school diploma requirement, he may only get high school graduate applicants through self-selection, particularly from the black community which is apprehensive of such requirements, and the numbers of black non-high school graduates screened out may not be apparent.

There are many ways of supplementing direct statistical data to overcome these problems. In the *Duke Power Company* case there was no direct data. The Court determined adverse effect by relying in part on studies of the same tests conducted in other places. Since the tests used by Duke were the same as those used in previously reported EEOC decisions, specific reference was made to the statistical findings in those decisions that 58% of the whites passed the tests while only 6% of the blacks did so. The Court also looked to census data for the State of North Carolina in assessing the high school diploma requirement. The 1960 census showed whites approximately three times as likely as blacks to have a high school education. While there was no specific evidence that this statewide data or the data from other Commission decisions reflected the relevant population at the Duke Power Company plant, the data was nonetheless sufficiently indicative of adverse racial impact to be relied upon. Finally the Court supported its findings of adverse impact by relying on non-statistical information, observing that the inferior segregated education of Negroes inevitably had an adverse effect on their ability to perform well in the testing process.

A similar approach was taken in Armstead v. Starkville Municipal Separate School District, 325 F. Supp. 560 (N.D. Miss. 1971), *aff'd in pertinent part and rev'd in part,* __ F.2d __ (5th Cir. 1972), 4 EPD Par. 7892, where a school board's use of the Graduate Record

Examination to select teachers for a Mississippi school district was held unlawful. The district court relied on specific data from the school district's own use of the test combined with data from the test publisher as to black and white statewide results on the test. It is interesting to note that although there was no explicit black-white break-down of statewide test results obtainable from the test publisher, the court was able to obtain a satisfactory estimate by comparing scores of graduates of primarily black colleges with those of primarily white colleges. In doing this the court was following the precedent of Hicks v. Crown Zellerbach Corp., supra, a Louisiana case, where the court accepted racial identification based on the high school attended by each tested person. The use of this technique of racial identification may be somewhat less fruitful in the North where historical lines of school segregation are less clear, but in many situations de facto patterns may be sufficient to establish significant statistical data.

The way is always open for an employer to adopt tests which are free of any adverse effects on protected minority groups. The Commission has for example found instances of no adverse impact from use of "pictorial reasoning" and manual dexterity tests (Unnumbered Decision, dated December 6, 1966; Decisions 71-1471, March 19, 1971; 71-1525, March 26, 1971) and an employer developed promotional test (Decision 71-1418, March 17, 1971). In each of these instances there was specific statistical data proving the lack of adverse impact. Absent such specific data, exonerating a test, it is fair to assume that any test which is shown to be similar in content to tests having known discriminatory impact is itself having such impact. This would probably include most verbal intelligence tests, as well as a wide range of other tests, because of the problems of inferior education referred to in the *Duke Power Co.* decision. As to other tests, an evaluation will have to be made based on all the evidence — direct and indirect —which is available.

The adverse impact of other selection criteria should be evaluated in the same fashion as tests. For example, in finding an arrest record criterion to have this impact, the court in Gregory v. Litton Systems, Inc., 316 F. Supp 401 (C.D. Calif. 1970), relied on various sources of official data on the national arrest rates of blacks and whites. The court in Carter v. Gallagher, 3 EPD Par. 8205 (D. Minn. March 9, 1971), *modified*, 452 F.2d 315 (8th Cir. 1971), *cert. denied*, __U.S.__(1972), 4 EPD Par. 7818, relied on police depart-ment data on arrest records, and police and correctional department data on local per-centages of convicted and incarcerated persons who are from minority groups, to find that an arrest record inquiry and a conviction record inquiry on an application form had an adverse impact on those minorities. In neither case was the data specific to the employer's situation, but, as with the statewide census data in the *Duke Power Company* case, it was sufficient to show the potential of adverse impact.

The EEOC has taken a similar approach, relying, for example, on published studies of relatively low average height of Mexican-Americans and women to show that a minimum height requirement has an adverse impact on these groups (Decision 71-1418, March 17, 1971; Decision 71-1529, April 2, 1971).

(2) Where Specific Discriminatory Policies Have Not Been Identified

COOPER AND RABB
EQUAL EMPLOYMENT LAW AND LITIGATION
230-237 (1972)

[In the materials above] . . . an approach was suggested for isolating specific discriminatory practices and mounting a challenge against them. In many instances, however, it will be impossible to produce any reliable information about the impact of individual aspects of an employer's practices. The equal employment lawyer should avoid that dilemma if at all possible. Every effort should be made to press defendants to produce useful data.

In this regard, the District Court's action in Chance v. Board of Examiners, 330 F. Supp. 203 (S.D.N.Y. 1971), *aff'd,* 458 F.2d 1167 (2d Cir. 1972), is instructive. The plaintiffs were able to produce various kinds of circumstantial data which indicated that something was amiss in the selection procedures for school supervisory personnel in New York. This included (1) a comparison between the low percentages of blacks and Puerto Ricans in those jobs and the high percentage in the school population; (2) a comparison between the New York City's minority group supervisor percentages and those in other major cities; and (3) an expert evaluation of the tests and procedures used which concluded that they had a discriminatory impact. However, the court was dissatisfied with the softness of all this data, and ordered the defendant to conduct a survey to determine the actual impact of its tests on various racial and ethnic groups. Where the court will not enter such an order, the plaintiff himself may be able to conduct a study as was done in Hicks v. Crown Zellerbach Corp., 319 F. Supp. 314 (E.D. La. 1970), *order issued,* 321 F. Supp. 1241 (E.D. La. 1971). But in some cases it remains impossible, despite everyone's best efforts, to generate meaningful data on specific practices.

Faced with this problem, courts have been willing to base a finding of adverse impact on overall data showing the percentages of blacks and whites hired as compared to the percentages of each in the available population. These courts have ruled that this statistical disparity creates a prima facie showing of discriminatory impact and thus invokes a requirement that the job relatedness of the overall selection process be established. This overall approach was taken, for example, in United States v. Ironworkers, Local 86, 443 F.2d 544 (9th Cir. 1971), *cert. denied,* __U.S.__(1971), 4 EPD Par. 7583. There a United States Court of Appeals found only one black member in each of several unions, with total memberships of over 900, despite the fact that the overall population in the general area was 7% black. This data, the court said, "raises an inference" of discrimination and shifts the "burden of going forward and the burden of persuasion" so as to make out a "prima facia case" of racial discrimination. The court emphasized that such use of statistical data had "particular application in Title VII cases."

The policy of the EEOC regarding statistical proof has been stated in several decisions. The EEOC has ruled that an inference of discrimination is reasonable whenever (1) there is a racially diverse population in an area, and (2) an employer has no Negroes in one or more major employment groupings for which persons are "hired regularly" under "standard entry requirements." (Decisions 71-1563, April 1, 1971; 71-1010, December 29, 1970). The same principle would also apply when there is only a token black work force in a heavily black community.

Some courts have gone a statistical step further. The United States Court of Appeals for the Eighth Circuit in Parham v. Southwestern Bell Telephone Co., 433 F.2d 421 (8th Cir. 1970), ruled that a gross disparity between numbers of minorities in an employer's work force (less than 2%) and numbers in the overall population (21% of the state population) can prove discrimination "per se". Put in non-legal terms, the court was so impressed by the statistical disparity that it refused even to hear any attempt by the employer to demonstrate that the disparity was caused by job related requirements. This is more than a rebuttable inference of discrimination based on statistics; it is a firm conclusion. This per se rule was also applied in Rios v. Enterprise Ass'n Steamfitters, Local 638, 326 F. Supp. 198 (S.D.N.Y. 1971), where the court was convinced of discrimination by the disparity between the small number of minorities in the union (28 blacks, 13 Spanish-surnamed) as compared to the total membership (4,000). Some courts after *Parham* have continued to interpret a demonstration of gross statistical disparity not as a per se violation but only as a prima facie showing of discrimination [Ochoa v. Monsanto Co., 335 F. Supp. 53 (S.D. Tex. 1971)], or in some cases as a matter for judicial discretion [(United States v. National Lead Co., 438 F.2d 935 (8th Cir. 1971)]. But there is no doubt that the per se rule will have increasing application as it becomes clear that no possible explanation can justify disparities of the magnitudes found in the *Parham* or *Rios* cases.

Where a per se case is made out, there is, of course, no need to explore the question of job relatedness or business necessity. In all other cases, however, that next question will be the crucial aspect of the inquiry. In most instances, the employer's justification will bring out certain specific practices or criteria which he uses in selecting employees but which were not mentioned earlier. This will lead naturally into the analysis of business justification for specific practices. . . .

In some cases, however, the employer's justification will be a claim, supported by some evidence, that no qualified persons are available even assuming he drops all exaggerated standards. There will ordinarily be some dispute over which standards are reasonable and which are exaggerated, again leading back into [a discussion of business necessity]. As to some jobs, particularly low level and unskilled jobs, it may well be that *no* qualifications are essential and all should be eliminated. But when skilled jobs and jobs at middle and upper management levels are involved, it is prima facie reasonable for an employer to seek certain indications of competence. How does one approach the case of a newsweekly which says that it has few women editors because relatively few women have sufficient background and experience in reporting to serve as editors? Or how does one approach the case of a law firm which says that it has few women lawyers because qualified women have not applied in sufficient numbers? To what extent, and in what manner can such an employer be shown to have acted in violation of fair employment laws?

Several approaches suggest themselves. First, the employer's recruitment procedures should be carefully scrutinized. These procedures can be viewed as part of the selection process and, if weighted against minorities or women, can make out a case of a specific discriminatory practice. This would apply, for example, where an employer interviews only at predominantly white or all-male colleges. To go back even one step further, past discriminatory policies may have resulted in the spread of a generally held belief within minority group communities that this particular employer will not, for example, hire blacks, thus severely curtailing the number of blacks who will ever apply for jobs with that company. Second, the employer's attitudes and policies can be probed for evidence of discriminatory biases. If incidents of overt bias, such as segregated facilities or references to racial or sexual stereotypes, can be unearthed, there will be strong evidence the make-up of the work force is not simply the result of a short labor force supply of minorities and women. Third, comparative data can be developed which shows that other similarly situated employers have better minority representation. This, again, is strong evidence that the situation could be better if the employer behaved better. Fourth, factual evidence on the available labor force supply can be gathered. That is, the plaintiff can attempt to show that sufficient qualified minority persons are available. This may be done either on the basis of general statistical data (e.g., "there are 700 qualified black plumbers in the relevant geographical area according to the Department of Commerce studies, yet you have none in your local union") or on the basis of specific examples (e.g., "John Jones is a qualified plumber and has unsuccessfully sought admission to your local union").

c. The Use of Documents and Expert Testimony

Statistics are not the only kind of evidence used in employment discrimination cases, of course. In the case study on sex segregation, the EEOC listed myriad company documents it had examined for evidence of sex discrimination; see AT&T: A Study in Sex Segregation, supra. Expert witnesses are frequently called to testify about complex issues; see, for example, Note: Expert Testimony in Pregnancy Cases, supra, and Note: Expert Testimony In Equal Pay Act Cases, Part III infra.

2. Intent

Employers often believe that they must have a discriminatory intent in order to be found in violation of Title VII. Cooper and Rabb point out the influence of this view.[176]

> As recently as 1967, the author of a leading article on American fair employment laws could caution his readers:
> "This means that the conduct which ultimately forms the basis of a finding of discrimination under the fair employment laws is prohibited only when it is coupled with a certain state of mind. 'Thus, discrimination is essentially an equivocal act accompanied and inspired by the mental element of prejudice. It is the motive that distinguishes the [prohibited] act, not the act itself.' However, a man is deemed to intend the natural consequences of his acts and therefore the act, the setting from whence it came as well as its consequences may be probative of the employer's intent. That is, circumstantial evidence may also establish the requisite general intent. As a result, the motive behind an employer's conduct will make a nice question of fact in each case — a question which must be resolved before an evaluation of the unlawfulness of the conduct can be ascertained." Bonfield, The Substance of American Fair Employment Practices Legislation, 61 Nw. L. Rev. 907, 956-57 (1967).
> This is the view that influenced virtually all fair employment enforcement efforts until the late 1960's, and, as a consequence, very little was accomplished. Factual problems of proof rendered the statutes and other provisions powerless against patterns and practices which grossly limited employment opportunities of blacks, women and other minority groups.

Griggs v. Duke Power Co., 401 U.S. 424, 91 S. Ct. 849, 28 L. Ed. 2d 158 (1971) supra, put an end to that view with its holding that "good intent or absence of discriminatory intent does not redeem employment procedures or testing mechanisms that operate as "built-in headwinds" for minority groups and are unrelated to measuring job capacity."[177] In fact, the accepted view now is that "the statute, read literally, requires only that the defendant meant to do what he did, that is, his employment practice was not accidental."[178]

3. Burden of Proof

A 1973 Supreme Court case defined the burden of proof for employment discrimination cases in the context of a difficult "one on one" case. "One on one" cases, where the plaintiff seeks to correct discrimination against him or herself only, rather than classwide discrimination, have been particularly troublesome to deal with because employers can so readily find excuses for the treatment of any individual. This decision should make it easier to win these cases by defining the shifting burden of proof and by permitting the use of evidence pointing to class discrimination in such cases.

McDONNELL DOUGLAS CORP. v. GREEN
411 U.S. 792, 93 S. Ct. 1817, 36 L. Ed. 2d 668 (1973)

Mr. Justice POWELL delivered the opinion of the Court.

The case before us raises significant questions as to the proper order and nature of proof in actions under Title VII of the Civil Rights Act of 1964.

Petitioner, McDonnell Douglas Corporation, is an aerospace and aircraft manufac-

---

176. Cooper and Rabb, supra, at 1.
177. 401 U.S. at 432.
178. Local 189, United Papermakers and Paperworkers v. United States, 416 F.2d 980, 996 (1969).

turer headquartered in St. Louis, Missouri, where it employs over 30,000 people. Respondent, a black citizen of St. Louis, worked for petitioner as a mechanic and laboratory technician from 1956 until August 28, 1964 when he was laid off in the course of a general reduction in petitioner's work force.

Respondent, a long-time activist in the civil rights movement, protested vigorously that his discharge and the general hiring practices of petitioner were racially motivated. As part of this protest, respondent and other members of the Congress on Racial Equality illegally stalled their cars on the main roads leading to petitioner's plant for the purpose of blocking access to it at the time of the morning shift change. . . .

On July 2, 1965, a "lock-in" took place wherein a chain and padlock were placed on the front door of a building to prevent the occupants, certain of petitioner's employees, from leaving. Though respondent apparently knew beforehand of the "lock-in," the full extent of his involvement remains uncertain.

Some three weeks following the "lock-in," on July 25, 1965, petitioner publicly advertised for qualified mechanics, respondent's trade, and respondent promptly applied for reemployment. Petitioner turned down respondent, basing its rejection on respondent's participation in the "stall-in" and "lock-in". Shortly thereafter, respondent filed a formal complaint with the Equal Employment Opportunity Commission, claiming that petitioner had refused to rehire him because of his race and persistent involvement in the civil rights movement, in violation of §§703(a)(1) and 704(a) of the Civil Rights Act of 1964, 42 U.S.C. §§2000e-(2)(a)(1) and 2000e-3(a)[4] The former section generally prohibits racial discrimination in any employment decision while the latter forbids discrimination against applicants or employees for attempting to protest or correct allegedly discriminatory conditions of employment. . . .

On April 15, 1968, respondent brought the present action, claiming initially a violation of §704(a) and, in an amended complaint, a violation of §703(a)(1) as well.[5] The District Court dismissed the latter claim of racial discrimination in petitioner's hiring procedures on the ground that the Commission had failed to make a determination of reasonable cause to believe that a violation of that section had been committed. The District Court also found that petitioner's refusal to rehire respondent was based solely on his participation in the illegal demonstrations and not on his legitimate civil rights activities. The court concluded that nothing in Title VII or §704 protected "such activity as employed by the plaintiff in the 'stall-in' and 'lock-in' demonstrations." 318 F. Supp., at 850.

On appeal, the Eighth Circuit affirmed that unlawful protests were not protected activities under §704(a), but reversed the dismissal of respondent's §703(a)(1) claim relating to racially discriminatory hiring practices, holding that a prior Commission determination of reasonable cause was not a jurisdictional prerequisite to raising a claim under that section in federal court. The court ordered the case remanded for trial of respondent's claim under §703(a)(1).

In remanding, the Court of Appeals attempted to set forth standards to govern the consideration of respondent's claim. The majority noted that respondent had established a prima facie case of racial discrimination; that petitioner's refusal to rehire respondent rested on "subjective" criteria which carried little weight in rebutting charges of discrimination; that though respondent's participation in the unlawful demonstrations might indicate a lack of a responsible attitude toward performing work for that employer, respondent should be given the opportunity to demonstrate that petitioner's reasons for refusing to rehire him were merely pretextual. In order to clarify the stand-

---

4. . . . Section 704(a) of the Civil Rights Act of 1964, 42 U.S.C. §2000e-3(a), in pertinent part provides:
"It shall be an unlawful employment practice for an employer to discriminate against any of his employees or applicants for employment . . . because he has opposed any practice made an unlawful employment practice by this subchapter. . . ."

5. Respondent also contested the legality of his 1964 discharge by petitioner, but both courts held this claim barred by the statute of limitations. Respondent does not challenge those rulings here.

ards governing the disposition of an action challenging employment discrimination, we granted certiorari, 409 U.S. 1036 (1972).

I. We agree with the Court of Appeals that absence of a Commission finding of reasonable cause cannot bar suit under an appropriate section of Title VII and that the District Judge erred in dismissing respondent's claim of racial discrimination under §703(a)(1). . . .

. . . Accordingly, we remand the case for trial of respondent's claim of racial discrimination consistent with the views set forth below.

II. The critical issue before us concerns the order and allocation of proof in a private, single-plaintiff action challenging employment discrimination. . . .

In this case respondent, the complainant below, charges that he was denied employment "because of his involvement in civil rights activities" and "because of his race and color." Petitioner denied discrimination of any kind, asserting that its failure to re-employ respondent was based upon and justified by his participation in the unlawful conduct against it. Thus, the issue at the trial on remand is framed by those opposing factual contentions. The two opinions of the Court of Appeals and the several opinions of the three judges of the court attempted, with a notable lack of harmony, to state the applicable rules as to burden of proof and how this shifts upon the making of a prima facie case. We now address this problem.

The complainant in a Title VII trial must carry the initial burden under the statute of establishing a prima facie case of racial discrimination. This may be done by showing (i) that he belongs to a racial minority; (ii) that he applied and was qualified for a job for which the employer was seeking applicants; (iii) that, despite his qualifications, he was rejected; and (iv) that, after his rejection, the position remained open and the employer continued to seek applicants from persons of complainant's qualifications.[13] In the instant case, we agree with the Court of Appeals that respondent proved a prima facie case. 463 F.2d 337, 353. Petitioner sought mechanics, respondent's trade, and continued to do so after respondent's rejection. Petitioner, moreover, does not dispute respondent's qualifications[14] and acknowledges that his past work performance in petitioner's employ was "satisfactory."

The burden then must shift to the employer to articulate some legitimate, nondiscriminatory reason for respondent's rejection. We need not attempt in the instant case to detail every matter which fairly could be recognized as a reasonable basis for a refusal to hire. Here petitioner has assigned respondent's participation in unlawful conduct against it as the cause for his rejection. We think that this suffices to discharge petitioner's burden of proof at this stage and to meet respondent's prima facie case of discrimination.

The Court of Appeals intimated, however, that petitioner's stated reason for refusing to rehire respondent was a "subjective" rather than objective criterion which "carries little weight in rebutting charges of discrimination," 463 F.2d., at 352, 5 FEP Cases, at 178. This was among the statements which caused the dissenting judge to read the opinion as taking "the position that such unlawful acts as Green committed against McDonnell would not legally entitle McDonnell to refuse to rehire him, even though no racial motivation was involved. . . ." Id., at 355, 5 FEP Cases, at 180. Regardless of whether this was the intended import of the opinion, we think the court below seriously under-estimated the rebuttal weight to which petitioner's reasons were entitled. Re-

13. The facts necessarily will vary in Title VII cases, and the specification above of the prima facie proof required from the complainant in this case is not necessarily applicable in every respect to differing factual situations.

14. We note that the issue of what may properly be used to test qualifications for employment is not present in this case. Where employers have instituted employment tests and qualifications with an exclusionary effect on minority applicants, such requirements must be "shown to bear a demonstrable relationship to successful performance of the jobs" for which they were used. Griggs v. Duke Power Co., 401 U.S. 424, 431 (1971). Castro v. Beecher, 459 F.2d 725 (CA1 1972); Chance v. Board of Examiners, 458 F.2d 1167 (CA2 1972).

spondent admittedly had taken part in a carefully planned "stall-in," designed to tie up access and egress to petitioner's plant at a peak traffic hour. Nothing in Title VII compels an employer to absolve and rehire one who has engaged in such deliberate, unlawful activity against it. In upholding, under the National Labor Relations Act, the discharge of employees who had seized and forcibly retained an employer's factory buildings in an illegal sit-down strike, the Court noted pertinently:

> We are unable to conclude that Congress intended to compel employers to retain persons in their employ regardless of their unlawful conduct — to invest those who go on strike with an immunity from discharge for acts of trespass or violence against the employer's property. . . . Apart from the question of the constitutional validity of an enactment of that sort, it is enough to say that such a legislative intention should be found in some definite and unmistakable expression. NLRB v. Fansteel Corp., 306 U.S. 240, 255, 4 LRRM 515, 519 (1939).

Petitioner's reason for rejection thus suffices to meet the prima facie case, but the inquiry must not end here. While Title VII does not, without more, compel rehiring of respondent, neither does it permit petitioner to use respondent's conduct as a pretext for the sort of discrimination prohibited by §703(a)(1). On remand, respondent must, as the Court of Appeals recognized, be afforded a fair opportunity to show that petitioner's stated reason for respondent's rejection was in fact pretextual. Especially relevant to such a showing would be evidence that white employees involved in acts against petitioner of comparable seriousness to the "stall-in" were nevertheless retained or rehired. Petitioner may justifiably refuse to rehire one who was engaged in unlawful, disruptive acts against it, but only if this criterion is applied alike to members of all races.

Other evidence that may be relevant to any showing of pretextuality includes facts as to the petitioner's treatment of respondent during his prior term of employment, petitioner's reaction, if any, to respondent's legitimate civil rights activities, and petitioner's general policy and practice with respect to minority employment.[18] On the latter point, statistics as to petitioner's employment policy and practice may be helpful to a determination of whether petitioner's refusal to rehire respondent in this case conformed to a general pattern of discrimination against blacks. Jones v. Lee Way Motor Freight, Inc., 421 F.2d 245, 2 FEP Cases 895 (CA 10 1970); Blumrosen, Strangers in Paradise: Griggs v. Duke Power Co., and the Concept of Employment Discrimination, 71 Mich. L. Rev. 59, 91-94 (1972).[19] In short, on the retrial respondent must be given a full and fair opportunity to demonstrate by competent evidence that the presumptively valid reasons for his rejection were in fact a coverup for a racially discriminatory decision.

The court below appeared to rely upon Griggs v. Duke Power Co., supra, in which the Court stated: "If an employment practice which operates to exclude Negroes cannot be shown to be related to job performance, the practice is prohibited." Id., at 431, 3 FEP Cases at 178. But Griggs differs from the instant case in important respects. It dealt with standardized testing devices which, however neutral on their face, operated to exclude

18. We are aware that some of the above factors were indeed considered by the District Judge in finding under §704(a), that "defendant's [here petitioner's] reasons for refusing to rehire the plaintiff were motivated solely and simply by the plaintiff's participation in the 'stall-in' and 'lock-in' demonstration." 318 F. Supp., at 850, 2 FEP Cases, at 1000. We do not intimate that this finding must be overturned after consideration on remand of respondent's §703(a)(1) claim. We do, however, insist that respondent under §703(a)(1) must be given a full and fair opportunity to demonstrate by competent evidence that whatever the stated reasons for his rejection, the decision was in reality racially premised.

19. The District Court may, for example, determine, after reasonable discovery that "the [racial] composition of defendant's labor force is itself reflective of restrictive or exclusionary practices." See Blumrosen, supra, at 92. We caution that such general determinations, while helpful, may not be in and of themselves controlling as to an individualized hiring decision, particularly in the presence of an otherwise justifiable reason for refusing to rehire. See generally, United States v. Bethlehem Steel Corporation, 312 F. Supp. 977, 992, 2 FEP Cases 545 (WDNY 1970), aff'd, 446 F.2d 652, 3 FEP Cases 589 (CA 2 1971). Blumrosen, supra, at 93.

many blacks who were capable of performing effectively in the desired positions. Griggs was rightly concerned that childhood deficiencies in the education and background of minority citizens, resulting from forces beyond their control, not be allowed to work a cumulative and invidious burden on such citizens for the remainder of their lives. Id., at 430. Respondent, however, appears in different clothing. He had engaged in a seriously disruptive act against the very one from whom he now seeks employment. And petitioner does not seek his exclusion on the basis of a testing device which overstates what is necessary for competent performance, or through some sweeping disqualification of all those with any past record of unlawful behavior, however remote, insubstantial or unrelated to applicant's personal qualifications as an employee. Petitioner assertedly rejected respondent for unlawful conduct against it and in the absence of proof of pretextual or discriminatory application of such a reason, this cannot be thought the kind of "artificial, arbitrary, and unnecessary barrier to employment" which the Court found to be the intention of Congress to remove. Griggs, p. 431.[21]

In sum, respondent should have been allowed to amend his complaint to include a claim under §703(a) (1). If the evidence on retrial is substantially in accord with that before us in this case, we think that respondent carried his burden of establishing a prima facie case of racial discrimination and that petitioner successfully rebutted that case. But this does not end the matter. On retrial respondent must be afforded a fair opportunity to demonstrate that petitioner's assigned reason for refusing to re-employ was pretextual or discriminatory in its application. If the District Judge so finds, he must order a prompt and appropriate remedy. In the absence of such a finding, petitioner's refusal to rehire must stand.

The cause is hereby remanded to the District Court for reconsideration in accordance with this opinion.

4. Use of Class Actions

Since race and sex discrimination are by definition class discrimination, the effective use of Title VII requires class actions. Class actions are easier to prove than "one on one" cases; they achieve greater results for the same input of time and money than do "one on one" cases, and they are ultimately the only way to force companies to undertake the major institutional changes that are needed to end employment discrimination. Unfortunately, clients rarely come into law offices seeking to eradicate class discrimination, and class actions do require greater time, effort, and responsibility of counsel.

The next excerpt discusses some of the features of the developing Title VII law relative to class actions.

COOPER AND RABB
EQUAL EMPLOYMENT LAW AND LITIGATION
337-350 (1972)

The use of class action techniques is an integral element of almost all effective equal employment litigation. Federal courts have recognized that antidiscrimination litigation

---

21. It is, of course, a predictive evaluation, resistant to empirical proof, whether "an applicant's past participation in unlawful conduct directed at his prospective employer might indicate the applicant's lack of a responsible attitude toward performing work for that employer." 463 F.2d at 353. But in this case, given the seriousness and harmful potential of respondent's participation in the "stall-in" and the accompanying inconvenience to other employees, it cannot be said that petitioner's refusal to employ lacked a rational and neutral business justification. As the Court has noted elsewhere: "Past conduct may well relate to present fitness; past loyalty may have a reasonable relationship to present and future trust." Garner v. Los Angeles Board, 341 U.S. 716, 720 (1951).

is public in character with the individual litigant serving as a private attorney general vindicating a strong Congressional policy to eradicate discrimination. See Jenkins v. United Gas Corp., 400 F.2d 28 (5th Cir. 1968); Oatis v. Crown Zellerbach Corp., 398 F.2d 496 (5th Cir. 1968); Newman v. Piggie Park Enterprises, Inc., 390 U.S. 400 (1968) (suit under Title II of the Act). Moreover, when a claimant is discriminated against on the basis of his race, sex, etc., he has been discriminated against on the basis of a class characteristic, and thus Title VII actions are inherently class actions. See Bowe v. Colgate-Palmolive Co., 416 F.2d 711 (7th Cir. 1969); Oatis v. Crown Zellerbach Corp., supra; Jenkins v. United States Gas Corp., supra; Hall v. Werthan Bag Corp., 251 F. Supp. 184 (M.D. Tenn. 1966). The attitude expressed by the court in *Jenkins,* supra, is typical. There the court observed that a Title VII suit is "more than a private claim by the employee. . . . When conciliation has failed the individual . . . takes on the mantle of the sovereign." (400 F.2d at 32.) "If classwide relief were not afforded expressly in any . . . order issued in employee's behalf, the result would be the incongruous one of the court . . . itself being the instrument of racial discrimination." (400 F.2d at 34.)

Consistent with this general view, the courts have been flexible in applying class action concepts to broaden the scope and effectiveness of a single suit. For example, it is now settled that a single plaintiff who has met the procedural prerequisites of 42 U.S.C. Sec. 2000e-5 (requiring that a complaint first be processed through the EEOC and any state agency) may maintain a class action in court on behalf of all others similarly situated, and the others need not meet those procedural prerequisites in order to obtain relief. Oatis v. Crown Zellerbach Corp., supra; Parham v. Southwestern Bell Telephone Co., 443 F.2d 421 (8th Cir. 1970) (a single charge of discrimination may serve to launch a full-scale inquiry into the employer's practices).

Likewise, the courts have, in general, been most liberal in determining the scope of a Title VII action growing out of an EEOC charge. The issues raised before the court may include not only those issues raised in the charge before the EEOC but also those issues which may reasonably be expected to come within the scope of an EEOC investigation growing out of the charge. Sanchez v. Standard Brands, 431 F.2d 455 (5th Cir. 1970); *Jenkins,* supra; *Oatis,* supra. The leading case establishing both the broad interpretation of this "reasonably-related" test and the broad scope of a Title VII class action in general has been Carr v. Conoco Plastics, Inc., 423 F.2d 57 (5th Cir.), *cert. denied,* 400 U.S. 951 (1970). In *Carr* several Negro males filed a complaint at EEOC alleging that the defendant refused to hire them because of their race. After exhausting their administrative remedies, the complainants filed a federal complaint seeking to enjoin across the board racial discrimination by Conoco. The company objected to the court's jurisdiction to consider other than the discriminatory hiring claims. The Fifth Circuit held for plaintiffs, stating:

> [a] suit brought pursuant to the Act by persons claiming that an employer has violated Section 703(a) (1) of the Act by refusing to hire them because of their race, may also allege and seek to enjoin other unlawful employment practices committed by the same employer, if those practices, although not directly injurious to them at the time of their application for employment, potentially affect them because of their race. The Court holds that they can.
>
> The plaintiffs here seek equal opportunity for employment, and charge defendants with discriminating against them on account of race. There can be no serious question but that plaintiffs have the right to bring the action for themselves and others similarly situated. Envisioning an equal opportunity for employment plaintiffs have the correlated right to enjoy nondiscriminatory practices within the plant.
>
> It is foolhardy to say that once plaintiffs have removed racial discriminatory practices at the door, they are required to start anew in order to remove those that exist on the inside. Such a practice would result in a multiplicity of suits and a waste of time and money for all interested parties. 423 F.2d 57, 65 (1970).

Since EEOC complaints are often filed by laymen without the advice of counsel the policy of a broadly construed EEOC complaint makes sense. Similar across the board suits directed not at an individual grievance but at a system-wide policy of discrimination have withstood attack in Johnson v. Georgia Highway Express, Inc., 417 F.2d 1122 (5th Cir. 1969) (discharged Negro employee allowed to maintain suit on behalf of all Negroes who may be affected by defendant's discrimination in hiring, firing, promotion and maintenance of facilities) and in *Jenkins,* supra (suit on behalf of all Negro employees of defendant).

This treatment of class actions by the federal courts seemed uniformly expansive through 1970, with consistently liberal opinions allowing ever broadening use of the class action mechanism to vindicate Title VII rights. However, several recent decisions have put the law in a state of flux and lawyers cannot wholly depend on a generous judicial interpretation to rescue a narrowly drawn EEOC charge. It is becoming increasingly important to carefully draw EEOC charges and shape issues as broadly as possible at the earliest stage. . . .

In order to maintain a class action under Title VII, the requirements of Rule 23 of the F.R.C.P. must be satisfied. First, the class must be so numerous that joinder of all members is impracticable. Rule 23(a) (1). This generally presents no problem in Title VII cases in light of the sweeping definition of the class. Second, there must be questions of law and fact common to the class. Rule 23 (a) (2). In *Johnson,* supra, the court noted that while it was true that there were different factual questions as to different employees, it was also true that these disparities were superseded by the "Damoclean threat of a racially discriminatory policy [which] hangs over the racial class [and] is a question of fact common to all members of the class." Hall v. Werthan Bag Corp., 251 F. Supp. 184 (M.D. Tenn. 1966). The court also sanctioned the liberal use of subclasses where issues diverged. See also Oatis v. Crown Zellerbach Corp., 398 F.2d 496 (5th Cir. 1968). Third, the claims of the named plaintiffs must be typical of those of the class. Rule 23(a) (3). It had, until recently,[1] consistently been held that the employment status of a complainant was not determinative of his capacity to represent a class of employees. Thus class actions on behalf of past, present and future employees have been maintained by individuals who were retired from employment (Hacket v. McGuire Bros., Inc., 445 F.2d 442 (3rd Cir. 1971)); who had been discharged from employment (*Johnson,* supra; Reyes v. Missouri-Kansas-Texas R.R. Co., 3 EPD Par. 8105 (E.D. Kan. 1971); Tipler v. DuPont Co., 443 F.2d 125 (6th Cir. 1971)); who had never been employed and had been denied employment by defendant (Carr v. Conoco Plastics, Inc., supra); and whose claims had become moot or had been held to lack merit (Parham v. Southwestern Bell Telephone Co., 433 F.2d 421 (8th Cir. 1970); Jenkins v. United Gas Co., 400 F.2d 28 (5th Cir. 1968)). Fourth, the named plaintiffs must fairly and adequately protect the interests of the class. Rule 23(a) (4). *Johnson* articulates the standard followed in making this determination:

> . . . [W]hether he will adequately represent the class is a question of fact to be "raised and resolved in the trial court in the usual manner . . ." Harris v. Palm Spring Alpine Estates, Inc., 329 F.2d 909, 913 (9th Cir. 1964). . . . The standard to be applied is not whether appellant will prevail but is as stated by Judge Medina:
> "An essential concomitant of adequate representation is that the party's attorney be qualified, experienced, and generally able to conduct the proposed litigation. Additionally, it is necessary to eliminate so far as possible the likelihood that the litigants are involved in a collusive suit or that plaintiff has interests antagonistic to those of the remainder of the class." Eisen v. Carlisle and Jacquelin, 391 F.2d 555 (2d Cir. 1968).
> 417 F.2d 1124-25.

---

1. See Huff v. N.D. Cass Co. [468 F.2d 172 (5th Cir. 1972)] and Tedford v. Airco Reduction Co. [4 FEP Cases 406, 690 (5th Cir. 1972)].

Similar standards were applied in Mack v. General Electric Co., 329 F. Supp. 72 (E.D. Pa. 1971), and the success or failure of plaintiff's individual claim was specifically rejected as a criterion of class relief in Parham v. Southwestern Bell Telephone Co., supra.

In addition to these general requirements of Rule 23(a), the plaintiff must also show that his case falls within one of the three categories of class actions described in subsections (b)(1), (b)(2) and (b)(3) of Rule 23. These are:

> *(b) Class Actions Maintainable.* An action may be maintained as a class action if the prerequisites of subdivision (a) are satisfied, and in addition:
> (1) the prosecution of separate actions by or against individual members of the class would create a risk of
> (A) inconsistent or varying adjudications with respect to individual members of the class which would establish incompatible standards of conduct for the party opposing the class, or
> (B) adjudications with respect to individual members of the class which would as a practical matter be dispositive of the interests of the other members not parties to the adjudications or substantially impair or impede their ability to protect their interests; or
> (2) the party opposing the class has acted or refused to act on grounds generally applicable to the class, thereby making appropriate final injunctive relief or corresponding declaratory relief with respect to the class as a whole; or
> (3) the court finds that the questions of law or fact common to the members of the class predominate over any questions affecting only individual members, and that a class action is superior to other available methods for the fair and efficient adjudication of the controversy. The matters pertinent to the findings include: (A) the interest of members of the class in individually controlling the prosecution or defense of separate actions; (B) the extent and nature of any litigation concerning the controversy already commenced by or against members of the class; (C) the desirability or undesirability of concentrating the litigation of the claims in the particular forum; (D) the difficulties likely to be encountered in the management of a class action.

The usual fair employment case is brought under subsection (b)(2), which refers to situations where "the party opposing the class has acted or refused to act on grounds generally applicable to class." Indeed the revisors' notes to the 1966 rule amendments referred to civil rights cases as the prototype of the (b)(2) class action.

A question is frequently raised about sending notice to class members early in the litigation. However, Rule 23 requires no notice in a (b)(2) action. The court is directed by Rule 23(c)(1) to make an early determination of the propriety of the class action, but notice to class members is required only in a (b)(3) variety of class action (one where the reason for class treatment is that common questions of law or fact predominate). Notice is in the discretion of the court in (b)(2) actions. Several recent decisions have taken advantage of this discretionary provision in requiring notice to all members of the class where practicable. See Arey v. Providence Hospital, 4 EPD Par. 7788 (D.D.C. 1972); Ostapowicz v. Johnson Bronze Co., 4 EPD Par. 7766 (W.D. Pa. 1972). Many fair employment cases also qualify under (b)(3) but it seems best to seek to have them classified as (b)(2). A (b)(3) classification would not only mean that notice would have to be given to all members (Rule 23(c)(2)) but also that each be given the chance to opt out of the action. This option-out could cause serious problems when later classwide injunctive relief is formulated. It is generally thought that a plaintiff may elect (b)(2) rather than (b)(3) if both are applicable.

It is incumbent on the Title VII lawyer in defining his or her class to take note of the fact that the overall picture is not quite as one-sidedly in favor of the use of class actions as might appear. The attorney who pursues a class action assumes a heavy responsibility. Rule 23(b)(2) provides that a final judgment in a class action "whether or not favorable to the class shall include and describe those whom the court finds to be members of the class." Judge Godbold, concurring in Johnson v. Georgia Highway Express, supra, warned that "an over-broad framing of the class may be so unfair to the absent members as to approach, if not amount to, deprivation of due process. . . . [W]hat of the catastrophic consequences if the plaintiff loses and carries the class down with him . . . ?" (417 F.2d at 1126.) Furthermore, the fact that Rule 23(c) requires no notice in a (b)(2) action and members of the class are not given a chance to opt out of the action may be unfair to individual members of the class.

These risks have led some to suggest that class actions ought possibly to be foregone in civil rights cases so as to provide opportunities for a second shot at the defendant, possibly in a more favorable forum, in the event the first action fails. In some cases where individual relief will in effect protect the entire class, the option of an individual action might be considered. For example, in an individual action challenging a seniority system, the remedy modifying the system will technically run only in favor of the named plaintiff. As a practical matter, however, the employer will probably modify the system as to all to avoid intraplant conflict and to avoid later suit by others; and if the employer does not cooperate, others are free to bring suit and establish their own rights. However, in most cases class actions offer too many advantages to pass up. For one thing a class action tends to open up the scope of the case so that the court will entertain discovery regarding sections of a plant where named plaintiffs do not work and even order relief as to such sections. And most important, the class action will lead to mandatory relief as to the entire class. This will permit any class members to take advantage of expeditious contempt proceedings in the event that classwide provisions of a remedial order are not adhered to in his behalf. Also, class actions prevent a multiplicity of suits which would place an onerous burden on the courts and constitute a waste of time and money for those fighting discrimination.

A further possible advantage of class actions, which has not yet become settled, is that of gaining damages for all class members. The most common example of this is back pay. While all courts agree that a class-wide order for injunctive relief is appropriate, and that back pay is an appropriate additional remedy to compensate for the period while the plaintiffs were suffering under discrimination, there is disagreement as to the appropriateness of awarding back pay to all class members in a single action. See King v. Georgia Power Co., 3 EPD Par. 8318 (N.D. Ga. 1971). This reluctance stems from the large sums involved,[2] and from the complexities of computing back pay for each class member since each has a somewhat different claim. However, in Bowe v. Colgate-Palmolive Co., 416 F.2d 711 (7th Cir. 1969), the court ordered back pay for the entire class, noting that it was "unable to perceive any justification for treating such a suit as a class action for injunctive purposes but not treat it so for purposes of other relief." Id. at 720. The court sanctioned a broad reading of 42 U.S.C. Sec. 2000e-5(g)'s affirmative action requirement to muster its full remedial power.

Another point to consider regarding classwide back pay claims is that the Advisory Committee Notes to Rule 23(b)(2) indicate that it "does not extend to cases in which the final relief relates exclusively or predominately to money damages." Thus the risk is raised that a damage claim will shift the case to the (b)(3) category and require troublesome notice and opting out.

Another issue in class action litigation is that of determining the scope of the class. This rests in the discretion of the trial judge who must balance the competing interests involved. Ultimately, practical considerations of manageability will dictate the outer limits of a class no matter how liberal a view is taken of Rule 23. Thus it is possible that an action against General Motors challenging its practices system-wide may make no sense in terms of the varied factual situations involved, in spite of common questions

---

2. It has been estimated that aggregate back pay claims in pending U.S. Steel fair employment litigation total $30 million. The NAACP Legal Defense Fund recently settled the case against Lorillard Co. with $500,000 in back pay for the class.

of law and fact. A plant-wide action, on the other hand, is not likely to present too unwieldy a situation and the use of sub-classes greatly increases the scope of the manageable class.

NOTE: A REFUSAL TO GRANT CLASSWIDE RELIEF

The Fifth Circuit suggested in a race case, Jenkins v. United Gas Corp., 400 F.2d 28 (5th Cir. 1968), that a court must award classwide relief where there is class discrimination. Subsequently, in a sex discrimination case, the Fifth Circuit refused to take this concept to its logical conclusion. The opinion in this case, Danner v. Phillips Petroleum Co., 447 F.2d 159 (5th Cir. 1971), is reprinted here, followed by the dissenting opinion from the denial of a rehearing and a rehearing en banc, 450 F. 2d 881 (5th Cir. 1971).

Danner v. Phillips Petroleum Company
447 F.2d 159 (5th Cir. 1971)

THORNBERRY, Circuit Judge: — In this sex discrimination case, Phillips Petroleum appeals from the judgment of the court below holding that Phillips' discharge of Mrs. Pauline Danner, the plaintiff below, was an unfair employment practice in violation of Title VII of the Civil Rights Act of 1964, 42 U.S.C.A. §2000e.

Mrs. Pauline Danner began working for Phillips Petroleum in March 1957. She was discharged by the company in January 1967. During the ten-year period she was employed at Phillips, Mrs. Danner performed the following tasks: (1) Testing plant water; (2) mixing chemicals for the water treatment; (3) cleaning the spark plugs for the plant engines; (4) doing the regular production figuring; (5) keeping the oil reports and the engine reports; (6) typing up the accident reports; (7) preparing and keeping up with the time sheets; (8) drawing diagrams and making the reports of leaks occuring in the field; (9) answering the telephone; and (10) cleaning the restrooms, washing the walls and woodwork, and burning the trash. The label Phillips placed on this conglomerate of tasks assigned to Mrs. Danner was "plant clerk." . . .

Although Mrs. Danner had been working for Phillips for almost ten years when she was discharged, she had no seniority rights and no bidding or "bumping" rights that would have enabled her to assert any rights to another job with Phillips. The trial court found, and the evidence on this point is uncontradicted, that none of the female employees at Phillips had seniority or bidding rights. Phillips claims that Mrs. Danner was discharged as part of an economy measure, and there is nothing in the Record to contradict this claim. According to Phillips' own witness, however, the reason Phillips discharged Mrs. Danner rather than some other employee in its economy move was that Mrs. Danner had no seniority or bumping privileges, and therefore could not assert any rights to another position with Phillips. . . . Had Phillips sought to discharge any of the men who replaced Mrs. Danner, the men would have been able to assert their seniority and bidding rights. On these facts, the trial court concluded that Mrs. Danner suffered sex discrimination. . . .

. . . Phillips argues that there is no evidence to support the trial court's conclusion that Mrs. Danner suffered sex discrimination.

Phillips does not dispute, however, that none of its women employees have seniority or bidding rights. This finding by the district court clearly is supported by the evidence; it is based on the testimony of one of Phillips' own witnesses, and it is uncontradicted.

This fact alone was enough to make out a prima facie case of sex discrimination against Phillips and to place the burden of explaining the fact upon Phillips.

Phillips' only explanation is that it is "company policy" not to give seniority and bidding rights to clerical employees because clerical jobs are not "unionized" jobs. Phillips' policy is to give all its non-union employees who hold "unionized" jobs the same benefits those employees would have if they were members of the union. Only the jobs of its "roustabouts" or utility men and its roughnecks are "unionized" jobs; thus only men holding those jobs possess seniority and bidding rights. And since there are no women "roustabouts" or roughnecks, Phillips explains, no women possess seniority or bidding rights.

The trial court concluded that Phillips' "company policy" did not show a sufficient business necessity to justify the net effect of that policy — which is to exclude all women employees from seniority benefits. We must agree with this conclusion.

A "policy" to limit company privileges to only one class of employees and to exclude others cannot survive in the name of "company policy" alone if the net effect of that policy is to exclude all women. Phillips has given no business justification for excluding its clerical employees from these rights. The excuse that clerical jobs are not "unionized" jobs is no excuse. For Phillips does not contend that its relations with the union will be affected in any way if it extends these privileges to clerical workers. It is difficult, moreover, to see how Phillips could make such a contention in view of the fact that the roustabouts and roughnecks who possess these rights were not union members; Phillips had extended the rights to these men as a matter of grace. Phillips gives no good reason why it should limit those privileges to roughnecks and roustabouts.[4] And when the policy which does so limit the privileges results in sex discrimination, it violates Title VII. . . .

We therefore find no error in the trial court's conclusion that Mrs. Danner suffered sex discrimination, and we affirm that part of the trial court's judgment awarding Mrs. Danner attorney's fees and lost wages from the time of her illegal termination, and ordering her reinstatement with rights of seniority and bidding status.

IV. CLASS ACTION RELIEF

In addition to awarding Mrs. Danner lost wages and ordering that she be reinstated, the trial court enjoined Phillips from discriminating against any other female because of sex, and retained jurisdiction of the case for the purpose of determining by appropriate proceedings that Phillips has initiated a proper seniority plan for its female employees. Phillips complains that this was an award of class action relief when none had been sought by Mrs. Danner and no basis for such relief has been established at the trial. We agree with Phillips on this point.

Class actions are very specialized types of suits, and "an allegation of class representation is attended by serious consequences." Philadelphia Electric Co. v. Anaconda American Brass Co., E.D. Pa. 1967, 42 F.R.D. 324, 328. Class actions are governed by the quite specific requirements of Rule 23 of the Federal Rules of Civil Procedure, and as a general rule, an action on behalf of unnamed persons must be brought in conformity with Rule 23. See 3B Moore's Federal Practice ¶23.02-2.

Rule 23 among other things, requires that the party suing establish himself as an adequate representative of the class,[6] and that the class be so large in number that it

---

4. At oral argument, Phillips pointed out that its engineers and geologists also possess no seniority and bidding rights, and contended that if the trial court's action is affirmed Phillips will be forced to extend these privileges to all its engineers and geologists, who according to Phillips do not wish to partake of the "bumping" practices of other employees because they prefer to work on a merit system. Phillips does not make this contention with respect to clerical workers, of course, nor do we think it plausibly could make such a contention in the face of Mrs. Danner's lawsuit. At any rate, we wish to make it clear that we have no intention of imposing seniority and bidding privileges upon employees who do not want them. That is one reason we have found that the district court erred in awarding class action relief in this case. See Part IV of this opinion. We have affirmed the action of the district court only to the extent that it affords relief to Mrs. Danner, who is neither an engineer nor a geologist, and who, as a clerical employee, clearly wishes to have the same employment privileges as the men who replaced her in her job. See Part IV of this opinion.

6. Mrs. Danner made no claim of representative status, nor any attempt to establish representative status

would be impracticable to join all members.[7] Moreover, the class itself must be identified.[8] In addition, once a court has determined that the suit is to be maintained as a class action, it may be required by subdivision (c)(2) of the Rule, or it may feel it advisable under subdivision (d)(2) of the Rule, to notify as many members of the class as possible of the existence of the suit and of those members' rights to be excluded from the suit.[9]

In the instant suit, none of the Rule 23 prerequisites have been satisfied. Mrs. Danner sued as an individual plaintiff; she established a prima facie case of sex discrimination against herself by proving that she had been discharged in a plant economy move because she possessed no seniority or bidding rights, and that no women in the plant had such rights. She showed further that the work she was doing was substantially similar to the work of men in the plant who had seniority and bidding rights, and that she was replaced by men who possessed those rights. Mrs. Danner, however, never took up the banner of women's liberation for all the female employees in the Phillips plant. This, of course, does not mean that female employees of Phillips may not take advantage of Mrs. Danner's judicial victory in the future, or, indeed, that they may not join together in a class action against Phillips if they feel one is justified. But if they decide to bring a class action, it must be brought and identified as such, and the predicate for class action relief must be carefully laid. In the meantime, Mrs. Danner's victory is for her alone to taste and enjoy. . . .

Danner v. Phillips Petroleum Company
450 F.2d 881 (5th Cir. 1971)

TUTTLE, Circuit Judge, dissenting: — After careful consideration of the petition for rehearing in this case, I respectfully dissent from the order of the court denying reconsideration of this court's action with respect to its reversal of the trial court's granting relief in favor of other female employees because of the fact that Mrs. Danner's suit was not initiated or maintained as a class action.

I would agree that the order of the trial court may have been over-broad in stating that it would retain jurisdiction to require "a proper seniority plan" for all female employees. In view, however, of the recognized fact that "whether in name or not, the suit is perforce a sort of class action for fellow employees similarly situated," see Jenkins v. United Gas Corporation, 5 Cir., 1968, 400 F.2d 28, 1 FEP Cases 364, 69 LRRM 2152, I do not feel that the trial court erred in its broad injunction against discriminations because of sex against "any other female," as well as plaintiff.

It was undisputed that in the kind of employment in which Mrs. Danner was engaged, she was in a position or classification which had no seniority or bumping rights, whereas male employees who were qualified to, and who actually undertook, to do her work after her discharge, were protected by seniority and bumping rights. It is also clear that other employees of the defendant corporation were in classifications, principally professional ones, as to which the employees, neither male nor female, had seniority or bumping rights. Thus it would appear that the trial court would not be justified in requiring the company to provide for a proper seniority plan for *all* defendant's female employees. The most that should be required would be that all defendant's female employees be afforded every right with respect to seniority or bumping that is enjoyed

---

in this suit. Moreover, her status as a representative of all women clerical employees or all women employees might have been questionable in light of some of the rather individualized aspects of her problem.

7. In this suit, there were only around 30 women employed in the Phillips plant.

8. There is no indication whether the district court's judgment would apply to all women, including women engineers and geologists, see note 4 supra, or only women clerical workers.

9. The district court might have found such a procedure very desirable in the instant case. See note 4 supra.

by any male employee capable of, classified for, or qualified to do the kind of work in which the female employee was engaged.

It is my view that the judgment of this court should be modified and the case remanded to the trial court, on this issue, for the purpose of requiring completely equal treatment with respect to female and male employees, in whatever classification or category of employment they might compete for. It should further be modified by reinstating the trial court's injunction preventing the defendant from discriminating against other females because of sex, a simple statement of the rights granted under the Act.

From the admitted facts in this case, it is plain that any other female holding a position similar to that of Mrs. Danner, would be equally prejudiced by the lack of bumping rights as was Mrs. Danner. The fact that such other person or persons was not named or referred to in Mrs. Danner's original complaint, as a member of a class of female employees, does not, it seems to me, deprive the trial court of the right of protecting the statutory rights of such female employees in its order. This precise issue has been decided as here suggested by the Seventh Circuit Court of Appeals in the case of Sprogis v. United Air Lines, Inc., No. 18481, decided June 16, 1971, 7 Cir., 1971, — F.2d — , 3 FEP Cases 621, 626-627. In that case the court said:

> As part of its decree, the district court retained jurisdiction to consider the possibility of extending relief to other stewardesses similarly discharged by United's enforcement of its no-marriage rule. Accordingly, the court ordered plaintiff to submit amended or supplemental pleadings, or suggestions on that matter, and gave United leave to respond. United attacks this portion of the decree as inconsistent with the policy of Rule 23 of the Federal Rules of Civil Procedure. It urges that the "class" aspect of a Title VII action must be established prior to judgment on the merits. We need not anticipate and resolve the array of issues which may arise in the determination of the propriety of class relief. In its present posture, this case presents the bald question of the court's power to grant such relief where justice requires such action. In our opinion, Rule 23 to the contrary notwithstanding, the district court possesses such power in Title VII cases.
>
> The vindication of the public interest expressed by the Civil Rights Act constitutes an important facet of private litigation under Title VII. In Bowe v. Colgate-Palmolive Co., 416 F.2d 711, 719, 2 FEP Cases 121, 223 (7th Cir. 1969), Judge Kerner recognized that such a suit is necessarily a class action "as the evil sought to be ended is discrimination on the basis of a class characteristic, i.e., race, sex, religion or national origin." See also Jenkins v. United Gas Corporation, 400 F.2d 28, 33, 1 FEP Cases 364, 69 LRRM 2152 (5th Cir. 1968). At stake, therefore, are the interests of the other members of that class, and the court has a special responsibility in the public interest to devise remedies which effectuate the policies of the Act as well as afford private relief to the individual employee instituting the complaint. Bowe v. Colgate-Palmolive Co., 416 F.2d at p. 715; Hutchings v. United States Industries, Inc., 428 F.2d 303, 311-312, 2 FEP Cases 725 (5th Cir. 1970); Parham v. Southwestern Bell Telephone Co., 433 F.2d 421, 428-429, 2 FEP Cases 1117 (8th Cir. 1970).
>
> Section 706(g) of the Act (note 9 supra) grants to federal courts plenary powers to fashion affirmative relief eradicating present discrimination and redressing the adverse consequences of past unlawful conduct. (Cf. Local 53 of International Ass'n of Heat & Frost I.G.A. Workers v. Vogler, 407 F.2d 1047, 1052-1053, 1 FEP Cases 577, 70 LRRM 2257 (5th Cir. 1969). In Bowe, we held that this power "should be broadly read and applied so as to effectively terminate the practice and make its victims whole." 416 F.2d at p. 721. In order to accomplish that result, we ordered that the "relief should be made available to all who were so damaged; whether or not they filed charges and whether or not they joined in the suit." Id.; cf. Griffin v. County School Board of Prince Edward County, 377 U.S. 218, 224.

I, of course, do not know whether there were any other persons similarly situated to Mrs. Danner in this case. I would, however, leave it to the trial court to determine whether there were female employees whose protection was properly the subject of the court's concern, once it appeared that as to women employees of Mrs. Danner's category there was a clear discrimination which would be equally injurious to any other person in her situation or one within the employment of Phillips Petroleum Company in which a similar disparity existed.

I would grant the rehearing for the purpose of remolding our judgment as indicated above.

Jenkins can be distinguished from *Danner* since *Jenkins* was explicitly brought as a class action. A more disturbing point of distinction is that the first case involved race discrimination, and the second, sex discrimination. However, *Danner* may only be part of a broader retreat from a liberal allowance of Title VII class actions, see Huff v. N.D. Cass Co., 468 F.2d 172 (5th Cir. 1972).

As for as the liberal Seventh Circuit view evidenced in the *Sprogis* opinion, it was defeated on remand. The district court disallowed a class action, primarily because costly back pay claims were involved. 4 EPD. ¶7920 (N.D. Ill. 1972).

G. REMEDIES

1. Injunctive Relief

a. Enjoining Violations, Affirmative Relief, and Quotas

COOPER AND RABB
EQUAL EMPLOYMENT LAW AND LITIGATION
410-413 (1972)

FORMULATING REMEDIAL ORDERS

All the effort that goes into building a case and proving violations is for naught if an effective remedy is not obtained. Fortunately the provisions of Title VII are very flexible on this score, permitting the court to order "such affirmative action as may be appropriate, which may include reinstatement or hiring of employees, with or without back pay." Sec. 706(g) 42 U.S.C.A. 2000(e)-5g. The general equity powers of the court would seem to authorize a similar scope of relief when legal theories other than Title VII are relied upon.

. . . [T]his remedial relief is not limited merely to stopping unlawful practices. An employer who has committed violations can be ordered to undertake corrective steps designed to right his wrong and compensate the victims of that wrong.

. A good example of the kinds of remedial points to consider is provided by the consent order entered in United States v. Household Finance Corporation, — F. Supp. — (N.D. Ill. 1972), 4 EPD Par. 7680. The order enjoins the defendant's testing program and requires that any new program conform to the EEOC Guidelines. But beyond that the order requires various affirmative steps to correct for past discrimination. These steps include immediate promotion of large numbers of persons with specific credentials, an affirmative recruitment program with specific publicity requirements (including modification of the defendant's standard recruiting brochure), and extensive reporting requirements.

The difficulties in structuring a remedy will be apparent from a few moments consideration of the papers in the women lawyers' action included earlier. Assuming that the allegations in those complaints are proved, how can they be effectively stopped through court order? Would it be sufficient merely to order that all discriminatory practices cease? If we are dealing with a specific objective practice, such as a test, that kind of prohibitive order has some effect; witness Chance v. Board of Examiners, [330 F. Supp. 203 (S.D.N.Y. 1971), *aff'd,* 458 F.2d 1167 (2d Cir. 1972)] . . . But where the practice results from subjective influences, the effect of such an order is to ask the employer to change his attitude, which is unlikely to work. Therefore it is necessary to consider measurable affirmative steps which the court can order into operation.

1. Hiring Quotas

One possibility for effectuating relief is a specific hiring quota. In Vogler v. McCarty, Inc., 2 EPD Par. 10, 182 (E.D. La. 1970), *aff'd,* 451 F.2d 1235 (5th Cir. 1971), the court ordered that specific persons be admitted to union membership and also that a quota of blacks be admitted. See Pars. A 5-9 and B 7 of this order. The Eighth Circuit en banc in Carter v. Gallagher, 452 F.2d 315 (8th Cir.), *cert. denied,* __ U.S. __ (1972), 4 EPD Par. 7818, disapproved an order that the next 20 persons hired by defendant be minority persons but approved a plan whereby a one minority to two white hiring procedure was to be pursued until at least twenty minority persons had been hired. Similar preferential quotas were also ordered in United States v. Household Finance Corp., *supra;* Castro v. Beecher, __ F.2d __, 4 EPD Par. 7783 (1st Cir. 1972); and Pennsylvania v. O'Neill, __ F. Supp. __, 4 EPD Par. 7858 (E.D. Pa. 1972). (It might also be noted that in both *Vogler* and *O'Neill* quotas were ordered by way of preliminary relief before a full trial.) Is there any reason why quotas are unsound or undesirable? How can they be squared with Sec. 703(j) of Title VII? These issues are raised by the Court of Appeals opinion in Carter v. Gallagher, [452 F.2d 315, 327 (8th Cir. en banc 1972), *cert denied,* 406 U.S. 950 (1972) (holding that §703(j) allows quotas to correct the effects of past discrimination). See also the discussion of goals versus quotas in Part IV, *infra.*]

b. Seniority and Transfer Adjustments

The formulation of relief which corrects all past discrimination can be an exceedingly complex matter. The next case illustrates the difficulty of adjusting seniority in a plant where employees received different job assignments on a weekly basis.

BOWE v. PALMOLIVE COMPANY
6 FEP Cases 1132, 1133-1136 (7th Cir. 1973)

FAIRCHILD, Circuit Judge: — This case involves job restrictions and a seniority system at the Jeffersonville plant of Colgate-Palmolive Company which produced results discriminatory against female employees. Many of the relevant facts appear in the 1967 decision of the district court, Bowe v. Colgate-Palmolive Company, 272 F. Supp. 332, 1 FEP Cases 201, 65 LRRM 2714 (S.D. Ind., 1967). The district court found that discrimination had occurred and awarded damages to twelve plaintiffs whose claims it considered properly before it.

On appeal, this court expanded the class entitled to pecuniary recovery, and decided, contrary to the district court, that Colgate's exclusion of women, but not men, from jobs requiring the lifting of more than 35 pounds was unlawful. The cause was remanded with directions to grant such injunctive relief as may be required to eliminate the discriminatory system and any residual effect. Those discriminatorily laid off were to be compensated and the district court was directed to ascertain the feasibility of computing the damage to those who, while not laid off, were denied the opportunity to bid on higher paying jobs. Bowe v. Colgate-Palmolive Company, 416 F.2d 711, 2 FEP Cases 121, 223 (7th Cir., 1969).

On remand, the district court, on February 25, 1970, 2 FEP Cases 463, issued a preliminary injunction which, among other things, opened all jobs without discrimination on the basis of sex. The ultimate judgment appears in an order dated May 7, 1971, as modified February 21, 1972, 6 FEP Cases 1123. It required adjustments in seniority of 17 female employees, required certain options to be given to all female employees, and awarded recovery of money to 54. Plaintiff Georgianna Sellers and others have appealed, claiming that the seniority adjustments and job-assignment options were inadequate to eliminate the residual effects of the past discriminatory systems. . . .

As will appear, we conclude that the portion of the judgment granting injunctional relief should be affirmed without modification. . . .

The seniority system, weekly job assignment system, and the restrictions making many jobs unavailable to women are described in the 1967 district court decision, 272 F. Supp. at 340 to 347. Unnecessary repetition will be avoided here.

Before the 1966 changes in the collective bargaining agreement, the so-called general labor jobs were reserved for men; finishing labor jobs for women. Only four of the seventeen departments contained jobs reserved for women. The majority of women were employed in TAF, the Toilet Articles Finishing Department. The highest rate for a finishing labor job was the same as the lowest rate for a general labor job. Thus women were confined to the work where the pay was, for the most part, lower than that for men.

During the same period, separate seniority rosters were maintained for men and women. It could happen that an employee of either sex might be forced out of the department where seniority was being gained, or be laid off, when employees of the other sex, with less seniority were not, but for various reasons this occurred more often to women than to men.

In April, 1966, the collective bargaining agreement was changed. The separate seniority rosters for men and women were combined and the designations of jobs as male or female were eliminated. Colgate, however, imposed the 35 pound lifting limitation, so that in practical effect, although all jobs were open to men, the better paying jobs which had previously been reserved for men remained, for the most part, closed to women.

After the first appeal, all jobs were opened to women, beginning in March, 1970. Because, however, the seniority rules would require that a new entrant in any department would start last on the list in the weekly competition for jobs, women employees largely remained in the departments where they had previously worked.

SENIORITY REMEDIES ORDERED BY THE DISTRICT COURT

The judgment contained, for the purpose of eliminating remaining disadvantages as a result of past discrimination, the following components:

1. *Adjustments in seniority.* A layoff in 1963 lasted more than one year and caused a number of women employees to lose seniority. The court ordered previously existing departmental, and in some cases, date-of-employment seniority restored to fourteen. The 1963 layoff was the last one before the effective date of Title VII which caused a loss of seniority as a result of discrimination. The court deemed it impractical to determine whether any earlier layoffs were discriminatory or to ascertain which employees would currently have more or less seniority if there had been no discrimination. Three additional women, who had lost seniority as a result of the 1963 layoff, had been laid off again in 1965, and had not been recalled, were re-entered at the bottom of the recall list and ordered to be given five years date-of-employment seniority if eventually recalled.

2. *Option to transfer to new Home department.* Each female employee was permitted to enter a new department of her choice where she would be given departmental seniority equal to her seniority in the department she was leaving. Colgate was required to set up an "exposure program" whereby women would be given an opportunity to visit and observe operations of the various departments, examine job descriptions, and be formally instructed in the nature of the work. Employees were to be paid for time spent

in the program including overtime rates for overtime. The transfer option had to be exercised within sixty days after completion of the program. Within sixty days after transfer, the employee could return to her former department and re-assert her position there.

3. *Option to select secondary department.* Each female employee was permitted, within sixty days after the completion of the program, to select a secondary department, in which she would, for one year, have department seniority of July 2, 1965, the effective date of Title VII, or her date-of-employment seniority, if less. Accordingly, if she were forced out of a department within one year, she could bid on jobs in her secondary department with 1965 seniority. This device was intended to establish parity with those men who had seniority in a secondary department as a result of involuntary transfers within one year.

CONTENTIONS OF THE APPELLANTS WITH RESPECT TO SENIORITY

Appellants contend that the adjustments and options granted were insufficient to eliminate the residual effects of past discrimination. . . . They contend that as a matter of law full relief to all members of the class demands the substitution of a seniority system based solely on date-of-employment seniority. . . .

Appellants rely on the principle, with which all parties and the district court agree, that Title VII proscribes practices which are neutral on their face, and even in intent, if they perpetuate the effects of past discrimination. Griggs v. Duke Power Co., 401 U.S. 424, 430, 3 FEP Cases 175 (1971); Local 189, United Papermak. & Paperwork. v. United States, 416 F.2d 980, 988, 1 FEP Cases 875, 71 LRRM 3070 (5th Cir., 1969); United States v. Bethlehem Steel Corporation, 446 F.2d 652, 659, 3 FEP Cases 589 (2d Cir., 1971); Robinson v. Lorillard Corporation, 444 F.2d 791, 795, 3 FEP Cases 653 (4th Cir., 1971); United States v. Jacksonville Terminal Company, 451 F.2d 418, 443, 3 FEP Cases 802 (5th Cir., 1971); Head v. Timken Roller Bearing Company, __F.2d__, 6 FEP Cases 813, (6th Cir., No. 72-1994, October 12, 1973). Reliance on departmental seniority for job assignment, as practiced at the Jeffersonville plant is neutral on its face. The key issue is whether the transfer and secondary department options adequately relieve the system of the tendency it would otherwise have of perpetuating the results of job restrictions discriminatory against female employees. The district court considered the options adequate and chose to preserve the system because scrapping it "would upset the rights, expectations, and seniority rank of every employee in the plant, male and female. . . . A majority of the employees in the plant [apparently both male and female] have voted against the adoption of a plant seniority system."

It appears that any tendency of the departmental seniority system to perpetuate previous discrimination arose from the concentration of women in departments where there were relatively few of the better paying jobs for which to compete. We conclude that the transfer option was an adequate equalizing remedy on this score, and the secondary department option corrected any imbalance in the enjoyment of seniority in a secondary department, surviving from past discrimination.

The factual complexity of industrial employment systems makes generalizations from the decided cases very dubious, and each situation must be considered separately. We note, however, the conclusion in other cases that Title VII does not necessarily require more than one bona fide opportunity to transfer to one's rightful place without loss of seniority. United States v. Hayes International Corporation, 456 F.2d 112, 119, 4 FEP Cases 411 (5th Cir., 1972); United States v. Jacksonville Terminal Company, supra, p. 458-9; United States v. Bethlehem Steel Corporation, supra, p. 666.

We think the district court could reasonably set sixty days as the period within which the transfer option could be exercised. Jobs at Colgate are assigned each week. Considerations applicable where assignments are permanent, and vacancies infrequent, do not apply to this case. The period began at the close of the exposure program, designed to make choice of department as meaningful as possible, and tending to lessen the effect of any ingrained psychological impediments discouraging exercise of the option.

Appellants contend that the 1965 seniority which a female employee was granted in the secondary department chosen by her failed to equalize the position of female and male employees. Most of the male employees, however, who enjoy seniority in more than one department have less seniority than the 1965 date chosen by the court. Only 10% of the male employees have seniority in more than one department. We are unable to say that this provision was inadequate.

Appellants also contend that as a result of past layoffs and transfers which reflect discrimination, female employees have less seniority in their department, and that this will put them at a continuing disadvantage. They argue that the use of date-of-employment seniority for all purposes is therefore necessary.

It is clear to all, as found by the district court, that it would be impossible to reconstruct the employment history of each employee as if no discrimination existed, and to determine in all instances whether a female employee would have been better or worse off vis-a-vis male employees. In each of the numerous instances of layoff or involuntary transfer, not only would it have to be shown that junior employees were retained, but the effect on the subsequent work history of the individual would have to be ascertained. Considerations other than pay differential doubtless often affected job preference at the time of weekly assignments. Any determination could only rest on speculation.

The district court has, however, taken account of the problem and attempted to make corrections in the seniority status of women where the determination was feasible. Restoration of seniority was ordered for fourteen women who lost as much as eleven years of seniority in a layoff occurring in 1963, the last major layoff causing a loss of seniority as a result of discrimination.

The impossibility of reconstructing "true" seniority for all employees, does not, we think, necessitate conversion of the entire system to date-of-employment seniority, as sought by appellants. Both men and women have widely disparate departmental and date-of-employment seniority as a result of past layoffs and transfers. Some of the disparity for both doubtless reflects the operation of the discriminatory element of the former system; some results solely from the operation of the collective bargaining contract without regard to sex.

A primary purpose of relief from residual effects of past discrimination, accorded to minority workers in other Title VII actions, has been to insure that they do not continue to be locked out of previously restricted jobs or departments. There is evident no inherent reason why this purpose is better served by a carryover of date-of-employment rather than departmental seniority. If date-of-employment seniority were to be required in the present case, it would be superimposed on over twenty years of gains and losses in departmental status of both males and females often reflecting no discrimination. In framing a remedy it is appropriate to recognize the value of individual expectations not based on advantages derived from past discrimination. See United States v. National Lead Company, 438 F.2d 935, 938, 3 FEP Cases 211 (8th Cir., 1971).

Given the alternatives available to the district court, the impossibility of a perfect solution, and the propriety of attempting to minimize damage of interests not in themselves built upon discrimination, we find no abuse of discretion in selection of remedies.

Note: Former Departmental Versus Date-of-Employment Seniority

In other seniority discrimination cases, courts have awarded date-of-employment seniority. See, e.g., Robinson v. Lorillard Corp., 444 F.2d 791 (4th Cir. 1971), supra Section C-1. *Robinson,* however, did not have a complex, weekly job assignment system under which both blacks and whites had built up "widely disparate departmental and date-of-employment seniority as a result of past layoffs and transfers."[179] In fact, the *Robinson* court noted that[180]

> We recognize Lorillard's point that changing the seniority system may frustrate the expectations of employees who have established departmental seniority but not employment seniority in the preferable departments. However, Title VII guarantees that all employees are entitled to the *same* expectations regardless of "race, color, religion, sex, or national origin." Where some employees now have lower expectations than their coworkers because of the influence of one of these forbidden factors, they are entitled to have their expectations raised even if the expectations of others must be lowered in order to achieve the statutorily mandated equality of opportunity.

Note that the *Bowe* court, supra, was unwilling to impose date-of-employment seniority because gains and losses in departmental seniority were sometimes nondiscriminatory, and "it is appropriate to recognize the value of individual expectations not based on advantages derived from past discrimination."[181] Nevertheless, *Bowe* can be criticized for failing completely to correct the effects of past discrimination. For example, individual women may have low former-department seniority, acquired solely because of discriminatory layoffs when they were limited to jobs in the four women's departments. Some men hired at the same time as these women may have longer departmental seniority built up, because they were allowed to avoid layoff by bidding for jobs in all seventeen departments — an advantage not then available to women. Whenever a woman in this position competes with a man in this position to avoid layoff in her new department, she will be laid off if her combined (former and new) departmental seniority is less than his — even if his seniority is longer because of past discrimination in his favor. This situation creates a difficult balancing of equities: whether to injure some men who have nondiscriminatory seniority benefits, or harm some women who may still suffer some effects of past discrimination. How would you resolve this issue?

It is possible that the court reached this result in part because of inadequate proof on the issue of how much discrimination was built into the prior departmental seniority of individual women. Apparently, no new evidence was introduced after the Seventh Circuit's first reversal and remand in the case. Bowe v. Colgate-Palmolive Co., 416 F.2d 711 (7th Cir. 1969).

NOTE: ADDITIONAL SOURCES

For a forthcoming review (in 1974 or 1975) of the case law on remedies, both in seniority and other contexts, write to the EEOC, General Counsel's Office, 1800 G Street, N.W., Washington, D.C. 20506, for a "Remedies Sourcebook" by David Zugschwerdt. To understand more completely the operation of the complex Cogate-Palmolive seniority system, see Bowe v. Colgate-Palmolive Co., 272 F. Supp. 332, 340-347 (S.D. Ind. 1967). Note also the time lag from that initial decision to the decision reprinted above.

---

179. 6 FEP Cases at 1136.
180. 444 F.2d at 800.
181. 6 FEP Cases at 1136.

c. Settlements Providing Comprehensive Relief

COOPER AND RABB
EQUAL EMPLOYMENT LAW AND LITIGATION
420, 421-426 (1972)

. . . [Q]uotas are not always a complete solution [to remedying discrimination], particularly in a case of professional hiring where subjective evaluation of credentials is important. Consider the following outline of a conciliation agreement suggested by New York City's Commission on Human Rights to a law firm accused of discriminating against women in its recruitment, hiring, and promotion practices. The complaint and Commission decision in this case are set out [in Part E-2 supra]. This agreement is neither in final form nor exhaustive in its scope, but it does indicate the nature of the remedies that will be sought in these and similar cases. Do you think the law firm in question found this proposed conciliation agreement acceptable? Why? How are courts likely to react when faced with plaintiffs seeking this type of broad remedial program? It is indeed probable that cases such as this soon will be in the federal courts; their outcomes could have a profound impact on the course of future Title VII litigation.

PROPOSED SETTLEMENT AGREEMENT
FOR THE CASE OF LAW FIRM SEX DISCRIMINATION

I. Statement of General Principles

II. Administration

One individual will be responsible for record keeping, reporting and other aspects of administering the agreement.

III. Selection Criteria

A. All selection criteria must be job related. Any job related criterion which causes a disparate rejection rate of female attorneys for employment or promotion may not be utilized unless the firm can show that no other criterion is available which is designed to measure the same qualification and which does not have such effect.

B. Examples of impermissible criteria include, but are not limited to, the following:

1. Marital or family plans
2. Child care arrangements
3. Spouse's job
4. Clerical skills
5. Professional seriousness of the applicant
6. Ability to work with or supervise members of the opposite or same sex
7. Ability to bring clients to the firm

C. The firm shall not assume that women are unsuited for employment with the firm because the position requires travel, client contact, overtime work, work in certain courts, labor or other negotiations, and other similar performance, or because of client preference for male attorneys, and no woman shall be rejected because of such assumptions.

D. No woman shall be required to possess other or higher qualifications for the position of attorney or partner than those of the least qualified incumbent at the date of the referenced complaint.

E. All selection criteria for hiring, promotion and assignment shall forthwith be validated for job-relatedness in accordance with the Guidelines on Employee Selection Procedure issued August, 1970 by EEOC. The validation study will be submitted to the Commission for its approval.

IV. Recruitment

A. Advertising

1. Brochures, prospectuses or other hiring materials distributed by and about the firm shall refer to "men and women" or "he/she" where appropriate. These materials shall clearly state the firm's interest in employing both men and women as well as minorities.

2. Any recruitment advertisements placed by the firm in any of the media shall clearly state "Male/Female".

B. Referral Sources

1. Requests for referrals from employment agencies shall state the firm's interest in employing women.

2. Advance notification of 30 days shall be given to such groups as the Women's Bar Associations and New Women Lawyers regarding vacancies for experienced attorneys.

C. Law Schools

1. The firm must recruit at law schools which have high percentages of female students, including but not limited to Columbia, N.Y.U., Harvard, Yale, Berkeley, Hastings and Rutgers.

2. Notification to placement offices of the firm's interest in recruiting at the school shall indicate the firm's interest in interviewing and hiring women.

3. The firm agrees to interview all female applicants who express an interest in the firm, who have complied with the procedure for obtaining an interview, and who meet any academic law school standard which the firm has established as a minimum qualification for an interview.

a. If the school pre-screens interviewees, the firm will request that sufficient time be allotted to it to enable it to see every female applicant meeting the firm's academic minimum qualification. If this is not possible, the firm will request that at least one out of every three interviewees be a woman.

b. If the school requires or allows the firm to pre-screen applicants, the firm agrees to interview, either on campus or at its offices, every female applicant who meets its minimum academic standard and, if this is not possible, to interview one female applicant for every two male applicants interviewed.

D. Record of firm's performance on the above shall be kept and reported to the Commission in prescribed form.

V. Hiring

A. Interviews

1. The firm will describe its non-discrimination policy to each female interviewee.

2. Interviewers will be required to record in writing and report their reasons for failing to recommend a female applicant for interview by the Hiring Committee.

3. The Hiring Committee will be required to record in writing and report its reasons for failing to invite for an in-house interview any female applicant recommended by a recruiter. Transportation costs and other courtesies extended to male applicants shall be extended to female applicants on an equal basis.

4. If the Hiring Committee fails to hire a female applicant after an in-house interview it will make a written record and report of its reasons.

B. Hiring Process

1. Applications from women will be accepted whether or not vacancies currently exist.

2. If the applicant is clearly unqualified for any position in the firm she will be promptly notified.

3. If she is qualified but not immediately hired her application will be kept in the Affirmative Action file for one year and she will be notified of vacancies arising during that time.

4. Offers to female applicants shall be made concurrently with offers made to similarly ranked men.

C. Hiring Commitment

1. One out of every two summer associates hired each summer shall be female.

2. One out of every three permanent associates hired shall be female.

D. Record of firm's performance on the above shall be kept and reported to the Commission.

VI. Assignment and Classification

A. All job assignments shall be made without regard to sex. Women shall be eligible for assignment to all jobs within the firm.

B. Women will be offered their choice of assignments and given the option to transfer among departments on the same basis as men.

VII. Promotion

A. Within 90 days the firm will accord partnership status to a woman.

B. Women associates shall advance in status on a basis equally applicable to male associates. Women asked to resign from the firm will be accorded the same treatment as similarly situated men. The firm will submit to the Commission its written reasons for requesting any woman's resignation from the firm.

C. If any female associate who has been admitted to practice six or more years and who has served two years or more with the firm is not offered partnership, the reasons for such action shall be justified in writing in each year that she is passed over in the partnership decision. If a woman is passed over an established number of times it will be considered a prima facie violation.

D. Goals and timetables will be established for female partners.

VIII. Terms and Conditions of Employment

A. Women will be assigned to work on cases on the same basis as are men and will travel and/or meet with clients as the cases demand.

B. Fringe Benefits

1. Medical, hospital, accident, life insurance, retirement benefits, profit-sharing and bonus plans shall be equally available to male and female attorneys, and will not be conditioned upon status as "head of household" or "principal wage earner."

2. Any benefits which are made available to wives and/or families of male attorneys will be made equally available to husbands and/or families of female attorneys, and any benefits made available to the wives of male attorneys shall be made equally available to female attorneys, whether or not the cost of such benefits is greater with respect to women.

3. Disabilities caused or contributed to by pregnancy, miscarriage, abortion, childbirth and recovery therefrom will be treated as other temporary disabilities for disability insurance or sick leave purposes.

4. Employees will be granted six months child-care leave for the birth of a child but an employee may elect to take a shorter leave.

C. Miscellaneous

1. Within 90 days of the execution of this agreement, the firm shall petition the Sky Club to revise its exclusionary policies toward women and if said Club does not comply with said request, the firm shall discontinue its practice of paying initiation or membership fees for members of the firm, so notifying the Sky Club.

2. Female attorneys in the firm shall be invited and encouraged to participate in all company-sponsored events.

IX. Relief for Complainant

The firm will pay the complainant the salary she would have earned during the summer of 1971, plus interest, minus her actual earnings that summer as well as $1,000 additional damages. In addition the firm will offer the complainant full-time employment as an associate commencing October 2, 1972.

X. Reporting

Detailed reports regarding the above enumerated activities will be submitted to the City Commission on Human Rights on a regular basis.

XI. Compliance

Reviews will be held by the Commission at regular intervals.

XII. Grievance Committee

A grievance committee will be established within the firm to handle sex discrimination complaints in a manner to be prescribed in the agreement.

In January 1973, the AT&T case, supra Section B-4-a, was settled by consent decree.[182] An article from Ms. Magazine describes some of the settlement's main features, as well as some serious criticisms that have been leveled against it.

WOHL, LIBERATING MA BELL
Ms. Magazine, 52, 92-97 (November 1973)

AT&T's troubles deepened when all the government agencies responsible for enforcing equal opportunity laws joined together in one action. Besides the EEOC, Bell had been under attack from the government on several flanks. The Department of Labor, for example, had been after Bell for more than five years in actions involving the Equal Pay Act. After one government agency almost made a settlement with Bell that would have seriously undercut the EEOC negotiations, the Labor Department suggested that all government agencies interested in civil rights enforcement get together. Ultimately, Bell faced a combination of the EEOC, the FCC, the Department of Labor, and the Department of Justice. "The AT&T case was the first to involve this kind of concerted action among government agencies," former EEOC chairman Brown said. "This is something we ought to continue to do." . . .

Some feminists have criticized the government's willingness to negotiate a consent decree rather than sue Bell in court. They charge that a formal court decision might have won more money and opportunities for women and minorities and that it would have set a more powerful precedent for future cases.

---

182. The decree was entered in a rather hasty federal court lawsuit, filed and settled in one day, brought to enforce Title VII, the Equal Pay Act (see Part III, infra) and Executive Order 11246 (see Part IV, infra). As a result, the EEOC proceedings before the FCC were withdrawn. In reading the description of the settlement, it should be kept in mind that some aspects of the settlement respond to laws other than Title VII; e.g., goals and timetables are required of government contractors under the executive order, although they are also an appropriate remedy in a Title VII lawsuit.

[An EEOC attorney],[183] however, defends the decision to sign rather than sue. "When we started the case, the EEOC didn't have the power to go to court," he said, "and when we obtained that right from Congress in March, 1972, the negotiations were pretty far along. Going back to a court case would have taken a lot of time and a lot of money, and it is not at all clear we would have won anything more."

Although he agreed that a consent decree does not have the same legal force as a court decision, he said, "All the major companies see the handwriting on the wall, and it's a big dollar sign. This case made it clear that the government can and will crack down on large companies that discriminate."

Left unsettled by the consent decree are more than 2,200 EEOC cases against Bell filed by individuals. When these are settled, women who have other complaints against Bell may sue in the courts. But by and large the EEOC will concentrate on enforcing its agreement. In effect, the government is saying this settlement is the best we can get.

How good is the government's best? In many ways it is very good indeed. The consent decree asserts control over virtually all official aspects of Bell's personnel policies. The company must desegregate everything from the recruiting booklet it sends to a high school in Seattle to the population and practices of its Manhattan headquarters offices.

Goals and timetables are the foundation for change. The Bell System has been divided into 700 geographical subdivisions called "establishments." Each will design its own affirmative action plan, using an EEOC formula to establish goals that reflect local hiring and job-pool conditions. New York City, for example, with its large Puerto Rican population, will have a far higher goal for Spanish Americans than Topeka, Kansas.

According to Bell, the systemwide goals for the end of 1975 are: 5 percent women in third-level management and above; 5.2 percent in skilled outside craft jobs, such as splicer; 9.6 percent in skilled inside craft jobs, such as switchperson; 12 percent in semiskilled outside craft jobs, such as installer-repairperson; and 35.1 percent in semiskilled inside craft jobs such as frameperson. Final goals have not been agreed upon, but samples include: 19 percent women in skilled and semiskilled outside craft jobs and 38 percent in skilled and semiskilled inside craft jobs. Many of these final goals are subject to renegotiation depending on changes in local job markets. While the intermediate 1975 goals seem shockingly low, the EEOC assures us that the ultimate goals can be renegotiated upward as more women enter the labor force.

Goals and timetables are nothing new in affirmative action plans, but the AT&T agreement dramatically expands their use by requiring that men be eligible for traditional "women's jobs." For example, about 10 percent of all new operators hired and 37.5 percent of new clerical workers must be male. These male hiring objectives — applied for the first time in this case — could have a major impact on sex stereotypes. . . .

The decree also offers women at Bell a chance to escape their job ghettos through the new upgrade-and-transfer plan. Under the decree, women and minority workers may apply for any company job. Company transfer bureaus will announce openings on a quarterly basis, and also report on how previous jobs were filled.

In an important step forward, seniority will be evaluated on the basis of an employee's years in the company rather than years in a specific job or department. Thus, a woman operator who has worked at Bell 20 years will not have to start at the bottom level of the craft jobs. She will have the same access as a man with 20 years' service and can jump a man with 19 years in a craft job.

Company seniority will also be the criterion for establishing employees' pay in-

183. An interesting omission from this account and other published articles about the settlement is the role of women law students and lawyers at EEOC in the development of the case. The white male task force leader, cited frequently in the article, apparently neglected to mention that feminist women had participated in the case. — Eds.

creases as they move up to better jobs. Formerly, pay increases were based on an employee's previous salary. But since women were invariably paid less than men, this system would have made it impossible for women workers ever to catch up to the pay of their male co-workers. Now John and Joan, who both worked at Bell for 15 years, will get the same pay when they become cable splicers, even though John made considerably more than Joan before.

The use of company seniority to determine promotions and pay increases was first developed in cases involving race discrimination, but the AT&T agreement is the first major action to apply this principle as a remedy for sex bias. Bell estimates that the new promotion pay plan will cost the company $36 million in additional wages in 1973.

The government has served notice that it wants these hiring and transfer goals to be met. One key provision rules out in advance a common excuse for affirmative action failure — testing. Bell may continue to use its carefully developed testing battery to select new employees. But the decree states that Bell must meet its goals whether or not it finds enough people to pass its tests. If too many fail, Bell must find other ways to select female and minority workers. . . .

The decree also includes creative approaches to ensure that Bell acts affirmatively. Special management-assessment centers are under way for those women college graduates who were hired into management but excluded from Bell's male-only accelerated executive training programs. Those women who prove their management potential can be targeted for rapid promotion. Unfortunately, because of legal technicalities, the number of women affected is very small — only about 2,000 female college graduates who were hired into management between July 2, 1965, and December 31, 1971. Many other women say they too need special assessments, but so far Bell hasn't made any promises.

AT&T will also be required to revise all company literature, from magazine ads to job descriptions, to eliminate sex and race stereotypes. You've probably noticed the ads showing Alana McFarlane at work as a repairperson atop a telephone pole — one result of this provision. Again, the EEOC hopes for a "ripple effect" that will change consciousness about female and minority workers throughout the society.

Finally, Bell must pay for its sins. The amount, $15 million, is the largest back-pay settlement in history, although it seems to diminish considerably when you realize that Bell had earnings of roughly $2.5 billion last year.

As part of the $15 million, the company has agreed to make "delayed restitution" — lump-sum payments ranging from $100 to $400 — to the first 10,000 female and minority employees who move from noncraft to craft jobs. "Delayed restitution is a new concept," [an] EEOC attorney . . . explained. "The law normally requires an individual to show she or he was discriminated against and personally lost money before the court will order back pay. But most operators never bothered to apply for craft jobs because they knew they would be turned down. The fact that they didn't apply doesn't mean that Bell didn't discriminate. This payment is a symbolic gesture for women who would have earned more if Bell's entire personnel structure had not been biased. We think this theory applies to a great many other companies."

Bell will also give a total of $500,000 to about 500 "switchroom helpers" at Michigan Bell. According to William J. Kilberg, Department of Labor solicitor, this payment may point the way to a new remedy for industry-wide wage discrimination.

So far, the attorney explained, the courts will rule unequal pay only if a woman can show she earns less than men who do the same job in her company. A company that hired only women for a particular job and paid them less than men who did the same job in other companies was safe from legal attack [under the Equal Pay Act].

Michigan Bell, technically an independent company, hired only women for the switchroom-helper job and paid them all the same. However, the same job at other Bell companies was called "frameman," was held only by men, and paid considerably more. In obtaining back pay for Michigan Bell's switchroom helpers, the government may have opened the way to ending the separate and lower wage scale that exists for women in ghettoized categories that cross company lines.

Also included in the $15-million back-pay settlement are those college women who successfully compete in the special management assessment centers, and the 3,000 women currently in craft jobs.

For all its considerable achievements, the consent decree encountered mixed reviews when it was announced in January, 1973. An immediate protest came from the Communication Workers of America, the union representing about 600,000 telephone company workers. CWA asked the court to delay implementing the decree because of alleged violations of the union's collective bargaining rights. . . .

Civil rights groups were generally enthusiastic, though with reservations. "The agreement does many, many good things for women and blacks," said William Wells, an attorney for the NAACP. "But it still doesn't go far enough. There are many areas where the EEOC documented discrimination that are left out."

One omission is the decree's failure to set goals at the highest levels of management. The government says this would be difficult because of the small numbers of positions involved, but some official pressure to move women and minorities beyond the middle management rank may be needed.

NOW said the agreement "vastly expanded job opportunities for females and minority males," but also indicated it wasn't totally satisfied. "Chicken feed" was president Wilma Scott Heide's verdict on the back-pay settlement, and NOW considered the goals and timetables "manifestly inadequate."

Sally Hacker, coordinator of the NOW task force on AT&T, argued that an ultimate goal such as 19 percent women in skilled outside craft jobs is entirely too low, given that women are 60 percent of the Bell work force and 53 percent of the population. Hacker also charged that the EEOC's "utilization plan," the formula used to develop goals, underestimates the potential number of women and minority workers. "For example, they don't consider housewives as part of the labor market," she explained.

The government decree also allowed Bell to evade key provisions of the EEOC's own guidelines on maternity benefits. The Commission has ruled that pregnancy should be treated like an illness or temporary disability when computing job benefits. Women who cannot work because of pregnancy are therefore entitled to disability pay, just as men are for hernias and prostate troubles.

Bell agreed to drop its rules requiring women to quit work at a specific time in their pregnancies — seven months, for example. But the company refused to provide disability pay for childbirth, estimating the rule could cost between $26 million and $58 million a year.

"We decided not to junk the whole agreement on this issue," [an EEOC] attorney . . . said, "It's now being litigated in the courts, and we're very optimistic about the result." (Meanwhile, NOW's Sally Hacker urges all Bell women who go on maternity leave to formally request disability benefits. If the court decides against Bell, those who apply now may be entitled to retroactive benefits.)

The decree also fails to include two Bell subsidiaries, Western Electric Company and Bell Telephone Laboratories. These companies were not involved in the original rate request before the FCC and could not be brought into the case. AT&T has said these companies already have affirmative action plans which they will voluntarily bring "substantially" into agreement with the decree. Whether or not this happens will be a key test of the company's good faith.

Finally, the decree does not demand the special assistance many women need to fully take their place in the work force. For example, child-care centers are not required. The company now operates two centers on an experimental basis and says it will open more "if they prove useful." But on an ominous note, AT&T recently closed a third center in Cleveland, Ohio. Data on the center is still being analyzed, but so far AT&T says it has found "no significant differences in absences or turnover between those who use the center and those who don't." What Bell apparently doesn't see is that a child-care center alone couldn't cure the problem of dead-end, low-paying jobs. And usefulness to employees who are parents should be the criterion — not Bell's perhaps unrealistic desire to cut down in employee turnover.

The decree also does not oblige Bell to encourage women to enter fields they have traditionally avoided. The company, for example, helped support a project to develop more black engineers. Similar programs for women are necessary. "Bell has helped create poor women's images," charges NOW's Sally Hacker. "Now they have an obligation to help change those images." . . .

AT&T, for its part, has accepted the consent decree with public grace. "Yes, I think it's a good agreement," said company president Robert D. Lilley. "All the litigation and questions are cleared up. It relieves the uncertainty and releases our energies to get the job done. That's what counts."

However, the AT&T chief said he has not yet read Unique Competence — an admission that earns him a gold star for honesty but somewhat undermines a claim to total involvement in the cause of ending discrimination. (NOW president Wilma Scott Heide has suggested the EEOC's landmark document be distributed to every Bell employee, an idea the company has pointedly ignored.)

And Lilley steadfastly denies that AT&T ever deliberately discriminated. The position of women at Bell, he says, "reflected the culture around us," adding that the rapid evolution in civil rights law made it difficult for the company to know what its obligations were. This defense won't wash with feminists who note that Bell, as a monopoly, created its own sex stereotypes from Emma Nutt onward.

Despite its insistence on innocence, the indications are that Bell's top management has begun to tackle its legal obligations. Back payments owed to craft women have been substantially completed. The revision of company literature is well under way and a series of one-hour meetings have been held to inform every employee of the decree's content — although a more intensive effort may be necessary for each employee to understand how this very complex agreement affects her or him. At least one company, New Jersey Bell, has opened a "hot line" so that employees who are afraid to ask their bosses about the settlement can get information.

AT&T has laid out the organization for its upgrade-and-transfer plan, and goals and timetables have been worked out for Bell's 700 establishments. The company said it is optimistic about meeting most hiring objectives. In the first quarter of 1973, for example, men comprised 16 percent of all new operator hires, well above the mandatory 10 percent hiring share. Males were 20 percent of all new clerical hires, a better reaction than Bell had expected, although still below the mandatory 37.5 percent share. Women also responded to new opportunities although female hires were still below the agreement targets.

"In this kind of business we're accustomed to thinking in accounting and engineering terms," said Gene Kofke, who is assistant vice-president in charge of equal employment at New Jersey Bell. "When you express something in quantitative terms, people seem to know what is expected of them, and they do it."

Some telephone company women agree. Geri Milek, network manager at New York Telephone, thinks that Bell will enforce the decree because "this is a straight-line organization. They really will follow through with what they are required to do by law."

But others are taking a wait-and-see attitude. "What's written on a piece of paper isn't what's important and what people at the top say doesn't matter all that much," said a woman training-specialist at AT&T. "This plan is going to work only if it is followed through, and that depends on a lot of white males down the ranks."

There's evidence that blatant discrimination still occurs even in the reformed Ma Bell. "My boss told me flatly that he doesn't believe in affirmative action," said an angry communications consultant at New York Telephone. "Later when I asked about a transfer to a line job, he told me women don't like that kind of work."

At a higher rank, one of the few women who has managed to achieve Level III management at Bell said she recently interviewed at two operating companies for promotion to Level IV. "I was told that even if I were accepted for the Fourth-Level job, I could not expect promotion to Level Five in the future. They said they had no intention of letting a woman break that barrier. They clearly thought I was some kind of freak and that I should be delighted with whatever they offered."

Furthermore, women at Bell still face the subtle sexism that undercuts morale and leadership ability. A woman who recently attended her first meeting with senior AT&T executives (all male) reported, "I went through that very, very excluded feeling. They clearly didn't know how to treat me. I felt like a piece of spinach in someone's teeth."

And sexism in the past cannot have left Bell women unscathed. Women's aspirations have been low because they have had to be, and second-class status has undoubtedly created poor self-images for many workers. "Now all of a sudden we're expected to raise our goals and develop attitudes and skills they didn't want us to have before," complained one chief operator.

Company-wide consciousness-raising or sensitivity training programs may ultimately be necessary to make equal employment a reality at Bell. In the past, the company has held a few such programs on race relations for selected employees.

Donald E. Liebers — AT&T personnel director in charge of employment and equal opportunity — does not rule out consciousness-raising as a future possibility. But, he stated, "Trying to change people's attitudes is not the way to make equal employment a reality. I think the way to do this is to establish targets and say we are going to meet those goals."

"You have to remember that people coming into the work force now have already developed according to a certain societal pattern," he continued. "It's a problem for us and it's a problem for women. I don't think it's entirely up to the business community to implement a social revolution."

No matter where responsibility for change should lie, there's little doubt that equal opportunity will come only if women insist on it. Women at AT&T have already organized the New York-based AT&T Alliance for Women, a management-recognized group that seeks to help the company meet its equal employment obligations. The mood at the Alliance is reformist rather than radical, but members say it is an effective pipeline, bringing women's concerns to the attention of management. In other Bell companies, women are beginning to organize on the Alliance model, and some underground and more aggressive feminist organizations are being discussed.

But the vast majority of women inside Bell will inevitably move gingerly toward reform. "This is an extremely hierarchical and conservative organization," said one feminist, who did not want her name used. "No one wants a radical or 'libber' tag stuck on them if they plan to get ahead."

NOW's Sally Hacker believes that "a great deal of pressure must continue to come from women outside Bell." While the EEOC is responsible for enforcing the decree, its resources are obviously limited. The NOW task force on AT&T is monitoring Bell's performance, and relevant information may be sent to Sally Hacker, c/o Drake University, Des Moines, Iowa 50311.

NOTE

Various documents from the AT&T settlement are reprinted in the Bureau of National Affairs FEP Manual 431:73. Included are the consent order, a model affirmative action program, and a model upgrading and transfer plan. A more technical discussion of the settlement than the Ms. article is Crothers, The AT&T Settlement, Women's Rights L. Rep. 5 (Summer 1973). Crothers also discusses a related case, decided after the

AT&T settlement had been filed: Leisner v. New York Telephone Co., 5 FEP Cases 732 (S.D.N.Y. 1973).[184]

> Female management employees in a class action sought injunctive relief against New York Telephone Company's use of non-validated tests and criteria to determine interests and qualifications for various jobs and training opportunities. Plaintiffs also alleged that these criteria have been applied more stringently with respect to women and they noted the wide discretion given to interviewers making these decisions.
>
> On the issue of whether or not the plaintiffs were barred by the consent decree [settling the AT&T case], Judge Constance Baker Motley held they were not barred for two reasons. The motions in this case were pending at the time the EEOC complaint was filed and the consent decree entered. And the court noted that the Second Circuit held in Williamson v. Bethlehem Steel Corp.,[81] that for purposes of res judicata or collateral estoppel, private citizens were not bound by a prior action brought by the Attorney General ". . . since they neither were parties to it . . . nor have interests such as to be in privity with the Attorney General. . . ."[82]
>
> The court in *Leisner* commented on future suits by individual plaintiffs: "The benefits of that decree [EEOC decree] are available . . . only to those who affirmatively elect to relinquish *any* complaint of discrimination against the Company in exchange for relief provided by the decree." (emphasis added)[83] Thus, if one accepts a lump sum payment under the consent decree, one may not bring suit on another claim of discrimination.
>
> *Leisner* is of particular interest, as the plaintiffs raise issues which highlight some of the inadequacies of the decree; an example of the allegedly non-job-related criteria for promotion of which the plaintiffs complain is the interviewers' definition of the requirement of "supervisory experience", necessary for promotion. Military experience is acceptable to meet this requirement, while teaching experience is not. Obviously, such a distinction has an adverse effect on women employees' promotion opportunities, while not being strictly prohibited under the consent decree.
>
> The court in *Leisner* held that "while the consent decree is a commendable step toward the enlargement of opportunities for women. . . . it is inadequate to protect the interests of the class in the action pending before this court."[84] The court found two areas in which this inadequacy appeared: "(I)t is not clear that (AT&T) is enjoined from discrimination on the basis of sex, as to individual employees, so long as it makes a good faith effort to comply with the broad goals of the Program,"[85] or "whether the decree actually enjoins use of criteria which disadvantage women and which are not both job-related and the only suitable means of screening unqualified applicants."[86]
>
> On this basis, the court granted a preliminary injunction which bars "the use of criteria for the filling of vacancies which are not utilized on an equal basis with respect to men and women, which the defendant cannot demonstrate to be predictive of success in the job, and for which the defendant cannot demonstrate that alternative suitable hiring, transfer or promotion procedures are unavailable . . ."[87]

Yet another action was brought against the New York Telephone Company by the New York State Attorney General under the state Human Rights Law, N.Y. Exec. Law §297. The settlement in that case, including the formulas used to set goals and timetables, is discussed in Rourke, The New York Telephone Settlement: A Study In Contrast, Women's Rights L. Rep. 15 (Summer 1973).

For a more complete discussion of the history and development of the AT&T settlement, see Shapiro, Women On The Line, Men At The Switchboard, The New York Times Magazine 26 (May 20, 1973).

---

184. Crothers, The AT&T Settlement, Women's Rights L. Rep. 5, 13 (Summer 1973).
81. 5 FEP Cas. 204 (2d Cir. Nov. 3, 1972).
82. 5 FEP Cas. at 205
83. *Leisner*, 5 FEP Cas. at 739.
84. Id. at 741.
85. Id. at 741-2.
86. Id. at 742.
87. Id.

d. Preliminary Injunctions

COOPER AND RABB
EQUAL EMPLOYMENT LAW AND LITIGATION
374-376 (1972)

STANDARDS FOR GRANTING THE INJUNCTION

The securing of prompt relief may often be as important as the scope of relief secured. The normal action in court moves very slowly; by the time that the complaint has been filed, pretrial motions heard and ruled upon, an answer filed, discovery conducted and trial completed, many months or even years will have elapsed. Although the availability of back pay relief somewhat mitigates the harshness of this delay, it is a problem which should not be tolerated if it can be avoided. A preliminary injunction (and/or a TRO) pursuant to Rule 65 of the Federal Rules of Civil Procedure is the usual device for expediting matters. Motion for summary judgment pursuant to Rule 56 may also be used but that is available only where there is no factual dispute — a rarity in the factually complex world of Title VII litigation.

The usual standard for granting a preliminary injunction is a showing of the probability of eventual success on the merits and irreparable injury because of delay. However, the courts have been relatively favorable to granting preliminary injunctions in Title VII cases, following the lead of the Fifth Circuit in United States v. Hayes International Co., 415 F.2d 1038 (5th Cir. 1969), which held that statistics showing blacks concentrated in poorer jobs could demonstrate "a preliminary showing that the company hiring practices violated Title VII," and that in such a situation it is not necessary to make an additional showing of irreparable injury.

> We take the position that in such a case, irreparable injury should be presumed from the very fact that the statute has been violated. Whenever a qualified Negro employee is discriminatorily denied a chance to fill a position for which he is qualified and has the seniority to obtain, he suffers irreparable injury and so does the labor force of the country as a whole. 415 F.2d at 1045.

Sometimes the very scope of relief sought in a preliminary injunction may make this issue the focus of the case and one that may be bitterly contested. Chance v. Board of Examiners, [330 F. Supp. 203 (S.D.N.Y. 1971), *aff'd,* 458 F.2d 1167 (2d Cir. 1972),] is a good example. In affirming the decision of the district court to grant the preliminary injunction, the United States Court of Appeals for the Second Circuit noted that "the impact of the interim order is sizeable," that "[w]e are dealing here not with abstractions but with people," and that "the injunction intrudes upon the operation of a school system in which clearly the local, rather than the federal, authorities, have primary responsibility." 458 F.2d 1167, 1178 (2d Cir. 1972). Nonetheless, the Second Circuit held that the order of the district court "was not improper" and it agreed that "there was a strong likelihood that plaintiffs would prevail on the merits at trial." Given the nature of the relief sought by the plaintiffs and the results of the extended hearings held on the motion for a preliminary injunction, it is apparent that the granting of the preliminary injunction has, in effect, contributed greatly to the ultimate disposition of the case.

This does not mean, however, that a preliminary injunction can be expected as a matter of course.

Note: Other Cases

After the above excerpt, Cooper and Rabb reprint two cases; although they involve similar facts, a preliminary injunction was granted in only one case. See Rios v. Enterprise Association Steamfitters, Local 638, 326 F. Supp. 198 (S.D.N.Y. 1971) (granting a preliminary injunction giving union membership to three of the four named plaintiffs), and Sims v. Sheetmetal Workers International Association, Local 65, 3 EPD ¶8278, 3 FEP Cases 712 (N.D. Ohio 1971) (denying a preliminary injunction giving union membership to three named plaintiffs).

Recently, academic women have begun to use Title VII to challenge denial of tenure and loss of jobs. Preliminary injunctions are particularly important to keep them on the faculty pending ultimate resolution of their claims. In Johnson v. University of Pittsburgh, 5 FEP Cases 1182 (W.D. Pa. 1973), the court granted a preliminary injunction restraining the university from discharging plaintiff or denying her tenure until her claim of sex discrimination was litigated. The court described the harm to plaintiff that would result if the injunction was not granted, as follows:[185]

> [W]e note that this is not the ordinary case of a salaried employee who is wrongfully discharged where a remedy in damages is adequate. Rather here we have a Ph.D with an outstanding professional reputation which will be unquestionably damaged by this. Her ability to get a job will certainly be impaired because of inability to secure recommendations from her present employers. It appears that jobs are very difficult to obtain at this time for people in this field and the mere fact of her discharge or failure to receive tenure from the University of Pittsburgh would naturally chill her chances of obtaining another position. Beyond this, we have the factor of the irreparable damage to plaintiff's reputation as a research scientist as the result of this discharge and also the effect upon the grant which the National Institution [sic] of Health has given to the University for research to be done by her. It was testified that while much of the equipment which had been purchased for this grant would not be destroyed nevertheless much of it would be rendered worthless, and the research already done on the project would be wasted. While the University has offered to transfer the grant to any other institute where plaintiff might get a job, nevertheless it is obvious that she is not going to get a job with any other institution and this is a futile gesture. We thus have very little difficulty in finding irreparable hardship to plaintiff.

Is the distinction the court draws between professional and salaried employees valid? It would seem to parallel the equitable exception of contracts for personal services from specific performance. Given the court's reliance on interrupted research, would the case for a preliminary injunction be harder to make out if the professor in question were in the humanities?

2. Back Pay

COOPER AND RABB
EQUAL EMPLOYMENT LAW AND LITIGATION
427-428 (1972)

BACK PAY AND OTHER DAMAGE REMEDIES

It has been suggested that the pursuit of intricate future remedies is fruitless because the orders are never strong enough to prevent recalcitrant employers from taking evasive action. If that observation is correct, then the back pay remedy may loom as most important because it is, in effect, a penalty for recalcitrance which generates a large

---

185. 5 FEP Cases at 1188.

deterrent effect. The 1972 amendments to Title VII, which limit back pay recoveries to two years before the date of filing charges (Sec. 706(g)), mitigate but do not eliminate the value of pursuing back pay. However, the back pay remedy is not without other problems, as [indicated by the decision in United States v. Wood Lathers, Local 46, 328 F. Supp. 429 (S.D.N.Y. 1971)]. . . . Back pay was ordered in this case as part of a contempt award after the Union had first violated a consent order. At the time of this writing, more than one year after the order was entered, a master appointed by the court has still not been able to figure out the appropriate back pay award for each member of the class.

Because of the potential effectiveness of monetary remedies, plaintiff's lawyers have considered "front pay" demands as well as back pay. A "front pay" award would consist of lost earnings which the class will suffer in the future because the employer cannot, as a practical matter, immediately place them in the jobs they should have had. Do you see any difficulties with this?

It should also be noted that a federal district court has recently held in a Title VII case that "a punitive damage remedy might in an appropriate case be a proper award." Tooles v. Kellog Co., 336 F. Supp. 142 (D. Neb. 1972). Though an uncommon and extraordinary remedy, punitive damages could, if pursued successfully in a few extreme cases, have a decided impact on Title VII litigation in some areas.[186] Are there valid reasons why, even as an unusual remedy, punitive damages may be denied in Title VII actions?

The decision in Bowe v. Palmolive Co., supra, also dealt with the issue of the adequacy of a back pay award. That portion of the opinion is presented here to demonstrate some of the factors that must be considered in the formula for computing back pay. The decision evidences a very generous approach to back pay; on this point, see also Bowe v. Colgate-Palmolive Co., 416 F.2d 711 (7th Cir. 1969) (holding that all members of the class are entitled to back pay, whether or not they have filed EEOC charges or joined in the federal law suit), and Robinson v. Lorillard Corp., 444 F.2d 791 (4th Cir. 1971).

BOWE v. PALMOLIVE COMPANY
6 FEP Cases 1132, 1133, 1136-1138 (7th Cir. 1973)

. . . Plaintiff Georgianna Sellers and others have appealed, claiming . . . that the back-pay awards did not reasonably represent the difference between the amount earned by the women and the amount they would have earned had no discrimination been practiced. . . .

. . . [W]e conclude . . . that the back-pay relief granted does not adequately compensate all members of the class for past discrimination. . . .

BACK PAY AWARD

The district court awarded money judgments for back pay in favor of 54 women. 31 were allowed compensation for a period of layoff in 1965, following the effective date of Title VII; 32 awards represented a differential between the amount received as wages for time worked since the effective date and the amount which would have been earned had the system not been discriminatory.

In each case the problem was to determine in some reasonable fashion "the highest rate of pay for such jobs as [the employee] would have bid on and qualified for if a nondiscriminatory seniority scheme would have been in existence." 416 F.2d at 721, 2

---

186. In late 1973, a district court judge awarded substantial punitive damages against the employer ($4,000,000) and the union ($250,000) in United States v. Detroit Edison Co., 365 F. Supp. 87 (E.D. Mich. 1973). — Eds.

FEP Cases at 127. As already observed, exact reconstruction of the work history of each employee had the system contained no discriminatory element is impossible. The district court chose a test period so as to determine on the basis of experience the jobs each employee would have performed in the absence of discrimination. The period selected was from March 9, 1970 through May 31, 1970, the twelve weeks beginning shortly after the preliminary injunction opening all jobs to women.

Women who obtained the better paid general labor jobs during the test period were awarded the difference between their actual pay for time since July 2, 1965 and an amount computed for the same period on the basis of their individual hourly rate during the test period, less adjustments for contractual increases. They did not, however, receive an upward adjustment in vacation or sick pay, or in the Christmas bonus.

All women who had been laid off in 1965, while men junior to them were retained, received an allowance for that period. Those who did not obtain general labor jobs during the test period, or who had ceased to be employed at Colgate, were paid at the higher of the two finishing labor rates.

We conclude that there were several deficiencies in the method used by the court to compute the amounts of and entitlement to back pay.

A principal deficiency is the selection of the test period. To be valid, the period must be one in which both current and residual discrimination was no longer in operation. It was only a week earlier that the preliminary injunction ordered Colgate to permit women to bid on all jobs. Because the seniority system required women to start as new employees in a new department, the segregation of women within a few departments remained frozen. While a woman could bid on the heavier and better paying jobs in her department, she was unable successfully to bid on those jobs in a different department. In TAF, where most of the women were employed, there were few general labor jobs available. The needs recognized by the court in providing the transfer and secondary department options were present, but those options were not yet available. The test period was therefore not representative for the purpose of determining the jobs in which female employees would have been employed had there been no discrimination in the system.

There were other deficiencies in the procedure for making the awards. Some members of the class who had worked for substantial periods after the effective date of Title VII, and thus been exposed to the discriminatory elements of the system, had resigned or retired before the test period. No differential allowance was made to them on the basis of comparability to others who did have experience in the test period, or on the basis of the average of those who had such experience, or otherwise. Leaving them out implies a presumption that they suffered no loss as a result of discrimination, and we think that to the extent any presumption is to be applied, it must be the opposite. Similarly the award of layoff back pay, based on the highest finishing labor rate, to women who were not employed during the test period implies an unwarranted presumption that they would not have chosen better paying jobs if they had had the opportunity.

There were others, still on the payroll, whose experience during the test period was, on account of illness or some other demonstrable reason, not fairly representative. In some instances aging between the effective date of Title VII and the test period may have been a substantial and reasonably demonstrable factor, since the opportunity for an employee to improve her earnings depended on her willingness to do heavier work. Colgate has really offered no justification for lack of adjustment for these factors, or for the failure to allow for the difference between vacation, sick pay, and bonus actually paid on the basis of the earnings received and those items if computed on the basis of test period earnings.

We conclude that there must be a new computation of both differential and layoff back pay awards. Appellants would apparently prefer an allowance based on the average earning rate of all male employees during the appropriate periods. Such an average, however, would reflect an assumption that the female employees would have chosen and been qualified to perform the heaviest jobs as often and to the same extent as male employees. Apparently there are jobs as to which that assumption would be inaccurate. It is claimed, also, that there are some jobs requiring technical skills that few or none of the female employees possessed. The record would not support a decision that the members of the class would be entitled as a matter of right of a computation based on average earning rate of men, just referred to.

Assuming, as is entirely probable, that experience during a test period is the best available basis for determination of what members of the class would have earned in the absence of discrimination, a new test period should be selected and used. The period should begin a reasonable time after the exercise of all transfer and secondary department options. It should be reasonably representative of plant operations. Members of the class should not be excluded from relief because they did not happen to be employed during the test period. In instances where the experience during the test period was not representative for some employee, adjustments should be made. Vacation, sick pay, and bonus should also be appropriately adjusted. Where resort to presumption is deemed necessary, the presumption should be in favor of the member of the class. Each class member should be allowed differential back pay for all time she worked from the effective date of Title VII until the beginning of the new test period.

The determination of damages for injury can rarely be exact. We are confident that in those instances where the district court finds that experience in the test period does not provide a reasonable and fair basis for an award, the court can devise a method for making a fair and reasonable approximation of the money loss for each individual, with a foundation as adequate as the law requires for an award of damages.

NOTE: DENIAL OF BACK PAY IN STATE LABOR LAW CASES

Although the award or denial of back pay is generally in the district court's discretion, many courts have been fairly generous in granting back pay. An important exception is in sex discrimination cases where the employers claim that state labor laws have caused them to discriminate. Many courts have been sympathetic to the notion that the companies should not be penalized by a back pay award because they were caught between two contradictory laws: Title VII telling them not to discriminate and the state laws commanding them to discriminate. See, e.g., Kober v. Westinghouse Electric Corp., 480 F.2d 240 (3d Cir. 1973); LeBlanc v. Southern Bell Telephone & Telegraph Co., 460 F.2d 1228 (5th Cir.), *cert. denied,* 409 U.S. 990, (1972); Manning v. Automobile Workers, Local 913, 466 F.2d 812 (6th Cir. 1972), *cert. denied,* 410 U.S. 946 (1973); *contra,* Shaeffer v. San Diego Yellow Cabs, Inc., 462 F.2d 1002 (9th Cir. 1972).

A disturbing element of these cases is the courts' reluctance to examine closely whether the discriminatory policies at issue were in fact caused by adherence to the state laws, or whether these laws provided a convenient cover-up for practices which the employers would have maintained even absent the laws. Consider, for example, the following excerpt from an EEOC amicus curiae brief.

Brief for the United States Equal Employment
Opportunity Commission as Amicus Curiae
20-24, Ridinger v. General Motors Corp., 474 F.2d 949 (6th Cir. 1972)

Back Pay Must Be Awarded Where Discrimination
Had No Relationship To . . . State Labor Laws.

While motive is normally a matter of fact, the lower court concluded from the pleadings alone that General Motors relied in "good faith" on statutes which were no longer valid, and concluded further that compliance with those statutes necessitated the alleged discrimination. These conclusions had no evidentiary basis; on the contrary, the pleadings clearly indicated that General Motors' assertions of reliance and causal connection were sham. . . .

First, the women alleged that they were denied ". . . [p]ayment of Saturday and Sunday overtime," and that they were not allowed to work ". . . six and seven days per week . . ." as were the male employees.

The Ohio maximum hours law states:

> In manufacturing establishments a female may not be employed more than forty-eight hours in any one week or nine hours in one day or on more than six days in a calendar week. Section 4107.46(A) (1).

Clearly, the statute allows women to work six days per week. . . . There is thus a factual dispute on whether Section 4107.46 caused General Motors to discriminate [as to the denial of overtime on the sixth day of the week], and the women should be given an opportunity to show that they were denied work and overtime pay for the sixth day of the week. Back pay should be awarded if they offer such evidence, for in that case, no defense of good faith compliance with a state statute could be raised as the statute does not require the alleged discriminatory practice.

Similarly, the women alleged that they suffered discrimination in regard to ". . . [a]dvancement and job transfer," and ". . . [c]ontinued maintenance of separate seniority rosters." More specifically, they claimed that women were not advanced ". . . to higher paying jobs when their seniority warranted transfer," nor were groups adjusted ". . . so as to upgrade female employees to eliminate the effects of the prior discrimination."

The court below refused to consider these claims, and the possible award of back pay if they should be proved, ostensibly because General Motors claimed in Commission proceedings that compliance with state law required it to discriminate in this fashion. The lower court noted that:

> In the Inland Manufacturing Company case [the proceedings before the Commission], employee Shaffer charged that General Motors violated the Act by maintaining sex-segregated employment classifications. *General Motors admitted this practice but contended that the employment classifications were required by Section 4107.43* Ohio Revised Code which prohibits females from performing work requiring frequent or repeated lifting of weights in excess of 25 pounds. (R.A. 54-55; J.A. 57-58). (Emphasis added) . . .

[S]ince there was no trial below, General Motors has never proved that the existence of the 25-pound weight ban necessitated sex-segregated employment classifications. On the contrary, it has admitted that its classifications were based on the fact that such jobs *"occasionally* required the lifting of weights in excess of 25 pounds. . . ." (Emphasis added). Since Section 4107.43 of the Ohio Revised Code only prohibits employment ". . . requiring *frequent or repeated lifting* of weights over twenty-five pounds" (Emphasis added), there is great doubt whether sex-segregated job classifications were in fact caused by compliance with Section 4107.43. The Company, at trial must, of course, establish the causal relationship [if] it seeks to use Ohio law as a defense.[15]

---

15. The Commission submits that to prove adequately this causal connection, General Motors would have to prove for each job from which women were excluded that: (1) the job required frequent or repeated lifting, and (2) no alternative method for lifting weights, while allowing women to perform the other functions of the job, could have been devised. Such alternative methods might have included restructuring the job to allow one or two men to take over completely the weight-lifting function; or better use of machinery. See Robinson v. Lorillard Corp., supra, 444 F.2d at 798, where the Fourth Circuit held, in a slightly different context, that ". . . there must be available no acceptable alternative policies or practices which would better accomplish the business purpose advanced, or accomplish it equally well with a lesser differential [sex] impact," and in a footnote to this text, that: "It should go without saying that a practice is hardly 'necessary'

Whether General Motors had a good faith belief that Title VII allowed it to comply with the Ohio labor laws is also an issue which must be resolved at trial. Its claim to have acted in good faith does not substitute for proof of that contention.

These cases, then, should be remanded for a trial on the disputed factual issues. If Defendants cannot prove that those discriminatory practices which are now colored by their claim of "reliance" on Ohio labor laws were in fact a direct and inevitable result of good faith compliance with those laws, the result is clear. They will have no defense to this action, and back pay must be awarded to the women Plaintiffs.

The Sixth Circuit did not even consider this issue in its opinion in the *Ridinger* case, and instead referred to its decision in Manning v. Automobile Workers, Local 913, 466 F.2d 812 (6th Cir. 1972), a companion case which held that it was not an abuse of discretion for a district court to deny back pay where there was no judicial ruling on the validity of the state laws and the EEOC had not handed down a definitive ruling. It is possible, of course, that the case was badly litigated, for the lower court decision was based on the pleadings alone, and the plaintiffs' attorney apparently did not stress in any way or introduce facts to show that many of General Motors' discriminatory practices were in no way compelled by adherence to the existing state law. However, even when plaintiffs have attempted to litigate this issue, the courts have rather blithely accepted the company's arguments. See, for example, the opinion in LeBlanc v. Southern Bell Telephone & Telegraph Co., 3 FEP Cases 1083 (E.D. La. 1971), *aff'd*, 460 F.2d 1228 (5th Cir.), *cert. denied*, 409 U.S. 990 (1972). The issue there involved women's exclusion from the position of test deskman, allegedly because the overtime requirements of that job were prohibited by the state maximum hours law. The court rejected plaintiffs' contentions that the company had violated the maximum hours law in other instances and that the overtime requirements of the job were artificially created. No one explored the issue of whether the company could have allowed women to handle the job during normal working hours, but restricted their overtime, as an alternative to the women's total exclusion from the job. See Note: AT&T's BFOQ Claims, Section B-4-a supra, which points out that some AT&T companies adopted this very approach, and that all AT&T companies could have eliminated sex segregation of jobs had they chosen to. These facts suggest that the court was very naive about the operation of sex discrimination at Southern Bell.

In all fairness, however, some of the blame for these decisions must be laid on the EEOC. The EEOC clearly waffled for about four years on whether state labor laws regulating women's work were invalid or not. Had the commission taken a strong stand on the issue from the very beginning, it may be that courts would now be more willing to grant back pay to the injured women workers.[187]

H. Miscellaneous Problems

1. Research Aids

Both the Bureau of National Affairs and Commerce Clearinghouse publish reporters collecting Title VII and other employment discrimination decisions, statutes, and regulations. The BNA looseleaf binder volumes are part of its Labor Relations Reporter series, and are titled Fair Employment Practice Cases (EEOC and court decisions) and Fair Employment Practice Manual (federal and state statutes and regulations); the bound

---

if an alternative practice better effectuates the intended purpose or is equally effective but less discriminatory." Id., n.7.

    187. Davidson, "Back Pay" Awards Under Title VII of the Civil Rights Act of 1964, 26 Rutgers L. Rev. 741 (1973), is a valuable and thorough article on the subject.

volumes are titled Fair Employment Practice Cases. The indices and case tables are in the Fair Employment Practice Cases binder if the FEP set was purchased separately, and otherwise in the Master Index Binder of the Labor Relations Reporter. The CCH loose-leaf binder volumes are not part of its Labor Law Reporter series, but are generally shelved near it in law libraries. They are titled Employment Practices Guide 1 (case tables, indices, statutes, and regulations), 2 (EEOC and court decisions), and 3 (state laws). Employment decisions under state law and the Fourteenth Amendment are also included in both the BNA and CCH reporters.

The EEOC also distributes a statutory index, which organizes Title VII decisions according to the sections of the act they construe. It is available from the Office of General Counsel, Equal Employment Opportunity Commission, 1800 G Street, NW, Washington, D.C. 20506.

Attorneys handling Title VII cases should also contact the EEOC General Counsel's office in Washington or local regional and district EEOC lawyers for advice on litigation tactics, discovery, expert witnesses, Title VII procedure, and the like, as well as citations which are not yet generally available.

Title VII has been the subject of law review articles too numerous to collect here. The text gives citations to some articles which may be helpful, but no attempt has been made to be comprehensive. Readers are urged to check the Index of Legal Periodicals for further references.

2. Other Laws

There are a wide variety of other laws prohibiting employment discrimination. At the federal level, these include the Age Discrimination in Employment Act of 1967; 42 U.S.C. §§1981 and 1983, the remedies derived from the Civil Rights Acts of 1866, 1870, and 1871; the Equal Pay Act of 1963 (infra); Executive Order 11246 (infra); Executive Order 11478 (prohibiting discrimination in federal government employment); and a variety of federal agency regulations, such as the Regulations on Nondiscrimination in Apprenticeship Programs of the Department of Labor, and the Civil Service Commission Regulations. BNA's Fair Employment Practice Manual and CCH's Employment Practices Guide set out the text of these federal laws as well as regulations and directives promulgated thereunder, and discussions of their provisions.

Most states have one or more laws prohibiting sex discrimination in employment. There are five main types of laws:[188]

> fair employment-practice laws, which are generally modeled on Title VII and offer the same kind of broad coverage; equal pay laws, modeled on the Equal Pay Act; state contract laws, which are modeled on Executive Order 11246, as amended by E.O. 11375, and which generally protect the employees of companies that hold contracts with the state government; state employees laws, which are sometimes modeled on Executive Order 11478 and prohibit the state government from discriminating against its own employees; and age discrimination laws, which are sometimes modeled on the Federal Age Discrimination Act or which may be included within other state antidis-crimination laws.

The Fair Employment Practice Manual (BNA) and 2 Employment Practices Guide (CCH) both reproduce each state's employment discrimination laws, except that BNA does not include equal pay laws. Ross, The Rights of Women, Appendix A, p. 291 (1973), includes a useful table categorizing the employment discrimination laws of each state, and providing citations. In addition, many cities and localities have their own antidis-crimination provisions and agencies, some of which are more effective than the state laws and enforcement bodies. For a list of such agencies, write for the Directory of State and

188. Ross, The Rights of Women 292 (1973).

Local Anti-discrimination Agencies, published by EEOC and updated on January 1 and July 1 of each year. It is available from Office of State and Community Affairs, EEOC, 1800 G Street, NW, Washington, D.C. 20506.

These laws vary widely in usefulness; many state laws in particular are extremely weak, and some have no enforcement mechanism at all. For a comparison of different federal question laws, see Peck, Remedies for Racial Discrimination in Employment: A Comparative Evaluation of Forums, 46 Wash. L. Rev. 455 (1971). While Peck's article discusses only race discrimination, most laws he discusses also include sex discrimination. See also Ross, supra, ch. 2 and Appendix A for useful discussions of the relative effectiveness of various laws.

3. Attorneys' Fees

Under 42 U.S.C. §2000e-5(k) reasonable attorneys' fees may, in the discretion of the court, be awarded to the prevailing party, and there has been considerable litigation about the extent of discretion which will be allowed the district judge. In a 1968 decision under Title II of the Civil Rights Act of 1964, Newman v. Piggie Park Enterprises, Inc., 390 U.S. 400, 88 S. Ct. 964, 19 L.Ed. 2d 1263 (1968), the Supreme Court spoke on the subject of attorneys' fees in language that is also applicable to Title VII cases:[189]

> When a plaintiff brings an action under [Title II], he cannot recover damages.
>
> If he obtains an injunction, he does so not for himself alone, but also as a "private attorney general," vindicating a policy that Congress considered of the highest priority. If successful plaintiffs were routinely forced to bear their own attorneys' fees, few aggrieved parties would be in a position to advance the public interest by invoking the injunctive powers of the federal courts. Congress therefore enacted the provision for counsel fees — not simply to penalize litigants who deliberately advance arguments they know to be untenable but more broadly to encourage individuals injured by racial discrimination to seek judicial relief under Title II.

This language was relied on, for example, in Clark v. American Marine Corp., 320 F. Supp. 709 (E.D. La. 1970), a successful Title VII suit, in which the court not only awarded the attorneys' fees requested, but also set forth standards according to which fees should be determined. The importance of requiring district judges to make findings of fact explaining their awards in terms of specific factors is illustrated by the history of the litigation in Lea v. Cone Mills. In that case, the district judge initially denied both back pay and attorneys' fees, among other reasons, because it was a test case. 301 F. Supp. 97 (M.D.N.C. 1969). The Fourth Circuit vacated and remanded the denial of counsel fees, holding that the case was governed by Newman v. Piggie Park, supra; that counsel fees were justified because plaintiffs' victory was an important one, opening the way for future employment of Negro females at the plant in question; and that the fact that plaintiffs' action was in the nature of a test case did not warrant denial of fees to counsel. On remand the plaintiffs requested $29,640 in attorneys' fees. In support of the request, counsel submitted an itemization of services which included time records showing 580 hours worked, and expert testimony that the time spent was reasonable. The judge awarded $10,000 in fees; the following statement was the only explanation of how the decision was made:[190]

> Gentlemen, one of the most disagreeable things, I guess, a Judge ever has to do is fix fees. Where there are minor parties in a personal injury suit, as to what the attorney should have, I guess it's appropriate to take into consideration that the attorney is working on a contingency fee basis and he doesn't get anything unless he wins. I don't

189. 390 U.S. at 402, 88 S. Ct. at 966, 19 L. Ed. 2d at 1265-1266.
190. Cooper and Rabb, Equal Employment Law and Litigation 452-453 (1972).

know. I will say this: I don't think there is anybody connected with the plaintiff's case that would deliberately misrepresent anything, but I think some of these items I just think wouldn't take that long. I will fix a fee in the sum of $10,000; and you can draw up an appropriate order.

On appeal, despite a lengthy brief discussing the standards which should have been considered,[191] the Fourth Circuit Court of Appeals affirmed, ruling that the district judge had not abused his discretion. A similar decision is Culpepper v. Reynolds Metals Co., 442 F.2d 1078 (5th Cir. 1971), *aff'g* 2 FEP Cases 873 (D. Ga. 1970). See also Weeks v. Southern Bell Telephone & Telegraph Co., 4 FEP Cases 918 (S.D. Ga. 1971), *aff'd*, 467 F.2d 95 (5th Cir. 1972), which falls between the *Lea* and *Clark* lines of cases; the court briefly discussed the standards it used but emphasized its own discretion in awarding counsel fees of $15,000 for 585 hours of work.

In Johnson v. Georgia Highway Express, 7 FEP Cases 1 (5th Cir. 1974), the conflict between the two lines of cases epitomized by *Clark* and *Lea* was decisively resolved in favor of requiring district judges to explain their awards by making findings of fact. The district court had awarded counsel fees of $13,500, based on $200 per attorney per day of six or seven hours of trial preparation and $250 per attorney per day in court. The court of appeals vacated and remanded for reconsideration in light of the following specific factors:[192]

(1) The time and labor required. Although hours claimed or spent on a case should not be the sole basis for determining a fee, they are a necessary ingredient to be considered. The trial judge should weigh the hours claimed against his own knowledge, experience, and expertise of the time required to complete similar activities. If more than one attorney is involved, the possibility of duplication of effort along with the proper utilization of time should be scrutinized. . . . It is appropriate to distinguish between legal work, in the strict sense, and investigation, clerical work, compilation of facts and statistics and other work which can often be accomplished by non-lawyers but which a lawyer may do because he has no other help available. Such non-legal work may command a lesser rate. Its dollar value is not enhanced just because a lawyer does it.

(2) The novelty and difficulty of the question. Cases of first impression generally require more time and effort on the attorney's part. Although this greater expenditure of time in research and preparation is an investment by counsel in obtaining knowledge which can be used in similar later cases, he should not be penalized for undertaking a case which may "make new law." Instead, he should be appropriately compensated for accepting the challenge.

(3) The skill requisite to perform the legal service properly. The trial judge should closely observe the attorney's work product, his preparation, and general ability before the court. . . .

(4) The preclusion of other employment by the attorney due to acceptance of the case. This guideline involves the dual consideration of otherwise available business which is foreclosed because of conflicts of interest which occur from the representation, and the fact that once the employment is undertaken the attorney is not free to use the time spent on the client's behalf for other purposes.

(5) The customary fee. The customary fee for similar work in the community should be considered. It is open knowledge that various types of legal work command differing scales of compensation. At no time, however, should the fee for strictly legal work fall below the $20 per hour prescribed by the Criminal Justice Act, 18 U.S.C.A. §3006A(d)(1), and awarded to appointed counsel for criminal defendants. As long as minimum fee schedules are in existence and are customarily followed by the lawyers in a given community, they should be taken into consideration.

(6) Whether the fee is fixed or contingent. The fee quoted to the client or the

191. Reproduced id. at 464-495.
192. 7 FEP Cases at 3-5.

percentage of the recovery agreed to is helpful in demonstrating the attorney's fee expectations when he accepted the case. . . . In no event, however, should the litigant be awarded a fee greater than he is contractually bound to pay, if indeed the attorneys have contracted as to amount.

(7) Time limitations imposed by the client or the circumstances. Priority work that delays the lawyer's other legal work is entitled to some premium. . . .

(8) The amount involved and the results obtained. Title VII, 42 U.S.C. §2000e-5(g), permits the recovery of damages in addition to injunctive relief. Although the court should consider the amount of damages, or back pay awarded, that consideration should not obviate court scrutiny of the decision's effect on the law. If the decision corrects across-the-board discrimination affecting a large class of an employer's employees, the attorney's fee award should reflect the relief granted.

(9) The experience, reputation, and ability of the attorneys. . . . An attorney specializing in civil rights cases may enjoy a higher rate for his expertise than others, providing his ability corresponds with his experience. Longevity per se, however, should not dictate the higher fee. If a young attorney demonstrates the skill and ability, he should not be penalized for only recently being admitted to the bar.

(10) The "undesirability" of the case. Civil rights attorneys face hardships in their communities because of their desire to help the civil rights litigant. Oftentimes his decision to help eradicate discrimination is not pleasantly received by the community or his contemporaries. This can have an economic impact on his practice which can be considered by the court.

(11) The nature and length of the professional relationship with the client. . . .

(12) Awards in similar cases. . . .

To put these guidelines into perspective and as a caveat to their application, courts must remember that they do not have a mandate under Section 706(k) to make the prevailing counsel rich. Concomitantly, the section should not be implemented in a manner to make the private attorney general's position so lucrative as to ridicule the public attorney general. The statute was not passed for the benefit of attorneys but to enable litigants to obtain competent counsel worthy of a contest with the caliber of counsel available to their opposition and to fairly place the economical burden of Title VII litigation. Adequate compensation is necessary, however, to enable an attorney to serve his client effectively and to preserve the integrity and independence of the profession. The guidelines contained herein are merely an attempt to assist in this balancing process.

See also Rock v. Norfolk & Western Ry. Co., 473 F.2d 1344 (4th Cir. 1973), remanding the issue of counsel fees for reconsideration in light of further proceedings and "findings to disclose the basis of the ultimate award." 473 F.2d at 1350.

Court awards of attorneys' fees in Title VII cases appear to be generally lower than the attorneys' fees arranged as part of out of court settlements. For example, in Bryan v. Pittsburgh Plate Glass Co., 6 FEP Cases 925 (W.D. Pa. 1973), the court approved a Title VII settlement which awarded $949,724 to the 371 members of the plaintiff class (including $17,500 to members of the class who were most active in the prosecution of the case) and $201,250 to various counsel. Although the opinion gives no information on the number of hours worked by the attorneys, it is highly likely that the rate of compensation is five or more times as high as the rate of approximately $19 to $35 per hour reflected in the judicial awards discussed above.

III. THE EQUAL PAY ACT

A. INTRODUCTION

MURPHY AND ROSS
LIBERATING WOMEN — LEGALLY SPEAKING
in Wasserstein and Green (eds.), With Justice For Some 112-113 (1971)

The 1960s gave rise to new legislation concerned with employment discrimination against women. The Equal Pay Act was designed to meet the widespread and blatantly discriminatory practice of paying women less than men for the same work. A government policy had already supported the principle of equal pay to women during both World Wars and the Korean War, when the female industrial work force became particularly valuable to the country. After each war, as the country returned to peacetime conditions, sex discrimination in wages also returned. Despite sustained efforts to obtain national legislation against this practice, it was not until 1963 that the Equal Pay Act was finally passed.

This law requires employers to pay equal salaries to a man and a woman when their jobs require equal skill, effort, and responsibility and are done under similar working conditions. It also forbids labor unions "to cause or attempt to cause" an employer to violate this requirement. Four exceptions are set forth in the statute. Different salaries paid to men and women do not violate the act if they are based on a merit system, a seniority system, a system measuring earnings by quality or quantity of production or on "any other factor other than sex."

The equal pay provision is enforced by the Labor Department's Division of Wages and Hours as part of the Fair Labor Standards Act. Labor Department inspectors routinely check for equal pay violations as well as investigate specific complaints. Women who have suffered pay discrimination can recover the difference between their wages and those paid to men for up to a two-year period. By April, 1970, seventeen million dollars had been recovered for over 50,000 employees.[1]

When necessary, the Labor Department (or the employee herself if the department fails to act) can sue to recover the wages due because of equal pay violations.

In fact, most of the litigation has been brought by the secretary of labor.

The act itself is an amendment to the Fair Labor Standards Act (FLSA), 29 U.S.C. §201 et seq., which provides for federal minimum wages and overtime pay; the Equal Pay Act thus inherited the enforcement process for the FLSA. The equal pay provisions are set forth in §206(d) of the FLSA:

> No employer having employees subject to any provisions of this section shall discriminate, within any establishment in which such employees are employed, between employees on the basis of sex by paying wages to employees in such establishment at a rate less than the rate at which he pays wages to employees of the opposite sex in such establishment for equal work on jobs the performance of which requires equal skill, effort, and responsibility, and which are performed under similar working condi-

---

1. From June 10, 1964, the effective date of the act, to June 30, 1973, the Labor Department found that about 142,600 workers (almost all of them women) were owed about 65.6 million dollars under the Equal Pay Act. Of this amount, employers had actually paid only about 31.5 million dollars — either through voluntary action after Labor Department investigation, out of court settlements, or court action. Although most cases are settled without the need for litigation, the Labor Department filed about 530 lawsuits in this period; less than a dozen were against unions. The number of employee lawsuits filed in this same period was minimal. (From a telephone conversation with Morag Simchak, Special Assistant to the Assistant Secretary of Labor for Employment Standards, July 13, 1973.) — Eds.

tions, except where such payment is made pursuant to (i) a seniority system; (ii) a merit system; (iii) a system which measures earnings by quantity or quality of production; or (iv) a differential based on any other factor other than sex: *Provided,* That an employer who is paying a wage rate differential in violation of this subsection shall not, in order to comply with the provisions of this subsection, reduce the wage rate of any employee.

The Equal Pay Act involves a complicated definition of wage discrimination, which has severely limited the impact of the statute, as the cases in this part illustrate, and has focused litigation on seemingly endless details about the nature of the particular work. The act has an even more fundamental defect: it does not apply to most forms of sex discrimination. Still, Equal Pay Act cases are important for several reasons. First, their intense focus on job details reveals much about the reality of the job situation of the blue-collar or low-paid white-collar woman worker, and the company psychology she faces. Many middle-class law students will have had no prior acquaintance with these facts, and will learn more from Equal Pay Act cases than they would learn from Title VII litigation, in which judicial opinions expose fewer concrete facts. Moreover, the cases dispel effectively the myth that litigation about sex discrimination in employment benefits primarily the middle-class professional woman. Finally, there are advantages to plaintiffs in suing under both the Equal Pay Act and Title VII, and it is therefore necessary to understand the technical details of equal pay litigation. This is true especially for those who plan to practice in the sex discrimination field because the bar has brought virtually no Equal Pay Act suits to date, and has shown a general ignorance of the act's intricacies.

B. The Plaintiff's Case

Generally the Equal Pay Act plaintiff must prove that the work of the men and women is equal. There are two tests for equal work: (1) the jobs must involve essentially the same duties; and (2) the performance of these duties must require substantially equal skill, effort, and responsibility, each of which is measured separately. These are the major factors examined in the existing litigation. The plaintiff also has the burden of proof as to whether men and women work under similar conditions, whether they work in the same establishment, and whether the unequal pay is based on sex. The cases which follow illustrate the application of most of these concepts.

1. Equal Work: "Substantially Equal" Rather than Identical

SHULTZ v. WHEATON GLASS COMPANY
421 F.2d 259 (3d Cir.),
cert. denied, 398 U.S. 905 (1970)

This appeal presents important problems in the construction of the Equal Pay Act of 1963 (29 U.S.C. §206(d)), which was added as an amendment to the Fair Labor Standards Act of 1938 (29 U.S.C. §§201 et seq.).

The Equal Pay Act prohibits an employer from discriminating "between employees on the basis of sex by paying wages to employees . . . at a rate less than the rate at which he pays wages to employees of the opposite sex . . . for equal work on jobs the performance of which requires equal skill, effort, and responsibility, and which are performed under similar working conditions, except where such payment is made pursuant to . . . (IV) a differential based on any other factor other than sex. . . ."

Invoking the enforcement provisions of the Fair Labor Standards Act the Secretary of Labor brought this action against Wheaton Glass Co., claiming that it discriminated against its "female selector-packers" on the basis of sex by paying them at an hourly rate of $2.14, which is 10% less than the $2.355 rate it pays to its "male selector-packers." The Secretary sought an injunction against future violations and the recovery of back pay for past violations. The company denied that the female selector-packers perform equal work within the terms of the Act. . . .

After an extensive trial the district court entered judgment for the defendant, holding that the Secretary had failed to carry his burden of proving that the wage differential was based upon sex discrimination. . . . The Secretary has appealed.

The company is one of the largest manufacturers of glass containers in the United States. Its plant at Millville, New Jersey, which is here involved, is called a "job shop" plant and manufactures glass containers to special order. Unlike the usual modern plants in the glass industry which make standard items in large quantities and employ automatic machinery, the company's job shop operation requires manual handling and visual inspection of the product.

Selector-packers are employed in the Bottle Inspection Department. They work at long tables and visually inspect the bottles for defects as they emerge on a conveyor from the oven, or "lehr." The defective products are discarded into waste containers. Those which meet the specifications are packed in cardboard cartons on a stand within arm's reach of the selector-packers and then lifted onto an adjacent conveyor or rollers and sent off to the Quality Control Department for further examination and processing. In the Bottle Inspection Department is another category of employees known as "snap-up boys," who crate and move bottles and generally function as handymen, sweeping and cleaning and performing other unskilled miscellaneous tasks. They are paid at the hourly rate of $2.16.

Prior to 1956, the company employed only male selector-packers. In that year, however, the shortage of available men in the Millville area forced the company to employ for the first time female selector-packers. On the insistence of the Glass Bottle Blowers Association of the United States and Canada, AFL-CIO, Local 219, with which the company had a collective bargaining agreement, there was, in the language of the district court, "carved out of the total job of selector-packer . . . a new role of female selector-packer." This new classification was written into the collective bargaining agreement, and pursuant to it female selector-packers were not to lift bulky cartons or cartons weighing more than 35 pounds. At the union's insistence a provision was added to the collective bargaining agreement that no male selector-packer was to be replaced by a female selector-packer except to fill a vacancy resulting from retirement, resignation, or dismissal for just cause.

On its face the record presents the incongruity that because male selector-packers spend a relatively small portion of their time doing the work of snap-up boys whose hourly rate of pay is $2.16 they are paid $2.355 per hour for their own work, while female selector-packers receive only $2.14. This immediately casts doubt on any contention that the difference in the work done by male and female selector-packers, which amounts substantially to what the snap-up boys do, is of itself enough to explain the difference in the rate of pay for male and female selector-packers on grounds other than sex.

The district court explored this difference in some detail. The court found that while male and female selector-packers perform substantially identical work at the ovens, the work of the male selector-packers is substantially different because they perform sixteen additional tasks. These consist of lifting packages weighing more than 35 pounds; lifting cartons which, regardless of weight, are bulky or difficult to handle; stacking full cartons; tying stacks of cartons; moving wooden pallets fully loaded with stacks of cartons; moving and placing empty pallets for later use; operating hand trucks near the ovens; positioning and adjusting portable roller conveyors and packing stands holding empty cartons for filling; collecting dump trays and tubs of rejected glassware; sweeping and cleaning work areas near the ovens; fitting and attaching metal clips to glass containers at the ovens; unjamming overhead carton conveyors and automatic belts; occasionally reinspecting, repacking and restacking glassware already delivered to the premises of customers; locating glassware in the warehouse, at times involving climbing over palletized cartons; and voluntarily working, when necessary, in excess of ten hours per day or of 54 hours per week.[5] The district court also found that the training period for men was six months, whereas the training period for women was three months.

The district court pointed to evidence submitted by the company that the male selector-packers spent an average of approximately 18 percent of their total time on this work, which was forbidden to women. It made no finding, however, that this was a fact, nor did it make any finding as to what percentage of time was spent by male selector-packers either on the average or individually in performing this different work. Indeed, it made no finding that all male selector-packers performed this extra work, but only that the extra work when not performed by snap-up boys was done by male selector-packers. There is, therefore, no basis for an assumption that all male selector-packers performed any or all of these 16 additional tasks.

Even if there had been a finding that all the male selector-packers performed all of the 16 additional tasks and that these consumed a substantial amount of their time, there would still be lacking an adequate basis for the differential in wages paid to male and female selector-packers. For there would be no rational explanation why men who at times perform work paying two cents per hour more than their female counterparts should for that reason receive 21½ cents per hour more than females for the work they do in common.

The district court, therefore, placed its conclusion on a factor of "flexibility." The company's job shop requires frequent shutdowns of the ovens when a customer's order is completed and before the run of a new order is begun. During such shutdowns the idled female selector-packers are assigned to what is known as the "Resort" area, where they inspect and pack glassware rejected by the Quality Control Inspection Department. Idled male selector-packers are similarly reassigned to the Resort area, but some of them are assigned to do work which otherwise would be done by snap-up boys.

The district court found that this availability of male selector-packers to perform the work of snap-up boys during shutdowns was an element of flexibility and deemed it to be of economic value to the company in the operation of its unique, customized plant. It is on this element of flexibility that the judgment of the district court ultimately rests.

Under the collective bargaining agreement the company could at any time assign selector-packers to perform the work of snap-up boys, although they would continue to receive their regular rate of pay. While this explains why male selector-packers would not have their pay reduced in performing work of snap-up boys, it does not run the other way and explain why their performance of the work of snap-up boys who receive only two cents per hour more than female selector-packers justifies their being paid 21½ cents per hour more than female selector-packers for performing selector-packer work.

Whatever difference may exist in the total work of male and female selector-packers because men also perform work of snap-up boys does not justify a class wage differential in the absence of any finding regarding the number of male selector-packers who perform or are available for the work of snap-up boys. While all male selector-packers receive the higher rate of pay, there is no finding that all of them are either available for or actually perform snap-up boys' work.

An even more serious imperfection in the claim of flexibility is the absence, as we have already indicated, of any finding or explanation why availability of men to perform work which pays two cents per hour more than women receive should result

5. It is argued that under New Jersey law, women are barred from working double shifts. But see *Wirtz v. Rainbo Baking Co. of Lexington,* 303 F. Supp. 1049 (E.D. Ky. 1967), holding that such a statutory restriction on the number of hours a female employee can work will not justify payment of lower wages. To the same effect as *Rainbo,* see the applicable regulation, 29 C.F.R. §800.163.

in overall payment to men of 21½ cents more than women for their common work. A 10% wage differential is not automatically justified by showing that some advantage exists to the employer because of a flexibility whose extent and economic value is neither measured nor determined and which is attained by the performance of work carrying a much lower rate of pay. In short, there is no finding of the economic value of the element of flexibility on which the district court justified the 10% discrimination in pay rate between male and female selector-packers.

There is, moreover, an additional element of significance with which the district court did not deal. Just as it has not been made clear by any finding that all male selector-packers perform or are available for the work of snap-up boys, so there is an absence of any finding on the ability of any female selector-packers to perform the work of snap-up boys. The fact that some female selector-packers, unlike some male selector-packers, may have been unwilling or unable to do the work of snap-up boys might justify a wage differential between them. But it would still leave open the question why the company did not include under its flexibility requirement the female selector-packers who are both able and willing to do the work of snap-up boys. There may have been some male selector-packers who were unwilling or even incompetent to do the work of snap-up boys. Yet because some of the class was willing and available to do the work of snap-up boys, all of the class received 21½ cents per hour more than all females, including those who might have been willing and able to do the work of snap-up boys when it was required.

These disparities in rates of pay under which snap-up boys performing physical labor receive a higher rate than female selector-packers while male selector-packers receive a much higher rate because they are available also to do some of the work of snap-up boys, take on an even more discriminatory aspect when viewed in the light of their history. For as the district court indicated, the classification of female selector-packers at the lowest rate of pay of these three categories was made at a time of labor shortage when the company was forced to hire women and the union insisted on conditions which would minimize their future competition against the men with whom they would now be working. The motive, therefore, clearly appears to have been to keep women in a subordinate role rather than to confer flexibility on the company and to emphasize this subordination by both the 10% differential between male and female selector-packers and the two cents difference between snap-up boys and female selector-packers.

The effect of such a motive and the evaluation of the distinction in the work done by male and female selector-packers requires us to turn to the construction of the Equal Pay Act of 1963. The Act was the culmination of many years of striving to eliminate discrimination in pay because of sex. Similar bills were before Congress for many years before the Act ultimately was adopted, and in its final form it bears evidence of the competing tendencies which surrounded its birth. There are problems of construction which leap up from the reading of its language. It has not been authoritatively construed by the Supreme Court and a study of its legislative history and the bills which preceded it yields little guidance in the construction of its provisions in concrete circumstances.

In adopting the Act, Congress chose to specify equal pay for "equal" work. In doing so, Congress was well aware of the experience of the National War Labor Board during World War II and its regulations requiring equal pay for "comparable" work. Under these regulations the National War Labor Board made job evaluations to determine whether inequities existed within a plant even between dissimilar occupations. Since Congress was aware of the Board's policy and chose to require equal pay for "equal" rather than "comparable" work, it is clear that the references in the legislative history to the Board's regulations were only to show the feasibility of administering a federal equal pay policy and do not warrant use of the Board's decisions as guiding principles for the construction of the Equal Pay Act.

On the other hand, Congress in prescribing "equal" work did not require that the jobs be identical, but only that they must be substantially equal. Any other interpretation would destroy the remedial purposes of the Act.

The Act was intended as a broad charter of women's rights in the economic field. It sought to overcome the age-old belief in women's inferiority and to eliminate the depressing effects on living standards of reduced wages for female workers and the economic and social consequences which flow from it.

Differences in job classifications were in general expected to be beyond the coverage of the Equal Pay Act. This was because in the case of genuine job classifications the differences in work necessarily would be substantial and the differences in compensation therefore would be based on the differences in work which justified them. Congress never intended, however, that an artificially created job classification which did not substantially differ from the genuine one could provide an escape for an employer from the operation of the Equal Pay Act.[12] This would be too wide a door through which the content of the Act would disappear.

This view is strengthened by the subsequent adoption of Title VII of the Civil Rights Act of 1964 which prohibits discrimination because of sex in the classification of employees as well as in their employment and compensation. Although the Civil Rights Act is much broader than the Equal Pay Act, its provisions regarding discrimination based on sex are in pari materia with the Equal Pay Act. This is recognized in the provision of §703(h) of the Civil Rights Act (42 U.S.C. §2000e-2(h)) that an employer's differentiation upon the basis of sex in determining wages or compensation shall not be an unlawful employment practice under the Civil Rights Act if the differentiation is authorized by the Equal Pay Act. Since both statutes serve the same fundamental purpose against discrimination based on sex, the Equal Pay Act may not be construed in a manner which by virtue of §703(h) would undermine the Civil Rights Act.

It is not necessary here, however, to delineate the precise manner in which these two statutes must be harmonized to work together in service of the underlying Congressional objective. For even if the Civil Rights Act is put aside, the Equal Pay Act alone does not permit artificial classification to prevent inquiry whether there exists a difference in pay for substantially equal work.

The district court held that the Secretary failed to carry his burden of proof that the company's wage differential is based on sex discrimination. In view of the facts which the district court found, we hold this conclusion to be erroneous. The Secretary met his burden of proof when he showed that male selector-packers received a pay rate 10% higher than female selector-packers although both performed identical work and that the additional work of snap-up boys which male selector-packers also performed was work which carried virtually the same rate of pay as that done by women. When to these circumstances are added the origin of the classification of female selector-packers and their reduced pay even below that paid to snap-up boys, the Secretary clearly established his prima facie case that the wage differential was based on sex and therefore discriminated against women. . . .

NOTE: THE IMPACT OF THE WHEATON GLASS DECISION

Wheaton Glass is a landmark decision, for it was the first circuit court decision construing the Equal Pay Act and it has been very influential in the development of later

---

12. The committee report accompanying the final version of the Act stated the effect of its language as it bore on job classification as follows: "This language recognizes that there are many factors which may be used to measure the relationships between jobs and which establish a valid basis for a difference in pay. These factors will be found in a majority of the job classification systems. Thus, it is anticipated that a *bona fide* job classification program *that does not discriminate on the basis of sex* will serve as a valid defense to a charge of discrimination." [Emphasis supplied.] H.R. Rep. No. 309, May 20, 1963.

Equal Pay Act cases. The most important aspect of the decision is its holding that jobs meriting equal pay need not be *identical,* but only *substantially equal.* As the court points out, a requirement of identical jobs would have nullified the practical effect of the act; under such an interpretation, companies could give men workers only a few extra insignificant duties in order to pay women workers less with impunity.

The lower court *Wheaton Glass* decision illustrates the effect of the identical job standard in its holding that the men and women were doing unequal work. The court particularly relied on the act's legislative history:[2]

> . . . The legislative history of the Act clearly reveals that Congress intended to substitute the word "equal" for the former word "comparable," thereby meaning "substantially identical" rather than merely "similar" work.[16] Additionally, it employed two dissimilar concepts when it used both words "equal" and "similar" within the same sentence, obviously attributing different meanings to each, i.e. "equal" to work and "similar" to conditions. When the proposed Bill for equal pay was carried over from the 87th to the 88th Congress, the word "equal" was recommended by the Sub-committee. Not only was "equal" subsequently adopted by Congress as the vital spinal cord in the body of the Act, but the Act, itself, was named the "Equal Pay Act of 1963" and mandated the equation of equal pay for equal work — not almost, not like, not comparable and not similar, but "equal." . . .

Compare this interpretation with that of Shultz v. Wheaton Glass Co., supra.

One commentator has pointed out that the *Wheaton Glass* appellate decision rejecting the "identical job" standard marked a real turning point in equal pay litigation. Until then, an unofficial count showed that the department had lost more Equal Pay Act suits (eleven) than it had won (four).[3] The commentator concluded:[4]

> The *Wheaton* case, often relied upon by many employers' attorneys and courts in its now reversed district court stage, presents a whole new context to the application and future enforcement of the Equal Pay Act. It has obviously made the Equal Pay Act a more viable instrument for change. . . .

And in fact, the *Wheaton Glass* "substantially equal" standard has been approved by all appellate courts which have construed equal work.[5]

2. Wirtz v. Wheaton Glass Co., 284 F. Supp. 23, 32 (D.N.J. 1968).

16. Since 1945 equal pay bills have been introduced in every session of Congress by members of both political parties without much success. The use of female help in World War II economy, during a shortage of male help, generated much agitation to secure a man's wage for a man's work performed by a female. However, much of the proposed legislation pivoted on the word "comparable" and was found be objectionable, as lacking sufficient objectivity regarding work performance. It was not until the 88th Congress, that enactment of the Equal Pay Act became possible by the significant change of "comparable" to "equal." Congresswoman Katherine St. George, who proposed the word "equal," stated that it connoted the Webster Dictionary definition of exactness in measure, quantity, number or degree, and like in value, quality, and status or portion, implying no difference in amount, number or value. (108 Cong. Rec. 14767). Such meaning of the St. George amendment was approved by the House (108 Cong. Rec. 14771), passed by the 87th Congress, but did not receive action by the Senate before the Session ended.

3. Murphy, Female Wage Discrimination: A Study of the Equal Pay Act 1963-1970, 39 U. Cin. L. Rev. 615, 623 n.47 (1970). The author points out, though, that the Labor Department achieved more success in voluntary compliance agreements and consent judgments than in trials. During the same period when it was losing so many trials, it collected 12.6 million dollars and distributed them to 36,000 women through the voluntary methods.

4. Id. at 628.

5. Hodgson v. Brookhaven General Hospital, 436 F.2d 719, 725 (5th Cir. 1970); Hodgson v. Corning Glass Works, 474 F.2d 226, 234 (2d Cir. 1973); Hodgson v. Fairmont Supply Company, 454 F.2d 490, 496 (4th Cir. 1972); Hodgson v. Miller Brewing Company, 457 F.2d 221, 224 n.7 (7th Cir. 1972); Hodgson v. Square D Company, 459 F.2d 805 (6th Cir. 1972), *cert. denied,* 20 Wage & Hour Cas. 937, *affirming the district court's holding of equal work at* 19 Wage & Hour Cas. 752, 64 CCH Lab. Cas. ¶32,397 (E.D. Ky. 1970; not otherwise reported); Shultz v. American Can Company, 424 F.2d 356, 360-361 (8th Cir. 1970); Hodgson v. Daisy Manufacturing Company, 317 F. Supp. 538, 551-552 (W.D. Ark. 1970), *aff'd per curiam,* 445 F.2d 823 (8th Cir. 1971).

Note: Reconciling Title VII with the Equal Pay Act

A troubling issue which recurs throughout many Equal Pay Act cases is the clear presence of Title VII violations, which the courts often ignore. For example, in the *Wheaton Glass* lower court decision, the court pointed out that the Wheaton Glass Company had employed no women selector-packers prior to 1956. After that date,[6]

> Defendant continued to employ women in the Bottling Department but, because of their limited utility, not to its entire satisfaction. It became evident that by reason of its dependence upon males for the performance of the total job cycle, and not merely for some supposed economic advantage, the existing employment of females did not provide the requisite flexibility, so crucially essential to its singular operation. Just as soon as the labor market permitted, hiring reverted solely to males, although women were abundantly available and it would have been economically more feasible to employ them, especially since their wage rate was 10 percent lower than that of the men. The uncontradicted testimony presented by the defendant was that not one female was hired between August 12, 1962 and May 12, 1966, a period of almost four years, during which time 1,279 males were hired. . . .
> [D]efendant was compelled to resort to the employment of females once again in May, 1966, when the male labor market had been exhausted.

In effect, the company proved its own violation of Title VII — a refusal to hire women over a period of four years; the company's motive was, of course, to show that male employees were more valuable.

The Equal Pay Act does not specifically authorize the secretary of labor to include Title VII claims in Equal Pay Act litigation, yet once a Title VII violation is proved — by the company, no less — should the court ignore it? As pointed out in Part II supra, the Fifth Circuit has suggested that it would be unconstitutional for a federal court to support discrimination by failing to order its eradication, once the court gains knowledge of a discriminatory policy. Jenkins v. United Gas Corp., 400 F.2d 28 (5th Cir. 1968). The Fifth Circuit thought that courts could do this in the exercise of equity powers. Other theories may support the court's power to remedy Title VII violations which are proved in the course of Equal Pay Act litigation. For example, the Federal Rules of Civil Procedure envisage courts which are not bound by legal technicalities, but which achieve justice for the parties. Thus, Rule 15(b) provides:

> When issues not raised by the proceedings are tried by express or implied consent of the parties, they shall be treated in all respects as if they had been raised in the pleadings. Such amendment of the pleadings as may be necessary to cause them to conform to the evidence and to raise these issues may be made upon motion of any party at any time, even after judgment. . . .

In addition, Rule 54(c) decrees that:

> . . . every final judgment shall grant the relief to which the party in whose favor it is rendered is entitled, even if the party has not demanded such relief in his pleadings.

The theory underlying federal court pendent jurisdiction would also support, by analogy, an Equal Pay Act court in remedying Title VII discrimination. Pendent jurisdiction allows a federal court to assume jurisdiction of a state claim which arises out of the same transaction forming the basis of the federal claim before the court. Pendent jurisdiction prevents multiple litigation on the same subject, and conserves judicial resources.[7] Should not a similar theory apply to two related federal claims?

---

6. 284 F. Supp. at 28.
7. See United Mine Workers of America v. Gibbs, 383 U.S. 715, 726, 86 S. Ct. 1130, 16 L. Ed. 2d 218 (1966): "Its [the doctrine of pendent jurisdiction] justification lies in considerations of judicial economy,

The argument should be even stronger in this context, since it is standing and not the court's subject matter jurisdiction which is involved. The court clearly has jurisdiction over the claim; the question is simply whether the circumstances are such that the secretary of labor has the interest necessary to give the litigation the concreteness required by Article III of the Constitution. Since he has already pursued the Equal Pay Act suit based on the same factual setting and thus demonstrated his stake in the outcome, he would seem to be the "proper party to request an adjudication" based upon the Title VII claim as well. Flast v. Cohen, 392 U.S. 83, 100, 88 S. Ct. 1942, 20 L. Ed. 2d 947 (1968).

As a practical matter, Labor Department lawyers have previously dealt with this problem by referring some Title VII violations to the EEOC, but since the EEOC had no power to bring suit until March 1972, this solution yielded few visible results. Now the Labor Department and EEOC can bring suits against the same defendant and move for consolidation of the cases; but, in the ordinary case, this seems unlikely to occur, given the lack of in-depth communication between the two agencies. In one case —the mammoth AT&T lawsuit, supra, Part II — government lawyers representing both EEOC and the Labor Department did cooperate, and the court papers settling the lawsuit showed both agencies as parties plaintiff. However, this cooperation materialized only in the final settlement stages after several years of independent action by each agency.

Litigation brought by individuals can, of course, allege violations of both the Equal Pay Act and Title VII in one lawsuit. But the act would be better enforced if the Labor Department were more aggressive in seeking remedies for Title VII violations proved during the trial of an Equal Pay Act claim and in taking joint action with the EEOC. At the least, the Labor Department should notify the aggrieved women of their right to sue under Title VII, when such a right becomes evident in an Equal Pay Act case.

As you read through the remaining Equal Pay Act cases, see how many Title VII violations you can spot.

2. Equal Skill, Effort, and Responsibility

The *Wheaton Glass* court did not analyze separately the skill, the effort, and the responsibility required by the male and female selector-packer positions. Other courts have increasingly turned to a detailed analysis of each factor. Of these, the most important is equal effort. Over and over again, employers have tried to justify higher wages for men because the men are assigned a few extra lifting duties; the courts have generally — but not always — rejected this subterfuge.

a. Equal Effort

HODGSON v. BROOKHAVEN GENERAL HOSPITAL
436 F.2d 719 (5th Cir. 1970)

. . . the Secretary of Labor brought this action to enjoin the defendant Brookhaven General Hospital from violating the provisions of the Equal Pay Act of 1963, 29 U.S.C. §206. The District Court made findings of fact and conclusions of law, holding that the

---

convenience and fairness to litigants. . . ." See also Astor-Honor, Inc. v. Grossett & Dunlap, Inc., 441 F.2d 627, 629 (2d Cir. 1971), and Leather's Best, Inc. v. S.S. Mormaclynx, 451 F.2d 800, 809 (2d Cir. 1971), in which the court relies upon these considerations to allow jurisdiction over a state claim against one party where it is closely related to a federal claim against another party. Similarly, in Rosado v. Wyman, 397 U.S. 397, 405, 90 S. Ct. 1207, 25 L. Ed. 2d 442 (1970), the Court cites "the conservation of judicial energy and the avoidance of multiplicity of litigation" to allow jurisdiction over the pendent state claim even where the federal claim has become moot.

hospital's male orderlies and female nurse's aides performed substantially equal work, and that defendant paid its aides at lower wage rates which had not been shown to have been based on any factor other than sex. . . .

The appellant hospital contends, among other things, that . . . (2) the Secretary of Labor failed to sustain the burden of proving that the aides and orderlies were doing "equal work" within the meaning of 29 U.S.C. §206(d)(1) . . . This case may set an important precedent for hospitals, and, accordingly, we have analyzed the issues in some detail. . . .

It has been the consistent practice of the hospital to hire men as "orderlies" and women as "nurse's aides." As the Trial Judge noted in her findings of fact:

> The primary [though not the sole] work performed by both aides and orderlies consists of (1) caring for the personal needs of patients, such as serving food and beverages, assisting with baths, oral hygiene, skin care, perineal care, (2) assisting patients with mechanics such as ambulations, turning, wheel chairs, bed pans, coughing, and deep breathing. Aides and orderlies are both responsible for observing and reporting intake and output of patients, dietary intake and preference, proper body elimination, attitude towards nursing care, change in patient's condition. Both are responsible for giving enemas, performing surgical preps and perilights, and seeing that all equipment used is cleaned and properly maintained. . . .

The Trial Judge found in effect that during most of the months in question, orderlies were hired at salaries higher than the salaries at which aides were hired, and that where an experienced aide and an experienced orderly had virtually equal seniority, the orderly was paid more than the aide. There is evidence in the record to support this finding.

Brookhaven concedes that the duties which occupied the better part of the time of both groups of employees demanded equal skill, effort and responsibility. Each orderly and aide was primarily responsible for routine care of the patients assigned to him,[2] and for the most part the employees on duty at any time were assigned approximately the same number of patients. Though some differences may have existed in working conditions, we think the Judge was correct in minimizing them.

Brookhaven contends, however, that the two roles were and are substantially distinguishable in terms of the "secondary and tertiary" duties the respective groups were called on to perform. First, it contends, orderlies were frequently called on to perform general hospital duties which aides were rarely called on to perform — duties requiring more than routine skill (catheterizations), effort (lifting heavy patients, bringing in stretcher patients, setting up traction, helping in the application of heavy casts, subduing violent patients, holding patients down in uncomfortable positions during spinal taps, moving TV sets and other heavy equipment, assisting in the emergency room, bringing up supplies), and responsibility (maintaining hospital security and preparing to assume leadership in the event of a fire). Second, it contends, orderlies were called on to perform duties for male patients assigned to aides which involved no special skill, effort, or responsibility, but which the patients simply preferred to have orderlies do. Among these tasks were bathing of the midsection, giving enemas, and preparing patients for abdominal surgery. Generally at Brookhaven the ratio of male patients to orderlies exceeded the ratio of female patients to aides. Thus, while orderlies were seldom assigned to female patients, aides were frequently assigned to male patients. By and large, the hospital contends, aides performed the more intimate services for their patients only; orderlies performed these services for their patients *and* patients assigned for other purposes to aides. . . .

At the close of the testimony, the Trial Judge had before her evidence which, if

---

2. Discrimination on the basis of sex must sometimes be justifiable when one writes in a language containing no neuter personal pronoun.

credited, indicated that even the least experienced aides and orderlies were called on from time to time to perform duties beyond the ambit of routine patient care. She had to determine whether those duties were distributed evenly among all aides and all orderlies so as to warrant comparison of aides and orderlies as classes; and if so, whether as a class the work of the aides was substantially equal to that of the orderlies in terms of skill, effort, and responsibility.

Focusing simply on the individual tasks performed over and above routine patient care, it seems clear that the Trial Judge was justified in finding in effect that those tasks performed only by aides require as much skill as the most skilled tasks performed by orderlies, and that the additional duties assigned to both groups involved substantially equal responsibility. The validity of the judgment thus depends on the application of the "equal effort" criterion.

The equal effort criterion has received substantial play in the reported cases to date. As the doctrine is emerging, jobs do not entail equal effort, even though they entail most of the same routine duties, if the more highly paid job involves additional tasks which (1) require extra effort, (2) consume a significant amount of the time of all those whose pay differentials are to be justified in terms of them, and (3) are of an economic value commensurate with the pay differential.[5] We are persuaded that this approach to the application of the statutory "equal effort" criterion is in keeping with the fundamental purposes of the Equal Pay Act, and adopt it here. Employers may not be permitted to frustrate the purposes of the Act by calling for extra effort only occasionally, or only from one or two male employees, or by paying males substantially more than females for the performance of tasks which command a low rate of pay when performed full time by other personnel in the same establishment.

The problem here is that the Trial Judge's findings of fact are not sufficiently thorough and specific to permit us to ascertain whether this test for equality of effort was satisfied in this case. In order to understand the problem it is necessary to examine the hospital's contentions fairly closely.

Aides and orderlies are assigned to a set group of individual patients, each of whom exerts a specific claim on their time and attention. When the male operator of a container-making machine downs tools to move supplies, his machine stands idle, while his female counterpart continues to operate hers. Cf. Shultz v. American Can Company–Dixie Products, 8 Cir., 1970, 424 F.2d 356. Here, the hospital contends, the situation is significantly different. Aides and orderlies care for approximately the same number of patients. In general, when an aide or an orderly is called away on an outside assignment, the same patient duties await him on his return. Because orderlies are called away far more frequently than aides, the hospital maintains, the typical orderly is required to compress into 75 per cent of his working time the routine patient duties which occupy something like 98 per cent of the working time of the typical aide. Brookhaven does not concede, and the Trial Judge did not clearly find, that routine patient duties are as exacting in terms of skill, effort, and responsibility as the outside duties. It contends, however, that in any event orderlies are called on to do a significantly greater volume of work.

The findings of the District Court fail to meet these contentions head on. Cf. Fortner v. Balkcom, 5 Cir., 1967, 380 F. 2d 816, 821. The Trial Judge made no findings with respect to the actual time orderlies and aides consumed in performing all duties other than routine care for their own patients. There was uncontradicted testimony,

5. See Shultz v. American Can Company, 8 Cir., 1970, 424 F.2d 356; Shultz v. Wheaton Glass Company, 3 Cir., 1970, 421 F.2d 259, cert. denied, 398 U.S. 905, 90 S. Ct. 1696, 26 L. Ed. 2d 64 (1970); see also Wirtz v. Rainbo Baking Company of Lexington, E.D. Ky., 1967, 303 F. Supp. 1049; Wirtz v. Meade Mfg. Inc., D. Kan., 1968, 285 F. Supp. 812. Compare the following three decisions, in which federal district courts have held for the defendant on the equal-effort issue: Wirtz v. Kentucky Baptist Hospital, W.D. Ky., 1969, 62 Lab. Cas. ¶32,296; Wirtz v. Koller Craft Plastic Products, Inc., E.D. Mo., 1968, 296 F. Supp. 1195; Wirtz v. Dennison Manufacturing Company, D. Mass., 1967, 265 F. Supp. 787.

corroborated to some extent by the testimony of individual orderlies and aides, to the effect that the general practice of the hospital was (1) to substitute orderlies for aides in the performance of intimate services for patients of the employee's own sex, rather than the reverse; and (2) to assign orderlies first to heavy work and work involving physical risk, calling on aides for this work only when orderlies were unavailable. Under the statute and the circumstances of the case, the existence of such practices is a material issue. There are no specific findings of fact to indicate how the Trial Judge resolved this issue. Her summary finding, Finding 18, is "but the most general [conclusion] of ultimate fact. It is impossible to tell from [it] . . . whether proper statutory standards were observed." Schneiderman v. United States, 320 U.S. 118, 129-130, 63 S. Ct. 1333, 1338-1339, 87 L. Ed. 1796 (1943).

Where "a full understanding of the question presented" may be had without specific findings, no remand is necessary. Janzen v. Goos, 8 Cir., 1962, 302 F.2d 421. This is not such a case. It is not the function of an appellate court in a nonjury case to supplement the Trial Judge's findings with its own. Kelley v. Everglades Drainage Dist., 319 U.S. 415, 421-422, 63 S. Ct. 1141, 1145, 87 L. Ed. 1485 (1943); S. S. Silberblatt, Inc. v. United States, 5 Cir., 1965, 353 F.2d 545, 550. Under these circumstances, we remand for further findings. . . .

IV. TITLE VII

Finally, appellee directs our attention to Title VII of the Civil Rights Act of 1964, 42 U.S.C. §§2000e et seq. Section 2000e-2(a)(2) declares it to be an unlawful employment practice for an employer "to limit, segregate, or classify his employees in any way which would deprive or tend to deprive any individual of employment opportunities . . . because of such individual's . . . sex. . . ." It is apparent that the purposes of this section and the Equal Pay Act are interrelated, and that the two provisions must in some way be "harmonized." See generally Kanowitz, Sex-Based Discrimination in American Law III: Title VII of the 1964 Civil Rights Act and the Equal Pay Act of 1963, 20 Hastings L. Rev. 305 (1968). At least one federal court of appeals has suggested that equal pay should be required for a "male" job and a "female" job which are in fact unequal if the reservation of the higher paid job to males would be impermissible under Title VII. See Shultz v. Wheaton Glass Company, 3 Cir., 1970, 421 F.2d 259, 266, *cert. denied,* 398 U.S. 905, 90 S. Ct. 1696, 26 L. Ed. 2d 64 (1970). We think that the present case illustrates very well the problems in such an approach.

The kind of "customer preference" reflected in the hospital's assignment of orderlies to perform certain services for male patients otherwise assigned to aides is cognizable under Title VII. See Diaz v. Pan American World Airways, S.D. Fla., 1970, 311 F. Supp. 559. But it is apparent that these duties do not account for a major proportion of the orderlies' work over and above routine patient care for the patients assigned directly to them. Nor is this a case such as Shultz v. Kentucky Baptist Hospital, W.D. Ky., 1969, 62 CCH Lab. Cas. ¶32,296, in which the duties which distinguished the orderly's job from the aide's quite evidently demanded unusual physical strength.

In Weeks v. Southern Bell Telephone & Telegraph Company, 5 Cir., 1969, 408 F.2d 228, this Court held that an employer violated 42 U.S.C. §2000e-2 when it foreclosed to women a job involving substantial physical effort on the assumption that few or no women possessed the necessary physical qualifications. If we were to adopt the approach of the Third Circuit in *Wheaton Glass,* supra, the *Weeks* analysis might be used here to sustain the Secretary of Labor's claim on behalf of the aides under the Equal Pay Act. We reject that approach because we believe it is destined to yield unfair results. "[O]n many jobs in which men are being paid higher wages than women because greater physical effort is apparently required, most women have not wanted or sought an opportunity to be so employed." Kanowitz, supra at 354, citing Wirtz v. Dennison Manufacturing Company, D. Mass., 1967, 265 F. Supp. 787 (1967). The purposes of the

Equal Pay Act and Title VII of the Civil Rights Act of 1964 are not well served by confounding the respective proofs required of plaintiffs. . . .

NOTE:
BROOKHAVEN'S IMPLICATIONS FOR OTHER AIDE-ORDERLY CASES

On remand, the district court found that the work of the aides and orderlies required equal effort, 65 CCH Lab. Cas. ¶32,520, 20 Wage & Hour Cas. 54 (N.D. Tex. 1971); the hospital appealed once more, but the Fifth Circuit ruled that the district court's finding of equal effort could be set aside under Federal Rule of Civil Procedure 52(a) only if it was "clearly erroneous," and that it was not. 470 F.2d 729 (5th Cir. 1972).

While the results in *Brookhaven* were favorable, the application to the findings on equal effort of the "clearly erroneous" standard for review leaves a disturbing amount of discretion to the district court. The maladministration of the act which can result from such unfettered discretion is revealed in another aide-orderly case, Hodgson v. Golden Isles Convalescent Homes, Inc., 468 F.2d 1256 (5th Cir. 1972), decided less than a month prior to *Brookhaven.* Like the Brookhaven General Hospital, the Golden Isles Convalescent Center alleged that orderlies performed many tasks not performed by aides; however, in this case the district court found in favor of the convalescent home as to the following tasks:[8]

> "A. Insertion of catheter, a skilled nursing function, which no aide would perform on males. B. Total lifting. C. Irrigation. D. Setting up a traction. E. Returning patients who had gone out of the building or who had simply wandered off. Acting as drivers to pick up patients. F. Primarily setting up oxygen tanks which required knowledge and skill.
> "In addition to performing the above different functions, the orderly at Golden Isles was required to 'float' to help in the rest of the nursing home. Aides were not required to 'float.' This was a substantial difference."
> The Secretary contends that these duties were performed by aides, that they did not differ greatly from aides' other duties, and that they were performed too infrequently to justify a conclusion that the work was unequal.

Despite the secretary of labor's arguments, the appellate court applied the "clearly erroneous" standard in favor of the home. It then concluded:[9]

> The Department of Labor apparently seeks to obtain a conclusive determination by the courts that, in hospitals and nursing homes across the country, aides and orderlies perform equal work. An amicus curiae brief informs us that numerous federal court actions throughout the country involve the "identical" issue raised in this case, i.e., whether nurse's aides perform work "equal" to that of orderlies, within the meaning of the Equal Pay Act of 1963. Some of these cases have been decided in favor of the hospital. E.g., Hodgson v. Good Shepherd Hospital, 327 F. Supp. 143 (E.D. Tex. 1971); Hodgson v. William and Mary Nursing Home, 65 L.C. ¶32,497 (M.D. Fla. 1971); and Shultz v. Royal Glades, Inc., 66 L.C. ¶32,548 (S.D. Fla. 1971). Some have decided that the work of orderlies and aides in the hospitals under consideration was equal. E.g., Shultz v. Brookhaven Hospital, 305 F. Supp. 424 (N.D. Tex. 1969); *reversed and remanded sub nom.* Hodgson v. Brookhaven General Hospital, 436 F.2d 719 (5th Cir. 1970), *on remand,* 65 L.C. ¶32,520 (N.D. Tex. 1971); Hodgson v. George W. Hubbard Hospital, 351 F. Supp. 1295 (M.D. Tenn.).
> These issues must be decided on a case-by-case basis under the facts of each case. They cannot be decided on an industry-wide basis. All aides in all hospitals do

8. 468 F.2d at 1257.
9. Id. at 1257-1259.

not perform identical functions. Nor do all orderlies in all hospitals perform identical functions. The functions for each classification may not even be substantially equal in different hospitals. The differences or similarities in each case must determine the ultimate outcome under the Equal Pay Act. For example, *Brookhaven* and *Hubbard,* supra, involved different facts than those found at Golden Isles. In *Brookhaven,* where there was a larger number of orderlies than in the case at bar, the court found that both orderlies and aides were assigned equal numbers of patients, that the primary duties of aides and orderlies were the same, and that the secondary and tertiary duties which were thought to distinguish the jobs either did not differ significantly from the primary responsibilities or were performed by aides as well as orderlies. In *Hubbard,* the proof showed that both female nurse's aides and male nurse attendants performed and assisted each other in performing as a unit, without regard to job classification, the task that the employer contended were performed only by the orderlies. Neither *Brookhaven* nor *Hubbard* presented the precise configuration of job functions and employee performances found at Golden Isles.

The legislative history of the Equal Pay Act underscores the necessity of case-by-case analysis. By substituting the term "equal work" for "comparable work," which was originally suggested, Congress manifested its intent to narrow the applicability of the Act. Cong. Rec. Vol. 19, Part 7 (88th Congress, 1st Sess.), at 8866, 8892, 8913-8917, 9192-9218, 9761-9762, 9854, and 9941. This legislative history is discussed extensively in Hodgson v. William and Mary Nursing Home, 65 L.C. ¶32,497 (M.D. Fla. 1971). It is not merely comparable skill and responsibility that Congress sought to address, but a substantial identity of job functions.

Furthermore, Congress intended to permit employers wide discretion in evaluating work for pay purposes. In the House Subcommittee Report on the Equal Pay Act, 109 Cong. Rec. 9209-9210 (1963), examples were debated to illustrate that a wage differential can be justified for employees who are available to perform an important differentiating task even though they do not spend large amounts of time at the task. Again, this approach requires examination of equal work claims in the light of practice in the particular employment.

We do not here decide whether the job of orderly should be open to females, or whether the job of nurse's aide should be open to males. Those questions are to be resolved in actions under Title VII of the Civil Rights Act of 1964, 42 U.S.C.A. §2000e (1970), in the manner pursued in Diaz v. Pan American World Airways, Inc., 442 F.2d 385 (5th Cir. 1971). Courts must be cautious not to apply improperly one Congressional act to achieve a purpose for which another act was intended. We here decline, nevertheless, to sanction the concept that only males can perform the work of an orderly. We decide only that the evidence supports the finding that the work done by the orderly at Golden Isles was sufficiently different from the work done by the aide to justify different pay scales. Having decided that, the extent of the difference is of no concern in this proceeding.

The Labor Department often pursues the strategy of obtaining a favorable appellate decision as to a type of occupation, and on the basis of precedent, negotiating settlements with other employers with similar practices. This seems like a wise use of limited agency resources, but the *Golden Isles* decision suggests that the courts may thwart the strategy through a rigid attention to detail and limited review. Indeed, the *Golden Isles* court's attempt to distinguish *Brookhaven* fails miserably; one cannot escape the conviction, after comparing the duties listed in each case, that a technical standard has been used as a device to enable a court's prejudices to prevail over fair wages for low-paid women workers.

NOTE: THE TITLE VII PROBLEM AGAIN

In the concluding paragraphs of the *Brookhaven* opinion, the Fifth Circuit attempts to deal with the problem of open Title VII violations, but the analysis is inadequate. First, about one and one-half years later, the court reversed the district court *Diaz* decision it cites in *Brookhaven* to justify — under a theory of customer preference — the hospital's assignment of orderlies to male patients for intimate care. (See Diaz v. Pan American World Airways, Part II-B supra.) And, although this practice has a surface plausibility in the interests of privacy, it loses much of that plausibility when it is recalled that the vast majority of female patients must commonly accept equally intimate services from male doctors. The difference between the two practices is that the female patient–male doctor relationship subordinates the female to the male, while the male patient–female aide relationship subordinates the male to the female. One is culturally acceptable; the other is not. But such cultural prejudices were precisely what Title VII was designed to overcome, and the hospital should not be allowed to violate Title VII by arbitrarily removing work from the female's job and then paying her less for what is left. The court seeks to avoid the implication that it is doing this by saying, "it is apparent that these [intimate care] duties do not account for a major proportion of the orderlies' work over and above routine patient care," yet the court had just cited these very duties as one of the two major facts creating a "material issue" involving equal effort, and thus necessitating remand.

The second major defect in the court's reasoning is that it ignores the implications of its own decision in *Weeks,* relying on the authority of one commentator's assertion that women have not wanted or sought heavy work. This despite the fact that in *Weeks* itself a woman wanted, and won, the right to "heavy" work. Since women have indeed sought heavy — i.e., higher paying — work over and over in Title VII cases, the court's refusal to prohibit the hospital from denying women heavy work, and then paying them less because of that, is indefensible. And by suggesting that, if the men were given *enough* extra work, the court would accept higher pay for the men, while refusing to look at the accompanying sex segregation of duties, the court actually encourages employers to differentiate the jobs and further violate Title VII.

In *Golden Isles,* the court simply abandons the effort to resolve the Title VII issue, saying that "Courts must be cautious not to apply improperly one Congressional act to achieve a purpose for which another act was intended." No attempt is made to explain how the purposes of Title VII and the Equal Pay Act differ.

NOTE: THE IMPORTANCE OF WEIGHT LIFTING

It is interesting that weight lifting is frequently offered as the extra duty which justifies increased pay for men. As a general proposition, our society does not reward, or particularly respect, physical exertion; e.g., administrators are paid more than garbage collectors. Yet in the context of male-female working relationships, physical exertion is used to justify higher pay — even where women are doing more highly skilled tasks in the time that the men devote to lifting.

This suggests that the real motive in paying men more for weight lifting is to maintain a dominant male–subordinate female hierarchy on the job. The hierarchy is a reflection of the structure of the larger society. One study of male managers' attitudes toward working women revealed a need to maintain this traditional structure: "Respondents were 174 males employed full-time in business or industry in the Rochester [New York] area in lower-, middle-, and upper-level management and staff positions."[10] These men were given a questionnaire to complete which contained 40 unfavorable statements about women (e.g., women cannot be aggressive in situations that demand it). For each statement, the respondent had to choose among 5 alternatives: 5 = strongly agree; 4 = agree; 3 = uncertain or don't know; 2 = disagree; 1 = strongly disagree. The

10. Bass, Krusell, and Alexander, Male Managers' Attitudes Toward Working Women, 15 Am. Behavioral Scientist 221, 224 (1971).

items were analyzed by separating them into 7 categories, or factors, relating to women workers' career orientation, supervisory potential, dependability, deference, emotionality, capability, and life style. The single statement with which the managers most strongly agreed was: "Women prefer working for a male boss" (mean — 3.9). Means were also computed for the broader categories, or factors. The authors of the study concluded:[11]

> . . . Analysis of the managers' responses revealed that certain factors influence their ability to accept women on an equal basis with men in the work situation.
> Of the seven factors, managers in this sample felt most strongly about deference. . . . That is, they felt that certain norms defined interaction between men and women — most notably, rules of etiquette and politeness between the two sexes in public. Implied in the managers' reactions to the items heavily loaded for the deference factor is that men and women have defined societal roles which govern their interaction. On the surface, deference does not seem to be that detrimental to the attainment of equality for women at work. However, the analysis of the next highest factor score sheds more light on the influence of the deference factor. Managers did not feel that women would make good supervisors. This does not appear to be because women were perceived as less capable than men (capability had the lowest mean factor score of all seven factors). Rather, the managers indicated that they felt that other men and women would prefer having male supervisors and that they themselves would be uncomfortable with a women supervisor. The problem seems to be that societal norms do not sanction the placement of women in dominant positions. The possibility of women becoming supervisors proved very uncomfortable for the managers.

A second sociological lesson that can be derived from the practice of paying men more for physical exertion such as weight lifting is that male chivalry has its price. Undoubtedly, one important reason for allocating lifting tasks to men is the cultural norm that strong men should take care of weak women. In return, however, men expect to receive greater power or privilege — which translates into higher pay in the job context. Of course, this aspect of the chivalry ideology is seldom discussed.

b. Mental Effort

An important variation on the effort theme appears in this case, involving a manufacturing company that assigned men and women workers to heavy and light work respectively in each of several job classifications.

HODGSON v. DAISY MANUFACTURING COMPANY
317 F. Supp. 538 (W.D. Ark. 1970),
aff'd per curiam, 445 F.2d 823 (8th Cir. 1971)

Defendant . . . admits that the respective job pairs require equal skill and that the women workers have always been excluded as a class from the higher paying male job classifications.[1] Defendant denies, however, that the wage differentials are discriminatory under the Act's equal pay provisions principally for the reason that the "heavy" or male jobs require greater physical effort. . . .

     . . . Prior to this action, Daisy designated its operations as either "male" or "female." Since this suit, defendant has redesignated "male" as "heavy" and "female" as "light," but has at all times excluded women as a class from the higher paying "male" or "heavy" designations. At all times, Daisy's male employees have been paid 10 cents

---

11. Id. at 232-233.
1. Plaintiff does not allege herein a violation of Title VII of the Civil Rights Act of 1964, 42 U.S.C. §2000e et seq. . . .

an hour more than their female counterparts. Other than press operators, all of the men in question have been paid an identical rate (now $2.10 an hour) and all of the women in question have been paid an identical rate (now $2.00 an hour). Male press operators, at $2.15 an hour, are paid 5 cents an hour more than the other men, and female press operators, at $2.05 an hour, are paid 5 cents an hour more than the other women. The men and women workers in question are paid strictly on an hourly basis, but 90 percent of them are governed by production quotas which the employees are expected to meet. . . . Quotas are established by timing the operation and then adjusting the hourly rate, if necessary, based upon the relative efficiency of the operator, then allowing a factor for fatigue, coffee breaks, cleanup, personal time, and "stock chasing" (material handling) if it applies to the operation. On "light" operations, the factor for fatigue, coffee breaks, cleanup and personal time is 15 to 20 percent. On "heavy" operations, it is usually 5 to 10 percent above the women's allowance, primarily as a result of material handling occasionally performed by male employees. Accordingly, the defendant generally sets substantially lower production quotas for operations designated as "heavy."

The system of production used by Daisy is based upon an engineering method which involves the analysis of the production of each part into a series of separate operations. Each separate operation performed on each part has its own production number and quota. For example, the production of the barrel for the model 1894 air rifle involves eight separate steps within the press department alone. It is not uncommon for an employee to work on many operations over a period of 60-90 days, but men work exclusively on operations designated "heavy" and women work exclusively on operations designated "light." Daisy has never, however, tested its women employees for "heavy" operations; it does not have or use preemployment tests for physical strength or stamina, or ability to lift weights; and it has never prescribed height or weight standards for any of the operations. Daisy offered no evidence as to how its "heavy" and "light" operations were originally chosen. . . .

[The court then examined the job of punch press operator.]

Defendant concedes that the work of male and female punch press operators requires equal skill and is performed under similar working conditions, but contends that the work of the males requires greater physical effort and job responsibility. The principal duties of the press operators are to feed metal blanks and gun parts into sundry punch presses, where they are formed, stamped, pierced, drawn, U-formed, closed, struck or re-struck and swaged; activate the press by depressing hand or foot controls; and, in the case of parts not automatically ejected by the press, remove the processed parts and stack them in containers for further processing. Women perform operations on every part which goes through the press department, most of which range in weight from a fraction of an ounce to a few ounces, and the largest parts, the barrels, weigh from about 9 ounces to one pound. . . . At the time of trial 28 women and 17 men worked in the press department.

Each press operator is charged with the responsibility of producing satisfactory work. At the end of the shift, each must do cleanup work, around his or her work area and enter the day's production on slips provided for this purpose. In addition, the male operators must roll their own containers of parts to the presses, either from another press or from a parts stockpile where wheeled containers full of parts are concentrated. When a female press operator completes an operation on a part, she places the part in a wheeled cart or gondola beside her press. If the next operation is performed by a male, he walks to the woman's press, a distance of a few feet, and rolls a container full of parts back to his own press. If, after a "heavy" operation is completed, the next operation is to be performed by a woman or in another department, a material handler or "stock chaser" rolls the container of parts to the appropriate location. If the next operation is not performed by a woman and the parts are not needed in another department, the male press operator rolls the parts to a stockpile. The material handling done by the male press operators involves a few trips per shift and accounts for approximately 3 to 4 percent of their work time. The company provides mechanical means for material handling, such as the wheeled cars or gondolas, and hydraulic jacks and hoists and, as a matter of company policy, Daisy's employees are not expected to do any heavy lifting or pushing by themselves, but are encouraged to get help and are in fact required to do so when lifting over fifty pounds.

Closing operations in the press department involve the use of a steel rod called an arbor or mandrel. The part to be closed is slid onto the mandrel, both are inserted into the mouth of the die, and when the press is activated the die molds or closes the part around the mandrel. After the die opens the part is stripped from the mandrel either automatically by another die operation on the same press, or manually by the operator. Manual stripping is accomplished by pulling the mandrel against a metal notch on the press. Both male and female press operators perform operations involving the use of mandrels, and both perform those which require the operator to manually strip the part from the mandrel.

Male press operators exert greater physical effort in performing some operations involving mandrels. Since mandrels form parts of varying sizes, they differ greatly in size and weight. Barrel size mandrels weigh up to 4½ pounds, while the smallest mandrels weigh only a few ounces. Daisy assigns only males to close the larger barrels and requires substantially lower quotas than those assigned to closing operations performed by females, in part because the presses strike the larger barrels three times in closing them instead of once in the case of barrels closed by females.

The company production manager testified that closing shot tubes is a "heavy" operation for the reason that they must be air tight, which results in close tolerance on the mandrel and requires the operator to exert considerable effort to strip the part. A male press operator testified that it is in fact difficult for him to strip the shot tube for a model 25 air rifle from the mandrel. It is, however, undisputed that females perform the closing operation on the shot tube for model 177 air rifles, which is classified as a "light" operation, and carries a substantially higher quota than the shot tube closing operations performed by males. As in the case of barrel closing operations, the lower male quotas are in part attributable to the fact that the presses strike the larger shot tubes several times.

Regarding the weight of the mandrels used in closing the larger air rifle barrels and the difficulty involved in stripping closed shot tubes from the mandrels used in those operations, it must be said that closing barrels and shot tubes amounts to less than 100 operations out of approximately 4,000 performed in the press department. There is also nothing in the record indicating how much of the males' work time is consumed in closing barrels and shot tubes and whether all male punch press operators spend approximately the same amount of time on such operations. In addition, the majority of mandrel operations performed by press operators of both sexes are performed with small mandrels, and male and female operators use many mandrels of the same size.

Male press operators regularly perform low-speed press operations not involving the use of mandrels, such as forming, U-forming and swaging, and are also assigned lower quotas than their female counterparts for these operations. Daisy apparently seeks to justify the lower male quotas for such operations by the fact that the males are required to bring their own stock to the presses. In any event, all high-speed press operations are performed by women, who are required to place the part used into the die by hand and then withdraw their hand from the die area, simultaneously activating the press by depressing a foot pedal. While the high-speed presses are equipped with a sweep guard, the press may "double-trip" on occasion and at times the sweep guard, because of continual use, becomes improperly coordinated with the closing of the die. When this happens, the female operator's hand may be caught as the die closes. Since Daisy began its operations at Rogers in 1958, seven female press operators have lost one or more fingers in die-closing accidents. There is no record of any male press operator being involved in a die-closing accident. Plaintiff introduced the testimony of an industrial psychologist who stated that the risk of injury to the women on high-speed presses is a factor which causes mental stress and fatigue; an industrial engineer who made an extensive study of the male and female operations at the Daisy plant testified that the risk of losing fingers necessitates a high degree of mental and visual attention for sustained periods; and a female punch press operator of eleven years experience testified that she felt fear every day she put her hand into the die.

The Secretary's Interpretative Bulletin regarding the Equal Pay Act defines "effort" as "the measurement of physical or *mental* exertion needed for the performance of a job." (Emphasis added.) 29 C.F.R. §800.127. The court agrees that job factors which cause mental fatigue and stress, as well as those which alleviate fatigue, all bear on the question of "effort" required by the job. Thus, "effort" embraces the total requirements of the job, and includes mental as well as physical exertion. It seems clear to the court that female press operators who are required to place their hands in the die in the course of operating high-speed presses expend significant mental exertion that is not required of their male counterparts.

Daisy also contends that greater job responsibility is required of its male press operators in that negligence in rolling containers of parts in work areas may result in lost time accidents to others. It is doubtful that the possibility of carelessness on the part of male press operators while engaged in material handling comes within the concept of job responsibility which is defined in 29 C.F.R. §800.129 as "concerned with the degree of accountability required in the performance of the job, with emphasis on the importance of the job obligation." More important, there is no record of a single accident involving material handling in the ten and one-half years defedant has operated its plant at Rogers, Arkansas. In short, there is no basis in fact for crediting male press operators with more job responsibility within the meaning of the Act.

In summary, male and female press operators have the same primary job function and perform essentially the same duties. Male press operators engage in occasional materials handling and exert greater physical effort in closing the larger shot tubes and barrels. Female press operators have substantially higher production quotas and exert greater mental effort when operating high-speed presses. The differences in job requirement between males and females are incidental and unsubstantial. . . .

[The court similarly concluded that men and women in the other contested job categories of paint line tender, subassembler, final assembler, inspector, and packer were performing equal work.

The court then discussed the issue, almost never referred to by courts, of unequal wage rates paid to *different* male and female jobs, where the female job requires equal or *greater* skill and responsibility than the male job.]

Daisy's defense, when closely scrutinized, rests primarily on the often repeated allegation that certain operations performed by the males require greater physical effort than that expended by the females. This basic argument possesses considerable merit and appeal, but the court is plainly unable to justify significant wage differentials based upon these sometimes additional and usually more physically difficult duties in the absence of evidence as to approximately how much work time such duties consume and whether all males receiving a given wage rate spend approximately the same amount of time in performing them. Shultz v. Wheaton Glass Co., [421 F.2d 259 (3d Cir.), *cert. denied,* 398 U.S. 905, 90 S. Ct. 1696, 26 L. Ed. 2d 64 (1970)]; Shultz v. American Can Co., [424 F.2d 356 (8th Cir. 1970)]. In addition, skill, job responsibility and working conditions must be weighed along with physical or mental effort. This rather obvious generalization carries particular import regarding stock chasing duties, to which the defendant has attempted to attach considerable weight in these proceedings. It must be remembered that while stock chasing requires substantial physical effort, it requires very little skill and entails minimal job responsibility. During the work time that the males spend stock chasing, the females are generally performing operations requiring substantially greater skill and job responsibility. In determining wage classifications, an employer cannot make jobs unequal by arbitrarily according greater weight to the physical effort required by a job than the weight or value accorded to skill, job responsibility and working conditions. It would be absurd to contend, apart from the statutory exceptions, that a male stock handler should be paid more than a female chemist or computer operator, simply because the job of the male requires greater physical effort. In the same vein, the court has considerable difficulty in rationalizing the fact that Daisy pays the male packers [primarily an unskilled job] more than the female punch press operators. [Male packers got $2.10 an hour; female packers, $2.00; male press operators, $2.15; female press operators, $2.05.]

NOTE: EQUAL PAY FOR DIFFERENT JOBS IF THE WOMAN'S JOB REQUIRES EQUAL SKILL, EFFORT, AND RESPONSIBILITY

The court's suggestion that male stock handlers cannot be paid more than female chemists has important implications. Jobs into which women have traditionally been segregated — such as secretary, typist, or telephone operator — are commonly undervalued for pay purposes throughout the United States. Because most companies do not hire men in such categories, the Equal Pay Act does not prohibit undervaluation of these services. However, Title VII might be interpreted to prohibit the practice, although no litigation to date has raised the issue. For instance, if plaintiffs could prove that a company paid men more for a manual job which required the same degree of skill, effort, and responsibility as a secretarial position, a court might realize that the company is evaluating on the basis of sex the economic worth of the two jobs.

Job evaluation plans offer one potential method of proof. A commentator explains their history and use.

Murphy, Female Wage Discrimination:
A Study of the Equal Pay Act 1963–1970
39 U. Cin. L. Rev. 615, 634-637 (1970)

4. THE USE OF JOB STUDIES

Congress chose the factors of skill, effort, responsibility, and working conditions to serve as the core of the Equal Pay Act standard primarily because these were the criteria used in standard job classification systems to evaluate jobs for classification and pay purposes. Briefly, a job evaluation or study takes two forms: (1) The traditional time and motion study, the objective of which is to find the best way to perform an operation or to set a production standard, and (2) the Kress method, which is used to identify the relative worth of each job to the company, and to provide a ranking or grading of jobs. Since the latter method has a similar objective to that of the Equal Pay Act, and since it uses the elements of skill, effort, responsibility, and working conditions, it is obviously the best method to compare male and female jobs.

Essentially, the job study quantifies work content, and thus is the most accurate way to determine equality of skill, effort, responsibility, and working conditions. The job study enters into the equal pay arena from two directions: (1) The results of job studies are offered by companies to show inquiring government investigators that their wage scales are soundly based, and to disprove sex as a factor in setting such rates.[99] (2) Job studies are presently being used by the Labor Department, through expert testimony, to show that the male-female jobs are equal and the male-female rates are discriminatory.[100]

99. E.g., Wirtz v. Multi-Products, Inc., 59 CCH Lab. Cas. ¶32,124 (N.D. Ill. 1968).
100. E.g., Shultz v. Hayes Indus., Inc., Civil No. 68-4 (N.D. Ohio April 14, 1970).

The Kress method of job study, used successfully by the Labor Department to prove a violation of the Equal Pay Act in Shultz v. Hayes Industries, Inc.,[101] is a trial lawyer's delight because it can be the most persuasive and exclusively important evidence of his case. The professional job evaluator, usually an engineer, observes the disputed jobs in action, taking detailed notes of what the females and males do in their respective assignments. Each of the elements are then subcategorized in the following manner and graded weights are given each element:

1. Skill (50 percent)
   (a) scholastic content
   (b) learning period
2. Effort (15 percent)
   (a) mental application
   (b) physical resistance overcome by operator
3. Responsibility (20 percent)
   (a) seriousness of errors
   (b) originality of problems
   (c) degree to which work is supervised
   (d) teamwork and public contacts required
   (e) supervision exercised by operator
4. Working Conditions (15 percent)
   (a) hazards and disagreeable conditions
   (b) expense to operator.

Using this analysis, each element of skill, effort, and the like is awarded a total number of points which are within a given predetermined weighted range. The job with the most points is eligible for a higher rate of pay.

To illustrate, in the *Hayes* case, the employees worked at a large power press, equipped with five dies in succession, and one piece of metal was moved through a sequence of operations by five different operators. The employer argued that one of the positions at the dies was more difficult than the other jobs, and thus an "A" (male) operator was assigned to this post at a higher rate than his four female colleagues, who were designated as "B" operators.

The job analysts, hired as expert witnesses by the Labor Department, made a quantitative job content study of the "B" jobs and the "A" jobs, based upon the Kress method, and assigned almost identical point values to all the positions at this press, concluding that the jobs were equal in skill, effort, and responsibility, and were performed under similar work conditions. While it is true that the Kress method involves some degree of subjectivity, it is the most rational way to compare jobs for equal pay purposes, so long as the study is performed by qualified analysts. The lay observations, conclusions, and unrefined impressions of Labor Department investigators, job foremen and managers, lawyers, and judges rank far below the degree of accuracy and scientific sophistication which a professional job study offers.

In the several cases where authentic job studies have been offered as evidence, the courts have given them significant weight. In Wirtz v. Multi-Products, Inc.,[104] where an impartial job evaluation had, well before the litigation commenced, established wage scale and job category grades, the court relied heavily on the evaluation in finding no discrimination. In Shultz v. Hayes Industries, Inc., the job evaluators, hired by the Labor Department as expert witnesses, clearly contributed to the court's findings that the male and female jobs were equal.[106]

101. Id.
104. 59 CCH Lab. Cas. ¶32,124 (N.D.Ill. 1968).
106. . . . See also Shultz v. Corning Glass Works, 63 CCH Lab. Cas. ¶32,363 (W.D.N.Y. 1970), where the plaintiff offered the defendant's job study as evidence of equality between male and female inspector jobs.

A word of caution about the utility of job studies should be noted because their use and acceptance is not universal. Job studies quantify, with point value, work content; but for equal pay purposes, the types of jobs being compared must be similar. Thus, the Labor Department's Interpretative Bulletin reads: "[T]he fact that jobs performed by male and female employees may have the same total point values under an evaluation system in use by the employer does not in itself mean that the jobs concerned are equal according to the terms of the statute."[107]

Similarly, in Krumbeck v. John Oster Mfg. Co.,[108] the court refused to accept the premise that jobs which are totally different in nature, but have the same total point value, should be considered equal. The court, in finding the jobs incomparable, indicated that the purpose of the Equal Pay Act would be misdirected if jobs were judged merely on their total point values, saying that you cannot compare a female bookkeeper with a male file clerk, even if their job content point totals, computed by a job evaluator, are equal.[109]

Despite certain misapplications of job studies, the fact remains that a professional job evaluation, based upon the Kress or a similar method, constitutes the best technique to evaluate jobs. Since Congress, in drafting the Equal Pay Act, chose the very same evaluation factors as used by professional job study analysts, the evidentiary impact of such job studies is no real phenomenon. Any employer, who reviews his wage structure and differential, and thereafter entertains a serious doubt as to its legality for equal pay purposes, should engage the services of a professional and independent job evaluator to compare the involved positions. When the study is completed, and the appropriate wage adjustments, if any, are made, the employer can have no better insurance against an equal pay lawsuit. . . .

Despite the *Daisy Manufacturing* court's suggestion, then, it appears unlikely that Equal Pay Act courts will require equal pay for different jobs with the same total point value. However, Title VII might well require this result. The major roadblock to such a decision is §703(h) of Title VII, often referred to as the Bennett Amendment:[12]

> It shall not be an unlawful employment practice under this subchapter for any employer to differentiate upon the basis of sex in determining the amount of the wages or compensation paid or to be paid to employees of such employer if such differentiation is authorized by the [Equal Pay Act].

The question would be whether undervaluing "women's work" in sex-segregated jobs is "authorized" by the Equal Pay Act, or whether it is even reached by the act. One could make a strong argument that the Equal Pay Act does not reach a comparison of *different* (unlike) jobs with equal economic worth, any more than it reaches job segregation; thus, undervaluation of different jobs is not "authorized" by the Equal Pay Act, just as job segregation is not.

This issue is one of major importance, for it is the only way rapidly to improve the economic position of the vast majority of women workers in the female job "ghetto." Opening up male jobs will help some women, but most will remain in their present job categories, if for no other reason than the time it will take to create "male job" vacancies. In the interval, the "ghetto" female worker deserves better pay.

Despite the defendant-employer's objections as to the admissability of the study, the court relied heavily on the findings of the employer's analyst because his study utilized the same criteria set forth in the Equal Pay Act (skill, effort, and responsibility, etc.) and the job study was made prior to the inception of the litigation. The job evaluator had found female and male inspector's work equal in point value, and the court found for equalized the wage structure, injunctive relief and a large back pay award might have been avoided.

107. 29 C.F.R. §800.121 (1970).
108. 63 CCH Lab. Cas. ¶32,350 (E.D. Wis. 1970).
109. Id. ¶32,350 at 44,267.
12. Section 703(h), 42 U.S.C. §2000e-2(h) (1970).

NOTE: EXPERT TESTIMONY IN EQUAL PAY ACT CASES

The *Daisy Manufacturing* case offers a representative sample of the kinds of expert testimony used in Equal Pay Act litigation. The government called five experts. The first, a research psychologist who worked for the Civil Service Commission, testified on women's strength and stamina. The Labor Department brief on appeal explains:[13]

> The testimony of Dr. Myers (A. 85-88) was offered for the purpose of showing the strength and stamina of women in general as determined by a civil service test given to women applicants for the position of mail handler. At the time Dr. Myers took the stand, it was thought that Daisy would contend that brawn alone made men more flexible and thus worth more as employees. As the case unfolded, however, Daisy made no such contention. . . . Under the civil service test for women mail handlers, applicants are required to lift, shoulder and carry, for a distance of 15 feet, 14 mail bags weighing up to 80 pounds; place the bags on a hand truck; pull the loaded truck for a distance of 15 feet; and then unload the truck — all within 10 minutes. Dr. Myers testifed that over 60 percent of the women taking the test had passed it.
>
> Daisy offered no rebuttal evidence on the physical capabilities of women to lift, shoulder and carry the type weights involved in Civil Service Test No. 915 which are considerably in excess of the physical tasks required of the Daisy males in question. As Daisy's Plant Manager acknowledged, the males are provided mechanical means for stock chasing, such as wheeled tables, "gondolas" or "coffins," and hydraulic jacks and hoists. As a matter of plant policy, they are not required to lift or push anything heavy by themselves, but are expected and encouraged to get help from other employees (A. 147). As an example of this policy, the plant manager testified as follows (A. 147):
>
> *Q.* Now suppose you have tote pans that weigh 100 pounds, what is your recommended procedure to a male employee, how is he supposed to lift the pan; he is a new employee and wants to know how you recommend that he handle the 100 pound tote pan?
> *A.* If he is required to lift it manually he is required to get someone else there to help him.
> *Q.* You don't want him to lift over 50 pounds.
> *A.* That is right.

Two psychology professors who had done research on fatigue and anxiety listened to the testimony of a male and a female punch press operator and then testified on the effort each exerted.[14]

> On the basis of the foregoing testimony, Dr. Sawyer testifed that in his opinion Mrs. Smith [a press operator who had lost one and a half fingers] exerts more effort than does Mr. Bunch [the male press operator] (A. 121). Handfeeding a high speed press with anxiety of fear of loss of fingers, he stated, makes for fatigue (A. 120, 121). The fatigue factor in repetitive operations is reduced by any movement away from a stationary position — be it to chase stock or whatever. It is a break in the routine or a change of pace (A. 121).
>
> Dr. DeKock agreed. At the outset, he explained that Mrs. Smith's job was more difficult because the male was permitted to stock chase which gave him a break from operating the press (A. 128). Dr. DeKock testified that his opinion that Mrs. Smith's job was "more demanding than that of the gentleman" (A. 128) was reached without regard to the fear or anxiety which may result from handfeeding a high-speed punch

13. Hodgson v. Daisy Manufacturing Company, Brief for the Secretary of Labor, 25-27, n.6, Nos. 20700, 71-1002 (8th Cir.).
14. Id. at 29-30.

press, but that consideration of this factor provided a further ground for the conclusion that the female operator exerted greater effort than the male. He explained that "it is an established fact that any kind of risk, bodily harm, is a stresser, is a fatiguer" (A. 129).

The fourth expert witness was a certified practitioner of the Methods Time Measurement Management Association, who analyzed the "heavy" and "light" jobs in three different ways. He used spring scale tests, the Methods Time Measurement system, and the National Metal Trades Association Job Evaluation Plan.[15]

Mr. Marek prepared a written report, analyzing the "heavy" and "light" operations in question. His report, received in evidence as Government Exh. 8, is based upon his observations and analyses conducted at Daisy's plant on three workshifts in June 1969, and a detailed study of the process books for the manufacture of three representative air rifles; the records of representative assignments for "heavy" and "light" operations; and the descriptions of 67 "heavy" and "light" operations prepared by Daisy after this suit was filed (A. 263-264). While at the Daisy plant, Mr. Marek inspected the presses, the tools, the gondolas, the hydraulic jacks and other equipment which the employees handle or operate. By the use of a spring scale, he was able to determine the physical effort involved in moving the gondolas and other wheeled vehicles — both the starting effort and the rolling or pushing effort — as well as lifting tote pans and the like. In the same way, he determined the withdrawal pressures on the so-called arbor operations. Mr. Marek's findings on material handling and arbor pressures are included in his report (Exhs pp. 73, 78, 83-85) and were considered in reaching his conclusion that the representative operations are equal for pay purposes in skill, effort, responsibility and working conditions, and that there is "no basis for classifying the jobs or operations as light or heavy (or male or female)" (Exhs p. 63, see also Exhs p. 86).

In addition to spring scale tests, Mr. Marek used the Methods Time Measurement system to analyze representative "light" and "heavy" press operations which he personally observed,[7] as well as those which are described in detail in the operation descriptions prepared by Daisy for this suit. His MTM findings in each case were that the women's press operations were "over paced" and required greater effort than the male press operations (Exhs pp. 65, 72, 82).

One pair of press operations which Mr. Marek found "representative" is the male operation of closing the Model 1894 magazine (quota: 550 per hour; arbor, about 3 pounds) compared to the female operation of U-forming the same part (quota: 1175 per hour) (Marek Report, Exhs pp. 63-65, 67-72). Mr. Marek made detailed observations of these operations and, applying the Methods Time Measurement system, rated the male operation at 98,560 TMU's per hour, or 98.5 percent of normal pace, while the woman's operation was rated 123,610 TMU's per hour, or 123.6 percent of normal pace (Exhs p. 79). By assuming the weights and number of stock chasing trips claimed by Daisy, Mr. Marek rated the male operation at 99,935 TMU's, or 99.9 percent of normal pace (ibid.). In explaining his conclusions, Mr. Marek stated that the woman's greater effort resulted from her much higher production quota, "the continuity of [her] operation and the fact that it does not contain the stock chasing element which is evaluated as a relief from fatigue and a resulting lower effort" (Exhs p. 65). . . .

In making his analysis of Daisy's male-female designations, Mr. Marek applied a second discipline for evaluating job requirements — i.e., the National Metal Trades Association Job Evaluation Plan, which is used to compare jobs in terms of skill, effort, responsibility and working conditions (see Exhs pp. 87-101). The NMTA plan assigns

15. Id. at 30-35.

7. The MTM system of analyzing jobs was prepared by the Methods Time Measurement Association, a nonprofit association of industrial engineers. It is based on detailed studies of the hand and body movements in all basic industrial jobs and the time required to perform each at a "normal pace," which is defined as "the rate an employee can perform a given job [or function] for an indefinite period without excessive fatigue" (see Exhs p. 57). These rates have been converted by the Association into Time Measurement Units (TMU's) on a scale of 100,000 units per hour as a "normal pace" or effort (ibid.).

numerical points under these factors and establishes a ranking of 12 labor grades (with a 21-point spread for each grade) for equitable wage rates.[8] Under this plan, "effort" is broken down into physical demand and mental or visual demand, with separate points for each.

In evaluating six representative press operations under the NMTA Plan, Mr. Marek found the male and female operations equal for pay purposes in terms of skill, effort, responsibility, and working conditions (Marek Report, Exhs pp. 70, 72, 86). While he found that an extra degree of effort was warranted for the physical demand involved in using the largest barrel-size arbor, he also found that an extra degree of effort, under mental or visual demand, was warranted for women operators who are required to put their hands into the die on high-speed press operations — with the result that the male "heavy" arbor operation and the female high-speed operations were rated as equal for pay purposes (Marek Report, Exhs p. 86, A. 241-243).

The fifth expert witness was an industrial engineer who had taught industrial engineering subjects, including job evaluation, for twenty years. His testimony was used principally to rebut the testimony of the company's expert witness — a job evaluator.

c. Skill, Effort, and Responsibility

In another aide-orderly case, the court rested on an analysis of all three factors — skill, effort, and responsibility. Some of the pertinent findings of fact and conclusions of law are excerpted here.

HODGSON v. GOOD SHEPHERD HOSPITAL
327 F. Supp. 143 (E.D. Tex. 1971)

FINDINGS OF FACT . . .

7. Permanent employees are placed on probation (training period) for three months. There are training courses for the aides conducted by Mrs. Elliott. There is a course of training for orderlies also by Mrs. Elliott, Medical Doctors and Senior Orderlies. This has not applied to orderlies having adequate prior training or experience. The training of the aides and orderlies differs in the following respects that the orderly is:

(1) Taught the art of moving and lifting heavy, obese and aged persons;
(2) Taught male catheterizations and related services by Urologists;
(3) Taught orthopedic services and use of, setting up traction equipment by senior orderly and by orthopedic surgeons;
(4) Taught the responsibility of Hospital wide service and knowledge of location of equipment of entire facility;
(5) Taught and trained for emergency room work by Doctors and senior orderlies;
(6) Taught Sterile procedures as opposed to aseptic procedures only taught to the aide by nursing personnel;

while Nurses Aides are not taught the above procedures.

8. Good Shepherd Hospital has had no policy prohibition against an orderly being a female or a male being a nurses aide though as a practical matter all aides have been females and all orderlies have been males. . . .

12. Wage Scale

(a) During the period from February 1, 1967 to the present date the following pay scales have been applied to orderlies:

---

8. The NMTA Job Evaluation Plan rests on the principle of equal pay for equal work. As stated in the Foreword of the plan: "Job Rating . . . provides a means for establishing and maintaining the equitable wage relationship between jobs which is fundamental to good industrial relations and sound wage administration."

1967 — 1.25 per hour
1968 — 1.25 per hour
    (1.52 per hour to experienced)
    (1.75 to Chief Orderly Murphy)
1969 — 1.52 per hour
    (2.08 to Chief Orderly Murphy)
1970 — 1.65 per hour
    (2.08 to Chief Orderly Murphy)

(Plaintiff stated in argument to Court Chief Orderly Murphy was not a proper subject for comparison purposes).

(b) During the period from February 1, 1967 to the present date the following pay scales have been applied to nurses aides:

1967 — 1.00 per hour
1968 — 1.16 per hour
    1.30 per hour
1969 — 1.36 per hour
    1.50 per hour
.1970 — 1.60 per hour

CONCLUSIONS OF LAW

The Court concludes that:

1. Plaintiff has not met its burden of proof to show the work and duties performed by Defendant's aides and orderlies are substantially identical. Even though all orderlies at this date are males and all aides are females, it is concluded that since February 1, 1967 the higher rate is paid to the orderly because he is an orderly performing the duties of an orderly which are different from those of an aide, and not because he is a male. See Wirtz v. Koller Craft Plastic Products, Inc., 296 F. Supp. 1195, 1199 [Paragraph (5).] Kilpatrick v. Sweet, D.C., 262 F. Supp. 561, 564.

2. Work performed by the orderlies during the period in question required greater and different skill, effort and responsibility from that of the aide.

A. SKILL — The orderly was trained to perform catheterizations and did perform them, while female catheterizations were performed only by licensed nurses not aides.[16] The orderly was trained in various duties to assist orthopedic surgeons in setting up traction equipment; helping in the application and removal of casts. The orderly was trained in the use of sterile procedures while the aide was limited to aseptic procedures. Orderlies were trained and skilled in the correct methods of lifting patients particularly critical, obese, or aged cases. These matters are illustrative and establish the difference of the skill required and employed by the orderly in his work, from the nurses aide and her work. *As to skill required of the orderly and aide jobs the Plaintiff has not shown that the work is substantially identical.* It is not enough to show "similarity" or that the work is "comparable."

B. EFFORT — The work of the orderly requires more effort in the area of lifting, handling equipment, moving, turning and transporting patients. The orderly has more work, is active a much greater per cent of his working time as shown by time and work studies. Also, in this area the strength and experience of the orderly is put to use in security, fire drills, disaster drills, handling of demented, drunk and unruly patients. Aides call for the help of the orderlies in these fields, an acknowledgment of the difference and strength and effort in respective jobs — not merely a requirement, but work that in many instances aides are physically unable to perform. *The Plaintiff has not met its burden of proof to show by the greater weight and degree of credible testimony that the nurses aide's work*

---

16. The court earlier noted that the hospital had prohibited aides from doing catheterizations, even on females, since Feb. 1, 1967. — Eds.

is "substantially equal" to the orderly's work as to the effort required. The lifting and strength demanding work of the orderly is not merely occasional but is shown to be one of the main functions that is demanded of the orderly with great frequency and regularity. Use of orderlies in the foregoing work is an operational necessity. The Hospital is dependent on the orderly for the performance of the job cycle. It is clear that from an economic standpoint the Hospital could have hired all aides and no orderlies if the jobs were identical and thus saved any pay differential. The Hospital was dependent upon the stronger, better trained orderlies, not by preference but as a matter of sound hospital management. During the entire time period the effort exerted by the orderly was substantially and significantly greater than that exerted by the aide. These additional duties are of economic value commensurate with the pay differential.

C. RESPONSIBILITY — The Plaintiff has not met its burden of proof in showing that the aide and orderly jobs were substantially equal and identical, as to responsibility. The orderly works out of Central Supply and his work carried him throughout the hospital. He was subject to emergency or "Stat" calls at all times wherever he might be. He had responsibility for storage and maintenance for various types of equipment with which he works. Important duties of the Orderly in the responsibility area were in the security, fire and disaster, emergency room and morgue areas. The aide had no responsibility in these areas and was assigned to a specific area or patients. The orderly had less supervision, was required to accept greater responsibilities and develop initiative in the performance of orderly duties. See Wirtz v. Muskogee Jones Store Company, D.C., 293 F. Supp. 1034. *The Court concludes that it is shown as a matter of law that the aide does not have the substantially identical and equal responsibilities of the orderly;* but that the latter has greater responsibility augmented in the field of traction and male catheterizations and sterile practices. . . .

The Court further concludes that Plaintiff has failed to establish that the jobs at issue during the period in question required equal skill, effort and responsibility under similar working conditions. The responsibility of the orderly to emergency throughout all floors of the Hospital during all of the time of his working period and furnishing security to patients and personnel in the emergency room and the psychiatric unit in themselves are added responsibilities that justify the difference in compensation. The presence of the orderly provided a psychological effect because they were strong, capable and efficient and gave a sense of security that an aide could not give. . . . [Emphasis added]

Did the court apply the same standard as that of the Third Circuit in Shultz v. Wheaton Glass Company, supra? In analyzing effort, did it apply the standard set forth in Hodgson v. Brookhaven General Hospital, supra?

3. Similar Working Conditions

Analysis of whether the working conditions are similar in positions held by men and by women has not figured prominently in Equal Pay Act litigation. However, in a few cases, the decision has turned on this factor; and the Second Circuit has handed down a major decision on the issue of whether night shift work creates dissimilar working conditions.

HODGSON v. CORNING GLASS WORKS
474 F.2d 226 (2d Cir. 1973)

. . . The controversy concerns the wages paid by Corning Glass Works ("Corning") to Class B, Class C, and General TV inspectors, in its A Factory, B & C Factory, and Pressware Plant at Corning, New York. Prior to 1925, Corning operated its plants only during the day, and found it unnecessary or undesirable to have a night shift. Between 1925 and 1930, however, the introduction of automatic production equipment made it necessary to institute a night inspection shift. Although, as the district judge found, Shultz v. Corning Glass Works, 319 F. Supp. 1161, 1170 W.D.N.Y. 1970), previously "women had filled most, if not all, of the inspection jobs on the day and afternoon shifts," New York law then prohibited the employment of women between 10:00 P.M. and 6:00 A.M., and thus Corning had to recruit male employees for a steady night shift. They demanded and received wages comparable to what they were earning on other, often more demanding jobs in the plant, which were approximately twice those paid to the female inspectors. The base rate for the inspectors on the night shift was 53 cents per hour, as against 24 to 28 cents per hour for the female inspectors on the day shifts.

Thus a situation was created where the night inspection shift was all male, the day shift virtually all female, and the males received wages significantly higher than the females. This state of affairs persisted until the effective date of the Equal Pay Act — and beyond it — except for one brief period when, because of labor shortages during World War II, New York allowed women to work at night; women employed by Corning on the night shift during that period received the same wages as the men when they performed the same work. In 1944 the Corning, New York plants were organized by the American Flint Glass Workers Union and a collective bargaining agreement was negotiated which provided for the company's first plant-wide night shift differential.[3] But this change in Corning's wage structure did not eliminate the higher base wage paid to male night inspectors since, in the case of the inspectors, the shift differential was superimposed upon the existing difference in wage scales. Similarly, although in 1953 New York changed its law to permit females over the agets of 21 to work after midnight in factories operating multiple shifts where the Industrial Commissioner found transportation and safety conditions to be satisfactory and granted approval,[4] the record does not reveal any application by Corning for such approval prior to 1966.

The Equal Pay Act became effective with respect to Corning's Corning, New York plants on June 11, 1964. Since Corning had previously maintained separate "male" and "female" rate schedules plant-wide, with the latter materially lower, the Act clearly called for action on its part. Corning therefore merged the separate schedules into one. However, so far as concerned the inspectors, this was a matter of theory only, since the day shift inspectors were assigned to lower wage groups, see 319 F. Supp. at 1165-1166. Thus, as the district court found, 319 F. Supp. at 1166, "the merger continued the historical difference in base hourly rates of the men and women inspectors working the three shifts."

Corning's first significant step toward eliminating the differential wage rates for male and female inspectors took place on June 1, 1966, when it opened the inspection jobs on the night shift to women, presumably with the approval of the State Industrial Commissioner. At this time Corning consolidated its theretofore separate male and female seniority lists, and women became eligible to bid for the higher paid night inspection jobs when vacancies occurred. It is undisputed that a considerable number of women took advantage of this opportunity; turnover in the night inspection jobs was substantial and over half the vacancies were taken by women. Still, the process required some time since women could not exercise their seniority to "bump" a less senior male night inspector.[6]

The last significant event was Corning's negotiation of a new collective bargaining

3. The record does not reveal whether, apart from the inspectors, Corning had paid more for night work before the institution of the plant-wide differential in the 1944 agreement. Corning suggested that there might have been other jobs performed by women during the day for which the company had to pay a higher wage to get men to perform at night. It seems relatively clear, however, that if a job had been performed on the day shift by men, men on the night shift would receive the same wage.

4. 1953 N.Y. Laws, Ch. 708, *amending* N.Y. Labor Law §172, *now* N.Y. Labor Law §173(3)(a)(1) (McKinney 1965).

6. In 1966 only 4 of 15 women requesting transfer to the night shift received this. The situation later improved so that 39 out of 61 requests were honored in 1967, and 42 out of 52 through November 7 in 1968.

agreement with the Flint Glass Workers Union, effective January 20, 1969. This abolished the separate base wage rates of day and night shift inspectors and increased the rate for all inspectors, so that the resulting base wage was the same for all three shifts and exceeded the wage rates on the steady night shift previously in effect. If the agreement had stopped at that point there could be no substantial claim of further violation of the Equal Pay Act. However, the agreement provided for a higher "red circle"[17] basic rate to every person employed before January 20, 1969, when working as an inspector on the night shift. At the time of the last hearing in the district court, over two years after the new agreement went into effect, all the night inspectors were being paid at the "red circle" rate; unless Corning changes its system, this is likely to continue for some time since at the date of the hearing over 500 laid-off inspectors had to be offered reemployment before any new inspectors could be hired.

The district court held that Corning had been in continuing violation of the Equal Pay Act; directed it to pay the night rate to all inspectors from November 1, 1964 . . . to January 20, 1969, and the "red circle" rate thereafter to all inspectors until true equalization was effected. . . . Corning claims that it was never in violation of the Equal Pay Act. . . .

Corning's most basic contention — one which, if sustained, would immediately end the case — is that work on a steady night shift is not performed under "working conditions" similar to work on day or afternoon shifts. To those uninitiated in the language of industrial relations, that would indeed seem to be true, and the District Court for the Middle District of Pennsylvania has so held. . . .

[However,] [t]he legislative history of the Equal Pay Act supports the construction that the time at which work is performed was not regarded as a "working condition" but rather as a proper subject for "a differential based on any other factor other than sex." The equal pay bills, H.R. 3861, 88th Cong., 1st Sess. (1963); S. 910, 88th Cong., 1st Sess. (1963), as originally introduced in Congress, would have required equal pay for "equal work on jobs the performance of which requires equal skills." Ezra G. Hester, then Corning's Director of Industrial Relations Research, testified before both House and Senate Committees in opposition to this formulation. He pointed out that most of industry was by then using formal job evaluation systems in order to establish equitable wage structures in their plants, and that most of these job classification systems considered three factors in addition to "skill," to wit, effort, responsibility, and working conditions. As an example, he cited his own company's plan, which was introduced into the record. Under "working conditions" the plan and the accompanying job evaluation sheets listed two factors: "surroundings" (requiring evaluation of exposure to elements, intensity, and frequency) and "hazards" (requiring evaluation of frequency of exposure to hazard, frequency of injury, and seriousness of injury); nothing was said about time of day worked or differences in shift.[8] Mr. Hester testified that "Other companies use similar job evaluation sheets," and urged the committees to amend the proposed legislation to conform to these industry practices. See Hearings on H.R. 3861 and Related Bills Before the Special Subcommittee on Labor of the House Committee on Education and Labor, 88th Cong., 1st Sess. 232-40 (1963); Hearings on S. 882 and S. 910 Before the

17. The term "red circle" is a common one in labor relations. It means that employees are guaranteed a current wage rate under a new wage agreement which would otherwise decrease their wage, or when they are temporarily reassigned to a lower-paying department; the current rate is "red-circled." — Eds.

8. Edward W. Noble, Corning's Manager of Job Evaluation, testifying in this case, gave a similar description of Corning's job evaluation plan and said specifically that the time of day was not considered to be a "working condition." See also the Dictionary of Occupational Titles (3d ed. 1965), published by the Manpower Administration of the Department of Labor. Volume II: Occupational Classification, at 656, defines working conditions as "the physical surroundings of a worker in a specific job," and gives the following examples: inside work v. outside work, exposure to heat, cold, wetness, humidity, noise, vibration, hazards (risk of bodily injury), fumes, odors, toxic conditions, dust and poor ventilation. It does not mention night work.

Subcommittee on Labor of the Senate Committee on Labor and Public Welfare, 88th Cong., 1st Sess. 96-104 (1963).

In response to this, the bill was rewritten in committee and placed in its present form. Five House Committee members thus explained the change, H. R.Rep. No. 309, 88th Cong., 1st Sess. 8 (1963), U.S. Code Cong. & Admin. News, p. 690:

> The concept of equal pay for jobs demanding equal skill has been expanded to require equal effort, responsibility, and similar working conditions as well. These factors are the core of all job classification systems and the basis for legitimate differentials in pay.

Earlier in the Report, at p. 3, U.S. Code Cong. & Admin. News, p. 689, the Committee had indicated where it thought shift differentials would fit into the statute:

> Three specific exceptions and one broad general exception are also listed. . . . As it is impossible to list each and every exception, the broad general exclusion ["differentials based on any other factor other than sex"] has also been included. Thus, among other things, shift differentials, restrictions on or differences based on time of day worked, hours of work, lifting or moving heavy objects, differences based on experience, training, or ability would also be excluded.

This persuasive explanation of how the bill took shape, and the evident understanding of the Committee, consistent with this explanation, of the structure of the amended bill, outweigh the point, strongly pressed by Corning, that Representative Goodell, who introduced the bill and had a hand in redrafting it, remarked during the course of an explanation of its provisions that "hours of work, difference in shift . . . would logically fall within the working condition factor." 109 Cong. Rec. 9209 (1963). . . .

Administrative interpretation by the Wage and Hour Administrator, which the Supreme Court has held entitled to deference, Skidmore v. Swift & Co., 323 U.S. 134, 140, 65 S. Ct. 161, 89 L. Ed. 124 (1944), further indicates that shift differentials are to be considered a legitimate exception to the Act rather than to reflect a difference in working conditions which would make the statute inapplicable. 29 C.F.R. §§800.100 et seq. set out the Administrator's interpretations of each of the provisions of the Equal Pay Act and each of the terms used in the Act. Under "similar working conditions," §800.132 says that "[g]enerally, employees performing jobs requiring equal skill, effort, and responsibility are likely to be performing them under similar working conditions," which in itself would seem to indicate that shift differences are not considered different working conditions since this is such a common situation. The only examples given of different working conditions are the salesman who works in a store as compared with the salesman who sells door to door, or one who does repair work in a shop as compared with one who does repair work in customers' homes. In contrast, the Administrator recognizes the legitimacy of night shift differentials in §800.145, under "Exceptions to Equal Pay Standard."

Finally, while the case law is not conclusive, the decisions, other than the recent one between the same parties in the Middle District of Pennsylvania . . . are more favorable to the Secretary's position on this issue than to Corning's. See Shultz v. American Can Co., . . . 424 F.2d 356; Hodgson v. Miller Brewing Co., . . . 457 F.2d at 224-225 & n.8; Wirtz v. Basic Inc., 256 F. Supp. 786 (D.Nev.1966).

Corning's impressive evidence that night work not only is less attractive than day work but often causes physical and emotional problems thus does not carry the day. While the statute indeed permits all this to be taken into account, it is relevant under the catch-all exception, with its requirement that the employer establish that the differential was based on a factor other than sex, rather than making night work a different "working condition" and eliminating application of the statute altogether. . . .

[After rejecting the company's factor other than sex argument, the court concluded:]

We thus approve the district court's holding that when the Equal Pay Act took effect, Corning was violating it by paying higher base wages to the male night inspectors. . . .

NOTE: OTHER CASES

The Labor Department sued Corning Glass Works plants in both New York and Pennsylvania. The Pennsylvania court found that working at night creates a dissimilar working condition. Since the case involved facts almost identical to those cited in the Second Circuit decision above, the reasoning leading to a contrary decision makes interesting reading. Hodgson v. Corning Glass Works, 341 F. Supp. 18 (M.D. Pa. 1972), aff'd, 480 F.2d 590 (3d Cir. 1973). For other decisions on the issue, read the cases cited in the Second Circuit opinion.

As this book went to press, the Supreme Court handed down an excellent decision by Justice Marshall affirming the Second Circuit decision above and reversing the Third Circuit. Corning Glass Works v. Brennan, — U.S. —, 94 S. Ct. 2223, — L. Ed. 2d — (1974). The Court held that the night shift work was performed under "similar working conditions" with the day shift work. It found that "similar working conditions" is a term of art with a specific meaning which does not include the time of day worked. [18] Instead,[19]

> . . . the element of working conditions encompasses two subfactors: "surroundings" and "hazards." "Surroundings" measure the elements, such as toxic chemicals or fumes, regularly encountered by a worker, their intensity, and their frequency. "Hazards" take into account the physical hazards regularly encountered, their frequency, and the severity of the injury they can cause.

Justice Stewart did not participate in the decision, and Justices Burger, Blackmun, and Rehnquist dissented.

NOTE: NIGHT WORK LAWS

As yet, no Title VII cases have considered the validity of "protective" night work laws, one of the many kinds of sex-based state "protective" labor laws. Notice that the facts cited in this opinion support the thesis that such laws have hindered women's employment opportunities. Until 1966 women were not able to bid on the higher-paying night shift jobs. Yet many women were willing to do this work during World War II, and many others sought to transfer to the jobs as soon as the opportunity became available in 1966. Obviously, higher pay would be one reason for doing so; in addition, night shift work provides greater flexibility for many families, since it allows one spouse to care for children at night while the other works, thus minimizing child care costs and providing the parental care that many parents prefer for their children. Given these factors, and the willingness to cease worrying about women's "safety" at night during World War II, one may be permitted some skepticism about the "protective" intentions of the supporters of this legislation. Once again, the effect of such laws is simply to preserve higher wages for men.

18. 94 S. Ct. at 2232.
19. Ibid.

C. ATTEMPTS TO "CURE" EQUAL PAY ACT VIOLATIONS

When the Equal Pay Act was passed, many employers realized it would affect their payrolls and adopted various strategies to avoid raising wages for large groups of women. The cases that follow illustrate some of these tactics, along with the company's legal arguments that their new employment policies had cured any equal pay violation. As the cases show, courts have not responded favorably to these arguments.

1. Segregating Workers by Sex

SHULTZ v. SAXONBURG CERAMICS, INC.
314 F. Supp. 1139 (W.D. Pa. 1970)

Defendant operates a plant in Saxonburg, Pennsylvania, which produces ceramic products. . . . [T]his action is concerned with the female employees of the Extrusion Department who have performed the job entitled "Extrusion Press Operator" and male employees who performed the job which defendant entitled "Extrusion Press Operator–Die Setter" prior to the December 14, 1965 reorganization. About 10-12 women and 3-4 men were involved.

Prior to December 14, 1965 females were assigned to the job "Extrusion Press Operator" and males were assigned to the job of "Extrusion Press Operator and Die Setter". The male job assignment received 30¢ per hour more than the female job assignment. It is the contention of the plaintiff here that the work done by the male "Extrusion Press Operator and Die Setter" and the work done by the female "Extrusion Press Operator" were equal and required equal pay. On December 14, 1965, those males formerly classified as "Extrusion Press Operator and Die Setter" were removed from all duties connected with the operation of the extrusion presses and were given a new job description as "Set-Up and Service". Thereafter, all the women employees continued to act as operators of the extrusion presses and their assignment was enlarged to include all presses, two of which were formerly operated by male employees only. The former male press operators were removed from all press operation duties and given the new set-up and service assignment. The basic 30¢ per hour differential in wages between the female operators and the former male operators was continued, but there is no contention by plaintiff that the work performed by the two new classifications after December 14, 1965 was equal. Defendant argues that the revision of the tasks between men and women and the installation of a plant-wide incentive system terminated defendant's duty to pay the women press operators the former higher male rate which men were paid when both men and women operated the presses.

The plaintiff alleges that the changes which defendant relies on have no bearing on the continued right of women press operators to have their pay raised to the former higher male rate which the males were paid as Extrusion Press Operators–Die Setters for work which was equal to the work performed by the female extrusion press operators. After the change of December 14, 1965 when all former male operators were removed to the new job classification, new male employees were hired as "Extrusion Press Operators" at the same pay rate as the female Extrusion Press Operators received.

From all of the testimony in the case it appears that for many years men and women extrusion press operators worked interchangeably, at least on presses 1, 2 and 4. The operation of the horizontal extrusion press (pug mill) and press No. 3 which was a press for larger products operated by a single operator seemed to have been assigned exclusively to male operators. In December 1959 the Commonwealth of Pennsylvania enacted an "Equal Pay Act" prohibiting pay differential for the same work on the basis of sex. At this time three duties were removed from the female extrusion press operators; the installing or removing of the G. C. holder (29 pounds) or the small holder adapter (18 1/2 pounds); knocking the clay plug into the cylinder when changing clay; and steering and pulling the rack wagon. These were operations which the female operators had previously performed and which they demonstrated their ability to perform during the trial of this case in the courtroom. This distinction in the tasks performed by the male operators and the female operators was one based upon weight lifting ability and physical effort required, although the female operators had performed these tasks before. Prior to the defendant's first labor contract, in 1961, the jobs were classified by sex as "Extrusion Press Operator — Male" and "Extrusion Press Operator — Female." In the 1961 labor contract the jobs were identified as "Extrusion Press Operator — Female" and "Extrusion Press Operator and Die Setter — Male". The additional description "and Die Setter" was added to the male job title beginning with the 1961 labor contract. Apparently this was in recognition of the three duties which were assigned exclusively to male press operators after 1959. The defendant continued to classify the female operators as "Extrusion Press Operator" and the men operators as "Extrusion Press Operator and Die Setter" until its September 1965 labor contract and from and after 1963 the hour rate between the male and the female operators provided 30¢ more per hour for the male operators. The effective date of the application of the statute in question to this case is June 11, 1964 and from that date until December 1965 no male was employed as an "Extrusion Press Operator" and no female was employed as an "Extrusion Press Operator and Die Setter". Up to September 1965 under the prevailing union contract the sexual designation of these jobs was preserved and there was no way that males could have been classified in the "Extrusion Press Operator" job or females classified in the "Extrusion Press Operator and Die Setter" job. It is through this history that the basic pattern of differences in the pay rates for males and females in this plant was established and in the opinion of the court was continued despite changes in job classifications which attempted to differentiate between the work assigned to the two sexes.

From and after December 14, 1965 there is no dispute that the jobs performed by the "Extrusion Press Operators" and the new description "Press Set-Up and Service", to which all males were removed, were different and unequal. However, the pattern of a 30¢ per hour pay differential under which the female operators had worked was not changed and the plaintiff argues that this job reclassification in effect resulted in a 30¢ per hour wage rate reduction for female workers because they had been entitled to the same pay rate as male operators from and after the effective date of the statute, June 11, 1964.

The essential distinction that defendant has attempted to draw between the work performed by male operators and by female operators ever since the adoption of the Pennsylvania Pay Law was based upon weight lifting and physical force. The most striking single illustration of this was the handling of the G. C. holder which weighs 29 pounds, and which has the size and shape of a bowling ball. At the trial one of the female operators demonstrated the facility with which she handled this appliance and it was shown that before the distinction in job classification was drawn the female operators had regularly handled this appliance. It was also testified that women had regularly performed all of the tasks prior to 1959 which were removed from their job classification that year and had performed them during the night shift when there was no male operator present to give any assistance. While the women were forbidden to take down or put up the G. C. holder into the machine the women operators stripped down the die assembly and installed or removed it from the G. C. holder and regularly carried the G. C. holder and the die holder and adapter to and from her work bench. As for the prohibition against women knocking the clay plug into the cylinder women regularly took the clay plug out of the cylinder as the male operator knocked it into the cylinder, and as for the prohibition against women pulling or steering the rack wagon women continued to aid by pushing the rack wagon as the male pulled it. . . .

[The court then concluded that the jobs of "Extrusion Press Operator" and "Extrusion Press Operator and Die Setter" were equal. The court continued:]

Throughout the entire trial of this case one element was outstanding. The women employees were shown to have been fully competent and capable of performance of all the functioning of the press operations, and did perform them prior to the restrictions of male-related functions first imposed in 1959 at the time of the enactment of the Pennsylvania Equal Pay Act, 43 P.S. §336.1 et seq.

Weight lifting restrictions imposed on female employees are no impediment to a finding that jobs performed by male and female employees are equal when only a small percentage of the total work time is taken up by the extra (i.e. weight-lifting and other physical activity) duties assigned to the male operators. . . .

Plaintiff contends that . . . [even though] men operators no longer operate these [extrusion press] machines, that the continued payment of the "old", lower rate to the female operators who are now exclusively operating the machines is an impermissible wage differential since it amounts to a wage reduction. We agree. This violation will continue until the company, by new contractual arrangement by voluntary action or by court order, raises, or is forced to raise, the wages of the female operators to that of the male operators as of the time the males ceased to operate the machines together with all increments to date. Wirtz v. Koller Craft Plastics Products, Inc., [296 F. Supp. 1049 (E.D. Ky. 1968)] 29 CFR §800.114 (c). See also Murphy v. Miller Brewing Co., 307 F. Supp. 829 (E.D. Wis. 1969).

CONCLUSIONS OF LAW

5. When male employees classified as "Extrusion Press Operator and Die Setter" were assigned on regular rotating shifts to work with female employees classified as "Extrusion Press Operator" on the same machines, doing substantially equal work, the female press operators were entitled, under the Act, to receive the same rate for operating these presses as the male employees were receiving.

6. During the period from June 11, 1964 to December 14, 1965, defendant violated the equal pay provisions of the Act by discriminating between employees on the basis of sex by paying female Extrusion Press Operators contract rates 30¢ an hour less than it paid male Extrusion Operators and Die Setters. . . .

7. The equal pay provisions of the Act apply where women are employed to do substantially the same work formerly performed by men, as well as where men and women perform equal work currently and interchangeably. . . .

8. The Act required the defendant to raise the hourly rate of female Extrusion Press Operators to equal the hourly rates which men formerly received or were awarded, including any contracted future increases, when the males performed the job of Extrusion Operator and Die Setter. Female Extrusion Press Operators were entitled to be paid the same basic hourly wage rate as was paid to the classification of male Extrusion Operator and Die Setter, including the applicable incentive rates computed on this base hourly rate.

9. Defendant has continued to violate the Act since December 14, 1965 by failing to pay female Extrusion Press Operators for their employment since December 14, 1965 the same hourly rates which male employees were entitled to receive for the job of Extrusion Operator and Die Setter. . . .

NOTE

Notice that the company tried segregation twice in its attempt to avoid equal wages. In 1959 it removed three tasks from the women's work, but the court found the jobs were still equal. Then in 1965 it segregated the workers sufficiently to give them unequal jobs, but this time the court ruled that equal pay is required for equal jobs held in immediate succession, as well as those held simultaneously by women and men. (On comparing a job held first by a man and then by a woman, see Hodgson v. The Behrens Drug Co., — F.2d — , 70 CCH Lab. Cas. ¶32,844 at 45,808, 20 Wage & Hour Cas. 1152 (5th Cir. 1973).)

Segregation has been tried by other companies. In a stipulation forming part of an Equal Pay Act settlement, a Sears, Roebuck and Co. store admitted that:[20]

> On June 22, 1964, all store managers in the Midwestern Territory were advised that the Equal Pay Act was in effect and that among the things they could do about it was to reassign workers or redesign jobs to segregate women's and men's work within the same establishment.

Of course, the conscious policy of segregating workers by sex not only indicated bad faith evasion of the Equal Pay Act, but also violated Title VII.

2. Integrating Jobs

SHULTZ v. AMERICAN CAN CO. — DIXIE PRODUCTS
424 F.2d 356 (8th Cir. 1970)

We are confronted here with a narrow but important question arising out of the administration of the Equal Pay Act. . . . Is the American Can Company discriminating against its female machine operators, who work exclusively on the AM-PM shifts, by paying operators on those shifts twenty cents an hour[1] less than males operating identical machines on the night shift? . . .

The wage differential between AM-PM and night shift operators is a historical one. When the plant was first opened, the first and second shifts comprised one department known as the AM-PM Shift Department, and the third shift comprised the Night Shift Department. Each department utilized the same machines but had separate seniority and separate job progression scales. Employment as an operator on the AM-PM shifts was specifically limited to women and employment on the night shift was specifically limited to men.

In October of 1965, the Company and Local 656, International Brotherhood of Pulp, Sulphite and Paper Mill Workers, representing the employees, entered into an agreement which purported to abolish the wage differential based on sex for all positions within the plant. The agreement expressly opened the night shift to women and the day shift to men but retained the wage differential between AM-PM operators and night operators at the then seventeen cents per hour. In January of 1966, the Union and the Company issued an interpretation of the amended collective bargaining agreement. The interpretation stated that in the event of a reduction in force, men would be permitted to "bump" AM-PM shift employees with less seniority. It gave a similar privilege to AM-PM employees. The AM-PM employees, however, were required to demonstrate, during a forty-five day trial period, that they could do all of the work required on the night shift, including loading the machines with paper. Transferring employees were to be paid the hourly rate applicable to the job to which they transferred. Five men had transferred to the AM-PM shifts when this case was tried in 1968. A few women had requested to be assigned to the night shift but, for reasons not material herein, their requests have not been granted.

The trial court concluded, on the basis of the above facts, that (1) the Company had ceased discriminating on June 10, 1965, by opening the AM-PM shifts to men and the night shift to women. . . .

---

20. Stipulation, ¶7, Hodgson v. Sears, Roebuck and Co., Civ. Act. File No. 2555 (W.D. Ky., April 25, 1972).

1. This twenty cents an hour pay differential is exclusive of "shift premium" paid to all employees on the PM and night shifts. No issue is raised as to the propriety or legality of these "shift premiums."

At the outset, we think it clear that the Company did not cure the alleged violation of the Equal Pay Act by agreeing to open the night shift to women. If in fact the work of the women was equal to that of the men, the Company became obligated to pay them the same scale as their male counterparts on the effective date of the Act, June 11, 1965. It could not relieve itself of that obligation by agreeing to allow some women to work on the night shift at a higher rate of pay at some future date when a vacancy occurred. . . . Nor could it achieve compliance by opening the AM-PM shifts to men at the lower rate. The statute expressly forecloses that possibility by providing that "an employer who is paying a wage rate differential in violation [of the Act] shall not, in order to comply with the provisions [of the Act] reduce the wage rate of any employee." 29 U.S.C.A. §206(d)(1). . . .

NOTE: OTHER CASES

The Second Circuit agreed fully with this stand, stating that:[21]

> . . . we cannot hold that Corning, by allowing some — or even many — women to move into the higher paid night jobs, achieved full compliance with the Act. Corning's action still left the inspectors on the day shift — virtually all women — earning a lower base wage than the night shift inspectors because of a differential initially based on sex and still not justified by any other consideration; in effect, Corning was still taking advantage of the availability of female labor to fill its day shift at a differentially lower wage rate not justified by any factor other than sex. We thus join with every other court of appeals which has considered the issue in holding that merely opening the higher paid jobs to women as vacancies arise is not sufficient to comply with the requirements of the Equal Pay Act. . . . Hodgson v. Square D. Co., 459 F.2d 805, 808-809 (6th Cir. 1972), *cert. denied,* 409 U.S. 967, 93 S. Ct. 293, 34 L. Ed. 2d 232 (1972); see also Hodgson v. Miller Brewing Co., [457 F.2d 221, 226-227 (7th Cir. 1972)].

3. *Segregating Workers, Followed by Re-Integrating Them*

HODGSON v. MILLER BREWING COMPANY
457 F.2d 221 (7th Cir. 1972)

These consolidated cases and appeals arise under . . . the Equal Pay Act of 1963. No. 18929 was filed October 15, 1965 by the three female plaintiffs, all laboratory technicians employed by defendant Miller Brewing Company (Miller), to recover back wages, liquidated damages and attorneys' fees under 29 U.S.C.A. §216(b). No. 18560 was commenced March 31, 1967 by the Secretary of Labor pursuant to 29 U.S.C.A. §217 to enjoin Miller from violating the equal pay provisions of the Act by paying discriminatory wages to its female laboratory technicians and by reducing the wage rates of certain male technicians. . . . The district court filed its opinion, reported as Murphy v. Miller Brewing Company, D.C., 307 F. Supp. 829 (1969), in favor of the three private plaintiffs and the Secretary of Labor. Judgment was entered enjoining Miller from violating the Act and ordering Miller to equalize the wage rates of all employees in the Analytical Laboratory with those in the [Packaging] Laboratory by increasing the former 70 cents per hour. . . . Miller has appealed. . . .

Miller is engaged in the production and sale of beer. . . .

These cases primarily involve employees in two main laboratory facilities —the Analytical Laboratory and the Packaging Laboratory. . . .

21. Hodgson v. Corning Glass Works, 474 F.2d 226, 235 (2d Cir. 1973), *aff'd,* 94 S. Ct. 2223 (1974).

During the period from January 1961 to January 1965, female laboratory technicians were restricted to work in the Analytical Lab. They were also restricted to working
only on the first shift from 8:00 A.M. to 4:00 P.M. in that laboratory. The other two shifts,
which were not always operated, were run by male technicians. The men who worked
on the other shifts in the Analytical Lab received 70 cents per hour more than the
women. This was in addition to a shift differential of 10 to 16 cents per hour.

After the effective date of the Equal Pay Act, men and women continued concurrently and interchangeably to perform the same tests and jobs in the Analytical Lab. On
occasion women trained the men to perform these tests. Despite this, women continued
to receive 70 cents per hour less than the men for the same work.

During the period July 10, 1964 to January 2, 1965, men were transferred out of
the Analytical Lab to the Packaging Lab. During the period of January 2, 1965 to October
31, 1966, Miller allowed only women to perform the work in the Analytical Lab. The
women continued to receive 70 cents per hour less than the men who had been transferred out.

After October 31, 1966, both men and women were allowed to work in the
Analytical Lab. At this time both men and women in the Analytical Lab received the
same lower rate which was 70 cents an hour less than what the men in the Analytical
Lab had previously received and than what technicians working in the Packaging Lab
received. After October 1966, women were permitted to transfer to the Packaging Lab
as vacancies arose. . . .

We agree with the district court's conclusion that "the working conditions in
the [Packaging] Lab are similar to the working conditions in the Analytical Lab, and there
is no substantial difference in terms of the skill, effort and responsibility required
between the jobs in the Analytical Lab and the [Packaging] Lab." Thus, we find that
the jobs in the two laboratories constitute "equal work" within the meaning of
§206(d). . . .

It is almost without question that Miller's wage differential between men and
women, who, we have found, performed equal work in the Analytical Lab, from the
effective date of the Equal Pay Act (June 11, 1964) to the date when all men had been
transferred out of the Analytical Lab (January 2, 1965) was in violation of §206(d). At
that juncture [the effective date of the act] Miller was required, in order to avoid
continued violation of the Act, to raise the wages of the women laboratory technicians
in the Analytical Lab by 70 cents per hour.

In order to circumvent this requirement, Miller instituted the following arrangement: (1) all men were transferred out of the Analytical Lab to the Packaging Lab and
women were restricted to working in the Analytical Lab; (2) women continued to receive
70 cents per hour less than the men had formerly earned in the Analytical Lab and now
earn in the Packaging Lab; (3) then, about one year later, the Analytical Lab was again
opened up to both male and female technicians with all receiving the lower women's
rate; and (4) at the same time, women were for the first time allowed to work at and
transfer to the higher paying Packaging Lab jobs.

As a result of this scheme, Miller arrived at the same result as if it had initially,
after the effective date of the Equal Pay Act, equalized pay in the Analytical Lab by
lowering the male employees wages by 70 cents per hour. Since that in substance is what
was accomplished, Miller violated §206(d). The proviso of §206(d) which Miller violated
is "[t]hat an employer who is paying a wage rate differential in violation of this subsection shall not, in order to comply with the provisions of this subsection, reduce the wage
rate of any employee. . . .

The second situation in which Miller has discriminated against the female Analytical Lab technicians is in paying them 70 cents per hour less than the male employees
in the [Packaging] Lab. We have already found that the jobs in these two laboratories
constitute "equal work" within the meaning of those terms in §206(d). It is irrelevant

that the male technicians in the Analytical Lab are now also receiving the lower wage or that the jobs in the [Packaging] Lab are now open to women at the higher rate, since we have found those circumstances to be part of a plan to circumvent the Act's requirement that the wages of the women in the Analytical Lab be raised. . . . [W]e conclude and hold that Miller has violated the Equal Pay Act and that its discriminatory practices did not cease with the removal of all male laboratory technicians from the Analytical Lab, or with the opening of all jobs in the Analytical Lab and [Packaging] Lab to both men and women. . . .

D. The Defendant's Case

Once the plaintiff has met his or her burden of proof, the burden shifts to the defendant, who can then try to establish an affirmative defense based on the second half of the act. Unequal pay for equal work does not violate the act if the "payment is made pursuant to (i) a seniority system; (ii) a merit system; (iii) a system which measures earnings by quantity or quality of production; or (iv) a differential based on any other factor other than sex. . . ."[22]

One commentator suggests some guidelines on how this language should be interpreted.

BERGER, EQUAL PAY, EQUAL EMPLOYMENT OPPORTUNITY
AND EQUAL ENFORCEMENT OF THE LAW FOR WOMEN
5 *Valparaiso U.L. Rev.* 327 (1971)

. . . The enumeration of these potential affirmative defenses in the statute should not be interpreted to mean that an employer may "discriminate . . . on the basis of sex" if he merely proves the existence of "a seniority system, a merit system or a system which measures earnings by quantity and quality of production". . . . These factors were enumerated in the statute simply to make it clear that a defendant may prove as a defense that the differential in wages was not in fact based on sex but was based on a non-discriminatory seniority system, a non-discriminatory merit system or a non-discriminatory system which measures earnings by quantity or quality of production. A sex-based system or a system in which sex plays any part *cannot* be considered as a proper defense under the Equal Pay Act. Otherwise, employers could escape the impact of the act by establishing a "seniority system" providing different seniority lines for men and women, a "merit system" that applied differently to men and women, or a system measuring earnings by quantity or quality of production which set different standards for men and women.

Unlike section 703(h) of the Civil Rights Act, the Equal Pay Act does not say that these systems must be "bona fide" or that they must not be the result "of an intention to discriminate. . . ." However, it is implicit in the Act, especially with its express intent to eliminate sex discrimination, that the seniority system, merit system or system rewarding quantity and quality of production must be bona fide and not a device for evading the Act. Any other conclusion would violate the cardinal rules of statutory construction — that a remedial statute must be liberally construed and given a meaning which effectuates its purposes. Accordingly, whether a defendant pleads one of the three systems mentioned as a defense or whether he claims the differential is based on some "factor other than sex," his defense will fail if sex is any part of the basis for the differential between men and women. . . .

Of course the defendant would always have the burden of proving that a wage

22. 29 U.S.C. §206(d).

differential shown to exist between his men and women employees was not based on sex but on a bona fide seniority system, merit system, system that establishes wages on the basis of quantity or quality of production or some other ground in which sex played no part. The facts which would tend to establish such defenses would ordinarily be known only to the defendant. "Plaintiff is not required to establish a negative factor especially when that factor is within the peculiar knowledge of defendant."

If the defendant fails to plead such a defense in his answer or by timely motion, he is regarded as having waived the right to make such defense under rule 12(h) of the Federal Rules of Civil Procedure. He therefore is not entitled to raise a defense on appeal or on remand that has been waived. Economically powerful employers and their attorneys are sometimes adroit about conceiving other defenses when their first defense fails and thereby exhausting impecunious plaintiffs and their counsel with interminable litigation. Accordingly, rule 12(h) is a good rule for plaintiffs' attorneys to remember in cases under either the Equal Pay Act or Title VII. . . .

1. The First Three Factors: Seniority, Merit, and Quantity or Quality of Production

None of these factors has been of any real importance in the litigation; excerpts from three cases illustrate their application. In Kilpatrick v. Sweet, 262 F. Supp. 561 (M.D. Fla. 1967), a rare private employee suit, the court awarded judgment for the defendant after finding both that the work was unequal and a seniority system justified higher pay.[23]

> . . . [T]he Defendants have shown through testimony that the 30 cent difference in pay was not based on the fact that the Plaintiff was a female. The facts show that the male employee, Lyndon Warren, had been employed with the Defendants for approximately two years longer than the Plaintiff and that the Defendants did have a de facto seniority system in effect at the time in question; that there were substantial differences in the work performed and the responsibility and skill involved between the jobs performed by the Plaintiff and Lyndon Warren. The sum total of the differences in work and longevity of service between the two employees certainly justified the difference in pay of thirty cents per hour.

The Second Circuit examined another seniority claim more critically in Hodgson v. Corning Glass Works, supra:[24]

> We come finally to Corning's contention that any violation was cured by the new collective bargaining agreement which became effective January 20, 1969. As previously indicated, this would clearly have been so if Corning had simply established a uniform day and night shift rate at least as high as the previous night shift rate, either with or without a plant-wide night differential. The problem stems from the "red circle" rate whereby any employee hired before January 20, 1969, receives a basic rate for night shift work some four to twelve cents per hour higher than for the day and afternoon shifts. Corning's contention that this is a differential based on seniority, another permitted exception, is belied by the fact that it is paid only for work on the night shift. We cannot disagree with the district judge, Hodgson v. Corning Glass Works, 330 F. Supp. 46, 50 (W.D.N.Y. 1971), that, on the facts of this case, "the 'red circle' rate paid to night shift inspectors perpetuates the discrimination of the 'supplemental escalating shift differential' " — the euphemism Corning has coined for the excess base wage rates paid to inspectors on the night shift.

---

23. 262 F. Supp. at 564.
24. 474 F.2d at 235, *aff'd sub nom.* Corning Glass Works v. Brennan, 94 S. Ct. 2223 (1974).

Similarly, the Fifth Circuit viewed with skepticism the defendant's claim of a merit system in Hodgson v. Brookhaven General Hospital, supra.[25]

> At trial the hospital objected to the exclusion of testimony by the Director of Nursing Services as to the qualifications, potential, and value of each aide and orderly as she perceived them. As to qualifications at the time of hiring, the hospital failed to demonstrate the relevance of such factors as formal education to the duties the employees were called on to perform. As to relative merit, however, the Act specifically provides that unequal pay for equal work is justified if administered pursuant to a "merit system." This statutory exception, if not strictly construed against the employer, could easily "swallow the rule." Cf. Shultz v. First Victoria National Bank, 5 Cir., 1969, 420 F.2d 648, 657. The employer must show that its "merit system" is administered, if not formally, at least systematically and objectively. Cf. 29 C.F.R. §800.144 (1970). The merit-system issue is so closely related to the equal-effort issue as to warrant the taking of additional evidence on the point if the hospital has anything better to offer than highly subjective evaluations of employee merit by hospital officials.

But see a sloppy decision upholding a merit "system" in Wirtz v. First Victoria National Bank, 63 CCH Lab. Cas. ¶32,378, 19 Wage & Hour Cas. 684 (S.D. Tex. 1970), aff'd per curiam, sub nom. Hodgson v. First Victoria National Bank, 446 F.2d 47 (5th Cir. 1971).

2. The Fourth Factor: "Any Other Factor Other than Sex"

This factor is the one most frequently raised in litigation. Companies have raised a variety of factors; we present a few of the most significant ones.

a. Training Programs

Employers often rely on training programs from which women have been excluded as a "factor other than sex" that justifies paying male employees more. As the following case demonstrates, the courts have dealt severely with this defense.

HODGSON v. BEHRENS DRUG COMPANY
475 F.2d 1941 (5th Cir. 1973)
cert. denied sub nom. Behrens Drug Co. v. Brennan, 414 U.S. 822 (1973)

RIVES, J. In this case brought by the Secretary of Labor under the Fair Labor Standards Act, the district court found that Behrens Drug Company (hereinafter Behrens) discriminated against certain female employees by compensating them at a lower rate than their male counterparts. Behrens appeals, arguing that each contested male-female wage differential rests on legitimate grounds — that the males involved are . . . participating in a bona fide training program. . . .

For many years Behrens has employed females in its Tyler division warehouse as "order clerks." The principal responsibilities of an "order clerk" include: arranging merchandise on the warehouse shelves, filling customer orders by gathering the requested stock and sending it along to the "checker," and restocking the shelves. (App. 211.) Behrens admitted and the district court found that certain male employees, designated "sales trainees," performed work substantially equal to that of the female "order clerks" during the period in question. (App. 211.)

Behrens acknowledged that the male "sales trainees" were paid a higher wage than

25. 436 F.2d at 726.

"order clerks" for doing the same work, but sought to justify this wage discrepancy as based on a bona fide training program, purportedly constituting a legitimate distinguishing factor other than sex.

29 U.S.C. §206(d)(1) recognizes four exceptions to the general prohibition of disparate wage payments between workers of the opposite sex. The first three exceptions to the Equal Pay Act are specific (a seniority system, a merit system, and a system which measures earnings by quantity or quality of production), but the last is stated in general terms — "any other factor other than sex," 29 U.S.C. §206(d)(1)(iv). 29 C.F.R. §800.148,[3] the Secretary's Interpretative Bulletin, expressly designates bona fide training programs as one factor other than sex which may validly produce a male-female wage gap. Behrens contends that its male "sales trainees" are all participants in a bona fide training program, providing a legitimate basis for their higher wage rate than that of female "order clerks."

In order to verify the structure of its training program, Behrens offered the testimony of its president, treasurer, Tyler division manager, and four salesmen.

Behrens' president, W. Lacy Clifton, admitted that his company's sales training program has never included a woman. (App. 553.) He sought to explain the program's male dominance by reference to its origin: "I would say that when this program was started (1946) that females were never considered as suitable for traveling. . . . You think about putting a female out on a job where she might have a flat tire at night." (App. 546.)

In recent years, Clifton claimed, inclusion of females in the sales training program has been considered, and one woman, Annette Neeley, was offered a sales job on a temporary basis. Miss Neeley turned the job down for reasons which are contested.[4] However, Clifton admitted that present company policy calls for active solicitation of young men as sales trainees, but not women, and Miss Neeley, while she was offered a sales job, was not offered a position as a sales trainee. (App. 554.)

The district court found and both parties, with minor exceptions, agree that the Behrens' sales training program has the following characteristics:

(1) No written or formal plan of training;

(2) a regular system of rotation through each of the different warehouse jobs with progression to the next position based on satisfactory familiarity with the position before it;

(3) no specific identifiable point of termination;[5]

(4) sales trainees are informed upon hiring that they are entering a training program;

3. "§800.148 *Examples — training programs.*

"Employees employed under a bona fide training program may, in the furtherance of their training, be assigned from time to time to various types of work in the establishment. At such times, the employee in training status may be performing equal work with non-trainees of the opposite sex whose wages or wage rates may be unequal to those of the trainee. Under these circumstances, provided the rate paid to the employee in training status is paid, regardless of sex, under the training program, the differential can be shown to be attributable to a factor other than sex and no violation of the equal pay standard will result. Training programs which appear to be available only to employees of one sex will, however, be carefully examined to determine whether such programs are, in fact, bona fide. In an establishment where a differential is paid to employees of one sex because, traditionally, only they have been considered eligible for promotion to executive positions, such a practice, in the absence of a bona fide training program, would be a discrimination based on sex and result in a violation of the equal pay provisions, if the equal pay standard otherwise applies."

4. App. p. 438. The Secretary contends that Miss Neeley refused the job because she was not offered an increase in pay or the incentive of the normal commission arrangement, while Behrens argues that pay was never discussed.

5. Behrens concedes that its training program lasts for an indefinite period of time, but argues that it ends at an identifiable point — when familiarity with all the warehouse jobs is satisfactorily accomplished and a sales position opens. This circuitous reasoning fails to focus upon an identifiable termination point. Theoretically, a job slot cannot be filled until the training program is successfully completed. Thus, to say that the program ends when the job slot opens implies that completion of the program is not a prerequisite to beginning a sales job. If that is true, then the program's validity is cast in a questionable light.

(5) some formal sales training, including meetings, study of sales literature and travel with current salesmen, is provided upon reaching the final job in rotation —the city order desk. (Although the district court made no express finding on this point, testimony to that effect appears at App. pp. 580-582.)

In addition, uncontradicted testimony established that a male trainee carries out productive work and rotates through the training program without regard to personnel needs, except that the final advance to the position of salesman is contingent upon an opening in that slot. (App. 561, 562.)

In the seminal case interpreting the bona fide training program exception to the Equal Pay Act, Shultz v. First Victoria National Bank, 5 Cir. 1969, 420 F.2d 648, this Court ruled that two separate male-dominated "executive training programs" for bank tellers did not constitute a factor other than sex which would permit payment of lower wages to female tellers not included in the training programs. Those particular programs were found to be merely "post-event justifications for disparate pay to men and women from the commencement of employment up through advancement." Shultz, supra, at 655.

The elements of the two bank training programs in Shultz, which that court listed as conclusive of their fatal imprecision, were:

(1) Employees were not hired with the knowledge that they were trainees.
(2) The plans were not in writing.
(3) The "rotation" of trainees through the various bank positions did not follow any definite sequence, but depended on personnel needs.
(4) No formal instruction was offered at either bank.
(5) Neither program had ever included a woman.
(6) Advancement to the next position was unpredictable and sporadic.

Faced with these amorphous bank training plans and strongly influenced by the fact that both programs excluded females, the Shultz court reasoned that judicial recognition of such programs would allow "the exception to swallow the rule" and effectively undermine the congressional purpose for passing the Equal Pay Act.

A cursory comparison of the training programs belatedly offered as justification for the unequal pay in Shultz with the program at issue here reveals that the latter is far more concrete than were the former. The Behrens training plan is not a post-event justification. Behrens' sales trainees enter employment with explicit knowledge of their training status. They rotate through the initial warehouse positions without regard to personnel needs, and they receive some formal sales training while serving as city order clerks.

Yet, because of the crucial weaknesses in the Behrens training program, which will be treated subsequently, coupled with the genuine concern for women's rights which prompted the Act, we feel that the principles enunciated in Shultz are applicable here.

The Behrens sales training program suffers from two principal weaknesses. First, the Behrens trainee's ultimate advancement to the position of salesman depends on, not only satisfactory completion of the training program, but also the fortuitous event of a sales opening. In other words, the termination point of the program is not determinable prior to its actual occurrence, and that termination point is subject to the vagaries of the business climate and the company's personnel needs.

Second, the Behrens program is male dominated. No woman has ever participated in the program. While it is true that the issue of whether trainee positions should be open to women is a question to be ultimately resolved only in an action under Title VII of the Civil Rights Act of 1964, 42 U.S.C. §2000c (1970), in the manner pursued in Diaz v. Pan American World Airways, Inc., 5 Cir. 1972, 442 F.2d 385; see Hodgson v. Golden Isles Nursing Home, 5 Cir. 1972, __ F.2d __ [No. 71-1994, Oct. 31, 1972], it is also true that "training programs which appear to be available only to employees of one sex will

. . . be carefully examined to determine whether such programs are, in fact, bona fide."
29 C.F.R. §800.148.

Male-dominated training programs subject to the close scrutiny required by §800.-
148 have failed to pass appellate tests with increasing frequency. See Hodgson v.
Security National Bank of Sioux City, 8 Cir. 1972, 460 F.2d 57, reversing a district court
decision ruling that a male-dominated bank management training program was bona
fide. See also Hodgson v. Fairmont Supply Co., 4 Cir. 1972, 454 F.2d 490, where the
Fourth Circuit (reversing the district court) found a violation of the Equal Pay Act, and
declined to recognize a sex-oriented sales training program. . . .

In light of . . . the clear purpose of the Equal Pay Act, a training program coterminus
with a stereotyped province called "man's work" cannot qualify as a factor other than
sex. Hodgson v. Fairmont Supply Co., supra at 498.

In the instant case, Behrens' president, Clifton, testified that women are not solic-
ited as sales trainees because "females were never considered as suitable for traveling."
This is a clear example of the attitude of male suitability designed to be nullified by the
Equal Pay Act.

Behrens' sales training procedure is not illusory, nor does it constitute a mere
post-event justification for disparate wage payments. Nevertheless, the program has
never included a female, and its completion — advancement to a sales job — is entirely
dependent on personnel needs. These two program characteristics compel the conclusion
that Behrens' training procedure is not a factor other than sex which should excuse
denial of equal pay to female workers and remove them from the aegis of the Equal Pay
Act.

> An exemption from the coverage of the Act "must be narrowly construed."
> Phillips, Inc. v. Walling, 324 U.S. 490, 493, 65 S. Ct. 807, 808, 89 L. Ed. 1095 (1945)
> and Mitchell v. Stenson, 1 Cir., 1954, 217 F.2d 210, 214. The exemptions must be
> applied only to those "plainly and unmistakably within its terms and spirit." Phillips,
> Inc. v. Walling, supra at 493. See also Arnold v. Ben Kanowsky, Inc., 361 U.S. 388,
> 392, 80 S. Ct. 453, 456, 4 L. Ed. 2d 393 (1960).

Hodgson v. Colonnades, Inc., 5 Cir. 1973, __ F.2d __ [No. 72-1029, January 16, 1973].

Until they reach the position of city desk clerk, Behrens' sales trainees participate
in no training activities independent of their regular, productive jobs. This fact reinforces
the conclusion that male trainees through most of the training period engage in exactly
the same activities as female nontrainees and do not warrant statutory exemption from
the Equal Pay Act.

Behrens advances two subsidiary arguments in support of its training program.
First, it contends that the term "bona fide training program" contained in 29 C.F.R.
§800.148 means simply "in good faith without fraud." Although the traditional, common law definition of "bona fide" may be as liberal as Behrens' claims, see Ware v.
Hylton, 3 U.S. (3 Dall.) 199, the term as used in the regulation at issue here must be
construed in light of the statute which that regulation implements. The Equal Pay Act
clearly mandates the demise of sex-based wage differences except in special, narrow
circumstances. A bona fide training program to constitute a valid exception to the Equal
Pay Act must represent more than an honest effort; such a program must have substance
and significance independent of the trainee's regular job.

Behrens also argues that to rule its "training program" invalid would discriminate
against small companies, like itself, who cannot maintain expensive, formal training
courses.[8] Certainly, a small corporation with limited resources need not implement as
elaborate a training program as those of the corporate giants. But the fact that a corpora-

---

8. We note in passing that the Equal Pay Act only applies to enterprises with an annual gross volume
of sales of over $1,000,000. 29 U.S.C. §203(s)(1). Thus, Behrens is only small in relation to the corporate giants.

tion is small does not relieve that corporation of its duty to establish a "bona fide training program," if it wishes to escape the mandate of the Equal Pay Act. In addition, all "training programs" which exclude females, whether originated by large companies or small, carry a stigma of suspect validity. . . .

. . . [T]he judgment is affirmed.

NOTE: OTHER TRAINING PROGRAM CASES

The landmark case on training programs, as the *Behrens* court points out, was its own decision in Shultz v. First Victoria National Bank, 420 F.2d 648 (5th Cir. 1969). The decisions on remand in *First Victoria National Bank* show that strong appellate decisions do not always guarantee good results in practice. The Fifth Circuit decision involved two banks: First Victoria National Bank and the American Bank of Commerce. After finding the training programs at both banks invalid, the Fifth Circuit remanded for more factfinding on whether the men and women were performing equal work and whether the pay difference could be justified under any exception other than training programs. In the *First Victoria National Bank* case, the district court promptly took the hint and found that the bank paid unequal wages pursuant to both unequal work assignments (the commercial teller position "required greater skill, effort and responsibility than the other teller positions") and its merit system for promotion. Wirtz v. First Victoria National Bank, 63 CCH Lab. Cas., ¶32,378, 19 Wage & Hour Cas. 684 (S.D. Tex. 1970). In an appeal from this decision, the Fifth Circuit affirmed per curiam, holding that the district court's findings were not clearly erroneous and therefore could not be overturned under Federal Rule of Civil Procedure 52(a). Hodgson v. First Victoria National Bank, 446 F.2d 47 (5th Cir. 1971).

As for the American Bank of Commerce, the same district court judge found the unequal wages to be justified because (1) the difference in pay was only slight; (2) a few women made slightly more than the men; (3) one male had supervisory responsibilities, making his job unequal; and (4) the men had individual additional responsibilities, making their jobs unequal. Wirtz v. American Bank of Commerce, 64 CCH Lab. Cas. ¶32,400, 19 Wage & Hour Cas. 774 (S.D. Tex. 1970). On this appeal, the court of appeals was not quite so content with the ruling, and rejected the first three arguments, including the fact that two women made more money than the men (the women had nine and ten years of experience, respectively, versus nine months and one year for the men). This meant a pay increase for seven to nine women tellers. However, the court accepted — under the Rule 52(a) clearly erroneous standard — the bank's fourth argument, that a male bookkeeper had to post a general ledger, which gave that job greater effort and responsibility than the female bookkeepers' job. Thus, the ten women bookkeepers were left at their former salary levels: $390 per month for a woman with nine years of experience, and $217-$290 per month for nine other women bookkeepers. The male bookkeeper, who had just been hired, earned $325-$350 per month, because of the general ledger posting task. Even this was not the end of the lawsuit, however, for the court still remanded for a determination on the issue of damages for the women tellers. Hodgson v. American Bank of Commerce, 447 F.2d 416 (5th Cir. 1971).

NOTE: THE CONTINUING ROLE OF SEX STEREOTYPES

The testimony in several training program cases reveals that bank officers still rely on the old stereotypes about women when making personnel decisions. In Hodgson v. Security National Bank of Sioux City:[26]

26. 460 F.2d 57, 62 (8th Cir. 1972).

Although the vice-president of the Bank testified that the management training program was open to both sexes, the Bank produced no testimony showing that it had ever offered management training to any woman. Its officers explained that females, who may have possessed college training and satisfactory prior working experience, were not considered for management training because of pregnancy or transfer of their husbands outside of the Sioux City area. These officers had commented to an investigator for the Labor Department that men possessed a greater potential for service to the Bank. In sum, the Bank claimed that, because of their sex or marriage status, none of the female employees hired during the period in question offered any potential for long-term employment. Thus, the Bank felt justified in soliciting and hiring women as tellers at a rate lower than men who did the very same work but carried the title of "management trainees."

A similar picture emerges in Hodgson v. Fairmont Supply Co.:[27]

Q. "Have you ever had any women in a training program?
A. Yes. Only for the — for their phase of the business, yes.
Q. What is their phase of the business?
A. Well, it depends on what a secretary or whether a stock clerk or whether a stock clerk or filing clerk, or what we hire them for.
Q. Well, what do you hire women for?
A. The things I just mentioned.
Q. All right. Have you ever had a woman in a sales training program?
A. No, ma'am." (App. 133).
Q. "Did JoAnn Fleming Chipps, or Mabel Villers attend any of these meetings?
A. We do not include any of our female help because they are not really being oriented for sales work really. They're performing clerical duties and this is really a training program." (App. 81).

b. Greater Average "Male" Profits

The following case illustrates the harm which can be produced by loose interpretation of the "any other factor other than sex" defense.

HODGSON v. ROBERT HALL CLOTHES, INC.
473 F.2d 589 (3rd Cir. 1972)
cert. denied sub nom. Brennan v. Robert Hall Clothes, Inc., 414 U.S. 866 (1973)

This case involves the application of the Equal Pay Act of 1963, 29 U.S.C. §206(d)(1) (1964). In view of the district court's well-written opinion reported at 326 F. Supp. 1264 (D. Del. 1971), we will not elaborate on the facts.

The Robert Hall store in question is located in Wilmington, Delaware. It sells clothing, and contains a department for men's and boys' clothing and another department for women's and girls' clothing. The store is a one-floor building, and the departments are in separate portions of it.

The merchandise in the men's department was, on the average, of higher price and better quality than the merchandise in the women's department; and Robert Hall's profit margin on the men's clothing was higher than its margin on the women's clothing. Consequently, the men's department at all times showed a larger dollar volume in gross sales, and a greater gross profit. Breaking this down, the salespeople in the men's department, on the average, sold more merchandise in terms of dollars and produced more gross profit than did the people in the women's department per hour of work.

The departments are staffed by full and part-time sales personnel. At all times, only

27. 454 F.2d 490, 498 (4th Cir. 1971).

men were permitted to work in the men's department and only women were permitted to work in the women's department. The complaint is not addressed to the propriety of such segregated employment.

. . . At all times, the salesmen received higher salaries than the saleswomen. Both starting salaries and periodic increases were higher for the males. . . .

PROCEDURAL HISTORY

. . . After a trial in late 1970, the district court filed its opinion on April 16, 1971. The court found that Robert Hall had a valid business reason for segregating its sales personnel, i.e., "the frequent necessity for physical contact between the sales persons and the customers which would embarrass both and would inhibit sales unless they were of the same sex." Hodgson v. Robert Hall, supra at 1269. However, it also found that this does not affect the application of the Equal Pay Act. It proceeded to hold that the sales personnel of each department performed equal work within the meaning of §206(d)(1).

The question then facing it was whether Robert Hall could prove that the wage "differential was based on any other factor other than sex." 29 U.S.C. §206(d)(1)(iv). Robert Hall contended that its wage differentials were based on economic factors, i.e., the higher profitability of the men's department allowed it to pay the men more, and the lower profitability of the women's department forced Robert Hall to pay the workers in that department less. In support of this contention, Robert Hall introduced evidence of sales and profit margins from which the district court was able to make the findings in the tables previously quoted.

The district court accepted Robert Hall's contention that economic benefit to the employer could be a factor other than sex on which a wage differential could be based. But it decided that the figures for the average performance of each department were not sufficient to meet Robert Hall's burden of proof. The court held that the relevant figures were those relating to the economic benefit produced by each individual sales person. Although Robert Hall in the ordinary course of business retained no records from which such performance could be calculated, fortuitously there were records available for two ten week periods out of the six years involved in this suit. Based on this evidence, the court compared the performances of the full-time male to the performances of the full-time female and compared the performances of the part-time males to those of the part-time females.[6] It found that the full-time male was responsible for more dollar sales per hour of work than was the full-time female. In regard to the part-time personnel, the court found:

> Two of Greenbank's part-time female employees, Alice Baker and C. Jarrell, were responsible for a higher per hour dollar volume of sales than three of the part-time male employees, McGonegal, Law and Layton, during the period from August 10, 1969 to October 18, 1969. A division of Jarrell's gross earnings (less incentive) by hours worked and a similar computation for the part-time salesmen discloses that Jarrell received a lower hourly rate than all three of these part-time salesmen, even though her gross sales per hour were more than that made by three of the five part-time salesmen.[7] Hodgson v. Robert Hall, supra at 1278.

On the basis of these findings, the district court held that the wage differential in favor of the part-time salesmen was not "supported by any economic benefits which defendants received from the job performances of the salesmen." Id. at 1278. Accord-

---

6. At the times covered by the record, there was only one full-time sales person of each sex. For the first ten-week period there were five part-time males and four part-time females. For the second, five males and three females.

7. Robert Hall claims that dollar volume of sales is not the most significant statistic. The most important statistic to it is the profit produced by the employee. While it is logical to assume that the salesmen could have produced more profit despite making fewer gross sales because of the higher profit margins on men's clothing, this statistic was not capable of calculation using the evidence available.

ingly, it found in favor of the secretary as to the part-time personnel (and awarded them back wages) and in favor of Robert Hall as to the full-time personnel. . . .

. . . The Secretary appeals from the decision adverse to the full-time female personnel . . . and Robert Hall appeals from the decision in favor of the part-time female personnel. . . .

"ANY OTHER FACTOR OTHER THAN SEX"

The initial question facing us is one raised by the Secretary. He contends that economic benefit to the employer cannot be used to justify a wage differential under §206(d)(1)(iv).

He argues that "any other factor" does not mean *any* other factor. Instead he claims it means any other factor other than sex which "is related to job performance or is typically used in setting wage scales." He contends that economic benefits to an employer do not fall within this exception.

He recognizes that the men's department produces a greater profit for Robert Hall. His contention is that the salesmen have nothing to do with producing this benefit since the district court found that the salesmen and saleswomen performed equal work. Since the saleswomen cannot sell the higher-priced clothing sold in the men's department, this cannot be used as a factor on which to base a wage differential. Otherwise, "the exception could swallow the rule." Shultz v. First Victoria National Bank, 420 F.2d 648 (5th Cir. 1969).

Robert Hall does not argue that "any other" means "any other" either. It claims that a wage differential is permissible if based on a legitimate business reason. As the district court found, economic benefits could justify a wage differential. We need go no further than to say the district court was correct to hold in this case that economic benefits to an employer can justify a wage differential.

The Secretary's argument is incorrect for several reasons. It ignores the basic finding of the district court that Robert Hall's segregation of its work force was done for legitimate business purposes. It is also inconsistent with the wording of the statute.

In providing for exceptions, the statute states that they will apply when the males and females are doing equal work. Congress thus intended to allow wage differentials even though the contrasted employers were performing equal work. However, two of the examples given as exceptions, (§206(d)(1)(ii) and (iii)), may be read to say that the contrasted employees really are not performing equal work. If, for example, some employees produce a greater quantity of work than others, pursuant to §206(d)(1)(iii), they may receive greater compensation.

The Secretary's test might be acceptable if §§206(d)(1)(ii) and (iii) stood alone. However, §§206(d)(1)(i) and (iv) indicate that there must be some factors upon which an employer may base a wage differential which are not related to job performance. We must point to the plain wording of the clause. It reads *"any* other factor. . . ." While the examples preceding §206(d)(1)(iv) necessarily qualify it to some extent, they do not narrow it to the degree for which the Secretary contends.

The Secretary recognizes this reasoning in §800.116(e) of his Wage-Hour Administrator's Interpretative Bulletin and §34d07 of his Field Office Handbook. In both of these the Secretary approves a commission system in which the amount of compensation is determined by the type of article sold.[9] The stated hypothesis is that the *sales people are*

---

9. The Bulletin states:

"Sec. 800.116(e) *Commissions.* The establishment of different rates of commission on different types of merchandise would not result in a violation of the Equal Pay provisions where the factor of sex provides no part of the basis for the differential. For example, suppose that a retail store maintains *two shoe departments, each having employees of both sexes,* [emphasis added] that the shoes carried in the two departments differ in style, quality and price, and that the male and female sales clerks in the one department are performing 'equal work' with those in the other. In such a situation, a prohibited differential would not result from payment of a lower commission rate in the department where a lower price line with a lower markup is sold than in the other department where the merchandise is higher priced and has a higher markup, if the employer can show that

performing equal work. Since this is given, the only basis for approving such a system has to be that the economic benefit to the employer is greater. As the Field Office Handbook states, "Such a difference in commission rates might be based on many factors such as sales volume, markup, cost of the items sold, type of merchandise sold, turnover in merchandise, and the ease of selling merchandise in each particular department." These are all factors of value to the employer. It might take no more effort or skill to sell two different pairs of ten dollar shoes; but if the employer makes a four dollar profit on one pair as opposed to a two dollar profit on the other, the Secretary apparently allows a higher commission rate. That the salary in this case is a base salary rather than a commission is not a significant distinction. The principle remains the same: the compensation is based on economic benefit to the employer, and the work performed is equal.

This would make good business sense. The saleswomen are paid less because the commodities which they sell cannot bear the same selling costs that the commodities sold in the men's department can bear. Without a more definite indication from Congress, it would not seem wise to impose the economic burden of higher compensation on employers. It could serve to weaken their competitive position. . . .

In addition, this case comes to us on a finding by the district court that "the jobs performed by salesmen and salesladies, respectively, are not reasonably susceptible of performance by both sexes because of the nature of the jobs." Hodgson v. Robert Hall Clothes, Inc., supra at 1269. Although the fact that the jobs in question require employment of one sex exclusively may not alone justify a wage differential, it does seem to be a factor that can be considered in evaluating the employer's justification for his differential.

The Secretary claims that his test is required by the Supreme Court's decision in Griggs v. Duke Power Co., Inc., 401 U.S. 424, 91 S. Ct. 849, 28 L. Ed. 2d 158 (1971). In *Griggs,* the Supreme Court interpreted Title VII of the Civil Rights Act to mean that if a job requirement operates to exclude a disproportionate number of blacks and the jobs in question formerly had been filled only by white employees as part of a longstanding practice of giving preference to whites, then the employer must show that the requirement is related to successful job performance to be able to use it. Although the Civil Rights Act and the Equal Pay Act are in para materia, . . . *Griggs* is not applicable to this case. Robert Hall's segregation of its sales force was related to job performance, as found by the District Court. The Secretary does not contend that the segregation is impermissible, but only that the pay must be equal. *Griggs* did not deal with justification of a wage differential and this is the issue we are considering.

BURDEN OF PROOF

The next question is whether Robert Hall proved that it received the economic benefits upon which it claimed it based its salary differentials. It is well-settled that the employer has the burden of proof on this issue. . . .

Robert Hall introduced evidence to show that for every year of the store's operation, the men's department was substantially more profitable than the women's department. . . .

---

the commission rates paid in each department are applied equally to the employees of both sexes in the establishment for all employment in that department and that the factor of sex has played no part in the setting of different commission rates." (519-20)

The Handbook reads:

"34d07 *Commissions.* IB 800.116(e) provides that the establishment of different rates of commission on different types of merchandise will not result in a violation of Sec 6(d) where the factor of sex provides no part of the basis for the differential. Thus, even though it is determined that salesmen and saleswomen are performing equal work in selling different merchandise in different departments the employer would not be in violation of Sec. 6(d) by paying different rates of commission on different merchandise where he can show that the differential is based on factors other than sex. Such a difference in commission rates *might be based on many factors such as sales volume, markup, cost of the items sold, type of merchandise sold, turnover in merchandise, and the ease of selling merchandise in each particular department.* If the employer applies such criteria in the same manner to employees of both sexes, the differential in rates would be based on factors other than sex." (488) (Emphasis added).

Robert Hall contends that this greater profitability is a sufficient reason to justify paying the sales people in its men's department more than it pays the salespeople in its women's department. It does not have to tie its compensation scheme into the performance of the individual sales person, and this is what the district court implicitly required.

We agree that the district's court's opinion implies that such a correlation is necessary. It compared the individual performances of the full-time male and the full-time female. It also compared the individual performances of the part-time workers. Hodgson v. Robert Hall Clothes, Inc., supra at 1278, 1280. . . . As we have mentioned, it was not Robert Hall's practice to retain records of individual performance. Fortuitously, the district court had before it the records of only two ten-week periods out of the six years in question here. Robert Hall questions the propriety of the district court's relying at all on these figures. It claims that these figures: (1) do not constitute a sufficient amount of evidence on which to base a finding; and (2) are not a representative sample.

Of course, it is the employer's burden to prove justification. Therefore, if the district court was correct in implicitly requiring Robert Hall to correlate wages with individual performance, Robert Hall cannot complain that there was not sufficient evidence available. This same reasoning applies to Robert Hall's complaint that the sample was not representative. Additionally, it does not seem unreasonable to us that in any comparison of individuals in these groups that there might be some saleswomen who had better statistics in some areas than some males had.[10] The question is whether the Equal Pay Act requires the employer to justify his base salary by correlating it to individual performance.

The overwhelming evidence which showed that the men's department was more profitable than the women's was sufficient to justify the differences in base salary. These statistics proved that Robert Hall's wage differentials were not based on sex but instead fully supported the reasoned business judgment that the sellers of women's clothing could not be paid as much as the sellers of men's clothing. Robert Hall's executives testified that it was their practice to base their wage rates on these departmental figures.

While no business reason could justify a practice clearly prohibited by the act, the legislative history . . . indicates a Congressional intent to allow reasonable business judgments to stand. It would be too great an economic and accounting hardship to impose upon Robert Hall the requirement that it correlate the wages of each individual with his or her performance. This could force it toward a system based totally upon commissions, and it seems unwise to read such a result into §206(d)(1)(iv). Robert Hall's method of determining salaries does not show the "clear pattern of discrimination," (Rep. Goodell, 109 Cong. Rec. 9203), that would be necessary for us to make it correlate more precisely the salary of each of its employees to the economic benefit which it receives from them. Robert Hall introduced substantial evidence. This is not a case where if we sustain the proof as justification for a wage differential "the exception will swallow the rule." Shultz v. First Victoria National Bank, 420 F.2d 648, 656, 657 (5th Cir. 1969).

The Secretary contends that our decision in Shultz v. Wheaton Glass Company, [421 F.2d 259 (3rd Cir. 1970), *cert. denied,* 398 U.S. 905 (1970)] supports the district court's decision not to rely on group averages to justify the wage differential. Cf. Hodgson v. Brookhaven General Hospital, 436 F.2d 719, 725 (5th Cir. 1970) and Shultz v. American Can Co., 424 F.2d 356, 358, 360-61 (8th Cir. 1970). We do not agree that *Wheaton* supports the district court. In that case the question, in part, was whether additional duties allegedly performed by certain males would justify paying males more than females. The courts held that the employers had failed to show that all of the males

10. See footnote 7.

performed the additional duties. Here all of the salesmen perform the same duties. One could analogize to *Wheaton Glass* and say that as the alleged justification there was the additional duties, the alleged justification here is the economic benefits. And as the employer there did not prove that each individual performed the duties here Robert Hall did not prove that each individual provided economic benefits. However, the nature of the proof required distinguishes the two cases. It would not have been difficult in *Wheaton* for the employer to have proved that each or most male workers performed the additional duties. That is not the case here.

Also, in *Wheaton Glass,* the court relied on the fact that there had been no finding that the women workers could not perform the additional duties allegedly performed by the men. Here there was a specific finding by the district court, unchallenged by the Secretary, that the women could not perform the work done by the men. . . .

The decision of that court will be affirmed as to the full-time personnel and reversed as to the part-time personnel. . . .

NOTE: THE IMPACT OF AVERAGING BY SEX

The court's opinion does not fully bring out the inequity for individual women of the company's use of sex-based averaging in computing profits by department. The following excerpt from the Brief for the Secretary of Labor examines the evidence more closely.[28]

The merchandise carried in the men's department is generally more expensive than that sold in the women's department (A. 272, 502, 510-511). For example, 60 percent of the men's coats and suits are priced above $39.95 whereas only 20 percent of women's coats and suits sell for more than $39.95 (A. 242, 420-432, 501, 502). As a result, the saleswomen must sell from 40 to 50 percent more items than the salesmen in order to generate the same volume of sales in dollars and cents (DX Nos. 20-23, 456, 462, 467, 473). Thus, as Mr. Silbert acknowledged, only "an excellent saleswoman might generate more sales than a very poor salesman, but normally, under normal circumstances, this would not happen" (A. 320). Compare, for example, the average dollar sales volume per hour of Mrs. Raker ($44.62) with that of Mr. Blawn ($48.95). Mrs. Raker, however, had to sell 8.18 items per hour in contrast to Mr. Blawn's 4.03 items. . . . Similarly, Mrs. Russell, who worked 184 hours during an earlier period, sold 4.8 items an hour (including 165 dresses, 106 coats, and 100 blouses), and had a sales volume of $33.22 per hour; in contrast, Mr. Layton, who worked 189.75 hours and sold 3.4 items an hour (including 48 suits, 2 coats, and 38 shirts), had a sales volume of $40.22 per hour (A. 456, 460, 462, 466). . . .

In an effort to justify the wage differential, defendants introduced several exhibits which purported to show the sales volume and profit ratio for each individual salesperson (A. 436, 451, 487). In fact, however, as the court below recognized (A. 333-334, 515-516, 552-553), most of these statistics were based on group averages and did not reflect the actual sales made by individual employees nor the profit attributable to such sales (A. 243-245, 233-234). Indeed, the only individual data introduced were sales figures for two short periods of time — from January 26, 1969, to April 12, 1969, and from August 10, 1969, to October 18, 1969 (DX Nos. 20-23, A. 456, 462, 467, 473). And these figures show that the sales volume of individual men and women varied considerably from person to person, regardless of sex and regardless of the fact that the gross sales of the men's department are higher than those of the women's department. Thus, during the period from August to October 1969, three of the women had a greater dollar sales volume per hour than three of the men, and one of the women (Mrs. Donofrio) had a greater dollar sales volume than four of the men (DX Nos. 22-23; A. 467, 477). . . .

28. Brief for the Secretary of Labor at 10-15, Hodgson v. Robert Hall Clothes, Inc., Nos. 71-1985, 761-1986 (3rd Cir. Feb. 1972).

The defendants had no evidence as to the profits generated by the sales of each salesperson (A. 321, 335, 336). Their Exhibit 41 (A. 487), which purports to show the gross profit per hour for salesmen versus the gross profit per hour for saleswomen, is a group average, as already noted. This group average was reached in three steps: (1) The gross profit in each department was determined by subtracting the cost of merchandise from total sales;[6] (2) total sales were divided into gross profits to get the ratio of sales to profits; and (3) the resulting percentage figure was then applied to the average sales per hour for salesmen and saleswomen to obtain their average "profitability" (A. 243-245, 302-303, 333-334, 437, 450-451, 524-538).

. . . Robert Hall's vice president, Mr. Silbert . . . admitted that the higher sales and profit figures for their men employees did not result from superior salesmanship (see A. 320) but from the fact that men's wearing apparel is more expensive and has a higher mark-up (A. 352-355).

Thus, women employees are assigned on the basis of sex to a department where, if they sell the same number of items of clothing as their male counterparts, they will necessarily produce a smaller profit for the company. This is because equivalent items of men's clothing produce a higher profit than women's clothing; the greater profitability of men's clothing derives from the fact that it costs the company less (Robert Hall manufactures its own men's clothing, but must purchase its women's clothing) and is also higher-priced merchandise than women's clothing. Nevertheless, if any individual woman manages to overcome this first form of built-in sex bias by superior saleswomanship and produces a greater profit than any individual man, she is still condemned to a lower wage because the female *group* profit experience is attributed to her. Meanwhile, a less competent male salesman wins a higher salary because the male *group* profit experience is attributed to him. The individual is judged by sex, rather than individual job performance — and this is the very nature of sex discrimination.

Notice also that the company was not able to produce any individual profit figures; it had only individual *sales* figures and sex-based group profit figures. Thus, one never knows whether any individual saleswoman has produced a higher profit for the company than any man earning more than she does (although we do know that individual women have produced higher sales volume per hour than some men). The court excuses the company's inability to correlate wages to the individual's profit performance (the alleged reason for the wage differential) by saying that it would be too onerous for the company to come forth with individual profit figures — although that is the only way to test the equity for individuals of the company's wage policy. Not all courts have been so overcome by the unfairness of forcing companies to justify wage differentials on an individual basis. In Wirtz v. Midwest Mfg. Corp., 58 CCH Lab. Cas. ¶32,070, 18 Wage & Hour Cas. 556 (S.D. Ill. 1968), the court refused to allow higher wages for men performing work equal to women's, despite the company's contention that it cost more to employ women due to higher insurance costs. The court replied:[29]

> The exception provided by section 6(d)(1)(iv) is inapplicable to defendant's claimed differences between the average cost of employing women employees *as a group* and the average cost of employing men employees *as a group*, as described in Findings 11 to 15, inclusive. A wage differential based on such claimed differences does not qualify as a differential based on any "other factor other than sex." The Department of Labor's Wage and Hour Administrator in section 800.151 of Interpretative Bulletin Part 800 states as follows:

6. The gross profit figures will always be greater for the men's department since much of its merchandise is manufactured by Robert Hall, and since, in computing gross profits, defendants use the actual cost of manufacturing, which, of course, does not include any profit to the manufacturing subsidiary (A. 336-340, 342-352). Robert Hall does not manufacture women's apparel.

29. 18 Wage & Hour Cas. at 560-561.

". . .To group employees solely on the basis of sex for purposes of comparison of costs necessarily rests on the assumption that the sex factor alone may justify the wage differential — an assumption plainly contrary to the terms and purpose of the Equal Pay Act. Wage differentials so based would serve only to perpetuate and promote the very discrimination at which the Act is directed, because in any grouping by sex of the employees to which the cost data relates, the group cost experience is necessarily assessed against an individual of one sex without regard to whether it costs an employer more or less to employ such individual than a particular individual of the opposite sex under similar working conditions in jobs requiring equal skill, effort and responsibility."

Note: Flaws in the Court's Reasoning and Labor Department Strategy

The essential point which the court misses is that the women's lower pay was based at least in part on the factor of sex, since all women were assigned on the basis of sex to a department where the profits they produced were necessarily lower than those which men could produce. The court may have had difficulty dealing with this issue because it found the sex segregation of the equal jobs reasonable; the lower court had noted that[30]

> Often the salesperson is required to assist with opening zippers; to touch the body of a customer near private parts in connection with measurements of the crotch, seat, waist, chest or inseam; to touch other areas of the body while assisting in the try-on of a garment, and to observe the customer in various stages of undress in connection with try-ons.

The court might have analyzed the situation more clearly without this privacy factor. For instance, imagine that men and women were assigned on the basis of sex to different factory machines, where each sex performed equal work but the product of the machines to which men were assigned earned a greater profit for the company than did the product of the machines to which women were assigned. A court might not find the greater average male profit "a factor other than sex" since it would be so obvious that women were not allowed the opportunity to work on the greater profit-making machines, and since there would be no problems like the invasion of privacy in *Robert Hall Clothes.*

The Labor Department regulations on commissions — which the court cites in footnote 9 to justify accepting profit as a "factor other than sex" — make this same point. The Labor Department supposition expressly assumes that both the lower- and higher-priced shoe departments have employees of both sexes; only then is a commission system paying higher rates in the higher-priced department legal. The court ignores the point that the higher commissions must be available to both sexes, and emphasizes instead that different commission rates can be based on cost factors (here, the price of the merchandise).

The essential point for the court, then, should have been that the pay differential was based on sex, and was therefore prohibited by the act since it was not a factor *other than sex.* Nowhere does the act allow wage differentials if the sex-based origin of the differential is reasonable, or one that might be allowed under the Title VII "BFOQ" standard. On the other hand, since the Equal Pay Act does not prohibit job segregation, the court would not have been forced to integrate the jobs — but should merely have awarded equal pay for what it had already found to be equal work.

Labor Department strategy may have been partly responsible for the result in this case. In its appellate brief, the department concentrated on the argument that "factors

30. Hodgson v. Robert Hall Clothes, Inc., 326 F. Supp. 1264, 1269 (D. Del. 1971).

other than sex" should be limited to factors which are related to the job performance of the worker. This is the argument the court spent most of its time refuting. Only one paragraph of the brief noted that the factor was sex-based, and the brief did not point out that the jobs could remain segregated even if equal pay were awarded. Do you think that the Labor Department should have used a different strategy? Would you answer the question differently if the department had succeeded in limiting the "any factor other than sex" defense to job performance factors?

Note: Retail Trade Litigation

The Labor Department is currently pursuing unequal pay in the retail trade industry on several fronts; the other cases have not involved the issue of the profitability of sex-segregated departments, and they have been much more successful than *Robert Hall Clothes.* So far the department has won decisions holding that salesmen in men's clothing departments and saleswomen in women's and children's clothing departments performed equal work, as did a male tailor and female seamstress, Brennan v. City Stores, Inc., 71 CCH Lab. Cas. ¶32,910, 21 Wage & Hour Cas. 69 (5th Cir. 1973); that men and women area supervisors of "hardlines" departments (all departments other than clothing) performed equal work, as did men and women area supervisors of "softlines" (clothing) departments (although the court rejected the Labor Department view that the jobs were equal even between hardlines and softlines; the Labor Department is asserting this view again on appeal), Shultz v. J.M. Fields, Inc., 335 F. Supp. 731 (M.D. Fla. 1971), *appeal pending* (5th Cir.); and, in a consent decree, that both men and women salespersons and men and women division managers performed equal work in varied hardline *and* softline departments, Hodgson v. Sears, Roebuck and Co., slip opinion, Civ. Act. File No. 2555 (W.D. Ky., April 25, 1972).
A news story indicates the impact these cases may have:[31]

Three equal-pay lawsuits involving women are scaring the daylights out of U.S. retailers as the cases move up inexorably through federal courts. No one has ever disputed that few women make fortunes as employees of retail establishments. Now the government is apparently on its way to proving that they do not even get an equal break with men. The cases concern Alabama, Florida and Delaware retail chains. If the stores lose — and so far they are losing — retailers may be forced to pay millions of dollars in additional wages to the women who make up almost half of their non-supervisory labor force across the nation.

"If the Labor Dept. tests the outer periphery of its power under this law (the 1968 Equal Pay Act), it could ruin any number of companies," says Eugene Keeney, president of the Washington-based American Retail Federation.

Neither a tight-lipped ARF nor a guardedly jubilant U.S. Labor Dept. will guess at the size of the bill that may come due. But the number of employees involved and their present earnings provide a clue.

More than 5-million women (and more than 6-million men) are employed in the Census Bureau category of retail trade. Full-time women workers average $4,062 a year; men, $8,639. Even allowing for the likelihood of greater seniority and expertise among the men, both legal justifications for higher pay, the $4,000-plus spread remains formidable. Used either as evidence of wage discrimination or as a guide to court-ordered correction of wage discrimination, the differential could produce dizzying increases in women's pay.

. . . the decision in the Loveman case, now heading for appeal in the U.S. Circuit Court in New Orleans,[32] unnerves retailers the most. If upheld, it would destroy the retailers' traditional rationale for paying differing wages: the assumption that different

31. Equal Pay for Women Hits Retailers, Business Week, Jan. 29, 1972, pp. 76-78.
32. The decision was later affirmed, Brennan v. City Stores, Inc., *supra.* — Eds.

departments of a store constitute different selling establishments. This assumption is nonsense, said Judge Frank M. Johnson, Jr., of the U.S. District Court in Montgomery, Ala.; a store is a single selling unit where men and women employed on jobs requiring "substantially equal skill, effort, and responsibility" must be paid the same wage.

Judge Johnson found "wholly unpersuasive and contrary to common sense" the defendant's argument that fitting a man's suit differs in kind from fitting a woman's suit. He ordered the stores to put $250,000 in escrow to cover two years of back wages (based on equalized pay scales), plus 6% interest for their women employees in case all appeals fail.

Judge Johnson's emphasis on equal pay for equal skill hits the nail right on the head, according to Labor Dept. lawyers. They have no intention of challenging genuine differences in qualifications, they say. "We are certainly willing to concede that a salesman of jewelry, who must know his gems, should be paid more than a clothing salesman," a spokesman says. . . .

IMPACT. Testimony on the wide discrepancy between what men and women earned in retailing bulked large in the Congressional hearings that led to passage of the 1963 act. Since then, says a Labor Dept. source, "retailers haven't done a thing except look at their stores and say that separate departments mean separate, differently paid jobs."

Retailers take another view of the situation. An ARF official insists that Esther Peterson, then head of the Labor Dept.'s Women's Bureau, promised that the Labor Dept. would be reasonable in interpreting the act for retailers because of its tremendous potential impact on the industry. The department is not being reasonable, he complains. Waiting several years for retailers to put their own house in order before stepping up legal pressure does not strike her as unreasonable, says Mrs. Peterson, now consumer adviser to the president of Giant Food, Inc.

Understandably, the industry would prefer to work out some accommodation with the Labor Dept. rather than face a series of all-or-nothing showdowns before the Supreme Court. Other equal-pay suits, including three against the nation's largest retailer, Sears, Roebuck & Co., are lined up behind the three that have already reached the appeals stage. Officials of the New York-based National Retail Merchants Assn. met quietly several months ago with Wage & Hour Div. representatives to explore possible wage guidelines acceptable to both parties, but nothing much came of the discussion. . . .

Says Edward Field, vice-president for personnel relations at Federated Department Stores, Inc., the country's largest department store chain: "The implications of the darn thing are quite broad."

They are so broad, in fact, that women employees at one Loveman's store reportedly broke a calculating machine trying to figure out how much money each would get if Judge Johnson's decision were upheld. It is probable that many retailers, using more sophisticated techniques, are making the same sort of calculations.

An interesting issue to consider is the extent to which jobs are equal among different departments in multidepartment stores. As the news story suggests, the stores want to be able to set different wages in every department. According to the same story, the Labor Department would not compare jobs in clothing departments to those in jewelry departments involving extremely expensive, valuable gems, because a jewelry salesman "must know his gems." In litigation, however, the department has sought to compare jobs between hardline and softline departments. It achieved this result in a settlement with a Kentucky Sears, Roebuck and Co. store, which agreed to equalize pay for sales personnel in departments carrying such varied items as clothing, paints and supplies, electrical table appliances, cosmetics, hardware and power tools, and yard good and patterns. Hodgson v. Sears, Roebuck and Co., supra. From a common-sense point of view, it seems hard to justify pay differences among such varied departments: is selling shoes really so different from, or more valuable than, selling toasters? Yet technically minded courts may be unwilling to go that far under the "skill, effort, and responsibility" formula of the Equal Pay Act. A middle ground might be found by picking broad categories within which jobs could be compared. For example, a Labor Department publication, The Retail Trade, Selected Department Store Occupations,[33] lists three major kinds of sales jobs: (1) salesperson — big ticket (i.e., high-priced) and specialty items (such as orthopedic shoes, fine jewelry, or major appliances); (2) salesperson — counter and customer selection (such as candy, books, and costume jewelry); and (3) salesperson — floor sales (such as housewares, sporting goods, or clothing). Perhaps the Labor Department will litigate equality of jobs within categories such as these, rather than attempt to show that all salespeople in a store do equal work.

A related issue to the choice of departments within which jobs are compared is the use of commission systems giving higher rates to sales personnel in high-priced departments than in low-priced departments. Where personnel in high-priced departments are predominantly male, the policy would probably violate Title VII and should be rejected under the Equal Pay Act as being sex-based (see Note: Flaws in the Court's Reasoning and Labor Department Strategy, supra). However, if male and female personnel are evenly distributed in each department, the current Labor Department guidelines find the practice legal under the Equal Pay Act. Yet if the work is indeed equal, why should employees be paid more simply because they are assigned to sell higher-priced items? Seen in this light, the Labor Department strategy to limit "factors other than sex" to those related to job performance is a good one; the practice could only be rejected under such an interpretation.

c. Other "Factors Other than Sex"

In the attempt to avoid equal pay, employers have litigated many other issues under the "factor other than sex" defense. For example, employers frequently contend that they are merely paying prevailing wage scales. The Fifth Circuit curtly responded:[34]

> Clearly the fact that the employer's bargaining power is greater with respect to women than with respect to men is not the kind of factor Congress had in mind. Thus it will not do for the hospital to press the point that it paid orderlies more because it could not get them for less.

Another court pointed out that a "defendant may not justify its discrimination by pointing to the conduct of others."[35]

Another rejected factor, similar to the training program defense, was a company policy of promoting employees into higher positions from a male job, but not from the equal female job. Shultz v. American Can Co. — Dixie Products, 424 F.2d 356, 362 (8th Cir. 1970). One court accepted the greater ambition and enthusiasm of a male salesman as a factor other than sex in Wirtz v. Oregon State Motor Assn., 57 CCH Lab. Cas. ¶32,010 (D. Ore. 1968). The supposed greater flexibility of male employees in their ability to perform extra, mostly weight-lifting, tasks was rejected in Shultz v. Wheaton Glass Co., 421 F.2d 259 (3rd Cir. 1970), and in Shultz v. Saxonburg Ceramics, Inc., 314 F. Supp. 1139, 1146 (W.D. Pa. 1970). In its guidelines, the Labor Department has rejected other factors, among them that it costs more on the average to employ women than it does men, 29 C.F.R. §800.151, and that men are heads of households, 29 C.F.R. §800.149.

33. U.S. Dept. of Labor, Manpower Administration, U.S. Employment Service (1972).
34. Hodgson v. Brookhaven General Hospital, 436 F.2d 719, 726 (5th Cir. 1970).
35. Hodgson v. City Stores, Inc., 332 F. Supp. 942, 950 (M.D. Ala. 1971), *aff'd sub nom.* Brennan v. City Stores, Inc., 71 CCH Labor Cas. ¶32,910, 21 Wage & Hour Cas. 69 (5th Cir. 1973).

E. UNION LIABILITY FOR EQUAL PAY ACT VIOLATIONS

The Equal Pay Act provides that[36]

> No labor organization, or its agents, representing employees of an employer . . . shall cause or attempt to cause such employer to discriminate against an employee in violation of [the Equal Pay mandate]. . . .

In general neither the Labor Department nor private litigants have sued unions under the act, although decisions often explicitly refer to union responsibility for wage discrimination. See, for example, Shultz v. Wheaton Glass Co., supra. Do you think labor unions should be sued? An argument against suing unions is that a back pay judgment against a union would eventually be paid out of the members' own pockets, including female members. Also, suing unions might alienate potential supporters of equal pay claims, whose resources would be far better deployed in support of Equal Pay Act litigation than in defending against an equal pay suit. On the other hand, successful litigation against some unions — including both back pay and injunctive relief —might convince other unions to take action to eliminate pay discrimination against their members. Consider these arguments in light of the following case.

HODGSON v. SAGNER, INC.
326 F. Supp. 371 (D. Md. 1971)

In this civil action, the Secretary of Labor is seeking an injunction against a clothing manufacturer and the union that represents its employees, seeking to restrain the defendants from violating the Equal Pay Act, and seeking further to restrain the withholding of certain unpaid back wages. The corporate defendant, Sagner, Inc. (the "Company"), manufactures men's clothing at its Frederick, Maryland, plant. The defendant Baltimore Regional Joint Board, Amalgamated Clothing Workers of America, AFL–CIO (the "Union") is the union which represents employees of Sagner. . . .

It is claimed by the Government that for a two-year period, from March 14, 1966 to March 14, 1968, the Company paid female cutters and female markers 40 cents per hour less than male cutters and markers. Fifteen female cutters and seven female markers are involved during the period in question. The Government claims that the amount of the underpayment for the entire period comes to $29,771.36, but since $7,442.84 (or one-quarter of this amount) was paid by the Company to these female cutters and markers in 1968, the amount claimed to be due in this action is $22,328.52, plus interest. . . .

In final argument, both the Company and the Union conceded that substantially equal work was being performed by both male and female employees involved and that the Company should have paid its female cutters and markers at the same hourly rate as it paid its male cutters and markers during the 2-year period after March 14, 1966. . . .

But this preliminary finding does not resolve the other questions presented in this case. The Company argues that it should not be held responsible for these payments due the female employees in question because the Union caused the discrimination. The Union argues, on its part, first that under the Act it cannot be compelled to pay back wages which have been withheld by the Company; and, second, that the facts here do not, in any event, establish that it caused the discrimination in question.

Taking up first the question of law raised by the Union, this Court must determine preliminarily whether, under the Act, a union which has caused a company to discriminate on the basis of sex can be held liable in damages for the payment of the wages illegally withheld. The Union here points out that the statute empowers the Court to

36. 29 U.S.C. §206(d)(2).

restrain the withholding of payments found by the Court to be due employees, but argues that since a union cannot be said to withhold payments due a company's employees, the only relief that the Court can grant against a union is prospective injunctive relief. In support of its argument, the Union relies on the cases of Wirtz v. Hayes Industries, Inc., 18 W.H. Cases 590 (N.D. Ohio 1968).

After reviewing that decision and considering the arguments advanced, this Court cannot agree with the Union's position, particularly under the facts of this case. If that position were correct, a union which had caused an employer to illegally withhold wages from its employees would be subject to no more than future restraint. Its past violation of the law would go uncorrected and unpunished; it could merely be prevented from breaking the law in the future. There is no apparent reason why a union which violates Section 206(d) should be treated any differently from an employer violator. Equitably, both should be subject to the same type of decree, which in order to give full relief would necessarily include a provision requiring the payment of wages illegally withheld or caused to be withheld as well as one prohibiting any future violation of the law.

Whether or not there is an express statutory basis for the ordering of this type of relief against the Union, this Court is satisfied that within its general equitable powers, it may, if it finds a violation of Section 206(d)(2), order an offending union to repay to the Government for distribution to the employees involved the wages that the Union caused to be wrongfully withheld. In support of this proposition, I would cite the case of Mitchell v. Robert De Mario Jewelry, Inc., 361 U.S. 288, 80 S. Ct. 332, 4 L. Ed. 2d 323 (1960). Any other result would not permit the enforcement of the Act by the Court in a manner consistent with the Congressional intention.

In the *Hayes* case, the language which is relied upon by the Union is pure dictum. The Government in the *Hayes* case had not sued the union and did not seek damages from the union. The Court found in connection with the third party claim being there asserted that the union had not caused the employer to establish the wage differential in question. Here, the Government relies on substantially different facts, and there is a direct claim against the Union. As to the Union, the Government argues that the Company was prepared to pay the entire amount of back wages due but that the Union bargained away the rights of the 22 employees involved in favor of some 100 other employees who were not due any back wages under the Act. Certainly, under facts such as those claimed to be present in this case, the Union, if indeed it did violate the Act, should not escape responsibility for making payment to the 22 employees involved who were denied their back wages allegedly because of union action.

In view of this Court's conclusion as to the law, the questions that remain to be resolved under the facts here, in addition to the question of prospective injunctive relief, are as follows:

1. Whether the Company alone is liable for the remaining amounts of back wages due;
2. Whether the Union alone is so liable;
3. Whether neither the Company nor the Union is so liable; and
4. Whether both the Company and the Union are so liable jointly and severally.

After hearing the evidence and reviewing the exhibits and the pleadings, this Court concludes that the Secretary of Labor is entitled to an injunction against both the Company and the Union and is further entitled to recover the full damages claimed from both of the defendants, jointly and severally.

For a full understanding of the facts which compel this conclusion, it is necessary to recount the events that transpired between October 30, 1967 and March 14, 1968, and in particular the details of the negotiations between the Company and the Union that took place during that period. On the former date, October 30, 1967, Mr. Sam Nocella, Manager of the Joint Board, wrote the Company and suggested that the Company was violating the Equal Pay Act. . . .

Meetings were thereupon arranged with Company officials to discuss this question. . . . Altogether, some five meetings were held between Company and Union representatives, including their attorneys, and as the negotiations proceeded, the Company's position changed from time to time. At one of the earlier meetings, it recognized its liability under the Equal Pay Act and stated that it was willing to pay one full year of wages to the female employees involved. At this stage in the negotiations, both the Company and the Union were in agreement that the Act had been violated and that substantial sums were owed to the 22 female cutters and markers in question. It was therefore incumbent on both parties at this stage to see that the amounts were properly computed and that all the amounts due under the law were paid to the 22 employees involved. Neither party fulfilled such duty. The Company, although realizing that under the law back wages were due, eventually paid only one-quarter of the total sum due. The Union, with a similar realization, proposed to the Company (and it is clear from the evidence that this was the Union's idea, not the Company's) that parts of the amounts due as back wages be paid to *other* employees.

The Union, from the outset, was not satisfied with merely the payment of the sums due the 22 female cutters and markers. The Union claimed during the negotiations that others in the cutting room would be dissatisfied and that there would be "problems" if only the 22 female employees received the payments. The Union argued that in addition, amounts should be paid to these other employees to avoid these "problems." The Company refused to go along with this proposal and insisted (shortly before agreement was reached) that it would pay no more than amounts due these female employees covered by the Act. As mentioned, it was the Union that initially proposed that only a part of the amounts calculated to be due to the 22 female cutters and markers be paid to those employees, with the remainder being distributed among the other employees in the cutting room as a wage increase until the end of the contract year.

Further negotiations ensued, and finally the Union's suggestion was accepted by Mr. Sagner, contrary to his attorney's advice. One-quarter of the amount legally due was paid by agreement to the 22 female cutters and markers. The remaining three-quarters was to be paid to the other 100-odd employees in the cutting room as a wage increase until the end of the current contract year.

These facts lead to the following conclusions:

1. That the Company did not relieve itself of the legal liability it had (and recognized) to the 22 female cutters and markers by entering into this agreement with the Union; and

2. That the Union caused the Company to discriminate against such female employees by inducing the Company to divert substantial sums due such employees and pay such sums to employees who were not then legally entitled to them.

I find that before the final agreement was reached between Mr. Nocella and Mr. Sagner, the Company was prepared to pay the full two years back pay to the female employees to whom it was due. The Union's refusal to agree to this proposal of the Company prevented such payment.

When the Company entered into the agreement proposed by the Union, it did so at its own risk. Indeed, the Company's experienced counsel advised that if all of the money were not paid to the 22 female cutters and markers, the Company might well have to pay certain sums twice. This was sound advice. Yet the Company's management chose to disregard it and ignore the clear legal obligation it had to make full retroactive payments to the employees entitled to them. Under the Fair Labor Standards Act, no agreement between a company and a union, even if arrived at as a result of collective bargaining negotiations, can be used as a defense by a company to the statutory requirements. See in this connection a number of cases that arose under other provisions of the Act: Johnson v. Dierks Lumber and Coal Co., 130 F.2d 115 (8th Cir. 1942); McNorrill

v. Gibbs, 45 F. Supp. 363 (E.D.S.C. 1942), and Tennessee Coal, Iron and R. Co. v. Muscoda Local No. 123, 137 F.2d 176 (5th Cir. 1943), affirmed 321 U.S. 590, 64 S. Ct. 698, 88 L. Ed. 949 (1944). This agreement then, reached in March, 1968, did not relieve the Company of its obligation to pay these female employees the full amount due them.

The Union's actions are even more difficult to comprehend. After recognizing the Company's obligations under the law to the female cutters and markers — even calling the Company's attention initially to the requirements of the law — the Union then went ahead and bargained such obligations away in favor of other employees in the cutting room. The Company owed nothing to those other employees, either under the law or under the existing collective bargaining agreement which did not expire until June 1, 1968. Yet it was the Union which suggested that the Company pay 75% of the amount legally due to these female cutters and markers to other employees not entitled to these sums by law or contract. Clearly, the Union violated the statute by insisting that the Company discriminate by not paying the female employees in question the full amount due them.

That the Union was well aware that its actions were legally questionable is indicated by what it did after agreement was reached. The Union sought to protect itself by means of presenting written waivers to the 22 female cutters and markers, whereby they purportedly surrendered their legal rights to the back pay due them. I find from the evidence that this device was the Union's idea, that it was carried out by the Union and that it was designed to protect the Union. . . .

These waivers in no way go to prove that the Union did not cause the Company to discriminate against the female employees in question. On the contrary, they are further proof of the Union's intent to violate the law, representing attempts by the Union to cover up the blatant manner in which it bargained away the legal rights of 22 union members in favor of windfall benefits conferred on 100 other union members. Perhaps the numbers involved in each respective group had something to do with the Union's actions here. . . .

The Union caused the entire amount not to be paid by the Company. The Company, for reasons of expediency, went along with the Union's proposal. The liability is therefore joint and several as to the entire amount claimed by the Government.

[The Fourth Circuit affirmed the decision, per curiam, stating "For reasons sufficiently indicated by the District Court, . . . we agree that the court was within its general equitable powers in imposing such liability upon the Union." Hodgson v. Baltimore Regional Joint Board, 462 F.2d 180 (4th Cir. 1972).]

F. Especially for Practitioners: Remedies and Pitfalls Under the Equal Pay Act

One theme of this part has been the superiority of Title VII over the Equal Pay Act because the first statute reaches a broad range of discriminatory practices, while the second reaches only wage discrimination. However, within the narrow context of wage discrimination, the Equal Pay Act does offer one basic advantage: plaintiffs can recover more money in back wages than under Title VII for that form of discrimination. This fact points up the necessity for examining all the relief available under both statutes. (See discussion of Title VII relief, Part II-G supra.)

1. Equal Pay Act Remedies

To understand Equal Pay Act remedies, the reader must first turn to the structure of the Fair Labor Standards Act (FLSA) of 1938, 29 U.S.C. §201 et seq., to which the Equal Pay Act was an amendment. In §§16 and 17, the FLSA provides for four different kinds of lawsuits:

(1) a §16(a) criminal prosecution for a willful violation of the FLSA or the Equal Pay Act;

(2) a §16(b) civil suit, brought by the aggrieved employees;

(3) a §16(c) civil suit, brought by the secretary of labor on behalf of aggrieved employees who file a written request for back wages with the secretary; and

(4) a §17 civil suit, brought by the secretary of labor on behalf of aggrieved employees.

The remedies in each kind of lawsuit are not uniform. In a §16(b) employee's lawsuit, they include: unpaid "equal," or back, wages; an additional equal amount as liquidated damages; and attorney's fees plus costs. In a §16(c) Department of Labor suit based on the employees' written request, they include: unpaid back wages; interest at 6 percent per year on the unpaid back wages; and costs.[37] In a §17 Department of Labor suit, they include: unpaid back wages; interest at 6 percent per year on the unpaid back wages; an injunction restraining future violations of the law; and costs.[38]

Two major points stand out immediately. Employees cannot win an injunction against future violations in a §16(b) lawsuit — a serious defect in the employees' remedy. And the Labor Department cannot win an injunction in a §16(c) suit (nor can it proceed without the employee's written request); consequently, the §16(c) suit is rarely used.

The monetary remedies above are further affected by the Portal-to-Portal Act of 1947, 29 U.S.C. §250 et seq., passed expressly by Congress in order to limit large back pay awards.[39] Section 6 of the Portal-to-Portal Act, 29 U.S.C. §255, provides a statute of limitations for equal pay actions that limits the time for which back wages can be recovered.[40] The time period commences two years prior to the filing of the Equal Pay Act complaint in federal court and continues up to the day of the court's order or the cessation of the practice; if the violation is willful, the time period commences three years prior to the filing. If the litigation lasts an undue time, this amount can grow to a large sum, especially when the liquidated damages in a §16(b) suit, or the interest in a §17 suit, are added to the original amount. In the landmark case of Shultz v. Wheaton Glass Co., supra, the award of back wages plus 6 percent interest came to $788,828 (back wages) and $112,233 (interest), or a total of $901,061, for 2168 employees, and that was just for the two-year, not the three-year willful violation time period.

The text of the FSLA provisions discussed above is as follows.

THE FAIR LABOR STANDARDS ACT OF 1938
29 U.S.C. §201 et seq., §§216, 217

§216(a). Any person who willfully violates any of the provisions of section 215 of this title [which makes it illegal for any person to violate section 6] shall upon conviction thereof be subject to a fine of not more than $10,000, or to imprisonment for not more

---

37. Section 16(c) does not provide for interest or costs, but it has been awarded in FLSA litigation. See, e.g., Mitchell v. DiVicenti Brothers, Inc. 42 CCH Lab. Cas. ¶31,091 (E.D. La. 1961); Goldberg v. Bailey dba Bailey's Aircraft Plastics, 42 CCH Lab. Cas. ¶31,097 (S.D. Cal. 1961).

38. For decisions holding that interest is available under §17 even though §17 does not specifically mention interest, see Hodgson v. Wheaton Glass Co., 446 F.2d 527, 534-535 (3d Cir. 1971), and Hodgson v. American Can Co., 440 F.2d 916, 921-922 (8th Cir. 1971). *American Can Co.* also awards costs, without discussion of the issue.

39. Congress reacted specifically to Tennessee Coal, Iron and R.R. Co. v. Muscoda Local 123, 321 U.S. 590, 64 S. Ct. 698, 88 L. Ed. 949 (1944), in which the Supreme Court held that under the FLSA miners must be paid for their travel time within mines, from the entrance to the working area and back to the entrance, or "portal-to-portal." The potential amount of money owed miners ran to 5 billion dollars, with the U.S. liable for 1½ billion dollars under wartime cost-plus contracts. Passage of the Portal-to-Portal Act prevented payment of these sums.

40. "Any action commenced on or after May 14, 1947, to enforce any cause of action for unpaid minimum wages . . . or liquidated damages, under the Fair Labor Standards Act of 1938, as amended. . . .

than six months, or both. No person shall be imprisoned under this subsection except for an offense committed after the conviction of such person for a prior offense under this subsection.

(b). Any employer who violates the provisions of section 206 . . . of this title shall be liable to the employee or employees affected in the amount of their unpaid minimum wages . . . and in an additional equal amount as liquidated damages. Action to recover such liability may be maintained in any court of competent jurisdiction by any one or more employees for and in behalf of himself or themselves and other employees similarly situated. No employee shall be a party plaintiff to any such action unless he gives his consent in writing to become such a party and such consent is filed in the court in which such action is brought. The court in such action shall, in addition to any judgment awarded to the plaintiff or plaintiffs, allow a reasonable attorney's fee to be paid by the defendant, and costs of the action. The right provided by this subsection to bring an action by or on behalf of any employee, and the right of any employee to become a party plaintiff to any such action, shall terminate upon the filing of a complaint by the Secretary of Labor in an action under section 217 of this title in which restraint is sought of any further delay in the payment of unpaid minimum wages . . . owing to such employee under section 206 . . . of this title by an employer liable therefor under the provisions of this subsection.

(c). The Secretary of Labor is authorized to supervise the payment of the unpaid minimum wages . . . owing to any employee or employees under section 206 . . . of this title, and the agreement of any employee to accept such payment shall upon payment in full constitute a waiver by such employee of any right he may have under subsection (b) of this section to such unpaid minimum wages . . . and an additional equal amount as liquidated damages. When a written request is filed by any employee with the Secretary of Labor claiming unpaid minimum wages . . . under section 206 . . . of this title, the Secretary of Labor may bring an action in any court of competent jurisdiction to recover the amount of such claim: *Provided,* That this authority to sue shall not be used by the Secretary of Labor in any case involving an issue of law which has not been settled finally by the courts, and in any such case no court shall have jurisdiction over such action or proceeding initiated or brought by the Secretary of Labor if it does involve any issue of law not so finally settled. The consent of any employee to the bringing of any such action by the Secretary of Labor, unless such action is dismissed without prejudice on motion of the Secretary of Labor, shall constitute a waiver by such employee of any right of action he may have under subsection (b) of this section for such unpaid minimum wages . . . and an additional equal amount as liquidated damages. Any sums thus recovered by the Secretary of Labor on behalf of an employee pursuant to this subsection shall be held in a special deposit account and shall be paid, on order of the Secretary of Labor, directly to the employee or employees affected. Any such sums not paid to an employee because of inability to do so within a period of three years shall be covered into the Treasury of the United States as miscellaneous receipts. In determining when an action is commenced by the Secretary of Labor under this subsection for the purposes of the statutes of limitations provided in section 255(a) of this title, it shall be considered to be commenced in the case of any individual claimant on the date when the complaint is filed if he is specifically named as a party plaintiff in the complaint, or if his name did not so appear, on the subsequent date on which his name is added as a party plaintiff in such action.

§217. The district courts, together with the United States District Court for the District of the Canal Zone, the District Court of the Virgin Islands, and the District Court of Guam shall have jurisdiction, for cause shown, to restrain violations of section 215

"(a) if the cause of action accrues on or after May 14, 1947 — may be commenced within two years after the cause of action accrued, and every such action shall be forever barred unless commenced within two years after the cause of action accrued, except that a cause of action arising out of a willful violation may be commenced within three years after the cause of action accrued. . . ." 29 U.S.C. §255.

of this title, including in the case of violations of section 215(a)(2) [which makes it illegal for any person to violate section 6] of this title the restraint of any withholding of payment of minimum wages . . . found by the court to be due to employees under this chapter (except sums which employees are barred from recovering, at the time of the commencement of the action to restrain the violations, by virtue of the provisions of section 255 of this title.

2. Equal Pay Act Pitfalls

The pleasant news of potential large recoveries in Equal Pay Act litigation is offset by a number of pitfalls provided in various sections of the Fair Labor Standards Act and the Portal-to-Portal Act. These are summarized briefly, with case annotations, in the material which follows. Subsection a describes defenses available in all Equal Pay Act civil suits; subsection b describes those unique to §16(b) suits; and subsection c, those unique to §16(c) suits.

a. All Lawsuits, Whether Brought Under §16(b), §16(c), or §17 of the FLSA

(1) *The Statute of Limitations Problem as a Potential Bar to Recovery and a Limitation on Back Wages.* Under the Portal-to-Portal Act statute of limitations, 29 U.S.C. §255, *supra*, Equal Pay Act suits must be commenced within two years of the violation, or within three years of a willful violation. As long as an employer continues to violate the Equal Pay Act, a lawsuit will be timely filed;[41] once he has stopped the illegal wage discrimination, however, the statute of limitations will start to run, and the suit will be barred after two years (or three where there is a willful violation). Discontinuing the wage discrimination will also shorten the time period for computing back wages, and thus the amount of back wages. For example, if the ABC Company stops discriminating on March 15, 1974 and suit is filed on June 15, 1975, the action is timely filed but recovery will be limited to the period from June 15, 1973 to March 15, 1974.

Notice also that the statute of limitations bars recovery for more than two years (or three, as the case may be) prior to filing the lawsuit, no matter how many years the discrimination has continued. Thus, if the ABC Company began paying unequal wages on Jan. 1, 1948 and continues to do so up to the date of filing an equal pay suit on Aug. 1, 1970, recovery will be limited to the period from Aug. 1, 1968 to the date of the court order, even though women employees have lost money for more than twenty other years.

(2) *Willfulness and the Three-Year Statute of Limitations.* Since a willful violation allows employees to recover for three years' back pay, rather than two years', the standard of willfulness becomes important. In Krumbeck v. John Oster Mfg. Co., 313 F. Supp. 257 (E.D. Wis. 1970), one Equal Pay Act court awarded back wages for the maximum three-year period. The finding of willfulness rested on a letter from the defendant company's attorney. The company maintained segregated male and female jobs, re-named, after passage of the Equal Pay Act, Inspector-Parts I (male) and Inspecter-Parts II (female). The court found:[42]

---

41. See Hodgson v. Behrens Drug Co., 70 CCH Lab. Cas. ¶32,844 at 45,809, 20 Wage & Hour Cas. 1152 (5th Cir. 1973), for a clear discussion of the continuing violation concept.

42. 313 F. Supp. at 264.

On June 15, 1964, the defendants' attorney wrote a letter to Mr. O'Donnel, the manager of industrial relations at Oster. (Def. Ex. 3.). This letter demonstrates that the defendant was generally mindful of its burdens under the new enactment. The second paragraph on page 3 states:

"With respect to the punch press operator job, it would seem that the problem of potential applicability of the equal pay standard could be avoided by up-grading the male employees performing the job on the basis of the additional physical effort and other additional factors involved in the male version of the job. . . ."

The defendants acted on this advice and did, on or before September 19, 1966 "upgrade" the male inspector's job to labor grade 9 by adding more factor points to the category of responsibility for safety of others. (Pl. Ex. 9.) However, the duties and responsibilities had not changed in any way to prompt such upgrading. (Tr. pp. 33, 145.) I conclude that the upgrading was done for the purpose of eluding the requirements of the Equal Pay Act.

While *Krumbeck* involved bad faith evasion of the act with definite knowledge of its applicability, a Fifth Circuit opinion indicates that much less is necessary to prove willfulness. Coleman v. Jiffy June Farms, Inc., 458 F.2d 1139 (5th Cir. 1972), *cert. denied sub nom.* Jiffy June Farms, Inc. v. Coleman, 409 U.S. 948 (1972), is the first federal appellate decision construing the willfulness standard after 1966 amendments added the three-year statute of limitations for a willful violation to the portal-to-portal limitations section. The decision involves the overtime provisions of the FLSA; it found a willful violation of the FLSA where an employer who had previously been paying overtime rates accepted a new and favorable wage settlement that provided for discontinuing overtime pay. Before agreeing to the settlement, the employer consulted his attorney, who assured him the settlement did not violate the FLSA. Despite the fact that he acted on legal advice, the court found a willful violation, stating that the test is whether:[43]

> there is substantial evidence in the record to support a finding that the employer knew or suspected that his actions *might* violate the FLSA. Stated more simply, we think the test should be: Did the employer know the FLSA was in the picture?

(3) Employer's Administrative Reliance Defense Against Back Wage Liability. Under §10 of the Portal-to-Portal Act, 29 U.S.C. §259,[44] any employer can totally avoid back pay liability if he pleads and proves that he acted "in good faith in conformity with and in reliance on" either (a) the written administrative regulations of the secretary of labor, or (b) his administrative practices or enforcement policies.

In Hodgson v. Square D Company, 459 F.2d 805 (6th Cir. 1972), the Sixth Circuit disallowed the administrative reliance defense in a narrow reading of §10. Square D asserted that an ambiguous letter of a regional director in the Labor Department hierarchy allowed it to use the wage policies in question; instead of examining the letter's ambiguity, the court found that a company could only rely on action taken by the administrator of the Wage and Hour Division of the Department of Labor, and not on a mere regional director.

43. 458 F.2d at 1142 (emphasis supplied).

44. "(a) In any action or proceeding based on any act or omission on or after May 14, 1947, no employer shall be subject to any liability or punishment for or on account of the failure of the employer to pay minimum wages . . . under the Fair Labor Standards Act of 1938, as amended . . . if he pleads and proves that the act or omission complained of was in good faith in conformity with and in reliance on any written administrative regulation, order, ruling, approval, or interpretation, of the agency of the United States specified in subsection (b) of this section, or any administrative practice or enforcement policy of such agency with respect to the class of employers to which he belonged. Such a defense, if established, shall be a bar to the action or proceeding, notwithstanding that after such act or omission, such administrative regulation, order, ruling, approval, interpretation, practice, or enforcement policy is modified or rescinded or is determined by judicial authority to be invalid or of no legal effect.

"(b) The agency referred to in subsection (a) of this section shall be —

"(1) in the case of the Fair Labor Standards Act of 1938, as amended — the Administrator of the Wage and Hour Division of the Department of Labor. . . ." 29 U.S.C. §259.

Another approach for plaintiff's attorneys faced with this defense would be to question closely and separately the pleading and proof for all three elements of the defense: (1) the employer acted in good faith; (2) his actions conformed to the administrative regulations; and (3) he relied on the regulation. Courts may be prone to accept the employer's bald assertion that he met all three requirements, but a good plaintiff's attorney should be able to counteract this by demanding proof.

b. §16(b) Employee Suits

(1) The Necessity for Written Consent To Be a Plaintiff. Section 16(b) suits can be brought as class actions, but any employee who wishes to be a party plaintiff must file a written consent with the court. 29 U.S.C. §216(b). This written consent is important because §7 of the Portal-to-Portal Act[45] effectively prohibits collecting back wages for any individual class member who has not filed the written consent. Thus, counsel in a large class action will have the burden of securing written consent from all members of the class in order to collect back wages for each member.

(2) Computation of Back Wages and the Statute of Limitations in Class Actions. The two- or three-year time period under the Portal-to-Portal Act must be computed individually for each class member, both for the amount of back wages and for the statute of limitations. Thus, if an individual woman is afraid to file written consent when the Equal Pay Act suit is commenced, but files when she sees that she could win some money, she is not deemed to start the action until the day of filing the consent. If the two years (or three, as the case may be) has already run by that time, the statute of limitations will bar her from recovering any money. Even if the statute has not run, waiting to file will reduce the money she can recover because the computation period will not start until two years prior to the filing of her written consent. For example, if a class action is filed on Jan. 1, 1974 and the judge finds an Equal Pay Act violation on Feb. 15, 1975, all women who had filed written consent by Jan. 1, 1974 will recover back wages for Jan. 1, 1972 to Feb. 15, 1975. However, if some women wait until Jan. 15, 1975 to file their consent, their recovery will be limited to the period of Jan. 15, 1973 to Feb. 15, 1975, or one year and 15 days less of back wages.

(3) Termination of the Employee's Right To Bring a §16(b) Suit. As soon as the secretary of labor brings a §17 lawsuit, all employees lose the right to file or join a §16(b) action, and thus to control the course of the proceedings. 29 U.S.C. §216(b).

(4) Discretionary Reduction of Liquidated Damages Based on the Employer's Good Faith Defense. The award of liquidated damages is not automatic. Under §11 of the Portal-to-Portal Act,[46] the court can refuse to award or can decrease the amount of liquidated damages if the employer proves to the court's satisfaction that he acted in good faith

45. "In determining when an action is commenced for the purposes of section 255 of this title, an action commenced on or after May 14, 1947 under the Fair Labor Standards Act of 1938, as amended . . . shall be considered to be commenced on the date when the complaint is filed; except that in the case of a collective or class action instituted under the Fair Labor Standards Act of 1938, as amended . . . it shall be considered to be commenced in the case of any individual claimant —
"(a) on the date when the complaint is filed, if he is specifically named as a party plaintiff in the complaint and his written consent to become a party plaintiff is filed on such date in the court in which the action is brought; or
"(b) if such written consent was not so filed or if his name did not so appear — on the subsequent date on which such written consent is filed in the court in which the action was commenced." 29 U.S.C. §256.
46. "In any action commenced prior to or on or after May 14, 1947 to recover unpaid minimum wages . . . or liquidated damages, under the Fair Labor Standards Act of 1938, as amended, if the employer shows to the satisfaction of the court that the act or omission giving rise to such action was in good faith and that he had reasonable grounds for believing that his act or omission was not a violation of the Fair Labor Standards Act of 1938, as amended, the court may, in its sound discretion, award no liquidated damages or award any amount thereof not to exceed the amount specified in section 216(b) of this title." 29 U.S.C. §260.

and had reasonable grounds to believe his actions did not violate the Equal Pay Act.

Krumbeck v. John Oster Mfg. Co., supra, illustrates a rejection of this Portal-to-Portal Act good faith defense.[47]

> Although the defendant claims that subsequent to June, 1966 sex has not been a factor in assigning jobs (Tr. p. 131), it is still difficult for a woman to get certain jobs which should be open to her. There is no posting system in the Oster plant, so women may not always know when an opening occurs. (Tr. p. 130.)
>
> The evidence shows that Eunice Casey was capable of performing tests on sheet steel, yet she was never given the opportunity; that work was reserved for males. (Tr. p. 220.) It is shown by the defendant's evidence (Def. Ex. 7), that the earliest any woman went to work in a previously all male job was September 13, 1966, more than two years after the applicability of the act. A two year delay in installing a female in previously all male jobs indicates that the defendant was exercising somewhat less than good faith. . . .
>
> I find that the defendant, John Oster Manufacturing Company, did not act in good faith and did not have reasonable grounds for believing that its dealings with Eunice Casey were consistent with the equal pay statute, and thus the defendant does not fall within the provisions of 29 U.S.C. §260.

Thus, the court awarded full liquidated damages (and for three years because of the prior finding of willfulness), rather than reduce or eliminate liquidated damages as a successful good faith defense allows. See also Hodgson v. Miller Brewing Co., 457 F.2d 221, 227-228 (7th Cir. 1972) (reliance on Labor Department investigator's statement and on state court decision did not create good faith bar to award of liquidated damages), *affirming sub nom.* Murphy v. Miller Brewing Co., 307 F. Supp. 829, 839 (E.D. Wis. 1969); and McClanahan v. Mathews, 440 F.2d 320, 322-323 (6th Cir. 1971) (an FLSA action for minimum wage and overtime pay violations). *McClanahan* also holds that if a §16(b) court denies liquidated damages pursuant to §11 of the Portal-to-Portal Act, it must then award interest on the back wages. However, the court may not award both liquidated damages *and* interest. *McClanahan,* supra; Hodgson v. Miller Brewing Co., 457 F.2d 221, 229 (7th Cir. 1971).

(Although the Portal-to-Portal Act contains no provision for a discretionary reduction or disallowance of a §17 interest award because of the employer's good faith, employers have advanced the argument. However, the courts have firmly rejected it. Hodgson v. Daisy Manufacturing Co., 445 F.2d 823 (8th Cir. 1971); Brennan v. City Stores, Inc., 71 CCH Lab. Cas. ¶32,910, 21 Wage & Hour Cas. 69 (5th Cir. 1973). Similarly, the courts have rejected employer contentions that their good faith barred a §17 award of back wages. Hodgson v. American Bank of Commerce, 447 F.2d 416, 422-423 (5th Cir. 1971); Shultz v. Mistletoe Express Service, Inc., 434 F.2d 1267, 1272-1273 (10th Cir. 1971) (an FLSA action for minimum wage and overtime pay violation).)

c. §16(c) Labor Department Suits, Brought upon Written Request of Employees

(1) Employee Waiver of Rights by Settlement of Suit. Section 16(c) authorizes the secretary of labor either to supervise the payment of unpaid back wages or to bring suit to collect them. If an employee accepts payment under a §16(c) supervised settlement, she waives her right to sue under §16(b) for a larger amount than the settlement or to sue for the equal amount as liquidated damages. 29 U.S.C. §216(c). Likewise, if an employee consents to the secretary's §16(c) lawsuit, she waives the same right to sue under §16(b). 29 U.S.C. §216(c).

---

47. 313 F. Supp. at 264.

(2) The Novel Question Proviso. The secretary is not allowed to sue under §16(c) in a "case involving an issue of law which has not been settled finally by the courts." After the Wheaton Glass Company suffered its first bad loss in its landmark litigation, the company tried to avoid back pay by asserting that this proviso also applied to the Labor Department's §17 lawsuit, and thus prohibited the *Wheaton Glass Co.* suit. The court flatly rejected this contention in Hodgson v. Wheaton Glass Co., 446 F.2d 527 (3rd Cir. 1971). See also Hodgson v. American Can Co., 440 F.2d 916 (8th Cir. 1971); Hodgson v. City Stores, Inc., 332 F. Supp. 942, 950-951 (M.D. Ala. 1971). (Anyone interested in the complicated legislative history of §§16(b), 16(c), and 17 of the FLSA should read the thorough *Wheaton Glass Co.* decision.)

3. §17 Injunctions

The granting or denial of injunctions against future violations of the Equal Pay Act in §17 lawsuits is a matter ordinarily left to the discretion of the trial court. See, e.g., Hodgson v. American Can Co., supra. An important issue arising within this context is whether the trial court may enjoin discrimination at all of a defendant's plants, where discrimination has been proved at only one or a few of these plants. The Fifth Circuit has upheld one very broad injunction, "that the defendant be . . . enjoined from engaging in any and all violations of"[48] the Equal Pay Act. Brennan v. City Stores, Inc., 71 CCH Lab. Cas. ¶32,910, 21 Wage & Hour Cas. 69 (5th Cir. 1973). And as this book went to press, the court had also decided to uphold an injunction "in any of" the J. M. Fields stores, where discrimination was proved as to 3 stores out of a chainstore enterprise of 66 discount department stores. Brennan v. J. M. Fields, Inc., 488 F.2d 443 (5th Cir. 1973). However, in the *Corning Glass Works* case, supra, Section B-3, the Second Circuit reversed the district court's company-wide injunction:[49]

> Not content with requiring the payment of back wages which, with interest, will exceed $600,000, the district court issued a sweeping injunction, broadly incorporating the words of the Act and applicable to all Corning plants (save that in Wellsboro, Pennsylvania), which we quote in the margin.[12]
>
> We see no justification for this. Corning had been found to have violated the Equal Pay Act only with respect to one class of employee at its three plants in Corning, New York. As indicated, the violations were largely a result of the New York law which until 1953 had prohibited the employment of women at night. The Secretary's case was by no means impregnable, and Corning had been endeavoring since 1966 — sincerely, if ineffectively — to bring itself into compliance. There was no evidence of widespread violations of the Act, either at the Corning plants or its 26 branch plants nationwide. The evidence rather was that the only other cases where a similar violation might exist were the inspection jobs in the plant at Wellsboro, Pennsylvania, which was excepted from the injunction because of a pending suit by the Secretary,

---

48. Hodgson v. City Stores, Inc., 332 F. Supp. 942, 951 (M.D. Ala. 1971).

49. 474 F.2d at 236-237, *aff'd on other grounds*, 94 S. Ct. 2223 (1974).

12. (1) The defendant shall not, contrary to section 6(d)(1) of the Act, discriminate on the basis of sex between employees employed within an establishment by paying wages to employees in such establishment at a rate less than the rate at which it pays wages to employees of the opposite sex in such establishment for equal work on jobs the performance of which requires equal skill, effort, and responsibility and which are performed under similar working conditions:

(2) The defendant shall not, contrary to section 6(d)(1) of the Act, reduce the wage rate of any employee in order to comply with the provisions of section 6(d)(1) of the Act:

(3) The defendant shall not, contrary to section 15(a)(1) of the Act, transport, offer for transportation, ship, deliver, or sell with knowledge that shipment or delivery or sale thereof in commerce is intended, any goods in the production of which any of its employees has hereafter been employed in violation of section 6(d)(1) of the Act:

(4) Defendants shall cease to withhold any amounts owing to any employee which have been withheld in violation of section 6(d)(1) of the Act.

and in a plant at Central Falls, Rhode Island, as to which the Secretary had also already instituted suit. Yet so broad an injunction put Corning under threat of contempt for any alleged violation of the Equal Pay Act in respect of any category of employee in all but one of Corning's many plants.

We agree with the point made by the Eighth Circuit, in another Equal Pay Act case, Hodgson v. American Can Co., 440 F.2d 916, 921 (1972), that absent a showing of a policy of discrimination which extends beyond the plants at issue here, there is no basis for a nationwide injunction. Moreover, the Supreme Court has held that "the mere fact that a court has found that a defendant has committed an act in violation of a statute does not justify an injunction broadly to obey the statute and thus subject the defendant to contempt proceedings if he should at any time in the future commit some new violation unlike and unrelated to that with which he was originally charged."

NLRB v. Express Publishing Co., 312 U.S. 426, 435-436, 61 S. Ct. 693, 699, 85 L. Ed. 930 (1941). Since there is no showing here of the "proclivity for unlawful conduct" or "record of continuing and persistent violations of the Act" found to justify such an injunction in McComb v. Jacksonville Paper Co., 336 U.S. 187, 192, 69 S. Ct. 497, 500, 93 L. Ed. 599 (1949), the injunction must be narrowed accordingly. While Hodgson v. First Fed. Savings & Loan Ass'n, 455 F.2d 818, 825-827 (5 Cir. 1972), relied on by the Secretary, may have been correctly decided on its own facts, we cannot subscribe, in the light of *Express Publishing* and our own views, to all that was there said.

The Corning Glass Works litigation is especially interesting because it proceeded on several fronts at once. The secretary of labor sued Corning in three separate suits, one involving its New York plants, one a Pennsylvania plant, and one a Rhode Island plant. In the first decision, Shultz v. Corning Glass Works, 319 F. Supp. 1161 (W.D.N.Y. 1970), the district court found equal pay violations but refused to enjoin further violations because it believed Corning had equalized all wages in the January 1969 collective bargaining agreement. A year later it found that in fact Corning had not equalized all wages, and issued the injunction, Hodgson v. Corning Glass Works, 330 F. Supp. 46 (W.D.N.Y. 1971). Both decisions were appealed to the Second Circuit, resulting in the decision above. Meanwhile, another federal court in Pennsylvania found, under facts almost identical with those in New York, that men working the night shift were subject to dissimilar working conditions, and therefore denied relief, Hodgson v. Corning Glass Workers, 341 F. Supp. 18 (M.D. Pa. 1972); the Third Circuit affirmed the decision, Brennan v. Corning Glass Workers, 480 F.2d 1254 (3rd Cir. 1973). The Rhode Island case, Hodgson v. Corning Glass Workers, C.A. 4036 (D.R.I. 1969), filed in November 1968, is still pending in district court, under an order staying proceedings until the Second Circuit decision.[50] The time, effort, and money which the Labor Department must have expended in all this litigation in order to achieve compliance by one company illustrates graphically the necessity for the national injunction denied by the Second Circuit. It may also suggest that the company has benefited enormously from paying unequal wages (the New York award alone — still unpaid — was for over $600,000), since maintaining litigation on all these fronts is obviously very expensive for the company, although not expensive enough to justify capitulating on the equal pay issue. On the other hand, the conflicting Second and Third Circuit opinions on the issue of whether night shift work creates dissimilar working conditions show the difficulty of enjoining a company in general terms from violating the Equal Pay Act.

---

50. Now that the Second Circuit has decided, in Hodgson v. Corning Glass Works, 474 F.2d 226 (1973), supra, the parties will probably stipulate to a stay of proceedings yet again, pending a Supreme Court decision resolving the similar working conditions issue.

4. The Importance of Combining Equal Pay Act and Title VII Lawsuits

As we have emphasized throughout this section, the Equal Pay Act has one severe drawback — it prohibits only wage discrimination, and even then a very narrowly defined wage discrimination. Moreover, unthinking equal pay courts have often ignored blatant violations of Title VII, and have even established legal standards which might encourage companies to violate Title VII by sex segregating workers. And as Part I of this chapter indicated, sex segregation is one of the primary sources of woman's low economic position in the labor market.

Yet for all that, there are reasons for using equal pay lawsuits — but in combination with Title VII claims. Since Title VII has no provision for liquidated damages or for a three-year willful violation statute of limitation, adding an equal pay claim to a Title VII suit can increase the amount of back wages recovered for wage discrimination, while allowing plaintiffs to reach all other forms of discrimination under Title VII. Conversely, since the Equal Pay Act has no provision for a §16(b) injunction, adding a Title VII claim (wage discrimination also violates Title VII) to the equal pay claim may enable plaintiffs to win an injunction against future wage discrimination. Similarly, it may be possible to avoid the Equal Pay Act necessity for written consent of all class action members, since Title VII does not require this. Another benefit from using the Equal Pay Act is that it provides for criminal penalties for a second violation, 29 U.S.C. §216(a), which may prove an effective deterrent if women make companies aware of it. Finally, even if plaintiffs should lose an Equal Pay Act claim because the jobs being compared are sufficiently different, Title VII offers the chance to recover back wages for the exclusion of low-paid women workers from the higher-paying job category.

In some situations, it may be valuable to bring lawsuits based solely on the Equal Pay Act. If women workers are interested only in wage discrimination, for instance, they can get to court — in either a §16(b) or §17 action — much faster by avoiding the procedural requirements of Title VII and the delays in EEOC action caused by the commission's large backlog of cases. This may be especially true for blue-collar workers, where the clearly defined job requirements, with little variation from worker to worker, and favorable equal pay precedents should make it easy to prove a case. (It is more difficult to prove professional white-collar discrimination, where subjective evaluation of a worker's abilities and individual variation in job content enter the picture much more than in the blue-collar market.) Even here, though, the class member written consent requirement of the Equal Pay Act and its lack of injunctive relief may outweigh the time disadvantages of a Title VII claim.

5. Miscellaneous Problems

a. Research Aids

Both the Bureau of National Affairs and Commerce Clearing House publish reporters collecting FLSA and Equal Pay Act decisions, statutes, and regulations. The BNA looseleaf binder volumes are part of its Labor Relations Reporter series, and are titled Wages And Hours (decisions) and Wage And Hour Manual (statutes and regulations); the bound volumes are titled Wage And Hour Cases (decisions). The CCH looseleaf binder volumes are part of its Labor Law Reporter series, and are titled Wages-Hours 1 (statutes and regulations) and Wages-Hours 2 (decisions); however, the bound volumes are titled Labor Cases (decisions). (CCH also publishes the Equal Pay Act statute, regulations, and decisions in its Employment Practices Guide series; however, it is better to use the Labor Law Reporter series because it includes FLSA materials, while EPG does not.)

Since the Equal Pay Act amends the FLSA, lawyers should be sure to check FLSA precedents in all procedural matters. In conducting trials, Labor Department lawyers in both the national and regional offices may be helpful in suggesting expert witnesses, the kinds of evidence to seek in discovery, and like matters.

The Equal Pay Act has not been the source of much law review commentary, but some articles are listed here:

1. Berger, Equal Pay, Equal Employment Opportunity and Equal Enforcement of the Law for Women, 5 Valparaiso U. L. Rev. 326 (1971);

2. Director, Construction and Application of Provisions of Equal Pay Act of 1963 (29 USC §206(d)) Prohibiting Wage Discrimination on Basis of Sex, 7 ALR Fed. 707 (1971);

3. Moran, Reducing Discrimination: Role of the Equal Pay Act, 93 Monthly Labor Rev. 30 (1970);

4. Murphy, Female Wage Discrimination: A Study of the Equal Pay Act 1963-1970, 39 U. Cin. L. Rev. 615 (1970);

5. Vladeck, The Equal Pay Act of 1963, 18 N.Y.U. Labor Conf. 381 (1965).

b. Attorney's Fees

The leading Equal Pay Act decision on attorneys' fees is Hodgson v. Miller Brewing Co., 457 F.2d 221 (7th Cir. 1972). *Miller* approved a $20,000 award of attorneys' fees to three women plaintiffs as within the trial court's discretion, despite the company's argument that the fees almost equaled the plaintiffs' total damages of $24,371.20. However, the court declined to remand for a further award of attorneys' fees for the appellate work. Lawyers in other circuits should check both FLSA and Title VII precedents on attorneys' fees.

c. Covered Employees

Many employees are not protected by the Equal Pay Act under a long list of exemptions to the FLSA; the full list is set forth at 29 U.S.C.§§213(a), 213(d), and 213(f). See also 29 U.S.C. §203. Executive, administrative, and professional workers, along with outside salesmen, were originally exempted also, but were brought under equal pay coverage by 1972 amendments to the act, Pub. L. 92-318, Title IX, §906(b)(1), 86 Stat. 375. With that addition of about 13 million workers, equal pay coverage rose to roughly 60 million workers out of a total work force of 84 million people.

State employees were brought under FLSA coverage in 1966, but in 1973 the Supreme Court held that a state employees' §16(b) overtime pay suit was barred by the Eleventh Amendment. Employees of the Department of Public Health and Welfare v. Department of Public Health and Welfare, 411 U.S. 279, 93 S. Ct. 1614, 36 L. Ed. 2d 251 (1973). The Court reasoned that it was not clear that the 1966 Congress had intended to deprive states of their constitutional immunity to suit in a federal forum because Congress had amended only the FLSA definitions of "employer" and "enterprise," and had not amended §16(b), the section authorizing employee lawsuits.

The decision may conceivably affect Title VII lawsuits brought by state employees, since state employees were first brought under Title VII coverage in 1972, Pub. L. 92-261, §§2(1), 2(2), 2(3), 4(a) (Mar. 24, 1972), 86 Stat. 104. However, unlike the 1966 FLSA amendments, the 1972 Title VII amendments expressly authorized state employees to sue, and it thus seems more likely that the *Employees* decision will not affect their Title VII rights.

d. State Laws

Many states have passed equal pay laws. For complete compilations, see the looseleaf binders in the BNA Labor Relations Reporter series entitled State Laws or the looseleaf binders in the CCH Labor Law Reporter series entitled State Laws (1, 2, and 3) or the looseleaf binder in the CCH Employment Practices Guide series entitled Employment Practices Guide 3. Some of these laws may be worth using in some situations; for instance, if an employee is exempted from federal equal pay coverage, she may nevertheless be covered by the applicable state law. Or state laws might provide longer statutes of limitations, thus increasing potential back pay recovery and allowing for later filing of suit. On the other hand, state agencies and courts tend to be more conservative in interpreting and applying employment discrimination laws, and this risk should be weighed before turning to a state law.

IV. EXECUTIVE ORDER 11246

The litany of federal legal weapons against employment discrimination always includes Executive Order 11246, which prohibits discrimination by employers who hold contracts with the federal government. The order originally reached race, color, religion, and national origin, but not sex, which was added to the order in October 1968 by Executive Order 11375. While the executive order appears on paper to provide substantial leverage against companies which discriminate, it has been largely ineffective, especially in eradicating sex discrimination. Nevertheless, the order provides a worthwhile study in the effect of political and administrative decision making on potentially powerful antidiscrimination commands.

Issued by the President, the orders are not statutes, and are without explicit congressional authority; yet they clearly bind the executive branch, and courts have declared that they have the force and effect of law.[1] Executive Order 11246 directs federal government agencies which contract with private companies or state and local governments to include nondiscrimination clauses in their contracts, and to monitor the employment policies of the contractors.

The first executive order concerning fair employment practices was issued by President Roosevelt in 1941.[2] Over the next thirty years other executive orders followed from Presidents Roosevelt, Truman, Eisenhower, Kennedy, and Johnson.[3] There were no enforcement powers, however, until 1961, and though succeeding orders have all provided for enforcement, there has been little action. The penalty provisions were never used under the Kennedy order, and in 1972 the Office of Federal Contract Compliance reported that, under the Johnson and Nixon administrations combined, sanctions were applied against only four companies[4] (none of them on the grounds of sex discrimination). As the Civil Rights Commission noted in 1970:[5]

> Despite the increasingly strong Presidential commitment to the goal of equal employment opportunity, despite the strength of the sanctions available to secure it, and despite the potential effectiveness of the Federal monitoring mechanisms, equal opportunity in Government contract employment, when measured in terms of actual employment of minorities, has not been achieved. Presidential commitment has not

1. The authority for the executive order is discussed at length in Contractor's Association of Eastern Pennsylvania v. Secretary of Labor, 442 F.2d 159, 162-166 (3d Cir. 1971), *cert. denied,* 404 U.S. 854 (1971).

2. Executive Order 8802, issued June 25, 1941, 6 Fed. Reg. 3109.

3. For a more complete account of the history of the current executive order and its predecessors, see U.S. Equal Employment Opportunity Commission, Legislative History of Titles VII and XI of the Civil Rights Act of 1964, 1-2 (1971).

4. Letter from Frederick L. Webber, Special Assistant for Legislative Affairs of the U.S. Department of Labor to Senator Edward Kennedy, July 1972, p. 3.

5. U.S. Commission on Civil Rights, Federal Civil Rights Enforcement Effort 134 (1970). The effectiveness of the contract compliance effort with regard to women was not included in the report because sex discrimination was not added to the commission's jurisdiction until 1972. The situation for women is, however, undoubtedly similar to that for minorities.

been realistically communicated to the community of Government contractors; sanctions rarely have been used; and the Federal monitoring mechanisms have not proved effective.

A. STRUCTURE AND ENFORCEMENT OF THE EXECUTIVE ORDER

1. Coverage

The executive order applies to any company or institution that contracts with the federal government and to subcontractors with the prime contractors. All branches of each company and institution are covered, even though only one branch may actually have made the contract.

The executive order is divided into two broad categories: nonconstruction (or procurements) contractors and federally assisted construction contracts. The first category covers only companies that contract with the government. The second category covers both companies that contract with the government and institutions that are applying for federal money for construction projects; in order to get such money, these institutions must establish certain agreements with their construction contractors.[6]

The category of procurements (or nonconstruction contracts) is huge, covering all kinds of supplies and services (e.g., utilities, transportation, research, insurance). One third of the nation's labor force is employed by companies which meet the executive order definition of government contractors.[7]

2. Requirements

All companies must agree to certain clauses, known as the equal employment opportunity (EEO) clauses, in their contracts with the government. Similarly, an applicant for federal construction money must agree to incorporate the same EEO clauses in its contracts with its construction contractors. Seven separate paragraphs set forth these contract terms; the most important reads as follows:[8]

> *The contractor will not discriminate against any employee or applicant for employment* because of race, color, religion, sex, or national origin. *The contractor will take affirmative action* to ensure that applicants are employed, and that employees are treated during employment, without regard to their race, color, religion, sex or national origin. Such action shall include, but not be limited to the following: employment, upgrading, demotion, or transfer; recruitment or recruitment advertising; layoff or termination; rates of pay or other forms of compensation; and selection for training, including apprenticeship. . . . [Emphasis added.]

In the other mandatory provisions, the contractor agrees to consider all job applicants without discrimination, to send labor unions notices of its equal opportunity obligations, to follow all the provisions of the executive order and of the secretary of labor's implementing regulations, to furnish reports and information to the secretary of labor, to accept certain penalties if it fails to meet these contract terms or to follow the Labor Department regulations, and to require any subcontractor to sign a contract which includes the antidiscrimination terms to which the contractor has agreed.

6. For the categories, see Part II of the executive order, Nondiscrimination in Employment by Government Contractors and Subcontractors, and Part III, Nondiscrimination Provisions in Federally Assisted Construction Contracts. Most of this account will be concerned with the obligations of contractors and subcontractors in procurement rather than construction contracts. In most cases, the obligations of applicants for federal construction funds and their contractors and subcontractors are the same.

7. U.S. Commission on Civil Rights, Federal Civil Rights Enforcement Effort 133 (1970).

8. 41 C.F.R. §60-1.4(1).

3. Enforcement Agencies

The order provides for enforcement by the secretary of labor, who in turn has created the Office of Federal Contract Compliance (OFCC) for this purpose. OFCC oversees fifteen compliance agencies, which carry out the direct enforcement effort; OFCC itself is not a large office.[9]

Each compliance agency is assigned several industries for which it is responsible. For instance, the Defense Department oversees ordnance, textiles, leathers, primary metals, machinery, motor vehicles, printing, and miscellaneous manufacturing industries. The Department of Health, Education, and Welfare oversees insurance, medical, legal and educational services, museums, and nonprofit organizations.[10] The compliance agency may or may not be the contracting agency, i.e., have contracts with the companies it monitors.

In general, OFCC is supposed to set overall policy directions, and the compliance agencies are to carry out the actual enforcement procedures. In fact, few of the compliance agencies have imposed sanctions, and OFCC has initiated most of the miniscule number of formal proceedings.[11] Monitoring has also been ineffective.[12]

4. Methods of Enforcement

Compliance reviews and complaint procedures[13] are the enforcement mechanisms. In theory, the appropriate compliance agency conducts periodic reviews of whether every contractor is discriminating or is taking "affirmative action." Any company negotiating a contract of $1,000,000 or more must pass a compliance review prior to the award. In actuality, compliance reviews are not conducted regularly; most contractors have never been reviewed, even for contracts of over a million dollars; there is evidence that many of the reviews that are conducted are ineffective.[14] The compliance agencies are so understaffed that it is impossible for them to do their jobs.

OFCC has also established a complaint procedure, under which any individual or group can charge a contractor with discrimination by writing to OFCC or to the compliance agency. Complaints must be filed within 180 days of the discrimination alleged, and may be made on a class or pattern, as well as an individual, basis.

Thus far, the courts have held that there is no private cause of action under the executive orders. The principal cases are Farmer v. Philadelphia Electric Company, 329 F.2d 3 (3d Cir. 1964), *aff'g* 215 F. Supp. 729 (D. Pa. 1963), a circuit court ruling that administrative remedies must be exhausted before any private action may be brought, and Farkas v. Texas Instrument Inc., 275 F.2d 629 (5th Cir. 1967), *cert. denied,* 389 U.S.

9. The Civil Rights Commission reported in 1971 that: "OFCC currently has a staff of 90, with 48 persons in the national office and 42 in field offices. Of the 58 professional OFCC staff members, 27 are in the national office, while 31 are assigned in the field. The authorization for Fiscal Year 1972 is 118, which represents an increase of 48 over the number authorized in Fiscal Year 1971." U.S. Commission on Civil Rights, The Federal Civil Rights Enforcement Effort: One Year Later 14 (1971).

10. For the complete list of all assigned industries, see OFCC Order No. 1, to Heads of All Agencies, Oct. 24, 1969. The list is reprinted in U.S. Commission on Civil Rights, Federal Civil Rights Enforcement Effort 195 n.278 (1970).

11. U.S. Commission on Civil Rights, Federal Civil Rights Enforcement Effort 215, 254 (1970).

12. According to the Civil Rights Commission: "To date, monitoring operations have progressed slowly because of manpower shortages. By April 1971, OFCC had reviewed some aspects of the operations of seven compliance agencies by conducting joint compliance reviews with them. Since April 1971, OFCC has conducted joint compliance reviews with only one other agency, the Department of the Treasury. Moreover, the value of these reviews has not been demonstrated since no record of improvements has been reported by OFCC. In any event, seven agencies remain to be reviewed." The Federal Civil Rights Enforcement Effort: One Year Later 16-17 (1971).

13. 41 C.F.R. Part 60-1, Subpart B, §§60-1.20 through 60-1.32.

14. U.S. Commission on Civil Rights, The Federal Civil Rights Enforcement Effort: One Year Later 17 (1971).

977 (1967), holding that the denial of administrative remedies is final and cannot be reviewed by the courts.[15]

However, in Hadnott v. Laird, 317 F. Supp. 379 (D.D.C. 1970), *aff'd,* 463 F.2d 304 (D.C. Cir. 1972), plaintiffs sought a different remedy under the executive order: a court order requiring federal officials to cancel federal contracts or debar discriminating employers from further contracts, rather than a court order requiring employers with federal contracts to cease discriminating (or requiring government officials to compel the employers to cease discriminating). The district court denied this relief on the grounds that the plaintiffs had not exhausted their administrative remedies under the executive order, that the doctrine of sovereign immunity barred the suit, and that action under Title VII of the Civil Rights Act of 1964 was also available to plaintiffs. The court of appeals did not reach the sovereign immunity question, and affirmed the lower court decision on the grounds of failure to exhaust administrative remedies. However, the court suggested that judicial review of administrative action (or inaction) might be available to plaintiffs in the future.[16]

> . . . [I]f plaintiffs go to the Office of Federal Contract Compliance and file a complaint . . . we are assured that one of several things will happen: (1) the Office of Federal Contract Compliance may actually reject the complaint on the ground that the matter has already been investigated, compliance assured, and the matter closed; (2) the OFCC may accept the complaint, reopen the investigation but deny plaintiffs any role in such investigation . . .; or (3) the OFCC may reopen the investigation, conduct an open hearing, in which plaintiffs are allowed to participate. In either eventuality, the plaintiffs will have definite administrative action to which to point when they then come into the United States District Court for review under the provisions of the Administrative Procedure Act.

The Administrative Procedure Act provides, in relevant part, that: "Every . . . final agency action for which there is no other adequate remedy in any court shall be subject to judicial review. . . ." 5 U.S.C. §1009.

While the court of appeals also referred to Title VII as an alternate remedy, the court recognized that it "is not an exclusive remedy, and that the action [under Title VII] is brought directly against the offending company rather than against government officials as plaintiffs have done here."[17]

The weapon of contract cancellation or debarment can be a powerful one. Litigants might well consider exhausting their administrative remedies under the executive order, and then proceeding to federal court under the Administrative Procedure Act, in hopes of obtaining these remedies against employment discrimination by government contractors.

5. Sanctions

The OFCC or the compliance agency has the authority to withhold funds on a contract until the contractor complies with its EEO obligations, to cancel a contract or

---

15. See also Gnotta v. United States, 415 F.2d 1271 (8th Cir. 1969) (opinion by Blackmun, J.), *cert. denied,* 397 U.S. 934 (1970); Freeman v. Schultz, 317 F. Supp. 376 (D.D.C. 1970), *aff'd,* 468 F.2d 120 (D.C. Cir. 1972); Braden v. University of Pittsburgh, 343 F. Supp. 836 (W.D. Pa. 1972), *vacated and remanded,* 477 F.2d 1 (3d Cir. 1973); CORE v. Commissioner, Social Security Admin., 270 F. Supp. 537 (D. Md. 1967); Davis v. Secretary, Dept. of Health, Education and Welfare, 262 F. Supp. 124 (D. Md. 1967); cf. Todd v. Joint Apprenticeship Committee, 223 F. Supp 12 (D. Ill. 1963), *vacated as moot,* 332 F.2d 243 (7th Cir. 1964). But see Thorn v. Richardson, 4 FEP Cases 299, 302, 4 EPD ¶7630, 7586 (W.D. Wash. 1971).

16. 463 F.2d at 308-309.

17. Id. at 311. The plaintiffs in *Hadnott* also argued for a direct federal right of action to compel contract cancellation or debarment on the basis of the Due Process Clause. The court of appeals took the position that such a holding would be "a bit unprecedented," id. at 310, unnecessary because of the remedies provided by the executive order, and premature. Ibid.

part of the contract, or to order the contractor debarred from future contracts with the government. A final penalty is to refer the company's case either to the Justice Department (for suit to enforce the EEO contract clause provisions, for Title VII suit, or for criminal prosecution), or to the EEOC (for Title VII suit).

In 1970, the Civil Rights Commission reported that debarment actions had been initiated by OFCC against seven companies, but that only three of the seven cases cited for hearing had actually gone to a formal hearing. Of these three, one had been taken to court, one had been settled by agreement with the company in question, and one had still not been decided by the hearing panel.[18]

In November 1971, the Commission reported that:[19]

> From July 1970 through September 1971, 640 "show cause" notices were issued to contractors. . . .
>
> While action against several other contractors has gone beyond the mere issuance of a "show cause" notice . . . , only one other sanction action has been initiated. . . . OFCC also has referred one case to the Department of Justice for litigation during the last six months.
>
> Since May 1971, there has been one bidder on a construction contract passed over and declared "nonresponsible" because his bid failed to include required goals and timetables for minority employment. OFCC estimates that as many as 15 percent of Federal contracts which are cleared . . . are delayed for some period of time until steps are taken by the contractors to come into compliance.

Given the magnitude of the problem, this is a sorry record.

6. Scope of the Obligations of Covered Employers

The obligations of covered employers are legally defined in a series of regulations issued by the OFCC and by the compliance agencies for particular industries. OFCC regulations for nonconstruction employers cover the obligations of government contractors and subcontractors (including compliance reviews and complaint procedures),[20] affirmative action programs,[21] testing,[22] and sex discrimination.[23] The most controversial regulations are those governing affirmative action plans, known as Revised Order No. 4. The Civil Rights Commission summarized the requirements of the original Order No. 4 as follows:[24]

> . . . Order No. 4 . . . states that any contractor required to develop affirmative action plans has not complied fully with the Executive Order until a program is developed and found acceptable by using standards and guidelines of Order No. 4. The new regulation sets forth three basic requirements and eight additional guidelines for acceptable affirmative actions plans.[274] The three basic obligations imposed on the

18. U.S. Commission on Civil Rights, Federal Civil Rights Enforcement Effort 215-216 (1970).
19. The Federal Civil Rights Enforcement Effort: One Year Later, supra, at 23.
20. 41 C.F.R. Part 60-1.
21. 41 C.F.R. Part 60-2, known as Revised Order No. 4.
22. 41 C.F.R. Part 60-3, which is the same as the EEOC guidelines on testing, 29 C.F.R. 1607.1 et seq.
23. 41 C.F.R. Part 60-20.
24. Federal Civil Rights Enforcement Effort, supra, at 190-192.
274. The eight additional guidelines are: I. Development or Reaffirmation of Company Policy of Non-Discrimination in all Personnel Actions. II. Formal Internal and External Dissemination of Company Policy. III. Establishment of Clear-cut Responsibilities — Line/Staff Relationship. IV. Identification of Problem Areas by Division, Department Location, and Job Classification. V. Establishment of Company Goals and Objectives by Division, Department, Location and Job Classification, Including Target Completion Dates. VI. Development and Execution of Action Oriented Programs Designed to Eliminate Problems and Further Designed to Attain Established Goals and Objectives. VII. Design and Implementation of Internal Audit and Reporting Systems to Measure Effectiveness of Total Program. VIII. Active Support of Local and National Community Action Programs. The Order also includes a procedure for the compliance agencies to follow when noncompliance is indicated.

contractors are: (1) to perform an analysis of minority utilization in all job categories, (2) establish goals and timetable to correct deficiencies, and (3) develop data collection systems and reporting plans documenting progress in achieving affirmative action goals.

The main difference between the original order, which was promulgated February 5, 1970, and the revised order, which was promulgated December 4, 1971, is the inclusion of women as well as minorities in the latter.[25]

B. The Controversy: Goals or Quotas?

An obvious target for criticism in the affirmative action regulations is the requirement that contractors establish numerical goals and timetables to correct deficiencies. The theory underlying the criticism is that numerical goals will lead to reverse discrimination. Two approaches have been taken to answer this charge: distinguishing goals from quotas, and pointing out the need for action to eradicate the effects of past discrimination. Consider the following analysis.

POTTINGER, THE DRIVE TOWARD EQUALITY
Change 24-29 (October 1972)

About two years ago, a previously unnoticed Executive Order prohibiting employment discrimination by Federal contractors (which includes most universities) was discovered by women's organizations and minority groups on a few East Coast campuses. Soon afterwards, the volume of formal complaints of sex and race employment discrimination in institutions of higher education rose sharply, and the Office for Civil Rights began constructing a systematic program of enforcement. During the early stages of this process, as the Office struggled to define law and policy and to obtain staff, the attention and support of women's and civil rights groups increased, while the higher education establishment remained unruffled.

When the Office made its presence on campuses felt, however — by deferring payment of some $23 million in Federal contracts to various universities pending compliance with the order — it began to raise the academic community's eyebrows. Today a significant and vocal segment of that community is actively challenging HEW's enforcement of Executive Order 11246 and the policies upon which it is based.

The reasons for this challenge are, as one might expect, more complex than the current dialogue on the subject would suggest. But every crusade must have its simplistic side — a galvanizing symbol, a bogeyman, a rallying cry. The word "quotas" serves these rhetorical purposes in the present case. Since quotas are not required or permitted by the Executive Order, they are for the most part a phony issue, but very much an issue nevertheless.

To understand the quotas issue one must first understand what the Executive Order is all about. In attempting to deal with employment inequities, Executive Order 11246 embodies two concepts: nondiscrimination and Affirmative Action.

Nondiscrimination means the elimination of all existing discriminatory treatment of present and potential employees. University officials are required under this concept

---

25. The long fight by feminist groups to get women included in Order No. 4 is described below by Bernice Sandler.

to ensure that their employment policies do not, if followed as stated, operate to the detriment of any persons on grounds of race, color, religion, sex or national origin. Typically, this means eliminating officially-sanctioned quotas restricting women and minorities, anti-nepotism policies that operate to deny equal opportunities to women, recruitment procedures that tend exclusively to reach white males and the like. In addition, the university must examine the practices of its decision-makers to ensure that nondiscriminatory policies are in fact implemented in a nondiscriminatory way. . . .

The concept of Affirmative Action requires more than mere neutrality on race and sex. It requires the university to determine whether it has failed to recruit, employ and promote women and minorities commensurate with their availability, even if this failure cannot be traced to specific acts of discrimination by university officials. Where women and minorities are not represented on a university's rolls, despite their availability (that is, where they are "under-utilized") the university has an obligation to initiate affirmative efforts to recruit and hire them. The premise of this obligation is that systemic forms of exclusion, inattention and discrimination cannot be remedied in any meaningful way, in any reasonable length of time, simply by ensuring a future benign neutrality with regard to race and sex. This would perpetuate indefinitely the grossest inequities of past discrimination. Thus there must be some form of positive action, along with a schedule for how such actions are to take place, and an honest appraisal of what the plan is likely to yield — an appraisal that the regulations call a "goal."

It is at this point that the issue of "quotas" rears its ugly head. What is a quota, and what is wrong with it? What is a goal, and what is right about it?

Historically, hiring quotas have been rigid numerical ceilings on the number of persons of a given racial, ethnic, religious, or sex group who could be employed by (or admitted to) an academic institution. If quotas were required or permitted by the Executive Order, they would operate as levels of employment that must be fulfilled if the university is to remain eligible for Federal contracts.

Some critics have assumed that the government is arguing that rigid numerical requirements would not constitute quotas under the Executive Order since, unlike traditional quotas, they would operate in *favor* of minorities and women rather than *against* them. But obviously, where the number of jobs is finite, as is true in all universities, a numerical requirement in *favor* of any group becomes by definition a restrictive ceiling or quota for all others. No one in the government is making an argument that *any* requirements in the form of quotas — for or against a defined class — are legitimate.

Once it is assumed that quotas are required, of course, there is no end to the horrors and hysteria that can be generated. University officials, it is said, will be obliged to hire regardless of merit or capability. Standards of excellence will crumble. Existing faculty will be fired and replaced wholesale. And if there are not enough qualified women engineers to fill the Engineering Department's quota, never mind; the positions will be filled with female home economics teachers (a favorite stereotype), and don't blame the university if the country's next suspension bridge looks like a plate of spaghetti. If there are not enough black surgeons to teach surgery, no matter; they'll be hired anyway, and when scores of hapless patients (hopefully Office for Civil Rights personnel) are left bleeding on the table, don't come to the universities for so much as a Band-Aid. If there are not enough qualified Chicano professors of Latin and Greek to fill their quotas, Latin and Greek can be dropped from the curriculum, and don't blame the universities for the fall of Western civilization.

Perhaps these charges would be worthy of debate if quotas were required. But they are not. Department of Labor guidelines state that goals "may not be rigid and inflexible quotas that must be met." HEW directives reflect the same policy. Furthermore, the Executive Order is a *Presidential* directive, and the President's prohibition of quotas is clear: "With respect to . . . Affirmative Action programs, I agree that numerical goals, although an important and useful tool to measure progress which remedies the effect of past discrimination, must not be allowed to be applied in such a fashion as to, in fact, result in the imposition of quotas. . . ."

What *is* required by the Executive Order is evidence of good faith and a positive effort to recruit and hire women and minorities. Since the road to exclusive white male faculties is paved with good intentions, however, we ask for something more than the mere promise of good behavior. Universities are required to commit themselves to defined, specific steps that will bring the university into contact with qualified women and minorities and that will ensure that in the selection process they will be judged fairly on the basis of their capabilities. Universities are also required to make an honest prediction of what these efforts are likely to yield over a given period of time, assuming that the availability of women and minorities is accurately approximated, and assuming that the procedures for recruitment and selection are actually followed.

This predictive aspect of Affirmative Action could be called any number of things: "level of expectancy"; "honest guesses"; "targets." They happen to be called "goals." The important point is not the term, but how it functions. Unlike quotas, goals are not the sole measure of a contractor's compliance. Good faith efforts and adherence to procedures that are likely to yield results remain the test of compliance. A university, in other words, would be required to make precisely the same level of effort, set and adhere to the same procedures, and take the same steps to correct the lack of women and minorities resulting from former exclusion, even if goals and timetables did not exist at all.

If goals are not designed to warp Affirmative Action toward quotas, what is the purpose of requiring them at all? There are two reasons:

— First, since a university cannot predict employment results in the form of goals without first analyzing its deficiencies and determining what steps are likely to remedy them, the setting of goals serves as an inducement to lay the analytical foundation necessary to guarantee nondiscrimination and the affirmative efforts required by the Executive Order.

— Second, goals serve as one way of measuring a university's level of effort, even if not the only way. If a university falls short of its goals at the end of a given period, that failure in itself does not require a conclusion of noncompliance (as would be the case if quotas were in use). It does, however, signal to the university that something has gone awry, and that reasons for the failure should be examined. If it appears, for example, that the cause for failure was not a lack of defined effort or adherence to fair procedures, then we regard compliance to have taken place. Perhaps the university's original goals were unrealistically high in light of later job market conditions. Or perhaps it faced an unforeseen contraction of its employment positions, or similar conditions beyond its control. On the other hand, if the failure to reach goals was clearly a failure to abide by the Affirmative Action program set by the university, compliance *is* an issue, and a hearing is likely to ensue. . . .

If goals are not quotas, and quotas really are not required, why the current fuss and confusion? . . .

Some critics object to goals not because they fail to understand how they differ from quotas, nor because they secretly want to throttle effort-oriented Affirmative Action. They object to the use of goals because of their fear that sound conceptual distinctions will be lost, and in actual practice, goals will be used as quotas, regardless of the law.

In confirmation of this fear, such evidence as a university official's letter is cited (but not condoned) by John Bunzel, the distinguished president of California State University at San Josè. . . .

[Pottinger is referring to an article by Bunzel entitled The Politics of Quotas, which was published in the same issue of Change magazine. The relevant portion (p. 30) follows:

Consider another troublesome issue. Does Affirmative Action mean that a university is expected to freeze or set aside faculty positions until women and members of certain minority groups are added to departments where they are now underrepresented even if this results in rejecting a better qualified applicant? The question is not hypothetical. Last spring a man received the following letter from a state university:

"I am sorry to report that although our Department saw you as our top candidate we will not be able to make you an offer for our new position.

"Our university is an Affirmative Action Employer and the Department must attempt to fill the new position with an individual from a recognized oppressed minority group. Although the Department initially viewed your ancestry as satisfying the requirements of Affirmative Action, consultation with our institutional advisors on the Affirmative Action Program indicated to us that your ancestry does not qualify you as an oppressed minority.

"I wish you the best of luck in your future, and I am deeply sorry we were not able to extend an offer to you."]

No one would agree more quickly than I that this form of "Affirmative Action-with-a-vengeance" is an outrageous and illegal form of reverse bias. I am not ready to agree, however, that blame for this petulant behavior must be laid to goals, or that valid distinctions between goals and quotas are too elusive for university officials to follow if they are sharply interested in equal opportunity.

More than once, we have discovered that what appears to be reverse discrimination born of a confusion about quotas is really nothing more than avoidance of a decision on the merits. A white male, like the person who received the letter quoted by Dr. Bunzel, is told that he was the "top candidate" for the job, when in fact that is not the truth. The personnel officer, lacking the fortitude to reject the applicant honestly, and shaking his head in mock sympathetic disgust, conveniently delivers the bad news as "Federally-required reverse discrimination." . . .

But even if the problem is widespread, or likely to become so, assuming that goals are the problem still misses the point. If, as our critics seem to imply, numbers of faculty and administrators are truly incapable of understanding and adhering to the distinction between a goal and a quota, or willfully commit reverse discrimination, are we ready to believe that these people will behave differently if goals are removed? To make the point that goals cannot operate in the real world without becoming quotas, critics must characterize university officials generally as ignorant, as spiteful, as unconcerned about merit, or as weaklings ready to collapse in the face of supposed whispered directions "from upstairs" to hire unqualified women and minorities because that is the easiest way to ensure a flow of Federal dollars. It is an unconscionable argument and an unfair condemnation of the academics' intelligence and integrity. . . .

Unfortunately, it is my impression that some critics who argue that goals are quotas are really not arguing against quotas at all. They understand the distinction between the two, and they understand that one need not inevitably become the other. Their insistence on crying "quota" to every discussion on Affirmative Action and their refusal to accompany their arguments with any alternatives that would appear to guarantee Affirmative Action without goals, lead to the conclusion that their real target is Affirmative Action itself. . . .

Attention to such matters as fair and adequate grievance procedures, anti-nepotism regulations, salary reviews and adjustments, training for non-academic personnel, safeguards against "clustering" or segregation of women, Chicanos, Jews, or others, guarantees of nondiscriminatory leave policies between men and women — these and other requirements have no bearing on hiring or promotion policies, goals, or quotas. Yet too many institutions are still failing to deal with them voluntarily. Instead, facile objections are raised to all Affirmative Action as constituting reverse discrimination and preferential treatment. And since these phrases ordinarily imply the evils of "quotas," the criticisms, no matter how simplistic or irrelevant, slide easily into a rhetorically appealing "anti-quota" posture.

The pathetic irony about those who say "never" to employment policy changes is the certainty with which they are inviting the very Federal presence which they and their colleagues deplore. Historically, universities throughout the country have understandably resisted government intervention into even the most trival aspects of university life, to keep out influence over their teaching, research, publication, and curricula. At the same time, however, there cannot be a university or college anywhere in the country today that does not know that where basic grievances exist, those who are aggrieved will turn to every available source for redress, including the Federal government. And surely they must know that if the university does not *voluntarily* deal with the issue, a vacuum is created which the government, like nature, abhors. Knowing this, it is deeply troubling to see the lethargy and paralysis with which so many universities have responded to even the most fundamental grievances presented. . . .

NOTE: JUDICIAL RESOLUTION OF THE CONTROVERSY

The following decision definitely established the legality of setting specific numerical goals and timetables in the enforcement of the executive order. At issue in the case was the Philadelphia Plan, a city-wide compliance program which set specific goals for all area bidders to meet, rather than proceeding on a company by company basis in the construction industry. This approach, which has been used in a number of cities, has only been followed in the construction industry, which has generally been treated by the OFCC separately from procurements contracts, and, as mentioned above, is governed by a separate part of the executive order.

CONTRACTORS ASSOCIATION OF EASTERN PENNSYLVANIA
v. SECRETARY OF LABOR
442 F.2d 159 (3d Cir.), cert. denied, 404 U.S. 854 (1971)

GIBBONS, Circuit Judge.

The original plaintiff, the Contractors Association of Eastern Pennsylvania (the Association) and the intervening plaintiffs, construction contractors doing business in the Philadelphia area (the Contractors), appeal from an order of the district court which denied their motion for summary judgment . . . and granted the cross-motion of the federal defendants for summary judgment. . . .

The complaint challenges the validity of the Philadelphia Plan, promulgated by the federal defendants under the authority of Executive Order No. 11246. That Plan is embodied in two orders issued by officials of the United States Department of Labor, dated June 27, 1969 and September 23, 1969, respectively. . . . In summary, they require that bidders on any federal or federally assisted construction contracts for projects in a five-county area around Philadelphia, the estimated total cost of which exceeds $500,-000, shall submit an acceptable affirmative action program which includes specific goals for the utilization of minority manpower in six skilled crafts: ironworkers, plumbers and pipefitters, steamfitters, sheetmetal workers, electrical workers, and elevator construction workers. . . .

The Executive Order empowers the Secretary of Labor to issue rules and regulations necessary and appropriate to achieve its purpose. On June 27, 1969 Assistant Secretary of Labor Fletcher issued an order implementing the Executive Order in the five-county Philadelphia area. The order required bidders, prior to the award of contracts, to submit "acceptable affirmative action" programs "which shall include specific goals of minority manpower utilization." The order contained a finding that enforcement of the "affirmative action" requirement of Executive Order No. 11246 had posed special problems in the construction trades. Contractors and subcontractors must hire a new employee complement for each job, and they rely on craft unions as their prime or sole source for labor. The craft unions operate hiring halls. "Because of the exclusionary practices of labor organizations," the order finds "there traditionally has been only a small number of Negroes employed in these seven trades." The June 27, 1969 order provided that the Area Coordinator of the Office of Federal Contract Compliance, in conjunction with the federal contracting and administering agencies in the Philadelphia area, would determine definite standards for specific goals in a contractor's affirmative action program. After such standards were determined, each bidder would be required to commit itself to specific goals for minority manpower utilization. The order set forth factors to be considered in determining definite standards, including:

(1) The current extent of minority group participation in the trade.
(2) The availability of minority group persons for employment in such trade.
(3) The need for training programs in the area and/or the need to assure demand for those in or from existing training programs.
(4) The impact of the program upon the existing labor force.

Acting pursuant to the June 29, 1969 order, representatives of the Department of Labor held public hearings in Philadelphia on August 26, 27 and 28, 1969. On September 23, 1969, Assistant Secretary Fletcher made findings with respect to each of the listed factors and ordered that the following ranges be established as the standards for minority manpower utilization for each of the designated trades in the Philadelphia area for [the years 1970-1973. See Table 2-6.]

[TABLE 2-6]

Identification of Trade	Range of Minority Group Employment			
	Until 12/31/70	for 1971	for 1972	for 1973
Ironworkers	5%–9%	11%–15%	16%–20%	22%–26%
Plumbers & Pipefitters	5%–8%	10%–14%	15%–19%	20%–24%
Steamfitters	5%–8%	11%–15%	15%–19%	20%–24%
Sheetmetal workers	4%–8%	9%–13%	14%–18%	19%–23%
Electrical workers	4%–8%	9%–13%	14%–18%	19%–23%
Elevator construction workers	4%–8%	9%–13%	14%–18%	19%–23%

The order of September 23, 1969 specified that on each invitation to bid each bidder would be required to submit an affirmative action program. The order further provided:

4. No bidder will be awarded a contract unless his affirmative action program contains goals falling within the range set forth . . . above. . . .
6. The purpose of the contractor's commitment to specific goals as to minority manpower utilization is to meet his affirmative action obligations under the equal opportunity clause of the contract. This commitment is not intended and shall not be used to discriminate against any qualified applicant or employee. Whenever it comes to the bidder's attention that the goals are being used in a discriminatory manner, he must report it to the Area Coordinator of the Office of Federal Contract Compliance of the U. S. Department of Labor in order that appropriate sanction proceedings may be instituted. . . .
8. The bidder agrees to keep such records and file such reports relating to the provisions of this order as shall be required by the contracting or administering agency. . . .

Plaintiffs contend that the Plan, by imposing remedial quotas, requires them to violate the basic prohibitions of Section 703(a), 42 U.S.C. §2000e-2(a):

> It shall be an unlawful employment practice for an employer —
> (1) to fail or refuse to hire . . . any individual . . . because of such individual's race . . . or
> (2) to . . . classify his employees in any way which would deprive . . . any individual of employment opportunities . . . because of such individual's race. . . .

Because the Plan requires that the contractor agree to specific goals for minority employment in each of the six trades and requires a good faith effort to achieve those goals, they argue, it requires (1) that they refuse to hire some white tradesmen, and (2) that they classify their employees by race, in violation of §703(a). This argument rests on an overly simple reading both of the Plan and of the findings which led to its adoption.

The order of September 23, 1969 contained findings that although overall minority group representation in the construction industry in the five-county Philadelphia area was thirty per cent, in the six trades representation was approximately one per cent. It found, moreover, that this obvious underrepresentation was due to the exclusionary practices of the unions representing the six trades. It is the practice of building contractors to rely on union hiring halls as the prime source for employees. The order made further findings as to the availability of qualified minority tradesmen for employment in each trade, and as to the impact of an affirmative action program with specific goals upon the existing labor force. The Department of Labor found that contractors could commit to the specific employment goals "without adverse impact on the existing labor force." Some minority tradesmen could be recruited, in other words, without eliminating job opportunities for white tradesmen.

To read §703(a) in the manner suggested by the plaintiffs we would have to attribute to Congress the intention to freeze the status quo and to foreclose remedial action under other authority designed to overcome existing evils. We discern no such intention either from the language of the statute or from its legislative history. Clearly the Philadelphia Plan is color-conscious. Indeed the only meaning which can be attributed to the "affirmative action" language which since March of 1961 has been included in successive Executive Orders is that Government contractors must be color-conscious. Since 1941 the Executive Order program has recognized that discriminatory practices exclude available minority manpower from the labor pool. In other contexts color-consciousness has been deemed to be an appropriate remedial posture. Porcelli v. Titus, 302 F. Supp. 726 (D.N.J. 1969), *aff'd,* 431 F.2d 1254 (3d Cir. 1970); Norwalk CORE v. Norwalk Redevelopment Agency, 395 F.2d 920, 931 (2d Cir. 1968); Offermann v. Nitkowski, 378 F.2d 22, 24 (2d Cir. 1967). It has been said respecting Title VII that "Congress did not intend to freeze an entire generation of Negro employees into discriminatory patterns that existed before the Act." Quarles v. Philip Morris, Inc., supra, 279 F. Supp. at 514. The *Quarles* case rejected the contention that existing, nondiscriminatory seniority arrangements were so sanctified by Title VII that the effects of past discrimination in job assignments could not be overcome.[47] We reject the contention that Title VII prevents the President acting through the Executive Order program from attempting to remedy the absence from the Philadelphia construction labor of minority tradesmen in key trades.

---

47. The federal courts in overcoming the effects of past discrimination are expressly authorized in Title VII to take affirmative action. 42 U.S.C. §2000e-5(g). See Vogler v. McCarty, 294 F. Supp. 368 (E.D. La. 1968), *aff'd sub nom.* International Ass'n Heat & Frost Insulation & Asbestos Workers v. Vogler, 407 F.2d 1047 (5th Cir. 1969).

Note: Women in Construction Work

Neither the Philadelphia Plan nor other executive order compliance efforts have dealt with the virtual exclusion of women from the construction industry,[26] which consistently provides some of the highest paying blue-collar work. For example, the 1970 Manpower Report of the President showed the gross average hourly earnings of production or nonsupervisory workers in the contract construction industry in 1969 at $4.77 an hour, as compared to gross average hourly wages for all privately employed production or nonsupervisory workers of $3.04.[27]

Note: The Ineffectiveness of Compliance Efforts in the Construction Industry

The Civil Rights Commission has been quite critical of the enforcement of the executive order with respect to construction contracts. For example, the commission has noted:[28]

> Of the five existing imposed plans, those in Philadelphia and Washington, D.C. are the oldest and the only ones for which employment data are available. In neither case have the results been encouraging. For example, in Washington, data for June and July, which are peak construction months, show 6 of the 12 skilled trades covered by the plan falling below minimum goals for minority employment under the plan. In Philadelphia, although nearly all second year goals for minority employment were being met as of October 1971, the progress has come about as a result of the use of more than 100 "show cause" notices and the issuance of one contract debarment order, the first in the history of the Executive Order. The massive enforcement activity required indicates that a new approach is called for since the Federal Government does not have the resources to cope with such noncompliance if encountered nationwide.

There are several types of plans in use in different cities at present. These differ from each other in the extent of their reliance on (1) negotiations among representatives of local management, labor, and minority groups to arrive at goals and timetables; (2) monitoring of compliance with the local plan by a minority community or communities; and (3) OFCC action. The last ranges from the imposition of goals and timetables on the basis of government factfinding hearings, as in the Philadelphia Plan, to approval of a hometown plan. Most of the voluntary plans are weaker than the imposed plans, like Philadelphia's, and are unlikely to be any more successful.[29]

> In addition to these local efforts, as of November, 1971, OFCC [had been considering] a "national construction plan" . . . for more than a year. This plan would establish minority employment goals and timetables for the major skilled construction crafts for every area of the country. By so doing, it would give compliance agencies a clear standard of required compliance, responding to a complaint made by many compli-

---

26. A striking example was provided in March 1971 by the experiences of two women who were, according to a Cleveland Press story of March 10, 1971, the first female construction workers in greater Cleveland. They were hired by the secretary of the Insana Construction Co., Sidney Simon, as common laborers installing sewers. Simon reportedly hired them after he heard feminists on a radio show complaining about their exclusion from men's jobs. "They got big mouths," said Simon. "So I figure, put up or shut up. I decide to let them start work in construction." He ran help-wanted ads, to which two women responded, and according to the press they were doing well on the job. But a week later they were fired, one day before they would have been eligible to join the union. The Women's Equity Action League is representing them in a Title VII action against the company.

27. U.S. Department of Labor, Manpower Report of the President, March 1970, Table C-6.

28. The Federal Civil Rights Enforcement Effort: One Year Later, supra, at 20.

29. Id. at 22. More detailed information on the plans can be found id. at 20-22.

ance agencies, e.g., [Department of Defense]. The proposed plan [had] been in the Office of the Solicitor, [Department of Labor] for more than six months, and no date [had] been set for its issuance.

The existence on a national basis of clear goals for compliance efforts could be of considerable importance. At the very least, noncompliance would be more easily identified by civil rights, feminist, and minority organizations, and the lack of enforcement by the government more easily challenged. If such a plan were to be promulgated, enforced, and extended to procurement as well as construction contracts, the result would be somewhat similar to the Galbraith Minority Advancement Plan discussed in Part I, supra. Unfortunately, the history of executive order enforcement to date suggests that case by case proceedings under Title VII of the Civil Rights Act of 1964, although far more time- and energy-consuming, are more likely than complaints to the OFCC to produce significant changes in employment practices.

C. A Case Study: Women's Use of Executive Order at Colleges and Universities

While the compliance effort has had some impact on particular industries in certain regions, in general the obligations of contractors have been seriously watered down by the lack of effective enforcement of the order. Some idea of the resulting situation can be obtained from the following account of the campaign by women's groups to obtain enforcement of the executive order at colleges and universities across the nation.

At the time women began to use the executive order on campus, there were virtually no other federal remedies for sex discrimination in the employment of educational personnel. Considering that there had been little enforcement of the executive order either on behalf of women or outside the construction industry prior to the complaints against univerisities made by the Women's Equity Action League (WEAL) in 1970, the women's organizations have had remarkable success. Yet many obstacles confront those who seek to challenge institutional sexism through administrative agency proceedings.

1. The Magnitude of the Problem

CARNEGIE COMMISSION ON HIGHER EDUCATION
OPPORTUNITIES FOR WOMEN IN HIGHER EDUCATION
109, 111-112, 113-115, 119 (1973)

. . . [W]omen represent about 46 percent of all undergraduates and about 37 percent of graduate students in higher education, but according to the most recent data available, they represented only 27 percent of college faculty members in 1971-72 (National Education Association, [Research: Salaries Paid and Salary-Related Practices in Higher Education, 1970-71] 1972). [See Chart 2-5.] However, there is a tendency for ratios of women to men to be much smaller in universities, and especially in highly research-oriented universities, than in other types of institutions. . . .

Perhaps the most surprising aspect of the status of women as faculty members, however, is the evidence that both the relative representation and status of women have deteriorated over the last 50 years. Chart [2-6] portrays what has happened to the relative representation of women in aggregative terms. . . .

This decline in the relative representation and status of women on college and university faculties is partly, but by no means wholly, explained by certain long-term trends . . . — changes in marriage and birthrates, the decline in the relative importance

Chart [2-5]
WOMEN AS A PERCENTAGE OF PERSONS AT SELECTED
LEVELS OF ADVANCEMENT WITHIN
THE EDUCATIONAL SYSTEM, 1970

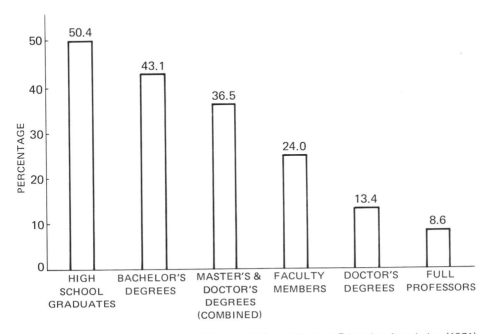

Sources: U.S. Office of Education (1971 and 1972); and National Education Association (1971).

Chart [2-6]
PROPORTION OF TOTAL FACULTY WHO WERE WOMEN,
1869–1959 (decade-to-decade changes)

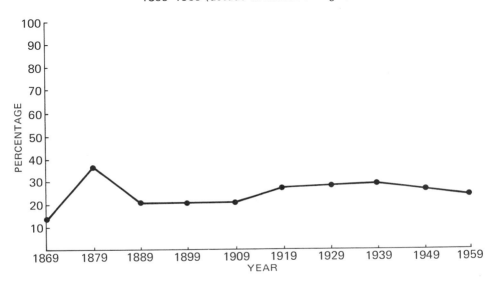

of women's colleges, and the long-term trend toward greater sex-differentiation of the fields in which men and women received the doctorate (only recently beginning to be reversed). There are also indications that the decline has been encouraged by the greatly increased emphasis on research, especially in the sciences, in the 1950s and 1960s. This trend was especially important, of course, in the universities that had long been leaders in the development of graduate education and research, but its influence clearly trickled down to less prestigious universities and four-year colleges, which showed an increasing tendency to regard the Harvards and Berkeleys as their models and to recruit faculty members with a record of research and publication or at least the potential for such a record in the future. All this militated against women, and especially married women. . . .

Not only were there relatively fewer women in highly selective research universities . . . but this was especially true in the higher ranks and in traditionally male fields. . . . For example, in these prestigious institutions, only 1 percent or fewer of the full professors were women in physical sciences and business; 2 percent were women in biological sciences and medicine-law; 3 percent were women in social sciences and humanities; and 6 percent in fine arts. Proportions were considerably higher in education (15 percent) and in the new professions (12 percent).

A factor in the lower status of women on college and university faculties is the smaller percentage of women who have doctor's degrees. The Carnegie Commission Survey of Faculty and Student Opinion, 1969, showed that about 83 percent of the male faculty members and 47 percent of the female faculty members in Research Universities I had doctor's degrees.

In other groups of universities smaller percentages of either sex had these advanced degrees. Sex differences in this respect were somewhat less pronounced in Liberal Arts Colleges I than in either universities or comprehensive universities and colleges. In two-year colleges, of course, relatively few faculty members of either sex held the doctorate.

Women were also considerably less likely to have tenure than men. This was, of course, related to their comparatively weak representation in the ranks that usually have tenure (associate and full professors). In addition, men tended to have tenure at a considerably earlier age than women. In part, this was explained by the fact that men are more heavily represented in such fields as the natural sciences, in which creativity tends to peak at an early age and which are highly competitive, so that promotion tends to take place early. . . .

One of the most significant manifestations of the women's movement among professional women has been the formation of a committee on the status of women in just about every professional field of any importance. . . . One of the first activities of many of these groups was to survey college and university faculties in the particular discipline to develop more adequate information on the status of women within that discipline. The results have in some cases revealed a more complete absence of women in the more prestigious departments in various fields than our data on Research Universities I would suggest. For example, one of the first reports of this type was presented by Professor Alice Rossi at the 1969 meeting of the American Sociological Association. The survey found, among other things, that there were no women among the 44 full professors in five leading sociology departments — Berkeley, Chicago, Columbia, Harvard, and Michigan (Rossi, [Status of Women in Graduate Departments of Sociology, 5 The American Sociologist, February 1970, pp. 1-12]). . . .

[In addition, the Commission presents extensive data on salary differences between male and female faculty members, which were analyzed to determine] whether these salary differences suggest discrimination against women or are explained by relatively objective factors such as the smaller percentage of women faculty members who have Ph.D.s. . . .

The data provide evidence of a pervasive pattern of lower compensation for women that is not explained by the predictor variables. . . .

In virtually all public institutions and in many private institutions that have formal salary structures, the discrimination does not take the form of paying a woman a lower salary than a man when she is in the same step of the same rank, but it does take the form of not moving her up through the steps and ranks as quickly. . . .

[At the outset, in presenting the major themes of the report, the Commission estimated that] on the average, women faculty members receive about $1,500 to $2,000 less per year than do men in comparable situations. . . . This adds up to about $150 to $200 million per year across the nation.

2. The National Campaign To End Sex Discrimination in Higher Education

SANDLER, A LITTLE HELP FROM OUR GOVERNMENT:
WEAL AND CONTRACT COMPLIANCE
in Rossi and Calderwood (eds.), Academic Women on the Move 440-456 (1973)

Late in 1969 the Women's Equity Action League (WEAL)[3] discovered that there was indeed a legal route to combat sex discrimination. In 1965 former President Lyndon Johnson issued Executive Order 11246[4] which prohibited discrimination by all federal contractors on the basis of race, color, religion, and national origin. Executive Order 11375, effective October 13, 1968, amended the original order to include discrimination based on sex. Unlike the former Title VII, Executive Order 11375 does not exempt educational institutions. Universities and colleges receive over 3 billion dollars annually, much of it in federal contract money. Most institutions, other than the very small ones, have federal contracts, and as federal contractors, they are subject to the sex discrimination provisions of the Executive Order.

On January 31, 1970, WEAL launched a national campaign to end discrimination against women in education by filing a historic class action complaint against all universities and colleges in the country. The charges were filed with the United States Department of Labor under Executive Order 11375. Until that time, the Executive Order had been used almost exclusively in cases concerning blue-collar workers in the construction industry (most notably in the "Philadelphia Plan"). Although the Executive Order had covered sex discrimination since October 1968, there was virtually no enforcement by the government until WEAL began its campaign. Governmental compliance agencies simply ignored the sex discrimination provisions of the Executive Order.

In its initial complaint in January 1970, WEAL charged an "industry-wide pattern" of discrimination against women in the academic community. Dr. Nancy E. Dowding, then president of WEAL, asked that the Department of Labor investigate the following areas: admission quotas to undergraduate and graduate schools, discrimination in financial assistance, hiring practices, promotions, and salary differentials. More than eighty pages of materials documenting these charges were submitted with the complaint to the Secretary of Labor. WEAL requested an immediate "class action" and compliance review of all institutions holding federal contracts. At the same time, specific charges were filed against the University of Maryland. Charges against more than 250 other institutions (about 10 percent of the nation's institutions of higher education) were subsequently filed by WEAL as word went out to women throughout the academic community. Among the institutions charged by WEAL were the University of Wisconsin, the Uni-

---

3. The Women's Equity Action League was incorporated in 1968 in Ohio for the purposes of promoting greater economic progress on the part of American women, and to establish solutions to economic, education, tax, and legal problems affecting women. It now has members in almost every state, and numerous state chapters.

4. The first Executive Order dealing with discrimination and federal contractors dates back to 1941, with successive presidents revising and strengthening the government's non-discrimination requirements for contractors. Historically, Executive Orders have been stronger and more far reaching than concurrent civil rights legislation.

versity of Minnesota, Columbia University, the University of Chicago, and the entire state university and college systems of California, Florida, and New Jersey. In October 1970, WEAL filed a class action against all the medical schools in the country. A similar class action against the nation's law schools also was filed by the Professional Women's Caucus in April 1971. The National Organization for Women (NOW) also filed charges against Harvard University and the entire state university system of New York. Additional complaints by individual women and women's campus associations have brought the number of formal charges filed against colleges and universities to more than 360 and the end is not in sight. . . .

[Under the Executive Order] all contractors with fifty employees and a contract of $50,000 or more must develop a *written* plan of affirmative action. The plan must include an analysis of the contractor's current employment of minority and female workers, an evaluation of opportunities for increasing their numbers if they are "underutilized," as well as specific numerical goals and timetables for correcting existing discrimination.

The responsibility for the enforcement of the Executive Order is divided among various governmental agencies. . . . The Department of Health, Education and Welfare, through its Office for Civil Rights, has been designated by OFCC as the agency responsible for enforcement of the Executive Order for all contracts with universities and colleges (regardless of the agency from which the contract originated).

One of the most useful aspects of the Executive Order is that any individual or group can file a complaint, and the complaint can be filed on the basis of a pattern of discrimination. Of equal importance is the applicability of the Executive Order to the *entire* institution, even if only one department is involved in the contract. The complainant need not be the individual or group suffering discrimination. (A typical letter of filing appears in the Appendix to this chapter). In some instances complaints have been based on extensive reports; in others, simply the number and percentage of women at each rank in several departments of an institution has served as the basis of a complaint. Regardless of the data included, the complainant can request a complete investigation of all hiring practices and policies, salary inequities, nepotism rules, and so on. . . .

HOW WEAL CHANGED FEDERAL POLICY REGARDING ENFORCEMENT OF THE EXECUTIVE ORDER

When WEAL filed its initial charges in January 1970, it was well aware that merely filing a complaint would not lead to action on the part of either the Department of Labor or HEW. Therefore, personal notes were sent to numerous senators and representatives who were thought to be potentially helpful. Various materials describing sex discrimination in education were enclosed, and the accompanying note pointed out that although the Executive Order applied, it had never been enforced with regard to sex discrimination, particularly sex discrimination in universities and colleges. Each legislator specifically was asked to write a note to the secretary of labor, requesting that the Executive Order be enforced with regard to sex discrimination in the academic community. Within a few weeks, more than twenty members of the Congress contacted the Secretary of Labor. On March 9, 1970, Congresswoman Martha Griffiths gave a speech in the House of Representatives detailing sex discrimination in education, describing WEAL's complaint, and criticizing the government for not enforcing its own rules and regulations as contained in the Executive Order. Some three weeks after Representative Griffiths' speech, the first investigation concerning sex discrimination began at Harvard University.

As more complaints were filed, additional letters from WEAL and women in the academic community were sent to legislators, asking them specifically to contact the secretary of labor or the secretary of health, education and welfare.[6] At one point the

6. Complaints may be filed with either the Department of Labor or the Department of Health, Education and Welfare. Most early complaints were filed with the Department of Labor because of their policy responsibility for the order, and because the writer was at the time a temporary employee of HEW.

Office for Civil Rights at HEW was receiving so much congressional mail that one person was assigned full-time to handle the correspondence. Similarly, at the Department of Labor more than 300 congressional letters were received within a short period of time. Letters to legislators serve a dual function: they sensitize congressional staffs to the problems of sex discrimination, and they are an effective prod to bureaucratic inaction. If anything moves the bureaucracy — and not much does — it's a series of inquiries from Capitol Hill. Five months after filing, in June 1970, there was a double payoff. HEW issued a memorandum to all field personnel requiring them to routinely include sex discrimination in all contract compliance investigations, regardless of whether or not there was a complaint involving sex discrimination. During the same month, the Department of Labor issued its long-awaited Sex Discrimination Guidelines for federal contractors. These guidelines, which deal with problems specific to women workers (such as maternity leave policies), had been in the works for nearly two years.

Equally important, investigations of college campuses began. When the first complaints were filed, there were no women in the contract compliance division of HEW's Office for Civil Rights. A woman investigator, Rose Brock, was hastily transferred from civil rights investigations and was given the responsibility of supervising compliance reviews concerning discrimination against women. Her dedication, experience, and persistence led to extensive documentation of sex discrimination charges in the early investigations, and she helped set the pattern for later compliance reviews.[7] Her findings also helped to convince some of the HEW staff of the extent of discrimination against women, and the blatant violations of the Executive Order on the campus.

When word of the investigations reached the academic community, many administrators and faculty reacted with disbelief and denial. They were quick to rationalize: "There are *no* qualified women." "Women don't *want* to be promoted." "There is discrimination at *some* institutions, but not at ours." When the first investigation began at Harvard, a slight shiver ran throughout the academic establishment, a shiver that increased perceptibly when new government contracts totaling almost four million dollars were delayed for two weeks when Harvard refused to grant HEW investigators access to personnel files. The delay, coupled with the threat of the additional loss of existing contracts as well, was sufficient to cause Harvard to change its mind and open its files to HEW investigators. Threats to sue the government evaporated when Harvard lawyers discovered that access to personnel files is one of the terms of the agreement voluntarily signed by Harvard and all other federal contractors.

To date, nearly 200 universities and colleges have been investigated. Many of these investigations have been conducted in almost absolute secrecy, with HEW investigators coming and going without the knowledge of concerned women. On some campuses however, particularly those where organized women's groups exist, the HEW investigations have been more open, and usually more thorough.

WHAT HAPPENS TO COMPLAINTS?

Typically, enforcement works like this: A complaint is filed with the Secretary of HEW[8] who refers it to the Office for Civil Rights. It is then forwarded to one of HEW's ten regional offices. Initially, priority was given to complaints of individuals and to preaward compliance reviews (contracts involving more than a million dollars cannot be awarded without a prior investigation regarding nondiscrimination and the adequacy of affirmative action programs). As HEW began to be swamped with individual complaints, the department shifted its emphasis to pattern complaints while continuing its preaward reviews. Meanwhile, the department's priorities and schedules continue to be affected by political pressure from representatives and senators, as well as the work load of the

7. Subsequently, all sex discrimination investigations were integrated into the regular compliance reviews.
8. Complaints filed with the Department of Labor are forwarded to HEW's Office for Civil Rights.

particular regional office. Reviews are scheduled on a quarterly basis but delays and last minute changes are typical. . . .

Requests for various kinds of information accompany the notice of an impending investigation by HEW. Until HEW finally sent out a memorandum to presidents of institutions of higher learning on October 4, 1972, to inform them of their responsibilities under the Executive Order (some four years after the order first went into effect) most institutions were surprised and caught unaware when they received notification of an investigation. Often, an institution will claim that the information HEW wants is "not available" for one reason or another. Negotiations with HEW and the threat of contract loss, as in the Harvard investigation, eventually produce the desired information, although often at the cost of postponed and delayed investigations.

The type of information requested has varied from school to school, depending upon the nature of the complaint, the particular investigator's predilections, the pressure (or lack of pressure) from Washington, the delay and avoidance tactics employed by the institution, and the activities of individual women and women's groups on campus. HEW has begun to codify the kinds of information it will require in all investigations of sex discrimination. At a minimum, they usually will ask for the following:

1. A listing of all employees (academic and nonacademic, full- and part-time, permanent and temporary, and student employees). The inventory must list employees by race, sex, ethnic origin, job category, rate of pay, status (e.g., full- or part-time; tenured, permanent, or temporary; and so on), number of hours if working part-time, date of hire, and date of last promotion. The data must be organized in two ways: by job category and organizational unit, such as academic departments.

2. A copy of the written affirmative action plan which details actions being taken to guarantee equal employment and any analysis or evaluation of the plan.

3. A listing of all persons hired (except in labor service categories) in a recent period (usually six months or a year depending upon circumstances), their job or position classification, date of hire, starting pay rate, race or ethnic origin, and sex.

4. Copies of tests and other criteria used in making selections for employment, upgrading, and promotion, and any validation studies which have been conducted on such criteria.

5. Copies of faculty manuals, administrative practices manuals, guides to personnel, or operational procedures or other issuances of the institution that describe matters affecting the employment or treatment of employees.

Investigators may request additional information that they believe to be pertinent. Sometimes these requests stem from suggestions made by concerned women on campus. The HEW team might also request a more detailed response to some of the items listed above. For example, they might ask to see the personnel files of a specific department in order to examine in greater detail the individual records of women and men applicants and employees. The review process may be completed in a whirlwind three weeks or drag on for many, many months. . . .

When the investigation is completed, a "letter of findings," detailing the results of the investigation is given to the institution, usually during a conference with the institution's head. The administrator may take exception to any or all of the findings if he or she can provide supporting data. In any event, the contractor must make a written commitment to correct "deficiencies" noted in the findings, and submit a written plan within thirty days. The plan then is reviewed by both the regional and Washington offices. The letter of findings is kept confidential by HEW, although the college or university is free to make its contents public if it wishes to do so. In actual practice, the delay between the letter of findings and HEW's acceptance of an affirmative action plan has dragged out in many cases to over a year. The delay has in part been caused not only by HEW staff shortages, conflicting policies, and other inefficiencies but also by the delaying tactics of the institutions.

At any point during the compliance review, either before or after the letter of findings has been submitted, HEW can delay the awarding of *new* contracts if they find that the institution is in noncompliance and that reasonable efforts to secure compliance by conciliation and conference are not working. Such delays are for a specific number of days within which the institution must move into compliance if they want new contracts. About forty institutions have had new contracts delayed for short periods for such reasons as not providing access to information, not developing a satisfactory affirmative action plan, not adjusting a verified complaint, and the like. One large university claimed it could not compile the data necessary for setting numerical goals and timetables for women and minorities. After innumerable delays, negotiations between the institution and HEW collapsed, and HEW finally withheld a large contract that was about to be awarded, and froze all new hiring for sixty days, with the exception of new women and new minority employees. By the end of the sixty days, the institution had collected the data it previously had been unable to obtain, and the target goals for women and minorities were developed.

Procedures for the termination or suspension of *existing* contracts and debarment from future contracts are far more formal, involving hearings before such sanctions are imposed; and, indeed, they have been initiated in only one instance. In November 1971, after two years of negotiating with HEW, Columbia University was notified that proceedings for debarment of future contracts would be initiated by HEW. Shortly after receiving HEW's notice, Columbia University complied with their requests, and the debarment proceedings were dropped. Ordinarily, the threat of such hearings, plus the actual delaying of new contracts has been sufficient to bring about compliance. . . .

The University of Michigan experience provides a good example of the kinds of problems that are encountered in the course of an investigation. Michigan was the first state university to be investigated. (Unlike many institutions which have kept HEW's activities and findings under wraps, Michigan openly publicized a good deal of its correspondence with HEW officials.) From its initial denial of discrimination at the university, Michigan administrators contacted officials at other institutions and educational associations to join with Michigan to sue HEW for violating the institution's rights. There were few, if any, takers, and the idea was dropped or postponed when attorneys realized that it would be difficult to establish a legal basis for such a suit.

Within a few days after HEW's investigation began, the compliance investigator publicly stated that there was no evidence of discrimination at Michigan because not one single woman had come forward to tell him how she personally had been discriminated against. This was a clear violation of HEW policy, and it ignored the fact that the complaint at Michigan was not an individual one, but a charge of a pattern of discrimination. WEAL immediately telegrammed the secretary of HEW demanding the investigator's resignation. While this was not forthcoming, he was removed from the investigation and a new person was assigned. The Michigan complaint was filed by a small but highly effective local feminist group called FOCUS. The act of filing encouraged campus women to band together in a new on-campus group called PROBE. FOCUS, PROBE, and WEAL together contacted every member of the Michigan congressional delegation as well as other members of Congress who were in a position to be of help.

Under the glare of congressional pressure, Washington subsequently monitored the Michigan investigation very closely, and a plan of affirmative action was adopted. It includes salary equity, back pay for women who have lost wages because of discriminatory treatment, revision of nepotism rules, increased recruitment of women for academic positions, and promotion of clerical and nonacademic women whose qualifications were equivalent to those of higher-level male employees. About one year after the plan was submitted, HEW notified the university that its plan was deficient in several respects.

Women's groups pointed out that Michigan's projections for additional women would increase the overall percentage of women on the faculty by only 2.5 percent after four years of so-called affirmative action. For example, the percentage of women at the rank of full professor at Michigan was 4.5 percent in 1970-1971, and projected to be 6.6 percent by 1973–1974–a mere 2.1 percentage increase, and still substantially below the current national figure of 8.7 percent. Once more the women protested, and HEW did not accept the numerical goals offered by the university.

When HEW insisted that the university recruit more women into its doctoral programs, the university protested strongly, and HEW retreated temporarily. HEW Secretary Elliot Richardson said in January 1971 that he would decide the issue "within a few weeks," and Michigan agreed to abide by his decision. As of June 1972, he had not yet issued any decision on this matter, nor is one expected. With the passage of the June 1972 Education Amendments Act, sex discrimination in admission to graduate programs is prohibited. The vigor of Michigan's struggle against admitting women on an equal basis suggests that the discrimination in admission must be far worse than women suspect.

Michigan personnel showed little sympathy to the issue. Fedele Fauri, one of Michigan's vice presidents was quoted as saying "We just want to get these bastards at HEW off our backs" (Zwerdling 1971:12). William Cash, the university's human relations director was quoted as saying "Once you let women know they've got you over a barrel they'll take everything they can get from you. Women just make life difficult"[9] (Zwerdling 1971:11). Such statements galvanized the women into action again. Although neither man was asked to resign, they and other officials have begun to pay greater lip service to nondiscrimination, and have been much more cautious in their remarks to the press.

EVALUATION OF CONTRACT COMPLIANCE
INVESTIGATION AND ENFORCEMENT

HEW officials, with notable exceptions, have been slow to understand the sex discrimination issue, and to accept it as part of HEW's responsibilities. Many men who joined HEW to work on civil rights simply do not see *women's* rights as part of that effort. When they speak of civil rights, they usually mean the rights of minorities only, and by minority, they often mean minority males. For example, the five-page letter of findings detailing the results of HEW's investigation at Harvard contained only *three paragraphs* that dealt with women. The rest dealt with male members of minority groups, although the investigation had been initiated to examine *sex* discrimination. None of the statistical data concerning women was included in the letter of findings, although a wealth of such data had been submitted with the official complaint. WEAL and several local groups actively dissented; letters went to HEW and to numerous senators and congressmen, whereupon HEW backtracked, saying that the letter of findings was only "preliminary" and that the study of discrimination against women was continuing. Similarly, when the Tufts plan of affirmative action was approved by HEW, WEAL quickly pointed out that there were no goals and timetables developed for women, although it was on the basis of a complaint of sex discrimination that Tufts had been investigated. Moreover, Tufts data were presented in such a way that the position of

---

9. One woman at Michigan bitterly commented that the university did not take sex discrimination as seriously as discrimination against minorities. She asked what would have happened to a university official if he had said, "Once you let *blacks* know they've got you over a barrel they'll take everything they can get from you. *Blacks* just make life difficult."

minority women was completely obscured: data were given for minority and non-minority employees in one column; in another column data were given for men and women faculty. There was no way of finding out if there were any minority women employed on the Tufts campus or what their status was. Under the Tufts plan every minority slot could have been filled with minority males, and Tufts nevertheless would have been in technical compliance. As a result of WEAL's pressure, the Tufts plan was amended to meet these criticisms.

WEAL and other groups have consistently asked that there be specific goals for minority women, in order to assure their fair treatment. Too often, minority recruiting has meant minority *males,* and too often, recruiting women has meant recruiting *white* women. In some instances, minority women are counted *twice* by the employer, once as minority and once as women, although only *one* salary is paid. Thus an employer with a goal of six slots for minorities, and six additional slots for women (or a total of twelve slots) could hire only six minority women, count them twice, and thereby fulfill the goals. Six of the original twelve slots would remain and could be filled by six white males. Unless goals are developed separately for minority females, either of the above evasions is likely to occur, both of which would be clear violations of the intent of the Executive Order.

Although the government was quick to praise its own efforts in the area of sex discrimination and hailed the Michigan affirmative action plan as a "landmark," WEAL and other women's groups were quick to point out the inconsistencies, inefficiencies, and blunders committed by both the Departments of Labor and HEW. A particular sore spot was Order No. 4, a set of guidelines issued for contractors by the Department of Labor in February 1970. This order details how affirmative action plans are to be written, and how goals and timetables are to be developed. The plan was clearly aimed at minorities, although there was no legal basis for excluding women. It had been developed without taking into account the sex discrimination provisions of the Executive Order; at the time of its writing, sex discrimination provisions of the order were not enforced (WEAL's first complaint had been filed just a few days prior to the issuance of Order No. 4). Women were quick to point out that affirmative action as detailed in Order No. 4 should apply to them as well. In fact, HEW campus investigations were proceeding on this assumption. The Department of Labor, through Arthur Fletcher, then assistant secretary of labor, assured women orally at several meetings that the order did indeed apply to them, but women were unable to obtain this statement in writing from any Department of Labor official. The department wavered, for at one point an internal memorandum was circulated within the department stating that Order No. 4 covered women workers; a few days later the memorandum was withdrawn, and Secretary Hodgson stated that Order No. 4 did *not* apply to women. Additional pressure from various members of the Congress and women's groups resulted in a new statement from the secretary on July 31, 1970. He stated that although the *concepts* of Order No. 4 applied to women, the *procedures* of the order did not, and that new procedures would need to be developed for women. He promised that the department would meet within a "few weeks" with women's groups and other interested parties to work out these procedures. The meetings were finally held, after much pressure, some nine months later in April and May of 1971. A Proposed Order No. 4 which includes women was issued for comment on August 31, 1971, again after much internal delay. On December 4, 1971, the Revised Order No. 4 finally was issued.

The Department of Labor, until late spring 1972, took the position that affirmative action plans did not have to be made public by the government or by contractors, although the latter were free to do so if they wished. In a letter to HEW dated June 10, 1971, Peter G. Nash, then solicitor of the Department of Labor, stated that "The contents of affirmative action programs would be useful to competitors with regard to contemplated changes in the contractor's processes, types of production, and overall business planning." Women's groups pointed out that it was difficult to see, for example, how

Harvard's affirmative action plan (of which only part has been released) would be of help to its competitors. Some colleges and universities such as the University of Michigan have made their plans public. Others have released only part of their plans; many have refused to disclose them. WEAL's testimony before Representative William Moorhead concerning affirmative action plans and the Freedom of Information Act, undoubtedly played a role in the Department of Labor's change of policy which now makes these plans available to interested parties. However, since the letter of findings also is kept confidential, it is all but impossible for women to find out what deficiencies exist on their campus, and what steps their institution is taking to correct these deficiencies.

Additional obstacles to full enforcement of the Executive Order are the understaffing of HEW's Office for Civil Rights and the relative lack of women on the contract compliance staff. Although the civil rights staff has expanded and additional positions have been requested, there is still an enormous backlog of cases and no end of new ones in sight. *More charges have been filed with HEW concerning sex discrimination than those of all the minority groups put together.* Yet there are very few women on the professional staff of HEW and virtually no women in policy-making positions. Nor are there enough women so that each compliance team has at least one woman. The director of the Office for Civil Rights has a special assistant for black affairs and a special assistant for Spanish-American affairs, but there is no special assistant to deal with the problems of women.

. . . [A]n institution charged with discrimination is not notified until just before the investigation is scheduled. Charging parties have not been notified when investigations are begun nor when they are finished; during some investigations no women or women's groups were contacted by HEW compliance teams. Moreover, policies are not uniform from one institution to another. What is sanctioned by one regional office may be viewed as a violation by investigators in another region.

Women's groups claim that HEW has shown much more concern with the educational establishment than with women's groups. HEW has met in secrecy with representatives of various educational associations in Washington, and has conducted regional meetings with presidents, vice-presidents, and personnel administrators of major universities and colleges. Only after substantial pressure did HEW finally meet for the first time with representatives of women's civil rights groups in the fall of 1971. Consequently WEAL and the Professional Women's Caucus have called for a Congressional investigation of HEW's handling of the sex discrimination investigations.

WE MAY HAVE COME A LONG WAY, BUT THERE'S STILL A LONG WAY TO GO

Despite obstacles, delays, and frustrations, the HEW investigations have nevertheless played a major role in changing the shape of attitudes toward women in the academic community. . . .

The very act of filing charges has helped to legitimize the issue and confirm the suspicion that "there really is discrimination." None of WEAL's charges of sex discrimination have ever been refuted, and the fact that a national organization has filed charges gives credence to the claim that the institution is indeed discriminating. As a result it has become far easier for women to band together both on the campus and in their professional organizations in order to fight sex discrimination. The very right to file charges frees women from being totally dependent upon the good will of their university to bring about change. Despite the image of the university as a just institution, it is far more likely to change as a result of pressure — pressure generated by the government and by women themselves. . . .

Changes have begun to be made throughout the academic community. The University of Wisconsin, as a result of HEW's investigation, decided to give 870 staff and faculty women "equity raises." The University of Maryland, the University of Maine, and other schools have allocated special funds to provide raises to women who have been discriminated against in the past. Numerous institutions have begun actively to seek out women for placement, albeit sometimes in token positions. At Harvard, Stanford, and Princeton, rules for full- and part-time employment have been revised in order to allow women (and men) to achieve tenure while working part-time. Nepotism rules have been eliminated in the State University system of New York (SUNY), and have been rewritten in numerous other institutions.

Nevertheless, on many campuses little has changed, and women remain second-class citizens. It is still dangerous for women to raise their voices in protest against discrimination, and numerous women have had their contracts terminated or their jobs abolished when they actively sought to end discriminatory policies. Although such firings are a violation of the Executive Order, HEW has been notoriously slow in getting these women reinstated. . . .

APPENDIX A: TYPICAL LETTER OF FILING[30]

The Honorable Caspar Weinberger
Secretary
Department of Health, Education and Welfare
Washington, D.C. 20201

Dear Mr. Secretary:

Please consider this letter as a formal charge of sex discrimination against _____ University. These charges are filed under Executive Order 11246 as amended, which forbids *all* federal contractors from discriminating on the basis of sex.

The charges are based on information attached to this letter giving the number of women in various units of the university. The figures detail a consistent and vicious pattern of discrimination against women at _____. For example, of 172 faculty in the College of Liberal Arts, not one woman is a full professor. Only *two* are associate professors. The remaining 44 women are in the lower ranks, without tenure. In the Psychology Department, where one would expect a substantial number of women because 23 percent of the doctorates awarded nationally go to women, there are *no* women on the faculty of 12. In the College of Education where one would also expect to find substantial numbers of women, only 5 of the 48 assistant, associate and full professors are women, although at the lowest level, fully half of the instructors are women (4 out of 8). In administration, women are present but mainly at the lower levels. There are no women deans whatsoever, nor are any of the officers of the university female.

The Women's Equity Action League requests an immediate full-scale compliance review, and that such review include an investigation of admission policies, financial aid to women students, placement of graduates, recruiting, hiring and promotion policies for all women staff and faculty, and salary inequities. We also ask that all current contract negotiations be suspended until such time as all inequities are eliminated and an acceptable plan of affirmative action is implemented. Please notify us when the compliance review begins.

Sincerely,

_____

The previous account was written by a woman who has been active in the feminist campaign for sex equality on campus since the beginning. The following excerpts from a report of the Carnegie Commission on Higher Education further detail the struggle.

30. "Note: Typically, copies of the letter are sent to the Secretary of Labor, numerous Senators and Congressmen, such as those from the institution's state, members of House and Senate Committees that deal with education, women members of Congress, and others that might be helpful. In most instances, Senators and Congressmen are asked to help, with a specific request that they write the Secretary of Health, Education and Welfare for his assistance in scheduling a compliance review. Copies also can be sent to the student newspaper and various members of the press. Charges are also filed simultaneously under Title IX, Title VII, and the Equal Pay Act." [This note follows the sample letter in Sandler's article. — Eds.]

In particular, these excerpts explain HEW's new guidelines for affirmative action at colleges and universities, provide case histories of compliance efforts at two major universities, and present selections from a number of college and university affirmative action plans.

In reading this material, particularly the affirmative action plans, consider whether or not such compliance efforts are likely to make a real difference in the employment practices of academia.

CARNEGIE COMMISSION ON HIGHER EDUCATION
OPPORTUNITIES FOR WOMEN IN HIGHER EDUCATION
129-135, 250-269 (1973)

In October 1972, the Office for Civil Rights sent to college and university presidents a detailed and explicit set of guidelines to be followed in implementing affirmative action on campuses. They apply to all educational institutions with federal contracts of over $10,000. They relate not only to women but also to members of minority groups, but we shall confine our discussion to their applicability to women. In general, the guidelines were greeted with relief in the academic community, because they showed more understanding of the special problems of academic employment than some earlier HEW actions had suggested.

Based chiefly on Executive Order 11246 (though provisions of Title VII are also pertinent), the guidelines emphasize the distinction between *nondiscrimination* and *affirmative action.* Nondiscrimination is defined as "the elimination of all existing discriminatory conditions, whether purposeful or inadvertent," on the basis of race, color, religion, national origin, or sex. Affirmative action goes beyond, ensuring "employment neutrality" in the area of deliberate and positive efforts on the part of institutions to rectify existing inequities that result from past discrimination.

To determine whether such inequities exist, and to what extent, a job analysis must be undertaken to identify "underutilization" of women, as determined by the availability of qualified women. The guidelines recognize that it is often difficult to determine figures for available academic personnel, because some faculty positions require highly specialized skills and because the recruitment pool for some institutions may be national or even international. They suggest that, in the case of senior-level positions, at least three data sources may be consulted: the National Science Foundation's National Register of Scientific and Technical Personnel,[3] the U.S. Office of Education's annual reports of earned degrees, and the National Research Council of the National Academy of Science. For junior-level positions, it is suggested that institutions consult the Office of Education's annual report of earned degrees for the past five years and data on current graduate school enrollments. In these ways, each institution can arrive at some estimate of the number of qualified women, by field, who make up the pool from which it may draw and, further, can assess the extent of their underutilization.

On the basis of this job analysis, the institution is further required to have an affirmative action plan that sets numerical goals consistent with the available pool and with projected turnover in employment and that specifies a time schedule for improving the situation. The guidelines stress that these goals are targets to be aimed at, not quotas that must be met within the specified time period.

The institution itself, not HEW, establishes the criteria for hiring, promotion, etc., and is required to make them "reasonably explicit" and available to applicants and employees. The individual departments or units at an institution must keep records that document reasons for employment decisions; in addition, a central institutional office

---

3. The Committee on the Status of Women in the Economics Profession has found the National Roster quite incomplete, especially because it tends to include only persons who are employed.

must audit and monitor the departments and units, making a formal report annually to the Office for Civil Rights (OCR) on the progress of the affirmative action program. OCR is empowered to examine the relevant documents with the intention of determining whether the institution has been making "good faith" efforts to implement its program.

Other important requirements (or recommendations) covered by the guidelines are (1) that institutions take active steps to identify and recruit women by using search committees that include women, by drawing on data provided by women's groups and disciplinary and professional associations, by advertising openings through channels that will reach women, and by stating in such advertising that they are equal opportunity employers; (2) that salaries be based on qualifications and merit rather than on ascriptive qualities; (3) that antinepotism rules be abolished; (4) that policies which prohibit a department from hiring its own graduate students be reconsidered, since they have often worked to the disadvantage of women; (5) that maternity leave be granted to women and parental leave for child rearing be granted to both sexes; and (6) that sound internal grievance procedures be developed. Finally, the institution must have a written policy of nondiscrimination and must publish its affirmative action plan. . . .

SOME CASE HISTORIES

In November 1970 it was reported that investigations of alleged employment discrimination against women were under way or had been completed at about 18 colleges and universities.[4] Since then there have been many more charges and investigations. There is little need to discuss the charges in detail. Enough has been said in the preceding section to provide an indication of the status of women on college and university faculties. One point worth repeating and often made by women pressing charges is that, in general, the more prestigious the institution, the fewer women are to be found in the higher ranks of its faculty.

One of the first institutions to be extensively involved in negotiations relating to charges of sex discrimination was the University of Michigan, whose president, Robben W. Fleming, is a labor lawyer with a long record of experience in arbitration and industrial relations. Following an investigation, it was reported that a contract awarded to the institution by the Agency for International Development was being held up. Shortly thereafter, HEW issued a list of nine requirements that the university would have to meet to continue its eligibility for federal contracts:

1. Achieve salary equity in every job category.
2. Compensate through payment of back wages each female employee who has lost wages due to discriminatory treatment. Payments must be retroactive to October 13, 1968 (the date of Executive Order 11246).
3. Achieve a ratio of female employment in academic positions at least equivalent to availability as determined by the number of qualified female applicants.
4. Increase ratios of female admissions to all Ph.D. graduate programs.
5. Increase the participation of women in committees involving the selection and treatment of employees.
6. Develop a written policy on nepotism which will ensure correct treatment of tandem teams.
7. Analyze the past effects of antinepotism policies and retroactively compensate (to October 13, 1968) any person who has suffered discrimination as a result.
8. Assure that female applicants for nonacademic employment receive consider-

---

4. These included Albany State College, Georgia; Borough of Manhattan Community College; Brooklyn College; Brown University; Georgia Institute of Technology; Georgia State University; Harvard University; Loyola University, Los Angeles; New Mexico State University; St. John's University, New York; Tufts University; University of Georgia; University of Pittsburgh; University of Michigan; University of San Francisco; University of Texas Medical School in Dallas; University of Vermont; and University of Wisconsin ("HEW Probing Alleged Employment Bias [Against Women on at Least 18 Campuses," *Chronicle of Higher Education*, Nov. 9, 1970)].

ation commensurate with their qualifications; also ensure that any conception of male and female job classifications is eliminated in recruitment procedures.

9. Assure that all present female employees occupying clerical and other nonacademic positions and possessing qualifications equal to, or exceeding, those of male employees occupying higher level positions be given primary consideration for promotion [Bazell, Sex Discrimination: Campuses Face Contract Loss Over HEW Demands, 170 Science 834-835 (Nov. 20, 1970)].

In January 1971, it was reported that the university and HEW had reached agreement and that several contracts that had been withheld were being approved. President Fleming had protested the third requirement listed above as "unworkable because it ignores the quality of applicants and lends itself to artificially increasing the number of women who apply." According to the university, HEW had agreed that other factors in addition to the percentage of applications should be considered. On the fourth provision, it was reported that the question of the ratio of women admitted to Ph.D. programs had been submitted to then-HEW Secretary Elliot L. Richardson for a ruling. The university contended that there were no Ph.D. programs in which admissions were specifically related to employment opportunities [U. of Michigan, HEW Agree on Plan to End Sex Bias, Chronicle of Higher Education, Jan. 11, 1971, p. 4]. We have been informed that the ruling was never issued. The legal situation relating to admission to Ph.D. programs has, of course, changed under the provisions of Educational Amendments of 1972, which ban discrimination by graduate and professional schools.

On January 4, 1971, President Fleming appointed a Commission for Women to evaluate and monitor fulfillment of the affirmative action goals. In November 1972, Science magazine reported that the commission was regarded by some women as too "establishment," but that it had "a secure place, an influential voice, and a no-nonsense chairwoman, lawyer Virginia Davis Nordin, who divides her time between the commission and her teaching job at the Center for Continuing Legal Education." . . .

We have been informed that Michigan's affirmative action plan has been revised several times, in an attempt to meet HEW objections, but that it has not yet (July 1973) received HEW approval.

Even more protracted than those of Michigan have been Columbia University's negotiations with the federal government. A series of negotiations began on January 31, 1969. Eleven months later the university submitted an affirmative action plan to the Office for Civil Rights. The plan was accepted with the condition that Columbia make a series of modifications. At that stage the concern was over employment opportunities for minority groups. It was only later, when charges were filed by a group of Columbia women, that the question of women was brought into the contention. According to J. Stanley Pottinger, then director of HEW's Office for Civil Rights, the requested modifications were never received, and, therefore, in February 1971, his office initiated a second review of Columbia's employment practices. In November 1971, it was reported that Pottinger was asking the department's general counsel to initiate action "to terminate all existing federal contracts with Columbia University and all of its divisions and to debar the University and all of its divisions from future participation in federal contracts." The action was reported to be the first time that the OCR had initiated formal proceedings to end all federal contracts with a university, although approval of contracts with about 35 institutions had been temporarily delayed [Semas, File an Acceptable Equal Employment Plan or Lose U.S. Contracts, Columbia Told, Chronicle of Higher Education, Nov. 15, 1971, p. 5].

In March 1972 the ban on federal contracts was lifted when Columbia submitted an interim affirmative action plan, and in September 1972 it was reported that the Office for Civil Rights was drafting a letter indicating acceptance of Columbia's "final affirmative action" plan, while "raising some areas of concern which will be negotiated out later." [Columbia Passes U.S. Test on Jobs, New York Times, September 2, 1972].

Excerpts from Columbia's plan, which was published in December 1972, are included in Appendix D.

However, in February 1973, it was reported that once again the federal government had held up a $1.9 million contract with Columbia, pending a meeting between the university and the OCR to determine if Columbia's affirmative action plan had been violated. A Columbia women's organization had complained to the OCR that two recent appointments had violated the plan [Columbia Contract Withheld, Chronicle of Higher Education, Feb. 26, 1973, p.2]. . . .

APPENDIX D. SELECTED PROVISIONS OF AFFIRMATIVE ACTION PLANS
OR COMMITTEE RECOMMENDATIONS ON AFFIRMATIVE ACTION,
SELECTED COLLEGES AND UNIVERSITIES

Sources:

1. Columbia University Affirmative Action Program (Condensed Version), December 1972.
2. Harvard University, University News Office, Release, May 4, 1973.
3. "The Status of Women at Oberlin," (excerpts and summaries from the Report and Recommendations from the Ad Hoc Committee on the Status of Women at Oberlin, Oberlin Alumni Magazine, pp. 6-13, March-April 1973 (most of the recommendations have been adopted).
4. Affirmative Action Plan of Stanford University, November 13, 1972.
5. New York State Education Department: Equal Opportunity for Women: A Statement of Policy and Proposed Action by the Regents of the University of the State of New York, Albany, N.Y., April 1972.
6. "University of California Affirmative Action Personnel Program: Policy and Guidelines," University Bulletin, vol. 21, pp. 88-94, January 22, 1973.

Goals and Timetables

Columbia:

In the following pages, goals for faculty recruitment are stated as targets for good faith efforts over a period of five years, because Columbia operates on a basis of five-year projections, annually updated under the master-planning requirements of New York State as well as under our own planning and budgetary policies. Annual changes in the composition of faculties and professional research staff will be identified, goals will be revised accordingly, and where there is opportunity to do so, attempts will be made to accelerate progress.

Goals are expressed in terms of new appointments only, not in terms of the composition of any faculty or school. For each of the schools or faculties, the number of new appointments has been estimated from projected terminations due to retirements, resignations, and expiration of terms of appointment, as adjusted for planned changes in faculty size. The University's goals are directly tied to the number of recruiting opportunities which result from the normal processes of faculty growth and attrition and which are possible to achieve through nondiscriminatory, nonpreferential hiring practices. . . . University policy proscribes recruitment efforts limited to any sex or ethnic group as well as faculty employment decisions based upon the treatment of sexual or ethnic identification alone as a qualification. . . .

Possible deficiencies are identified by comparing the percentage of women . . . in the nation's potential professoriate, by specialty, with the percentage on the various schools and faculties at Columbia utilizing that specialty. Where statistical discrepancies appear, the problem arises as to whether or not they are deficiencies indicative of discrimination requiring corrective action. Two possibilities exist: that the discrepancy arises primarily from a practice within the University or that it results from a cause external to the University, such as, perhaps, an occupational mobility pattern in which women leave good positions to accommodate changes in the job location of husbands or a traditional family pattern which has impeded professional advancement. The University's goals are therefore expressed not in terms of single or fixed numbers but as a range of possible actions on new appointments resulting from recruitment policies which include active search for talent among women and minorities. One point on this range is the number of new appointments that would result if the current profile of a given school or faculty were to continue unchanged; the other point on this range is the number of new appointments that would result if appointment at the rate of availability in the national pool were accomplished.

In schools or faculties whose profiles indicate that Columbia's recruitment meets or exceeds the national pool availability rate, the University's goals range from a "low option" — appointment of women and minorities at less than Columbia's profile but still at the national pool average — to a "high option" — such appointments at Columbia's traditionally high rate of utilization of women and minorities.

In schools or faculties whose profiles suggest underutilization of women or minorities, the range of possible personnel actions similarly reflects a "low option" — appointments which maintain the current rate of utilization — and a "high option" — new appointments at the national pool rate. In these cases, where women or minorities have been attracted to Columbia at a rate less than their availability in the national pool, Columbia's stated goal is to move toward parity of utilization by employing the "high option".

Columbia undertakes these "high option" goals with the specific understanding that goals are targets for good faith effort and are not inflexible quotas. . . .

The numerical goals required by Executive Order 11246 which result from the application of these principles have been calculated by school or faculty. . . .

For the faculty of Philosophy . . . 28 tenured and 79 nontenured full-time faculty openings are projected to occur from 1972 to 1977. With a national pool of approximately 20 percent women and a 1971-72 full-time faculty composition of 24 percent women, the goal for this faculty ranges from 19 to 25 appointments of women over the next five-year period, of which three to six would be in the tenure ranks.

For the faculty of Political Science . . . it is estimated that approximately 28 tenured and 41 nontenured full-time positions will be filled in the next 5 years. . . . With a national pool of approximately 10 percent women, a goal of seven new appointments of faculty women is indicated, three to tenure rank. . . .

Three other large professional schools — Business, Engineering, and Law — have far smaller national pools of women, varying from 1.9 percent to 5.5. percent, on which to draw for faculty recruitment. With an aggregate of 23 tenured and 48 nontenured full-time positions opening up in the next five years, a goal of six tenured or nontenured appointments of women to these faculties is projected. . . .

Harvard:

Harvard University has completed a comprehensive affirmative action program report establishing University wide goals for hiring women and minority-group members during the next two academic years, and promising updated goals every two years. . . .

Outlined for the first time in this report are the "utilization analyses" — procedures now used by the University's academic and administrative departments to determine the size of the labor pools in their areas and the percentage of women and minorities in these pools. . . .

The detailed charts of hiring goals through June 30, 1975, include annual projections of how many women and members of minority groups will hold jobs in a specific category, how many such jobs there will be and how many of this total will become available over the two-year period, through turnover and expansion.

For instance, 14 women and 32 members of minority groups now hold full professorships, out of a total of 743 professorships in all faculties. By June of 1974, the number of professorships is projected to rise to 757, including one more woman professor and two more from minority groups. By June of 1975, projections show 18 women and 36 minority group professors out of a total of 761.

The number of women in the rank of Associate Professor — now 14 of 280 — is projected to increase by half, to 21 (of 294) by 1974 and to 24 (of 302) by 1975. . . .

Of the 109 Assistant Professorships expected to become available by 1974-75, 17 are expected to go to women and members of minority groups, bringing the 1975 projected totals at this rank to 57 women and 35 minority group members out of 566 posts. . . .

Oberlin:

Recommendation 4: The faculty must commit itself to the goal of increasing the rate of hiring women for regular positions on the faculty such that, within a three-year period, the percentage of women on the faculty will reflect *as a minimum* the percentage of women in the candidate pool. Further, as positions become available, *each department* will make strong efforts to hire one or more women.

Stanford:

An analysis has been made of the representation of women, Blacks, Chicanos, and Orientals on the professorial faculty. . . . The results are summarized here.

There will be eighteen Blacks, nine Chicanos, and nineteen Orientals on the professorial faculty in the 1972–73 academic year, as counted in July. . . . While these numbers are small in comparison to the total faculty of approximately one thousand, they are not disproportionate with the number of available Ph.D.'s. The figure of eighteen Blacks is consistent with estimates that fewer than two percent of the Ph.D. degrees awarded in the decade beginning in 1960 were received by Blacks. Similarly, the figure of nine Chicanos is appreciable considering that there are fewer than two hundred Chicano Ph.D. degree holders in the United States. The figure of nineteen Orientals cannot currently be analyzed, since there are no appropriate statistics.

There will be sixty-four women on the professorial faculty in 1972–73. Analysis suggests that some departments may have fewer women than might be expected based on a statistical analysis of female Ph.D. holders in the field.

The faculty affirmative action officer met with individual deans and department chairmen in spring 1972 to discuss problem areas and goals. Six departments were identified as problem areas, so far as numbers of women were concerned, and specific five-year hiring goals were established.

Stanford has a substantial number of women employed in nonprofessorial academic positions, such as lecturer or instructor. An analysis of the number of women and ethnic minorities in these positions is a high priority item for 1972–73. The question is being considered in three different ways. A faculty committee on the professoriate is currently reviewing the entire faculty structure. The faculty affirmative action officer has been assigned responsibility to review procedures for making certain that appointments and salary scales of given individuals are appropriate for them. And the faculty affirmative action officer, and other members of the provost's staff, are examining the ongoing appointment procedures with particular concern for new nonprofessorial appointments. . . .

Search Procedures

Columbia:

The availability of documentation to establish that nondiscriminatory procedures have been followed, and positive steps have been taken to include qualified women and minority groups in academic recruitment efforts, is necessary for approval of the proposed offers of appointments. The required documentation consists of the following: (1) Statement of standard search and evaluation procedures. A general statement describing the standard procedures followed by the school or department in identifying and evaluating candidates for appointment should be filed. . . . This general statement should indicate school or department practice concerning the use and selection of search committees, how the school or department makes position openings known, whether seminar or class appearances and student reports are used to evaluate candidates, and the manner in which the department or school decides upon particular candidates. . . . (2) Search report. A brief report of the specific search for the candidate for whom clearance is requested should accompany each clearance request. This report . . . should identify the institutions and professional groups canvassed, the relevant professional files or registries utilized and the names and institutional affiliations of the individuals consulted, including women and minority professionals in the discipline. The report should also identify the media communication utilized in making the position opening known.

Harvard:

"In order to increase the representation of minority persons and women in the professional ranks, the various faculties have been expanding their candidate searches and have instituted measures to ensure that all sources of potential minority and women professors are sought out. . . ."

These measures include checking such information sources as learned and professional societies and examining information issued by the President's Office on women and minorities with the appropriate qualifying degrees. The report also suggests consultation with "female and minority scholars," and the inclusion of "women and minority-group members in the department" on the committees screening candidates for tenured appointments.

Oberlin:

Recommendation 3: Departments must be required to include qualified women among the candidates interviewed for faculty positions or to show convincing evidence that it was not possible for them to do so.

Stanford:

The faculty search is central to faculty affirmative action. Search committees at Stanford are encouraged to consult with their University resources — women and minority group members on campus — for advice on candidates who might otherwise be missed.

Search committees are expected to inform all universities with significant activity in the field for which a vacancy exists of a faculty position for which they seek candidates. In addition, search committees are expected to inform committees for minorities and women within appropriate professional societies of the opening. Finally, search committees have been and will be encouraged to advertise the opening for which they seek candidates in appropriate professional journals.

University of California:

Current methods of recruitment and search for candidates for appointment shall be reviewed, and new or modified methods shall be introduced in order to broaden the scope of the search. Priority shall be given to the effective recruitment of minority and women applicants for those occupational categories and employing units where underutilization has been determined to exist.

Special Affirmative Action Funding

Stanford:

Because the Stanford University faculty is not expected to grow appreciably during the next decade, it is particularly important to provide a special means for increasing the proportion of women and ethnic minority group members on the faculty. The Faculty Affirmative Action Fund serves that purpose exclusively. It is especially useful for the general purpose of hiring individuals who are outstanding scholars and teachers who may be expected to contribute significantly to the University's educational needs, but who do not fit exactly the specifications for an existing faculty opening. . . .

. . . The Fund was announced in December 1971 with a budget of $75,000 of annually recurring . . . "budget-base money." Once the funds are allotted to support an appointment they continue within the budget of a given department for the duration of the individual's appointment. The Fund was used to support partially or completely the appointment of sixteen faculty members [in 1971–72] and involved considerably more than the designated $75,000 because of special opportunities.

Salary Equity

Columbia:

Average salaries of officers of instruction and officers of research as of 1971 were analyzed to identify salary differences between men and women and between minority groups and others. Among full-time officers of instruction, 57 cases were found out of a possible 111 in which there were salary differences larger than 5% among members of the identified groups holding the same rank. . . . Twenty-two of these cases were discrepancies in favor of women or minority groups. Of the remaining 35, in which the difference was in favor of men or majority group members, the large majority were accounted for by differences in length of time in rank or by merit considerations. The small remaining number of differences has been corrected or will be corrected by salary adjustments in the next fiscal year (1972–73).

Columbia's nondiscriminatory salary policies are strongly evident also in part-time faculty salaries. Here, the mean salaries of men and women and minority group members approach absolute equality, with all discrepancies favoring women and minorities. . . .

Oberlin:

Recommendation 1: That the appropriate bodies of the College undertake immediately to determine what members of the Faculty have suffered salary and rank inequities, to take positive steps to eliminate those inequities within a two-year period, and to consider ways of compensating for past inequities.

Stanford:

During the 1971–72 academic year, the salary of every female faculty and teaching staff member was reviewed to assure that it was equal to that of males with equal duties and accomplishments. Where discrepancies were found, salaries were increased accordingly.

Part-time Employment

Oberlin:

Recommendation 6: It is recommended that there be created a category of part-time full status faculty described as follows: to have responsibility for at least one credit-bearing course approved by the department or by EPPC, to be hired through the regular hiring process, to have no employment elsewhere; to hold a regular academic rank appropriate to training and experience; to receive a salary proportionate to the fraction of responsibility at the rank held and to be eligible for full or prorated support for research and other professional activities; to assume all normal faculty non-teaching responsibilities, including participation in departmental and faculty meetings with the right to vote, prorated advising, service on committees, and other administrative duties; to be eligible for multiple year contracts, and for tenure; to be considered as eligible candidates for full-time positions as they become available.

Recommendation 7: Departments, deans, and councils are strongly urged to be open to the possibilities of creating part-time full status faculty who may wish part-time full status employment for reasons such as health, family, research, or the desire for partial retirement.

Stanford:

In September 1971, the provost reaffirmed existing University policy: "There is no University wide policy which prohibits the appointment of regular faculty members — tenured or nontenured — at any rank on a part-time basis." . . . This clarification of existing policy was important to affirmative action for women. . . . the memorandum specifically notes ". . . regular part-time appointments offer the possibility of appointing noted scholars who are not available full time, faculty members who wish to assume an active role in child rearing. . . ."

Lecturers

Oberlin:

Recommendation 5: It is recommended that the category of lecturer be abolished. [The report included the following discussion of the reasons for this recommendation.]

In April 1970, the faculty of Oberlin voted to abolish its 40-year-old anti-nepotism rule. The report of the Committee on Concurrent Employment of Family Members . . . concluded with a brief analysis of the connection between the status of lecturer and the discriminatory effects of the anti-nepotism rule on married women. The Committee asked that the College re-examine its policy with regard to lecturers.

The Committee on the Status of Women investigated the status of lecturers as well as the larger question of the status and definition of part-time teaching at Oberlin. Part-time teaching appointments in the past have provided only marginal or subprofessional status. At present regular faculty appointments are not usually made on a part-time basis. Nor is there, as the Colish report points out, any "provision in the lecturer rank as it is currently conceived for raises providing systematic rewards for experience and professional growth, for leaves of absence or for other fringe benefits. Lecturers do not have a vote in faculty meetings, although the matters decided . . . often have a direct bearing on their working conditions. . . .

The heritage of the anti-nepotism rule leaves us with some unfinished business. Because the rule strengthened associations between part-time teaching and marginal status, its effects are still felt in attitudes toward, and definitions of, part-time teaching positions. . . .

In the next decade, male as well as female academics may begin to feel the need for more flexible schedules and for new definitions of "regular" faculty status. Foreseeing that the opportunity for part-time full status teaching appointments will allow both men and women to create a greater variety of individual life and career patterns than is now possible, the Committee recommends the granting of full professional status to fully qualified women and men who wish, as the needs of departments allow, to teach part-time.

Delay of Tenure

Stanford:

In order to make Stanford University a more attractive institution for women faculty, and to assure that untenured female faculty have an appropriate opportunity to develop and prove themselves as scholars, the following statement was appended to the Statement of Policy on Appointment and Tenure. . . .

> A faculty member who gives birth while serving under an appointment which accrues time toward tenure by length of service may, subject to any necessary reappointment, have the time after which tenure would be conferred by length or service extended by one year. No more than two such extensions shall be allowed.

University of the State of New York:

Colleges and universities should encourage adequate career opportunities for women faculty members and administrators by such arrangements as . . . authorizing maternity leaves, with guarantee of job reservation and the postponement of tenure decisions by length of leave. . . .

Antinepotism Policies

Columbia:

Employment opportunities are offered to spouses and other relatives on a competitive basis. The University policy states a negative preference in cases where the job is under the immediate supervision of a spouse or close relative. Even in these cases, however, no prohibition is expressed, and a number of instances can be cited where close relatives work in the same University department.

Harvard:

The nepotism policy declares that members of the same immediate family "should not" work for each other in the same unit, with exceptions made at the discretion of the appropriate dean or vice-president.

Stanford:

It is the policy of Stanford University to seek for its faculty the best possible teachers and scholars, who are judged to be so in a national (or international) search preceding each appointment and promotion. There are no bars to the appointment of close relatives to the faculty, in the same or different departments, so long as each meets this standard. . . . No faculty member . . . shall vote, make recommendations, or in any way participate in the decision of any matter which may directly affect the appointment, tenure, promotion, salary, or other status or interest of a close relative.

University of the State of New York:

Colleges and universities should encourage adequate career opportunities for women faculty members and administrators by such arrangements as . . . eliminating nepotism rules.

University of California:

[Note: The issue of modifying the formerly strict antinepotism rules has been much debated at the University of California in recent years. The rules were liberalized somewhat in July 1971, and the policy then adopted is included here in full as it appears in the University personnel manual. We have been informed, however, that additional changes are under consideration.]

Policy. The employment of near relatives in the same department is permitted when such employment has been authorized in accordance with the following subsections. Such concurrent employment may arise under the following circumstances:

1. Two employees already holding positions in the same department subsequently become near relatives.

2. Simultaneous appointment of near relatives in the same department is recommended.

3. Appointment of one who is the near relative of an individual already employed in the same department is recommended.

Definition. Near relatives include parents and children, husband, wife, brother, sister, brother-in-law, sister-in-law, mother-in-law, father-in-law, son-in-law, daughter-in-law; and step relatives in the same relationship.

Standards. In searching for qualified candidates for a new or vacant position in a department, those persons responsible for recruitment shall not disqualify a candidate by reason of near relationship to an appointee already in the department or by reason of near relationship when simultaneous appointment of near relatives in the same department is recommended. When the recommended appointment involves such near relationship, this fact shall be noted in the recommendation, and an analysis of the possible conflict of interest or other disadvantage in the situation shall be forwarded through normal channels with the recommendation in sufficient time to permit complete review of the case before the proposed effective date.

Restriction. A member of the University staff shall not participate in the processes of review and decision-making on any matter concerning appointment, promotion, salary, retention, or termination of a near relative.

Authority. Each Chancellor (or, for positions under his jurisdiction, a Vice President) is authorized to approve an appointment in which a near-relative relationship in a department is involved or when simultaneous appointment of near relatives in the same department is recommended if, after review of the cases, he considers the appointments to be justified and in the best interest of the University. Such review and approval by the Chancellor or Vice President is also required to authorize the continuance of the appointments of two members in the same department when a near-relative relationship is established between them.

This authority may not be redelegated.

Maternity Leave

Columbia:

Any employee with at least six month's service who is pregnant shall be eligible for unpaid maternity leave. . . . Such leave shall not exceed nine months in duration. . . . No employee shall be discharged by reason of pregnancy or direct medical results thereof while on maternity leave. Each employee, upon return to active status, shall be reemployed in the same position or in a position of equivalent rank and salary.

Harvard:

This latter policy [maternity leave] has been amended to grant a pregnant woman sick pay earned during her period of employment "for the period she is physically unable to work because of childbirth." Previously, maternity leaves of absence were taken without pay.

Oberlin:

Recommendation 16: The Committee recommends the establishment of a uniform maternity leave policy to apply to *all* females employees of the College. We support a policy which would grant women up to one month paid maternity leave and up to two additional months of unpaid child care leave, without penalty or loss of seniority.

Stanford:

The University has revised its operating policy on maternity leave to establish maternity leave as a right, and guarantees the same or comparable position to a person returning from maternity leave. . . . Stanford's health plans have been changed to extend existing maternity benefits to unwed mothers. . . . Stanford's health plans have been modified to include benefits for abortion.

University of the State of New York:

Colleges and universities should encourage adequate career opportunities for women faculty members and administrators by such arrangements as (1) authorizing maternity leaves, with guarantee of job reservation and the postponement of tenure decisions by length of leave. . . .

Students

Oberlin:

Recommendation 8: It is recommended that all faculty and other College personnel recognize the existence of differential treatment as experienced by students and examine their own attitudes and practices in this regard. Conscientious attempts must be made by all members of the College community to rectify existing attitudinal and functional inequities in the treatment of students. Students should be counseled according to their capabilities. This is particularly important as more students enter fields not in accordance with traditional sexual stereotypes and where few if any female role models exist. . . .

University of the State of New York:

There must be no quota limitations on the admission of women in coeducational colleges, universities and professional schools. Admission standards must be the same for men and women, and individuals who meet the qualifications for admission must be accepted on the first come first served basis. . . . Loans, scholarships and fellowships must be available to all students without regard to sex.

Note: The Backlash

The case studies presented by Sandler and the Carnegie Commission of contract compliance efforts at Michigan and Columbia contain only faint hints of the storm which was generated in the academic community over affirmative action requirements in federal contracts. The article by Pottinger alludes to some of the criticisms, but the most vehement to date were from a political scientist at the University of California in Berkeley, writing in Commentary magazine. His article attacking HEW's efforts was followed by a contentious batch of letters to the editor, called the Pottinger papers. Selections from the original article and from some of the letters are printed below.

Seabury, HEW and the Universities
53 Commentary 38-44 (February 1972)

. . . In the dynamics of competition between race and sex for scarce places on university faculties, a new hidden crisis of higher education is brewing. As universities climb out of the rubble of campus disorders of the 1960's, beset by harsh budgetary reverses, they now are required to redress national social injustices within their walls at their own expense. Compliance with demands from the federal government to do this would compel a stark remodeling of their criteria of recruitment; their ethos of professionalism, and their standards of excellence. Refusal to comply satisfactorily would risk their destruction. . . .

As the federal government of the United States moves uncertainly to establish equitable racial patterns in universities and colleges, it does so with few guidelines from historical experience. The management, manipulation, and evaluation of quotas, targets, and goals for preferential hiring are certainly matters as complex as are the unusual politics which such announced policies inspire. How equitably to assuage the many group claimants for preference, context-by-context, occasion-by-occasion, and year-by-year, as these press and jostle among themselves for prior attention in preference, must by now occasion some puzzlement even among HEW bureaucrats. . . .

Fifteen years ago, David Riesman in his Constraint and Variety in American Education pointed to certain qualities which distinctively characterized avant-garde institutions of higher learning in this country. The world of scholarship, he said, "is democratic rather than aristocratic in tone, and scholars are made, not born." . . . In America, the relative decline of ethnic and social-class snobberies and discrimination, combined with immense expansion of the colleges, drew into scholarship a great majority whose backgrounds were distinctly unscholarly. . . . In contrast to his European counterparts, the American scholar found few colleagues among the mass of under-graduates on the basis either of "a common culture or a common ideology in the political or eschatological sense." Paradoxically this democratization of the university (with its stress not on status but upon excellence in performance) had not begun in rank-and-file small colleges of the nation, which were exemplars of America's ethnic, religious, and cultural diversity. Rather it had come out of those innovating institutions which, in quest of excellence, either abandoned or transcended much of their discriminatory sociological parochialism. It was the denominational college, where deliberate discrimination according to sex, religion, color, and culture continued to be practiced in admissions and faculty recruitment, which made up the rear of the snake-like academic procession. The egalitarianism of excellence, a democracy of performance, was an ethos consummated by the avant-garde. Riesman labelled the disciplines of the great universities the "race-courses of the mind." . . .

The greatest boost to America's universities came in the 1930's from European emigré scholars whose powerful influence (notably in the sciences and social sciences) is still felt even today. As exemplars of learning, their impact upon young and parochial American students was profound. Thanks in part to them, by the 1950's the great American universities attained an authentic cosmopolitanism of scholarship matched by no other university system in the world. And the outward reach of American higher education toward the best the world of scholarship could offer generated an inward magnetism, attracting to itself the most qualified students who could be found to study with these newly renowned faculties.

This system of recruitment also left a myriad of American sociological categories statistically underrepresented in the highest precincts of American higher education. Today, with respect to race and ethnicity, blacks, Irish, Italians, Greeks, Poles, and all other Slavic groups (including Slovaks, Slovenes, Serbs, Czechs, and Croatians) are underrepresented. On faculties, at least, women are underrepresented. Important religious categories are underrepresented. . . .

The best universities, which also happen to be those upon which HEW has chiefly worked its knout, habitually and commonsensically recruit from other best institutions. The top universities hire the top 5 per cent of graduate students in the top ten universities. This is the "skill pool" they rely upon. Some may now deem such practices archaic but they have definitely served to maintain quality. Just as definitely they have not served to obtain "equality of results" in terms of the proportional representation of sociological categories. Such equality assumes that faculties somehow must "represent" designated categories of people on grounds other than those of professional qualification. . . .

If departments abandon the practice of looking to the best pools from which they can hope to draw, then quality must in fact be jeopardized. To comply with HEW orders, every department must come up not with the *best* candidate, but with the best-qualified *woman* or *non-white* candidate. For when a male or a white candidate is actually selected or recommended, it is now incumbent on both department and university to *prove* that no qualified woman or non-white was found available. Some universities already have gone so far in emulating the federal bureaucracy as to have installed their own bureaucratic monitors, in the form of affirmative-action coordinators, to screen recommendations for faculty appointments before final action is taken.

A striking contradiction exists between HEW's insistence that faculties prove they do not discriminate and its demand for goals and timetables which require discrimination to occur. For there is no reason to suppose that equitable processes in individual cases will automatically produce results which are set in the timetables and statistical goals universities are now required to develop. If all that HEW wishes is evidence that universities are bending over backward to be fair, why should it require them to have statistical goals at all? Do they know something no one else knows, about where fairness inevitably leads?

Yet another facet of HEW's procedures goes to the very heart of faculty due process: its demand of the right of access to faculty files, when searching for evidence of discrimination. Such files have always been the most sacrosanct documents of academia, and for good reason: it has been assumed that candor in the evaluation of candidates and personnel is best guaranteed by confidentiality of comment; and that evasiveness, caution, smoke-screening, and grandstanding — which would be the principal consequences of open files — would debase standards of judgment. In the past, universities have denied federal authorities — the FBI for instance — access to these files. Now HEW demands access. And it is the recent reluctance of the Berkeley campus of the University of California to render unto this agent of Caesar what was denied to previous agents, which occasioned the HEW ultimatum of possible contract suspension: $72 million. One might imagine the faculty would be in an uproar, what with Nixon's men ransacking the inner temple. But no. In this as in other aspects of this curious story, the faculty is silent. . . .

Some of us in the league of lost liberals are still wont to say that the Constitution is color-blind. Yet now under the watchful eye of federal functionaries, academic administrators are compelled to be as acutely sensitive as Kodachrome to the outward physical appearance of their faculty members and of proposed candidates for employment. . . .

While deans, chancellors, and personnel officials struggle with these momentous matters, faculties and graduate students with few exceptions are silent. HEW is acting in the name of social justice. Who in the prevailing campus atmosphere would openly challenge anything done in that name? Tenured faculty perhaps consult their private interests and conclude that whatever damage the storm may do to less-protected colleagues or to their job-seeking students, prudence suggests a posture of silence. Others perhaps, refusing to admit that contending interests are involved, believe that affirmative action is cost-free, and that all will benefit from it in the Keynesian long run. But someone *will* pay: namely very large numbers of white males who are among those distinguishable as "best qualified" and who will be shunted aside in the frantic quest for "disadvantaged qualifiables."

The inequities implied in affirmative action, and the concealed but real costs to individuals, would probably have had less damaging effects upon such highly-skilled graduate students had they been imposed in the early 1960's. Then, the sky was the limit on the growth and the affluence of higher education. If a pie gets bigger, so may its slices enlarge; nobody *seems* to lose. Such is today not the case. The pie now shrinks. One West Coast state college, for example, last year alone lost nearly 70 budgeted faculty positions due to financial stringency. Yet this same college has just announced the boldest affirmative-action program in California higher education. "Decided educational advantages can accrue to the college," it said, "by having its faculty as well as its student body be more representative of the minority population of the area. *It is therefore expected that a substantial majority of all new faculty appointments during the immediate academic years will be from minorities, including women, until the underutilization no longer exists.*" (Italics added.) Departments which refuse to play the game will have their budgets reviewed by university officials.

It is hard to say how widely such pernicious practices have been institutionalized in other colleges and universities. But were they to be generalized across the nation, one thing is certain: either large numbers of highly-qualified scholars will pay with their careers simply because they are male and white, *or,* affirmative action will have failed in its benevolent purposes. . . .

It seems superfluous to end this chronicle of woe with mention of another heavy cost — one not so immediately visible — in the forceful administration of affirmative-action hiring goals. This is that men will be less able to know, much less sustain, the professional standards by which they and others judge and are judged. . . .

Selected Letters from Readers:
The Pottinger Papers, HEW, Affirmative Action
and the Universities
53 Commentary 13-15, 16-18 (May 1972)

To the Editor of Commentary: . . .

(10) Mr. Seabury talks about HEW's access to personnel files, speaking of the "sacrosanct documents of academia," and the need for confidentiality. He does not mention that HEW employees cannot reveal these documents to anyone without losing their jobs. The information is exempt from the Freedom of Information Act and is protected from disclosure by 5 U.S.C. 552(b)(7) U.S. Code.

As I mentioned earlier, the institution, of course, has agreed to show these documents when it signed the contracts in the first place. If Mr. Seabury knows how to tell if discrimination against women and minorities has occurred without allowing examination of personnel files, I wish he would let the rest of us know how to do this.

(11) Mr. Seabury worries about the impact of such affirmative action on white males. Of course, it will be harder for some of them to get jobs. For years white males have used their sex and color as a way of keeping the competition (non-white, non-males) from competing with them in the first place. Well-qualified males will now have to compete with well-qualified women and minorities. Hiring that is in line with the government's policy is on the basis of ability; the best-qualified person is hired regardless of sex or color or national origin, even if that person turns out to be white and male. The intent is not to give preference to any group, but to see that all groups are considered equally. In a recent consent decree in the Libby Owens Ford case, the judge stated that when discrimination ends, some people may indeed lose something, but what they lose is what they were not entitled to in the first place.

Discrimination against women is the last socially acceptable prejudice. It has gone unchallenged and unchecked, particularly in the academic world, for too many years. I assume that Mr. Seabury likewise condemns such discrimination. What he would suggest doing about it remains to be seen.

Bernice Sandler

Executive Associate and Director
Project on the Status and Education of Women
Association of American Colleges
Washington, D.C.

To the Editor of Commentary:

Paul Seabury's article . . . is filled with fine examples of the emotive use of language: women who attempt to utilize the Civil Rights Act are "horning in"; the inclusion of women in the Act is termed "a fit of inspired raillery," "a perverse stratagem," "a fall-back strategy"; HEW investigators are "Nixon's men ransacking the inner temple"; statistics demonstrating compliance with the law are "body counts." The article offers as evidence quotations from vague, unverifiable sources: "a white third-year law student," "an enthusiastic affirmative-action administrator," "a Women's Commission lady" at Michigan. . . . Finally, and most important, it . . . omits any relevant evidence. First of all, Mr. Seabury never mentions the fact that the goal is representation of minorities on faculties in proportion to their number in a *relevant* community. For a university teaching position, a relevant community would not be the local community in which the university is situated (although this might be the relevant community for non-teaching positions) or the total population of the United States, but might be the total pool of Ph.D.'s produced in the field in a given period, or the number of graduate students in that particular university at a given time. Universities are asked to supply their *own* affirmative-action plan, subject to HEW approval. An example of a possible plan is set forth in the recommendations of the Report of the Committee on the Status of Women in the Faculty of Arts and Sciences (Harvard University, April, 1971):

> The Harvard Faculty should strive to achieve a percentage of women in its tenured ranks equal to the percentage of women receiving Ph.D.'s from Harvard ten years ago (9.6 per cent in 1959-60) and a percentage of women in the nontenured ranks equal to the percentage of women receiving Ph.D.'s from Harvard today (19 per cent in 1968-69).

By blurring over the notion of relevant community, Mr. Seabury is able to raise an unnecessary specter of Jewish suffering: the fact that Jews make up about 3 per cent of the population but a much higher percentage of certain professions does not mean that Jews are therefore necessarily "overrepresented" in these professions (as Norman Podhoretz seems to feel in "Is It Good for the Jews?" [February]). In terms of relevant communities, they may be fairly represented, or even underrepresented.

Secondly, by omitting facts about the available pool of qualified female Ph.D.'s, and by omitting data about the relative achievements of men and women in graduate schools and their later relative achievements in teaching and publishing, Mr. Seabury masks the absurdity of his basic unexamined assumption: that the hiring of women is equivalent to the hiring of unqualified or poorly-qualified applicants, and that increasing numbers of women on faculties will decrease quality. . . .

Paul Seabury teaches at a top university. According to his own statement, it is therefore reasonable to infer that he was one of the top 5 per cent of the graduates of one of the top ten universities. I assume that he is white, from the concern he shows for white males. Therefore, he represents the uppermost elite, the select group of "best-qualified" white males. If this is the best that the system can do, we should be thankful indeed that we have HEW to provide us with an instrument of change.

Nancy Demand

Wellesley, Massachusetts

To the Editor of Commentary:

Commentary is to be congratulated on the publication of Paul Seabury's "HEW & the Universities." Discriminatory hiring and promotion practices exist in higher education and some of us have fought these effectively with appropriate professional procedures. Now HEW is engaged in a national campaign fiscally bulldozing the country's colleges and universities into the establishment of new forms of sex and racial discrimination, all in the name of "equal opportunity." George Orwell merely imagined things;

this is the story of our own government — Republicans as well as Democrats — openly engaged in the use of fiscal and bureaucratic pressure to compel the majority to comply with clearly illegal quota schemes which are verbally camouflaged as "affirmative action." If this campaign is allowed to stand unchallenged, what shall we be able to do or say when an articulate and determined majority decides to avail itself of the precedents established by "liberal" administrators?

Harry D. Gideonse

Chancellor
New School for Social Research
New York City

To the Editor of Commentary:
. . . I was at the University of Michigan when HEW first raised the specter which Paul Seabury discusses so well and which plagues all of us who are in the position of having to recruit faculty for our respective institutions. The imposition of subtle, but nonetheless real, quotas, ... will ultimately do a disservice to those who have in the past been discriminated against. Given the limited number of members from minority groups, including women, available for academic positions, we find ourselves engaged in a mad rat-race of recruitment. Clearly, there are not now sufficient numbers to meet the quotas that have been established. Thus, to satisfy the rather futile criteria established by HEW, the concept of quality must go by the board. . . .
The time has come, as Mr. Seabury has indicated, for those of us on faculties . . . to rise up and express concern for the future of our universities. . . .

Ronald S. Tikofsky

Director, Division of Social Sciences
Florida International University
Miami, Florida

Paul Seabury writes:
A friend of mine, wise to the ways of opinion journals, once convinced me not to write a letter jibing at something an author had written. Just remember, he said, that whatever you write the author has the last word. My situation is now reversed. . . .
Exemplar that I may be of the white male trash whom Nancy Demand sees as cluttering up higher education, permit me to tug an imaginary forelock and respond to some of her comments.
My evidence, she writes, is based upon "vague, unverifiable sources." My sources, however, are specific and verifiable. I would be willing, though not glad, to supply her with the particulars of the three instances she cites. In each of them I did not want to cause public embarrassment to the individuals mentioned.
Her main point, however, is that quotas should be devised for women and minorities in proportion to their number of a *relevant* community. Very good. Departments in truly cosmopolitan universities seek to recruit the best they can find from all over the world. (This, incidentally, distinguishes American universities from many European ones which are quite strict in discriminating against foreigners.) The relevant community of mathematicians, for example, knows no national boundaries. Where do we get race and sex data for this community? Can UNESCO supply it? Might we, when such data were stacked up in print-outs, possibly discover that HEW's criteria would require us to prefer Chinese, Russians, and Frenchmen? Perhaps, were Miss Demand in charge of supply, she might determine the relevant community in more parochial ways — as Harvard, being Harvard, apparently has. (Would Harvard's formula, which she approvingly cites, appeal to her if Notre Dame also used it?) I suspect that each group claiming to speak for women or minorities really, if given the choice, would prefer a "relevant-community" formula most consistent with its perceived interests.
Finally, Miss Demand evidently knows more of my mind and its "unexamined assumptions" than I do. How could I assume that increasing the numbers of women on

faculties will decrease (or, for that matter, increase) quality? The question of quality turns entirely on the competence of the individuals chosen, and not on irrelevant statistical criteria established by HEW and forbidden by the Civil Rights Act. . . .

One trouble which I perhaps did not sufficiently stress in my article is that HEW's policies — in addition to the damage which they directly create — also inspire "do-it-yourself" affirmative-action programs which exceed in their boldness anything which HEW, in a crunch, might settle for in pursuit of its own purposes. If there are instances, and they are not known to me, where HEW has enjoined a university for too-blatant "benign quotas," it would be interesting to hear of them. We might then begin to see what standards of its own HEW is developing, to accord with the standards of the Civil Rights Act.

A limerick I have written sums up my view of this whole sorry matter:

> *There was an old dog from LaGrange*
> *Who developed a case of the mange;*
> *But cured this disease*
> *With remarkable ease*
> *By roasting himself on the range.*

The basic difference of opinion between proponents of affirmative action, such as Bernice Sandler, and opponents, such as Paul Seabury, seems to be whether or not there are qualified women and minorities who have been denied jobs because of discrimination. If there are proportionally as many talented women and minorities as men and Anglos in the pool of potential faculty, universities should be able to meet their goals without serious difficulty. If there are not, then meeting the goals *would* require reverse discrimination.

But there may well be serious psychological interferences to a fair determination of whether women, and other minorities as well, are qualified. For example, Fidell sent one of two forms to 228 chairmen of graduate programs in university psychology departments, describing in ten paragraphs the professional behavior and resumes of young psychologists, with the forms differing only in that feminine first names were attached to four paragraphs of Form A and to a different four paragraphs of Form B.[31] Respondents were asked to rate the desirability of each candidate and indicate the level at which such a person would be offered a position. Sixty-eight percent of the forms were returned. Women were offered lower levels of appointment than men for 7 of 8 paragraphs and rated less desirable than men for 6 of 8 paragraphs. Goldberg did a somewhat similar study by asking college students to rate a number of professional articles from each of six fields.[32] The articles were arranged in two equal sets of booklets and were exactly the same except that female authorship was ascribed to those in one set and male authorship to the other. Goldberg's subjects were all women, who consistently rated the worth of the articles as considerably lower when they were allegedly done by women. Sandra and Daryl Bem replicated the study with men and women students and got the same results.[33] It seems likely that the powerful sexual biases, which studies such as these measure, must have a significant impact on academic hiring, promotion, and tenure decisions.

Another difficulty in determining "qualifications" is that some criteria are facially neutral, but discriminatory in practice, and not job-related. For instance, would a law school faculty's preference for hiring Supreme Court law clerks be discriminatory, in light of the fact that as of 1972 less than five women had held this position? Could an affirmative action plan provide that this particular criterion is not

---

31. Fidell, L. S., Empirical Verification of Sex Discrimination in Hiring Practices in Psychology, 25 American Psychologist 1094 (1970).

32. Goldberg, Are Women Prejudiced Against Women? Trans-action 28-30 (April 1968).

33. Bem and Bem, Training the Woman to Know Her Place: The Power of a Nonconscious Ideology, in D.J. Bem, Beliefs, Attitudes and Human Affairs (1970).

to be set? Could the schools prove that Supreme Court clerks are better professors?

In answering this question, consider the EEOC Guidelines on Employee Selection Procedures, 29 C.F.R. §1607.1 et seq. They define "test" broadly to include "specific qualifying or disqualifying personal history or background requirements, [and] specific educational or work history requirements."[34] The guidelines further provide that:[35]

> The use of any test which adversely affects hiring, promotion, transfer or any other employment or membership opportunity of classes protected by Title VII constitutes discrimination unless (a) the test has been validated and evidences a high degree of utility as hereinafter described, and (b) the person giving or acting upon the results of the particular test can demonstrate that alternative suitable hiring, transfer or promotion procedures are unavailable for his use.

The concept of validation is technical; the interested reader should refer to the guidelines and to Cooper and Rabb, Equal Employment Law and Litigation, Materials for a Clinical Law Course 75-229 and Appendix B (both on employer selection procedures generally) (Employment Rights Project, Columbia Law School 1972). Basically, a test must be shown by empirical data to be "predictive or significantly correlated with important elements of work behavior which comprise or are relevant to the job or jobs for which candidates are being evaluated."[36]

To the extent that facially neutral but discriminatory and non-job-related standards (the Supreme Court clerkship requirement might be one example) are being used to evaluate potential faculty members, those who hire may believe that there are fewer qualified women or minorities among the pool of potential candidates than in fact there are.

A final point is the resistance of colleges and universities to rationalizing their procedures. As the Carnegie Commission has observed:[37]

> The charge is frequently made by academic women, with considerable justification, that the recruitment methods used by departments and schools tend to favor men. The typical procedure in prestigious departments is for the department chairman or the chairman of the department's personnel committee to visit the ten to a dozen most distinguished departments in his field at other universities and to interview advanced candidates for the Ph.D. Women charge that the candidates who are recommended for interview under these procedures tend to be the men being trained by faculty members who want to see them placed in prestigious institutions, where their performance will redound to the credit of the department in which they have been trained. Whether or not these faculty members are less interested in their women students, it is charged, they are likely to think that women will not acquire distinguished records through their future research and publication activities. . . .
>
> Less distinguished departments will tend to recruit among more graduate schools than leading departments do, because their chances of hiring from the most prestigious departments are less good. But, in general, academic recruitment procedures tend to be somewhat "cosy." Especially among the more prestigious departments, openings are not publicized. Interviews with prospective candidates are conducted either at the candidate's university, at the university doing the hiring (by invitation), or at professional association meetings. Even at the association meetings, however, it is frequently very difficult for jobseekers to discover which departments have openings. . . .

White male academics, having been hired under this system, and benefiting from its continuation, probably believe sincerely that it produces the best qualified individuals. When confronted with statistics that are sufficient under Title VII and under the

34. 29 C.F.R. §1607.2.
35. 29 C.F.A. §1607.3.
36. 29 C.F.R. §1607.4(c).
37. Carnegie Commission on Higher Education, Opportunities for Women, supra, at 119-120.

executive order to make out a prima facie case of discrimination, they are often resistant to the suggestion that they consider more rational procedures which will probably more accurately identify qualified individuals, but at the expense of the "Old Boy" network.

NOTE: REALISTIC GOALS

In evaluating the efforts made by universities, and predicting their impact on the extensive sex segregation and sex discrimination in academia, consider the following:

> *The Carnegie Commission on Higher Education*
> *Opportunities for Women in Higher Education*
> *124-125, 230-235 (1973)*

As the rate of increase of enrollments in higher education declines in the 1970s, it will become increasingly difficult to correct sexual and racial imbalances on college and university faculties. Elizabeth Scott has developed projections of percentages of faculty members who will be women in future years in universities, four-year colleges, and two-year colleges, on the basis of several assumed ratios of women to men among newly hired faculty members and several projected turnover rates. The projections are presented in Appendix C. . . . Chart [2-7] shows the growth path in the percentage of faculty members of universities who will be women from 1970 to 1990 for six different initial percentages of faculty who are women, on the assumption that the proportion of new hires who are women is a constant 30 percent. This chart is particularly appropriate for assessing the situation in individual universities, because some have ratios of women to men that are considerably lower or higher than the average 15 percent for universities. Chart [2-8] shows the average growth path for universities on the basis of four different assumptions about the percentage of women among new hires. Only when 100 percent of the new hires are women will the percentage of all faculty members who are women reach 50 percent in the 1980s. To reach an average percentage of 30 percent women in 1990, universities as a whole would have to maintain a constant proportion of women among new hires of 50 percent.

In practice, maintaining a hiring rate of 50 percent women is inconceivable for universities, or for any other group of institutions that normally recruits largely, or almost entirely, among holders of doctor's degrees. As we have seen, women have represented only 13 to 14 percent of the recipients of doctor's degrees in the last few years. The proportion varies by field, of course, but even in such fields as English and education, women make up only 20 to 30 percent of the Ph.D. recipients. . . . Only in nursing, in which the number of Ph.D.'s awarded is extremely small, and in home economics do women represent a large majority of Ph.D. recipients. In setting goals for its affirmative action program for the next five years, Columbia University mentioned pools ranging from about 2 to 5 percent women in such fields as business administration, engineering, and law to 47 percent in social work. (Women represented only 36 percent of the recipients of doctor's degrees in social work in 1970, but a good many faculty members in schools of social work, especially those who supervise field work, do not have doctor's degrees.) Intermediate between these extremes, pools of 20 percent women in the humanities, 10 percent in the social sciences, and 10 percent in the natural sciences were mentioned. In setting its actual goals, Columbia took into account not only these percentages, but also existing percentages of women among faculty members in these groups of fields [Columbia University, Affirmative Action Program, Condensed Version, 6-7 (December 1972)].

The projections in Appendix C suggest that it is exceedingly important for universities and colleges to take vigorous steps to correct imbalances in the immediate future,

Chart [2–7]
WOMEN AS A PERCENTAGE OF FACULTY MEMBERS,
PROJECTED 1970–1990 IN UNIVERSITIES;
CONSTANT HIRING 30 PERCENT WOMEN.
COMPARISON OF DIFFERENT INITIAL PERCENTAGES IN 1969

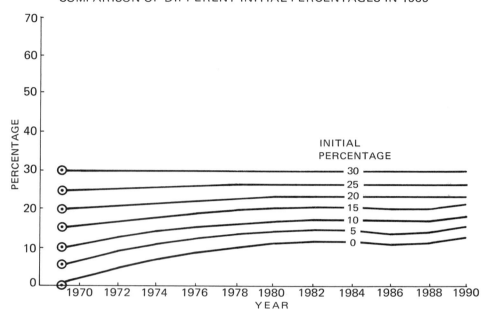

Chart [2–8]
WOMEN AS A PERCENTAGE OF FACULTY MEMBERS,
PROJECTED, 1970 TO 1990, IN UNIVERSITIES;
INITIAL PERCENTAGE IN 1969 EQUAL TO 14.67.
COMPARISON OF DIFFERENT RATES OF HIRING WOMEN

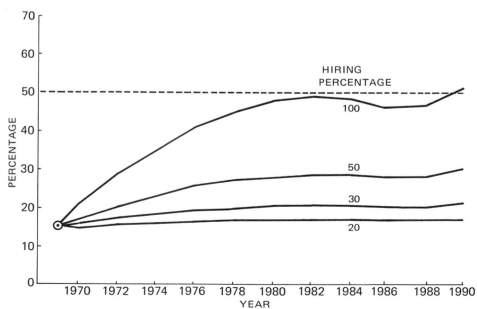

while enrollment increases continue to stimulate modest increases in the demand for faculty members. The most rapid increases in enrollment, in fact, are occurring in two-year colleges, where sexual imbalances on faculties are least serious. As in the case of graduate students, it would have been far easier to provide increased opportunities for women on faculties a decade ago, when enrollments were rising exceedingly rapidly. . . .

Most plans focus on raising the percentage of women *among new hires* to the percentage of women among the pool of individuals qualified for the jobs. An alternative which would more rapidly change the university situation would be to increase the percentage of women among new hires until the representation of women *on the faculty* was the same as the percentage of women in the potential applicant pool.

There are two main justifications for rejecting this idea: first is the principle of equality of treatment on an individual basis. If the percentage of women to be hired were higher than the percentage of women in the pool of potential applicants, there would be sex-based discrimination against male job applicants, who would necessarily be hired in a lower percentage than their representation in the pool would normally require. The second justification is that sex integration should be achieved without threatening present employees' jobs, and thus goals can only be set in relation to job vacancies and new jobs.

Aside from the political obstacles, what are the arguments for and against disregarding either of these principles? One argument for faster hiring of women might be the need to break the cycle of discrimination by reaching a level of female employment sufficient (a) to change the "male" image of prestigious jobs and encourage young women to undergo the lengthy training necessary for faculty and high administrative positions, and (b) to insure that women will be on faculties and in the administration in large enough numbers that they can begin to affect hiring practices and other university policies directly. An argument against abandoning the principle of equality of treatment on an individual basis is that it is the standard which feminists are trying to substitute for discrimination against women on the basis of averages and sex-based stereotypes. On the other hand, the women who do have Ph.D's may be a more select and therefore a more highly qualified group than the men with Ph.D's, so individual equity might produce a higher percentage of women on faculties than their percentage in the potential applicant pool.

The low goals set by some universities are another limit on the amount of change that university affirmative action plans can be expected to produce. Consider the following figures about the percentage of women at Harvard University:[38]

	Full professors	Full and associate professors
1959–60, whole university	0.94	2.2
1968–69, whole university	0.5	1.5
1970, Faculty of Arts & Sciences	0	0
May 1973, whole university	1.9	2.7
Harvard University Affirmative Action Goal: June 1975, whole university	2.4	4.0
Doctorates, Harvard University 1959–60: 9.6%	—	—

38. The figures for 1959–69 are not strictly comparable with those for 1973–75, because faculty nomenclature was revised in 1969–70. Bynum and Martin, The Sad Status of Women Teaching at Harvard, or "From What You Said, I Would Never Have Known You Were a Woman," Radcliffe Quarterly 13 (June 1970).
  Source: The figures for 1959–69 are from Bynum & Martin, id. at 12-13. The other figures are taken from Harvard's Affirmative Action plan, as reported in Harvard University, University News Office, Release, May 4, 1973. The percentage of doctorates statistic is quoted from Nancy Demand's letter to the Editor of Commentary, 53 Commentary 14 (May 1972), which cited the Report of the Committee on the Status of Women in the Faculty of Arts and Sciences (Harvard University, April 1971) as the source.

Since Harvard starts from an extremely low level of employment of women, even the tiny increases are improvements. On the other hand, the numbers remain so low that the university still will have achieved only token employment of women at the higher levels of its faculty by June 1975, and probably for many years thereafter. Note that, according to the Carnegie projections, a university that starts at a low percentage of women must hire them at a very high rate, possibly 30 or more percent of new hires, to increase the proportion of women on the faculty even to 10 percent. Harvard and the other universities do not at present seem to be planning affirmative action on that scale, much less carrying it out.

Note also, in the plans reproduced at pages 537 ff., supra, the typical failure to give figures on the percentages of women in the pool of potential faculty, to analyze the pool by field and year of Ph.D., or to break down hiring goals by rank and department. Without these figures, it is difficult for women's groups to evaluate the institution's performance in relation to its goals, or to put pressure on the individuals or committees within departments who actually do the hiring.

There are a number of other questions raised by the affirmative action plans excerpted above. In reference to faculty hiring, shouldn't HEW request statistics on percentages of women and men discovered by search procedures, so that the procedures themselves could better be evaluated? Under some of the plans excerpted, the onus is upon the few existing women and minority faculty members to find new women and minority faculty. Not only is this an inadequate method, but the extra committee work which is often involved can interfere with scholarly plans and advancement in the profession. Many universities, moreover, emphasize procedural reform rather than department- and rank-specific goals and timetables.

Think about procedural reforms in faculty hiring which might produce truly fruitful searches. Which of the institutions whose plans are excerpted seems most committed to meaningful change? Which the least? But in evaluating the plans, remember that the apparent differences may not be real, but may reflect only varying degrees of effectiveness by the public relations staffs of the institutions.

NOTE:
JOB TRAINING PROGRAMS — THE UNIVERSITY'S RESPONSIBILITY?

The Carnegie Commission on Higher Education (which itself includes only 2 women out of 19 members) comments that the HEW guidelines for affirmative action on campus "were greeted with relief . . . because they showed more understanding of the special problems of academic employment than some earlier HEW actions had suggested."[39] This understanding may be at the expense of meaningful affirmative action. Revised Order No. 4 refers to "the existence of training institutions capable of training persons in the requisite skills" and "the degree of training which the contractor is reasonably able to undertake as a means of making all job classes available to women" as factors for consideration in the analysis of utilization of women and minorities and in the setting of goals levels.[40] Yet neither the HEW guidelines nor the affirmative action plan excerpts presented by the commission[41] refer to the possibility that universities could increase the percentage of women in the nation's potential professoriate by ac-

39. Carnegie Commission on Higher Education, Opportunities for Women in Higher Education 129 (1973).

40. 41 C.F.R. §§60-2.11 and 60-2.12.

41. Possible exceptions are the affirmative actions plans of Oberlin, which refers to the need for sex-neutral treatment of male and female students, and of the University of the State of New York, which provides for sex-neutral admissions and financial aid. Sex discrimination in admissions by sex-integrated schools is now prohibited by Title IX of the Education Amendments of 1972, but there is no requirement of affirmative action.

tively recruiting more women for their existing "training" programs — i.e., graduate and undergraduate programs in various fields. Universities could also initiate training programs for women who have the potential for college teaching, research, or administration, but who are not presently trained for such employment or whose training is outdated. Compare this lack with the Galbraith Minority Advancement Plan, supra Part I, which sets goals in reference to the percentage of women in the labor force rather than the percentage of women who already have the requisite training for executive jobs, and provides for federal grants to assist state governments and educational institutions in providing executive and specialized training for women, blacks, and Spanish-speaking individuals.

NOTE: COLLEGE AND UNIVERSITY MATERNITY LEAVE PROVISIONS AND THE EEOC AND OFCC GUIDELINES

Notice that several of the affirmative action plans excerpted above are not sex-neutral in their maternity, part-time employment, or delay of tenure provisions. For example, Stanford allows women who give birth to delay tenure decisions by one year, regardless of the length of leave they actually take or how much of the leave is for medical reasons, without giving the same option to fathers or adoptive parents who want to take childrearing leave or to employees of either sex who suffer other temporary disabilities which cause them to need reduced work loads for a period of time. Likewise, a number of universities have adopted special maternity leave policies, rather than creating or extending temporary disability leave policies to cover pregnancy-related disabilities on an equal basis with other temporary disabilities.

At this writing, the OFCC guidelines provide that:[42]

> (1) Women shall not be penalized in their conditions of employment because they require time away from work on account of childbearing. When, under the employer's leave policy the female employee would qualify for leave, then childbearing must be considered by the employer to be a justification for leave of absence for female employees for a reasonable period of time. For example, if the female employee meets the equally applied minimum length of service requirements for leave time, she must be granted a reasonable leave on account of childbearing. The conditions applicable to her leave (other than the length thereof) and to her return to employment, shall be in accordance with the employer's leave policy.
>
> (2) If the employer has no leave policy, childbearing must be considered by the employer to be a justification for a leave of absence for a female employee for a reasonable period of time. Following childbirth, and upon signifying her intent to return within a reasonable time, such female employee shall be reinstated to her original job or to a position of like status and pay, without loss of service credits.

The EEOC guidelines provide that:[43]

> (a) A written or unwritten employment policy or practice which excludes from employment applicants or employees because of pregnancy is in prima facie violation of Title VII.
>
> (b) Disabilities caused or contributed to by pregnancy, miscarriage, abortion, childbirth, and recovery therefrom are, for all job-related purposes, temporary disabilities and should be treated as such under any health or temporary disability insurance or sick leave plan available in connection with employment. Written and unwritten employment policies and practices involving matters such as the commencement and duration of leave, the availability of extensions, the accrual of senior-

---

42. 41 C.F.R. §60-20.3(g).
43. 29 C.F.R. §1604.10.

ity and other benefits and privileges, reinstatement, and payment under any health or temporary disability insurance or sick leave plan, formal or informal, shall be applied to disability due to pregnancy or childbirth on the same terms and conditions as they are applied to other temporary disabilities.

(c) Where the termination of an employee who is temporarily disabled is caused by an employment policy under which insufficient or no leave is available, such a termination violates the Act if it has a disparate impact on employees of one sex and is not justified by business necessity.

Some of the sex-discriminatory maternity policies in the affirmative action plans excerpted above conform to the OFCC guidelines, but none conform to the EEOC guidelines. Although universities and colleges were not covered by Title VII in the employment of educational personnel, and public educational institutions were not covered at all, until March 24, 1972, all of the affirmative action plans quoted were published after that time. How could the policies be redrafted to provide the same substantial benefits for women who give birth, yet avoid discriminating on the basis of sex? Consider the possibility of giving men the same childrearing leave benefits as women have. This would conform with the EEOC guidelines which prohibit discrimination "between men and women with regard to fringe benefits," 29 C.F.R. §1604.9(b).

The differences in the OFCC and EEOC guidelines reflect one of the sad facts about the federal civil rights enforcement effort — the lack of a unified approach. New OFCC guidelines have been proposed, however, which are much closer to the EEOC guidelines:[44]

(1) Women shall not be rejected for employment, suspended from employment, or required to take leave involuntarily solely on account of the condition of pregnancy.

(2) Medically verifiable disabilities caused or contributed to by pregnancy, miscarriage, abortion, childbirth and recovery therefrom are for all job-related purposes temporary disabilities and shall be treated as such under any health or sick leave plans available in connection with employment. Written and unwritten employment policies and practices involving matters such as the commencement and duration of leave, the availability of extensions, the accrual of seniority and other benefits and privileges, reinstatement and payments under any health or temporary disability insurance policies or sick leave plans, formal or informal, shall be applied to disability due to pregnancy or childbirth on the same terms and conditions as they are applied to other temporary disabilities.

(3) Where the termination of or the refusal to reinstate an employee who is temporarily disabled is caused by an employment policy under which insufficient or no leave is available, such a termination or failure to reinstate violates Executive Order 11246, as amended, if it has a disparate impact on employees of one sex and is not justified by business necessity.

NOTE: OTHER LEGAL TOOLS FOR TEACHERS AND STUDENTS

When the Women's Equity Action League first invoked the executive order against universities and colleges, Title VII did not cover professional and administrative employees, and there were no other laws to protect either teachers or students at the university level. The effort under the order has been a valuable organizing and consciousness-raising tool, but given the inadequacy of enforcement, and the new laws, it seems likely that the order will fade as a method of challenging sex discrimination. The following list of other laws could be used by teachers and students, in addition to the executive order, to combat sex discrimination on the campus: The first two are usually the most effective protections for employees of educational institutions.

44. Proposed Revision of Guidelines, 41 C.F.R. Part 60-20, 38 F.R. 35336, 35338 §60-20.3(h) (December 27, 1973).

Title VII of the Civil Rights Act of 1964: As amended on March 24, 1972, this covers educational personnel of educational institutions, as well as employees of state or local governmental units. See Part II of this chapter.

The Equal Pay Act of 1963: As amended by the Education Amendments of 1972, this covers executive, administrative, and professional workers, as well as many other categories of workers. See Part III of this chapter.

Title IX of the Education Amendment of 1972: This forbids some private and public schools from discriminating on the basis of sex against employees or students and is described below in Chapter Five, Part II. The major disadvantages of this statute are that it allows a great deal of sex discrimination, especially in admissions, and that it is enforced in a manner similar to the executive order. Agencies that provide federal funds — whether as grants, contract payments, or loans — to particular institutions may cut off federal assistance to those institutions and may refuse to award such assistance in the future if they find that the institution discriminates. Women may ask a United States court of appeals to review the agency action. Since HEW is the main grantor, it will be the chief enforcement agency.

Titles IV and IX of the Civil Rights Act of 1964: These titles concern the power of the Attorney General to bring litigation and to intervene in litigation begun by others charging sex discrimination in violation of the Equal Protection Clause of the Fourteenth Amendment. See Chapter Five, Part II, for a brief account of these provisions.

The Public Health Service Act: Schools and training programs in the health services and hospitals that operate medical schools, training programs, or internships and that receive funds under Titles VII and VIII of this act (and most do) are specifically prohibited from discriminating against students on the basis of sex. The remedy is a cancellation of federal financial assistance under these titles. This act is described in greater detail in Chapter Five, Part II.

NOTE: FUTURE USE OF THE EXECUTIVE ORDER

Now that both the Equal Pay Act and Title VII cover employees at all levels at universities and colleges, the executive order should never be relied on to the exclusion of proceedings under the other two laws, which are much more effective. However, action under the executive order as an accompaniment to Title VII and Equal Pay Act suits can still be useful for mobilizing universities to make public commitments. The order should also be used against government contractors generally, in conjunction with other antidiscrimination legal actions. Although universities and other nonprofit institutions are more sensitive to the moral suasion which has provided a large proportion of the small clout of executive order actions so far, banks and other profit-making institutions may also be sufficiently concerned about their public images, not to mention the withholding of federal contract monies, to take heed of executive order complaints. Women should also consider proceedings in federal court to compel government agencies to cancel contracts with employers who discriminate, as discussed above in Section A-4, as one route to make the executive order more effective.

However, it should be clear that the present government has no intention of attacking sex segregation and other fundamental problems through the use of the executive order sanctions. Perhaps lawsuits in the future will be effective in forcing use of these weapons.

CHAPTER THREE

SEX ROLE DISCRIMINATION IN THE LAW OF THE FAMILY

I. INTRODUCTION: FROM STATUS TO CONTRACT?

Courts and commentators define and discuss marriage as a contract. Thus, one might expect that the terms of the relationship would be the subject of bargaining and agreement between the parties, and enforcement through the courts. But, in fact, parties to a marriage are not allowed to define their legal relationships, and if they attempt to do so, their agreements will not be enforced. A marriage "contract" thus exists only in the narrow sense that the parties decide whether to marry. Once they are married, the law dictates their roles; in marrying, they enter a predetermined civil status.

Over time, the incidents of the marriage status have changed, but the marriage relationship has moved only slightly closer to a genuine contract. This introduction will first examine the changes and then consider why they do not effect a contract model, although the theory that marriage is a contract nevertheless persists. Finally, we will raise the question of whether marriage should be a contract, or whether there should be, instead, a dramatic change in its status incidents.

At common law, the status of a married man was clearly more desirable than that of a married woman.[1] The man was the head of the family and alone represented it to the outside world. Economically, marriage, as enforced by law, cost the man very little, and the advantages, financial and otherwise, to him of marriage could be considerable.

A married man was the head of his household and sole guardian of his children, his wife, and their property, as well as of his own. He owned his wife's and children's services, and had the sole right to collect wages for their work outside the home. He owned his wife's personal property outright, and had the right to manage and control all of his wife's real property during marriage, which included the right to use or lease property, and to keep any rents and profits from it. She could not sell her property

---

1. For somewhat more detailed accounts of the legal position of married men and women at common law, see Clark, Law of Domestic Relations 219-229 (1968) and Kanowitz, Women and the Law 35-99 (1968). Clark refers to 3 Holdsworth, History of English Law 520-533 (3d ed. 1923), 2 Pollock and Maitland, History of English Law 399-436 (2d ed. 1898), and Bromley, Family Law 400-408 (2d ed. 1962) for good general accounts of the law on this subject. See also Moynihan, Introduction to the Law of Real Property 52-58, 229-235, 236 (1962): and see also Johnston, Sex and Property: The Common Law Tradition, the Law School Curriculum, and Developments Toward Equality, 47 N.Y.U.L. Rev 1033, 1044, nn. 30, 31 (1972), citing 1 Am. L. of Prop. §5.1-5.74 (A.J. Casner ed. 1952); 1 Bishop, Commentaries on the Law of Married Women (1873); and Kenny, Effects of Marriage on Property 7-98 (1879). The summary presented here describes in broad outline the common law duties and rights of spouses without reference to various reforms that took place at equity after the fifteenth century, some of which are described below, or the extensive changes in married women's property rights made by statute in the nineteenth century in the United States. It should not be relied upon without reference to the above sources.

without his consent. He could enforce his wife's choses in action (claims that she might assert in law or in equity), and if he reduced them to possession during marriage, they became his absolutely. He also had the right to curtesy: the inheritance of a life estate in all his wife's property if the couple had a child born alive. He had the responsibility of supporting his wife and children (whether or not he fathered them); however, he had almost complete control over the amount of support he paid during cohabitation; no court would question his judgment. He was answerable for his wife's torts and debts (whether committed or incurred before or during marriage), but he could also sue in his wife's name for any harm done to her.

A married woman, by contrast, was merely a part of the body of the family of which the husband was the head. (She was sometimes sentimentally referred to as its "heart.") Both single and married women were denied many rights and duties accorded to male citizens, and had essentially no public life, but single women at least attained a degree of independence in the private sphere. By marriage, however, a woman became a legal nonperson, both publicly and privately. According to Blackstone:[2]

> By marriage, the husband and wife are one person in law: . . . [T]he very being or legal existence of the woman is suspended during marriage, or at least is incorporated . . . into that of the husband, under whose wing, protection, and *cover* she performs everything; and is therefore called, in our law-French a *feme-covert;* . . . and her condition during her marriage is called her *coverture.* Upon this principle, of a union of person in husband and wife, depend almost all the legal rights, duties, and disabilities, that either of them acquire by the marriage.

As Justice Black once stated, "This rule has worked out in reality to mean that though the husband and wife are one, the one is the husband."[3] The wife's status has been compared to that of a slave[4] or, at best, a ward of her husband.[5]

By marriage, a woman lost the power to make enforceable contracts with other persons, including her husband, to retain her wages from work outside the home, to be paid for domestic work in the home, to sue and be sued, to manage and control her real property, to own personal property, to assert her claims in law or in equity or to receive the proceeds, to make a will, or to choose her own domicile. She was bound to accept her husband's sexual advances, whether friendly or forcible, was obligated to perform domestic services for him and their children in the home of his choice, and was subject to physical as well as economic restraint by her husband. By marriage a woman gained a largely unenforceable right to support, immunity from liability for certain debts, torts, and crimes, and dower: the right to inherit a life estate in one third of the property her husband owned or acquired at any time during marriage, a right that vested upon marriage.[6]

At common law, neither the man nor the woman could directly enforce some incidents of the status of marriage during cohabitation; for example, a wife could not get a court order for support during cohabitation, nor could the husband get specific

2. 1 Blackstone, Commentaries on the Laws of England *442.
3. United States v. Yazell, 382 U.S. 341, 359, 86 S. Ct. 500, 510, 15 L. Ed. 2d 404, 414 (1966) (dissenting opinion).
4. Crozier, Marital Support, 15 Boston U. L. Rev. 28, 33–34 (1935).
5. Johnston, supra, at 1047; 2 Pollock and Maitland, supra, at 406, cited in Clark, supra, at 219.
6. Because dower vested upon marriage, the wife's interest "could not be barred without her consent through transfers of the husband's land inter vivos or by will." Johnston, supra, at 1046. As a result, the wife had some limited protection against the husband's mismanagement of his property during his lifetime. However, "a widow had no claim on any of her husband's personalty except under the rules of intestate succession. He could bequeath this property by will and defeat her claim; even if he died intestate, her claim would be subordinate to claims of his creditors." Id. Notice also that the husband's right to a life estate in his wife's real property if the couple had a child born alive extended to all of her property, whereas her rights were limited to one third of his property, regardless of the birth of children to the couple.

performance of her duty to render services.[7] However, the husband was given such extensive control over his wife's person, income, and property, which *was* enforceable,[8] that he was undoubtedly able to coerce her into obedience if she became rebellious. Of course, not all husbands used their authority over their wives to the fullest extent possible, but the fact that great power was available to any husband who chose to use it necessarily influenced the relative social, economic, and political positions of men and women.

By marriage, both spouses assumed duties that neither could change and a status that they could not terminate. Although the wife was subject to her husband's control, he did not have the power to emancipate her. Both husband and wife were required to cohabit solely with the other for life, or until serious fault on the part of one justified the other in living apart. And even after separation, the marriage continued to govern the legal status of each for life; neither could remarry.

Not only did marriage create a new legal status for each party; the status it created was patriarchal, with the husband given authority and power, and the wife commanded to obey him. Although marriage today is still a patriarchal, status-based institution, the more feudal aspects of the husband-wife relationship at common law have been eliminated. The biggest substantive changes have concerned the property rights of the parties, the ownership of the services of the wife, and the availability of divorce. Some states have adopted a community property system, under which each spouse owns one half of all income and property acquired during the marriage — thus tending toward a partnership status for each spouse.[9] The majority of states give ownership and control of property and income to the spouse who acquires it, eliminating most of the status aspects of property relations during marriage.[10] Divorce is increasingly available and, in a number of states, on a no-fault basis, so that spouses are no longer imprisoned in the status of marriage once they enter it.[11]

7. Clark, supra, §6.1 at 186; Paulsen, Support Rights and Duties Between Husband and Wife, 9 Vand. L. Rev. 709, 735 (1956).

8. The wife could not bring charges against the husband for rape or assault and battery because she could not sue in her own name and because rape was defined as forcible intercourse by a man with "a woman not his wife." See Chapter 4, I. The husband could go to court to get control of her property, its profits and rents, and her wages. He could have her forcibly returned to him if she ran away. Mansfield, The Legal Rights, Liabilities and Duties of Women 273 (1845); Rose, On Legal Discrimination, Speech delivered at the Second Worcester Women's Rights Convention, 1851, in Kraditor (ed.), Up From the Pedestal 222, 225 (Quadrangle ed. 1968); Declaration of Sentiments, Seneca Falls Convention (1848), in Kraditor at 185. According to Blackstone, he could legally "restrain his wife of her liberty, in case of any gross misbehavior." 1 Blackstone, supra, at *445. If she committed adultery, he could kill her lover and be acquitted on the grounds that it was a crime of passion. This is still a defense to a prosecution for murder in three states. See Kanowitz, supra, at 92-93 and Note, Sex Discrimination in the Criminal Law: The Effect of the Equal Rights Amendment, 11 Am. Crim. L. Rev. 469, 500-501 (1973).

9. Partnership *status* should be clearly distinguished from a business partnership, in which the parties are free to determine by contract the "rights, powers, duties, and responsibilities" — including financial rewards — of each partner. By partnership status system we mean one which mandates an equal and sex-neutral division of rights and responsibilities between spouses. As will be discussed below, no community property state maintains a complete partnership status system of marriage. All either retain incidents of patriarchal status, e.g., the husband's right to manage the community property during marriage in Louisiana, Nevada, and Idaho; or use semicontractual concepts in some areas, e.g., California allows the spouses to decide how to split up property on divorce rather than mandating a 50-50 division.

10. But note that contractual freedom does not always advance the economic interests of wives. Since most women are still precluded from acquiring either any independent income or one equivalent to their husbands' incomes, the community property system provides definite advantages. On the other hand, in some community property states, the husband's right to manage and control community property during marriage includes the wife's income acquired after marriage, while married women who work for pay in common law states at least have the right to manage and control their own salaries.

11. There is some evidence, however, that one result of no-fault divorce is to decrease the amount of alimony, child support, and property awards to wives, demonstrating again that a contractual system is not necessarily the most advantageous, in the short run at least, to women. See infra, Parts VI and VII.

By the elimination of some status relationships altogether, or the substitution of partnership status for patriarchal status, marriage appears more like a contractual relationship, at the core of which is a reciprocal exchange of support and domestic services. In reality, however, the reforms have merely deprived the husband of some of his economic power, without changing the underlying patriarchal structure of the institution. There is still no contract because the law, not the parties, defines the obligations of each spouse. Furthermore, the obligations of support and services are absolute, and not dependent upon performance by the other spouse. Nor is their legal status that of partners, because the law still prescribes sex-differentiated marital roles and male domination.

Although marriage is not legally a contractual relationship, it might be argued that people are free to create their own marital roles, which could be quite different from those contemplated by the law. But this option does not amount to liberty of contract because the courts will not enforce the parties' agreement either during the marriage or after it has terminated. The parties are thus free to contract only as long as they agree. It is a strange contract indeed that vanishes as soon as it is breached. Likewise, the completeness of the state's power to enforce its view of marriage in the divorce proceeding is a significant restraint on the parties' freedom to control their relationship. Finally, parties who agree to contract in marriage confront social and economic, as well as legal, forces that strongly reinforce the patriarchal tradition in marriage. As we shall see in this chapter, even aside from domestic relations law, the government contributes significantly to the promotion of traditional roles in marriage through its affirmative policies and programs.

Marriage was not a contract at common law and has not become contractual despite considerable reforms of some areas of domestic relations and property law. Nor is the relationship "contractual" in the nonlegal sense that the parties can easily deviate from the roles contemplated by the law. Yet people continue to describe marriage as a contract, and so do courts, thus masking its patriarchal structure. As Clark points out, the conservatism of rules of marital behavior is "reinforced by the reciprocal nature of the duties imposed" because the contractual image makes it "easier to treat deviations as evidence of moral fault and of breach of faith."[12] The aura of fairness imparted to the marriage relation by the idea that it is contractual is especially powerful in our society, which protects the sanctity of contracts in the Constitution, and defines its political existence in terms of social contract ideology.[13]

The persistence of the contract theory raises the question of whether marriage should be changed so that it in fact fits the model. The idea is appealing because it allows great individual freedom and is egalitarian in assuming that men and women will be able to negotiate as equals. But in reality, since most women are conditioned to exercise less control over their lives than are men, they might accept grossly unfair bargains in order to get married. A partnership status in which the law mandated identical rights and responsibilities for each partner might better advance the goals of justice and equality in marriage.

In order to analyze competing theories about the ideal legal structure for marriage, one must examine not only the practical effects of particular reforms, but also the underlying assumptions of the theories themselves. The materials presented later in this chapter show that contractual patriarchal status and partnership status concepts are often mixed together in domestic relations law. However, for the present, they will be considered as wholly separate entities.

These are the underlying assumptions of contract law, as explained by McDowell:[14]

12. Clark, supra, §6.1 at 181-182.
13. See the U.S. Const. art. I, §10, and the Declaration of Independence.
14. Contracts in the Family, 45 Boston U. L. Rev. 43 (1965).

The prototype on which the modern law of contract has been built is the business deal. Some of the assumptions which have been made about the realities of commercial transactions are: (1) The parties are sufficiently mature and well-informed to be aware of the risks in the particular transaction. (2) The parties are sufficiently equal in bargaining power to be able to negotiate about whether consent will be given and also about the terms of the agreement. (3) The major motivation for the agreement is the deal itself and the bargained-for exchange. (4) The deal is so isolated that the court can ignore the effect of the parties' relationship on the formation of the agreement and can also discount the effect of enforcing the contract on the subsequent relations of the parties.

The fourth assumption in the above paragraph is misleadingly expressed. The primary reason the courts ignore the effect of enforcement on the relationship of the parties is not that the deal is necessarily isolated, but rather that the business system requires that contracts be enforced, more or less regardless of the impact of enforcement on the continuing relationship between the parties. The prospect of enforcement is part of the parties' understanding in making the deal. Either party has the choice of suing to enforce the contract, or making some compromise that will preserve the relationship.

A fifth assumption behind contract law is that no harm sufficient to justify restricting liberty of contract will result from the parties' free negotiations and judicial enforcement in case of breach. In other words, the system assumes either that there is no state (or unrepresented third party) interest that might be injured by the transaction, or that the state interest will be advanced by the transaction (or, in the long run, by the results of the process of individual bargaining).

The assumptions underlying the status theory of marriage are not as clear as those of the law of contract. When status-based relationships predominated in society, questions about why law and society were structured in a certain way, on the rare occasions such questions arose, would probably have been answered by invoking God's will. Since rationalistic, democratic, and utilitarian notions have replaced natural law theory in our jurisprudence, the status theory has acquired a new rationale. Societal good or state interests are the asserted justifications for denying individuals the power to control the terms, conditions, and duration of their relationships.[15] This "state interest" can be supported by any one of several assumptions, each contradicting one of the premises of contract theory: (1) that the parties are unaware of the risks of their transaction, either through love's blindness, immaturity, or lack of information; (2) that the parties have unequal bargaining positions, and the state must protect the weaker of the two; (3) that the establishment and maintenance of marital relationships is more important than any particular agreement or the freedom of the individual, and individual parties must consequently be denied enforcement, which might be destructive to their marriages; or (4) that the parties are likely to harm the interests of third parties by their agreement (their children, for example). These premises are the ones most frequently cited to justify a status theory of marriage. Of course, tradition is also a factor in its retention.

Both the patriarchal and the partnership status theories of marriage accept the necessity for the state to impose terms and conditions on marriage, but the similarity stops there. The patriarchal system gives one party authority over the other and apportions duties and responsibilities on the basis of sex. This avoids controversies which, it is believed, would be destructive to the relationship; as one judge put it, you cannot have a majority rule in a marriage.[16] It is also a way for the strong (the husband) to protect the weak (the wife). The partnership theory gives neither spouse authority over the other, and gives each sex the same rights, powers, duties, and responsibilities. It assumes, moreover, that the best protection for the "weak" wife is to give her more power, not less.

---

15. The increasing influence of social control on the law of contracts is discussed in F. Kessler and G. Gilmore, Contracts 12 (2d ed. 1970).

16. Estate of Wickes, 128 Cal. 270, 278, 60 P. at 870 (1900).

With this background, the reader should turn to the following materials. Parts II, III, and IV consider marriage: its socioeconomic reality, its legal structure, and alternatives to traditional marital forms. Parts V, VI, and VII contain parallel examinations of divorce. Part VIII deals with the impact of the proposed Equal Rights Amendment on domestic relations law, and Part IX considers the influence of government programs and policies on family structures. In evaluating present institutions and proposed reforms, the reader should decide which set of assumptions — those underlying the contractual, patriarchal status, or partnership status systems — she or he accepts in each area of marriage and divorce law, for in large part one's assumptions will determine what legal framework one advocates.

II. A SOCIOLOGICAL OVERVIEW OF MARRIAGE

A. STATISTICAL INTRODUCTION

Marriage is the most viable and important form of social organization in this country. Of the generation in their late twenties and early thirties in the 1960s, 97 percent of the women and 96 percent of the men had been, were, or would be married.[1] The percentage of married people in the United States has risen decade by decade.[2] A study by the Census Bureau of 1971 data shows that about 95.7 percent of all women forty-five to forty-nine years of age in 1970 had been married at least once by 1971. Almost three fourths of the women who had ever been married were still married to their first husbands.[3]

Marriages are usually homogamous, that is, like marrying like. Carter and Glick found that "About three-fourths of the married couples in the United States in 1960 comprised a husband and wife of the same national origin."[4] The same data showed that in the early 1960s 99.8 percent of the Caucasian population were married to Caucasians and almost all blacks (99 percent) were married to blacks.

Also, by measures of education and class, husbands and wives tend to be very close, although Bernard observes:[5]

> Within that common background, men tend to marry women slightly below them in such measurable items as age, education, and occupation, and presumably, in other as yet unmeasurable items as well. The result is that there is no one for the men at the bottom to marry, no one to look up to them. Conversely, there is no one for the women at the top to look up to; there are no men who are superior to them. The result is . . . that the never-married men tend to be "bottom of the barrel," and the women "cream of the crop."

In addition to individual reasons and the desire to fulfill social expectations, women's motives for marrying include pregnancy and economic need. Recent data suggest that[6]

1. Bernard, The Future of Marriage 158 (1972).
2. Carter and Glick, Marriage and Divorce: A Social and Economic Study 40-70 (1970). This study is the most comprehensive found by the authors in terms of collection and analysis of statistics. Its data are mostly from the mid-sixties, however, although the authors predict the continuance of all the major trends that they saw.
3. U.S. Bureau of the Census, Current Population Reports, Series P-20, No. 239, "Marriage, Divorce and Remarriage by Year of Birth: June 1971" 1 (1972).
4. H. Carter and Glick, supra, at 392.
5. Bernard, supra, at 33.
6. Wachtel, Options of the Single Pregnant Woman, in 4 Review of Radical Political Economics 86, 92, and Table 1, p. 96 (July 1972), quoting figures from Kovar, Interval from First Marriage to First Birth, United

Pregnancy [may be] a major factor in the decision to get married, particularly among younger women. Overall in the United States in the period between 1964 and 1966 about 20 percent of all first births occurred to women who had been married less than eight months. The proportion of first births conceived before marriage is highest with the youngest age group (15-19), about 32 percent, and declines to a low of less than two percent for women aged 30-44.

Many of these unmarried pregnant women would prefer abortion, if readily available, to marriage. Wachtel found that the marriage rates of young women declined in California and in Maryland as abortions became easier to obtain.[7] In 1973 national statistics showed a decline in the birth rate and an increase in the age of marriage as abortion became more widely available.[8]

Using 1960 Census data, Havens found a strong direct relation between economic attainment (occupational status and income) and unmarried (either never married or divorced) status. She hypothesized that[9]

> If one rejects the common notion that females with high incomes are simply the "marital rejects" or "pathetic misfits" of society, then a possible interpretation is that these females are less willing to enter into and/or maintain marital commitments. In other words, many of these females may choose not to be married.

The hypothesis that women marry in part for economic reasons is a logical one in view of the widespread sex discrimination in the labor market, making it difficult for a woman on her own to have a comfortable living.

Almost all married people have at least one child. There has been measurable change in the first sixty years of this century in this regard. Fully 26 percent of women born in the first decade of the 1900s did not have children; 73 percent of the women who did not have children were married. Only 10 percent of the women born in the 1930s and 1940s are expected not to have children, and only 60 percent of these women who are expected not to have children are expected to be married.[10] This trend toward increased childbearing seems to have halted in the early years of the 1970s, when the birth rate declined substantially — 4 percent from 1972 to 1973 alone.[11] However, married people with at least one child will probably remain in the majority in the married population for quite some time.

The number of children in the family bears an inverse relationship to the education of the wife. Thus, as of 1969, the number of children born during the lifetime of women ever married, thirty-five to forty-four years old, ranged from 4.16 for women who had

---

States, 1964-66 Births (paper presented at the meetings of the Population Association of America, April 16-18, 1970, available from the National Center for Health Statistics). See also Carter and Glick, supra, at 423, n.1.

7. Id. at 93. Wachtel's data cast some doubt on the hypothesis that women get pregnant either in order to force their boyfriends to marry them or after having decided to get married anyway. It is also possible that the decline in marriage rates is due to the lesser effectiveness of getting pregnant as a strategy to trick a man into marriage because men are also aware of the alternative of abortion. Id. at 92, n.11.

If in the future the greater availability of abortions causes a decrease in early marriage, it seems likely that the divorce rate will also decline, since teenage marriages have the highest rate of divorce of all marriages.

8. "Women are getting married later (38 percent in the 20-24 age group were single in 1973, compared to 28 percent in 1960). . . . [There were] about 700,000 legal [abortions] in 1973. . . .

"According to the National Center for Health Statistics, the 1973 birth rate was 15.0 births for every 1,000 persons, a 4 per cent decrease from the previous year. The fertility rate, which is the average number of children born to a family, dropped to 1.9 from 2.03 in 1972." Birth Rates Are Lower Than Ever, New York Times, April 21, 1974, §4, at 8.

9. Havens, Women, Work and Wedlock: A Note on Female Marital Patterns in the United States, 78 Am. J. Sociology 975, 980 (1973).

10. Carter and Glick, supra, at 144-145.

11. Statistics from the National Center for Health Statistics reported in Birth Rates Are Lower Than Ever, New York Times, April 21, 1974, §4, at 8.

completed less than eight years of school, to 2.90 for high school graduates, to 2.73 for college graduates.[12]

Although the majority of wives still do not work outside the home, a substantial and growing minority do. As of 1972, 41 percent of all wives were in the labor force.[13] These nineteen million working wives comprised over 60 percent of the female labor force, which is approximately 40 percent of the total work force. As of March 1971, 29.6 percent had children under six — and 49.4 percent had children between the ages of six and seventeen.[14]

There has always been a marked statistical difference between black and white wives in terms of participation in the labor force. In March 1971, this difference was about 12 percent (white wives had a 39.7 labor participation rate, and black wives a 52.5 percent rate).[15] This gap, however, had been as much as 20 percent in the late 1940s and 1950s. The most obvious reason for this greater participation in the labor force is the pervasive race discrimination that causes black husbands to earn less than white husbands. Another possible factor is that black wives are younger, on the average, than white wives,[16] and there has historically been some differential in labor force participation in terms of age; i.e., among younger people, a larger proportion tend to be in the labor force. It also appears that black wives tend more than white wives to work outside the home even when they have preschool age children and when their husbands make relatively high incomes. For example, as of March 1969, among families with preschool age children, 44 percent of black wives, but only 27 percent of white wives, were in the work force. For the same period, among families where the husband's yearly income was $10,000 or more, about half of the black wives worked, compared to about a third of the white wives similarly situated.[17]

Education is also directly related to labor force participation by married women. Over half of those married women who had completed four years of college were in the labor force in March 1971. Among wives who were high school graduates, 44 percent were in the labor force, compared with 33 percent of those who had completed eleven years of school or less.[18]

The work of wives in the labor force clearly makes a difference in the family's well-being:[19]

> When a wife did not work during the year, median family income in 1968 was about $8,175. If she worked at all median income was $10,485; or about $13,600 if she

12. Waldman and Gover, Marital and Family Characteristics of the Labor Force, Monthly Labor Review 4, 6 (April 1972). "Wives" is used throughout this overview to mean those in a "going marriage," with husband present.

13. Ibid. In an earlier article, Waldman pointed out that the addition of large numbers of wives to the labor force has been quite a dramatic change. "Since 1960, nearly half of the increase in the labor force was accounted for by married women. In early 1970, over 18 million married women were working or looking for work, representing about 60 percent of the female labor force. In 1940, these figures were only about 4.2 million, and 30 percent. The 30 year increase of about 320 percent in the number of working wives far outstrips the 50 percent increase in the size of their population." Waldman, Changes in the Labor Force Activity of Women, Monthly Labor Review 10, 11 (June 1970).

"Today, nearly two out of every five American workers are women. Most of these women are married and half are over 39 years old. If asked why they work, there is a good chance they would say that they are supplementing family income to provide their children with a college education, or to help buy or furnish a new home, or to pay for an additional car.

"In 1920, the typical working woman was single, about 28 years old, and from the working class." Id. at 10.

14. Waldman and Gover, supra, at 4, 7, Table 3. These figures represent an 11 percent increase from 1960 for mothers of children under six, and a 10.4 percent increase for mothers of children between six and seventeen.

15. Id. at 4.

16. Id. at 6.

17. Waldman, supra, at 10, 12.

18. Waldman and Gover, supra, at 4, 6.

19. Waldman, supra, at 10, 15-16.

worked all year at a full-time job. A wife's earnings thus appear to be a family's vital link to the maintenance of the "good life," as opposed to one with few options other than life's . . . necessities.

B. The Traditional Marriage

There is a rich body of sociological literature on the reality of marriage for couples who maintain traditional sex roles. Bernard collects data and also presents the results of her own research. Her thesis is that each spouse is involved in a marriage separate and different from the other and that, on the whole, the husband's marriage is far healthier for him than the wife's is for her.

Of the husband's marriage, Bernard writes as follows.

BERNARD, MARRIAGE: HERS AND HIS
Ms. Magazine 46, 47-49, 110, 113 (December 1972)[20]

The superiority of married men over never-married men is impressive on almost every index — demographic, psychological, or social.

After middle age the physical health of married men is better than that of never-married men. But regardless of age, married men enjoy better mental health and fewer serious symptoms of psychological distress. To take an extreme example, in the United States, the suicide rate for single men is almost twice as high as for married men.

Some men do not marry because they do not want to, for whatever reason, and some because no one wants to marry them. In either case, we are faced with the inevitable, and insoluble chicken-and-egg, cause-and-effect question. This selectivity factor is undoubtedly part of the explanation of the superiority married men show over the unmarried, and cannot therefore be ignored in evaluating the impact of marriage. But the weight of the evidence explaining differences by marital status seems to me to be overwhelmingly on the side of the beneficent effects which marriage has on men rather than on the initial superiority of the married men. Are married men so much better off than the never-married because marriage is good for them or because the less good prospects were selected out of the married population in the first place?

By comparing the married with the widowed, we minimize the selective factor, for the widowed did once choose marriage or were chosen by someone. Such comparisons give us an indication of the value of marriage by showing what happens to men who are deprived of it by death. They are miserable. Widowers show more than expected frequencies of psychological distress, and their death rate is very high. . . .

Other studies have shown that more single than married men suffer from inertia, passivity, antisocial tendencies, greater moral conflict, and a history of stressful childhoods.

I have emphasized only the documentable, research-based evidence of the benefits of marriage. But every happily married man will be able to add a dozen more: marriage is more comfortable than bachelorhood; sex is always available; responsibility is a rewarding experience. It is reassuring to have a confidante. And then there is love, friendship, and personal service. . . .

The benefits of marriage for men do not come without costs. . . .

Economic responsibilities and sexual restrictiveness are the two major costs men feel they pay to maintain a haven. Many husbands therefore name two areas of potential improvement of the state of matrimony. One would be to relieve them from the respon-

---

20. The material concerning "his" marriage is an excerpt from Bernard, The Future of Marriage (1972).

sibility for the entire support of wives and children, and the other to make sexual variation more feasible. Both seem to be in the process of realization. . . .

[As compared to the generally rosy picture of the husband's marriage, Bernard presents a rather alarming description of the wife's.]

Years ago, I propounded a "shock theory" of marriage. It was my idea that marriage introduced such profound discontinuities into the lives of women as to constitute a genuine emotional health hazard.

There are some standardized "shocks" that are almost taken for granted. For example, one analyst cites the conflict the bride experiences between her attachment to her parental family and her attachment to her new husband. Another shock marks the end of the romantic idealization when the honeymoon is over and disenchantment sets in. The transition from the best-behavior presentation of the self during courtship to the daily lack of privacy in marriage (hair curlers, the unshaven face) presents its own kind of shock. So does the change that occurs when the wife ceases to be the catered-to and becomes the caterer. Discontinuities such as these demand a redefinition of the self, with the assumption of new role obligations. . . .

Some of the shocks that marriage may produce have to do with the lowering of status that it brings to women. For, despite the possibilities of a woman's "marrying up," becoming a wife is a step down in the eyes of society.

. . . Alice Rossi warns us that "the possibility must be faced . . . that women lose ground in personal development and self-esteem during the early and middle years of adulthood, whereas men gain ground in these respects during the same years." For it is the husband's *role* — not necessarily his own wishes, desires, or demands — that proves to be the key to the marriage and requires the wife to be accommodating.

This in turn tallies with the common finding that wives make more of the adjustments called for in marriage than do husbands. The psychological and emotional costs of these adjustments show up in the increasing unhappiness of wives with the passage of time and in their increasingly negative and passive outlook on life.

One of the basic differences in the wife's and the husband's marriages results from lifestyle — namely, the almost complete change in occupation that marriage brings in her life but not in his. For most women today there are certain years in a marriage when a wife becomes a *housewife.* Even those women who work outside the home are still, in traditional marriages, housewives too. After a nine-to-five day on the job these women tackle the cleaning, cooking, and laundry with the blind obedience of an ordained domestic. Few deny the economic and sociological importance of housework and homemaking. But housewives are not in the labor force. They are not paid for the services that they perform.

The low status of the wife's work has ramifications all through her marriage. Since the husband's work is higher than hers in status, earnings, and degree of competition, his needs have to be catered to first.

Eventually the difference in the work of wives and husbands has alienating effects on the relationship. They may not share the same kinds of problems. The couple who began their marriage at the same early stage of their development may find that they and their interests have grown apart in later years. Most often the husband's horizons expand and the wife's contract. "The idea of imprisoning each woman alone in a small, self-contained, and architecturally isolating dwelling is a modern invention," Philip Slater reminds us. "In our society the housewife may move about freely, but since she has nowhere in particular to go and is not part of anything, her prison needs no walls."

Isolation has negative psychological effects on people. It encourages brooding; it leads to erratic judgments, untempered by the leavening effect of contact with others. It renders one more susceptible to psychoses, and heightens one's sense of powerlessness.

We have a ready-made life experiment to demonstrate that it is the role of housewife rather than the fact of being married which contributes heavily to the poor mental and emotional health of wives. By comparing married housewives with married working women, we find that wives who are rescued from the isolation of the household by outside employment show up very well. They may be neurotic, but they are less likely than full-time housewives to be psychotic. In nearly all symptoms of psychological distress — from headaches to heart palpitations — the working women are overwhelmingly better off. In terms of the number of people involved, the housewife syndrome might well be viewed as Public Health Problem Number One. Ironically, the woman suffering from it is not likely to elicit much sympathy. Her symptoms of psychological distress are not worth anyone's attention. Only advertisers take the housewife seriously, and to them she seems only a laughable idiot with a full wallet and an insatiable need for approval. But it's even simpler than that. In truth, being a housewife makes a woman sick.

If we were, in fact, epidemiologists and we saw bright, promising young people enter a certain occupation and little by little begin to droop and finally succumb, we would be alerted at once and bend all our research efforts to locate the hazards and remove them. But we are complacent when we see what happens to women in marriage. We put an enormous premium on their getting married, but make them pay an unconscionable price for falling in with our expectations.

If the wife's marriage is really so pathogenic, why do women marry at all? There is a wide variety of reasons: emancipation from the parental home; babies; pressure of social expectations; the absence of any better alternatives.

The real question is not why do young women marry, but why, in the face of all the evidence, do more married than unmarried women report themselves as happy? As, in fact, they do.

The anomaly may be explained by the fact that happiness is interpreted in terms of conformity. Those who do not marry are made to feel failures. Escape from being "an old maid" is one definition of happiness.

Such conformity to the norm of marriage is not merely imposed from the outside. Women have internalized the norms prescribing marriage. And since marriage is set up as the *summum bonum* of life for women, they interpret their achievement of marriage as happiness, no matter how unhappy the marriage itself may be. "I am married, am I not? Therefore I must be happy."

Another way to explain the anomaly of depressed, phobic, and psychologically distressed women reporting themselves as happy may be that they are interpreting happiness in terms of adjustment. The married woman has supposedly adjusted to the demands of marriage; she is reconciled to them. She interprets her reconciliation as happiness, no matter how much she is paying for it in terms of psychological distress.

Another way to solve the paradox of depressed wives reporting their marriages as happy is to view the socialization process as one which "deforms" women in order to fit them for marriage. . . .

"But what about love? Isn't that what marriage is all about?" the young bride cries. "None of what you say has even included the word!" . . . Love is, in fact, so important to women that they are willing to pay an exorbitant price for it.

But the basic question is, does the satisfaction of these needs for love and companionship have to extort such excessive costs? Can marriage — for women — ever become more often for better than for worse? Perhaps if the ceremonial vows were supplemented with guarantees of human fulfillment, then marriage could become an arena for "enlargement" rather than for "dwindling" into wifely despair.

Another finding reported in Bernard's book is the negative impact of having children on both the husband and the wife. She explains:[21]

21. Bernard, The Future of Marriage 57 (1972).

It is true that divorce is more common among childless couples — though even this is less true than it was formerly — because it is psychologically and emotionally easier to get a divorce if there are no children, and the financial burden on the husband is less onerous. Children may also provide substitute personal satisfactions for unhappy marital relationships. . . .

But, contrary to all the cliches, childless marriages that do survive are happier than marriages with children. Mothers far more than childless wives find marriage restrictive; slightly fewer are very happy. Far more . . . report problems in the marriage; considerably fewer report satisfaction in the marital relationship; and more feel dissatisfied with themselves. . . .

The benign effect of childlessness is even more marked in the husbands' marriages than in the wives'. . . . [M]ore fathers felt marriage to be restrictive, and more reported problems. Twice as many fathers as childless men felt dissatisfied with themselves; three times as many, inadequate.

C. THE ROLE OF HOUSEWIFE

What explains the negative impact on women of the roles of housewife and mother? In the excerpts above, Bernard highlights some of the disadvantages of the housewife's role — that it is low in status, unpaid, and isolated. In this regard, it is informative to see the skill level allocated to the job of housewife in comparison to other occupations by the U.S. Department of Labor. The Dictionary of Occupational Titles, a Labor Department publication that defines some 22,000 occupations and serves as a standard reference for government and industry, rates occupations on a skill scale from a high of 1 to a low of 887. Scott has pointed out that homemakers, foster mothers, child care attendants, home health aides, nursery school teachers, and practical nurses are listed at a skill level of 878. A marine mammal handler, on the other hand, has a ranking of 328, a hotel clerk 368, and a barber 371. She comments, "obviously, 'women's work' doesn't measure up."[22]

As for the effect of childrearing on women's lives, Bernard notes:[23]

It is not necessary to invoke esoteric psychiatric mechanisms to interpret the strains introduced by a first child at any age. The sheer fatigue factor, including sleeplessness, would be enough to account for much of it. Young mothers "develop a transient but recurring state called the 'tired mother syndrome,'" Beverly Jones notes. "In its severe form it is, or resembles, a psychosis. . . . They complain of being utterly exhausted, irritable, unable to concentrate. They may wander about somewhat aimlessly, they may have physical pains. They are depressed, anxious, sometimes paranoid, and they cry a lot."

There are reverberations in the marital relationship: "The greater burden of parental responsibilities is," Burgess and Wallin found, "borne by the mother. Mothers who report that they find their duties too much for them may be expressing indirectly dissatisfaction with the extent to which their husbands are assuming their share of responsibility. Even if this dissatisfaction is not present, the irritability of harassed mothers with their children may manifest itself in their marital relationships. . . ."

The husband's marriage may suffer also. The sex relationship may be interfered with, as Burgess and Wallin noted, social activities curtailed, customary routines of postwork relaxation upset, and his "monopoly on his wife's attentions and ministrations . . . inevitably shattered with the advent of a child."[24] In fact, Daniel Hobbs reported the stress of the first child to be greater for the husband's than for the wife's

---

22. Scott, A.C. The Value of Housework: For Love or Money?, Ms. Magazine 57 (July 1972). See also Briggs, Guess Who Has the Most Complex Job?, in Chapter Two, I-A, supra.

23. Bernard, The Future of Marriage 65 (1972).

24. As pointed out to one of the authors by Ms. Rhea Schwartz, the wife's marriage may also suffer if the sex relationship is interfered with or social activities are curtailed — Eds.

marriage. But for both, the sheer weight of coping with problems would be enough to weigh heavily on any relationship.

Recent studies on the amount of time spent by family members on household chores shed additional light on the matter. Economists at the Chase Manhattan Bank estimate that the average housewife does 99.6 hours of housework a week, including 44.5 hours a week as a nursemaid, with the remaining 55.1 hours apportioned among eleven other categories.[25] Walker, in another study,[26] reports that the average time used for household work by homemakers in the 1296 upstate New York families surveyed was about 49 hours per week. Those with no children in the home averaged about 35 hours per week. As the number of children increased, so did the amount of time spent by the homemaker. Her time averaged about 49 hours a week in families with 1 child, 56 hours in families with 2, 3, and 4 children, and about 63 hours in families with 5 or more children. The ages of the children also make a difference. The average time varied from 65.1 hours for homemakers if the youngest child was less than 1 year old to 42 hours if the youngest was 12 to 17 years of age.

Walker reports that women who work outside the home spend less time on housework than women who do not. She hypothesizes that[27]

> The reduced homemaking time for gainfully employed homemakers probably reflects, in part, more effective use of time and a tendency to eliminate some household work. But it undoubtedly reflects even more the fact that the gainfully employed homemakers, as a group, had fewer children — small children especially — than the full-time homemakers.

Another notable finding is that time spent by husbands on household work averaged only 11.2 hours per week, and did not increase with the hours of their wives' paid employment.[28] On the other hand, the more hours women worked outside the home, the longer their average working day. If time spent on volunteer work as well as paid employment and household tasks is counted, the working week averaged about 63 hours for full-time homemakers and 70 hours for women employed 30 or more hours a week.[29] Men averaged a working week of about 64 hours.

Similarly, Robinson and Converse report on the basis of a study of time budgets in the United States in 1965-1966 that the total time spent by married workers on paid work, commuting to work, housework, and family tasks averaged 66.5 hours a week for men and 71.4 hours for women.[30] Among working couples with children, fathers averaged 1.3 hours more free time each weekday and 1.4 hours more on Sunday than mothers. As noted above, Burgess and Wallin confirm that the mother bears the greater burden of parental responsibilities.

25. A. C. Scott, supra, at 59.
26. Walker, "Time-use Patterns for Household Work Related to Homemakers' Employment," speech, Agricultural Outlook Conference, Washington, D.C., Feb. 18, 1970. See also Walker, Time Spent in Household Work by Homemakers, Family Economics Review 5 (September 1969), and Walker, Homemaking Still Takes Time, 61 J. Home Economics 621 (1969).
27. Walker in Family Economics Review, supra, at 5.
28. Walker, Time Used by Husbands For Household Work, Family Economics Review 8 (June 1970). But see the studies reported in Nye and Hoffman, The Employed Mother in America, Part III, The Husband-Wife Relationship (1963), which suggest that the division of labor between spouses is strongly affected by the wife's employment.
29. Walker, Time Spent in Household Work by Homemakers, supra, at 5. See also Hall and Schroeder, Time Spent on Household Tasks, Journal of Home Economics 23-29 (January 1970), reporting that in a survey of Seattle, Washington homemakers (based on a 20 percent response from a random sample of 1200 homemakers), the average weekly hours spent on all home-associated tasks ranged from 39 for those who worked for pay 40 hours or more a week, to 54 for those who were not employed.
30. Robinson and Converse, Summary of U.S. Time-Use Survey, Survey Research Center Monograph (University of Michigan, 1966), cited in Hedges and Barnett, Working Women and the Division of Household Tasks, Monthly Labor Rev. 9, 10 (April 1972).

It is clear that housework is an unusually time-consuming occupation. When that feature is combined with the other negative characteristics previously mentioned, the effect of the housewife role on married women who do not have outside jobs is not very surprising.

Joel Roach's article, "Confessions of a House-Husband," which is excerpted below, convincingly describes the effect of the housespouse role on one's emotional well-being and intellectual effectiveness.[31] He became a househusband for a few months when his wife and he decided to reverse their roles in order to allow her to finish a job outside of the home.

> There was something of a shock for me in discovering the sheer quantity of the housework, and my standards of acceptable cleanliness fell rapidly. It became much easier to see my insistence on neatness as an inherited middle-class hang-up now that I had to do so much of the work myself. . . . I enjoyed it, at first. When not interrupted by the children I could, on a good day, do the kitchen and a bedroom, a load of laundry, and a meal in a little over two hours. Then I'd clean up after the meal and relax for a while with considerable satisfaction. . . .
>
> But within a few weeks that satisfaction and that enthusiasm began to erode a little more each time I woke up or walked into the house, only to find that it all needed to be done again. Finally, the image of the finished job . . . was crowded out of my head by the image of the job to do all over again. I became lethargic, with the result that I worked less efficiently; so that even when I did "finish," it took longer and was done less well, rendering still less satisfaction. At first I had intellectual energy to spare, thinking about my teaching while washing dishes; pausing in the middle of a load of laundry to jot down a note. But those pauses soon became passive daydreams, fantasies from which I would have to snap myself back to the grind, until finally it was all I could do to keep going at all. I became more and more irritable and resentful.
>
> Something similar happened even sooner and more dramatically to my relationship with our three children. I soon found myself angry with them most of the time. . . . [W]ith a six-year-old, a four-year-old, and a one-year-old, someone would need me every five to 15 minutes . . . In everything I tried to do, I was frustrated by their constant demands and soon came, quite simply, to hate them; and to hate myself for hating them; and at some level, I suspect, to hate Jan for getting me into this mess. My home life became a study in frustration and resentment.
>
> I soon reached the conclusion that if I was going to keep house and take care of the children, I might as well give up doing anything else at the same time if I hoped to maintain any equilibrium at all. So I deliberately went through my housekeeping paces in a daze, keeping alert for the children but otherwise concentrating on whatever was before me, closing down all circuits not relevant to the work at hand. . . .
>
> Things went on this way for quite some time. . . . I began to perceive my condition as normal, and I didn't notice that my professional work was at a standstill. Then Jan became involved in community organizing, which took up more and more of her time and began to eat into mine, until finally I found myself doing housekeeping and child care from eight to 16 hours a day, and this went on for about eight weeks. . . .
>
> I can pinpoint the place in time when we saw the necessity for a more careful adjustment of responsibilities, defining duties and scheduling hours more precisely and adhering to them more faithfully. It was at a moment when it became clear that Jan's work was beginning to pay off and her group scored a definite and apparently unqualified success. I went around the house for a full day feeling very self-satisfied, proud of her achievement, *as if it were my own*, which was fine until I realized, somewhere near the end of the day, that much of that sense of achievement resulted from the fact that I had no achievement of my own. I was getting my sense of fulfillment, of self-esteem, *through her*, while she was getting it *through her work*. It had happened: I was a full-fledged househusband.
>
> A similar moment of illumination occurred at about the same time. Jan had spent

31. 1 Ms. Magazine 25 (November 1972).

the afternoon with a friend while I took care of the children and typed a revision of the bibliography for the book I was trying to finish at the time, the kind of drudgery more prosperous authors underpay some woman to do. By the time Jan got home I was in a state of benumbed introversion, and when she began to talk about the substance of her afternoon's conversation, I was at first bored and finally irritated. Before long I was snapping at her viciously. She sat there looking first puzzled, then bewildered, and finally withdrawn. In a kind of reflexive self-defense she cut me off emotionally and went on thinking about whatever was on her mind. As I began to run down, I realized that what she had been trying to talk about would normally be interesting and important to me, yet I had driven her away. Then I looked at her and suddenly had the really weird sensation of seeing myself, my own isolation and frustration when I used to come home and try to talk to her. I realized that I was in her traditional position and felt a much fuller understanding of what that was. In that moment, on the verge of anger, an important part of what we had been doing to each other for all those years became clearer than it had ever been to either of us.

III. THE LAW OF THE ONGOING MARRIAGE

A. MERGER OF THE WIFE'S LEGAL IDENTITY INTO HER HUSBAND'S

1. Married Women's Domicile

KANOWITZ, WOMEN AND THE LAW
46-52 (1969)

To most non-lawyers, the word "domicile" conveys the idea of a home. In legal contemplation, while "home" and "domicile" are often synonymous, the latter word has a more technical meaning. The Restatement of the Conflict of Laws defines domicile as a "place where a person has a settled connection for certain legal purposes, either because his home is there *or because it is assigned to him by law.'*[75] Elsewhere domicile has been described as "a relationship which the law creates between an individual and a particular locality or country."[76]

The distinction between "residence" and "domicile" is also important. A person's domicile may be in one state or territory and his actual residence in another.[77] In effect, a domicile is the place where a person lives and has his true, permanent home, to which, whenever he is absent, he has an intention of returning.[78] The question of a person's domicile is largely one of intent.[79]

The areas of law in which a person's domicile may be important are many and varied. Domicile of a party or a decedent often determines whether a court has jurisdiction to hear and decide certain kinds of legal questions: e.g., divorce suits,[80] probate matters,[81] and guardianship proceedings.[82] In other types of cases, though the parties'

---

75. Restatement, Conflict of Laws §9 (1934).

76. In re Schultz' Estate, 316 Ill. App. 540, 45 N.E.2d 577, 582 (1942), *rev'd on other grounds* 384 Ill. 148, 51 N.E.2d 140 (1943).

77. Wells v. People, 44 Ill. 40 (1867).

78. Peirce v. Peirce, 379 Ill. 185, 39 N.E.2d 990 (1942).

79. Id.

80. See Williams v. North Carolina, 317 U.S. 287 (1942).

81. See, e.g., Ives v. Salisbury's Heirs, 56 Vt. 565 (1884); Tripp v. Tripp, 240 S.C. 334, 126 S.E.2d 9 (1962).

82. See, e.g., Restatement, Conflict of Laws §149 (1934), "The status of a guardian and ward is created and terminated by the state of the domicil of the ward; but cf. Paulsen & Best, Appointment of a Guardian

domiciles may not affect the court's basic jurisdiction (i.e., its power or authority to hear a particular case), it may be of importance in determining whether the court should nevertheless entertain the action (the question of venue).[83] The availability of many rights and privileges of citizenship also depend upon a person's domicile. These include the right to vote,[84] to hold and, therefore, to run for public office,[85] to receive welfare assistance,[86] or to qualify for free or limited tuition at state-operated educational institutions.[87] Some obligations of citizenship — e.g., jury duty and the taxability of personal and intangible property — are also determined by the juror's[88] or taxpayer's[89]. domicile, respectively.

From the foregoing, it should be evident that the location of a person's domicile may have important practical, as well as legal, consequences. Ideally, free choice of domicile should be possible. For the most part, that has in fact been the situation. Adult women who are unmarried and adult men, regardless of their marital status, have the legal right to establish or change a former domicile freely. This type of domicile —not surprisingly called a "domicile of choice"[90] — can be acquired by those who are authorized to do so by actually residing in a particular locality and, at the same time, intending to remain there.[91]

Where married women are concerned, however, the rule is otherwise. Though exceptions have been carved out in recent years, the general rule persists that a wife's domicile follows that of her husband.[92] This means that by operation of law, when a woman marries, she "loses her domicile and acquires that of her husband, no matter where she resides, or what she believes or intends."[93] In choosing the domicile of his family and wife, the husband must of course act reasonably. He cannot, for example, insist that the only place for his wife to live is in his parents' home.[94] As long as his

---

in the Conflict of Laws, 45 Iowa L. Rev. 212, 215 (1960), "The case law has generally rejected the Restatement principle."

83. The word "residence" is sometimes intended to convey the meaning of "domicile." In federal court actions, the jurisdictional basis of which is solely the diverse citizenship of the parties, proper venue is in the district of either the plaintiff's or the defendant's residence. 28 U.S.C. §1391(a) (1948). For most other federal court cases, the only district in which the action may be brought is the one in which "all defendants reside." 28 U.S.C. §1391(b) (1948).

84. See, e.g., Brown v. Hows, 163 Tenn. 178, 42 S.W.2d 210 (1931); Berry v. Wilcox, 44 Neb. 82, 62 N.W. 249 (1895).

85. See, e.g., Bigney v. Secretary of Commonwealth, 301 Mass. 107, 16 N.E.2d 573 (1938).

86. See, e.g., Georgia v. Waterville, 107 Vt. 347, 178 Atl. 893 (1935). Some courts have recently divided over whether state residency requirements for welfare recipients violate constitutional provisions, including the equal protection guarantee. Compare B.__v. S.__, reported at 8 Wel. L. Bull. 11 (May, 1967). Should the U.S. Supreme Court hold such requirements to be unconstitutional, see Shapiro v. Thompson, *prob. juris. noted*, 389 U.S. 1032 (1968), other areas in which domicile or residency now play an important role may also be affected.

87. See 55 Am. Jur. Universities and Colleges §16 (1946).

88. See State v. Wimby, 119 La. 139, 43 So. 984 (1907).

89. See Commonwealth v. Kernochan, 129 Va. 405, 106 S.E. 367 (1921).

90. See Goodrich, Conflict of Laws 40 (4th ed. Scoles 1964).

91. Id.

92. New York Trust Co. v. Riley, 24 Del. Ch. 354, 16 A.2d 772 (1940), affirmed 315 U.S.343 (1941). Though "domicile" and "nationality" are distinct concepts, they are not entirely unrelated. Under the laws of many countries a woman loses her nationality automatically upon marriage to an alien or if she acquires her husband's nationality by the marriage. U.N. Dept. of Economic and Social Affairs, Nationality of Married Women *passim* (1963). In this connection, a Convention on the Nationality of Married Women has been proposed by the United Nations and signed by a number of countries. See United Nations Commission on the Status of Women, Legal Status of Married Women 100-103 (1958). The Convention generally eliminates the automatic loss of citizenship for a woman who marries an alien. In the United States, prior to September 22, 1933, American women lost their citizenship by marrying an alien, although American men who married aliens did not lose theirs. U.S. Inter-American Commission of Women, A Comparison of the Political Rights of Men and Women in the United States (74th Congress, 2d session, Senate Document No. 270) Washington, 1936 [hereinafter cited as Comparison]. Under present American law, marriage of a United States national to an alien does not affect nationality, whether the national be a man or a woman, unless he or she makes a formal renunciation of nationality before a court. Id.

93. In re Paullin, 92 N.J. Eq. 419, 113 Atl. 240 (1921).

94. Hoffhines v. Hoffhines, 146 Md. 350, 126 Atl. 112 (1924).

selection of a domicile is a reasonable one, however, that choice is his to make, and his wife is legally bound to abide by it.

This rule can cause much hardship. If a married woman owns personal property in State X, it may be taxed at the higher rate of State Y, her husband's domicile, though she is residing in State X with her husband's consent. Similarly, where a married woman is, for any reason, living in a different state from her husband (a not uncommon situation in this day and age), her right to vote or run for public office may be rendered meaningless by the rule that attributes her husband's domicile to her.

Apart from these practical problems, the continued enshrinement into law of a rule that accords to only one of the spouses, the husband, the right to decide a question of such intimate concern to both husband and wife is obviously inconsistent with the spirit and intent of the Married Women's Acts.

In recognition of the difficulties created by the traditional rule, four states (Arkansas, Delaware, Hawaii and New Hampshire) permit married women to acquire an independent domicile for all purposes.[95] A married woman may also acquire a separate domicile in 42 states if she is living apart from her husband for cause.[96] This exception is justified by some courts on the ground that the general rule is founded upon the concept of a unified marriage relationship. That unity having been destroyed by the husband's misconduct amounting to grounds for divorce or separation, the wife is allowed to acquire a domicile of her own.[97] Where husband and wife are living apart by mutual agreement, however, or if the husband consents to the separation, only 18 of the last-mentioned 42 states permit a married woman to acquire a separate domicile.[98]

In all states, married women are permitted to acquire a separate domicile for the purpose of instituting divorce proceedings.[99] Having done so, they may then claim the same separate domicile for other purposes — e.g., to establish their citizenship in a particular state in order to sustain federal court jurisdiction based upon the parties' "diversity of citizenship" though the action is for tort damages only.[100] Finally, in addition to the four states previously mentioned as permitting married women to acquire separate domiciles for all purposes, some states allow married women to establish their own domicile for limited purposes only: 15 states for purposes of voting, 6 for election to public office, 5 for jury service, 7 for taxation, and 5 for probate.[101] . . .

American courts have in recent times assigned various reasons to justify the traditional rule which forces a husband's domicile upon his wife. Some have frankly acknowledged its origins in the theoretical identity of husband and wife at common law.[105] Recognizing, perhaps, that this fiction was supposed to have been rejected by the passage of the married women's acts, these courts have at times urged additional policy reasons of a more logical nature in support of the rule. Thus, in Estate of Wickes, the California Supreme Court stated:

> The subjection of the wife to the husband *was not the only reason for the rule.* Parties marrying contract to live together. The husband obligates himself to furnish a proper

95. [Report of the Committee on Civil and Political Rights to the President's Commission on the Status of Women (CCPR) (1963)] 20. The statistical summary of state laws governing married women's domicile is derived from Table 2, CCPR 21, which, in turn, was prepared by the Women's Bureau, Department of Labor. The figures reflect the situation as of March 6, 1963.

96. Id.

97. See Burns v. Burns, 145 Neb. 213, 15 N.W.2d 753 (1944); Smith v. Smith, 205 Ore. 650, 289'P.2d 1086 (1955); but cf. Galvin v. Dailey, 109 Iowa 332, 80 N.W.420 (1899); and Harrison v. Harrison, 20 Ala. 629 (1852).

98. CCPR 20.

99. Id.

100. Williamson v. Osenton, 232 U.S.619 (1913).

101. CCPR 20.

105. See, e.g., Younger v. Gianotti, 176 Tenn. 139, 138 S.W.2d 448 (1940), Estate of Wickes, 128 Cal. 270, 60 Pac. 867 (1900).

home for his wife and to maintain her there in a degree of comfort authorized by his circumstances, and they mutually agreed to live there together. It is a matter of great public concern that this should be so. In this association there can be no majority vote, and the law leaves the ultimate decision to the husband.[106]

Similarly, describing the reasons for the common law rule, the Tennessee Supreme Court, in Younger v. Gianotti, stated:

> The rule of the common law that the domicile of the wife follows that of the husband was based on (1) the doctrine of marital unity, and (2) that public policy demanded that the family unity be protected by allowing one family to have only one domicile.[107]

Other courts have completely denied the part played by the common law fiction of the unity of husband and wife in the development of the rule. Instead, they have sought to assign allegedly modern social reasons as its only basis. Thus, in Carlson v. Carlson,[108] the Arizona Supreme Court offers as "sound reasons" for the rule the following:

> The law imposes upon the husband the burden and obligation of the support, maintenance and care of the family and almost of necessity he must have the right of choice of the situs of the home. There can be no decision by a majority rule as to where the family home shall be maintained, and a reasonable accompaniment of the imposition of the obligations is the right of selection. The violation of this principle tends to sacrifice the family unity, the entity upon which our civilization is built. *The principle is not based on the common law theory of the merger of the personality of the wife with that of the husband; it is based on the theory that one domicile for the family home is still an essential way of life.*[109]

Whether presented as additional or substituted arguments for the common law fictional unity of the spouses, these "policy reasons" are, in the light of modern day sociological and legal conditions, specious and unrealistic.

At one time in Anglo-American legal history, when divorces were virtually impossible to procure, the married woman's domicile rule was no doubt an effective determinant when questions of the family home's location arose within the family itself. If the spouses could not agree, the husband decided where he and his wife and his children should live. If the wife was unhappy with the decision she could protest. But if he insisted, she went along. Legally, there was nothing she could do to alter the decision.

Today — now that divorces are relatively simple to procure — the husband's unilateral right to choose the family domicile has practical significance only with reference to third parties, such as creditors who seek to sue the wife. And, of course, it affects the wife's rights with regard to the matters discussed earlier. As for resolving the question of the family domicile within the family itself, however, the rule, as a practical matter, can have no meaningful influence at all. . . .

What of the frequently encountered phrase in these cases that a "majority vote" is impossible in this situation? This theme runs through many judicial and statutory rules that discriminate on the basis of sex. It assumes that for marital partners to pull in opposite directions on certain matters would be intolerable. The power to make

---

106. Estate of Wickes, 128 Cal. 270, 278, 60 Pac. at 870. (Emphasis supplied.)
107. 176 Tenn. at 140; 138 S.W.2d at 449.
108. 75 Ariz. 308, 256 P.2d 249 (1953).
109. 75 Ariz. at 309; 256 P.2d at 250. (Emphasis supplied.)

important decisions is therefore given to only one of the spouses. Yet consistently the one who is given this power is always the husband, never the wife.

Various reasons have been urged in support of this arbitrary allocation of decision-making power. In the *Carlson* case, the court invokes the husband's support obligation as justifying his unilateral right to decide matters of family domicile. Aside from the fact that the almost exclusive obligation of the husband to support the family may have become in modern America an impediment to true legal equality of the sexes the argument assumes the primacy of economic considerations in the marriage relationship. As suggested earlier, however, other factors may be equally important in deciding where a family should make its home.

The suggestion in the cases that a family should have one home only under all circumstances also overlooks the frequency of family separations caused by a husband's military service. Somehow marriages survive and often thrive under these conditions. This is by no means to suggest that as a general rule husband and wife should live apart from one another. But husbands and wives live together because they want to, and not because the law tells them that they must. Certainly, where spouses decide, amicably and for whatever reasons, that each should maintain a separate domicile, the law should allow them this choice. More than a "majority vote," such a choice by husband and wife would in fact constitute a "unanimous vote." . . .

NOTE

It is important to realize what is involved in the decisions of 18 states to give married women equal rights with married men to establish, change, and retain legal domicile for some purposes. This means that the state will no longer attach a particular legal consequence outside the marriage relation to the wife's obligation to cohabit with her husband in the home and location of his choice. It does *not* mean that the parties may contract as to who shall select the marital residence or that the wife who has no other grounds for divorce may refuse to follow the husband to the residential location of his choice without thereby giving him grounds for divorce.

2. The Surnames of Married Women and Legitimate Children

In the United States custom, and occasionally law, dictate that a woman adopt the surname of her husband upon marriage. This is a manifestation of the traditional merger of the two persons, in which the identity of the woman, symbolized by her name, is lost. But the custom has more than symbolic significance as, for instance, divorced women learn when seeking to establish lines of credit in their newly resumed birth names. The following is a brief examination of the history and current state of the law as to the names of married women.

a. Historical Background

Through the common law concept of coverture, a married woman's legal identity was merged into that of her husband, with numerous legal consequences, such as the termination of her right to bring suit on her own behalf and of her ability to acquire her own domicile. However, it was apparently not until Victorian times that her loss of identity generally included the loss of both her first and last names. And even then, it was a matter of widespread custom, *not* law, in England.[1]

1. See Eiven, A History of British Surnames 391 (London 1941); 19 Halsbury's Laws of England 829 (3d ed. 1957); M. Turner-Samuels, The Law of Married Women 345 (1957), citing cases. See also Reany, The

In the United States, there are numerous cases and statutes dealing with the names of married women, but most of them have arisen in contexts remote from that of a woman seeking to retain a separate identity within marriage.[2] Frequently, the cases arose in the context of a lawsuit in which a married woman who had assumed her husband's surname had been sued, served with legal notice, or noticed by publication in her birth-given surname. In order to avoid suit or notice, the woman would argue that her legal name, and the only name under which she could be expected to receive notice by publication, was her husband's surname. The courts, seeing a need for consistent practice, and being aware that the prevailing custom was for married women to assume their husband's surnames, usually ruled that a married woman's legal as well as customary surname was that of her husband.[3] In cases involving women who did not use their husband's surnames, the courts have generally ruled that their legal names were their birth-given names. However, such cases did not arise very often.[4]

The use of the husband's proper name and surname with the prefix "Mrs." to designate a married woman received similarly inconsistent treatment. If the issue arose in a case where there was possible confusion between the woman and her husband, or among successive wives, the court was liable to require that the woman use her own proper name, or even her own proper name and birth-given surname.[5] If no such confusion was involved, the courts usually ruled that the Mrs. John J. Doe form was adequate, though not preferred.[6]

Similarly, state statutes often require, imply, or assume that upon marriage a woman takes her husband's surname. Since most women followed the customary practice, there was no need for the state legislatures to settle by statute the issue of whether the change was legally required. But it probably seemed important to establish procedures for recording in women's voter registrations, driver's licenses, and the like the changes of name that customarily were made. The results of the attempts of state legislatures to deal with the customary change of surname upon marriage were summarized as follows by the Women's Rights Project of the American Civil Liberties Union.

MEMORANDUM ON THE RIGHT OF MARRIED WOMEN TO RETAIN OR REGAIN THEIR BIRTH NAMES
The Women's Rights Project of the American Civil Liberties Union
Memorandum to Affiliates and Liaison People 2-3 (September 1972)

Only Hawaii has a statute specifically requiring [that] "Every married woman shall adopt her husband's surname as a family name." Hawaii Rev. Laws, tit. 31 §574-1.[1] In the other states, despite detailed provisions on the subject of marriage and divorce and

---

Origins of English Surnames 82-85 (1962); Mordacque, History of the Names of Men, Nations and Places (1964); and Pine, The Story of Surnames 23 (1966).

2. See Hughes, And Then There Were Two, 23 Hast. L.J. 233 (1971), and Carlson, Surnames of Married Women and Legitimate Children, 17 N.Y.L.J. 552 (1971).

3. See, e.g., Chapman v. Phoenix National Bank, 85 N.Y. 437 (1881) and Freeman v. Hawkins, 77 Tex. 498, 14 S.W. 364 (1890).

4. See, e.g., Lane v. Duchac, 73 Wis. 646, 41 N.W. 962 (1889) and State ex rel. Krupa v. Green, 114 Ohio App. 497, 177 N.E.2d 616 (1961). But cf. In re Kayaloff, 9 F. Supp. 176 (S.D.N.Y. 1934), and People ex rel. Rago v. Lipsky, 327 Ill. App. 63, 63 N.E. 2d 642 (1945). As Carlson, supra, at 555-558, points out, one situation is particularly likely to give rise to the idea that married women may not use their birth-given surnames instead of their husband's surnames: cases involving married women who have assumed their husbands' surnames for some but not all purposes. The fact that a court, given a choice between two surnames, chooses the husband's surname as a married woman's legal name does not necessarily mean that the same court would deny the right to use her premarriage surname to a married woman who used that name consistently.

5. See, e.g., Wilty v. Jefferson Parish Democratic Executive Comm., 245 La. 145, 157 So. 2d 718 (1963). But see Baumann v. Baumann, 250 N.Y. 382, 165 N.E. 819 (1929).

6. See, e.g., Koley v. Williams, 265 Mass. 661, 164 N.E. 444 (1929) and Kelle v. Crab Orchard Rural Fire Protection Dist., 164 Neb. 593, 83 N.W. 2d 251 (1957).

1. Puerto Rico has a similar statute. P.R. Laws Ann. tit. 31, §287 (1967).

husband and wife, no statute expressly requires a wife to assume her husband's surname.

However, the implication that married women must use their husbands' surnames underlies or appears to underlie statutes in force in several states. The clearest example is a name change statute that excludes married women entirely. For example, the Iowa Code §674.1 reads: "Any person, under no civil disabilities, who has attained his or her majority and is unmarried, if a female, desiring to change his or her name, may do so as provided in this chapter." The implication is present too in statutes providing that when a married man changes his surname, the surname of his wife also changes.

Voter registration laws of two varieties provide some support for the argument that, upon marriage, a woman assumes her husband's name as a matter of law: re-registration requirements and Miss/Mrs. prefix requirements. The first type, effective in a majority of the states, typically calls for report to the Board of Elections of the names of female persons who marry. The voter then receives a notice that her registration is cancelled and in order to vote she must re-register in her married name. . . .

In a few states . . . a woman must precede her name with the prefix "Miss" or "Mrs." for the purpose of voter registration. . . .

Implicitly recognizing that most women adopt their husbands' surnames upon marriage, many states provide by statute that upon awarding a divorce the court may change the name of the wife back to her former name. The Indiana statute is typical: "The court upon granting a divorce may allow the wife to resume her maiden name or previous married name, whether the wife be plaintiff or defendant in such action." Ind. Ann. Stat. §3-1225. Some states restrict this provision to women who do not have minor children or to those who were not at fault in the divorce. In practice, however, a divorce-related order authorizing a woman to resume her birth name is within the judge's discretion and factors such as children in her custody and the names they bear may enter into his or her determination.

b. Challenges to Legal Requirements that a Married Woman Assume Her Husband's Surname

(1) In the 1920s and 1930s.[7] In 1921, a league was formed to secure the common law right of women to retain their own names at marriage, naming itself for Lucy Stone, the feminist leader, who had kept her own name when she married Henry B. Blackwell in 1855.[8] Over the next ten years, the Lucy Stone League and the National Woman's Party tangled with the Passport Office, the Copyright Office and the Comptroller General of the United States (with the latter, over the right to use one's birth-given surname on the government payroll).[9] The women won all three battles eventually, and three prominent New York newspapers editorialized in their favor.[10] During this period, the attorneys general of several states issued opinions supporting the rights of married women to keep their birth-given surnames.[11]

7. This account relies heavily on MacDougall, Married Women's Common Law Right to Their Own Surnames, 1 Women's Rights L. Rep. 2 (Fall/Winter 1972-73).

8. Id. at 5.

9. Id. at 5-7.

10. The New York Times, the New York Tribune, and the New York World. MacDougall, id. at 5-6; Stannard, Married Women v. Husbands' Names 6 (1973), available from Germainbooks, 91 St. Germain Avenue, San Francisco, Ca. 94114, in paperback for $2.00. The women lost the fight with the Comptroller General in the 1920s when Marjorie Jarvis, the woman who had raised the issue, failed to pursue her case. However, on August 15, 1939, the Comptroller General rendered an opinion authorizing the use of birth-given surnames by married women on government payrolls. 2 Women Today, Aug. 21, 1972. Until 1966, the Code of Federal Regulations provided that a married woman could be issued a passport in her premarriage surname provided that she used it consistently and submitted two affidavits from persons who had known her for ten years that she had always used that name and no other. 22 C.F.R. §51.20 (1938). This provision was deleted in 1966 when the entire passport section was revised. MacDougall, id. at 6.

11. See, e.g., 13 Op. Atty. Gen. 632 (Wisconsin, 1924); and Biennial Report of Atty. Gen. 824 (Michigan, 1929-30). This history is recounted in MacDougall, supra, and will not be explored in detail here.

(2) In the 1960s and 1970s. Recently women in many states have begun asserting their rights to keep their own surnames during marriage, both by using the formal name change procedure (including one innovative petition for establishment, rather than change, of name) and by suing to obtain the right to register to vote, obtain driver's licenses, or run for election in their own surnames. They have met with varied results. Wendy Forbush, whose case was discussed in Chapter One, V, attacked on equal protection grounds the Alabama law which was interpreted as requiring the use of the husband's surname on driver's licenses. A three-judge court rejected her claim, in the context of Alabama's simple inexpensive name change procedure, and the Supreme Court affirmed without opinion. Forbush v. Wallace, 401 U.S. 970, 92 S. Ct. 1197, 31 L. Ed. 2d 246 (1972), *aff'g mem.* 341 F. Supp. 217 (M.D. Ala. 1971). She had accepted the interpretation offered by Alabama that the common law of the state required her to change to her husband's surname. Other cases have been litigated on the theory that, though the common law and custom allow and even encourage the change, it is not required. Courts in both Ohio and Maryland have so ruled. In Krupa v. Green, 114 Ohio App. 497, 177 N.E.2d 616 (1961), the court stated: "It is only *by custom,* in English speaking countries that a woman, upon marriage, adopts the surname of her husband in place of the surname of her father. The State of Ohio follows this custom, but there exists no law compelling it."[12] The Maryland court held in Stuart v. Board of Supervisors, 266 Md. 440, 447, 295 A.2d 223, 227 (1972):

> Consistent with the common law principle referred to in Maryland cases, we hold that a married woman's surname does not become that of her husband where, as here, she evidences a clear intent to consistently and nonfraudulently use her birth given name subsequent to her marriage.... [W]e believe the rule we enunciate today is founded upon the English common law.

In both *Krupa* and *Stuart,* married women who had never used their husbands names were allowed to retain their pre-marriage names without formal proceedings.

In general, the case law as far as a woman's right to choose her own surname or to maintain a surname different from that of her husband appears to be in a state of flux, with the possibility of choosing one's own surname clearly open, through one proceeding or another, to women in most states. As of this writing, legislation which would allow married women to retain their father's surnames or choose other surnames[13] has been introduced in several states. It seems clear that to the extent that present statutes are interpreted to require married women to take their husband's surnames, they will be held to be invalid under the federal equal rights amendment.

Because the law is in a period of transition, it is important that a woman who wishes to use a surname of her choice other than the surname of her husband seek information and assistance from those with experience in this area. A number of useful articles and handbooks are now available,[14] and there are a number of organizations

---

12. 114 Ohio App. at 501, 177 N.E.2d at 619.

13. Legislation has been introduced in Wisconsin, Washington, Illinois, California, and Massachusetts. The 1969 Wisconsin bill read:

"(1) Any woman named on a marriage license may, at the time the license is issued, elect to retain her maiden name or another permissible previous name. Such election shall be made in writing and signed by her on a form provided under S. 245.20 and shall be attached to the copy of the marriage license retained by the county clerk.

"(2) A name retained by a woman under the section shall be that woman's name for all legal purposes including business affairs and elections to public offices." (Wis. Assembly Bill No. 781 (1969).)

As yet none of the legislation has passed, although the increasing frequency of its introduction and the prospect of imminent passage of the Equal Rights Amendment make it likely that eventually some states will have such statutes. It is important that these laws be scrutinized carefully so that existing common law rights to use the name of one's choice not be abrogated by statutory change. Further information on legislation which has been introduced can be obtained from the Center for a Woman's Own Name, infra.

14. In addition to the ACLU memorandum reproduced in part above, Married Women v. Husbands' Names, supra, and the article by MacDougall, supra, see also Center for a Woman's Own Name, Booklet for

which may be able to provide assistance, particularly the Center for a Woman's Own Name.[15]

c. Surnames of Children

Another area of the law of names in which changes are being sought is the naming of children. Some courts have held that fathers have a direct and protectible interest in having children bear their surnames, even when custody of the children has been awarded to the mother.[16] However, it is quite common for a divorced or separated mother to change the surnames of the children of whom she has custody to a surname different from that of their natural father.[17] Unless the father objects, such a common law change of name by custom and usage will be effective. Similarly, in most states, if the parents agree, a child can be given a surname other than its father's either on the birth certificate, by formal name change proceedings, or by the common law method of using the new surname consistently for a period of time.[18]

According to the Center for a Woman's Own Name, however,[19]

> Although the law may clearly allow you to name your children as you please in your state, custom is so entrenched and prejudice against the concept of children born to married couples being named for their mothers or children born to unmarried couples being given names other than those of their mothers is so great in many areas that you may have to take legal action to enforce your rights in naming your children and their rights to change their names.

The suggestion above that expert help be obtained therefore applies even more strongly to those seeking to give nontraditional surnames to children.

3. The Effect on Credit of the Merger of Identity

Seven areas of discrimination against women have been identified in the commercial credit area:[20]

> 1. Extinction of a woman's individual credit upon marriage, and the requirement that her husband join in her application, if she is to retain her own credit cards after marriage.
> 2. Requiring a married woman, who is objectively a better credit risk than her husband, to list financial information about her husband and have him join in a credit card application without requiring a married man to do the same for his wife.
> 3. Extinction of a woman's credit after divorce because all credit during marriage was in her husband's name, regardless of the wife's contribution to her husband's credit rating.

Women Who Wish to Determine Their Own Names After Marriage (1974), available from the Center for $2.00 plus 25¢ postage, 261 Kimberley, Barrington, Ill. 60010; and Ross, The Rights of Women, ch. 9 and Appendix: Chart C (1973).

15. Both Married Women v. Husbands' Names, the Booklet for Women Who Wish to Determine Their Own Names After Marriage, and The Rights of Women, all supra, list further sources of information and assistance.

16. See, e.g., cases cited in 53 A.L.R.2d 914 (1957); Warms v. Warms, 252 Cal. App. 2d 130, 60 Cal. Rptr. 88 (1967); King v. Newman, 421 S.W.2d 149 (Tex. 1967). Where the father has been guilty of severe misconduct, or when there is some unusual benefit to the child from bearing a name other than his or her father's, the name change has been granted. See, e.g., In re Fein, 51 Misc. 2d 1022, 274 N.Y.S. 2d 547 (N.Y. City Civ. Ct. 1966); In rel Almasnino, 204 Misc. 53, 122 N.Y.S. 2d 277 (N.Y. City Civ. Ct. 1952).

17. See Booklet for Women Who Wish to Determine Their Own Names After Marriage, supra, at 18.

18. Id. at 16-18.

19. Id. at 16.

20. These areas were listed in the testimony of the Pennsylvania Commission on the Status of Women at hearings on proposed changes in the Federal Deposit Insurance Corporation regulations, Washington, Dec. 20, 1972. See Penn. Commission on the Status of Women, Credit Report 67 (1973).

4. Refusal of mortgage institutions to consider a wife's income, or such institutions' refusal to grant an unmarried woman a mortgage regardless of her income.

5. Resistance by credit institutions to granting credit based in whole or in part upon court-ordered support payments.

6. Resistance by credit institutions to providing credit for widows.

7. Application of different and stricter standards for women than for men in determining whether to grant credit.

The topic will be briefly discussed in this chapter because these particular discriminations spring from the primal stereotypical thinking about woman's place: all women are or will become wives, and all wives will be controlled by their husbands and thus are bad individual credit risks; all women either are or will be controlled by nature and will become mothers who leave the labor force, making them poor credit risks for long-term ventures. As well as being based on stereotypes, those attitudes reinforce the situation from which the stereotypes arose in the first place. Unable to obtain loans for education, starting their own businesses, or buying their own homes, women are more likely to end up married and out of the labor force.

a. *Discounting of Women's Income*

The most egregious of the identified forms of discrimination is the discounting of a woman's income in considering all loans, particularly mortgage loans. "The ability to obtain mortgage credit to purchase a home can mean more to a family than merely the adequacy of its shelter. It can mean living in a decent neighborhood, having access to good educational, health, and recreational facilities, or even access to a decent job."[21] Lenders are straightforward in stating that they believe women's incomes are unreliable because they may have children and leave the labor force. That the experience of a woman's income being partly or wholly discounted is widespread became recently evident in hearings before federal agencies and a congressional committee.[22] Revealed at the hearings were the results of a survey conducted by the Federal Home Loan Bank Board on lending practices of 100 institutions. One question was what credit they would allow for a working wife's income if she was age twenty-five, had two school-age children, and worked full time as a secretary. Fully 25 percent of the institutions responded that they would count none of her income, 22 percent indicated that they would give full credit, and the rest would give partial credit.[23]

This discrimination falls most heavily on minority women, 52 percent of whom are in the labor force and whose income must especially be counted for mortgage loans if their families are to have decent housing. Another distressing aspect of the discrimination is that it apparently is not based on any empirical study of actual performance. In fact, economists have testified that the few studies that exist show the risk of default

21. Steven Rohde, Statement before the National Commission on Consumer Finance, Hearings, p. 2, Washington, May 22, 1972 (representing the Center for National Policy Review, School of Law, Catholic University).

22. National Commission on Consumer Finance (NCCF), Hearings, May 22, 23, 1972. Federal Deposit Insurance Corporation (FDIC), Hearings on Proposed Rulemaking, Dec. 20, 1972. Oversight Hearings on 15 U.S.C. §§1601-81(t) (Truth In Lending Act) before the Subcomm. on Consumer Affairs of the House Comm. on Banking and Currency, 93d Cong., 1st Sess. (Oct. 30, Nov. 6, Nov. 13, 1973), hereinafter Oversight Hearings. At all of these hearings, witnesses from public interest and feminist organizations presented extensive examples of sex discrimination in the consumer and credit and loan areas, and also suggested existing mandates and regulations that would allow federal agencies to act, even without new legislation.

23. The survey was made by the board, apparently on its own initiative, but it did not release the results until the United States Commission on Civil Rights made public the existence of the survey, and public interest groups demanded the release of the figures. They were released in March 1972. Of the 100 banks surveyed, 74 responded. Stephen Rohde, in NCCF Hearings, id. at 4.

or substantial delinquency to be less in two-earner than in single-earner families.[24]

Many lending institutions require as a regular part of the application procedure that women supply information, and sometimes proof, about their capacity and intention to have children. The trade magazine American Banker recently surveyed the banking commissioners of all states to ascertain whether such information was requested. Among the 37 states that responded, there was wide disagreement about the propriety and the discriminatory nature of such questions. The director of the Department of Financial Institutions in Indiana stated, for instance, "[Y]ou trade your privacy a little bit to get a loan anyway. I think it's discrimination but justified."[25]

Single women are also clearly discriminated against by lending institutions in obtaining substantial personal or mortgage loans. This seems to spring from the notion that the life of the single or divorced woman is likely to change, i.e., that she will get married or remarried and then presumably move out of the job market.[26]

b. Credit Card Application and Issuance

The problems that have been identified with credit card applications and issuance have taken a number of forms. Most serious is the requirement of some credit issuers that a married woman's account actually be in her husband's name — in other words, he is the responsible party and, in effect, she is not allowed to maintain her own account and pay for it from her own or family resources. This policy may arise from the fear that otherwise the husband's assets will not be reachable for the wife's debts, and from the assumption that she is unlikely to have her own assets, or any need for her own line of credit. A more likely reason for the policy is that "it is expensive for [creditors] to open two accounts per family and, as between the husband and the wife, they prefer to deal with the man."[27]

A second kind of problem is that many credit institutions require a married woman to list information about her husband on her credit applications. A third credit requirement, of lesser significance but which some women consider unnecessary and insulting, is the listing of a married woman as Mrs. John Doe, when she would prefer to be simply Mary Doe, or use some other surname, such as her birth-given name or one of her own choosing. One advantage to a married woman of credit in a name which does not indicate her marital status is that she need not apply for new credit on divorce, and therefore avoids giving creditors an opportunity to deny her credit because of their biases against divorcees.

c. The Effect of State Laws on the Creditworthiness of Married Women

An explanation which is commonly offered for discrimination against married women in the granting of credit is the effect of certain state laws governing the marital relationship. The main statutes which are thought to be inconsistent with the granting of credit to wives are those which require a husband to support his wife; those in community property states which give control of the community property to the hus-

24. Herzog and Earley, Home Mortgage Delinquency and Foreclosure, National Bureau of Economic Research, New York, 1970, as quoted by Rohde, id. at 11. See also the testimony of Josephine McElhone, The Economic Rationale for Mortgage Lending Standards Affecting Women Borrowers, in NCCF Hearings, supra, May 22, 1972.

25. Bishopric, Women Begin to Get Action on Complaints of Discrimination in Granting of Credit, American Banker, 1,6 (July 13, 1973).

26. Rohde, in NCCF Hearings, supra, at 13-15, substantiates the discrimination against single persons applying for loans and mortgages.

27. Gates, Credit Discrimination Against Women: Causes and Solutions, 27 Vand. L. Rev. 409, 414-415 (1974), citing a statement by a spokesman for Sears, Roebuck and Company in Business Week, Jan. 12, 1974, at 77.

band; laws prohibiting alienation of jointly owned property or assignment of one spouse's wages without the consent of both spouses; and multiple agreement laws, which prohibit the maintenance by creditors of separate accounts for husband and wife. On closer examination, it becomes evident that a large number of the laws which allegedly require creditors to discriminate do not have this effect, while the effect of others has been exaggerated.

The common law doctrine that a husband must support his wife is thought to present a problem because it obligates husbands for the purchase of necessaries by their wives. Many people mistakenly believe that this doctrine requires creditors to proceed against the husband rather than against the wife even when the wife has signed in her own name for the purchases. Creditors use this interpretation as an excuse to seek information on the husband in acting on a married woman's credit application or even to insist on granting credit solely to him. However, in the majority of states, the doctrine of necessaries, or the family expense statutes which have amended it in over twenty states, do not have the claimed result. In fact, in some cases it gives the creditor an additional remedy against the husband if he is unable to obtain satisfaction from the wife.[28] In most states, it in no way diminishes the ability of the wife to bind herself.

Similarly, in all of the community property states, except Louisiana and California, a wife retains control of her own earnings, and in California, a wife can retain control of her earnings if she does not commingle her property with community property. Thus, the community property laws do not justify denying credit to a wife whose earnings would be sufficient to grant a man or single woman credit.[29] Only in Louisiana would the community property system be a bar to a married woman's creditworthiness.[30]

Ownership by a tenancy by the entirety means that neither the husband nor the wife can alienate real property without the consent of the other. Tenancies by the entirety and laws requiring the consent of both spouses to wage assignments as collateral for debts only affect situations where the property is serving as security for a loan. Ownership by tenancies by the entirety exists in twenty-one states, and the number is decreasing.[31] In many of those states, a couple can choose to hold real property in other forms of joint ownership, for example as joint tenants.

Multiple agreement laws serve the public policy of minimizing the aggregate finance charge a lender may impose on a family unit by a flat prohibition on more than one account per family. The law does not require that the account be in the husband's name; it is the bias of the creditors that creates a preference for the husband. Thus, if the husband and wife decide that the wife should be the one to get credit, or if she independently applies for credit before her husband does, these statutes would be no bar. However, to minimize the constraints imposed on one spouse by the economic activities of the other, these laws could be amended to provide that the combined finance charge on accounts of the husband and wife not exceed a certain percentage.[32]

Although most of the community property laws, laws governing tenancies by the entireties, and multiple agreements laws do not justify sex discrimination, they fre-

---

28. Id. at 414 For further discussion of the doctrine of necessaries, see Section C, The Support-Services Reciprocity, infra.

29. Id. at 415. In Arizona, New Mexico, and Washington, property laws actually improve the creditworthiness of wives who have no or small independent incomes as compared to wives in similar situations in common law property states. In these three states, with the exception of certain transactions (notably those concerning joint commercial property in New Mexico, and real estate transactions in all three states), both spouses have independent power to bind the community. Ariz. Rev. Stat. §25-214 (1973); N.M. Stat. Ann. §§7-4A-7.1, 57-4A-8 (1973); Wash. Rev. Code §26.16.030 (Supp 1972). Therefore, both spouses are equally creditworthy from a legal point of view regardless of which spouse earned the income on which credit is based.

30. La. Civ. Code art. 2404 (West 1971).

31. See Kulzer, Property and the Family: Spousal Protection, 4 Rutgers-Camden L. J. 195 (1973), as cited in Testimony of Margaret Gates of the Center for Women Policy Studies 8, n.17, in Oversight Hearings, supra, November 13, 1973.

32. Gates, supra, at 415-416.

quently do justify different treatment on the basis of marital status. If legislation is passed which covers marital status discrimination as well as sex discrimination in the granting of credit, these types of property laws either will have to form the basis for exceptions to the prohibition on marital status discrimination or will have to be changed.

From the above analysis, it is evident that most of the difficulty women encounter in obtaining credit is neither legally mandated nor made economically necessary by state property laws.[33] Creditors' simple assertions that they are a problem may be based on a failure to understand the impact of the married women's property acts (which are discussed in Section B, infra), or an unwillingness to accept women as financially responsible individuals. To the extent that the laws do pose problems in particular states, there have been a number of encouraging developments. Many statutes, particularly the discriminatory community property statutes, are being changed pursuant to state equal rights amendments, and none which are sex specific will survive the impact of the federal Equal Rights Amendment after it has been ratified and goes into effect. Some of the remaining problems are amenable to change through legislation; others through information on their limits and effect. The combination of laws and doctrines differs from state to state, leaving to feminists the task of deciding what changes are needed and working to have them implemented. Some of this work has already begun, as the following discussion of proposed and enacted state and federal laws and regulations illustrates.

d. Possible Legal Solutions

GATES, CREDIT DISCRIMINATION AGAINST WOMEN:
CAUSES AND SOLUTIONS
27 Vand. L. Rev. 409, 420-427 (1974)

B. *State Laws Prohibiting Discrimination in Credit Practices.* Twenty-two states and the District of Columbia now have laws prohibiting sex discrimination in the extension of credit; most of these states also prohibit marital status discrimination.[53] Because the majority of these laws were enacted less than a year ago, it is difficult to evaluate their effectiveness at this time, but a few observations can be made.

Many of these state laws do not prohibit all types of discrimination. For example, the statutes of six states apply only to sex discrimination and therefore might not be interpreted to include some of the offensive practices that affect married women.[54] The West Virginia law applies only to public accommodations,[55] and the Illinois law covers only retail credit or credit cards.[56] Nine state nondiscrimination statutes apply to public accommodations and expressly or implicitly cover only some credit establishments.[57]

33. One exception may be the restrictions on the ability of married women to do business or engage in certain kinds of transactions without judicial authorization. See Section B-3, infra, for a discussion of the few laws of this type which still exist.

53. See Appendix B [a chart, not here reproduced, which summarizes the provisions of state laws prohibiting discrimination on the basis of sex or marital status in the granting of credit. The twenty-two states are Alaska, California, Colorado, Connecticut, Florida, Illinois, Kansas, Maryland, Massachusetts, Minnesota, New Jersey, New York, Oregon, Pennsylvania, Rhode Island, South Dakota, Texas, Utah, Vermont, Washington, West Virginia, and Wisconsin].

54. Alaska, Kansas, South Dakota, Texas, Utah and West Virginia. Both Colorado and Minnesota have separate statutes for consumer credit and home financing. Marital status is covered only under the home financing statutes. . . .

55. Although discrimination in the granting of mortgage credit by banks can usually be covered under a public accommodations statute, language in the West Virginia law suggests that discrimination on the basis of sex in home financing is not prohibited. W. Va. Code §5-11-2 (1971).

56. Ill. Pub. Act 78-839, §1a, *amending* Ill. Stat. Ann. ch. 121 1/2, §385.

57. Alaska, District of Columbia, Kansas, New Jersey, New York, Oregon, South Dakota, Utah, West Virginia. . . .

The enforcement provisions of these laws fall into two basic categories: those that extend a private right of action for damages;[58] and those that provide for an administrative remedy.[59] The Oregon, Washington, Massachusetts, and District of Columbia laws include both provisions and permit the complainant to choose which to pursue. Three states explicitly provide for injunctive relief in addition to one of the above remedies,[60] and Wisconsin has a criminal sanction of a 1,000-dollar fine instead of the right to a civil action. The Illinois law was enacted without any enforcement provisions. Six states provide for attorneys' fees and/or court costs[61] and punitive damages may be awarded in Oregon and Florida.

C. *Existing Federal Remedies.* Unlike the reform of property laws, legal prohibitions against discriminatory credit practices do not have to be left to the states. The federal government has legislative authority under the commerce clause to control credit practices.[62] Prior to a discussion of proposed federal legislation, it is useful to explore existing federal remedies in order to assess their adequacy and the consequent need for legislation.

1. *Constitutional Litigation.* At least one suit, Hoberman v. Manufacturers' Hanover Trust Co.,[63] has been filed[64] in a federal court challenging the discriminatory credit practice of discounting a married woman's income for the purpose of computing family income for a home mortgage. The cause of action in *Hoberman* arose in New York where at that time the Executive Law forbade sex, but not marital-status, discrimination by banks in mortgage lending and provided an administrative remedy.[65] Plaintiff's attorneys, however, preferred the forum of a federal district court to the cumbersome state administrative process.[66] Plaintiffs allege discrimination on the basis of sex in violation of the fourteenth and fifth amendments, and an important threshhold issue is whether sufficient state and federal involvement to raise claims under these amendments exists.[67] Plaintiffs are expected to argue that because the defendant bank's activities are regulated by both state and federal agencies, the requisite "state action" is present.[68] Assuming that state action will be found, the *Hoberman* decision will turn on whether defendant's justifications for discounting the income of a married woman can withstand the degree of scrutiny that the court chooses to apply to a classification according to sex.[69]

2. *Regulation by Federal Agencies.* The issue being litigated in *Hoberman* is subject to regulation by several federal agencies. On December 17, 1973, the Federal Home Loan

---

58. California, Colorado, Florida, Texas, Utah. . . .

59. Alaska, Connecticut, Kansas, Maryland, Minnesota, New Jersey, New York, Rhode Island, South Dakota, West Virginia. . . .

60. California, Utah, Washington. . . .

61. Colorado, Florida, Massachusetts, Oregon, Texas, Washington.

62. Consumer Credit Protection Act, 15 U.S.C. §1601 *et seq.* (1970).

63. Civil No. 73-3279 (S.D.N.Y., filed July 26, 1973).

64. The case had not reached trial at the time of this writing.

65. New York Executive Law §296(5)(e) (McKinney 1972), *repealed by* Act of Feb. 6, 1974, Bill No. A-9359, that specifically prohibits arbitrary discounting of a married woman's income.

66. Spokeswoman for the feminist law firm of Bellamy, Blank, Goodman, Kelly, Ross and Stanley, which represents plaintiffs and has received a foundation grant to litigate in the area of sex discrimination in credit.

67. Plaintiffs claim jurisdiction under 28 U.S.C. §§1331, 1337, 1343. They have pleaded violations of 42 U.S.C. §§1981, 1982, 1983. The court is asked to find state action for the purposes of §1983 in the regulation of the bank by the New York State Banking Department and the Board of Governors of the Federal Reserve System.

68. While the requisite state action might be found in the case of a bank or savings and loan association, it is doubtful that other types of creditors could be reached on constitutional grounds. But see, The Discredited American Woman: Sex Discrimination in Consumer Credit, 6 Calif. Davis L. Rev. 61, 78-79 (1973).

69. The Supreme Court in its most recent application of the Equal Protection Clause to a sex discrimination case was divided as to whether the "rational basis" test or the "suspect classification" test should be employed. The majority found that even under the most lenient test the Air Force regulation denying to dependents of servicewomen benefits granted to dependents of servicemen was unconstitutional. Four Justices, however, did adopt the "suspect classification" test saying that sex discrimination, like racial discrimination, must be subjected to strict judicial scrutiny. Frontiero v. Richardson, 411 U.S. 677 (1973).

Bank Board published a policy statement concerning nondiscrimination by its member organizations.[70] The guidelines required that "[e]ach loan applicant's credit worthiness . . . be evaluated on an individual basis without reference to presumed characteristics of a group,"[71] and they specifically discourage the discounting of a working wife's income.[72] The Board found that "such discrimination is contrary to the principle of, and may in fact violate, constitutional provisions which guarantee equal protection of the law for all persons."[73] Although it has no legislative mandate to deal specifically with sex discrimination, the Board said that it had issued the guidelines on discounting married women's income under its authority to enforce provisions of the Civil Rights Act of 1968,[74] which prohibits discrimination in housing against minority groups, because "a larger proportion of minority group families rely on the wife's income to afford housing and other necessities."[75]

Other financial regulatory agencies — the Federal Deposit Insurance Corporation (FDIC), the Board of Governors of the Federal Reserve System and the Comptroller of the Currency — have been asked to issue rules prohibiting sex discrimination in lending policies.[76] The FDIC held hearings in December 1972 to consider the need for and its authority to issue such regulations. Although more than a year has elapsed, the FDIC has not yet announced its decision as to either issue.

The Federal Housing Administration (FHA)[77] and the Veterans Administration (VA)[78] provide mortgage insurance or guarantee for housing-related loans with low down payments. In 1965 the FHA revised its underwriting manual to include the following liberalized policy with respect to a wife's income:

> The principal element of mortgage risk in allowing the income of working wives as effective income is the possibility of its interruption as maternity leave. Most employers recognize this possibility and provide for maternity leave, with job retention, as an inducement of employment. With strong motives for returning to work any failure to do so after maternity leave would probably be due to causes which would be unpredictable and would represent such a very small percentage of volume that it could be accepted as a calculated risk.[79]

In 1970 the FHA counted all of the wife's income in 91 percent of the loans actually extended for new single-family homes.[80] The percentage of applicants who were rejected as the result of discounting the wife's income is not known.

The VA, on the other hand, persisted until mid-1973 in a more restrictive policy[81]

---

70. 38 Fed. Reg. 34653 (1973). The FHLBB regulates all federally chartered savings and loan associations as well as many other institutions. 12 U.S.C. §§1437-42 (1970).

71. 38 Fed. Reg. 34653 (1973).

72. Id.

73. Id.

74. 42 U.S.C. §§3601-31 (1970).

75. 38 Fed. Reg. 34653 (1973).

76. In February and March 1972 the Center for National Policy Review filed comments on behalf of 30 civil rights and public interest groups with all these agencies arguing that the agencies have authority under the Constitution and the Housing Act of 1949 to promulgate regulations prohibiting sex discrimination. A petition for rulemaking was also filed before the Board of Governors of the Federal Reserve System by the Institute for Public Interest Representation of the Georgetown University Law Center, May 15, 1973.

77. 12 U.S.C. §§1702-06(d) (1970). The FHA, an agency of the Department of Housing and Urban Development, insures a variety of housing related loans whose loan-to-value ratios are low and are, therefore, more subject to default than those in which a large down payment has been made.

78. 38 U.S.C. §§201-44 (1970). The VA provides mortgage insurance on low down payment loans as well as other benefits to veterans.

79. VII FHA Underwriting Manual, Home Mortgages, §71924.

80. The Center for National Policy Review, The Catholic University of America, School of Law, Washington, D.C., Memorandum to the VA, VA's Restrictive Credit Practices — Comparative Analysis with Policies of Other Federal Agencies (April 1973).

81. DVB Manual M-26-1, Ch. 5, §IV, ¶5.11c(5) stated that a wife's income could be "considered" if facts indicated that it was reasonable to conclude that her employment would continue in the "foreseeable future."

and, in addition, obtained considerable adverse publicity because in order to comply with VA guidelines lenders were demanding affidavits from wives stating that they were practicing birth control and did not intend to have children.[82] A VA circular dated July 18, 1973, urged lenders to adopt a new policy:

> In consideration of present day social and economic patterns, the Veterans Administration will hereafter recognize in full both the income and expenses of the veteran and spouse in determining ability to repay a loan obligation. VA regional offices have been instructed that there shall not be any discounting of income on account of sex or marital status in making such determinations.[83]

The federal secondary mortgage markets — the Federal National Mortgage Association (FNMA)[84] and the Federal Home Loan Mortgage Corporation (FHLMC)[85] —issue nondiscriminatory underwriting guidelines for use in their conventional mortgage purchase programs in 1971. The contract of FNMA (Fannie Mae) includes a warranty that the seller of the mortgage did not discriminate against the mortgagor on the basis of race, color, creed, religion, sex, age, or national origin, but it does not include marital status.[86] The FNMA also requires that, with respect to a wife's income, "[t]he key determination to be made is whether the circumstances reasonably indicate that the income, jointly or severally, will continue in a manner sufficient to liquidate the debt under the terms of the note and mortgage."[87] The guidelines do not explain the use of "reasonably" in this sentence or give examples of circumstances that would indicate that the income is stable.

FHLMC (Freddie Mac) has issued more specific rules to the same effect:

> If there are two borrowers both of whom have full time employment, a determination should be made as to whether both will probably work for several years (normally at least 20% of the time).[88]

The guidelines permit discounting of fifty percent of one income, however, when it is judged that one person is likely to stop working during the first few years of the mortgage. Significantly, temporary maternity leave is exempted from that provision.

These guidelines will not abolish the practice of discounting a wife's income unless FNMA and FHLMC check the practices of the institutions with which they deal and refuse to buy loans from those who discriminate.[89]

3. *Proposed Federal Legislation.* Because the efficacy of existing judicial remedies and regulatory prohibitions of sex discrimination in the granting of credit remains uncertain, there has been considerable activity in both houses of Congress aimed at providing a comprehensive, effective remedy. On July 23, 1973, by a 90-0 vote, the Senate unanimously passed the Equal Credit Opportunity Act[90] as an amendment to the Truth in

---

82. E.g., Wife Says Loan Tied to No-Child Vow, Washington Post, Feb. 24, 1973 at A-1. In an information bulletin entitled Wives' Income (DVB 1B 26-73-1, Feb. 2, 1973), the VA said it did not require or condone solicitation of such affidavits.

83. DVB Circular 23-73-24, July 18, 1973, announcing Change 42; DVB Manual M-26-1, Ch. 5, §IV, Credit Standards.

84. 12 U.S.C. §§1716-19 (1970). FNMA is a secondary mortgage market for both conventional loans, id. §1717(b)(2), and loans insured by FHA and VA, id. §1717(b)(1). FNMA purchases mortgages from commercial and savings banks.

85. 12 U.S.C. §§1451-59 (1970). FHLMC, like FNMA, buys conventional FHA and VA mortgages, id. §1454, but it deals primarily with federal savings and loan associations, federal home loan banks and state chartered banks which are members of the Federal Home Loan Bank system.

86. FNMA Conventional Selling Contract Supplement, §701(s) (Nov. 1972).

87. Id. §311.03(c).

88. FHLMC-Sellers Guide Conventional, Part V, Credit Underwriting.

89. FNMA's guidelines are likely to be more effective than FHLMC's because of their loans while FHLMC's clientele, the savings and loans, characteristically hold their mortgages as investments.

90. S. 2101, Title III, 93d Cong., 1st Sess. (1973).

Lending Act.[91] The Act includes provisions of S. 1605,[92] introduced by Senator William Brock, and of S. 867,[93] introduced by Senator Harrison Williams. The operative language of the Senate Act is:

> It shall be unlawful for any creditor or card issuer to discriminate on account of sex or marital status against any individual with respect to the approval or denial of any extension of consumer credit or with respect to the terms thereof or with respect to the approval, denial, renewal, continuation, or revocation of any open end consumer credit account or with respect to the terms thereof. Section 104 of this title does not apply with respect to any transactions subject to this section.[94]

Section 104[95] excepts credit for business or commercial purposes, credit transactions of more than 25,000 dollars, and transactions in securities or commodities accounts by a broker-dealer registered with the Securities and Exchange Commission. The removal of these exceptions clearly strengthens the Equal Credit Opportunity Act, since the unavailability of business loans for women is becoming more evident.[96]

As an amendment to the Truth in Lending Act, the law would be enforced through a number of federal agencies. The Board of Governors of the Federal Reserve System would be empowered to issue regulations, including compliance guidelines, which would be enforced by the Federal Trade Commission, with respect to most consumer credit transactions. Other enforcement agencies would include the United States Treasury Department, the Federal Deposit Insurance Corporation, the Federal Home Loan Bank Board acting directly or through the Federal Savings and Loan Insurance Corporation, the Bureau of Federal Credit Unions, the Civil Aeronautics Board, the Department of Agriculture and the Interstate Commerce Commission.[97]

Fortunately, enforcement by this unwieldy conglomerate is augmented by the Truth in Lending Act provision for civil liability.[98] The existing law provides for a 100-dollar minimum recovery for violations of the disclosure requirements of the Act. This minimum liability provision has caused courts to disallow class actions rather than award 100 dollars to each member of an enormous class and thereby ruin businesses for technical infringements of the law.[99] Therefore, the Equal Credit Opportunity Act amends the Truth in Lending Act to allow a maximum recovery of 100,000 dollars or one percent of the creditor's net worth, whichever is less, in class action suits.[100] The Senate Committee believes this amendment is necessary to provide meaningful penalties that will induce compliance with the law and which the courts will not be reluctant to impose.[101]

The Consumer Affairs Subcommittee of the House Banking and Currency Committee currently has before it several bills that are similar to the one approved by the Senate.[102]

---

91. 15 U.S.C. §§1601-81t (1970).
92. S. 1605, 93d Cong., 1st Sess. (1973).
93. S. 867, 93d Cong., 1st Sess. (1973).
94. S. 2101, Title III, 93d Cong., 1st Sess. §181 (1973).
95. 15 U.S.C. §1603 (1970).
96. Of 33,948 loans made by the Small Business Administration (SBA) in fiscal year 1973, only 123 went to women according to a synopsis of a study done for the SBA by Jeanne Wertz, Women Entrepreneurs and SBA (March 21, 1973).
97. 15 U.S.C. §1607(a) (1970). Section 203 of S. 2101, Title II, however, would remove the Interstate Commerce Commission and add the Farm Credit Administration.
98. 15 U.S.C. §1640(a) (1970).
99. The leading case is Ratner v. Chemical Bank New York Trust Co., 54 F.R.D. 412 (S.D.N.Y. 1972).
100. S. 2101, Title II, 93d Cong., 1st Sess. §208 (1973).
101. S. Rep. No. 278, 93d Cong., 1st Sess. 14-15 (1973).
102. H.R. 5414, H.R. 5599, H.R. 10109, H.R. 10162, H.R. 10311, H.R. 10603, H.R. 10675. The following bills have been referred to the Subcommittee on Bank supervision and insurance: H.R. 248, H.R. 3210, H.R. 3375, H.R. 10824.

The entire credit area is susceptible to pressure by those who are willing to fight individual instances of discrimination, and the increasing popular press coverage of the topic should have an effect. The Wall Street Journal quoted a high executive of a major retailing firm as saying: "This was sort of a shocker to us. Our business is primarily oriented to women. I'm afraid we didn't really know we had a problem."[34]

B. MARITAL PROPERTY LAW

1. *Introduction*

Common law marriage was patriarchal and status-based. In feudal times, this arrangement of the family comported with the structure of most other social institutions. But over the years new contractual forms for exchanges of services, property, and income evolved in all major areas of human intercourse — except marriage. In the institution of marriage alone, cultural traditions, religious norms, and perhaps the self-interest of the men who governed society prevented contractual reforms from taking hold. Only in property law were there any changes bringing the marriage relationship closer to the modern approach. Reforms were limited to the treatment of the wife's property, however, without any re-examination of the other status aspects of marriage. Thus, for example, the wife gained the right to collect, control, and own her wages from work outside the home, and the right to own and manage her real property, but did not gain the right to be paid for her work inside the home (which she was still legally obligated to do), or the right to participate in the management and control of the household or property held jointly with her husband. On the other hand, the husband lost the right to income from his wife's services or property, but he still has at least a theoretical obligation to support his wife.

The materials that follow provide a brief historical account of reforms in marital property law both at equity and by statute, and a summary of the discriminatory provisions that remain today in both common law and community property states.[35] Section C describes the economic arrangements of marriage that have not been reformed, the sex-differentiated obligations to perform domestic services and to provide support.

2. *Early Reforms*

The first efforts to ameliorate the harsh effects of the common law on married women were through equity. Between 1400 and 1800, the Court of Chancery evolved a number of devices to mitigate the property consequences of marriage at common law. The three major reforms that benefited wives were (1) the enforcement of provisions in antenuptial contracts reserving the wife's property to her use during marriage; (2) the recognition of the wife's separate estate in equity through the enforcement of a trust for her benefit against her husband; and (3) the development of a wife's equity to a settlement, so that if the husband sought the aid of equity in gaining possession of his wife's property or personalty, the Court of Chancery would require him to do equity —i.e., set aside some of her own property for her benefit.[36]

---

34. Wall Street Journal, July 18, 1972, at 23 (cont. from p. 1).

35. See also references cited in n. 1, Part I, supra.

36. See Johnston, Sex and Property: The Common Law Tradition, the Law School Curriculum, and Developments Toward Equality, 47 N.Y.U.L. Rev. 1033 (1972).

"Equity courts also came to the aid of husbands by exempting the husband's equitable interests from the wife's claim for dower. Eventually, lawyers were able to frustrate dower rights on all real property through the use of this exemption. The goal of the Chancellor was apparently to increase the alienability of land; prior to this equitable reform, dower attached to all the property interests owned by the husband at any time during the marriage, and could only be released by a time consuming and costly fictitious law suit." Id. at 1054. "Meanwhile, the Chancery Court ruled that the widower's right to curtesy extended to his wife's equitable interests!" Id. at 1055.

The benefits of such equitable intervention were available of course only to wives whose families had the wealth, legal counsel, and bargaining power to make antenuptial agreements and to litigate to enforce rights to separate property. Furthermore the equitable subterfuges did not change the basic subservience of wives to husbands. In using the trust device, in fact, equity classified married women with idiots and infants.[37] Johnston explains the underlying rationale of the equitable remedies as follows:[38]

> In 1581, equity laid the foundation for recognition of a wife's separate estate. When funds had been placed in the hands of a trustee for a married woman's benefit, pursuant to a separation agreement, it was held that she could enforce this trust free of her husband's intervention. This holding was later extended to validate trusts created for the sole benefit of married women who were still living with their husbands. Although these trusts assured wives of greater independence from their husbands, they did not necessarily permit them to exercise control over the trust property — such was the province of the trustee.[74] The married woman's appeal to the chancellor's conscience rested not on the notion that she rightfully deserved control over her own property, but rather on whether her husband, father or other "protector" had fulfilled his responsibility as trustee. But at least the wife was entitled to the *benefit* of the assets, and could enforce her rights against the trustee in a court of equity.

One result was that the equitable remedies were used only in extreme cases.

The unavailability of equity to the majority of people, and the complicated nature of the equitable remedies with their numerous exceptions and qualifications, were some of the reasons for the legislative reforms known as the Married Women's Property Acts, which were passed in various forms in all the states in the nineteenth century. The impetus for the reforms came both from the women's rights movement and from male lawyers and legislators.[39] However, the conservative legislators recognized the potential implications of the laws for the status of women generally so that the proponents had an uphill battle even to get piecemeal changes in the common law system. In the end, most of the acts were designed to establish simpler statutory procedures to replace the cumbersome equitable protections for women's separate property, while changing as little as possible the underlying institution of marriage.

JOHNSTON, SEX AND PROPERTY: THE COMMON LAW TRADITION, THE LAW SCHOOL CURRICULUM, AND DEVELOPMENTS TOWARD EQUALITY
47 N.Y.U.L. Rev. 1033, 1062-1070 (1972)*

1839-1895: THE MARRIED WOMEN'S PROPERTY LEGISLATION

. . . [Let us] take a look at some of the significant events in one of the most influential states — New York.

Although New York's first married woman's property act was not adopted until

---

37. Kanowitz, Women and the Law 40 (1968).

38. Johnston, supra, at 1052-1053.

74. The trustee owed fiduciary duties to the female beneficiary, of course. She was entitled to the benefit of the trust res in accordance with the settlor's manifested intent. But legal ownership, with the power to initiate decisions about buying, selling, managing and investing the trust estate belonged solely to the trustee.

39. See Kanowitz, supra, at 42-45; Clark, Law of Domestic Relations 219, n. 5, citing D. John-Stevas, Women in Public Law, printed in Graveson and Crane, A Century of Family Law 256 (1957); Pankhurst, Suffragette Movement (1931); 29 Encyc. Americana 89-96 (1963); 15 Encyc. Social Sciences 439-450 (1934). Myra Bradwell, of Bradwell v. Illinois, 83 U.S. (16 Wall.) 130, 21 L. Ed. 442 (1873), supra, Chapter One, I, drafted much of the married women's property legislation that was passed in Illinois. 1 James, Wilson, and Boyer, Notable American Women 225 (1971). But see Walter, The Legal Condition of Women, in C. Haar (ed.), The Golden Age of American Law 316-317 (1965).

* This selection is reprinted with the permission of the New York University Law Review.

1848, a proposal for giving married women control over their separate property was discussed at the State Constitutional Convention of 1846.[122] Its proponents contended that it would make property settlements for married women easier and less costly to effectuate. They argued that the social values of utility and egalitarianism would both be served: the proposal would provide greater protection against wastrel husbands, and it would be available to people of more limited means. . . . The proponents strove mightily to convince their brethren that the proposal was not a challenge to the assumptions of male supremacy essential to the concept of marital unity. One commentator later explained:

> It is also worthy of remark that in all this spirit of legislative innovation there is a recognition of the inherent incapacity of women, as a rule, to deal judiciously with their own property or to act with even ordinary wisdom in the making of contracts.[125]

Experience with the civil law system was offered to allay fears that departure from the unity doctrine would spell the end of marriage itself.[126]

These arguments were unavailing, however; the majority of the delegates sensed that disruption of the family would inevitably follow in the wake of any proliferation of separate property interests that could cause dissention between husband and wife. Charles O'Conor opined that one distinctive feature of English common law was the "gospel precept, that the twain should be one flesh."[127] References to the civil law were met with such great hostility that George Simmons went so far as to quote Thomas Jefferson's proposition "that it was owing to the separate interest of wife and husband in France that about half the annual increase of the population of Paris was illegitimate."[128] Arphaxed Loomis summed up the general fear that the proposed change in the property aspect of the marriage relationship would "change the whole face of society," although his further conclusion that it "would result in all property descending in the female line, and being tied up in families, secure from the reach of creditors and from alienation,"[129] was somewhat idiosyncratic. Robert Morris was no doubt accurate in his charge that mercenary considerations lay behind this defense of a unity doctrine "which proceeded on the assumption that the harmony of a family consisted in the man's pocketing all the cash."[130] However mixed their motives may have been, opponents of the provision viewed it as a dangerous first step toward catastrophic social change. . . .

Two years later, in 1848, the New York legislature enacted a statute assuring to the married woman control over all real and personal property which came to her either before or during coverture. It further specified that the income from such property would

---

122. "All property of the wife, owned by her at the time of her marriage, and that acquired by her afterwards, by gifts, devise, or descent, or otherwise than from her husband, shall be her separate property. Laws shall be passed providing for the registry of the wife's separate property, and more clearly defining her rights thereto, as well as to property held by her with her husband." S. Croswell & R. Sutton, Debates and Proceedings in the New York State Convention, for the Revision of the Constitution 811 (1846) [hereinafter Debates]. See generally 2 Journal of the Convention of the State of New York 1357 (1846); W. Bishop & W. Atree, Report of the Debates and Proceedings of the Convention for the Revision of the Constitution of the State of New York 156 (1846).

125. Mister, Law of Married Women, 20 Amer. L. Rev. 356, 360 (1886).

126. Cf. Bishop & Atree, supra note 122, at 1059-60 (remarks of Ira Harris).

127. Debates, supra note 122, at 811.

128. Id. at 813.

129. Id.

130. Id. at 812.

remain hers and could be invested in her own name, free of her husband's control and immune from liability for his debts.[131] This statute broke new ground: it not only extended the benefits of the separate estate in equity to all married women as an inherent incident of their marital status, but also, by eliminating the necessity for a trustee, conferred upon them the powers of management and control.[132]

In the following year, married women were granted the power to convey or devise real estate in the same manner and with the same effect "as if [they] were unmarried."[133] The statute, however, received a restrictive interpretation in White v. Wager.[134] In that case, the wife was sole owner of a tract of land by inheritance from her parents. She purported to convey it to her husband, the defendant, by a quitclaim deed executed one day before her death, and he later conveyed it to plaintiff for a valuable consideration. In this action to recover the consideration paid, the plaintiff contended that the deed from defendant's wife had conveyed nothing, relying on the common law rule that, since husband and wife were one, they could not convey real property to one another. Defendant pleaded the statute of 1849, arguing that by enabling his late wife to convey to him "as if she were unmarried," it had abrogated the common law disability.[135] The court held for plaintiff, however, stating that "[w]e would not expect to find in a law, passed professedly to shield the property of married women from the control of their husbands, a provision making it more easy for the latter to acquire such control."[136]

The holding is difficult to assess. Given the availability of remedies to nullify transfers procured by fraud or undue influence, the protectionist rationale may seem disingenuous at first glance. On the other hand, the decision could be praised as a sensible recognition of the substantial degree of control that husbands still retained over their wives, and an honest attempt to restrain husbands from using that power to undermine the legislative grant to married women of greater control over their property. If this was the court's motivation, however, the holding in White v. Wager could be of scant help: surely an authoritarian husband could coerce an indirect, or "straw," conveyance as easily as a direct one. The decision was in effect overruled by the legislature in 1887.[137]

It was not until 1860 that married women in New York acquired the rights to conduct a separate business, to contract with respect thereto as if they were unmarried and to keep their own earnings.[138] Restrictive judicial interpretations made it clear, however, that where husband and wife "live together, and work together where they live, the presumption is that her services are performed in her relation of wife and that

---

131. Law of Apr. 7, 1848, ch. 200, §§1, 2, [1848] N.Y. Laws 307, as amended N.Y. Dom. Rel. Law §50 (McKinney 1964):

"The real and personal property of any female who may hereafter marry, and which she shall own at the time of marriage, and the rents issues and profits thereof shall not be subject to the disposal of her husband, nor liable for his debts, and shall continue her sole and separate property, as if she were a single female.

"The real and personal property and the rents issues and profits thereof of any female now married shall not be subject to the disposal of her husband; but shall be her sole and separate property as if she were a single female, except so far as the same be liable for the debts of her husband heretofore contracted."

132. See W. Bullock, The Law of Husband and Wife in New York 99 (1897).

133. Law of Apr. 11, 1849, ch. 375, §1, [1849] N.Y. Laws 528, as amended N.Y. Gen. Oblig. Law §3-301 (McKinney 1970).

134. 25 N.Y. 328 (1862).

135. Id. at 333.

136. Id. at 332. It was also held that the common law rule that gifts from husband to wife were invalid was unaffected by the statutes of 1848 and 1849. Bullock, supra note 120, §135.

137. Law of June 6, 1887, ch. 537, §1, [1887] N.Y. Laws 667, as amended N.Y. Gen. Oblig. Law §3-309 (McKinney 1970).

138. Law of Mar. 20, 1860, ch. 90, §2, [1860] N.Y. Laws 157, as amended N.Y. Gen. Oblig. Law §3-301 (McKinney 1970).

the business is the husband's."[139] This confirmed the continuation of the husband's dominance of jointly undertaken business enterprises.[140]

Even more significant, however, was the judicial conclusion that the married women's acts did not deprive

> the husband of his common-law right to avail himself of a profit or benefit from his wife's services. The law has never recognized the wife's right to compensation from her husband on account of the peculiar nature of her services for him whether done in or outside of the household. While he may not, as a matter of right, require her services outside of the household, yet such services as she does render him, whether within or without the strict line of her duty, belong to him. If he promises to pay her for them it is a promise to make her a gift which she cannot enforce by a suit against him.[141]

> . . .

As a whole, these New York married women's property acts now seem considerably less than revolutionary. Nevertheless, this legislation of 1847-48 and 1860-62 was described in 1874 as the most "radical and startling innovation" that had ever been effected in the law.[142] Finally, in 1884, the freedom to contract was extended to all of a married woman's separate property.[143] She was not permitted to contract with her husband, however, until 1892.[144]

In summary, it required almost a half-century of piecemeal legislation for the married woman in New York to achieve substantial control over her realty, personalty, and earnings. The above account is vastly oversimplified, however; at any point in time, many issues pertaining to a wife's control over her property were subject to considerable doubt and uncertainty. . . .

With all of its limitations, the New York legislation is an example of the bolder of the two general patterns into which early married women's property legislation[149] could be placed. The other set of statutes had a much more limited goal: insulation of a married woman's separate property from claims of her husband's creditors. This was sometimes accomplished by declaring every husband trustee of his wife's separate property for her benefit. Thus, while she acquired the right to the benefit of it, he was permitted to retain much the same control over her property as before; this constituted an extremely modest advance in the wife's status.

Nevertheless, even this mild "reform" was sometimes accompanied by the same attitudes of legislative caution and judicial distrust as its more forthright counterpart. . . . It was not until 1877, in fact, that Connecticut finally enacted laws giving married women control of their property. These were similar to statutes adopted in New York almost three decades earlier.[151]

139. Bullock, supra note 120, §86. See generally id. §§92-93.

140. The statute of 1860 did not affect the wife's power to employ her husband as managing agent of her separate business. Buckley v. Wells, 33 N.Y. 518, 520-21 (1865); Bullock, supra note 120, §91.

141. Bullock, supra note 120, §146 (footnotes omitted), citing Porter v. Dunn, 131 N.Y. 314 (1892); see Whitaker v. Whitaker, 52 N.Y. 368 (1873).

142. Note, Contracts of Married Women, 10 Albany L.J. 49 (1874).

143. Law of May 28, 1884, ch. 381, [1884] N.Y. Laws 465, as amended N.Y. Gen. Oblig. Law §3-301 (McKinney 1970).

144. Law of May 14, 1892, ch. 594, [1892] N.Y. Laws 1138, as amended N.Y. Gen. Oblig. Law §3-301 (McKinney 1970).

149. In a number of states, early legislation was later consolidated and incorporated into the state constitution.

151. Act of Mar. 16, 1877, ch. 114, [1875-80] Conn. Acts 211, as amended Conn. Gen. Stat. Ann §§46-9, 46-10 (1960):

"In case of marriage on or after the twentieth of April, 1877, neither husband nor wife shall acquire, by force of the marriage, any right to or interest in any property held by the other before, or acquired after, such marriage, except as to the share of the survivor in the property, as provided by law. The separate earnings of the wife shall be her sole property. She shall have power to make contracts with third persons, and to convey

The development of new marital property doctrine through the process of piece-meal legislative change is observable in a number of other states, notably Alabama, California, Illinois, Maine, Maryland, Massachusetts, Mississippi, North Carolina, and Pennsylvania.[152] It is clear that a characteristic pattern of restrictive judicial interpretations of this legislation complicated the process and retarded the rate of change.[153] . . .

. . . By the end of the nineteenth century, the law of marital property had emerged as a jumbled patchwork reflecting no coherent policy or philosophy concerning the status of married women. . . . It cannot be denied, however, that the changes effected between 1839 and 1895 constituted by far the most significant advance in the status of married women with respect to property of any period [up to that time]. . . .

From an historical perspective, the passage of the married women's property acts was not entirely a haphazard, uncoordinated development which produced a jumble of laws. One historian has found that the reforms resulted, at least in part, from a well-organized, coordinated campaign by the women's rights movement.

RAPAPORT, RELATIONSHIP OF THE WOMEN'S MOVEMENT TO THE PASSAGE OF MARRIED WOMEN'S PROPERTY ACTS IN THE MID-NINETEENTH CENTURY
Manuscript, Stanford Law School Library (May 1973)

. . . The several steps of this campaign were so well executed as to dispel any possibility of random activity. The large numbers of progressive laws passed in those states where the movement flourished before the Civil War — amongst them the states of New York, Massachusetts, Pennsylvania, Ohio, New Jersey, Indiana, Wisconsin, Kansas — confirms to some extent the effectiveness of the campaign. The claim is not that the Women's Rights movement was responsible for all early progressive law; for this is clearly contradicted by the experience in Mississippi,[1] Michigan,[2] and Maine.[3] The claim is instead that the women's rights activities were critically important in influencing enactment of the most favorable laws for women in the shortest period of time.

Reform of the property laws was one of the major subjects of the women's rights conventions which were held nationally every year from 1850 to 1860, with the exception of 1855. Local women's rights conventions were also held across the country. From

---

to them her real and personal estate, as if unmarried. Her property shall be liable to be taken for her debts, except when exempt from execution, but in no case shall be liable to be taken for the debts of the husband. The husband shall not be liable for her debts contracted before marriage, nor upon her contracts made after marriage, except as provided in the following section.

"All purchases made by either husband or wife in his or her own name, [in case of marriages on or after the twentieth of April, 1877,] shall be presumed, in the absence of notice to the contrary, to be on his or her private account and liability; but both shall be liable when any article purchased by either shall have in fact gone to the support of the family, or for the joint benefit of both, or for the reasonable apparel of the wife, or for her reasonable support, while abandoned by her husband. It shall, however, be the duty of the husband to support his family, and his property when found shall be first applied to satisfy any such joint liability; and the wife shall in equity be entitled to an indemnity from the property of the husband, for any property of her own that shall have been taken, or for any money that she shall have been compelled to pay, for the satisfaction of any such claim."

152. See 2 Bishop . . . §§591-610, 626-45, 686-98, 712-18, 719-26, 727-41, 751-61, 786-95, 799-809.

153. See, e.g., Warren, Husband's Right to Wife's Services, 38 Harv. L. Rev. 421 and 622 (1925). Warren attributes this judicial attitude partly to "the distrust with which changes in family law are commonly viewed," and also to the fact that "the interpretations of these acts frequently fell into the hands of judges who as young lawyers had been educated in the legal supremacy of the husband." Id. at 423.

1. Mississippi Laws, 1839, C.46, p. 72.

2. Michigan Acts, 1844, No.66, p. 77.

3. Maine Acts, 1844, C.117, p. 104. A discussion of the above three laws is Brown, Memorandum on the Mississippi Woman's Law of 1839, 42 Michigan L. Rev. 1110 (1944).

the conventions would flow signature-collecting campaigns on petitions seeking property law reform and then often another women's rights convention would be summoned for the same time and in the same city as the legislature was convened, and the women would seek to present the petition, or address the legislators.

. . . In Ohio, for example, the Salem Convention of April, 1850, was called to meet at the same time as the Ohio Constitutional Convention. The high point of the meeting was the presentation to the Constitutional Convention of a memorial demanding reform of the marital property law.[4] Later, in 1861, three leaders of the Ohio Women's Rights organization were called by the state senate to explain the thousands of petitions sent to the state legislature. Soon after, a senate committee recommended approval of reform legislation on marital property.[5] Similarly, in Massachusetts, in May, 1853, Lucy Stone, Theodore Parker, Wendell Phillips, and Thomas W. Higginson addressed a committee of the Constitutional Convention in support of a petition with two thousand signatures which requested that state laws be equalized between the sexes in the matters of property and suffrage.[6]

Perhaps the most famous appearances before a state legislature in these early years were Elizabeth C. Stanton's two speeches to the New York State Legislature. Both opportunities resulted from the strategy of convening an Albany convention each year while the legislature was in session. . . . As a result of the efforts of male allies, hearings on the subject of legal disabilities of women were conducted in both branches of the legislature. If the legislators wanted more information, there were the convention's regular sessions which were open to the public. Finally, upon invitation, Mrs. Stanton addressed the joint judiciary committees in the senate chamber. The key theme of the address was the need to expand married women's property rights.[7]

Although no new laws resulted from this first encounter, the impact of the Albany Convention was considerable. Both the official community of the state and the women themselves realized the special effect of this first meeting in the state capitol. Reflecting the view of the politician, The Albany Transcript summed up the activities:

> Thus has ended the first Convention of women designed to influence political action. On Monday the 6,000 petitions will be presented in the Legislature, and [a copy of Mrs. Stanton's] address be placed on the member's tables. Whatever may be the final disposition of the matter, it is well to make a note of this first effort to influence the Legislature.[8]

At the same time Mrs. Stanton, field general as well as speechmaker, was able to report that

> it was decided to hold a series of conventions in all the counties and chief cities of the state, in order to roll up mammoth petitions with which to bombard the legislature at every annual session. . . . A number of able speakers joined in the work, and the State was thoroughly canvassed every year until the war, and petitions presented by the thousands until the bill securing the civil rights of married women was passed in March, 1860.[9]

As a consequence of this continuous activity, Mrs. Stanton was again asked to appear before the New York Legislature. The occasion for the address was delicate since an amendment to the Property Bill of 1848, greatly improving women's legal status, was before the Senate. Rising to the occasion, Mrs. Stanton addressed a full joint session of the legislature for over an hour with great success. Even more important, the next day

---

4. Elizabeth C. Stanton et al., History of Woman Suffrage 105 (Rochester, New York, 1887).
5. Ibid., pp. 169-70.
6. Ibid., pp. 248-49.
7. Alma Lutz, Created Equal: A Biography of Elizabeth Cady Stanton (New York, 1940), p. 92.
8. Stanton, p. 606.
9. Stanton, p. 619.

the amendment bill passed the legislature and was signed by Governor Morgan.[10]

Evaluation of the precise role of the Women's Rights movement in enacting married women's property law is a difficult task. The difficulty lies in discerning the multiplicity of influences on the members of a legislative body. In addition to the efforts of the feminists through their petition and convention campaign there is the role of individual male legislators who, either on their own or in alliance with the women, pressed hard for reforms. Some examples are Judges Hertell and Fine, both early friends of the women's rights cause, who were responsible for the New York Property Bill of 1848;[11] and there was Robert Dale Owen, son of the founder of New Harmony, Indiana, who must get most of the credit for married women's property reform in Indiana in the early 1850s.[12]

It also appears that many men at the time had some sympathy towards property reform for women; although the concern reflected self-interests almost as much as the desire to improve the civil rights of women. Fathers who had estates to bequeath to their daughters could see the advantage of securing to women certain property rights that might limit the legal power of profligate husbands. This motive for reform was widely held amongst the wealthy Dutch farmers of the Hudson valley.[13] From their perspective, husbands with extensive business interests could see the advantage of allowing the wife to hold separate property, settled on her in time of prosperity, that might not be seized for his debts. Therefore in several states some men championed early reform measures.

Nevertheless, the Women's Rights movement had undeniable impact on the enactment of married women's property laws in the 1840s and 50s. Both the comprehensiveness and liberality of the reform legislation of the states where the women were most active far surpass the laws of states outside the movement's direct influence. In particular, the legislators of New York, Ohio, New Jersey, Massachusetts, Pennsylvania, Indiana, Wisconsin, and Kansas, were pressed to go farther towards genuine reform more quickly than their counterparts in other states. In these states, statutes effectively moderating or completely abolishing the common law were passed before the hardships of the Civil War preempted the legislators' attentions.[14] Another group of states — where feminist activity was minimal — including Connecticut, Delaware, Maryland, New Hampshire, Vermont, and West Virginia — did not alter the common law until after 1865. Finally, south of the Mason-Dixon line — where women's rights activities only started during reconstruction — reform in married women's property law did not come, except for Mississippi,[15] until the 1870s, 80s, and 90s.

3. Contemporary Marital Property Law in the Common Law States

JOHNSTON, SEX AND PROPERTY:
THE COMMON LAW TRADITION, THE LAW SCHOOL
CURRICULUM, AND DEVELOPMENTS TOWARD EQUALITY
47 N.Y.U.L. Rev. 1033, 1070-1086 (1972)

MARITAL PROPERTY LAW FROM 1895 TO DATE

In this part of the discussion, the impact of married women's legislation on [four] separate aspects of marital property rights will be investigated: (1) the wife's right to her

10. Lutz, Created Equal, pp. 109-110.
11. National American Woman Suffrage Association, Victory: How Women Won It, 1840-1940 (New York, 1940), p. 11.
12. Stanton, p. 293.
13. Lutz, Created Equal, p. 37.
14. See 2 J. P. Bishop, Law of Married Women (1873). The law of the individual states in 1875 is summarized in §§591-829 of this volume.
15. Miss. Laws, 1839, C.46, p. 72.

earnings; (2) her power to contract and carry on a business; (3) her power to transfer property free of her husband's consent; . . . and (5) tenancy by the entirety.

1. Wife's Right to her Earnings

Vernier's study, published in 1935, concluded that in all of the non-community property states with the exception of Georgia, and perhaps Vermont, married women had gained sole control over their earnings outside the home.[142] Georgia reversed its position in 1943, by statute.[143] Vernier's doubts about Vermont were based on a 1904 decision[144] hinting that the statute securing to a married woman the sole control over her personal property whether acquired before or during the marriage[145] did not alter the common law concerning a wife's outside earnings. No subsequent authority supporting this suggestion can be found; indeed, it has apparently been ignored.[146] Thus, it would appear that all of the non-community property states have repudiated the common law as to earnings from activities outside the home.

Vernier found the situation very different, however, with respect to the value of the services a wife performs *inside* the home: "In the main the courts have jealously guarded the right of the husband to the wife's services in the household. . . ."[147] Clearly, neither legislators nor judges read the married women's property acts as conferring upon married women a property right, enforceable against their husbands, in the value of their own labor within the home. . . .

2. Wife's Power To Contract and To Engage in Business Activity

Although legislation in a number of states expressly terminated the common law disability of married women to contract or to conduct a business, remnants of the old law persist to this day in some jurisdictions. A survey published in 1913 noted that at least five states still required a husband's consent as a prerequisite to his wife's engaging in business activity; in six others, a formal court petition and judicial order were required before a wife could act as a sole trader.[152] Other jurisdictions still restricted the exercise of a wife's power to contract in various ways, either voiding the contract altogether or requiring her to act only with her husband's consent.

By 1935, the situation had not changed significantly. Vernier lists thirty-five states that permitted wives to contract as if unmarried; of the remaining fifteen,[153] thirteen were non-community property jurisdictions.[154] He found eleven states that restricted in various ways the power of a married woman to engage in business, seven of which were non-community property jurisdictions.[155]

The situation was just about the same in 1965. According to the Government's brief

---

142. III C. Vernier, American Family Laws 193 (1935) (hereinafter referred to as Vernier). In all community property states except Louisiana, the wife's earnings would be community property and therefore subject to the husband's control. Id. §178.

143. Ga. Code Ann. §53-512: "A husband living with his wife shall not be entitled to, and shall not receive the salary or wages of his wife, except by her consent."

144. Monahan v. Monahan, 77 Vt. 133, 59 A. 170 (1904).

145. This statute now appears as Vt. Stat. Ann. tit. 15 §66 (1958).

146. See National League of Women Voters, Survey of the Legal Status of Women 203 (1930) (hereinafter referred to as Survey), in which the question "Does a wife own her wages earned outside her home?" was answered affirmatively on the authority of Vt. Gen. L. 1917 ch. 164 §3524, the predecessor to the statute cited supra note 145.

147. Vernier 195.

152. L. Foster, The Legal Rights of Women 46-70 (1913).

153. Vernier included Alaska and Hawaii in his survey, but excluded the District of Columbia.

154. Vernier 34-36.

155. Id. at 333-36. A very similar pattern is revealed by 2 Williston on Contracts §269A (3d ed. Jaeger 1959), which lists eleven states in which a married woman cannot contract with her husband or cannot be a surety.

in United States v. Yazell, twelve states, of which seven were non-community property, "limit in some degree the capacity of women to contract."[156] Some of these restrictions, such as the prohibition of surety contracts for the husband's debts, seem to be aimed at protecting women against economic coercion by their husbands. Others, such as the requirement that a wife file public notice or receive a court order before acting as a sole trader, were probably designed to give notice to creditors who might otherwise have assumed that the husband would be responsible for the wife's contractual obligations. Whatever their motivation, these restrictions seem squarely in conflict with the equality principle. As Vernier put it:

> It seems needless to suggest that the wife should be given the same power to bind herself by contract that the husband enjoys. Her common-law immunity from liability on her promises was never regarded as a privilege or protection, but rather as a natural consequence of a total incapacity. The wife neither needs nor desires privilege or protection today. To restrict her power to contract on either theory is hardly consistent with modern standards.[157]

In the Yazell case, the Small Business Administration had granted a loan to the defendant and her husband for use in their business, secured by a chattel mortgage on their merchandise. They defaulted on the loan, and the mortgage foreclosure proceeding did not produce sufficient funds to pay the debt. Action was brought against both of them to recover the deficiency. The wife defended on the ground that, under Texas law (her state of domicile), she was under a disability to contract since she had not obtained the requisite court order. This defense was sustained at the district and circuit court levels, and the Supreme Court affirmed. . . .

3. The Power To Convey Land

A 1913 survey listed at least twenty states in which a married woman's conveyance was inoperative without the joinder of her husband.[164] Of course, in a number of states where curtesy or a statutory substitute was in effect, the husband's signature would be necessary to transfer an unencumbered fee simple. But the laws now under discussion were different: the husband's assent was essential to the validity of the wife's transfer of her *own* interest. Such laws apparently reflect legislative acceptance of the stereotype of the wife as ward of her husband,[165] perhaps augmented by recognition of the fact that for various reasons, husbands not infrequently place title to their separate property in the name of their wives. In any event, these laws violate the equality principle.

A 1930 survey showed that the number of states with such restrictions had decreased to nine.[166] In 1935, Vernier found the number to be eight: Alabama, Florida, Indiana, Kentucky, New Jersey, North Carolina, Pennsylvania, and Texas.[167] Seven of these states have by now eliminated the requirement of the husband's joinder in the wife's conveyance: New Jersey, in 1934;[168] Kentucky, in 1942;[169] Pennsylvania, in

---

156. United States v. Yazell, 382 U.S. 341, 351 (1966).

157. Vernier 36.

164. Foster, op. cit. supra note 152, at 46-70.

165. See, e.g., Ferguson v. Kinsland, 93 N.C. 337, 339 (1885): "The requirement that the husband should execute the same deed with his wife, was to afford her his protection against the wiles and insidious acts of others. . . ."

166. Survey 21-228.

167. Vernier §183.

168. N.J. Stat. Ann. tit. 37 §2017 (1968).

169. Ky. Rev. Stat. §404.030 (1972). In May v. May, 311 Ky. 74, 223 S.W.2d 362 (1949), it was held that this statute has no retroactive effect.

1957;[170] North Carolina, in 1965;[171] Indiana, in 1967;[172] Florida, in 1968;[173] and Texas, in 1969.[174]

Apparently, Alabama is the lone holdout;[175] . . .

5. Tenancy by the Entireties

As already noted, at common law a devise or conveyance to husband and wife created a tenancy by the entireties. The four unities of time, title, interest, and possession necessary for a joint tenancy were also required for a tenancy by the entireties.[193] In addition, a valid marriage had to be in existence at the time of the transfer. If all of these five requirements were met, a tenancy by the entireties arose unless the transferror manifested an intent that the grantees should hold as joint tenants or tenants in common.[194]

Tenants by the entireties hold, it is said, *pur tout et non pur my:* This means that individual interests in the estate are not recognized, in contrast with the joint tenancy.[195] The estate can be severed and converted into a tenancy in common by divorce. It can be terminated by: (1) transfer of each spouse's interest to a third party; (2) transfer of the interest of either spouse to the other;[196] or (3) death of one spouse, in which case the survivor owns the entire undivided interest.[197]

At common law, entireties property was under the exclusive control of the husband. He had the sole privilege of occupancy; he was entitled to all of the income; he could alienate these rights without the wife's consent; and his creditors could levy against them.[198] As a practical matter, only the wife's right of survivorship was hers absolutely and free of unilateral disposition by her husband. This result was consistent with the other property incidents of the common law marital relationship; in fact, it was almost identical to the husband's right of *jure uxoris* in his wife's separate realty.

The tenancy by the entireties was originally received by all but three of the common law jurisdictions.[199] Subsequently, it has been subjected to considerable modification.[200] In this connection, the married women's property acts have had a particularly significant impact. . . .

The threshold question is: does a statute guaranteeing to married women the

170. Pa. Stat. Ann. tit. 48 §32.1 (Purdon 1965).

171. N.C. Const. Art. X §6 was amended by deleting the provision stating that a married woman's property can, "with the written consent of her husband, [be] conveyed by her as if unmarried" and substituting for it the provision that a married woman's property can be "conveyed by her subject to such regulations and limitations as the General Assembly may prescribe." In 1965, N.C. Gen. Stat. §39-7 was amended to abolish the requirement of the husband's joinder, except for the purpose of releasing his statutory life estate as surviving spouse.

172. Ind. Stat. Ann. §38-102 (supp. 1972).

173. Fla. Const. Art. X §5 (1968): "There shall be no distinction between married women and married men in the holding, control, disposition, or encumbering of their property, both real and personal; except that dower or curtesy may be established and regulated by law." In 1970, Fla. Stat. Ann. §708.08 (supp. 1972) was amended so as to conform to the constitutional change.

174. Tex. Code Ann. §5.21 (1971) states that "each spouse has the sole management, control, and disposition of his or her separate property."

175. See Ala. Code tit. 34 §73 (Michie 1959).

193. 2 A.L.P. 25.

194. For criticism of the notion that husband and wife have no separate legal existence and are therefore incapable of holding otherwise than as tenants by the entireties, see id. at 24 n.8.

195. Id. at 27; J. Cribbett, Principles of the Law of Property 92-94 (1962); C. Moynihan, Preliminary Survey of the Law of Real Property 136 (1940).

196. The common law disability of the spouses to transfer property to each other has been widely abrogated by statute. Vernier §182.

197. In the event that the order of death cannot be ascertained, one-half of the property passes through the estate of each spouse. Uniform Simultaneous Death Act §3 (1940).

198. 2 A.L.P. 28.

199. They are Connecticut, Nebraska, and Ohio. Phipps, Tenancy by the Entireties, 24 Temple L.Q. 24, 32 (1951) (hereinafter referred to as Phipps).

200. Several states have omitted tenancy by the entireties from the list of permitted co-tenancies. Others have interpreted the tenancy by the entirety as the equivalent of a joint tenancy. Phipps at 32-33; 2 A.L.P. at 31; Vernier §171.

management and control of their separate property affect the tenancy by the entirety at all? In three jurisdictions, the judicial answer was no.[201] The rationale was that husband and wife do not hold *separate* interests in a tenancy by the entireties. This conclusion logically follows from a literal interpretation of *pur tout et non pur my*. These three courts therefore concluded that the tenancy by the entireties was entirely outside the purview of the married women's acts and was not affected by them.

For all its apparent logical consistency, this holding is anomalous. The legislatures had clearly manifested an intention to abolish *jure uxoris;* it seems strange indeed that they would not also have intended to abolish those incidents of tenancy by the entireties that were virtually identical to *jure uxoris.* . . .

. . . [T]hese holdings may reflect the judges' determination to retain tenancy by the entirety because of its social utility. It is a convenient method of ownership for husband and wife that exempts the property from attachment by creditors of either spouse individually and then automatically confers sole ownership on the surviving spouse without the necessity for a will or for administration of the decedent spouse's estate. . . .

In the states wherein these acts *were* held to affect the tenancy by the entireties, Phipps noted two divergent judicial views. One was that the statutes had struck a death blow to the concept of marital unity, and *a fortiori*, to the tenancy based on it. This conclusion seems particularly compelling in states whose statutes provided that henceforth a married woman would be able to manage and control her property *as if unmarried.* This view was accepted in at least nine states, wherein it was held that the married women's acts had abolished the tenancy by the entireties.[204]

Seventeen other states took the intermediate position that the married women's legislation had altered some of the incidents of the tenancy by the entirety, but had not abolished it altogether.[205] These courts all started with the same premise: the married women's act mandates equality between husband and wife in determining the incidents of entireties ownership. They differed, however, in the *level* at which equality was reached. Some held that the wife's interest must be increased to the point where she can exercise incidents of ownership formerly exercisable by the husband alone; others concluded that the husband's interest should be reduced to parity with the wife's disability to act alone.

The issue of greatest concern seems to have been the exposure of entireties property to claims of creditors of either spouse individually. Some states held that each spouse was entitled to possession of one-half of the property, and one-half of the income; their individual creditors were permitted to attach these interests. Other states held that *neither* party had the exclusive right to possession or income, and therefore did not permit creditors of either spouse alone to levy on entireties property so long as both were alive. . . .

Unfortunately, the tenancy by the entireties law of some states still seems inconsistent with the equality principle. As an example of this, we shall now look at some of the Tennessee statutes and decisions. . . .

[Here Johnston discusses the history of the impact of Tennessee's Married Women's Act on tenancies by the entirety. Between 1913, when the Married Women's Act[40] was passed, and 1966, the Supreme Court of Tennessee seemed to have accepted the position taken by twenty other states that although the tenancy by the entirety was not eliminated, the Married Women's Acts had abrogated the husband's common law right to sole and complete control of the property during the marriage.[41] In 1966, however, the court took the position that the husband is solely entitled to rents and

201. They were Massachusetts, Michigan, and North Carolina. See Phipps at 29-31.

204. Phipps at 28-29.

205. Id. at 31-32.

40. Tenn. Acts 1913, ch. 26. This statute now appears as Tenn. Code Ann. §36-601 (1951).

41. Alfred v. Bankers and Shippers Ins. Co., 167 Tenn. 278, 68 S.W.2d 941 (1934), interpreting Tenn. Acts 1919, ch. 26; Cartwright v. Gracosa, 216 Tenn. 18, 390 S.W.2d 204 (1965); and Irwin v. Dawson, 197 Tenn. 314, 273 S.W.2d 6 (1954).

profits from entireties property on the ground that to rule otherwise would disrupt and injure the marriage relationship and "no doubt" bring it to an end.[42] This view was reaffirmed in 1968 and again in 1971.[43]]

4. History of Community Property

In contrast to the common law system of property as revised by the Married Women's Property Acts, some states have a system of community property. Its features are summarized by Foote, Levy, and Sander as follows:[44]

> . . . [T]he system of community property which is in force in such states as Arizona, California, Idaho, Louisiana, Nevada, New Mexico, Texas, and Washington, as well as in a number of civil law countries around the world, purports to give legal recognition to marriage as an economic partnership. It does this by establishing a new class of property (community property) consisting in essence of the assets or income (other than gifts or bequests) received by the spouses during the marriage.[37] This community property, in which each of the spouses has a legally defined interest, is normally managed by the husband,[38] subject to certain restrictions to assure the appropriate protection of the wife's cointerest. In addition, each spouse continues to own and manage his or her own separate property. Upon dissolution of the marriage by death or divorce, each spouse is theoretically entitled to his or her separate estate plus one half of the community. In practice, however, this rule is subject to a variety of exceptions and qualifications.[39]
>
> Such an oversimplified statement of the essence of the community property system is misleading in that it fails to take account of the subtle variations between differing versions as well as the myriad complexities which necessarily arise within any particular system.[40] In some states, for example, the income derived during the marriage from separate property is treated as community property; in others it is not. This rule has obvious significance in a case where a husband's wealth is largely inherited and he has little or no earned income. If this occurs in a state where the husband's unearned income is regarded as his separate property, the wife may be worse off than she would be in a common law state.
>
> The complexities which commonly arise are such as might naturally be anticipated whenever a new type of property interest is given legal recognition. Suppose, for example, one of the spouses receives compensation on account of a personal injury. Or suppose new assets are purchased in part with separate property and in part with community property. How are such transactions to be viewed? Generally speaking, the answers are arrived at by a weighty presumption that assets acquired during the marriage are community property — and by a host of technical rules and exceptions.
>
> One of the most troublesome and confusing aspects of community property concerns the rights of creditors. In most of the community property states, the community is liable for all postnuptial debts incurred by the husband but not those incurred by the wife unless she was her husband's agent; a few states embark upon

42. In re Guardianship of Plowman, 217 Tenn. 487, 398 S.W.2d 721 (1966).

43. Mitchell v. Sinclair Refining Co., 221 Tenn. 516, 428 S.W.2d 299 (1968), Weaks v. Gress, 225 Tenn. 593, 474 S.W.2d 424 (1971). See also Phipps, supra, at 39-41, Chapman v. Mitchell, 23 N.J. Misc. 358, 44 A.2d 416 (1948), and cases cited in 38 A.L.R.2d 1447 n. 1 (1954).

44. Foote, Levy, and Sander, Cases and Materials on Family Law 320-321 (1966).

37. California has recently created an additional category known as quasi-community property consisting of property similar to community property but acquired while the recipient was domiciled outside California. 1 The California Family Lawyer §4.1 (California Practice Handbook No. 17, 1961). In many jurisdictions, the spouses may by antenuptial agreement elect to avoid community property treatment.

38. In some states the wife is given control over her own earnings. 2 American Law of Property §7.21 (Casner ed. 1952).

39. In some states the court has power upon divorce on the grounds of adultery or extreme cruelty to divide the community in such proportion as it may deem just; in others it has this power in any divorce proceeding. See id. §7.35.

40. In general, see id., pt. 7.

the hopeless task of distinguishing between community and separate obligations.[41] But even in the majority group, there are occasional exceptions, such as that community property consisting of the wife's earnings will not be subject to the husband's debts. The rules with respect to antenuptial debts of the spouses are, if anything, more complex.

Here is Younger's explanation of the historical origins of the community property system.

YOUNGER, COMMUNITY PROPERTY, WOMEN, AND THE LAW SCHOOL CURRICULUM
48 N.Y.U.L. Rev. 211, 214-222 (1973)

. . . [T]he English rejected the marital community in the thirteenth century;[18] it arrived in the New World, therefore, as part of the civil law systems of the Spanish and the French. At one time it enjoyed fairly wide recognition in America, existing "in every one of the southern tier of states" as well as a number of those northern ones which formed part of the Northwest Territory.[19] In lasting impact, however, the civil law community was no match for the English common law. In some jurisdictions it was viewed as a transplanted but rootless "exotic"[20] and was soon displaced. In others — Louisiana, Texas and California — it was retained despite the omnipresence of the rival system in other areas of law.[21] In still other states — Nevada, New Mexico, Arizona, Washington and Idaho — it was adopted anew after a test of married life under common law property rules.[22] In Louisiana the civil law governed not only marital property but everything else as well;[23] in Texas it applied to marital property, land and civil procedure;[24] and in California,[25] Nevada,[26] New Mexico,[27] Arizona,[28] Washington,[29] and Idaho,[30] it governed marital property only. The common law was the source of all other rules.[31]

It is not always clear why the states rejected, retained or adopted the marital

---

41. Is it a community obligation, for example, if a tort judgment is entered against the husband for negligent operation of his automobile while driving to a dance without his wife? See id. §7.31.

18. 3 Holdsworth [A History of English Law (4th ed. 1935)] at 524.

19. Lobingier [The Marital Community: Its Origin and Diffusion — A Problem of Comparative Law, 14 A.B.A.J. 211 (1928)], at 215.

20. See, e.g., Chadwick v. Tatem, 9 Mont. 354, 370, 23 P. 729, 733 (1890); see also McVoy v. Hallett, 11 Ala. 864 (1847); MaGee v. Doe, 9 Fla. 382, 398 (1861).

21. The story is well and accurately told in Morrow, Matrimonial Property Law in Louisiana, in Matrimonial Property Law 28 (W. Friedmann ed. 1955); Kirkwood, Historical Background and Objectives of the Law of Community Property in the Pacific Coast States, 11 Wash. L. Rev. 1 (1936); Loewy, The Spanish Community of Acquests and Gains and Its Adoption and Modification by the State of California, 1 Calif. L. Rev. 32 (1912); McKnight, Texas Community Property Law — Its Course of Development and Reform, 8 Calif. Western L. Rev. 117 (1971); McMurray, The Beginnings of the Community Property System in California and the Adoption of the Common Law, 3 Calif. L. Rev. 359 (1915).

22. See Hill, Early Washington Marital Property Statutes, 14 Wash. L. Rev. 118 (1939); Jacob, The Law of Community Property in Idaho, 1 Idaho L.J. 1, 7 (1931); Kirkwood, supra note 21; Lyons, Development of Community Property Law in Arizona, 15 La. L. Rev. 512 (1955).

23. It was embodied in "A Digest of the Civil Laws Now in Force in the Territory of Orleans, with alterations and amendments adapted to its present system of Government," subsequently known as the Louisiana Code of 1808. Louisiana became a state in 1812. The 1808 Code, essentially French, was revised as a result of Cottin v. Cottin, 2 Mart. 398 (La. 1817). The product was the Code of 1825. See Morrow, supra note 21.

24. See McKnight, supra note 21, at 119 n.9.

25. See Loewy, supra note 21, at 32-33; McMurray, supra note 21.

26. See Kirkwood, supra note 21, at 9.

27. See id.

28. See Lyons, supra note 22.

29. See Hill, supra note 22.

30. See Jacob, supra note 22.

31. See authorities cited in notes 21-22 supra.

community.[32] Of the retaining states, Louisiana was the first to take a firm stand by prohibiting acceptance of the common law as a unit in the Constitution of 1812.[33] Texas formally retained the marital community in 1840[34] and California followed suit in 1850;[35] together the two influenced its adoption in the other five community states.[36] Only in California, however, does the record show that the relative merits of common law and community systems were actually discussed. The occasion was the California Constitutional Convention of 1849; the focal point was the proposed inclusion in the state constitution of a provision defining the wife's separate estate.[37] One delegate made his personal preferences crystal clear: he saw the constitutional definition and the community system as a way to attract wives. Calling on all fellow bachelors at the Convention to vote accordingly, he anticipated the migration of rich, marriageable women to California.[38] Another delegate lent his support for a less selfish reason: the common law "annihilated" married women. While he himself could "stand" the system, he entreated the Convention not to impose its "despotic provisions" on wives.[39] The advocates of the common law rallied to its defense. To this group there was nothing more natural than the notion of woman's inferior place. Delegate Lippit, citing the sad example of France, described its capital as a "spectacle of domestic disunion" where, he assured the Convention, two-thirds of the married couples were living apart. Civil law principles caused such disorder by "setting the wife up as an equal, in everything whatever, to the husband" and "raising her from the condition of head clerk to partner."[40] Delegate Botts was even more emphatic. In his eyes, common law marital rules were "beautiful," "admirable" and "beneficial"; husbands were better protectors of wives than the law; the opposition's plan "to make the wife independent of the husband" was contrary to "nature" and "wisdom"; and the "doctrine of woman's rights" was the doctrine of "those mental hermaphrodites, Abby Folsom, Fanny Wright, and the rest of that tribe."[41]

32. See Kirkwood, supra note 21, at 9-11.

33. La. Const. art. IV, §11 (1812).

34. Texas adopted the common law by the Act of Jan. 20, 1840, §1, [1839] Laws of Tex. Republic 1-2 (now Tex. Rev. Civ. Stat. Ann. art. 1 (1969)), but also affirmed its system of community property within the same Act of Jan. 20, 1840, §4, [1839] Laws of Tex. Republic 4 (now Tex. Family Code Ann. §5.01(b) (1972)).

35. California adopted the common law by the Act of Apr. 13, 1850, ch. 95, [1850] Stats. of Cal. 219 (now Cal. Civ. Code §22.2 (West 1954)), but also affirmed its system of community property in a separate piece of legislation, Act of Apr. 17, 1850, ch. 103, §2, [1850] Stats. of Cal. 254 (now Cal. Civ. Code §687 (West 1954)).

36. See Kirkwood, supra note 21, at 4, 11.

37. The controversial provision read as follows: "All property, both real and personal, of the wife, owned or claimed by her before marriage, and that acquired afterwards by gift, devise or descent, shall be her separate property, and laws shall be passed more clearly defining the rights of the wife, in relation as well to her separate property as that held in common with her husband. Laws shall also be passed providing for the registration of the wife's separate property."

A substitute was also proposed: " 'Laws shall be passed more effectually securing to the wife the benefit of all property owned by her at her marriage, or acquired by her afterwards, by gift, demise [sic], or bequest, or otherwise than from her husband.' " J. Browne, Report of the Debates in the Convention of California, on the Formation of the State Constitution 257 (1850).

38. Id. at 259 (remarks of Mr. Halleck).

39. Id. at 265 (remarks of Mr. Jones).

40. Id. at 261. France was similarly cited as a bad example at the New York Constitutional Convention of 1846. See Johnston [Sex and Property: The Common Law Tradition, the Law School Curriculum, and Developments toward Equality, 47 N.Y.U.L. Rev. 1033 (1972)] at 1064.

41. Browne, supra note 37, at 259-60. Short biographies of Fanny Wright and Abby Folsom appear in 2 The National Cyclopaedia of American Biography 319-20, 394 (1899). That of the latter is particularly amusing: "She was looked upon as a harmless fanatic on the subject of free speech, and was frequently removed from meetings and conventions on account of her determined desire to speak. On one occasion she was carried out of the hall in a chair by Wendell Phillips, Oliver Johnson, and one other man, when she remarked that she was more fortunate than her Lord, for he had only one ass to ride, but she had three to carry her. Emerson called her "that flea of conventions." After her marriage with Mr. Folsom of Massachusetts, she lived a retired life, rarely appearing in public. . . ." Id. at 394.

Both factions were overreacting, for the community system, as it ultimately developed in this country, offered nothing for married women to celebrate or married men to fear. Basically, it created a community. The members, of course, were husband and wife. Community property, or "common" property as it was called in early American statutes, included everything acquired by either spouse after marriage, except for gifts and inheritances.[42] Common property was said to belong to both spouses as partners in marriage.[43] In theory, it followed, the wife's interest in the common property was that of a full "partner" — a startling contrast to the common law in which all was vested in the husband.[44] In practice, however, the two systems had like effect. The wife was a decidedly inferior partner; in fact, her partnership interest began at the partnership's end.[45] While the marriage and the community lasted, the husband was vested with the sole management and control of its assets, generally enjoying the same power of disposition over them as he had over his separate estate.[46] Until dissolution of the marriage and the community, the wife's interest seemed suspended.[47] As the Louisiana Code frankly provided, she had "no sort of right" in community assets "until her husband be dead."[48] She was then entitled to sue his heirs if she could prove he had fraudulently sold community assets in order to injure her.[49] The exact nature of the wife's interest gave rise to much discussion, since courts then,[50] as now,[51] felt the need to match theory and

42. See, e.g., Law of Dec. 30, 1865, ch. 31, §2, [1865] Laws of Ariz. 60 (now Ariz. Rev. Stat. Ann. §25-211 (1956)); Act of Apr. 17, 1850, ch. 103, §2, [1850] Stats. of Cal. 254 (now Cal. Civ. Code §687 (West 1954), §§5107-08 (West 1970)); Act of Jan. 2, 1867, ch. 9, §2, [1867] Laws of Idaho 66 (now Idaho Code §§32-903, 32-906 (1963)); Act of Mar. 7, 1865, ch. 76, §2, [1864] Stats. of Nev. 239 (now Nev. Rev. Stat. §§123.130, 123.220 (1967)); Act of Mar. 20, 1901, ch. 62, §§1-3, [1901] Laws of N.M. 112-13 (now N.M. Stat. Ann. §§57-3-4, 57-3-5, 57-4-1 (1962)); Act of Jan. 20, 1840, §4, [1839] Laws of Tex. Republic 4 (now Tex. Family Code Ann. §5.01(b) (1972)); Act of Nov. 14, 1873, §2, [1873] Laws of Wash. Territory 450 (now Wash. Rev. Code Ann. §§26.16.010, 26.16.020 (1961), §26.16.030 (West Supp. 1972)). In Louisiana the community was broader. See Tit. V, ch. 2, §4, art. 64, [1808] Civil Laws of La. [Code] 336 (now La. Civ. Code Ann. art. 2402 (West 1971)).

43. See, e.g., Ord v. De La Guerra, 18 Cal. 67, 74 (1861) ("matrimonial copartnership"); Childers v. Johnson, 6 La. Ann. 634, 637 (1851) ("conjugal partnership"); Mabie v. Whittaker, 10 Wash. 656, 662, 39 P. 172, 174 (1895) (" 'marriage makes the man and woman partners' ").

44. See Johnston, [supra, note 40] at 1045.

45. Its end, of course, comes on dissolution of the marriage by death or divorce. . . . Most often, on the husband's death the wife took one-half. With respect to divorce, in some jurisdictions the division could be unequal if one party was at fault. Typical provisions governing those events were Law of Dec. 30, 1865, ch. 31, §§11-12, [1865] Laws of Ariz. 61 (now Ariz. Rev. Stat. Ann. §§14-203, 25-318 (1956)); Tit. V, ch. 2, §4, art. 68, [1808] Civil Laws of La. [Code] 336 (now La. Civ. Code Ann. art. 2406 (West 1971)); Act of Mar. 7, 1865, ch. 76, §§11-12, [1864] Stats. of Nev. 240-41 (now Nev. Rev. Stat. §123.250 (1967), §125.150 (1971)).

46. Act of Dec. 30, 1865, ch. XXXI, §9, [1865] Laws of Ariz. 61 (now Ariz. Rev. Stat. Ann. §25-211 (1956)); Act of Apr. 17, 1850, ch. 103, §9, [1850] Stats. of Cal. 254 (now Cal. Civ. Code §§5114, 5115 (West 1970)); Act of Jan. 9, 1867, ch. 9, §9, [1867] Laws of Idaho 67 (now Idaho Code §32-912 (1963)); Tit. V, ch. 2, §4, art. 66, [1808] Civil Laws of La. [Code] 336 (now La. Civ. Code Ann. art. 2404 (West 1971)); Act of Mar. 7, 1865, ch. LXXVI, §9, [1864] Stats. of Nev. 240 (now Nev. Rev. Stat. §123.230 (1967)); Act of Jan. 20, 1840, §4, [1839] Laws of Tex. Republic 4 (repealed 1869); Act of Nov. 14, 1873, §9, [1873] Laws of Wash. Territory 452 (repealed 1972). The first territorial legislation on community property was not passed in New Mexico until 1901. For a summary of the husband's powers over the community before that time, see Reade v. de Lea, 14 N.M. 442, 448-51, 95 P. 131, 132-33 (1908). The 1901 statute gave all married persons the same property rights and powers to sue, be sued or convey as those already possessed by unmarried persons of legal age. Act of Mar. 20, 1901, ch. LXII, §5, [1901] Laws of N.M. 113 (repealed 1907). Husband and wife both had to join in conveyances of community reality, id. §6, until, in 1907, the husband was again made manager and controller of the community "with the like absolute power of disposition, other than testamentary, as he has of his separate property." Act of Mar. 18, 1907, ch. XXXVII, §6, [1907] Laws of N.M. 48 (now N.M. Stat. Ann. §57-4-3 (1962)).

47. At best, she had a mere expectancy. Packard v. Arellanes, 17 Cal. 525, 538 (1861).

48. Tit. V, ch. 2, §4, art. 66, [1808] Civil Laws of La. [Code] 336 (repealed 1825, but substance preserved in La. Civ. Code Ann. art. 2404 (West 1971)).

49. Id.

50. See, e.g., Packard v. Arellanes, 17 Cal. 525 (1861).

51. See United States v. Mitchell, 403 U.S. 190 (1971).

practice so as to justify the law's preference for husbands. Some were forthright: the husband, they said, was made manager of the community because the community property was really his.[52] According to others, the husband was given control of the community not because he was its exclusive owner, but because someone must manage it and the law chose him.[53] Of course, both spouses might have been designated joint managers of community assets,[54] or management responsibilities might have been apportioned between them.[55] Neither of these schemes, however, was part of early American law.

The other aspect of the community system which differed theoretically from the common law was its clear recognition of wife's separate estate — the very thing that struck terror into Delegates Lippit and Botts[56] at the California Convention. So important was this concept thought to be that the framers in Texas,[57] California[58] and Nevada[59] were not content to leave its definition to statute. They included it in their state constitutions. The Texas provision, parent to and prototype of the rest, provided that:

> [a]ll property both real and personal of the wife, owned or claimed by her before marriage, and that acquired afterwards by gift, devise, or descent, shall be her separate property; and laws shall be passed more clearly defining the rights of the wife, in relation as well to her separate property, as that held in common with her husband. . . .[60]

If the wife seemed thus endowed with a separate estate, she was not to be permitted to use it. Its management, like that of her interest in the community, was vested by law in the husband.[61] Written consent of both spouses, however, was required for its sale.[62] Louisiana alone stood true to the Spanish heritage, allowing the wife to administer her

---

52. E.g., Packard v. Arellanes, 17 Cal. 525, 538 (1861): "The title to such property rests in the husband, and for all practical purposes he is regarded by the law as the sole owner."

53. E.g., Warburton v. White, 176 U.S. 484, 490, 492 (1900).

54. That was the scheme of the NOW bill, [2 Women's Rights L. Rptr. 17 (Spring, 1972)], and is presently the law with respect to part of the community in Texas. See note 133 infra.

55. That is presently true of part of the community in Texas. [Tex. Family Code Ann. §5.22(a) (1972).]

56. See text accompanying notes 40-41 supra.

57. Tex. Const. art. VII, §19 (1845).

58. Cal. Const. art. XI, §14 (1849).

59. Nev. Const. art. IV, §31 (1864).

60. Tex. Const. art. VII, §19 (1845). Other states included similar definitions in their statutes. Act of Dec. 30, 1865, ch. XXXI, §1, [1865] Laws of Ariz. 60 (now Ariz. Rev. Stat. Ann. §25-211(A) (1956)); Act of Jan. 2, 1867, ch. 9, §1, [1867] Laws of Idaho 65-66 (now Idaho Code §32-903 (1963)); Act of Nov. 14, 1873, §1, [1873] Laws of Wash. Territory 451 (repealed 1972).

61. Clay v. Power, 24 Tex. 304 (1859); Act of Dec. 30, 1865, ch. XXXI, §6, [1865] Laws of Ariz. 61 (repealed 1901); Act of Apr. 17, 1850, ch. 103, §6, [1850] Stats. of Cal. 254 (repealed 1872); Act of Jan. 2, 1867, ch. IX, §6, [1867] Laws of Idaho 66 (repealed 1903); Act of Mar. 7, 1865, ch. LXXVI, §6, [1864] Stats. of Nev. 239 (repealed 1973); Act of Nov. 14, 1873, §6, [1873] Laws of Wash. Territory 451-52 (repealed 1972). This also seems to have been the state of affairs in New Mexico before 1884. See Strong v. Eakin, 11 N.M. 107, 122-26, 66 P. 539, 543-44 (1901). Section 8 of the Arizona, California, Nevada and Washington laws ironically gave her an action against her husband for mismanagement of her separate property and the appointment in his stead of a trustee. Act of Dec. 30, 1865, ch. XXXI, §8, [1865] Laws of Ariz. 60-61 (repealed 1901); Act of Apr. 17, 1850, ch. 103, §8, [1850] Stats. of Cal. 254 (repealed 1872); Act of Mar. 7, 1865, ch. LXXVI, §8, [1864] Stats. of Nev. 240 (repealed 1973); Act of Nov. 14, 1873, §8, [1873] Laws of Wash. Territory 452 (repealed 1881). Sections 3, 4 and 5 required her to file an inventory of her separate property to protect it from her husband's creditors. Act of Dec. 30, 1865, ch. XXXI, §§3-5, [1865] Laws of Ariz. 60 (repealed 1901); Act of Apr. 17, 1850, ch. 103, §§3-5, [1850] Stats. of Cal. 254 (now Cal. Civ. Code §5114 (West 1970)); Act of Mar. 7, 1865, ch. LXXVI, §§3-5, [1864] Stats. of Nev. 239 (now Nev. Rev. Stat. §§123.140, 123.150, 123.160 (1967)); Act of Nov. 14, 1873, §§3-5, [1873] Laws of Wash. Territory 450-51 (repealed 1879). In Texas it had to be registered to achieve the same effect. Act of Apr. 29, 1846, §6, [1846] Laws of Tex. 154 (now Tex. Family Code Ann. §5.03 (1972)).

62. See Act of Dec. 30, 1865, ch. XXXI, §6, [1865] Laws of Ariz. 61 (repealed 1901); Act of Apr. 17, 1850, ch. 103, §6, [1850] Stats. of Cal. 254 (repealed 1872); Act of Mar. 7, 1865, ch. LXXVI, §6, [1864] Stats. of Nev. 239-40 (repealed 1873); Act of Feb. 3, 1841, §1, [1840-41] Laws of Tex. Republic 144-45 (repealed 1913); Act of Nov. 14, 1873, §6, [1873] Laws of Wash. Territory 451-52 (repealed 1881).

own paraphernal property.[63] But there, too, the husband's authorization or, if he failed to give it, that of the court was required for sale.[64] In California the restriction on the wife's power to sell her separate property was soon attacked. How could the husband's consent be required in view of the state constitution? The California Supreme Court considered the question and upheld the restriction.[65] Conceding that the framers, by defining the wife's separate estate, "swept out of existence many of the disabilities of the wife and some of the most important rights of the husband," the court unaccountably found the state legislators free to restore them.[66]

In justification of American lawmakers, it might be said that in making the husband manager of the community, they were merely following Spanish law, expressing legitimate concern for the rights of creditors or giving effect to the reality of most marriages in which the husband was the sole wage-earner and provider. In making him manager of the wife's separate estate as well, they ignored the Spanish law and had no other excuses with which to justify their action. In fact, they were influenced by the common law and its insistence on the husband's superior place. Thus they acted purely on the basis of sex. . . .

Thus, by the turn of the century, the stage was set for forty-two common law and eight community property states; and so it remained except for short-lived conversions to community property by the then territory of Hawaii and the states of Michigan, Nebraska, Oklahoma, Oregon and Pennsylvania.[76] These departures were motivated by the hope of securing tax advantages for married residents,[77] not by legislative concern for women's rights.

5. Some Features of Contemporary Community Property Law

YOUNGER, COMMUNITY PROPERTY, WOMEN, AND THE LAW SCHOOL CURRICULUM
48 N.Y.U.L. Rev. 230-240 (1973)

A. THE WIFE'S INTEREST IN THE COMMUNITY DURING MARRIAGE

Statutes and cases in all community property states repeatedly refer to the wife's interest in the community as "present" and "existing" during marriage and "equal" to the husband's.[130] Despite such assertions and popular lay opinion, it is simply not true that the community property system treats the husband and wife as equals with respect to property they have acquired during the marriage. To be sure the husband's superior powers have diminished since the system's reception: he has lost control over his wife's

---

63. This was defined as "all the effects of the wife which are no part of her dowery." Tit. V, ch. 1, art. 12, [1808] Civil Laws of La. [Code] 324 (now La. Civ. Code Ann. art. 2383 (West 1971)). She was also given the right to administer and enjoy these effects. Tit. V, ch. 2, §3, art. 58, [1808] Civil Laws of La. [Code] 334 (now La. Civ. Ann. art. 2384 (West 1971)).

64. Tit. V, ch. 2, §3, art. 58, [1808] Civil Laws of La. [Code] 334 (repealed to the extent that husband's authorization is required for sale, 1916).

65. Dow v. The Gould & Curry Silver Mining Co., 31 Cal. 629 (1867).

66. Id. at 641-42.

76. Principles [W. deFuniak and M. Vaughn, Principles of Community Property (2d ed. 1971)] §53.1, at 89.

77. Id.

130. See, e.g., United States v. Malcolm, 282 U.S. 792 (1931) (California); Bender v. Pfaff, 282 U.S. 127 (1930) (Louisiana); Hopkins v. Bacon, 282 U.S. 122 (1930) (Texas); Goodell v. Koch, 282 U.S. 118 (1930) (Arizona); Poe v. Seaborn, 282 U.S. 101 (1930) (Washington); Estate of Williams, 40 Nev. 241, 161 P. 741 (1916); Beals v. Ares, 25 N.M. 459, 185 P. 780 (1919); Arnold v. Leonard, 114 Tex. 535, 273 S.W. 799 (1925); Cal. Civ. Code §5105 (West 1970); Nev. Rev. Stat. §123.220 (1967).

earnings and personal injury recoveries in a number of jurisdictions,[131] the exclusive statutory managerial label in Washington[132] and Texas,[133] and the first court test of the system's constitutionality in Arizona.[134] Yet he remains exclusive manager of the community in six of the eight community property states[135] and his wife's interest in community assets remains distinctly less valuable than, and inferior to, his.

[A discussion follows of United States v. Mitchell, 403 U.S. 190, 91 S. Ct. 1763, 29 L. Ed. 2d 406 (1971), in which Louisiana wives were held liable for taxes due on community income derived from community property they had never received, although the Court agreed with the Fifth Circuit's view of Louisiana law that their interest in the property was so "evanescent" that they could not be considered owners.]

. . . A superior court judge has recently applied the *Reed* case to the community

131. In California, the wife's earnings remain part of the community, but she is given control over their management. This control is lost, however, if she commingles her earnings with community property managed by her husband. Cal. Civ. Code §5124 (West 1970). The same is true of personal injury recoveries, except that the husband may use them to reimburse himself or the community for the wife's medical expenses. Id. If they are received after certain kinds of separation or if they are the fruits of an action by one spouse against the other, however, they are not community but separate property. Id. §5126 (West Supp. 1972); id. §5109 (West 1970). Notwithstanding any statutory grant of management to the husband, id. §§5125, 5127 (West 1970), the wife is entitled to management and control of the whole community to the extent necessary to fulfill her duty to support her children. Id. §5127.5 (West Supp. 1970). In Texas, the wife's earnings remain part of the community, but she is given control. Tex. Family Code Ann. §5.22(a)(1) (1972). Personal injury recoveries attributable to loss of earning capacity are community property; the rest are separate property of the injured spouse, who has control of both. Id. §§5.01(a)(3), 5.22(a)(3). Mingling with community property controlled by the husband results in joint control. Id. §5.22(b). In Idaho, the wife's earnings remain part of the community, but she is given control. Idaho Code §32-913 (1963). Her personal injury recoveries are community property and are under the husband's control. Labonte v. Davidson, 31 Idaho 644, 175 P. 588 (1918). In Louisiana, the wife's personal injury recoveries are her separate property but her husband's are part of the community. La. Civ. Code Ann. arts. 2402, 2334 (West 1971). See text accompanying notes 292-96 infra for a more detailed discussion of this point. In New Mexico, the cause of action attributable to medical expenses, loss of services to the community and the loss of earnings due to personal injury belongs to the community; however, the cause of action for personal injury to the wife (and for resultant pain and suffering) is her separate property and therefore hers to control. Soto v. Vandeventer, 56 N.M. 483, 245 P.2d 826 (1952). In both Louisiana and New Mexico, the wife's earnings remain in the community under the management of the husband. La. Civ. Code Ann. art. 2404 (West 1971); N.M. Stat. Ann. §57-4-3 (1962). Nevada makes a division of personal injury recoveries like that in New Mexico if the spouses sue jointly; if the wife sues alone, the whole recovery is hers. Nev. Rev. Stat. §41.170 (1969). As to the wife's earnings, Nev. Rev. Stat. §123.190 (1967) shockingly provides: "When the husband has allowed the wife to appropriate to her own use her earnings, the same, with the issues and profits thereof, is deemed a gift from him to her, and is, with such issues and profits, her separate property."

A wife is in complete control of her earnings and accumulations when they are being used for the care and maintenance of the family. Id. §123.230(2) (1967). In Arizona, the wife has no control over her earnings or personal injury recoveries. Both are part of the community managed by the husband. Ariz. Rev. Stat. Ann. §25-211 (1956); see Tinker v. Hobbs, 80 Ariz. 166, 294 P.2d 659 (1956). But see Fahey v. Nelson, No. 134285, (Ariz. Super. Ct. Apr. 4, 1973) [hereinafter *Fahey*]. In Washington, recoveries for injuries by a third-party tortfeasor are community property. If the tortfeasor is the other spouse, special damages are recoverable by the community and the injured spouse may recover half the general damages for loss of future earnings and the entire amount of the general damages for pain, suffering and emotional distress as separate property. Freehe v. Freehe, 81 Wash. 2d 183, ___, 500 P.2d 771, 777 (1972); Schneider v. Biberger, 76 Wash. 504, 136 P. 701 (1913). A statute giving the wife control over the "wages of her personal labor," Wash. Rev. Code Ann. §26.16.130 (1961), was recently repealed, ch. 108, §8, [1972] Wash. Laws, 2d Extraord. Sess. 247. The wife's earnings remain community property which "[e]ither spouse, acting alone, may manage and control." Wash. Rev. Code Ann. §26.16.030 (Supp. 1972). One wonders if this is a step forward or backward for the earning wife.

132. In Washington, either spouse acting alone may "manage and control community property, with a like power of disposition" over his or her separate property. But neither may bequeath more than half of the property, make gifts, convey or contract with respect to realty, create certain security interests or deal in certain business assets without the other's consent. Wash. Rev. Code Ann. §26.16.030 (Supp. 1972).

133. In Texas, each spouse now has "sole management, control and disposition of the community property that he or she would have owned if single." Tex. Family Code Ann. §5.22(a) (1972). Over the rest of the community their powers are joint. Id. §5.22(b).

134. *Fahey*, supra note 131. See text accompanying notes 147-50 infra.

135. [Arizona, California, Idaho, Louisiana, Nevada and New Mexico. But see *Fahey*, supra n. 131.]

property system of Arizona,[147] declaring unconstitutional statutes[148] which make the husband exclusive manager of community personalty and disable wives from making contracts binding it. The successful challenge was made by two wives[149] who argued that the combination of husbands' managerial powers and their inability to contract with respect to community assets operated to deprive them of credit. One, separated from her husband for seven years, could not borrow money for necessaries because her husband was not available to co-sign the loan and his whereabouts were unknown. The other, a Ph.D. teaching at the University of Arizona and earning more than $15,000 a year, could not obtain a charge account without her husband's signature. The court found that the statutes discriminated "solely on sex" by requiring "dissimilar treatment for men and women who are similarly situated." This unequal result denied plaintiffs equal protection in violation of both the federal and state constitutions.[150] The decision is welcome and long overdue. But until it is affirmed on the several appeals it is likely to undergo, it can have little effect on wives' rights to control the community assets which they are supposed to own. Most jurisdictions deny them these rights.

In Texas when he is the sole wage-earner,[151] and all other states[152] save Washington[153] and hopefully Arizona,[154] the husband has sole control of most of the community personalty. He can sell it, encumber it and, in three states, give it away, all without his wife's consent.[155] One California wife tested her "ownership" against her husband's management rights.[156] She took and secreted $30,000 in community funds, refusing her husband's demands to return them. When he sued to get them back, the trial court sustained his wife's demurrer, but the appellate court reversed, holding:

> The right of the husband thus conferred to manage, control and dispose of community personal property is invaded by his wife when she deprives him thereof by taking, secreting and exercising exclusive control over community funds. A husband has a cause of action against his wife for such an invasion and violation of his right in the premises with attendant appropriate remedies.[157]

147. *Fahey*, supra note 131.

148. Ariz. Rev. Stat. Ann. §§25-211(B) (1956), 25-214(A) (Supp. 1972). See note 175 infra.

149. There was a third unsuccessful plaintiff-wife who complained of the community's liability for taxes attributable to her husband's business in which she never participated. The court denied her relief because no written protest or objection to payment of the taxes was ever filed. *Fahey*, supra note 131, at 1.

150. *Fahey*, supra note 131, at 2. The test used by the court in reaching this decision is not altogether clear. Judge Fenton relied on *Reed*, in which the Supreme Court used a strict rational basis test to strike a statute that discriminated arbitrarily between men and women similarly situated. He also relied on Shapiro v. Thompson, 394 U.S. 618 (1969), in which the Court mandated use of a compelling state interest test when suspect classifications are made by the state. Although sex has not been declared a suspect classification by the Supreme Court, other courts have found it to be so. Sail'er Inn, Inc. v. Kirby, 5 Cal. 3d 1, 485 P.2d 529, 95 Cal. Rptr. 329 (1971).

151. See Tex. Family Code Ann. §5.22(a) (1972).

152. Cal. Civ. Code §5125 (West 1970) (but he needs her written consent for gifts and for any disposition of the furniture, furnishings or fittings of the home, or her or the children's clothing); Idaho Code §32-912 (1963); La. Civ. Code Ann. art. 2404 (West 1971); Nev. Rev. Stat. §123.230 (1967); N.M. Stat. Ann. §57-4-3 (1962).

153. See Wash. Rev. Code Ann. §26.16.030 (Supp. 1972).

154. See text accompanying notes 146-50 supra.

155. See statutes cited in notes 151 & 152 supra. The three states which permit gifts are Nevada, Louisiana and Texas. This unilateral power extends to community personalty and realty, of which the husband has sole control in Texas, to movables — but not immovables — in Louisiana, and to personalty and realty (except homestead, see text accompanying note 164 infra) in Nevada. The gifts are not supposed to be excessive or in fraud of the wife; however, a husband was allowed to give away an opera house in Nixon v. Brown, 46 Nev. 439, 214 P. 524 (1923). For other authorities, see Azar v. Azar, 239 La. 941, 120 So. 2d 485 (1960); Oliphint v. Oliphint, 219 La. 781, 54 So. 2d 18 (1951); La. Civ. Code Ann. art. 2404 (West 1971); Tex. Family Code Ann. §5.22(a) (1972). In Arizona, the husband also seems to have the power to dispense gifts which take effect on the death of either spouse. See Gaethje v. Gaethje, 7 Ariz. App. 544, 549, 441 P.2d 579, 584 (1968). On a husband's power to give community property to a trustee, see Land v. Marshall, 426 S.W.2d 841 (Tex. 1968); Cal. Civ. Code §5113.5 (West Supp. 1972).

156. Wilcox v. Wilcox, 21 Cal. App. 3d 457, 98 Cal. Rptr. 319 (Dist. Ct. App. 1971).

157. Id. at 459, 98 Cal. Rptr. at 320.

The wife's interest in community realty is almost as nebulous. In all community property states, with the exceptions of Texas[158] and Washington,[159] the husband is manager.[160] In four states, his wife is required to join with him before he can sell, encumber or convey any community realty.[161] The same is true in Washington, when the husband is managing,[162] and in Texas when the property is under joint control or homestead.[163] In the two remaining states, joinder is required only if the husband is dealing with the family homestead;[164] if not, he is virtually free to do as he pleases.[165] On its face, the joinder requirement seems adequate to protect the wife's interest; but courts have diluted its content. The requirement has been held expendable in a number of borderline transactions.[166] Even when joinder is clearly required, failure to obtain it may not render a transaction void. . . . [See Sander v. Wells, 71 Wash. 2d 25, 246 P.2d 481 (1967).]

California has a similar rule incorporated in a statute:[172] though the wife's joinder is required for conveyance of community realty, if the husband who holds record title to it conveys to a bona fide purchaser who has no knowledge of the marriage, the conveyance is presumed to be valid. Actions to avoid conveyances by such husbands must be brought within one year from the filing of the deed for record.[173] Thus the burden is put on the wife, who has neither management nor control of the realty, nor knowledge of her husband's transactions concerning it, somehow to protect what she "owns."

As manager of the community, the husband makes contracts on its behalf.[174] A wife is generally not empowered to do so[175] except when her husband consents,[176] is incapacitated, is incompetent, has disappeared[177] or has failed to provide necessaries.[178] A typical case[179] involved a wife who wanted to buy a graduation present to give to her minor son. Although the husband opposed it, saying he would take no part in the transaction, the wife nevertheless bought and presented the gift. When she defaulted

158. See Tex. Family Code Ann. §5.22 (1972).

159. See Wash. Rev. Code Ann. §26.16.030 (Supp. 1972).

160. Pendleton v. Brown, 25 Ariz. 604, 221 P. 213 (1923); Cal. Civ. Code §5127 (West 1970); Idaho Code §32-912 (1963); La. Civ. Code Ann. art. 2404 (West 1971); Nev. Rev. Stat. §123.230 (1967); N.M. Stat. Ann. §57-4-3 (1962).

161. Ariz. Rev. Stat. Ann. §33.452 (1956); Cal. Civ. Code §5127 (West 1970), Idaho Code §32-912 (1963); N.M. Stat. Ann. §57-4-3 (1962).

162. Wash. Rev. Code Ann. §26.16.030(3) (Supp. 1972).

163. Tex. Family Code Ann. §§5.22, 5.81 (1972).

164. La. Civ. Code Ann. art. 2404 (West 1971); La. Rev. Stat. Ann. §§9:2801, 9:2802 (1951); Nev. Rev. Stat. §123.230(1) (1967). But see Mullikin v. Jones, 71 Nev. 14, 278 P.2d 876 (1955).

165. He may not, however, convey community immovables inter vivos by gratuitous title in Louisiana. La. Civ. Code Ann. art. 2404 (West 1971). As to gifts of realty in Nevada and Texas, see note 155 supra.

166. E.g., Reimann v. United States, 315 F.2d 746 (9th Cir. 1963) (soil bank conservation reserve contract not an encumbrance, and wife need not join); Janes v. LeDeit, 228 Cal. App. 2d 474, 39 Cal. Rptr. 559 (Dist. Ct. App. 1964) (wife's joinder not needed to settle boundaries); Martin v. Butter, 93 Cal. App. 2d 562, 209 P.2d 636 (Dist. Ct. App. 1949) (wife's joinder not needed to modify or terminate contract for sale of realty); McDonald v. Bernard, 87 Cal. App. 717, 262 P. 430 (Dist. Ct. App. 1927) (wife's joinder not needed in an agreement to pay broker's commission). But see Geoghegan v. Dever, 30 Wash. 2d 877, 194 P.2d 397 (1948) (agreement to pay broker's commission was "encumbrance"; wife's joinder needed).

172. Cal. Civ. Code §5127 (West 1970).

173. Id.

174. Principles, [W. deFuniak and M. Vaughn, Principles of Community Property (2d ed. 1971)] §116.

175. See, e.g., Ariz. Rev. Stat. Ann. §25-214(A) (Supp. 1972), which provides: "Married women of the age of eighteen years and upwards have the same legal rights and are subject to the same legal liabilities as men of the age of eighteen years and upwards except the right to make contracts binding the common property of the husband and wife." This statute has recently been declared unconstitutional by a lower state court. *Fahey,* supra note 131.

176. See, e.g., Cal. Civ. Code §5116 (West 1970); N.M. Stat. Ann. §57-4-2 (1962).

177. See, e.g., N.M. Stat. Ann. §57-4-5 (1962); Tex. Family Code Ann. §5.25(a) (1972).

178. See, e.g., Ariz. Rev. Stat. Ann. §25-215 (1956).

179. Watson v. Veuleman, 260 So. 2d 123 (La. App. 1972).

in her payments, the dealer sought to hold her husband liable on the ground that the purchase price was a community debt. The court disagreed: only the husband, not the wife, could obligate the community unless the wife was its agent or her husband ratified her act. The court refused to find either agency or ratification from the spouses' relationship.[180] Yet the courts have no difficulty, aided as they are by statute, in reaching a similar conclusion in favor of the husband; in fact, any debt incurred by a married man is presumed to be a community obligation.[181]

Similarly, as manager, husband has been the appropriate plaintiff in suits on behalf of the community and the required defendant in suits against it.[182] The rule has even been applied in actions to recover damages for injuries to wife's person or reputation in states where such awards are considered community property. The reasoning behind the rule that the husband is a necessary plaintiff has been explained in a leading Arizona case:

> It is not because a *cause* of action ever existed in him, for that belonged to the person actually injured. As was said . . . the injury did not accrue to the husband; "it was wholly personal to the wife. It was her body that was bruised; it was she who suffered the agonizing, mental and physical pain." The husband merely *represents* the community as a guardian would represent a minor child; he has no more individual and personal cause of action than a guardian. . . .[183]

The court's language leads logically to the opposite conclusion — i.e., that wives should sue for themselves unless, of course, one views them as incompetent. . . . [See also Few v. Charter Oak Fire Ins. Co., 463 S.W.2d 424 (Tex. 1971).]

In exercising his still very substantial powers over the community, the husband is not supposed to act in fraud or injury of his wife.[190] He is said to be a fiduciary, although this status may "not require that [he] be as prudent as a trustee or that he keep complete and accurate records of income received and disbursed."[191] Furthermore, if the husband does exceed his powers to the detriment of his wife, she may, except in Louisiana,[192] sue him during marriage or proceed against his transferees. Such actions, of course, require knowledge of what has been done: this the wife may never acquire.

These safeguards do not secure equality of result between husbands and wives in relation to their interests in community property. To say, as courts and legislatures persist in doing, that the wife, during marriage, has a "present," "existing" and "equal" interest in the community with her husband is hypocrisy.

180. "The fact that Mrs. Veuleman did all the paper work in the family and paid all of the bills does not justify a holding that she acted as agent for the community." Id. at 126. In a later case reaching the same result, the same court said, quoting a law professor, that "a presumptive mandate in such terms in favor of the wife would make her the *alter ego* of the husband in all things and therefore violate the division of authority between husband and wife in all matrimonial regimes." American Nat'l Bank v. Rathburn, 264 So. 2d 360, 363 (La. App. 1972).

181. E.g., Hofmann Co. v. Meisner, 17 Ariz. App. 263, __, 497 P.2d 83, 87 (1972). As the court put it in Kerr v. Cochran, 65 Wash. 2d 211, 223, 396 P.2d 642, 649 (1964), "[t]he *presumption* is that the wife is not acting for or on behalf of the community, whereas the husband is *presumed* to be acting for or on behalf of the marital community." (emphasis added).

182. See generally Principles, supra note 3, §124. Compare Principles with Tex. Family Code Ann. §4.04 (1972) and Wash. Rev. Code Ann. §4.08.040 (Supp. 1972).

183. Fox Tucson Theatres Corp. v. Lindsay, 47 Ariz. 388, 392, 56 P.2d 183, 184 (1936).

190. E.g., Weinberg v. Weinberg, 67 Cal. 2d 557, 563, 432 P.2d 709, 712, 63 Cal. Rptr. 13, 16 (1967). But cf. Nixon v. Brown, 46 Nev. 439, 214 P. 524 (1923).

191. Williams v. Williams, 14 Cal. App. 3d 560, 567, 92 Cal. Rptr. 385, 389 (Dist. Ct. App. 1971).

192. In that state she can only bring four kinds of actions as the marriage continues. La. Rev. Stat. Ann. §9:291 (West 1965). They are for (1) a separation of property, (2) restitution and enjoyment of paraphernal property, (3) separation from bed and board and (4) divorce. Id. As to (1), the court of appeals in Mitchell v. Commissioner, 430 F.2d 1, 6 n.6 (5th Cir. 1970), said: "Although the wife may obtain a judicial separation of property without dissolution of the marriage, this remedy is difficult to obtain and somewhat illusory because the wife must show prior mismanagement and thus the funds may have already been dissipated."

6. Estates and Trusts

Few laws relating to estates and trusts discriminate on their face against women. Rather, these laws combine with the facts that men usually control a married couple's property, that the wife is likely to outlive the husband, and that there are devices enabling the husband to control the property after his death, to give estate and gift provisions a markedly discriminatory potential in individual cases.

a. The Laws of Intestacy: The Forced Share

PLOVER, TRUSTS AND THE MISTRUSTED WIDOW
2-7 (unpublished paper, Geo. Wash. U. Law School 1971;
revised and reorganized with the permission of the author)

In most of the forty-two states which retain the common law property laws, dower and curtesy have been abolished ,[5] and the main protection afforded a surviving spouse against complete disinheritance is a "statutory elective" or "forced" share. Under these statutes, a surviving spouse may elect to take a certain share of the decedent's estate — usually one-third — in lieu of any provision (or lack of provision) in the decedent's will. [This share is based upon the wife's contribution or "marital rights." However, the amount which a wife recovers depends upon what is left in the estate on the husband's death, not upon the wife's contributions or her needs; and the laws which give the husband either the title to or the control over property acquired during marriage allow substantial waste of the probate estate before death.]

Most [common law] states (except the Dakotas) have attempted by statutes to protect a surviving spouse against intentional diminution of the probate estate. There are statutes which limit the amount of an estate which a testator may give to charitable institutions, either by limiting the size of such share relative to the total estate, or by providing that such a gift is invalid if it is not made (or, if the gift is testamentary, if the will is not executed) prior to a certain time period before the testator's death.[6] Others, such as New York, prescribe exactly what assets, whether or not part of the probate estate, are to be included in computing the value of the statutory elective share.[7] Also, case law has provided that "an heir cannot be disinherited by language alone. Unless the property to which he or she is heir is given to someone else, it is still intestate and the heirs take it as intestate property."[8] So unless a testator specifically gives his property to others, either by inter vivos gift or by will, the property may pass as intestate property, and under most state intestacy statutes the surviving spouse is an heir who is entitled to a specific portion, if not all, of intestate property.

The Uniform Probate Code recommends that the surviving spouse can elect to take one-third of the "augmented estate." The augmented estate would not include funeral and administration expenses, family allowances and exemptions, and certain other claims, but would include the value of transfers made by the decedent during marriage which are essentially will substitutes. Property which the decedent had given to the surviving spouse and property derived from the decedent which the surviving spouse has, in turn, given away in a will-like substitute, would not be included in the aug-

5. Uniform Probate Code, Section 2-113. [Common law dower and curtesy were clearly discriminatory: curtesy consummate entitled the surviving husband to a life estate in all of the wife's real estate; dower entitled a surviving spouse to a life estate in only one-third of the husband's realty. On the other hand, curtesy required, in addition to marriage and survivorship, the live birth of a child; there was no similar prerequisite to the validity of a widow's dower claim. — Eds.]

6. Ritchie, Alford and Effland, . . . [Cases and Materials on Decedents' Estates and Trusts, 4th ed. 1971], p. 123.

7. Ibid. at 116; New York Decedent Estate Law Section 18a (1966).

8. Ness v. Lunde, 394 Ill. 286, 68 N.E.2d 458.

mented estate.[9] Also, under the Uniform Probate Code, election of a statutory share does not result in a loss of any benefits to the surviving spouse under the will; the benefits are charged against the elective share.[10]

The Restatement (Second) of Trusts provides that equitable interests of a decedent are included in determining the statutory distributive share of a deceased spouse.[11] . . .

. . . [T]he community property states have [also] enacted statutes to prevent a husband from disposing of all community property before his death, thereby leaving his wife with one-half of zero in these states (which have neither dower nor elective share statutes). In California, any gift of community personal property, to be valid, must be consented to, in writing, by the wife.[17]

b. Testate Succession: The Widow's Election in Community Property States

The husband's superior rights of control of the marital property extend, in many states, beyond the grave, in the form of superior rights to devise marital property.[45] Two examples are analyzed by Younger:[46]

> If the wife owns half of the community during marriage, she should also have the right to leave it by will. This rule is followed in every community property state except New Mexico, where her interest expires at her death and the whole community goes to her husband.[193] On his death, however, he has full testamentary powers over his share.[194]
>
> A different inequity exists in the law of California. There the husband has continuing power over his wife's share of the community pending administration of her estate.[195] He need not transfer it to her personal representative except to the extent necessary to carry her will into effect.[196] He is free, in the interim, to change its form, though not its status.[197] When the wife's personal representative needs the property

9. Uniform Probate Code, Section 2-202.
10. Ibid. Section 2-206.
11. Restatement (Second) of Trusts, Section 146A (1959).
17. 13 Stanford Law Review 610 (1961).
45. E.g., N.M. Stat. Ann. §29-1-8 (1962) provides: "Upon the death of the wife, the entire community property, without administration, belongs to the surviving husband, except such portion thereof as may have been set apart to her by a judicial decree, for her support and maintenance, which portion is subject to her testamentary disposition, and in the absence of such disposition, goes to her descendants, or heirs, exclusive of her husband."
But id. §29-1-9 provides: "Upon the death of the husband, the entire community property goes to the surviving wife, subject to the husband's power of testamentary disposition over one-half [1/2] of the community property. In the case of the dissolution of the community by the death of the husband the entire community property is subject to the community debts, the husband's debts, funeral expenses of the husband, the family allowance and the charge and expenses of administration."
46. Younger, Community Property, Women and the Law School Curriculum, 48 N.Y.U.L. Rev. 211, 240-241 (1973).
193. N.M. Stat. Ann. §29-1-8 (1954) provides: "Upon the death of the wife, the entire community property, without administration, belongs to the surviving husband, except such portion thereof as may have been set apart to her by a judicial decree, for her support and maintenance which portion is subject to her testamentary disposition, and in the absence of such disposition, goes to her descendants, or heirs, exclusive of her husband."
194. Id. §29-1-9 (Supp. 1971) provides:
"Upon the death of the husband, the entire community property goes to the surviving wife, subject to the husband's power of testamentary disposition over one-half of the community property. In the case of the dissolution of the community by the death of the husband the entire community property is subject to the community debts, the husband's debts, funeral expenses of the husband, the family allowance and the charge and expenses of administration."
195. Cal. Prob. Code Ann. §§202, 203 (West 1956). Compare Nev. Rev. Stat. §123.260 (1957).
196. Cal. Prob. Code Ann. §§202, 203 (West 1956).
197. Chuba v. Fishbein, 13 Cal. App. 3d 382, 91 Cal. Rptr. 683 (Dist. Ct. App. 1970).

for distribution under the wife's will, he may demand it from her husband. Before then, however, he may have substantial difficulty in establishing either its status as community property or its value.[198] It remains, though the wife has willed it, subject to her husband's debts.[199] Similarly, when the husband dies, under either New Mexico or California law, the entire community is first subject to his separate debts. Only after his creditors get their share does the wife get hers.[200] No justification for these niggling but nevertheless damaging distinctions has been offered and none can be convincingly made. They are created by statute and linger as unpleasant remnants of the husband's lifetime managerial powers.

However, the more pervasive discrimination exists in the "Widow's Election" statutes of community property states.[47] Under these statutes, the husband may devise even his wife's half of the community property, and force his wife to take what he provided or the problematical "forced share":[48]

> Aside from [the husband's] lifetime powers, the doctrine of election operates to dilute the protections which the law displays as [the wife's]. As it originated in equity election compelled a choice between inconsistent benefits only. Perverted now, it makes [the wife] choose between consistent benefits designed for her protection in her dependent state. Modern forced share statutes, for example, reverse the common law presumption that a gift in [the husband's] will is in addition to [the wife's] dower.[1] Unless [the husband] expresses his intention that [the wife] is to take both, [she] must choose between her statutory share and whatever he has left her. Some jurisdictions stretch the perversion further, holding that where [the husband] dies partially intestate [the wife's] decision to take against the will precludes her from taking as [her husband's] distributee.[2]

In some states, an election to take a "forced share" also is an election against homestead, exemption, and family allowance rights.[49] As Younger notes,[50]

> Such an election seems particularly inappropriate in the case of community property since the wife's interest is not described as inchoate during her husband's life but as present, equal and existing. How then can the husband dispose of it or require her to elect whether to keep it?

c. Bypassing the Estate: The Trust

A frequently used device with considerable potential for discrimination is the trust. The trust may be used both to reduce the property included in the "estate," and thereby limit the wife's forced share, and by explicit provision to force the wife to elect between the division of property which the husband chose and her forced share, a choice which is often accompanied by severe penalties. Once again, while the trust provisions are equally applicable to men and women, the fact of male control over the property and the likelihood that the husband will predecease the wife make use of this device by the husband much more likely.

198. Id.
199. Cal. Prob. Code Ann. §202 (West 1956).
200. Cal. Prob. Code Ann. §202 (West 1956); N.M. Stat. Ann. §29-1-9 (Supp. 1971).
47. See Wren, The Widow's Election in Community Property States, 7 Ariz. L. Rev. 1 (1965).
48. Trusts and Estates, Dec. 1972, p. 944.
1. See generally 5 Page on Wills §47.7 (1962).
2. Id. §47.43 n. 6.
49. Homestead rights protect the equity in a family house from attachment by creditors, up to a fixed limit. Exemption rights provide the surviving spouse with the same protections for household furnishings and other family personalty. The family allowance provides the survivor with a percentage of the estate for living expenses, before the appropriate share passes through probate.
50. Younger, supra, at 241.

d. Inter Vivos Trusts

Stated simply, the way in which such a trust may be used discriminatorily is for the husband to put substantial assets into a trust, and make someone other than the wife its beneficiary. A trust bypasses probate and can be drafted so that the settlor retains considerable control over the trust property during his lifetime. When he dies, the trust assets are not included in arriving at the widow's share.

Apparently, discriminatory uses of the trust device have been sufficiently frequent so that there is a body of case law and even some legislation which attempt to provide for situations in which an inter vivos trust to a third party beneficiary can be reached and included in computing the value of the widow's forced share, but none of the tests are based on clearly definable standards of application, and there is little assurance of consistency.[51]

> Probably the most equitable solution yet to inter vivos attempts to defeat a widow's statutory elective share are the New York, Ohio, and Pennsylvania statutes which explicitly extend the statutory share of a surviving spouse to certain non-testamentary transfers. For example, the New York statute sets forth these inter vivos dispositions to be treated as testamentary provisions for the purpose of election by the surviving spouse: 1) gifts causa mortis; 2) "Totten" trusts; 3) disposition of property held by the decedent with another as joint tenants with right of survivorship or as tenants by the entirety; and 4) revocable trusts.[52]

51. "One such test was stated in the leading case of Newman v. Dore [275 N.Y. 371, 9 N.E.2d 966, 112 A.L.R. 643], where the court held that ... whether ... [the] trust unlawfully invaded the contingent expectant interest of the wife and could be reached by the widow's forced share ... [depended upon] whether the transfer was 'real' or 'illusory,' based on the degree of control retained by the settlor. If the transfer were illusory, it could be reached under the forced share statutes. But since the court also said that motive and intent were unsatisfactory tests of validity, and failed to set forth any helpful guidelines as to how to determine what was 'real' and what 'illusory,' this test is too vague to be of use in many cases other than those in which there is obvious, outright fraud. The power to revoke the trust, in whole or in part, standing alone, has not been held to render a trust illusory; the power of beneficial enjoyment retained by the settlor does not, of itself, render a trust illusory; nor does the power to control the trustee, by itself, make a trust illusory.

"Other courts have held that an inter vivos transfer will be set aside if it was made for the purpose of defeating the claim of the surviving spouse. But intention is very difficult to prove once the testator is dead. [Ritchie, Alford, and Effland, Cases and Materials on Decedents' Estates and Trusts 412 (4th ed. 1971).]

"Still other states have held that no single test should be used; the court should examine all aspects of the transaction, including the size of the estate; other provisions for the surviving spouse; whether or not she has independent means; the time interval between the transfer and the death of the transferor; the completeness of the transfer; the extent of control retained by the transferor; motive; possible fraud, etc. [Whittington v. Whittington, 205 Md. 1, 106 A.2d 72, 49 A.L.R.2d 521] This rule also has no clearly definable standards of application. The Restatement states that 'Where, however, an outright gift would not operate to deprive the wife of her distributive share, a trust created under the same circumstances would be equally ineffective.' [Restatement (Second) of Trusts, Section 57, comment c] . . .

"In some common-law states 'Totten' trusts (revocable savings bank trusts where the depositor holds the money as trustee for another) can be reached by the creditors of an insolvent decedent but may be immune from the elective share of a surviving spouse. [H. Tweed and W. Parsons, Lifetime and Testamentary Estate Planning 43 (7th ed. 1969)] . . .

"Where the widow herself is the beneficiary of the inter vivos trust, she can assert her forced share against the will and still retain the trust benefits, as she can where she is the beneficiary of her husband's life insurance policy or holds property with her husband jointly with the right of survivorship. But in a prominent casebook on decedent's estates and trusts, the authors point out that 'the draftsman can provide against this possible windfall to the wife by a provision reducing her benefits under the trust if she elects to take against the will.' [Ritchie, Alford, and Effland, supra, at 639.]

"Scott on Trusts states that 'Although a surviving spouse is not entitled to an elective share of an irrevocable inter vivos trust, some courts have held, as to revocable trusts, it is against statutory policy to allow the decedent to have the practical advantages of entire ownership as long as he lives and yet to deprive the surviving spouse of a distributive share.' [A. Scott, The Law of Trusts, Vol. I, Section 57.5, p. 512 (3d ed. 1967)] . . ." Plover, supra, at 8-11.

52. Plover, supra, at 11.

e. Testamentary Trusts for the Benefit of the Wife

While the tax laws provide a strong incentive for leaving property in trust,[53] the prime basis for such disposition, as expressed in treatises on estate planning, is the assumption that a trustee would automatically be more capable of managing the funds and making them productive than the wife. An article from Trusts and Estates is typical:[54]

> ... It has been my experience that a woman unaccustomed to the use and management of money will shortly adjust her life with inescapable tragic consequences based on certain illusions which she will certainly harbor. In due course she will unconsciously make an election between absurd niggardliness or ridiculous extravagances. She will be her own worst enemy as she functions under one or the other equally untenable illusions of poverty or wealth. . . .
>
> ... [W]e can create an atmosphere for our beloved widow to live with them [the devils of Senility, Sentiment and Sickness] with a measure of harmony and affection and without sacrificing Security and Independence. We accomplish this through the use of a proper trust, preferably with an institutional trustee, designed and drawn with her happiness, comfort, and peace of mind foremost in our thoughts.

A twist on the testamentary trust device in community property states is the widow's election trust. Although the widow of a decedent in a community property state is entitled to one half of the community assets outright, she may be put to an election of either collecting her half or enjoying the benefits of the entire estate in trust.[55] If she elects the trust arrangement, then at her death the property continues in trust for others or is distributed as directed in the husband's original will. The point is that she does not have control over the property at any point from her husband's death to her own. A widow's election trust must be established explicitly in the husband's will and the wife must agree to it.

NOTES

1. The Report of the Task Force on Family Law and Policy to the Citizen's Advisory Council on the Status of Women[56] has recommended that appropriate legislation should protect either spouse against the improper alienation of property by the other. Legal

---

53. . . . [T]he incentive, simply stated, is this: a device called the marital deduction was enacted to allow a testator to leave approximately half of his property to his wife free of estate taxation. This marital deduction was originally intended to put the common-law states on a par with the community property states, where the wife's half of community property was actually owned by her and was not considered to 'pass' to her on her husband's death, and, therefore, was not included in the husband's taxable estate. But even though this half of the marital property was not included in his taxable estate at his death, because of the marital deduction provision, this same half was included in the wife's taxable estate when she died, since it was then property owned by her and transferred by her upon her death. In order to get around having this 'second half' of the marital property taxed in the wife's estate at her death, the husband could put half of the marital property into trust for his wife at his death. She would be paid the income of the trust for her life and, on her death, the principal would be paid to the children, or others. In this way the wife did not 'own' the property placed in trust and it was not included in her taxable estate on her death. The 'second' tax was avoided (or, at least, deferred until the death of the persons receiving the trust principal) by simply putting the property in trust." Plover, supra, at 14.

54. Holberg, Trusted Wife — Trusteed Widow, Trusts and Estates 1100-1104, December 1968.

55. In California, Washington, Arizona and Texas, all community property states, it is true generally that the husband can dispose in his will of all the community property and leave the wife something else instead. If his expressed intention is to cause an election, she may choose the gift in the will or her half of the community property. See Wren, The Widow's Election in Community Property States, 7 Ariz. L. Rev. 1 (1965).

56. Parts IB and ID, pp. 3-6 (1968).

control of alienation could be limited to (1) requiring consent of the other spouse or of the court to sale by the owner-spouse of the home, and (2) requiring consent to excessive gifts made from the kind of property which would be combined and divided equally under the following formula: At the death of a spouse: (a) deduct separate property, (b) deduct from each spouse's property his or her debts, and (c) add the remainder together and divide it equally. After this division, the inheritance laws would apply, but only to the deceased's half. Would this suggestion lessen the discriminatory potential of present laws?

2. It may be that "family lawyers," that is, those who represent both the husband and wife and advise them on the disposition of their property, should be more alert to the possibility that the loss of control over property is against the wife's interest. Of course, if there is even a possibility of a conflict of interest, the lawyer should not represent both people.

C. THE SUPPORT-SERVICES RECIPROCITY

At the core of the marriage status is an economic exchange: the man's support for the woman's services. To facilitate the exchange, the law has established and continues to support sex-differentiated roles of breadwinner and housewife-nursemaid.

The cases which follow have been selected because they dramatically illustrate both the major principles of support law and common judicial attitudes in this area. The factual situations involved are often unusual, however, and should not be taken as representative samples of domestic relations litigation.

1. Support and Services During an Ongoing Marriage

McGUIRE v. McGUIRE
157 Neb. 226, 59 N.W.2d 336 (1953)

MESSMORE, J.

The plaintiff, Lydia McGuire, brought this action in equity in the district court for Wayne County against Charles W. McGuire, her husband, as defendant, to recover suitable maintenance and support money, and for costs and attorney's fees. Trial was had to the court and a decree was rendered in favor of the plaintiff.

The district court decreed that the plaintiff was legally entitled to use the credit of the defendant and obligate him to pay for certain items in the nature of improvements and repairs, furniture, and appliances for the household in the amount of several thousand dollars; required the defendant to purchase a new automobile with an effective heater within 30 days; ordered him to pay travel expenses of the plaintiff for a visit to each of her daughters at least once a year; that the plaintiff be entitled in the future to pledge the credit of the defendant for what may constitute necessaries of life; awarded a personal allowance to the plaintiff in the sum of $50 a month; awarded $800 for services for the plaintiff's attorney; and as an alternative to part of the award so made, defendant was permitted, in agreement with plaintiff, to purchase a modern home elsewhere. . . .

The record shows that the plaintiff and defendant were married in Wayne, Nebraska, on August 11, 1919. At the time of the marriage the defendant was a bachelor 46 or 47 years of age and had a reputation for more than ordinary frugality, of which the plaintiff was aware. She had visited in his home and had known him for about 3 years prior to the marriage. After the marriage the couple went to live on a farm of 160 acres located in Leslie precinct, Wayne County, owned by the defendant and upon which he had lived and farmed since 1905. The parties have lived on this place ever since. The plaintiff had been previously married. Her first husband died in October 1914, leaving surviving him the plaintiff and two daughters. He died intestate, leaving 80 acres of land in Dixon County. The plaintiff and each of the daughters inherited a one-third interest therein. At the time of the marriage of the plaintiff and defendant the plaintiff's daughters were 9 and 11 years of age. By working and receiving financial assistance from the parties to this action, the daughters received a high school education in Pender. One daughter attended Wayne State Teachers College for 2 years and the other daughter attended a business college in Sioux City, Iowa, for 1 year. Both these daughters are married and have families of their own.

On April 12, 1939, the plaintiff transferred her interest in the 80 acre farm to her two daughters. The defendant signed the deed.

At the time of trial plaintiff was 66 years of age and the defendant nearly 80 years of age. No children were born to these parties. The defendant had no dependents except the plaintiff.

The plaintiff testified that she was a dutiful and obedient wife, worked and saved, and cohabited with the defendant until the last 2 or 3 years. She worked in the fields, did outside chores, cooked, and attended to household duties such as cleaning the house and doing the washing. For a number of years she raised as high as 300 chickens, sold poultry and eggs, and used the money to buy clothing, things she wanted, and groceries. She further testified that the defendant was the boss of the house and his word was law; that he would not tolerate any charge accounts and would not inform her as to his finances or business; and that he was a poor companion. The defendant did not complain of her work but left the impression to her that she had not done enough. On several occasions the plaintiff asked the defendant for money. He would give her very small amounts, and for the last 3 or 4 years he had not given her money nor provided her with clothing, except a coat about 4 years previous. The defendant had purchased the groceries the last 3 or 4 years, and permitted her to buy groceries, but he paid for them by check. There was apparently no complaint about the groceries the defendant furnished. The defendant had not taken her to a motion picture show during the past 12 years. They did not belong to any organizations or charitable institutions, nor did he give her money to make contributions to any charitable institutions. The defendant belongs to the Pleasant Valley Church which occupies about 2 acres of his farm land. At the time of trial there was no minister for this church so there were no services. For the past 4 years or more, the defendant had not given the plaintiff money to purchase furniture or other household necessities. Three years ago he did purchase an electric, wood-and-cob combination stove which was installed in the kitchen, also linoleum floor covering for the kitchen. The plaintiff further testified that the house is not equipped with a bathroom, bathing facilities, or inside toilet. The kitchen is not modern. She does not have a kitchen sink. Hard and soft water is obtained from a well and cistern. She has a mechanical Servel refrigerator, and the house is equipped with electricity. There is a pipeless furnace which she testified had not been in good working order for 5 or 6 years, and she testified she was tired of scooping coal and ashes. She had requested a new furnace but the defendant believed the one they had to be satisfactory. She related that the furniture was old and she would like to replenish it, at least to be comparable with some of her neighbors; that her silverware and dishes were old and were primarily gifts, outside of what she purchased; that one of her daughters was good about furnishing her clothing, at least a dress a year, or sometimes two; that the defendant owns a 1929 Ford coupé equipped with a heater which is not efficient, and on the average of every 2 weeks he drives the plaintiff to Wayne to visit her mother; and that he also owns a 1927 Chevrolet pickup which is used for different purposes on the farm. The plaintiff was privileged to use all of the rent money she wanted to from the 80-acre farm, and when she goes to see her daughters, which is not frequent, she uses part of the rent money for that purpose, the defendant providing no funds for such use. The defendant ordinarily raised hogs on his farm, but the last 4 or 5 years has leased his farm land to tenants, and he generally keeps up the fences and the buildings. At the present time the plaintiff is not able to raise chickens and sell eggs. She has about 25 chickens. The plaintiff has had three abdominal operations for which the defendant has paid. She selected her own doctor, and there were no restrictions placed in that respect. When she has requested various things for the home or personal effects, defendant has informed her on many occasions that he did not have the money to pay for the same. She would like to have a new car. She visited one daughter in Spokane, Washington, in March 1951 for 3 or 4 weeks, and visited the other daughter living in Fort Worth, Texas, on three occasions for 2 to 4 weeks at a time. She had visited one of her daughters when she was living in Sioux City some weekends. The plaintiff further testified that she had very little funds, possibly $1500 in the bank which was chicken money and money which her father furnished her, he having departed this life a few years ago; and that use of the telephone was restricted, indicating that defendant did not desire that she make long distance calls, otherwise she had free access to the telephone.

It appears that the defendant owned 398 acres of land with 2 acres deeded to a church, the land being of the value of $83,960; that he has bank deposits in the sum of $12,786.81 and government bonds in the amount of $104,500; and that his income, including interest on the bonds and rental for his real estate, is $8000 or $9000 a year. There are apparently some Series E United States Savings Bonds listed and registered in the names of Charles W. McGuire or Lydia M. McGuire purchased in 1943, 1944, and 1945, in the amount of $2500. Other bonds seem to be in the name of Charles W. McGuire, without a beneficiary or co-owner designated. The plaintiff has a bank account of $5960.22. This account includes deposits of some $200 and $100 which the court required the defendant to pay his wife as temporary allowance during the pendency of these proceedings. One hundred dollars was withdrawn on the date of each deposit.

The facts are not in dispute. . . .

[The court then reviewed a series of cases from Nebraska and other jurisdictions which held that where the spouses are living separate and apart, or where the husband is guilty of such abusive conduct as to entitle the wife to move out, or where the husband has deserted the wife, she may maintain an action for separate maintenance.]

It becomes apparent that there are no cases cited by the plaintiff and relied upon by her from this jurisdiction or other jurisdictions that will sustain the action such as she has instituted in the instant case.

With reference to the proposition that the parties are living under the same roof, [the cases have held] that while a wife had no right to the interference of the court for her maintenance until her abandonment or separation, there might be an abandonment or separation, within the sound construction of the statute, while the parties continued to live under the same roof, as where the husband utterly refused to have intercourse with his wife, or to make any provision for her maintenance, and thus he might seclude himself in a portion of his house, take his meals alone or board elsewhere than in his house, and so as effectively separate himself from his wife and refuse to provide for her as in case of actual abandonment, although in whatever form it might exist there must be an abandonment. . . .

In the instant case the marital relation has continued for more than 33 years, and the wife has been supported in the same manner during this time without complaint on her part. The parties have not been separated or living apart from each other at any time. In the light of the cited cases it is clear, especially so in this jurisdiction, that to maintain an action such as the one at bar, the parties must be separated or living apart from each other.

The living standards of a family are a matter of concern to the household, and not for the courts to determine, even though the husband's attitude toward his wife, according to his wealth and circumstances, leaves little to be said in his behalf. As long as the home is maintained and the parties are living as husband and wife it may be said that the husband is legally supporting his wife and the purpose of the marriage relation is being carried out. Public policy requires such a holding. It appears that the plaintiff is not devoid of money in her own right. She has a fair-sized bank account and is entitled to use the rent from the 80 acres of land left by her first husband, if she so chooses. . . .

Reversed and remanded with directions to dismiss.

YEAGER, J., dissenting. . . . There is and can be no doubt that, independent of statutes relating to divorce, alimony, and separate maintenance, if this plaintiff were living apart from the defendant she could in equity and on the facts as outlined in the record be awarded appropriate relief. . . .

If relief is to be denied to plaintiff under this principle it must be denied because of the fact that she is not living separate and apart from the defendant and is not seeking separation.

In the light of what the decisions declare to be the basis of the right to maintain an action for support, is there any less reason for extending the right to a wife who is denied the right to maintenance in a home occupied with her husband than to one who has chosen to occupy a separate abode?

If the right is to be extended only to one who is separated from the husband equity and effective justice would be denied where a wealthy husband refused proper support and maintenance to a wife physically or mentally incapable of putting herself in a position where the rule could become available to her.

It is true that in all cases examined which uphold the right of a wife to maintain an action in equity for maintenance the parties were living apart, but no case has been cited or found which says that separation is a condition precedent to the right to maintain an action in equity for maintenance. Likewise none has been cited or found which says that it is not.

In primary essence the rule contemplates the enforcement of an obligation within and not without the full marriage relationship. . . .

I think however that the court was without proper power to make any of the awards contained in the decree for the support and maintenance of the plaintiff except the one of $50 a month.

From the cases cited herein it is clear that a husband has the obligation to furnish to his wife the necessaries of life. These decisions make clear that for failure to furnish them the wife may seek allowances for her support and maintenance. However neither these decisions nor any others cited or found support the view contended for by plaintiff that the court may go beyond this and impose obligations other than that of payment of money for the proper support and maintenance of the wife.

There is no doubt that plaintiff had the right to charge her husband with her necessaries of life and that recovery could be had therefor. No award of a court of equity was necessary to establish this right. Nothing was accomplished by the declaration of that right. The provision relating thereto therefore had no proper place in the decree. . . .

As pointed out the district court made an allowance of $50 a month. In the light of generally well-known present day economy the conclusion is inevitable that this award is insufficient for the maintenance of the plaintiff. The record before us however does not supply adequate information upon which this court could make a finding as to what would be sufficient.

. . . [A]ccordingly this phase of the case should be remanded to the district court for the taking of evidence in order that finding may be made as to what would be adequate for plaintiff's suitable maintenance. . . .

NOTES

1. This case illustrates the most important principle of support during an ongoing marriage. Unless the parties separate, the wife's right is to what her husband chooses to give her, not what he can afford or what a court thinks reasonable under the circumstances. As Blanche Crozier put it,[57]

> Depending on his personality and hers, the chances — which have nothing to do with legal rights — may be either that she will with difficulty get an inadequate subsistence or that she will live in idleness and luxury. This is precisely the situation in which property finds itself; it may be overworked and underfed, or it may be petted and fed with cream, and that is a matter for the owner to decide.

If this case seems unfair to you, would you have the same reaction to a case brought by a poor farmer without children whose wife had inherited $150,000 twenty years ago which she refused to spend? In most states, he would have no legal right to a share of her separate estate during marriage unless he was on the verge of going on welfare, although she might be liable for debts he incurred for items used in their household, if he was able to persuade any merchants to extend credit to him in the first place. Are there any circumstances in which a 50-50 division of property, however and whenever acquired, enforceable during an ongoing marriage, would seem unfair to you? Should the party who earns the money or inherits it have a superior claim to it, or the right to a larger share?

There are contract theory overtones in the court's statements that Lydia McGuire put up with the present state of affairs for 33 years, and that she knew her husband was frugal before she married him. She got what she bargained for, which had apparently been enough until now. Note also the ages of the parties; in the normal course of events, Lydia would probably inherit all her husband's money fairly soon. The court may have seen no reason to intervene in a situation which might resolve itself shortly.

2. The dissenting judge states that Lydia McGuire could "in equity and on the facts outlined in the record" be awarded a judgment against her husband if she were living in a separate abode. In Nebraska, separate maintenance is awarded without explicit authority, on the basis of inherent equitable jurisdiction, and as a result is not limited as it is in many states to cases in which the wife has grounds for divorce or legal separation.[58] However, even in Nebraska, as a general rule, the husband must be shown to be in some way at fault before a support order will be made.[59] Unless the wife can prove some wrongdoing on her husband's part, she will not be able to get a support order in most states whether she leaves or she stays.[60]

The rationale for this position was recently explained by a court in the District of Columbia. In the case of Lee v. Lee, 267 A.2d 824 (D.C. 1970), where the wife had left the marital domicile without just cause or excuse, the court held that her "desertion" was a bar to her claim for separate maintenance and support. In the court's view, "to hold otherwise would encourage families to separate rather than remain together to resolve their differences." 267 A.2d at 826. Do you think many women in Lydia McGuire's situation would leave their husbands in order to get a court order for support, if that

---

57. Crozier, Marital Support, 15 Boston U.L. Rev. 28, 33 (1935).
58. See Clark, Law of Domestic Relations 196-197 (1968), and Sinn v. Sinn, 138 Neb. 621, 294 N.W. 381 (1940) cited id., at 196, n. 49.
59. Robinson v. Robinson, 164 Neb. 413, 82 N.W. 2d 550 (1957), cited in Clark, id. at 197, n. 53. A few states have statutes authorizing separate maintenance when the parties live apart by mutual consent, however. Clark, id. at 197, n.59.
60. But see Miller v. Miller, 320 Mich. 43, 30, N.W.2d 509 (1948), in which the Michigan Supreme Court upheld an award of separate maintenance and a decree of equal separation on the grounds of extreme cruelty to a wife whose husband was still living with her.

were a possibility? Consider this question again after reading Parts V and VI, infra.

3. Judge Yeager argues that the lower court's decree that Ms. McGuire was legally entitled to use her husband's credit for certain items was superfluous, since she already "had the right to charge her husband with her necessaries of life."[61] In legal theory, he is correct. In practice, the doctrine is not much help to women in Lydia McGuire's situation. Presumably it was because of her inability to get credit that she sought the court order in the first place.

Clark describes the operation of the doctrine of necessaries as follows:[62]

> At common law, the customary method for enforcing the husband's duty to support his family was for the wife or child to buy what they needed and charge it to the husband. According to what became the doctrine of necessaries, the husband was thereby responsible directly to the merchant who supplied goods to the wife or child.

In defining necessaries, the courts apply the same standards that they profess to employ in making maintenance awards after the parties are separated or divorced. A good statement of the standard, taken from a maintenance case, follows:[63]

> Where the parties are man and wife, it is obvious that they are normally expected to live together. That does not mean that she is to sleep in the garage, eat with the cook and wear castoffs. It commonly contemplates not only sharing the same residence, but eating at the same table, enjoying the ministrations of the same servants — if they have servants — and wearing such apparel as befits her husband's station.

The husband is liable whether or not he has given his consent.[64] However, he is not liable if the items are not necessaries,[65] if he has already supplied her with the items themselves or the means to purchase them, or if the parties are living apart through no fault of the husband.

The merchant supplies necessaries at his financial peril. He bears the burden of proof as to all the factors controlling liability, even though the information which would enable him to evaluate the risk involved is not available to him. According to Clark,[66]

> The doctrine of necessaries may once have been an effective way of supporting wives and children (though one doubts it). Today, however, it is hedged about with so many limitations that few merchants would wish to rely on it. More importantly, it is of least value to those most in need of support, those wives and children too poor to be able to get credit. For these reasons the doctrine is of little practical value in the solution of the non-support problem.

61. R.R.S. (Neb.) §42-201 (Clark, supra, at 186-187, n. 59.). Cf. Dreamer v. Oberlander, 122 Neb. 335, 240 N.W. 435 (1932), noted in Brown, 18 Va. L. Rev. 680 (1932), holding that wife has no personal liability, and that only property she held at the time the contract was made can be reached.
62. Clark, supra, at 189.
63. Dupont v. Dupont, 34 Del. Ch. 267, 274, 103 A.2d 234, 238 (1954).
64. The wife's ability to pledge her husband's credit for necessaries has sometimes been referred to as the "agency of necessity," but this involves a confusion between agency theory and the doctrine of necessaries per se. The marital relation does not automatically make the wife an agent of the husband, although it may make proof of agency in accordance with the ordinary principles of agency law easier. If the wife is acting under the apparent or explicit authority as the agent of the husband, his liability for her purchases is not limited to necessaries, and the husband's defenses against liability under the doctrine of necessaries, which are discussed below, do not apply. Conversely, if the items purchased are necessaries, the husband is liable whether or not he has given his consent. See Clark, supra, §6.3.
65. Items which have been held to be necessaries in particular cases include "not only food, clothing, and shelter; . . . medical . . . dental, . . . and legal services, . . . [and] furniture and household goods; [but even a] wife's funeral expenses and, . . . [in one case,] a mink coat." Clark, supra, at 190. See also Brown, The Duty of the Husband to Support the Wife, 18 Va. L. Rev. 823, 830-835 (1932).
66. Clark, supra, at 192.

The inadequacy of the doctrine of necessaries from a creditor's point of view has led almost half the states to adopt family expense statutes which alter the common law support obligations between husband and wife in relation to third parties. Without such statutes, in the common law states, the wife's separate property, including her earnings, was not available to creditors for satisfaction of debts her husband incurred. Likewise, the husband was not liable either for debts his wife incurred on her own credit, or for debts she incurred in his name but without his consent unless the items she purchased were shown to be necessaries. Family expense statutes[67]

> generally provide that the expenses of the family and of the education of children are chargeable against the property of both husband and wife and (under some statutes) that they may be held jointly or severally liable for such expenses.

These statutes thus improve the position of family creditors to the extent that they are enabled to reach a secondary source of repayment. However, such statutes have had little impact on the ability of married women to get credit without their husbands' consent either in their own or their husbands' names. First, in many states creditors still have to prove that the items were necessaries, that the husband neglected to provide necessaries for the family, or that the items were actually used by the family. Second, such statutes don't solve the basic problems (a) that the creditors are not willing to advance credit on the basis of a working wife's income alone because they expect her both to get pregnant and to stop working and (b) that many women have neither independent income nor enforceable legal rights to a share of their husband's incomes.

4. In forming your opinion about the result in *McGuire,* remember that the wife has in theory as much control over whether or not she will perform household services for her husband as her husband has over how much of his money he will devote to her support during cohabitation, because she can exchange her services either for her husband's support or in the labor market for her own salary. This increase in her bargaining power is an indirect consequence of the provisions in the Married Women's Property Acts giving women the right to receive wages for their work outside the home and the right to own, manage, and control property. The wife's power to grant or withhold her services from her husband and their children, and to work for her own money instead, is in practice limited by many factors. They include discrimination against her in the labor market, cultural stereotypes and norms about appropriate sex roles, the impact of joint taxation of married couples, and the lack of adequate day care facilities. However, if the wife nonetheless refuses to do housework, the courts will not intervene during an ongoing marriage, just as they would not intervene between the McGuires.

5. What problems would there be if women could get court orders like the one Lydia McGuire sought? Remember that the wife's duty to perform domestic services is unenforceable because under contract law, specific performance is not available for personal service contracts, and most women have too little money to make suing for damages attractive. Therefore, even if both parties could go to court, only the wife would have an effective legal remedy. This problem could be avoided by allowing the husband to withhold support until his wife fulfilled her obligations, and granting enforcement of

---

67. Clark, supra, at 186. Under most of the statutes, the wife's liability to the creditor does not absolve the husband of the ultimate responsibility to support her and their children; if an outsider recovers the cost of goods and services from the wife, she is entitled to reimbursement from the husband, in the absence of proof that she intended to make a gift or a nonreimbursable contribution to household expenses. See generally Clark, supra, §6.2; 3 Vernier, American Family Law §160 (1935); Annot., Liability of Married Woman for Necessaries, 15 A.L.R. 833, 856 (1921). Nebraska's family expense statute, R.R.S. 1943 §42-201 (1968), provides that the wife's separate property and 10 percent of her wages are liable for necessaries furnished the family only after execution against her husband's property and wages has been returned unsatisfied.

support to the wife if she had. But what standard could the court use to decide whether or not she had done her duty? See Glover v. Glover, infra, Part VI-D, and Lazzarevich v. Lazzarevich, infra, Section 2-c, for two different models of what can happen when the courts have occasion to evaluate a wife's housekeeping.

Note also that litigation like that involved in *McGuire* would not be an effective remedy for the majority of people, who, for financial and other reasons, have limited access to lawyers and courts.

HARDY v. HARDY
235 F. Supp. 208 (D.D.C. 1964)

KEECH, D. J.

This is an action by plaintiff husband against his defendant wife and her attorney, in four counts (Counts 1 and 2 being against both defendants, and Counts 3 and 4 being against defendant wife only).

Plaintiff husband and defendant wife have been married since 1939. From its inception the marriage has been subject to frequent controversies, including the filing of this suit in 1961.

From 1948 to 1958, plaintiff gave his wife approximately $125 per week to cover household expenses. Mrs. Hardy took any excess in these funds and invested it in securities in her own name. In January of 1961, plaintiff discovered such use of this excess. Subsequently, plaintiff and defendant wife discontinued residing together, and sold their house in Kenwood, Maryland, which they held as tenants by the entireties. (An action for divorce instituted by plaintiff prior to this action is pending in the Circuit Court of Montgomery County, Maryland.) This action seeks to recover the proceeds of the sale of the Kenwood home and to impress a trust on securities held by defendant wife which were purchased with a portion of the aforesaid household funds. . . .

As to Count 3: From the year 1948 until 1958, plaintiff turned over to his wife approximately and irregularly $125 per week. With these funds, the wife paid the normal household running expenses, such as food, gas, electricity, cleaning, window washing, laundry, and newspapers, as well as her personal needs. She also paid a maid $35 per week, and a yard man $10 per week. Any savings over and above these expenditures, the exact figure not known, were utilized by the defendant wife for a period of years for the purchase of securities to be held in her sole account. During this period, the maid was discharged and the wife performed at least some if not all of the maid's work.

Mrs. Hardy testified that at the time the maid was dismissed there was an agreement that she (Mrs. Hardy) should do all the cleaning and cooking herself, and retain the money saved by her efforts. However, she does not claim that it was a contract. Nor could it be since a wife may not contract for the performance of her marital duties. Rather, she maintains that it was a gift; that there was an understanding that she should keep what she saved so long as she continued the necessary operations of the house.

The court finds that there was no gift of the household savings to Mrs. Hardy. To constitute a valid gift, the courts have held, three essential elements must be shown: (1) delivery, (2) intent to make a gift, and (3) absolute disposition of the subject matter of the gift. There is here no dispute as to delivery. The plaintiff denies having made a gift to the defendant wife. The latter's testimony in this regard was most equivocal. The plaintiff asserts that, until he discovered, in 1961, his wife's stock portfolio, he had no knowledge that there were any such savings. There was no showing of intent to make a gift. The court recognizes that such household allowances generally comprehend expenditures by the wife for personal needs such as clothes, entertainment and transportation. Such expenses are within the obligation of the husband to support and maintain his wife. Acquiescence in these expenditures does not indicate an acquiescence in the use of such funds for the creation of a portfolio of securities for the wife's sole account. To hold otherwise would be to invite disruptive influences in the home. As for the third element, there was likewise no showing of an absolute disposition of any part of the money advanced by the plaintiff to the defendant.

The court finds that Mrs. Hardy did in fact appropriate certain household funds, and commingle them with her own funds which were invested in stocks and bonds. It is therefore necessary to endeavor to determine the amount so appropriated. . . . The only practical method available, under the evidence, by which to determine the amount of household funds appropriated by defendant wife is to deduct, from the total value of Mrs. Hardy's portfolio as of October 30, 1964, contributions made by her from her personal savings and a legacy from her mother. . . . The record shows that as of 1964 the securities held by defendant wife in her own account aggregated $20,000 to $25,000. There is no proof that the defendant's account was ever greater than its present value. The record further shows that the defendant wife had $7,000 of her own money coming from Victory Bonds and the net figure of $3,000 coming to her through the estate of her mother, which she invested in her security account. The court concludes that, from the securities account of defendant wife with Ferris & Company on the date of this opinion, . . . there should be deducted the $10,000 which the court finds to be her personal contribution to the portfolio. This makes no allowance for dividends which may have been realized on her contribution to the portfolio. Where one mixes trust funds with his own the whole is to be treated as trust property, except so far as he may be able to distinguish what is his. Bird v. Stein, 258 F.2d 168, 177 (5th Cir., 1958). Defendant has failed to make a showing as to what were the earnings on her part of the securities acquired.

The court therefore finds for the plaintiff as to Count 3. The account of the defendant wife with Ferris & Company will be impressed with a trust in favor of the plaintiff, as of October 30, 1964. . . .

NOTES

1. This case apparently stands for the principle that a wife who deceives her husband in financial matters should not be allowed to keep the proceeds of her wrongdoing. It seems reasonable to discourage husbands and wives from stealing from each other. But what if Ms. Hardy had secretly saved the money over the years and then bought a mink coat just before the parties separated? Or suppose that she had charged the coat to his account at a local store without his knowledge or consent, and the store had sued Mr. Hardy and recovered the purchase price on the theory that it was a "necessary." What result in Mr. Hardy's suit for recovery of the coat? Consider separately the effect on the court's ruling of the nature of the item (i.e., whether it is a consumer good or a financial asset) and the process by which it was acquired. An interesting question is whether one could successfully establish the principle that even for a wife in an ongoing marriage, financial assets of some kind are a "necessary" if her standard of living "according to the station of the parties" is to be protected in the event of widowhood or divorce.

2. In evaluating transactions between husband and wife, the courts usually employe a rebuttable presumption that money, property, or services transferred from one spouse to the other are gifts.[68] This presumption is especially strong with regard to

---

[68]. The major exception to this rule is that when "the wife pays for land and title is taken in the husband's name, a gift is not presumed and a resulting trust in the wife's favor is created." Clark, supra, at 225. Some courts have also refused to apply the presumption of gratuity to advances of cash from the wife to the husband unless the advances were for family expenses. Van Inwegen v. Van Inwegen, 4 N.J. 46, 71 A.2d 340 (1950). See generally Clark, supra, at 224-225 and McDowell, Contracts in the Family, 45 Boston U. L. Rev. 43, 58 (1965).

transfers of money or property from husband to wife and with regard to the performance of services by the wife for her husband. The court's failure to apply this presumption in the *Hardy* case suggests how strongly the court reacted to Ms. Hardy's course of action.

3. If Ms. Hardy had invested money without her husband's knowledge or consent in securities in both their names, would the court have reacted differently? If so, then should the court have split the securities between Mr. and Ms. Hardy rather than awarding them to him? In a community property state that would have been the result, because money and property acquired by either party other than by gift, devise, or inheritance during the marriage is first divided equally between the spouses, after which maintenance may be awarded to the wife (in some states, to either spouse) or the children if necessary. In a common law state, the property, rather than being divided equally, is first allocated to whichever party earned or inherited it, and then the issue of alimony and property transfers in lieu of alimony is considered. Note that the divorce action between the Hardys was a separate matter, so it is theoretically possible that some of the securities were later awarded to her as lump sum alimony.

4. By treating support payments like an expense account rather than like wages, the court sharply limits a married woman's ability to acquire financial security. The majority of married women do not have jobs outside the home, do not have inherited wealth, and do not have much money saved from before marriage. Most of those who do hold outside jobs are in low-paying occupations. Therefore, the major sources of wealth for most married women are their husbands. Yet even if a woman persuades her husband to turn over half his paycheck each month, the courts will not treat it as wages for the housework she has done. In order to provide for her own future, she must not only get her husband to give her extra money, but be able to prove in court that it was neither wages, which she may not be paid, nor support money, which she would have to return, but a gift.

YOUNGBERG v. HOLSTRUM
252 Iowa 815, 108 N.W.2d 498 (1961)

GARFIELD, C.J.

This is a suit in equity by Dale M. Youngberg, individually and as trustee for certain defendants who joined with him, for specific performance of an alleged oral agreement between William R. Holstrom, deceased, and his predeceased wife, Nettie C., to make mutual wills. . . .

[October 16, 1942, William and Nettie executed reciprocal wills, each providing that "all of my property . . . I may own at the time of my death" be bequeathed to the other "absolutely and forever." In addition, William's will provided that if his wife predeceased him or left any of his property undisposed of at her death, his property would go for the benefit of their nieces and nephews, the children of Nettie's brother.

The plaintiff in the case is the representative of these nieces and nephews.]

Will and Nettie were married May 19, 1923. Nettie was then thirty-five, Will forty-two. Will had been married before and divorced. The two lived together, mostly on the 160-acre farm here in controversy, until Nettie died April 20, 1943, from cancer she had had about a year. They had no children. July 1, 1947, Will married Lillie with whom he lived until his death May 3, 1959. Lillie had a daughter, Mary Louise Wittmer, by a previous marriage. These two are defendants-appellees.

November 2, 1957, Will executed a later will . . . [which] gives Lillie testator's personalty, three fifths of his real estate and income from the rest of it for life. . . . After Will's death this will was probated and Lillie was appointed executrix.

Some members of the court would hold it is not shown by clear and satisfactory proof that Will and Nettie orally agreed to make irrevocable wills. . . . [W]e may assume, without so holding, proof of such an agreement is sufficient.

But it does not follow that plaintiff is entitled to specific performance of the agreement. The trial court held consideration for it was insufficient to call for such a decree. We think this conclusion was not an abuse of discretion and concur in it.

Will acquired the 160 acres in controversy February 1, 1909. In September 1920 the land was mortgaged for $17,700 to secure a note Will signed at least partly for his brother in the purchase of "Blue-sky" stock. In 1929 we held the mortgage invalid and it was released. The farm was then mortgaged for $14,000, released in 1938, then mortgaged for $12,000, released March 29, 1946, nearly three years after Nettie died. When she died Will's bank balance was $200. When Will died 16 years later the balance in a joint account in the names of Will and Lillie was $11,422. Will also acquired, evidently at least five years after Nettie died, the residence of his parents in the town of Strafford, valued at $12,500, by paying liens and taxes against it and other obligations of the parents. Will claimed the amounts paid were not far from the value of the property. Plaintiff sought to include this property in the present suit.

Except for some household furniture and a piano that Nettie had when she married Will (it was her first marriage) she never had property of her own. Nor, so far as appears, did she have any prospect of acquiring any, when the wills were made or thereafter, except from her husband if he should predecease her. Aside from the furniture, to which we will refer later, Will acquired nothing under Nettie's will.

In arguing consideration for the agreement was sufficient appellants seem to rely most on evidence that Nettie performed the usual duties of a farm wife, such as raising poultry, at times hogs, and had a big garden. It is true Nettie, as well as Will, worked hard and were happily married. Reliance is also placed on the fact Nettie inherited from her father $3346, much of which was probably used to pay a note signed by her and Will for $2500 borrowed from her brother-in-law soon after their marriage to pay for remodeling the house on the farm. Two hundred twenty-seven dollars of this inheritance was received more than 18 years before the 1942 wills were made and the remaining $3119 was received and the $2500 note was paid about 15 years before then. It is also said Nettie gave up her opportunity to receive a deed to the farm. . . .

. . . [I]t cannot be claimed any benefit to testator from the disposition made of Nettie's inheritance or from her performing the usual duties of a farm wife was in any way related to the alleged oral agreement to make the first wills. Aside from the technical consideration the mutual promises to make wills may have supplied, there is nothing but a moral obligation at best arising from past services and an advancement from Nettie to her husband. There was no legal obligation to pay for the services nor to repay the advancement. Nor is it shown Nettie expected to be paid or that testator expected to pay her.

An important precedent on the question of consideration as applied to the present case is Dullard v. Schafer, 251 Iowa 274, 278, 100 N.W.2d 422, 425, cited in Levis v. Hammond [251 Iowa 567, 576, 100 N.W.2d 638, 644]. There a father agreed in writing to leave all his property to his son for the stated consideration that the latter had "deported himself as a dutiful and loving son, and has thereby contributed to his father's acquisition and maintenance of the property." We held the consideration was inadequate to warrant a decree of specific execution of the contract and that denial of such relief was not an abuse of discretion. This from the opinion is applicable here (pages 283, 284 of 251 Iowa, page 428 of 100 N.W.2d):

"A recitation of past services, especially those where there is nothing to show that payment therefor was contemplated by the parties when rendered, are by one line of authorities, including Iowa, declared insufficient to support a subsequent executory promise. . . . It may be said generally that we favor the rule that unless it is made to satisfactorily appear that the services rendered were not intended originally to be gratuitous, no obligation arose, even though some benefit had been derived by the promisor and detriment suffered by promisee. . . ."

It is not to be inferred from the above that an agreement by testator, if there were such, to pay for Nettie's services would be valid. It is well settled that a husband's agreement to pay for services within the scope of the marital relation is without consideration and contrary to public policy. . . . Most, if not all, of Nettie's services were within the scope of the marital relation.

Our conclusion that use of Nettie's inheritance, with her consent, to repay money borrowed to remodel the dwelling on the farm, without any contract by Will to repay Nettie, is insufficient consideration for the alleged agreement in suit also finds support in [cited cases].

It is true that when Nettie died she left some household furniture which Will sold. It does not appear how much it brought. It is unlikely it was enough to pay costs of administration, expenses of Nettie's last sickness and funeral (she died following an operation for cancer for which she was hospitalized in Des Moines), and cost of a marker at her grave. Will paid these costs and expenses. He was entitled to reimbursement therefor from Nettie's estate, if she left any. . . .

The contention Nettie gave up her opportunity to receive a deed to the farm in return for the alleged agreement to make mutual wills needs little comment. There is evidence Will consulted his attorney, Mr. Lund, about making a deed to Nettie. . . .

. . . [I]t appears Mr. Lund advised Will against making a deed and the advice was accepted. Nettie had no enforceable right to a deed and of course gave up no such right, in return for the alleged agreement or otherwise. . . .

The right to make a will as a person chooses is a valuable one of which he should not be deprived by such an agreement as plaintiff seeks to enforce unless it is supported by adequate consideration and is fair and reasonable. Here, as we have tried to explain, Will received no real benefit from the claimed agreement or Nettie's will.

Incidentally, the trial court thought the equities are with the surviving spouse and her daughter. Lillie lived with Will 12 years, lacking less than two months. There is no evidence of undue influence or inequitable conduct on her part in relation to the second will, nor that Will was not in full possession of his faculties. The will we are asked to uphold leaves to plaintiff full power to designate the nieces and nephews of Will and Nettie (whose death occurred nearly 18 years ago) who are to receive the property. Under this will plaintiff could designate as beneficiaries only Nettie's nieces and nephews and exclude Will's. There is no evidence to show what the relationship was, whether cordial or otherwise, between Will and any of Nettie's nieces or nephews, nor that any of them have any claim upon his bounty.

After full consideration of all contentions urged the decree is Affirmed.

LARSON, J. (dissenting). . . .

Will purchased the 160-acre farm involved herein in 1909, married Nettie in 1923, and they lived and worked together, mostly on this farm, until her death on April 20, 1943, less than a year after the execution of the mutual wills on October 16, 1942. At the time of their marriage the farm was heavily mortgaged, but it was all paid within three years after Nettie's death and more than a year before he married Lillie.

Can it be denied, under these circumstances, that by the joint efforts of Will and Nettie over a period of 19 years the estate held by Will at the time of the execution of the mutual wills was not created or built up? To me it is unjust and unrealistic to say that Nettie had no interest in this farm which equity would recognize in an action to enforce the contractual or mutual wills. . . .

. . . Surely a court of equity will look beyond the bare title in such cases and, if it finds an adequate consideration, actual or equitable, it will decree performance of the wills not revoked during the life of the parties. . . .

. . . [B]y such will Nettie surrendered her statutory inchoate right in the property of her husband, and also gave up her right to pass her estate to someone other than those mentioned in the mutual wills. . . .

NOTES

1. This case illustrates the maxim that hard cases make bad law. Ordinarily mutual wills are in themselves sufficient consideration for each other.[69] Although the majority calls it "technical consideration," the dissenting judge rightly points out that Nettie surrendered significant rights in making the will in question. Apparently, however, disinheriting Will's second wife by enforcing his agreement with his first wife was too much for the court. Note, however, that Lillie would have gotten at least one third of all Will's real and personal property as a forced share even if his first will had been upheld.[70]

2. Although Chief Justice Garfield bent the law of estates to find for Lillie, the domestic relations law he used is fairly straightforward. As we have already noted, the wife cannot recover from her husband for domestic services she performs for him. This is so both because it is her duty to perform them, and because services in excess of her obligation (to the extent that it is measurable) are presumed to be gratuitous.[71] Therefore, her services as a farm wife were not valid consideration for the agreement, since performance of a pre-existing duty, or a gift, cannot be consideration for a contract.[72]

It is also traditional to treat advances of money by the wife to the husband as gifts, although the presumption is rebuttable, and less strong than the presumption as to the husband's gifts of money or property to the wife.[73] Thus the court's ruling that Nettie's advance of money from her separate estate to pay off a debt on the farm was a gift rather than valid consideration was not unprecedented. On the other hand, the discussion between Will and his attorney about giving Nettie a deed and the subsequent making of mutual wills might instead have been treated as evidence rebutting the presumption of gratuity, especially if the court had been disposed to uphold the agreement to make mutual wills.

3. The court's unwillingness to treat payments from husband to wife as wages for a woman's domestic services or to treat a wife's services as valid consideration for a contract is part of their hostility toward interpersonal contracts in marriage. The following cases and materials illustrate both legal principles and judicial attitudes in this area.

2. The Ability of Spouses To Contract Freely

a. Interspousal Agreements About Property in Common Law States

One of the major areas in which contractual freedom or partnership status relations have replaced patriarchal status relations is marital property law.[74] Spouses are permitted

---

69. 97 C.J.S. Wills §1367 a and b. *Contra:* In re Johnson's Estate, 233 Iowa 782, 10 N.W.2d 664 (1943).

70. Iowa Code Ann. §633.238 (1966), which gives the surviving spouse an election against the will for one third of all real estate the testator ever owned, for all personal property he held as head of a family, and for one half of all other personal property.

71. A similar set of assumptions applies to the husband's transfers of money or property to his wife, as we noted above. However, it is usually easier to rebut the presumptions of duty and gratuity with regard to services; see, e.g., Hardy v. Hardy, supra.

72. This problem would not have arisen if Iowa had recognized the contribution of wives to the acquisition of family property through a community property system. In that case, Nettie would have had a legal right to half the farm, and the passage of that half to Will upon her death would have been consideration for their agreement. In Iowa, Nettie had no legal right to a share in property her husband acquired during the marriage unless they divorced or she survived him.

73. See Clark, supra, at 224-225 and note 2 to Hardy v. Hardy, supra.

74. In fact, the enforcement of antenuptial contracts about property rights was one of the equitable reforms which preceded the married women's property acts. Johnston, Sex and Property: The Common Law

to contract relatively freely about property rights which flow from marriage by law, both in community property and common law property jurisdictions, although enforcement is still denied to contracts about other aspects of their relationship.[75] The rules in common law and community property jurisdictions are somewhat different and are therefore treated separately.

KARP, ANTENUPTIAL AGREEMENTS: A VEHICLE FOR CHANGING MARITAL ROLES
7-11, Unpublished paper, Geo. Wash. U. Law School (Fall 1971)

"Antenuptial agreements are not against public policy, but on the contrary, if freely and intelligently made, are regarded as generally conducive to marital tranquility and the avoidance of disputes as to property."[10] Consequently, they are regarded with favor by the law.[11] All courts today recognize that antenuptial agreements as to property are enforceable as long as the parties have complied with the [special] requirements concerning [their] execution. . . .[12,13]

. . . [S]uch agreements may contain a release by [either] spouse [of] rights that would normally flow from the marriage. . . . Accordingly, prospective spouses may relinquish their distributive shares in each other's estates; the husband may bar his curtsey and the wife her dower rights; and they may give up their right of election to take against the other's estate. Under the agreement, either spouse may transfer money and/or property to the other before or after the marriage takes place. . . .[14]

The idea behind the agreement is to leave each spouse free to control and enjoy [his/her] wealth as though [he/she] were not married. . . . [However, although] [t]he law of contracts is generally applicable to antenuptial agreements,[15] . . . the parties are not considered to be dealing at arm's length with one another. . . .

> A valid antenuptial agreement contemplates a *fair and reasonable provision* therein for the wife, or absent such provision, a *full and frank disclosure to the wife,* before the signing of the agreement, of the husband's worth, or absent such disclosure a general and *approximate knowledge* by her of the prospective husband's property. [Emphasis supplied.][22]

Tradition, The Law School Curriculum, and Developments Toward Equality, 47 N.Y.U.L. Rev. 1033, 1052 (1972).

75. The term antenuptial agreement is limited by definition to contracts about property rights and interests. In re Carnevale's Will, 248 App. Div. 62, 289 N.Y.S. 185, 188-189 (1936).

10. Scuss v. Schukat, 358 Ill. 27, 192 N.E. 668, 671, 95 A.L.R. 1461 (1934).

11. See, Baugher v. Barrett, 128 Ind. App. 233, 145 N.E.2d 297, (1957); Lightman v. Magid, 54 Tenn. App. 701, 394 S.W.2d 151 (1965); Clark, Law of Domestic Relations 27 (1968).

12. Klein, "A 'Check List' for the Drafting of Enforceable Antenuptial Agreements," 19 U. Miami L. Rev. 615, 616 (1965).

13. The Klein article, [id.] at 635-636, contains a check list for the draftsman of an antenuptial agreement: (1) the agreement should be in writing; (2) it should be signed in the presence of three witnesses; (3) before the agreement is committed to writing, the wife should be represented by counsel of her own choice; (4) it should be executed as far in advance of the wedding as is possible; (5) it should state that it's entered into in consideration of marriage; (6) it should contain a statement of the husband's approximate worth; (7) it should contain a recital that each party made full disclosure to the other concerning the nature and extent of their property; (8) it should clearly state the rights that each party is relinquishing in the property and estate of the other; (9) provision made should be substantial enough to satisfy the test of adequacy; (10) a no alimony provision should be avoided; (11) it should state clearly the intention of the parties; and (12) the wife should read the agreement in the presence of witnesses.

These suggestions follow, as we shall see later, the view of the courts that the husband will attempt to cheat the wife out of something which is rightfully hers by the status of marriage, and that the wife is an idiot thoroughly incapable of understanding what's going on in a transaction concerning property.

14. See, [2] Lindey, Separation Agreements and Ante-nuptial Contracts (1967), at 90-26 and case cited therein.

15. Baucher v. Barrett, 128 Ind. App. 233, 145 N.E.2d 298 (1957).

22. [Del Vecchio v. Del Vecchio, 143 So.2d 17], 20 [(Fla. 1962)].

Most of the agreements that have reached the courts have been attacked on the grounds that the prospective husband failed to disclose the nature and extent of his property.[23] The courts are mainly concerned with assuring that there is no overreaching on the part of the husband.[24]

b. Contracting in Community Property States

YOUNGER, COMMUNITY PROPERTY, WOMEN AND THE LAW SCHOOL CURRICULUM
48 N.Y.U.L. Rev. 211, 248-250 (1973)

In ruling on the validity of both antenuptial and postnuptial agreements, courts in jurisdictions which allow them also take a protective attitude toward wives. Husbands may have to comply with extra formalities,[263] and clearly and convincingly prove that neither the terms[264] nor the agreements themselves are fraudulent, coerced or unfair.[265] In community property states such agreements must overcome still another hurdle: a presumption that everything acquired after marriage belongs to the community. In re Estate of Harber[266] is a recent example. When the husband and wife made their postnuptial agreement, approximately $300,000 worth of property was in the wife's name and $800,000 in the husband's. Under the agreement, the wife was to get some realty in Arizona purchased for $43,000, $25,000 of which she had contributed herself, and $100,000 in cash. All other property was to become the sole property of her husband. The wife never received the cash; she received only a promissory note. The couple nevertheless lived under the agreement for 24 years during which time the wife executed deeds to her husband in about 175 different real estate transactions. When the husband died, his wife claimed for the first time, in an action for determination of heirship, that his entire estate was community property. Despite the written agreement, the fact that the couple had conformed to it for 24 years and the absence of evidence of fraud or coercion, the court held that all the property in the husband's estate was community in nature. Conceding that a married woman was " 'as fully capable of managing her affairs as a man under the same circumstances' "[267] and "that married couples should not be deprived of the right by contract to divide their property as they please, both presently and prospectively,"[268] it found that the husband's executors had not proved by "clear and convincing evidence that the agreement was not fraudulent or coerced, or that it was not unfair or inequitable."[269]

Clearly, wives are still considered less competent than husbands and in need of protection — and so they are, if dependent. In light of their legal casting in that role, stringent standards for upholding postnuptial if not antenuptial property agreements may be warranted. When these standards are met, wives by agreement can convert

23. Klein ["A 'Checklist' for the Drafting of Enforceable Antenuptial Agreements," 19 U. Miami L. Rev. 615], 623 [(1965)].

24. In re Cantrell's Estate, 154 Kan. 545, 119 P.2d 483 (1941); see also, [2] Lindey [Separation Agreements and Ante-nuptial Contracts], 90-44 [1967].

263. Compare La. Civ. Code Ann. art. 2328 (West 1971) with N.Y. Gen. Oblig. Law §5-701(3) (McKinney 1964). But see Nevins v. Nevins, 129 Cal. App. 2d 150, 157, 276 P.2d 655, 659-60 (Dist. Ct. App. 1954).

264. See, e.g., In re Estate of Harber, 104 Ariz. 79, 88, 449 P.2d 7, 16 (1969).

265. Id. On the whole subject of antenuptial agreements, see 2 A. Lindey, Separation Agreements and Ante-Nuptial Contracts §90 (1967 & Supp. 1972).

266. 104 Ariz. 79, 88, 449 P.2d 7, 16 (1969).

267. Id. at 86, 449 P.2d at 14, quoting Hall v. Weatherford, 32 Ariz. 370, 378, 259 P. 282, 285 (1927).

268. 104 Ariz. at 87, 449 P.2d at 15.

269. Id. at 88, 449 P.2d at 16.

holdings in community to separate property, joint tenancies or tenancies in common.[270] In addition to their power to contract away the community, spouses by agreement may also alter the rights to manage and control it.[271] Thus, they can vest control of the community in the wife, making her, rather than her husband, the managing partner. This is sometimes done.[272] As manager, the wife presumably has the same duties and responsibilities as the husband would have in the same position.

c. Other Types of Interspousal Agreements

GRAHAM v. GRAHAM
33 F. Supp. 936 (E.D. Mich. 1940)

TUTTLE, J.

This is a suit by a man against his former wife upon the following written agreement alleged to have been executed September 17, 1932, by the parties:

"This agreement made this 17th day of September, 1932, between Margrethe Graham and Sidney Graham, husband and wife. For valuable consideration Margrethe Graham hereby agrees to pay to Sidney Graham the sum of Three Hundred ($300.00) Dollars per month each and every month hereafter until the parties hereto no longer desire this arrangement to continue. . . .

"This agreement is made to adjust financial matters between the parties hereto, so that in the future there will be no further arguments as to what money said Sidney Graham shall receive."

The parties were divorced on July 11, 1933. While the writing itself recites no consideration but merely states that it is made to prevent future arguments as to the amount of money the husband is to receive from his wife, the complaint alleges that the plaintiff had quit his job in a hotel at the solicitation of the defendant who wanted him to accompany her upon her travels, she paying his expenses, and that he was desirous of returning to work but that the defendant in order to induce him not to do so entered into this agreement. The total amount claimed until November 7, 1939, is $25,500, with interest at five per cent per annum from the time each monthly installment of $300 became due. The defendant in her answer alleges that she has no recollection of entering into the agreement and she denies that she ever induced plaintiff to give up his hotel work alleging that on the contrary his abandonment of work and continued reliance upon her for support was always distasteful to her. The answer further alleges that at the time of divorce the parties entered into a written settlement agreement under which defendant (plaintiff in the divorce suit) paid plaintiff (defendant in the divorce suit) $9000 and each party surrendered any and all claims he or she might have in the property of the other.

270. See, e.g., In re Ivers' Estate, 4 Wash. 2d 477, 486-87, 104 P.2d 467, 471 (1940); Ariz. Rev. Stat. Ann. §33-431 (1956); Cal. Civ. Code §5104 (West 1970); Nev. Rev. Stat. §123.030 (1971). It seems to be the practice, at least in California, for community real property to be held in joint tenancy. See Griffith, Community Property in Joint Tenancy Form, 14 Stan. L. Rev. 87, 88-90 (1961). The state legislature has shown its disapproval of the practice with respect to single-family residences acquired during marriage by creating a presumption, effective on dissolution of the marriage or legal separation, that such property is community property. Cal. Civ. Code §5110 (West Supp. 1972). Joint tenancy, like a tenancy in common, gives the wife the opportunity to control what she owns herself. "So far as the husband is concerned," says Professor deFuniak, it is "far more disadvantageous than holding property in community." Principles, supra note 3, §134, at 333. Community property, however, enjoys a tax advantage on the death of a spouse which a joint tenancy does not. On the death of one spouse, the share of the surviving spouse, as well as that of the decedent, gets a "stepped-up" basis. 26 U.S.C. §1014(b)(6) (1970). As to joint property, see Treas. Reg. §1.1014-2(b)(2) (1960). This, no doubt, helps its survival.
271. Munger v. Boardman, 53 Ariz. 271, 280, 88 P.2d 536, 539 (1939).
272. See, e.g., id.

Subsequent to filing her answer, the defendant filed a motion to dismiss the complaint on the grounds that her promise was without consideration; that the alleged contract was not within the power of a married woman under Michigan law to make; that, since under its express provisions it was to continue only until the parties no longer desired the arrangement to continue, it was terminated by the divorce and settlement agreement. . . . I . . . assume all of the allegations of the bill of complaint to be true. . . .

. . . A married woman has no general power to contract, but can contract only in relation to her separate property. . . . The limitation applies to contracts of married women with their husbands as well as with third parties. . . . In general, the Michigan Supreme Court in deciding whether an agreement is within a married woman's contractual capacity looks to the nature of the consideration, requiring it to be for the benefit of her separate estate. . . . [T]he promise of the defendant here consists of a general executory obligation unrelated to specific property and since the consideration is not for the benefit of her separate estate, but if anything to its detriment, it would appear that the contract is beyond the capacity of a married woman under Michigan law to make.

However, I do not rest my decision on this ground, but rather upon the broader ground that even if the contract is otherwise within the contractual power of the parties it is void because it contravenes public policy. Under the law, marriage is not merely a private contract between the parties, but creates a status in which the state is vitally interested and under which certain rights and duties incident to the relationship come into being, irrespective of the wishes of the parties. As a result of the marriage contract, for example, the husband has a duty to support and to live with his wife and the wife must contribute her services and society to the husband and follow him in his choice of domicile. The law is well settled that a private agreement between persons married or about to be married which attempts to change the essential obligations of the marriage contract as defined by the law is contrary to public policy and unenforceable. . . .

Thus, it has been repeatedly held that a provision releasing the husband from his duty to support his wife in a contract between married persons, or those about to be married, except in connection with a pre-existing or contemplated immediate separation, makes the contract void. . . . Even in the states with the most liberal emancipation statutes with respect to married women, the law has not gone to the extent of permitting husbands and wives by agreement to change the essential incidents of the marriage contract.

The contract claimed to have been made by the plaintiff and defendant in the case at bar while married and living together falls within this prohibition. Under its terms, the husband becomes obligated to accompany his wife upon her travels; while under the law of marriage the wife is obliged to follow the husband's choice of domicile. . . . The contract, furthermore, would seem to suffer from a second defect by impliedly releasing the husband from his duty to support his wife . . . . The present contract does not expressly contain such a release, but if the husband can always call upon his wife for payments of $300 per month he is in practical effect getting rid of his obligation to support his wife. The plaintiff seems to place this construction on the contract since his claim makes no deduction from the promised $300 per month for support of his wife. . . .

The law prohibiting married persons from altering by private agreement the personal relationships and obligations assumed upon marriage is based on sound foundations of public policy. If they were permitted to regulate by private contract where the parties are to live and whether the husband is to work or be supported by his wife, there would seem to be no reason why married persons could not contract as to the allowance the husband or wife may receive, the number of dresses she may have, the places where they will spend their evenings and vacations, and innumerable other aspects of their personal relationships. Such right would open an endless field for controversy and bickering and would destroy the element of flexibility needed in making adjustments to new conditions arising in marital life. There is no reason, of course, why the wife cannot voluntarily pay her husband a monthly sum or the husband by mutual understanding quit his job and travel with his wife. The objection is to putting such conduct into a binding contract, tying the parties' hands in the future and inviting controversy and litigation between them. . . .

The case is also to be distinguished from a group of cases which hold that a married woman can properly contract with her husband to work for him outside the home and be compensated by him for her services (although it appears that this is contrary to the weight of authority). See annotations in 14 A.L.R. 1013 and 23 A.L.R. 18. The ground on which the contract has been upheld in those cases is that it covered services outside the scope of the marriage contract; the promises did not, as here, involve the essential obligations of the marriage contract, and no question of public policy was therefore involved. . . .

[Complaint dismissed.]

NOTES

1. Both ex-husbands and ex-wives can be injured by the ban on interspousal contracts which go to the heart of the marital relationship, as Hardy v. Hardy and Graham v. Graham illustrate. If Ms. Graham had sued Mr. Graham to recover money she had paid him in the past pursuant to this agreement, should she have been able to recover? After all, Ms. Graham could argue that she was paying pursuant to an illegal contract and never intended a gift. If she made the payments believing she had a legal obligation to do so, wasn't she in the same position as Mr. Hardy, who had made what he thought were legally required support payments which turned out to be contributions to his wife's portfolio? It is possible that the court would be more sympathetic to Mr. Graham's mistake of law than to Ms. Hardy's deceit as to the facts.

Is the argument for Mr. Graham made stronger or weaker by the fact that his wife had no legal duty to support him?

2. McDowell noted three common types of husband-wife contracts in addition to antenuptial agreements dealing with property: (1) an "adjustment of obligations" agreement, which fixes the amount of support due or settles the rights and duties of the parties in some disputed area, like the contract in Graham v. Graham: (2) "above and beyond the call of duty" agreements in which one of the spouses promises for consideration to perform a marital duty to an unusually high degree, e.g., the wife promises to nurse an invalid husband, "when the motives of love and affection or of family obligation might not be strong enough"; (3) the "reconciliation agreement" in which one party has left or threatens to leave and the other makes promises in order to induce the injured party to stay or return.[76] The attitudes of the courts toward the different types of contracts range from a grudging willingness to provide enforcement if certain conditions are met, to undisguised hostility.

Because the first two kinds of agreements are clear attempts by marriage partners to substitute private contractual arrangements for status incidents of marriage, there are numerous reported decisions denying them enforcement. For example, the courts have refused to enforce agreements:

     — to obtain a divorce[77]
     — to refrain from sexual relations[78]

---

76. McDowell, Contracts in the Family, 45 Boston U. L. Rev. 43, 52-53 (1965).
77. In re Duncan's Estate, 87 Colo. 149, 285 P. 757 (1930).
78. Restatement of Contracts (1932), §587 (1932), Illustration 1 provides: "A and B who are about to marry agree to forego sexual intercourse. The bargain is illegal."

— to refrain from cohabitation[79]

— not to have children[80]

— to exclude children of the wife's prior marriage from the household[81]

— to bind the husband to reside in a particular location[82]

— to permit the wife to choose the marital domicile[83]

— to raise children in a particular religion[84]

— to relieve the husband of his obligation to support his wife[85]

— to limit the husband's liability for support in the event of separation or divorce[86]

— to keep the husband's mother in the household indefinitely[87]

— to have the husband pay his wife for his care[88]

— in which the sole consideration for the contract was the wife's services in the family home and farm.[89]

The third transaction type, the reconciliation agreement, which usually involves the departure or threatened departure of the wife and the husband's promise to induce her to return, is the most common and has met the most favor with the courts:[90]

> If her [the wife's] cause for leaving him [the husband] would not be grounds for legal separation or divorce, the courts say that her return is a duty under the marriage which obligates her to live with her husband and thus her promise to return is no consideration and the agreement is against public policy.[34] If the wife, however, had cause for legal separation or divorce, not only will her forbearance from bringing such action and her return to the husband be consideration for his promise, but such agreements are enthusiastically supported by public policy.[35] The reason for this one hundred and eighty degree turn in policy is clear if we assume that the over-riding

79. Mirizio v. Mirizio, 242 N.Y. 74, 150 N.E. 605, 44 A.L.R. 714 (1926); Gelin v. Gelin, N.Y.L.J., Feb. 20, 1928, p. 2467 (N.Y. Sup. Ct.) noted in 41 Harv. L. Rev. 925 (1928).

80. Pilpel and Zavin, Your Marriage and the Law 36 (1964).

81. Mengal v. Mengal, 103 N.Y.S.2d 992 (1951).

82. Marshak v. Marshak, 115 Ark. 51, 170 S.W. 567 (1914); Isaacs v. Isaacs, 71 Neb. 537, 99 N.W. 268 (1904).

83. Graham v. Graham, 33 F. Supp. 936 (E.D. Mich. 1940).

84. Hackett v. Hackett, 150 N.E.2d 431 (Ohio 1958); Wood v. Wood, 168 A.2d 102 (Del. 1961).

85. Kershner v. Kershner, 244 App. Div. 34, 278 N.Y.S. 501 (1935), *aff'd per curiam*, 269 N.Y. 654 200 N.E. 43 (1936); Smith v. Smith, 154 Ga. 702, 115 S.E. 73 (1922); In re Ryan's Estate, 134 Wis. 431, 114 N.W. 820 (1908); Garlock v. Garlock, 279 N.Y. 337, 18 N.E.2d 521 (1939). Cf. Graham v. Graham, 33 F. Supp. 936 (E.D. Mich. 1940).

86. Fricke v. Fricke, 257 Wis. 124, 42 N.W.2d 500 (1950); In re Ryan's Estate, 134 Wis. 431, 144 N.W. 820 (1908); Fincham v. Fincham, 160 Kan. 683, 165 Pac. 2d 209 (1946); Scherba v. Scherba, 340 Mich. 228, 65 N.W.2d 758 (1954).

87. Koch v. Koch, 95 N.J. Super. 546, 232 A.2d 157(1967).

88. Tellez v. Tellez, 51 N.M. 416, 186 P.2d 390 (1947).

89. Youngberg v. Holstrom, 252 Iowa 815, 108 N.W.2d 498 (1961) supra; Sprinkle v. Ponder, 233 N.C. 312, 64 S.E.2d 171 (1951) (dictum); Frame v. Frame, 120 Tex. 61, 36 S.W.2d 152 (1931); 16 Minn. L. Rev. 443 (1932). Most of the citations in this and the preceding twelve footnotes were taken from Karp, Antenuptial Agreements: A Vehicle for Changing Marital Roles (unpublished paper, Geo. Wash. U. Law School, 1971).

90. McDowell, supra, at 50.

34. Litwin v. Litwin, 375 Ill. 90, 30 N.E.2d 619 (1940); In re Kesler's Estate, 143 Pa. 386, 22 Atl. 892 (1891); Campbell v. Prater, 64 Wyo. 293, 191 P.2d 160 (1948). See cases cited in annotation at 149 A.L.R. 1015-16 (1944).

35. Young v. Cockman, 182 Md. 246, 34 A.2d 428 (1943); Polson v. Stewart, 167 Mass. 211, 45 N.E.737 (1897); Duffy v. White, 115 Mich. 264, 73 N.W. 363 (1897) (the husband left the home and his wife made the promise to secure his return); Adams v. Adams, 91 N.Y. 381 (1883); Darcey v. Darcey, 29 R.I. 384, 71 Atl. 595 (1909). Contra, Hill v. Hill, 217 Ala. 235, 115 So. 258 (1928) and Oppenheimer v. Collins, 115 Wis. 283, 91 N.W. 690 (1902) (where a third party creditor was claiming the subject matter of the contract between the spouses). See cases cited in annotation at 149 A.L.R. 1013-15 (1944). The principle applies a fortiorari to a reconciliation agreement made by parties in the interlocutory period following a divorce. Angell v. Angell, 84 Cal. App. 2d 339, 191 P.2d 54 (1948).

policy is to protect the marriage. In [this] group of cases, we have a foundering marriage and the contract is an attempt to obtain a reconciliation.

These cases operate with two black and white categories. If the marriage has not reached the point where one of the parties has a legal cause of action for separation or divorce, it is assumed to be a harmonious relationship.

Under yet a fourth type of agreement, the wife provides nondomestic services to her husband in return for wages or a partnership interest. The following case illustrates prevalent judicial attitudes toward this type of contract.

EGGLESTON v. EGGLESTON
228 N.C. 668, 47 S.E.2d 243 (1948)

SEAWELL, J.

The plaintiff brought this suit against her husband for alimony without divorce under G.S., 50-16, joining with this cause of action . . . a cause of action to have herself declared a business partner with her husband and to have her rights under the partnership adjudicated and an account taken. . . .

. . . The case then proceeded to trial, the issues being answered as to both causes of action unfavorably to the plaintiff . . . .

The evidence by which plaintiff sought to show the alleged partnership may be summarized as tending to show the following facts and conditions:

When they first moved into the filling station on the Draper road and started business she helped display the stock; while defendant went out into the "territory" plaintiff was in charge of the filling station, worked there with no assistance except casual help from little boys to whom plaintiff paid small sums; plaintiff had access to the funds, taking in the money and keeping it in the cash drawer; she put her "inheritance money," about $125.00, in the business at this early stage; she sometimes bought, but buying was mostly done by defendant. As more filling stations were added plaintiff went and put up signs in the windows, displayed stock and helped them get set up in the business. She worked regularly during this period, living in the service station for 15 years, and except for a short period of time and vacations in the summer, was there continually, often being compelled to let her housework go. She had often gone without food all day except what she could pick up at the filling station. She sold things out of stock, serviced cars, putting in gas and oil; carried water from the pump in tubs, as there was, for a long time, no running water; washed cars, often making $5.00 a day in this way. Plaintiff handled the paid and unpaid bills, made out statements and sent them out. Later plaintiff took a bookkeeping course and learned to type, and thereafter kept books for the business. After plaintiff and defendant moved into the new home in 1940 until 1946, while plaintiff did not go to the filling station every day because of her illness, the help came to her to inquire about the business and for direction in matters with which she was familiar, and she continued in charge during Mr. Eggleston's absence. Between 1940 and 1946, when they separated, she went down and did book work. During 1945 plaintiff and her brother, Pickett Parker, did the book work together. Plaintiff took part in the conduct of the tire business. . . .

All this proffered evidence was rejected upon objection made seriatim by defendant, and in the same manner plaintiff excepted.

The plaintiff then testified that during the year 1945, she was not certain of the date, defendant came into the kitchen where she was cooking supper, put his arm around her, started kissing her and told her she was his business partner. "I asked him what he meant and I said I had been his business partner for twenty years. He said I had always been worried about losing a great deal of the business at his death, and he had fixed it so I would not even have to pay inheritance tax on my part of the partnership. He talked to me about it and ten days or two weeks later he signed — he said of course I would have to pay income [tax] since I was a partner in the business and he brought some papers in for me to sign. I signed three different sheets, I think, income papers and different papers, and a blank check."

After identification, plaintiff then introduced in evidence copies of the joint partnership income tax returns made by herself and husband for the calendar year 1945 to the Federal and State taxing authorities, respectively. These returns manifest a taxable net income for that year of $20,801.29 and indicate that Mattie P. Eggleston, the plaintiff, and Frank Eggleston, the defendant, were partners upon equal shares in the business, entitling each to one-half of said net income. The partnership appears as "Eggleston Brothers Filling Station." . . .

. . . [I]t is necessary to turn to the evidence of the plaintiff as above noted — principally her own testimony — of the dealings between herself and husband with relation to the business in which she claims partnership.

This evidence was excluded apparently upon the theory that her complaint setting up the creation of the partnership restricts her to the transactions involved in the filing of the income tax returns, and especially to its organization on January 1, 1945. . . . Its exclusion was error. . . . In our view of the case the whole evidence directed to the existence of the partnership must be taken together, and so taken was competent to be submitted to the jury for their consideration and evaluation.

Under the common law as a consequence of the fictional merger of husband and wife into one person, and other disabilities of the wife incident to coverture, there could be no contract and, therefore, no business partnership between husband and wife. That incapacity has been removed in many states by the enactment of "Married Women's Acts," — statutes directly or impliedly giving them the power or the right to contract. The broad general powers of contract given under most of these statutes has in many instances been extended by judicial interpretation to authorize the formation of partnerships with the husband. . . .

"A contract, express or implied, is essential to the formation of a partnership." 40 Am. Jur., Partnership, p. 135, sec. 20, see notes 14, 15. But we see no reason why a course of dealing between the parties of sufficient significance and duration may not, along with other proof of the fact, be admitted as evidence tending to establish the fact of partnership provided it has sufficient substance and definiteness to evince the essentials of the legal concept, including, of course, the necessary intent. . . .

It is proper to say here that the services rendered by the wife to her husband are presumed to be gratuitous. The presumption is not conclusive and may be overcome by evidence tending to show that the services were not gratuitous. That was a matter for the jury. . . .

. . . [I]t is not necessary to a partnership that property or capital involved in it should belong in common to the parties to the contract. On the contrary, a familiar type of partnership, as indicated by the evidence in this case, occurs where the services of the one party [are] balanced against the capital furnished by the other. . . .

New trial.

NOTES

1. If Mattie Eggleston was her husband's partner in the filling station, why wasn't Nettie Holstrum her husband's partner in their farm? Courts in most states have been willing to enforce agreements under which the wife provides nondomestic services to her husband in return for wages or a partnership interest.[91] However, the services

91. See, e.g., Hull v. Hull Bros. Lumber Co., 186 Tenn. 53, 208 S.W.2d 338 (1948); Reid v. Reid, 216 Iowa 882, 249 N.W. 387 (1933) (semble); McCarthy v. McKechnie, 152 Me. 420, 132 A.2d 437 (1957); Flynn v. State

performed must be clearly of the kind which are not customarily performed by one spouse for the other as part of the marital relation. Apparently, the duties of a farm wife were not sufficiently nonmarital to satisfy the Iowa court (which, as we have noted, was already strongly disposed to rule against Nettie in favor of Will's second wife).

2. A second distinction between the two cases is that Ms. Eggleston had better proof of a partnership agreement than did Nettie Holstrum's nieces and nephews. This written proof is important because of the court's biases against contracts between spouses other than those about property. In fact, the concern of the courts to scrutinize all agreements between actual or prospective marriage partners for fairness, which was discussed in connection with antenuptial agreements about property, is in effect inverted in its application to contracts between marriage partners involving the exchange of nondomestic services for valuable consideration. In regard to contracts about property, the courts focus on whether or not an otherwise valid contract involved overreaching by the wealthier spouse, usually the husband. In regard to contracts about nondomestic services, the courts seek to protect the spouse from whom payment for the services is sought, also usually the husband, from being held answerable in contract for services which were originally tendered as a gift or performed as a marital duty by the employee-spouse. To accomplish this result, the courts often use the rebuttable presumption we have already mentioned that the services rendered were gratuitous.[92] As a result, only in a case as relatively clear as Eggleston v. Eggleston is enforcement likely.

3. When the wife works outside the home, presumably her husband gets less of her services in the home. This need not result in unfairness to the husband, however. He can redress the balance between them, during an ongoing marriage, by reducing his payments for her support as her wages from outside work increase, or by requiring her to pay for the household help necessitated by her outside work. If the wife cannot get support from her husband for the full value of the domestic services she performs, she, theoretically at least, has the option of working less in the home and more outside. The reality of this option is somewhat undercut by marketplace discrimination against women, particularly working mothers.

4. Is it reasonable to allow the wife to recover for her nondomestic services in the husband's business and yet deny her recovery for domestic services? The major grounds for differentiating between the two situations seem to be (1) that the former exchange

---

Compensation Comm'r, 141 W.Va. 445, 91 S.E.2d 156 (1956). Re partnership agreements, see McGehee v. McGehee, 227 Miss. 170, 85 So. 2d 799 (1956); Klotz v. Klotz, 202 Va. 393, 117 S.E.2d 650 (1961); Annot., 157 A.L.R. 652 (1945).

However, a few states have taken the opposite approach, and prohibit husband-wife employment contracts, apparently because they can't make this distinction. See, e.g., Miss. Code Ann. §454 (1956); Bendler v. Bendler, 3 N.J. 161, 69 A.2d 302 (1949), in which the court refused to award workman's compensation to a husband who worked for a regular weekly salary in his wife's embroidery business and was injured on the job, on the grounds of the illegality of a hiring contract between husband and wife; Ladden v. Ladden, 59 N.J. Super. 502, 158 A.2d 189 (1960); Blaechinska v. Howard Mission & Home for Little Wanderers, 130 N.Y. 497, 29 N.E. 755 (1892). Other early cases are discussed in Husband's Right to Wife's Services, 38 Harv. L. Rev. 421, 422 (1925). New Jersey has changed its position to the extent of allowing the wife the status of employee for workman's compensation purposes when she works for a partnership of which her husband is a member. Felice v. Felice, 34 N.J. Super. 388, 112 A.2d 581 (1955). Other courts have limited the right to recover to cases in which the wife can prove a contract, and will not allow recovery on the basis of an implied obligation to pay her for services rendered. Ferris v. Barrett, 250 Iowa 646, 95 N.W.2d 527 (1959); Brodsky v. Brodsky, 132 Neb. 659, 272 N.W. 919 (1937); Dorsett v. Dorsett, 183 N.C. 354, 111 S.E. 541 (1922); 32 Yale L.J. 188 (1922). See also Sprinkle v. Ponder, 233 N.C. 312, 64 S.E.2d 171 (1951). Re partnership agreements, see Annot. 157 A.L.R. 652 (1945); Clark, supra, §7.2, at 226-227, n.47.

92. For the presumption that services rendered are gratuitous as between spouses, see Andrews v. English, 200 Okla. 667, 199 P.2d 202 (1948); Jennings v. Conn., 194 Ore. 686, 243 P.2d 1080 (1952). As between parent and child, see McDowell, supra, at 56, n.44; for other family contracts, id. at 58, n.53.

is at the heart of the marital relationship, in which the courts should not intervene, while the latter is outside it, and (2) that it is more difficult to evaluate domestic services than services performed in a business. As to the first contention, litigation about a wife's contract for employment in her husband's business is probably as destructive to the marital relationship as litigation about a support-services agreement. As to the second, consider the following case.

LAZZAREVICH v. LAZZAREVICH
88 Cal. App. 2d 708, 200 P.2d 49 (1948)

VALLEE, J.

Plaintiff commenced the action on August 14, 1946. The first cause of action sought recovery of the reasonable value of work and services performed by plaintiff for defendant from July, 1935, to April, 1946, in maintaining a home for defendant and their son, "cooking for him, washing defendant's clothes, and performing the entire household services for defendant," during all of which period she "believed that she was the legal wife of defendant." The second cause of action sought recovery of contributions made by plaintiff to the household expenses from January 17, 1943 to June 13, 1945, consisting of earnings received by plaintiff while employed in a defense plant and during the period she believed she was defendant's lawful wife. Defendant . . . alleged . . . that the services rendered by plaintiff in his behalf were voluntarily rendered without any agreement or understanding that she would be compensated therefor; and that plaintiff had been fully compensated for all services rendered by her in his behalf.

The Settled Statement reveals the following facts: The parties were married in Los Angeles on March 18, 1921. One child, a daughter, was born, the issue of this marriage. Subsequently [the husband] filed an action for divorce in Los Angeles County. An interlocutory decree was granted . . . on March 18, 1932. On September 6, 1933, without the husband's knowledge or request, his attorney had a final decree of divorce entered. [The husband and wife] became reconciled in July of 1935. . . . Thereafter, on April 23, 1936, a son was born to the parties. As an aftermath of domestic difficulties which arose between them, plaintiff, on August 1, 1945, consulted her attorneys about a divorce. On August 10, 1945 she was informed by them that the court records disclosed the entry of a final decree of divorce on September 6, 1933. Plaintiff testified that she would not have lived with defendant if she had not believed that she was his wife. During the periods from July, 1935, to August, 1945, and from October, 1945, to April, 1946, plaintiff performed the usual household duties of a wife, excepting that during the period from January 17, 1943, until June 13, 1945, she worked in a defense plant. During this latter period . . . she contributed all of her salary, $172.50 a month, to the household expenses. . . .

The court found . . . that the reasonable value of the services rendered . . . over and above the value of support and maintenance furnished her by the defendant, was $50 per month, . . . during the period of twenty-nine months during which she rendered less service by reason of working in a defense plant . . . the reasonable value of her services, over and above the value of support and maintenance furnished her by defendant, was $25 per month. . . .

. . . The court concluded that: (1) plaintiff was entitled to recover the reasonable value of the services rendered for defendant during the period she lived with him under the mistaken belief that she was still married to him and for contributions made to him within that period, except that recovery for services rendered and for contributions made prior to August 14, 1944, was barred by the statute of limitations. . . .

Upon his appeal defendant contends that the plaintiff is not entitled to a judgment for the value of her services or for contributions because she has received one-half of all the property acquired by the parties after their reconciliation and that he, therefore, has not been unjustly enriched. This contention is not tenable.

The rights and remedies afforded a woman who cohabits with a man, believing in good faith that they are validly married, may be epitomized generally as follows:

(1) In some jurisdictions she has an action in damages for deceit against her putative husband in those cases where by fraud or misrepresentation he has induced her to enter into the supposed marriage relation. . . .

(2) In those jurisdictions in which the community property doctrine prevails, it is generally recognized that a de facto spouse is entitled to the rights accorded a lawful spouse in the property acquired during the de facto marriage. . . .

(3) In some jurisdictions, including California, the deluded woman is permitted to recover the reasonable value of her services over and above the value of the support and maintenance furnished her by her supposed husband. Sanguinetti v. Sanguinetti, 9 Cal. 2d 95, 100, 69 P.2d 845, 111 A.L.R. 342. . . .

In Sanguinetti v. Sanguinetti, supra, 9 Cal. 2d 95, at page 100, 69 P.2d 845, 847, 111 A.L.R. 342, the court said:

". . . The basis of recovery for services in the above-cited cases is quasi-contractual. The supposed husband has been unjustly enriched by the amount by which the reasonable value of the services rendered to him by his de facto wife exceed the amount devoted by him to her support and maintenance. . . . The law raises the promise to pay in such cases." . . .

A different result must obtain as to services performed by plaintiff after August 10, 1945. As we have noted, the parties separated on August 1, 1945. On August 10, 1945, plaintiff discovered that the final decree of divorce had been entered on September 6, 1933. On October 1, 1945, she went to live with defendant and continued to do so until April 1, 1946. The essence of the right of a putative wife to recover for services rendered the putative husband is her belief in the validity of a marriage between them. After August 10, 1945, plaintiff was no longer an innocent, deluded, putative wife. . . . In the absence of an express agreement that plaintiff would be compensated for services performed after that date she has no right to compensation therefor. . . .

. . . Under the findings, plaintiff is entitled to recover the sum of $10,277.50 from defendant as follows: For services rendered, $5,275.00, being ninety-one months at $50.00 a month and twenty-nine months at $25.00 a month; for contributions, $5,002.50, being twenty-nine months at $172.50.

NOTES

1. This case suggests both that it is possible to evaluate the domestic services rendered by one spouse to the other and that domestic services are sometimes worth more than the support for which they are exchanged in a traditional marriage. Thus, the application of the principles of quasi-contract, rather than the assumptions underlying the view of marriage as a status, would in many marriages result in quite different conclusions, probably more favorable to the wife. Consider, however, when you are reading the materials on the law of divorce, infra, to what extent the concept of unjust enrichment is expressed in the law of alimony.

2. It seems unfair for Ms. Lazzarevich to get half of the community property in addition to an award of back pay. The justification appears to be, first, that this is but slight compensation to her for the discovery that her "marriage" has in reality been an illicit relationship. Second, since a wife can get both an award of her half of the community property and an award of separate maintenance, why shouldn't Ms. Lazzarevich? The difference is that alimony usually is based in part on the ability of the ex-husband to pay and on the need of the ex-wife, while this quasi-contractual award does not take these factors into account. Note also the court's sex-differentiated view about who

suffers when a marriage is discovered to be an illicit relationship. It seems unlikely that a putative husband could recover the excess value of his support over the wife's services, even if her lawyer had been responsible for the mix-up instead of his.

3. To avoïd putting mistresses in a position the same as or better than wives, the courts have generally limited quasi-contractual recovery to cases in which the putative spouse did not know the true situation. A "Catch-22" example of this limitation of the doctrine is Willis v. Willis, 49 P.2d 670 (Wyo. 1935). A woman first brought suit for divorce, claiming that she had been the common law wife of the defendant. In the divorce case, the defendant claimed that she was employed as a domestic servant. Upon losing this case, she then filed for compensation for services rendered while she lived with the defendant. The court held:[93]

> . . . It appears to be a well-settled rule "that a woman who knowingly and voluntarily lives in illicit relations with a man cannot recover on an implied contract for services rendered him during such relationship. Not only does the relationship as of husband and wife negative that of master and servant, but, such cohabitation being in violation of principles of morality and chastity, and so against public policy, the law will not imply a promise to pay for services rendered under such circumstances."

d. Consortium

The sex-linked allocation of roles within marriage has had another legal consequence which should be discussed in an examination of the support-services reciprocity. At common law only the husband could sue for loss of consortium in cases where a third party had negligently injured his spouse. Consortium is the right of one spouse to the other's services or support, companionship, affection, and sexual attentions. Denying the wife's right to sue for negligent invasion of consortium was another index of her subordinate position in the marriage, and signified that in the eyes of the law the most fundamental marital rights were unimportant for her.

Logically, the Married Women's Property Acts should have changed this situation, either by extending the right to sue to the wife or by eliminating the husband's cause of action. But this did not happen in most states until the 1950s.

HITAFFER v. ARGONNE COMPANY
183 F.2d 811 (D.C. Cir. 1950)

CLARK, C. J.

Appellant's husband was injured while in appellee's employ. As a result thereof he suffered and sustained severe and permanent injuries to his body and in particular in and about his abdomen, and as a consequence appellant has been deprived of his aid, assistance, and enjoyment, specifically sexual relations. . . .

Subsequently, the instant action was filed by the wife. The defendant-appellee thereupon moved for a summary judgment on the grounds that the court lacked jurisdiction and the complaint failed to state a cause of action. The motion was granted and judgment entered for appellee. This appeal has followed to test the validity of that order. . . .

Although this is the first time this question has been presented to this court, we are not unaware of the unanimity of authority elsewhere denying the wife recovery under these circumstances. . . .

One group of cases base their results on the theory that although in the abstract

---

93. 49 P.2d at 681.

the term "consortium" contains, in addition to material services, elements of companionship, love, felicity, and sexual relations, in cases of injury to the consortium resulting' from negligence the material services are the predominant factor for which compensation is given. From this point they variously argue: (1) That since the wife has no right as such to her husband's services, she has no cause of action, although, of course, the husband, having always been entitled to his wife's services, still has a right of action; (2) That the Emancipation Acts, having given a wife a right to the fruits of her own services, have placed the husband in the same position as the wife in number (1) so that neither may bring an action, except that a husband may recover for monies actually expended. The difficulty with adhering to these authorities is that they sound in the false premise that in these actions the loss of services is the predominant factor. . . .

Consortium, although it embraces within its ambit of meaning the wife's material services, also includes love, affection, companionship, sexual relations, etc., all welded into a conceptualistic unity. And, although loss of one or the other of these elements may be greater in the case of any one of the several types of invasions from which consortium may be injured, there can be no rational basis for holding that in negligent invasions suability depends on whether there is a loss of services. . . .

Another group of cases which similarly appear to place principal emphasis on the element of services in these actions hold that in negligent invasions of the consortium the wife has no cause of action because the husband, who is under a legal duty to support his wife according to his station in life, recovers in his action for the tort as an element of his damages, for any impairment of his ability to perform his obligation, and thus the wife indirectly recovers for the value of any loss of her consortium. Any other conclusion, they reason, would result in a double recovery. The husband, on the other hand, is allowed the action when the wife is injured, because she is under no corresponding duty to him. Of course, as we have already pointed out, there is no foundation for the statement that the predominant factor involved in negligence cases of this type is the element of material services. For that reason we cannot accept their argument. There is more to consortium than the mere services of the spouse. Beyond that there are the so-called sentimental elements to which the wife has a right for which there should be a remedy. We do agree, however, that if the wife is allowed to sue, there could be a double recovery in regard to the service element of consortium, if the husband's recovery is not taken into account in measuring the wife's damages and we shall deal with the problem hereinafter in more detail.

Other cases following the reasoning of the foregoing authorities have realized, however, that the sentimental elements of the consortium are injured in negligent invasions. Thus, in order to deny the wife a right to recover for love, affection, conjugal relations, etc., they have variously concluded: (1) That in negligence cases the purpose of the damages is to compensate the injured person for the direct consequences of the wrong. The injury to the wife is indirect and so not compensable; (2) That her injuries are too remote and consequential to be capable of measure; (3) That the common law recognized no cause of action for the loss of the so-called sentimental elements of consortium and the acts have given the wife no new cause of action; and (4) That no action for loss of consortium was ever allowed in which there was no showing of the loss of some services, and since the wife cannot show such a loss she has no action. None of these cases commend themselves to us on the basis of their logic. . . .

Finally, there are a few cases which hold that the wife's interest in the marital relation is not a right of property or derived from a contract of bargain and sale and it lies in an area into which the law will not enter except of necessity. But be that as it may for those jurisdictions, we are nonetheless here committed to a different rule. . . .

Furthermore, we can conceive of no reasons for denying the wife this right for the reason that in this enlightened day and age they simply do not exist. . . .

It can hardly be said that a wife has less of an interest in the marriage relation than does the husband or in these modern times that a husband renders services of such a different character to the family and household that they must be measured by a standard of such uncertainty that the law cannot estimate any loss thereof. The husband owes the same degree of love, affection, felicity, etc., to the wife as she to him. He also owes the material service of support, but above and beyond that he renders other services as his mate's helper in her duties, as advisor and counselor, etc. . . .

It is therefore the opinion of this court that in light of the existing law of this jurisdiction, in light of the specious and fallacious reasoning of those cases from other jurisdictions which have decided the question, and in light of the demonstrable desirability of the rule under the circumstances, a wife has a cause of action for loss of consortium due to a negligent injury to her husband.

This result poses no problems in ascertaining the wife's damages. Simple mathematics will suffice to set the proper quantum. For inasmuch as it is our opinion that the husband in most cases does recover for any impairment of his duty to support his wife, and, since a compensable element of damages must be subject to measure, it is a simple matter to determine the damages to the wife's consortium in exactly the same way as those of the husband are measured in a similar action and subtract therefrom the value of any impairment of his duty of support. . . .

NOTES

1. The position taken by the D.C. Court of Appeals in the *Hitaffer* case now prevails in twenty jurisdictions.[94] A number of states which, shortly after it was introduced in the

94. Ark.: Missouri Pac. Transp. Co. v. Miller, 227 Ark. 351, 299 S.W.2d 41 (1957).
Colo.: Colo. Rev. Stat. Ann. §90-2-11(1963).
Del.: Yonner v. Adams, 3 Storey 229, 167 A.2d 717 (Del. Super. 1961); Stenta v. Leblang, 185 A.2d 759 (Del. 1962).
Ga.: Brown v. Georgia-Tennessee Coaches, Inc., 88 Ga. App. 519, 77 S.E.2d 24 (1953); Hightower v. Landrum, 109 Ga. App. 510, 136 S.E.2d 425 (1964). Cf. Louisville & Nashville R. Co. v. Lunsford, 216 Ga. 289, 116 S.E.2d 232 (1960).
Ill.: Dini v. Naiditch, 20 Ill. 2d 406, 170 N.E.2d 881 (1960).
Ind.: Troue v. Marker, 253 Ind. 284, 252 N.E.2d 800 (1970), overruling Miller v. Sparks, 136 Ind. App. 148, 189 N.E.2d (1963); McVickers v. Chesapeake & O. R. Co., 194 F.Supp. 848 (E.D. Mich. 1969) (Indiana law).
Iowa: Acuff v. Schmidt, 248 Iowa 272, 78 N.W.2d 480 (1956).
Md.: Deems v. Western Maryland Ry. Co., 247 Md. 95, 231 A.2d 514 (1967), overruling Coastal Tank Lines v. Canoles, 207 Md. 37, 113 A.2d 82 (1955).
Mich.: Montgomery v. Stephan, 359 Mich. 33, 101 N.W.2d 227 (1960).
Minn.: Thill v. Modern Erecting Co., 284 Minn. 508, 170 N.W.2d 865 (1969), overruling Hartman v. Cold Spring Granite Co., 247 Minn. 515, 77 N.W.2d 651 (1956).
Mo.: Novak v. Kansas City Transit Co., 365 S.W.2d 539 (1963); Manning v. Jones, 349 F.2d 992 (8th Cir. 1965).
Mont.: Duffy v. Lipsman-Fulkerson & Co., 200 F. Supp. 71 (D. Mont. 1961); Dutton v. Hightower & Lubrecht Const. Co., 214 F. Supp. 298 (D. Mont. 1963).
Neb.: Luther v. Maple, 250 F.2d 916 (8th Cir. 1958); Guyton v. Solomon Dehydrating Co., 302 F.2d 283 (8th Cir. 1962), *cert. denied,* 371 U.S. 817, 83 S. Ct. 32, 9 L. Ed. 2d 58 (1962); Cooney v. Moomaw, 109 F. Supp. 448 (D. Neb. 1953).
N.J.: Ekalo v. Constructive Service Corp. of America, 46 N.J. 82, 215 A.2d 1 (1966) (wife may sue if she joins her claim with that of her husband).
N.Y.: Millington v. Southeastern Elevator Co., 22 N.Y.2d 498, 293 N.Y.S.2d 305, 239 N.E.2d 897 (1968), overruling Kronenbitter v. Washburn Wire Co., 4 N.Y.2d 524, 176, N.Y.S.2d 354, 151 N.E.2d 898 (1958).
Ohio: Clouston v. Remlinger Oldsmobile Cadillac, Inc., 22 Ohio St. 2d 65, 258 N.E.2d 230 (1970).
Ore.: §108.010 Ore. Rev. Stat. §108.010 (1973); Ross v. Cuthbert, 239 Ore. 429, 397 P.2d 529 (1964).
Pa: Hopkins v. Blanco, 224 Pa. Super. 116, 302 A.2d 855 (Super. Ct. 1973), *appeal allowed,* No. 7, January Term 1974 (Pa. Sup. Ct., August 14, 1973) (decision based on the commonwealth's equal rights amendment), overruling Neuberg v. Bobowicz, 401 Pa. 146, 162 A.2d 662 (1960), and Brown v. Glenside Lumber & Coal Co., 429 Pa. 601, 240 A.2d 822 (1968).
S.D.: Hoekstra v. Helgeland, 78 S.D.82, 98 N.W.2d 669 (1959).

Hitaffer case, rejected the idea that a wife should have an action for loss of consortium have recently reconsidered and reversed themselves, and it appears likely that more states will follow suit. For discussion of the arbitrariness of denying a cause action for loss of consortium to the wife as a means of avoiding double recovery, see Johnston and Knapp, Sex Discrimination by Law: A Study in Judicial Perspective, 46 N.Y.U.L. Rev. 675, 735-736 (1971), criticizing Misunkas v. Union Carbide Corp., 399 F.2d 847 (7th Cir. 1968).

2. After the passage of the Married Women's Acts, nine states abolished the husband's right to recover for negligent interference with consortium.[95] In addition to placing the sexes in an equal position before the law, this position also satisfied the desires of many judges and legislators to limit recovery throughout the law of torts to pecuniary and physical damage, as distinguished from more intangible emotional or psychological injuries.[96]

3. In at least two cases, federal district courts have ruled that the failure to grant the wife a right to recover for negligent interference with consortium by a state which grants such a right to the husband is a denial of equal protection of the laws. Both cases were later overruled by the Seventh Circuit in Misunkas v. Union Carbide Corp., 399 F.2d 847 (1968), which was in turn mooted by changes in state law.[97] One state court has extended recovery to wives on equal protection grounds, while a number of other courts have denied equal protection challenges, so the constitutional issue remains unresolved.[98]

Wis.: Moran v. Quality Aluminum Casting Co., 34 Wis. 2d 542, 150 N.W.2d 137 (1967) (conditions relief on joinder with husband's claim).

This list is an updated version of Clark, Law of Domestic Relations 275 n.31 (1968).

95. Calif.: West v. City of San Diego, 54 Cal. 2d 469, 6 Cal. Rptr. 289, 353 P.2d 929 (1960), 48 Cal. L. Rev. 882 (1960), 8 U.C.L.A.L. Rev. 985 (1960), purporting to rely on West's Ann. Civ. Proc. Code (Cal.) §427, holding the husband may recover for loss of services only.

Conn.: Marri v. Stamford St. Ry. Co., 84 Conn. 9, 78 A. 582 (1911).

Kan.: Kan. Stat. Ann. §23-205 (1964), as construed in Clark v. Southwestern Greyhound Lines, 144 Kan. 344, 58 P.2d 1128 (1936).

Mass.: Rodgers v. Boynton, 315 Mass. 279, 52 N.E.2d 576 (1943), and Feneff v. N.Y. Cent. R.R., 203 Mass. 278, 89 N.E. 436 (1909).

N.C.: Helmstetler v. Duke Power Co., 224 N.C. 821, 32 S.E.2d 611 (1945).

R.I.: Martin v. United Electric Rys. Co., 71 R.I. 137, 42 A.2d 897 (1945).

Utah: Black v. United States, 263 F. Supp. 470 (D. Utah 1967).

Va.: Va. Code Ann. §55-36 (1959).

Wash.: Hawkins v. Front St. Cable Ry. Co., 3 Wash. 592, 28 P. 1021 (1892) (husband may recover only for loss of services).

From Clark, Law of Domestic Relations 273, n. 16 (1968).

96. Clark, supra, at §10.5; Johnston and Knapp, Sex Discrimination by Law: A Study in Judicial Perspective, 46 N.Y.U.L. Rev. 675, 736 (1971).

97. Karczewski v. Baltimore & Ohio R.R., 274 F. Supp. 169 (N.D. Ill., 1967); Owen v. Illinois Baking Corp., 260 F. Supp. 820 (W.D. Mich. 1966), overruled in effect by Misunkas v. Union Carbide Corp., 399 F.2d 847 (7th Cir. 1968), now mooted by state rules in Illinois, Wisconsin, and Indiana following Hitaffer v. Argonne Co., 183 F.2d 811 (D.C. Cir. 1950).

98. No-recovery rule does not deny equal protection of the laws: Krohn v. Richardson-Merrell, Inc., 219 Tenn. 37, 406 S.W.2d 166 (1966), *cert. denied*, 386 U.S. 970 (1967); Seagraves v. Legg, 147 W. Va. 331, 127 S.E.2d 605 (1962). Cf. Gates v. Foley, 247 So. 2d 40, 42 n.1 (Fla. 1971); Umpleby v. Dorsey, 10 Ohio Misc. 288, 277 N.E.2d 274 (1967); Bronfield v. Seybolt Motors, Inc., 109 N.H. 501, 256 A.2d 151 (1969); Copeland v. Smith Dairy Products Co., 288 F. Supp. 904 (N.D.N.J. 1968).

No-recovery rule denies equal protection of the laws: Clem v. Brown, 3 Ohio Misc. 167, 207 N.E.2d 390 (1965).

See Kanowitz, Women and the Law 160-167 (1968); Note, Equal Protection: The Wife's Action for Loss of Consortium, 54 Iowa L. Rev. 519 (1968). See also Note, Judicial Treatment of Negligent Invasion of Consortium, 61 Colum. L. Rev. 1341 (1961); Holbrook, The Change in the Meaning of Consortium, 22 Mich. L. Rev. 1 (1923); Lippman, The Breakdown of Consortium, 30 Colum. L. Rev. 651 (1930); Pound, Individual Interests in the Domestic Relations, 14 Mich. L. Rev. 177 (1916); Clark, Law of Domestic Relations 272 (1968);

IV. PROPOSALS FOR CHANGING THE LAW OF THE ONGOING MARRIAGE

A. Expanding the Scope of Contracts Between Spouses

1. Introduction: Past Attempts To Contract

Attempts to replace the marriage contract prescribed by the state with more egalitarian commitments date back as far as the first third of the nineteenth century. The following are two early examples.[1]

ROBERT DALE OWEN AND MARY JANE ROBINSON MARRIAGE DOCUMENT (1832)

New York, Tuesday, April 12, 1832

This afternoon I enter into a matrimonial engagement with Mary Jane Robinson, a young person whose opinions on all important subjects, whose mode of thinking and feeling coincide more intimately with my own than do those of any other individual with whom I am acquainted. . . . We have selected the simplest ceremony which the laws of this State recognize. . . . This ceremony involves not the necessity of making promises regarding that over which we have no control, the state of human affections in the distant future, nor of repeating forms which we deem offensive, inasmuch as they outrage the principles of human liberty and equality, by conferring rights and imposing duties unequally on the sexes. The ceremony consists of a simply written contract in which we agree to take each other as husband and wife according to the laws of the State of New York, our signatures being attested by those friends who are present.

Of the unjust rights which in virtue of this ceremony an iniquitous law tacitly gives me over the person and property of another, I can not legally, but I can morally divest myself. And I hereby distinctly and emphatically declare that I consider myself, and earnestly desire to be considered by others, as utterly divested, now and during the rest of my life, of any such rights, the barbarous relics of a feudal, despotic system, soon destined, in the onward course of improvement, to be wholly swept away; and the existence of which is a tacit insult to the good sense and good feeling of this comparatively civilized age.

Robert Dale Owen

I concur in this sentiment.

Mary Jane Robinson

HENRY B. BLACKWELL AND LUCY STONE PROTEST (1855)

While acknowledging our mutual affection by publicly assuming the relationship of husband and wife, yet in justice to ourselves and a great principle, we deem it a duty to declare that this act on our part implies no sanction of, nor promise of voluntary obedience to such of the present laws of marriage, as refuse to recognize the wife as an independent, rational being, while they confer upon the husband an injurious and unnatural superiority, investing him with legal powers which no honor-

---

Prosser, Handbook of the Law of Torts 910 (3d ed. 1964).

1. Kraditor, ed., Up From the Pedestal 148-150 (Quadrangle ed. 1970).

able man would exercise, and which no man should possess. We protest especially against the laws which give to the husband:

1. The custody of the wife's person.

2. The exclusive control and guardianship of their children.

3. The sole ownership of her personal property, and use of her real estate, unless previously settled upon her, or placed in the hands of trustees, as in the case of minors, lunatics, and idiots.

4. The absolute right to the product of her industry.

5. Also against laws which give to the widower so much larger and more permanent an interest in the property of his deceased wife, than they give to the widow in that of the deceased husband.

6. Finally, against the whole system by which "the legal existence of the wife is suspended during marriage," so that in most States, she neither has a legal part in the choice of her residence, nor can she make a will, nor sue or be sued in her own name, nor inherit property.

We believe that personal independence and equal human rights can never be forfeited, except for crime; that marriage should be an equal and permanent partnership, and so recognized by law; that until it is so recognized, married partners should provide against the radical injustice of present laws, by every means in their power.

We believe that where domestic difficulties arise, no appeal should be made to legal tribunals under existing laws, but that all difficulties should be submitted to the equitable adjustment of arbitrators mutually chosen.

Thus reverencing law, we enter our protest against rules and customs which are unworthy of the name, since they violate justice, the essence of law.

(Signed) Henry B. Blackwell

Lucy Stone

2. Current Approaches to Contract During Marriage

Recently a number of commentators have renewed the idea that prospective spouses should design their marriage contracts. Some people further urge that there be legal enforcement for such contracts both during the marriage and upon its possible dissolution. Proposed contracts cover topics such as surnames, domicile, mutual disclosures of property, background and income, sexual relations (including attitudes toward adultery, having or adopting children, responsibility for birth control and its methods), the upbringing of children, relations with their prospective in-laws, support obligations both during marriage, upon divorce, and in estate planning, career plans and obligations, division of household tasks, conditions of marriage dissolution, and interpretation, modification, and enforcement of the contract, often with a provision for compulsory arbitration or marriage counseling. "Dotting all the i's might prevent some unions . . . but that is just the point." [2]

A number of feminists have published the agreements which govern their own marriages, often negotiated after several years of marriage and dealing primarily with household and childrearing tasks. Selected provisions from several modern agreements follow.[3]

The contracts excerpted are

(1) a proposed antenuptial agreement based in part on the contracts used by the Los Angeles conciliation court, designed by a law student (Knisely);

(2) Donald and Ina's contract, an antenuptial agreement composed by a domestic relations lawyer and a thrice-married novelist and essayist for a hypothetical couple composed of Donald, a twenty-nine year old previously married and divorced sales manager for an electronics firm, who makes $20,000 a year, and Ina, a twenty-one year old previously single assistant interior decorator, who makes $6300 a year;

(3) the Shulmans' contract, an agreement for adjustment of household and child-

---

2. Mannes and Sheresky, A Radical Guide to Wedlock, Saturday Review, July 29, 1972 at 33.

3. The provisions are divided up by topics; not all the provisions relating to each topic of each of the four contracts are included; nor are all the topics they cover represented here.

rearing obligations, written during marriage by a feminist free-lance writer and a man with a traditional office job, who had been married to each other ten years and had two children; and

(4) a contract by Lenore Weitzman, a sociologist, an antenuptial agreement which includes options for group, homosexual, and term marriages.

a. Agreements About Housework and Child Care

THE LAW STUDENT'S CONTRACT
KNISELY, THE MARRIAGE CONTRACT, A BLUEPRINT
Res Ipsa Loquitur 34 (Fall 1971)

Assignment of responsibility for children for named period and recompense therefor. The parties hereby declare that the pleasures, duties, and responsibilities of raising the children of the marriage shall always be made mutual insofar as practicable, but that while each child of the marriage is less than __ years old, the primary responsibility for that child shall belong to _____, and for undertaking this sometimes onerous responsibility at the expense of other interests, said party shall be recompensed by _____ in whatever ways as are mutually agreeable, whether in real or personal property or in an understanding and compassion going far beyond that already required by the marriage itself. This recompense shall in no way diminish the responsibility of _____to provide for and assist _____ however possible in regaining as soon as possible that level of independence desired.

DONALD AND INA'S CONTRACT
MANNES AND SHERESKY
A RADICAL GUIDE TO WEDLOCK
Saturday Review, July 29, 1972 at 33[3a]

(c) It is the parties' present intention that Ina continue to work, health permitting, until such time as she may become pregnant. The parties have no exact intentions concerning the employment of Ina after the birth of any child or children, although Ina has expressed the feeling that simply caring for children would not be sufficiently stimulating to her. Donald's inclination at the present time is that he would prefer for Ina to discontinue any full-time employment if she had a child, but he would not insist upon it.

Both parties agree that any subsequent employment of Ina after the birth of a child should be such that it would permit her to spend reasonable periods of time with the child and that it should not entail any evening or weekend hours.

THE SHULMANS' CONTRACT
SHULMAN, A MARRIAGE AGREEMENT
Up From Under, August/September 1970 at 5[4]

As parents we believe we must share all responsibility for taking care of our children and home—not only the work, but the responsibility. At least during the first year of this agreement, *sharing responsibility* shall mean:

1. Dividing the *jobs* (see "Job Breakdown" below); and
2. Dividing the *time* (see "Schedule" below) for which each parent is responsible.

3a. Copyright © 1972 by the Saturday Review.

4. This agreement was reprinted in Edmiston, How to Write Your Own Marriage Contract, 1 Ms. Magazine, Spring 1972 at 72.

In principle, jobs should be shared equally, 50-50, but deals may be made by mutual agreement. If jobs and schedule are divided on any other than a 50-50 basis, then either party may call for a re-examination and redistribution of jobs or a revision of the schedule at any time. Any deviation from 50-50 must be for the convenience of both parties. If one party works overtime in any domestic job, she/he must be compensated by equal extra work by the other. For convenience, the schedule may be flexible, but changes must be formally agreed upon. The terms of this agreement are rights and duties, not privileges and favors.

II. JOB BREAKDOWN

(A) Children

1. Mornings: Waking children; getting their clothes out, making their lunches; seeing that they have notes, homework, money, passes, books, etc.; brushing their hair; giving them breakfast; making coffee for us.

2. Transportation: Getting children to and from lessons, doctors, dentists, friends' houses, park, parties, movies, library, etc. Making appointments.

3. Help: Helping with homework, personal problems, projects like cooking, making gifts, experiments, planting, etc.; answering questions, explaining things.

4. Nighttime: Getting children to take baths, brush their teeth, go to bed, put away their toys and clothes; reading with them; tucking them in and having night-talks; handling if they wake and call in the night.

5. Babysitters: Getting babysitters, which sometimes takes an hour of phoning.

6. Sickcare: Calling doctors, checking out symptoms, getting prescriptions filled, remembering to give medicine, taking days off to stay home with sick child; providing special activities.

7. Weekends: All above, plus special activities (beach, park, zoo, etc.).

(B) Housework

8. Cooking: Breakfasts; dinners; (children, parents, guests).

9. Shopping: Food for all meals; housewares; clothing and supplies for children.

10. Cleaning: Dishes daily; apartment weekly, bi-weekly, or monthly.

11. Laundry: Home laundry; making beds; drycleaning (take and pick up).

III. SCHEDULE

(The numbers on the following schedule refer to Job Breakdown list.)

1. Mornings: Every other week each parent does all.

2. and 3. Transportation and Help: Parts occurring between 3:00 and 6:30 pm, fall to wife. She must be compensated (see 10 below). Husband does all weekend transportation and pickups after 6:00. The rest is split.

4. Nighttime (and all Help after 6:30): Husband does Tuesday, Thursday, and Sunday. Wife does Monday, Wednesday, and Saturday. Friday is split according to who has done extra work during the week.

5. Babysitters must be called by whoever the sitter is to replace. If no sitter turns up, the parent whose night it is to take responsibility must stay home.

6. Sickcare: This must still be worked out equally, since now wife seems to do it all. (The same goes for the now frequently declared school closings for so-called political protest, whereby the mayor gets credit at the expense of the mothers of young children. The mayor only closes the schools, not the places of business or the government offices.)

7. Weekends: Split equally. Husband is free all of Saturday, wife is free all of Sunday, except that the husband does all weekend transportation, breakfasts, and special shopping.

8. Cooking: Wife does all dinners except Sunday nights; husband does all weekend breakfasts (including shopping for them and dishes), Sunday dinner, and any other

dinners on his nights of responsibility if wife isn't home. Breakfasts are divided week by week. Whoever invites the guests does shopping, cooking, and dishes; if both invite them, split work.

9. Shopping: Divide by convenience. Generally, wife does local daily food shopping, husband does special shopping for supplies and children's things.

10. Cleaning: Husband does all the house-cleaning, in exchange for wife's extra childcare (3:00 to 6:30 daily) and sick care. Dishes: same as 4.

11. Laundry: Wife does most home laundry. Husband does all dry cleaning delivery and pick up. Wife strips beds, husband remakes them.

b. Financial Arrangements

THE LAW STUDENT'S CONTRACT
KNISELY, THE MARRIAGE CONTRACT (cont.)

Real and Personal Property

A. The parties hereby agree that all real and personal property acquired after the date of their marriage, and all rents and profits derived from property acquired prior to the marriage, shall be held jointly as community property, and the parties further agree to manage jointly or separately all matters relating to the acquisition, use, and disposition of each share of said community property, real and personal.

B. The parties hereby express their manifest intention to discuss openly and frankly all things, especially any differences or prospective differences concerning the aforementioned community. . . .

C. The parties hereby agree . . . that each party is entitled to a regular and equitable share of the joint disposable income, for which shares they shall in no way be accountable to each other, and that the size of this share, or allowance, is a matter which shall be openly discussed and jointly agreed upon as described in Section B, supra.

D. The parties hereby recognize the need for current wills to aid in the distribution of the joint property upon death of either party, and agree to execute new wills at intervals not exceeding five years.

Contractual Relationships

The parties hereby agree to consult with each other in all contractual matters which have a substantial impact on either party or upon the marriage itself; this shall include any and all purchases (exclusive of those made from the allowances, . . . supra) costing more than $100.00. More particularly, and by way of example and not limitation, parties agree to attempt to seek mutual agreement as to the location, employer, and hours to be worked for each job of each party, and the location, type, and price of the housing to be enjoyed by the parties, including the decision whether to rent or to buy, and the type, brand, cost and frequency of purchase of any and all automobiles to be purchased or leased by either party.

SHULMAN, A MARRIAGE AGREEMENT (cont.)

[Preface: Our agreement is designed for our particular situation only in which my husband works all day at a job of his choice, and I work at home on a free-lance basis during the hours the children are in school (from 8:30 till 3:00). . . .

Now, as my husband makes much more money than I do, he pays for most of our expenses.]

I. PRINCIPLES

We reject the notion that the work which brings in more money is the more valuable. The ability to earn more money is already a privilege which must not be compounded by enabling the larger earner to buy out of his/her duties and put the burden on the one who earns less, or on someone hired from outside.

We believe that each member of the family has an equal right to his/her own time, work, value, choices. As long as all duties are performed, each person may use his/her extra time any way he/she chooses. If he/she wants to use it making money, fine. If he/she wants to spend it with spouse, fine. If not, fine.

WEITZMAN'S CONTRACT
WEITZMAN, A PROPOSAL FOR LEGAL PARTNERSHIPS
Unpublished manuscript, U. Calif.-Davis (March 1972)[4a]

Control of the Community Property

The partners will elect the way in which they choose to handle the management and control of community property. Several suggestions for how this may be done follow:

a. All community property and income may be managed and controlled jointly (by the entire membership in a group marriage).

b. Expenses for running the household could be deducted from income accrued each year, and the remaining property split equally among the partners. Each partner would then have exclusive management and control of [her or his] property. . . .

c. If the marriage consists of more than three people the group might wish to designate or hire someone to handle the day to day management of the community property.

d. In the case in which option b is elected, expenses for the normal maintenance of the household and the partnership would be deducted from the income and community property before individual shares are prorated. . . .

1. rent, electric, gas, telephone
2. cleaning expenses
3. child care (more on this later)
4. health, accident and other medical insurance
5. social security payments (based on share of earnings)
6. Pension plan: part of the partnership income might go into an insurance plan—or be held in trust—with annuity payable later. . . .

c. Termination of the Contract

WEITZMAN'S CONTRACT
WEITZMAN, A PROPOSAL FOR LEGAL PARTNERSHIPS
(cont.)

Grounds for Termination

a. Partners could write their own provisions for the termination of the contract.

b. They might contract to a distribution of specific items in the community property, so long as the overall distribution was equitable.

4a. This is a summary of a much longer article, Weitzman, Legal Regulation of the Marriage Contract: Tradition and Change; A Proposal for Individual Contracts and Contracts-In-Lieu of Marriage, 62 Calif. L. Rev. — (June, 1974).

Fee for Termination

a. Partners might contract for a termination fee to be paid upon dissolution to the non-income earning partner (or to the partner with less income earning power).

1. For example, if, as part of the agreement a woman chooses to forgo further education and career opportunities to stay home and care for the children and household, it might be stipulated that she receive a lump sum termination fee to compensate for her loss in earning ability for the sake of the marriage.

2. Or, for example, if one partner supports the other through school, and the marriage then terminates, the receiving partner may then be obligated to reimburse the first one for the educational expenses.

b. Alternatively, the partners might contract for a termination fee to be paid by the partner who wishes to dissolve the partnership before a certain date/after a certain date/or whenever they specify. . . .

c. Partners might want to insure the termination fee, or buy a bond to guarantee it, etc.

d. Partners may specify that the termination fee must be paid as a lump sum, over time, etc.

e. The termination fee agreement would be treated as any other enforceable financial contract.

The State's interest in Dissolution

a. The state shall not determine any grounds for dissolution.

b. Any individual may apply for separation from the family. In the case of a two person marriage this would imply the dissolution of the marriage. . . .

DONALD AND INA'S CONTRACT
MANNES AND SHERESKY
A RADICAL GUIDE TO WEDLOCK (cont.)

Article IV. Future Support

(a) In the event that either party desires a separation (by mutual agreement or legal decree) or a divorce during the first five years of marriage, provided there is no surviving child born of the marriage, neither party will request support from the other unless he or she is in dire need thereof, and then only for such temporary periods as may be deemed necessary in accordance with Article VIII hereof.

(b) If either party desires to separate after the first five years of marriage or if, at the time of a request for separation during the first five years, a child of the marriage is alive, either party may request support, which shall be granted or denied by arbitration in accordance with Article VIII hereof. . . . [A list of factors to be considered by the arbitrator, bearing on need, fault, earning capacity and other obligations (e.g., to Donald's son by a prior marriage) are omitted.]

Article VI. Future Ownership of Property

(a) Donald and Ina have agreed that all property now standing in the name of either shall continue to be held in the individual names of the parties owning such property.

(b) Upon the marriage of Donald and Ina, they will create a joint-checking account and a joint-savings account to which each shall contribute in the same proportion as their earnings shall bear to each other. In the event that either party decides to seek a separation or divorce within a period of thirty-six months from the date of their marriage or at any time prior to the birth of a child, the proceeds of such checking and savings accounts shall be divided in the same proportion in which such funds were contributed by the parties. If either party seeks a separation or divorce after the birth of a child or at the end of said thirty-six-month period, whichever is earlier, such proceeds shall be divided between the parties equally.

(c) In the event that Ina is unable to find employment or is involuntarily unemployed or is unable to work during a period of maternity or illness, her contributions to the joint funds during the period of such unemployment, illness, or maternity shall be deemed to have been made in direct proportion to the contributions previously made by her during the period immediately preceding such unemployment, illness, or maternity.

(d) All questions concerning the investment of the joint funds of Donald and Ina in securities or real estate shall be decided jointly by the parties, and the ownership and division of such real or personal property should be made in accordance with paragraphs (a) and (c) hereof.

(e) The parties do not contemplate a different division of property, real or personal, whether or not either or both may later be guilty of any marital misconduct as defined by the laws of the State of Illinois. Any property not held in accordance with the terms of this article by either of the parties shall be deemed to be held in trust for the other party, and no additional private or oral understanding between the parties concerning the division of property between them is to be deemed valid until agreed to in writing in accordance with paragraph (f) hereof.

(f) In the event that either Donald or Ina subsequently wishes to change the rules by which their property shall be divided, the party desiring such change shall notify the other in writing and by registered mail at least one hundred and twenty days prior to such proposed change. If the other party does not wish to make such change, he or she may notify the other party in writing within the one hundred and twenty days. The matter shall be resolved by arbitration in accordance with the terms of Article VIII hereof. In making a determination the arbitrator shall fully inquire into the facts and circumstances surrounding the reasons for the proposed change. No modification of existing financial arrangements shall be made if it is determined that a substantial reason for such proposed change is that the party seeking modification has the imminent expectation of coming into a sudden period of prosperity from which the other party is to be excluded. The arbitrator may consider such other factors as he wishes in order to do substantial justice between the parties, but he may not order that any modification of the rules by which the parties have agreed to divide the property be made retroactive to the period preceding the written request for modification.

Article VII. Matters of Estate

After thirty-six months of marriage each party agrees to leave the other at least 40 percent of his or her entire estate, and each agrees to make no attempt to assign, transfer, or otherwise dispose of, without valuable consideration, any portion of his or her estate with the intention of depriving the other of the benefits of this agreement.

d. Children and Sexual Relations

THE LAW STUDENT'S CONTRACT
KNISELY, THE MARRIAGE CONTRACT *(cont.)*

Alternative "c": Current intention to have issue. The parties to this marriage contract, _____ and _____, do hereby freely and mutually declare their agreement that healthy and happy children are a reasonable, valid and joyous product of their union, but that the spacing of the births of said children is a matter of valid concern to all parties, and to that end the methods of contraception to be used by each party prior to the birth of the last expected child unless otherwise agreed shall be:

party:_____   method:_____
party:_____   method:_____

Further, the parties agree that after the birth of the last expected child, the methods of contraception to be used by each party unless otherwise agreed shall be:

party:_____   method:_____
party:_____   method:_____

Marriage as monogamous.

Choose one alternative:

Alternative "a": The parties hereby declare that their marriage is based on strict, mutual monogamy.

Alternative "b": The parties hereby declare that their marriage is not based on strict, mutual monogamy, and in this regard is subject to separate agreement between them.

DONALD AND INA'S CONTRACT
MANNES AND SHERESKY
A RADICAL GUIDE TO WEDLOCK (cont.)

(d) Both Donald and Ina have expressed opposition to adultery. Donald has stated he would immediately divorce Ina if such an act occurred on her part, regardless of the circumstances. Ina has said that, although she does not wish to solicit such conduct on the part of Donald, nevertheless she is unable to determine her attitude toward adultery on Donald's part in advance of knowing what the circumstances might be. If the act were an isolated "meaningless' episode, Ina's opinion is that she would rather not know of it because she does not know how it would affect her relationship with Donald.

Both parties have agreed that in the event either engages in any serious or prolonged affair with anyone else, he or she is under an obligation to disclose that fact to the other.

Both Donald and Ina believe that their sex life together is sufficiently pleasurable and knowledgeable at present so that no serious adjustment need be made by either. Ina has expressed the belief that her sex life with Donald will become more pleasurable, and somewhat less tense, after marriage and after each party has had more "experience" with each other. She denied, however, having any apprehension concerning future sexual relations with Donald.

(e) The parties intend to have two or three children of their own. It is their desire to have such children sometime after the next two years, although the possibility of having a child prior to that time does not cause any particular anxiety in either of them. In the event Ina becomes accidentally pregnant the parties' present inclination is to have such a child and not seek an abortion. Both parties feel, however, that any decision on abortion should be left entirely to the discretion of Ina.

Donald and Ina have discussed and have rejected the following notions: marriage of limited duration, separate vacations, separate beds, divorce by reason of the physical incapacity of the other, divorce by reason of the inability of Ina to bear children.

WEITZMAN'S CONTRACT
WEITZMAN, A PROPOSAL FOR LEGAL PARTNERSHIPS
(cont.)

Sexual Access

Sexual relations might not be governed at all by the marriage contract. Thus, adultery would not in any way violate the contract. Sexual relations would be subject to the consent of individual participants (whether marital partners or not) in each individual interaction. This would also eliminate the current doctrine that a husband "can't" rape his wife. Some marital partners may want the security and exclusive commitment of sexual monogamy. They might wish to contract for this, with specific penalties to be imposed for failure to live up to the agreement.

Responsibility for Children

a. Some partnerships might want to agree beforehand not to have any children or to agree initially not to have children, but to allow the option of periodic review of the decision.

[Partners should specify responsibility for birth control, contingency plans and responsibility should birth control fail, financial responsibility for an abortion if necessary, and for maternity costs, compensation, and arrangements. If a woman agrees to an abortion in advance and later changes her mind, the contract might then provide for her to assume the major responsibility for maternity and child care costs.]

b. All partners might agree to be equally responsible for the care and support of the children. In this case they would probably agree to be responsible to provide for the child's support even after marital dissolution. Such support would be irrespective of custody, and could be guaranteed by each partner by a signed "wage deduction" statement, security of personal property, etc.

c. Partners might agree that specific people would be responsible for the child's support exclusively. One might expect this situation to arise more frequently in a large group marriage in which not all partners want to be equally responsible for children. On the other hand, the partnership might stipulate that only those who agree to responsibility can enter the partnership.

d. Partners might agree that specific people would be responsible for the care of the child for the first 5 (?) years. The responsibility for care is distinct from that of support, but both provide crucial areas of concern for the partnership.

e. In the case of option d, the partners might want to write a presumption for custody in favor of the caretaker if the partnership dissolves while the child is young.

f. Provisions with regard to support and maintenance of the children may or may not take into consideration biological parenthood, at the option of the contracting parties.

3. The Value of Marriage Contracts

Is it anomalous that the parties can agree on their separation and divorce relations and not on the terms of their marriage? The justification is, of course, that the parties deal at arm's length during predivorce negotiations and not during marriage. But, proponents of marriage contracts argue that spouses and prospective spouses need to be more hardheaded, or at least more open with each other about the details of their relationship, and that a formal contract would encourage this result.

But notice the number of unresolved issues in the law student's and Donald and Ina's contracts, as contrasted to that of the Shulmans. The law student argued that "no contract can succeed which attempts to detail who will do the supper dishes every Tuesday for fifty years."[5] Yet apparently it is the recurrence of this kind of issue which prompts already married couples to make formal agreements.[6] Perhaps a reasonable contract can only be drafted after a period of living together.

5. Knisely, supra, at 33.

6. In addition to the Shulman's contract, supra, see also Burton, I'm Running Away from Home but I'm Not Allowed to Cross the Street (1972), as excerpted in 1 Ms. Magazine, February 1973 at 73, 75; Edmiston, supra, at 66-72; and Bernard, The Future of Marriage ch. 5 (1972).

How much impact do you think a formal agreement before marriage can have on the behavior of marriage partners? Would a formal agreement inhibit the woman who thinks at the outset of marriage that she would like to care for children full time and later discovers that she is equally committed to her career and wants her husband to take on equal childcare responsibilities? How likely do you think it is that the majority of people will take the trouble or have the mind-set to write their own marriage contracts?

McDowell studied attempts by married couples to adjust their obligations through formal contracts and found that the vast majority of agreements did not reach the courts until after the marriage had dissolved.[7] One could surmise from this fact that the contracts had little effect on the marriage while it lasted. Yet legal enforcement is not necessarily the measure of the value of contracts during the marriage. Making a contract causes the parties to discuss issues and to reach agreement before failure to communicate destroys the marriage. A contract may also change the day-to-day balance of power and responsibility; a wife who knows that she and her husband have a written agreement that she owns half of his income could well feel freer to spend it. If her husband is unwilling for her to control one half his salary, they could agree to share housework so that each can earn a salary. Finally, a contract negotiated before or during marriage, enforced by arbitration between the two partners during cohabitation and by the courts upon dissolution, may be the fairest basis for resolving the relationship of the couple.

But as to the argument that the contract will promote more egalitarian relationships during marriage, remember the studies showing that the husbands of working wives did not do a significantly larger share of the housework than husbands of wives who do not work. In other words, women who had greater economic independence did not necessarily have more egalitarian relationships as to household responsibilities. On the other hand, the studies have not been uniform in this finding. Several have suggested that not only does the division of household tasks become more egalitarian, but also that the husband's power increases in relation to decision making in areas associated with the role of housewife, while the working wife's power increases in relation to major economic decisions.[8] Do you think that the amount of money the wife makes and the prestige of her job affect the husband's willingness to take over some of the household services she would otherwise perform? In that case, an end to sex discrimination in the labor market would be crucial to changing sex roles in marriage.

4. The State's Interest in the Contract

Would it be a good idea for the state to require that people desiring to marry prepare and file with the clerk of the court a detailed marriage contract as a condition of receiving a marriage license? In other words, does the state have an interest in encouraging or enforcing contracts made before or during marriage? The answer may be yes, if one accepts the proposition that frank antenuptial negotiations would discourage people from making mistakes in marriage, and thus lower the divorce rates.[9] Fewer divorces would also mean that there would be fewer single-parent families.[10] If a high

7. McDowell, Contracts in the Family, 45 Boston U. L. Rev. 43, 52 (1965), reporting that, at the time of suit, the marital relationship had ended by divorce or death of one of the spouses in 70 percent of the reported suits to enforce "adjustment of obligations" agreements between spouses.

8. See Nye and Hoffman, The Employed Mother in America, Part III (1963), especially Blood, The Husband-Wife Relationship 282, 285-295.

9. See also Bradway, Why Pay Alimony? 32 Ill. L. Rev. 301, 303 (1937), infra, Part VII, ascribing a similar deterrent effect to divorce insurance.

10. Of course, single-parent families also result from sexual relations outside marriage. As the section on welfare demonstrates, most states take the position that forcing people to get married and stay married, or to support their sexual partners and children if they are not married, is a good way to minimize welfare costs. This view of the state's interest is not affected one way or the other by encouraging and enforcing private

divorce rate and nontraditional family structures are considered to be social costs, the state may have some interest in using its powers to promote contracts between parties.

In arguing for state support of privately designed marriage contracts, Knisely writes:[11]

> At the present time, the state interest in marriage centers around three goals: (1) assuring children of their physical necessities, (2) reducing or eliminating profligate, immoral behavior, and (3) attempting to assure that no party to a marriage will be left as a public charge, as long as the other party can support him. The state interest is pursued by preserving all or nearly all existing marriages, rather than by attempting to assure better marriages *ab initio*. . . .
>
> Now that there are greater expectations of marriage, the end structure is proving insufficient. Remedial law is ineffective compared with preventive law or social policy. . . .
>
> If there is a state interest in marriage, it should be in facilitating and fostering the preservation of healthy, happy marriages. Certainly in this era of expanding governmental benefits for individuals there is no reason to preserve a bad marriage on any economic grounds. The literature is full of references to the ill effects on children of parents staying together only "for the sake of the kids." Marriage does not seem much of a bar to profligate, immoral behavior, either, and there is certainly no proved nexus between such behavior and any legitimate state interest.
>
> In fact, one can argue that the legitimate state interest is to discourage a marriage if it is likely to prove unsuccessful; the divorce process is expensive, the time lost from economically productive activity during marital discord is surely more than that lost via immoral behavior, the children if any produced by an unsuccessful marriage may not prove as happy/productive/useful to the state as those produced by a successful marriage, and there is no dearth of children. If one can argue that a bad marriage is worse than no marriage at all, then the state should make marriage harder to get into and easier to get out of. . . .
>
> . . . [T]he state could be sure that all parties are informed about the current legal obligations resulting from marriage. . . .
>
> More important, the state should allow every individual couple to delineate for themselves the basic requirements of marriage; where not inconsistent with the state interest, they should specify their legal obligations as well. The state should have to demonstrate the undesirability of certain provisions in marriage contracts. Since the state is really providing the couple with what amounts to a contract of adhesion, it should be strictly construed against the state. . . .

B. ALTERATION OF THE ECONOMIC AND SOCIAL STRUCTURE OF THE HOUSEWIFE ROLE[12]

1. Introduction

The only change that makes sense is one that gradually embraces communal feeding, group dining rooms, kibbutz living and big commercial cleaning enterprises. Instead of bedmaking, we'll have big single sheets that you throw over the bed. In addition,

---

marriage contracts, except to the extent that antenuptial negotiations would encourage people to decide not to have children when they can not support them.

11. Knisely, The Marriage Contract: A Blueprint, Res Ipsa Loquitur, Fall 1971 at 33.

12. The term "housewife" is used throughout to highlight the fact that almost all of the people in this occupation are women. The authors do not, however, believe that this occupational sex segregation is desirable. Some of the proposals discussed in this section might increase the number of men performing this role, in which case a sex-neutral term would be desirable. "Housespouse" is one possibility, although the rhyming makes its widespread use unlikely.

you'll have men come through the house with large power vacuums and blow the dust off the joint once a week. But what's extremely important is communal eating. What there should be in New York is a whole series of apartments without dining rooms and without kitchens. Depending on the cost of the apartment, one dines either cafeteria style or in a dining room. This would eliminate shopping, washing up, meal planning and preparation — more than half of household work.[13]

The above proposal, made by John Kenneth Galbraith, obviously would require tremendous architectural and economic reorganization, as well as social change. Aside from these utopian aspects, what is especially interesting is the extent to which this proposal discounts the value of the personal service aspect of a housewife's work. The savings in human effort accomplished in Galbraith's scheme for the "abolition" of housework are accomplished through the substitution of impersonal service for personal service. Although the amount of human effort required to maintain each individual is lower in the centralized system described by Galbraith than in the present system of nuclear households, this is in part because the extra effort involved in tailoring those services to each individual's needs has been eliminated.

In the article excerpted below, Galbraith discusses the value to the economy of the housewife's work, which he calls the management of consumption. In terms of the analysis he presents, consider what the impact on the economy would be of simplifying and industrializing housework.

GALBRAITH
HOW THE ECONOMY HANGS ON HER APRON STRINGS
2 Ms. Magazine 74, 75 (May 1974)

The decisive contribution of women in the developed industrial society is rather simple — or at least it becomes so, once the disguising myth is dissolved. It is, overwhelmingly, to facilitate a continuing and more or less unlimited increase in consumption.

The test of success in modern economic society is the annual rate of increase in Gross National Product. . . .

Increasing production, in turn, strongly reflects the needs of the dominant economic interest. The most powerful interest in modern economic society is the modern great corporation. . . .

Economic growth requires manpower, capital, and materials for increased production. It also — a less celebrated point — requires increased consumption, and if population is relatively stable this must be increased per capita consumption. . . . And there is a further and an equally unimpeachable truth which, in economics at least, has been celebrated scarcely at all: just as the production of goods and services requires management or administration, so does their consumption. The one is not greatly less essential than the other. The higher the standard of living — that is to say, the larger the house, the more numerous the automobiles, the more elaborate the attire, the more competitive and costly the social rites — the more demanding the administration.

In earlier times, this administration was the function of a subordinate and menial servant class. Industrialization, to its great credit, everywhere liquidates this class. . . . [I]t is an absolute imperative that substitute administrative talent be found. This, in the modern industrial societies — the nonsocialist societies in any case — is the vital function that women have now been induced to perform.

13. John Kenneth Galbraith, quoted in Edmiston, While We're at It, What About Maids' Lib?, New York Magazine, June 28, 1971, 24 at 30.

In the remainder of his article, Galbraith argues that consumption by the "upper-bracket housewife" is particularly important for maintaining consumption throughout the economy. He then discusses the means by which this economic function is concealed from women: the identification of increased consumption with increasing happiness; the practice of ignoring the tasks and costs associated with consumption; the avoiding of any accounting of the housewife's contribution to the economy; and the use of the concept of the household to obscure the division of roles between the spouses according to which the wife bears the burden of managing consumption and the husband makes the decisions about the level of consumption which they will reach.

The following two subsections of this section are devoted to discussing the viability of paying wages for housework, and the possible consequences of such a wage system. In reading them, consider the implications of Galbraith's analysis of the larger social and economic function of the housewife's role as consumption manager.

2. Wages for Housewives

Over 75 years ago, Charlotte Perkins Gilman thoroughly debunked the idea that wives earn their support as economically independent beings, either by helping their husbands in their professions or by their work as housekeepers and nursemaids; her position is still valid today.

GILMAN, WOMEN AND ECONOMICS
11-15 (1898)[14]

. . . [I]n the closest interpretation, individual economic independence among human beings means that the individual pays for what he gets . . . gives to the other an equivalent for what the other gives him. . . .

Women consume economic goods. What economic product do they give in exchange for what they consume? . . . A man happy and comfortable can produce more than one unhappy and uncomfortable, but this is as true of a father or a son as of a husband. To take from a man any of the conditions which make him happy and strong is to cripple his industry. . . . But those relatives who make him happy are not therefore his business partners. . . .

Grateful return for happiness conferred is not the method of exchange in a partnership. The comfort a man takes with his wife is not in the nature of a business partnership, nor are her frugality and industry. A housekeeper, in her place, might be as frugal, as industrious, but would not therefore be a partner. . . .

If the wife is not, then, truly a business partner, in what way does she earn from her husband the food, clothing and shelter she receives at his hands? By house service, it will be instantly replied. . . .

. . . The labor of women in the house, certainly, enables men to produce more wealth than they otherwise could; and in this way women are economic factors in society. But so are horses.

. . . [T]he horse is not economically independent, nor is the woman. If a man plus a valet can perform more useful service than he could minus a valet, then the valet is performing a useful service. But, if the valet is the property of the man, is obligated to perform this service, and is not paid for it, he is not economically independent. . . .

To take this ground and hold it honestly, wives, as earners through domestic service, are entitled to the wages of cooks, housemaids, nursemaids, seamstresses, or housekeepers, and to no more. This would of course reduce the spending money of the wives of the rich, and put it out of the power of the poor man to "support" a wife at

14. This book is also available in a Harper Torchbook edition, published in 1966.

all, unless, indeed, the poor man faced the situation fully, paid his wife her wages as house servant, and then she and he used their funds in support of their children. He would be keeping a servant; she would be helping keep the family. But nowhere on earth would there be "a rich woman" by these means. Even the highest class of private housekeeper, useful as her services are, does not accumulate a fortune. She does not buy diamonds and sables and keep a carriage. Things like these are not earned by house service.

But the salient fact in this discussion is that, whatever the economic value of the domestic industry of women is, they do not get it. The women who do the most work get the least money, and the women who have the most money do the least work. Their labor is neither given nor taken as a factor in economic exchange. It is held to be their duty as women to do this work; and their economic status bears no relation to their domestic labors, unless an inverse one. . . .

To be the only workers operating under a status-based system in a wage labor economy is at best an uncomfortable position. The difficult question is whether it is possible or desirable to substitute wage payments for support payments. Although systems for paying housewives have been outlined in broad terms, there have been no concrete proposals with supporting economic analyses. Jessie Bernard suggests, for instance, that wives could be paid from some fund like Social Security, to which the husband's employer contributed.[15] Scott proposes that:[16]

> . . . the law assure the wife a salary for the housework she performs. This salary would reflect the value of her individual services, what she could be earning in the labor market, or the official minimum wage. She could receive a percentage of her husband's salary to be paid by him or paid directly by his employer in the same way as the military sends allotment checks to the wives of servicemen who are stationed overseas. If she is paid by her husband, her salary would not be subject to tax, since it was already taxed once when the husband received it. Since the husband would in fact be the "employer," he would be expected to pay the basic household expenses of food, clothing, and shelter, allowing his wife to spend her salary as she chose, on her own personal needs, on her family, savings, or investment. If she worked outside the home and did all the housework, too, she would get paid for both jobs. If a husband and wife each did half of the housework, they would receive no household salary, or they could split a salary. A husband who refused to pay his wife for housework could be taken to domestic court for a determination of her proper salary.

Or, even more simply, the government could simply make payments to the women of the country for housework.[17]

There are practical and conceptual problems with each idea. Payment by the husband does not really differ from the present system. While wage contracts could be made enforceable during marriage, people would be reluctant to litigate during an ongoing marriage, and a woman's ability to negotiate a decent salary for herself would be determined by her husband's income and achievements rather than by her own ability at the job. Few men earn enough money to pay even the minimum wage for a 40-hour week of housework and child care (in 1973, $3,328 a year at $1.60 an hour), much less

15. Bernard, supra, at 258.

16. A. C. Scott, The Value of Housework: For Love or Money?, Ms. Magazine, July 1972 at 56, 57-58.

17. This suggestion was made, for instance, by Tillmon, Welfare Is A Women's Issue, Ms. Magazine, Spring 1972, reprinted in Klagsburn, ed., The First Ms. Reader 51 (1973). See also the similar proposals in Report of the Marriage and Family Committee of the National Organization for Women, Suggested Guidelines in Studying and Comments on the Uniform Marriage and Divorce Act 2 (1971); Ross, The Rights of Women 267-274 (1973); Warrior, Slavery or Labor of Love, in Koedt and Firestone, Notes from the Third Year 68, 70-71 (1971). Cf. Benston, The Political Economy of Women's Liberation, reprinted in Tanner (ed.), Voices from Women's Liberation 281-282 (1970), and Mitchell, Woman's Estate, Part II (1971).

salaries based on estimates of the true value of the work. Finally, what about women in the occupation "housewife" who do not have spouses to pay them?

Having employers pay the wives of their employees would create a high disproportion between the cost of employing a single and a married person. Also, women without husbands or with unemployed husbands would not be covered.

Because of the high cost, any government program would probably provide payments only to poor and husbandless women, which means that the same political and economic factors which depress welfare payments would also keep down housewives' wages. Payments only to the poor might also encourage dissolution and nonformation of families among the poor and working class.[18]

Perhaps most fundamentally, payment to housewives would not necessarily eliminate the major problems with the occupation itself. The job has long hours, isolated working conditions, few vacations or breaks, and little chance for promotion. Experience qualifies the worker for few other jobs. Decent pay might help solve the problem of long hours and lack of vacations because women could use some of their new income to hire substitutes, and additional income would enable housewives to pay for further job training after their children leave home, or to work part time while their young children were in day care. The isolated working conditions, the monotony of many of the tasks, and the dead-end job structure would remain for both paid housewives and domestic workers, as for employees in many other jobs. Thus, it might be that paying housewives would only reinforce the tendency in modern times to force people into boring repetitive tasks. And it would have the additional disadvantage of institutionalizing the concept of women's work, effecting, for instance, the continuation of the system in which the father is uninvolved in child care; he could leave the responsibility entirely to the newly compensated mother.[19]

On the other hand, paying housewives would have such profound effects on the society that it is difficult to draw definite conclusions. If the wages were high, the pay for women's work in general might be driven up, so that it would become attractive for men to stay home. Whatever the wage, there would be increased status for housewives as a result of the use of wage rather than support concepts.

The method of payment would also make a difference. If women were paid only if they did their own housework, the disincentive effect on women taking outside jobs would be considerable. If, however, the government paid for all housework by vouchers, so that housewives could choose to do their own work or use the vouchers to pay someone else, the system could be made neutral as to the choice between staying home and working at an outside job. Such a neutral system could have other positive effects on the professionalization of domestic work; Susan Edmiston has pointed out that under the present system[20]

> The status of the professional household worker derives inevitably from the status of housewives: the professional must compete with unpaid labor, and therefore the wage at which she prices herself out of the market is very low. Improvements sufficient to make this occupation attractive to other than "cast-off" women will cost so much that the number of people able to afford it will be reduced even further. Potential consumers will simply turn back to the free labor available in their own homes; every housewife is a potential scab, willing to moonlight at two jobs, if necessary.

Wages for housewives might also mitigate the impact of divorce on women who have performed the traditional role. Having received incomes during marriage, they might have assets with which to cushion the impact of divorce.

18. For a discussion of the theory of income maximization and the current welfare system, see Bernstein, Welfare in New York City, City Almanac, February 1970 at 8-9.
19. Bernard, supra, at 258.
20. Edmiston, supra, at 30.

3. The Value of Housework

Deciding how much housewives would be paid is important for developing realistic proposals for wages for housework, and for ascertaining the overall cost of such proposals. Even if no system of pay for housewives is ever adopted, it is important to estimate the worth of their work, both because it will make the society more conscious of the work's value, and because accurate estimates will assist women in making trade-offs between working at home and taking outside jobs. Also, if it is possible to estimate the value of housework, the aggregate amount could be added into the gross national product, thus eliminating the bias which results from including the value of women's services when they work outside the home and not their nonmarket work within it.[21] A close look at the true value of housework might also be useful in arguing for other reforms which would improve women's situations, such as federally subsidized day care, modified community property systems, tax reforms, and favorable welfare work regulations.

In a classic free market model, each employee negotiates with her or his employer about the prices to be paid and the services to be rendered. But the market mechanism will not work for setting housewives' wages. First, since no such market now exists, initial estimates must be made in some other way. Second, the amount, type, and quality of work done by housewives is profoundly affected by personal and familial considerations. Thus, although housewives vary in the quality and quantity of work they do, the consumers of their services would be unlikely to hire or fire them on this basis. Furthermore, if a system of payment by government vouchers existed, the interests of the housewives, spouses, and children would be in obtaining the highest possible wages from the government for the housework, not in establishing a fair return for the work. Of course, all wages are often influenced by factors outside the traditional market model, such as oligopoly and monopoly power (including unionization of employees), state regulation (such as minimum wage laws or licensing), and personal relationships between the parties. Nonetheless, housewifery is extreme in the degree to which a system of individual bargaining for wages is not viable.

One alternative to individual negotiations would be collective bargaining between housewives and the government, with wages varying in relation to standardized measures of quantity and quality of work done, such as numbers of children, years in the occupation, and skill levels. However, such a system would be more a matter of political bargaining, like that involved in setting social security payment levels, than a market process which would accurately reflect the relative value of housework in the economy.

Assuming that market determination of wages for housework is not a likely possibility, some other means must be found for attaching a reasonable value to the work which housewives do. There are two major possibilities: determining the replacement cost of housework; and ascertaining the value which housewives and their families place on their work, by noting what salaries are sufficient to induce them to take jobs outside the home. For calculations of the first type, there are several sources. Included here are calculations made by Chase Manhattan Bank economists, geared toward determining the error in GNP which results from the exclusion of housework (Table 3-1); the results of a study by Cornell researchers on time spent on housework and its value; and a selection from a lawyers' handbook on wrongful death tort actions, on how to prove the value and replacement costs of a housewife's services. These are followed by Kreps' calculations of the value of housework, based on the salaries that various housewives forgo as a result of choosing not to work for pay. Kreps hypothesizes that these salaries may be seen as the maximum value placed on a housewife's services by the wife and her family.

---

21. Kreps, Sex in the Marketplace: American Women at Work 66-68 (1971).

TABLE 3–1. WOMAN'S WORK

Job	Hours per week	Rate per hour	Value per week
Nursemaid	44.5	$2.00	$89.00
Dietitian	1.2	4.50	5.40
Food buyer	3.3	3.50	11.55
Cook	13.1	3.25	42.58
Dishwasher	6.2	2.00	12.40
Housekeeper	17.5	3.25	56.88
Laundress	5.9	2.50	14.75
Seamstress	1.3	3.25	4.22
Practical nurse	.6	3.75	2.25
Maintenance man	1.7	3.00	5.10
Gardener	2.3	3.00	6.90
Chauffeur	2.0	3.25	6.50
TOTAL			$257.53
			or $13,391.56 a year*

Source: Scott, The Value of Housework: For Love or Money?, Ms. Magazine, July 1972 at 59. Compiled by Chase Manhattan Bank, 1972.

*Considerably more than what 83.8 percent of all American workers were able to earn in 1970.

WALKER AND GAUGER
THE DOLLAR VALUE OF HOUSEHOLD WORK
Department of Consumer Economics and Public Policy,
N.Y. State College of Human Ecology, Cornell Univ. at 5, 9 (1973)

[Using a survey of almost 1400 families in upstate New York, Walker and Gauger calculated the monetary value of average time contributions of family members to household operations when the wife worked outside the home and when she did not, broken down by the ages and number of children.]

To put a monetary value on time contributed by family members it was necessary to assign wage rates to these hours.

In deriving hourly values for pricing various household work tasks, we identified workers in the marketplace who perform services similar to the household tasks normally engaged in by family members. These workers included cooks, dishwashers, cleaning women, "handymen," washing-machine operators, laundry workers, clothing-maintenance specialists, child-care women, homemaker aides and accounting clerks. Then we obtained wage rates for each task by contacting public and private employment agencies in central New York State and by consulting publications of the United States Bureau of Labor Statistics. In 1971, when these wage rates were obtained, rates for the various job categories in the Syracuse, New York, area ranged from $1.65 per hour for a dishwasher to $2.50 an hour for a cleaning woman. Those paid at $1.85 per hour included washing-machine operator, clothing-maintenance specialist and homemaker aide. The hourly rate was $2.00 for a cook, presser and handyman; it was $2.33 and $2.40, respectively, for an accounting clerk and child-care woman. These rates would vary somewhat according to where a family lives.

Once hourly rates were assigned, we applied them to the amount of time spent by each family member in the 1,378 upstate New York families surveyed. The household tasks given a dollar value were marketing, management and record keeping; food preparation, aftermeal cleanup; house care and maintenance, yard and car care; washing, ironing and special care of clothing; physical and other care of family members.

Our dollar estimates of the value of household work were consistently conservative, and they provide a minimum estimate of value. Time spent in child care, for instance, was valued at the rates for a child-care woman, not at the rates for a worker with specialized education in child development. We attempted to assign what it would cost to hire someone to do the task in question, not what is would cost to replace the family member doing it. For instance, bill-paying and other money-management tasks might, in one family, be handled by a wife who is a licensed accountant, but we figured all such tasks at accounting-clerk pay rates. Another reason that the values estimated are conservative is that it would be difficult to hire someone at these rates for the relatively small amounts of time devoted to some of the tasks.

Families were categorized by the employment status of the wife, number of children and age of the youngest child (or in childless families the age of the wife). We calculated the money value of the contributions of husbands, wives and children 12 to 17 years old for each of the tasks.... Contributions of children 6 to 11 years of age were not calculated since both the quantity and quality of the work of this age group are hard to evaluate. The time given by older family members to teach the younger children to work was included as educational activities in the family care category, and time thus spent was priced for the older worker.

TABLE 3–2. AVERAGE WEEKLY DOLLAR VALUE OF TIME CONTRIBUTED
BY VARIOUS MEMBERS IN ALL HOUSEHOLD TASKS
(All values expressed to nearest dollar)

Number of children	Wife's age	Employed-wife households			Nonemployed-wife households		
		Wife	Husband	12–17 year-olds	Wife	Husband	12–17 year-olds
0	under 25	$50	$20	—	$74	$13	—
	25–39	53	20	—	86	17	—
	40–54	62	11	—	88	22	—
	55+	62	17	—	78	30	—
	Youngest child's age						
2	12–17	68	24	$17	107	25	$13
	6–11	79	23	14	108	24	11
	2–5	91	27	18	122	25	12
	1	94	55	*	132	26	*
	under 1	119	24	*	146	24	*
4	12–17	87	19	19	91	16	13
	6–11	79	14	11*	117	22	16
	2–5	*	*	*	135	22	12
	1	*	*	*	131	29	15
	under 1	*	*	*	161	32	*

*Averages not calculated because there were fewer than 4 cases.

[The research] shows that the value of household work for the wife tends to increase as the number of children increases. The age of the youngest child also has a strong effect, regardless of family size. Total household contributions of employed wives are less than that of their nonemployed counterparts. These daily values for family members were used to arrive at dollar estimates by the week, month and year.... [Table 3-2, reproduced here, shows the average weekly amount.][22]

22. Figures for households with 1 child, with 3 children, with 5-6 children, and with 7-9 children have been omitted. In all categories relating to families with 5 or more children, there were fewer than four or no cases of employed wives. — Eds.

SPEISER, RECOVERY FOR WRONGFUL DEATH,
ECONOMIC HANDBOOK
196-202 (1970)

§12:2. *The unemployed housewife.*

When we come to the matter of deceased unemployed housewives, we encounter unique problems. On the one hand, there is no doubt that an economic loss has been experienced by those survivors who were dependent upon the housewife's services.[1] But, on the other hand, not all of the lost values can be assessed using money as a measuring rod. The following items illustrate losses of valuable considerations that are not readily amenable to economic analysis and measurement: conjugal bliss (where compensable), companionship, custodianship of home and hearth. . . . The reason is clear: there is no market in which these values are traded and therefore no market price to use in their evaluation.

§12:3. *Lost service values of economic worth.*

Other lost values can and should be measured, with the caveat that there is so much overlapping among them that separate assessment of their worth is at least very difficult. Consider Table [3-3] of values that can be measured in money terms, but are very hard to separate out because a wife performs a combination of the services they represent,

TABLE [3-3]. ROLES OF WIFE AND MOTHER AND THEIR OCCUPATIONAL EQUIVALENTS

Roles assumed by a wife and mother	Similar occupations
Housekeeper	Household Worker, Domestic
Nurse	Registered Nurse, Practical Nurse
Counsellor	Teacher, Psychotherapist
Money manager	Bookkeeper, Accountant, Home Economist
Family chauffeur	Chauffeur, Taxi Driver
Mrs. "Fixit"	Carpenter, Plumber, Electrician
Cook	Cook, Chef, Dietician
Dishwasher	Dishwasher
Clothes-washer	Laundress, Laundry Worker

a combination that is not easily specified. The first column suggests some of the various roles usually assumed by a wife and mother; the second column shows an occupation whose earnings provide a close economic value equivalent, *provided a substitute could be hired at going market rates of pay to work the number of hours and the various hours required by the household.*

The nine roles and corresponding occupations are by no means exhaustive of a housewife's activities. Taken together, they simply illuminate some of the many facets of what being a housewife means. Moreover, the second column shows that it is feasible to state occupations for which wage equivalents can be found. There are, however, three major difficulties that may render dubious, at least in some instances, the use of this approach to the measurement of economic loss for a decedent housewife:

1. It is frequently difficult, sometimes impossible, to determine how many hours a day a housewife or mother spends in her various roles. On a given day, she may spend 6 hours as housekeeper, 10 minutes as nurse, 2 hours as cook, 18 minutes as chauffeur, and so on. On another day, the time allocated to different roles may change radically.

---

1. In the rare instances where a wife (and/or mother) was a slovenly or "worthless' housekeeper, a bad cook, and a poor companion, the surviving husband (and/or children) may have experienced no palpable loss from her demise. Less uncommonly, a wife (and/or mother) may have suffered during her lifetime from so severe an illness or disability that, aside from companionship, she was unable to perform the usual wifely (and/or motherly) chores. Here, again, the survivors may have incurred little or no measurable economic loss as a result of her death.

There may be little possibility of getting a meaningful norm or average. This means that supporting factual testimony of substance would be required.

2. If one attempted to hire persons for odd numbers of hours and fluctuating numbers of hours and minutes, the cost would be prohibitive. That is, one may hire a housekeeper for a *given* number of days or hours *each week* and expect to pay about $2.00 an hour in several of the suburbs of New York City in 1969. But one would have to pay that housekeeper a much higher hourly rate if he imposed the burden of working an hour and a half on Monday, seven hours on Tuesday, none on Wednesday, and so forth. Thus the typical rates of pay in the market might be deemed inapplicable to situations of employment where hours and days of employment would vary enormously.

3. The quality of the service rendered by a housewife determines the equivalent market grade within corresponding occupations. Specifically, this approach of fragmenting the services of a housewife in roles and occupations requires a decision that, in her role as, say, Nurse, decedent was the equivalent of an experienced practical nurse; as counsellor, like a psychiatric social worker; as Mrs. "Fixit", the equivalent of a mixture of apprentice carpenter, master plumber, and so on.

The conclusion is that the piecemeal reckoning of lost values for decedent housewives is not usually practical. A different approach is frequently called for.

§12:4. Sketch of a practical approach.

Of all the occupations women fill, the one that most nearly resembles, in outward appearance, the role of housewife is that of "Experienced Female Private Household Worker, Living In." As will be spelled out in the next section, this occupation can be the cornerstone upon which an evaluation of lost services can be based. Succinctly stated, the economic loss to survivors is estimated as the wages and social security payments required for a household worker over the period of the survivors life expectancies with appropriate allowance for wage trends, discounting to present value, and the time period during which survivors might fairly have been expected to have benefited from the housewife's services.

Suppose there are surviving minor children. Is not the value of a mother's care of her children greater than the value of the family's housekeeper? The answer is obviously yes. To make some allowance for this greater value, we may select an occupation that fairly resembles the role a mother fills in the raising of her children, namely, "Elementary School Teacher." Following this reasoning, we estimate the loss to the survivors as the wage earned by an Elementary School Teacher over the minority years of the children. Again, wage trends and discounting must be allowed for.

For a deceased woman who is survived by both husband and minor children, the two economic proof approaches to estimating the measures of loss may be combined. During the more demanding years when the children are being raised — for example, until the youngest reaches age 18 — decedent's services would be valued as equivalent to the earnings of a school teacher. Thereafter, for the remaining years of the *husband's* s life expectancy, her services could be valued as equivalent to the earnings of an experienced household worker.

This relatively simple and direct approach to the measurement of lost wife, or wife and mother, values has much to commend it. For one thing, it uses as yardsticks occupations in which millions of women are actually employed. The triers of the facts can understand, follow and apply it. It also takes into account the probability that decedent may have become gainfully employed in one of these, or similar, occupations without importantly affecting the appraisal. The major shortcomings of this procedure are: it explicitly omits many of the roles of a housewife; it generally understates the number of hours a housewife works and the extensiveness of her responsibilities; it makes no allowance for part-time, gainful employment to which millions of women are increasingly attracted while they are yet wives and mothers. Despite these shortcomings and the near certainty of underestimation, the procedure is to be recommended when a more piecemeal approach is not susceptible to supporting proof.

§12:5. *Illustrative case; housewife and mother.*

A housewife, her husband, and week-old son lived in a state where there is no "limit" on death damages. She was killed in an accident in 1965. The following data provide the initial base for the measurement of economic loss: [The ages and life expectancies of the family members at the time of the accident were wife: age, 22.3 years, life expectancy, 54.4 years; husband: age, 26.3 years, life expectancy, 44.4 years; son, age, 0.0 years, life expectancy, 67.6 years.] Next, it is determined from the regional office of the Bureau of Labor Statistics in the area that the wage in 1965 for an Experienced Female Private Household Worker, Living In, in the particular city and vicinity, is $50 weekly for an eight-hour day for 5.5 days a week. For a full seven-day week, the wage becomes $64. On an annual basis, multiplying $64 a week by 52 weeks, the wage is $3,328.

To project the economic loss of household services (excluding child-raising) to the survivors, we advance the annual loss of $3,328 over husband's life expectancy of 44.4 years. In this case, the appraiser assumed that the rate of increase in wages for household workers in the area was equal to the prevalent discount rate, namely, 4 percent. Therefore the two factors of discounting and earnings increase cancel, and the projection is simply the product of $3,328 times 44.4 years, or $147,763. This sum of $147,763 is the "discounted value" of economic loss of the value of decedent's services as housekeeper.

The undiscounted economic loss would amount to $3,328 increasing annually at a compound rate of 4 percent for 44.4 years, or $407,300.

Are there deductions or additions to this discounted loss of $147,763? The answer is: none of consequence other than social security payments. The household worker will have to be fed and sheltered just as the wife whose services she is attempting to replace. Therefore, there is no saving from the husband's income on outlays for food and shelter. There are savings in terms of clothing and other miscellaneous expenditures which a husband may be expected to make for his wife but not for his housekeeper. But these are at least offset by such other considerations as the fact that the household worker will be providing services over an eight-hour day, not the ten or sixteen hours a wife works.

To this point, all we have evaluated are the ordinary household services rendered by a wife. Can we make allowance for the services a wife renders in rearing her children? On the assumption that the nearest equivalent occupation whose market value we can ascertain is the salary of an Elementary School Teacher in the area, we can estimate this lost value. During the 18 years when the only child may be considered a minor, this value seems most appropriate. A teacher would be hired as a teacher whether there were one pupil or twenty-five, if the law required the furnishing of a teacher.

The most recent census data (as of 1965) is provided by the census of 1960, reporting 1959 information and showing the average salary of an Elementary School Teacher in the area as $4,726. Advancing this salary for 6 years to the year of accident, 1965, at a growth rate of 4 percent, gives an annual average salary of $5,978.

Now, for the 18 years of the child's minority, we proceed, as before, to arrive at an undiscounted loss of $159,430, and a loss discounted at 4 percent of $107,600.

Next we face the problem whether the household services provided by the hired household worker, living in, are in addition to the loss just estimated, that is, the child-raising function represented by the salary of an Elementary School Teacher; or, if the household worker's services should be taken in sequence. Of course, the truth lies in between these approaches — which is why Table [3-4] shows both approaches, namely:

TABLE [3-4]. SUMMARY OF ECONOMIC LOSS FOR A DECENT HOUSEWIFE

	Undiscounted	Discounted at 4%
I. Assuming the market equivalent of an Elementary School Teacher and Household Worker, *in sequence:*		
A. Teacher for the first 18 years when the child is a minor	$159,430	$107,600
B. Household Worker for the 26.4 years remaining of husband's life expectancy	321,200	87,860
Total loss, assumption I	$480,630	$195,460
II. Assuming the market equivalent of an Elementary School Teacher and a Household Worker to be *additive:*		
A. Teacher for the first 18 years when the child is a minor	$159,430	$107,600
B. Household Worker for 44.4 years of husband's life expectancy	407,300	147,763
Total loss, assumption II	$566,730	$255,363

I. The assumption that for the first 18 years the loss is projected only as the salary of an Elementary School Teacher, then *followed by* 26.4 years of loss as the wage equivalent of a household worker, or, alternatively,

II. The assumption that the values are *additive*, meaning that we add the losses of the two values:

A. 18 years of salary equivalent to that of an Elementary School Teacher plus

B. 44.4 years of wages of a household worker.

As to assumption I, the only row of figures in the Table below not already discussed is the second row, I, B, where the estimate is made for the household worker who is assumed to be hired in 1983, that is, 18 years after 1965 when the services of the Elementary School Teacher are no longer included. To calculate the loss from 1983 for 26.4 years when only the household worker's services are required, the following steps are taken:

1. In 1983, when the child is considered no longer dependent, the *undiscounted* salary of a household worker will have risen from its 1965 level of $3,328 to a level of $6,742. (The multiplicative factor of 4 percent for 18 years is 2.026.)

2. The cumulative *undiscounted* loss for the 26.4 years of the husband's then remaining life expectancy is determined as $321,200. (The factor of 4 percent growth, cumulating for 26.4 years, is 47.64.) This value is the first entry in the second row in I.

3. The discounted value of economic loss shown in the same second row is as straightforward as in earlier calculations — where the rate of growth of wages is assumed equal to the discount rate. Thus, the 1965 wage of $3,328 is simply multiplied by the 26.4 years of husband's remaining life expectancy to yield $87,860.

Finally, we turn our attention to the "additive formula" in II, then to the two discounted estimates of economic loss. Between these the best estimate lies. Our conclusion is that the true discounted loss to survivors lies between $195,460 and $255,363.

KREPS, SEX IN THE MARKETPLACE:
AMERICAN WOMEN AT WORK
65-74 (1971)

The degree of . . . [married women's] responsiveness to wage incentive turns on the perceived value of the alternative use of the wife's time. In the absence of information on the value a family places on the wife's nonmarket services, the elasticity of married women's labor supply is difficult to estimate. It is clear that their supply (and that of other groups of secondary workers) is more elastic than that of primary workers. The reason for this greater elasticity is important to note, although it is of course self-evident: men's alternative to market work is free time, which may or may not have utility, whereas a wife's alternatives are free time and nonmarket work, the latter having utility in most instances. Thus when a man goes to work, no loss in value is imputed to the free time he gives up. On the contrary, any loss in the time from work is considered a loss in income, or forgone earnings. But married women's nonmarket services are of value; problems of analysis arise from the fact that we do not know, household to household, precisely what value.

The maximum value placed on a nonworking wife's services can be deduced from the salary that does in fact induce her to take a job. Similarly, there is some theoretical minimum below which wives at work will withdraw from their jobs, and devote their time to home work. The asking price is higher, the greater the value attached to home work and this value obviously varies at different stages of a family's life cycle, each stage making a different set of demands on the wife's time. Between families in the same stage, however, the values also differ; the presence of children in Negro families has been less of a deterrent to the wife's market work than children have been in white families, where the need for income was less pressing. For any given family size and age composition, the relative value imputed to the wife's home work is obviously lower, the greater the perceived need for additional income. . . .

[Kreps' discussion of the desirability of including the aggregate value of housework in the GNP, including cites to estimates placing that value at around one fourth of the GNP, is omitted.]

Attempts to impute a dollar value to nonmarket work done by wives are hampered by a lack of data on the prices of many services which are typically performed primarily in the home, and by our inability to attach monetary values to certain intangible qualities usually associated with having a wife and mother in the home: companionship, attention, interest in the family's welfare, continuity of relationship with young children. An alternative approach is to estimate the opportunity costs of the wife's home work by supposing that its value equals the foregone earnings in the labor market. . . .

The rough estimates of the opportunity costs of wives' nonmarket work, which follow, indicate one method of approach, but more importantly, they indicate the data needed for an accurate appraisal of the gains and losses that may be occasioned by changes in wives' labor force status.

Housework done by wives. American women, especially married ones, do most of the housework. James Morgan and his associates estimate that married women spend an average of forty hours per week in this endeavor.[7] Adding these hours to those which women spend in market work gives a total workweek in excess of that reported by male heads of families [Chart 3-1]. The wife typically did 2053 hours of unpaid household work in a year.

---

7. Morgan, Sirageldin, and Baerwaldt, *Productive Americans*, p. 102. The authors also note that women do 70 percent of all housework done by family members.

[Chart 3-1]

AGGREGATE HOURS OF REGULAR HOUSEWORK AND WORK
FOR MONEY DONE BY VARIOUS FAMILY MEMBERS
IN 1964 (in millions of hours)

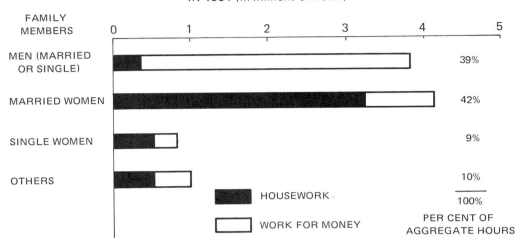

Source: Morgan, Sirageldin, and Baerwaldi, op. cit., p. 103.

Hourly earnings of wives who work. Sirageldin's estimates of the hourly earnings of wives who worked in 1964, by age and educational groups . . . [show that age] and education were the major determinants of the rate earned, the range being from an average of $1.14 per hour for wives aged eighteen to twenty-four with less than twelve grades of school completed, to $3.50 per hour for those aged 45-54 with college degrees.

Annual earnings of wives. [When average] hourly earnings [were] translated into annual salaries (at the 2,053 hours per year estimated by Morgan et al). . . . the range was wide: from $2340 per year to $7186. The opportunity cost for a thirty-year-old housewife to remain at home engaged in housework was $2566 if she had less than twelve years of education, or $5892 if she had a college degree; a fifty-year-old wife with a college degree was foregoing $7186; and so on. The opportunity cost of women's services is highest in the forty-five to fifty-four year age group for those with less than twelve years of school or with college degrees; for the high school graduate, the cost is highest in the thirty-five to forty-four age bracket.

Sirageldin estimates that the average value of unpaid output for the American family was $3929, or about fifty percent of its disposable income, in 1964.[8] Approximately ninety percent of this estimated production was in the form of housework, giving a value of $3536 for housework per family. As [chart 3-1] shows, married women do most of this work — about ten times as many hours per week as married men.

Numbers of nonworking wives. Given the rough indicators of opportunity costs for women not in the labor force, . . . we raise the question: what would be the effect on GNP if all the nonworking wives (aged eighteen and over) without children of preschool age came to be employed in market jobs?

[Oppenheimer's estimates, from the Female Labor Force, p. 172, indicate that not] counting the single, widowed, and divorced women, the total number of married women who remained outside the labor force and who could theoretically have taken jobs, was

8. Sirageldin, *Non-Market Components*, p. 53.

almost 26 million. This figure excludes married women with children of preschool age.

Aggregate cost of foregone earnings. [Tentative rough estimates of the earnings that might have accrued to various age and educational groups of married women not then employed, had they been in market jobs in 1960] indicate, for example, that if all forty-five to fifty-four year old married women who had college degrees and who were engaged in nonmarket activities had been employed in paying jobs, their total earnings would have been over five billion dollars. Similarly, if all twenty-five to thirty-four year-old nonworking married women with up to 12 years of education had been engaged in market activity, their earnings would have been three billion dollars. The foregone earnings of married women in all age and educational groups total roughly $105 billion; this addition would have raised the 1960 GNP of $622.6 [billion] by over one-sixth.

MAXIMUM CONTRIBUTION OR MAXIMUM PAY?

Many questions can be raised regarding the foregoing calculations, not the least of which are questions of the method and the validity of the data used. The use of average hourly earnings for women of any particular group, rather than some sort of declining marginal wage as women are added to the labor force, will offend economists. We have used the pools of potential female workers in 1960, and made only a rough correction for wage changes backward from 1964 to 1960. A more reliable dollar estimate of the value of wives' home work could be made, based perhaps on 1970 census data.

NOTES

1. With the exception of Kreps' calculations, the above estimates are all based on replacement costs. But most of the time, a man left with children and no wife is likely to remarry rather than hire a long-term replacement — a fact which highlights the problems of using wage contract analysis to deal with spousal relations.

2. Discuss in light of your own experience what is involved in the occupation of housewife/mother. How much is it worth? What factors should be taken into account in setting rates of pay: number of children? number of household appliances? education and options of the housewife? the degree of her housework and childrearing skills?

3. How would you evaluate the work done by a housewife who also works outside the home? Would your answer vary depending on whether or not she hired a housekeeper to replace her in the home, or used day care facilities?

4. Another figure which can be viewed as a social estimation of the value of woman's work in the home is the maximum tax deduction for childcare and housekeeping expenses of $400 per month. See Part IX-A, infra, for an explanation of this deduction and its limitations.

C. THE SHARED-ROLE PATTERN

BERNARD, THE FUTURE OF MARRIAGE
248-265 (1972)

. . . [T]o achieve [relief from the entire responsibility for child care and for housekeeping] involves changing not only relations in the bedroom and the household but in the world outside as well. Bringing about changes here will call for change all along the line, in offices and shops and factories and hospitals and schools, in construction sites and laboratories and libraries, and in every other place where people work at jobs of any kind.

"A new kind of life style." One way to achieve such changes proposed by Susan Brownmiller is "a new kind of life style in which a husband and wife would each work half-day and devote the other half of the day to caring for their children." I like the idea very much. It seems to me to fit the conditions of modern life and to offer the best trade-off between security and challenge for both partners. With one stroke, it alleviates one of the major grievances of men (sole responsibility for the provider role) and of women (exclusive responsibility for housework and child care). It seems to me to be most in line with what is actually happening in our society. It is both the most conservative design for the future and the most radical.

Shared, not reversed, roles. We are in such an intellectual bind when thinking about sex that we can think only in terms of polarities. Thus, when we think of change at all we think in terms of reversals. If men are not to be the providers, then women must be; if women are not to take care of children, then men must. But role reversal is not role sharing.

There is, of course, nothing inherently wrong with reversed roles, if that is what the partners prefer. . . .

Reversing roles, however, is not the same as sharing them. There undoubtedly are men who would enjoy household management — on a large enough scale it has long been an honorable male profession in the form of stewardship — as there are women who do. All power to them; there should certainly be no sanctions against such reversal. It is a legitimate option. But it violates some of the basic tenets of role sharing: that children should have the care of both parents, that all who benefit from the services supplied in the household should contribute to them, and that both partners should share in supporting the household. . . .

Shared parenthood. Sharing responsibility for the household is only one part of the new pattern. If female "personhood" is a goal of the Women's Liberation Movement, so also is male parenthood. When or if there are no children, role sharing is not too much of a problem. It is when there are preschool children that the real test comes, because sharing roles also means sharing the child-care and the child-rearing function as well as the work of the household. . . .

The respectable objection to the idea is that it would cost too much. A man can earn so much more doing what he does than the woman could in the labor force. Precisely; this is an unassailable argument under the present status quo. If the wife is to share in the provider role, she has to be free from discrimination in the world of work. She has to be trained to her optimum capacity, and given as good a chance as her husband to put it to use. Her time at work has to be worth as much as that of her — or anyone's — husband doing the same work. Now turn to the vast literature on sex discrimination in education, access to employment, and promotion. It explains why it is cheaper to assign child care exclusively to mothers. They aren't worth as much as fathers in the labor force.

This economic argument, however, is only the most respectable one, not necessarily the most powerful one. The most powerful arguments are rarely expressed or, for that matter, even recognized.

Fears and nightmares. Some men would welcome role sharing enthusiastically as partial relief from the dull and unrewarding work that now takes forty hours of their lives each week. They would be willing to exchange half of those hours for work around the home, even for child care. But some men will fight it. They are the men who love their work — even, admittedly in some candid cases, more than they love their families.

A sample of tycoons, for example, did admit to Stanley Talbot that they preferred to spend their time on their job than to spend it with their families. And B. F. Skinner, the psychologist, said on a television program that he had told his daughters that if he had to choose between saving his work and saving them, he would save his work. No hard feeling, he assured them, just a matter of priorities. Such men will not willingly surrender even one hour of their work. Still they are quite willing to ask women to do so, women who would like to spend as much time on work that enthralls them as the men do themselves. In such cases it is not so much aversion to housework or child care that is the stumbling block but the aversion to any loss of time from their work. This is a form of self-indulgence they are not prepared to curtail. It is very difficult for wives to persuade such careerist husbands that they are being paid twice over, once in the form of freedom from domestic cares and once in the form of rewarding work. Such husbands and wives will have to hassle out this one by themselves.

The counterparts of the work-intoxicated men are the thousands, perhaps even millions, of women who do not want to be anything but housewives. And of course that option should not be foreclosed. In cases where this is a genuine preference, so be it. Coercion could not be justified. Still the research evidence is that almost all women — as many as four-fifths in one study and at least a third of another — say that they would prefer to enter the labor force if adequate provision could be made for the care of their children, and even more would do so if the work was part-time only.

There are other fears that are aroused by the shared-role idea. Some men, like the informant in a 1969 Gallup poll, fear the loss of the comfort and services provided by a full-time housekeeper. "Women," he said, "should stay home and take care of their families. . . . A woman's obligation is still to make a home for her husband." The increasing participation of wives in the labor force may, further, have an impact on the husband's marriage by making independence more possible for wives, and, through independence, reducing the superiority which the structure of marriage has traditionally accorded to husbands. An income of her own improves the position of the wife in the marriage. . . .

The brighter side. . . . Right off, the sharing of the provider role by the wife relieves the husband of the sole responsibility for it, and immediately removes one of the grievances men have expressed against marriage as now structured. Not only does the increased participation of the wife in the labor force ameliorate the financial load the husband has to bear, but it also has benign effects on the wife as well. Her mental health is improved. She becomes less susceptible to the housewife syndrome in the form of symptoms of psychological distress. Less concentrated on her children, she is less likely to succumb to depression when the children no longer fully occupy her. Among educated women — and more and more women are going to be educated — work outside the home improves marriage. This is especially true of part-time work.

Employment seems to make it possible for disturbed women to hold out longer before they become mentally ill enough to be hospitalized. Taking the work of mothers out of the home has a tranquilizing and fulfilling effect on many of them which may ruffle, but at the same time salvage, their marriages. The nature of the job makes a difference, to be sure; wives who are very satisfied with their jobs are less likely to express marital dissatisfaction than those who are not.

Not the least advantage of the participation of fathers in child care and child rearing is the effect it has on them. If the nurturing quality in women is related to the function they perform in the care of children, it is an excellent idea to permit men also to come under this benign influence. It would mark a great advance in human relations if men came to have a chance to develop this nurturing quality as well as women. . . .

How feasible is the shared-role pattern? All this talk about sharing roles assumes that it is feasible. But obviously it depends on the availability of jobs with flexible hours, and that, in turn, depends on the organization of industry. The shared-role model of marriage will not come because it improves the mental health of women or relieves stress from men or because it is good for children. It will have to have more hardheaded justification. It does have.

We have noted several times that the technologists have as much to say about the future — of marriage as well as other relationships — as anything else. They are now telling us that by 1990 a twenty-hour, four-day week could produce the same annual increase in gross national product as we now produce with a forty-hour, five-day week. With increased productivity, industry could afford to pay the same wages to workers for half time as presently for full time.

Hours of work are not determined by natural law laid down in the beginning of time. They are an institutionalized matter, subject to change. The current direction of change is toward the four-day, forty-hour, three-day weekend week. Workers spend ten hours working during four days and then have the rest of the week off. From the point of view of marital role sharing, this is not a good kind of schedule. But as an encouragement of experiment, it is good; it makes innovation more acceptable. The four-day week is profitable for many firms; in the automobile industry it has been seen as a way to improve quality control. And in some cases it improves productivity to such an extent that hours can be cut below the customary forty. The drift toward the four-day work week may be inevitable, although as yet only less than seven hundred out of the five million firms in this country have adopted it. But the number is increasing rapidly, and Riva Poor, who has studied the movement in detail, believes it "could herald a new era of innovation in which this particular innovation in work scheduling is only one. The rapidity with which the public has adopted this new idea could be a harbinger of increased receptivity to change and improvement."

To be sure, the first reaction to any radical innovation is that it is impossible, it just can't be done. Most of us are like the physicist who declared that it was impossible to throw a curve ball; then, when a pitcher finally did, he went to work to show how, of course, it was possible to throw a curve ball.

Large-scale rescheduling of hours of work in industry has been shown to be possible, even profitable. But how about service occupations? This is, indeed, a crucial question, for an increasing proportion of the labor force is engaged in services and a decreasing proportion in physical production. Different approaches may be called for. Interestingly, it is in the professional services that the most reassuring experiments are being reported. . . .

There are even beginnings of experiments on the part of employing agencies. One approach is being made in academia, where part-time appointments are on the drawing board and are even being tried out. Such part-time appointments would be optional; they would have all the dignity, status, and fringe benefits accorded to full-time appointments — not as they so often are now, underpaid, last-minute emergency appointments to handle unexpectedly large introductory enrollments. They would be attractive enough to appeal to both men and women and to the top as well as to the lower ranks in the academic structure.

One example of this new concept in operation is that of William and Patricia Dean at Gustavus Adolphus College in St. Peter, Minnesota. They have a single contract with the college, both teaching part time, permitting them to be at home with the family and also providing the opportunity for each to pursue professional interests as well, he in the religion department, and she in area studies.

This is Patricia's statement: "We asked for the arrangement because of my problems in dealing with the pressures of home responsibilities, in addition to a job. We have two children, seven and two. The most sensible and just solution seemed to be for my husband to assume more of the family responsibilities, but he could not do so unless he were released from some of his teaching duties. Accordingly, a proposal was presented to the college for each of us to work part time, between us teaching a full load.

The college was willing to endorse it as an experimental and potential solution to problems facing parents who both want to work. The college has benefited in this venture we believe because we each bring more energy to our courses as a result of the new arrangement. Although the experiment was undertaken as a solution to my problems, my husband has discovered some unanticipated advantages. He feels fresher in the classroom, has as much or more time for research as before, and has gained a more intimate relationship with his children. The preschool child, in particular, has benefited from the arrangement; he appears equally attached to both parents and has a lessened dependence on his mother. The elder child has the advantage of living with a more satisfied mother."

Here is William's statement: "First, I should admit that it is still disconcerting to deviate from a role I have always accepted as normal and to watch men drive off to work and see myself remain in the neighborhood with the women. But my positive reactions are more important. First, I have traded one course, of a three-course teaching load, for a morning's work at home. The loss of a course gives me about as much working time as I lose at home. I think I will have about the same amount of time for extracurricular research as I have previously had. Second, I find my professional working day less tedious, probably because it is now limited to a long afternoon and a couple of hours picked up in the evening or in the morning while at home. In retrospect, it seems that it was the third course, or the last three hours of work, that dried me out and drove down what productivity I may have. Third, I sense an unforeseen benefit in the new arrangement. I think a man who sees his children only in the evening or on the weekends has a more restricted experience with them than he may realize. I, at least, have felt a new kind of intimacy with my preschool child, partly because I am alone with him and partly because it is during the calm of the morning. I think, for example, of silently driving through the hills, on an errand in the morning, with my two-year-old son on the front seat with me, sucking his thumb and holding his blanket. Finally, a much anticipated benefit is the alleviation of my feelings of guilt. I do not have to live with the realization that my occupational responsibilities are forcing a capable and professionally trained woman to work full time on a house and children that are half mine. Nor must I see her work outside of the home while already working full time in the home." The male sociologists who, like Ira Reiss, "doubt very much if males in our society will change very drastically in their sharing of the mother and wife roles" may be projecting too indiscriminatingly their own biases. . . .

. . . The shared-role pattern was already being viewed in Sweden as the basis for policy. It was beneficial for children as well as for their parents, for it would let the child have two parents rather than, as now all too often only, in effect, one. "The greatest disadvantage with the male sex-role," the Swedish prime minister noted, "is that the man has too small a share in the upbringing of the children." Children suffer from lack of contact with the father. Contact of children with men was advocated not only in the home but also in infant schools, kindergartens, and regular schools.

Nor was this merely political palaver. It was a bona fide statement of policy. In 1968, the government of Sweden had already proclaimed that it was "necessary to abolish the conditions which tend to assign certain privileges, obligations, or rights to men. No decisive change in the distribution of functions and status as between the sexes can be achieved if the duties of the male in society are assumed a priori to be unaltered. . . . The division of functions as between the sexes must be changed in such a way that both the man and woman in a family are afforded the same practical opportunities of participating in both active parenthood and gainful employment." And, astonishingly, the prime minister of Sweden reported in 1970 that "Swedish trade unions and management organizations have worked out plans to make it possible for men to share the child care with women.". . . .

In light of Galbraith's analysis presented at the outset of this section, consider what would be the impact of Bernard's proposal on consumption levels. Reversing the question, to what extent and in what ways might corporate pressure for high consumption levels interfere with the shared role model?

V. A SOCIOLOGICAL OVERVIEW OF DIVORCE

A. STATISTICAL PATTERNS OF DIVORCE

Writing in 1956, Goode estimated that "the experience of divorce is likely to occur to one-fifth to one-sixth of the men and women who live out an average life span," and to one-fourth to one-fifth of all people who ever marry.[1] A Census Bureau report based on 1971 data confirms this estimate, and suggests that the percentage of ever-married people experiencing divorce is rising.[2] By 1955, when ever-married women born in 1920-1924 were in their early thirties, about one in ten had already had her first marriage end in divorce. By comparison, of women born in 1935-1939, 15.8 percent had had their first marriages end in divorce by 1970.[3] In other words, at the same ages, their divorce rate was 50 percent higher than that of women born 15 years earlier. According to the Census Bureau extrapolations, about a fourth of the women in their middle thirties in 1971 will have had their first marriages end in divorce by the time they reach fifty years of age in the 1980s, as contrasted to the one sixth of women born in 1920-1924 who had their first marriages end in divorce by 1971.[4]

A consistent statistical finding is that the divorce rate for men declines as income and education rise.[5] For women, the correlation is reversed as to incomes.[6] The effect of education on divorce for women is similar to, though slightly less consistent than, the effect for men.[7] Divorce rates for blacks are higher than for whites; as to black men, this may correlate with discrepancies in income and education which result from discrimination. Teenage marriages are more likely to end in divorce; one probable explanation for the unusually high divorce rate among women born in 1935-1939 is that the peak of early marriages occurred in 1955 among women of that birth cohort.[8]

1. Goode, Women in Divorce 56 (Free Press ed. 1965) (originally published under the title After Divorce).
2. U.S. Bureau of the Census, Current Population Reports, Series P-20, No. 239, Marriage, Divorce, and Remarriage by Year of Birth: June 1971, 1 (1972).
3. Id. at 5.
4. Ibid. The number of divorces per year per 1000 married persons and per 1000 persons regardless of marital status is also on the rise. See U.S. Public Health Service, Vital and Health Statistics, Series 21, No. 20, Increases in Divorces, United States — 1967, 2, 12, Table 1 (1970); Paul Glick, Assistant Chief, Demographic and Social Statistics Programs, Population Division, U.S. Bureau of the Census, quoted in Milius, Affluence and Education Reduce the Divorce Rate, The Washington Post, Sept. 22, 1972, at A-1, A-18. Note that the latter figure is particularly affected by changes in the age distribution of the population, as well as by the percentage of the population which is married, a figure itself affected by the age distribution of the population. See Carter and Glick, Marriage and Divorce: A Social and Economic Study 59-61 (1970).
5. See, e.g., U.S. Bureau of the Census, Marriage, Divorce, and Remarriage by Year of Birth: June 1971, supra, Detailed Tables, especially 11, 13. Milius, supra, at A-1, A-18, interpreted this report as follows: "In 72 percent of families with annual incomes of under $5,000 both husband and wife had been married only once. The corresponding figure was 77 percent for families with incomes between $5,000 and $10,000, and 81 percent for families in the $10,000 to $15,000 bracket. It was 83 percent for families with incomes of $15,000 and over. The percentages applied only to families in which the husband was 35 to 54 years old. A similar pattern held true for education." See also Carter and Glick, supra at 57, Table 3.10 (divorce rates by race); 72, Table 3.17; 73, Fig. 3.8; 74-76 (divorce rates and education); 204, Table 7.17; 266 (divorce rates and income); and Goode, supra, ch. 4, Socioeconomic Factors and Divorce. See also references cited by Havens, Women, Work and Wedlock: A Note on Female Marital Patterns in the United States, 78 Am. J. Sociology 975 (1973).
6. Around annual incomes of $10,000, the divorce rates begin to go back down slightly. See Havens, id.; Carter and Glick, supra, at 264, Table 8.33 and 266, Table 8.34.
7. Carter and Glick, supra, at 72-73, 402-403.
8. On the association of early marriage with high divorce rates, see, e.g., U.S. Bureau of the Census,

In a 1965 sample of divorce cases in 22 states, the wife was the plaintiff and the husband the defendant in 71.4 percent of the cases. This proportion was similar in earlier years.[9] The wife also has a better chance of winning the divorce than the husband. In a 1963 sample covering 22 states, of divorce cases in which decrees were granted, "the wife as plaintiff lost only about 2 percent of the time (i.e., the husband was granted the decree); whereas the husband as plaintiff lost about 10 percent of the time (i.e., the wife was granted the decree)."[10] It is possible that these figures reflect a bias of the legal system toward granting divorces to wives rather than husbands, and a consequent choice by husbands and wives mutually seeking divorce that the wife be the plaintiff. However, Goode, reporting on a 1948 study of a random sample of over 400 recently divorced women, found that in 62 percent of the cases it was the wife who had suggested divorce first, and in 55 percent of the cases the wife both suggested the divorce first and continued to insist that a divorce be obtained.[11]

B. STATISTICAL PATTERNS OF REMARRIAGE

A very high proportion of divorced people remarry, thus making the percentage of divorced people in the United States at any one time lower than the divorce rate would indicate. This is illustrated by Table 3-5.

TABLE 3-5. PERCENT MARRIED AND PERCENT DIVORCED,
FOR PERSONS 14 YEARS OLD AND OVER,
by color and sex: United States, 1960

	Percent married		*Percent Divorced*	
	Men	*Women*	*Men*	*Women*
White	69.9	66.5	2.1	2.7
Nonwhite[a]	62.1	60.1	2.4	3.6

Source: Carter and Glick, Marriage and Divorce: A Social and Economic Study 71, Table 3.16 (1970), based on U.S. Bureau of the Census, U.S. Census of Population: 1960, General Population Characteristics, United States Summary, Final Report PC (1)-1B, Table 49.

a. The term "nonwhite" is used instead of "black" because the available data combines figures for all races other than Caucasian into a single category.

Note the sex and race differences, however; white people and men are more likely to be married or remarried, and nonwhite people and women are more likely to be and remain divorced.

According to the Census Bureau study, among ever-married women born in 1920-1924 whose first marriages had ended by 1971, approximately three out of five women had remarried at least once.[12] However, the remarriage rates in certain age groups are much higher. Goode estimated that about 94 percent of all women divorced by age 30 will eventually remarry.[13] In one study he found that, about two years after divorce, 80

Marriage, Divorce, and Remarriage by Year of Birth: June 1971, supra, at 4-5, Table D. On the peak of early marriage in 1955, see id., cover table.

9. U.S. Public Health Service, Divorce Statistics Analysis, United States, 1964-65, National Center for Health Statistics, Series 21, No. 17, 8-9 (1969).

10. U.S. Public Healthe Service, Divorce Statistics Analysis, United States, 1963, National Center for Health Statistics, Series 21, No. 13, (1967).

11. In 25 percent of the cases it was the husband who first suggested the divorce and in 13 percent the decision was mutual. In 14 percent of the cases the husband both suggested the divorce and continued to insist on it, and in 31 percent there was some combination of husband and wife suggestion and insistence. Goode, supra, at 147, 149.

12. U.S. Bureau of the Census, Marriage, Divorce, and Remarriage by Year of Birth: June 1971, supra, at 4-7.

13. Goode, supra, at 277.

percent of women between 20 and 24 years of age had already remarried, while only 46 percent of those over 46 had remarried by then.[14]

A larger proportion of eligible men than women remarry, and they also do so more quickly than women do. Crude evidence are the facts that a larger proportion of men than women are married, and a larger proportion of women than men are divorced at any point in time. More specifically, statistics show that, in almost every age group and every time period after divorce, the remarriage rates of men are higher than those of women.[15] Rates calculated without direct reference to age are also different for men and women. For example, among people in the first through fifth year of divorce in 1966, the probability was 243 remarriages per 1000 divorced men and 192 remarriages per 1000 divorced women.[16]

Another index of the differential tendency of men and women to remain married or to remarry quickly is the percentage of adult years spent living with a spouse, calculated by cumulating years spent with the spouses of the first and all subsequent marriages. "Among men, nearly 68 percent of the entire adult life in 1964 . . . was spent as a married man with wife present. Among women, the corresponding figure . . . [was] about 62 percent in 1964.[17] Over time, the percentages have increased, but the differential between them has also increased.[18]

In evaluating these figures, remember that men die younger than women on the average. In the older age brackets, this can have a substantial effect on remarriage rates and the percentages married, divorced, and widowed. First, there are more women of marriageable age than men. The percentages of married, divorced, and widowed are calculated as a percentage of all members of each sex. Therefore, although the numbers of men and women married are equal, the number of men who are married shows up as a higher percentage of all men than the same number of married women in relation to all women. Second, this differential is compounded by the greater remarriage possibilities for men it creates. The results are a rise in men's remarriage rates and in the percentage of men reporting themselves married, as compared to women, and a decrease in the percentage of men reporting themselves as divorced or widowed, as compared to women.[19]

14. Id. at 279.

15. The only exception is divorced women between 14 and 24, who remarry at a faster rate than do divorced men of the same age — and faster than any other group in the population. U.S. Bureau of the Census, Current Population Reports, Series P-20, No. 223, 55, Table 8 (1971), and U.S. Public Health Service, Vital and Health Statistics, Series 21, No. 20, Increases in Divorces, United States — 1967, 10, Table J (1970). However, divorced men aged 25-29, who are probably marrying and divorcing women somewhat younger than themselves, had a marriage rate closer to the rate of divorced women 14-24 years of age, although still not as high. Note that the remarriage rates for divorced people are always higher than the marriage rates of single or widowed persons, sometimes as much as four or more times as high. Id.

16. U.S. Bureau of the Census, Current Population Reports, Series P-20, No. 223, 55, Table 8 (1971). The proportion of divorced men was 35 to every 1000 married couples in 1970, and of divorced women, 60 to every 1000 married couples. Id. at 2. Likewise, analyzing the marital status of people who had first married from 3 to 20 years ago and whose first marriages were dissolved by 1960, Carter and Glick found that the percentages of white men who had remarried were generally higher than of nonwhite men, nonwhite women, and white women. However, nonwhite men, followed closely by white women, had the highest remarriage rate for the group whose first marriages had taken place from 3 to 5 years ago. Nonwhite women had a lower remarriage rate than the other three categories in every group of marriages studied: 28.8 percent of white women and 36.1 percent of nonwhite women whose first marriages took place between 1960 and 1944 and had dissolved by 1960 had not remarried as of 1960. Carter and Glick, supra, at 239, Table 8.15.

17. Id. at 63, Table 3.12; 64. These ratios were calculated with reference to a hypothetical stationary population in the United States, 1964 and 1940.

18. In 1940, the figure for men was 59 percent and for women, 56 percent. Ibid.

19. For example, Carter and Glick discuss the influence of the mortality rate on the variation of remarriage rates by sex for persons 45 to 64 years old:

"For this age group the remarriage rate for widowers (70.1 per 1,000) was more than four times as high as the rate for widows (16.2); but in numbers of reported remarriages for persons in this age group, the approximately 27,000 widows who remarried exceeded the 22,000 widowers who remarried in 1963." Id. at 47-48.

The relationship of income and education to remarriage rates is also quite interesting. Among men, according to 1960 Census data, the income and education levels were highest among those still married to their first spouse, next among those recently divorced or remarried, and lowest among the "total divorced" and the separated group. Among women, the pattern was slightly more complicated. The women still married and living with their first husbands and the "total divorced" group had the highest education levels; next the recently divorced, then the remarried, and finally the separated. The income levels showed the "total divorced" the highest, next the recently divorced, then the remarried, then the separated, and finally the still married and living with their first husbands.[20] Carter and Glick state that "the data taken as a whole are consistent with the hypothesis that . . . divorced women who are weak on ability to support themselves are the most likely to remarry."[21]

In sum, many people get divorced, and most of them remarry. If one is a man, the higher one's income and education, the more one is likely to stay married, or to remarry and to stay remarried. If one is a woman, higher income and education have the opposite effect. White people have lower rates of divorce and higher rates of remarriage than members of other racial groups. The divorce rate is on the rise, but so is the proportion of the population which ever marries or is married at any one time. Women are more likely than men to seek divorces, and less likely to remarry. However, their remarriage possibilities are also fewer, since the disproportion of women to men in the population is high in older age groups.

C. THE SOCIAL IMPACT OF DIVORCE ON THE INDIVIDUAL

In his major study of the institution, Goode discusses the effect of divorce on the individual.[22] He rejects the common comparison to the experience of bereavement (i.e., loss of partner, economic and status changes, sexual deprivation), mainly because "divorce is preceded by a long period of conflict whose effect is to reduce the emotional attachment between the spouses, and thereby to make the finality of the divorce less upsetting than that of bereavement."[23] On the other hand, he notes: "Those who divorce do usually feel that they have been through an unfortunate experience", and he finds that "trauma" is not an inapt description of the effect of divorce. In addition, there is societal disapproval of divorce, and individuals usually feel that they have failed in some way:[24]

> Divorce occupies a very particular place among the predictable tragedies of living. . . . [It] is viewed as the willed result of a definable decision by the participants. They have violated a civil contract to remain together, broken a moral compact of monogamy, and assailed the myth that the romantic love of marriage must continue throughout life. If, in addition, there are children of the marriage, the parents have

---

Likewise, for the previously widowed, the marriage rate was 10.2 for women and 38.4 for men, but the *number* of widows who remarried exceeded the number of widowers who remarried by a ratio of 10 to 9. Id. at 46.

Another figure which reflects differential mortality is the percentage of women reporting themselves as divorced, which includes an unknown number of women whose ex-husbands have since died, and who would therefore be reported as widowed "but for" the divorce. Id. at 64-65. Nonetheless, the marriages of these women ended in divorce some time earlier than they would have ended in death, and the consequences for them of the dissolution of their marriages were those of divorce, and later those of divorce complicated by the death of the ex-husband, not those of widowhood. Therefore, these women are appropriately included in our discussion of the differential impact of divorce on women and men.

20. Id. at 268, Table 8.35 and accompanying text.
21. Id. at 269.
22. Goode, supra, at 203-204.
23. Id. at 185.
24. Id. at 203-204.

(in cold blood, anger, or desperation) decided to destroy their prospect of a permanent home. This the parents have done with the merely selfish aim of personal happiness, or the avoidance of unhappiness. The tragedy is, then, one they have wished on themselves.

Though still socially discouraged, divorce is an increasingly common experience. It has a strong impact on the lives of all parties concerned, but probably affects wives most profoundly. Since marriage occupies a central rather than a secondary position in most women's lives and identities, divorce would logically be more traumatic for them. Second, the changes divorce makes in the lives of women who have played the traditional role of housewives (or must now play it as a result of obtaining child custody) may be longer lasting than the changes for men. A woman may have to support herself when she has not done so for many years, while assuming virtually sole responsibility for the children. The husband's position after divorce is more often like his bachelor days. He may have heavier financial responsibilities, of course, but he is also likely to have a higher income than before his marriage. Because he does not have the children with him, he will have a greater opportunity to establish another romantic relationship.

D. The Economic Impact of Divorce on the Individual

1. Child Custody

In 1965, children were involved in almost 60 percent of all divorces.[25] Estimates of the percentage of cases in which the wife obtains custody of the children of the marriage vary, but all place the figure between 80 and 95 percent.[26] The younger the children of divorced or separated parents, the more likely they are to be with their mothers.[27]

2. Alimony and Child Support

Excerpts from an article about the divorce of an upper middle-class couple reflect many commonly held notions about the economic significance of the separation to the man and woman:[28]

> [The Husband]
> While Phil is getting by, it's true he is in no position to play the big spender.

25. U.S. Public Health Service, Divorce Statistics Analysis, United States, 1964-65, National Center for Health Statistics, Series 21, Number 17, at 12 (1969).

26. According to Jacobson, the mother receives custody in about four fifths of all cases. American Marriage and Divorce 131 (1959). In Goode's study, the mother received custody in 94.8 percent of the cases; the father, in 2.4 percent; with split custody, shared custody, grandparental and other arrangements making up the remaining 2.8 percent. Supra, at 311. "In the cases involving children which went through the divorce courts of Cook County (Chicago), during 1940-50, about 86 percent of the women obtained custody. Nine percent of the fathers obtained custody, and in 5 percent of the cases there was some other arrangement." Id. at 312, citing Robson, The Law and Practice of Divorce — The Judge's Point of View, in University of Chicago Law School Conference on Divorce 4 (Conference Ser. No. 9, 1952). Similar results were obtained by Marshall and May in studies of divorce in Ohio and Maryland in the 1920s. Ibid.

According to the U.S. Census Bureau, of the 8.438 million children under 18 living with only one parent in March 1970, approximately 91 percent were living with their mothers, and 9 percent with their fathers; of the children of divorced parents, about 93 percent were living with their mothers, and only about 7 percent with their fathers. Calculations based on U.S. Bureau of the Census, Current Population Reports, Series P-20, No. 212, Marital Status and Family Status: March 1970, 20, Table 5, Presence of Parent, by Marital Status of Parent, for Persons Under 18 Years Old Living with Only One Parent, by Age and Race, March, 1970.

27. Only 5 percent of all children under 5 living with one parent only were with their fathers, while 11 percent of children between 14 and 17 in this category lived with their fathers only. Ibid.

28. Klein, Breaking Up, in The Wall Street Journal, June 4, 1970, pp. 1, 10, 22.

He is still repaying the $2,000 he borrowed from his father to pay off household bills soon after he split with Joan. The closest Phil has to property is his $9,000 equity in his former house, and he will receive that only if Joan sells the house or occupies it with a new husband. . . .

. . . [S]ix months after the divorce Joan was back in court asking for more money (the judge initially granted her $400 a month in child support) on the ground that Phil's income had climbed $2,500 to $17,000 yearly. . . . He fought the request but lost and now pays Joan $435 a month.

Counting [that] . . . and visits to a psychologist by his son Bryan, six, his total monthly support bill is about $500. That's almost half (his) . . . monthly takehome pay of $1,100. . . . Of the remaining $600, Phil pays $133 a month in rent . . . and $15 for the life insurance that he must maintain as a part of the divorce settlement. . . . Debt repayment comes to $100 a month.

[The Wife]
As a secretary to two top executives of a manufacturing firm, her base pay is $140 a week and she regularly boosts that by putting in overtime, sometimes as much as $100 worth a week. Last year she earned $8,800, and she expects to top $11,000 this year. . . . [W]ith the $5,200 in child support, it puts her income at over $16,000, well above the $12,000 Phil has left after he pays the child support.

Joan says that kind of money is more than enough for her needs, even after the $60 a week she pays her live-in housekeeper. In the past year she bought a new car, put $450 into a mutual fund and repaid much of the $1,350 borrowed from her mother during the separation.

According to the Wall Street Journal, Phil has gotten the worse end of the divorce, for he ends up with $12,000 to Joan's $16,200. To make the comparison fair, two adjustments should be made. First, Joan has the use of the house, half of which is legally Phil's; a crude way to reflect the advantage this gives her is to adjust her income by adding in half of Phil's monthly rent, or $804 a year. Second, if child support accurately reflects the expenditures for the children's needs, it should not be counted as income for either of them. If we deduct child support from Joan's "income," and make the rent adjustment described, their postdivorce incomes are roughly equal.[29]

Note also the bias in the Wall Street Journal's reporting. Her debt repayment is listed as evidence that she has more than enough money for her needs; his debt repayment is described as an expense. Also note that she is underpaying her housekeeper. Finally, she is working probably as hard as Phil is or harder because of her daily responsibility for the children and all her overtime. She is certainly not an alimony drone.

Although this case study was presented in the popular press as prototypic, actually it is quite unusual. Despite her ten years out of the labor force, Joan has a job which is high paying, especially in comparison to other "women's" jobs. Phil's income alone is much higher than the United States median *family* income of $8500.

The relatively high economic standing of this couple is not the only unusual aspect of their divorce. It is also relatively rare for the wife actually to be receiving alimony or child support regularly. Data is unavailable on the total number of women receiving or entitled to alimony or child support payments, but the figures which do exist are very suggestive as to the frequency with which in particular domestic relations courts alimony and child support are sought and granted, and payments made.[30] Consider the following.

29. This is an equitable result in partnership status terms. However, it may seem unfair to some that Joan and Phil end up with the same income despite the fact that Phil earns a larger salary in his job than she does in hers.

30. Few of these studies take into account the probability that there were property division transfers rather than or in addition to alimony and child support. There are no adequate statistics on the frequency with which the courts order property division transfers, the economic significance of such transfers for the parties to the divorce, or the relationship of property division to other kinds of transfers. In any event, property

a. Percentage of Cases in Which Payments Were Sought or Ordered, and Amounts Awarded

In six studies reporting data collected between 1922 and 1965, alimony was requested in from 3.7 to 27 percent of the cases, and awarded in from 2 percent to 16.5 percent of the cases.[31] In the one study which reported both property and child support awards as well as alimony, the percentages were only slightly higher.[32] In the same study, done in the 1930s, there was also evidence that wives without child custody were unlikely to receive either money or property.[33] A study in Chicago showed that one third of the minor children involved in divorces in 1949 and 1950 were awarded no child support at all.[34]

Data reported in various studies, which was collected between 1931 and 1965, show child support payments (or child support and alimony payments combined) averaging from $33 to $140 a month, with a substantial minority of children awarded no payments at all or amounts under $10 a week.[35]

---

division transfers are probably a significant possibility in only a small percentage of marriage dissolutions. See infra, Part VI-B-1, footnote 8.

31. Alimony was requested in 7 percent of 12,000 Chicago divorce cases. Virtue, Family Cases in Court 92 (1956). In 1922, the last year the Census Bureau kept alimony data, alimony was decreed in 15 percent of a nationwide sample of cases. Jacobson, American Marriage and Divorce 126 (1959). (Both sources as cited in Nagel and Weitzman, Women as Litigants, 23 Hast. L. J. 171, 190, n. 50 (1971).) Alimony was requested in 3.7 percent and granted in 6.6 percent of 3000 Maryland cases in 1929; alimony was sought in 27.5 percent of 6800 divorces granted in Ohio in 1930, and granted in 16.5 percent. 1 Marshall and May, The Divorce Court 18, 311 (1932); 2 id at 322-323 (1933), as cited in Foote, Levy, and Sander, Cases and Materials on Family Law 937, n.n. 36 and 37 (1966). The following estimates were made by domestic relations judges surveyed: alimony waived in 10 percent of all divorces; temporary alimony granted in less than 10 percent of all divorces; permanent alimony granted in less than 2 percent of all divorces. Quoted in Quenstedt and Winkler, What Are Our Domestic Relations Judges Thinking?, Monograph No. 1, A.B.A. Section of Family Law, July 1965, pp. 2-6, as excerpted in the Citizen's Advisory Council on the Status of Women, The Equal Rights Amendment and Alimony and Child Support Laws 4 (1972). In a Kansas study, alimony was granted in 3 cases out of 17. Hopson, The Economics of a Divorce: A Pilot Empirical Study at the Trial Court Level, 11 Kan. L. Rev. 107 (1962).

32. Marshall and May reported that in the Ohio study child support was awarded in 19.4 percent of the cases, although it was only sought in the original petition in 13 percent; property settlements were awarded in 12.4 percent of the cases, although only sought in 9.9 percent. 2 Marshall and May, supra, at 322-323.

33. In the Ohio study, the wife received money or property in 75 percent of the 2058 cases in which she was given custody of the children, but this proportion dropped to 19 percent in the 4528 cases in which she did not receive custody of children. 2 Marshall and May, supra, at 330-331, 333-334, 340, as discussed in Foote, Levy, and Sander, supra, at 937, n. 37.

34. Robson, The Law and Practice of Divorce — The Judge's Point of View, in University of Chicago Law School Conference on Divorce 4 (Conference Ser. no. 9, 1952). There is little data on the number of women legally entitled to receive alimony pursuant to privately negotiated separation or divorce settlement agreements. Estimates of the percentage of private settlements in divorce cases range from about 25 percent (1 Marshall and May, supra, at 220-221, cited in Foote, Levy, and Sander, supra, at 938, n. 39) to 45 percent (Hopson, supra, at 118). Common sense would suggest that private agreements would be more common among higher-income people, and therefore that the proportion of private agreements which include alimony payments would be higher than the proportion of court-ordered financial settlements which include alimony. However, Hopson, in the Kansas study mentioned above, found that nine of his seventeen agreements were in cases where the parties had from $2000 assets down to "nothing," and that, overall, in only three cases of the seventeen was there alimony in the popular sense of the word. Id. at 115, 126. Furthermore, the considerable percentage of privately negotiated agreements which *are* incorporated into court decrees is probably reflected in the court data presented above. Finally, what the parties bargain for is probably affected to a great extent by information from their lawyers about what they could expect to get through litigation of the financial issues, so the limited availability of alimony in court makes alimony by private agreement less available.

35. See 2 Marshall and May, supra, at 330-331, 333-334, 340, reported in Foote, Levy, and Sander at 937; Gellhorn, Children and Families in the Courts of New York City 341, 343-344; Goode, supra, at 221-222, citing also Robson, supra; data from Quenstedt and Winkler, supra, at 2-3, as reported in The Equal Rights Amendment and Alimony and Child Support Laws, supra, at 6-8.

b. Enforcement and Compliance with Child Support and Alimony Payments

A 1955 study of families receiving aid to dependent children, though obviously unrepresentative of the population as a whole, illustrates some of the frustrations inherent in the enforcement of private support obligations among those with insufficient means for self-support. Child support payments . . . had been ordered or agreed to in 42 percent of the . . . families where the now absent father had once been on the scene, married to the mother of the child. But in only about half of these cases (and only 18.3 percent of the total cases) was any support actually received from the father. The total contributed annually by these fathers was estimated at . . . only about 10 percent of the total public assistance funds expended on these families. Almost one out of every ten fathers was either currently or had at some time in the past been imprisoned for criminal nonsupport.[36]

Table 3-6, prepared by Nagel and Weitzman, illustrates the low levels of enforcement and compliance with child support orders which are apparently typical. Nagel and Weitzman's calculations are consistent with data reported by Goode and by Gellhorn.[37]

36. Foote, Levy, and Sander, supra, at 938, discussing Kaplan, Support from Absent Fathers of Children Receiving ADC 1955, at 7, 15-16, 24-26, 75 (Table A-50) (U.S. Bureau of Public Assistance Rep. No. 41, 1960).
37. Goode reported that in a Detroit study done in 1948, "in a substantial proportion of cases, the child support payments are not met. . . . In somewhat less than half of the cases there is apparently continuity of payments." Women in Divorce, supra, at 222. Excluding cases in which the wife did not have full custody, the ex-husband continued to make payments "always" in only 35 percent of the cases, "usually" in 14 percent of the cases, "once in a while" in 11 percent of the cases, and "rarely or never" in 40 percent of the cases. Id. Even among ex-husbands who apparently had steady employment, 26 percent rarely made child support payments, as compared to 38 percent of ex-husbands who had frequently been unemployed during the marriage. Goode found that the amount of the ex-husband's earnings had no apparent relationship to continuity of payments. Id at 223.
As might be expected, wives who had remarried were less likely to receive child support payments regularly, even though their remarriages had no legal effect on their former husbands' responsibility to support the children of their earlier marriages. Goode reports that "30 percent of the wives who have remarried received their payments always, as against 45 percent of the not remarried." Id at 226.
Gellhorn, in his study of the family court of New York County in 1951-52, also found evidence that defaults on payments are common. Gellhorn, Children and Families in the Courts of New York City 343-344 (1954).
The reasons that fathers do not comply with support orders are not clear. One reason might be that the orders are too high and do not sufficiently consider the ability of the father to pay. But data available, although extremely limited, does not indicate that this is the problem.
One study (based on analysis of new child support cases during the period December 7 through December 18, 1970 in five California counties, comprising 527 fathers of welfare children and 103 fathers of nonwelfare children) of the characteristics of nonsupporting fathers shows an occupational distribution similar to that of the entire male population — not a predominance of low-income occupations, and not a very high proportion of unemployed (9 percent were reported as unemployed, in the recession year of 1970). Five percent were described as professional or semiprofessional, another 5 percent as proprietor/manager/official, and 8 percent as craftsmen or foremen.
The same study appears to refute several other commonly held beliefs about nonsupporting fathers:
"They have not disappeared. Usually they were living in the same county as their children.
"They are not supporting many other children. Ninety-two percent of the nonsupporting fathers had a total of 3 or fewer children.
"Only 13 percent were married to other women, with another 1 percent each divorced or separated from another or of unknown marital status. The nonwelfare fathers were more likely to have remarried; the welfare fathers were more likely to be still married to the 'complaining witness.'
"The amount of child support awarded was not unreasonably large. For those nonsupporting fathers who were already under court order to contribute to their children's support, the typical payment ordered was $50 a month. In 33 percent of the *nonwelfare* cases, the order called for $50 or less."
Winston and Forsher, Nonsupport of Legitimate Children by Affluent Fathers as a Cause of Poverty and Welfare Dependence 15-16 (Rand Corp. 1971).

TABLE 3-6. THE PROBABILITY OF A DIVORCED WOMAN COLLECTING ANY CHILD SUPPORT
MONEY
(by years since the court order)

Years since court order	Number of open cases	Full compliance	Partial compliance	No compliance	Non-paying fathers against whom legal action was taken
One	163	38%	20%	42%	19%
Two	163	28	20	52	32
Three	161	26	14	60	21
Four	161	22	11	67	18
Five	160	19	14	67	9
Six	158	17	12	71	6
Seven	157	17	12	71	4
Eight	155	17	8	75	2
Nine	155	17	8	75	0
Ten	149	13	8	79	1

Source: Nagel and Weitzman, Women as Litigants, 23 Hast. L.J. 171, 190 (1971); based on data from Eckhardt, Deviance, Visibility, and Legal Action: The Duty to Support, 15 Social Problems 470, 473–474 (1968).

The amount and enforcement of support payments must be considered in light of the cost of raising a child. The Citizens Advisory Council on the Status of Women reports:[38]

> The average cost at 1969 prices of rearing a child in a two child urban family with both parents present ranges, according to Department of Agriculture estimates, from $1,400 per year on a low-cost budget in the north central area of the U.S. to $2,100 per year on a moderate-cost budget in the south. In a divided family with the mother working food costs would be higher, and there would be added child care costs.[2]

Thus, assuming a cost per child of $1500 per year (a conservative estimate), the father is providing less than half the child support in all families where child support awards are less than $60 per child per month. And of course when the awards are not complied with fully, or at all, the father may be supplying far less than half the child's support. Families in which this is the case are probably in the majority among the divorced and separated.

3. Other Indices of the Economic Position of Separated and Divorced People

a. Labor Force Participation Rates

According to Waldman and Gover:[39]

> The chance for divorced and separated women to be in the labor force is gener-ally much greater than for wives or widows. In March 1971, 70 percent of all divorcees,

38. Citizens Advisory Council on the Status of Women, Women in 1971, Appendix C, The Equal Rights Amendment and Alimony and Child Support Laws, at 47 (1972).
2. Information from Agricultural Research Service, Consumer and Food Economics Research Division, U.S. Dept. of Agriculture — excerpt from Family Economics Review, December 1970 and talk by Jean L. Pennock at the 47th Annual Agricultural Outlook Conference, February 18, 1970.
39. Waldman and Gover, Marital and Family Characteristics of the Labor Force, Monthly Labor Review, April 1972, at 7, with corrections and supplementary tables, U.S. Bureau of Labor Statistics Reprint 2798.

including those who were not family heads, and 50 percent of all separated women were in the labor force, compared with about 41 percent of all wives and only 26 percent of all widows.

Among the most obvious elements that account for the differences in labor force rates are the presence and age of children, and the need for self support. In March 1971, the proportion of divorcees with preschool age children (13 percent) was considerably lower than for married (20 percent) or separated women (24 percent).

Even so, with children under 6 years old, divorcees had a much greater labor force participation rate — 62 percent — than the other mothers of young children — 30 and 41 percent, respectively — suggesting that many either receive no child support payments or find them insufficient.

It is interesting that the labor force participation rates of divorced men and women are very close; of all divorced white men, 74.0 percent were in the labor force in 1960, the comparable figure for nonwhite men was 73.4; for white women 71 percent and for nonwhite women 69.4 percent. Thus, divorced women participated in the labor force 94.6 to 95.9 percent as much as divorced men. From 35 to 65 years of age, the labor force participation rates of men and women stayed quite close. However, white women between 20 and 24 dropped to 84.2 percent of white men of that age, and nonwhite women in that age group dropped to 74.7 percent of nonwhite men of that age. Divorced women's labor force participation rates stayed relatively low throughout the childbearing and childraising years of 20 to 35, ranging between a low for nonwhite women 20-24 years of age of 58.9 percent and a high for white women 30-34 years of age of 78.2 percent. Men's labor force participation rates were at their highest in these years, ranging up to 88.6 percent for white men and to 81.3 percent for nonwhite men.[40]

b. The Economic Status of One-Parent Families

The economic status of families with children and only one adult present provides important data about the consequences of marriage dissolution for men and for women. This is so because a large proportion of divorced and separated people have children under eighteen. A substantial minority of these divorced parents do not remarry, and for all, there is some period of time before remarriage. As noted in Section D-1, supra, few men are ever in the situation of running a single-parent household. Therefore this discussion will concentrate on the position of "female-headed"[41] single-parent families, as compared with two-parent families and as compared with divorced and separated men who have not remarried (and who will be assumed not to have children in their custody).

The following data were presented by Stein in a Monthly Labor Review article:[42]

— 3.4 million of the 5.6 million families headed by women include children under eighteen: 2.3 million families headed by divorced or separated women, 0.9 million by widows, and 0.2 by single women. An average female-headed family with children under eighteen includes 2.4 children.

— "By March 1970, about three-fifths of the 3.4 million families with children headed by women were already on welfare and the rolls were still rising."

— "The median income of the families of 8 million children who were being brought up by their mothers — or other female relatives — was $4,000 in 1969. This contrasts with a median family income of $11,600 for the 60 million children living with both parents. . . . Although husband-wife families tend to be larger than families headed

---

40. Carter and Glick, supra, at 258, Table 8.28 (1970).

41. As mentioned previously, the use of the terms "female-headed" to mean families with no male adult present, and "male-headed" to mean families with both a male and a female adult present, is itself sexist. Therefore, a neutral term, such as two-parent family, will be substituted where possible.

42. Stein, The Economic Status of Families Headed by Women, from the December 1970 Monthly Labor Review, U.S. Bureau of Labor Statistics Reprint 2703, at 3-5.

by women, the differences in income between the two types of families far exceed any differences in need."

— "In 1969, 47 out of every 100 poor families with children were headed by women. In 1959, the proportion was 28 out of 100."

In comparison with divorced and separated men, divorced and separated women have considerably lower incomes. In 1959, white divorced and separated men exceeded white divorced and separated women by $800 to $1000 in median income each year; nonwhite divorced and separated men exceeded nonwhite divorced and separated women by about $800 per year.[43] If the incomes of people in these segments of the population increased between 1959 and 1971 in proportion to the changes in income of the working population as a whole, the gaps have increased rather than decreased over time.[44] Since divorced and separated women with young children have lower labor force participation rates than those without young children, it is likely that divorced and separated women with one or more children in their households have even lower incomes relative to divorced and separated men than the comparison of all divorced women and all divorced men suggests.

4. *Summary*

As will be further discussed in Part VI, *infra*, the upper middle-class divorce is overrepresented both in the personal experience of most lawyers and judges and in the reported law on divorce. As a result, many people believe that most divorced women are financially well off at the expense of their ex-husbands. Yet the data suggest that, in the majority of cases, divorced women are in fact worse off financially than their ex-husbands and that rarely is either spouse richer after divorce.

E. Conclusions and Analyses

As was pointed out in Parts II and III, *supra*, women are forced into a subordinate position in marriage — legally, psychologically, and economically — by a combination of job discrimination, outmoded patriarchal status concepts in marriage and property law, and government programs which discriminate against married women, especially those with children, both in and out of the labor force. The divorce laws make a bad situation worse. The right of support for the wife and children is in many, if not most, cases meaningless in practice. Child care, even more necessary for divorced or separated women with children than for married women, is not available to either group, and child care costs are still discriminatorily treated for income tax purposes. Sex discrimination in the labor market remains a serious problem, coupled with race discrimination for black women, of whom a larger proportion than of white women are separated or divorced. As a result, women who head one-parent households are poor in gross disproportion to their percentage of the population, despite their considerably higher labor force participation rates.

It seems paradoxical, then, that women seek divorces in larger numbers than do men. Goode suggests that the higher percentage of women than men responsible for initiating and pursuing legal divorce proceedings does not necessarily mean that the wife initiated the conflict leading to the divorce. He posits that it is more usual for the husband to be the first to wish to escape from the marriage. This is so because of his greater freedom in the world outside the home, which gives him attractive alternatives

43. Carter and Glick, *supra*, at 266, Table 8.34.
44. The President's Economic Report to Congress, January 1973, as discussed in Chapman, *Job Bias Affecting Women Found To Drop Only Slightly*, The Washington Post, Jan. 31, 1973, at A-1, A-14.

to his present family relationships.[45] The strategy of conflict, by which the husband can reduce his guilt over ending the marriage once he has already decided he wants out, is to "make himself so obnoxious that his wife is willing to ask for and even insist upon divorce."[46] Viewed in this light, the question is not whether divorce is good for women, but whether divorce is a preferable alternative to a particular woman's current marital situation.

It is also understandable that so many divorcees remarry, or that they have remarriage as a goal.[47] Goode lists a number of reasons supporting this form of "adjustment" to divorce, including not only the simple economic fact that men can earn more than women, but more complex factors, such as the woman's conflicts about going to work, especially when there are likely to be no adequate arrangements for child care and the expected income is inadequate to cover child care expenses; social pressures to get married as a result of the couple-based structure of adult society; demands from the children that the mother remarry; and the inconvenience of sexual pleasure outside marriage, especially when there are children.[48]

At a more profound level, Goode describes how the role of mother as institutionalized in our society virtually requires the remarriage of divorcees who have young children. The focus of the kinship institutions of our society is the care and status of children. This means that relationships through children determine most kinship relationships of adults. This is particularly true for women with small children, because "mother" is a primary status. That is, the status of mother is one in comparison with which all other role obligations are residual and must wait until those of mother are satisfied. As Goode explains, "the legitimacy of *non*maternal responsibilities is questioned unless it can be shown that the maternal responsibilities themselves are being met; and the clarity and moral force of this prescription are greater than for [the] other statuses [of a mother]."[49] In our society, motherhood is defined to require mothers to raise their children with fathers or father substitutes, to stay at home while their children are young, and not to relinquish custody of their children to others. Achieving these goals is difficult for most divorcee-mothers; their divorces disrupt to a high degree the kinship institutions which surround themselves and their children, and interfere with the mother status they are expected to place before all other roles. Goode adds:[50]

> In our own society the structural disruptions created by a high divorce rate without explicit postdivorce institutions are accentuated by (1) the fairly general disapproval of divorce, particularly when children are involved; and (2) the perhaps increasing structural importance of the nuclear family as the primary kinship unit, that is the family composed of parents and children, and with few strong ties with further generations or collateral relatives. . . .

Goode describes the resulting situation as a high degree of status ambiguity for the divorcee-mother. Her primary role as mother as defined by her society is in conflict with the practical consequences of her divorce. The legal and social definitions of her status as a divorcee are somewhat ambiguous, and do not provide institutionalized support for combining the role with that of mother. He concludes:[51]

> The kinship institutions do not, then, make provision for the consequences of divorce, *within* its structure. But, *by the very fact that there are no such provisions, no set of status*

45. Goode, supra, at 133-135.
46. Id. at 135-136.
47. Id. at chs. 15 and 19.
48. Id. at ch. 15.
49. Id. at 209.
50. Id. at 208.
51. Id. at 216.

privileges and stigmata, which would allow the divorcee to play easily the mother role outside marriage, the institutional patterns create pressures toward new marriages, while offering some positive inducements in the same direction. There is thus as yet little direct institutionalization of postdivorce adjustment. But the larger kinship patterns nevertheless force very similar behavior on divorcees, by making difficult or inconvenient any other status than that of married mother.

It is thus that our society has been able to bear such a high rate of divorce without specific, direct kinship prescriptions for handling the problems that are created by the dissolution of a marriage. Although the rate of divorce is high, the existing kinship institutions indirectly move both child and mother back into relatively well-defined statuses. . . .

The fact that many divorcees remarry does not eliminate all cause for concern about the differential impact of marriage and divorce on women and men. First, many divorcees do not remarry (not to mention separated women who are not legally able to remarry), and all remain unmarried for some period of time. Second, the fact that marriage and remarriage are desirable options for women could be interpreted as highlighting the fact that women's alternatives in general are not good.

VI. THE LAW OF DIVORCE

A. A Brief History of American Divorce Law

FOOTE, LEVY, AND SANDER
CASES AND MATERIALS ON FAMILY LAW
172, 646-648 (1966)

"The Catholic Church taught from the very beginning the indissolubility of marriage, and by the tenth century this doctrine had become embodied in the civil law of every Christian country."[6] In England, of course, the ecclesiastical courts were eventually successful in asserting jurisdiction over the entire province of marriage, and at a very early period "the marriage law of England was the canon law."[7] The Church insisted that marriages be relatively easy to enter . . . but impossible to dissolve. Yet an ecclesiastical court could and would declare that a marriage had never existed (although the marriage had to be "void ab initio" to avoid the implication that it was being dissolved). Thus the apparent indissolubility of marriage was

> softened by the wide discretion exercised by the Church in annulling marriages. There was no valid marriage if the parties were within the forbidden degrees of consanguinity or affinity, these degrees being stretched by the medieval canonists to an astonishing extent. . . . The annulling of marriages between parties within the prohibited degrees became a flourishing business of the Church, and for sufficient payment a flaw could be found in almost every union. . . .[8]

Before 1857, since exclusive jurisdiction in matrimonial matters in England was in the ecclesiastical courts, the only judicial decree which was available was separation a mensa et thoro (from bed and board) without right of remarriage. 1 Holdsworth, A History of English Law 622-624 (6th ed. 1938). Although for a brief period after the

---

6. 2 U. Toronto L.J. at 320, Selected Essays on Family Law at 231.
7. 2 Pollock & Maitland 367-368. (2d ed. 1899).
8. Comment, 171 Law Times 462, 463 (1931).

Reformation these courts took the position that they could grant an absolute divorce, in 1602 this opinion was overruled, and for the next two and one-half centuries the only method of divorce granting the right of remarriage was by a prolonged and very expensive procedure culminating in a private act of Parliament. See generally id. at 621-625. During this period, although the ecclesiastical courts were no longer subject to Rome, they applied the principles of canon law in which they had been steeped for many centuries. Because of the continuing force of these principles in the evolution of modern civil law, a brief review of the major canon law provisions is necessary.

. . . [U]nder canon law . . . the underlying doctrine is that a "valid and consummated marriage of baptized persons can be dissolved by no human power and for no cause other than death" (Canon 1118). Marriage involves, moreover, the duty that "Spouses must live together unless a justifying reason excuses them from doing so" (Canon 1128). For a discussion of the strict construction given to this and other relevant canons, see Genuario, Rotal Criteria for Granting Separations, 22 Jurist 333 (1962). The Sacred Roman Rota, highest judicial authority in the Church, has been quoted as stating (id. at 344):

> "It has been the constant jurisprudence of this Sacred Tribunal . . . that great caution should be used in granting separations from bed and board, because separation is directly opposed to the very purpose and ends of marriage; it gives rise to scandal; it destroys the family; it exposes the consorts to the danger of incontinence; and it inflicts a severe loss on children, if there are any. . . . There is no one who does not know that if *divortium semiplenum* is easily granted, the way is made easy for *divortium plenum*. For matrimony exists also as a remedy for concupiscence and, if common life is dissolved by separation, immediately it opens the door to adulterous amours and illicit associations."

Permanent separation can be granted only for adultery, with the proviso that the spouse granted the right to live separately has not "given consent to the offense, caused it, or expressly or tacitly condoned it, or has himself also been guilty of the same offense" (Canon 1129). A temporary separation, good only until "the reason for the separation ceases to exist," is available if "one of the spouses joins a non-Catholic sect, or procures the non-Catholic rearing of the children, or leads a criminal or disgraceful life, or creates for the other a serious threat to the latter's soul or body, or makes the common life unduly burdensome by cruelty" (Canon 1131).

Under canon law, therefore, separation is relief for the innocent spouse from the duty of cohabitation because of the guilt of the other spouse. For the offending spouse it is a punitive measure, and for neither is there any possibility of remarriage. This is the seedbed from which our civil law has sprung. With respect to the abolition in 1857 of the ecclesiastical courts and the establishment of absolute divorce *a vinculo matrimonii* for adultery, Holdsworth quotes with approval the observation:

"Not the least part of the merit and success of the Act of 1857 is due to the skill which, while effecting a great social change, did so with the smallest possible amount of innovation." 1 Holdsworth, History of English Law 624 (,6th ed. 1938). This minimum of innovation was accomplished by incorporating into the law of absolute divorce the jurisprudence which had grown up around separation.

In America both the assertion of civil jurisdiction and the utilization of canonical principles for separation as grounds for absolute divorce came much earlier than in England. Haskins has noted that in Massachusetts "the absence of a separate ecclesiastical court in the colony almost necessarily entailed its taking jurisdiction over divorce." He continues:

[T]he colonists appear to have abandoned the conception of the divorce a mensa et thoro and to have granted divorces a vinculo in the same types of situations in which the bishops' courts issued a mensa decrees. A decree of separation was incompatible with colonial ideas, constantly expressed in the legislation and court records, that the unattached individual was a potential danger to the community. If a marriage was effectively to be dissolved for practical purposes, it was thought wiser both for the parties and for the community that they be free to settle themselves in new marriages than to pose continual threats to the stability of other households. . . .[9]

But even with this earlier and more radical development, the thread of a common history is apparent to anyone comparing current American legislation with canon law and the jurisprudence of the English ecclesiastical courts.

Professor Kanowitz has pointed out that, from the very first, divorces were granted on sex-discriminatory grounds:[1]

> Between the reign of Charles II and 1857, when the Matrimonial Causes Act was enacted to permit total divorces to be granted by the newly-established Court of Divorce and Matrimonial Causes, absolute divorces were frequently granted by act of Parliament.[345] From 1715 to 1800, for example, at least 134 divorces were granted in this manner.[346] In only five cases, however, were they granted on the petition of wives.[347] Professor Madden has observed that in "all of these cases there were aggravating circumstances, in addition to adultery on the part of the husband, which would make future reconciliation impossible. Thus different standards of morality were enforced between the sexes.[348]
>
> Even with the passage of the Matrimonial Causes Act of 1857, the practice of requiring aggravating circumstances for a wife to be granted a divorce for the husband's adultery but not in the reverse situation was continued. This state of affairs persisted for another 66 years in England until, finally, under the Matrimonial Causes Act of 1923, a wife was permitted to maintain a petition for adultery alone.[349]

Today absolute divorce is available in every state, and in many states the identification of fault as the basis of divorce has been replaced by new no-fault grounds, such as voluntary separation for some specified time, or "irretrievable breakdown." Even in states which do not have such new liberal grounds, couples often agree to allege as fictions the appropriate grounds for divorce.[2] And, of course, "the great mobility of middle class Americans [permits] them to go to a state which has liberal grounds for divorce, or abroad, when they want to dissolve a marriage."[3]

Despite the recent reforms and the ability of many people to get divorced by evading restrictive state laws,[4]

> the statutory grounds for divorce which remain in effect in most states are of concern because they still control in contested divorce situations, because they affect the economic and personal relations of the parties even in consent divorces, and because there is evidence that they cause a disproportionate amount of difficulty to poor people.

9. Haskins, Law and Authority in Early Massachusetts 195 (1960).

1. Kanowitz, Women and the Law 94 (1969).

345. Keezer, Marriage and Divorce 297 (3d ed. Moreland 1946).

346. Jacobs & Goebel, Domestic Relations 337, 338 (4th ed. 1961).

347. Madden [Handbook of the Law of Persons and Domestic Relations (1931)].

348. Id.

349. Jacobs & Goebel, supra note [346] at 412.

2. Brown, Emerson, Falk and Freedman, The Equal Rights Amendment: A Constitutional Basis for Equal Rights for Women, 80 Yale L.J. 871, 949 (1971).

3. Id.

4. Id.

Furthermore, the fault background of divorce law sometimes affects judicial behavior even in states with reformed laws.

B. Sex Discrimination in Divorce Grounds

BROWN, EMERSON, FALK, AND FREEDMAN
THE EQUAL RIGHTS AMENDMENT:
A CONSTITUTIONAL BASIS
FOR EQUAL RIGHTS FOR WOMEN
80 Yale L.J. 871, 949-950 (1971)

In the past many grounds for divorce were highly sex discriminatory; today only a few apply solely to one sex or the other. These are non-age, pregnancy by a man other than husband at time of marriage,[178] nonsupport,[179] alcoholism of husband if and only if accompanied by wasting of his estate to the detriment of his wife and children,[180] wife's unchaste behavior (without actual proof of adultery),[181] husband's vagrancy,[182] wife's absence from state for ten years without husband's consent,[183] wife's refusal to move with husband without reasonable cause,[184] wife a prostitute before marriage,[185] husband a drug addict,[186] indignities by husband to wife's person,[187] and wilful neglect by husband.[188]

Except for nonsupport . . . all the sex discriminatory grounds for divorce listed above are anachronisms, surviving in only one or two states. . . .

Of the thirty states which allow a woman a divorce for nonsupport, only two — Arkansas and North Dakota — give a husband whose wife has failed to support him a cause of action.[189]

C. The Concepts of Alimony, Child Support, and Property Division

The "alimony drone" is a persistent stereotype. The common view is that the courts award overly generous alimony to women who could earn livings but who prefer to sit home munching chocolates and enjoying their ex-husbands' money, while the ex-husbands slave to support two households. The reality is a good deal more complex.

178. A ground for divorce in at least thirteen states: Alabama, Arizona, Georgia, Iowa, Kentucky, Mississippi, Missouri, New Mexico, North Carolina, Oklahoma, Tennessee, Virginia, and Wyoming. See, e.g., N.C. Gen. Stat. §50-5(3) (1966); Va. Code Ann. §20-91(7) (Cum. Supp. 1970).
179. A ground for divorce in thirty states: Alabama, Alaska, Arizona, Arkansas, California, Colorado, Delaware, Hawaii, Idaho, Indiana, Kansas, Maine, Massachusetts, Michigan, Montana, Nebraska, Nevada, New Hampshire, New Mexico, North Dakota, Oklahoma, Ohio, Rhode Island, South Dakota, Tennessee, Utah, Vermont, Washington, Wisconsin, and Wyoming. Report on Family Law 66. See, e.g., Cal. Civ. Code Ann. §105 (West 1954); Mass. Gen. Laws Ann. ch. 208, §1 (1969).
180. Kentucky only. Ky. Rev. Stat. §403.020(3)(a) (1960). The husband can get a divorce for his wife's alcoholism without any qualifications.
181. Kentucky only. Ky. Rev. Stat. §403.020(4)(c) (1960).
182. Missouri and Wyoming. Mo. Ann. Stat. §452.010 (1949); Wyo. Stat. Ann. §20-38, Ninth (1957).
183. New Hampshire only. N.H. Rev. Stat. Ann. §458-7, XII (1965).
184. Tennessee only. Wife must remain wilfully absent for two years. Tenn. Code Ann. §36-801(8) (1955).
185. Virginia only. Va. Code Ann. §20-91(8) (Cum. Supp. 1970).
186. Alabama only. Ala. Code tit. 34 §20(6) (1959).
187. Tennessee only. Tenn. Code Ann. §36-802 (1955).
188. Montana only. Mont. Rev. Codes Ann. §21-115 (1967).
189. Ark. Stat. Ann. §34-1202, Ninth (Cum. Supp. 1969); N.D. Cent. Code §14-05-07 (1960).

Some women undoubtedly do get unduly high alimony payments. As the statistics in Part V, supra, show, however, the majority of women get no alimony, and those who do, do not collect for very long. And most alimony and child support payments are extremely low, so that even women who are getting payments from their ex-husbands often contribute more to their own and their childrens' support than the fathers do.

Much of the "law" of divorce is, of course, appellate opinions. These opinions may serve to reinforce the alimony drone stereotype because of the socioeconomic status of the people who appeal divorce cases. Generally, middle- and upper-income people are the only ones who can pay for an appeal and who have sufficient property to make extended litigation worthwhile. Awards to the ex-wives of middle- and upper-income men, which are naturally higher than the average, thus make a larger impact on the consciousness of lawyers and the public than the more common situation of splitting a modest income in order to support two households. In addition, most cases which reach appellate courts are contested divorces in which one spouse thinks that enough injustice has been done to make reversal a possibility. Thus, extreme fact situations are overrepresented in the reported law.

A third reason for the persistence of the myth of the alimony drone is the common practice of labeling as alimony interspousal transfers which actually are spent to support the children. To understand this facet, the reader must first know that there are three main kinds of transfers of money and property between ex-spouses: alimony (or separate maintenance), child support, and property division.[5] In theory the three are quite different. Alimony and separate maintenance are for the support of the wife, and child support is for the minor children of the parties. Property division sometimes serves to settle disputes about which property is joint and which is separate and the shares each should get of joint property. However, property transfers can also serve the functions of alimony or child support.

In addition to these differences in function, there are other distinctions among the types of property transfers.[6] Alimony is deductible from the income of the payor spouse and is treated as income to the recipient spouse for income tax purposes, giving it some of the benefits of a joint tax return. In general, alimony payments cease upon the remarriage of the recipient spouse. Historically, alimony was available only to the wife, but now awards are made to the husband in many states. Alimony may be paid as a lump sum or periodically.

Child support is not legally affected by the remarriage of either spouse, but ceases for each child when he or she reaches some specific age, usually between fifteen and twenty-one years. Child support payments are taxable as income to the payor spouse (who gets to take the dependent deduction only if he provides more than half of that child's support) and not to the recipient spouse. Alimony awards are generally modifiable by the court, sometimes even if the parties have provided otherwise by private agreement. Child support awards are always modifiable, since the welfare of the children is the paramount consideration.

Property division is usually accomplished through single-transaction transfers. Whatever the payment arrangements, payments pursuant to a property division are final

---

5. The following discussion of types of interspousal transfers and their principal characteristics is based primarily on Clark, Law of Domestic Relations ch. 14, §§14.1 et seq. See also Foote, Levy, and Sander, Cases and Materials on Family Law 631-682, 924-957 (1966) and Paulsen, Wadlington, and Goebel, Cases and Other Materials on Domestic Relations 521-612 (1970).

6. There are also differences in enforcement mechanisms, which are discussed in Section E-3, infra. Of particular importance is the fact that alimony and child support obligations, including accumulated arrears, are not dischargeable in bankruptcy and are not subject to the constitutional prohibition against imprisonment for debt. Property settlement payments, on the contrary, are generally held to be debts dischargeable in bankruptcy, and failure to make such payments cannot constitutionally be punished by imprisonment. See, e.g., Bradley v. Superior Court, 48 Cal. 2d 509, 310 P.2d 634 (1957), for discussion of the law on this point. It seems unlikely, however, that these considerations play much of a role in the negotiation of most divorce settlement agreements.

as of the date of the decree and are unaffected by the remarriage of either spouse, the age of the children, or other changes in circumstances. While some courts do not have the legal authority to award property to which one spouse has legal title to the other pursuant to a divorce decree, the power to award lump sum alimony may amount to the same thing.[7] Also, the parties can agree to a property division instead of alimony even if the courts do not have the power independently to make such an award. The majority of divorcing couples have very little property, however.[8]

Because the label applied to interspousal transfers pursuant to a divorce or separation has so much practical significance, it is a common subject of bargaining between the parties. One arrangement is for the recipient spouse to agree to have some of the child support money labeled "alimony" in return for higher total payments. Since this is the form of mislabeling which is the most beneficial to the parties viewed as an economic unit (because of its income tax consequences), it is the most common. Thus, from a functional point of view, payments labeled as alimony are often child support.

A fourth reason that the average amount of alimony is believed to be higher than it is in actuality is the practice, common among payor spouses, lawyers, judges, and the public, of comparing the income of the payor spouse, minus alimony, child support, property transfer payments, and income taxes, to the income of the recipient spouse, before taxes and including child support. This favors husbands, usually the payor spouses, and encourages the idea that divorce settlements are unfair to men.

Probably the most important reason for the popular belief that alimony is unfair to the payor spouse is the fact that alimony is a noncontractual concept in a largely contractual society. Originally, alimony was a means of continuing the status of marriage despite the end of marital cohabitation. The English ecclesiastical courts, whose concept of alimony was the foundation for modern law on this subject, granted only divorces *a mensa et thoro* (from bed and board), the equivalent of legal separations:[9]

> The alimony of the canon law was grounded on a husband's duty to support his wife, a duty deemed to be continuing because the decree *mensa et thoro* did not dissolve the marriage but merely effected a physical separation, the husband retaining, of course, the control of the wife's property.

Alimony was usually not awarded if the wife was at fault, although such an award could be made.[10] The wife's right to alimony was a substitute for maintenance in her husband's household. Therefore the quantum of her recovery was alimony sufficient to maintain her in accordance with the previous standard of living of the parties.

In modern law, the status-based system for awarding alimony has been supplemented by other approaches. The two main themes of the reported cases are need and fairness. The practical need for financial transfers may be the result of any of three causes: (1) the inability of the spouse with custody of the children to support them alone, often as a result of that spouse's continued performance of domestic services in the form of child care after divorce; (2) one spouse's past performance of the traditional role of housewife, which has prevented her or him from acquiring assets (whether in the form of contractual rights, savings, unemployment or old age insurance, or property) or maintaining or improving her or his wage-earning capacity to protect her/himself in the event of marriage dissolution; (3) physical or emotional disabilities of either spouse, including advanced age, whether or not the result of marital roles and fortunes.

In such situations, the law provides that the wage-earning spouse be required to support the other before the state's resources are tapped. In England, during the seven-

---

7. See Clark, supra, at 449.

8. Of the 425 divorced women interviewed in 1948 in Detroit, 40 percent reported no property, with another 35 percent reporting property worth $1999 or less. Goode, Women in Divorce 217-221 (1956).

9. Paulsen, Wadlington, and Goebel, supra, at 529.

10. Id. at n. 2.

teenth century, a dual system of family law existed.[11] With regard to poor people, the Elizabethan Poor Laws established a responsibility of kin and neighbors to the destitute person, with the primary goal of minimizing public cost. For the well-to-do, the ecclesiastical courts enforced the responsibility of the estranged husband for his wife, with the goal of giving limited financial protection to middle- and upper-class married women whose husbands had wronged them. The concept of need (and the reciprocal concept of the husband's ability to pay) was expressed with regard to the latter group only insofar as it was contained in the standard of the husband's station in life. In the United States, need has increasingly become a primary element of middle-class family law, as well as of welfare law. One result has been an increasing tendency to consider the wife's earning capacity and property in setting alimony. A second has been the implementation of a "rehabilitative" focus for alimony. Alimony awarded on this basis looks to the rapid return to independence of the divorced person who was formerly supported. The return will, if necessary, be at a lower standard of living than she or he had enjoyed with the ex-spouse.

The theme of fairness is expressed in various moral judgments about the parties, their behavior and situations, and their roles. Since colonial times, fault concepts have played a larger part in the award of alimony in the United States than they did in the English ecclesiastical courts. The determination of guilt has continued to be a significant determinant of the financial settlements of many contested divorces, despite the increasing trend to grant divorces on a no-fault basis. It is still fairly common for a court to award substantial alimony to the ex-wife of an upper-class adulterer, even though the wife could adequately support herself. She is given continuing financial benefits of her past marital status for a variety of reasons: to punish her ex-husband, to discourage conduct like his by making divorce expensive, or to compensate her for the loss of status resulting from his wrongful behavior. Other opinions have a more contemporary aura, and talk about the broken marriage as a dissolving partnership. These courts serve the ideal of fairness by considering the parties' respective contributions to the marriage as one factor in the award of alimony. In the main, however, their awards are still based primarily on need and ability to pay.

In sum, the concepts of fault, need, ability to pay, and just compensation play greater or lesser parts depending on the amount of money available, the strength of the trial judge's feelings about the conduct of the parties, and the respective situations of the ex-spouses. This interplay is reflected in Clark's summary of contemporary rationales for alimony:[12]

> [A]limony acts indirectly to protect the children of divorce, it prevents the wife from becoming a financial burden to the community, it eases the hardship of transition from marriage to single status, it compensates the wife for services rendered, and to some extent it gives tangible form to moral judgments about the relative fault of the spouses.

Most of these methods of deciding whether and how much alimony will be awarded would produce quite different results from the measures of damages used in a contractual system. For example, if the quasi-contractual standard of quantum meruit were used, the wife might get the value of the services she had performed less the support she had received. The wife of a wealthy man might owe her husband money upon divorce, whereas the wife of a poor man would be owed much more than one third or one half of his income. This is not to say that the wife of a rich man does not perform services, such as entertaining, decorating, and hiring servants, but that the value of her services is much less likely in a market sense to be worth a substantial portion of a

---

11. Ten Broek, California's Dual System of Family Law: Its Origin, Development, and Present Status, 16 Stan. L. Rev. 257-317, 900-981 (1964); 17 id. 614-682 (1965).

12. Clark, supra, at 442.

wealthy man's income. Gilman, in the passage quoted in Part IV-B-2, supra, makes the point also that it is likely that the money goods and perquisites received by a rich wife from her husband reflect her value as a conspicuous consumption item herself, rather than being very close to wages for services performed.

A practical system that would often produce different results from our present one would be giving the homemaking spouse in an ongoing marriage a stated share of the breadwinner's income on a yearly basis, rather than waiting until the dissolution of the marriage to compensate her or him for services rendered.

A serious problem with our present system is that it encourages the idea that a spouse who is awarded alimony does not deserve so much: first, because alimony payments do not vary with the value of the recipient spouse's contribution to the marriage; and second, because judges make quite different awards of alimony in apparently similar situations. With such a system, it is certainly possible that an ex-spouse gets money she or he does not "deserve," at least in reference to marketplace or contractual principles. This does not mean that most women who get alimony have not worked for the payments they receive. Most people would agree that child care and housekeeping involve work, and most women who get alimony have performed or are still performing such services. The problem is that the legal system for awarding alimony obscures this fact. And in a society whose financial dealings are based primarily on quid pro quo, transfers only indirectly related to services performed are suspect.

The increasing social acceptability of divorce exacerbates the anger felt by many people toward a situation in which women, particularly, get money based on status rather than earned in a contractual system. When divorce was viewed as immoral, people were more willing to see the party who wanted out pay for his or her action through the court's granting or withholding high alimony. Now it is fairly widely agreed that if spouses want to end their marriage, they should be able to do so relatively easily.

This does not necessarily mean, however, that marriage has lost importance as an institution. Rather, the societal and legal emphasis has shifted from encouraging people to stay married at whatever cost to encouraging divorced people to find better partners for a second try. One important way to promote remarriage is to minimize ex-spouses' obligations to each other. The change in social goals from punishing divorce toward social neutrality toward divorce and toward encouraging remarriage has caused widespread criticism of alimony, which is associated with the adjudication of guilt and which usually prolongs the relationship between ex-spouses. The needs to compensate housespouses for services rendered or for damages suffered in the course of marriage, to obtain for the children the financial benefits of having two parents, and to pay the housespouse for continuing child care services — functions that alimony has performed in the past, even though it was not always awarded on this basis — are often discounted in the reaction against the status-maintenance and fault-oriented aspects of traditional divorce law.

Criminal nonsupport and desertion statutes, and the use of civil and criminal contempt powers to punish failure to comply with a court order for child support or alimony, also contribute indirectly to the myth of the alimony drone. Statistics on the frequency with which the sanction of imprisonment is used to enforce child and spousal support obligations are not available. However, jail terms are sometimes imposed and are available as sanctions in every jurisdiction.[13] This probably increases public sympathy for spouses who must pay alimony or child support and reinforces the tendency for people to be suspicious of those who receive it.[14]

13. See Clark, supra, at 200, n. 2; Model Penal Code §207.14, Comment at 189 (Tent. Draft No. 9, 1959); Model Penal Code §230.5 (Proposed Official Draft, 1962). In the three states which do not penalize by statute a man's desertion or nonsupport of his wife, it is likely that criminal or civil contempt powers enable the courts to imprison those who fail to comply with a court order for spousal support or alimony. Clark, supra, at 465.

14. The law generally provides that a man can be required to get a job to conform to a court order for support, that alimony and child support arrearages are not dischargeable in bankruptcy, and that imprisonment

Male prejudice is a final possibility in the consideration of why the alimony drone myth persists. Male bias against alimony would not be surprising, since most alimony is paid by men. If men do see alimony as basically unfair, this view would surely influence the overwhelmingly male legal system.

The following cases illustrate the variety of standards that judges use to set alimony awards, and certain additional aspects of divorce law which give rise to sex discrimination.

D. Judicial Standards for the Award of Alimony

SKIFF v. SKIFF
277 A.2d 284 (D.C.C.A. 1971)

Kern, A. J.

The parties to this appeal were married each for the first time, in Washington, D.C. in 1950. They have no children. In 1969 they separated and the husband obtained a divorce, ex parte, in Florida. While the husband's divorce suit was pending there the wife commenced an action for separate maintenance in the District of Columbia Court of General Sessions. The husband was personally served and defended in that action. The trial court, after hearing testimony by the parties and their witnesses, entered findings that:

The separation was not caused by any misconduct on the part of the wife,

the husband had failed to support his wife from the time he left her although he was able to do so,

during their 19 years of marriage she had made substantial contributions to the family support,

as of April 15, 1970, his annual income would be $19,704,

the income she could reasonably expect in 1970 from her own sources was "approximately $13,000 to $14,000," and the amount she needed annually to maintain her customary station in life was "on the order of $17,000 to $18,000,"

she is now 50 years of age, suffers from asthma, and has not worked since 1954, and,

he is 46, in good health and employed by the State Department as a foreign service officer. The trial court awarded her support and maintenance in the amount of $200 per month and counsel fees in the amount of $1500.

The husband, appellant before us, attacks the award of separate maintenance on numerous grounds, only two of which merit extended discussion. Appellant vigorously argues that in view of the evidence that appellee owned securities inherited from her parents of a value of at least $370,000, the trial court abused its discretion in ordering appellant, who had virtually no net worth, to pay any support to appellee. . . .

We have recognized that the wife's own financial resources constitute one factor among several which the trier of fact must evaluate in determining the amount of maintenance, if any, which will be required of a husband. . . . However, when all the relevant and material factors are considered upon this record we cannot say that the trial court abused its discretion in awarding appellee maintenance. She had made a substan-

---

for nonsupport does not violate the constitutional prohibition on imprisonment for debt. See Clark, supra, at 469, 472 n. 75, 466. It is also common for state welfare laws and officials to require women to file both civil and criminal nonsupport actions against their absent spouses as a condition of receiving welfare. See Citizens' Advisory Council on the Status of Women, Report of the Task Force on Family Law and Policy 19 (1968). These features, the rationales for which are fairly complex and not widely understood, increase the apparent unfairness of nonsupport laws and judicial contempt powers.

tial contribution to the parties' way of life during their 19-year marriage and there was no evidence that she had failed to meet her wifely obligations. She was 50 years of age and a chronic asthmatic who had no marketable job skill and had not worked in more than 15 years. He is four years younger than she and regularly employed by the State Department in a position that pays more than $19,000 a year. Her anticipated expenses presently exceed her anticipated income and she is not obliged to deplete her inheritance to support herself when her husband is able but refuses to support her. See Foley v. Foley, [184 A.2d 853] at 855; Klotz v. Klotz, 203 Va. 677, 127 S.E.2d 104 (1962). In the *Foley* case relied upon by appellant, the wife's annual income *exceeded* her expenses and her husband's earning power had been substantially *reduced* because he had developed a heart ailment. . . .

We do not by our decision today rule out a further examination and re-evaluation by the trial court of the parties' respective financial positions if appellant in the future demonstrates a change of circumstances. For example, we note testimony by appellee's broker that her holdings are being shifted from speculative, growth-type securities to those which will produce more annual income for her.[7] It may be that what appellee has in fact earned from her investments and actually required for her living expenses during the twelve months between trial and decision of this appeal will be relevant and material to what support and maintenance appellant should have to pay in the future. . . .

NOTES

1. Is it reasonable for a court to award alimony to a woman worth more than a third of a million dollars, with no children, from a salaried employee making less than $20,000 a year? Despite her fifteen years out of the labor force, Ms. Skiff could probably get a job paying at least $5000 a year, the salary necessary to enable her to maintain the style of life to which she was accustomed, after the income from her securities is applied to that end. The decision appears sex-discriminatory, since presumably a man whose income from investments was insufficient to meet his needs would be required to seek employment or deplete his capital rather than being awarded alimony. The logic behind such sex-differentiated treatment was actually expressed by an English court:[15]

> It has been suggested that because she was working before the marriage and is still young, and as there are no children of the marriage, she ought at once to go back into the position she was in before the marriage and start earning her living, with as far as I can see only one object, to reduce the amount of money which the husband should pay to her, his wife. I do not accept that view. She may have been lucky, or, at any rate thought that she was lucky at the time, in marrying someone who brought about an improvement in her financial and possibly her social position; but it has been through no fault of hers that their married life together has come to an end, and I see no reason whatever why the wife should go back to earning in order to reduce the husband's liability to maintain her. . . .

This approach includes both the goal of maintaining sex roles in marriage regardless of the parties' individual circumstances and abilities, and the idea that fault in causing the dissolution of marriage is relevant in deciding whether or not to award alimony. One can of course question both the idea that either party is ever blameless in the dissolution

---

7. It is not necessary to the disposition of this appeal to determine whether a wife's failure to maximize the annual income from her securities might be analogous to a husband who seeks to reduce the support he must pay his wife by retiring from gainful employment, see Appleton v. Appleton, 191 Pa. Super. 95, 155 A.2d 394 (1959); Grant v. Grant, 61 Misc. 2d 968, 307 N.Y.S.2d 153 (N.Y.C. Family Ct. 1969), or by not fully utilizing his earnings capacity. See Knutson v. Knutson, 15 Wis. 2d 115, 111 N.W.2d 905 (1961).

15. Le Roy-Lewis v. Le Roy-Lewis, [1955] P. 1, 3 [1954], 3 W.L.R. 549, 551, as quoted in Foote, Levy, and Sander, supra, at 909.

of a marriage and the desirability of having courts inquire into the fault of the parties at all. In the instant case, the decision does not reveal what or who was responsible for the Skiffs' decision to separate, or how strongly the factor of fault may have influenced the trial court.

Second, despite the court's reference to the wife's customary station in life as the standard for setting alimony, the court order can be viewed as a reasonable attempt to treat the parties' respective incomes as mutual resources in a partnership. In fact, the court divided the Skiffs' income almost evenly between them; Mr. Skiff ended up from $1000 to $2000 ahead. A third possibility is that the court was influenced to award Ms. Skiff alimony by her substantial contributions to the family resources during the marriage. Since it was the husband's legal duty to support his wife, her contributions could be viewed as analagous to a loan, giving her a moral claim, if probably not a legal one, to repayment in the form of alimony.

2. The *Skiff* case is unusual. Astor v. Astor, 89 So. 2d 645 (Fla. 1956) also represents an extreme. In that case, a twenty-six year old woman who had earned $65 per week prior to her six-week long marriage to John Jacob Astor, a multimillionaire, was awarded $250 per week in support and $12,500 in attorneys fees. Cf. Hempel v. Hempel, 225 Minn. 287, 30 N.W.2d 594 (1948), in which a woman who had previously earned $180 a month was awarded $750 a month and the use of a new Cadillac as temporary alimony after a marriage to a millionaire, in which cohabitation lasted less than four weeks.

GLOVER v. GLOVER
314 N.Y.S.2d 873, 64 Misc. 2d 374 (1970)

Levine, J.

Petitioner, a most attractive, articulate and youthful looking woman, apparently in her forties, but fiery, volatile, ruthless, self-centered, cunning and uncompromising, sues the respondent herein contending that since November, 1969 he has refused and neglected to provide fair and reasonable support for her. Petitioner also contends that respondent was physically abusive to her and in particular on June 6, 1970 when without provocation he allegedly kicked her in the lower part of her spine, requiring X-rays and medical treatment, when all she did, she claims, was to ask him for her weekly allowance.

Respondent, a practicing attorney for 30 years, vehemently denies these allegations and claims that petitioner has been guilty of such gross misconduct that she is not entitled to support from him on a means basis.

Petitioner and respondent were married on May 20, 1962, approximately eight years ago. There are no children of the marriage.

While much of the testimony was in sharp contradiction between the parties, some critical issues were admitted by petitioner. The court, however, has had the special advantage of seeing, hearing and observing the manner of the witnesses on the stand, and evaluating their credibility.

[T]he court . . . finds that the petitioner did indeed grossly misconduct herself toward her husband.

The court finds that petitioner, who was obsessed with the desire to be in business for herself despite the respondent's repeated requests to her to give up her business ventures and take care of the home, and despite the fact that he had already yielded to petitioner and given her no less than $2000, for her business ventures which he opposed, went behind respondent's back and approached several of his legal clients and friends to loan her money or co-sign loans for her. (Petitioner admitted approaching at least five whose names are in the record.)

In addition and most reprehensibly the court finds that petitioner told a number of respondent's clients that he was not a good lawyer and that they should not do business with him. (Petitioner admitted that she may have made deprecating remarks about her husband as a lawyer.) . . .

. . . On several occasions respondent was compelled to entertain clients alone at his home and cook the dinner for them, since petitioner, who was aware of the social engagements, came home several hours late, and on two occasions, corroborated by a witness for respondent who was present as a guest, came home at about 12 midnight. The testimony evidences further social and business relationships outside the home when petitioner failed to show up on time and respondent was required to entertain his clients and their wives alone.

Further exacerbations of the marital strain between the parties were the result of petitioner's preoccupation with animals which resulted in dispossess proceedings against her and respondent because of charges of barking emanating from the apartment at all hours of the day and night, because of the urination and defecation by the dogs on the terrace of this apartment (one of the respondent's witnesses testified that petitioner's home was a mess and that the dog vomited in the living room when he was present in the apartment on August 14, 1970, corroborating in part testimony by respondent that the apartment was constantly in a mess).

Adding up all of this testimony, together with other testimony in the record, the court concludes that the petitioner's misconduct has been so gross as to warrant a denial of her support by respondent on a means basis. One who would destroy her husband professionally and hence financially ought not to be permitted to look to him for support and share in his income on a means basis. . . .

While the court finds that the conduct of the petitioner drove the respondent to distraction, the respondent failed to establish by medical or other evidence that such misconduct so endangered his physical or mental well being as would render it unsafe or improper for petitioner to cohabit with respondent, and accordingly the court is not mandatorily required to deny petitioner support on a means basis.

However, the court does find that the petitioner's misconduct was so grievous and loathsome that in the exercise of discretion it orders no support for petitioner on a means basis. . . .

Having denied petitioner support on a means basis, the court now turns to consideration of support of petitioner on a public charge basis, should this eventuate, despite the court's finding that the petitioner is fully able to support herself. It will be noted that the petitioner has had excellent background as a sales representative, interior decorator, and real estate saleswoman, and is attractive, articulate and youthful. However, since at the moment petitioner claims not to have any income, the court directs her support by respondent on a public charge basis for a period not to exceed four weeks from the date hereof for which purpose the attorneys for both sides are directed to confer with the Department of Social Services to agree upon a sum. Should the attorneys fail to come to agreement within one week after receipt of the decision and order herein, either attorney may petition the court for fixing of this sum. Should petitioner not be gainfully employed after four weeks from date, she may petition the court for the continuance of this order of support on a public charge basis. . . .

NOTE

This case can be characterized as a demonstration of the principle that marital fault defeats a claim for alimony. Cf. Flanagan v. Flanagan, in which a Maryland court of appeals stated, "The greater the degree of fault on the part of the wife, the greater the need she must show to entitle her to an award of alimony." 42 U.S.L.W. 2283 (Nov. 21, 1973). It is unusual, however, in the kinds of marital wrongs which were held to defeat the wife's application; normally adultery or serious cruelty would have to be shown. Nonetheless, because of the extensive discretion given the judge by most statutes, this kind of ruling is always a possibility.

The case can also be seen as turning on the idea that, since support is an exchange for domestic services, the wife's refusal to stay home and perform the housewife role is a breach of contract justifying the husband's refusal to support her. In this context, note that the presence of children would have prevented the court from looking solely to the wife's activities during the marriage. If child custody upon divorce was awarded to her, she would be continuing to provide services in the form of child care after divorce. Unless the judge were hostile enough to the wife to deny her child custody, he would be unlikely to deny support to her and the children, despite her lousy housekeeping and her independent ideas.

A third basis for the holding would be the court's belief that Ms. Glover could support herself adequately and therefore did not need alimony. This ground would certainly have been less controversial than those upon which the court strongly relied.

In re MARRIAGE OF DENNIS
35 Cal. App. 3d 279, 110 Cal. Rptr. 619 (1973)

Kaus, P. J.

This dispute concerns an award of spousal support. Rose Sherman Dennis ("wife") appeals from an interlocutory judgment of dissolution of marriage from Earle Spiliotis Dennis ("husband").

Facts

The parties were married in October 1946. They have one child, a son, born in 1953. They were separated in December 1970. The dissolution hearing was held in July and December 1971. The interlocutory judgment provided, in relevant part, as follows: the wife was to have custody of the son, who attended and lived at college; the community assets of $5,255 were divided; the interests in the family home, worth about $30,000 were also divided. The wife was awarded spousal support of $200 a month for the first year, and $100 a month for the following three years. Support would then terminate. Child support of $150 a month until the son reached his "majority" was also awarded.

The couple were married for about 25 years. The wife was about 50 years old. She had been keeping some of the monthly $150 in temporary child support to cover her son's costs when he stayed with her on weekends.

The husband's gross income was $1,250 a month; his net was $866. The wife was not employed outside the home. She had not been employed for some 25 years. In the past she had worked as a riveter. Her only source of income during the years of their marriage had been about $6.00 a week, doing sewing. She had to give up that work because "it impaired the health of [her] eyes." Although she could "see now that [she] had [her] eyes improved," with glasses, she could "not do very close work." She was not trained to do any other work, except riveting. She had not attempted to get any training: "I raised a family." The trial court found that the wife had the ability to earn a living as a seamstress.

The wife did not want to go to work. The only thing that would make her do so was "starvation." She agreed that she wanted her husband to support her "for the rest of [her] life." She testified that she spent 24 hours a day maintaining her home. In response to the question, "What do you do around home for 24 hours a day?" She answered, "I live there."

The husband's estimated monthly expenses were $816 a month. The wife claimed monthly expenses of $372[2] which would be increased by $200 if the marital home were sold.

Contentions

The wife wanted spousal support in the amount of $225 a month for an indefinite period. As noted, she was awarded $200 a month for the first year, and $100 a month for the next three years. She contends that the trial court abused its discretion both in the amount of spousal support awarded and the period for which it was awarded. We disagree with the first contention but, with qualifications, agree with the second.

I

Both parties rely on In re Marriage of Rosan, 24 Cal. App. 3d 885, 101 Cal. Rptr. 295. The facts of *Rosan* must be closely compared with the facts in this case. In *Rosan,* the total community property amounted to about $54,000. (24 Cal. App. 3d at p. 889.) In this case, the total community, including the family home, adds up to about $35,000. In *Rosan,* the husband's average monthly net income was more than $2,000 plus expenses of $150 a month. (Id., at p. 888.) In this case, the husband's average monthly net income is about $866 a month. The husband's expenses in both cases are roughly comparable. In *Rosan,* the wife had custody of a 15 year old boy, and, for a while, an older, emotionally disturbed child. (Id., at pp. 891, 893.) In this case, the 18 year old son lives at college, except for weekends; the wife does not pay any of his expenses, except to give him some of the $150 child support that the husband pays to her.

In *Rosan,* the parties had been married for some 17 years, during which time the wife, who was not employed, was accustomed "to a high standard of living." (Id., at p. 894, 101 Cal. Rptr. at p. 301.) In this case, the parties were married for about 25 years; nothing in the record suggests that the parties lived other than modestly.

The trial court in *Rosan* ordered $150 a month child support, and alimony of $400 a month for one year, $300 a month for the second year, and $200 a month for the third — and final — year. The appellate court found that the award was inadequate. (Id., at p. 891.)

The *Rosan* court, in evaluating the amounts fixed by the trial court for spousal support, focused on (1) the length of marriage; (2) the lifestyle of the parties; (3) the wife's absence of training *and* her "uncontroverted testimony" that she intended to undertake training; (4) the support needed for the minor child in her custody; and (5) the ability of the husband to pay such spousal support. (24 Cal. App. 3d at p. 895.)

The wife in this case points out that the ratio of the husband's income in *Rosan* to spousal support, an average of $300 a month over a three-year period, is comparable to the ratio in this case, an average of $125 a month spousal support over a four year period, and that, based on *Rosan,* the trial court abused its discretion in this case.

We disagree. First, in *Rosan,* the husband's income exceeded his estimated expenses by at least $1,000 a month. (24 Cal. App. 3d at p. 894.) Second, the son in *Rosan* was younger, living with the wife, and might have placed greater limitations on the wife's options in pursuing a career. Third, in *Rosan,* there was substantial evidence of a high standard of living. The final and critical factor is the wife's unwillingness in this case — short of "starvation" — to work. The importance of this factor is made clear in *Rosan:*

"It may be inferred from the express reference in Civil Code, section 4801, subdivision (a) to the factor of the supported spouse's ability to engage in gainful employment that the supported spouse is to be encouraged to seek such employment. . . .

"When evidence exists that the party to be supported has unreasonably delayed or refused to seek employment consistent with her or his ability, of course, that factor

---

2. The wife was unclear or confused concerning her expenses. In her petition for dissolution, she claimed $642 a month in expenses. She was confused in testifying whether her monthly needs included, or excluded, $150 in child support, and the extent to which she should include various outstanding bills.

may be taken into consideration by the trial court in fixing the amount of support in the first instance or in modification proceedings. [Citation.] However, where there is no evidence of any unreasonable delay or willful refusal of the supported spouse to seek employment consistent with her or his health and parental responsibilities and when the other party has the ability to pay the needed support, it is inappropriate to make an order for support in an amount substantially less than that needed. [Citing Webber v. Webber, 33 Cal. 2d 153, 159, 199 P.2d 934.]" (24 Cal. App. 3d at pp. 896-897, 101 Cal. Rptr. at p. 303.)

The parties hereto separated in December 1970. At the dissolution hearing held one year later, the wife testified that she had done nothing about obtaining training and that she did not want to work. . . .

It is true that the wife, aged 50, had not been employed in 25 years, that her only income had been $6.00 a week for doing "alterations," and that she had had to give up that work because her "eyes became very weak." However, the wife's testimony regarding her corrected vision is somewhat equivocal. Moreover, there is absolutely no evidence that she was physically disabled from performing any work or that she had any responsibilities that required her presence in the home.

In the circumstances, the trial court's award of alimony did not constitute an abuse of discretion.

The wife next contends that the trial court, in awarding alimony, neglected to consider that the family home, owned free and clear and worth about $30,000, would be sold, requiring her to pay rent. The contention is without merit. . . . The wife estimated that rent would cost her an additional $200 a month, or $2,400 a year. She estimated that she would net $12,000 from the sale of the house. Discounting both inflation, if any, and interest on the proceeds of the sale, the property award will cover her rent for a period of five years. It was not unreasonable for the trial court to determine that within five years, the wife should be sufficiently self-supporting to be able to pay rent.

II

We agree, however, that the trial court should not have ordered termination of spousal support at the end of four years, without reserving jurisdiction to modify its order at that time. (Civ. Code, §4801, subd. (d).) Although the evidence indicates that the wife was unwilling, rather than unable, to support herself, it should be remembered that she is 50 years old and has not been employed for some 25 years. There was also evidence that the wife's ability to support herself as a seamstress might be affected by the condition of her eyes.

It is possible that difficulties not contemplated at this time will frustrate even a good faith attempt by the wife to become wholly or partially self-supporting. *Rosan,* 24 Cal. App. 3d at pp. 897-898, certainly indicates that after a lengthy marriage a retention of jurisdiction to modify spousal support should be the norm and that the burden of justification is on the party seeking termination.

That burden is not met here. The court had no real assurance that at the end of the four year period the wife will be unable to show that in spite of sincere efforts on her part, she cannot support herself adequately. It was not warranted in burning its bridges.

The interlocutory judgment must be modified to provide that the trial court retain continuing jurisdiction to extend the spousal support period beyond the termination date of January 31, 1974, upon a proper showing of incapacity by the wife. . . .

NOTES

1. This decision highlights the problems with the housewife role in marriage. Ms. Dennis is out of a job after twenty-five years of apparently steady work at home, with neither pension rights nor skills derived from her work which would enable her to get other employment. Had she stayed married, her normal expectation would probably have been to retire after her children had left home. Because her marriage has dissolved, she must instead support herself by seeking employment in another occupation; her status-based expectations of being supported for the rest of her life are not being fulfilled. Consider though whether the court has compensated her on a quasi-contract basis for her past contributions. There are no explicit calculations in the opinion about the value of her contribution as versus the cost of her support. However, the property division probably includes some return for her uncompensated work at home, since there is no evidence that she had purchased any of the community property. On the other hand, it is at least arguable that her husband's earning capacity was a major asset of the community, and that this limited support award discounts her right to a share in that asset.

If you were deciding the *Dennis* case, what basis for allocating income and property would you use and why?

2. In Beard v. Beard, 262 So. 2d 269 (Fla. App. 1972), an appellate court overturned an award of $100 per week from a husband who earned $9500 annually after taxes to a forty-eight year old wife, who had the use of the fully furnished marital home, did not have custody of the only one of their three children who was still at home, had already received alimony for one year after the divorce, had been briefly employed shortly after the parties had separated, and was an alcoholic. The parties had been married for twentyone years at the time of their separation. While this decision may have been fair under all the circumstances, the remarks of the court in making the decision illustrated the tendency of male judges to deny the economic costs that the traditional marriage role has placed on women faced with divorce after many years of marriage. For example,[16]

> In the earlier days of our civilization the female members of society were known as the weaker sex whose destiny it was to remain always in the home and occupy themselves exclusively in providing for the needs and comforts of the family. Their educational opportunities were generally limited, and their experience in the world of commerce and industry was almost nonexistent. Under these circumstances, when the family tie was severed by divorce, the policy of the law looked with compassion, tenderness and mercy upon the defenseless and almost helpless wife who was seldom equipped through education, training, or experience to fend for herself and provide the necessities of life for her support and maintenance.
>
> Such conditions as related above no longer exist. In this era of women's liberation movements and enlightened thinking, we have almost universally come to appreciate the fallacy of treating the feminine members of our society on anything but a basis of complete equality with the opposite sex. Any contrary view would be completely anachronistic. In this day and time, women are as well educated and trained in the arts, sciences, and professions as are their male counterparts. The law properly protects them in their right to independently acquire, encumber, accumulate, and alienate property at will. They now occupy a position of equal partners in the family relationship resulting from marriage, and more often than not contribute a full measure to the economic well-being of the family unit. Whether the marriage continues to exist or is severed through the device of judicial decree, the woman continues to be as fully equipped as the man to earn a living and provide for her essential needs. The fortuitous circumstance created by recitation of the marriage vows neither diminishes her capacity for self-support nor does it give her a vested right in her husband's earnings for the remainder of her life.

16. 262 So. 2d at 271-272.

2. The decision in the *Dennis* case has a distinctly rehabilitative focus. The following statute similarly illustrates the tendency of courts and legislators to tie alimony to the rapid return of the wife to the labor market rather than to the balance of equities growing out of the now defunct marriage:[17]

> Upon a decree of nullity or divorce, the court may restore to the wife all or any part of her estate, and may assign to her such part of the estate of her husband, or order him to pay such sum of money, as may be deemed just, provided that in cases in which no children are involved, or in which the children have reached the age of majority, said order shall be effective for not more than three years from the date thereof, but such order may be renewed, modified or extended if justice requires for periods of not more than three years at a time. . . .

E. OTHER ASPECTS OF ALIMONY AND CHILD SUPPORT LAWS WHICH CAUSE SEX DISCRIMINATION

1. The Denial to Men of Alimony

The power to award alimony to the husband exists only where there is specific statutory authority, since the husband had no common law right to support on which such an award could be based. The Task Force on Family Law and Policy of the Citizens' Advisory Council on the Status of Women reported that in 1968 more than one third of the states permitted alimony to be awarded to either spouse.[18] Some of the states which have adopted "no-fault" divorce laws have, like Florida, made the right to alimony or separate maintenance sex-neutral.[19] But even in states where alimony can be awarded to either spouse, it is not clear that the same standards are applied to determine alimony awards for husbands as for wives.

In evaluating the significance of this sex discrimination, remember that more men than women have adequate means for self-support and that few fathers get custody of their children. Thus, the number of men who would qualify for alimony, and whose wives would be able to pay alimony, is considerably smaller than the comparable number of women.

2. The Effect of Remarriage on Alimony Payments

Usually when a woman remarries, she loses her right to alimony. When a man remarries, his alimony payments to his first wife are sometimes reduced. In some states, case law provides that the mere fact of remarriage and assumption of financial responsibilities to a new family is not enough to justify a modification of alimony,[20] but in other states, the courts do reduce or eliminate alimony in order to "put both wives on the same footing."[21] While the latter view may be more practical, the difference between the financial consequences of the wife's and the husband's remarriage is striking. It is certainly possible that a wife's remarriage would increase rather than decrease her financial responsibilities. It follows that equal treatment of the payor and recipient spouses with regard to remarriage may require that the courts be able to order one ex-spouse to continue to pay alimony to the other despite the remarriage of the recipient.

17. N.H. Rev. Stat. Ann. §458:19 (1955).
18. Report 7 (1968). Clark, supra, at 448, lists Alaska, Iowa, North Dakota, Massachusetts, Ohio, Oregon, Utah, Virginia, and Washington as states which allow alimony awards to either spouse.
19. See, e.g., Lefler v. Lefler, 264 So. 2d 112 (Fla. 1972), construing Fla. Stat. Ann. §61.08 (1971).
20. Clark, supra, at 459, nn. 57, 58, and Warren v. Warren, 218 Md. 212, 146 A.2d 34 (1958).
21. Clark, supra, at 459, n. 60, and Covert v. Covert, 48 Misc. 2d 386, 264 N.Y.S.2d 820 (1965).

This seems especially reasonable in those cases in which alimony is, in effect, back wages or restitution for damages suffered in the course of marriage.

3. Enforcement Mechanisms for Support and Alimony

The means of enforcement for alimony and child support include ordinary contract remedies where a private agreement has been negotiated, execution and garnishment once a judgment has been obtained, civil contempt proceedings, criminal prosecution for nonsupport, original court proceedings in the payor spouses's state of residence if different from the jurisdiction which made the original award, proceedings in the courts of another state pursuant to the original judgment based on either full faith and credit or comity, the Uniform Enforcement of Foreign Judgments Act (in eight states) and the Uniform Reciprocal Enforcement of Support Act (in all states).[22] In addition, people can be and are sent to jail for nonsupport and failure to make court-ordered alimony or child support payments. Although women can be jailed in all states for failing to support their children and in some states for failing to support their husbands if their husbands cannot support themselves,[23] it appears that almost all of the people actually imprisoned are men.

The sanction of imprisonment is severe and its imposition primarily on men is sex-discriminatory. Even if the obligations of support are extended to both women and men on a sex-neutral basis, it is an open question whether the sanction of imprisonment should be retained, at least in its present form.[24] Of course, even if the obligation to provide support is made sex-neutral in all jurisdictions, in practice it seems likely that it will continue to fall more often on men than on women, at least for the near future.

On the other hand, the data on compliance with support and alimony orders, presented in Part V, supra, suggest that the other sanctions for nonsupport are not very effective, at least as presently designed and administered. To the extent that it is women who more often are owed support and men who are under an obligation to provide it, even when obligations are determined in accordance with a functional rather than a rigid sex role standard for the division of labor, it is sex discriminatory for the society to fail to enforce that obligation.

There may be some sex discrimination in the application of the support standard in that men are often required to take jobs, or to work at the highest-paying job available, in order to pay alimony or child support.[25] When women are ordered to make payments to former husbands, their resources are more often evaluated on the basis of actual rather than potential earnings. The overall sex-discriminatory impact of this differentiation is probably not great, however, in light of the better job opportunities available to men.[26]

F. Child Custody

The best interest of the child is the universally enunciated standard for awarding custody. Although facially sex-neutral, in practice these words are often interpreted to mean that the mother should have custody, especially if the children are young, and

22. See Clark, supra, at 465-481, 507-520, 553-572.

23. Id. at 186, 187-188, 200-201, 507. See also Note, Sex Discrimination in the Criminal Law: The Effect of the Equal Rights Amendment, 4 Am. Crim. L. Rev. 469, 476-477 (1973).

24. For the suggestions that this sanction should be used only as a last resort see, e.g., Clark, supra, at 201; Report of the Task Force on Family Law and Policy to the Citizen's Advisory Council on the Status of Women 18-19 (1968), and Model Penal Code §207.14, Comment (Tent. Draft No. 9, 1959).

25. See, e.g., Johnson v. Johnson, 319 P.2d 1107 (Okla. 1957); Brandt v. Brandt., 36 Misc. 2d 901, 233 N.Y.S.2d 951 (1962).

26. See also Part IX-C, infra, for examples of women being virtually forced into the labor market, as a condition of welfare.

sometimes there is a statutory policy in favor of this disposition as well. However, the basic standard is one which gives the trial court broad discretionary powers.

The courts award the children to the mother on the basis of sexual stereotypes about childrearing capability and interest. By the same token, judges often react against a mother who deviates from tradition by committing adultery or working outside the home, behavior which would be less inflammatory if engaged in by the father. A subsidiary problem is the courts' practice of comparing the natural mother and the father's new wife, rather than the mother and father, as potential child caretakers. This is a logical result of the traditional sex-based division of labor in the family, but it does seem unfair that the natural mother really does not have the option of marrying a new spouse to care for her children while she works, in order to get custody of them.

BUNIM v. BUNIM
298 N.Y. 391, 83 N.E.2d 848 (1949)

DESMOND, J.

On the trial of this divorce suit the wife admitted numerous deliberate adulteries (with a man who was married and had children), attempted to rationalize and justify those adulteries, denied any repentence therefor, committed perjury in swearing to denials in her answer, see Civil Practice Act, §1148, and, as found by both courts below, testified to a deliberately false story as to consent by plaintiff (a reputable and successful physician) to the adulteries. With all that in the record, custody of the two children of the marriage (eleven and thirteen years old at the time of the trial) has been, nonetheless, awarded to the defendant.

There is an affirmed finding below that the husband is a fit and proper person to have such custody, and no such finding as to the wife, but a finding that "the interests and welfare of the children, the issue of said marriage, will be best served by awarding the custody to the defendant." We see in this record no conceivable basis for that latter finding, unless it be the testimony of the two daughters that, though they love their father, they prefer to live with their mother. Unless that attitude of these adolescent girls be controlling as against every other fact and consideration, see, contra, People ex rel. Glendening v. Glendening, 259 App. Div. 384, 19 N.Y.S.2d 693, affirmed 284 N.Y. 598, 29 N.E.2d 926, this judgment, insofar as it deals with custody, is unsupported and unsupportable.

. . . We hold that there was here such abuse of discretion as to be error of law, with consequent jurisdiction to review, and duty to reverse, in this court.

. . . [A] decision . . . cannot be one repugnant to all normal concepts of sex, family and marriage. The State of New York has old, strong policies on those subjects. . . . Our whole society is based on the absolutely fundamental proposition that: "Marriage, as creating the most important relation in life," has "more to do with the morals and civilization of a people than any other institution" Maynard v. Hill, 125 U.S. 190, 205, 8 S. Ct. 723, 726, 31 L. Ed. 654. Defendant here, in open court, has stated her considered belief in the propriety of indulgence, by a dissatisfied wife such as herself, in extramarital sex experimentation. It cannot be that "the best interests and welfare" of those impressionable teen-age girls will be "best served" by awarding their custody to one who proclaims, and lives by, such extraordinary ideas of right conduct. . . .

LOUGHRAN, C.J., and LEWIS and CONWAY, JJ., concur with DESMOND, J.

FULD, J. (dissenting).

This case involves a problem as perplexing as any in the field of human relationships, and, while a different result could, of course, have been reached below, I hesitate to stamp as an abuse the discretion exercised by the Special Term judge, and affirmed by four justices of the Appellate Division, only after the most painstaking and conscientious consideration.

Especially in a case such as this, the judge who sees and hears the witnesses, who is face to face with the children and the parents, is in a far better position to make a decision calling for the exercise of discretion than is the appellate judge whose only source of guidance is the cold print, the lifeless pages, of the record. . . .

The primary and paramount concern of the trial judge was the welfare and happiness of the children. Would it better serve their interests and their well-being to place them with their mother or with their father? Bearing directly on that issue was evidence that the father was inordinately preoccupied with his professional duties; that, as a result, he gave little of his time or of himself to the children; and that not infrequently he treated them brusquely, impatiently and even intemperately. Likewise pertinent was proof that the wife was ever a good and devoted mother; that her indiscretions were unknown to the children; that she was deeply devoted to the children and truly concerned with their welfare; and that, for their part, the children returned her affections with an attachment that was, in the language of the trial court, "almost Biblical" in its intensity.

With such evidence — and there was more of like import — in the record, the decision at Special Term and the judgment of the Appellate Division awarding custody to the mother cannot be said to be completely beyond the pale of permissible discretion.

I would affirm the judgment.

[DYE, J., concurs in this dissent.]

NOTES

1. The contrast between the majority opinion and Judge Fuld's dissent points up the tendency of some judges to abandon the difficult task of balancing the factors relevant to the best interests of the children when a moral issue arises about the conduct of the mother. The record in this case[27] contains strong evidence to support the trial court's award of custody to the mother, including the facts that when the father had custody of the children he was away from home most of the time and relegated the children to the care of a governess, with whom the children were extremely unhappy. Yet the majority does not even reach the question of the fitness of the father as a nurturing parent (as opposed to the traditional provider role) because of its outraged reaction to the mother's moral views and behavior.

2. This case illustrates how judges pick facts from the record to support their point of view. Because of this selectivity, written opinions of courts do not necessarily reflect what may actually have motivated the custody award. Research into the records of a large number of cases would be required for any definitive statement about the factors which most often influence judges strongly, and those which are most often ignored.

SHAW v. SHAW
402 S.W.2d 222 (Ark. 1971)

HARRIS, C. J.

This appeal involves the custody of James Kello Shaw, five year old son of Gloria Fay Shaw (Morrow), appellant herein, and Homer Kello Shaw, appellee. Mr. Shaw was granted a divorce from Mrs. Shaw on January 15, 1968, and the custody of James Kello was awarded to both parents, each to have the custody and control for six months of the year until the child became of school age. Appellee was directed to pay the sum of $15.00 per week as child support during each whole or partial week in which the child

27. Excerpted in Goldstein and Katz, The Family and the Law 682-697, 928-953 (1965).

was in the custody of Mrs. Shaw. In September, 1969, Mr. Shaw filed a motion to modify the decree, asserting that his ex-wife refused to permit him to talk with his child by telephone or otherwise contact him during the time she had custody; that appellant's husband, James Morrow, had attacked him at a time when he was trying to see the child; that it would be to the best interest of the child for appellee to be given complete custody. Mrs. Morrow answered, denying the allegations and asking that full time custody be given to her. On trial, after hearing a number of witnesses, the court found that Mr. Shaw had been deprived of freedom of contact with the child; that continued controversy arose between the parties, including personal difficulties of violence with appellant's present husband, all occurring in the presence of the child. The court further found by the testimony "that the environment, as well as the activities of this defendant, are not conducive to being in the best interest of the minor child. Further, the defendant lives in an apartment complex and is employed, having to leave the minor child in a kindergarten or with other persons. On the other hand, the plaintiff has other minor children in his home which is near to the home of his parents where the minor child of the parties has resided for a portion of his lifetime, and this is in a rural community with an environment of churches, family life, and wholesome farm life, and all of which lends itself for better growth and development of minor child concerned. In addition, the plaintiff's present wife did not work when the minor child lived with the plaintiff prior to this hearing and would not work if the child were again in their home, so that this child would have a normal home family life at all times."

Custody was accordingly placed with the father, subject to the right of reasonable visitation to the mother at all reasonable times. . . .

. . . Some facts seem to be definitely established. Shaw has also remarried and his present wife has a child by a previous marriage, and the Shaws also have a child of their own. Mr. Shaw's parents live about half a mile from their son and his wife, and she (the elderly Mrs. Shaw) has kept the children when the two were working. Mrs. Homer Shaw stated that she had worked during the period when her husband did not have custody of James Kello, as a matter of helping him meet the support payments, but she did not work when he had custody of the boy, and would quit her job if he were given the absolute custody. Reverend John Holt, pastor of the church attended by the Shaws, testified that appellee was very active in his church, and regularly attended with his wife and children.

Mrs. Morrow and her husband have an apartment in Little Rock, where they are employed by Life and Time, Inc., Family Publication Service. Mr. Morrow is sales manager of Arkansas and Mrs. Morrow is employed as secretary and assistant manager. During the time when the Morrows had custody of James Kello, he was left at a nursery while they were at work. Admittedly, appellant fell in love with Morrow while she was still married to Shaw. . . . Admittedly, she knew that Morrow was also married and the father of two children. After becoming divorced, appellant lived with Morrow in Little Rock as husband and wife for a month or two before marriage. Her stated reason was "because I loved him, and at the time he wasn't able to obtain his divorce and we did move in together and lived together". In fact, Mr. and Mrs. Roe Neal, the couple who "stood-up" with them when they were married, both testified that previous to the marriage they thought appellant and Mr. Morrow were already married, Mrs. Neal stating that they already lived at the same address, and went by the name of Mr. and Mrs. Morrow at work and "every place". . . .

Mr. Neal also testified that on one occasion, Mrs. Morrow (before her marriage) called his wife and said that her husband was leaving to go out to a club, "he was going drinking that night" and wanted to know if Mrs. Neal could visit with her. He took his wife to the Morrow Home and his wife went upstairs, but returned screaming that appellant was hollering "I'm going to kill myself"; appellant had a "bunch of pills, and she was hollering that if Jim didn't love her—if she couldn't have him, nobody else could get him, and she was going to take those pills". He said that he finally got the pills away from her. Mrs. Morrow denied any intent to commit suicide, stating "Well, during this time I was away from my child and wasn't getting to see him. When I did call and talk to him I was being harassed and everything, and my nerves were upset. I was taking a light sedative".

Be that as it may, we certainly cannot agree that the chancellor's findings were incorrect. This is not to say that one cannot do wrong, and later change for the better. We do think however that this evidence was pertinent to the custody issue, inasmuch as the events mentioned occurred only about eighteen months before the custody hearing. Entirely aside from that however, it would appear that the child would be in more suitable surroundings with his father. There, according to the evidence, he would be looked after during the day by appellee's second wife, it being remembered also that his grandparents live in close proximity to the Shaw home. Also, he would be living with the two children heretofore mentioned. Mrs. Morrow herself testified that "Mr. Shaw is a good daddy to his child". She said that he worked and provided for James Kello and was good to him. Her only criticism was "He didn't give the child the time that I thought he should have". It definitely appears from the evidence that the welfare of the child would be best served with the custody in the father. . . .

. . . after reviewing the record, we hold that the order placing custody in appellee was entirely correct.

Affirmed.

NOTE

Obviously, many factors influenced the judge in making this child custody award, but the fact that the mother worked while the father's second wife did not was certainly significant to him. Is this reasonable in a society where an increasing percentage of mothers work, even during marriage? Even if the argument is made that a judge should take into account the presence of a woman playing the traditional role, is he justified in preferring a stepmother chosen by the father to a nursemaid or day care center chosen by the mother? Note also that whether the stepmother or the mother goes to work may depend only on how much money the father gives to his former wife.

The next case is more in line with contemporary realities about working mothers, though sex discriminatory in other respects.

PELLEGRIN v. FRIEDLEY
237 So. 2d 696 (La. Ct. App. 1970)

DOMENGEAUX, J.

Donovan F. Pellegrin and Ann Friedley were married in New Orleans on December 19, 1964, and of this marriage one child was born, Cal James Pellegrin, who is now four years of age. Mrs. Pellegrin had another child, seven, by a former marriage which appears to have been a putative marriage. On April 9, 1969, Mr. Pellegrin filed a petition for separation from bed and board alleging abandonment and cruel treatment on the part of his wife and praying for custody of his minor son, Cal J. Pellegrin. Alleging that his wife was an unfit mother he also prayed that a rule nisi be issued ordering the defendant to show cause why he should not be given custody of their son pendente lite. Following the trial of this rule on April 25, 1969, the trial judge rendered judgment discharging and dismissing the rule and thus retaining custody of the child in Mrs. Pellegrin. Plaintiff has appealed that judgment to this court.

The record discloses that the defendant wife earns her living as a barmaid in a less than desirable establishment. There is, however, nothing in the evidence which would lead us to believe that she engages in any sort of immoral conduct. She uses the money that she earns to pay the rent on a one-room apartment for herself and to pay a baby sitter to care for her two children. This baby sitter lives with her retired husband in a five-room home, with a fenced-in back yard, located in a reasonably pleasant residential neighborhood. The two boys live in the baby sitter's home and have their own room therein. The older boy attends school and is escorted to and from school each day by the baby sitter's sister. Mrs. Pellegrin testified, and her testimony was corroborated by the baby sitter, that she visits with her children every day, plays with them, and takes them out for walks, purchasing sweets for them, etc.

The law of this state is clear in commanding that the custody of minors pending the outcome of a suit for separation or divorce *shall* be granted to the wife, whether she be plaintiff or defendant, unless there are *strong* reasons to deprive her of it. LSA-C.C. art. 146. . . . Considering the manner in which this mother is caring for her children we see no such strong reasons. She has not been shown to be unfit and the welfare of the children is being looked after. The fact that due to the necessity for working she must keep the boys in a home other than her own is not a sufficiently good reason to deprive her of custody. . . . The boys enjoy a wholesome home atmosphere and see their mother daily.

NOTES

1. For a similar decision, see Baker v. Baker, 122 Ga. App. 639, 178 S.E.2d 295 (1970), in which the court commented, apparently with approval, on the mother's working at night rather than going on welfare, although her work meant she left her children with a neighbor.

2. Do you think the court in *Pellegrin* would have reached the same result had it not been for the strong statutory policy in favor of granting custody to the mother, and if the suit had concerned permanent rather than temporary custody?

HAMMETT v. HAMMETT
239 So. 2d 778 (Ala. Ct. Civ. App. 1970)

WRIGHT, J.

This is an appeal from a decree of divorce by which the parties were each granted a divorce on complaint and cross-complaint. The authority for such decree is Title 34, Section 22(1), Code of Alabama 1940. This is the statute which permits a final divorce after there has been a decree of separate maintenance in effect for more than two years. By its decree, the trial court granted custody of three minor children, ranging in age from eight to thirteen years, to the mother-appellee, with reasonable visitation rights to the father-appellant.

The only error assigned is that the court erred in granting custody of the children to the mother rather than to the father.

Appellant is retired from military service after some thirty years service. His career in the service was that of cook and NCO in charge of general mess. Appellee, during most of the marriage years, worked as a beautician and is presently so employed. Appellant has suffered several heart attacks and is also a diabetic. His physical condition appears to have stabilized, but he is not able to be regularly employed. His income consists of retirement benefits and social security. His children receive $27.50 a month each from social security. He has purchased and lives in a comfortable home in Prattville, Alabama. Appellee is regularly employed as a beautician in Montgomery.

Following the decree of separate maintenance in 1966, appellee worked from early morning until late afternoon. The children were either alone or in the care of a sitter or watched by a neighbor. Appellant often met them in the afternoon after school, and had them with him on weekends. Appellant fully complied with the terms of the separate maintenance decree, and supplemented it by purchasing clothes and other necessities for the children.

Shortly before the filing of the petition for divorce by appellant, the appellee and the children moved back into the home in Prattville. Appellee testified that the return was at the request of appellant and the children, and was for the purpose of reconciliation. Appellant testified that the return was on appellee's own initiative and not at his request. However, appellant accepted the return, prepared meals and cared for the children. They were entered in school in Prattville and were living there at the time of the decree.

There was no order in the decree requiring appellee to move after the divorce, and insofar as the record discloses they may all still be living in the same residence, including appellee. . . .

. . . [F]or the purpose of this appeal some undisputed facts should be set out.

At the time of the decree in June 1969, the children were fourteen, twelve and eleven years of age. The oldest and youngest are girls and the other a boy. Throughout this marriage appellant had done substantially all the cooking for the family and had continued to do so after they returned home in 1968. Appellant is not employed and stays at home. Appellee is employed and is gone from home all day, six days a week. When questioned by the court the children expressed a desire to live with their father rather than their mother. The mother had discipline problems with the children, particularly with the boy. Appellant has an excellent home near the schools where the children are enrolled, located in Prattville "the best place to live in the United States."

The testimony was without serious conflict as to appellant or appellee being a fit and proper person to have custody of the children.

We have very carefully read and considered the testimony in this case. . . . It is obvious that the decision of the court concerning the custody of the children was reached after serious consideration. It is only after equally serious study and consideration that we have concluded that the award of the custody of these children to appellee is plainly wrong and does not represent the best interest of the children — which is the paramount matter for consideration. . . .

To summarize the evidence which forces us to our decision — the children prefer to live with their father. The father has prepared their meals almost exclusively since their birth. He is free to be at home with them at all times. He is undisputedly fitted morally and financially to provide them with a good home. The mother, whether from necessity or inclination, has worked throughout the children's lives, all day and every day, except Sunday, leaving their care to someone else. She, admittedly, cannot cook for them as well as the father. The children are enrolled in schools near the home of appellant. The children are in need of parental discipline. . . .

. . . In the event there is not involved a child of such tender years as to be peculiarly dependent upon the mother, there is no rule requiring that custody be granted to the mother rather than the father, when either is a fit and proper custodian. From the facts in the instant case, it rather appears that the children are peculiarly dependent upon the father. In making such statement and in rendering this decision, we do not intend to appear derogatory to the appellee as a mother. We are certain she has attempted to do her best for her children under difficult circumstances. We are further certain that the trial court will insure that she has every opportunity, consonant with the welfare of the children, to be with them and have them with her. . . .

Reversed and remanded with directions.

NOTE

This case suggests that judges are greatly influenced by the advantage to the child of a parent at home, and that the parent who will stay home will win the custody award. Ordinarily this preference for the parent who plays the housespouse role operates to the advantage of the mother. But the advantage is counterbalanced by the father's ability to acquire a new mate and offer a traditional "two-parent" home. Although the mother can marry again and be supported in the role of housewife herself, her chances are less than her husband's unless she is young. (See Part V-B, supra.)

As families turn more and more to sharing child care, housework, and work outside the home, how will judges resolve the issue of child custody without the easy determinant of who can provide a housespouse?

VII. ALTERNATIVES TO TRADITIONAL DIVORCE LAW

A. No-Fault Divorce

A major effort to reform divorce laws has been made by the National Conference of Commissioners on Uniform State Laws. The Uniform Marriage and Divorce Act sets one ground for divorce: that the court find that "the marriage is irretrievably broken" (§305). This finding may be made even though one of the parties denies it. "A finding of irretrievable breakdown is a determination that there is no reasonable prospect of reconciliation." The act specifically abolishes all previously existing defenses, "including but not limited to condonation, connivance, collusion, recrimination, insanity, and lapse of time" (§§303(e), 503). Following is the commentary which explains this approach, and the other sections and commentary of the act which would effect significant changes in traditional divorce law.

NATIONAL CONFERENCE OF COMMISSIONERS
ON UNIFORM STATE LAWS
THE UNIFORM MARRIAGE AND DIVORCE ACT
30-43, 46-47, 56 (1971)

SECTION 305. [IRRETRIEVABLE BREAKDOWN.]

Comment

. . . The traditional grounds for divorce, which assumed that one party had been at fault by committing an act giving rise to a cause of action for divorce, are abolished. The legal assignment of blame is here replaced by a search for the reality of the marital situation: whether the marriage has ended in fact. The public policy embodied in this section was recognized in DeBurgh v. DeBurgh, 39 Cal. 2d 858, 863-44; 250 P.2d 598, 601 (1952) (Traynor, J.): "when a marriage has failed and the family has ceased to be a unit, the purposes of family life are no longer served and divorce will be permitted." . . .

This section makes the determination of whether the marriage is irretrievably broken, in all cases, a matter for determination by the court, "after hearing," which means "upon evidence." . . .

Because the defense of recrimination and other concepts associated with fault are abolished by the Act (sections 303(e) and 503), the court may not refuse to find that the marriage has broken down irretrievably merely because of petitioner's conduct during the marriage. If the court decides to adjourn the matter as provided in subsection (b) (2), it may suggest that the parties seek counseling during the period of adjournment. The waiting period must be no shorter than thirty days and, if possible in light of the court's calendar, no longer than sixty days after the previous hearing. The court must make its final decision as to whether the marriage is irretrievably broken at the adjourned hearing. The section does not contemplate more than one adjourned hearing, although certainly a hearing not completed at one session may be continued. The power of either party, or of the court, to require a conciliation conference, is in aid of the policy to encourage conciliation, and, in appropriate cases, resort to counseling, without invoking the controversial tool of compulsory counseling.

Section 305 intentionally makes no distinction between childless marriages and those with minor children. If the parties establish that their marriage has broken down irretrievably, the court is not authorized to make a contrary finding because of the impact of a dissolution of the marriage upon the minor children. Under former law, if the parties established the existence of a ground for divorce and no defenses existed, the court lacked jurisdiction to deny the divorce simply because of its views about divorce or the impact of divorce on minor children. There is no intention to change this rule. . . .

SECTION 306. [SEPARATION AGREEMENT.]

(a) To promote amicable settlement of disputes between parties to a marriage attendant upon their separation or the dissolution of their marriage, the parties may enter into a written separation agreement containing provisions for disposition of any property owned by either of them, maintenance of either of them, and support, custody, and visitation of their children.

(b) In a proceeding for dissolution of marriage or for legal separation, the terms of the separation agreement, except those providing for the support, custody, and visitation of children, are binding upon the court unless it finds, after considering the economic circumstances of the parties and any other relevant evidence produced by the parties, on their own motion or on request of the court, that the separation agreement is unconscionable.

(c) If the court finds the separation agreement unconscionable, it may request the parties to submit a revised separation agreement or may make orders for the disposition of property, maintenance, and support.

(d) If the court finds that the separation agreement is not unconscionable as to disposition of property or maintenance, and not unsatisfactory as to support:

(1) unless the separation agreement provides to the contrary, its terms shall be set forth in the decree of dissolution or legal separation and the parties shall be ordered to perform them, or

(2) if the separation agreement provides that its terms shall not be set forth in the decree, the decree shall identify the separation agreement and state that the court has found the terms not unconscionable.

(e) Terms of the agreement set forth in the decree are enforceable by all remedies available for enforcement of a judgment, including contempt, and are enforceable as contract terms.

(f) Except for terms concerning the support, custody, or visitation of children, the decree may expressly preclude or limit modification of terms set forth in the decree if the separation agreement so provides. Otherwise, terms of a separation agreement set forth in the decree are automatically modified by modification of the decree.

Comment

An important aspect of the effort to reduce the adversary trappings of marital dissolution is the attempt, made by Section 306, to encourage the parties to reach an amicable disposition of the financial and other incidents of their marriage. This section entirely reverses the older view that property settlement agreements are against public policy because they tend to promote divorce. Rather, when a marriage has broken down irretrievably, public policy will be served by allowing the parties to plan their future by agreeing upon a disposition of their property, their maintenance, and the support, custody, and visitation of their children.

Subsection (b) undergirds the freedom allowed the parties by making clear that the terms of the agreement respecting maintenance and property disposition are binding upon the court unless those terms are found to be unconscionable. The standard of unconscionability is used in commercial law, where its meaning includes protection against one-sidedness, oppression, or unfair surprise. . . .

. . . In the context of negotiations between spouses as to the financial incidents of their marriage, the standard includes protection against overreaching, concealment of assets, and sharp dealing not consistent with the obligations of marital partners to deal fairly with each other.

In order to determine whether the agreement is unconscionable, the court may look to the economic circumstances of the parties resulting from the agreement, and any other relevant evidence such as the conditions under which the agreement was made, including the knowledge of the other party. . . .

The terms of the agreement respecting support, custody, and visitation of children are not binding upon the court even if these terms are not unconscionable. The court should perform its duty to provide for the children by careful examination of the agreement as to these terms in light of the standards established by Section 309 for support and by Part IV for custody and visitation.

Subsection (c) envisages that, if the court finds the agreement unconscionable, it will afford the parties the opportunity to negotiate further. If they are unable to arrive at an agreement that is not unconscionable, the court, on motion of either party, may decide the issues of property disposition, support, and maintenance in light of the standards established in Sections 307 through 309. The court's power to make orders for the custody and visitation of the children is set forth in Part IV.

Subsection (d) permits the parties, in drawing the separation agreement, to choose whether its terms shall or shall not be set forth in the decree. In the former event, the provisions of subsection (e), making these terms enforceable through the remedies available for the enforcement of a judgment, but retaining also the enforceability of them as contract terms, apply. This represents a reversal of the policy of the original 1970 Act, which required a choice between "merging" the agreement in the judgment and retaining its character as a contract. Strong representations as to the undesirability of such a choice, in the light of foreign doctrines as to the enforceability of judgments, as compared with contract terms, in this area of the law, made by persons and groups whose expertise entitled them to respect, led the Conference, in 1971, to change its former decision.

There still remains a place for agreements the terms of which are not set forth in the decree, if the parties prefer that it retain the status of a private contract, only. In this instance, the remedies for the enforcement of a judgment will not be available, but the court's determination, in the decree, that the terms are not unconscionable, under the ordinary rules of res adjudicata, will prevent a later successful claim of unconscionability. Such an agreement, unless its terms expressily so permit, will not be modifiable as to economic matters. Other subjects, relating to the children, by subsection (b) do not bind the Court.

Subsection (f) allows the parties to agree that their provisions as to maintenance and property division will not be modifiable or can be modified only in accordance with the terms of the agreement, even though those terms are included in the decree. If the court finds that these are not unconscionable, it may include them in its decree. The effect of including in the decree a provision precluding or limiting modification of the terms respecting maintenance or property division is to make the decree nonmodifiable or modifiable only in the limited way as to those terms. Subsection (f) thus permits the parties to agree that their future arrangements may not be altered except in accord with their agreement. Such an agreement maximizes the advantages of careful future planning and eliminates uncertainties based on the fear of subsequent motions to increase or decrease the obligations of the parties. However, as stated in the subsection, this does not apply to provisions for the support, custody, or visitation of children. . . .

SECTION 307. [DISPOSITION OF PROPERTY.]

In a proceeding for dissolution of the marriage, or for legal separation, or in a proceeding for disposition of property following dissolution of the marriage by a court which lacked personal jurisdiction over the absent spouse or lacked jurisdiction to dispose of the property, the court shall assign each spouse's property to him. It also shall divide the marital property without regard to marital misconduct in just proportions considering all relevant factors including:

(1) contribution of each spouse to acquisition of the marital property, including contribution of a spouse as homemaker;

(2) value of the property set apart to each spouse;

(3) duration of the marriage; and

(4) economic circumstances of each spouse when the division of property is to become effective, including the desirability of awarding the family home or the right to live therein for reasonable periods to the spouse having custody of any children.

(b) For purposes of this Act, "marital property" means all property acquired by either spouse subsequent to the marriage except:

(1) property acquired by gift, bequest, devise, or descent;

(2) property acquired in exchange for property acquired before the marriage or in exchange for property acquired by gift, bequest, devise, or descent;

(3) property acquired by a spouse after a decree of legal separation;

(4) property excluded by valid agreement of the parties; and

(5) the increase in value of property acquired before the marriage.

(c) All property acquired by either spouse after the marriage and before a decree of legal separation is presumed to be marital property, regardless of whether title is held individually or by the spouses in some form of co-ownership such as joint tenancy, tenancy in common, tenancy by the entirety, and community property. The presumption of marital property is overcome by a showing that the property was acquired by a method listed in subsection (b).

Comment

Subsection (a) establishes standards for the court's disposition of property in four kinds of proceedings: (1) dissolution of marriage; (2) legal separation; (3) independent proceedings for property disposition following an earlier proceeding for dissolution of the marriage in which the court had lacked jurisdiction over the person of the absent spouse; and (4) independent proceedings for property disposition following an earlier proceeding for dissolution of marriage in which the court made no disposition, equitable or otherwise, of property located in the enacting state. In all four kinds, the court is directed first to set apart to each spouse all of his or her property that is not defined as marital property by subsection (b), and secondly to divide the marital property between the parties in accord with the standards established by the section. The court may divide the marital property equally or unequally between the parties, having regard for the contributions of each spouse in the acquisition thereof, the length of the marriage, the value of each spouse's nonmarital property, and the relative economic position of each spouse following the division. The court is directed not to consider marital misconduct, such as adultery or other nonfinancial misdeeds, committed during the marriage, in making its division. If the parties have reached a mutually satisfactory property settlement agreement which is not unconscionable (see Section 306) the court will not be called upon to make a disposition under this section.

Community property states which require an equal division of community property on termination of marriage may wish to substitute that rule in this section. . . .

Subsection (b) defines marital property only for the purposes of division on dissolution of marriage or legal separation. No attempt is made to regulate the respective interests of the spouses in property during the existence of the marriage. . . .

SECTION 308. [MAINTENANCE.]

(a) In a proceeding for dissolution of marriage or legal separation, or a proceeding for maintenance following dissolution of the marriage by a court which lacked personal jurisdiction over the absent spouse, the court may grant a maintenance order for either spouse only if it finds that the spouse seeking maintenance:

(1) lacks sufficient property, including marital property apportioned to him, to provide for his reasonable needs, and

(2) is unable to support himself through appropriate employment or is the custodian of a child whose condition or circumstances make it appropriate that the custodian not be required to seek employment outside the home,

(b) The maintenance order shall be in such amounts and for such periods of time as the court deems just, without regard to marital misconduct, and after considering all relevant factors including:

(1) the financial resources of the party seeking maintenance, including marital property apportioned to him, and his ability to meet his needs independently, including the extent to which a provision for support of a child living with the party includes a sum for that party as custodian;

(2) the time necessary to acquire sufficient education or training to enable the party seeking maintenance to find appropriate employment;

(3) the standard of living established during the marriage;

(4) the duration of the marriage;

(5) the age, and the physical and emotional condition of the spouse seeking maintenance; and

(6) the ability of the spouse from whom maintenance is sought to meet his needs while meeting those of the spouse seeking maintenance. . . . The dual intention of this section and Section 307 is to encourage the court to provide for the financial needs of the spouses by property disposition rather than by an award of maintenance. Only if the available property is insufficient for the purpose and if the spouse who seeks maintenance is unable to secure employment appropriate to his skills and interests or is occupied with child care may an award of maintenance be ordered. . . .

SECTION 309. [CHILD SUPPORT.]

In a proceeding for dissolution of marriage, legal separation, maintenance, or child support, the court may order either or both parents owing a duty of support to a child of the marriage to pay an amount reasonable or necessary for his support, without regard to marital misconduct, after considering all relevant factors including:

(1) the financial resources of the child;

(2) the financial resources of the custodial parent;

(3) the standard of living the child would have enjoyed had the marriage not been dissolved;

(4) the physical and emotional condition of the child, and his educational needs; and

(5) the financial resources and needs of the noncustodial parent. . . .

SECTION 311. [PAYMENT OF MAINTENANCE OR SUPPORT TO COURT.]

(a) Upon its own motion or upon motion of either party, the court may order at any time that maintenance or support payments be made to the [clerk of court, court trustee, probation officer] as trustee for remittance to the person entitled to receive the payments.

(b) The [clerk of court, court trustee, probation officer] shall maintain records listing the amount of payments, the date payments are required to be made, and the names and addresses of the parties affected by the order.

(c) The parties affected by the order shall inform the [clerk of court, court trustee, probation officer] of any change of address or of other condition that may affect the administration of the order.

(d) If a party fails to make a required payment, the [clerk of court, court trustee, probation officer] shall send by registered or certified mail notice of the arrearage to the obligor. If payment of the sum due is not made to the [clerk of court, court trustee, probation officer] within 10 days after sending notice, the [clerk of court, court trustee, probation officer] shall certify the amount due to the [prosecuting attorney]. The [prosecuting attorney] shall promptly initiate contempt proceedings against the obligator.

(e) The [prosecuting attorney] shall assist the court on behalf of a person entitled to receive maintenance or support in all proceedings initiated under this section to enforce compliance with the order. The person to whom maintenance or support is awarded may also initiate action to collect arrearages.

(f) If the person obligated to pay support has left or is beyond the jurisdiction of the court, the [prosecuting attorney] may institute any other proceeding available under the laws of this State for enforcement of the duties of support and maintenance.

Comment

This section establishes a procedure for payment of support or maintenance orders through a court officer and for enforcement by the appropriate prosecuting attorney. The section is modeled on similar provisions in North Dakota, Wisconsin, and other states and is intended to make use of the state's remedy of civil contempt as an effective device for the enforcement of support and maintenance. Under subsection (f), the person to whom a decree for maintenance or support is awarded also may initiate action to collect arrearages. In this action the person might be represented by personal counsel, by a legal aid society or other public agency, or, by a "friend of the court", as envisaged by the Uniform Reciprocal Enforcement of Support Act. Subsection (f) correlates this procedure with the Uniform Reciprocal Enforcement of Support Act so that enforcement can be obtained even though the obligor is beyond the jurisdiction of the court.

SECTION 312. [ASSIGNMENTS.]

The court may order the person obligated to pay support or maintenance to make an assignment of a part of his periodic earnings or trust income to the person entitled to receive the payments. The assignment is binding on the employer, trustee, or other payor of the funds 2 weeks after service upon him of notice that it has been made. The payor shall withhold from the earnings or trust income payable to the person obligated to support the amount specified in the assignment and shall transmit the payments to the person specified in the order. The payor may deduct from each payment a sum not exceeding [$1.00] as reimbursement for costs. An employer shall not discharge or otherwise discipline an employee as a result of a wage or salary assignment authorized by this section.

Comment

This section is modeled on similar provisions in Wisconsin and California and provides an additional method of assuring that obligations for support and maintenance will be met when due. The Section goes beyond existing law in authorizing an assignment of trust income as well as periodic earnings. In states which permit spendthrift trusts, for purposes of support and maintenance, to be attacked, this section will also apply to spendthrift trusts. Each state should insert in the bracket the sum it deems sufficient to meet the cost to the payor of deducting the sums due from each payment. . . .

SECTION 316. [MODIFICATION AND TERMINATION OF PROVISIONS
FOR MAINTENANCE, SUPPORT AND PROPERTY DISPOSITION.]

(a) Except as otherwise provided in subsection (f) of Section 306, the provisions of any decree respecting maintenance or support may be modified only as to installments accruing subsequent to the motion for modification and only upon a showing of changed circumstances so substantial and continuing as to make the terms unconscionable. The provisions as to property disposition may not be revoked or modified, unless the court finds the existence of conditions that justify the reopening of a judgment under the laws of this state.

(b) Unless otherwise agreed in writing or expressly provided in the decree, the obligation to pay future maintenance is terminated upon the death of either party or the remarriage of the party receiving maintenance.

(c) Unless otherwise agreed in writing or expressly provided in the decree, provisions for the support of a child are terminated by emancipation of the child but not by the death of a parent obligated to support the child. When a parent obligated to pay support dies, the amount of support may be modified, revoked, or commuted to a lump sum payment, to the extent just and appropriate in the circumstances.

Comment

Subsection (a) makes each installment under an order for periodic support or maintenance final and non-modifiable when it falls due. The accrued installments cannot be modified retroactively, and future installments can be modified only as to those falling due after a motion for modification has been filed. The purpose of thus making each installment final and non-modifiable when it becomes due is to give each past due installment the status of a final judgment entitled to full faith and credit in other states pursuant to the decisions of the Supreme Court. . . .

Except where the decree, incorporating the agreement of the parties, provides to the contrary [see Section 306(f)], future installments may be modified, but the person seeking modification must show that circumstances have changed since the date of the original order so that the order is unconscionable at the time the motion is made and will continue to be unconscionable unless modified. This strict standard is intended to discourage repeated or insubstantial motions for modification. In accordance with presently existing law, the provisions of the decree respecting property disposition may not be altered unless the judgment itself can be reopened for fraud or otherwise under the laws of the state. There is no intention to change this law. If the judgment was rendered by another state, normal full faith and credit law would allow it to be reopened in the forum state if it can be reopened under the laws of the rendering state. . . .

SECTION 402. [BEST INTEREST OF CHILD.]

The court shall determine custody in accordance with the best interest of the child. The court shall consider all relevant factors including:

(1) the wishes of the child's parent or parents as to his custody;

(2) the wishes of the child as to his custodian;

(3) the interaction and interrelationship of the child with his parent or parents, his siblings, and any other person who may significantly affect the child's best interest;

(4) the child's adjustment to his home, school, and community; and

(5) the mental and physical health of all individuals involved.

The court shall not consider conduct of a proposed custodian that does not affect his relationship to the child.

Comment

This section, excepting the last sentence, is designed to codify existing law in most jurisdictions. It simply states that the trial court must look to a variety of factors to determine what is the child's best interest. The five factors mentioned specifically are those most commonly relied upon in the appellate opinions; but the language of the section makes it clear that the judge need not be limited to the factors specified. Although none of the familiar presumptions developed by the case law are mentioned here, the language of the section is consistent with preserving such rules of thumb. The preference for the mother as custodian of young children when all things are equal, for example, is simply a shorthand method of expressing the best interest of children —and this section enjoins judges to decide custody cases according to that general standard. The same analysis is appropriate to the other common presumptions: a parent is usually preferred to a non-parent; the existing custodian is usually preferred to any new custodian because of the interest in assuring continuity for the child; preference is usually given to the custodian chosen by agreement of the parents. In the case of modification, there is also a specific provision designed to foster continuity of custodians and discourage change. . . .

The last sentence of the section changes the law in those states which continue to use fault notions in custody adjudication. There is no reason to encourage parties to spy on each other in order to discover marital (most commonly, sexual) misconduct for use in a custody contest. This provision makes it clear that unless a contestant is able to prove that the parent's behavior in fact affects his relationship to the child (a standard which could seldom be met if the parent's behavior has been circumspect or unknown to the child), evidence of such behavior is irrelevant. . . .

SECTION 506. [LAWS NOT REPEALED.]

This Act does not repeal: [Here should follow the acts not to be repealed, including any acts regulating or prescribing:

(1) the contents of and forms for marriage licenses and methods of registering marriages and providing for license or registration fees;

(2) the validity of premarital agreements between spouses concerning their marital property rights;

(3) marital property rights during a marriage or when the marriage terminates by the death of one of the spouses;

(4) the scope and extent of the duty of a parent to support a child of the marriage;

(5) custody of and support duty owed to an illegitimate child;

(6) the Uniform Child Custody Jurisdiction Act; and

(7) any applicable laws relating to wage assignments, garnishments, and exemptions other than those providing for family support and maintenance].

NOTE: FEMINIST COMMENTARY ON THE ACT

Some feminists have criticized no-fault divorce on the ground that in practice it reduces the amount of maintenance awarded to women.[1] One reason for this may be that the act removes one of the wife's bargaining weapons, i.e., threatening or seeking divorce on a fault ground. The argument is that lower payments to women are unjust in a society where labor market discrimination condemns most women to earn less than their husbands, and where the traditional structure of marriage encourages women to leave work, and thus decreases their wage-earning capacity if they seek to re-enter the market after divorce. The act could be revised to meet this objection by a directive to

---

1. For other criticisms of the act, see Report of the Marriage and Family Committee of the National Organization for Women, Suggested Guidelines in Studying and Comments on the Uniform Marriage and Divorce Act (1971).

the judge to award money for training and education, and related expenses such as day care, so that the woman can bring her earning capacity up to a level commensurate with that of her former husband.

Section 308(b)(2) of the Uniform Act does mention the time necessary for training and education in order to obtain appropriate employment as one of the relevant factors in determining the amount of maintenance. But "appropriate employment" is not defined. Is a wife who has stayed home raising children while the husband has advanced in a lucrative career entitled to be trained as a secretary, or as a medical doctor? And if she is old enough that prolonged training seems unrealistic because of her few remaining years in the work force, or because of the age and sex discrimination practiced by educational institutions, is she entitled to maintenance as a supplement to her earnings, so that her standard of living will be comparable to her husband's? Is she entitled to such a supplement even though she will never be able to earn enough herself to continue the standard? The information in Parts V and VI, supra, suggests that judges do not now believe that women are entitled to live at a standard comparable to that of their former husbands; nothing in the act would change this approach. On the other hand, isn't it good from a feminist perspective to encourage women toward economic independence and away from reliance on maintenance, as the Uniform Act does?

Although the act does not fully meet the problem of compensating a woman for the loss in wage-earning capacity she may have suffered during marriage, it does deal with other feminist concerns. Section 307, for instance, directs the court to consider the contribution of the homemaker spouse in dividing the property. The section does not, however, set any standards for this evaluation, which could result in a downgrading of the contribution traditionally made by the woman. Those who see marriage as a partnership might prefer a mandatory 50-50 division of the property, as is done in some community property states.

The enforcement provisions of §§311 and 312 are practical and creative, and if the courts follow through on them, they could go far toward solving the problems of defaults on maintenance and child support payments.

What do you think of the sex-neutral standard for awarding the custody of children in §402? Is it undercut by the commentary? What comments from a feminist perspective could be made on the other sections, particularly §306?

NOTE: OTHER REACTIONS TO THE UNIFORM ACT

Three states have substantially accepted the act, although no state has adopted it in toto.[2] Several other states have followed the act's approach and adopted a no-fault, marriage breakdown standard as the basis of divorce.[3]

The major controversies in the legal community about the act have not centered on feminist issues, but rather have been about the content of the words "irretrievable breakdown," the authority of the judge to deny dissolution, even if both parties seek the divorce, the lack of mandatory counseling or conciliation procedures, and the divi-

2. Colorado, Colo. Rev. Stat. Ann. §§46-1-10 to 46-1-33 (Supp. 1971); Kentucky, ch. 182 [1972] Ky. Acts 740-57; Nebraska, Legislative Bill 820 [1972] Neb. Laws, 82nd Legislature, 2d Sess. 246-55.

3. The no-fault states are California, Cal. Civ. Code §4506 (West 1970); Iowa, Iowa Code Ann. §598.17 (Supp. 1972); Colorado, Colo. Rev. Stat. Ann. §46-1-10 (Supp. 1971); Florida, Fla. Stat. Ann. §61.052 (Supp. 1972-73); Michigan, Mich. Comp. Laws Ann. §552.6 (Supp. 1972); Oregon, Ore. Rev. Stat. §107.025 (Supp. 1971); Kentucky, Ky. Ch. 182, §6 [1972] Ky. Acts 744; Nebraska, Legislative Bill 820, §15 [1972] Neb. Laws. 82nd Legislature, 2d Sess. 249-250. Three other states have merely added a no-fault ground to the list of fault grounds: Idaho, Idaho Code §32-603 (Supp. 1971); New Hampshire, N.H. Rev. Stat. Ann. §458.7-a (Supp. 1971); and North Dakota, N.D. Cent. Code §14-05-03 (1971).

sion only of property acquired during the marriage. The Family Law Section of the American Bar Association was quite critical of the act on such grounds.[4]

B. Divorce Insurance

The idea of divorce or dissolution insurance has been suggested by Henry Foster of New York University Law School, who is a member of the ABA's Family Law Council; the National Organization for Women; and Diana DuBroff, a New York lawyer.[5] Consider the following more detailed proposals.

BRADWAY, WHY PAY ALIMONY?
32 Ill. L. Rev. 295, 301-306 (1937)

Let us first consider the substitution of a new set of concepts. The marital relation has been likened to a partnership. It approximates more closely a corporation because most marriages must have the approval of the state before they are valid and a divorce may be obtained only by permission of the state. If the legal concepts in the economic aspect of family life were expressed in terms now applied to a corporation the subject would be clearer and ready for critical study and improvement.

A corporation deals with three groups of persons — creditors, stockholders and employees. To the first it pays its debts under well recognized legal rules. To the second go dividends in orderly fashion. To the third are awarded wages for services rendered. The economic relations of the wife to the husband can be expressed in terms of debts, dividends and wages without doing violence to her legal rights or his. If she brings to the marriage money or property amassed elsewhere, her rights in it may be defined as those of a creditor. If she contributes to the social or economic improvement of the family by extraordinary services or skills a dividend could reward her insofar as such imponderables may be translated into material values. But for her ordinary services wages would seem a businesslike return.

The use of the wages concept has been urged by many feminists, but apparently not as a part of the analogy between the family and the corporation. The market value of wages is determinable. As long as the family remains a going concern the wife's wages ordinarily would be a matter of domestic adjustment. But when the family disintegrates, the wife's rights might be protected by something like unemployment insurance.

2. *Modifications in Administrative Machinery.* There is nothing unusual in utilizing the insurance device to solve social problems. A long list of precedents show that it is practicable and that it has an inherent flexibility which should make possible an adaptation to a somewhat novel situation. The question is whether it can be adapted to the

4. Report and Recommendations on the Uniform Marriage and Divorce Act, 5 F.L.Q. 123 (1971)

5. Loercher, Women Heft Law as Equality Weapon, The Christian Science Monitor, April 3, 1973, at 6. Cf. A. C. Scott, The Value of Housework: For Love or Money?, 1 Ms. Magazine at 58 (July 1972). Scott explains the connection between wages for housework and divorce insurance as follows:

". . . [M]any feminists worry that the idea would only reinforce the association of housework with 'woman's work,' and make the eventual goal of abolishing sex roles more difficult than ever to achieve. 'The husband would just be employing his wife as a servant,' complains one activist, 'and who wants that?'

"Some advocates overcome this objection by suggesting that the salary need not be actually paid unless the marriage is dissolved. At that time the wife's 'back wages' could be awarded to her as a sort of 'severance pay.' Others have suggested that the portion of the family income allotted to the wife as salary be used to buy an annuity or pension, payable if the marriage went aground — a sort of forced savings against the possibility of divorce. And in that event, instead of receiving alimony, with all its connotations of charity, the wife would receive accrued income, or reparations, for the labor she had put into the job of marriage. The New York Chapter of NOW is extending that idea by pushing for family insurance. In cases of divorce, such an insurance policy would guarantee the homeworking wife an income, determined by number of children and length of marriage."

domestic relations field. An illustration will suggest some of the administrative problems and bring up tentative proposals for their solution.

Let us assume that an insurance fund has been established with all the necessary administrative details; that it offers a policy or variety of policies of insurance to husbands and wives promising to pay the wife a certain sum or sums upon the event of the dissolution of the family; that it will function when the wife, unable to live adequately upon the normal returns for her services in the home, is faced with an appeal to the charity of friends or the public authorities administering the poor laws; that the wife must elect either the present system, or the insurance plan, but not both.

M and W, planning to marry, or already married, and being convinced that the possibility of domestic dissolution with the consequent unemployment of the wife for an uncertain period is a contingency as worth guarding against as the illness or death of the breadwinner, the burning of the residence or the theft of the family possessions, come to the office of an insurance company and make application. They have decided that it is more businesslike to accept the insurance protection than to rely upon the older methods.

They desire to know, first of all, the nature of the fund out of which the insurance will be paid. Public and private insurance funds, sustained by premiums, by taxation and otherwise, have engaged the attention of experts in the field for a sufficiently long time so that several working models are available, any one of which geared to the local conditions of a particular jurisdiction, should offer adequate service.

The second question will relate to the cost of the protection. After a reasonable period of experimentation it is possible for any insurance company to arrive at an actuarial figure for premiums, on certain classes of risks. While it is usual for the insured to pay the premiums, it is not unknown for the beneficiary to undertake the burden. In cases where the individual does not have sufficient funds to meet the payments, group insurance, paid by the employer, or a group of individuals on a cooperative basis or even by the state is not unknown.

The nature of the policy next engages attention. This would be in the form of a promise by the insurance agency, public or private, to pay certain monies in a certain manner upon the happenings of the contingency. The amount of the policy may be a matter for individual agreement. There is much to be said, however, for the arrangement, now in effect in workmen's compensation policies, which provides for a return to the beneficiary or his family at a schedule based upon the wages earned, and the nature of the disability, whether temporary or total. The manner of distribution of the money upon the happening of the contingency, whether in a lump sum or installments, may also be the subject of individual preference. It is likely, however, that the state may desire some voice in the matter since the purpose of the plan is to protect the public from the need to pay for the wife's support. The duration of the liability of the fund, whether for a term or an endowment basis or otherwise, may be adjusted to fit the particular family.

The next step is to make the application. From a business standpoint this is important because it presents the facts which enable the insurance fund to determine whether or not the applicant is an insurable risk. It is the practice of insurance companies not to accept the application at its face value, but to make a thorough investigation of the applicant to prevent fraud, and for other reasons. Hence one finds physicians on the staffs of insurance companies. Other business organizations also probe into the financial ability of a prospective customer, his credit rating and other personal matters. Some of the small loan companies of the country employ a social worker to aid in obtaining the social background of the prospective borrower and to investigate any difficulties which occur during the continuance of the loan.

In the light of these established practices there is little novelty in the proposal that part of the application procedure for unemployment insurance for the wife should be an investigation by a trained social worker as to the social stability of the family. There seems no better way to determine whether it is an insurable risk. The technique of such an investigation is well known to trained social workers, and they are able to secure a maximum of information with a minimum of annoyance to those being investigated. Experience should permit the erection and maintenance of reasonable standards here as in other business relations. It is possible that during an experimental period the executives of the insurance fund will require periodic renewals of the application on which occasions the fund may relieve itself from liability in the event of fraud or a threatened domestic instability. During the continuance of the policy there may be occasional social investigations and perhaps we may hear the slogan, "See your social worker twice a year," just as we now find life and health insurance companies advising their clients to have periodic conferences with physicians and dentists. When group insurance in this field has become well established there may be organized supervision which will tend, by preventive means, to keep families from disintegration. The analogy is to preventive work in the medical field.

The insured will look forward to certain contingencies: the ending of the term when the contract will cease and determine; the death of the husband when the policy may provide a payment to the wife as in ordinary endowment life insurance; the death of the wife, when the policy may provide an endowment return to the husband; the continuance of the marriage for a certain number of years, when an endowment may be payable to both parties. Such matters may render the plan more attractive to individual families.

What will happen when the family breaks down? A breakdown may mean a domestic quarrel, a desertion, or a divorce. Through its periodic social investigations the insurance fund should have advance notice, and it is assumed that all sorts of preventive efforts will have been made. When the contingency, in spite of everything, does occur, the following steps are in order:

1. A filing of a claim by the wife.
2. A social investigation of the claim by the insurance fund.
3. The approval or rejection of the claim.

If the claim is approved, payments will be made at once. If it is rejected, the wife may sue the insurance company presenting such facts as she may have to support the contention that the contingency has occurred and that it is bona fide. . . . This, roughly, is the plan both as to theory and practice. Attention should now be given to some obvious criticisms.

The first possible snag is the problem of regimentation. Will people voluntarily submit their personal affairs to investigation by social workers and others, no matter how tactful and able? There are several reasons why they may. The applicant may come to believe that the business advantages of the plan outweigh considerations of privacy. Since, in an earlier day, individuals submitted to supervision by families and church officials, the proposal is not novel, rather it is a return to fundamentals. If standards of living were more clearly defined and the causes of breakdown statistically presented, individuals might be aroused to a sense of pride in keeping the rate of marriage dissolutions in their home community at a lower rate than in the neighboring city.

A second snag is the possibility that frauds may be perpetrated upon the fund so extensive and ingenious as to discourage its operation. It is difficult to see how such frauds would be greater than those now attempted in other forms of insurance. Since they are being met and insurance companies still show a profit, it is likely that ingenuity, backed by an enlightened self interest, will find a solution. The social work investigation should reduce the possibility of fraud to a minimum and the offenders could be prosecuted criminally with more effect than a wife can bring to bear upon her husband.

A third snag is the possibility that romantically inclined persons will resent what may appear to them a commercialization of the marriage relation. If this were the only occasion dragging the domestic intimacies before the light of publicity, the argument would be stronger. Domestic matters are spread abroad in the columns of every newspaper and many magazines. Court proceedings receive wide attention. A generation which has learned to discuss sex without distress of mind or spirit, and to seek aid from advice-to-the-lovelorn columnists is not likely to be frightened by the instant proposal. When an engagement is announced insurance agents flock to the prospective bridegroom and discuss with him such dismal subjects as death, illness, accidents. Since young love can see a business value in protecting the family from such spectres, it would seem that there is nothing scandalously shocking in the suggestion that protection should be afforded the wife, if a family dissolution should occur.

The fourth snag is the possibility that the proposed device will free the husband from a sense of obligation to his family, and that a general exodus will ensue. There seems to be no real reason to fear such a catastrophe. While the present proposal is not intended to solve the whole problem of family disintegration, it is not so revolutionary as to upset established habits. The proposal is voluntary, not compulsory. If the husband and wife do not elect it, there are still the existing rules and machinery. If they take the insurance it does not necessarily mean that they abandon all marital ties. No doubt some men will seek their freedom who today are restrained by a fear of the consequences. Yet one cannot call this an unmitigated evil. A family held together only by fear is not a healthy social organism such as the state desires. How can it perform adequately the tasks which the state requires of it, such as the rearing of children?

TOMPKINS, REPORT OF THE SUBCOMMITTEE ON THE FAMILY LAW PROCESS — MARRIAGE INSURANCE*

Society has become uncomfortably aware of the contradictory purposes of the law in relation to the family. The legislature, desiring to focus on given areas in order to achieve a coherent synthesis and, to receive suggestions for the implementation of these goals in practice, has appointed this committee "to consider the problems raised, for nearly one million citizens annually, by alimony decrees and more specifically to advise the legislature concerning the establishment of state or private alimony insurance."

The Committee was guided in its deliberations by acknowledging that the functions, or purposes of awarding periodic payments by one party to another subsequent to divorce include: (1) Punishment of the party "at fault," that is, the party held responsible at law "for causing" the divorce or breakup; (2) Maintaining continued contact between the parties so that they might be induced to reconcile and to remarry; (3) Supporting either party with or without fault, and any children of the marriage.

The stimulating and rewarding task of ordering and summarizing the ideas rising from this committee's discussion fell to me, as secretary.

The Committee proposed that each couple — subsequent to the marriage ceremony — should apply for a marriage insurance policy for a certain minimum coverage. Premium payments should be determined by actuarial standards taking into account: age, homogeneity of religious and cultural background, prior status, and any other factors statistically related to the divorce rates. In the event of divorce, insurance payments should be paid to either or both parties or to any party awarded alimony, thereby relieving the party obligated to provide alimony of such payments to the extent of coverage.

The Committee found no serious legal barriers to the insurance plan; our legal system has long upheld insurance as a manifestation of the freedom to contract.

(1) Some members, while accepting wholeheartedly the principles underlying free-

---

*Excerpts from a paper submitted by Roger Tompkins, following a hearing in a class on The Family and the Law, during his third term as a student at the Yale Law School (1962). Printed with permission of the author [in Goldstein and Katz, The Family and The Law 633-637 (1965)].

dom of contract, pointed out that since no one can have a business or property interest in divorce, alimony insurance cannot be "an insurable interest" and must, therefore constitute a wager. They reminded the committee that wagering contracts in the form of insurance have been banned in England since the early seventeenth century and that the American courts early adopted this proscription. . . .

The minority further argued that the dangers are even greater [than] in the case of life insurance. They quoted the Supreme Court in Warnock v. Davis, 104 U.S. 755 (10), which struck down an agreement giving nine tenths of the policy's proceeds to a trust association because the association had no insurable interest.

> It is not easy to define with precision what will in all cases constitute an insurable interest . . . [but must be such] as will justify a reasonable expectation of advantage or benefit from the continuance of [the insured's] life [: for example] either pecuniary or of blood or affinity. [O]therwise the contract is a mere wager, by which the party taking the policy is directly interested in the early death of the assured. Such policies have a tendency to create a desire for the event. They are, therefore, independently of any statute on the subject, condemned, as being against public policy. [Id. at 779].

It is preposterous some members argued, to think that divorce or alimony constitute an insurable interest.

But the majority of the Committee replied that not alimony or divorce, but rather marriage was the interest to be insured. Such insurance contains certain elements of investment, as well as indemnity insurance. As Professor Vance, discussing life insurance, noted: "[W]hen made in good faith, for the purpose of accumulating a fund for the support after the death of the insured, of those dependent upon him, the contract is one that encourages industry and thrift, and tends to relieve society of the burden of caring for its helpless members." [The Law of Life Insurance 8-27 (2d ex. 1930)] When a couple insures their marriage they invest against the contingency of its dissolution at the same time they protect the property interest of continued support in case of dissolution. By gearing premiums and payments to earning power, and by setting a maximum, as well as minimum schedule of payments, it is possible to make the continuation of marriage more lucrative than its dissolution. Moreover, the affection and security which many held to be the essence of marriage, will no doubt be an incentive to continuation of the marriage. And it may be possible to induce such continuation further by allowing the policy to be converted into a retirement or life insurance scheme at a set date. All of these interests not only constitute property and more, which one may wish to insure or invest, but also serve to offset any inducement to dissolve the marriage. Thus the Committee concluded that any such plan should be called MARRIAGE not alimony, insurance.

(2) Nevertheless, even if one has an insurable interest in post-divorce support, it was objected that such a scheme might be an incentive to divorce by inducing marriage solely for the purpose of financial gain. . . .

To avoid inducing such fraud the Committee recommended a clause allowing a two year period from its operative date during which the insurer could establish a reasonable presumption of fraud. The insurer shall have the burden of pleading and proving the charge, unless the accused party alone shall have access to necessary evidence or unless the court shall call forth the accused on a doctrine of *res ipsa loquitur*. After the two year period, however, there shall be an irrebuttable presumption of non-fraud.

(3) Another member switched the argument to a less obvious danger. He reasoned that if the scheme does not induce fraud, it will certainly remove an effective deterrent to divorce. The couple's financial problems cared for, they will surely not think twice about divorce. They will make no effort to stay together, to make the marriage work. The overriding interest insured would be in divorce in order to collect, and not in the continuation of the marriage. Furthermore, since there is no deterrent to divorce in the

form of authorized sanction, as the crime of arson in fire insurance or murder in life insurance, the proposed policy would surely induce, or fail doubly to deter, contemplated divorce. . . .

The Committee acknowledged that financial considerations as a deterrent to divorce might be weakened in some cases. But in others the financial security offered by the policy might enable the parties to make an unclouded decision concerning their capacity to live together in a meaningful relation. Insofar as people have control over whether they can continue living together, by minimizing the risk of financial pressure, the scheme allows the parties to view their position with somewhat less anxiety than is already imposed upon them. The increased burden of insecure financial future might actually cause persons to leap into divorce — without considering whether their relationship is or could become meaningful — simply in order to reduce anxiety or to secure punishment to satisfy severe guilt feelings. Moreover, because of affection and stability that constitute a meaningful relation, it was felt that the parties would always struggle to attain that relationship even though they could receive certain minimal payments upon dissolution of the marriage. And, furthermore, failing the establishment of such a relationship parties should not be deterred from or handicapped in establishing another marriage.

(4) Even if the inducement and non-deterrent arguments are not true, some argued, is it not possible that by admitting the possibility of divorce through providing for it, the state is tacitly sanctioning the moral evil of a family dissolution? And in doing so, is not the state cutting against its primary interest of keeping the parties together in their marital relation? The law has always been averse to interfering with the marital relation, either to promote or obstruct it. In White v. Equitable Nuptial Benefit Union, 76 Ala. 251 (1884), the court refused to allow any contracts inducing or deterring marriage and in speaking of a marriage-broker contract for the purpose of procuring a marriage partner declared:

> Although they may not be a fraud on either party, such contracts are held to be void, and a public mischief, forasmuch as they are calculated to bring to pass mistaken and unhappy marriages, to countervail parental influence in the training and education of children, and to tempt the exercise of an undue and pernicious influence, for selfish gain, in respect to the most sacred of human relations. (Id. at 258.)

In that case the court struck down an insurance policy — providing that after three months, the insured, upon marrying, would receive monthly benefits — as an inducement to postpone marriage indefinitely, declaring that,

> all conditions in deeds or wills and all contracts, executory or executed, that create a general prohibition of marriage, are contrary to public policy and to "the common weal and good order of society." The rule rests upon the proposition, that the institution of marriage is the fundamental support of national and social life, and the promoter of individual and public morality and virtue; and that to secure well-assorted marriages, there must exist the utmost freedom of choice. Neither is it necessary there shall be positive prohibiting. If the condition is of such nature and rigidity in its requirements as to operate as a probable prohibition, it is void.

Moreover, the law absolutely refuses to sanction any agreement tending to disrupt the harmony of a marriage. In Metropolitan Life Ins. Co. v. Smith, 22 Ky. Law Rep. 868, 59 S.W. 24 (1900) the wife obtained a life insurance policy on her husband without his consent and paid the premiums out of her housekeeping money which he had given her. The court declared that,

> it was against public policy for . . . the wife [to] obtain insurance upon her husband's life without his knowledge and consent. . . . [I]f such practice was indulged in, it might

be a fruitful source of crime. . . . It seems to us that it is not only illegal and against public policy for any insurance company to engage in such insurances as unquestionably existed in this case, but it is also to be condemned for the further reason that the tendency is to induce the wife to use money for insurance purposes that ought to be applied to the purchase of food and raiment for the family. It is also likely to produce discord in the family. [59 S.W. at 25.]

The majority of the Committee however argued that marriage insurance comports with the overall objective of minimal state intervention in the family — whether to encourage or discourage marriage or its dissolution. By insuring minimal alimony payments the insurance plan will reduce state intrusion by eliminating substantive enquiry into the fault of either party. The Committee observed that the lack of funds arising either because a party cannot pay alimony or because he must pay alimony, may well be the very sort of detriment to *re*-marriage which the dissenting member abhors.

(5) Finally it was argued that since the law forbids insurance covering loss caused by the wilful destruction of the property insured, benefits to any person found at fault in a divorce action should be forbidden because the insurance would be for "wilfully destructive" conduct.

In Burt v. Union Central Life Ins. Co., 187 U.S. 362, a case concerning a life insurance contract, the court declared:

> It cannot be that one of the risks covered by a contract of insurance is the crime of the insured. There is an implied obligation on his part to do nothing to wrongfully accelerate the maturity of the policy. Public policy forbids the insertion in a contract of a condition which would tend to induce crime, and as it forbids the introduction of such stipulation, it also forbids the enforcement of a contract under circumstances which cannot be lawfully stipulated for. [Id. at 574.]

The majority of the Committee replied that it was erroneous to equate the concept of "fault" in crime and tort with the concept in divorce. Whatever a finding of fault in divorce may mean, it cannot be relied on as a finding of *the cause* of the breakdown of so highly a complex interrelationship as marriage. Except in rare instances, placing the burden of wilful marital destruction exclusively on one party, oversimplifies the nature of the relationship and is clearly unrelated to defrauding the insurer, which is already met by the two-year provision of the plan.

The Committee recognized the apparently unromantic aspects of the marriage insurance plan, but nevertheless believed that it is responsive to a reality which must not be denied. Furthermore it provides a partial solution to the unanticipated and crippling financial risks accompanying marriage. Many problems remain. Nothing in this plan resolves the difficulties of distributing family assets at the time of divorce. Moreover, we have not considered whether payments should cease for the beneficiaries who remarry; how long payments should continue; whether marriage insurance should be extended to provide for the care and education of children, or for optional medical expenses or for its conversion to a retirement or a life insurance plan.

Whether the policy — whatever its coverage — should be compulsory or voluntary; whether it should be administered by the state — in a deductible payment scheme similar to social security — or operated solely by private companies are important decisions requiring further study.

Of course, we have assumed that alimony is desirable; we have only argued about its form. If the goal of welfare legislation is to secure minimum financial standards for each individual, we might ask why alimony payments, in any form, should be allowed to raise divorced persons above that minimum. Should alimony therefore be abolished, or does something in the nature of the marital relationship compel us to retain it?

NOTE

The first proposal excerpted above is analogous to private insurance and the second to public programs such as old age, survivors, and disability insurance under the Social Security Act. One problem with the first scheme is the likelihood that those who most need insurance will not be able to get it. Couples whose marriages are predictably unstable but who are likely to have children by the time their marriage dissolves, e.g., those who marry at an early age, are unlikely to be insurable. Poor and working-class people who, in the event of divorce, have insufficient resources to support two households probably would be unable to afford the insurance.

As to the second scheme, if it is compulsory, and if benefits are not proportional to contributions to the program, it, like OASDI, is more like a regressive tax than an insurance program. On the other hand, if benefits are proportional to contributions, the program will provide little protection for the poor and working-class people who need it most. If the program were like OASDI, would it be worth accepting the regressive tax structure in order to give the aura of legitimacy imparted by the insurance concept to government payments to separated and divorced women? Note that such a scheme would still mean two categories of recipients: widowed, divorced, and separated women getting insurance, and unwed mothers getting welfare.

VIII. THE EFFECT OF THE EQUAL RIGHTS AMENDMENT ON FAMILY LAW

Both proponents and opponents of the Equal Rights Amendment have agreed that domestic relations law will be a major area affected. The following excerpt discusses changes which will be required.

BROWN, EMERSON, FALK, AND FREEDMAN
THE EQUAL RIGHTS AMENDMENT:
A CONSTITUTIONAL BASIS
FOR EQUAL RIGHTS FOR WOMEN
80 Yale L.J. 871, 936-954 (1971)

1. Laws Affecting the Act of Marriage

The statutory requirements for a lawful marriage are generally very simple. They include in most states a valid license, a waiting period before issuance of the license, a medical certificate, proof of age, parental consent for parties below the age of consent, and a ceremony of solemnization. Of these, only age requirements for marriage with and without parental consent involve widespread discrimination on the basis of sex.[136] A 1967 survey of state marriage laws by the United States Department of Labor showed that only ten states set the same minimum age for marriage (age below which marriage, even with parental consent, is prohibited) for men and women. Only eighteen states set

---

136. In general the requirements for physical examination before marriage apply equally to men and women. In Washington, however, only men are required to answer questions about contagious venereal disease. Wsh. Rev. Code §26.04.210 (Supp. 1970). Such a distinction is based on the Victorian fiction that only men will engage in premarital intercourse. The underlying health reasons for requiring men to be examined apply equally to women. Although physical examination is presumably for protection of the new spouse, the requirement of examination for venereal disease is a useful public health measure. It obviously should not be struck down where it applies unequally to men and women, but rather extended to women, as it already has been in most states.

the same age of consent (age at which marriage is permitted without parental consent) for both men and women.[137] In every state with an age differential, the minimum age for men was one to three years higher than the minimum age for women.[138]

Since the minimum marriage age in all states is now well above the normal age of puberty, physical capacity to bear children can no longer justify a different statutory marriage age for men and women. Instead, there seem to be two current rationales for the higher marriage age for men. One is that, mentally and emotionally, women mature earlier than men. Maturity is such a relative and subjective concept that a court could never use it as a test for an inborn characteristic distinguishing all women from all men. Furthermore, mere estimates of emotional preparedness founded on impressions about the "normal" adolescent boy and girl are based on the kind of averaging which the Equal Rights Amendment forbids. The other rationale for the age difference is that men should not be distracted during adolescence from education and other preparation for earning a living. This rationale is obviously untenable: the law should give as much encouragement to women to prepare themselves to earn a living as it gives to men.[139]

Under the Equal Rights Amendment, a court challenge to the age differential would most likely be made by a man suing to require issuance of a license to him at the lower women's age. Faced with such a challenge to the state law a court would have to find, for the reasons just discussed, that the marriage age differential did not meet the strict criteria of the unique physical characteristics tests required by the Equal Rights Amendment. Once it had concluded that a state could not constitutionally set one marriage age for men, and one for women, a court would be able to increase the marriage age for women upward to match the age for men, on the theory that the state should be equally solicitous of a woman's training as a man's. Or a court might find that the legislature had pegged the age for men unreasonably high and revise the marriage age for men downward to correspond to the marriage age for women. A legislature reconsidering laws about the minimum age for marriage, either before or after a court challenge, would have to set a single age for men and women after weighing the policy considerations underlying the age limit. These considerations might indicate the higher age, the lower age, or an age in between the two.[140]

2. Merger of the Woman's Legal Identity into Her Husband's

a. *Name Change.* The [idea] that a woman [will] assume her husband's name at the time she marries him is based on long-standing American social custom. . . .

The Equal Rights Amendment would not permit a legal requirement, or even a legal presumption, that a woman takes her husband's name at the time of marriage. In a case where a married woman wished to retain or regain her maiden name or take some new name, a court would have to permit her to do so if it would permit a man in a similar situation to keep the name he had before marriage or change to a new name. Thus, [any laws or rules interpreted as] requiring name change for the married woman would

137. See Citizens' Advisory Council on the Status of Women, Report of the Task Force on Family Law and Policy, Appendix B at 62 (1968) (hereinafter cited as Report on Family Law). The states which set the same age of consent are: Connecticut, Florida, Georgia, Hawaii, Kentucky, Louisiana, Michigan, Mississippi, Nebraska, North Carolina, Ohio, Pennsylvania, Rhode Island, South Carolina, Tennessee, Virginia, West Virginia and Wyoming. See, e.g., Ky. Rev. Stat. §402.210 (1969); Pa. Stat. Ann. tit. 48, §1-5(c) (1965).

138. The original basis for this differential was the presumption that women reached puberty earlier than men. The common law ages of consent — 14 for males, 12 for females — represented estimates of the ages when children became physically capable of producing children. Kanowitz [Women and the Law (1969)] at 10.

139. For a decision sustaining legislative judgment about age of majority differentials under current constitutional doctrines, see Jacobson v. Lenhart, 30 Ill. 2d 225, 195 N.E.2d 638 (1964).

140. The considerations which should shape a legislature's judgment in setting a minimum marriage age are outlined in [Levy, Uniform Marriage and Divorce Legislation: A Preliminary Analysis (1969)] at 24-25. The drafters of the Uniform Marriage and Divorce Act chose the lower "women's" ages of 18 for marriage without parental consent and 16 for marriage with consent. Uniform Marriage and Divorce Act §203(1).

become legal nullities. A man and woman would still be free to adopt the same name, and most couples would probably do so for reasons of identification, social custom, personal preference, or consistency in naming children. However, the legal barriers would have been removed for a woman who wanted to use a name that was not her husband's.

Some state legislatures might decide there was a governmental interest, such as identification, in requiring spouses to have the same last name. These states could conform to the Equal Rights Amendment by requiring couples to pick the same last name, but allowing selection of the name of either spouse, or of a third name satisfactory to both.[143] Similarly, statutes which now permit the judge in a divorce case to use discretion in determining whether to allow a woman to resume her maiden name or to take a new name would be extended under the Equal Rights Amendment to cover all men, or at least men who had changed their names at marriage. Moreover, any state coercion regarding an individual's choice of name might still be open to attack under developing constitutional principles of due process and privacy.

In a state where both spouses were required to have the same last name, the children would simply take their parents' name. If the state had no requirement that husband and wife take the same name, it could either require that parents choose one of their names for their children, or it could decide to have no rule at all. The Amendment would only prohibit the states from requiring that a child's last name be the same as his or her father's, or from requiring that a child's last name be the same as his or her mother's.

b. *Domicile.* . . . A court suit challenging discriminatory domicile rules could arise after a woman had been denied some right or benefit because her husband's domicile had been imputed to her.[146] In such a suit a court would have to hold that the Equal Rights Amendment requires rules governing domicile to be the same for married women as for married men. Extending women's dependent status to men would simply create a circular situation with each spouse's domicile dependent on the other's. Thus, equal treatment of men and women for purposes of domicile implies giving married women the same independent right to choice of domicile as married men now have. A court would probably resolve the inequality by striking down whatever statute or portion of a statute sets out a special rule for married women. It would leave standing the general domicile law which would automatically be extended to married women. For similar reasons, a court would do away with the rule that refusal to accompany or follow a husband to a new domicile amounts to desertion or abandonment.[147] A husband would no longer have grounds for divorce in a wife's unjustifiable refusal to follow him to a new home, unless the state also permitted the wife to sue for divorce if her husband unjustifiably refused to accompany her in a move. . . .

With respect to children, the traditional rule is that the domicile of legitimate children is the same as their father's.[149] Even those states which permit a married woman to have a separate domicile from her husband appear to retain this rule with respect to the child's domicile.[150] The Equal Rights Amendment would not permit this result.

---

143. The West German federal government has recently proposed legislation along these lines. Part of a large-scale reform of family and divorce legislation, "the bill breaks an ancient tradition of male priority in family names. It will permit marriage partners to adopt the wife's maiden name if they choose or to use it in combination with the husband's surname." Binder, Bill in Bonn Encourages German Penchant for Double Names, N.Y. Times, May 20, 1971, at 2, col. 3.

146. See also Clarke v. Redeker, 259 F. Supp. 117 (S.D. Iowa 1966), in which a man wanted to adopt his wife's domicile to get the benefit of lower tuition at the state university.

147. See Annot., 29 A.L.R.2d 474 (1953), citing cases from 29 states which held that a wife's refusal to follow her husband to a new domicile is desertion by her and grounds for divorce proceedings.

149. Madden [Handbook of the Law of Persons and Domestic Relations (1931)] at 453. Illegitimate children follow the domicile of their mothers.

150. The law on children's domicile is confused because the states have failed to integrate the statutes removing women's civil disabilities with those which determine children's domicile. Thus the provisions of Arkansas law defining a woman's domicile as independent from that of her husband, Ark. Stat. Ann. §§34-

Either by legislative action or judicial determination, a state would have to devise a sex-neutral basis for determining the child's domicile. The most reasonable domicile would be the place the child actually lives most of the time. If the family lives together but one of the parents is domiciled in a separate place, the child's domicile should be the place of family residence. If the parents live apart, then the child's domicile should be the domicile of the parent with whom he or she lives most of the time. Alternatively, the state could allow the child to determine his or her own domicile on the basis of where he or she actually lives or works, if apart from both parents.

3. Rights of Husbands and Wives Inter Se . . .

a. *Rights of Consortium.* . . . The Equal Rights Amendment would not permit men to have a greater right than women to recover for loss of their spouse's services and companionship. . . .

More fundamentally, however, the Equal Rights Amendment would prohibit enforcement of the sex-based definitions of conjugal function, on which the discriminatory consortium laws are based. Courts would not be able to assume for any purpose that women had a legal obligation to do housework, or provide affection and companionship, or be available for sexual relations, unless men owed their wives exactly the same duties. Similarly, as discussed more fully below, men could not be assigned the duty to provide financial support simply because of their sex.

b. *Allocation of The Duty of Family Support between Husband and Wife.* In all states husbands are primarily liable for the support of their wives and children, although the details of this liability and the possible defenses vary. A wife may be liable for supporting her husband in many states, but generally only if the husband is incapacitated or indigent. In most states the mother is liable for support of the children only if the father refuses or fails to provide for their support.[154]

Criminal nonsupport laws are the legal system's most heavy-handed technique for enforcing the husband's current duty of support. Nonsupport was not an indictable offense at common law.[155] But criminal statutes in all but three states now penalize a man's desertion or nonsupport of his wife, and all American jurisdictions set criminal penalties for nonsupport of young children.[156] While these laws typically penalize either parent who fails to provide support for a minor child, the duty of interspousal support is placed solely on the man.[157]

The child-support sections of the criminal nonsupport laws would continue to be valid under the Equal Rights Amendment in any jurisdiction where they apply equally

---

1307 to 1309 (1962), enacted in 1941, did not affect Arkansas' adherence to the common law rule "that the last domicile of the deceased father of an infant constitutes his legal domicile. . . ." Bell v. Silas, 223 Ark. 694, 268 S.W.2d 624 (1954). The impact of Wisconsin's 1965 law titled "Women to have equal rights," Wis. Stat. Ann. §246.15 (Supp. 1970) on the law of children's domicile has not yet been judicially determined. The most recent Wisconsin case on the subject, Town of Carlton v. State Dept. of Public Welfare, 271 Wis. 465, 74 N.W.2d 340 (1956), followed the traditional rule, embodied in Wisconsin's public assistance statute, that "the domicile of a minor child . . . is that of its father." 271 Wis. at 469. Cf. Alaska Stat. Ann. §25.15.110 (1962) (removing women's civil disabilities) as compared with Alaska Stat. Ann. §25.05.040 (1962) (giving fathers preference in child custody).

154. The support laws also favor male children in seven states, since the right to support is terminated when the child reaches the age of majority, 39 Am. Jur. Parent and Child §§35, 40 (1942), and this age is set higher for males than for females. The following statutes set age of majority at 18 for females and 21 for males: Ark. Stat. Ann. §57-103 (1947); Idaho Code Ann. §32-101 (1963); Nev. Rev. Stat. §129.010 (1963); N.D. Cent. Code §14-10-01 (1960); Okla. Stat. Ann. tit. 15 §13 (1966); S.D. Comp. Laws Ann. §26-1-1 (1967); Utah Code Ann. §15-2-1 (1953). The implicit premise of these laws — that girls will be or should be married by the time they are 18 and no longer dependent on parents' support — is obviously improper under the Equal Rights Amendment. The considerations involved in equalizing the ages would be the same as for the minimum marriage age, discussed [above].

155. R. Perkins, Criminal Law 604 (1969).

156. See, e.g., Model Penal Code §207.14, Comment 2 at 189 (Tent. Draft No. 9, 1959).

157. E.g., Uniform Desertion and Nonsupport Act, 10 Uniform Laws Annotated 1 (1922).

to mothers and fathers. However, the sections of the laws dealing with interspousal duty of support could not be sustained where only the male is liable for support. Applying rules of narrow construction of criminal laws, courts would have to strike down nonsupport laws which impose the duty of support on men only. Legislatures might decide not to re-enact any husband-wife criminal nonsupport laws. Criminal sanctions against the husband are widely recognized as poor compensation for a wife's unpaid domestic labor and discriminatory treatment against her in the labor market; a legislature might choose to use its resources for a more direct attack on these problems. Alternatively, a state legislature could adopt a law which makes no distinctions on the basis of sex, like the Model Penal Code's nonsupport provision.[158]

With regard to civil enforcement of support laws, courts could take a more flexible approach. The Equal Rights Amendment would bar a state from imposing greater liability for support on a husband than on a wife merely because of his sex. However, a court could equalize the civil law by extending the duty of support to women. With regard to child support this is already the rule in Iowa, where father and mother are under the same legal duty to support the children. . . .[159]

The Equal Rights Amendment would *not* require mathematically equal contributions to family support from husband and wife in any given family. A functional definition of support obligations, based on current resources, earning power, and nonmonetary contributions to the family welfare, would be permissible and practical under the Equal Rights Amendment, so long as the criteria met the tests of reasonable classification described above in Part III(C)[161] If husband and wife had equal resources and earning capacity, neither would have a claim for support against the other. However, if one spouse were a wage earner and the other spouse performed uncompensated domestic labor for the family, the wage-earning spouse would owe a duty of support to the spouse who worked in the home. Creating in each spouse equal liability for support might give creditors an advantage in some instances where they would not currently be able to reach the wife's resources. If this extra liability created hardship for families, the legislature could make rules limiting the extent of creditors' access to a family's resources.

c. *Ownership of Property.* The law has attempted to recognize women's contribution to the family by giving each spouse an interest in property acquired during the marriage. Two different systems have been adopted in the United States for distributing property rights within a family — the community property system and the common law system. In both systems the woman's right matures primarily upon separation or death of her spouse. As both systems currently operate, they contain sex discriminatory aspects which would be changed under the Equal Rights Amendment.

(1) *Community Property.* . . . Under the Equal Rights Amendment, laws which vest management of the community property in the husband alone, or favor the husband as manager in any way, would not be valid.[166] In the absence of new legislation, the courts would leave decisions about disposition of the community property to be made jointly by husband and wife. This would be consistent with the general judicial preference to allow married couples to work matters out between themselves.

158. "A person commits a misdemeanor if he persistently fails to provide support which he can provide and which he knows he is legally obliged to provide to a spouse, child, or other dependent." Model Penal Code §230.5 (Proposed Official Draft, 1962).

159. Picht v. Henry, 252 Iowa 559, 107 N.W.2d 441 (1961).

161. See the discussion [reprinted in Chapter One, VI-C-1, supra].

166. Similarly, laws which give the husband greater testamentary power over the community property would also fall. For example, in New Mexico, if the wife dies first the husband gets all the community property, but if the husband dies first, the wife has a legal right to bequeath only half the community property, the rest to be distributed as the husband decrees in his will. N.M. Stat. Ann. §§29-1-8 (1953), 29-1-9 (Supp. 1969). This law would clearly violate the Equal Rights Amendment. The inequality could be resolved either by giving the wife all the community property if the husband dies first, or by limiting the surviving husband's share to one half the community property as the wife's share is now limited. The latter is more consistent with the practice in the common law states.

Legislatures might prefer to follow the example of the recent amendment of the Texas community property law. The new Texas law provides that

> each spouse shall have sole management, control and disposition of that community property which he or she would have owned if a single person.[167]

Rather than leaving decisions about the community property to husband and wife together, this rule would give the spouse who had earned or been given property the power to dispose of it. This rule obviously favors the wage-earning spouse, who in most instances under current conditions will be the man. Thus it would require scrutiny as a rule neutral on its face, which falls more heavily on one sex than the other.[168] The Texas law also states that property of one spouse which is mixed or combined with property of the other spouse is subject to the joint control of husband and wife unless they agree otherwise. This part of the law would certainly be valid under the Equal Rights Amendment.

(2) *Common Law Ownership.* The other forty-two states have a common law basis for distributing marital property. However, Married Women's Property Acts in every state have modified the harsh common law principles that gave the husband complete control over his wife's property and the products of her labors. . . . Except for qualifications relating to the right of a surviving spouse to inherit, therefore, each spouse now owns his or her separate property free of legal control of the other spouse.

The Married Women's Property Acts did not automatically abolish the common law estates of dower and curtesy, but today most states have abandoned these cumbersome devices for protecting the interests of widows and widowers, and others have modified them substantially. In their place, the states have substituted other forms of protection of a marital share of the property of one or both spouses. All states except North Dakota and South Dakota give the woman a nonbarrable share in her husband's estate, but a number of states fail to give the husband a corresponding legal claim in his wife's estate.[170] The widow's allowance or family allowance, homestead, and limitation on gifts to charity are other devices to protect a surviving spouse against complete disinheritance.

Where these devices give the surviving husband rights equal to the surviving wife, they would be valid under the Equal Rights Amendment.[171] In the many states, however, where the wife still has a protected position, the discriminatory laws would either be invalidated or extended. Where a legal device has proved to be a useful protection, legislatures would probably be inclined to extend its coverage to men, but where the technique has provided little real protection, the legislature could take the opportunity for review provided by the Equal Rights Amendment to revise or repeal the law.

d. *Grounds for Divorce.* . . . In the past many grounds for divorce were highly sex discriminatory; today only a few apply solely to one sex or the other. . . .

Except for nonsupport and pregnancy, all the sex discriminatory grounds for divorce . . . are anachronisms, surviving in only one or two states, and are not deserving of extended discussion here. In each instance, a court could invalidate such a provision without doing any serious harm to the overall structure of the state's divorce law. On the other hand, the court could also extend the law to the opposite sex without risking serious criticism that it was usurping legislative authority. Even without the pressure of

---

167. Texas Rev. Codes Ann., Family Code, tit. 1, §5.22 (Pamphlet, 1969).

168. See the discussion in Part III (C) [reprinted in Chapter One, VI-C-1, supra]. The Texas law creates a situation similar to the rule in common law jurisdictions concerning control of property, and would be upheld if the common law system were upheld.

170. See W. MacDonald, Fraud on the Widow's Share 21-24 (1960).

171. The Uniform Probate Code, approved by the National Conference of Commissioners on Uniform State Laws and the American Bar Association, gives a "surviving spouse" an elective share of one-third in the decedent's estate. Uniform Probate Code §2-201.

the Equal Rights Amendment, these provisions are likely to be dropped or extended to the opposite sex in the course of divorce law reform. . . .

. . . Like the duty of support during marriage and the obligation to pay alimony in the case of separation or divorce, nonsupport would have to be eliminated as a ground for divorce against husbands only, or else extended to the wife where the husband was without resources and the wife had the financial capacity to support him.

The laws that grant a husband a divorce because at the time of marriage he did not know his wife was pregnant by another man would be subject to strict scrutiny under the unique physical characteristics tests. As with paternity laws, the argument can be made that the ease of identifying the mother of a child, as opposed to the difficulty of identifying the father, is a kind of unique physical characteristic which justifies different rules regarding the relationship of mothers and fathers to illegitimate children. However, no reason exists for distinguishing between the duties and obligations of the mother and the father when the father of an illegitimate child has acknowledged paternity or has been adjudged the father in a paternity proceeding. Furthermore, the divorce laws are not based primarily upon the physical act of giving birth but upon other considerations. The laws derive, at least in major part, from the fact that any child born of a woman during marriage is presumed to be her husband's child. Whether the husband claims the child or not, the law imposes on him the duty to support the child and gives the child his name. In this respect the law places an unequal burden on the husband, for his wife receives no corresponding obligations to support or nurture any children her husband may conceive. Since the Equal Rights Amendment would require men and women to bear equal responsibility for the support and nurture of their children, it eliminates most of the justification for giving men alone this ground of divorce. The Equal Rights Amendment would permit resolution of the disparity either by giving a woman a claim for divorce if, at the time of marriage, she did not know that her husband had impregnated another woman, or by abolishing the ground altogether.

e. *Alimony.* . . . The Equal Rights Amendment would not require that alimony be abolished but only that it be available equally to husbands and wives. This result is consistent with the recommendations of Robert Levy to the Special Committee on Divorce of the National Conference of Commissioners on Uniform State Laws, who concludes,

> [T]he distinction [permitting alimony for wives but not husbands] is an historical idiosyncrasy; there is no principled reason for maintaining the distinction between husbands and wives; almost all recent commentators and official studies of divorce-property doctrines have recommended that the distinction be abolished.[193]

Alimony laws could be written to grant special protection to a spouse who had been out of the labor force for a long time in order to make a non-compensated contribution to the family's well-being. Similarly the laws could provide support payments for a parent with custody of a young child who stays at home to care for that child, so long as there was no legal presumption that the parent granted custody should be the mother.[194] In short, as long as the law was written in terms of parental function, marital contribution, and ability to pay, rather than the sex of the spouse, it would not violate the Equal Rights Amendment.

The maintenance provisions of the Uniform Marriage and Divorce Act serve as an example of the kind of law which would be valid under the Equal Rights Amendment.

193. Levy, *supra* note [140] at 147.

194. See for an example of this assumption, Family Law Committee, Connecticut Bar Association, Proposal for Revision of the Connecticut Statutes Relative to Divorce, 44 Conn. Bar J. 411 (1970). Section 18 provides that when assessing alimony, "in the case of a *mother* to whom the custody of minor children has been awarded, the desirability of the *mother* securing employment" should be a consideration. Id. at 429 (emphasis added).

The Act provides for maintenance to be paid from one spouse to the other if the spouse seeking maintenance lacks sufficient property to provide for his reasonable needs and is unable to support himself through appropriate employment, or is the custodian of a child whose condition or circumstances make it appropriate that the parent not seek employment outside the home. The amount and duration of payments for maintenance are to be determined after the court considers the financial resources of the party seeking maintenance, the time necessary to acquire sufficient training to enable the party to find appropriate employment, the standard of living established during the marriage, the duration of the marriage, the age and physical and emotional condition of the spouse seeking maintenance, and the ability of the spouse from whom maintenance is sought to meet his or her own needs while making maintenance payments.[195]

f. *Custody of Children.* At common law the father, if living, was the natural guardian of his child and as such was nearly always entitled to custody of the children in case of separation or divorce.[196] Some states, including California and Utah, changed this by statute which prefers the mother if the child is young.[197] Others, including Missouri, Florida, Minnesota, New York, and Colorado, give both spouses equal right to custody of the children.[198] In most states there is no statute favoring one parent or the other; rather, preference for the mother or father exists as a result of judicially created presumptions in favor of the mother for girls and young children and in favor of the father for older boys.[199]

The Equal Rights Amendment would prohibit both statutory and common law presumptions about which parent was the proper guardian based on the sex of the parent. Given present social realities and subconscious values of judges, mothers would undoubtedly continue to be awarded custody in the preponderance of situations, but the black letter law would no longer weight the balance in this direction.

4. Summary

The present legal structure of domestic relations represents the incorporation into law of social and religious views of the proper roles for men and women with respect to family life. Changing social attitudes and economic experiences are already breaking down these rigid stereotypes. The Equal Rights Amendment, continuing this trend, would prohibit dictating different roles for men and women within the family on the basis of their sex. Most of the legal changes required by the Amendment would leave couples free to allocate privileges and responsibilities between themselves according to their own individual preferences and capacities. By and large these changes could be made by courts in the process of adjudicating claims under the Amendment. In any area where the legislature felt that sudden extension of the law to men and women alike would cause undue hardship, it could pass new legislation basing marital rights and duties on functions actually performed within the family, instead of on sex.

NOTE: A CONTRARY VIEW OF THE AMENDMENT'S IMPACT ON FAMILY LAW

In light of the small number of significant changes in existing domestic relations law which the amendment would require, is it not possible that, in the family law area,

195. Uniform Marriage and Divorce Act, §§308(a)-(b).
196. See Madden, supra note [149] at 456-57; Clark [Domestic Relations (1968)] at 584. The father could be deprived of custody only when he was shown to be corrupt or to be endangering the child.
197. Cal. Civ. Code Ann. §4600(a) (West 1970); Utah Code Ann. §30-3-10 (1953).
198. Mo. Stat. Ann. §452.120 (1952); Fla. Stat. Ann. §61.13 (West 1969); Minn. Stat. Ann. §518.17 (1969); N.Y. Dom. Rel. Law §70 (McKinney 1964); Colo. Rev. Stat. 46-1-5(7) (1967).
199. See Clark, supra note [196] at 585. In 90 percent of custody cases the mother is awarded the custody. Drinan, The Rights of Children in Modern American Family Law, 2 J. Fam. L. 101, 102 (1962).

the amendment will be largely symbolic and hortatory? Yet opponents of the amendment have argued that one of its worst aspects is its impact on present family structure.

For instance, Phyllis Schlafly, a dedicated political conservative and antifeminist, contends that the amendment will require elimination of support and alimony rights for women. As the excerpt above indicates, the theory of the amendment adopted by Congress does not require this result, even where the courts are left with the final decision. More importantly, legislators can choose among many alternatives for making divorce laws sex neutral. Furthermore, it should be remembered that the question of support is mostly academic to an ongoing marriage, since the courts generally will not award support while the parties are living together.

On the other hand, there are undoubtedly some women who have gotten high alimony awards under a sex-based standard whose awards would not be as substantial under a sex-neutral standard. It is important for feminists not to discount the reality that some individual women will lose benefits as a result of the amendment, while recognizing that the size of the benefits lost and the number of women adversely affected is much smaller than ERA opponents argue. It will also be necessary for women to lobby for the kinds of sex-neutral laws which are in women's best interest, if the predictions of the Yale article and the expectations of congressional sponsors of the ERA are to be fully realized. Already the Uniform Marriage and Divorce Act, a suggested reform of major importance raised long before serious hopes for passage of the ERA, has taken a sex-neutral approach.

IX. THE INFLUENCE OF GOVERNMENT PROGRAMS AND POLICIES ON FAMILY STRUCTURE

This part of Chapter Three concerns the impact on sex roles within the family of four areas of governmental action: the federal income tax laws; the old age, survivors, and disability insurance program (Social Security); the welfare program; and government-funded child care. To a greater or lesser extent, government policy in all four areas promotes conformity to traditional sex roles. The income tax and Social Security programs both operate to discourage women from working outside the home during marriage. The inadequacy of government funding for child care programs has a similar effect, especially on middle-class women. These effects are mild, however, when compared to the impact of welfare and child care programs on poor people. These programs enforce harsh restrictions on mothers and children who do not have men to support them, while denying welfare altogether to families with a male "breadwinner" whose income is inadequate for their needs. Discussion of these four programs is included in this chapter because it is important to consider the cumulative effect of both state domestic relations laws and affirmative governmental programs in evaluating the impact of law on family structure.

A. INCOME TAXATION

Income tax policy supports the traditional model of marriage, in which the wife renders domestic services in the home, and the husband is the sole wage earner. Four features of the tax laws have, in the past, operated to make it disadvantageous for a married woman to work: the aggregation of dual incomes for tax purposes; income splitting whereby half of a single income is attributed to each spouse, and the individual tax rate applied; the disallowance, as a substantial deduction, of child care or housekeeping expenses and other costs of replacing the working wife in the home; and the application to housework of the general approach of failing to tax imputed income. An attempt to modify the effects of the second and third policies above was made in the Revenue Act of 1971. But it appears that those provisions will not go far toward encouraging married women to enter the labor force. In this section, we will briefly consider the effect of each of the four policies on the married woman's decision to work.

1. Aggregation

Blumberg, in her article focusing on sexism in the tax code, articulates the meaning and effect of aggregation of incomes as follows:[1]

> Aggregation . . . is based on the indisputable economic unity of the family. Since resources are generally pooled by spouses, their ability to pay taxes is best measured in terms of family rather than individual income. Aggregation creates, however, a strong work disincentive for potential or actual secondary family earners. The secondary earner's first dollar of income is effectively taxed at the primary earner's highest or "marginal" rate. Assume that a husband earns $12,000 taxable income. At 1970 rates, he is taxed 14 percent of his first thousand dollars of taxable income, 15 percent of the second thousand, 16 percent of the third thousand, etc. His final or twelfth thousand is taxed at 22 percent. Any dollar that he earns in excess of $12,000 will be taxed at 25 percent, his marginal rate. If his wife decided to work, her very first dollar will be taxed at her husband's marginal rate. As the husband's income increases, so will his marginal rate and the wife's work disincentive. Filing separate returns is not an economically practical solution.

2. Income Splitting

Income splitting allows the spousal income, after aggregation, to be divided, the individual tax rate applied, and then the tax liability multiplied by two. Clearly, the greatest advantage of this procedure lies with the family with one wage earner, or to one in which the secondary income (usually the woman's) is substantially less than the primary income. Income splitting was first made available to all married couples nationwide in 1948. Even then, the treatment of each spouse's half of the aggregated spousal income was not the same as that accorded similar income earned by a single person. Each single taxpayer was entitled to a maximum standard deduction (in 1948, $1000; by 1972, $2000). Married people filing a joint return are entitled to only one maximum standard deduction between them, instead of the two they would have had as single persons. According to McCaffrey, "Husbands and wives whose earnings were approximately equivalent may have lost more from the denial of separate standard deductions than they gained from income splitting."[2] In 1951, Congress further decreased the relative advantages to married couples of income splitting, by creating[3]

> a special class of taxpayers called "heads of households," defined (with some exceptions) as the single taxpayer who maintains and shares a home with a single child, grandchild or with another person with respect to whom he is entitled to a deduction for personal exemptions. These taxpayers were then given a special rate schedule which entitled them to about half of the benefit of income splitting.

---

1. Blumberg, Sexism in the Code: A Comparative Study of Income Taxation of Working Wives and Mothers, 21 Buffalo L. Rev. 49, 52-53 (1971).
2. McCaffrey, Computation of Tax at 4, in Barton, Blumberg, and McCaffrey, Tax Law Materials Prepared for the AALS Symposium on the Law School Curriculum and the Legal Rights of Women, Oct. 20-21, 1972, Part I, Income Tax.
3. Id. at 3.

In 1969, in response to the complaints of single taxpayers that married couples had an unfair tax advantage, and a showing that in some instances single persons paid as much as 42 percent more tax on the same income as married people, Congress enacted a new tax structure that creates a different and lower rate for single individuals. Thus, at the effective date of the Reform Bill, four tax tables went into effect in increasing order of progressivity: for married persons filing jointly, for heads of households, for individuals, and for married persons filing separate returns. Two-earner couples are still limited to one maximum standard deduction and are also limited to one low-income allowance (new form of the standard deduction).[4] Although these new rates decrease the inequity between single taxpayers and the spouses in a single-earner family, they have created a new inequity: a tax disincentive to marriage for single working people.

Nussbaum and McCaffrey have prepared extensive charts and tables on the effect of the new tax schedules on various family models.[5] For example, Nussbaum calculates a tax cost of marriage of $717 for spouses who each earn $12,000, have one child, and choose the standard deduction. The tax cost of marriage can be as high as $2,285 for spouses who each make $20,000, have one child, and choose the standard deduction, and it continues to rise as income rises. The percentage differential between the taxes of married and single people with similar incomes for some families goes up to 49.3 percent. In contrast, the tax benefit of marriage for two-earner families in which the wife earns between 25 and 50 percent of family income reaches a maximum of $418 for a couple with five children in which each spouse earns $6,000 and they itemize deductions.[6]

For families with children, these figures reflect the impact both of the provisions summarized above and of the limitations on §214 child care deductions, discussed below. The latter strongly increase the tax cost of marriage for working parents with combined incomes over $18,000.

Both professors reach similar conclusions, summarized by Nussbaum as follows:[7]

> The principal conclusion to be drawn from these data is that the income tax structure discriminates against working wives by imposing a penalty on most marriages where both husband and wife work. The size of this tax cost of marriage, TCM, is greater if there are children and it generally increases with income. In addition, there is a tendency for TCM to increase as the wife's share of family income increases, though it declines somewhat after reaching a peak in the neighborhood of 40 percent of family income.
>
> The income splitting provisions of the American tax system [have] been regarded as somewhat unusual in the preferential treatment of married couples. Yet this

---

4. As McCaffrey explains,
"The 1969 Act also . . . increased the standard deduction to the lower of 15 percent or $2000 [I.R.C. §141] and restricted tax on earned income to a maximum of 50 percent [I.R.C. §1348]. . . . [T]hese major reforms can work to the substantial disadvantage of a married taxpayer. . . . The maximum tax can be used by a married taxpayer only if he files a joint return with his spouse. The effect of this requirement is to subject income from property owned by one spouse to tax rates above 50 percent regardless of the rates that would be applicable to such income if included on the owner's separate return."
Id. at 5. Both the increase in the value of the standard deduction, and the high value of the new low income allowance (presently worth $1300) raise the cost to the married taxpayer of the old provision limiting married couples to one standard deduction and the new provision limiting them to one low-income allowance. The effect of these changes in the standard deduction and the low-income allowance is reflected in Nussbaum's material on the tax cost of marriage, discussed below. The increase in some married persons' tax rates for income from property as a result of the maximum tax on earnings is not.
5. Nussbaum, The Tax Structure and Discrimination Against Working Wives, 25 National Tax J. 183 passim (1972); McCaffrey, supra, at 8-11, Tables I-IV.
6. Nussbaum, supra, at 188-189; McCaffrey, supra, at Tables I and IV. The differential of 49.3 percent is for spouses who each earn $4,000, have one child, and use the standard deduction. The earned income referred to throughout is adjusted gross income; all couples are assumed to have only earned income. Married couples are compared to unmarried couples with the same income and number of dependents.
7. Nussbaum, supra, at 191.

preferential treatment is applied only to the one income family, to the family without children which itemizes deductions and has some income inequality between the spouses, and to the family without children which chooses the standard deduction and has a great deal of income inequality between the spouses. In addition, the preferential treatment has been reduced somewhat by the institution of lower marginal tax rates for single individuals than for married couples with the same per capita taxable income.

One author has suggested that "the two-job family may be the true exception to the rule that two people can live more cheaply (per capita) than one. And why should two people, each with a job, pay higher taxes because they choose to marry and live together?" If a wife and mother chooses to confine herself to the home there is a net advantage to being married; if she chooses to remain in the labor force she is penalized for being married. Thus the tax structure, in the process of discriminating against working wives, is inconsistent in its treatment of married couples vis-à-vis single persons. It should be noted that, so long as married couples are required to lump their incomes and the tax rates are progressive, equality between married persons and single persons cannot be achieved (unless husband and wife have equal incomes). Either single or married persons will be "discriminated" against. The irony of the present tax structure is that single individuals are discriminated against vis-à-vis the one income couple and the two income couple is discriminated against vis-à-vis the single individual.

3. Child Care Expenses

Before 1954, child care expenses were not allowed as deductions for wage earners, a policy based on a 1937 case, Smith v. Commissioner, 40 B.T.A. 1038 (1939), *aff'd mem.,* 113 F.2d 114 (2d Cir. 1940). Ms. Smith tried to deduct the cost of a nursemaid for her child while she was working. The Board of Tax Appeals refused to allow the deduction, stating:[8]

> Petitioners would have us apply the "but for" test. They propose that but for the nurses the wife could not leave her child; but for the freedom so secured she could not pursue her gainful labors; and but for them there would be no income and no tax. This thought evokes an array of interesting possibilities. The fee to the doctor, but for whose healing service the earner of the family income could not leave his sickbed; the cost of the laborer's raiment, for how can the world proceed about its business unclothed; the very home which gives us shelter and rest and the food which provides energy, might all by an extension of the same proposition be construed as necessary to the operation of business and to the creation of income. Yet these are the very essence of those "personal" expenses the deductibility of which is expressly denied.

Blumberg points out the error in the logic of the Board:[9]

> The cost of child care necessary to enable a parent to pursue gainful employment is not analogous to the cost of medical care, food and shelter. One does not seek medical care, food or shelter in order to be gainfully employed, but rather to sustain one's corporal existence. Child care, on the other hand, is an expense that Mrs. Smith need not have incurred had she not been employed. It is not a sine qua non of human survival or comfort but an expense which necessarily arises only when both parents are employed. Nor is expenditure for child care analogous, as the Board suggests, to expenditure for personal servants. Employment of household servants generally represents a discretionary expense unrelated to (or at least not required by) the fact of the taxpayer's employment. A working mother's provision for child care is a nondiscretionary expense directly related to the fact of her employment.

8. 40 B.T.A. at 1038-1039.
9. Blumberg, supra, at 64.

It was not until 1954 that any child care deduction was enacted, and that was very restrictive. The Revenue Act of 1971 greatly liberalized the child care deduction, but the major feminist commentators on tax reform believe that the latest provision is far from ideal. Blumberg analyzes its provisions and the problems it fails to meet.

BLUMBERG
HOUSEHOLD AND DEPENDENT CARE SERVICES: §214
Barton, Blumberg, and McCaffrey, Tax Law Materials Prepared for the AALS Symposium on the Law School Curriculum and the Legal Rights of Women, Oct. 20-21, 1972, 19-34

(2) The Current Provision . . .

1. Who is eligible for the deduction?

An individual who maintains a household which includes a person under the age of 15 who is a §151(e) dependent of the taxpayer OR a dependent or spouse of the taxpayer who is physically or mentally unable to care for himself.

2. What is deductible?

Expenses incurred for care of the dependent or spouse AND expenses for services provided in taxpayer's household but only if such expenses are incurred to enable the taxpayer to be gainfully employed.

3. Limitations on the amount deductible.

(1) Up to $400 per month may be deducted for services provided *in* the taxpayer's household.

(2) With respect to services provided outside taxpayer's household, expenditures incurred for care only (as opposed to household services) may be deducted to the extent of $200 per month for one individual, $300 for two, and $400 per month for three or more.

4. Income limitations.

If the adjusted gross income of the taxpayer exceeds $18,000, the amount otherwise deductible shall be reduced by one half the excess adjusted gross income.

For purposes of the income limitation, the adjusted gross income includes both the income of the taxpayer and his spouse. In order to claim a §214 deduction a working couple must file a joint return.

5. Special rules.

(1) "Substantially full-time" employment requirement for married couples only.

(2) Disallowance of deduction for payments to certain relatives.

(3) Deductible expenses for certain dependents reduced by dependent's gross income and disability payments.

(a) Eligibility for the Deduction

The new provision . . . tends . . . to deny the deduction to many divorced spouses. In order to be a "qualifying individual," a child under the age of 15 must be a 151(e) dependent.[65] Section 151(e) incorporates by reference §152(e) which provides that the parent *not* having custody shall claim the child as dependent if the decree of divorce or separate maintenance provides that such parent shall be entitled to the §151 deduction and such parent pays at least $600 support per year, or if the noncustodial parent pays at least $1200 support and the custodial parent is unable to clearly establish he (most likely "she") provided more than $1200.

When the noncustodial parent qualifies for the dependent deduction under 152(e), he cannot take a §214 deduction because he does "maintain a household" which includes

65. [P.L. 92-178,] §214(b)(1)(A)(1971).

the dependent.[66] Nor, of course, is any dependent care expenditure necessary to enable *him* to work.[67] The employed custodial parent, presumably the wife, who does incur such expenses cannot claim them because the child is not, by virtue of 152(e), her 151(e) dependent.

The simplest solution, that suggested by Hjorth, would change the requirement that the "qualifying individual" be a dependent of the taxpayer to provide instead that such individual must be a dependent or a person who would be a dependent of the taxpayer absent §152(e). Until this inequitable feature is cured, it is advisable for working couples seeking separation or divorce to denominate agreement or decree payments as "alimony" rather than "child support."[69]. . .

While §214 does make such an adjustment for taxpayers who hire a maid to replace the "lost housewife," it does not make any adjustment for taxpayers who replace the lost household services in other ways. The provision allows for deduction of expenses incurred for household services (other than dependent *care*) only if they are provided in the taxpayer's household. When a maid is hired, the maximum deduction is a generous $400 per month.

Yet there are many reasons why a taxpayer might not choose to hire a maid and many other effective ways to obtain the same services. . . .

. . . Consider the task of laundering. If a maid performs these services in the taxpayer's home, the expense is deductible. But if the taxpayer has the same work done by a commercial laundry or takes the family's wash to a laundromat or purchases an automatic washer and drier, no deduction is permitted. Consider the task of food preparation. If the maid prepares meals, the expense is deductible. But if the working couple brings home prepared food or the family eats out more frequently than they would if one spouse were not employed, the additional expense is not deductible.

It is true that Congress intended that §214 would open up new job opportunities in the area of domestic services and would, therefore, remove individuals from the public welfare rolls. But increased participation by mothers in the labor force and deductibility of extra-household service expenditure would also open new job opportunities in service industries, e.g., commercial laundries, restaurants, take-out food establishments and home appliance factories.

The main objection to allowing deduction for such a variety of extra-household expenses would seem to be the difficulty of taxpayer record-keeping and the administrative difficulty in determining whether such expenses were actually incurred and whether they were necessitated by the taxpayer's employment. This is certainly a legitimate objection to itemized deductions. It does not, however, go to the basic issue of whether the likelihood of such expenses should be taken into account in determining tax liability.
. . .

(c) Limitations on the Amount Deductible

While the provision allows deduction of $400 per month for dependent care and household services provided in the household, deductible extra-household expenses are limited in kind and amount. The expenditure must be made for care and the limit is $200 per month for one child, $300 for two and $400 for three or more. One commentator suggests that while the provision appears to discriminate against day care centers, the discrimination is more illusory than real so long as adequate day care can be purchased for $200 per month. He does not consider whether day care centers generally offer a 50

66. Id. §214(a).
67. Id. §214(a) and (b)(2).
69. So long as the husband pays "alimony" rather than "child support," the wife can almost always claim the children as §151(e) dependents. See, e.g., Carole F. Brown, T.C. Memo 1972-47. This approach is generally the best. Substantial "child support" payments could also jeopardize the custodial spouse's head of household status. Int. Rev. Code of 1954 §2(b)(1) (as amended by Tax Reform Act of 1969, P.L. 91-172 §803). For succinct discussion of tax benefits obtainable by proper decree terminology, see 1972 CCH Fed. Tax Rep., Vol. 7, 8246.

percent reduction to the second and third children and waive all fees for any additional children.

While the statute would appear to allow the mother of one child to deduct $200 monthly for day care expenditure and $200 monthly for household services provided in the home, the parent of three children who spends the $400 limit for day care will be unable to deduct anything for household services. In order to stay within the deduction limit and maximize the services received, the taxpayer is induced to hire a maid to perform both dependent care and housekeeping services. While this inducement would be present on the basis of cost alone, the limit on deductibility will increase its effect. This is an undesirable result for those who believe that professional group day care is preferable to a maid's custodial care with respect to both the quality of child care and the creation of new employment opportunities.

(d) The Income Limitation

When the taxpayer's adjusted gross income exceeds $18,000, deductible expenses actually incurred are to be reduced by one-half the excess. Thus the taxpayer who earns $21,000 and spends $4000 can deduct only $2500. In the case of working couples, the income limitation refers to their combined adjusted gross income.

In contrast to former §214, the final version of the current act placed an income limitation on both single and married taxpayers. The limitation is objectionable in its application to all taxpayers and particularly objectionable insofar as it applies to the joint income of married couples. It is not at all clear why the deduction should be denied to upper-middle and upper income taxpayers. . . .

The limitation seems particularly unfair to married couples. Insofar as it represents a congressional determination that individuals earning more than $18,000 but less than $27,600 can partially afford to absorb the loss of the deduction and individuals earning more than $27,600 can entirely afford to absorb the loss, it would seem that the limitation on the joint income of working couples should be set at a higher figure simply because their general expenses are likely to be greater. Stated otherwise, while an individual earning more than $18,000 might be considered affluent, the same cannot be said of a working couple whose joint income reaches that figure.

But there is a more basic objection to the joint treatment of spousal income. It tends to deter the secondary earner, i.e., the wife, from working at all. The effect of the joint income limitation is to deny relief at the income level at which the disincentive effect of other Code provisions is most marked. The wife's earnings are taxed from the very first dollar (because her husband has already claimed all available exemptions and deductions); her applicable tax rate begins at her husband's marginal rate. As her husband's earnings increase, so does the rate at which her earnings are taxed. As their joint income exceeds $18,000 the family also begins to lose its eligibility for the dependent care deduction. Section 214 thus loses its potential to ameliorate the disincentive created by other Code provisions at the level at which their effect is most severe. While fixing the joint spousal income limitation at a rate appreciably higher than the limitation for unmarried individuals would recognize the fact that two must earn more than one to be as wealthy as one, such an approach would not meet the deterrent problem. If the income limitation is retained at all, it should refer to individual income and in the case of married couples, the referent income should be that of the secondary earner, i.e., the lesser earner, presumably the wife. If this approach were adopted, it would be reasonable to lower the income limitation for the secondary family earner to the level at which the estimated cost of dependent care would not be likely to deter the taxpayer from continuing or seeking employment. For example, if maximum dependent care costs are estimated to be $4800 per year, $12,000 might be a reasonable income limitation for secondary family earners. It would be better, however, to entirely abolish the limitation.

Finally, the deduction should probably serve to reduce only the secondary earner's taxable income. The cost of dependent care is not "necessary" for the employment of the primary earner. It is incurred because the other spouse is also gainfully employed. The deduction should not, therefore, result in a tax savings at the couple's joint marginal rate. Instead the savings should be determined by the marginal rate applicable to the individual whose employment necessitated the expense.[89]

(e) Special Rules

There are two special rules that are significant for working couples.[90] The first allows the deduction only when both spouses are employed on a "substantially full-time basis."[91] There is no such requirement for unmarried individuals. The second disallows deduction for amounts paid to certain relatives or to persons who live in taxpayer's household and receive over half their support from him.[92]

The Senate Report defines substantially full-time employment as employment "for three-quarters or more of the normal or customary work week."[93] The "work week" should probably be understood to be that customary in taxpayer's trade or profession. If some sort of national average had been intended, Congress would probably have specified a thirty-five or forty hour work week.

The requirement probably reflects congressional feeling that expenditure for household services is not necessary when one spouse is a part time worker. Yet there is no reason to disallow the deduction for dependent care expenses since they are still necessary for taxpayer's gainful employment. Also, insofar as the taxpayer employs a maid to perform both services while she is gainfully employed, it is arguable that the entire deduction should be allowed. Housework in a household with dependents is a continuing task and not one allocable to certain days of the week. While the spouse is employed part time her family is losing imputed service income at the same rate as the family in which both spouses are employed full time. The only proper restraint would be a requirement that part time earners show that their work hours match the periods for which they purchased dependent care and household services. Finally, whatever the merits of the "substantially full time" employment requirement, there is no reason to apply it solely to married couples.

Section 214 disallows deduction of payments made to two classes of persons: any near relative of taxpayer whether or not claimed by taxpayer as a dependent and whether or not resident in taxpayer's household, and any person who lives in taxpayer's household and for whom taxpayer furnishes more than half support.[95] While the latter exclusion is arguably justifiable on the ground that a person supported by taxpayer and living in his household will or should provide such services without charge, the exclusion of nondependent relatives seems unwarranted. As a general principle, intrafamilial cooperation should be encouraged rather than discouraged. Also, this provision is likely to primarily affect lower income taxpayers who are unable to afford the cost of purchasing services from the open labor market. It is suggested that insofar as this exclusion is retained at all, it should be restricted to payments made to resident dependents of taxpayer. . . .

---

89. Just as the husband's income should not determine the wife's eligibility for the deduction, so the husband's income should not affect the amount of tax savings realized from the deduction. Such an approach would probably necessitate the filing of separate returns or, even better, a return to individual taxation of all taxpayers. See Blumberg [21 Buffalo Law Review] at 80-83 and 85-88.

90. There is another special rule which reduces the amount of deductible expenditure when the qualifying individual is someone other than a child under 15, §214(e)(5). Since this paper is primarily concerned with the issue of child care, this rule will not be treated.

91. Int. Rev. Acts 1971, P.L. 92-178, §214(e)(2).

92. Id., §214(e)(4).

93. S.R. No. 92-437. See also Conf. Rept. No. 92-708.

95. Note 91 supra, §214(e)(4). Relatives include sons and stepsons, daughters and stepdaughters, brothers, sisters, fathers, mothers, stepfathers and stepmothers, nieces and nephews, aunts and uncles, and various in-laws.

C. ALTERNATIVE MECHANISMS FOR TAKING DEPENDENT CARE
EXPENDITURE INTO ACCOUNT IN COMPUTING TAX LIABILITY

As a preliminary matter, it is suggested that any deduction (or allowance) should effectively be a §62(a) deduction rather than an itemized deduction which is unavailable if the taxpayer takes the optional standard deduction or the low income allowance.[97] Itemized deductions are granted largely for expenditures which are personal and discretionary. The optional standard deduction and low income allowances should, therefore, be understood as a compensatory measure for taxpayers who either cannot afford or choose not to make such expenditures.[98] As such, their election should not serve as a bar to deduction of expenses which are necessary to taxpayer's gainful employment.

It is suggested that the most appropriate treatment of household and dependent care expenses incurred for the purpose of enabling taxpayer to be gainfully employed requires separate mechanisms for taking into account these two varieties of expenditure. Dependent care expenditure is clearly identifiable. The expense is either incurred or it is not incurred. The variety of ways in which it can be incurred is limited. Insofar as the expense purchases both dependent care and household services, e.g., a maid, a reasonable allocation can be made.[99] If the expense is not incurred at all because taxpayer's dependents do not require care, taxpayer has not suffered any loss of housewifely imputed service income. It is suggested, therefore, that dependent care expenses should be taken into account as itemized expenses, giving rise to either a deduction at taxpayer's marginal rate or a tax credit at a fixed percentage of actual expenditure.

On the other hand, household services (or, more properly, replacement of lost housewifely imputed service income) are not susceptible to accurate or convenient accounting. A two earner family may choose to replace the lost imputed income by hiring a maid or by purchasing services from a variety of commercial establishments or, if they can afford neither, by simply giving up their leisure time. Each approach represents an "expense" which should be taken into account. But only the first is readily ascertainable. It is suggested that the most appropriate method of accounting for such expenditure is an allowance giving rise to either a deduction or a credit. The allowance should reflect the difference between average two earner family and one earner family expenditure for household services.[102] While this discussion has been primarily concerned with the two earner family, such an allowance would be equally appropriate for unmarried taxpayers with §214 dependents. . . .

4. Imputed Income

The value of various services that the taxpayer performs for himself has never been included in the tax base. The most notable example of this is the work of the housewife. Because the actual cost of paying others to do housework is great, and there is no actual and no tax cost in doing it herself, the wife is discouraged from entering the work force. The effect has been described by McCaffrey:[10]

> The housewife who performs services at home adds substantially to the economic welfare of her family with no corresponding increase in the family's tax base. Her functions may include those of nurse, house cleaner, cook, seamstress, launderer,

97. The §62(a) approach was taken in the Senate version but was changed in conference to the effect that the deduction could only be taken as an itemized deduction. Conf. Rept. No. 92-708.

98. For more extensive discussion, see Blumberg [21 Buffalo L. Rev.] at 60-62.

99. As was done under the former section. Treas. Reg. §1.214-1(f)(2)(1956).

102. See, e.g., the Community Council of Greater New York, Budget Service, Annual Price Survey and Family Budget Costs discussed by J. N. Morgan in Income and Welfare in the United States 189 (1962).

10. McCaffrey, Gross Income Concepts — Imputed Income 2-3 in Barton, Blumberg, and McCaffrey, Tax Law Materials Prepared for the AALS Symposium on the Law School Curriculum and the Legal Rights of Women, Oct. 20-21, 1972, Part I, Income Tax.

gardener, and decorator. In addition, she may effect savings for her family by acquiring the ability to shop for and prepare food and clothing more economically than the wife who is employed outside the home. Although the value of these services is not the only instance of tax free imputed income in our economy, the exclusion of this kind of imputed income is particularly significant since those who perform these services probably constitute the largest single occupation in our economy and certainly the largest occupation producing imputed income. The failure to reflect the value of these services in the housewife's taxable income results in an inequitable distribution of the tax burden between one and two earner families and acts to deter wives from entering the work force.

The decision of a wife to remain at home or to engage in "gainful" employment, if rationally made, must take into account the fact that the economic position of her family will only be improved to the extent that her after-tax wages exceed the value of the services she previously performed at home. If she is unable to earn an amount sufficient to pay for substitute household services and to pay taxes accruing on her wages, economic factors may dictate a decision to remain at home. In such a case the tax law has not played the neutral role most economists would agree it should play.

Any attempt to include imputed income in the tax base is probably administratively impractical, but an alternative is to provide an earned income deduction, on the theory that an employee's cost of earning income should be excluded from his taxable income in order to put him on a par with recipients of unearned income. The child care deduction is an example of an earned income deduction. But it is only the beginning of a real incorporation of this principle into the United States tax system. Blumberg argues that even were an earned income deduction not allowed for all workers, it should be for women:[11]

> . . . First, since most families have at least one earner, failure to provide an earned income allowance for the first family earner distributes a burden, albeit inequitable, equally among families. Since, however, most families do not have two earners, such families bear an extra burden. Secondly, the working wife is likely to incur more employment-related expenses than the primary earner. In addition to normal commuting, clothing and lunch costs, she is also likely to incur housekeeping and child care expenses. Thirdly, since the wife's first dollar is effectively taxed at her husband's marginal rate, she has less disposable income with which to defray her cost of earning income. Finally, providing the wife with an earned income allowance would tend to mitigate the work disincentive of income aggregation. Thus, if the revenue cost of an earned income allowance for all workers is judged to be excessive, consideration should still be given to earned income allowances for working wives and mothers.[1]

NOTES

1. It is clear that current tax policy creates disadvantages for married women entering the labor force. But is it also clear that the disadvantage is a disincentive? What about the argument that people work for reasons and goals other than economic advantage — for example, power, interest, and prestige? Read and discuss the following response to the above statement:[12]

11. Blumberg, Sexism in the Code: A Comparative Study of Income Taxation of Working Wives and Mothers, 21 Buffalo L. Rev. at 62 (1971).

64. Pechman [Federal Tax Policy (1966)] estimated in 1966 that a 10 percent rate reduction, that is, a 10 percent earned income exemption for every taxpayer, would result in an annual revenue cost of $5 billion. However, a relatively small deduction for working wives, 10 percent of earned income with a limit of $2,000, would cost about $500 million a year. Id. at 88-90. That is approximately the amount of revenue loss resulting from the 1969 single person's rate return. . . . Had the excessive differential between the joint and the individual tables been resolved by raising the joint rates rather than lowering the individual rates, the resulting revenue profit would have covered the cost of a modest working wives' allowance.

12. Blumberg, supra, at 89-90.

Studies involving the work motivation of male professionals and executives . . . should probably not be used to measure the effect of tax disincentive on wives.[163]

Firstly, male executives are likely to work for different reasons or, more precisely, to feel comfortable articulating certain non-monetary motivations. A male executive or professional says that he likes the power, prestige, or sense of identity that he obtains from work.[165] While the same factors may motivate a wife to work, she generally does not feel comfortable expressing them. A desire for power and prestige is unfeminine. She is supposed to find her identity at home and she is expected to enjoy staying at home. She says, therefore, that she works primarily to supplement family income. If she is not substantially adding to family income, she ought not, by her own articulated criterion, be working. Any wife contemplating work or actually working will compare her disposable income (after taxation without exemptions at her husband's marginal rate) with the additional expenses incurred because of her daily departure from the home. If the difference is not great (and under our present system of taxation and prevalent pattern of wage discrimination, it is not likely to be), the wife may well stop working regardless of the unarticulated non-monetary benefits that she and her family derive from her work.

Secondly, the male executive is the primary family earner. He and his family expect him to be employed. Even if he can choose between early retirement and continued employment, he is likely to opt for a continuation of his life pattern. Unlike the wife, he has no reentry problem. Between his first job and his final retirement, it is unlikely that a male will ever consider the possibility of not working. His wife's initial employment is likely, however, to have been terminated by marriage or childbearing. Her reentry into the labor market is generally the result of a considered and often discretionary choice.

Thirdly, the studies involved general tax increases. The larger resultant tax burden did not imply any societal judgments regarding the desirability of the taxpayer's gainful employment. But the disincentive provisions not only reflect national policy; they also express it normatively. The married woman who is instructed to claim "0" exemptions, informed that child care expenses are disallowed because her family is not poor, and taxed at her husband's marginal rate is effectively told that her proper place is the home. . . .

2. The foregoing materials are obviously oversimplified, and limited to the effect of tax policy on nontraditional marriage roles. This limited treatment reflects two judgments by the authors: first, that the technical questions of tax law and policy cannot be extensively handled except in the context of a tax course, and second, that patchwork changes in tax policy (which, practically, are all that are available at this time) are extremely limited instruments for changing the status of women in society. For full analysis of the issues, and consideration of other comparative tax effects on the family and single persons, see, in addition to the materials cited in this section: Oldman and Temple, Comparative Analysis of the Taxation of Married Persons, 12 Stan. L. Rev. 585 (1960); Groves, Taxing the Family Unit: The Carter Commission's Proposals and U.S. Practice, 22 Nat. Tax J. 109 (1969); Hearings on Revenue Revisions, 1947-1948 —Tax Treatment of Family Income before the House Committee on Ways and Means, 80th Cong., 1st Sess. 846-874 (1947); U.S. Citizens' Advisory Council on the Status of

163. [The author cites such studies as] C. Hall, Effects of Taxation: Executive Compensation and Retirement Plans (1951); C. Long, The Labor Force Under Changing Income and Employment (1958); T. Sanders, The Effects of Taxation on Executives (1951); Break, Income Taxes and Incentive to Work: An Empirical Study, 47 Am. Econ. Rev. 530 (1957).

165. George Break in his article, Income Tax and Incentives to Work: An Empirical Study . . . studies male self-employed English solicitors and accountants to determine whether a high marginal tax rate influenced their decision to assume additional work. The author determined that the most important incentive factors were: attractiveness of the work itself; ambition to make a professional reputation; and rejection of the concept of idleness. He concluded "that contrary to the frequently repeated injunctions of so many financial commentators, solicitude for the state of work incentives does not under current conditions justify significant reductions in the role of progressive income taxation. Indeed, it would appear that, in the United States at least, income tax rates could be raised considerably, especially in the middle and upper-middle income ranges, without lowering unduly the aggregate supply of labor." Break . . . at 549.

Women, Task Force on Social Insurance and Taxes (1968); Thorson, An Analysis of the Sources of Continued Controversy Over the Treatment of Family Income, 18 Nat. Tax J. 113 (1965).

B. The Social Security Program (OASDI)

1. *Women and Social Security*

C. S. BELL, WOMEN AND SOCIAL SECURITY:
CONTRIBUTIONS AND BENEFITS
Paper prepared for hearings
on economic problems of women, Joint Economic Committee (July 25, 1973)

As the social security system has evolved it has developed conflicting goals. Although it is still known as a system of social insurance, present methods of calculating benefits and determining benefit eligibility mean that social security is almost entirely a tax and transfer system, with significant redistributional effects on income. Probably the two more serious criticisms of the system are first, that its "contributions," which should be honestly termed taxes, pose a highly regressive burden on employed earners. Second, the relation between contributions and benefits, quite apart from the deliberate weighting of payments to assist covered earners with low wages, treats some people more favorably than others. Inequities exist for those who choose to retire young, for those who choose to work between the ages of 65 and 72, and for married couples with two earners.

These circumstances of regressivity and the inequities of benefit payments have special import for women because women as workers receive low incomes. The fact that full-time earners who are women receive about 58 percent of the earnings of their male counterparts cannot be repeated too often. That the differential in the earnings in turn reflects differential opportunities for employment, or discrimination in occupations, has been established by empirical research. The result of confining women to so-called women's jobs can best be summarized by remembering that the 58 percent fraction just quoted represents a substantial decline since the mid-1950s. . . .

. . . If women had higher incomes, then we would not need to be concerned about the special impact of social security on them either as workers or as beneficiaries. But women typically earn low wages when they are employed which means that women as retirees or disabled workers can receive only low benefits. As dependents, women have other rights to benefits, but dependency is also highly associated with being poor, and with insecurity.

Secondly, we should look at the special problems of social security for women because of the rapid increase in the number of women who are wage-earners and therefore contributors to social security funds. The labor force participation of married women and of mothers with young children, who are currently the fastest growing group, can be expected to remain high and probably to increase slightly in the future. Consequently their contributions — the social security taxes they pay — will add more and more to the system's total revenues. . . .

At the moment, social security works to transfer income from men to women; women beneficiaries outnumber the men who receive social security payments, and male earners as taxpayers outnumber the women who pay social security contributions. Calculations for December 1971, however, show that although women represented 52 percent of the beneficiaries, the sums they received amounted to only 46 percent of the total benefits. It is also true that over the past few years women have accounted for less than 30 percent of the social security taxes collected from workers and the self-employed. While this proportion may hold in the future (as long as the earnings differential between men and women is allowed to persist), nevertheless the absolute amount withheld from womens' earnings has steadily grown. The median earnings of women workers covered by social security has doubled since 1955 and will undoubtedly continue to rise. Furthermore, because very few women earn more than the social security base income, their contribution to the system represents a larger share of what they earn than is true for men. In all probability these circumstances will continue, so we may pay special attention to women as taxpayers under the system.

The regressive nature of the social security tax for women because of their low earnings as workers can be simply expressed. In 1971 the social security base, the maximum amount of earnings for which contributions were required, was $7800. Forty-five percent of all of the men who worked in that year earned over $8000. By contrast less than 9 percent of the working women earned such amounts. Anyone earning over $8000 obviously contributed a maximum to the social security system but of course the impact of the tax becomes successively smaller at earning levels above the social security base: the tax is, therefore, regressive. This regressive nature of the tax affects all but a small minority of women but only about half of the men workers. The latest rise in the social security tax base and those planned for the future will mean that about 85 percent of all workers will have all of their earnings counted for social security. But this proportion represents, of course, more than 85 percent of the women who work — probably 95-96 percent — and considerably less than 85 percent of the men who work.

It follows that corresponding to the gap in earnings between men and women there is an equally significant gap in social security benefits received by men and women. As of December 1971 the average monthly benefits paid to men without reduction for early retirement amounted to $156.39. Some 7.9 million men received such benefits. For 6 million women with similar benefits the average monthly sum was $126.24. A similar differential can be found in the benefit payments to disabled workers and their families. The average amount paid to a male worker (with no dependents) was $152.60; the disabled women workers averaged $124.90. It is of course true that the formula weighting benefits in favor of low wage earners means that the differential between men and women as beneficiaries is much smaller than that between men and women as earners. The 1970 median earnings for women workers covered by the system amounted to $2734, some 45 percent of the median earned by men, while the women's average benefit provided about 80 percent of the sum received by men. Yet much of this redistribution of income would be unnecessary if women could earn higher incomes in the first place. If, in fact, the earnings differential persists, the amount of income redistributed will grow as more and more women become eligible for retired worker benefits. During the past five years about one million men but over one and one-half million women were added to the group of people eligible for these benefits.

The latest amendments to the Social Security Act provide a minimum benefit amount especially designed to remedy the situation of those who have been employed in low wage jobs. (The present benefits also exceed, of course, the figures just quoted for 1971.) The special minimum will not benefit women to any great extent because it is weighted by the worker's years of coverage in excess of ten years up to a maximum of thirty years. Since many women have low earnings but have also not always worked in covered jobs, they will be excluded by these provisions.

But of course most women receive benefits under the social security system not in terms of their own eligibility as retired or disabled workers, but as dependents of some other earner. This leads to the most basic problem inherent in the system. People have dual roles as individuals and as members of a family. Social security taxes are levied on the individual as a wage earner. Social security benefits may be paid to people in their capacity as retired workers but far more frequently people receive payments based on their status as family members. Two different units of analysis exist, therefore, as well as two different units toward which to direct policy: the individual and the family. . . .

As far as social security goes, this definition of women in terms of the family means that most women receive benefits as a dependent, either wife or widow. The notion of dependency implicitly assumes that the family is supported by the man as husband (or father) and that the woman is therefore dependent upon male income and male earnings for her financial support. In recent years this has become far less true than previously. But the ambiguity persists not only in the system but in the language used by various analysts as well as by the social security administration itself. In the pamphlet "Your Social Security", a hand-out which is designed presumably as the simplest form of information, social security is described as "the basic income-maintenance program" of the country and also as a "basic income insurance plan." These two are not exactly synonymous. In particular, the income which is being maintained refers to family income, the worker plus dependents, whereas the income which is insured refers to the individual earner. The pamphlet further confuses the issue by repeated use of the term *"the* family earner." I stress the singular article here because it is important to realize that most families do not have a single earner. Out of 53 million families in 1971 only 17.8 million or 37 percent derived their income exclusively from the earnings of the head of the family. This obviously includes women heads of the family as well as men heads. But the point is that 63 percent of the families obtained income from more than one "family earner."

That social security taxes are regressive, and that this regressivity bears more heavily on women (who earn low wages) than on men, means also that the taxes are more regressive for families with two or more earners. And such families are in the majority in this country. For most families, the sums paid in social security taxes exceed the sums paid as personal income taxes. Some numerical examples may help here. In 1971 there were 20 million families with both husband and wife at work; median earnings for the husband amounted to $8858, for the wife to $3325. The total family earnings, of $12,183, would have required payment of social security taxes of $578, almost $175 more than a person earning, on an individual basis, the sum of $12,183. With today's contribution rate, the impact is far more severe. Given the same earnings, the social security tax burden would amount to $712.70, or about 6 percent of income. Again, if the total had been earned by one individual, the tax contribution would have been almost $200 less.

The Social Security Administration rightly emphasizes that workers' contributions provide income security for their survivors, in the case of early death, and that retirement benefits are not the only way to judge the return on social security taxes. Yet neither survival nor retirement benefits bear the same relation to contributions when two or more earners provide the family income as they do in the case of the single earner.

The question of dual earners (most families, some 20 million, have two rather than one or three people earning income) involves, of course, both men and women, yet it is appropriate to discuss this as a problem for the woman worker rather than the man for several reasons. First, there is the simple fact that very few men receive benefits based on their wives' earnings. As of December, 1971, only 12,000 husbands and widowers received such benefits, compared with about 7 million wives and widows. Next, although some 6 million women were retired workers, entitled to benefits on their own behalf in 1971, over one million of them received supplementary payments because they were entitled to larger sums as the wives of retired workers. For any of these women, the relation between her tax contribution and the benefit she received was negative: her payments to the social security system had effectively vanished. Of course, they had in actuality been transferred to other beneficiaries, rather than disappearing altogether. Then, some unknown fraction of the 4 million women receiving benefits as widows and mothers presumably had worked, and therefore paid social security taxes, on which the return was negative.

It is also true that the workingwoman whose husband is paying social security taxes knows that she is entitled, as his dependent, to retirement and survivor's benefits just as the women at home who are not gainfully employed. She senses, therefore, and she is quite correct, an inequity of cost/benefits between herself and women not employed outside the home. The inequity can be quantified by calculating the differential benefit. For example, if a retired man's earnings history were such that benefits payable to him amounted to $354.50 he would be entitled to another $177.30 if he were married, for the sum payable to a couple at that level is $531.80. If his wife had established her own eligibility, say to a monthly benefit of $250.60, she would of course receive that sum, rather than the lower figure, so that total family benefits would be higher for many couples where both had covered earnings than where only one did. But the marginal payment to the woman amounts to only $73.30, the difference between what she would be entitled to as a wife and what she would receive as a retired worker. The return figured in this way looks very small indeed to an employed woman.

Commissioner Ball remarked at a Senate hearing earlier this year that the question of how workingwomen are treated under the system would probably continue to demand attention. The difficulty has been that almost every remedy proposed implies another type of inequity from the one that already exists. To allow a married man the benefit payable to a couple while simultaneously paying his wife as a retiree clearly contradicts the notion of dependency. If the woman has earned income, and established her own rights to benefits, then she is not dependent. But to continue the present practice of simply making up the difference between a woman's benefit as a wife and her benefit as a retired worker means that the married workingwoman has contributed at a heavier tax rate than other women or than married men. The real burden of the social security tax, when both contributions and benefits are considered, is greater for women.

The only equitable solution to the problem seems to be to recognize the non-paid work performed in the home by a married woman to be economic work, and to allow such women to accumulate credits under the social security system. This would enable all benefits to be paid to individuals on the basis of their work and the benefits they had earned accordingly.

The following precedents exist for treating this suggestion with some seriousness. First, non-contributory wage credits already exist in the social security system, although they are accummulated for men. Members of the uniformed services receive wage credits of $300 for each quarter in which the serviceman receives military pay during the period January 1957 through December 1967. Such credits already exist for military service after 1967. It would seem appropriate that the women who provide services at home could also be allowed wage credit. Secondly, the 1972 changes in the Act provided social security coverage for non-paid members of religious orders. Here the order itself in effect takes responsibility for its members (who have taken the vow of poverty) as pseudo-employees. The wages calculated for the purposes of social security will be the "fair market value of any board, lodging, clothing, and other perquisites furnished to the member (but not less than $100/month)."[1] In this second instance contributions are made on behalf of the employee by the employer; in the case of servicemen the credits are non-contributory. Either approach could be taken to recognizing the work performed by women at home.

Other precedents for such a calculation exist in social security systems abroad. The clearest example is the situation in Belgium where a special payment (under the Family Allowances for Children plan) can be obtained by an adult daughter up to the age of 25 who stays at home to be housekeeper rather than seeking gainful employment. Such a woman qualifies if the mother of the children is absent or is incapable of caring for

---

1. Social Security Bulletin, March 1973, vol. 36, no. 3, p. 18.

the family and if there are four children of whom three receive family allowances. The qualifications do not detract from the principle that what is going on here is the recognition of unpaid work at home as economic work entitled to economic support by the social security system.

In West Germany the social security system credits women with hypothetical wage contributions during any periods of maternity. All workers can be credited with similar hypothetical contributions if they suffer extended illness or unemployment, or if education interrupts their employment. Here the size of the contribution is based on the previous earnings of the worker and since a differential between men and women is as typical of West Germany and other European countries as it is here, women's gains are not very great. If non-contributory wage credits were accumulated for women working at home, they would presumably be counted at a standard rate, perhaps with additional allowances depending on the size of the family. It would be possible to supplement the contributions, however, if the law permitted voluntary social security contributions for the woman employed at home. Such a provision exists in West Germany, Great Britain, and other countries. If wage credits were accumulated for the woman employed at housekeeping and child care at home, with actual dollar contributions or with hypothetical contributions, then social security benefits could be paid to individuals qua individuals rather than as dependents of covered earners.

The economic value of work performed at home is rapidly becoming apparent with every effort to understand our welfare system and to analyze properly the suggestions for welfare reform that have been made. To argue that welfare should not be paid those who are able to earn an income but chose not to do so leads to the question, what about the woman with children? Should she be required to work or should she be entitled to welfare because she is raising her children? The provision of day dare centers is obviously a minimum if women with small children are to be required to register for work or for work training as a prerequisite for receiving welfare. Once the actual costs and benefits of day care are realistically examined, it becomes crystal clear that institutional day care in centers is far more costly and probably less beneficial to the parent, the child, and society, than day care in the home. But this argument, turned the other way around, also indicates that the value of the services performed by women at home are much greater than the sums received (especially if the amount is zero).

The Social Security Administration also recognizes the economic value of this kind of women's work in some rather naive remarks about how women's social security contributions can benefit their children. The children of working women who died before retirement age (about 300,000 children in December 1971) obviously benefit directly but the S.S.A. points out that "child's benefits based on a mother's earnings record are also very valuable when her husband survives her and he must employ someone to help care for the children in the home."[2] Obviously a woman who has to be replaced by a paid employee must be doing something useful.

The other implicit recognition of the value of the woman's unpaid work at home comes from the present provisions of the social security law for divorced women. The 1965 Ways and Means Committee report recommending social security benefits for the divorced wives of eligible workers included the following description of purpose. The legislation would provide "protection mainly for women who have spent their lives in marriages . . . especially housewives who have not been able to work and earn social security benefit protection of their own — from loss of benefit rights."[3] What the law does is to tacitly recognize that married women perform economically important work in the household, even if it is not paid for in monetary terms. That the payment to the wife of a retired worker is called a dependent's benefit while the divorced wife is clearly

2. U.S. Department of Health, Education and Welfare, Social Security Administration, Office of Research and Statistics, Research Report No. 42, United States Printing Office, Washington, 1973, p. 88.
3. Report on HR 6675, HR 213, 89th Congress, March 29, 1965, p. 94.

not dependent upon the man makes no difference. The extension of these benefits to a divorced woman accepts the reasoning that married women are entitled to support in exchange for the services they have rendered as well as for the services they are currently rendering.

On the other hand, the present law still confines divorced women to a position of dependency. First, the marriage must have lasted twenty years for the woman to be entitled to benefits from her ex-husband's contributions. Any such flat limitation poses the "threshold" problem: why should the woman who was divorced after nineteen and one-half years be entitled to nothing? As of June 1971 there were 21 million women who had been married over 20 years and not quite as many who had been married for a shorter period of time. But 6,139,000 women had been married between 15 and 20 years and another 5 million had been married at least 10 but not yet 15 years. There seems to be no rationale for requiring a 20 year "sentence" before becoming eligible for pension and parole. The second requirement for divorced wives to benefit is that their former husbands must be receiving social security payments themselves. Hence the woman is dependent on the decision of a man no longer part of her family rather than on her own decisions.

One remedy for both these situations would allow payments of social security benefits to divorced wives on a kind of sliding scale reflecting the length of marriage, with a minimum number of years (or quarters) of marriage required. . . .

However, these problems of divorced women, and the much weightier problems of the inequitable tax/benefit treatment of married couples with two earners, could be far more simply solved by recognizing the economic value of women's employment at home. If all benefit payments were tied strictly to earnings, as has been recommended by some analysts, it could then correctly be termed an income maintenance *or* income insurance system. If the income distribution that resulted appeared inequitable, then transfers to correct the situation would be called for. But these would be financed out of general tax revenue rather than a payroll tax. Whether such changes are made or not, I believe that wives who are fully employed at home should be granted coverage under the social security system, and should be eligible for benefits earned on the basis of their own work. Their contributions should be hypothetical, and perhaps they should be supplemented with voluntary contributions. But they should be eligible for income maintenance because they have earned it, not because they are dependent.

2. Importance of OASDI Protection for Women

CITIZENS' ADVISORY COUNCIL ON THE STATUS OF WOMEN
REPORT OF THE TASK FORCE
ON SOCIAL INSURANCE AND TAXES
54-56 (1968)

LONG-TERM INSURABLE RISKS THAT WOMEN FACE
AND EXTENT OF PRESENT PROTECTION

Old Age

The number of women facing the problem of security in old age is becoming increasingly significant. There were 2.3 million more women than men 65 and over in 1965 — almost 10.5 million women in all. Although the numbers of old people of both sexes will keep increasing, the proportion of the aged formed by women 65 and over will be 3 percent larger in 1980. New projections place the number of women 65 and over between 13.5 and 14 million, or at nearly 4 million more than the number of men in that age bracket.

Not only do more women than men reach age 65, but women live longer after age 65 than do men. Estimates for 1965 place the life expectancy of women beyond 65 at 16.2 years, or 3.3 years longer than men.

Moreover, a smaller proportion of aged women than aged men are in the labor force. The labor force participation rate of women 65 and over is expected to increase slightly from 9.5 percent in 1965 to 9.9 percent in 1980. In contrast, the rate for men 65 and over is assumed to continue its steady decline, falling from 26.9 percent in 1965 to 21.9 percent in 1980.

These three factors — the greater number, the longer life expectancy, and the low rate of employment of women 65 and over — point to an even greater number of women than men for whom adequate protection for old age needs to be provided.

Since women on the average earn less when working than men, they cannot make as adequate provisions for old age as men. This is true even for those who work throughout a normal lifetime. But the majority of women, because of marriage and motherhood, are out of the labor market for some years at least, and they find it even more difficult to achieve adequate old-age security on the basis of their own earnings.
. . .

Extent of Protection Provided

Social insurance is the most common source of income for women 65 and over. Nearly three-fourths of the aged women in the country received some income in 1962 from public retirement programs — that is, social security, railroad retirement, and Federal, State and local government employee retirement systems. . . . That social insurance was not meeting all the income needs of aged women is indicated by the fact that in 1962 14 percent of the aged women were drawing public assistance. Generally, these women were more advanced in age; they had grown up and raised their families when it was far less common for women to work. For some, their husbands also never worked in social security covered employment. Even among social security women beneficiaries, the data for 1962 showed that 8 percent needed public assistance to supplement their benefits. . . .

The median annual income of all women 65 and over was only $913 in 1966, as compared with $2,144 for men. Even after excluding those women having no income, the median annual income was only $1,085. Among all aged women, only 45 percent had incomes of $1,000 or more. . . .

3. Other Proposals

The Citizen's Advisory Council Task Force on Social Insurance and Taxes considered four proposals to eliminate the inequitable treatment of married working women:[13]

> Eliminate the benefit for wives, with an appropriate increase in benefits for all workers.
> Separate benefits into two parts: A social benefit determined in the light of presumptive need and payable to all the aged and a wage-related benefit paid on the basis of covered work.
> Build a working woman's benefit on top of, instead of in lieu of, a wife's benefit.
> Move toward a concept of family earnings as a base for computing family benefits.

The council concluded that most forms of the first and third proposals would be too expensive, and recommended[14]

13. Citizens' Advisory Council on the Status of Women, Report of the Task Force on Social Insurance and Taxes 72 (1968).
14. Id. at 77.

that for the immediate future the retirement benefit provisions be amended to offer as an option to husbands and wives that their earnings be combined for purposes of benefit determination, up to the maximum under law. To avoid prohibitive administrative complications and substantial additional costs, we suggest that the option be limited to retirement benefits in cases where no dependents' benefits are payable and that it be available only to couples who have both reached retirement age and have had at least 10 years of simultaneous double wage credits. Both would, of course, have to join in the exercise of the option.

They also recommended that serious consideration be given to the second proposal, and that aged widows and dependent widowers be entitled to the same benefit the worker would have received at the same age, had he lived. (Widows and dependent widowers currently receive about 80 percent of the covered worker's benefit.) The representative of the AFL-CIO on the task force dissented from the first two proposals. He noted that the effect of allowing income aggregation for Social Security purposes for married people was to create a new inequity between married working women and single working women, and commented as follows on the "double decker" idea:[15]

> . . . The establishment of a "double decker" system would inevitably lead to inclusion of a means test in the lower "deck" program. The AFL-CIO has long been opposed to the adoption of any means test in the social security program, and we see no need to encourage study of a proposal that, if adopted, would cause that result. Instead, we would favor raising the minimum benefit to a more adequate level as well as boosting substantially the entire benefit structure. To help finance these higher benefits, we favor gradual introduction of a general revenue contribution into the system so that eventually the financial cost would be borne by equal contributions of employers, employees and the Federal Government. . . .

Note that neither the income aggregation nor the double decker proposal recognizes unpaid housework as work for Social Security purposes.[16]

GRUENWALD v. GARDNER
390 F.2d 591 (2d Cir.), cert. denied, 393 U.S. 982 (1968)

ANDERSON, J.

After receiving notice of the old age assistance benefits awarded him in the amount of $80.50, pursuant to the provisions of the Social Security Act, the plaintiff requested reconsideration on the ground that Congress had established different and discriminatory criteria for the computation of benefits for men and women at age 62 as a result of the application of 42 U.S.C. §415(b)(3). Because the plaintiff, a male, elected, as he was entitled to do, to have his benefit payments commence 36 months prior to his attaining his 65th birthday, his primary insurance of $100.60 was reduced by 20 percent. A female, with a history of equal earnings, retiring at age 62 would have had a primary insurance amount of $115.60 and would have been entitled to monthly payments of $92.50. The years of an individual's highest earnings are used in computing the "average monthly wage," §415(b)(2)(B), which determines the primary insurance amount under §415. The statute provides for the computation of a female wage earner's average monthly wage on the basis of three years less than that used in the computation for a

15. Statement of William Schnitzler, id. at 84-85.
16. On Social Security credits for housewives, see Women and Social Security, the Report of the Women's Action Program, U.S. Dept. of Health, Education and Welfare 91-93 (1972); Bell, Social Security: Society's Last Discrimination, in Business and Society Rev., Autumn 1972, No. 3 at 45; Walker, Sex Discrimination in Government Benefit Programs, 23 Hast. L. J. 277, 279 (1972); and The Report of the Committee on Social Insurance and Taxes, President's Commission on the Status of Women 37 (1963).

male. §415(b)(3)(A) and (C). This eliminates years of lower earnings and increases the average monthly wage and the primary insurance amount for the female.[17]

The Appeal Council confirmed the computation of plaintiff's benefits and refused to apply the measure applicable to women under the same circumstances. The plaintiff then commenced this action pursuant to 42 U.S.C. §405(g) to have the determination of the Hearing Examiner and Appeals Council reviewed and the 1961 Amendment to the Social Security Act, §415(b)(2)(A)-(3)(A,C), declared unconstitutional. The District Court granted the defendant's motion for summary judgment from which the plaintiff has appealed.

The appellant concedes that women, as a class, earn less than men, that their economic opportunities in higher age groups are less,[1] and that higher benefits will operate as an inducement for their earlier retirement, but disputes "the unequal treatment of two individuals solely because of sex" and argues that a "classification must rest upon a difference which is real. . . ." Quaker City Cab Co. v. Com. of Pennsylvania, 277 U.S. 389, 406, 48 S. Ct. 553, 556, 72 L. Ed. 927 (1928) (dissenting opinion). Yet the "two sexes are not fungible," Ballard v. United States, 329 U.S. 187, 193, 67 S. Ct. 261 (1946), and special recognition and favored treatment can constitutionally be afforded women. See Hoyt v. Florida, 368 U.S. 57, 7 L. Ed. 2d 118 (1961); Muller v. Oregon, 208 U.S. 412, 28 S. Ct. 324, 52 L. Ed. 551 (1908). It is only the "invidious discrimination" or the classification which is "patently arbitrary [and] utterly lacking in rational justification" which is barred by either the "due process" or "equal protection" clauses. Fleming v. Nestor, 363 U.S. 603, 611, 80 S. Ct. 1367, 1373, 4 L. Ed. 2d 1435 (1960); Williamson v. Lee Optical Co., 348 U.S. 483, 489, 75 S. Ct. 461, 99 L. Ed. 563 (1955). A classification or regulation, on the other hand, "which is reasonable in relation to its subject and is adopted in the interests of the community is due process." West Coast Hotel Co. v. Parrish, 300 U.S. 379, 391, 57 S. Ct. 578, 582, 81 L. Ed. 703 (1937). . . .

There is here reasonable relationship between the objective sought by the classification, which is to reduce the disparity between the economic and physical capabilities of a man and a woman — and the means used to achieve that objective in affording to women more favorable benefit computations. There is, moreover, nothing arbitrary or unreasonable about the application of the principle underlying the statutory differences in the computations for men and women. Notwithstanding the favorable treatment granted to women in computing their benefits, the average monthly payments to men retiring at age 62 still exceeds those awarded women retiring at that age. Social Security Bulletin, Annual Statistical Supplement 1965, U.S. Dept. of Health, Education and Welfare, at 47, 56, 64, 69. Social Security Bulletin, Annual Statistical Supplement 1963, supra at 47.

The appellant's case was well and forcefully presented but the trend of authority makes it clear that the variation in amounts of retirement benefits based upon differences in the attributes of men and women is constitutionally valid. The appellant does not

17. "Under present law, retirement benefits for men are figured differently, and less advantageously, than benefits are for women. Three more years are used in computing benefits for a man than are used for a woman of the same age. This difference in the treatment of men and women can result in significantly lower benefits being paid to a retired man than are paid to a retired woman with the same earnings. For example, take the case of a man and a women each of whom reaches age 65 and retires in 1971. The woman's benefit would be $220.40 a month under present law, while the man's benefit would be only $213.10 a month. If both workers retire at age 62 in 1971, the woman's benefit would be $170.50 a month while the man's benefit would be only $163.60 a month." H. R. Rep. No. 231, 92d Cong., 1st Sess. 45 (1971), as quoted in Levy and Atwood, Social Welfare Legislation 12-13, in Kay, Levy, Atwood, and Gehrels, Family Law Materials (AALS Symposium on the Law School Curriculum and the Legal Rights of Women, October 20-21, 1972). — Eds.

1. In 1965 there were over two and one-half times as many male workers age 60-64 as there were females age 60-64, Social Security Bulletin, Annual Statistical Supplement 1965. U.S. Dept. of Health, Educa. and Welfare, at 34-35; the median earnings of the male workers was nearly twice that of the females. Id. at 36-37. In 1959, 1960, and 1961, median earnings for male workers with taxable incomes was also approximately twice the median earnings of females. [Annual Statistical Supplement 1965.] Ibid.

press his argument that the section in question is violative of the Civil Rights Act of 1964, 42 U.S.C. §2000e et seq. (1964), 78 Stat. 253 (1964), but we find that that contention is also without merit.

The judgment of the District Court is affirmed.

4. Proposed Reforms

LEVY AND ATWOOD, SOCIAL WELFARE LEGISLATION
In Kay, Levy, Atwood, and Gehrels, Family Law Materials
AALS Symposium on the Law School Curriculum and
the Legal Rights of Women, Oct. 20-21, 1972, 15, 32, 37-39

[a] H.R. 1, the Nixon Administration's proposal for extensive modification of the Social Security Act, would alter the result in Gruenwald. It provides that determination of the insured's "average monthly wage" will be based on the same number of work years (three) prior to retirement for both male and female workers. H.R. 1, Section 107, 92d Cong., 1st Sess. (1971).

Senator Fong, in the course of Senate debate on the Equal Rights Amendment, 118 Cong. Rec. S4401 (daily ed. March 21, 1972), argued:

> I am advised that if the H.R. 1 computation of benefits, based on an age 62 computation for both men and women, graded on the last three years of earnings is to be applied only prospectively, the cost for the 12-month period beginning July 1972 will amount to an additional $6 million.
>
> But, if the computation is to be equal, under the equal rights amendment, it must be applied to those men presently on the rolls and receiving benefits as well as those men and women who will become eligible in fiscal year 1973. That, I am informed unofficially, will cost in the neighborhood of an additional $1 billion for the first few years.

. . .

[b] H.R. Rep. No. 231, 92nd Cong., 1st Sess. 49 (1970) explains a combined earnings provision included in H.R. 1:

[H.R. 1] would permit the payment of benefits based on the combined earnings of a married couple [Section 110]. . . .

The earnings of the man and wife in each year would be combined up to the maximum amount of annual earnings that is creditable for social security purposes for the year. . . .

The total benefits payable to a couple would be equal to 150 percent (75 percent for each member) of the amount that would be paid to a single person with an average monthly wage equal to the couple's combined wage. This 150 percent total is equal to what is paid to a couple under present law and would be divided equally between the husband and the wife, and each would be paid an old-age insurance benefit. If either were entitled to disability insurance benefits, the disability benefit would be paid up to age 65, as under present law.

[c] Section 104 of H.R. 1 codifies the recommendations of both the President's Commission on the Status of Women and the Citizen's Advisory Council that the widow's benefit be equal to the amount that the wage earner would have received at the same age had he lived. What arguments can be made for and against the change?

[d. In Clark v. Celebrezze, 344 F.2d 479 (1st Cir. 1965), the first Circuit Court of Appeals considered and rejected a widower's challenge to the denial of OASDHI survivor's benefits to him on the basis of his deceased wife's social security coverage because she was not furnishing one-half of his support in the month she applied for benefits, although she was at other times. The court did not comment on the equal protection issues arguably raised by the application of a dependency requirement to widowers of insured wage earners when none is applied to widows of insured wage earners, nor apparently had the plaintiff raised the question.]

The President's Task Force on Women's Rights and Responsibilities in its report, *A Matter of Simple Justice,* p. 11 (1970) recommended:

> The Social Security Act should be amended to: "Provide benefits to husbands and widowers of disabled and deceased women workers under the same conditions as they are provided to wives and widows of men workers. . . ."

The Task Force commented (id. at 11):

> Under current law a wife or widow receives a benefit based on her husband's earnings without meeting any test of dependency. A husband or widower of a woman worker is entitled to a benefit only if he proved he receives one-half or more of his support from his wife.
>
> The death or disablement of a wife in a two-income family will leave the husband with increased responsibility for the children and less income with which to meet the needs. With almost two-fifths of all husband-wife families following a new pattern of economic interdependence, it is time for the social security program to adapt to the new sociological conditions and climate.

. . . Note that as long as husbands as a class are higher wage earners than are wives, eliminating the dependency requirement for husbands and widowers may produce additional (or any) benefits only for husbands and widowers with marginal, below OASDHI maximum, or below "retirement test" incomes.

[e] In a letter to Senator Fong (Hawaii), H.E.W. Secretary Richardson identified the following areas in which the Social Security Act treats men and women in different fashion (118 Cong. Rec. 4404 daily ed., March 21, 1972):

> Certain divorced wives are eligible for wife's benefits as wives if they meet a test of dependency on their former husbands; a divorced husband is not eligible on the earnings record of his former wife (42 U.S.C. 402(b), (c)). Likewise, after death, a widow is eligible if she *is not married,* regardless of dependency; a widower is eligible only if dependent and only if he *has not re-married.* Again, a divorced wife is eligible if dependent; a divorced husband is not eligible (sec. 402(e), (f). Provision is also made for mothers' insurance benefits but not for fathers' benefits (sec. 402(g)). (Distinguish this last *from parent's benefits, section* 402 (h)).
>
> In determining net earnings from self-employment, the income from community property generally is considered the husband's income (sec. 411(a)(5)). . . .
>
> A transitional provision which provides benefits for individuals with less than the normally required quarters of coverage covers individuals and their wives and widows, but not husbands and widowers (sec. 427).

H.R. 1 modifies only some of the disparities mentioned by Secretary Richardson. Section 120 of H.R. 1 removes the dependency test for divorced wives, divorced widows and surviving divorced mothers. (Under the present Social Security provision, a woman in these categories is entitled to benefits based on her ex-husband's account only if (1) she was receiving at least one-half of her support from her former husband; (2) she was receiving substantial contributions from her former husband pursuant to a written agreement; or (3) there was a court order in effect providing for substantial contributions to her support by her former husband.) However, the proposed section does not provide similar rights for divorced husbands, divorced widowers, or surviving divorced fathers. Should a divorced man be entitled to benefits based on his wife's earnings record?

... H.R. 1 retains the "dependency" test for husband's and widower's benefits about which the President's Task Force complained.

C. WOMEN AND WELFARE[18]

1. Introduction

SPARER, THE RIGHT TO WELFARE
In Dorsen (ed.), The Rights of Americans:
What They Are, What They Should Be, 65-66, 82 (1970-1971)

The history of the American welfare system traverses more than three hundred years and several cumulative stages, each growing into or co-existing with the next. These stages are represented by the "poor laws" dating from early colonial times, the purely state and local categorical[19] efforts dating from the early twentieth century (particularly the mother's aid "movement"), the federally funded categorical programs, dating from 1935, and the era of struggle over the "legal rights of the welfare poor" which commenced in 1965, and moved haltingly over the course of five very intense years until 1970, when its first phase was completed. . . .

The struggle to establish a legal right to an adequate welfare grant, without onerous conditions and with fair administration, for all persons in need of financial assistance began as an offshoot of the now defunct "war on poverty." Two forces have led the struggle, sometimes cooperating, sometimes working independently, never quite sure of their proper relationship to each other and — consequently — weaker in their joint effect. One of these forces is composed of lawyers (funded primarily by the federal government's Office of Economic Opportunity); the other is the organized recipients in the various local welfare rights organizations and the National Welfare Rights Organization (NWRO). Organized recipients are not new to the American scene. . . . Never before, however, had welfare organization developed among mothers, nor had there been comparable organization on a national scale. And yet, even by its own claims, the organized recipient movement today numbers only 75,000 out of some 12 million welfare recipients (and, depending upon the definition, some 25 to 50 more million American poor).

Organized recipients have historical precedents; organized effort by lawyers to represent recipients has none. It is even hard to find an analogy, in all the varied areas of American litigation, to the manner in which welfare litigation sprang into being on a national scale with no prior history, encountered a series of successes on issues where defeat was widely predicted, beneficially affected hundreds of thousands of people, became an area of legal practice with its own complexities, professional fraternity, and law school impact, and within five years reached a rather distinct outline of how far it could develop. . . .

The legal strategy, as it emerged over the first few years, consisted of planned assaults against the four major characteristics of the welfare system: (1) the innumerable tests for aid and exclusions from aid, most of which were unrelated to need; (2) procedures which reduced the welfare recipient to a "client," stripped of constitutional and

---

18. In preparing this section, the authors have relied heavily on materials from Edward V. Sparer's course, Income Security, at the University of Pennsylvania Law School, and on Cases and Materials on Welfare Law, prepared by the Center on Social Welfare Policy and Law (1972).

19. The term "categorical" as applied to welfare programs means programs which require not only that the applicant be needy but also that she or he belong to a particular category in order to receive aid. For example, to get Aid to Families with Dependent Children, an adult must be a needy caretaker of needy dependent children as defined in the Federal Social Security Act and applicable state law; adults who are not in this category cannot get aid under the program. — Eds.

other rights assumed by other citizens and forced into dependency upon the welfare agency's whim; (3) the state and local character of the welfare system, which, among other things, is responsible for the numerous welfare "residence" rules [and] for the continuing major reliance on state and local funding; and (4) the inadequate and often shockingly low amount of the money grant. If the assaults as planned were to succeed, the nature of the American welfare system would be changed, something akin to a "right to live" would gradually emerge, and a better society would result.

     . . . [T]he main legal battles carried on during the first five years of the struggle for a legal right to welfare . . . present a very mixed picture. There have been more legal victories than defeats, but the latter have gone to the heart of the effort to change the system.

     The Supreme Court has decided cases in all of the areas Sparer lists. King v. Smith, 392 U.S. 309, 88 S. Ct. 2128, 20 L. Ed. 2d 1118 (1968) infra, struck down one variety of the "innumerable tests for aid and exclusion from aid." Wyman v. James, 400 U.S. 309, 91 S. Ct. 381, 27 L. Ed. 2d 408 (1971), which allowed states to make warrantless searches by welfare officials a condition of receiving aid, was a crucial and disappointing decision in the area of personal dignity for welfare recipients. Shapiro v. Thompson, 394 U.S. 618, 89 S. Ct. 1322, 22 L. Ed. 2d 600 (1969), invalidating state residency requirements, was a victory in the struggle to federalize welfare. And Dandridge v. Williams, 397 U.S. 471, 90 S. Ct. 1153, 25 L. Ed. 2d 491 (1970), supra, Chapter One, IV, was a key defeat, both in the fight for adequate money grants and in the effort to get a strict standard of review applied to poverty classifications.

     The overwhelming majority of welfare recipients are female,[20] which means that welfare victories and defeats have had a major impact on the rights and status of women. It also means that state and federal governments have necessarily dealt with women's role in society, in their constant efforts to cut welfare expenditures. Overt sexism has occurred, for instance, in the definition of eligibility, and eligibility requirements will be the chief focus of the materials in this section; the program primarily discussed will be Aid to Families with Dependent Children (AFDC), which is the largest of the categorical assistance programs.

     The study of welfare eligibility reveals that a primary consequence of sexism is grinding economic deprivation,[21] and that perhaps the problems of poverty will never be solved in American society without fundamental changes in sex roles. Yet in considering the materials which follow, the student should remember that the struggles against sexist policies in welfare have been part of a broad movement on behalf of poor people, and that sexism has had adverse effects on poor men as well as on poor women. Furthermore, the sexism of welfare programs and administrators is not always an end in itself. In the short run, for example, sexist policies may enable government officials

---

     20. In 1967, the mother without the father was present in 70.1 percent of AFDC families; the father without the mother was present in only 1 percent of the families. Both parents were present in 17.8 percent of AFDC families. National Center for Social Statistics, Findings of the 1967 AFDC Study, Part I, NCSS Rept AFDC-3 (67), Table 16 (July 1970). 1971 statistics were similar. National Center for Social Statistics, Findings of the 1971 AFDC Study, Part I, DHEW Pub. No. (SRS) 72-03756, p. 4 (1971).

     21. Chapter Two, I, and Chapter Three, V, supra. The following statistics confirm these findings:

     In 1960, 26 percent of poor people were women aged 16 to 64, while men aged 16 to 64 were only 16.8 percent. Children and the elderly made up the balance. Office of Planning, Research and Evaluation, Office of Economic Opportunity, The Poor in 1970: A Chartbook, Chart 1 (1970).

     In 1963, by one measure 47 percent and by another measure 40 percent of all poor families were headed by women. Women headed only 11 percent of all families regardless of income. Oshansky, Counting the Poor: Another Look at the Poverty Profile, Social Security Bulletin, January 1965, p. 12.

     Of the over six million families headed by women in March 1972, 34 percent had incomes below the low-income level in 1971. The comparable proportion for families with a male head was 7 percent. Women's Bureau, Facts About Women Heads of Households and Heads of Families 8 (April 1973).

to cut down the welfare rolls or to minimize welfare costs. In the long run, sexist policies reinforce work norms (which are themselves sexist) and help to maintain class- and race-based inequities in the distribution of political power, wealth, and social status.[22] In short, although welfare is to a large extent a "woman's problem," the defects of the welfare system can best be understood if other legal and political analyses are used in conjunction with feminist criticism.[23]

2. Family Structure and Eligibility for AFDC

State and federal governments have taken two basic approaches in their efforts to reduce welfare rolls. The first, examined in this subsection, has been to define the problem of poverty in terms of the absence of male breadwinners, and then to attempt to replace the breadwinner, either by supplementing the family's income or by trying to force one of the mother's past or present sexual partners to play the role. The second approach, considered in the following subsection, has been to discount the AFDC mother's role as child caretaker and encourage or force her to shoulder the breadwinning responsibility herself. These descriptions oversimplify, of course; more complete discussions follow later in this part.

KING v. SMITH
392 U.S. 309, 88 S. Ct. 2128, 20 L. Ed. 2d 1118 (1968)

Mr. Chief Justice WARREN delivered the opinion of the Court.

Alabama, together with every other State, Puerto Rico, the Virgin Islands, the District of Columbia, and Guam, participates in the Federal Government's Aid to Families With Dependent Children (AFDC) program, which was established by the Social Security Act of 1935. 49 Stat. 620, as amended, 42 USC §§301-1394. This appeal presents the question whether a regulation of the Alabama Department of Pensions and Security, employed in that Department's administration of the State's federally funded AFDC program, is consistent with Subchapter IV of the Social Security Act, 42 USC §§601-609, and with the Equal Protection Clause of the Fourteenth Amendment. At issue is the validity of Alabama's so-called "substitute father" regulation which denies AFDC payments to the children of a mother who "cohabits" in or outside her home with any single or married able-bodied man. . . . A properly convened three-judge District Court[3]

22. For example, Cloward and Piven, in Regulating the Poor: The Functions of Public Welfare, pp. xv-xvii (1970), argue that "relief programs are initiated to deal with dislocations in the work system that lead to mass disorder, and are then retained (in an altered form) to enforce work. . . .

" . . . The giving of relief goes far toward defining and enforcing the terms on which different classes of men are made to do different kinds of work; relief arrangements in other words, have a great deal to do with maintaining social and economic inequities."

According to these authors, the sexist welfare policies which exclude most poor men from the AFDC rolls are promulgated in order to enforce work. "Thus, relief systems ordinarily exclude able-bodied men (as well as at times, able-bodied women and children) no matter how severe their destitution or prolonged their unemployment. Even though on the edge of starvation, potential workers are ordinarily kept in the labor pool." Id. at 126.

23. Readers are urged to study the major sources cited in this section for discussion of the political economy of welfare from other perspectives, e.g., Cloward and Piven, Regulating the Poor: The Functions of Public Welfare (1970); Sparer, The Right to Welfare, in Dorsen (ed.), The Rights of Americans: What They Are, What They Should Be 65 (1970-1971); Center on Social Welfare Policy and Law, Materials on Welfare Law (1972).

3. Since appellees sought injunctive relief restraining the appellant state officials from the enforcement, operation and execution of a statewide regulation on the ground of its unconstitutionality, the three-judge court was properly convened pursuant to 28 USC §2281. See Alabama Public Service Comm'n v. Southern R. Co. 341 U.S. 341, 343, n.3, 95 L. Ed. 1002, 1005, 71 S. Ct. 762 (1951). See also Florida Lime Growers v. Jacobsen, 362 U.S. 73, 4 L. Ed. 2d 568, 80 S. Ct. 568 (1960); Allen v. Grand Central Aircraft Co., 347 U.S. 535, 98 L. Ed. 933, 74 S. Ct. 745 (1954). Jurisdiction was conferred on the court by 28 USC §§1343(3) and (4). The

... found the regulation to be inconsistent with the Social Security Act and the Equal Protection Clause. . . . [F]or reasons which will appear, we affirm without reaching the constitutional issue.

I

The AFDC program is one of the three major categorical public assistance programs established by the Social Security Act of 1935. . . . The category singled out for welfare assistance by AFDC is the "dependent child," who is defined in §406 of the Act, 49 Stat. 629, as amended, 42 USC §606(a) (1964 ed., Supp. II), as an age-qualified[6] "needy child . . . who has been deprived of parental support or care by reason of the death, continued absence from the home, or physical or mental incapacity of a parent, and who is living with" any one of several listed relatives. Under this provision, and, insofar as relevant here, aid can be granted only if "a parent" of the needy child is continually absent from the home. Alabama considers a man who qualifies as a "substitute father" under its regulation to be a nonabsent parent within the federal statute. The State therefore denies aid to an otherwise eligible needy child on the basis that his substitute parent is not absent from the home.

Under the Alabama regulation, an "able-bodied man, married or single, is considered a substitute father of *all the children of the applicant . . .* mother" in three different situations: (1) if "he lives in the home with the child's natural or adoptive mother for the purpose of cohabitation"; or (2) if "he visits [the home] frequently for the purpose of cohabiting with the child's natural or adoptive mother"; or (3) if "he does not frequent the home but cohabits with the child's natural or adoptive mother elsewhere." Whether the substitute father is actually the father of the children is irrelevant. It is also irrelevant whether he is legally obligated to support the children, and whether he does in fact contribute to their support. What is determinative is simply whether he "cohabits" with the mother.

The testimony below by officials responsible for the administration of Alabama's AFDC program establishes that "cohabitation," as used in the regulation, means essentially that the man and woman have "frequent" or "continuing" sexual relations. With regard to how frequent or continual these relations must be, the testimony is conflicting. One state official testified that the regulation applied only if the parties had sex at least once a week; another thought once every three months would suffice; and still another believed once every six months sufficient. The regulation itself provides that pregnancy or a baby under six months of age is prima facie evidence of a substitute father.

Between June 1964, when Alabama's substitute father regulation became effective, and January 1967, the total number of AFDC recipients in the State declined by about 20,000 persons, and the number of children recipients by about 16,000, or 22%. As applied in this case, the regulation has caused the termination of all AFDC payments to the appellees, Mrs. Sylvester Smith and her four minor children.

Mrs. Smith and her four children, ages 14, 12, 11, and 9, reside in Dallas County, Alabama. For several years prior to October 1, 1966, they had received aid under the AFDC program. By notice dated October 11, 1966, they were removed from the list of persons eligible to receive such aid. This action was taken by the Dallas County welfare authorities pursuant to the substitute father regulation, on the ground that a Mr. Williams came to her home on weekends and had sexual relations with her.

---

decision we announce today holds Alabama's substitute father regulation invalid as inconsistent with Subchapter IV of the Social Security Act. We intimate no views as to whether and under what circumstances suits challenging state AFDC provisions only on the ground that they are inconsistent with the federal statute may be brought in federal courts. See generally Note, Federal Judicial Review of State Welfare Practices, 67 Col. L. Rev. 84 (1967).

6. A needy child, to qualify for the AFDC assistance, must be under the age of 18, or under the age of 21 and a student, as defined by HEW. 79 Stat. 422, 42 USC §§606(a)(2)(A) and (B) (1964 ed., Supp II).

Three of Mrs. Smith's children have not received parental support or care from a father since their natural father's death in 1955. The fourth child's father left home in 1963, and the child has not received the support or care of his father since then. All the children live in the home of their mother, and except for the substitute father regulation are eligible for aid. The family is not receiving any other type of public assistance, and has been living, since the termination of AFDC payments, on Mrs. Smith's salary of between $16 and $20 per week which she earns working from 3:30 a.m. to 12 noon as a cook and waitress.

Mr. Williams, the alleged "substitute father" of Mrs. Smith's children, has nine children of his own and lives with his wife and family, all of whom are dependent upon him for support. Mr. Williams is not the father of any of Mrs. Smith's children. He is not legally obligated, under Alabama law, to support any of Mrs. Smith's children. Further, he is not willing or able to support the Smith children, and does not in fact support them. His wife is required to work to help support the Williams household.

II

The AFDC program is based on a scheme of cooperative federalism. . . . It is financed largely by the Federal Government, on a matching fund basis, and is administered by the States. States are not required to participate in the program, but those which desire to take advantage of the substantial federal funds available for distribution to needy children are required to submit an AFDC plan for the approval of the Secretary of Health, Education, and Welfare (HEW). . . . The plan must conform with several requirements of the Social Security Act and with rules and regulations promulgated by HEW.

One of the statutory requirements is that "aid to families with dependent children . . . shall be furnished with reasonable promptness to all eligible individuals. . . ." 64 Stat. 550, as amended, 42 USC §602(a)(9) (1964 ed., Supp. II). As noted above, §406(a) of the Act defines a "dependent child" as one who has been deprived of "parental" support or care by reason of the death, continued absence, or incapacity of a "parent." 42 USC §606(a) (1964 ed., Supp. II). In combination, these two provisions of the Act clearly require participating States to furnish aid to families with children who have a parent absent from the home, if such families are in other respects eligible. See also Handbook, pt. IV, §2200(b)(4).

The State argues that its substitute father regulation simply defines who is a nonabsent "parent" under §406(a) of the Social Security Act. 42 USC §606(a) (1964 ed., Supp. II). The State submits that the regulation is a legitimate way of allocating its limited resources available for AFDC assistance, in that it reduces the caseload of its social workers and provides increased benefits to those still eligible for assistance. Two state interests are asserted in support of the allocation of AFDC assistance achieved by the regulation: first, it discourages illicit sexual relationships and illegitimate births; second, it puts families in which there is an informal "marital" relationship on a par with those in which there is an ordinary marital relationship, because families of the latter sort are not eligible for AFDC assistance.[13]

We think it well to note at the outset what is *not* involved in this case. There is no question that States have considerable latitude in allocating their AFDC resources, since each State is free to set its own standard of need and to determine the level of benefits by the amount of funds it devotes to the program. See [U.S. Advisory Commis-

13. Commencing in 1961, federal matching funds have been made available under the AFDC subchapter of the Social Security Act for a State which grants assistance to needy children who have two able-bodied parents living in the home, but who have been "deprived of parental support or care by reason of the unemployment . . . of a parent." 42 USC §607. Participation in this program for aid to dependent children of unemployed parents is not obligatory on the States, and the Court has been advised that only 21 States participate. Alabama does not participate.

sion Report on Intergovernmental Relations, Statutory and Administrative Controls Associated with Federal Grants for Public Assistance (1964)] at 30-59. Further, there is no question that regular and actual contributions to a needy child, including contributions from the kind of person Alabama calls a substitute father, can be taken into account in determining whether the child is needy. In other words, if by reason of such a man's contribution, the child is not in financial need, the child would be ineligible for AFDC assistance without regard to the substitute father rule. The appellees here, however, meet Alabama's need requirements; their alleged substitute father makes no contribution to their support; and they have been denied assistance solely on the basis of the substitute father regulation. Further, the regulation itself is unrelated to need, because the actual financial situation of the family is irrelevant in determining the existence of a substitute father.

Also not involved in this case is the question of Alabama's general power to deal with conduct it regards as immoral and with the problem of illegitimacy. This appeal raises only the question whether the State may deal with these problems in the manner that it has here — by flatly denying AFDC assistance to otherwise eligible dependent children.

Alabama's argument based on its interest in discouraging immorality and illegitimacy would have been quite relevant at one time in the history of the AFDC program. . . .

A significant characteristic of public welfare programs during the last half of the 19th century in this country was their preference for the "worthy" poor. Some poor persons were thought worthy of public assistance, and others were thought unworthy because of their supposed incapacity for "moral regeneration." H. Leyendecker, Problems and Policy in Public Assistance 45-57 (1955); Wedemeyer & Moore, The American Welfare System, 54 Calif. L. Rev. 326, 327-328 (1966). This worthy-person concept characterized the mothers' pension welfare programs,[17] which were the precursors of AFDC. See W. Bell, Aid to Dependent Children 3-19 (1965). Benefits under the mothers' pension programs, accordingly, were customarily restricted to widows who were considered morally fit. See Bell, supra, at 7; Leyendecker, supra, at 53.

In this social context it is not surprising that both the House and Senate Committee Reports on the Social Security Act of 1935 indicate that States participating in AFDC were free to impose eligibility requirements relating to the "moral character" of applicants. H.R. Rep. No. 615, 74th Cong. 1st Sess., 24 (1935); S. Rep. No. 628, 74th Cong., 1st Sess., 36 (1935). See also 79 Cong. Rec. 5679 (statement by Representative Jenkins) (1935). During the following years, many state AFDC plans included provisions making ineligible for assistance dependent children not living in "suitable homes." See Bell, supra, at 29-136 (1965). As applied, these suitable home provisions frequently disqualified children on the basis of the alleged immoral behavior of their mothers. Ibid.[18]

In the 1940s, suitable home provisions came under increasing attack. Critics argued, for example, that such disqualification provisions undermined a mother's confidence and authority, thereby promoting continued dependency; that they forced destitute mothers into increased immorality as a means of earning money; that they were habitually used to disguise systematic racial discrimination; and that they senselessly punished impoverished children on the basis of their mothers' behavior, while inconsistently permitting them to remain in the allegedly unsuitable homes. In 1945, the predecessor of HEW produced a state letter arguing against suitable home provisions and recommending their

17. For a discussion of the mother's pension welfare programs, see J. Brown, Public Relief 1929-1939, at 26-32 (1940).

18. Bell quotes a case record, for example, where a mother whose conduct with men displeased a social worker was required, as a condition of continued assistance, to sign an affidavit stating that, "I . . . do hereby promise and agree that until such time as the following agreement is rescinded, I will not have any male callers coming to my home nor meeting me elsewhere under improper conditions." Bell, supra, at 48.

abolition. See Bell, supra, at 51. Although 15 States abolished their provisions during the following decade, numerous other States retained them. Ibid.

In the 1950s, matters became further complicated by pressures in numerous States to disqualify illegitimate children from AFDC assistance. Attempts were made in at least 18 States to enact laws excluding children on the basis of their own or their siblings' birth status. See Bell, supra, at 72-73. All but three attempts failed to pass the state legislatures, and two of the three successful bills were vetoed by the governors of the States involved. Ibid. In 1960, the federal agency strongly disapproved of illegitimacy disqualifications. See Bell, supra, at 73-74.

Nonetheless, in 1960, Louisiana enacted legislation requiring, as a condition precedent for AFDC eligibility, that the home of a dependent child be "suitable," and specifying that any home in which an illegitimate child had been born subsequent to the receipt of public assistance would be considered unsuitable. Louisiana Acts, No. 251 (1960). In the summer of 1960, approximately 23,000 children were dropped from Louisiana's AFDC rolls. Bell, supra, at 137. In disapproving this legislation, then Secretary of Health, Education, and Welfare Flemming issued what is now known as the Flemming Ruling, stating that as of July 1, 1961,

> *A State plan . . . may not impose an eligibility condition that would deny assistance with respect to a needy child on the basis that the home conditions in which the child lives are unsuitable, while the child continues to reside in the home.* Assistance will therefore be continued during the time efforts are being made either to improve the home conditions or to make arrangements for the child elsewhere.

Congress quickly approved the Flemming Ruling, while extending until September 1, 1962, the time for state compliance. 75 Stat. 77, as amended, 42 USC §604(b). At the same time, Congress acted to implement the ruling by providing, on a temporary basis, that dependent children could receive AFDC assistance if they were placed in foster homes after a court determination that their former homes were, as the Senate Report stated, "unsuitable because of the immoral or negligent behavior of the parent." S. Rep. No. 165, 87th Cong., 1st Sess., 6 (1961). See 75 Stat. 76, as amended, 42 USC §608.

In 1962, Congress made permanent the provision for AFDC assistance to children placed in foster homes and extended such coverage to include children placed in child-care institutions. 76 Stat. 180, 185, 193, 196, 207, 42 USC §608. See S. Rep. No. 1589, 87th Cong., 2d Sess., 13 (1962). At the same time, Congress modified the Flemming Ruling by amending §404(b) of the Act. As amended, the statute permits States to disqualify from AFDC aid children who live in unsuitable homes, provided they are granted other "adequate care and assistance." 76 Stat. 189, 42 USC §604(b). See S. Rep. No. 1589, 87th Cong., 2d Sess., 14 (1962).

Thus, under the 1961 and 1962 amendments to the Social Security Act, the States are permitted to remove a child from a home that is judicially determined to be so unsuitable as to "be contrary to the welfare of such child." 42 USC §608(a)(1). The States are also permitted to terminate AFDC assistance to a child living in an unsuitable home, if they provide other adequate care and assistance for the child under a general welfare program. 42 USC §604(b). See S. Rep. No. 1589, 87th Cong., 2d Sess., 14 (1962). The statutory approval of the Flemming Ruling, however, precludes the States from otherwise denying AFDC assistance to dependent children on the basis of their mothers' alleged immorality or to discourage illegitimate births.

The most recent congressional amendments to the Social Security Act further corroborate that federal public welfare policy now rests on a basis considerably more sophisticated and enlightened than the "worthy-person" concept of earlier times. State plans are now required to provide for a rehabilitative program of improving and correcting unsuitable homes . . . to provide voluntary family planning services for the purpose of reducing illegitimate births . . . and to provide a program for establishing the paternity of illegitimate children and securing support for them. . . .

In sum, Congress has determined that immorality and illegitimacy should be dealt with through rehabilitative measures rather than measures that punish dependent children, and that protection of such children is the paramount goal of AFDC. In light of the Flemming Ruling and the 1961, 1962, and 1968 amendments to the Social Security Act, it is simply inconceivable, as HEW has recognized, that Alabama is free to discourage immorality and illegitimacy by the device of absolute disqualification of needy children. Alabama may deal with these problems by several different methods under the Social Security Act. But the method it has chosen plainly conflicts with the Act.

III

Alabama's second justification for its substitute father regulation is that "there is a public interest in a State not undertaking the payment of these funds to families who because of their living arrangements would be in the same situation as if the parents were married, except for the marriage." In other words, the State argues that since in Alabama the needy children of married couples are not eligible for AFDC aid so long as their father is in the home, it is only fair that children of a mother who cohabits with a man not her husband and not their father be treated similarly. The difficulty with this argument is that it fails to take account of the circumstance that children of fathers living in the home are in a very different position from children of mothers who cohabit with men not their fathers: the child's father has a legal duty to support him, while the unrelated substitute father, at least in Alabama, does not. We believe Congress intended the term "parent" in §406(a) of the Act, 42 USC §606 (a), to include only those persons with a legal duty of support.

The Social Security Act of 1935 was part of a broad legislative program to counteract the depression. Congress was deeply concerned with the dire straits in which all needy children in the Nation then found themselves. In agreement with the President's Committee on Economic Security, the House Committee Report declared, "the core of any social plan must be the child." . . . The AFDC program, however, was not designed to aid all needy children. The plight of most children was caused simply by the unemployment of their fathers. With respect to these children, Congress planned that "the work relief program and . . . the revival of private industry" would provide employment for their fathers. . . . As the Senate Committee Report stated: "Many of the children included in relief families present no other problem than that of providing work for the breadwinner of the family." [S. Rep. No. 628, 74th Cong., 1st Sess., 17 (1935).] Implicit in this statement is the assumption that children would in fact be supported by the family "breadwinner."

The AFDC program was designed to meet a need unmet by programs providing employment for breadwinners. It was designed to protect what the House Report characterized as "[o]ne clearly distinguishable group of children." H.R. Rep. No. 615, 74th Cong., 1st Sess., 10 (1935). This group was composed of children in families without a "breadwinner," "wage earner," or "father," as the repeated use of these terms throughout the Report of the President's Committee, Committee Hearings and Reports and the floor debates makes perfectly clear. To describe the sort of breadwinner that it had in mind, Congress employed the word "parent." 49 Stat. 629, as amended, 42 USC §606(a). A child would be eligible for assistance if his parent was deceased, incapacitated or continually absent.

The question for decision here is whether Congress could have intended that a man was to be regarded as a child's parent so as to deprive the child of AFDC eligibility despite the circumstances: (1) that the man did not in fact support the child; and (2) that he was not legally obligated to support the child. The State correctly observes that the fact that the man in question does not actually support the child cannot be determinative, because a natural father at home may fail actually to support his child but his presence will still render the child ineligible for assistance. On the question whether the man must be legally obligated to provide support before he can be regarded as the child's parent, the State has no such cogent answer. We think the answer is quite clear: Congress must have meant by the term "parent" an individual who owed to the child a state-imposed legal duty of support.

It is clear, as we have noted, that Congress expected "breadwinners" who secured employment would support their children. This congressional expectation is most reasonably explained on the basis that the kind of breadwinner Congress had in mind was one who was legally obligated to support his children. We think it beyond reason to believe that Congress would have considered that providing employment for the paramour of a deserted mother would benefit the mother's children whom he was not obligated to support.

By a parity of reasoning, we think that Congress must have intended that the children in such a situation remain eligible for AFDC assistance notwithstanding their mother's impropriety. AFDC was intended to provide economic security for children whom Congress could not reasonably expect would be provided for by simply securing employment for family breadwinners. We think it apparent that neither Congress nor any reasonable person would believe that providing employment for some man who is under no legal duty to support a child would in any way provide meaningful economic security for that child.

A contrary view would require us to assume that Congress, at the same time that it intended to provide programs for the economic security and protection of *all* children, also intended arbitrarily to leave one class of destitute children entirely without meaningful protection. Children who are told, as Alabama has told these appellees, to look for their food to a man who is not in the least obliged to support them are without meaningful protection. Such an interpretation of congressional intent would be most unreasonable, and we decline to adopt it.

Our interpretation of the term "parent" in §406(a) is strongly supported by the way the term is used in other sections of the Act. Section 402(a) (10) requires that, effective July 1, 1952, a state plan must: "provide for prompt notice to appropriate law-enforcement officials of the furnishing of aid to families with dependent children in respect of a child who has been deserted or abandoned by a *parent.*" . . . The "parent" whom this provision requires to be reported to law enforcement officials is surely the same "parent" whose desertion makes a child eligible for AFDC assistance in the first place. And Congress obviously did not intend that a so-called "parent" who has no legal duties of support be referred to law enforcement officials (as Alabama's own welfare regulations recognize), for the very purpose of such referrals is to institute nonsupport proceedings. . . . Whatever doubt there might have been over this proposition has been completely dispelled by the 1968 amendments to the Social Security Act, which provide that the States must develop a program: "(i) in the case of a child born out of wedlock who is receiving aid to families with dependent children, to establish the *paternity of such child and secure support for him,* and (ii) in the case of any child receiving such aid who has been deserted or abandoned *by his parent, to secure support for such child from such parent (or from any other person legally liable for such support).* . . .''

[Discussion of other provisions relating to support proceedings is omitted.]

The pattern of this legislation could not be clearer. Every effort is to be made to locate and secure support payments from persons legally obligated to support a deserted child. The underlying policy and consistency in statutory interpretation dictate that the "parent" referred to in these statutory provisions is the same parent as that in §406(a). The provisions seek to secure parental support in lieu of AFDC support for dependent children. Such parental support can be secured only where the parent is under a state-imposed legal duty to support the child. Children with alleged substitute parents who owe them no duty of support are entirely unprotected by these provisions. We think that these provisions corroborate the intent of Congress that the only kind of "parent," under §406(a), whose presence in the home would provide adequate economic protection for a dependent child is one who is legally obligated to support him. Consequently, if Alabama believes it necessary that it be able to disqualify a child on the basis of a man who is not under such a duty of support, its arguments should be addressed to Congress and not this Court.

[The concurring opinion of Mr. Justice Douglas, reaching the same result on constitutional grounds, is omitted.]

Note: Sexism in the Statutory Design of AFDC

There is ample evidence that the AFDC program was designed with conventional sex roles in mind. Until 1961, for instance, only single-parent families were eligible at all for AFDC. In that year, the unemployed parent program (AFDC-UP) was inaugurated. As late as 1969, only 24 states had AFDC-UP programs, and the eligibility requirements were so stringent that less than 100,000 families were in it.[24] In addition, in 1967, the AFDC-UP program was restricted to families in which the unemployed parent is the father. Thus, in two families, in each of which one parent works part time at an identical below subsistence salary and the other parent is unemployed, the family in which it is the father who is unemployed is eligible for assistance (in states with AFDC-UP), and the family in which it is the mother who is unemployed are not.[25] In addition, it is very difficult for the few men who head single-parent families to get welfare assistance.[26] Thus, as a practical matter, the federal-state public assistance programs operate on the factually incorrect assumption that having a father at home and needing income supplementation are mutually exclusive. It is true that there are more poor families which are female-headed[27] than there are male-headed single-parent or two-parent, one-wage-earner families in poverty. It is also true that because of sex discrimination in the labor market and lack of adequate child care facilities women are, on the average, less able to earn enough money to support a family. But it is also true that not all men make enough money to maintain their families above the welfare standard. A program which assumes that a male parent at home means economic self-sufficiency mistakes the average for the individual case. Some observers think that the purpose of this across-the-board, contrary-to-fact assumption is to pressure able-bodied men to work, however unsafe, badly paid, or unpleasant the jobs.[28] Whatever its rationale, this type of sexism inevitably results in hardship for many children.

Corollary to the proposition that the father is solely responsible for support is the idea that there are two mutually exclusive kinds of parental functions — breadwinning and child care. And although the Social Security statute is in terms asexual, the legislative history is replete with assumptions about which parent will play which role. Thus, in surveying the history in King v. Smith, Chief Justice Warren concluded: "The AFDC program was . . . designed to protect . . . '[one] clearly distinguishable group of children' . . . composed of children in families without a 'breadwinner', 'wage earner', or 'father'."[29]

24. The President's Commission on Income Maintenance Programs, Federal Public Assistance Programs (1969) in Gordon (ed.), Problems in Political Economy: An Urban Perspective 244, 246 (1971).
25. 42 U.S.C. §607. See Senate Comm. on Finance, Social Security Amendments of 1967, S. Rep. 744, 90th Cong., 1st Sess. 160 (1967).
26. See discussion of Graham v. Shaffer, 17 Ariz. App. 497, 498 P.2d 571 (Ct. App. 1972), infra this note.
27. The use of the terms "female-headed" to mean families with no male adult present, and "male-headed" to mean families with both a male and a female adult present, is itself sexist. Therefore, a neutral term, such as two-parent family, will be substituted for "male-headed" where possible.
28. Cloward and Piven, Regulating the Poor: The Functions of Public Welfare (1970); The President's Commission on Income Maintenance Programs, supra.
29. 392 U.S. at 328.

It is possible for a father to get aid from AFDC as the caretaking relative for a needy dependent child or children; in 1971, 1 percent of AFDC children had a father and no mother present in their homes. However, a recent case shows the reluctance of state welfare officials to accept such role reversals. In Graham v. Shaffer, 17 Ariz. App. 497, 498 P.2d 571 (Ct. App. 1972), the Arizona Court of Appeals ruled that a father who refused employment because he wanted personally to care for his nine-year old son, of whom he had custody, was not eligible for assistance under the AFDC program. The Arizona statute adds an additional provision to the Social Security Act's definition of "dependent child": a "dependent child" is "a needy child . . . who has been deprived of parental support or care by reason of the death, *unemployment of the supporting parent as defined and prescribed by federal statutes relating to welfare,* continued absence from the home, or physical or mental incapacity of a parent."[30]

In Arizona, then, a dependent child is either one who is deprived of parental support or care by reason of the death, absence, or incapacity of a parent, or one who is deprived by the unemployment of his supporting parent. The father had supported his son prior to the divorce and was therefore the "supporting parent." The court found that the absence of the mother was insufficient for eligibility, in effect construing "deprived of parental support or care by reason of the . . . absence . . . of a parent" to mean only the absence of the supporting parent. In response to the father's claim of eligibility under the unemployment criterion, the court ruled that because the father refused to accept free day care and any job to which his son could not accompany him, he and his son were ineligible for AFDC assistance. The court commented: "We believe . . . 'The child has not been deprived of a wage-earning parent — the wage-earning parent has deprived the child.' "[31]

Apparently, a needy child in Arizona, whose father had previously been the "supporting parent" but who had left home, would have been eligible for AFDC without regard to the previous employment history or present employment opportunities of her or his mother. The upshot of the case is that a father in a single-parent family who stays home with his children is wilfully depriving them of parental support; a mother in a single-parent family who makes the same choice is performing a proper role.[32]

NOTE: SEXISM IN THE ADMINISTRATION OF AFDC

The administrators of the AFDC program have long been ambivalent about the mother who has "failed" to get a man to support her and her children. The woman who assumes the federally supported caretaker role is in all states subject to various kinds of harassment. As Johnnie Tillmon, past president of the National Welfare Rights Organization, put it,[33]

30. ARS §46-101, subsec. 4 (emphasis supplied). The italicized portion is not in the federal definition.

31. 498 P.2d at 575. The court was quoting a section of the brief for the state. The Arizona Supreme Court refused to review the case and the U.S. Supreme Court dismissed the case for want of jurisdiction without ruling on Shaffer's equal protection challenge. Shaffer v. Graham, 410 U.S. 977 (1973).

32. The Arizona statute, as interpreted by the Shaffer Court, is presumably in conflict with the Social Security Act. However, the results of applying the Arizona statute and of applying the federal government's work rules under the work incentive (WIN) program are quite similar. Under WIN, recipients of both sexes with no children under six must accept proffered work or training or be cut off welfare. Since there is a sex-based priority for WIN referral which requires men to be referred before women, Mr. Shaffer would almost certainly have been offered work or training under the WIN program. Had he failed to conform to the work requirement, his AFDC grant would have been terminated. However, his son would have remained on the rolls, whereas under the Arizona statute both the father and the son were denied assistance. The federal work program is described in further detail in Subsection 3, Welfare and Work, infra.

33. Tillmon, Welfare is a Woman's Issue, Ms. Magazine, Spring, 1972, reprinted in Klagsburn (ed.), The First Ms. Reader 51, 52-53 (1973). For other commentaries comparing welfare to marriage, see, e.g., Leo, ADC: Marriage to the State, in Koedt and Firestone (eds.), Notes from the Third Year 66 (1971), and Glassman, Women and the Welfare System, in Morgan (ed.), Sisterhood is Powerful 102 (1970).

> The truth is that AFDC is like a super-sexist marriage. You trade in *a* man for *the* man. But you can't divorce him if he treats you bad. He can divorce you, of course, cut you off any time he wants. But in that case, *he* keeps the kids, not you.
>
> *The* man runs everything. In ordinary marriage, sex is supposed to be for your husband. On AFDC, you're not supposed to have any sex at all. You give up control of your own body. It's a condition of aid. You may even have to agree to get your tubes tied so you can't never have more children just to avoid being cut off welfare.
>
> *The* man, the welfare system, controls your money. He tells you what to buy, what not to buy, where to buy it, and how much things cost. If things — rent, for instance — really cost more than he says they do, it's just too bad for you. He's always right. Everything is budgeted down to the last penny; and you've got to make your money stretch.
>
> *The* man can break into your house any time he wants to poke into your things. You've got no right to protest. You've got no right to privacy when you go on welfare.

State governments have been very inventive in harassing various groups with the aim of excluding them from the welfare rolls. Regulations like that in King v. Smith, which focus on the relationship of an AFDC mother to sexual partners, have been particularly widely used: The justifications, offered for such policies have been (1) that the man in question contributes to the support of the mother or children so that they are no longer "needy," (2) that he does not contribute to their support, but should, and (3) that the policy will discourage sex and therefore illegitimate births. If the policies fail to get indigent women to conform to welfare department or legislative standards of morality, they do achieve a second goal — cutting the welfare rolls.

In King v. Smith, the Supreme Court recounted the history of suitable home rules, illegitimacy qualifications, and man-in-the-house rules in AFDC and its predecessors. More recent state tactics in this area are (1) requiring AFDC recipients to cooperate in paternity or nonsupport proceedings as a condition of aid; (2) creating an irrebuttable presumption that the mother's sexual partner pays child support when he is not legally required to do so, or does not do so in fact; and (3) in at least one state, making it a criminal offense for a man to share lodgings or meals with a welfare recipient without sharing expenses.

a. The Requirement that Action Be Brought

The memorandum reproduced in part below, issued by one state welfare department to its social workers, typifies the policies and practices that have sprung up in many states.

WEST VIRGINIA DEPARTMENT OF WELFARE
MEMORANDUM ON SUPPORT FROM ABSENT PARENTS
March 1972

I. INTRODUCTION — DEPRIVATION FACTOR OF ABSENCE

Over the past several months, this agency has recognized the value of and made considerable effort toward the control of the assistance caseload. The goal for this plan is to enable the agency to provide more adequate support for those recipients who have no recourse but assistance in meeting their basic human needs. The steps in the plan include elimination of fraud and ineligibility, a concentrated effort at employment of employable recipients and pursuit of alternative means of support (resources) by recipients. It is within this latter category that the pursuit of the resource of child support is included. . . .

Often overlooked in discussions of seeking support payments from absent parents are the benefits beyond those which are monetary. It is unfortunate, but we do not have access to statistics pointing out the number of families that are reunited yearly as a result of our third party involvement in keeping family ties intact through efforts to obtain support for AFDC children. A second overlooked, but very important benefit often reaped from our encouragement to mothers to establish paternity and maintain ties with the fathers of their children, is that of establishing the childrens' present and future rights to inheritance, benefits from Social Security, Veterans Administration, etc. Thirdly, we have no way to measure the impact on a child who, although he may not have benefit of his father's presence in the home, can see that his father had concern enough to assist financially in providing for his needs.

Approximately 15,000 assistance cases in West Virginia are active on the basis of the deprivation factor of absence of the father. Of this number, two-thirds are on file with the Deserting Parent Unit indicating desertion or paternity not established.

There is no reason to believe that a peak has been reached in this area, because the agency is only now becoming cognizant of the potential available to recipients via support payments. The resources available to us in locating absent parents and obtaining support are expanding, as is our capability of using these resources. Because of these very favorable circumstances, we are establishing, as a goal for 1972-73, a 100 percent increase in the support payments available from absent parents.

VI. CAUSES OF ABSENCE — PATERNITY NOT ESTABLISHED

1. Definition
    a. Paternity *has not been* legally *established.*
    b. Paternity *has not been acknowledged in writing.*
2. Required payee action
    a. The unmarried mother must identify the father of the child and express a willingness to take necessary steps to establish paternity and/or obtain support — *except* in the following situations:
        (1) Due to mental limitations, the mother is not competent to identify the father.
        (2) Pregnancy resulted from rape by an unknown person.
        (3) The child is over three years of age, no bastardy warrant has been filed and there is no evidence of paternity which could be used in court to support a charge of non-support of an illegitimate child.
    b. The unmarried mother must sign C-3 forms and assist in providing Information necessary for completion of the deserting parent summary.
    c. The unmarried mother must, within 30 days after pre-approval home visit:
        (1) Obtain notarized statement from the father acknowledging paternity and agreeing to support (FC-13 may be used); or
        (2) File a bastardy warrant through a justice of the peace; or
        (3) Agree to contact and follow the advice of the prosecuting attorney.

Regulations compelling an AFDC applicant to disclose the name of, or bring suit against, the alleged father of her child as a condition of aid are among many eligibility standards which have received judicial scrutiny over the years since King v. Smith. The question which has framed judicial inquiry is the extent to which the federal Social Security Act precludes state eligibility standards which are narrower than those of the federal statute. Initially, the Supreme Court took the position that states could not exclude from AFDC persons eligible for assistance under the federal statute unless there had been congressional authorization as evidenced by the terms of the Social Security Act or its legislative history.[34] Using this standard, states attempted to rationalize various

34. The major cases were Townsend v. Swank, 404 U.S. 282, 92 S. Ct. 502, 30 L. Ed. 2d 448 (1971), and Carleson v. Remillard, 406 U.S. 598, 92 S. Ct. 1932, 32 L. Ed. 2d 352 (1972).

paternity and support action requirements by use of the federal Notice to Law Enforcement Officials (NOLEO) requirements of §402 of the Social Security Act, which required states to institute paternity proceedings in cases where an AFDC child is born out of wedlock.[35] A number of district courts considered the issue and struck down requirements that the mother name the father of the potential AFDC child, or institute a criminal support action against him as a condition of eligibility, and three of the decisions were affirmed summarily by the Supreme Court.[36]

However, on April 30, 1973, HEW adopted a new regulation which, while reaffirming the position that a child may not be denied benefits for the refusal of his parent to assist in the establishment of paternity for a child born out of wedlock or in seeking support from a person having a legal duty to support the child, permits the state to exclude from AFDC parents or caretakers who refuse such assistance.[37] And, on June 21, 1973, the Supreme Court decided New York State Dep't of Social Services v. Dublino, 413 U.S. 405, 93 S. Ct. 2507, 37 L. Ed. 2d 688. In *Dublino,* the Court overturned a lower court decision which had ruled that the WIN program had preempted New York's state work requirements for AFDC recipients. This decision is amenable to at least two conflicting interpretations. HEW attorneys argue that *Dublino* is an acknowledgment by the Supreme Court of the right of the states to impose eligibility conditions beyond those authorized by the Social Security Act, when required by administrative necessity or justified by underlying state welfare purposes — hence a radical departure from the *King-Townsend-Remillard* line of cases.[38] A contrary view, which has been adopted by a number of lower courts,[39] is that *Dublino* is not a rejection of the *King-Townsend-Remillard* test, but rather an application of the test "to uphold a particular eligibility rule that the Court found to have been authorized by Congress."[40]

As of this writing, it is not clear which interpretation will ultimately prevail, but the importance of the outcome is evident. A Connecticut decision rendered soon after *Dublino* suggests that the combined impact of the HEW regulation and adoption of the HEW interpretation of the *Dublino* decision can be drastic. In Doe v. Norton, 365 F. Supp. 65 (D. Conn. 1973), a three-judge court upheld a Connecticut statute which requires all

35. Title 42, U.S.C. §602(a)(17)(A)(i) and (ii) provides:

"(A) for the development and implementation of a program under which the State agency will undertake — (i) in the case of a child born out of wedlock who is receiving aid to families with dependent children, to establish the paternity of such child and secure support for him, and (ii) in the case of any child receiving such aid who has been deserted or abandoned by his parent, to secure support for such child from such parent (or from any other person legally liable for such support), utilizing any reciprocal arrangements adopted with other States to obtain or enforce court orders for support. . . ."

36. Doe v. Shapiro, 302 F. Supp. 761 (D. Conn. 1969), *appeal dismissed,* 296 U.S. 488, *rehearing denied,* 397 U.S. 970 (1970); Doe v. Harder, 310 F. Supp. 302 (D. Conn.), *appeal dismissed for want of jurisdiction,* 399 U.S. 902 (1970); Story v. Roberts, 352 F. Supp. 473 (M.D. Fla. 1972); Doe v. Ellis, 350 F. Supp. 372 (D.S.C. 1972); Doe v. Gillman, 347 F. Supp. 483 (N.D. Iowa 1972); Doe v. Levine, 347 F. Supp. 357 (S.D.N.Y. 1972); Saiz v. Hernandez, 340 F. Supp. 165 (D. N. Mex. 1972); Saddler v. Winstead, 332 F. Supp. 130 (N.D. Miss. 1971); Doe v. Swank, 332 F. Supp. 61 (N.D. Ill.), *aff'd summarily sub nom.* Weaver v. Doe, 404 U.S. 987 (1971); Taylor v. Martin, 330 F. Supp. 85 (N.D. Cal. 1971), *aff'd summarily sub nom.* Carleson v. Taylor, 404 U.S. 980 (1972); Meyers v. Juras, 327 F. Supp. 579 (D. Ore.), *aff'd summarily,* 404 U.S. 803, *rehearing denied,* 404 U.S. 961 (1971).

37. 45 C.F.R. §233.90(b)(4), effective July 2, 1973.

38. Memorandum of Points and Authorities in Opposition to Plaintiff's Motion for Summary Judgment and in Support of Defendant's Motion for Summary Judgment, National Welfare Rights Organization v. The United States Dept. of Health, Education and Welfare, Civ. Action No. 264-73 (D.D.C., filed Feb. 13, 1973). This view of the law was also urged on the Supreme Court by HEW in the *Dublino* case; see Brief for the United States as Amicus Curiae at 9, New York State Dep't of Social Services v. Dublino, 413 U.S. 405, 93 S. Ct. 2507, 37 L. Ed. 2d 688 (1973).

39. Doe v. Lukhard, 363 F. Supp. 823, 827, n. 5 (E.D. Va. 1973), aff'd — F. 2d — (No. 73-2179, 4th Cir., Feb. 26, 1974); Green v. Stanton, 364 F. Supp. 123, 126-127 (N.D. Ind. 1973); Shirley v. Lavine, 365 F. Supp. 818, 824 (N.D.N.Y. 1973).

40. Memorandum of Points and Authorities in Opposition to Defendants' Motion for Summary Judgment and Reply Memorandum in Support of Plaintiff's Motion for Summary Judgment at 15, National Welfare Rights Organization v. The United States Dept of Health Education and Welfare, Civ. Action No. 264-73 (D.D.C. filed Feb. 13, 1973).

mothers of children born out of wedlock or found not to be the issue of a marriage terminated by judicial decree to name the putative father to the welfare commissioner if the child is a recipient of public assistance, to the town selectman if the child receives general assistance, or to a guardian or guardian ad litem for the child, on pain of being held in contempt of court and fined not more than $200 and/or imprisoned for not more than one year.[41] The court relied heavily on the new HEW regulations and on *Dublino* in ruling that the statute did not conflict with the Social Security Act. The court also distinguished the statute from those previously invalidated in Connecticut and elsewhere on the grounds that (a) while it separates mother and child, it does not deny either food, clothing, or shelter, and does not per se add an additional eligibility requirement for AFDC, and (b) that it applies across the board to all mothers of illegitimate children. The court went on to uphold the statute against a variety of constitutional challenges, including arguments that it infringed the mother's right to privacy and that it denied the children equal protection of the laws as a discriminatory classification based upon illegitimacy.

Although the state could search birth records to identify all mothers of illegitimate children and require them to name the putative fathers of their children, it seems likely that the statute will be used primarily against mothers of illegitimate children who apply for welfare assistance. Even if the statute is broadly enforced, it will certainly have the effect in fact, if not in law, of establishing assistance in paternity suits as an additional condition of eligibility for AFDC.

b. "Man Assuming the Role of Spouse" Statutes

After the Supreme Court invalidated "man in the house" rules, many states tried assuming that the income of a stepfather or other sexual partner of the mother was available to meet the children's needs, whether or not he in fact contributed to their support. In Solman v. Shapiro, 300 F. Supp. 409 (D. Conn.), *aff'd mem.*, 396 U.S. 5 (1969), the court ruled that states could not consider a stepparent's income in determining the eligibility of a child for assistance unless the man in question was legally obligated to support the child under state law, or actually contributed to the support of the child. Subsequently, in ruling on California's MARS (man assuming the role of spouse) statute, the Supreme Court held that the obligation of support which the state imposed on the mother's sexual partner must be established by a statute of general applicability, and not one for welfare recipients only. Lewis v. Martin, 397 U.S. 552, 90 S. Ct. 1282, 25 L. Ed. 2d 561 (1970). A California court subsequently ruled that the mother's interest under community property law in the stepparent's income could not be considered in determining the needs of the children unless it was shown to be actually available to the mother for such use. Camp v. Carleson, No. 216154 (Sup. Ct., Sacramento County, Feb. 15, 1972).

According to the Center for Social Welfare Policy and Law,[42]

> Taken together, King v. Smith, Solman v. Shapiro, and Lewis v. Martin clearly stand for the proposition that except for the income of a parent . . . income which is not in fact made available for purposes of providing support for recipients of aid may *never* be considered in determining eligibility and computing the amount of the welfare grant.[43]

41. Public Act 439, §4 (1971), Conn. Gen. Stats. §52-440b.

42. 2 Center for Social Welfare Policy and Law, Cases and Materials on Welfare Law VI-113 (1972).

43. Since *Solman* depends upon a finding that state plans for distribution of AFDC aid "must conform" with federal laws (300 F. Supp. at 413), whereas the subsequent case of New York State Dep't of Social Services v. Dublino, 413 U.S. 405, 93 S. Ct. 2507, 37 L. Ed. 2d 688 (1973), depends upon a finding that parallel provisions of the Social Security Act did not preempt New York's work rules, it might be argued that *Dublino* undermines *Solman.* In *Solman,* however, there was a direct conflict between the provisions, which was not the case in *Dublino.* In fact, in *Dublino,* the Court finds evidence that Congress did not intend to preempt the field, 93 S. Ct. at 2514, n. 17, and remands for the express purpose of allowing the lower court to consider the possibility of conflict in particular provisions, 93 S. Ct. at 2518. Similarly, in *Lewis* the holding was based upon a direct conflict

c. Imposing Criminal Penalties on the "Man in the House"

STATE v. BEARCUB
1 Ore. App. 579, 465 P. 2d 252 (1970)

LANGTRY, J.

The defendants, before their marriage, were jointly indicted under ORS 418.140, for unlawfully sharing public assistance.

They demurred separately to the indictment on grounds that no crime was stated and that every statute can embrace only one subject and this statute is "buried in a chapter relating to child welfare services." Each demurrer was sustained.

ORS 418.140 provides:

(1) No male person over the age of 18 years . . . shall habitually accept subsistence or lodging in the dwelling place of any female householder, who is the recipient of aid. . . .

Sandra [Bearcub] contends that only a male can be prosecuted under this statute; hence, no crime can be stated under it as to her. The state contends that a female can be guilty of the crime by aiding and abetting the male who violates the statute. ORS 161.220 makes principals of all persons concerned in the commission of a crime.

1. In State v. Fraser, 105 Or. 589, 209 P. 467 (1922), a corporation and its president were alleged to have violated the Blue Sky Law. The court said that a person who cannot alone commit a particular crime, can, by aiding and abetting another against whose class the statute is directed, become criminally liable under the statute. This case and State v. Case, 61 Or. 265, 122 P. 304 (1912), cited therein, might be authority for the state's contention but for the fact that ORS 418.140 indicates the statute is directed only at the male. Subsection (2) makes it a defense if "the person accused has fully paid to the female householder" the costs of subsistence, etc. By this language of the statute, the legislature obviously intended that only the male would be accused. It would be absurd if the female householder, in this case, Sandra, who was receiving welfare aid, could be accused under the statute, but have a good defense by paying her welfare money from one of her pockets into another. The first demurrer was correctly sustained.

2. The trial court sustained Ernest [Bearcub's] demurrer on grounds that are not clear from the transcript. Apparently, it was sustained because ORS 418.140 is part of an act having to do with civil as distinguished from criminal matters. The state points out that this is common and unchallenged practice in drafting statutes, and defendants' brief concedes that this ground is insufficient. But defendant contends for the first time on appeal that classifying males and females differently under this act is unreasonable and a violation of the equal protection provisions of state and federal constitutions. The defendant says, "Surely a male should have equal rights with a female to live as a lodger in the household of a female and recipient, without being a criminal."

3. The Creator took care of classifying men and women differently, and if the legislature accepts these differences in a matter like this, we are not prepared to say that the classifications thus made were without good reason.

Against the defendant Ernest Bearcub the indictment was good and the demurrer should have been overruled. The cause is remanded for further proceedings consistent with this opinion.

Affirmed in part, reversed in part.

---

between state regulations and HEW regulations, and the Court finds the latter to be consistent with the Social Security Act provisions in question. 397 U.S. at 558. — Eds.

A similar result to that obtained in Oregon under the statute described in the case above is now obtained in California under the successor to the MARS statute invalidated in Lewis v. Martin, 397 U.S. 552, 90 S. Ct. 1282, 25 L. Ed. 2d 561 (1970). The new statute was passed after the litigation in the *Lewis* case had begun, and was described by the Court in a footnote as follows:[44]

> On September 3, 1969, the Governor of California signed into law a new §11351.5 of the California Welfare and Institutions Code, which becomes effective November 10, 1969. It leaves unchanged §11351 and implementing regulations insofar as they apply to a stepfather, but repeals the old §11351 insofar as it applied to "an adult male person assuming the role of spouse." Under the new law, a MARS "shall be required to make a financial contribution to the family which shall not be less than it would cost him to provide himself with an independent living arrangement." The new law also provides that, under regulations to be promulgated by the State Welfare Department, the MARS and the mother will be required to present the Department with "all the facts in connection with the sharing of expenses. . . ."

The statute is interpreted to require the MARS to pay the amount he would have to pay in an independent living arrangement as calculated by the state Welfare Department, even if his share of expenses in the household where he actually lives is less. Thus he is required to subsidize the expenses of the welfare recipients with whom he lives. If he is unwilling to do so, the state threatens prosecution under a statute making it a misdemeanor to use welfare funds in a manner inconsistent with the best interests of the children on whose behalf the welfare grant is made.[45]

What constitutional challenges could be made to the above procedure?

3. Welfare and Work

a. The History of Work Rules Under the AFDC Program

In general, the AFDC program has placed less emphasis on work outside the home than have programs designed primarily for men, such as workmen's compensation, unemployment insurance, AFDC-UP, and aid to the permanently and totally disabled. Thus it is fair to say that the sex of the welfare recipients has often determined whether they will be made to work. Yet the difference is only one of degree; many women, like many men, have been encouraged or required to enter the marketplace as a condition of receiving public assistance.

ROSENHEIM, VAGRANCY CONCEPTS IN WELFARE LAW
54 Calif. L. Rev. 511, 545-546 (1966)

. . . It has repeatedly been said that AFDC was established for a needy group which like the other original public assistance categories was outside the labor market. The [Mother's Pension Laws] forerunners of AFDC, we are told, were predicated on the desire to foster the mother's invaluable presence in the home as child caretaker,[119] and possibly were stimulated in the early depression years by labor's wish to limit the ranks

44. 397 U.S. at 554, n. 2.
45. Cal. Welf. & Inst. Code §11480 (West 1972).
119. The classic formulation of the case in favor of outdoor relief for mothers and children is found in the initial resolution of the Conference on the Care of Dependent Children, Proceedings 9-10 (1909). See also U.S. Social Security Board, Social Security in America 233-34 (1937).

of those seeking employment principally to males.[120] These Mother's Pension Laws were enacted to afford financial aid outside of the almshouse or poor farm for dependent children.[121]

It is not clear, however, whether AFDC, or its precursors, was designed to wholly eliminate maternal employment or to offer an alternative to the prevailing mode of child care for dependent children, namely institutionalization.[122] We may mislead ourselves by speaking of the history of AFDC as though the original impetus was to provide a choice between employment and nonemployment. It might better be characterized as offering mothers an alternative to institutionalization of their children or to starvation where employment was not a live possibility or brought insufficient income for the entire family. The latter possibility is supported by our knowledge that working women do not represent a new phenomenon, though undeniably our attitudes toward the acceptable reasons for women seeking employment have broadened. Lower-class women generally have been expected to work when the possibility was open to them.[123]

In 1956, Congress added a new dimension to the AFDC program by providing funds to enable states to extend services as well as financial aid to recipients.[46] Services that focused more or less directly on getting adult welfare recipients to work were only one part of the 1956 congressional mandate; they were later to become more important. In 1962 further amendments to the Social Security Act "placed heavy emphasis on service programs to the family[9] and in effect compelled the states to provide them."[47] These amendments also inaugurated, on a small scale, a community work and training program (CWT). Although the program was primarily for unemployed fathers (covered by AFDC in states with AFDC-UP programs), states were allowed to open the program to eligible mothers.[48]

The federal-state CWT program was not the only work program for AFDC recipients. By 1967, at least twenty-two jurisdictions had work requirements, known as "employable mother" rules, for AFDC recipients.[49] HEW's official position on work rules was that women receiving AFDC should be given monetary aid and supportive services sufficient to "make it possible for a mother to choose between staying at home to care for her children and taking a job away from home." The federal administrators

120. In many states during the depression mothers were classed as unemployables. Bookman, A Community Program for Reducing Unemployment and Relief, 11 Social Service Rev. 367 (1937). This author argues against such a designation for mothers or other groups (that is, those between fifty and sixty-five, the physically handicapped) because of its stigmatizing effect and its deterring the rehabilitative programs which he espouses. Id. at 365-67.

121. See New York State Comm. on Relief for Widowed Mothers, Report, extracted in 2 Arendt, The Child and the State 251-253 (1938).

122. Proponents of Mother's Pension Laws stressed the greater expense of the alternative, institutionalization. Id. at 252-53. The Commission on the Support of Dependent Minor Children of Widowed Mothers of Massachusetts recommended that aid be limited to young children in a good family, believing that "the widow without children, or with children grown up is in a situation that she can generally manage." Id. at 251. Note that under AFDC, with its more liberal coverage, the number of one child families supported was larger than under Mother's Pension programs. Lundberg, Unto the Least of These 178 (1947).

123. Peterson, [Working Women, in The Woman in America 671 (Daedalus, Spring 1964)], at 671-73; see also Rossi, Equality Between the Sexes, in The Woman in America 615 (Daedalus, Spring 1964) (*"for the first time in the history of any known society, motherhood has become a full-time occupation for adult women"*; italics in original). Compare Bureau of Family Services, U.S. Dept. of Health, Educ. & Welfare, Handbook of Public Assistance Administration, pt. IV, §3401.1, expressing very measured approval of mothers' working.

46. See the discussion in Rosenheim, supra, at 546-548.

9. The services envisioned were primarily those of casework counseling. That is, the welfare caseworker became obliged to do more than simply provide a check; he was supposed to become more involved in solving the recipient family's problems, be they childrearing, housework, budgeting, or whatever. See S. Rep. No. 1589, 87th Cong., 2d Sess. 7 (1962).

47. Comment, The Failure of the Work Incentive (WIN) Program, 119 U. Pa. L. Rev 485, 486 (1971).

48. Id. at 487.

49. Brief of the United States as Amicus Curiae, Appendix A, Woolfolk v. Brown, 325 F. Supp. 1162 (E.D. Va. 1971).

explained in the Handbook of Public Assistance Administration how the welfare agencies were to implement this position:[50]

> The role of the public assistance agencies is, by assistance and other services, to help the mother arrive at a decision that will best meet her own needs and those of her children. Such help will involve consideration with families of such factors as the welfare of children during the mother's absence from the home and of the type of substitute child care arrangements the mother can or wishes to make if she takes full- or part-time work. Consultation service should also be available that will help the mother determine what increased costs will be involved in taking a job; for instance, clothes, lunches, transportation costs and other necessary expenses involved in the mother's absenting herself from home. In some instances, a part of the potential wages will be required to provide supervision for the children in their home or in a day-care facility. The opportunity to discuss these conditions will necessarily influence decisions since it will often be apparent that anticipated earnings will not, in all cases, provide the essentials for family life.

Unfortunately, the statement of official policy did not mold reality in states with work rules. Georgia is a dramatic example. During periods designated as times of full employment, usually when farm workers were needed, the state cut off welfare, whether or not welfare recipients actually had jobs and whether or not the wages they received were sufficient to meet their needs according to welfare standards. These practices were challenged in Anderson v. Schaefer, *decided sub nom.* Anderson v. Burson.[51] Plaintiffs contended that the Georgia work rule denied equal protection of the laws in that it distinguished between welfare recipients on the basis of the source of their income, denied due process of law because individual hearings were not held before welfare was cut off, conflicted with the purpose of the Social Security Act to enable mothers to stay home and care for their children, and had a racially discriminatory purpose and effect.[52] Under the pressure of the suit, the state agreed to stop presuming that employment was available to everyone during certain seasons, and eliminated its rule placing the burden of proof on the recipient to establish the unavailability of employment. The court ruled on equal protection grounds that the state must also stop automatically cutting women with full-time jobs off welfare and must instead supplement earned income on the same basis as income from other sources. However, the court upheld the right of the state to require welfare recipients to take jobs as a condition of aid, stating that there was "no federally protected right of a mother to refuse employment while receiving assistance and remaining home with her children."[53]

GOLD, COMMENT, THE FAILURE OF THE WORK INCENTIVE (WIN) PROGRAM
119 U. Pa. L. Rev 485, 487, 489 (1971)

[In 1967, Congress passed amendments to the Social Security Act which included the Work Incentive (WIN) program] without serious congressional criticism of conditioning welfare eligibility on a willingness to work. The goal, as stated in §430 of the Act, was to restore the families of individuals enrolled in the program to

> independence and useful roles in their communities. It is expected that individuals participating in the program . . . will acquire a sense of dignity, self-worth, and

---

50. Bureau of Family Services, U.S. Dep't of Health, Educ. & Welfare, Handbook of Public Assistance Administration, pt. IV, §3401.1.

51. 300 F. Supp. 401 (N.D. Ga. 1968).

52. Brief for Plaintiffs on Their Motions for a Temporary Restraining Order and Preliminary Injunction, Preliminary Statement at 2-6, Anderson v. Schaefer, opinion *sub. nom.* Anderson v. Burson, 300 F. Supp. 401 (N.D. Ga. 1968).

53. 300 F. Supp at 403.

confidence which will flow from being recognized as a wage-earning member of society and that the example of a working adult in these families will have beneficial effects on the children in such families.

. . .

WIN is administered by HEW and the Department of Labor. Each department is responsible for different aspects of the program. The process begins when the state welfare agency evaluates adult AFDC recipients to determine which are "appropriate" for referral to the program. Federal regulations require that the states evaluate individuals in a specified order, beginning with AFDC unemployed fathers. Mothers and other caretaker relatives who volunteer for WIN and are currently in a program under title V of the Economic Opportunity Act or in a CWT [community work and training] program are evaluated next. Presumably these individuals are already motivated to work or to be trained and have access to child care programs. The third group comprises "[d]ependent children and essential persons age 16 or over who are not in school, at work, or in training, and for whom there are no educational plans under consideration." Mothers who volunteer but are not already in existing training programs constitute the next group if they have no pre-school-age children, and the fifth group if they do. Thereafter, the state welfare agency may evaluate for referral any other recipients.

Of the five groups, the regulations require assessment of only the first (unemployed fathers) and third (youth and essential persons 16 or over). States need not assess any other individuals, but if they do, they must follow the prescribed order.

Welfare caseworkers interview recipients and ostensibly select for enrollment in WIN only those most likely to succeed in the program. . . .

Recipients found appropriate by the state agencies are next referred to the Local Bureau of Employment Services (under the supervision of the Department of Labor), which conducts its own assessment of appropriateness. . . .

. . . [I]ndividuals are separated into three "priorities." Those who are immediately employable and have work skills needed in the local labor market, or who can enter on-the-job training positions in existing federal programs, are either found employment or placed in federal manpower programs. These enrollees receive supportive services (such as counseling) for a minimum of ninety days and, in computing their welfare needs, may disregard the first thirty dollars of their earned income and one third of the remainder.

The second priority includes enrollees needing special training to be employable. Enrollees in this priority fall into either occupational or pre-occupational training. . . . All enrollees in this second priority receive a monthly incentive payment of thirty dollars in addition to their welfare grants.

Recipients who cannot benefit from training and for whom jobs in the economy cannot be located — but who have nonetheless been found appropriate for WIN — are placed in "special works projects," the third priority. Public agencies or private nonprofit agencies organized for public purpose can employ these enrollees, who "in most instances . . . would no longer receive a welfare check." Instead, they receive a payment from an employer for services performed. A supplemental grant will be made, if necessary, to bring their wages to a level 20 percent above their welfare grant level. They are also reimbursed for any expenses incurred due to participation in the program. If an enrollee's employability development plan bogs down, he may be sidetracked, perhaps for months, in a "holding" status; no incentive payments are made to these enrollees.

In 1969, President Nixon first proposed the Family Assistance Plan (FAP). Designed to replace AFDC and the WIN program, the provisions of FAP as originally introduced can be summarized as follows:[54]

54. Abramovitz, Nixon's Welfare Proposals: Poor Laws in the Space Age, AIM Newsletter, Oct. 15, 1969, p. 19.

... (1) a national minimum income of $1600 a year for a family of four, (2) compulsory work or training for out-of-work heads of families (except mothers of pre-school children) who receive this welfare benefit, (3) an extension of the work incentive program from some to all states, (4) provision of assistance to families where the father is present, (5) use of an affidavit[55] method by all, not just some states, (6) possible elimination of food stamps for families who receive the $1600 benefit, (7) creation of more day-care centers, (8) transference of the administration of the public assistance program from state and local welfare departments to the federal Social Security Administration, (9) re-organization of job-training programs with a decreased role for the Office of Economic Opportunity (O.E.O.) and an increased role for state and local employment offices, (10) promises of increased federal aid for state welfare departments.

In late 1971, after sharp criticism and numerous revisions, the program was dropped by the Administration. Despite the demise of the proposed federal floor on financial assistance for all poor families, the work programs of FAP and a later addition, the Opportunities for Families (OFF) Program, were enacted in December 1971 in the form of the Talmadge Amendments to the Social Security Act.[56]

The House and Senate Conference Committee reports stated very directly the desired effects of the amendments. Excerpts are reprinted below.

JOINT EXPLANATORY STATEMENT
OF THE COMMITTEE OF CONFERENCE
H.R. Rep. No. 747, 92d Cong., 1st Sess. 6-9 (1971)

IMPROVEMENT OF WORK INCENTIVE PROGRAM

Amendment No. 1. — This amendment made a number of changes in the Work Incentive Program to:

Require an individual, as a condition of eligibility for welfare, to register for the WIN program unless the person is:

(1) a child under age 16 or attending school;
(2) ill, incapacitated or for advanced age;
(3) so remote from a WIN project that his effective participation is precluded;
(4) caring for another member of the household who is ill or incapacitated; or
(5) the mother or other relative of a child under the age of six who is caring for the child. Mothers who are not required to register must be told of their opportunity to volunteer to participate.

Increase Federal matching for the WIN program from 80 percent to 90 percent.

Require the welfare agency to designate a separate administrative unit to make arrangements for supportive services needed by welfare recipients in order to participate in WIN program and to refer recipients so prepared to the Labor Department for participation in the WIN program.

Penalize a State if its welfare agency prepares and refers to Labor Department less than 15 percent of registrants in a year by reducing Federal matching one percent for Aid to Families with Dependent Children for every percentage point the proportion of registered individuals the State welfare agency prepares and refers is under 15 percent.

Increase from 75 percent to 90 percent Federal matching for supportive services, including child care, provided to enable welfare recipients to work or participate in WIN program.

---

55. This refers to the fact that many states investigate each welfare applicant instead of relying on the applicants' affidavits as to their income, resources, and family situation. — Eds.
56. Act of Dec. 28, 1971, Pub. L. No. 92-223, §3, 81 Stat. 877.

Require that not less than 40 percent of expenditures under the WIN program be for on-the-job training and public service employment. . . .

Require Labor Department in handling WIN referrals to accord priority in the following order, taking into account employability potential:

(1) unemployed fathers;
(2) dependent children and relatives age 16 or over who are not in school, working, or in training;
(3) mothers who volunteer for participation; and
(4) all other persons.

The conference agreement includes the Senate amendment with the following changes:

Exempts from the registration requirement a mother in a family where the father registers.

Makes clear that the WIN unit in the State welfare agency is to provide child care and other supportive services to persons required to be registered with the Secretary of Labor, and to certify when such persons are so prepared. . . .

Sets the following order of priority in handling Work Incentive Program participants: (1) unemployed fathers; (2) mothers who volunteer for participation; (3) other mothers and pregnant women under nineteen years of age; (4) dependent children and relatives age sixteen or over who are not in school, working, or in training; and (5) all other persons.

Deletes requirement of jointly developed employability plan for each Work Incentive Program recipient.

Provides 100 percent Federal funding for the first year of public service employment, 75 percent funding in the second year, 50 percent in the third year and no Federal funding thereafter.

Sets effective date of July 1, 1972, for increased Federal matching for WIN training, public service employment, and supportive services (including child care for WIN participants) rather than January 1, 1972.

Deletes requirement to collect and publish certain WIN statistical data.

The conferees agreed to direct the Secretary of Labor to prepare and publish monthly the following information, by age group and sex, about the operations of the WIN program:

(1) the number of individuals registered, the number of individuals receiving each particular type of work training services, and the number of individuals receiving no services;

(2) the number of individuals placed in jobs by the Secretary, and the average wages of the individuals placed;

(3) the number of individuals who begin but fail to complete training, and the number of individuals who register voluntarily but do not receive training or placement;

(4) the number of individuals who obtain employment following the completion of training, and the number whose employment is in fields related to the particular type of training received;

(5) the number of individuals who obtain employment following the completion of training, their average wages, and the number retaining employment 3 months, 6 months, and 12 months following the completion of training;

(6) the number of individuals in public service employment by type of employment, and the average wages of such individuals; and

(7) the amount of savings under the AFDC program realized by reason of the operation of the WIN program.

After WIN was enacted, state work rules were challenged because they were more restrictive than those of the WIN program. Some courts struck down such state work rules and programs.[57] But in New York State Dep't of Social Services v. Dublino, 413 U.S. 405, 93 S. Ct. 2507, 37 L. Ed. 2d 688 (1973), the Supreme Court overruled a three-judge court's broad holding that the WIN program pre-empted all other work rules; the Court remanded the case to the district court for consideration of whether the particular rules in question contravened the provisions or purposes of the WIN program. The New York state rules in question covered all mothers for whose children alternative child care was available, regardless of their ages; and required all recipients to obtain a certificate every two weeks from the state employment agency certifying that work was not available, to pick up their welfare checks in person twice a month instead of getting them in the mail, and to report for all interviews and employment available. The impact on recipients is illustrated by the following excerpt from the complaint in *Dublino:*

COMPLAINT, DUBLINO v. NEW YORK STATE DEPT. OF SOCIAL SERVICES
Opinion reported, 348 F. Supp. 290 (2d Cir.)
rev'd, 413 U.S. 405, 93 S. Ct. 2507, 37 L. Ed. 2d 688 (1973)

29. Plaintiff Virginia Michael has been notified that she is an "employable person" under N.Y. Soc. Serv. L. §131(4), has reported to the County Department in Buffalo to obtain an identification card, and has been scheduled for an appointment on July 14, 1971, to pick up her check at the Buffalo SES office. Buffalo is 22 miles from Mrs. Michael's home; she will have to take an 8:20 A.M. bus to Buffalo, and will have to wait until 2:30 P.M. for the return bus to her home in Alden, New York, arriving at 3:40 P.M. Round trip bus fare from Alden is $1.40 and, because of the schedule, Mrs. Michael will have to purchase lunch in Buffalo. The "flat grant" for Mrs. Michael under ADC is approximately $1.65 per day.

30. Mrs. Michael has been informed by her caseworker that her two oldest children, ages 19 and 18, both high school graduates, will also be required to report to the Buffalo office of SES twice monthly, necessitating a further high expenditure of their benefits.

31. Although Mrs. Michael has been informed that she will receive a "special check" on July 1 to tide her and her family over until she receives her regular check at the SES office on July 14, this "special check" will not include an allotment for rent. Mrs. Michael's rent is due on July 1, and she is afraid that her landlord will take action against her for failure to pay her rent when due.

32. Plaintiff Janie Lee Phillips lost her leg in 1965, in a farm incident. She is fitted with an artificial limb, but because of its heaviness she has great difficulty in walking more than 100 yards. Plaintiff Phillips has been notified that she is an "employable person" under N.Y. Soc. Serv. L. §131(4), and has reported to the County Department to obtain an identification card. Because of her handicap, Plaintiff Phillips had to take a taxi to the County Department. She will also have to take a taxi to the SES office, where she is required to report on July 12.

33. Plaintiff Phillips pays rent for each month on the 16th of the month. Although she will receive her check, including one half of her rent allotment, on the 12th of July, she will not receive her second rent allotment until July 27, her next appointment at SES.

57. Woolfolk v. Brown, 325 F. Supp. 1162 (E.D. Va. 1971), *aff'd,* 456 F.2d 652 (4th Cir. 1972); Jefferies v. Sugarman, 71 Civ. 2060 (S.D.N.Y. June 30, 1972), *rev'd and remanded in light of Dublino,* 481 F.2d 414 (2d Cir. 1973); Dublino v. New York State Dep't of Social Services, 348 F. Supp. 290 (W.D.N.Y.), *rev'd,* 413 U.S. 405, 93 S. Ct. 2507, 37 L. Ed. 2d 688 (1973); Bueno v. Juras, Civ. No. 71-420 (D. Ore. May 27, 1973).

Plaintiff Phillips receives $72 in public assistance every two weeks; her rent is $50.00 per month. Mrs. Phillips is afraid that she will be unable to pay her rent when due and that her landlord will take action against her.

34. Plaintiff Maria Marfoglia has been notified that she is an "employable person" under N.Y. Soc. Serv. L. §131(4) and has reported to the County Department to obtain an identification card. At the time she was required to so report, Mrs. Marfoglia had no money for bus fare or for babysitters, and so she and her six children walked three miles to the offices of the County Department. Mrs. Marfoglia is concerned about the requirement that she travel to the SES office every two weeks and also about the possibility that she may be required to accept employment. Mrs. Marfoglia feels that adequate child care is not available for her children. Her sister cannot care for Mrs. Marfoglia's children, being busied with her own five children, and Mrs. Marfoglia's mother, age 67, is ill. Mrs. Marfoglia, who is divorced, does not want to leave her children in the care of a stranger, as she feels this will have a detrimental effect on their upbringing. Mrs. Marfoglia has been scheduled for an appointment on July 2, 1971 to pick up her check at the SES office in Buffalo, some two miles from her home.

35. None of the above Plaintiffs received any notice prior to their receipt of the letter informing them that they had been deemed "employable." No discussion had been had with any caseworker or other official as to any Plaintiff's availability for work or as to any problems which might arise as a result of the obligations incurred by them because of their being found "employable." Each of the Plaintiffs is under immediate threat of referral to a work project by reason of the determination that she is "employable."

Compulsory work and training programs raise many questions about permissible reasons for refusing work. May a welfare recipient refuse a job because of the kind of work? the working conditions? the inadequacy of child care arrangements? the availability of more desirable work? long hours? pay below the minimum wage? pay inadequate to meet family's needs? the distance from home to job? Can strikers refuse work and still get welfare? What kind of training will be provided? Can WIN volunteers complain of their discriminatory exclusion from training or work opportunities? A further question is whether procedures adequate to assure fair answers to any of the first questions in individual cases will be established.

Some of the problems these programs pose will be discussed in subsections b and c below, which examine current state and federal work programs from a feminist perspective. For a more general analysis of compulsory work programs for the recipients of government benefits, see I Center on Social Welfare Policy and Law, Materials on Welfare Law, ch. 5 (1972); Gold, Comment, The Failure of the Work Incentive (WIN) Program, 119 U. Pa. L. Rev. 485 (1971); Rosenheim, Vagrancy Concepts in Welfare Law, 54 Calif. L. Rev. 511, 545-552 (1966).

b. Tracking into Certain Types of Jobs and Training

The available evidence indicates that men and women are channeled into different kinds of work within the WIN program. The Women's Action Program of the U.S. Department of Health, Education and Welfare reported:[58]

A Department of Labor study of WIN participants[59] found there were significant variations both in the types of employment attained by men and women, and in their average hourly earnings. The median hourly wage for men was $2.48 per hour, while

58. U.S. Dept of Health, Education and Welfare, The Women's Action Program 74 (1972).
59. A survey of 4623 employed WIN participants, Office of Manpower Management Data Systems Manpower Admin., U.S. Dep't of Labor, Results of Special Occupational and Wage Survey of Employed WIN Program Participants in Follow-Up Status Conducted in Six States as of August 31, 1969, at 7. — Eds.

for women it was $2.03. Median gross weekly earnings for male WIN participants was $99.20; female WIN participants earned $81.20 per week.

The differential in the wage rates is directly related to the job categories in which the participants obtained employment. Almost three-quarters of all women were employed in the relatively low-paid clerical and sales and service categories. In contrast, male employment was more evenly distributed throughout the various occupational groupings. The problem with the WIN program, therefore, begins at the initial referral stage when men are given priority over women, and becomes manifest as women are shunted off to jobs at the lowest end of the social and economic scale.

Tracking also occurs in state work programs. In addition to discrimination in work and training programs between men and women, there is discrimination between blacks and whites. For example, plaintiffs in Anderson v. Burson, 300 F. Supp. 401 (N.D. Ga. 1968), a lawsuit challenging the "employable mother" regulation in Georgia, made the following preliminary statement:[60]

> [In this brief] we examine the *actual* purpose and function of the "employable mother" regulation. There we set forth our grounds for contending that the regulation was conceived in racial discrimination and has had the purpose and effect of (1) cutting Negro mothers off the welfare rolls as distinguished from white mothers; (2) preserving a cheap source of Negro woman and child labor for domestic and agricultural work. The discrimination is effected under the vague standards of the regulation, which allow the Defendants to virtually pick and choose, at their whim, the needy mothers and children who are to be excluded. As we intend to demonstrate at the trial of of this action, domestic work and field work is seldom deemed "suitable" and "available" for white AFDC applicants and recipients; such work is deemed a function for Negro women and children.

The Mississippi State Advisory Committee to the United States Commission on Civil Rights reported similar practices in that state.

WELFARE IN MISSISSIPPI, A REPORT OF THE MISSISSIPPI STATE ADVISORY COMMITTEE TO THE UNITED STATES COMMISSION ON CIVIL RIGHTS
29, 31-32 (1969)

A number of persons who spoke before the Advisory Committee made it clear that the immediate effect of an employable mother rule, under the vague standards of a formulation such as Mississippi's, is to transfer to the welfare worker the power to determine for whom, at what job, for what pay, and under what conditions the mother must work. . . .

A social worker — a native Mississippian — permitted a transcript of an interview to be read to the Committee, describing a conversation with two of her fellow workers in a local welfare office:

> The workers felt that the employable mother policy stated that any woman who could work must, or her check would be cut off. They responded to the question of who decided who could work by saying that they felt anyone without a very serious physical problem could work. They felt that Negro mothers always had farmed out their children to neighbors and relatives, or at least "communal care" and that they certainly could continue to do so. Therefore, they felt that child care plans were not . . . a problem.

---

60. Brief for Plaintiffs on Their Motions for a Temporary Restraining Order and Preliminary Injunction at 5-6, Anderson v. Schaefer, opinion reported *sub nom.* Anderson v. Burson, 300 F. Supp. 401 (N.D. Ga. 1968).

When the problem of the availability of jobs was raised, these workers laughingly said that there are always white women looking for maids, baby-sitters, laundresses, and so forth. They admitted that there were industrial or agricultural blue collar jobs paying a decent wage for women. Domestics, according to these workers, make about $15 a week for a six-day, eight hour shift. When the interviewer commented that this was around $60 monthly the workers added that any employer would also give employees left-over food, used clothing, and furniture, thereby raising the total. The job expenses within limitations are subtracted from the worker's income. However, the allowance for clothing is usually the extent of these deductions as the woman would walk to work, receive lunch, and, according to the workers, would never have to pay for child care.

When asked how they personally enforced the policy, the workers agreed that their enforcement fluctuated as to rigidity. They both have high case loads, spend most of their time either doing clerical work or investigating absent fathers. Employability is thus one of the less frequently considered items. Both say that they periodically become irritated by some of the "lazy bitches" who sit home in leisure, while they, the workers, work and try to live "decently." During those times they go on a rampage, flipping through their cases, and deciding who should be working. Then they "hound" those mothers weekly until they get a job, threatening them with the termination of their case if they don't find work. They thought it quite amusing that they could always go on one of their enforcement drives whenever one of their friends needed household help.

WOOLFOLK v. BROWN
325 F. Supp. 1162, 1164 (E.D. Va. 1971),
aff'd, 456 F.2d 652 (4th Cir. 1972)

It was the general practice of the Bedford welfare office to keep a list of available jobs on hand and to offer positions deemed suitable to welfare recipients. [Goode depos. 27.] No definable standards of suitability exist. (Id., 28.) No job training is available to persons offered work rule jobs (Id., 29.) The ineligibility which flows from refusal to accept a job is considered "rather permanent." However, if one reapplies for benefits, the question of need is re-examined, and in practice aid will be granted if the job is not still available. (Id., 46-47.)

The three Calloway plaintiffs, sisters, were offered the same job in the course of a single telephone call (Carson depos., 82). This was . . . a babysitting job, an opening for one person, involving caring for two small children at a home some fifteen to twenty miles distant from the Calloway plaintiffs' residence (Carson depos., 82). When they each in turn declined the offer, on April 8, 1970, their cases were submitted to the welfare board; aid was terminated at the April 17th welfare board meeting. . . .

The local welfare office was aware from earlier unrelated contacts with the prospective employer of his general situation. The procedure to determine the suitability of the employment was extremely informal in other respects as well:

Q. Is an accepted procedure in your office to offer jobs over the telephone?

A. No, we do not generally do it this way. The man had to have someone that day or was trying to find someone that day. We knew something about his home situation, and we knew the Calloway girls, and we felt that this was a job one of them could do because one of them had said when she worked the other two would take care of her children. And this was the plan for each one; if one wouldn't go then we tried the others.

As illustrated by the above materials, many state work programs lack both substantive guidelines for the exercise of administrative discretion and procedural safeguards for the recipients; even when administrative procedures and standards are prescribed, welfare caseworkers have considerable informal power over their clients' decisions about work.[61]

When the power to decide who will work and at what jobs resides in local caseworkers, many abuses result — not the least of which is the expression of racial and sexual biases about suitable work. In addition, the sex segregation of the labor market contributes to tracking women welfare recipients into low-paid, low-status work; programs to combat this effect do not exist.

A further problem is the tracking of welfare recipients per se into certain levels of training and employment. A glaring example is New York State's policy of denying welfare assistance to otherwise eligible individuals who are enrolled in college, although assistance is granted to recipients in vocational or prevocational programs of similar or greater duration. The following case describes the state's policies and their asserted rationale.

JEFFERIES v. SUGARMAN
345 F. Supp. 172 (S.D.N.Y. 1972)

Before Hays, Circuit Judge, and Tyler and Tenney, District Judges.

Hays, Circuit Judge:

In this class action Mrs. Jefferies challenges the validity of New York Social Services Law §131(4) (McKinney's Consol. Laws, c. 55, Supp. 1971 and regulations adopted pursuant thereto, 18 N.Y.C.R.R. §§385.1, 385.7). Mrs. Jefferies claims that the application of these provisions allows mothers who are enrolled in "vocational" training programs to receive welfare benefits if they are otherwise eligible, and denies such benefits to mothers who, except that they are enrolled in an "academic" course of instruction, are similarly situated and that these provisions thus applied violate her rights to due process and equal protection of the law, infringe her first amendment rights by penalizing her for going to college, and conflict with the federal Aid to Families with Dependent Children program, 42 U.S.C. §601 et seq. (1970). Maxine Handel, Pearl Woods, and Alice Woods (hereinafter referred to as the Westchester plaintiffs), were permitted to intervene over the defendants' objections.[4]

Mrs. Jefferies purports to represent the class of "parents of minor children who are otherwise eligible for public assistance [AFDC] but who are denied such assistance on the grounds that they are enrolled in 'academic' rather than 'vocational' education programs and [are] therefore deemed available for employment." She is the mother of one child, and the father is absent. Before September, 1969 she was employed as a typist at a salary of $125 per week, and was not receiving any public assistance. She left her job to enter Queens Community College with the aim of becoming a teacher, aided by a full-tuition scholarship under the federally sponsored "College Discovery Program." She received emergency assistance from the New York City Department of Social Services from September 11 to December 11, 1969, at which time benefits to both her and

---

61. See Handler, *Controlling Official Behavior in Welfare Administration*, 54 Calif. L. Rev. 479, 493-495 (1966).

4. A Mrs. Patricia Carson also moved to intervene, but the court did not rule on her motion at the time of argument. Mrs. Carson and her husband, the parents of an infant child, are both enrolled in four-year college programs and are studying to become teachers. Neither has employment skills, and the family has been receiving AFDC benefits since July 1970. In 1971 Mrs. Carson, but not her husband, was informed by the New York City Department of Social Services that her public assistance would be discontinued unless she left college to seek employment. Mrs. Carson asserts that the only difference between her situation and that of her husband is that he is enrolled in the SEEK program (a special program of the City University of New York providing remedial assistance to students to enable them to earn college degrees) while she is not.

Mrs. Carson thus challenges state practices in addition to those challenged by the main plaintiffs, and we therefore deny her motion to intervene. To the extent that she *is* a member of plaintiffs' class, her rights are determined in accordance with this opinion.

her child were terminated, pursuant to the provisions of state law challenged here, because she refused to accept employment. In a Decision After Fair Hearing, benefits for the child were reinstated, but the denial of benefits to Mrs. Jefferies was affirmed. The defendants urge that since she already has shown the ability to be self-supporting, she is not "otherwise eligible for welfare" and thus does not adequately represent the class she claims to represent. We disagree; since her child is "both needy and dependent," Doe v. Swank, 332 F. Supp. 61, 63 (N.D. Ill.) (three-judge court), *aff'd mem. sub nom.* Weaver v. Doe, 404 U.S. 987, 92 S. Ct. 537, 30 L. Ed. 2d 539 (1971); Doe v. Shapiro, 302 F. Supp. 761, 764 (D. Conn. 1969) (three-judge court), *appeal dismissed as untimely docketed,* 396 U.S. 488, 90 S. Ct. 641, 24 L. Ed. 2d 677 (1970), the household is within the purview of the AFDC program, and she has standing to raise the issue of whether she can be denied benefits for refusal to accept employment while attending college, while those attending vocational schools and who refuse employment continue to receive benefits.

The Westchester intervenors are in a different situation, and they perhaps present the issues in this case more clearly than does Mrs. Jefferies. They have from three to six minor children each and, since their husbands left the home, have continuously been receiving welfare benefits even when they have been employed. Thus, unlike Mrs. Jefferies, they have no history of being self-supporting in the regular economy. Each of them, with the approval of her caseworker, enrolled as a full-time student in a four-year college program, with a specific vocational objective. In June, 1971 each was advised that her welfare benefits would be terminated unless she enrolled in vocational training courses under the federal Work Incentive Program (WIN), 42 U.S.C. §§602(a)(19), 630 et seq. (1970).

By now it is well settled that legislative classifications in the welfare area are not subject to the rule requiring "strict scrutiny." "If the classification has some 'reasonable basis,' it does not offend the Constitution simply because the classification 'is not made with mathematical nicety or because in practice it results in some inequality.'" Dandridge v. Williams, 397 U.S. 471, 485, 90 S. Ct. 1153, 1161, 25 L. Ed. 2d 491 (1970), quoting Lindsley v. Natural Carbonic Gas Co., 220 U.S. 61, 78, 31 S. Ct. 337, 55 L. Ed. 369 (1911). See also Jefferson v. Hackney, U.S., 92 S. Ct. 1724, 32 L. Ed. 2d 285 (1972). Applying this standard to the case at hand, we cannot find that the "academic-vocational" distinction embodied in New York's welfare practices violates the equal protection clause. See Money v. Swank, 432 F.2d 1140 (7th Cir. 1970). Plaintiffs urge that the distinction is irrational in view of the purpose of the AFDC program to make families self-supporting, because college graduates are more employable than persons who have merely received vocational training. The statistics cited to us show that of approximately 25,000 welfare recipients receiving vocational training, only about 2,000 have become employed, and of those many continue to receive assistance, though this is principally because of the income exemption provisions of the Work Incentive Program, 42 U.S.C. §602(a)(8)(A)(ii) (1970). However, this proves only that the WIN program in New York is not working very well, not that it would work any better if the state disregarded the distinction between academic and vocational training.

Furthermore, it appears from the deposition of defendant Wyman, and from the regulations, 18 N.Y.C.R.R. §385.1(4) (a recipient is not "employable" if enrolled in an approved "two-year college program with a specific vocational objective") that the distinction in New York is really between two-year and four-year programs. It is urged that even this classification operates irrationally, since some recipients will need pre-vocational training before they enter a two-year program, and thus will receive assistance for more than two years, while a recipient who has less than two years of a four-year program to complete is denied benefits. However, it is clear that the distinction is based upon the state's desire to use its limited welfare funds to secure at least some useful training to a larger number of people, and not to assist persons whose education has gone beyond a certain point. We cannot say that such a policy is irrational. It is true that there is dictum in Townsend v. Swank, 404 U.S. 282, 291-292, 92 S. Ct. 502, 30 L.

Ed. 2d 448 and n. 8 (1971) that might be thought to be contrary, but at least as applied to these facts it is entitled to little or no weight.

The plaintiffs' contention that New York is infringing on their first amendment rights is plainly frivolous and need not detain us further.

Having found the plaintiffs' constitutional claims to be without merit, we remand the case to Judge Tenney, who sought the three-judge court, for consideration of the pendent statutory claims. . . .

TENNEY, District Judge (concurring in part and dissenting in part):

Although I concur with the majority's disposition of plaintiffs' first amendment claims, I must dissent from their holding under the fourteenth amendment.

Under the Supreme Court's ruling in Dandridge v. Williams, 397 U.S. 471, 90 S. Ct. 1153, 25 L. Ed. 2d 491 (1970), the test for determining whether a state welfare classification is violative of equal protection is the traditional "rational basis" test:

> In the area of economics and social welfare, a State does not violate the Equal Protection Clause merely because the classifications made by its laws are imperfect. If the classification has some "reasonable basis," it does not offend the Constitution simply because the classification "is not made with mathematical nicety or because in practice it results in some inequality." (Citation omitted.) Id. at 485, 90 S. Ct. at 1161.

The Dandridge Court gave great weight to the fact that states have finite resources to devote to social welfare and that the federal Social Security Act gives them great latitude in dispensing them. As long as "a solid foundation for the regulation can be found" (Id. at 486, 90 S. Ct. at 1162.) in the state's legitimate purpose in enacting the regulation, no constitutional violation will ensue.

Dandridge, therefore, sets forth four factors to be considered in determining whether a state welfare classification is violative of equal protection: (1) the state's legitimate purpose in enacting the challenged regulation; (2) the means used to effect that purpose; (3) whether the means used are rationally related to the purpose sought to be achieved; and (4) whether the means used are such as to ensure the fiscal integrity of the state's welfare program — i.e., whether the means used are economically sound.

In *Dandridge,* the purpose of the challenged regulation was to provide the greatest amount of aid to the largest number of needy people by the most economic method. The means used to effect that purpose was a maximum grant system whereby the state was able to provide grants to a larger *number* of family units by reducing the *amount* of the grants provided to very large family units. Clearly, the means were rationally related to the purpose of the regulation, and moreover, were such as to ensure the fiscal integrity of the state's welfare program.

Applying the foregoing analysis to the instant case, the purpose of the federal AFDC-WIN program and accompanying state regulations which embody the academic-vocational distinction is to "help . . . [AFDC recipients] to attain or retain capability for . . . *maximum* self-support and personal independence" (emphasis added) (42 U.S.C. §601) and to restore "the families of . . . individuals [receiving AFDC] to independence and useful roles in their communities." 42 U.S.C. §630. The means adopted by the state to effect that purpose is to provide public assistance benefits to those enrolled in two-year college programs or vocational training courses, but not to those enrolled in four-year college programs.

The instant case differs from *Dandridge,* however, in that the means used by the state to effect the legitimate statutory purpose are not rationally related to the ends sought to be achieved, and moreover, are not such as to ensure the fiscal integrity of the state's welfare program.

Townsend v. Swank, 404 U.S. 282, 92 S. Ct. 502, 30 L. Ed. 2d 448 (1971) supports this view, for although that case was decided on statutory grounds, the Court strongly questioned the rationality of the academic-vocational distinction:

The majority [of the court below] justified the classification as designed to attain the twin goals of aiding needy children to become employable and self-sufficient, and of insuring fiscal integrity of the State's welfare program. We doubt the rationality of the classification as a means of furthering the goal of aiding needy children to become employable and self-sufficient; we are not told what basis in practical experience supports the proposition that children with a vocational training are more readily employable than children with a college education. Id. at 291, 92 S. Ct. at 508.[2]

The statistics cited to this Court with regard to the rationality of the academic-vocational distinction show that as of March 1971, 25,900 AFDC recipients had been referred to the WIN program since its inception in 1967. Of these 25,900, only 1,921 have successfully completed their training and are employed. Of these 1,921, a "predominant" number are still receiving welfare assistance. Depos. of Comm'r Wyman by Phillips, Ass't Comm'r, at 23-25. It is apparent, therefore, that the academic-vocational distinction is not rationally related to the legitimate statutory purpose of enabling AFDC recipients to become financially independent and off the welfare roles.

The majority insists that these statistics show only that the WIN program is not working very well, but to me they demonstrate not only the irrationality of the academic-vocational distinction, but also unsound fiscal policy.

This latter point is particularly evident when one examines the way in which the academic-vocational distinction operates. Theoretically, the state sets forth two conditions an AFDC recipient must meet in order to qualify for assistance while engaged in training under either the WIN program or the state work rule: (1) her program must be of a maximum duration of two years, and (2) it must lead to a specific vocational objective. Although specifying a two-year maximum, the state actually provides benefits to AFDC recipients engaged in training for more than two years if, for instance, the recipient needs pre-vocational training to complete her basic literacy or to obtain her high school equivalency certificate. But New York has clearly demonstrated that it does not provide public assistance benefits to enable a recipient to matriculate at a four-year college, even if she has less than two years to complete for her degree, *solely* because she would be engaged in academic rather than vocational training. Depos. of Comm'r Wyman by Phillips, Ass't Comm'r, at 37.

So while the state is willing to provide benefits for more than two years to a welfare recipient who, even after receiving vocational training, is not likely to get off the welfare rolls, it is unwilling to provide such assistance for four years or less to enable a recipient who has the requisite aptitude to obtain a degree that would ensure her becoming financially independent.[3] I find this irrational.

It is just this latter situation which is presented most sharply by the Westchester intervenors. Each of the three Westchester intervenors is estranged from her husband; each has from three to six minor dependent children; each has a long history of receiving public assistance, even while employed; and two of the three have one year of college credit acquired some years ago. All three were encouraged by their respective caseworkers to enroll in four-year college programs *precisely because* vocational training would never generate the income necessary to enable them to become financially independent.

The majority holds that the academic-vocational distinction "is based upon the state's desire to use its limited welfare funds to secure at least some useful training to a larger number of people." But I question the "usefulness" of vocational training for

2. The Court further stated that "a classification which channels one class of people, poor people, into a particular class of low paying, low status jobs would plainly raise substantial questions under the Equal Protection Clause." Townsend v. Swank, supra, 404 U.S. at 292 n. 8, 92 S. Ct. at 908.

3. It is important to note that the instant case is distinguishable from Money v. Swank, 432 F.2d 1140 (7th Cir. 1970), cited by the majority in support of its holding that the academic-vocational distinction does not violate the equal protection clause. There, as in Napper v. Wyman, 305 F. Supp. 429 (S.D.N.Y. 1969) (which has a similar holding), the plaintiffs sued the state for tuition grants. Here, plaintiffs seek only living expenses; their tuition is completely financed by scholarships and loans.

those AFDC recipients, like the plaintiffs herein, for whom such training will not make it possible for them to become financially independent, and who, moreover, possess the intellectual capacity to pursue a course of study which would ensure such a result.

I am not suggesting that the state be required to provide public assistance benefits to *all* AFDC recipients who desire to enroll in four-year college programs. Whether any particular AFDC recipient would be accorded benefits while pursuing academic training should depend, as it has in the past,[4] upon that recipient's intellectual capabilities and on whether the degree she seeks is tied to a specific vocational objective to ensure her becoming self-supporting and off the welfare rolls. An across-the-board denial of public assistance to those AFDC recipients enrolled in four-year academic programs, while providing such assistance to those enrolled in vocational training programs, is not rationally related to the state's legitimate interest in providing training for welfare recipients to enable them to become financially independent, and does little to ensure the fiscal integrity of its welfare program.

On the basis of the foregoing analysis, I would find for the plaintiffs.[62]

If the state may channel welfare recipients into certain kinds of education and jobs even where better training or employment would be of equal cost to the state, what limits are there on the state's control over the work that recipients may be required to do? If prostitution were legal, as it is in Nevada, could a state require a woman to take a job as a prostitute as a condition of eligibility? If not, what distinguishes such work from the jobs as a household domestic, a topless waitress, a Playboy Bunny, a receptionist in a large office, a secretary or a field worker?

c. Sex-Based Referral Priorities in the WIN Program

WALKER, SEX DISCRIMINATION
IN GOVERNMENT BENEFIT PROGRAMS
23 Hast. L.J. 277, 287-289 (1971)

. . . Mothers . . . are not "appropriate" for referral unless there is adequate care for their children.[53]

The child care requirement can work against women in two ways. Since the states

---

4. It appears that until the end of 1969, the Department of Social Services did authorize attendance at four-year colleges for individual welfare recipients on a discretionary basis. Depos. of Comm'r Wyman by Phillips, Ass't Comm'r, at 3-4.

62. On remand, Judge Tenney ruled that the WIN program preempted the state work rules. Jefferies v. Sugarman, 71 Civ. 2060 (S.D.N.Y. June 31, 1972), a decision that was reversed and remanded in light of *Dublino*, 481 F.2d 414 (2d Cir. 1973). — Eds.

53. See id. In California as of April 1970 there were the following number of day nurseries licensed by the State Department of Social Welfare and therefore qualifying as adequate child-care plans for WIN mothers:

1,042	proprietary (private, for profit)
429	nonprofit
620	church affiliated
2,091	total number of nurseries

The capacity of the nurseries was:

45,044	proprietary
15,543	nonprofit
28,786	church affiliated
89,373	total number of children

Human Relations Agency, California Dep't of Social Welfare, AR-1-12, Public Welfare in California, table 41 (1969-1970). The inadequacy of the available care is clear, as there are 808,570 children who received welfare in fiscal year ending June 30, 1970. Id., table 1.

have great discretion in determining what is adequate care, a state may have a very lenient definition of suitable care which would make nearly every AFDC mother "appropriate" for mandatory referral to WIN. This could mean that even mothers without adequate care for their children would be forced to leave them and go into WIN. Or, a state may have such a narrow definition of adequate care that no mother would be considered appropriate for referral, even though the mother herself felt her children were well cared for and she wanted to go to WIN. These are extreme examples, but they illustrate the need for reasonable federal guidelines on child care to be applied to all state WIN plans so that mothers will receive equitable, uniform treatment from state to state.

The other aspect of WIN that can discriminate against women is the requirement that unemployed fathers on AFDC *must* be referred to WIN within thirty days after the family begins receiving assistance, and that these fathers be given first priority in the WIN program.[54] If WIN programs had adequate space for all the men who *must* be referred,[55] and all the women who *want* to be referred,[56] there would be no problem of discrimination, as every woman who wanted to participate could do so. This, however, is not the case, as funds for the program are limited, and therefore the number of participants is also limited.[57] Because the men get first priority on referral, they fill the available places, and make it difficult, if not impossible, for the women to participate.

For example, in California's Alameda County no women have been enrolled in the WIN program since April 1969. There are 457 women now in the program, but they were enrolled when the program was initiated. Since that time, all vacancies have been filled by men.[58] As of March 1971 there were 1103 women on the waiting list for WIN, some of whom have been waiting as long as two years.[59] In an interview with the author, the director of the Alameda County WIN program[60] expressed his opinion that more women were interested in WIN than those currently on the waiting list, but they know they have no chance of getting into the program and do not bother signing up. The director stated it was cheaper to have men in WIN than women, because men do not require a child care allowance. Women who participate in the program have all child care expenses paid by WIN. The cost averages about $100 per family. Women also need more money than men for transportation as they often have to take children to a babysitter or nursery school.[61]

Despite the fact that women are more costly to train, the director felt experience had shown that the program was more successful with women. A higher percentage of women than men complete the training (which may be basic education courses, junior college, or vocational training) and a higher percentage of women obtain and keep jobs related to their training.[62] Men, on the other hand, take the first job offered them and seem less interested in the training.[63]

From the standpoint of cutting costs, it is more profitable to the states to have men participate in WIN because their training allowance is generally lower and they drop out

54. See 42 U.S.C. §607 (Supp. V, 1970). The WIN program has been challenged for discrimination against women in violation of the equal protection clause. Hawk v. Richardson, Civil No. 71-1754 (C.D. Cal., filed July 28, 1971).

55. In California, July 1969 to June 1970, 27,936 men were referred to WIN. Human Relations Agency, California Dep't of Social Welfare, AR-1-12, Annual Statistical Report Series, table 60 (1969-70).

56. In California, from July 1969 to June 1970, 16,112 women were referred to WIN. Id.

57. In California the WIN normal capacity for active training participants at any one time is 16,800 slots. Id., table 61.

58. Alameda County Dep't of Social Welfare, Statistical Report of the Alameda Dep't of Social Welfare (1971).

59. Id.

60. Interview with Mr. Vancy Bulluck, Vocational Supervisor II, Vocational Services Section, Alameda County Welfare Department, in Alameda, California, Apr. 1971.

61. Id.

62. Id.

63. Id.

more quickly to take jobs.[64]Once men have a job, their families must go off public assistance, and the state can therefore reduce the welfare rolls. Women, however, may stay on AFDC after completing WIN and getting a job.[65] Since women's wages are usually low,[66] they generally cannot earn enough to meet their families' needs, and hence must continue on aid.[67]

In excluding women from WIN by giving men priority for participation, the legislators have saved money at the expense of women. What the legislators are saying by this is that they are not particularly concerned with increasing a person's chances in life by training them for better opportunities, rather their specific concern is with getting people off welfare and saving the state money. Since women will probably stay on welfare anyway, even after training, their participation in WIN is given lower priority. The fact that the large majority of families on welfare are headed by women[68] who are unable to break out of the poverty cycle because they lack such training seems to be overlooked.

Statistics show a national pattern of enrollment in WIN similar to that of Alameda County. As of April 30, 1970, only 71 percent of WIN enrollees were women,[63] although 95 percent of all adult AFDC recipients were women.[64]

THORN v. RICHARDSON
4 FEP Cases 299 (W.D. Wash. 1971)

BOWEN, J.

This action was brought by the two plaintiff women for themselves and on behalf of a class of women welfare recipients. Both women plaintiffs are heads of households receiving public assistance. They sought entrance into the WIN program, authorized under the Social Security Act (42 U.S.C. §632(a)). That is a federally funded, state

---

64. See text accompanying notes 61-63 supra.

65. In California, 3,185 AFDC-U (unemployed father) cases were closed in the period July 1969–June 1970 because of employment or increased earnings within 6 months following participation in WIN. However, only 1,101 of the cases where women were the WIN participants were closed during the same period. Annual Statistical Report Series, supra note 55, table 61.

66. The median income for a white female in 1959 was $1,441 as compared with $4,103 for a white male. A nonwhite female had a median income of $909. H. Miller, U.S. Bureau of the Census, Income Distribution in the United States (A 1960 Census Monograph) 198 (1966).

67. Under the federal provisions, deprivation due to unemployment of the parent is limited to the unemployment of the father. 42 U.S.C. §5607(a) (1964). Thus, the employment of the father may eliminate the source of deprivation on which aid is predicated. However, the employment of the mother may not eliminate the source of deprivation under statutes based on the federal requirement and under California provisions when another source of deprivation exists. See California Dep't of Social Welfare, Public Social Services Manual of Policies & Procedures 42-301.1 (1967) and accompanying interpretation. "Aid, services, or both shall be granted . . . to families of related children under the age of 18 years . . . in need thereof because they have been deprived of parental support or care due to: (a) The death, physical or mental incapacity, or incarceration of a parent; or (b) The divorce, separation or desertion of a parent or parents and resultant continued absence of a parent from the home for these or other reasons: or (c) The unemployment of a parent or parents." Cal. Welf. & Inst'ns Code §11250 (West 1956); *accord,* California Dep't of Social Welfare, Public Social Services Manual of Policies & Procedures 42-301.1 (1967).

68. In California, in 1970, 972,646 persons (adults and children) receiving AFDC were in women-headed families, as opposed to 168,440 persons in families where the father was present and unemployed. Public Social Services Manual, supra note 67, app. J. For the national picture, in 1969, AFDC mothers were present in 92 percent of the families receiving aid. Eppley, The AFDC Family in the 1960's, Welfare in Review, Sept.-Oct. 1970, table 12.

63. U.S. Dep't of Labor, The Work Incentive Program: First Annual Report of the Department of Labor to the Congress on Training and Employment under Title IV of the Social Security Act, Table 2, June 1970.

64. Division of Program Review & Analysis, Office of Evaluation, U.S. Dep't of Labor, WIN Program Review After One Year 2, Oct. 22, 1969.

operated program providing job training and employment opportunities to persons on public assistance.

The plaintiffs attack the system of referral which give priority to the participation of male welfare recipients over female welfare recipients applying for the program. As a result of this priority the plaintiffs have not received job training while males who have applied at a later date than plaintiffs have. Had plaintiffs been males rather than females they would have received job training by now.

The named plaintiffs have each become indebted for the sum of $1500.00 to receive job training. In order to continue her job training, plaintiff Croply must become further indebted for the sum of $500.00.

The Court is asked to determine the lawfulness of certain policies and practices of the defendants appearing at 45 C.F.R. §220.35(a)(3), WAC 388-57-055 and BWTP Manual §406 under applicable standards of the Fifth and Fourteenth Amendments to the Constitution; Title VII of the Civil Rights Act of 1964, 42 U.S.C. §2000(e); Title IV of the Civil Rights Act of 1964, 42 U.S.C. §§601 et seq., 42 U.S.C. §1983 and pertinent contracts between the United States Department of Labor [DOL] and the Washington State Department of Employment Security [DES].

The Court approves and adopts as made by the Court the proposed findings and conclusions and proposed order made and suggested by plaintiffs, as follows:

FINDINGS OF FACT

1. This Court hereby incorporates herein as findings of fact all of the facts which were admitted by all parties in the Amended Pretrial Orders as amended and the Court further finds that;

2. The WIN program provides recipients of AFDC with job training and employment opportunities;

3. All of the defendants, in their official capacities and as respective heads of their departments, jointly administer the WIN program;

4. All of the defendants issued and applied regulations which, on their face and as applied, discriminate against women by giving a priority to unemployed fathers;

5. The plaintiffs are members of a class of women who have been discriminated against as a result of the application of these regulations;

6. This discrimination against the plaintiffs is based solely upon sex, i.e., the fact that the plaintiffs are women;

7. All of the defendants herein, in their official capacities and as heads of their respective departments, have actively participated in this discrimination against the plaintiffs herein;

8. The plaintiffs applied for the WIN program, but because they are women they have not been considered for enrollment in the WIN program. Had the plaintiffs been males rather than females, they would have been considered for enrollment in the WIN program by now;

9. As a result of this discrimination, plaintiff Shelley G. Thorn has been forced to incur indebtedness in the sum of $1500;

10. As a result of this discrimination plaintiff Dolores Cropley has been forced to incur indebtedness in the sum of $2000.00;

11. As a result of this discrimination, both plaintiffs have been greatly frustrated and humiliated;

12. The discrimination against the plaintiffs and the class they represent has resulted from the collaboration, cooperation, and joint action of all the defendants;

13. As a result of the discrimination based on sex, the WIN program in the State of Washington contains a disproportionately large number of men, to the detriment and exclusion of the plaintiffs and the class which they represent;

From the foregoing Findings of Facts, the Court hereby makes and enters the following:

CONCLUSIONS OF LAW

A. Social Security Act — Statutory Claim

1. The regulations which have been adopted and applied by all defendants, on their face, require the giving of a priority based upon sex.

2. The Social Security Act, 42 U.S.C. §602 et seq. neither permits nor requires the adoption and application by the defendants of the challenged regulations which give a priority to unemployed fathers.

3. The Social Security Act, 42 U.S.C. §602 et seq. requires the WIN program to be administered without regard to sex.

4. The regulations as adopted and applied by the defendants exceed the authority of the Social Security Act, 42 U.S.C. §602 et seq.

5. The plaintiffs are entitled to judgment in the nature of mandamus, under 28 U.S.C. §1361, requiring defendants HEW and DOL to administer the WIN program in compliance with the provisions of the Social Security Act, 42 U.S.C. §602 et seq.; directing defendants HEW and DOL to eliminate the challenged regulations; and directing defendants HEW and DOL to require their agents, DES and DSHS [Washington State Department of Health and Social Services], to eliminate their challenged regulations; . . .

C. Equal Protection and Due Process of Law

9. The regulations, as adopted and applied by all the defendants, violate the rights of plaintiffs, and the class which they represent, to due process and equal protection of law under the Fifth and Fourteenth Amendments to the United States Constitution.

10. The regulations, as adopted and applied by all of the defendants, set up classifications based solely upon sex, which deny plaintiffs and the class which they represent, an equal opportunity to participate in the WIN program.

11. The classifications based solely upon sex, contained in the regulations adopted and applied by all defendants, are without a rational basis as is required by the Fifth and Fourteenth Amendments to the United States Constitution.

12. The reasons given by defendants for adopting and applying the challenged regulations do not provide, as a matter of law, a rational basis for said regulations.

13. The regulations adopted and applied by all defendants create a suspect classification based upon sex and encroach upon the fundamental rights of plaintiffs and the class they represent.

14. The defendants have failed to show a compelling federal or state interest justifying the adoption and application of the challenged regulations.

[The court also held that the regulations violated Title VII of the Civil Rights Act of 1964 (42 U.S.C. §2000(c) et seq.), Executive Orders 11246, 11375, and 11478, and state laws against sex discrimination.]

From the foregoing Findings of Fact and Conclusions of Law, the Court hereby finds and concludes that the plaintiffs are entitled to judgment, relief, and equitable reimbursement against defendants in the amounts above stated and the defendants are hereby ordered

1. To make referral to and to enroll referees in the WIN program without regard to the challenged priority schedules.

2. To eliminate in those areas of the State of Washington where the priority schedules have had the effect of discriminating against women, enrollment of unemployed fathers until mothers who have already applied for WIN are considered for enrollment.

3. To require that mothers presently waiting to be considered for the WIN program be considered in order of their date of application. Each local DES office shall maintain a single chronological list containing the names of all persons referred to WIN.Referees

shall be selected for consideration for enrollment from that list regardless of the DSHS office which processed his or her referral. This procedure shall continue at least until all those women, whose participation in WIN has been delayed by the challenged priority schedules, have been considered for the program.

4. To take affirmative action to recruit, refer and enroll women interested in WIN until such time as the proportion of women to men in the program equals that proportion which would result from enrollment of AFDC recipients in order of when they applied rather than according to the challenged enrollment priorities.

5. To give notice to all members of the class that consideration for enrollment in WIN will take place starting with the earliest date of application by said member and that women will be given a preference in said consideration until the proportionate number of women in the program is as described in paragraph "4".

6. Defendants DES and DSHS shall supply plaintiffs' counsel with copies of the monthly statistical reports, compiled on the state level and for Seattle in the normal course of administering WIN, to show whether this court's order is being complied with.

7. To enroll Shelley Thorn and Dolores Cropley in the WIN program retroactively to the date of each plaintiff's entry in the training program in which she is currently enrolled.

8. Pursuant to "7" above, to reimburse plaintiff Shelley G. Thorn for the indebtedness of $1500.00 which she has been forced to incur as a result of the discrimination herein.

9. Pursuant to "7" above, to reimburse plaintiff Dolores Cropley for the indebtedness of $2000.00 which she has been forced to incur as a result of the discrimination herein.

10. To pay the reasonable attorney's fees of plaintiff Dolores Cropley in the amount of $2962.50.

11. To pay plaintiffs' costs incurred in bringing this action, in the amount of $1114.30, all of which payments as ordered in paragraphs 8, 9, 10 and 11 herein shall be paid to plaintiffs by defendants Department of Health, Education and Welfare and Social and Health Services, with each Department paying one-half of such equitable reimbursement, attorneys fees and costs.

The ruling of the court in *Thorn* that the Social Security Act requires the WIN program to be administered without regard to sex is interesting, since the act itself explicitly requires individuals to be evaluated for WIN referral in an order based on sex, and permits states to limit the groups they assess to unemployed fathers and youth and essential persons sixteen years or over. The new list of priorities for referral under the WIN program, as set forth in the Joint Explanatory Statement of the Committee of Conference, supra §C-3-d, continues to place unemployed fathers ahead of both unemployed mothers who volunteer for the program and those who do not; it also provides that mothers are exempt from registration for the program if the father registers. Is it possible that in establishing a priority of men over women for the WIN program that Congress simply did not anticipate the possibility that some women would need or prefer to work outside the home? The emphasis placed on the problems of women who are denied job training or are subject to more stringent state work rules because of the sex-based referral priorities of the WIN program should not obscure the discriminatory impact of the sex-based priorities on male welfare recipients. In any household in which an adult male has registered for work or training, the adult females do not have to register. This discriminates against groups of men or women who share living arrangements but who do not gain exemptions from the registration requirement for one adult when another adult registers; it removes from adult recipients the choice of who is to work outside the home if only one need do so; and it discriminates against families in which a female adult recipient works part time for a subsistence wage, because it does not exempt male adults from the work requirement on that account, whereas if the roles are reversed, the female adults are exempted.

1 CENTER FOR SOCIAL WELFARE POLICY AND LAW
MATERIALS ON WELFARE LAW
V-97 (1972)

WIN OR WIP? — THE FEDERAL WORK PROGRAM FOR AFDC

As is noted in Wexler's article on Practicing Law for Poor People [79 Yale L.J. 1049 (1970)], the initial reaction to the enactment of the AFDC Work Incentive Program (WIN) in 1967 focused primarily on the coercive feature of the program and its potential for harassment of recipients. This reaction is clearly understandable in light of the previous history of welfare work programs and much of the tenor of the congressional interest in these programs. It is also clear that the program was so used in some instances. However, as Wexler notes, it soon became apparent that more recipients had reason to complain by reason of their exclusion from WIN or the poor quality of the program, than because of compelled participation. . . .

To a certain degree, the potential for real abuse was curbed by the Department of Labor's establishment of criteria for job placements which required an entry-level wage of at least $1.60 an hour and an opportunity for improvement in skill or earnings. In addition, whether as the result of choice or the combination of labor market conditions and client skills, the program placed primary emphasis on training. These factors, in themselves, limited the numbers of people who could be compelled to participate. As of January 31, 1972, the total number of enrollees since the inception of the program was only 350,322, and a significant number of these had never been required to actually participate.

This, of course, does not mean that the use of work requirements as a punitive device did not continue in AFDC for . . . states continued to impose their own work requirements contemporaneously with WIN. However, by and large, the WIN program itself did not serve as the vehicle for overt abuse of recipients although it did continue many of the subtle forms of repression to which recipients have been subjected. Thus, recipients were denied training by reason of nonestablishment of WIN projects, women were denied an opportunity for training by discriminatory enrollment practices, etc. . . .

BLONG, TALMADGE—NARROWING THE EMPLOYABILITY
GAP OR EXPLOITATION OF ASSISTANCE CLIENTS?
1 Center on Social Welfare Policy and Law, Materials on Welfare Law
V-160 (1972)

. . . [I]t is clear . . . that primary emphasis will be placed on getting people into any kind of a job with little, if any, concern for its ability to offer long term employment at adequate income levels.

This problem will be even worse than is suggested by the WIN standards themselves, since HEW and DOL are continuing to take the position that states can impose work requirements in addition to the WIN program.[65] Thus, the "Registrant Pool" will be "available to recruiters from other manpower programs, the Employment Service, and potential employers" and, apparently, it is intended that states could even include individuals exempt from WIN registration in a state work program. This means that

---

65. The government agencies' position was upheld by the U.S. Supreme Court in New York State Dep't of Social Services v. Dublino, 413 U.S. 405, 93 S. Ct. 2507, 37 L. Ed. 2d 688 (1973). — Eds.

individuals whom Congress has deliberately freed from compulsory work, e.g., mothers of children under six, or who have not yet been selected for appraisal, possibly because they have deliberately been passed over in the selection process, or who have been appraised and determined to be "in circumstances so extreme as to preclude any effective assistance from [WIN] participation," could be required to accept jobs that do not even meet WIN standards. Furthermore, a state would not be required to follow WIN standards in determining the appropriateness of the job or whether the individual had good cause to refuse and [it] would apparently be permitted to impose more punitive sanctions for noncooperation than those allowed under WIN, e.g., New York does not provide any post-hearing counseling in the state work program and imposes a 30 day suspension for individuals who failed to comply, even if the individual is willing to immediately cooperate. The effect of such [an] approach is aptly summarized in Labor Secretary Hodgson's recent statements on congressional workfare proposals: "this would disrupt our labor market and channel the poor into nonproductive jobs. There would be a field day for the manipulators out to exploit whatever they can." N.Y. Times, April 29, 1972, at p. 16.

As Blong suggests, the result of WIN's sex-based referral policies is likely to be proportionately more women than men in the less desirable state work programs. In a *Thorn*-type case, the forced participation in a relatively dead-end job could be alleged as an injury suffered by plaintiffs because of the government's sex-discriminatory policies.

d. Discounting the Housewife Role

WORK IN AMERICA
Report of a Special Task Force to the Secretary of HEW
(O'Toole Report) 142-143 (1972)

Should Welfare Mothers be Required to Take a Job?

The question of whether the mother in a fatherless family (76 percent of AFDC families) should take a job or not is a complex one. It is not even clear that anyone other than the mother has the legal or moral right to make that decision, or that anyone other than the mother can make the decision that is best for her and her children. Some mothers prefer outside jobs to keeping house and raising children; others prefer to stay home. To force all AFDC mothers to do one or the other is to do violence to what we know about human development and family relationships: mothers who work because they prefer to work, and mothers who stay home because they prefer to stay home, probably make better and happier mothers (and children) than those who do one or the other because of circumstances or coercion. It follows that the public interest and the interests of the mother and her children will be best served if the mother herself makes the choice. This choice, of course, must be essentially a free one: a decision either way must not carry with it any special penalties, rewards or forfeitures.

The easiest part of the problem has to do with those women now on AFDC — perhaps a majority — who, other things being equal, would prefer to work and support their families. But other things are not equal. They do not take jobs because there aren't suitable child care facilities, or because the costs associated with having a job and paying for child care often leave them with less than they would be receiving on welfare. These women do not need to be coerced into the labor force; they need the freedom to join it: adequate child care facilities and a decent job at a living wage.

The more difficult part of the problem lies with those AFDC mothers who choose to remain home and raise their children themselves. More accurately, the problem lies not with them but rather with our system of public values regarding women and women's roles and our definition of work. When we say to the AFDC mother, for example, "You must go to work or take work-training in order to be eligible for public assistance," we are, in effect, telling her that, from society's point of view, she is not now working, that keeping house and raising children are not socially useful, at least not as useful as "a job." But we are able to make this judgment of the AFDC mother who stays home and raises her children only because we make this same judgment of all house-wives.

Thus, the public devaluation of keeping house and raising children is, for the AFDC mother, only a special case of the more general problem faced by women throughout our society. Indeed, it is one of the principal sources of the deep discontent experienced by women in all social classes. The failure of society to acknowledge housekeeping and childrearing as socially useful work on a par with paid employment makes it increasingly difficult for the married woman who is "just a housewife" to see herself as a valued contributor in the eyes of her family, her neighbors, and the larger society. The pressures generated by such social values tend to push women into the labor force in their search for recognition as full and valued participants in society. The result is that some women who would perhaps prefer to remain at home are, in effect, pushed into the labor force against their will.

It is with the AFDC mother who would prefer to stay home that the social undervaluing of housekeeping and childrearing appears in its clearest, most perfect form. In this case, it is precisely the social undervaluing of housekeeping and childrearing that provides the rationale for telling her that she must take a job to be eligible for welfare, and also for the notion that she is "getting something for doing nothing."

The clear fact is that keeping house and raising children is work — work that is, on the average, as difficult to do well and as useful to the larger society as almost any paid job involving the production of goods or services. The difficulty is not that most people don't believe this or accept it (we pay lip service to it all the time) but that, whatever our private and informal belief systems, we have not, as a society, acknowledged this fact in our public system of values . . . and rewards.

As noted above, mothers or other caretakers of young children[66] are exempted from WIN's registration requirement. This may indicate that Congress believes that home care is preferable for young children. In any event, child care outside the home is not widely available for the very young. The exemption can also be viewed as a recognition of the greater amount of work involved in the care of younger children. As noted in Part II, supra, the average number of hours a woman spends on housework each week increases in inverse proportion to the age of the children she cares for.

4. Strategies for Ending Sexism in the Welfare Laws

[The assumptions implicit in the 1967 Social Security Amendments are] that a working parent imparts respect for a work ethic . . . to the children in the family. . . . that many AFDC recipients were not working because of either indolence or lack of training; that is, many recipients were immediately employable, or at least immediately trainable for work. . . . that WIN's training program would raise the vocational skills of recipients to employable levels . . . that the economy is sufficiently flexible to absorb immediately recipients who could work right away as well as recipients whom the program would train; and finally, that the jobs obtained through the WIN program would enable the recipients to earn enough money to leave the relief rolls.[67]

66. Caretaker relatives of children under six are exempted from the registration requirement, but must be told of their opportunity to volunteer to participate. See Joint Explanatory Statement of the Committee of Conference, H.R. Rep. No. 747, 92d Cong., 1st Sess. 6 (1971), supra, Part V-C-3-a.

67. Gold, Comment: The Failure of the Work Incentive (WIN) Program, 119 U. Pa. L. Rev. 485, 487-489 (1971).

In a detailed critique of the WIN program, analyzing its first two years, the same commentator highlights the inaccuracy of these assumptions. One obvious flaw is the failure to identify and confront the problems which face the poor women who are the overwhelming majority of adult AFDC recipients. Aside from other limitations of the "workfare" approach, it can never provide a meaningful alternative to welfare dependency unless it includes an intelligent strategy for dealing with two facets of the lives of poor women: the massive discrimination against them in the labor market, and the responsibility that the majority of them bear for the care of young children. A newspaper columnist reported as follows on a study by Ferman and Miller of a random sample of welfare and nonwelfare poor people. It graphically illustrates the folly of relying on work to get people, especially women, off welfare under present conditions.

WICKER, THE POOR AND THE WORK ETHIC
The New York Times, July 13, 1973, at 35

What is the difference between the "working poor," who are not despised in America, and the "welfare poor," who are? Is it that the working poor have jobs? Or that those jobs will lead them inevitably out of poverty? Or that they are motivated by the "work ethic" while the welfare poor take handouts?

Well, the working poor do have jobs, but so do many of the welfare poor. But in neither case is there much chance that work will lead the worker out of poverty. As for the work ethic, both the working poor and the welfare poor usually have it in about the same degree, but it doesn't do them much good because the only jobs available are low-paid and lead nowhere.

If a working-poor person or a welfare-poor person also happens to be a woman, she's even worse off; because even within the desperate world of the low-wage earner, sexism is rampant and women are given the least desirable jobs and paid the smallest wages.

These are some of the major conclusions in an important study of a random sample of more than a thousand low-wage earners and welfare recipients in Detroit. Commissioned by the Department of Labor, the study was made by Louis A. Ferman, research director of the Institute of Labor and Industrial Relations at the University of Michigan, and Joe A. Miller, now of the Pennsylvania State University faculty.

Mr. Ferman and Mr. Miller have found, to put it simply, that most of what the public thinks about welfare recipients is a stereotype with little basis in fact; and that since much Congressional and administrative policymaking is based on the same stereotype, most programs to "get people off welfare" — let alone what is left of those to "get people out of poverty" — are going nowhere.

Their study found, perhaps most importantly, that among the Detroit poor (who were nearly 85 percent women) "there were few differences between the working welfare recipients and nonrecipient low-wage workers with respect to personal characteristics or background." And for either category, work "did not appreciably alter the economic resources or life situation."

In fact, "if the nonrecipient low-wage workers were a standard, then getting off welfare completely would not really improve" life for the so-called welfare poor. Besides, a surprising number of them *are* working — 94 percent of the male welfare recipients studied had worked more than 50 percent of the time covered by the study as against only 90 percent of male nonrecipients. Among women, a majority of both recipients and nonrecipients had worked at least half the time. Moreover, the jobs held by low-wage workers were mostly full time — but so poorly paid and dead-end as to leave the workers still in poverty, often earning less than the "combined value of services and cash from welfare."

The Ferman-Miller study isolated a set of characteristics that tend to keep too many Americans in poverty, whether of the working or welfare variety — rural origins with poor educational opportunity; migration to the city or elsewhere; lack of skills and training. These problems are compounded for racial minorities and for women. For these people good jobs are usually not available, no matter how much they want to work; for them, too, welfare can be of substantial assistance, and many take advantage of it without losing their desire to work and rise.

The study notes a substantial difference in the problems of male and female welfare recipients. Contrary to stereotype, the women do not have large numbers of children, but they do tend to be the only workers in their families and they work for the lowest wages. The men, on the other hand, usually make much better wages and sometimes are helped by a working wife or older child, but have such large families that they cannot adequately support them. In that situation, increased earnings for a female recipient is a possible solution; but it is not a likely solution for the male recipient, who probably needs — as Mr. Ferman and Mr. Miller argue — a family allowance plan.

They conclude that in any sensible approach to the poverty problem, "The emphasis should not be on welfare recipient versus nonrecipient — meaningless categories — but rather on male workers versus female workers. Second, the emphasis should be shifted from the concept of a welfare problem to that of a labor market problem."

Obviously, if far more women than men are in the poverty class, whether welfare or working, any effective program will have to "result in well-paying, prestigious careers for women as well as men." Just as obviously, if there are no real differences between the working and the welfare poor, the problem is not to get some people off welfare but to get far more people out of an economic dead end. Mr. Ferman and Mr. Miller favor "restructuring the low-wage market" through unionization; surely their study also points straight to the need for an income assistance and maintenance plan.

The substantially lower wages of the women who have participated in the WIN program are additional evidence of sex discrimination in employment as an obstacle for economic self-sufficiency for AFDC women.

Solving the problems of work incentives and income maintenance in relation to family structure and sex roles is a vital step for our society. Unfortunately, congressional action in this area has so far been grossly inadequate to the task. The present strategy, as reflected in the WIN program, is to shore up the two-parent family. This is to be done by emphasizing jobs and training for men. While both men and women are required to register for referral, wives in families where a man has registered are exempted, presumably as an incentive for families to stay together. Women who do not have a man to register in their stead must register unless they have very young children at home. Since many states do not have AFDC-UP programs, and because, in any case, the training and job referral program is inadequate, the program is unlikely to make two-parent, single-breadwinner families into a ticket off welfare for very many welfare recipients. What it will do, when coupled with the state work programs which apparently will be allowed to coexist with WIN, is to increase the power of administrators over welfare recipients.

Yet an adequately financed and administered program, providing jobs and training primarily to men and increasing incentives for poor families to form two-parent households, is certainly one major work-oriented approach to the problems of women on welfare. A second is to enable women to support themselves and their children by attacking sex discrimination in the labor market and by providing child care outside the home.

Both approaches can be either progressive or reactionary depending on the specific details of their design and administration, especially whether they are compulsory or voluntary and whether they are combined with each other or pursued separately. Aside from such questions as the sexism of training men to the exclusion of women and vice versa, and the problems involved in pressuring or requiring parents to entrust the care of their young children to others, both approaches require major changes in our social and economic system. First, under present economic conditions, it is doubtful whether enough jobs can be provided for poor people of either sex with pay adequate for the costs both of child care and of self-support. Therefore, under a voluntary program, it is likely that a large number of people would choose to remain on welfare rather than the low-status, poorly paid jobs that might be available to them. Under a compulsory program, needy people would be coerced into jobs no one else would take, and still require governmental assistance (which might not be forthcoming) to obtain a decent standard of living. Second, the changes required to end sex segregation and discrimination in the labor market are enormous, and may be impossible without a reorganization and redefinition of work throughout the society.

D. Child Care

1. Introduction

Many people think that the major purpose of marriage and the family is to bear and rear children. Thus a chapter in family law must consider the issues raised by the question: who should care for children during their waking hours? Until recently, the answer took three class-related forms. Upper-class women hired maids, governesses, or nannies. Middle-class women stayed home to care for their children, possibly sending three-and four-year-olds to nursery school for a few hours a day to prepare them for kindergarten. Poor women who had to work left their children with relatives or neighbors, or alone. In all three forms, the mother was primarily responsible for the children's care, either arranging for it or doing it herself. Organized extended day care outside the home by someone other than the mother was considered an unfortunate consequence of poverty or national mobilization in wartime.[68]

In the last decade, the view that outside child care is undesirable has been increasingly attacked — probably out of necessity. There has been a significant rise in the percentage of the labor force composed of women with children who work outside the home. As their numbers increase, filling their need for child care seems more reasonable. The statistics are impressive:[69]

> In March 1971, the labor force participation rate of married women, husband present, with children less than six years old was 30 percent.[1] In the same survey month, the labor force participation rates for divorced or separated women with children under six were even higher, 62 percent and 41 percent respectively.[2] The labor force participation rate for mothers with pre-school children has increased by

---

68. Until the 1960s and 1970s, the only occasions in which the political scene featured a concern over day care were during the Depression and during World War II. Even at the height of wartime day care efforts, however, programs were inadequate to the need. Chafe reports one journalist's estimate "that out of 662 war areas needing child-care facilities in the summer of 1943 only sixty-six had operating programs." He continues:

"As of February 2, 1944, some 65, 717 children were enrolled in federally supported facilities, and at the height of its effectiveness in the spring of 1945, the Lanham Act offered assistance to only 100,000. From one point of view, the figures represented significant progress. . . . On the other hand, the number of children receiving supervision in federal centers represented less than 10 percent of those needing it, and only one-third of the number cared for in Great Britain, a country with less than half the population of the United States." Chafe, The American Woman 170 (1972).

For a fascinating discussion of the political struggles about the nature and scope of the government's wartime and postwar role in the provision of day care and its relation to the economic position of women, see id. at 161-173 and 186-87.

69. Strober, Some Thoughts on the Economics of Child Care Centers, Research Paper No. 143, Graduate School of Business, Stanford University, March 1973, p. 1.

1. Elizabeth Waldman and Kathryn R. Gover, "Marital and Family Characteristics of the Labor Force," Monthly Labor Review, April 1972, p. 7.

2. Ibid.

ten percentage points since 1960.[3] It has been the most rapidly rising labor force participation rate during the past decade.[4] Overall, in March 1971, 10 per cent of the female labor force, 3.2. million women, had pre-school children.[5] Or, looking at it from the children's standpoint, in March 1970, 5.8 million children under six had working mothers.[6]

Another reason for the growing interest in extra-family child care has been the national debate generated by the women's movement about the desirability of traditional sex roles. In particular, feminints have questioned the benefits to children, and highlighted the costs to women, of full-time motherhood. Increasing numbers of women have agreed.[70] A third factor was the realization that poverty can permanently cripple children at an early age. Institutionalized access to poor children would allow the government or other agencies to reach mental and physical defects or developmental retardation. The idea of using child care programs to better meet the needs of poor children was reinforced by information about the inadequacy of the arrangements that working mothers were making for the care of their children. Strober described the situation as follows.

STROBER, SOME THOUGHTS ON THE ECONOMICS OF CHILD CARE CENTERS
Research Paper No. 143, Graduate School of Business, Stanford University, March 1973, 7-8

In the present system of child care arrangements of working mothers, child care centers play a very small role. According to the 1970 Westinghouse study, child care centers provide care for only 10.5 percent of the pre-school children of working mothers.[31] Family day care homes provide 19 percent of the care. The bulk of the care, however, (50 percent) is provided in the child's own home; 18.4 percent by the father, 18.9 percent by other relatives, 7.3 percent by a nonrelative and 5.2 percent by mother during nonschool hours. Five percent of all children under age six have no special arrangements made for their care. Some of these children spend the day at their mother's work place; others are simply latch-key children who look after themselves.[32]

Dissatisfaction with present arrangements is documented in the nonscientific but poignant testimony provided by the National Council of Jewish Women study. We read of mothers and fathers who work at night and try, during the day, to simultaneously

3. See U.S. Dept. of Labor, Women's Bureau, Handbook on Women Workers, U.S. Govt. Printing Office, Washington D.C., 1969, p. 41.

4. Ibid.

5. Ibid., calculated from figures in Table 1, p. 5 and p. 7.

6. Elizabeth Waldman and Kathryn R. Gover, "Children of Women in the Labor Force," Monthly Labor Review, July 1971, p. 24.

70. In its April 1972 issue, Redbook magazine published a six-page questionnaire on attitudes toward women's liberation. More than 120,000 completed questionnaires were returned, out of which 2500 were selected on a random basis for analysis: 73.9 percent of all respondents agreed with the statement that "Raising a child provides many rewards, but as a full-time job it cannot keep most women satisfied"; 65.1 percent agreed that "The housewife/mother role does not really provide women with enough opportunity for self-fulfillment"; 35.6 percent thought it was great that a mother of two small children had an arrangement whereby she worked full time at a job she enjoyed and left her children in a day care center run by trained teachers of whom she approved. However, only 21.2 percent disagreed with the statement that "Little children need full-time mothers." Tavris and Jayaraine, How Do You Feel About Being a Woman? The Results of a Redbook Questionnaire, reprinted from Redbook, January 1973, questions 22, 25, 30, 33.

31. Westinghouse [Learning Corporation and Westat Research, Inc. Day Care Survey, 1970 (1971); excerpts from Survey reprinted in Committee on Finance, U.S. Senate, Child Care Data and Materials, June 1971, p. 89] pp. 175, 178-180. This figure is, however, almost double the 5.6 percent figure for 1965. See Seth Low and Pearl G. Spindler, Child Care Arrangements of Working Mothers in the United States, U.S. Govt. Printing Office, Washington, D.C., 1968.

32. Ibid.

sleep and provide care. We read of older brothers and sisters who rotate their days of school attendance to provide babysitting for younger siblings. We find that children are sometimes left with certain neighbors or babysitters even though mothers know that these arrangements are physically harmful to their children. And we note that mothers of sick children must miss work or leave ill children alone in order to provide necessary income. . . .

It would appear . . . that dissatisfaction [with present child care arrangements] is warranted. The Council Study rated 35 percent of all proprietary centers as "fair" in the sense of meeting basic physical needs but having very little, if any, developmental services; 50 percent of these centers, rated "poor," didn't even do that much. Fifty percent of family care homes were rated "fair"; 11 percent were "poor." Nonprofit centers, while providing more superior care than other arrangements, were still rated "fair" in 50 percent and "poor" in 10 percent of the cases.[34]

2. Federal Child Care Legislation

The three factors discussed above have brought about a "day care movement" supported by feminists, unions, and civil rights, church, and professional groups seeking federal support for day care. In 1971, these forces finally succeeded in winning passage of a comprehensive day care bill. Key provisions were the consolidation of child care funding and services in the Department of Health, Education and Welfare and the Aid to Families with Dependent Children program. The legislation developed models for community and parent participation, and included funding of two billion dollars with significant increases planned for subsequent years;[71] it was vetoed by President Nixon, with a message which revealed the federal administration as still deeply committed to the traditional family with its concomitant sex role division of tasks.

MESSAGE OF THE PRESIDENT VETOING THE
ECONOMIC OPPORTUNITY AMENDMENTS OF 1971
(S. 2007), *Weekly Compilation of Presidential Documents*
1635, Dec. 9, 1971

. . . [T]he most deeply flawed provision of this legislation is Title V, "Child Development Programs."

Adopted as an amendment to the OEO legislation, this program points far beyond what this Administration envisioned when it made a "national commitment to providing all American children an opportunity for a healthful and stimulating development during the first five years of life."

Flaws in Child Care Plans

Though Title V's stated purpose, "to provide for every child a full and fair opportunity to reach his full potential" is certainly laudable, the intent of Title V is overshadowed by the fiscal irresponsibility, administrative unworkability, and family-weakening implications of the system it envisions. We owe our children something more than good intentions.

Specifically, these are my present objections to the proposed child development program:

First, neither the immediate need nor the desirability of a national child development program of this character has been demonstrated.

---

34. Keyserling [Windows on Day Care, National Council of Jewish Women, New York, 1972], p. 5.
71. The Comprehensive Child Development Act of 1971, adopted by Congress as part of the Economic Opportunity Amendments of 1971, S. 2007, H.R. 10351, 92d Cong., 1st Sess. (1971). Many of the provisions of the 1971 legislation were incorporated in the Comprehensive Headstart, Child Development, and Family Services Act of 1972, discussed infra.

Second, day-care centers to provide for the children of the poor so that their parents can leave the welfare rolls to go on the payrolls of the nation, are already provided in H.R. 1, my work fare legislation. To some degree, child development centers are a duplication of these efforts. Further, these child development programs would be redundant in that they duplicate many existing and growing Federal, state and local efforts to provide social, medical, nutritional and education services to the very young.

Third, given the limited resources of the Federal budget, and the growing demands upon the Federal taxpayer, the expenditure of $2 billion in a program whose effectiveness has yet to be demonstrated cannot be justified. And the prospect of costs which could eventually reach $20 billion annually is even more unreasonable.

Family Goal in Jeopardy

Fourth, for more than two years this Administration has been working for the enactment of welfare reform, one of the objectives of which is to bring the family together. This child development program appears to move in precisely the opposite direction.

Fifth, all other factors being equal, good public policy requires that we enhance rather than diminish both parental authority and parental involvement with children — particularly in those decisive early years when social attitudes and a conscience are formed and religious and moral principles are first inculcated.

Sixth, there has yet to be an adequate answer provided to the crucial question of who the qualified people are, and where they would come from, to staff the child development centers.

Seventh, as currently written, the legislation would create, ex nihilo, a new army of bureaucrats.

Eighth, the states would be relegated to an insignificant role.

Ninth, for the Federal Government to plunge headlong financially into supporting child development would commit the vast moral authority of the National Government to the side of communal approaches to child rearing over against the family-centered approach.

This President, this Government, is unwilling to take that step.[72]

A new version of the vetoed bill, titled the Comprehensive Headstart, Child Development, and Family Services Act (S. 3617), was introduced but defeated in 1972. The general design of the new bill was for a national office of child development (located in the Department of Health, Education and Welfare) which would make grants to both states and other public and private nonprofit organizations and entities which submitted plans for child development centers. The legislation required that the plans "shall set

----

72. The emotion surrounding the daycare issue is further illustrated by the remarks of some congressmen and senators in the debate over the 1971 Child Development Act. This section of the legislation was by far the most heatedly and lengthily debated.

"Have American parents forgotten their primary responsibility? Dogs spend time with their puppies, lionesses teach their cubs how to survive. . . . Yet, there are some who are only too willing to send our young away from us before they know what it is to be human. . . .

"Children should grow up with their mothers — not with a series of caretakers and nurses' aides. . . ." (Senator Carl T. Curtis (R. Neb.) 117 Cong. Rec. 44138, 44139, Dec. 2, 1971.)

". . . Communist Russia and Socialist nations have long had such programs. So long, in fact, that experience with such programs in Communist Russia has occasioned serious second thoughts on the ultimate value of such programs because of their admitted tendency to undermine the family as the basic unit of society. . . .

". . . The idea that the taxpayers of the Nation should be made to bear the cost of conditioning our children to respond like robots to programmed behavior patterns is intolerable to think about. Such programs, however, are implicit in the term "comprehensive child development.," (Senator James B. Allen (D. Ala.) 117 Cong. Rec. 44135, 44136, Dec. 2, 1971.) — Eds.

forth a comprehensive program for providing child care services" which should meet more than twenty requirements, among them that a plan:

(1) provides that programs or services under this title shall be provided only for children whose parents or legal guardians request them;
(8) provides that to the extent feasible each program within the prime sponsorship area will include children from a range of socioeconomic backgrounds;
(12) provides for direct parent participation in the conduct, overall direction, and evaluation of programs;
(13) includes to the extent feasible a career development plan for paraprofessional and professional training, education, and advancement on a career ladder.

The design of the bill also provided for governance of the day care centers by councils, at least 50 percent of whose members would be parents of the children in the program.

The most important differences from the 1971 Act included paring down the costs and decreasing the numbers and types of agencies and organizations eligible for grants, as well as making it clear that the only children eligible for full-time day care were those whose parents were out of the home full time. Different versions of day care bills vary as to financial eligibility for the programs, although all emphasize that the bulk of the funds are to be spent for economically disadvantaged families.[73]

A major source of controversy has been whether the centers should be open to middle-class people. President Nixon's bill, H.R. 1, would have essentially limited day care to those on welfare or the very poor. Many congressional liberals wanted to give priority to the poor on the ground that their needs were more pressing than those of lower-middle or middle-income women. (Of course, women who are called "middle-income" are usually so only on the basis of their husband's earnings; their own incomes would qualify many of them as poor people.) Yet restricting day care to the poor assumes that most middle-income women either want to stay home, ought to stay home, or have no difficulty finding day care services at prices they can afford.

Another important issue, from a feminist perspective, is raised by the provision limiting full-day day care to those children whose parents are both employed full-time. This is another way of limiting options for women (and men who decide to take responsibility for child care) by denying them the chance to mix child raising with outside activities. This limitation has an impact on both the present and the future employment opportunities of a parent with primary responsibility for child care, since outside activities one or two days a week could lead to a better outside job once the children are in school all day.

3. Toward New Arrangements for Childrearing

CENTER FOR THE STUDY OF PUBLIC POLICY
AN IMPACT STUDY OF DAY CARE
Grant CG 1081, on contract from the Office of Economic Opportunity, 173-181 (1971)

. . . Current critiques of child care arrangements come from three major groups: child development experts, womens' rights groups, and political groups on both left and right who want to help people get off welfare. This section considers each of these three critiques of the status quo; the following section will present what alternatives they seem to imply.

73. A definition of "economically disadvantaged" by the Bureau of Labor Statistics is an urban family of four or more with an income of $6,900 or less.

CHILD DEVELOPMENT PERSPECTIVE

Recent research and findings of child psychologists and educators in early child-hood development have consistently suggested that the earliest years of life are the crucial formative period for a child's physical, cognitive, emotional, and social develop-ment. Environmental conditions during this period such as health, nutrition, and hous-ing, exposure to new experiences and new people, warm and secure relationships with adults, are all extremely important in fostering learning potential, self-confidence and identity, and social skills.

This emphasis has led to a closer look at the environments in which children are presently being raised. . . . [m] any . . . [of which have been found to be] developmentally inadequate and far too many are physically unsafe. . . .

It can also be said that many family situations seem to be developmentally inade-quate, even when a parent is home all day and can supervise the child. Parental indiffer-ence, ineptitude, or even cruelty toward children is often cited; it has been suggested that some of these parents might use child care facilities, to the benefit of their children, were they available.

The idea that child care may have benefits for *all* children is relatively new. Many people have feared that the separation of mother and child can be detrimental to a child's security, and have argued that separation should occur only under extreme circum-stances. The emotional deprivation observed in children in orphanages and foster homes has often been attributed to the fact of separation from the real mother rather than to what happens to the child within those settings. Furthermore, the idea of "day care" has often been seen as a service for poor families where mothers must work and have no choice but to put their children in the care of others. This viewpoint has often implied that a "good" mother is one who is with her child twenty-four hours a day and that a mother who needs or desires to have outside help is somehow "bad" or inadequate.

Much of the pressure for new child care arrangements comes, then, from those who are concerned about the environments in which children grow up. There is much contro-versy, however, over what should happen to children in these arrangements.

The provision of physical and emotional security is least problematic. A good child care facility can offer safe and attractive surroundings with adults who are sensitive to children. Many children from low-income areas lack sufficient attention to their nutri-tional and medical needs; a child care facility is an ideal setting for providing for these needs.

Students of cognitive and social growth in young children go further to suggest that pre-school programs of certain types, in fact, enhance the development of children and that child care could be used as an opportunity to make up for developmental deficien-cies in the home. Lower-class children seem to benefit from early attention to the development of cognitive and learning skills; such pre-school programs might help reduce class differences in readiness for school. This hypothesis would imply that a pre-school component should be included in all child care centers. A center should have specially trained teachers and a curriculum aimed at the development of competence in specific cognitive, social, and emotional skills.

There is considerable disagreement, however, over whether pre-school programs actually work, and if so, which kinds (e.g., traditional nursery school, Montessori, Bereiter-Englemann, etc.) work best. Certain programs seem to affect certain kinds of children in positive ways. There is some evidence, for example, that lower-class children improve their language proficiency in highly structured, cognitive programs. This evi-dence does not necessarily imply that such programs ought to be incorporated into a child care system. The research indicates that some children benefit from some programs, but it cannot yet identify exactly what is causing the result. Long-term effects of these programs have not been verified. And even if we had this information, there is a real question as to what the goals of child care should be; it is quite possible that a successful cognitive program might, in fact, be inapporpriate for young children in terms of their overall development, and that programs stressing social and emotional growth would produce greater benefits in the long run. Given this uncertainty, it would not make sense to require that child care arrangements include any specific pre-school curricula.

When proponents of federally subsidized child care argue that subsidies would improve the environments in which most poor children grow up, the argument is usually based on observation of a small number of high quality child care centers with many pre-school components, highly trained, carefully selected staff, ample budget, and a generally appealing atmosphere. These centers are then contrasted to the oppressive conditions which prevail in the most disorganized low-income families, and especially in families where the mother works and a variety of ad hoc arrangements have to be made for looking after the children. Such a comparison inevitably suggests that children in bad family situations would be better off in good child care centers, and that if federal subsidies helped move them into such centers, the next generation would have been well served.

The flaw in this line of reasoning is that although child care centers with good programs may be better than the worst families, it does not follow that all, or even most, child care centers would be better for children than most parents. Massive federal subsidies would mean a rapid increase in the child care arrangements, but not necessarily a similar increase in quality over what now exists. Indeed, it would probably be hard to ensure any real attention to child development in all centers. And even if we could guarantee the quality of all child care arrangements, we still would not know whether child care was most appropriate for any particular child or family. Yet, subsidies would increase the economic incentives to the more responsible parents to place their children in a child care facility and find jobs, rather than taking care of their own children. There is no reason to suppose that under these circumstances the child would be better off. He [or she] might well be worse off.

Indeed, if one's objective were to improve the quality of the environment of low-income children, it might well make sense to try to encourage fewer mothers to work, rather than more. Mothers who work often do so out of economic necessity and their children are often harmed by the inadequate arrangements which are available. These children would be better off if they were placed in an institutional child care facility. But they might also be better off if their parents were paid enough for looking after them, and no longer had to neglect the children in order to take jobs the parents might not want.

Hence, from the standpoint of child development, persuasive arguments can be made for supporting mothers directly and allowing them to take more adequate care of their own children. These arguments can be summarized as follows:

1. Although it is clearly true that some mothers now need child care services and that some existing arrangements are harmful to children, the appropriate solution is not necessarily to institute a new and expensive system to provide quality care outside the home exclusively. Rather, the best answer may be to make available enough money and enough guidance to enable mothers to choose to take care of their own children if they wish. Many might prefer to do so if they could afford it, and many might do a better job with their own particular children than a child care staff could do.

2. Americans, rich or poor, do not need or want to have the government decide what is good for them or their children. They want the resources to be able to conduct their own lives and assist in the growth of their children. Poor parents want this freedom for precisely the same reasons that middle-class parents want it. If parents choose to raise their own children on a full-time basis, this choice should be available as an economically sensible alternative.

On the other hand, the arguments for an expanded and improved child care program are compelling:

1. To the extent that existing arrangements both in the home and away from it are

harmful to chidren, alternative settings, which are safe and developmentally adequate, should be available.

2. Child care arrangements can ensure that proper attention is paid to medical and nutritional needs and can provide an enriched environment through peer group relations and pre-school programs not usually available in the home.

The pros and cons of this controversy are complex. The essential question is whether it makes more sense for the federal government to assist American families, especially poor families, by providing improved supplemental services outside the home, by shoring up the family directly, or with some balance of both. Careful examination of the research findings shows them inconclusive on this point. In the absence of clear evidence, making any a priori decision seems unreasonable. Instead, parents should be free to choose what they themselves prefer. If child care were a paid job, and if various types of child care were also available outside the home, parents could decide for themselves over time whether they were more satisfied working outside the home and entrusting their children to a trained staff, or whether they preferred to be full-time caretakers for their own children.

WOMEN'S RIGHTS PERSPECTIVE

Strong pressure for governmental subsidies for child care has come from groups concerned with the status of women. In general, the argument is that women will have equal opportunities in education and employment only when care for children outside the home is both widely available and recognized by society as legitimate.

The specific arguments made by women's groups vary greatly and reflect different attitudes toward the relative responsibilities of mothers, parents, and the society for raising children. Some groups argue that the state ought to take complete responsibility for child care and establish twenty-four-hour-a-day children's houses on the model of the Israeli kibbutzim. Others argue that the state ought to exert pressure for more equal division of responsibility between parents, perhaps by encouraging a twenty-hour work week so that both parents have the option of holding a job and raising their children. Still others would leave the primary responsibility for child-rearing in the family, to be divided as the parents desired, but would ask the state to make alternative arrangements available. Common to all positions, however, is a desire for state-subsidized child care of sufficient legitimacy and quality that mothers have a real choice of careers.

It is not evident whether more opportunities for women will be generated through putting money into the provision of services outside the home or through allocating funds in direct support of full-time parenthood. It could be argued that women should have free, nearby care available at all times in order to allow them to take jobs outside the home. It can also be argued that child care by the parent in the home is as much a job as any other, and that a system of full-time child care which excludes parental care provides disincentives for mothers to stay home with their children, the job they might really prefer. Many women, especially women who prefer caring for their own children to any other job, would see such a child care system as a further degradation of their status rather than an enhancement of it.

In conclusion, then, it is not clear whether the road to equal rights for women involves getting more women into jobs outside the home, or providing more monetary rewards and status for staying home, or both. It seems best therefore for this decision to be left to mothers themselves by providing both options. Arrangements should be such that a mother could, with equal economic and status advantage, make arrangements for care of her child outside the home or care for the child herself. In this way, all modes of womanhood and motherhood would be equally possible, and a woman's relationship to her family and her children would be more a matter of choice.

ECONOMIC PERSPECTIVE

Many of those who advocate federal subsidies for child care anticipate that such subsidies will help reduce the welfare rolls. Some hope for this development because they want to cut overall public expenditures. Others feel that public expenditures are essential if the families in question are to maintain an adequate standard of living, but that these expenditures should take a form which allows the recipients more dignity and discourages the kinds of dependency and passivity which welfare often fosters among recipients.

The issue of whether it will be cheaper to provide child care rather than welfare is difficult to resolve, given our present state of knowledge. There are some families, especially those with only one child, in which the provision of heavily subsidized or free child care would enable the mother to get a job and in which the job would pay enough for the family to escape from dependency on welfare. Such employment would not necessarily lower overall public spending, however. Most of these families would still not be able to afford to pay anything more than a nominal fee for the child care services they would continue to need in order to keep their jobs, and thus, the need for subsidized child care would remain. Large-scale, federally funded child care programs would almost inevitably have to meet "quality" requirements and therefore be likely to cost at least $2000 per year per pre-school child, and perhaps as much as $1000 per year per primary school child. The overall cost of child care for many families in many states would thus exceed the current cost of welfare.

Furthermore, unskilled women are unlikely to earn more than $4000 per year in the labor force. This low wage means that many unskilled mothers would be earning less than would be spent on child care for their children. Public spending could be kept lower by paying these mothers a competitive wage to care for their own children at home than by providing expensive care outside the home.

On the other hand, subsidized child care services may prove to be less expensive than welfare in the very long run. Child care allows mothers the time to gain education, training, and work experience. Presumably, such preparation and experience will enable them to get higher paying jobs, the benefits of which will continue long after their children no longer need child care. The possible benefits of child care in addition to growing up in a family which has escaped welfare may affect children's ability to perform well in school, and thus increase opportunities in their adult life. If so, child care may contribute positively to breaking the poverty cycle, and public spending may thereby eventually be reduced.

In any case, child care cannot be considered as a simple substitute for welfare; if jobs are not available for those who would prefer to work, a family is far worse off without welfare than with it, even if it has access to child care.

The argument that child care subsidies are better for the recipients than welfare subsidies is more plausible than the argument that child care is cheaper than welfare. But here too the case is hardly unequivocal. If a woman prefers working to caring for children, and if she can get a decently paid job, it is no doubt better to enable her to work. She may get more money; she may get more satisfaction; and her children may be better taken care of. On the other hand, the jobs available to untrained, unskilled women are limited, the wages are likely to be low, and the work is likely to be routine, disagreeable, and often psychologically debilitating. It is hard to believe that all parents would prefer such jobs to taking care of their own children, or would gain more dignity and self-reliance from them. Furthermore, the opportunities for education and training, let alone the availability of any job, skilled or unskilled, are limited, and some women may have no choice but not to work.

In psychological terms, the effect of federal subsidies for approved child care but not for parents' taking care of their own children could be somewhat perverse. One can imagine situations in which educated mothers from the suburbs leave their children each morning to commute to the central city, where they hold professional jobs at professional wages, running child care centers for the poor. Meanwhile, the uneducated mothers of these children, having dropped the children at a professionally managed child care center, commute to the suburbs, where they have badly paid domestic jobs in the homes of the professional women who run child care centers. Whether this kind of arrangement makes economic or psychological sense is open to serious question.

In general, people prefer to earn their own way by holding a job. But taking care of children is work by any normal standard and ought to be considered a job in which a parent can take pride like any other. The option of paying parents might be a step towards rescuing the role of "parent" as a respectable and useful one in modern America. Given all the factors which must be considered in order to determine the best solution for any particular family, it seems most appropriate to make available both the options of child care and parent payment, and let the individual family choose for itself.

DIVERSITY OF CHILD CARE ARRANGEMENTS

The lines of argument presented above lead to the conclusion that the ideal system of federal subsidies for child care would give parents a choice between taking a job caring for their own children and taking some other job while their children were cared for by others. Such a system provides poor parents with alternative forms of supplementary income and might in the long run be a more effective and efficient way of attacking the poverty cycle than either institutional day care or income transfers alone.

BOURNE, WHAT DAY CARE OUGHT TO BE
The New Republic, Feb. 2, 1972, pp. 18, 19-23

[DAY CARE]

Day care has been, and still is, primarily the bailiwick of the social welfare profession. Licensing of private day nurseries is generally done by departments of social welfare (though this varies from state to state); family day care homes are "caseloads" and the most significant federal support for day care comes from social security legislation administered by welfare departments. Virtually all federal support for day care has been explicitly for, and limited to, welfare or near-welfare children.

The backbone of the official day care services system is the licensed family day-care home. (The backbone of the "real" day care system is, by the way, the *unlicensed* family day care home and the babysitter — often grandmother or sister-in-law.) Care for 50 percent or more of the children whose parents work is by unofficial (i.e., unlicensed) arrangements.

A family day care home is simply a situation where a woman (usually a mother) cares for a few children in her own home. Licensing procedures generally set limits on the number of children she may accommodate and set standards for the physical condition and characteristics of the house in hopes of ensuring the health and safety of the children. Licensing is theoretically contingent upon an acceptable rating by the social worker of the woman's emotional and intellectual suitability for the task of nurturing and caring for young children.

Family day care homes vary widely in type and quality of care provided. Many writers' favorite day care horror story is of a day care home with children tied to beds. Less frequently recounted are the instances of first-rate mini-nursery schools in an atmosphere of affection and freshly baked cookies. Day care homes often care for children during hours that no group program would contemplate — the split shift is a reality with which it is difficult for group programs to come to terms.

Private day nurseries, run for profit, and licensed (or not), are also a long-standing day care tradition. As with day care homes, licensing standards have related primarily to the adequacy of physical facilities and some minimum staff-child ratio of 1-to-10 or-12. The service provided is basically babysitting, whether you are poor and receiving care courtesy of the welfare department, or whether you are paying yourself.

Federal involvement in day care began during the Depression as part of WPA. But the first significant full-day group care program was created by the Lanham Act in 1941 to provide care for the children of mothers who were desperately needed in the war economy. This program was implemented with astonishing speed (and mixed results) and dismantled just as quickly when the war ended. Continuation of these programs was contingent upon state willingness to assume responsibility — California was the one state to do so and its Children's Centers programs, operated by school districts, and paid for by state funds and sliding-scale parent fees, now make it unique in extent and quality of day care services.

The primary source of federal support for day care has been Title 4A of the Social Security Act, as amended in 1967. Under the AFDC Section, state welfare departments are enabled to provide day care benefits to every AFDC family and to those judged as past and potential recipients. These funds are disbursed on a three-to-one local matching-share basis; thus their use is contingent upon the willingness of state, county, city or some private source to provide one-quarter of the costs. Welfare agencies may use these funds to pay present providers (e.g., licensed family day care homes and day nurseries) or may contract with a private non-profit group to provide new services.

The second piece of Title 4A is the Work Incentive Program (WIN); it allows payment, again on a three-to-one matching basis, for day care services when the mother is enrolled in a WIN training program. This program makes no provision for expansion of services, it just pays for what is already there *if* you are lucky enough to find it. As soon as the mother has finished her training, WIN day care support ceases.

Title 4B of the Social Security Act, as amended, 1967, provides something called child welfare services. Grants are made to state welfare departments to provide services to children regardless of financial status. This program expended only $1.5 million in 1970 (as contrasted to $94 million under Title 4A, AFDC), and even some knowledgeable welfare department day care specialists have not heard of it.

The Economic Opportunity Act (1964) provides money for day care through two programs: the Concentrated Employment program, which authorizes day care funds in conjunction with manpower training programs administered by local community action agencies, and the Migrant Children program.

In addition, a wide variety of federal legislation includes a day care clause —that is, funds *may* be used for day care services, for planning, for facilities, for staff training and so on. Usually funds, which *may* be used for day care, are used instead in one of the many other allowable ways, but some programs such as Model Cities have begun to make a substantial contribution to new day care services. Because federal funding operates on a kind of "find me if you can" philosophy, the ferreting out of these many hidden sources of support has been limited to those few communities and groups who are highly skilled in the ways of grantsmanship.

In looking back over this brief review of federal participation in the support of day care services, three points stand out: 1) the federal government has gone to some pains to stay out of the business or *providing* day care services; they will *pay for services* that are provided by a local public agency or a nonprofit group. Funds are circuitously routed via state and county agencies (and are contingent upon their commitment to pay a share) to make sure that there is no such thing as what Governor Reagan has called "federal kindergartens." 2) Funding is, with the one exception of an almost invisible program, explicitly for and limited to the welfare or near-welfare population. 3) Funds for day care for the poor are almost always contingent upon participation in the labor force or some training program in preparation for participation in the labor force. Federal participation in day care has been explicitly and almost solely linked to programs designed to limit the welfare rolls.

There is one irony in this chronicle of federal participation: in order for any provider of services to receive federal funds, he must meet what are called the Federal Interagency Guidelines. The irony is that the bureaucrats assigned the task of setting these standards came up with a requirement of a staff/child ratio of one-to-five (as opposed to the 1-to-10 or -12 usual in state-licensed custodial programs), and they require an educational, nutritional and parent-participation component among others. Programs that meet the government's own standards, then, cross dangerously over the line into child-rearing as defined by President Nixon. And, as we shall see, programs that meet the government's standards are costly.

[NURSERY SCHOOLS]

The nursery school movement has stressed the importance of the early years, not so much as a time for learning (learning to read before the first grade was seen as an evil that inhibited the child's proper experience of childhood), but as a time for critical emotional development. Children needed to learn to play with their peers, to cooperate, to tolerate those restrictions on their freedom arising from their membership in a community. They needed to learn to relate to adults other than their parents, to be provided with alternative role models and to be provided with a variety of experiences essential to emotional and cognitive development. Nursery schools were not about education; they were about child development.

Public support for nursery schools has been only through state university programs where the nursery school is operated as a laboratory for teacher training. Fees in these schools are usually far below actual cost and sometimes an effort is made to grant scholarships in order to obtain a socioeconomic mix. But by and large the values associated with the nursery school have been held by, and been limited to, the middle class.

[COMPENSATORY EDUCATION]

Only recently have the education and learning theorists captured the middle-class imagination. Again, ability to pay limits such experiences to middle- and upper-class children. There is an irony to these expensive preschool learning centers — they developed in emulation (albeit grossly misinterpreted emulation) of a public program for the poor.

In 1964, as part of the War on Poverty, a bright-eyed hope-filled new program was begun called Head Start. Putting down Head Start as misguided boondoggle is now chic with both the right and the left. Its payoffs in terms of its stated goals have certainly not been proven — nor disproven. But the influence of Head Start is undeniable. A program of compensatory education for "culturally disadvantaged" children, it was part and parcel of an attempt at basic social reform. Head Start was premised on success in the educational system as the key to social mobility of the poor and was seen by its creators as one essential piece of a *many-faceted* strategy to break the locked-in class structure of American society.

Interestingly enough, its creators and early administrators were rarely educators, but rather psychologists, psychiatrists and physicians. Like the nursery school movement, the thrust of Head Start was child development. The key to achievement in school was not seen to be so much a matter of giving children a literal "head start" in learning to read, but rather a catching up on what middle-class children had learned at home. The middle-class child's advantage was seen as being a matter of the "coping" skills he had acquired.

Originally comprising summer programs, then full-year, half-day and now often full-year, full-day programs, Head Start was endowed with the best the academic research establishment in a hopeful era could muster. But the latest in learning theories, in motor and cognitive skill development techniques, in educational games and toys were just part of the picture. A staff-child ratio of at least one-to-five was essential. The children were to be given nourishing meals, dental care, eye checks, screenings for early detection of physical or psychological handicaps. A salient part of the program was the involvement of parents — both in setting policy for their community's center and in the classroom. This effort to pull the community and home environment into a reciprocal link with the "school" was deemed essential, but its implementation was also largely uncharted waters and was thus one of the most vulnerable components of the program. (Another OEO program confronts this issue even more directly. Parent Child Centers serve children from before birth to about age three. Mothers are expected to be with their children most of the time and are given instruction in child-rearing while caring for their children.)

Head Start, with its high visibility, high costs and high pretentions, has inevitably come in for criticism from every direction. Money-savers met the Westinghouse evaluation study (which showed, by their criteria, the "head start" fading out by the second or third grade) with glee. Liberals met the same findings with despondency. It is not uncommon for Americans to substitute educational reform for basic social reform and then to castigate the schools for having been unable to reform the nation's social class structure.

The groups for whom Head Start was created have also criticized it, though for the most part continuing to participate and take pride in it. Their complaint that Head Start's "compensatory" ideology, based on a theory of "cultural deprivation," was patronizing, unfair and counter-productive has largely been accepted by even those who designed the program. Their plea that Head Start *must* be run by those participating is an increasing imperative. Concerns about participation have centered around Head Start much more than around the custodial day care services to which the poor have usually been treated. Like it or not, Head Start has guts — highly controversial programs usually do. Head Start's guts lie in the degree to which it may supplant parental child-rearing responsibility. The recipients are right to be vehemently concerned that they maintain effective control of such a program. Their response, as opposed to President Nixon's, is not to avoid the problem with custodial care, but rather to struggle for ways of shaping and controlling high-quality educational and developmental programs so that they conform to their own child-rearing values.

[ANALYSIS]

We have seen that day care really means: 1) *care and protection of children while their parents work.* This tradition of day care has steadfastly avoided anything which will *appear* to be a usurpation of the family's child-rearing role. 2) *Nursery school in full-day form.* Here child-rearing functions are also carefully not usurped. It is a complement to and extension of the family environment. Nursery schools are often of the cooperative genre with the mother participating at least one morning a week and perhaps even taking classes in child development. 3) *Compensatory education.* Here we are not raising the child *for* the parents, but *making up* for what is seen as inadequate parental child-rearing. Some effort as in Head Start and especially in Parent Child Centers is made to educate the parents in the ways of child-rearing.

There are a number of programs around the country which effectively combine care and protection, child development and education. Though often growing out of the compensatory education tradition, these programs do not think of themselves as appropriate only to the poor, but rather to early childhood education for all children. The education profession has taken charge of this new definition of child care, but the education profession is no more acceptable a purveyor of day care services to many groups than is the welfare profession. Child development skills are hardly one of the fortes of our school system, and our schools have been notoriously disconnected from and unresponsive to the child's family environment.

When one reads over what has been written about day care since it became a popular topic, one begins to get some feel that we are coming to a rough consensus about what day care ought to be. It should of course care for and protect our children; it should connect the child's worlds of home and day care; it should provide an environment that fosters his development of a sense of self, self-worth and security, and his ability to get what he wants and needs from the environment around him; and one which stimulates and develops his cognitive and sensory abilities. But when we take a closer look, we are not at all close to an agreement on what day care ought to be. The disagreement is wide on what *kind* of child care we want and on how much we are willing to spend for it.

States-righters on the right and decentralists on the left don't want the federal government to take charge of day care because that would destroy local autonomy. John Birchers on the right and radicals on the left don't want the public sector at any level to have anything to do with it because it would be an usurpation of individual freedom. Some groups on the right want the state to take over child-rearing functions for the poor in order to create a well-behaved lower class; some groups on the left think it is the state's responsibility to provide free child-rearing institutions for everyone who wants them.

Some minority groups want a way into the system and say the state must provide institutions that will facilitate this; others don't want any middle-class establishment inculcating values into their kids. Some want their young children to play and explore freely in their preschool years; others want their children to sit up straight and learn to read early.

The diversity of views could be spun out almost indefinitely. There is only one common denominator: care for the children of working mothers. Beyond that there is no possibility of agreeing on a definition. The common denominator is the lowest common denominator. The coalition that has formed around day care is really a coalition based on the needs of women in the labor force, *not* a coalition based on the needs of young children. — The second point on which there is a seeming consensus but, in fact, a wide disagreement, is on the amount of money we are willing to invest in care for children. Let us take a very rough look at day care costs, with school systems as a reference point.

An extravagant school district like Berkeley, California, spends about $1400 per year per child. The national average is more like $800. The *cheapest* custodial day care in California costs $1200 per year per child. As with schools, the costs are in the teachers. The $1200 day nursery figure pays for a program which employs an adult (usually an untrained one) for every 10 or 12 children. Federal Interagency Guidelines, mentioned earlier, require one adult for every five children; all instructors must have academic degrees. Israeli programs operate on a one-to-four ratio. An OEO funded study of "exemplary" day care programs and systems around the country shows that those which maintain a one-to-five adult/child *contact-hour ratio* and which have first-rate educational developmental, health and parent involvement components are costing between $2500 and $3500 per year per child.

The major emphasis of federal legislation and administration proposals as of this writing is on enabling welfare women to work — or to make sure they have no excuses not to. An AFDC grant in San Francisco for a woman with two children (not including food stamps and medical coverage) is about $2400 per year. The cheapest child care for her two children would be $1200 each. Perhaps the administration hopes to be able to benefit the poor by paying for excellent child care rather than welfare support on the theory that the public will more willingly pay for quality child care than they will for feckless women. Perhaps. Or perhaps there are ways of cutting the costs of child care. There are. Schools have an adult-child contact-hour ratio of one-to-30 or-40. The middle class would, of course, not stand for such a thing. But they could and would pay if they were confronted with such an alternative.

The most striking thing to emerge from a cursory look at child care costs is the importance which staff/child ratios make. It is difficult to imagine how one adult can even "care-for and protect" more than five children at once, especially five children between the ages, of, say, two and four — unless, of course, we were able to deal with them as we now do with older children in schools. Ask any mother! We might well define "quality" in these terms as a minimum for all styles of day care — custodial, nursery or educational — but we will find that the costs of even custodial care are then up around $2500 per year per child. Now let us look again at the groups that have formed a coalition of sorts around day care and ask whether they would be willing to pay at such a rate.

Will those in favor of getting welfare women out to work be willing to pay $5000 for care for a woman's two children in order to save $2400 on her AFDC grant? Will a woman whose earning power is $6000-8000 be willing to spend $5000 of it for child care in the private market? If she isn't, can the franchisers now entering the business with enthusiasm make a profit? Will industry and labor unions be willing to provide that magnitude of fringe benefit?

The common denominator in the case of costs, then, will very likely again be the lowest common denominator. But there are two choices that fall within an acceptable price range: one is the present low-cost, low-quality custodial system mixed with a few low-profile, high-quality programs like full-day Head Start, like some of the California Children's Centers or some Title 4A programs; the other alternative is an extension of kindergarten, in its present format, to include children from six months to five years old.

It would seem that if we are to have quality day care services in the public *or* private sector — quality even in the most limited sense of a reasonably adequate adult/child ratio — we will have to be willing to assume at least a portion of its costs for all who use it, as yet another public responsibility. I am not optimistic about the possibilities of our doing this, simply because of our long-term national unwillingness to make meaningful investments in future generations. If we are even to find a basis of agreement upon which to do so it seems to me that we must find ways of giving that support in such a way that communities and groups may shape their own services in consonance with their own values and goals for their children. Those groups who argue most fervently that the nuclear family is an anachronistic child-rearing institution would be appalled and outraged if their children were subjected to child-rearing practices that shaped them into compulsively achieving, productive, fiercely competitive adults.

Since we as a nation disapprove of relinquishing responsibility for child-rearing to professionals — if not "disapprove" in some ideological sense, then at least are skeptical and mistrustful of the ability of anybody else to do it as we would like — then perhaps the only kind of child care system that can come into being is one that parents can trust and influence to raise their children as they would like. And if the development of a system which provides real choices and a real diversity of styles of care to the parents of young children is to come about, then we may have to be willing to think of the rearing of children as a task with real economic value and thus be willing to pay a woman or a man $7000 a year to stay home and care for their two preschool children. And if men were mothers — or at least agreed to take a full share in the responsibility for rearing children — my guess is that this country would come to care in a meaningful sense for its future generations much more quickly and happily.

In the long run, then, given some critical value shifts, and given the invention of new mechanisms for disbursing public funds in such a way that effective client control can be combined with some acceptable modicum of public accountability. I can envision the possibilities of a network of quality child care services that would be acceptable.

In the short run, however, I am pessimistic. I feel that neither the public sector *nor* the private individual is, at this point, willing to spend sums on the order of $2500 to $3500 per year per child during the working day — willing, that is, if the issue is drawn solely around the needs of children. I would argue that day care must be placed in the larger context of national priorities in pragmatic American style. We have seen that lawmakers have been willing to pay for child care if it is a means to a valued end, such as getting women off the welfare rolls and into the labor force. Perhaps we must, for the time being, accept these kinds of national priorities and play on them.

One of the current critical deterrents to the expansion of services, for instance, is the unavailability of construction and start-up funds. If we were to create an FHA-style, long-term guaranteed mortgage arrangement, we would provide large-scale capital to day care at very low actual cost to the government and with high appeal to the nation's bankers. We might also embellish on the tax credit and deduction theme. Employers who hire people from the welfare rolls, for instance, might be given tax credits if they pay for day care services for the children of those workers. A day care program might be granted credits on their building mortgages when they take welfare or near-welfare children. And allowed personal income tax deductions for working parents could be extended — most critically to benefit the lower middle class.

Welfare and near-welfare women could be employed as operators of family day care homes if some funds could be found for rehabilitating and equipping their homes and for training and supportive services. Another avenue is the exploitation of adult education funds linking instruction in "child development" with the operation of nursery or day care.

Perhaps most promising would be a linking of national concern over wage stability with day care. When the Scandinavians were faced with the problem of limiting wages in order to maintain a competitive position in the world economy, they substituted social benefits, which generate activity in the economy without inflationary stress, for wage increases. Free or subsidized child care services seen as substitution for wage increases might be politically acceptable.

We might also spend less of our energy pressuring the legislative branch for new appropriations, and more on finding effective mechanisms at the local level for ferreting out and combining existing federal, state and private funds. Techniques for watchdogging the bureaucracies that administer existing funds are also crucially needed; too often their reluctance to produce implementing regulations and their propensity to alter the intent of legislation by the way in which they write these regulations, block, tie-up and limit the use of funds authorized by the legislative branch at all levels of government.

This strategy of piecemeal picking and poking at the present system may strike those who have hoped for a bold and straightforward initiative as incredibly depressing. I would argue simply that a politically acceptable bold initiative at this point in history would have to take such a form that it would be a genuine disservice to the nation's children.

NOTE: FURTHER MATERIALS
WHICH ARGUE FOR AND AGAINST EXTENDED DAY CARE

There is a substantial literature on whether, and how early, day care should be given. One of the best sources is Chandler, Lourie, and Peters, Early Child Care: The New Perspectives, (1968). This book, which has excellent bibliographies, contains theoretical material, as well as four studies of various modes of day care that are or were in operation. Other good sources for consideration of the philosophical, social, and psychiatric arguments for and against early child care are Ruderman, Child Care and the Working Mother, (1968); Mead, Some Theoretical Considerations in the Problem of Mother-Child Separation, 24 Am. J. Orthopsychiatry (1954); Provence, A Guide to the Care of Infants in Groups, (1967); Shakow, Research in Child Development: A Case Illustration of the Psychologist's Dilemma, 29 Am. J. Orthopsychiatry (1959); Women's Bureau, Child Care Arrangements of the Nation's Working Mothers (1965). See also Women's Bureau, Day Care Facts (May 1970); Bettelheim, The Children of the Dream (1969); Sidel, Women and Child Care in China (1972); Evans, Shub, and Weinstein, Day Care: How to Plan, Develop and Operate a Day Care Center (1971); Note, The Proposed Federal Child Care Corporation, 119 U. Pa. L. Rev. 878 (1971); Low and Spindler, Child Care Arrangements of Working Mothers in the United States, Children's Bureau Publication No. 461 (1968); Joint Hearings on the Comprehensive Child Development Act of

1971 Before the Subcommittee on Employment, Manpower and Poverty and the Sub-committee on Children and Youth of the Senate Comm. on Labor and Public Welfare, 92d Cong., 1st Sess. (3 pts. 1971); Hearings on the Comprehensive Child Development Act of 1971 Before Select Subcommittee on Education, House Committee on Education and Labor, 92d Cong., 1st Sess. (1971); S. Rep. No. 92-331 and Conf. Rep. No. 92-682 (On Economic Opportunity Amendments of 1971), 92d Cong., 1st Sess. (1971); Day Care Services: Industry's Involvement, Women's Bureau Bulletin 296 (1971); Keyserling, Windows on Day Care: Report on the Findings of Members of the National Council of Jewish Women on Day Care Needs and Services in Their Communities (1972).

4. Other Government Policies Affecting Day Care

Two government policies, other than the issue of direct funding, affect day care: income tax deductions for the costs of day care; and federal, state, and local regulation of day care centers.

a. Income Tax Provisions

Income tax provisions have a profound impact on day care and day care's correlative effect on the sex role system. Full deductions for child care, for instance, in effect are an indirect subsidy, with the benefits designed primarily for the middle-income couple to whom deductions can make an economic difference. These provisions are discussed in detail in Section A of this part, supra. Here we will only briefly summarize their effects and limitations.

Until 1972, the deductions allowed for child care were minimal. Deductions were classified as personal expenses, were limited to $600 per year for one child or $900 for two or more children under thirteen years of age, and were available to widows, widowers, and separated and divorced persons regardless of income. A married working woman or a husband whose wife was incapacitated could only claim the deduction if she or he filed a joint return with the spouse. Furthermore, the deduction was reduced $1 for each $1 of combined adjusted gross income exceeding $6000. In 1972, a new law was passed which greatly increased the significance of day care deductions. Deductions (for both child care and household services) were still classified as personal expenses, but the amount of the deduction was increased to $200 per month for one child, $300 per month for two children, and $400 per month for three or more children. (The limits per child do not apply if the care is inside the home, although the maximum amount per month remains $400.) In order to qualify, both parents must be employed full time, the child care expenses must be incurred in order to allow both to work, and the child care payments must not be made to a relative. Finally, anyone making a gross income of more than $18,000 must subtract one half of the excess above $18,000 from the amount of the deduction.

Two examples, taken from an Internal Revenue Service publication, show how the deductions are applied. Note that in the IRS's own examples, the expenditures for child care exceed the maximum allowable in both cases:[74]

> *Example 1: Child Care Outside the Home.* You are a widow. You maintain a household for yourself and one preschool child, are gainfully employed full time, file Form 1040 with adjusted gross income of less than $18,000 for the tax year, and itemize your deductions.
>
> During a month you incur and pay for employment-related expenses of $150 for household services within your home and $300 child care expenses at a nursery school.

74. Your Federal Income Tax 99 (1973).

Your deductions would be computed as follows:

Household expense	$150
Add: Child care outside home ($300, but limited to maximum for 1 child)	200
Allowable deduction for the month	$350

If instead, your household expenses are $250 for the month, your deduction would be:

Household expenses	$250
Add: Child care outside home ($300, but limited to maximum for 1 child)	200
Total expenses	$450
Allowable deduction for the month (maximum)	$400

Example 2: Adjusted Gross Income Adjustment. You are married. With your spouse you maintain a household that includes 2 preschool dependent children. Both you and your husband, or wife, are gainfully employed full time. You file a joint Form 1040 with $19,200 adjusted gross income for the tax year and you itemize your deductions.

During a month you incur and pay employment-related expenses of $450 for a housekeeper who cares for your preschool children in your home and also does your cleaning, laundry, and some cooking.

Your deduction is computed as follows:

Household/child care in the home ($450, but limited to maximum)	$400
Reduction required for excess over $18,000 adjusted gross income ($19,200 − $18,000 = 1,200 ÷ 24)	50
Allowable deduction for the month	$350

Clearly, there are a number of important restrictions still built into the law reflecting biases about women's proper role. Even though the child care expenditures are required to be "employment-related" in order to be deductible, they are defined as personal rather than business expenses; this restricts both the income of those who can claim the deduction and the amount of the deduction, unlike a business expense where the sole test is whether the payments are ordinary and necessary expenses incurred in the production of income. The reason for so defining and limiting the child care deduction is that most Congressmen believe women ought to stay home. They work for pleasure, for luxuries, and so on — therefore, child care is a personal expense, which can and ought to be restricted. Thus, the woman's net after-tax income is artificially limited in comparison to that of the businessman. (This is so if a couple allocates the cost of child care to the wife's income, as many couples do; if the couple splits the costs, then the income of each spouse is artificially held down.)

A second issue important to feminists is the limitation of the deduction to those couples where the wife is working substantially full time (generally, at least three fourths of the normal work week). This is a disincentive for the wife who works only part time or who performs volunteer work; she still must pay for child care in order to do so, and the government in effect says that neither job is very valuable. It also discourages experimentation with new sex role divisions of labor within marriage. The couple who wish each to take a part-time job and combine it with shared part-time child-rearing will be disadvantaged in comparison with either a couple who both work full time and get the child care deduction, or a couple in which one spouse works full time and one stays home (who get the greatest advantages from income aggregation and the joint return).

Another problem is the prohibition against pay to relatives for child care. Grandmothers and aunts, whom the parents would often prefer, are expected to work for nothing. If they will not do so, the parents must either forgo the deduction or employ a stranger.

Finally, as Senator Mondale has pointed out, the provisions do not help many couples. In his Introductory Remarks on the 1972 Act, he stated:[75]

> Some people would like us to believe that the day care needs of the near poor and working parents have been adequately met by the recently enacted liberalization of income tax deductions for child care. In fact, the President suggested as much in his veto message of the child development bill, but the facts do not support this optimism.
>
> In response to my inquiry concerning the tax savings under this new income tax deduction, the Treasury has provided the following information:
>
> A family of four with an income of $5,000 which spends $500 for child care would realize no tax savings;
>
> A family of four with a $7,000 income which spends $700 for child care would realize a savings of only $77;
>
> A family of four with a $10,000 income which spends $1,000 for child care would realize only $190 tax savings;
>
> A family of four with an income of $18,000 and child care expenses of $1,000 would save $250 in taxes.
>
> That it is precisely why the bill we are introducing today retains the fee schedule from last year's conference report which provides free services for families with incomes up to $4,320, modest fees for families with incomes between $4,320 and $6,960, and a sliding scale of fees above that level.

b. Federal, State, and Local Regulation of Day Care

Health and safety regulation of day care centers is another major governmental policy affecting the availability of the services. Each state regulates day care, and many cities also impose restrictions. Regulations cover such varied subjects as a definition of what constitutes a regulated day care center; standards for physical facilities and the amount of space per child; requirements for the professional training for staff members; the age of children who may be cared for; the number of children the center may care for; a minimum staff-child ratio; and the kinds of insurance the center must carry.

Needless to say, the requirements set vary widely from state to state. For example, Montana requires that teachers have certain defined personality characteristics, while Kentucky requires that the center director and all teachers have a bachelor's degree in early childhood education, and that assistant teachers have a high school degree plus either two years of college or previous experience. In Indiana, children under three are barred from centers; Georgia lets in children of any age; and North Dakota "discourages" children under two. Children must have 100 square feet of outdoor space in Kansas, New Jersey, and North Carolina; 40 square feet in Florida or Utah; sufficient space in Oregon; and 200 square feet in Wyoming.[76]

As Bourne points out, supra, there are also federal standards — the Federal Interagency Guidelines — which local groups that receive federal funding must meet. These are often more restrictive than the state regulations. Thus, the federal government wants a one-to-five staff-child ratio for children three years of age, and one-to-seven for four and five year olds; while the states are often satisfied with one-to-ten or one-to-twelve.[77]

In some states, the effect of the often irrational and always uncoordinated structure of regulation is to drive up the costs of day care, further restricting its availability. Moreover, the regulations often bear little or no relationship to the child's real needs. Women in states where arbitrary regulations are a problem may want to litigate, arguing that by setting standards which prevent day care centers from being established, the state is interfering with the parents' right to control the upbringing of their children.[78]

75. 118 Cong. Rec. S1972 (daily ed. Feb. 17, 1972).
76. Westinghouse Learning Corporation and Westat Research, Inc., Day Care Survey, 1970 (1971).
77. Federal Interagency Childcare Requirements, 45 C.F.R. §71 (1973).
78. But see Evans, Shub, and Weinstein, Day Care, ch. 2 (1971).

CHAPTER FOUR

WOMEN AND THE CRIMINAL LAW

I. INTRODUCTION

Issues rising from women's involvement in the criminal process — as victim, as accused, and as prisoner — have not been closely examined. This chapter will consider the subjects of rape, prostitution, and convicted women, for several purposes. First, it is useful to study the problems of women in relation to criminal law because, peculiarly, this branch of the law reflects society's current notions, prejudices, and concerns about groups within it. In the administration of the laws against rape, most dramatically, are exhibited deeply ambivalent attitudes toward women. The picture of innocence violated coexists with the version of the fantasied rape. In the dealings of police investigators and prosecutors with rape victims is revealed the suspicion that women universally (unconsciously) desire to be raped, inviting it by careless or calculated actions. Rules of evidence are especially devised for cases involving sexual assaults on women: sometimes the victim's sworn testimony is insufficient for conviction. The penalties for rape are severe, indicating society's concern to protect women, yet no other victim is so often treated by the entire criminal law system as deserving what she got.

How society views the criminal woman can best be seen in the form and administration of the laws against prostitution. Prostitution cases are petty, the grist of the criminal justice system. Yet today there are women in jail who are virtually serving life sentences in small "bits" for prostitution offenses. And as anyone knows who has ever been in a "women's court,"[1] the interchange among court personnel, spectators, the police, and defendants creates a lewd and degrading atmosphere unmatched even by "drunk courts."

It seems likely that right to privacy and equal protection arguments will be raised in prostitution cases with increasing frequency and success, perhaps effecting for all practical purposes the decriminalization of prostitution. Decriminalization, however, would leave the society with questions about whether the prostitute's life is essentially degraded, quite apart from the criminal stigma, and if so, what to do about it. Such hard questions are made more difficult because so little is known about who prostitutes are, and much of the stereotypical thinking which is done about women generally also appears in descriptions of prostitutes. They are seen as whores with hearts of gold, nymphomaniacs, or high class call girls who have rationally chosen to make money rather than be secretaries. No serious attention has been given to whether these and like stereotypes have any basis in reality. The only certainty is that in criminal courts and most assuredly in women's jails, those accused of prostitution are almost all poor, physically debilitated, and often addicted to heroin or alcohol.

---

1. The New York City courts which processed prostitution cases were literally so denominated until very recently.

As for women in prison, it is true that less than one percent of the nation's federal and state prisoners are women. But at the end of 1970 this was more than 5000 people, almost all poor, almost all from racial minorities, and almost all accused or convicted of nonviolent crimes. Their problems are important in themselves, are different from those of men prisoners, and were hidden until the general interest in women's rights brought them to light.

Another reason for a chapter on women and the criminal law is that consideration of the problems of women in relationship to any body of law benefits from an increasingly unified and organized feminist perspective. Such a perspective can provide fresh insights and new arguments. To use an example from prison law, a feminist approach is responsible for the following allegations in a complaint filed in a civil rights suit against a women's detention center:[2]

> Upon information and belief, the only vocational training or job counseling available . . . consists of a "self-teaching" typing program, a weekly lesson in cooking economically, a weekly sewing class, and a drug program recently instituted in which only nine women are enrolled. All of the programs are available only to a limited number of women. . . . [T]he absence of adequate vocational, educational and recreational programs results in incarceration without rehabilitation. The fact that the only programs which do exist, i.e., limited access to typing exercises, sewing and cooking, are sex-tracked, providing training only in areas traditionally defined as a woman's job, discriminated against plaintiffs because they are women.

In sum, a study of women and the criminal law is a worthy undertaking because there is a fresh feminist perspective from which to make analysis and because the form and administration of criminal laws affecting women are a measure of how far we are from realizing an egalitarian society.

II. RAPE

A. DEFINITION OF THE CRIMES OF RAPE AND STATUTORY RAPE

Rape, at common law, is unlawful carnal knowledge of a woman without her consent. Any sexual penetration, however slight, is sufficient to complete the crime if the other elements are present.

"By force and against her will" is the phrase often used in the definitions but, as unlawful carnal knowledge of a woman who is insensibly drunk at the time is held to be rape unless she had consented in advance, it is obvious that no more is required than that the deed be done without her consent. Sexual intercourse by a man with his lawful wife is not unlawful, and hence is not rape, even if she does not consent. But while a husband cannot rape his wife, he can be guilty of the crime of rape committed upon her. That is, if A should aid B in having sexual intercourse with A's wife without her consent, both A and B would be guilty of rape.[1]

---

2. Garnes v. Taylor, Civ. No. 159-72 (D.D.C. 1972). This complaint is more fully quoted in Part IV-A-2, infra.

1. Perkins, Criminal Law 152 (2d ed. 1969). Two recent cases in Israel (El Fakir v. Attorney General, (1964) vol. 4, 18 P.D. 200; Katib v. Attorney General, (1966) vol. 2, 20 P.D. 136) have challenged the assumption, virtually universal in the Western world, that forced intercourse is one of a woman's matrimonial duties:

"In my view this doctrine does not do justice to the dignity of man nor to the dignity of matrimony, and in Israel it should not be adopted except by express order of the legislature. . . . A wife is not like a 'captive taken with the sword' (Gen. XXXI, 26) in her husband's house and she has the same right of corporal freedom as he. . . ." ((1964) vol. 4, 18 P.D. 200 at 219.)

In a 1963 dissent from a denial of certiorari,[2] Justice Goldberg suggested that the death penalty was excessive in rape cases where "a value other than life" was being protected. Exactly what is the value that the rape statutes are designed to protect? The California statute, enacted in 1872, specifically states: "The essential guilt of rape consists in the outrage to the person and feelings of the female. Any sexual penetration, however slight, is sufficient to complete the crime."[3]

Even more straightforward in its definition of the values protected by rape statutes was a Comment appearing in the Yale Law Journal entitled Forcible and Statutory Rape: An Exploration of the Operation and Objectives of the Consent Standard:[4]

> All societies seek to control and direct sexual energy in order to maintain their group structure and function. Unchanneled, the sex drive threatens to disrupt patterns of social and family organization. Properly controlled, on the other hand, sexual energy moves people into relationships and activities which sustain the group. The channeling of sexuality into marriage is crucial to all societies and espoused as a desirable goal by virtually all component sub-groups. In our society, sexual taboos, often enacted into law, buttress a system of monogamy based upon the "free bargaining" of the potential spouses. Within this process, the woman's power to withhold or grant sexual access is an important bargaining weapon. Beyond the use of sexuality in marriage, it is difficult to generalize on the socially approved allocation of sexual energy. However, many sub-groups and individual members of society, more or less overtly, recognize the approriateness of non-marital relationships fostered by the woman's decision to participate in sexual union. In all cases the law of rape protects the woman's discretion by proscribing coitus contrary to her wishes. . . .
>
> The consent standard in our society does more than protect a significant item of social currency for women; it fosters, and is in turn bolstered by, a masculine pride in the exclusive possession of a sexual object. The consent of a woman to sexual intercourse awards the man a privilege of bodily access, a personal "prize" whose value is enhanced by sole ownership. A man may fear loss of the woman's sexual consent to a competitor. Against the potential seducer, the threatened lover is supposed to employ devices such as the manly art of wooing or recrimination of the woman to restore the relationship and maintain his masculine self-esteem. These devices, however, may do little to allay his anxiety. And he may not be able to resort to direct action against his competitor without a symbolic admission of impotence. Hence the fear and passion aroused by the threat of deposal may be "displaced," directed against a more socially acceptable target — the rapist. An additional reason for the man's condemnation of rape may be found in the threat to his status from a decrease in the "value" of his sexual "possession" which would result from forcible violation. Rape seems to arouse in most people a feeling of disgust, perhaps generated by the repressions surrounding aggressive sex; and the disgust may spread to the body of the victim who is somehow thought to be contaminated by the experience. Words

---

An article in the Israel Law Review surveys the approach of other nations and finds that Russia and other communist countries take the view that "marriage does not abolish the sexual freedom of women, and the husband has no right to compel his wife to have sexual relations with him." (Livney, On Rape and the Sanctity of Matrimony, 2 Israel L. Rev. 415, 420 (1967).)

When a couple is not legally divorced, but separated, does the traditional definition of rape still assure the estranged husband forced sexual access to his legal wife? The answer may be yes, at least in some jurisdictions. See, e.g., Baugh v. State, 402 S.W.2d 768 (Texas Ct. App. 1966). In order to protect women separated from their husbands, the definition of rape as an act which does not occur in marriage should be changed. The change should also have an educative effect on society as a declaration of all women's right to sexual self-determination. In practical terms, however, rape within marriage, like other forms of intra-spousal violence, is not controllable by legal sanctions as long as the marriage continues. See Truninger, Marital Violence: The Legal Sanctions, 23 Hast. L. J. 259 (1971), for a discussion of the uselessness of the criminal sanction, peace bonds, and any other legal device, because of both the disinterest of enforcing authorities and the ultimate unwillingness of spouses to pursue definitive remedies against each other, short of divorce.

2. Rudolph v. Alabama, 375 U.S. 889, 84 S. Ct. 155, 11 L. Ed. 2d 119 (1963).

3. California Penal Code §263.

4. Comment, 62 Yale L.J. 55, 70-73 (1952).

like "ravaged" and "despoiled" used to describe the rape victim reflect the notion of a stain attaching to the body of the girl. The man responds to this undercutting of his status as "possessor" of the girl with hostility toward the rapist; no other restitution device is available. The law of rape provides an orderly outlet for his vengeance.

It is commonly provided by statute that unlawful carnal knowledge is a crime committed upon a girl under a certain age (called the age of consent) even if she consents. To distinguish between this and the other type of rape, the first is often called "statutory rape" or "carnal knowledge of a child" and the other "common law rape," or "forcible rape."

The so-called "age of consent" varies in the different jurisdictions. An early English statute fixed the age at twelve. Modern statutes usually provide a substantially higher age — not infrequently eighteen.[5]

Statutes prohibiting intercourse with young girls involve protection of values in addition to those discussed in the law journal excerpt above. The commentary to the Model Penal Code explains why statutory rape should be regarded as a separate crime.[6]

> Special treatment of consensual intercourse with a child is warranted not only because the immature require protection and to prevent the outrage to parental and community feelings, but also because an adult male's proclivity for sex relations with children is a recognized symptom of mental aberration, called pedophilia. On the other hand, statistics of arrest and conviction do not demonstrate unusual recidivism such as one might expect of mentally ill offenders. Moreover, a single instance of sexual relations with a child does not establish mental aberration. Another factor to be considered is that extremely young victims may not make competent witnesses.
>
> There appear to be three significant categories involving the age of the female: (1) pre-puberty victims with a considerable probability of aberration in the male agressor, (2) the period of puberty, when the girl arrives at physical capacity to engage in intercourse, but remains seriously deficient in comprehension of the social, psychological, emotional and even physical significance of sexuality, so that it is still realistic to regard her as victimized, and (3) the period of later adolescence when the chief significance of the behavior is its contravention of the moral standards of the community.

It should be noted that on the basis of this analysis the Model Penal Code sets the age of consent at ten, much lower than most jurisdictions.

B. THE PROSECUTION AND DEFENSE OF A RAPE CASE

From the viewpoint of those concerned with the inequality of women in American society, there are two problems with the structure and operation of laws designed to prevent and punish rape. First, the criminal sanction cannot possibly deter in the case of rape because it often happens that rapes are not reported,[7] not fully prosecuted, and

5. Perkins, supra at 152.

6. Commentary, Model Penal Code §207.4(d) (1962). The Model Penal Code is an attempt by a distinguished group of lawyers, the American Law Institute, to bring rationality and coherence to the variant penal laws of this country. The section on sexual offenses was first presented to the institute in 1955, accompanied by an extensive commentary. It was not significantly changed in the 1962 final version, which relied on the earlier commentary. The Code is not intended to be typical of the law now in effect in most jurisdictions, although it draws for its formulation upon the experience of the states as well as on the common law.

Not mentioned in the Model Penal Code, but a factor which also must be an underlying concern in the passage of statutory rape laws, is the possibility of physical harm to a prepubertal child from intercourse.

7. President's Commission on Law Enforcement and the Administration of Justice: The Challenge of Crime in a Free Society 21 (1967). The Commission found that forcible rapes occur at 3½ times the reported rate.

1970 Uniform Crime Reports 14 (1971). The Uniform Crime Reports are the most widely publicized and consulted sources on the incidence of crime in the United States, although they are far from totally reliable. They are generally gathered from local police agencies, whose criteria for categorizing crimes varies. The raw statistical problem is compounded by the fact that not every local agency participates in the FBI's reporting

even when they are fully reported and prosecuted frequently convictions are not obtained.[8] Statistics bear out the thesis that the criminal justice system operates particularly poorly on the crime of rape. Forcible rapes increased 146 percent from 1960 to 1971[9] and during 1972 rose sharply while the incidence of other serious crime declined.[10]

The second major problem is with the administration of the rape laws: the victim is subjected to peculiar pressures, humiliations, and traumatic occurrences in the very process of prosecuting the crime. This occurs because the rape jurisprudence, that is, the case law, evidentiary requirements, the instructions, and the operation of the jury itself, is based on a deeply suspicious view of both the nature of women and sexual intercourse. The materials in this section are designed for the study of both of these problems and of possible solutions.

1. The Issue of Nonconsent: The Ambiguous Circumstance and the Ambivalent Victim

PEOPLE v. DEFRATES
33 Ill. 2d 190, 210 N.E.2d 467 (1965)

UNDERWOOD, J.

After a bench trial in the criminal court of Cook County, the defendant, Walter DeFrates, was found guilty of rape and sentenced to the penitentiary for a term of 10 to 25 years. The appellate court, with one justice dissenting, affirmed the judgment of

---

program. For instance, as late as 1967, 148 of New Jersey's police departments were not making reports. Mandel, Problems with Official Drug Statistics, Narcotics Cases: Prosecution and Defense 549, 500 n.3 (1970). See generally, Zeisel, The FBI's Biased Sampling, 29 Bull. Atomic Scientists 38 (1973).

The Uniform Crime Reports figures do not, moreover, even represent the total number of complaints brought to the attention of the police which do report to the FBI. Rather, they indicate the number *founded* as rapes, that is, determined to be valid complaints by the police. Rape traditionally has a lower founding rate than other serious crimes. In 1971, for example, 82 percent of rape complaints were founded compared to 96 percent of all crimes covered in the reports. The FBI attributes the low figure for rape "to the question of the use of force or threat of force frequently complicated by a prior relationship between victim and offender." This could be interpreted to mean that there are variations in the definition of rape utilized by police agencies at the investigative level. But data on the lack of "founding" for rape complaints is more often taken to indicate that there are many false reports of rape. Notably, such a conclusion was drawn by the National Commission on the Causes and Prevention of Violence in a staff report noting that it was very difficult to assess the reported increase in the crime of rape between 1958 and 1968, one reason being that "many of the cases reported by the police, and hence the UCR (Uniform Crime Reports) may actually be unfounded." 11 Crimes of Violence: A Staff Report 59 (December 1969). The support for this statement is a task force report which simply states without any authority that "[i]n the case of forcible rape some police departments regularly conclude that as many as 50% of the complaints received were not offenses." Task Force Report: Crime and Its Impact — An Assessment, President's Commission on Law Enforcement and Administration of Justice 25 (1967).

Some district attorneys think that the Women's Movement has encouraged more rape victims to report and prosecute rapes; rape centers in large cities across the country similarly encourage victims to acknowledge rapes and to bring the attacks and attackers to public attention. If such efforts have had an effect, at least part of the dramatic statistical increase in reported rapes could reflect an increased willingness to report rather than a greater incidence of the crime.

8. Federal Bureau of Investigation data for 1970 shows that 28.8 adults were prosecuted for rape per 100 offenses, that 36.1 adults were found guilty of rape per 100 trials, with 18.4 adults found guilty of lesser offenses. Acquittals or dismissals per 100 trials of rape cases numbered 46.5 (cited in Note, 81 Yale L.J. 1365 n.38). This should be compared with an acquittal or dismissal rate of 38.3 adults per 100 armed robbery trials. Statistic furnished by Uniform Crime Reporting, Federal Bureau of Investigation.

Good evidence of the disinclination of juries to convict in rape cases is also found in Kalvan and Zeisel, The American Jury 142 (1966), discussed in detail in Note: Jury Behavior in Rape Cases Generally, infra this section.

9. 1971 Uniform Crime Reports 61 (1972).

10. Federal Bureau of Investigation, Uniform Crime Reporting (January-June 1972). During this period, robbery decreased 4 percent compared to a 14 percent increase in forcible rapes. Even in categories which showed increases (e.g., burglary: 4 percent, aggravated assault: 6 percent), the increases were substantially less than that for forcible rape.

conviction (53 Ill. App. 2d 277, 203 N.E.2d 188) and we have granted defendant's petition for leave to appeal. The critical issue is whether the proof establishes beyond all reasonable doubt that an act of sexual intercourse was forcible and against the will of the complaining witness.

Defendant was a heating and air conditioning engineer who, on at least six occasions between October, 1961, and April 12, 1962, had been in the family home of the prosecutrix to service equipment. It appears that a familiarity with the prosecutrix and her husband was established beyond what would normally be expected to arise from the relationship, and that defendant, for some reason or other, submitted a bill only for the first call he made in October, 1961. During the first week of April, 1962, he was asked by the husband of the prosecutrix to adjust some fans, but this work had not been done when the husband went away on a business trip which extended through April 12. Remaining home alone were the prosecutrix and three daughters, aged eleven, ten and eight years. According to the prosecutrix she received a telephone call from defendant at about 2:45 A.M. on the morning of April 12, and he stated that he had just made another call in the vicinity and was coming over to make the service call her husband had requested. She said that she told him her husband was not home and sought to dissuade him, but that defendant insisted upon doing the work then. After defendant had hung up, prosecutrix testified that she took off her pajamas, and put on underpants, a brassiere, a slip, shoes, and a "brunch" coat which extended below her knees.

When defendant arrived at the residence about 3:00 A.M., he was admitted by the prosecutrix, and there was agreement that he first inspected heating equipment in various parts of the house in the company of the prosecutrix, and that he then requested and was given a drink of liquor by the prosecutrix in the kitchen, though she stated she did so reluctantly and only after defendant had insisted he was cold. Continuing her testimony, the prosecutrix testified that defendant returned to the kitchen after having been in the basement, and put his arms around her and asked for a kiss, a request that was first denied but subsequently granted when defendant inquired if he would have to use force and started choking her until she could not breathe. Defendant then proposed sexual intercourse and, when this proposal was refused, he took her by the shoulders and "marched" her to the basement. There, when he ordered her to take her dress off, she did so and also removed her underclothing with defendant's assistance. At this time defendant gave her a choice of committing the sexual act either on the basement floor or "up in the bed," whereupon she chose the latter, but stated she "was not marching through this house nude with the children awake." Defendant then allowed her to put on her house coat and once again took hold of her shoulders and "marched" her from the basement to her bedroom where, on his order, she removed her house coat and got into bed.

They remained in the bedroom until 5:45 A.M., or for approximately two hours. Prosecutrix testified there was an initial act of vaginal intercourse which was accomplished only after defendant had inquired: "Do I have to force you again?" and had ignored her pleas that she was suffering from being treated for a vaginal condition which caused her great pain. Later, over her protests, she said that defendant subjected her to an act of anal intercourse and to a second act of vaginal intercourse. She testified that when she "screamed into the pillow" during the anal intercourse, defendant said: "Shut up or I'll beat you up." In the intervals between these sexual activities, defendant talked about a wide variety of subjects, and as he did so kept one leg locked over the body of the prosecutrix and an arm over her chest, exerting pressure whenever she tried to arise. Shortly before 5:45 A.M., according to the prosecutrix, she left the room on the pretext that she wanted to shut off the children's alarm clocks before they rang. Instead, she awakened the three children and ran with them to the house of a next-door neighbor where they were admitted once the neighbors were aroused. About 7:00 A.M. the police were called and at their suggestion the prosecutrix was sent to a hospital for examination.

Defendant's version of the incident and the background leading to it was entirely different. He testified that he had been a frequent visitor at the home after October, 1961, both socially and in a business capacity, and that after his second visit he had been intimate with the prosecutrix on numerous occasions. His business made service calls on a 24-hour basis and he stated that when he had returned to his office about 3:00 A.M. on the morning of April 12, he was given a list of calls and told that the prosecutrix had called several times since midnight. He said that he telephoned her and complied with a request that he come over; that he checked a heating unit that was vibrating; and that he had a few drinks in the kitchen, after which he and the prosecutrix started "fooling around" and then went to a bedroom. Defendant denied that he had used force, or that he had committed unnatural acts, but testified that he had engaged in two acts of sexual intercourse with the consent and co-operation of the prosecutrix. He said that he then fell asleep until 5:45 A.M., at which time he was awakened by the prosecutrix who told him it was daylight and that he should get out of the house, whereupon he dressed and left in his car which had been parked in the driveway.

For the People, the oldest daughter testified that she had been awake when defendant was in the house, that she had seen him with her mother near a thermostat located just outside her bedroom door, and also that she had seen defendant with his hands on her mother's shoulders as they went into the mother's bedroom. With respect to the testimony of this witness, the prosecutrix testified that defendant had spoken to the daughter when he went to check the thermostat immediately after his arrival at the house. Defendant agreed that he had spoken to the girl, but stated that he had done so as he and the prosecutrix were on their way to the bedroom, the only time he was on the upper floor. A police officer, who had responded to the original call, told of seeing a spot on the prosecutrix's neck, while the nextdoor neighbor told of being awakened about 6:00 A.M., of finding the prosecutrix and her children at the door, and of her distraught condition and immediate complaint of rape. For the defense an employee of the heating company testified that prior to 3:00 A.M. on the morning of April 12, a woman had telephoned for defendant at least six times.

Where, as here, the charge is forcible rape, it must be proved beyond a reasonable doubt that the act of intercourse was performed forcibly and against the will of the complaining witness. And while useless or foolhardy acts of resistance are not necessary, if the prosecutrix has use of her faculties and physical powers, the evidence must show such resistance as will demonstrate that the act was against her will. . . . Voluntary submission by the female, while she has the power to resist, no matter how reluctantly yielded, amounts to consent and removes from the act an essential element of the crime of forcible rape. . . .

In apparent recognition of the fact that the evidence shows no outcry or attempt to escape, and little, if any, physical resistance on the part of the prosecutrix, the People seek to justify these failures on the grounds that she was paralyzed by fear for her own safety and that of her daughters, and that she was so remote from human help that an outcry or attempt to escape would have been futile and unavailing. . . . To our minds her election to have intercourse in a bed rather than the floor, her indignant remark that she would not parade nude through the house, and the fact that she walked from the basement to the bedroom is not the demeanor of one paralyzed by fear. What is more, it is difficult to conceive that such a fear would have consumed her for the entire two hours that was spent in the bedroom before she allegedly perpetrated a ruse to escape.

Considering the record as a whole, we are constrained to say that the testimony of the prosecutrix is not sufficiently convincing to lead to an abiding conviction of guilt, and was such that it required corroboration by some other testimony, fact or circumstance. . . .

The prosecutrix testified that she was being treated for a vaginal infection which gave her great pain, and the People argue it is inconceivable that she would have consented to sexual intercourse. Yet, no medical testimony was offered to corroborate this fact. . . .

We are not unmindful that the prosecutrix made an immediate complaint of rape to her neighbors; however, the events which preceded it cause the complaint to lose much of its weight. Further, it may as well be accounted for by a belated sense of guilt occurring when a dalliance unintentionally extended into the daylight hours and the prosecutrix felt the need to explain the presence of defendant's auto on the driveway and his departure from the home in case they had been observed. In this regard, the prosecutrix testified that defendant's car was gone when, immediately after her complaint, the wife of the neighbor looked out the window. Had defendant been in bed and undressed when the prosecutrix said she left him, we think it doubtful he could have risen and departed within the short period encompassed by the prosecutrix's testimony.

[Conviction reversed.]

NOTE: SUFFICIENCY OF THE EVIDENCE OF NONCONSENT

The court is finding, in effect, that the prosecution failed to present sufficient evidence of force by the defendant or nonconsent by the victim. Think about the kind of evidence which would be sufficient and how it would be adduced. Courts sometimes give illustrations of evidence which they would consider probative on the issue:

> In rape prosecutions, evidence of the prosecutrix should be carefully considered in determining whether she consented, and ordinarily proof of failure to make an outcry, offer resistance and complain tends to show consent. Commonwealth v. Berklowitz, 133 Pa. Super. 190, 2 A.2d 516; Commonwealth v. Bolles, 160 Pa. Super. 148, 80 A.2d 729. We are of the opinion that events leading up to allegations of rape are important in the final determination whether consent was given or force was used.[11]

> As to available means to a female of resistance we have said that nature has given her hands and feet with which she can strike and kick, teeth to bite, and a voice to cry out. Oleson v. State, 11 Neb. 276, 9 N.W. 38, 38 Am. Rep. 366.[12]

NOTE: INSTRUCTIONS ON FORCE OR NONCONSENT

The court in a jury trial (which *DeFrates* was not) instructs on each element of the government's case, including the element of force or nonconsent. Two issues are present in formulating an expression of what the government must prove about nonconsent: how much resistance is necessary, and what evidence is sufficient to prove resistance. A typical, if somewhat elaborate, instruction on nonconsent is that in State v. Dizon.[13]

> The law of rape demands that the sexual act be accomplished against the will of the female, which means without her consent. In the ordinary case, when the female is awake, of mature years, of sound mind, and not in fear, a failure by her to oppose the act is consent.
>
> The degree of resistance on the part of the woman must be proportioned to the outrage, and the amount required necessarily depends on the circumstances, such as the number and the relative strength of the parties, the age of the female, the physical and mental condition of the female, the uselessness of resistance, and the degree of force used.
>
> The female need resist only until physical penetration occurs, at which time the crime is complete; and her failure to resist after that is immaterial, and she need resist only until resistance becomes so useless as to warrant its cessation.
>
> Mere verbal protestations and a pretense of resistance are not sufficient to show want of consent. If the female fails to take such measures to frustrate the execution

11. Commonwealth v. Goodman, 182 Pa. Super. 205, 211, 126 A.2d 763, 765-766 (1956).
12. Frank v. State, 150 Neb. 745, 754, 35 N.W.2d 816 (1949).
13. State v. Dizon, 147 Hawaii 444, 390 P.2d 759 (1962).

of the male's design as she is able to make and are called for under the circumstances, the inference may be drawn that she did in fact consent.

And if you should find that although initially the idea of the act was completely abhorrent to her, but that she did in fact ultimately consent prior to penetration, then you cannot find the defendant guilty of rape.

The fact that consent was reluctantly given is immaterial if in fact it was given.

If you should find, however, that the female yielded to overpowering force the same is to be construed as submission and not consent.

The facts in *Dizon* are summarized by the appellate court as follows:[14]

> The prosecutrix was a first-grade school teacher at Waialua Elementary School. On Sunday, March 19, 1961, she was alone in her classroom . . . cutting letters spelling "Happy Easter" with a pair of scissors when suddenly she beheld a completely nude man advancing toward her on tiptoes. He was masked and his arms were raised over his head in a menacing manner. Startled and horrified she attempted to retreat but the furniture obstructed her way. When the man was upon her, she struck out with the scissors in her hand and inflicted on his right palm a laceration. A struggle ensued and as both fell to the floor, he wrenched the scissors from her hand and threw it across the room.
>
> The defendant, admittedly the assailant, was nineteen years old, six feet tall and weighed about one hundred sixty-five pounds, while the prosecutrix was fifty-eight years old, five feet two inches in height, and weighed about one hundred twelve pounds. Moreover, the prosecutrix had sustained a fracture of her tenth thoracic vertebra about two years prior to this incident and was not completely relieved from such ailment. . . .
>
> Testifying further as to what occurred when the assailant advanced toward her, she said: "I got past the area of two lockers, backing and backing, when he came upon me, seized me. We grappled. . . . I struggled, I talked. I remember talking constantly. . . ."
>
> Turning deaf ears to her plea, the assailant forcibly removed her clothes, first her blouse by ripping off the buttons and then her pedal pushers and panties, leaving only the camisole which fit so tightly that he could not remove it. "I kept trying to get up and my right shoulder, constantly pushed down," she testified. Finally subduing her, he consummated the carnal attack.

On these facts, the defendant sought the following instruction:[15]

> In the absence of threats, or other things which make resistance impossible, there must be not only an entire absence of mental consent or assent, but there must be the most vehement exercise of every physical means or faculty within the woman's power to resist penetration and a persistence in such resistance until the offense is consummated.
>
> The term "rape" imports not only force and violence on the part of the man, but resistance on the part of the woman. There must be force, actual or constructive, and resistance.
>
> In the absence of proof of resistance, consent is presumed. Mere general statements of the complainant that she resisted are not sufficient but the specific act of resistance must be shown. The dissent and repulsion must be shown beyond a reasonable doubt. . . .

Without directly stating it, the standard of nonconsent sought by the defendant's proposed instruction is clearly that of "resistance to the utmost." This was the standard in some jurisdictions until recent times, but has been almost universally rejected in favor of a standard of reasonable resistance under the circumstances.

A sidelight on the issue of resistance is what the courts do in cases where the

---

14. 390 P.2d at 761-762.
15. 390 P.2d at 763-764.

woman is drunk, drugged, sleeping, or defrauded, and so offered no resistance at the time of intercourse. Some, mostly older, decisions find that force was not proved in such cases, and therefore the evidence was insufficient.[16] Other courts assume nonconsent in instances where the woman was not in a condition to refuse;[17] and still others speak of fraudulent acts or verbal threats as the use of "constructive force."[18]

NOTE: JURY BEHAVIOR ON THE ISSUE OF FORCE

The elaborateness of the court's instruction on the element of force, and sometimes the tone and tenor in which it is given, may cause a jury to exaggerate this requirement. But even aside from the court's interpretation of the law on sufficient evidence of force or nonconsent and the standard for its application, juries often have their own ideas about the issue. In some instances, juries have in effect erected a requirement that the victim physically resist and suffer substantial consequences of such resistance. Such a case occurred recently in Washington, D.C. In the trial, two students at George Washington University testified to separate instances of rape and sodomy committed on each of them by a stranger. There were positive identifications and medical evidence as to force, including in one case large bruises. The jury apparently believed that there had been sexual contact between the defendant and the women but that they had not resisted sufficiently, and found the defendant not guilty. Newspaper accounts of an interview with a juror who explained the verdict related:[19]

> In general, [the juror] said, one of the strong factors in the jury's decision was "women speaking as women and what they would do under the same circumstances." There were eight women on the jury.
> [The juror] said the women felt the two coeds could have used their teeth, fingernails and feet to resist "violence of this type."

In this case, the women involved gave interviews concerning the trial:[20]

> A 19-year-old George Washington University coed, her alleged attacker acquitted by a jury, complained yesterday that the trial proceedings had made her feel more like a defendant than a plaintiff.
> "I wasn't on trial. I don't see anything I did wrong," she said. "I screamed. I struggled. How could they have decided that he was innocent, that I didn't resist. It's preposterous." . . .
> The roommate of the woman who accused [the defendant] of attacking her in the campus washroom said yesterday it "was obvious something was wrong when she came screaming out of the room. Her hair and clothes were messed up and she had red marks on her neck. I saw all the bruises."
> "I told all this at the trial," the roommate said. "I told them she was hysterical and that I saw the guy running out of the bathroom. I thought the case was all sewn up."
> The woman who accused [the defendant] of raping her in Lisner Auditorium said she was even more surprised to find out that the jury expected more proof of forced intercourse and fear of death on her part.
> "I thought he had a gun, and I didn't want to be killed," she said. "The only consent I gave was consent in that I didn't want to be killed."

16. See, e.g., Thomas v. State, 227 Ind. 42, 83 N.E.2d 788 (1949); Harris v. State, 88 Okla. Crim. 413, 204 P.2d 310 (1949).

17. See, e.g., Davis v. Commonwealth, 186 Va. 936, 45 S.E.2d 167 (1947); People v. Kinne, 25 Cal. App. 2d 112, 76 P.2d 714 (1938).

18. See, e.g., State v. Thompson, 227 N.C. 19, 40 S.E.2d 620 (1946).

19. Washington Post, Dec. 1, 1972, p. A16.

20. Washington Post, Dec. 2, 1972, p. E1.

The standard instruction on force in the District of Columbia, which was given in this case, is: "You may not find that the complaining witness submitted out of fear of death or grave bodily harm simply because she said she was afraid. Such fears must be shown to have been reasonable in light of the circumstances at the time and the conduct of the defendant as shown by the objective evidence."[21] As a practical matter, many juries are unwilling to find sufficient evidence of force unless there is the use of a weapon or evidence of physical resistance by the victim.

NOTE: JURY BEHAVIOR IN RAPE CASES GENERALLY

The attitude of juries toward rape cases, especially when there is no evidence of physical violence other than the intercourse itself, is often very exacting toward the woman. Kalven and Zeisel, in their monumental study of the operation of the American jury,[22] found that in forcible rape cases, it was common for juries to import notions of the contributory fault of the victim. They found that: "The jury . . . does not limit itself to [the issue of whether there was consent at the moment of intercourse]; it goes on to weigh the woman's conduct in the prior history of the affair. It closely, and often harshly, scrutinizes the female complainant and is moved to be lenient with the defendant whenever there are suggestions of contributory behavior on her part."[23]

The method used in the jury study, which analyzed jury reaction to many crimes other than rape, was to follow 3576 trials with a questionnaire to the trial judge to determine whether he would have reached the same result as the jury did, and if not, what factors he thought influenced the jury. The overall results revealed that in more than 75 percent of the cases, judges would have reached the same conclusion as the jury.[24] But in rape cases where there was no extrinsic violence, where there was prior acquaintance of the victim and the defendant, or where there was only one assailant, the judge and the jury would have reached the same result only 40 percent of the time, with the jury acquitting and the judge convicting in 60 percent of the cases.

Typical of the fact patterns in which the jury acquitted when the judge would have convicted are the following:[25]

> The complaining witness alleged after several beers she entered car with defendant and three other men and was driven to cemetery where act took place.
> Woman involved went to public dance and was picked up by defendant. Then went to night club and permitted defendant to take her home over unfrequented road . . . woman involved twice married and divorced, age 33.
> Prosecutrix and defendant strangers to each other; met each other at dance hall. He undertook to take her home . . . rape occurred in lonely wooded area, she drinking but not drunk. He much more under influence.

2. Lack of Force (Consent) as a Defense

The prosecution is concerned with evidence of force or nonconsent and, as we have seen in the foregoing section, the defense at trial may try, by cross-examination and on appeal, to establish that such evidence was insufficient. In addition, at trial the main thrust of the defense case is often to present evidence that the victim consented, which is different in form and content from that given through direct or cross-examination on the issue of resistance.

---

21. Standard Jury Instructions, District of Columbia (collected by ther Junior Bar Association of the District of Columbia Bar).
22. Kalven and Zeisel, The American Jury (1966).
23. Id. at 250.
24. Id. at 56.
25. Id. at 250.

a. The Woman's Character as Evidence of Her Consent

In virtually every jurisdiction, evidence about the woman's character is admissible in most circumstances. The theory of allowing this kind of evidence is that an "unchaste" woman, that is, one who had previously consented to intercourse, would likely have done so on the occasion in question. Wigmore explains the theory as follows:[26]

. . . The classical opinion in favor of admissibility is the following:

1838, COWEN, J., in People v. Abbott, 19 Wend. 194: "The prosecutrix is usually, as here, the sole witness to the principal facts, and the accused is put to rely for his defence on circumstantial evidence. Any fact tending to the inference that there was not the utmost reluctance and the utmost resistance is always received. . . . The connection must be absolutely against the will; and are we to be told that previous prostitution shall not make one among those circumstances which raise a doubt of assent? That triers should be advised to make no distinction in their minds between the virgin and a tenant of the stew, — between one who would prefer death to pollution, and another who, incited by lust and lucre, daily offers her person to the indiscriminate embraces of the other sex? And will you not more readily infer assent in the practised Messalina in loose attire, than in the reserved and virtuous Lucretia? . . .[After referring to evidence of common prostitution as admissible:] It has been repeatedly adjudged that in the same view you may also show a previous voluntary connection between the prosecutrix and the prisoner. Why is this? Because there is not so much probability that a common prostitute or the prisoner's concubine would withhold her assent as one less depraved; and may I not ask, does not the same probable distinction arise between one who has already submitted herself to the lewd embraces of another, and the coy and modest female severely chaste and instinctively shuddering at the thought of impurity? Shall I be answered that both are equally under the protection of the law? That I admit, and so are the common prostitute and the concubine. If either have in truth been feloniously ravished, the punishment is the same. But the proof is quite different. It requires that stronger evidence be added to the oath of the prosecutrix in one case than in the other."

The reasoning of the exclusionary rule is presented in the following passage:

1895, SIDDON, J., in Rice v. State, 35 Fla. 236, 17 So. 286: "The fact that a woman may have been guilty of illicit intercourse with one man is too slight and uncertain an indication to warrant the conclusion that she would probably be guilty with any other man who sought such favors of her. If she was a woman of general bad reputation for chastity, or had been guilty of acts of lewdness with the defendant, the case would be different. In the first instance, the evidence would bear directly upon the question as to whether such a woman would be likely to resist the advances of any man; and, in the second, as to whether having yielded once to the sexual embraces of the defendant, she would not be likely to yield again to the same person. The greatest objection to such testimony is that it introduces collateral issues, which have no direct bearing upon the defendant's guilt."

The better view is that which admits the evidence. Between the evil of putting an innocent or perhaps an erring woman's security at the mercy of a villain, and the evil of putting an innocent man's liberty at the mercy of an unscrupulous and revengeful mistress, it is hard to strike a balance. But, with regard to the intensity of injustice involved in an erroneous verdict, and the practical frequency of either danger, the admission of the evidence seems preferable. In the opposing judicial opinions the writers respectively assume that the man is innocent and that the woman is wronged; and on these inconsistent assumptions, the conclusion reached by each is fair enough. . . .

Most authorities agree that the previous chastity of the victim, whether proved by specific acts or reputation, should only be raised in a case where consent is at issue. There is some authority, however, for allowing the unchastity of the victim to be shown as affecting her general credibility as a witness.[27]

26. 1 Wigmore, Evidence §200 (3d ed. 1940).
27. Id. at §§62, 200.

b. The Evidentiary Rule in Practice

FRANK v. STATE
150 Neb. 745, 35 N.W.2d 816 (1949)

The court stated the facts of the case, as follows:

Defendant in the fifth contention questioned the sufficiency of the state's evidence to sustain the verdict and judgment. In that connection, we have examined the record, and without specifically reciting its sordid details, decide that there was competent evidence from which the jury could have reasonably concluded: That three young men, including defendant, in conformity with a preconceived plan, accosted prosecutrix at 10:30 P.M. on a side street, forced her into a car, and drove rapidly away to a city park. There they manhandled her, removed some of her underclothing, forced her out of the car, and pulled her over to a haystack nearby. Another car then entered the park some distance away so, deciding that it was not a safe or proper place, they put prosecutrix back in the car, and drove out into the country and down a lane, across a wheat field into a ravine. There they forced her out of the car, threw her to the ground, and while two of the young men held her the other assaulted her, completing an act of intercourse by force and against her will, thereafter he and another held her while a second one likewise assaulted her, and completed the sexual act, after which he assisted in holding her while the third attempted the act but was unable to do so. They then put her in the car and drove back to town, letting her out a half block from her home.

At home the mother and sister noticed the condition of her clothing, whereupon she was questioned and tearfully told substantially the foregoing story to them. Her coat was littered with hay, the shoulder straps were torn from her clothing, the buttons were torn from her blouse, and there was blood on her slip and blouse.

. . . [D]efendant complained that the trial court confined evidence adduced in defendant's behalf to the general reputation of the prosecutrix for morality and erroneously sustained defendant's objection to and overruled defendant's offer to prove by direct evidence specific unchaste or immoral acts and conduct by her with others, thus precluding him from adducing such evidence relating to the immoral character of prosecutrix. . . .

In that connection, in Redmon v. State, 150 Neb. 62, 33 N.W.2d 349, this court recently concluded that in cases wherein a woman charges a man with a sex offense, immorality has a direct connection with veracity, and that direct evidence of the general reputation of the prosecutrix for sexual morality may be shown by defendant, who is not restricted to proof of general reputation of the witness for truth and veracity.

Therein, it was also concluded not only that cross-examination of the prosecutrix should be as unrestrained and searching as is consistent with rules of law, but that it was also prejudicial error to exclude any direct competent evidence not too remote in time, showing specific immoral or unchaste acts and conduct by her with others, not only for the purpose of being considered by the jury in deciding the weight and credibility of her testimony generally, but for the purpose of inferring the probability of consent and discrediting her testimony relating to force or violence used by defendant in accomplishing his purpose and her claimed resistance thereto. See, also, State v. Wood, 59 Ariz. 48, 122 P.2d 416, 140 A.L.R. 361, and annotations 364; 3 Wigmore on Evidence, (3d ed.), s. 924a, p. 459, s. 979, p. 537. Concededly, there is authority to the contrary, but the foregoing is the modern realist rule, and we deem it the better one. Reversed.

Evidence of prior acts of unchastity with men other than the defendant may be introduced through extrinsic evidence in the defendant's own case, as well as through cross-examination. A magazine article described the form such a cross-examination may take.

GRIFFIN, RAPE: THE ALL-AMERICAN CRIME
Ramparts Magazine 26, 31-32 (September 1971)

. . . Mr. Plotkin, a 36-year-old jeweler, was tried for rape last spring in a San Francisco Superior Court. According to the woman who brought the charges, Plotkin, along with three other men, forced her at gunpoint to enter a car one night in October 1970. She was taken to Mr. Plotkin's fashionable apartment where he and the three other men first raped her and then, in the delicate language of the S.F. Chronicle, "subjected her to perverted sex acts." She was, she said, set free in the morning with the warning that she would be killed if she spoke to anyone about the event. She did report the incident to the police who then searched Plotkin's apartment and discovered a long list of names of women. Her name was on the list and had been crossed out.

In addition to the woman's account of her abduction and rape, the prosecution submitted four of Plotkin's address books containing the names of hundreds of women. Plotkin claimed he did not know all of the women since some of the names had been given to him by friends and he had not yet called on them. Several women, however, did testify in court that Plotkin had, to cite the Chronicle, "lured them up to his apartment under one pretext or another, and forced his sexual attentions on them."

Plotkin's defense rested on two premises. First, through his own testimony Plotkin established a reputation for himself as a sexual libertine who frequently picked up girls in bars and took them to his house where sexual relations often took place. He was the Playboy. He claimed that the accusation of rape, therefore, was false — this incident had simply been one of many casual sexual relationships, the victim one of many playmates. The second premise of the defense was that his accuser was also a sexual libertine. However, the picture created of the young woman (fully 13 years younger than Plotkin) was not akin to the light-hearted, gay-bachelor image projected by the defendant. On the contrary, the day after the defense cross-examined the woman, the Chronicle printed a story headlined, "Gruelling Day For Rape Case Victim." (A leaflet passed out by women in front of the courtroom was more succinct, "rape was committed by four men in a private apartment in October; on Thursday, it was done by a judge and a lawyer in a public courtroom.")

Through skillful questioning fraught with innuendo, Plotkin's defense attorney . . . portrayed the young woman as a licentious opportunist and unfit mother. [He] began by asking the young woman (then employed as a secretary) whether or not it was true that she was "familiar with liquor" and had worked as a "cocktail waitress." The young woman replied (the Chronicle wrote "admitted") that she had worked once or twice as a cocktail waitress. The attorney then asked if she had worked as a secretary in the financial district but had "left that employment after it was discovered that you had sexual intercourse on a couch in the office." The woman replied, "That is a lie. I left because I didn't like working in a one-girl office. It was too lonely." Then the defense asked if, while working as an attendant at a health club, "you were accused of having a sexual affair with a man?" Again the woman denied the story, "I was never accused of that."

Plotkin's attorney then sought to establish that his client's accuser was living with a married man. She responded that the man was separated from his wife. Finally he told the court that she had "spent the night" with another man who lived in the same building.

At this point in the testimony the woman asked Plotkin's defense attorney, "Am I on trial? . . . It is embarrassing and personal to admit these things to all these people. . . . I did not commit a crime. I am a human being." The lawyer, true to the chivalry of his class, apologized and immediately resumed questioning her, turning his attention to her children. (She is divorced, and the children at the time of the trial were in a foster home.) "Isn't it true that your two children have a sex game in which one gets on top of another and they — " "That is a lie!" the young woman interrupted him. She ended her testimony by explaining "They are wonderful children. They are not perverted."

The jury, divided in favor of acquittal ten to two, asked the court stenographer to read the woman's testimony back to them. After this reading, the Superior Court acquitted the defendant of both the charges of rape and kidnapping.

Another illustration, taken from an actual trial transcript, is an extreme example of the cross-examination of a rape victim on the issue of consent, in circumstances in which it was uncontested that the intercourse occurred in a public place and that the woman and the defendant were strangers. The form of the questions illustrates the examination by leading questions to which a victim-witness will routinely be subjected.

TRANSCRIPT, UNITED STATES v. THORNE
(D.D.C. 1969)

[EXCERPTS FROM DIRECT TESTIMONY]

Questions by [The Prosecutor]:

Q. Are you employed, Miss?
A. Yes.
Q. Where are you employed?
A. Department of State.
Q. In what capacity are you employed?
A. I am a secretary at the American Embassy in Bonn.
Q. How long have you been at the American Embassy in Bonn?
A. Since September of 1967.
Q. How long have you been employed by the Department of State. . . ?
A. Since July, 1966.
Q. I take it then that in July of 1967 you were employed as a secretary for the Department of State?
A. Yes.
Q. Where were you stationed July the 22nd and July the 23rd of 1967?
A. Washington.
Q. And did you have a local address on July the 22nd and 23rd?
A. Yes.
Q. What was your local address?
A. 1715 N Street, Northwest.
Q. Is that anywhere near the Francis Junior High School?
A. Well, it's on the other side of Connecticut Avenue from Francis Junior High School.
Q. I want to direct your attention . . . to the evening of July the 22nd, 1967. Were you in the company of anyone approximately at eleven o'clock that evening?
A. Yes.
Q. Whose company were you in?
A. Toby. . . .
Q. Is that the individual that stood up and identified himself to the jury this afternoon?
A. Yes.
Q. Now where had you been with [him] on the evening of July the 22nd and also on the morning hours of July the 23rd . . . ?
A. We were at his house. He lived in a house with several other roommates and we were over there for dinner.

Q. Approximately how many people were there for dinner that evening?

A. Five.

Q. Now where was [Toby] working at that time, if you know?

A. Bureau of the Budget.

Q. Were you with [him] after midnight on July the 23rd, 1967?

A. Yes.

Q. That is on the early morning hours —

A. Yes.

Q. — of July the 23rd. Where were you with him then?

A. We were in the area of Francis Junior High School.

Q. Now I want to direct your attention to your time in the area of the Francis Junior High School. What, if any, area did you go to specifically while you were in that field area of Francis Junior High School?

A. We walked around towards the pool, towards the playground area where the swings are. . . .

Q. All right. And what, if anything, happened while you were walking in that general area?

A. Three people started to follow us, three men, three fellows. . . .

Q. Now what, if anything, did you do at the time that they were walking behind you?

A. They started walking faster and we started walking faster and then we started to run.

Q. Now during the course of this running, what, if anything, happened?

A. Well, Toby stopped and I ran on and then I was grabbed from behind.

Q. How were you grabbed at this time . . . ?

A. One hand from behind me around my face and the other hand on my head, my hair, and I was pulled back.

Q. Now at this time was [Toby] next to you?

A. No, he had stopped. I ran past Toby. He stopped.

Q. All right. What, if anything, did you see and what, if anything, did you do at this time that you were grabbed?

A. Why, I was screaming and I was struggling and he was pulling me by the hair and he pulled me back and I was being dragged back into the — behind the school.

Q. Did you see [Toby] at the time that you were being brought back?

A. I never saw Toby again until the police came.

Q. Now approximately what time would you say it was that you were first grabbed by this person?

A. It was after — it was probably a little after one. . . .

Q. Now at the time that you were being dragged back, was this by one individual or more than one?

A. One. One the first time, but the other one joined him. . . .

Q. Now what, if anything, else happened to you aside from just being pulled back into the field area? What, if anything else was done to you?

A. I was thrown on the ground.

Q. All right. What happened at the time you were thrown on the ground?

A. And then the other fellow joined us and he said, "Not here," and he grabbed my other arm and they picked me up and they dragged me further and as they were dragging me they were ripping at my clothes.

Q. What clothing was ripped off you or taken off you?

A. My — my girdle and — my pants and stockings were ripped to shreds and — my girdle was caught at my ankles so as I was being dragged I couldn't move my feet really, they were all stopping moving back. I was dragged back towards where the pool is in a hole in the fence.

Q. All right. What, if anything, happened when you got to the hole in the fence?

A. Well, when we got to the hole in the fence the third one joined us and I was thrown down on the ground there again and they had taken my purse at this time and were going through my purse and then they picked — then they picked me up again and someone held the hole in the fence, the barbed wire, and one got through and pulled me through. . . .

Q. All right. How did you get through the fence area, aside from someone picking it up? Did you just walk through?

A. No. There was another person went through first and he pulled — and then they pushed me down by the hole and the other person grabbed my arm and pulled me through.

Q. Were you saying anything at this time?

A. I was pleading with them to leave me alone.

Q. Now, what's on the opposite side of this fence? What, if anything, occurred at this time?

A. Then I was dragged down — there is a little — there is a little platform and just a slide down the hill. I was dragged down the hill and then someone got on top of me and — but nothing could happen because we kept sliding together down the hill so they dragged me all the way back up the hill to just right on — on the flat — flat area.

Q. Now, what happened, if anything, up on the top of this knoll area on the flat ground?

A. I was raped by all three of them.

Q. You say raped. Specifically, did they have intercourse with you?

A. Yes

Q. All three of them?

A. Yes.

Q. Was there penetration? In other words, did they actually insert their penis into the vaginal area?

A. Yes.

Q. Were you saying anything or doing anything at this time to them?

A. Yes.

Q. What did you say and what did you do, if anything?

A. I asked them to please leave me alone and I was screaming and I was crying, too.

Q. What, if anything, did any of them do to you during the course of the time that they were having relations with you?

A. One of them hit me. (Crying.) And they kept saying that if I ever told anybody that they would kill me. . . .

A. One was always sort of watching by the fence across toward the field.

Q. Were you held down in any way?

A. Yes. . . .

Cross-Examination

Q. Where were you living at the time . . . of this incident?

A. 1715 N Street, Northwest.

Q. On the night in question, you were out on a date, is that correct?

A. That is true, sir.

Q. With Toby . . . ?

A. Yes.

Q. You were at his home for a drink and dinner, is that correct?

A. That is true, yes.

Q. Now, I think you indicated that there were other people present at the dinner at his home.

A. Yes, his roommates were there.

Q. His roommates?

A. Yes.

Q. Was it a dinner party that you were attending?

A. No. We were to go to a movie that night. That was the arrangements that were made, but they came back late that afternoon from where they had been and they hadn't eaten. So he came over and picked me up and I ate with them while they were having dinner. Actually, I had already eaten.

Q. Had you had a drink?

A. One drink.

Q. One beer?

A. No, I don't think it was a beer.

Q. I'm sorry?

A. I am not quite sure what it was now, but I don't think it was beer.

Q. Had you had more than one drink?

A. No.

Q. During the course of the dinner?

A. No, I don't think so.

Q. Did you have any drinks after the dinner?

A. No.

Q. You say it was too late to go to the movie?

A. That is true.

Q. What happened?

A. So we went out for a walk.

Q. Where did Toby live?

A. O Street, Northwest.

Q. And what? 20th, 21st and O, where did he live?

A. I am not sure of the exact address now. I'm sorry. I had never been there before.

Q. Was this your first date with Toby?

A. First technical date. I had met him several times before. He was a friend of my roommate's. They had gone to school together and he used to come over and play tennis, to pick her up to play tennis, and I had met him at breakfast one time, and he was at my going away party and we all, a group of us went to a concert once.

Q. Now, you left his home at about what time?

A. About midnight, I think.

Q. Midnight. You were walking down what street?

A. O Street.

Q. To about what? 23rd?

A. I am not familiar with the streets in that area, but there is one that goes around like this, you know, that comes in like that.

Q. On the front of Francis Junior High School almost from the front of the establishment?

A. No. It was by the tennis court.

Q. By the tennis court. With your boyfriend?

A. Yes.

Q. Now, as I recall your testimony . . . you stated that you were dragged from time to time during the course of your being in the company of these three young men. Isn't that correct?

A. That's true, sir.

Q. Were you dragged on your back or on your stomach or on your side?

A. I was standing up, but when my clothes were ripped off me, my girdle was down at my ankles so my feet were together and I wasn't exactly walking. I was, you know, my feet were together because of the girdle.

Q. Had you lost your footing?

A. Had I lost my footing? If I was being pulled, I lost my footing, yes, sir.

Q. So there came a time when you were being dragged along the ground, is that correct?

A. No. I was being held up by the arms like this and my feet were being dragged. I was being moved. . . .

Q. Isn't it a fact . . . that you walked the entire way from the point where you met the man to the point where you went to the fence, to the opening in the gateway?

A. I don't think you can say that, no.

Q. You were on your feet, weren't you?

A. But I couldn't have walked without someone pulling me with my girdle at my ankles. I would have had to hop.

Q. At what point in your trek across that field did your girdle come off?

A. I can't pinpoint that. I'm sorry.

Q. Isn't it a fact . . . that the point when your girdle came off, you assisted in taking of that girdle off?

A. Assisted? I wouldn't use the word "assisted."

Q. Did you participate in taking that girdle off?

A. No. I might have had my hands down there, yes, but I didn't participate.

Q. Did you in any way pull that girdle down?

A. No, I wouldn't say that, sir.

Q. The girdle wasn't ripped, was it?

A. No, it wasn't.

Q. Your dress wasn't ripped, either, was it?

A. No.

Q. Nor were your underpants ripped?

A. No, they were not ripped.

Q. Now, at all times, you had your dress on you, isn't that correct?

A. That is true, sir.

Q. Now, did you assist in the taking of your pants off?

A. No, sir.

Q. What effort if any did you make toward taking that girdle off of your body?

A. Effort? I don't understand.

Q. Isn't it a fact . . . that you helped those men take that girdle off your body?

A. That's not true.

Q. Isn't it a fact, further, that you did not resist their taking off those underpants from your body?

A. That's not true. That's not true.

Q. There were no grass stains on this dress, were there . . . ?

A. I haven't really examined the dress, sir.

Q. At the time . . . you went down the embankment with the young men, isn't it a fact that at one point when the two of you started slipping down this embankment that you said to that young man, "don't hurt yourself," or "be careful," or words to that effect?

A. No. I don't remember ever saying that.

Q. Isn't it a fact . . . at least certainly between the second and the third intercourse you took time out to brush away the excesses of fluid that were around your vaginal area?

A. No, that's not true.

Q. Isn't it a fact . . . that upon the occasion of at least the third intercourse you assisted the third man in the completion of the sexual act to the extent of assisting him in penetrating you?

A. No, that's not true, sir. . . .

Q. One more question. . . . Is it not a fact that on the occasion of the third intercourse, you said to the man, "come on, come on"? (Short pause) Did you hear my question?

A. Yes, I heard your question, sir. [No answer]

NOTES

1. An alert prosecutor might have objected to this line of cross-examination on the ground that the defendant's story, as presented through the leading questions on cross-examination, was so inherently incredible that it did not offer a sufficient basis for the cross-examination. On the other hand, under the Sixth Amendment, a defendant has the right to confront the witness against him, and denial of this kind of cross-examination would raise constitutional problems, particularly were defense counsel to argue that his client planned to take the stand and swear to the story embodied in the leading questions of the cross-examination.

The history of the case is a further illustration of the harrowing experience for the victim-witness in a sexual assault case. The trial resulted in a hung jury. When the retrial was scheduled, a psychiatrist testified for the victim that she could not mentally or physically withstand further testimony in the case. The court found her "legally unavailable," and ordered the trial to proceed on the reading of her testimony from the prior transcript. The unexplained absence of the victim resulted in another hung jury, and the government did not further prosecute the defendant.

2. Think about the kinds of questions and answers and the witnesses that would be presented both on the issue of a victim's reputation and on the issue of prior unchaste acts. There are cases where, because the woman appears particularly sympathetic, the defense attorney will not pursue such questions for tactical reasons. And, of course, in many instances, defense lawyers are inadequately prepared, particularly when they represent the indigent accused; and therefore they neither cross-examine to the limits permitted by the law, nor present witnesses. But in an effectively defended case where consent is an issue, questions about chastity will generally be asked on cross-examination and witnesses will be presented for the defense.

It is even possible that issues of chastity and the woman's character may be inserted into a case when consent is not an issue; for instance, through innuendo in cross-examination of the victim about her activities immediately prior to the attack (e.g., "Now you say that you had several drinks at a tavern after work? That was at a tavern on Atlantic Avenue? And of course you knew when you went in that it would be dark outside when you came out? And you knew, didn't you, that the bus stop is a block away? You often have a drink after work, don't you? And do you often make new acquaintances in this tavern? And some of them are men, no doubt?") Certainly, every lawyer who has prosecuted or defended rape cases knows that the jury is always interested in and curious about the woman's history. The unspoken issue is: "How much did she lose by being raped?"

c. Duty of the Feminist Lawyer

Rules of evidence and cases in most jurisdictions clearly allow the admission of the kind of evidence outlined above. An attorney defending a rape case would be remiss in his duty to his client in failing to present it, if his investigation reveals any basis for it. In light of this fact, some feminist attorneys, both men and women, have argued that they would not or could not represent a defendant charged with rape, particularly where the defense is consent. Arguably, however, professional duty might be dependent on the lawyer's sex. Some experienced trial lawyers feel that an accused rapist enjoys an unjustified advantage when he is represented by a woman. The jury psychology is that no nice woman *would* represent a man who actually did what the defendant is alleged to have done. What do you think of this argument?

d. The "Law" of Consent

As the foregoing materials show, the defense often does present evidence of lack of force in its own case: the reputation of the victim, prior acts of intercourse, and often the defendant's account of the incident are examples of such evidence. But, to reiterate, these are examples of evidence of "nonforce," rather than of consent, because conceptually consent is not a defense to a rape charge. If intercourse were accomplished by force, and the woman consented to the force, the crime would nevertheless be rape: it is hornbook criminal law that "consent to a physical assault, particularly a violent one, is uniformly held to constitute no defense."[28]

A famous analogy is sadomasochistic beating, in which cases hold that consent of the victim is no defense.[29] Williams[30] and Hart[31] on one side, and Lord Devlin[32] on the other, have debated in their writings whether consent should in fact be a defense in such a case, or whether when there is consent, no crime has been committed at all. Williams has written in response to Devlin:[33]

> Lord Devlin's philosophy naturally implies that the consent of a person against whom force is used is no excuse to the person who uses the force, if the use of the force is regarded as immoral notwithstanding the consent. The fact that it is used against a willing victim is immaterial. His words on this particular matter are as follows: "Subject to certain exceptions inherent in the nature of particular crimes, the criminal law has never permitted consent of the victim to be used as a defence. In rape, for example, consent negatives an essential element. But consent of the victim is no defence to a charge of murder. It is not a defence to any form of assault that the victim thought his punishment well deserved and submitted to it; to make a good defence the accused must prove that the law gave him the right to chastise and that he exercised it reasonably."
>
> I do not know of any specific legal authority for the last statement, which the learned author does not confine to chastisements causing grievous bodily harm. Let it be supposed that an employer detects his servant in dishonesty, and gives him the alternative of either being dismissed or submitting to moderate chastisement. Lord Devlin seems to assume that if the servant submits to the chastisement the employer can be charged with battery, even though no grievous bodily harm is caused. If this proposition is to be relevant to the general question of the enforcement of morals, it must be assumed that the chastisement is immoral even though the servant accepted it — which may not be obvious. On what principle does such conduct fall within the domain of the criminal Law? . . . Is it not inherent in the conception of assault and battery that the victim does not consent? It is because the definition of this crime involves absence of the victim's consent the burden of proving this absence rests on the prosecution. Why, then, does Lord Devlin assume that there is a distinction in this respect between rape and assault?

e. Changing the Operation of the Laws Regarding Force and Nonconsent

The rules which admit evidence of reputation and prior acts of intercourse should be changed, because they are based on outmoded conceptions of human behavior. Today, a woman's consensual intercourse on some occasions with some men simply does not raise an inference of consent on another occasion with another man. In a mobile,

---

28. Kadish and Paulsen, Criminal Law and Its Processes 15 (2d ed. 1969).

29. Rex v. Donovan, 2 K.B. 498 (1934); People v. Samuels, 58 Cal. Rptr. 439 (Dist. Ct. of App. 1967).

30. Williams, Consent and Public Policy, 1962 Crim. L. Rev. 74.

31. Hart, Law, Liberty and Morality 30-34 (1963).

32. Devlin, The Enforcement of Morals (Maccabaian Lecture in Jurisprudence of the British Academy 1959).

33. Williams, supra footnote 30, at 74-75.

sexually active society, moreover, there is no such thing as a "reputation for unchastity." Such unwarranted evidence could be eliminated from rape trials in two ways. First, in particular cases, objection could be made to the evidence on the ground of irrelevancy with a trial memorandum citing sociological and psychological works about current sexual mores. But in the ordinary course this objection would be made by the government attorney, and prosecutors' offices, particularly in the criminal trial division, are still overwhelmingly male and have often proved insensitive to the need to protect rape victims from irrelevant questioning on the witness stand.

As an alternative to relying on the prosecution to make the argument for exclusion of irrelevant evidence, a lawyer for the victim could review before trial evidence which might be introduced and make appropriate motions for its exclusion. A rape victim who could afford it could employ her own attorney, who could then seek to play this role. Otherwise, such a lawyer for the victim would have to be court-appointed and compensated. A procedure whereby the victim-witness is represented by counsel is unusual and is not provided for by the rules of most courts, yet there are analogues to the procedure. For instance, courts often appoint counsel to advise a witness who appears to be verging on self-incrimination. Courts may also appoint an attorney to represent the child's interest in a divorce action. This practice has been legislated in Wisconsin, and grew specifically from a judicial recognition that the two contesting parties in a divorce action would not always properly litigate the best interests of the children.[34] The analogy is direct to rape cases in which the prosecution is concerned with proving its case (often with limited resources), not with protecting the woman-witness from humiliation.

Legislation could bring about the revision of evidence law in regard to consent. A statute might simply declare that evidence of unchastity or prior consensual intercourse, at least with men other than the defendant, is inadmissible under most circumstances.

It should be borne in mind, however, that there are cases and circumstances in which evidence of sexual promiscuity would clearly be relevant. The famous case of Giles v. Maryland, 386 U.S. 66 (1967), is one such instance, in which the defendants' testimony of consensual intercourse was undermined because they were strangers to the young girl who was the alleged victim, and racially different from her. But had it been known to the defense and the jury that the girl was extremely promiscuous sexually and had intercourse with strangers consensually on other occasions, the verdict might well have been different. It would be necessary for legislation to explicate the circumstances in which evidence of promiscuity should be admissible.

A memorandum which spells out a procedure for testing the relevance of evidence of prior sexual history follows.

AMSTERDAM AND BABCOCK
PROPOSED POSITION ON ISSUES RAISED BY THE
ADMINISTRATION OF LAWS AGAINST RAPE
Memorandum for the ACLU of Northern California (April 1974)

Before any evidence of sexual experience, practices or attitudes of the complaining witness may be presented in open court, either by cross-examination or by extrinsic proof, the evidence should be heard by the judge in a closed voir dire proceeding and screened for relevance under appropriate standards. If defense counsel proposes to mention such evidence in opening argument or in the interrogation of prospective jurors, the voir dire proceeding must be held prior to the argument or interrogation, as the case may be. No exploration of the complainant's sexual history or attitudes in open court should be permitted until after the judge has explicitly found, by written order, that one or more of the specified standards of admissibility is met; and then the line of examina-

---

34. Wendland v. Wendland, 29 Wis. 2d 145, 138 N.W.2d 185 (1965).

tion should be controlled by the judge so as to exclude extraneous material and protect the complainant from harassment and from unnecessary embarrassment.

THE HEARING

Counsel should be forbidden to mention or elicit any form of evidence regarding the complainant's sexual history, experiences, practices or attitudes (other than those immediately connected with the alleged rape itself) unless expressly authorized by order of the court following a voir dire hearing. The hearing will be in a closed courtroom or in the judge's chambers; and only the judge, counsel for the prosecution and defense, the defendant, the witness through whom the evidence is offered, the court reporter, and court personnel necessary for the maintenance of security should be present. If the hearing includes questioning of the complaining witness, the judge shall ensure that such questioning is conducted in a manner that is not harassing or unduly embarrassing.

DETERMINATION AS TO ADMISSIBILITY

After hearing the evidence or the line of cross-examination proffered by the defense, and any cross or redirect examination as the case may be, the judge should make a ruling on its admissibility. The evidence or cross-examination should not be admitted unless the court enters a written order containing one or more of the following findings:

(1) The evidence or cross-examination tends to show consensual sexual intercourse between the complainant and the defendant within six months preceding or following the alleged rape.

(2) The evidence or cross-examination tends to show that the defendant, at the time of the alleged rape, knew of prior sexual activity of the complainant which would reasonably lead him to believe that she was consenting to sexual intercourse under the circumstances of their encounter.

(3) The evidence or cross-examination tends to show that the complaining witness has, on direct examination, affirmatively misrepresented the nature of her sexual experience on occasions other than that of the alleged rape.

(4) The evidence or cross-examination tends to show that the complaining witness has engaged in consensual sexual activity with any person under particular and characteristic circumstances sufficiently similar to those of the encounter with the defendant so as to establish that she consented to sexual intercourse with the defendant or that she acted in such a way as to lead him to believe that she consented.

(5) The evidence or cross-examination tends to show that the complainant has a motive for fabricating a charge of rape.

If, for the purpose of applying these standards, it is necessary for the judge to inform himself of the factual theory of the defense, a representation of that theory by defense counsel should be sufficient. Defense counsel should not be required to state the evidence by which he proposes to establish this theory, but should be expected to make a representation only upon an adequate factual basis.

PRESENTATION OF EVIDENCE IN OPEN COURT

If the judge makes a ruling that evidence is admissible, he shall give appropriate instructions to counsel concerning the scope of the examination of witnesses that is to be permitted. The permitted examination should be limited to proof of matters relevant under the standards set forth in the preceding paragraph, and should be conducted in such a manner as to avoid eliciting extraneous matter or harassing or unduly embarrassing the complainant. Counsel's examination should not be so confined as to preclude following up answers with appropriately probing questions, but should be limited to eliciting the matter that the court has ruled admissible.

When evidence of prior sexual history has been admitted, the court shall, as part of its instructions to the jury at the close of all the evidence, inform the jury as follows:

> There has been testimony about the sexual experience of the complainant in this case. You are to judge this testimony by the same standards of credibility which you apply to all other evidence. Even if you find it credible, you should not infer that, because a woman has consented on prior occasions to sexual intercourse, she necessarily consented with the defendant on the particular occasion at issue in this case. The testimony has been admitted for your consideration together with all the other evidence on the issue[s] of [whether she consented] [whether the defendant reasonably believed that she consented] [whether her complaint of rape is credible].

Commentary

The procedure suggested above is based upon a practice that was used successfully for a time in the District of Columbia to pre-screen possible prejudicial prior-crime evidence offered to impeach the testimony of a criminal defendant. In our experience, the procedure worked well in the District; and we believe that, as we have adapted it, it should work well in California rape cases. It is, quite frankly, a compromise between the legitimate interests of the complainant and those of the criminal accused; but we think that it is the best compromise that can be worked out.

A rape complainant will still be required to answer questions about her sexual experience and attitudes, and ample room will be allowed for the defense to inquire fully on these subjects, but the inquiry will be conducted in a closed hearing that is not conducive to the harassment and denigrating innuendo often employed in open court before a jury. After the evidence has been fully developed, the judge will rule upon its admissibility pursuant to standards that are designed to allow the presentation of all relevant defensive evidence while excluding unwarranted prying into the sexual privacy of the complainant or unduly badgering or embarrassing modes of examination. This approach accepts the premise that there are some circumstances in which a complainant's sexual history, experience and attitudes are relevant on the issues of force and consent. The best example perhaps is the famous *Giles* case in Maryland, where two black youths claimed that they had had consensual intercourse with a white girl who was a stranger to them. Their story was unbelievable in the absence of evidence (which the Supreme Court of the United States held must be produced to the defense) that the complainant had had consensual sexual intercourse with strangers on many other occasions. A less obvious but common example is the case in which a complainant has been carefully coached by the prosecutor to project a false image of sexual innocence from the witness stand. We believe it must be recognized that there *are* situations in which the sexual history of the complainant is relevant to the issues in a rape prosecution, and that the ACLU should not support crudely drafted legislation which ignores this fact. On the other hand, concerns for privacy and against sexual discrimination require that irrelevant prying into the complainant's sex life, unwarrantedly wholesale exploration of her sexual behavior, and rude, roughshod manners of examination should be eliminated.

The standards of admissibility that we propose are intended to strike the balance. We are not committed to their precise language, but strongly favor the approach of enumerating an exclusive list of sorts of evidence that is admissible; and we are satisfied with our present enumeration pending its criticism by others within the ACLU's policy-making process. We have considered other approaches and concluded that they are less satisfactory: a "presumption" against admissibility of evidence of prior sexual activity, for example, coupled with a requirement that the judge pre-screen such evidence under the standard of "relevancy" or Evidence Code §352.[2] We are loath to employ devices

---

2. §352. *Discretion of court to exclude evidence.* The court in its discretion may exclude evidence if its probative value is substantially outweighed by the probability that its admission will (a) necessitate undue consumption of time or (b) create substantial danger of undue prejudice, of confusing the issues, or of misleading the jury.

such as "presumptions" against the relevance of defensive evidence in criminal cases because of the propensity of such devices, once recognized, to spread dangerously into other areas (informers, "national security"), where it is thought by some that defendants ought not be allowed to pry. We are also loath to leave determinations of general "relevancy" to judges who are too frequently male and too frequently imbued with unreal and insensitive attitudes toward women's sexual attitudes and experiences. We are still more loath to utilize procedures or standards that would effectively require advance notice or disclosure of defenses by a criminal defendant or preclude the defendant's development of all relevant facts prior to a ruling on their admissibility. Some of our particular standards — for example, the six-month cut-off on evidence of sexual relations between complainant and defendant that are not otherwise relevant — are necessarily approximative and arbitrary. It is worth consideration whether the desirable flexibility of looser standards (e.g., "recent" sexual activity between complainant and defendant) warrants their obvious risks.

This memorandum was prepared to aid an American Civil Liberties Union Board to take a position on pending legislation in California. Do you think it is a successful compromise between the rights of the defendant and those of the victim?

3. The Requirement of Corroboration: Testimonial Disability of the Victim

UNITED STATES v. WILEY
492 F.2d 547 (D.C. Cir. 1973)

WISDOM, Circuit Judge: David Wiley, the appellant, and Eugene Cunningham, a co-defendant, were arrested on March 17, 1971, in connection with an alleged sexual assault on the same date on twelve-year old Maxine Lewis. By a two-count indictment filed May 25, 1971, they were charged with carnal knowledge (22 D.C. Code §2801) and taking indecent liberties with a minor child (22 D.C. Code §3501(a)). Wiley was tried separately on May 22, 1972. After a jury trial the trial court dismissed the indecent liberties count and submitted the case to the jury on the charge of carnal knowledge. The jury found Wiley guilty, and on August 18, 1972, he was sentenced to a term of four to twelve years. The principal issue on appeal is whether there was sufficient corroborative evidence to take the case to the jury. We find that there was not sufficient corroborative evidence and therefore reverse.

I

At about 5:00 p.m. on March 17, 1971, Maxine Lewis arrived at 240 W Street, N.W. to meet a friend, Sandra Wiggins, with whom Miss Lewis planned to visit a relative in the hospital. She was invited inside the apartment by Wiley's girl friend, Delores Smith. There, she encountered Eugene Cunningham, a friend of another woman who also lived in the apartment. Miss Lewis testified that Cunningham came and sat next to her. He "started feeling all over me and I try to get away from him, but I couldn't". Miss Smith went to a bedroom in the back of the apartment and returned with Wiley, who looked as though he had been sleeping. Miss Lewis testified that Wiley grabbed her by the legs while Cunningham was choking her. They dragged her into the bedroom, closed the door, put a dresser across it, and threw her on the bed. Cunningham was holding her in a choking grip and Wiley was holding her legs and pulling her clothes off. She testified that Cunningham then "had sex with me". After Cunningham finished, "David had sex with me". On closer questioning, Miss Lewis stated that the penis of each man had penetrated her and that each ejaculated. As soon as Wiley and Cunningham had finished she went to the bathroom to "fix [herself] up", then ran out of the apartment, leaving her coat behind.

Miss Lewis found a telephone booth to call the police, but then saw Wiley and Cunningham approaching. She hung up the telephone and fled. Shortly afterwards she noticed a police officer on a scooter talking to some people, but she was too embarrassed to approach him and continued on her way. She finally managed to call the police from a public telephone at 4th and U Streets, N.W. When Officers Dye and Kraigler responded to her call, Miss Lewis told these officers that she had been raped by Wiley and Cunningham.

Miss Lewis also testified about her relationships with the people involved in the incident. She had seen Wiley four or five times before the day of the assault, and he had "never said nothing to me out of the way". She stated that she had never dated Wiley or Cunningham and had only spoken a few words to either. When asked how she got along with Miss Smith, she replied: "She used to accuse me of doing things that I didn't do . . . like something missing of hers, like food stamps or some money, I always get the blame," although she never took any of Miss Smith's things. On cross-examination, she testified that she was angry at Miss Smith for not helping her during the incident but that she hadn't mentioned this fact to Miss Smith. She further testified that she could have known that Miss Smith wasn't going to help her "by the way she probably set him [either Wiley or Cunningham] up to do it".

Two police officers testified at trial about the events following Miss Lewis' departure from the apartment. Officer James Gordon, the police officer on the scooter, stated that on March 17 he was about two blocks from 240 W Street, N.W., when he noticed Miss Lewis. He said:

> I observed a young lady coming off the intersection of 4th and Elm Streets, appeared to be crying. I noticed it was cold and she didn't have a coat, blouse was deranged on her, so I took notice of her and I think she took notice of me, so I made no effort to see what the problem was, she didn't come over.

Minutes later, Officer Gordon heard a radio run to check for a possible criminal assault at 4th and U Streets; he went around the corner to check the report, and talked to Miss Lewis. She pointed down the street toward the alleged suspects. Officer Gordon then passed the two men whom Miss Lewis later identified as Wiley and Cunningham.

Officer Kaigler testified that he was patrolling in a scout car with his partner, Officer Norman Dye. At 5:39 P.M., They received a radio run for a possible criminal assault. They went to the corner of 4th and U Streets, N.W., where they found Miss Lewis. Officer Kaigler stated:

> She was a young lady, she appeared to be upset, she was crying as she walked up to the car. We asked the young lady did she call the police and she indicated she did.

Miss Lewis and the officers drove in the car toward the apartment. En route, she pointed out Cunningham and Wiley on the street and named them. Officer Kaigler testified that when Wiley and Cunningham saw the car coming, they turned down another block. The police stopped Wiley and Cunningham, and Miss Lewis identified them; they were arrested. Miss Lewis was then taken to a hospital where a doctor examined her.

Sandra Wiggins, the friend whom Miss Lewis was to meet at the apartment, testified that during that evening she was riding in a car when she saw Miss Lewis "standing at 4th and U by some phone booths". Miss Wiggins did not stop.

Wiley took the stand in his own behalf. He testified that on March 17 he had been asleep in one of the bedrooms of the apartment since 12:00 or 1:00 P.M. when Miss Smith awakened him and asked him to tell Cunningham to leave Miss Lewis alone. Wiley got up, and when he saw that Cunningham was bothering Miss Lewis, told him to stop it. Wiley then went back to sleep. Later, he was awakened by Cunningham. Both left the apartment to visit Cunningham's girl friend to get some money. Wiley stated that he did not see Miss Lewis in a telephone booth during their walk. En route, they were arrested by the police. Wiley stated that he did not see the police car until he was stopped.

Wiley expressly denied that he had helped Cunningham take Miss Lewis into the bedroom, that he himself had gone into the bedroom with Miss Lewis, and that he ever had sexual relations with Miss Lewis. Wiley stated that he did not hear Miss Lewis run out of the apartment crying, nor did he hear any argument in the bedroom while he was asleep. Also, he testified that Miss Lewis and Miss Smith "got along as I seen", and that he and Miss Lewis were good friends. As to the relationship between Miss Lewis and Cunningham, Wiley stated that Cunningham was "always picking at her", that he was "messing with her, all the time, arguing". He further testified that although they made repeated attempts, neither he nor his mother had been able to locate Miss Smith to have her testify.

Wiley was arrested on March 17, 1971. After a preliminary hearing on March 26, 1971, Wiley was indicted on May 25, 1971. Subsequent events delayed the trial date until May 22, 1972. By that time, Cunningham had fled the jurisdiction. Dr. Matthews, who had examined the complainant on the date of the incident, was not subpoenaed by the Government on May 22, 1972, because he was on vacation. Indeed, no medical testimony was introduced at trial.

At the close of the Government's case, the defense moved for a judgment of acquittal on the indictment on the ground that there was insufficient corroboration of the complainant's testimony. As noted, the trial court later dismissed the charge of indecent liberties and submitted the case to the jury on the charge of carnal knowledge. The court also submitted an aiding and abetting instruction.

The jury returned a verdict of guilty. After the trial court denied a motion for acquittal n.o.v. or for a new trial, Wiley appealed.

II

It is established law in this jurisdiction that a person may not be convicted of a "sex offense" on the uncorroborated testimony of the alleged victim. Bailey & Humphries v. United States, 132 U.S. App. D.C. 82, 405 F.2d 1352 (1968); Duckett v. United States, 133 U.S. App. D.C. 305, 410 F.2d 1004 (1969); United States v. Medley, 146 U.S. App. D.C. 396, 452 F.2d 1325 (1971). The corroboration requirement provides an essential safeguard in such cases where the risk of unjust conviction is high. Complainants all too frequently have "an urge to fantasize or even a motive to fabricate". Coltrane v. United States, 135 U.S. App. D.C. 295, 418 F.2d 1131, 1135 (1969). Typically, the "innocent as well as the guilty have only their own testimony upon which to rely", and the nature of the charges "poses an unusual threat to the reliability of a judgment on credibility of the allegedly defiled vis a vis the alleged defiler". 418 F.2d 1135.

This Circuit has avoided imposing rigid rules concerning corroboration. See United States v. Terry, 137 U.S. App. D.C. 267, 422 F.2d 704, 708 (1970). In general, the degree of corroboration required will vary according to the danger of fabrication by a particular complainant. With respect to the corpus delicti, for example, it is not always necessary to introduce independent evidence to corroborate each and every element of the offense. Rather, "independent corroborative evidence will be regarded as sufficient when it would permit the jury to conclude beyond a reasonable doubt that the victim's account of the crime was not a fabrication". United States v. Gray, — U.S. App. D.C. —, — F.2d — (No. 72-1776, March 30, 1973). See United States v. Terry, supra; United States v. Huff, 143 U.S. App. D.C. 163, 165-66, 442 F.2d 885, 887-88 (1971); United States v. Jones, — U.S. App. D.C. —, — F.2d — (Nos. 71-1691, 72-1284, March 15, 1973). The quantum of proof required will depend upon such factors as the age and impressionability of the complainant and the presence or absence of any apparent motive. United States v. Gray, supra. This flexible approach to the corroboration rule focuses attention on the facts of each case. For example, scrutiny must be exercised where, as here, the complainant is a young girl. Courts have exhibited a "traditional skepticism" towards accusations of children. Wilson v. United States, 106 U.S. App. D.C. 226, 271 F.2d 492 (1959). In such cases, the offense may not be established by the testimony of the victim alone.

Applying this standard to the present case, we find that there was not sufficient corroboration to warrant submission of the case to the jury. The elements of the offense of carnal knowledge are: (1) penetration, (2) with a child under the age of sixteen. D.C.C.E. §22-2801, ¶2; Wheeler v. United States, 93 U.S. App. D.C. 159, 211 F.2d 19, 21 (1953), cert. denied, 347 U.S. 1019 (1954). In its instruction to the jury, the trial court set forth the principal corroboration testimony introduced:

> The testimony of Officer Gordon, that shortly after the alleged event he saw the complaining witness on the street in a disheveled condition, crying and upset, and without a coat, although it was a cold day, and that she told him she had been attacked and pointed at a group of people a block and a half away in which she said two of them were the people involved in this offense.
>
> And the testimony of Officer Kaigler that shortly after the alleged attack he saw the complaining witness on the street, that she appeared upset, crying, and reported that she had been raped by this defendant and by Cunningham.

Corroboration, therefore, consisted of testimony of the two officers to the effect that (1) the complainant was crying and upset, (2) her clothing was disheveled, (3) she had no coat even though it was a cold day, and (4) the complainant's prompt report of the alleged incident to the officers. Although this evidence may corroborate the occurrence of some event, it does not corroborate sexual intercourse.

The most effective corroboration of the complainant's testimony would have been medical evidence. Here, Miss Lewis was examined by a doctor shortly after the alleged incident. Notwithstanding the importance of the medical evidence, the Government went to trial without having subpoenaed the examining physician. The Government was well aware of the significance of that evidence and had subpoenaed the doctor on the three prior dates set for trial. At the time of the fourth and final trial date, the doctor was on vacation. The Government's decision to proceed without him was irresponsible. Medical evidence may not be an indispensable prerequisite to conviction where other independent evidence is introduced to corroborate sexual intercourse.[1] But in the instant case, no such evidence was presented. As a practical matter, the Government's case rested almost exclusively on the testimony of the child. Any inference that sexual intercourse or penetration occurred must be based on her bare accusation. In these circumstances, the traditional purpose of the corroboration requirement — avoidance of fabricated charges — requires reversal of the defendant's conviction.

Nor was the evidence sufficient to warrant submission of the case to the jury on the theory that the defendant was an aider and abettor in Cunningham's act of carnal knowledge. The elements of the offense of aiding and abetting are: (1) guilty knowledge on the part of the accused; (2) that an offense was committed by someone; and (3) that

---

1. See Bailey & Humphries v. United States, supra (carnal knowledge); Coltrane v. United States, supra (sodomy); United States v. Green, 139 U.S. App. D.C. 75, 429 F.2d 754 (1970) (rape); Carter v. United States, 138 U.S. App. D.C. 349, 427 F.2d 619, 623 (1970) (rape); Johnson v. United States, 138 U.S. App. D.C. 174, 426 F.2d 651, 652-3 (1970), cert. denied, 401 U.S. 846 (1971) (rape); Washington v. United States, 136 U.S. App. D.C. 54, 419 F.2d 636, 637 (1969) (rape); Gass v. United States, 135 U.S. App. D.C. 11, 416 F.2d 767, 769 (1969) (rape); Duckett v. United States, 133 U.S. App. D.C. 305, 410 F.2d 1004, 1005 (1969) (carnal knowledge); Borum v. United States, 133 U.S. App. D.C. 305, 409 F.2d 433, 437-8 (1967) (rape), cert. denied, 395 U.S. 916 (1969); Thomas v. United States, 128 U.S. App. D.C. 233, 387 F.2d 191 (1967) (carnal knowledge); McGuinn v. United States, 89 U.S. App. D.C. 477, 191 F.2d 477, 478 (1951) (rape); Ewing v. United States, 77 U.S. App. D.C. 14, 135 F.2d 633 (1942), cert. denied, 318 U.S. 776 (1943) (rape).

the defendant assisted or participated in the commission of the offense. United States v. Harris, 140 U.S. App. D.C. 270, 435 F.2d 74, 88, n.40 (1970), cert. denied, 402 U.S. 986 (1971). Even when the evidence is viewed in the light most favorable to the Government, it is clear that there was insufficient corroboration proved in this case to show that carnal knowledge was committed by anyone — either Wiley or Cunningham. The defendant's alleged assistance or participation in any act of carnal knowledge is similarly uncorroborated.

We therefore conclude that the defendant's conviction must be Reversed. For this reason, we need not consider the other issues raised by the defendant.

BAZELON, Chief Judge, concurring: The requirement of corroboration in sex offenses, particularly rape, has come under sharp attack in recent years. Feminists have found the requirement unjust to women and prosecutors have argued that it makes convictions too difficult to obtain. These criticisms force us to examine the origins of the current views on corroboration. . . . [Most citations in the concurrence are omitted.]

Numerous justifications have been advanced for the requirement of corroboration in sex cases. An examination of these rationales reveals a tangled web of legitimate concerns, out-dated beliefs, and deep-seated prejudices.

The most common basis advanced for the requirement is that false charges of rape are more prevalent than false charges of other crimes. A statement such as this is extremely difficult to prove, and little or no evidence has bee adduced to support it. Two reasons are generally given for the belief that unfounded rape charges are common. It is argued, first, that women often have a motive to fabricate rape accusations and second, that women may fantasize rapes.

It is contended that a woman may fabricate a rape accusation because, having consented to intercourse she is ashamed and bitter, or because she is pregnant and feels pressured to create a false explanation, or because she hates the man she accuses or wishes to blackmail him. It is said to be relatively easy to create a false description of rape in convincing detail.

There are, however, countervailing reasons not to report a rape. One said to be a victim of rape may be stigmatized by society, there may be humiliating publicity, and the necessity of facing the insinuations of defense counsel may be a deterrent. Moreover, those claiming to have been raped may be treated harshly by the police and by hospitals. One result of all of these obstacles is that rape is one of the most under-reported of all crimes. . . .

In addition to fabricated rapes, it has been suggested that women may report fantasized rapes. Both the causes and prevalence of rape fantasies have been hotly disputed and it is not established that any significant number of rape charges arise out of fantasies. To the extent that rape charges do so arise, that could be the result of an inferior and oppressed status of women that is now being eroded. . . .

In addition to the problem of false charges, the corroboration requirement is justified on the theory that rape is a charge unusually difficult to defend against. In 1680 Lord Chief Justice Hale wrote, in one of the most oft-quoted passages in our jurisprudence, that rape "is an accusation easily to be made and hard to be proved, and harder to be defended by the party accused, tho never so innocent." The same theme has been echoed by modern commentators and courts. The usual absence of eyewitnesses damages the defendant as well as the complainant. Juries are said to be unusually sympathetic to a woman wronged, thus weakening the presumption of innocence.

Again, there is little hard evidence with which to test this theory. What studies are available suggest that a defendant is unlikely to be convicted of rape on the uncorroborated testimony of the complainant in those jurisdictions that do not require corroboration. Thus juries may be more skeptical of rape accusations than is often supposed. . . .

Still another basis for the corroboration requirement lies in "the sorry history of racism in America." There has been an enormous danger of injustice when a black man accused of raping a white woman is tried before a white jury. Of the 455 men executed for rape since 1930, 405 (89 per cent) were black. In the vast majority of these cases the complainant was white.

All of the safeguards that developed in this context should not be automatically applied today. Juries are more integrated than in the past and racial prejudice may be at a somewhat lower level. Numerous rape victims are black and their interests, as well as those of white women, may have been slighted by the concern for black defendants.

A final theory of the corroboration requirement is that it stems from discrimination against women. It is said that traditional sex stereotypes have resulted in rape laws that protect men rather than women. Penalties are high because a "good" woman is a valued possession of a man. Corroboration is required because to a "good" woman rape is "a fate worse than death" and she should fight to the death to resist it. If no such fight is put up, the woman must have consented or at least enticed the rapist, who is therefore blameless. In sum it is said to be the "male desire to 'protect' his 'possession' which results in laws designed to protect the male — both the 'owner' and the assailant — rather than protecting the physical well-being and freedom of movement of women."

This point of view, which has been expressed by men as well as women, may well have some validity. It would be surprising if entrenched notions of sexuality did not play a role in the law of crimes dealing with sexual violations. Corroboration rules may be structured, for example, to protect male rather than female defendants. This could explain the fact that conviction for soliciting for homosexual purposes requires corroboration while soliciting for heterosexual prostitution does not.

Ultimately modern notions of sexual equality may help break down those aspects of rape law which stem from unjust discrimination against women.

III

Analyzing all of these justifications in order to separate the valid from the invalid is no easy task. As I have said in another context, we are in that terrible period known as "meanwhile." We know enough to be troubled but not enough to know how to resolve our troubles. As evidence, mores, and attitudes change we too must remain open to change. Next year or twenty years from now available information may require a different approach. But at least for the immediate present, I find that the flexible corroboration rule developed by this Court provides the best accommodation of numerous conflicting considerations. There may still be the possibility of special fabrication problems relating to rape, particularly where, as in this case, the complainant is young. There are still severe penalties for rape. There is still racism in our society and that racism may be particularly likely to surface in a case involving alleged sexual violations.

To guard against these possible dangers we retain a corroboration rule which provides that "independent corroborative evidence will be regarded as sufficient when it would permit the jury to conclude beyond a reasonable doubt that the victim's account of the crime was not a fabrication." United States v. Gray, Slip Opinion No. 72-1776 (D.C. Cir. March 30, 1973) at 2. We adhere to no absolute tests or concrete guidelines. We only require evidence of the crime of probative value outside of the complainant's testimony. In cases such as this one where that evidence is lacking the dangers to the defendant outweigh the difficulties created for the prosecution. . . .

Wilkey, Circuit Judge, dissenting: . . . In my view, the errors of the majority are clearly demonstrable as two:

1. The requirement of specific medical corroboration of one single fact conflicts with our previous decisions, and leads with inevitable logic to the conclusion that no rape conviction is sustainable without medical testimony confirming penetration, despite the established medical view that in many instances after the event a medical examination cannot determine one way or another whether forcible penetration took place; and

2. In the circumstances of this case, given the uncontradicted testimony of the 12 year old victim on the question of forcible penetration and the testimony of appellant Wiley, the majority has focused on the wrong issue on which corroboration is relevant.

I. THE STANDARD OF CORROBORATION IN THIS JURISDICTION. . . .

Our most recent decision is United States v. Gray, 30 March 1973.[5] *Gray* requires the affirmance of Wiley's conviction here, for precisely the same issue as to the absence of medical corroboration of the complainant's testimony as to sexual intercourse was raised in *Gray*.

> Appellant urges that corroboration of the corpus delicti requires independent evidence tending to establish each and every material element of the offense. Specifically, he contends that because the Government's proof as to penetration rested wholly on the complainant's testimony, his conviction must be reversed. Although there are statements in Allison v. United States, and United States v. Bryant, that support appellant's position, our more recent decisions make it clear that *Allison* and *Bryant* no longer reflect the controlling law. (citations omitted) Simply put, the principle emerging from these cases is that the independent corroborative evidence will be regarded as sufficient when it would permit the jury to conclude beyond a reasonable doubt that the victim's account of the crime was not a fabrication.[6]

While it may be argued, or denied, that the overall corroborative circumstances were stronger in *Gray* than in Wiley's case, corroboration here (particularly when analysis is made of what question needed corroboration, see III.B. infra) was strong enough at least to go to the jury.

Gray is one of many cases establishing that medical proof of forcible penetration may be impossible to obtain. "Although gynecological examination of the prosecutrix was inconclusive, she testified unequivocally that her attacker had achieved penetration."[7]

And, as to the real contested issue in Wiley's case — not whether the offense was committed but who committed it — we said in *Gray:* "Corroboration is also required as to identification of the assailant; but our cases have traditionally recognized that, as to this element, a lesser standard of proof is required. And where there is a convincing identification, one that minimizes the danger of mistake or falsification, no further corroboration is required. (Citations omitted) Here the victim identified appellant to police by name."[8] And so the victim here pointed out Wiley to officers on the street. . . .

II. CORROBORATION OF WILEY'S GUILT

First, the evidence to be corroborated. The testimony of the 12 year old victim as to the sexual assault in the apartment is, to my mind, clear, coherent, and without any internal contradictions. It is fairly set forth in Judge Wisdom's opinion. In the interest of brevity, it will not be repeated here, but we should not forget that the victim provided a complete documentation of every essential detail, unshaken on cross-examination, and uncontradicted except by the bare denial of the appellant.

Second, appellant *Wiley's testimony does not contradict the victim's assertion that a sexual assault took place.* Indeed, appellant confirms it. According to his story, he was awakened by Miss Smith (Wiley's girlfriend) who asked him to stop Cunningham from taking indecent liberties with the 12 year old. ". . . *he saw* that Cunningham was bothering Miss Lewis (the victim), told him to stop it." (Majority opinion, p. 5) Wiley says he then went back to sleep; the victim says he participated in the rape. At no time did Wiley testify that Cunningham did not, or could not, have raped the girl.

With this as the basic evidence, how much corroboration was needed *to send the case to the jury?* here is what the District Judge had:

1. The victim reported the offense immediately. After fleeing the apartment, she

---

5. No. 72-1776, Circuit Judges Leventhal and Robb, Senior District Judge Jameson [(30 March 1973)].
6. Id., slip op. at 2.
7. Id., slip op. at 3.
8. Id., slip op. at 4.

found a phone booth, started to call, but on seeing Wiley and Cunningham approaching, hung up and slipped away. She *was* seen at this time by Officer Gordon, who noticed her because she was crying, obviously upset, had a disarrayed blouse, and was not wearing a coat although it was a cold day. She found another phone, called the police. When Officers Dye and Kraigler arrived, she pointed out Wiley and Cunningham by name, and stated she had been raped by them.

2. Her crying and other visible signs of emotional distress, noted first without suggestion by Officer Gordon, then by Officers Dye and Kraigler.

3. Her disheveled clothing and her disarranged blouse, noted by all officers.

4. Her being on the street on a cold day without a coat, sufficiently odd to attract Officer Gordon's attention.

5. Finding the coat in the apartment at 240 W. Street, N.W., from whence she had fled, and claimed to have left the coat in her haste and emotional distress.

6. The complete absence of any motive on the victim's part to fabricate a story of Wiley's guilt. A portion of appellant's own testimony confirms this; he claimed "that he and Miss Lewis were good friends." (Majority opinion, p. 5) She, the victim, testified that Wiley "never said nothing to me out of the way". (Majority opinion, p. 3) . . .

[III] FOCUS ON THE WRONG ISSUE ON WHICH CORROBORATION WAS IMPORTANT

The majority opinion asserts "[t]he most effective corroboration of the complainant's testimony would have been medical evidence," and "[t]he Government's decision to proceed without [the doctor] was irresponsible."[20] Just what would the evidence of the examining physician have added to the certainty or uncertainty that appellant Wiley raped the victim? We know that the victim was raped, at least by Cunningham. The jury had the victim's testimony to this, and Wiley's testimony does not contradict it. Furthermore, although of course the jury did not have this, we now judicially know that Cunningham did commit this offense; this fact was judicially established in United States v. Cunningham, No. 994-71, U.S. District Court for the District of Columbia, now on appeal in this Court, No. 73-1283. This was a separate trial of Wiley's co-defendant, Cunningham, charged and tried in the same numbered case as Wiley.

So we know the victim was *raped by Cunningham.* Granting that the jury had only the victim's testimony (uncontradicted as to the rape by Cunningham), the question before the jury was and here is, *was she also raped by Wiley?* The physician's testimony could not have answered that question. At the most, he could have testified to penetration and sperm in the vagina. But who was responsible? Cunningham, or Cunningham *and Wiley?* Wiley's defense was *not* that the rape did not, or could not have occurred; his defense was that he was asleep in the other room while Cunningham was with the 12 year old victim.

Obviously the jury disbelieved Wiley's story on the critical issue. The physician's testimony would not have been even relevant to the critical issue raised by Wiley: Was it Wiley who *also* raped the victim?

I am not overlooking the well understood principle that every element of an offense must be *proved* — but the law in this jurisdiction is that *not every element* of a sexual offense need be *corroborated.*[21] *Every element was* PROVED. The 12 year old victim's testimony was clear and unequivocal; she was raped by *both* Cunningham and Wiley, there was penetration and ejaculation by *both.* As to Cunningham, her story was not only clear and

---

20. . . . Government counsel had had the examining physician under subpoena and in courthouse attendance for three prior settings of the case. The doctor wasted numerous hours without the case ever going to trial. So, for any subsequent setting, the prosecuting attorney made an agreement with the doctor to appear without subpoena when called by phone. On the critical day the doctor was away on vacation. Record p. 49. Both sides had made motions for continuance, the Government because of the flight of co-defendant Cunningham, and the prosecution did not anticipate being put to trial, hence the failure to alert the doctor.

21. United States v. Gray, supra note 1, slip op. at 2; United States v. Jones, supra, note 4 at 1217-18; United States v. Terry, 137 U.S. App. D.C. at 271-72, 422 F.2d at 708-09 (1970); United States v. Huff, 143 U.S. App. D.C. at 166, 442 F.2d at 888 (1971).

unequivocal, it was uncontradicted. In the offense of rape there must be corroboration, and Wiley denied his participation in the criminal act. I submit there *was* sufficient corroboration in all the surrounding, undisputed circumstances, both as to the occurence of the rape and Wiley's participation. But looking at what the majority considers the critical point, insufficient corroboration, what is the specific corroboration my colleagues point to as essential, "most effective", and missing: the physician's testimony. *But the physician's testimony could never have corroborated the victim's testimony on the issue in dispute: whether Wiley, in addition to Cunningham, did accomplish penetration and thereby perpetrate a rape.*

Since the victim's testimony as to the rape having been perpetrated was uncontradicted by any witness, including appellant Wiley, and certainly was strongly supported by all attendant circumstances, the corroboration needed here is not corroboration of the rape having taken place, but of Wiley's participation therein. Consider what would have been the position of appellant Wiley and all the evidence before the jury, if the absent physician had appeared and testified to both penetration and sperm in the victim's vagina. Wiley's testimony would not, could not, have been different. He never testified Cunningham did not, could not, have raped the 12 year old girl. Wiley testified that he "got up, and when he saw that Cunningham was bothering Miss Lewis, told him to stop it. Wiley then went back to sleep. Later, he was awakened by Cunningham." By then Miss Lewis had left the apartment and Wiley did not see her.

The absent physician's testimony thus in no way could have corroborated any fact disputed by appellant Wiley. The vital corroboration needed here is as to Wiley's participation; medical testimony could not supply this; any needed corroboration of the victim's clear and unequivocal testimony *is supplied* by all the attendant circumstances.

I trust and would sustain the jury verdict here.[23] Thus I respectfully dissent.

Wiley is an example of the application of a judicially created corroboration requirement. In some jurisdictions, the requirement that "something more" is necessary than the sworn and cross-examined testimony of the victim may take the form of a legislatively created evidentiary rule. The Model Penal Code phrases a corroboration requirement as follows:[35]

> *Testimony of Complainants.* No person shall be convicted of any felony under this Article upon the uncorroborated testimony of the alleged victim. Corroboration may be circumstantial. In any prosecution before a jury for an offense under this Article, the jury shall be instructed to evaluate the testimony of a victim or complaining witness with special care in view of the emotional involvement of the witness and the difficulty of determining the truth with respect to alleged sexual activities carried out in private.

Corroboration has no fixed content. Nor is it clear exactly what fact or facts must be corroborated. Possibilities are the corpus delicti (meaning, variously, the fact of penetration, the fact of forcible penetration, or the lack of consent), the identification of the accused as the attacker, or all of the material testimony of the complainant. (This last would seem to mean that her credibility must be generally sustained in some way.)

---

23. The portion of Chief Judge Bazelon's opinion directly relevant to Wiley's case is this: "Juries are more integrated than in the past and racial prejudice may be at a somewhat lower level. Numerous rape victims are black and their interests, as well as those of white women, may have been slighted by the concern for black defendants." Concurring opinion, supra at [848].

35. Model Penal Code §213.6(6). Law review commentary with citations to statutorily and judically created corroboration requirements include: Comment, Forcible and Statutory Rape: An Exploration of the Operation and Objectives of the Consent Standard, 62 Yale L.J. 55 (1953); Note, Necessity for Corroboration of Prosecutrix's Testimony in Prosecution for Rape, 3 Vill. L. Rev. 220 (1958); Myers, Reasonable Mistake of Age: A Needed Defense to Statutory Rape, 64 Mich. L. Rev. 105, 126 (1965); Dworkin, The Resistance Standard in Rape Legislation, 18 Stan. L. Rev. 680 (1966); Comment, Corroborating Charges of Rape, 67 Colum. L. Rev. 1137 (1967); Comment, The Corroboration Rule and Crimes Accompanying a Rape, 118 U. Pa. L. Rev. 458 (1970); Younger, The Requirement of Corroboration in Prosecutions for Sex Offenses in New York, 40 Ford. L. Rev. 276 (1971).

A law journal article summarized the current status of the law on corroboration, with extensive citations, as follows:[36]

> . . . [S]even jurisdictions have adopted the rule — five by statute[13] and two by judicial decision[14] — that the testimony of a female complainant must be corroborated in order to sustain a conviction for rape.[15] . . . [E]ight have taken an intermediate position, requiring only limited corroboration[17] or corroboration under certain circumstances.[18]

Even in jurisdictions where there is no explicit corroboration requirement, a trial court ruling on a motion for a judgment of acquittal, or an appellate court, may in effect create such a requirement by holding the victim's testimony insufficient though technically corroborated, if such testimony is incredible, contradictory, or improbable.[37]

Any reading of cases on corroboration would lead one to agree with the law journal notewriter who concluded:[38]

> . . . Decisions abound qualifying the . . . apparent rigorousness of the black-letter, which recites that the uncorroborated testimony is sufficient to sustain a conviction, and demonstrate that in practice a reviewing court will consider the peculiar circumstances of each case and will require that the prosecutrix's testimony in a sense be corroborated by bringing together a number of surrounding facts and circumstances tending to prove the truth of the testimony.[9] It has been stated that the testimony

36. The Rape Corroboration Requirement: Repeal Not Reform, 81 Yale L.J. 1365, 1367-1368 (1972).

13. Ga. Code Ann. §26-2001 (rev. ed. 1971); Idaho Pen. and Corr. Code §18-907(4) (Supp. 1971); Iowa Code Ann. §782.4 (1950); Law of May 22, 1972, ch. 373, §1, N.Y. Sess. Law News 195th Sess., June 10, 1972, at 811; V.I. Code Ann. tit. 14, §1706 (1964).

14. Only two jurisdictions, the District of Columbia and Nebraska, appear to apply a full corroboration requirement in the absence of legislation. [See 81 Yale L.J. at 1369. — Eds.]

15. The historical bases of the statutory and case law rules vary among American jurisdictions imposing a corroboration requirement. New York's statutory rule may be traced back as far as 1886, Law of June 15, 1886, ch. 663 §1 [1886], N.Y. Laws 109th Sess. 953, and it has its roots in earlier statutes requiring corroboration of the female's testimony in charges of seduction under promise of marriage. See, e.g., Law of Mar. 22, 1848, ch. 111, §1 [1848] N.Y. Laws 71st Sess. 148. Georgia's earlier common-law rule, the precursor of its present statutory rule, see note 13 supra, appears to have been adopted in the mistaken belief that it had been the prevailing rule in England. See Davis v. State, 120 Ga. 433, 435, 48 S.E. 180, 181 (1904). In other states the imposition of the requirement may be linked to the reversal of the common-law rule excluding parties to a lawsuit from testifying. See, e.g., Mathews v. State, 19 Neb. 330, 337, 27 N.W. 234, 237 (1886). Following this reversal, the courts could hear the defendant expressly deny the allegations of the complainant. At this time they adopted the rule that an accusation must be corroborated where the defendant denies the accusation of the complaining witness in a charge of rape. In still other states the requirement developed from the application to rape cases of the requirement that any conviction must be based upon sufficient evidence; this requirement became formalized over the course of decisions into a rule of law. In the District of Columbia, for example, Kidwell v. United States, 38 App. D.C. 566, 573 (1912), which noted that those decisions affirming a conviction on the testimony of the complainant all involved cases in which there was corroborating circumstantial evidence, later became cited for the proposition that corroboration of the testimony of the complainant was required in every case as a matter of law. See, e.g., Calhoun v. United States, 399 F.2d 999, 1001 (D.C. Cir. 1968).

17. Two states require limited corroboration in the sense of facts and circumstances which coincide with and tend to establish the truth of the complainant's testimony. See Territory v. Hayes, 43 Hawaii, 58, 62 (1958); State v. Baca, 56 N.M. 236, 241-42, 242 P.2d 1002, 1006 (1952).

18. Six states, through statutes or judicial decisions, have limited the application of the corroboration requirement to specific factual circumstances. See Mass. Gen. Laws ch. 272, §11 (1968) (applies to, inter alia, certain specified non-forcible rapes); State v. Artez, 286 Minn. 545, 546, 176 N.W.2d 81, 82 (1970) (corroboration important when complainant is minor); Miss. Code Ann. §2360 (1956) (applies only to specific statutory rape); State v. Thomas, 351 Mo. 804, 818, 174 S.W.2d 337, 345 (1943) (corroboration required in those cases where complainant is mature woman and case is weak); Tenn. Code Ann. §39-3706 (Supp. 1971) (applies only to specific statutory rape); Wright v. State, 364 S.W.2d 384, 387 (Tex. Cr. App. 1963) (corroboration required only in those cases where a belated complaint was made).

37. See, e.g., Alvarado v. State, 63 Ariz. 511, 164 P.2d 460 (1945); Commonwealth v. Oyler, 130 Pa. Sup. Ct. 405, 197 A. 508 (1938); and Bradley v. Commonwealth, 196 Va. 1126, 86 S.E.2d 828 (1955).

38. Note, 3 Vill. L. Rev. 220, 221 (1958).

9. Kidwell v. United States, 38 App. D.C. 566 (1912); State v. Gibbs, 45 Idaho 760, 265 Pac. 24 (1928);

must be of a clear and convincing nature,[10] and not contain numerous and material contradictions and inconsistencies[11] nor be inherently improbable or incredible.[12]

NOTE: INSTRUCTIONS ON CORROBORATION

Conceptually, the corroboration requirement could be considered a measure of the sufficiency of the prosecution's case. Courts in jurisdictions which have an explicit corroboration requirement seem, however, to regard it as an element of the government's case. United States v. Greene, 429 F.2d 754, (D.C. Cir. 1970). However conceptualized, a corroboration instruction is given which is quite separate from the instruction on force. (See Note: Instructions on Force or Nonconsent, supra.) The corroboration instruction is also separate from and in addition to the general cautionary instruction commonly given in rape cases to the effect:[39]

> A charge such as that made against the defendant in this case is one which is easily made and once made difficult to defend against, even if the person accused is innocent. Therefore, the law requires that you examine the testimony of the female person named in the Information with caution.

Thus, in a rape case there may be at least three special instructions given, one on the amount of force necessary, one on corroboration, and one on the care and caution with which the victim's testimony must be regarded. In addition to such standard instructions, defense counsel who have submitted evidence of consent may be granted instructions on how that evidence is to be assessed. The cumulative effect of these instructions is to advise the jury that the accuser in a rape case carries a unique testimonial burden and disability.

a. Corroboration Gone Amok: The New York Experience

The *Wiley* case, supra, is an example of the highly technical review of the evidence and the reversals of jury verdicts which an explicit corroboration requirement often occasions. The requirement also affects the trial level, making prosecutors less willing fully to charge and try cases unless there is "strong" corroboration.

The experience in the last decade in New York is instructive as to the effect of a corroboration requirement carried to its logical limits. New York has had a statutory corroboration requirement since 1909.[40] Especially in recent years the requirement has

---

Upton v. State, 192 Miss. 339, 6 So. 2d 129 (1942); State v. Goodale, 210 Mo. 275, 109 S.W. 9 (1908); Wiedeman v. State, 141 Neb. 579, 4 N.W.2d 566 (1942); State v. Ellison, 19 N.M. 428, 144 Pac. 10 (1914); Ganzel v. State, 185 Wis. 589, 201 N.W. 724 (1925); Rex v. Berry, 18 Cr. App. Rep. 65 (Eng. 1924).

10. People v. Vaughn, 390 Ill. 360, 61 N.E.2d 546 (1945); Morris v. State, 9 Okla. Crim. Rep. 241, 131 Pac. 731 (1913); Brown v. State, 127 Wis. 193, 106 N.W. 536 (1906).

11. State v. Connelly, 57 Minn. 482, 59 N.W. 479 (1894); State v. Tevis, 234 Mo. 276, 136 S.W. 339 (1911); Woodruff v. State, 74 Okla. Crim. Rep. 289, 125 P.2d 211 (1942); Blumenthal v. State, 98 Tex. Crim. Rep. 601, 267 S.W. 727 (1925).

12. State v. Moe, 68 Mont. 552, 219 Pac. 830 (1923); Mares v. Territory, 10 N.M. 770, 65 Pac. 165 (1901); DeWitt v. State, 79 Okla. Crim. Rep. 136, 152 P.2d 284 (1944); Self v. State, 62 Okla. Crim. Rep. 208, 70 P.2d 1083 (1937).

39. This is based on a form of words quoted in 1 Hale, Pleas of the Crown 633, 635 (1680); the particular wording in the text is from Oregon v. Stocker, 503 P.2d 501 (Ore. Ct. App. 1972).

40. Until 1967 the New York statute provided that no "conviction can be had for rape or defilement upon the testimony of the female defiled, unsupported by other evidence." N.Y. Consol. Laws c.88, §2013 (1909). When the cases which are discussed in the text were decided, the New York corroboration requirement read as follows:

"A person shall not be convicted of any offense defined in this article, or of an attempt to commit the same, solely on the uncorroborated testimony of the alleged victim. This section shall not apply to the offense of sexual abuse in the third degree." N.Y. Penal Law §130.15 (1967).

resulted in exacting review of rape convictions by appellate courts. It was said that corroboration was required of every aspect of the crime, including penetration and the identification of the defendant. People v. Page, 162 N.Y. 272, 274-275, 56 N.E. 750, 751-752 (1900); People v. Croes, 285 N.Y. 279, 34 N.E.2d 320 (1941). Increasingly technical standards were applied to the sufficiency of the evidence to meet the various aspects of corroboration. People v. Radunovic, 21 N.Y.2d 186, 287 N.Y.S.2d 33, 234 N.E.2d 212 (1967).

In light of their frequent inability to meet the stringent corroboration requirement, New York prosecutors started routinely charging, in addition to rape, lesser offenses for which no corroboration was required. The appellate court responded by holding that when the victim's testimony, if corroborated, would prove a rape, any lesser sexual assault must also be corroborated. People v. Radunovic, supra. *Radunovic* was followed by a case in which the accusation was made that the defendant raped the woman, and virtually in the act of raping her, removed a coin purse from her brassiere. There was no corroboration of either offense. The court of appeals sustained the robbery conviction on the ground that it need not be corroborated because robbery is not the kind of crime necessarily included within a sexual offense. People v. Moore, 29 App. Div. 2d 570, 286 N.Y.S.2d 296 (1967). Logically however, as the dissenters and critical commentary pointed out,[41] if the purpose of the corroboration requirement is to create a testimonial disability of the victim because of the possibilities of false accusation and of undue sympathy for her, then there is no way to distinguish between the evidentiary requirements for nonsexual and sexual crimes committed at the same time as a rape.

The difficulties inherent in distinctions such as that drawn between *Radunovic* and *Moore* and the dramatic acquittal rates in rape cases led the prosecutor's office to seek legislative change in the corroboration requirement. The Chief Assistant District Attorney of Queens County wrote a law review article calling for complete abolition of the corroboration requirement, noting that: "Since the effective date of the new Penal Law, September 1, 1967 [the most recent version of New York's stringent corroboration

41. Note, The Corroboration Rule and Crimes Accompanying a Rape, 118 U. Pa. L. Rev. 458 (1970). In criticizing *Moore*, this modern notewriter evinced the ancient extreme distrust of women:

"The majority overlooked the fundamental purpose of the statutory corroboration requirement: to give defendants special protection in an area filled with false accusations. A woman disposed to fabricate an allegation of a sexual attack might easily add to her story accusations of assault, robbery, or other crimes, particularly if she is aware of the need for corroboration. The majority failed to extend the corroboration rule to these additional accusations because it wished to avoid imposing on women what it believed to be an unwarranted testimonial disability. To realize this latter goal, however, the majority was forced to adopt an untenable position: although a woman's testimony concerning the facts of an alleged consummated rape are too untrustworthy to support a rape conviction, the same uncorroborated testimony will support a conviction for all crimes not "intrinsically related to the rape." What the majority failed to recognize is that the imposition of a testimonial disability is the core of the corroboration requirement; such a disability is the only protection the defendant has against the judge and jury's susceptibility to prejudice.

"The *Moore* court did not assign sufficient importance to the danger that a jury might convict the defendant of crimes tried with the rape accusation when the jury believes the defendant guilty of the sexual attack but is prevented by the corroboration requirement from returning a guilty verdict on the rape charge. Regardless of what instructions a jury is given, the jurors will probably assess the credibility of the complainant concerning the rape charge and, if they believe her story, be influenced by the sexual attack in reaching a verdict on the other crimes. Frustrated by their inability to punish the defendant for the serious sexual offense and emotionally prejudiced against him, the jurors might convict on the other crimes even though they did not believe beyond a reasonable doubt that the defendant committed them. . . .

"The facts of *Moore* are particularly compelling. The uncorroborated testimony of the prosecutrix that she was forcibly raped indicates that her assailant was too fully occupied with her violent resistance to have formed a specific larcenous intent. It would require crediting Moore with extraordinary presence of mind and powers of concentration to find him capable of forming such an intent. Affirming a conviction in such circumstances encourages prosecutors to press charges for "intrinsically unrelated" offenses allegedly committed with a rape in the hope that jurors will convict of the unrelated offenses in order to punish the defendant for the alleged rape. Although this practice might result in a crude kind of justice in some cases and remove dangerous individuals from the streets, it cannot be tolerated within a system that purports to consider a man innocent until proven guilty." Id. at 469-471.

requirement], there has not been a conviction after trial for any sex felony . . . in Queens, the second most populous county of the State (2.3 million inhabitants)."[42]

As a result of the efforts of the prosecutor's office, New York's corroboration statute was revised in 1972 to provide that corroboration need not be required of the actual completion of a sexual act (thus semen on the victim's underwear would corroborate the fact of penetration), and to directly overrule *Radunovic* and related cases.[43]

b. The Purposes of Corroboration Requirements

COMMENT
118 U. Pa. L. Rev. 458, 459-460 (1970)

[T]he prosecution of the crime [of rape] often results in a deadlock between the uncorroborated accusation of the female complainant and the insistent denial of the alleged ravisher.

When such a deadlock occurs in other criminal prosecutions, the presumption of the defendant's innocence assures acquittal. But in rape cases, normal operation of that presumption is seriously impaired. The incidence of false accusations and the potential for unjust convictions are perhaps greatest with sexual offenses.[12] Woman often falsely accuse men of sexual attacks to extort money, to force marriage, to satisfy a childish desire for notoriety, or to attain personal revenge. Their motives include hatred, a sense of shame after consenting to illicit intercourse, especially when pregnancy results, and delusion.[13] In cases of delusion, the woman may describe the attack in remarkably convincing detail, for she herself believes her story but fails to appreciate the significance and consequences of the accusation. "Most women," according to a prominent psychiatrist, "entertain more or less consciously at one time or another fleeting fantasies or fears that they are being or will be attacked by a man. Of course, the normal woman who has such a fantasy does not confuse it with reality, but it is . . . easy for . . . neurotic individuals to translate their fantasies into actual beliefs and memory falsifications. . . ."[14] These neurotic individuals can often deceive the most astute judges and jurors into believing that the imagined attack actually occurred.

In the law review article above, the chief authority for the proposition that a corroboration requirement is necessary to protect against the malicious or fantasied charge of rape is a passage and the sources from Wigmore's treatise on Evidence, in which he argues that the dangers of miscarriage of justice inherent in a rape prosecution are so grave that a psychiatric examination of the woman or girl should be ordered in every case. This passage has been cited literally thousands of times, often as sole author-

---

42. Ludwig, The Case for Repeal of the Sex Corroboration Requirement in New York, 36 Brooklyn L. Rev. 378, 386 (1970). See also Hechtman, Supplementary Practice Commentary to N.Y. Penal Law §130.00: "In a recent typical year, only 18 rape convictions were obtained in the courts of New York versus thousands of complaints," citing Governor's approval memorandum No. 6, May 22, 1972.

43. N.Y. Penal Law §130.00 (1972).

12. According to what little legislative history can be found, the objective of New York's corroboration statute is "to protect against false accusations and to prevent unjust convictions. . . ." New York Law Revision Commission, Communication and Study Relating to Sexual Crimes 76 (1937). . . . The report may be found in State of New York, Report of the Law Revision Commission for 1937, at 401-514.

13. See generally Thomas v. United States, 370 F.2d 621 (9th Cir. 1967) (suggesting the likelihood of false accusation is the only justification for a corroboration rule); Wedmore v. State, 237 Ind. 212, 227, 143 N.E.2d 649, 656 (1957) (dissenting opinion); People v. Smallwood, 306 Mich. 49, 10 N.W.2d 303 (1943); Note, Forcible and Statutory Rape: An Exploration of the Operation and Objectives of the Consent Standard, 62 Yale L.J. 55, 68-70 (1952).

14. Dr. Karl A. Menninger, as quoted in 3 Wigmore §924a at 464; see Psychiatric Opinions, [as to Credibility of Witnesses: A Suggested Approach, 48 Calif. L. Rev. 648,] 674 n.159 [(1960)].

ity for the proposition that the victim's accusation in a sex offense case, without more, should not sustain a conviction:[44]

> . . . Modern psychiatrists have amply studied the behavior of errant young girls and women coming before the courts in all sorts of cases. Their psychic complexes are multifarious, distorted partly by inherent defects, partly by diseased derangements or abnormal instincts, partly by bad social environment, partly by temporary physiological or emotional conditions. One form taken by these complexes is that of contriving false charges of sexual offenses by men. The unchaste (let us call it) mentality finds incidental but direct expression in the narration of imaginary sex incidents of which the narrator is the heroine or the victim. On the surface the narration is straightforward and convincing. The real victim, however, too often in such cases is the innocent man; for the respect and sympathy naturally felt by any tribunal for a wronged female helps to give easy credit to such a plausible tale.
>
> No doubt any judge of a criminal court and any prosecuting attorney can corroborate this with instances from his own observation. But the lamentable thing is that the orthodox rules of evidence in most instances prevent adequate probing of the testimonial mentality of a woman witness, so as to reveal the possible falsity of such charges. Judging merely from the reports of cases in the appellate courts, one must infer that many innocent men have gone to prison because of tales whose falsity could not be exposed. And the situation of injustice has become the more extreme, because in some states the so-called age of consent has been raised to 16 or 18 years (thus making consent immaterial below that age). . . .

The psychological literature upon which the sweeping statements in this text are based consists of five case studies from a 1915 textbook,[45] and of letters and monographs from four psychiatrists, all dated before 1933 (the date of publication of the Wigmore treatise).[46] The authorities supporting this part of the text have never been updated in revisions and supplements to Wigmore, and the inadequacy of some of them is apparent on their face.[47] Yet courts and commentators which have dealt with the danger of false accusations of sexual offenses have done little more than cite Wigmore.[48]

44. 3A Wigmore, Evidence §924a (Chadbourn rev. 1970).

45. Healy, The Individual Delinquent, originally printed by Little, Brown & Company (1950), reprint Patterson Smith Reprint Series in Criminology, Law Enforcement and Social Problems, No. 85 (1969). Of the five cases cited by Wigmore, one has nothing to do with sexual misconduct; another involves only an "announcement" that "immoral advances" had been made; a third involved a seven-year-old accuser who may have been protecting a family member. Only the remaining two dealt with false criminal charges of sexual misconduct.

46. How and in what context the three letters were received by Wigmore is not explained in the treatise. The relevant citation states merely that they were obtained "through the courtesy of Dr. Harold S. Hulburt, consulting psychiatrist, Chicago." 3A Evidence §924a, n.3 (Chadbourn rev. 1970).

47. One Dr. Otto Mönkemöller is particularly worth noting for his description of problems encountered with the female witness in the sex case. "The most dangerous witnesses in prosecutions for morality offenses are the youthful ones (often mere children) in whom the sex instinct holds the foremost place in their thoughts and feelings. This intensely erotic propensity often can be detected in the wanton facial expression, the sensuous motions, and the manner of speech. But on the other hand one must not be deceived by the madonna-like countenance that such a girl can readily assume; nor by the convincing upturn of the eyes, with which she seeks to strengthen her credibility. To be sure, the coarse sensuousness of her demeanor, coupled with a pert and forward manner, usually leaves no doubt about her type of thought. Even in her early years can be seen in countenance and demeanor the symptoms of the hussy-type, which in later years enable one at first glance to recognize the hardened prostitute. With profuse falsities they shamelessly speak of the coarsest sex-matters. . . . When the sex-urge is strongly developed, then if some man comes within their vicinity, they may dally with a secret wish to have some sex-relation with him, and then his most harmless conduct is transformed by these sex-imaginative witnesses into acts which charge him as criminal. . . . In male youths this particular sex disposition plays a far smaller part." Dr. Otto Mönkemöller, Psychology and Psychopathology of Testimony, 333 (1933), cited in 3A Wigmore, §924a at 743-744 (Chadbourn rev. 1970). The work has apparently never been translated into English.

48. See generally Watkins, Do Women Fantasize Rape? An Evaluation of the Literature (unpublished paper, Stanford Law School 1973).

Close examination of Wigmore's sources themselves — and of the occasional "case study" that appears over the years — indicates that, though the evidence that some young girls are dangerous sexual "fantasts" is inconclusive at best, it may be possible for young girls bringing false charges to mislead some authorities in the criminal process. But there is no evidence that the judge or jury are among those misled. In fact, in three of the case studies relied on by Wigmore the young "victims" were sent for psychiatric examination because someone in the system suspected they were lying long before trial.

Although most of the psychological studies of fantasied rape, at least those which find their way into legal commentary and opinions, seem to concern young girls, the corroboration requirement also applies to charges made by mature women. The psychological literature which purports to account for false charges by adult women has been summarized as follows:[49]

> The underlying idea of the psychoanalytic school of thought is the tendency for victimization as a universal condition of every woman. It assumes the idea of "polymorphic perverse" characteristic of humans.[2] Reflected in women is the tendency for passivity and masochism,[3] and a universal desire to be violently possessed[4] and aggressively handled by men.[5] Some writers even claim that there is a universal wish among women to be raped[6] or at least to be forcefully seduced by strangers.[7]
>
> Entering the role of a victim may alleviate anxiety and mollify the feelings of guilt which the forbidden wishes evoke,[8] and it will allow a taste of the "sweetness of stolen waters."[9] Sometimes the very fear of rape may activate a "riddance rape," whereby those who suffer from such fear may get rid of anxiety by doing the very thing that is feared, or the victim may yield to being raped in order "to get it over with."[10] Whatever is one's judgment on such views,[11] it follows that rape may be a primarily pleasurable event or provides a secondary gain as a liberating experience.[12]

A law review article reflected on the psychiatric literature:[50]

> Many psychiatrists and physicians once considered fantasies of rape to be extremely common among women.[78] Dr. Karl A. Menninger has said that such fantasies are so common that they may be considered universal.[79] The most frequent explanation for these fantasies is that they represent "an unrealized wish or unconscious, deeply suppressed sex-longing or thwarting."[80] . . .

49. This passage is from Amir, Patterns in Forcible Rape, 253-254 (1971).

2. S. Freud, "Three Essays on the Theory of Sexuality," Collected Papers (1949).

3. H. Deutsch, Psychology of Women (1944), vol. 1; O. Fenichel, The Psychoanalytic Theory of Neuroses (1945); S. L. Halleck, "The Physician's Role in Management of Victims of Sex Offenses," 180 Journal of American Medical Association 273-278 (1962).

4. Jenkins, "The Making of Sex Offenders," 30 Focus 129-131 (1951), p. 131; Murray, Explorations in Personality (1933), p. 135.

5. Alexander, Fundamentals of Psychoanalysis (1948), p. 127; Ferenczi, "Sex and Psychoanalysis," Collected Papers (1916), vol. 2.

6. Eidelberg, The Dark Urge (1961), chapt. 1.

7. Abraham, "The Experiencing of Sexual Traumas as a Form of Sexual Activity," (1907), Selected Papers, 47 (1927); S. Freud, New Introductory Lectures in Psychoanalysis (1933), p. 151.

8. Abrahamsen, The Psychology of Crime (1960), p. 161; Alexander, Fundamentals of Psychoanalysis (1948), p. 122.

9. Eidelberg, supra, p. 15.

10. Slovenko and Phillips, "Psychosexuality and the Criminal Law," 15 Vanderbilt L. Rev. 797 (1961-62).

11. On the logical and scientific merit of psychoanalytic theory, see Hook, Psychoanalysis: Scientific Method and Philosophy (1960), esp. chaps. 1, 4.

12. Devereaux, "The Awarding of the Penis as a Compensation for Rape," 38 International Journal of Psychoanalysis 398 (1957); Factor, "A Woman's Psychological Reaction to Attempted Rape," 23 Psychoanalytic Quarterly 243 (1954).

50. The Rape Corroboration Requirement: Repeal Not Reform, 81 Yale L.J. 1365, 1376-1378 (1972).

78. See, e.g., sources cited in 3A J. Wigmore, . . . §924(a), at 736-46 [Chadbourne rev. ed. 1970]; M. Guttmacher & H. Weihofen, Psychiatry and the Law 375 (1952); W. Overholser, The Psychiatrist and the Law 53 (1953).

79. K. Menninger, quoted in 3A J. Wigmore, supra note 78, §924(a), at 744.

80. W. Lorenz, quoted in id. 745-46. See also W. White, quoted in id. 745.

Perhaps the most carefully considered theory that purports to explain these fantasies has been propounded by the psychoanalyst Helene Deutsch. She assimilated rape fantasies to a theory of female masochism,[82] a corollary to Freud's concept of "penis envy."[83] She contended that fantasies of violent sexual intercourse without consent are a manifestation of the "attraction of suffering [that] is incomparably stronger for women than for men."[84] Because the theories of penis envy and female masochism are rooted in the physiology of women and hence are considered characteristic of "normal" female psychology, Deutsch's theory predicts a high frequency of rape fantasies, many of which become public accusations.[85]

Deutsch's theory, however, has been largely discredited in recent years.[86] Some have criticized her, as well as Freud, for using clinical experience with abnormal patients to derive theories of normal female psychology.[87] Others have criticized her for failing to consider the social context in which women live.[88] The effect of any biological characteristic is very strongly conditioned, perhaps even dominated,[89] by the culture-complex in which the particular woman has developed. If these cultural factors are considered, and if today's culture is compared with that in which Freud and even Deutsch developed their theories, the incidence of female masochism very likely will be far less than it may ever have been in the past.[90]

Thus, whatever may have been the former validity of the theory that female masochism will lead women to fantasize rape incidents, its currency today has been

---

82. See 1 H. Deutsch, [The Psychology of Women], 239-78 [1944].

83. See generally S. Freud, Femininity, in 22 The Standard Edition of the Complete Psychological Works of Sigmund Freud 112-35 (J. Strachey ed. & transl. 1964); Female Sexuality, in 21 The Standard Edition of the Complete Psychological Works of Sigmund Freud 225-43 (J. Strachey ed. and transl. 1961); Some Psychical Consequences of the Anatomical Distinction Between the Sexes, in 19 id. 248-58.

84. 1 H. Deutsch, [The Psychology of Women], at 274 [1944] (emphasis removed from original).

85. See id. 256.

86. For a thorough review of the literature regarding psychoanalytic theories of female development see S. Weisskopf, The Psychoanalytic Theory of Female Development (unpublished Ph.D. thesis in Harvard University Library 1972). Weisskopf concludes that the Freudian theory of female development is inadequate; it is based on critical assumptions which are not valid and employs certain important constructs for which there is no evidence. Id. 133, 150.

87. See, e.g., K. Horney, Feminine Psychology 215-17 (1967); K. Millet, [Sexual Politics] 179 [1970]; Weisstein, "Kinder, Kuche, Kirche" as Scientific Law: Psychology Constructs the Female, in Sisterhood is Powerful 205, 209-13 (R. Morgan ed. 1970).

88. See, e.g., K. Horney, supra note 87, at 229-33; K. Millet, supra note 87, at 179, 187; C. Thompson, Psychoanalysis: Evolution and Development 131 (1950); Weisstein, supra note 87, at 208-09, 213-18.

89. See Weisstein, supra note 87, at 209: "Compared to the influence of the social context within which a person lives, his or her history or 'traits,' as well as biological makeup may simply be random variations, 'noise' superimposed on the true signal which can predict behavior."

90. Karen Horney, a neo-Freudian psychoanalyst, suggests several social factors which predispose to the appearance of female masochism:

1. Blocking of outlets for expansiveness and sexuality;

2. Restriction in the number of children, inasmuch as having and rearing children supplies the woman with various gratifying outlets (tenderness, achievement, self-esteem), and this becomes all the more important when having and rearing children is the measuring rod of social evaluation;

3. Estimation of women as beings who are, on the whole, inferior to men (insofar as it leads to a deterioration of female self-confidence);

4. Economic dependence of women on men or on family, inasmuch as it fosters an emotional adaptation in the way of emotional dependence;

5. Restriction of women to spheres of life that are built chiefly upon emotional bonds, such as family life, religion, or charity work;

6. Surplus of marriageable women, particularly when marriage offers the principal opportunity for sexual gratification, children, security, and social recognition. K. Horney, supra note 87, at 230.

An analysis of these factors suggests that the frequency of occurrence of female masochism will decline as inhibitions on female sexual expression are lifted, as women acquire legal, economic and educational equality with men, as the economic dependence of women on men and the family is lifted, as restrictions upon female employment and community involvement disappear, and as marriage and the family cease to be the exclusive foci of female life. Clara Thompson, another neo-Freudian psychoanalyst, argues further that many of these cultural changes have occurred and that, as a result, "a new type of woman is emerging, a woman . . . whose characteristics differ from those described by Freud." C. Thompson, Interpersonal Psychoanalysis 238 (1964).

largely eroded, and will be increasingly eroded as women acquire social, legal and economic equality with men. Insofar as the corroboration requirement in rape cases has been justified by the danger of false rape charges brought by fantasizing women, it is linked to a psychological theory that fails to take into account the changing role of women in American society.

Another image of women's psyche used to support the necessity of the corroboration requirement is that of the malicious accuser, satisfying her own motives of revenge, blackmail, or guilt assuagement, through a rape accusation and prosecution. But sexual offenses are not the only ones subject to false and malicious accusation, and usually cross-examination at trial and presentation of evidence in the defense case are considered sufficient to uncover bias and prejudice. Is it something about the nature of the sexual exchange which makes it peculiarly subject to false accusation? Or is the fear of false accusation based on a deep suspicion about the nature of women?

The corroboration requirement must be put in the perspective of its extremely inadequate premises. At the same time, even people most concerned about the status of and attitudes toward women reflected in the administration of the rape laws acknowledge that there are some instances of malicious, fabricated, or exaggerated charges of rape. *DeFrates,* supra, may be an example of a case involving such motives. Yet the elaborate screening through which charges of rape pass, starting with often disbelieving or cynical police, through grand juries and prosecutors, makes it somewhat unlikely that many false charges would even get to the trial stage, much less survive cross-examination at trial to lead to conviction. In considering whether there are, in fact, many false charges of rape, one article outlined the "disincentives" to make the charge:[51]

> There are several factors . . . which discourage accusations of rape, whatever their motive. For example, there are the stigma that attach to the victim of an incident culturally defined as sordid,[61] and the humiliation caused by some forms of publicity associated with such charges.[62] Also to be considered are the necessity of confronting the assailant[63] and the reluctance to face the barbs and insinuations of the defense attorney.[64] There is, in addition, the fear of retaliation from the accused rapist or his

51. The Rape Corroboration Requirement: Repeal Not Reform, 81 Yale L.J. 1365, 1374-1375 (1972).

61. Rape seems to arouse in most people a feeling of disgust, perhaps generated by the repressions surrounding aggressive sex; and the disgust may spread to the body of the victim who is somehow thought to be contaminated by the experience. Note, Forcible and Statutory Rape: An Exploration of the Operation and Objective of the Consent Standard, 62 Yale L.J. 55, 73 (1952). See K. Millet, Sexual Politics 44 (1970).

62. K. Millet, supra note 61, at 44. See Toll, Rape: Reliving the Horror Eases the Pain, Chicago Tribune, Apr. 16, 1972, §5, 2, col. 4, for a report of a forum on rape in Chicago. The humiliation of the rape experience was reflected in one woman's statement: "I would never say I was raped. I would always say I was attacked. . . . Even talking about it now. I feel ashamed, as if I admit I did something wrong." In some states this publicity is reduced by criminal statutes prohibiting the naming or identification of a victim of a rape or a similar sexual assault. See, e.g., Fla. Stat. Ann. §794.03 (1965); Ga. Code Ann. §26-9901 (rev. ed. 1971); Wis. Stat. Ann. §942.02 (1958).
Women's descriptions of their rape experiences related at a "Speak-Out on Rape" organized by New York City women's groups in 1970 illustrated the humiliation which comes from simply reporting a rape to the police: "Police reactions described at the meeting were a sorry lot. Disbelief. Ridicule. Questioning along voyeuristic lines. Or just plain lack of interest." Sheehy, Nice Girls Don't Get Into Trouble, 4 New York, Feb. 15, 1971, at 26, 28.
For an account of a typical rape situation as told by the victim to a journalist, see The Story of Maxwell Kent — Rapist, [Washington Post, June 18, 1967, §C,] at 1, col. 1. Perhaps the most striking feature of this account is the callousness of the police toward the victim.

63. The embarrassment of the victim in relating the details of her assault in a public trial may be reduced with no harm to the accused by conducting the trial with less publicity than cases ordinarily are. For example, the trial may be held in the petit jury room rather than the larger court room. For discussion of this possibility, see Dutton v. State, 123 Md. 373, 387, 91 A. 417, 422-23 (1913).

64. See, e.g., Griffin, Rape: The All-American Crime, 10 Ramparts, Sept. 1971, at 26, 31-32, for a description of a particularly brutal defense examination of the sexual mores of the complainant in a rape case. But see Wigmore's suggestion that there be wide-open admissibility of evidence bearing on the complainant's moral and mental qualities. 3A J. Wigmore, Evidence §924(b), at 747-48 (Chadbourne rev. ed. 1970). Such a rule would make testifying to a rape even more unpleasant than it is at present.

friends.[65] Finally, there is the deterrent effect of the existence of the corroboration requirement itself, at least to the extent that a potential complainant may be aware of it.

These disincentives are so powerful that many real victims of rape avoid reporting incidents. . . . Even if she reports the offense, a complaining witness may refuse to prosecute, in large part to avoid having to relive a traumatic and humiliating experience for the benefit of the judge and jury. A study in Detroit, for example, showed that in nearly thirty-three percent of the rape offenses reported to the police, the complainant subsequently refused to prosecute her assailant, and charges had to be dropped.[70]

In light of the inadequate and dated psychiatric literature and other empirical data regarding the frequency of false charges of rape, it seems inappropriate to approach all victims on the assumption that the false charge is the major danger to be avoided in the administration of rape laws.

NOTE: PSYCHIATRIC EXAMINATION AS AN ALTERNATIVE TO THE CORROBORATION REQUIREMENT

One suggestion for screening out possible false complaints of rape is to require accusers to submit to a psychiatric examination. Again, such a broad approach seems totally unsupported by any indication that the problem of false charges is so grave that every person alleging rape should be subjected to a psychiatric interview, which can be a painful invasion of privacy. Some states have, however, adopted a middle course, requiring such an examination when the defendant can make some showing that it is indicated.

BALLARD v. SUPERIOR COURT OF SAN DIEGO COUNTY
64 Cal. 2d 159, 410 P.2d 838 (1966)

TOBRINER, J. Petitioner is a physician charged with the rape of a patient to whom he allegedly administered an intoxicating narcotic or anesthetic substance in order to prevent resistance, a violation of Penal Code §261, subdivision 4. He petitions for writs of mandate and prohibition. . . .

On October 6, 1964, the prosecutrix lodged a complaint with the San Diego Police Department, accusing petitioner of having performed an act of sexual intercourse upon her on October 4 without her consent and while she could not resist because of the drugs which he had administered to her. The police then gave the prosecutrix a lie detector test; a police physician examined her.

The day after the victim filed the charges the police furnished her with an electronic microphone to conceal in her purse and instructed her to go to petitioner's office in order to obtain incriminating statements from him. The officers placed a device in a police car outside the physician's office for the purpose of recording the statements. Thereby the officers did obtain from petitioner several incriminating statements.

On October 8, a police expert determined that the victim's clothing contained semen stains. On October 13, October 16, and November 4, after a specially equipped electronic recording device had been attached to her telephone, the victim, in the presence of the police, called petitioner, asking questions concerning the incident. During these telephone conversations petitioner made several incriminating statements, which the police recorded. . . .

---

65. J. MacDonald, Rape: Offenders and Their Victims, at 27, 72-73 (1971).

70. L. Laughlin, The Disposition of Sex Complaints at the Level of Police Investigation 6, 58 (unpublished master's thesis in Wayne State University Library 1950). See also J. MacDonald, supra at 94-96.

Petitioner contends that the trial court should not have denied his request for an order requiring the complaining witness to undergo a psychiatric examination for the purpose of determining whether her mental or emotional condition affected her veracity. The resolution of this issue raises the dual problems of the judicial treatment of psychiatric testimony for the limited purpose of impeachment of the complaining witness in a sex violation case as well as the propriety of a psychiatric examination of such a witness.

A number of leading authorities have suggested that in a case in which a defendant faces a charge of a sex violation, the complaining witness, if her testimony is uncorroborated, should be required to submit to a psychiatric examination. (3 Wigmore, Evidence (1940) §924a, and authorities collected therein; Report of the A.B.A. Committee on the Improvement of the Law of Evidence 1937-1938; Juviler, Psychiatric Opinions as to Credibility of Witnesses: A Suggested Approach (1960), 48 Cal. L. Rev. 648, 673; Comment, Pre-Trial Psychiatric Examination as Proposed Means for Testing the Complainant's Competency to Allege a Sex Offense (1957), U. Ill. L. F. 651; Note, Psychiatric Aid on Evaluating Credibility of Rape Complainant (1950) 26 Ind. L.J. 98). . . .

In urging psychiatric interviews for complaining witnesses in sex cases, some prominent psychiatrists have explained that a woman or a girl may falsely accuse a person of a sex crime as a result of a mental condition that transforms into fantasy a wishful biological urge. Such a charge may likewise flow from an aggressive tendency directed to the person accused or from a childish desire for notoriety. (See authorities collected in: 3 Wigmore, Evidence, §§924a, 934a, 963; Juviler, Psychiatric Opinions as to Credibility of Witnesses: A Suggested Approach, 48 Cal. L. Rev. 648, 674; Comment, Psychiatric Evaluation of the Mentally Abnormal Witness (1950), 59 Yale L.J. 1324, 1338; Note, Psychiatric Impeachment in Sex Cases (1949), 39 J. Crim. L., C. & P.S. 750; see also Overholser, The Psychiatrist and the Law (1953) 51-54; Ploscowe, Sex and the Law (1951) 187-190.)[6] . . .

This concern is stimulated by the possibility that a believable complaining witness, who suffers from an emotional condition inducing her belief that she has been subjected to a sexual offense, may charge some male with that offense. Thus, the testimony of a sympathy-arousing child may lead to the conviction of an unattractive defendant, subjecting him to a lengthy prison term. . . .

We submit however, that a general rule requiring a psychiatric examination of complaining witnesses in every sex case or, as an alternative, in any such case that rests upon the uncorroborated testimony of the complaining witness would, in many instances, not be necessary or appropriate. Moreover, victims of sex crimes might be deterred by such an absolute requirement from disclosing such offenses.

Rather than formulate a fixed rule in this matter we believe that discretion should repose in the trial judge to order a psychiatric examination of the complaining witness in a case involving a sex violation if the defendant presents a compelling reason for such an examination.[12] . . .

We therefore believe that the trial judge should be authorized to order the prosecutrix to submit to a psychiatric examination if the circumstances indicate a necessity for an examination. Such necessity would generally arise only if little or no corroboration supported the charge and if the defense raised the issue of the effect of the complaining witness' mental or emotional condition upon her veracity. . . .

The complaining witness should not, and realistically cannot, be forced to submit to a psychiatric examination or to cooperate with a psychiatrist. In the event that the witness thus refuses to cooperate, however, a comment on that refusal should be permitted.

6. *"Pseudologia phantastica* is described as a medical condition involving a mixture of lies with imagination. Not infrequently, this is the basis of alleged sexual assault. Girls assert that they have been raped, sometimes recounting as true a story they have heard, falsely naming individuals or describing them." (1 Gray's Attorneys' Textbook of Medicine (3d ed. 1950) 940.)

12. Since this court has developed the rules of criminal discovery in the absence of legislation (Louisell, Modern Cal. Discovery (1963) 396-397), we may allow the trial judges such authority in appropriate cases. (See State v. Butler, [27 N.S. 560,] 143 A.2d 530, 553 [(1958)].)

NOTE

What kinds of reasons might a defense lawyer offer for seeking a psychiatric examination of the witness? Would you, as a judge, consider the following reasons sufficient?

(1) The prosecutrix has an IQ below 100 and was considered a behavior problem when she was in school.

(2) The prosecutrix has made two complaints of rape against other men in the past five years.

(3) The prosecutrix has been under analysis for the past three years, visiting a psychiatrist once a week; 80 percent of the cost has been paid by her Blue Cross plan.

(4) The prosecutrix has been hospitalized on three occasions in the last decade for severe depression, and on one such occasion had shock treatment.

(5) The prosecutrix has sought several times to withdraw from the prosecution of the case, stating that she is not strong enough to go through with it.

Note: Abolition or Modification of the Corroboration Requirement

Rules of evidence can always be established or changed through legislation. The instruction to the jury to regard the woman's testimony with care and caution, which often operates as a corroboration requirement even in jurisdictions which do not have a formal requirement, could simply be abolished. An effort to abolish the cautionary instruction in California was phrased as follows:[52]

> In any prosecution under [the sexual assault provisions] of the Penal Code, or for assault with intent to commit any crime defined in any such section, the credibility of the victim or prosecutrix shall be determined pursuant to Section 780, as in the case of any other witness, and the court shall not give a cautionary instruction concerning the nature of the offense.

In jurisdictions which have a judicially or legislatively created corroboration requirement, it could either be removed from the books by legislative fiat, or be substantially revised and refined to prevent its misapplication. For instance, part of the problem with the corroboration requirement is its application to *all* rapes, even those in which the victim and defendant did not know each other, so that the woman's motive to lie or falsely accuse becomes a strange fiction indeed. A model statute could provide for corroboration only when there was evidence of prior contact between the defendant and the victim, or some other basis for believing the charge could be fabricated. A model statute might also specifically detail the kind and degree of evidence which would furnish corroboration.

Note: A Special Evidence Rule Which Benefits the Prosecution

In cases of sexual assault, certain evidence is allowed which would probably be designated hearsay in other contexts. This is the evidence that the victim made a complaint.[52] McCormick states:[53]

---

52. Assembly Bill No. 61, introduced by Assemblyman McAlister to the California Legislature, 1973–74 session, Jan. 11, 1973.

52. See 4 Wigmore, Evidence, §§1134–1140 (2d ed.).

53. McCormick, Evidence 109–110 (1954).

... Under the presently prevailing practice the state may prove the fact of complaint, made within a reasonable time, to rebut the inference which might otherwise be drawn, unfavorable to the complainant's testimony, if complaint were not mentioned. Note however that it is only the *fact* of complaint of ravishment (including time, place, and person to whom made) that may be proven but not the "details". . . .

McCormick goes on to note that occasionally "details" of the complaint are admitted as "excited utterances," and as a matter of practice, trial judges often exercise their discretion to admit such testimony in circumstances where the utterance would not usually be considered sufficiently close in time to the happening to be exempt from the hearsay rule. The form such evidence may take appears in Baber v. United States, 324 F.2d 390 (D.C. Cir. 1963), in which the victim first testified about an attempted rape:[54]

> The father, called as the next witness, testified that he was awakened by the noise of a door rattling or slamming. Shortly thereafter he heard his daughter; she "hollered, fussing." He went downstairs and asked his daughter what was wrong. . . . The witness then gave as much of his daughter's statement as he could recollect.
>
> . . .
>
> Two police officers followed the father to the stand. They had arrived at the scene about 25 minutes after the incident. Over objection, they were allowed to testify in considerable detail concerning the statement that the complaining witness made to them.[55]

See also the facts of Frank v. State, supra Section B-2-b, in which the relatives of the victim were allowed to testify to her account of the incident to them.

The question is whether the relaxation of the hearsay rules to allow testimony about the complaint in rape cases balances or compensates for the corroboration requirement and special instructions regarding the victim's testimony, making reform unnecessary. Do you think it does?

4. Possible Solutions for the Maladministration of the Laws Against Rape

a. Reconsideration of Penalties

Criminal law is the civilized tool for deterring and punishing aberrant behavior. Yet, although rape is everywhere defined as a crime and extreme penalties are assigned to it on the books,[56] the tool has clearly failed to function. One possible reason is that the very extremity of the penalties has prevented their genuine enforcement, and that this, in turn, has reduced the deterrent effect of the criminal sanction.

Death was a possible penalty for rape until recent times in many jurisdictions.[57] Two of the cases in which the Supreme Court struck down a discretionary death penalty as cruel and unusual punishment involved convictions for rape.[58] The argument made

---

54. 324 F.2d at 391.

55. In *Baber,* however, the appellate court found the admission of the police officer's testimony doubtful, but that it was, in any event, harmless error.

56. At this writing, thirty states provide a possible life sentence for rape, and in many other jurisdictions 30, 40, or 50 years is a common maximum. Some states provide a minimum sentence as well, e.g., Virginia (no less than 5), Code of Va. §18.1-43; and Washington (no less than 5), Wash. Stat. §9.79010. Others add the condition that a rape sentence be spent at hard labor, e.g., South Carolina, S.C. Stat. §16-72. Some states provide for the possibility of substantial fines, as well as prison time, e.g., New Jersey (up to $5000), N.J. Stat. §2A.138-1; New Mexico (up to $10,000), N.M. Crim. Code §40A-29-2.3.

57. Prior to the death penalty cases, cited in the following note, sixteen states provided the most extreme penalty for rape.

58. Jackson v. Georgia, 408 U.S. 238, 92 S. Ct. 2726, 33 L. Ed. 2d 346 (1972); Branch v. Texas, 408 U.S. 238, 92 S. Ct. 2726, 33 L. Ed. 2d 346 (1972).

by appellants in these cases was that the sentence was disproportionate when imposed to protect a value other than life. The majority of the Court declined to separate the issues raised by the death penalty in rape and in murder cases, and did not discuss the issue. But in dissent Justice Powell stated:[59]

> . . . I find it quite impossible to declare the death sentence grossly excessive for all rapes. Rape is widely recognized as among the most serious of violent crimes. . . . It is widely viewed as the most atrocious of intrusions upon the privacy and dignity of the victim; never is the crime committed accidentally; rarely can it be said to be unpremeditated; often the victim suffers serious physical injury; the psychological impact can often be as great as the physical consequences; in a real sense, the threat of both types of injury is always present.

The response in many states to the Supreme Court's opinion in the death penalty cases has been legislation enacting mandatory death penalties for some crimes, including rape. It is certain that in the testing of such legislation against constitutional standards, the disproportionality argument will again arise. Prior to the death penalty cases in the Supreme Court, the Fourth Circuit adopted the proposition that death in some circumstances is a disproportionate penalty for rape. The case raises basic questions about what is the "proper" penalty for the crime.

RALPH v. WARDEN, MARYLAND PENITENTIARY
438 F.2d 786 (4th Cir. 1970)

BUTZNER, Circuit Judge:
William Ralph, convicted of rape in 1961 by a three-judge court sitting without a jury, was sentenced to death. . . . In 1964, Ralph claimed on appeal that the death penalty violated the Eighth Amendment. . . . [W]e noted in Snider v. Peyton, 356 F.2d 626, 627 (4th Cir. 1966):

> There is extreme variation in the degree of culpability of rapists. If one were sentenced to death upon conviction of rape of an adult under circumstances lacking great aggravation, the Supreme Court might well find it an appropriate case to consider the constitutional questions tendered to us. Even an inferior court such as ours might find the question not foreclosed to it if the actual and potential harm to the victim was relatively slight.

The hypothetical case we envisioned in *Snider* is before us now. Armed with a tire iron, Ralph broke into the victim's home late at night. Threatening her and her young son, who was asleep in another room, with death if she did not submit, he forcibly committed rape and sodomy. The prosecuting witness was neither of tender years nor aged, but she was frail and unquestionably her fear was genuine. The physician who thoroughly examined her shortly after the crime testified that he found "no outward evidence of injury or violence" nor any signs of unusual psychological trauma. . . .

On these facts, it is appropriate to consider the constitutional implications of capital punishment for a rape that has neither taken nor endangered life. Cf. Rudolph v. Alabama, 375 U.S. 889, 84 S. Ct. 155, 11 L. Ed. 2d 119 (1963) (Goldberg, J., dissenting from a denial of certiorari). A critic of Mr. Justice Goldberg's dissent correctly noted: "There is a sense in which life is always endangered by sexual attack, just as there is a sense in which it is always endangered by robbery or by burglary of a dwelling, or by any physical assault." We use the term, however, in another sense — that there are rational gradations of culpability that can be made on the basis of injury

---

59. 408 U.S. at 458-459, 92 S. Ct. at 2838-2839, 33 L. Ed. 2d at 476.

to the victim. For example, Nevada distinguishes for purposes of punishment rape which results in substantial bodily harm. Nev. Rev. Stat. §200.363 (1968). . . .

. . . Despite the lack of controlling precedent, we believe the Supreme Court has fashioned a workable objective standard for determining whether punishment is cruel and unusual. As early as 1892, Mr. Justice Field suggested that the prohibition of the Eighth Amendment is directed not only against torture or barbarism, "but against all punishments which by their excessive length or severity are greatly disproportioned to the offenses charged."[7]. . .

An objective indication of society's "evolving standards of decency" can be drawn from the trend of legislative action. As Mr. Justice Stone noted, "The social policy and judgment expressed in legislation . . . would seem to merit that judicial recognition which is freely accorded to the like expression in judicial precedent." The precedent to be gathered from the course of legislation on capital punishment is unmistakable. Generally, laws authorizing capital punishment are justified as efficient, economical means of protecting society by permanently removing a criminal who otherwise might offend again and as deterrents to other persons. Many people also consider death to be just retribution for serious crimes. Therefore, when legislators abolish the death penalty for a certain crime, we may fairly assume that they deem it excessive and that the aims of punishment may be achieved by less severe measures.

The most recent instance of the abolition of capital punishment occurred in July 1970, when, in a bill designed to cope with the rising crime rate in the District of Columbia, Congress eliminated death as a penalty for rape.[13] On the other hand, within the special maritime and territorial jurisdiction of the United States, rape is still punishable by death or imprisonment. Significantly, however, in only one year out of the last forty has the federal government executed anyone for that crime. Moreover, the National Commission on Reform of Federal Criminal Laws has recommended repeal of the death penalty for rape. This, too, is the recommendation of the Model Penal Code.

Congressional action in recently repealing the death penalty for rape in the District of Columbia follows a worldwide trend. Presently the United States is one of only four nations in which rape is punishable by death, and in this country 34 states punish rape only by imprisonment. In none of the 16 remaining states is death mandatory, but it is retained as a sentencing alternate. It appears, therefore, that the overwhelming majority of the nations of the world, legislatures of more than two-thirds of the states of the union, and Congress, as evidenced by its amendment of the District of Columbia Code, now consider the death penalty to be an excessive punishment for the crime of rape.

In theory a minority of jurisdictions accept the death penalty for rape because it

---

7. O'Neil v. Vermont, 144 U.S. 323, 329, 12 S. Ct. 693, 699, 36 L. Ed. 450 (1892) (Field, J., dissenting). O'Neil had been convicted of 307 separate offenses of selling intoxicating liquor. His fines and costs aggregated $6,638.72, and the judgment provided that if this sum were not paid, he should be imprisoned for 54 years and 204 days. Mr. Justice Harlan, who was joined by Mr. Justice Brewer in a separate dissent, also wrote that the punishment was cruel and unusual in view of the character of the offenses. The majority did not dispute the dissenters on this point. They held, instead, that the issue of cruel and unusual punishment presented a state and not a federal question. However, it is now settled that the Eighth Amendment's prohibition of cruel and unusual punishment is applied to the states by the Fourteenth Amendment. Robinson v. California, 370 U.S. 660, 82 S. Ct. 1417, 8 L. Ed. 2d 758 (1962).

13. D.C. Court Reform and Criminal Procedure Act of 1970, Pub. L. No. 91-358, §20, 84 Stat. 473, 600, amending D.C. Code Ann. §22-2801 (1970). The legislative history indicates that the background for the amendment is United States v. Jackson, 390 U.S. 570, 88 S. Ct. 1209, 20 L. Ed. 2d 138 (1969), which held the death penalty provision in the federal kidnapping law was unconstitutional because it tended to coerce a defendant to either plead guilty or be tried without a jury. The District of Columbia death penalty for rape suffered the same defect. Instead of amending the statute to retain the death penalty under proper procedures, Congress abolished it for rape, while retaining it for other crimes. See H.R. Rep. No. 91-907, 91st Cong., 2d Sess. (1970).

remains a part of their criminal codes, but the extreme infrequency of execution belies the argument. Maryland executed twenty-four persons for rape between 1930 and 1947, and since 1948 no one has been put to death in Maryland for that crime. The infrequency of execution in Maryland does not differ significantly from the practice in other states that still retain the death penalty. Throughout the United States, 455 persons have been executed for rape since 1930. From an average of twenty a year in the 1940's, executions dropped to ten a year in the 1950's and less than six a year in the early part of the 1960's. No one has been put to death in the United States for rape since 1964.[21] . . .

Infrequent imposition of the death penalty for rape not only indicates that it is excessive, it also suggests that it is meted out arbitrarily. In 1960, the year Ralph committed the offense, 15,560 reports of rape were recorded in the United States.[22] From 1960–1968 there were 190,790 rapes reported. In contrast to the frequency of the commission of rape, the imposition of the death penalty is extremely rare. In 1961, the year in which Ralph was convicted, 21 persons were sentenced to death for rape, and in the period 1960–1968, 101 convicted rapists received death sentences. During the same period of time 28 prisoners were actually executed for the crime. The high incidence of the crime compared with the low incidence of the death penalty suggests the lack of a rational ground for selecting the prisoners on whom the death penalty is inflicted.[23] This is particularly true when, as here, the harshest penalty is imposed on a rapist whose act is not marked with the great aggravation that often accompanies this crime.[24]

We conclude, therefore, that two factors coalesce to establish that the death sentence is so disproportionate to the crime of rape when the victim's life is neither taken nor endangered that it violates the Eighth Amendment. First, in most jurisdictions death is now considered an excessive penalty for rape. This has been demonstrated by the legislative trend to abolish capital punishment for this crime and by the infrequency of its infliction in jurisdictions that still authorize it. Second, when a rapist does not take or endanger the life of his victim, the selection of the death penalty from the range of punishment authorized by statute is anomalous when compared to the large number of rapists who are sentenced to prison. Lest our opinion be given a breadth greater than is necessary for the decision of this case, we do not hold, despite the argument of the amicus curiae, that death is an unconstitutional punishment for all rapes.

HAYNSWORTH, Chief Judge, on the Petition for Rehearing:

The harm done the victim may or may not bear upon the moral guilt of her attacker. If there is lasting physical injury, it probably will, but it well may not if the lasting harm is psychological. But the nature, degree and duration of the harm have long been recognized as important criteria in determining the appropriateness of punishment. The

21. No one has been executed in this country for any crime since 1967. At the end of 1968, 479 prisoners remained under sentence of death. United States Dep't of Justice, Bureau of Prisons, National Prisoner Statistics No. 45, Capital Punishment 1930–1968, at 7, 26 (1969). Stays have been granted for many reasons, both procedural and substantive, and they, of course, do not conclusively establish that society repudiates capital punishment for all crimes. The reluctance to carry out death sentences, however, is symptomatic of a national and worldwide trend away from capital punishment. See Witherspoon v. Illinois, 391 U.S. 510, 520, 88 S. Ct. 1770, 20 L. Ed. 2d 776 (1967); Capital Punishment (Sellin ed. 1967); United Nations, Dep't of Economic and Social Affairs, Capital Punishment (1968). More fundamentally, though, the doubts about capital punishment demonstrate concern over the effectiveness of our entire penal system.

22. Statistics on reported offenses are derived from FBI, Uniform Crime Reports, Crime in the United States, 1960 through 1968. Firgures on death sentences and executions are from the United States Dep't of Justice, National Prisoner Statistics.

23. See Goldberg & Dershowitz, Declaring the Death Penalty Unconstitutional, 83 Harv. L. Rev. 1773, 1790 (1970).

24. Ralph contends that he arbitrarily received the death penalty because he is black and his victim was white. In support, he calls attention to statistics that illustrate a high correlation of race to death sentences in rape cases. See United States Dep't of Justice, Bureau of Prisons, National Prisoner Statistics No. 45, Capital Punishment 1930–1968, at 10 (1969); Howard, Administration of Rape Cases in the City of Baltimore and the State of Maryland (1967). But there remain too many variables for us to conclude that the statistics prove that Ralph received the death penalty because he is black. Cf. Maxwell v. Bishop, 398 F.2d 138 (8th Cir. 1968), vacated and remanded on other grounds, 398 U.S. 262, 90 S. Ct. 1578 (1970).

difference between murder and attempted murder is a fortuitous accident without relevance to the assailant's moral culpability, but in every jurisdiction which retains capital punishment for murder, the survival of the victim avoids all possibility of imposition of the death penalty.

BOREMAN, Circuit Judge, with whom BRYAN, Circuit Judge joins, dissenting from the majority's refusal to grant rehearing en banc:

. . . [F]oremost, the very facts recited in rather abbreviated form in the court's opinion are contrary to the decision as rendered:

> Armed with a tire iron, Ralph broke into the victim's home late at night. Threatening her and her young son, who was asleep in another room, with death if she did not submit, he forcibly committed rape and sodomy.

But there are other facts and circumstances which properly may be taken into consideration. Ralph entered the victim's home in the dead of night and as he entered through the garage and basement he pulled out the fuse box to make certain that he would be operating in the dark and thus make identification more difficult. He picked up a metal tire tool which he carried with him to the victim's bedroom and which was later found there. It was apparent that he had had the victim's home under surveillance before breaking in at 2 o'clock in the morning and his visit appears to have been carefully planned and premeditated. It was obvious that he was bent on rape and was prepared to resort to such violence as might be necessary. The victim was not selected at random. She was a small, frail woman and Ralph threatened that if she made an outcry he would kill her and her young son asleep in the next room. To me, this is an aggravated case, not only because of the threats of death to the victim and her son which put her in mortal fear but also for the reason that before the crime of rape was perpetrated the defendant performed perverted and degrading acts upon the person of the victim and then subjected her to further degradations and perversions. . . .

. . . Is the court's decision to be construed as saying that the victim in the instant case had to be hit over the head with the tire iron for her life to be endangered? The crime of rape is a crime of force against the consent of the victim and while force is an element of the crime there is the clear alternative, intimidation, which may be by threats of immediate great bodily harm accompanied by the apparent power of execution. To be bashed with a tire iron certainly constitutes great bodily harm and intimidation is the inescapable result when, in the face of a threat of death, a man armed with a tire iron has the immediate and apparent power of executing the threat. Furthermore, there are other dangers to the life and health of the victim inherent in Ralph's attack which should not be lightly disregarded. What about the possibility of pregnancy and of infecting the victim with a loathsome disease? Is it only when the attack does not produce the possible dire results that the death penalty becomes cruel, inhuman and unusual punishment?

Ralph, in which the death penalty was ordered although the defendant did not take a life, is the clearest case for the "proportionality" argument. But the same argument could be made when long prison sentences are meted out for rapes which do not involve "extrinsic" violence, i.e., no infliction of physical harm other than the act itself. In Workman v. Commonwealth, 429 S.W.2d 374 (Ky. Ct. App. 1968), for instance, life imprisonment without the possibility of parole was held excessive for the crime of rape committed by fourteen-year-olds.

The proportionality approach to cruel and unusual punishment has also been used in situations involving crimes other than rape. See, e.g., People v. Lorentzen, 387 Mich. 167, 194 N.W.2d 827 (1972), holding excessive a mandatory minimum sentence of twenty years for selling marijuana; Cannon v. Gladden, 203 Ore. 629, 281 P.2d 233 (1955), in which a sentence of life imprisonment for assault to commit rape was voided on disproportionality grounds.

In interpreting the state constitution's cruel and unusual clause to cover a punishment "so disproportionate to the crime for which it is inflicted that it shocks the conscience and offends fundamental notions of human dignity," the California Supreme Court set out a number of factors which would be considered on the issue of disproportionality.[60] One of these factors is the nature of the offender or the offense with particular reference to the nonviolence of the offense (although, relying on *Ralph,* the court noted that nonviolence is not an absolute requirement for a punishment to be found disproportionate). A second test of disproportionality offered by the court is the comparison of the challenged penalty with punishments prescribed in the same jurisdiction for different and arguably more serious offenses. A third method of inquiry is the comparison of punishment prescribed with that given in other jurisdictions for the same offense. The court used these techniques in declaring that a possible life penalty maximum was cruel and unusual for a second conviction for indecent exposure.

The death penalty for rape must also be considered in light of its discriminatory enforcement. Of the sixteen jurisdictions that as of 1972 still imposed the death penalty for the crime of rape, four were Southern or border states.[61] The actual imposition of the death penalty in rape cases in the South has been overwhelmingly on black men for the rape of white women. The Federal Bureau of Prisons' National Prisoner Statistics for executions during the period 1930–1970 reveals that more than eight times as many blacks as whites were put to death for rape, although the numbers of blacks and whites executed for murder were almost identical.[62] So significant is the racially discriminatory factor in rape cases that the argument was made in one of the death penalty cases, *Maxwell v. Bishop,* 398 F.2d 138 (8th Cir. 1968), 398 U.S. 262 (1970), that blacks sentenced to death for raping white women are denied equal protection of the laws. This argument was not discussed by any opinion of the court.

In assessing extreme penalties for rape, another factor to be considered is their effect on the administration of the laws. Such penalties probably help to account for the mistreatment of the victim by police, prosecutors, and the criminal justice system generally. When the stakes are excessively high, the system becomes distorted in its protection of the accused, and concomitantly harsh in its efforts to be certain that the victim is telling the truth. This effect was explicitly recognized by the American Bar Association in 1938 when it passed a resolution supporting mental examinations for a prosecutrix in a rape case in virtually all circumstances. The report stated: "The penalties for sex-crimes are very severe — justly so, in most cases. But the very severity of the penalty calls for special procedural precautions to protect an innocent accused from condemnation by unreliable testimony."[63]

Societal ambivalence toward rape and its victims is expressed in the high maximum penalties for rape accompanied by a panoply of special instructions and evidentiary rules which decrease the possibility that there will be convictions and that these penalties will ever be imposed. Actually, in fact, the extreme penalties are unevenly applied, and where there are no aggravating circumstances and the victim and defendant are of the same race, the actual sentence given and served is far below the maximum.[64] But the existence

60. In Re Lynch, 8 Cal. 3d 410, 105 Cal. Rptr. 217, 503 P.2d 921 (1972).

61. Nevada also imposed the penalty but only in the event of "substantial bodily harm," Nev. Rev. Stat. §200.363 (1967). The federal government also authorized the death penalty for rape.

62. 1971 National Prisoner Statistics No. 46, pp. 12-13. These figures do not include those blacks lynched for alleged rapes of white women over the same period of time. See Violence in America, Historical and Comparative Perspectives — A Staff Report to the National Commission on the Causes and Prevention of Violence 106 (1969).

63. Quoted in Commentary to Model Penal Code §207 (1962), supra Part II-A at footnote 6.

64. Ploscowe, Sex and the Law 190-191 (1951), records the practice of judges to sentence far below the maximum in "non-aggravated" rape cases. "Only one-fourth of all defendants convicted of rape in California superior courts in 1951 were committed to a state authority for care and treatment. The majority were given the lesser penalties of placement in jail or on probation. . . ." California Sex Crimes Report at 16 (1950-1953).
Both of these sources are quoted in the Commentary to the Model Penal Code §207.6 (Tent. Draft No. 4, 1955) as authority for the statement that there is a judicial tendency to avoid "the extreme sanctions permitted by present [rape] statutes."

and possibility of the harsh penalties is the basis for the special instructions and evidentiary rules, as well as, arguably, for the disinclination of juries to convict. The actual infliction of the possible very severe penalties may also occasion an unusually close review in the appellate court. One wonders, for instance, in DeFrates, supra, whether a six-month sentence would have stirred such a skeptical regard of the victim's testimony as the ten to twenty-five years actually imposed. Realistically and fairly, efforts such as those suggested in other sections of this chapter to abolish the special rules concerning the trial of rape cases should be accompanied by a reassessment of the penalty for the crime. If the penalty were brought into line with that for aggravated assaults in most jurisdictions, there would be less need felt for special evidentiary rules and instructions to protect the accused against the risk of too high a penalty in comparison to the crime. Lowering the penalties should in itself increase the conviction rate because juries will no longer be overly concerned with the possible drastic consequences of conviction.

Any consideration of penalties and their revision and effect on the conviction rate is, of course, made within the context of traditional beliefs about the purposes and effects of the criminal law, i.e., that deterrence, punishment, and rehabilitation are derived from justly convicting those who are guilty. Even those who do not accept this proposition, however, and therefore are troubled by feminist efforts to change rape laws in order to increase convictions, would assent to the proposition that as long as there is a criminal law system, it should not discriminate so baldly against one type of victim and operate differentially as to one kind of crime.

b. General Revision of Sexual Assault Laws Pursuant to the Equal Rights Amendment

If the Equal Rights Amendment is ratified, the decade after its passage will be propitious for reconsidering all aspects of sexual assault laws, including revision of the penalties for rape. The amendment should cause the review, and repeal or revision, of sex-discriminatory provisions. Since most statutes define rape as committed only by men, the extreme penalties for this kind of an assault are arguably sex-discriminatory. In any event, the general reconsideration of the wording and structure of sexual assault laws, which the amendment should occasion, would logically also involve a re-evaluation of the penalties.

Opponents of the Equal Rights Amendment have argued that it will mean total abolition of all rape and sexual assault laws designed to protect women and young girls. On the other hand, it has been urged that laws written in terms of one sex only may be retained under the amendment if they are based on a unique physical characteristic pertaining to all members of one sex and to no members of the opposite sex.[65] Rape laws would meet this requirement if viewed as written to give women's vaginas special protection from assault. The excerpt that follows provides a fuller explanation of this theory and discusses the possible effect of the amendment on other sexual assault laws.

BROWN, EMERSON, FALK, AND FREEDMAN
THE EQUAL RIGHTS AMENDMENT:
A CONSTITUTIONAL BASIS
FOR EQUAL RIGHTS FOR WOMEN
80 Yale L.J. 871, 955-959 (1971)

Insofar as rape is defined as penetration into the vagina by the penis, courts could uphold forcible rape laws which limit liability to men as based on a unique physical

---

65. Brown, Emerson, Falk, and Freedman, The Equal Rights Amendment: A Constitutional Basis for Equal Rights for Women, 80 Yale L.J. 871, 955-959 (1971).

characteristic of men.[205] Laws which define rape as forced sexual intercourse could also be sustained if a court defined sexual intercourse as an act done only by a man and a woman together, and if the statute clearly and appropriately defined women as the sole victims of rape.[206] Using the criteria . . . for determining whether a law bears the necessary close relationship to a unique physical characteristic,[66] a court could conclude that, on balance, the law should be sustained. Among other things, the court might find that rape is an extremely traumatic event for the victim; that most men are capable of penetration, and therefore, rape; that a major proportion of sexual assaults consist of sexual intercourse forced by men; that penetration by a man's penis carries with it the possibility of unwanted pregnancy for the victim and forcible penetration carries high danger of injury to the victim; that a criminal penalty is an appropriate way of deterring rape; and that, accompanied by procedural and substantive rights, the law is sufficiently narrow and specific in its scope to be upheld.

Similarly, insofar as a court could find that the rape laws are intended to give special protection from assault to women's vaginas, it could sustain the laws even though their protection is limited to women. A court would conduct an inquiry analogous to that described above for determining whether, under the unique physical characteristics tests, the rape laws could properly be limited to female victims. All or nearly all women's genitals differ from all or nearly all men's genitals in that they can be penetrated in an act of sexual assault against the victim's will. Rape laws could thus be sustained as a legislative choice to give one part of the body (unique to women) special protection from physical attack. By contrast, the statutes which include penetration "per anum and per os" in the definition of rape, could not justifiably be limited to female victims because no physical characteristic unique to women is being protected by these laws. A court could choose between invalidating these broader rape laws or else limiting them to penetration of a woman's genitals. In the case of such a serious offense, courts would probably choose to retain the central and valid portion of the law and invalidate only the part referring to "penetration per anum and per os." Alternatively, the legislature could extend the laws to cover the designated assaults on all persons, regardless of sex.

Rape is only one of a number of nonconsensual sexual acts which are penalized throughout the United States.[208] Laws governing such offenses are based on two related sets of concerns. The first is that unwanted sexual contact may be imposed on a person in ways ranging from physical force and threats to more subtle coercion in the form of deception and abuse of positions of trust and authority. The second range of concerns is that particular groups in the population may be especially susceptible to such sexual coercion. By merging these two aspects of the problem of sexual assault, traditional laws provide highly uneven and irrational coverage permeated by sex discrimination.

With a few notable exceptions, laws which punish sexual intercourse per se as a

205. Statutes which define rape as "penetration" mostly fail, with Victorian delicacy, to specify what instruments of penetration are included. The common law antecedents of the rape statutes, as well as contemporary case law, indicate that courts have limited the application of rape laws to penetration by a man's penis. However, penetration of a woman's vagina may be made by many instruments other than a man's penis, and with equally devastating consequences for the victim's psyche. Whether or not pregnancy has resulted from the rape is immaterial under current laws; similarly, sterility is not a defense for a man accused of rape. Thus a court might conclude there is no rational reason for differentiating such assaults, of which women are as capable as men, and hold the rape laws invalid unless they extend to women assailants as well as men.

206. The Model Penal Code, §213.1 (Proposed Official Draft, 1962) adopts this definition of rape.

66. See Chapter One, V-C, for a discussion of unique physical characteristics. — Eds.

208. A few states still have statutes which extend the concept of "sexual assault" to the use of obscene or insulting language in the presence of a woman. For instance, Alabama penalizes "any person who in the presence or hearing of any girl or woman, uses abusive, insulting, or obscene language." Ala. Code, tit. 14, §11 (1958). See also Mich. Comp. Laws Ann. §750.337 (1968); Ariz. Rev. Stat. §13-377 (1956). A variation on the same theme is a Georgia libel law which forbids anyone to utter or circulate "any defamatory words or statements derogatory to the fair fame or reputation for virtue of any virtuous female," Ga. Code Ann. §26-2104 (1953). Such laws, based on a stereotyped view that women are morally pure, yet morally fragile, rather than on any unique physical characteristic of women which actually distinguishes them from men, would be invalidated under the Equal Rights Amendment.

constructive assault rest on the premise that the female party is incapable of giving meaningful consent.[209] Best known among these are the statutory rape laws, which punish men for having sexual intercourse with any woman under an age specified by law, frequently sixteen.[210] . . .

These laws suffer from a double defect under the Equal Rights Amendment. First, they single out women for special protection from sexual coercion, even where men in similar circumstances are equally in need of protection; in this sense the laws are "underinclusive."[213] To be sure, the singling out of women probably reflects sociological reality: in this society, young women, who learn both that marriage is the most important goal for them and that they may pursue it only passively, are undoubtedly more susceptible than young men to the lures of persons who want to take sexual advantage of them. Likewise, in this society, the bad reputation and illegitimate child which can result from an improvident sexual liaison may be far more ruinous to a young woman's psychological health than similar conduct is to a young man's. But the Equal Rights Amendment forbids finding legislative justification in the sexual double standard, and requires such statutes to be framed in terms of the general human need for protection rather than in terms of crude sexual categories.

Second, traditional laws protecting all women of a particular age or status against sexual assault are "overinclusive" to the extent that they punish sexual activity when unwanted penetration of the vagina is not involved. It might be argued that statutory rape laws and other laws which render a woman's consent inoperative should be sustained on the same theory that forcible rape laws are upheld: that the legislature wished to give special protection to young women's genital organs.[214] However, it is unlikely that such claims could withstand close court scrutiny under the unique physical characteristics tests. In particular, a court would be unable to find a close correlation between the activity being regulated (consensual sexual intercourse) and the justifying physical basis (susceptibility of the vagina to unwanted penetration).[215]

Even if it found noncoerced sexual intercourse rarely physically harmful to post-

209. The few statutes which declare young or helpless males incapable of consent are: Colo. Rev. Stat. Ann. §40-2-25(1)(k) (1963) (intercourse with male under 18 solicited by female); Ill. Ann. Stat. ch. 38, §§11-4 and 11-5 (Smith-Hurd 1964) (indecent liberties with a child and contributing to the delinquency of a child, regardless of sex); Ind. Ann. Stat. §10-4203 (1956) (intercourse with male over 14 knowing he is epileptic, imbecile, feeble minded or insane); Ky. Rev. Stat. §435.100 (1970) (carnal knowledge of male child under 18); Mich. Comp. Laws Ann. §§750.339-340 (1968) (debauching a male under 15); Wash. Rev. Code Ann. §9-79.020 (1961) (sexual intercourse with male under 18).

210. See, e.g., 44 Am. Jur. Rape §17 (1942). Some states make an exception for intercourse with women who are not virgins, e.g., Fla. Stat. §794.05 (1961).

213. See, e.g., the report of the Carroll County, Maryland, grand jury calling for legislation to prevent mental and physical harm to unsuspecting, unprepared adolescents by forced, coerced or seduced sexual activity which may warp the development of such children as useful citizens to society." The report was prompted by evidence presented to the grand jury that two women elementary school teachers had seduced boys 11 and 12 years old. The grand jury concluded that the Maryland criminal code provided no statute under which the teachers could be indicted and called for state legislation "giving male juveniles equal protection under the laws." Washington Post, Jan. 2, 1971, at 3, col. 2. The Royal Commission on the Status of Women in Canada has reached a similar conclusion. Its recent Report recommended "that the Criminal Code be amended to extend protection from sexual abuse to all young people, male and female, and protection to everyone from sexual exploitation either by false representation, use of force, threat, or the abuse of authority." Report of the Royal Commission on the Status of Women in Canada ch. 9, par. 42, at 374 (1970).

214. It is true that statutory rape may involve breaking the hymen, but very few states consider the victim's chastity material to the question of guilt. Moreover, statistical reports show that few statutory rape complainants are virgins. See Schiff, Statistical Features of Rape, 14 J. For. Sci. 102 (1969).

215. The law in most states presumes that a sixteen year old girl can consent to marriage (with her parents' approval), and, by implication, to sexual relations, while an unmarried girl of sixteen is legally presumed to be incapable of giving consent to a single act of sexual intercourse. However, there are no physical differences between the sexual acts involved. . . . [T]he minimum marriage age is not based on a unique physical characteristic of women. Therefore, the statutory rape law, which also deals with consensual sexual relations, cannot be justified as based on such a unique characteristic. There are, of course, social and psychological differences between marital and extramarital sexual relations, and the state may recognize them through sex-neutral legislation about extramarital sexual intercourse involving either young men or young women.

pubescent girls, a court might find that sexual intercourse is physically dangerous to girls who have not reached puberty. Upon finding such a fact situation, the court would conclude that the class of women victims is defined too broadly. If it made such a determination, a court could limit the operation of the statutory rape laws to pre-pubescent children. In the alternative, the court could strike down the law altogether because of its overbreadth and because it fails to base its sex difference upon a unique physical characteristic of women.

If invalidated, some of the laws, such as the seduction laws, which derive from outdated standards of courting and morality, would probably not be resuscitated. Upon reexamination, legislatures might decide that the existing kidnap laws or other unlawful restraint laws already penalize any serious offensive deception or decoying, and that further penalties would be duplicative. Legislatures would be free, however, to extend the laws against sexual coercion to protect men as well as women. This is particularly likely where sexual relations with pre-adolescent children are involved.[216]

NOTE

What is the basis for the argument made in the article that vaginas need special protection? In spite of the author's disclaimer, doesn't the argument ultimately depend on the possibility of impregnation; and if so, can this possibility, which is statistically remote in a single instance of intercourse, sustain laws which differentiate sexual assaults made against women?

Revision of the statutory rape laws, also discussed in the article, would be a healthy development for the general administration of all rape laws. To some extent, corroboration requirements and the suspicion of victims which permeates the system are based on the image of a man led astray by a young temptress. Lowering the age of consent would eventually alter the reality of that image, and thus affect the treatment of all women victims.

If sexual assault laws were revised to bring the penalties into line with those accorded other aggravated assaults, the Model Penal Code provides a starting point for consideration. It separates degrees of seriousness of sexual assaults and assigns a sliding scale of penalties. The code's approach is certainly more thoughtful and consistent than the laws in regard to sexual assault in most jurisdictions. Sections of the code and excerpts from a commentary explaining its approach are set out below. Read the materials with these questions in mind: Would this penalty scale ameliorate the present problems of administration of the rape laws? What improvements, from a feminist perspective, could be made?

MODEL PENAL CODE
(Proposed Official Draft, 1962)

ARTICLE 213. SEXUAL OFFENSES

Section 213.1. Rape and Related Offenses.

(1) *Rape.* A male who has sexual intercourse with a female not his wife is guilty of rape if:

(a) he compels her to submit by force or by threat of imminent death, serious bodily injury, extreme pain or kidnapping, to be inflicted on anyone; or

---

216. Some states already have laws that protect all children, regardless of sex. For example, Illinois has merged its statutory rape law into laws prohibiting indecent liberties with any child or contributing to any child's sexual delinquency. Ill. Ann. Stat. ch. 38, §11-4 (Smith-Hurd Supp. 1971) and ch. 38, §11-5 (Smith-Hurd 1964).

[For an alternative theory of the impact of the Equal Rights Amendment on rape laws, see Eastwood, The Double Standard of Justice: Women's Rights Under the Constitution, 5 Val. L. Rev. 281, 313 (1971). — Eds.]

(b) he has substantially impaired her power to appraise or control her conduct by administering or employing without her knowledge drugs, intoxicants or other means for the purpose of preventing resistance; or

(c) the female is unconscious; or

(d) the female is less than 10 years old.

Rape is a felony of the second degree unless (i) in the course thereof the actor inflicts serious bodily injury upon anyone, or (ii) the victim was not a voluntary social companion of the actor upon the occasion of the crime and had not previously permitted him sexual liberties, in which cases the offense is a felony of the first degree. Sexual intercourse includes intercourse per os or per anum, with some penetration however slight; emission is not required. [Felonies of the first degree are punishable by a possible maximum of life imprisonment, with a minimum of not less than a year nor more than ten years. Felonies of the second degree are punishable by a maximum of ten and a minimum of one year.]

(2) *Gross Sexual Imposition.* A male who has sexual intercourse with a female not his wife commits a felony of the third degree [punishable by a maximum of five and a minimum of one year] if:

(a) he compels her to submit by any threat that would prevent resistance by a woman of ordinary resolution; or

(b) he knows that she suffers from a mental disease or defect which renders her incapable of appraising the nature of her conduct; or

(c) he knows that she is unaware that a sexual act is being committed upon her or that she submits because she falsely supposes that he is her husband.

Section 213.3 Corruption of Minors and Seduction.

(1) *Offense Defined.* A male who has sexual intercourse with a female not his wife, or any person who engages in deviate sexual intercourse or causes another to engage in deviate sexual intercourse, is guilty of an offense if:

(a) the other person is less than [16] years old and the actor is at least [4] years older than the other person; or

(b) the other person is less than 21 years old and the actor is his guardian or otherwise responsible for general supervision of his welfare; or

(c) the other person is in custody of law or detained in a hospital or other institution and the actor has supervisory or disciplinary authority over him; or

(d) the other person is a female who is induced to participate by a promise of marriage which the actor does not mean to perform.

(2) *Grading.* An offense under paragraph (a) of Subsection (1) is a felony of the third degree. Otherwise an offense under this section is a misdemeanor.

Section 213.4. Sexual Assault.

A person who subjects another not his spouse to any sexual contact is guilty of sexual assault, a misdemeanor, if:

(1) he knows that the contact is offensive to the other person; or

(2) he knows that the other person suffers from a mental disease or defect which renders him or her incapable of appraising the nature of his or her conduct; or

(3) he knows that the other person is unaware that a sexual act is being committed; or

(4) the other person is less than 10 years old; or

(5) he has substantially impaired the other person's power to appraise or control his or her conduct, by administering or employing without the other's knowledge drugs, intoxicants or other means for the purpose of preventing resistance; or

(6) the other person is less than [16] years old and the actor is at least [four] years older than the other person; or

(7) the other person is less than 21 years old and the actor is his guardian or otherwise responsible for general supervision of his welfare; or

(8) the other person is in custody of law or detained in a hospital or other institution and the actor has supervisory or disciplinary authority over him.

Sexual contact is any touching of the sexual or other intimate parts of the person of another for the purpose of arousing or gratifying sexual desire of either party.

The 1955 comentary explained the code's approach to the definitions and grading of sexual offenses:

MODEL PENAL CODE
(Tentative Draft No. 4, 1955)

[Comment to §207.4, which appears as §213.4 of the approved 1962 draft, supra:]

Background and General Scheme of Proposed Section.

It is everywhere regarded as a serious offense for a male to have intercourse with a female other than his wife by means of force, threats, or certain forms of fundamental deception. The chief problems are (i) to decide and express what shall be the minimum amount of coercion or deception to be included here, i.e., drawing the line between rape-seduction, on the one hand, and illicit intercourse on the other; and (ii) to devise a grading system that distributes the entire group of offenses rationally over the range of available punishments. The latter problem is especially important because: (1) the upper ranges of punishment include life imprisonment and even death; (2) the offense is typically committed in privacy, so that conviction often rests on little more than the testimony of the complainant; (3) the central issue is likely to be the question of consent on the part of the female, a subtle psychological problem in view of social and religious pressures upon the woman to conceive of herself as victim rather than collaborator; and (4) the offender's threat to society is difficult to evaluate.

We know very little about "rapists" as a class, if indeed they constitute a single group. The intelligence of sex offenders is reported to be average, but the I.Q. of rapists falls below that level. Rape is most often committed by males between the ages of sixteen and thirty; and forcible rape especially is the crime of younger men. Among possible motivations for forcible rape Karpman has suggested: (a) male need for female resistance to achieve potency, (b) sadism, masochism or narcissism, (c) male hostility to the female and compensatory force to overcome feelings of sexual inadequacy, (d) overdevelopment of normal male aggressiveness, (e) aggressive criminality based upon a desire to pillage and plunder with rape as merely another act of plunder. Recidivism in statutory and forcible rape is said to be negligible in comparison with other offenses. The grouping of statutory and forcible rapists together in attempts to characterize "the rapist" makes available statistics of little use in identifying the offender who merits the ultimate sanction.

The classification proposed in the text is based on the following rationale: the extreme punishment of first degree felony is reserved for situations which are the most brutal or shocking, evincing the most dangerous aberration of character and threat to public security, and which also provide some objective support for the complainant's testimony of non-consent. The remaining offenses embraced in common law rape or the usual statutory first degree are classified as second degree felonies. Subsections (2) and (3) delineate certain categories in which it appears desirable and safe to set even lower limits on punishment. . . .

[Comment to §207.6, which appears as §213.4 of the approved 1962 draft, supra:]

Sexual Assault.

Introduction. Section 207.6 deals with acts of sexual aggression which, with some exceptions, do not involve the peculiarly resented element of "penetration." The range of activity covered extends from unauthorized fondling of a woman's breast to homosexual manipulation of a young boy's genitals, digital penetration of a girl by an older man, and sadist or masochistic flagellation. The common law made no special provision for indecent assault, treating these as varieties of common assault and battery. At least as early as 1861, English legislation distinguished indecent assault from common assault by providing higher penalties for the former. American legislation has not generally differentiated sexual from other assaults, except that assaults with intent to rape or commit sodomy have been classified as aggravated. A few states have statutes on "gross lewdness" which, unlike most such statutes, cover private as well as public indecency. However, in recent years especially, there has been enacted in most states special legislation on taking sexual liberties with children. . . .

NOTES

1. Note that where the woman is not seriously injured, is a voluntary social companion of the man, and has permitted him previous intimacies, there is no possibility of a charge of first-degree rape. Do you think that this is right?

2. Rather than maintaining the possibility of life imprisonment for the most extreme sexual assaults, another approach to rescaling the penalties would be simply to reduce the maximum for rape to ten or fifteen years. Under such a penalty system, if physical violence were done in addition to the rape, or if a weapon were used, such acts would be the basis for additional charges, which would, of course, have the potential for increasing the penalties in aggravated cases.

3. In addition to the sections on rape printed above, the code includes a section on "deviate sexual intercourse"[67] (per os, or anum, or with an animal), often known as sodomy, which tracks the rape sections. Section 213.2 does not apply to consensual relations between adults and designates so-called deviate sexual intercourse as a second-degree felony in the instance of the use of force or its equivalent. A third-degree felony is committed, if one who engages in deviate sexual intercourse does so by means of threats that would prevent resistance by an average person if he knows that the other person suffers from a mental disease or defect, or if he knows the other person is unaware that a sexual act of this nature is being committed upon him. The crime can be committed by both men and women, but not within marriage.

c. Civil Remedies Against Rapists

One avenue open to an individual victim of rape is to bring a civil suit on a tort theory against the rapist, or against third parties who might be held responsible, e.g., the owners of an inadequately lighted public building. Such a proceeding would involve much of the same evidence as a criminal case, including the possibility of a "consent defense". But the burden of proof is less in a civil case, and, especially if there is physical harm, significant recoveries are possible. Realistically, however, civil suits are not an alternative route to justice for most rape victims. The suits are slow-

---

67. Model Penal Code §213.2 (1962).

moving and costly, and few rapists are wealthy enough to pay substantial damages.

Some states have enacted crime victim compensation plans which offer a theoretically possible remedy for a rape victim. But none of these plans is very well developed, and all are based on rather primitive tort concepts, measuring damages by the cost of the injury. In most circumstances, this means that pain and suffering is either excluded from compensation or undercompensated. As pointed out by one commentator:[68]

> . . . [I]n some crimes, particularly forcible rape . . . the unliquidated claim for compensation for pain and suffering is all that the victim generally has. Thus, it would appear to mock the victim and play havoc with consistency to urge the compensation of a forcible rape victim . . . and in the next breath to reject her claim for pain and suffering.

d. Nonlegal Solutions

Many of the problems in the administration of rape laws are not susceptible to solution by a change in the form, structure, or wording of laws. A common experience for rape victims, for instance, is inadequate medical treatment and unsympathetic attitudes by police officers, which range from disbelieving to voyeuristic.[69] To deal with these aspects of the problem, women across the country have formed self-help groups to aid victims and to negotiate with hospital administrators and police departments in order to change procedures. Suggestions which are made by such groups and often adopted include allowing the woman to be accompanied by a friend, or volunteer from the rape crisis center, during the initial examinations and interviews after a rape; counseling women on the advisability of taking an abortifacient; special training for police officers in dealing with rape cases and victims; and the availability of policewomen for taking rape reports.

Such efforts have historical antecedents. A feminist publication of 1878[70] described aid to rape victims by feminists, whose activity included lending emotional support and financial assistance, encouraging victims to testify, and advocating the position that women's word in court should have as much weight as men's.

Another nonlegal solution to the problem of the maladministration of the rape laws is to seek change in the disrupted and deeply unsatisfactory relationship between the sexes:[71]

> . . . Feminists are at least beginning to spell it out for them, but too many men do not realize that the slogan "An End to Rape" does not so much refer to grand rapes committed on the crime-ridden streets of the cities as to the daily brutalization of contact between brother and sister, father and daughter, teacher and pupil, doctor and patient, employer and employee, dater and datee, fiance and fiancee, husband and wife, adulterer and adulteress, the billions of petty liberties exacted from passive and wondering women. The solution is not to be found in the castration or killing of the rare rapists who offend so crazily that they can be caught and punished but in the correction of our distorted notions of the nature of sexual intercourse, which are also the rationale of the law of rape as a felony.
>
> Women are now struggling to discover and develop their own sexuality, to know their own minds and bodies and to improve the bases upon which they can attempt communication with men. . . . [T]he stereotype of seduction, conquest, the chase and all [should be abandoned].

---

68. Note, A Modest Proposal to Insure Justice for Victims of Crime, 50 Minn. L. Rev. 285, 306 (1965).
69. The investigatory process of a rape case is described in Note: The Victim in a Forcible Rape Case: A Feminist View, 11 Am. Crim. L. Rev. 335, 349-351 (1973).
70. Alpha, Feb. 11, 1878, p. 6.
71. Germaine Greer, Seduction is a Four-Letter Word, in Playboy Magazine, June 1973, p. 228.

Support for the view that many of the problems with the administration of rape laws arises from men's ambivalent feelings about the crime is found in a letter written under a pseudonym, in a jocular tone, but whose message is quite serious:[72]

> I have read a lot of professor stuff on how to stop rapes the last couple of years. I am not saying I have the answer but since I have some general experience from the streets maybe what I say might be a part answer.
>
> Everyone knows that most rapes are never told to the police. I'd say that on the blocks where I use to live maybe ten girls and women anyone would want to rape would tell the police. And that's out of maybe 150 girls. And, of course, most girls who tell the police are treated like whores even if they are not. But, the worse thing about it from the girls viewpoint is that almost no one is convicted and most rapers are treated like heroes by the people who count — their friends. . . .
>
> Here is how my weapon works and as you can see it is probably legal.
>
> When a woman is raped, if she uses my weapon, she goes to the police and instead of charging rape she charges *Indecent Exposure.* All she has to say is that a man grabbed her, took out his penis and showed it to her and that's all. She says nothing about rape. The advantages of doing this are:
>
> 1. The police have no respect for guys who take out their penis in front of women and will immediately try to find the guy. More important, the police will not treat the woman like a whore or ask her any embarrassing questions about who screws her.
>
> 2. The woman is not embarrassed before her friends or husband.
>
> 3. The raper who is picked up is very humiliated since his friends think he is a sick guy who can't even screw a woman. And, when he goes to jail he will be picked on by the inmates as a sick guy.
>
> 4. The raper will probably plead guilty since any lawyer will tell him that juries don't need much evidence to convict guys of sick sex crimes like Indecent Exposure.
>
> 5. Even if the case goes to trial the woman's background will not be examined since it has nothing to do with the crime or any defense to the crime.
>
> 6. Although Indecent Exposure is usually only a misdemeanor the raper has to register as a sex offender wherever he goes and in many states, like California, a second conviction is a felony.
>
> The only disadvantage to reporting a rape as an Indecent Exposure is that the penalty is much greater if you are convicted of rape. But, since most women don't report rapes, those who do are embarrassed, and few rapers are convicted, the odds are much better on Indecent Exposure. To put it another way, you are a probably winner with Indecent Exposure and a sure loser with rape.
>
> Some people may ask, is this legal? In my opinion it probably is since it's the very thing the District Attorney does all the time when he lets a guy plead guilty to a lesser crime like disturbing the peace instead of assault with a deadly weapon. Since all the legal elements of the crime of Indecent Exposure are part of virtually every rape, the woman doesn't even have to lie. All she does is not report the rest of the crime. The funny part of it is the raper can't afford to say it wasn't Indecent Exposure and was really rape — since if he does he gets convicted of a felony.

III. PROSTITUTION

A. THE PATTERN OF LAWS

A summary of the various criminal sanctions against prostitution in the United States follows.

72. *A Street Man's Answer to Rape: Humiliate the Raper,* by Willie Williams, unpublished anonymous letter, on file in the Stanford University Library.

*GEORGE, LEGAL, MEDICAL, AND PSYCHIATRIC
CONSIDERATIONS IN THE CONTROL OF PROSTITUTION*
60 Mich. L. Rev. 717, 719-732 (1962)

CONTROL THROUGH CRIMINAL SANCTIONS

State and Local Control. State and local legislation is abundant, covering all kinds of conduct directly and indirectly involved in prostitution. While no classification of statutes will serve completely all fifty-one American jurisdictions, in general the statutes cover the following classes of persons or activities:

(a) *The female prostitute.* At common law an act of prostitution was not in itself criminal, though to walk the streets at night for the purpose of solicitation may have been. Statutes and ordinances reach either the woman herself because of what she is, the preliminary negotiations with the prospective customer or the act of prostitution itself. In the common-law tradition, preserved in statutes in most jurisdictions, one who holds the status of vagrant is punishable for that fact alone, without the necessity of any particular criminal act being alleged and proved. In many states and cities "common prostitutes" are comprehended within the statutory language, and in other statutes the term "lewd and dissolute persons" will include them. Although recent authority casts doubt on the constitutionality of some of the traditional language defining criminal status, there is enough tradition surrounding the term "common prostitute" that it will probably survive as constitutionally valid unless and until crimes of status per se are held to deny due process of law. Streetwalking is often punishable under statute or local ordinance, as is solicitation by the woman herself. A prostitute who enters a restaurant, bar or the like, or who remains there after being ordered out by the proprietor may be punished. The woman who takes her customer to a hotel room, room or apartment for the purpose of committing an act of prostitution often violates a statute or ordinance. Being an inmate of a house of prostitution is itself criminal.

Instead of or in addition to punishing the prostitute as such or the activities preliminary to specific acts of prostitution, legislation penalizes such acts themselves. In some states those who "commit prostitution" are punishable without the offense being further defined. Other states define prostitution in such terms as "indiscriminate sexual intercourse with males for compensation," any act of sexual intercourse or any act of deviate sexual conduct for money, "the offering or receiving of the body for sexual intercourse for hire and the offering or receiving of the body for indiscriminate sexual intercourse without hire," or some similar definition which may or may not be limited to "normal" heterosexual intercourse or to compensated intercourse. Such statutes commonly punish "lewdness" and "assignation" as alternatives to "prostitution." The most common interpretation is that these terms are intended "to cover commercialized vice cases which might be commonly understood as such by the layman but which might slip through a strict legal definition of 'prostitution.' " . . .

Although prostitutes might accommodate non-prostitute women who wish to engage in homosexual relations, such conduct is not reflected in the legal materials. Should it occur it would be punishable as sodomy in most states.

(b) *The male prostitute.* Although their conduct less often comes to the attention of the public than does that of female prostitutes, in every metropolitan area there are actual or feigned homosexuals who cater for compensation to the desires of other homosexuals. . . . If the basic prostitution statute applies to "any person" or to "any man or woman" who performs or engages in "lewdness" it is probably adequate to cover such "professional" homosexuality, although such prosecutions are not reflected in the appellate decisions. The soliciting statute is often broad enough to cover solicitation to an act of homosexuality, but homosexual solicitation itself may be directly prohibited. Special statutes or ordinances may reach those who loiter about public toilets or other public places, since this is conduct through which homosexual contacts are commonly made. Indecent exposure or lewd touching statutes are probably also applicable to homosexual solicitation and enticement. Approximating "status crimes" are those ordinances which prohibit persons from appearing in the dress of the opposite sex. Other ordinances are patently aimed at places of entertainment where both male and female homosexuals congregate.

Whether or not such special statutes exist or are applied to homosexual prostitutes, in every state except Illinois and New York homosexual acts are punished as sodomy whether or not they are private, whether or not they are between adults and whether or not they are mutually consented to. The consummated act is therefore clearly criminal. The importance of the solicitation, prostitution, loitering and indecent liberties statutes, therefore, lies in their law enforcement role. . . .

(c) *The pander.* The pander or procurer is the individual who places a woman in a house of prostitution or supervises her career. The woman is not considered an accomplice, and her testimony therefore need not be supported under a general accomplice statute. Because of the blackmail possibilities inherent in this as well as other sex crimes, however, legislation occasionally requires specific corroboration. The character of the woman is immaterial; she may already be a hardened prostitute. However, there must be some kind of physical or moral coercion present before the crime of pandering is committed, since this is the only substantive element which distinguishes the usual case of pandering from that of solicitation or receiving the earnings of a prostitute (i.e., pimping). . . .

There are also numerous related statutes covering interstate or intrastate transportation of women for prostitution. Many statutes penalizing the operation of houses of prostitution also are closely related to pandering.

(d) *The pimp.* Pimping as defined by statute consists of soliciting persons to become the customers of prostitutes, the traditional definition, or of living off or receiving the earnings of prostitutes. Occasionally treatment discriminations are made between the two kinds of conduct, one being punished more heavily than the other. Ordinarily compensation must be forthcoming before the crime can be committed, though if no money or other consideration actually passes, the crime of attempted solicitation may have been committed. When receiving earnings is made criminal, money need only be received from one who is known to be a prostitute. The amount received need not form all or a substantial part of the income of the pimp.

Partaking in part both of statutes prohibiting pandering and those prohibiting pimping are those which penalize husbands who cause or permit their wives to commit prostitution, and parents or others who cause or permit children to remain in a house of prostitution or to engage in prostitution. . . .

(e) *Those who facilitate prostitution.* The persons most obviously facilitating prostitution are operators of houses of prostitution. Laws are in effect in every jurisdiction which make it a criminal offense to own or operate such a house. In addition, activities incidental to the running of such a business fall within the broad language of statutes applicable to pandering and pimping. But beyond this it is common to reach by state statute those whose otherwise legitimate operations may be knowingly misused to facilitate prostitution. Thus criminal penalties lie against one who leases premises with knowledge that they are to be used for purposes of prostitution or who permits known prostitution to continue. Holders of liquor licenses may be guilty of a criminal offense by permitting known prostitutes to frequent their premises. Persons connected with employment agencies who send women to places which they know or on reasonable inquiry could have determined to be of ill repute or houses of prostitution or assignation commit criminal acts. Drivers of taxicabs who knowingly transport prostitutes or customers of prostitutes also commit criminal acts in a number of jurisdictions.

Even more detailed control measures are embodied in local ordinances, reaching activities which at first glance seem unconnected with prostitution, but which in fact play a major role in the suppression of prostitution. Counterpart ordinances to state statutes are common controlling lessors of rooms and apartments and operators of hotels who may rent to prostitutes and others about to engage in illicit sexual activity. Liquor licensees may be under strict control at the local level as to whom they permit on their premises. Owners and operators of dancing academies, public dance halls and rental halls commit criminal acts if prostitutes are permitted on the premises, if solicitation occurs or if lewd conduct takes place. Because the old bordello may today appear in the guise of a Turkish or other public bath, a massage parlor or a place where physical therapy is administered, ordinances are common prohibiting employees of such establishments from serving or attending patrons of the opposite sex or nude patrons in the presence of persons of the opposite sex. Call girl operations may masquerade as escort agencies, and so special ordinances sometimes control the operation of these enterprises. Control of taxicab drivers at the local level is also common. The ordinance may apply to all businesses. Such ordinances form the mainstay of local law enforcement, even though ordinance prosecutions are rarely revealed in the appellate decisions.

(f) *The customer.* Statutes which directly penalize the act of patronizing a prostitute are not common, though they do exist. More often, activity of the customer may violate a collateral statute in broad terms. Fornication statutes, where they exist, apply to any act of sexual intercourse between persons who are not married to each other, except as the legislature or courts add the requirement of public, open or notorious cohabitation. Solicitation statutes or ordinances include the man who initiates contact with a prostitute. Where houses of prostitution exist, those who frequent or loiter about them are guilty of a crime. Statutes or ordinances often penalize anyone who enters any place for purposes of illicit intercourse or lewdness. Appellate courts, however, have not shown overwhelming enthusiasm toward the application of such statutes, particularly those which penalize persons "loitering" in a house of prostitution, to a male who has a single act of intercourse with a prostitute. Lacking any of these statutes, the male's conduct may still amount to aiding and abetting an act of prostitution, thus making him vicariously responsible for the woman's act. In any event, the invocation of these statutes is less likely to be designed to punish the male or control his future activities than it is to coerce him to cooperate with the prosecuting authorities by testifying against the woman.

Federal control. Federal legislation is directed chiefly at control of interstate prostitution and at exclusion and deportation of alien prostitutes. The most important statute is the Federal White Slave Act, or Mann Act, which penalizes anyone who knowingly transports in interstate or foreign commerce "any woman or girl for the purpose of prostitution or debauchery, or for any other immoral purpose, or with the intent and purpose to induce, entice, or compel such woman or girl to become a prostitute or to give herself up to debauchery, or to engage in any other immoral practice. . . ."

The United States also cooperates in the repression of international traffic in women and children. It became a party to the international convention for suppression of the white slave traffic of 1904 and adopted the amending agreement of 1949. However, treaties do not under American law create criminal liability directly, and so the only implementing legislation other than the Mann Act is that which bars the entry of alien prostitutes and authorizes deportation of those who are convicted of crimes involving moral turpitude within five years after their entry.

B. THE PATTERNS OF LAW ENFORCEMENT

1. Low Visibility Decisions: The Harassment Arrest

Enforcement of prostitution laws varies from jurisdiction to jurisdiction in the methods used and in the vigor of arrests and prosecutions. Yet certain patterns and flaws in enforcement are much the same everywhere. A typical enforcement method was described under the heading of "harassment" arrests in an American Bar Foundation Study of the criminal justice system in Detroit.

DONALD M. McINTYRE (ed.)
LAW ENFORCEMENT IN THE METROPOLIS
84, 86-87 (Chicago: American Bar Foundation 1967)[1]

In harassment arrests, as distinguished from other arrests, the police officer does not intend to prosecute the arrestee; nor does he intend to undertake an investigation to gather additional evidence. His purpose is twofold: (1) to impose an extra-legal sanction against suspects for the deterrent effect it will have on them individually and (2) to disrupt an organized crime operation by incarcerating their members, however temporarily. Because these are the objectives, the officer effecting the arrest does not try to justify the arrest in terms of evidence. The arrestee is released by the police department without further processing, with the exception of prostitutes, who are first subject to medical examination. There are a number of minor exceptions to these generalizations, but most of them hold for all arrests made for purposes of harassment.

Harassment arrests made in Detroit primarily attempt to control prostitution, gambling, illegal liquor sale, and accosting by homosexuals. A study was conducted of harassment arrests in one of Detroit's fifteen precincts having a very high crime rate. In a six-month period 3047 arrests were made for prostitution, but only 75 of those arrested were prosecuted. . . .

. . . There are provisions in both the state law and the city ordinances for the compulsory physical examination of prostitutes, but they have little applicability in practice. The state statute, by its terms, applies only to persons arrested and charged with committing an act of prostitution;[108] a valid arrest is a prerequisite to its applicability. The city ordinance provides that a person known or reasonably suspected of being a common prostitute "shall be subject to arrest and to examination. . . ."[109] This provision is ambiguous, at best, for a number of reasons. The police arrest prostitutes to keep them on the run, not primarily to control venereal disease. There is no directive from the commissioner of health to the police to make such arrests in his behalf. There is no attempt by the police to make the arrests at a time when examination facilities are available, nor is there an attempt to make examination facilities available during the hours when most of the arrests are made. Finally, when a prostitute is arrested, she is booked for a violation of the disorderly persons statute, which does not necessarily reflect the precise reason for the arrest. . . .

Prostitutes and transvestites. The decision to arrest for harassment was sometimes made by the police officer on his beat, but in high-crime areas several officers were frequently assigned to "picking up" prostitutes under the harassment program. Within their own group they affectionately referred to themselves as the "whore squad." . . .

Almost all harassment arrests of prostitutes were made in one particular precinct in Detroit. Moreover, within the precinct, the program was restricted to a relatively small area in which prostitution flourished. Full-fledged brothels, as such, were rare. Instead, the prostitutes solicited their trade on the street and escorted their patrons to rooms in their own homes or in nearby accommodations which they rented. Prostitutes stood on street corners, in doorways, or walked the street. In the winter, when the survey was conducted, it was noted that most of these women could be distinguished by their

1. This working paper was edited by Donald M. McIntyre, Jr.
108. The state statute provides that "every person arrested and charged with committing an act of prostitution . . ." in violation of a number of specific provisions of the statute "shall be examined by the local health officer . . . to determine whether such person is afflicted with venereal disease." It provides that any such person taken into custody may be detained until the examination is completed for a period not to exceed 5 days. Mich. Stat. Ann. §14.345(3) (1956).
109. The city ordinance provides that "all persons known to be common prostitutes or reasonably suspected and believed to be such . . . shall be deemed to be suspected cases [of venereal disease] and shall be subject to arrest and to examination at such places and times as the Commissioner of Health may direct. . . ." Detroit Compiled Ordinances, ch. 173 VIII, §1 (1954).

expensive-looking water-resistant coats and high boots. To the eyes of the police officers, this was the uniform of the trade. Women known to have prior arrests for prostitution were stopped by the police, asked to get into the police car, and taken to headquarters. . . .

Women thought to be prostitutes because of their dress, actions, or past records were not immune from harassment even in the shelter of public places such as restaurants. Officers in one case observed a suspect in a restaurant and proceeded to ask her name and address and whether she had ever been "D.P.I.'d." The girl said that she had never been picked up by the police, never been brought into a police station, and never been in a courtroom. She appeared to be ignorant of the meaning of D.P.I. The officer said, "You'd better come with us anyway," and they asked her to enter the car. This girl was released later. In a similar case that was observed, the girl was known to the police as a prostitute. . . .

Male homosexuals are arrested for purposes of harassment, especially when they are encountered on the street dressed in female attire. One of the reasons why these individuals (whom the police referred to as "fags") are harassed is because the police have found, from past experience, that they are responsible for absconding with funds given them by men who believe them to be prostitutes. For this reason transvestites are arrested in the same manner as women prostitutes.

2. The Decoy Arrest

Another pattern of enforcement involves an arrest procured by an officer acting as a "decoy." The kind of testimony and proceeding that results from these arrests is illustrated in the following case.

STATE v. PERRY
249 Ore. 76, 436 P.2d 252 (1968)

Defendant appeals from a judgment of conviction of the crime of vagrancy in being a common prostitute (ORS 166.060).

A police officer with the vice division of the Portland Police Bureau struck up a conversation with defendant in a Portland bar. He asked her if she knew the whereabouts of a certain girl (a prostitute with whom he had previously made contact). Defendant said, "Maybe I better be talking to you." The rest of the episode was described by the police officer as follows:

[T]hen she says, "Are you looking for a girl?" Or a lady, one of the two. And I says, "Yeah, I guess I am."

And she says, "Well how much do you want to spend?" And I says, "How much will it cost me?" And then she told me it would cost me $20. So I asked her, "Well, what will I get for $20?" And she says, "Well, whatever you want." So then I asked her what was her specialty. She says, "Well, half and half, straight lay." I says, "How about a straight lay for the $20?" So then she asked me if she could finish her drink and I says, "Sure."

And then we went on to a conversation — I asked her where we were going to go and she says, "We can go next door to the Anna Maria Hotel." So I says, "Okay." Then she finished the drink and we proceeded out. She took the lead and I went after her.

On the way over to the hotel, I told the defendant, I says, "I'm married." I says, "I don't want any of this to get out. Is this place all right?" And she says, "Yeah. They don't ask any questions in here. They know what's going on. So, it's all right."

And when we went in, she paid the $4 for the room and signed the register. It was either Mr. and Mrs. James Smith or John Smith. I can't recall the first name she used right now. But, then, he gave us the key to the room. I believe it was 203. . . . [A]pproximately 15 minutes had passed by, between the time we left or when I first made contact and the time that we went into the hotel. Approximately. I couldn't be sure, though. . . . The man registered us in at the desk. We went up to Room 203. When we were in there, I asked her, I says, "Do you want the money now or after we're finished?" And she says, "I want it now." So, I gave her the $20.

And she says, "Okay. Go ahead and get undressed." In the meantime, while she's saying this, she was disrobing herself. I disrobed down to my shorts. She says, "Come over here and be washed." She took ahold of my private area and washed it, and I told her I was a vice officer and she was under arrest.

Defendant contends that ORS 166.060 is unconstitutionally vague, providing no standard by which to determine who is a "common prostitute."

It is important to note that ORS 166.060(d) does not purport to proscribe and make punishable a specific act of prostitution; it defines the crime in terms of the defendant's status or condition. The crime "consists not in proscribed action or inaction, but in the accused's having a certain personal condition or being a person of a specified character." We can see no way of construing subsection (d) of the statute as proscribing only the specific act of prostitution. The state makes out its case under the statute only if it can prove that the defendant has the status of a "common prostitute."

Logically, proof of status could be supplied by evidence of prior acts of prostitution and it would not be necessary to prove that the accused engaged in the particular act of prostitution for which she was ostensibly arrested.

It is not necessary for us to decide whether prior acts of prostitution alone, without proof of the specific act of prostitution for which the accused is arrested, would constitute sufficient proof of the crime defined by ORS 166.060(d) because, in the present case, the evidence of defendant's acts and the circumstances surrounding the arrest clearly demonstrated that she was a "common prostitute."

It is defendant's position that the state is required to prove multiple acts of sexual intercourse for gain in order to make out the charge of vagrancy as a common prostitute and that this evidence was lacking in the present case since there was proof only of a single act of solicitation at the time of the arrest. Although the crime of vagrancy as a common prostitute requires proof of a personal condition or status normally characterized by a continuing course of conduct, it does not follow that the condition or status can be proved only by showing that the accused engaged in a series of acts. If a virgin moves into a house of prostitution, her first act of intercourse for gain places her in the status of a common prostitute, and she thereby becomes a vagrant under ORS 166.060(d). Her status is shown by the "circumstances under which she performed the single act." . . .

The feature which distinguishes a prostitute from other women who engage in illicit intercourse is the indiscrimination with which she offers herself to men for hire. The term "common" is frequently used to describe this indiscrimination, and thus the term becomes a redundancy in the expression "common prostitute." There was ample evidence in the case at bar from which the jury could decide that defendant was a person who offered to engage indiscriminately in illicit intercourse. The manner in which she approached officer Wright, the language she used, her knowledge of the arrangement with the hotel, her modus operandi after she and Wright were in the hotel room, and other circumstances provide the basis for an inference that she indiscriminately offered herself to men for sexual purposes.

In State v. Gustin, 244 Or. 531, 532, 419 P.2d 429 (1966), we held that a single offer of illicit intercourse, without more, was not sufficient to sustain a charge under ORS 166.060(d). The case was presented in the trial court on a stipulation of facts which simply recited that on a certain date in the city of Portland the accused "did offer to engage in an act of illicit sexual intercourse, for money, with one Robert D. Colyer, not being [her husband]. . . ." Although a woman who will offer to engage in illicit intercourse for money with one man is likely to offer her body indiscriminately to others for the same purpose, it is not necessarily so, and without proof from which indiscriminate sexual activity can be inferred the crime defined in ORS 166.060(d) is not established. . . .

NOTES

1. Anyone who has ever been in a court in which prostitution cases are routinely processed or tried could testify to the degradation of the law enforcement officers, defendants, and the criminal justice system itself. For instance, as in *Perry,* the officers always testify that they stopped short of the act of intercourse. When the defendants take the stand, they uniformly testify that the officer initiated and completed the sexual act. The trial itself is often treated as pro forma and as a passing courtroom entertainment. As with most other crimes, however, prostitution charges are not usually tried; convictions are obtained on guilty pleas. Fines are imposed and the women defendants are soon back at work; or if a woman has a long record, she may receive a 60- or 90-day sentence. A series of these can amount to a life sentence on the installment plan. But the point is that neither the trial nor the guilty plea is treated by the system as a matter of any serious concern.

2. The credibility of the testimony is most difficult to assess when the charge is solicitation, and there is no evidence of steps taken to perform the act of intercourse. In Kelly v. United States, 90 U.S. App. D.C. 125, 194 F.2d 150 (1952), a male defendant was charged with offering to commit sodomy. The appellate court reversed a conviction, finding the word of the police officer that such solicitation had occurred insufficient to support the charge:[2]

> The public has a peculiar interest in the problem before us. The alleged offense, consisting of a few spoken words, may be alleged to have occurred in any public place, where any citizen is likely to be. They may be alleged to have been whispered, or to have occurred in the course of a most casual conversation. Any citizen who answers a stranger's inquiry as to direction, or time, or a request for a dime or a match is liable to be threatened with an accusation of this sort. . . . There is simply no protection, except one's reputation and appearance of credibility, against an uncorroborated charge of this sort. At the same time, the results of the accusation itself are devastating to the accused. . . . [W]hile technically this offense is a minor misdemeanor . . . in the practical world of everyday living it is a major accusation.

The reasoning has not been generally applied to the "few spoken words" that also constitute the offense of soliciting for prostitution. See, e.g., Wajer v. United States, 222 A.2d 68 (D.C. Ct. App. 1966). But also see United States v. Moses, Cr. No. 1778-72, 41 U.S.L.W. 2298, 12 Cr. L. Rptr. 2198 (Super. Ct. D.C. 1972), discussed infra in Section D-8-b-1. Are there ways to prevent the degradation of law enforcement personnel involved in regulation of prostitution, or is it inherent in the process?

C. The Federal Attempt To Regulate Prostitution

Many of the problems inherent in the enforcement of laws against prostitution are illustrated by the history of the Mann Act, 35 Stat. 825-827 (1910), 18 U.S.C. §§2421-2422, forbidding the interstate transportation of women for purposes of prostitution, debauchery, or any other immoral purpose. There have been thousands of prosecutions under the Act, and in terms of uneven, uncertain, and unequal enforcement of the laws,

---

2. 194 F.2d 150, 153-154 (1952).

it has no parallel in the federal statutes.[3] Yet the problems of enforcement and interpretation of the Mann Act are similar, only writ somewhat larger, to those often encountered with local prostitution statutes. The first problem arises from confusion about the purpose of criminal laws against prostitution. Are they meant to accomplish the elimination of an offense against public decorum? protection of the individual herself from a prostituted existence? avoidance of theft crimes associated with prostitution? The Mann Act came from a legislative history clearly expressing its purpose; yet its enforcement immediately reached beyond the initial purpose.

LEVI, AN INTRODUCTION TO LEGAL REASONING
24-47 (1949)

The Mann Act was passed during a period when large American cities had illegal but segregated "red-light" areas. It was believed that women were procured for houses of prostitution by bands of "white slavers" who "were said to operate from coast to coast, in town and country, with tentacles in foreign lands, east and west and across the American borders. The most sensational of these were said to be the French, Italian, and Jewish rings who preyed on innocent girls of their respective nationalities at ports of entry into the United States or ensnared them at the ports of embarkation in Europe and even in their home towns." It was thought that the girls were young; many of them were supposed to be "scarcely in their teens."[58] They were forced or lured into the business. It was thought that they had previously been virtuous, and while supposedly many of them had been aliens, it was also believed that they represented "our" women. Once captured, the woman disappeared from her own community, was brutally treated, whipped with rawhide, and became, as the House Report said, practically a slave in the true sense of the word. . . .[59]

Yet while it was said that "the traffic at which this bill strikes is admitted to be abhorrent to all men," and "the time will never arrive when there will be a change of sentiment with respect to its infamy and depravity,"[69] there was confusion both as to the facts and as to the legislation proposed.

For example, Congressman Richardson said he knew of the complaint about the traffic but "it may be that there is a good deal of exaggeration about it." Many of the situations described in the House Report had to do with conditions in Illinois. But the "law in Illinois has been strengthened and there had been many prosecutions under it."[70] Congressman Adamson noted that "the Chairman of the Committee on Immigration and Naturalization . . . stated . . . that the white slave traffic had practically been stamped out of our large cities." An examination of the instances cited, Adamson thought, would show that they could be handled under existing laws.[71] And despite the descriptions of immorality, the truth was that society was getting better and "we are vastly better morally than the rest of the world." On the other hand, Congressman Russell, as his contribution on the facts, told the House the story of a Negro who was supposed to have purchased his third white wife "out of a group of twenty-five that were offered for sale in Chicago."[72] . . .

The Mann Act was passed after there had been many extensive governmental

3. The nadir of the act's enforcement may have occurred in Cleveland v. United States, 329 U.S. 14, 67 S. Ct. 13, 91 L. Ed. 12 (1946), when the convictions of Mormons who traveled with their plural wives were upheld. The Court found polygamy to be immoral because it was "a notorious example of promiscuity." 329 U.S. at 19. This case is noted with a history of the Mann Act's interpretation in Interstate Immorality: The Mann Act and the Supreme Court, 56 Yale L. J. 718 (1947).

58. Reckless, Vice in Chicago 40 (1933).
59. H.R. Rep. 47, 61st Cong., 2d Sess. (1909).
69. 45 Cong. Rec. 1039 (1910).
70. Ibid., at 810.
71. Ibid., at 1031.
72. Ibid., at 821.

investigations. Yet there was no common understanding of the facts, and whatever understanding seems to have been achieved concerning the white-slave trade in retrospect seems incorrectly based. The words used were broad and ambiguous. There were three key phrases: "prostitution," "debauchery," and "for any other immoral purpose." . . .

. . . Athanasaw v. United States[87] upheld the application of the Act through the word "debauchery" to a defendant who had caused a girl to be transported from Georgia to Florida for the ostensible purpose of appearing as a chorus girl in a theater operated by the defendant. There was evidence of improper advances made to the girl upon her arrival; the advances were related to her membership in the theater group. The Supreme Court held that debauchery as used in the Act did not mean only sexual intercourse but "was designed to reach acts which might ultimately lead to that phase of debauchery which consisted in 'sexual actions.' " . . .

Then in 1915 the Supreme Court apparently held that the Act was not confined to cases where the woman was "practically a slave."[89] The Court had before it an indictment of a woman for conspiracy. The conspiracy charged was between the woman and one Laudenschlager that Laudenschlager should "cause the defendant [the woman] to be transported from Illinois to Wisconsin for the purpose of prostitution." It was urged that since the woman could not commit the substantive crime of violating the Mann Act, for she would be the victim transported, she could not be guilty of conspiracy to commit that crime. But Justice Holmes held that she could be. He did not agree that the woman victim would never be under the prohibition of the Mann Act. He said, "Suppose, for instance that a professional prostitute, as well able to look out for herself as was the man, should suggest and carry out the journey within the act of 1910 in the hope of blackmailing the man, and should buy the railroad tickets, or should pay the fare from Jersey City to New York, she would be within the letter of the act of 1910 and we see no reason why the act should not be held to apply." Therefore "we see equally little reason for not treating the preliminary agreement as a conspiracy that the law can reach, if we abandon the illusion that the woman always is the victim. The words of the statute punish the transportation of a woman for the purpose of prostitution even if she were the first to suggest the crime." . . .

It became clear in the *Caminetti* cases[90] in 1917, when the Supreme Court applied the phrase "for any other immoral purpose," that organized traffic did not have to be involved either. The indictments considered in *Caminetti* involved the transportation of women for the purpose of paid cohabitation or for the purpose of having them become mistress and concubine. But the indictments did not involve commercialized and organized vice. . . . Not only was the vice not organized and commercialized, but the women were not inexperienced victims. In one case, while there was conflicting testimony before the jury, there was some evidence that the woman was doing the pursuing. Another case was described by counsel as follows:

> . . . the woman was a public prostitute and made no pretense of virtue. Hays happened to meet her at Oklahoma City while attending a cattlemen's convention there, and after his return to his home another woman telegraphed the Oklahoma woman to come to Kansas, sending her the money with which to buy the ticket. In response to that message the woman went from Oklahoma City to Wichita, where she met and entertained Hays. We may justly censure the man for associating with those loose women, but that was the extent of his offense, for there is not, so far as the woman in this case is concerned, a single aggravating circumstance; and yet this man of good standing in the community where he lives, with a wife and children dependent on him, has been sentenced to the penitentiary for eighteen months,

87. 227 U.S. 326 (1913).
89. United States v. Holte, 236 U.S. 140 (1915).
90. Caminetti v. United States, 242 U.S. 470 (1917).

stripped of his civil rights, his wife deprived of his support, his boy and girl forever branded as the children of a convict, and all for no better reason than that he made a mistake which the State of Kansas might have adequately punished by a fine. To subject American citizens to such punishments for such offenses will brutalize the American people in time, and to suppose that the American Congress intended such a result impeaches its wisdom as well as its sense of justice.[93]

[The result would be] . . . that for every man who can be convicted under this statute, when charged with only an immorality, two men will submit to extortion and pay blood-money to save themselves, their families, and their friends from the humiliation which an exposure of their mistakes would bring.[94]

According to Justice Day, there was "no ambiguity in the terms of this Act." The words "immoral purpose" had been interpreted by the Court in a related and earlier act and that interpretation "must be presumed to have been known to Congress when it enacted the law here involved." Under the *Bitty* case[98] "immoral purpose" included importing a woman for the purpose of concubinage. The Act there read "[t]hat the importation into the United States of any alien woman or girl for the purpose of prostitution, or for any other immoral purpose, is hereby forbidden. . . ."[4] And the Court had then said that " . . . the immoral purpose charged in the indictment is of the same general class or kind as the one that controls in the importation of an alien woman for the purpose strictly of prostitution. The prostitute may, in the popular sense, be more degraded in character than the concubine, but the latter none the less must be held to lead an immoral life, if any regard whatever be had to the views that are almost universally held in this country as to the relations which may rightfully, from the standpoint of morality, exist between man and woman in the matter of sexual intercourse. . . ."[5]

At the very least, *Caminetti* set the direction of the Mann Act to include more than white slavery; at most it imported into the statute all acts commonly thought to be sexually immoral. The suggested definition of "any other immoral purpose" went far beyond the facts to include those things which "common understanding" or views "almost universally held in this country" would regard as immoral in the matter of sexual intercourse.

Enforcement of laws against prostitution often reveal an inherent ambiguity in the societal image of women. Is the prostitute a weak preyed-upon creature, or an evil being acting from choice? The Mann Act has historically adopted the former view. In spite of Justice Holmes's observations quoted in the discussion of *Holte,* supra, that there could be circumstances in which women could be prosecuted under the Mann Act, in fact, no such convictions have been upheld. In 1932 Gebardi v. United States, 287 U.S. 112, 53 S. Ct. 35, 77 L. Ed. 206 (1932), specifically held that women could not be punished under the ordinary circumstances of a Mann Act violation. In that case, a man and willing woman were indicted for conspiracy to violate the act. The court said:[6]

Congress set out in the Mann Act to deal with cases which frequently, if not normally, involve consent and agreement on the part of the woman to the forbidden transportation. In every case in which she is not intimidated or forced into the transportation, the statute necessarily contemplates her acquiescence. Yet this acquiescence, though an incident of a type of transportation specifically dealt with by the statute, was not made a crime under the Mann Act itself. . . . [W]e perceive in the

---

93. Ibid., at 18, 19.
94. Ibid., at 20.
98. United States v. Bitty, 208 U.S. 393 (1908).
4. 34 Stat. 898, Pt. 1. — Eds.
5. 208 U.S. 393, 402 (1908). — Eds.
6. 287 U.S. at 121-123.

failure of the Mann Act to condemn the woman's participation in those transporta-
tions which are effected with her mere consent, evidence of an affirmative legislative
policy to leave her acquiescence unpunished. We think it a necessary implication of
that policy that when the Mann Act and the conspiracy statute came to be construed
together, as they necessarily would be, the same participation which the former
contemplates as an inseparable incident of all cases in which the woman is a voluntary
agent at all, but does not punish, was not automatically to be made punishable under
the latter. It would contravene that policy to hold that the very passage of the Mann
Act effected a withdrawal by the conspiracy statute of that immunity which the Mann
Act itself confers.

It is not to be supposed that the consent of an unmarried person to adultery with
a married person, where the latter alone is guilty of the substantive offense, would
render the former an abettor or a conspirator, compare In re Cooper, 162 Cal. 81, 85,
121 P. 318, or that the acquiescence of a woman under the age of consent would make
her a co-conspirator with the man to commit statutory rape upon herself. Compare
Queen v. Tyrrell, [1894] 1 Q.B. 710. The principle, determinative of this case, is the
same.

On the evidence before us the woman petitioner has not violated the Mann Act
and, we hold, is not guilty of a conspiracy to do so. As there is no proof that the man
conspired with anyone else to bring about the transportation, the convictions of both
petitioners must be
Reversed.

The view of the prostitute as a creature too weak to resist, even in the face of
evidence that she was the instigator of the prostitution scheme, is persistent and common
in modern prosecutions under the Mann Act.

WYATT v. UNITED STATES
362 U.S. 525, 80 S. Ct. 901, 4 L. Ed. 2d 931 (1960)

HARLAN, J., delivered the opinion of the Court.

Petitioner was tried and convicted of knowingly transporting a woman in interstate
commerce for the purpose of prostitution, in violation of the White Slave Traffic Act.
. . . At the trial, the woman, who had since the date of the offense married the petitioner,
was ordered, over her objection and that of the petitioner, to testify on behalf of the
prosecution.[1]

First. Our decision in Hawkins v. U.S., 358 U.S. 74, established for the federal
courts the continued validity of the common-law rule of evidence ordinarily permitting
a party to exclude the adverse testimony of his or her spouse. However, as that case
expressly acknowledged, the common law has long recognized an exception in the case
of certain kinds of offenses committed by the party against his spouse. . . . [I]t cannot
be seriously argued that one who has committed this "shameless offense against wife-
hood," id., at p. 257, should be permitted to prevent his wife from testifying to the crime
by invoking an interest founded on the marital relation or the desire of the law to protect
it. . . .

Second. The witness-wife, however, did not testify willingly, but objected to being
questioned by the prosecution, and gave evidence only upon the ruling of the District
Court denying her claimed privilege not to testify. We therefore consider the correctness
of that ruling. . . .

While the question has not often arisen, it has apparently been generally assumed

---

1. Although the record is ambiguous as to the fact and time of petitioner's marriage, we shall consider
established, as the Court of Appeals did, the sequence of events stated in the text. Further, the Court of Appeals
noted that, while the record did not clearly establish that the petitioner, as well as his wife, claimed a privilege
with respect to her testimony, it would assume that he had. 263 F.2d 304, 308. We accept that assumption.

that the privilege resided in the witness as well as in the party. *Hawkins* referred to "a rule which bars the testimony of one spouse against the other unless *both* consent," supra, at 78. (Emphasis supplied.) . . .

As Wigmore puts it, [8 Wigmore, Evidence §2239 (3d ed. 1940)] at p. 264: "[W]hile the defendant-husband is entitled to be protected against condemnation through the wife's testimony, the witness-wife is also entitled to be protected against becoming the instrument of that condemnation, the sentiment in each case being equal in degree and yet different in quality." In light of these considerations, we decline to accept the view that the privilege is that of the party alone.

Third. Neither can we hold that, whenever the privilege is unavailable to the party, it is ipso facto lost to the witness as well. It is a question in each case, or in each category of cases, whether, in light of the reason which has led to a refusal to recognize the party's privilege, the witness should be held compellable. Certainly, we would not be justified in laying down a general rule that both privileges stand or fall together. We turn instead to the particular situation at bar.

Where a man has prostituted his own wife, he has committed an offense against both her and the marital relation, and we have today affirmed the exception disabling him from excluding her testimony against him. It is suggested, however, that this exception has no application to the witness-wife when she chooses to remain silent. The exception to the party's privilege, it is said, rests on the necessity of preventing the defendant from sealing his wife's lips by his own unlawful act, see United States v. Mitchell, [137 F.2d 1006 (2d Cir. 1943)], at 1008-1009; Wigmore, op. cit., supra, §2239, and it is argued that where the wife has chosen not to "become the instrument" of her husband's downfall, it is her own privilege which is in question, and the reasons for according it to her in the first place are fully applicable.

We must view this position in light of the congressional judgment and policy embodied in the Mann Act. "A primary purpose of the Mann Act was to protect women who were weak from men who were bad." Denning v. United States, 247 F. 463, 465. It was in response to shocking revelations of subjugation of women too weak to resist that Congress acted. See H.R. Rep. No. 47, 61st Cong., 2d Sess., pp. 10-11. As the legislative history discloses, the Act reflects the supposition that the women with whom it sought to deal often had no independent will of their own, and embodies, in effect, the view that they must be protected against themselves. Compare 18 U.S.C. §2422 (consent of woman immaterial in prosecution under that section). It is not for us to re-examine the basis of that supposition.

Applying the legislative judgment underlying the Act, we are led to hold it not an allowable choice for a prostituted witness-wife "voluntarily" to decide to protect her husband by declining to testify against him. For if a defendant can induce a woman, against her "will," to enter a life of prostitution for his benefit — and the Act rests on the view that he can — by the same token it should be considered that he can, at least as easily, persuade one who has already fallen victim to his influence that she must also protect him. To make matters turn upon ad hoc inquiries into the actual state of mind of particular women, thereby encumbering Mann Act trials with a collateral issue of the greatest subtlety, is hardly an acceptable solution. . . .

Mr. Chief Justice WARREN, with whom Mr. Justice BLACK and Mr. Justice DOUGLAS join, dissenting.

Last Term this Court held that a wife could not voluntarily testify against her husband in a criminal prosecution over his objection. Hawkins v. United States, 358 U.S. 74. The Court finds the case at bar so different from *Hawkins* that it approves overriding not only the husband's objection, but also the wife's. In both cases the husband was prosecuted for violation of the Mann Act, 18 U.S.C. §2421. The only relevant difference is that here the wife herself was the person allegedly transported by the husband for purposes of prostitution. Morally speaking, this profanation of the marriage relationship adds an element of the utmost depravity to the ugly business of promoting prostitution.

Legally speaking, however, this does not warrant the radical departure from the *Hawkins* rule which the Court now sanctions.

. . . The defendant may not claim the privilege where he is charged with "certain kinds of offenses committed . . . against his spouse," and the Court believes that the instant case involves this type of crime. It apparently recognizes, moreover, that the policy behind this exception may be effectuated in the ordinary situation by giving the injured party the *option* to testify, without *compelling* her to testify. In this case, however, it concludes that the wife "should be assumed" to be under the sway of the husband to such an extent that she cannot be entrusted with that choice. Consequently, the trial court — and the prosecutor — must be given the power to protect her against herself by forcing her to testify.

The fatal defect in this conclusion lies in the Court's evaluation which finds no support in the record and which cannot properly be justified by any legislative enactment.

The Court does not and could not rely upon the record to prove that petitioner's wife was somehow mesmerized by him when she was on the witness stand. The evidence, in point of fact, strongly suggests that the wife played a managerial role in the sordid enterprise which formed the basis for the prosecution.[2] Apparently this was the jury's view, since the jurors asked the judge whether it would "make any difference or — if the woman had anything to do with the instigation or planning. . . ." The judge, of course, instructed them that this would be immaterial, but the jury nevertheless unanimously recommended leniency. Thus this case is a strange vehicle for the Court to use in announcing its "lack of independent will" theory. Presumably it is to be regarded as the exception which proves the rule.

The sole ground assigned by the Court for its decision is that it is a necessary application of the "legislative judgment underlying the [Mann] Act," which "reflects the supposition that the women with whom [Congress] sought to deal often had no independent will of their own, and embodies, in effect, the view that they must be protected against themselves." In support of this hypothesis, the Court cites legislative history and the fact that, under 18 U.S.C. §2422, a companion provision to §2421, the consent of the woman does not relieve the defendant of criminal responsibility. This equation of the legislative judgment involved in fashioning a criminal statute with the judgment involved in the Court's restriction of the husband-wife privilege is, I submit, entirely too facile, for it overlooks the critically different nature of these problems. . . .

The testimonial privilege, however, presents questions of quite a different order, since there is a significant interest traditionally regarded as supporting the privilege, as we recognized in *Hawkins* — the preservation of the conjugal relationship. And where the wife refuses to testify, there is strong evidence that there is still a marital relationship to be protected. . . .

NOTES

1. In Hawkins v. United States, 358 U.S. 74, 79 S. Ct. 136, 3 L. Ed. 2d 125 (1958), also a Mann Act prosecution, although the wife was not the prostituted woman, the Court had said:[7]

> The basic reason the law has refused to pit wife against husband or husband against
> wife in a trial where life or liberty is at stake was a belief that such a policy was

2. The most important testimony regarding the petitioner's purpose in providing for his wife's transportation was given by a hotel bellboy, who related various conversations which he had with the petitioner. The clerk also testified as to his conversations with the wife, and there is little if anything to distinguish the evidence relating to the wife from that relating to the husband.

7. 358 U.S. 74, 77-78 (1958).

necessary to foster family peace, not only for the benefit of husband, wife and children, but for the benefit of the public as well. Such a belief has never been unreasonable and is not now. Moreover, it is difficult to see how family harmony is less disturbed by a wife's voluntary testimony against her husband than by her compelled testimony. In truth, it seems probable that much more bitterness would be engendered by voluntary testimony than by that which is compelled. But the Government argues that the fact a husband or wife testifies against the other voluntarily is strong indication that the marriage is already gone. Doubtless this is often true. But not all marital flare-ups in which one spouse wants to hurt the other are permanent. The widespread success achieved by courts throughout the country in conciliating family differences is a real indication that some apparently broken homes can be saved provided no unforgivable act is done by either party. Adverse testimony given in criminal proceedings would, we think, be likely to destroy almost any marriage.

Hawkins was a case in which the couple were not even living together at the time of the trial and, in fact, had not lived together much.[8] Thus, there was even less of a marriage potentially to be saved than in *Wyatt.* Can the two cases be reconciled as a matter of legal reasoning? What is the view of women, and particularly of women who become prostitutes, that is implicit in *Wyatt?*

2. Think about the emotional and psychological stress placed on the witness-wife by the situation, like that in *Wyatt,* in which she is forced to have a hand in her husband's conviction for a felony. Under the guise of protecting the woman from the overweening influence of the man who has led her into prostitution, the court is actually subjecting her to severe hardship.

3. The image of the prostituted woman exemplified in *Wyatt* coexists with the view that the great danger of the Mann Act is the possibility of blackmail. See, e.g., United States v. Beach, 324 U.S. 193, 199-200, 65 S. Ct. 602, 605, 89 L. Ed. 865, 869 (1945) (Murphy, J., dissenting). Justice McKenna, dissenting in *Caminetti,* wrote: "Blackmailers of both sexes have arisen, using the terrors of the construction now sanctioned by this court as a help — indeed, the means — for their brigandage. The result is grave and should give us pause."[9] The scheming, dominating blackmailer and the weak-as-water victim hardly seem compatible, but they live together in cases interpreting the Mann Act.

D. DECRIMINALIZATION OF PROSTITUTION

1. Who Is the Prostitute?

Abandonment of the prostitution laws is one solution to the problems of their enforcement and moral ambiguity. Once denominated "legalization," this proposal is now more often referred to as decriminalization. Before the merits of decriminalization can be discussed, however, it is necessary to focus on who would be affected by that change: Who is the prostitute?

Prostitution has many faces. The structure of the profession, from heroin-addicted streetwalker to highly paid call girl, has often been described. But these descriptions do not adequately reveal who these women are and how they feel about their lives. Where there is descriptive material, it is based on courtroom and prison observations. But those arrested for prostitution must be a fraction of those who practice it. Certainly the people who serve time are an even smaller proportion of the whole. Yet on the basis of what

8. Id. at 82 n.4.
9. 242 U.S. 470, 501, 502 (1918).

he saw in the courtroom, a New York judge delivered the following staggering generality about the identities of prostitutes:[10]

> The route by which they have entered upon a life of prostitution varies, but certain factors are constantly encountered: seduction in adolescence by a friend or a relative; illegitimate children; inadequate, drunken, criminal or abusive parents; broken homes; low economic and moral standards in the home; low intelligence; emotional instability; poor vocational training; menial and uninteresting jobs; recent immigration to this country.

A somewhat different picture of the life of a prostitute is presented in another work.

MILLET, PROSTITUTION: A QUARTET FOR FEMALE VOICES
*in Gornick and Moran (eds.), Women in Sexist Society
60-125 (Basic Books, Inc. 1971)*

The way that I got into it was like this. I was just broke and I had never liked to be in debt to anyone. I have a thing about it — being in debt. I've never liked to be financially dependent on anyone. I've always had this thing. What happened was I borrowed ten dollars from someone, and then I realized, after I borrowed it, that I couldn't pay it back. I had no way of knowing that I'd ever be able to pay it back — it was a man that I'd slept with too. So that's how I got into it. I just decided . . . I'm not going to be poor any more. I'd never been poor and I wasn't used to it. I was an undergraduate on a scholarship. My father was doing the worst he'd done in years. He couldn't afford to give me any money. They would have gone out of their way to give me money — my folks — especially if they'd known what I was doing to get it.

. . . So I just went on the street. The thing that broke the ice had actually happened years before at a concert of Miles Davis. Davis was playing in a club, and someone outside wanted to take me. You know, asked me if I wanted to go in. And I knew that if I went in with him I'd have to sleep with him. But I figured it was worth it; I wanted to see Miles Davis. I had no feeling for this guy; I just wanted the ticket to get in there. I realized I'd whored — there was no way of denying the truth to myself. So when the time came a few years later and I was absolutely broke, I was ready. . . .

. . . Often I really couldn't understand the customer, couldn't understand what he got out of this, because I really felt I was giving nothing. What he got was nothing. I could never see myself in his position, doing what he was doing. I would think it would be humiliating to buy a person, to have to offer somebody money. I felt the poor guy's gotta buy it; I felt sorry for him. He's really hard up. But then I remember he could be not so hard up as to have to buy, really; he wanted instead to have something so special you gotta buy it. I did not always see the gesture of buying someone as arrogance because I did not feel that controlled by the customer. I felt I was the boss because I could say no to the deal. I didn't want even the involvement of being a kept woman because then it's control again. When you're living with someone, that's when I really felt controlled. Then you can't refuse. People I've lived with, men I've lived with — I really felt that they had power because I couldn't say no to them. Because then I could lose them and, if I did, I would lose my whole life — lose my whole reason for living. . . .

. . . I don't think you can ever eliminate the economic factor motivating women to prostitution. Even a call girl could never make as much in a straight job as she could at prostitution. All prostitutes are in it for the money. With most uptown call girls, the

10. Ploscowe, Sex and the Law 227 (1962).

choice is not between starvation and life, but it is a choice between $5,000 and $25,000 or between $10,000 and $50,000. That's a pretty big choice: a pretty big difference. You can say that they're in this business because of the difference of $40,000 a year. A businessman would say so. Businessmen do things because of the difference of $40,000 a year. Call girls do go into capitalism and think like capitalists. . . . If you tell me that being in the life is beating yourself up psychologically, I can't help but resent that. Because psychologically I've suffered so much more in other situations, been humiliated much more in other situations. I think the money had a lot to do with my feeling freer. I didn't feel I was taking nearly so much shit when I was in the life as I do now that I am a teaching assistant. As a teaching assistant I am really put down and I don't make nearly as much money. True, it carries a certain social status that's a lot higher than that of a prostitute, but you pay for it, you really pay for it. I worked long hours for little money and I took shit. I was in tears so much more in graduate school, infuriated and sick. I didn't get an ulcer when I was a prostitute. That happened when I was in graduate school.[11]

New York Magazine printed the results of a journalistic investigation of the life of prostitution in one section of the city.

SHEEHY, CLEANING UP HELL'S BEDROOM
New York Magazine, Nov. 13, 1972, pp. 56, 57, 62, 65

Five million people cross Hell's Bedroom every day. It was formerly called the 18th Precinct, a predictable sewer which carried a reputation as the nation's leading district in reported crime. Last May its boundaries were extended and now it is called Midtown North. The territory is: 43rd to 59th Streets, Lexington Avenue clear west to the Hudson River. The heaviest concentration of prostitution activity has shifted west to Eighth Avenue, from 49th to 51st Streets, right across from the hotels — safe, convenient. The crossbeam of Hell's Bedroom is 49th Street, and that is where it begins.

The code on the street is simple: survival of the fastest. The police are genuine competition but rather sporting, as a rule. Cops who ride the vans are in this game year after year, just like the pross. Faces grow familiar. The girls give the cops fond nicknames like Muscles and Lurch and McGillah the Gorilla; the cops give the sporting girls a break now and then — "If you have any dope or weapons, get rid of them before we get to the precinct." A loose system of ethics operates among these experienced players. Serious working girls, for instance, refer respectfully to one another as "dedicated women." They work the street from six to twelve hours a day, seven days a week, every week of winter as well as summer. Midtown North alone has 1,200 such hard-core working girls. When the heat is on they may be pushed up, down or across town temporarily, but they always come back to the territory where their first pimp turned them out. Which is why the dedicated women survive every cleanup.

The tie that binds is more than sentimental. Like any good salesperson, a working girl wants to be where her steady customers can find her. Even then it takes a long while to learn a territory, its faces and places, cops and plainclothes. . . .

The ugly combat is not between these two professional teams. It is played out on the street every night, after midnight, when the marginal hustlers come up from their concrete holes like worms in a warm rain to prey on the pross. Now the dedicated woman must compete with ripoff artists and fly-by-night whores who will mug or cut another girl as soon as a trick, and the "jive bitches" . . . who are on the street just for kicks,

---

11. This excerpt accurately reflects one view expressed by this former prostitute. However, her statements as a whole indicated a marked ambivalence about the extent of "free choice" exercised by prostitutes and about the relative happiness of their lives. — Eds.

and the summer runaways from Connecticut who undercut fixed street prices, and the . . . female impersonators who do a brisk business as prostitutes in the hallways along Ninth and Tenth. . . .

I was introduced to Sergeant Hanson, supervisor of the original precinct task force [leading a crackdown on prostitution]. He looked tired. He had been playing a futile game for eight months. His experience with midtown prostitutes confirmed my own observations: over 60 percent are white. Most seem to come from Minneapolis with a baby on their knee, or at least pregnant. The young white girls are rarely on drugs. Some are very intelligent. All are better-looking than average. . . .

The long thin girl was wearing long thin earrings — ivory elephants dangling on gold chains — for good luck. We found her near dawn in the deserted canyon of Eighth Avenue. She was swaying gracefully by the curbstone like some exotic nightbloom that grows wild in cement and survives on city poisons. She has left five years of her life on these pavingstones. To show for it she has 27 direct prostitution arrests, one grand larceny conviction and a vague memory of being picked up by the pross van roughly 1,500 times. . . .

It is a silly question to ask a prostitute why she does it. The top salary for a teacher with a B.A. in New York City public schools is $13,950; for a registered staff nurse $13,000; for a telephone operator about $8,000. The absolute daily minimum a pimp expects a streetwalker to bring in is $200 a night. That comes to easily $70,000 a year. These are the highest-paid "professional" women in America. . . .

But rare is the streetwalker who keeps any of her money. This leaves everyone, including police who have spent years riding the pross van, confounded. And so I ask again, as I have asked so many girls: How much of this money do you turn over to your pimp, and why?

"I give him *all* of it." Valerie, the former addict who has had only nine months in this game, breaks in with her half-lunatic eyes blazing. "I never had a man before. I worked independent. But I love it, I love it! Because he gives me en-ee-thing I want, a new outfit, silver jewelry. I've only got one wife-in-law, and I'm the first one of his girls she's ever gotten along with. We both have separate apartments on the East Side. He spends tonight with me, tomorrow with her and so on. That's why I know whatever we have together is mine, all *mine.*"

To Valerie (as to most street girls), the pimp is still sacred, a super-being created in her own desperate brain in whom she is investing all hopes, dreams and goals for the future. She wears his beatings proudly as symbols of affection. He is the father-substitute; he disciplines, he cares. She submits gladly to his sadistic lovemaking. The pimp as lover takes her money, tricks her, gives her raw sex but denies her an ounce of emotion, and drops her ten minutes later for another woman — exactly reversing the sado-masochistic process she must play with her own tricks. In this way she can reaffirm herself (at least every other night) as that adoring, devoted, sacrificial lamb — the "feminine" woman. Prostitutes are unbelievably romantic. There is one sentence they all utter with total conviction: "I couldn't stand to live and sleep with someone I didn't love — *I gotta love him!*"

Are there prostitutes who were not driven to their behavior in one fashion or another, but who entered the work by rational choice? Are there people who find it a satisfying and profitable way of life, and who are as happy as others in our society? Would both groups increase if prostitution were to be decriminalized and if sex were "permitted to be used by women to their own benefit and under conditions of fair protection, like any other asset which they may possess"?[12] There is a lack of real information to assist in answering these questions. If the answers are negative, and if prostitutes are in an essentially degraded and unhappy position, then other arguments must be considered. Issues are raised about the function of the criminal law in "protecting people from themselves," in enforcing morality generally, and about the effect

12. Rene Buyon, quoted in Benjamin and Masters, Prostitution and Morality 33 (1964).

of "decriminalization" as condonation and encouragement of the status of prostitution.

2. Overuse of the Criminal Sanction

KADISH, THE CRISIS OF OVERCRIMINALIZATION
7 Am. Crim. L.Q. 17, 21-22, 29-30 (1968)

Although there are social norms beyond private immorality — in commercialized sex, spread of venereal disease, exploitation of the young, and the affront of public solicitation, for example — the blunt use of the criminal prohibition has proven ineffective and costly. Prostitution has perdured in all civilizations; indeed, few institutions have proven as hardy. The inevitable conditions of social life unfailingly produce the supply to meet the ever-present demand. As the Wolfenden Report observed: "There are limits to the degree of discouragement which the criminal law can properly exercise towards a woman who has deliberately decided to live her life in this way, or a man who has deliberately chosen her services." The more so, one may add, in a country where it has been estimated that over two-thirds of white males alone will have experience with prostitutes during their lives. The costs, on the other hand, of making the effort are similar to those entailed in enforcing the homosexual laws — diversion of police resources; encouragement of use of illegal means of police control (which, in the case of prostitution, take the form of knowingly unlawful harassment arrests to remove suspected prostitutes from the streets; and various entrapment devices, usually the only means of obtaining convictions); degradation of the image of law enforcement; discriminatory enforcement against the poor; and official corruption.

To the extent that spread of venereal disease, corruption of the young, and public affront are the objects of prostitution controls, it would require little ingenuity to devise modes of social control short of the blanket criminalization of prostitution which would at the same time prove more effective and less costly for law enforcement. Apparently, the driving force behind prostitution laws is principally the conviction that prostitution is immoral. Only the judgment that the use of the criminal law for verbal vindication of our morals is more important than its use to protect life and property can support the preservation of these laws as they are. . . .

The plain sense that the criminal law is a highly specialized tool of social control, useful for certain purposes but not for others; that when improperly used it is capable of producing more evil than good; that the decision to criminalize any particular behavior must follow only after an assessment and balancing of gains and losses — this obvious injunction of rationality has been noted widely for over 250 years, from Jeremy Bentham[51] to the National Crime Commission, and by the moralistic philosophers[53] as well as the utilitarian ones.[54] And those whose daily business is the administration of the criminal law have, on occasion, exhibited acute awareness of the folly of departing from it. The need for restraint seems to be recognized by those who deal with the criminal laws, but not by those who make them or by the general public which lives under them. One hopes that attempts to set out the facts and to particularize the perils of overcriminalization may ultimately affect the decisions of the legislatures. But past experience gives little cause for optimism.

Perhaps part of the explanation of the lack of success is the inherent limitation of any rational appeal against a course of conduct which is moved by powerful irrational drives. Explaining to legislatures why it does more harm than good to criminalize drunkenness or homosexuality, for example, has as little effect (and for the same reasons)

---

51. Bentham, Principles of Morals and Legislation 281-288 (Harrison ed., 1948).
53. Devlin, The Enforcement of Morals 17 (1959). It is noteworthy that, as a practical matter, Lord Devlin became convinced of the undesirability of continuing to consider consenting homosexuality a crime. See Dworkin, Lord Devlin and the Enforcement of Morals, 75 Yale L.J. 986, 987 n.4 (1966).
54. E.g., H.L.A. Hart, The Morality of the Criminal Law, chap. ii (1964).

as explaining to alcoholics or homosexuals that their behavior does them more harm than good. It may be that the best hope for the future lies in efforts to understand more subtly and comprehensively than we do now the dynamics of the legislative (and, it must be added, popular) drive to criminalize. The sociologists, the social psychologists, the political scientists, the survey research people, and no doubt, others will have to be conscripted for any effort of this kind. A number of studies have already appeared which have revealed illuminating insights into the process of conversion of popular indignation into legislative designation of deviancy,[56] the nature of the competitive struggles among rival moralities, and the use of the criminal law to solidify and manifest victory.[57] We also have a degree of understanding of the effect of representative political processes on the choice of sanctions and the dynamics of law enforcement by the police.[58] Perhaps by further substantial research along these lines — research which would put the process of over-criminalization by popularly elected legislators itself under the microscope —we will understand better the societal forces which have unfailingly produced it.[59] Understanding, of course, is not control, and control may prove as hopeless with it as without it. But scientific progress over the past one hundred years has dramatized the control over the physical environment which comes from knowledge of its forces. It may prove possible to exert in like manner at least some measure of control over the social environment. It is an alternative worth pursuing.

3. The Argument that Criminal Penalties Should Be Retained

Prostitution appears as an offense in the Model Penal Code in the following form.

THE MODEL PENAL CODE
(Proposed Official Draft, 1962)

Section 251.1. Prostitution and Related Offenses.

(1) Prostitution. A person is guilty of prostitution, a petty misdemeanor, if he or she:

(a) is an inmate of a house of prostitution or otherwise engages in sexual activity as a business; or

(b) loiters in or within view of any public place for the purpose of being hired to engage in sexual activity. . . .

————————

The following excerpts from the Commentary upon the 1959 Draft, which also rejected decriminalization, offered these reasons for the approach taken:

COMMENTS TO MODEL PENAL CODE §207.12
(Tentative Draft No. 9, 1959)

Although prostitution appears to respond to a widespread demand, and despite indications that a substantial proportion of prostitutes are victims of social and psychic

56. H. S. Becker, Outsiders: Studies in the Sociology of Deviance (1963); Kai Erikson, Sociology of Deviance in Social Problems 457 (J. Simpson ed., 1965).

57. Gusfield, Symbolic Crusade: Status Politics and the American Temperance Movement (1963); Joseph Gusfield, The Symbolic Process in Deviance Designation (Ms. 1967).

58. Westley, Violence and the Police, 59 Amer. J. Sociology 34 (1953); Skolnick, Justice Without Trial (1966), chap. iii.

59. Under a Ford Foundation grant for a Program of Criminal Law and Social Policy, the Earl Warren Legal Center and the Center for the Study of Law and Society of the University of California (Berkeley) are attempting to undertake studies of this kind.

conditions beyond their control, most students of the problem favor penal repression of commercialized sex. Religious and moral ideas undoubtedly are the main force behind the demand for repression; but utilitarian arguments are also available. Prostitution is an important source of venereal disease, although some contend that the "amateurs" to whom men turn in lieu of prostitutes present a greater danger in this respect. It has been observed that prostitution is a source of profit and power for criminal groups who commonly combine it with illicit trade in drugs and liquor, illegal gambling and even robbery and extortion. Prostitution is also a source of corrupt influence on government and law enforcement machinery. Its promoters are willing and able to pay for police protection; and unscrupulous officials and politicians find them an easy mark for extortion. Finally, some view prostitution as a significant factor in social disorganization, encouraging sex delinquency and undermining marriage, the home, and individual character. . . .

   . . . Many of the issues between those who favor repression and those who would tolerate some prostitution cannot be resolved on the basis of available evidence. However, on the question of medical risk, the record is persuasive that inspection of licensed prostitutes would give no assurance against venereal infection. . . . Accordingly, the Institute's proposals on prostitution, embodied in Section 207.12, pursue the same basic policy of repressing commercialized sexual activity, as does present American law. . . .

4. The Position of the Women's Rights Movement on Prostitution

   The women's rights movement today is ambivalent about prostitution, recognizing it as essentially degrading to women and yet concerned that women alone bear the almost entire burden of criminalization. One attempt to synthesize a feminist position follows:[13]

>   . . . [But w]e are opposed to legalization because it is the ultimate in degradation for women and legally sanctions this kind of abuse of women by men. It would mean forced examinations, licensing, and inspections. Women who did not comply with the regulations would, of course, still be subject to arrest. From the evidence of countries that have legalized prostitution, this would be most women. We do not want women photographed, fingerprinted, and identified for life by this trade. At least now women are free to move in and out of it according to need. As long as prostitution exists we want it as free as possible from any male regulation and laws that would punish women for it. This does not mean that we are in favor of prostitution, any more than we support the institution of marriage. Needless to say, this is what the women's movement is all about: women getting together and creating enough power to throw off these institutions (and the functions particular to them) which oppress us all. But this must begin with every woman who can do so leaving these institutions now, even if it means a lower standard of living or months of emotional distress. Sacrifice and courage are necessary to change the world significantly. Therefore, we call upon all women who possibly can to leave prostitution as we have called upon women to leave marriage. Those who cannot leave now must begin to work at a plan to achieve independence. This will not only weaken the institution but will strengthen the women's movement. Finally, right now it is important for prostitutes to realize our common oppression as women and to become actively involved in the movement. We must all work together to devise an effective strategy for action.

   Historically, the women's movement had a more certain perspective on prostitution. Many of the reformers who were active in abolitionist and suffrage campaigns in the late 1800s were also ardently opposed to any type of legalization or regulation of

---

13. Kearon and Mehrhof, Prostitution, in Notes from the Third Year: Women's Liberation 71, 74-75 (Koedt and Firestone, eds. 1971).

prostitution. The barroom and the brothel were considered to be interconnected vices, and "Purity reform from its inception demonstrated a dependence upon the older temperance reform. The two reforms were of great importance in the emergence of a social morality in the Nineteenth century. If drink and prostitution were the 'twin evils,' temperance and social purity were the twin forces to combat them."[14]

Prostitution was not a serious problem in America until the early nineteenth-century rise of urbanization. In 1833 the Society for Moral Reform, directed toward suppression of prostitution, was organized in New York. But:[15]

> [N]o movement clearly designated as social purity appeared. The failure can be correlated with the primitive condition of the women's rights movement. Purity reform and the women's rights movement paralleled each other in the course of development. Purity reform utilized the reform structure erected by women. The women's rights movement implemented and coordinated its activities. . . .

The two major forms of action taken by women's rights advocates in response to prostitution were to arrange club meetings and societies for the rescue and reform of fallen women and to petition and speak against all efforts to regulate or legalize prostitution. Grace Dodge and Frances Willard were among leading women's rights advocates who also devoted themselves to suppressing prostitution.[16]

> Prostitution blocked the attainment of equal rights for women. Implied in the institution was the idea that woman was obligated to satisfy the physical appetites of man. The corollary of the belief was that man had a right to satisfy his appetites while women were obligated, unless prostitutes, to maintain a strict chastity. Within that context prostitution was considered a defensive buffer for the protection of the family and respectable womanhood. Women reformers condemned the system.

In the early twentieth century, feminists grew more concerned about the economic motivation of prostitution, and linked their drives against prostitution with efforts to improve the pay and working conditions of women in noncriminal businesses. They wanted to change the situation in which "[L]ust is a better paymaster than the mill owner or the tailor."[17]

5. The Nevada Experiment

Nevada is the only state which, in some counties, has effected legalization. Regulation of prostitution is left to county option where the population is less than 200,000. The population restriction means that prostitution is illegal in Las Vegas, Reno, Lake Tahoe, and Carson City. But in other parts of the state, there are about forty licensed houses. A popular magazine recounted the cleanliness of the prostitutes and their surroundings and described their good spirits.[18] Very little else has been written about the experiment. In Storey County, Nevada, it must be considered a success from some viewpoints, however; the licensing fees for houses of prostitution are one-fifth of the annual county budget.

6. The New York City Experiment

From 1967 to 1969, the city of New York experimented unsuccessfully with a reduced penalty system for prostitution. The legislature changed the classification of

14. Pivar, The New Abolitionism: The Quest for Social Purity, 1876–1900, 26 (Ph.D. dissertation University of Pennsylvania 1965). Much of the history in this note is based on Pivar's excellent account, which also includes an extensive bibliography.
15. Id. at 29.
16. Id. at 205.
17. See, e.g., Addams, A New Conscience and An Ancient Evil (1913).
18. Astor, Legal Prostitution Spreads in Nevada, Look Magazine, June 29, 1971, p. 26.

the offense from a misdemeanor to a violation carrying a penalty of fifteen days in jail. The experiment caused a public uproar and, according to the New York Times of January 27, 1969, "[s]treetwalkers from across the country have swarmed into New York." There were allegations that competition was causing prostitutes to become extremely aggressive and that muggings and robberies were increasingly connected with sexual solicitation. In 1969, the maximum penalty for prostitution was increased to ninety days.

This experiment did not really amount to a "decriminalization" of prostitution, because the increased population of prostitutes apparently resulted in more, rather than fewer, arrests for the crime. The New York City Police Department reported a 61 percent increase in prostitution arrests in the first six months of 1969, as compared to the same period in 1967. But the New York experiment may be instructive about the practicability of decriminalization in a multijurisdiction country.

One of the members of a mayoral committee established to study the New York situation submitted the following arguments against the reduced penalties.

LINDSAY, PROSTITUTION — DELINQUENCY'S TIME BOMB
16 Crime & Delinquency 151, 153-156 (April 1970)[19]

The new Penal Code's shortened sentence not only increased prostitution but also made it impossible for the House of Detention for Women to give to those committed even the emergency *physical* rehabilitation they needed — to withdraw an inmate from drugs, clean her clothing or fit her to new clothing, give her a hairdo, extract an aching tooth. As for social casework, psychiatric examination or treatment, job training, or lengthy medical attention — impossible! The usual sentence was ten or fifteen days, but from that were subtracted all time spent awaiting trial in jail and one day off for every six "good behavior" days served on the sentence. If, after this computation, the days of release were to fall on a Saturday, a Sunday, or a legal holiday, actual release would be effected on the preceding day. It was plain to see that the commitment was merely a bookkeeping exercise, a recording of admissions and discharges. No real help could be given to even the most needy or the most eager to receive it. Certainly there was no time in which to establish any motivation for change.

Before the ten-day and fifteen-day sentences went into effect, the prostitute could make use of a jail sentence when life became too burdensome — when, say, her pimp became too importunate or intractable, or she became ill and tired, or her drug habit reached insatiable proportions. It was simple to "cruise a bull" and rest up in jail. The misery of the life of a prostitute, and especially of the prostitute-addict, is inconceivable to inhabitants of the "square" world. Many confide that their sojourns in the House of Detention for Women are the only calm, strengthening periods of their lives. As their discharge date comes closer, many become extremely nervous and apprehensive and deliberately break the rules, the loss of "good time" enabling them to stay another day or two. . . .

A Proposal for Effective Treatment

First, give us time to do the job. The ninety-day sentence is not much more realistic than the fifteen-day sentence, but at least it is more humane and more dignified.

Some may say, "Why any sentence? Why not a voluntary or outpatient kind of treatment?" Simply because the prostitute will not come to treatment voluntarily. Harold Greenwald, a court psychologist specializing in prostitute behavior, states that he has not been able to recruit even one prostitute for voluntary treatment, although it is free

19. Reprinted with permission of the National Council on Crime and Delinquency. The author served as Superintendent of the House of Detention for Women of the Department of Correction in New York City from 1964 to 1968 and was a member of the Mayor's Committee on Prostitution and chairperson of its Subcommittee on Rehabilitation in 1967.

and readily available. There are many reasons for this: (1) Fear of the pimp. (2) Fear of ridicule by one's companions and sister prostitutes. (3) A lifetime of failure and disappointment resulting in an inability to identify with the "square" world. (4) The frequent complication of drug addiction. (5) Remnants of pride which will not admit to emotional bankruptcy or inability to control one's own life. (6) Unavailability or inadequacy of substitute satisfactions. . . .

. . . We need a halfway house. The expertise, the skills, and the resources of Correction Department personnel should not continue to be wasted within the confines of prison walls. In prison the inmate can be taught to live in *prison,* but teaching her to live in the *world* requires the teacher to enter the world with her.

What kind of house should it be? Warm, alive, comfortable, but with sufficient structure and rules to continue the discipline learned in correctional custody. "Self-government" is not for these inmates — at least not at first. What must be there are protection, structure, schedules, and the certain knowledge that someone is "in charge" and that this someone possesses sufficient authority to instruct, protect, and care enough to take the place of the loving authority most of these residents never had in their lives before. Perhaps a large brownstone where a sheltered workshop might be maintained would be the most suitable facility. All inmates will not immediately be able to leave the residence to work; shocking as it may sound, *some* of these inmates are so psychologically damaged that they should never leave the residence to live elsewhere or to work. These inmates could be employed in cooking or maintenance. . . . [M]ost inmates [would] return gradually to normal, self-sustaining lives in the outside community, except that the halfway house would always be there for counseling or for companionship —a cup of tea, a visit "home" with a child to show off, an evening of cards or TV in companionship with others, and the opportunity to offer and receive encouragement.

Success depends on two circumstances:

1. The person (social worker, correctional officer, teacher) who provided the motivation must continue contact throughout the transferral period.

2. Other residents undergoing the transferral process must serve as reinforcement for the process and provide the necessary social contact without which the transferral period would be unbearably bleak.

7. "Rehabilitating" the Prostitute

> WINICK AND KINSIE, THE LIVELY COMMERCE:
> PROSTITUTION IN THE UNITED STATES
> 287, 289-292 (Quadrangle/New York Times Book Co. 1971)[20]

. . . [I]f there will always be prostitutes and clients, why shouldn't civilized people accept it? But a major issue about prostitution is whether it serves a true social function, and whether fulfillment of this function makes it impossible for prostitutes to achieve any reasonable amount of human happiness. It could be argued, for example, that slavery was functional in the United States before the Civil War; yet however functional it might have been, it clearly violated the slaves' humanity. Similarly, the American dream of making equality meaningful for all would clearly seem to be violated by segregating a group of women whose primary work is meeting the sexual needs of men on an anonymous cash basis. Respect for human beings and for the ideal of giving every person an opportunity to achieve, in John Dewey's phrase, the greatest quality as well as quantity of experience, is clearly inconsistent with condoning prostitution.

[This work goes on to outline possible forms which a rehabilitative program for prostitutes could take, with an optimistic view of the possibilities.]

20. Reprinted by permission of Quadrangle/The New York Times Book Co. from The Lively Commerce by Charles Winick and Paul M. Kinsie. Copyright © 1971 by Charles Winick.

The hopelessness that surrounds much discussion of prostitution and what to do about it used to characterize official and unofficial attitudes toward drug addiction as recently as ten years ago.[8] But in the last decade public and governmental opinion has become aroused, many new programs have been developed, and a wide range of innovative ideas is now being explored. New York State, with more than half the country's drug addicts, did not have a program or even one bed available for them in 1959; today it has thousands of beds and an annual budget of more than $100 million for treatment and rehabilitation. An aroused public opinion, such as occurred in the case of addiction after a half-century of inertia, may suggest a model for a similar breakthrough in prostitution.

As reformers in the field of addiction have had to accept interim goals while public opinion evolves, it may be possible to take some intermediate steps toward an ultimately more humane and civilized approach to prostitution. The model of addiction suggests what could be a useful contemporary viewpoint toward prostitution. Modern approaches to the drug problem stress a lack of sympathy for addiction and drug abuse but a sympathetic attitude toward the addict, offering him every assistance. Educational programs seek to deter future drug users, and control procedures attempt to make illicit drugs unavailable. At the same time the addict is regarded as a person with an illness who should get every kind of help and support in coping with it.

A similarly enlightened attitude toward prostitution would include disapproval for the practice but every possible assistance to the women who work in it. A realistic goal would be to maximize opportunities for those women who wish to leave prostitution. It would be unrealistic to force all women who are identified as prostitutes to submit to treatment. Treatment might be mandatory for prostitutes who have venereal disease or are juveniles. Other women would enter treatment voluntarily. The great range of personality and background found among prostitutes makes it unlikely that any one program would meet the needs of all. The problem calls for extensive experimentation with different approaches to rehabilitation to determine the kinds of women who respond best to each approach. A panel composed of specialists in resocialization might determine the most constructive approach to each case. An administrative procedure for handling such cases outside the usual system of criminal justice is a possibility that ought to be explored.

The best time to try to cope with incipient prostitution is doubtless around the time of adolescence. Girls who experience a diffusion of identity or a negative identity, and who have problems with intimacy, may, as we have seen, move into prostitution as a way of coping with events or internal psychological pressures. An emotionally disturbed promiscuous adolescent, young female delinquent, or unwed mother often appears to be drifting toward prostitution. Programs designed to identify and help such persons are likely to be successful if introduced before the girl has become entrenched in a career of prostitution. Working with girls who exhibit such characteristics could prove far more rewarding than have previous attempts to rehabilitate older prostitutes. Such girls might receive an intensive period of preparation for treatment and rehabilitation.

A thoughtful rehabilitation program is needed because vocational training by itself is unlikely to enable a former prostitute to hold a job. Milieu therapy, perhaps in a halfway-house situation, may be one way of effecting a radical change in personality and outlook. The discipline and routine of an ordinary job may be overwhelming for a prostitute who has a low threshold of frustration and has not received special preparation.

In the rehabilitation of narcotics addicts one particularly effective approach is to employ former addicts as therapeutic personnel. Many have developed vocations as dedicated therapists and, at the same time, contributed toward the opening of new career possibilities for other addicts. They have the respect of addicts because there can be no

8. C. Winick, "Tendency Systems and the Effects of a Movie Dealing with a Social Problem," Journal of General Psychology, 1963, 68, 289-305.

doubt that they know the score and have firsthand experience of what they are talking about. Similarly, former prostitutes might make excellent therapists in the rehabilitation of women "in the life." Such an approach might generate as much public support as Daytop and Synanon were able to develop for drug addicts. Indeed, some of the female members of those same institutions who have been prostitutes might serve as a beginning cadre.

Resocialization of prostitutes in various European countries has had a success rate that in recent years has ranged from 33 to 75 per cent. France, Spain, and Italy have successfully used fairly large halfway houses, and England has had a favorable experience with smaller facilities. Most countries have reported that prostitutes under twenty-two and over twenty-eight are most likely to respond to retraining and reeducation. The experiences of those European countries that have mounted effective programs to reintegrate the prostitute into the community can provide valuable clues.

The most effective of these European resocialization programs have helped the former prostitute to enter a new "friendly circle" to replace the group from which she had been withdrawn. Both residential and nonresidential treatment has been successful. Every effort is made to train the woman for work which involves graded increases in responsibility. Women who have experienced years of submission need to strengthen their personalities by identification with a shared responsibility. Resocialization centers avoid placing the women in traditional jobs for "reclaimed women," such as laundry and domestic work.

War experience has proved that private and government agencies can work together effectively to implement sound rehabilitation programs. Creative experimentation in the rehabilitation of prostitutes is long overdue. Such programs need to be established and carefully evaluated. Some approaches will undoubtedly fail, others will have only partial success. But we must begin to provide facilities on almost a compensatory basis, recognizing that we have neglected prostitution since World War II. Such programs would explore the feasibility of retraining pimps as well as prostitutes. The relationship of prostitute to pimp makes it important for the latter to be included in any efforts at resocialization.

In recent years there has been a vigorous controversy over the nature and direction of instruction in family-life education and sex education. Although the subject is still controversial and is not fully accepted in some quarters, there is reason to believe that it will become more firmly established in the near future. As it reaches more young people, such instruction should help the next generation to be more realistic and honest about prostitution. Perhaps long before then, enlightened approaches to the problem of prostitution will ease the heavy social, criminal, and judicial burden which it has long placed on so many American communities.

NOTE

Isn't the possibility of voluntary programs unrealistic? How would "an administrative procedure for handling [prostitution cases] outside the usual system of criminal justice" work? In the last analysis, isn't the criminal sanction necessary for identifying those who need rehabilitation and convincing them to seek it? Even assuming that the answer to this question is affirmative and that ideal programs like those discussed in the above passage existed, is there sufficient reason for retaining the criminalization of prostitution?

8. *Decriminalization Through Litigation*

It is unlikely that legislatures in many jurisdictions would find it politically feasible to decriminalize prostitution, even if they desired to do so. Decriminalization could be accomplished in effect, however, by attacking the application of the laws through litigation. This section presents some of the arguments that could be made against typical prostitution laws and includes related materials.

a. Equal Protection Arguments

WILSON v. STATE
278 Ind. 569, 278 N.E.2d 569, cert. denied, 408 U.S. 928 (1972)

Defendant [asks] that this Court declare a statute under which she was charged unconstitutional as being violative of Article IV, §22 of the Constitution of the State of Indiana, the applicable portions thereof being as follows: "The General Assembly shall not pass local or special laws, in any of the following enumerated cases, that is to say: . . . For the punishment of crimes and misdemeanors. . . ."

It is the defendant's position hereunder that the statute, being applicable to females only is special, inasmuch as the acts proscribed thereby could be committed as well by males. . . .

"This section of the Constitution is not violated by the involved act, because it applies to all who come within its provisions, generally and without exceptions, and it rests upon an inherent and substantial basis of classification. 'A law which applies generally to a particular class of cases is not local or special. The Constitution does not require that the operation of a law shall be uniform, other than that its operation shall be the same in all parts of the state under the same circumstances.' " 226 Ind. 279 at 290, 79 N.E.2d 537 at 543.

Finding no error, the judgment of the trial court is affirmed.

Arterburn, C.J., and Givan and Hunter, J.J., concur.

DeBruler, J., dissents with opinion.

DeBruler, J. (dissenting). Appellant is a woman. She offered to commit sexual intercourse with an undercover vice squad officer for ten dollars. She was convicted of violating I.C. 1971, 35-30-1-1, being Burns §10-4220, and was sentenced to the Women's Prison for a term of not less than two nor more than five years.

The prostitute statute reads as follows: "Prostitute. Any female who frequents or lives in a house or houses of ill fame, knowing the same to be a house of ill fame, or who commits or offers to commit one or more acts of sexual intercourse or sodomy for hire, shall be deemed guilty of prostitution, and on conviction thereof shall either be fined not less than one hundred dollars nor more than five hundred dollars, and imprisonment not to exceed 180 days or such person may be imprisoned in the Indiana women's prison not less than two years nor more than five years." . . .

. . . Secondly, the case of State v. Griffin (1948), 226 Ind. 279, 79 N.E.2d 537, cited by the majority supports appellant's contention that the statute is unconstitutional. In that case a statute made it unlawful for male persons to visit a gaming house. There the classification was based solely upon sex and it was found not to violate this same provision of our Constitution. However, the basis of that Court's decision was in part the existence of a different but corollary statute making it a crime for a female person to visit a house of ill fame, and the Court interpreted the phrase "house of ill fame" to include gaming houses. Therefore the Court held that in fact the statute provided for essentially similar treatment for men and women. In the case before us now, there has never been a corollary statute making it a crime for a man to commit or offer to commit sexual intercourse or sodomy for hire. The basis of the Court's decision there was that the classification "male persons" in the statute complained of dissolved when a corollary statute was found treating "female persons" in the same manner.

Although admittedly not argued by appellant, two recent cases compel a determination of unconstitutionality in this case. In Troue v. Marker (1969), Ind., 252 N.E.2d 800, this Court struck down a classification based on sex which had been erected at common law. In that case we abrogated the doctrine which denied a wife the right to recover damages for loss of consortium of her husband. In requiring that the law respond to the demands of our society that women be treated equally with men we said:

"The common law must keep pace with changes in our society, and in our opinion the change in the legal and social status of women in our society forces us to recognize a change in the doctrine with which we are concerned in this opinion." 252 N.E.2d at 804.

That arbitrary distinction between men and women at common law prevented a wife from recovering money damages for her loss. The arbitrary distinction between men and women erected by the prostitute statute subjects the female prostitute to five years imprisonment while her male counterpart violates no law. The need for a reasoned and timely response to this appellant's claim of discrimination is even more compelling than that in Troue v. Marker, supra. In Reed v. Reed (1971), 404 U.S. 71, 92 S. Ct. 251, 30 L. Ed. 2d 225, the United States Supreme Court held that an Idaho statute favoring males over females for the offices of personal representative in probate estates was in violation of the equal protection clause of the Fourteenth Amendment. Under that statute women were not entirely disqualified to serve. Men were to be preferred. It seems to me that if the equal protection clause prohibits that kind of different treatment of women, it would likewise prohibit this State from punishing female prostitutes and at the same time sanction male prostitution.

That part of the prostitute statute making it a crime for a female person to commit or offer to commit an act of sexual intercourse or sodomy for hire should be declared unconstitutional.

The argument which was rejected in *Wilson* was accepted in Minnesota v. Woods, No. 443072 (Minneapolis, Minn. Mun. Ct. Dec. 21, 1971), in which a municipal court struck down an ordinance providing that "no female shall offer or submit her body indiscriminately, for sexual intercourse" because it found no legislative justification for allowing a male to so offer his body while prohibiting the female. A similar statute in Portland was also struck down; see City of Portland v. Sherrill, No. M-47623 (Multnomah County, Ore. Cir. Ct. Jan. 10, 1967). A very recent and thorough opinion upholding an equal protection argument and striking down the Alaska statute defining prostitution as "the giving or receiving of the body by a female for sexual intercourse for hire," Alaska Stat. §11.40.210, is Alaska v. Fields (Dist. Ct. Alaska 3d Jud. Dist. 1973). See also the discussion of United States v. Moses, infra Section D-8-b(1), 41 U.S.L.W. 2298, 12 Cr. L. Rptr. 2198.

It seems clear that the Equal Rights Amendment would invalidate prostitution laws that are written in terms which make only women subject to prosecution.[21]

> . . . There is no unique physical characteristic of women which would justify outlawing prostitution when it is done by women, and not when it is done by men. Earlier beliefs that women are the carriers of venereal disease because of their sex have no scientific basis. Ideas that women who sell access to their bodies are social problems, whereas men who do the same thing are not, derive their only rationality from a social double standard which may not enter into legislative or judicial determinations under the Equal Rights Amendment. . . .
>
> If prostitution laws were redefined to cover male prostitutes, then the courts would be unlikely to find a per se violation of the Equal Rights Amendment in the fact that prostitution laws penalize the "seller" but not the "buyer." In general,

21. Brown, Emerson, Falk, and Freedman, The Equal Rights Amendment: A Constitutional Basis for Equal Rights for Women, 80 Yale L.J. 871, 962-965 (1971).

regulating the conduct of the seller and not the buyer is a rational governmental choice, although in the case of prostitution such a choice may not make sense, even in terms of effective deterrence. Nevertheless, prostitution laws which penalize only the seller would be subject to judicial scrutiny as classifications which fall more heavily on one sex than the other. Thus, to sustain its laws, a state would bear a heavy burden of demonstrating the rationality of regulating only the seller and not the buyer in a prostitution transaction. Reformed penal laws have already begun to regulate patrons as well as prostitutes. It is likely, and desirable, that legislatures in removing the sex bias from their laws, will follow this lead.[22]

The efficacy of laws that punish the customer is open to question, on the basis of New York's experience with such laws. A reformed penal law, which makes the customers of prostitutes also liable to criminal punishment, went into effect on September 1, 1967.[23]

> Those who watched the enforcement of the "patron clause" soon realized that New York's "johns" (the trade name for patrons) had little to fear . . . ; of the total prostitution and patronizing convictions, less than 1% were for patronizing. With neither the police nor the judges treating it seriously, the clause, as described by Judge Amos Basel of the New York Criminal Court, didn't make sense. "We don't have the will to make it hold, so it makes the law a joke."

b. Right to Privacy Arguments

A law review article written with the express purpose "to provide attorneys with the basis of lodging a legal attack against the prostitution statutes in their jurisdictions" sets out the structure and background of the privacy argument.

ROSENBLEET AND PARRIENTE
THE PROSTITUTION OF THE CRIMINAL LAW
11 Am. Crim. L. Rev. 373, 421 (1973)

In launching a constitutional attack on prostitution laws based upon a privacy argument, it is helpful to view the statutes as falling into three categories: (1) status statutes, (2) overt action statutes, and (3) negotiation and soliciting statutes. The privacy argument must be adapted to the type of statute under attack. Where the status or act itself is proscribed, the right of privacy is direct. Where, however, the jurisdiction does not make prostitution per se, illegal, but outlaws the preliminary negotiations[216] and all other prostitution-related activity,[217] the argument is somewhat different: though not

---

22. Some British Columbian courts, in interpreting the Canadian Bill of Rights, which prohibits discrimination on account of sex, have found a vagrancy-prostitution statute phrased in female terms to be unlawful. Regina v. Lavoie, 16 D.L.R.3d 647 (1971); 1 W.W.R. 690 (B.C. Co. Cr.), noted in 6 U.B.C.L. Rev. (1971).

23. Roby and Kerr, The Politics of Prostitution, in the Nation, April 10, 1972, p. 465.

216. See, e.g., D.C. Code Ann. §22-2701 (1967) (prohibits invitations for purpose of prostitution).

217. See, e.g., D.C. Code Ann. §22-2704 (1967) et seq:

Sec.

22-2704. Abducting, secreting, or enticing child from her home for purposes of prostitution — Harboring such child.

22-2705. Pandering — Inducing or compelling female to become prostitute or engage in prostitution — Penalty.

22-2706. Compelling female to live life of prostitution against her will — Penalty.

22-2707. Procurer — Punishment for receiving money or other valuable thing for arranging assignation or debauchery — Penalty.

22-2708. Punishment for causing wife to live in prostitution.

22-2709. Punishment for detailing inmate in disorderly house for debt there contracted.

directly making the activity unlawful, the state has effectively infringed on the individual's right of privacy by proscribing all associated activity.

One of the earliest statements of a "privacy" notion came more than a century ago from the British political writer, John Stuart Mill. In his work, On Liberty, Mill reflected on an individual's liberty of action vis à vis society:

> That the only purpose for which power can be rightfully exercised over any member of a civilized community, against his will, is to prevent harm to others. His own good, either physical or moral, is not a sufficient warrant.[218]

This philosophy was reflected in an early Supreme Court case, Union Pacific Railway Co. v. Botsford,[219] in which the Court stated:

> No right is held more sacred, or is more carefully guarded, by the common law, than the right of every individual to the possession and control of his own person, free from all restraint or interference of others, unless by clear and unquestionable authority of law.[220]

The Supreme Court reaffirmed the above-quoted passage from *Botsford* recently in Terry v. Ohio, a fourth amendment case.[221] In addition to the restatement of the *Botsford* principle in a fourth amendment context, the Supreme Court has over the years expanded this principle in a variety of decisions interpreting the Constitution to protect certain rights relating to sex, marriage, child-rearing and child-bearing.[222]

22-2710. Procurer for house of prostitution — Penalty.

22-2711. Procurer for third persons — Penalty.

22-2712. Running house of prostitution — Penalty.

22-2713. Premises occupied for lewdness, assignation, or prostitution declared nuisance.

22-2714. Abatement of nuisance under section 22-2713 by injunction — Temporary injunction — Effect of injunction.

22-2715. Abatement of nuisance under section 22-2713 — Trial — Dismissal of complaint — Prosecution to judgment — Costs.

22-2716. Trials for violating injunction granted under section 22-2714 — Punishment.

22-2717. Order of abatement — Sale of property — Entry of closed premises punishable as contempt.

22-2718. Disposition of proceeds of sale.

22-2719. Bond for abatement — Order for delivery of premises — Effect of release.

22-2720. Tax for maintaining such nuisance.

22-2722. Keeping bawdy or disorderly houses.

218. J. S. Mill, On Liberty 13 (Bobbs-Merrill ed. 1956). The Millian position has stirred a heated debate over the legal enforcement of morality. The principal participants in this debate have been Lord Patrick Devlin, H. L. A. Hart and Ronald Dworkin. See P. Devlin, The Enforcement of Morals (1st ed. 1959); H. Hart, The Concept of Law (1961); H. Hart, Law, Liberty and Morality (1963); Dworkin, Lord Devlin and the Enforcement of Morals, 75 Yale L.J. 986 (1966); Hart, Social Solidarity and the Enforcement of Morality, 35 U. Chi. L. Rev. 1 (1967). A recent commentary on this debate appears in Sartorius, The Enforcement of Morality, 81 Yale L.J. 891 (1972).

219. 141 U.S. 250 (1891).

220. Id. at 251.

221. 392 U.S. 1, 9 (1968).

222. See, e.g., Meyer v. Nebraska, 262 U.S. 390 (1923) (where the Supreme Court struck down, on fourteenth amendment grounds, a state statute which sought to support the primacy of the English language by prohibiting the teaching of modern foreign languages to school children below the eighth grade); Pierce v. Society of Sisters, 268 U.S. 510 (1925) (in which the Court relied on the fourteenth amendment as guaranteeing the liberty of parents and guardians to direct the upbringing and education of children under their control and vindicated the right of private school attendance despite a state law requiring that students be educated in public schools); Skinner v. Oklahoma *ex rel.* Williamson, 316 U.S. 535 (1942) (where the Court unanimously voided an Oklahoma statute requiring compulsory sexual sterilization for habitual criminal offenders as violative of the Equal Protection Clause of the fourteenth amendment); Loving v. Virginia, 388 U.S. 1 (1967)

The most significant case directly relying on a right of privacy dealt with a Connecticut statute (on the books since the Civil War) prohibiting the use and prescription of contraceptive drugs or devices. Griswold v. Connecticut[223] declared this prohibition to be unconstitutional, and gave rise to the doctrine of penumbral rights — the idea that specific guarantees in the Bill of Rights have "penumbras, formed by emanations from those guarantees that help to give them life and substance."[224] Writing the opinion of the Court, Justice Douglas deduced a constitutionally protected right of privacy as implicit within the penumbra of the enumerated rights.[225] A concurring opinion in *Griswold,* by Justice Goldberg (joined by Chief Justice Warren and Justice Brennan) related the right of privacy to the ninth amendment.[226]

     . . . The Supreme Court just last term, in a 6-1 decision, made it clear that the right of privacy enunciated in *Griswold* was not confined to the marital relationship. In Eisenstadt v. Baird,[229] a Massachusetts criminal statute[230] prohibited the distribution of contraceptives to unmarried individuals except to prevent the spread of disease. In holding the statute unconstitutional, Justice Brennan, writing for the majority, reflected on *Griswold* and attempted to further define the privacy concept:

> It is true that in *Griswold* the right of privacy in question inhered in the marital relationship. Yet the marital couple is not an independent entity with a mind and heart of its own, but an association of two individuals each with a separate intellectual and emotional makeup. If the right of privacy means anything, it is the right of the *individual,* married or single, to be free from unwarranted governmental intrusion. . . .[231]

It is generally recognized that constitutional rights are not immune from all governmental regulation.[232] Over the years, a number of tests have been devised to determine whether there is a justification for state intrusion into an area of constitutionally protected freedoms.[233] *Griswold* employs the compelling state interest test — determining

---

(where the Supreme Court asserted that the freedom to marry, long recognized as one of the vital personal rights essential to the orderly pursuit of happiness by free men, was unreasonably interfered with by a state anti-miscegenation law which violated the Equal Protection and Due Process Clauses of the fourteenth amendment.)

    223. 381 U.S. 479 (1965).

    224. Id. at 484.

    225. 381 U.S. at 484-86.

    226. ". . . I believe that the right of privacy in the marital relation is fundamental and basic — a personal right retained by the people within the meaning of the Ninth Amendment." 381 U.S. 479, 499 (Goldberg, J., concurring).

    229. 405 U.S. 438 (1972).

    230. Mass. Gen. Laws ch. 272, §§21, 21A (1932).

    231. 405 U.S. at 543.

    232. See, e.g., New York Times Co. v. United States, 403 U.S. 713 (1971); Schenck v. United States, 249 U.S. 47 (1919); Reynolds v. United States, 98 U.S. 145 (1878).

    233. One such test is a "balancing" test — determining whether the protected relationship or activities outweigh the state's interest as carried out in its legislation. The balancing test was first utilized in a free speech context in American Communications Ass'n v. Douds, 339 U.S. 382, 399 (1950). For a favorable analysis of the test, see Karst, Legislative Facts in Constitutional Litigation, 1960 Sup. Ct. Rev. 75. A critical approach to the test appears in Meiklejohn, The Balancing of Self Preservation Against Political Freedom, 49 Calif. L. Rev. 4 (1961) and in Frantz, The First Amendment in the Balance, 71 Yale L.J. 1424 (1962). A second test is the "rational relation" test — determining whether the challenged statute bears a rational relationship to the state's interest. The rational relation test has been closely tied to the Equal Protection clause of the fourteenth amendment, specifically when a legislative classification is challenged as being without rational and substantial relation to the object of the legislation. See, e.g., McGowan v. Maryland, 366 U.S. 420, 425 (1965). Another test is the "less restrictive alternative" test — determining whether, even though the statute bears a rational relationship to the activity sought to be controlled, the end could be achieved by less restrictive means. See Shelton v. Tucker, 364 U.S. 479, 488 (1960), where Justice Stewart wrote: "[E]ven though the governmental purpose be legitimate and substantial, that purpose cannot be pursued by means that broadly stifle fundamental personal liberties when the end can be more narrowly achieved. The breadth of legislative abridgment must be viewed in the light of less drastic means for achieving the same basic purpose." See also Aptheker v.

whether the statutory classification is not only rationally related to a valid public purpose but additionally whether it is necessary to the achievement of a compelling state interest.[234] Justice Goldberg emphasized this requirement of a compelling state interest which overrides the private rights of an individual in his concurring opinion in *Griswold*:[235]

> In a long series of cases this Court has held that where fundamental personal liberties are involved, they may not be abridged by the States simply on a showing that a regulatory statute has some rational relationship to the effectuation of a proper state purpose. "Where there is a significant encroachment upon personal liberty, the State may prevail only upon showing a subordinating interest which is compelling." Bates v. Little Rock, 361 U.S. 516, 524. The law must be shown "necessary, and not merely rationally related, to the accomplishment of a permissable state policy." McLaughlin v. Florida, 379 U.S. 184, 196.

The logical question then follows: What is the state interest in placing statutory restrictions on prostitution? Several possibilities exist:[236] (1) The claim that prostitution is the cause of great increases in venereal disease; (2) An alleged link between prostitution and organized crime; (3) The theory that prostitution is in some way connected to other crime-related activities and is a significant factor in increasing such crimes as robbery, assault, and narcotic possession and sale; and (4) the notion that streetwalkers offend public decency and that the regulation of immorality is necessary to safeguard the general welfare. All of these possibilities fall short of providing a particular and specific interest which is compelling enough to permit the state to encroach upon personal liberty and invade an individual's zone of privacy.

The claim that prostitution is the cause of an increase in venereal disease is highly suspect. A recent three year study in Washington[237] in which all women arrested as prostitutes in the Seattle area were inspected found no more than one or two out of hundreds with infectious syphillis and fewer than six percent infected with gonorrhea. The age group which suffers the highest rate of V.D. ranges from 15 to 30 years of age. This is not the age group which most frequently patronizes prostitutes; 84 percent of reported V.D. cases came from the 15-30 age group, whereas prostitutes interviewed in Seattle reported that 70 percent of their customers were between 30 and 60 years of age. The findings in Seattle are consistent with the general conclusion reached throughout the United States that the spread of venereal disease is not a consequence of prostitution.[238]

The rationale that organized crime is involved in prostitution activity appears to

---

Secretary of State, 378 U.S. 500, 508 (1964); Struve, The Less-Restrictive-Alternative Principle and Economic Due Process, 80 Harv. L. Rev. 1463 (1967); Comment, Less Drastic Means and the First Amendment, 78 Yale L.J. 464 (1969). A fourth possible test is the "absolute right" test — determining whether the rights restricted are absolute and therefore not subject to infringement. This test is generally found used in a first amendment context. See Meiklejohn, The First Amendment as an Absolute, 1961 Sup. Ct. Rev. 245.

234. Bates v. Little Rock, 361 U.S. 516, 524 (1959). See also Shapiro v. Thompson, 394 U.S. 618, 634 (1968) (state statutes in Connecticut, Pennsylvania and the District of Columbia refusing welfare payments to claimants with less than one year's residency held unconstitutional "because any classification, which serves to penalize the exercise of [the right to travel], unless shown to be necessary to promote a compelling governmental interest, is unconstitutional); Sherbert v. Verner, 374 U.S. 398 (1962) (state of South Carolina unable to show compelling state interest to uphold a statute prohibiting claimant from obtaining compensation because claimant would not work on Saturday, the sabbath of her faith).

235. 381 U.S. at 497.

236. These rationales are discussed in a variety of writings. See, e.g., W. LaFave, Arrest: The Decision to Take a Suspect into Custody, Chapter 22 (1965); L. Tiffany, D. McIntyre & D. Rotenberg, Detection of Crime, Chapter 16 (1967); The Flatfoot Floozies, Newsweek 99 (May 18, 1970); Put Your Clothes Back On Honey, You're Under Arrest, Washingtonian 43 (Aug. 1970).

237. Burnstin & James, Prostitution in Seattle, 6 Wash. State Bar News 5 (Aug.-Sept. 1971).

238. See H. Benjamin & R. Masters, Prostitution and Morality, (1964); Should Prostitution Be Legalized?, Sexual Behavior, January 1972, at 72.

be unfounded. The President's Commission on Law Enforcement and Administration of Justice has rebutted such a contention:

> Prostitution . . . play[s] a small and declining role in organized crime's operations. . . . Prostitution is difficult to organize and discipline is hard to maintain.[239]

The President's Commission on Crime in the District of Columbia also downplayed a possible tie between prostitution and organized crime in the District of Columbia:

> Prostitution exists in the District, as in every city, but it is not considered by law enforcement officials to be a significant problem. It most often involves street walkers and call girls who operate on an individual basis, or in conjunction with other women with whom they share the expense of an apartment and telephone.[240]

These views were reiterated in an interview with Lieutenant Charles Rinaldi, head of the morals squad of the District of Columbia Metropolitan Police Force:

> There is no real organization of call girls here in Washington. Maybe there's a loose network, but only infrequently do you find one pimp with a couple of girls working for him. The Mafia isn't around here . . . Anyway, prostitution just isn't profitable enough in Washington to keep any organization interested.[241]

To arrest and criminally prosecute a prostitute because crime-related activity *might* be involved either directly or indirectly seems antithetical to the notions of due process, equal protection, and individual liberty. The Supreme Court recently voided a vagrancy statute in Florida which made extravagant presumptions about certain individuals. In Papachristou v. City of Jacksonville,[242] Justice Douglas wrote for a unanimous Court:

> A presumption that people who might walk or loaf or loiter or stroll or frequent houses where liquor is sold, or who are supported by their wives or who look suspicious to the police are to become future criminals is too precarious for a rule of law. The implicit presumption in these generalized vagrancy standards — that crime is being nipped in the bud — is too extravagant to deserve extended treatment. Of course, vagrancy statutes are useful to the police. They are nets making easy the roundup of so-called undesirables. But the rule of law implies equality and justice in its application. Vagrancy laws of the Jacksonville type teach that the scales of justice are so tipped that even-handed administration of the law is not possible. The rule of law, evenly applied to minorities as well as majorities, to the poor as well as to the rich, is the great mucilage that holds society together.[243] . . .

The final justification for a state interest in prostitution controls is probably the most frequently heard. "Apparently, the driving force behind prostitution laws is principally the conviction that prostitution is immoral."[247] There appears a dramatic picture of the citizenry being physically assaulted and verbally abused by hordes of lecherous streetwalkers. Such a picture is a mere fiction:

> Because of the nature of prostitution, there is no victim, in the usual sense of the word, who is willing to testify against the prostitute. In addition, the prostitute takes care to operate in such a way that those citizens who might make a report

239. President's Commission of Law Enforcement and Administration of Justice, The Challenge of Crime in a Free Society 189 (1967).
240. President's Commission on Crime in the District of Columbia, Report 133 (1966).
241. Put Your Clothes Back on Honey, You're Under Arrest, Washingtonian 43 (Aug. 1970).
242. 405 U.S. 156 (1972).
243. Id. at 171.
247. Kadish, The Crisis of Overcriminalization, 374 Annals 157, 162 (1967).

to the police will not observe the conduct which constitutes the prostitution offense. As a consequence, to convict a prostitute, a police officer must pose as a man to be solicited. . . .

. . .

In all cases, the prostitute tries to avoid offending the average member of the community. Even the streetwalker limits her activity to geographic areas and times of night that are apt to produce customers. Furthermore, the actual solicitation is difficult to detect because it is often an innocent-looking, inobtrusive, quiet conversation.[248] . . .

Even assuming that there are some instances where individuals are annoyed by advances in public by either a female or a male,[251] there are statutes already in existence to adequately deal with this problem.[252] In fact, the private citizen does not even complain about prostitution and solicitation. The complaining witness in the cases is most probably a police officer and not the private citizen.[253]

Prostitution, both in the preliminary solicitation and negotiations and in the act itself, is overwhelmingly a private, consensual affair between individuals who wish to make their own decisions as to how to control their sexual lives and use their bodies.[254] It seems highly incongruous that a woman is being given the right to undergo an abortion (where the health, safety, and life of the mother as well as the fetus is at stake) because courts are finding the states to be without a compelling interest to prohibit abortion while at the same time repressive legislation permits the arrest, prosecution, and incarceration of a female either because of her status as a prostitute, or her verbal communication of that fact to another consenting individual. . . .

The decisions in the abortion cases, Doe v. Bolton, 410 U.S. 179, 93 S. Ct. 739, 35 L. Ed. 2d 201 (1973), and Roe v. Wade, 410 U.S. 113, S. Ct. 705, 35 L. Ed. 2d 147 (1973), further strengthen the privacy argument. The Court held that the "right of privacy, whether it be founded in the Fourteenth Amendment's concept of personal liberty and restrictions upon state action, as we feel it is, or, as the District Court determined, in the Ninth Amendment's reservation of rights to the people, is broad enough to encompass a woman's decision whether or not to terminate her pregnancy." Roe v. Wade, 410 U.S. at 153. In concurring, Justice Douglas dealt with the content of the right to privacy, finding that anti-abortion statutes invaded the right to privacy because "childbirth may deprive a woman of her preferred life style and force upon her a radically different and undesired future." 410 U.S. 209, 214 (Douglas, J., concurring). Such statements of the right to privacy would surely encompass the right of the woman to control the use and function of her body, even to prostitute it, if that is her decision.

---

248. L .Tiffany, D. McIntyre & D. Rotenberg, Detection of Crime 214-15 (1967).

251. What about the other side of the coin? Women are likely to find themselves harassed by catcalls, off-color remarks, solicitations, whistles, and other offensive behavior from "respectable" men. While some women may view the attention as complimentary rather than degrading, it is not uncommon for a woman to be annoyed, uncomfortable, and even outraged by this "invasion of privacy." When a woman engages in similar conduct, she may be arrested for solicitation or loitering for the purposes of prostitution.

252. See, e.g., D.C. Code Ann. §22-1121 (1967) (makes unlawful the provocation of a breach of peace by acting in such a manner as to annoy, disturb, interfere with, obstruct, or be offensive to others).

253. In the District of Columbia, the complaining witness in the cases brought under D.C. Code Ann. §22-2701 (1967) is always a police officer.

254. In 1957 a report was issued by the Wolfenden Committee in England, considering the extent to which homosexual behavior and female prostitution should come under the condemnation of the criminal law. The Report of the Committee on Homosexual Offences and Prostitution, at 79, stated: "Prostitution in itself is not, in this country, an offense against the criminal law. Some of the activities of prostitutes are, and so are the activities of some others who are concerned in the activities of prostitutes. But it is not illegal for a woman to 'offer her body to indiscriminate lewdness for hire,' provided that she does not, in the course of doing so, commit any one of the specified acts which would bring her within the ambit of the law. Nor, it seems to us, can any case be sustained for attempting to make prostitution in itself illegal. . . ."

(1) United States v. Moses

In United States v. Moses, Cr. No. 17778-72 (D.C. Super. Ct. 1972), 41 U.S.L.W. 2298, 12 Cr. L. Rptr. 2198, five women (represented by the authors of the article quoted above, who were then at Georgetown Law School practicing under a student practice rule) were charged with violations of a statute proscribing solicitation for prostitution. The defendants contended that the statute enjoining invitation, persuasion, or enticement to prostitution or other lewd or immoral conduct, constituted an infringement of their rights of privacy, free speech, and equal protection of the laws. These arguments were upheld in an opinion which concluded, first, that the verbal conduct involved in soliciting for prostitution was protected by the First Amendment. The court then indicated that, "if the statute prohibited an evil which Congress had a right to prevent," First Amendment rights might have to give way, but that "the statutory proscription against fornication, sodomy and adultery engaged in by consenting adults is an unconstitutional invasion of the right to privacy. . . ." The court held that the right to privacy encompassed "the constitutional right of the individual to control the use and function of his or her own body" and could not be encroached upon to prevent conduct that was itself uninjurious to the public:

> The only injury which actually is traceable to consensual acts of prostitution between adults is the sense of indignation spawned in certain other persons . . . [a] harm . . . not of an order cognizable by the law.

In addition to finding that the anti-solicitation statute infringed the defendants' rights of privacy and expression, the court also discussed unequal protection of the laws. Because the statute was utilized predominantly to prosecute females, despite the use of the term "person" in its language, District of Columbia Superior Court Judge Charles Halleck decided that

> . . . no reason has been advanced, and none may be found, to distinguish between the female who engages in such transactions with men, and the other possible combinations of participants who make analogous arrangements.

The court termed the factor of sex in the law's enforcement "arbitrary and unrelated," and it concluded that sex-biased application of the statute served no compelling state interest.

In United States v. Wilson, Judge Norman, of the same court, dismissed the prosecutions against women under the facially sex-neutral District of Columbia prostitution statute, holding:[24]

> The evidence adduced at the hearing demonstrates beyond any doubt that the quoted portion of Sec. 22-2701 is enforced exclusively against females. . . .
> Lt. Hersey testified unequivocally that it is neither the policy nor the practice of his agency to make any effort to arrest male persons who are on the streets looking for females with whom they can engage in sexual acts at a price. Although his office does presently employ two female undercover officers, they are used exclusively either as back-up officers or in connection with the enforcement of the so-called "pimp" statute. Female undercover agents are not used for the purpose of ferreting out those males who are on the streets seeking to engage in sex with females for a price. No female non-police officer informants are used for such purposes. When police officers are investigating suspected bawdy houses, and they observe males and females together going in and coming out of such houses, the police officers identify and interview the females but do not seek to identify or interview the males. In searches of

24. 15 Cr. L. Rptr. 2001 (D.C. Super. Ct. March 14, 1974).

the houses or apartments of so-called "call girls," or of suspected bawdy houses, the police have seized lists of male customers; yet they have made no effort to pursue those leads to determine whether any or all of these male customers may have violated Sec. 22-2701.

Lt. Hersey also testified that in calendar year 1973, the Metropolitan Police Department made 550 arrests under the provision of Sec. 22-2701 now before the Court. He testified that all 550 persons arrested were females; none were males. He testified further that in each of these 550 instances the complaining witness — that is, the person who was allegedly solicited — was a male police officer who was put on the street for that purpose. . . .

This case represents a classic example of our historic double standard under which one set of standards is applied to females and another set of standards to males. Under police policy, what warrants criminal prosecution for a female does not warrant criminal prosecution for a male. The Constitution does not condone this result. . . .

The government in this case has fallen far short of providing a reasonable justification for the discrimination. Its primary contention is that if female undercover agents were to be used in enforcing the statute against male offenders, there would be a danger of entrapment. This contention borders on the absurd. If the police department has trained male undercover agents in the art of capturing female offenders without entrapping them, no reason has been advanced nor does any come to mind why the same art cannot be taught to females. The suggestion that the mere placing of an attractive female on the street constitutes an entrapment of males must be rejected.

Moses and *Wilson* are unique in the far reach of their holdings, and are under appeal by the government.

(2) Laws Against Consensual Sodomy

Right to privacy arguments similar to those outlined above are being used by homosexual men who are bringing increasing pressure on courts and legislatures to repeal laws criminalizing consensual private sexual activity between adults. Eight states have removed from their books laws concerning consensual sodomy,[25] and the revision is recommended by the Model Penal Code.[26] Although sodomy statutes apply to both homosexual and heterosexual behavior, they are most often applied against homosexuals. The existence of such laws results in employment and other discrimination against those who identify themselves as homosexuals because there is an assumption that they must be violating the law.[27]

Organizations composed mainly of homosexual men have actively lobbied for repeal of sodomy statutes. At the annual meeting of the American Bar Association in 1973, the following resolution was adopted by both the Assembly and the House of Delegates:[28]

25. Colorado, Connecticut, Delaware, Hawaii, Illinois, North Dakota, Ohio, and Oregon are the states.

26. American Law Institute, Model Penal Code §207, Comment 227-78 (Tent. Draft No. 4, 1955). The Code also urges repeal of laws against adultery and fornication, and, of course, the arguments are the same.

27. See Matter of Kimball, 399 N.Y.S.2d 302, 40 App. Div. 2d 252 (2d Dept. 1973), a case in which an acknowledged homosexual applied for admission to the Bar. The court stated: "Accordingly, so long as this statute is in effect (Penal Law §130.38), homosexuality, which, in its fulfillment, usually entails commission of such a statutorily prescribed act, is a factor which could militate against the eligibility of an applicant for admission to the Bar who proposes to pursue this way of life in disregard of the statute." 40 App. Div. 2d at 257. See the discussion of discrimination against homosexuals in Report of the Commission on Sex and Law and the Committee on Civil Rights of the Association of the Bar of the City of New York, Intro. 475, 28 Record of the Association of the Bar of the City of New York 148 (1973). See also, Government Created Employment Disabilities and the Homosexual, 82 Harv. L. Rev. 1738 (1969); The Consenting Adult Homosexual and the Law: An Empirical Study of Enforcement and Administration in Los Angeles County, 13 U.C.L.A.L. Rev. 643 (1969).

28. House of Delegates proceedings, Annual Meeting, 59 A.B.A.J. 1131 (1973).

Be it resolved, that the legislatures of the several states are urged to repeal all laws which classify as criminal conduct any form of non-commercial sexual conduct between consenting adults in private, saving only those portions which protect minors or public decorum.

The wording of this resolution reflects the effort to distinguish the arguments for repeal of sodomy statutes from those for decriminalization of prostitution, thus the reference to public decorum and noncommercial activities. Yet the arguments about the difficulty of enforcement and the primacy of the right to privacy are indistinguishable from those made for decriminalization of prostitution. Do you think the success of homosexual men in attacking laws which are discriminatorily enforced against them will necessarily or possibly have an effect on prostitution laws?

c. Other Arguments

Statutes prescribing punishment for prostitution are often vulnerable to attack on grounds of vagueness or overbreadth. See, e.g., Ricks v. United States, 228 A.2d 316, 414 F.2d 1097 (1968); Detroit v. Bowden, 6 Mich. App. 514, 149 N.W.2d 771 (1967); People v. Williams, 55 Misc. 2d 774, 286 N.Y.S.2d 575 (1967) (holding as to an antiloitering statute that it was "the judgment of the officer and not the activity of the defendant [which] constitutes the crime").

A statute which prohibits prostitution per se arguably punishes a status or condition, rather than criminal acts. See, e.g., the statute as interpreted in State v. Perry, supra Section B-2, which punished "common prostitutes." The principle that the law cannot validly punish a person for a status has been invoked in relation to the Eighth and Fourteenth Amendments. Robinson v. California, 370 U.S. 660, 82 S. Ct. 1417, 8 L. Ed. 2d 758 (1962), held that a statute which punished narcotics addicts for that condition amounted to prohibitions of a status, and that this was cruel and unusual punishment. Lambert v. California, 355 U.S. 225, 78 S. Ct. 240, 2 L. Ed. 2d 228 (1957), held that a municipal ordinance requiring ex-felons to register was unconstitutional because it failed to give notice to ex-felons and because it did not punish any specific criminal act in violation of due process of law.

The broadest interpretation of Robinson, which could be urged in a prostitution case, was outlined by Rosenbleet and Parriente, as follows:[29]

> . . . One starts from the position that the concept of cruel and unusual punishment is not static, and that prohibitions must conform to modern concepts of what society accepts as cruelty and what is unusual at the present time.[42] Today there are several approaches to evaluating a particular punishment.[43] One approach considers whether the punishment is disproportionate to the offense.[44] A second weighs the severity or harshness of the sanction against the "broad and idealistic concepts of dignity, civilized standards, humanity, and decency."[45] And a third approach relates to equal protection arguments, so that "a penalty . . . should be considered 'unusually' imposed [in an eighth amendment sense] if it is

29. Rosenbleet and Parriente, supra Section D-8-b, at 379-380.

42. Trop v. Dulles, 356 U.S. 86, 100 (1958). See also Furman v. Georgia, 408 U.S. 238 (1972); Weems v. United States, 217 U.S. 349 (1910); United States v. Dickerson, 337 F.2d 343 (6th Cir. 1964); Rhem v. McGrath, 326 F. Supp. 681 (S.D.N.Y. 1971).

43. The first two approaches are discussed generally in Wheeler, Toward a Theory of Limited Punishment: An Examination of the Eighth Amendment, 24 Stan. L. Rev. 838 (1972).

44. See, e.g., Robinson v. California, 370 U.S. 660 (1962); Weems v. United States, 217 U.S. 349 (1910); Lollis v. New York State Dep't of Social Services, 322 F. Supp. 473 (S.D.N.Y. 1970); Jordon v. Fitzharris, 257 F. Supp. 674 (N.D. Cal. 1966).

45. Jackson v. Bishop, 404 F.2d 571, 579 (8th Cir. 1968) (Blackmun, J.). See also Trop v. Dulles, 356 U.S. 86, 100-01 (1958); Weems v. United States, 217 U.S. 349 (1910); Lee v. Tahash, 352 F.2d 970, 972 (8th Cir. 1965); People v. Lorentzen, 387 Mich. 167, 194 N.W. 2d 828 (1972).

administered arbitrarily or discriminatorily."[47] If courts are to be guided, in determining eighth amendment rights, by "contemporary human knowledge,"[48] and by "public opinion . . . enlightened by a humane justice,"[49] then, regardless of which approach is used, an argument may be made that punishing a female for prostitution by subjecting her to *any* criminal sanction falls within contemporary prohibitions of the eighth amendment. Significantly, soon after the decision in *Robinson,* a commentator remarked:

> "*Robinson v. California* may have established in the eighth amendment a basis for invalidating legislation that is thought inappropriately to invoke the criminal sanction, despite an entire lack of precedent for the idea that a punishment may be deemed cruel not because of its mode or even its proportion but because the conduct for which it is imposed should not be subject to the criminal sanction."[50]

Application of the *Lambert* and *Robinson* lines of argument to test the constitutionality of prostitution statutes is, however, complicated by qualifications that have since been placed upon those decisions. In Powell v. Texas, 392 U.S. 514, 88 S. Ct. 2145, 20 L. Ed. 2d 1254 (1968), the Court indicated its unwillingness to protect, under the *Robinson* principle, a chronic alcoholic who was prosecuted for public drunkenness; the Court emphasized that Powell's act of drinking and of being in public distinguished his situation from that of Robinson. *Powell* thus appears to limit the possible application of the "status" defense to arrests of prostitutes that are unaccompanied by charges of specific acts. See also Perkins v. North Carolina, 234 F. Supp. 333 (D.N.C. 1964), in which the court decided that punishment of a male homosexual for an act of fellatio was distinguishable from punishment for status.

IV. WOMEN AND GIRLS UNDER SENTENCE

A. PRISONS FOR WOMEN

1. Introduction

Who are the prisoners?[1]

> . . . Mounting evidence supports the conclusion that the criminal justice system as a whole screens out the middle class offender, while leaving the poor, and often racial minorities to be dealt with by imprisonment.[10] Although statistics are virtually nonexistent to prove or disprove this observation as it relates to women, anyone who has spent time in women's prisons would agree that they are not institutions for the rich. The few statistics that are available support this conclusion. For example, a survey of prisoners at the two federal prisons for women undertaken by the Women's Bureau of the Labor Department revealed that "[m]ost women offenders come from the city ghettos. A disproportionate number are from minority populations. . . . They

47. Goldberg & Dershowitz, Declaring the Death Penalty Unconstitutional, 83 Harv. L. Rev. 1773, 1790 (1970).
 48. Robinson v. California, 370 U.S. 660, 666 (1962).
 49. Weems v. United States, 217 U.S. 349, 378 (1910).
 50. Packer, Making the Punishment Fit the Crime, 77 Harv. L. Rev. 1971 (1964).
 1. Singer, Women and the Correctional Process, 11 Am. Crim. L. Rev. 295, 297 (1973).
 10. See generally R. Goldfarb & L. Singer, After Conviction, Chapter 8 (. . . 1973).

are poor — very poor."[11] A recent study of the District of Columbia Women's Detention Center concluded that "the criminal justice system of the District appears to penalize black female offenders with disproportionate severity. At every stage in the criminal justice process, black women are retained in the system at higher rates than white women. Thus, although the female population of the district aged 18 and over is only 63% black, first bookings into the Women's Detention Center are 73% black, returns to WDC from initial court hearings are 83% black, cases sentenced for 30 days or more are 92% black, and cases sentenced for 3 months or longer are 97% black."[12] Similar findings, although less detailed, emerged from a study of women prisoners in Pennsylvania.[13]

Historically, the overwhelming majority of women in prison have been convicted of prostitution, narcotics, or theft offenses (with many of the theft offenses drug-related). Recent arrest statistics indicate that the pattern of female crime may be changing. The 1972 Uniform Crime Reports showed that there was a 219 percent increase in arrests of women for major crimes from 1960 to 1971, while for men the increase was 83 percent. For robbery the increase of arrests of women was 227 percent.

Of the approximately 16,000 adult women incarcerated on any one day in the United States, about 800 are inmates of the two federal reformatories for women. Six thousand are in state institutions, and roughly 8000 are held in the more than 3500 local jails scattered throughout the country. Women serving sentences in state institutions are housed in separate institutions in twenty-eight jurisdictions, including Puerto Rico and the District of Columbia. Twenty-four state facilities for women are under the control of the wardens of male prisons in other states.[2]

2. Conditions in Women's Prisons

Conditions in women's prisons have not been widely studied. However, the following excerpts from a complaint reveal the inmates' views about their circumstances.

COMPLAINT, GARNES v. TAYLOR
Civil Action No. 159-72 (D.C. Dist. Ct. 1972)

COMPLAINT FOR PERMANENT INJUNCTION, DECLARATORY JUDGMENT, AND OTHER RELIEF

II

The Parties

3. Plaintiffs Lana Phoebe Garnes, Queenie E. Harper, Jeannette Nickens, Annabelle Armedes Callen and Deborah H. Williams are citizens of the United States. Each is presently incarcerated in the Women's Detention Center.

(a) Lana Phoebe Garnes has been incarcerated since January 7, 1972, because she does not have money enough to post a $1,000 bond. Queenie E. Harper has been incarcerated since January 10, 1972, because she does not have 10 percent of $500 to post as a condition of her release on personal recognizance. They are each charged with a criminal offense but have not been convicted by a court or jury. They are being held in a penal institution because they are financially unable to meet the monetary terms of release set for them.

11. Statement of Elizabeth Koontz, Director, Women's Bureau, U.S. Department of Labor, Before the D.C. Commission on the Status of Women, Nov. 4, 1971.

12. Barros, Slavin, McArthur & Adams, Movement and Characteristics of Women's Detention Center Admissions, Research Rep. No. 39, ii (1971).

13. American Association of University Women, Report on the Survey of 41 Pennsylvania County Court and Correctional Services for Women and Girl Offenders (1969).

2. Figures were provided by the U.S. Department of Labor, Women's Bureau, Washington, D.C.

(b) Jeannette Nickens is serving a sentence of one year after pleading guilty in September 1971 to a misdemeanor of false pretenses, 22 D.C. Code §1301.

(c) Annabelle Armedes Callen was sentenced to ninety days for soliciting for lewd and immoral purposes, 22 D.C. Code §2701, in January 1972.

(d) Deborah Williams was sentenced under the Federal Youth Corrections Act, 18 U.S.C. §5010, in March 1971 but instead of being transferred to a Youth Corrections Act facility, she has been confined in the Women's Detention Center serving her sentence. . . .

III

Statement of the Claim

11. Upon information and belief, the building at 1010 North Capitol Street which houses the Women's Detention Center was not designed for, and is not suitable for, a residential facility. The building became a jail for women after originally being used by the Metropolitan Police Department as a temporary holding facility for women. Located on a busy and noisy street, the building has extremely limited space for recreation, meetings, classes or visiting, and a small courtyard provides the only outdoor recreational facility available to plaintiffs. Upon information and belief, the building is infested with roaches, living conditions are generally unhygienic, and the lighting is dim and inadequate.

12. Upon information and belief, the Women's Detention Center was constructed to house at full capacity fifty (50) women. During December 1971, the last full month for which statistics are available, the average daily population was 118.

13. Upon information and belief, the crowded conditions in the Women's Detention Center have resulted in the housing together, in the same cell-rooms and dormitories, of convicted women and women awaiting trial, of sick and healthy women and of lesbians and heterosexuals.

14. Upon information and belief, there is at the Women's Detention Center inadequate and limited counseling or treatment programs for narcotics addicts and alcoholics although over sixty percent of the inmates in 1970, the last full year for which statistics are available, had histories of drug use or alcoholism.

15. Upon information and belief, there is at the Women's Detention Center inadequate access to a medical doctor, prenatal or other regular care.

16. Upon information and belief, the only vocational training or job counseling available at the Women's Detention Center consists of a "self-teaching" typing program, a weekly lesson in cooking economically, a weekly sewing class, and Project New Hope, instituted in December 1971, in which nine women were enrolled as of January 21. All of the programs are available only to a limited number of women.

17. Upon information and belief, women accused of misconduct are confined in "control cells" or the "hole", which are often cold, inadequately furnished and dirty. When so confined, women are not allowed regular baths, recreation, reading material, vocational training, visits or telephone calls.

18. Upon information and belief, no written rules inform inmates of the type of conduct which will result in confinement as described in paragraph 17.

19. By terms of a consent order entered in Campbell v. Rodgers, Civil Action No. 1462-71, United States District Court for the District of Columbia, men confined in the District of Columbia Jail cannot be placed in treatment segregation cells unless the safety of one or more persons is threatened.

20. Upon information and belief, women are subjected to confinement in "control cells" without a disciplinary hearing before an impartial official with prior due process procedural safeguards, that is, without adequate notice of charges, representation by counsel or other spokesperson, confrontation of her accusers, right to cross-examine, and written records of a hearing decision, reasons therefor and evidence relied upon.

21. By terms of a consent order entered in Campbell v. Rodgers, supra paragraph 19, men confined in the District of Columbia Jail are accorded an administrative hearing within twenty-four hours from the beginning of confinement in treatment segregation cells. At the hearing, they are entitled to representation and the representative is furnished in advance of the hearing with a brief description of the events which led to confinement in the segregation cells.

22. Upon information and belief, the library has no current books or magazines and only a few out-of-date legal materials.

23. Official regulations concerning inmates' mail state that all outgoing and incoming letters are subject to censorship, including letters to and from attorneys, and that inmates may not discuss institutional affairs nor mention the name of any member of the personnel, except that of the Superintendent in their letters or communications.

The regulations further state that all letters to members of Congress, the Corporation Counsel, Commissioner, or other Government officials shall be referred to the Classification and Parole Office as Special Purpose Letters, implying that such letters will be individually considered and subject to additional delay and censorship. (Women's Detention Center, "Inmate Information Bulletins", February 1971.)

24. Regulations of the Women's Detention Center state that requests for books, educational material, and the like, should be forwarded to the Educational Specialist for approval, and that books or educational material will not be received through the mail or accepted from anyone without prior approval. (Women's Detention Center, "Inmates Information Bulletins", February 1971)

25. Official regulations pertaining to social visits to inmates at the Women's Detention Center state that inmates are permitted two one-hour visits per week, and that social visits are restricted to those persons on an approved visiting list. (Women's Detention Center, "Inmate Information Bulletins", February 1971)

26. Defendants acting together, by their intentional acts and omissions, under the color of law, are violating 42 U.S.C. §§1983 and 1985 in that plaintiffs are thereby subjected to a deprivation of Fifth and Fourteenth Amendment rights to due process of law and equal protection of the laws, Eighth Amendment rights to be free from cruel and unusual punishment, Sixth Amendment rights to effective legal assistance, and First, Fourth, Ninth and Fourteenth Amendment rights to privacy in the following manner:

(a) Each plaintiff is confined in a cell-room or dormitory which is overcrowded and violates minimal architectural standards as well as standards established by the American Correctional Association for correctional institutions.

(b) The health and safety of each plaintiff is threatened by the lack of adequate medical care.

(c) The absence of adequate vocational, educational and recreational programs results in incarceration without rehabilitation. The fact that the only programs which do exist, i.e., limited access to typing exercises, sewing and cooking, are sex-tracked, providing training only in areas traditionally defined as a woman's job, discriminates against plaintiffs because they are women.

(d) The overcrowding, which causes the mingling of convicted and unconvicted women, lesbians and heterosexuals, the limited access to the community, as well as other conditions of confinement combine to create severe psychological pressure in all plaintiffs.

(e) Each plaintiff is subject to disciplinary confinement in the Control Cells of the Women's Detention Center without adequate notice, hearing rights and representation.

(f) Each woman is subject to confinement in the Control and Adjustment Cells without the benefits of notice and representation accorded men similarly situated at the District of Columbia Jail.

(g) The censorship of her incoming and outgoing mail, including legal correspondence, violates each plaintiff's constitutional rights to free expression, privacy and effective assistance of counsel.

(h) Each plaintiff is denied adequate contact with her children and family as well as with the general community by the censorship of reading material, the limitations on visits, and the lack of access to telephone, newspapers, and other means of communication.

(i) The incarceration of plaintiffs Garnes and Harper, who have not been convicted, violates their rights under the First, Fifth and Eighth Amendments to the United States Constitution in that they are suffering the same severe, punitive and restrictive conditions constituting punishment to which convicted persons are subject, notwithstanding that they are presumed innocent, and that there is no basis for punishing them at all.

(j) The incarceration of plaintiff Williams, who is serving a sentence under the Federal Youth Corrections Act (18 U.S.C. §5010), violates her constitutional rights under the Fifth, Eighth and Fourteenth Amendments and her statutory rights under the Federal Youth Corrections Act (18 U.S.C. §5005 et seq.) in that she is suffering non-rehabilitative, punitive and restrictive confinement, instead of the special rehabilitative treatment intended by the Federal Youth Corrections Act.

(k) The incarceration of plaintiff Callen, who has been convicted of prostitution, violates her constitutional rights under the First, Fourth, Eighth, Ninth and Fourteenth Amendments in that she is imprisoned under the most restrictive conditions of confinement, i.e., twenty-four hour surveillance and deprivation of liberty, for acts which are non-criminal, or which if committed by men would result in less onerous sentences.

27. Defendants, each within the scope of his or her authority and under color of law, and as a matter of custom and practice, enforced and administered the practices and policies constituting the violations alleged in paragraph 26.

28. There is an actual and continuing controversy requiring a declaration of the rights of the named plaintiffs and the members of the class and sub-classes which they represent. There is no adequate remedy at law.

29. The existence and continuation of the unconstitutional practices, policies, acts and omissions alleged herein have subjected and will continue to subject the class to irreparable suffering and injury unless defendants, and each of them, are enjoined by this Court from continuing such practices, policies, acts and omissions and are required to perform their respective duties according to law.

IV

Prayer For Relief

Wherefore, plaintiffs, on behalf of themselves and all other prisoners at the Women's Detention Center who are similarly situated, pray:

1. That the Court allow this case to proceed under Rule 23, Federal Rules of Civil Procedure as a class action on behalf of all women incarcerated at the Women's Detention Center, with sub-classes of:

(a) women who have not been convicted of any offense;

(b) women serving sentences on offenses other than prostitution;

(c) women serving sentences for prostitution; and

(d) women serving Federal Youth Corrections Act sentences.

2. That all members of the class be notified by defendants of the pendency of this action by posting one copy of the complaint in a conspicuous place in each section of the Center and that several attorneys and their assistants designated by plaintiffs' attorneys and several attorneys designated by defendants' attorneys be permitted to move through the Women's Detention Center so as to answer questions by members of the class.

3. That the Court order defendants to permit corrections experts designated by plaintiffs to inspect the Women's Detention Center and all of its facilities and to report to all parties and the Court on the results of their inspection.

4. That the Court declare that by the individual and collective effect of their acts, practices and omissions, the defendants:

(a) are subjecting plaintiffs and the class they represent to punishment without due process of law and to cruel and unusual punishment within the meaning of the Fifth, Eighth and Fourteenth Amendments of the United States Constitution;

(b) are subjecting plaintiffs and the class they represent to summary discipline without due process of law in violation of the Fifth, Sixth and Fourteenth Amendments;

(c) are depriving plaintiffs and their class of the equal protection of the laws to which they are entitled under the Fifth and Fourteenth Amendments;

(d) are depriving plaintiffs and their class of their rights to effective assistance of counsel, in violation of the Sixth and Fourteenth Amendments; and

(e) are subjecting plaintiffs and their class to an invasion of their right to privacy as guaranteed by the First, Fourth, Fifth, Ninth and Fourteenth Amendments.

6. That the Court order that, within sixty days, defendants submit to the Court a plan for assuring that plaintiffs and the class they represent are confined under conditions which, as to the sub-class of pretrial detainees, will accord them all of the rights and privileges of the innocent, and as to sub-classes of convicted women will accord them equal protection of the laws, protection from cruel and unusual punishment and protection from invasion of their privacy. More specifically, the plaintiffs and the class they represent should be assured by the plan:

(a) That the isolated, twenty-four hour controlled, traditional "jail" which is the Women's Detention Center will be abolished as the primary facility for women and that instead plans will be made for centers to meet the particular needs of women offenders. Such centers would involve small-group living in a normal community setting, with conscious efforts made to involve the women prisoners with the community. Specifics as to how such a plan would be implemented and the budgetary considerations should be part of the plan submitted to the Court.

(b) That if the Women's Detention Center is to be retained at all, the cells and dormitories be kept in safe and sanitary conditions, and that each cell ward and dormitory contain no more prisoners than the designed capacity of the particular location.

(c) That programs designed for narcotics addict treatment, treatment of alcoholics, rehabilitation of short-term offenders and consideration of the special problems of those accused of and convicted of prostitution offenses, be submitted as part of the plan.

(d) That prisoners be accorded essential preventive medical practices and receive adequate and sound medical, dental and mental health care.

(e) That increased library facilities, including current legal materials, be made part of the plan.

(f) That visiting conditions be established which ensure decency, comfort, privacy of conversations, conjugal rights and that no limitations be placed on persons a woman may see, communicate with, and receive communication from.

(g) That no censorship be exercised on incoming or outgoing mail, newspapers, books and periodicals; that the only control on incoming mail be for inspection of contraband such as drugs or weapons; that adequate phones be installed and the prisoners have access to them in order to make local outgoing calls without charge.

(h) That a code of intra-center behavior providing for inmate rights be promulgated and provided to every prisoner upon entry into the Center.

(i) That no discipline be effected without first affording the woman notice, a hearing, the assistance of counsel, the confrontation of accusers, the right to cross-examine, written records of a hearing decision, reasons therefor and evidence relied upon, and a hearing before an impartial official.

7. That upon a finding that the plan will eliminate the constitutional violations outlined in this complaint, the Court will order the implementation of the plan.

8. That the Court appoint as an impartial advisor a recognized expert in the field of corrections to evaluate the plans submitted pursuant to paragraph 6 and to report to the Court about the suitability of the plans and their efficacy to eliminate the constitutional violations described in the complaint.

9. That the Court enter its order permanently directing defendants to allocate funds and to take such further steps as may be necessary and appropriate within their powers for the implementation of the provisions contained in paragraph 6 above.

10. That if a satisfactory plan cannot be submitted and implemented, the defendants be enjoined and restrained from incarcerating or detaining any and all of the plaintiffs and members of the class they represent in the Women's Detention Center and further enjoined from transferring plaintiffs and their class to an alternative facility unless defendants can provide evidence satisfactory to the Court that the alternative does not suffer from the conditions herein complained of and that it is accessible to visitors and counsel.

11. That the Court retain jurisdiction over defendants until such time as the Court is satisfied that the practices, policies, acts and omissions alleged herein no longer exist and will not recur.

NOTES

1. As a tactical matter, do you think it was wise to seek the total elimination of the institution? As counsel for the women in prison, what evidence and testimony would you use to substantiate the complaint?

2. It is generally thought that women's prisons are more humane and less security-conscious than men's institutions. The idea that the institutions are basically different in nature received judicial sanction in Wark v. Robbins, 458 F.2d 1295 (1st Cir. 1972), state ct. op., *sub nom.* Wark v. State, 266 A.2d 62 (Me. 1970), *cert. denied,* 400 U.S. 952 (1970), which upheld a more severe sentence for escape from a men's institution. On appeal from a denial of federal habeas corpus, the court found that "on this record we think it likely that one venturing escape from the State Prison, with the attendant risks of violence and danger to inmates, prison personnel and the outside community is not similarly circumstanced to one venturing escape from the Women's Reformatory."[3] The court quotes the district court, which held that "a classification based not merely upon the distinctive attributes of the sexes, but more importantly upon the character of the institution from which the prisoner escapes, is neither arbitrary nor unreasonable, and in no way a denial of Equal Protection."[4]

The basis for the First Circuit's conclusion was an earlier opinion in the same case from the Maine Supreme Court. On appeal from denial of postconviction relief, that court had held that the legislature could "on the basis of long experience" conclude that even women sentenced for serious offenses could be "effectively confined in an institution which lacks the high walls, armed guards and security precautions of a prison." The Maine court continued:[5]

> By the same token the Legislature could reasonably conclude that the greater physical strength, aggressiveness and disposition toward violent action so frequently displayed by a male prisoner bent on escape from a maximum security institution presents a far greater risk of harm to prison guards and personnel and to the public than is the case when escape is undertaken by a woman confined in an institution designed primarily for reform and rehabilitation. Viewing statutory provisions for punishment as in part a deterrent to criminal conduct, the Legislature could logically and reasonably conclude that a more severe penalty should be imposed upon a male prisoner escaping from the State Prison than upon a woman confined at the "Reformatory" while serving a State Prison sentence who escapes from that institution.

3. Id. at 1296.
4. Ibid. See also Johnson and Knapp, Sex Discrimination By Law: A Study in Judicial Perspective, 46 N.Y.U.L. Rev. 675, 729-730 (1971).
5. Wark v. State, 266 A.2d 62, 65 (Me. 1970), *cert. denied,* 400 U.S. 952 (1970).

B. Prisons for Girls

The ideal of rehabilitation and treatment has failed as much in juvenile institutions as elsewhere. A provocative study of the juvenile detention system in Connecticut suggests that the most egregious failures may well have been in institutions for girls.

ROGERS, "FOR HER OWN PROTECTION . . .":
CONDITIONS OF INCARCERATION FOR FEMALE
OFFENDERS IN THE STATE OF CONNECTICUT
7 J. Law and Society Ass'n 223, 230-239 (1972)

Connecticut presents a perfect case study of differential correctional treatment for young male and female offenders. The state controls two juvenile correctional institutions: the Long Lane School (LLS) in Middletown for girls and the Connecticut School for Boys (CSB) in Meriden. Both facilities have existed practically side-by-side for over a century under state management, yet they have evolved in markedly different ways. The boys' school has been in the throes of constant turmoil and consequently under severe public scrutiny throughout most of its operation. The administrators of the "farm for girls," on the other hand, have run a very tight ship and take pride in their undisrupted tradition. As a result, the Connecticut School for Boys has bungled its way (albeit ineptly) into the twentieth century while the Long Lane School still prepares women to re-enter the community as nineteenth century domestics.

A legacy of stereotypic "old maid" administrators and a "female-only" staff policy at Long Lane until 1971 has compounded the institutional inbreeding. In a recent report issued by the superintendent describing the development of the school, Long Lane was cited as providing "for girls in need of protection, education and training." . . .

. . . [I]n a brochure boasting of the institution's treatment orientation, the former superintendent writes:

> — pre-vocational training with special emphasis on homemaking since the girls will eventually be homemakers, religious training, extra-curricular activities through Girl Scouts, Tri-Hi-Y, Garden Club, 4-H Club, Acrobatics Club, etc., all continue to give youngsters an opportunity to taste success and raise their usually low self-esteem.

The following study is based on a year's experience (from June, 1970 to May, 1971) in the Connecticut Department of Children and Youth Services as Special Assistant in the Commissioner's office; interviews with judges and other officials of the "Juvenile Justice System"; juvenile court and departmental records and other relevant official documents, and discussions with myriads of the state's "wayward girls." . . .

COTTAGE LIFE ENVIRONMENT

The appearance of the Long Lane School in Middletown is much like a nineteenth century girls' finishing school. A low hedge surrounds the "campus" and the grounds are well landscaped with manicured flower beds and low shrubbery. Planting and grazing fields surround most of the farm which lies on the outskirts of Wesleyan University campus. Several small brick "cottages" are used as residential buildings which have a homey enough atmosphere until one notes the bars on the windows. . . .

Cottages are staffed by housemothers (usually elderly) who live in a small suite on the main floor on a five days on, five days off shift. There are no male cottage personnel at Long Lane, the official reason being that the girls would be embarrassed to cross the hallways to the bathrooms if they were not fully clothed. At Meriden, cottage "parents" staff all living units full time, so that the boys are able to relate to both male and female adult figures. Several studies have shown that many girls' delinquency problems stem from poor rapport with their fathers (Johnson and Szurek, 1952; Michlin, 1970). Yet at Long Lane they are expected to resolve these difficulties in an all-female living situation.

Girls are assigned to small individual rooms furnished with a bed and a bureau which they may decorate within limits. When girls are in the rooms, the doors are closed and "belled." (A main signal board downstairs will sound a bell for any room when the door is opened.)

As opposed to the boys' school where the residents' biggest complaint is "no privacy" because of their large dormitory arrangements, at Long Lane the girls spend extraordinary amounts of time locked in these rather cramped quarters. Because of the shift arrangement for staff working hours at the girls' school, all girls must be in their rooms for 8:30 P.M. bedtime. . . . Since the boys' school has round-the-clock coverage, boys at Meriden are allowed to stay up later and watch television or participate in recreational activities until eleven o'clock or so.

Since the cottage staff at Long Lane is not officially on duty from 8:30 P.M. to 6:00 A.M., girls are "belled in," given a bottle to urinate in, and expected not to bother the staff again until early morning wake-up. Girls are then lined up in the doorways and "excused" to go to the bathroom, one at a time, under close supervision, supposedly to cut down on "chicking" behavior (an undeveloped form of adolescent homosexual activity). The girls resent this whole procedure and find it degrading. The American Correctional Association Consultants' study, done at the request of Commissioner Wayne R. Mucci almost a year ago, recommended that "girls should have complete privacy in the use of the bathroom area." (American Correctional Association, 1970: 25).

The cottages at Long Lane also contain two isolation rooms, which are solitary confinement cells, usually poorly heated and barren. A housemother was once reprimanded for giving a *staff* mattress pad to a girl for warmth, when she noticed her shivering during isolation during the winter. The ACA report remarks that these rooms are "inappropriate to have in the cottage setting," and cited them as "extremely disruptive and threatening to the other girls" (American Correctional Association, 1970: 34). No such rooms exist at CSB within the cottages.

Other discrepancies in daily living regulations include restrictions on: home newspapers (girls not allowed to receive any "upsetting" literature); mail (girls' mail is closely guarded both in terms of approved addresses and contents, to be written twice a week to "parents or approved relatives" — the boys have no such restrictions); smoking (due to the lack of a "sprinkler system at Long Lane to safeguard against fires," girls are forbidden to smoke, but staff can and are given careful instructions about flushing their butts "so as not to tempt the girls who clean up," and of course boys can at Meriden and are even encouraged to smoke to relieve their tensions); gum chewing is prohibited for girls at Long Lane.

Girls at Long Lane quickly lose interest in their appearances, which they blame on the absence of men, the institutional laundry and clothing service (baggy pants and house frocks) and the high starch diet which is prepared in each cottage's kitchen. The food, incidentally, is excellent and was cited by the boys as CSB as the *only* part of the girls' school which they'd like to adopt. . . .

DISCIPLINARY SYSTEM

Discipline plays a prominent role at Long Lane. The girls' school, for instance, has a special category of counselors whose sole responsibility is meting out discipline and counseling the girls about proper behavior. One counselor is assigned to each cottage at Long Lane and runs the weekly house council meetings there. These meetings are the school's answer to the student government concept. They begin by a recitation of the Long Lane pledge and the counselor's calling on a girl to enumerate the Seven Ideals [including self-respect, self-control, loyalty and courtesy].

Disciplinary reports are then read about individual girls in the cottage. Written reports submitted by the cottage staff to the counselors are grounds for loss of "status" at Long Lane. Status is determined by the following stages: (1) "New Girl" for the first month; (2) "Trial Citizen" after one month if no serious disciplinary problems; (3) "Citizen" after two months (if she has been clear of discipline, she then becomes eligible to go on a monthly visit home); (4) "Honor Girl" after one good month on Citizenship Status (then can be elected vice-president of her cottage and go off-grounds for church; (5) "Honorable Mention" after four months if she has been a Citizen and an Honor Girl for one full month each. These girls may get a three-hour pass to go off-grounds once a month and may be elected House President. Finally, there is Loss of Privilege Status where girls may get knocked down to the bottom rung and have to start all over again earning "privileges."

A detailed description of the rules and regulations governing the girls is unnecessary here. Suffice it to say that there are many; that there is considerable latitude for staff to interpret them; that they are often picayune and present an invitation to the girls to violate them. Disciplinary action for these infractions can be "lock," 5:30 bedtime, 7:30 bedtime, loss of privileges (seeing movies, going off-grounds with staff, etc.) or loss of Status. . . . ["Lock"] is carried out in the so-called DP rooms located in the Kimball Infirmary at the School. DP rooms have wire fences for doors and steel cots. They are also used for girls with behavioral problems. Often, if the Connecticut Valley Mental Hospital will not accept a transfer from Long Lane, a girl will have to be forcibly detained in one of these cages. Girls attempting suicide have been handcuffed to the cots. Pregnant girls who "act out" have been similarly restrained. . . .

Discipline at the boys' school is far less harsh, at least structurally. Connecticut School for Boys has been in a state of constant turmoil since the new Department took over, and the institutional staff is generally confused and disjointed—not sure *which* rules to follow or enforce any more. The school was the subject of a brutality investigation conducted by the Hartford office based on complaints by the boys of corporal punishment. Because there is very little supervisory control at CSB, chaos has reigned supreme with staff and boys doing pretty much as they like. There have been incidents of staff striking boys and boys assaulting staff, but it has been said that practically no disciplinary *system* of any kind exists at the boys' school.

Recently, with the help of the Yale Psycho-Educational Clinic, a modified form of "token economy" based on earning points for specific privileges and having them taken away for misbehavior has been instituted in two "experimental" cottages at Meriden. Efforts are now being made to develop a new approach to discipline at CSB which will be uniformly enacted and will be far less repressive than that at Long Lane.

Usually the damage done to the girls is a more covert psychic brutality, with the more aggressive, non-institutionalized individuals being systematically squelched and a passive, obedient girl emerging as the finished product.

TREATMENT

Clinical services at Long Lane are minimal. The social workers handle mostly parole cases and put out the fires of immediate institutional crisis. The counselors handle discipline. There is one full-time psychologist who spends much time administering tests and one part-time psychiatrist who is at the school on Saturday mornings. . . .

The medical services are poor at best. Treatment by an aging doctor and two nurses often consists of aspirin or "a shot to quiet her down." Very little dietary help is available to girls who have weight problems. Sex education is forbidden by law. . . .

. . . If a girl is pregnant upon commitment by the Juvenile Court (several more become pregnant on runaway), she is allowed to remain in a cottage until the seventh month of her pregnancy at which time she must move into the infirmary. Girls are taken to Middlesex Hospital in Middletown for delivery, kept in a ward overnight, then returned to Long Lane for six more weeks to be "medically cleared." Babies are usually given up for adoption.

The prevailing attitude at the school is very much a "pay to the piper" one. Pregnancy is seen as "getting what she deserves" and staff hope that if girls are made to live through one in such a punitive surrounding, then perhaps "it" won't happen again. Consider the comments of the following young unwed mother, who had been committed to Long Lane because she couldn't get along with her step-father, ran away from the school, got pregnant and was returned to "live out her pregnancy," and was finally released two years later to a foster home after turning the mirrors away so that she wouldn't even see the baby in the delivery room.

> I am presently in this "unmentionable" [a twist on the staff's designation of "UM" for unmarried] situation. Maybe if we don't talk about it it will go away. Unfortunately this is not so. People say that motherhood is such a beautiful thing. Don't you believe it. . . .
> Citizenship is an honor. How does an "unmentionable" feel about this? What privileges of Citizenship are retained when she is in this condition? Off campus privileges are denied. Reasons are given. The school is responsible for the girl's health. Some girls feel that the true reason is that people are ashamed of their condition. It is hard to understand this denial of privileges. Each "unmentionable" girl is an individual, and should be treated as such. It would be a tremendous uplift for pregnant girls to enjoy the full benefits of Citizenship.

Abortions are anathema to the staff at Long Lane. Many girls have done serious damage to themselves trying to induce miscarriages. This whole area of treatment for young pregnant women is coming under review by the new Commissioner. Any new policy, however, is subject to political approval.

The American Correctional Association's Consultant Report (1970: 61) decried the "complete lack of a professional approach in the child care program at the Long Lane School." Services provided at the boys' school, however, are not that much better. There are three psychologists and two part-time psychiatrists at the Connecticut School for Boys (when the positions are filled). Theoretically this should allow for much more therapy, both group and individual, than at Long Lane. Nevertheless in the past the clinical staff at CSB has spent more time consulting with other staff and instigating and resolving staff in-fighting than working with the boys. The boys' school also has the supportive services of the Yale Psycho-Educational Clinic, and under their auspices, a new training program is beginning in Meriden for institutional personnel.

EDUCATIONAL AND VOCATIONAL "REHABILITATION"

Compared to CSB, the girls at Long Lane are better off in their academic program, although it still has serious shortcomings. There are girls at Long Lane Cady School (accredited) who have received high school diplomas—something unheard of at the boys' school. Yet the relative effectiveness of the LLS academic program may work an extra hardship on the girls in terms of opportunities to return home. Since the academic program at Meriden is so poor, the staff feels no hesitation in letting boys have extended vacations, trips and early home placements. Girls are often kept at Long Lane, not because of behavioral problems, but "to complete a successful academic program." Very little effort is made to arrange special academic programming in the community for Long Lane girls whose behavior warrants their release. . . .

The most blatant forms of sexual stereotyping are evidenced in vocational programming at each institution. The ACA consultants indicated that "vocational and work assignments at both schools are . . . pretty much of the conventional type." (American Correctional Association, 1970: 48). Their report did not even comment on the obvious discrepancies *between the types* of training and work programs at CSB and Long Lane.

In the section of the report on vocation education, the following trades are listed for the girls: sewing, cooking, cosmotology (grooming), laundry work, home economics, janitorial, storeroom, gardening and horticulture; side-by-side with the boys' list: print shop, woodworking, small engines, auto mechanics, bakery, electronics. A forestry training program is also underway and boys assist carpenters and painters at CSB on local jobs. As usual the boys have a good paper program which falls somewhat short of its potential in practice—the girls don't even have that.

Changing the LLS vocational offerings entails changing the philosophies and expectations of the female staff there. They take pride in their mission to turn out good homemakers. All their reports emphasize this role. In a state progress report under the heading of "Industries or Work Program," Long Lane has simply written "not applicable." The Commissioner's office continually receives memos from LLS describing their "vocational programs" which would be a great source of amusement (at the author's obvious obliviousness) were it not for the young female "trainees" involved:

> Sewing, cooking, waitress training, housekeeping, horticulture and beauty culture are some of the areas offered for training. . . . In depth training is not possible but it is hoped that some experience in one or two of these areas may prove beneficial in selecting an area of vocational interest.

Furthermore, boys are paid for their work at CSB (albeit 15¢/hour), girls are not. It apparently never occurred to anyone to rectify this inequity until the girls starting complaining to the former Commissioner. A request has been submitted to the 1971 Connecticut Legislature to provide funding for this purpose (allow higher wages for *both* schools) as of July, 1971, the new fiscal year.

When vocational programming for young women is viewed in conjunction with female unemployment statistics, its importance takes on additional weight. As Sarah Gold stressed in her study of similar conditions in New York: "Unemployment has been shown to be a significant factor in the occurrence of juvenile delinquency. . . . Girls consistently have a higher rate of unemployment than boys, and non-white girls have the highest unemployment rate of any group in the country" (Gold, unpublished paper, 1970; Eldefonso, 1967: 41). Young girls often leave Long Lane and turn to prostitution or premature marriage because they are simply not prepared to do anything else. . . .

As the Long Lane administration freely admits, "no overall, structured recreation program exists." The boys' school has had recreational personnel on the staff who have been more or less active over the years. CSB has a pool (which a few girls were allowed to use periodically last summer) and baseball and basketball teams. Most boys in Meriden spend their free time clustered around pool tables in the basement of every cottage. This winter some fifty volunteers from the University of Connecticut have started coming to Meriden in the evenings to engage the boys in a greater variety of activities. (At least the boys have this time available at night—by the time such volunteers could get to Long Lane, the girls would probably have to go to bed!)

The girls look forward to the summer, when an influx of young "summer staff" come to the school and beach trips, picnics and more energetic events are arranged. This summer, the wife of the CSB recreational supervisor has been hired to develop a similar program at Long Lane. Hopefully, several aides will be assigned to work with her. In the past summers, cottage groups have been able to go to the beach only once every three weeks, and then they are so closely monitored (must cluster on blankets around staff, only go to the water when accompanied by staff, ask the staff to buy them ice cream, because girls aren't allowed to carry their own money, etc.) that much of the fun is undercut. . . .

For the most part, "recreation" at Long Lane consists of a few unstructured hours in the cottages when girls may watch TV, listen to records or the radio, read, play table games, etc. Movies are shown once a week and have traditionally been of such poor quality that girls either sleep, talk, or ask to be excused from the auditorium to return to their room. Trips to movies in the surrounding community are usually impossible to schedule due to the 8:30 bedtime. . . .

The author's observation that an adequate educational program at the girl's institution tended to make for longer incarceration is borne out in other areas. Generally, when institutions are improved, and particularly when "model" prisons are built, the commitment rate increases dramatically.[6]

C. THE EFFECT OF SEX SEGREGATION ON PRISON CONDITIONS

1. The Yale Law Journal Study

Through a grant from the Ford Foundation, editors of the Yale Law Journal made personal visits and an extensive telephone survey of adult penal institutions in order to study the effects of sex segregation. The results of the study appear in The Sexual Segregation of American Prisons, 82 Yale Law Journal 1229 (1973), which concludes that in most respects state and federal governments operate entirely different systems for men and women, and that treatment disparities arise both from differences in scale and from sexual stereotyping. For instance, women's institutions are fewer and thus geographically spread within a jurisdiction; they are also smaller. "These factors have generated a variety of treatment differentials, particularly with regard to the remoteness of each institution, the heterogeneity of its populations, and the level of institutional service."[7] The geographic factor usually means that women prisoners are farther than men prisoners from their homes and families. The study also found that "[m]any of the most important differences between male and female prisons, while undoubtedly aggravated by scale considerations, are generated at least in part by legislative and administrative sexual stereotyping."[8] Differential treatment is found in physical surrounding (generally more individualistic and "homey" for women), recreational facilities (less for women), institutional staff (more staff per inmate in women's institutions), and rehabilitative and industrial programs (less variety and depth for women).

There have been some legal challenges to the effects of sexual segregation in prison systems. Dawson v. Carberry, No. C-71-1916 (N.D. Cal., filed September 1971), attacked a practice whereby sentenced men were allowed to work in the community during the day, while no such program existed for women convicted of the same, or less serious, crimes as the men. This was said by the state to be a result of the high administrative cost of running such a program for the comparatively few women who would be involved. After a full hearing, the court recessed the matter, pending efforts by the prison administrators to develop a similar program for women. In Commonwealth v. Stauffer, 214 Pa. Super. 113, 251 A.2d 718 (1969), the challenge was to a system in which women were imprisoned in the penitentiary for the same crimes for which men were sent to jail, because there was no jail facility for women. The court held that mixing women misdemeanants, sometimes first offenders, with the hardened criminals likely to be in penitentiaries, violated equal protection, because similarly situated men were not so treated. The woman was ordered returned to the county jail.

2. The Equal Rights Amendment and Sex-Segregated Prisons

In the past five years litigation about prison conditions has exploded.[9] Little attention, however, has been paid to women's prisons. More resources and concern might be

---

6. Nagel, The New Red Barn: A Critical Look at the Modern American Prison 180 (1973).

7. Note, The Sexual Segregation of American Prisons, 82 Yale L.J. 1229, 1232 (1973).

8. Id. at 1237.

9. See, e.g., Johnson v. Avery, 393 U.S. 483, 89 S. Ct. 747, 21 L. Ed. 2d 718 (1969); Lee v. Washington, 390 U.S. 333, 88 S. Ct. 994, 19 L. Ed. 2d 1212 (1968); Jackson v. Bishop, 404 F.2d 571 (8th Cir. 1968); Jackson v. Godwin, 400 F.2d 529 (5th Cir. 1968); Jones v. Peyton, 294 F. Supp. 173 (E.D. Va. 1968); Wright v. McMann, 387 F.2d 519 (2d Cir. 1967). See also discussion of these and other prison cases in Hirschkop and Millemann, The Unconstitutionality of Prison Life, 55 Va. L. Rev. 795 (1969). This litigation explosion has also engendered the Prison Law Reporter, published by the American Bar Association, which provides monthly coverage of case developments.

directed to women prisoners if sex segregation of prisons were ended. Passage of the Equal Rights Amendment will certainly assure that there will be litigation on the issue.

The issue of sex segregation in prisons was treated almost exclusively as a "scare" argument during the congressional debate over the amendment. Harvard law professor Paul Freund offered as a reason to oppose the Amendment the fact that it would require sex integration of prisons and that this was undesirable.[10] Other commentators theorized that the constitutional right of privacy could insulate prisons from the reach of the amendment.[11]

A recent article on the sex segregation of prisons opines flatly that passage of the Equal Rights Amendment would mean integration:[12]

> Despite claims to the contrary by opponents of the ERA,[155] Congress clearly passed the Amendment in the belief that it would be balanced against the right of privacy, and that as a result the sleeping and toilet facilities of public institutions could continue to be sexually segregated.[156] This conclusion is by no means self-evident, since no court has yet found a right of sexual privacy with regard to such facilities, much less extended such a right to prisoners. Nevertheless, the right of an inmate to disrobe and perform personal functions out of the presence of inmates of the opposite sex is probably inferrable from the reasoning of earlier privacy and prisoners' rights cases, at least where no legitimate security or rehabilitative interests dictate to the contrary.[157]

10. Freund, The Equal Rights Amendment Is Not the Way, quoted by Senator Ervin, at 118 Cong. Rec. §1502 (daily ed. Feb. 9, 1972).

11. See, e.g., Brown, Emerson, Falk, and Freedman, The Equal Rights Amendment: A Constitutional Basis for Equal Rights for Women, 80 Yale L.J. 871, 901 (1971).

12. Note, The Sexual Segregation of American Prisons, 82 Yale L.J. 1229, 1259-1262 (May 1973).

155. Senator Ervin's position is explained in his Senate Minority Report:

"I believe that the absolute nature of the Equal Rights Amendment will, without a doubt, cause all laws and state-sanctioned practices which in any way differentiate between men and women to be held unconstitutional. Thus, all laws which separate men and women, such as separate schools, restrooms, dormitories, prisons, and others will be stricken. . . . The proponents of the ERA mention that the Constitutional right to privacy will protect and keep separate items such as public restrooms; however, this assertion overlooks the basic fact of constitutional law construction: The most recent constitutional amendment takes precedence over all other sections of the Constitution with which it is inconsistent. Thus, if the ERA is to be construed absolutely, as its proponents say, then there can be no exception for elements of publically imposed sexual segregation on the basis of privacy between men and women." S. Rep. No. 92-689, [92d Cong., 1st Sess. (1972), hereinafter cited as S. Rep. No. 92-689,] at 45-46.

Professor Freund took a similar position. He testified before the Senate Judiciary Committee that the strict model of racial equality would require that there be no segregation of the sexes in prisons, reform schools, public restrooms, and other public facilities. See Senate Hearings, [Hearings on S.J. Res. 61 and S.J. Res. 231, Before the Sen. Comm. on the Judiciary, 91st Cong., 2d Sess. 225 (1970), hereinafter cited as Senate Hearings,] at 74. See also Freund, The Equal Rights Amendment Is Not the Way, 6 Harv. Civ. Rts.-Civ. Lib. L. Rev. 234-40 (1971).

156. The Senate Report states that the "constitutional right of privacy established by the Supreme Court in Griswold v. Connecticut" would permit a separation of the sexes with respect to such places as public toilets and the sleeping quarters of public institutions, even after passage of the Amendment. S. Rep. No. 92-689, . . . at 12. The proponents of the ERA also noted the privacy exception throughout the hearings and floor debate. See, e.g., 118 Cong. Rec. §4394 (daily ed. March 21, 1972) (remarks of Senator Gurney); Senate Hearings, [supra note 155], at 97 (remarks of Senator Cook); [Hearings Before Subcom. 4 of the House Comm. on the Judiciary, 92d Cong., 1st Sess (1971) hereinafter cited as House Hearings], at 40 (remarks of Congresswoman Griffiths), 86-87 (remarks of Congressman Mikva); 118 Cong. Rec. H9386 (daily ed. Oct. 12, 1971) (remarks of Congressman Ashley).

In addition to this constitutional right to privacy, the Senate Report also refers to the "traditional power of the state to regulate cohabitation and sexual activity by unmarried persons." S. Rep. No. 92-689, [supra note 155], at 12. This power, according to the Report, would permit the state to segregate the sexes with respect to such facilities as sleeping quarters at coeducational colleges, prison dormitories and military barracks. However, except for a few cryptic references during the House Hearings, see, e.g., House Hearings, [supra] at 289-90, 305, there is no other mention of the doctrine in the legislative history. The legal basis for the doctrine, the general police power, is, of course, as pervasive as any of the reserved powers of the states, but it is not of constitutional dimension. Consistent interpretation of the ERA requires that no state interest, not even under the police power, be allowed to justify a law or regulation containing a sex-based classification.

157. Congress based this perceived right of sexual privacy on the Supreme Court's decision in Griswold v. Connecticut, 381 U.S. 479 (1965). See note 156 supra. The Court has since expanded and clarified the right

Although there is no discussion of the Eighth Amendment[158] in the legislative history of the ERA, that constitutional right cannot be overlooked in an analysis of the rights of prison inmates. The courts have held that prisoners have an Eighth Amendment right to be free from physical abuse at the hands of both state officials[159] and fellow prisoners.[160] The latter right stems from the affirmative duty of prison officials to minimize violence among inmates.[161] Such constitutional principles must also be accommodated within the framework of the ERA. . . .

---

of privacy, see Roe v. Wade, 93 Sup. Ct. 705 (1973); Eisenstadt v. Baird, 405 U.S. 438 (1972), but it has not yet been called on to determine whether that right encompasses a prisoner's unwillingness to disrobe or shower in the presence of the opposite sex. The Ninth Circuit, however, has indicated that the *unincarcerated* person has such a right. In Ford v. Story, 324 F.2d 450 (9th Cir. 1963), in which a police officer photographed the nude body of a rape victim over her objection and then circulated the photographs among the stationhouse personnel, that court said "We cannot conceive of a more basic subject of privacy than the naked body. The desire to shield one's unclothed figured [sic] from view of strangers, and particularly strangers of the opposite sex, is impelled by elementary self-respect and personal dignity." Id. at 455. On the nexus between the right of privacy and basic human dignity, see Bloustein, Privacy as an Aspect of Human Dignity: An Answer to Dean Prosser, 39 N.Y.U.L. Rev. 962 (1964); Singer, Privacy, Autonomy, and Dignity in the Prison: A Preliminary Inquiry Concerning Constitutional Aspects of the Degradation Process in Our Prisons, in 1 Practising Law Institute, Prisoner's Rights 147 (1972).

Of course, prisons are not noted for the degree to which they protect the dignity and self-respect of their inmates. See Singer, supra, at 149-51. However, elements of personal freedom which are protected by the Constitution can only be denied to prisoners if they conflict with compelling security or other penal interests. See Barnett v. Rodgers, 410 F.2d 995, 1003 (D.C. Cir. 1969) . . . ; 1 Practising Law Institute, Prisoner's Rights 117 (1972); Tucker, Establishing the Rule of Law in Prisons: A Manual for Prisoners' Rights Litigation, 23 Stan. L. Rev. 473, 508-09 (1971). Moreover, constitutional rights may only be abridged if there exist no less drastic means of satisfying such penal interests. See Barnett v. Rodgers, supra, at 1003; Practising Law Institute, supra, at 117.

These principles have led one commentator to conclude that a wide variety of current prison practices violate the inmate's constitutional right of privacy. See Singer, supra. Whether or not the courts accept this position, they would probably recognize that no significant prison interest would be served by the sexual integration of institutional living quarters. On the contrary, security and rehabilitation would probably demand, and the states would probably so require on their own, the same segregation dictated by the right of privacy. . . . Barnett v. Rodgers, supra, at 1002: "Treatment that degrades the inmate, invades his privacy, and frustrates the ability to choose pursuits through which he can manifest himself and gain self-respect erodes the very foundations upon which he can prepare for a socially useful life."

Congress therefore could have reasonably found that prisoners retain a right to disrobe and perform personal functions out of the presence of inmates of the opposite sex, and that this right would require the segregation of living quarters in otherwise integrated institutions. However, even if the courts, as final arbiters of constitutional interpretation, accept this conclusion, they will find little guidance in the legislative history concerning the manner in which privacy and the ERA would interact in particular situations. . . .

Concerning the persons affected by the right of privacy, it is interesting to note that the male institution at San Quentin now employs two female guards, whose duties have thus far been limited to the gun towers, visiting rooms, and gates. Telephone conversation with Lee E. DeBord, Information Officer, California State Prison at San Quentin, March 30, 1973. Even this limited use of female guards, who *may* be called on to conduct skin searches and oversee showers, is being challenged in court by a male inmate. N.Y. Times, March 30, 1973, at 33, col. 8. It seems clear that certain treatment personnel, such as physicians and perhaps even counselors, must be allowed greater "intimacy" with the prisoner than would be afforded a fellow inmate. Custody officers appear to fall somewhere between these two extremes on a continuum of permissible "invasions." In each case, the court should balance the degree of humiliation (loss of dignity and thus privacy) involved, the prison's interest in causing that humiliation, and the feasibility of the less drastic method of having same-sex staff conduct the "invasion" at issue.

158. U.S. Const. amend. VIII.

159. Wiltsie v. California Dept. of Corrections, 406 F.2d 515 (9th Cir. 1968) (beating with fists and billy clubs); Jackson v. Bishop, 404 F.2d 571 (8th Cir. 1968), *modifying* 268 F. Supp. 804 (E.D. Ark. 1967) (whipping with strap).

160. Kish v. County of Milwaukee, 441 F.2d 901 (7th Cir. 1971); Gates v. Collier, 349 F. Supp. 881 (N.D. Miss. 1972); Holt v. Sarver, 309 F. Supp. 362 (E.D. Ark. 1970), *aff'd,* 442 F.2d 304 (8th Cir. 1971). It should be noted that both *Kish* and *Holt* dealt in part with claims of homosexual rape, a problem analogous to that of sexual assault in integrated institutions.

161. In Gates v. Collier, 349 F. Supp. 881 (N.D. Miss. 1972), a federal district court held that a wide range of practices and conditions at the Mississippi State Penitentiary constituted a deprivation of Eighth Amendment rights. The court held that the inmates had been subjected to cruel and unusual punishment because of the failure of penitentiary officials to provide adequate protection against physical assaults, abuses, indignities, and cruelties by other inmates, by placing excessive numbers of inmates in barracks without adequate

Would "Separate but Equal" Treatment Be Permitted Under the ERA?

In Brown v. Board of Education,[162] the Supreme Court invalidated the doctrine of "separate but equal" in the racial context on the grounds that separate, by its very nature, could not be equal. As noted above, however, the Court has not yet made the same determination concerning sexual segregation; nevertheless, the ERA would appear to compel such a result.[163]

The framework developed by Professor Emerson simply does not accommodate a "separate but equal" approach, since that doctrine, just as in the case of race, could be used to keep one sex in a subordinate position.[164] Although there has not been extensive study in the area, the existing evidence does tend to show that sexually separate facilities are rarely equal.[165]

Although most of the debate before Congress concerning sexual segregation dealt with schools,[166] there is evidence that Congress contemplated and, by its refusal to revise the ERA, intended that the Amendment would require sexual integration of all public institutions, including prisons.[167] The constitutional exceptions described

---

classification or supervision, and by assigning custodial responsibility to incompetent and untrained inmates. *Accord,* Holt v. Sarver, 309 F. Supp. 362 (E.D. Ark. 1970), *aff'd,* 442 F.2d 304 (8th Cir. 1971).

162. 347 U.S. 483 (1954).

163. A "freedom of choice" arrangement cannot be so easily rejected. In the context of school segregation, the Supreme Court refused to accept a freedom of choice plan, but only because in the instant case such plans had failed to "effectuate conversion of a state-imposed dual system to a unitary, nonracial system." Green v. County School Board, 391 U.S. 430, 440-41 (1968). Arguably, a state would not be discriminating against either sex if it maintained three equally desirable institutions — one for men, one for women, and one mixed —and gave each inmate the choice of incarceration in an integrated or a segregated institution.

Such an arrangement would, however, be both doctrinally and practically unacceptable. While the Court in *Green* conceded the theoretical legality of "freedom of choice" plans, it was referring to a system in which each pupil could select among *all* institutions in the district. The designation of one institution as "male" and another as "female" must be seen as inherently inimical to the "unitary" system envisioned in *Green,* and would also appear to be a sexual classification at odds with the basic principle of the ERA. Furthermore, the single-sex prisons would have to be equally desirable to afford each sex an "equal" choice, and the integrated prison would have to be at least as desirable to insure that the state was not covertly encouraging segregation. The cost of maintaining such "equal" institutions would undoubtedly deter all but the largest states, which would also probably be deterred by the degree to which such a tripartite system would limit the geographic and rehabilitative classification of inmates.

164. Brown, Emerson, Falk & Freedman, [The Equal Rights Amendment; A Constitutional Basis for Equal Rights for Women, 80 Yale L.J. 871 (1971)], at 902-03.

165. . . . An analysis of coordinate "brother-sister" colleges reveals similar findings. See C. Jencks & D. Reisman, The Academic Revolution 305 (1968). See also House Hearings, [supra note 156], at 272 (remarks of Dr. Bernice Sandler).

166. Congresswoman Martha Griffiths totally rejected the notion of "separate but equal" in this context. House Hearings, [supra note 156] at 47.

167. Congressman Edwards questioned then Assistant Attorney General Rehnquist as to whether the various correctional institutions throughout the country would have to be integrated if the ERA were enacted. Mr. Rehnquist replied that the requirement of integration would be "a very permissible interpretation." House Hearings, [supra note 156] at 3220. In a subsequent letter to Congressman Edwards, Mr. Rehnquist qualified his testimony by explaining that the question could not be fully answered with any certainty: "[A]t a minimum it would appear permissible under the proposed amendment to separate men and women to the extent necessary to prevent further crimes, such as rape and prostitution, as male prisoners are now to some degree separated to prevent homosexual assaults. It has been further suggested by supporters of the amendment that separation would be permissible to the extent necessary to protect a competing right of privacy. To what extent recognition of the necessity of some degree of separation of some prisoners could be generalized to permit separation of all prisoners or maintenance of separate systems is, we believe, uncertain." Letter reprinted in House Hearings, [supra note 156], at 329.

Professor Philip Kurland, an opponent of the ERA, testified that the Amendment would make it unconstitutional for the federal government or state governments to maintain separate prisons for men and women and separate reformatories for boys and girls. See Senate Hearings, [supra note 155], at 99. However, Professor Kurland also noted that there are some, albeit old fashioned, notions of privacy that might properly justify a policy of "separate but equal" facilities. See 118 Cong. Rec. S4570 (daily ed. March 22, 1972).

Congressman Edwards noted that the Director of the U.S. Bureau of Prisons responded very affirmatively to a question concerning the possible integration of prisons under the Amendment. The Director felt that the prisons should be integrated now — "for good penology, good corrections and decent living. . . ." House Hearings, [supra note 156] at 306.

above would not bar such integration: Privacy does not require the segregation of entire institutions,[168] and the right to be secure from physical abuse can also be accommodated, as has been required in the racial context, in far less drastic ways.

Is sex integration in prisons feasible or desirable? What practical problems are raised by the severe disproportion between men and women? Could these be minimized by classification by offense or otherwise?

D. DIFFERENTIAL SENTENCING OF WOMEN AND MEN

The small amount of litigation which has occurred over women's prisons has centered around the validity of longer sentences imposed on women. The following case outlines the history of differential sentencing.

1. The History

STATE v. HEITMAN
105 Kan. 481, 181 P. 630 (1919)

BURCH, J. The defendant was convicted of keeping a liquor nuisance [for which the possible sentence was a fine of $100 to $500 and imprisonment for thirty days to six months]. She was sentenced to pay a fine of $100, and was committed to the state industrial farm for women until discharged according to law. She appeals from the portion of the judgment assessing penalty. . . .

. . . [Her jail] commitment was adjudged under the provisions . . . reading as follows:

> Every female person, above the age of eighteen years, who shall be convicted of any offense against the criminal laws of this state, punishable by imprisonment, shall be sentenced to the state industrial farm for women, but the court imposing such sentence shall not fix the limit or duration of the sentence. The term of imprisonment of any person so convicted and sentenced shall be terminated by the state board of administration, as authorized by this act, but such imprisonment shall not exceed the maximum term provided by law for the crime for which the person was convicted. . . .

The detention portion of the defendant's sentence was therefore indeterminate, with a maximum limit of six months. If the defendant had been a man, the sentence would have been to the county jail for some definite period within the maximum and minimum limits fixed by the statute in 1901. . . .

. . . The defendant asserts that sex does not constitute a just and reasonable ground for substituting an indeterminate sentence, within a stated limit, to the industrial farm for women, in place of a definite sentence, within the same limit, to the county jail. . . .

Individuals cannot be studied en masse. They may be classified into groups, on the basis of common characteristics; but the individual cannot be assigned to his proper group until he has been segregated, and his lack of endowments have been considered in the light of his heredity and environment.

The method which has just been described must be employed in affixing punishment. . . .

168. House Hearings, [supra note 156] at 402 (testimony of Professor Emerson). . . .

The one unqualifiedly reprobated and repudiated punitive institution is the county jail. It has no defenders, except local officials, jealous of centralized authority, and the sheriff, elected irrespective of qualification to rehabilitate men and women, even if he had facilities and opportunity, and whose compensation depends in part on fees for keeping and boarding prisoners. There is no opportunity for segregation, differentiation, and proper classification. There is no opportunity for discipline at all, much less discipline appropriate to individual need. There is nothing but detention, and detention in caged and demoralizing idleness, injurious to body and mind, crushing to the spirit, and tending to moral contamination and induration, rather than to moral upbuilding. . . .

Another relic of the stone age of penological theory and practice is the definite sentence for a fixed period for a specific crime. It has been well said that it is just as stupid, and infinitely more cruel, to sentence misdemeanants to jail for fixed periods as it would be to sentence sick people to a hospital for fixed periods. All penologists agree that the definite sentence should be abolished, because, if the primary object be to return to society as future assets those who are present liabilities, there must be classification, and there must be time, according to susceptibility and capability, for the remedial, reformatory, and educational processes to have their effect. In a given case, the period of detention may be quite short; but, according to need, the brain must be cooled, the nerves nourished and quieted, the clouded or deadened conscience cleared or quickened, the weakened will strengthened, the disordered mind, with its confused notions of right and morality, stabilized, and fresh impulses given outward, away from the old self, forward to new and hopeful things, and upward to self-respect and self-control.

Comprehension of the fact that punishment ought to fit, in some degree, not simply the crime, but the offender, led the Legislature to adopt the system of maximum and minimum penalties found in the Crimes Act and related statutes. Clearer comprehension led it to adopt, in recent years, the indeterminate sentence for felonies, except murder and treason (1903), and the parole system (1907). . . .

Long ago the Legislature made the first and most obvious classification of delinquents, and provided for segregation of youthful offenders, and treatment of boys and girls in separate corrective institutions. By enactment of the industrial farm statute, the Legislature made the next most obvious classification, based on the distinction between male and female, and abolished the county jail and the penitentiary as places for the reformatory treatment of women.

The industrial farm law puts into practice the most advanced tenets of the new penology. The farm is under supervision of the state board of administration, the central body having control of all correctional, charitable, and educational institutions of the state. The superintendent is a woman. The farm is in fact a farm, and the buildings are constructed on the cottage plan. Provision is made against overcrowding, and there are no cells or bars or restraining walls. Careful classifications are made, according to the results of searching physical, mental, and moral diagnosis, and complete records are kept of all facts throwing light on cause of detention, proper plan of treatment, and progress of the individual. Medical and surgical treatment is administered. The discipline is educative and reformative, and the work includes agriculture, dairying, poultry raising, manufacturing, and practice of domestic arts and sciences. Small wages are allowed, and provision is made for parole and final discharge whenever compatible with the welfare of society, with full restoration of all civil rights.

It required no anatomist, or physiologist, or psychologist, or psychiatrist to tell the Legislature that women are different from men. In structure and function human beings are still as they were in the beginning "Male and female created He them." It is a patent and deep-lying fact that these fundamental anatomical and physiological differences affect the whole psychic organization. They create the differences in personality between men and women, and personality is the predominating factor in delinquent careers. It was inevitable that, in the ages during which woman has been bearer of the race, her unique and absolutely personal experiences, from the time of conception to the time when developed offspring attains maturity, should react on personality, and produce what we understand to be embraced by the term "womanhood." Woman enters spheres of sensation, perception, emotion, desire, knowledge, and experience, of an intensity and of a kind which man cannot know.

It is not worth while discussing the necessity of preventing promiscuous association of the sexes in prison. There must be complete segregation. Female wards in men's prisons, and female annexes to men's prisons, merely separate the sexes. They do not differentiate the problems of the delinquent female from the problems of the delinquent male. In 1869 the Legislature of the state of Indiana undertook to do this, by establishing a separate prison for women, to be officered and managed by women, and conducted according to the reformatory method as then apprehended. Since 1869 some 13 other states have established separate institutions for the treatment of delinquent women, on the definite principle of reclamation as opposed to naked punishment. The industrial farm with buildings constructed on the cottage plan, has become an accepted type, and the indeterminate sentence has been almost, though not quite, universally adopted. . . .

The judgment of the district court is affirmed.

All the Justices concurring.

NOTE

The opinions's analogy to the treatment and rehabilitation of juveniles is common. See In Re Dunkerton, 104 Kan. 481, 179 P. 347 (1919); Ex parte Gosselin, 141 Me. 412, 44 A.2d 882 (1945); Platt v. Commonwealth, 256 Mass. 539, 152 N.E. 914 (1926); Ex parte Brady, 116 Ohio 512, 157 N.E. 69 (1927). Typical is this decisive language from *Dunkerton*:[13]

> The purpose of the act of 1917 is to ameliorate the condition of women who have been convicted of an offense punishable by imprisonment. Under the act women are not subject to the debauching influence of the county jail and of the penitentiary and of the close confinement therein, but are placed in a field where labor is pleasant and restraint is limited, and where the evil influence of other persons convicted of crime is minimized. The act seeks to improve, to educate, and to build up, not to punish. The court is asked to say that the law is unconstitutional because in accomplishing these objects it imposes restraint on women different from that imposed on men. . . . The Legislature may very properly determine that women convicted of crime shall be less severely punished than men convicted of the same crime. The number of women that commit crimes is much smaller than the number of men committing similar crimes, and that fact may be taken into consideration by the Legislature, and punishment may be prescribed which recognizes that difference.

2. Contemporary Challenges

COMMONWEALTH v. DANIELS (I)
210 Pa. Super. 156, 232 A.2d 247 (1967)

Opinion by JACOBS, J., June 16, 1967:
. . . Jane M. Daniels, was tried . . . without a jury on charges of burglary, aggravated robbery, carrying a concealed deadly weapon, and possession of a firearm after conviction of a crime of violence. She was found guilty of robbery on May 3,

---

13. In re Dunkerton, 104 Kan. 481, 483-484 (1919).

1966, and . . . sentenced . . . to a one to four year prison term in Philadelphia County Prison. On June 3, 1966, thirty-one days after the imposition of this sentence, Judge Stern vacated the original sentence and resentenced appellant to an indefinite term of imprisonment in the State Correctional Institution at Muncy. In accordance with the Muncy Act, the sentence was a general one fixing no maximum or minimum. From that sentence appellant appealed to this court, contending that her sentence to an indeterminate term at Muncy is improper since the applicable statute provides for an unconstitutional distinction between males and females as to sentencing. . . . It is clear to us that the legislature intended to make sentence to Muncy the sole method of incarceration for any woman convicted of a crime punishable by more than a year of imprisonment. . . .

The Muncy Act does provide a different sentence for women than for men convicted of the same crime. Where a woman is sentenced to imprisonment the sentence is a general one to the institution at Muncy and the limits of the imprisonment are not fixed in the sentence.

A male offender sentenced to imprisonment for robbery is sentenced under [an act which provides] for an indefinite term, but directs the judge to fix the minimum and maximum limits with the further proviso that the maximum may not exceed the maximum prescribed by law for such offense and the minimum shall never exceed one-half of the maximum prescribed by the judge. . . .

. . . The legislature in enacting the Muncy Act has decided that women as a class are to be treated differently than men as to the term and manner of incarceration for crimes. The fact that legislation might impose greater burdens on one class of citizens does not in itself violate the Equal Protection Clause. . . . In a recent case the Supreme Court of this state held that imposing the added burden of oral exams on women candidates for police sergeant did not violate the Equal Protection Clause. Wells v. Civil Service Commission, 423 Pa. 608, 225 A.2d 554 (1967). A classification by the legislature would violate the Equal Protection Clause only if it did not rest upon a difference between the classes that bore a reasonable relation to the purposes of the legislation. E.g., McLaughlin v. State of Florida, 379 U.S. 184, 85 S. Ct. 283, 13 L. Ed. 2d 222 (1964); Hoyt v. State of Florida, 368 U.S. 57, 82 S. Ct. 159, 7 L. Ed. 2d 118 (1961); Milk Control Commission v. Battista, [413 Pa. 652, 198 A.2d 840 (1964)]. The test stated by our Supreme Court is that a classification violates the Equal Protection Clause if it is shown to be arbitrary or utterly lacking in rational justification. Milk Control Commission v. Battista, supra. Of course, where fundamental rights and personal liberties may be affected by a classification, as they are here, the classification must be closely scrutinized and carefully confined. Harper v. Virginia State Board of Elections, 383 U.S. 663, 86 S. Ct. 1079, 16 L. Ed. 2d 169, 174 (1966).

Is there a rational basis for the classification, i.e., a reasonable connection between the classification by sex and the purpose of the legislation? The broad purpose of the legislation was to provide for the punishment and rehabilitation of prisoners. Different types of incarceration for the same crimes are regularly imposed both for classes of individuals (e.g., juveniles, sex offenders, recidivists, criminally insane), as well as among separate individuals where judicial discretion in imposing sentence may be allowed by the legislature. The only requirement for different classes of persons is that the class exhibits characteristics that justify the different treatment. . . . This court is of the opinion that the legislature reasonably could have concluded that indeterminate sentences should be imposed on women as a class, allowing the time of incarceration to be matched to the necessary treatment in order to provide more effective rehabilitation. Such a conclusion could be based on the physiological and psychological makeup of women, the type of crime committed by women, their relation to the criminal world, their roles in society, their unique vocational skills and pursuits, and their reaction as a class to imprisonment as well as the number and type of women who are sentenced to imprisonment rather than given suspended sentences. Such facts could have led the legislature to conclude that a different manner of punishment and rehabilitation was necessary for women sentenced to confinement. . . .

In effect, appellant presents us with arguments against the legislation without supporting data and asks us to reweigh the wisdom of the act of the legislature. This we cannot do. . . .

Judgment of sentence affirmed.

Opinion by HOFFMAN, J. (dissenting):

In my view, the Muncy Act constitutes an arbitrary and invidious discrimination against women offenders as a class.

The statute concededly requires longer sentences for women than for men convicted of the same crime. In the case of women offenders, the judge is precluded from exercising his discretion so as to achieve an equitable matching of crime and punishment. All women sentenced for offenses punishable by imprisonment for more than one year *must* be sentenced to the maximum permissible term. Men, on the other hand, *may* be sentenced to lesser terms.

Furthermore, the statute robs the trial judge of his discretion in the area of sentencing, and therefore lends itself to arbitrary and erratic administration of non-judicial authorities. Thus, in theory, a woman sentenced under the provisions of the Muncy Act receives no minimum sentence. In practice, however, she will be required to spend a substantial period of time in prison before referral for parole, because of the rigid schedules of "time to be served" established by the Muncy authorities.[1]

In the instant case, the trial judge attempted to sentence the defendant to a term of one to four years. Were it not for the fact that she is a woman, she would have become eligible for parole in one year. Even if never released on parole, she would have been discharged after four years. Because of the mandatory language of the Muncy statute, however, she may serve a term whose maximum is 10 years. Because of the scheme of parole referral in force at Muncy, she will probably serve a minimum of three years at that institution. It is therefore apparent that the Act imposes heavier sentences on women in general and has worked to impose a more severe punishment on defendant Daniels in particular. . . .

In my view, the "any rational basis" formula is inadequate to test the validity of the Muncy Act against the present challenge. That doctrine derives from a number of cases upholding economic regulatory measures or statutes not directly impinging on personal liberties or fundamental rights. . . .

. . . The Supreme Court, in Skinner v. State of Oklahoma, 316 U.S. 535, 541, 62 S. Ct. 1110, 86 L. Ed. 1655 (1942), has already spoken on the question. In *Skinner,* an Oklahoma statute required the sterilization of "habitual criminals." That term included all persons three times convicted of felonies involving moral turpitude, but excepted persons convicted of embezzlement. The Court struck down the statute, as offensive to the Equal Protection clause, observing: "When the law lays an unequal hand on those who have committed intrinsically the same quality of offense . . . it has made as an invidious a discrimination." Again in McLaughlin v. State of Florida, supra at 192 of 379

---

1. According to a letter from the Superintendent of Muncy to the Voluntary Defender, the schedule is as follows:

SENTENCE	TIME TO BE SERVED
3 years	18 to 20 months
5 years	2 to 2½ years
7 years	2½ to 3 years
10 years (robbery)	2½ to 3½ years
12 years (voluntary manslaughter)	4 to 4½ years
15 years	3½ to 4½ years

U.S., at 290 of 85 S. Ct., the Court stated: "[in the context of a criminal statute] where the power of the state weighs most heavily on the individual or the group, *we must be especially sensitive to the policies of the Equal Protection Clause . . . were intended . . . to subject all persons 'to like punishments, pains, penalties . . . and exactions of every kind, and to no other.' "* [emphasis supplied]

To justify such discriminatory treatment, the Commonwealth must demonstrate more than the fragmentary and tenuous theories presented to us. Absent any compelling psychological, statistical, or scientific data, we cannot, nor should we, sanction a legislative scheme which is patently arbitrary and manifestly unfair.[1]

The recent decision by the Supreme Court in Application of Gault, 387 U.S. 1, 87 S. Ct. 1428, 18 L. Ed. 2d 527 (1967) reflects a similar concern that high-minded ideals may obscure a harsh reality. In considering the nature of the Juvenile Court, the Supreme Court stated: "[T]he highest motives and most enlightened impulses led to a peculiar system for juveniles, unknown to our law in any comparable context. The constitutional and theoretical basis for this peculiar system is — to say the least — debatable. And in practice . . . the results have not been entirely satisfactory. Juvenile court history has again demonstrated that unbridled discretion, however benevolently motivated, is frequently a poor substitute for principle and procedure."

Similarly, under the guise of special rehabilitative treatment for women, the legislature, in the Muncy statute, has adopted a system which accomplishes little more than the imposition of harsher punishment for women offenders. As such, it denies them the Equal Protection of the laws guaranteed by the Constitution of the United States.

For these reasons, I would reverse.

COMMONWEALTH v. DANIELS (II)
430 Pa. 642, 243 A.2d 400 (1968)

. . . In these appeals, appellants attack the Constitutionality of the Muncy Act. . . .

Appellant Daisy Douglas and a co-defendant, Richard Johnson, were charged with aggravated robbery and conspiracy. They were tried without a jury and both found guilty as charged. Johnson was given *a sentence of from four to ten years* in the Eastern State Penitentiary, and Daisy Douglas was given *an indeterminate sentence to Muncy.* She filed a petition for relief under the Post Conviction Hearing Act, *alleging that she had been denied the Equal Protection of the Laws* by having been sentenced under the Muncy Act. The hearing Judge denied Daisy's petition. . . . We consolidated her appeal with that of Jane Daniels. . . . The Judge sentencing a woman under the Muncy Act is given no right or power to impose a shorter maximum sentence than the maximum punishment proscribed by statutory law for the criminal offense committed, nor a sentence with a minimum of one-half the maximum punishment, nor indeed any sentence except an indeterminate sentence as above set forth. Thus, women are deprived of the right to have a Judge fix (a) a maximum sentence less than the maximum prescribed by law for the offense

1. Philadelphia District Attorney Arlen Specter has filed a candid and persuasive brief in support of the conclusion that the Muncy Act is unconstitutional. He offers the following excerpt from the work of a leading criminologist of fifty years ago to illustrate the philosophy underlying the statute:

"There is little doubt in the minds of those who have had much experience in dealing with women delinquents, that the fundamental fact is that they belong to the class of women who lead sexually immoral lives. . . .

"[Such a statute] would remove permanently from the community the feebleminded delinquents who are now generally recognized as a social menace, and would relieve the state from the ever increasing burden of the support of their illegitimate children. Furthermore, . . . such a policy, thoroughly carried out, would do more to rid the streets . . . of soliciting, loitering, and public vice than anything that could be devised. There is nothing the common prostitute fears so greatly as to know that if she offends and is caught she will be subject to the possibility of prolonged confinement."

committed, or (b) a minimum-maximum sentence, with its inherent advantages, which right the appellants correctly assert is given to the Judge in the sentencing of men under the Act of 1911, [P.L. 1055, §6, as amended, 19 P.S. §1057] . . .

Regardless of the facts and circumstances involved in each case, whether extenuating or otherwise, a Judge in sentencing a woman has no discretion in fixing the maximum period during which she must be imprisoned. On the other hand, a Judge in sentencing a man under the Act of June 19, 1911, supra, may and does consider extenuating facts and factors. It is clear, therefore, that an arbitrary and invidious discrimination exists in the sentencing of men to prison and women to Muncy, with resultant injury to women. . . .

. . . A classification by sex alone would not, per se, offend the Equal Protection Clause of the United States Constitution. For example, there are undoubtedly significant biological, natural and practical differences between men and women which would justify, under certain circumstances, the establishment of different employment qualification standards. Over the years, both the Supreme Court of the United States and this Court have upheld laws which differentiate between the employment of men and women. . . .

We are convinced, however, that the considerations and factors which would justify a difference between men and women in matters of employment, as well as in a number of other matters, *do not govern* or justify the imposition of a longer or greater sentence of women than is imposed upon men for the commission of the same crime. In particular, we fail to discern any reasonable and justifiable difference or deterrents between men and women which would justify a man being *eligible* for a shorter maximum prison sentence than a woman for the commission of the same crime, especially if there is no material difference in their records and the relevant circumstances.

NOTES

1. Judge Hoffman's dissent in *Daniels* is a more satisfactory opinion than the decision of the Pennsylvania Supreme Court, because the underlying basis of his finding is explicitly stated. Is he saying that the "rehabilitative ideal" for incarceration has failed so badly that it will no longer lend a rational basis to legislative classifications? Would the argument in the case be any different if women received the definite and men the indefinite sentence?

2. The year after *Daniels* was decided, a federal judge granted habeas corpus because he found that a Connecticut statute similar to the one in Pennsylvania had resulted in unconstitutional detention:[14]

> . . . The state seeks to justify [the statute, Conn. Gen. Stat. §17-360] by noting that it is one among a number of provisions in that title of the General Statutes dealing with "Humane and Reformatory Agencies and Institutions" as distinguished from the "Penal Institutions" authorized in Title 18, and that it is, therefore, "part of the integral whole which constitutes the State's attempt to provide for women and juveniles a special protection and every reformative and rehabilitative opportunity." Respondent's Brief at 18. This purports to be a way of concealing the abrasive nature of imprisonment under the charming image of an educational institution. But this should not blind one to the fact that the institution is still a place of imprisonment.
>
> There are a number of things that could well be said in defense of separate institutions for women, but merely calling the State Farm for Women a reformatory, and, therefore, distinguishable from the penal system does not make it so. What Mr. Justice Fortas noted in the recent case of In re Gault, 387 U.S. 1, 87 S. Ct. 1428, 18

14. United States ex rel. Robinson v. York, 281 F. Supp. 8 (D. Conn. 1968).

L. Ed. 2d 527 (1967), with regard to juvenile institutions is equally applicable here:
"It is of no constitutional consequence — and of limited practical meaning — that the institution to which he is committed is called an Industrial School. The fact of the matter is that, however euphemistic the title, a 'receiving home' or an 'industrial school' for juveniles is an institution of confinement in which the child is incarcerated for a greater or lesser time. His world becomes 'a building with whitewashed walls, regimented routine and institutional hours. . . .' His world is peopled by guards, custodians, state employees, and 'delinquents' confined with him for anything from waywardness to rape and homicide." (387 U.S. at 27, 87 S. Ct. at 1443).

Moreover, none of the special features which might justify distinguishing the state's treatment of juveniles from that it accords adults exist in the case of commitment of adult women to the State Farm. E.g., Conn. Gen. Stats. §17-72 (adjudication of juvenile court that a child is delinquent is not a criminal conviction); Conn. Gen. Stats. §17-73 (delinquency proceedings inadmissible as evidence in some criminal prosecutions); Conn. Gen. Stats. §17-67 (juvenile court hearings held in private); Conn. Gen. Stats. §17-66 (pre-hearing investigations).

Even assuming, as the state alleges, that there is a difference in the quality of treatment and conditions of incarceration at the Farm, those facts are not enough to justify a longer period of imprisonment for adult women as opposed to adult men. Of course, imprisonment need not be all of one kind. There are ample reasons for separate institutions, and the state may permissibly introduce priorities and coordination between them; but if it matters what kind of facilities are provided, it matters even more that there shall be no invidious discrimination with respect to the length of imprisonment.

In Connecticut the predominant criterion for judgment imposed on those convicted of violating its criminal laws continues to be punishment.

3. The *Daniels* court comes close to finding sex a suspect classification, since the opinion necessarily rejects the "reasonable relationship" test applied by the court below. Both *Daniels* and *Robinson* have, however, been interpreted as applying the rational basis test. In both United States ex rel. Sumrell v. York, 288 F. Supp. 955 (D. Conn. 1968), and Liberti v. York, 28 Conn. Supp. 9, 246 A.2d 106 (1968), Connecticut sentencing schemes that permitted longer sentences for females than for males convicted of the same crimes were found to violate equal protection due to their lack of rational basis. In Liberti v. York, a Connecticut superior court reasoned that a "legitimate basis" for that state's sex-differential sentencing statute could have saved the statute from violation of equal protection, but it concluded that[15]

[the scheme] . . . assumes that a greater period of restraint is necessary in the case of women and that they require a longer period of rehabilitation to again become useful members of society. Factually and statistically there is no basis for any such finding.

4. State v. Costello, 59 N.J. 334, 282 A.2d 748 (1971), involved a statutory scheme which required that women convicted of crimes punishable by five years or less be sentenced to the Women's Correctional Institution for the maximum prescribed by law. For an offense punishable by more than five years, a woman must have received the five years, or any term in excess of five, which was not greater than the maximum. Men sentenced either for more or less than five years must have received a minimum and a maximum number of years. The clear result of the statutory scheme was that in many cases women served longer sentences than men. The New Jersey Supreme Court did not find a denial of equal protection, but instead remanded the case to give the state an opportunity to demonstrate "that the statutory scheme rests on a solid basis from the standpoint of both societal benefit and the welfare of the affected females themselves."[16] Because of the terms of the remand, *Costello* can be read as looking away from the broad

15. 246 A.2d at 107 (1968).
16. State v. Costello, 59 N.J. at 345, 282 A.2d at 754 (1971).

holdings of both *Daniels* and *Robinson.* Yet the words of remand were in apparent conflict with other of the court's language which applied the compelling state interest test to the issue.[17] At least one New Jersey court has apparently read the opinion as making sex a suspect classification. In State v. Palendrano, 120 N.J. Super. 336, 341, 293 A.2d 747, 752 (1972), *Costello* was cited as authority for the decision that a New Jersey statute that made criminal the status of a "common scold" constituted an "obvious" and "senseless" denial of equal protection, since by legal definition only females could be "common scolds."

5. Although *Daniels* and *Robinson* are important precedents, they involve only two states, and *Robinson* is the decision of a single district court judge. Sentencing statutes and the practices of parole boards in many other jurisdictions would doubtless reveal situations similar to those in *Robinson* and *Daniels,* if challenged in litigation. In 1968 and 1969, for instance, women in Washington, D.C., sentenced indeterminately under the Federal Youth Corrections Act, 18 U.S.C. §5010 et seq., were likely to spend at least eighteen months in custody in the women's prison, while the average incarceration for men sentenced under the same statute was six months.[18] This and comparable situations easily arise from the fact that the institutions for men and women are separate, with separate administrations and parole boards.

6. The picture of differential sentencing would not be complete without noting that there is considerable "reverse discrimination" in the way women are treated by the criminal justice system. For example, female prisoners are prohibited from hard labor in many parts of the American penal system, and corporal punishment is less prevalent for female than for male prisoners.

Observers of the criminal justice system point out that judges are more likely to use probation or suspended sentences for women than for men, although few statistics are available on the differential rates of arrest, conviction, and sentencing. Statistics which are available show that in 1970 nearly four million men and boys were arrested, as compared to 675,000 women and girls, a ratio of about 6 to 1.[19] But entrance to state and federal penal or treatment institutions during the same year numbered 75,692 males and 3659 females, a ratio of nearly 21 to 1.[20]

These figures may be partly explained by the less frequent involvement of women in violent crime. However, statistics from California, acknowledged by the National Commission on Violence as having the best crime reporting system in the United States, indicate that the factor of chivalry toward women in sentencing occurs even when comparing arrests and convictions for the same crime.[21] These statistics led the commission to conclude that the increasing ratio of men to women, from arrest to imprisonment, is due ultimately to the norms of American society, which lead to pity and protection rather than punishment for the female offender.[22]

17. "In our view disparate sentencing treatment based on sex falls in the category of special treatment given a selected class which 'impinges seriously on fundamental personal interests' [quoting 82 Harv. L. Rev.'s description of a suspect classification] and therefore the burden rests on the State to show a substantial justification for the female sentencing scheme . . . , empirically grounded to the greatest extent possible." Id. at 754-755. On remand, the defendant's sentence was reconsidered and lowered, and there was no occasion to pursue it further.

18. Gertner, Memorandum on Differential Sentencing 10-13 (unpublished paper, Yale Law School, 1971).

19. 1970 Uniform Crime Reports 124, Table 26.

20. National Prisoner Statistics, Bull. No. 47, Prisoners in State and Federal Institutions for Adult Felons 6, Table 36 (1972).

21. National Commission on Violence, Crimes of Violence: A Staff Report, Vol. 13, p. 845.

22. Id. at 845-846.

E. DIFFERENTIAL TREATMENT OF GIRLS AND BOYS BY THE JUVENILE JUSTICE SYSTEM

MATTER OF PATRICIA A.
31 N.Y.2d 83, 335 N.Y.S.2d 33 (1972)

Chief Judge FULD. The appellant Patricia A. has been adjudicated a person in need of supervision (referred to at times as PINS) pursuant to section 712 (subdiv. [b]) of the Family Court Act. Such a person is there defined as "a male less than sixteen years of age and a female less than eighteen years of age who does not attend school in accord with the provisions of part one of article sixty-five of the Education Law [relating to truancy or other nonattendance] or who is incorrigible, ungovernable or habitually disobedient and beyond the lawful control of parent or other lawful authority." The appellant, sixteen years old at the time of her PINS adjudication, contends, first —as does fifteen-year-old Tomasita in the companion appeal (Matter of Tomasita N., — N.Y.2d — , also decided today) — that the statute offends against the requirement of due process in that it is unconstitutionally vague and, second, that it discriminates against the sixteen and seventeen-year-old female in violation of the Equal Protection Clause of the state and federal constitutions. We treat each claim separately. [The Court ruled that the challenged statute was not void for vagueness.]

Discrimination by the state between different classes of citizens must, at the very least, "have some relevance to the purpose for which the classification is made." (Baxstrom v. Herold, 383 U.S. 107, 111; see also, Stanley v. Illinois, [405 U.S. 645 (1972)]; Eisenstadt v. Baird, [405 U.S. 438 (1972)]; Reed v. Reed, 404 U.S. 71, 76; Matter of Jesmer v. Dundon, 29 N.Y.2d 5, 9; Seidenberg v. McSorley's Old Ale House, 308 F. Supp. 1253; Sailer Inn v. Kirby, 5 Cal. 3d 1; Matter of Louise B., 68 Misc. 2d 95.) Phrased somewhat differently, the classification "must be reasonable, not arbitrary, and must rest upon some ground of difference having a fair and substantial relation to the object of the legislation, so that all persons similarly circumstanced shall be treated alike." (Reed v. Reed, 404 U.S. 71, 76, supra.)

The object of the PINS statute is to provide rehabilitation and treatment for young persons who engage in the sort of conduct there proscribed. This affords no reasonable ground, however, for differentiating between males and females over sixteen and under eighteen. Girls in that age bracket are no more prone than boys to truancy, disobedience, incorrigible conduct and the like, nor are they more in need of rehabilitation and treatment by reason of such conduct.

The argument that discrimination against females on the basis of age is justified because of the obvious danger of pregnancy in an immature girl and because of out-of-wedlock births which add to the welfare relief burdens of the state and city is wholly without merit. If that were a legislative purpose, males, as well as females, would, of course, be subject to the same restrictions: There would be no reason to exempt from the PINS definition, the sixteen and seventeen-year-old boy responsible for the girl's pregnancy on the out-of-wedlock birth. As it is, the conclusion seems inescapable that lurking behind the discrimination is the imputation that girls who engage in sexual misconduct ought more to be censured, and their conduct subject to greater control and regulation, than boys.

Somewhat similar moral presumptions have been squarely rejected as a basis or excuse for sexually discriminatory legislation (see Stanley v. Illinois, . . . supra; Eisenstadt . . . supra). Thus, in the *Stanley* case, the Supreme Court reversed a determination of the Illinois high court upholding a statute which made the children of unwed fathers wards of the state upon the death of the mother. It was a denial of equal protection, the court decided, to refuse a hearing to unmarried fathers as to their fitness to have custody of their children and, in effect, to presume that such fathers, as opposed to unwed mothers and other parents, are unsuitable and neglectful parents. . . . If an unwed father may not lose the custody of his children without the hearing to which unmarried mothers and other parents would be entitled, by a parity of reasoning, a girl of sixteen or seventeen may not be subject to a possible loss of liberty for conduct which would be entirely licit for sixteen and seventeen-year-old boys.

Consequently, since there is no justification for the age-sex discrimination, so much of section 712 (subdiv. [b]) of the Family Court Act as encompasses girls between the ages of sixteen and eighteen must be stricken as unconstitutional.

Judges Burke, Bergan, Breitel and Gibson concur with Chief Judge Fuld; Judges Scileppi and Jasen dissent. . . .

NOTES

1. An attack similar to that in Matter of Patricia A. was made against an Oklahoma statute by a young man over sixteen, but under eighteen, who sought the benefits of treatment as a juvenile on the ground that a girl would be so treated. In Lamb v. State, 475 P.2d 829 (Ct. Crim. App. Okla. 1970), the lower court upheld the age distinction on the basis of "the demonstrated facts of life." This reasoning was not found compelling by the Tenth Circuit, which found that the record did not show that the age distinction was based on a reasonable classification. Lamb v. Brown, 456 F.2d 18, 20 (10th Cir. 1972). Ultimately, the legislature raised to eighteen the age at which people would be treated as juveniles.

2. Singer summarizes the statistical evidence in the differential treatment of boys and girls:[23]

> Several years ago, a study of the treatment of female offenders in four countries concluded that while in every case fewer women than men were sent to prison, the misbehavior of girls was considered more serious and consequently was more strictly repressed than that of boys.[14] The limited data available for the United States appears to support this ironic conclusion. While some screening out of girls similar to that noted for women does appear to take place,[15] officials seem willing to institutionalize girls for far less serious offenses than those for which they confine boys. According to the President's Commission on Law Enforcement and Administration of Justice, more than half of the girls directed to juvenile court in 1965 were referred for conduct that would not be criminal if committed by adults; only one-fifth of the boys were referred for such conduct.[16] Evidence collected from Connecticut institutions indicated that while only 18 percent of the boys had been committed for "juvenile" offenses that would not be criminal if committed by adults, 80 percent of the girls were committed for similar involvements.[17] Similarly, more than 80 percent of the girls

23. Singer, Women and the Correctional Process, 11 Am. Crim. L. Rev. 295, 297-299 (1973).
14. Bertrand, The Myth of Sexual Equality Before the Law, in Quebec Society of Criminology Proceedings: 5th Research Conference on Delinquency and Criminality 129 (1967).
15. In 1970, more than 870,000 boys and 234,000 girls under eighteen, a ratio of 3.7 to 1, were arrested in the jurisdictions reporting to the Uniform Crime Reports. See 1970 Uniform Crime Reports, p. 124, Table 26. Few statistics are available on a national basis to reveal what happens to these minors after their arrest. In California, which does keep statistics, the ratio of boys to girls among first commitments to the Youth Authority in 1971 was 5.6 to 1, while the ratio of those given probation was approximately 2.5 to 1. Figures furnished by the California Youth Authority, 1972.
16. President's Commission on Law Enforcement and Administration of Justice, The Challenge of Crime in a Free Society 56 (1967).
17. Olson, ". . . For Her Own Protection . . ." A Case Study of the Conditions of Incarceration for Female Juvenile Offenders in the State of Connecticut 5 (1971) (unpublished paper, Yale Law School) [hereinafter cited as Olson]. The cited paper has since been published as Rogers, "For Her Own Protection. . . .": Conditions of Incarceration for Female Juvenile Offenders in the State of Connecticut, 7 Law & Soc'y Rev. 223 (1972).]

incarcerated in a state institution in New Jersey were "criminals without crimes," having been committed for such offenses as running away from home; being incorrigible, ungovernable, and beyond control of parents; being truant; being promiscuous; engaging in sexual relations; and becoming pregnant.[18]

There is some evidence that, although girls are institutionalized for less serious delinquency on the average than boys, they in fact spend longer periods of time in institutions. In 1964, the nationwide median length of stay in institutions for girls was 10.7 months; for boys it was 8.2 months.[19] More recently, girls in Connecticut spent an average of seven months in an institution, while boys stayed for an average of five months.[20] In New York, girls averaged 12-month stays, while boys averaged 9.3 months.[21] Although there is no clear explanation for this disparity, observers have attributed it tentatively to the fear of pregnancy occurring in young girls.[22]

---

18. See Lerman, Child Convicts, 8 Transaction 35 (1971). This pattern also appears in other states. See generally W. Reckless, The Crime Problem (1967), citing Clark, Systematic Comparison of Female and Male Delinquency 22-24, 1961 (Ph. D. dissertation, Ohio State University) (74 percent of the girls to go through juvenile court were complained about for being "wayward").

In Gesicki v. Oswald, 336 F. Supp. 371 (S.D.N.Y. 1971) (wayward minor statute held invalid as impermissible punishment of a status), the court cited typical examples of girls to whom the wayward minor statute, N.Y. Code Crim. Proc. §§913-(a)(5)-(6), applied:

"Esther Gesicki was expelled from school because the school principal charged her with 'sexual promiscuity' and later adjudicated a wayward minor. She was placed in a foster home. When her social worker refused to allow her to return home . . . [to her mother] Esther ran away. She then was sent to Albion and later to Bedford Hills for violating probation.

"When her social worker pressured her to give up the illegitimate child for adoption and she refused, Marion Johnson was adjudicated a wayward minor. . . . Her social worker allegedly told her: 'If you had signed the adoption papers, you wouldn't be going to Albion.'

"Dominica Morelli, the first of eight children, grew up in a broken home. Her mother remarried four times, and one of her stepfathers sexually assaulted her. After her mother, an alcoholic, was found to be unfit, all the children were placed in foster homes. When Dominica ran away, her mother secured a warrant for her arrest. Dominica was allowed to remain at home, but was placed under a curfew. She has no recollection of being placed on probation. After she journeyed to Williamsport, Pennsylvania, with a friend and without her mother's permission (she was suspected of having attended a drug party), she was charged with violating probation." Id. at 375 n.5.

19. U.S. Dep't of Health, Education & Welfare, Children's Bureau, Statistics on Public Institutions for Delinquent Children — 1964 (1965).

20. Olson, supra note 17, at 5.

21. Gold, Equal Protection for Juvenile Girls in Need of Supervision in New York State, 46 N.Y.L.F. 57 (1971).

22. Olson, supra note 17, at 6-7. "The major reason for the persisting inequality and confinement periods between the two institutions lies in the attitudes of the staff who prepare the six-month case summaries for the Commissioner to review. In the case of the staff at [the boys' institution], they are often anxious to see the boys return to the community and tend to have plans worked out at their five-month 'progress meetings' at school. At [the girls' institution], the staff often insists that a girl finish her academic term, even though her behavior would warrant release, or they may fear 'summer temptations' if a girl is released over the summer with nothing to 'keep her occupied,' or they may keep a girl through a pregnancy and for two months afterwards until she is 'medically cleared.' " Id.

CHAPTER FIVE

WOMEN'S RIGHTS TO CONTROL THEIR REPRODUCTIVE CAPACITIES, OBTAIN EQUAL EDUCATION AND GAIN EQUAL ACCESS TO PLACES OF PUBLIC ACCOMMODATION

This chapter brings together materials in three seemingly diverse areas. Yet all three involve application of constitutional doctrine; for instance, concepts of state action are central to the developing law in each category, as is the meaning of the privacy right. Yet none of the topics is most usefully studied under the rubric of constitutional law. Rather, investigation in each area stirs fundamental policy questions for the women's movement. What are the ultimate goals? What is "good" for women? Are there priorities among goals, and if so, is there any way to set them? How much harm may be done to individual women in the short range in the effort to realize grand ends? And how much harm is too much? Because these materials relate to each other in raising such questions in three extremely different contexts, they have been placed together in this chapter.

I. THE RIGHT OF WOMEN TO CHOOSE WHETHER TO BEAR CHILDREN

ROE v. WADE
410 U.S. 113, 93 S. Ct. 756, 35 L. Ed. 2d 147 (1973)

Mr. Justice BLACKMUN delivered the opinion of the Court.

This Texas federal appeal and its Georgia companion, Doe v. Bolton, post. . . , present constitutional challenges to state criminal abortion legislation. The Texas statutes under attack here are typical of those that have been in effect in many States for approximately a century. The Georgia statutes, in contrast, have a modern cast and are a legislative product that, to an extent at least, obviously reflects the influences of recent attitudinal change, of advancing medical knowledge and techniques, and of new thinking about an old issue.

We forthwith acknowledge our awareness of the sensitive and emotional nature of the abortion controversy, of the vigorous opposing views, even among physicians, and of the deep and seemingly absolute convictions that the subject inspires. One's philosophy, one's experiences, one's exposure to the raw edges of human existence, one's religious training, one's attitudes toward life and family and their values, and the moral standards one establishes and seeks to observe, are all likely to influence and to color one's thinking and conclusions about abortion.

In addition, population growth, pollution, poverty, and racial overtones tend to complicate and not to simplify the problem.

Our task, of course, is to resolve the issue by constitutional measurement free of emotion and of predilection. We seek earnestly to do this, and, because we do, we have inquired into, and in this opinion place some emphasis upon, medical and medical-legal history and what that history reveals about man's attitudes toward the abortive procedure over the centuries. We bear in mind, too, Mr. Justice Holmes' admonition in his now vindicated dissent in Lochner v. New York, 198 U.S. 45, 76 (1905):

> It [the Constitution] is made for people of fundamentally differing views, and the accident of our finding certain opinions natural and familiar or novel and even shocking ought not to conclude our judgment upon the question whether statutes embodying them conflict with the Constitution of the United States.

I

The Texas statutes that concern us here are Arts. 1191-1194 and 1196 of the State's Penal Code.[1] These make it a crime to "procure an abortion," as therein defined, or to attempt one, except with respect to "an abortion procured or attempted by medical advice for the purpose of saving the life of the mother." Similar statutes are in existence in a majority of the States. . . .

II

Jane Roe, a single woman who was residing in Dallas County, Texas, instituted this federal action in March 1970 against the District Attorney of the county. . . .

Roe alleged that she was unmarried and pregnant; that she wished to terminate her pregnancy by an abortion "performed by a competent, licensed physician, under safe, clinical conditions"; that she was unable to get a "legal" abortion in Texas because her life did not appear to be threatened by the continuation of her pregnancy; and that she could not afford to travel to another jurisdiction in order to secure a legal abortion under safe conditions. She claimed that the Texas statutes were unconstitutionally vague and

---

1. "Article 1191. Abortion

"If any person shall designedly administer to a pregnant woman or knowingly procure to be administered with her consent any drug or medicine, or shall use towards her any violence or means whatever externally or internally applied, and thereby procure an abortion, he shall be confined in the penitentiary not less than two nor more than five years; if it be done without her consent, the punishment shall be doubled. By 'abortion' is meant that the life of the fetus or embryo shall be destroyed in the woman's womb or that a premature birth thereof be caused.

"Art. 1192. Furnishing the means

"Whoever furnishes the means for procuring an abortion knowing the purpose intended is guilty as an accomplice.

"Art. 1193. Attempt at abortion

"If the means used shall fail to produce an abortion, the offender is nevertheless guilty of an attempt to produce abortion, provided it be shown that such means were calculated to produce that result, and shall be fined not less than one hundred nor more than one thousand dollars.

"Art. 1194. Murder in producing abortion

"If the death of the mother is occasioned by an abortion so produced or by an attempt to effect the same it is murder.

"Art. 1196. By medical advice

"Nothing in this chapter applies to an abortion procured or attempted by medical advice for the purpose of saving the life of the mother."

The foregoing Articles, together with Art. 1195, comprise Chapter 9 of Title 15 of the Penal Code. Article 1195, not attacked here, reads:

"Art. 1195. Destroying unborn child

"Whoever shall during parturition of the mother destroy the vitality or life in a child in a state of being born and before actual birth, which child would otherwise have been born alive, shall be confined in the penitentiary for life or for not less than five years."

that they abridged her right of personal privacy, protected by the First, Fourth, Fifth, Ninth, and Fourteenth Amendments. By an amendment to her complaint Roe purported to sue "on behalf of herself and all other women" similarly situated. . . .

The usual rule in federal cases is that an actual controversy must exist at stages of appellate or certiorari review, and not simply at the date the action is initiated. United States v. Munsingwear, Inc., 340 U.S. 36 (1950); Golden v. Zwickler, [394 U.S. 103 (1969)]; SEC v. Medical Committee for Human Rights, 404 U.S. 403 (1972).

But when, as here, pregnancy is a significant fact in the litigation, the normal 266-day human gestation period is so short that the pregnancy will come to term before the usual appellate process is complete. If that termination makes a case moot, pregnancy litigation seldom will survive much beyond the trial stage, and appellate review will be effectively denied. Our law should not be that rigid. Pregnancy often comes more than once to the same woman, and in the general population, if man is to survive, it will always be with us. Pregnancy provides a classic justification for a conclusion of non-mootness. It truly could be "capable of repetition, yet evading review." Southern Pacific Terminal Co. v. ICC, 219 U.S. 498, 515 (1911). See Moore v. Ogilvie, 394 U.S. 814, 816 (1969); Carroll v. President and Commissioners, 393 U.S. 175, 178–179 (1968); United States v. W. T. Grant Co., 345 U.S. 629, 632-633 (1953).

We therefore agree with the District Court that Jane Roe had standing to undertake this litigation, that she presented a justiciable controversy, and that the termination of her 1970 pregnancy has not rendered her case moot. . . .

V

The principal thrust of appellant's attack on the Texas statutes is that they improperly invade a right, said to be possessed by the pregnant woman, to choose to terminate her pregnancy. Appellant would discover this right in the concept of personal "liberty" embodied in the Fourteenth Amendment's Due Process Clause; or in personal, marital, familial, and sexual privacy said to be protected by the Bill of Rights or its penumbras, see Griswold v. Connecticut, 381 U.S. 479 (1965); Eisenstadt v. Baird, 405 U.S. 438 (1972); id., at 460 (White, J., concurring); or among those rights reserved to the people by the Ninth Amendment, Griswold v. Connecticut, 381 U.S., at 486 (Goldberg, J., concurring). Before addressing this claim, we feel it desirable briefly to survey, in several aspects, the history of abortion, for such insight as that history may afford us, and then to examine the state purposes and interests behind the criminal abortion laws.

VI

It perhaps is not generally appreciated that the restrictive criminal abortion laws in effect in a majority of States today are of relatively recent vintage. Those laws, generally proscribing abortion or its attempt at any time during pregnancy except when necessary to preserve the pregnant woman's life, are not of ancient or even of common law origin. Instead, they derive from statutory changes effected, for the most part, in the latter half of the 19th century.

1. *Ancient attitudes.* These are not capable of precise determination. We are told that at the time of the Persian Empire abortifacients were known and that criminal abortions were severely punished. We are also told, however, that abortion was practiced in Greek times as well as in the Roman Era, and that "it was resorted to without scruple." The Ephesian, Soranos, often described as the greatest of the ancient gynecologists, appears to have been generally opposed to Rome's prevailing free-abortion practices. He found it necessary to think first of the life of the mother, and he resorted to abortion when, upon this standard, he felt the procedure advisable. Greek and Roman law afforded little protection to the unborn. If abortion was prosecuted in some places, it seems to have been based on a concept of a violation of the father's right to his offspring. Ancient religion did not bar abortion.

2. *The Hippocratic Oath.* What then of the famous Oath that has stood so long as the ethical guide of the medical profession and that bears the name of the great Greek

(460(?)–377(?) B.C.), who has been described as the Father of Medicine, the "wisest and the greatest practioner of his art," and the "most important and most complete medical personality of antiquity," who dominated the medical schools of his time, and who typified the sum of the medical knowledge of the past? The Oath varies somewhat according to the particular translation, but in any translation the content is clear: "I will give no deadly medicine to anyone if asked, nor suggest any such counsel; and in like manner I will not give to a woman a pessary to produce abortion," or "I will neither give a deadly drug to anybody if asked for it, nor will I make a suggestion to this effect. Similarly, I will not give to a woman an abortive remedy."

Although the Oath is not mentioned in any of the principal briefs in this case or in Doe v. Bolton, post, it represents the apex of the development of strict ethical concepts in medicine, and its influence endures to this day. Why did not the authority of Hippocrates dissuade abortion practice in his time and that of Rome? The late Dr. Edelstein provides us with a theory: The Oath was not uncontested even in Hippocrates' day; only the Pythagorean school of philosophers frowned upon the related act of suicide. Most Greek thinkers, on the other hand, commended abortion, at least prior to viability. See Plato, Republic, V. 461; Aristotle, Politics, VII, 1335 b 25. For the Pythagoreans, however, it was a matter of dogma. For them the embryo was animate from the moment of conception, and abortion meant destruction of a living being. The abortion clause of the Oath, therefore, "echoes Pythagorean doctrines," and "[i]n no other stratum of Greek opinion were such views held or proposed in the same spirit of uncompromising austerity."

Edelstein then concludes that the Oath originated in a group representing only a small segment of Greek opinion and that it certainly was not accepted by all ancient physicians. He points out that medical writings down to Galen (130–200 A.D.) "give evidence of the violation of almost every one of its injunctions." But with the end of antiquity a decided change took place. Resistance against suicide and against abortion became common. The Oath came to be popular. The emerging teachings of Christianity were in agreement with the Pythagorean ethic. The Oath "became the nucleus of all medical ethics" and "was applauded as the embodiment of truth." Thus, suggests Dr. Edelstein, it is "a Pythagorean manifesto and not the expression of an absolute standard of medical conduct."

This, it seems to us, is a satisfactory and acceptable explanation of the Hippocratic Oath's apparent rigidity. It enables us to understand, in historical context, a long accepted and revered statement of medical ethics.

3. *The Common Law.* It is undisputed that at the common law, abortion performed *before* "quickening" — the first recognizable movement of the fetus in utero, appearing usually from the 16th to the 18th week of pregnancy — was not an indictable offense. The absence of a common law crime for pre-quickening abortion appears to have developed from a confluence of earlier philosophical, theological, and civil and canon law concepts of when life begins. These disciplines variously approached the question in terms of the point at which the embryo or fetus became "formed" or recognizably human, or in terms of when a "person" came into being, that is, infused with a "soul" or "animated." A loose consensus evolved in early English law that these events occurred at some point between conception and live birth. This was "mediate animation." Although Christian theology and the canon law came to fix the point of animation at 40 days for a male and 80 days for a female, a view that persisted until the 19th century, there was otherwise little agreement about the precise time of formation or animation. There was agreement, however, that prior to this point the fetus was to be regarded as part of the mother and its destruction, therefore, was not homicide. Due to continued uncertainty about the precise time when animation occurred, to the lack of any empirical basis for the 40–80 day view, and perhaps to Acquinas' definition of movement as one of the two first principles of life, Bracton focused upon quickening as the critical point. The significance of quickening was echoed by later common law scholars and found its way into the received common law in this country.

Whether abortion of a *quick* fetus was a felony at common law, or even a lesser crime, is still disputed. Bracton, writing early in the 13th century, thought it homicide. But the later and predominant view, following the great common law scholars, has been that it was at most a lesser offense. In a frequently cited passage, Coke took the position that abortion of a woman "quick with childe" is "a great misprision and no murder." Blackstone followed, saying that while abortion after quickening had once been considered manslaughter (though not murder), "modern law" took a less severe view. A recent review of the common law precedents argues, however, that those precedents contradict Coke and that even post-quickening abortion was never established as a common law crime.[26] This is of some importance because while most American courts ruled, in holding or dictum, that abortion of an unquickened fetus was not criminal under their received common law, others followed Coke in stating that abortion of a quick fetus was a "misprision," a term they translated to mean "misdemeanor." That their reliance on Coke on this aspect of the law was uncritical and, apparently in all the reported cases, dictum (due probably to the paucity of common law prosecutions for post-quickening abortion), makes it now appear doubtful that abortion was ever firmly established as a common law crime even with respect to the destruction of a quick fetus.

4. *The English statutory law.* England's first criminal abortion statute, Lord Ellenborough's Act, 43 Geo. 3, c. 58, came in 1803. It made abortion of a quick fetus, §1, a capital crime, but in §2 it provided lesser penalties for the felony of abortion before quickening, and thus preserved the quickening distinction. This contrast was continued in the general revision of 1828, 9 Geo. 4, c. 31, §13, at 104. It disappeared, however, together with the death penalty, in 1837, 7 Will. 4 & 1 Vic., c. 85, §6, at 360, and did not reappear in the Offenses Against the Person Act of 1861, 24 & 25 Vic., c. 100, §59, at 438, that formed the core of English anti-abortion law until the liberalizing reforms of 1967. In 1929 the Infant Life (Preservation) Act, 19 & 20 Geo. 5, c. 34, came into being. Its emphasis was upon the destruction of "the life of a child capable of being born alive." It made a willful act preformed with the necessary intent a felony. It contained a proviso that one was not to be found guilty of the offense "unless it is proved that the act which caused the death of the child was not done in good faith for the purpose only of preserving the life of the mother."

A seemingly notable development in the English law was the case of Rex v. Bourne, [1939] 1 K.B. 687. This case apparently answered in the affirmative the question whether an abortion necessary to preserve the life of the pregnant woman was excepted from the criminal penalties of the 1861 Act. In his instructions to the jury Judge Macnaghten referred to the 1929 Act, and observed, p. 691, that that Act related to "the case where a child is killed by a willful act at the time when it is being delivered in the ordinary course of nature." Id., at 91. He concluded that the 1861 Act's use of the word "unlawfully," imported the same meaning expressed by the specific proviso in the 1929 Act even though there was no mention of preserving the mother's life in the 1861 Act. He then construed the phrase "preserving the life of the mother" broadly, that is, "in a reasonable sense," to include a serious and permanent threat to the mother's *health,* and instructed the jury to acquit Dr. Bourne if it found he had acted in a good faith belief that the abortion was necessary for this purpose. Id., at 693–694. The jury did acquit.

---

26. C. Means, The Phoenix of Abortional Freedom: Is a Penumbral or Ninth-Amendment Right About to Arise from the Nineteenth-Century Legislative Ashes of a Fourteenth-Century Common-Law Liberty?, 17 N.Y.L. Forum 335 (1971) (hereinafter "Means II"). The author examines the two principal precedents cited marginally by Coke, both contrary to his dictum, and traces the treatment of these and other cases by earlier commentators. He concludes that Coke, who himself participated as an advocate in an abortion case in 1601, may have intentionally misstated the law. The author even suggests a reason: Coke's strong feelings about abortion, coupled with his reluctance to acknowledge common law (secular) jurisdiction to assess penalties for an offence that traditionally had been an exclusively ecclesiastical or canon law crime. See also Lader 78-79, who notes that some scholars doubt the common law ever was applied to abortion; that the English ecclesiastical courts seem to have lost interest in the problem after 1527; and that the preamble to the English legislation of 1803, 43 Geo. 3, c. 58, §1, at 203, referred to in the text, infra, states that "no adequate means have been hitherto provided for the prevention and punishment of such offenses."

Recently Parliament enacted a new abortion law. This is the Abortion Act of 1967, 15 & 16 Eliz. 2, c. 87. The Act permits a licensed physician to perform an abortion where two other licensed physicians agree (a) "that the continuance of the pregnancy would involve risk to the life of the pregnant woman, or of injury to the physical or mental health of the pregnant woman or any existing children of her family, greater than if the pregnancy were terminated," or (b) "that there is a substantial risk that if the child were born it would suffer from such physical or mental abnormalities as to be seriously handicapped." The Act also provides that, in making this determination, "account may be taken of the pregnant woman's actual or reasonably forseeable environment." It also permits a physician, without the concurrence of others, to terminate a pregnancy where he is of the good faith opinion that the abortion "is immediately necessary to save the life or to prevent grave permanent injury to the physical or mental health of the pregnant woman."

5. *The American law.* In this country the law in effect in all but a few States until mid-19th century was the pre-existing English common law. Connecticut, the first State to enact abortion legislation, adopted in 1821 that part of Lord Ellenborough's Act that related to a woman "quick with child." The death penalty was not imposed. Abortion before quickening was made a crime in that State only in 1860. In 1828 New York enacted legislation that, in two respects, was to serve as a model for early anti-abortion statutes. First, while barring destruction of an unquickened fetus as well as a quick fetus, it made the former only a misdemeanor, but the latter second-degree manslaughter. Second, it incorporated a concept of therapeutic abortion by providing that an abortion was excused if it "shall have been necessary to preserve the life of such mother, or shall have been advised by two physicians to be necessary for such purpose." By 1840, when Texas had received the common law, only eight American States had statutes dealing with abortion. It was not until after the War Between the States that legislation began generally to replace the common law. Most of these initial statutes dealt severely with abortion after quickening but were lenient with it before quickening. Most punished attempts equally with completed abortions. While many statutes included the exception for an abortion thought by one or more physicians to be necessary to save the mother's life, that provision soon disappeared and the typical law required that the procedure actually be necessary for that purpose.

Gradually, in the middle and late 19th century the quickening distinction disappeared from the statutory law of most States and the degree of the offense and the penalties were increased. By the end of the 1950's, a large majority of the States banned abortion, however and whenever performed, unless done to save or preserve the life of the mother. The exceptions, Alabama and the District of Columbia, permitted abortion to preserve the mother's health. Three other States permitted abortions that were not "unlawfully" performed or that were not "without lawful justification," leaving interpretation of those standards to the courts. In the past several years, however, a trend toward liberalization of abortion statutes has resulted in adoption, by about one-third of the States, of less stringent laws, most of them patterned after the ALI Model Penal Code, §230.3, set forth as Appendix B to the opinion in Doe v. Bolton, post — .

It is thus apparent that at common law, at the time of the adoption of our Constitution, and throughout the major portion of the 19th century, abortion was viewed with less disfavor than under most American statutes currently in effect. Phrasing it another way, a woman enjoyed a substantially broader right to terminate a pregnancy than she does in most States today. At least with respect to the early stage of pregnancy, and very possibly without such a limitation, the opportunity to make this choice was present in this country well into the 19th century. Even later, the law continued for some time to treat less punitively an abortion procured in early pregnancy.

6. *The position of the American Medical Association.* The anti-abortion mood prevalent in

this country in the late 19th century was shared by the medical profession. Indeed, the attitude of the profession may have played a significant role in the enactment of stringent criminal abortion legislation during that period.

An AMA Committee on Criminal Abortion was appointed in May 1857. It presented its report, 12 Trans. of the Am. Med. Assn. 73-77 (1859), to the Twelfth Annual Meeting. That report observed that the Committee had been appointed to investigate criminal abortion "with a view to its general suppression." It deplored abortion and its frequency and it listed three causes "of this general demoralization":

> The first of these causes is a wide-spread popular ignorance of the true character of the crime — a belief, even among mothers themselves, that the foetus is not alive till after the period of quickening.
> The second of the agents alluded to is the fact that the profession themselves are frequently supposed careless of foetal life. . . .
> The third reason of the frightful extent of this crime is found in the grave defects of our laws, both common and statute, as regards the independent and actual existence of the child before birth, as a living being. These errors, which are sufficient in most instances to prevent conviction, are based, and only based, upon mistaken and exploded medical dogmas. With strange inconsistency, the law fully acknowledges the foetus in utero and its inherent rights, for civil purposes; while personally and as criminally affected, it fails to recognize it, and to its life as yet denies all protection. Id., at 75-76.

The Committee then offered, and the Association adopted, resolutions protesting "against such unwarrantable destruction of human life," calling upon state legislatures to revise their abortion laws, and requesting the cooperation of state medical societies "in pressing the subject." Id., at 28, 78.

In 1871 a long and vivid report was submitted by the Committee on Criminal Abortion. It ended with the observation, "We had to deal with human life. In a matter of less importance we could entertain no compromise. An honest judge on the bench would call things by their proper names. We could do no less." 22 Trans. of the Am. Med. Assn. 258 (1871). It proffered resolutions, adopted by the Association, id., at 38-39, recommending, among other things, that it "be unlawful and unprofessional for any physician to induce abortion or premature labor, without the concurrent opinion of at least one respectable consulting physician, and then always with a view to the safety of the child — if that be possible," and calling "the attention of the clergy of all denominations to the perverted views of morality entertained by a large class of females —aye, and men also, on this important question."

Except for periodic condemnation of the criminal abortionist, no further formal AMA action took place until 1967. In that year the Committee on Human Reproduction urged the adoption of a stated policy of opposition to induced abortion except when there is "documented medical evidence" of a threat to the health or life of the mother, or that the child "may be born with incapacitating physical deformity or mental deficiency," or that a pregnancy "resulting from legally established statutory or forcible rape or incest may constitute a threat to the mental or physical health of the patient," and two other physicians "chosen because of their recognized professional competence have examined the patient and have concurred in writing," and the procedure "is performed in a hospital accredited by the Joint Commission on Accreditation of Hospitals." The providing of medical information by physicians to state legislatures in their consideration of legislation regarding therapeutic abortion was "to be considered consistent with the principles of ethics of the American Medical Association." This recommendation was adopted by the House of Delegates. Proceedings of the AMA House of Delegates, 40-51 (June 1967).

In 1970, after the introduction of a variety of proposed resolutions, and of a report from its Board of Trustees, a reference committee noted "polarization of the medical profession on this controversial issue"; division among those who had testified; a difference of opinion among AMA councils and committees; "the remarkable shift in testimony" in six months, felt to be influenced "by the rapid changes in state laws and by the judicial decisions which tend to make abortion more freely available;" and a feeling "that this trend will continue." On June 25, 1970, the House of Delegates adopted preambles and most of the resolutions proposed by the reference committee. The preambles emphasized "the best interests of the patient," "sound clinical judgment," and "informed patient consent," in contrast to "mere acquiescence to the patient's demand." The resolutions asserted that abortion is a medical procedure that should be performed by a licensed physician in an accredited hospital only after consultation with two other physicians and in conformity with state law, and that no party to the procedure should be required to violate personally held moral principles. Proceedings of the AMA House of Delegates 221 (June 1970). The AMA Judicial Council rendered a complementary opinion.

7. *The position of the American Public Health Association.* In October 1970, the Executive Board of the APHA adopted Standards for Abortion Services. These were five in number:

> a. Rapid and simple abortion referral must be readily available through state and local public health departments, medical societies, or other nonprofit organizations.
>
> b. An important function of counseling should be to simplify and expedite the provision of abortion services; it should not delay the obtaining of these services.
>
> c. Psychiatric consultation should not be mandatory. As in the case of other specialized medical services, psychiatric consultation should be sought for definite indications and not on a routine basis.
>
> d. A wide range of individuals from appropriately trained, sympathetic volunteers to highly skilled physicians may qualify as abortion counselors.
>
> e. Contraception and/or sterilization should be discussed with each abortion patient. Recommended Standards for Abortion Services, 61 Am. J.Pub.Health 396 (1971).

Among factors pertinent to life and health risks associated with abortion were three that "are recognized as important":

> a. the skill of the physician,
> b. the environment in which the abortion is performed, and above all
> c. the duration of pregnancy, as determined by uterine size and confirmed by menstrual history. Id., at 397.

It was said that "a well-equipped hospital" offers more protection "to cope with unforeseen difficulties than an office or clinic without such resources. . . . The factor of gestational age is of overriding importance." Thus it was recommended that abortions in the second trimester and early abortions in the presence of existing medical complications be performed in hospitals as in-patient procedures. For pregnancies in the first trimester, abortion in the hospital with or without overnight stay "is probably the safest practice." An abortion in an extramural facility, however, is an acceptable alternative "provided arrangements exist in advance to admit patients promptly if unforeseen complications develop." Standards for an abortion facility were listed. It was said that at present abortions should be performed by physicians or osteopaths who are licensed to practice and who have "adequate training." Id., at 398.

8. *The position of the American Bar Association.* At its meeting in February 1972 the ABA House of Delegates approved, with 17 opposing votes, the Uniform Abortion Act that had been drafted and approved the preceding August by the Conference of Commis-

sioners on Uniform State Laws. 58 A.B.A.J. 380 (1972). We set forth the Act in full in the margin.[40] The Conference has appended an enlightening Prefatory Note.[41]

VII

Three reasons have been advanced to explain historically the enactment of criminal abortion laws in the 19th century and to justify their continued existence.

It has been argued occasionally that these laws were the product of a Victorian social concern to discourage illicit sexual conduct. Texas, however, does not advance this justification in the present case, and it appears that no court or commentator has taken the argument seriously. The appellants and amici contend, moreover, that this is not a proper state purpose at all and suggest that, if it were, the Texas statutes are overbroad in protecting it since the law fails to distinguish between married and unwed mothers.

A second reason is concerned with abortion as a medical procedure. When most criminal abortion laws were first enacted, the procedure was a hazardous one for the woman. This was particularly true prior to the development of antisepsis. Antiseptic

---

40. "UNIFORM ABORTION ACT

"Section 1. [*Abortion Defined; When Authorized.*]

"(a) 'Abortion' means the termination of human pregnancy with an intention other than to produce a live birth or to remove a dead fetus

"(b) An abortion may be performed in this state only if it is performed:

"(1) by a physician licensed to practice medicine [or osteopathy] in this state or by a physician practicing medicine [or osteopathy] in the employ of the government of the United States or of this state, [and the abortion is performed [in the physician's office or in a medical clinic, or] in a hospital approved by the [Department of Health] or operated by the United States, this state, or any department, agency, or political subdivision of either;] or by a female upon herself upon the advice of the physician; and

"(2) within [20] weeks after the commencement of the pregnancy [or after [20] weeks only if the physician has reasonable cause to believe (i) there is a substantial risk that continuance of the pregnancy would endanger the life of the mother or would gravely impair the physical or mental health of the mother, (ii) that the child would be born with grave physical or mental defect, or (iii) that the pregnancy resulted from rape or incest, or illicit intercourse with a girl under the age of 16 years of age].

"Section 2. [*Penalty.*] Any person who performs or procures an abortion other than authorized by this Act is guilty of a [felony] and, upon conviction thereof, may be sentenced to pay a fine not exceeding [$1,000] or to imprisonment [in the state penitentiary] not exceeding [5 years], or both.

"Section 3. [*Uniformity of Interpretation.*] This Act shall be construed to effectuate its general purpose to make uniform the law with respect to the subject of this Act among those states which enact it.

"Section 4. [*Short Title.*] This Act may be cited as the Uniform Abortion Act.

"Section 5. [*Severability.*] If any provision of this Act or the application thereof to any person or circumstance is held invalid, the invalidity does not affect other provisions or applications of this Act which can be given effect without the invalid provision or application, and to this end the provisions of this Act are severable.

"Section 6. [*Repeal.*] The following acts and parts of acts are repealed:

"(1)

"(2)

"(3)

"Section 7. [*Time of Taking Effect.*] This Act shall take effect _____."

41. "This Act is based largely upon the New York abortion act following a review of the more recent laws on abortion in several states and upon recognition of a more liberal trend in laws on this subject. Recognition was given also to the several decisions in state and federal courts which show a further trend toward liberalization of abortion laws, especially during the first trimester of pregnancy.

"Recognizing that a number of problems appeared in New York, a shorter time period for 'unlimited' abortions was advisable. The time period was bracketed to permit the various states to insert a figure more in keeping with the different conditions that might exist among the states. Likewise, the language limiting the place or places in which abortions may be performed was also bracketed to account for different conditions among the states. In addition, limitations on abortions after the initial 'unlimited' period were placed in brackets so that individual states may adopt all or any of these reasons, or place further restrictions upon abortions after the initial period.

"This Act does not contain any provision relating to medical review committees or prohibitions against sanctions imposed upon medical personnel refusing to participate in abortions because of religious or other similar reasons, or the like. Such provisions, while related, do not directly pertain to when, where, or by whom abortions may be performed; however, the Act is not drafted to exclude such a provision by a state wishing to enact the same."

techniques, of course, were based on discoveries by Lister, Pasteur, and others first announced in 1867, but were not generally accepted and employed until about the turn of the century. Abortion mortality was high. Even after 1900, and perhaps until as late as the development of antibiotics in the 1940's, standard modern techniques such as dilation and curettage were not nearly so safe as they are today. Thus it has been argued that a State's real concern in enacting a criminal abortion law was to protect the pregnant woman, that is, to restrain her from submitting to a procedure that placed her life in serious jeopardy.

Modern medical techniques have altered this situation. Appellants and various amici refer to medical data indicating that abortion in early pregnancy, that is, prior to the end of first trimester, although not without its risk, is now relatively safe. Mortality rates for women undergoing early abortions, where the procedure is legal, appear to be as low as or lower than the rates for normal childbirth. Consequently, any interest of the State in protecting the woman from an inherently hazardous procedure, except when it would be equally dangerous for her to forgo it, has largely disappeared. Of course, important state interests in the area of health and medical standards do remain. The State has a legitimate interest in seeing to it that abortion, like any other medical procedure, is performed under circumstances that insure maximum safety for the patient. This interest obviously extends at least to the performing physician and his staff, to the facilities involved, to the availability of after-care, and to adequate provision for any complication or emergency that might arise. The prevalence of high mortality rates at illegal "abortion mills" strengthens, rather than weakens, the State's interest in regulating the conditions under which abortions are performed. Moreover, the risk to the woman increases as her pregnancy continues. Thus the State retains a definite interest in protecting the woman's own health and safety when an abortion is proposed at a late stage of pregnancy.

The third reason is the State's interest — some phrase it in terms of duty — in protecting prenatal life. Some of the argument for this justification rests on the theory that a new human life is present from the moment of conception. The State's interest and general obligation to protect life then extends, it is argued, to prenatal life. Only when the life of the pregnant mother herself is at stake, balanced against the life she carries within her, should the interest of the embryo or fetus not prevail. Logically, of course, a legitimate state interest in this area need not stand or fall on acceptance of the belief that life begins at conception or at some other point prior to live birth. In assessing the State's interest, recognition may be given to the less rigid claim that as long as at least *potential* life is involved, the State may assert interests beyond the protection of the pregnant woman alone.

Parties challenging state abortion laws have sharply disputed in some courts the contention that a purpose of these laws, when enacted, was to protect prenatal life. Pointing to the absence of legislative history to support the contention, they claim that most state laws were designed solely to protect the woman. Because medical advances have lessened this concern, at least with respect to abortion in early pregnancy, they argue that with respect to such abortions the laws can no longer be justified by any state interest. There is some scholarly support for this view of original purpose. The few state courts called upon to interpret their laws in the late 19th and early 20th centuries did focus on the State's interest in protecting the woman's health rather than in preserving the embryo and fetus. Proponents of this view point out that in many States, including Texas, by statute or judicial interpretation, the pregnant woman herself could not be prosecuted for self-abortion or for cooperating in an abortion performed upon her by another. They claim that adoption of the "quickening" distinction through received common law and state statutes tacitly recognizes the greater health hazards inherent in late abortion and impliedly repudiates the theory that life begins at conception.

It is with these interests, and the weight to be attached to them, that this case is concerned.

VIII

The Constitution does not explicitly mention any right of privacy. In a line of decisions, however, going back perhaps as far as Union Pacific R. Co. v. Botsford, 141 U.S. 250, 251 (1891), the Court has recognized that a right of personal privacy, or a guarantee of certain areas or zones of privacy, does exist under the Constitution. In varying contexts the Court or individual Justices have indeed found at least the roots of that right in the First Amendment, Stanley v. Georgia, 394 U.S. 557, 564 (1969); in the Fourth andFifth Amendments, Terry v. Ohio, 392 U.S. 1, 8-9 (1968), Katz v. United States, 389 U.S. 347, 350 (1967), Boyd v. United States, 116 U.S. 616 (1886), see Olmstead v. United States, 277 U.S. 438, 478 (1928) (Brandeis, J. dissenting); in the penumbras of the Bill of Rights, Griswold v. Connecticut, 381 U.S. 479, 484-485 (1965); in the Ninth Amendment, id., at 486 (Goldberg, J., concurring); or in the concept of liberty guaranteed by the first section of the Fourteenth Amendment, see Meyer v. Nebraska, 262 U.S. 390, 399 (1923). These decisions make it clear that only personal rights that can be deemed "fundamental" or "implicit in the concept of ordered liberty," Palko v. Connecticut, 302 U.S. 319, 325 (1937), are included in this guarantee of personal privacy. They also make it clear that the right has some extension to activities relating to marriage, Loving v. Virginia, 388 U.S. 1, 12 (1967), procreation, Skinner v. Oklahoma, 316 U.S. 535, 541-542 (1942), contraception, Eisenstadt v. Baird, 405 U.S. 438, 453-454 (1972); id., at 460, 463-465 (White, J., concurring), family relationships, Prince v. Massachusetts, 321 U.S. 158, 166 (1944), and child rearing and education, Pierce v. Society of Sisters, 268 U.S. 510, 535 (1925), Meyer v. Nebraska, supra.

This right of privacy, whether it be founded in the Fourteenth Amendment's concept of personal liberty and restrictions upon state action, as we feel it is, or, as the District Court determined, in the Ninth Amendment's reservation of rights to the people, is broad enough to encompass a woman's decision whether or not to terminate her pregnancy. The detriment that the State would impose upon the pregnant woman by denying this choice altogether is apparent. Specific and direct harm medically diagnosable even in early pregnancy may be involved. Maternity, or additional off-spring, may force upon the woman a distressful life and future. Psychological harm may be imminent. Mental and physical health may be taxed by child care. There is also the distress, for all concerned, associated with the unwanted child, and there is the problem of bringing a child into a family already unable, psychologically and otherwise, to care for it. In other cases, as in this one, the additional difficulties and continuing stigma of unwed motherhood may be involved. All these are factors the woman and her responsible physician necessarily will consider in consultation.

On the basis of elements such as these, appellants and some amici argue that the woman's right is absolute and that she is entitled to terminate her pregnancy at whatever time, in whatever way, and for whatever reason she alone chooses. With this we do not agree. Appellants' arguments that Texas either has no valid interest at all in regulating the abortion decision, or no interest strong enough to support any limitation upon the woman's sole determination, is unpersuasive. The Court's decisions recognizing a right of privacy also acknowledge that some state regulation in areas protected by that right is appropriate. As noted above, a state may properly assert important interests in safeguarding health, in maintaining medical standards, and in protecting potential life. At some point in pregnancy, these respective interests become sufficiently compelling to sustain regulation of the factors that govern the abortion decision. The privacy right involved, therefore, cannot be said to be absolute. In fact, it is not clear to us that the claim asserted by some amici that one has an unlimited right to do with one's body as one pleases bears a close relationship to the right of privacy previously articulated in the Court's decisions. The Court has refused to recognize an unlimited right of this kind in the past. Jacobson v. Massachusetts, 197 U.S. 11 (1905) (vaccination); Buck v. Bell, 274 U.S. 200 (1927) (sterilization).

We therefore conclude that the right of personal privacy includes the abortion decision, but that this right is not unqualified and must be considered against important state interests in regulation.

We note that those federal and state courts that have recently considered abortion law challenges have reached the same conclusion. A majority, in addition to the District Court in the present case, have held state laws unconstitutional, at least in part, because of vagueness or because of overbreadth and abridgement of rights. Abele V. Markle, 342 F. Supp. 800 (Conn. 1972), appeal pending; Abele v. Markle, — F. Supp. — (Conn. Sept. 20, 1972), appeal pending; Doe v. Bolton, 319 F. Supp. 1048 (ND Ga. 1970), appeal decided today, *post* — ; Doe v. Scott, 321 F. Supp. 1385 (ND Ill. 1971), appeal pending; Poe v. Menghini, 339 F. Supp. 986 (Kan. 1972); YWCA v. Kugler, 342 F. Supp. 1048 (NJ 1970); Babbitz v. McCann, 310 F. Supp. 293 (ED Wis. 1970), appeal dismissed, 400 U.S. 1 (1970); People v. Belous, 71 Cal. 2d 954, 458 P.2d 194 (1969), cert. denied, 397 U.S. 915 (1970); State v. Barquet, 262 So. 2d 431 (Fla. 1972).

Others have sustained state statutes. Crossen v. Attorney General, 344 F. Supp. 587 (ED Ky. 1972), appeal pending; Rosen v. Louisiana State Board of Medical Examiners, 318 F. Supp. 1217 (ED La. 1970), appeal pending; Corkey v. Edwards, 322 F. Supp. 1248 (WDNC 1971), appeal pending; Steinberg v. Brown, 321 F. Supp. 741 (ND Ohio 1970); Doe v. Rampton, — F. Supp. — (Utah 1971), appeal pending; Cheaney v. Indiana, —Ind. — , 285 N.E.2d 265 (1972); Spears v. State, 257 So. 2d 876 (Miss. 1972); State v. Munson, — S.D. — , 201 N.W.2d 123 (1972), appeal pending.

Although the results are divided, most of these courts have agreed that the right of privacy, however based, is broad enough to cover the abortion decision; that the right, nonetheless, is not absolute and is subject to some limitations; and that at some point the state interests as to protection of health, medical standards, and prenatal life, become dominant. We agree with this approach.

Where certain "fundamental rights" are involved, the Court has held that regulation limiting these rights may be justified only by a "compelling state interest," Kramer v. Union Free School District, 395 U.S. 621, 627 (1969); Shapiro v. Thompson, 394 U.S. 618, 634 (1969), Sherbert v. Verner, 374 U.S. 398, 406 (1963), and that legislative enactments must be narrowly drawn to express only the legitimate state interests at stake. Griswold v. Connecticut, 381 U.S. 479, 485 (1965); Aptheker v. Secretary of State, 378 U.S. 500, 508 (1964); Cantwell v. Connecticut, 310 U.S. 296, 307-308 (1940); see Eisenstadt v. Baird, 405 U.S. 438, 460, 463-464 (1972) (White, J., concurring).

In the recent abortion cases, cited above, courts have recognized these principles. Those striking down state laws have generally scrutinized the State's interest in protecting health and potential life and have concluded that neither interest justified broad limitations on the reasons for which a physician and his pregnant patient might decide that she should have an abortion in the early stages of pregnancy. Courts sustaining state laws have held that the State's determinations to protect health or prenatal life are dominant and constitutionally justifiable.

IX

The District Court held that the appellee failed to meet his burden of demonstrating that the Texas statute's infringement upon Roe's rights was necessary to support a compelling state interest, and that, although the defendant presented "several compelling justifications for state presence in the area of abortions," the statutes outstripped these justifications and swept "far beyond any areas of compelling state interest." 314 F. Supp., at 1222-1223. Appellant and appellee both contest that holding. Appellant, as has been indicated, claims an absolute right that bars any state imposition of criminal penalties in the area. Appellee argues that the State's determination to recognize and protect prenatal life from and after conception constitutes a compelling state interest. As noted above, we do not agree fully with either formulation.

A. The appellee and certain amici argue that the fetus is a "person" within the language and meaning of the Fourteenth Amendment. In support of this they outline at length and in detail the well-known facts of fetal development. If this suggestion of personhood is established, the appellant's case, of course, collapses, for the fetus' right to life is then guaranteed specifically by the Amendment. The appellant conceded as much on reargument. On the other hand, the appellee conceded on reargument that no case could be cited that holds that a fetus is a person within the meaning of the Fourteenth Amendment.

The Constitution does not define "person" in so many words. Section 1 of the Fourteenth Amendment contains three references to "person." The first, in defining "citizens," speaks of "persons born or naturalized in the United States." The word also appears both in the Due Process Clause and in the Equal Protection Clause. "Person" is used in other places in the Constitution: in the listing of qualifications for representatives and senators, Art. I, §2, cl. 2, and §3, cl. 3; in the Apportionment Clause, Art. I, §2, cl. 3;[53] in the Migration and Importation provision, Art. I, §9, cl. 1; in the Emolument Clause, Art. I, §9, cl. 8; in the Electors provisions, Art. II, §1, cl. 2, and the superseded cl. 3; in the provision outlining qualifications for the office of President, Art. II, §1, cl. 5; in the Extradition provisions, Art. IV, §2, cl. 2, and the superseded Fugitive Slave cl. 3; and in the Fifth, Twelfth, and Twenty-second Amendments as well as in §§2 and 3 of the Fourteenth Amendment. But in nearly all these instances, the use of the word is such that it has application only postnatally. None indicates, with any assurance, that it has any possible pre-natal application.[54]

All this, together with our observation, supra, that throughout the major portion of the 19th century prevailing legal abortion practices were far freer than they are today, persuades us that the word "person," as used in the Fourteenth Amendment, does not include the unborn.[55] This is in accord with the results reached in those few cases where the issue has been squarely presented. . . . Indeed, our decision in United States v. Vuitch, 402 U.S. 62 (1971), inferentially is to the same effect, for we there would not have indulged in statutory interpretation favorable to abortion in specified circumstances if the necessary consequence was the termination of life entitled to Fourteenth Amendment protection.

This conclusion, however, does not of itself fully answer the contentions raised by Texas, and we pass on to other considerations.

B. The pregnant woman cannot be isolated in her privacy. She carries an embryo and, later, a fetus, if one accepts the medical definitions of the developing young in the human uterus. See Dorland's Illustrated Medical Dictionary, 478-479, 547 (24th ed. 1965). The situation therefore is inherently different from marital intimacy, or bedroom possession of obscene material, or marriage, or procreation, or education, with which *Eisenstadt, Giswold, Stanley, Loving, Skinner, Pierce,* and *Meyer* were respectively concerned. As we have intimated above, it is reasonable and appropriate for a State to decide that at some point in time another interest, that of health of the mother or that of potential human life, becomes significantly involved. The woman's privacy is

53. We are not aware that in the taking of any census under this clause, a fetus has ever been counted.

54. When Texas urges that a fetus is entitled to Fourteenth Amendment protection as a person, it faces a dilemma. Neither in Texas nor in any other State are all abortions prohibited. Despite broad proscription, an exception always exists. The exception contained in Art. 1196, for an abortion procured or attempted by medical advice for the purpose of saving the life of the mother, is typical. But if the fetus is a person who is not to be deprived of life without due process of law, and if the mother's condition is the sole determinant, does not the Texas exception appear to be out of line with the Amendment's command?

There are other inconsistencies between Fourteenth Amendment status and the typical abortion statute. It has already been pointed out that in Texas the woman is not a principal or an accomplice with respect to an abortion upon her. If the fetus is a person, why is the woman not a principal or an accomplice? Further, the penalty for criminal abortion specified by Art. 1195 is significantly less than the maximum penalty for murder prescribed by Art. 1257 of the Texas Penal Code. If the fetus is a person, may the penalties be different?

55. Cf. the Wisconsin abortion statute, defining "unborn child" to mean "a human being from the time of conception until it is born alive," Wis. Stat. §940.04(6) (1969), and the new Connecticut statute, Pub. Act No. 1 (May 1972 special session), declaring it to be the public policy of the State and the legislative intent "to protect and preserve human life from the moment of conception."

no longer sole and any right of privacy she possesses must be measured accordingly.

Texas urges that, apart from the Fourteenth Amendment, life begins at conception and is present throughout pregnancy, and that, therefore, the State has a compelling interest in protecting that life from and after conception. We need not resolve the difficult question of when life begins. When those trained in the respective disciplines of medicine, philosophy, and theology are unable to arrive at any consensus, the judiciary, at this point in the development of man's knowledge, is not in a position to speculate as to the answer.

It should be sufficient to note briefly the wide divergence of thinking on this most sensitive and difficult question. There has always been strong support for the view that life does not begin until live birth. This was the belief of the Stoics. It appears to be the pre-dominant, though not the unanimous, attitude of the Jewish faith. It may be taken to represent also the position of a large segment of the Protestant community, insofar as that can be ascertained; organized groups that have taken a formal position on the abortion issue have generally regarded abortion as a matter for the conscience of the individual and her family. As we have noted, the common law found greater significance in quickening. Physicians and their scientific colleagues have regarded that event with less interest and have tended to focus either upon conception or upon live birth or upon the interim point at which the fetus becomes "viable," that is, potentially able to live outside the mother's womb, albeit with artificial aid. Viability is usually placed at about seven months (28 weeks) but may occur earlier, even at 24 weeks. The Aristotelian theory of "mediate animation," that held sway throughout the Middle Ages and the Renaissance in Europe, continued to be official Roman Catholic dogma until the 19th century, despite opposition to this "ensoulment" theory from those in the Church who would recognize the existence of life from the moment of conception. The latter is now, of course, the official belief of the Catholic Church. As one of the briefs amicus discloses, this is a view strongly held by many non-Catholics as well, and by many physicians. Substantial problems for precise definition of this view are posed, however, by new embryological data that purport to indicate that conception is a "process" over time, rather than an event, and by new medical techniques such as menstrual extraction, the "morning-after" pill, implantation of embryos, artificial insemination, and even artificial wombs.

In areas other than criminal abortion the law has been reluctant to endorse any theory that life, as we recognize it, begins before live birth or to accord legal rights to the unborn except in narrowly defined situations and except when the rights are contingent upon live birth. For example, the traditional rule of tort law had denied recovery for prenatal injuries even though the child was born alive. That rule has been changed in almost every jurisdiction. In most States recovery is said to be permitted only if the fetus was viable, or at least quick, when the injuries were sustained, though few courts have squarely so held. In a recent development, generally opposed by the commentators, some States permit the parents of a stillborn child to maintain an action for wrongful death because of prenatal injuries. Such an action, however, would appear to be one to vindicate the parents' interest and is thus consistent with the view that the fetus, at most, represents only the potentiality of life. Similarly, unborn children have been recognized as acquiring rights or interests by way of inheritance or other devolution of property, and have been represented by guardians ad litem.[66] Perfection of the interests involved, again, has generally been contingent upon live birth. In short, the unborn have never been recognized in the law as persons in the whole sense.

X

In view of all this, we do not agree that, by adopting one theory of life, Texas may override the rights of the pregnant woman that are at stake. We repeat, however, that

---

66. D. Louisell, Abortion, The Practice of Medicine, and the Due Process of Law, 16 UCLA L. Rev. 233, 235-238 (1969); Note, 56 Iowa L. Rev. 994, 999-1000 (1971); Note, The Law and the Unborn Child, 46 Notre Dame Law. 349, 351-354 (1971).

the State does have an important and legitimate interest in preserving and protecting the health of the pregnant woman, whether she be a resident of the State or a nonresident who seeks medical consultation and treatment there, and that it has still *another* important and legitimate interest in protecting the potentiality of human life. These interests are separate and distinct. Each grows in substantiality as the woman approaches term and, at a point during pregnancy, each becomes "compelling."

With respect to the State's important and legitimate interest in the health of the mother, the "compelling" point, in the light of present medical knowledge, is at approximately the end of the first trimester. This is so because of the now established medical fact, . . . that until the end of the first trimester mortality in abortion is less than mortality in normal childbirth. It follows that, from and after this point, a State may regulate the abortion procedure to the extent that the regulation reasonably relates to the preservation and protection of maternal health. Examples of permissible state regulation in this area are requirements as to the qualifications of the person who is to perform the abortion; as to the licensure of that person; as to the facility in which the procedure is to be performed, that is, whether it must be a hospital or may be a clinic or some other place of less-than-hospital status; as to the licensing of the facility; and the like.

This means, on the other hand, that, for the period of pregnancy prior to this "compelling" point, the attending physician, in consultation with his patient, is free to determine, without regulation by the State, that in his medical judgment the patient's pregnancy should be terminated. If that decision is reached, the judgment may be effectuated by an abortion free of interference by the State.

With respect to the State's important and legitimate interest in potential life, the "compelling" point is at viability. This is so because the fetus then presumably has the capability of meaningful life outside the mother's womb. State regulation protective of fetal life after viability thus has both logical and biological justifications. If the State is interested in protecting fetal life after viability, it may go so far as to proscribe abortion during that period except when it is necessary to preserve the life or health of the mother.

Measured against these standards, Art. 1196 of the Texas Penal Code, in restricting legal abortions to those "procured or attempted by medical advice for the purpose of saving the life of the mother," sweeps too broadly. The statute makes no distinction between abortions performed early in pregnancy and those performed later, and it limits to a single reason, "saving" the mother's life, the legal justification for the procedure. The statute, therefore, cannot survive the constitutional attack made upon it here.

This conclusion makes it unnecessary for us to consider the additional challenge to the Texas statute asserted on grounds of vagueness. See United States v. Vuitch, 402 U.S. 62, 67-72 (1971).

XI

To summarize and to repeat:

1. A state criminal abortion statute of the current Texas type, that excepts from criminality only a *life saving* procedure on behalf of the mother, without regard to pregnancy stage and without recognition of the other interests involved, is violative of the Due Process Clause of the Fourteenth Amendment.

(a) For the stage prior to approximately the end of the first trimester, the abortion decision and its effectuation must be left to the medical judgment of the pregnant woman's attending physician.

(b) For the stage subsequent to approximately the end of the first trimester, the State, in promoting its interest in the health of the mother, may, if it chooses, regulate the abortion procedure in ways that are reasonably related to maternal health.

(c) For the stage subsequent to viability the State, in promoting its interest in the potentiality of human life, may, if it chooses, regulate, and even proscribe, abortion except where it is necessary, in appropriate medical judgment, for the preservation of the life or health of the mother.

2. The State may define the term "physician," as it has been employed in the

preceding numbered paragraphs of this Part XI of this opinion, to mean only a physician currently licensed by the State, and may proscribe any abortion by a person who is not a physician as so defined.

In Doe v. Bolton, post, procedural requirements contained in one of the modern abortion statutes are considered. That opinion and this one, of course, are to be read together.[67]

This holding, we feel, is consistent with the relative weights of the respective interests involved, with the lessons and example of medical and legal history, with the lenity of the common law, and with the demands of the profound problems of the present day. The decision leaves the State free to place increasing restrictions on abortion as the period of pregnancy lengthens, so long as those restrictions are tailored to the recognized state interests. The decision vindicates the right of the physician to administer medical treatment according to his professional judgment up to the points where important state interests provide compelling justifications for intervention. Up to those points the abortion decision in all its aspects is inherently, and primarily, a medical decision, and basic responsibility for it must rest with the physician. If an individual practitioner abuses the privilege of exercising proper medical judgment, the usual remedies, judicial and intra-professional, are available. . . .

[The concurring opinion of Mr. Justice Stewart is omitted.]

Mr. Justice REHNQUIST, dissenting.

The Court's opinion brings to the decision of this troubling question both extensive historical fact and a wealth of legal scholarship. While the opinion thus commands my respect, I find myself nonetheless in fundamental disagreement with those parts of it that invalidate the Texas statute in question, and therefore dissent.

I

. . . We know only that plaintiff Roe at the time of filing her complaint was a pregnant woman; for aught that appears in this record, she may have been in her *last* trimester of pregnancy as of the date the complaint was filed.

Nothing in the Court's opinion indicates that Texas might not constitutionally apply its proscription of abortion as written to a woman in that stage of pregnancy. Nonetheless, the Court uses her complaint against the Texas statute as a fulcrum for deciding that States may impose virtually no restrictions on medical abortions performed during the *first* trimester of pregnancy. In deciding such a hypothetical lawsuit, the Court departs from the longstanding admonition that it should never "formulate a rule of constitutional law broader than is required by the precise facts to which it is to be applied." Liverpool, New York & Philadelphia S. S. Co. v. Commissioners of Emigration, 113 U.S. 33, 39 (1885). See also Ashwander v. TVA, 297 U.S. 288, 345 (1936) (Brandeis, J., concurring).

II

Even if there were a plaintiff in this case capable of litigating the issue which the Court decides, I would reach a conclusion opposite to that reached by the Court. I have difficulty in concluding, as the Court does, that the right of "privacy" is involved in this case. Texas, by the statute here challenged, bars the performance of a medical abortion by a licensed physician on a plaintiff such as Roe. A transaction resulting in an operation such as this is not "private" in the ordinary usage of that word. Nor is the "privacy"

67. Neither in this opinion nor in Doe v. Bolton, post, p. 179, do we discuss the father's rights, if any exist in the constitutional context, in the abortion decision. No paternal right has been asserted in either of the cases, and the Texas and the Georgia statutes on their face take no cognizance of the father. We are aware that some statutes recognize the father under certain circumstances. North Carolina, for example, N.C. Gen. Stat. §14-45.1 (Supp. 1971), requires written permission for the abortion from the husband when the woman is a married minor, that is, when she is less than 18 years of age, 41 N.C.A.G. 489 (1971); if the woman is an unmarried minor, written permission from the parents is required. We need not now decide whether provisions of this kind are constitutional.

that the Court finds here even a distant relative of the freedom from searches and seizures protected by the Fourth Amendment to the Constitution, which the Court has referred to as embodying a right to privacy. Katz v. United States, 389 U.S. 347 (1967).

If the Court means by the term "privacy" no more than that the claim of a person to be free from unwanted state regulation of consensual transactions may be a form of "liberty" protected by the Fourteenth Amendment, there is no doubt that similar claims have been upheld in our earlier decisions on the basis of that liberty. I agree with the statement of Mr. Justice Stewart in his concurring opinion that the "liberty," against deprivation of which without due process the Fourteenth Amendment protects, embraces more than the rights found in the Bill of Rights. But that liberty is not guaranteed absolutely against deprivation, only against deprivation without due process of law. The test traditionally applied in the area of social and economic legislation is whether or not a law such as that challenged has a rational relation to a valid state objective. Williamson v. Lee Optical Co., 348 U.S. 483, 491 (1955). The Due Process Clause of the Fourteenth Amendment undoubtedly does place a limit, albeit a broad one, on legislative power to enact laws such as this. If the Texas statute were to prohibit an abortion even where the mother's life is in jeopardy, I have little doubt that such a statute would lack a rational relation to a valid state objective under the test stated in Williamson, supra. But the Court's sweeping invalidation of any restrictions on abortion during the first trimester is impossible to justify under that standard, and the conscious weighing of competing factors that the Court's opinion apparently substitutes for the established test is far more appropriate to a legislative judgment than to a judicial one.

The Court eschews the history of the Fourteenth Amendment in its reliance on the "compelling state interest" test. See Weber v. Aetna Casualty & Surety Co., 406 U.S. 164, 179 (1972) (dissenting opinion). But the Court adds a new wrinkle to this test by transposing it from the legal considerations associated with the Equal Protection Clause of the Fourteenth Amendment to this case arising under the Due Process Clause of the Fourteenth Amendment. . . .

While the Court's opinion quotes from the dissent of Mr. Justice Holmes in Lochner v. New York, 198 U.S. 45, 74 (1905), the result it reaches is more closely attuned to the majority opinion of Mr. Justice Peckham in that case. As in *Lochner* and similar cases applying substantive due process standards to economic and social welfare legislation, the adoption of the compelling state interest standard will inevitably require this Court to examine the legislative policies and pass on the wisdom of these policies in the very process of deciding whether a particular state interest put forward may or may not be "compelling." The decision here to break pregnancy into three distinct terms and to outline the permissible restrictions the State may impose in each one, for example, partakes more of judicial legislation than it does of a determination of the intent of the drafters of the Fourteenth Amendment.

The fact that a majority of the States reflecting, after all, the majority sentiment in those States, have had restrictions on abortions for at least a century is a strong indication, it seems to me, that the asserted right to an abortion is not "so rooted in the traditions and conscience of our people as to be ranked as fundamental," Snyder v. Massachusetts, 291 U.S. 97, 105 (1934). Even today, when society's views on abortion are changing, the very existence of the debate is evidence that the "right" to an abortion is not so universally accepted as the appellants would have us believe.

To reach its result the Court necessarily has had to find within the scope of the Fourteenth Amendment a right that was apparently completely unknown to the drafters of the Amendment. As early as 1821, the first state law dealing directly with abortion was enacted by the Connecticut legislature. Conn. Stat. Tit. 22, §§14, 16 (1821). By the time of the adoption of the Fourteenth Amendment in 1868 there were at least 36 laws enacted by state or territorial legislatures limiting abortion. While many States have amended or updated their laws, 21 of the laws on the books in 1868 remain in effect today. Indeed, the Texas statute struck down today was, as the majority notes, first enacted in 1857 and "has remained substantially unchanged to the present time." Ante, at — .

There apparently was no question concerning the validity of this provision or of any of the other state statutes when the Fourteenth Amendment was adopted. The only conclusion possible from this history is that the drafters did not intend to have the Fourteenth Amendment withdraw from the States the power to legislate with respect to this matter.

III

Even if one were to agree that the case which the Court decides were here, and that the enunciation of the substantive constitutional law in the Court's opinion were proper, the actual disposition of the case by the Court is still difficult to justify. The Texas statute is struck down in toto, even though the Court apparently concedes that at later periods of pregnancy Texas might impose these selfsame statutory limitations on abortion. My understanding of past practice is that a statute found to be invalid as applied to a particular plaintiff, but not unconstitutional as a whole, is not simply "struck down" but is instead declared unconstitutional as applied to the fact situation before the Court. Yick Wo v. Hopkins, 118 U.S. 356 (1886); Street v. New York, 394 U.S. 576 (1969).

For all of the foregoing reasons, I respectfully dissent.

DOE v. BOLTON
410 U.S. 179, 93 S. Ct. 739, 35 L. Ed. 2d 201 (1973)

Mr. Justice Blackmun, delivered the opinion of the Court. . . .

I

. . . As the appellants acknowledge, the 1968 statutes are patterned upon the American Law Institute's Model Penal Code, §230.3 (Proposed Official Draft, 1962), reproduced as Appendix B, post — . The ALI proposal has served as the model for recent legislation in approximately one-fourth of our States. The new Georgia provisions replaced statutory law that had been in effect for more than 90 years. Georgia Laws 1876, No. 130, §2, at 113. The predecessor statute paralleled the Texas legislation considered in Roe v. Wade, ante, and made all abortions criminal except those necessary "to preserve the life" of the pregnant woman. . . .

Section 26-1201, with a referenced exception, makes abortion a crime, and §26-1203 provides that a person convicted of that crime shall be punished by imprisonment for not less than one nor more than 10 years. Section 26-1202(a) states the exception and removes from §1201's definition of criminal abortion, and thus makes noncriminal, an abortion "performed by a physician duly licensed" in Goergia when, "based upon his best clinical judgment . . . an abortion is necessary because

> (1) A continuation of the pregnancy would endanger the life of the pregnant woman or would seriously and permanently injure her health, or
> (2) The fetus would very likely be born with a grave, permanent, and irremediable mental or physical defect, or
> (3) The pregnancy resulted from forcible or statutory rape.[5]

Section 26-1202 also requires, by numbered subdivisions of its subsection (b), that, for an abortion to be authorized or performed as a noncriminal procedure, additional conditions must be fulfilled. These are (1) and (2) residence of the woman in Georgia; (3) reduction to writing of the performing physician's medical judgment that an abortion is justified for one or more of the reasons specified by §26-1202(a), with written concur-

---

5. In contrast with the ALI model, the Georgia statute makes no specific reference to pregnancy resulting from incest. We were assured by the State at reargument that this was because the statute's reference to "rape" was intended to include incest. Tr. of Oral Rearg. 32.

rence in that judgment by at least two other Georgia-licensed physicians, based upon their separate personal medical examinations of the woman; (4) performance of the abortion in a hospital licensed by the State Board of Health and also accredited by the Joint Commission on Accreditation of Hospitals; (5) advance approval by an abortion committee of not less than three members of the hospital's staff; (6) certifications in a rape situation; and (7), (8), and (9) maintenance and confidentiality of records. There is a provision (subsection (c)) for judicial determination of the legality of a proposed abortion on petition of the judicial circuit law officer or of a close relative, as therein defined, of the unborn child, and for expeditious hearing of that petition. There is also a provision (subsection (e)) giving a hospital the right not to admit an abortion patient and giving any physician and any hospital employee or staff member the right, on moral or religious grounds, not to participate in the procedure.

II

On April 16, 1970, Mary Doe, 23 other individuals (nine described as Georgia-licensed physicians, seven as nurses registered in the State, five as clergymen, and two as social workers), and two nonprofit Georgia corporations that advocate abortion reform, instituted this federal action in the Northern District of Georgia against the State's attorney general, the district attorney of Fulton County, and the chief of police of the city of Atlanta. The plaintiffs sought a declaratory judgment that the Georgia abortion statutes were unconstitutional in their entirety. They also sought injunctive relief restraining the defendants and their successors from enforcing the statutes.

Mary Doe alleged:

> (1) She was a 22-year-old Georgia citizen, married, and nine weeks pregnant. She had three living children. The two older ones had been placed in a foster home because of Doe's poverty and inability to care for them. The youngest, born July 19, 1969, had been placed for adoption. Her husband had recently abandoned her and she was forced to live with her indigent parents and their eight children. She and her husband, however, had become reconciled. He was a construction worker employed only sporadically. She had been a mental patient at the State Hospital. She had been advised that an abortion could be performed on her with less danger to her health than if she gave birth to the child she was carrying. She would be unable to care for or support the new child.
>
> (2) On March 25, 1970, she applied to the Abortion Committee of Grady Memorial Hospital, Atlanta, for a therapeutic abortion under §26-1202. Her application was denied 16 days later, on April 10, when she was eight weeks pregnant, on the ground that her situation was not one described in §26-1202(a).[7]
>
> (3) Because her application was denied, she was forced either to relinquish "her right to decide when and how many children she will bear" or to seek an abortion that was illegal under the Georgia statutes. This invaded her rights of privacy and liberty in matters related to family, marriage, and sex, and deprived her of the right to choose whether to bear children. This was a violation of rights guaranteed her by the First, Fourth, Fifth, Ninth, and Fourteenth Amendments. The statutes also denied her equal protection and procedural due process and, because they were unconstitutionally vague, deterred hospitals and doctors from performing abortions. She sued "on her own behalf and on behalf of all others similarly situated."

The other plaintiffs alleged that the Georgia statutes "chilled and deterred" them from practicing their respective professions and deprived them of rights guaranteed by the First, Fourth, and Fourteenth Amendments. These plaintiffs also purported to sue on their own behalf and on behalf of others similarly situated. . . .

---

7. In answers to interrogatories, Doe stated that her application for an abortion was approved at Georgia Baptist Hospital on May 5, 1970, but that she was not approved as a charity patient there and had no money to pay for an abortion. App. 64.

The District Court, per curiam, 319 F. Supp. 1048 (ND Ga. 1970), held that all the plaintiffs had standing but that only Doe presented a justiciable controversy. On the merits, the court concluded that the limitation in the Georgia statute of the "number of reasons for which an abortion may be sought," id., at 1056, improperly restricted Doe's rights of privacy articulated in Griswold v. Connecticut, 381 U.S. 479 (1965), and of "personal liberty," both of which it thought "broad enough to include the decision to abort a pregnancy," id., at 1055. As a consequence, the court held invalid those portions of §§26-1202(a) and (b)(3) limiting legal abortions to the three situations specified; §26-1202(b)(6) relating to certifications in a rape situation; and §26-1202(c) authorizing a court test. Declaratory relief was granted accordingly. The court, however, held that Georgia's interest in protection of health, and the existence of a *"potential* of independent human existence" (emphasis in original), id., at 1055, justified state regulation of "the manner of performance as well as the quality of the final decision to abort," id., at 1056, and it refused to strike down the other provisions of the statutes. It denied the request for an injunction, id., at 1057. . . .

III

Our decision in Roe v. Wade, ante — , establishes (1) that, despite her pseudonym, we may accept as true, for this case, Mary Doe's existence and her pregnant state on April 16, 1970; (2) that the constitutional issue is substantial; (3) that the interim termination of Doe's and all other Georgia pregnancies in existence in 1970 has not rendered the case moot; and (4) that Doe presents a justiciable controversy and has standing to maintain the action. . . .

. . . We conclude . . . that the physician-appellants, who are Georgia-licensed doctors consulted by pregnant women, also present a justiciable controversy and do have standing despite the fact that the record does not disclose that any one of them has been prosecuted, or threatened with prosecution, for violation of the State's abortion statutes. The physician is the one against whom these criminal statutes directly operate in the event he procures an abortion that does not meet the statutory exceptions and conditions. The physician-appellants, therefore, assert a sufficiently direct threat of personal detriment. They should not be required to await and undergo a criminal prosecution as the sole means of seeking relief. . . .

The parallel claims of the nurse, clergy, social worker, and corporation-appellants are another step removed and as to them, the Georgia statutes operate less directly. Not being licensed physicians, the nurses and the others are in no position to render medical advice. They would be reached by the abortion statutes only in their capacity as accessories or as counselor-conspirators. We conclude that we need not pass upon the status of these additional appellants in this suit, for the issues are sufficiently and adequately presented by Doe and the physician-appellants, and nothing is gained or lost by the presence or absence of the nurses, the clergymen, the social workers, and the corporations. See Roe v. Wade, ante, at — .

IV

The appellants attack on several grounds those portions of the Georgia abortion statutes that remain after the District Court decision: undue restriction of a right to personal and marital privacy; vagueness; deprivation of substantive and procedural due process; improper restriction to Georgia residents; and denial of equal protection.

A. Roe v. Wade, ante, sets forth our conclusion that a pregnant woman does not have an absolute constitutional right to an abortion on her demand. What is said there is applicable here and need not be repeated. . . .

C. Appellants argue that §26-1202(a) of the Georgia statute, as it has been left by the District Court's decision, is unconstitutionally vague. This argument centers in the proposition that, with the District Court's having stricken the statutorily specified reasons, it still remains a crime for a physician to perform an abortion except when, as

§26-1202(a) reads, it is "based upon his best clinical judgment that an abortion is necessary." The appellants contend that the word "necessary" does not warn the physician of what conduct is proscribed; that the statute is wholly without objective standards and is subject to diverse interpretation; and that doctors will choose to err on the side of caution and will be arbitrary.

The net result of the District Court's decision is that the abortion determination, so far as the physician is concerned, is made in the exercise of his professional, that is, his "best clinical" judgment in the light of *all* the attendant circumstances. He is not now restricted to the three situations originally specified. Instead, he may range farther afield wherever his medical judgment, properly and professionally exercised, so dictates and directs him.

The vagueness argument is set at rest by the decision in United States v. Vuitch, 402 U.S. 62, 71-72 (1971), where the issue was raised with respect to a District of Columbia statute making abortions criminal "unless the same were done as necessary for the preservation of the mother's life or health and under the direction of a competent licensed practitioner of medicine." That statute has been construed to bear upon psychological as well as physical well-being. This being so, the Court concluded that the term "health" presented no problem of vagueness. "Indeed, whether a particular operation is necessary for a patient's physical or mental health is a judgment that physicians are obviously called upon to make routinely whenever surgery is considered." 402 U.S., at 72. This conclusion is equally applicable here. Whether, in the words of the Georgia statute, "an abortion is necessary," is a professional judgment that the Georgia physician will be called upon to make routinely.

We agree with the District Court, 319 F. Supp., at 1058, that the medical judgment may be exercised in the light of all factors — physical, emotional, psychological, familial, and the woman's age — relevant to the well-being of the patient. All these factors may relate to health. This allows the attending physician the room he needs to make his best medical judgment. And it is room that operates for the benefit, not the disadvantage, of the pregnant woman.

D. The appellants next argue that the District Court should have declared unconstitutional three procedural demands of the Georgia statute: (1) that the abortion be performed in a hospital accredited by the Joint Commission on Accreditation of Hospitals:[11] (2) that the procedure be approved by the hospital staff abortion committee; and (3) that the performing physician's judgment be confirmed by the independent examinations of the patient by two other licensed physicians. The appellants attack these provisions not only on the ground that they unduly restrict the woman's right of privacy, but also on procedural due process and equal protection grounds. The physician-appellants also argue that, by subjecting a doctor's individual medical judgment to committee approval and to confirming consultations, the statute impermissibly restricts the physician's right to practice his profession and deprives him of due process.

1. *JCAH Accreditation.* The Joint Commission on Accreditation of Hospitals is an organization without governmental sponsorship or overtones. No question whatever is raised concerning the integrity of the organization or the high purpose of the accreditation process. That process, however, has to do with hospital standards generally and has no present particularized concern with abortion as a medical or surgical procedure. In Georgia there is no restriction of the performance of nonabortion surgery in a hospital not yet accredited by the JCAH so long as other requirements imposed by the State, such as licensing of the hospital and of the operating surgeon, are met. See Georgia Code §§88-1901(a) and 88-1905 (1971) and 84-907 (Supp. 1971). Furthermore, accreditation by the Commission is not granted until a hospital has been in operation at least one year. The Model Penal Code, §230.3, Appendix B hereto, contains no requirement for JCAH

11. We were advised at reargument, Tr. of Rearg. 10, that only 54 of Georgia's 159 counties have a JCAH accredited hospital.

accreditation. And the Uniform Abortion Act (Final Draft, August 1971), approved by the American Bar Association in February 1972, contains no JCAH accredited hospital specification. Some courts have held that a JCAH accreditation requirement is an over-broad infringement of fundamental rights because it does not relate to the particular medical problems and dangers of the abortion operation. Poe v. Menghini, 339 F. Supp. 986, 993-994 (Kan. 1972); People v. Barksdale, 96 Cal. Rptr. 265, 273-274 (Cal. App. 1971).

We hold that the JCAH accreditation requirement does not withstand constitutional scrutiny in the present context. It is a requirement that simply is not "based on differences that are reasonably related to the purposes of the Act in which it is found." Morey v. Doud, 354 U.S. 457, 465 (1957).

This is not to say that Georgia may not or should not, from and after the end of the first trimester, adopt standards for licensing all facilities where abortions may be performed so long as those standards are legitimately related to the objective the State seeks to accomplish. The appellants contend that such a relationship would be lacking even in a lesser requirement that an abortion be performed in a licensed hospital, as opposed to a facility, such as a clinic, that may be required by the State to possess all the staffing and services necessary to perform an abortion safely (including those adequate to handle serious complications or other emergency, or arrangements with a nearby hospital to provide such services). Appellants and various amici have presented us with a mass of data purporting to demonstrate that some facilities other than hospitals are entirely adequate to perform abortions if they possess these qualifications. The State, on the other hand, has not presented persuasive data to show that only hospitals meet its acknowledged interest in insuring the quality of the operation and the full protection of the patient. We feel compelled to agree with appellants that the State must show more than it has in order to prove that only the full resources of a licensed hospital, rather than those of some other appropriately licensed institution, satisfy these health interests. We hold that the hospital requirement of the Georgia law, because it fails to exclude the first trimester of pregnancy, see Roe v. Wade, ante, p. __, is also invalid. In so holding we naturally express no opinion on the medical judgment involved in any particular case, that is, whether the patient's situation is such that an abortion should be performed in a hospital rather than in some other facility.

2. *Committee Approval.* The second aspect of the appellants' procedural attack relates to the hospital abortion committee and to the pregnant woman's asserted lack of access to that committee. Relying primarily on Goldberg v. Kelly, 397 U.S. 254 (1970), concerning the termination of welfare benefits, and Wisconsin v. Constantineau, 400 U.S. 433 (1971), concerning the posting of an alcoholic's name, Doe first argues that she was denied due process because she could not make a presentation to the committee. It is not clear from the record, however, whether Doe's own consulting physician was or was not a member of the committee or did or did not present her case, or, indeed, whether she herself was or was not there. We see nothing in the Georgia statute that explicitly denies access to the committee by or on behalf of the woman. If the access point alone were involved, we would not be persuaded to strike down the committee provision on the unsupported assumption that access is not provided.

Appellants attack the discretion the statute leaves to the committee. The most concrete argument they advance is their suggestion that it is still a badge of infamy "in many minds" to bear an illegitimate child, and that the Georgia system enables the committee members' personal views as to extramarital sex relations, and punishment therefore, to govern their decisions. This approach obviously is one founded on suspicion and one that discloses a lack of confidence in the integrity of physicians. To say that physicians will be guided in their hospital committee decisions by their predilections on extramarital sex unduly narrows the issue to pregnancy outside marriage. (Doe's own situation did not involve extramarital sex and its product.) The appellants' suggestion is necessarily somewhat degrading to the conscientious physician, particularly the obstetrician, whose professional activity is concerned with the physical and mental welfare, the woes, the emotions, and the concern of his female patients. He, perhaps more than anyone else, is knowledgeable in this area of patient care, and he is aware of human frailty, so-called "error," and needs. The good physician — despite the presence of rascals in the medical profession, as in all others, we trust that most physicians are "good" — will have a sympathy and an understanding for the pregnant patient that probably is not exceeded by those who participate in other areas of professional counseling.

It is perhaps worth noting that the abortion committee has a function of its own. It is a committee of the hospital and it is composed of members of the institution's medical staff. The membership usually is a changing one. In this way its work burden is shared and is more readily accepted. The committee's function is protective. It enables the hospital appropriately to be advised that its posture and activities are in accord with legal requirements. It is to be remembered that the hospital is an entity and that it, too, has legal rights and legal obligations.

Saying all this, however, does not settle the issue of the constitutional propriety of the committee requirement. Viewing the Georgia statute as a whole, we see no constitutionally justifiable pertinence in the structure for the advance approval by the abortion committee. With regard to the protection of potential life, the medical judgment is already completed prior to the committee stage, and review by a committee once removed from diagnosis is basically redundant. We are not cited to any other surgical procedure made subject to commmittee approval as a matter of state criminal law. The woman's right to receive medical care in accordance with her licensed physician's best judgment and the physician's right to administer it are substantially limited by this statutorily imposed overview. And the hospital itself is otherwise fully protected. Under §26-1202(e) the hospital is free not to admit a patient for an abortion. It is even free not to have an abortion committee. Further, a physician or any other employee has the right to refrain, for moral or religious reasons, from participating in the abortion procedure. These provisions obviously are in the statute in order to afford appropriate protection to the individual and to the denominational hospital. Section 26-1202(e) affords adequate protection to the hospital and little more is provided by the committee prescribed by §26-1202(b)(5).

We conclude that the interposition of the hospital abortion committee is unduly restrictive of the patient's rights and needs that, at this point, have already been medically delineated and substantiated by her personal physician. To ask more serves neither the hospital nor the State.

3. *Two-Doctor Concurrence.* The third aspects of the appellants' attack centers on the "time and availability of adequate medical facilities and personnel." It is said that the system imposes substantial and irrational roadblocks and "is patently unsuited" to prompt determination of the abortion decision. Time, of course, is critical in abortion. Risks during the first trimester of pregnancy are admittedly lower than during later months.

The appellants purport to show by a local study of Grady Memorial Hospital (serving indigent residents in Fulton and DeKalb Counties) that the "mechanics of the system itself forced . . . discontinuation of the abortion process" because the median time for the workup was 15 days. The same study shows, however, that 27% of the candidates for abortion were already 13 or more weeks pregnant at the time of application, that is, they were at the end of or beyond the first trimester when they made their applications. It is too much to say, as appellants do, that these particular persons "were victims of [a] system over which they [had] no control." If higher risk was incurred because of abortions in the second rather than the first trimester, much of that risk was due to delay in application, and not to the alleged cumbersomeness of the system. We note, in passing, that appellant Doe had no delay problem herself; the decision in her case was made well within the first trimester.

It should be manifest that our rejection of the accredited hospital requirement and, more important, of the abortion committee's advance approval eliminates the major grounds of the attack based on the system's delay and the lack of facilities. There remains, however, the required confirmation by two Georgia-licensed physicians in addition to the recommendation of the pregnant woman's own consultant (making under the statute, a total of six physicians involved, including the three on the hospital's abortion committee). We conclude that this provision, too, must fall.

The statute's emphasis, as has been repetitively noted, is on the attending physician's "best clinical judgment that an abortion is necessary." That should be sufficient. The reasons for the presence of the confirmation step in the statute are perhaps apparent, but they are insufficient to withstand constitutional challenge. Again, not other voluntary medical or surgical procedure for which Georgia requires confirmation by two other physicians has been cited to us. If a physician is licensed by the State, he is recognized by the State as capable of exercising acceptable clinical judgment. If he fails in this, professional censure or deprivation of his license are available remedies. Required acquiescence by co-practitioners has no rational connection with a patient's needs and unduly infringes on the physician's right to practice. The attending physician will know when a consultation is advisable — the doubtful situation, the need for assurance when the medical decision is a delicate one, and the like. Physicians have followed this routine historically and know its usefulness and benefit for all concerned. It is still true today that "[r]eliance must be placed upon the assurance given by his license, issued by an authority competent to judge in that respect, that he [the physician] possesses the requisite qualifications." Dent v. West Virginia, 129 U.S. 114, 122-123 (1889). See United States v. Vuitch, 402 U.S., at 71.

E. The appellants attack the residency requirement of the Georgia law, §§26-1202(b)(1) and (b)(2), as violative of the right to travel stressed in Shapiro v. Thompson, 394 U.S. 618, 629-631 (1969), and other cases. A requirement of this kind, of course, could be deemed to have some relationship to the availability of post-procedure medical care for the aborted patient.

Nevertheless, we do not uphold the constitutionality of the residence requirement. It is not based on any policy of preserving state-supported facilities for Georgia residents, for the bar also applies to private hospitals and to privately retained physicians. There is no intimation, either, that Georgia facilities are utilized to capacity in caring for Georgia residents. Just as the Privileges and Immunities Clause, Const. Art. IV, §2, protects persons who enter other States to ply their trade, Ward v. Maryland, 79 U.S. (12 Wall.) 418, 430 (1870); Blake v. McClung, 172 U.S. 239, 248-256 (1898), so must it protect persons who enter Georgia seeking the medical services that are available there. See Toomer v. Witsell, 334 U.S. 385, 396-397 (1948). A contrary holding would mean that a State could limit to its own residents the general medical care available within its borders. This we could not approve.

F. The last argument on this phase of the case is one that often is made, namely, that the Georgia system is violative of equal protection because it discriminates against the poor. The appellants do not urge that abortions should be performed by persons other than licensed physicians, so we have no argument that because the wealthy can better afford physicians, the poor should have non-physicians made available to them. The appellants acknowledged that the procedures are "nondiscriminatory in . . . express terms" but they suggest that they have produced invidious discriminations. The District Court rejected this approach out of hand. 319 F. Supp., at 1056. It rests primarily on the accreditation and approval and confirmation requirements, discussed above, and on the assertion that most of Georgia's counties have no accredited hospital. We have set aside the accreditation, approval, and confirmation requirements, however, and with that, the discrimination argument collapses in all significant aspects. . . .

Criminal Code of Georgia
(The italicized portions are those held unconstitutional by the District Court)

Chapter 26-12. Abortion

26-1201. Criminal Abortion. Except as otherwise provided in section 26-1202, a person commits criminal abortion when he administers any medicine, drug or other substance whatever to any woman or when he uses any instrument or other means whatever upon any woman with intent to produce a miscarriage or abortion.

26-1202. Exception. (a) Section 26-1201 shall not apply to an abortion performed by a physician duly licensed to practice medicine and surgery pursuant to Chapter 84-9 or 84-12 of the Code of Georgia of 1933, as amended, based upon his best clinical judgment that an abortion is necessary *because:*

(1) A continuation of the pregnancy would endanger the life of the pregnant woman or would seriously and permanently injure her health; or

(2) The fetus would very likely be born with a grave, permanent, and irremediable mental or physical defect; or

(3) The pregnancy resulted from forcible or statutory rape.

(b) No abortion is authorized or shall be performed under this section unless each of the following conditions is met:

(1) the pregnant woman requesting the abortion certifies in writing under oath and subject to the penalties of false swearing to the physician who proposes to perform the abortion that she is a bona fide legal resident of the State of Georgia.

(2) The physician certifies that he believes the woman is a bona fide resident of this State and that he has no information which should lead him to believe otherwise.

(3) Such physician's judgment is reduced to writing and concurred in by at least two other physicians duly licensed to practice medicine and surgery pursuant to Chapter 84-9 of the Code of Georgia of 1933, as amended, who certify in writing that based upon their separate personal medical examinations of the pregnant woman, the abortion is, in their judgment, necessary *because of one or more of the reasons enumerated above.*

(4) Such abortion is performed in a hospital licensed by the State Board of Health and accredited by the Joint Commission on Accreditation of Hospitals.

(5) The performance of the abortion has been approved in advance by a committee of the medical staff of the hospital in which the operation is to be performed. This committee must be one established and maintained in accordance with the standards promulgated by the Joint Commission on the Accreditation of Hospitals, and its approval must be by a majority vote of a membership of not less than three members of the hospital's staff; the physician proposing to perform the operation may not be counted as a member of the committee for this purpose.

(6) If the proposed abortion is considered necessary because the woman has been raped, the woman makes a written statement under oath, and subject to the penalties of false swearing, of the date, time and place of the rape and the name of the rapist, if known. There must be attached to this statement a certified copy of any report of the rape made by any law enforcement officer or agency and a statement by the solicitor general of the judicial circuit where the rape occurred or allegedly occurred that, according to his best information, there is probable cause to believe that the rape did occur.

(7) Such written opinions, statements, certificates, and concurrences are maintained in the permanent files of such hospital and are available at all reasonable times to the solicitor general of the judicial circuit in which the hospital is located.

(8) A copy of such written opinions, statements, certificates, and concurrences is filed with the Director of the State Department of Public Health within ten (10) days after such operation is performed.

(9) All written opinions, statements, certificates, and concurrences filed and maintained pursuant to paragraphs (7) and (8) of this subsection shall be confidential records and shall not be made available for public inspection at any time.

(c) Any solicitor general of the judicial circuit in which an abortion is to be performed under this section, or any person who would be a relative of the child within the second degree of consanguinity, may petition the superior court of the county in which the abortion is to be performed for a declaratory judgment whether the performance of such abortion would violate any constitutional or other legal rights of the fetus. Such solicitor general may also petition such court for the purpose of taking issue with compliance with the requirements of this section. The physician who proposes to perform the abortion and the pregnant woman shall be respondents. The petition shall be heard expeditiously and if the court adjudges that such abortion would violate the constitutional or other legal rights of the fetus, the court shall so declare and shall restrain the physician from performing the abortion.

(d) If an abortion is performed in compliance with this section, the death of the fetus shall not give rise to any claim for wrongful death.

(e) Nothing in this section shall require a hospital to admit any patient under the provisions hereof for the purpose of performing an abortion, nor shall any hospital be required to appoint a committee such as contemplated under subsection (b)(5). A physician, or any other person who is a member of or associated with the staff of a hospital, or any employee of a hospital in which an abortion has been authorized, who shall state in writing an objection to such abortion on moral or religious grounds shall not be required to participate in the medical procedures which will result in the abortion, and the refusal of any such person to participate therein shall not form the basis of any claim for damages on account of such refusal or for any disciplinary or recriminatory action against such person.

26-1203. Punishment. A person convicted of criminal abortion shall be punished by imprisonment for not less than one nor more than 10 years.

APPENDIX B

American Law Institutes, Model Penal Code

Section 230.3. Abortion.

(1) *Unjustified Abortion.* A person who purposely and unjustifiably terminates the pregnancy of another otherwise than by a live birth commits a felony of the third degree or, where the pregnancy has continued beyond the twenty-sixth week, a felony of the second degree.

(2) *Justifiable Abortion.* A licensed physician is justified in terminating a pregnancy if he believes there is substantial risk that continuance of the pregnancy would gravely impair the physical or mental health of the mother or that the child would be born with grave physical or mental defect, or that the pregnancy resulted from rape, incest, or other felonious intercourse. All illicit intercourse with a girl below the age of 16 shall be deemed felonious for purposes of this subsection. Justifiable abortions shall be performed only in a licensed hospital except in case of emergency when hospital facilities are unavailable. [Additional exceptions from the requirement of hospitalization may be incorporated here to take account of situations in sparsely settled areas where hospitals are not generally accessible.]

(3) *Physicians' Certificates; Presumption from Non-Compliance.* No abortion shall be performed unless two physicians, one of whom may be the person performing the abortion, shall have certified in writing the circumstances which they believe to justify the abortion. Such certificate shall be submitted before the abortion to the hospital where it is to be performed and, in the case of abortion following felonious intercourse, to the prosecuting attorney or the police. Failure to comply with any of the requirements of this Subsection gives rise to a presumption that the abortion was unjustified.

(4) *Self-Abortion.* A woman whose pregnancy has continued beyond the twenty-sixth week commits a felony of the third degree if she purposely terminates her own pregnancy otherwise than by a live birth, or if she uses instruments, drugs or violence upon herself for that purpose. Except as justified under Subsection (2), a person who induces or knowingly aids a woman to use instruments, drugs or violence upon herself for the purpose of terminating her pregnancy otherwise than by a live birth commits a

felony of the third degree whether or not the pregnancy has continued beyond the twenty-sixth week.

(5) *Pretended Abortion.* A person commits a felony of the third degree if, representing that it is his purpose to perform an abortion, he does an act adapted to cause abortion in a pregnant woman although the woman is in fact not pregnant, or the actor does not believe she is. A person charged with unjustified abortion under Subsection (1) or an attempt to commit that offense may be convicted thereof upon proof of conduct prohibited by this Subsection.

(6) *Distribution of Abortifacients.* A person who sells, offers to sell, possesses with intent to sell, advertises, or displays for sale anything specially designed to terminate a pregnancy, or held out by the actor as useful for that purpose, commits a misdemeanor, unless:

(a) the sale, offer or display is to a physician or druggist or to an intermediary in a chain of distribution to physicians or druggists; or

(b) the sale is made upon prescription or order of a physician; or

(c) the possession is with intent to sell as authorized in paragraphs (a) and (b); or

(d) the advertising is addressed to persons named in paragraph (a) and confined to trade or professional channels not likely to reach the general public.

(7) *Section Inapplicable to Prevention of Pregnancy.* Nothing in this Section shall be deemed applicable to the prescription, administration or distribution of drugs or other substances for avoiding pregnancy, whether by preventing implantation of a fertilized ovum or by any other method that operates before, at or immediately after fertilization.

[The concurring opinion (in both *Roe* and *Doe*) of Mr. Chief Justice, Burger is omitted.]

Mr. Justice Douglas, concurring.

While I join the opinion of the Court, I add a few words.

The questions presented in the present cases go far beyond the issues of vagueness, which we considered in *United States* v. *Vuitch*, 402 U.S. 62. They involve the right of privacy, one aspect of which we considered in *Griswold* v. *Connecticut*, 381 U.S. 479, 484, when we held that various guarantees in the Bill of Rights create zones of privacy.[2]

The Griswold case involved a law forbidding the use of contraceptives. We held that law as applied to married people unconstitutional:

> We deal with a right of privacy older than the Bill of Rights — older than our political parties, older than our school system. Marriage is a coming together for better or for worse, hopefully enduring, and intimate to the degree of being sacred. Id., 486.

The District Court in *Doe* held that *Griswold* and related cases "establish a constitutional right to privacy broad enough to encompass the right of a woman to terminate an unwanted pregnancy in its early stages, by obtaining an abortion." 319 F. Supp., at 1054.

---

2. There is no mention of privacy in our Bill of Rights but our decisions have recognized it as one of the fundamental values those amendments were designed to protect. The fountainhead case is Boyd v. United States, 116 U.S. 616, holding that a federal statute which authorized a court in tax cases to require a taxpayer to produce his records or to concede the Government's allegations offended the Fourth and Fifth Amendments. Mr. Justice Bradley, for the Court, found that the measure unduly intruded into the "sanctity of a man's home and the privacies of life." Id., at 630. Prior to *Boyd,* in Kilbourn v. Thompson, 103 U.S. 168, 190, Mr. Justice Miller held for the Court that neither House of Congress "possesses the general power of making inquiry into the private affairs of the citizen." Of *Kilbourn,* Mr. Justice Field later said, "This case will stand for all time as a bulwark against the invasion of the right of the citizen to protection in his private affairs against the unlimited scrutiny of investigation by a congressional committee." In re Pacific Railway Comm'n, 32 F. 241, 253 (cited with approval in Sinclair v. United States, 279 U.S. 263, 293). Mr. Justice Harlan, also speaking for the Court, in ICC v. Brimson, 154 U.S. 447, 478, thought the same was true of administrative inquiries, saying the Constitution did not permit a "general power of making inquiry into the private affairs of the citizen." In a similar vein were Harriman v. Interstate Commerce Comm'n, 211 U.S. 407; United States v. Louisville & Nashville R.R., 236 U.S. 318, 335; and Federal Trade Comm'n v. American Tobacco Co., 264 U.S. 298.

The Supreme Court of California expressed the same view in People v. Belous, 71 Cal. 2d 954, 963.

The Ninth Amendment obviously does not create federally enforceable rights. It merely says, "The enumeration in the Constitution of certain rights shall not be construed to deny or disparage others retained by the people." But a catalogue of these rights includes customary, traditional, and time-honored rights, amenities, privileges, and immunities that come within the sweep of "the Blessings of Liberty" mentioned in the preamble to the Constitution. Many of them in my view come within the meaning of the term "liberty" as used in the Fourteenth Amendment.

First is the autonomous control over the development and expression on one's intellect, interests, tastes, and personality.

These are rights protected by the First Amendment and, in my view, they are absolute, permitting of no exceptions. See Terminiello v. Chicago, 337 U.S. 1; Roth v. United States, 354 U.S. 476, 508 (dissent); Kingsley Pictures Corp. v. Regents, 360 U.S. 684, 697 (concurring); New York Times Co. v. Sullivan, 376 U.S. 254, 293 (Black, J., concurring, in which I joined). The Free Exercise Clause of the First Amendment is one facet of this constitutional right. The right to remain silent as respects one's own beliefs, Watkins v. United States, 354 U.S. 178, 196-199, is protected by the First and the Fifth. The First Amendment grants the privacy of first-class mail, United States v. Van Leeuwen, 397 U.S. 249, 253. All of these aspects of the right of privacy are rights "retained by the people" in the meaning of the Ninth Amendment.

Second is freedom of choice in the basic decisions of one's life respecting marriage, divorce, procreation, contraception, and the education and upbringing of children.

These rights, unlike those protected by the First Amendment, are subject to some control by the police power. Thus, the Fourth Amendment speaks only of "unreasonable searches and seizures" and of "probable cause." These rights are "fundamental," and we have held that in order to support legislative action the statute must be narrowly and precisely drawn and that a "compelling state interest" must be shown in support of the limitation. E.g., Kramer v. Union Free School District, 395 U.S. 621; Shapiro v. Thompson, 394 U.S. 618; Carrington v. Rash, 380 U.S. 89; Sherbert v. Verner, 374 U.S. 398; NAACP v. Alabama, 357 U.S. 449.

The liberty to marry a person of one's own choosing, Loving v. Virginia, 388 U.S. 1; the right of procreation, Skinner v. Oklahoma, 316 U.S. 535; the liberty to direct the education of one's children, Pierce v. Society of Sisters, 268 U.S. 510, and the privacy of the marital relation, Griswold v. Connecticut, supra, are in this category.[4] Only last Term in Eisenstadt v. Baird, 405 U.S. 438, another contraceptive case, we expanded the concept of *Griswold* by saying:

4. My Brother Stewart, writing in Roe v. Wade, supra, says that our decision in *Griswold* reintroduced substantive due process that had been rejected in Ferguson v. Skrupa, 372 U.S. 726. *Skrupa* involved legislation governing a business enterprise; and the Court in that case, as had Mr. Justice Holmes on earlier occasions, rejected the idea that "liberty" within the meaning of the Due Process Clause of the Fourteenth Amendment was a vessel to be filled with one's personal choices of values, whether drawn from the laissez faire school, from the socialistic school, or from the technocrats. *Griswold* involved legislation touching on the marital relation and involving the conviction of a licensed physician for giving married people information concerning contraception. There is nothing specific in the Bill of Rights that covers that item. Nor is there anything in the Bill of Rights that in terms protects the right of association or the privacy in one's association. Yet we found those rights in the periphery of the First Amendment. NAACP v. Alabama, 357 U.S. 449, 462. Other peripheral rights are the right to educate one's children as one chooses, Pierce v. Society of Sisters, 268 U.S. 510, and the right to study the German language, Meyer v. Nebraska, 262 U.S. 390. These decisions, with all respect, have nothing to do with substantive due process. One may think they are not peripheral to other rights that are expressed in the Bill of Rights. But that is not enough to bring into play the protection of substantive due process.

There are, of course, those who have believed that the reach of due process in the Fourteenth Amendment included all of the Bill of Rights but went further. Such was the view of Mr. Justice Murphy and Mr. Justice Rutledge. See Adamson v. California, 332 U.S. 46, 123, 124 (dissenting opinion). Perhaps they were right; but it is a bridge that neither I nor those who joined the Court's opinion in *Griswold* crossed.

It is true that in *Griswold* the right of privacy in question inhered in the marital relationship. Yet the marital couple is not an independent entity with a mind and heart of its own, but an association of two individuals each with a separate intellectual and emotional makeup. If the right of privacy means anything, it is the right of the *individual,* married or single, to be free from unwarranted governmental intrusion into matters so fundamentally affecting a person as the decision whether to bear or beget a child. Id., at 453.

This right of privacy was called by Mr. Justice Brandeis the right "to be let alone." Olmstead v. United States, 277 U.S. 438, 478 (dissenting opinion). That right includes the privilege of an individual to plan his own affairs, for, " 'outside areas of plainly harmful conduct, every American is left to shape his own life as he thinks best, do what he pleases, go where he pleases.' " Kent v. Dulles, 357 U.S. 116, 126.

Third is the freedom to care for one's health and person, freedom from bodily restraint or compulsion, freedom to walk, stroll, or loaf.

These rights, though fundamental, are likewise subject to regulation on a showing of "compelling state interest." We stated in Papachristou v. City of Jacksonville, 405 U.S. 156, 164, that walking, strolling, and wandering "are historically part of the amenities of life as we have known them." As stated in Jacobson v. Massachusetts, 197 U.S. 11, 29:

> There is, of course, a sphere within which the individual may assert the supremacy of his own will and rightfully dispute the authority of any human government, especially of any free government existing under a written constitution, to interfere with the exercise of that will.

In Union Pacific R. Co. v. Botsford, 141 U.S. 250, 252, the Court said, "The inviolability of the person is as much invaded by a compulsory stripping and exposure as by a blow."

In Terry v. Ohio, 392 U.S. 1, 8-9, the Court, in speaking of the Fourth Amendment stated, "This inestimable right of personal security belongs as much to the citizen on the streets of our cities as to the homeowner closeted in his study to dispose of his secret affairs."

Katz v. United States, 389 U.S. 347, 350, emphasizes that the Fourth Amendment "protects individual privacy against certain kinds of governmental intrusion."

In Meyer v. Nebraska, 262 U.S. 390, 399, the Court said:

> Without doubt, it [liberty] denotes not merely freedom from bodily restraint but also the right of the individual to contract, to engage in any of the common occupations of life, to acquire useful knowledge, to marry, establish a home and bring up children, to worship God according to the dictates of his own conscience, and generally to enjoy those privileges long recognized at common law as essential to the orderly pursuit of happiness by free men.

The Georgia statute is at war with the clear message of these cases — that a woman is free to make the basic decision whether to bear an unwanted child. Elaborate argument is hardly necessary to demonstrate that child birth may deprive a woman of her preferred life style and force upon her a radically different and undesired future. For example, rejected applicants under the Georgia statute are required to endure the discomforts of pregnancy; to incur the pain, higher mortality rate, and aftereffects of childbirth; to abandon educational plans; to sustain loss of income; to forgo the satisfactions of careers; to tax further mental and physical health in providing childcare; and, in some cases, to bear the lifelong stigma of unwed motherhood, a badge which may haunt, if not deter, later legitimate family relationships.

Such a holding is, however, only the beginning of the problem. The State has interests to protect. Vaccinations to prevent epidemics are one example, as *Jacobson* holds. The Court held that compulsory sterilization of imbeciles afflicted with hereditary forms of insanity or imbecility is another. Buck v. Bell, 274 U.S. 200. Abortion affects another. While childbirth endangers the lives of some women, voluntary abortion at any time and place regardless of medical standards would impinge on a rightful concern of society. The woman's health is part of that concern; as is the life of the fetus after quickening. These concerns justify the State in treating the procedure as a medical one.

One difficulty is that this statute as construed and applied apparently does not give full sweep to the "psychological as well as physical well-being" of women patients which saved the concept "health" from being void for vagueness in United States v. Vuitch, supra, at 72. But apart from that, Georgia's enactment has a constitutional infirmity because, as stated by the District Court, it "limits the number of reasons for which an abortion may be sought." I agree with the holding of the District Court, "This the State may not do, because such action unduly restricts a decision sheltered by the Constitutional right to privacy." 319 F.Supp., at 1056.

The vicissitudes of life produce pregnancies which may be unwanted, or which may impair "health" in the broad *Vuitch* sense of the term, or which may imperil the life of the mother, or which in the full setting of the case may create such suffering, dislocations, misery, or tragedy as to make an early abortion the only civilized step to take. These hardships may be properly embraced in the "health" factor of the mother as appraised by a person of insight. Or they may be part of a broader medical judgment based on what is "appropriate" in a given case, though perhaps not "necessary" in a strict sense.

The "liberty" of the mother, though rooted as it is in the Constitution, may be qualified by the State for the reasons we have stated. But where fundamental personal rights and liberties are involved, the corrective legislation must be "narrowly drawn to prevent the supposed evil," Cantwell v. Connecticut, 310 U.S. 296, 307, and not be dealt with in an "unlimited and indiscriminate" manner. Shelton v. Tucker, 364 U.S. 479, 490. And see Talley v. California, 362 U.S. 60. Unless regulatory measures are so confined and are addressed to the specific areas of compelling legislative concern, the police power would become the great leveller of constitutional rights and liberties.

There is no doubt that the State may require abortions to be performed by qualified medical personnel. The legitimate objective of preserving the mother's health clearly supports such laws. Their impact upon the woman's privacy is minimal. But the Georgia statute outlaws virtually all such operations — even in the earliest stages of pregnancy. In light of modern medican evidence suggesting that an early abortion is safer healthwise than childbirth itself, it cannot be seriously urged that so comprehensive a ban is aimed at protecting the woman's health. Rather, this expansive proscription of all abortions along the temporal spectrum can rest only on a public goal of preserving both embryonic and fetal life.

The present statute has struck the balance between the woman and the State's interests wholly in favor of the latter. I am not prepared to hold that a State may equate, as Georgia has done, all phases of maturation preceding birth. We held in *Griswold* that the States may not preclude spouses from attempting to avoid the joinder of sperm and egg. If this is true, it is difficult to perceive any overriding public necessity which might attach precisely at the moment of conception. As Mr. Justice Clark has said:[6]

> To say that life is present at conception is to give recognition to the potential, rather than the actual. The unfertilized egg has life, and if fertilized, it takes on human proportions. But the law deals in reality, not obscurity — the known rather than the unknown. When sperm meets egg, life may eventually form, but quite often it does not. The law does not deal in speculation. The phenomenon of life takes time to

6. Religion, Morality and Abortion: A Constitutional Appraisal, 2 Loy. U. (L.A.) L. Rev. 1, 10 (1969).

develop, and until it is actually present, it cannot be destroyed. Its interruption prior to formation would hardly be homicide, and as we have seen, society does not regard it as such. The rites of Baptism are not performed and death certificates are not required when a miscarriage occurs. No prosecutor has ever returned a murder indictment charging the taking of the life of a fetus.[7] This would not be the case if the fetus constituted human life.

In summary, the enactment is overbroad. It is not closely correlated to the aim of preserving pre-natal life. In fact, it permits its destruction in several cases, including pregnancies resulting from sex acts in which unmarried females are below the statutory age of consent. At the same time, however, the measure broadly proscribes aborting other pregnancies which may cause severe mental disorders. Additionally, the statute is overbroad because it equates the value of embryonic life immediately after conception with the worth of life immediately before birth.

III

Under the Georgia Act the mother's physician is not the sole judge as to whether the abortion should be performed. Two other licensed physicians must concur in his judgment.[8] Moreover, the abortion must be performed in a licensed hospital;[9] and the abortion must be approved in advance by a committee of the medical staff of that hospital.[10]

Physicians, who speak to us in *Doe* through an amicus brief, complain of the Georgia Act's interference with their practice of their profession.

The right of privacy has no more conspicuous place than in the physician-patient relationship, unless it be in the priest-penitent relation.

It is one thing for a patient to agree that her physician may consult with another physician about her case. It is quite a different matter for the State compulsorily to impose on that physician-patient relationship another layer or, as in this case, still a third layer of physicians. The right of privacy — the right to care for one's health and person and to seek out a physician of one's own choice protected by the Fourteenth Amendment — becomes only a matter of theory not a reality, when a multiple physician approval system is mandated by the State.

The State licenses a physician. If he is derelict or faithless, the procedures available to punish him or to deprive him of his license are well known. He is entitled to procedural due process before professional disciplinary sanctions may be imposed. See In re Ruffalo, 390 U.S. 544. Crucial here, however, is state-imposed control over the medical decision whether pregnancy should be interrupted. The good-faith decision of the patient's chosen physician is overridden and the final decision passed on to others in whose selection the patient has no part. This is a total destruction of the right of privacy between physician and patient and the intimacy of relation which that entails.

The right to seek advice on one's health and the right to place his reliance on the physician of his choice are basic to Fourteenth Amendment values. We deal with fundamental rights and liberties, which, as already noted, can be contained or controlled only by discretely drawn legislation that preserves the "liberty" and regulates only those phases of the problem of compelling legislative concern. The imposition by the State of group controls over the physician-patient relation is not made on any medical procedure apart from abortion, no matter how dangerous the medical step may be. The oversight

7. In Keeler v. Superior Court, 2 Cal. 3d 619, 470 P.2d 617, the California Supreme Court held in 1970 that the California murder statute did not cover the killing of an unborn fetus, even though the fetus be "viable," and that it was beyond judicial power to extend the statute to the killing of an unborn. It held that the child must be "born alive before a charge of homicide can be sustained." Id., at 639, 470 P.2d, at 630.

8. See Ga. Code Ann. §26-1202(b)(3).

9. See id., §26-1202(b)(4).

10. Id., §26-1202(b)(5).

imposed on the physician and patient in abortion cases denies them their "liberty," viz., their right of privacy, without any compelling, discernable state interest.

Georgia has constitutional warrant in treating abortion as a medical problem. To protect the woman's right of privacy, however, the control must be through the physician of her choice and the standards set for his performance.

The protection of the fetus when it has acquired life is a legitimate concern of the State. Georgia's law makes no rational, discernible decision on that score. For under the Act the developmental stage of the fetus is irrelevant when pregnancy is the result of rape or when the fetus will very likely be born with a permanent defect or when a continuation of the pregnancy will endanger the life of the mother or permanently injure her health. When life is present is a question we do not try to resolve. While basically a question for medical experts, as stated by Mr. Justice Clark,[12] it is, of course, caught up in matters of religion and morality.

In short, I agree with the Court that endangering the life of the woman or seriously and permanently injuring her health are standards too narrow for the right of privacy that are at stake.

I also agree that the superstructure of medical supervision which Georgia has erected violates the patient's right of privacy inherent in her choice of her own physician.

Mr. Justice WHITE, with whom Mr. Justice REHNQUIST joins, dissenting. At the heart of the controversy in these cases are those recurring pregnancies that pose no danger whatsoever to the life or health of the mother but are nevertheless unwanted for any one or more of a variety of reasons — convenience, family planning, economics, dislike of children, the embarrassment of illegitimacy, etc. The common claim before us is that for any one of such reasons, or for no reason at all, and without asserting or claiming any threat to life or health, any woman is entitled to an abortion at her request if she is able to find a medical advisor willing to undertake the procedure.

The Court for the most part sustains this position: During the period prior to the time the fetus becomes viable, the Constitution of the United States values the convenience, whim or caprice of the putative mother more than the life or potential life of the fetus; the Constitution, therefore, guarantees the right to an abortion as against any state law or policy seeking to protect the fetus from an abortion not prompted by more compelling reasons of the mother.

With all due respect, I dissent. I find nothing in the language or history of the Constitution to support the Court's judgment. The Court simply fashions and announces a new constitutional right for pregnant mothers and, with scarcely any reason or authority for its action, invests that right with sufficient substance to override most existing state abortion statutes. The upshot is that the people and the legislatures of the 50 States are constitutionally disentitled to weigh the relative importance of the continued existence and development of the fetus on the one hand against a spectrum of possible impacts on the mother on the other hand. As an exercise of raw judicial power, the Court perhaps has authority to do what it does today; but in my view its judgment is an improvident and extravagant exercise of the power of judicial review which the Constitution extends to this Court.

The Court apparently values the convenience of the pregnant mother more than the continued existence and development of the life or potential life which she carries. Whether or not I might agree with that marshalling of values, I can in no event join the Court's judgment because I find no constitutional warrant for imposing such an order of priorities on the people and legislatures of the States. In a sensitive area such as this, involving as it does issues over which reasonable men may easily and heatedly differ, I cannot accept the Court's exercise of its clear power of choice by interposing a constitutional barrier to state efforts to protect human life and by investing mothers and doctors with the constitutionally protected right to exterminate it. This issue, for the most part,

---

12. *Religion, Morality and Abortion: A Constitutional Appraisal,* 2 Loy. U. (L.A.) L. Rev. 1, 10 (1969).

should be left with the people and to the political processes the people have devised to govern their affairs.

It is my view, therefore, that the Texas statute is not constitutionally infirm because it denies abortions to those who seek to serve only their convenience rather than to protect their life or health. Nor is this plaintiff, who claims no threat to her mental or physical health, entitled to assert the possible rights of those women whose pregnancy assertedly implicates their health. This, together with United States v. Vuitch, 402 U.S. 62 (1971), dictates reversal of the judgment of the District Court.

Likewise, because Georgia may constitutionally forbid abortions to putative mothers who, like the plaintiff in this case, do not fall within the reach of §26-1202(a) of its criminal code, I have no occasion, and the District Court had none, to consider the constitutionality of the procedural requirements of the Georgia statute as applied to those pregnancies posing substantial hazards to either life or health. I would reverse the judgment of the District Court in the Georgia case.

Note: Political and Constitutional Perspectives

The first case invalidating an abortion statute was handed down in 1969; within only four years, the Supreme Court had called into question the criminal abortion statutes of every state.[1] Given the powerful moral judgment embodied in anti-abortion legislation, the move from almost total prohibition to constitutional protection for a woman's right to choose has been breathtaking. The Court's decision was made in the face of the fierce and continuing opposition of many Catholics and members of other religious groups who believe that abortion is literally murder. Although the revolutionary change cannot be briefly or easily explained, several factors clearly played a role, including fundamental changes in sexual morality and dramatic improvements in contraceptive technology. The long fight waged by advocates of birth control paved the legal path. Although early pioneers of the use of contraception, such as Margaret Sanger, rejected abortion,[2] the litigation which their struggle produced culminated in the landmark decisions of Griswold v. Connecticut, 381 U.S. 479, 85 S. Ct. 1678, 14 L. Ed. 2d 510 (1965), and Eisenstadt v. Baird, 405 U.S. 438, 92 S. Ct. 1029, 31 L. Ed. 2d 349 (1972), which extended the constitutional right of privacy to cover contraceptive freedom and made the *Roe* and *Doe* decisions possible. Their struggle also changed attitudes by promoting the idea that potential parents, particularly women, should be able to choose whether and when to have children. The renascent women's movement also was important. There was a nationwide litigation campaign against abortion laws, which was inspired and directed by women who viewed this as a key issue for the current movement. Across the country, literally hundreds of cases of all kinds were brought to court, with cooperation among people differing in abilities and interests, but united in the idea that there must be access to abortion if women were ever to be truly equal. The attacks on abortion laws in all their forms were varied and creative. In Connecticut, for instance, there was a mammoth class action, joining as plaintiffs 1000 women of all interests and places in life.[3] Some actions were, of course, defenses for doctors who had performed abortions, or for counselors who had aided in giving advice. Others were brought by women who sought abortions and had been refused. These cases, their variety and notoriety, created a climate of opinion, a receptivity to the issues — in short, had an

---

1. Not even the states with liberalized abortion statutes, such as Hawaii and New York, conformed in all respects to the Supreme Court's mandate.

2. Sanger, Margaret Sanger, An Autobiography 217 (Dover ed. 1971).

3. During the litigation, all nonpregnant female plaintiffs' claims were dismissed. However, the litigation was supported by their organization, Women vs. Connecticut, and was successful in Abele v. Markle, a series of court decisions invalidating successive anti-abortion statutes passed by the Connecticut legislature. One of the series of decisions in Abele v. Markle is reported at 351 F. Supp. 224 (D. Conn. 1972).

educative effect which allowed (and "caused" is not too strong a word) the Supreme Court decisions.[4] A mere listing of those who filed amicus briefs in the Supreme Court indicates the broad base of the movement for change and the extent to which the issue was joined between pro- and anti-abortion forces. In addition to the briefs for appellants and appellees, briefs were filed by the attorney generals of Arizona, Connecticut, Kentucky, Nebraska, and Utah; for the Association of Texas Diocesan Attorneys; for Americans United for Life; for Women for the Unborn et al.; for the American College of Obstetricians and Gynecologists et al.; for Certain Physicians, Professors and Fellows of the American College of Obstetrics and Gynecology; for Planned Parenthood Federation of America, Inc., et al.; for the National Legal Program on Health Problems of the Poor et al.; for the State Communities Aid Ass'n; for the National Right to Life Committee; for the American Ethical Union et al.; for the American Association of University Women et al.; for New Women Lawyers et al.; for the California Committee to Legalize Abortion et al.; for Robert L. Sassone, and by Ferdinand Buckley pro se.[5] Other factors which have contributed to the political climate that made the abortion decisions possible are the increasing participation of women in the labor force, aspirations for a life materially more comfortable or with more social options than traditional family life permits, and concern about world population growth.

Roe v. Wade and Doe v. Bolton, supra, not only are rather astonishing decisions politically but are doctrinally extremely difficult. Extraordinarily vague about their constitutional foundation, the decisions are unusually explicit about issues not directly before the court. Ely has observed:[6]

> A number of fairly standard criticisms can be made of *Roe*. A plausible narrower basis of decision, that of vagueness, is brushed aside in the rush toward broader ground. The opinion strikes the reader initially as a sort of guidebook, addressing questions not before the Court and drawing lines with an apparent precision one generally associates with a commissioner's regulations. On closer examination, however, the precision appears largely illusory. Confusing signals are emitted, particularly with respect to the nature of the doctor's responsibilities and the permissible scope of health regulations after the first trimester. The Court seems, moreover, to get carried away on the subject of remedies: Even assuming the case can be made for an unusually protected constitutional right to an abortion, it hardly seems necessary to have banned during the first trimester *all* state regulation of the conditions under which abortions can be performed.

Ely goes on to make what he regards as a far more significant criticism:[7]

> What is frightening about *Roe* is that this super-protected right [a woman's freedom to choose an abortion] is not inferable from the language of the Constitution, the framers' thinking respecting the specific problem in issue, any general value derivable from the provisions they included, or the nation's governmental structure. Nor is it explainable in terms of the unusual political impotence of the group judicially protected vis-à-vis the interest that legislatively prevailed over it.[8] And that, I believe — the predictable early reaction to *Roe* notwithstanding ("more of the same Warren-

4. The impact of the women's movement on the legal situation is described in Goodman, Schoenbrod, and Stearns, Doe and Roe, Where Do We Go From Here?, 4 Women's Rights L. Rep. 20 (Spring 1973), and in Hole and Levine, The Rebirth of Feminism 278-308 (1971). The enormous number of court cases involved is demonstrated in a pre-*Roe* listing in Vergata et al., Abortion Cases in the United States, 2 Women's Rights L. Rep. 50-55 (Spring 1972).

5. Roe v. Wade, 410 U.S. at 115-116; Doe v. Bolton, 410 U.S. at 181.

6. Ely, The Wages of Crying Wolf: A Comment on Roe v. Wade, 82 Yale L.J. 920, 922 (1973).

7. Id. at 935-936.

8. Ely is here apparently comparing the political power of fetuses with the political power of women. It is at least arguable that the political impotence of women, the group most affected by anti-abortion legislation, vis-à-vis men, the group which dominates the legislatures and the courts, provides some justification for judicial intervention. — Eds.

type activism") — is a charge that can responsibly be leveled at no other decision of the past twenty years.

He concludes by comparing the decision to Lochner v. New York, 198 U.S. 45, 45 S. Ct. 539, 49 L. Ed. 937 (1905), supra Chapter One, II-A, and its progeny, and charging the Court with a failure to live up to its constitutional responsibilities.

Although the constitutional rhetoric, and indeed the doctrinal underpinning, of *Roe* and *Doe* may be flawed, the result of the decisions is not so surprising when considered in context. The last ten years have seen a series of cases which protect the individual's rights involved in decisions about procreation. As the Court stated in *Roe,* the right of privacy includes "only personal rights that can be deemed 'fundamental' or 'implicit in the concept of ordered liberty,' " 410 U.S. at 152, and has "some extension to activities relating to marriage, procreation, contraception, family relationships, and child rearing and education," 410 U.S. at 152-153 (citations omitted). In both *Roe* and LaFleur v. Cleveland Board of Education, 42 U.S.L.W. 4186 (U.S. Jan. 21, 1974), the Supreme Court listed a series of cases, described in *LaFleur* as those recognizing "that freedom of personal choice in matters of marriage and family life is one of the liberties protected by the Due Process Clause of the Fourteenth Amendment": among them are Loving v. Virginia, 388 U.S. 1, 87 S. Ct. 1817, 18 L. Ed. 2d 1010 (1967) (interracial marriage); Griswold v. Connecticut, 381 U.S. 479, 85 S. Ct. 1678, 14 L. Ed. 2d 510 (1965) (the rights of married persons to use contraceptives); Pierce v. Society of Sisters, 268 U.S. 510, 45 S. Ct. 571, 69 L. Ed. 1070 (1925), and Meyer v. Nebraska, 262 U.S. 390, 43 S. Ct. 625, 67 L. Ed. 2d 1042 (1923) (the rights of parents to send their children to private schools *(Pierce)* or to have them learn German *(Meyer))*; Prince v. Massachusetts, 321 U.S. 158, 88 L. Ed. 645 (1944) (the right of a state to restrict street vending by children despite a claim of religious immunity by Jehovah's Witnesses); and Eisenstadt v. Baird, 405 U.S. 438, 92 S. Ct. 1029, 31 L. Ed. 2d 349 (1972) (the rights of unmarried persons to access to contraceptive information). Another case which demonstrates the Court's concern in this area is Stanley v. Illinois, 405 U.S. 645, 92 S. Ct. 1208, 31 L. Ed. 2d 551 (1972), holding that the state cannot deprive unwed fathers of child custody without a hearing like that granted other parents. These cases use constitutional methodologies ranging from traditional equal protection *(Loving)* to due process hearing rights *(LaFleur)* to privacy *(Griswold).* Aside from the question of methodology, however, is there constitutional justification for special judicial protection of individual rights related to procreation, child rearing, marriage, and the family?

The "rightness" of the decisions has been argued not only in context, but as constitutional law, by Laurence H. Tribe.[9] He urges that the decisions should be viewed as an exercise in constitutional role allocation, rather than a return to Lochnering. In his view, judicial intervention vis-à-vis the legislature in order to assert individual control over the abortion decision is justified by the "excessive entanglement" of religion in the legislative processes around abortion. This entanglement is inevitable where, as in abortion legislation, no secular reason for governmental involvement exists, yet the legislature is unable to refrain from acting because of the intense political pressure generated by the religious controversy. In contrast, no such justification existed for judicial intervention in the *Lochner* series of cases.

As to the other scholarly criticisms of the decision, the arbitrariness of the lines drawn by the Supreme Court, and the opinions' "guidebook" quality, two points can be made. First, the unusually detailed opinion in Roe suggests that the Court desired to settle as many of the issues as possible at one time rather than invite prolonged litigation. Perhaps, in the Court's view, it was fast becoming the center of a polarizing debate from which it desired to remove itself as expeditiously as possible. And in fact, as the following notes show, the most politically heated controversies about

---

9. The Supreme Court, 1972 Term, Foreword: Toward a Model of Roles in the Due Process of Life and Law, 87 Harv. L. Rev. 1 (1973).

abortion have moved from the courts to the legislatures, at least for the time being.

Second, because a continuous biological process is involved in conception and birth, any drawing of lines must be inexact. In a difficult confrontation between biology, law, and politics, the Court managed to draw lines which have at least some relation to common sense and the conclusions of current science. Yet, in the end, the Court's very reliance on current scientific knowledge may mean that the decision will be subject to challenge at some time when more precise information is available about viability, or there are more advanced techniques for maintaing a fetus outside of the womb.

NOTE: THE DOCTOR'S ROLE

In both *Roe* and *Doe,* the Supreme Court emphasized the role of the physician:[10]

> The decision vindicates the right of the physician to administer medical treatment according to his professional judgment up to the points where important state interests provide compelling justifications for intervention. Up to those points the abortion decision in all its aspects is inherently, and primarily, a medical decision, and basic responsibility for it must rest with the physician. If an individual practitioner abuses the privilege of exercising proper medical judgment, the usual remedies, judicial and intra-professional, are available.

In Doe v. Bolton, supra, the Court, in invalidating a series of limitations on abortion, such as two-doctor concurrence and committee approval requirements, focused on the right of the physician to administer medical care in accordance with his best judgment. For example, the Court commented that[11]

> The statute's emphasis . . . is on the attending physicians' "best clinical judgment that an abortion is necessary." That should be sufficient. . . . The attending physician will know when a consultation is advisable — the doubtful situation, the need for assurance when the medical decision is a delicate one, and the like. Physicians have followed this routine historically and know its usefulness and benefit for all concerned. It is still true today that "[re]liance must be placed upon the assurance given by his license, issued by an authority competent to judge in that respect, that he [the physician] possesses the requisite qualifications."

This emphasis on the doctor's rights and responsibilities raises some interesting issues. At the outset, the doctor's right to refuse to do an abortion seems to be clearly established. In fact, in *Doe,* the statute, in a provision which was not challenged, explicitly protected his right to refrain for moral or religious reasons. As Note: Legislative Responses to the Decisions, infra, reports, many states and the federal government have similarly acted to protect the right of physicians and other health personnel to refuse to participate in abortions. Even without statutory authority, however, the language of both *Roe* and *Doe* would seem to support the physician's right to refuse to perform abortions as well as his right to perform them. This is a good protection both for the civil liberties of health professionals and for the health of women seeking abortions.

The application of so-called conscience clauses to health institutions, however, will often conflict with the doctors' and the women's rights. See Note: Refusal by Institutions To Make Facilities Available, infra, especially the discussion of Watkins v. Mercy Medical Center, 364 F. Supp. 799 (D. Idaho 1973).

While feminists may be uncomfortable with the emphasis in the opinions on the doctor's rather than the woman's rights, the substitution of the individual physician's judgment for that of the state legislature or the hospital abortion committee goes far

10. Roe v. Wade, supra, 410 U.S. at 165-166.
11. 410 U.S. at 199-200.

toward abortion on demand, certainly in the first trimester and perhaps later in pregnancy as well. This is true because the opinion contains no guide to the exercise of the doctor's best judgment, and response to a patient's expressed desires would probably seem to many the best basis on which to act. Some language of the Court's in an earlier abortion case, United States v. Vuitch, 402 U.S. 62, 91 S. Ct. 1294, 28 L. Ed. 2d 601 (1971), may indicate how wide really is the room for the play of the doctor's "best clinical judgment" during the entire course of the pregnancy.

Vuitch was an example of a major type of abortion litigation, a statutory attack based on vagueness. In *Vuitch,* the Court reversed the judgment of the District Court for the District of Columbia, which had dismissed indictments against a physician on the ground that a statute prohibiting abortion unless "done as necessary for the preservation of the mother's life or health" (D.C. Code Ann. §22-201) was unconstitutionally vague. Justice Black in the majority opinion presaged the reliance of *Roe* and *Doe* on the physician's judgment:[12]

> The trial court apparently felt that the term was vague because there "is no indication whether it includes varying degrees of mental as well as physical health." 305 F. Supp., at 1034. . . . [G]eneral usage and modern understanding of the word "health" . . . includes psychological as well as physical well-being. Indeed Webster's Dictionary, in accord with that common usage, properly defines health as the "[s]tate of being . . . sound in body [or] mind." Viewed in this light, the term "health" presents no problem of vagueness. Indeed, whether a particular operation is necessary for a patient's physical or mental health is a judgment that physicians are obviously called upon to make routinely whenever surgery is considered.

Still, Justice Douglas in dissent was troubled that a doctor's judgment concerning health could nevertheless be reviewed by jurors who might give the words meaning "drawn from their own predilictions and prejudices" in a criminal proceeding, with resultant liability to a physician of one to ten years.[13] He argued:[14]

> I agree with the Court that a physician — within the limits of his own expertise — would be able to say that an abortion at a particular time performed on a designated patient would or would not be necessary for the "preservation" of her "life or health." That judgment, however, is highly subjective, dependent on the training and insight of the particular physician and his standard as to what is "necessary" for the "preservation" of the mother's "life or health."
>
> The answers may well differ, physician to physician. Those trained in conventional obstetrics may have one answer; those with deeper psychiatric insight may have another. Each answer is clear to the particular physician. If we could read the Act as making that determination conclusive, not subject to review by judge and by jury, the case would be simple.

Justice Stewart's answer to this, in an opinion dissenting in part, could form the basis for how courts come to regard the regulation of even late-term abortions.[15]

> [W]hen a physician has exercised his judgment in favor of performing an abortion, he has, by hypothesis, not violated the statute. To put it another way, I think the question of whether the performance of an abortion is "necessary for the . . . mother's life or health" is entrusted under the statute exclusively to those licensed to practice medicine, without the overhanging risk of incurring criminal liability at the hands of a second-guessing lay jury. I would hold, therefore, that "a competent licensed practitioner of medicine" is wholly immune from being charged with the commission of a criminal offense under this law.

12. 402 U.S. at 71-72.
13. Id. at 75.
14. Id. at 74, 78-80.
15. Id. at 96, 97.

Although the total reliance on the doctor's discretion exampled by Justice Stewart in theory would make even abortion in the third trimester freely available, this result is unlikely in practice, because of the reluctance of doctors to do abortions at a period when the distinction is so blurred between abortion and induced labor.

NOTE: LEGISLATIVE RESPONSES TO THE DECISIONS

In effect, *Roe* and *Doe* invalidated the criminal abortion statutes of all 50 states. In the year following the decisions, more than 200 bills about abortion were introduced in state legislatures. But only 23 states succeeded in passing any legislation at all, and only 11 attempted comprehensive laws in the area.[16] Much of what did pass was a result of campaigns by those who opposed the decision, so that, for instance, the new abortion laws of Rhode Island and Utah were almost immediately declared unconstitutional.[17] Rhode Island provided for example that "in the furtherance of public policy of said state, human life, and, in fact, a person within the language and meaning of the Fourteenth Amendment to the Constitution of the United States, commences to exist at the instance of conception."[18] Provisions in the laws of other states which are arguably unconstitutional include a requirement that first trimester abortions be performed in hospitals or other licensed facilities (e.g., ch. 766, [1973] Stat. Nev.; Ind. Ann. Stat. §10-108(a)(1) (Supp. 1973)); the requirement of consent to the abortion by the parent of a minor woman (e.g., Ind. Ann. Stat. §10-108(a)(2) (Supp. 1973)) or the "father" of the fetus (e.g., 8 Utah Code Ann. §76-7-304(5) (Supp. 1973)); and the provision that no public assistance or medical grant can be used for an abortion (e.g., 8 Utah Code Ann. §76-7-314 (Supp. 1973)). Residency requirements also continued to be enacted, although the opinion in *Roe* decisively invalidated them (e.g., 7 Tenn. Code Ann. §39-301(f) (Supp. 1973)).

The Commissioners on Uniform Laws responded to the decisions by revising the Uniform Abortion Act. The revised act is reprinted below. (Note that one of the factors cited by the Supreme Court in support of its decision in *Doe* was the approval of the Uniform Abortion Act by the American Bar Association, and its enactment, more or less in toto, by four states.)[19] The Revised Uniform Act is notably more detailed than the prior version. Read it carefully and consider whether it is model legislation from a feminist perspective. Is Section 4 a necessary or desirable provision? One question is whether the emergency situation specified justifies the total discretion granted the physician. What is the relationship between Section 3 and Section 4 of the Act?

Think about other provisions which might be included in a model act. Would you want to define the life or health of the woman for third trimester purposes? Would the following definition be correct in light of the opinion? Possible to legislate?

> After the twenty-fourth week of gestation, an abortion shall be performed only to save the life or health of the pregnant patient. Such decision must be based on the best clinical judgment of the woman's physician, taking into account but not limited to such factors as the well-being of the patient in light of her age, physical, emotional, psychological and familial condition.

---

16. See the summary of legislation in 2 Family Planning/Population Reporter 143 (Dec. 1973).

17. Doe v. Israel, 482 F.2d 156 (1st Cir. 1973), denying stay of district court decision pending appeal; Doe v. Rampton, 366 F. Supp. 189 (D. Utah 1973).

18. Preamble, Rhode Island Criminal Abortion Statute, R.I. Gen. Laws §11-3-1 et seq., quoted in Doe v. Israel, 358 F. Supp. 1193, 1195 (D.R.I. 1973). The spirit of much of the state legislation enacted in response to *Roe* and *Doe* is captured in Section 1 of Publ. L. No. 322, [1973] Acts Ind. 1740, which declares that "it is not the intent of the Indiana General Assembly, in enacting this legislation . . . to indicate that it approves of abortion, except to save the life of the mother. The General Assembly is, however, controlled to a certain extent by recent Supreme Court decisions. . . ."

19. 410 U.S. at 194.

REVISED UNIFORM ABORTION ACT (1973)
9 Uniform Laws Ann. (Master ed. Supp. 1974) §§1-10

Section 1. [*Definitions.*] As used in this Act:

(1) "Abortion" means the termination of human pregnancy with an intention other than to produce a live birth or to remove a dead embryo or fetus.

(2) "Hospital" means a hospital approved by the [state department of health] or operated by the United States, this State, or any department, agency, or political subdivision thereof.

(3) "Medical facility" means a facility other than a hospital, such as a medical clinic, that has adequate staff and services necessary to perform an abortion safely, to provide after-care, and to cope with any complication or emergency that might reasonably be expected to arise therefrom, or that has arrangements with a nearby hospital to provide those services.

(4) "Licensed physician" means a physician licensed to practice medicine [or osteopathy] in this state, or a physician practicing medicine [or osteopathy] in the employ of the government of the United States or of this State, or any department, agency, or political subdivision thereof.

Section 2. [*Limitations on Abortions.*] An abortion may be performed in this State only under the following circumstances:

(1) During the first [12] [13] [14] weeks of pregnancy by a woman upon herself upon the advice of a licensed physician or by a licensed physician.

(2) After the first [12] [13] [14] weeks of pregnancy and before the fetus is viable, by a licensed physician and in a hospital or medical facility.

(3) After the fetus is viable, by a licensed physician, in a hospital, and in the medical judgment of the physician the abortion is necessary to preserve the life or health of the woman.

Section 3. [*Consent Required.*] Consent to an abortion must first be given by the woman or, if she is mentally incapable of giving consent, by a parent or guardian or by order of the [appropriate] court. A woman is not incapable by reason of her minority of giving consent to an abortion under this Act.

Section 4. [*Exceptions to Requirements.*] If, in the medical judgment of the physician, an abortion is immediately necessary to preserve the life of the woman, it may be performed anywhere and, if the woman is unable to consent for any reason, without her consent.

Section 5. [*Express Objection.*] In no event may any abortion be performed under this Act upon a woman over her express objection, except that if she is under [12] [13] [14] years of age and the [appropriate] court finds the abortion is necessary to preserve her life or health, it may order the abortion to be performed.

Section 6. [*Participation in Abortion Not Required.*] No physician, nurse, hospital or medical facility employee, or any other individual is under any duty or required to participate in an abortion. An individual who participates or refuses to participate in an abortion permitted under this Act may not for that reason be discriminated against in employment or professional privileges.]

Section 7. [*Penalty.*] Any person who knowingly performs or procures an abortion other than as permitted by this Act is guilty of a [felony] and, upon conviction thereof, may be sentenced to pay a fine not exceeding [$1,000] dollars or to imprisonment in the [state penitentiary] not exceeding [5] years, or both.

Section 8. [*Application and Construction.*] This Act shall be applied and construed to effectuate its general purpose to make uniform the law with respect to the subject of this Act among states enacting it.

Section 9. [*Short Title.*] This Act may be cited as the Revised Uniform Abortion Act.

Section 10. [*Severability.*] If any provision of this Act or the application thereof to any person or circumstance is held invalid, the invalidity does not affect other provisions or applications of this Act which can be given effect without the invalid provision or application, and to this end the provisions of this Act are severable.

Note: The Federal Congress

Much of the focus of anti-abortion activities shifted to Congress after the *Doe* and *Roe* decisions. A lobbying campaign, which has included a volume of vehement letters and photographs of embryos and fetuses, as well as delegations, phone calls, and personal visits, has produced a number of proposals for overturning the decisions or making difficult their implementation.

Measures introduced in the first year after the decision are summarized below.[20] It is likely that the opposition will continue to take forms similar to these.

There have been two major types of constitutional amendments proposed. One is a "states rights" model like H.R.J. Res. 427, which has been sponsored by 24 representatives and has no companion measure in the Senate. The amendment reads, in part:

> Nothing in this Constitution shall bar any state or territory or the District of Columbia, with regard to any area over which it has jurisdication, from allowing, regulating, or prohibiting the practice of abortion.

The second type is "right to life" proposals, first introduced in the House by Rep. Lawrence J. Hogan (R,Md.) (H.R.J. Res. 261) and in the Senate by Sen. Jesse A. Helms (R,N.C.) (S.J. Res. 130) and by Sen. James L. Buckley (R,N.Y.) (S.J. Res. 119). The Hogan and Helms amendments are identical. They have 19 sponsors in the House and one in the Senate. The Buckley amendment differs somewhat in form and substance. It has 7 cosponsors in the Senate, and 4 House members have proposed similar measures. The Helms-Hogan amendment reads, in part:

> Neither the United States nor any state shall deprive any human being, from the moment of conception, of life without the due process of law; nor deny to any human being, from the moment of conception, within its jurisdiction, the equal protection of the laws.

The Buckley amendment reads, in part:

> With respect to the right to life, the word "person" as used in this article and in the fifth and fourteenth articles of amendment to the Constitution of the United States, applies to all human beings, including their unborn offspring at every stage of their biological development, irrespective of age, health, function or condition of dependency.

Unlike the Hogan-Helms amendment, S.J. Res. 119 would allow an exception "in a medical emergency when a reasonable medical certainty exists that continuation of pregnancy will cause the death of the mother." Whereas, under the Hogan-Helms amendment "the moment of conception" is regarded as occurring at fertilization, the Buckley formulation is less specific.

Five floor amendments to reduce the availability of abortion were introduced in 1973 during the consideration of a variety of measures. None was considered in committee prior to adoption by at least one house; none was the subject of hearings. Two eventually became law in modified versions; the others are still pending in one house or in conference.

---

20. These summaries are based on the Washington Memo (Jan. 22, 1974) of the Planned Parenthood–World Population Organization, which does an excellent job of monitoring the activities of the well-organized anti-abortion forces.

The Church amendment, added with some modifications to the Health Programs Extension Act of 1973 (P.L. 93-45), permits institutions which are wholly or partially federally funded to refuse to perform abortion or sterilization procedures. The amendment, sponsored by Sen. Frank Church (D,Idaho), applies not only to religiously affiliated institutions which may have, as a fundamental tenet of religious doctrine, opposition to abortion, but to any institution which declines to perform these surgical procedures on the basis of "religious beliefs or moral convictions." This amendment poses some constitutional problems, which are discussed below in Note: Refusal by Institutions To Make Facilities Available.

As proposed by Sen. Jacob K. Javits (R,N.Y.), Sen. Church's "conscience clause" also includes a section prohibiting discrimination against doctors and other medical personnel who support abortion and sterilization, or perform the procedures elsewhere, by institutions which themselves refuse to perform sterilizations or abortions. The P.L. 93-45 amendment has been offered again by Sen. Church as an amendment to the Social Security legislation. It was one of the Senate-passed amendments which the Social Security conferees decided not to consider prior to the Christmas recess.

The Helms amendment to the 1973 Foreign Assistance Act (P.L. 93-189) would have prohibited the use of United States funds in overseas population programs to perform abortions (for any reasons, even to save the woman's life), to pay for abortifacient drugs and devices (a category poorly defined, perhaps including the widely used intrauterine devices), and to support abortion-related research. The last two clauses were dropped in conference; the first was modified. The amendment to P.L. 93-189 reads:

> None of the funds made available to carry out this part shall be used to pay for the performance of abortions as a method of family planning or to motivate or coerce any person to practice abortions.

Still pending is an amendment to the legal services bill by Rep. Hogan, which was one of 24 amendments the House adopted restricting poverty lawyers from engaging in certain types of litigation. Senator Helms led the Senate filibuster on the bill, and the Senate failed to act on it before the recess. The amendment forbids poverty lawyers to

> provide legal assistance with respect to any proceeding or litigation which seeks to provide a nontherapeutic abortion or to compel any individual or institution to perform an abortion, or assist in the performance of an abortion, contrary to the religious beliefs or moral convictions of such individual or institution.

Also pending is an amendment to the Social Security legislation by Sen. Buckley, adopted during floor consideration of H.R. 3153, which would prohibit the use of Medicaid funds to pay for abortion procedures, for any reasons.

Note that most of the measures would not affect the availability of abortion for those who can afford to travel and to pay for their own medical care. Yet, "there is considerable evidence that the poor and the minorities . . . experience a greater rate of unwanted pregnancies than the general population. . . . Partial statistics from New York, California and Maryland, where abortion has been available for some time, indicate that a minimum of 30% of abortions to New York City residents were for Medicaid-eligible women; the proportion was similar in Maryland and even higher in California (38%)."[21] Equal protection challenges to laws restricting access to abortion are thus the most likely line of attack. Note, however, that the Supreme Court has not been particularly responsive to this argument in the abortion area. In *Roe,* equal protection was strongly briefed, but not mentioned by the Court's opinion. In *Doe,* equal protection was one of the bases for invalidating restrictive hospital regulations and, again, the Court did not directly

---

21. Washington Memo, supra at 4.

confront the argument's implications, saying that since "we have set aside the accreditation, approval, and confirmation requirements . . . the discrimination argument collapses in all significant aspects." 410 U.S. at 201. Of course, the equal protection argument is in no way foreclosed by anything in *Doe* or *Roe*.

What other constitutional or statutory attacks might be made on the legislative proposals outlined above? In the notes which follow, the discussion of some of the cases decided or begun since *Roe* and *Doe* delineates some of the possibilities.

NOTE: REFUSAL BY INSTITUTIONS
TO MAKE FACILITIES AVAILABLE

A major issue is whether, or under what circumstances, a health institution can refuse its facilities for abortion or sterilization. Much of the state abortion legislation passed since the federal decisions has provided that hospitals have an institutional "right to refuse," and usually no distinction has been made between private and public hospitals. As to public hospitals, however, it seems clear on the basis of *Roe* and *Doe* themselves that there is no right to deny facilities. Such a denial would be a state regulation interfering with the doctor-patient decision, which *Roe* and *Doe* forbid. The Georgia statute in *Doe* did have a "conscience clause" which was allowed to stand; however, it had not been challenged by plaintiffs. In the context of the case, the clause was ambiguous and the Court spoke of its application to "denominational" hospitals, and to individual doctors and other staff. (Note also that the conscience clause of the Revised Uniform Abortion Act, supra, speaks in terms of individuals rather than of institutions.)

An important case decided before *Roe* and *Doe* further supports the theory that public hospitals cannot, without due process, refuse the use of their facilities. In McCabe v. Nassau County Medical Center, 453 F.2d 698 (2d Cir. 1971), a woman sought injunctive and declaratory relief and damages against a hospital which had refused to sterilize her because she had only four children, when the hospital required that women her age (twenty-five) have five or more before voluntary sterilization would be permitted. After suit was filed, the hospital abandoned its position and permitted the operation, and the district court dismissed the case. The United States court of appeals reversed, ruling that the claim for damages was not moot, that the federal courts had jurisdiction, and that the plaintiff's constitutional claims were not frivolous. The court summarized the plaintiff's case as follows:[22]

> The essence of plaintiff's claim is [that] . . . Defendants' refusal to sterilize plaintiff was based not on medical factors peculiar to her case but on an arbitrary age-parity formula. . . . Plaintiff argues that through use of the age-parity rule defendants violated her constitutional rights by attempting to decide for her that she must subject herself to the possibility of pregnancy, despite the risk to her health, and by attempting to decide how many children she and her husband should have and by what means they may prevent conception. We need not determine whether plaintiff's contentions are sound, particularly without a full development of the facts, but it is a massive understatement to say that they are not frivolous.

Likewise, in Hathaway v. Worcester City Hospital, 475 F.2d 701 (1st Cir. 1973), and Nyberg v. City of Virginia, 361 F. Supp. 932 (D.Minn. 1973), courts held that public facilities may not make irrational distinctions among surgical procedures, allowing some and banning others which cause no greater risk to the patient or demand on staff or facilities. Such strong precedents, and the mandate of *Roe*, make it unlikely that public hospitals will be able to deny access to their facilities for abortions, although in light of

22. 453 F.2d at 704.

the legislation in many states individuals may find it necessary, at least in the next few years, to litigate in order to vindicate their rights.

On the other hand,[23]

> Private, or nongovernmental, hospitals outnumber public hospitals by more than two to one. There are 4,838 nongovernmental hospitals and 2,159 federal, state and local government hospitals.[5] If all private hospitals were permitted to refuse to allow abortions and sterilizations, the availability of those procedures would be severely limited, and in many areas, impossible to obtain, since a parochial or private hospital may be the only medical facility available.

Whether the Fourteenth Amendment precedents such as those cited above apply to private hospitals depends, of course, on whether there is some sense in which the state is acting through the hospitals. In a number of cases, courts have held that the receipt of federal funds allocated on the basis of a state plan for providing hospital care to its citizens involves the hospital in the performance of a public function, and hence constitutes state action. See, e.g., Simkins v. Moses H. Cone Memorial Hospital, 323 F.2d 959 (4th Cir. 1963).

In one case, a United States court of appeals declined to apply the *Simkins* precedent to abortion. In Doe v. Bellin Memorial Hospital, 479 F.2d 756 (7th Cir. 1973), the Seventh Circuit ruled that a nondenominational private hospital could refuse to perform abortions despite its acceptance of financial support pursuant to the Hill-Burton Act, the same legislation involved in *Simkins*, because its refusal was not proven to be directly or indirectly influenced by the state or by persons acting under color of state law. The court commented that[24]

> [t]here is no evidence . . . that any condition related to the performance or nonperformance of abortions was imposed upon the hospital. Unlike the situation in *Simkins* . . . on which plaintiffs place heavy reliance, this record does not reflect any governmental involvement in the very activity which is being challenged. We find no bases for concluding that by accepting Hill-Burton funds the hospital unwittingly surrendered the right it otherwise possessed to determine whether it would accept abortion patients.

On the other hand, a district court ruled that even a denominational hospital could not refuse its facilities for abortion when alternatives were not available and the hospital was receiving federal funds. Taylor v. St. Vincents Hospital, Civ. No. 1090, (D. Mont. Oct. 27, 1972). As a result, anti-abortion forces drafted the Church Amendment to the Health Programs Extension Act of 1973[25] specifically to change the interpretation of state action when abortion is involved. The amendment provides, in pertinent part:[26]

> The receipt of any grant, contract, loan, or loan guarantee under the Public Health Service Act [including Hill-Burton], the Community Mental Health Centers Act, or the Developmental Disabilities Services and Facilities Construction Act by any individual or entity *does not authorize any court or any public official or other public authority to require* . . . such entity to —
>
> (A) make its facilities available for the performance of any sterilization procedure or abortion if the performance of such procedure or abortion in such facilities is prohibited by the entity on the basis of religious beliefs or moral convictions. . . .

---

23. Gutman, Can Hospitals Constitutionally Refuse to Permit Abortions and Sterilizations?, 2 Family Planning /Population Reporter 146 (1973).

5. Congressional Record, Government Printing Office, March 27, 1973, p. S5724.

24. 479 F.2d at 761.

25. Pub. L. No. 93-45, §401(b) (Jun. 18, 1973), 87 Stat. 96, codified at 42 U.S.C.A. §300a-7 (Supp. 1974).

26. Pub. L. No. 93-45, §401(b), 42 U.S.C.A. §300a-7(a) (Supp. 1974) (emphasis supplied).

An almost immediate consequence of the passage of this amendment was a reversal of the *Taylor* decision. Taylor v. St. Vincents Hospital, Civ. No. 1090 (D. Mont. Oct. 26, 1973), dissolving preliminary injunction of Oct. 27, 1972. See also Watkins v. Mercy Medical Center, 364 F. Supp. 799 (D. Idaho 1973), in which a district court upheld a Catholic hospital's refusal to reappoint to its medical staff an otherwise qualified physician who would not agree to a directive prohibiting staff physicians from performing sterilizations or abortions in the hospital. Although the hospital was constructed with the help of Hill-Burton funds, the court, relying heavily on the Health Programs Extension Act of 1973, ruled that Dr. Watkins could not force the hospital to allow him to perform abortions and sterilizations in its facilities.

Think about the constitutional attacks which could be made on the Church Amendment. Equal protection is one of the strongest arguments where there are not other facilities nearby and the plaintiff is a poor or rural woman who cannot travel easily. Equal protection has long been pressed in the abortion litigation, and although, as noted supra, the Supreme Court in *Doe* and *Roe* largely ignored this aspect of the briefs, it seems likely that the real life situation, in which only the poor were effectively denied abortion, had an impact on the decisions.

The First Amendment clauses protecting free exercise and prohibiting establishment of religion provide another ground for challenging the Church Amendment. The argument would be that the grant of authority to hospitals to implement their religious or moral beliefs by denying access for abortion denies religious freedom to doctors and pregnant women whose moral or religious beliefs permit or even require abortion, and amounts to an establishment of religion. Would this argument be weakened if alternative facilities were available? Alternatives were not available in either Doe v. Bellin Memorial Hospital, supra, or Taylor v. St. Vincents Hospital, supra, but were available in *Watkins,* supra.

In this connection, note the conflict between political realities and legal doctrine under the Establishment Clause. Popular support for the right of denominational hospitals, particularly those affiliated with the Catholic Church, to refuse to do abortions and sterilizations, whether or not they get federal or state funds, is probably significantly greater than for similar rights for private hospitals without religious affiliation. However, under the First Amendment, Congress cannot give benefits to those whose beliefs derive from an organized religious group which it withholds from those with similar beliefs but no religious affiliation, for that would be to favor organized religion over other moral beliefs, and thus to establish religion or impede its free exercise. See United States v. Seeger, 380 U.S. 163, 188, 85 S. Ct. 850, 13 L. Ed. 2d 733 (1965) (Douglas, J., concurring). Therefore, in order to enable denominational hospitals to refuse to do abortions, Congress must exempt all private hospitals whose religious or moral beliefs forbid or discourage abortion or sterilization.

Another problem with the Church Amendment is that it appears to be an attempt to usurp the judicial function by limiting the concept of state action legislatively. This is a violation of separation of powers, and might run afoul of Article III. Ironically, this amendment may actually strengthen the argument that private hospitals are imbued with state action, in that it reflects "governmental involvement in the very activity which is being challenged," Doe v. Bellin Memorial Hospital, 479 F.2d at 761. Alternatively, it may be characterized as an attempt to limit the power of federal courts to grant remedies in a particular class of cases. Some of the constitutional problems listed above also arise under this interpretation, but the power of Congress is greater than it is in relation to the definition of state action.

It should be noted that, quite aside from direct funding like that under the Hill-Burton program, which is affected by the Church Amendment, hospitals are extensively involved with both the federal and state governments through Medicare and Medicaid, charter arrangements, licensing, and regulations. The network of regulatory patterns for any hospital would support a strong argument for state action.

In any event, however, the practical effect of the Church Amendment on litigation will be substantial unless and until the Supreme Court resolves the issues it poses, or the Church Amendment is repealed.

NOTE: MEDICAID REIMBURSEMENT

At the least, *Roe* and *Doe* decided that abortion should be regarded as normal medical treatment, prescribed by the doctor in consultation with his patient. Yet a continuing issue has been the attempt by legislatures and welfare officials to place restrictive conditions on the availability of medicaid and other welfare payments for abortions, which necessarily interfere with the doctor-patient decision. Typical of the provisions are those currently being challenged in a suit filed in Pennsylvania: the state will pay for the abortion only if there is a likelihood of deformity, the conception was a result of rape, or the abortion is necessary to preserve the life or health of the mother. The abortion must be performed in a hospital, and two doctors must concur with the attending physician that the abortion should be performed.[27] The similarity of these limitations and those invalidated in Doe v. Bolton is striking. Another common practice is to attempt to restrict the considerations which the physcian can take into account in prescribing abortion, for example, by confining payment to abortions which are "medically indicated."[28]

Every court which has considered such provisions has found them unconstitutional, mainly as a denial of equal protection. Doe v. Rose, No. C-197-73 (D. Utah July 27, 1973), invalidated a rule providing that medical assistance reimbursement was available only where the abortion was required for therapeutic reasons, and where prior authorization had been obtained from the state agency. In Doe v. Wohlgemuth, Civ. No. 73-846 (W.D. Pa. Oct. 9, 1973), the court ordered that welfare officials be temporarily restrained from applying payment restrictions to poor women who sought inpatient hospital abortions.

The equal protection considerations were eloquently stated in Klein v. Nassau County Medical Center, 347 F. Supp. 496 (E.D.N.Y. 1972), which arose shortly after New York liberalized its abortion law, and before the Supreme Court decisions in *Roe* and *Doe*.[29] In *Klein,* the plaintiffs challenged the Department of Welfare's administrative letter ruling that elective abortions are not medically indicated and therefore refusing payment. The court stated:[30]

> The directive, and the State statute, if interpreted as mandating the Commissioner's directive, would deny indigent women the equal protection of the laws to which they are constitutionally entitled. They alone are subjected to State coercion to bear children which they do not wish to bear, and no other women similarly situated are so coerced. Other women, able to afford the medical cost of either a justifiable abortional act or full term child birth, have complete freedom to make the choice in light of the manifold of considerations directly relevant to the problem uninhibited by any State action. The indigent is advised by the State that the State will deny her medical assistance unless she resigns her freedom of choice and bears the child. She is denied

27. These provisions are under attack in Doe v. Wohlgemuth, Civ. Action No. 73-1564 (E.D. Pa., filed July 12, 1973), and Doe v. Wohlgemuth, Civ. Action No. 73-846 (W.D. Pa. Oct. 9, 1973). The former also challenges the refusal of the Department of Public Welfare to reimburse for outpatient abortions and its failure to provide family planning services mandated by Titles XIX and IVA of the Social Security Act.

28. This is the sort of limitation that was involved in Klein v. Nassau County Medical Center, infra.

29. On appeal from the decision in *Klein,* the Supreme Court vacated the judgment and remanded for consideration in light of *Roe* and *Doe,* Nassau County Medical Center v. Klein, 412 U.S. 925, 93 S. Ct. 2748, 37 L. Ed. 2d 152 (1973) (mem.) On remand, the three-judge district court reconciled the minor differences between *Doe* and *Roe* and the standards applied in the original *Klein* decision, — F. Supp. — (1974).

30. 347 F. Supp. at 500-501.

the medical assistance that is in general her statutory entitlement, and that is otherwise extended to her even with respect to her pregnancy. She is thus discriminated against both by reason of her poverty and by reason of her behavioral choice. No interest of the State is served by the arbitrary discrimination; it reflects no genuine exclusion from benefit by operation of a classification founded on an identifiable state interest served by the denial of medical assistance. Certainly the denial of medical assistance does not serve the State's fiscal interest, since the consequence is that the indigent may then apply for prenatal, obstetrical and post partum care and for prenatal support for the unborn child.

NOTE: CONSENT REQUIREMENTS

The Court in *Roe* expressly left open the question of whether the potential father has any role or rights in decisions regarding abortion. Can an argument be made that the father's interest increases as pregnancy matures, like the escalating state interest described in *Roe?* Perhaps there should be some difference between the recognition accorded the interest of the cohabitating father and the separated or divorced father, or the disappeared father. How does an essentially undefined interest of one person fit with the "fundamental right" of another?

In Coe v. Gerstein, No. 72-1842-Civ-JE (S.D. Fla. Aug. 13, 1973), a three-judge United States district court held unconstitutional the section of the state's abortion law which specified that a married woman needed the written consent of her husband for an abortion, unless the couple was voluntarily separated, and that a woman under eighteen needed the written consent of her parent or guardian.[31] The court said that under *Roe* and *Doe*

> [T]he state has no authority to interfere with a woman's right of privacy in the first trimester to protect maternal health nor can it interfere with that right before the fetus becomes viable in order to protect potential life. It follows inescapably that the state may not statutorily delegate to husbands and parents an authority the state does not possess . . . a state which has no authority to regulate abortion in certain areas simply cannot constitutionally grant power to husbands and parents to regulate in those areas.

In an earlier case, a Florida court of appeals upheld a lower court ruling that a "potential putative father" did not have the right to restrain the pregnant woman from having an abortion, despite the man's desire to marry the woman and assume all the financial and other obligations for the care and support of the child if it were born. The court pointed out that if the father could prohibit a woman from having an abortion, he also could force her to have one or to use contraceptives, which would be "ludicrous."[32] Jones v. Smith, No. 73-560 (D.C. App. Fla., 4th Dist. May 15, 1973.)

Note that what is involved in various consent provisions is a decision by the state to give one or more people authority to veto a particular woman's abortion decision — i.e., to compel her to carry her pregnancy to term. Thus, any consent requirement involves the state in legislating in favor of pregnancy and against abortion. Can the potential father's interest in compelling a woman to become pregnant in the first place be distinguished from his interest in compelling continuation of a first or second trimester pregnancy? Note that the traditional remedy for a woman's refusal to bear children with her husband is annulment or divorce.

31. The account of this case and the one following are based on Florida, Consent, Facility Requirements for Abortion Invalidated, 2 Family Planning/Population Reporter 109 (1973).
32. See also Doe v. Bellin Memorial Hospital, 479 F.2d at 758-759, in which the court ruled that a woman seeking to compel a hospital to perform an abortion need not join the putative father as an indispensable party to the decision.

Parental consent provisions for minors may have a different legal basis than the husband's or putative father's consent requirements. Theoretically, parents' power to withhold consent is designed to protect the best interests of their daughter, who is legally presumed incapable of making the decision. The requirement of parental consent is in practice imposed by most hospitals for operations other than abortion to protect themselves from tort litigation.

State legislatures have begun to lower the age of majority or to authorize minors to consent to medical treatment in various situations, especially treatment for venereal disease.[33] However, some statutes explicitly exclude abortion from their coverage. Note also that the new lower age of majority, which is usually eighteen, is not low enough to solve the problem for many pregnant minors. The constitutionality of parental consent requirements has been raised in several cases, including Coe v. Gerstein, supra, in which the court invalidated the Florida parental consent requirement along with the spousal consent provision. In Washington v. Koome,[34] a doctor performed an abortion upon a sixteen-year-old woman who was ten weeks pregnant. She had petitioned the juvenile court for permission to have the abortion. Her petition was opposed by her parents and by the Catholic Childrens Services, her temporary legal guardian. The juvenile court judge's order granting her petition was stayed by the chief justice of the Washington Supreme Court.[35] Dr. Koome went ahead with the abortion because of his belief that the consent requirement was unconstitutional. He was arrested, tried, and convicted. An appeal is pending before the Supreme Court of Washington.

Can it be argued as a matter of law that it is never in the best interests of a pregnant minor who desires an abortion early in pregnancy to be compelled to carry her pregnancy to term? If so, wouldn't all parental consent requirements be invalidated?

What about a woman whose parents want her to have an abortion but who wants to have the child? In re Smith, 16 Md. App. 209, 295 A.2d 239 (1972), was an unsuccessful attempt by a woman to compel her sixteen-year-old daughter to have an abortion. Cindy Lou Smith and her boyfriend had tried to get married but were unable to do so without parental consent. Her mother obtained an order from the juvenile court adjudging Cindy in need of supervision, placing her in her mother's custody, and specifically ordering her to obey her mother by submitting to the abortion. The Maryland Court of Appeals reversed, basing its action on a statute conferring on minors the same rights as adults to seek treatment and advice concerning pregnancy.[36] Supposing there had been no statute which could be interpreted to reach this result, what grounds could the appellate court have used to reverse the juvenile court order? Should the result be affected by the age of the pregnant woman?[37]

Sterilization procedures for females raise legal issues about whose consent is necessary very similar to those involved in abortion decisions. As abortion and sterilization have become much more available in the 1970s, the possibility has emerged that minors particularly, as well as other women, might be coerced into the operations. The coercion can take the form of psychological pressure on girls, economic pressure for poor women in fear about future welfare payments, refusal to perform other medical procedures related to reproduction unless consent is given to sterilization, and withholding of information about the procedures actually being performed. A highly publicized case

33. For an account of 1973 legislative efforts in this area, see Analysis: An Overview of 1973 Legislation, Minors, 2 Family Planning/Population Reporter 142, 144 (1973) and Legislative Record, id. at 149, 152.

34. Information on this case is based on an account in Davidson, Ginsberg, and Kay, Sex Based Discrimination, Text, Cases and Materials 415-416 (1974), itself based on information obtained from Mr. Raymond J. Lee, the attorney for Dr. Koome.

35. In re Hagans, No. 42529 (Wash. S. Ct. Aug. 14, 1972).

36. See also Ballard v. Anderson, 4 Cal. 3d 873, 95 Cal. Rptr. 1, 484 P.2d 1345 (1971), reaching a similar result under the California statute.

37. For a detailed study of the right of minors to decide whether to have an abortion, see Pilpel and Zuckerman, Abortion and the Rights of Minors, 23 Case W. Res. L. Rev. 779 (1972).

arose in Alabama when two young, black, mentally retarded sisters were sterilized by a federally funded family planning clinic. Relf v. Weinberger, Civ. Action No. 1557-73 (D.D.C. Oct. 5, 1973). Following publicity about the case, the Department of Health, Education, and Welfare declared a moratorium on the use of any federal funds for sterilization of people under twenty-one until regulations governing such operations could be established.[38] A well-developed parental consent provision could be considered an appropriate tool for lessening the chance of coercion of minors. Does the fact that the sterilization procedure is irreversible for women in most cases make parental consent for minors more reasonable than in the abortion situation?

II. THE RIGHT TO EQUAL EDUCATIONAL OPPORTUNITY

A. INTEGRATION OF THE SEXES

Most cases in the education area of sex discrimination law have been brought under the Equal Protection Clause. At present, although there are some additional statutory resources for challenging sexism in education, constitutional litigation using the legal theories discussed in Chapter One is still the most powerful tool available. However, while the legal framework is familiar, the policy issues that are raised in educational litigation are unusual, and merit separate consideration. One of the most interesting of these issues is whether there should be sex-segregated public or private schools or educational programs at any level. Women's colleges and sex-segregated athletic programs, discussed herein, are two of the most controversial areas of educational policy. Both raise the difficult and fascinating question of whether there are any situations in which limits on competition and interaction between men and women advance the goal of sex equality.

1. Sex-Segregated Educational Institutions

WILLIAMS v. McNAIR
316 F. Supp. 134 (D.S.C. 1970)

Before Haynsworth, Chief Judge and Hemphill and Russell, District Judges.
RUSSELL, District Judge:
This is an action instituted by the plaintiffs, all males, suing on behalf of themselves and others similarly situated, to enjoin the enforcement of a state statute which limits regular admissions to Winthrop College, a State supported college located at Rock Hill, South Carolina, to "girls". . . .
The parties have stipulated the facts involved in the controversy and have submitted the cause to the Court on their respective motions for judgment. The stipulation of facts is adopted as the Findings of Fact herein.
. . . South Carolina has established a wide range of educational institutions at the college and university level consisting of eight separate institutions, with nine additional regional campuses. The several institutions so established vary in purpose, curriculum,

---

38. See United States, Sterilization Controversy Continues, Government Sued, 2 Family Planning/Population Reporter 114 (1973), and United States, Sterilization Suit Against DHEW Dismissed, id. at 141, discussing Relf v. Weinberger, and reporting also on the policy of three obstetricians in Aiken, South Carolina who "had adopted a policy of refusing to deliver the babies of welfare women who had two or more children unless the women agreed to be sterilized at the time of delivery. Aiken County Hospital records show that last year 18 of the 34 deliveries paid for by Medicaid also included sterilizations. 16 of the 18 women were black." Id. at 114.

and location. Some are limited to undergraduate programs; others extend their offerings into the graduate field. With two exceptions, such institutions are co-educational. Two, by law, however, limit their student admissions to members of one sex. Thus the Citadel restricts its student admission to males and Winthrop, the college involved in this proceeding, may not admit as a regular degree candidate males. There is an historical reason for these legislative restrictions upon the admission standards of these two latter institutions. The first, the Citadel, while offering a full range of undergraduate liberal arts courses and granting degrees in engineering as well, is designated as a military school, and apparently, the Legislature deemed it appropriate for that reason to provide for an all-male student body. Winthrop, on the other hand, was designed as a school for young ladies, which, though offering a liberal arts program, gave special attention to many courses thought to be specially helpful to female students.

The Equal Protection Clause of the Fourteenth Amendment does not require "identity of treatment" for all citizens, or preclude a state, by legislation, from making classifications and creating differences in the rights of different groups. It is only when the discriminatory treatment and varying standards, as created by the legislative or administrative classification are arbitrary and wanting in any rational justification that they offend the Equal Protection Clause. Specifically, a legislative classification based on sex, has often been held to be constitutionally permissible. . . . [Here follow the citations of ten Supreme Court and lower federal court opinions, *inter alia* Heaton v. Bristol, 317 S.W.2d 86 (Tex. Civ. App. 1958), *cert. denied,* 359 U.S. 230, and Allred v. Heaton, 336 S.W.2d 251 (Tex. Civ. App. 1960), *cert. denied,* 364 U.S. 517, both of which involved denial of the right of women to attend an all-male state-supported college.]

[T]he issue in this case is whether the discrimination in admission of students, created by the statute governing the operation of Winthrop and based on sex, is without rational justification.

It is conceded that recognized pedagogical opinion is divided on the wisdom of maintaining "single-sex" institutions of higher education but it is stipulated that there is a respectable body of educators who believe that "a single-sex institution can advance the quality and effectiveness of its instruction by concentrating upon areas of primary interest to only one sex." The idea of educating the sexes separately, the plaintiffs admit, "has a long history" and "is practiced extensively throughout the world." It is no doubt true, as plaintiffs suggest, that the trend in this country is away from the operation of separate institutions for the sexes, but there is still a substantial number of private and public institutions, which limit their enrollment to one sex and do so because they feel it offers better educational advantages. While history and tradition alone may not support a discrimination, the Constitution does not require that a classification "keep abreast of the latest" in educational opinion, especially when there remains a respectable opinion to the contrary; it only demands that the discrimination not be wholly wanting in reason. Any other rule would mean that courts and not legislatures would determine all matters of public policy. It must be remembered, too, that Winthrop is merely a part of an entire system of State-supported higher education. It may not be considered in isolation. If the State operated only one college and that college was Winthrop, there can be no question that to deny males admission thereto would be impermissible under the Equal Protection Clause. But, as we have already remarked, these plaintiffs have a complete range of state institutions they may attend. They are free to attend either an all-male or, if they wish, a number of co-educational institutions at various locations over the State. There is no suggestion that there is any special feature connected with Winthrop that will make it more advantageous educationally to them than any number of other State-supported institutions. They point to no courses peculiar to Winthrop in which they wish to enroll. It is true that, in the case of some, if not all, of the plaintiffs, Winthrop is more convenient geographically for them than the other State institutions. They, in being denied the right to attend the State college in their home town, are treated no differently than are other students who reside in communities many miles distant from any State supported college or university. The location of any such institution must necessarily inure to the benefit of some and to the detriment of others, depending upon the distance the affected individuals reside from the institution.

Under these circumstances, this Court cannot declare as a matter of law that a legislative classification, premised as it is on respectable pedagogical opinion, is without any rational justification and violative of the Equal Protection Clause. It might well be that if the members of this Court were permitted a personal opinion on the question, they would reach a contrary conclusion. Moreover, it may be, as plaintiffs argue, that the experience of the college in admitting in its summer and evening classes male students, has weakened to some extent the force of the legislative determination that the maintenance of at least one all-female institution in the state system has merit educationally. The evaluation of such experience, however, is not the function or prerogative of the Courts; that falls within the legislative province and the plaintiffs must address their arguments to that body and look to it for relief. After all, flexibility and diversity in educational methods, when not tainted with racial overtones, often are both desirable and beneficial; they should be encouraged, not condemned.

It is suggested by the plaintiffs that this conclusion is contrary to the ruling in Kirstein v. Rector and Visitors of University of Virginia (D.C. Va. 1970), 309 F. Supp. 184. The Court there very pointedly remarked, however, that "We are urged to go further and to hold that Virginia may not operate any educational institutions separated according to the sexes. We decline to do so." Page 187, 309 F. Supp. There the women-plaintiffs were seeking admission to the University of Virginia and it was conceded that the University occupied a preeminence among the State-supported institutions of Virginia and offered a far wider range of curriculum. No such situation exists here. It is not intimated that Winthrop offers a wider range of subject matter or enjoys a position of outstanding prestige over the other State-supported institutions in this State whose admission policies are co-educational.

Let judgment be entered for the defendants.

———————

This case was affirmed without a substantive opinion by the Supreme Court, with Justice Harlan writing a short dissenting opinion on the issue of whether direct appeal to the Supreme Court was available. 401 U.S. 951, 91 S. Ct. 976, 28 L. Ed. 2d 235 (1971).

Note: Other Cases

Johnston and Knapp provide the following account of the three major cases about sex-segregated colleges which preceded Williams v. McNair:[1]

> Although the dominant form of public education in the United States today is obviously "coeducation" (both sexes taught in the same schools and usually in the same classes), a number of public institutions of higher learning are not coeducational. In recent years a few courts have been called upon to decide the validity of a state educational policy providing for separation of the sexes; overall, the results represent at best a limited recognition of the right to equal educational opportunity regardless of sex.
>
> Two such cases have come before the Texas Court of Civil Appeals. In 1958, in Heaton v. Bristol,[153] female plaintiffs had sought to enter Texas A. & M., an all-male

---

1. Johnston and Knapp, Sex Discrimination By Law: A Study in Judicial Perspective, 46 N.Y.U.L. Rev. 721-723 (1971).

153. 317 S.W.2d 86 (Tex. Civ. App. 1958), *cert. denied,* 359 U.S. 230 (1959).

institution. Reversing the lower court, the appellate court held — despite uncontroverted findings by the trial court that Texas A. & M. offered several courses of study not available at any other public institution of higher learning in the state — that no constitutional right of the plaintiffs had been violated. First, it was not shown that plaintiffs desired to take any of the courses unique to that institution. Nor was the court impressed by plaintiffs' argument that, by denying them the right to attend this particular institution, which was most near their homes and thus most convenient, the state had denied them equal protection. Finally, the court relied upon the existence of compulsory military training at Texas A. & M. as evidence of its unsuitability for females and pointed to the lack of any precedent upholding plaintiffs' position.

To determine whether there is unequal treatment of the sexes, the court stated, one must view the state's entire higher education system. The court concluded that the Texas system did make "ample and substantially equal provision for the education of both sexes."[154] In the court's view, the question was simply whether the state may constitutionally maintain, along with sixteen coeducational institutions, two which are not coeducational — one male, one female:

"We think undoubtedly the answer is Yes. Such a plan exalts neither sex at the expense of the other, but to the contrary recognizes the equal rights of both sexes to the benefits of the best, most varied systems of higher education that the State can supply."[155]

A similar action was brought two years later in Allred v. Heaton,[156] and in that case, at least one of the plaintiffs declared her desire to enroll in floriculture, one of the courses apparently not available at any other campus in the Texas university system. The court, possibly dubious of her good faith since she had once declared an intention to study law, held that, since the applicants (relying on the stated policy of exclusion) had not submitted applications for admission, they were precluded from relief. In affirming generally its earlier position with respect to sex-segregated education, the court indicated in dictum that should the plaintiff in fact apply for admission to study floriculture, she should not be excluded solely on the basis of her sex.[157] Upon rehearing, the college moved to strike that paragraph from the court's opinion, as constituting dictum. The court granted the motion without comment. This was not the only dictum in the opinion, however; consider the following:

"Surely the Supreme Court of the United States will not attempt to interfere with the public policy of the sovereign states of this nation in the management and control of their respective education systems so long as such systems do not discriminate against color or race."[158]

A far different view of the constitutional issues was expressed in Kirstein v. Rector and Visitors of the University of Virginia,[159] a 1970 decision involving the College of Arts and Sciences of the University of Virginia at Charlottesville. A three-judge federal district court held that refusal to admit women to the college was a denial of equal protection, since the college offered courses of instruction not found elsewhere in the state and because its degree had greater "prestige" than that of any other state college. The court did, however, deny plaintiffs' claim for relief, on the ground that a plan for implementing coeducation at the campus had already been adopted. The court expressly declined to decide whether it was impermissible for the state to operate *any* institution of higher learning restricted to one sex, on the ground that plaintiffs lacked standing to raise the issue. The court was also careful to skirt — in a footnote — the question of whether the ghost of Plessy v. Ferguson[160] still walks: "We need not decide on the facts of this case whether the now discountenanced principle of "separate but equal" may have lingering validity in another area — for the facilities elsewhere are not equal with respect to these plaintiffs."[161]

154. Id. at 99.
155. Id. at 100.
156. 336 S.W.2d 251 (Tex. Civ. App.), *cert. denied,* 364 U.S. 517 (1960).
157. Id. at 262-63.
158. Id. at 261.
159. 309 F. Supp. 184 (E.D. Va. 1970).
160. 163 U.S. at 537 (1866).
161. 309 F. Supp. at 187 n.1. . . .

After Williams v. McNair, supra, the Massachusetts district court decided Bray v. Lee, 337 F. Supp. 934 (D. Mass. 1972), a suit by female students in the Boston public school system challenging the use of a higher cut-off score for girls than for boys on the entrance examination for the Boston Boys and Girls Latin Schools. The court ruled that the use of different standards was a denial of equal protection, and ordered the admission of all female applicants who would have been admitted had one standard been used for both sexes, and who still wanted to be admitted. The sex segregation of the schools was not challenged.

ROSS, THE RIGHTS OF WOMEN
119-122 (1973)

There are important lessons to be learned from comparing the successful suits with the failures. The most important single factor in explaining the women's success in desegregating the University of Virginia was the thorough documentation of the discrepancies in education available to men and to women in the state. Among the shocking differences discovered by ACLU [American Civil Liberties Union] lawyers: The men's college offered the highest average faculty salaries in the state. The state appropriation per student at the men's college was more than double that at each of the two women's colleges. Men had access to sophisticated astronomy and science facilities; women did not. Men could take degrees in astronomy, Latin-American studies, and nine foreign languages — all unavailable to women. The men's college offered a far greater variety of courses in almost every department, especially in government, astronomy, economics, English, history, physics, geology, geography, sociology, and anthropology. In short, the lawyers showed in detail that the state reserved its highest quality educational facilities "For Men Only."

The lawyers topped this factual survey by extensive questioning of university officials to see whether they could offer any cogent reasons for excluding women. Even the judge was embarrassed by the answers the school officials gave: allowing women to use dormitories built for men would not be feasible because women needed more dimunitive furniture; the shower heads were set at the wrong height; and so on, *ad ridiculum.*

In contrast, lawyers for the men who unsuccessfully tried to enter Winthrop College in South Carolina apparently conceded that there was no difference between the quality of education available at Winthrop and that available at other public colleges in the state, which included the all-male Citadel and several integrated schools. Since the men failed to document any disparity, it is impossible to tell from the court's opinion whether Winthrop offered an identical education to that of the male school. However, the law establishing Winthrop had emphasized that the school should offer certain "courses thought to be especially helpful to female students." These included:

> . . . stenography, typewriting, telegraphy, bookkeeping, drawing . . . , designing, engraving, sewing, dressmaking, millinery, art, needlework, cooking, housekeeping and such other industrial arts as may be suitable to their sex and conducive to their support and usefulness.

The men's school, the Citadel, is an engineering and military school. Thus, there were clear differences between the two schools, and, at the very least, women in South Carolina were deprived of some forms of education available only at the Citadel. Yet the men never pointed to such facts, and indeed, may not have been able to, if Winthrop offered the same courses as the other schools. Instead, the men sought to show that maintaining single-sex schools was inherently lacking in rational justification and thus violated the Equal Protection clause. This is analogous to whites' saying that "separate but equal" schools for whites and blacks inherently violate the Equal Protection clause, rather than showing in detail that the schools are not, *in fact,* equal. The time may not be ripe for men — or women — to challenge segregation per se. First, they must build up the cases that all illustrate cogently just how unequal *in fact* are the opportunities for women.

A second explanation for the loss of the lawsuit in South Carolina may be that men challenged segregation at the female school. . . . [Perhaps the plaintiffs' attorneys should have joined female plaintiffs and challenged the segregation at the Citadel in the same suit.] As already pointed out, the Citadel did offer opportunities in engineering and military training, which women were deprived of. Had the attack on sex segregation [included women trying to enter the all male school] the result might have been entirely different. The reason is, as some feminists believe, that since society offers most of its advantages to men, a lawsuit brought on behalf of men will not evoke much sense of injustice. Courts that might be moved to attack discrimination against women could find a man's suit a mere diversion and leave a discriminatory law standing.

In light of the Texas A. & M. cases, do you agree that it would have been good litigation strategy to add a woman's challenge to a military school to this lawsuit?

NOTE: IS EDUCATION A FUNDAMENTAL RIGHT?

In a long series of cases both preceding and following Brown v. Board of Education, 347 U.S. 483, 74 S. Ct. 686, 98 L. Ed. 873 (1954), the Supreme Court recognized "the vital role of education in a free society." San Antonio Independent School District v. Rodriguez, 411 U.S. 1, 30, 93 S. Ct. 1278, 1295, 36 L. Ed. 2d 16, (1973). Before *Rodriguez,* it appeared possible that education would be held "fundamental for purposes of examination under the Equal protection Clause," id. which would mean that all discrimination in this area would be subject to strict review by the courts. But that case, upholding the financing of public schools by local property taxation, effectively foreclosed this possibility. Justice Powell, for the majority, commented as follows:[2]

> Nothing this Court holds today in any way detracts from our historic dedication to public education. We are in complete agreement with the conclusion of the three-judge panel below that "the grave significance of education both to the individual and to our society" cannot be doubted. But the importance of a service performed by the State does not determine whether it must be regarded as fundamental for purposes of examination under the Equal Protection Clause. Mr. Justice Harlan, dissenting from the Court's application of strict scrutiny to a law impinging upon the right of interstate travel, admonished that "[v]irtually every state statute affects important rights." Shapiro v. Thompson, 394 U.S. 618, 655, 661, 89 S. Ct. 1322, 1342, 1345, 22 L. Ed. 2d 600 (1969). In his view, if the degree of judicial scrutiny of state legislation fluctuated depending on a majority's view of the importance of the interest affected, we would have gone "far toward making this Court a 'super-legislature.'" Ibid. We would indeed then be assuming a legislative role and one for which the Court lacks both authority and competence.
>   . . . It is not the province of this Court to create substantive constitutional rights in the name of guaranteeing equal protection of the laws. Thus the key to discovering whether education is "fundamental" is not to be found in comparisons of the relative societal significance of education as opposed to subsistence or housing. Nor is it to be found by weighing whether education is as important as the right to travel. Rather, the answer lies in assessing whether there is a right to education explicitly or implicitly guaranteed by the Constitution. [Citations omitted.]
>   Education, of course, is not among the rights afforded explicit protection under

2. 411 U.S. at 30-37.

our Federal Constitution. Nor do we find any basis for saying it is implicitly so protected. As we have said, the undisputed importance of education will not alone cause this Court to depart from the usual standard for reviewing a State's social and economic legislation. It is appellees' contention, however, that education is distinguishable from other services and benefits provided by the State because it bears a peculiarly close relationship to other rights and liberties accorded protection under the Constitution. Specifically, they insist that education is itself a fundamental personal right because it is essential to the effective exercise of First Amendment freedoms and to intelligent utilization of the right to vote. . . .

. . . The Court has long afforded zealous protection against unjustifiable governmental interference with the individual's rights to speak and to vote. Yet we have never presumed to possess either the ability or the authority to guarantee to the citizenry the most *effective* speech or the most *informed* electoral choice. That these may be desirable goals of a system of freedom of expression and of a representative form of government is not to be doubted. These are indeed goals to be pursued by a people whose thoughts and beliefs are freed from governmental interference. But they are not values to be implemented by judicial intrusion into otherwise legitimate state activities.

Even if it were conceded that some identifiable quantum of education is a constitutionally protected prerequisite to the meaningful exercise of either right, we have no indication that the present levels of educational expenditure in Texas provide an education that falls short. Whatever merit appellees' argument might have if a State's financing system occasioned an absolute denial of educational opportunities to any of its children, that argument provides no basis for finding an interference with fundamental rights where only relative differences in spending levels are involved and where — as is true in the present case — no charge fairly could be made that the system fails to provide each child with an opportunity to acquire the basic minimal skills necessary for the enjoyment of the rights of speech and of full participation in the political process.

Furthermore, the logical limitations on appellees' nexus theory are difficult to perceive. How, for instance, is education to be distinguished from the significant personal interests in the basics of decent food and shelter? Empirical examination might well buttress an assumption that the ill-fed, ill-clothed, and ill-housed are among the most ineffective participants in the political process and that they derive the least enjoyment from the benefits of the First Amendment.

NOTE: SEX SEGREGATION AND RACIAL INTEGRATION

An interesting issue which has arisen in a few cases is the constitutionality of sex separation in plans for the desegregation of racially segregated schools. Sixteen cases in which sex separation was proposed by a school board as part of a desegregation plan are cited in the Constitutionality of Sex Separation in School Desegregation Plans, 37 U. Chi. L. Rev. 296, 297 n.14 (1970). This note, which considered the question in some detail, argues that

> while the sex separation device selectively integrates the races, it may be racially discriminatory in that (1) it perpetuates a vestige of the racial caste system — the separation of opposite-sex members of the two races — and/or (2) this separation results in harms similar to those recognized in *Brown* as inherent in a system of pure racial segregation.

The article concludes:

> The use of sex separation in school desegregation plans raises three important issues of constitutional dimension. These include the extent to which the scheme perpetuates the racial discrimination forbidden by *Brown,* the validity of the sex classification, and the limits of the fundamental freedom to associate. Given the presence of these issues in the use of the sex separation schemes and the burden of

proof normally placed on the school boards in plan evaluation, it would seem that better justifications than those which have thus far been advanced would be needed if the boards are to persuade the courts of the validity of this particular scheme. In the final analysis, the courts, in evaluating the sex-separation plans, will be primarily concerned with the existence of racial discrimination in the use of the device. If the courts do not overturn the use of sex separation in school desegregation plans, they will be sanctioning racial discrimination by validating plans which perpetuate a vestige of the racial caste system and foster the very harms declared unconstitutional over fifteen years ago in the *School Desegregation Cases.*

NOTE: STATE ACTION, PRIVATE COLLEGES, AND SEX SEGREGATION

All the cases discussed thus far concern public schools. If sex segregation in public schools were held unconstitutional by the Supreme Court, should the same decision be reached as to private schools? Will it be? From a legal point of view, one's answers to these questions depend in large part on whether or not one believes that private schools are sufficiently imbued with state action that constitutional restrictions ought to or will be applied.

The courts have drawn a sharp line between public and private schools from the Dartmouth College case, Trustees of Dartmouth College v. Woodward, 17 U.S. (4 Wheat) 518 (1819), until recent years. But meanwhile the concept of state action has been progressively broadened. As O'Neil has explained:[3]

> The Supreme Court has frequently defined the core concept of state action: "Conduct that is formally 'private' may become so entwined with governmental policies or so impregnated with a governmental character as to become subject to constitutional limitations placed upon state action."[47] The scope of the doctrine is broad if its contours are sometimes imprecise: "[T]he Fourteenth Amendment forbids States to use their governmental powers [for discriminatory purposes] where there is state participation through any arrangement, management, funds or property."[48]
>
> The grounds for finding state action are many and varied. Three lines of decisions, however, dominate. First, there are cases in which private conduct is subject to the fourteenth amendment because of governmental aid and support — through cash payments, donations or loans of land or buildings, special tax exemptions, or some combination of these ingredients.[49] Second, state action may be found without any public financial support where a private entity holds an inherently governmental power — with the control that a company town,[50] an exclusive bargaining agent,[51] or a political primary in a one-party state[52] possesses over those persons whose lives are significantly affected by it. Sometimes such power is exercised merely by governmental acquiescence; where government has actually delegated the power to the private actor,[53] or mandated its use by him,[54] a lesser impact will warrant a finding of state action. Finally, one recent case suggests the fourteenth amendment will reach

3. O'Neil, Private Universities and Public Law, 19 Buff. L. Rev. 155, 168-169 (1970).
47. Evans v. Newton, 382 U.S. 296, 299 (1966).
48. Cooper v. Aaron, 358 U.S. 1, 4 (1958).
49. See Sams v. Ohio Valley General Hosp. Ass'n, 413 F.2d 826 (4th Cir. 1969); Eaton v. Grubbs, 329 F.2d 710 (4th Cir. 1964); Simkins v. Moses H. Cone Memorial Hosp., 323 F.2d 959 (4th Cir. 1963); Kerr v. Enoch Pratt Free Library, 149 F.2d 212 (4th Cir. 1945); cf. Smith v. Holiday Inns of America, Inc., 336 F.2d 630 (6th Cir. 1964).
50. Marsh v. Alabama, 326 U.S. 501 (1946). Cf. Amalgamated Food Employees Union v. Logan Valley Plaza, Inc., 391 U.S. 308 (1968).
51. Steele v. Louisville & Nashville R.R., 323 U.S. 192, 208-09 (1944) (Murphy, J., concurring).
52. Smith v. Allwright, 321 U.S. 649 (1944). Cf. Terry v. Adams, 345 U.S. 461 (1953).
53. Boman v. Birmingham Transit Co., 280 F.2d 531 (5th Cir. 1960); Flemming v. South Carolina Elec. & Gas. Co., 224 F.2d 752 (4th Cir. 1955).
54. Peterson v. City of Greenville, 373 U.S. 244 (1963). Cf. Lombard v. Louisiana, 373 U.S. 267 (1963).

private action which is merely encouraged, condoned or reinforced by government without financial support, delegation, or exercise of quasi-public power.[55]

He goes on to explain:[4]

> The case for extending the fourteenth amendment to the private campus relies upon an application of these precepts. It focuses specifically upon two pervasive attributes of private higher education — substantial governmental involvement through financial support and regulation, and the exercise of essentially governmental or public powers. This thesis presupposes that John Marshall entertained an inaccurate view of private colleges — both in finding the private sector so readily separable from the public, and in characterizing the mission of Dartmouth College as an essentially private responsibility. The section which follows will suggest that public and private components have been so intermingled in private colleges and universities that they are no longer realistically separable; and that the function of private higher education is so essentially public that a governmental standard should judge its performance.

In addition, O'Neil points out that in fiscal year 1967, "the federal government provided some form of financial support or assistance to 2056 institutions of higher learning, roughly 80% of the total number of colleges and universities of all types.[76]"[5]

O'Neil explores at some length the question of the proper treatment of "private" schools in light of such factors as "substantial public support for general educational needs [and] other fiscal and economic benefits [to 'private' schools]," "special governmental regulation and supervision" and a "significant degree of interdependence between public and private sectors" in education (id. at 181-186). He concludes that what is needed is not "a rigid public-private distinction" (id. at 156), but a constitutional matrix in which[6]

> The extent to which a federal court may inquire into the acts and decisions of a private institution of higher learning [w]ould depend upon the particular degree of its governmental involvement and/or interdependence.[141] This is one dimension of the grid, upon which all institutions can be arranged according to the various specific factors we have examined here. The other dimensions consists of the relief sought, or the institutional decision under challenge. It does not take much to hold a college sufficiently "public" that it may not constitutionally refuse to admit an otherwise qualified black student solely because of race. It is not much harder to find unconstitutional a private university's rejection of an invited speaker because of his unorthodox political views.[142] (Where the university does in fact dominate the community and is the major source of entertainment, culture and recreation, this result seems to follow quite directly from Marsh v. Alabama.[143] It is a little less obvious in the case of the urban university or small private college where forums for unpopular speakers exist within easy reach of the faculty and student body).

For illustrative purposes, O'Neil uses his matrix to resolve a number of problems.

55. Reitman v. Mulkey, 367 U.S. 369 (1967).

4. O'Neil, supra, at 169.

76. Federal Support to Universities and Colleges — Fiscal Year 1967 23 (1969).

5. O'Neil, supra, at 173.

6. Id. at 189.

141. The Supreme Court cautioned in Burton v. Wilmington Parking Authority, 365 U.S. 715, 722 (1961): "Only by sifting facts and weighing circumstances can the nonobvious involvement of the State in private conduct be attributed its true significance."

142. Cf. Brooks v. Auburn Univ., 296 F. Supp. 188 (M.D. Ala. 1969); Snyder v. Board of Trustees of Univ. of Ill., 286 F. Supp. 927 (N.D. Ill. 1968); Dickson v. Sitterson, 280 F. Supp. 486 (M.D.N.C. 1968); Van Alstyne, Political Speakers at State Universities: Some Constitutional Considerations, 111 U. Pa. L. Rev. 328 (1963).

143. 326 U.S. 501 (1946).

One example he gives concerns the "innovative potential of private higher education".[7]

> ... Antioch's black dormitory and black studies program suggest a possible example. Dr. Kenneth Clark has argued that Antioch's tolerance of racial separatism is unwise —so unwise that he quit the Board of Trustees in protest. But unwisdom does not always denote unconstitutionality. Federal officials responsible for policing Title VI of the 1964 Civil Rights Act have come eventually to this view in the Antioch case, and have uneasily allowed the black studies program to go forward on an effectively segregated basis.[150] The Civil Rights Office of HEW has also permitted Northwestern to operate what amounts to an all-black dormitory wing.[151]
>
> Such practices as these would be very vulnerable in the public sector, at least as the fourteenth amendment is currently understood. But who is to say the courts may not someday decide that complete freedom of choice for blacks and other minority groups is closer to the purpose of the equal protection clause than is the neutrality on which we now insist? The outcome of that debate, into which we are just now moving, may depend very much on practical experience with just such voluntarily segregated programs as Antioch and Northwestern are now running. Since it is clear that the public sector cannot undertake such experiments, the laboratory must be the private campus. A too rigid application of the state action concept to private colleges and universities would preclude such innovation, even for benign purposes. Perhaps the solution is to have the federal courts ready and willing to review the case of an Antioch student expelled because he supports, or opposes, the black studies program; but not quite prepared to hold that Antioch cannot try the program at all simply because Kent State may not.

What arguments can be made for and against the use of state action doctrine to invalidate sex segregation in "private" colleges which receive substantial public funding or other special government benefits or supervision?

2. The Social Policy Debate

In Brown v. Board of Education, 34 U.S. 483, 74 S. Ct. 686, 98 L. Ed. 873 (1954), the Supreme Court concluded that race segregation in the public schools deprived children of the minority group of equal educational opportunities, even though the physical facilities and other "tangible" aspects of the segregated institutions were equal. In reaching this conclusion, the Court relied in part on a number of psychological and sociological studies documenting the impact of race segregation on members of the minority race.

There were two barriers to obtaining a similar ruling in the *McNair* case. First, as Ross pointed out in the excerpt reprinted above, plaintiffs were members of the dominant, not the subordinate group. Second, as plaintiffs conceded, "recognized pedagogical opinion is divided on the wisdom of maintaining 'single-sex' institutions of higher learning."

In fact, plaintiffs stipulated that "there is a respectable body of educators who believe that 'a single-sex institution can advance the quality and effectiveness of its instruction by concentrating upon areas of primary interest to only one sex.'" Do you think this was a wise decision from a litigative point of view? Strategic questions aside, do you agree that single-sex institutions "can advance the quality and effectiveness of instruction," or promote other valid social or educational goals?

The following materials present the history and sociology of women's higher education in the United States, and policy arguments for and against sex-segregated education. In reading them, consider whether, or under what circumstances, either public or private sex-segregated educational institutions should be opposed or encouraged.

7. O'Neil, supra at 192.
150. See N.Y. Times, May 3, 1969, p. 1, col. 7-8; CCH College & Univ. Rep. ¶14,881 (HEW 1969).
151. See Chronicle of Higher Ed., June 10, 1968, p. 8.

a. History and Sociology of Sex-Segregated Education

GRAHAM, WOMEN IN ACADEME
169 Science 1284 (1970)

[In] the first two centuries of higher education in the United States . . . women were simply excluded from collegiate precincts. From the founding of Harvard in 1636 to the opening of Oberlin in 1837, it was not possible for a young woman to attend college in this country. By the mid-19th century, some American colleges had begun to admit women to their classes, in response to pressures similar in some respects to those affecting higher education in the United States today. One source of the pressure was ideological—the conviction that women were entitled to the same educational opportunities as men. From this stimulus, which, significantly, was contemporaneous with the abolition movement, came the establishment of certain colleges designed specifically for women, and of others which admitted both men and women. But the major impetus for women's higher education came in the second half of the 19th century, a time of dire economic need for many colleges, caused chiefly by shrinking masculine enrollments. The sag in college attendance was attributed to the Civil War, to economic depressions, and to dissatisfaction with the college curriculum. College trustees and presidents saw women as potential sources of tuition revenues that would permit the colleges to remain open. The principal reason, then, for the 19th-century breakthrough in admitting women to colleges with men was economic rather than ideological, and these circumstances were not highly conducive to developing plans that would take particular account of the educational needs of women. Even such state institutions as the University of Wisconsin first admitted women during the Civil War when many men students had joined the army.

After the Civil War very few colleges were established solely for men, the major exception being Roman Catholic institutions. The most important women's colleges were still in the East, where traditional institutions of the Ivy League—as it would later be called—dominated the educational scene; these, on the whole, saw no need to include women. In the West, where endowments were small or nonexistent and the financial pressures were greater, resistance to the admission of women was much less. There the critical institutions were state universities, and by the turn of the century most were coeducational. There, too, the denominational colleges, limited as they were in endowments and dependent upon tuition, and now in competition with the less expensive public institutions, frequently became coeducational. The argument is sometimes made that the important role the women on the frontier played is substantially responsible for the greater degree of coeducation in the West. Although this may have been a factor, it seems not to have been as determining a one as the economic considerations, or as the nascent women's rights movement, which was heavily centered in the East. Well into the 20th century the single-sex colleges in the East remained the prestigious places for young women to be educated.

By 1920 women constituted 47 percent of the undergraduates in the country and were receiving roughly 15 percent of the Ph.D.'s. In 1930 the proportion remained about the same. Today women constitute only 40 percent of the undergraduate student body and receive about 10 percent of the doctorates. The total number of students, of course, has increased enormously during these years. Although the percentage of women receiving doctorates is rising gradually from a low in the late 1950's and early 1960's, it still has not reached the high attained in the late 1920's. Various studies have also shown that between 75 and 90 percent of the "well-qualified" students who do not go on to college are women.

In the present movement toward coeducation at some of the well-known single-

sex colleges, particularly Princeton, Yale, Vassar, and Sarah Lawrence, economic considerations are again an important basis for the decision to admit members of the opposite
sex. The current financial dilemmas of many colleges and universities are well known,
but the cure is no longer simply a matter of enlarging the student body. Although these
institutions are not short of applicants, some of them at least believe that the most
outstanding high school graduates are choosing other, coeducational colleges because of
a desire not to be isolated from young persons of the opposite sex. This is an economic
argument of a rather more sophisticated type, based on considerations of human capital.
In some cases the admission of women follows by several decades the abolition of quotas
for Jews and, more recently, the initiation of efforts to admit blacks. Again, the parallel
with the mid-19th century is striking: the women's rights advocates rode the coattails
of the abolitionists much as the current feminists are trailing the black power movement.

b. Arguments Against Single-Sex Schools

JENCKS AND RIESMAN
FEMINISM, MASCULINISM AND COEDUCATION
The Academic Revolution 291-311 (1968)

THE RISE OF COEDUCATION

Although Oberlin admitted women in 1837, and Elmira Female College was
founded in 1855, American higher education remained a virtually all-male affair until
after the Civil War.[1] Not only were women thought generally incapable of intellectual
self-discipline and rigor, but the attempt to impose it on them was thought debilitating
to both mind and body. (This may not have been wholly delusory, given the character
of nineteenth-century academic life.) The men who controlled job opportunities had no
interest in hiring women in any but menial roles, and men looking for wives were also
unlikely to be impressed by a girl's educational qualifications.[2] The lack of advanced
educational opportunity for women was thus paralleled by lack of incentive.

It is hard to say what effect the absence of women had on pre–Civil War colleges.
These colleges certainly gave short shrift to many of the presumptively feminine virtues,
such as warmth, compassion, sensitivity to other people, and even aesthetic sensibility.
But the same could be said of all nineteenth-century America. It was a very "masculine"
time, in which the virtues of the frontier and the market place seemed more glamorous
than those of the hearth. Nonetheless, the arid pedantry and tyrannical discipline of
most nineteenth-century colleges probably would have been more difficult to maintain
if coeducation had become common earlier.

After the Civil War the attack on sex segregation and exclusion in higher education
accelerated very rapidly. This attack was, of course, part of a broader feminist movement, which affected almost every aspect of American life. This movement had much
in common with other "minority" struggles against "majority" oppression. Male prejudice and protectiveness were the enemy, but success depended on finding liberal male
allies to serve as a fifth column in the seats of power. This was not always easy. While
most men had little to lose from female emancipation in any direct and self-interested
sense, many certainly *felt* they had something to lose in a larger psychological sense.

1. It is interesting to note, however, that the U.S. Office of Education's first survey of higher education
reported that women had received 1,378 of the 9,371 Bachelor's awarded in 1870: see [U.S. Bureau of the
Census, Historical Statistics of the United States: Colonial Times to 1957, Series H 330-332 (1960)]. We suspect
that many of the 1,378 women in question received degrees from academies that were more nearly secondary
schools than colleges.
2. One partial exception to this rule was the public school movement which hired women to "keep
school" and established secondary-level normal schools to train them. Here economy triumphed over ideology.

Feminism was one of the many nineteenth-century movements Joseph Gusfield has termed symbolic crusades, and both its advocates and opponents often saw it as a threat to a traditional pattern of life. The fury of male opposition was thus akin to that of modern squares who see the hippies as a threat to the American way of life, even though the hippies' decision to opt out actually serves the interests of those scrambling for scarce places at the "top" of the occupational and social pyramids. Yet like other minorities the feminists often found that their worst enemies were not men, relatively few of whom felt personally threatened by female emancipation even when they opposed it for traditionalistic reasons. The most dangerous opposition often came from other women, who interpreted the feminists' program as an indictment of the kind of femininity they themselves had adopted. Docile subordinate "Uncle Toms" of this variety still play a major role in the war between the sexes.

Another important similarity between feminism and other minority revolts was the feminists' tendency to accept virtually all the assumptions and aspirations of their oppressors, with the single exception of anti-feminism. Thus the leaders of the feminist movement were strikingly masculine in outlook and manner and often asserted their "independence" by adopting hitherto male clothing, speech, and the like. They struggled to gain entry into male careers and male social life. In a more general sense, their aim was to establish their right to deny the difference between the sexes when they chose.

The necessity of winning male allies and the tendency to emulate male models had important consequences for the higher education of women. The feminists' primary objective was to open traditionally male institutions to women. Since men controlled the nation's economic resources, "piggy-backing" on male colleges was a more promising approach to finance than setting up new colleges exclusively for women. And since men still defined what was academically respectable and what was not, integration also provided much the best guarantee of true equality. This strategy was re-enforced by the fact that sexual segregation proved economically ruinous in many small school districts, and was therefore generally (though never quite universally) rejected at the elementary and secondary level. This set a pattern that residential higher education found it natural, if not quite necessary, to follow. By the end of the nineteenth century most public colleges and universities had opened their doors to women, even in states where women still did not have the vote. In the Midwest and Far West, moreover, even the private colleges had mostly gone coed. . . .

Still, the triumph of coeducation has not obliterated either the persistent differences between the sexes or the persistent myths of difference, which simultaneously enhance and obscure the reality. As a result, women are by no means universally integrated with men even inside nominally coeducational institutions. Academically, the men tend to study the more quantitative subjects, such as science and engineering, while women are concentrated in seemingly qualitative fields like psychology, sociology, and the humanities. There is a further division along occupational lines, with men going into areas like economics, law, and business while women turn to education, nursing, and home economics.[10]

In the social sphere, too, segregation has been at least partially preserved. Most coeducational colleges have separate deans of men and women. They justify this partly on the grounds that students would find it hard to discuss personal problems with somebody of the opposite sex, but it is notable that college psychiatric services make no comparable effort to segregate their clientele. The real reason for separating students by sex seems to be that the dean of women is expected to look (and often act) like a maternal disciplinarian, keeping college girls in line in a way that is not thought necessary for men. Women are almost always subject to tighter rules than men, and violations

---

10. Home economics began as a prehousewife course, but it has increasingly become a kind of female engineering, requiring considerable scientific training and turning out dietitians, institutional managers, and the like. The heads of home economics departments are now often men, though male students are still rare.

are usually taken more seriously. (Several state universities, for example, have a policy that if girls are out after hours their parents must be notified immediately.)

Residential segregation has also been almost universal in coeducational colleges, though off-campus housing has usually been integrated and a few mixed dormitories are now being built. The most culturally elaborated version of such segregation has been the fraternity-sorority system, which arose in the late nineteenth century at about the time coeducation became common and has begun to decline only in the last decade. The "Greek" system may, indeed, have been as much a response to the problem of segregating and organizing relations between the sexes as to that of the relations between classes and ethnic groups, though the two are obviously related. (John Finley Scott has shown how sororities systematically dissuade girls from choosing the "wrong" husband, or indeed from choosing any husband at all during their first college years.[11] Sororities differ in this respect from fraternities, which exercise far less control over their members. . . .

. . . Nonetheless, the fraternity-sorority system has served in a general way to preserve nineteenth-century definitions of proper sexual roles, keeping them considerably more polarized than the twentieth-century avant garde thought necessary or desirable. The recent decline of the Greek system at predominantly upper-middle class colleges and universities seems in turn to reflect upper-middle class rejection of stylized sexual distinctions and agendas. Fraternities and sororities seem to be doing quite well, on the other hand, at colleges catering primarily to first-generation collegians—though even there undergraduates' increasing tendency to pair off in protomarital relationships leads a good many to drop their membership after an initial year or two. . . .

The slowly increasing similarity between the attitudes and behavior permitted men and women has obviously not eliminated all the basic differences between them, nor is it likely to do so. . . .

But while the modal responses of men and women will probably remain quite different, the *range* of permissible responses for each sex may continue to widen, and the two distributions may increasingly overlap. The average woman is unlikely ever to be as career-oriented as the average man, and the average man is unlikely ever to be as emotionally expressive as the average woman. But America may be sufficiently pluralistic and tolerant for some women to pursue careers with the same passion that men do, for these women to be accepted in their jobs on the same basis as men, and for them not to feel guilty about it. Conversely, men may eventually feel largely free of the exigencies of the occupational world, quite willing to be economically dependent if they can find others willing to support them, and eager to live the emotionally less fettered life available to many women. This latter development is more remote, but its beginnings can be seen in many bohemias, both on and off campus.

Some might argue that this pluralistic dream also requires the preservation of at least a few traditional masculine subcultures, where those who cling to an older ethos can find comfort and a sense of sexual superiority. Perhaps this is true. Yet no principle can be pushed to its logical conclusion without crushing all other principles, and none can be applied except in a particular historical context. The pluralistic argument for preserving all-male colleges is uncomfortably similar to the pluralistic argument for preserving all-white colleges, and we are far from enthusiastic about it. The all-male college would be relatively easy to defend if it emerged from a world in which women were established as fully equal to men. But it does not. It is therefore likely to be a witting or unwitting device for preserving tacit assumptions of male superiority — assumptions for which women must eventually pay. So, indeed, must men. We are generally skeptical about the claim that oppressors suffer as much from their prejudices as the oppressed, especially when they never see their victims face to face. But we do

11. See Scott, [The American College Sorority: Its Role in Class and Ethnic Endegamy, American Sociological Review, 30 (June 1965), 514-527].

feel reasonably confident that men pay a price for arrogance vis-à-vis women. Since they almost always commit a part of their lives into a woman's hands anyway, their tendency to crush these women means crushing a part of themselves. This may not hurt them as much as it hurts the woman involved, but it does cost something. Thus while we are not against segregation of the sexes under all circumstances, we are against it when it helps preserve sexual arrogance. Historical and social context are critically important here. The reader will see later that we do not find the arguments against women's colleges as persuasive as the arguments against men's colleges. This is a wholly contextual judgment. If America were now a matriarchy (as some paranoid men seem to fear it is becoming) we would regard women's colleges as a menace and men's colleges as a possibly justified defense.[13]

Whatever their merits, however, men's colleges persist, especially in the Northeast but also to a lesser extent in the South. These colleges are almost all private, and about half of them are Catholic. They enroll about 5 per cent of America's male undergraduates.[14] We know of no men's colleges founded in recent years except the Air Force Academy, but then relatively few private colleges of any sort are being founded. Existing men's colleges show some tendency to become coeducational, but the rate of integration is glacial. The percentage of men attending men's colleges is probably declining, but this is mainly because the percentage in the private sector as a whole is declining.

Princeton is the only first-rank university whose graduate schools take virtually no women on principle, and even it makes a few exceptions. But many graduate schools and departments are strongly prejudiced against women applicants and end up with a largely male student body. . . .

When one turns from the graduate to the undergraduate scene, the persistence of all-male enclaves is both more common and harder to rationalize. A number of Universities that admit women to their graduate departments (e.g. Yale, Johns Hopkins, Cal Tech, the University of Virginia, Georgetown) do not admit them to the undergraduate college. Others, like Tufts, the University of Pennsylvania, and the University of Richmond, have separate undergraduate colleges for women, which allow the men to segregate themselves in non-academic affairs. A variety of "coordinate college" relationships also exist, ranging from the near integration of Harvard and Radcliffe (which have separate governing boards but a common faculty and largely integrated extracurricular activities) through the looser ties of Columbia and Barnard (which have a common board, adjacent campuses, but separate facilities) to the almost complete separation of the University of Virginia and Mary Washington (which have a common board but are in different towns). A number of exclusively undergraduate liberal arts colleges have no women at all (e.g. Amherst, Claremont, Dartmouth, Hamilton, Haverford, Holy Cross, Randolph-Macon). A number of technical institutions follow the same policy de facto.

The results seem to us usually unfortunate. Stag undergraduate institutions are prone to a kind of excess. Many are notable for athletic overemphasis and for a narrow Philistine pragmatism, whether in the engineering or business administration programs. (We have no prejudice against either of these fields, only against teaching them or anything else in a mindless, complacent way that rules out all alternatives as "soft" or "unrealistic.") These stag institutions preserve earlier collegiate styles, like the Jazz Age pride in holding hard liquor one can still find at the University of Virginia, the teen-age muscularity of Princeton or Notre Dame, or the John Wayne militarism of Texas A &

13. Since black America is in some respects more of a matriarchy than white a stronger case can perhaps be made for Negro men's colleges than for white ones. Morehouse is, however, the only test case, though Lincoln in Pennsylvania was all male until recently.

14. [Simon and Grant, Digest of Educational Statistics (1965)], table 70, lists 20 public colleges for men, 57 private non-sectarian ones, 38 Protestant ones, 131 Catholic ones, and 7 "others." For statistics on first-time enrollment at Catholic and non-sectarian men's colleges, see Astin, Panos, and Creager, [Supplementary National Norms for Freshmen Entering College in 1966; American Council on Education Research Reports, Vol 2, No. 3 (1967)].

M. There are still many women of all ages who find such delayed maturity charming, and who are as enamored of athletes and moneyed arrogance as are their male classmates. Nonetheless, it seems to us that girls are seldom quite as complacent as men about their college lives, if only because the dilemmas of being adult women are more obvious and less easily repressed. . . .

We have been struck even in coeducational colleges by the extent to which men will come to class unprepared and then hold forth, counting on improvisation, luck, and gall to get them through. In contrast, while male professors are fond of stories about coeds who do no work and count on private charm or tears to save the day, such girls seem to us atypical. In general, girls are likely to talk in class only when they have done the work and feel some confidence they are right.

Yet it is true that, by pre-empting the "safe" ground in this way, girls may sometimes push their male classmates into exaggerated know-nothing postures, which they hope will dramatize their masculinity and help them escape the danger of subordination to "feminine" facts and reading lists. . . .

This kind of posturing takes place whether or not girls are physically present in the classroom; it is a response born of coeducational elementary and secondary schools, of predominantly women teachers, and of American culture generally. Yet we would argue that it is a response more likely to be overcome in coeducational than in all male colleges. In mixed colleges the boys are more likely to learn that their attractiveness to girls is not really dependent on being radically different from them, but rather the reverse. This reassures them about exploring seemingly "feminine" behavior like doing assignments, getting excited about books, and developing aesthetic sensitivity. Such reassurance is probably harder to come by if girls are seen only on weekends and never in academic or extracurricular settings.

THE WOMEN'S COLLEGES

While most of the major bulwarks of masculinism have today fallen to coeducation, their collapse was so slow in some parts of the country that advocates of women's education felt obliged to establish "separate but equal" colleges for their daughters. Elmira was the first of these, but it was eclipsed in 1865 by Vassar. The 1870s saw Smith and Wellesley opened, and by the end of the 1880s all of today's leading northeastern women's colleges, now known as "the Seven Sisters," were in operation. Like other minority-group colleges, the Seven Sisters offered instruction almost identical to the leading Eastern men's colleges of the time. (Radcliffe, indeed, depended on the Harvard faculty from the start and made no effort to develop its own program.) But unlike most other minority-group institutions, the women's colleges found that, while they were hard pressed to compete for the most desirable instructors, they were able to get students just as talented and often more easily educable than those at the established institutions. As a result, Bryn Mawr and perhaps some of the other leading women's colleges set standards of undergraduate academic competence that no male college would match for many years.

The early success of the feminist colleges in meeting male payrolls is so unlike the history of other minority-group colleges that it deserves additional comment. One factor was certainly the size of the female minority: women's colleges had a far broader base from which to start than did Catholic colleges, Negro colleges, public colleges, and so forth. Women were, moreover, a "minority" with the same parental backgrounds as the male "majority," and had never suffered the same degree of exclusion as most minorities. Not only was their upbringing in many cases more conducive to academic success than the upbringing of other minorities, but even in 1870 they were more likely to finish secondary school. The women's colleges thus began with a much larger pool of potentially able recruits than did other special-interest colleges. These recruits were, moreover, in some ways temperamentally better suited to academic work than was the male majority that had designed and dominated the system. Female students did not feel obliged to establish their sexual identity by rebelling against adult authority, and they were relatively willing to do large quantities of academic work in a fairly methodical way.

In their early years the aggressively feminist colleges recruited predominantly female faculties, partly because it was hard to get men and partly because they felt an obligation to offer careers to their more scholarly alumnae. Once the first flush of female emancipation had worn off, however, and fear of spinsterhood had reasserted itself the recruitment of women to academic careers began to fall off.[20] Discrimination against women on coeducational college faculties also became less obvious, so the women's colleges felt less of an obligation to discriminate in reverse. These colleges are also aware that college-age girls dislike spending all their time with other women, and they may see male faculty as a way of reducing the resemblance to a nunnery. Whatever the reason, the Seven Sisters and other women's colleges have increasingly male faculties and often male presidents as well. These faculties have conventional academic training and qualifications, and they offer curricula that differ in no important respect from those of comparable men's colleges.[21]

The Seven Sisters are not the only models for American women's colleges. In the South, academic competence and competition with men's colleges have been less emphasized, and the production of moderately cultured Southern womanhood more heavily stressed. A college like Winthrop in South Carolina (one of the few remaining public women's colleges) embodies this outlook, while Sweet Briar, Mary Baldwin, and Hollins struggle sporadically against it. Randolph-Macon Woman's College and Goucher seem more academically competitive and sympathetic to "Northern" norms, though the level of effort and of sophistication is lower than in the Seven Sisters and social grace seems more cultivated. Yet even the most "feminine" of these colleges has done little to develop a distinctive curriculum, and it would be hard to show that their extracurricular traditions had a very different influence from those of coeducational Southern colleges. The same must, in general, be said of private junior colleges for women, such as Briarcliff (now going four-year), Pine Manor, and Bradford. It must also be said of most of the Catholic women's colleges. . . . A few of these seem more effective than any of their male rivals, but most are entirely undistinguished.

There have been a few experimental women's colleges, of which Bennington and Sarah Lawrence are the best known. These two were set up in the late 1920s and early 1930s after the Seven Sisters and similar ventures had proven that women could compete with men on men's terms. They sought to move undergraduates into new cultural areas that male colleges had traditionally shunned. In the humanities they emphasized artistic as well as academic competence, hiring composers as well as musicologists, novelists as well as literary scholars, dancers as well as historians. They also stressed the social rather than the scientific aspects of the social sciences, placing more emphasis on ethics and politics than on methodology. And in all areas they developed a pedagogy that stressed small rather than large groups, catering to girls' hunger for personal contact and support. . . .

Less aggressively intellectual experiments have been tried in California. Lynn White, Jr., for example, aroused the fury of the feminists by writing a book called *Educating Our Daughters* in which he argued that women should study subjects like ceramics and not necessarily be expected to master the intricacies of a professionalized academic discipline. While he was never fully able to impose this vision on Mills College,

20. Historical Statistics, [supra n. 1] Series H 319, shows that the proportion of college faculty who were women rose steadily until the 1930s, reaching 30 percent. It then began to decline slowly, and has now returned to its level around 1900, about 20 percent. Most of these women are in low-ranking jobs and/or low-ranking institutions.

21. One partial exception to this rule is the emphasis on the performing arts at Bennington, Sarah Lawrence, and some other women's colleges. Yet this innovation has now been copied at coed colleges like UCLA and San Francisco State.

of which he was president, Scripps developed somewhat along these lines. In Missouri, Stephens Junior College (now a four-year institution) had rather similar aims. In New England, Simmons College took a different tack, emphasizing vocational competence and turning out girls who could get on in female careers. All these colleges had a common impulse to provide women with education that would be neither identical to that usually given men nor a watered-down version of it.

As a result of all these varied efforts there are now something like 275 independent women's colleges, of which about 200 are four-year institutions. Two-thirds of these 200 are Roman Catholic, most of the rest non-sectarian. The number seems to be growing steadily, but this is largely due to the multiplication of marginal Catholic colleges for women. (We know of no non-Catholic four-year college for women founded in recent years.[23] With a few dozen exceptions, all women's colleges are relatively impoverished. Even the relatively affluent Seven Sisters are poor by comparison with their Ivy League counterparts. In principle, women's colleges should do fairly well from bequests, since women usually outlive their husbands and could then give to their own rather than their husbands' colleges. But tax laws encourage husbands to give away their money before they die, or to tie it up in trusts for their children, and sentiment often encourages a widow to memorialize her husband at his college rather than herself at her own. Men's colleges also benefit from the fact that their alumni are often business colleagues, and are therefore in a good position to put pressure on one another on behalf of alma mater, whereas women have less chance to exploit such fraternal solidarity.

Like other special-interest institutions, the women's colleges have remained largely dependent on the national (and predominantly male) graduate schools, both to define their objectives and to train their faculty. Only one women's college, Bryn Mawr, has made a successful effort to establish doctoral instruction, and even Bryn Mawr has achieved national distinction only in the humanities. . . .

Lacking legitimation from the graduate schools, efforts to establish "feminine" curricula have seldom proved very durable. Indeed, the very idea of such programs seems patronizing to the die-hard feminists and ridiculous to the traditional masculinists. Just as the academic disciplines have no time for "Catholic biology" or "Negro political science," so, too, they give short shrift to "women's mathematics" or "women's literature." In most ways, this is fair enough. But there are special problems in persuading American women they can do mathematics, and special possibilities open to the teacher of literature who has a class composed entirely of women. Sensitive teachers usually recognize and respond to this, but nobody writes about it; there is no systematic body of theory and experience to help a teacher deal with it; and no effort is made to train teachers to recognize or solve these problems. So long as women feel they are still less than fully equal, they seem, in Diana Trilling's phrase, to insist on an education at least as bad as that given men.

The feminist revolution is in this sense like the other "missed" revolutions Paul Goodman speaks of, which are incomplete. Yet it has gone far enough so that there is little value in further demonstrations of the fact that women can beat men at the latter's game. What is needed is rather the reverse: an attempt to restore the respectability of the "feminine" virtues and to see what they might contribute to the various academic disciplines. This would be most interesting not in traditionally somewhat feminine fields like literature and the arts, but in fields like the natural sciences and economics, which might benefit from perspectives other than those of the aggressively virile.

For this and other reasons there may still be some advantages to educating women separately from men. Women worried about their femininity are understandably fearful of seeming too bright or too competent in direct competition with male classmates. . . .

---

23. There is at least one partial exception. Pitzer College has been established as part of the Claremont group, partly to equalize the sex imbalance created by the presence of Claremont Men's College and Harvey Mudd's male engineers.

[D]ocile and passive women sometimes clam up entirely when confronted with aggressive young men in a coeducational college, whereas they may discover some of their resources in a sexually sheltered setting.[25]

Yet the advantages of segregation for women are equivocal. Men are almost always vicariously present for girls, just as whites are for American Negroes, even if they are physically missing. Girls in women's colleges seem to worry as much about being really feminine as girls in coeducational colleges, and perhaps more. And getting seriously committed to an academic discipline seems to threaten their sense of femininity no matter where they are. A few certainly feel more inhibited in front of boys, but others seem to be liberated by the discovery that they can talk to boys in class on a non-sexual basis without losing their "after hours" appeal. Similarly, while some girls may flourish when they do not have to compete with boys, others evidently need the stimulus of male rebellion and aggressiveness. As a result, the academic case for sex segregation is moot.[26]

When one turns from the curriculum to the extracurriculum, many similar ambiguities arise. If one looks at girls working on college newspapers, for example, it could theoretically be argued that an exclusively female college forces girls to take charge and discover their talents, whereas a coed college encourages them to play subsidiary roles. Some women's college papers lend credence to this thesis (e.g. the Vassar Miscellany or Immaculate Heart Comment). In general, however, the girls who run newspapers at women's colleges appear even less willing to be combative or entrepreneurial than those in coeducational colleges. They create papers that, instead of liberating their staffs from conventional definitions of femininity, seem to re-enforce them. On coeducational campuses, on the other hand, the newspaper is more often a mix of masculine and feminine staff, skills, and attitudes. Girls often rise to the top of these papers, and despite the pseudo-professionalism and front-page posing into which their male colleagues sometimes push them, they usually get a broader view of themselves and their powers than they would on a girls' college paper.

The dilemmas confronting women in extracurricular activities are, of course, mainly a reflection of larger dilemmas confronting all American women. Such dilemmas can and sometimes should be postponed by staying within the shelter of a single-sex college. But they cannot be avoided indefinitely, as women's college graduates quickly discover. The question is thus not *whether* to integrate but *when*. Our own view is that sex segregation is more likely to be helpful in junior or senior high school than in college. But there are doubtless exceptions, and we would hate to see women's colleges entirely eliminated just because they do not seem to suit the majority. The fact that these colleges cannot solve most of their girls' problems must not be taken as proof of their worthlessness, for coed colleges cannot do so either. So long as the tensions and ambiguities of adult womanhood remain unresolved and seemingly unresolvable, *no* college will be able to do very much. Certainly we have difficulty imagining any system of undergraduate education that would prepare girls for the full range of roles and problems they may encounter after graduating.

25. See Riesman, "Some Continuities" [Some Continuities and Discontinuities in the Education of Women, in Abundance for What? (1964)]. This essay, originally a lecture at Bennington College in 1956, makes a stronger case for sex segregation than either of us would be willing to make today. Donald R. Brown has argued the same case in the Yale Daily News of April 15, 1966. Proposing geographic but not curricular or extracurricular proximity, he writes: "In a certain sense, young women deserve the opportunity to compete with each other in order to develop their capacity for leadership rather than having constantly to compete with the cultural scale weighted against them as it is in the coeducational institutions. Male students in coed universities are in the position of running a race against cultural cripples, if you will." The relative handicaps under which women compete vary according to social class, region, ethnicity, and religion, so that it is hard to reach any general conclusion.

26. This impression is supported by Astin, [Productivity of Undergraduate Institutions, 136 Science (April 13, 1962), 129-135], which shows that a woman's chances of earning a Ph.D. are not significantly influenced by whether she attends a women's or a coed college. The odds are, of course, low in either case.

Taking all things into account, we are inclined to conclude that women's colleges are probably an anachronism. They try to separate women from men at a time when most women rightly want proximity. The reasons why women shun women's colleges are clear. The complete emancipation of women may or may not be desirable, but it certainly does not appear to be imminent. A woman's adult life is still in large measure shaped by her choice of a husband — and by her ability to persuade the husband she chooses to choose her. She is expected to go where his career takes him, regardless of how it affects hers; to have children, and in most cases to take considerable time off from her career to see them through their childhood; to adapt her leisure life to her husband's pocketbook and perhaps even to his tastes and career needs. Her husband may, for all practical purposes, marry his job or his golf rather than his spouse; she is almost always married to her husband in a far more complete sense. Most undergraduate girls realize this, and their hopes and fears for the future rightly reflect it. Such worries may be dysfunctional in the sense that they compound the problem, but they are hardly irrational. So long as they persist, undergraduate women will be male-oriented, and women's colleges will have a hard time competing with coed ones for students. There is no objective evidence that women's college alumnae are less likely to marry the right man; but most girls want to explore the possibilities during their undergraduate years, and most think this will be easier if men are around all the time.

Even the girl who wants to put the marriage question aside for four years is unlikely to find a women's college appealing. She may, for example, be interested in preparing for a profession. But she will usually expect to go to a coeducational graduate school to prepare for it, and she will only rarely see her professional ambitions in combative feminist terms. She will accept the fact that work is a man's world and will be interested in learning to accommodate and make her way in that world, not in challenging or changing it. Most women find it easier to come to terms with male dominance at an integrated college than at a segregated one.[29]

None of this means that Smith, Bryn Mawr, or Sarah Lawrence is about to go begging for applicants. The small private women's colleges with established academic and social credentials are, on the contrary, almost certain to be inundated with impressively qualified prospects.

. . . Despite their success by these and other conventional indices, however, the elite women's colleges feel very much on the defensive. They lose many of their most promising prospects to Harvard-Radcliffe, Stanford, and even Cornell and Middlebury.

In good part, of course, the difficulties confronting the women's colleges are those of the private sector as a whole, and especially the private liberal arts college. But even within this context, the majority of the women's colleges seem to be in special difficulty. We have not been able to find any trend data on the proportion of women enrolling in women's colleges. But we have the strong impression that the proportion (probably less than 10 per cent)[30] is declining even faster than the proportion in the private sector as a whole. This does not mean that many women's colleges will fold, but it does mean they will grow much less rapidly than coeducational colleges and that they will exert a declining influence on coming generations.

---

29. Wrapped up in these attitudes is a certain degree of female self-hatred, which leads many women to say that they cannot stand women — a statement virtually no men would make about their own sex. (It is also notorious that women prefer male bosses.) Mary Haywood's "Were There but World Enough and Time . . ." [Harvard Univ. Dept. of Social Relations Library, undergraduate honors thesis, 1960], documents the low priority Radcliffe girls give same-sex friendships in contrast to the exigencies of premarital involvements and other career concerns. It should be added that as male college students become less boorish and boyish, many also become engrossed in cross-sex relations and limit their ties to same-sex "buddies."

30. Estimated from Astin, Panos, and Creager, Supplementary National Norms [supra n. 14].

JOHNSTON AND KNAPP, SEX DISCRIMINATION BY LAW: A STUDY IN JUDICIAL PERSPECTIVE
46 N.Y.U.L. Rev. 675, 723-726 (1971)

The most recent case to call into question a state's operation of sex-segregated educational facilities is Williams v. McNair [supra]. . . .

The district court in *Williams* was careful to avoid the kind of overt sexist rhetoric that has marred court opinions in many sex-discrimination cases, and at first blush the decision seems not only predictable but reasonable in light of the general availability of quality coeducation in the state. But closer examination may be in order. The statute establishing Winthrop College described its curriculum as follows: "such education as shall fit them [young women] for teaching" and also "stenography, typewriting, telegraphy, bookkeeping, drawing (freehand, mechanical, architectural, etc.), designing, engraving, sewing, dressmaking, millinery, art, needlework, cooking, housekeeping and such other industrial arts as may be suitable to their sex and conducive to their support and usefulness," together with such other subjects "as the progress of the times may require."[164] To evaluate this case, it may be useful to return to the racial analogy:

1) May the state properly operate only one college, for whites only? Clearly not. Could it operate only one, and only for men? The *Williams* opinion concedes that it could not.

2) Could it operate only two colleges, one for whites and one for blacks? Again, clearly not. Could it operate only two colleges, one for women and one for men? The *Williams* opinion is silent. In view of the long history of male dominance, we suggest that the adoption of such a scheme by a male-dominated legislature would at least raise a constitutional question. If accompanied by different curricula, clearly reflecting stereotypical attitudes about sex roles, a strong inference would arise that the scheme reflected an assumption that women are inherently incapable of education on an equal basis with men — just as clearly as the race-segregated schools of the South indicated a similar belief about the races.

3) Can the state operate separate schools for the races, so long as it maintains at least some school where the races *are* mixed? Any plan where the white citizens of a state were given the option of education in black-free state colleges would seem in clear violation of the school segregation decisions,[165] *whether or not* any integrated schools were also available. Should the same result follow in a sex-segregation case?

To the *Williams* court and apparently to the Supreme Court as well, the answer is clear: no violation here. But consider the facts of *Williams:* In addition to its coeducational colleges, South Carolina operates two sex-segregated institutions — Winthrop, a school apparently designed to produce secretaries and homemakers, and the Citadel, a military school offering a full range of liberal arts and engineering degrees. To pursue the race analogy a bit further, suppose that South Carolina, in addition to operating one or more racially mixed institutions, should maintain two other colleges. One, Dred Scott Institute, would offer degrees in agriculture, music, dance and physical education; it would accept only black students. The other, Calhoun College, would offer degrees in nuclear physics, medicine, law, engineering and business administration; only whites need apply. Even assuming that all of these studies were available at a biracial institution in the state, would such a scheme survive constitutional scrutiny?

It is difficult to see how; indeed, any other answer is unthinkable. And yet, the maintenance of two institutions for the sexes in South Carolina, one for male warriors and the other for female domestics, is different only in that the assumptions it reflects about individual capabilities and aspirations are more widely shared. The role of a housewife or a secretary is an honorable and productive one; so of course is the role of

164. Id. at 136 n.3.
165. See Green v. County School Bd., 391 U.S. 430 (1968); Goss v. Board of Educ., 373 U.S. 683 (1963).

a champion athlete or a tenant farmer. To attack the attitudes reflected in the *Williams* decision is not to denigrate the individuals for whom such stereotypes happen to be accurate; it is to attack the arrogant assumption that merely because these stereotypes are accurate for some individuals, the state has a right to apply them to all individuals — and, indeed, to shape its official policy toward the end that they shall *continue* to be accurate for all individuals.

DE RIVERA, ON DE-SEGREGATING STUYVESANT HIGH
Morgan (ed.), *Sisterhood is Powerful* 366-371 (1970)

Before I went to John Jay High School I hadn't realized how bad the conditions were for students. One of the things that changed my outlook was being involved with the hostilities of the New York City teacher strikes in the fall of 1968. Students were trying to open the school and the teachers were preventing them. I was disillusioned by the low-quality, high-pay teaching we received afterwards, and soon became involved with expressing my discontent.

It was then I found that students had no rights. We had no freedom of the press: many controversial articles were removed from the newspapers by the teacher-editors. We were not allowed to distribute leaflets or newspapers inside our school building, so that press communication was taken away from us. We also had no freedom of speech. Many teachers would put us down in class for our political ideas and then would not let us answer their charges. If we tried to talk with other students during a free period about political issues, we were told to stop. The school was a prison — we were required by state law to be there, but when we were there we had no rights. We had to carry ID cards and passes. We could be suspended; we were considered guilty before proven innocent.

It was this treatment which made me as a student want to change the schools. When I talked to students from other public high schools in the city, I found they had been oppressed within the schools in much the same way.

I have been writing about the student's plight in general because it was my first encounter with oppression. It is such a familiar experience to me now, that I think I can try to define it. Oppression, to me, is when people are not allowed to be themselves. I encountered this condition a second time when I realized *woman's* plight in the high schools. And for the second time I tried to help change the schools so that I and other girls would not be hurt.

The first time it really occurred to me that I was oppressed as a woman was when I began to think of what I was going to be when I was older. I realized I had no real plans for the future — college, maybe, and after that was a dark space in my mind. In talking and listening to other girls, I found that they had either the same blank spot in their minds or were planning on marriage. If not that, they figured on taking a job of some sort *until* they got married.

The boys that I knew all had at least some slight idea in their minds of what career or job they were preparing for. Some prepared for careers in science and math by going to a specialized school. Others prepared for their later jobs as mechanics, electricians, and other tradesmen in vocational schools. Some just did their thing in a regular, zoned high school. It seemed to me that I should fill the blank spot in my mind as the boys were able to do, and I decided to study science (biology, in particular) much more intensively. It was then that I encountered one of the many blocks which stand in the woman student's way: discrimination against women in the specialized science and math high schools in the city.

Many years before women in New York State had won their right to vote (1917), a school was established for those high-school students who wish to specialize in science and math. Naturally it was not co-ed, for women were not regarded legally or psychologically as people. This school, Stuyvesant High School, was erected in 1903. In 1956, thirty-nine years after New York women earned the right to vote, the school was renovated; yet no provision was made for girls to enter.

There are only two other high schools in New York which specialize in science and math: Brooklyn Technical, a school geared towards engineering, and Bronx High School of Science. Brooklyn Tech moved from the warehouse, where its male-only classes were started, into a modern building in 1933. It was renovated in 1960, yet still no provision was made for girls.

This left only Bronx Science. Bronx High School of Science is the only school where girls can study science and math intensively — it is co-ed. It became so in 1946, the year it moved into a new building. However, although it admits girls, it still discriminates against them; it admits only one girl to every two boys.

Out of these three schools I could try out for only one. This one, Bronx Science, is one and one-half hours travel time from my home. It presents very stiff competition because of the discriminatory policy which allows only a certain number of girls to enter, and also because all the girls who would otherwise be trying out for Stuyvesant or Brooklyn Tech have Bronx Science as their only alternative. I became disgusted with this, not only for my sake, but for all the girls who hadn't become scientists or engineers because they were a little less than brilliant or had been put down by nobody having challenged those little blank spots in their minds. After talking about it with my parents and friends, I decided to open up Stuyvesant and challenge the Board of Education's traditional policy.

I took my idea to Ramona Ripston, co-director of the National Emergency Civil Liberties Committee, and she accepted it warmly. Pretty soon I became involved in trying to get an application for the entrance exam to Stuyvesant filled out and sent. It was turned down and we — NECLC, my parents, and I — went to court against the principal of Stuyvesant and the Board of Ed.

The day on which we went to court was the day before the entrance exam was scheduled to be given. The Board of Ed granted me the privilege of taking the test for Bronx Science (which is the same as the one given for Stuyvesant), and the judge recognized that the results of this test would be used in another court hearing to resolve whether or not I would be admitted. Five days after the other students had received their results, we found out that I had passed for entrance into both Stuyvesant and Bronx Science.

We went to court again a couple of months later, in April. Our judge, Jawn A. Sandafer, seemed receptive to our case, but he reserved his decision. Later we were told that he wished an open hearing for May 13. This was a great break for us because if what the judge needed was public support, we had many important people who were willing to argue in my favor. However, on April 30 the New York City Board of Education voted to admit me to Stuyvesant High School in the Fall. The superintendent had wanted to continue the court fight.

This seemed a victory to us at first, but in actuality it would have been better if we could have continued the case and received a court order. We hoped to establish that public funds could not be used to support institutions of learning which discriminate against women. Such a ruling would have been the key to opening up the other sexually segregated high schools in New York City.

There are a great many battles yet to be fought. Aside from being discouraged to study for a career, women are discouraged from preparing for jobs involving anything *but* secretarial work, beauty care, nursing, cooking, and the fashion industry. During my fight over Stuyvesant, I investigated the whole high-school scene, and found that out of the twenty-seven vocational high schools in the city, only *seven* are co-ed. The boys' vocational schools teach trades in electronics, plumbing, carpentry, foods, printing (another example of Board of Ed traditional policy — there is hardly any work for a hand-typesetter today), etc. The girls are taught to be beauticians, secretaries, or health aides. This means that if a girl is seeking entrance to a vocational school, she is pressured to feel that certain jobs are masculine and others feminine. She is forced to conform to the Board of Education's image of her sex. At the seven co-ed vocational schools, boys can learn clerical work, food preparation, and beauty care along with the girls. But the courses that would normally be found in a boys' school are not open to girls. There are only two schools where a girl can prepare for a "masculine" job. Charles Evans Hughes High School in Manhattan is coed for teaching technical electronics. Newtown High School offers an academic pre-engineering course of study for boys and girls. However, this school is zoned for the Borough of Queens only.

In conclusion, there are three types of schools, twenty-nine in number, that the Board of Ed has copped out on. These schools are composed of the specialized science and math school Brooklyn Tech, twenty vocational schools which teach students their trade according to what sex they are, and the eight traditionally non-co-ed academic schools.

These eight academic schools are zoned schools which admit only boys or only girls. The argument against these schools is that "separate but equal" is not equal (as established with regard to race in the Brown Decision). The psychological result of the school which is segregated by sex — only because of tradition — is to impress upon girls that they are only "flighty females" who would bother the boys' study habits (as a consequence of girls not being interested in anything but the male sex). This insinuates immaturity on the part of girls — and certainly produces it in both sexes. A boy who has never worked with a girl in the classroom is bound to think of her as his intellectual inferior, and will not treat her as if she had any capacity for understanding things other than child care and homemaking. Both sexes learn to deal with each other as non-people. It really messes up the growth of a person's mind.

Out of the sixty-two high schools in New York City, twenty-nine are now sexually segregated. I believe that it is up to the girls to put pressure on the Board of Education to change this situation. I myself cannot live with oppression.

All girls have been brought up by this society never being able to be themselves — the school system has reinforced this. My desire at this time is to change the educational situation to benefit *all* the students. But I'm afraid changes *could* be made that benefited male students, leaving the status of females pretty much as it is. Female students share the general oppressive conditions forced upon everyone by the System's schools, plus a special psychological discrimination shown to women by the schools, the teachers, *and* their fellow students. So, since I don't want *my* issues to get swallowed up in the supposed "larger" issues, I'm going to make women's liberation the center of my fight.

c. Arguments in Favor of Maintaining Some Schools for Women Only

CARNEGIE COMMISSION ON HIGHER EDUCATION
OPPORTUNITIES FOR WOMEN IN HIGHER EDUCATION
70-75 (1973)

Women's colleges have played a unique role in the development of higher education for women. Many of them were established in the middle and latter part of the nineteenth century, when many private colleges and universities, and some public institutions, were exclusively male. Over the decades, however, the proportion of institutions that were exclusively male declined sharply, the proportion of those for women declined more slowly, and coeducational institutions came to be overwhelmingly predominant in higher education (Table [5-1]). According to a study recently published by the Educational Testing Service, about half of the women's colleges existing in 1960 became coeducational or went out of business between 1960 and

TABLE [5-1]. INSTITUTIONS OF HIGHER EDUCATION, BY SEX STATUS,
Selected Years, 1870–1970

Year	Number of institutions	Sex status			
		Total (percent)	Men only	Women only	Coeducational
1870	582	100	59	12	29
1890	1,082	100	37	20	43
1910	1,083	100	27	15	58
1930	1,322	100	15	16	69
1960	2,028	100	12	13	76
1970	2,573	100	6	8	86

Sources: Newcomer ([A Century of Higher Education for American Women] 1959, p. 37); and U.S. Office of Education ([Digest of Educational Statistics, 1971] 1972, p. 86).

1972. Moreover, in 1960 three out of every five women's colleges were Catholic, and they were the women's institutions most affected by developments of the last decade. By 1972 their numbers had dropped from 185 to 73, chiefly as a result of a shift to coeducational status ("Number of Women's Colleges Down," [Chronicle of Higher Education, May 7,] 1973). The total number of women's colleges was down to 146, and they enrolled less than 10 percent of all female students.

Not only has the number of women's colleges declined, but the proportion of men on their faculties and in their administrative ranks has steadily increased. This has come about, at least in part, because of the increasing proportion of women scholars who are married and who are not available to teach in women's colleges because they prefer jobs in areas where their husbands are employed. In the 1960s, the trend of increasing numbers of male staff was also probably encouraged by enrollment of male students in courses on women's college campuses under various types of exchange relationships with neighboring male or coeducational institutions. These arrangements doubtless made the women's colleges more attractive to male teachers.

In the last few years, however, there have been signs of resistance to these trends, at least among some of the more highly selective women's colleges, and the women's movement clearly has played a role in stimulating this growing resistance. Recently, Mount Holyoke, Smith, and Wellesley have all made carefully considered decisions to remain single-sex institutions. "While the conditions that historically justified the founding of women's colleges have clearly changed to some extent," the Mount Holyoke Trustees Committee on Coeducation concluded in the fall of 1971, "they remain in the less tangible but still potent areas of attitude, feeling, spirit" (Bird, ["Women's Colleges and Women's Lib," Change, April] 1972, p. 65). The Smith report commented that "at the present time, when the status and roles of women in American society are being reexamined with a view to their improvement, an important option that should remain open to women is attendance at a college of the highest caliber in which women are unquestionably first-class citizens" (ibid.).

In announcing Wellesley's decision to remain a women's college, President Barbara Newell said:

> The research we have clearly demonstrates that women's colleges produce a dispro-
> portionate number of women leaders and women in responsible positions in society;
> it does demonstrate that the higher proportion of women on the faculty the higher
> the motivation for women students (Kovach, ["Wellesley Says It Won't Go Coed,"
> New York Times, Mar. 9,] 1973).

Various studies have shown that women who attend women's colleges have academic records superior to those of their coeducational sisters, on the basis of such
measures as persistence, proportion going on to graduate education, and proportion

receiving Ph.D.'s.[10] In their study [The Educational and Vocational Development of College Students], Astin and Panos (1969, p. 144) concluded:

> Both men and women are more likely to drop out of college if they attend a coeducational institution. . . . The largest single environmental effect observed among the noncoeducational institutions occurs in the men's colleges (technological institutions excepted) which tend to steer students out of potential careers in engineering and physical science and [into] careers in law. Women's colleges do not show many pronounced effects on the various student outcomes, except for a slight tendency to channel students out of education and teaching and into the natural sciences. Colleges for men and colleges for women both have a slight tendency to stimulate the student's interest in majoring in arts and humanities and in attending graduate school. . . .

In an analysis of bachelor's degrees awarded in 1969, we found that about 13 percent of those graduating from the Seven Sister colleges,[11] as compared with about 7 percent of all women receiving bachelor's degrees that year, were awarded degrees in the natural sciences and mathematics.[12]

Clearly, these differences cannot be attributed solely to the impact of women's colleges on their students. To some extent, they result from the characteristics of women who enroll in women's colleges. The most selective women's colleges, for example, have long had exceptionally able students. Yet there are reasons for believing that the experience of attending a women's college is partially responsible. In women's colleges, female students are not reluctant to participate actively in class discussion for fear of losing their feminine appeal in the eyes of male students. They have far greater opportunity to gain experience in leadership roles in campus organizations and activities than women in coeducational institutions, where the top leadership positions nearly always go to men.

In a recent analysis of random samples [from] three editions of Who's Who of American Women, Tidball (["Perspective on Academic Women and Affirmative Action," 54 Educational Record 130–135] 1973) found that the number of women achievers per 1,000 women enrolled was about twice as high among graduates of women's colleges as among graduates of coeducational institutions. (Ratios . . . were computed for . . . the five decades . . . from 1910 to 1960.) She also found evidence that the larger proportion of achievers among graduates of women's colleges was related to the larger proportion of women on [their] faculties. . . .[13] In addition, there was a high negative correlation between the ratio of men to women among undergraduates in coeducational institutions and the ratio of women achievers among their graduates.

10. Information supplied by Alexander W. Astin on the basis of unpublished data from studies conducted by the American Council on Education.

11. Barnard, Bryn Mawr, Mount Holyoke, Radcliffe, Smith, Vassar, and Wellesley.

12. The difference was largest in physical sciences and smallest in mathematical sciences. Comparisons between the seven women's colleges and all undergraduate programs are complicated by the fact that nearly half of all the bachelor's degrees awarded were in education and "other" (chiefly professional programs), whereas in the seven women's colleges only 4.1 percent of the degrees awarded were in these categories. On the other hand, more than half of the degrees awarded in the women's colleges were in arts and humanities, compared with 28 percent of all bachelor's degrees awarded to women, and the proportion of degrees in the social sciences was considerably higher in the women's colleges than among all degrees awarded to women. As we have suggested earlier, in liberal arts colleges men and women preparing for teaching tend to major in liberal arts subjects rather than in education. Even so, the data do suggest that women are less inhibited from majoring in the natural sciences and mathematics in women's colleges.

In a comparison of degrees awarded in 1956, Newcomer [A Century of Higher Education for American Women 95 (1959)] found that substantially larger proportions of degrees in the physical sciences and mathematics were awarded to women in women's colleges than in state universities.

13. That is, when the number of achievers per 1,000 women faculty members was computed for both the graduates of women's colleges and the graduates of coeducational institutions, there was no significant difference between the two ratios.

In a similar analysis of data from such sources as American Men of Science and the Dictionary of American Biography, Newcomer [supra], p. 195, showed that women's colleges over the relevant period accounted for 16 percent of all women students enrolled and 34 percent of all women scholars.

These accomplishments of the graduates of women's colleges are worthy of emphasis, not only as they bear on decisions of women's colleges to continue or abandon their single-sex status, but also — and far more significantly in terms of potential influence — as they suggest how changes in policies and faculty attitudes in coeducational institutions could affect the accomplishments of their women students.

A basic need is for women to overcome their feelings of hesitancy about entering traditionally male fields and participating actively in class discussion in coeducational institutions, but this change will come slowly and will probably depend more on changes in early acculturation than on what happens in higher education. Some observers believe that the women's movement is making matters more difficult for shy women. Typically it is their more aggressive sisters who are actively pushing for change, and shy women tend to draw away from participation in aggressive activities. Equally basic is the need for administrators, faculty members, and counselors to adopt positive and encouraging attitudes toward aspirations of qualified women to develop their capacities and, when they wish, to major in traditionally male fields. As a transitional measure, until women are better prepared psychologically to compete with men in the classroom, there is a case for experimentation with special sections for women in large introductory courses.[14]

An emerging problem for women's colleges is the absence from their curricula of such traditionally male professional subjects as business administration and engineering, in which their students would like to major. Whether students should be encouraged to major in business administration at the undergraduate stage is questionable, however.[15] On the other hand, certain courses like accounting may usefully be taken by undergraduate economics majors. We believe that women's colleges would be well advised to enter into arrangements, wherever possible, with neighboring male or coeducational institutions to enable their students to enroll in accounting courses or to undertake an engineering program rather than attempting to develop their own programs in these fields. The cost per student is high in a field like engineering, particularly when the number of students is small, because there are appreciable economies of scale.

Another quite different realm in which women frequently have greater opportunities in women's colleges is competitive sports. In coeducational institutions, women are now seeking and sometimes aggressively demanding, opportunities to participate in athletic training and to participate in some of the competitive sports formerly regarded as male preserves.[16]

SANDLER
A FEMINIST APPROACH TO THE WOMEN'S COLLEGE
Speech Before the Southern Association of Colleges for Women,
Nov. 30, 1971

What . . . is the justification for an all-women's college? If a women's college is to indeed serve a unique purpose, it must do something different from the predominant institutions in our society. . . .

[A] women's college must have *more* than just the same noble aims of the coeduca-

14. Recently 10 women at Harvard successfully insisted on the organization of a separate section of the introductory physics course for them [Women Physicists are Bucking the Tide At Harvard, Boston Globe, Nov. 24, 1972].

15. Two influential studies of higher education in business conducted in the late 1950s concluded that it was preferable for students preparing for a business career to gain a broad liberal arts background at the undergraduate stage, with some emphasis on economics and other social sciences, and to postpone specilization in business until the graduate education stage (Gordon and Howell [Higher Education in Business], 1959; and Pierson [The Education of American Businessmen], 1959).

16. In The Lonely Crowd, Riesman (1969, pp. 81-82) called attention to the importance of "antagonistic cooperation" and the role of competitive sports in encouraging this trait.

tional institutions. Just as a woman, in order to succeed, must be *twice* as good in order to earn half as much, so it is with our women's colleges: in order to succeed they must do *more* than our other institutions, and they must do it *better.*

A women's college must provide a settling and a framework in which young women can flourish and develop in ways in which they cannot readily do so at other institutions. *If a women's college is to be truly useful to the women who attend it, it must act as a counterbalance to those trends in our society that hurt the development of women. . . .*

The women's colleges must deliberately set out to provide a different kind of experience from what young women would find elsewhere. The coeducational institutions are not particularly sensitive or appreciative of women and their talents. Although women have been admitted to institutions of higher learning for more than a hundred years, it looks like many colleges have still not gotten used to the idea, judging from the more than 350 formal charges of sex discrimination that have been filed against universities and colleges. Indeed, the typical college program is aimed at the young, unmarried male student. Young women, who need higher grades in the first place in order to be accepted at many coeducational institutions, are not infrequently discouraged, both subtly and overtly, from pursuing academic excellence: "You'll only get married," "Are you really serious about political science?," "Education is wasted on women," and "Frankly, we have too many women students in this department already."

In contrast, the women's college must be acutely aware that it is a women's institution, serving women. It must provide a singular atmosphere where women examine and evaluate their lives as women, where students and faculty together deliberately and consciously set out to explore what it means to be a woman in our society. It must be a place where the patterns of discrimination against women are discussed and analyzed.

Often it has been said that women can be helped most by providing them with good counseling, and that this is what women need in order to raise their aspirations and vocational sights. While better counseling would be helpful, it does not make most of our young women change their lives or reevaluate their vocational plans unless something else occurs. Blacks did not need better counseling in order to raise their aspirations; *what they needed was a keen sense of the discrimination they face, and the knowledge that overcoming the barriers of discrimination was indeed possible.*

When women begin to examine their lives *as women in our society* — when they see how discrimination against women has affected themselves, when they confront their own experiences as women — then it is possible for them to begin to build new sources of strength within themselves.

It is in this area — re-examining the role of women — that women's studies courses can be of enormous help. Anyone who has looked at the extensive reading lists of many of these courses knows that they are not frivolous but highly academic, enriching the perspectives in traditional fields. For many young women (and for men, too) these courses serve a very real purpose in helping women to examine themselves as women for the first time in their lives and how they see themselves. By confronting themselves as women, they can begin to deal with the contradictions and conflicts in their lives. For this purpose, the women's studies courses serve a unique role, for unlike many academic courses, they are directly relevant to the lives of students. They are consciousness raising with intelligence and without hysteria. . . .

Equally important, the women's college must increasingly be concerned with *the problems of all women,* and not just those of the traditional college student. It must reach out actively to older women who want to return to the campus, to poor women who want and need education, to black women and other minority women who need a special helping hand. . . . The women's college can play a major role in bridging the gap between different groups of women. It must reorganize itself so that its concern is truly that of *all* women and not just that of young women who fit the standard mold of the young college student. For example, part-time studies need to be encouraged, so that women with family responsibilities can still complete their education. Courses need to be given in the evening as well as in the traditional daytime hours. Saturday courses, short-term courses and off-campus courses need to be explored. Part-time scholarships need to be developed so that women who can only attend on a part-time basis can still obtain the financial support they need. Students who have dropped out because of marriage or whatever reasons should find the door open if they wish to return. Certainly the transfer of credits, and the development of a degree in absentia would ease the burden of those students who move and cannot easily return to complete their degree, or who started elsewhere and need help in finishing. Residency requirements need to be revamped, again so that women are not penalized but are encouraged to return to school. Dormitory arrangements for married women with children need to be worked out. Child care services need to be developed so that mothers can continue their education. Regulations forbidding married students or pregnant students must be abolished, for their effect is punitive and not helpful to anyone, certainly least of all to women.

What is indeed needed in both the women's colleges and in the coeducational institutions is a thorough reevaluation of all policies and practices and how these policies and practices affect women *as women.*

By reaching out into the community toward all women, and by making it easier for all women to attend college, the student body will change, for it will include a mixture of women at all ages, with differing economic backgrounds and interests. Such a mixture can only be beneficial. Young women, instead of being isolated for four years with other young women very much like themselves, will have an expanded opportunity to have contacts with a variety of people, and thereby increase their opportunities for evaluating more realistically their own future plans. The lockstep of the four-year college would be broken, as women could enter and leave, *without penalty,* as the differing tempos and requirements of their lives demanded.

One of the often extolled virtues of a women's college is the opportunity for leadership. When young men and young women work together on extracurricular projects they typically follow the pattern that is "normal" for our society: the men play the role of leader, and the women become the secretaries, note-takers and the coffee makers. . . . In the women's college, women students can be the editor of the yearbook, direct student plays, be president of the student body, and act as leaders in innumerable activities.

Nevertheless, the women's college must make an especial effort to increase leadership opportunities for its students. To do this, it must treat its students as responsible, active adults. We are all likely to respond in terms of the expectations people have of us. If we treat our women students as passive and unable to make decisions concerning their own lives, then they may indeed act this way. Women students need to be encouraged to play a large role in decision making on their campuses. The movement to give students a greater voice in the running of campus affairs is particularly important in the women's colleges if we are to help counteract the notions that women are passive and need to be dominated by others. We need to treat women the way we want them to behave. Increased student governance in the women's college would serve another purpose. It would lay to rest once and for all the outdated image of women's colleges as a place to "protect" and "take care" of "little girls."

The women's college must serve another critical function by providing role models of women actively engaged in the world of work, particularly in academic life. . . .

Traditionally, and fortunately, women's colleges have had a high proportion of women on their faculty. I recently read of a study which estimated the chances of a student's having a woman history teacher. In a coeducational liberal arts college, the probability is only 5-1/2%; in a women's college the student has a 33% chance of having a woman history teacher.

Yet many of the women's colleges have shown a disturbing tendency that echoes what happens in coeducational institutions. Some of these schools are just as discriminatory in their hiring and promotion policies as are the male-dominated coeducational institutions. Women's institutions should be a model employer for women. . . .

I think, too, that we need to see more women as presidents of women's colleges. . . .

Unless women's colleges change, the economic problems that beset them will not go away. The unique program that a women's college can offer is that of a female environment which deliberately sets out to create a climate that helps women discover and examine their role as women in society — a campus that is responsive to all women, and brings together on the campus women of varying ages, varying races, and varying backgrounds; a campus that acknowledges that women are often treated unfairly and differently in our society; a campus that actively seeks to provide a climate in which women can grow to be full human beings.

Matina Horner reported that[8]

> for women . . . the desire to achieve is often contaminated by what I call the *motive to avoid success*. I define it as the fear that success in competitive achievement situations will lead to negative consequences, such as unpopularity and loss of femininity. . . . When fear of success conflicts with a desire to be successful, the result is an inhibition of achievement motivation.

In Horner's opinion, her research findings suggested "that most women will fully explore their intellectual potential only when they do not need to compete — and least of all when they are competing with men." If she is right, doesn't this data strengthen the argument for single-sex schools for women only?

There is another way to look at her findings, however. It is hardly surprising that many women are discouraged from doing as well as they can by social stereotypes that achievement is unfeminine. The question is what to do about this problem.

One option is to segregate women and men educationally and thus shelter women from competition. There are a number of problems with this alternative. First, if work roles are sex-integrated, women lose their protection from competition with men as soon as they leave school. Of course, work roles can also be sex-segregated. Unfortunately, as the material in Chapter Two, Part I suggested, sex segregation in the labor market is intimately linked to sex discrimination in wages and status.

A second alternative is to challenge the idea that success is unfeminine. The question then becomes: Which setting is best for changing the social stereotypes about femininity and masculinity? Sandler and others have suggested that women's colleges are best equipped to perform this function, "to act as a counterbalance to those trends in our society that hurt the development of women." There are two assumptions in this contention: first, that women's colleges are most likely, because of their history and constituency, to devote the resources necessary to achieve this goal; and second, that an all-female environment is best for achieving it. As to the first, it is probably true. On the other hand, concomitant with sex segregation, which accounts for women's colleges' greater willingness to support the aspirations of women, are smaller budgets and less adequate facilities than those of all-male or integrated schools of comparable status. It is a difficult question whether this trade-off is worthwhile. As to the second assumption, while it may seem easier to deal with sexism by shutting out men, this is probably at best a short-run solution. In a segregated school, one cannot confront the cultural barriers that cause women to defer to men as effectively as at an integrated school, because half of the people who share these attitudes are not present. At a coeducational school, aware teachers, administrators, and students could confront the issue head on and thus help both women and men overcome sex role problems that affect their education and leadership opportunities while in school.

However the debate over integration and segregation is resolved, women's colleges account for too small a proportion of the total enrollment in higher education to affect the majority of college-bound women. Whether or not women's colleges make strong institutional commitments to the educational and occupational equality of women, and

8. Fail: Bright Women, Psychology Today Magazine, Nov. 1969, pp. 38, 62.

whether or not they decide to go "coed," the policies of coeducational institutions will also have to be challenged and changed.

3. Sex-Segregated Athletic Programs

Lawsuits challenging the male domination of sports may be the best illustration of female impatience with women's place. The issues in the sports litigation raise physiological and philosophical questions with few analogies in other areas: whether "segregation" or "integration" is the most desirable pattern; whether contact sports should be treated separately; whether direct male-female physical competition should be encouraged; and what forms of equalization are appropriate in an area where physical differences between the sexes have some relevance.

The number of cases is increasing and they reflect a growing restiveness about discouragement of female sports activity. Since most sports for young people are school-connected or -sponsored, unequal treatment in games can often be challenged in the same way as other state-condoned discrimination, as the following cases illustrate.

BRENDEN v. INDEPENDENT SCHOOL DISTRICT
477 F.2d 1292 (8th Cir. 1973)

Before LAY, HEANEY and STEPHENSON, Circuit Judges.

HEANEY, C. J. This is a civil rights action brought under 42 U.S.C. §1983 to enjoin enforcement of a rule promulgated by the Minnesota State High School League which bars females from participating with males in high school interscholastic athletics. The rule states:

> Girls shall be prohibited from participation in the boys' interscholastic athletic program either as a member of the boys' team or a member of the girls' team playing the boys' team.
> The girls' team shall not accept male members.

Minnesota State High School League Official Handbook, 1971-72. Athletic Rules for Girls, Article III, Section 5.

The complaint charges that this rule discriminates against females in violation of the Equal Protection Clause of the Fourteenth Amendment to the United States Constitution.

The plaintiffs are Peggy Brenden and Antoinette St. Pierre, female high school students at Minnesota public high schools. . . .

The plaintiffs desired to participate in non-contact interscholastic sports: Brenden in tennis; St. Pierre in cross-country skiing and cross-country running. Neither of their schools provided teams for females in the respective sports. They did, however, provide such teams for males. Both plaintiffs would have liked to qualify for positions on the teams which have been established for males, but they were precluded from doing so on the basis of the above quoted rule. The trial court found that both were excellent athletes, and that neither would be damaged by competition with males.

The court, after a trial on the merits, granted relief stating:

> In summary, the Court is confronted with a situation where two high school girls wish to take part in certain interscholastic boys' athletics: where it is shown that the girls could compete effectively on those teams, and where there are no alternative competitive programs sponsored by their schools which would provide an equal opportunity for competition for these girls; and where the rule, in its application, becomes unreasonable in light of the objectives which the rule seeks to promote. Brought to its base, then, Peggy Brenden and Tony St. Pierre are being prevented from participating on the boys' interscholastic teams in tennis, cross-country, and cross-

country skiing solely on the basis of the fact of sex and sex alone. The Court is thus of the opinion that in these factual circumstances, the application of the League rules to Peggy Brenden and Tony St. Pierre is arbitrary and unreasonable, in violation of the equal protection clause of the fourteenth amendment. For this reason, the application of the rule to these girls cannot stand. . . . To implement this decision, it is ordered.

    1. That Peggy Brenden and Tony St. Pierre be declared eligible to compete on their respective teams at their respective high schools.

    2. That the Minnesota State High School League is enjoined from imposing any sanctions upon either St. Cloud Technical High School or Hopkins Eisenhower High School for compliance with this Court order, and that no sanctions are to be imposed on any other public high schools for engaging in interscholastic competition with St. Cloud Technical High School and Hopkins Eisenhower High School.

Brenden v. Independent School District 742, 342 F.Supp. 1224, 1234 (D.Minn. 1972).

    We affirm the decision of the trial court.

    Having stated what this case is about, we would also like to emphasize what it is not about. First, because neither high school provided teams for females in the sports in which Brenden and St. Pierre desired to participate, we are not faced with the question of whether the schools can fulfill their responsibilities under the Equal Protection Clause by providing separate but equal facilities for females in interscholastic athletics. See generally, Note, Sex Discrimination in High School Athletics, 57 Minn. L. Rev. 339, 366-370 (1972). Second, because the sports in question are clearly non-contact sports, we need not determine if the High School League would be justified in precluding females from competing with males in contact sports such as football. See, Cynthia Morris et al., etc. v. Michigan State Board of Education et al., etc., 472 F.2d 1207 (6th Cir. 1973). . . .

    . . . In evaluating a claim that state action violates the Equal Protection Clause, the following three criteria must be considered:

    . . . [I] the character of the classification in question; [II] the individual interests affected by the classification; [III] and the governmental interests asserted in support of the classification. . . .

Dunn v. Blumstein, 405 U.S. 330, 335, 92 S. Ct. 995, 999, 31 L. Ed. 2d 274, 280 (1972).

I. SEX-BASED CLASSIFICATIONS

    In 1961, President Kennedy, having found that "prejudices and outmoded customs act as barriers to the full realization of women's basic rights," established the President's Commission on the Status of Women. Executive Order 10980 (December 14, 1961). That Commission, the President's Task Force on Women's Rights and Responsibilities, congressional hearings and critical studies have confirmed the serious nature of discrimination on account of sex.

    In recent years, Congress and the Executive have acted to eliminate discrimination based on " 'stereotyped characterizations of the sexes'," Phillips v. Marietta Corp., 400 U.S. 542, 91 S. Ct. 496, 27 L. Ed. 2d 613 (1971) (Marshall, J., concurring). See, Title VII of the Civil Rights Act of 1964, the Equal Pay Act, and Title IX of the Education Amendments of 1972. The jurisdiction of the Civil Rights Commission has been extended to include discrimination on the basis of sex. Finally, Congress has passed the Equal Rights Amendment and transmitted it to the states.

    In recent years, courts, too, have become sensitive to the problems of sex-based discrimination. In 1963, the Presidential Commission on the Status of Women recommended that:

    Early and definitive court pronouncement, particularly by the United States Supreme Court, is urgently needed with regard to the validity under the Fifth and Fourteenth

Amendments of laws and official practices discriminating against women, to the end that the principle of equality becomes firmly established in constitutional doctrine.

There is no longer any doubt that sex-based classifications are subject to scrutiny by the courts under the Equal Protection Clause and will be struck down when they provide dissimilar treatment for men and women who are similarly situated with respect to the object of the classification. Reed v. Reed, 404 U.S. 71, 77, 92 S. Ct. 251, 30 L. Ed. 2d 225 (1971). See, Moritz v. C.I.R., 469 F.2d 466 (10th Cir. 1972). Compare, Green v. Waterford Board of Education, 473 F.2d 629 (2nd Cir. 1973), and LaFleur v. Cleveland Board of Education, 465 F.2d 1184 (6th Cir. 1972), with Mrs. Susan Cohen v. Chesterfield County School Board et al., etc., 474 F.2d 395 (4th Cir. 1973) (en banc). Furthermore, discrimination on the basis of sex can no longer be justified by reliance on "outdated images . . . of women as peculiarly delicate and impressionable creatures in need of protection from the rough and tumble of unvarnished humanity." Seidenberg v. McSorleys' Old Ale House, Inc., 317 F. Supp. 593, 606 (S.D.N.Y. 1970). . . .

In this case, it is unnecessary for this Court to determine whether classification based on sex are suspect and, thus, can be justified only by a compelling state interest because the High School League's rule cannot be justified even under the standard applied to test nonsuspect classifications. See, Eisenstadt v. Baird, 405 U.S. 438, 92 S. Ct. 1029, 31 L. Ed. 2d 349, 359 n.8 (1972). . . .

Discrimination in education has been recognized as a matter of the utmost importance. . . . In particular, "[d]iscrimination in education is one of the most damaging injustices women suffer. It denies them equal education and equal employment opportunity, contributing to a second class self image." A Matter of Simple Justice, The Report on the President's Task Force on Women's Rights and Responsibilities 7 (April, 1970). See, American Women, The Report of the President's Commission on the Status of Women (1963).[6] The President's Task Force also concluded that "discrimination based on sex in public education should be prohibited by the Fourteenth Amendment." A Matter of Simple Justice, supra at 8. Congress has also recognized the importance of all aspects of education for women by declaring:

> No person in the United States shall, on the basis of sex, be excluded from participation in, be denied the benefits of, or be subjected to discrimination under any education program or activity receiving Federal financial assistance. . . .

Title IX of the Education Amendments of 1972, 86 Stat. 235, §901(a), P.L. 92-318 (June 23, 1972) U.S. Code Cong. & Admin. News p. 444.

Discrimination in high school interscholastic athletics constitutes discrimination in education. The Supreme Court of Minnesota has stated that:

> . . . [I]nterscholastic activities . . . [are] today recognized . . . as an important and integral facet of the . . . education process, see, Bunger v. Iowa High School Athletic Assn, 197 N.W.2d 555 (Iowa 1972); Kelley v. Metropolitan County Bd. of Ed. of Nashville and Davidson County, 293 F. Supp. 485 (M.D. Tenn. 1968). . . .

Thompson v. Barnes, 200 N.W.2d 921, 926 n. 11 (Minn. 1972). The court in *Thompson* pointed out that this was also the position of the Minnesota High School League. See, Behagen v. Intercollegiate Conference of Faculty Rep., 346 F. Supp. 602 (D. Minn. 1972). The National Federation of State High School Athletic Associations has taken the position that:

6. The failure to provide educational opportunity for women has long been criticized in this country. For instance, Abigail Adams, writing in revolutionary war America, "spoke often and sometimes sharply in her letters about the discrimination between boys and girls with respect to educational privileges, a disparity she could only attribute to men's 'ungenerous jealousy of rivals near the throne'." Quoted in James & James & Boyer, Notable American Women 1607-1950: A Biographical Dictionary (1971).

> Interscholastic athletics shall be an integral part of the total secondary school educational program that has as its purpose to provide educational experiences not otherwise provided in the curriculum, which will develop learning outcomes in the areas of knowledge, skills and emotional patterns and will contribute to the development of better citizens. Emphasis shall be upon teaching "through" athletics in addition to teaching the "skills" of athletics.

1970–1971 National Federation of State High School Athletic Associations Official Handbook 9.

Furthermore, the High School League recognizes that interscholastic sports are just as valuable for females as for males. See, Haas v. South Bend Community School Corporation, 289 N.E.2d 495, 500 (Ind. 1972).

The importance of interscholastic athletics for females as part of the total educational process has been recently emphasized by the Minnesota State Board of Education. Its recent statement of policy and proposed action, Eliminating Sex Bias in Education (September 1972), states that:

> . . . [O]ur educational system has helped perpetuate the division of the sexes into predetermined roles and has failed to provide freedom from discrimination because of sex. . . .
>
> The practice of stereotyping and socializing men and women into "masculine" "feminine" roles has resulted in prejudice, dominance, discrimination and segregation harmful to the human development of both sexes. . . .
>
> The State Board of Education is concerned about four areas in particular: discrimination in hiring and promoting, *sex requirements for boys and girls to participate in sports and extra-curricular activities,* sex bias in curricular and teaching materials, and providing in-service training for administrators and teachers to overcome the habits and practices of teaching stereotyped social roles. (Emphasis added.)

In view of these circumstances, we must conclude that at the very least, the plaintiffs' interest in participating in interscholastic sports is a substantial and cognizable one. Thus, this case is properly before a federal court to determine if the High School League's actions are in conformity with the Equal Protection Clause. See, Cynthia Morris et al., etc. v. Michigan State Board of Education, [430 F.2d 1155 (1970)]; Mitchell v. Louisiana High School Athletic Association, 430 F.2d at 1158; Bucha v. Illinois High School Athletic Association, 351 F. Supp. 69 (N.D. Ill. 1972); Reed v. The Nebraska School Activities Association, [341 F. Supp. 258 (D. Neb. 1972)]; Graves v. Walton County Board of Education, 300 F. Supp. 188, 199 (M.D. Ga. 1968), aff'd, 410 F.2d 1152, 1153 (5th Cir. 1969). See generally, 36 Mo. L. Rev. 406-408 (1971).

III. THE HIGH SCHOOL LEAGUE'S INTEREST

Because the defendant high schools have not provided teams for females in tennis and cross-country skiing and running, the effect of the High School League's rule is to completely bar Brenden and St. Pierre from competition in these non-contact interscholastic sports, despite their being fully qualified. The High School League argues, however, that its rule is justified in order to assure that persons with similar qualifications compete among themselves. They state that physiological differences between males and females make it impossible for the latter to equitably compete with males in athletic competition.[7]

In evaluating the High School League's justification for their rule, we will, as we

7. " . . . As testified to by defendants' expert witnesses, men are taller than women, stronger than women by reason of a greater muscle mass; have larger hearts than women and a deeper breathing capacity, enabling them to utilize oxygen more efficiently than women, run faster, based upon the construction of the pelvic area, which when women reach puberty, widens, causing the femur to bend outward, rendering the female incapable of running as efficiently as a male. . . ." Brenden v. Independent School District 742, 342 F. Supp. 1224, 1233 (D. Minn. 1972).

have indicated, apply the equal protection standard for evaluating non-suspect classifications. That standard is set forth in Reed v. Reed, 404 U.S. at 76, 92 S. Ct. at 254.

> . . . A classification "must be reasonable, not arbitrary, and must rest upon some ground of difference having a *fair and substantial* relation to the object of the legislation, so that all persons in similar circumstances shall be treated alike." . . . (Citation omitted and emphasis added.)

It has been pointed out that in applying this standard, the Supreme Court's definition of what constitutes a rational relationship has become more rigorous, and that the Court has become "less willing to speculate as to what unexpressed legitimate state purposes may be rationally furthered by a challenged statutory classification." Green v. Waterford Board of Education, supra, 473 F.2d at 633.

We recognize that because sex-based classifications may be based on outdated stereotypes of the nature of males and females, courts must be particularly sensitive to the possibility of invidious discrimination in evaluating them, and must be particularly demanding in ascertaining whether the state has demonstrated a substantial rational basis for the classification. Compare, Reed v. Reed, supra, with Gunther, The Supreme Court, 1971 Term — Foreword: In Search of Evolving Doctrine on a Changing Court: A Model for a Newer Equal Protection, 86 Harv. L. Rev. 1, 34 (1972). See, Wark v. Robbins, 458 F.2d 1295, 1297 n.4 (1st Cir. 1972); Sex Discrimination in High School Athletics, supra at 346-349, 370. This is especially true where the classification involves the interest of females in securing an education.

We believe that in view of the nature of the classification and the important interests of the plaintiffs involved, the High School League has failed to demonstrate that the sex-based classification fairly and substantially promotes the purposes of the League's rule.

(A)

First, we do not believe the High School League has demonstrated a sufficient rational basis for their conclusion that women are incapable of competing with men in non-contact sports. The trial court specifically found that the plaintiffs were capable of such competition and the evidence indicates that the class of women, like the class of men, includes individuals with widely different athletic abilities. As the Fifth Circuit has recognized in activities requiring physical strength, technique may be just as important as physical capacity. Weeks v. Southern Bell Telephone Company, 408 F.2d 228, 236 (5th Cir. 1969). And, "[t]echnique is hardly a function of sex." Ibid. at 236. Furthermore, the record indicates that in non-contact sports, such as those involved here, factors such as coordination, concentration, agility and timing play a large role in achieving success. No objective evidence was introduced comparing males and females with respect to these factors. See, Sex Discrimination in High School Athletics, supra at 363.

Essentially, the testimony of those witnesses who concluded that females were wholly incapable of competing with men in interscholastic athletics was based on subjective conclusions drawn from the physiological difference between the sexes by individuals who were not themselves familiar with mixed competition. This subjective testimony is particularly susceptible to discrimination based on stereotyped notions about the nature of the sexes.

Furthermore, the High School League failed to show that it had established any objective nondiscriminatory minimum standards for evaluating qualifications for non-contact interscholastic athletics. The record indicates, in fact, that the schools had adopted no cut policies allowing male students, no matter *how untalented,* to participate in the non-contact interscholastic sports involved here.

We note that there is at least one systematic study of mixed competition in non-contact sports. In 1969, a rule of the New York State Department of Education prohibiting competition between males and females in non-contact sports was challenged. The Department reports: ·

> Faced with the need for valid supporting data, the Education Department gathered all the evidence it could find on the matter. Very little was reported in professional literature. In the limited number of experiences that came to its attention wherein girls competed on boys' teams (primarily at the college level), the only negative factor reported was that it was not yet socially acceptable for a girl to defeat a boy in athletic competition. Discussion with various medical personnel elicited a unanimous expression that there are no medical reasons to prohibit girls from competing on boys' teams in selected non-contact sports. Thus, it became clear that the Department had little or nothing to support its traditional position. It was then suggested that a moratorium be declared on a decision until some evidence could be gathered through experience. Thus, the experimental project came into being.

University of the State of New York, The State Department of Education, Division of Health, Physical Education and Recreation, Report on Experiment: Girls on Boys Interscholastic Athletic Teams, March 1969–June 1970, 1 (February, 1972).

The Department then conducted an experiment in which one hundred schools over a sixteen-month period maintained athletic teams on which both males and females participated. The results of the experiment were overwhelmingly favorable to continuing mixed competition:

> Should the practice of allowing girls to compete on boys' athletic teams be continued? Eighty percent of the principals, directors, women physical educators, coaches, and physicians involved in the experiment voted in favor of continuing the practice, either as an experiment or as legal policy. Slightly more than 90 percent of the boy team members, girl participants, parents, coaches and opposing coaches also favored continuation of the practice. . . .

Id. at 4. As a result of the experiment, New York amended its rules to allow females to compete with males.[8]

(B)

Second, even if we assume, arguendo, that, on the whole, females are unlikely to be able to compete with males in non-contact interscholastic sports, this fact alone

---

8. New York has determined that:

(4) Girls may participate on the same team with boys in interscholastic competition in the sports of archery, badminton, bowling, fencing, golf, gymnastics, riflery, rowing (but only as coxswain), shuffleboard, skiing, swimming and diving, table tennis, tennis, and track and field, provided the school attended by a girl wishing to participate in any such sport does not maintain a girls' team in that sport. In exceptional cases, the principal or the chief executive officer of a school may permit a girl or girls to participate on a boys' team in a designated sport or sports, notwithstanding the fact that the school maintains a girls' team in that sport or sports." Section 135.4 of the Regulations of the Commissioner of Education.

New York is not alone in having concluded that mixed competition is feasible. A new Michigan statute states:

"Female pupils shall be permitted to participate in all noncontact interscholastic athletic activities, including but not limited to archery, badminton, bowling, fencing, golf, gymnastics, riflery, shuffleboard, skiing, swimming, diving, table tennis, track and field and tennis. Even if the institution does have a girls' team in any non-contact interscholastic athletic activity, the female shall be permitted to compete for a position on the boys' team. Nothing in this subsection shall be construed to prevent or interfere with the selection of competing teams solely on the basis of athletic ability." M.C.L.A. 340.379(2). Pub. Act No. 138 (Mich. May 22, 1972).

Even in Minnesota, mixed competition exists in St. Paul pursuant to an exemption from the usual League rule. See, Brenden v. Independent School District 742, supra 342 F. Supp. at 1234 n.17.

In addition, recently groups such as the National Collegiate Athletic Association and the Big Eight Athletic Conference have eliminated provisions in their rules which prohibited females from competing in interscholastic activities with men.

would not justify precluding qualified females like Brenden and St. Pierre from such competition. Reed v. Reed, supra. Cf., Stanley v. Illinois, 405 U.S. 645, 92 S. Ct. 1208, 31 L. Ed. 2d 551 (1972).

In *Reed,* the Court found unconstitutional a portion of the Idaho probate code which granted males a mandatory preference over females in competing for the right to administer an estate without regard for the individual qualifications of the female applicant. One of the reasons which the Idaho Supreme Court gave for upholding the statute was that the "legislature when it enacted the statute evidently concluded that in general men are better qualified to act as an administrator than are women." Reed v. Reed, 465 P.2d 635, 638 (Idaho 1970). Because of this, in the Idaho Supreme Court's opinion, eliminating females from consideration "is neither an illogical or arbitrary method devised by the legislature to resolve an issue that would otherwise require a hearing as to the relative merits . . . of the two or more petitioning relatives." Id. at 638.

The United States Supreme Court did not discuss the validity of the assumption that women are less qualified than men to be administrators of estates. Nonetheless, it concluded that the preference for men was arbitrary:

> . . . To give a mandatory preference to members of either sex over members of the other, merely to accomplish the elimination of hearings on the merits, is to make the very kind of arbitrary legislative choice forbidden by the Equal Protection Clause of the Fourteenth Amendment. . . .
>
> By providing dissimilar treatment for men and women who are . . . similarly situated, the challenged section violates the Equal Protection Clause. . . .

Reed v. Reed, supra 404 U.S. at 76–77, 92 S. Ct. at 254.

In our view, *Reed* precludes a state from using assumptions about the nature of females as a class, to deny to females an individualized determination of their qualifications for a benefit provided by the state.

In the present case, the underlying purpose of the High School League's rule is, as we have indicated, to insure that persons with similar qualifications will compete with each other. Yet, females, whatever their qualifications, have been barred from competition with males on the basis of an assumption about the qualifications of women as a class. The failure to provide the plaintiffs with an individualized determination of their own ability to qualify for positions on these teams is under *Reed,* violative of the Equal Protection Clause. See, Note, Sex Discrimination in High School Athletics, supra.

The High School League argues that invalidation of its rule will have an adverse impact on the future development of opportunities for females in interscholastic sports. This argument is too speculative to have merit, particularly in view of the recent statement of the Minnesota State Board of Education calling on its local boards to provide equal education opportunity for females, see Eliminating Sex Bias in Education, supra, and the League's own stated commitment to interscholastic athletics for females. This argument certainly can not be used to deprive Brenden and St. Pierre of their rights to equal protection of the law. With respect to these two females, the record is clear. Their schools have failed to provide them with opportunities for interscholastic competition equal to those provided for males with similar athletic qualifications. Accordingly, they are entitled to relief See, Haas v. South Bend Community School Corporation, [289 N.E.2d 495 (Ind. 1972)].

We are, of course, always reluctant to invalidate state and local action as unconstitutional. We have, however, no choice where a group of citizens has been deprived of the equal protection of the law. The likelihood of similar state action in this area being found unconstitutional in the future will be minimized if the League and the local school board affirmatively respond to the request of the Minnesota Department of Education to:

> . . . Review all State Board rules and regulations and take steps to eliminate all sex-based requirements for courses and extra-curricular activities for students.

[And] . . . Provide equal access for all pupils to local school facilities, programs, equipment, staff services, and financial resources.

Eliminating Sex Bias in Education, supra at 6.

Affirmed.

BUCHA v. ILLINOIS HIGH SCHOOL ASSOCIATION
351 F. Supp. 69 (N.D. Ill. 1972)

MEMORANDUM OPINION AND JUDGMENT ORDER

AUSTIN, District Judge.

I. Facts

Plaintiffs are two female students at Hinsdale Center Township High School who were excluded from trying out for and participating on the school's interscholastic swimming team solely because of their sex. They allege that this discrimination is necessitated by the rules of the Illinois High School Association (the "IHSA"), which is an unincorporated association of approximately 790 Illinois high schools that regulates interscholastic sports among its members. Three IHSA by-laws are challenged in this action. The first is a rule prohibiting member schools from conducting interscholastic swimming competition for girls. Since the commencement of this suit that by-law has been amended to allow interscholastic swimming meets for girls,[1] but those contests are subject to the second challenged by-law, which places limitations on girls' athletic contests that are not applicable to those available to the boys.[2] Moreover, it is asserted that the girls' contests are purposely conducted in a manner that emphasizes intramural, multi-sport activities which are devoid of the concentration and competitive emphasis that is characteristic of boys' extracurricular sports. Finally, plaintiffs challenge a recent amendment to the IHSA by-laws which completely prohibits competition between members of the opposite sex. . . .

. . . The relevant inquiry here is whether the challenged classification is rational, Reed v. Reed, 404 U.S. 71, 92 S. Ct. 251, 30 L. Ed. 2d 225 (1971), and this court finds that it is rational even under plaintiffs' description of the facts. . . .

High school interscholastic sports are properly a part of a school's overall educational program because they promote an interest in athletics and thereby encourage the students to participate in activities that benefit them physically and mentally. Clearly, both boys and girls benefit from participation in athletics, so it is appropriate to note at this point that this case does not deal with the total absence of a girls' athletic program. Rather, what is questioned is a matter of degree and professional judgment, that is, given the uncontroverted existence of a statewide athletics program open to all girls, plaintiffs assert that the decision of Illinois' physical educators to conduct separate athletic con-

---

1. By-law A-II-14 as amended states:

"No school belonging to this Association shall permit girls to participate in interscholastic athletic contests with the following specific exceptions: Interscholastic contests in archery, badminton, bowling, fencing, golf, gymnastics, swimming, tennis and track and field may be permitted, and sports days may be held in basketball, field hockey, soccer, softball and volleyball provided: that each sport included in sports days is taught by a girls' physical education teacher as part of the girls' physical education curriculum and intramural program; that no girl shall participate in more than one sport at any sports day; that no school shall be permitted to enter girls in more than four sports days in the same sport during a school year; and that all such athletic contests and sports days be conducted under the rules prescribed by the Illinois League of High School Girls' Athletic Associations."

2. The restrictions applicable only to girls include a prohibition on organized cheering, a one dollar limitation on the value of awards, and a prohibition on overnight trips in conjunction with girls' contests.

tests for the sexes and to provide a different program for each sex is not rationally related to the overall educational objectives in sponsoring sporting events. With that proposition this court is not prepared to agree.

Since the instant inquiry probes only the *rationality* of separate programs for the sexes, this court takes judicial notice of the fact that at the pinnacle of all sporting contests, the Olympic games, the men's times in each event are consistently better than the women's. In the hearing on the motion for a preliminary injunction in this matter, it was shown that the times of the two boy swimmers sent to the state championship contest from Hinsdale were better than those ever recorded by either of the named plaintiffs. Moreover, plaintiffs' claim that the physical and psychological differences between male and female athletes are "unfounded assumptions" is refuted by expert testimony presented and received in a case which plaintiffs themselves cite in their favor. All of these facts lend substantial credence to the fears expressed by women coaches and athletes in defendants' affidavits that unrestricted athletic competition between the sexes would consistently lead to male domination of interscholastic sports and actually result in a decrease in female participation in such events. This court finds that such opinions have a rational basis in fact and are a constitutionally sufficient reason for prohibiting athletic interscholastic competition between boys and girls in Illinois.

Similarly, the uncontroverted existence of a bona fide athletic program for girls coupled with the physical and psychological differences noted above also support the rationality the IHSA's decision to conduct girls' interscholastic sports programs different from the boys'. Plaintiffs cite the affidavit of the Associate Secretary of the Committee on the Medical Aspects of Sport of the American Medical Association, who reported that a trial study of integrated athletic teams in New York revealed no harmful consequences on either the boys or girls and was indeed beneficial to the participants. This merely reinforces my opinion that judicial restraint is appropriate here, for the question of what is the best program for girls' sports is one upon which even the experts apparently disagree. Moreover, what is the best program is not properly an issue here, since this case presents only the question of what is a constitutionally permissible program.

Finally, plaintiffs cite sex discrimination cases dealing with equal employment opportunity under Title VII of the 1964 Civil Rights Act, 42 U.S.C. §2000e (1970). These cases are simply inapposite because that statute represents a special legislative exception to the previously controlling rational relationship test that would otherwise apply.

Note: Equal Status for Women's Teams or Equal Rights for Individual Athletes?

Most of the early cases have involved situations where there was a boys' team but no girls' team. The courts would have a more difficult question if there were separate teams for each sex in each sport, and girls still desired to compete on boys' teams. See, e.g., Bucha v. Illinois High School Association, supra. One commentator who is a feminist and civil liberties lawyer suggests that "separate but equal" is the only way to guarantee fair treatment to female athletes.[9]

> Because girls have not enjoyed the same physical and psychological opportunities as boys to develop athletically, I believe that resources must be made available for at least two interscholastic teams per sport: one for girls and one for boys. While sex-segregated teams may sound like the long-discredited separate-but-equal doctrine, it is through a process of careful elimination that this policy emerges as the most viable. The four other alternatives listed below are simply *not* equitable:
> 1. A system involving ability-determined first- and second-string teams will

9. Fasteau, Giving Women a Sporting Chance, Ms. Magazine, July 1973, p. 58.

undoubtedly result in two mostly male teams and no greatly increased participation for females.

2. A first-string team that is sex-integrated to absorb top talent of both sexes plus a second-string all-girl team would increase girls' participation but it runs afoul of boys' rights by excluding them from the second team.

3. If the first-string team is based solely on ability and the second-string team members are evenly divided, boys and girls, the system ends up favoring boys again by assuring them representation on what amounts to one and one-half out of two teams.

4. The quota solution requiring half boys and half girls presents both practical and psychological problems: intrateam ostracizing of the girls who dilute the overall performance, and interteam exploitation of the "weaker" sex members of the opposing team.

So we're left with the separate-but-equal solution. While it may penalize the outstanding female athlete who must play on girls' teams regardless of whether she qualifies for the boys' team, it has the singular advantage of giving boys and girls an equal opportunity to compete interscholastically. This is, in my view, an adequate response to the argument that in sports, as in other areas, women should be compensated for past discriminations. The contention that women should be allowed to try out for men's teams, even if there are comparable women's teams, is potentially unfair to the men who can't make the men's teams but might make the women's teams. Even more importantly, it cheats the women's team which would lose its best athletes to the male squads, thus setting women's sports back even farther.

Where girls' sports are taken seriously at the high school and college level, the results are striking. Throughout Iowa, for instance, girls' basketball draws the bigger crowds. The coaching is excellent, and the facilities and equipment are first-rate. Because women's basketball is a matter of state pride, high school and college women in Iowa eagerly try out without feeling the traditional stigma and scorn so frequently associated with women's sports.

Marcia Federbush of Michigan suggests an Olympic-style system to solve the inevitable imbalances of participation, resource allocation and spectator interest: the girls' varsity and the boys' varsity would *together* constitute the school's varsity team. On the same day or evening both teams would play their counterparts from another school (alternating the game order since the second game is inevitably the star attraction). At the end of the two games the point scores would be totaled. If the boys' basketball squad won 75-70 and the girls' basketball team lost with a score of 60-80, the final school score would amount to a 15-point loss.

The girls' and boys' teams would travel together and use the same facilities. They would enjoy equally skilled (and equally paid) coaching staffs, equal budgets, game schedules, uniforms, equipment, combined publicity attention, and a shared spotlight.

Clearly, when interdependence leads to team success, the primary advantage would be the shared commitment in *two* strong separate-but-equal teams.

Another commentator strongly disagrees:[10]

There are three reasons why the separate but equal doctrine should be rejected in sex discrimination in athletics cases. First, with respect to non-contact sports, no intimate body contact is required so there is no justification for separation on that basis. Second, separation of the sexes in athletics does not only imply inferiority for women, it is premised on it. Third, separate girls' teams can never be equal in fact to boys' teams. The high school leagues themselves proved this with their physiological data. Although that data may not be valid as applied to specific individuals, it is valid for women generally. It follows then that the girls' team will generally be less skilled as a whole than the boys' team. Thus the boys' team will always have the "prestige" factor which was determinative in *Kirstein*. As long as this prestige factor obtains, boys' and girls' teams will never be truly equal. The exceptional female athlete would still not be afforded equal treatment with male athletes of the same ability. . . .

10. Note, Sex Discrimination in High School Athletics, 57 Minn. L. Rev. 339, 369, 371 (1972).

The significance of sex discrimination in athletics cases extends beyond the immediate changes which they will cause in high school athletic programs. A basic tenet of equality is that people should be treated as individuals and not on the basis of commonly-held stereotypes. One such stereotype posits that women cannot perform physical tasks as well as men because of their physiological disabilities. A sound and well-reasoned holding that such assumptions are insufficient to justify differences in treatment without an individualized determination would be a step forward in the area of women's rights.

The question is difficult: What best serves the interests of women — promoting to the fullest the exceptional female athletes, or providing resources for good segregated teams so that all women will have a chance to play? There are political and legal problems with the inconsistency of allowing sports programs premised on sex-based averaging (for the good of women in general), while arguing for individualized determinations in the application of state "protective" labor legislation or armed services regulations (where the physical and psychological factors may also be thought to apply.) Should the individual women who do not fit the stereotypes be held back in order to benefit their "average" sisters? Perhaps the decision should be left to the women athletes themselves.

A fundamental problem with sex segregation is that it maintains the cultural differences between male and female athletics. Female sports have fallen into a noncompetitive unrigorous mold which does not develop skills to the fullest and which also fails to provide much fun.[11] Note, for example, in *Bucha*, the mention and incidental approval of "a prohibition on organized cheering" at girls' sports, a one-dollar limitation on the value of awards,[12] and a prohibition on overnight trips. The court also approves a rule which limits each girl to participating in only one sport on a "sports day" and which limits the school to four sports days in each sport each year. There is little question that rules like these maintain the inferiority of women's sports, or that it will be more difficult to break down the sex stereotyped patterns unless sex segregation is ended.

Another alternative to simply abolishing any consideration other than athletic ability for team selection might be height and weight limits, with rules permitting individuals to compete above their levels if they demonstrate sufficient skill. The resulting sports program would be scrutinized to ensure that the neutral rules on which the system was based did not fall more heavily on women than on men. Thus, a school would have to spend its sports money in such a way as to ensure that both men and women participated in equivalent numbers and with roughly equal facilities and expenditures per capita, while allowing students to participate on the basis of their individual characteristics and preferences rather than sex-based averages.

NOTE: SEX DISCRIMINATION IN ATHLETIC EXPENDITURES

The disparities in the amount of money spent by colleges and school systems for sports activities are shocking. For example, Billie Jean King testified in Senate hearings in November 1973 to the following athletic budgets:[13]

11. This perception is supported by an account of women's status in athletics by Post, Female Athletics: From the Dark Age of Discrimination to an Era of Legislative-Judicial Enlightenment (unpublished student paper, Georgetown University Law Center, Fall 1973). Post's work has also been helpful in the preparation of the rest of this section on athletics.

12. The limitation on the amount of awards is typical of the problems of women's athletics, from almost nonexistent athletic scholarships for women to the enormous disparities in prize money in the professional golf and tennis circuits. See Hearings on S. 2518 Before the Senate Committee on Labor and Public Welfare, 92nd Cong., 1st Sess., Nov. 9, 1973, Testimony of Ms. Billie Jean King; Gilbert and Williamson, Sport is Unfair to Women, Part I, Sports Illustrated, May 25, 1973 at p. 92; and Collins, Billie Jean King, Ms. Magazine, July 1973 at p. 42.

13. Hearings on S. 2518, supra footnote 12, Testimony of Ms. Billie Jean King.

Fairfield, Pennsylvania
(Kindergarten–Twelfth; 800 students)
> *Female:* $460
> *Male:* $19,880

University of Washington
(41 percent women; 26,000 undergraduates)
> *Female:* 0.9 percent of a total budget of $2 million — $18,000

Vassar
(1400 women; 700 men)
> *Female:* $2,000
> *Male:* $4,750

Syracuse Public Schools
> 1969
>> *Female:* $200
>> *Male:* $90,000
>
> 1970
>> *Female:*   0
>> *Male:* $87,000

New Brunswick, N.J. (senior high school)
> *Female:* $2,250
> *Male:* $25,575

Must public schools spend equal amounts on sports activities for boys and girls? Could disparities be justified on the basis of differences in demand among boys and girls? Would a requirement of equality be served if funds for boys' sports went into traditional competitive sports, while equivalent funds for girls went into activities geared especially for them, such as modern dance and exercise? Note that there is discrimination against boys who are interested in the latter activities, as well as that against girls who want to play sports traditionally reserved for boys.

In New Haven, Connecticut, women high school students and teachers recently obtained a favorable settlement in a suit challenging "a systematic pattern of sex discrimination" in the funding of varsity sports.[14] The suit was brought when teachers who had been coaching basketball, track, softball, and volleyball at two local high schools submitted a budget request to the city. The city budgeted $121,000 for men's varsity teams and refused to budget anything for women. The settlement provides that teams will be established for women in all sports sanctioned by the Connecticut Interscholastic Athletic Conference for which there is sufficient demand. The schools will immediately provide teams in basketball at one high school and softball, track and field, tennis, and volleyball at all three high schools, with a budget limitation for volleyball of $1000 for each school. *Wright v. City of New Haven,* Civ. No. 15927 (D. Conn., Order of Jan. 18, 1974). Apparently, the suit does not foreclose women from seeking admission to all-male teams when there is not sufficient demand for the establishment of a separate women's team.

NOTE: CONTACT SPORTS

The distinction between contact and noncontact sports has been fairly important in the litigation. For example, in Morris v. Michigan State Board of Education, 472 F.2d 1207 (6th Cir. 1973), the court of appeals ordered the district court to amend its preliminary injunction against preventing or obstructing girls from participating fully in varsity

14. This account of the background of the lawsuit is based on Henderson, Sports Victory in the Court of Law, Modern Times, Jan. 1974. The attorney was Michael Avery of Roraback, Williams and Avery, New Haven, Conn., assisted by Cookie Polan and Susan Kovac, a Stanford law student specializing in sex discrimination cases on an externship program.

interscholastic athletics because of their sex by inserting the word "noncontact" between "interscholastic" and "athletics." The court of appeals observed that there was no case or controversy with regard to contact sports. The courts' unwillingness to order integration of contact sports is a significant limitation on sex equality, since baseball and basketball are classified as contact sports along with wrestling, boxing, and football. As a legal matter, can the categories of contact and noncontact sports stand without more rigid definition?

What concerns underlie this distinction? Two possibilities are attitudes about the sexuality of close physical contact between the sexes, and the belief that all women are too fragile to play contact sports with men. As to the first issue, does the constitutional right to privacy justify sex segregation in contact sports? Can sports be distinguished on the basis of the kind of physical contact involved — e.g., segregate wrestling but not basketball? Does the age of the athletes make any difference?

As to the fragility of women, Fasteau argues:[15]

> That only noncontact sports are considered suitable for sex-integration is non-sensical. As one proponent for the integration of contact sports puts it: "If we are worried about girls' breasts and internal organs then give them chest and belly protectors. We haven't spared our male football players any expense in that department. We can't declare that because we think many or even most girls cannot or will not play in certain sports that *none* may therefore be allowed to."

In terms of the fragility of sexual organs, a better argument could probably be made for excluding men from contact sports than for excluding women. Passing the question of whether young people should be societally encouraged to engage in the violence inherent in contact sports, isn't it sexist to allow boys to risk head injuries and broken bones in football and not girls? Under the Equal Rights Amendment, if a showing could be made that smaller people ran a higher risk of injury in certain sports than larger people, could schools exclude students below a certain height and weight from participation, even if more women were thereby excluded? What about the availability of less drastic (i.e., sex-neutral) alternatives, such as changing the rules of a game to make it less violent?

NOTE: PHYSICAL EDUCATION CLASSES

The cases discussed thus far have concerned interscholastic athletic programs and not physical education classes, which are a required part of high school curricula in most states and are almost universally sex-segregated. What are the arguments for and against sex integration of physical education classes? Do they differ from the arguments for and against sex-integrated interscholastic competition?

NOTE: ATHLETIC PROGRAMS NOT RELATED TO EDUCATIONAL INSTITUTIONS

The movement to obtain better athletic opportunities for women has not been limited to public schools. The demands and protests of professional women athletes in golf and tennis have been widely publicized, as well as the efforts of women to become jockeys, all of which have met with considerable success.[16] A successful suit has also

15. Fasteau, supra footnote 9, at 103.

16. See, e.g., Gilbert and Williamson, Sport is Unfair to Women, Part I, Sports Illustrated, May 25, 1973 at p. 94; Part II, June 4, 1973, at p. 45; Part III, June 11, 1973, at p. 60; Collins, Billie Jean King, Ms. Magazine, July 1973, p. 39.

been brought to compel the Little League to allow girls as well as boys to participate. National Organization for Women v. Little League, Inc., Docket No. OJO5SB-0493 (N.J. Div. on Civ. Rts., January, 1974). The suit was brought under New Jersey's statute forbidding sex discrimination in public accommodations, so the case did not make law on whether or not the league is sufficiently imbued with state action to be reached under the Fourteenth Amendment Equal Protection Clause. See also *Magill v. Avonworth Baseball Conference,* 364 F. Supp. 1212 (W.D. Pa. 1973), in which a federal district court upheld the discrimination on the grounds that the league was not imbued with state action and that baseball was a contact sport.

B. Other Educational Practices Which Can Be Challenged Under the Equal Protection Clause

The Citizens' Advisory Council on the Status of Women recently outlined many problems needing attention in the area of education. In any local community, the council would look for[17]

> . . . the degree of sex discrimination . . . with respect to (1) schools restricted to one sex, (2) courses of study in co-educational schools restricted to one sex, (3) the per capita expenditure of funds by sex for physical education courses and physical education extra curricular and other extra curricular activities, (4) sex sterotyping in textbooks, library books, and other curriculum aids, (5) school activities, such as hall patrols, safety squads, room chores, etc., and (6) promotion of teachers.

Guidance counselors also offer sex-stereotyped advice about jobs and careers to students. Many of the same problems exist in colleges and graduate schools. Additional problems at that level include restrictive quotas on the admission of women and unequal scholarship aid. A number of studies of sex discrimination in schools have been written in recent years; for a useful list, see Citizens' Advisory Council on the Status of Women, The Need for Studies of Sex Discrimination in Public Schools, Appendix: Useful Publications (revised September 1972). Lawsuits are beginning to be brought on some of these issues as well; see, for example, Sanchez v. Baron, C.A. No. 69-C-1615 (E.D.N.Y.) challenging exclusion of women from certain public school classes.

In addition, suits have been brought against the exclusion of pregnant students or unwed mothers; see Perry v. Grenada Municipal Separate School District, 300 F. Supp. 748 (N.D. Miss. 1969); Ordway v. Hargraves, 323 F. Supp. 1155 (D. Mass. 1971); Shull v. The Columbus Municipal Separate School District, 338 F. Supp. 1376 (N.D. Miss. 1972); Farley v. Reinhard, No. 15569 (N.D. Ga. Sept. 22, 1971), 5 Clearinghouse Rev. 620 (1972); and Smith v. The Columbus Municipal Separate School District No. E C 71-3-K (N.D. Miss., Order dated Jan. 15, 1971), all requiring equal treatment for pregnant or unwed mothers except *Perry,* which allowed a hearing on the student's moral fitness. A lawsuit has also successfully contested the requirement that women students under twenty-one live in dormitories where no such requirement was imposed on men, Mollere v. Southeastern Louisiana College, 304 F. Supp. 826 (E.D. La. 1969).

A woman in Kentucky challenged restrictions on hours for women under twenty-one at a state college, where women students needed parental consent to have the regulation waived, and men did not, but the suit was unsuccessful. Robinson v. Board of Regents, 475 F.2d 707 (6th Cir. 1973). Culminating in the Supreme Court victory of LaFleur v. Cleveland Board of Education, __ U.S. __, 94 S. Ct. 791, __ L. Ed. 2d __ (1974), many lawsuits sought to invalidate rules requiring pregnant teachers to take a set period of leave before and after childbirth; see cases cited supra Chapter One, V. At least one

17. Women in 1971, 19-20 (1972).

suit seeking to extend the right to childbearing leave to male teachers has been brought; see Danielson v. Board of Higher Education, 4 FEP Cases 885 (S.D.N.Y. 1972) (opinion denying motion to dismiss).

C. Avenues of Attack Other Than the Equal Protection Clause

1. Federal Laws

a. Titles VI and IX of the Civil Rights Act of 1964, 42 U.S.C. 2000c et seq. (1973 Supp.)

Title IV was recently amended to allow suits by the United States Attorney General on equal protection grounds against sex discrimination in public schools, colleges, and universities. In the past, such suits have been primarily concerned with racial desegregation and, incidentally, with other types of racial discrimination, primarily in elementary and secondary schools. Title IX was also amended to extend to cases of sex discrimination the Attorney General's power to intervene on behalf of the United States in litigation already begun by others claiming denial of the equal protection of the laws under the Fourteenth Amendment.

b. Title IX of the Education Amendments of 1972

ROSS, THE RIGHTS OF WOMEN
131-135 (1973)

Title IX . . . forbids some private and public schools from discriminating on the basis of sex. . . . [It] covers any school — from the preschool level through graduate education — that received federal funds. However, it does *not* reach religious schools if a particular religion's tenets require the sex discrimination that the school practices. (If the religion's tenet does not require sex discrimination, then the school's practices are reached.) Title IX also exempts military schools, which are defined as schools training individuals for the U.S. military services or for the merchant marine.

> . . . Discrimination is defined very broadly: No person in the United States shall, on the basis of sex, be excluded from participation in, be denied the benefits of, or be subject to discrimination under any education program or activity receiving Federal financial assistance. . . .

The agencies administering this law — principally, the Department of Health, Education, and Welfare (HEW) — will publish regulations defining the discriminatory practices much more explicitly. . . .

. . . [However] Title IX specifically allows many schools to engage in discriminatory practices as to both admissions and living facilities. First, and of principal significance, it allows several kinds of educational institutions to discriminate in admissions policies. Presumably, this allows schools either to exclude women completely, to set up quota systems to limit their enrollment, or to demand that women meet higher admissions standards than men. The schools that may discriminate include preschool, elementary and secondary schools, whether public or private*; private undergraduate colleges (such as Harvard, Yale or Princeton); and public undergraduate colleges that have always been single-sex institutions.[20] In addition, any institution that was once a single-sex school and has begun to integrate under a Federally approved plan is given seven full years after the effective date of the Title (July 1, 1972) to continue to discriminate in admissions. Title IX in effect licenses many of the schools that practice the most blatant forms of discrimination to continue doing so. In fact, the only institutions prohibited from using discriminatory admissions policies are public and private vocational schools at all levels, integrated public undergraduate colleges, and public and private graduate and professional schools. Even in these categories, any school that has begun integrating under an approved plan has the seven-year grace period to continue to discriminate in admissions.[21]

Title IX specifically allows a second discriminatory practice — segregating living facilities by sex. . . .

. . . Any Federal agency that awards money — whether as grants, loans, or contracts — to a school can cancel that assistance if it finds that the school discriminates. The agency may also refuse to award such assistance in the future. Although many Federal agencies administer grant programs to educational institutions, HEW is the main grantor and as such will be the chief enforcement agency.

The threat of a cut-off of Federal money is a powerful weapon since many schools depend on this money for a major portion of their budget. Of course, HEW must be willing to make this threat and to carry through in the event of non-compliance if the law is to be effective. It remains to be seen whether HEW will be willing to do so.

It is important to understand the limitation of Title IX sanctions. There is no way for either women or HEW to force the school directly to stop discriminating — except insofar as a loss of federal money provides leverage to achieve that. If the school is willing to forego Federal aid, it can continue discriminating. Thus, Title IX differs greatly from the Equal Protection clause, under which a court can order a school to cease discriminating if the requisite "state action" is found to exist. In some circumstances, HEW can recommend that the Justice Department bring suit against an offending school. In that case, of course, a court could order the school to stop discriminating; however, this remedy is not the normal one under Title IX. . . .

Once HEW receives [a] . . . charge, it is required to investigate and conduct a

---

*Vocational schools at these levels, however, may *not* discriminate in their admission policies.

20. The number of single-sex public undergraduate colleges is fairly small. It includes the following all-female schools: Texas Women's University; Mississippi State College for Women; Longwood College (Va.); Radford College (Va.); Douglass College (N.J.) and Winthrop College (S.C.). The list of all-male public undergraduate schools is larger: Maine Maritime Academy; Massachusetts Maritime Academy; New Mexico Military Institute; State University of New York Maritime College; The Citadel Military College (S.C.); Virginia Military Institute; Air Force Institute of Technology; U.S. Air Force Academy; U.S. Coast Guard Academy; U.S. Merchant Marine Academy; U.S. Naval Academy; U.S. Naval Post-graduate School; California Maritime Academy. These male schools are exempt from Title IX coverage in two ways: they are military schools; and they have always been single-sex, public undergraduate colleges.

21. The seven-year grace period comes from a technically confusing section of the Title — Section 901(a)(2). Readers interested in full details should consult the HEW regulations when they are published and, if still confused, the HEW Office of the General Counsel. For the present purpose it is enough to know two things. First, all the schools whose discriminatory admissions policies are prohibited — professional, graduate, vocational and integrated public undergraduate schools — had one year from the effective date of the Title, or until July 1, 1973, to continue discriminatory admissions policies. After that, they must have stopped discrimination in admissions. Second, if a woman suspects discrimination in admissions, she should always file charges of sex discrimination with HEW even if the school claims it has the seven-year grace period. The school might not qualify for the grace period because it has no Federally approved plan, because it failed to submit the plan on time (by July 1, 1973), or because it began the process of integration too long ago. Or the school might not be adhering to its own plan and thus could still violate Title IX. So when in doubt, complain to HEW.

hearing to determine whether the school discriminates. (Whether this requirement is more theoretical than real remains to be seen.) Women may participate in these hearings only as witnesses or as [amicus curiae] . . . but if they are unhappy with the results, they can ask a U.S. Court of Appeals to review the HEW action. Sometimes women's organizations may also be allowed to participate as [amicus curiae]. . . .

c. The Public Health Service Act (PHSA)

ROSS, THE RIGHTS OF WOMEN
139-140 (1973)

. . . Under a recent amendment to the Public Health Service Act, sections 799A and 845[23] specifically prohibit schools and training programs in the health professions from discriminating against students on the basis of their sex. The prohibition applies only to schools and programs receiving financial assistance under Titles VII and VIII of the Public Health Service Act, but the vast majority of these schools do receive such assistance. The prohibition also applies to hospitals insofar as they operate medical schools, training programs, or even internships. Thus, women — or men — may now protest and seek legal redress if a hospital refuses to hire women interns, if a medical school limits its enrollment of women or refuses to admit people over 30 (which affects women more than men), or if a nursing school refuses to admit men.

. . . The Department of Health, Education and Welfare must cancel any Federal financial assistance — whether in the form of a grant, a loan guarantee, or a subsidy on interest payments — received under Titles VII or VIII of the Public Health Service Act by a school or program that discriminates. Theoretically, cancellation can occur in three ways. If the school fails to give HEW a written assurance that it will not discriminate, HEW *must* cut off or refuse to award the funds. HEW also conducts routine reviews to check for discrimination. Finally, someone can file a complaint with HEW, charging a program with discrimination. HEW would then conduct a hearing and cancel any financial assistance if it finds discrimination. Although women will not be allowed to participate in these hearings except as witnesses or [amici curiae] they will be able to ask a Federal court to review HEW action.

NOTE: THE RIGHTS OF TEACHERS

All school employees are protected from sex discrimination by Title IX. The PHSA provisions protect only those teachers and employees who work directly with students. Both Title VII of the 1964 Civil Rights Act and the Equal Pay Act have recently been amended to protect teachers against sex discrimination. Executive Order 11246, as amended by E.O. 11375, forbids sex discrimination in employment, hiring, and training by federal contractors, which includes most educational institutions, and requires affirmative action to correct discrimination. These last three antidiscrimination laws are discussed in Chapter Two.

23. For copies of these sections of the law and the HEW regulations, which will be published at 45 C.F.R. Part 83, write to: Office of Civil Rights, HEW 330 Independence Avenue, S.W., Washington, D.C.

2. State Laws

ROSS, THE RIGHTS OF WOMEN
142-143 (1973)

A few states have at least cursory provisions outlawing some forms of discrimination. They include Alaska, Illinois, Indiana, Massachusetts, and New York. A few other states have laws prohibiting educational discrimination on the basis of race, religion, or national origin, but not sex. . . . It is difficult to know how effective these state laws are. Some, administered by state civil rights agencies, provide for a complaint procedure and full enforcement powers. Others merely forbid some forms of discrimination and provide no apparent enforcement mechanism.

III. PUBLIC ACCOMMODATIONS: DISCRIMINATION AGAINST WOMEN IN PUBLIC PLACES

A. Introduction

Many places of public accommodation have been traditionally less than public when it comes to accommodating female customers. Escorted or single, rich or poor, women have encountered unexpected hostility or outright exclusion at hotels, bars, restaurants, and clubs throughout the country, despite the claims of these and other establishments to be open to members of the general public. Exclusion and segregation are variously defended as necessary to discourage prostitution, to protect women themselves, or, just as often, to protect the all-male atmosphere. The constitutional rights of privacy and freedom of association are sometimes asserted in this debate, but these principles need the most refined application when they are invoked against the principle of equality to ensure the maintenance of the all-male, or, for that matter, the all-female preserve.

Although sex discrimination in employment is barred by Title VII of the 1964 Civil Rights Act, no mention of sex appears in Title II, which bars discrimination in public accommodations. This can be explained by a combination of reasons, including the level of consciousness of sex bias at the time of the passage of the act and the fact that, almost overwhelmingly, exclusion from public accommodations in the United States has been on the basis of race. Still, instances of discrimination in public places, such as restaurants and bars, have affected women sufficiently to cause a turn to statutory remedies in several states.

A congressional statute barring sex discrimination in public accommodations would be based on the power of the federal government, derived from the Constitution. In Heart of Atlanta Motel, Inc. v. United States, 379 U.S. 241, 85 S. Ct. 348, 13 L. Ed. 2d 258 (1964), the Supreme Court probed for the constitutional basis of federal power to bar discrimination against blacks:[1]

> The legislative history of the [1964 Civil Rights Act] indicates that Congress based the Act on §5 and the Equal Protection Clause of the Fourteenth Amendment as well as its power to regulate interstate commerce under Art. I, §8, cl. 3, of the Constitution.
> The Senate Commerce Committee made it quite clear that the fundamental object of Title II was to vindicate "the deprivation of personal dignity that surely

1. 379 U.S. at 249-250, 85 S. Ct. at 13, L. Ed. 2d at 264.

accompanies denials of equal access to public establishments." At the same time, however, it noted that such an objective has been and could be readily achieved "by congressional action based on the commerce power of the Constitution." S. Rep. No. 872, [88th Cong., 2d Sess., February 10, 1964] at 16-17. Our study of the legislative record, made in the light of prior cases, has brought us to the conclusion that Congress possessed ample power in this regard, and we have therefore not considered the other grounds relied upon. This is not to say that the remaining authority upon which it acted was not adequate, a question upon which we do not pass, but merely that since the commerce power is sufficient for our decision here we have considered it alone. Nor is §201(d) or §202, having to do with state action, involved here and we do not pass upon either of those sections.

Thus even where race, the historic concern of the Equal Protection Clause, was involved, the Court preferred the Commerce Clause to the Fourteenth Amendment as a basis for federal power to intervene in a traditionally state domain. But in this and in a companion case, Justices Douglas and Goldberg concurred separately, arguing that the decision should rest on both grounds. Consider whether or not both grounds would form a valid basis for a statute barring sex discrimination. Could a woman bring an action against a restaurant that had refused to serve her on the basis of her sex by claiming violations of the unexercised commerce power? Why not? Would such a suit be possible if Congress were to amend Title II to include sex-based discrimination? Is discrimination by sex more or less amenable to congressional legislation under the Commerce Clause than race or color discrimination? Religious discrimination? National origin discrimination? What factors keep classification by sex from being exactly analogous to other classifications for purposes of the exercise of congressional power in this area?

What effects would the ratification of the Equal Rights Amendment have on Title II?

B. The Judicial Response

When courts have struggled with sex discrimination in public accommodations without statutory support, the results have been uneven.

SEIDENBERG v. McSORLEYS' OLD ALE HOUSE, INC.
317 F. Supp. 593 (S.D.N.Y. 1970)

Mansfield, District Judge.

Two determined ladies, both board members of the National Organization for Women ("NOW"), have brought this suit pursuant to 42 U.S.C. §1983[1] challenging defendant's 115-year practice of catering to men only. They claim that defendant's refusal to serve women at its bar constitutes a denial of rights secured by the Equal Protection Clause of the Fourteenth Amendment.[2] Both parties have moved for summary judgment. For reasons stated in detail below, plaintiffs' motion is granted and defendant's denied.

The essential facts are not in dispute. Defendant McSorleys' Old Ale House, Inc.

---

1. Title 42 U.S.C. §1983 provides that "Every person who, under color of any statute, ordinance, regulation, custom, or usage, of any State or Territory, subjects, or causes to be subjected, any citizen of the United States or other person within the jurisdiction thereof to the deprivation of any rights, privileges, or immunities secured by the Constitution and laws, shall be liable to the party injured in an action at law, suit in equity, or other proper proceeding for redress."

Title 28 U.S.C. §1343(3) establishes original jurisdiction in the district courts to entertain civil actions based upon §1983.

2. ". . . No State shall . . . deny to any person within its jurisdiction the equal protection of the laws."

is a New York corporation operating a bar located at 15 East 7th Street in New York City. While food may be purchased on the premises, the complaint specified, and it is conceded, that McSorleys' is "primarily a bar which serves alcoholic and non-alcoholic beverages." On January 9, 1969, plaintiffs, unescorted by any male companions, entered McSorleys' and seated themselves at the bar. Their request for service was refused by the bartender, who informed them that it was McSorleys' policy, and had been for 114 years, to refuse to serve women under any conditions. Their repeated requests for service were met with similar refusals. Thereupon they were escorted by the bartender to the door and voluntarily departed, wisely choosing to stage this battle of the sexes in the courthouse rather than resort to militant tactics. Their action accords with the principle that an ale house, with its "nut-brown drafts," should be treated as a peaceful center and source of happiness, once described by Johnson as "the throne of human felicity."

On June 24, 1969, plaintiffs commenced this action under 42 U.S.C. §1983, seeking both a declaratory judgment that defendant's refusal to serve women is illegal, discriminatory and unconstitutional, and an injunction against continuation of defendant's practice. Following Judge Tenney's denial of a motion to dismiss the complaint, 308 F. Supp. 1253 (S.D.N.Y. 1969), defendant filed its answer on December 15. These motions for summary judgment ensued.

Plaintiffs' action must stand or fall on the applicability of 42 U.S.C. §1983. We are in accord with Judge Tenney's conclusion that §201(a) of the Civil Rights Act of 1964, 42 U.S.C. §2000a(a), guaranteeing to all persons the full and equal enjoyment of public accommodations without discrimination on account of race, color, religion or national origin, applies neither to discrimination on the basis of sex, DeCrow v. Hotel Syracuse Corp., 288 F. Supp. 530, 532 (N.D.N.Y. 1968), nor to discrimination in a bar or tavern whose principal business is the sale of alcoholic beverages rather than food. Cuevas v. Sdrales, 344 F.2d 1019, 1020-1023 (10th Cir. 1965), cert. denied, 382 U.S. 1014, 86 S. Ct. 625, 15 L. Ed. 2d 528 (1966). . . .

There being "no genuine issue of material fact" between the parties, 6 J. Moore, Federal Practice ¶56.04[1] (2d ed. 1966), plaintiffs are entitled to summary judgment if they can establish that defendant was acting under color of state law in its continuing practice of refusing service to women, and that such refusal has denied plaintiffs the equal protection of the laws secured by the Fourteenth Amendment to the Constitution.

Beginning with Mr. Justice Bradley's opinion for the Court in the Civil Rights Cases, 109 U.S. 3, 3 S. Ct. 18, 27 L. Ed. 835 (1883), the principle has become firmly embedded in our constitutional law that the Equal Protection Clause of the Fourteenth Amendment reaches "only such action as may fairly be said to be that of the States. That Amendment erects no shield against merely private conduct, however discriminatory or wrongful." Shelley v. Kraemer, 334 U.S. 1, 13, 68 S. Ct. 836, 842, 92 L. Ed. 1161 (1948). No simple or precise test for distinguishing between state action and private action has, however, yet been devised. . . . [State action] may occur through the action of a state's executive body, its administrative and regulatory agencies, its legislature, or its courts. Lombard v. Louisiana, 373 U.S. 267, 273, 83 S. Ct. 1122, 10 L. Ed. 2d 338 (1963); Robinson v. Florida, 378 U.S. 153, 156, 84 S. Ct. 1693, 12 L. Ed. 2d 771 (1964); Avery v. Midland County, 390 U.S. 474, 479, 88 S. Ct. 1114, 20 L. Ed. 2d 45 (1968); Shelley v. Kraemer, 334 U.S. 1, 14-15, 68 S. Ct. 836, 92 L. Ed. 1161 (1948). The state need not expressly or specifically authorize, command or support the discriminatory conduct. Where the state has become sufficiently involved, its inaction, acquiescence or continuation of its involvement under circumstances where it could withdraw, may be sufficient. Burton v. Wilmington Parking Authority, 365 U.S. 715, 725, 81 S. Ct. 856, 6 L. Ed. 2d 45 (1961). Accordingly the issue has usually been resolved — almost always in favor of finding state action — by reference to the *kind* and *degree* of state involvement alleged. The issue has been posed in terms of whether "to some *significant extent* the State in any of its manifestations" has become involved in the discriminatory practice under attack. Burton

v. Wilmington Parking Authority, 365 U.S. 715, 722, 81 S. Ct. 856, 860, 6 L. Ed. 2d 45 (1961) (emphasis added). . . .

In approaching the task of "sifting facts and weighing circumstances," it is important to consider the purpose and function of the state action limitation. A finding of no state action does not eliminate the discrimination; it is a determination that regardless of the discrimination the Federal Government is not to be permitted to interfere. The function of the state action concept is to bar the Fourteenth Amendment from being used to govern purely private life and private decisions. The right of equal protection must be balanced against the countervailing rights of individual freedom of association and freedom of choice that govern in private matters. A person still has the right to invite to his home only those guests whom he or she chooses, whether they be all black, white, men, women, old or young. Under the Fourth Amendment a person's home remains his or her castle. Likewise, that person may, in a private transaction, sell his belongings to whomever he pleases. But once a property, facility or transaction becomes significantly impregnated with a state character the Equal Protection Clause controls. Burton v. Wilmington Parking Authority, supra.

In determining whether state involvement has risen to the level of "significance" for state action purposes, therefore, inquiry should focus upon the alleged sphere of privacy and autonomy in need of protection from federal intervention, as well as upon the customary search for some causal relation, however tenuous, between state activity and the discrimination alleged. For instance, a state lessee may not exclude black persons from its restaurant. Burton v. Wilmington Parking Authority, 365 U.S. 715, 81 S. Ct. 856, 6 L. Ed. 2d 45 (1961). The use of state courts to enforce purely private easements by owners of land prohibiting black occupancy has been held to constitute state action. Shelley v. Kraemer, 334 U.S. 1, 68 S. Ct. 836, 92 L. Ed. 1161 (1948). If the state engages in conduct having the effect of encouraging, tolerating or acquiescing in the discrimination, the Fourteenth Amendment may be invoked. Reitman v. Mulkey, 387 U.S. 369, 87 S. Ct. 1627, 18 L. Ed. 2d 830 (1967).[7]

Turning to the case before us, we are asked to find state action in the licensing of McSorleys' Old Ale House under the New York State Alcoholic Beverage Control Law. No other state involvement in the policy complained of is alleged by plaintiffs. There was no state enforcement of the refusal to serve, cf. Shelley v. Kraemer, 334 U.S. 1, 68 S. Ct. 836, 92 L. Ed. 1161 (1948); Griffin v. Maryland, 378 U.S. 130, 84 S. Ct. 1770, 12 L. Ed. 2d 754 (1964), no use of state property, cf. Burton v. Wilmington Parking Authority, 365 U.S. 715, 81 S. Ct. 856, 6 L. Ed. 2d 45 (1961); Boman v. Birmingham Transit Co., 280 F.2d 531 (5th Cir. 1960), 292 F.2d 4 (5th Cir. 1961), and no performance of a governmental function, cf. Terry v. Adams, 345 U.S. 461, 73 S. Ct. 809, 97 L. Ed. 1152 (1953); Evans v. Newton, 382 U.S. 296, 86 S. Ct. 486, 15 L. Ed. 2d 373 (1966), or the like. . . .

. . . The reasoning in favor of finding state action is that the state license enables the private licensee to engage in discriminatory conduct in the exercise of its franchise rights. To put it another way, without the state license to serve beer, defendant here could never have discriminated in the sale of beer. The license, it is argued, becomes a license to discriminate. See Justice Douglas' concurring opinions in *Garner, Lombard* and *Reitman,* supra. The opposing view is that in the absence of further evidence the license

7. While the growth of the state action concept has taken place almost entirely in the peculiarly sensitive context of "the sordid business of racial discrimination," Adickes v. S. H. Kress & Co., 398 U.S. 144, 90 S. Ct. 1598, 26 L. Ed. 2d 142 (June 2, 1970) (Brennan, J., concurring), we can see no reason in logic for applying different principles to a case involving discrimination on the basis of sex.

"Granted 'that the post–Civil War amendments ought to be taken as applying with a highly special force to the racial field,' 81 Harvard Law Review at 70, this would seem to go to the constitutionality rather than the existence of state action. Why would there not equally be 'state action' when the state refuses to prevent discrimination on the ground of religion, sex or age, even though in those cases the discrimination may be more easily justified?" H. Friendly, The Dartmouth College Case and the Public–Private Penumbra 35 n.50.

neither relates to nor authorizes discrimination in the exercise of the rights granted. It does not constitute the licensee an administrative agency of the state, and the state, as licensor, does not dictate to the licensee whom it must serve.[8] In rebuttal the advocates of state action reply that no such state authorization was found in the landlord-tenant relationship in Burton v. Wilmington Parking Authority, supra.

We believe that the present case is distinguishable from those licensing cases where courts have shied away from finding state action, because here we are not dealing merely with a bare state licensor-licensee relationship. In addition we are faced with a *pervasive* regulation by the state of the activities of the defendant, a commercial enterprise engaged in voluntarily serving the public except for women. Furthermore, the state has continued annually to renew defendant's license over the years despite its open discrimination against women, without making any effort in the exercise of the broad authority granted it, to remedy the discrimination or revoke the license which defendant must have in order to practice it. These circumstances convince us that the state's participation here is significant, as distinguished from situations where the licensor-licensee relationship is not accompanied by any extensive state regulation and the licensee is not a commercial establishment or has not offered its facilities or services to the public generally.[9]

For many years there has been no inherent right to engage in the sale of intoxicating beverages. The business has long been considered one peculiarly fraught with danger to the community, and the power of a state to eliminate traffic in liquor within its borders altogether, as well as to impose any limitations thereon short of absolute prohibition, or even to arrogate to itself the entire business of distributing and selling liquor to its citizens, e.g., 47 Penna. Stats. Ann. §§1-104, 2-207, 2-208, 3-301, 3-305 (1969), is unquestioned. While state regulation of traffic in liquor is of course subject to certain limits imposed by the Due Process and Equal Protection clauses of the Fourteenth Amendment, as well as by the Commerce Clause, nevertheless the state's regulatory power in this area is far broader than in the case of an ordinary lawful business essential to the conduct of human affairs. . . . It is in this context that the State of New York's relationship to McSorleys' as a liquor licensee must be examined.

8. Of the 10 state action cases we have been able to find in which a licensing argument figured significantly in the court's decision, only one, later reversed on appeal, has found state action in a mere licensor-licensee relationship. Mitchell v. Delaware Alcoholic Beverage Control Commission, 193 A.2d 294 (Del. Super.), rev'd, 196 A.2d 410 (Del. Super. 1963). See also State v. Brown, 195 A.2d 379, 384 (Del. Super. 1963). In one other case, Anderson v. Moses, 185 F. Supp. 727, 732-734 (S.D.N.Y. 1960), a license agreement providing for regulation of a restaurant concession in "meticulous detail," 185 F. Supp. at 732, contributed to a finding of state action. In addition, however, the concession's land, building and physical facilities were all owned by the City of New York, 185 F. Supp. at 733, rendering a finding of state action almost a foregone conclusion. The remaining cases have rejected the licensing rationale, holding variously that a license must be distinguished from a "franchise" or special privilege granted by the state, Madden v. Queens County Jockey Club, 296 N.Y. 249, 254-256, 72 N.E.2d 697, cert. denied, 332 U.S. 761, 68 S. Ct. 63, 92 L. Ed. 346 (1947), or that the licensing act in question simply conditioned the licensee's right to engage in purely private action, Weyandt v. Mason's Stores, 279 F. Supp. 283, 287 (W.D. Pa. 1968), cited with approval in Van Daele v. Vinci, 294 F. Supp. 71, 74 (N.D. Ill. 1968); Jones v. Alfred H. Mayer Co., 255 F. Supp. 115, 127 (E.D. Mo. 1966), aff'd, 379 F.2d 33, 45 (8th Cir. 1967), rev'd on other grounds, 392 U.S. 409, 88 S. Ct. 2186, 20 L. Ed. 2d 1189 (1968), or that it did not render the licensee an administrative agency of the State, Madden v. Queens County Jockey Club, 296 N.Y. 249, 254-256, 72 N.E.2d 697, cert. denied, 332 U.S. 761, 68 S. Ct. 63, 92 L. Ed. 346 (1947); Watkins v. Oaklawn Jockey Club, 86 F. Supp. 1006, 1016 (W.D. Ark. 1949), aff'd, 183 F.2d 440 (8th Cir. 1950), or that it did not authorize state officials to control the management of the business or to dictate who should be served, Williams v. Howard Johnson's Restaurant, 268 F.2d 845, 847-848 (4th Cir. 1959); Slack v. Atlantic White Tower System Inc., 181 F. Supp. 124, 129 (D. Md.), aff'd, 284 F.2d 746 (4th Cir. 1960); Simkins v. Moses H. Cone Memorial Hospital, 211 F. Supp. 628, 636-637 (M.D.N.C. 1962), rev'd on other grounds, 323 F.2d 959 (4th Cir. 1963), cert. denied, 376 U.S. 938, 84 S. Ct. 793, 11 L. Ed. 2d 659 (1964); Wood v. Hogan, 215 F. Supp. 53, 57-58 (W.D. Va. 1963) (distinguishing between licenses used as a means of regulating a business and licenses for mere tax purposes).

9. For cogent objections to findings of state action based upon the bare fact of licensing alone, absent such further consideration of the extent of state involvement in the challenged activity and the public character of the enterprise involved, see Lewis, The Sit-In Cases: Great Expectations, in The Supreme Court Review 1963, at 101, 116-118 (P. Kurland ed. 1963), and P. Freund, On Law and Justice 17-18 (1968).

Section 2 of the Alcoholic Beverage Control Law (McKinney's Consol. Laws, c. 3-B, 1970) ("ABC Law") sets forth the state policy and purpose underlying liquor regulation in New York:

> It is hereby declared as the policy of the state that it is necessary to regulate and control the manufacture, sale and distribution within the state of alcoholic beverages for the purpose of fostering and promoting temperance in their consumption and respect for and obedience to law. It is hereby declared that such policy will best be carried out by empowering the liquor authority of the state to determine whether public convenience and advantage will be promoted by the issuance of licenses to traffic in alcoholic beverages, the increase or decrease in the number thereof and the location of premises licensed thereby, subject only to the right of judicial review hereinafter provided for. It is the purpose of this chapter to carry out that policy in the public interest. The restrictions, regulations and provisions contained in this chapter are enacted by the legislature for the protection, health, welfare and safety of the people of the state.

Section 17 of the law grants to the State Liquor Authority ("SLA") power to issue, revoke, cancel or suspend for cause any of the 36-odd classes of licenses and permits provided for in the law (see §§50, 58, 60, 75 and 90); to limit in its discretion the number of licenses of each class — except hotel and restaurant licenses for on-premises consumption (see §64(1), (5)) — to be issued within the state; to inspect any premises where alcoholic beverages are manufactured or sold; to hold hearings, subpoena witnesses for examination under oath, and require production of any books or papers relevant to its inquiry; and to prohibit the sale of alcoholic beverages, without prior notice, in time of public emergency.

Defendant McSorleys' is the holder of a retail beer license for on-premises consumption issued under §55 of the Law. As such it is subject to a wide variety of provisions affecting the operation of its business. At the most elementary level, the personal qualifications of liquor licensees are subject to SLA review. The issuance of a license is a privilege afforded only to those of "high standing and character," Belden v. State Liquor Authority, 294 N.Y.S.2d at 851; Rios v. State Liquor Authority, 302 N.Y.S.2d at 81, and since license renewals are judged by the same standards applied to applications for new licenses, Wager v. State Liquor Authority, 4 N.Y.2d at 468, 176 N.Y.S.2d at 312, 151 N.E.2d at 870; Farina v. State Liquor Authority, 20 N.Y.2d 484, 491, 285 N.Y.S.2d 44, 49, 231 N.E.2d 748 (1967), a licensee may be deprived of the right to operate his business if the SLA determines that he has demonstrated sufficiently undesirable propensities. See SLA Rule 53.1(n) (McKinney App. 1970). Review of the SLA's exercise of discretion in refusing to issue or renew a license, moreover, is limited to the question whether its action was arbitrary and capricious. Wagner v. State Liquor Authority, supra; Farina v. State Liquor Authority, supra. Similarly a license may be revoked, cancelled or suspended pursuant to §118 for any of the multitude of causes listed in Rule 53.1, with review only slightly less limited than in the case of refusals to issue or renew. Farina v. State Liquor Authority, supra. We do not believe that the Authority's revocation or refusal to renew a license because of the licensee's discrimination in the exercise of the rights granted would be set aside as arbitrary or capricious.

In this respect the case before us is distinguishable from Coleman v. Wagner College, 429 F.2d 1120 (2d Cir., June 22, 1970), where the court, in refusing to find state action on the record before it, noted that the state had not reserved the power to approve or disapprove disciplinary regulations adopted by private colleges pursuant to §6450 of the State Education Law, McKinney's Consol. Laws. c. 16. Here the SLA is granted broad authority to revoke or refuse a license for reasons deemed by it to serve the "public convenience and advantage," which could include the prevention of unjustified discrimination in the exercise of the rights granted.

Besides limiting liquor licenses to persons meeting certain standards of character and behavior, the law imposes restrictive physical standards on premises licensed for the sale and consumption of alcoholic beverages. . . .

Most relevant to our inquiry, however, are the numerous provisions of the law directly regulating various aspects of a liquor licensee's day-to-day operations. For example, §§65 and 82 prohibit sales to minors, intoxicated persons, and habitual drunkards. Sections 105-a and 106(5), together with Rule 60.1, prescribe the hours during which alcoholic beverages may be sold and consumed on licensed premises. Section 100 2-a provides that no retailer of alcoholic beverages, except the holder of a grocery store beer license, shall employ any person under the age of 18 on licensed premises in any capacity requiring the handling of liquor. Section 102(2) forbids license holders to employ, in any capacity, any person who has been convicted of a felony or of any of a series of enumerated offenses and has not received either an executive pardon or the written approval of such employment from the SLA. Section 100(5) forbids retail licensees to sell alcoholic beverages on credit, and subsection (6) prohibits licensees from selling or purchasing alcoholic beverages by way of warehouse receipts, except as provided by Part 64 of the SLA Rules. Section 112 and Part 81 of the Rules set forth the terms and conditions of surety company bonds required of all licensees and permitees under the law. Section 17(8) gives the SLA power to prescribe forms of "all reports which it deems necessary to be made by any licensee or permitee," and §106(12) requires that retail licensees for on-premises consumption maintain on the premises precise records of daily purchases and sales, available for inspection by any authorized representative of the SLA.

The effect of this pervasive regulatory scheme goes beyond the immediate and extensive control over the operation of the businesses of liquor licensees. In addition, the general restrictions with which the retail sale of alcohol is hedged about, and in particular the restrictions imposed upon applications for new licenses, operate to limit competition to a degree sufficient to render the issuance of a license a commercially valuable privilege granted by the state to the licensee. At one time, indeed, it was the affirmative policy of the State of New York to foster and protect a monopolistic position for liquor licensees, on the theory that high, stable liquor prices would encourage temperance. Note, The New York State Liquor Market: The Rocky Road to Competition, 54 Cornell L. Rev. 113, 114 (1968).

. . . The standard applied by the Liquor Authority in passing upon applications for licenses under §55 (on-premises beer licenses) is that set forth in §2 of the law, which empowers the Authority to determine

> whether public convenience and advantage will be promoted by the issuance of licenses to traffic in alcoholic beverages, the increase or decrease in the number thereof and the location of premises licensed. . . .

The Authority's exercise of this broad power as reviewed by state courts reveals a tendency, notwithstanding the 1964 amendments, to protect the economic interests of established licensees by renewing their licenses and by denying applications of new entrants, at least where existing licensees have made substantial investments and there has been no growth in community population or usage. Forman v. State Liquor Authority, 17 N.Y.2d 224, 270 N.Y.S.2d 401, 217 N.E.2d 129, on remand, 52 Misc. 2d 641, 276 N.Y.S.2d 537 (Sup. Ct. 1966), rev'd, 28 A.D.2d 684, 282 N.Y.S.2d 452 (2d Dep't 1967), aff'd, 21 N.Y.2d 984, 290 N.Y.S.2d 909, 238 N.E.2d 215 (1968); William H. Van Vleck, Inc. v. Klein, 50 Misc 2d 622, 271 N.Y.S.2d 64, 67, 69 (Sup. Ct. 1966).

Thus, while it can no longer be said that liquor licensees in New York enjoy the benefits of a state-created monopoly, cf. the bus franchise involved in Boman v. Birmingham Transit Company, 280 F.2d 531 (5th Cir. 1960), 292 F.2d 4 (5th Cir. 1961); Karst & Van Alstyne, Comment: Sit-Ins and State Action, 14 Stan. L. Rev. 762, 775 (1962), the licensing practices of the SLA still operate to restrict competition between vendors of alcoholic beverages, thus conferring on license holders a significant state-derived economic benefit approximating the state support provided by the lease involved in Burton v. Wilmington Parking Authority, 365 U.S. 715, 724, 81 S. Ct. 856, 6 L. Ed. 2d 45 (1961).

Other significant factors revealing state involvement appear in the present case. Each year McSorleys' is required by §109 of the ABC Law to apply for renewal of its license. In addition to the information required to be furnished annually in support of these applications for renewal, it is also required to maintain detailed records, and its premises may be visited and inspected from time to time by ABC inspectors pursuant to §17. Since McSorleys' has pursued a uniform policy over the last 115 years of refusing service to women, it would be rather extraordinary if the SLA had not become aware of its discriminatory policy. Indeed the state has issued a renewal of its current license, to go into effect on June 30, 1970, with knowledge of the discrimination forming the basis of the present suit. The state's apparent acquiescence is a factor that has been considered elsewhere in resolving the issue of state action. Reitman v. Mulkey, 387 U.S. 369, 87 S. Ct. 1627, 18 L. Ed. 2d 830 (1967); Burton v. Wilmington Parking Authority, supra, 365 U.S. at 725, 81 S. Ct. 856.

Another criterion suggested for determining whether state involvement is to be deemed significant, whether the conduct may reasonably be viewed "as authorized by an agency of the state," see concurring opinion of Judge Friendly in Coleman v. Wagner College, supra (429 F.2d at 1127), commenting on Burton v. Wilmington Parking Authority, is also met here. McSorleys' prominently displays its state license to be seen by all visitors pursuant to §114 of the ABC Law, which provides:

> Before commencing or doing any business for the time for which a license has been issued said license shall be enclosed in a suitable wood or metal frame having a clear glass space and a substantial wood or metal back so that the whole of said license may be seen therein, and shall be posted up and at all times displayed in a conspicuous place in the room where such business is carried on, so that all persons visiting such place may readily see the same.

As we noted earlier in discussing the purpose of the state action limitation upon federal remedies under §1983, it is relevant to a finding of "state action" vel non to consider the nature of the alleged sphere of privacy and autonomy in need of protection from federal intervention. The question in a case like that before us is not whether *any* state involvement can be found; manifestly it can. The question is whether the state involvement that is undeniably present is involvement of a kind and extent that is "significant" in terms of present-day state action doctrine. One of the facts to be sifted and circumstances to be weighed in determining the true significance of state involvement, Reitman v. Mulkey, 387 U.S. 369, 378, 87 S. Ct. 1627, 18 L. Ed. 2d 830 (1967), is surely the context of that involvement, the nature of the activity in which state sanctions or control or support are felt.

Defendant's policy of refusing service to women hardly represents an exercise of individual choice in the use of private property. McSorleys' is open to the public. Any one of the male sex who is over 18 and neither drunk nor disorderly may enter and purchase a drink. The success of the business depends, in fact, upon large numbers of individuals doing precisely that, and a continuing invitation is extended to as many males as can, consistent with fire regulations, be served on the premises. In this significant respect defendant differs from a private men's club, which does not purport, and is not required, to serve the public.[20]

---

20. This distinction is reflected in the provisions of the Alcoholic Beverage Control Law, which regulate private-club licensees more loosely in certain respects than licensees whose premises are open to the public. Compare, for instance, Rule 47.7(d), prescribing those alterations in premises licensed under §55 which are considered "substantial" and which require payment of a fee and written permission from the Authority, with

Furthermore, it is meaningless to conceive of McSorleys' policy as in any sense an expression of personal preference on the part of a property owner. As the title of this action indicates, McSorleys' is corporately owned. Its decision to exclude women is a business decision. The proverbial right of a homeowner to choose whom he shall invite to dinner is in no sense bound up in McSorleys' freedom to exclude women. We deal with property voluntarily serving the public, devoted to a business in which volume of patronage is essential to commercial success. When a state licenses such an enterprise, in an area peculiarly subject to state regulation, pursuant to a statute imposing pervasive controls upon the conduct of the business, and under circumstances in which state licensing practices endow the license with a certain franchise value as well, the state's involvement in the operation of defendant's business, and hence by implication in the exclusionary practice under attack,[21] rises to the level of significance within the meaning of *Burton,* and requires McSorleys' to comply with the proscriptions of the Fourteenth Amendment "as certainly as though they were binding covenants written into the [license] itself." 365 U.S. at 726, 81 S. Ct. at 862.

We turn to the question of whether defendant's practice of refusing service to women denies plaintiffs the equal protection of the laws. The answer turns on whether such discrimination is without foundation in reason. It is only irrational or arbitrary distinctions or classifications that are forbidden by the Fourteenth Amendment.

Although the difference between the sexes has been the source of more poetry and prose than almost any other phenomenon of life, discrimination based on sex will be tolerated under the Equal Protection Clause only if it bears a rational relation to a permissible purpose of the classification. For instance, in Muller v. Oregon, 208 U.S. 412, 28 S. Ct. 324, 52 L. Ed. 551 (1908), the Supreme Court took account of differences in physical structure, strength and endurance of women in upholding a state work-hour limitation for women only. In Hoyt v. Florida, 368 U.S. 57, 82 S. Ct. 159, 7 L. Ed. 2d 118 (1961), home and family responsibilities were held to justify a jury duty exemption for women. Gruenwald v. Gardner, 390 F.2d 591 (2d Cir.), cert. denied sub nom. Gruenwald v. Cohen, 393 U.S. 982, 89 S. Ct. 456, 21 L. Ed. 2d 445 (1968), upheld Social Security Act provisions favoring women in computation of benefits as reasonably related to the legislative objective of redressing the imbalance in economic opportunity and achievement between men and women. Conversely sex-based discriminations have been nullified when no persuasive difference between women and men could be offered to justify the difference in treatment. See, e.g., United States ex rel. Robinson v. York, 281 F. Supp. 8 (D. Conn. 1968), invalidating a statute providing that women, but not men, could be

---

§(f) of the same Rule, listing only three such types of alterations in the case of club licensees. Similarly all nonsubstantial alterations may be made by a club without securing the permission of the Authority, Rule 47.3(f), while an eating place beer licensee like McSorleys' must secure permission for all but certain excepted alterations, Rules 47.1, 47.3(d).

License fees are half the retail on-premises amount for all clubs except luncheon and golf clubs, for which specific reduced rates are set. Section 66(4). Sales on credit, forbidden on the part of retail licensees generally, are permitted by club licensees to members and their guests, as well as by hotel licensees to registered guests and by off-premises wine licensees to duly organized churches, synagogues and other religious organizations. Section 100(5). And §100(4) provides that temporary portable bars are permitted without payment of the usual additional fee in hotels, restaurants and clubs at functions "to which members of the general public are not admitted."

21. The state involvement in this case is sufficiently pervasive, and defendant's operations sufficiently unitary, to escape the state action problems pointed out by Judge Friendly in Powe v. Miles, 407 F.2d 73, 81 (2d Cir. 1968). The court rejected the argument that state financial aid to Alfred University's Ceramics College could provide a basis for finding state action in the University's suspension of students from the University at large, and the argument that state regulation of educational standards within the University could be held to implicate the state generally in University policies toward demonstrations and discipline. Our case, like Burton v. Wilmington Parking Authority, avoids the *Powe* part-whole problem, and involves the state far more extensively and intimately in the management of defendant's business than the limited state regulation of educational standards in *Powe* involved New York in the operation of Alfred University.

committed to the state farm for indefinite terms exceeding the statutory maxima provided by the substantive statutes under which they were convicted; White v. Crook, 251 F. Supp. 401 (M.D. Ala. 1966), declaring unconstitutional a statute excluding women from jury service; and Karczewski v. Baltimore & O.R.R., 274 F. Supp. 169 (N.D. Ill. 1967), overturning the Indiana practice of denying women the right to sue for loss of consortium.[22]

In the case before us no difference between men and women, as potential customers of the defendant, has been offered as a rational basis for serving the one and not the other. It may be argued that the occasional preference of men for a haven to which they may retreat from the watchful eye of wives or womanhood in general to have a drink or pass a few hours in their own company, is justification enough; that the simple fact that women are not men justifies defendant's practice. The answer is that McSorleys' is a public place, not a private club, and that the preferences of certain of its patrons are no justification under the Equal Protection Clause. Such preferences, no matter how widely shared by defendant's male clientele, bear no rational relation to the suitability of women as customers of McSorleys'.

Nor do we find any merit in the argument that the presence of women in bars gives rise to "moral and social problems" against which McSorleys' can reasonably protect itself by excluding women from the premises. Social mores have not stood still since that argument was used in 1948 to convince a 6–3 majority of the Supreme Court that women might rationally be prohibited from working as bartenders unless they were wives or daughters of male owners of the premises. Goesaert v. Cleary, 335 U.S. 464, 69 S. Ct. 198, 93 L. Ed. 163 (1948). Quite apart from the differences between tending a bar and being served at one, we take judicial notice that the vast majority of bars and taverns do cater to both sexes. Without suggesting that chivalry is dead, we no longer hold to Shakespeare's immortal phrase "Frailty, thy name is woman." Outdated images of bars as dens of coarseness and iniquity and of women as peculiarly delicate and impressionable creatures in need of protection from the rough and tumble of unvarnished humanity[23] will no longer justify sexual separatism. At least to this extent woman's "emancipation" is recognized.

Finally, we note defendant's argument that it is unreasonable to impose upon it by judicial mandate the modifications in its sanitary facilities that would be required if it is directed to cater to women as well as men. As defendant's brief puts it, "Such collateral rules and regulations as would be necessary to make the overall mandate viable and workable, are most feasibly arranged by the enactment of laws by the legislature." Precisely such "collateral rules and regulations" have already been spelled out in the municipal codes dealing with health and sanitation, and are observed as a matter of course by the "vast majority of bars and taverns" mentioned above in which customers

---

22. But see Miskunas v. Union Carbide Corp., 399 F.2d 847 (7th Cir. 1968), cert. denied, 393 U.S. 1066, 89 S. Ct. 718, 21 L. Ed. 2d 709 (1969).

23. See, e.g., the concurring opinion of Mr. Justice Bradley in Bradwell v. State of Illinois, 83 U.S. (16 Wall.) 130, 141-142, 21 L. Ed. 442 (1872), in which he stated:

"Man is, or should be, woman's protector and defender. The natural and proper timidity and delicacy which belongs to the female sex evidently unfits it for many of the occupations of civil life. The constitution of the family organization, which is founded in the divine ordinance, as well as in the nature of things, indicates the domestic sphere as that which properly belongs to the domain and functions of womanhood. The harmony, not to say identity, of interests and views which belong, or should belong, to the family institution is repugnant to the idea of a woman adopting a distinct and independent career from that of her husband. . . . The paramount destiny and mission of woman are to fulfill the noble and benign offices of wife and mother. This is the law of the Creator. And the rules of civil society must be adapted to the general constitution of things, and cannot be based upon exceptional cases."

This view, expressed on the dawn of Victorianism, hardly reflects the view expressed by Socrates to the effect that "Woman, once made equal to man, becometh his superior," or that of Tennyson: "The woman's cause is man's. They rise or sink together; dwarfed or godlike, bond or free; if she be small, slight-natured, miserable, how shall men grow?"

of both sexes are served. Defendant should have no difficulty in ascertaining exactly what the law requires of it in this area.

Plaintiffs' motion for summary judgment is granted. . . .

NOTES

1. The court in *Seidenberg* assumes jurisdiction under 42 U.S.C. §1983 (and 28 U.S.C. §1343(3)), the section of the 1871 Civil Rights Act generally invoked by plaintiffs, very often blacks, alleging deprivation of their civil rights. Should this section be applied to sex discrimination, in view of the fact that women were considered but excluded from protection when the Fourteenth Amendment was passed? Though DeCrow v. Hotel Syracuse Corp., 288 F. Supp. 530 (N.D.N.Y. 1969), had held that a complaint seeking to enjoin refusal of service to women did not state a §1983 claim, the *Seidenberg* court declined to follow this ruling, and no appeal was taken. Outside of the Second Circuit, it has been expressly held that §1983 is not limited to actions alleging discrimination on the grounds of race, color, religion, or national origin, at least where damages are the remedy sought,[2] and that it reaches any invidious or unreasonable discrimination.[3] In Holmes v. New York City Housing Authority, 398 F.2d 262 (2d Cir. 1968) (on motion to dismiss), the Second Circuit found §1983 jurisdiction over violations of federal due process rights alleged by a class defined only in terms of the alleged deprivation —an implied recognition that §1983 reaches any substantial constitutional claim under the Equal Protection Clause. In Eisen v. Eastman, 421 F.2d 560 (2d Cir. 1969), Judge Friendly conceded that plaintiffs classified only by their relation to a state welfare scheme should be able to invoke §1983. Such plaintiffs have in fact done so; e.g., King v. Smith, 392 U.S. 309, 88 S. Ct. 2128, 20 L. Ed. 2d 1118 (1968) (finding jurisdiction under §1343(3) without discussion), and Shapiro v. Thompson, 394 U.S. 618, 89 S. Ct. 1322, 22 L. Ed. 2d 600 (1969) (assuming jurisdiction, apparently under §1983 and §1343(3), without mention of basis).

2. Note how much time and effort the court had to devote to finding state action before it could reach the merits of the case. The *Seidenberg* court quoted the Supreme Court's warning that designing a "precise formula for recognition of state responsibility under the Equal Protection Clause" was an "impossible task." What then can be predicted about the usefulness of the state action concept to bar sex discrimination as a general matter? Is there a more precise route?

3. Note that the district court expressly rejects the argument that the personal preferences of customers can justify discriminatory practices despite the Equal Protection Clause. Similar rulings (though based more narrowly on statute) have been made with respect to areas of the law other than that concerned with public accommodations. See, e.g., Diaz v. Pan American World Airways, Inc., 442 F.2d 385 (5th Cir. 1971) supra Chapter Two, II-B; Cooper and Rabb, Equal Employment Law and Litigation 298-304 (1972).

Though the court in *Seidenberg* commented that "[t]he Supreme Court has never passed upon a licensing theory of state action," it then went on to find that "the present case is distinguishable from those licensing cases where courts have shied away from finding state action" and that, in the circumstances of this case, "the state's participation is significant." Since this case was decided, however, the Supreme Court has ruled on such a licensing theory of state action involving regulations of the Pennsylvania Liquor Authority in a suit brought under §1983, Moose Lodge No. 107 v. Irvis, 407 U.S. 163,

---

2. Bonnano v. Thomas, 309 F.2d 320 (9th Cir. 1962); Scher v. Board of Education of West Orange, 424 F.2d 741 (3rd Cir. 1970).

3. Nanez v. Ritger, 304 F. Supp. 354 (E.D. Wis. 1969); Basista v. Weir, 340 F.2d 74 (3rd Cir. 1965).

92 S. Ct. 1965, 32 L. Ed. 2d 627 (1972), which follows. As you read, consider the following questions: Can *Moose Lodge* be distinguished from *Seidenberg?* Are these differences of legal significance? What remains of *Seidenberg* after *Moose Lodge?*

MOOSE LODGE NO. 107 v. IRVIS

407 U.S. 163, 92 S. Ct. 1965, 32 L. Ed. 2d 627 (1972)

Mr. Justice Rehnquist delivered the opinion of the Court.

Appellee Irvis, a Negro (hereafter appellee), was refused service by appellant Moose Lodge, a local branch of the national fraternal organization located in Harrisburg, Pennsylvania. Appellee then brought this action under 42 U.S.C. §1983 for injunctive relief in the United States District Court for the Middle District of Pennsylvania. He claimed that because the Pennsylvania liquor board had issued appellant Moose Lodge a private club license that authorized the sale of alcoholic beverages on its premises, the refusal of service to him was "state action" for the purposes of the Equal Protection Clause of the Fourteenth Amendment. He named both Moose Lodge and the Pennsylvania Liquor Authority as defendants, seeking injunctive relief that would have required the defendant liquor board to revoke Moose Lodge's license so long as it continued its discriminatory practices. Appellee sought no damages.

A three-judge district court, convened at appellee's request, upheld his contention on the merits, and entered a decree declaring invalid the liquor license issued to Moose Lodge "as long as it follows a policy of racial discrimination in its membership or operating policies or practices." Moose Lodge alone appealed from the decree. . . .

The District Court in its opinion found that "a Caucasian member in good standing brought plaintiff, a Negro, to the Lodge's dining room and bar as his guest and requested service of food and beverages. The Lodge through its employees refused service to plaintiff solely because he is a Negro." 318 F. Supp. 1246, 1247. It is undisputed that each local Moose Lodge is bound by the constitution and general bylaws of the Supreme Lodge, the latter of which contain a provision limiting membership in the lodges to white male Caucasians. The District Court in this connection found that "[t]he lodges accordingly maintain a policy and practice of restricting membership to the Caucasian race and permitting members to bring only Caucasian guests on lodge premises, particularly to the dining room and bar." Ibid.

The District Court ruled in favor of appellee on his Fourteenth Amendment claim, and entered the previously described decree. Following its loss on the merits in the District Court, Moose Lodge moved to modify the final decree by limiting its effect to discriminatory policies with respect to the service of guests. Appellee opposed the proposed modification, and the court denied the motion.

The District Court did not find, and it could not have found on this record, that appellee had sought membership in Moose Lodge and been denied it. Appellant contends that because of this fact, appellee had no standing to litigate the constitutional issue respecting Moose Lodge's membership requirements, and that therefore the decree of the court below erred insofar as it decided that issue.

Any injury to appellee from the conduct of Moose Lodge stemmed, not from the lodge's membership requirements, but from its policies with respect to the serving of guests of members. Appellee has standing to seek redress for injuries done to him, but may not seek redress for injuries done to others. Virginian R. Co. v. System Federation, 300 U.S. 515, 558 (1937); Erie R. Co. v. Williams, 233 U.S. 685, 697 (1914). While this Court has held that in exceptional situations a concededly injured party may rely on the constitutional rights of a third party in obtaining relief, Barrows v. Jackson, 346 U.S. 249 (1953),[1] in this case appellee was not injured

---

1. Our recent opinion in Sierra Club v. Morton, 405 U.S. 727, referred to a similar relationship between the standing of the plaintiff and the argument of which he might avail himself where judicial review of agency action is sought. Id., at 737.

by Moose Lodge's membership policy since he never sought to become a member. . . .

Moose Lodge is a private club in the ordinary meaning of that term. It is a local chapter of a national fraternal organization having well-defined requirements for membership. It conducts all of its activities in a building that is owned by it. It is not publicly funded. Only members and guests are permitted in any lodge of the order; one may become a guest only by invitation of a member or upon invitation of the house committee.

Appellee, while conceding the right of private clubs to choose members upon a discriminatory basis, asserts that the licensing of Moose Lodge to serve liquor by the Pennsylvania Liquor Control Board amounts to such state involvement with the club's activities as to make its discriminatory practices forbidden by the Equal Protection Clause of the Fourteenth Amendment. The relief sought and obtained by appellee in the District Court was an injunction forbidding the licensing by the liquor authority of Moose Lodge until it ceased its discriminatory practices. We conclude that Moose Lodge's refusal to serve food and beverages to a guest by reason of the fact that he was a Negro does not, under the circumstances here presented, violate the Fourteenth Amendment.

In 1883, this Court in *The Civil Rights Cases,* 109 U.S. 3, set forth the essential dichotomy between discriminatory action by the State, which is prohibited by the Equal Protection Clause, and private conduct, "however discriminatory or wrongful," against which that clause "erects no shield," Shelley v. Kraemer, 334 U.S. 1, 13 (1948). That dichotomy has been subsequently reaffirmed in Shelley v. Kraemer, supra, and in Burton v. Wilmington Parking Authority, 365 U.S. 715 (1961).

While the principle is easily stated, the question of whether particular discriminatory conduct is private, on the one hand, or amounts to "state action," on the other hand, frequently admits of no easy answer. "Only by sifting facts and weighing circumstances can the nonobvious involvement of the State in private conduct be attributed its true significance." Burton v. Wilmington Parking Authority, supra, at 722.

Our cases make clear that the impetus for the forbidden discrimination need not originate with the State if it is state action that enforces privately originated discrimination. Shelley v. Kraemer, supra. The Court held in Burton v. Wilmington Parking Authority, supra, that a private restaurant owner who refused service because of a customer's race violated the Fourteenth Amendment, where the restaurant was located in a building owned by a state-created parking authority and leased from the authority. The Court, after a comprehensive review of the relationship between the lessee and the parking authority concluded that the latter had "so far insinuated itself into a position of interdependence with Eagle [the restaurant owner] that it must be recognized as a joint participant in the challenged activity, which, on that account, cannot be considered to have been so "purely private' as to fall without the scope of the Fourteenth Amendment." 365 U.S., at 725.

The Court has never held, of course, that discrimination by an otherwise private entity would be violative of the Equal Protection Clause if the private entity receives any sort of benefit or service at all from the State, or if it is subject to state regulation in any degree whatever. Since state-furnished services include such necessities of life as electricity, water, and police and fire protection, such a holding would utterly emasculate the distinction between private as distinguished from state conduct set forth in *The Civil Rights Cases,* supra, and adhered to in subsequent decisions. Our holdings indicate that where the impetus for the discrimination is private, the State must have "significantly involved itself with invidious discriminations," Reitman v. Mulkey, 387 U.S. 369, 380 (1967), in order for the discriminatory action to fall within the ambit of the constitutional prohibition.

Our prior decisions dealing with discriminatory refusal of service in public eating places are significantly different factually from the case now before us. Peterson v. City of Greenville, 373 U.S. 244 (1963), dealt with the trespass prosecution of persons who "sat in" at a restaurant to protest its refusal of service to Negroes. There the Court held that although the ostensible initiative for the trespass prosecution came from the proprietor, the existence of a local ordinance requiring segregation of races in such places was tantamount to the State having "commanded a particular result," 373 U.S., at 248. With one exception, which is discussed infra, at 178-179, there is no suggestion in this record that the Pennsylvania statutes and regulations governing the sale of liquor are intended either overtly or covertly to encourage discrimination.

In *Burton,* supra, the Court's full discussion of the facts in its opinion indicates the significant differences between that case and this:

> The land and building were publicly owned. As an entity, the building was dedicated to "public uses" in performance of the Authority's "essential governmental functions." [Citation omitted.] The costs of land acquisition, construction, and maintenance are defrayed entirely from donations by the City of Wilmington, from loans and revenue bonds and from the proceeds of rentals and parking services out of which the loans and bonds were payable. Assuming that the distinction would be significant, [citation omitted] the commercially leased areas were not surplus state property, but constituted a physically and financially integral and, indeed, indispensable part of the State's plan to operate its project as a self-sustaining unit. Upkeep and maintenance of the building, including necessary repairs, were responsibilities of the Authority and were payable out of public funds. It cannot be doubted that the peculiar relationship of the restaurant to the parking facility in which it is located confers on each an incidental variety of mutual benefits. Guests of the restaurant are afforded a convenient place to park their automobiles, even if they cannot enter the restaurant directly from the parking area. Similarly, its convenience for diners may well provide additional demand for the Authority's parking facilities. Should any improvements effected in the leasehold by Eagle become part of the realty, there is no possibility of increased taxes being passed on to it since the fee is held by a tax-exempt government agency. Neither can it be ignored, especially in view of Eagle's affirmative allegation that for it to serve Negroes would injure its business, that profits earned by discrimination not only contribute to, but also are indispensable elements in, the financial success of a governmental agency. 365 U.S., at 723-724.

Here there is nothing approaching the symbiotic relationship between lessor and lessee that was present in *Burton,* where the private lessee obtained the benefit of locating in a building owned by the state-created parking authority, and the parking authority was enabled to carry out its primary public purpose of furnishing parking space by advantageously leasing portions of the building constructed for that purpose to commercial lessees such as the owner of the Eagle Restaurant. Unlike *Burton,* the Moose Lodge building is located on land owned by it, not by any public authority. Far from apparently holding itself out as a place of public accommodation, Moose Lodge quite ostentatiously proclaims the fact that it is not open to the public at large.[2] Nor is it located and operated in such surroundings that although private in name, it discharges a function or performs a service that would otherwise in all likelihood be performed by the State. In short, while Eagle was a public restaurant in a public building, Moose Lodge is a private social club in a private building.

With the exception hereafter noted, the Pennsylvania Liquor Control Board plays absolutely no part in establishing or enforcing the membership or guest policies of the club that it licenses to serve liquor.[3] There is no suggestion in this record that Pennsyl-

2. The Pennsylvania courts have found that Local 107 is not a "place of public accommodation" within the terms of the Pennsylvania Human Relations Act, Pa. Stat. Ann., Tit. 43, §951 et seq. 1964. Pennsylvania Human Relations Comm'n v. The Loyal Order of Moose, Lodge No. 107, Ct. Common Pleas, Dauphin County, aff'd, 220 Pa. Super. 356, 286 A.2d 374 (1971).

3. Unlike the situation in Public Utilities Comm'n v. Pollak, 343 U.S. 451 (1952), where the regulatory agency had affirmatively approved the practice of the regulated entity after full investigation, the Pennsylvania Liquor Control Board has neither approved nor endorsed the racially discriminatory practices of Moose Lodge.

vania law, either as written or as applied, discriminates against minority groups either in their right to apply for club licenses themselves or in their right to purchase and be served liquor in places of public accommodation. The only effect that the state licensing of Moose Lodge to serve liquor can be said to have on the right of any other Pennsylvanian to buy or be served liquor on premises other than those of Moose Lodge is that for some purposes club licenses are counted in the maximum number of licenses that may be issued in a given municipality. Basically each municipality has a quota of one retail license for each 1,500 inhabitants. Licenses issued to hotels, municipal golf courses, and airport restaurants are not counted in this quota, nor are club licenses until the maximum number of retail licenses is reached. Beyond that point, neither additional retail licenses nor additional club licenses may be issued so long as the number of issued and outstanding retail licenses remains at or above the statutory maximum.

The District Court was at pains to point out in its opinion what it considered to be the "pervasive" nature of the regulation of private clubs by the Pennsylvania Liquor Control Board. As that court noted, an applicant for a club license must make such physical alterations in its premises as the board may require, must file a list of the names and addresses of its members and employees, and must keep extensive financial records. The board is granted the right to inspect the licensed premises at any time when patrons, guests, or members are present.

However detailed this type of regulation may be in some particulars, it cannot be said to in any way foster or encourage racial discrimination. Nor can it be said to make the State in any realistic sense a partner or even a joint venturer in the club's enterprise. The limited effect of the prohibition against obtaining additional club licenses when the maximum number of retail licenses allotted to a municipality has been issued, when considered together with the availability of liquor from hotel, restaurant, and retail licensees, falls far short of conferring upon club licensees a monopoly in the dispensing of liquor in any given municipality or in the State as a whole. We therefore hold that, with the exception hereafter noted, the operation of the regulatory scheme enforced by the Pennsylvania Liquor Control Board does not sufficiently implicate the State in the discriminatory guest policies of Moose Lodge so as to make the latter "state action" within the ambit of the Equal Protection Clause of the Fourteenth Amendment.

The District Court found that the regulations of the Liquor Control Board adopted pursuant to statute affirmatively require that "every club licensee shall adhere to all the provisions of its constitution and by-laws."[4] Appellant argues that the purpose of this provision "is purely and simply and plainly the prevention of subterfuge," pointing out that the bona fides of a private club, as opposed to a place of public accommodation masquerading as a private club, is a matter with which the State Liquor Control Board may legitimately concern itself. Appellee concedes this to be the case, and expresses disagreement with the District Court on this point. . . .

. . . Appellee stated upon oral argument, though, and Moose Lodge conceded in its brief[5] that the bylaws of the Supreme Lodge have been altered since the lower court decision to make applicable to guests the same sort of racial restrictions as are presently applicable to members.[6]

Even though the Liquor Control Board regulation in question is neutral in its terms, the result of its application in a case where the constitution and bylaws of a club required

4. Regulations of the Pennsylvania Liquor Control Board §113.09 (June 1970 ed.).

5. Brief for Appellant 10.

6. Section 92.1 of the General Laws of the Loyal Order of Moose presently provides in relevant part as follows:

"Sec. 92.1 — *To Prevent Admission of Non Members* — There shall never at any time be admitted to any social club or home maintained or operated by any lodge, any person who is not a member of some lodge in good standing. The House Committee may grant guest privileges to persons who are eligible for membership in the fraternity consistent with governmental laws and regulations. A member shall accompany such guest and shall be responsible for the actions of said guest, and upon the member leaving, the guest must also leave. It is the duty of each member of the Order when so requested to submit for inspection his receipt for dues to any member of any House Committee or its authorized employee."

racial discrimination would be to invoke the sanctions of the State to enforce a concededly discriminatory private rule. State action, for purposes of the Equal Protection Clause, may emanate from rulings of administrative and regulatory agencies as well as from legislative or judicial action. Robinson v. Florida, 378 U.S. 153, 156 (1964). Shelley v. Kraemer, 334 U.S. 1 (1948), makes it clear that the application of state sanctions to enforce such a rule would violate the Fourteenth Amendment. Although the record before us is not as clear as one would like, appellant has not persuaded us that the District Court should have denied any and all relief.

Appellee was entitled to a decree enjoining the enforcement of §113.09 of the regulations promulgated by the Pennsylvania Liquor Control Board insofar as that regulation requires compliance by Moose Lodge with provisions of its constitution and bylaws containing racially discriminatory provisions. He was entitled to no more. The judgment of the District Court is reversed, and the cause remanded with instructions to enter a decree in conformity with this opinion.

Reversed and remanded.

Mr. Justice DOUGLAS, with whom Mr. Justice MARSHALL, joins, dissenting.

My view of the First Amendment and the related guarantees of the Bill of Rights is that they create a zone of privacy which precludes government from interfering with private clubs or groups.[1] The associational rights which our system honors permit all white, all black, all brown, and all yellow clubs to be formed. They also permit all Catholic, all Jewish, or all agnostic clubs to be established. Government may not tell a man or woman who his or her associates must be. The individual can be as selective as he desires. So the fact that the Moose Lodge allows only Caucasians to join or come as guests is constitutionally irrelevant, as is the decision of the Black Muslims to admit to their services only members of their race.

The problem is different, however, where the public domain is concerned. I have indicated in Garner v. Louisiana, 368 U.S. 157, and Lombard v. Louisiana, 373 U.S. 267, that where restaurants or other facilities serving the public are concerned and licenses are obtained from the State for operating the business, the "public" may not be defined by the proprietor to include only people of his choice; nor may a state or municipal service be granted only to some. Evans v. Newton, 382 U.S. 296, 298-299.

Those cases are not precisely apposite, however, for a private club, by definition, is not in the public domain. And the fact that a private club gets some kind of permit from the State or municipality does not make it ipso facto a public enterprise or undertaking, any more than the grant to a householder of a permit to operate an incinerator puts the householder in the public domain. We must, therefore, examine whether there are special circumstances involved in the Pennsylvania scheme which differentiate the liquor license possessed by Moose Lodge from the incinerator permit.

Pennsylvania has a state store system of alcohol distribution. Resale is permitted by hotels, restaurants, and private clubs which all must obtain licenses from the Liquor Control Board. The scheme of regulation is complete and pervasive; and the state courts have sustained many restrictions on the licensees. See Tahiti Bar Inc. Liquor License Case, 395 Pa. 355, 150 A.2d 112. Once a license is issued the licensee must comply with many detailed requirements or risk suspension or revocation of the license. Among these

---

1. It has been stipulated that Moose Lodge No. 107 "is, in all respects, private in nature and does not appear to have any public characteristics." App. 23. The cause below was tried solely on the theory that granting a Pennsylvania liquor license to a club assumed to be purely private was sufficient state involvement to trigger the Equal Protection Clause. There was no occasion to consider the question whether, perhaps because of a role as a center of community activity, Moose Lodge No. 107 was in fact "private" for equal protection purposes. The decision today, therefore, leaves this question open. See Comment, Current Developments in State Action and Equal Protection of the Law, 4 Gonzaga L. Rev. 233, 271-286.

requirements is Regulation §113.09 which says: "Every club licensee shall adhere to all of the provisions of its Constitution and By-laws." This regulation means, as applied to Moose Lodge, that it must adhere to the racially discriminatory provision of the Constitution of its Supreme Lodge that "[t]he membership of lodges shall be composed of male persons of the Caucasian or White race above the age of twenty-one years, and not married to someone of any other than the Caucasian or White race, who are of good moral character, physically and mentally normal, who shall profess a belief in a Supreme Being."

It is argued that this regulation only aims at the prevention of subterfuge and at enforcing Pennsylvania's differentiation between places of public accommodation and bona fide private clubs. It is also argued that the regulation only gives effect to the constitutionally protected rights of privacy and of association. But I cannot so read the regulation. While those other purposes are embraced in it, so is the restrictive membership clause. And we have held that "a State is responsible for the discriminatory act of a private party when the State, by its law, has compelled the act." Adickes v. Kress & Co., 398 U.S. 144, 170. See Peterson v. City of Greenville, 373 U.S. 244, 248. It is irrelevant whether the law is statutory, or an administrative regulation. Robinson v. Florida, 378 U.S. 153, 156. And it is irrelevant whether the discriminatory act was instigated by the regulation, or was independent of it. Peterson v. City of Greenville, supra. The result, as I see it, is the same as though Pennsylvania had put into its liquor licenses a provision that the license may not be used to dispense liquor to blacks, browns, yellows — or atheists or agnostics. Regulation §113.09 is thus an invidious form of state action.

Were this regulation the only infirmity in Pennsylvania's licensing scheme, I would perhaps agree with the majority that the appropriate relief would be a decree enjoining its enforcement. But there is another flaw in the scheme not so easily cured. Liquor licenses in Pennsylvania, unlike driver's licenses, or marriage licenses, are not freely available to those who meet racially neutral qualifications. There is a complex quota system, which the majority accurately describes. . . . What the majority neglects to say is that the Harrisburg quota, where Moose Lodge No. 107 is located, has been full for many years.[2] No more club licenses may be issued in that city.

This state-enforced scarcity of licenses restricts the ability of blacks to obtain liquor, for liquor is commercially available *only* at private clubs for a significant portion of each week.[3] Access by blacks to places that serve liquor is further limited by the fact that the state quota is filled. A group desiring to form a nondiscriminatory club which would serve blacks must purchase a license held by an existing club, which can exact a monopoly price for the transfer. The availability of such a license is speculative at best, however, for, as Moose Lodge itself concedes, without a liquor license a fraternal organization would be hard pressed to survive.

Thus, the State of Pennsylvania is putting the weight of its liquor license, concededly a valued and important adjunct to a private club, behind racial discrimination. . . .

Mr. Justice BRENNAN, with whom Mr. Justice MARSHALL joins, dissenting.

When Moose Lodge obtained its liquor license, the State of Pennsylvania became an active participant in the operation of the Lodge bar. Liquor licensing laws are only

2. Indeed, the quota is more than full, as a result of a grandfather clause in the law limiting licenses to one per 1,500 inhabitants. Act No. 702 of Dec. 17, 1959, §2. There are presently 115 licenses in effect in Harrisburg, and based on 1970 census figures, the quota would be 45.

3. Hotels and restaurants may serve liquor between 7 A.M. and 2 A.M. the next day, Monday through Saturday. On Sunday, such licenses are restricted to sales between 12 A.M. and 2 A.M., and between 1 P.M. and 10 P.M. Pennsylvania Liquor Code, §406(a). Thus, such licensees may serve a total of 123 hours per week. Club licensees, however, are permitted to sell liquor to members and guests from 7 A.M. to 3 A.M. the next day, seven days a week. Ibid. The total hours of sale permitted club licensees are 140, 17 more than are permitted hotels and restaurants. (There is an additional restriction on election-day sales as to which only club licensees are exempt. Ibid.)

incidentally revenue measures; they are primarily pervasive regulatory schemes under which the State dictates and continually supervises virtually every detail of the operation of the licensee's business. Very few, if any, other licensed businesses experience such complete state involvement. Yet the Court holds that such involvement does not constitute "state action" making the Lodge's refusal to serve a guest liquor solely because of his race a violation of the Fourteenth Amendment. The vital flaw in the Court's reasoning is its complete disregard of the fundamental value underlying the "state action" concept. That value is discussed in my separate opinion in Adickes v. Kress & Co., 398 U.S. 144, 190-191 (1970):

> The state-action doctrine reflects the profound judgment that denials of equal treatment, and particularly denials on account of race or color, are singularly grave when government has or shares responsibility for them. Government is the social organ to which all in our society look for the promotion of liberty, justice, fair and equal treatment, and the setting of worthy norms and goals for social conduct. Therefore something is uniquely amiss in a society where the government, the authoritative oracle of community values, involves itself in racial discrimination. Accordingly, . . . the cases that have come before us [in which] this Court has condemned significant state involvement in racial discrimination, however subtle and indirect it may have been and whatever form it may have taken [,] . . . represent vigilant fidelity to the constitutional principle that no State shall in any significant way lend its authority to the sordid business of racial discrimination.

Plainly, the State of Pennsylvania's liquor regulations intertwine the State with the operation of the Lodge bar in a "significant way [and] lend [the State's] authority to the sordid business of racial discrimination." The opinion of the late Circuit Judge Freedman, for the three-judge District Court, most persuasively demonstrates the "state action" present in this case:

> We believe the decisive factor is the uniqueness and the all-pervasiveness of the regulation by the Commonwealth of Pennsylvania of the dispensing of liquor under licenses granted by the state. The regulation inherent in the grant of a state liquor license is so different in nature and extent from the ordinary licenses issued by the state that it is different in quality.
>
> It had always been held in Pennsylvania, even prior to the Eighteenth Amendment, that the exercise of the power to grant licenses for the sale of intoxicating liquor was an exercise of the highest governmental power, one in which the state had the fullest freedom inhering in the police power of the sovereign. With the Eighteenth Amendment which went into effect in 1919 the right to deal in intoxicating liquor was extinguished. The era of Prohibition ended with the adoption in 1933 of the Twenty-first Amendment, which has left to each state the absolute power to prohibit the sale, possession or use of intoxicating liquor, and in general to deal otherwise with it as it sees fit.
>
> Pennsylvania has exercised this power with the fullest measure of state authority. Under the Pennsylvania plan the state monopolizes the sale of liquor through its so-called state stores, operated by the state. Resale of liquor is permitted by hotels, restaurants and private clubs, which must obtain licenses from the Liquor Control Board, authorizing them "to purchase liquor from a Pennsylvania Liquor Store [at a discount]." . . .
>
> . . . It would be difficult to find a more pervasive interaction of state authority with personal conduct. The holder of a liquor license from the Commonwealth of Pennsylvania therefore is not like other licensees who conduct their enterprises at arms-length from the state, even though they may have been required to comply with certain conditions, such as zoning or building requirements, in order to obtain or continue to enjoy the license which authorizes them to engage in their business. The state's concern in such cases is minimal and once the conditions it has exacted are met the customary operations of the enterprise are free from further encroachment. Here

by contrast beyond the act of licensing is the continuing and pervasive regulation of the licensees by the state to an unparalleled extent. The unique power which the state enjoys in this area, which has put it in the business of operating state liquor stores and in the role of licensing clubs, has been exercised in a manner which reaches intimately and deeply into the operation of the licensees.

In addition to this, the regulations of the Liquor Control Board adopted pursuant to the statute affirmatively require that "every club licensee shall adhere to all the provisions of its constitution and by-laws". As applied to the present case this regulation requires the local Lodge to adhere to the constitution of the Supreme Lodge and thus to exclude non-Caucasians from membership in its licensed club. The state therefore has been far from neutral. It has declared that the local Lodge must adhere to the discriminatory provision under penalty of loss of its license. It would be difficult in any event to consider the state neutral in an area which is so permeated with state regulation and control, but any vestige of neutrality disappears when the state's regulation specifically exacts compliance by the licensee with an approved provision for discrimination, especially where the exaction holds the threat of loss of the license.

However it may deal with its licensees in exercising its great and untrammeled power over liquor traffic, the state may not discriminate against others or disregard the operation of the Equal Protection Clause of the Fourteenth Amendment as it affects personal rights. Here the state has used its great power to license the liquor traffic in a manner which has no relation to the traffic in liquor itself but instead permits it to be exploited in the pursuit of a discriminatory practice. 318 F. Supp. 1246, 1248-1250 (MD Pa. 1970).

This is thus a case requiring application of the principle that until today has governed our determinations of the existence of "state action": "Our prior decisions leave no doubt that the mere existence of efforts by the State, through legislation or otherwise, to authorize, encourage, or otherwise support racial discrimination in a particular facet of life constitutes illegal state involvement in those pertinent private acts of discrimination that subsequently occur." Adickes v. Kress & Co., 398 U.S., at 202 (separate opinion of Brennan, J.). See, e.g., Peterson v. City of Greenville, 373 U.S. 244 (1963); Burton v. Wilmington Parking Authority, 365 U.S. 715 (1961); Evans v. Newton, 382 U.S. 296 (1966); Hunter v. Erickson, 393 U.S. 385 (1969); Lombard v. Louisiana, 373 U.S. 267 (1963); Reitman v. Mulkey, 387 U.S. 369 (1967); Robinson v. Florida, 378 U.S. 153 (1964); McCabe v. Atchison, T. & S.F.R. Co., 235 U.S. 151 (1914).

I therefore dissent and would affirm the final decree entered by the District Court.

NOTES

1. Insofar as the *Moose Lodge* decision can be limited in application to admittedly private clubs, it is possible to reconcile it with a case like *Seidenberg*, which relied, at least in part, on the fact that McSorleys' was engaged in voluntarily serving the public. The Court says that "Moose Lodge is a private club in the ordinary meaning of that term"; it distinguishes Burton v. Wilmington Parking Authority by noting that "while Eagle was a public restaurant in a public building, Moose Lodge is a private social club in a private building."

Whether an establishment is public or private is often an important issue in this area. See Daniel v. Paul, 395 U.S. 298, 89 S. Ct. 1697, 23 L. Ed. 2d 318 (1969); see generally Van Alstyne, Civil Rights: A New Public Accommodations Law for Ohio, 22 Ohio St. L.J. 683 (1961). Courts usually give several factual grounds for holding that an organization is not entitled to be treated as a club, the most important of which fall into three categories:

Procedure for obtaining membership. If whites are admitted with little formality, for instance by simply paying a fee, the club is difficult to distinguish from a segregated facility open to the public. Lackey v. Sacoolas, 411 Pa. 235, 191 A.2d 395 (1963). A lack of genuine qualifications for membership (other than race) or little attempt to restrict the number of members may also be fatal. Castle Hill Beach Club v. Arbury, 208 Misc. 35, 142 N.Y.S.2d 432 (1955); 2 N.Y.2d 596, 142 N.E.2d 186 (Ct. App. 1957). Even a high initiation fee will not save an association if it is insufficiently exclusive on any basis other than race. Smith v. Montgomery Y.M.C.A., 316 F. Supp. 899 (M.D. Ala. 1970).

Use of the club by nonmembers. If persons who are not guests are regularly admitted without becoming members, the organization will usually be held not to be a bona fide private club. See Gillespie v. Lake Shore Golf Club, 91 N.E.2d 290 (Ohio Ct. App. 1950).

Participation by members in the governance of the organization. The courts appear to require some bond between members stronger than mere patronage of the same facility. They inquire whether policy decisions are made by the members or instead merely reflect decisions made by a manager, owner, or a small group of directors. Gillespie v. Lake Shore Golf Club, supra. In one case, a lack of general membership meetings was held to be crucial. United States v. Northwest Louisiana Restaurant Club, 256 F. Supp. 151 (W.D. La. 1966). In others, the court found evidence that the principal support of the club was not the members' desires to associate with each other, but that their only common interest was in the activity of the club's sponsors, e.g., use of a restaurant or a private beach. Norman v. City Island Beach Co., 126 Misc. 335, 213 N.Y.S. 379 (Sup. Ct. 1926); Castle Hill Beach Club v. Arbury, supra.

2. Consider the impact of *Moose Lodge* on the development of the state action tool as a way to eliminate discriminatory practices. Justice Rehnquist in *Moose Lodge* accepted the case-by-case formula of Burton v. Wilmington Parking Authority, that "[o]nly by sifting facts and weighing circumstances can the non-obvious involvement of the State in private conduct be attributed its true significance. "Under prior cases, among the most significant factors was the degree of state involvement as measured by the detail of regulation. But in this case, the Court said:[4]

> However detailed this type of regulation may be in some particulars, it cannot be said to in any way foster or encourage racial discrimination. Nor can it be said to make the State in any realistic sense a partner or even a joint venturer in the club's enterprise.

Does the view seem consistent with or a revision of the developing methodology for finding state action? Recall that the court in *Seidenberg* indirectly cited the Pennsylvania liquor control statute as one that was in some ways even more strict and pervasive than the New York liquor licensing statute held in that case to amount to state action. Can the New York statute be considered state action now that the Pennsylvania statute and regulations have been ruled to be otherwise?

3. Women often seek entry into what purport to be private clubs for reasons other than a desire to socialize. The impact of private club discrimination on executive hiring and promotion has been studied in depth by the American Jewish Committee and the University of Michigan's Institute for Social Research. The committee launched a campaign against private club discrimination because it considered it "central to the problem of anti-semitism, producing harmful results far beyond personal affronts and embarrassment. . . . It served to perpetuate the infection of bigotry and implied the inferiority and undesirability of an entire group of Americans."[5] The rise of separate-but-equal Jewish clubs was, the committee found, "an unwholesome response to the barriers which the majority had erected against the full and equal participation of Jews in American life."[6] The authors concluded that social club membership is often the tail that wags the dog,

4. 407 U.S. at 176-177.
5. Slawson and Bloomgarden, The Unequal Treatment of Equals 3 (1965).
6. Ibid.

controlling entry into the "elite."[7] The committee's findings as to religious discrimination may prove to have strategic impact on job opportunities for women:[8]

> Social clubs have long been part of the American way of life. Not only do they provide pleasant amenities for members, they are gathering places for the establishment . . . where respected and important members of the community come together both socially and professionally. Thus the opportunity to join such a club may be a necessity for continued success in employment and other critical areas. Because social club discrimination on the basis of religion does not stop there, [it helps to foster] an attitude that spills over from the social sphere to business, the professions, politics, and many other areas of life. Thus, the drive against social club discrimination is not a matter of social climbing or even of ambition and the desire to get ahead. It is an integral part of the mounting pressure for true equality.

4. What are the implications of *Moose Lodge* for women seeking to bring legal actions against places of *public* accommodation that discriminate on the basis of sex? How would your answer differ if there were specific statutory provisions prohibiting such discrimination? Could a statute be framed that would not eliminate all truly private clubs?

C. Results and Developments Under Statutory Formulas

Is statutory reform a more effective way to secure equal rights for women in public accommodations? What can a statute accomplish that a judicial ruling cannot? Though, as noted above, sex has not yet been included in Title II of the Civil Rights Act of 1964, a growing number of states now have statutes which specifically prohibit discrimination on the basis of sex in places of public accommodation.[9]

New York City was one of the earliest jurisdictions specifically to include sex in its statute prohibiting discrimination in places of public accommodation. The following article, indicating why that statute was felt to be necessary, gives some idea of the encounters that have led women to seek statutory remedies.

HARKINS, SEX AND THE CITY COUNCIL
New York Magazine, April 27, 1970, vol. 3, no. 17, pp. 10-11

In this most liberal of cities, a woman has no legally guaranteed right to enter a restaurant, rent an apartment, purchase a building, or sleep in a hotel; the owners may lawfully exclude her simply for being female.

A state law has banned discrimination in places of public accommodation on racial or religious grounds since 1895. But a bill that would have extended the coverage to women has just died in committee in the Assembly. Thomas Laverne, who sponsored a companion public-accommodations bill in the State Senate, acknowledges that it's a controversial issue: "The silent majority is strong among men. There seems to be something sacred about our men's bars and lunchroom arrangements."

Those "sacred" men's bars and lunchrooms are the embodiment of a strong idea: that discrimination on the ground of sex is reasonable, even natural — not as harmful, somehow, as racial or religious bias. It's a point of view even a Northern legislator (who

---

7. See E.D. Baltzell, The Protestant Establishment (1964).

8. Dale, The Closed Society (American Jewish Committee pamphlet 1969).

9. See, e.g., Ind. Rev. Stat. §§40-2307 to 40-2314 (Supp. 1972); Mont. Rev. Codes §64-301 (Amend. 1971); N.H. Rev. Stat. Ann. §354-A:8 (Supp. 1972); N.J. Stat. Ann. §10:5-4 (Supp. 1974); and W. Va. Code §5-11-9 (1967). A more complete list of laws as of 1972 appears in Ross, The Rights of Women 342, Chart B (1973).

wouldn't dare endorse racism) will unashamedly put on the public record. Back in 1964, when the Civil Rights Bill was on the floor of the House, someone offered an amendment extending its protection to women. The idea seemed so irrational, so unpalatable, that Representative James Corman was stung into frankness: "Mr. Chairman, I stand exposed here by the maker of this amendment because he has finally reached the point where I become a segregationist. Custom and usage in our state [California] carefully segregates certain facilities provided for men and women. I do not think we should stop that practice at all, and I hope if the amendment is offered at this point that it be defeated." It was offered at that point — and defeated.

Six years after the Civil Rights Law went into effect, "custom and usage" still operate — even in New York. Three Brooklyn girls, looking for an apartment to share, run into so much trouble finding a landlord who will rent to them that they write a letter to the State Attorney General pleading for help. Two women, applying for two single rooms at the Abbey Victoria Hotel, are asked if they are with their husbands. They say they're not; the clerk tells them to find rooms somewhere else. Three middle-aged women from Utica, in New York for a holiday, are turned away from the nine o'clock show at a large nightclub; they have reservations, but the maitre d' won't seat them because there is no man escorting them. The ladies leave, perplexed, and call the Attorney General's office in the morning. "We've had dozens of calls from women complaining about the renting problem and the restaurant problem," says George Zuckerman, Assistant Attorney General in charge of the state's Civil Rights Bureau. "But we have to tell them there's no remedy under existing law."

Well, there's finally hope for a remedy. In addition to a bill — passed in the final days of the State Assembly session — which forbids housing bias on the ground of sex, there's a broader bill (covering sex and marital status) before the City Council. Its sponsor, Carol Greitzer, has also introduced legislation banning discrimination in public accommodations because of sex. If there's enough public pressure to get it passed, her public-accommodations bill will give women the same legal protection that racial minorities have enjoyed for 75 years. . . .

Last month there was a joint hearing on the two city bills (Mrs. Greitzer's) and the two bills before the State Legislature (sponsored by Senator Laverne and Assemblywoman Constance Cook). It was an orderly morning; the bra-burners stayed away. The women who showed up to testify were dignified and decorous witnesses.

They'd had the same kind of angering experiences. At a business conference upstate, a field representative for the OEO, meeting with her colleagues late into the night, missed the last bus back to New York. When she applied for a room at the nearest hotel, she was told, "We don't give a room to a woman coming in off the street at one o'clock in the morning" (the old woman-equals-prostitute equation). A lawyer from the Women's Bar Association came to the hearing to recount her embarrassment at finding herself and her male colleagues, headed for a business lunch at Whyte's Restaurant, turned away from the main dining room. They all had to trudge upstairs to a less desirable dining room where the lady was acceptable. "Many of these Wall Street restaurants advertise in the New York Law Journal," she said. "They invite the patronage of attorneys, so they're the site of important business meetings. But they embarrass any woman attorney who attempts to attend the meetings by refusing service to the entire party because of her presence." (Eighty lawyers — most of them women — have written to Carol Greitzer protesting this practice, a hallowed but humiliating example of Representative Corman's "custom and usage.")

A writer and a psychiatrist, both women, meeting at a midtown restaurant, were refused a drink at the bar (they'd decided to skip lunch, since they had a long wait for a table and the psychiatrist had a plane to catch). The manager told them they could have a drink only if they found a man to sit at the bar with them. "I find it humiliating, as a mother of three — in my forties — to be told that I must indulge, in effect, in sexual provocation in order to have a drink with a colleague at noontime," the writer testified.

Another writer and her friend had a similar experience at the Russian Tea Room's bar — this time, though, at six in the evening. "We sat there for an hour and the men who were at the bar thought this was absurd. When I asked whether if I had gone out on 57th Street and picked up some man and come in with him, I would have been served, I was told I would." Another field representative for the OEO, waiting for a bus from Port Authority Terminal, stopped in at Sardi's at 1:30 in the afternoon, planning to have a drink and examine some papers she was carrying. The bartender wanted to serve her ("She seems like a very nice girl," she heard him whisper to his customers) but he had to refuse her or lose his job. She was offended enough to make an issue of it (most women don't): "*Why* can't you serve me?" "Because you are a woman," he said.

"Because you may be a prostitute," is probably the honest answer. According to Preston David, director of the City Commission on Human Rights, "Discriminatory establishments justify exclusion of unescorted women on the basis that they wish to discourage prostitutes. . . . The commission believes that any harm the public-accommodations bill might permit is far outweighed by the damage done to all women now being denied access to these facilities." Whether it's reasonable for a restaurant or nightclub or cocktail lounge to prejudge, and bar, 4 million New Yorkers because X per cent may be prostitutes, our city councilmen will soon have the opportunity to decide.

One voice was raised in opposition at the hearing. It belonged to John Redding Jr., representing the Real Estate Board of New York (Manhattan), who appeared against the housing bill. Mr. Redding expressed the opinion that the rights of landlords should be interfered with only in some matter *seriously* affecting the public interest, and added that, although discrimination against single girls was rare, "it seems to me that under certain circumstances it might be a reasonable thing for a landlord to do for the protection of his property."

It was unclear from Mr. Redding's testimony what it was that landlords and tenants have to fear from the presence of a single woman in a building (the prostitute equation again?). But it *was* clear that, since Manhattan landlords seem to want to keep their right to discriminate, women need the protection of a strong housing law. . . .

Women who do care about restaurant discrimination see it not so much as a practical problem but a legal and philosophical question affecting the status of women — and therefore not a frivolous matter. Congress established, with the passage of the Civil Rights Law, that a privately owned restaurant loses some of its private character when it opens its doors to the public; the owner loses the right to discriminate against whole classes of people. There are no special rooms in public restaurants closed to, say, blacks or Puerto Ricans. Strange, then, that the right of the *majority* of New Yorkers to service everywhere should still be controversial. . . .

Well, the right to single out women as unwelcome is stubbornly held, and if the City Council bills fail, it will be because our legislators follow a curious, self-contradictory course of logic: A: there's hardly any bias against women, and therefore no need for a law, and anyway, B: in *this* matter, at least, shouldn't a man be allowed his prejudices?

NEW YORK CITY LAW PROHIBITING SEX DISCRIMINATION IN PLACES OF PUBLIC ACCOMMODATION
N.Y.C. Admin. Code c. 1, tit. B, §B1-7.0-2

It shall be unlawful discriminatory practice for any person, being the owner, lessee, proprietor, manager, superintendent, agent or employee of any place of public accommodation, resort or amusement, because of the *race, creed, color, national origin or sex* of any person directly or indirectly, to refuse, withhold from or deny to such person any of the accommodations, advantages, facilities or privileges thereof, or, directly or indirectly, to publish, circulate, issue, display, post or mail any written or printed communication, notice or advertisement, to the effect that any of the accommodations, advantages, facilities and privileges or any such place shall be refused, withheld from or denied to any person on account of race, creed, color, national origin or sex or that the patronage or custom thereat of any person belonging to or purporting to be of any particular race, creed, color, national origin, or sex is unwelcome, objectionable or not acceptable, desired or solicited. *Notwithstanding the foregoing the provisions of this paragraph shall not apply, with respect to sex, to places of public accommodation, resort or amusement where the Commission grants an exemption based on bona fide considerations of public policy.* [Emphasis added.]

Note that the law gives the New York City Commission on Human Rights the authority to grant exemptions to the law "based on bona fide considerations of public policy." Consider the reasons why exemptions as to sex might be granted, but not as to race, creed, color, or national origin.

D. The New York City Commission on Human Rights Hearings

In accordance with its mandate to grant appropriate exemptions, the New York City Commission held public hearings to help it decide on classes of facilities that should be exempt, reserving the right to decide on additional classes and individual cases as the need arose.

What kinds of places of public accommodation should be entitled to such exemption? What are "bona fide considerations of public policy"? By what criteria should "public policy" be measured? Seeking answers to such questions, the commission sent out a letter to individuals, groups, businesses, and corporations likely to be interested in exemptions from the new law and invited testimony on the following subjects:[10]

> I. Residences limited to one sex, other than those whose main purpose is to provide health or social services.
> Speakers should be prepared to address themselves to the following considerations among others:
> Type of sleeping accommodations provided; type of, location and number of bathroom accommodations provided; nature of and reasons for need for protective segregation by sex; availability of alternate accommodations for the excluded sex; economic, psychological and sociological effects of exclusion; anticipated economic, sociological, or other effects of change in existing practices.
> II. "Ladies Days" (reduction of admission fees for one sex at certain times in bars and at ball fields or on transportation facilities).
> Speakers are urged to address themselves to the social, psychological and economic effects on both sexes and on the proprietors of public accommodations of existing practices and the anticipated effects of rendering such practices unlawful.
> Speakers also are urged to bring out in their testimony any additional factors they feel should be considered in the determination of exemptions.
> III. In view of the clear intent of the law, the Commission will not entertain applications for exemption for bars and eating places which exclude one sex entirely from their premises at all times or at certain hours.
> Speakers may also raise and discuss at the hearing, areas of possible exemption other than those outlined above.

Does the exclusion of residences whose "main purpose is to provide health or social services" imply an automatic exemption? Should it? On what statutory or policy basis?

Based on the first requests for exemptions, the commission hearings focused on single-sex hotels, bars that excluded or restricted women, and differential admission

10. Letter from New York City Commission on Human Rights, Dec. 29, 1970.

pricing at sports events, dance halls, and other facilities. Witnesses included patrons and representatives of various organizations seeking exemption from the new law, as well as expert sociologists and architects who were asked to give their opinions on the likely effects of the law and the proposed rationale for exemptions therefrom.

Parts of the testimony of one of the invited experts pointed up the significance as well as the delicacy of designing public policy when the underlying social values and the relevant institutions are still in the process of basic change. Professor S. M. Miller, a sociologist invited by the commission to testify, put the changes mandated by the new law into a historical framework and concluded that exclusionist practices directed against women, whatever their purpose in former years, are no longer functional:[11]

> . . . I think the kind of hearings that are going on now are an effort to review the changes which have taken place in American life and to see whether many of the institutional practices continue to make sense today, particularly in light of our concern about eliminating inequalities and eliminating discrimination in American life.
>
> A number of practices grew up at one time which supposedly made sense, and sociologists say were functional, because they dealt with the special position of women in American society. They presumed that women had relatively little knowledge about sex, that men were very raucous and difficult, outrageous in their forward demands, and consequently women had to be protected.
>
> You get an index of how things have changed when you think of Booth Tarkington's novel, "Seventeen," which if it were published today one would have to call "Twelve" because the sexual outlook which a youth had at seventeen is now held by boys at a younger age; and what would have been called extraordinary precocity at that time is the normal way people today develop.
>
> So what may have had at some time some gain or function now becomes ways of denigrating women in society, forms that tend to discrimination and to stigma. So we have separatist institutions which once had a history of being formed in order to keep women protected and now to a large extent have more the function of saying women are very different from the rest of society, can't be integrated with society, have to be warehoused in institutions.
>
> I think now we have to question whether the separatism has any function at all, question whether it had any function at any time. Presently it tends to stigmatize the people who live in these institutions and makes it very difficult to develop new kinds of cross-sexual institutions. . . .

Still, Miller was bothered by withdrawing altogether the single-sex choice, particularly in light of the testimony of residents of a women's hotel:[12]

> I find it very difficult. It seems to me people should have choice, but at the same time there are other feelings I have about the openness of institutions which this would violate. And I must confess confusion on this particular question, whether we should have complete elimination except on health or like grounds, [or] whether we should have some choice available.

Should the option of sexual exclusivity be available in some facilities? Consider the following possibilities.

1. Single-Sex Hotels

Testimony from the staff and residents of a women's hotel raised a fair cross section of the various rationales and competing considerations in offering one type of accommodation to both sexes. Serving women exclusively since it was built in 1927, the Barbizon

---

11. Transcript of Hearings on Exemptions to Sex Discrimination in the Public Accommodations Law, New York City Commission on Human Rights, Jan. 14, 1971. (Available at Commission.)
12. Id. at 159.

Hotel argued that admission of males "would completely destroy the character of the house as a home for women."[13]

>   *Mr. David:* How do you distinguish your population from the population of any hotel in the city . . . ?
>
>   *Mr. Sherry:* We distinguish them only solely because we cater exclusively to women, and for the most part, as you have heard the testimony, young women who are attending school in New York. And the average hotel does cater to whoever comes, whoever is able and willing to pay the price without any particular bargaining.
>
>   *Commissioner Norton:* The use of the term application —
>
>   *Mr. Sherry:* Checking in.
>
>   *Commissioner Norton:* When people come to this hotel they check in as in any other hotel rather than fill out an application?
>
>   *Mrs. Sibley:* No, they fill out an application, giving references.
>
>   *Commissioner Norton:* But is the application filled out any differently from the application you fill out at the Hilton or other hotels?
>
>   *Mr. Sherry:* No. The only thing we want to be sure, we have references so if somebody does develop a problem, we have somebody to contact. In other words, we ask the name of the parent and address and telephone number of who to contact in case of emergency. In that respect we do differ, and for the purpose I earlier mentioned.
>
>   *Miss Meyers:* You don't have references in terms of checking social references?
>
>   *Mrs. Sibley:* Yes, we do.
>
>   *Miss Meyers:* You check those references?
>
>   *Mrs. Sibley:* Yes.
>
>   *Miss Meyers:* Before the person is admitted?
>
>   *Commissioner Norton:* How can that happen when the person comes off the street with a suitcase?
>
>   *Mrs. Sibley:* Usually we take them without checking the references, then check them out afterwards.
>
>   *Miss Meyers:* How do you check the references?
>
>   *Mrs. Sibley:* We write to the people they give as references. We get them in writing, in letters. . . .
>
>   *Miss Meyers:* Would you say that your standards for — if you don't like to use the word eviction, your standards for asking girls to leave for a reason other than the nonpayment of rent would be any different from a normal hotel's standards?
>
>   *Mr. Sherry:* I would say not. We use normal hotel standards for proper behavior in a hotel. . . .
>
>   *Miss Meyers:* Do you have any guidance activities for the young ladies?
>
>   *Mrs. Sibley:* Guidance? We have social activities.
>
>   *Miss Meyers:* What type of social activities do you have?
>
>   *Mrs. Sibley:* We have tea every afternoon. Occasionally we have a movie, a concert, a lecture, a play, a travelogue, that sort of thing; bridge parties.
>
>   *Miss Meyers:* Do you have any protective techniques besides the physical protection?
>
>   *Mrs. Sibley:* I don't understand the question.
>
>   *Miss Meyers:* I would like to go on about the guidance activities.
>
>   *Mrs. Sibley:* They are not guidance activities.
>
>   *Miss Meyers:* But they are social activities?
>
>   *Mrs. Sibley:* Yes.
>
>   *Miss Meyers:* Well, is this in any way similar to a private club?
>
>   *Mr. Sherry:* Yes, I would say so.
>
>   *Miss Meyers:* The Barbizon may be in a way similar to a private club?
>
>   *Mrs. Sibley:* Yes.
>
>   *Miss Meyers:* You have social references?
>
>   *Mrs. Sibley:* Yes.
>
>   *Miss Meyers:* There is no official membership procedure?

13. Id. at 33-35, 37-40, 44-45, 184-185.

Mrs. Sibley: Yes.

Miss Meyers: It is a private corporation?

Mr. Sherry: It is an ordinary business corporation. . . .

. . . You mentioned a protective device, you know. And my young friend to my immediate left over here reminded me that we do have the telephone available, you know, as a protective device at all times for them.

Commissioner Norton: That of course is present in normal commercial hotels. . . .

Commissioner Colgate: . . . It does seem to me, however, that one of the basic, elemental policies of the Barbizon has been to serve in loco parentis; that you are assuming a responsibility for these young ladies.

Mr. Sherry: Yes.

Commissioner Norton: I am not sure that the term should be used lightly. In the legal sense, is it indeed true that you accept legal responsibility for these young women in this city?

Mr. Sherry: No, we don't accept a legal responsibility in the strict sense of loco parentis, naturally. But we do hold ourselves out to the parents, you know, as responsible and reliable people to whom they can reasonably entrust their children. And that of course is grounded upon such practices as have been pointed out.

Now if a young lady comes home much too late in the evening — 1:00 o'clock, 2:00 o'clock, 3:00 o'clock in the morning — and not necessarily in a straight path, then we do speak to her about it.

Miss Meyers: Do you speak to the parents about it?

Mr. Sherry: Not necessarily. It depends again on judgment. And if it happens too frequently, we certainly do. . . .

Mr. Bick: . . . I am not so happy about the Barbizon situation. I think there is a social class issue that clouds the issue somewhat.

Commissioner Norton: Why do you think that is?

Mr. Bick: I think the Barbizon tends to be an exclusive hotel which caters primarily to middle and upper class white women who go there because their families feel this is a good place to meet other women and other men of the same class. This is a social club. I think the club aspect of it that was brought out in the testimony is not totally without some substance.

Commissioner Litter: What is the objection to that? Don't people want to go to the Waldorf instead of the Lancaster? Should they be prevented from going to the Waldorf?

Mr. Bick: I don't say they should. I'm just asking, is it a question here of sex or class?

What references in the testimony of hotel representatives give credence to Bick's argument that the Barbizon is a "social club"? Can it be argued that the hotel was seeking the advantages of both a public accommodation and a private club at the same time? What are the elements of each? Does the testimony from hotel residents that follows corroborate the notion of an admixture of public and private elements?[14]

Miss Minrath: I feel [the Barbizon] is the safest place. It is a place where I feel very comfortable. It's almost a home away from home, yet I have independence away from my parents, I have the social life I enjoy. I like being back in New York.

I feel protected there. I don't have to worry about phone calls. And we have a great phone call system at the Barbizon. I can ask the operator to have no phone calls accepted up to, I think 12 hours, except my parents. Or no one can pick up the phone — they have to ask for me directly, they can't just pick up the phone and ask for my room number.

When I say good-bye to my date — that is, good night — in the lobby, I don't have to go through a big ordeal. Well, it's true.

Miss Meyers: If there were men, selected men, assuming that the policy of selection would continue but that the differentiation would no longer be sexual — in other

14. Id. at 52-56, 60-64, 104-105.

words, you would still have your phone calls screened through the switchboard, men who came late as permanent residents might have references checked, and so on — assuming everything remained the same but the introduction of the male sex on either certain corridors or mixed up, depending on how that worked out, took place, would you feel the quality of your life and protection would materially change?

Miss Minrath: Yes, I would.

Miss Meyers: Would you care to explain that?

Miss Minrath: I feel if men move into the Barbizon, it would do nothing but destroy it, and it would cause an awful lot of problems. I don't think segregation of floors or bathrooms or showers or what have you would do anything. When I close my door at night I'm not worried about someone breaking in. I really feel that way very strongly.

Miss Meyers: Have you stayed in other hotels?

Miss Minrath: No.

Miss Meyers: You don't have any experience in a normal hotel?

Miss Minrath: No, not really.

Miss Meyers: Do you think that in a normal hotel people break down doors?

Miss Minrath: I don't know.

Miss Meyers: I am just asking.

Miss Minrath: I just don't want to have to get on an elevator and be embarrassed by someone. I mean, sometimes you can be in the coffee shop and, you know, you can be solicited more or less by someone that comes in off the street. And I feel — in the lobby, too, sometimes they have been asked to not loiter, and they've been asked to leave the hotel. And I really feel very protected there.

Miss Meyers: Do you have any difficult experiences — you don't have to describe them — when you had your own apartment?

Miss Minrath: Well, yes, we did, both my roommate and I. Many times we would find that, you know, the boys down the hall wanted to come over, and they constantly wanted to borrow a cup of sugar, and they would come in and stay three or four hours. There wasn't the privacy that we enjoy.

In the Barbizon we can talk to the girls across the hall or run around with just a robe on or something like that. And I do enjoy this more or less.

Miss Meyers: Do you do that frequently?

Miss Minrath: In the Barbizon?

Miss Meyers: In the Barbizon. I am just wondering about the quality of life in the Barbizon, about the communal living. Do you run around the halls?

Miss Minrath: Not the Barbizon Hotel, my particular corridor.

Miss Meyers: I did not mean downstairs, I meant in your corridor.

Miss Minrath: Yes.

Miss Meyers: Is there that quality?

Miss Minrath: Yes, there's a definite freedom where three or four of us can have our doors open and talk back and forth and girls can mingle in a room. And I'm on a floor where there's mostly professional women. . . .

Miss Sick: I live there for safety because I'm a student. And I'm from Pennsylvania. The Barbizon was referred to me by the school I'm attending, and it's — I think it's one of the best hotels. I feel safe there no matter if I'm away for — like Christmas vacation I was away two weeks. I came back and everything was okay in my room and nothing was touched.

In an apartment I would feel — maybe there was vandals or something like that.

Commissioner Norton: Is it your impression that if you were in another hotel where men also were allowed . . . that this would not have been the case — you would not have come back and found your belongings together?

Miss Sick: I don't know. Just like running around the rooms, like Carol said, you have freedom to walk to your room, back and forth to rooms in your robe without having some male seeing.

Miss Kimaagre: Another thing I would like to say. I have a girl friend who was in New York, who was staying at the Martinique Hotel, and she was raped at 3:00 o'clock in the morning in the hotel. This man said there had been a fire, and just barged in. I haven't been worried till now, but I don't want that to happen.

Commissioner Norton: Where is the Martinique?

Miss Kimaagre: At Broadway and 32nd Street. A lot of girls who can't afford other hotels are staying there.

Mr. Sherry: One of the most serious problems of the large commercial hotels in the City of New York is probably safety. The number of thefts in the hotels is almost incredible. And the measure is that we are not able to cope with it; even the best assistance of the Police Department is not quite adequate. This is true even of the luxury hotels. . . .

Mr. Weitz: Mr. Sherry, are you saying that crime is primarily a function of males?

Mr. Sherry: I would say in the largest measure in the City. of New York, our experience in the hotels has been that the vast majority of the thieves that have been apprehended have been males. . . .

Mr. Weitz: Assuming, Mr. Sherry, that your male guests were subjected to the same sort of screening and the same close supervision and same evaluation that is given to your female applicants, would you be given the same kind of problem?

Mr. Sherry: I hope not.

Mr. Weitz: In other words, you don't think it is inevitable, assuming what I have stated, that there would be discrimination against male guests of the quality I have described?

Mrs. Sibley: If there were male guests taken in as transients, they would not be screened.

Mr. Sherry: The assumption here is that they would be screened, you know.

Mrs. Sibley: Not for two or three nights, the way the permanent guests are.

Mr. Sherry: With respect to that question, the other aspect of it is the important one. And I just learned, you know, that the real concern of the young people in the hotel is their privacy, the freedom with which they can go around and about informally and which they would be deprived of. . . .

Mrs. Grietzer: As to the intent of the legislation, initially, when I first had the bill drafted, it only covered the situation of restaurants and bars. And the various women's rights groups suggested that I change the wording from, I think it talked about eating establishments initially, to public accommodations because in other jurisdictions the law was expressed this way. And I did that.

So I made the change, not really knowing at the time exactly what all of these other ramifications were going to be. And there was not at the time the intent to cover the places such as the Barbizon in this particular legislation. And I think it was brought out by me in questioning at the Council Committee hearings, and when I was interviewed by the press I so stated, that I did not think that the hotels were going to be included or covered by the nature of the bill. . . . And I mentioned that the hotels and the Y's and the Barbizon were examples that we gave as men's residences and women's residences that would not be covered.

I don't have any opinion one way or the other at this time on whether hotels should be covered or not eventually. However, I do think that there would have to be considerably more research done on the subject.

NOTES

1. Compare the reasons advanced for desiring an all-female atmosphere with the advantages men seek from an all-male atmosphere. Are there ways, short of excluding all members of either sex, to control female prostitutes from bars or male criminals from hotels? What are they?

2. The sponsor of the bill apparently intended limited sexual integration of public accommodations. Was the language of the bill appropriate to achieve that end? The commission apparently did not think so, for it did not grant the requested exemptions for single-sex residential hotels. Instead, it announced that an exemption would be granted "to such portion of places of public accommodation, resort or other amusement where the patrons customarily disrobe, including but not limited to locker rooms, dressing rooms, toilets or shower rooms containing multiple facilities, turkish baths, steam

rooms, saunas, and hospital wards." This exception was interpreted to allow segregation of residential hotels by floor, to protect the privacy of patrons in the corridors between their bedrooms, and in using the common bathroom facilities. This was not sufficient to prevent a strong movement among residents of single-sex residential hotels which eventually resulted in the passage of an explicit exemption.[15] This later provision was introduced by the same councilwoman as the original bill.

The relevant portions of the amended law are reproduced below; the italicized portions were among a series of amendments signed into law February 7, 1973.[16]

> 5(a) It shall be an unlawful discriminatory practice for the owner, lessee, sublessee, assignee, or managing agent of, or other person having the right to sell, rent, or lease a housing accommodation, constructed or to be constructed, or any agent or employee thereof:
>
> (1) To refuse to sell, rent, lease or otherwise deny to or withhold from any person or group of persons such a housing accommodation because of race, creed, color, national origin, sex or marital status of such person or persons.
>
> (2) To discriminate against any person because of his race, creed, color, national origin, sex or marital status in the terms, conditions or privileges of the sale, rental or lease of any such housing accommodation or in the furnishing of facilities or services in connection therewith.
>
> (3) To print or circulate or cause to be printed or circulated any statement, advertisement or publication, or to use any form or application for the purchase, rental or lease of such a housing accommodation or to make any record or inquiry in connection with the prospective purchase, rental or lease of such a housing accommodation which expresses, directly or indirectly, any limitation, specification or discrimination as to race, creed, color, national origin, sex or marital status, or an intent to make any such limitation, specification or discrimination.
>
> The provisions of this paragraph (a) shall not apply: (1) to the rental of a housing accommodation in a building which contains housing accommodations for not more than two families living independently of each other, if the owner or members of his family reside in one of such housing accommodations, or (2) to the rental of a room or rooms in a housing accommodation, if such rental is by the occupant of the housing accommodation or by the owner of the housing accommodation and he or members of his family reside in such housing accommodation or (3) *to the restriction of the rental of rooms in a rooming house, dormitory or residence hotel to one sex if such housing accommodation is regularly occupied on a permanent, as opposed to transient, basis by the majority of its guests.* . . .
>
> 10. *The provisions of this section shall not be applicable for dormitory-type residences designed for occupancy by members of the same sex.*

3. The passage of this amendment, in response to pressure from women and without active opposition by feminists groups, highlights the difficulties of drawing lines between the protection of the privacy of individuals and the elimination of sex discrimination. Do you think this exemption delineates an appropriate sphere of privacy? Note that this exemption does not apply to transients or to hotels that cater to the general public. Would this exemption, if applied to facilities imbued with state action, be consistent with the Equal Rights Amendment? The difficulty of finding analogues to single sex residential hotels in the public sphere lends credence to the theory of the amendment's proponents that privacy can be adequately protected without adopting exceptions to the principle of absolute sex equality in the public sphere.

15. After the first New York City law was passed, New York State amended §296.2 of its Human Rights Law to include sex as a prohibited basis for discrimination in places of public accommodation, exempting single sex hotels by directing that "this subdivision shall not apply to the rental of rooms in a housing accommodation which restricts such rental to individuals of one sex." N.Y. Exec. §296.2 (McKinney 1972).

16. N.Y.C. Admin. Code c. 1, tit. B, §§B1-7.0-5(a), B1-7.0-10.

Other provisions prohibited discrimination on the basis of marital status in transactions relating to land, commercial space, publicly-assisted and private housing accommodations, and their financing. N.Y.C. Admin. Code c. 1, tit. B, §§B1-7.0-3, B1-7.0-5(b)-(d).

2. Bars and Restaurants

As the sponsor of the original New York City law prohibiting sex discrimination in public accommodations testified, she was primarily concerned about the restrictive practices of bars and restaurants. These, of course, are places where professional and business-related connections often occur. The following testimony demonstrates a concern to eliminate prostitution — a mounting problem in cities such as New York —as the underlying reason for excluding women. As you read the testimony, can you think of ways to discourage prostitution without excluding all women?[17]

> *Mr. Sherry:* . . . It has been found from experience over a long period of observation ever since, of course, the regulation of traffic in alcoholic beverages that hotel bars and bars generally, public bars, have been places of public accommodation not only for the legitimate purpose of taking refreshment but also for the illegitimate purpose of making contacts for the purpose of sexual intercourse.
>
> Now the closer the people of the opposite sex at the bar are permitted to get to each other, the easier it is for these women who are engaged in that sort of activity to make the solicitation. Which of course immediately exposes the hotel keepers to the very great danger of the loss of their licenses, which is the very heart of their business. So it is for the purpose of protecting the legitimacy of their lawful business that they have established a practice that women are not to stand at the bar. But they are permitted to be in the same room and are served exactly the same way, except that they don't stand at the bar. That is for their protection as well as the protection of the good name and reputation and legitimacy of the whole operation itself. . . .
>
> *Mr. Sherry:* But with respect to hotels, I would respectfully submit the thought I would very much like to have the Commission bear in mind: In a hotel — take any of the hotels that are known to you — there may be as many as five, six separate dining rooms. Each serves a purpose, and each has a character of its own. There's a bar which is the so-called stand-up bar, and that usually is restricted either through the day or at least part of the day to members of one sex — usually to men, although I should imagine it can easily be restricted for certain hours of the day or certain times of the year to women, as the case may be, particularly if there is a convention of women in the hotel at the time.
>
> Now as long as the hotel maintains adequate and proper and indiscriminative service to both sexes throughout the establishment so that no woman can ever complain or would complain that she is not being served with either food or beverages, I respectfully question the policy of eliminating or forbidding a hotel to maintain a men's bar. I can't see personally the wisdom of taking away this prerogative from men, if that's what they want to do, nor yet the prerogative of the hotel keeper to exercise his otherwise unrestricted freedom to provide such accommodations to men solely because the men want that sort of accommodation and it is good business for the hotel keeper and a privilege for the men to have it.
>
> *Commissioner Norton:* You realize, Mr. Sherry, you are going beyond the Hotel Association, which goes to the single character of bars without stools, and you wish to add, I take it —
>
> *Mr. Sherry:* This is not on behalf of the Association. I am really submitting my own thinking for your consideration, that a distinction should be made between a restaurant which is a single bar and perhaps one dining room which is available to the public, and a hotel which has a variety of accommodations, each having its own character but which does not discriminate — perish the thought — against women.
>
> *Mr. Barry:* Let me make it really clear. We do not intend to argue in favor of separate bars and separate facilities in hotels. We have no complaint about that at all. Our only intention here was to make a comment so it be known when you do make your guidelines that there is some problem with regulations and so that hotel bars and

17. Transcripts of Hearings on Exemptions to Sex Discrimination in the Public Accommodations Law, *supra* footnote 11, at 76-77, 101-102.

restaurants might deal with the problem of solicitation, regulations which might be based on sex, such as women standing at bars.

Also I really don't know of anything right now where there would be another example, but this is one practice which is brought up which would be affected by this law, and we only secure understanding of this problem at this time. We have no intention of arguing in favor of separate accommodations in hotels. We understand, and we feel it is not right ourselves.

Miss Meyers: In relation to the problem of women sitting or standing at the bar as opposed to sitting at a table, in anticipation of this line of discussion, we have received a letter from the State Liquor Authority which I would like to read into the record at this time to clarify the law on this subject. . . .

"The purpose of this letter is to set forth the law applicable to the question raised by your Miss Joy Meyers in her letter dated January 11, 1971, addressed to Senior Investigator Harry Watson.

"Section 106, subd: F, of the Alcoholic Beverage Control Law provides:

" 'No person licensed to sell alcoholic beverages shall suffer or permit any gambling on the licensed premises, or suffer or permit such premises to become disorderly.'

" 'Disorderly' premises are not defined by the statute.

"That the operation of premises in a disorderly manner constitutes cause for the revocation, cancellation or suspension of a liquor license has been uniformly recognized by the courts in adjudicating upon a wide range of particular facts and circumstances falling within the general prohibition against the operation of a premises in a disorderly manner.

"To suffer or permit a solicitation for prostitution to occur in a licensed premises constitutes a disorder within the meaning of the above statement. Licensees are expected to supervise their premises in such a way that these as well as all other disorders do not occur therein.

"There is no provision whatsoever that prohibits the sale of alcoholic beverages to unescorted females, as long as their conduct is not such as to constitute a disorder."

This is signed Eli Ratner of the State Liquor Authority. I spoke to Mr. Ratner about this letter yesterday, and he informally advised me that the establishment would, in order to lose its license, be required to have had reason to believe that there was an act of prostitution occurring; that a mere pickup would not be cause for revocation of a liquor license and that the record of the establishment — in other words, a long record with no blemishes and so on — would be considered in any disqualification that they may have. . . .

Mr. Weitz: Mr. Barry, have any members of your Association reported to you any difficulty with respect to solicitation for the purpose of prostitution by male homosexuals?

Mr. Barry: Yes.

Mr. Weitz: They have?

Mr. Barry: Yes. This is part of the problem, and it's growing.

Mr. Weitz: Do you have any sense of that in your proposal to the Commission?

Mr. Barry: I think I stated "solicitation by males or females." I meant to. Well, I just want to make the statement. But I would like to make it clear that this is a problem, and it is a growing problem, and it is a problem which the hotels are very concerned about because it is just one more problem in maintaining the order of the bar.

Mr. Weitz: You have no specifics to suggest for our consideration with respect to male homosexuals?

Mr. Barry: No.

Miss Meyers: I assume that you are developing techniques in self-protection for protecting yourself against solicitation by male homosexuals.

Would not whatever techniques you develop also apply to female homosexuals, which would not necessitate the drastic measure of barring all unescorted females? In other words, you are going to have to develop some technique for male homosexuals.

Mr. Barry: I think the novelty of the problem creates a problem. And here, I am not quite so sure I know how to handle it. It's becoming a much greater problem recently. And in just conversations with hotel managers, they are more confused on how to handle that than they have suggestions. . . .

Did you recognize a "separate but equal" argument in this testimony? Compare the legitimate concern about prostitutes here with the legitimate concern of the Barbizon residents about criminals. In both cases the exclusion is based on what is probably a correct perception that the excluded group contains within it the offending group: most prostitutes are women; most criminals are men. Does the strong statistical probability justify the exclusion as the most efficient way to run a business? How would you argue against this?

3. Ladies' Days

Differential pricing of accommodations takes various forms — offering a reduction in fare for the wife, but not the husband, on a business trip, discounting tickets for women but not men at public events, and so on. Particularly when these offerings take the form of Ladies' Days, they have been trivialized as virtually harmless to men and beneficial to women. But consider this exchange at the commission hearings:[18]

> *Miss Meyers:* What is your estimate as a sociologist of the effect on women of having a Ladies' Day at ball parks? Do you think they are significantly damaged by it?
> *Mr. Miller:* I don't know if it is damaging. I think it reinforces stereotypes.
> *Commissioner Norton:* What is the stereotype being reinforced here?
> *Mr. Miller:* Unathletic. Improvident. And also the notion of silly. Ladies' Day is a silly day. You expect to have silliness going on with a lot of shrieking and silliness because "that is the way women behave on public occasions."

Are there arguments against this preference in pricing for women? The arguments pro and con were made before the New York State Human Rights Appeal Board in the following case.

ABOSH v. NEW YORK YANKEES, INC.

No. CPS-25284, Appeal No. 1194 (N.Y. State Human Rights Appeal Board, July 19, 1972)

Complainant-appellant (hereinafter referred to as appellant) alleges in his verified complaint that on September 4, 1971, he attempted to gain entrance to a ball game at 1:00 P.M. by paying "the same entrance fee as the female spectators on Ladies Day." He claims that he was denied a discount ticket and refused entrance to the Yankee Stadium because of his male sex. He charges respondents with unequal terms, conditions and privileges at a public accommodation, resort or amusement in violation of the Human Rights Law.

The record shows that respondent New York Yankees, Inc., . . . during the 1970-71 baseball season . . . scheduled 11 Ladies' Days, a national tradition for about 100 years, to encourage the attendance of women at the Yankee Stadium, when the price of admission for women was less than for male patrons.

On that point the record shows that a $.50 admission ticket sold to female patrons provided a dollar discount on the applicable price for a bleacher seat ($1.50), which also applied towards an exchange for a general admission seat ($2.50) or a box seat ($4.00) at the exchange booth of the Stadium.

[R]espondents contend that Section 296.2 does not require uniform pricing nor purport to regulate admission prices in a place of public accommodation and that even if appellant was refused a $.50 ticket because he was not a woman that he was not barred from the accommodations, advantages or privileges of the Stadium.

It would seem then that the purchase price of that ticket under Section 296.2

---

18. Id. at 200-201.

entailed more than entry rights in that the purchase price of a ticket for a female patron on September 4, 1971 represented the cost of obtaining not only entry rights but also the accommodations, advantages, facilities or privileges available at the Stadium — including the intrinsic dollar discount intertwined in her ticket.

Here, the fact that the Legislature omitted in Section 296.2 the use of the words "terms" and "conditions" as respondents argued, does not necessarily mean that the word "privileges" as used in Section 296.2 detracts from the legislative intent to accord men the same inherent privileges available to women in an admission ticket to the Yankee Stadium on "Ladies Day."

Presumably, the Legislature did not contemplate its exclusive application to women nor limit its usage only to women as respondents here would have us believe.

It would further appear that the statutory criterion on sex is extensive to both men and women and that it accords no preferential treatment or privileges to women over men.

With respect to respondents' argument that "Ladies Day" is a business concept to promote commercial patronage and that the difference in price of $1.00 is neither irrational nor arbitrary, the record shows that in the 1970-71 season, the average attendance on "Ladies Day" was 350 women at a Stadium which holds a capacity crowd of 65,000 persons (par. 2-3, p. 2, Division's Conference Report dated October 18, 1971).

In light of that spotty attendance, it would appear that respondents' variations in price for comparable seats to encourage women who might otherwise not attend were irrational and futile and did not justify respondents' arbitrary pricing based on sex as a business concept.

The record further shows that at the Conference held at the Division on November 4, 1971, respondents argued that "Ladies Day" also encouraged "the women of the United States to build stronger bonds with the male members of their families" (par. 3, p. 1) and that "Baseball is a family sport — a sort of Mom and Pop deal" (lines 4-5, par. 8, p. 2).

Respondents' argument, although praiseworthy, is untenable in that it presupposes intact families where every woman has a man to take care of her. Unfortunately, that is not the case in America today, where 11.5% of all families are headed by women and where 40% of all working women are either single, divorced, deserted, widowed, separated or abandoned.

Apparently, respondents here realized that the stereotyped characterizations of a woman's role in society that prevailed at the inception of "Ladies Day" in 1876 have ceased to be relevant in a modern technological society where women and men are to be on equal footing as a matter of public policy.

And, presumably, no woman who really cherishes her hard fought rights of equality under the Human Rights Law would accept preferential treatment at the expense of her male counterpart.

Perhaps, in their unending quest to serve best the social interests of the public, a Community Day at reduced prices irrespective of sex, rather than a Ladies Day with its attendant pricing based on sex, might well accomplish respondents' social concerns without violating the public policy of this State as embodied in the sex prohibition of Section 296.2.

After considering all the proposed exemptions discussed above, the New York City Commission on Human Rights denied all except the exemption for portions of facilities where patrons customarily disrobe. Do you agree with this outcome?

INDEX